THE
Jewish Encyclopedia

A DESCRIPTIVE RECORD OF

THE HISTORY, RELIGION, LITERATURE, AND CUSTOMS OF THE JEWISH PEOPLE FROM THE EARLIEST TIMES TO THE PRESENT DAY

Prepared by More than Four Hundred Scholars and Specialists

UNDER THE DIRECTION OF THE FOLLOWING EDITORIAL BOARD

CYRUS ADLER, PH.D. (*Departments of Post-Biblical Antiquities ; the Jews of America*).

WILHELM BACHER, PH.D. (*Departments of the Talmud and Rabbinical Literature*).

GOTTHARD DEUTSCH, PH.D. (*Department of History from 1492 to 1905*).

RICHARD GOTTHEIL, PH.D. (*Departments of History from Ezra to 1492 ; History of Post-Talmudic Literature*).

EMIL G. HIRSCH, PH.D., LL.D. (*Department of the Bible*).

JOSEPH JACOBS, B.A. (*Departments of the Jews of England and Anthropology; Revising Editor*).

KAUFMANN KOHLER, PH.D. (*Departments of Theology and Philosophy*).

HERMAN ROSENTHAL (*Department of the Jews of Russia and Poland*).

ISIDORE SINGER, PH.D. (*Department of Modern Biography from 1750 to 1905*).

CRAWFORD H. TOY, D.D., LL.D. (*Departments of Hebrew Philology and Hellenistic Literature*).

ISAAC K. FUNK, D.D., LL.D.
Chairman of the Board

FRANK H. VIZETELLY, F.S.A.
Secretary of the Board

WILLIAM POPPER, M.A., PH.D.
Associate Revising Editor ; Chief of the Bureau of Translation

ISIDORE SINGER, Ph.D.
Projector and Managing Editor

ASSISTED BY AMERICAN AND FOREIGN BOARDS OF CONSULTING EDITORS

NEW EDITION

COMPLETE IN TWELVE VOLUMES

EMBELLISHED WITH MORE THAN TWO THOUSAND ILLUSTRATIONS

FUNK AND WAGNALLS COMPANY
NEW YORK AND LONDON

Bas-relief from the Arch of Titus at Rome

Showing Spoils from the Temple of Jerusalem

(Candlestick, Table of Showbread and Trumpets)

THE
Jewish Encyclopedia

A DESCRIPTIVE RECORD OF

THE HISTORY, RELIGION, LITERATURE, AND CUSTOMS OF THE JEWISH PEOPLE FROM THE EARLIEST TIMES TO THE PRESENT DAY

Prepared by More than Six Hundred Scholars and Specialists

UNDER THE DIRECTION OF THE FOLLOWING EDITORIAL BOARD

CYRUS ADLER, PH.D. (*Departments of Post-Biblical Antiquities ; the Jews of America*).

WILHELM BACHER, PH.D. (*Departments of the Talmud and Rabbinical Literature*).

GOTTHARD DEUTSCH, PH.D. (*Department of History from 1492 to 1906*).

RICHARD GOTTHEIL, PH.D. (*Departments of History from Ezra to 1492 ; History of Post-Talmudic Literature*).

EMIL G. HIRSCH, PH.D., LL.D. (*Department of the Bible*).

JOSEPH JACOBS, B.A. (*Departments of the Jews of England and Anthropology; Revising Editor*).

KAUFMANN KOHLER, PH.D. (*Departments of Theology and Philosophy*).

HERMAN ROSENTHAL (*Department of the Jews of Russia and Poland*).

ISIDORE SINGER, PH.D. (*Department of Modern Biography from 1750 to 1906*).

CRAWFORD H. TOY, D.D., LL.D. (*Departments of Hebrew Philology and Hellenistic Literature*).

ISAAC K. FUNK, D.D., LL.D.
Chairman of the Board

FRANK H. VIZETELLY, F.S.A.
Secretary of the Board

WILLIAM POPPER, M.A., PH.D.
Associate Revising Editor ; Chief of the Bureau of Translation

ISIDORE SINGER, Ph.D.
Projector and Managing Editor

ASSISTED BY AMERICAN AND FOREIGN BOARDS OF CONSULTING EDITORS

NEW EDITION

VOLUME XII

TALMUD—ZWEIFEL

NEW YORK AND LONDON
FUNK AND WAGNALLS COMPANY

COPYRIGHT 1905, 1909, 1916 AND 1925, BY

FUNK & WAGNALLS COMPANY

All rights of translation reserved

[Printed in the United States of America]

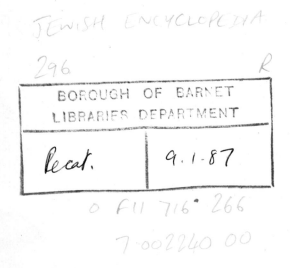
XII.3.25

SYSTEMS OF TRANSLITERATION AND OF CITATION OF PROPER NAMES *

A.—Rules for the Transliteration of Hebrew and Aramaic.

1. All important names which occur in the Bible are cited as found in the authorized King James version; *e.g.*, *Moses*, not Mosheh; *Isaac*, not Yiẓḥaḳ; *Saul*, not Sha'ul or Shaül; *Solomon*, not Shelomoh, etc.

2. Names that have gained currency in English books on Jewish subjects, or that have become familiar to English readers, are always retained and cross-references given, though the topic be treated under the form transliterated according to the system tabulated below.

3. Hebrew subject-headings are transcribed according to the scheme of transliteration; cross-references are made as in the case of personal names.

4. The following system of transliteration has been used for Hebrew and Aramaic:

א *Not noted at the beginning or the end of a word; otherwise' or by dieresis; e.g., Ze'eb or Meïr.*

ב	*b*	ז	*z*	ל	*l*	פ	*with dagesh, p*	שׁ	*sh*

ב	*b*	ז	*z*	ל	*l*	פ *with dagesh, p*	שׁ *sh*
ג	*g*	ח	*ḥ*	מ	*m*	פ *without dagesh, f*	שׂ *s*
ד	*d*	ט	*ṭ*	נ	*n*	צ *ẓ*	ת *t*
ה	*h*	י	*y*	ס	*s*	ק *ḳ*	
ו	*w*	כ	*k*	ע	*'*	ר *r*	

NOTE: The presence of dagesh lene is not noted except in the case of *pe*. Dagesh forte is indicated by doubling the letter.

5. The vowels have been transcribed as follows:

ָ *a*	ֻ *u*	ַ *a*	ֵ *e*	וֹ *o*
ֵ *e*	ֻ *e*	ֹ *o*	ִי *i*	
ִ *i*	ְ *e*	ָ *a*	ו *u*	

Ḳameẓ ḥaṭuf is represented by *o*.

The so-called "Continental" pronunciation of the English vowels is implied.

6. The Hebrew article is transcribed as *ha*, followed by a hyphen, without doubling the following letter. [Not *hak-Kohen* or *hak-Cohen*, nor *Rosh ha-shshanah*.]

B.—Rules for the Transliteration of Arabic.

1. All Arabic names and words except such as have become familiar to English readers in another form, as *Mohammed, Koran, mosque*, are transliterated according to the following system:

ﺀ *See א above*	خ *kh*	ش *sh*	غ *gh*	ن *n*
ب *b*	د *d*	ص *ṣ*	ف *f*	ه *h*
ت *t*	ذ *dh*	ض *ḍ*	ق *ḳ*	و *w*
ث *th*	ر *r*	ط *ṭ*	ك *k*	ي *y*
ج *j*	ز *z*	ظ *ẓ*	ل *l*	
ح *ḥ*	س *s*	ع *'*	م *m*	

2. Only the three vowels—a, i, u—are represented:

ـَ *a*	ـِ *i*	ـُ *u*

No account has been taken of the *imālah; i* has not been written *e*, nor *u* written *o*.

---

* In all other matters of orthography the spelling preferred by the STANDARD DICTIONARY has usually been followed. Typographical exigencies have rendered occasional deviations from these systems necessary.

3. The Arabic article is invariably written *al*, no account being taken of the assimilation of the *l* to the following letter; *e.g.*, *Abu al-Salt*, not *Abu-l-Salt*; *Nafis al-Daulah*, not *Nafis ad-Daulah*. The article is joined by a hyphen to the following word.

4. At the end of words the feminine termination is written *ah*; but when followed by a genitive, *at*; *e.g.*, *Risalah dhat al-Kursiyy*, but *Hi'at al-Aflak*.

5. No account is taken of the overhanging vowels which distinguish the cases; *e.g.*, *'Amr*, not *'Amru* or *'Amrun*; *Ya'ḳub*, not *Ya'ḳubun*; or in a title, *Kitab al-Amanat wal-I'tiḳadat*.

C.—Rules for the Transliteration of Russian.

All Russian names and words, except such as have become familiar to English readers in other forms, as *Czar, Alexander, deciatine, Moscow*, are transliterated according to the following system :

А а	*a*	Н н	*n*	Щ щ	*shch*
Б б	*b*	О о	*o*	Ъ ъ	mute
В в	*v*	П п	*p*	Ы ы	*y*
Г г	*h, v,* or *g*	Р р	*r*	Ь ь	half mute
Д д	*d*	С с	*s*	Ѣ ѣ	*ye*
Е е	*e* and *ye* at the beginning.	Т т	*t*	Э э	*e*
Ж ж	*zh*	У у	*u*	Ю ю	*yu*
З з	*z*	Ф ф	*f*	Я я	*ya*
И и I i	*i*	Х х	*kh*	Ѳ ѳ	*F*
К к	*k*	Ц ц	*tz*	Ѵ ѵ	*œ*
Л л	*l*	Ч ч	*ch*	Й й	*i*
М м	*m*	Ш ш	*sh*		

Rules for the Citation of Proper Names, Personal and Otherwise.

1 Whenever possible, an author is cited under his most specific name; *e.g.*, Moses Nigrin under *Nigrin*; Moses Zacuto under *Zacuto*; Moses Rieti under *Rieti*; all the Ḳimḥis (or Ḳamḥis) under *Ḳimḥi*; Israel ben Joseph Drohobiczer under *Drohobiczer*. Cross-references are freely made from any other form to the most specific one; *e.g.*, to Moses *Vidal* from Moses *Narboni*; to Solomon Nathan *Vidal* from Menahem *Meïri*; to Samuel *Kansi* from Samuel Astruc *Dascola*; to Jedaiah *Penini* from both *Bedersi* and *En Bonet*; to *John* of Avignon from Moses de *Roquemaure*.

2. When a person is not referred to as above, he is cited under his own personal name followed by his official or other title; or, where he has borne no such title, by "of" followed by the place of his birth or residence; *e.g.*, *Johanan* ha-Sandlar; *Samuel* ha-Nagid; *Judah* he-Ḥasid; *Gershom* of Metz; *Isaac* of Corbeil.

3. Names containing the words *d', de, da, di, van, von, y, of, ben, ha-, ibn** are arranged under the letter of the name following this word; *e.g.*, de Pomis under *Pomis*, de Barrios under *Barrios*, Jacob d'Illescas under *Illescas*. The order of topics is illustrated by the following examples :

Abraham of Augsburg	Abraham de Balmes	Abraham ben Benjamin Aaron
Abraham of Avila	Abraham ben Baruch	Abraham ben Benjamin Zeeb
Abraham ben Azriel	Abraham of Beja	Abraham Benveniste

* When IBN has come to be a specific part of a name, as IBN EZRA, such name is treated in its alphabetical place under "I."

NOTE TO THE READER.

Subjects on which further information is afforded elsewhere in this work are indicated by the use of capitals and small capitals in the text; as, ABBA ARIKA; PUMBEDITA; VOCALIZATION.

LIST OF ABBREVIATIONS

[Self-evident abbreviations, particularly those used in the bibliographies, are not included here.]

Ab ....Abot, Pirḳe
Ab. R. N...........Abot de-Rabbi Natan
'Ab. Zarah.........'Abodah Zarah
ad loc...............at the place ; to the passage cited
A.H..................in the year of the Hegira
Allg. Zeit. des Jud..Allgemeine Zeitung des Judenthums
Am. Jew. Hist. Soc.American Jewish Historical Society
Am. Jour. Semit. ⎰
  Lang.......... ⎱ American Journal of Semitic Languages
Anglo-Jew. Assoc...Anglo-Jewish Association
Apoc...............Apocalypse
Apocr..............Apocrypha
Apost. Const.......Apostolical Constitutions
'Ar................'Arakin (Talmud)
Arch. Isr..........Archives Israélites
Aronius, Regesten ⎰ Aronius, Regesten zur Geschichte der Juden
   ⎱ in Deutschland
A. T..............Das Alte Testament
A. V..............Authorized Version
b...................ben *or* bar *or* born
Bacher, Ag. Bab. ⎰
  Amor ..... ⎱ Bacher, Agada der Babylonischen Amoräer
Bacher, Ag. Pal. ⎰ Bacher, Agada der Palästinensischen Amo-
  Amor ...... ⎱ räer
Bacher, Ag. Tan....Bacher, Agada der Tannaiten
B. B...............Baba Batra (Talmud)
B.C................before the Christian era
Bek................Bekorot (Talmud)
Benzinger, Arch....Benzinger, Hebräische Archäologie
Ber................Berakot (Talmud)
Berliner Fest-⎰
  schrift.. ...... ⎱ Festschrift zum 70ten Geburtstag Berliners
Berliner's ⎰ Berliner's Magazin für die Wissenschaft des
  Magazin. ...... ⎱ Judenthums
Bibl. Rab..........Bibliotheca Rabbinica
Bik................Bikkurim (Talmud)
B. Ḳ...............Baba Ḳamma (Talmud)
B. M...............Baba Meẓi'a (Talmud)
Boletin Acad. Hist. ⎰ Boletin de la Real Academia de la Historia
   ⎱ (Madrid)
Brit. Mus..........British Museum
Brüll's Jahrb..... ⎰ Brüll's Jahrbücher für Jüdische Geschichte
   ⎱ und Litteratur
Bulletin All. Isr...Bulletin of the Alliance Israélite Universelle
c ....about
Cant...............Canticles (Song of Solomon)
Cat. Anglo-Jew. ⎰ Catalogue of Anglo-Jewish Historical Ex-
  Hist. Exh...... ⎱ hibition
Cazès, Notes Bi-⎰ Cazès, Notes Bibliographiques sur la Littéra-
  bliographiques . ⎱ ture Juive-Tunisienne
C.E................common era
ch..................chapter *or* chapters
Cheyne and Black, ⎰ Cheyne and Black, Encyclopædia Biblica
  Encyc. Bibl.... ⎱
Chwolson Jubilee ⎰ Recueil des Travaux Rédigés en Mémoire
  Volume........ ⎱ du Jubilé Scientifique de M. Daniel Chwol-
   son, 1846-1896
C. I. A............Corpus Inscriptionum Atticarum
C. I. G............Corpus Inscriptionum Græcarum
C. I. H............Corpus Inscriptionum Hebraicarum
C. I. L............Corpus Inscriptionum Latinarum
C. I. P............Corpus Inscriptionum Peloponnesi
C. I. S............Corpus Inscriptionum Semiticarum
comp...............compare
Curinier, Dict. ⎰ E. E. Curinier, Dictionnaire National des
  Nat............ ⎱ Contemporains
d...................died
D..................Deuteronomist
De Gubernatis, ⎰ De Gubernatis, Dizionario Biografico degli
  Diz. Biog....... ⎱ Scrittori Contemporanei
De Gubernatis, ⎰ De Gubernatis, Dictionnaire International
  Ecrivains du Jour ⎱ des Ecrivains du Jour
De le Roi, Juden-⎰ De le Roi, Geschichte der Evangelischen
  Mission .... ⎱ Juden-Mission
Dem ....Demai (Talmud)
Derenbourg, Hist. ⎰ Derenbourg, Essai sur l'Histoire et la Géo-
   ⎱ graphie de la Palestine, etc.
De Rossi, Dizio-⎰ De Rossi, Dizionario Storico degli Autori
  nario.......... ⎱ Ebrei e delle Loro Opere
De Rossi - Ham-⎰ De Rossi-Hamberger, Historisches Wörter-
  berger, Hist. ⎱ buch der Jüdischen Schriftsteller und
  Wörterb. ...... Ihrer Werke
Driver, Introduc-⎰ S. R. Driver, An Introduction to the Liter-
  tion........... ⎱ ature of the Old Testament
E..................Elohist
Eccl ....Ecclesiastes
Ecclus. (Sirach)....Ecclesiasticus
ed..................edition
'Eduy ....'Eduyot (Talmud)
Eisenberg, Biog. ⎰ Ludwig Eisenberg's Grosses Biographisches
  Lex .... ⎱ Lexikon der Deutschen Bühne im XIX.
   Jahrhundert
Encyc. Brit........Encyclopædia Britannica
Eng ....English

Epiphanius, Hæres.Epiphanius, Adversus Hæreses
'Er................'Erubin (Talmud)
Ersch and ⎰ Ersch and Gruber, Allgemeine Encyklopädie
  Gruber, Encyc.. ⎱ der Wissenschaften und Künste
Esd ....Esdras
et seq..............and following
Eusebius, Hist. Eccl.Eusebius, Historia Ecclesiastica
Ewald, Gesch ....Ewald, Geschichte des Volkes Israel
Frankel, Mebo.....Frankel, Mebo Yerushalmi
Fürst, Bibl. Jud....Fürst, Bibliotheca Judaica
Fürst, Gesch. des ⎰ Fürst, Geschichte des Karäerthums
  Karäert.... ... ⎱
Gaster, Hist. of ⎰ Gaster, Bevis Marks Memorial Volume
  Bevis Marks.... ⎱
   ⎰ Geiger, Urschrift und Uebersetzungen der
Geiger, Urschrift. ⎰ Bibel in Ihrer Abhängigkeit von der In-
   neren Entwicklung des Judenthums
Geiger's Jüd. Zeit. ⎰ Geiger's Jüdische Zeitschrift für Wissen-
   ⎱ schaft und Leben
Geiger's Wiss. ⎰ Geiger's Wissenschaftliche Zeitschrift für
  Zeit. Jüd. Theol. ⎱ Jüdische Theologie
Gesch..............Geschichte
Gesenius, Gr.......Gesenius, Grammar
Gesenius, Th......Gesenius, Thesaurus
Gibbon, Decline ⎰ Gibbon, History of the Decline and Fall of
  and Fall........ ⎱ the Roman Empire
Ginsburg's Bible.. ⎰ Ginsburg's New Massoretico-Critical Text
   ⎱ of the Hebrew Bible
Giṭ ....Giṭṭin (Talmud)
Graetz, Hist.......Graetz, History of the Jews
Grätz, Gesch......Grätz, Geschichte der Juden
Güdemann, ⎰ Güdemann, Geschichte des Erziehungs-
  Gesch .... ⎱ wesens und der Cultur der Abendländi-
   schen Juden
H..................Holiness Code
Hag ....Haggai
Ḥag ....Ḥagigah (Talmud)
Ḥal ....Ḥallah (Talmud)
Hamburger, ⎰ Hamburger, Realencyclopädie für Bibel
  R. B. T........ ⎱ und Talmud
Hastings, Dict. ⎰ Hastings, Dictionary of the Bible
  Bible........... ⎱
Heb................Epistle to the Hebrews
Hebr...............Masoretic Text
Herzog-Plitt or ⎰ Herzog-Plitt or Herzog-Hauck, Real-Ency-
  Herzog - Hauck, ⎰ klopädie für Protestantische Theologie und
  Real-Encyc.... ⎱ Kirche (2d and 3d editions respectively)
Hirsch, Biog. Lex. ⎰ Hirsch, Biographisches Lexikon der Hervor-
   ⎱ ragenden Aerzte Aller Zeiten und Völker
Hor ....Horayot (Talmud)
Ḥul ....Ḥullin (Talmud)
ib..................same place
idem...............same author
Isr. Letterbode.....Israelitische Letterbode
J ....Jahvist
Jaarboeken ....Jaarboeken voor de Israeliten in Nederland
Jacobs, Sources.. ⎰ Jacobs, Inquiry into the Sources of Spanish-
   ⎱ Jewish History
Jacobs and Wolf, ⎰ Jacobs and Wolf, Bibliotheca Anglo-Judaica
  Bibl. Anglo-Jud. ⎱
Jahrb. Gesch. der ⎰ Jahrbuch für die Geschichte der Juden und
  Jud............ ⎱ des Judenthums
Jastrow, Dict..... ⎰ Jastrow, Dictionary of the Targumim, Tal-
   ⎱ mudim, and Midrashim
Jellinek, B. H......Jellinek, Bet ha-Midrash
Jew. Chron........Jewish Chronicle, London
Jew. Encyc ....The Jewish Encyclopedia
Jew. Hist. Soc. Eng.Jewish Historical Society of England
Jew. World ....Jewish World, London
Josephus, Ant......Josephus, Antiquities of the Jews
Josephus, B. J......Josephus, De Bello Judaico
Josephus, Contra Ap.Josephus, Contra Apionem
Josh ....Joshua
Jost's Annalen.....Jost's Israelitische Annalen
Jour. Bib. Lit......Journal of Biblical Literature
J. Q. R.............Jewish Quarterly Review
J. R. A. S..........Journal of the Royal Asiatic Society
Justin, Dial. cum ⎰ Justin, Dialogus cum Tryphone Judæo
  Tryph .... ⎱
Kaufmann Ge-⎰ Gedenkbuch zur Erinnerung an David Kauf-
  denkbuch...... ⎱ mann
Kautzsch, Apo-⎰ Kautzsch, Die Apokryphen und Pseudepi-
  kryphen........ ⎱ graphen des Alten Testaments
Kayserling, Bibl. ⎰ Kayserling, Biblioteca Española-Portugueza-
  Esp.-Port.-Jud.. ⎱ Judaica
Kayserling, Die ⎰ Kayserling, Die Jüdischen Frauen in der
  Jüdischen Frau-⎰ Geschichte, Literatur und Kunst
  en .... ⎱
Ker ....Keritot (Talmud)
Ket ....Ketubot (Talmud)
K. H. C...........⎰ Kurzer Hand-Commentar zum Alten Testa-
   ⎱ ment, ed. Marti
Ḳid ....Ḳiddushin (Talmud)
Kil ....Kil'ayim (Talmud)
Ḳin................Ḳinnim (Talmud)

Kohut Memorial Volume........	Semitic Studies in Memory of A. Kohut
Krauss, Lehnwörter	Krauss, Griechische und Lateinische Lehnwörter im Talmud, Midrasch, und Targum
Kuenen, Einleitung............	Kuenen, Historisch-Kritische Einleitung in die Bücher des Alten Testaments
Larousse, Dict....	Larousse, Grand Dictionnaire Universel du XIXe Siècle
l.c.	in the place cited
Levy, Chal. Wörterb........	Levy, Chaldäisches Wörterbuch über die Targumim
Levy, Neuhebr. Wörterb......	Levy, Neuhebräisches und Chaldäisches Wörterbuch über die Talmudim und Midraschim
Lewysohn, Z. T....	Lewysohn, Zoologie des Talmuds
lit	literally
Löw, Lebensalter	Löw, Die Lebensalter in der Jüdischen Literatur
LXX	Septuagint
m	married
Ma'as.	Ma'aserot (Talmud)
Ma'as. Sh.	Ma'aser Sheni (Talmud)
Macc.	Maccabees
Maimonides, Moreh.	Maimonides, Moreh Nebukim
Maimonides, Yad ..	Maimonides, Yad ha-Ḥazaḳah
Mak.	Makkot (Talmud)
Maksh.	Makshirin (Talmud)
Mas	Masorah
Massek.	Masseket
McClintock and Strong, Cyc....	McClintock and Strong, Cyclopædia of Biblical, Theological, and Ecclesiastical Literature
Meg.	Megillah (Talmud)
Me'i.	Me'ilah (Talmud)
Mek.	Mekilta
Men.	Menaḥot (Talmud)
Mid.	Middot (Talmud)
Midr.	Midrash
Midr. Teh.	Midrash Tehillim (Psalms)
Miḳ.	Miḳwa'ot (Talmud)
M. Ḳ.	Mo'ed Ḳaṭan (Talmud)
Monatsschrift.....	Monatsschrift für die Geschichte und Wissenschaft des Judenthums
Mortara, Indice..	Mortara, Indice Alfabetico
Müller. Frag.Hist. Græc..........	Müller, Fragmenta Historicorum Græcorum
Munk, Mélanges .	Munk, Mélanges de Philosophie Juive et Arabe
Murray's Eng. Dict.	A. H. Murray, A New English Dictionary
Naz	Nazir (Talmud)
n.d.	no date
Ned.	Nedarim (Talmud)
Neg	Nega'im
Neubauer, Cat. Bodl.Hebr.MSS.	Neubauer, Catalogue of the Hebrew MSS. in the Bodleian Library
Neubauer, G. T.	Neubauer, Géographie du Talmud
Neubauer, M. J. C.	Neubauer, Mediæval Jewish Chronicles
n.p.	no place of publication stated
N. T.	New Testament
Oest.Wochenschrift.	Oesterreichische Wochenschrift
Oh	Ohalot (Talmud)
Onḳ	Onḳelos
Orient, Lit.	Literaturblatt des Orients
O. T.	Old Testament
P	Priestly Code
Pagel, Biog. Lex.	Pagel, Biographisches Lexikon Hervorragender Aerzte des Neunzehnten Jahrhunderts
Pal. Explor. Fund.	Palestine Exploration Fund
Pallas Lex.	Pallas Nagy Lexicon
Pauly-Wissowa, Real-Encyc	Pauly-Wissowa, Real-Encyclopädie der Classischen Altertumswissenschaft
Pes	Pesaḥim (Talmud)
Pesh.	Peshito, Peshiṭta
Pesiḳ	Pesiḳta de-Rab Kahana
Pesiḳ. R.	Pesiḳta Rabbati
Pirḳe R. El.	Pirḳe Rabbi Eli'ezer
Proc	Proceedings
Publ	Publications
R	Rab or Rabbi or Rabbah or Redactor
Rahmer's Jüd. Lit.-Blatt.	Rahmer's Jüdisches Litteratur-Blatt
Regesty	Regesty i Nadpisi
R. E. J.	Revue des Etudes Juives
Rev. Bib.	Revue Biblique
Rev. Sém.	Revue Sémitique
R. H.	Rosh ha-Shanah (Talmud)
Rios, Estudios.	Amador de los Rios, Estudios Históricos, Políticos y Literarios, etc.
Rios, Hist.	Amador de los Rios, Historia ... de los Judios de España y Portugal
Ritter, Erdkunde.	Ritter, Die Erdkunde im Verhältnis zur Natur und zur Geschichte des Menschen
Robinson, Later Researches	Robinson, Later Biblical Researches in Palestine and the Adjacent Regions ... 1852
Robinson, Researches	Robinson, Biblical Researches in Palestine, Mt. Sinai, and Arabia Petræa ... 1838
Roest, Cat. Rosenthal. Bibl.	Roest, Catalog der Hebraica und Judaica aus der L. Rosenthal'schen Bibliothek
R. V	Revised Version
Salfeld, Martyrologium.........	Salfeld, Das Martyrologium des Nürnberger Memorbuches
Sanh	Sanhedrin (Talmud)
S. B. E.	Sacred Books of the East
S. B. O. T.	(Sacred Books of the Old Testament) Polychrome Bible, ed. Paul Haupt
Schaff-Herzog, Encyc	Schaff-Herzog, A Religious Encyclopædia
Schiller-Szinessy, Cat. Cambridge	Catalogue of the Hebrew Manuscripts Preserved in the University Library, Cambridge
Schrader, C. I. O. T.	Schrader, Cuneiform Inscriptions and the Old Testament, Eng. transl.
Schrader, K. A. T.	Schrader, Keilinschriften und das Alte Testament
Schrader, K. B.	Schrader, Keilinschriftliche Bibliothek
Schrader, K. G. F.	Schrader, Keilinschriften und Geschichtsforschung
Schürer, Gesch.	Schürer, Geschichte des Jüdischen Volkes
Sem.	Semaḥot (Talmud)
Shab	Shabbat (Talmud)
Sheb.	Shebi'it (Talmud)
Shebu	Shebu'ot (Talmud)
Sheḳ	Sheḳalim (Talmud)
Sibyllines	Sibylline Books
Smith, Rel. of Sem.	Smith, Lectures on Religion of the Semites
Soc. Bibl. Arch.	Society of Biblical Archæology
Stade's Zeitschrift	Stade's Zeitschrift für die Alttestamentliche Wissenschaft
Steinschneider, Cat. Bodl.	Steinschneider, Catalogue of the Hebrew Books in the Bodleian Library
Steinschneider, Cat. Leyden....	Steinschneider, Catalogus Codicum Hebræorum Bibliothecæ Academiæ Lugduno-Batavæ
Steinschneider, Cat. Munich ...	Steinschneider, Die Hebräischen Handschriften der K. Hof- und Staats-Bibliothek in München
Steinschneider, Hebr. Bibl.	Steinschneider, Hebräische Bibliographie
Steinschneider, Hebr. Uebers...	Steinschneider, Hebräische Uebersetzungen
Strack, Das Blut..	Strack, Das Blut im Glauben und Aberglauben der Menschheit
Suk	Sukkah (Talmud)
s.v.	under the word
Ta'an	Ta'anit (Talmud)
Tan	Tanḥuma
Targ	Targumim
Targ. Onḳ.	Targum Onḳelos
Targ. Yer.	Targum Yerushalmi or Targum Jonathan
Tem	Temurah (Talmud)
Ter	Terumot (Talmud)
Test. Patr.	Testaments of the Twelve Patriarchs
Toh	Tohorot
Tos	Tosafot
Tosef	Tosefta
Tr.	Transactions
transl	translation
Tristram, Nat. Hist.	Tristram, Natural History of the Bible
T. Y	Ṭebul Yom (Talmud)
'Uḳ	'Uḳzin (Talmud)
Univ. Isr.	Univers Israélite
Virchow's Archiv	Virchow's Archiv für Pathologische Anatomie und Physiologie, und für Klinische Medizin
Vulg	Vulgate
Weiss, Dor.	Weiss, Dor Dor we-Dorshaw
Wellhausen, I. J. G.	Wellhausen, Israelitische und Jüdische Geschichte
Winer, B. R.	Winer, Biblisches Realwörterbuch
Wisdom	Wisdom of Solomon
Wolf, Bibl. Hebr.	Wolf, Bibliotheca Hebræa
W. Z. K. M.	Wiener Zeitschrift für die Kunde des Morgenlandes
Yad	Yadayim (Talmud)
"Yad"	Yad ha-Ḥazaḳah
Yalḳ	Yalḳuṭ
Yeb	Yebamot (Talmud)
Yer.	Yerushalmi (Jerusalem Talmud)
YHWH	Yahweh, Jehovah
Zab	Zabim (Talmud)
Z. D. M. G.	Zeitschrift der Deutschen Morgenländischen Gesellschaft
Z. D. P. V.	Zeitschrift des Deutschen Palästina-Vereins
Zeb	Zebaḥim (Talmud)
Zedner, Cat. Hebr. Books Brit.Mus.	Zedner, Catalogue of the Hebrew Books in the British Museum
Zeit. für Assyr.	Zeitschrift für Assyriologie
Zeit. für Hebr. Bibl.	Zeitschrift für Hebräische Bibliographie
Zeitlin, Bibl. Post-Mendels.	Zeitlin, Bibliotheca Hebraica Post-Mendelssohniana
Zunz, G. S.	Zunz, Gesammelte Schriften
Zunz, G. V.	Zunz, Gottesdienstliche Vorträge
Zunz, Literaturgesch	Zunz, Literaturgeschichte der Synagogalen Poesie
Zunz, Ritus	Zunz, Die Ritus des Synagogalen Gottesdienstes
Zunz, S. P.	Zunz, Synagogale Poesie des Mittelalters
Zunz, Z. G.	Zunz, Zur Geschichte und Literatur

CONTRIBUTORS TO VOLUME XII

A.............**Cyrus Adler, Ph.D.,**
President of the American Jewish Historical Society; Former President of the Board of Directors of the Jewish Theological Seminary of America; Assistant Secretary of the Smithsonian Institution, Washington, D. C.

A. Bü........**Alexander Büchler, Ph.D.,**
Rabbi, Keszthely, Hungary.

A. Fe........**Alfred Feilchenfeld, Ph.D.,**
Principal of the Realschule, Fürth, Bavaria, Germany.

A. Ga........**Abraham Galante,**
Formerly Editor of "La Buena Esperanza," Smyrna; Cairo, Egypt.

A. Kai.......**Alois Kaiser,**
Cantor, Temple Oheb Shalom, Baltimore, Md.

A. Ke........**A. Kecskemeti,**
Rabbi, Makow, Hungary.

A. Ki.........**Alexander Kisch, Ph.D.,**
Rabbi, Meysel Synagoge, Prague, Bohemia, Austria.

A. Ku.......**A. Kurrein, Ph.D.,**
Rabbi, Teplitz, Bohemia, Austria.

A. Lew......**Abraham Lewinsky, Ph.D.,**
Chief Rabbi, Hildesheim, Hanover, Germany.

A. Lu........**Abraham Lubarsky,**
New York City.

A. M. F......**A. M. Friedenberg, B.S., LL.B.,**
Counselor at Law, New York City.

A. M. H.....**A. M. Hyamson,**
London, England.

A. M. Ho...**A. M. Hofmann,**
United States National Museum, Washington, D. C.

A. P..........**A. Porter** (*Office Editor*),
Formerly Associate Editor of "The Forum," New York; Revising Editor of "Standard Cyclopedia"; New York City.

A. Pe........**A. Peiginsky, Ph.D.,**
New York City.

A. S..........**Abram Simon,**
Rabbi, Hebrew Congregation, Washington, D. C.

A. S. I.......**Abram S. Isaacs, Ph.D.,**
Professor of German Language and Literature, New York University Graduate Seminary, New York City; Rabbi, B'nai Jeshurun Congregation, Paterson, N. J

A. S. W......**A. S. Waldstein, B.A.,**
New York City.

A. Tä. ....**Aaron Tänzer, Ph.D.,**
Rabbi, Hohenems, Tyrol, Austria.

A. V. W. J..**A. V. W. Jackson, Ph.D., Lit.D., LL.D.,**
Professor of Indo-Iranian Languages, Columbia University, New York City.

B. P..........**Bernhard Pick, Ph.D., D.D.,**
Pastor of St. John's Lutheran Church, Newark, N. J.

B. R..........**Baer Ratner,**
Author, Wilna, Russia.

C. I. de S....**Clarence I. de Sola,**
President of the Federation of Canadian Zionists; Belgian Consul, Montreal, Canada.

C. J. F.......**Charles J. Freund,**
Rabbi, Congregation B'nai Israel, Salt Lake City, Utah.

C. L..........**Caspar Levias, M.A.,**
Formerly Instructor in Exegesis and Talmudic Aramaic, Hebrew Union College, Cincinnati, Ohio.

D.............**Gotthard Deutsch, Ph.D.,**
Professor of Jewish History, Hebrew Union College, Cincinnati, Ohio.

D. P..........**David Philipson, D.D.,**
Rabbi, B'ne Israel Congregation; Professor of Homiletics, Hebrew Union College, Cincinnati, Ohio.

E. A. V......**Ernest A. Vizetelly,**
Author of "Emile Zola, Novelist and Reformer"; London, England.

E. C..........**Executive Committee of the Editorial Board.**

E. Co........**Ernst Cohn,**
Berlin University, Berlin, Germany.

E. G. H......**Emil G. Hirsch, Ph.D., LL.D.,**
Rabbi, Sinai Congregation; Professor of Rabbinical Literature and Philosophy, University of Chicago; Chicago, Ill.

E. K..........**Eduard König, Ph.D., LL.D.,**
Professor of Old Testament Exegesis, University of Bonn, Germany.

E. L.........**Eude Lolli** (*deceased*),
Late Chief Rabbi; Professor of Hebrew at the University of Padua, Italy.

E. Me........**Eduard Meyer, Ph.D.,**
Professor of Ancient History, University of Berlin, Germany.

E. Ms........**E. Mels,**
New York City.

E. N.........**Eduard Neumann, Ph.D.,**
Chief Rabbi, Nagy-Kanizsa, Hungary.

E. O. A. M..**E. O. Adelbert Marx, Ph.D.,**
Professor, Heidelberg, Germany.

E. Sc........**Emil Schlesinger, Ph.D.,**
Rabbi, St. Gallen, Switzerland.

F. C..........**Frank Cramer, B.Sc.,**
New York City.

F. C. C......**Frederick C. Conybeare, M.A.,**
Late Fellow of University College, Oxford, England.

F. H. V......**Frank H. Vizetelly, F.S.A.,**
Associate Editor of the STANDARD DICTIONARY; author of "The Preparation of Manuscripts for the Printer," New York City.

F. L. C.....**Francis L. Cohen,**
Chief Minister, Sydney, N. S. W., Australia.

F. N. L......**Florence N. Levy,**
New York City.

F. S. W......**Franklin S. Wilson, M.A.,**
New York City.

F. T. H......**Frederick T. Haneman, M.D.,**
Brooklyn, N. Y.

G.............**Richard Gottheil, Ph.D.,**
Professor of Semitic Languages, Columbia University, New York; Chief of the Oriental Department, New York Public Library; New York City.

G. A. B......**George A. Barton, Ph.D.,**
Professor of Biblical Literature and Semitic Languages, Bryn Mawr College, Bryn Mawr, Pa.

G. L.........**Goodman Lipkind, B.A.,**
Rabbi, New York City.

G. Se........**G. Selikovitch,**
Journalist, New York City.

H. B.........**H. Brody, Ph.D.,**
Rabbi; Coeditor of the "Zeitschrift für Hebräische Bibliographie"; Nachod, Bohemia, Austria.

H. C.........**Henry Cohen,**
Rabbi B'nai Israel Congregation, Galveston, Tex.

H. F.........**Herbert Friedenwald, Ph.D.,**
Formerly Superintendent of the Department of Manuscripts, Library of Congress, Washington, D. C.; Recording Secretary of the American Jewish Historical Society; Philadelphia, Pa.

H. L.........**Harry Levi,**
Wheeling, W. Va.

H. L. R.......**Harry L. Rosenthal,**
Ardwick, Manchester, England.

H. M.......**Henry Malter, Ph.D.,**
Professor of Talmud and Instructor in Judæo-Arabic Philosophy, Hebrew Union College, Cincinnati, Ohio.

H. Ma......**Hillel Malachowsky,**
Teacher, New York City.

H. R.........**Herman Rosenthal,**
Chief of the Slavonic Department of the New York Public Library, New York City.

H. S.........**Henrietta Szold,**
Secretary of the Publication Committee of the Jewish Publication Society of America, New York City.

I. A. H......**Isaac A. Hourwich, Ph.D.,**
Expert Special Agent of the Bureau of the Census, Department of Commerce and Labor, Washington, D. C.

I. Be........**Immanuel Benzinger, Ph.D.,**
Professor of Old Testament Exegesis, University of Berlin, Germany; Jerusalem, Palestine.

I. Br........**Isaac Broydé** (*Office Editor*),
Doctor of the University of Paris, France; formerly Librarian of the Alliance Israélite Universelle, Paris, France; New York City.

I. Gi........**Ignatio Guidi,**
Professor of Hebrew Language and Comparative Semitic Philology, University of Rome, Italy.

I. H.........**Isidore Harris, A.M.,**
Rabbi, West London Synagogue, London, England.

I. K.........**Isidor Kahan,**
Rabbi, Znaim, Moravia, Austria.

I. L. B.......**I. L. Bril,**
Associate Editor of the "American Hebrew"; New York City.

I. Lév.......**Isaac Lévy,**
Chief Rabbi, Bordeaux, France.

I. Lö........**Immanuel Löw, Ph.D.,**
Chief Rabbi, Budapest, Hungary.

I. M. C.......**I. M. Casanowicz, Ph.D.,**
United States National Museum, Washington, D. C.

I. M. P......**Ira Maurice Price, Ph.D., LL.D.,**
Professor of Semitic Languages and Literature, University of Chicago, Chicago, Ill.

I. R..........**I. Rosenberg, Ph.D.,**
Thorn, Prussia.

I. Sa........**I. Sachs,**
Paris, France.

I. Sc........**Ignaz Schipper, Ph.D.,**
Szczakowa, Galicia, Austria.

J...........**Joseph Jacobs, B.A.,**
Formerly President of the Jewish Historical Society of England; Corresponding Member of the Royal Academy of History, Madrid; New York City.

J. D. E......**Judah David Eisenstein,**
Author, New York City.

J. de H......**J. de Haas,**
Journalist, New York City.

J. D. P.......**John Dyneley Prince, Ph.D.,**
Professor of Semitic Languages, Columbia University, New York.

J. F. McL...**J. F. McLaughlin, M.A., B.D.,**
Professor of Oriental Languages and Literature, Victoria College, Toronto, Canada.

J. G. L........**J. G. Lipman, Ph.D.,**
Assistant Agriculturist, New Jersey State Experiment Station, New Brunswick, N. J.

J. Go.........**Julius Gottlieb, M.A., Ph.D.,**
New York City.

J. Hy........**J. Hyams,**
Bombay, India.

J. Ka........**Jacques Kahn,**
Rabbi, Paris, France.

J. Leb........**Joseph Lebovich,**
Harvard University, Cambridge, Mass.

J. Si..........**Jakob Singer,**
Rabbi, Temesvar, Hungary.

J. So..........**Joseph Sohn,**
Musical Critic on the "American and Journal," New York City.

J. Z. L.......**Jacob Zallel Lauterbach, Ph.D.** (*Office Editor*).
Rabbi, Cong. Agudat Achim, Peoria, Ill.

K.............**Kaufmann Kohler, Ph D.,**
Rabbi Emeritus of Temple Beth-El, New York; President of the Hebrew Union College, Cincinnati, Ohio.

L. B...........**Ludwig Blau, Ph.D.,**
Professor, Jewish Theological Seminary; Editor of "Magyar Zsidó Szemle"; Budapest, Hungary.

L. G...........**Louis Ginzberg, Ph.D.,**
Professor of Talmud, Jewish Theological Seminary of America, New York City.

L. Grü.......**Lazarus Grünhut,**
Director of Orphan Asylum, Jerusalem, Palestine.

L. H. G......**Louis H. Gray, Ph.D.,**
Assistant Editor of the "Orientalische Bibliographie" and "The New International Encyclopedia"; Newark, N. J.

L. Hü.......**L. Hühner, A.M., LL.B.,**
Counselor at Law, New York City.

L. K........**Lesser Knoller, Ph.D.,**
Rabbi; Principal of the Bildungsanstalt für Jüdische Lehrer; Hanover, Germany.

L. La........**Laura Landau,**
New York City.

L. Lew......**Louis Lewin, Ph.D.,**
Rabbi, Pinne, Posen, Germany.

L. Loe......**Louis Loewenstein,**
Troy, N. Y.

L. N. D......**Lewis N. Dembitz, D.H.L.,**
Counselor at Law, Louisville, Ky.

L. N. Le.....**Lilian N. Levy,**
New York City.

L. R..........**Louis Roth,**
New York City.

L. V..........**Ludwig Venetianer, Ph.D.,**
Rabbi, Ujpest, Hungary.

L. Wi.......**Leo Wise,**
Editor of the "American Israelite," Cincinnati, Ohio.

M. B.........**Moses Beer,**
Berlin, Germany.

M. C.........**M. Caimi,**
Corfu, Greece.

M. Fi........**Maurice Fishberg, M.D.,**
Surgeon to the Beth Israel Hospital Dispensary; Medical Examiner to the United States Hebrew Charities, New York City.

M. Fr........**M. Franco,**
Principal, Alliance Israélite Universelle School, Gallipoli, Turkey.

M. H. H.....**M. H. Harris, Ph.D.,**
Rabbi, Temple Israel of Harlem, New York City.

M. K........**Meyer Kayserling, Ph.D.** (*deceased*),
Late Rabbi, Budapest, Hungary.

M. L. B......**Moses Löb Bamberger, Ph.D.,**
Rabbi; Lecturer on Rabbinics, Jewish Seminary, Würzburg, Bavaria, Germany.

M. L. M.....**Max L. Margolis, Ph.D.,**
Professor of Biblical Exegesis, Hebrew Union College, Cincinnati, Ohio.

M. L. S......**M. L. Stern, Ph.D.,**
Rabbi, Triesch, Moravia, Austria.

M. Lw.......**M. Lewin, Ph.D.,**
Rabbi, Wreschen, Posen, Germany.

M. R........**Max Rosenthal, M.D.,**
Visiting Physician, German Dispensary, New York City.

M. Ri........**M. Richtmann, Ph.D.,**
Budapest, Hungary.

M. Sa........**Max Samfield, Ph.D.,**
Rabbi, Children of Israel Congregation; Editor of the "Jewish Spectator," Memphis, Tenn.

M. Sal.......**Marcus Salzman,**
Wilkesbarre, Pa.

M. Sc........**Max Schloessinger, Ph.D.,**
Librarian and Lecturer on Biblical Exegesis, Hebrew Union College, Cincinnati, Ohio.

M. Sel......**Max Seligsohn** (*Office Editor*),
Doctor of the University of Paris, France; New York City.

M. Si.......**Moritz Silberstein, Ph.D.,**
Rabbi, Wiesbaden, Nassau, Germany.

M. W. M....**Mary W. Montgomery, Ph.D.,**
New York City.

M. Z........**M. Zametkin,**
New York City.

N. D........**Newell Dunbar, B.D.,**
Author, Newark, N. J.

N. E. B. E...**N. E. B. Ezra,**
Shanghai, China.

N. Sl........**N. Slouschz,**
Doctor of the University of Paris, France; Lecturer on Neo-Hebraic Literature, University of Paris, France.

N. T. L......**N. T. London,**
New York City.

P. S. M......**Percival S. Menken,**
New York City.

P. Wi.......**Peter Wiernik,**
Journalist, New York City.

R. N........**Regina Neisser,**
Author, Breslau, Silesia, Germany.

S..............**Isidore Singer, Ph.D.,**
MANAGING EDITOR, New York City.

S. Hu........**S. Hurwitz,**
New York City.

S. J..........**S. Janovsky,**
Counselor at Law, St. Petersburg, Russia.

S. K..........**S. Kahn,**
Rabbi, Nîmes, France.

S. Kr........**Samuel Krauss, Ph.D.,**
Professor, Normal College, Budapest, Hungary.

S. Led......**Sampson Lederhändler,**
New York City.

S. Man......**S. Mannheimer, B.L.,**
Instructor, Hebrew Union College, Cincinnati, Ohio.

S. O.........**Schulim Ochser, Ph.D.** (*Office Editor*),
Rabbi, New York City.

S. Sa........**Siegmund Salfeld, Ph.D.,**
Rabbi, Mayence, Hesse, Germany.

S. S. W.....**Stephen S. Wise, Ph.D.,**
Rabbi, Temple Beth Israel, Portland, Ore.

S. We.......**Samuel Wessel, Ph.D.,**
Rabbi, Sarajevo, Bosnia.

T.............**Crawford Howell Toy, D.D., LL.D.,**
Professor of Hebrew, Harvard University, Cambridge, Mass.

T. F. J.......**T. F. Joseph,**
Rabbi, Temple de Hirsch, Seattle, Washington.

T. K........**Theodor Kroner, Ph.D.,**
Rabbi, Stuttgart, Württemberg, Germany.

T. L.........**Theodor Lieben, Ph.D.,**
Secretary of the Israelitische Kultusgemeinde, Vienna, Austria.

U. C.........**Umberto Cassuto,**
Editor of "La Rivista Israelitica," Florence, Italy.

V. C.........**Vittore Castiglione,**
Chief Rabbi, Rome, Italy.

V. E.........**Victor Rousseau Emanuel,**
New York City.

V. R.........**Vasili Rosenthal,**
Krementchug, Russia.

W. B.........**Wilhelm Bacher, Ph.D.,**
Professor, Jewish Theological Seminary, Budapest, Hungary.

W. M.-A....**W. Muss-Arnolt, Ph.D.,**
Assistant Professor of Biblical Philology, University of Chicago, Chicago, Ill.

W. M. M....**W. Max Muller, Ph.D.,**
Professor of Bible Exegesis, Reformed Episcopal Theological Seminary, Philadelphia, Pa.

W. N........**Wilhelm Nowack, Ph.D.,**
Professor of Old Testament Exegesis, University of Strasburg, Germany.

W. Sa........**W. Salzberger, Ph.D.,**
Erfurt, Germany.

LIST OF ILLUSTRATIONS IN VOLUME XII.

N. B.—In the following list subjects likely to be sought for under various headings are repeated under each heading. Cross-references in this list are to other items in the list, not to articles in the Encyclopedia.

TIKTIN, ABRAHAM	WEIL, GUSTAV	WISSOTZKI, KALONYMOS
TOURO, JUDAH	WEIL, HENRY	WOLF, JOHANN CHRISTOPH
VALABRÈGUE, MARDOCHÉE-GEORGES	WEISS, ISAAC HIRSCH	WOLF, SIMON
VAMBÉRY, ARMINIUS	WERTHEIMER, JOSEPH	ZANGWILL, ISRAEL
VAN OVEN, JOSHUA	WESSELY, NAPHTALI HIRZ	ZUNZ, LEOPOLD
WAHRMAN, MORITZ	WISE, ISAAC MAYER	

THE

JEWISH ENCYCLOPEDIA

TALMUD (תלמוד): Name of two works which have been preserved to posterity as the product of the Palestinian and Babylonian schools during the amoraic period, which extended from the third to the fifth century C.E. One of these compilations is entitled "Talmud Yerushalmi" (Jerusalem Talmud) and the other "Talmud Babli" (Babylonian Talmud). Used alone, the word "Talmud" generally denotes "Talmud Babli," but it frequently serves as a generic designation for an entire body of literature, since the Talmud marks the culmination of the writings of Jewish tradition, of which it is, from a historical point of view, the most important production.

"Talmud" is an old scholastic term of the Tannaim, and is a noun formed from the verb "limmed" = "to teach." It therefore means primarily

The Name. "teaching," although it denotes also "learning"; it is employed in this latter sense with special reference to the Torah, the terms "talmud" and "Torah" being usually combined to indicate the study of the Law both in its wider and in its more restricted sense, as in Pe'ah i. 1, where the term "talmud Torah" is applied to study as a religious duty. On the other hand, the learning acquired by study is also called "talmud," so that Akiba's pupil Judah ben Ilai could say: "He from whom one derives the greater part of his knowledge ["talmudo"] must be regarded as the teacher" (Tosef., B. M. ii., end; Yer. B. M. 8d; B. M. 33a has "ḥokmah" instead of "talmud"). To designate the study of religion, the word "talmud" is used in contrast with "ma'aseh," which connotes the practise of religion. Akiba's view that on this account the "talmud" ranked above the "ma'aseh" was adopted as a resolution by a famous conference at Lydda during the Hadrianic persecution (see Sifre, Deut. 41; Ḳid. 40b; Yer. Pes. 30b; Cant. R. ii. 14). The two terms are contrasted differently, however, in the tannaitic saying (B. B. 130b), "The Halakah [the principles guiding decisions in religious law] may not be drawn from a teaching of the master ["talmud"] nor be based upon an act of his ["ma'aseh"], unless the master expressly declare that the teaching or act under consideration is the one which is applicable to the practise."

In the second place, the word "talmud"—generally in the phrase "talmud lomar"—is frequently used in tannaitic terminology in order to denote instruction by means of the text of the Bible and of the exegetic deductions therefrom. In the third place, the noun "talmud" has the meaning which

alone can be genetically connected with the name "Talmud"; in tannaitic phraseology the verb "limmed" denotes the exegetic deduction of a halakic principle from the Biblical text (for examples see R. H. ii. 9; Sifre, Num. 118); and in harmony with this meaning of the word "talmud" denotes that exposition of a halakic saying which receives an exegetic confirmation from the Biblical text. Of the terms, therefore, denoting the three branches into which the study of the traditional exegesis of the Bible was from earliest times divided by the Tannaim (see JEW. ENCYC. iii. 163, s.v. BIBLE EXEGESIS), "midrash" was the one identical in content with "talmud" in its original sense, except that the Midrash, which includes any kind of Biblical hermeneutics, but more especially the halakic, deals with the Bible text itself, while the Talmud is based on the Halakah. The Midrash is devoted to Biblical exposition, the result being the Halakah (comp. the phrase "mi-kan ameru" [= "beginning here the sages have said"], which occurs frequently in the tannaitic Midrash and which serves to introduce halakic deductions from the exegesis). In the Talmud, on the other hand, the halakic passage is the subject of an exegesis based on the Biblical text.

In consequence of the original identity of "Talmud" and "Midrash," noted above, the former term is sometimes used instead of the latter in tannaitic

Relation to Midrash. sentences which enumerate the three branches of traditional science, Midrash, Halakah, and Haggadah (see Ber. 22a [comp. M. Ḳ. 15a and Yer. Ber. 6c, 39]; Ḳid. 30a; Suk. 28a; B. B. 134a; Ab. R. N. xiv. [comp. Masseket Soferim, xvi. 8]; Yer. B. Ḳ. 4b, 31 [comp. Sifre, Deut. 33]; Tosef., Soṭah, vii. 20 [comp. Yer. Soṭah 44a]), while sometimes both "Talmud" and "Midrash" are used (M. Ḳ. 21a; Ta'an. 30a); it must be noted, however, that in the editions of the Babli, "Gemara" is usually substituted for "Talmud," even in the passages here cited. The word "Talmud" in all these places did not denote the study subsequently pursued by the Amoraim, but was used instead of the word "Midrash," although this did not preclude the later introduction of the term "Talmud" into tannaitic sayings, where it either entirely displaced "Midrash" or was used side by side with it.

After the term "Talmud" had come to denote the exegetic confirmation of the Halakah, it was applied also to the explanation and exposition of halakic passages in general. As early as the end of the tannaitic period, when the halakot were finally redacted by the patriarch Judah I. and were designated as "Mishnah," a term originally applied to the entire system of traditional learning, the Talmud was developed as a new division of this same science; and it was destined to absorb all others. In a baraita dating, according to the amora Johanan, from the days of Judah I. (B. M. 33a; comp. Yer. Shab. 15c, 22 *et seq.*), the Mishnah and the Talmud are defined as subjects of study side by side with the "Miḳra" (Bible), the study of the Talmud being mentioned first. To this baraita there is an addition, however, to the effect that more attention should be given to the Mishnah than to the Talmud. Johanan explains this passage by the fact that the members of Judah's academy, in their eagerness to investigate the Talmud, neglected the Mishnah; hence the patriarch laid stress upon the duty of studying the Mishnah primarily. In these passages the word "Talmud" is used not in its more restricted sense of the establishment of halakot by Biblical exegesis, but in its wider signification, in which it designates study for the purpose of elucidating the Mishnah in general, as pursued after Judah's death in the academies of Palestine and Babylon. This baraita is, furthermore, an authentic document on the origin of the Talmud.

Three classes of members of the academy are mentioned in an anecdote referring to Judah I. (B. B. 8a): (1) those who devoted themselves chiefly to the Bible ("ba'ale Miḳra"); (2) those whose principal study was the Mishnah ("ba'ale Mishnah"); and (3) those whose main interest lay in the Talmud ("ba'ale Talmud"). This is the original reading of the passage, although the editions mention also the "ba'ale Halakah" and the "ba'ale Haggadah" (see below). These three branches of knowledge are, therefore, the same as those enumerated in B. M. 33a. Tanḥum b. Ḥanilai, a Palestinian amora of the third century, declared, with reference to this threefold investigation ('Ab. Zarah 19b): "Let the time given to study be divided into three parts: one-third for the Bible, one-third for the Mishnah, and one-third for the Talmud." In Ḳid. 33a this saying is quoted in the name of the tanna Joshua b. Hananiah, although this is probably a corruption of the name of Jose b. Ḥanina (amora). Yudan, a Palestinian amora of the fourth century, found in Eccl. xi. 9 an allusion to the pleasure taken in the three branches of study, Miḳra, Mishnah, and Talmud.

The old trichotomy of traditional literature was changed, however, by the acceptance of the Mishnah of Judah I., and by the new study of the Talmud designed to interpret it. The division termed "Halakot" (singular, "Halakah") in the old classification was then called "Mishnah," although in Palestine the Mishnah continued to be designated as "Halakot." The Midrash became a component part of the Talmud; and a considerable portion of the halakic Bible hermeneutics of the Tannaim, which had been preserved in various special works, was incorporated in the Babylonian Talmud. The Haggadah (plural, "Haggadot") lost its importance as an individual branch of study in the academies, although it naturally continued to be a subject of investigation, and a portion of it also was included in

The Three Subjects of Study.

the Talmud. Occasionally the Haggadah is even designated as a special branch, being added as a fourth division to the three already mentioned. Ḥanina ben Pappa, an amora of the early part of the fourth century, in characterizing these four branches says: "The countenance should be serious and earnest in teaching the Scriptures, mild and calm for the Mishnah, bright and lively for the Talmud, and merry and smiling for the Haggadah" (Pesiḳ. 110a; Pes. R. 101b; Tan., Yitro, ed. Buber, p. 17; Massek. Soferim, xvi. 2). As early as the third century Joshua ben Levi interpreted Deut. ix. 10 to mean that the entire Law, including Miḳra, Mishnah, Talmud, and Haggadah, had been revealed to Moses on Sinai (Yer. Pes. 17a, line 59; Meg. 74d, 25), while in Gen. R. lxvi. 3 the blessings invoked in Gen. xxvii. 28 are explained as "Miḳra, Mishnah, Talmud, and Haggadah." The Palestinian haggadist Isaac divided these four branches into two groups: (1) the Miḳra and the Haggadah, dealing with subjects of general interest; and (2) the Mishnah and the Talmud, "which can not hold the attention of those who hear them" (Pesiḳ. 101b; see Bacher, "Ag. Pal. Amor." ii. 211).

According to a note of Tanḥuma ben Abba (of the latter part of the 4th cent.) on Cant. v. 14 (Cant. R. *ad loc.*), a student must be familiar with all four branches of knowledge, Miḳra, Mishnah, Halakah (the last-named term used here instead of "Talmud"), and Haggadah; while Samuel b. Judah b. Abun, a Palestinian amora of the same century, interpreted Prov. xxviii. 11 as an allusion to the halakist ("man of the Talmud") and to the haggadist ("man of the Haggadah"; Yer. Hor. 48c; see also Pesiḳ. 176a; Lev. R. xxi., Talmud and Haggadah). Here may be mentioned also the concluding passage of the mishnaic treatise Abot (v., end): "At the age of five to the Bible; at the age of ten to the Mishnah; at the age of fifteen to the Talmud." This is ascribed by many to the ancient tanna Samuel ha-Ḳaṭon (see Bacher, "Ag. Tan." i. 378), although the sequence of study which it mentions is evidently that which was customary during the amoraic period (comp. also the saying of Abaye in Ket. 50a).

The following passages from the Babylonian Talmud may likewise serve to illustrate the special usage which finally made the word "Talmud" current as the name of the work. Samuel, one of the earliest Babylonian amoraim, interpreted the words of Zech. viii. 10, "neither was there any peace to him that went out or came in," as applying to the restlessness of one who turns from the Talmud and confines himself to the study of the Mishnah (Ḥag. 10a). Johanan, the younger Palestinian contemporary of Samuel, extends the allusion to "him also who turns from one Talmud to study another," referring here to Babli and to Yerushalmi. It is very possible that he had noticed that in the case of his numerous Babylonian pupils the transition from the mishnaic exegesis which they had acquired at home to that of the Palestinian schools was not made without disturbing their peace of mind. Allusions to the "Talmud of Babylon" by two prominent Babylonians who settled in Palestine (Ze'era and Jeremiah) have likewise been preserved (B. M. 85c; Sanh. 24a); and they confirm Johanan's conception of the meaning of the term.

In Babylonia the Aramaic noun " gemar " (emphatic state, " gemara ") was formed from the verb גמר (which does not occur in Palestinian texts), having the meaning of "learn." This substantive accord-

The Gemara. ingly designates that which has been learned, and the learning transmitted to scholars by tradition, although it is used also in a more restricted sense to connote the traditional exposition of the Mishnah; and it therefore gained currency as a designation of the Talmud. In the modern editions of the Babylonian Talmud the term "Gemara " occurs very frequently in this sense; but in nearly every case it was substituted at a later time for the objectionable word "Talmud," which was interdicted by the censor. The only passage in which "Gemara " occurs with the meaning of "Talmud " in the strict sense of that term and from which it was not removed by the censor is 'Er. 32b, where it is used by Naḥman bar Jacob, a Babylonian amora of the second half of the third century. For further details see Bacher, " Gemara," in " Hebrew Union College Annual," pp. 26–36, Cincinnati, 1904, where the word is shown to have been used for "Talmud " from the geonic period (see also *idem*, " Die Terminologie der Amoräer," pp. 31 *et seq.*, Leipsic, 1905). The later editions of the Talmud frequently substitute for the word " Gemara " the abbreviation ש״ס (Aramaic, שתא סדרי = "the six orders of the Mishnah "), which has come to be, with the pronunciation "Shas," a popular designation for the Babylonian Talmud.

Here may be mentioned the term "Shem'ata " (שמעתא), which was used in Babylonia to designate the halakic portion of the Talmud, and which was thus contrasted with "Haggadah " (see Ḥag. 26a; Soṭah 20a; Sanh. 38b; comp. also M. Ḳ. 23a, where "Shemu'ah," the Hebrew form, occurs in a baraita). In the tenth century this word was used in Mohammedan circles to designate Jewish tradition as well as its chief source, the Talmud; so that Mas'udi refers to Saadia Gaon as an "ashma'ti " (*i.e.*, a believer in the tradition), using this term in contrast to "Karaite " (see Pinsker, " Liḳḳuṭe Ḳadmoniyyot," i. 5). A " Kitab al-Ashma'ah " (*i.e.*, " Talmud ") is also mentioned (" Z. D. M. G." lviii. 659).

The theorem that the Talmud was the latest development of traditional science has been demonstrated by this discussion of the meaning and the use of the word itself. The Talmud accordingly dates from the time following the final redaction of the Mishnah; and it was taught in the academy of Judah I. as the commentary on the tannaitic Halakah. The editorial activity which, from the mass of halakic material that had accumulated since Akiba's Mishnah, crystallized the Talmud in accordance with the systematic order introduced by that teacher, implied the interpretation and critical examination of the Halakah, and was, therefore, analogous to Talmudic methodology.

There were, likewise, many elements of tannaitic tradition, especially the midrashic exegesis of the Bible, as well as numerous halakic interpretations, lexicographical and material, which were ready for incorporation into the Talmud in its more re-

stricted meaning of the interpretation of the Mishnah of Judah I. When this Mishnah became the standard halakic work, both as a source for decisions of questions of religious law, and, even more especially, as a subject of study in the academies, the Talmud interpretation of the mishnaic text, both in theory and in practise, naturally became the most important branch of study, and included the other branches of traditional science, being derived from the Halakah and the Midrash (halakic exegesis), and also including haggadic material, though to a minor degree. The Talmud, however, was not an independent work; and it was this characteristic which constituted the chief difference between it and the earlier subjects of study of the tannaitic period. It had no form of its own, since it served as a running commentary on the mishnaic text; and this fact determined the character which the work ultimately assumed.

The Talmud is practically a mere amplification of the Mishnah by manifold comments and additions; so that even those portions of the Mishnah which

Relation to Mishnah. have no Talmud are regarded as component parts of it and are accordingly included in the editions of Babli. The history of the origin of the Talmud is the same as that of the Mishnah—a tradition, transmitted orally for centuries, was finally cast into definite literary form, although from the moment in which the Talmud became the chief subject of study in the academies it had a double existence, and was accordingly, in its final stage, redacted in two different forms. The Mishnah of Judah I. was adopted simultaneously in Babylon and Palestine as the halakic collection par excellence; and at the same time the development of the Talmud was begun both at Sepphoris, where the Mishnah was redacted, and at Nehardea and Sura, where Judah's pupils Samuel and Rab engaged in their epoch-making work. The academies of Babylon and of Palestine alike regarded the study of the Mishnah and its interpretation as their chief task. The Amoraim, as the directors and members of these academies were called (see AMORA), became the originators of the Talmud; and its final redaction marked the end of the amoraic times in the same way that the period of the Tannaim was concluded by the compilation of the Mishnah of Judah I. Like the Mishnah, the Talmud was not the work of one author or of several authors, but was the result of the collective labors of many successive generations, whose toil finally resulted in a book unique in its mode of development.

Before entering into any discussion of the origin and peculiar form of the Talmud, the two recensions of the work itself may be briefly described. The general designation of the Palestinian Talmud as " Talmud Yerushalmi," or simply as " Yerushalmi," is precisely analogous to that of the Palestinian Targum. The term originated in the geonic period, when, however, the work received also the more precise designations of " Talmud of Palestine," " Talmud of the Land of Israel," " Talmud of the West," and " Talmud of the Western Lands." Yerushalmi has not been preserved in its entirety; large portions of it were entirely lost at an early date, while other parts exist only in fragments. The editio princeps (ed. Bomberg, Venice, 1523 *et seq.*), on which all later editions are based, terminates with the following remark: "Thus far we have found what is contained in this Talmud; and we have endeavored in vain to obtain the missing portions." Of the four manuscripts used for this first edition (comp. the note at the conclusion of Shab. xx. 17d and the passage just cited), only one is now in existence; it is preserved in the library of the University of Leyden (see below). Of the six orders of the Mishnah, the fifth, Ḳodashim, is missing entirely from the Palestinian Talmud, while of the sixth, Ṭohorot, it

The Palestinian Talmud. contains only the first three chapters of the treatise Niddah (iv. 48d–51b). The treatises of the orders of the Mishnah are arranged in the following sequence in this Talmud; the pagination also is given here, in parentheses, to indicate the length of the several treatises:

the treatise Niddah ends abruptly after the first lines of ch. iv.

Maimonides expressly states in the introduction to his commentary on the Mishnah that in his time Yerushalmi was extant for the entire first five orders (comp. Abraham ibn Daud, ed. Neubauer, "M. J. C." i. 57); therefore he must have seen the Yerushalmi of the order Ḳodashim, although he himself does not quote it in his commentary on this order (see Frankel, "Mebo," p. 45b). Except for the treatise Niddah, on the other hand, there was, according to Maimonides (*l.c.*), no Yerushalmi for the sixth order. A South-Arabian work of the fifteenth century, however, quotes the Gemara "on 'Uḳzin in the Gemara of the people of Jerusalem," which is said to contain a passage on the zodiac (see Steinschneider, "Catalog der Hebräischen Handschriften der Königlichen Bibliothek zu Berlin," p. 65, Berlin, 1878). The author of this quotation, therefore, knew Yerushalmi for the last treatise of the sixth order,

PAGES FROM A MANUSCRIPT OF THE JERUSALEM TALMUD.
(From the Cairo Genizah.)

I. **Zera'im:** Berakot (2a–14d); Pe'ah (15a–21b); Demai (21c–26c); Ki'layim (26d–32d); Shebi'it (33a–39d); Terumot (40a–48b); Ma'aserot (48c–52a); Ma'aser Sheni (52b–56d); Ḥallah (57a–60b); 'Orlah (60c–63b); Bikkurim (63c–65d).

II. **Mo'ed:** Shabbat (2a–18a); 'Erubin (18a–26d); Pesaḥim (27a–37d); Yoma (38a–45c); Sheḳalim (45c–51b); Sukkah (51c–55d); Rosh ha-Shanah (56a–59d); Beẓah (59d–63b); Ta'anit (63c–69c); Megillah (69d–75d); Ḥagigah (75d–79d); Mo'ed Ḳaṭan (80a–83d).

III. **Nashim:** Yebamot (2a–15a); Soṭah (15a–24c); Ketubot (24c–36b); Nedarim (36c–42d); Gittin (43a–50d); Nazir (51a–58a); Ḳiddushin (58a–66d).

IV. **Nezikin:** Baba Ḳamma (2a–7c); Baba Meẓi'a (7c–12c); Baba Batra (12d–17d); Sanhedrin (17d–30c); Makkot (30d–32b); Shebu'ot (32c–38d); 'Abodah Zarah (39a–45b); Horayot (45c–48c).

VI. **Ṭohorot:** Niddah (48d–51b).

In order ii. the last four chapters of Shabbat are missing from the Palestinian Talmud, while the treatise Sheḳalim has been incorporated into the editions of the Babylonian Talmud from Yerushalmi, and is found also in a Munich manuscript of Babli. In order iv. the treatises Abot and 'Eduyot are missing in both Talmudim, and the concluding chapter of Makkot is wanting in Yerushalmi. In order vi.

although it is possible that the passage quoted may have been in the lost portion of the treatise Niddah, and that the name "'Uḳzin" may have been used instead of "Ṭohorot." For further details on the missing sections of Yerushalmi see Frankel, *l.c.* pp. 45a *et seq.*; Weiss, "Dor," iii. 232; Buber, in Berliner's "Magazin," v. 100–105; and Strack, "Einleitung in den Talmud," pp. 63–65. The mishnaic text on which the Palestinian Talmud is based has been preserved in its entirety in a manuscript belonging to the library of the University of Cambridge, and has been edited by W. H. Lowe ("The Mishnah on Which the Palestinian Talmud Rests," Cambridge, 1883).

The Palestinian Talmud is so arranged in the editions that each chapter is preceded by its entire mishnaic text with the paragraphs numbered, this being followed by the Talmud on the several paragraphs. In the first seven chapters of Berakot the paragraphs are designated as "First Mishnah" (מתני' א), "Second Mishnah," etc.; while in the remaining chapters and all the other treatises the paragraphs are termed "halakot" (א הלכה). In the early chapters the mishnaic text of each paragraph is repeated entire in the Talmud at the beginning of the paragraph; but later only the first words are prefaced to the Talmudic text. Even in cases where there is no Talmud the designation of the paragraph and the beginning of the mishnaic text are given. The editio princeps seems to have borrowed this arrangement from the manuscripts, although the system is much more simple in the fragment of Yerushalmi edited by Paul von Kokowzoff in the "Mémoires de la Société Archéologique de St. Petersbourg" (xi. 195-205), which contains some paragraphs of the sixth and eighth chapters of Baba Ḳamma. This fragment begins with the concluding lines of the Talmudic text of ch. v.; but between them and the beginning of ch. vi. the Mishnah is lacking, so that the superscription, "Chapter vi.," is followed immediately by the Talmudic text. There is no reference to the beginning of the paragraph, either in the first or in the succeeding paragraphs; nor is there any explanation of the fact that paragraphs 4 and 7 of ch. viii. have no Talmud. It is clear, therefore, that the manuscript to which this fragment belonged contained only the Talmudic text, thus presupposing the use of a special copy of the Mishnah. It is likewise noteworthy that in the first two chapters of Berakot the sections of the Talmudic text on some of the paragraphs are designated in the editions by the word "piska" (section),

The Style of the Ye- rushalmi. a term found occasionally also in other portions of the text of Yerushalmi. The style of Yerushalmi may be indicated by a brief analysis of a few sections, such as Ber. i. 1; R. H. i. 1, 2; Giṭ. ii. 1; and B. B. i. 6.

Ber. i. 1: The text of this paragraph, which begins the Mishnah, is as follows:

"During what time in the evening is the reading of the 'Shema'' begun? From the time when the priests go in to eat their leaven [see Lev. xxii. 7] until the end of the first watch of the night, such being the words of R. Eliezer. The sages, however, say until midnight, though R. Gamaliel says until the coming of the dawn."

The Talmud on this paragraph (2a, line 34-3a, line 3) contains three sections, which correspond to the three opinions and the contents of which are as follows: (1) A citation, from a baraita, of another tannaitic regulation defining the Mishnah that governs the reading of the "Shema'" in the evening; two sayings of Jose (a Palestinian amora of the 4th cent.), serving to elucidate the baraita (2a, 34-45). Remarks on the position of one who is in doubt whether he has read the "Shema'," with analogous cases, according to Jeremiah, whose views were transmitted by Ze'era II. (4th cent.), the first case being decided according to the baraita already mentioned (2a, 45-2b, 4). Another passage from the baraita, designating the appearance of the stars as an indication of the time in question; explanation of this baraita by Abba bar Pappai (transmitter, Phinehas; both of the 4th cent.); other passages on the appearance of the stars as bearing on the ritual, together with a dialectic explanation by Jose b. Abin (second half of the 4th cent.) and a saying by

Judah b. Pazzi (2b, 5-31). A baraita on the division between day and night, and other passages bearing on the same subject (ib. lines 31-41). The meaning of "ben ha-shemashot" (twilight), and an answer by Tanhuma b. Abba (latter part of the 4th cent.), together with another solution given by a baraita (ib. lines 41-46). Discussion of this baraita by Aḥa and Jose (4th cent.); reference by Mani to a question dealing with this subject which he addressed to Hezekiah of Cæsarea (4th cent.) from Mishnah Zab. i. 6, and the answer of the latter (2b, 46-2c, 9). Amoraic sayings and a baraita on the beginning of the day (ib. lines 9-20). A sentence of tannaitic origin in no way related to the preceding matters: "One who prays standing must hold his feet straight," and the controversy on this subject between Levi and Simon (3d cent.), the one adding, "like the angels," and the other, "like the priests"; comments on these two comparisons (2c, 20-31). Further discussion regarding the beginning of the day, introduced by a saying of Ḥanina's (3d cent.); haggadic statements concerning the dawn; a conversation between Ḥiyya the Elder and Simeon b. Ḥalafta (latter part of the tannaitic period); cosmological comments: dimensions of the firmament, and the cosmic distances expressed in units of 50 and 500 years, together with similar haggadic material, chiefly tannaitic in origin; Haggadic sayings on Gen. i. 6, introduced by a saying of Abin's (4th cent.), and including sayings by Rab, Judah b. Pazzi, and Ḥanina;

Examples. Haggadic material on Isa. xl. 22, introduced by a controversy between Johanan and Simeon b. Laḳish (3d cent.), and on Gen. ii. 4 (2c, 31-2d, 11). On the second part of the first mishnaic sentence; the views of Judah I. and Nathan on the number of the night-watches, and an exegetic discussion of them, with an allusion to Ps. cxix. 62 ("at midnight"), as well as haggadic material concerning David and his harp, with especial reference to Ps. lvii. 9 (2d, 11-44).

(2) Assi in the name of Johanan: "The ruling of the sages ["until midnight"] is the valid one, and forms the basis for the counsel given by Jose [4th cent.] to the members of the academy" (ib. lines 45-48). Baraita on the reading of the "Shema'" in the synagogue; a question bearing on this matter, and Huna's answer in the name of the Babylonian amora Joseph (ib. lines 48-52), an illustration being given in an anecdote regarding Samuel b. Naḥman, together with a haggadic saying by him (ib. lines 52-58). A contradictory view by Joshua b. Levi, together with pertinent haggadic sayings to the effect that the "Shemoneh 'Esreh" must follow immediately the after-benediction of the "Shema'" (ib. lines 59-73).

(3) R. Gamaliel's view compared with an analogous opinion of Simeon b. Yoḥai, together with a question which remains unanswered (2d, 74-3a, 3).

R. H. i. 1, 2: These two paragraphs, which are combined into one in Babli, deal with the commencement of the four seasons (new years): Nisan 1, Elul 1, Tishri 1, and Shebaṭ 1 (or 15). The Talmud on par. 1 is found in 56a, 44-56d, 52, and that on par. 2 in 56d, 52-57a, 30.

Talmud on par. 1: (a) The "new year of the kings." Exegetic deductions and elucidations, beginning with the interpretation of Ex. xii. 1; Johanan's explanation of II Chron. iii. 2; a controversy between Hananiah and Mani regarding the same verse; an explanation by Aḥa of Ex. xii. 1; a baraita by Samuel on the same verse; and similar material (56a, 44–56b, 10). Ḥanina's saying that even the years of Gentile kings were dated from Nisan, and the confirmation thereof by Biblical passages from Haggai and Zechariah, together with the contradictory view of the Babylonian amora 'Efa or Ḥefa; remarks and objections by Jonah and Isaac (56b, 10–29). Jonah on the practical importance of the new year for dating business documents (*ib.* lines 29–33). On the new year in the chronology of the kings of Israel and Judah, together with an interpretation of I Kings ii. 11, and several haggadic passages referring to David (*ib.* lines 33–52).

(*b*) The "new year of the feasts." Statement that according to Simeon b. Yoḥai Nisan 1 marks the beginning of the year for the sequence of the feasts; a tannaitic midrash of considerable length on Lev. xxiii. 38, and a reply by Ela (4th cent.) to a question bearing on this matter; additional remarks and objections by amoraim of the fourth century, together with the citation of a saying by the scholars "of that place" (*i.e.*, Babylonia; 56b, 52–56c, 15); various discussions on kindred subjects, especially those whose content involved halakic exegesis (56c, 15–56d, 14).

(*c*) The "new year for tithes of cattle," declared by Meïr to be Elul 1. Proof by the Babylonian amora Huna, who deduced an opposing view from Ps. lxv. 14; the relation between Ben 'Azzai, who is mentioned in a baraita belonging to this passage, and Akiba (*ib.* lines 14–33); interpretation of Mishnah Bek. vii. 7 as being analogous in content; a citation by Mani of a halakic exegesis by his father, Jonah (*ib.* lines 33–52).

Talmud on par. 2: (*a*) Tishri 1, the "new year for the counting of the years." Deductions from Biblical passages; discussion on the subject between Jonah and the members of the college; Jonah's quotation of Ḥanina's saying on the names of the months, and a saying of Simeon b. Laḳish on the names of the angels (56d, 52–77). (*b*) The "new year for the Sabbatical years and the years of jubilee." Biblical inference (56d, 77–57a, 2). (*c*) The "new year for the planting of trees." Explanation and exegetical deduction (*ib.* lines 3–14). (*d*) The "new year for vegetables." Elucidation and discussion (*ib.* lines 14–23). (*e*) The "new year for trees," this section being supplemented by an example from a tannaitic account of Akiba's practise, with explanations (*ib.* lines 23–30).

Giṭ. ii. 1: Inadequate attestation of the preparation of a bill of divorce. The Talmud on the passage (44a, 34–71); a special case in the Mishnah shown to contain the opinion of Judah b. Ilai (*ib.* lines 34–40); two casuistic questions by Jose and the Babylonian amora Ḥisda, and the **Further** answers furnished by the Mishnah (*ib.* **Examples.** lines 40–50); a more detailed discussion of another question of similar content, with reference to a controversy between Johanan and Simeon b. Laḳish, together with notes thereon by Ammi and Ze'era, and a discus-

sion concluding with a comment by Mani (*ib.* lines 50–71).

B. B. i. 6: (*a*) A short exegetic proof by Ela, based on Prov. xviii. 11 (12d, 71 *et seq.*). (*b*) A baraita dealing with analogous matter, together with a remark by Jose b. Abin (*ib.* lines 72–75).

Although this analysis of the contents of four parts of Yerushalmi gives no adequate idea of the structure of the entire work, it will serve to show the difference between its several parts in regard both to their length and to their amplifications of the simple explanations of the Mishnah. A comparison of the portions of the Palestinian Talmud here summarized with the corresponding sections of Babli, as given below, is especially instructive.

Yerushalmi, when regarded as a work of literature, is noteworthy for a textual peculiarity which is characteristic of it, though found also in Babli, namely, the large number of literal repetitions. Entire passages, sometimes whole columns, of the Talmud are found in two, occasionally in three, separate treatises, in which they differ from each other by mere variants, most of them due to corruptions of the text. These repetitions throw some light on the redaction of the Talmudic text, since they prove that before the editing of the treatises was undertaken a uniform mass of material was already at hand in a definitely revised form; they likewise show that in the compilation of the Talmud one portion was explained by another, as was natural in view of the character of the contents. The opportunity was gladly seized, moreover, to repeat didactic material in passages where it did not **Passages** strictly belong. These repetitions are **Repeated.** obviously of great value in the textual criticism of the Talmud. Since sufficient attention has never yet been paid to this phenomenon of Yerushalmi, a list is here given of those passages of the first order, Zera'im, which are repeated in other orders. It must be noted, however, that this list includes neither citations based on passages of another treatise nor parallel passages consisting of a single sentence.

(*a*) Passages from the order i. repeated in the order ii.:

Ber. 3b, lines 10–55 = Shab. 3a, 69–3b, 20. Ber. 4a, 30–56 = Sheḳ. 47a, 13–59 = M. Ḳ. 83c, 40–83d, 8. Ber. 5a, 33–62 = M. Ḳ. 82b, 14–47. Ber. 5d, 14–20 = Shab. 3a, 55–61. Ber. 5d, 65–6a, 9 = M. Ḳ. 83a, 5–27. Ber. 6c, 4–17 = Yoma 44d, 58–68. Ber. 6d, 60–67 = Meg. 73d, 15–22. Ber. 7b, 70–7d, 25 = Ta'an. 67c, 12–67d, 47. Ber. 7d, 75–8a, 59 = Ta'an. 65c, 2–69. Ber. 8c, 60–69 = R. H. 59d, 16–25. Ber. 9a, 70–9b, 47 = Ta'an. 63c, 66–63d, 44. Ber. 9c, 20–31 = Meg. 75c, 8–19. Ber. 9c, 49–54 = Meg. 75b, 31–36. Ber. 10a, 32–43 = Pes. 29c, 16–27. Ber. 11c, 14–21 = Pes. 37c, 54–71. Ber. 12c, 16–25 = 'Er. 22b, 29–37. Ber. 12c, 44–62 = Suk. 24a, 6–21 = Meg. 72a, 15–31. Ber. 13d, 72–14a, 30 = Ta'an. 64a, 75–64b, 35. Pe'ah 15a, 67–15b, 21 = Ḥag. 76b, 24–53. Pe'ah 17a, 39–72 = Ḥag. 76b, 13–47. Pe'ah 18d, 16–33 = Sheḳ. 46a, 48–67. Pe'ah 18d, 66–19a, 5 = Sheḳ. 48c, 75–48d, 13. Pe'ah 21a, 25–29 = Sheḳ. 48d, 55–58. Dem. 22a, 31–40 = Sheḳ. 48d, 40–49. Kil. 29b, 27–61 = 'Er. 19c, 15–49 = Suk. 52a, 40–73. Kil. 29b, 62–76 = Suk. 52a, 73–52b, 11. Sheb. 34c, 27–49 = M. Ḳ. 80b, 26–52. Sheb. 38a, 50–60 = Shab. 3c, 55–65. Ter. 44a, 32–38 = Shab. 44d, 4–10. Ter. 45d, 42–51 = Shab. 3d, 2–15 (comp. 'Ab. Zarah 41d, 13–28). Ter. 46a, 41–46b, 35 = Pes. 28a, 34–28b, 37. Ma'as. 49a, 22–28 = Suk. 53d, 43–53. Ma'as. 49b, 14–32 = Shab. 6b, 17–36. Ma'as. 49b, 39–48 = Beẓah 62b, 72–62c, 6. Ma'as. Sh. 53b, 6–44 = Yoma 45c, 2–36 (comp. Shebu. 32b, 56–34c, 3). Ma'as. Sh. 54b, 48–58 = Sheḳ. 51b, 15–25. Ma'as. Sh. 55a, 23–55 = 'Er. 24c, 33–66. Ma'as. Sh. 55d, 62–67 = M. Ḳ. 80b, 72–80c, 10. Ḥal. 57c, 16–20 = R. H. 57b, 60–63.

(b) Passages from the order i. repeated in the order iii. :

Ber. 6a, 35–6b, 17 = Naz. 56a, 12–68. Ber. 6b, 51–56 = Ḳid. 61c, 11–17. Ber. 9d, 3–19 = Giṭ. 47b, 49–63. Ber. 11b, 42–68 = Naz. 54b, 2–27. Ber. 14b, 45–70 = Soṭah 20c, 40–64. Pe'ah 15b, 41–47 = Ket. 32c, 10–16. Pe'ah 15c, 7–16 = Ḳid. 61a, 75–61c, 10. Dem. 25b, 60–25c, 7 = Ḳid. 63a, 75–63b, 21. Kil. 32a, 64–32d, 7 = Ket. 34d, 74–35b, 56. Sheb. 36b, 25–68 = Ḳid. 61c, 56–61d, 17. Ter. 40c, 42–40d, 6 = Yeb. 13c, 70–13d, 32. Ter. 42b, 44–53 = Naz. 53d, 16–27. Ter. 44c, 9–44d, 44 = Ket. 27b, 5–27c, 39. Ma'as. Sh. 55a, 69–55b, 13 = Giṭ. 47d, 55–70. 'Orlah 61b, 8–38 = Naz. 55c, 32–63. Bik. 64a, 32–44 = Yeb. 9b, 71–9c, 8.

(c) Passages from the order i. repeated in the order iv. :

Ber. 3a, 52–69 = Sanh. 30a, 65–30b, 8 = 'Ab. Zarah 41c, 46–63. Ber. 6b, 20–41 = Sanh. 20a, 43–60. Pe'ah 16b, 22–25, 43–60 = Sanh. 27c, 38–60. Sheb. 35b, 26–40 = 'Ab. Zarah 44b, 27–41. Sheb. 39b, 14–38 = Mak. 31a, 33–50. Ter. 45c, 24–45d, 11 = 'Ab. Zarah 41a, 18–41b, 3. Ter. 47c, 66–47d, 4 = 'Ab. Zarah 41c, 13–23. Ma'as. Sh. 54d, 71–55a, 8 = Sanh. 19a, 63–76. Ma'as. Sh. 56c, 9–18 = Sanh. 18d, 13–22. 'Orlah 62b, 49–62c, 10 = 'Ab. Zarah 45a, 32–45b, 10.

The following parallel passages from the second and fourth orders may also be mentioned on account of their length: Shab. 9c, 62–9d, 59 = Sanh. 24c, 19–24d, 14; Shab. 14d, 10–15a, 1 = 'Ab. Zarah 40d, 12–41a, 4.

Despite these parallel passages in the four orders of Yerushalmi, which might be regarded as a proof of the uniform redaction of the entire work, there is proof to the contrary, which shows that the first two orders differ in origin from the third and fourth. While the first and second contain a large number of baraitot with the introductory formula "Samuel transmits [תני שמואל]," there is not a single baraita by Samuel in the third and fourth orders. These latter two include, on the other hand, many controversies between Mani and Abin, two amoraim of the second half of the fourth century, while Ze-ra'im and Mo'ed contain very few (see Bacher, "Ag. Pal. Amor." iii. 398). The redaction of Yerushalmi is discussed in further detail below.

The haggadic portions of Yerushalmi are also characteristic of its style. As in Babli, they frequently have only a slight bearing, sometimes none at all, on the subject of the mishnaic section and its Talmudic interpretation, being added to the passages in which they are found either because they were mentioned in the academy on account of some subject under discussion, or because, in the process of the redaction of the treatise, this haggadic material, which was valued for some special reason, seemed to fit into the Talmudic text at the passage in question. Many haggadic portions of Yerushalmi are likewise found almost word for word in the earlier works of Palestinian midrashic literature, especially in Genesis Rabbah, Leviticus Rabbah, Pesiḳta di-Rab Kahana, Ekah (Lamentations) Rabbati, and Midrash Shemuel. These parallel passages do not always prove actual borrowing; for the same earlier source may have been used in the redaction both of Yerushalmi and of the midrashic works. The haggadot of the Palestinian Talmud were collected and annotated by Samuel ben Isaac Jaffe Ashkenazi in his "Yefeh Mar'eh" (Venice, 1589), and they were translated into German by Wünsche ("Der Jerusalemische Tal-

The Haggadot of the Yerushalmi.

mud in Seinen Haggadischen Bestandtheilen," Zurich, 1880).

Linguistically, the Palestinian Talmud is Aramaic, in so far as its framework (like the elucidations of the mishnaic text by the members of the academies and the amoraic discussions connected with them) is redacted in that language; the greater portion of the terminology is in like manner Aramaic. The same dialect is employed in general for the narrative sections, including both the haggadot and the accounts of the lives of the sages and their pupils. The Aramaic portion consequently comprises all that is popular in origin or content. The Hebrew sections, on the other hand, include the halakic sayings of the Tannaim, the citations from the collections of baraitot, and many of the amoraic discussions based on the tannaitic tradition, together with other sayings of the Amoraim. This linguistic usage is due to the fact that both in Palestine and in Babylon the Halakah was for the most part elucidated and expanded by the Amoraim themselves in the language in which it had been transmitted by the Tannaim. In the academy the Hebrew of the Mishnah held its place side by side with the Aramaic, thus giving to the latter a certain coloring, especially from a lexicographic point of view. Hebrew was retained in great measure also in the amoraic Haggadah. The Aramaic, which assumed a fixed literary form in Yerushalmi, is almost the same as that of the earlier Palestinian midrashic works, differing from them only in a few peculiarities, mostly orthographic. This idiom, together with that of the Palestinian Targum on the Pentateuch, has been analyzed in G. Dalman's "Grammatik des Jüdisch-Palästinischen Aramäisch" (Leipsic, 1894; 2 ed. 1905).

The first complete edition of the Babylonian Talmud (תלמוד בבלי) was printed at Venice, 1520–23, by Daniel Bomberg, and has become the basis, down to the present day, of a very large number of editions, including that of Basel, 1578–81, which, with the changes and omissions made by the censor, exerted a powerful influence on later texts until the edition of Frankfort-on-the-Main, 1720–22, with its additions, became the model of all subsequent editions of the Talmud (see below). The external form of Babli was determined by the editio princeps. While the first edition of Yerushalmi, in its two columns on each folio page, contains only the text, the editio princeps of Babli adds the commentary of Rashi on one margin and the tosafot on the other, together with kindred matter. Especially noteworthy is the fact that the first edition of Babli has a pagination which has been retained in all subsequent editions, thus rendering it possible to quote passages with exactness, and to find citations readily. The mishnaic treatises which have no Babylonian Talmud are included in the editions of the Talmud, together with commentaries, and these same tractates are likewise found in the only complete manuscript of Babli (that at Munich), where they form an appendix, although they precede the post-Talmudic treatises, which are likewise contained in the editions. It has been noted above that the editions of Babli contain the Yerushalmi for the treatise

Editions of the Babli.

Sheḳalim; and this is also the case in the Munich manuscript.

The following list gives the names of the treatises of Babli which have been preserved, together with the sequence generally followed in the editions, and the number of folios in each tractate, the pagination always beginning with fol. 2. Of the 570 leaves of the Munich codex, containing about eighty lines to a page, 490 belong to Babli; this gives an approximate idea of the size of this Talmud. The amount of text on each page of the editions, however, varies greatly on account of the varying length of the commentary of Rashi and the tosafot which accompany it; but the number of leaves shows the comparative lengths of the several treatises.

I. **Zera'im:** Berakot (64).

II. **Mo'ed:** Shabbat (157); 'Erubin (105); Pesaḥim (121); Beẓah (40); Ḥagigah (27); Mo'ed Ḳaṭan (29); Rosh ha-Shanah (35); Yoma (88); Sukkah (56); Ta'anit (31); Megillah (32).

III. **Nashim:** Yebamot (122); Ketubot (112); Ḳiddushin (82); Giṭṭin (90); Nedarim (91); Nazir (66); Soṭah (49).

IV. **Nezikin:** Baba Ḳamma (119); Baba Meẓi'a (119); Baba Batra (176); 'Abodah Zarah (76); Sanhedrin (113); Shebu'ot (49); Makkot (24); Horayot (14).

V. **Ḳodashim:** Zebaḥim (120); Menaḥot (110); Bekorot (161); Ḥullin (142); 'Arakin (34); Temurah (34); Keritot (28); Me'ilah (22); Tamid (9).

VI. **Ṭohorot:** Niddah (73).

Babli thus contains but one treatise each of the first and sixth orders; of the second, Sheḳalim (see above) is lacking; and there is no Talmud on 'Eduyot or Abot either in Babli or Yerushalmi. The fifth order of Babli contains neither Middot nor Ḳinnim, nor the third, fifth, sixth, and seventh chapters of Tamid. It is incorrect, however, to speak of missing portions of the Babylonian Talmud, since in all probability the sections which it omits were entirely disregarded in the final redaction of the work, and were consequently never committed to writing (for a divergent opinion see Weiss, "Dor," iii. 271). It will be shown further on that the mishnaic treatises lacking in Babli were subjects of study in the Babylonian academies.

Missing Gemaras.

In the editions the Babylonian Talmud is so arranged that each paragraph of the Mishnah is followed by the portion of the Talmud which forms the commentary on it; the portions are frequently divided into sections, rubricked by the successive sentences of the mishnaic paragraph on which they are based, although an entire paragraph occasionally serves as a single text. Thus Babli on Ket. ii. 1 (16a–18b) is divided into six sections; but there is no division into sections for ii. 2 (18b–20b), ii. 3 (20b–22a), ii. 5 (23b), and ii. 9 (27b–28a). There are three sections for ii. 4 (23a); two for ii. 6 (23b–26a), ii. 7 (26b–27a), and ii. 8 (27a, b); and eight for ii. 10 (28a, b). In the Munich codex, which is based on a manuscript of the middle of the ninth century (see Lewy in "Breslauer Jahresbericht," 1905, p. 28), the text of the entire chapter of the Mishnah is written in large characters on the inner portion of the page, separated from the Talmudic text, which is in a different script. In the fragments in the Bodleian Library, Oxford, written in 1123 and containing a portion of the treatise Keritot (see "J. Q. R." ix. 145), each chapter is headed by the entire mishnaic text on which it is based. Then follow the sections of the

Talmud, each beginning with the word 'מתני and the first part of the mishnaic paragraph in question, although some sections are marked by the superscription 'פים (= פיסקא). The superscription גמרא, which in the editions marks the beginning of the Talmud on each paragraph of the Mishnah, is found neither in the Munich codex nor in the Bodleian fragments. Most of the manuscripts containing one or more treatises of Babli, and described by R. N. Rabbinovicz in the introductions to vols. i., iv., viii., ix., and xi. of his "Diḳduḳe Soferim," are so arranged that the entire mishnaic text is placed at the beginning of the chapter; and this is also occasionally the case in the editions, as in the first chapter of the treatise Sanhedrin. In a St. Petersburg manuscript said to date from 1112 the paragraphs are repeated in their proper places (*ib.* viii. 3). A number of codices in the Vatican Library are arranged partly in the one way and partly in the other (xi. 13, 15, 17, 18), while the system adopted in the printed texts occurs in manuscripts also (see *ib.* iv. 6, 8; xi. 20). It may be mentioned as a curious circumstance that in one manuscript of the Vatican (*ib.* xi. 19), containing the treatise Pesaḥim, many passages are vocalized and accented, as is also the case in a Bodleian fragment of Yerushalmi on Berakot ("J. Q. R." ix. 150). A fragment of considerable length in the Cambridge Library, and possibly the earliest extant manuscript of Babli, also contains the treatise Pesaḥim; it has been edited by Lowe ("The Fragment of Talmud Babli of the Ninth or Tenth Century," Cambridge, 1879); and in its four folios it includes the text of fols. 7a, below –9a, middle, and 13a, below –16a, above, of the editions. The pages are divided into two columns; and the entire mishnaic text precedes the chapter; the several sections, even those beginning with a new paragraph of the Mishnah, have an introduction only in the case of the first word of the mishnaic passage in question, with the word 'מתני as superscription.

Earliest Manuscript of the Babli.

The character of Babli and its divergencies from Yerushalmi may best be illustrated by a citation of its commentary on the same passages of the Mishnah as those contained in the sections of the Palestinian Talmud already analyzed.

Ber. i. 1 (divided in Yerushalmi into four paragraphs, but in Babli forms one only, the explanations of which are given in 2a–9a; for the purposes of the present comparison, only those discussions in Babli which refer to that part of the Mishnah which in Yerushalmi forms the first paragraph are here summarized): (*a*) The initial question of the Mishnah and its basis; two divergent answers, together with an objection and its refutation (2a; all anonymous). The initial statement of the Mishnah, and an interpretation of Lev. xxii. 7 based on a baraita on this verse and concluding with a note of Rabbah b. Shela (2b), and the method of teaching this interpretation in Palestine. The contradictions between the statement of the Mishnah and three baraitot which are successively stated and dialectically refuted (all anonymous). A discussion of the third baraita (3a). The opinion of R. Eliezer ("until the end of the first watch of the night"), and the problem whether

three or four night-watches were implied; a haggadic baraita with a saying of R. Eliezer on the three watches of the night, together with a discussion of it. A haggadic excursus of some length, beginning with Rab's saying regarding the three watches of the night, and containing a baraita (a poem by Jose b. Ḥalafta) and a disquisition on it (3b). Further details of the night-watches, beginning with a controversy between Judah I. and Nathan (in a baraita); a haggadic saying of Joshua b. Levi transmitted by Zeriḳa and Ammi, this section concluding with a saying of Ashi. Another saying of Joshua b. Levi, transmitted in like manner, together with two versions of a comment by Abba b. Kahana. Discussion of the first saying of Joshua b. Levi, beginning with the rising of David "at midnight" (Ps. cxix. 62), and devoted in the main to the connotation of the word "neshef" (ib. cxix. 147), together with sayings of Babylonian amoraim. The way in which David knew when midnight had arrived, and concerning his harp (4a). Further details regarding David, Ps. lvii. 9, and Ex. xi. 4, with an exegesis by Ashi, which concludes the entire discussion. Additional haggadic material concerning David, and a controversy between the Palestinian haggadists Levi and Isaac on Ps. lxxxvi. 2 with reference to Ps. cxix. 62, together with comments and citations of a kindred nature.

(b) Dialectic exposition of the relation of the view of the scholars to the opinions of R. Eliezer and R. Gamaliel, together with the citation of a baraita (4b). A controversy between Johanan and Joshua b. Levi on the sequence of the "Shema'" and prayer, based on a sentence in this baraita ("the 'Shema'' is read: prayer is offered"), together with a discussion devoted chiefly to exegetic inferences. An objection alleged by Mar b. Rabina and based on a passage in the Mishnah, and a haggadic saying of Eleazar b. Abina to the effect that he who recites Ps. cxlv. thrice daily is assuredly a son of the

Examples world to come, the citation being
from made in this place on account of an
the Babli. aphorism of similar content given by
Johanan in the course of the same
debate. A discussion of these matters, and a saying of Johanan on Ps. cxlv., together with another haggadic aphorism by Eleazar b. Abina on the angels Michael and Raphael, and its elucidation. The view of Joshua b. Levi on the evening "Shema'," which should be recited in bed (5a), and amoraic sayings on the same subject, together with a confirmation, by a citation of Ps. iv. 6, of the ruling of Joshua b. Levi; a haggadic saying of Simeon b. Laḳish transmitted by Levi b. Laḥma, as well as another aphorism of this scholar transmitted by the same authority. A haggadic saying by Isaac on reading the "Shema'" in bed, and a comment by Ashi, followed by another haggadic aphorism by Isaac based on Job v. 7; interpretation of this verse as denoting afflictions sent by God ("yissurim"), against which the study of the Torah gives protection; haggadic sentences on the Law. A long series of haggadic sayings by Palestinian and Babylonian amoraim, and especially by Johanan, regarding affliction (5b), with anecdotes from Palestine and Babylon. A baraita with a saying of Abba Benjamin regarding prayer

before retiring, and its elucidation, together with three other baraitot and haggadic sayings of Abba Benjamin regarding prayer (6a), regarding demons (with various sayings of Babylonian authors), and praying in the synagogue. A haggadic saying by Isaac on the last subject transmitted by Rabin b. Adda, together with a saying of Ashi and additional elucidations, followed by another aphorism transmitted by Rabin in the name of Isaac regarding the "phylacteries of God," and by a discussion of the subject by Babylonian amoraim, the view of Ashi standing last. A third haggadic saying of Isaac, of similar transmission, concerning prayer in the synagogue (6b), and a series of aphorisms of a like nature, the first being by Johanan, and the second by Huna transmitted by Ḥelbo. These, interspersed with other sayings, are followed by five more aphorisms transmitted by Ḥelbo in the name of Huna and regarding departure from the synagogue, the Minḥah prayer, participation in marriage festivities, the fear of God, and the refusal to return a salutation. A series (7a) of five haggadic sayings transmitted by Johanan in the name of Jose ben Ḥalafta: the prayer offered by God, pacification of an angry neighbor, discipline of one's own conscience, three requests of Moses, and the teaching that a threat or promise by God is not recalled, even though given only conditionally, and that neither, therefore, is ever unfulfilled. After a number of sayings, partly tannaitic and partly amoraic in origin, come six haggadic aphorisms (7b) transmitted by Johanan in the name of the tanna Simeon ben Yoḥai, the second treating of the same subject as the corrresponding one in the previous series. To these sayings are appended various aphorisms and elucidations, followed by a conversation between Naḥman b. Jacob and Isaac, in which the latter cites a sixth saying, concerning prayer in the synagogue, transmitted by Johanan in the name of Simeon ben Yoḥai. Additional haggadic aphorisms (8a) on this subject as well as on the importance of the synagogue, followed by three sayings of 'Ulla transmitted by Ḥiyya b. Ammi, and by various aphorisms on the reading of the Torah in the synagogue (8b) and other kindred matters. This portion is concluded by the instructions which Joshua b. Levi gave to his sons, and by the analogous instructions which Raba gave to his children, as well as by elucidations of details of these teachings and by sayings of a similar import.

(c) In the name of Samuel, Judah declares that the opinion of R. Gamaliel is authoritative. A baraita giving a similar view by Simeon ben Yoḥai, followed by an interpretation of it with a final decision by Joshua ben Levi, and by another version of the relation to it of the ruling of Joshua ben Levi. The section (9a) terminates with an opinion on this baraita by a scholar who had come from Palestine to Babylon.

R. H. i. 1 (§§ 1–2 in Yerushalmi; the Talmud on these sections is contained in 2a–15b): (a) Ḥisda's answer to the question as to the practical importance of the "new year of the kings," with a citation of the mishnaic passage (Sheb. x. 5) regarding antedated and postdated promissory notes. A baraita on the reckoning of regnal years, and its elucidation (2b), together with hermeneutic deductions from the Bible regarding Nisan as the beginning of the regnal year, introduced by an inference of Johanan based on I Kings vi. 1 as compared with Num. xxxiii. 38, Deut. i. 3, 4, Num. xxi. 1 (3a), and similar passages, preference being finally given to Eleazar's deduction founded on II **Further** Chron. iii. 2. A baraita giving the **Examples.** deduction of Johanan. The assertion of Ḥisda that the regnal years of non-Israelitish kings were reckoned from Tishri, together with Biblical passages in confirmation of this view, beginning with Neh. i. 1 and its hermeneutic exposition (3b), the conclusion being formed by a variety of haggadic material on the Persian kings mentioned in the Bible (4a).

(b) Ḥisda's answer to the query why Nisan 15, the first day of the Feast of Passover, was not made the "new year of the feasts," while a baraita shows that this view was promulgated by Simeon ben Yoḥai himself. Another baraita (4b) on the ritual order of the festivals, together with exegetic deductions from the views contained therein and additional discussions, concluding with an elucidation (5a) of other halakic and exegetic sayings on festivals and sacrifices. Baraita (5b) on Deut. xxiii. 22 et seq., and a detailed discussion, followed by a similar section (6a, b) on Deut. xxiii. 24. Baraita (7a) on Nisan 1 and its four meanings, the first being deduced from Ex. xii. 2 and Deut. xvi. 1, although an objection caused Lev. xxiii. 39 to be regarded by Ḥisda as the basic passage, while Zech. i. 7 was cited to refute an allegation made by Rabina, additional Biblical passages being quoted by the Babylonian amoraim 'Ulla, Kahana, and Ashi; the section is concluded by a deduction of the three other meanings of Nisan 1 (7b) mentioned in the baraita.

(c) The signification of Elul 1 as the "new year for tithes of cattle," as taught by R. Meïr. The various origins of the sentences collected in R. H. i. 1, together with a saying by Joseph, followed by a series of aphorisms of later Babylonian amoraim, and one by Ashi (8a). Johanan's deduction, from Ps. lxv. 14, of the double view concerning the new year for tithes of cattle, and its dialectic elucidation.

Second half of the mishnaic paragraph: (a) The question regarding the practical utility of the new year for the counting of the years, answered by Pappa in exactly the same way as Ḥisda had solved the question concerning the new year of the kings; solution of the discrepancy and further elucidations of the principle that Tishri 1 was the new year for the counting of the years. Two baraitot on Ps. lxxxi. 4 et seq. (8b).

(b) An inference regarding the year of jubilee, based on Lev. xxv. 4; and the obviation of the difficulty presented by Lev. xxv. 9 (with reference to the Sabbatical year) by means of a baraita on the following verse, together with two other baraitot on the same subject (9a) and an elucidation of Tishri 10, concluded by a baraita on Lev. xxv. 11 and its interpretation (9b).

(c) Biblical deduction regarding the planting of trees and a baraita thereon, with an inference drawn from the Bible by Johanan (10a), and an elucidation of another baraita cited in explanation of the first. Johanan's deduction from Gen. viii. 13 regarding the opposing views of R. Meïr and R. Eleazar (10b)

as to whether a day may be reckoned like a year, thus introducing a baraita containing the controversy between R. Eliezer and R. Joshua on the month of Creation, the former arguing for Tishri and the latter for Nisan; exegetic haggadot of considerable length (11a–12a) on this section.

(d) A baraita stating that "tithes" and "vows" as well as "vegetables" belong to Tishri 1, together with interpretations by hermeneutics and other methods (12b), and with discussions of the subject by the Palestinian and Babylonian schools, and halakic exegeses (13a–14a).

(e) An argument by Hoshaiah transmitted by Eleazar (14a), and a baraita recording the practise of R. Akiba (14b–15b), as well as elucidations of it. Another baraita on Shebaṭ 15, with a controversy between Johanan and Simeon ben Laḳish, and a discussion of it.

Giṭ. ii. 1 (the Talmud on this section is contained in 15a–17a): (a) The purpose of the entire paragraph, although its content is immediately apparent from the opening sentence of the mishnaic treatise.

(b) The problem of the connotation of "the half" of the bill of divorce, and Ashi's answer.

(c) The law regarding a case in which only "the half" of a bill of divorce is signed by witness in the presence of the bearer; the more rigorous interpretation of it by Ḥisda and subsequent modifications by Raba and (15b) Ashi, as well as a dialectic discussion of these three sayings. Analogous cases from other branches of the Halakah and casuistic questions bearing on them (16a), concluding with one by Pappa which remains unanswered.

(d) Case in which one of the bearers of a bill of divorce witnesses the engrossing of the document and the other the signature; exact definition given by Johanan and transmitted by Samuel b. Judah (16b); the answer of the latter to the objection of Abaye, although another version of the entire affair makes Ashi the author of the objection; controversy on the subject between Hoshaiah and 'Ulla. Anecdote of a visit made by Judah b. Ezekiel to Rabbah bar bar Ḥana during an illness of the latter, and their conversation on a problem connected with Giṭ. i. 1.

(e) The case in which the engrossing of a bill of divorce is witnessed by one and the signature by two persons (17a), and the exact definition of such an event, given by Johanan and transmitted by Ammi, the section being concluded by a discussion between Ammi and Assi.

B. B. i. 6 (the Talmud on this section is contained in 7b–11a): (a) "One who is part owner of a courtyard is obliged to contribute to the **Legal** cost of the gateway as well as of the **Example.** door itself"; the citation of a legend concerning Elijah to prove that a gateway is not necessarily a subject for praise, concluded by a casuistic definition of the case presupposed by the Mishnah.

(b) According to R. Simeon b. Gamaliel, "Every courtyard is not adapted to a gateway"; a baraita containing the complete version of this saying.

(c) According to R. Simeon b. Gamaliel, "One who dwells in a city is obliged to contribute toward the building of the walls and the doors," etc.; a baraita containing the complete version of this saying. Johanan's answer to the query advanced by Eleazar concerning the method of levying contributions, followed by a second version of the same account. The patriarch Judah II. and the scholars contributed toward building the wall, although the legality of this action was questioned by Simeon b. Laḳish on the basis of a haggadic deduction from Ps. cxxxix. 18, while Johanan proposed another verse, Cant. viii. 10, to aid in the solution of the problem (8a); Rabbah's interpretation of this passage of Canticles. An instance of contributions on the part of the scholars of Babylonia, and the proof of their illegality furnished by the exegesis of three Biblical passages, taken respectively from the Pentateuch, the Prophets, and the Hagiographa. Pappa's proof that a certain tax was imposed on orphans, and a discussion of it, followed by a tannaitic account (half Aramaic) by Judah I. of the support of scholars during a time of famine.

(*d*) "How long must one dwell in a city to have equal rights with its citizens? Twelve months"; a conflicting baraita which speaks of thirty days; Rabbah's solution of this contradiction, while Johanan reconciles the discrepancy between the period of twelve months and that given in another baraita. The saying of Johanan as to the liability of scholars to taxation, and various statements regarding the practise of the Babylonian sages. The way in which Joseph (4th cent.) expended a sum of money sent him by the mother of King Sapor, together (8b) with an interpretation of Jer. xv. 2. Baraita on the mode of levying taxes for the poor, and the right of assessment of municipal taxes. The rule of the Mishnah (Sheḳ. v. 2) that the smallest number of persons who may be entrusted with raising taxes is two, and its Biblical basis according to Naḥman b. Jacob, together with sayings and examples bearing on this matter. An interpretation of Dan. xii. 3 as referring to the collectors and trustees of the tax for the poor, followed by two baraitot on these collectors and Abaye's statements regarding the practise of Rabbah b. Naḥmani, as well as (9a) by a note of Ashi and an opinion of Rabbah. Baraita on the auditing of the accounts of the trustees of the tax for the poor, and elucidations of it. Notes and anecdotes illustrating Mishnah Pe'ah viii. 7 (on the amount to be given to the poor), followed by haggadic passages on the importance of almsgiving, among these aphorisms being one cited by Rabbah as transmitted to Eleazar by a certain 'Ulla with a curious surname, which forms the basis of an anecdote. Further haggadic passages on the charity of Eleazar, Isaac, and others. A baraita giving R. Meïr's answer (10a) to the question why God Himself does not nurture the poor, followed by an account of the conversation on this subject between R. Akiba and Tineius Rufus. Sermon by Judah b. Shalom (Palestinian amora of the 4th cent.) on Jer. lvii. 17, and anecdotes from the lives of Johanan b. Zakkai and Pappa. Haggadic sayings by tannaim and amoraim on alms. The vision of Joseph b. Joshua b. Levi (10b) of the future life, together with baraitot on the interpretation of Prov. xiv. 34 by Johanan b. Zakkai and his scholars as well as by Gamaliel II. and the other sages of Jabneh. The charity of the mother of Sapor, and two baraitot:

one (11a) the story of the beneficence of Benjamin ha-Ẓaddiḳ; the other an account of the generosity of King Monobaz.

(*e*) "If one obtains a dwelling-place in the city, he immediately receives equal rights with the citizens"; an opposing view by Simeon b. Gamaliel transmitted in two versions.

This analysis of four different passages of the Babylonian Talmud shows, in the first place, that the framework, as in the Palestinian Talmud, is formed by a running interpretation of the Mishnah, despite the heterogeneity of the material which is interwoven with it. The Talmud, however, is not a mere commentary on the Mishnah, since, in addition to its haggadic portions, it contains a varied mass of halakic material, connected only loosely, if at all, with the contents of the mishnaic paragraphs in question; and while the Talmud sometimes adheres closely to the text of such a paragraph, its commentary on a single section of the Mishnah is often expanded into the compass of a small book. In this respect Babli is much more free than Yerushalmi, which is more concise in other regards as well; the wider interests of the former and its greater variety and length are due at least in large part to the fact that the Babylonian academies enjoyed a longer existence and hence its redaction extended over a more protracted period.

The fact that the Haggadah is much more prominent in Babli, of which it forms, according to Weiss ("Dor," iii. 19), more than one-third, while it constitutes only one-sixth of Yerushalmi, was due, in a sense, to the course of the development of Hebrew literature. No independent mass of haggadot developed in Babylon, as was the case in Palestine; and the haggadic writings were accordingly collected in the Talmud. The most curious example of this is a midrash on the Book of Esther, found at the end of the first chapter of the treatise Megillah (pp. 10b–17a). Except for the fact that the text of this section naturally alludes to the Book of Esther, the midrash has no connecting-link with the preceding portion of the Talmud. It is a true midrashic compilation in the style of the Palestinian midrashim, introduced by sixteen proems (mostly by Palestinian authors), and followed by exegeses and comments on individual verses of Esther in the order of the text, each preceded by a catchword (for further details on this midrash see Bacher, "Ag. Bab. Amor." p. 119). A fragment of a similar compilation on Lamentations, treating of a few verses of the first two chapters, is found in the last chapter of Sanhedrin (104, 4 *et seq.*), this fragment being inserted there on account of the preceding casual allusion to the Babylonian exile (*ib.* p. 120). The treatise Giṭṭin (55a–58a) contains a haggadic compilation on the destruction of Jerusalem, its elements being found partly in the Palestinian literature, partly in Ekah Rabbati, and partly in the treatise Ta'anit of the Jerusalem Talmud. This haggadah, which begins with a saying by Johanan, is appended to the brief halakic elucidation of the first sentence of the mishnaic paragraph on the law of the Sicarii (Giṭ. v. 6), mentioning those who fell in the war against

PAGE FROM AN UNKNOWN EDITION OF TRACTATE BABA MEẒI'A OF THE BABYLONIAN TALMUD, PRINTED PROBABLY BY SONCINO BEFORE 1500.

(By courtesy of Prof. Solomon Schechter.)

the Romans. In Babli such haggadic interpolations, often of considerable length, are extremely frequent, while the very content of the mishnaic paragraphs often affords a basis for lengthy haggadic excursuses. Thus the last (in Yerushalmi, next to the last) chapter of Sanhedrin is made the foundation for a mass of haggadic comments,
Haggadah of the Babli. most of them only loosely connected by an association of ideas with the text of the passages of the Mishnah to which they are assigned. In this exceptionally long chapter of Babli (pp. 90a–113b) only that portion (111b–112b) which refers to the Law in Deut. xiii. 12 *et seq.* is halakic in nature. The haggadic conclusion of the first chapter of Soṭah furnishes the basis for further Talmudic comments in the style of the Haggadah (8b, 14a); so that, for example, the interpretation of Ex. ii. 4, cited in the Mishnah (11a), is followed (11a–13b) by an independent section which forms a running midrash on Ex. i. 8–ii. 4. Additional examples may be found in nearly every treatise of the Babylonian Talmud. The haggadic sections of this Talmud, which form an important part of the entire work, have been collected in the very popular "'En Ya'aḳob" of Jacob ibn Ḥabib (1st ed. 1516), as well as in the rarer "Haggadot ha-Talmud" (Constantinople, 1511; comp. Rabbinovicz, "Diḳduḳe Soferim," viii. 131); and they have been translated into German by A. Wünsche ("Der Babylonische Talmud in Seinen Haggadischen Bestandtheilen," 3 vols., Leipsic, 1886–89).

An important factor in the composition of the Talmud, and consequently one it is necessary to consider in a discussion of its literary form, is the frequent juxtaposition of several sayings ascribed to one and the same author. These sayings, which are frequently linked together by the name of their common transmitter as well as by that of their author, were evidently taught in this connected form in the academies, thus finding their way into the appropriate passages of the Talmudic text. Such groups of aphorisms are extremely frequent in Babli; and several of them are found in the passage from Ber. 2a–9a which has been analyzed above (regarding Yerushalmi see Frankel, "Mebo," p. 39a). Other circumstances which must be considered in discussing the composition of the text of the Talmud are set forth in the account of its origin and redaction given below.

The remarks already made concerning the relation of the Hebrew and the Aramaic elements in the vocabulary of Yerushalmi apply with little modification to Babli, although the Aramaic of the latter is more nearly akin to the Syriac (the eastern Aramaic dialect then current in Babylonia) and is even more closely related to Mandæan (see Nöldeke, "Mandäische Grammatik," p. xxvi., Halle, 1875;
Style and Language. on the Persian elements in the vocabulary of Babli see JEW. ENCYC. vii. 313b, *s.v.* JUDÆO-PERSIAN). In regard to Greek and Latin terms Levy makes the incomprehensible statement ("Neuhebr. Wörterb." iv. 274a) that "no Greek or Latin words are found in the Babylonian Talmud." This is, however, incorrect; for a large number of words

from the Latin and Greek (see Krauss, "Lehnwörter," i. p. xxiii.) are employed in the Talmud, both in the tannaitic passages found in Babli, and in the sayings of Palestinian as well as of Babylonian amoraim, such as Rab (see Bacher, *l.c.* p. 32). On the exegetic terminology as applied in Biblical and traditional hermeneutics, see Bacher, "Terminologie der Amoräer," Leipsic, 1905. An interesting linguistic peculiarity of Babli is the fact that tannaitic traditions, especially stories, are occasionally given entirely in Aramaic, or an anecdote, begun in Hebrew, is continued in Aramaic (such as the story, designated by תנו רבנן as a baraita, concerning Joshua b. Peraḥyah and his pupil Jesus [Sanh. 107b]).

The contents of the Talmud—this term being restricted to Babli, although much which applies to it holds true of Yerushalmi as well—fall into the two main divisions of Halakah and Haggadah. Although, as stated above, the Mishnah itself frequently furnishes the ground for the inclusion of haggadic elements in the Talmud, and although the
The Halakah in Babli. subjects discussed in the Halakah frequently lead of themselves to haggadic treatment, the Haggadah occupies only a secondary position in the Talmud, since this is, both in origin and in purpose, a halakic work, and was intended to serve as a commentary on the chief authoritative work of the tannaitic Halakah, the Mishnah of Judah I. Those portions, therefore, which treat of the interpretation of the Mishnah are the substance of the Talmud. This interpretation, however, was not merely theoretical, but was primarily devoted to a determination of the rules applying to the practise of the ceremonial law; on the other hand, the development of the Halakah had not ceased in the academies of the Amoraim, despite the acceptance of the Mishnah, so that the opinions and the decisions of the Amoraim themselves, even when they were not based merely on an interpretation of the Mishnah and other tannaitic halakot, became the subject of tradition and comment. In addition to the Mishnah, furthermore, the Midrash (the halakic exegesis of the Bible) and the Halakah in the more restricted sense became the subject of tradition and of study, and were preserved in different collections as being the other results of the tannaitic period. In this way the Talmud, in its strict connotation of the interpretation of the Mishnah, was increased by an inexhaustible mass of material, which afforded the amoraic academies a basis both for the interpretation and for the criticism of the Mishnah; for since the Talmud deals with the criticism of the Mishnah, not only in text and meaning, but also in its relation to the baraitot, these baraitot themselves were frequently interpreted in the same way as were mishnaic passages (*e.g.*, R. H. 10a, 12b, 29a), and were supplied with their Talmud. Moreover, the Talmud was further augmented by the inclusion within it of the views which the scholars expressed in the course of their public, judicial, and other activities, as well as by the data regarding their private lives and their religious practises which were discussed and memorized in the academies. If this brief sketch of the Talmud as regards its halakic con-

tents be supplemented by the statement that the sayings of the several amoraim as well as the opposing views of their contemporaries and the members of the academies, whether teachers or pupils, are frequently recorded in connection with the report of the discussions of the academies, a more complete view of the nature of the Talmud and a better conception of its form may be gained.

The real framework of the Talmud, however, on which the entire structure was built, was, as noted above, provided by the questions, comments, and discussions which are based on individual paragraphs of the Mishnah, and which are anonymous, or not ascribed to any author. Appended to these passages and interspersed among them are sayings whose authors are named; and this class frequently preponderates greatly. The anonymous framework of the Talmud may be regarded as the **The Framework Anonymous.** warp resulting from the united activity of the members of the academy, and upon which the woof of the Talmud was interwoven and developed during three centuries, until its final redaction gave it definitive form. The Talmud is really the work of the body of scholars in the academies, who devoted themselves to it generation after generation, and kept its traditions alive. Although many members of the academies—the great as well as the small, teachers as well as pupils—are mentioned as the authors of various sayings and decisions, and as taking part in the discussions and controversies, some of them being deemed scholars worthy of record on account of a single remark, the background of the Talmud, or rather the background for those elements regarding whose authorship statements are made, was formed by the united efforts of those who labored to produce that work. The manifold objections and refutations introduced by the word "metibi" (= "they object"), and the questions (generally casuistic in nature) preceded by the formula "ibba'ya lehu" (= "they have asked") refer to this body of scholars, regardless of the date at which they lived.

This allusion to the anonymous framework of the Talmud suggests the problem of its redaction, which is partially answered by the allusion itself; for the work began with the inception of the collection, and the first amoraim laid the foundation for the task, which was carried on by succeeding generations, the final result being the Talmud in its present form. The system of mishnaic hermeneutics, which was in a sense official, and was at all events sanctioned by the lectures delivered in the academy, was determined as early as the first generation, and remained valid thenceforth. It is interesting to notice that the only certain occurrence of the word "Gemara" in the sense of "Talmud" ('Er. 32b) is found in connection with an account which throws a flood of light upon the first stages of the redaction of the Talmud. This account begins with the interpretation of 'Er. iii. 4, and is as follows: "R. Ḥiyya b. Abba, R. Assi [Palestinian amoraim in Babylon], and Rabba b. Nathan sat; and beside them sat also Rab Naḥman. They sat and said [here follows a dialectic discussion on the nature of the place of the tree mentioned in the paragraph of the Mishnah]. Then R. Naḥman said: 'It is correct; and Samuel also has approved of this explanation.' Then the first three asked: 'Hast thou established this explanation in the Gemara?' [i.e., "Hast thou included it as a fixed element in the Talmud? Naḥman answers in the affirmative, whereupon a confirmatory amoraic tradition is added; and, in the name of Samuel, Rab Naḥman interprets the mishnaic passage under consideration in the light of that exegesis]." The term "ḳaba'" ("establish") was used in a later age by Sherira Gaon to designate the incorporation of portions that were used to make up the Talmud into its text (see Lewy, "Interpretation des Ersten Abschnitts des Palästinischen Talmud-Traktates Nesikin," p. 4; Bacher, in "Hebrew Union College Annual," 1904, p. 34), while in the Talmud itself the word was applied to the redaction of tannaitic traditions (see R. H. 32a, above; Ḳid. 25a; Sanh. 21b; Zeb. 114b). This account, which dates from the beginning of the amoraic period in the Academy of Nehardea, is, curiously enough, an isolated instance; for among the many dates and accounts which the Talmud contains in **Redaction.** reference to the academy and its members, there is no direct statement concerning the redaction of the text, either in its earlier stages or at its conclusion, although certain statements on divergent traditions of amoraic sayings and discussions afford an idea of the way in which the Talmudic text emerged from the various versions given by the scholars and schools that transmitted it. These statements, which have been collected by Lewy (l.c. pp. 4–14), use the verb "tanni" ("pa'el" from תני) in referring to lectures on the Talmudic text as well as amoraic sayings or discussions on them (Bacher, "Terminologie der Amoräer," p. 239). Thus it is stated (Shab. 48b; B. B. 86a) that at Sura a certain interpretation was given in the name of Ḥisda and at Pumbedita in that of Kahana. There are a number of other similar statements concerning traditions, in regard to differences, as between Sura and Pumbedita, and between Sura and Nehardea, in the wording of the amoraic sayings and in their ascribed authorship (Giṭ. 35a). Especially frequent is the mention of amoraim of the fourth and fifth centuries as transmitters of these divergent statements, either two amoraim being named as authorities for two different versions, or an amora being cited as opposing another version to an anonymous tradition. As examples of the former may be mentioned Rabba and Joseph (Zeb. 25b), Pappa and Zebid (Shab. 66b), Kahana and Tabyomi (Ned. 16b), Ashi and Mar Zuṭra (Shab. 119a), and Rabina and Aḥa (Ket. 31b); while many other instances are cited by Lewy (l.c.).

Particularly interesting are the cases in which a divergent account is presented before Ashi, and thus before the one who projected the definitive redaction of the Talmud, Ashi appearing in all these cases as representing the version first given. Thus the amora Mordecai said to Ashi: "Thou teachest thus; but we teach differently" (Men. 42b; Ber. 5a). In addition to such statements, which are ascribed to members of the Babylonian academies, and which indicate divergencies in amoraic tradition, the extant text of the Talmud contains also a number of other variants, which are included without such statements. These are introduced by such formulas as "And if you will say" (ואי תימא), referring to other authorities, or "There are those who say," or "There are those who teach," and similar phrases. The expression "another version" (לישנא אחרינא) frequently appears in the text as a superscription to a divergent account (Naz. 9b; B. Ḳ. 59a; Ḥul. 119b; Tem. 5a, 6a, 9b, 11b, 30b [comp. Frankel in "Monatsschrift," 1861, x. 262]; Niddah 29a, 38a). All these instances afford an idea, even though but an imperfect one, of the gradual development of the Talmudic text. To comprehend why only practically a single Talmud was produced, despite the various academies, the great number of authoritative transmitters of the mass of material, and the number of generations that collaborated on the work, it must be borne in mind that there was a continual interchange of ideas between the academies, and that the numerous pupils of the successive generations who memorized the Talmud, and perhaps committed at least a part of it to writing, drew from a single source, namely, the lectures of their masters and the discussions in the academies; further, that, since the work on the Talmud was continued without interruption along the lines laid down by the first generation of amo-

Technical Terms for Tradition. raim, all succeeding generations may be regarded as one body of scholars who produced a work which was, to all intents and purposes, uniform. This unity finds its expression in the phraseology adopted in the anonymous framework of the Talmud, which terms the authors "we," exactly as a writer speaks of himself as "I" in an individual work. Examples of this phraseology occur in the following formulas: והוינן בה ("We then raised the question"; see Shab. 6b, 71a, 99b; Yoma 74a, 79b; Suk. 33a; Meg. 22a; Yeb. 29b; Ḳid. 49a; Giṭ. 60b; Shebu. 22b; 'Ab. Zarah 35a, 52b; Niddah 6b); ורמינהו ("We have opposed [another teaching to the one which has been quoted]"); תנן ("We have learned," or, in other words, "have received by tradition"), the conventional formula which introduces mishnaic passages; and, finally, מנא לן ("Whence have we it?"), the regular preface to an inquiry regarding the Biblical basis of a saying. In all these formulas the "we" denotes the authors of the Talmud regarded as a collective unity, and as the totality of the members of the academies whose labors, covering three centuries of collaboration, resulted in the Talmud. It was in the Babylonian Academy of Sura, moreover, that the final redaction of the Talmud took place, the very academy that took the lead in the first century of the amoraic period; and the uniformity of the Talmud was thus assured, even to the place of its origin.

The statements already made concerning the continuous redaction of the Babylonian Talmud apply with equal force to the Yerushalmi, this fact being expressed by Lewy (l.c. pp. 14–15) in the following words: "In Palestine, as in Babylon, there may have been different Talmudim in the various schools at different periods. . . . Similarly in the Palestinian Talmud different versions of amoraic sayings are quoted in the names of different authors, from which

it may be inferred that these authors learned and taught different Talmudim." Lewy speaks also (l.c. p. 20) of several redactions which preceded the final casting of the Palestinian Talmud into its present form. The actual condition of affairs can scarcely be formulated in these terms, however, since the divergencies consist, for the most part, of mere variants in certain sentences, or in the fact that there were different authors and transmitters of them; and although many of these deviations are cited by R. Jonah and R. Jose, who lived and taught contemporaneously at Tiberias, this fact scarcely justifies the assumption that there were two different Talmudim, one taught by Jonah and the other by Jose; it will nevertheless be evident, from the statements cited above, that the Talmud existed in some definite form throughout the amoraic period, and that, furthermore, its final redaction was preceded by other revisions. It may likewise be assumed that the contemporaneous schools of Tiberias, Sepphoris, and Cæsarea in Palestine taught the Talmud in different redactions in the fourth century. Lewy assumes, probably with correctness, that in the case of Yerushalmi the treatise Neziḳin (the three treatises Baba Ḳamma, Baba Meẓi'a, and Baba Batra) was taken from a redaction differing from that of the other treatises. (Allusion has already been made to a difference of content between the first two and the last two orders of the Yerushalmi.) With regard to Babli, Frankel has shown ("Monatsschrift," x. 194) that the treatise Tamid, in which only three chapters out of seven are accompanied by a Talmud, belongs to a different redaction from that of the other treatises; and he endeavors to show, in like manner (ib. p. 259), both "that the redactor of the treatise Ḳiddushin is not identical with that of Baba Batra and Nedarim," and "that the redactor of the treatise

Date of Redaction. Giṭṭin is not the same as that of Keritot and Baba Batra." However, as these remarks refer to the final redaction of the Talmud, they do not touch upon the abstract unity of the work as emphasized above. It is sufficient to assume, therefore, that the final redaction of the several treatises was based on the versions used in the different academies. It may be postulated, on the whole, that the Palestinian Talmud received its present form at Tiberias, and the Babylonian Talmud at Sura (comp. the passages in Yerushalmi in which הכא [= "here"] refers to Tiberias, and those in Babli in which the same word denotes Sura [Lewy, l.c. p. 4]).

The chief data regarding the academies of Palestine and Babylon, whose activity resulted in the Talmud, have been set forth elsewhere (see JEW. ENCYC. i. 145–148, s.v. ACADEMIES), so that here stress need be laid only on those events in the history of the two schools and of their teachers which are especially noteworthy in connection with the origin and the final redaction of the two Talmudim. It may be said, by way of preface, that the academies of Palestine and Babylon were in constant intercommunication, notwithstanding their geographical position. Many prominent Babylonian scholars settled permanently in Palestine, and many eminent Palestinians sojourned in Babylon for some time,

בני צרות רב בריך ליה לבריה בפומ' בני חם שמע טב' מעיד אני לכם שמם כהנן גדולי נדוני'
בני במי ר' דוסא הוורה אחותו של מל של רדוסא שהיה מתלמירי ב'ם היתירן כדרכנו לקחו ועמדו על פתחו של ריה וה'ג כן מחל גדול היה וכובדו' חכמ' שהוא התירן קמו
צרות אני מעיד לכם שמע תא שמע ביחו ר' דוס'
בן ארכינס הותרו צרת הבת לאחין שמע מינ'
עשו שמע מינה גופא התירו ביתו ר' דוסא הר כב'
התירו צרות הבת לאחין והיה הדבר קשה
לחכמים מפני שזקן גדול הוד ועיניו קמו
מלאו לבית המדרש אמ' מי ילך ויודיעו אמר
להן ר' יהושע אני אלך ואחריו מי ר' אלעזר בן
עזריה ואחריו ר' עקיבא הלכו ועמדו על
פתח ביתו נכנסה שפחתו אמרה לו ר' חכמי
ישרא' באין אצלך אמ' לה יכנסו ונכנסו תפסו
לר יהושע והושיבוהו על מטה של זהב אמר
ליה ר' אמור לתלמידך אחד וישב אמ' לו מי הו
ר' אלעז' בן עזריה אמ' לו וליש לו בן לעזריה חבירנו
קרא עליו המקרא הזה נער הייתי גם זקנתי לא
ראיתי צדיק נעזב וזרעו מבקש לחם תפסו
והושיבו על מטה של זהב אמר ליה הרבי אמור
לתלמידך אחד וישב אלו מי הוא עקיבא בן
יוסף אמ' ליה אתה הוא עקיבא בן יוסף ששמך
הולך מסוף העולם ועד סופו שב בני שב כמוך
ירבו בישראל התחילו מסבבים אותו בהלכו
עד שהגיעו לצרת הבת אלו ליה צר הבת מהו

אמר להן מחלוקת בית שמאי ובית הלל הלכה כדברי מי אל הלכה כבה אמרו ליה ר
והלא משמך אמרו הלכה כב"ש אמ' להם דוסא שמעתם או בן הרכינס שמעתם אל
ר' חיי חיי סתם שמענו א' להם את קטן מי יש לי בכור שטן הוא ויונתן שמו והוא מתלמי'
שמאי וחזהירו שלא יקפח אתכ' בהלכו לפי שיש עמו ג' מאות תשובו' בצר הבת שהי'
מותר' אבל מעיד אני עלי שמים וארץ שעל מדוכה זו ישב חגי הנביא ואמר ג' דברים
צרת הברת אסורה עמון ומואב מעשרין מעשר עני בשביעית ומקבלין גרים מן
הקרדויים ומן התרמודים תנא כשנכנסו נכנסו בפתח אח' וכשיצאו יצאו בשלשה
פתחים פגע בו ר' עקיבא אקשי ליה ואוקמי אמ' ליה אתה הוא עקיבא ששמך הולך
מסוף העולם ועד סופו אשריך שזכית לשם ועדיין לא הגעת לרועי בקר א"ל ר' עקיבא
ואפילו לרועי צאן : עמון ומואב מעשרין מעשר עני בשביעית דאמר מר הרבה
כרכים כבשו עולי מצרים ולא כבשום עולי בבל וקרושה ראשונה קדשה לשעתה
ולא קרשה לעתיד לבא והניחום כדי שיסמכו עליהן עניים בשביעות ומקבלים גרים
מן הקרדויים והתרמודים איפ'וה וה' תני רמי בר יחזקאל אין מקבלים גרים מן הקרדו'
אמר רב אשי קרתויים איתמר כדאמר אינשי קרתוי' פסולים ואיבא דאמרי תני רמי
בר יחזקאל אין מקבלים גרים מן הקרתויים מאי לאו היינו קרתויים היינו קרדויים
אמר רב אשי לא קרתויים לחוד וקרדויי לחוד כדאמרי אינשי קרתוי' פסולי ר' יוחנן
וסביא דאמרי תרויהו אין מקבלים גרים מן התרמודים ומי אמר רבי יוחנן הכי והתנן
כל הבאים מן הרקם טהורים ורבי יהודה מטמא מפני שהם גרים וטועים
מבין הגוים טהורים והוינן בה   קפסיק

PAGE FROM THE FIRST COMPLETE EDITION OF THE BABYLONIAN TALMUD, PRINTED BY BOMBERG, VENICE, 1520–23.

(From the Sulzberger collection in the Jewish Theological Seminary of America, New York.)

or even for a considerable portion of their lives. In the second half of the third century Babylonian students sought the Palestinian schools with especial frequency, while many pupils of Johanan went during the same period to Babylon; and in the troublous days of the fourth century many Palestinian scholars sought refuge in the more quiet regions along the Euphrates. This uninterrupted association of scholars resulted in an active interchange of ideas between the schools, especially as the activity of both was devoted in the main to the study of the Mishnah. The Jerusalem Talmud accordingly contains a large number of sayings by Babylonian authorities, and Babli quotes a still larger number of sayings by Palestinian scholars in addition to the proceedings of the Palestinian academies, while it likewise devotes a very considerable space to the halakic and haggadic teachings of such Palestinian masters as Johanan, Simeon b. Laḳish, and Abbahu. Anonymous Palestinian sentences are quoted in Babli with the statement, "They say in the West"; and similar maxims of Babylonian origin are quoted in Yerushalmi in the name of "the scholars there." Both the Talmudim thus acquired more traits in common than they had formerly possessed despite their common foundation, while owing to the mass of material which Babli received from the schools of the Holy Land it was destined in a measure to supplant the Palestinian Talmud even in Palestine.

The history of the origin of Yerushalmi covers a period of two centuries. Its projector was Johanan, the great teacher of Tiberias, who, together with his pupils and contemporaries, some of them of considerable prominence, laid the foundations for the work which was continued by succeeding generations. The extreme importance of Johanan in the genesis of the Palestinian Talmud seems to have been the basis of the belief, which first found expression in the twelfth century, although it is certainly older in origin, that he was the author of Yerushalmi (see Frankel, "Mebo," p. 47b). As a matter of fact, however, almost a century and a half elapsed after the death of Johanan (279) before this Talmud received its present form, but it was approximated to this form, toward the end of the fourth century, by Jonah and Jose, the two directors of the Academy of Tiberias. Their joint halakic sentences, controversies, and divergent opinions on the utterances of their predecessors are **Activity of** scattered throughout Yerushalmi; but **Jonah** the conclusion that Jose redacted it **and Jose.** twice, which has been drawn from certain statements in this Talmud, is incorrect (Frankel, *l.c.* p. 101a; Weiss, "Dor," iii. 113 *et seq.*, 211; see Lewy, *l.c.* pp. 10, 17; Halevy, "Dorot ha-Rishonim," ii. 322). Jonah's son Mani, one of the scholars most frequently named in Yerushalmi, seems, after studying at Cæsarea, where noteworthy scholars were living in the fourth century, to have raised the school of Sepphoris to its highest plane; and a large number of the sayings of the "scholars of Cæsarea" was included in Yerushalmi (see "Monatsschrift," 1901, pp. 298–310). The only other halakist of importance among the Palestinian amoraim is Jose b. Abin (or Abun). According to Frankel (*l.c.* p.

102a), he occupied about the same position in regard to the redaction of Yerushalmi as was held by Ashi in regard to that of Babli (see also Weiss, *l.c.* iii. 117). The final redaction of the Talmud was reserved for the succeeding generation, probably because the activity of the Academy of Tiberias ceased with the discontinuance of the patriarchate (*c.* 425). This was the time during which Tanḥuma b. Abba (see Bacher, "Ag. Pal. Amor." iii. 502) made his collection and definite literary arrangement of the haggadic exegesis of the amoraic period.

The beginnings of the Babylonian Talmud are associated both with Nehardea, where the study of the tradition had flourished even before the close of the tannaitic period, and with Sura, where Rab founded a new academy which soon surpassed Nehardea in importance. Rab and Samuel, who respectively presided with equal distinction over the two schools, laid the foundation of the Babylonian Talmud through their comments on the Mishnah and their other teachings. Their views are frequently contrasted in the form of controversies; but on the other hand they are often mentioned as the common authors of sentences which were probably transmitted by certain pupils who had heard them from both masters. One of these pupils, Judah b. Ezekiel, when asked to explain some of the more obscure portions of the Mishnah, subsequently alluded plaintively to the "hawayyot" of Rab and Samuel, meaning thereby the questions and comments of the two masters on the entire Mishnah (Ber. 20a and parallels). In like manner, scholars of the fourth century spoke of the hawayot of Abaye and Raba, which formed, as it were, the quintessence of the Talmud, and which, according to an anachronistic addition to an old baraita, were even said to have been included in the branches of knowledge familiar to Johanan b. Zakkai (Suk. 28a; B. B. 134a).

The pupils of Rab and Samuel, the leading amoraim of the second half of the third century—Huna, Ḥisda, Naḥman b. Jacob, Sheshet, and the Judah mentioned above, who is especially prominent as a transmitter of the sayings of his two teachers—added a mass of material to the Talmud; and the last-named founded the Academy of Pumbedita, where, as at Sura, the development of the Talmud was continued. Pumbedita was likewise the birthplace of that casuistic and hair-splitting method of interpreting and criticizing halakic passages which forms the special characteristic of the Babylonian Talmud, although the scholars of this academy devoted themselves also to the study of the collections of tannaitic traditions; and at the beginning of the fourth century the representatives of the two movements, "Sinai" Joseph and Rabbah, the "uprooter of mountains," succeeded their master Judah and became the directors of the school. Their sayings and controversies, together with the still more important dicta and debates of their pupils Abaye and Raba, form a considerable part of the material of the Talmud, which was greatly increased at the same time by the halakic and haggadic sentences brought from Palestine to Babylon. All the six orders of the Mishnah were then studied as is stated by Raba (not Rabba; see Rabbinovicz, "Diḳduḳe Soferim," on Ta'anit, p. 144), although in Judah's time the lectures had been confined to the fourth order, or, according to the view of Weiss ("Dor," iii. 187), which is probably correct, to the first four orders (comp. Meg. 28b; Ta'an. 24a, b; Sanh. 106b; Raba's pupil Pappa expresses a similar view in Ber. 20a).

Activity of Raba.

Rab's activity marks the culmination of the work on the Talmud. The time had now come when the preservation and arrangement of the material already collected were more important than further accretions. Naḥman b. Isaac, pupil and successor of Raba (d. 352), whom he survived but four years, expressed the task of the epigoni in the following words (Pes. 105b): "I am neither a sage nor a seer, nor even a scholar as contrasted with the majority. I am a transmitter ["gamrana"] and an arranger ["sadrana"]." The combination of the former term with the latter, which occurs only here, very concisely summarizes the activity of the redactor. It is clear that Naḥman b. Isaac actually engaged in this task from the fact that he is mentioned as the Babylonian amora who introduced MNEMONICS ("simanim"), designed to facilitate the memorizing and grouping of Talmudic passages and the names of their authors. The mnemonics ascribed to him in the Talmud (see J. Brüll, "Die Mnemonotechnik des Talmuds," p. 21; Bacher, "Ag. Bab. Amor." p. 134), however, constitute only a very small part of the simanim included in the text of that work. These again form but a remnant of the entire mass of what N. Brüll ("Jahrb." ii. 60) terms the "mnemotechnic apparatus," of which only a portion was included in the printed text of the Talmud, although many others may be traced both in the manuscripts of the Talmud and in ancient citations (see N. Brüll, l.c. pp. 62 et seq., 118 et seq.). The material, to which the epigoni of the second half of the fourth century had added little, was now ready for its final redaction; and it was definitively edited by ASHI (d. 427), who during his long period of activity infused fresh life into the Academy of Sura. In view of his recognized authority, little was left for the two succeeding generations, except to round out the work, since another redaction was no longer possible. The work begun by Ashi was completed by Rabina (Abina), whose death in 499 marks, according to an ancient tradition, the end of the amoraic period and the completion of the redaction of the Talmud.

The date at which the Talmud was committed to writing is purely conjectural. The work itself contains neither statements nor allusions to show that any complete or partial copy of the work redacted and completed by Ashi and Rabina had been made in their days; and the same lack of information characterizes both Yerushalmi and the Mishnah (the basis of both the Talmudim), as well as the other works of the tannaitic period. There are, however, allusions, although they are only sporadic, which show that the Halakah and the Haggadah were committed to writing; for copies were described as being in the possession of individual scholars, who were occasionally criticized for owning them.

This censure was based on an interdiction issued in the third century, which forbade any one to commit the teachings of tradition to writing or to use a manuscript of such a character in lecturing (see Giṭ. 60a; Tem. 14b). Replying to the scholars of Kairwan, Sherira Gaon in his letter (ed. Neubauer, "M. J. C." i. 26) alludes to this prohibition as follows: "In answer to your question asking when the Mishnah and the Talmud were respectively committed to writing, it should be said that neither of them was thus transmitted, but both were arranged [redacted] orally; and the scholars believe it to be their duty to recite them from memory, and not from written copies." From the second part of this statement it is evident that even in Sherira's time the "scholars," a term here restricted to the members of the Babylonian academies, refrained from using written copies of the Talmud in their lectures, although they were sufficiently familiar with it to be able to recite it from memory. The statement that the exilarch Naṭronai (8th cent.), who emigrated to Spain, wrote a copy of the Talmud from memory (see Brüll, "Jahrb." ii. 51), would show that the scholars of the geonic period actually knew the work by heart. Although this statement is not altogether free from suspicion, it at least proves that it was believed to be within the powers of this exilarch to make a copy of the Talmud without having an original at hand. This passage also throws light upon the period of the development and redaction of the Talmud, during which the ability to memorize the mass of material taught in the schools was developed to an extent which now transcends conception.

Committed to Writing.

On the other hand, Sherira's statement shows that his denial of the existence of the Talmud and the Mishnah in written form was limited to an officially recognized redaction; for manuscripts of the kind mentioned by him were then current, as they had been in the geonic period, despite the interdiction; for they were used at least as aids to study, and without them the Talmud could not possibly have been memorized. In like manner, this prohibition, in the light of Sherira's words, does not preclude the existence of private copies of portions of the traditional literature, even in earlier times. The concealed rolls ("megillot setarim") with halakic comments which Rab found in the house of his uncle Ḥiyya (Shab. 6b; B. M. 92a), as well as the note-books ($\pi i \nu a \kappa \epsilon \varsigma$) mentioned at the beginning of the amoraic period and in which such scholars as Levi b. Sisi, Joshua b. Levi, Ze'iri, and Ḥilfai or Ilfa (Shab. 156a; Yer. Ma'as. 49d, 60b; Men. 70a) entered sentences, some of them halakic in character, indicate that such personal copies were frequently used, while the written Haggadah is repeatedly mentioned. It may therefore be assumed that the Mishnah and other tannaitic traditional works were committed to writing as early as the time of the Amoraim. In like manner, there may have been copies of the amoraic comments on the Mishnah, as aids to the memory and to private study. In the early part of the fourth century Ze'era disputed the accuracy of the halakic tradition taught by the Babylonian amora Sheshet; and as he based his suspicions on Sheshet's blindness, he evidently believed that it was impossible for the Babylonian scholar to confirm and verify his knowledge by the use of written notes (see Bacher, "Ag. Pal. Amor." iii. 4). When Ashi undertook the final redaction of the Talmud he evidently had at his disposal notes of this kind, although Brüll (*l.c.* p. 18) is probably correct in ascribing to Rabina the first complete written copy of the Talmud; Rabina had as collaborators many of the SABORAIM, to whom an ancient and incontrovertible tradition assigns numerous additions to the Talmudic text.

When Rabina died a written text of the Talmud was already in existence, the material contributed by the Saboraim being merely additions; although in thus extending the text they simply continued what had been done since the first redaction of the Talmud by Ashi. The Saboraim, however, confined themselves to additions of a certain form which made no change whatsoever in the text as determined by them under the direction of Rabina (on these saboraic additions as well as on other accretions in Babli, see the statements by **No Formal** Brüll, *l.c.* pp. 69–86). Yet there is no **Rati-** allusion whatever to a formal sanction **fication.** of the written text of the Talmud; for neither did such a ratification take place nor was a formal one at all necessary. The Babylonian academies, which produced the text in the course of 300 years, remained its guardians when it was reduced to writing; and it became authoritative in virtue of its acceptance by the successors of the Amoraim, as the Mishnah had been sanctioned by the latter and was made the chief subject of study, thus becoming a basis for halakic decisions. The traditions, however, underwent no further development; for the "horayot," or the independent exegesis of the Mishnah and the halakic decisions based on this exegesis, ceased with Ashi and Rabina, and thus with the completion of the Talmud, as is stated in the canon incorporated in the Talmud itself (B. M. 86a). The Mishnah, the basal work of halakic tradition, thenceforth shared its authority with the Talmud.

Among the Jews who came under the influence of western Arabic culture the belief that the Talmud (and the Mishnah) had been redacted orally was superseded by the view that the initial redaction itself had been in writing. This theory was first expressed by R. Nissim of Kairwan ("Mafteah," p. 3b), although even before his time the question addressed, as already noted, to Sherira Gaon by the Jews of Kairwan had shown that they favored this view, and the gaon's response had received an interpolation postulating the written redaction of the Talmud.

The definitive redaction of the Babylonian Talmud marks a new epoch in the history of the Jewish people, in which the Talmud itself becomes the most important factor, both as the pivotal point of the development and the manifestation of the spirit of Judaism, and as a work of literature deeply influenced by the fortunes of those who cherished it as their palladium. On the internal history of Judaism the Talmud exerted a decisive influence as the recognized source for a knowledge of tradition and as the authoritative collection of the traditional religious doctrines which supplemented the Bible; indeed, this influence and the efforts which were made to escape from it, or to restrict it within certain limits, constitute the substance of the inner history of Judaism. The Babylonian academies, which had gradually become the central authority for the entire Jewish Diaspora, found their chief task in teaching the Talmud, on which they based the answers to the questions addressed to them. Thus was evolved a new science, the interpretation of the Talmud, which produced a literature of wide ramifications, and whose beginnings were the work of the Geonim themselves.

The Talmud and its study spread from Babylon to Egypt, northern Africa, Italy, Spain, France, and Germany, regions destined to become the abodes of **Influence** the Jewish spirit; and in all these **of the** countries intellectual interest centered **Talmud.** in the Talmud. The first great reaction against its supremacy was Karaism, which arose in the very stronghold of the Geonim within two centuries after the completion of the Talmud. The movement thus initiated and the influence of Arabic culture were the two chief factors which aroused the dormant forces of Judaism and gave inspiration to the scientific pursuits to which the Jewish spirit owed many centuries of marvelous and fruitful activity. This activity, however, did not infringe in the least on the authority of the Talmud; for although it combined other ideals and intellectual aims with Talmudic study, which it enriched and perfected, the importance of that study was in no wise decried by those who devoted themselves to other fields of learning. Nor did the speculative treatment of the fundamental teachings of Judaism lower the position of the Talmud; for Maimonides, the greatest philosopher of religion of his time, was likewise the greatest student of the Talmud, on which work he endeavored to base his philosophic views. A dangerous internal enemy of the Talmud, however, arose in the Cabala during the thirteenth century; but it also had to share with the Talmud the supremacy to which it aspired.

During the decline of intellectual life among the Jews which began in the sixteenth century, the Talmud was regarded almost as the supreme authority by the majority of them; and in the same century eastern Europe, especially Poland, became the seat of its study. Even the Bible was relegated to a secondary place, and the Jewish schools devoted themselves almost exclusively to the Talmud; so that "study" became synonymous with "study of the Talmud." A reaction against the supremacy of the Talmud came with the appearance of Moses Mendelssohn and the intellectual regeneration of Judaism through its contact with the Gentile culture of the eighteenth century, the results of this struggle being a closer assimilation to European culture, the creation of a new science of Judaism, and the movements for religious reform. Despite the Karaite inclinations which frequently appeared in these movements, the great majority of the followers of Judaism clung to the principle, authoritatively maintained by the Talmud, that tradition supplements the Bible; and the Talmud itself re-

PAGE FROM TRACTATE ḲIDDUSHIN OF THE BABYLONIAN TALMUD, SABBIONETTA, 1559.

(From the Sulzberger collection in the Jewish Theological Seminary of America, New York.)

tained its authority as the work embodying the traditions of the earliest post-Biblical period, when Judaism was molded. Modern culture, however, has gradually alienated from the study of the Talmud a number of Jews in the countries of progressive civilization, and it is now regarded by the most of them merely as one of the branches of Jewish theology, to which only a limited amount of time can be devoted, although it occupies a prominent place in the curricula of the rabbinical seminaries. On the whole Jewish learning has done full justice to the Talmud, many scholars of the nineteenth century having made noteworthy contributions to its history and textual criticism, and having constituted it the basis of historical and archeological researches. The study of the Talmud has even attracted the attention of non-Jewish scholars; and it has been included in the curricula of universities.

The external history of the Talmud reflects in part the history of Judaism persisting in a world of hostility and persecution. Almost at the very time that the Babylonian saboraim put the finishing touches to the redaction of the Talmud, the emperor Justinian issued his edict against the abolition of the Greek translation of the Bible in the service of the Synagogue, and also forbade the use of the δευτέρωσις, or traditional exposition of Scripture.

Edict of Justinian. This edict, dictated by Christian zeal and anti-Jewish feeling, was the prelude to attacks on the Talmud, conceived in the same spirit, and beginning in the thirteenth century in France, where Talmudic study was then flourishing. The charge against the Talmud brought by the convert Nicholas Donin led to the first public disputation between Jews and Christians and to the first burning of copies of the work (Paris, 1244). The Talmud was likewise the subject of a disputation at Barcelona in 1263 between Moses ben Naḥman and Pablo Christiani. In this controversy Naḥmanides asserted that the haggadic portions of the Talmud were merely "sermones," and therefore devoid of binding force; so that proofs deduced from them in support of Christian dogmas were invalid, even in case they were correct. This same Pablo Christiani made an attack on the Talmud which resulted in a papal bull against it and in the first censorship, which was undertaken at Barcelona by a commission of Dominicans, who ordered the cancelation of passages reprehensible from a Christian point of view (1264). At the disputation of Tortosa in 1413, Geronimo de Santa Fé brought forward a number of accusations, including the fateful assertion that the condemnations of pagans and apostates found in the Talmud referred in reality to Christians. Two years later, Pope Martin V., who had convened this disputation, issued a bull (which was destined, however, to remain inoperative) forbidding the Jews to read the Talmud, and ordering the destruction of all copies of it. Far more important were the charges made in the early part of the sixteenth century by the convert Johann Pfefferkorn, the agent of the Dominicans. The result of these accusations was a struggle in which the emperor and the pope acted as judges, the advocate of the Jews being Johann Reuchlin, who was opposed by the

obscurantists and the humanists; and this controversy, which was carried on for the most part by means of pamphlets, became the precursor of the Reformation. An unexpected result of this affair was the complete printed edition of the Babylonian Talmud issued in 1520 by Daniel Bomberg at Venice, under the protection of a papal privilege. Three years later, in 1523, Bomberg published the first edition of the Palestinian Talmud. After thirty years the Vatican, which had first permitted the Talmud to appear in print, undertook a campaign of destruction against it. On New-Year's Day (Sept. 9), 1553, the copies of the Talmud which had been confiscated in compliance with a decree of the Inquisition were burned at Rome; and similar burnings took place in other Italian cities, as at Cremona in 1559. The CENSORSHIP of the Talmud and other Hebrew works was introduced by a papal bull issued in 1554; five years later the Talmud was included in the first Index Expurgatorius; and Pope Pius IV. commanded, in 1565, that the Talmud be deprived of its very name. The first edition of the expurgated Talmud, on which most subsequent editions were based, appeared at Basel (1578–1581) with the omission of the entire treatise of 'Abodah Zarah and of passages considered inimical to Christianity, together with modifications of certain phrases. A fresh attack on the Talmud was decreed by Pope Gregory XIII. (1575–85), and in 1593 Clement VIII. renewed the old interdiction against reading or owning it. The increasing study of the Talmud in Poland led to the issue of a complete edition (Cracow, 1602–5), with a restoration of the original text; an edition containing, so far as known, only two treatises had previously been published at Lublin (1559–76).

Attacks on the Talmud. In 1707 some copies of the Talmud were confiscated in the province of Brandenburg, but were restored to their owners by command of Frederick, the first king of Prussia. The last attack on the Talmud took place in Poland in 1757, when Bishop Dembowski, at the instance of the Frankists, convened a public disputation at Kamenetz-Podolsk, and ordered all copies of the work found in his bishopric to be confiscated and burned by the hangman.

The external history of the Talmud includes also the literary attacks made upon it by Christian theologians after the Reformation, since these onslaughts on Judaism were directed primarily against that work, even though it was made a subject of study by the Christian theologians of the seventeenth and eighteenth centuries. In 1830, during a debate in the French Chamber of Peers regarding state recognition of the Jewish faith, Admiral Verhuell declared himself unable to forgive the Jews whom he had met during his travels throughout the world either for their refusal to recognize Jesus as the Messiah or for their possession of the Talmud. In the same year the Abbé CHIARINI published at Paris a voluminous work entitled "Théorie du Judaïsme," in which he announced a translation of the Talmud, advocating for the first time a version which should make the work generally accessible, and thus serve for attacks on Juda-

אלא אמר רב אשי *שלש מחיצות ולחי אחד זה מבוי שאינו מפולש ג' מחיצות בלא לחי זהו מבוי המפולש ואפילו לרבי אליעזר דאמר בעינן לחיים הני מילי לאוכלין ומשקין אבל לספר תורה בחד לחי סגי:

מתני' ב*מצילין *מזון ג' סעודות הראוי לאדם לאדם הראוי לבהמה לבהמה כיצד נפלה דליקה בלילי שבת מצילין מזון ג' סעודות בשחרית מצילין מזון ב' סעודות במנחה מזון סעודה אחת ר' יוסי אומר לעולם מצילין מזון שלש סעודות:

גמ' מכדי בהיתרא קטרח נציל טפי אמר רבא *מתוך שאדם בהול על ממונו אי שריית ליה אתי לכבויי א"ל אביי אלא הא דתניא *נשברה לו חבית בראש גגו מביא כלי ומניח תחתיה *ובלבד שלא יביא כלי אחר ויקלוט כלי אחר ויצרף התם מאי גזירה איכא ה"נ גזירה שמא יביא כלי דרך רה"ר גופא ג*נשברה לו חבית בראש גגו מביא כלי ומניח תחתיה ובלבד שלא יביא כלי אחר ויקלוט כלי אחר ויצרף ד*נזדמן לו אורחין מביא כלי אחר וקולט כלי אחר ומצרף ולא יקלוט ואחר כך יזמין אלא יזמין ואח"כ יקלוט °ואין מערימין בכך משום רבי יוסי בר יהודה אמרו מערימין לימא בפלוגתא דרבי אליעזר ור' יהושע קמיפלגי דתניא *אותו ואת בנו שנפלו לבור רבי אליעזר

[לעיל מג. ע"ש]

[לקמן קכ:]

רש"י

אלא אמר רב אשי כו'. בין רבנן ובין בן בתירא כר' אליעזר סבירא להו דבעי ג' מחיצות וב' לחיים בעלמא והכא לגבי ספר אמרי רבנן מודה ר' אליעזר בלחי אחד ובן בתירא אמר דמודה ר' אליעזר אף בלא לחי: בחד לחי סגי ליה. מילתא דרבנן קא מפרשי:

מתני' נפלה דליקה בלילי שבת. קודם אכילה: שחרית. קודם סעודה: לעולם הוא מציל. הואיל ויומא בר הכי הוא ובהיתרא טרח דהא בני טלטול נינהו ולחצר המעורבת ואפי' טובא הוה שרי ליה אי לאו משום גזירה וכדמפרש בגמרא: **גמ'** מכדי בהיתרא קטרח. חזו לטלטול ולחצר המעורבת: ואי שריית ליה. לאתחולי בהצלה טולי האי מתוך שהוא בהול מיכשי ליה שבת ואתי נמי לכבויי: ויקלוט. קילוח השפל מן האויר: ויצרף. סמוך לגג כעין שאיבה אלא שאינו ראוי לשאוב שהגג חלק והיין אינו בגומא מצרף כלי לגג שיזוב מן הגג לכלי והוא אוחז הכלי בידו: התם מאי גזירה איכא. כיון דמידי דהתירא הוא אמאי לא יקלוט ויצרף: שמא יביא כלי כו'. מתוך שהוא מחזר על כלים הרבה ישכח ויביא: ולא יקלוט ואח"כ יזמין. אורחים דבשעת קליטה לא מיבעיא ליה: אין מערימין בכך. לזמן אורחים שאינן צריכין לאכול ויותירו: שנפלו לבור. בי"ט ואין שניהם ראוים לשחיטה ביום אחד: ואינו שוחטו. שמותר לו עלילה שמא חברו שמן ממנו: עד כאן לא קאמר ר' אליעזר. דאין מערימין: הציל פת נקיה. לשלש סעודות: לא יציל פת הדראה. פת קיבר שניטל הדרה לפי שאין ערמה כשרה לומר פת הדראה נוחה לי:

תוספות

הא דתניא נשברה לו חבית בראש גגו. הקשה הרב פורת אמאי לא פריך ממתניתין דריש חבית (לקמן קמג:) דתנן חבית שנשברה מצילין ממנה מזון שלש סעודות ואומר לאחרים בואו והצילו לכם ובלבד שלא יספוג ותירץ דההיא איכא למימר כגון שהחבית בכרמלית דחיישינן שמא יעביר כלי ד' אמות בכרמלית אבל בהך ברייתא קתני בהדיא בראש גגו ור"י תירץ דהתם מיירי כשנשפך היין לארץ דחיישינן שמא יספוג אומר ה"ר שמואל בשם ר"ת דדוקא נשברה לו חבית אבל נסדקה ועושה טיף טיף מותר להביא כלים לקלוט ולצרף דאינו בהול כל כך להביא כלים דרך רה"ר כמו כשנשברה:

כלי אחר ויקלוט כלי אחר ויצרף. אומר ר"י דזו אף זו קתני לא מבעי לקלוט דמינכר שמציל דאסור אלא אפילו לצרף דלא מינכר כולי האי שהוא מציל אסור: **הציל** פת נקיה לא יציל פת הדראה. אומר ר"י כשחל י"ט של פסח מלות מסולת נקיה שיש לו די לצורך י"ט אין אופין אחריהן פת של הדראה אלא מתחילה יעשה של הדראה ואחרי כן יעשה הנקיה:

אבל לא משבת ליום הכפורים. פירש בקונטרס למוצאי יוה"כ וא"ת פשיטא דחול גמור הוא ומ"ש משבת למוצאי שבת וי"ל דמצוה לאכול במוצאי יוה"כ כדפי' לעיל(ב) (דף קיד:) ועוד לפי שהתענו מותר יותר אי כמי ליום הכפורים עצמו קאמר ולהאכיל התינוקות:

והתנא דבי רבי ישמעאל כל מלאכת עבודה לא תעשו. וא"ת ואמאי מייתי קרא

יז א מיי' פי"ז מהל' שבת הלכה ב ופכ"ג הלכ"ו סמג לאוין סה ועשין א טור ש"ע או"ח סימן של"ד סעיף יז וסימן שסג סעיף א ג יד:

יח ב מיי' פכ"ג שם הלכ"א וסמג שם טור וש"ע או"ח סימן שלד סעיף א:

יט ג מיי' פרק כ"ב שם הלכה טו סמג שם טוש"ע או"ח סימן שלה סעיף ב:

כ ד מיי' שם טור ש"ע שם סעיף ג:

כא ה מיי' פ"ב מהלכות יו"ט הלכה ד טור ש"ע או"ח סימן תמח סעיף י:

כב ו מיי' פכ"ג מהלכות שבת הלכה כח טור ש"ע או"ח סימן שלד סעיף ג:

כג ז מיי' שם טור ש"ע שם סעיף ד:

כד ח מיי' פכ"ב שם הל"א סמג שם טור וש"ע או"ח סימן רנד סעיף ה:

כה ט טוש"ע או"ח סי' רנ סעיף א:

כו י כ מיי' פ"ל שם הלכה ט סמג עשין ל טור ש"ע או"ח סימן רעד סעיף א ב וסימן רפט סעיף א:

כז ל טוש"ע או"ח סימן שלד סעיף ב בהג"ה:

כח מ מיי' וסמג שם טוש"ע או"ח סימן רנא סעיף א:

הגהות הב"ח

(א) גמ' והא תנא דבי ר' ישמעאל לא תעשו. נ"ב עי' בפי' ר"א דמילה דף קלא ע"ב דגורס קרא דכל מלאכת עבודה לא תעשו:

(ב) תוס' ד"ה אבל וכו' כדפי' לעיל. נ"ב בס"פ אלו קשרים ממש וכ"כ התוס' סוף יומא דף

PAGE FROM TRACTATE SHABBAT OF THE ROMM EDITION OF THE BABYLONIAN TALMUD, WILNA, 1886.

J. E., Vol. XII.

ism. In a like spirit modern anti-Semitic agitators have urged that a translation be made; and this demand has even been brought before legislative bodies, as in Vienna. The Talmud and the "Talmud Jew" thus became objects of anti-Semitic attacks, although, on the other hand, they were defended by many Christian students of the Talmud.

In consequence of the checkered fortunes of the Talmud, manuscripts of it are extremely rare; and the Babylonian Talmud is found entire only in a Munich codex (Hebrew MS. No. 95), completed in 1369, while a Florentine manuscript containing several treatises of the fourth and fifth orders dates from the year 1176. A number of Talmudic codices containing one or more tractates are extant in Rome, Oxford, Paris, Hamburg, and New York, while the treatise Sanhedrin, from Reuchlin's library, is in the grand-ducal library at Carlsruhe. In the introduction to vols. i., iv., viii., ix., and xi. of his "Dikduke Soferim, Variæ Lectiones in Mischnam et in Talmud Babylonicum," which contains a mass of critical material bearing on the text of Babli, N. Rabbinovicz has described all the manuscripts of this Talmud known to him, and has collated the Munich manuscript with the printed editions, besides giving in his running notes a great number of readings collected with much skill and learning from other manuscripts and various ancient sources. Of this work, which is indispensable for the study of the Talmud, Rabbinovicz himself published fifteen volumes (Munich, 1868-86), containing the treatises of the first, second, and fourth orders, as well as two treatises (Zebahim and Menahot) of the fifth order. The sixteenth volume (Hullin) was published posthumously (completed by Ehrentreu, Przemysl, 1897). Of the Palestinian Talmud only one codex, now at Leyden, has been preserved, this being one of the manuscripts used for the editio princeps. Excepting this codex, only fragments and single treatises are extant. Recently (1904) Luncz discovered a portion of Yerushalmi in the Vatican Library, and Ratner has made valuable contributions to the history of the text in his scholia on Yerushalmi ("Sefer Ahabat Ziyyon we-Yerushalayim"), of which three volumes have thus far appeared, comprising Berakot, Shabbat, Terumot, and Hallah (Wilna, 1901, 1902, 1904).

The first edition of Babli (1520) was preceded by a series of editions, some of them no longer extant, of single treatises published at Soncino and Pesaro by the Soncinos. The first to appear was Berakot (1488); this was followed by the twenty-three other tractates which, according to **Early** Gershon Soncino, were regularly stud- **Editions.** ied in the yeshibot. The first edition by Bomberg was followed by two more (1531, 1548), while another was published at Venice by Giustiniani (1546-51), who added to Bomberg's supplements (such as Rashi and the Tosafot, which later were invariably appended to the text) other useful marginal glosses, including references to Biblical quotations and to parallel passages of the Talmud as well as to the ritual codices. At Sabionetta in 1553, Joshua Boaz (d. 1557), the author of these marginalia, which subsequently were added to all editions of the Talmud, undertook a new and

magnificent edition of the Talmud. Only a few treatises were completed, however; for the papal bull issued against the Talmud in the same year interrupted the work. As a result of the burning of thousands of copies of the Talmud in Italy, Joseph Jabez published a large number of treatises at Salonica (1563 et seq.) and Constantinople (1583 et seq.). The mutilated Basel edition (1578-81) and the two editions which first appeared in Poland have been mentioned above. The first Cracow edition (1602-5) was followed by a second (1616-20); while the first Lublin edition (1559 et seq.), which was incomplete, was followed by one giving the entire text (1617-39); this was adopted for the Amsterdam edition (1644-48), the partial basis of the edition of Frankfort-on-the-Oder (1697-99). Many useful addenda were made to the second Amsterdam edition (1714-19), which was the subject of an interesting lawsuit, and which was completed by the edition of Frankfort-on-the-Main (1720-22). This latter text has served as the basis of almost all the subsequent editions. Of these the most important are: Prague, 1728-39; Berlin and Frankfort-on-the-Oder, 1734-39 (earlier ed. 1715-22); Amsterdam, 1752-65; Sulzbach, 1755-63, 1766-70; Vienna, 1791-1797, 1806-11, 1830-33, 1840-49, 1860-73; Dyhernfurth, 1800-4, 1816-21; Slawita, Russia, 1801-6, 1808-13, 1817-22; Prague, 1830-35, 1839-46; Wilna and Grodno, 1835-54; Czernowitz, 1840-49; Jitomir, 1858-64; Warsaw, 1859-64, 1863-67 et seq.; Wilna, 1859-66; Lemberg, 1860-65 et seq.; Berlin, 1862-68; Stettin, 1862 et seq. (incomplete). The edition of the Widow and Brothers Romm at Wilna (1886) is the largest as regards old and new commentaries, glosses, other addenda, and aids to study.

Two other editions of Yerushalmi have appeared in addition to the editio princeps (Venice, 1523 et seq.), which they closely follow in columniation— those of Cracow, 1609, and Krotoschin, 1866. A complete edition with commentary appeared at Jitomir in 1860-67. The latest edition is that of Piotrkow (1898-1900). There are also editions of single orders or treatises and their commentaries, especially noteworthy being Z. Frankel's edition of Berakot, Pe'ah, and Demai (Breslau, 1874-75).

A critical edition of Babli has been proposed repeatedly, and a number of valuable contributions have been made, especially in the huge collections of variants by Rabbinovicz; **"Variæ** but so far this work has not even been **Lectiones"** begun, although mention should be **and Trans-** made of the interesting attempt by M. **lations.** Friedmann, "Kritische Edition des Traktates Makkoth," in the "Verhandlungen des Siebenten Internationalen Orientalisten-Congresses, Semitische Section," pp. 1-78 (Vienna, 1888). Here the structure of the text is indicated by such external means as different type, sections, and punctuation. The edition of Yerushalmi announced by Luncz at Jerusalem promises a text of critical purity.

The earliest allusion to a translation of the Talmud is made by Abraham ibn Daud in his historical "Sefer ha-Kabbalah" (see Neubauer, "M. J. C." i. 69), who, referring to Joseph ibn Abitur (second half of 10th cent.), says: "He is the one who translated the entire Talmud into Arabic for the calif Al-Ḥakim." The tradition was therefore current among the Jews of Spain in the twelfth century that Ibn Abitur had translated the Talmud for this ruler of Cordova, who was especially noted for his large library, this tradition being analogous to the one current in Alexandria in antiquity with regard to the first Greek translation of the Bible. No trace, however, remains of Joseph Abitur's translation; and in all probability he translated merely detached portions for the calif, this work giving rise to the legend of his complete version. The need of a translation to render the contents of the Talmud more generally accessible, began to be felt by Christian theologians after the sixteenth century, and by Jewish circles in the nineteenth century. This gave rise to the translations of the Mishnah which have been noted elsewhere (see Jew. Encyc. viii. 618, *s.v.* Mishnah). In addition to the complete translations mentioned there, single treatises of the Mishnah have been rendered into Latin and into modern languages, a survey being given by Bischoff in his "Kritische Geschichte der Thalmud-Uebersetzungen," pp. 28–56 (Frankfort-on-the-Main, 1899). Twenty treatises of Yerushalmi were translated into Latin by Blasio Ugolino in his "Thesaurus Antiquitatum Sacrarum," xvii. (1755), xxx. (1765); and the entire text of this Talmud was rendered into French by Moïse Schwab ("Le Talmud de Jérusalem," 11 vols., Paris, 1871–1889). The translation by Wünsche of the haggadic portions of Yerushalmi has already been mentioned; and an account of the translations of single portions is given by Bischoff (*l.c.* pp. 59 *et seq.*). In 1896 L. Goldschmidt began the translation of a German version of Babli, together with the text of Bomberg's first edition; and a number of volumes have already appeared (Berlin, 1898 *et seq.*). The insufficiency of this work apparently corresponds to the rapidity with which it is issued. In the same year M. L. Rodkinson undertook an abridged translation of the Babylonian Talmud into English, of which seven volumes appeared before the translator's death (1904); Rodkinson's point of view was quite unscholarly. Of translations of single treatises the following may be mentioned (see Bischoff, *l.c.* pp. 68–76): Earlier Latin translations: Ugolino, Zebaḥim, Menaḥot (in "Thesaurus Antiquitatum Sacrarum," xix.), Sanhedrin (*ib.* xxv.); G. E. Edzard, Berakot (Hamburg, 1713); F. B. Dachs, Sukkah (Utrecht, 1726). Noteworthy among the Jewish translators of the Talmud are M. Rawicz (Megillah, 1863; Rosh ha-Shanah, 1886; Sanhedrin, 1892; Ketubot, 1897); E. M. Pinner (Berakot, 1842, designed as the first volume of a translation of the entire Talmud); D. O. Straschun (Ta'anit, 1883); and Sammter (Baba Meẓi'a, 1876). Their translations are entirely in German. Translations published by Christian scholars in the nineteenth century: F. C. Ewald (a baptized Jew), 'Abodah Zarah (Nuremberg, 1856); in 1831 the Abbé Chiarini, mentioned above, published a French translation of Berakot; and in 1891 A. W. Streane prepared an English translation of Ḥagigah. A French version of several treatises is included in J. M. Rabbinovicz's works "Législation Civile du Talmud" (5 vols., Paris, 1873–79) and "Législation Criminelle

du Talmud" (*ib.* 1876), while Wünsche's translation of the haggadic portions of Babli (1886–89) has been mentioned above.

To gain a comprehensive view of the Talmud it must be considered as a historical factor in Judaism as well as a literary production. In the latter aspect it is unique among the great masterpieces of the literatures of the world. In form a commentary, it became an encyclopedia of Jewish faith and scholarship, comprising whatsoever the greatest representatives of Judaism in Palestine and in Babylon had regarded as objects of study and investigation and of teaching and learning, during the three centuries which elapsed from the conclusion of the Mishnah to the completion of the Talmud itself. When the Mishnah, with the many ancient traditions to which it had given rise since the latter centuries of the Second Temple, was incorporated into the Talmud as its text-book, the Talmud became a record of the entire epoch which was represented by the Jewish schools of Palestine and Babylon, and which served as a stage of transition from the Biblical period to the later aspect of Judaism. Although the Talmud is an academic product and may be characterized in the main as a report **Function** (frequently with the accuracy of min- **in** utes) of the discussions of the schools, **Judaism.** it also sheds a flood of light on the culture of the people outside the academies. The interrelation between the schools and daily life, and the fact that neither teachers nor pupils stood aloof from that life, but took part in it as judges, instructors, and expounders of the Law, caused the Talmud to represent even non-scholastic affairs with an abundance of minute details, and made it an important source for the history of civilization. Since, moreover, the religious law of the Jews dealt with all the circumstances of life, the Talmud discusses the most varied branches of human knowledge—astronomy and medicine, mathematics and law, anatomy and botany—thus furnishing valuable data for the history of science also.

The Talmud, furthermore, is unique from the point of view of literary history as being a product of literature based on oral tradition and yet summarizing the literature of an entire epoch. Aside from it, those to whose united efforts it may be ascribed have left no trace of intellectual activity. Though anonymous itself, the Talmud, like other products of tannaitic and amoraic literature, cites the names of many authors of sayings because it was a universal practise to memorize the name of the author together with the saying. Many of these scholars are credited with only a few sentences or with even but one, while to others are ascribed many hundreds of aphorisms, teachings, questions, and answers; and the representatives of Jewish tradition of those centuries, the Tannaim and the Amoraim, received an abundant compensation for their renunciation of the fame of authorship when tradition preserved their names together with their various expositions, and thus rescued even the least of them from oblivion. The peculiar form of the Talmud is due to the fact that it is composed almost entirely of individual sayings and discussions on them, this circumstance being a result of its origin:

מסורת הש"ס | עין משפט נר מצוה

גמ' *הוון בעיי מימר מליח לעולם הא לשעה לא אמר ר' יודן מן מה דתנינן הרי עלי כבשר מלוח וביין נסך. הדא אמרה מליח לשעה מלוח הוא. אי זהו מלוח לשעה כיי דתני כיצד הוא עושה נותן את האיברים על גבי המלח והופכן. אמר ר' אבא מרי שנייא היא שאם משהא הוא אותן שהן נמלחין. ויידא אמרה דא דמר ר' חייה בר אבא *הנוטל זיתים מן המעטן טובל אחד במלח ואוכל הדא אמרה מלוח הוא לשעה מלוח הוא. הרי עלי כתרומה אם בתרומת הלשכה נדר אסור הא בתרומת תודה מותר. ואם של גורן מותר. הא בתרומת תודה אסור. הכא את אמר אסור והכא את אמר מותר. נישמעינה מן הדא כחלת אהרן וכתרומתו מותר. הא בתרומת תודה אסור. וחכמים אומרים סתם תרומה ביהודה אסורה ובגליל מותרת. שאין אנשי גליל מכירין תרומת הלשכה. אבל אם היו מכירין כתם אסור. סתם חרמין ביהודה מותרין ובגליל אסורין שאין בני גליל מכירין חרמי כהנים. אבל אם היו מכירין סתמן מותר. הכא את אמר מותר. וכא את אמר אסור. אמר רבי אלעזר תרין תניין אינון. אמר רבי ירמיה
הד

קרבן העדה

גמ' תמן בעי מימר. סברוהו למימר לא מיקרי בשר מלוח אלא אם נמלח שיהי' לעולם במליחתו אבל אם נמלח לשעה לא מיקרי בשר מלוח: הדא אמרה. זאת אומרת אפי' מלוח לשעה מיקרי מלוח דהא קרבנות אינן נמלחין אלא לשעה כדמסיק ואפילו הכי תנן במתני' דמיקרי בשר מלוח: כיי דתני. כי הא דתני בת"כ ומייתי לה במנחות פ"ג: כילד הוא עושה. במליחת הקרבנות: והופכן. תוך המלח שיהא המלח בכל צדדיו: ה"ג שנייא היא שאם משהא וכו'. נ"פ שאני התם בקרבנות שמשהה את האיברים תוך המלח שיקלט טעם המלח נמצא שהן מלוחים לעולם: ויידא אמרה דא. והיכן אמר דבר זה שמלוח לשעה הוי מליחה: דאמר רחב"א הנוטל זיתים וכו'. מתני' היא פ"ד דמעשרות: טובל אחד אחד במלח. שאין קובע למעשר אלא מלח ולירוף שתים הלכך תנן בסיפא אם מלח ונתן לפניו חייב שמעינן מיהא אם לירף שתים אע"ג דאוכלן מיד חייב דה"ל מלוח ש"מ דמלוח לשעה הוי מלוח: הא כתרומת תודה. ארבעה לחם שתורמין מלחמי תודה וניתנו לכהן אסור: הכא את אמר אסור וכו'. דיוקא דרישא וסיפא קשיין אהדדי מרישא משמע כתרומת הידה מותר ומסיפא משמע דאסור: נישמעינה מן הדא. כלומר ממתני' דהכא ליכא למשמע מינה לא איסור ולא היתר אלא ממתני' דריש פרקין איכא למשמע דאסור דתנן כחלת אהרן וכתרומתו מותר ש"מ דוקא כתרומת אהרן הוא דמותר הא כתרומת תודה אסור: אבל אם היו מכירין. אע"ג דמספקא לן אי כתרומת הלשכה אי כתרומת הגורן נדר סתם אסור דספיקא לחומרא: הכא את אמר מותר וכו'. דיוקא דרישא וסיפא קשיין אהדדי ברישא משמע ספיקא לחומרא ובסיפא משמע לקולא: תרין תניין אינון. תרין תנאים הן רישא ר' יהודה דסובר ספיקא לחומרא וסיפא ראב"ל דסובר ספיקא לקולא:
חד

פני משה

גמ' הוון בעיי מימר. היו רוצין בני הישיבה מתחילה לומר מלוח לעולם נקרא מלוח וג"מ לנודר מן המלוח כדתנן לקמן פ"ו ועלה דהתם קאי הא מלוח לשעה לא: אמר ר' יודן. לא היא דמן מה דתנינן במתני' הרי עלי כבשר מלוח ואברי הקרבן לא היו נמלחין אלא לשעה כדלקמן ש"מ מלוח לשעה נמי נקרא מלוח: איזהו מלוח לשעה. שאסור בנודר וילפת לה מבשר מלוח דמתני': כהאי דתני. בברייתא דקדשים ומייתי לה בבבלי מנחות דף כ"א: כילד הוא עושה. במליחת אברי הקרבנות נותן כו' ושם גרים נותן המלח ע"ג האבר וחוזר והופכו ונותן עליו מלח: שנייא היא. התם דלאו מלוח לשעה מיקרי שהרי אם משהה אותן כך במלחן ואינו מקריבן ודאי הן נמלחין לגמרי ואכתי לא ידעינן הי המלוח לשעה דקאמרת ומנא לך דמיקרי מלוח: ויידא אמרה. ומהיכן שמענו זה: דא. מן ההיא דאמר ר' חייה כלומר ר' חייה למד לנו מן ההיא מתני' דתנן במס' מעשרות: הנוטל זיתים מן המעטן. מקום שצוברין שם הזיתים נקרא מעטן: טובל אחד אחד במלח ואוכל. דלא הוי קבע הואיל וטבלן א' אחד ומותר לאכול אכילת עראי בלא מעשר אלמא שנקרא מלוח במה שטובל לפי שעה: הדא אמרה מלוח לשעה מלוח הוא. כלומר ש"מ אפילו מלוח לשעה בכה"ג נקרא מלוח ואסור בנודר מן המלוח: הרי עלי כתרומה כו'. ומדייק הש"ס דברישא משמע דוקא בתרומת הלשכה אסור דהוי דבר הנדור: הא בתרומת תודה. תרומת לחמי תודה שהיה נוטל הלה אחת מכל עשר חלות של כל מין שבה ואם התפיס בה מותר דדבר אסור מיקריא ובסיפא קתני של גורן דוקא מותר דמשמע הא בתרומת תודה אסור וקשיא דיוקא דרישא וסיפא אהדדי הכא את אמר אסור והכא את אמר מותר: נישמעינה מן הדא. כלומר מהא ודאי ליכא למישמע מינה אלא מהא דתנן ריש פרקין כחלת אהרן וכתרומתו מותר ושמע מינה הא כתרומת תודה אסור דהוי דבר הנדור שמנדרין תודה ולהמה. וכן משמע ממסקנת הבבלי פרק קמא דף י"ב לפי שינויא בתרא דהתם: וחכמים אומרים כו'. ומקשי נמי דיוקא דרישא לסיפא דקהני טעמא דסתם תרומה בגליל מותר שאין מ רין תרומת הלשכה ומסתמא דעתן לגורן הוא אבל אם היו מכירין לתרומת הלשכה סתם תרומה אסור אפי' בגליל מספיקא אלמא דספיקא לחומרא והדר קתני בחרמין סתם חרמין כו'. דמשמע אבל אם היו מכירין חרמי כהנים סתמן מותר מספיקא אלמא ספיקא לקולא הכא כו': תרין תניין אינון. כתנאי אזלא רישא וסיפא דמתני' ימני משנה זו לא שנה זו דמר אזיל בספיקא להומרא ומר אזיל לקולא. וכן מוקי לה בבבלי דף י"ט כתנאי: רבי ירמיה. קאמר לעולם
חד.

רידב"ז

ובגליל אסורין שאין אנשי בני גליל מכירין את חרמי הכהנים אבל אם היו מכירין סתמא מותר הכא את אמר מותר וכא את אמר אסיר דקס"ד אם היו מכירין אלו ואלו הי' מותרין וברישא אם היו מכירין אלו ואלו אסורין וקשיא מרישא לסיפא ע"ז אמר רבי אליעזר תרי תניין אינון ורבי ירמי' משני דלעולם חד תנא הוא ולעולם סתם נדרים להחמיר ואם הי' מכירין אלו ואלו מותרין והא דתני שאין אנשי גליל מכירין את חרמי הכהנים לא תידוק מינה אם הי' מכירין אלו ואלו מותרין ז"א אלא משום דבחרמים איכא פליגתא דתנאי אם סתם חרמים. הוא לבד"ה אי דסתם חרמים הוא לכהנים וע"כ אנשי גליל אסורין בחרמים דאיפסק הלכתא עם מנהגי כמ"ד סתם חרמים לבד"ה אבל למאן דאמר סתם חרמים לכהנים הי' מותרין ולא תידוק הא אם היו מכירין אלו ואלו מותרין ז"א דבחרמים ליכא אלו ואלו אלא הי סתם חרמים לבד"ה אי סתם חרמים לכהנים והכי קאמר במתניתין דאין אנשי גליל מכירין בחרמי כהנים לא נהגו כמאן דאמר סתם חרמים לכהנים הא אם הי' מכירין חרמי כהנים כלומר אם היו מכירין והי' נוהגין כמאן דאמר סתם חרמים לכהנים או אף בגליל מותר וזה שייך בחרמים דשם ליכא אלו ואלו אלא או כמאן דאמר סתם לבד"ה או כמאן דאמר סתם חרמים לכהנים לפיכך מדייק התנא דבגליל אסורין שאין מכירין חרמי כהנים ונהג בגליל כמאן דאמר סתם חרמים לבד"ה אבל אי סבירא ליה כמ"ד סתם חרמים לכהנים או פשיטא דמותר ע"ז קאמר ר"י בשם רבי הילא דז"א דלא אתיא כמאן דאמר סתם חרמים לבד"ה ולא תלי יהודה וגליל בפלוגתא דהתנאים אי סתם חרמים לבד"ה או לכהנים ולא משום דנהגו ביהודה כהאי תנא ובגליל כהאי תנא אלא כל עיקר הגפ"מ שבין יהודה לגליל הוא משום דבגליל היו רגילין בחרם עכן וביהודה לא היו רגילין בחרם עכן ופליג על האוקימתא דר' ירמי' ודוק:

רב

תוס' הרי"ד

לשמים לענין מעילה דלא נתקדש ע"י קדושתו האימורין דהא בחיים אין מועלין בו דלא הוי קדשי שמים מחיים והא דכ' התוס' ז"ל במס' כריתות דף כ"ג ע"ב ד"ה בולדות דבקק"ל אפילו דליכא מעילה קודם זריקה מ"מ איסורא מיהא איכא הוא ע"כ משום דכיון דעומד בע"כ להיות קדשי שמים ע"י זריקה ע"כ הוי עליו איסור דמעילה והרא"י דהא בבשר אין עליו איסור לעולם אפילו איסורא בעלמא כדמדייק בגמ' במס' מעילה דף ז' ע"ב על הבשר דאין בו מעילה הא איסורא איכא ומשני ליואלין ורע"ס עיי"ש א"כ מוכח דע"כ בבשר ליכא איסורא בלל אפילו לאחר זריקה וע"כ הא דתנינן בשר קק"ל לפני זריקת דמים אין מועלין בהם ובאימורין דע"כ מדייקינן מעילה הוא דליכא הא איסורא איכא עיי"ש בגמ' הוא ע"כ על האימורין אבל לא על הבשר והא דנקט בשר הוא משום דבעי למתני אימורין לפיכך תני בשר כדאיתא שם בסוגיא מתחלה משום דנסיב רישא מועלין וה"ה אפילו איסורא ליכא עיי"ש היטב. בסוגיא ותמצא כן לפיכך אין לנו למימר דתל הקדש על אימורין רק בדבר שהוא בעצמו הקדש לשמים והרי בידו להקדש סוכה לשמים בירושלמי הנ"ל אבל בהקדש הזה שאין בידו להקדישו לשמים רק נתקדש מאיליו ע"י הזריקה והזריקה מקדש להקדש זה הקדש לשמים מהיכי תיתי דיחול על אימורין אם לא דסבירא ליה דאתפ"א ומהסוגיא הזאת מוכח גם כן כדברינו דע"כ כל מידי דבר אכילה דהוי קדשי ד' מועלין ע"כ על אכילתו דילפינן מתרומה דהל"כ מנ"ל להוכית דרבי סבירא ליה דאתפ"א בקדשים מהאי דחלב אימא דמועיל בחלב רק על הנאה לחוד בלא אכילה אלא ע"כ כיון דמידי דבר אכילה נהרבי למעילה ע"כ דמועלין גם על אכילה דגמרינן מתרומה כנ"ל וכזה טוחא להבין הרמב"ם ז"ל בפ"ד דשבועות ה"ע שבועה שלא אוכל ככר זו או שלא אוכל אותה כיון שאכל ממנה כזית חייב שבועה שלא אוכלנה ואכלה אינו חייב עד שאכל את כולה אמר שבועה שלא אוכל ככר זו שבועה שלא אוכלנה ואכלה אינו חייב אלא אחת ובה"י וכן אם אמר שבועה שלא אוכל היום וחזר ונשבע על הככר שלא יאכלנה ואכלה כולה באותו היום אינו חייב אלא אחת וכן כל כיוצא בזה שאין שבועה חלה. על השבועה אבל אם נשבע על הככר שלא יאכלנה וחזר ונשבע שלא יאכל כלום או שלא יאכל ככר זו ואכלה כולה חייב שתים, שבשבועה שנשבע תחלה שלא אוכלנה אינו. חייב עד שיאכל כולה וכשחזר ונשבע שלא יאכל או שלא יאכל אותה משאכל ממנה כזית. חייב כו' עכ"ל ז"ל עיי' בכ"מ ז"ל שכבא דרישא בה"ע וככא דסיפא בה"י אבל אם נשבע על הככר שלא יאכלנה הוא כמאה וגמ' ומ"ש במליעתא וכן אם אמר שבועה שלא אוכל היום הוא נלמד מבבא דרישא ולכאורה יש לדקדק מדוע בה"י כתב וכן אם אמר שבועה שלא אוכל היום וחזר ונשבע על הככר שלא יאכלנה כו' כתב בדיוק שלא אוכל היום ולא כתב דבר והפוכו כמו שמסיק אבל אם נשבע על הככר שלא יאכלנה וחזר ונשבע שלא יאכל כלום מדוע לא כתב ברישא שבועה שלא יאכל כלום וחזר ונשבע על הככר שלא יאכלנה למה נקט שלא יאכל היום. [ומכל שכן לפי' הראב"ד ז"ל דפירש שלא יאכלנה הוא ג"כ היום] ועל פי דברינו ניחא דאי כנשבע שלא יאכל כלום למה לא חל השבועה שני' הא כהשבועה לא חל על החפץ רק על גופו דגברא ולמה לא חל השבועה שני' בעל הככר הא ל"ל דאין איסור חל על איסור כנ"ל ע"כ מדייק שלא יאכל היום ולא אסר גוף האכילה רק היום ותל האיסור על היום ונמצא דלא חל השבועה שני' על היום הזה והוי כמו …
[illegible]

Page from the Latest Edition of the Jerusalem Talmud, Printed at Piotrkow, 1899–1903.

(In the possession of J. D. Eisenstein, New York.)

the fact that it sought especially to preserve the oral tradition and the transactions of the academies allowed the introduction only of the single sentences which represented the contributions of the teachers and scholars to the discussions. The preservation of the names of the authors of these apothegms, and of those who took part in the discussions, transactions, and disputations renders the Talmud the most important, and in many respects the only, source for the period of which it is the product. The sequence of generations which constitute the framework of the history of the Tannaim and Amoraim may be determined from the allusions contained in the Talmud, from the anecdotes and stories of the academies, and from other valuable literary material, which exhibit the historical conditions, events, and personages of the time, not excepting cases in which the facts have been clothed in the garb of legend or myth. Although it was undertaken with no distinctly literary purpose, it contains, especially in its haggadic portions, many passages which are noteworthy as literature, and which for many centuries were the sole repositories of Jewish poetry.

After the completion of the Talmud as a work of literature, it exercised a twofold influence as a historical factor in the history of Judaism and its followers, not only in **Its** regard to the guidance and formula-**Authority.** tion of religious life and thought, but also with respect to the awakening and development of intellectual activity. As a document of religion the Talmud acquired that authority which was due to it as the written embodiment of the ancient tradition, and it fulfilled the task which the men of the Great Assembly set for the representatives of the tradition when they said, "Make a hedge for the Torah" (Ab. i. 2). Those who professed Judaism felt no doubt that the Talmud was equal to the Bible as a source of instruction and decision in problems of religion, and every effort to set forth religious teachings and duties was based on it; so that even the great systematic treatise of Maimonides, which was intended to supersede the Talmud, only led to a more thorough study of it. In like manner, the Shulḥan 'Aruk of Joseph Caro, which achieved greater practical results than the Mishneh Torah, of Maimonides, owed its authority to the fact that it was recognized as the most convenient codification of the teachings of the Talmud; while the treatises on the philosophy of religion which strove as early as the time of Saadia to harmonize the truths of Judaism with the results of independent thinking referred in all possible cases to the authority of the Talmud, upon which they could easily draw for a confirmation of their theses and arguments. The wealth of moral instruction contained in the Talmud exercised a profound influence upon the ethics and ideals of Judaism. Despite all this, however, the authority enjoyed by it did not lessen the authority of the Bible, which continued to exercise its influence as the primal source of religious and ethical instruction and edification even while the Talmud ruled supreme over religious practise, preserving and fostering in the Diaspora, for many centuries and under most unfavorable external conditions, the spirit of deep religion and strict morality.

The history of Jewish literature since the completion of the Talmud has been a witness to its importance in awakening and stimulating intellectual activity among the Jews. The Talmud has been made the subject or the starting-point of a large portion of this widely ramified literature, which has been the product of the intellectual activity induced by its study, and to which both scholars in the technical sense of the word and also a large number of the studious Jewish laity have contributed. The same faculties which had been exercised in the composition of the Talmud were requisite also for the study of it; the Talmud therefore had an exceedingly stimulating influence upon the intellectual powers of the Jewish people, which were then directed toward other departments of knowledge. It is a noteworthy fact that the study of the Talmud gradually became a religious duty, and thus developed into an intellectual activity having no ulterior object in view. Consequently it formed a model of study for the sake of study.

The Talmud has not yet entirely lost its twofold importance as a historical factor within Judaism, despite the changes which have taken place during the last century. For the majority of Jews it is still the supreme authority in religion; and, as noted above, although it is rarely an object of study on the part of those who have assimilated modern culture, it is still a subject of investigation for Jewish learning, as a product of Judaism which yet exerts an influence second in importance only to the Bible.

The following works of traditional literature not belonging to the Talmud have been included in the editions of Babli: ABOT DE-RABBI NATAN; DEREK EREẒ RABBAH; DEREK EREẒ ZUṬA; KALLAH; SEMAḤOT; SOFERIM.

BIBLIOGRAPHY: The manuscripts, editions, and translations have been discussed in the article. For an introduction to the Talmud the following works may be mentioned in addition to the general ones on Jewish history: Weiss, *Dor*, iii.; Halevy, *Dorot ha-Rishonim*, ii., Frankfort-on-the-Main, 1901; H. L. Strack, *Einleitung in den Talmud*, 2d ed., Leipsic, 1894 (covers the Mishnah also and contains an extensive bibliography of the Talmud); M. Mielziner, *Introduction to the Talmud*, Cincinnati (also gives good bibliography of the Talmud; the second part of this work contains a clear discussion of the hermeneutics and the methodology of the Talmud). On the Palestinian Talmud: Z. Frankel, *Mebo*, Breslau, 1870; J. Wiener, *Gib'at Yerushalayim*, Vienna, 1872 (reprinted from *Ha-Shaḥar*); A. Geiger, *Die Jerusalemische Gemara*, in his *Jüd. Zeit.* 1870, pp. 278-306 (comp. *Monatsschrift*, 1871, pp. 120-137); I. Lewy, *Interpretation des Ersten Abschnitts des Palästinischen Talmud-Traktates Nesikin*, in *Breslauer Jahresbericht*, 1895, pp. 1-19. On the Babylonian Talmud: Z. Frankel, *Beiträge zur Einleitung in den Talmud*, in *Monatsschrift*, 1861, pp. 168-194, 205-212, 258-272; N. Brüll, *Die Entstehungsgeschichte des Babylonischen Talmuds als Schriftwerkes*, in his *Jahrb.* 1876, ii. 1-123. On the earlier works introductory to the Talmud: J. H. Weiss, in *Bet Talmud*, i., ii., Vienna, 1881, 1882; Samuel b. Hophni, *Madkhal ila 'al-Talmud* (= "Introduction to the Talmud"); this is the earliest work bearing the title and is known only through a quotation in the lexicon of Ibn Janaḥ, *s.v.* דרך); Samuel ha-Nagid, *Mebo ha-Talmud* (forming an appendix to the first volume of modern editions of the Talmud); Joseph ibn 'Aḳnin, an introduction to the Talmud (Hebr. transl. from the Arabic), edited in the *Jubelschrift des Breslauer Seminars zum Siebzigen Geburtstage Frankels*, 1871. For other works on the subject see TALMUD HERMENEUTICS; a list is given in Jellinek, *Ḳontres ha-Kelalim*, Vienna, 1878. General articles on the Talmud in reviews and encyclopedias: Emil Deutsch, in *Quarterly Review*, 1867, frequently reprinted and translated; J. Derenbourg, in Lichtenberg's *Encyclopédie des Sciences Religieuses*, 1882, xii. 1007-1036; Arsène Darmesteter, in *R. E. J.* xviii. (*Actes et Conferences*, pp. ccclxxxi.-dcxlii.); S. Schechter, in Hastings, *Dict. Bible*, extra vol., 1904, pp. 57-66; E. Bischoff, *Talmud-Katechismus*, Leipsic, 1904. On the literature of the Talmud commentaries see TALMUD COMMENTARIES. On grammatical and lexicographical aids to the study of the Talmud see JEW. ENCYC. vi.

80, *s.v.* GRAMMAR, HEBREW, and *ib.* iv. 580-585, *s.v.* DICTION-
ARIES, HEBREW. On the terminology of the Talmud see,
in addition to the works on Talmudic methodology: A.
Stein, *Talmudische Terminologie, Alphabetisch Geordnet,*
Prague, 1869; W. Bacher, *Die Exegetische Terminologie der
Jüdischen Traditionslitteratur:* part i., *Die Bibelexege-
tische Terminologie der Tannaiten,* Leipsic, 1899 (original
title, *Die Aelteste Terminologie der Jüdischen Schriftaus-
legung*); part ii., *Die Bibel- und Traditionsexegetische
Terminologie der Amoräer,* ib. 1905.

W. B.

TALMUD COMMENTARIES: The commen-
taries on the Talmud constitute only a small part of
halakic literature in comparison with the responsa
literature and the commentaries on the codices. At
the time when the Talmud was concluded the traditional literature was still so fresh in the memory
of scholars that there was no need of writing Talmudic commentaries, nor were such works undertaken in the first period of the gaonate. Palṭoi Gaon
(c. 840) was the first who in his responsa offered verbal
and textual comments on the Talmud. Ẓemaḥ b.
Palṭoi (c. 872) paraphrased and explained the passages
which he quoted; and he composed, as an aid to the
study of the Talmud, a lexicon which Abraham
Zacuto consulted in the fifteenth century. Saadia
Gaon is said to have composed commentaries on the
Talmud, aside from his Arabic com-
Earliest mentaries on the Mishnah (Benjacob,
Attempts. "Oẓar ha-Sefarim," p. 181, No. 430).
According to the Karaite Solomon b.
Jeroham, a commentary on Yerushalmi by Ephraim
b. Jacob existed as early as the time of Saadia, al-
though this is highly improbable (Pinsker, "Liḳ-
ḳuṭe Ḳadmoniyyot," Supplement, p. 4; Poznanski,
in "Kaufmann Gedenkbuch," p. 182).

The last three great geonim, Sherira, Hai, and
Samuel b. Ḥofni, did much in this field. Most of
Sherira's comments were explanations of difficult
terms. Many of these are quoted by Abu al-Walid
(Bacher, "Leben und Werke des Abulwalid Mer-
wân ibn Gānāḥ," etc., p. 85). It appears from the
quotations in the "'Aruk" that Hai Gaon wrote
commentaries on at least eleven treatises (Kohut,
"Aruch Completum," xiii. *et seq.*). Abu al-Walid
quotes Hai's commentary on Shabbat (Bacher, *l.c.*
p. 87). In the eleventh century commentaries on
the Talmud were composed not only in Babylon but
also in Africa, Spain, and Germany. In the first
half of that century Nissim b. Jacob, of Kairwan in
northern Africa, composed his "Kitab Miftaḥ Ma-
ghaliḳ al-Talmud" (Hebr. title, "Sefer Mafteaḥ Man-
'ule ha-Talmud" = "Key to the Locks of the Talmud"), a commentary in which he explains difficult
passages by references to parallel ones and occasionally to Yerushalmi also. The work of Hananeel
b. Ḥushiel corresponds more to a commentary in the
exact sense of the term. He sums up the Talmudic
discussions, perhaps in order to facilitate the halakic
decision, devoting his attention principally to determining the correct text of the Talmud. The first
teachers in Spain, Enoch ben Moses, Joseph ibn
Abitur, Isaac ibn Ghayyat, and Isaac Albargeloni,
are also known to have composed commentaries on
the Talmud (Weiss, "Dor," iv. 276 *et seq.*). Naḥmani quotes Talmudic comments from a work by
Samuel ha-Nagid (Benjacob, *l.c.* No. 481). According to a not entirely authenticated statement (*ib.*
No. 247), the famous exegete Abraham ibn Ezra

composed a commentary on the treatise Ḳiddushin. In Germany, Gershom b. Judah engaged in
similar labors, though his commentaries have come
to light only in the last century: they appear to
have been the chief sources used by Rashi (1040-
1105), the greatest commentator of the Talmud.
Although Rashi drew upon all his predecessors, yet
his originality in using the material offered by them
has always been admired. His commentaries, in
turn, became the basis of the work
Rashi. of his pupils and successors, who composed a large number of supplemen-
tary works that were partly in emendation and
partly in explanation of Rashi's, and are known
under the title "tosafot." These works were printed
together with Rashi's commentaries in the first editions of single Talmud treatises, and then in the
collective editions. The tosafot included in the
present editions are taken from various collections.
There are tosafot of Sens, tosafot of Evreux, tosafot of Touques, etc. (Winter and Wünsche, "Die
Jüdische Litteratur," ii. 465). Instead of the simple,
strictly logical method of exegesis a dialectic method
showing great acumen is frequently employed
in the tosafot. Originating in the German and
French schools, and thence adopted by the Spanish
and Arabic, it found in the following centuries (13th
to 15th) brilliant representatives in Moses b. Naḥman,
Solomon ben Adret, and others in Spain, as well as
in various scholars in Turkey, although the Oriental
Jews generally followed the simple method of Talmud study. The commentators are called "rishonim" (elders) down to the sixteenth century, and
subsequently "aḥaronim" (juniors).

In the sixteenth century the hair-splitting dialectic study of the Talmud known as the PILPUL came
to the fore. The method called "ḥilluḳ," originating
in Augsburg and Nuremberg, claimed chief attention, especially through the influence of Jacob POLLAK
of Poland, that country becoming in the course of
the century the principal center of the study of the
Talmud. Special rules were formulated for composing the ḥillukim (Jellinek, in Keller's "Bikkurim," i. 3). It is frequently inti-
Method mated in subsequent pilpulistic works
of that the author himself regards his
Ḥilluḳim. expositions as artificial, though he
believes them to contain a grain of
truth. This method still dominates to some extent
the study of the Talmud in the eastern countries of
Europe. But Jewish science demands a scientific
treatment of the Talmud — an examination of its
sources and parallel passages from a historical,
archeological, and philological point of view, a
methodical analysis of its text, and a comparative
study of it by the side of other monuments of
antiquity.

The Palestinian Talmud was studied much less
than the Babylonian, although occasional comments
on Yerushalmi are found in Alfasi and other earlier
authorities, especially in the commentary of Samson
of Sens on the mishnaic order Zera'im. The first
connected commentary on many treatises of Yerushalmi was composed in the seventeenth century by
R. Joshua Benveniste, who had at hand R. Solomon
Sirillo's commentary on certain treatises. Elijah

Fulda commentated in 1710 the order Zera'im and part of the order Neziḳin. The greater part of

Palestinian Talmud.

Yerushalmi was edited about the middle of the eighteenth century by Mendelssohn's teacher David Fränkel; and a complete commentary was written by Moses Margolioth. Noteworthy as commentators in the nineteenth century are Nahum Trebitsch and Zacharias Frankel.

The commentaries on Babli may be divided into: (1) "perushim," running commentaries accompanying the text; (2) "tosafot" (additions), glosses on Rashi's commentary; (3) "ḥiddushim" (novellæ), explicit comments on certain passages of the Talmud text; and (4) "haggahot," or marginal glosses. As appears from the following chronological list, the treatises Seder Mo'ed, Nashim, and Ḥullin, which deal particularly with the religious life and which were therefore made special subjects of study and instruction, were most frequently commentated, while the Seder Ḳodashim is less often made the subject of comment. In the subjoined list only the edited commentaries are enumerated, no note being taken of treatises on which there are no commentaries. The letter "W" indicates the Wilna (Widow & Brothers Romm) Talmud edition of 1886.

CHRONOLOGICAL LIST OF COMMENTATORS ON BOTH TALMUDIM.

ELEVENTH CENTURY.

Nissim b. Jacob (d. 1040), Sefer Mafteaḥ (see above; Ber., Shab., 'Er.), ed. I. Goldenthal, Vienna, 1847; m W.

Gershom b. Judah (d. 1040), perush (Ber., Ta'an., B. B., entire Seder Ḳodashim excepting Zeb.); in W.

Hananeel b. Ḥushiel (d. 1050), perush (Seder Mo'ed, Seder Neziḳin excepting B. B.); in W.

Solomon b. Isaac (Rashi), commentary on thirty treatises; in all editions.

TWELFTH TO FIFTEENTH CENTURY.

Samuel b. Meïr, commentary on Baba Batra from the third section and on the last section of Pesaḥim; in all editions.

Isaac b. Nathan, commentary on Makkot; in all editions, beginning with 19b.

Eliezer b. Nathan, commentary on Nazir; in W.

Jacob Tam (d. 1171), ספר הישר, on thirty-one treatises, Vienna, 1811.

Isaac b. Samuel of Dampierre, tosafot to Ḳiddushin; in W.

Joseph ibn Migash, ḥiddushim (Sheb., Salonica, 1759; B. B., Amsterdam, 1702).

Moses b. Maimon, perush (R. H.), Paris, 1865.

Judah Sir Leon (d. 1224), tosafot (Ber., in ברכה משולשת), Warsaw, 1863.

Samson of Sens, tosafot (Shab., 'Er., Men., in all editions; Soṭah in W.).

Perez, tosafot (Beẓah, Ned., Naz., Sanh., Mek., Me'i., in all editions; B. Ḳ., Leghorn, 1819).

Moses of Evreux, tosafot (Ber.); in all editions.

Samuel of Evreux, tosafot to Soṭah, ib.

Samuel of Falaise, tosafot to 'Abodah Zarah, ib.

Baruch, tosafot to Zebaḥim, ib.

Meïr Abulafia (d. 1244), יד רמה (B. B., Salonica, 1803; Sanh., ib. 1798).

Judah b. Benjamin ha-Rofe, perush (Sheḳ.); in W.

Peraḥyah b. Nissim (c. 1250), ḥiddushim, in מעשה רוקח, Venice, 1752.

Isaiah di Trani (c. 1250), tosafot (i., B. Ḳ., B. M., B. B., 'Ab. Zarah, Niddah, Shab., Ḥag.; ii., 'Er., R. H., Yoma, Suk., Meg., M. Ḳ., Pes., Beẓah, Ned., Naz., Lemberg, 1862; Ket., Giṭ., in W.).

Jonah Gerondi (d. 1263), ḥiddushim (Sanh., in סם חיים), Leghorn, 1801.

Moses b. Naḥman (d. c. 1270), ḥiddushim (Ber., 'Er., Pes., M. Ḳ., Ḥag., R. H., Suk., Ta'an., Meg., in לקוטות הרמב"ן, Salonica, 1791; Shab., in אוצר נחמד, Presburg, 1837; Yeb., Homburg, 1700; Ket., Metz, 1765; Giṭ., Niddah, in חמשה שטות, Sulzbach, 1762; B. B., Venice, 1723).

Todros ha-Levi (d. 1283), אוצר הכבוד (on the haggadot), Novidvor, 1808; ḥiddushim (Meg., Yoma, in סם חיים), Leghorn, 1801.

Aaron ha-Levi (d. 1293), ḥiddushim (Ket., Prague, 1742; Beẓah, in מראה האופנים, Leghorn, 1810).

Meïr of Rothenburg (d. 1293), tosafot to Yoma; in all editions.

Solomon b. Adret (d. 1310), ḥiddushim (Shab., R. H., Meg., Yeb., Ned., B. Ḳ., Ḥul., Constantinople, 1720; Sheb., Salonica, 1729; Niddah, Altona, 1737; Men., Warsaw, 1861; 'Er., ib. 1895).

Yom-Ṭob b. Abraham, ḥiddushim (Sheb., Salonica, 1805; 'Er., Ta'an., M. Ḳ., Ket., B. M., Amsterdam, 1729; R. H., Königsberg, 1858; Yoma, Constantinople, 1754; Meg., Warsaw, 1880; Yeb., Leghorn, 1787; Ḳid., Sabbionetta, 1553; Giṭ., Salonica, 1758; 'Ab. Zarah, in אורין תליתאי, ib. 1759; Sanh., in לשון חכמים, Leghorn, 1781; Sheb., in מעשה הצדיקים, ib. 1780; Mak., Sulzbach, 1762; Ḥul., Prague, 1735; Niddah, Vienna, 1868).

Menahem Me'iri (c. 1300), בית הבחירה (Shab., Leghorn, 1794; Yoma, ib. 1760; Meg., Ḥag., Ta'an., Prague, 1810; Ned., Naz., Soṭah, Beẓah, Berlin, 1859; Yeb., Salonica, 1794).

Asher b. Jehiel (d. 1327), perush (Ned., Naz.), in W.; tosafot (Ber., in ברכה משולשת, Warsaw, 1862; Suk., Jerusalem, 1903; R. H., ib. 1871; Meg., ib. 1884; 'Ab. Zarah, ib. 1888; Giṭ., Constantinople, 1711; B. M., Dyhernfurth, 1823; Sanh., Ḥul., in חמשה שטות, Sulzbach, 1762; Sheb., Venice, 1608; Niddah, under the title תורת שלמים, Venice, 1741); Aaron ha-Levi, הרא"ה (חידושי, Ḳid., Husiatyn, 1902; 'Er., מהר"ם חלאווה חידושי (Pes.), Jerusalem, 1873.

Isaac Aboab (d. 1493), ḥiddushim (in the responsa of Moses Galante), Venice, 1608.

SIXTEENTH CENTURY.

Jacob be-Rab (d. 1546), ḥiddushim (Ket., Ḳid.), in his responsa, Venice, 1663.

1549. Joshua Boaz Baruch, the indexes עין משפט נר מצוה, תורה אור, Venice.

1552. Mattathias Delacrut, ḥiddushim ('Er.), Lublin.

1561. Joseph ibn Leb, ḥiddushim (Ket., B. Ḳ., Sheb., Constantinople, 1561; Giṭ., ib. 1573).

Solomon Luria (d. 1573), ים של שלמה (Beẓah, Lublin, 1636; Yeb., Altona, 1740; Ḳid., Berlin, 1766; Ket., Lemberg, 1862; Giṭ., Berlin, 1761; Ḥul., Cracow, 1615); חכמת שלמה on nineteen treatises, Cracow, 1581.

1573. Judah b. Moses, מסורת תלמוד ירושלמי, Constantinople.

1577. Jacob (מוהרי ק"ש), תולדות יעקב (Beẓah), Jerusalem, 1865.

1587. Samuel Jaffe Ashkenazi, יפה מראה, on the haggadot of Yerushalmi, Venice, 1590.

Abraham Burjil, לחם אבירים (Yeb., Ket., B. Ḳ., Bik.), ib. 1605.

1591. Joseph ibn Ezra, עצמות יוסף (Ḳid.), Salonica.

Bezaleel Ashkenazi, שטה מקובצת (Ber., Warsaw, 1863; Beẓah, Constantinople, 1731; Ket., ib. 1738; Naz., Leghorn, 1774; Soṭah, ib. 1800; B. Ḳ., Venice, 1762; B. M., Amsterdam, 1726; B. B., Lemberg, 1809; Seder Ḳodashim, excepting Ḥul., in W.).

SEVENTEENTH CENTURY.

1602. Samuel b. Eleazer, ḥiddushim (Ket., Giṭ.), Prossnitz.

1603. Jedidiah Galante, ḥiddushim (Beẓah, Yeb., Giṭ., B. Ḳ., 'Ab. Zarah), Venice.

1608. Abraham Ḥayyim Shor, תורת חיים ('Er., Pes., B. Ḳ., B. M., B. B. Sanh., Sheb., 'Ab. Zarah, Ḥul.), Lublin; צאן קדשים (Seder Ḳodashim), Wandsbeck, 1729.

Mordecai Jaffe (d. 1611), מסורות חדשות (glosses); in W.

Moses b. Isaiah, ḥiddushim (Zeb.), Berlin, 1701.

1612. Samuel Edels, ḥiddushim (מהרש"א on all treatises), Lublin.

1614. Issachar Bär (Hor., Ker., Soṭah, Ḥul.), באר שבע, Venice.

1619. Meïr Lublin, מאיר עיני חכמים (on most of the treatises), ib.

Isaac ha-Levi, ḥiddushim (Sheb., Beẓah, Yeb., Ḳid., Ket., 'Ab. Zarah, Ḥul.), Neuwied, 1736.

Abraham di Boton (d. 1625), ḥiddushim (B. Ḳ., in מהררי נמרים), Venice, 1599.

Joseph di Trani (d. 1639), ḥiddushim (Ḳid.), ib. 1645.

Joel Sirkes (d. 1640), haggahot; in W.

Joshua b. Solomon (d. 1648), מגני שלמה (Shab., Pes., Beẓah, Yeb., Ket., Ḳid., B. Ḳ., Ḥul.), Amsterdam, 1715.

Lipmann Heller (d. 1654), מלאכת יום טוב (notes); in W.

1652. Ḥiyya Rofe, מעשי חייא (on nineteen treatises), Venice.

1660. Mordecai Kremsier, קטרת המזבח (on the haggadot of Ber.), Amsterdam.

1662. Joshua Benveniste, שדה יהושע (Yer. Zera'im, Constantinople, 1662; Mo'ed, Nashim, Neziḳin, ib. 1754).

Meïr Schiff b. Jacob, ḥiddushe halakot (i., ii., Sheb., Be-
zah, Ket., Giṭ., B. Ḳ., B. M., B. B., Sanh., Zeb., Ḥul.),
Zolkiev, 1826, and in the editions.

Joshua Höschel (d. 1663), ḥiddushim (B. Ḳ., B. M., B. B.),
Frankfort-on-the-Main, 1725.

1664. Solomon Algazi, לחם סתרים ('Ab. Zarah, Ber., Ḥul., Venice, 1664; תאוה לעינים, Salonica, 1655; and זהב שיבה,
Constantinople, 1683; on haggadot).

1669. Aaron Samuel Kaidanover, ברכת הזבח (Zeb., Men., 'Er.,
Ker., Tem., Me'i.), Amsterdam, 1669; תפארת שמואל
(Pes., Beẓah, Yeb., Ket., Giṭ., B. Ḳ., B. M., Ḥul.), Frank-
fort-on-the-Main, 1696.

1670. Jonah Teomim (d. 1699), קיקיון דיונה (on thirteen treatises), Amsterdam.

1671. Moses Benveniste of Segovia, שפתי ישנים (Ber., Seder Mo'ed), Smyrna.

Ḥayyim ben Israel Benveniste (d. 1673), המרא וחיי (Sanh.),
Leghorn, 1802.

1682. Samuel Eliezer b. Judah, ḥiddushe aggadot, Frankfort.

1686. Isaac Benjamin Wolf, ḥiddushim (B. M.), *ib.*

Moses ibn Ḥabib (d. 1696), שמות בארץ (R. H., Yoma,
Suk.), Constantinople, 1727.

1693. Moses b. Simeon, פנים מסבירות (Ber., Seder Mo'ed),
Prague.

1698. Judah b. Nissan, בית יהודה (Yeb., Ket., Ḳid., Giṭ., B. Ḳ.,
B. M., B. B., Ḥul.), with ḥiddushim of David Oppenheim,
Dessau.

1698. Naphtali Cohen, ברכת יהודה (Ber.), Frankfort.

1699. Samuel Ẓarfati, דברי שמואל (Ber., 'Er., Beẓah, R. H., B.
Ḳ., Hor.), Amsterdam.

Meïr Schiff b. Soloman, דרך אניה בלב ים (Ber., Sheb., Be-
zah, Pes., Men.), Fürth, 1798.

Baruch Angel, ḥiddushim (Ket., Giṭ., B. Ḳ., B. M., Sheb.,
'Ab. Zarah, Ḥul.), Salonica, 1717.

Nehemiah b. Abraham Feiwel Duschnitz, דברי נב"א (on
twelve treatises), Amsterdam, 1694.

Judah Liva b. Bezaleel גור מריה (Shab., 'Er., Pes.), Lemberg, 1861.

EIGHTEENTH CENTURY.

1700. Joseph b. Jacob, ראש יוסף (on the haggadah), Amsterdam.

Elijah Spira (d. 1712), אליהו רבה (Ḳid., Ket., Giṭ., B. Ḳ.,
B. M., Ḥul.), Fürth, 1768.

Abraham Broda (d. 1717), אשל אברהם (Pes., Giṭ., B. M.,
B. B.), Frankfort-on-the-Main, 1747; תולדות אברהם
(Ḳid., Ket.), Fürth, 1769; ḥiddushim (B. Ḳ., B. M.,
Sanh. in חדושי הגאונים), Offenbach, 1723.

1710. Elijah b. Judah, perush on Yer. Zera'im and Sheḳ., Amsterdam, 1710; B. Ḳ., B. M., B. B., Frankfort, 1742.

1710. Abraham Naphtali Spitz, מלא רצון (on most of the treatises), Frankfort-on-the-Main.

1711. Samuel Shotten, כוס הישועות (Seder Neziḳin, excepting
Hor.), *ib.*

1714. Akiba b. Judah Löb, האהל עולם (Ket.), *ib.*

1715. Meïr Eisenstadt (d. 1744), פנים מאירות (part i., Zeb., Shab.,
Ḥul., Amsterdam, 1715; part ii., Giṭ., Sulzbach, 1733;
part iii., Ḳid., Beẓah, *ib.* 1738; also B. Ḳ., Sudilkov, 1832).

Joseph ha-Kohen Tanuji (d. 1720), בני יוסף (B. Ḳ., B.M.,
'Ab. Zarah), Leghorn, 1793.

1720. Solomon Kohen, ḥiddushim (on eleven treatises), Wilmersdorf.

1725. Samuel di Avila, כתר תורה (Naz.), Amsterdam.

Menahem Nahum b. Jacob, זכרון מסהן (on fourteen treatises), Dyhernfurth, 1726.

1728. Johanan Kremnitzer, אורה מישור (Naz.), Berlin.

1728. Elijah b. Jacob, ברכת אליהו (Pes., Ḳid., Ket., Giṭ., B. Ḳ.),
Wandsbeck.

Elijah ha-Kohen (d. 1729), אגדת אליהו (Yer. Zera'im),
Smyrna, 1755.

1729. Judah of Gross-Glogau, קול יהודה (on most of the treatises), Amsterdam.

1729. Jacob b. Joseph Reischer, עיון יעקב (on haggadot), Wilmersdorf.

1730. Menahem Manuele, זרע ברוך (on most of the treatises),
Wandsbeck.

1731. Isaac b. David, פני יצחק (Ber., Seder Mo'ed), Amsterdam.

Jacob b. Joseph Kremer, זרע ישראל (R. H., Amsterdam,
1731; Meg., Altona, 1735).

Aryeh Löb b. Asher, גבורות ארי (Ta'an.), Wilna, 1862;
טורי אבן (R. H., Ḥag., Meg.), Metz, 1781.

1733. Selig b. Phoebus, עולת אהרן (on haggadot), Offenbach.

1733. Ephraim b. Samuel, לוית חן (on most of the treatises),
Altona.

1737. Ẓebi Hirsch b. Joshua, גאון צבי (Yeb., Ket., Ḳid., B. Ḳ.,
B. M., Ḥul.), Prague.

1739. Jacob Joshua Falk (d. 1756), פני יהושע (Ket., Giṭ., Ḳid.,
Amsterdam, 1739; Ber., Shab., Pes., R. H., Suk., Frank-
fort-on-the-Main, 1752; B. Ḳ., B. M., *ib.* 1756; Ḥul.,
Mak., Sheb., Fürth, 1780).

1740. Shabbethai b. Moses, מנחת כהן (on most of the treatises),
Fürth.

1741. Israel b. Moses, נצח ישראל (on the mathematical passages), Frankfort-on-the-Oder.

1743. David Fränkel, קרבן עדה and שירי קרבן (Yer. Seder
Mo'ed, Dessau, 1743; Seder Nashim, *ib.* 1757).

1750. Moses Margolioth, פני משה (Yer. Nashim, Amsterdam,
1750; Neziḳin, Leghorn, 1770).

1751. Jacob Samosc, חרות יעקב (Ber., Suk., Beẓah, Ḳid., B. Ḳ.,
B. M., Sheb.), Rödelheim.

1755. Aaron b. Nathan, שם אהרן (on most of the treatises),
Zolkiev.

1756. Ḥayyim Joseph David Azulai, שער יוסף (Hor.), Leghorn.

Akiba Eger (d. 1758), משנת דרבי עקיבא (Ber., Shab., 'Er.,
Pes., Beẓah, Suk., Yeb., Ket., Ḳid., Giṭ., Seder Neziḳin,
Seder Ḳodashim, Niddah), Fürth, 1781.

1757. Joseph b. Meïr Teomim (d. 1793), פורת יוסף (Yeb., Ket.),
Zolkiev, 1757; ראש יוסף (Ḥul., Frankfort-on-the-Oder,
1794; Sheb., Meg., Lemberg, 1863).

1760. Isaiah Berlin, קשות מיושב and אומר השכחה (notes on all
the treatises; ḥiddushim on Naz.), n.p.; haggahot in W.

1763. Joseph Darmstadt, (Ber., Beẓah, Meg.), Carlsruhe.

Jonathan Eybeschütz (d. 1764), הסרי יהונתן (on most of the
treatises), Piotrkow, 1897.

1766. Isaac Ashkenazi, גבול יהודה (Giṭ., Ket., B. Ḳ.), Salonica.

1766. Isaac Nuñez-Vaez, שיח יצחק (Yoma, Leghorn, 1766; Ḥag.,
ib. 1794).

Jacob Emden (d. 1776), glosses; in W.

1776. Elijah Sidlov, עטרת אליהו (Zeb., Men., Tem.), Fürth, 1776.

1776. Eleazar Kallir (d. 1801), אור חדש (Pes., Frankfort-on-the-
Oder, 1776; Ḳid., Vienna, 1799).

Judah Lissa, מראה כהן (Zeb.), Frankfort-on-the-Main,
1776; מנחת כהן (Men.), Prague, 1788.

1777. Itzig b. Samson, קרבן אשם (Yoma, Beẓah, Sheb., Ḥul.,
'Ar., Tem., Me'i., Ker.), Sulzbach.

1778. Saul b. Aryeh (d. 1790), בית תלמוד (on fourteen treatises),
Amsterdam.

1778. Raphael Peiser, אור לישרים (Pes., Shab., Beẓah, Ket., R.
H., Ḥul.), Dyhernfurth, 1778; גולת התחתית (Ḳid., Giṭ.),
ib. 1805.

1781. Eliezer de Avila, מגן גבורים (i., B. M., Hor.; ii., Ket., Ḳid.,
Leghorn, 1781–85).

1784. Nathan Maas, בנין שלמה (Sanh., Offenbach, 1784; 'Ab.
Zarah, *ib.* 1796).

1784. Ezekiel Landau צל"ח = ציון לנפש חיה (Pes., Prague,
1784; Ber., *ib.* 1791; Beẓah, *ib.* 1799; Sheb., 'Er., Warsaw, 1879; R. H., Yoma, Suk., Ta'an., Ḥag., Meg., *ib.*
1890; Ḥul., Zeb., Men., *ib.* 1891); glosses; in W.

Elijah Wilna (d. 1797), glosses and elucidations of both
Talmudim in various editions.

1785. Moses Katz, דרבונו זהב (Sheḳ.), Fürth.

1786. Phinehas Horwitz, הפלאה (part i., Ket., Offenbach, 1786;
part ii., Ḳid., *ib.* 1801; part iii., Ber., Munkacs, 1895).

1786. Meïr Barby, ḥiddushe halakot (i., Beẓah, Pes., Ḳid., Ket.,
Dyhernfurth, 1786; ii., Yoma, Suk., Giṭ., Ḥul., Sheb.,
Prague, 1793).

Uziel Meisels, עץ הדעת טוב (Sheb.), Lemberg, 1886.

1788. Wolf Lasch, קדושת ישראל (i., ii., Ket., Ḳid., Giṭ., Brünn,
1788; Vienna, 1829).

1789. Joseph David Sinzheim, יד דוד (Ber., entire Seder Mo'ed),
Offenbach.

David Schiff (d. 1792), לשון הזהב (on most of the treatises),
ib. 1822.

1791. Levi Pollak, עמודי שטים לבית לוי (B. Ḳ., B. M., B. B.,
Sheb., 'Ab. Zarah), Prague.

1792. Isaac b. Ẓebi, טהרות הקדש (Zeb.), Lemberg.

1792. Meïr Spitz, כתית למאור (R. H., Yoma, Suk., Meg.,
Ta'an.), Vienna.

1794. Judah Najar, אלפי יהודה (Sheb.), Leghorn, 1794; שמחת
יהודה (Ker.), Pisa, 1816.

1796. Baruch b. Samuel Zanwil, זרע שמואל (Ket.), Vienna,
1796.

1796. Joseph b. Moses, מעשה חושב (B. Ḳ.), Lemberg.

1799. Elijah Ventura, כבא דשבט (on twenty-one treatises),
Salonica.

Aryeh Judah Löb Teomim, אילת אהבים (Ber., Shab., Pes.,
Beẓah, Ḥul., Ḳid., Sheb.), Zolkiev, 1802.

Ḥayyim Shabbethai Lago, שמחת עולם (Ber., Pes., Ḳid., Sanh., Ḥul.), Salonica, 1801.

Abraham b. Jacob Mutal, נזיר (Naz.), n.p., 1821.

Ḥayyim Abraham b. Samuel, ḥiddushim (Shab., R. H., Suk., Ḥul.), Salonica, 1804.

NINETEENTH AND TWENTIETH CENTURIES.

1801. Ẓebi Hirsch Horwitz, מחנה לוי (14 treatises), Offenbach.

1801. Eleazar Karpeles, מאבני המקום (Hor.), Prague; ערכי עיי (Ḥul., 'Ar.), *ib.* 1815.

1802. Bezaleel Ronsburg, הורה גבר (Hor.), Prague; מעשי ר"ב notes, in W.

1802. Eleazar Löw, שמן רוקח (Ber., Pes., Beẓah, Prague.

1804. Abraham Aryeh Kahana, אור הנערב (on most of the treatises), Ostrog.

1810. Meïr Schlesinger, דברי מאיר (Shab., R. H., Giṭ., B. M.), Prague.

1811. Jacob Simeon Shabbethai, מתח אלהים (Meg., Ta'an.), Pisa, 1821; אביר יעקב (Ker.), *ib.* 1811.

1814. Jacob Günzburg, זרע יעקב (Ber., Shab.), Prague.

1815. Benedetto Frizzi, פתח עינים (on haggadot), Leghorn.

1821. Nahum Trebitsch, שלום ירושלים (Yer. Seder Mo'ed), Vienna.

1822. David Deutsch, אהל דוד (on most of the treatises), Vienna, 1822, 1825; Presburg, 1836; Ungvar, 1867.

Moses Sofer, חירושי חתם סופר (Beẓah, Piotrkow, 1898; B. B., *ib.* 1896; Shab., Vienna, 1889; Ḥul., Giṭ., *ib.* 1893; Pes., Jerusalem, 1894); haggahot in W.

1822. Gabriel Cohen, עיני ישראל (B. B., Sheb.), Vienna.

1823. Jacob Lissa, בית יעקב (Ket.), Hrubisov.

1824. Marcus Hirsch, דרך המלך (Seder Mo'ed excepting Shab., 'Er., Ḥag.), Prague.

Shalom Ullmann (d. 1825), דברי ו"ש (on most of the treatises), Vienna, 1826.

Akiba Eger (d. 1837), דרוש וחרוש (Ber., Seder Mo'ed, Yeb., Ket.), Warsaw, 1892; חדושי ר' עקיבא איגר (B. M., Giṭ.), Berlin, 1858; notes in W.

1826. Ẓebi Hirsch Leipnik, קב ונקי לשר השמן (Ber., Shab., 'Er., Pes., Beẓah, Ket., Ḳid., Giṭ., B. M., Ker., Zeb.), Ofen.

Isaac Ardit, יקר הערך ('Ar.), Salonica, 1828.

1829. Jacob Weiler, בית יעקב ('Er.), Zolkiev.

Aaron Kuttner (d. 1829), משחת אהרון (Nid.), Paks, 1901.

Cosman Wodianer (d. 1831), נחלת יהושע (2 parts, on most of the treatises), ed. Bacher, Vienna, 1890.

Ẓebi Hirsch Heller, חירושי טוב גיטין (Giṭ.), Zolkiev, 1844.

1834. Solomon Kluger, מי נדה (Niddah), Zolkiev, 1834; בגדי יום טוב (Beẓah), Lemberg, 1891.

Ezekiel Binet (d. 1836), תורת יחזקאל (Shab., Pes., Beẓah, Ḳid., Giṭ., Mek., Ḥul.), Paks, 1899.

Wolf Bär Schiff (d. 1842), מנחת זכרון ('Er.), Cracow, 1894.

Koppel Reich, חירושי יעבץ על חולין, Presburg, 1837.

Benjamin Rapoport, עדות לישראל (Mak.), Vienna, 1839.

1840. Hirsch Chajes, haggahot; in W.

Aryeh Judah b. Akiba, לב אריה (Ḥul.), Lemberg, 1861.

1850. Samuel Freund, עת לחננה (Seder Mo'ed), Prague.

1850. Jacob Ettlinger (d. 1869), ערוך לנר (Ker., Altona, 1850; Yeb., *ib.* 1854; R. H., Sanh., Warsaw, 1873); עטור בכורים (Suk.), Altona, 1858.

1851. David b. Samuel, קרשי דוד (Seder Ḳodashim), Leghorn, 1851; ידי דוד (Naz.), Algiers, 1853.

1851. Isaac Kamarun, פני זקן (Shek.), Lemberg.

1854. Nathan Coronel, בית נתן (Ber.), Vienna.

1857. Issachar Bär ben Sinai, מנחת עני (on most of the treatises), Vienna, 1857.

1859. Wiesner, scholia on Babli (part i., Ber., Prague, 1859; part ii., Shab., *ib.* 1862; part iii., 'Er., Pes., *ib.* 1867).

1860. Zeeb Ettinger and Joseph Nathansohn, עין משפט, נר מערבי, ציון וירושלים, גליון הש"ס (glosses, etc., on Yer.), Jitomir.

1861. Ezekiel b. Moses, בנין יחזקאל (Ket., Ned.), Warsaw. Mordecai Müller, בן אורי (Shab.), Vienna.

1862. Weissman Chajes, Solomon Brann, Judel Slabatki, notes on Yer., Krotoschin.

1864. Mordecai Herzka, דברי חכמים (Ber.), Vienna. Issachar Präger, מוצל מאש (Giṭ.), Lemberg.

1867. A. Krochmal, ירושלים הבנויה (notes on Yer.), Lemberg.

1867–97. Rabbinovicz, דקדוקי סופרים, i.–xvi. (variant readings on the entire Talmud), Munich and Przemysl.

1869. Aryeh Löb Zunz, גרש ירחים (Giṭ.), Warsaw. Joshua Eizik, נועם הירושלמי (Yer. Seder Neziḳin), Wilna.

1874. Zacharias Frankel, אהבת ציון (i., Yer. Ber., Beẓah; ii., Dem.), Breslau, 1874–75.

1876. Asher Cohen, ברכת ראש (Naz.), Warsaw.

1877. Raphael Schlesinger, חירושי רפאל (Sanh., Sheb.), Berlin.

1878. Naphtali Ẓebi ha-Levi, בית לוי (Giṭ.), Przemysl.

1880. I. Ḥayyim Deiches, נתיבות ירושלים (Yer. B. Ḳ.), Wilna.

1883. Benjamin Ḥeshin, אמתחת בנימין (Seder Neziḳin, Ḳodashim), Warsaw.

1888. Meïr Friedmann, notes on his edition of Mak., Vienna.

1888. A. Schmidl, על צרי הרף (Ḳid.), in "Oẓar ha-Sifrut," ii.–iii.

1888. Simon Sidon, שבט שמעון (Beẓah), Vienna.

1895. I. Lewy, interpretation of the first three sections of Yer. Neziḳin, Breslau, 1895–1902.

1897. S. L. Brill, "Aus den Talmudischen Randnoten des . . . von Ludwig Blau," in "Monatsschrift." 1897.

1899. Isaac Chajes, שיח יצחק (Mak.), Podgorze.

1897–1903. Joseph Dünner, haggahot (i., 'Er., Beẓah, Suk.; ii., Ket., Ḳid., Giṭ.; iii., Sanh., Mak., Sheb., Hor.), Frankfort.

1901. Dob Baer Ratner, אהבת ציון וירושלים (on Yer. Ber., Shab., Ter., Ḥal.), Wilna, 1901–4.

1905. Sal. Friedländer, פירוש and תוספות (on Yer. Yeb.), Szinervareya.

BIBLIOGRAPHY: Weiss, *Dor*, iv., v., Vienna, 1887, 1891; Zunz, *Z. G.* pp. 29–59, Berlin, 1845; Jellinek, *Ḳorot Seder ha-Limmud*, in Keller's *Bikkurim* (Vienna), i. 1–26. ii. 1–19; idem, *Ḳontres ha-Mefaresh*, Vienna, 1877; Frankel, *Introductio in Talmud Hierosolymitanum*, pp. 138–141, Breslau, 1870; Steinschneider, *Cat. Bodl.* passim; Zedner, *Cat. Hebr. Books Brit. Mus.* passim; Fürst, *Bibl. Jud.* passim.

W. B.   M. Rɪ.

TALMUD HERMENEUTICS: The science which defines the rules and methods for the investigation and exact determination of the meaning of the Scriptures, both legal and historical. Since the Halakah, however, is regarded simply as an exposition and explanation of the Torah, Talmud hermeneutics includes also the rules by which the requirements of the oral law are derived from and established by the written law. These rules relate to: (*a*) grammar and exegesis; (*b*) the interpretation of certain words and letters and superfluous words, prefixes, and suffixes in general; (*c*) the interpretation of those letters which, in certain words, are provided with points; (*d*) the interpretation of the letters in a word according to their numerical value (see GEMAṬRIA); (*e*) the interpretation of a word by dividing it into two or more words (see NOṬARIḲON); (*f*) the interpretation of a word according to its consonantal form or according to its vocalization; (*g*) the interpretation of a word by transposing its letters or by changing its vowels; and (*h*) the logical deduction of a halakah from a Scriptural text or from another law.

Classes of Rules.

Compilations of such hermeneutic rules were made in the earliest times. The tannaitic tradition recognizes three such collections, namely: (1) the seven RULES OF HILLEL (baraita at the beginning of Sifra; Ab. R. N. xxxvii.); (2) the thirteen RULES OF R. ISHMAEL (baraita at the beginning of Sifra; this collection is merely an amplification of that of Hillel); and (3) the thirty-two RULES OF R. ELIEZER B. JOSE HA-GELILI. The last-mentioned rules are contained in an independent baraita which has been incorporated and preserved only in later works. They are intended for haggadic interpretation; but many of them are valid for the Halakah as well, coinciding with the rules of Hillel and Ishmael.

It must be borne in mind, however, that neither Hillel, Ishmael, nor Eliezer ben Jose ha-Gelili sought to give a complete enumeration of the rules of interpretation current in his day, but that they omitted from their collections many rules which were then followed. For some reason or other they restricted themselves to a compilation of the principal methods of logical deduction, which they called "middot" (measures), although the other rules also were known by that term (comp. Sifre, Num. 2 [ed. Friedmann, p. 2a]).

All the hermeneutic rules scattered through the Talmudim and Midrashim have been collected by Malbim in "Ayyelet ha-Shaḥar," the introduction to his commentary on the Sifra, and have been arbitrarily reckoned at 613, to correspond with the 613 commandments. The antiquity of the rules can be determined only by the dates of the authorities who quote them; in general, they can not **Dates of the Rules.** safely be declared older than the tanna to whom they are first ascribed. It is certain, however, that the seven middot of Hillel and the thirteen of Ishmael are earlier than the time of Hillel himself, who was the first to transmit them. At all events, he did not invent them, but merely collected them as current in his day, though he possibly amplified them.

The Talmud itself gives no information concerning the origin of the middot, although the Geonim regarded them as Sinaitic (הלכה למשה מסיני; comp. R. Samson of Chinon in his "Sefer ha-Keritot"). This can be correct only if the expression הלכה למשה מסיני means nothing more than "very old," as is the case in many Talmudic passages. It is decidedly erroneous, however, to take this expression literally and to consider the middot as traditional from the time of Moses on Sinai.

The middot seem to have been first laid down as abstract rules by the teachers of Hillel, though they were not immediately recognized by all as valid and binding. Different schools interpreted and modified them, restricted or expanded them, in various ways. Akiba and Ishmael and their scholars especially contributed to the development or establishment of these rules. Akiba devoted his attention particularly to the grammatical and exegetical rules, while Ishmael developed the logical. The rules laid down by one school were frequently rejected by another because the principles which guided them in their respective formulations were essentially different. According to Akiba, the divine language of the Torah is distinguished from the speech of men by the fact that in the former no word or sound is superfluous. He established two principles broadening the scope of the rule of his teacher NAHUM OF GIMZO, who had declared that certain particles, like את, גם, and אף, were inclusive and certain others, such as אך, רק, and מן, were exclusive. These two principles are: (1) אין רבוי אחר רבוי אלא למעט (= "one inclusion added to another is equivalent to an exclusion"; Sifra, Ẓaw, Pereḳ, 11 [ed. Weiss, p. 34d]); and (2) לשונות רבויין הן (= "words are amplifications"; Yer. Shab. xix. 17a). Hence he interprets the following forms of expression as amplifications: an infinitive before a finite verb, e.g., הכרת תכרת (Sanh. 64b); the doubling of a word, e.g., איש איש (Yeb. 71a); and the repetition of a term by a synonym, e.g., ודבר ואמר (Yer. Soṭah viii. 22b). Ishmael, on the contrary, lays down the principle, דברה תורה כלשון בני אדם (= "the Torah speaks in the language of men"; Sifre, Num. 112).

The Bible may, therefore, have employed superfluous words and sounds; and forced values should not be assigned to them for the purpose of deducing new rules therefrom. The same statement holds with regard to the repetition of an entire section. Ishmael is of the opinion that "the Torah at times repeats a whole section of the Law in order to give a new application to it" (כל פרשה שנאמרה במקום אחד וחזרו ונשנה במקום אחר לא שנאה אלא בשביל דבר שנתחדש בה; Sifre, Num. 2, according to the reading of Elijah Wilna). It is not necessary, therefore, to draw a new inference from every repetition. Thus, for instance, in Num. v. 5-8 the Torah repeats the section on אשם נזלות in Lev. v. 20-26 (vi. 1-7, A. V.) for the purpose of teaching the new ruling that in certain cases recompense for sin shall be made directly to the priests. Akiba asserts, on the other hand (in Sifre, l.c., according to the reading of Elijah Wilna), that "Everything that is said in a section so repeated must be interpreted" (= כל מה שנאמר בה צריך להדרש), and that new deductions may be drawn from it. According to this view, in Num. v. 5-8, for example, a new meaning must be **Akiba's Rules.** sought in the repetition of the Law. According to Akiba, the traditional vocalization in the Bible of a word which may be read in various ways is well founded (יש אם למקרא); and he deduces many rules from the meanings which such words have according to traditional pointing. This rule had been formulated before Akiba by a tanna named R. Judah ben Ro'ez, who is not mentioned elsewhere, and of whom, consequently, nothing more is known (comp. Sanh. 4a).

Ishmael, in opposition to Akiba, follows the principle יש אם למסורת, i.e., that the tradition regarding only the consonantal text is authoritative, and that rules may be deduced only from that text. A single example will serve to illustrate the difference between the methods of the two schools. In Lev. xxi. 11, in the law which forbids a priest to defile himself by touching a corpse, the word נפשת is written defectively. Since the traditional reading indicates the plural, "nafshot," Akiba draws the conclusion that a quarter-log of blood, the minimum quantity by which a priest may be rendered unclean through contact with a single corpse, also defiles him when it issues from two bodies. According to Ishmael, however, this minimum quantity defiles a priest only when it issues from a single corpse; for the word, according to the consonantal text, is to be read in the singular "nafshat" (comp. Sanh. 4a, b, Ḥul. 72a, and Tosafot to both passages).

According to Akiba, laws may be deduced from the juxtaposition of two legal sections, since "every passage which stands close to another must be explained and interpreted with reference to its neighbor" (כל פרשה שהיא סמוכה לחבירתה למדה הימנה; Sifre, Num. 131). According to Ishmael, on the contrary, nothing may be inferred from the position of the individual sections, since it is not at all certain that every single portion now stands in its proper place. Many a paragraph which forms, strictly speaking, the beginning of a book and should stand in that position, has been transposed to the middle.

Ishmael explains the occurrence of a section in a place where it does not properly belong (ולמה נכתב כאן) by declaring that "there is no first or last in the Scriptures" (אלא מפני שאין מקדם ומאחר בתורה), not as due to any special reason (Mek., ed. Weiss, p. 48a; Eccl. R. i.; comp. Pes. 6b, where R. Pappa defines this principle in such a manner that it does not contradict Ishmael's rules concerning "Kelal u-feraṭ"). Eliezer b. Jose ha-Gelili expanded this rule in his baraita and divided it into two parts (Nos. 31 and 32). The opposition between the schools of Ishmael and Akiba lessened gradually, and finally vanished altogether, so that the later tannaim apply the axioms of both indiscriminately, although the hermeneutics of Akiba predominated. In this way all the principles cited above obtained general recognition.

A more detailed discussion of the seven rules of Hillel and of the thirteen of Ishmael may now be given, together with certain other important canons of Talmud hermeneutics.

1. Ḳal (ḳol) wa-ḥomer: The first rule of Hillel and of Ishmael, called also "din" (conclusion). This is the argument "a minori ad majus" or "a majori ad minus." In the Baraita of Eliezer b. Jose ha-Gelili this rule is divided into two (Nos. 5 and 6), since a distinction is made between a course of reasoning carried to its logical conclusion in the Holy Scriptures themselves ("ḳal wa-ḥomer meforash") and one merely suggested there ("ḳal wa-ḥomer satum"). The completed argument is illustrated in ten examples given in Gen. R. xcii. The full name of this rule should be "ḳal wa-ḥomer, ḥomer we-ḳal" (simple and complex, complex and simple), since by it deductions are made from the simple to the complex or vice versa, according to the nature of the conclusion required. The major premise on which the argument is based is called "nadon," or, at a later period, "melammed" (that which teaches); the conclusion resulting from the argument is termed בא מן הדין, or, later, "lamed" (that which learns). The process of deduction in the ḳal wa-ḥomer is limited by the rule that the conclusion may contain nothing more than is found in the premise. This is the so-called "dayyo" law, which many teachers, however, ignored. It is formulated thus: דיו לבא מן הדין להיות כנדון ("The conclusion of an argument is satisfied when it is like the major premise"). The discovery of a fallacy in the process of deduction is called "teshubah" (objection), or, in the terminology of the Amoraim, "pirka." The possibility of such an objection is never wholly excluded, hence the deduction of the ḳal wa-ḥomer has no absolute certainty. The consequences of this are: (a) that the conclusions have, according to many teachers, no real value in criminal procedure, a view expressed in the axiom that the conclusion is insufficient to punish the violator of an inferred prohibition (אין עונשין מן הדין; Sifre, Num. 1); (b) that very often a passage is interpreted to mean something which may be inferred by means of a ḳal wa-ḥomer (מילתא דאתיא בק"ו טרח וכתב לה קרא; Pes. 18b; Yoma 43a).

2. Gezerah shawah ("Similar laws, similar verdicts"): The second rule of Hillel and of Ishmael, and the seventh of Eliezer b. Jose ha-Gelili. This may be described as argument by analogy, which infers from the similarity of two cases that the legal decision given for the one holds good for the other also. The term "gezerah shawah" originally included arguments based on analogies either in word or in fact. Before long, however, the latter class was designated as "heḳḳesh," while the phrase "gezerah shawah" was limited to analogy in the case of two different Biblical laws containing a word common to both. The gezerah shawah was originally restricted to a δὶς λεγόμενον, i.e., a word occurring only in the two passages offering the analogy. Since such a word is found nowhere else, there is no reason to assume that it bears different meanings in the two passages. The gezerah shawah consequently attaches to the word in the one passage the entire sequence of ideas which it bears in the other. Such a gezerah shawah is purely lexicographical, as seeking to determine the exact signification of a word by comparison with another passage in which the full meaning of such word is clear. The rule thus demonstrates itself. An example will illustrate this more clearly. The phrase מלק את ראשו ("to wring off the head") occurs only twice in the Pentateuch, namely, in Lev. i. 15 and ib. v. 8. In the latter passage, however, the meaning of the phrase is more closely defined by ממול ערפו ("from the neck"). The Sifra (ed. Weiss, p. 9a) concludes, therefore, that the nearer definition, "from the neck," in the second passage, is part of the concept of the word מלק, and, consequently, that in the former passage, also, מלק means "to wring the head from the neck." At a later period, however, the gezerah shawah emerged from these narrow bounds and inferred the identity of legal requirements from the identity of their terminology, even when such terminology occurred in many passages besides the two which formed the analogy. Thereby the gezerah shawah lost its inherent power of demonstration; for it is wholly unreasonable to attribute to a word a meaning which happens to be associated with it in a single passage, when various other passages connect ideas entirely different with the same word. Since, moreover, each individual teacher might choose which two expressions he would select for a gezerah shawah, contradictory conclusions might be drawn, which would each have the same claim to validity, since both were obtained by a gezerah shawah. Consequently, in order to be binding, a gezerah shawah was obliged to conform to two requirements which, on the one hand, greatly restricted its application, and, on the other, gave legal decisions thus obtained the value of those deduced from a superfluous word in the Holy Scriptures. These conditions are: (a) אין אדם דן גזירה שוה מעצמו ("No one may draw a conclusion from analogy upon his own authority"; Pes. 66a; Niddah 19b). This rule, however, is not to be regarded as implying that every gezerah shawah must have been handed down from Sinai, as Rashi (on the various passages) and many expositors who followed him explained it, but that the use of this method of hermeneutics is to be permitted only to an entire board or council, and is to be employed only when its results agree with the traditional halakah, which thereby acquires the importance of a law implied in the Scriptures. In Yerushalmi this rule reads: אדם דן גזירה שוה לקיים תלמודו ואין אדם דן נ״ש לבטל תלמודו ("From a gezerah shawah conclusions may be deduced which support tradition, but not such as are opposed to tradition"; comp. Maimonides in the introduction to his "Mishneh Torah"). (*b*) The words of the text which form the basis of the deduction from analogy must be free, *i.e.*, they must be superfluous and non-essential, or they may not be used (מופנה להקיש ולדין היומן נזירה שוה). This limitation of the gezerah shawah, however, to superfluous words is not generally recognized. Akiba considers the gezerah shawah valid when neither of the two words is superfluous (אינו מופנה כלל). According to Ishmael, it is sufficient if the analogy is free on one side (מופנה מצד אחד), *i.e.*, if one of the two words forming the basis of the analogy is pleonastic. Eliezer alone requires both words to be superfluous (מופנה משני צדדים; comp. Hoffmann, "Zur Einleitung in die Halachischen Midrashchim," p. 6).

3. Binyan ab mi-katub ehad ("A standard from a passage of Scripture"): A certain passage serves as a basis for the interpretation of many others, so that the decision given in the case of one is valid for all the rest.

4. Binyan ab mi-shene ketubim ("A standard from two passages of Scripture"): By this rule a decision in two laws having a characteristic in common (הצד השוה) is applied to many other laws which have this same characteristic. Ishmael unites rules 2 and 4 in his third rule, while the same combination forms the eighth rule of Eliezer b. Jose ha-Gelili.

5. Kelal u-ferat and **ferat u-kelal** ("General and particular, particular and general," *i.e.*, limitation of the general by the particular, and vice versa): According to Ishmael, this principle has eight special applications, and thus includes eight separate rules in his scheme (Nos. 4–11). This method of limitation is one of the main points of difference between Ishmael and Akiba. According to the former, who follows his teacher R. Neḥunya b. ha-Ḳanah, the particular is only an elucidation of the preceding general expression, so that the latter includes only what is contained in the particular (כלל ופרט אין בכלל אלא מה שבפרט). But if still another general follows the particular, the two general expressions are defined by the intermediate particular, so that the law applies only to what is like the particular (כלל ופרט וכלל אי אתה מרבה אלא כעין הפרט). Akiba, on the contrary, applies the rule of increase and decrease (רבוי ומיעוט) which had been taught him by his teacher Nahum of Gimzo. According to this principle, the general followed by a particular subsumes everything which is like the particular (Sanh. 45b, 46a). If, however, another general term follows the particular, the former subsumes also what is not similar to the latter. The two general terms are decreased in only one respect by the intermediate particular (רבוי ומיעוט ורבוי ריבה הכל; ומאי מיעט מיעט דבר אחד; Shebu. 26a; comp. also Rashi on Sanh. *l.c.*).

6. Ka-yoze bo mi-maḳom aḥer ("Like that

XII.—3

in another place"): The explanation of a Biblical passage according to another of similar content.

7. Dabar ha-lamed me-'inyano ("Something proved by the context"): Definition from the context. Ishmael omits rule 6 entirely, and has another (No. 13) instead which is not found in Hillel, and which reads thus: שני כתובים המכחישים זה את זה עד שיבא הכתוב השלישי ויכריע ביניהם ("If two passages contradict each other, this contradiction must be reconciled by comparison with a third passage"). The method of solution of such opposing statements by the help of a third passage is a point of divergency between Ishmael and Akiba. According to the latter, the third sentence decides in favor of one of the two contradictory statements (Mek., ed. Weiss, 6a); according to the former, it modifies the interpretation of both. With regard to the meaning of words which are pointed in the text, Simeon b. Eleazar laid down the rule that if the pointed part of the word (נקודה) is equal to the unpointed part (כתב) in length, the word must not be interpreted at all; but if one part is longer than the other, such part must be interpreted (Gen. R. lxxviii.). Concerning the interpretation of words by a change of letters or vowels the rule is: אל תקרא ("Do not read so, but so"). Under this rule the integrity of the text itself is not assailed, the changes made being only for the purpose of explanation.

To support a halakic decision, and more especially to find a point of departure in the Haggadah, the traditional reading of a word is altered by transposition of its consonants or by substitution of others which are related to them, or the consonant-group is retained with alteration of its vowels, the last method being the most frequent. A halakic example of this form of hermeneutics is the interpretation of the word "kapot" (bough; Lev. xxiii. 40) as though it were "kaput" (bound; Sifra, ed. Weiss, p. 102d; Suk. 32a). It is noteworthy, moreover, that only the Tannaim derived new halakot with the aid of these rules, while the Amoraim employed them only in advancing haggadic explanations or in establishing the old halakot of the Tannaim.

BIBLIOGRAPHY: Saadia Gaon, Commentary on the thirteen middot of R. Ishmael, published by Schechter in *Bet Talmud*, iv. 237 *et seq.*, and in the *Œuvres Complètes*, ix. 73–83; Rashi, Commentary on the thirteen rules, in Kobak's *Jeschurun*, vi., Hebrew part, pp. 38–44, 201–204; the remaining commentaries on the thirteen rules are enumerated by Jellinek in *Ḳonṭres ha-Kelalim*, Nos. 163–175; R. Samson of Chinon, *Sefer Keritut*, Warsaw, 1854; Malachi Kohen, *Yad Mal'aki*, Berlin, 1852; Aaron ibn Ḥayyim, *Middot Aharon*; R. Solomon Algazi, *Yabin Shemu'ah*; Jacob Hirsch Jolles, *Melo ha-Ro'im*, part ii.; Hirsch Chajes, *Mebo ha-Talmud*, Zolkiev, 1845; Malbim, *Ayyelet ha-Shaḥar*; Frankel, *Hodegetica in Mischnam*, pp. 19 and 108–109, Leipsic, 1859; I. H. Weiss, *Dor*, i. 164–168, ii. 105; Mordecai Plungian, *Sefer Talpiyyot*, Wilna, 1849; H. S. Hirschfeld, *Halachische Exegese*, Berlin, 1840; idem, *Hagadische Exegese*, ib. 1847; Grätz, *Hillel und Seine Sieben Interpretationsregeln*, in *Monatsschrift*, i.; M. Mielziner, *The Talmudic Syllogism or the Inference of Kal Vechomer*, in *Hebrew Review*, i., Cincinnati, 1880; Hoffmann, *Zur Einleitung in die Halachischen Midraschim*, pp. 4–11, Berlin, 1887; idem, *Ein Midrasch über die Dreizehn Middot*, in *Berliner Festschrift*, pp. 55–71; S. Landau, *Ansichten des Talmud und der Geonim über den Werth der Midraschischen Schriftauslegung*, Hanover, 1888; Dobschütz, *Die Einfache Bibelexegese der Tannaim*, Halle, 1893; A. Schwartz, *Die Hermeneutische Analogie*, Vienna, 1897; idem, *Der Hermeneutische Syllogismus*, ib. 1901.
W. B.   J. Z. L.

TALMUDIC LAW: The development of thousands of years is represented by the Jewish law as it is found in the Shulḥan 'Aruk, Ḥoshen Mishpaṭ, of Joseph Caro (16th cent.), as well as in numerous other works which elaborate or elucidate individual passages in various ways. The history of the Hebrew code falls into three chief epochs: (1) the Pentateuch, (2) the Talmud, and (3) post-Talmudic literature. The Pentateuch forms the basis of the Talmud, while the latter serves in its turn as a foundation for post-Talmudic law, which

Three Historical Periods of Jewish Law.

has tenaciously maintained its validity in less cultured countries to the present day. Although these three periods are closely related in so far as the later epochs were developed from the earlier, they must be regarded as mutually independent, since they represent different phases of evolution. As controverting the theory which formerly prevailed, especial stress must be laid upon the fact that in the course of time the changes both in material and in spiritual life profoundly modified Jewish law, the stages of whose evolution are linked together only by the legal fictions common to all history of law. It may accordingly be said that there were three judiciary systems: the Mosaic, the Talmudic, and the rabbinic. The Talmudic code is generally termed the "Mosaic-Talmudic," since the authorities of the Talmud took the Mosaic law as their basis. From the point of view of judicial history, however, the Talmud must be regarded as an independent structure; and it is therefore more correct to use the simple term "Talmudic law." The present article excludes all reference to rabbinic law, and discusses only those aspects of the Mosaic system which facilitate an intelligent comprehension of the Talmudic code.

The Torah, revealed by God, was the basis of the code; and God Himself was consequently the Supreme Source of law. The Talmud, like the Torah, drew no distinction between religious and secular law, thus conforming to the general custom of ancient peoples, especially in the East.

Religious and Secular Law.

One result of this peculiarity was the wide range and close articulation of the Talmudic system, since the commandments of religion influenced secular law, and modified civil relations in so far as any infraction of them was punishable. It is impossible, therefore, to differentiate sharply between religious and secular law. Everything pertaining to the former is discussed more properly under HALAKAH, and is, therefore, omitted here so as to render possible a brief outline of secular jurisprudence and a citation of parallels with other systems. While the application of modern legal categories to Talmudic law is foreign to its nature, it can not be avoided; a careful check, however, must be kept upon this method. In like manner a careful distinction must be drawn between the civil and the penal codes of Talmudic law. While the civil code was actually enforced, the penal code was a dead letter; for the Romans, about 30 C.E., had withdrawn all criminal jurisdiction from the Jews (Sanh. 41a; Yer. Sanh. i. 1, vii. 2; Mommsen, "Römische Geschichte," v. 512). After the destruction of the Temple, in the year 70, jurisdiction in civil cases as well seems to have been given to the Roman courts (Mommsen, l.c. p. 548; Frankel, "Der Gerichtliche Beweis nach Mosaisch-Talmudischem Rechte," pp. 45, 142;

Civil and Penal Codes.

idem, "Zeitschrift für die Religiösen Interessen," i. 153, 189), although this can have been only a temporary measure, and, in view of the power possessed by the parties involved to refuse to submit to such a court, can never have been rigidly enforced. Civil jurisdiction may be regarded, therefore, as a right which really existed, while criminal law was, for the most part, merely theoretical from the very beginning. Survivals from the period of independence, Pentateuchal laws, and the penal codes of foreign rulers are the component elements of the criminal law of the Talmud. Very frequent, moreover, are the instances in which exegeses of Biblical passages served as sources, often elucidating laws which were never actually enforced. The origin of the Talmudic penal code explains the majority of its peculiarities as well as its weaknesses and its merits. The merits consist chiefly in leniency. Thus, for example, while the code recognized capital punishment and the frequency of its infliction as ordered by the Pentateuch, it rendered the death-sentence practically impossible, since this penalty was so conditioned by requirements of proof of malice aforethought that finally guilt could no longer be proved. Capital punishment, even for murder, was so abhorrent to the authorities of tradition that its infliction was to be prevented by all legal means (Mak. i. 10 et passim). In view of these circumstances and principles, the penal law in general and its theoretical development in particular aimed at strengthening moral consciousness and at rousing a sense of guilt. In like manner, the punishments inflicted were mild. Thus, a thief was obliged to return twice the value of the stolen goods, while early Roman law visited a thief caught in the act with a terrible penalty, which was extended under the empire to other forms of theft as well. The Germans frequently punished theft with death or at least with amputation of a hand or a foot.

The impetus to the development of the Talmudic code was given by the study of the divine law, the precepts of which had to be expounded and elucidated even to the least dot on the smallest letter. No other people ever honored its national literature so highly or guarded it so carefully as the Jews did the teachings of Moses. Numerous scholars of the Law consequently arose, who may be regarded as jurists both individually and collectively. Every place of any size had its bet ha-midrash, where men of all vocations gathered daily for discussions. The result of five centuries of this activity was the Talmudic code. The civil law was intelligible even to laymen, and it was, moreover, interpreted by scholars; consequently its development was essentially practical, not merely theoretical as was that of the criminal code. These scholars, all working without compensation, evolved a legal system which in scope and excellence stands far above the period of civilization for which and in which it was created. The wealth of Talmudic law and its comparative freedom from defects are best seen when it is compared with a compendium of modern law, such as Josef Kohler's "Einführung in die Rechtswissenschaft" (2d ed., Berlin, 1905).

The history of the Jews explains the fulness of development in the code of civil law, its deficiencies as regards public law, and the entire absence therefrom of international law. In civil law the most noteworthy features are the provisions relating to persons, property, claims, family es-

Absence of Commercial Law.

tates, and inheritance. A distinct branch of commercial law, such as has been highly developed among modern nations, does not exist in the Talmudic code, although regulations concerning commerce are not lacking; for in Talmudic times the Jews were not as distinctly a commercial nation as they became in the post-Talmudic and medieval periods. Indeed, the highly developed system of damages, as, for instance, in the case of injuries by animals (Kohler, *l.c.* p. 96), characterizes them as an agricultural people. The following is a list of the various legal articles in THE JEWISH ENCYCLOPEDIA:

While the foregoing list will give an idea of the extent of the Talmudic code, an estimate of its value compared with other systems may be gained by a perusal of the following list of rubrics which do not occur in the Talmud. The pages cited in parentheses are those of Kohler's above-mentioned work:

Associations (p. 81 ; societies only)
Bankruptcy (p. 145)
Bills of Exchange and Kindred Matters (p. 88 ; promissory notes only)
Commercial Firms (p. 79)
Counterfeiting (p. 155)
Defamation of Character, Slander, Calumny, etc. (p. 174 ; no specific penalty was fixed for these crimes ; they were branded as most immoral ; and the severest divine punishment was invoked upon the offender)
Embezzlement (included under theft, and does not constitute a specific crime ; p. 175)
Insurance (pp. 66 *et seq.*)
Joint-Stock Companies (p. 68)
Lawful Duels (as ordeals, which ceased in Italy in the thirteenth century ; p. 170)
Lex Talionis (p. 161)
Limited Liability Companies and Financial Trusts (p. 82)
Maritime Law (p. 87 ; river law, however, existed)
Ordeals (p. 133)
Pardon (p. 166)
Secrets of Manufacture and Commerce (p. 172)

The penal code made no provision for a public prosecutor or for torture, although the latter was employed in Europe until the last quarter of the eighteenth century. A few examples will serve to show the lofty standard of the civil and marriage codes of the Talmud. According to Talmudic law, the agent was equal in all respects to the party he represented; and the Jews even allowed betrothal, itself a contract, to take place by proxy (*ib.* p. 32). On this subject Kohler says (*l.c.* p. 27): "Representation is an institution of elaborate development, introduced at a comparatively recent period by legal regulation. It is a creation of the highest type, rendering it possible for one to own a fortune of millions without having to administer it in person." Among other ancient peoples the debtor was held responsible for his debt with liberty, life, and limb, the law relating to debt being based on the value of the debtor; Talmudic law, however, agrees with modern codes, which permit the debtor neither to be sold as a slave nor to be deprived of his liberty in any other way. The payment of a debt was a moral, not a legal, obligation (B. B. 174a and parallel passages; comp. Kohler, *l.c.* p. 58).

High Development of Talmudic Law.

The Jewish laws relating to family life did not recognize the unlimited authority of the head of the household as did Roman law, but, on the contrary, a son who had attained his majority (13 years) might hold property in his own name. In the Christian world this was not the case until after the reign of Justinian (*ib.* p. 93). The law of inheritance, as in modern codes, recognized the system based on kinship. Jewish law restricted the prohibitions against consanguineous marriages, and permitted divorce. With regard to these cardinal points of marriage legislation, modern codes, in opposition to canon law, adopt the same point of view as Judaism, probably because derived from the Roman law. There are numerous legal questions and even judicial principles in which modern views coincide with those of the Talmud, and to which a general allusion may be made.

The Talmud has been completed for 1,400 years; and the greater part of the legal material which it contains is more than 2,000 years old. It is therefore self-evident that foreign elements from the great civilized nations of the ancient world must have exercised an influence on it. Following the chronological order, mention should first be made of the Assyro-Babylonian elements. With regard to the relation of the Mosaic law to the code of Hammurabi, see HAMMURABI and the literature there cited, as well as numerous later works. There can be no doubt that the Assyro-Babylonian laws outlived the state by centuries, while their influence was felt even in the Christian period, and may still be traced in Talmudic law. The most common terms for written contracts, "sheṭar" and "geṭ," are Babylonian; and clay tablets were still used in Talmudic times for promissory notes (Blau, "Althebräisches Buchwesen," p. 18). A receipt was called "zober," *i.e.*, "zebiru" in Assyrian contracts. Giṭ. 86a gives

Assyro-Babylonian Influence.

the text of a contract regarding the sale of slaves, the first part of which is apparently Assyrian in origin. Even in post-Talmudical literature, as in the "Sefer ha-Sheṭarot" of Judah b. Barzillai (ed. Halberstam, Berlin, 1898), there are distinct reminiscences of Babylonian formulas. The contracts included in this work number more than seventy, and in them the phrase "the contracting party has made all stipulations 'in accordance with his pleasure'" recurs in all varieties of terminology (*e.g.*, pp. 9 *et seq.*). The same formula appears in Babylonian contracts, this example, like others, being furnished by Pick ("Assyrisches und Talmudisches Kulturgeschichte und Lexicalische Notizen," pp. 22, 30).

Incomparably greater was the influence exerted by Greco-Roman jurisprudence in later days. The lingua Franca of the East, even during the period of Roman sovereignty, was the κοινή; so that about seventy of the seventy-seven foreign legal terms that are found in the Talmud (Löw, in Krauss, "Lehnwörter," ii. 630), are Greek, only the remaining few being Latin. As a rule the Jews learned Roman law from the actual practise of the courts and not from legal writings only. Greek terms are used for document, will, protocol, guardian, contract, hypothec, purchase, accusation, accuser, attorney, and the like; and Latin words for legacy, bill of indictment, divorce, etc. Roman law, with its high development, exercised a much greater influence on the Talmudic system than has hitherto been shown, thorough investigations having as yet been made only sporadically. Frankel ("Gerichtlicher Beweis," pp. 58 *et seq.*) thinks that the majority of the legal cases in Talmudic law have parallels in the Roman code. "The same subjects are often treated in both, and form a basis for the application of the legal principles. This resemblance was due to the conditions and requirements of the time; and for the same reason many legal provisions are common to both codes." The difference between the two lies, in his view, "in the divergent mental processes of Orientals and Occidentals, so that Talmudic law formulated anew the very parts it borrowed from the Roman code. The Oriental in his method of investigation is characterized by acuteness and facility of comprehension; so that he is guided in his legal enactments by the vivacity of his mind rather than by a principle. . . . The Occidental is marked by thoughtfulness: he desires a universal concept, not a schematized nexus or a reduction to some principle. He therefore combines the law into a harmonious whole, while the code of the Oriental consists of disconnected parts."

Influence of Roman Law.

Although this characterization is in the main correct, it must be borne in mind that Frankel underestimates the influence of the Roman code on the Talmud. Several Talmudists of the early part of the second century were so deeply versed in the Roman civil law that they decided cases according to it if they were so requested. Constantin l'Empereur of Oppyck, in his "De Legibus Ebræorum Forensibus" (1637; reprinted by Surenhuis in his "Mischna," iv.), was the first to compare the Roman and Talmudic systems, although he did not postulate any adaptation from the one code by the other.

Subsequently Zunz ("Etwas über die Rabbinische Litteratur," 1818), Jost ("Gesch." iv. 144, and appendix), Frankel (*l.c.*), Krochmal ("Moreh Nebuke ha-Zeman," 1845), and others (comp. Blau, "Concursus Vitiorum" [in Hungarian], pp. 8, 11, 13) made similar comparisons.

The Jews lived for a time both under the ancient Persian régime of the Achæmenidæ (550–330 B.C.)

Influence of Persian Law.
and under the neo-Persian dynasty of the Sassanids (250–500 C.E.). Persian law has, therefore, also been a factor, although the present knowledge both of the Achæmenian and the Sassanid codes is insufficient for an estimate of the extent of their influence on the Jews. The Talmud, on the other hand, characterizes the legal system of the Sassanids as a superficial one, and quotes some extracts in support of its assertions, *e.g.*, the creditor may seize the security (B. B. 173, borrowed from Turkish law). See further Frankel, *l.c.* p. 56, where the theory is advanced that Sassanid law influenced the code of the Babylonian Talmud.

Among the compilations of Talmudic law, the "Mishneh Torah," or religious code, of Maimonides

Compilations of Talmudic Law.
took a foremost place. Superior in system and arrangement to its predecessors and successors alike, even though its author did not codify the law of the Talmud in the strict sense of the term, but only the rabbinico-legal system as formulated at the time, it served as an authority for subsequent centuries. The Christian literature on the subject in the sixteenth and seventeenth centuries, and, to a great extent, even the modern literature of the nineteenth century, are dependent upon this work, even in cases where the treatises are termed "Mosaic-Talmudic." The authors who combined Talmudic and legal knowledge were, generally speaking, rare; for the majority were either Talmudists or jurists, but not both.

In recent times Rapoport has begun a systematic compilation of Talmudic law (the laws of inheritance, endowments, obligations, etc.); and his work has been favorably received by the eminent historian of jurisprudence, Josef Kohler of Berlin. Rapoport, however, has not drawn a sharp distinction between the three chief epochs, the Mosaic, the Talmudic, and the rabbinic, nor has he paid sufficient heed to the historical criticism contained in traditional literature. Much work still remains to be done in this field.

BIBLIOGRAPHY: Ludovicus de Compiègne de Veille, *Hebreorum de Connubiis Ius Civile et Pontificium seu ex R. Mosis Majemonidae Secundae Legis sive Manus Fortis Eo Libro, Qui Est de Re Uxoria, Tractatus Primus*, Paris, 1673; Surenhuis, *Dissertatio de Natura Pandectarum Hebraicarum*, Amsterdam, 1704; Spencer, *De Legibus Hebreorum Ritualibus*, three books, Leipsic, 1705; four books, Tübingen, 1732; Frankel, *Die Eidesleitung der Juden*, Dresden, 1840; idem, *Der Gerichtliche Beweis nach Mosaisch-Talmudischem Rechte*, Berlin, 1846; Hirsch Bär Fassel, *Zedek u-Mishpaṭ*, Vienna, 1848; idem, *Mishpeṭe El: Das Mosaisch-Rabbinische Civilrecht*, etc., Nagy-Kanizsa, 1852–54; idem, *'Asot Mishpaṭ: Das Mosaisch-Rabbinische Gerichtsverfahren in Civilrechtlichen Sachen*, etc., *ib.* 1859; idem, *We-Shafeṭu we-Hizẓilu: Das Mosaisch-Rabbinische Strafrecht*, etc., *ib.* 1870; Saalschütz, *Das Mosaische Recht*, 2 vols., 2d ed., Berlin, 1852–53; M. Duschak, *Das Mosaisch-Talmudische Eherecht, mit Besonderer Rücksicht auf die Bürgerlichen Gesetze*, Vienna, 1864; idem, *Josephus Flavius und die Tradition*, *ib.* 1864; I. Wiesner, *Der Bann in Seiner Geschichtlichen Entwickelung auf dem Boden des Judenthums*, Leipsic, 1864; Bruns-Sachau, *Syrisch-Römisches Rechtsbuch* (comp. Perles in

Z. D. M. G. xxxv.); Samuel Mayer, *Die Rechte der Israeliten, Athener und Römer*, 3 vols., Leipsic and Treves, 1866–1876; Leopold Auerbach, *Das Jüdische Obligationsrecht nach den Quellen und mit Besonderer Berücksichtigung des Römischen und Deutschen Rechts Systematisch Dargestellt*, vol. i., *Umrisse der Entwickelungsgeschichte des Jüdischen Rechts; Die Natur der Obligation*, Berlin, 1870; J. Fürst, *Das Peinliche Rechtsverfahren im Jüdischen Alterthume*, Heidelberg, 1870; M. Schmiedl, *Die Lehre vom Kampf ums Recht*, Vienna, 1875; S. Spitzer, *Das Heer- und Wehrgesetz der Alten Israeliten, Griechen und Römer*, 2d ed., Vinkovce, 1879; M. Bloch, *Das Mosaisch-Talmudische Polizeirecht*, Budapest, 1879 (English transl., Cincinnati, 1880); idem, *Die Civilprozess-Ordnung nach Mosaisch-Rabbinischen Rechte*, Budapest, 1882; idem, *Das Mosaisch-Talmudische Erbrecht*, Budapest, 1889; idem, *Der Vertrag nach Mosaisch-Talmudischem Rechte*, *ib.* 1893; idem, *Das Mosaisch-Talmudische Besitzrecht*, *ib.* 1897; idem, *Das Mosaisch-Talmudische Strafgerichtsverfahren*, *ib.* 1901; idem, *Die Vormundschaft nach Mosaisch-Talmudischem Rechte*, *ib.* 1904; Israel Michel Rabbinovicz, *Législation Civile du Thalmud*, Paris, 1880; O. Bähr, *Das Gesetz über Falsche Zeugen nach Bibel und Talmud*, Berlin, 1882; M. Mielziner, *The Jewish Law of Marriage and Divorce*, Cincinnati, 1884; Elijah Benamozegh, *Israël et Humanité: Demonstration du Cosmopolitisme dans les Dogmes, les Lois, etc.*, Leghorn, 1885; I. Klein, *Das Gesetz über das Gerichtliche Beweisverfahren nach Mosaisch-Thalmudischem Rechte*, Halle-on-the-Saale, 1885; L. Blau, *A Bűnhalmazat Elmélete a Hébereknél Szentírásuk és Hagyományuk Szerint*, Budapest, 1887; D. Fink, *Miggo als Rechtsbeweis im Babylonischen Talmud: Ein Beitrag zur Kenntniss der Talmudischen Methodologie*, Leipsic, 1891; D. Farbstein, *Das Recht der Unfreien und der Freien Arbeiter nach Jüdisch-Talmudischem Recht, Verglichen mit dem Antiken, Speciell mit dem Römischen Recht*, Frankfort-on-the-Main, 1896; F. Kanter, *Beiträge zur Kenntniss des Rechtssystems und der Ethik Mar Samuels Rectors der Hochschule zu Nehardea und Babylonien*, Bern, 1895; S. Mandl, *Der Bann: Ein Beitrag zum Mosaisch-Rabbinischen Strafrechte Dargestellt nach der Bibel und der Rabbinischen Litteratur*, Brünn, 1898; I. Ziegler, *Die Königsgleichnisse des Midrasch Beleuchtet Durch die Römische Kaiserzeit (Die Jurisdiction der Kaiser)*, pp. 101–132, Breslau, 1903; H. Pick, *Assyrisches und Talmudisches Kulturgeschichte und Lexicalische Notizen*, Berlin, 1903; Rapoport, *Der Talmud und Sein Recht*, in *Zeitschrift für die Vergleichende Rechtswissenschaft*, xiv.–xvi.; C. H. W. Johns, *Babylonian and Assyrian Laws, Contracts, and Letters*, Edinburgh, 1905; I. Telski, *Die Innere Einrichtung des Grossen Synedrions zu Jerusalem und Ihre Fortsetzung im Späteren Palästinensischen Lehrhause bis zur Zeit des R. Jehuda ha-Nasi: Ein Beitrag zum Verständnisse und Würdigung der Aeltesten Talmudischen Quellen*, Breslau, n.d.

W. B.   L. B.

TALMUD TORAH: Public free school for poor and orphaned boys, who are there given an elementary education in Hebrew, the Scriptures (especially the Pentateuch), and the Talmud (Halakah), and are thus prepared for the YESHIBAH. The Talmud Torah school is known simply as the Talmud Torah, and has the essential elements of the ḤEDER, the latter being a private self-supporting school.

In the remotest time of Jewish history the father was the sole teacher of his children (Deut. xi. 19). The institution known as the "be rab" or "bet rabban" (house of the teacher), or as the "be safra" or "bet sefer" (house of the book), is supposed to have been originated by Ezra and his Great Assembly, who provided a public school in Jerusalem to secure the education of fatherless boys of the age of sixteen years and upward. But the school sys-

Origin of Schools.
tem did not develop till JOSHUA BEN GAMLA the high priest caused public schools to be opened in every town and hamlet for all children above six or seven years of age (B. B. 21a). Strict discipline was observed. Rab, however, ordered Samuel b. Shilat to deal tenderly with the pupils, to refrain from corporal punishment, or at most to use a shoe-strap in correcting pupils for inattention. A stupid pupil was made monitor until able to grasp the art

of learning. Raba fixed the number of pupils at twenty-five for one teacher; if the number was between twenty-five and forty an assistant teacher ("resh dukana") was necessary; and for over forty, two teachers were required. The expense was borne by the community. There is a difference of opinion regarding the qualification of the "melammed" (teacher). Raba preferred one who taught his pupils much, even though somewhat carelessly, while R. Dimi of Nehardea preferred one who taught his pupils little, but that correctly, as an error in reading once adopted is hard to correct (*ib.*). It is, of course, assumed that both qualifications were rarely to be found in one person. Only married men were engaged as teachers.

Girls were invariably excluded from the Talmud Torah, first because teaching them is not obligatory, and second because they are "light-minded." R.

Girls Excluded. Eliezer said: "Whosoever teaches his daughter the Torah is as one who teaches her frivolity" (Soṭah 21b). Maimonides, however, held that the prohibition refers to the Talmud, and not to the Bible ("Yad," Talmud Torah, i. 13). Girls were mostly taught privately, and received a fair education. The teaching in the Talmud Torah consumed the whole day, and in the winter months a few hours of the night besides. Teaching was suspended in the afternoon of Friday, and in the afternoon of the day preceding a holy day. On Sabbaths and holy days no new lessons were assigned; but the work of the previous week was reviewed on Sabbath afternoons by the child's parent or guardian (Shulḥan 'Aruk, Yoreh De'ah, 245).

The Talmud Torah did little for the religious teaching and training of the pupils; this was left to parents or guardians. The main object of the early schools was to instruct the pupil in the laws of Moses and in the knowledge of the rabbinical writings, more from a literary than from a practical standpoint. In later times, influenced in a measure by the Christian parochial schools of the thirteenth century, the reading of the prayers and benedictions and the teaching of the principles of the Jewish faith were included. In almost every community an organization called "Ḥebra Talmud Torah" was formed, whose duty was to create a fund and provide means for the support of public schools, and to control all teachers and pupils.

R. Asher b. Jehiel (1250–1328) decided to allow withdrawals from the funds of the Talmud Torah for the purpose of meeting the annual tax collected by the local governor, since otherwise great hardships would fall upon the poor, who were liable to be stripped of all their belongings if they failed in the prompt payment of their taxes (Responsa, rule vi., § 2). On the other hand, money from the general charity fund was at times employed to support the Talmud Torah, and donations for a synagogue or cemetery were similarly used (*ib.* rule xiii., §§ 5, 14).

Samuel di Medina (1505–89) ruled that in case of a legacy left by will to a Talmud Torah and guaranteed by the testator's brother, the latter was not held liable if the property had been consumed owing to the prolonged illness of the deceased (Responsa,

Ḥoshen Mishpaṭ, No. 357). A legacy for the support of a yeshibah and Talmud Torah in a certain town, if accompanied by a provision that it may

In the Responsa. be managed "as the son of the testator may see fit," may be transferred, it was declared, to a yeshibah elsewhere (*ib.* Oraḥ Ḥayyim, i., No. 60; see also "Paḥad Yiẓḥak," *s.v.* קדש, p. 43a).

Solomon b. Abraham ha-Kohen (16th cent.) decided that it requires the unanimous consent of the eight trustees of a Talmud Torah to engage teachers where a resolution has been passed that "no trustee or trustees shall engage the service of a melammed without the consent of the whole" (Responsa, ii., No. 89, ed. Venice, 1592).

As a specimen of the medieval organization of these schools that of the Cracow schools may be selected. From the congregational record (pinḳes) of Cracow in 1551 it appears that the Talmud Torah society controlled both private and public schools. It passed the following taḳḳanot: (1) The members shall have general supervision over the teachers and shall visit the Talmud Torah every week to see that the pupils are properly taught. (2) No melammed

The Pinḳes Record. may teach the Pentateuch except with the translation "Be'er Mosheh" (Judæo-German transl. by Moses b. Issachar, Prague, 1605), "which is in our vernacular"; for the advanced pupils he shall use no other than the Rashi commentary. (3) A melammed in the primary class shall teach not more than twenty-five pupils and shall have two assistants. (4) One melammed shall not compete with another during the term of his engagement, and shall not seek to obtain a pupil in charge of another teacher, even at the expiration of the term, unless the father or the guardian of the pupil desires to make a change. (5) The members of the Ḥebra Talmud Torah shall hire a competent and God-fearing melammed, with an assistant, for poor and orphaned boys at the bet ha-midrash. (6) The melammed and assistant shall teach pupils the alphabet (with the vowels), the Siddur, the Pentateuch (with the "Be'er Mosheh" translation), the Rashi commentary, the order of the prayers, etiquette, and good behavior—every boy according to his grade and intelligence; also reading and writing in the vernacular. The more advanced shall be taught Hebrew grammar and arithmetic; those of the highest grade shall study Talmud with Rashi and Tosafot. (7) Boys near the age of thirteen shall learn the regulations regarding tefillin. (8) At the age of fourteen a boy who is incapable of learning Talmud shall be taught a trade or become a servant in a household.

The income of the society was derived from several sources: (*a*) one-sixth of the Monday and Thursday contributions in the synagogues

Sources of Income. and other places of worship; (*b*) donations at circumcisions from guests invited to the feast; (*c*) donations at weddings from the groom and the bride and from invited guests; (*d*) one-tenth of the collections in the charity-box known as the "mattan ba-setar." The election of officers was made by ballot—three gabba'im, three vice-gabba'im, and a treasurer. Only learned and honorable men over thirty-six years of age were eligible for election. The taḳḳa-not regulating these sources of the Talmud Torah's income were in existence in the time of R. Moses Isserles. R. Joel Sirkes, rabbi of Cracow in 1638, indorsed these regulations and added many others, all of which were confirmed at a general assembly of seventy representatives of the congregations on the 25th of Ṭebet, 5398 (1638; F. H. Wetstein, "Ḳadmoniyyot," document No. 1, Cracow, 1892).

The Talmud Torah organization in Rome included eight societies in 1554, and was reconstituted Aug. 13, 1617 (Rieger, "Gesch. der Juden in Rom," p. 316, Berlin, 1895). Later, certain synagogues assumed the name "Talmud Torah," as in the case of one at Fez in 1603 (Ankava, "Kerem Ḥemed," ii. 78, Leghorn, 1869) and one at Cairo. This was probably because the school was held in or adjoined the synagogue.

The Sephardim conducted their schools more methodically. The one in Amsterdam was highly praised by R. Sheftel b. Isaiah Horowitz ("Wawe ha-'Ammudim," p. 9b, appended to "Shelah," Amsterdam, 1698). Shabbethai Bass, in the introduction to his "Sifte Yeshanim" (p. 8a, *ib.* 1680), describes this Talmud Torah and wishes it might serve as a model for other schools. He says: "It is built near the synagogue, and has six rooms, each accommodating a separate class under a me-

Curriculum. lammed. The first class is for small boys who are learning to read their prayers. In the second class they learn the Pentateuch from beginning to end, with the musical accents. In the third, they translate the Pentateuch into the vernacular and use the Rashi commentary, divided into the regular weekly sidrot. In the fourth, they learn the Prophets and the Hagiographa, with the proper accents and translation. In the fifth, they learn grammar and begin upon a series of halakic excerpts from the Talmud, the text being in Hebrew and the explanations in the vernacular. Before the approach of a holy day they memorize the laws in the Shulḥan 'Aruk pertaining to that holy day. The sixth class is preparatory to the yeshibah in the bet ha-midrash and is conducted by the ḥakam-rabbi. In this class every day one halakah, with the commentaries of Rashi and the Tosafot, is studied, and compared with the conclusions in the codes of Maimonides, Asheri, and Caro. The hours of study are from 8 to 11 in the morning, and from 2 to 5 in the afternoon; in winter, till the Minḥah prayer. The expense of maintaining this school is defrayed from a fund contributed by the members of the Ḥebra Talmud Torah. This Sephardic school made an exception to the rule of keeping the pupils in Talmud Torah all day, and a few hours of the night in the short winter days."

The Talmud Torah at Nikolsburg, Moravia, from 1724 to 1744, gave poor boys an education equal to that which was offered their more fortunate companions. The studies consisted of Siddur, Ḥumesh (Pentateuch), and Talmud (Güdemann, "Quellenschriften zur Gesch. des Unterrichts und der Erziehung bei den Deutschen Juden," p. 275). The schools in eastern Europe retained the ancient type and methods of the Ashkenazic schools up to the middle of the nineteenth century, when a movement

for improvement and better management took place in the larger cities. Thus at Odessa, in 1857, the Talmud Torah, which had existed ever since the city was chartered, was reorganized into a model school by distinguished pedagogues. In 1881 S. J. Abramowitch was appointed principal over 400 pupils. In 1904 two branches were

The Modern Talmud Torah. opened in the suburbs with an additional 400 pupils. The boys are furnished text-books and clothing free. The expenses are about 20,000 rubles annually. There is a Talmud Torah in every city within the Pale in Russia. The income is derived from the Jewish tax on meat and from private contributions.

In Jerusalem the Talmud Torah of the Sephardim, called "Tif'eret Yerushalayim," was reorganized by the ḥakam bashi R. Raphael Meïr Panejil in 1891, with 300 pupils and 13 teachers; there the boys learn Arabic and arithmetic in addition to other subjects, which range from the alphabet to the Talmud. The time of study is from sunrise to sunset. The largest contributions for the support of the school come from the Sassoons in Bombay and Calcutta, through the meshullaḥim. The Ashkenazic Talmud Torah and yeshibah 'Eẓ Ḥayyim, with 35 teachers and over 1,000 pupils, succeeded the school established by R. Judah he-Ḥasid of Siedlce. It was started with a fund contributed by Hirsch Wolf Fischbein and David Janover in 1860. The annual expenditure is about $10,000, over half of which is collected in the United States. At Jaffa the Talmud Torah and yeshibah Sha'are Torah was organized in 1886 by N. H. Lewi, with 9 teachers and 9 classes for 102 boys. Its expenses are about $2,000 yearly, mostly covered by donations from abroad.

In America the Machzikei Talmud Torah in New York was organized in 1883 by Israel (Isidor) Rosenthal. It maintains schools on its own premises at

In America. 225–227 East Broadway. It instructs over 1,100 boys at a yearly expense of about $12,000. On Jan. 22, 1905, the society opened a branch at 67 East 7th street, to which Jacob H. Schiff donated $25,000. The society is managed by a board of directors and a committee of education. The studies comprise elementary Hebrew, the reading of the prayers, the translation of the Pentateuch into Yiddish and English, and the principles of the Jewish faith and practise. The time of study occupies only two hours per day, after public-school hours, as all pupils attend the city schools for secular education. There are several other Talmud Torahs in New York; and similar institutions exist in all cities of the United States and Canada that have a large Jewish population. See EDUCATION; ḤEDER; PEDAGOGICS; YESHIBAH.

BIBLIOGRAPHY: Judah Löb, *'Omer mi-Yehudah*, Brünn, 1790; Zederbaum, *Die Geheimnisse von Berditchev*, pp. 38–44, Warsaw, 1870 (a sketch); Brandstädter, sketch in *Ha-Eshkol*, v. 70–84.

J.   J. D. E.

TAM, JACOB. See JACOB BEN MEÏR TAM.

TAM, JACOB B. DAVID IBN YAḤYA: Portuguese-Turkish rabbi and physician; born in Portugal in the second half of the fifteenth century;

died in Constantinople between 1534 and 1542. His father, David b. Solomon (d. Constantinople, 1504), one of the most prominent members of the great Yaḥya family, fled from Portugal to Naples in 1493, and thence went to Constantinople about 1497. Tam, who accompanied his father on both journeys, was recognized as a Talmudical authority, and presumably he succeeded Elijah MIZRAḤI as rabbi of the Turkish capital. It is stated that he was the body-physician of Sultan Sulaiman and a renowned authority on Mohammedan law, but there is reason to believe that his admirers exaggerated his importance. Tam's 213 responsa, which, under the name "Ohole Tam," form a part of "Tummat Yesharim" (edited by Benjamin b. Abraham MOTAL, Venice, 1622), constitute all that has been preserved of his writings. The preface to "Yosippon," attributed to him and first published in the Constantinople edition of 1510, is really the work of Judah Leon b. Moses Mosconi (see JEW. ENCYC. vii. 260, s.v. JOSEPH BEN GORION). Tam had two sons, **Joseph** and **Gedaliah**, and a grandson, **Tam b. Gedaliah**, whose actual name, as in the case of his grandfather, was Jacob.

BIBLIOGRAPHY: Benjacob, *Oẓar ha-Sefarim*, p. 217; Carmoly, *Dibre ha-Yamim li-Bene Yaḥya*, pp. 23–25, Frankfort-on-the-Main, 1850; Fürst, *Bibl. Jud.* iii. 4; Fuenn, *Keneset Yisrael*, p. 237, Warsaw, 1886; Steinschneider, *Cat. Bodl.* No. 7288.
s.   P. WI.

TAMAN: Peninsula between the Black Sea and the Sea of Azof; now included in the Russian province of Kuban. It contains the Cossack settlement of Taman, with a population of 4,291.

The peninsula was the seat of prosperous Greek colonies at the beginning of the Christian era. That a large number of Jews lived there at that time and subsequently is testified to by the Byzantine historian Theophanes (d. 817) in his "Chronographia." In 680 (or 679) Taman was captured by the Chazars, and was then known as Tame, from which originated the Russian Tmutarakan. The peninsula and the settlement near the site of the present town of Taman were known also under other names, among them Matega (by the Venetians). In 965 the Chazars were expelled from Taman by the Russian prince Swyatoslaw, a Russian colony being established at Tmutarakan; and in 1016 they were driven from their remaining Crimean possessions. In 1475, at the time of the conquest of the Crimea by Mohammed II., Taman was under the rule of the Guizolfis, descendants of the Genoese Jew Simeon de Guizolfi (see GUIZOLFI, ZACHARIAS).

In the excavations made on the Taman peninsula after the middle of the nineteenth century there were discovered about sixty tombstones which once marked Jewish graves. The inscriptions on two of these tombstones were partly deciphered; on the others only single Hebrew letters could be made out. All of them bear Jewish symbols — candelabra, shofar, and lulab. Of the two partly deciphered inscriptions one belongs to the fourth or fifth century, and contains the name of Menahem, son of Amtz; the other dates back to the eighth or ninth century, and contains the words "in this grave lies the body of Mir[iam]." A marble slab which forms a part of the wall in the lodge of the synagogue in

Theodosia bears the name of the "respected Joshua, the son of Meïr of Taman Ashkenazi," who died on Wednesday, the 27th of Ṭebet, 5269 (Dec. 31, 1508). See CRIMEA; KAFFA; KARAITES; KERTCH.

BIBLIOGRAPHY: *Regesty i Nadpisi*, vol. i.; A. Fabr, *Drevny Byt, etc.*, Odessa, 1861; Löwe, *Die Reste der Germanen am Schwarzen Meere*, Halle, 1896.
H. R.   J. G. L.

TAMAR: 1. City mentioned in the vision of Ezekiel (Ezek. xlvii. 19) as one terminus of the southern boundary-line of Canaan, which extended thence through Meriboth-kadesh to the Mediterranean. According to Ezek. xlviii. 28, moreover, this entire district was to belong to the tribe of Gad. A comparison of this boundary-line with that given in Num. xxxiv. 3–5 shows that Tamar was probably situated in the border-land of Moab, near the Dead Sea.

2. Same as HAZAZON-TAMAR.
S.   S. O.

TAMAR: 1.—Biblical Data: Daughter-in-law of Judah. After the death of her husband, Er, she married his brother Onan; but when he also died, Judah sent her back to her father's house, fearing to let her marry his third son, Shelah. When Tamar saw that Shelah, having reached maturity, did not marry her, she disguised herself and met Judah on his way to Timnath. Supposing her to be of questionable virtue, he approached her and entered into relations with her that resulted in her pregnancy. As a pledge of payment, he left with her his staff, seal, and belt. When her condition was discovered, and she was about to be burned to death in punishment for unchastity, she confronted her father-in-law with the tokens he had left with her, declaring that she was with child by the man to whom they belonged. She bore him the twins Zarah and Pharez (Gen. xxxviii.).

——In Rabbinical Literature: Tamar was the daughter of Shem, the son of Noah. Shem was a priest, and when Tamar was charged with fornication (Gen. R. lxxxv. 11) she was condemned to be burned to death in conformity with Lev. xxi. 9.

In the house of Judah, her father-in-law, she was extremely virtuous and timid, and used to keep her face constantly covered with a veil, so that Judah failed to recognize her when he saw her sitting by the roadside (Soṭah 10b; Gen. R. lxxxv. 9). Tamar prayed to God that she might not go barren from Judah's house, and resolved upon the course which she subsequently pursued (Gen. R. lxxxv. 8). In reply to Judah's questions she declared that she was not a Gentile, and that she was unmarried (Gen. R. lxxxv. 9; Soṭah 10a). When she had become pregnant she was not at all ashamed of her condition, but boasted to all that she would be the mother of kings and redeemers (Gen. R. lxxxv. 11). When charged with unchastity, she was unwilling to assert directly that she was with child by her father-in-law, for she feared that such a disclosure might humiliate him, and she was ready to die rather than incriminate him (Ber. 43a; Soṭah 12b). She was willing, however, indirectly to cause him to confess, and therefore sent him the articles which he had left her as a pledge, and which had been taken from her by Samael and restored by Gabriel. After her innocence had been proved, Judah continued to live with her in marital relations (Soṭah 10b).

2.—Biblical Data: Sister of Absalom, and the victim of the passion of her half-brother Amnon. At the suggestion of Jonadab, his confidant, Amnon feigned illness, and Tamar was sent by the king to his apartment to prepare food for him. Amnon took advantage of this opportunity to dishonor her forcibly, after which he drove her away. Weeping and lamenting, she went to her brother Absalom, in whose house she remained. Absalom avenged his sister two years later by killing Amnon (II Sam. xiii.).

——In Rabbinical Literature: Tamar was the natural daughter of David by a captive whom he married after she had abjured her Gentile religion, and who became the mother of Absalom. Because of her illegitimacy it would have been lawful for her to marry Amnon, the son of David, and she therefore besought him (II Sam. xiii. 13) not to dishonor her, but to ask the king to bestow her on him as his wife, a request which would surely have been granted (Sanh. 21a).

s.   J. Z. L.

TAMARISK: Tree, several species of which are found in and around Palestine. The Hebrew term for the tamarisk is doubtful. The word אשל, which occurs three times in the Old Testament, is interpreted by modern scholars as meaning "a tamarisk," and is so rendered in the Revised Version. Abraham planted a "tamarisk-tree" (R. V.) in Beer-sheba (Gen. xxi. 33; A. V. gives "a grove"). "Saul was sitting . . . under the tamarisk-tree in Ramah" (I Sam. xxii. 6, R. V.). Finally, the bones of Saul and his sons were buried "under the tamarisk-tree in Jabesh" (I Sam. xxxi. 13, R. V.). The parallel passage of I Chron. x. 12 has אלה, which is rendered "oak-tree" by both the English versions (R. V., margin, "terebinth"). Therefore אשל in the last-mentioned passage is rendered "tree" in the Authorized Version.

s.   M. Sel.

TAMID (in full, 'OLAT TAMID): Treatise in the Mishnah and the Babylonian Gemara; devoted chiefly to the regulations regarding the morning and evening burnt offerings (comp. Ex. xxix. 38–42; Num. xxviii. 3–8), but dealing also with other ceremonies in the ritual of the Temple which are binding on the priests and the Levites. In most editions this treatise stands ninth in the order Ḳodashim, and it is divided into seven chapters (six in Lowe's edition of the Mishnah), containing thirty-four paragraphs in all.

Ch. i.: The priests kept watch in three places in the Temple; where the young priests were on guard, and where the older ones slept who held the keys (§ 1); all who sought admission to remove the ashes from the altar were obliged to prepare themselves by a ritual bath before the officer appeared; when he appeared and when he called upon the priests to draw lots (§ 2); the mutual greetings of the priests (§ 3); how the one chosen by lot to remove the ashes from the altar performed his duties (§ 4).

Ch. ii.: How the other priests continued the task of cleansing the altar (§ 1); the piling of the ashes, in the center of the altar, into a hillock, which was considered an adornment (§ 2); the supply of fuel for the altar and the kind of wood used (§ 3); the arrangement of the wood and fire in layers (§§ 4–5).

Ch. iii.: The drawing of lots for various official duties, such as slaying the tamid, sprinkling its blood, and cleansing the altar and the candlestick (§ 1); the announcement of the time of slaying the morning sacrifice (§ 2); the bringing of the sacrificial lamb, which was given to drink from a golden cup before it was killed; who was charged with taking it to the place of sacrifice (§§ 3–5); the mode of cleansing the inner altar and the candlesticks, together with the statement, in conformity with Ezek. xliv. 2, that no man ever passed through the postern on the southern side of the large door; how the opening of this great portal was heard as far as Jericho, as was the sound of the trumpets and other music of the Temple (§§ 6–9).

Ch. iv.: The ritual for killing and dismembering the sacrificial lamb; how the parts of the sacrifice were brought to the altar.

Ch. v.: The daily morning prayer in the Temple, which was supplemented on the Sabbath by a benediction on the division of priests who then completed their duties (§ 1); the drawing of lots for offering incense; the question as to whether one might make this offering twice, and the mode of burning the incense (§§ 2–5); the "magrefah," a musical instrument used in the Temple (see ORGAN), and the various priestly and Levitical meanings of the signals given on it (§ 6).

Ch. vi.: Additional details in regard to offering incense.

Ch. vii.: The ritual used in case the high priest himself performed the sacrifice; the mode in which he pronounced the benediction on the people; the divergency of this benediction from that bestowed by the priests outside the Temple, and the music which accompanied the high priest's performance of his functions (§§ 1–3); enumeration of the Psalms sung by the Levites in the Temple on the various days of the week (§ 4).

Although the extant Babylonian Gemara covers only ch. i., ii., and iv. of Tamid, it contains several sayings and ethical maxims of importance, as well as stories and legends of much interest. The following saying may be cited as a specimen (29a): "The Pentateuch and the writings of the Prophets and the mishnaic sages contain many exaggerated expressions which can not be taken literally, such as, 'The cities are great and walled up to heaven'" (Deut. i. 28). On the legends contained in this treatise concerning Alexander the Great, his conversation with the sages of the South, his journey to Africa, and his adventures among the Amazons and at the gate of paradise, see JEW. ENCYC. i. 342 et seq., s.v. ALEXANDER THE GREAT.

w. b.   J. Z. L.

TAMMUZ (Assyrian, "Dumuzi"): Babylonian deity supposed to be referred to in Ezek. viii. 14. He is regarded as the husband, or sometimes as the son, of the goddess Ishtar, who descended to Hades every year in the fourth month, named after him, and remained there till the following spring. He is accordingly supposed to represent the spirit of the spring vegetation; and there was a period of mourning in Babylonia to mark the discontinuance of growth. It has been suggested that the fast of the Seventeenth of Tammuz was a survival in Jewish folk-lore of the mourning for Tammuz; while the myth of Adonis in classical literature has also been associated with the legend. The reference in Ezekiel to the women weeping for Tammuz certainly shows a trace of a cult in early Israel; but how far it extended it is difficult to say. W. Robertson Smith attempted to associate the Tammuz-worship with the sacrificial rites connected with "the king of the woods."

BIBLIOGRAPHY: Frazer, *Golden Bough*, 2d ed., i. 360 *et seq.*; Jastrow, *Religion of the Babylonians and Assyrians*, p. 549, Boston, 1898; W. Robertson Smith, *Rel. of Sem.* p. 411; Barton, *Sketch of Semitic Origins*, pp. 211 *et seq.*
S.   J.

TAMMUZ (תמוז): Fourth ecclesiastical and tenth civil month of the Hebrew calendar. It consists of twenty-nine days, and corresponds to part of June and part of July. During the last years of the Second Temple the 14th of Tammuz was declared a feast-day in commemoration of a victory gained by the Pharisees over the Sadducees in a dispute regarding the interpretation of the Law (Ta'an. iv. 6). The 17th of Tammuz is the public fast-day called "Shib'ah 'Asar be-Tammuz," in commemoration of the breaking down of the walls of Jerusalem by Nebuchadnezzar. As stated in Jer. xxxix. 2, this catastrophe occurred on the 9th day of the month; the 17th was selected because, during the siege of Jerusalem by Titus, a similar catastrophe happened on that day (Ta'an. 26a; Shulḥan 'Aruk, Oraḥ Ḥayyim, 549).

According to the Megillat Ta'anit (iv. 6), four other calamities had overtaken the people of Israel on the 17th: the breaking of the tables of the Law by Moses, the cessation of the perpetual offering, the burning of the Torah and the erection of an idol in the sanctuary by Apostomus (comp. Josephus, "Ant." xx. 5, § 4; *idem*, "B. J." ii. 12, § 2), and the discontinuance of the sacrifices. With the 17th begin the three weeks of mourning over the destruction of Jerusalem, which end with the 9th of Ab. During this period it is forbidden to celebrate marriages, to cut the hair, to bathe, etc. (Shulḥan 'Aruk, Oraḥ Ḥayyim, 551). The pious fast every day during these three weeks (*ib.*). The 27th of Tammuz is the anniversary of the burning of the tanna Ḥanina ben Teradion during the Hadrianic persecutions (additions to Megillat Ta'anit, ed. Neubauer, in "M. J. C." ii. 24).

J.   I. Br.

TANG, ABRAHAM: English author; flourished in London in the latter half of the eighteenth century. In 1773 he published a philosophic commentary on Ecclesiastes which gives evidence of some classical scholarship. The mythology of Greece and of Rome is presented in this commentary in a very clear and concise manner; and the "Anthologia Græca," Ovid, Vergil, and Seneca are frequently cited. Tang wrote also an exposition of the Talmudical passages in which the sayings

of the "Ancients of Athens" are quoted (London, 1772); this work was dedicated to R. Moses of Minsk.

BIBLIOGRAPHY: *Jew. Chron.* Dec. 19, 1884.
J.   G. L.

TANGIER. See Morocco.

TANḤUM B. ELIEZER: Lithuanian rabbi and merchant; born 1746; died in Grodno Jan. 12, 1819. He was the son of R. Eliezer of Urle (Orle), in the government of Grodno, and succeeded his father in that rabbinate. Later he occupied the position of "rosh bet din" at Grodno, where his father had been called as rabbi. Upon his failure to secure the rabbinate of Grodno after the death of his father (1791), Tanḥum engaged in business, in which he was very successful. There is a tradition that he enjoyed the confidence of the last king of Poland and that he was well thought of by Emperor Alexander I. His signature is first under the resolutions adopted by the Jewish delegates who met in Wilna in 1818 to select three deputies to reside permanently in St. Petersburg and represent Jewish affairs before the government (see Jew. Encyc. i. 345, *s.v.* Alexander I.). Tanḥum left several works in manuscript under the collective title "Neḥamat Ẓiyyon"; these in 1860 were in possession of his grandson Elijah Pereẓ of Wilna. His son was Issachar Bär b. Tanḥum.

BIBLIOGRAPHY: Fuenn, *Ḳiryah Ne'emanah*, pp. 35, 236, Wilna, 1860; Friedenstein, '*Ir Gibborim*, pp. 54, 69–70, Wilna, 1880.
E. C.   P. Wi.

TANḤUM BAR ḤANILAI (or **ILAI**): Palestinian amora of the third century, although his father's name suggests a Babylonian origin. He transmitted the sayings of Joshua ben Levi, Johanan, and Bar Ḳappara. In the Babylonian Talmud he appears as the author of decisions which in the Jerusalem Talmud are attributed to older authorities. Thus, in Sanh. 93a he is said to be the author of a decision which in Pesiḳ. xi. (ed. Buber, p. 99a) is ascribed to Eleazar b. Pedat. On the other hand, halakic sentences of his have been preserved in the Jerusalem Talmud (Ma'as. 48b; Ḥag. 76a; Ter. 41c; Shab. 5d; Ta'an. 65a). Among those who transmitted sayings of his were Abbahu (Cant. R. ii. 7) and Tanḥuma (Pesiḳ. R. 112).

It appears from Yer. Ta'an. 65a, b that Tanḥum bar Ḥanilai was active as a preacher, and that he once preached with Abba bar Zabdai and Josefa. He died during a Ḥanukkah festival (Yer. M. Ḳ., end). His sayings were of a high ethical and moral character: "God speaks thus to Israel: 'My daughter [*i.e.*, the Torah] is in thy hands; thy daughter [soul] is in My hands. If thou protect Mine, then will I protect thine'" (Tan., Ki Tissa, end). With regard to the prohibition against certain kinds of food, he said: "A physician once visited two sick people; the one who had no hope of recovery was permitted to eat everything, while the one who had every prospect of recovery was allowed only certain foods. So God treats the Jews; because they have hope of a future life, He gives them certain dietary laws; while the heathen, who have no part in the life to come, are permitted to eat of all things" (Lev. R. xiii. 2).

Tanḥum bar Ḥanilai's haggadah is especially characteristic because of his system of connecting the last words of one Bible paragraph with the opening words of the next, as Lev. i. 16 with ii. 1 (Lev. R. iii. 4), Lev. xii. 2 *et seq.* with xiii. 2 *et seq.* (Lev. R. xv. 5), Ps. xciv. 1 with xciii. 5 (Midr. Teh. *ad loc.*), and Num. v. 12 *et seq.* with v. 2 *et seq.* (Num. R. ix. 4). Haggadic sayings of his are quoted in the following places: Sanh. 7a, 100a; 'Ab. Zarah 18b, 19b; B. M. 86b; Shab. 22a; Ḥag. 7a; Ber. 8b, 13b; Meg. 15b; Mak. 10a; Yer. Ta'an. 68c; Gen. R. iv. 6, xci., beginning; Pesiḳ. R. 21, end; Ex. R. xlii., end; and Lev. R. xxvi. The Midrash Mishle begins with a procœmium by Tanḥum bar Hanilai, although his name is not mentioned in any other part of the book. He is mentioned twice in the Pirḳe Rabbi Eli'ezer (xxxix., xlix.) by the name of Tanḥum.

BIBLIOGRAPHY: Heilprin, *Seder ha-Dorot*, ii. 283a; Bacher, *Ag. Pal. Amor.* iii. 627-636 and Index; Frankel, *Mebo*, p. 131a.
W. B. S. O.

TANḤUM B. ḤIYYA: Palestinian amora of the third century; a pupil of Simeon b. Pazzi, whose sayings he transmits. In the Babylonian Talmud he is constantly referred to as R. Tanḥum b. Ḥiyya of Kefar 'Akko (M. Ḳ. 25b; Yeb. 45a), of which place he was a native; he resided, however, in Tiberias, where on one occasion, with the aid of Aḥa, the lord of the castle, he ransomed some Jewish women who probably had been taken there by Roman troops (Yeb. 45a). He was a member of the commission which determined the intercalations of the calendar (Yer. Sanh. 6c). He was on terms of friendship with Assi, who visited him (Yer. Shab. 6c), and he maintained friendly relations with Hananiah b. Papa (Yer. M. Ḳ. 83c). Tanḥum was wealthy and philanthropic. It is recorded that when his mother purchased meat for the household a similar quantity was always purchased for distribution among the poor (Lev. R. xxxiv. 1).

Only three halakic sayings by him have been preserved (Bek. 57b; Yer. Meg. 75a, twice); but several of his haggadic utterances are extant. The following may be mentioned: "When one who has learned, taught, and observed the Law fails to prevent the evil which it is in his power to prevent, or to confirm the good which it is in his power to confirm, then shall smite him the curse pronounced [Deut. xxvii. 26] over those who fail to confirm 'all the words of this law'" (Yer. Soṭah 21d). He interpreted Prov. vi. 32 ("Whoso committeth adultery with a woman lacketh understanding") as referring to those who seek office for the sake of gain (Pesiḳ. R. 22 [ed. Friedmann, p. 111a]). Tanḥum was the author also of a prayer to be read by any one who has had an ominous dream (Yer. Ber. 9a). It was told in Babylon that when Tanḥum died all the statues in Tiberias moved from their places (M. Ḳ. 25b, according to the correct reading in Rabbinovicz's "Variæ Lectiones," *ad loc.*).

BIBLIOGRAPHY: Frankel, *Mebo*, pp. 130b, 131a; Bacher, *Ag. Pal. Amor.* iii. 636-639.
W. B. J. Z. L.

TANḤUM BAR JEREMIAH: Palestinian amora of the fourth century; pupil of R. Manis the Elder. In the town of Ḥefer in Galilee he once ren-

dered a legal decision on a religious question, whereupon his attention was called to the fact that his action was unwarranted, since his teacher resided within twelve miles of that place. Only one halakic decision of his—regarding the liturgy—is extant (Yer. Ber. 7b). He was the author of several haggadic sentences (Midr. Teh. to Ps. xxxi.; Gen. R. iv. 8; Lam. R. ii. 1; and Pesiḳ. 163b).

BIBLIOGRAPHY: Bacher, *Ag. Pal. Amor.* iii. 751-752; Frankel, *Mebo*, p. 131a; Heilprin, *Seder ha-Dorot*, ii. 192b.
E. C. S. O.

TANḤUM BEN JOSEPH YERUSHALMI: Oriental philologist and exegete of the thirteenth century. He was a scholar of great merit and was one of the last representatives of the rationalistic school of Biblical exegesis in the Orient; he is called by modern writers "the Ibn Ezra of the East." He lived in Palestine, perhaps for a time in Egypt also, and had a son, Joseph, who maintained a correspondence with David, the grandson of Maimonides (comp. Brody in "Sammelband," 1893, issued by the Meḳiẓe Nirdamim). Tanḥum's very existence was unknown to European scholars until the eighteenth century, when fragments of his works were brought from the Orient by Pocock, who published some of them in his "Porta Mosis." Tanḥum skilfully handled the Arabic language, in which he composed his works; he possessed some knowledge of Greek, and was well versed in philosophy and natural science. He was the author of "Kitab al-Ijaz wal-Bayan," consisting of commentaries on the Biblical books, with an introduction entitled "Kulliyyat" giving a sketch of Hebrew grammar and an account of the philologists of the Middle Ages.

With the exception of those on Ezra and Nehemiah, the commentaries are found in manuscript, complete or in fragments, in the libraries of St. Petersburg, Oxford, and London; and they are known also through quotations made either by the author himself or by later writers. The commentaries which have been published are: "Ad Libros V. T. Commentarii Arabici Specimen una cum Annott. ad Aliquot Loca Libri Judicum" (ed. Ch. F. Schnurrer, Tübingen, 1791); "Commentarii in Prophetas Arabici Specimen," etc. (ed. Theodor Haarbrücker, Halle, 1842); "Commentarii Arabici in Lamentat." (ed. Cureton, London, 1843); "Commentaire sur le Livre de Habakkouk, Publié en Arabe avec une Traduction Française par Salomon Munk" (in Cahen's French Bible, vol. xvii.); "Arab. ad Libros Samuelis et Regum Locos Graviores, Edidit et Interpretationem Latinam Adjecit Th. Haarbrücker" (Leipsic, 1844); on Joshua, by the same editor (published with the "Blätter aus der Veitel-Heine-Ephraim Lehranstalt," Berlin, 1862); extracts from the commentary on Judges, published by Goldziher in his "Studien," 1870; on Ḳohelet (ed. Samuel Eppenstein, Berlin, 1888); on Jonah (ed. Kokowzow, in the "Rosen-Festschrift," St. Petersburg, 1897). In his commentaries, Tanḥum, being a decided adversary of midrashic exegesis, endeavored to give a philological or a philosophical interpretation of the Scriptural text. He quotes the prominent exegetes from Saadia down to Abraham ibn Ezra.

Tanḥum wrote also "Al-Murshid al-Kafi," a lexicon giving in alphabetical order the etymologies and significations of all the vocables found in Maimonides' "Mishneh Torah," and of a great number of those found in the Mishnah. The main sources used are the "'Aruk" and Maimonides' commentary on the Mishnah. The author quotes Saadia, Ibn Janaḥ, Dunash, Moses ibn Ezra, and other prominent philologists. Specimens of the "Murshid," still extant in manuscript (Bagdad, Jerusalem, and Oxford), have been published by Wilhelm Bacher under the title "Aus dem Wörterbuche Tanchum Jerushalmi's" (Strasburg, 1903).

BIBLIOGRAPHY: Steinschneider, *Cat. Bodl.* col. 2666; idem, *Die Arabische Literatur der Juden*, p. 174; Goldziher, *Studien über Tanchum*, Leipsic, 1870; Poznanski, in *R. E. J.* xl., xli.; idem, in *Zeitschrift für Hebräische Bibliographie*, v. 122, 184; idem, in *Z. D. M. G.* lv. 603; Harkavy, *Studien*, iii. 43; idem, *Ḥadashim gam Yeshanim*, vi. 2; Grätz, *Gesch.* vii. 144, note 2.
W. B.   I. Br.

TANḤUM OF NAVE. See Tanḥuma B. Abba.

TANḤUMA B. ABBA: Palestinian amora of the fifth generation; one of the foremost haggaḏists of his time. He was a pupil of Ḥuna b. Abin (Num. R. iii.; Gen. R. xli.), from whom he transmits halakic (Yer. Ḥal. 57d; Shab. 10c) as well as haggadic sayings (Yer. Pe'ah 15b; Shab. 11d; 'Ab. Zarah 43a). He received instruction also from Judah b. Shalom (Midr. Teh. to Ps. cxix. 2) and R. Phinehas (Yer. Sheḳ. 49d). According to Bacher, he resided in Nave, a town in Peræa (comp. Neubauer, "G. T." p. 23).

Of Tanḥuma's life the Babylonian Talmud relates the following incident, probably based on an actual occurrence. The emperor—a Christian ruler no doubt being meant—said to Tanḥuma, "Let us all become one people." To this the latter replied, "Yes; but since we are circumcised we can not become like you; whereas you, by having yourself circumcised, may become like us." The emperor thereupon said, "You have answered me correctly; but he who worsts the king must be thrown to wild beasts." This was done, but the animals did Tanḥuma no harm. An unbeliever who stood by remarked that perhaps they were not hungry, whereupon he himself was thrown after Tanḥuma and was instantly torn to pieces (Sanh. 39a).

Retort to the Emperor.

With regard to Tanḥuma's public activity, the only fact known is that he ordered a fast on account of a drought. Two fasts were held, but no rain came, whereupon Tanḥuma ordered a third fast, saying in his sermon: "My children, be charitable unto each other, and God will be merciful unto you." On this occasion one man gave money to his divorced wife, who was in need; Tanḥuma thereupon lifted his face toward the heavens and prayed: "Lord of the Universe, this hard-hearted man took pity on his wife when he saw that she was in need, and helped her, although not obliged to do so; how much more shouldest Thou, the Gracious and Merciful, be filled with pity when Thou seest Thy beloved children, the sons of Abraham, Isaac, and Jacob, in need." As soon as he had ceased praying, rain came, and the world was relieved of its distress (Gen. R. xxxiii.; Lev. R. xxxiv.).

Tanḥuma is not often mentioned as a halakist: a few remarks on and explanations of halakic teachings are ascribed to him in the Palestinian Talmud (Yer. 'Er. 26c; Pes. 37b, d; Yoma 44d; Sheḳ. 47c; Ta'an. 67a), while the Babylonian Talmud mentions an objection raised by him against a halakic thesis advanced by the Palestinian schools (Ḥul. 55b). As a haggadist, on the other hand, he is frequently mentioned, and the numerous haggadic sentences of his which are still preserved touch every province of the Haggadah. He often points out the Scriptural bases for the sayings of older authors, always using the characteristic formula of introduction: "I give the reason"; that is, "I cite the Biblical authority" (Yer. Ber. 12c; Gen. R. iv. 3; Lev. R. xxi.). He also explains and annotates older sayings (Gen. R. xxiv.), adjusts differing traditions (Lev. R. xxiv. 5), and varies the text of old haggadic sentences (Gen. R. xliii. 3). His own haggadic teachings differ but little from those of his contemporaries, although some of his interpretations approach the simple exegetic method. An example of this is furnished by his interpretation of Eccl. iii. 11, where he explains the word "ha-kol" as meaning "the universe" (Gen. R. ix. 2).

His Haggadot.

Tanḥuma often made use of symbolism to illustrate his thought. Some of his haggadic utterances may be quoted: "Just as the spice-box contains all kinds of fragrant spices, so must the wise youth be filled with all kinds of Biblical, mishnaic, halakic, and haggadic knowledge" (Cant. R. v. 13). On Isa. xlv. 3 Tanḥuma said: "Nebuchadnezzar grudged his son and successor Evil-merodach his treasures, wherefore he filled iron ships with gold and sunk them in the Euphrates. When Cyrus conquered Babylonia and decided to rebuild the Temple in Jerusalem, and diverted the river into another channel, and 'the treasures of darkness, and hidden riches of secret places' were given to him" (Esth. R. iii. 1).

Tanḥuma often held religious disputations with non-Jewish, especially Christian, scholars; and he himself tells of one which took place in Antioch (Gen. R. xix. 4). He was asked concerning Gen. iii. 5, where the word "Ke-Elohim [yode'e ṭob wa-ra']" seems to point to a plurality of gods. Tanḥuma replied that such a construction was refuted by the immediately preceding words, "yodea' [singular] Elohim." His frequent intercourse with non-Jews led him to formulate the following rule: "When a non-Jew greets you with a blessing, answer him with an 'Amen'" (Yer. Ber. 12c; Suk. 54a). The Pesiḳta Rabbati contains about eighty proems said to have originated with Tanḥuma, and beginning with the phrase "Thus said R. Tanḥuma." A great number of proems bearing his name are found also in the Midrash Tanḥuma. In addition to these proems several lengthy sections of the Pesiḳta Rabbati as well as of the Midrash Tanḥuma are followed by the note "Thus explained [or "preached"] R. Tanḥuma." See Tanḥuma, Midrash.

Polemics.

BIBLIOGRAPHY: Weiss, *Dor*, iii. 142–144; Frankel, *Mebo*, p. 131a, b; Buber, *Einleitung zum Midrash Tanḥuma*, pp. 3a, 4a; Bacher, *Ag. Pal. Amor.* iii. 465–514.
W. B.   J. Z. L.

TANḤUMA, MIDRASH: Name given to three different collections of Pentateuch haggadot; two are extant, while the third is known only through citations. These midrashim, although bearing the name of R. Tanḥuma, must not be regarded as having been written or edited by him. They were so named merely because they consist partly of homilies originating with him (this being indicated by the introductory formula "Thus began R. Tanḥuma" or "Thus preached R. Tanḥuma") and partly of homilies by haggadic teachers who followed the style of R. Tanḥuma. It is possible that R. Tanḥuma himself preserved his homilies, and that his collection was used by the editors of the midrash. The three collections were edited at different times; they will, therefore, be treated in chronological order.

Three Midrashim.

Tanḥuma A: The collection published by Buber (Wilna, 1885), who gathered the material from several manuscripts. This collection, consisting of homilies on and haggadic interpretations of the weekly sections of the Pentateuch, is the oldest of the three, as well as perhaps the oldest compilation of its kind arranged as a running commentary on the Pentateuch. It is even older than Bereshit Rabbah, which quotes several of its decisions. This midrash (Tanḥuma) was edited in the fifth century, before the completion of the Babylonian Talmud, to which work it nowhere refers. On the contrary, a passage in the Babylonian Talmud seems with probability to indicate that the redactor of that work had referred to the Midrash Tanḥuma. This passage (Ḳid. 33b) says that two amoraim differed in their interpretations of the words "and [they] looked after Moses, until he was gone into the tabernacle" (Ex. xxxiii. 8). One amora interpreted the words in a complimentary sense, while the other held that the people looked after Moses and made unfavorable remarks about him. The favorable interpretation only is given in the Talmud, while the adverse opinion is referred to with the words "ki de-ita" (as it is said). Inasmuch as the adverse view is given in the Tanḥuma Peḳude (ed. Buber, p. 65a), it is extremely probable that the words "ki de-ita" in the Talmud have reference to the former work, or that the reference originally read "ki de-ita be-Tanḥuma" (as it is said in the Tanḥuma), the words "be-Tanḥuma" having been eliminated later.

The homilies contained in Midrash Tanḥuma A begin with the words "As the Scriptures say" or sometimes "As it is written." Then follow a verse (in most cases taken from the Hagiographa), its explanation, and a homily on the particular passage of the Pentateuch referred to. Several of the homilies on the first, third, and fourth books of the Pentateuch begin with brief halakic dissertations bearing on the passages to which the homilies refer. The halakic treatises consist of a question introduced with the words "Yelammedenu rabbenu" (May our teacher instruct us), and of a reply beginning with the phrase "Kak shanu rabbotenu" (Thus have our teachers instructed us); the replies are always taken from either a mishnah or a baraita. Many of the homilies close with words of hope and encouragement regarding the future of

the Jews; but several of them are abbreviated and not entirely completed, this curtailment being apologized for in the words "Much more might be said on this subject, but we shall not tire you" (Noaḥ xxvi. 27b), or "This passage has been elucidated by several other interpretations and expositions, but in order not to tire you we quote only that which is necessary for to-day's theme" (Ḥuḳḳat xvi. 57a).

Although essentially a haggadic midrash, Tanḥuma A contains many halakic sayings. In addition to its sixty-one introductions to homilies, which contain halakic questions and answers, there are several halakic rules and decisions quoted throughout the work. These halakic passages were taken from the Mishnah or the Baraita, and not from the Babylonian Talmud; indeed, many of the decisions given are in opposition to those of the latter work (comp. Buber, Introduction, pp. 15 et seq.). The haggadic contents of the midrash are also very extensive and varied; it contains, too, simple explanations of Scriptural passages; several refutations of heretics; explanations of the differences between "ḳere" and "ketib" and between words written "plene" (male) and defectively ("ḥaser"); interpretations according to noṭarikon and gemaṭria; several narratives and parables; and numerous aphorisms, moral sayings, and popular proverbs.

Contents.

Some of the aphorisms and proverbs may be cited here: "One may not give an honest man an opportunity to steal, much less a thief" (Wayishlaḥ xii. 85b). "The office seeks those that would escape it" (Wayiḳra iv. 2b). "If you yield not to wickedness it will not follow you nor dwell by you" (Tazria' xi. 20b). "Do the wicked no good in order that thou reap not that which is evil" (Ḥuḳḳat i. 50a).

This Tanḥuma midrash has been referred to in many other midrashim, as, for example, all the Rabbot, Pesiḳta de-Rab Kahana, Pesiḳta Rabbati, and in the midrashim to Samuel, Proverbs, and Psalms, which all quote passages from it. The Geonim also and the older rabbinical authorities made use of it, and cited halakic as well as haggadic sentences from it (comp. Buber, l.c. pp. 37 et seq.). The first to refer to this midrash by the name of Tanḥuma, however, was Rashi, who mentions it in several passages of his commentary, and quotes from it. Most of Rashi's quotations are taken from Tanḥuma A (see Buber, l.c. pp. 44 et seq.).

Tanḥuma B, or Yelammedenu: This second midrash with which the name of Tanḥuma is associated is known as the "Yelammedenu" from the opening words of the halakic introductions to the homilies — "Yelammedenu rabbenu" (May our teacher instruct us). It is referred to also under the name of Tanḥuma, though by only a few authorities, as Hai Gaon and Zedekiah ben Abraham (Buber, l.c. pp. 44a, 50a). The reason for this confusion of names may be found in the fact that a later collection of midrashim (Tanḥuma C) included a great part of the material contained in the Yelammedenu, especially that referring to the second book of the Pentateuch. The Yelammedenu, which contains several passages from Tanḥuma A, is often cited in the "'Aruk," and has been extensively referred to by the redactor of the Yalḳuṭ. Other old rabbinical authorities refer to the Yelammedenu by that name, and quote passages from it; but otherwise the work has been completely lost.

Tanḥuma C: The third haggadic midrash to the Pentateuch bearing the name of Tanḥuma contains many passages taken from A and B. It is, in fact, an amended edition of the two earlier works, with various additions by later authors. Its homilies on Genesis are original, although they contain several revised passages from Tanḥuma A as well as from the Yelammedenu, the Babylonian Talmud being largely drawn upon for additional interpretations and expositions. The part referring to Exodus is borrowed almost entirely from the Yelammedenu, with the exception of the Wayaḳhel and Peḳude sections, which contain homilies not embodied in the lost work. For the portions to the books of Leviticus, Numbers, and Deuteronomy the redactor of this midrash has made extensive use of the material that he found in Tanḥuma A, which he has revised and supplied with numerous additions. The first authority to cite this midrash was Rashi, who in some passages of his commentary refers to

Literary History. Tanḥuma C and not to the A collection (comp. Buber, *l.c.* pp. 44 *et seq.*). Because of the fact that the third midrash contains much of the material of the lost Yelammedenu, the two works were often confounded. Some authorities believed that it was the Tanḥuma C and not the Yelammedenu which had been lost (Menahem de Lonzano, in "Ma'arik," *s.v.* "Tanḥuma"; comp. Azulai, "Shem ha-Gedolim," ii.). Others erroneously considered this midrash identical with the Yelammedenu, thinking the work had a double title; and the first editions of Tanḥuma C appeared, therefore, under the title "Midrash Tanḥuma, Called Also the Yelammedenu."

Tanḥuma C was first published at Constantinople in 1522, and was reprinted without emendation at Venice in 1545. The third edition, which served as a basis for all the later editions, was published at Mantua in 1563 by Meïr b. Abraham of Padua and Ezra of Fano. This edition contains several additions, consisting of single sentences as well as of entire paragraphs, which Ezra of Fano selected from two of the original manuscripts and also from the Yalḳuṭ. Ezra indicated the added matter by marking it with open hands, but in the following editions these marks were omitted, so that it is no longer possible to distinguish between original contents and material added by revisers. Ezra of Fano further added to his edition an index of all halakic decisions, as well as of the legends and parables contained in this midrash; this index has been retained in all later editions.

BIBLIOGRAPHY: Zunz, *G. V.* pp. 226–238; Solomon Buber's *Introduction* (*Mebo*) to his edition of the *Midrash Tanḥuma*, Wilna, 1885; Theodor, in *Monatsschrift*, 1885–86; Bacher, *Ag. Pal. Amor.* iii. 500–514; Weiss, *Dor*, iii. 268–273; A. Epstein, *Ḳadmut ha-Tanḥuma*, in *Bet Talmud*, v. 7–23; L. Grünhut, *Sefer ha-Liḳḳuṭim*, iv.–vi., Jerusalem, 1900.
W. B. J. Z. L.

TANḤUMA B. SKOLASTIḲAI: Palestinian teacher of the Law. His period is not known, but according to a conjecture (see "'Aruk," *s.v.* "Askolastika") he was the son of that Joshua b. Hana-

niah who in Gen. R. lxiv. 10 is called "Askolastikus." Tanḥuma is mentioned but once in the Palestinian Talmud, namely, in Ber. 7d, where it is said that he read the following prayer: "May it be Thy will, O Lord my God, and the God of my fathers, that the evil desire which dwells within our hearts shall be destroyed. Thou hast created us to do Thy bidding, and we are constrained to follow Thy will. Thou desirest it, and we also desire it, but the yeast in our dough [*i.e.*, the tendency toward evil] hinders us. Thou knowest that we do not possess strength enough to withstand it; let it therefore be Thy will to destroy and suppress it, so that we may do according to Thy will with all our hearts." According to Frankel ("Mebo," 131b), Tanḥuma b. Skolastiḳai is identical with Tanḥuma b. Abba (comp. Bacher, "Ag. Pal. Amor." iii. 470).

BIBLIOGRAPHY: Heilprin, *Seder ha-Dorot*, ii., Warsaw, 1882.
W. B. J. Z. L.

TANḤUMA B. YUDAN: Palestinian amora of the fourth century, some of whose haggadic utterances have been preserved. The words ואחר כבוד in Ps. lxxiii. 24 are interpreted by him as implying that on account of the honor in which Esau held his father, Isaac, the recognition of Jacob's merit in this world was delayed (Pesiḳ. R. xxiii. 124a). On account of the different meanings of the two names of God he declared (Yer. Ber. 14b), with reference to Ps. lvi. 2, that he praised the name of God regardless of whether it indicated severe justice ("middat ha-din") or mild grace ("middat ha-raḥamim"). From the fact that in Judges vi. 24 (see margin) God is given the name of "Peace" he deduces that it is forbidden to use the word "peace" as a term of greeting in an unclean place (Lev. R. ix., end). Two other sayings of Tanḥuma b. Yudan are really transmitted baraita sentences (Yer. Ber. 11d [comp. Frankel, "Mebo," p. 24b]; Yer. Yoma 38b; in the latter passage it is noted that the saying is contained in a baraita).

BIBLIOGRAPHY: Frankel, *Mebo*, p. 131a; Bacher, *Ag. Pal. Amor.* iii. 752–753; Heilprin, *Seder ha-Dorot*, ii. 192a.
W. B. J. Z. L.

TANNA. See TANNAIM AND AMORAIM.

TANNA DEBE ELIYAHU: Composite name of a midrash, consisting of two parts, whose final redaction took place at the end of the tenth century of the common era. The first part is called "Seder Eliyahu Rabbah" (thirty-one chapters); the second, "Seder Eliyahu Zuṭa" (fifteen chapters). A distinct reference to this midrash occurs in the Talmud in Ket. 106a: "Elijah used to come to R. Anan, upon which occasions the prophet recited the

Origin of the Name. Seder Eliyahu to him. When, however, R. Anan had given this decision [one previously narrated in the Talmud] the prophet came no more. R. Anan fasted in consequence, and begged forgiveness, whereupon the prophet came again; but R. Anan had such great fear of Elijah that, in order to avoid seeing him, he made a box and sat in it until the recitation was over" (but see JEW. ENCYC. i. 552, *s.v.* ANAN). Hence, according to Rashi, the midrash has the two names, "Rabbah" for the earlier, and "Zuṭa" for the later lectures. Anan was a

Babylonian amora of the third century. The collection of baraitot concerning him, referred to in this midrash, is cited in the Babylonian Talmud under the title "Tanna debe Eliyahu" (see below); and the utterances in question are found in the midrash itself. The tosafot to Ketubot (106a, *s.v.* והיינו) say that the midrash consists of a large book and a small one. R. Nathan in his "'Aruk" (*s.v.* סדר, ii.) says: "The midrash contains baraitot which the prophet taught to Anan, and consists of two parts, a large seder with thirty chapters, and a small seder with twelve chapters; and all of the Tanna debe Eliyahu cited in the Talmud is to be found in these baraitot." The inner connection between these two midrashim is a loose one, and it is only in sections 5 to 10 that the second refers to the first.

The underlying theme of the Tanna debe Eliyahu, which, with many interruptions, runs through the whole work, is the evolution of the world-system. The midrash calls the single periods of the history of man "shiṭṭot" (series). The first series, which deals with the beginning of the world and extends to the moment when man was driven out of Eden, consists of two subsections, (*a*) "Ma'aseh Merkabah" and (*b*) "Ma'aseh Bereshit." The six series of the world-system, however, were created in the divine mind even before **The Underlying Principle of the Book.** any being, with the exception of Israel, existed. They were: (1) the divine law (תורה); (2) hell (גיהנם) and (3) paradise (גן עדן), or punishment and reward in the future world; (4) the throne (כסא הכבוד), or the divine government of the world; (5) the name of the Messiah (שם המשיח), or the restoration of the universe when about to be destroyed; and (6) the Temple (בית המקדש), or the dependence of man upon God. Even before these six foundations, however, Israel was, as stated above, already in being in the divine mind, because without Israel there could have been no Torah (Friedmann, "Seder Eliyahu," p. 161).

The second series embraces the period from the expulsion of man from Eden to the Flood. In the ten generations from Adam to Noah man did not adhere to "meekness," did not do what was right (*ib.* p. 80), but fell lower and lower until he practised violence, theft, immorality, and murder. For this reason his destruction became a necessity (*ib.* p. 190).

The third series extends from the Flood to King Manasseh of Judah. It treats of the time of the study of the Law, of the priestly office, of the kingdom, and of the end of Israel's prosperity through the evil administration of Manasseh. In the days of Abraham the period of "tohu wa-bohu" (confusion) ceases and the 2,000 years of law begin. This time is divided into the following periods: **The Periods of Jewish History.** (1) the sojourn of the children of Israel in Egypt, the Exodus, to Joshua; (2) the kingdom of love extending to Samuel; (3) the kingdom of fear, to the time of Elijah; (4) the kingdom of truth, to the time of Jeroboam II.; (5) the time of Israel's salvation from oppression under Hezekiah; (6) from the time of Hezekiah to the reign of Manasseh (see Friedmann, "Mebo," v. 108).

The fourth series is filled with "meekness" (*ib.* p. 163). Whoever studies the Torah receives "meekness" as a reward. In addition there is a second recompense, which is the Mishnah. In this introduction of the Mishnah there is a trace of apology intended for those who believe that only the Torah was delivered on Sinai. The fifth series extends from King Manasseh to the building of the Second Temple (*ib.* p. 163). The last series treats of the future. God, surrounded by all the saints, sits in His bet ha-midrash and counts up the generations of the different periods of time, what they have learned, and what reward they shall receive therefor (*ib.* p. 4). The future of these saints will be like the beginning of the life of man (*ib.* p. 164).

These six series are again divided into three main periods: (1) the present world; (2) the Messianic period; and (3) the future world. **The Three Periods.** These are subdivided into: (*a*) 2,000 years of confusion ("tohu"); (*b*) 2,000 years of the Torah; (*c*) 2,000 years of the Messiah; (*d*) inauguration of a general peace; (*e*) the future world (*ib.* p. 115).

Besides this fundamental idea both parts of the midrash emphasize the importance of virtue, of a religious life, and of the study of the Law, and exhort to repentance and almsgiving, greater tolerance toward both Jews and non-Jews, diligent study and respect for scholars, modesty and humility, and the avoidance of non-Jewish manners and customs. The midrash, further, attempts to prove that all human life is based on the two extremes, toil in the sweat of the brow, and the regaining of the freedom of the soul. Hence it begins with the expulsion of Adam from Eden (Gen. iii. 24), and closes with the same theme. The cherubim in Eden are identified with man, and are the symbol of the reward of well-doing; the flaming sword is hell, the punishment for evil-doing. The way to the tree of life is said to be "derek erez" (good behavior); while the guarding of the tree of life is like the guarding of the word of God. By derek erez the midrash understands that which is fitting, useful, and honest; and these three qualities are the fundamental principles upon which the human world-system and society rest. An example of derek erez in this midrash is the following: The princes of the Philistines possessed derek erez, because when the Philistines wished to convey the Ark to the Israelites they would not send it back without sacrifices (I Sam. vi. 3; Friedmann, *l.c.* p. 58). On the other hand, the inhabitants of Beth-shemesh did not possess it, inasmuch as instead of bowing before the Ark they rejoiced and danced before it boldly, so that misfortune came upon them and 50,000 of them fell (*ib.*).

The opposite of derek erez is "to walk in the crooked way," *i.e.*, to do unworthy deeds and to give oneself up to immorality. Yet no nation of the world, with the exception of Egypt, has sunk so low as this. In ordinary life, how- **Quality of Derek Erez.** ever, the transgression of a command or prohibition, indecency, or even theft is a most pronounced opposite of derek erez; and every father of a family should strive to preserve those depending on him from these vices, because they belong to those evils which might bring about the destruction of the world.

The twelve chapters of the second part of the midrash are characterized by the fact that the narratives showing why in this world things often go amiss with the good and well with the wicked, are commonly introduced by the words "It happened" (מעשה) or "Once on a time" (פעם אחת). The midrash is sometimes interspersed with very beautiful prayers (see, for example, Friedmann, *l.c.* pp. 6, 18, 19, 28).

The Tanna debe Eliyahu is the only haggadic work which contains a rabbinic-karaitic polemic. In the second chapter of the second part is an account of a meeting of the author with a Karaite, who possesses a knowledge of Scripture, but not of the Mishnah; the differences discussed, however, are not important. The polemical attitude is much more noticeable in ch. xv. of the first part. There the following points are treated in detail: (1) washing the hands (comp. Ḥul. 106a; Shab. 62b; Soṭah 4b); (2) slaughtering (comp. Ḥul. 27a); (3) partaking of human blood (comp. Ker. 20b); (4) prohibition against eating fat (comp. Lev. vii. 23; Ker. 4b; Pinsker, "Liḳḳuṭe Ḳadmoniyyot," p. 20); (5) robbery from a Jew and from a non-Jew (comp. B. Ḳ. 113b); (6) degrees of relationship as bearing on marriage (comp. "Eshkol ha-Kofer," p. 117b); (7) grades of purity (comp. *ib.* p. 111b; Shab. 13a). Unlike other polemics, this one is not couched in acrimonious terms; but it adopts a mild, conciliatory tone.

As to the time of the composition of the work, all scholars agree in assigning it to the end of the tenth

Composed in the Tenth Century.

century; but as to the place where it was written, authorities differ. Whereas certain scholars (*e.g.*, Zunz, Rapoport, Bacher, Oppenheim, and Hochmuth) suppose Babylonia or Palestine, Güdemann is of the opinion that the work was written in Italy, or at least that its author must have been an Italian who had traveled a great deal and had been as far as Babylon, who learned there of the polemic between the Rabbinites and Karaites, but who abstained from mentioning Europe or Italy because he considered he would be likely to create a greater impression among his fellow countrymen by relating observations which he had made abroad. Furthermore, the fact that he knew nothing of Babylonia beyond its name shows that he could not have been a native of that region. Derenbourg also places the origin of the work in Rome. Grätz goes farthest of all, by simply identifying the Babylon of the midrash with Rome, and the fights of Gog and Magog described in the work with the devastating invasion of the Hungarians into Italy from 889 to 955. The most radical opponent of this view is Friedmann. For him all arguments concerning the age of the Tanna debe Eliyahu and against its identification with the Seder Eliyahu mentioned in Ket. 10b, are only superficial and only apparently sound; and he accordingly assigns the origin of the work "eo ipso" to Babylonia.

The age of the midrash is approximately ascertainable by three data contained in the book itself. (1) In ch. ii. the author speaks of the seventh century of the 2,000 years of the Messianic period as having

passed; this period began in 242 C.E., hence the time of writing must have been the tenth century. (2) The second datum relates to the temporal reckoning of the jubilees, and is treated by Rapoport in "Toledot de-R. Natan," p. 144. (3) The third datum (ch. xxx.) indicates that nine centuries had passed since the destruction of the Temple; hence the last redaction of the midrash falls in the interval between 968 and 984.

Of especially original midrashim contained in the work a few may be noticed here. On the passage "and set me down in the midst of the valley which was full of bones" (Ezek. xxxvii. 1–11) it is said, "Instead of 'bones' [עצמות] should be read 'tree of death' [עץ מות]; for it was the same tree which, through Adam's disobedience, brought death to him and to all his descendants" (v. 24).

Examples of Exegesis.

"'And this man went up out of his city yearly' [I Sam. i. 3]: from these words it appears that Elkanah went to Shiloh four times a year, three times in accordance with the legal prescription, and once in addition, which last journey he had assumed voluntarily" (Friedmann, *l.c.* p. 47). "On the day of Adam's death his descendants made a feast, because on account of his age he had long been a burden to himself and to them" (*ib.* p. 81). "'I will not execute the fierceness of mine anger' [Hos. xi. 9]: God has sworn to His people that He will not give them in exchange for another people, nor change them for another nation" (Friedmann, *l.c.* p. 127). "'The fool hath said in his heart, there is no God' [Ps. xiv. 2]: a man may not say in his heart, 'This world is a tohu wa-bohu; I will give myself up to sensual pleasures and will retire from the world'" (xxiii. 127–128). "From the words 'Israel was holiness unto the Lord' [Jer. ii. 3] it follows that the holiness of God, of the Sabbath, and of Israel is the same" (Friedmann, *l.c.* p. 133).

The passages in the Talmud cited in Tanna debe Eliyahu are: Shab. 13a; Pes. 94a, 112a; Meg. 28b; Ḳid. 80b; 'Ab. Zarah 5b, 9a; Sanh. 92a; Tamid 32a. Those cited in the Talmud under "Ṭanu Rabbanan" and found also in this midrash are: Shab. 88b and Giṭ. 36b = Tanna debe Eliyahu (ed. Friedmann), p. 78; Pes. 49a = *ib.* p. 30; Pes. 49a = *ib.* p. 68; Suk. 52a = *ib.* p. 20; R. H. 18a = *ib.* p. 53; Meg. 14a = *ib.* p. 82; Ḳid. 82a = *ib.* p. 101; B. Ḳ. 97b = *ib.* p. 21; B. B. 90b = *ib.* p. 77; B. B. 147a = *ib.* p. 157; Sanh. 19a = *ib.* p. 147; Sanh. 43b = *ib.* p. 102; Sanh. 109a = *ib.* p. 168; Sanh. 39a = *ib.* p. 132; Yeb. 62b = *ib.* p. 78. Furthermore, in the midrash are found sentences of the following amoraim: Johanan, Joshua b. Levi, R. Abbahu, and Eleazar.

The first edition of the midrash appeared at Venice in the year 1598, prepared from a copy dated

Editions.

1186. In 1677 an edition by Samuel b. Moses Haida, with changes in the text and with a commentary (בעורין דאשא זקוקין דנורא), appeared in Prague. The text itself was presented in a "nusḥa ḥadasha" (new text) and in a "nusḥa yeshana" (old text), being wholly distorted from its original form by Talmudic and cabalistic interpolations. This edition consists of three parts, the first two of which contain the text of the Rabbah and the Zuṭa (thirty-one and twenty-nine chapters respectively). These two parts are preceded by prefaces bearing the titles "Mar Ḳash-shisha" or "Sod Malbush ha-Neshamah" (Mystery of the Clothing of the Soul) and "Mar Yanuḳa" or "Sod Ḥaluḳa de-Rabbanan" (Mystery of the Clothing of the Rabbis). Then follows an introduction (common to part ii. and part iii.), with the title "Sha'ar Shemuel" (Gate of Samuel), and a third part consisting mainly of an exegesis of ch. xx.

The following editions are specially to be recommended, namely: that by Jacob b. Naphtali Herz of Brody, with a commentary, "Yeshu'at Ya'aḳob" (Zolkiev, 1798); that by Abraham b. Judah Löb Schick, with the commentary "Me'ore Esh" (Sidl-kov, 1835); that by Isaac Elijah b. Samuel Landau, with a commentary, "Ma'aneh Eliyahu" (Wilna, 1840). Among the best editions is the Warsaw one of 1880 containing both texts. The latest edition appeared in Vienna in 1900 and 1903, under the titles "Seder Eliyahu Rabbah" and "Seder Eliyahu Zuṭa," after a Vatican manuscript of the year 1073, critically revised, and with a commentary entitled "Me'ir 'Ayin," and a voluminous introduction by M. Friedmann. In this edition Seder Eliyahu Zuṭa is divided into fifteen chapters.

BIBLIOGRAPHY: Bacher, in *Monatsschrift,* xxiii. 267 *et seq.*; *idem,* in *R. E. J.,* xx. 144-146; T. Derenbourg, in *R. E. J.* ii. 134 *et seq.,* iii. 121-122; Friedmann, introduction (*Mebo*) to his ed. of *Seder Eliyahu;* Grätz, *Gesch.* 3d ed., v. 294-295; Güdemann, *Gesch.* ii. 50, 52 *et seq.,* 300-303; Hochmuth, in *Neuzeit,* 1868, Nos. 23 *et seq.;* Oppenheim, *Bet Talmud,* i. 304 *et seq.;* Rapoport, *Toledot de-Rabbi Natan,* in *Bikkure ha-'Ittim,* x. 43; J. Theodor, in *Monatsschrift,* xliv. 380-384, 550-561; Zunz, *G. V.* ii. 119-124, Frankfort-on-the-Main, 1892.
W. B. S. O.

TANNAIM AND AMORAIM: The name "tanna" is derived from the Aramaic "teni" or "tena" (= "to teach"), and designates in general a teacher of the oral law, and in particular one of the sages of the Mishnah, those teachers of the oral law whose teachings are contained in the Mishnah and in the Baraita. The term was first used in the Gemara to indicate a teacher mentioned in the Mishnah or in a baraita, in contradistinction to the later authorities, the Amoraim. Not all the teachers of the oral law who are mentioned in the Mishnah are called tannaim, how-
The Name. ever, but only those belonging to the period beginning with the disciples of Shammai and Hillel and ending with the contemporaries of Judah ha-Nasi I. The authorities preceding that period are called "zeḳenim ha-rishonim" (the former elders). In the time of the Amoraim the name "tanna" was given also to one well versed in the Mishnah and the other tannaitic traditions.

The period of the Tannaim, which lasted about 210 years (10-220 C.E.), is generally divided by Jewish scholars into five or six sections or generations, the purpose of such division being to show which teachers developed their principal activity contemporaneously. Some of the tannaim, however, were active in more than one generation. The following is an enumeration of the six generations and of the more prominent tannaim respectively belonging to them:

First Generation (10-80 C.E.): Principal tannaim: the Shammaites (Bet Shammai) and the

Hillelites (Bet Hillel), 'Aḳabya b. Mahalaleel, Rabban Gamaliel the Elder, Ḥanina, chief of the priests ("segan ha-kohanim"), Simeon b. Gamaliel, and Johanan b. Zakkai.

Second Generation (80-120): Principal tannaim: Rabban Gamaliel II. (of Jabneh), Zadok, Dosa b. Harkinas, Eliezer b. Jacob, Eliezer b. Hyrcanus, Joshua b. Hananiah, Eleazar b. Azariah, Judah b. Bathyra.

Third Generation (120-140): Principal tannaim: Ṭarfon, Ishmael, Akiba, Johanan b. Nuri, Jose ha-Gelili, Simeon b. Nanos, Judah b. Baba, and Johanan b. Baroḳa. Several of these flourished in the preceding period.

Fourth Generation: This generation extended from the death of Akiba (c. 140) to that of the patriarch Simeon b. Gamaliel (c. 165). The teachers belonging to this generation were: Meïr, Judah b. Ilai, Jose b. Ḥalafta, Simeon b. Yoḥai, Eleazar b. Shammua, Johanan ha-Sandalar, Eleazar b. Jacob, Nehemiah, Joshua b. Ḳarḥa, and the above-mentioned Simeon b. Gamaliel.

Fifth Generation (165-200): Principal tannaim: Nathan ha-Babli, Symmachus, Judah ha-Nasi I., Jose b. Judah, Eleazar b. Simeon, Simeon b. Eleazar.

Sixth Generation (200-220): To this generation belong the contemporaries and disciples of Judah ha-Nasi. They are mentioned in the Tosefta and the Baraita but not in the Mishnah. Their names are: Polemo, Issi b. Judah, Eleazar b. Jose, Ishmael b. Jose, Judah b. Laḳish, Ḥiyya, Aḥa, Abba (Arika). These teachers are termed "semi-tannaim"; and therefore some scholars count only five generations of tannaim. Christian scholars, moreover, count only four generations, reckoning the second and third as one (Strack, "Einleitung in den Talmud," pp. 77 *et seq.*).

For the term "amora" and a list of the generations of amoraim, see AMORA.
W. B. J. Z. L.

The following list enumerates all the zeḳenim ha-rishonim, tannaim, and amoraim mentioned in the Talmudic-Midrashic literature, those who are well known and frequently mentioned as well as those whose names occur once only in the Mishnah and Tosefta or in the Talmud and Midrash. To this pretannaitic period belong the so-called "pairs" ("zugot") of teachers: Simeon the Just and Antigonus of Soko; Jose ben Joezer and Jose ben Johanan; Joshua ben Peraḥyah and Nittai of Arbela; Judah ben Tabbai and Simeon ben Sheṭaḥ; Shemaiah and Abtalion; Hillel and Shammai.

Stars indicate that separate articles appear under the names so marked.

LIST OF TANNAIM.

Abba Benjamin	Abba Kohen of Bardala
*Abba Doresh	*Abba Saul
Abba Eleazar b. Dula'i	*Abba Saul b. Baṭnit
Abba Eleazar b. Gamaliel	Abba Yudan of Sidon
*Abba Gorion of Sidon	*Absalom the Elder
*Abba Ḥanin	*Abtalion
*Abba Jose b. Dosetai	Abtolemus
*Abba Jose b. Ḥanin	Abtolos
*Abba Jose of Maḥoza	Admon
Abba Jose Torti	*Aḥa I.
Abba Joseph the Horonite	Aḥai b. Josiah

*'Aḳabya b. Mahalaleel
*Akiba b. Joseph
*Antigonus of Soko
Antoninus
Azariah
*Baba ben Buṭa
Baitos b. Zonin
*Bar Ḳappara
*Ben Bag-Bag
Ben Buḳri
Ben Paṭuri
Benaiah
*Benjamin (an Egyptian proselyte)
Dosa
Dosa b. Harkinas
*Dosetai
*Dosetai b. Judah
*Dosetai of Kefar Yatmʼ
*Dosetai b. Yannai
*Eleazar ben Aḥwai
*Eleazar ben 'Arak
*Eleazar b. Azariah
*Eleazar ben Dama
Eleazar ben Hananiah ben Hezekiah
*Eleazar b. Ḥarsom
*Eleazar b. Ḥisma
*Eleazar b. Jacob
*Eleazar b. Jose
*Eleazar b. Judah of Bartota
Eleazar b. Judah of Kefar Obelim
*Eleazar ha-Ḳappar
*Eleazar b. Mattai
*Eleazar of Modi'im
*Eleazar ben Peraṭa I.
*Eleazar ben Peraṭa II.
Eleazar b. Phinehas
Eleazar b. Pilai (or Piabi)
*Eleazar b. Shammua
*Eleazar b. Simeon
Eleazar b. Yannai
*Eliezer ben Hyrcanus
*Eliezer b. Isaac
*Eliezer b. Jacob (1st cent.)
*Eliezer b. Jose ha-Gelili
Eliezer b. Judah (contemporary of Judah I.)
*Eliezer b. Taddai
*Eliezer b. Zadok, I.
*Eliezer b. Zadok, II.
*Elisha ben Abuyah
*Ephraim Maḳsha'ah
*Eurydemus ben Jose
*Gamaliel I.
*Gamaliel II. (of Jabneh)
*Gamaliel III. (b. Judah I.)
*Ḥalafta
Ḥalafta b. Ḥagra
Ḥalafta b. Jose
*Ḥalafta b. Karuya
*Ḥalafta of Kefar Hananiah
*Ḥanan, Abba
*Ḥanan the Egyptian
Ḥanan b. Menahem
*Hananiah (n e p h e w of R. Joshua)
Hananiah b. 'Adai
*Hananiah b. 'Aḳabya
*Hananiah b. 'Aḳashyah
*Hananiah b. Ḥakinai
Hananiah b. Hezekiah b. Garon
*Hananiah b. Judah
*Hananiah of Ono
*Hananiah (Ḥanina) b. Teradion
Hananiah of Ṭibe'im
*Ḥanina
*Ḥanina b. Adda
*Ḥanina b. Antigonus
*Ḥanina b. Dosa

*Ḥanina b. Gamaliel II.
Ḥanina Segan ha-Kohanim
Hezekiah Abi 'Iḳḳesh
*Ḥidḳa
*Hillel
*Ḥiyya bar Abba (Rabbah)
Ḥiyya b. Eleazar ha-Ḳappar
Ḥiyya b. Naḥmani
Huzpit the Meturgeman
Ilai
Isaac
Ishmael b. Eleazar b. Azariah
*Ishmael b. Elisha
*Ishmael b. Johanan b. Baroḳa
*Ishmael b. Jose b. Ḥalafta
*Jacob of Kefar Ḥiṭṭaya
*Jacob b. Ḳorshai (R. Jacob)
Jaddua (Babylonian pupil of
*Jeremiah   [R. Meïr)
Jeshebab
*Johanan b. Baroḳa
Johanan b. Dahabai
*Johanan b. Gudgada
*Johanan ben ha-Ḥoranit
Johanan b. Joseph
Johanan ben Joshua
Johanan b. Josiah
Johanan b. Matthias
*Johanan b. Nuri
*Johanan ha-Sandalar
*Johanan b. Torta
*Johanan ben Zakkai
Jonathan b. Abtolemus
Jonathan b. Bathyra
Jonathan b. Joseph
Jonathan b. Meshullam
*Jonathan ben Uzziel
Jose (son of the Damascene)
*Jose b. 'Aḳabya
Jose b. Assi
Jose b. Eleazar
Jose b. Eliakim
Jose b. Elisha
*Jose ha-Gelili
Jose b. Gilai
Jose b. Gurya
*Jose b. Ḥalafta
Jose b. Ḥanina
Jose b. Ḥoram
*Jose ben Joezer
*Jose ben Johanan
Jose ben Josiah
*Jose (Ise) ben Judah
Jose b. Ḳazrata
Jose b. Kippor
Jose b. Ḳisma
*Jose ha-Kohen
Jose b. Menahem
Jose b. Meshullam
Jose of Modi'im
Jose b. Petros
Jose b. Shammai
Jose b. Yasyan
Jose b. Zimra
Joshua b. Akiba
Joshua b. Bathyra
Joshua ha-Garsi
*Joshua b. Hananiah
Joshua b. Hyrcanus
Joshua b. Jonathan
Joshua b. Kaposai
*Joshua b. Ḳarḥa
Joshua b. Mamal
Joshua b. Matthias
*Joshua b. Peraḥyah
Joshua b. Ziruz
*Josiah
*Judah I. (ha-Nasi)
Judah b. Agra
*Judah b. Baba
*Judah b. Bathyra
Judah b. Dama
Judah b. Doroteus
Judah b. Gadish

Judah b. Gamaliel
Judah b. Gerim
Judah b. Hananiah
*Judah ben Ilai
Judah b. Jair
Judah b. Johanan b. Zakkai
Judah b. Jose
Judah ha-Kohen
*Judah ben Laḳish
Judah b. Naḳosa
Judah b. Nehemiah
Judah b. Ro'eẓ
Judah b. Shammua
Judah b. Simeon
Judah b. Ṭabbai
Judah b. Temah
Levi ha-Saddar
*Levi b. Sisi
Levitas of Jabneh
*Mattithiah b. Ḥeresh
Mattithiah b. Samuel
*Me'asha
*Meïr
Menahem of Galya
Menahem b. Jose
Menahem b. Nappaḥa
Menahem b. Sagnai
Mona
Monobaz
*Nahum of Gimzo
Nahum ha-Lablar
*Nahum the Mede
*Nathan
Nehemiah
Nehemiah of Bet Deli
Nehorai
Neḥunya b. Elinathan
Neḥunya b. Gudgada
*Neḥunya ben ha-Ḳanah
*Nittai of Arbela
*Onias ha-Me'aggel
*Onḳelos
Pappias
*Pappos b. Judah
Perida
*Phinehas ben Jair
Polemo
*Reuben ben Strobilus
J.

Samuel the Younger
Shammai
Shela
Shemaiah
Simai
Simeon (brother of Azariah)
*Simeon b. 'Aḳashyah
Simeon b. Akiba
Simeon b. Azzai
Simeon b. Bathyra
*Simeon b. Eleazar
Simeon b. Gamaliel I.
Simeon b. Gamaliel II.
Simeon b. Gudda
Simeon b. Ḥalafta
*Simeon b. Ḥanina
Simeon he-Ḥasid
Simeon b. Hillel
*Simeon b. Jehozadak
*Simeon b. Jose b. Lekonya
*Simeon b. Judah of Kefar 'Ikos
*Simeon b. Judah ha-Nasi I.
Simeon the Just
Simeon b. Kahana
*Simeon of Ḳitron
*Simeon b. Menasya
*Simeon of Mizpah
*Simeon ben Nanos
*Simeon b. Nethaneel
*Simeon ha-Paḳoli
*Simeon ben ha-Segan
*Simeon ben Sheṭaḥ
*Simeon Shezuri
*Simeon of Shiḳmona
*Simeon b. Tarfon
*Simeon of Teman
*Simeon b. Yoḥai
Simeon b. Zoma
*Symmachus
*Ṭarfon   [Rome
*Theodosius (T h e u d a s) of
*Yannai
Zachariah b. Abkulas
Zachariah b. Ḳabutal
Zachariah b. ha-Ḳazẓab
*Zakkai

J. Z. L.

LIST OF AMORAIM.

[Babylonian and Palestinian amoraim are distinguished respectively by the initials B and P in parentheses; the figures indicate the centuries to which they belonged. For amoraim whose names are preceded by the dagger-sign, see also JEW. ENCYC. s.v. YIẒḤAḲ.]

*Aaron (B)
Aaron (B)   [P]
Abba (father of Abba Mari;
Abba (father of Ḥiyya; B)
*Abba bar Abba (B)
Abba b. Abimai (B)
*Abba of Acre (P)
Abba b. Aḥa (P)
Abba Arika (B)
Abba of Bira (P)
*Abba b. Bizna (P)
Abba of Cæsarea (P)
*Abba of Carthage (P)
Abba b. Eliashib (P)
Abba b. Hamnuna (P)
Abba bar Ḥana (P and B)
Abba Ḥanan (B)
Abba b. Ḥanina
Abba b. Ḥilefai (P)
*Abba b. Ḥiyya (P)
Abba b. Huna (B)
Abba b. Huna (B)
Abba b. Ilai (P)
Abba b. Isa (P)
Abba b. Isaac (P)
Abba b. Jacob (B)
Abba b. Jacob (P)

*Abba bar Jeremiah (B)
Abba b. Jonah (P)
Abba b. Joseph (B)
Abba b. Judah (P)
Abba b. Kahana (P)
Abba b. Levi (B)
Abba b. Lima
Abba b. Mar Papa (B)
Abba Mari (P)
Abba Mari (P)
Abba Mari (P)
Abba Mari (brother of Jose; P)
Abba b. Mari (?)
*Abba bar Memel (P)
Abba b. Mina (P)
Abba b. Naḥman (B)
Abba of Narsoh
Abba b. Nathan (P)
Abba bar Papa (P)
*Abba b. Pappai (P)
Abba b. Safra (P)
Abba b. Samuel Rabbah
Abba b. Shila
Abba b. Taḥlifa (P)
Abba Umana (B)
Abba b. Zabda (B)
*Abba b. Zabdai (P)

Abba b. Ze'era (P)
Abba Zuṭi
Abba b. Zuṭra (P)
Abbahu (P)
Abbahu (father of Samuel)
Abbahu b. Aḥa (P)
Abbahu b. Bebi (B)
Abbahu b. Ehi (B)
Abbahu b. Geniba (B)
Abbahu b. Zuṭarti (B)
Abbai (called Naḥmani; B)
Abbai b. Abbin (B)
Abbai b. Benjamin (P)
Abbai the Elder (B)
Abdima b. Ḥama (B)
*Abdima b. Hamdure (P)
Abdima b. Ḥisda (B)
Abdima b. Neḥunya (P)
*Abdima of Sepphoris (P)
Abdimi (brother of Jose)
Abdimi (father of Isaac)
*Abdimi of Ḥaifa
*Abiathar
*Abimi (B)
*Abimi b. Abbahu (P)
Abimi the Colleague
*Abimi of Hagrunya
Abimi the Nabatæan
Abimi b. Papi (B)
Abimi b. Tobi (P)
Abin (the pupil of Johanan)
*Abin (Rabin) b. Abba (P)
*Abin ben Adda (B)
Abin b. Bisna (P)
Abin b. Ḥinana (B)
*Abin b. Ḥiyya (P)
Abin b. Ḥuna (B)
*Abin b. Kahana (P)
Abin ha-Levi (P)
Abin Naggara
Abin b. Naḥman (B)
Abin of Nashikiya
Abin the Old
*Abin b. Rab Ḥisda (P)
Abin b. Samuel
Abin of Sepphoris
*Abin b. Tanḥum (P)
Abina I. (P)
Abina II. (B)
Abina III. (B)
Abram of Ḥuza (B)
Abudemi (grandson of To-
bi; P)
Abudemi b. Tanḥum (P)
Abudemi b. Tobi (P)
*Adda b. Abimi (P)
Adda b. Abin (B)
Adda b. Aḥa (B)
*Adda b. Ahabah (B)
Adda of Be Zeluḥit
*Adda of Cæsarea
Adda b. Isaac (B)
Adda of Jaffa
Adda Karḥina
*Adda b. Matnah (B)
*Adda b. Minyomi (B)
Adda of Naresh
Adda b. Papa (B)
Adda b. Simi (B)
*Adda b. Simeon (P)
Adda of Sura
Afes (Efes) (P; 1)
Aggara or Agra (B)
Aḥa (brother of R. Jose)
Aḥa b. Abba (B)
Aḥa b. R. Abba (B)
Aḥa b. Abba b. Aḥa (B)
Aḥa b. Abbai (B)
Aḥa b. Abin (P)
*Aḥa b. Adda (B)
Aḥa b. Aḥa (B)
Aḥa b. Ahaba (P)
Aḥa b. Ami (B)
Aḥa b. Ashi (B)

Aḥa b. Awira (B)
*Aḥa b. Awya (B)
Aḥa b. Azza (B)
*Aḥa Bardala
Aḥa of Be Ḥusa
Aḥa b. Bebi (B)
Aḥa b. Bizna (P)
Aḥa of Carthage
Aḥa of Carthage (P)
*Aḥa of Difti
Aḥa of Galilee
*Aḥa b. Ḥanina (P)
Aḥa b. Haya (B)
Aḥa b. Hoshaiah (P)
*Aḥa b. Ḥuna (B)
Aḥa of Ḥuzal
*Aḥa b. Iḳa (B)
*Aḥa b. Isaac (P)
*Aḥa b. Jacob (B)
Aḥa b. Jose (P)
*Aḥa b. Joseph (B)
Aḥa b. Ḳaṭṭina (B)
Aḥa the Long (B)
*Aḥa b. Minyomi (B)
Aḥa b. Naḥman (B)
Aḥa b. Papa
Aḥa b. Phinehas (B)
Aḥa of Porsika
Aḥa b. Rabbina (B)
Aḥa Saba
Aḥa Sar ha-Birah
*Aḥa b. Shila (P)
*Aḥa b. Taḥlifa (B)
*Aḥa b. 'Ula (B)
Aḥa b. Yeba
Ahabah b. Ze'era (P)
*Aḥadboi (B)
*Aḥadboi b. Ammi (B)
Aḥadboi b. Matnah
Ahilai (B)
Aibu (name of several Pal-
estinian amoraim)
Alexa (P)
Alexandra b. Haga (P)
*Alexandri (P)
*Alexandri (P)
Ammi (P)
Ammi (father of Samuel)
Ammi b. Abba (B)
Ammi b. Abin (B)
Ammi b. Ada (B)
Ammi b. Aḥa (B)
Ammi the Babylonian
Ammi b. Ḳarḥa (P)
Ammi b. Matnah (B)
Ammi b. Nathan (B)
Ammi b. Tobi
Ammi of Wadina (P; 3)
*Amram R. (B; 3)
*Amram Ḥasida (B)
Anan b. Ḥiyya (B)
Anan b. Joseph (B)
Anan b. Taḥlifa (B; 2)
*'Anani b. Sason (P; 3)
Armania (P; 1)
*Ashi (B; 6)
Ashi b. Abin (B; 4)
Ashi of Awira? (6)
Ashi of Ḥuzal (B; 4)
Ashi the Old (B; 1)
*Ashyan bar Jakim (P; 4)
*Ashyan Naggara
*Ashyan b. Nidbak (P)
*Assi I. (B)
*Assi II. (P)
Assi of Nehor Bal (B)
*Awia Saba
*Awira (B; 3)
Babahu (B)
Bali (B; 4)
Banna'ah or Bannayah (P;
1)

Banna'ah b. 'Ula (B; 4)
Baruka of Ḥuza (B; 5)
Baruna (B; 2)
Batha (B and P; 3)
Beba b. Abba (P; 3)
*Bebai b. Abaye (B; 5)
*Bebai b. Abba (B)
Bebai b. Ashi (B; 6)
Bebai b. Mesharshiya (P; 5)
*Benjamin b. 'Ashtor (P; 3)
*Benjamin b. Giddel (P; 4)
Benjamin Ḥiyya (B)
*Benjamin b. Japhet (P; 3)
*Benjamin b. Levi (P; 3)
Beotes (P; 3)
Berechiah (P; 5)
*Berechiah (P; 2)
Berechiah b. Abba (P)
Berechiah b. Ḥamma
Berechiah ben Ḥelbo (P; 4)
Berechiah b. Judah (P)
Berechiah Saba
Berechiah b. Simeon (P; 2)
Berim (P; 2)
Berna or Bera (B; 4)
Bisa or Bisna (P; 1)
*Bisna (P; 4)
Bisna b. Zabda (P)
Budia (B; 6)
Burakai (P; 5)
*Daniel, Ḥayyaṭa (P)
*Daniel b. Ḳaṭṭina (B)
Dari b. Papa (B)
*Dimi (brother of Rab Safra;
B; 4)
Dimi b. Abba (B)
Dimi b. Abui
*Dimi b. Ḥinena (B; 5)
*Dimi b. Huna of Damharia
(B; 6)
*Dimi b. Isaac (B; 4)
*Dimi b. Joseph (B; 3)
*Dimi b. Levai (B; 4)
Dimi b. Naḥman (B; 5)
*Dimi of Nehardea (B)
Dimi b. Sheshna
Dosetai (father of Aftoriki)
Dosetai of Beri
Dosetai b. Maton
Elai b. Berechiah (P)
Elai b. Eliezer (B; 2)
*Eleazar b. Abina (P)
Eleazar b. Antigonus (P; 2)
Eleazar of Basra (P)
*Eleazar of Hagrunya (B; 4)
Eleazar b. Ḥagya
Eleazar b. Ḥanina (P)
*Eleazar b. Jose II. (P; 5)
*Eleazar b. Malai (P; 3)
Eleazar b. Maram (Miriam or
Maron?) (P; 4)
Eleazar b. Marinus (P)
*Eleazar b. Menahem (P; 3)
Eleazar the Nabatæan
Eleazar of Nineveh (B; 3)
*Eleazar b. Pedat (P; 3)
Eleazar of the South (P; 5)
Eleazar b. Yannai (P; 2)
Eleazar Ze'era (the little)
Eliakim (B; 5)
Eliehoenai (P)
Ezekiel
Gadda (B; 4)
Gamaliel b. Elai (P; 4)
Gamaliel b. Ḥanina (P; 4)
Gamaliel Zoga (P; 2)
Gamda
*Gebiha of Argizah (B; 5)
*Gebiha of Be Katil (B; 5)
Gedaliah
Geniba (B; 1)
Gershom (P; 5)
Gidal or Giddul (B; 2)
Gidal b. Minyomi

Gidal of Naresh
Giddul b. Benjamin (P; ẓ)
Giddul b. Menaschi (B; 5)
Giora (proselyte)
Gorion (P; 2)
Gorion of Asparak (B; 3)
Gorion b. Astion (B)
Ḥabiba (B; 1)
Ḥabiba of Ḥuza (B; 6)
Ḥabiba b. Joseph (B; 4)
Ḥabiba of Sora (B; 6)
Ḥabiba b. Surmaki (B and
P; 4)
Ḥagga (B; 4?), contempo-
rary of R. Naḥman
Ḥagga (pupil of R. Huna;
B; 4)
Ḥagga of Sepphoris (P; 2)
Haggai (P; 3)
Haggai Kusmai (?)
Haggai of the South (P; ?)
Hagra (Haggaria; P; 2)
Ḥalafta of Cæsarea (P)
*Ḥalafta of Huna (P; 1)
*Ḥalafta Ḳaroya (the Bible
reader)
Ḥalafta of Radfa (P; 2)
Ḥalfa b. Idi (P)
Ḥama (grandfather of Raba)
Ḥama b. Adda
Ḥama b. Ashi (P)
*Ḥama b. Bisa (P)
Ḥama b. Buzi (B; 5)
Ḥama b. Gurya (B; 3)
*Ḥama b. Ḥanina (P; 2)
Ḥama b. Joseph (P; 2)
Ḥama b. Mari
Ḥama of Nehardea (B; 5)
Ḥama b. Osha'ya (P; 2)
Ḥama b. Papa (P; 5)
Ḥama b. Rabbah (P; 4)
Ḥama b. Tobia (B; 6)
Ḥama b. 'Uḳba (P; 3)
Hamnuna (B; 2)
*Hamnuna I. (B; 3)
*Hamnuna II. (B; 3, 4)
Hamnuna b. Ada b. Ahabah
(B; 6)
Hamnuna of Babylonia
Hamnuna b. Joseph (B; 4)
Hamnuna b. Rabbah of Pash-
ronia (B)
*Hamnuna Zuṭa
Ḥana b. Adda
Ḥana b. Aḥa
Ḥana of Bagdad
*Ḥana b. Bizna
Ḥana of Carthage
*Ḥana b. Ḥanilai
Ḥana b. Ḥinena
Ḥana b. Judah
Ḥana b. Ḳaṭṭina
Ḥana of Kefar Teḥumim
Ḥana b. Lewai
Ḥana Sha'onah
Hanan b. Abba (B; 2)
Hanan b. Ammi
Hanan of Be Zeluḥit
Hanan b. Ḥisda (B; 4)
Hanan of Nehardea (B; 2)
Hanan b. Rabbah (B; 2)
Hanan b. Taḥlifa (B; 4)
Hanan b. Zabdi (P; 1)
Hanana (B; 3)
*Hananeel (B; 2)
Hananeel b. Papa (B)
Hananiah (B)
Hananiah (B; 4)
Hananiah (B)
*Hananiah (P; 3, 4)
Hananiah b. Aibu (P)
Hanilai of Ḥuza
Ḥanilai b. Idi

Ḥanina (B ; 6)
*Ḥanina b. Abbahu (P ; 4)
Ḥanina b. Abdimi (B)
*Ḥanina b. 'Agul (P ; 3)
Ḥanina of Akra
Ḥanina of Anat
Ḥanina b. Andrai (P)
Ḥanina b. Atal
Ḥanina b. Bebai (B ; 5)
*Ḥanina b. Ḥama (P ; 1)
Ḥanina b. Hillel (B)
Ḥanina b. Ḥiyya (B ; 3)
Ḥanina of Ḥuza
*Ḥanina b. Iḳa
Ḥanina b. Isi (P ; 3)
Ḥanina b. Joseph (P ; 1)
Ḥanina Ḳara (the Bible reader)
*Ḥanina Katoba (the writer)
*Ḥanina b. Papa (B)
*Ḥanina b. Pazi (P)
Ḥanina b. Samson (P)
Ḥanina b. Samuel (P ; 2)
Ḥanina Sholḳa (the cook)
Ḥanina b. Sisi (P ; 1)
*Ḥanina of Sura
Ḥanina of Sura near the Euphrates
Ḥanina b. Tiba
Ḥanina of Tirta or Tarna
*Ḥanina b. Torta
Ḥanina b. Uri
*Ḥasa
Henaḳ
Hezekiah (B)
Hezekiah (P)
Hezekiah Akkaya
Hezekiah b. Ḥiyya
Hezekiah of Hukuk
Ḥilfa (P ; 2)
Ḥilfa (grandson of Abbahu ; 4)
Hilkiah (father of Minjamin ; B)
Hilkiah b. Awia (B)
Hilkiah of Hagrunya (B)
Hilkiah b. Tobia (B ; 3)
Hilkiah of the South (B)
Hillel (P ; 3)
Hillel (B ; 6)
Hillel (son-in-law of Jose ; P ; 6)
*Hillel b. Berechiah (P)
Hillel b. Helena (P)
Hillel of Kifra (P ; 5)
Hillel b. Pazi (P ; 4)
Hillel b. Samuel b. Naḥman (P ; 4)
Hillel b. Vales (Valens ; P ; 3)
Ḥinena (father of Yanta)
Ḥinena b. Abin
Ḥinena b. Assi
Ḥinena b. Kahana (B ; 3)
Ḥinena b. Rabbah (B ; 4)
Ḥinena b. Shelamya (B ; 2)
Ḥinena b. Shila (B ; 1)
Ḥinena of Wardan
*Ḥisda (B ; 3)
Ḥisda b. Abdami
Ḥisda b. Joseph (B ; 4)
Ḥiyya
Ḥiyya (P and B ; 4)
Ḥiyya b. Abba (B and P ; 3)
Ḥiyya b. Abbahu (B)
Ḥiyya b. Abbui (B ; 4)
*Ḥiyya b. Adda (P)
Ḥiyya b. Adda (P ; 5)
Ḥiyya b. Adda of Joppa (P)
Ḥiyya b. Ammi (B ; 4)
Ḥiyya b. Amram (B)
Ḥiyya Arika (the tall one)
Ḥiyya b. Ashi (B ; 2)
Ḥiyya b. Assi (B)
Ḥiyya b. Awia (B ; 3)

Ḥiyya of Ctesiphon (B ; 3)
Ḥiyya of Difta (B ; 3)
*Ḥiyya b. Gammada (P)
Ḥiyya b. Garya (B)
Ḥiyya of Hagra (B ; 3)
Ḥiyya b. Ḥanina (B)
Ḥiyya b. Huna (B ; 5)
Ḥiyya of Hurmis (B ; 4)
Ḥiyya b. Isaac (P)
Ḥiyya b. Isaac (P ; 5)
Ḥiyya b. Jacob (B)
Ḥiyya b. Joseph (B and P ; 2)
Ḥiyya b. Joshua ? (B ; 4)
Ḥiyya b. Judah
Ḥiyya b. Judah (B ; 3)
*Ḥiyya Ḳara (the Bible reader)
Ḥiyya of Kefar Teḥumim (P ; 4)
Ḥiyya b. Lulianos (P ; 5)
Ḥiyya b. Luliba (P ; 4)
Ḥiyya b. Matnah (B ; 3)
*Ḥiyya b. Moria (P ; 5)
Ḥiyya b. Naḥman (P ; 3)
Ḥiyya b. Nathan (B ; 4)
Ḥiyya b. Papa (P ; 3)
Ḥiyya of Parwada (B ; 3)
Ḥiyya b. Rab (B ; 2)
Ḥiyya b. Rabbah (B ; 4)
Ḥiyya b. Shabbethai (P ; 4)
Ḥiyya b. Tanḥum (P ; 4)
Ḥiyya b. Tiba
Ḥiyya b. Titus (P ; 4)
Ḥiyya b. 'Uḳba (P)
Ḥiyya b. Yannai (P)
Ḥiyya b. Zarnaki (P ; 2)
*Huna (B)
Huna b. Abin (B ; 5)
Huna b. Aḥa
Huna b. Ashi (B ; 2)
Huna b. Berechiah
Huna of Damharia
Huna of Diskarta
Huna b. Geniba
Huna b. Halob (B ; 4)
*Huna b. Ḥanina (B ; 4)
Huna of Hauran
Huna b. Hillel (P)
Huna b. Hiwan (B ; 6)
Huna b. Ḥiyya (B)
Huna b. Ida (B ; 6)
Huna b. Iḳa (B ; 6)
Huna b. Ilai
Huna b. Jeremiah (B ; 5)
*Huna b. Joshua (B ; 5)
Huna b. Judah (B ; 4)
Huna b. Ḳaṭṭina (B ; 3)
Huna b. Lewai (B)
Huna b. Manoah (B ; 5)
Huna Mar b. Awia (B ; 5)
Huna b. Marẹmor (B ; 6)
Huna b. Matnah (B ; 4)
Huna b. Minyomi (B ; 3)
Huna b. Moses (B ; 4)
Huna b. Naḥman (B ; 4)
*Huna b. Nathan (B ; 7)
Huna b. Nehemiah (B ; 6)
Huna b. Papi
Huna b. Phinehas (B)
Huna of Porsica
Huna b. Rabbah (B ; 6)
Huna b. Saḥḥora (B ; 4)
Huna of Sepphoris
Huna of Sura
Huna b. Taḥlifa (B ; 5)
Huna b. Torta
Huna b. Zuṭi (B ; 6)
Hunya Jacob of Apretaim
Ishmael (father of Judah ; P ; 3)
Ishmael b. Abba (P ; 2)
Ishmael b. Jacob (P)
Ishmael b. Kathriel (P ; 1)
Ishmael of Kefar Yama (P ; 3)
Isaac (B ; 6)

Isaac (father of Samuel)
Isaac b. Abba (B ; 2)
Isaac b. Abba (B ; 4)
Isaac b. Abdimi I. (P ; 1)
Isaac b. Abdimi II. (B ; 3)
Isaac b. Abin
†Isaac b. Adda (B)
Isaac b. Aḥa (B)
Isaac b. Ammi (P)
Isaac b. Ammi (B ; 4)
Isaac b. Ashi (B , 2)
Isaac b. Ashya (B ; 5)
†Isaac ha-Babli
Isaac Berrabi
Isaac b. Bisna (B ; 2)
†Isaac of Carthage
Isaac Dibaha
Isaac b. Elai
Isaac b. Eliashib (P ; 4)
†Isaac b. Eleazar (P ; 4)
Isaac of Gufta
†Isaac b. Ḥaḳola
Isaac b. Ḥalub (B ; 3)
Isaac b. Ḥanina (B ; 3)
†Isaac b. Ḥiyya (P ; 2)
Isaac b. Jacob
Isaac b. Jonathan (P ; 4)
Isaac b. Joseph (P ; 2 and 3)
Isaac b. Judah (B ; 3)
Isaac b. Ḳappara (P)
Isaac Kaskasa
Isaac of Kefar 'Itos
Isaac Krispa
Isaac b. Levi
†Isaac of Magdala
†Isaac b. Marion (P ; 3)
Isaac b. Menahem (P)
Isaac b. Mesharshiya (B, P ; 6)
Isaac b. Naḥmani (P ; 3)
Isaac b. Naphtali (B ; 6)
†Isaac Nappaḥa (the smith)
Isaac b. Ostiya (P)
†Isaac b. Parnak
Isaac Paska
†Isaac b. Phinehas (B and P ; 3)
Isaac b. Rabbah b. bar Ḥana (B ; 4)
†Isaac b. Redifa (P ; 4)
Isaac b. Samuel (B ; 2)
Isaac b. Shila (B)
Isaac b Simeon (P)
†Isaac b. Tabla (P ; 4)
Isaac b. Teradion
†Isaac b. Ze'era or Sita (P ; 4)
Jabez   [Jacob]
Jacob (grandson of Aḥa b.
Jacob (grandson of Samuel)
*Jacob b. Abba I.
*Jacob b. Abba II.
*Jacob b. Abbuha
*Jacob b. Abina
Jacob b. Adda
Jacob b. Adda b. Athaliah
Jacob of Adiabene
*Jacob b. Aḥa (B ; 3)
Jacob b. Aḥa (P)
*Jacob b. Aḥa (P ; 4)
Jacob b. Aḥa b. Idi
Jacob b. Ammi
Jacob of Armenia
Jacob b. Dosai
Jacob of Emaus
Jacob of Gebula
Jacob b. Ḥama   [tus]
Jacob b. Hapiliti (Hippoly-
Jacob b. Ḥisda
Jacob b. Idi
Jacob b. Idi b. Oshaya
Jacob b. Ise (Jose)
*Jacob of Kefar Ḥanin
Jacob of Neboria
Jacob of Nehar-Peḳod
Jacob of Rumania
Jacob b. Sisai

Jacob of the South
Jacob b. Taḥlifa
Jacob b. Yannai
Jacob b. Yoḥai
*Jacob b. Zabdai
Jehiel
Jeremiah (B ; 6)
Jeremiah (B and P ; 2)
*Jeremiah b. Abba (B ; 3)
Jeremiah b. Aḥa (B)
*Jeremiah of Difte
Jeremiah of Gufta
Jeremiah Rabba (the great)
Jeremiah Safra (the scribe)
Jeremiah of Shebshab
Jeremiah of the South
Jeremiah b. Taḥlifa (B)
Johanan (son of the smith)
Johanan (brother of Safra ; B)
Johanan Antonarta
Johanan b. Kassarta
Johanan of Maḥuka (P ; 1)
*Johanan b. Meriya (P ; 5)
*Johanan b. Nappaḥa
Johanan b. Rabbina (B ; 5)
Johanan Safra of Gufta
Johanan b. Shila (P)
Joḥani (B ; 1)
*Jonah (P ; 4)
Jonah of Bosra (P ; 5)
Jonah b. Taḥlifa (B ; 4)
Jonathan (P ; 1)
Jonathan b. 'Akmai (P ; 3)
Jonathan b. Amram (P ; 1)
*Jonathan of Bet Gubrin (P)
Jonathan b. Eliezer
Jonathan b. Haggai (P)
Jonathan b. Ḥila (P)
Jonathan b. Isaac b. Ahor (P)
Jonathan Kefa (P ; 4)
Jose b. Abba or Abai
*Jose b. Abin
Jose b. Ashyan
Jose b. Bebai
Jose of Cæsarea
Jose b. Elai
Jose b. Eliakim
Jose the Galilean (amora)
Jose b. Gezira
Jose b. Ḥananiah
Jose b. Ḥanina
Jose of Kefar Dan
Jose of Kefar Gufta
Jose Kuzira
*Jose b. Jacob
Jose b. Jason
Jose b. Jose
Jose b. Joshua
*Jose b. Ḳazrata
*Jose of Malaḥaya
Jose the Mede
Jose b. Menashya
Jose of Nahar Bul
Jose b. Nathan
*Jose b. Nehorai
Jose of Oni
Jose b. Pazi
Jose b. Petros
Jose Resha
Jose b. Saul
Jose of the South
Jose b. Tanḥum
Jose of Yodkarat
Jose of Zaitur
Jose b. Zebida
Jose b. Zemina
Jose b. Zimra
Joseph b. Abba
Joseph b. Ammi
Joseph b. Ḥabu
Joseph b. Ḥama
Joseph b. Ḥanin
Joseph b. Ḥiyya
*Joseph b. Joshua b. Levi

Joseph b. Menasya of Dewil
Joseph b. Minyomi
Joseph b. Nehunya
Joseph b. Rabba
Joseph b. Salla
Joseph b. Samuel
Joseph b. Shemaiah
Joseph of Sidon
Joshua (brother of Dorai ; P)
Joshua b. Abba
*Joshua b. Abin (P)
Joshua b. Benjamin
Joshua b. Beri (P)
Joshua b. Boethus
Joshua of Gizora (P ; 4)
Joshua b. Idi
*Joshua (ha-Kohen) b. Nehemiah (P)
*Joshua b. Levi
Joshua b. Levi b. Shalum
Joshua b. Marta (B ; 1)
Joshua b. Naḥman
*Joshua b. Nehemiah
Joshua of Ona (P)
Joshua b. Pedaya
*Joshua of Shiknin
Joshua of the South
Joshua b. Tanḥum
Joshua b. Timi (P)
Joshua of 'Uzza
Joshua b. Zidal (P ; 1)
Josiah
Josiah of Huẓal
Josiah of Usha　　　　[sida]
Judah (brother of Sola Ha-
Judah b. Aḥitai
Judah b. Aibu
*Judah b. Ammi
Judah b. Ashi
Judah b. Ashtita
Judah b. Astira
Judah b. Bisna
Judah b. Buni
Judah of Difte
Judah of Diskarta
*Judah b. Ezekiel
Judah of Gallia
Judah b. Gamda
Judah b. Ḥabiba
Judah of Hagrunya
Judah b. Ḥama
Judah b. Ḥanina
Judah b. Ḥiyya
Judah b. Huna
Judah b. Idi
Judah b. Isaac
Judah b. Ishmael
Judah b. Joshua
Judah Klaustra
Judah b. Levi
Judah b. Menashya
Judah b. Meremar
Judah Mosparta
Judah b. Naḥmani
Judah b. Oshaya
Judah b. Pazi
Judah b. Pedaiah
Judah b. Samuel
Judah b. Shalum
Judah b. Shila
*Judah b. Simeon
Judah b. Simeon b. Pazi
Judah of Soporta
Judah b. Titos
Judah b. Zabda
Judah b. Zebina
Judah b. Zeruya
Justa Ḥabra (the Colleague ; P)
Justa b. Judah (P)
Justa of Shunem (P ; 5 and 6)
Justa b. Simeon (P ; 4)
Justina (P ; 3)
Kadi

Kahana (B)
Kahana (B and P)
Kahana (brother of Judah)
Kahana (father-in-law of Me-
sharshiya)
Kahana b. Ḥanina
Kahana b. Jeremiah
Kahana b. Malkai
Kahana b. Malkiya
Kahana b. Nathan
Kahana b. Nehemiah
*Kahana b. Taḥlifa
Ḳarna
*Ḳaṭṭina
Kiris of Urmia
Krispa
Kruspedai
Levanti
Levi b. Berechiah
Levi of Biri
Levi b. Buta
Levi b. Ḥaita
Levi b. Ḥama
Levi b. Ḥini
Levi b. Ḥiyya
Levi b. Huna
Levi b. Isaac
*Levi b. Laḥma
Levi b. Panti
Levi b. Parta
Levi b. Pitam
Levi b. Rabbi
Levi Saba
Levi b. Samuel
Levi b. Samuel b. Naḥman
Levi of Sandaria
Levi b. Seira
*Levi b. Sisi
Levi of Suki
Luda
Lulianos of the South
Lulianos of Tiberias
Malkio
Maluk of Arabia
Mana of Sepphoris
Mana of Shab
Mana b. Tanḥum
Manasseh
Manasseh b. Zebid
Mani b. Jonah
Mani b. Patish
Mar b. Ashi
Mar Johanya (B ; 4)
Mar b. Joseph
Mar Kashshisha
Mar b. Rabina
Mar Yanka　　　　[Isar]
Mari (son of the proselyte
Mari b. Abbuh
Mari b. Bisnaa
Mari b. Ḥisda
Mari b. Huna
Mari b. Kahana
Mari b. Mar
Mari b. Phinehas
Mari b. 'Uḳba
Marino
Marinus
Marinus b. Oshaya
Marion
Matnah
Mattatya b. Judah
Matun
Menahem of Gallia
Menahem b. Nopaḥ
Menahem b. Simai
Menahem Tolomia
Menashya
Menashya of Dewil
Menashya b. Gada
Menashya b. Jacob
Menashya b. Jeremiah
Menashya b. Judah
Menashya b. Menahem

Menashya b. Raba
Menashya b. Taḥlifa
Meremar
Meremar b. Ḥanina
Mesharshiya b. Ammi
Mesharshiya b. Idi
Mesharshiya b. Dimi
Mesharshiya b. Nathan
Mesharshiya b. Paḳod
Mesharshiya b. Raba
Mesharshiya of Tosnia
Minyomi
Mona
Mordecai
Naḥman b. Ada
Naḥman b. Baruk
Naḥman b. Gurya
Naḥman b. Ḥisdai
Naḥman b. Isaac
*Naḥman b. Jacob
Naḥman b. Kohen
Naḥman b. Minyomi
Naḥman b. Papa
Naḥman b. Parta
Naḥman b. Rabbah
Naḥman b. Samuel
Naḥman b. Zabda
Nahum (brother of Ila)
Nahum (servant of Abbahu)
Naḥumi
Naḥumi b. Zechariah
Naphtali
Nasah
Nathan (father of Huna)
Nathan (brother of Ḥiyya)
Nathan b. Abba
Nathan b. Abbai
Nathan b. Abin
Nathan b. Ammi
Nathan b. Asya
Nathan b. Berechiah
Nathan of Bira
Nathan b. Mar 'Uḳba
Nathan b. Mar Zuṭra
Nathan b. Minyomi
Nathan b. Oshaya
Nathan b. Tobia
*Nathan de Ẓuẓita (exilarch)
Nehemiah
Nehemiah b. Ḥiyya
Nehemiah b. Huna
Nehemiah b. Joseph
Nehemiah b. Joshua
Nehilai
Nehorai
Nehorai b. Shemaiah
Niha b. Saba
Niḳomeki
Osha'ya (Hoshaiah)
Paddat
Paddaya
Panda
*Papa
Papa b. Abba
Papa b. Aḥa
Papa b. Hanan of Be Zeluḥit
Papa b. Joseph
Papa b. Naḥman
Papa Saba
Papa b. Samuel
Parnak
Pazi
*Pereda
Philippi
Phinehas
Phinehas b. Ammi
*Phinehas b. Ḥama
Phinehas b. Hananiah
Phinehas b. Ḥisda
Phinehas of Joppa
Phinehas ha-Kohen
Phinehas b. Mari
Phinehas b. Zakkai
*Raba b. Ada

*Raba b. Joseph b. Ḥama
Raba b. 'Ula
Rabbah b. Abba
*Rabbah b. Abuha
Rabbah b. Aḥa
Rabbah b. Aḥilai
Rabbah b. Aḥini
Rabbah b. Ammi
Rabbah b. Ashi
Rabbah b. Bar Ḥanah
Rabbah of Barnash
Rabbah b. Baruna
Rabbah b. Ḥaklai
*Rabbah b. Hanan
Rabbah b. Ḥanina
*Rabbah b. Ḥiyya
*Rabbah b. Huna
Rabbah b. Idi b. Abin
Rabbah b. Ihi or Iti
Rabbah b. Ilai
Rabbah b. Isaac
Rabbah b. Ishmael
Rabbah b. Isi
Rabbah b. Jeremiah
Rabbah b. Jonathan
Rabbah b. Kahana
Rabbah b. Ḳisma
Rabbah of Kubaya
Rabbah b. Lema
Rabbah b. Lewai
Rabbah b. Marion
*Rabbah b. Matnah
Rabbah b. Meḥasya
Rabbah b. Mesharshiya
Rabbah b. Minyomi
Rabbah b. Papa
*Rabbah of Parziḳi
Rabbah b. Raba
Rabbah b. Saba
*Rabbah b. Safra
*Rabbah b. Samuel
*Rabbah b. Shela
Rabbah b. Shumni
Rabbah b. Simi
Rabbah b. Taḥlifa
Rabbanai
Rabbanai of Ḥuza
*Rabina I.
*Rabina II.
Rabina III.
Rafram
*Rafram I. (b. Papa)
*Rafram II.
Raḥbah or Reḥabah
Raḥmai
Rakish b. Papa
Rammi b. Abba
Rammi b. Berechiah
Rammi b. Ezekiel
Rammi b. Ḥama
Rammi b. Judah
Rammi b. Papa
Rammi b. Rab
Rammi b. Samuel
Rammi b. Tamre
Rammi b. Yeba
Redifa
Reuben
Romanus
Safra
Safra b. Se'oram
Safra b. Tobia
Safra b. Yeba
Saḥḥorah
Salla Ḥasida (the pious)
Samlai
Samlai of Bira
Samlai of Cæsarea
Samlai of Lydda
Samma b. Aibu
Samma b. Asi
Samma b. Ḥalkai
Samma b. Jeremiah
Samma b. Judah

Samma b. Mari
Samma b. Mesharshiya
Samma b. Rabbah
Samma b. Rakta
Samuel (brother of Bere-
chiah)
Samuel (brother of Osha'ya)
Samuel (brother of Phinehas
b. Hama)
Samuel b. Abba
Samuel (Mar) b. Abba b.
Abba
Samuel b. Abba of Hagrunya
*Samuel b. Abbahu
Samuel b. Abdimi
Samuel b. Abin
Samuel b. Ada
Samuel b. Aha
Samuel b. Ahitai
Samuel b. Ahunai
*Samuel b. Ammi
*Samuel b. Anaya
Samuel b. Bisna
Samuel of Cappadocia
Samuel of Difte
Samuel b. Gedaliah
Samuel b. Halafta
Samuel b. Hananiah
Samuel b. Hanina
*Samuel b. Hiyya
Samuel b. Ika
Samuel b. Isaac
Samuel b. Jacob
*Samuel b. Jose b. Bun
Samuel b. Judah of India
Samuel b. Kattina
Samuel b. Marta
Samuel b. Nadab
*Samuel b. Nahmani
*Samuel b. Nathan
Samuel b. Papa
Samuel Podagrita
Samuel b. Raba
Samuel b. Rabbi
Samuel Saba
Samuel b. Shaba
Samuel b. Shilot
Samuel b. Simi
Samuel of Sofatta
Samuel b. Sustra or Susreta
Samuel b. Sutar
Samuel b. Yeba
Samuel b. Zadok
Samuel of Zarkonya
Samuel b. Ze'era
Samuel b. Zutra
Saul of Nawah
Se'oram
Shaba
Shabbethai
Shabbethai b. Marinus
Shabbethai of Saduki
Shalemya
Shalman of Be Zeluhit
Shalman b. Levi
Shappir
Shayin
Shazbi
Shela
Shela b. Abina
Shela b. Isaac
*Shela of Kefar Tamarta
Shela Mari
Shela of Shalomya
Shemaiah
Shemaiah b. Zera
Shephatiah
Sherebiah
Shesha b. Idi b. Abin
*Sheshet
Sheshet b. Joshua
Sheshet of Kartiza
Sheshna b. Samuel
Sidor

Simeon b. Abba
Simeon b. Abishalom
Simeon b. Aibu
Simeon b. Bisna
Simeon b. Hillel b. Pazi
Simeon b. Hiyya
Simeon b. Hiyya of Huza
Simeon b. Jacob of Tyrus
*Simeon b. Jakim
Simeon b. Jasina
*Simeon b. Jehozadak
Simeon b. Jonah
Simeon b. Joshua
Simeon the Judge
Simeon b. Kana or Sana
Simeon b. Karsena
Simeon b. Kisma
*Simeon b. Lakish
Simeon b. Levi
Simeon b. Me'asha
Simeon b. Narshiyah
Simeon b. Nezira
*Simeon b. Pazi
Simeon the Pious
Simeon the Scribe
Simeon of Shiloh
Simeon b. Simeon
Simeon b. Tahlifa
Simeon of Tospata
*Simeon b. Yannai
Simeon b. Zachariah
Simeon b. Zebid
Simeon b. Zirud
Simi b. Abba
Simi b. Ada
Simi b. Ashi
Simi of Birtadeshore
Simi b. Hezekiah
Simi b. Hiyya
Simi of Mahaza
Simi of Nehardea
Simi b. 'Ukba
Simi Ze'era
Sisai
Surhab b. Papa
Tabala
*Tabi
Tabi (grandson of Mar Tabi)
Tabi, Mar
Tabut
Tabut Rishba
*Tabyome (B)
Tabyome (P)
Tabyome II. (B)
Taddai
Tahlifa
Tahlifa (father-in-law of Ab-
bahu)
Tahlifa (father-in-law of Aha)
Tahlifa (father of Huna)
Tahlifa b. Abdimi
Tahlifa b. Abimi
Tahlifa b. Abina
Tahlifa b. Bar Hana
Tahlifa of Cæsarea
Tahlifa b. Gazza
Tahlifa b. Hisda
Tahlifa b. Imo
Tahlifa Ma'araba (the Pales-
tinian)
Tahlifa b. Samuel
Tanhum b. Ammi
Tanhum of Bosra
*Tanhum b. Hanilai
Tanhum b. Hanina
*Tanhum b. Hiyya
Tanhum b. Hiyya b. Abba
Tanhum b. Hiyya of Kefar
Agin
Tanhum b. Hiyya of Kefar
Ako
*Tanhum b. Jeremiah
*Tanhuma b. Abba
*Tanhuma b. Judah

Tanhum of Parwad
Tanhum b. Skolastikai
Tanhuma
Tarayya
Tayyefa Simmuka
Tobi b. Isaac
Tobi b. Kattina
Tobi b. Kisna
Tobi b. Mattanah
Tobi b. Nehemiah
Totai
'Ukba b. Abba
'Ukba b. Hama
'Ukba b. Hiyya
'Ukba, Mar
'Ukba of Meshan
'Ukba of Pashronya
'Ukba, Rabbana
Ulla b. Abba
Ulla b. Ashi
Ulla of Biri
Ulla of Cæsarea
Ulla Hazzana
Ulla b. Hinena
Ulla b. Idi
Ulla b. Ilai
Ulla b. Ishmael
Ulla b. Menasya
Ulla b. Rab
Ulla Rabbah
Uzziel (grandson of Uzziel
Rabbah)
Uzziel b. Nehunya
*Yannai
*Yannai (grandson of Yannai
the Elder)
Yannai b. Ammi
Yannai of Cappadocia
*Yannai b. Ishmael
Yannai b. Nahmani
Yannai Ze'era (the little
one)
Yeba (father-in-law of Ash-
yan)
Yeba Saba (the old one)
Yemar
Yemar of Difte
Yemar b. Hashwai
Yemar Saba (the old one)

J.

Yemar b. Shazbi
Yemar b. Shelmia
*Yudan (father of Mattaniah)
Yudan b. Aibu
Yudan of Cappadocia
*Yudan of Magdala
*Yudan b. Phila
Yudan of Saknin
Yudan b. Shakli
Zabda
Zabda (father of Abba)
*Zabda b. Levi
*Zakkai
Zakkai of Alexandria
*Zakkai the Butcher (Tab-
baha)
Zakkai the Great (Rabbah)
Zakkai of Kabul
*Zakkai of Shab
*Zebid
Zebid of Nehardea
Zebid b. Osha'ya
Zebulun b. Don (B)
Zechariah
Zechariah (son - in - law of
Joshua b. Levi)
*Ze'era (P)
Ze'era b. Abbahu (P)
Ze'era b. Hama (P)
Ze'era b. Hanina (P)
Ze'era or Zera (B and P)
Zemina (P)
*Zerika
Zerika (brother-in-law of Ze-
rikan)
Zerikan
Zuga
Zuga or Zawwa of Adiabene
Zuti
Zutra b. Huna   [Ashi]
Zutra, Mar (the colleague of
Zutra, Mar (the great)
Zutra, Mar (the pious)
Zutra b. Mari
Zutra b. Nahman
Zutra b. Rishba
Zutra b. Samuel
Zutra b. Tobia
Zutra b. Ze'era

L. G.

TANNENBAUM, ABNER: Yiddish and Hebrew journalist; born at Schirwind, East Prussia,
March 1, 1848. He studied in Kamenetz-Podolsk
and in the Kishinef Lyceum, and was awarded a
diploma by the Imperial University of Odessa for
his historical and geographical studies. He chose a
commercial career, and, after having held various
positions, became manager of a wholesale drug business. In 1887 he emigrated to New York, where he
devoted himself to journalism. He died July 24, 1913.

Tannenbaum translated into Yiddish several of
the works of Jules Verne, among which may be
mentioned "Kalt und Warm," London, 1895, and
"Gesucht und Gefunden," New York, 1896. He was
especially known as a popularizer, among Russian
immigrants, of the secular sciences, having written
extensive treatises on historical topics, natural
science, etc., in almost all Yiddish periodicals of the
United States. He was the author of a "History of
the Jews in America" (2 parts, New York, 1905)
and of a "Commercial, Industrial, and Agricultural
Geography of the United States" (ib. 1905).

J.   L. LA.

TANUJI, ISHMAEL HA-KOHEN: Egyp-
tian rabbi and author of the sixteenth century. He
was a descendant of the Tanuji (from "Tanjah" =

"Tangiers") family of Tunis, to which belonged R. Samuel ha-Kohen and his son R. Judah, both rabbis of Jerusalem. In 1543 he wrote a book, popular in style, entitled "Sefer ha-Zikkaron" and containing halakic decisions on current topics (Ferrara, 1555). As the chief of the Egyptian rabbis he appended his name to an approbation of the responsa of R. Elijah ben Ḥayyim (Ranaḥ). There still exists in Egypt a synagogue in which Ishmael ha-Kohen Tanuji had been wont to pray, and which is therefore called by his name (see JEW. ENCYC. v. 72a, line 1).

BIBLIOGRAPHY: Azulai, *Shem ha-Gedolim*, i. 111; Fuenn, *Keneset Yisrael*, p. 674.
G. N. T. L.

TANYA: Collection of ritual laws and customs, published first at Mantua, 1514, then at Cremona, 1565, and later in two other editions. The epigraph of the Mantua edition reads as follows: "'Minhag Abot Sefer Tanya' was terminated in the month of Siwan, 5074 of Creation" (= 1314). This is interpreted by Dukes ("Orient, Lit." v. 219), to mean that the work was originally called "Minhag Abot" and that it was composed in 1314. Buber (introduction to his edition of "Shibbole ha-Leḳeṭ"), however, proves that 1314 is a misprint for 1514, which is the date of the first edition. Steinschneider supposes that the "Minhag Abot" mentioned by Abraham ha-Levi in his treatise "Ha-Hora'ah" (see "Oẓar Neḥmad," ii. 152) is the same as "Tanya." This book is arranged in the same way as the "Shibbole ha-Leḳeṭ," which, as well as its author, Zedekiah ben Abraham, is often quoted. The author of the "Tanya," besides, frequently cites as his teachers Benjamin b. Abraham (Zedekiah's brother) and Judah b. Benjamin; and in certain places the expression "I, Jehiel the scribe," is found. These details gave rise to a discussion among different authorities as to the authorship of the book, which is variously ascribed to Judah b. Benjamin, to a pupil of his, and to Jehiel b. Asher b. Jekuthiel.

Among the opinions of modern scholars that of Osias Schorr may be mentioned, namely, that the "Tanya" is simply a copy of the "Shibbole ha-Leḳeṭ," called "Tanya" after its initial word, but written in such a way as to make it appear the copyist's own composition; *e.g.*, in many places Schorr declares the copyist ascribes this or that to the "Shibbole ha-Leḳeṭ" to make it appear that he took only so much from that work. Where the author of the "Shibbole" refers to "my brother Benjamin" the copyist of the "Tanya" omits the words "my brother." The copyist for the most part confined his attention to the Law, neglecting the customs. He also added extracts from Maimonides' "Yad."

BIBLIOGRAPHY: Azulai, *Shem ha-Gedolim*; Benjacob, *Oẓar ha-Sefarim*, p. 657, No. 660; Conforte, *Ḳore ha-Dorot*, p. 21a; Schorr, in *Ziyyon*, i. 147-148; *idem*, in *He-Ḥaluẓ*, i. 103-105; Steinschneider, *Cat. Bodl.* col. 2771.
W. B. M. SEL.

TÄNZER, AARON: Austrian rabbi; born at Presburg, Hungary, Jan. 30, 1871; studied at the Presburg Rabbinerschule, and Oriental philology and history at the University of Berlin (Ph.D. 1895). In 1896 he was called to Hohenems as chief rabbi of Tyrol and Vorarlberg; and in 1904 he became

rabbi of Meran (Tyrol). He is the author of "Die Religionsphilosophie Josef Albo's," Frankfort-on-the-Main, 1896; "Der Israelitische Friedhof in Hohenems," Vienna, 1901; "Judenthum und Entwickelungslehre," Berlin, 1903; and "Geschichte der Juden in Tirol und Vorarlberg," vol. i., *ib.* 1903-4.
S.

TAPPUAH: 1. City in the Shefelah, described as lying between the towns of En-gannim and Enam; probably situated north of the Wadi al-Sunṭ, and identical with the modern 'Artuf (Josh. xv. 34). **2.** City in Ephraim, marking the western boundary of the tribe (Josh. xvi. 8). **3.** The land of Tappuah, which belonged, with the exception of the city of the same name, to the tribe of Manasseh (Josh. xvii. 8). It was one of the thirty-one districts whose kings were vanquished by the Jews when they first invaded Palestine (Josh. xii. 17). **4 (En-tappuah)**. Southern boundary of the tribe of Manasseh (Josh. xvii. 7). **5.** Son of Hebron (I Chron. ii. 43).

BIBLIOGRAPHY: Schwarz, *Palestine*, pp. 89, 102, Philadelphia, 1850.
J. S. O.

TARASCON (Hebrew, טראשקון, טאראשקן): City in the department of Bouches-du-Rhône, France. In 1276 King Charles I. intervened in behalf of its Jews against the inquisitors, who had obliged them to enlarge the wheel-shaped badge worn by them, and had extorted large sums from them in the guise of a fine. Several Jews who were expelled from Languedoc in 1306 went to Tarascon, where they were cordially received; but in 1308 Charles II., on the complaint of Christians, forbade Jews to hold public office. Queen Jeanne, however, took the Tarascon Jews under her protection (1348 and 1378); and her daughter, Marie de Blois, treated them still more favorably, making no distinction whatever between her Jewish and her Christian subjects (1390). Louis II. of Anjou exempted them (1400) from all new taxes, and granted them a special letter of protection ("sauvegarde"), by the terms of which the other inhabitants of Tarascon were enjoined to provide for their defense and for the preservation of their property. Louis III. appointed conservators of these privileges in order to remove the Jews from the arbitrary jurisdiction of the courts.

In 1454 King René issued a decree mitigating the severity of the edict of Charles I. relative to the wearing of the badge; but in 1460, at the request of the syndics, he ordered that no Jew should thenceforth hold public office, on pain of a fine of fifty marks in silver. In 1475 he obliged the Jews of the city to pay him a subsidy of 8,000 florins. Owing to their letter of protection of 1400, the Jews of Tarascon did not suffer during the bloody excesses committed in Provence in 1484 by a band of reapers; and in 1489 the municipal council, in conformity with the "sauvegarde," took steps which enabled the Jewish inhabitants to escape from the populace, which had attacked their quarter.

This quarter was commonly called the "Carrière des Juifs," or simply the "Carrière," though the names "Juzataria" and "Juateria" also occur occasionally. It included, on the one side, the portion of the Rue du Château between the royal court and the château of King René, and, on the other side, the portion which separated the traverse, now the Rue des Juifs, from the monastery of the Benedictines of St. Honorat. When some Jews settled outside of the Carrière a royal decree of 1377 ordered them to return to their former domicil, on pain of a fine of 100 livres. In case of necessity, however, the Jews were permitted to go outside as far as the Rue des Baptêmes, but the condition was made that they should construct no gate or other opening to this street near the Church of St. Marthe.

The exact site of the synagogue is unknown. In 1368 the community paid to the public treasury a tax of 10 oboles for the possession of this building. In the Middle Ages the community had two cemeteries, one of them situated on the island of Tarnègue near the old commandery of St. Antoine, and the other outside of the Condamine gate between the road to Maillane and that to St. Georges. In 1526 the latter became the property of the city, which erected a pest-house on the plot.

The following scholars of Tarascon are known: R. Eliezer and his brother Joshua, Solomon of Salon, Israel of Valabrègue, Immanuel ben Jacob (Bonfils), Joseph Caspi, Don Bonafous, Samuel b. Judah and his brother En Bondavi of Marseilles; also the following physicians: Comprat Asser, Bonjuhas Guassin, Rossel, Ferrier, Bellant, Nathan, Jacob of Lunel, Orgier, Maystre Aron, Mosse Meyr, and Joseph b. Joseph.

BIBLIOGRAPHY: Arnaud Camille, *Essai sur la Condition des Juifs en Provence*, pp. 24, 36, 37, 39, 52; Bardinet, *Revue Historique*, 1880; Blancard, *Inventaire Sommaire des Archives Départementales des Bouches-du-Rhône*, B. 142; Bédarride, *Les Juifs en France*, pp. 317, 320; Bondurand, *Les Coutumes de Tarascon*, pp. 53, 64, 65, 80, 84, Nîmes, 1892; Bouche Hon, *Histoire de Provence*, II., book ix., section iv.; Depping, *Les Juifs dans le Moyen Age*, pp. 198, 206, 207; Gross, *Gallia Judaica*, pp. 249-250; S. Kahn, *Les Juifs de Tarascon*, pp. 3-57 (reprinted from *R. E. J.* 1889); Nostradamus, *Histoire de Provence*, part 6; Renan-Neubauer, *Les Rabbins Français*, pp. 477, 561, 688; idem, *Les Ecrivains Juifs Français*, pp. 692 et seq.; *Revue des Langues Romanes*, 1897, pp. 224-226.

S.   S. K.

ṬARFON (Greek, Τρύφων; Yer. Bik. 64c): Tanna of the third generation, living in the period between the destruction of the Temple and the fall of Bethar. He was of priestly lineage, and he expressly states that he officiated in the Temple with the priests (Yer. Yoma iii. 7); in the pride of his rank he used to demand the heave-offering even after the Temple had fallen (Tosef., Ḥag. iii., end). His devotion to his mother was such that he used to place his hands beneath her feet when she was obliged to cross the courtyard barefoot (Ḳid. 61b), while his generosity made him return to the father the redemption-money for the first-born, although it was his priestly perquisite (Tosef., Bek. vi. 14). Once, in a time of famine, he took 300 wives so that they might, as wives of a priest, exercise the right of sharing in the tithes (Tosef., Ket. v. 1). On one occasion, when from his window he saw a bridal procession evidently of the poorer classes, he requested his mother and sister to anoint the bride that the groom might find more joy in her (Ab. R. N. xli., end). Although he was blessed with riches, he possessed extraordinary modesty; in one instance he deeply regretted having mentioned his name in a time of peril, since he feared that in using his position as teacher to escape from danger he had seemingly violated the rule against utilizing knowledge of the Torah for practical ends (Ned. 62b).

Although as a halakist R. Ṭarfon was an adherent of the school of Shammai, only two passages describe him as following its teachings (Yeb. 15b; Yer. Sheb. iv. 20), and he always inclined toward leniency in the interpretation of those halakot of Shammai which had not actually been put into practise (Kil. v. 6; Yeb. xv. 6; Ket. v. 2); often he decided in direct opposition to the Bet Shammai when it imposed restrictions of excessive severity (Yeb. xv. 47; Naz. v. 5). R. Ṭarfon **As Halakist.** was also the author of independent halakot, one being on the form of benediction when quenching thirst with water (Ber. vi. 8), and another on the benediction for the eve of the Passover (Pes. x. 6). The majority of his rulings, however, deal with subjects discussed in the orders Nashim, Ḳodashim, Ṭohorot, and Neziḳin. In those found in Ṭohorot his tendency is always toward severity, while in Neziḳin are found his sayings on lost objects and usufruct (B. M. iv. 3, v. 7), the payment of debts, the money due a woman when she receives a bill of divorce (Ket. ix. 2, 3), and damage caused by cattle (B. Ḳ. ii. 5, and the baraitot connected with this passage, p. 26). If he had belonged to the Sanhedrin, the death-penalty would have been abolished (Mak. i. 10; comp. Frankel, "Der Gerichtliche Beweis," p. 48, Berlin, 1846). R. Ṭarfon engaged in halakic controversies with R. Akiba (Ket. 84a; Pes. 117, 118), but the two agreed with regard to a tosefta (Miḳ. i.; Ḳid. 66; Yer. Yoma i. 1; Ter. iv. 5; Mak. i. 10; Ker. v. 3), with R. Simeon (Men. xii. 5; possibly, however, an error for R. Akiba), and R. Eleazar ben Azariah (Yad. iv. 3). Other sayings of his have been preserved which were accepted without controversy (Pes. 117a, 118a; Giṭ. 83a); and two of his apothegms are especially noteworthy as indicating his intense earnestness: "The day is short, the labor vast, the toilers idle, the reward great, and the Master urgent" (Ab. i. 15); "It is not thy task to complete the work, neither art thou a free man that thou canst withdraw thyself; if thou hast learned much, great shall be thy reward, for He that doth hire thee will surely repay thee for thy toil; yet the requital of the pious is in the future" (Ab. i. 17). In the discussion as to the relative importance of theory and practise, Ṭarfon decided in favor of the latter.

When Eliezer ben Hyrcanus was sick, and a deputation was sent to him, R. Ṭarfon acted as the spokesman, addressing him as follows: "Master, thou art of more worth to Israel than the sun, for **Incidents of His Life.** that gives light only on earth, while thou dost shed thy rays both in this world and in the world to come" (Sanh. 101a; Mek., Baḥodesh, xi. [ed. Weiss, p. 80a]). In like manner he led a number of scholars in a visit to R. Ishmael ben Elisha, upon the death of the sons of the latter (M. Ḳ. 28b); and when Jose the Galilean, R. Ṭarfon, R. Eliezer ben Azariah, and R. Akiba assembled to decide on the disputed sayings of Eliezer ben Hyrcanus, Ṭarfon was the first speaker (Tosef., Giṭ. vii.; Giṭ. 83a). He was one of those whose names occurred in the deposition of Gamaliel II., and it is expressly stated that he was addressed as "brother" by the other scholars. He is said to have dwelt at Jabneh, although it is evident that he lived also in Lydda (Ta'an. iii. 9; B. M. iv. 3; Ḥag. 18a).

R. Ṭarfon was accustomed to open his haggadic discourses with a halakic question (Tosef., Ber. iv. 16). In his own upper chamber at Jabneh it was decided that benevolence should be practised according to the injunction of Ps. cvi. 3 (Esth. R. vi. 2, 5). Ṭarfon held that God did not allow His glory to overshadow Israel until the people had fulfilled a task (Ab. R. N. ii.), and that death can overtake one only when he is idle (comp. Gen. xlix. 33).

On festivals and holy days R. Ṭarfon was accustomed to delight his wife and children by preparing for them the finest fruits and dainties (Yer. Pes. 37b). When he wished to express ap-

Domestic Life. proval of any one, he would say, "'A knop and a flower' [Ex. xxv. 33]; thou hast spoken as beautifully as the adornments of the candlestick in the Temple"; but when it was necessary to upbraid another, he would say, "'My son shall not go down with you'" (Gen. R. xci.), repeating the words of Jacob to his sons in Gen. xlii. 38. When he perceived that his two nephews, whom he was instructing personally, were becoming careless, he interrupted his lecture and regained their attention by saying, "Then again Abraham took a wife, and her name was Johanna" (instead of Keturah; Gen. xxv. 1), whereupon his pupils interrupted him by exclaiming, "No, Keturah!" (Zeb. 26b). His chief scholars were R. Judah ('Er. 45b; Yeb. 101b), Simeon Shezari (Men. 31b), and Judah ben Isaiah ha-Bosem (Ḥul. 55b).

R. Ṭarfon was extremely bitter against those Jews who had been converted to the new faith; and he swore that he would burn every book of theirs which should fall into his hands (Shab. 116a), his feeling being so intense that he had no scruples against destroying the Gospels, although the name of God occurred frequently in them.

BIBLIOGRAPHY: Frankel, *Hodegetica in Mischnam*, pp. 101–105, Leipsic, 1859; Brüll, *Einleitung in die Mischna*, i. 100–103, Frankfort-on-the-Main, 1876; Bacher, *Ag. Tan.* pp. 342–352; Hamburger, *R. B. T.* ii. 1196; Derenbourg, *Hist.* pp. 379 *et seq.* A list of the mishnayot which mention R. Ṭarfon is given by Schürer, *Gesch.* ii. 378, note 137; of the Tosefta passages in which his name occurs, by Zuckermandel in his edition of the Tosefta; of similar sections in the Mekilta, Sifra, and Sifre, by Hoffmann, *Zur Einleitung in die Halachischen Midraschim*, p. 85, Berlin, 1887.

W. B. S. O.

TARGUM: The Aramaic translation of the Bible. It forms a part of the Jewish traditional literature, and in its inception is as early as the time of the Second Temple. The verb תרגם, from which the noun תרגום is formed, is used in Ezra iv. 7 in reference to a document written in Aramaic, although "Aramit" (A. V. "in the Syrian tongue") is added. In mishnaic phraseology the verb denotes a translation from Hebrew into any other language, as into Greek (see Yer. Ḳid. 59a, line 10, and Yer. Meg. 71c, line 11; both statements referring to the Greek version of Aquila); and the noun likewise may refer to the translation of the Biblical text into any language (see Meg. ii. 1; Shab. 115a). The use of the term

"Targum" by itself was restricted to the Aramaic version of the Bible (see Bacher, "Die Terminologie der Tannaiten," pp. 205 *et seq.*). In

Name. like manner, the Aramaic passages in Genesis, Jeremiah, Daniel, and Ezra were briefly called "Targum," while the Hebrew text was called "Miḳra" (see Yad. iv. 5; Shab. 115b).

As an interpretation of the Hebrew text of the Bible the Targum had its place both in the synagogal liturgy and in Biblical instruction, while the reading of the Bible text combined with the Targum in the presence of the congregation assembled for public worship was an ancient institution which dated from the time of the Second Temple, and was traced back to Ezra by Rab when he interpreted the word "meforash" (Neh. viii. 8) as referring to the Targum (Meg. 3a; Ned. 37b; comp. Yer. Meg. 74d, line 48; Gen. R. xxxvi., end). The rules for reading the Targum are formulated in the Halakah (see Meg. iii. and the Talmud *ad loc.*; Tosef., Meg. iv.). The Targum was to be read after every verse of the parashiyyot of the Pentateuch, and after every third verse of the lesson from the Prophets. Excepting the Scroll of Esther, which might be read by two persons in turn, only one person might read the Targum, as the Pentateuch or prophetic section also was read by a single person. Even a minor might read the Targum, although it was not fitting for him to do so when an adult had read the text. Certain portions of the Bible, although read, were not translated (as Gen. xxxv. 22), while others were neither read nor translated (as Num. vi. 24–26; II Sam. xi.–xiii.). The reader was forbidden to prompt the translator, lest any one should say that the Targum was included in the text of the Bible (Ulla in Meg. 32a). With regard to the translation of Biblical passages, Judah ben Ilai, the pupil of Akiba, declared that whosoever rendered a verse of the Bible in its original form was a liar, while he who made additions was a blasphemer (Tosef., Meg., end; Ḳid. 49a; comp. the geonic responsum in Harkavy, "Responsen der Geonim," pp. 124 *et seq.*, and the quotation from Midr. ha-Gadol in "J. Q. R." vi. 425). A passage in Ab. R. N. (Recension B, xii. [ed. Schechter, p. 24]) referring to R. Akiba's early training says that he studied the Bible and the Targum; but allusions to the Targum as a special subject of study in connection with the Bible are excessively rare. It must be assumed, however, that the Targum was an integral part of the Biblical course of study designated as "Miḳra"; and Judah b. Ilai declared that only he who could read and translate the Bible might be regarded as a "ḳaryana," or one thoroughly versed in the Bible (Ḳid. 49a). In Sifre, Deut. 161 the Targum is mentioned as a branch of study intermediate between the Miḳra and the Mishnah.

The professional translator of the text of the Bible in the synagogue was called "targeman" ("torgeman," "metorgeman"; the common pronunciation being METURGEMAN; see Meg. iv. 4). His duties naturally formed part of the functions of the communal official ("sofer") who had charge of Biblical instruction (see Yer. Meg. 74d). Early in the fourth century Samuel ben Isaac, upon entering a synagogue, once saw a teacher ("sofer") read the Targum from a book, and bade him desist. This anecdote shows that there was a written

Liturgical Use. Targum which was used for public worship in that century in Palestine, although there was no definitely determined and generally recognized Targum, such as existed in Babylonia. The story is told (Yer. Ber. 9c) that Jose b. Abin, an amora of the second half of the fourth century, reprehended those who read a Targum to Lev. xxii. 28 which laid a biased emphasis on the view that the command contained in that verse was based on God's mercy (this same paraphrase is still found in the Palestinian Targum); see also the statements on the erroneous translation of Ex. xii. 8, Lev. vi. 7, and Deut. xxvi. 4 in Yer. Bik. 65d; as well as Yer. Kil. viii., end, on Deut. xiv. 5; and Meg. iii. 10 on Lev. xviii. 21. In addition to the anecdotes mentioned above, there were earlier indications that the Targum was committed to writing, although for private reading only. Thus, the Mishnah states (Yad. iv. 5) that portions of the text of the Bible were "written as a Targum," these doubtless being Biblical passages in an Aramaic translation; and a tannaitic tradition (Shab. 115a; Tosef., Shab. xiv.; Yer. Shab. 15c; Massek. Soferim v. 15) refers to an Aramaic translation of the Book of Job which existed in written form at the time of Gamaliel I., and which, after being withdrawn from use, reappeared in the lifetime of his grandson Gamaliel II. The Pentateuchal Targum, which was made the official Targum of the Babylonian schools, was at all events committed to writing and redacted as early as the third century, since its Masorah dates from the first half of that century. Two Palestinian amoraim of the same century urged the individual members of the congregation to read the Hebrew text of the weekly parashah twice in private and the Targum once, exactly as was done in public worship: Joshua ben Levi recommended this practise to his sons (Ber. 8b), while Ammi, a pupil of Johanan, made it a rule binding on every one (*ib.* 8a). These two dicta were especially instrumental in authorizing the custom of reciting the Targum; and it was considered a religious duty even in later centuries, when Aramaic, the language of the Targum, was no longer the vernacular of the Jews. Owing to the obsolescence of the dialect, however, the strict observance of the custom ceased in the days of the first geonim. About the middle of the ninth century the gaon Naṭronai

Disuse. ben Hilai reproached those who declared that they could dispense with the "Targum of the scholars" because the translation in their mother tongue (Arabic) was sufficient for them (see Müller, "Einleitung in die Responsen der Geonen," p. 106).

At the end of the ninth or in the beginning of the tenth century Judah ibn Ḳuraish sent a letter to the community of Fez, in which he reproved the members for neglecting the Targum, saying that he was surprised to hear that some of them did not read the Targum to the Pentateuch and the Prophets, although the custom of such a perusal had always been observed in Babylonia, Egypt, Africa, and Spain, and had never been abrogated. Hai

Gaon (d. 1038) was likewise much astonished to hear that the reading of the Targum had been entirely abandoned in Spain, a fact which he had not known before (Müller, *l.c.* p. 211); and Samuel ha-Nagid (d. 1056) also sharply criticized the scholars who openly advocated the omission of the reading of it, although according to him the Targum was thus neglected only in the northern provinces of that country (see the responsum in Berliner, "Onḳelos," ii. 169). As a matter of fact, however, the custom did entirely cease in Spain; and only in southern Arabia has it been observed until the present time (see Jacob Saphir, "Eben Sappir," i. 53b; Berliner, *l.c.* p. 172), although the Targum to the hafṭarot, together with introductions and poems in Aramaic, long continued to be read in some rituals (see Zunz, "G. V." pp. 410, 412; *idem*, "Literaturgesch." pp. 21 *et seq.*; *idem*, "Ritus," pp. 53, 60 *et seq.*, 81; Bacher, in "Monatsschrift," xxii. 220-223). In the synagogues of Bokhara the Persian Jews read the Targum, together with the Persian paraphrase of it, to the hafṭarah for the last day of Passover (Isa. x. 32-xii.; see "Zeit. für Hebr. Bibl." iv. 181).

The Aramaic translations of the Bible which have survived include all the books excepting Daniel and Ezra (together with Nehemiah), which, being written in great part in Aramaic, have no Targum, although one may have existed in ancient times.

Targumim to the Pentateuch: 1. Targum Onḳelos or **Babylonian Targum:** The official Targum to the Pentateuch, which subsequently gained currency and general acceptance throughout the Babylonian schools, and was therefore called the "Babylonian Targum" (on the tosafistic name "Targum Babli" see Berliner, *l.c.* p. 180; "Mordekai" on Giṭ. ix., end, mentions an old "Targum Babli" which was brought from Rome). The title "Targum Onḳelos" is derived from the well-known passage in the Babylonian Talmud (Meg. 3a) which discusses the origin of the Targumim: "R. Jeremiah [or, according to another version, R. Ḥiyya bar Abba] said: ' The Targum to the Pentateuch was composed by the proselyte Onḳelos at the dictation of R. Eliezer and R. Joshua.' " This statement is undoubtedly due to error or ignorance on the part of the scholars of Babylonia, who applied to the Aramaic translation of the Pentateuch the tradition current in Palestine regarding the Greek version of Aquila. According to Yer. Meg. 71c, "Aquila the proselyte translated the Pentateuch in the presence of R. Eliezer and R. Joshua, who praised him in the words of Ps. xlv. 3." In this passage, moreover, R. Jeremiah is described as transmitting the tradition on the authority of R. Ḥiyya bar Abba. There is no doubt that these accounts coincide; and the identity of אונקלוס הגר and עקילס הגר is also clear, so that Onḳelos and Aḳylas (Aquila) are one and the same person (but see ONḲELOS). In the Babylonian Talmud only the first form of the name occurs; the second alone is found in the Palestinian Talmud; while even the Babylonian Talmud mentions Onḳelos as the author of the Targum only in the passage cited. The statements referring to Onḳelos as the author of the Aramaic translation of the Pentateuch originated in the post-Talmudic period, although they are based entirely on Meg. 3a. The first citation of a targumic passage (on Gen. xlv. 27) with the direct statement "Onḳelos has translated" occurs in Pirḳe R. El. xxxviii. The gaon Sar Shalom, writing in the ninth century, expressed himself as follows on the Targum Onḳelos: "The Targum of which the sages spoke is the one which we now have in our hands; no sanctity attaches to the other Targumim. We have heard it reported as the tradition of ancient sages that God wrought a great thing [miracle] for Onḳelos when He permitted him to compose the Targum." In a similar fashion Maimonides speaks of Onḳelos as the bearer of ancient exegetic traditions and as a thorough master of Hebrew and Aramaic (see Bacher, "Die Bibelexegese Moses Maimunis," pp. 38–42). The designation "Targum Onḳelos" was accordingly established in the early portion of the geonic period, and can no longer be effaced from the terminology of Jewish learning.

The accepted Targum to the Pentateuch has a better claim to the title "Targum Babli" (Babylonian Targum), as has already been explained. It is noteworthy, moreover, that the Jews of Yemen received this Targum, like that to the Prophets, with the Babylonian punctuation (see Merx, "Chrestomathia Targumica"); and the colophon of a De Rossi codex states that a Targum with Babylonian punctuation was brought to Europe (Italy) from Babylon in the twelfth century, a copy with the Tiberian punctuation being made from it (see Berliner, *l.c.* ii. 134). In the **Babylonian Influence.** Babylonian Talmud the accepted Targum is called "our Targum," thus connoting the Targum of Babylonia or of the Babylonian academies (Ḳid. 49a, "Targum didan," for which Maimonides, in his "Yad," Ishut, viii. 4, substitutes "Targum Onḳelos"). Passages from the Targum are cited with great frequency in the Babylonian Talmud with the introductory remark "As we translate" (Berliner *l.c.* p. 112), and the Babylonian geonim also speak of "our Targum" as contrasted with the Palestinian Targum (see Hai Gaon in Harkavy, *l.c.* Nos. 15, 248).

The Targum Onḳelos, moreover, shows traces of Babylonian influence in its language, since its vocabulary contains: (1) Aramaic words which occur elsewhere in the Babylonian vernacular, *e. g.*, the Hebrew ראה ("to see") is always translated by חזא, and not by the Palestinian חמא, while the Hebrew סביב ("round about") is rendered by חזור חזור and not by סחור סחור; (2) Aramaic words used to render Greek words found in the Palestinian Targum; (3) a few Persian words, including "naḥshirkan" (hunter; Gen. xxv. 27); and "enderun" (*ib.* xliii. 30) instead of the Greek κοιτών found in the Palestinian Targum. These peculiarities, however, justify only the assumption that the final redaction of the Targum Onḳelos was made in Babylonia; for its diction does not resemble in any other respects the Aramaic diction found in the Babylonian Talmud; indeed, as Nöldeke has shown ("Mandäische Grammatik," p. xxvii.), "the official Targum, although redacted in Babylonia, is composed in a dialect fundamentally Palestinian." This statement is confirmed by the text of the Targum

Onḳelos, by the results of historical investigations of its origin, and by a comparison of it with the Palestinian Targum. These researches into its history show that the Targum which was made the official one was received by the Babylonian authorities from Palestine, whence they had taken the Mishnah, the Tosefta, and the halakic midrashim on the Pentateuch. The content of the Targum shows, moreover, that it was composed in Palestine in the second century; for both in its halakic and in its haggadic portions it may be traced in great part to the school of Akiba, and especially to the tannaim of that period (see F. Rosenthal in "Bet Talmud," vols. ii.–iii.; Berliner, *l.c.* p. 107). The Targum Onḳelos can not be compared unqualifiedly with the Palestinian Targum, however, since the latter has been preserved only in a much later form; moreover the majority of those fragments which are earliest seem to be later than the redaction of the Targum Onḳelos. Yet even in this form the Palestinian Targum to the Pentateuch furnishes sufficient evidence that the two Targumim were originally identical, as is evident from many verses in which they agree word for word, such as Lev. vi. 3, 4, 6–7, 9, 11, 18–20, 22–23. The difference between the two is due to two facts: (1) the Pentateuchal Targum of the tannaitic period was subjected to a thorough and systematic revision, which may have taken place in Palestine, this revision of subject-matter being followed by a textual revision to make it conform with the vernacular of the Babylonian Jews; and (2) the version of the Targum resulting from this double revision was accepted and committed to writing by the Babylonian academies.

Despite the fact that the Targum was thus reduced to a fixed form in Babylonia, the Palestinian meturgemanim had full license to revise and amplify it, so that the final redaction as it now exists in the so-called "Targum pseudo-Jonathan" (and this is true in even a greater degree of the "Fragmenten-Targum" mentioned below), though it was made as late as the seventh century, approximates the original Targum much more closely both in diction and in content, and includes many elements earlier than the Targum bearing the **Peculiarities.** name of Onḳelos and belonging to its final form to the third century.

The Masorah on the Targum Onḳelos is first mentioned in the "Patshegen," a commentary on this same Targum, written in the thirteenth century; it was edited by Berliner (1877), and reedited in alphabetical order by Landauer ("Letterbode," viii., ix.). This Masorah contains statements concerning the divergencies between the schools of Sura and Nehardea, exactly as the Talmud (Zeb. 54a; Sanh. 99b) alludes to controversies between Rab and Levi over individual words in the Targum. The system followed in the revision of the subject-matter which resulted in the Targum Onḳelos becomes clear when the latter is compared with the Palestinian Targum. The principal object being to conform the Targum as closely as possible to the original text both in diction and in content, explanatory notes were omitted, and the Hebrew words were translated according to their etymological meaning, although the geographical names were retained in their Hebrew form almost without exception, and the grammatical structure of the Hebrew was closely followed. The paraphrastic style of translation affected by the Targumim generally, in order to obviate all anthropomorphisms in reference to God, is observed with special care in the Targum Onḳelos, which employs paraphrases also in the poetic sections of the Pentateuch and in many other cases. In some instances the original paraphrase is abbreviated in order that the translation may not exceed the length of the text too greatly; consequently this Targum occasionally fails to represent the original, as is evident from paraphrases preserved in their entirety in the Palestinian Targum, as in the case of Gen. iv. 7, 10; xlix. 3, 22; Ex. xiv. 15; Num. xxiv. 4; and Deut. xxix. 17. An example of an abbreviated paraphrase is found also in the Targum Onḳelos to Deut. i. 44, as compared with the paraphrase in Soṭah 48b made by a Babylonian amora of the third century.

2. The Palestinian Targum (Targum Yerushalmi): A responsum of Hai Gaon, already cited with reference to the Targumim, answers the question concerning the "Targum of the Land of Israel [Palestine]" in the following words: "We do not know who composed it, nor do we even know this Targum, of which we have heard only a few passages. If there is a tradition among them [the Palestinians] that it has been made the subject of public discourse since the days of the ancient sages [here follow the names of Palestinian amoraim of the third and fourth centuries], it must be held in the same esteem as our Targum; for otherwise they would not have allowed it. But if it is less ancient, it is not authoritative. It is very improbable, however, in our opinion, that it is of later origin" (comp. "R. E. J." xlii. 235). The following statement is quoted ("Kol Bo," § 37) in the name of R. Meïr of Rothenburg (13th cent.) with reference to the Targum: "Strictly speaking, we should recite the weekly section with the Targum Yerushalmi, since it explains the Hebrew text in fuller detail than does our Targum; but we do not possess it, and we follow, moreover, the custom of the Babylonians." Both these statements indicate that the Palestinian Targum was rarely

Supposed Authorship.	found in the Middle Ages, although it was frequently quoted after the eleventh century (see Zunz, "G. V." pp. 66 *et seq.*), especially in the "'Aruk" of

Nathan b. Jehiel, which explains many words found in it. Another Italian, Menahem b. Solomon, took the term "Yerushalmi" (which must be interpreted as in the title "Talmud Yerushalmi") literally, and quoted the Palestinian Targum with the prefatory remark, "The Jerusalemites translated," or "The Targum of the People of the Holy City." After the fourteenth century Jonathan b. Uzziel, author of the Targum to the Prophets, was believed to have been the author of the Palestinian Targum to the Pentateuch also, the first to ascribe this work to him being Menahem Recanati in his commentary on the Pentateuch. This error was probably due to an incorrect analysis of the abbreviation י״ת (= "Targum Yerushalmi"), which was supposed to denote "Targum Jonathan." The statement in the Zohar (i. 89a, on Gen. xv. 1) that

Onḳelos translated the Torah, and Jonathan the Miḳra, does not mean, as Ginsburger thinks ("Pseudo-Jonathan," p. viii.), that according to the Zohar Jonathan translated the entire Bible, and thus the Pentateuch; but the word "Miḳra" here refers to the Prophets (see "R. E. J." xxii. 46). It is possible, however, that the view, first advanced by Recanati, that Jonathan composed also a Targum on the Pentateuch, was due to a misinterpretation of the passage in the Zohar. Azariah dei Rossi, who lived in the sixteenth century, states ("Me'or 'Enayim," ed. Wilna, p. 127) that he saw two manuscripts of the Palestinian Targum which agreed in every detail, one of which was entitled "Targum Yerushalmi" and the other "Targum Jonathan b. Uzziel." The editio princeps of the complete Palestinian Targum was printed from the latter (Venice, 1591), thus giving currency to the erroneous title.

In addition to the complete Palestinian Targum (pseudo-Jonathan) there exist fragments of the Palestinian Targum termed "Targum Yerushalmi"; but of these fragments, comprised under the generic term "Fragment-Targum," only those were until recently known which were first published in Bomberg's "Biblia Rabbinica" in 1518 on the basis of Codex Vaticanus No. 440. A few years ago, however, Ginsburger edited under the title "Das Fragmententhargum" (Berlin, 1899) a number of other fragments from manuscript sources, especially from Codex Parisiensis No. 110, as well as the quotations from the Targum Yerushalmi found in ancient authors. This work rendered a large amount of additional material available for the criticism of the Palestinian Targum, even though a considerable advance had already been made by Bassfreund in his "Fragmenten-Targum zum Pentateuch" (see "Monatsschrift," 1896, xl.). The general views concerning the Palestinian Targum and its relation to Onḳelos have been modified but slightly by these new publications. Although the relation of the Targum Yerushalmi to Onḳelos has already been discussed, it may be added here that the complete Palestinian Targum, as it is found in the pseudo-Jonathan, is not earlier than the seventh century; for it mentions Ayeshah ('A'ishah) (or, according to another reading, Khadija [Ḥadijah]) and Fatima, the wife and daughter of Mohammed, as wives of Ishmael, who was regarded as Mohammed's ancestor. It originated, moreover, at a period when the Targum Onḳelos was exercising its influence on the Occident; for the redactor of the Palestinian Targum in this form combined many passages of the two translations as they now exist in the Targum Yerushalmi and the Targum Onḳelos (see "Z. D. M. G." xxviii. 69 *et seq.*), besides revealing his dependence on the Onḳelos in other respects as well. The fragments of the Targum Yerushalmi are not all contemporaneous; and many passages contain several versions of the same verses, while certain sections are designated as additions

Relation to Onḳelos.	("tosefta"). The text of the majority of the fragments is older than the pseudo-Jonathan; and these remnants, which frequently consist of a single

word only or of a portion of a verse, have been fused according to a principle which can no longer be recognized; but they may have consisted in part of glosses written by some copyist on the margin of the Onḳelos, although without system and thus without completeness. Many of these fragments, especially the haggadic paraphrases, agree with the pseudo-Jonathan, which may, on the other hand, be older than some of them. In like manner, haggadic additions were made in later centuries to the text of the Targum, so that an African manuscript of the year 1487 alludes to the capture of Constantinople by the Turks in 1453. Early in the twelfth century Judah ben Barzillai wrote as follows with regard to these additions: "The Palestinian Targum contains haggadic sayings added by those who led in prayer and who also read the Targum, insisting that these sayings be recited in the synagogue as interpretations of the text of the Bible." Despite the numerous additions to the Palestinian Targum, and notwithstanding the fact that the majority of the fragments are of later date than Onḳelos, both pseudo-Jonathan and the fragments contain much that has survived from a very early period; indeed, the nucleus of the Palestinian Targum is older than the Babylonian, which was redacted from it.

Targum to the Prophets: 1. The Official Targum to the Prophets: Like the Targum Onḳelos to the Pentateuch the Targum to the Books of the Prophets gained general recognition in Babylonia in the third century; and from the Babylonian academies it was carried throughout the Diaspora. It originated, however, in Palestine, and
Targum was then adapted to the vernacular of
Jonathan. Babylonia; so that it contains the same linguistic peculiarities as the Targum Onḳelos, including sporadic instances of Persian words (e.g., "enderun," Judges xv. 1, xvi. 12; Joel ii. 16; "dastaka" = "dastah," Judges iii. 22). In cases where the Palestinian and Babylonian texts differ, this Targum follows the latter ("madinḥa'e"; see Pinsker, "Einleitung in die Babylonische Punktuation," p. 124). It originated, like the Targum to the Pentateuch, in the reading, during the service, of a translation from the Prophets, together with the weekly lesson. It is expressly stated in the Babylonian Talmud that the Targum accepted in Babylonia was Palestinian in origin; and a tannaitic tradition is quoted in the passage already cited from Megillah (3a), which declares that the Targum to the Prophets was composed by Jonathan b. Uzziel "from the mouths of Haggai, Zechariah, and Malachi," thus implying that it was based on traditions derived from the last prophets. The additional statements that on this account the entire land of Israel was shaken and that a voice from heaven cried: "Who hath revealed my secrets to the children of men?" are simply legendary reflections of the novelty of Jonathan's undertaking, and of the disapprobation which it evoked. The story adds that Jonathan wished to translate the Hagiographa also, but that a heavenly voice bade him desist. The Targum to Job, which, as already noted, was withdrawn from circulation by Gamaliel I., may have represented the result of his attempts to translate the Hagiographa (see Bacher, "Ag. Tan." i. 23 et seq.; 2d ed., pp. 20 et seq.). JONATHAN B. Uz-

ziel is named as Hillel's most prominent pupil (comp. JEW. ENCYC. vi. 399, s.v. HILLEL); and the reference to his Targum is at all events of historical value, so that there is nothing to controvert the assumption that it served as the foundation for the present Targum to the Prophets. It was thoroughly revised, however, before it was redacted in Babylonia. In the Babylonian Talmud it is quoted with especial frequency by Joseph, head of the Academy of Pumbedita (see Bacher, "Ag. Bab. Amor." p. 103), who says, with reference to two Biblical passages (Isa. viii. 6 and Zech. xii. 11): "If there were no Targum to it we should not know the meaning of these verses" (Sanh. 94b; M. Ḳ. 28b; Meg. 3a). This shows that as early as the beginning of the fourth century the Targum to the Prophets was recognized as of ancient authority. Hai Gaon apparently regarded Joseph as its author, since he cited passages from it with the words "Rab Joseph has translated" (commentary on Ṭohorot, quoted in the "'Aruk"; see Kohut, "Aruch Completum," ii. 293a, 308a). As a whole, this Targum resembles that of Onḳelos, although it does not follow the Hebrew text so closely, and paraphrases more freely, in harmony with the text of the prophetic books. The Targum to the Prophets is undoubtedly the result of a single redaction.

2. A Palestinian Targum (Targum Yerushalmi): This Targum to the prophetic books of the Bible is frequently cited by early authors, especially by Rashi and David Ḳimḥi. The Codex Reuchlinianus, written in 1105 (ed. Lagarde, "Prophetæ Chaldaice," 1872), contains eighty extracts from
Targum the Targum Yerushalmi, in addition
Yeru- to many variants given in the margin
shalmi. under different designations, many of them with the note that they were taken from "another copy" of the Targum. Linguistically they are Palestinian in origin. Most of the quotations given in the Targum Yerushalmi are haggadic additions, frequently traceable to the Babylonian Talmud, so that this Palestinian Targum to the Prophets belongs to a later period, when the Babylonian Talmud had begun to exert an influence upon Palestinian literature. The relation of the variants of this Targum to the Babylonian Targum to the Prophets is, on the whole, the same as that of the fragments of the Palestinian Targum to the Onḳelos; and they show the changes to which the targumic text was subjected in the course of centuries, and which are shown also both by the earliest editions of the Targum to the Prophets and by their relation to the text of the Codex Reuchlinianus. This question is discussed in detail by Bacher, "Kritische Untersuchungen zum Prophetentargum" ("Z. D. M. G." xxviii. 1–58). Additions ("tosefta") to the Targum to the Prophets, similar in most cases to those in the Targum Yerushalmi, are also cited, especially by David Ḳimḥi. The chief extant portion of this Palestinian Targum is the translation of the haftarot (see Zunz, "G. V." pp. 79, 412).

Targum to the Hagiographa: The Babylonian Targumim to the Pentateuch and that to the Prophets were the only ones which enjoyed official recognition; so that even in Babylonia there was no authorized Targum to the Hagiographa, since this portion of the Bible furnished no sidrot for public worship. This fact is mentioned in the legend, already noted, that Jonathan ben Uzziel was forbidden to translate the Hagiographa. Nevertheless, there are extant Targumim on the hagiographic books; they are, for the most part, Palestinian in origin, although the Babylonian Talmud and its language influenced the Targumim on the Five Megillot.

1. To the Psalms and to Job: These Targumim form a separate group, and, in view of their entire agreement in diction, hermeneutics, and use of the Haggadah, may have a common origin. In no other Targum, excepting the Targum Sheni to Esther, does ἄγγελος, the Greek word for "angel," occur. In rendering Ps. xviii., the Targum to Psalms avails itself of the Targum to II Sam. xxii., although it does not reproduce the linguistic peculiarities found in the Babylonian recension of the latter. The Targum to Psalms contains an interesting dramatization of Ps. xci., cxviii., and cxxxvii., while both in it and in the Targum to Job the two constant themes are the law of God and its study, and the future life and its retribution. In Ps. cviii. 12 the parallel construction in the two sections of the verse is interpreted in such a way as to mention Rome and Constantinople as the two capitals of the Roman empire, thus indicating that the work was composed before the fall of Rome in 476. The Targum to Job iv. 10 (where שֵׁנִי is read instead of שִׁנֵּי) also seems to allude to the division of the empire; and this hypothesis is confirmed by the presence of a Greek and a Latin word in the Targum to Job, which in all cases renders "nagid" or "nadib" by ἄρχων (on this word as an official title in the Jewish communities, see Schürer, "Gesch." ii. 518), and translates "ḥanef" by "delator," a term which was applied in the Roman empire to the vilest class of informers. Characteristic of both these Targumim is the fact that they contain more variants from the Masoretic text in vowel-points and even in consonants than any other Targum, about fifty of them occurring in the Targum to Psalms, and almost as many being found in the Targum to Job, despite its relative brevity. A number of these variants occur also in the Septuagint and in the Peshiṭta, thus affording a confirmation of the early date of composition assigned to the two Targumim. Both of these contain, moreover, a number of variants, fifty verses of Job having two, and sometimes three, translations, of which the second is the original, while the later reading is put first (for a confirmation of the statements in "Monatsschrift," xx. 218, see Perles, *ib.* vii. 147, and "R. E. J." xxi. 122). The Targum to Psalms, like that to Job, is quoted by Naḥmanides under the title "Targum Yerushalmi" (Zunz, "G. V." p. 80).

2. To Proverbs: This Targum differs from all other Judæo-Aramaic translations of the Bible in that it shows Syriac characteristics, and also agrees in other respects with the Peshiṭta, to which, according to Geiger ("Nachgelassene Schriften," iv. 112), one-half of it corresponds word for word. This Targum contains scarcely any haggadic paraphrases. It may be assumed either that its author used or, rather, revised the Peshiṭta, or, with a greater degree of probability, that the Targum to Proverbs was derived from the same source as the Peshiṭta of that book, the Syriac version itself being based on a translation originally intended for Jews who spoke the Syriac dialect. This Targum also is quoted in the "'Aruk" and by Naḥmanides as "Targum Yerushalmi" (Zunz, *l.c.*).

3. To the Five Megillot: These Targumim are alike in so far as all of them are essentially detailed haggadic paraphrases. This is especially the case in the Targum to Canticles, in which the book is interpreted as an allegory of the relation between God and Israel and of the history of Israel. In the "'Aruk," the first work to cite these Targumim, the Targum to Canticles is once (*s.v.* פלטיא) called "Targum Yerushalmi"; and Rashi applies the same name (Targ. Yer. to Deut. iii. 4) to the second Targum on Esther, the so-called "Targum Sheni," which may be termed, in view of its length, and of the fact that it betrays eastern Aramaic influences in its diction, an Aramaic midrash on Esther. This last-named work, which is quoted as early as the Massek. Soferim (xiii. 6), has proved extremely popular. The Book of Esther is the only one of the hagiographic books which has a Targum noticed by the Halakah, rules for its reading having been formulated as early as the tannaitic period. The other "scrolls," however, were also used to a certain extent in the liturgy, being read on festivals and on the Ninth of Ab, which fact explains the discursiveness of their Targumim.

4. To Chronicles: This Targum follows the Palestinian Targumim both in language and in its haggadic paraphrases, although it shows the influence of the Babylonian Talmud also. It remained almost wholly unknown, however, not being cited even in the "'Aruk," nor included in the first editions of the Targumim. It was first published in 1680 (and 1683) by M. F. Beck from an Erfurt codex of 1343; and it was again edited, by D. Wilkins in 1715, on the basis of a Cambridge manuscript of 1347, this edition containing a later revision of the targumic text.

Among the apocryphal additions to Esther the "Ḥalom Mordekai" (Dream of Mordecai) has been preserved in a Targum which is designated in a manuscript as an integral portion of the Targum to the Hagiographa. This passage, divided into fifty-one verses in Biblical fashion, has been printed in Lagarde's edition of the Targumim ("Hagiographa Chaldaice." pp. 352-365) and in Merx's "Chrestomathia Targumica," pp. 154-164 (see Bacher in "Monatsschrift," 1869, xviii. 543 *et seq.*). On the Targum to the Book of Tobit, known to Jerome, and preserved in a recension published by A. Neubauer ("The Book of Tobit," Oxford, 1878), see Dalman, "Grammatik des Jüdisch-Palästinensischen Aramäisch," pp. 27-29). It is probable, moreover, that a complete Aramaic translation of Ben Sira once existed (*ib.* p. 29).

The view prevailed at an early time that the amora Joseph b. Ḥama, who had the reputation of being thoroughly versed in the Targumim to the Prophets, was the author of the Targumim to the

Hagiographa. In the Masseket Soferim (*l.c.*) a quotation from the Targum Sheni to Esth. iii. 1 is introduced by the words "Tirgem Rab Yosef" (Rab Joseph has translated); and a manuscript of 1238, in the municipal library of Breslau, appends to the "Dream of Mordecai" the statement: "This is the end of the book of the Targum on the Hagiographa, translated by Rab Joseph." The manuscript from which the copyist of the Breslau codex took the "Dream of Mordecai," together with this colophon, included therefore all the Targumim to the Hagiographa, excepting that to Chronicles, the one to Esther standing last (see "Monatsschrift," xviii. 343). In his commentary on Ex. xv. 2 and Lev. xx. 17, moreover, Samuel ben Meïr, writing in the twelfth century, quoted targumic passages on Job and Proverbs in the name of R. Joseph. The belief that Joseph was the translator of the Hagiographa was due to the fact that the phrase frequently found in the Talmud, "as Rab Joseph has translated," was referred to the Targum to the Hagiographa, although it occurred only in passages from the Prophets and, according to one reading (Soṭah 48b), in a single passage of the Pentateuch. The Palestinian characteristics of the hagiographic Targumim, and the fact that the translations of the several books are differentiated according to the grouping noted above, prove that the view is historically baseless. The Tosafot (to Shab. 115a, below), since they ascribed a tannaitic origin to the Targum to the Hagiographa (comp. Tos. to Meg. 21b), naturally refused to accept the theory of Joseph's authorship.

Bibliography: Editions—Targum to the Pentateuch: Onḳelos, editio princeps, Bologna, 1482; Sabbionetta, 1557 (reprinted by Berliner, *Targum Onḳelos*, Berlin, 1884); pseudo-Jonathan, Venice, 1591; *Fragment-Targum*, in *Biblia Rabbinica*, Appendix, *ib.* 1518. Targum to the Prophets: editio princeps, Leiria, 1494; Venice, 1518; Lagarde, *Prophetæ Chaldaice*, Leipsic, 1872. Prætorius has edited *Joshua* and *Judges* on the basis of manuscripts from Yemen with superlinear punctuation (1900, 1901; see *Theologische Literaturzeitung*, xxv. 164, xxvi. 131); Alfr. Levy, *Ḳohelet*, Breslau, 1905. Targum to the Hagiographa: Venice, 1517; Lagarde, *Hagiographa Chaldaice*, Leipsic, 1873. On the editions of the Targum to Chronicles see above. *Targum Sheni*, ed. L. Munk, Berlin, 1876. The polyglot and rabbinical Bibles (see Berliner, *l.c.* ii. 187–190), as well as numerous other editions. The three Targumim to the Pentateuch were translated into English by J. W. Etheridge (London, 1862, 1865); and German translations of considerable length are given by Winter and Wünsche, *Die Jüdische Litteratur*, i. 63–79.
On the Targum in general: the various introductions to the Bible: Zunz, *G. V.* pp. 61–83; Z. Frankel, *Einiges zu den Targumim*, in *Zeitschrift für die Religiösen Interessen des Judenthums*, 1846, iii. 110–111; Geiger, *Urschrift*, pp. 162–167; idem, *Nachgelassene Schriften*, iv. 98–116; G. Dalman, *Grammatik des Jüdisch-Palästinensischen Aramäisch*, pp. 21–27; Hamburger, *R. B. T.* ii. 1167–1195; E. Nestle, in *Bibeltext und Bibelübertragungen*, pp. 163–170, Leipsic, 1897; Buhl, *Kanon und Text des Alten Testaments*, 1891, pp. 168–184.
On the Targumim to the Pentateuch: Luzzatto, *Oheb Ger*, Vienna, 1830 (see Cracow ed. 1895); Levy, *Ueber Onḳelos*, etc., in Geiger's *Wiss. Zeit. Jüd. Theol.* 1844, vol. v.: Fürst, in *Orient, Lit.* 1845; A. Geiger, *Das Nach Onḳelos Benannte Babylonische Targum*, in his *Jüd. Zeit.* ix. 85–194; A. Berliner, *Das Targum Onḳelos*, ii., Berlin, 1884; Anger, *De Onḳelo Chaldaico*, Leipsic, 1846; M. Friedmann, *Onḳelos und Akylas*, Vienna, 1896; Schönfelder, *Onḳelos und Peschitta*, Munich, 1864; Maybaum, *Die Anthropomorphien und Anthropopathien bei Onḳelos*, etc., Breslau, 1870; S. Singer, *Onḳelos und das Verhältniss Seines Targum zur Halacha*, Frankfort-on-the-Main, 1881; H. Barnstein, *The Targum of Onḳelos to Genesis*, London, 1896; E. Kautzsch, *Mittheilungen über eine Alte Handschrift des Targum Onḳelos*, Halle, 1893; A. Merx, *Anmerkungen über die Vocalisation der Targume*, in *Verhandlungen des Fünften Orientalistencongresses*, ii. 1, 145–188; G. B. Winer, *De Jonathanis in Pentateuchum Paraphrasi Chaldaica*, Erlangen, 1823; H. Petermann, *De Indole Targumi Paraphraseos Quem Jonathanis Esse Dicitur*, Berlin, 1831; S. Baer, *Geist des Yeruschalmi*, in *Monatsschrift*, 1851–52, i. 235–242; Seligsohn and

Traub, *Ueber den Geist der Uebersetzung des Jonathan b. Usiel zum Pentateuch*, *ib.* 1857, vi. 69–114; Seligsohn, *De Duabus Hierosolymitanis Pentateuchi Paraphrasibus*, Breslau, 1858; S. Gronemann, *Die Jonathan'sche Pentateuchübersetzung in Ihrem Verhältnisse zur Halacha*, Leipsic, 1879; W. Bacher, *Ueber das Gegenseitige Verhältniss der Pentateuch-Targumim*, in *Z. D. M. G.* 1874, xxviii. 59–72; J. Bassfreund, *Das Fragmenten-Targum zum Pentateuch*, in *Monatsschrift*, 1896, xl. 1–14, 49, 67, 97–109, 145–163, 241–252, 352–365, 396–405; M. Neumark, *Lexikalische Untersuchungen zur Sprache des Jerusalemischen Pentateuch-Targum*, Berlin, 1905.
On the Targum to the Prophets: Z. Frankel, *Zu dem Targum der Propheten*, Breslau, 1872; H. S. Levy, *Targum to Isaiah i., with Commentary*, London, 1889; Cornill, *Das Targum zu den Propheten*, i., in Stade's *Zeitschrift*, vii. 731–767; idem, *Das Buch des Propheten Ezechiel*, 1886, pp. 110–136; H. Weiss, *Die Peschitha zu Deutero-Jesaja und Ihr Verhältniss zum . . . Targum*, Halle, 1893; M. Sebök (Schönberger), *Die Syrische Uebersetzung der Zwölf Kleinen Propheten und Ihr Verhältniss zum . . . Targum*, Breslau, 1887.
On the Targum to the Hagiographa: W. Bacher, *Das Targum zu den Psalmen*, in *Monatsschrift*, 1872, xxi. 408–416, 462–673; idem, *Das Targum zu Hiob*, ib. 1871, xx. 208–223, 283 *et seq.*; S. Maybaum, *Ueber die Sprache des Targum zu den Sprüchen und Dessen Verhältniss zum Syrer*, in Merx's *Archiv*, ii. 66–93; T. Nöldeke, *Das Targum zu den Sprüchen*, ib. pp. 246–249; H. Pinkusz, *Die Syrische Uebersetzung der Proverbien . . . und Ihr Verhältniss zum Targum*, in Stade's *Zeitschrift*, 1894, xiv. 65–141, 161–162; A. Abelesz, *Die Syrische Uebersetzung der Klagelieder und Ihr Verhältniss zum Targum*, Giessen, 1896; A. Weiss, *De Libri Job Paraphrasi Chaldaica*, Breslau, 1873; A. Posner, *Das Targum Rischon zu dem Biblischen Buche Esther*, ib. 1896; S. Gelbhaus, *Das Targum Sheni zum Buche Esther*, Frankfort-on-the-Main, 1893; J. Reis, *Das Targum Sheni zu dem Buche Esther*, in *Monatsschrift*, 1876, xxv.; 1881, xxx.; P. Cassel, *Zweites Targum zum Buche Esther*, Leipsic, 1885; M. Rosenberg and K. Kohler, *Das Targum zur Chronik*, in Geiger's *Jüd. Zeit.* 1870, viii. 72–80, 135–163, 263–278.
Hebrew works on the Targum: the commentaries *Patshegen* of the thirteenth century, printed in the Wilna edition of the Pentateuch, 1874; N. Adler, *Netinah la-Ger*, in the same edition; S. B. Scheftel, *Bi'ure Onḳelos*, ed. I. Perles, Munich, 1888; Abraham ben Elijah of Wilna, *Targum Abraham*, Jerusalem, 1896. Other Hebrew works: Isaiah Berlin, *Mine Targima*, Breslau, 1831: Wilna, 1836; H. Chajes, *Imre Binah*, Zolkiev, 1849; B. Berkowitz, *'Oṭeh Or*, Wilna, 1843; idem, *Leḥem we-Simlah*, ib. 1850; idem, *Ḥaliſot u-Semalot*, ib. 1874; idem, *Abne Ziyyon*, ib. 1877; J. Reifmann, *Sedeh Aram*, Berlin, 1875; idem, *Ma'amar Darke ha-Targumim*, St. Petersburg, 1891.

W. B.

TARNOPOL: Polish town in eastern Galicia, formerly Austria; on the Sereth, founded in 1540 by the Polish hetman Johann Tarnowski. Polish Jews were admitted, and soon predominated; during the sixteenth and seventeenth centuries there were 300 Jewish families in the city. Among the towns destroyed by Chmielnicki during his march of devastation from Zloczow through Galicia was Tarnopol, the large Jewish population of which carried on an extensive trade. Shortly afterward, however, when the Cossacks had been subdued by John Casimir II., of Poland, the town began to prosper anew, and its Jewish population exceeded all previous figures. It may be noted that Ḥasidism at this time dominated the community, which opposed any introduction of Western culture. During the troublous times in the latter part of the eighteenth century the city was stormed (1770) by the adherents of the Confederacy of Bar, who massacred many of its inhabitants, especially the Jews.

After the second partition of Poland, Tarnopol came under Austrian domination; and Joseph Perl was able to continue his efforts to improve the condition of the Jews there, which he had begun under Russian rule. In 1813 he established a Jewish school which had for its chief object the instruction of Jewish youth in German as well as in Hebrew and various other branches. The controversy between the Ḥasidim and the Maskilim which this school caused resulted four years later in a victory for the latter, whereupon the institution received official recognition and was placed under communal control. Since 1863 the school policy has gradually been modified by Polish influences, and very little attention has been given to instruction in German. The Tempel für Geregelten Gottesdienst, opened by Perl in 1819, also caused dissensions within the community, and its rabbi, S. J. Rapoport, was forced to withdraw. This dispute also was eventually settled in favor of the Maskilim. In 1905 rabbi of the Tempel was Dr. Taubeles, who officiated also as a teacher of religion in the local gymnasium. In the year 1921 the Jewish community numbered about 12,000 in a total population of 30,921. The Jews are engaged principally in an active import and export trade with Russia through the border city of Podwoloczyska.

BIBLIOGRAPHY: *Allg. Zeit. des Jud.* 1839, iii. 606; A. Bresler, *Joseph Perl*, Warsaw, 1879, *passim*; Orgelbrandt, in *Encyklopedja Powszechna*, xiv. 409; J. H. Gurland, *Le-Korot ha-Gezerot*, p. 22, Odessa, 1892; *Meyers Konversations-Lexikon.*

J. S. O.

TARNOW: Town of Polish Galicia. An organized community existed there in the middle of the sixteenth century. The Jews were, for the most part, under the jurisdiction of the lords of Tarnow, the city being the hereditary possession of the latter. In 1637 Ladislaus Dominik granted the Jews a privilege placing them under the jurisdiction of the castle, assuring them of protection, and permitting them to engage in commerce on the same footing as other citizens. In 1654, however, popular jealousy, combined with the intrigues of the magistracy, secured the abrogation of this privilege; but when the town was brought to the verge of ruin in 1670 by the plague, conflagrations, and attacks of the Swedes, Alexander Janusz, its overlord, was forced to restore the privilege to the Jews in the interest of the town. This privilege was confirmed by Michael Radziwill in the same year, by Stanislaus Koniecepolski in 1676, and by Katarina Radziwill in 1681 and 1684.

In 1670 Janusz succeeded in effecting the following agreement between the Jewish inhabitants and the magistrate and the gilds: (1) the Jews should pay 30 per cent of all municipal taxes; (2) they should purchase goods only from the gilds within the town, except at the annual and weekly fairs; (3) they should surrender to the gilds a certain percentage of all goods purchased in the markets for retail purposes.

When misfortune on misfortune had reduced Tarnow to ruins early in the eighteenth century, its revival was due to the Jews, who paid, in accordance with a decree of Paul, Prince Sanguszko, then the lord of Tarnow, about three-fourths of all the taxes of the municipality (1730), receiving in return certain commercial privileges. Scarcely had the town been reestablished by these measures when the citizens, and even more eagerly the Christian gilds, resumed their attacks upon the Jews and the Jewish gilds, which had been organized about that time. This crusade was headed by the clergy, who insisted on Jewish isolation, although they maintained profitable business relations with the synagogue of Tarnow.

In 1765 the community numbered 2,325 persons, but it ceased to exist on the partition of Poland (1772). The population of Tarnow in 1921 was 35,725.

s. I. Sc.

TARRAGONA (טרגונה, טרכונה): Capital of the province of Tarragona, Spain; the ancient **Tarraco.** It was called the "City of the Jews" by Edrisi (ed. Conde, p. 64), and contained a community at an early date, as is shown by Jewish coins discovered in the course of excavations there some decades ago (Helfferich, "Der Westgothische Arianismus," p. 68, Berlin, 1860). The Jews' quarter was in the street now known as Plaza de las Monjas de la Enseñanza; and their cemetery was near the Plaza del Milagro. When the Count of Barcelona won Catalonia from the Moors, he granted rights and privileges to the Jews of Tarragona, whose ghetto contained ninety-five houses in 1239. They elected their own administrators, and engaged in commerce, industry, and brokerage, their circumstances and their taxes being similar to those of their coreligionists at Barcelona and other Catalonian cities. In 1322 the Archbishop of Tarragona confiscated the property of the Jews of the city, and in 1348 almost 300 Jews were killed at Tarragona and the neighboring Solsona, while in 1391 the community suffered the same fate as that of Barcelona, many of its members being slain. Even after this Tarragona was the residence of a number of Jews, who were noted for their piety. Isaac Arama officiated for some time as rabbi there; and a certain D. Benjamin was city physician. Two tombstones with Hebrew inscriptions, dating from the years 1300 and 1302, have recently been found at Tarragona: one (1½ meters wide and 43 centimeters high) marks the grave of Ḥayyim b. Isaac, who died in the month of Nisan, 1300; and the other commemorates Hananiah b. Simeon ארלבי, perhaps Alrabi.

Tarragona must not be confounded with Tarazona in Aragon, where the philosopher and apologist Shem-Ṭob ben Isaac ibn Shaprut lived for a time, and where there was a small but wealthy community, which paid a poll-tax of 145 "sueldos jaqueses" in 1282, and one of 200 "sueldos" in the middle of the fourteenth century.

BIBLIOGRAPHY: Solomon ben Adret, *Responsa*, Nos. 391, 452, 1234; Isaac ben Sheshet, *Responsa*, Nos. 210, 226, 515; Rios, *Hist.* i. 245 *et seq.*; ii. 14, 297; iii. 229; Joseph ha-Kohen, *'Emeḳ ha-Baka*, p. 66 (where שרכונה should be read instead of ארלקונה; see Wiener's German translation, pp. 53, 185); *R. E. J.* xiii. 241; *Boletin Acad. Hist.* xliii. 460 *et seq.*; Fidel Fita, *La España Hebrea*, i. 175.

G. M. K.

TARRASCH, SIEGBERT: German physician and chess-master; born at Breslau March 5, 1862; studied medicine at the universities of Berlin, Halle, and Nuremberg, in which last-named city he engaged in practise as a physician. Tarrasch has been one of the most successful of modern chess-players, as the following list shows. In the tournaments at Manchester, Dresden, and Leipsic he lost but a single game.

1884. Nuremberg, first prize.	1889. Breslau, first prize.
1885. Hamburg, tied for second prize.	1890. Manchester, first prize.
	1892. Dresden, first prize.
1887. Frankfort-on-the-Main, divided fifth and sixth prizes.	1894. Leipsic, first prize.
	1805. Hastings, fourth prize.
	1896. Nuremberg, fourth prize.

In 1893 he played a drawn match with Tchigorin, 9 games all, 4 being drawn. In 1905, at Nuremberg, he played with Marshall a match of eight games up (draws not counted) in which the American player won only one game.

Tarrasch is an able writer on chess; and his annotations of games evince great analytical power. For some time he was joint editor with Gottschall of the "Schachzeitung." He has published "Dreihundert Schachpartieen Gespielt und Erläutert" (Leipsic, 1894).

Bibliography: *Meyers Konversations-Lexikon*; C. T. Blaushard, *Examples of Chess Master-Play*, 2d series, London, 1894.

s.   A. P.

TARREGA: City of Catalonia. Jews were among its inhabitants when the counts of Barcelona took Catalonia from the Moors. They enjoyed certain privileges, which were confirmed in 1332 and later. At the special request of the king the community was permitted in 1346 to build a new synagogue 80 feet long, 50 feet wide, and 60 feet high; also a school. On this occasion Pedro Montell, vicar of the Bishop of Vich, assured the Jews that, in conformity with canonical law, their cemeteries should not be desecrated, nor they themselves disturbed on their holy days; further that any one found guilty of acting contrary to this assurance would be strictly punished. Three years later, on the Ninth of Ab (July 26), the citizens of Tarrega attacked the Jews, killing more than 300, throwing their bodies into a pit, and plundering their houses. The survivors, robbed of all their possessions, fled, and remained hidden until the danger had passed.

Many Jews of Tarrega were killed during the persecutions of 1391; but a small community continued to dwell in the town, and it sent delegates to the funeral services held for King James at Cervera. In the civil war of 1462 some Jews of Tarrega and Cervera were killed and their possessions confiscated.

Bibliography: Rios, *Hist.* ii. 162 *et seq.*; Jacobs, *Sources*, Nos. 1001, 1189; Joseph ha-Kohen, '*Emek ha-Baka*, p. 66.

J.   M. K.

TARSHISH: In the genealogical table of the Noachidæ, Tarshish is given as the second son of Javan and is followed by Kittim and Dodanim (Gen. x. 4; I Chron. i. 7). As with all these names, Tarshish denotes a country; in several instances, indeed, it is mentioned as a maritime country lying in the remotest region of the earth. Thus, Jonah flees to Tarshish from the presence of Yhwh (Jonah i. 3, iv. 2). With Pul, Tubal, and Javan, it is mentioned as one of the remote places that have not heard of Yhwh (Isa. lxvi. 19, comp. lx. 9; Ps. lxxii. 10; Ezek. xxxviii. 13). Any large vessel capable of making a long sea-voyage was styled a "ship of Tarshish," though this did not necessarily mean that the vessel sailed either to or from Tarshish (Ps. xlviii. 7; I Kings x. 22, xxii. 48; Isa. ii. 16; *et al.*). It seems that in parallel passages referring to Solomon's and Jehoshaphat's ships (I Kings *l.c.*) the author of Chronicles did not understand the meaning of "ships of Tarshish" (II Chron. ix. 21, xx. 36).

XII.—5

Tarshish appears to have had a considerable trade in silver, iron, tin, and lead (Jer. x. 9; Ezek. xxvii. 12). It gave its name, besides, to a precious stone which has not yet been satisfactorily identified (see Gems). The Targum of Jonathan renders the word "Tarshish" in the prophetical books by "sea," which rendering is followed by Saadia. Moreover, the term "ships of Tarshish" is rendered by Jewish scholars "sea-ships" (comp. LXX., Isa. ii. 16, πλοῖα θαλάσσης). Jerome, too, renders "Tarshish" by "sea" in many instances; and in his commentary on Isaiah (*l.c.*) he declares that he had been told by his Jewish teachers that the Hebrew word for "sea" was "tarshish." In Isa. xxiii. 1 the Septuagint, and in Ezek. xxvii. 12 both the Septuagint and the Vulgate, render "Tarshish" by "Carthage," apparently suggested by Jewish tradition. Indeed, the Targum of Jonathan renders "Tarshish" in I Kings xxii. 48 and Jer. x. 9 by "Afriki," that is, Carthage.

Josephus ("Ant." i. 6, § 1), apparently reading "Tarshush," identifies it with Tarsus in Cilicia. This identification was adopted by Bunsen and Sayce ("Expository Times," 1902, p. 179); but it seems from Assyrian inscriptions that the original Hebrew name of Tarsus was not "Tarshush." Bochart (in his "Phaleg"), followed by many later scholars, identifies Tarshish with Tartessus, mentioned by Herodotus and Strabo as a district of southern Spain; he thinks, moreover, that "Tartessus" is the Aramaic form of "Tarshish." On the other hand, Le Page Renouf ("Proc. Soc. Bibl. Arch." xvi. 104 *et seq.*) refutes this theory, declaring beside that Tartessus never really existed. Renouf's opinion is that "Tarshish" means a coast, and, as the word occurs frequently in connection with Tyre, the Phenician coast is to be understood. Cheyne (in "Orientalische Litteraturzeitung," iii. 151) thinks that "Tarshish" of Gen. x. 4, and "Tiras" of Gen. x. 2, are really two names of one nation derived from two different sources, and might indicate the Tyrsenians or Etruscans. Thus the name may denote Italy or the European coasts west of Greece.

s.   M. Sel.

TARSUS: Turkish town in the vilayet of Adana, 12 miles from the Mediterranean, on the River Cydnus. During the Roman period it was the capital of Cilicia. It was important on account of its commerce and its textile products, and was famed for its schools of rhetoric. In Tarsus, as in Cilicia generally, the original population was Semitic, a fact reflected in the tradition that the city was a Phenician colony (Dio Chrysostom, "Orationes," xxxiii. 40), while on Phenician coins it was often called "Taraz" (תרז). Josephus ("Ant." i. 6, § 1), in agreement with rabbinical literature (Gen. R. xxxvii. 1; Yer. Meg. 71b; Targ. Yer. to Gen. x. 4), identified the city with Tarshish (Gen. x. 4), and accordingly believed it was to Tarsus that Jonah wished to flee ("Ant." ix. 10, § 2). A monument to Jonah was discovered in Tarsus in 1876; but it doubtless dates from the Christian period.

The Hellenization of the city began in the days of Alexander the Great; this influence was fully felt by the Jews, who had been colonized at Tarsus by the Seleucids about 170 B.C. During the reign of Antiochus Epiphanes a revolt of these colonists proved a factor in Jewish history (II Macc. iv. 30–38). Nothing further is known regarding the Jews of this city, although it later became famous as the birthplace of SAUL OF TARSUS, who lived there for a time (Acts ix. 11, xi. 25, xxi. 39, xxii. 3) and claimed Roman citizenship in virtue thereof. Ramsay, followed by Schürer, has proved (see Hastings, "Dict. Bible," ii. 105, s.v. "Diaspora") that a Jew could not have been a citizen in a Greek town unless the sovereign had ordered that the Jews of the city in question form a separate gens, an event which must have happened in Tarsus, probably, as Ramsay thinks, at the instance of Antiochus Epiphanes ("Expository Times," xvi. 18 et seq.).

The city of Tarsus is frequently mentioned by the Rabbis. There R. Jose ben Jasian boarded a vessel (Eccl. R. vii. 11), and R. Nahum ben Simai lectured (Pesiḳ. R. 15 [ed. Friedmann, p. 78a]). The Rabbis allude to the inhabitants and the language of Tarsus in connection with Bigthan and Teresh (Esth. ii. 21), although the exact meaning of this passage is not clear. The presence of Jews in Tarsus is further evidenced by inscriptions: one in Rome names a certain Asaphat of Tarsus (Levy, in "Jahrbuch für die Gesch. der Juden," ii. 287), and an epitaph found at Jaffa was inscribed to the memory of one Judah ben Joseph of the same city (Schürer, "Gesch." 3d ed., iii. 17). Mention is likewise made of one Isaac, elder of the synagogue of the Cappadocians at Tarsus, who was a dealer in linen ("Pal. Explor. Fund, Quarterly Statement," No. 110, p. 18), proving not only the existence of a Jewish community at Tarsus but also Jewish participation in mercantile pursuits. In the Middle Ages the town came under the dominion of the Isaurians and other barbarians, later falling into the hands of the Arabs and Turks, who deprived it of its importance. In 1905 the permanent population was about 7,000.

BIBLIOGRAPHY: Ritter, Erdkunde, ii. 197–220; Winer, B. R.; Boettger, Lexicon zu Flavius Josephus; S. Krauss, in Monatsschrift, xxxix. 53; Hastings, Dict. Bible.
J.   S. KR.

TARTAK: Deity mentioned but once in the Bible (II Kings xvii. 31). His name occurs together with that of NIBHAZ or Nibhan, who was a divinity of the Avites, a tribe colonized by Sargon on Israelitish soil. In the Babylonian Talmud (Sanh. 63a; comp. Yalḳuṭ Shim'oni, 234) R. Judah, transmitting a saying in the name of Abba Arika, states that Tartak was worshiped in the form of an ass. All attempts to identify this god have thus far proved unsuccessful. No similar divinity is found among the Babylonians or Assyrians; and an Egyptian parallel exists only in so far as the ass was sacred to the god Typhon and was sacrificed to him.
E. C.   S. O.

TARTAN (Assyrian, "tartanu," "turtanu"): Title of an Assyrian official; twice mentioned in the Bible. A tartan, accompanied by a "rabsaris" and a "rab-shakeh," was sent to Jerusalem by Sennacherib to command Hezekiah to surrender the city (II Kings xviii. 17); and another is mentioned as Sar-

gon's envoy to Ashdod in the year of a prophecy of Isaiah (Isa. xx. 1). The title was borne only by the two generals next to the king; thus there were a "tartanu rabu" (great tartan) and a "tartanu shanu" (second tartan). It is no longer possible to identify the tartans mentioned in the Bible, although the names of three of these officials are known: Ashur-isku (?)-udannim in 720 (the first year of Sargon's reign), Ilu-ittea in 694 (the beginning of the reign of Sennacherib), and Bel-emuranni in 686.

BIBLIOGRAPHY: Delitzsch, Assyriologisches Handwörterbuch.
S.   S. O.

TARTAS, DAVID. See CASTRO TARTAS, DAVID B. ABRAHAM.

TARTAS, ISAAC DE CASTRO. See CASTRO TARTAS, ISAAC.

TARYAG MIẒWOT. See COMMANDMENTS, THE 613.

TASHLIK: Propitiatory rite, the name of which is derived from the passage (Micah vii. 18–20) recited at the ceremony. In illustration of the sentence "Thou wilt cast all their sins into the depths of the sea," it is customary to congregate near a running stream on the afternoon of New-Year's Day, when Micah vii. 18–20 is recited and penitential prayers are offered. The prayers and hymns used are given in Emden's Siddur ("Bet Ya'aḳob," ii. 54b, 55a, Warsaw, 1881).

When and where the custom was first introduced is problematical. Kalman Schulman (in "Ha-Meliẓ," 1868, viii., No. 14) is of the opinion that it is referred to in Josephus ("Ant." xiv. 10, § 23), in the decree of the Halicarnassians permitting Jews to "perform their holy rites according to the Jewish laws and to have their places of prayer by the sea, according to the customs of their forefathers." The Zohar, perhaps, refers to the custom when it says that "whatever falls into the deep is lost forever; . . . it acts like the scapegoat for the ablution of sins" (Zohar, Leviticus, p. 101a, b). But the fact that the Talmud, the geonic literature, and the early casuistic authorities are silent on this custom gives the impression that it originated not earlier than the fourteenth century, with the German Jews. The first direct reference to it is by R. Jacob Mölln (d 1425) in "Sefer Maharil" (p. 38a, Warsaw, 1874); where, by the midrashic haggadah of the "Sefer ha-Yashar," he explains the minhag as a reminder of the "'Aḳedah" incident; i.e., Satan, by throwing himself across Abraham's path in the form of a deep stream, endeavored to prevent him from sacrificing Isaac on Mount Moriah; Abraham and Isaac nevertheless plunged into the river up to their necks and prayed for divine aid, whereupon the river disappeared (comp. Tan., Wayera, 22). Mölln, however, forbids the practise of throwing pieces of bread to the fish in the river during the ceremony, especially on the Sabbath, being opposed to carrying the bread without an 'ERUB. This shows that in his time tashlik was duly performed, even when the first day of New-Year fell on the Sabbath, though in later times the ceremony was on such occasions deferred till the second day. The significance of the fish is thus explained by R. Isaiah Horowitz

TASHLIK CEREMONY IN GALICIA

("Shelah," p. 214b): (1) they illustrate man's plight, and also arouse him to repentance: "As the fishes that are taken in an evil net" (Eccl. ix. 12); (2) as fishes have no eyebrows and their eyes are always wide open, they symbolize the guardian of Israel, who slumbereth not. Moses Isserles gives this explanation: "The deeps of the sea saw the genesis of Creation; therefore to throw bread into the sea on New-Year's Day, the anniversary of Creation, is an appropriate tribute to the Creator" ("Torat ha-'Olah," iii. 56).

The cabalistic practise of shaking the ends of one's garments at the ceremony, as though casting off the "ḳelippot" (lit. "shells"; i.e., the clinging demons of sin), has caused many who are not cabalists to denounce the whole custom, as it created the impression among the common people that by literally throwing their sins into the river to be swept away by the stream, they might escape them without repenting and making amends. The Maskilim in particular have ridiculed the custom and characterized it as heathenish. The best satire on this subject is by Isaac Erter, in his "Ha-Ẓofeh le-Bet Yisrael" (pp. 64-80, Vienna, 1864), in which Samael watches the sins of the hypocrites dropping into the river. The Orthodox Jews of New York perform the ceremony in large numbers from the Brooklyn and Manhattan bridges.

BIBLIOGRAPHY: *Shulḥan 'Aruk, Oraḥ Ḥayyim*, 583, 2, Isserles' note; Baer's *Siddur*, *'Abodat Yisrael*, p. 407; Moses Brück, *Rabbinische Ceremonialgebräuche*, § 4, Breslau, 1837; I. Abrahams, in *Jew. Chron.* Sept. 27, 1889.
s. J. D. E.

TATNAI (R. V. **Tattenai**): Governor of Cœle-Syria under Darius Hystaspes (Ezra v. 3). He was one of those who tried to prevent Zerubbabel and Jeshua from continuing the building of the Temple, and who sent to Darius asking that search be made in the royal archives to ascertain whether there was any foundation for the claim put forward by the Jews that Cyrus had given them permission to rebuild the sanctuary.

According to Eduard Meyer ("Entstehung des Judenthums," p. 32, Halle, 1896; comp. also Justi, "Iranisches Namenbuch"), the Old Persian name was probably "Thithinaya" or "Thathanaia." Both the Septuagint and Josephus ("Ant." xi. 4, §§ 5, 6, 7) transcribe the name by Σισίνης.

s. S. O.

TAUBE, DIE. See PERIODICALS.

TAUBER-BISCHOFSHEIM. See BISCHOFS-HEIM-ON-THE-TAUBER.

TAUBES, AARON MOSES B. JACOB: Rumanian rabbi and author; born in Lemberg 1787; died in Jassy 1852. He became rabbi of Sniatyn and its districts in 1820, and in 1841 was appointed rabbi of Jassy, where he remained until his death. His works are: (1) "To'afot Re'em," responsa on the four parts of the Shulḥan 'Aruk. Among these are some written to his son R. Samuel and some to his grandson R. Shalom Taubes (Zolkiev, 1855). (2) "Ḳarne Re'em," novellæ on the Talmud, mentioned in "She'elat Shalom," No. 254. (3) Novellæ on Alfasi (according to Walden in his "Shem ha-Gedolim he-Ḥadash," Let. A, No. 129), which remained in

manuscript. He corresponded on halakic subjects with Rabbi Solomon Kluger and with Rabbi Jacob Ornstein, author of "Yeshu'ot Ya'aḳob."

BIBLIOGRAPHY: Buber, *Anshe Shem*, p. 27.
E. C. N. T. L.

TAURIDA, RUSSIA. See CRIMEA.

TAUSIG, CARL: Polish pianist and composer; born at Warsaw Nov. 4, 1841; died at Leipsic July 17, 1871. He received his early musical education from his father, Aloys T. Tausig (1820-85), who was a pupil of Thalberg and a composer of brilliant pianoforte music. When Carl was fourteen years of age his father took him to Weimar to study under Liszt, whose favorite pupil he soon became. In 1858 he made his début in public at an orchestral concert conducted by Bülow at Berlin; and during the following two years he gave concerts in various German cities. After a sojourn at Dresden he went to Vienna (1862), where, however, his classical programs and his artistic views failed to find acceptance. He married in 1865 and settled in Berlin, where he opened a Schule des Höheren Klavierspiels, and occasionally gave pianoforte recitals. Shortly before his death he made several concert tours through Germany and Russia, and was everywhere received with enthusiasm.

Carl Tausig ranks with Liszt and Rubinstein as one of the three greatest pianists of the nineteenth century. He was one of the stanchest champions of the "music of the future," and a close personal friend of Richard Wagner. It was he who formulated a plan for raising 300,000 thaler for building the Bayreuth Theater, and who "with his exceptional endowment and splendid energy seemed to regard the execution of this plan as his own particular task" (Richard Wagner, "Gesammelte Schriften," ix. 385). An epitaph composed by Wagner (*l.c.* p. 386) was inscribed on Tausig's tombstone.

Of Tausig's original compositions and numerous arrangements of classical works the following may be mentioned: "Deux Etudes de Concert," replacing an earlier pianoforte transcription of his symphonic ballad "Das Geisterschiff"; "Ungarische Zigeunerweisen," a composition for pianoforte; "Nouvelles Soirées de Vienne"; "Tägliche Studien," finger exercises of high value; a selection of studies from Clementi's "Gradus ad Parnassum"; a transcription of Bach's "Toccata und Fuge für die Orgel in D moll"; and adaptations of Weber's "Aufforderung zum Tanz," of six Beethoven quartets, and of Wagner's "Die Meistersinger von Nürnberg."

BIBLIOGRAPHY: *Musikalisches Wochenblatt*, ii. 488-490, Leipsic, 1871; Grove, *Dictionary of Music and Musicians*; Richard Wagner, *Gesammelte Schriften*, ix. 385, 386; Baker, *Biographical Dictionary of Music*; Kohut, *Berühmte Israelitische Männer und Frauen*.
s. J. So.

TAUSSIG, EDWARD DAVID: American naval officer; born at St. Louis, Mo., Nov. 20, 1847. Educated in the St. Louis schools, he entered the United States Naval Academy at Annapolis in 1863, graduating in 1867, since which date he was in active service. In 1868 he was appointed ensign; 1870, master; 1872, lieutenant; 1892, lieutenant-commander; 1902, captain; and rear-admiral in 1908. He served on the Pacific and European stations and in the coast-survey until 1898, when he was made commander of the "Bennington." He took possession of Wake Island for the United States, and was placed in charge of Guam when that island was ceded by Spain on Feb. 1, 1899. During the following year he served in the Philippines, and during the early part of 1900 in China, assuming command of the "Yorktown" in June of the latter year. From Nov., 1901, to May, 1902, he served in the navy-yard at Washington, D. C., and at Boston, and was then appointed commander of the "Enterprise." In 1903 he was commander of the navy-yard at Pensacola, Fla. Retired in 1909.

Although of Jewish descent, Taussig was brought up in the Unitarian Church. He died Jan. 29, 1921.

BIBLIOGRAPHY: *Who's Who in America*, 1905.
A. F. T. H.

TAUWITZ, EDUARD : German composer; born Jan. 21, 1812, at Glatz; died July 26, 1894, at Prague. While studying law at the University of Breslau he devoted himself to music under the direction of Wolf and Mosovius. At the same time he took charge of the Akademische Gesangverein. Having decided not to follow a juridical career, he left Breslau in 1837 to accept a call to Wilna as director of the orchestra of the theater there. In 1840 he went in the same capacity to Riga, but in 1843 returned to Breslau, and two years later accepted a similar position in Prague, where he also taught music. On the death of Leopold Zwonar he succeeded him as the director of the Sophienakademie.

Tauwitz was a very prolific composer of songs; he wrote in addition two operettas, "Schmolke und Bakel" and "Bramante." Of his songs the following are worthy of special mention: "Zwölf Soldatenlieder für Vier- und Fünfstimmigen Männergesang" and "Zweiundzwanzig Banner- und Schwertlieder für Vierstimmigen Männergesang."

BIBLIOGRAPHY: Wurzbach, *Biographisches Lexikon*; *Fremdenblatt* (Vienna), 1863, No. 72; Lumir, *Belletristicky Tydennik*, 1851, p. 623.
S.

TAW (ת): The twenty-second letter of the Hebrew alphabet. Its name is connected with "taw" = "sign" (see ALPHABET). "Taw" has a twofold pronunciation: (1) a soft, lisping sound uttered with a gentle expiration, like the Greek "theta" and the English "th" in "thin," and (2) a hard, attenuated sound without expiration, like the English "t"; the latter pronunciation is indicated by a "dagesh lene" in the letter. In the classification of letters (consonants) as it is found for the first time in "Sefer Yezirah" (iv. 3), the "taw" is included in the group of linguals דטלנת, which are formed at the upper edge of the tongue. According to modern phonetic terminology, "taw" is a surd mute dental, corresponding to which is the sonant dental "d." "Taw" sometimes interchanges with the lingual "tet" and the dental "shin." It occurs both as a radical and as a formative element. As a numeral "taw" has (in the later period) the value 400.

T. I. BR.

TAWUS, JACOB B. JOSEPH : Persian translator of the Bible; flourished in the sixteenth century. The polyglot Pentateuch printed at Constantinople in 1546 included a Persian translation in Hebrew characters, in addition to the Targum of Onḳelos and the Arabic rendering by Saadia Gaon. In his preface the editor of the polyglot referred to this version as "a Persian translation which a wise and learned man, R. Jacob b. Joseph Tawus, has made for us"; this is followed by a statement indicating that the translator or the translation had been brought to Constantinople by Moses Hamon, the physician of Sulaiman I. Of the two interpretations, the view which makes the word "hebi'o" refer to the translator, thus implying that Jacob Tawus went to Constantinople at the request of Moses Hamon, is probably correct, as the editor expressly says "us"; the version accordingly seems to have been made by Tawus at Constantinople specifically for this polygot. Except for these data, nothing is known concerning the translator, whose name denotes "peacock." About 1570, however, a certain Jacob ben Issachar Tawus is described in a responsum of R. Moses Alshech (No. 103) as a thorough Talmudist. According to Zunz (in Geiger's "Wiss. Zeit. Jüd. Theol." iv. 391), this Jacob ben Issachar was a nephew of the translator, a view which is far more plausible than that of Kohut, who seeks to identify him with the translator himself by substituting the name Issachar for Joseph ("Kritische Beleuchtung," etc., p. 10). When Moses Hamon accompanied Sulaiman on his first Persian campaign (1534-35), he may have induced the scholarly Persian Jew to return with him to Constantinople (see Grätz, "Gesch." ix. 34). Jacob Tawus based his work on the old traditions of the Judæo-Persian Bible translations (see JEW. ENCYC. vii. 317), although he was influenced in many passages by the Targum of Onḳelos and Saadia's Arabic version, as well as by the commentaries of Rashi and Ibn Ezra. His version, transcribed in Persian characters, was reprinted in 1657 in the fourth volume of the London Polyglot, with a Latin translation by Thomas Hyde; but it remained almost unnoticed until Munk recognized its true character, and determined its date in his "Notice sur R. Saadia Gaon" (Paris, 1838). The work is apparently known to a certain extent among the Jews of Persia, inasmuch as Simeon Ḥakam, the latest Judæo-Persian translator of the Pentateuch, states in the preface to his "Miḳra Meforash" (Jerusalem, 1901, vol. i.) that he remembered seeing as a youth a copy of the Constantinople Polyglot of the Pentateuch in his native place, Bokhara, although he became acquainted with the translation by Tawus only when he found it in the London Polyglot at Jerusalem.

BIBLIOGRAPHY: Kohut, *Kritische Beleuchtung der Persischen Pentateuch-Uebersetzung des Jacob b. Joseph Tawus*, Leipsic, 1871; A. Geiger's review of the same in *Jüd. Zeit.* x. 103-113.
W. B.

ṬAWWAH, ABRAHAM BEN JACOB IBN : Algerian Talmudist; flourished at Algiers in the sixteenth century. On his mother's side he was a grandson of Solomon b. Simeon Duran, and therefore a descendant of Naḥmanides and a great grandson of Simeon b. Zemaḥ Duran I., to all of whom as his ancestors he refers frequently in his responsa. Ṭawwah was the contemporary of Solomon b. Zemaḥ Duran and of his brother Simeon b. Zemaḥ Duran II., the latter's son Zemaḥ having been Ṭawwah's pupil. Of Ṭawwah's responsa thirty-five were inserted in the fourth part of Simeon b. Ẓemaḥ Duran's responsa entitled " Ḥuṭ ha-Meshullash "; others are quoted in part and also copied by various authorities. Judah 'Ayyash quotes a part of Ṭawwah's responsa, entitled " Nofek," in his " Bet Yehudah " (p. 113a) and his " Maṭṭeh Yehudah " (p. 20b), and Solomon Ẓeror, in his " Peri Ẓaddiḳ," No. 10, quotes that part of his responsa entitled " Sappir." It may be concluded that Abraham ibn Ṭawwah divided his responsa into twelve parts, calling them after the precious stones in the high priest's breastplate.

BIBLIOGRAPHY: Fuenn, *Keneset Yisrael*, p. 35; Michael, *Or ha-Ḥayyim*, No. 100.
E. C. M. SEL.

TAX-GATHERERS (מוכסין): During the Egyptian government of Palestine the taxes of each city were annually leased to the highest bidder (Josephus, " Ant." xii. 4, § 3). The lessee paid into the royal treasury a fixed annual sum; and whatever the revenue yielded in excess was his gain, whereas if the sum was not realized he had to bear the loss. Under Ptolemy IV., Philopator, all the royal revenues from Cœle-Syria, Phenicia, and Judea were leased by Joseph ben Tobiah, nephew of the high priest Onias II. He held the office of tax-collector for twenty-two years, and was succeeded by his son Hyrcanus. How exacting the tax-collectors must have been may be judged from the fact that in spite of the increase of the annual rental from 8,000 to 16,000 talents, Joseph and Hyrcanus were still able to accumulate immense riches. The former, according to Josephus (*ib.* § 4), beheaded twenty distinguished citizens of Ascalon and Scythopolis for refusing to pay their taxes, and then confiscated their possessions. However, both father and son showed great leniency toward their coreligionists; and their accumulated wealth raised the material condition of Judea.

In Palestine Under Egyptian Rule.

Under the government of Palestine by the Syrian kings all the taxes were collected by state officials. The Romans left to the governors or procurators the collection of the regular taxes, such as the land-tax and poll-tax, but leased the customs duties, the market tolls, and similar special imposts. The lessees were generally Roman knights; but there were among them Jews also. Mention is made of a Jewish tax-gatherer named John, who headed a deputation sent to Florus by the inhabitants of Cæsarea (Josephus, " B. J." ii. 14, § 5). The fact that they were helping the Romans in the exaction of the heavy taxes imposed upon the Jews, combined with the rapacity of some tax-collectors who, taking advantage of the indefiniteness of the tariffs, overcharged the taxpayer, rendered this class of officials hateful to the people. Hence the stringent Jewish legislation which classified the tax-collectors with robbers. Thus, for instance, it was forbidden to take payment in coin from the treasury of the tax-gatherer or to receive alms from it, because the money had been gained by robbery (B. Ḳ. x. 1; " Yad," Gezelah, § 5; Shulḥan 'Aruk, Ḥoshen Mishpaṭ, 370, 389). The tax-gatherer was ineligible to serve as judge or

In the Talmud.

even as a witness (Sanh. 25b). If one member of a family was a tax-gatherer, all its members were liable to be considered as such for the purposes of testimony, because they would be likely to shield him (Sheb. 39a).

During the Middle Ages the position of tax-collector was often filled by Jews. Mention is made of Jewish tax-collectors in France as early as the sixth century (Gregory of Tours, " Historia Francorum," vii. 23). In 587 the Council of Mâcon issued among other prohibitions one against farming the taxes to Jews. That this prohibition was disregarded is seen from the fact that the Council of Meaux (849) deemed it necessary to renew it. The collection of Jewish taxes was always entrusted to Jews; during the reign of Charles V. (1364–80) Menassier of Vesoul was receiver-general of the Jewish taxes for the north of France, and Denis Quinan for Languedoc. The kings likewise often entrusted to Jews the position of receiver-general of taxes. Among the renowned receivers mention may be made of Joseph Pichon, Joseph of Ecija, and Samuel ibn Waḳar, all of whom paid with their lives for the riches they had accumulated in office. Until the regency of John I. of Castile (1385) Jews held the position of tax-receivers in Portugal also.

In the Middle Ages.

In Germany the Jews were very early excluded from all public offices; and it can not be ascertained whether they ever filled there the position of tax-receiver. It seems, however, that such Jewish officials existed in Austria in the thirteenth century; for in a document dated 1257 two Jews are mentioned as the king's financiers. In Hungary the Jews were excluded from the office in 1279 by the Council of Buda. The higher Polish nobility, however, depended largely on the Jews for tax-collectors; until lately the Russian government also made use of Jewish tax-gatherers (" sborschiki ") for the collection of taxes from the Jews; and it still leases to the highest bidder the special Jewish taxes, such as that on kasher-meat (" korobka "), and on the candles used for Sabbath and for other religious purposes. Until the middle of the seventeenth century the customs duties were generally leased by the Turkish government to Jews. According to Manasseh ben Israel (1656), " the viceroy of Egypt has always at his side a Jew who bears the title 'ṣarraf bashi,' or 'treasurer,' and who gathers the taxes of the land. At present Abraham Alkula holds the position." Alkula was succeeded by Raphael Joseph Halabi, the rich friend and protector of Shabbethai Ẓebi (Grätz, " Gesch." x. 34). See PUBLICAN.

BIBLIOGRAPHY: For the tax-gatherers in Judea: Wünsche, *Neue Beiträge zur Erläuterung der Evangelien*, 1878, p. 71; Hamburger, *R. B. T.* ii., s.v. *Zoll*; Schürer, *Gesch.* i. 478 *et seq.*; Herzfeld, *Handelsgeschichte der Juden*, pp. 161 *et seq.*
J. I. BR.

TAXATION.—**Biblical Data:** The Bible gives scant information concerning the secular or political taxes of the Jews. Practically all that can be gathered is the following: Just as Abraham (Gen. xiv. 20) voluntarily gave a tenth " of all " (*i.e.*, according to the context, of the whole spoil taken in war), so the Israelitish and foreign subjects of the kings of Israel voluntarily brought presents to their rulers.

These gifts were withheld by churlish people only (comp. I Sam. x. 27), but were given by all others (*ib.* xvi. 20; II Sam. viii. 2, 11 *et seq.*; xii. 30; I Kings x. 10, 25; II Kings iii. 4; II Chron. ix. 24; Isa. xvi. 1; Ps. lxxii. 10). A chief source of the king's income consisted in his landed possessions (I Chron. xxvii. 25 *et seq.*; II Chron. xxvi. 10); but a money- or poll-tax is not mentioned among the royal prerogatives, even in the detailed description of them with which Samuel tried to deter the people from choosing a king (I Sam. viii. 11-17). The census of the people which was ordered by David (II Sam. xxiv. 1 *et seq.*) was intended perhaps to furnish a basis for a methodical distribution of the military burdens and taxes; but Solomon was the first monarch to systematize the furnishing of foodstuffs (I Kings iv. 7-28), and to demand toll from the merchants (*ib.* x. 15), and he, moreover, made the lot of the people an inordinately heavy one (xii. 4), probably imposing an additional money-tax. The later kings again received only voluntary gifts from their subjects, as is recorded of the time of Jehoshaphat and Hezekiah (II Chron. xvii. 5, xxxii. 23), a money-tax being levied in time of war only, when the demands of victorious enemies had to be satisfied (II Kings xv. 20, xxiii. 35).

The repugnance of the free Israelites to the payment of a money-tax was overcome by the postexilic foreign rulers. Although the Persian kings exempted the priests and Levites (Ezra vii. 24), they demanded toll (הלך) and other imposts which likewise had to be paid in money (Ezra iv. 13; Neh. v. 4: "We have borrowed money for the king's tribute"). The taxes often grew to be an especially heavy burden under the Ptolemaic and Seleucidan kings. These rulers employed tax-farmers, who, of course, endeavored not only to collect the taxes, but also to derive a large personal profit in addition (I Macc. xi. 28, xiii. 15; Josephus, "Ant." xii. 4, §§ 1, 4 *et seq.*). Josephus (in the passage just cited) narrates that Joseph, the son of Tobias, accumulated great wealth as a tax-farmer, although he had to pay to the Egyptian king Euergetes the enormous sum of 16,000 talents. The Seleucidan kings likewise demanded a poll-tax (I Macc. x. 29: φόρους, according to "Ant." xii. 3, § 3, denoting what is paid per head).

This tax was imposed by the Roman rulers also. Julius Cæsar, it is true, showed himself very lenient toward the Jews, and even was considerate with regard to the Sabbatical year ("Ant." xiv. 8, § 3); but under Augustus conditions changed. During the latter's reign a "descriptio orbis" was completed, in which the property of the inhabitants of the whole Roman empire was set down. He chose twenty of the most eminent men, and sent them into all the countries of the subjugated peoples, to make a list of persons and property; moreover he wrote with his own hand a "breviarium totius imperii," which contained a list of the number of citizens carrying arms and of the allies, of the tributes or taxes, etc. This census was introduced into Judea when Herod's son Archelaus was removed, in the year 760 of the foundation of Rome, and was exiled to Vienna in Gaul; it is mentioned in Matt. xxii. 17. The precise amount of this tax is not known, nor can

it be estimated with certainty from the fact that the denarius is called the "coin of the census" (A. V. "tribute money") in Matt. xxii. 19; for these words may mean also "a sample of the Roman coins with which the tribute is paid." In any case the tax imposed by the Romans was high and oppressive.

Refusal to pay taxes involved rebellion against the suzerainty of the Romans, as in the case of Judas the Gaulonite in the year 760 of the foundation of Rome ("Ant." xviii. 1, § 1).

BIBLIOGRAPHY: I. Benzinger, *Arch.* 1894, pp. 174, 221, 308 *et seq.*; Franz Walter, *Die Propheten in Ihrem Socialen Berufe*, 1900, p. 26.

E. G. H.   E. K.

——**Middle Ages:** A direct result of the persecutions of the Jews in the eleventh and twelfth centuries was that they came under the immediate protection of the rulers; this, in turn, led to their becoming KAMMERKNECHTE. The imperial rights

Transferred to Nobles and Church Dignitaries. were often transferred to minor rulers. Thus, the widow of Duke Roger of Apulia bequeathed to the church of Salerno the revenues derived from the Jews; and in like manner the Jews of Bohemia, in the twelfth century, came under the immediate protection of the Bohemian princes. In the thirteenth century the Jews became at times the wards of the ecclesiastical potentates also, to whom they were then obliged to pay their taxes. For example, in 1209 the taxes paid by the Jews of the archbishopric of Mayence fell into the coffers of Archbishop Siegfried; in 1212 the Jewish taxes for Provence were paid to the church of Arles.

The assessment of taxes to be paid by individual members of the communities was the duty of the elders, who took into consideration both the property owned by each member and his yearly income. Particularly wealthy Jews, by placing themselves under the personal protection of the ruler, sometimes escaped communal taxes; this aroused the anger of the communities and caused them to complain to the emperor. As a rule only Jewish

Special Taxes. physicians and such Jews as had rendered the state special services were exempt from taxation. The following twelve taxes, which may almost be termed "official," were generally levied upon German Jews of medieval times:

(1) The Coronation Tax: When this tax was introduced is not known; but the Jews of the entire German empire were compelled to pay a certain sum whenever a new ruler ascended the throne. At the coronation of Philip the Fair the Jews of Champagne paid a tax of 25,000 florins French money; while the Jews of Italy, upon the accession of a pope, paid a tribute consisting of one pound of pepper and two pounds of cinnamon.

(2) Taxation on Dress: In 1405 the Jews of several German and French cities were allowed to purchase exemption from wearing the Jewish badge by payment of a higher annual tax (Weizsäcker, "Reichstagsacten," v. 637).

(3) The Golden Opferpfennig: Introduced by Ludwig the Bavarian (1342). The income derived from this tax amounted in the fourteenth century

to 30,000 gulden. Beginning with the seventeenth century it was gradually abolished (see OPFER-PFENNIG, GOLDENER).

(4) Judengeleitsgeld: For each safe-conduct a payment of 1 turnose was exacted, and even a Christian, if traveling with a Jew, had to pay this fee.

(5) Landfrieden Protection Tax: This was one of the heaviest taxes imposed upon the Jews, and was paid only when the latter had been publicly assured that protection had been granted them, as, for example, by Henry IV. (1103) and Henry of Hohenstaufen (1254), by the cities of Worms, Mayence, and Oppenheim (1260), and by Archbishop Werner of Mayence (1265).

(6) The Leibzoll (see JEW. ENCYC. vii. 669).

(7) The Real Estate and Building Tax: Levied as early as the ninth century. When a Jew purchased a house or a lot he placed himself under the protection of the local church or monastery, to which he paid a certain tribute: for a house, one-tenth of the income derived from it; for a lot, a certain quantity of barley, wheat, and wine. The custom of acquiring real property under the protection of the Church was rendered more difficult during the thirteenth century, measures against it being taken in Normandy, 1222, in northern Germany, 1240, in Gascony, 1288, and by Charles of Valois, 1324. Toward the middle of the fifteenth century it fell entirely into disuse.

(8) The Reichssteuer: Imposed by the emperor Wenceslaus (1383). The right to levy taxes upon the Jews was granted to cities only on condition that one-half of the income thus derived should be paid into the treasury of the state. A similar Jewish tax existed in France from the middle of the fourteenth century.

(9) Royal and Papal Protection Tax: From the twelfth century the popes granted letters protecting the Jews against the severity of their overlords. The amounts paid for these privileges varied from 1,000 to 3,000 marks for each letter. Such taxes were received by popes Alexander III., Clement III., Innocent III. (1199), Honorius III. (1217), Gregory IX. (1235), Innocent IV. (1246), and Innocent V. The same class of tax was imposed in England for the renewal of charters; e.g., 4,000 marks were paid to John in 1200.

(10) The Servitium: Sum paid in lieu of personal services. It was first paid in Spain and in France in the middle of the thirteenth century, especially under Charles the Wise, when exemption from statute labor might be purchased with money. It was collected also in Germany, especially in Cologne.

(11) The Tenth Pfennig: Levied upon all German Jews within the jurisdiction of the archbishops of Mayence. The fact that the archbishops had this prerogative caused a rupture between John II. and Emperor Rupert (1403-4); eventually an agreement was reached by which the emperor acquired the right to levy the tax.

(12) The Third Pfennig: Imposed by the Nuremberg Reichstag (Aug. 9, 1422) to defray the expenses of the Hussite war. It was levied on all Jews of the German empire, which, for that purpose, was divided into four districts presided over by Margrave Bernhard of Baden, Palsgrave John of Neumarkt, Landgrave John of Lupfen, and Freiherr della Scala of Bavaria.

Besides these regular taxes, however, the Jews were often forced to pay extra tributes. Noteworthy instances of such extra taxation occurred under Conrad IV. and Ludwig the Bavarian, but especially under Emperor Sigismund (1416, 1418, 1423). The specifically Jewish taxes, in various forms, continued to be levied until the nineteenth century, and were not abolished until the Jews had been generally accorded full civic rights. It should be added that, while more onerous, taxes on Jews were, as a rule, not more numerous than those levied on all citizens possessing means. See SPAIN; TALLAGE.

BIBLIOGRAPHY: Stobbe, Die Juden in Deutschland, passim; Nübling, Die Judengemeinden des Mittelalters, passim; Aronius, Regesten, passim; Depping, Die Juden im Mittelalter, passim, Stuttgart, 1834; Wiener, Regesten, passim.
J.　　　　　　　　　　　　　　　　　　S. O.

TAXO: The mysterious name of "the man of the tribe of Levi" who, under a Roman governor in the time of Herod, according to the Assumptio Mosis, ix. 1–7, underwent martyrdom with his seven sons amidst the cruel persecution of the Zealots (vi.–viii.). He exhorted his sons thus: "Let us die rather than transgress the commands of the Lord of Lords, the God of our Fathers, for if we do this and die our blood will be avenged before the Lord." Here the story breaks off abruptly. It appears, however, that Josephus ("Ant." xiv. 15, § 5) refers to this martyrdom of Taxo during Herod's cruel onslaught against the Zealots, when he states that "one old man was caught within one of these caves with seven children and a wife, and rather than permit any of these to surrender he killed them all and finally himself, preferring, as he said, death to slavery, and reproaching Herod with the meanness of his family although he was king." Charles, in the "Assumptio Mosis" (1897), thinks that "Taxo" (תכסא) is a corruption of the word הקנא ("the Zealot"), and that the Samaritan legend of Moses in Heidenheim's "Vierteljahrschrift" (1871, iv. 210), in speaking of a "Levite" who would be a zealous battler for the congregation "and die and after three days rise again," refers to the same Taxo mentioned in the "Assumptio Mosis." According to Gen. R. lvii. end, "Taḥash" ("Taḥshon") signifies a rebel.

K.

TAYLOR, CHARLES: English Christian Hebraist; born in London 1840; educated at King's College, London, and St. John's College, Cambridge, of which he is now master. In 1874 he published an edition of "Coheleth"; in 1877 "Sayings of the Jewish Fathers," an elaborate edition of the Pirḳe Abot (2 ed., 1897); and in 1899 a valuable appendix giving a list of manuscripts. This is probably the most important contribution to rabbinic learning of any living Christian Hebraist. Taylor discovered the Jewish source of the "Didache" in his "Teaching of the Twelve Apostles," 1886, and has published also "Essay on the Theology of the Didache," 1889.

Taylor took great interest in Professor Schechter's work in Cairo, and the genizah fragments presented to the University of Cambridge are known as the Taylor-Schechter Collection. He was joint editor with Schechter of "The Wisdom of Ben Sira," 1899. He published separately "Cairo Genizah Palimpsests," 1900. He died on August 12, 1908.

He has published also several works on geometry.

BIBLIOGRAPHY: *Who's Who in England.*
J.

ṬAYYIB: Tunisian family, first known in the second half of the seventeenth century. The more prominent members are the following:

Abraham Ṭayyib: Grandson of Abraham b. Isaac Ṭayyib (see below); lived at the end of the eighteenth century. He was the author of "Ḥayye Abraham" (Leghorn, 1826), a commentary on the treatises Shabbat, Pesaḥim, Megillah, Ta'anit, Mo'ed Ḳaṭan, Yebamot, Ketubot, Ḳiddushin, Baba Ḳamma, Sanhedrin, Makkot, Shebu'ot, 'Abodah Zarah, and 'Arakin. Appended to it are notes on Maimonides' "Yad," on Alfasi, and on Rashi to the Pentateuch.

Abraham ben Isaac Ṭayyib (surnamed **Baba Sidi**): Rabbi of Tunis, where he died in 1741. He was a companion of Zemaḥ Zarfati and one of the teachers of Isaac Lombroso, chief rabbi of Tunis. He was the author of novellæ on the treatises of the order Ḳodashim, printed in Jacob Faitusi's "Mizbaḥ Kapparah" (Leghorn, 1810). Other novellæ of his are to be found in Joseph Tanuji's "Bene Yosef" (Salonica, 1726).

Ḥayyim ben Abraham Ṭayyib: Rabbi of Tunis, and author of "Derek Ḥayyim" (printed with his father's Ḥayye Abraham"), a commentary on Pesaḥim, Ketubot, Ḳiddushin, Baba Meẓi'a, and Ḥullin.

Isaac ben Benjamin Ṭayyib: Rabbi and cabalist of Tunis; died in 1830. He was the author of: (1) "'Erek ha-Shulḥan," novellæ on the four divisions of the Shulḥan 'Aruk, Oraḥ Ḥayyim (Leghorn, 1791; preface by Joseph Sarko, who seems to have been Isaac's teacher), Yoreh De'ah (*ib.* 1798), Ḥoshen Mishpaṭ (*ib.* 1815; Tunis, 1890–92), and Eben ha-'Ezer (Leghorn, 1844); (2) "Wawe ha-'Ammudim" (*ib.* 1837), a commentary on Eliezer of Metz's "Sefer Yere'im," cabalistic in spirit and containing quotations from cabalistic works; (3) "Ḥuḳḳot ha-Pesaḥ" (*ib.* 1853), novellæ on the part of the Shulḥan 'Aruk containing the laws regarding the Passover feast; (4) "Sefer ha-Zikkaron" (Tunis, 1892), in two parts, the first being a collection of Isaac's divers notes, and the second a cabalistic commentary on Abot and on the Pesaḥ Haggadah.

BIBLIOGRAPHY: D. Cazès, *Notes Bibliographiques*, pp. 307 *et seq.*, Tunis, 1893; Fürst, *Bibl. Jud.* iii. 406.
J.
M. Sel.

ṬEBET: Tenth ecclesiastical and fourth civil month; it invariably has twenty-nine days. The name, like those of the other months, appears to be taken from the Assyro-Babylonians, who called their tenth month, described as the month of violent rains, "Ṭebetu" (Delitzsch, "Wörterbuch," p. 298). This month fell near the close of the rainy season in Palestine, to which fact the gloss in Ta'an. 6b alludes, holding that the year will be fertile if Ṭebet be "ugly" (*i.e.*, rainy). The observation that that year will be a good one in which Ṭebet is "widowed" (*i.e.*, rainless) presupposes that a sufficient precipitation had preceded the month, the rainy season

normally beginning with the month of Ḥeshwan (the 8th month).

Of notable events and dates connected with this month, the following are among the more important:

Ṭebet 1 and 2: Seventh and eighth days of Ḥanukkah. Ṭebet 5: See Ezek. xxxiii. 21; R. H. 18b. Ṭebet 8: Day on which the translation of the Septuagint was completed, when the earth was shrouded in darkness for three days ("Megillat Ta'anit," end). Ṭebet 9: Fast-day, but for reasons not known (*ib.*; Shulḥan 'Aruk, Oraḥ Ḥayyim, 580); it is said to have been the day on which Ezra died (*ib.*), and Abu Ḥusain Joseph ibn Nagdela was killed on this day (1066). Ṭebet 10: Fast-day, commemorating the beginning of the siege of Jerusalem under Nebuchadnezzar (see Jer. lii. 4; II Kings xxv. 1; Ezek. xxiv. 1; R. H. 18b); when this fast-day falls on the Sabbath, it is observed on the day following. Ṭebet 12: Ezekiel received a revelation (Ezek. xxix. 1). Ṭebet 20: Death of Moses Maimonides (1204). Ṭebet 24: The discomfiture of the Sadducean party (B. B. 115b) by Johanan ben Zakkai (according to "Megillat Ta'anit," this occurred on the 24th of Ab). Ṭebet 25: Said to have been the day of Alexander the Great's appearance before the walls of Jerusalem (Yoma 60a). Ṭebet 28: Another anti-Sadducean feast-day ("Megillat Ta'anit," x.); on this day the majority of the Sanhedrin passed over to the Pharisees.
E. G. H.

ṬEBUL YOM: Name of a treatise in the Mishnah and in the Tosefta; in most editions of the Mishnah it is tenth in the order Ṭohorot. According to Lev. xv. 5 *et seq.*, one who takes the prescribed bath still remains unclean until sunset. The degree of uncleanness in such a case is slight, and according to rabbinical interpretation neither the "ḥallah" nor sanctified flesh is rendered unclean by being touched by such a person, even before sunset; it is merely rendered unfit ("pasul"). Profane or unsanctified things may be touched by him without fear. The treatise Ṭebul Yom more closely defines the degree of uncleanness attaching to such a person, and stipulates also how far the purity of anything is affected by his touch. The treatise comprises four chapters, containing twenty-six paragraphs in all.

Ch. i.: Regulations concerning bread and other things which are of such a form that if a ṭebul yom or any other uncleanness touches part of them the whole is rendered unclean.

Ch. ii.: Concerning liquids touched by a ṭebul yom; when such contact renders the whole unfit, and when it affects only the part touched.

Ch. iii.: Continuation of ch. ii.: regulations concerning liquids easily rendered unclean.

Ch. iv.: Regulations concerning utensils touched by a ṭebul yom; enumeration of halakic rules which have undergone changes in the course of time; of the halakic regulations which R. Joshua declared were introduced by the sages ("soferim"), and which he was unable to explain.

In the Tosefta the treatise is divided into two chapters.
W. B.
J. Z. L.

TEDESCHI, MARCO: Italian rabbi and poet; born at Piova, Piedmont, in 1817; died at Triest in

1870. He removed to Vercelli with his father (d. 1836), who had been appointed rabbi there; and in 1838 he went to Turin to study under R. Hillel Cantoni. He was successively elected rabbi of Nizza-Monferrato, Saluzzo, Asti, and Triest. His principal poems were published by Vittorio Castiglione in the "Yelid Kinnor" (Drohobycz, 1886). He translated from the French "Les Prières d'un Cœur Israélite." Marco Tedeschi was celebrated as a preacher.

s.   V. C.

TEDESCHI, MOSES ISAAC: Italian translator, Biblical commentator, and teacher; born at Triest June 6, 1821; died there June 17, 1898. He lectured on Biblical exegesis in the Tamud Torah of his native city, and occasionally delivered sermons on holy days. He was the author of the following works: "Ho'il Mosheh," comprising commentaries on the Earlier Prophets (Göritz, 1870), the Book of Job (Padua, 1877), the Psalms (Leghorn, 1880), the Five Megillot and the Book of Proverbs (ib. 1880), the Pentateuch (ib. 1881), the Minor Prophets (Triest, 1887), the books of Daniel, Ezra, and Nehemiah, and Chronicles (Przemysl, 1889); "Musar Melakim," a collection of ethical homilies based on the Pirḳe Abot (Triest, 1878); "Zeker Rab," an Italian translation of the didactical prose-poem of Mussafia (Padua, 1878); "Oẓar Nirdefe Leshon 'Ibri," on Hebrew synonyms (ib. 1879); "Simḥat ha-Regel," homilies and glosses on the Targum to Proverbs. The author's autobiography is appended to the last-named work. He published also, in "Ha-Asif" (1886), an introduction to the Minor Prophets.

BIBLIOGRAPHY: Zeitlin, *Bibl. Post-Mendels.* p. 394.

s.   M. B.

TEDESCO, IGNAZ AMADEUS: Austrian pianist; born at Prague 1817; died at Odessa Nov. 13, 1882; a pupil of Triebensee and Tomaschek at Prague. He made numerous successful concert tours, especially in southern Russia, and settled at Odessa, although he lived for a short time at Hamburg (1848) and London (1856).

As a pianist Tedesco was distinguished for his fine technique; he was called the "Hannibal of octaves." In recognition of his ability he was appointed pianist to the Grand Duke of Oldenburg. He wrote brilliant salon music, comprising a pianoforte concerto, caprices de concerts, mazurkas, nocturnes, rhapsodies, waltzes, and transcriptions.

BIBLIOGRAPHY: Champlin, *Cyc. of Music and Musicians*; Illustrirte Zeitung, 1850, i. 346; Baker, *Dict. of Music and Musicians.*

s.   J. So.

TEFILLIN. See PHYLACTERIES.

TEHERAN: Capital and commercial center of Persia; situated about seventy miles south of the Caspian Sea. The chief development of the city took place within the last half of the nineteenth century, under Shah Naṣir al-Din, whose court physician, J. E. POLAK, was a Jew. The antiquity of Teheran is not great, since its existence can hardly be traced beyond the twelfth century. It appears gradually to have taken the place of the ancient Rai, which sank slowly into oblivion and is now a mass of ruins in the suburbs of Teheran. Rai itself had a long history, being the ancient metropolis of Media mentioned in the Apocrypha as Rages (Tobit

Interior of the Great Synagogue at Teheran.
(From a photograph by E. N. Adler.)

i. 14 *et seq.*) or Ragau (Judith i. 15), in the Avesta and Old Persian inscriptions as Ragha or Raga (Vendidad, i. 15; Yasna, xix. 18; Behistun, ii. 70-74, iii. 1-10), and in the classics as Rhagæ (Strabo, §§ 1, 3, 19, etc.). It is mentioned as an emporium of Jewish trade by Ibn Khordadhbeh, 817 (see JEW. ENCYC. iv. 189, *s.v.* COMMERCE).

Teheran covers a considerable area, as the wall which surrounds it is eleven miles in circuit and is pierced by twelve gates. The Europeans reside in the northern section of the city, where the foreign legations are located. The Jews live in a quarter of their own. In their daily life they are subject to much the same restrictions and disabilities as the Gabars and the Armenians; and they were formerly liable to acts of persecution which resulted in reducing them to a state of misery, ignorance, and degradation. A riot against them occurred in Teheran as late as May 16, 1897. The Alliance Israélite

Universelle has accomplished a great deal toward removing this condition of affairs by bettering the position of the Jews in the community and by establishing schools for the education of the children. The Alliance report for 1904 shows a combined attendance of nearly 400 pupils at the two schools, established six years previously for boys and for girls. The occupations of the Jews in Teheran, as elsewhere in Persia, are largely those of traders, silversmiths, wine-merchants, and petty dealers. Teheran has a total population estimated at 250,000, including about 5,000 Jews.

Bibliography: Curzon, Persia and the Persian Question, i. 300–353, London, 1892; Benjamin, Persia and the Persians, Boston, 1886; Basset, Land of the Imams, New York, 1887; Wilson, Persian Life and Customs, New York, 1895; Brugsch, Im Lande der Sonne, Berlin, 1886; Univers Israélite, Aug. 12, 1904; Bulletin de l'Alliance Israélite, 1897, p. 76.

J.   A. V. W. J.

TEḤINA, ABBA (called also **Teḥina ben Perisha** ["the Pharisee"] or **Ḥasida** ["the pious one"]): A leader of the Zealots. Together with Eleazar ben Dinai, he is mentioned in the remarkable dictum of Johanan ben Zakkai concerning the Zealots: "Since the murderers have increased, the expiation ceremony of the 'eglah 'arufah [the heifer whose neck is broken for a murder the perpetrator of which is unknown; Deut. xxi. 1–9] has come into abeyance because of the many murders by these only too well-known Zealots. Such murderers are Eleazar ben Dinai and Teḥina, who was formerly called 'the Pharisee' and later on received the name of 'the Murderer'" (Soṭah ix. 9; Sifre, Deut. 205).

Synagogue of Asher the Physician at Teheran.
(From a photograph by E. N. Adler.)

This Teḥina has aptly been identified by Derenbourg ("Essai sur l'Histoire et la Géographie de la Palestine d'Après les Thalmuds et les Autres Sources Rabbiniques," i. 279–280, Paris, 1867) with the Abba Teḥina Ḥasida of Eccl. R. ix. 7. Derenbourg, however, takes the epithet "Ḥasid" to be ironical; but he ignores the very nature of the passage to which he refers and which is as follows: "Teḥina the Essene [Ḥasid] with the title Abba [see Kohler, "Abba, Father," in "J. Q. R." xiii. 567–575], returning to his native town on Friday afternoon shortly before the beginning of the Sabbath, and carrying upon his shoulder a bundle containing the provisions for his household for the Sabbath, met a disease-stricken man unable to move,

who asked him to have pity on him and bring him into the town, where his wants might receive the necessary attention. This placed Teḥina in a quandary: he was afraid if he left his bundle he might lose all his Sabbath provisions; and if he did not aid the sick man, he (Teḥina) would be accounted as guilty of death. His better impulses proving victorious, he carried the sick man to a safe place, and then went back for his bundle. Meanwhile it had grown dark; and the people, seeing him carry a bundle on Sabbath eve, wondered, saying, 'Is this Abba Teḥina the Pious?' Teḥina himself was in doubt as to whether he had really violated the Sabbath, when a miracle happened: God caused the sun again to shine forth to show that the Sabbath had not yet begun, as it is written (Mal. iii. 20 [A. V. iv. 2]): 'But unto you that fear my name shall the sun of righteousness arise with healing in his wings.'" Later the punctilious Essene became a fierce Zealot (see Zealots).

Eleazar ben Dinai is mentioned by Josephus several times, while Teḥina is not. He has been identified with the Alexander mentioned together with Eleazar b. Dinai by that author (Josephus, "B. J." ii. 12, § 4; see Eleazar ben Dinai); but Alexander appears to be identical with Amram, cited as companion of Ben Dinai in "Ant." xx. 1, § 1 (comp. Cant. R. iii. 5: "In the days of Amram [?] and in the days of Ben Dinai they attempted to bring about the Messianic time by violence"; see Grätz, "Gesch." 3d ed., iii. 431), whereas it is quite possible that Teḥina is identical with Ἀννιβας who was executed by order of Fadus (Josephus, "Ant." l.c.; Grätz, l.c. p. 278).   K.

TEḤINNAH. See Devotional Literature.

TEITELBAUM, MOSES: Austrian Ḥasid; died July 17, 1841. According to Löw, he signed his name **Tamar**, this being the equivalent of **Teitelbaum**, which is the Yiddish for **Dattelbaum** = "palm-tree." He officiated as rabbi, first in Przemysl, and later in Sátoralja-Ujhely, to which latter place he was called in 1809. In Ujhely he founded a Ḥasidic congregation which was independent of the Galician leaders. In 1822 Teitelbaum was suspected of having supplied amulets to certain Jewish culprits who had been cast into prison for libel, in order to assist them in escaping. When called upon to vindicate himself he declared that the amulets in question served only as substitutes for the mezuzah and that their only purpose was to protect their bearers against demons.

Teitelbaum enjoyed an enviable reputation, even R. Moses Sofer paying him homage. He was the author of: "Yismaḥ Mosheh" (1849; 2d ed. 1898), homilies on the Torah; "Tefillah le-Mosheh," commentaries on the Psalms; and "Heshib Mosheh," a collection of responsa.

BIBLIOGRAPHY: Walden, *Shem ha-Gedolim he-Ḥadash*, p. 101; Löw, *Gesammelte Schriften*, ii. 76, 84, 91.

s.　　　　　　　　　　　　　　　　　　L. V.

TEIXEIRA, TEIXEYRA, TEXEIRA, or **TEIXARA:** Noble Portuguese Marano family, originally bearing the surname of **Sampayo.** In accordance with a decree of King Philip IV. of Spain, its coat of arms—azure, a cross potencée or— was included in the Spanish roll of arms. In the patent, dated 1643, conferring nobility on Diego Teixeira his armorial bearings are blazoned as follows: Quarterly, 1 and 4, or, an eagle displayed purple; 2 and 3, checky or and sable (sixteen fields); bordure gules, charged by eight "S's" argent. This coat of arms was exchanged by the family, with the exception of a few members, for another, probably that of the De Mattos, with whom they intermarried, the new bearings being: Gules, a fir-tree sinople, rooted argent between two lions rampant, affronte, or, armed azure.

The family was known also

Jewish School at Teheran.
(From a photograph by E. N. Adler.)

as **Teixeira de Mattos,** and members of it, distinguished for their riches, philanthropy, commercial activity, and influence, have resided until very recently in Hamburg, Holland, London, Vienna, and Venice.

Diego Teixeira Sampayo (Abraham Senior Teixeira): Portuguese Marano; left Portugal for Antwerp in 1643; died at Hamburg Jan. 6, 1666. After a brief residence at Antwerp he settled in Hamburg, professing Catholicism until Good Friday in 1647 or 1648, when he and his wife openly acknowledged Judaism, while Diego, who was approaching seventy, together with his two sons, one of whom was born out of wedlock, was circumcised by a rabbi. The imperial government thereupon demanded the surrender of Diego's person and the confiscation of his estate, but the senate of Hamburg

energetically opposed this demand (M. Grunwald, "Portugiesengräber," p. 124). Diego Teixeira, who never added "de Mattos" to his name, was known in Hamburg only as the "rich Jew." He rode in an ornate carriage upholstered with velvet, had liveried servants, and kept a princely house, which, in 1654, was for some time the residence of Queen Christina of Sweden, to whom Diego had been recommended by the Spanish ambassador D. Antonio Pimentel, and by whom he was held in high esteem. He always took a keen interest in the affairs of his coreligionists; and at his intercession in 1657 King Frederick III. of Denmark granted them privileges, which were later confirmed by Christian V. For several years he was the head of the Spanish-Portuguese community in Hamburg, and at his son's wedding he presented the congregation with a ewer and a basin of silver plated with gold, while in 1659 he contributed 15,000 marks for the erection of a synagogue. It was he who supplied the copper roofing for the great Church of St. Michael in Hamburg, and when the elders asked for his bill he requested them to accept it receipted without payment. There still exist two benevolent institutions founded by Diego Teixeira and his wife, Sara d'Andrade (d. Dec. 5, 1693): Zur Ausstattung Dürftiger Jungfrauen and Zur Auslösung von Gefangenen.

BIBLIOGRAPHY: Archenholtz, *Mémoire de Christine de Suède*, i. 450, iii. 228, Amsterdam, 1651; Grätz, *Gesch.* x. 23; D. H. de Castro, *Keur van Grafsteenen*, pp. 104 *et seq.*; Grunwald, *Portugiesengräber*, pp. 123 *et seq.* (the epitaphs being given on p. 86).

Manuel Teixeira (Isaac Ḥayyim Senior Teixeira): Only son of Diego Teixeira and Sara d'Andrade; born in Lisbon about 1625; died at Amsterdam June 5, 1705. He was twice married, his second wife being Esther Gomez de Mesquita, whom he wedded at Hamburg April 7, 1654. Like his father, he was the financial agent and resident minister of Queen Christina of Sweden, retaining this position until 1687, as is proved by the patent of dismissal given him by her (Archenholtz, "Mémoire de Christine de Suède," iv.). Christina esteemed her ambassador so highly for his integrity and discretion that when the magistracy of Hamburg attempted to prevent him from leaving the city the queen regarded their action as a personal affront. She considered Teixeira's opinions and advice of such value that she recommended her ambassador Rosenbach to follow his counsels, "for they are wise and clever, and I approve of them," while in one of her letters to Count Wassenau the queen said: "Teixeira has written you a letter so clever and sagacious that King Solomon himself could not have improved upon it. I can only add that you must do all things as he bids you, and undertake nothing in opposition to his views. . . . Be careful not to do anything without his sanction" (Archenholtz, *l.c.* iii. 399, 465).

During her repeated visits to Hamburg, Queen Christina always took up her residence in Teixeira's house, which was situated in the most beautiful portion of the town, on the Jungfernstieg; she remained there for an entire year in 1661. When she revisited Hamburg in July, 1666, and instead of accepting the hospitality of the municipal council became the guest of Teixeira, the rabble, instigated by the clergy, endeavored to storm the house. For more than a quarter of a century Teixeira served the queen faithfully, and, even when, in 1685, he refused to advance further sums on her appanage, her governor-general, Olivekraus, did not succeed in disgracing him; on the contrary, she maintained a correspondence with him until her death.

Although Manuel Teixeira, like his father, kept a princely house and moved in the highest circles, he was a faithful adherent of Judaism, and supported a Talmud Torah in which Jacob Sasportas was employed as teacher. Like many other Jews of Spanish-Portuguese extraction, he was a follower of Shabbethai Ẓebi. In 1670, when the Jews were threatened with expulsion from Vienna and from the Austrian domains, Teixeira, in response to the appeal of the Vienna community, advocated their cause with great devotion. He accordingly wrote to several of his friends among the grandees of Spain and invoked the aid of Cardinal Azzolino at Rome, the confidential friend of Queen Christina, while at his request the queen herself wrote to the papal nuncio in Vienna and sent Teixeira letters for the dowager empress and for the empress. Manuel must have removed to Amsterdam before 1699, since in that year he was head of the Spanish-Portuguese congregation in that city.

BIBLIOGRAPHY: *Jahrbuch für Israeliten,* vii. 1-13, Vienna, 1860; Grätz, *Gesch.* x. 227, 263; xxii. *et seq.*; J. Sasportas, *Ohel Ya'akob,* responsum No. 77; *Zeitschrift des Hamburger Geschichtsvereins,* ii. 409 *et seq.*; D. H. de Castro, *Keur van Grafsteenen,* pp. 104 *et seq.*; *Jew. Chron.* Aug. 11, 1905; Diamant, in *Magyar Zsidó Szemle,* vi. 269 *et seq.*, 323 *et seq.*
S.   M. K.

TEIXEIRA, PEDRO : Portuguese traveler; born at Lisbon of Marano parents; died about the middle of the seventeenth century either at Verona (according to De Barrios, who is followed by Wolf, Zunz, and others) or at Antwerp (according to Barbosa Machado), whither he had removed from Venice. A man of education and a close observer, he traveled for eighteen months through the Philippines, China, and parts of America, and, after spending two years at Lisbon, undertook a scientific journey to India, Persia, and other countries. As a result he published "Relaciones de Pedro Teixeira d'el Origen, Descendencia, y Sucesion de los Reyes de Persia, y de Hormuz, y de un Viage Hecho por el Mismo Autor Dende la India Oriental Hasta Italia

por Tierra " (Antwerp, 1610), containing a history of the kings of Persia according to Persian sources, as well as a fund of information on the Jews of Aleppo, Bagdad, and other cities, with notes on Jewish monuments. It served as a guide for Thomas de Pinedo and others, and has been translated into English by W. J. Sinclair, and edited by D. Fergeson; the latter also supplied the edition with an introduction.

BIBLIOGRAPHY: Barrios, *Relacion de los Poetas Españoles,* p. 58; Wolf, *Bibl. Hebr.* iii. 922; Zunz, *G. S.* i. 188; Barbosa Machado, *Biblioteca Lusitana,* iii. 622; Kayserling, *Pedro Teixeira: Eine Reiseskizze als Einleitung zu J. J. Benjamin, Acht Jahre in Asien und Africa,* Hanover, 1858 (English transl. *ib.* 1859); idem, *Bibl. Esp.-Port.-Jud.* p. 105.
S.   M. K.

TEḲI'AH. See SHOFAR.

TEKOA : City of southern Judea, frequently mentioned in the Old Testament. The "wise woman" who brought about the recall of Absalom was a resident of the city (II Sam. xiv. 2 *et seq.*), and it was also the home of the prophet Amos (i. 1), the herdsman and the gatherer of sycamore fruit. The fortification of Tekoa by Rehoboam (II Chron. xi. .6) gave it strategic importance. In the post-exilic period its inhabitants were CALEBITES (I Chron. ii. 24); and they aided Nehemiah in rebuilding the wall (iii. 5, 27).

The site of Tekoa is fixed by Biblical data. It was in the south (Jer. vi. 1), and in the vicinity of the valley of Berachah ("blessing "), near the desert to which it gave its name (II Chron. xx. 20, 26; I Macc. ix. 33). The place is still more accurately localized in Josh. xv. 60, where the Greek text of a passage lost in the Hebrew places it, together with Beth-lehem and other towns of the hill-country of Judah, south of Jerusalem. According to the "Onomasticon" of Eusebius and Jerome, it lay twelve Roman miles (eighteen kilometers) south of that city and to the east of Beth-lehem on the edge of the desert. The site of the city is represented by the modern Khirbat Taḳu'ah, a mass of scantily inhabited ruins, with ancient cisterns and tombs and the remains of a church, lying on a hill which commands a wide landscape. Since the days of Jerome the grave of Amos has been shown there. The Mishnah speaks in high praise of the oil of Tekoa; and medieval Arabic authors mention its honey.

E. C.   I. BE.

TEḲUFAH (lit. "turn," "cycle"): Season of the year. The four teḳufot are: (1) Teḳufat Nisan, the vernal equinox (March 21), when the sun enters Aries; this is the beginning of spring, or "'et ha-zera'" (seed-time), when day and night are equal; (2) Teḳufat Tammuz, the summer solstice (June 21), when the sun enters Cancer; this is the summer season, or "'et ha-ḳaẓir" (harvest-time), when the day is the longest in the year; (3) Teḳufat Tishri, the autumnal equinox (Sept. 23), when the sun enters Libra, and autumn, or "'et ha-baẓir"
Seasons. (vintage-time), begins, and when the day again equals the night; (4) Teḳufat Ṭebet, the winter solstice (Dec. 22), when the sun enters Capricornus; this is the beginning of

winter, or "'et ha-horef" (stripping-time), when the night is the longest during the year. Each teḳufah, according to Samuel Yarḥinai, marks the beginning of a period of 91 days and 7½ hours.

that has been boiled or used in salting or pickling. The danger in unused water may be avoided by putting in it a piece of iron or an iron vessel ("Bet Yosef" on the "Ṭur," and Isserles' note to Shulḥan

TABLE OF THE TEḲUFOT DURING 1905-14.

Year.	Teḳufat Ṭebet.	Day in Ṭebet.	Teḳufat Nisan.	Day in Nisan.	Teḳufat Tammuz.	Day in Tammuz.	Teḳufat Tishri.	Day in Tishri.
1905	10.30 a.m. Fri., Jan. 6....	29	6 p.m. Fri., April 7	3	1.30 a.m. Sat., July 8.....	5	9 a.m. Sat., Oct. 7	8
1906	4.30 p.m. Sat., Jan. 6....	9	12 p.m. Sat., April 7	13	7.30 a.m. Sun., July 8....	14	3 p.m. Sun., Oct. 7.......	18
1907	10.30 p.m. Sun., Jan. 6. ..	21	6 a.m. Mon., April 8	24	1.30 p.m. Mon., July 8 ...	26	9 p.m. Mon., Oct. 7	30
1908	4.30 p.m. Tues., Jan. 7...	4	12 a.m. Tues., April 7....	6	7.30 p.m. Tues., July 7 ...	9	3 a.m. Wed., Oct. 7......	12
1909	10.30 a.m. Wed., Jan. 6 ..	13	6 p.m. Wed., April 7.....	17	1.30 a.m. Thur., July 8...	19	9 a.m. Thur., Oct. 7......	22
1910	4.30 p.m. Thur., Jan. 6..	25	12 p.m. Thur., April 7 ...	28*	7.30 a.m. Fri., July 8.....	1	3 p.m. Fri., Oct. 7.......	4
1911	10.30 p.m. Fri., Jan. 6,...	7	6 a.m. Sat., April 8	10	1.30 p.m. Sat., July 8 ...	12	9 p.m. Sat., Oct. 7.......	16
1912	4.30 a.m. Sun., Jan. 7 ...	17	12 a.m. Sun., April 7	20	7.30 p.m. Sun., July 7....	23	3 a.m. Mon., Oct. 7......	26
1913	10.30 a.m. Mon., Jan. 6..	27	6 p.m. Mon., April 7....	1	1.30 a.m. Tues., July 8 ...	3	9 a.m. Tues., Oct. 7......	6
1914	4.30 p.m. Tues., Jan. 6..	8	12 p.m. Tues., April 7....	12	7.30 a.m. Wed., July 8 ...	14	3 p.m. Wed., Oct. 7......	17

*Adar II.

It will be noticed that the teḳufot fall from fourteen to eighteen days later than the true solar equinox or solstice; this, however, does not interfere with the calendar, which follows the figures of R. Ada.

An ancient and widely believed superstition is connected with the teḳufot. All water that may be in the house or stored away in vessels in the first hour of the teḳufah is thrown away in the belief that the water is then poisoned, and if drunk would cause swelling of the body, sickness, and sometimes death. Several reasons are advanced for this. Some say it is because the angels who protect the water change guard at the teḳufah and leave it unwatched for a short time. Others say that Cancer fights with Libra and drops blood into the water. Another authority accounts for the drops of blood in the water at Teḳufat Nisan by pointing out that the waters in Egypt turned to blood at that particular moment. At Teḳufat Tammuz, Moses smote the rock and caused drops of blood to flow from it. At Teḳufat Tishri the knife which Abraham held to slay Isaac dropped blood. At Teḳufat Ṭebet, Jephthah sacrificed his daughter (Abudarham, "Sha'ar ha-Teḳufot," p. 122a, Venice, 1566).

The origin of the superstition can not be traced. Hai Gaon, in the tenth century, in reply to a question as to the prevalence of this custom in the "West" (i.e., west of Babylon), said it was followed only in order that the new season might be begun with a supply of fresh, sweet water. Ibn Ezra ridicules the fear that the teḳufah water will cause swelling, and ascribes the belief to the "gossip of old women" (ib.). Hezekiah da Silva, however, warns his coreligionists to pay no attention to Ibn Ezra's remarks, asserting that in his own times many persons who drank water when the teḳufah occurred fell ill and died in consequence. Da Silva says the principal danger lies in the first teḳufah (Nisan); and a special announcement of its occurrence was made by the beadle of the congregation ("Peri Ḥadash," on Oraḥ Ḥayyim, 428, end). The danger lurks only in unused water, not in water

Superstition.

'Aruk, Oraḥ Ḥayyim, 455, 1; "Be'er Heṭeb," to Yoreh De'ah, 116, 5). R. Jacob Mölln required that a new iron nail should be lowered by means of a string into the water used for baking maẓẓot during the Nisan teḳufah ("Sefer Maharil," p. 6b, ed. Warsaw).

See CALENDAR; MONTH; SUN, BLESSING OF.

J.　　　　　　　　　　　　　　　J. D. E.

TELASSAR (תְּלַאשַׂר): City, along with Gozan, Haran, and Reseph, which Rabshakeh mentions as having been conquered by Sennacherib's predecessors (II Kings xix. 12; Isa. xxxvii. 12). This city was inhabited by the Bene 'Eden. The cuneiform inscriptions mention a Bit-Adini, located in the upper Mesopotamian country, which may be identical with the Biblical place. "Telassar" is probably, as Schrader holds, the same name as "Til-Ashshuri" (the hill of Ashur), and may have been given to any place on which a temple was built. One such place is found east of the Tigris, as shown by Schrader; and another, mentioned by Tiglath-pileser III., was probably in Babylonia. Esarhaddon, too, mentions one near the land of the Mitanni. Telassar, then, being a possible general name, is located in at least three sections of the great Mesopotamian valley by as many separate cuneiform documents.

E. C.　　　　　　　　　　　　　I. M. P.

TELCS, EDUARD : Hungarian sculptor; born at Baja May 12, 1872. At the age of twelve he went to Budapest and studied decorative art, but he soon left that city for Vienna, where he was educated for four years in the Allgemeine Bildhauerschule, winning the Füger gold medal with his "St. Boniface Striking Down the Banner of Wotan." He next entered Professor Zumbusch's school, where he studied for three years, gaining the school's first prize with his "Two Drinkers," which later won a medal of the second class at the World's Fair in Antwerp. Telcs attracted particular attention in 1900 by being awarded, for his monument in honor of Empress Elizabeth of Austria, first prize among many competitors. In the year 1905 he made a statue of the poet Vörösmarty to be erected in

Budapest, and another of Kossuth in Kecskemet, having been awarded both these commissions as a result of competition.

s.   L. V.

TELESINUS: Jew of Telesia, who lived at Rome about 480. Not only did Pope Gelasius refer to him, in a letter to Bishop Quingesius, as a " vir clarissimus " and his most deserving friend, but he recommended Telesinus' relative Antonius (Antius) to the bishop. Telesinus, moreover, is mentioned in papal documents as the physician of Pope Gelasius. Of late it has been denied that Telesinus was physician in ordinary to Gelasius or even a physician at all.

BIBLIOGRAPHY: Berliner, *Gesch. der Juden in Rom,* ii. 4; Vogelstein and Rieger, *Gesch. der Juden in Rom,* i. 128, and note.
s.   A. M. F.

TELL EL-AMARNA: Name derived from the Beni 'Amran or El-Amarna Bedouins, and now given to the extensive ruins and rock-cut tombs which are the last relics of the ancient royal city of Khut Aten. These ruins are in middle Egypt, on the east bank of the Nile, near the villages of Hagg Ḳandîl on the south and Et-Tell on the north. They are the ruins of a city built by Amenophis IV., of the eighteenth Egyptian dynasty. Shortly after the beginning of his reign, Amenophis broke away from the worship of all gods except Aten, the god of the solar disk. He accordingly removed from Thebes, which for cen-
turies had been the Egyptian capital,
Of the and built a new city, in which ancient
Eighteenth traditions and invested religious inter-
Dynasty. ests should not be able to oppose his reforms. He selected the site now known as El-Amarna, in the Hermopolitan nome in central Egypt, in which a royal palace and a temple of Aten were soon surrounded by residences of nobles and of others who would naturally follow in the train of royalty. After the death of Amenophis the old religion reasserted itself, the royal residence was soon moved back to Thebes, and the city which he had been at so much pains to build fell into decay. As the reign of Amenophis was less than twenty years, the occupation of his new capital can not have been long. Its site was never reoccupied, so that the course of the streets of Khut Aten and the plans of the ancient palaces and houses may still be traced in the mound.

The position of the palace of Amenophis was discovered by Petrie during his excavation at El-Amarna in 1891–92. It is indicated on the mound to-day by a building erected to preserve some painted stucco pavements which once formed a part of the palace. These paintings, as well as those in the neighboring tombs, prove that the artists of the time of Amenophis had emancipated themselves from ordinary Egyptian conventions, and represented objects much more naturally than had hitherto been the case.

The attention of the modern world was first called to El-Amarna by the discovery, accidentally made by a peasant woman late in 1887, of more than 300 cuneiform tablets, which turned out to be letters written to Amenophis III. and Amenophis IV. by kings of various Asiatic countries and by Egyptian

officials or vassals in Phenicia, Syria, and Palestine. This correspondence opened vistas of Oriental history that had been entirely unsuspected. Kadash-
man-Bel and Burnaburiash, kings of
The Babylon; Ashuruballit, a king of As-
El-Amarna syria; Dushratta, a king of Mittani,
Tablets. and a king of Alashia (supposed to be Cyprus)—all had friendly correspond-
ence with the Egyptian kings. An entirely new conception of international relations at this period was thus acquired; and the remarkable fact was established that the language of diplomatic intercourse was then the cuneiform Babylonian. The majority of the letters were from vassals or officials in places like Gebal, Tyre, Sidon, Lachish, Jerusalem, etc.
—letters which proved that even in writing to Egyptians the natives of this region used Babylonian cuneiform. Thus a long domination of these countries by Babylonian influence, before the Egyptian conquest by Thothmes III., was evident. The contents of the letters afford a vivid picture of the way in which the Asiatic empire of Egypt was disintegrating under the weak administration of Amenophis IV.

Amenophis IV. had an Asiatic mother. He was accordingly more interested in preserving these letters than most Egyptian kings would have been; those which had been written to his father he took to his new capital, while those which were written to himself were stored in the same archive, where they remained until 1887. After their discovery the British Museum purchased 87 of them, the Berlin Museum 160 (a considerable number being fragments), the Gizeh Museum at Cairo obtained 60, while about 20 were purchased by private persons.

BIBLIOGRAPHY: Baedeker, *Egypt,* pp. 203 *et seq.,* Leipsic, 1902; Budge, *History of Egypt,* iv. 117–141, 184–241, London, 1902; Bezold, *The Tell-El-Amarna Tablets in the British Museum,* London, 1891; *Oriental Diplomacy,* London, 1893; Winckler, *Der Thontafelfund von El-Amarna,* Berlin, 1889; *Die Thontafeln von Tell-El-Amarna* (vol. v. of Schrader, *K. B.*).
E. C.   G. A. B.

TELLER, LEOPOLD: Hungarian actor; born at Budapest April 3, 1844. For a time he studied medicine at the University of Vienna, but in 1862 he went to Laibach, where he joined a theatrical company. During the following ten years he played at small theaters in Iglau, Klagenfurt, Troppau, Budapest, Leipsic, and Liebenstein; and from 1874 to 1890 he was a member of the " Meininger," and appeared in such rôles as *Shylock, Iago, Gessler, Franz Moor,* and *Marinelli.* On leaving the " Meininger " he secured an engagement at the Stadttheater in Hamburg, where his principal rôles were *Graf Trast, Doctor Crusius,* and *Graf Menges.* In 1899 he retired from the stage, and settled as teacher of elocution in Hamburg. He has written a play entitled " Wintersonnenwende," which has met with considerable success.

BIBLIOGRAPHY: Eisenberg, *Biog. Lex.*
s.   F. T. H.

TELLER, PROBST. See FRIEDLÄNDER, DAVID.

TELLHEIM, CAROLINE. See BETTELHEIM, CAROLINE VON.

TEMAN : Originally, the name of a tribe and then of a district of the Edomites. In Biblical genealogy it is the name of the eldest son of Eliphaz, the first-born of Esau, and one of the "dukes" of Edom (Gen. xxxvi. 11, 15, 42; I Chron. i. 36, 53). The genealogy here noted proves that Teman was one of the most important of the Edomite tribes, and this is confirmed by the fact that "Teman" is used as a synonym for Edom itself (Amos i. 12 ; Obad. 9; comp. Jer. xlix. 20, 22; Hab. iii. 3). The Teman-ites were famed for their wisdom (Jer. xlix. 7; Baruch iii. 22); Eliphaz, the oldest and wisest of the friends of Job, is described as a member of this tribe (Job ii. 11 *et passim*).

Teman is referred to in Obad. 9 as a part of the mount of Esau, while Amos i. 12 mentions it in con-nection with the Edomitic "palaces of Bozrah"; Ezek. xxv. 13 speaks of it in contrast to the southern boundary Dedan. The "Onomasticon" of Eusebius (260, 155) mentions a region called Thaiman, in Geba-lene (the GEBAL of Ps. lxxxiii. 8 [A. V. 7]), and thus in the district of Petra, noting also an East Teman, a town with a Roman garrison fifteen (according to Jerome, five) miles from Petra.

E. C.   I. BE.

TEMERLS, JACOB BEN ELIEZER (known also as **Jacob Ashkenazi**): German Talmudist and cabalist; born at Worms at the end of the six-teenth century; died at Vienna about 1667. At an early age Temerls went to Poland, and for some years directed a Talmudical school at Lublin. Thence he removed to Kremenetz, where he passed the greater part of his life. In his old age he settled at Vienna, where he remained until his death. He enjoyed a high reputation both as a Talmudist and as a cabalist, and was lauded by his contem-poraries for his great piety. He is said to have fasted forty years, during which period he never left the bet ha-midrash.

Temerls was the author of "Sifra di-Ẓeni'uta de-Ya'aḳob," containing a cabalistic commentary on the Pentateuch and rules for the study of the Cab-ala (Amsterdam, 1669). He left in manuscript: "She'elot u-Teshubot," a collection of responsa, quoted in "Emunat Shemuel" (§ 53); a comprehen-sive commentary on the Pentateuch and the Megillot, quoted by himself in his "Sifra di-Ẓeni'uta de-Ya'aḳob"; a commentary on the "Idrot"; a com-mentary on difficult passages in the Babylonian and Palestinian Talmuds; explanations of some passages of the Zohar, the books of the Prophets, and the Hagiographa; and a dissertation on Luria's cabalistic writings.

BIBLIOGRAPHY : Nepi-Ghirondi, *Toledot Gedole Yisrael*, pp. 210, 350 (where Jacob is confounded with the brother of Shab-bethai Bass); Steinschneider, *Cat. Bodl.* col. 1258; Fuenn, *Keneset Yisrael*, p. 581; Dembitz, *Kelilat Yofi*, ii. 117.
S.   I. BR.

TEMESVAR : Hungarian city. The oldest gravestone in the Jewish cemetery is dated 1636, and was erected in memory of Azriel Assach of Salonica. Between 1552 and 1716 large numbers of Spanish Jews settled in Temesvar, where the Turkish gov-ernment received them with favor; but after the capture of the city in 1716 by Prince Eugene their treatment became less favorable, for Temesvar and its district were annexed to Hungary and adminis-tered as an Austrian province. In 1718 the pro-vincial government ordered the expulsion of the Jews from the city on the charge of being Turkish spies. The order was not strictly enforced, how-ever, on account of the influence of Moses Lopez Pereira Diego d'AGUILAR, the founder of the Se-phardic community; Maria Theresa even permitted five other Spanish Jewish families to settle in the city. D'Aguilar presented to the Sephardic com-munity mantles of the Law and silver crowns for the scrolls of the Torah. At that time the Span-ish Jews had a society for the promotion of the study of the Bible, while another association re-ceived official recognition from the Count of Wallis, the commander-in-chief of the citadel.

As in Bohemia and Moravia, the Jews of Temesvar were oppressed by the restrictions formulated by Maria Theresa in 1776. Only forty-nine were per-mitted to reside in the city. They were restricted to a single community, headed by a dayyan and a rabbi; nor might they contract mar-**Residence** riages or leave the city without the **Limited.** permission of the authorities. Only eight were allowed to engage in com-merce; and the distinction between Ashkenazim and Sephardim was abolished, the whole Jewry being comprised under the term "protected Jews of the cities and counties of the Banat." Jews from other places were forbidden to enter the city except for commercial purposes, when they were required to pay a daily tax of five groschen for protection, and were obliged to leave the city at night. Jews were forbidden either to have Christian servants or to live in the houses of Christians, and were compelled to reside in a ghetto in the citadel, their quarter being bounded by the streets now called Varoshaz, Szerb, Erzsibet, and Jenö. Marriages might be performed only by the rabbi of Temesvar, and all Jews who died in the province were to be buried in the ceme-tery of the city. It was not until the reign of Jo-seph II. (1780–90) that the condition of the Jews of Temesvar began to improve.

The community's most important society, next to the charitable organization, is the Jewish Women's Club of the citadel, one of the oldest societies of Hungary, founded by Sarolta Fischel in 1846. This is the famous Jewish society which gave Louis Kos-suth 800 crowns for patriotic purposes on the out-break of the Hungarian revolution. During the oc-cupation of Bosnia and Herzegovina this society rendered valuable aid by sending food to the wounded; and at the time of the flood at Szegedin, in 1879, it materially assisted the poor, especially by maintaining a soup-kitchen. The commu-nity supports two other women's clubs, founded in 1847 and 1869 respectively, as well as the Talmud Torah (a charitable organization), the Maskil el Dal, and a ḥebra ḳaddisha, the last-named established in 1748, although its hospital in the citadel has since been demolished.

Temesvar has had the following rabbis: Jacob Moses of Belgrade (Sephardi; 1739); Eliezer Lip-mann, author of the commentary "Migdal Dawid" (1748); Jonathan Trebitsch, chief rabbi of Transyl-vania (1752); Johanan b. Isaiah (1775); Zebi Hirsch

b. Israel (Hershele Ḥarif; 1782); and David b. Ẓebi Oppenheim (1801), and his son David Hirsch Oppenheim, author of "'Ene ha-Da'at" (Budapest, 1829). The rabbinate of Temesvar has always included the entire district composed of Lugos, Versecz, Karansebes, Pancsova, and Nagy Becskerek. In

city possesses a synagogue in the Moorish style, built in 1865. There is a small Sephardic synagogue in the citadel, but the Spanish Jews in Temesvar are now very few, and their old place of worship, the Judenhof, founded in 1760, has been demolished to make room for the new Reform synagogue.

SYNAGOGUE AT TEMESVAR, HUNGARY.
(From a photograph.)

1863 Moritz Hirschfeld was elected rabbi, and was succeeded by Moritz Löwy. Since 1860, however, internal dissensions have divided the community into factions, with the Reform rabbi, Moritz Löwy, at the head of the one in the city, and the Orthodox rabbi, Jakob Singer, leading that in the citadel.

The latter contains a synagogue in the Renaissance Gothic style, designed by Leopold Baumhorn; the

The earliest Jewish census at Temesvar was taken in 1739, when there were 139 Ashkenazim and 81 Sephardim (46 families altogether). In 1755 there were 23 Jewish families in the city; 53 in 1772; 76 in 1776; and 72 in 1781. In 1840 the Jewish population of the city was about 1,200, of whom 750 lived in the citadel, 340 in the city, and about 50 in the suburbs. In 1858 the number was 2,202; in 1890,

4,870; and in 1914 about 10,000 (including Jewish soldiery). The total population of Temesvar in 1920 was 72,555.

BIBLIOGRAPHY: M. Löwy, *Skizzen zur Geschichte der Juden in Temesvár*; Jakob Singer, *Adata a Bánati Zsidók Törten*, Budapest, 1905.

s.
J. Si.

TEMPLE, ADMINISTRATION AND SERVICE OF:

The affairs of the Second Temple were managed by a board of fifteen appointed officers ("memunnim"). The Mishnah records the following names of officers of the Temple without stating their respective periods of activity; but it is presumed they were those appointed in the time of Agrippa: (1) Johanan b. Phinehas, in charge of the seals given in exchange for money to purchase sacrifices; (2) Ahijah, of libations; (3) Mattithiah b. Samuel, of allotments (*i.e.*, the selection of priests for the day); (4) Pethahiah, of the nests of fowls (for sacrifices); (5) Ben Ahijah, of the health department (treating especially a disease of the bowels caused by the bare feet touching the cold marble pavement); (6) Nehunya, of the digging of wells (for the pilgrims on the highways leading to Jerusalem); (7) Gebini (Gabinimus), of announcements (the Temple crier); (8) Ben Geber, of the gates (opening and closing them); (9) Ben Babi, of the wicks for the candlestick ("menorah"); (10) Ben Arza, of the cymbals (leading the music of the Levites); (11) Hugras (Hugdas) b. Levi, of the musical instruments; (12) the Garmu family, of the preparation of the showbread; (13) the Abṭinas family, of the incense; (14) Eleazar, of the curtains; and (15) Phinehas, of the vestments (Sheḳ. v. 1; comp. Maimonides, "Yad," Kele ha-Miḳdash, vii. 1).

Officers.

Seven trustees ("amarkelim") and three cashiers ("gizbarim") had charge of the Temple treasury. In the courts were thirteen contribution-boxes in the shape of shofarim, with narrow necks and broad bases (Sheḳ. vi.). The half-shekel contribution for public sacrifices, etc., was demanded on the first of Adar and was payable by the twenty-fifth of the same month (*ib.* i. 1, 3). There was a special room, called "Lishkat Ḥashsha'im" (Secret Chamber), for anonymous donations, out of which fund the worthy poor were supported. Into the Vessel Chamber the people threw donations of silver and gold vessels. Every thirty days this chamber was opened by the cashiers, who selected such vessels as could be utilized in the Temple, the rest being sold and the proceeds applied to a fund for repairing the Temple building ("bedeḳ ha-bayit"; *ib.* v. 4).

The priestly officials were: the high priest, his deputy ("segan"), and his two attendants ("ḳatoliḳin" = "catholicus").

A strict watch over the Temple was maintained, the guard being composed of three priests and twenty-one Levites. The priests were stationed one at the Chamber of the Flame ("Bet ha-Niẓoẓ"), one at the Chamber of the Hearth ("Bet ha-Moḳed"), and one at the Chamber (attic) of Abṭinas (see diagram, page 95). The Levites kept guard as follows: one at each of the five gates of the mount entrances; one at each of the four corners within the mount enclosure; one at each of the five impor-

tant gates of the courts; one at each of the four corners within the court; one at the Chamber of Sacrifice; one at the Chamber of Curtains; and one behind the "Kapporet" (Holy of Holies). The captain of the guard saw that every man was alert, chastising a priest if found asleep at his post, and sometimes even punishing him by burning his shirt upon him, as a warning to others (Mid. i. 1).

Priestly Guard.

The priests were divided into twenty-four patrols ("mishmarot"), which were changed every week. The patrol was quartered partly in the Chamber of the Flame and principally in the Chamber of the Hearth, both of which were on the north side of the inner court ("'azarah"). The latter chamber was a capacious one, surmounted by a dome. Half of the chamber extended outside the court to the "ḥel," a kind of platform surrounding the courts, which was considered as secular, in contrast to the sacred premises within, where the priests were not allowed to sit down, much less to sleep. A fire was always kept burning in the outer extension, at which the priests might warm their hands and bare feet. Here also they might sit down and rest for a while. At night the elder priests slept here on divans placed on rows of stone steps one above another. The younger priests slept on cushions on the floor, putting their sacred garments under their heads and covering themselves with their secular clothing (Tamid i. 1). The elder priests kept the keys of the Temple, putting them at night under a marble slab in the floor; to this slab a ring was attached for lifting it. A priest watched over or slept on the slab until the keys were demanded by the officer in the morning.

The king when visiting the Temple had no rights beyond those of the ordinary Israelite; only the kings of the house of David were privileged to sit down in the 'azarah (Soṭah 41b; Tamid 27a).

The major Sanhedrin, composed of 71 members, sat in the Chamber of Hewn Stone ("Lishkat ha-Gazit") on the extreme north of the priests' hall. Two tribunals of minor Sanhedrin, each composed of twenty-three members, sat one by the south gate of the mount and one in front of the hall on the north side.

The Judiciary.

The sessions were held from the morning sacrifice till that of the afternoon. On Sabbaths and holy days, to facilitate increased business the major Sanhedrin sat outside on the ḥel (Sanh. 88b), and the minor Sanhedrin assembled in the bet ha-midrash situated on the mount (Tosef., Ḥag. ii.).

Entrance within the enclosure of the mount was permitted to any one who was decently attired and who carried no burden. Israelites when ritually unclean and Gentiles were not allowed to pass beyond the "soreg," a fence which surrounded the courts at a distance of ten cubits. The outer court, called "'Ezrat Nashim" (Women's Hall), was for the use of ordinary Israelites. The priests' hall was reserved for the priests and Levites; occasionally, however, men and women presenting sin-offerings, sacrifices on which they were required to place the hands ("semikah"), made use of it. At the festivals, to accommodate the large crowds, all Israelites were permitted to enter

Local Divisions and Water-Supply.

the priests' hall, on which occasion the curtain of the vestibule was raised to show the people the interior of the "Hekal" (see PILGRIMAGE). The people, though tightly packed, were able to find sufficient space in which to prostrate themselves, this being one of the miracles associated with the Temple. The people crowded to within eleven cubits behind the Holy of Holies (Yoma 21a).

Another phenomenon was the water-supply. A spring rising below the Holy of Holies from an opening as narrow as the antennæ of a locust increased when it reached the entrance to the Hekal to the size of a warp-thread; at the entrance to the vestibule it assumed the size of a woof-thread; and

rah, being unfit for service till sunset of the same day.

The order of the priests' daily service in the Temple was as follows: One of the priests arose early and bathed before the arrival of the officer, who usually came about cockcrow. The officer knocked at the door of the Chamber of the Hearth, and the priests opened it. He called for the priest who had bathed, and ordered him to **Order of** decide by lot which of the priests should **Service.** serve that day. The officer then took the keys and entered through the wicket ("pishpush") of the door to the 'azarah, followed by the priests who formed the patrol, each

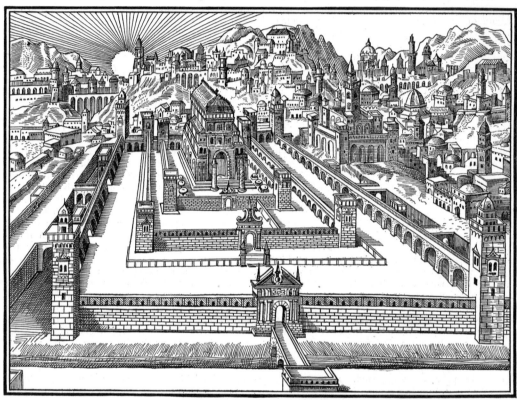

THE TEMPLE AT JERUSALEM.
(From a Passover Haggadah, printed at Amsterdam, 1695.)

at the house of David it became an overflowing brook (Yoma 77b, 78a). This spring is referred to in the passage "And behold, waters issued out from under the threshold of the house . . . at the south side of the altar" (Ezek. xlvii. 1, 2); it was the mysterious spring that filled the bath of Ishmael the high priest, situated by the attic of Abṭinas on the south of the court, at the water-gate. There was another bath, in a passage under the Chamber of the Hearth, for the use of any ordinary priest who might become ritually unclean. This was reached by a winding staircase. The priest, having bathed, dried himself by the fire; he then dressed and returned to his comrades above, with whom he waited until the gates were opened, when he left the 'aza-

holding two torches. The patrol was divided into two sections; one going through the colonnade on the east, and one on the west, the sections meeting on the south side at the chamber where they prepared the "ḥabittin" (the baked cake for the meal-offering). The priests now asked one another "Is all well?" and received the answer "All is well." The officer assigned by lot the making of the ḥabittin. Similarly he selected a priest to clean the altar of ashes, his comrades uttering the warning: "Be careful not to touch the sacred vessels before thou sanctifiest [by washing] thy hands and feet at the laver; and see that the coal-shovel ["maḥtah"] is in its place [near the "kebesh," the inclined plank or bridge leading to the altar]." Proceeding without

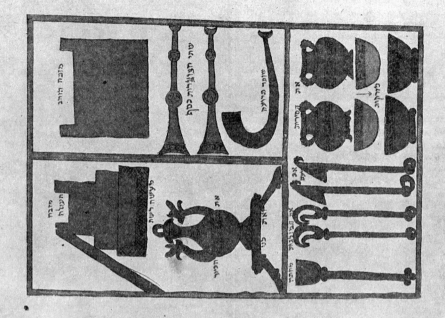

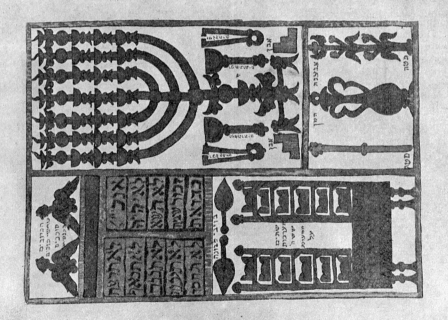

UTENSILS OF THE TEMPLE.

(From an illuminated Hebrew manuscript of the 13th century in the Bibliothèque Nationale, Paris.)

any light save that of the pyre ("ma'arakah") on the altar, he disappeared below, and was next heard operating the machinery for raising the laver from the well. This consisted of a wooden wheel and shaft and a chain, a device designed by the high priest Ben Ḳaṭṭin. The noise caused by this operation fixed the time for washing hands and feet. The priest took the silver "maḥtah" and ascended the altar; pushing the large coals aside, he took a shovelful of ashes and charred wood, and, descending, turned northward and deposited the ashes in a heap on the floor three handbreadths from the "kebesh," where also the ashes from the golden altar and the candlestick were placed. The authorities disagree as to the disposition of the ashes: some say they fell through a grate in the floor; others, that they were removed later. Observing his act, the priest's comrades hurried to wash their hands and feet at the laver. They then took large shovels ("magrefot") and made a heap ("tappuaḥ") of the ashes of the altar in the center, other priests meanwhile using flesh-hooks to place aside the portions of the sacrifices that had not been consumed during the night. When the heap of ashes was sufficiently large it was removed outside the city. The priests now brought pieces of all kinds of wood except olive and vine, and built a new pyre, on which they replaced the unconsumed portions of the sacrifices. For a second pyre, intended for the burning of incense, they selected the best fig-wood. Having lit the two pyres, they descended from the altars.

The officer then ordered the priests to decide by lot who should slaughter the sacrificial victim, who should sprinkle the blood, who should clean the ashes from the golden altar and from the golden candlestick, and who should attend to the sacrifices in detail. This being done, the officer commanded: "Go ye and see if it is time to commence the sacrificial service!" Mounting to an eminence of the Temple, they looked toward the east, till at length one shouted, "Barḳai!" (the morning light has appeared). Mattithiah b. Samuel said

The Tamid Sacrifice. they asked him, "Has the light in the east reached Hebron?" and he answered, "Yes." The mention of Hebron was made to honor the memory of the patriarchs buried there. The officer then said: "Go and fetch a lamb from the Chamber of the Lambs" (situated at the northeast corner of the 'azarah). The priests entered also the Vessel Chamber and took therefrom ninety-three vessels of silver and gold. The lamb was now examined by the light of torches to see whether it was free from blemishes; and water from a golden cup was given it to drink. The priest selected by lot then dragged the animal to the abattoir, north of the altar. Meanwhile other priests advanced with the "ṭeni," a gold dish in the shape of a basket of a "tarḳab" measure; the "kuz," a gold pitcher; and two keys wherewith to open the Hekal, one from the outside and one from within through the wicket or lattice of a cell on the north side of the vestibule. The bolt was thrown back and the doors unlocked, causing a noise which was heard a long distance and which was the signal for the shoḥeṭ to slaughter the perpetual morning sacrifice ("tamid shel shaḥarit") at the abattoir, while

the priest in the Hekal carefully gathered up all the ashes of the golden altar into the ṭeni, put this on the floor, and went out. The priest with the kuz cleared the candlestick of ashes, leaving the two lights nearest to the east to burn till the evening. If he found them extinguished he renewed and relighted them, after which he trimmed the other lamps. In front of the candlestick were three marble steps, on the top one of which the priest stood to trim and light the lamps. When he had finished he put the kuz on the second step and went out. On the first step the tongs and snuff-dishes were placed (Maimonides, "Yad," Bet ha-Beḥirah, iii. 11). The ṭeni was removed by the priest chosen to remove the ashes of the altar after the incense had been offered; the kuz, by the priest who in the afternoon attended to the two lights of the candlestick that had been burning all day.

The slaughter of the lamb was effected as follows: The front legs were bound to the hind legs, the head pointing south with its face toward the west. The

The Abattoir. shoḥeṭ stood facing the west. The morning tamid was slaughtered at the northwest corner, that of the afternoon at the northeast corner, of the altar at the second ring. There were twenty-four rings, in four rows, fixed to the floor on hinges; in these the heads of the animals were held in position. The priest who received the blood in a basin stood facing the south. He sprinkled the blood on both sides of the northeast and southwest corners of the altar. The removal of the hide and the dissection of the carcass were shared by the priests, and were followed by the meal-offering (Lev. vi. 13). This accomplished, the priests went to the Chamber of Hewn Stone. There the officer directed them to recite one benediction ("Ahabah Rabbah") and to read the Ten Commandments and the "Shema'," after which they blessed the people. On Sabbaths they blessed also with "love, brotherhood, peace, and friendship" the patrol that was about to go off duty.

Finally, the priests drew lots for the incense service, and the various assignments were made, only those who had not been previously selected being admitted to the ballot. The priests

The Incense Service. that were not to share in the service of the day now removed their priestly garments and then, having delivered them to an attendant who placed them in the proper lockers, dressed themselves in their secular clothes and retired from the 'azarah till their next turn.

During the sacrifice the Levites were at their stations on the steps leading to the priests' hall, and in front of the dukan; but they did not commence their music until the libation at the conclusion of the service. The musical instrument called the "magrefah," somewhat similar to the organ, stood between the altar and the vestibule. Its tones, which could be heard a long distance, were the signal for the priests to prostrate themselves: this took place after the incense-offering.

Special honor was paid to the high priest. He was attended by three priests: one on his right, one on his left, and one holding up the breastplate adorned with precious stones. The high priest entered the Hekal alone, and after the curtain was lowered, he prostrated himself and retired. The officer who waited in the vestibule, on hearing the sound of the bells on the hem of the high priest's garment, raised the curtain. After **Honor to** the high priest had left, the officer **the High** who acted as sagan entered the Hekal **Priest.** and prostrated himself; and on his retirement the other priests entered and followed his example. In case the high priest desired to offer the incense he was assisted by the officer and two attendants.

At the conclusion the priests bearing the five empty vessels—the basket, pitcher, ladle, spoon, and cover—used in the service of the altar, and those carrying the candlestick and incense, stood in line on the staircase of the vestibule, and, raising their hands as high as their shoulders, recited the priestly benediction.

The high priest then offered the libation of wine ("nesakim"). The officer stood in the corner with kerchief (flag) in hand, and two priests with silver trumpets by the table, the cymbals meanwhile playing between them. The trumpeters sounded "teḳi-'ah, teru'ah, te-

Greek Inscription, Found on Site of Temple Area, Forbidding Gentiles to Enter Within the Inner Temple Walls.
(In the museum at Constantinople.)

ḳi'ah"; the high priest commenced the ceremony of the libation; the officer unfurled the kerchief; the cymbals clashed; and the Levites sang hymns accompanied by music. During the pauses the trumpet sounded "teḳi'ah," and the people in the 'azarah prostrated themselves; at every pause a teḳi'ah and a prostration. The order of the daily Psalms from Sunday to Saturday was as follows: Ps. xxiv., xlviii., lxxxii., xciv., lxxxi., xciii., xciv.
J. J. D. E.

TEMPLE OF HEROD: In the eighteenth year (20–19 B.C.) of his reign Herod rebuilt the Temple on a more magnificent scale. There are many evidences that he shared the passion for building by which many powerful men of that time were moved. He had adorned many cities and had erected many heathen temples; and it was not fitting that the temple of his capital should fall beneath these in magnificence. Probably, also, one of his motives was to placate the more pious of his subjects, whose sentiments he had often outraged.

The Jews were loth to have their Temple pulled down, fearing lest it might not be rebuilt. To demonstrate his good faith, Herod acccumulated the materials for the new building before the old one was taken down. The new Temple was rebuilt as rapidly as possible, being finished in a year and a half, although work was in progress on the outbuildings and courts for eighty years. As it was unlawful for any but priests to enter the Temple, Herod employed 1,000 of them as masons and carpenters.

The Temple proper as reconstructed by Herod was of the same dimensions as that of Solo-**Dimen-** mon, viz.: 60 cubits long, 20 cubits **sions.** wide, and 40 cubits high. This space was divided into the Holy of Holies and the "Hekal." The former measured 20 × 20 cubits; the latter, 20 × 40 ("B. J." v. 5, § 5). At the entrance to the outer Temple hung a veil embroidered in blue, white (byssus), scarlet, and purple; the outer Temple was separated from the Holy of Holies by a similar curtain. The outer curtain was folded back on the south side, and the inner one on the north side, so that a priest in entering the Holy of Holies traversed the outer Temple diagonally. The Holy of Holies was quite empty. In the Holy Place stood the altar of incense, near the entrance to the Holy of Holies the seven-branched golden CANDLESTICK to the south, and the table of showbread to the north. Above the gate of the Temple were golden vines and grape-clusters as large as a man ("Ant." xv. 11, § 3; "B. J." v. 5, § 4). The Temple building had an upper story similar in size to the lower ("B. J." v. 5, § 5). Side-structures, as in Solomon's Temple, afforded space for three stories of chambers on the north, south, and west sides of the Temple. These chambers were connected by doors; and trap-doors afforded communication from those of one story to those of the story immediately above or below. The whole breadth of the structure including the side-buildings was 70 cubits (Mid. iv. 7).

East of Herod's Temple there was, as in Solomon's, a porch, 100 cubits wide, 100 cubits high, and 20 cubits deep, thus extending 15 cubits on either side of the Temple ("B. J." v. 5, § 4). Its gateway, which had no gates, was 20 cubits broad and 70 cubits high. Over this gateway Herod erected a golden eagle, which was afterward pulled down by the Jews ("Ant." xvii. 6, § 2). The front of the porch was covered with gold ("B. J." v. 5, § 4); and it was most brilliant when the rays of the morning sun fell upon it.

In front of the Temple, 22 cubits distant from the porch, stood the altar of burnt offering, constructed of unhewn stones. Its length and breadth were each 50 cubits, and its height 15 cubits ("B. J." v. 5, § 5). To the north of the altar twenty-four rings were fixed in the ground, to which the sacrificial animals were tied. Near by were eight pillars supporting cedar beams, on which the carcasses of the animals were hung. There were also eight marble tables for preparing sacrificial flesh

J." v. 5, § 2). If the first part of this account is true, only the length of the Temple area was enlarged, the width remaining the same. It is more probable that Herod enlarged the area in both dimensions, though it is possible that it had been enlarged to the size of a square stadium by one of the Hasmoneans. The size to which Herod increased the area was almost that of the present Ḥaram enclosure. The sacred territory has been increased since the time of Herod only on the north.

In order to obtain space for this area on the top of a hill the sides of which sloped so steeply, it was necessary to extend artificially the surface of the hill itself. This was done, especially to the south,

SUBSTRUCTURE OF TEMPLE OF HEROD, NOW CALLED "SOLOMON'S STABLES."
(From a photograph by the American Colony at Jerusalem.)

(Mid. iii. 5, v. 2; Tamid iii. 5; Sheḳ. vi. 4). On the south was a bronze laver for the priestly ablutions (Mid. iii. 6; Yoma iii. 10).

If sacred tradition compelled Herod to conform closely to the ancient plan of the holy house, allowing him to vary little from precedents **The Temple Courts.** save in its façade, his Grecized taste and his genius for building found ample scope in the Temple courts and cloisters. First of all, he greatly enlarged the Temple area. Josephus says that before the time of Herod the Temple area was square, each side being a stadium ("Ant." xv. 11, § 3—conflicting with the statement of Hecatæus, see JEW. ENCYC. xii. 97b), and that Herod so enlarged the courts that the perimeter was increased to six stadia ("B.

where the massive masonry (called by the Arabs "Solomon's Stables") which Herod constructed to support a pavement on a level with the surface of the hill farther to the north may still be seen. The whole was surrounded by a battlemented wall ("B. J." iv. 9, § 12). The number of gates which this wall contained is somewhat uncertain, as Josephus and the Mishnah differ. The former says ("Ant." xv. 11, § 5) that there were four gates in the western wall. Probably one of these was at the southwest corner and led to the upper city over the bridge where Robinson's arch may still be seen. This bridge, broken down by Pompey, was reconstructed; indeed, the remains of the arch in the modern wall are evidence that it was rebuilt. Probably there was another gate some 600 feet farther to the north,

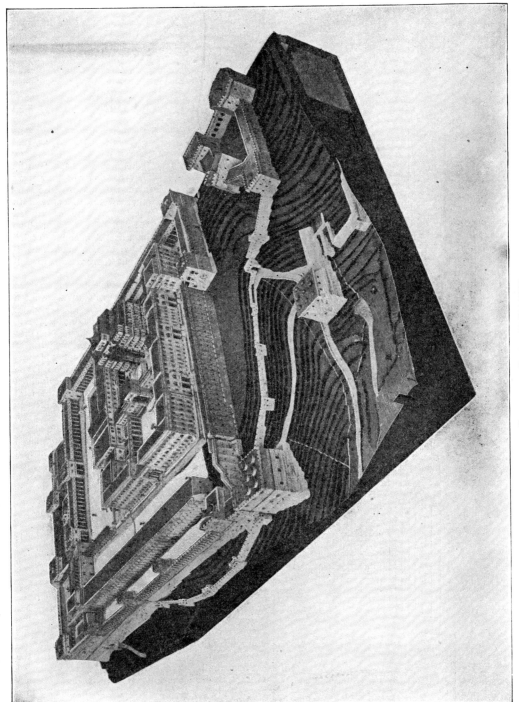

VIEW OF THE TEMPLE OF SOLOMON.
(Reconstructed by Schick.)

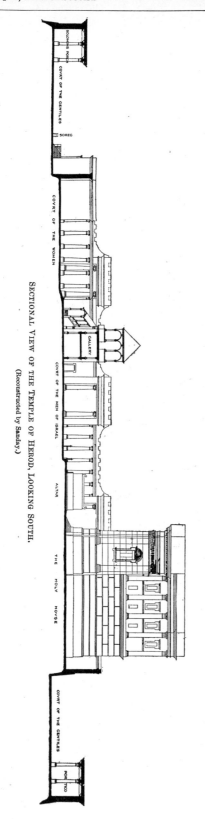

SECTIONAL VIEW OF THE TEMPLE OF HEROD, LOOKING SOUTH.

(Reconstructed by Sanday.)

where Wilson's arch (comp. Warren and Conder, "Jerusalem," pp. 195 *et seq.*) supported a causeway across the valley to the city. The gates in the south wall may be more easily traced. Josephus says ("Ant." xv. 11, § 5) that it had gates in the middle; these the Mishnah calls "gates of Huldah," and they may still be traced in the substructures of the present wall. From them a double tunnel leads by an inclined plane under the modern mosque Al-Aḳṣa to the level of the Temple courts. About 250 feet farther to the east a triple gate may also be traced. Josephus does not mention this; but perhaps it was the second Huldah gate of the Mishnah.

Around the entire interior of this wall were ranged porticoes or cloisters. The finest were those on the south. They consisted of four rows of Corinthian columns of white marble; and there were 162 columns in all. The ceilings were of carved wood ("Ant." xv. 11, § 5; "B. J." v. 5, § 2). The eastern cloister was known as "Solomon's Porch" (John x. 23; Acts iii. 11, v. 12); it must accordingly have been believed that there were here Solomonic substructures.

The Cloisters.

The open space beyond the cloisters was paved with various kinds of stone, probably forming a mosaic. This outer court was, strictly speaking, not a part of the Temple. Its soil was not sacred, and it might be entered by any one. Some distance within, one came to an interior court which was raised 15 cubits above the other. Access to it was gained by means of fourteen steps. This was the beginning of the sanctuary. It probably coincided with the elevated court still to be seen in the central part of the Ḥaram area. This raised court was surrounded by a terrace 10 cubits in breadth ("B. J." v. 5, § 2). A breastwork of stone ran around the whole at the level of the steps. On it were placed at frequent intervals inscriptions in Greek and Latin forbidding a non-Jew to enter farther on pain of death. One of these has been recovered. It reads: "No foreigner may pass within the lattice and wall around the sanctuary. Whoever is caught, the guilt for the death which will follow will be his own" (comp. "Pal. Explor. Fund, Quarterly Statement," 1871, p. 132; Benzinger, "Arch." p. 404; Nowack, "Lehrbuch der Hebräischen Archäologie," ii. 77). This enclosure was penetrated by nine gates. Four of these were on the north, four on the south, and one on the east, the western side having none. The eastern part of this court was separated from the western, and formed the court of the women. Women might pass beyond the court of the Gentiles into this court alone. The Temple proper might be entered by men only. One of the four gates on the north and one on the south gave entrance to the women's hall, as did likewise the sole gate which led on the east from the court of the Gentiles. The remaining six of the nine gates led into the court of the men. A large gate led from the court of the women into the court of the men. The gates had double doors which were covered with silver and gold donated by a certain Alexander of Alexandria. The gate on the east was especially magnificent, and was

The Gates.

covered with Corinthian bronze. The greatest of all the gates was, however, the "gate of Nicanor," which led from the court of the women into the court of the men. It was the "great gate," its height being 50 cubits and its breadth 40 cubits ("B. J." v. 5, § 3); fifteen steps led up to it from the women's court. Whether this gate or the one directly east of it in the eastern wall of the women's court was the gate "Beautiful" of Acts iii. 2 can not now be determined. Each gate was porch-like in form.

Along the enclosing wall of the men's court was a series of chambers for storing utensils, vestments, and other articles. Within this western court, or court of the men, was another raised platform, to which access was gained by twelve steps, and on which the Temple, as already described, was situated. On the north the fortress which had existed from the time of Nehemiah was rebuilt and named "Antonia" in honor of Mark Antony. It was connected with the Temple by a secret passage ("Ant." xv. 11, § 7).

The construction of all this work occupied, according to John ii. 20, forty-six years; in reality, however, it was not completed until the procuratorship of Albinus (62–64 C.E.), more than eighty years after its commencement. Less than a decade later (70) it was destroyed by fire during the siege of Jerusalem by Titus.

Column from the Temple of Herod.
(From a photograph by the Palestine Exploration Fund.)

BIBLIOGRAPHY: Josephus, *Ant.* especially xv. 11; idem, *B. J.* especially v. 5; idem, *Contra Ap.* i. 22; Nowack, *Lehrbuch der Hebräischen Archäologie*, 1894, ii. 71–83; Benzinger, *Arch.* 1894, pp. 399–404; Schick, *Die Stiftshütte, der Tempel in Jerusalem und der Tempelplatz der Jetztzeit*, 1896; Sanday, *Sacred Sites of the Gospels*, 1903, pp. 58–63, 107–117.

E. C.   G. A. B.

TEMPLE OF MOUNT GERIZIM. See GERIZIM, MOUNT.

TEMPLE OF ONIAS. See LEONTOPOLIS.

TEMPLE, PLAN OF SECOND: The plan and description of the Second Temple according to Talmudic sources were as follows:

Mount Moriah, known as the "Har ha-Bayit" (Mount of the House), had an area of 500 × 500 cubits or ells (1 cubit = 21.85 inches). It was lowest on the east side, rising gradually to its highest point on the west, and was walled on all sides. The main entrance was on the south, and consisted of two gates near the center, the one on the right for admission, and the other for exit. The two gates were named "Huldah," after the prophetess who used to preach there to the people; the space on this side being the greatest, 265 cubits in width. The next largest space, 115 cubits, was on the east side. The eastern gate was called "Shushan" because it bore a model of Susa, the capital of Persia, in recognition of the permission given by that government to rebuild the Temple. The entrance on the north was through the "Tadi" gate, *i.e.*, the gate of obscurity or privacy, it being used only by those who were ceremonially unclean and by mourners and those under the ban. The space on this side was 100 cubits. The space on the west was the least of all, measuring only 63 cubits to the court wall. The gate on this side was called "Ḳiponus," meaning "garden bower," from the fact that Joshua planted on its site the herbs, etc., from which the ingredients for the incense were derived. Each gate was 10 cubits wide and 20 cubits high. The height of the walls above the gates is not recorded; but it does not appear that they were raised much above the lintels. The Tadi gate had no lintel, but was triangular in shape, this distinguishing it as a private entrance. The walls were all 5 cubits thick and of a uniform height. From the eastern side of the mount, which, as stated above, was the lowest, a flight of steps, consisting of thirty-nine of a rise of ½ cubit each and one of 1 cubit (total, 20½ cubits), gave access to the floor of the Hekal, which was nearly level with the top of the eastern wall, rendering it easy for the priest to observe the inside of the Holy of Holies while standing on Mount Olivet opposite the eastern gate, when he sprinkled the ashes of the red heifer in the direction of the Sanctuary.

A reticulated fence of sticks, called "soreg," 10 handbreadths in height and at a distance of 10 cubits from the outer wall of the courts, surrounded the

Temple. This fence was on the edge of the foundation of the platform called "ḥel," which was between the fence and the courts. The soreg

The Soreg. served as a barrier beyond which Gentiles and the ceremonially unclean might not pass (Kelim i. 8); and it was provided with a guarded entrance opposite each gate of the courts. The exclusion of Gentiles angered the Greeks, who, when they gained control over the Jews, made thirteen openings in the soreg; but after the Maccabean victory these breaches were repaired.

women (hence its name), especially during the celebration of the water libation at the close of the first day of Sukkot, when the women occupied the galleries above (see GALLERY). This court contained four unroofed chambers, one at each corner, each measuring 40 × 40 cubits. They

The Courts. were used as follows: (1) that on the southeast as the Chamber of the Nazarites, where, after the expiration of their terms, the Nazarites cooked their peace-offerings and burned their superfluous hair; (2) that on

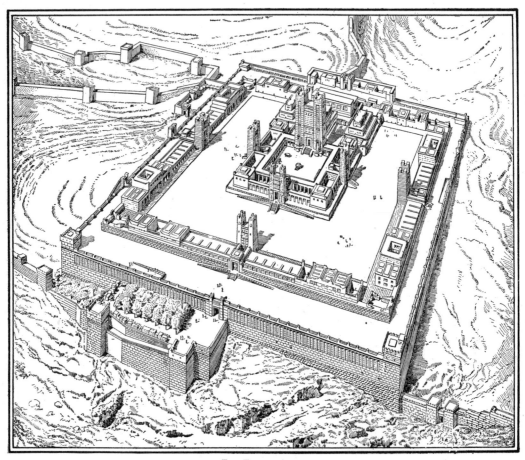

THE TEMPLE AREA.
(Reconstructed by Chipiez.)

Leading up from the ḥel to the courts were twelve marble steps, each of ½ cubit rise. These steps were protected from the sun and rain; and on them the people sat and rested (Pes. 13b).

Within the soreg were the courts: the outer court, known as "'ezrat nashim" (women's hall), to the east, and the inner court, the Temple enclosure, to the west. The two together measured 135 × 322 cubits, the dimensions of the outer court being 135 × 135 cubits and those of the inner one 135 × 187 cubits. The Temple service was conducted in the inner court, the outer one being used mainly for the gathering of the people, including

the northeast as the Chamber of Wood, where fuel for the altar and the hearth was stored; (3) that on the northwest as the Chamber of the Lepers, where, after they had been cured and had bathed on the eighth day of their purification, lepers remained prior to their admittance to the inner court for the anointing of their toes, etc.; (4) that on the southwest as the Chamber of Oils, in which oil for the candlestick and the meal-offering, as well as wine for the libation, was kept.

The inner court, with the Nicanor gate in the center, was 7½ cubits higher than the outer one, and was connected with the latter by fifteen steps (each of ¼ cubit rise). On these steps the Levites sang the "hymns of degrees," fifteen in number (Ps. cxx.–cxxxv.), corresponding with the number of steps (Yoma 38a); these were recited at the festival of the rejoicing of the water (Suk. 51b). Several chambers built under the inner court opened on either side of the staircase into the outer court below; among these were two music chambers for the Levites. In the inner court above were two chambers, one on each side of the Nicanor gate. On the right was the Chamber of Phinehas, the vestment-keeper, who had charge of the priests' lockers built in the wall and who arranged for the 24 patrols ("mishmarot"; Tamid v. 3). To the left was the Chamber of the Pancake-Makers ("'ose ḥabittim"), where twelve cakes were prepared daily, six for the morning and six for the afternoon sacrifice (ib. i. 3). The high priest had a special chamber called "lishkat parhedrin" (πάρεδροι = "assessors") = "the Counselors' Chamber" (Yoma 10a). The inner court was divided. On the east was the Israelites' hall ("'ezrat Yisrael"), 135 × 11 cubits; and on the

The Hall of the Priests. west the priests' hall ("'ezrat kohanim"). Slats or sticks, also a step of 1 cubit rise, divided the priests' hall from that of the Israelites. In front of the priests' hall stood the dais (DUKAN), three stone steps, from the highest of which the priests blessed the people. This hall contained also several chambers (Mid. v. 16).

The space between the priests' hall and the vestibule of the Temple proper was 54 cubits. The altar occupied 32 cubits, leaving 22 cubits vacant. The space of 135 cubits along the width of the 'azarah, from north to south, was made up as follows: 8 cubits space from the wall; 12½ cubits for the four rows of posts on which the slaughtered sacrificial victims were hung and flayed; 4 cubits for the eight marble tables, in two rows, on which the animal sacrifices were washed (ib. iii. 2); 4 cubits between the tables and the rings; 24 cubits for the twenty-four rings, in four rows, to which the animals were secured for slaughtering (ib. v. 2); 8 cubits between the rings and the altar; 32 cubits for the altar; 30 cubits for the "kebesh" (plank or bridge) leading up to the altar; and 12½ cubits to the southern wall. In front of the kebesh were two tables. The laver stood southwest of the altar.

On the north of the 'azarah was the Chamber of the Hearth ("Bet ha-Moḳed"), which extended to the ḥel, and part of which was used as a shelter for the patrol. This chamber was capacious and was surmounted by a dome. Four small chambers opened into it: (1) the one in which the sacrificial lambs were kept, on the southwest; (2) that in which the showbread was made, on the southeast; (3) a chamber in which the stones of the altar defiled by the Greeks were preserved (I Macc. ii. 25), on the northeast; (4) the bath-chamber, on the northwest. A row of slats or sticks divided the Bet ha-Moḳed, separating the sacred part within the court from the secular part in the ḥel. In the bath-chamber was a trap-door leading to a bath and lavatory below (ib. i. 6; Tamid iii. 3).

The vestibule was 6 cubits higher than the 'azarah, and was connected with it by twelve steps, each of ½ cubit rise. The front wall of the vestibule was 100 cubits long from north to south; its thickness was 5 cubits; and its height up to the Hekal was 100 cubits (ib. iv. 7). The entrance to the vestibule was 20 cubits wide and 40 cubits high. It had in place of doors a richly embroidered

The Vestibule. curtain. The lintel of this entranceway consisted of five superimposed oaken beams artistically carved. The lower one extended 1 cubit on each side over the entrance, which was 20 cubits wide; the second beam extended 2 cubits, or 1 cubit beyond the first; and so on to the fifth, which extended 5 cubits on each side, bringing its total length to 30 cubits. A row of stones separated each beam from the next (ib. iii. 4). Cross-beams of cedar stretched from the vestibule wall to that of the Hekal. From the ceiling of the vestibule were suspended golden chains, up which the young priests climbed to see the crowns in the windows of the Hekal, such as the crowns of Helem, Tobijah, Jedaiah, and Hen ben Zephaniah "for a memorial in the Temple of the Lord" (Zech. vi. 14; Mid. iii. 5). From the cedar cross-beams was suspended a golden vine on the branches of which various donors hung nuggets of gold and precious vessels. The vine was a symbol of Israel. The dimensions of the vestibule were 11 cubits from east to west and 70 cubits along the Hekal (ib. iv. 7). In it stood two tables: one of marble, to the right, on which were laid the loaves of showbread prior to their being taken into the Hekal; and one of gold, to the left, on which the old loaves were temporarily placed (Sheḳ. vi. 4; Men. xi. 7). On each side, north and south of the vestibule, was a Chamber of Knives ("Bet Ḥalifot"), each chamber being 11 × 15 × 8 cubits; evidently they were used for other purposes besides the storing of the sacrificial knives. A wicket on either side of the vestibule gave entrance to the closets or cells around the Hekal. The southern wicket, however, was always closed.

The Temple proper, known as the Hekal, had an entrance 10 × 20 cubits, with a double door. The thickness of the walls was 6 cubits. The height of the Hekal was 100 cubits, made up as follows: foundation 6 cubits; inner height 40; paneling (entablature) 1; receptacle for water, which might drop through a leak in the roof, 2; beams 1; concrete of ceiling 1; attic 40; paneling 1; receptacle for dripping 2; beams 1; concrete of ceiling 1; balustrade 3; device to exclude the ravens 1 (ib. vi. 5). It

The Hekal. is thus seen that the Hekal was a two-story building, the upper story being of the same size as that below. The Hekal proper was 20 × 40 × 40 cubits. Besides the golden table to the right, on which every Sabbath the showbread was placed, and the seven-branched candlestick to the left, were five tables along the north and five tables along the south, with five menorot on each side, which Solomon had added to the Temple. The golden altar stood between the showbread-table and the candlestick, a little nearer the vestibule. The Hekal had windows near the top.

The dimensions of the Holy of Holies were 20 × 20 × 40 cubits. It was divided from the Hekal by two curtains. The outer one was folded back to the right; the inner, to the left. There was a space of 1 cubit between the two, which was considered doubtful ground, it being uncertain whether it belonged to the Hekal or to the Holy of Holies; hence the space was named "ammah ṭeraḳsin" ($\tau\acute{a}\rho\alpha\xi\iota\varsigma$ = "confusion"). Nearly in the center of the Holy of Holies, somewhat toward the west, was the foundation-stone ("eben shetiyyah"), on which was placed the Ark of the Covenant. In the Second Temple the Ark was missing, and the eben shetiyyah was there exposed to the extent of three thumb-breadths (about 6 inches) from the ground.

Thirty-eight cells surrounded the Hekal. There were fifteen, in three rows of five cells each on the

thick, which surrounded the cells; this space on the north and south sides was a "mesibbah" (winding passageway). A bridge reached from this passage to the upper cells on the northwest. From **Cells and** the upper cells southwest the bridge **Attic.** stretched upward to the southeast corner of the Hekal, connecting with the attic, whence a trap-door and staircase led down to the roof of the Hekal (*ib.* iv. 5). On the south side a leader carried off the rain from the roofs of the Hekal and of the upper cells (*ib.*).

The use of the attic above the Hekal and of the 38 cells is not mentioned in the Talmud, but there is no doubt that they were built for defense and for

COURT OF PRIESTS.
(Reconstructed by Chipiez.)

north side, and the same number on the south. The bottom row was 5 cubits deep; the second, 6 cubits; and the third, 7 cubits. The length of the cells from east to west is not recorded; but it is presumed to have been about 8 cubits. On the west side of the Hekal were eight cells in three rows, namely, two of three cells each and one, the uppermost, of two. Their depth corresponded with that of those on the sides. Three doors in each cell connected it with the side and upper cells, except in the case of the two corner cells on the northeast and southeast, each of which had 1 (2 ?) in addition, connecting with the Hekal and the vestibule. The door of the southeast cell to the vestibule was, however, never used (*ib.* iv. 7). The cells had bay windows. The thickness of the walls was 5 cubits, and there was a space of 3 cubits between the lower cells and the wall, 5 cubits

the storage of weapons, etc., when necessary. The two chambers for knives in the vestibule are significant in this connection.

It appears that there was a colonnade or veranda inside the courts; the size of it is not recorded.

BIBLIOGRAPHY: *Middot*, passim; Maimonides, *Yad, Bet ha-Beḥirah*, passim; Jacob de Leon, *Tabnit Hekal*, Amsterdam, 1650; Israel Lipschütz, *Ẓurat Bet ha-Miḳdash* (annexed to his commentary on *Middot*); Menahem Ḥayyim Lewinsohn, *Binyan Nezaḥ*, Warsaw, 1875; Israel Elijah Plotkin, *Bi'ur Ben Shelomoh*, St. Petersburg, 1875; Joshua J. Kolbo, *Binyan Ariel*, Vienna, 1883; idem, *The Glorious Temple and City of Jerusalem*, London, 1884; James Fergusson, *The Temple of the Jews*, London, 1878.
J.   J. D. E.

TEMPLE IN RABBINICAL LITERATURE: Mount Moriah, on which the Temple was erected, is known by tradition as the spot where Adam was born and where he built an altar to God; where Cain and Abel offered their sacrifices; and

HOLY OF HOLIES OF THE TEMPLE AT JERUSALEM.

(Reconstructed by Chipiez.)

where Noah built an altar after the Flood (Gen. viii. 20). Abraham offered Isaac as a sacrifice on this "mount of the Lord" (*ib.* xxii. 14); David purchased the spot from Araunah "to build an altar unto the Lord" (II Sam. xxiv. 21); and finally it was chosen as the site of the permanent altar in the Holy of Holies of Solomon's Temple (Maimonides, "Yad," Bet ha-

of Judah and Benjamin. The area of the mount, the halls, and the chambers of the courts were assigned to Judah; but the vestibule ("ulam"), the Hekal, and the Holy of Holies were built on the lot of Benjamin. However, a strip of land running into the Hekal, on which stood the altar, belonged to Judah. According to another authority, Jerusa-

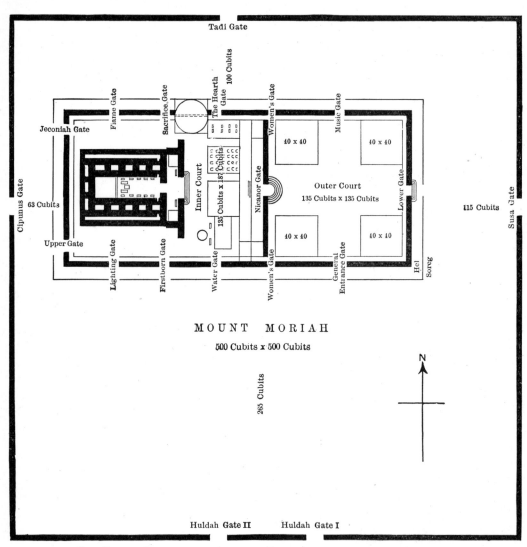

PLAN SHOWING POSITION OF THE TEMPLE ON MOUNT MORIAH ACCORDING TO THE TALMUD.
(Designed by J. D. Eisenstein, New York.)

Beḥirah, ii. 2). The stone on which rested the Ark of the Covenant was called "eben shetiyyah" = "the foundation-stone," on which the world was based (Yoma 54b). The west side of the mount was selected for the Temple site because the Shekinah rests in the west (B. B. 25a), and also in opposition to the rite of the heathen, who worship the sun in the east (Maimonides, "Moreh," iii. 45).

Site.

Mount Moriah was allotted by Joshua to the tribes

lem was not divided among the tribes, and Mount Moriah became their common property.

King David proposed to build the Temple; and he designed the plans and prepared the materials. God would not, however, allow him to build it because he had been a man of war and had shed blood (I Chron. xxviii. 3); but its erection was entrusted to Solomon, who, being a man of peace, was well fitted to construct an edifice representing peace. The people, being aware of this fact, anxiously

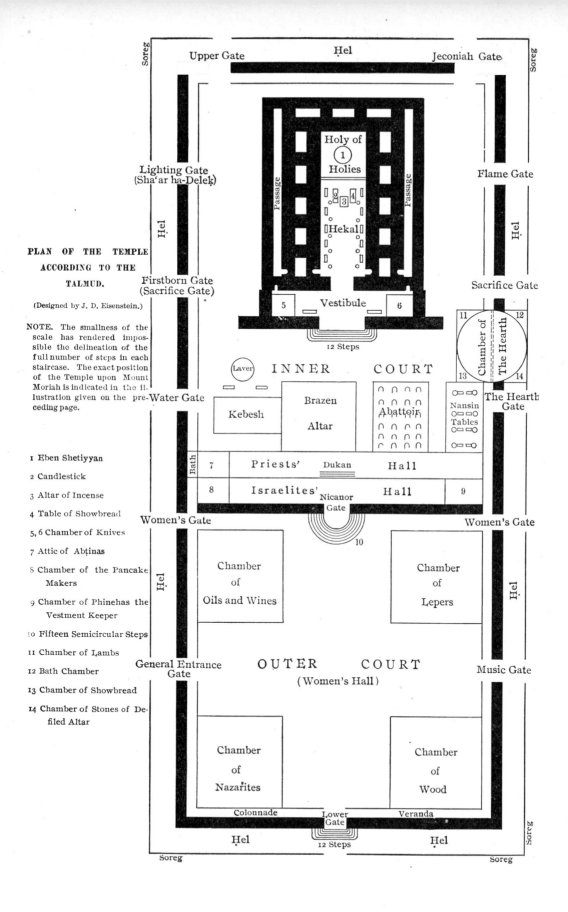

PLAN OF THE TEMPLE ACCORDING TO THE TALMUD.

(Designed by J. D. Eisenstein.)

NOTE. The smallness of the scale has rendered impossible the delineation of the full number of steps in each staircase. The exact position of the Temple upon Mount Moriah is indicated in the illustration given on the preceding page.

1 Eben Shetiyyan
2 Candlestick
3 Altar of Incense
4 Table of Showbread
5, 6 Chamber of Knives
7 Attic of Abṭinas
8 Chamber of the Pancake Makers
9 Chamber of Phinehas the Vestment Keeper
10 Fifteen Semicircular Steps
11 Chamber of Lambs
12 Bath Chamber
13 Chamber of Showbread
14 Chamber of Stones of Defiled Altar

awaited Solomon's accession. A haggadah says David once overheard the people say: "How soon will the old man die, that his son may commence to build the Temple and we may visit the house of the Lord?" Their talk pleased David somewhat; and he chanted: "I was glad when they said unto me, Let us go into the house of the Lord" (Ps. cxxii. 1). The Almighty consoled David, assuring him that "A day in thy courts is better than a thousand" (*ib.* lxxxiv. 10); that is, God prefers one day of David's study of the Law in the courts of learning to 1,000 offerings of sacrifice in the Temple by Solomon (Mak. 10a). In the same sense Raba said: "One who is engaged in the study of the Law need bring neither a burnt offering, a sin-offering, nor a meal-offering" (Men. 110a), showing the tendency of the Talmudists to belittle the importance of sacrifices.

David was apprehensive lest his enemies should assign his sin with Bath-sheba as the reason for God's refusal to allow him to build the Temple: he therefore appealed for divine intervention, praying, "Show me a token for good; that they which hate me may see it, and be ashamed" (Ps. lxxxvi. 17). God granted his wish when Solomon had finished the Temple and was about to bring in the Ark to the Holy of Holies. At this moment the doors slammed and could not be opened. Solomon thereupon recited twenty-four hymns and cried: "Lift up your heads, O ye gates . . . ye everlasting doors; and the King of glory shall come in" (*ib.* xxiv. 7). But no response came. Finally he prayed, "O Lord God, turn not away the face of thine anointed: remember the mercies of David thy servant" (II Chron. vi. 42); and immediately the doors opened of themselves. Then the enemies of David were cast down, and their faces turned black, the people being convinced that the sin of David had been forgiven (Shab. 30a).

Everything connected with the Temple is distinguished as "yedid" = "amiable," "beloved." A Talmudic epigram runs: "Solomon, who was named Jedidiah [= "God's beloved"; II Sam. xii. 25], had built the Temple [Tabernacle], referred to as 'amiable' [Ps. lxxxiv. 1] and situated in the lot of Benjamin 'the beloved' [Deut. xxxiii. 12], in honor of God, who is 'beloved' [Isa. v. 1], in order that the sins of Israel who is 'dearly beloved' [Jer. xii. 7] might be forgiven" (Men. 53a, b).

Through the agency of Ashmedai, Solomon acquired the SHAMIR, either a worm or an exceedingly hard stone, which hewed or cut with perfect ease all kinds of granite, marble, and glass necessary in building the Temple (Giṭ. 68b). Indeed, its mere touch cleft the hardest substance in existence (Soṭah 9a). In size the shamir was no larger than a grain; and it had been preserved since the Creation. R. Oshaya (Hoshaiah) declared that Solomon planted in the Temple various kinds of aromatic trees of gold, bearing fruit which, when the heathen entered the Temple, withered away, but which the Almighty will restore in the future Temple: "It shall blossom abundantly . . . the glory of Lebanon shall be given unto it" (Isa. xxxv. 2; Yoma 21b). "Lebanon" is the poetic name of the Temple, because the latter was built of cedars of Lebanon.

Solomon's Temple was an artistic structure of the highest conception. In its commanding position on the mount, in the pleasing effect of its white stone ornamented with cedar-wood, and in its symmetrical proportions it surpassed Herod's Temple, though the latter exceeded the former in mere magnificence. "One who did not see Herod's Temple missed seeing the most beautiful building in the world. It was constructed entirely of polished granite interspersed with dark-colored marble, with beveled edges, set in plaster. Herod even proposed to fill up the edges with gold; but the Rabbis advised him to abstain from doing so, as the white plaster combined with the granite and marble gave the Temple the appearance of waves of the sea" (Suk. 57b). Thus it is evident that Herod was somewhat gaudy in his taste and that his Temple was less artistic in design and coloring than that of Solomon. Two views are expressed in commenting on the verse "The glory of this latter house shall be greater than that of the former" (Hag. ii. 8). One is that the Temple was more beautiful than its predecessor, while the other says it was only "greater" in years, alluding to the fact that it stood 420 years, whereas that of Solomon existed for 410 years only (Mid. iv. 6; B. B. 3a).

The sacredness of Solomon's Temple was greater than that of Herod's, as the latter lacked five important accessories: (1) the Ark and the "kapporet" (mercy-seat, cherubim), (2) the divine fire, (3) the Shekinah, (4) the Holy Spirit, and (5) Urim and Thummim (Yoma 21b). It lacked also the pot of manna and Aaron's staff alongside the Ark, the jar of holy oil, and the coffer with jewels of gold presented by the Philistines as a trespass-offering on returning the Ark (I Sam. vi. 8). King Josiah, anticipating the fall of the Temple, concealed these sacred objects (Yer. Sheḳ. vi. 1). Evidently they were hidden in the subterranean passage under the Temple, where, it is claimed, were buried also, as soon as the Temple was finished, all the parts of the Tabernacle (Soṭah 9a). A priest in the Temple once noticed that the flooring under his feet was uneven; and he showed it to a comrade, with a view to investigation. No sooner had he spoken about it, however, than a spark issued from a crevice in the floor and killed him. The priests then surmised that the Ark was buried in that place. R. Hoshaiah says that the priest pounded the floor with a hammer, whereupon a fire arose and consumed him (Yer. Sheḳ. vi. 2; Yoma 54a). In the Second Temple two curtains, instead of the cedar-wood partition of the First Temple, separated the Hekal from the Holy of Holies. The First Temple was destroyed on account of three sins, namely, bloodshed, immorality, and idolatry. In the Second Temple there were learning, obedience to the commandments, and charity, but there were also enmity and malevolence among the people, which outweighed the three great sins for which the First Temple was destroyed (Yoma 9b).

After the destruction of the Temple the Rabbis endeavored to enshrine its memory in the hearts of the Jews. As a reminiscence of its usage ("zeker le-miḳdash ") R. Johanan b. Zakkai ordered that the celebration of the lulab be continued for seven days during the Sukkot festival as had been the custom in the Temple, although in Temple times the celebration was observed outside the sanctuary on one day only (Suk. iii. 12). As a sign of mourning for the destruction of the Temple, one should not whitewash or paint his house entirely, but should leave a space about one cubit square above the door (B. B. 60b). See SANCTUARY.

J.   J. D. E.

TEMPLE, THE SECOND: The Temple of Solomon was destroyed by Nebuchadnezzar in 586 B.C. (II Kings xxv. 9). It is usually supposed that its sacred site was desolate and unused for fifty years, until the accession of Cyrus made the rebuilding of the Temple possible. This view is shown by Jer. xli. 5 to be mistaken; for two months after the city was destroyed a company of men from Samaria, Shechem, and Shiloh came to keep the Feast of Ingathering at Jerusalem. It is true that Giesebrecht (*ad loc.*) argues that the men were bound for Mizpah and not for Jerusalem; but if that be so the whole narrative is meaningless. No reason is known why at this date men from a distance should go to Mizpah to worship. More probably they were on their way to Jerusalem, when the messenger from Mizpah enticed them into that town. It is probable, therefore, that, though the building was in ruins, the site of the Temple was used by the poor Hebrews resident in Palestine as a place of worship all through the Exile.

With the accession of Cyrus in 538 it became possible—that monarch replacing the old Assyro-Babylonian policy of transportation by a policy of toleration—for the Jews to resuscitate their religious institutions. The Chronicler, who wrote much of the Book of Ezra, represents Cyrus as issuing a decree for the rebuilding of the Temple at Jerusalem; but this assertion is of doubtful authority. The Aramaic document in Ezra relates that the sacred vessels which Nebuchadnezzar had carried away were delivered to Sheshbazzar with authority to take them back and rebuild the Temple (Ezra v. 14, 15). It states also that Sheshbazzar "laid the foundations of the house," but it is doubtful if any building was then done, as the house remained unbuilt in the time of Haggai, twenty years later. The Chronicler (Ezra iii. 1) declares that Zerubbabel (whom he puts in place of Sheshbazzar, thus placing him twenty years too early) "builded the altar of the God of Israel, to offer burnt offerings thereon"; but as Haggai (ii. 14) declared that all which was offered here was unclean, it is altogether probable that the altar was the same that had been used throughout the Exile, and that the Chronicler's statement is a mistake.

In the second year of the reign of Darius Hystaspes (519) the real rebuilding began. The people were aroused to the effort by the preaching of Haggai and Zechariah; and in the course of three years the rebuilding was accomplished. It is now generally recognized that the representation in the Book of Ezra, that the work was begun immediately

The Decree of Cyrus.

The Rebuilding.

XII.—7

upon the accession of Cyrus and was then interrupted by opposition from Israel's neighbors, is unhistorical.

Of the dimensions of this Temple there are given but few data. Hecatæus, a Greek writer contemporary with Alexander the Great, is quoted by Josephus (" Contra Ap." i. 22) as saying that the Temple area was enclosed by a wall a plethra, or 500 Greek feet, in length and 100 Greek cubits in breadth, *i.e.*, 485½ × 145½ English feet. The altar was built of unhewn stones in conformity with the precepts of the Law (comp. I Macc. iv. 44 *et seq.*). The dimensions of the building were probably the same as those of Solomon's Temple, though the edifice was apparently at first lacking in ornament. It was probably because the building was less ornate that the old men who had seen the former Temple wept at the sight of its successor (Ezra iii. 12; Josephus, "Ant." xi. 4, § 2). Nehemiah in rebuilding the city wall followed the lines of the former wall, and it is altogether likely that the old lines were followed in building the walls of the Temple also. The statement in Ezra vi. 3 that Cyrus gave permission to make the Temple 60 cubits high and 60 cubits broad has probably no connection with its actual dimensions: how the statement arose can now be only conjectured. The authorities for this period make no mention of the palace of Solomon. If the wall of the Temple was at this period less than 500 feet long, the whole Temple court occupied but about one-third the length of the present Ḥaram area, and less than half its width (comp. Baedeker, "Palestine and Syria," ed. 1898, p. 39). It is probable that the site of Solomon's palace either lay desolate or was covered by other dwellings.

Dimensions.

The Temple was surrounded by two courts (I Macc. i. 22, iv. 48); but until the time of Alexander Jannæus (104–79 B.C.) it would seem that these were separated by a difference of elevation only. That ruler surrounded the inner court with a wall of wood because the Pharisees, with whom he was unpopular, had pelted him with citrons while officiating at the altar at the Feast of Tabernacles (comp. "Ant." xiii. 13, § 5). The inner court contained chambers for storing the garments of the priests (I Macc. iv. 38, 57). The stone altar of burnt offering probably occupied the site of the bronze altar in Solomon's Temple.

The Temple, or Holy Place, seems to have had two veils or curtains at its front (*ib.* iv. 51). It had also one holy candlestick, a golden altar of incense, and a table of showbread (*ib.* i. 21, 22). Separated from the Temple by another veil was the Holy of Holies (Josephus, "B. J." v. 5, § 5). According to Josephus, this contained nothing; but, according to the Mishnah (Mid. iii. 6), the "stone of foundation" stood where the Ark used to be, and the high priest put his censer on it on the Day of Atonement. According to the Babylonian Talmud (Yoma 22b), the Second Temple lacked five things which had been in Solomon's Temple, namely, the Ark, the sacred fire, the Shekinah, the Holy Spirit, and the Urim and Thummim.

In the time of Nehemiah there were two towers,

Furniture of the Temple.

named respectively Hananeel and Meah, which probably formed parts of a fortress on the site afterward occupied by the tower Antonia (comp. Neh. xii. 39, and Mitchell in "Jour. Bib. Lit." xxii. 144). The small size of the Temple area at this period makes it improbable that this fortress adjoined the Temple court. The "gate of the guard" (Neh. xii. 39) was probably an entrance into the Temple court on the north side. From the time of Zerubbabel to the time of Antiochus Epiphanes the history of this Temple was comparatively uneventful. Sirach (Ecclus.) l. 1 *et seq.* says that "Simon, son of Onias, the great priest," repaired the Temple and fortified it; but the text of the passage is corrupt. In the year 168 Antiochus, as a part of a policy to enforce Hellenistic practises on the Jews, robbed the Temple of its candlestick, golden altar, table of showbread, and veils (these being its distinctive furniture), and compelled the high priest to sacrifice swine upon its altar. This led to the Maccabean revolt (comp. I Macc. i.), as a result of which the Jews after three years regained possession of their Temple and rededicated it. They carefully replaced the stone altar of burnt offering with stones which had not been defiled, and replaced the other characteristic articles of furniture (*ib.* iv. 43–56). Judas Maccabeus at this time fortified the Temple with high walls and towers (*ib.* iv. 60, vi. 7); so that thenceforth the Temple was the real citadel of Jerusalem. These walls were pulled down by Antiochus V. (*ib.* vi. 62), but were restored by Jonathan Maccabeus ("Ant." xiii. 5, § 11). The fortifications were afterward strengthened by Simon (I Macc. xiii. 52). At the time of the rededication, in the year 165, the front of the Temple was decorated with gilded crowns and shields (*ib.* iv. 57).

At some time during the ascendency of the Hasmonean dynasty a bridge was built across the Tyropœon valley to connect the Temple with the western hill ("Ant." xiv. 4, § 2). This bridge was probably situated at the point where Robinson's arch (so called because its nature and importance were first discovered by Prof. Edward Robinson; see his "Biblical Researches," ed. 1856, i. 287 *et seq.*) may still be seen. The nature and purpose of this bridge have been regarded as obscure problems; but there can be little doubt that the structure was intended to afford easy access to the Temple from the royal palace which the Hasmoneans had built on the western hill ("Ant." xx. 8, § 11). From this palace the movements of people in the Temple courts could be seen, as Josephus records; and as the Hasmoneans were high priests as well as monarchs, the purpose of the bridge is clear.

In 63 B.C. Pompey, the Roman general, captured Jerusalem and had a hard struggle to take the Temple ("Ant." xiv. 4). In the conflict the bridge was broken down. In exploring Jerusalem Sir Charles Warren found its remains, or the remains of its successor, lying in the ancient bed of the Tyropœon valley eighty feet below (comp. Warren and Conder, "Jerusalem," p. 184, London, 1884). Pompey did not harm the Temple itself or its furniture; but nine years later Crassus plundered it of all its gold ("Ant." xiv. 7, § 1). In 37 B.C Herod during his

siege of Jerusalem burned some of the cloisters about the courts, but did not otherwise harm the Temple (ib. 16, § 2).

BIBLIOGRAPHY : See TEMPLE OF HEROD.
E. C.   G. A. B.

TEMPLE OF SOLOMON.—**Biblical Data:** David, according to II Sam. vii. 2 *et seq.*, desired to build a temple for YHWH, but was not permitted to do so, although, according to the Chronicler (I Chron. xxii. 14 *et seq.*), he prepared for the building a large quantity of material, which he later gave to his son Solomon. David also purchased a thrashing-floor from Araunah the Jebusite (II Sam. xxiv. 21 *et seq.*), on which he offered sacrifice; and there Solomon afterward built his Temple (II Chron. iii. 1). In preparation for the building Solomon made an alliance with Hiram, King of Tyre, who furnished him with skilled workmen and, apparently, permitted him to cut timber in Lebanon. Solomon began to build the Temple in the fourth year of his reign; its erection occupied seven years (I Kings vi. 37, 38).

The structure was 60 cubits long, 20 cubits wide, and 30 cubits high (I Kings vi. 2). It faced the east (Ezek. xlvii. 1). Before the Temple stood a porch 20 cubits long (corresponding to the width of the Temple) and 10 cubits deep (I Kings vi. 3). II Chron. iii. 4 adds the curious statement (probably corrupted from the statement of the depth of the porch) that this porch was 120 cubits high, which would make it a regular tower. The stone of which the Temple was built was dressed at the quarry, so that no work of that kind was necessary within the Temple precincts (I Kings vi. 7). The roof was of cedar, and the whole house was overlaid with gold (I Kings vi. 9, 22).

The structure was three stories in height. The wall was not of equal thickness all the way up, but had ledges on which the floorbeams rested. Around the structure was a series of chambers, of varying size because of the differences in the thickness of the wall. Those of the lowest story were 5 cubits in depth; those of the second 6; and those of the third, 7. The Temple was also provided with windows of fixed latticework (I Kings vi. 4, 6, 8, 10). At the rear of this edifice was the Holy of Holies, which was in form a perfect cube, each of its dimensions being 20 cubits. The interior was lined with cedar and overlaid with pure gold. The Holy of Holies contained two cherubim of olive-wood, each 10 cubits high (I Kings vi. 16, 20, 21, 23–28) and each having outspread wings 10 cubits from tip to tip, so that, since they stood side by side, the wings touched the wall on either side and met in the center of the room (comp. CHERUB). According to II Chron. iii. 14, a veil of variegated linen separated the Holy of Holies from the rest of the Temple.

The rest of the building, the Holy Place, was of the same width and height as the Holy of Holies, but 40 cubits in length. Its walls were lined with cedar, on which were carved figures of cherubim, palm-trees, and open flowers, which were overlaid with gold. Chains of gold further marked it off from the Holy of Holies. The floor of the Temple was of fir-wood overlaid with gold. The door-posts, of olive-wood, supported folding-doors of fir. The doors of the Holy of Holies were of olive-wood. On both sets of doors were carved cherubim, palm-trees, and flowers, all being overlaid with gold (I Kings vi. 15 *et seq.*).

Before the Temple, Solomon erected two bronze pillars, called Jachin and Boaz. Each of these was 18 cubits in height, and was surmounted by a capital of carved lilies, 5 cubits high. Before the Temple, a little to the southeast (I Kings vii. 39), there stood the molten sea, a large laver 10 cubits in diameter, ornamented with knops. This laver rested on the backs of twelve oxen (*ib.* vii. 23–26). The Chronicler gives its capacity as "three thousand baths" (II Chron. iv. 5–6) and states that its purpose was to afford opportunity for the ablutions of the priests.

The Pillars.

Another article of Temple furniture is described as a "base." It was a portable holder for a small laver, and was made of bronze, provided with wheels,

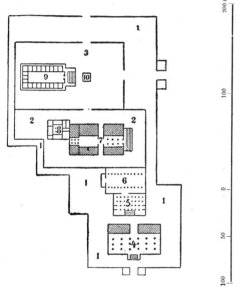

PLAN OF THE ROYAL BUILDINGS ERECTED BY SOLOMON ON THE TEMPLE MOUND (ACCORDING TO STADE).

1. Great court. 2. Middle court. 3. Temple court. 4. House of Lebanon. 5. Porch of pillars. 6. Throne porch. 7. Royal palace. 8. Harem. 9. Temple. 10. Altar.

and ornamented with figures of lions, cherubim, and palm-trees. These vessels especially excited the admiration of the Jews. The author of the books of the Kings describes their minute details with great interest (I Kings vii. 27–37). Each of these "bases" supported a laver which held "forty baths" (I Kings vii. 38). From II Kings xvi. 14 it is learned that a brazen altar stood before the Temple. II Chron. iv. 1 says that this altar was 20 cubits square and 10 cubits high; according to I Kings vii. 48 there stood before the Holy of Holies a golden altar of incense and a table for showbread. This table was of gold, as were also the five candlesticks on each side of it. The implements

The Vessels.

for the care of the candles—tongs, basins, snuffers, and fire-pans—were of gold; and so were the hinges of the doors. The Temple was surrounded by a court, which was separated from the space beyond by a wall of three courses of hewn stone, surmounted by cedar beams (I Kings vi. 36). The Chronicler calls this the court of the priests (II Chron. iv. 9).

The Temple did not stand alone; it was part of a splendid pile of buildings which Solomon constructed in immediate connection with it. This pile included Solomon's own residence, the palace of Pharaoh's daughter, the throne-room, the "porch of pillars," and "the house of the forest of Lebanon" (I Kings vii. 1–8). These were so arranged that in entering the palace enclosure one came first to the "house ot the forest of Lebanon," with its splendid pillars, then to the inner "porch of pillars," the hall of state, or throne-room, Solomon's private dwelling, and, lastly, to the palace of Pharaoh's daughter. For the splendor of these buildings Solomon was indebted to Phenician architects and workmen (I Kings vii. 40–47).

E. C.   G. A. B.

——**Critical View :** When the Temple was constructed it was, together with Solomon's palace, by far the most splendid pile of buildings that the Hebrews had ever seen. Even to this day, as one comes from the surrounding country to Jerusalem, the city seems magnificent, although in comparison with a European capital it is far otherwise. Similarly the influence of environment may be seen in the description of Solomon's Temple. With the lapse of time Israel's fortunes declined, and the age of Solomon seemed even more glorious in comparison with later obviously decadent periods; and this increased the tendency to exaggerate the splendor of the Temple. Moreover, religious reforms made some of the arrangements of the Temple seem unorthodox, and various scribes seem to have amplified its description; as they did not always have the same point of view, present accounts are confused to a degree (comp. Stade's "Zeitschrift," 1883, pp. 129 *et seq.*). One of the exaggerations of later times probably produced all those statements which declare that the inner parts of the Temple and all its implements were overlaid with gold (comp. Kittel, "Königsbücher," in Nowack, "Hand-Kommentar," pp. 46–55).

Exaggerations in Account.

As a result of editorial reworking of the description, the narrative in Kings contains no account of the great brazen altar which stood before the Temple. Ex. xx. 24 *et seq.* provided that an altar might be made of earth or unhewn stone; and as it offended a later age to think that Solomon made an altar of bronze, its description was removed from I Kings vii. Nevertheless it is recorded elsewhere (*ib.* viii. 64; II Kings xvi. 14) that it was a part of the furniture of the original Temple. Later scribes, too, are responsible for those statements which represent David as desiring to build the Temple, and as making preparation for it. Had he desired to build it he certainly could have done so. But in his reign the nomadic idea still prevailed, and a tent was thought to be YHWH's proper dwelling (comp. II Sam. vii. 6). Later generations, to whom the Temple seemed a necessity, could not understand why so venerated a man as David did not build it; hence these statements.

There can be no doubt that the Temple of Solomon was situated upon the more easterly of the two hills which form the site of the present Ḥaram area in Jerusalem, in the center of which area is the Mosque of Omar. Fergusson, Trupp, Lewin, and W. R. Smith held that the Temple was built in the southwest corner of the present Ḥaram area; but the view is false. That site is a part of an artifi-

It was probably a sacred place of the Jebusites before David's time, though II Sam. xxiv. connects its consecration with an incident in David's reign. Solomon's palace probably lay to the south of the Temple. The most probable arrangement of the buildings is that suggested by Stade ("Gesch. des Volkes Israel," i. 314, 315).

The Biblical text makes it clear that Solomon received from Hiram, King of Tyre, much aid in constructing his buildings. As· the Hebrews were an agricultural people, this aid probably involved not

INTERIOR OF THE "DOME OF THE ROCK" SHOWING TRADITIONAL SITE OF HOLY OF HOLIES.
(From a photograph by the American Colony at Jerusalem.)

cial extension of the level of the Temple area over the Tyropœon valley, and probably was not made before the time of Herod. The most probable site of the Temple is just west of the "Dome of the Rock" in the center of the Mosque of Omar. The bronze altar was probably on this rock. The mosque was built over a rock the traditions of which were sacred; probably the site was the same as that of the temple which Hadrian erected to Jupiter. This in turn was on the site of Herod's temple, which would naturally be on that of Solomon's. The persistency of sacred sites in the East makes this most likely.

The Site.

only material (cedar-wood, etc.), but architectural direction and skilled craftsmen. The architectural features will be considered later. Among the details which were probably copied from Tyre were the two pillars Jachin and Boaz. Herodotus (ii. 44) says that the temple at Tyre contained two such, one of emerald and the other of fine gold. In the same way the ornamentation of palm-trees and cherubim were probably derived from Tyre, for Ezekiel (xxviii. 13, 14) represents the King of Tyre, who was high priest also, as being in the "garden of God." Probably both at Tyre and at Jerusalem the cherubim and palm-tree ornaments were survivals of an earlier conception—that the abode of God was a "garden of Eden." The Tyrians, therefore, in their temple imitated to some extent the primitive garden, and Solomon borrowed these features (comp. PARADISE). Similarly, the bronze altar was a Phenician innovation; and probably the same is true of the bronze implements which were ornamented with palm-trees and cherubim. The Orthodox Israelitish altar was of earth or unhewn stone. The Decalogue of Ex. xx. (Elohist) prohibited the making of graven images, while that of Ex. xxxiv. (Jahvist) prohibited the making of molten gods; and the Deuteronomic expansions prohibited the making of any likeness whatever. All these are, to be sure, later than Solomon's time; but there is no reason to believe that before that time the Hebrews had either the skill or the wealth necessary to produce ornamentation of this kind.

Several temples in Babylonia, many in Egypt, and some of the Phenicians are now known. In Babylonia the characteristic feature was a "ziggurat," or terraced tower, evidently intended to imitate a mountain. The chamber for the divine dwelling was at its top. The early Egyptian temples consisted of buildings containing two or three rooms, the innermost of which was the abode of the deity. A good example is the granite temple near the sphinx at Gizeh. The Middle Empire (12th dynasty) added obelisks and pylons, and the New Empire (18th dynasty) hypostyle halls. The Phenician temples varied somewhat in form, and were surrounded by courts. Solomon's Temple was not a copy of any of these, but embodied features derived from all of them. It was on the summit of a hill, thus expressing the Babylonian idea of the divine abode; it was surrounded by courts, like the Phenician temples and the splendid temple of Der al-Bakri at Thebes, while its general form reminds one of Egyptian sanctuaries. The two pillars Jachin and Boaz had their parallel not only at Tyre but at Byblus, Paphos, and Telloh (see, however, De Sarzec, "Découvertes en Chaldée," pp. 62–64). In Egypt the obelisks expressed the same idea. All these were phallic emblems, being survivals of the primitive Hamito-Semitic "mazzebah" (comp. W. R. Smith, "Rel. of Sem." 2d ed., p. 208; Schmidt, "Solomon's Temple," pp. 40 *et seq.*). Jachin and Boaz were really isolated columns, as Schick has shown ("Die Stiftshütte, der Tempel in Jerusalem," etc., pp. 82 *et seq.*), and not, as some have supposed, a part of the ornamentation of the building. Their tops were crowned with ornamentation as if they were lamps; and W. R. Smith supposed (*l.c.* p. 488) that they may have been used as firealtars. This assumes that they contained cressets for burning the fat.

The chambers which surrounded the Holy Place in Solomon's Temple are said in I Chron. xxviii. 12 to have been storehouses for the sacred treasure. These are paralleled in Babylonian and Egyptian temples by similar chambers, which surrounded the naos, or hypostyle hall, and were used for similar purposes. The "molten sea" finds its parallel in Babylonian temples in a great basin called the "apsu" (deep). As the ziggurat typified a mountain, so the apsu typified the sea. The Temple thus became a miniature world. This apsu was used as early as the time of Gudea and continued in use till the end of Babylonian history; it was made of stone and was elaborately decorated (comp. Jastrow, "Rel. of Bab. and Assyria," p. 653).

In Solomon's Temple there was nothing to correspond to the hypostyle hall of an Egyptian temple; but this feature was introduced into Solomon's palace. The "house of the forest of Lebanon" and the "porch of pillars" remind one strongly of the outer and the inner hypostyle hall of an Egyptian temple.

Solomon's Temple was, then, a fine example of an Oriental temple. Although it had features in common with the temples of all the races kindred to the Jews, it combined those features in a new and independent way, so that the Temple at Jerusalem was one of the most interesting architectural products of the Hamito-Semitic religious life.

The Temple of Solomon was in reality an innovation in Israel. It was a part of a regal magnificence which was foreign to the national life, and which had to be introduced from outside and patterned on foreign models; and it was looked upon with little favor by many of his subjects. Moreover, the Temple was erected upon a site but recently conquered from the Jebusites, and which for the Israelites had no sacred associations. Other sites—those of Shechem, Beth-el, Hebron—were consecrated by patriarchal tradition (Gen. xxii. 2 is the product of a later time), but Jerusalem was unhallowed by such associations, and its sanctuary was full of foreign innovations. When Jeroboam revolted and erected Beth-el and Dan into royal sanctuaries he perpetuated a ritual of a simpler and more national character (comp. I Kings xii. 28). The Temple at Jerusalem was in reality Solomon's chapel—a part of that regal pile of buildings which he had constructed not so much for the use of his subjects as for his personal aggrandizement. It was later events, such as Sennacherib's invasion, Isaiah's conception that Jerusalem was inviolable, the Deuteronomic reform (which made all sanctuaries except that at Jerusalem illegal), and, above all, the tragic events of the Exile, which made this Temple supremely sacred in the thought of Jews of later times.

BIBLIOGRAPHY: Stade, *Gesch. des Volkes Israel*, i. 311 *et seq.*, Berlin, 1889; Nowack, *Hebräische Archäologie*, ii. 38 *et seq.*, Leipsic, 1894; Benzinger, *Arch.*; Schick, *Die Stiftshütte, der Tempel in Jerusalem und der Tempelplatz der Jetztzeit*, Berlin, 1896; Emanuel Schmidt, *Solomon's Temple in the Light of Other Oriental Temples*, Chicago, 1902.
E. C.   G. A. B.

TEMPLER, BERNHARD: Austrian theologian; born at Brzesko, Galicia, May 1, 1865; educated at the University and the Bet ha-Midrash of Vienna, and at the Hochschule für die Wissenschaft des Judentums at Berlin. At the age of fifteen he began contributing articles to various Hebrew periodicals, and two years later he published his "Dober Ṭob" (Lemberg, 1882), novellæ and commentaries on obscure Talmudic passages. Of other works from his pen may be mentioned: "Peḳuddat ha-Ẓaddiḳim" (Cracow, 1883), comments on Biblical passages; and

" Die Unsterblichkeitslehre (Psychologie, Messianologie und Eschatologie) bei den Jüdischen Philosophen des Mittelalters " (Leipsic, 1895).

BIBLIOGRAPHY: *Deutsch-Oesterreichisches Künstler- und Schriftsteller-Lexikon*, p. 488, Vienna, 1902; *Drohobyczer Zeitung*, 1904, No. 15.
S.

TEMURAH (" Exchange "): Treatise in the Mishnah, Tosefta, and Babylonian Talmud mainly concerned with the regulations in Lev. xxvii. 10, 33 regarding the exchange of consecrated things. In most editions of the Mishnah this treatise is the sixth in the order Ḳodashim. It is divided into seven chapters, containing altogether thirty-four paragraphs.

Ch. i. : Regarding those who are allowed to make an exchange; things that may be exchanged, and things that may not be exchanged (§§ 3–6). Regulations concerning drawn water which is unfit for the miḳweh; concerning water for sprinkling, and a field in which there is a grave that can not be found (§§ 4–5).

Ch. ii. : In what ways the sacrifices of the congregation are different from the sacrifices of individuals (§§ 1–2). Difficulties connected with consecrated objects in general which do not affect objects consecrated through temurah and vice versa (§ 3).

Ch. iii. : Sacrifices in which the young of the sacrificial animal is equivalent to the sacrificial animal itself; sacrifices in which this is not the case (§§ 1–2). What must be done when some one consecrates a female animal for a sacrifice for which only a male animal is appropriate (§§ 3–4). In what ways the first-born and the tenth are different from other sacrificial animals (§ 5).

Ch. iv. : The young of a sin-offering; temurah in connection with a sin-offering; other regulations concerning sin-offerings. Cases in which the bringer of the sin-offering dies before the sacrifice is made; in which the sin-offering has been lost and found again; in which a sin-offering with a blemish is consecrated.

Ch. v. : How, an animal being pregnant, its young may be consecrated while still unborn (§§ 1–3). The form of words with which a temurah is made.

Ch. vi. : Things that may not be placed on the altar (§§ 1–4). The young of animals which may not be placed on the altar may be sacrificed; sacrificial animals which have become unfit (" ṭerefah ") through sickness may not be redeemed (§ 5).

Ch. vii. : In what ways things which have been consecrated for the altar are different from things which are dedicated only for the maintenance of the Temple, and in what ways they are similar (§§ 1–3). What sacrificial objects must be burned and what buried; in this connection are enumerated other unconsecrated things which must be partly burned and partly buried (§§ 4–6).

The Tosefta to this treatise is divided into four chapters, and contains various additions to and amplifications of the Mishnah. The Gemara of the Babylonian Talmud contains, in addition to the discussions and explanations of the Mishnah, many interesting haggadic utterances. Of these, two deserve special notice: (1) the saying concerning the custom of not writing down sentences of oral teaching, and how this was abrogated because if it had been adhered to the oral teaching would have been forgotten (14b), and (2) that concerning the numerous halakic utterances which were forgotten in the days of mourning for the death of Moses (16a).
W. B. J. Z. L.

TEMURAH, MIDRASH (or **MIDRASH TEMUROT**): Ethical haggadic work consisting of three chapters. Its tendency is to prove that changes and differences are necessary to the world's welfare, and that earthly contrasts—as wealth and poverty, beauty and ugliness—serve to harmonize the whole, thus giving evidence of the divine wisdom. From this purpose the work has derived its name.

In the third chapter of the Midrash Temurah, Ps. cxxxvi. is interpreted as referring to the changes in human life mentioned in Eccl. iii. 1–8. The first and second chapters introduce R. Ishmael and R. Akiba as lecturers; and for that reason this midrash was erroneously ascribed to those two tannaim. Certain passages in the work indicate that it was not written until the end of the twelfth or the beginning of the thirteenth century. According to Jellinek, the author of the Midrash Temurah made use of the works of Ibn Ezra as well as of Galen's dialogue on the soul; this would show that he could not have lived before the latter part of the twelfth century. The literary style of the work, which contains in the initial chapter later Hebraisms as well as some medical terms, also points to the twelfth century. The first chapter includes anthropological, and the second cosmogonic, passages. The first author to refer to this work as the Midrash Temurah was Gedaliah ibn Yaḥya, in his " Shalshelet ha-Ḳabbalah " (ed. Amsterdam, p. 24b). The midrash was first printed by Azulai, after part ii. of his " Shem ha-Gedolim " (Leghorn, 1786); later it was reprinted with the Agadat Bereshit (Zolkiev, 1804). The last-named edition is that included by A. Jellinek in his " Bet ha-Midrash " (i. 106–114).

BIBLIOGRAPHY: Zunz, *G. V.* (ed. Brüll, Frankfort-on-the-Main, 1892), pp. 124–125; Jellinek, in *B. H.* i. 20–21 (German part).
W. B. J. Z. L.

TEN : The art of counting was founded on the number of the fingers and toes, which constituted the basis for the quinary, decimal, and vigesimal systems, according to whether one hand was used or two, or whether the toes were included or not. Among the ancient Hebrews the decimal system prevailed, as is shown by the Hebrew names for the numbers from one to ten. In the later development likewise the number ten preserved its importance as a higher unity, although the number seven, which was, like three, a sacred number, predominated in religious usage.

Ten forms a basal unit in the round numbers of the measurements of Noah's ark, and is clearly present in the dimensions of the Tabernacle

Bible. (Ex. xxvi.–xxvii.) and of both Solomon's and Ezekiel's temples (I Kings vi., vii. ; Ezek. xl.–xlii.), and in the number of the commandments (Ex. xx. ; Deut. v.); and possibly it served to measure the week (Gen. xxiv. 55; comp. Dan. i. 14). It appeared also in the ritual for the

Day of Atonement (Lev. xvi. 29), which was observed on the tenth day of the seventh month, and in the celebration of the Passover (Ex. xii. 3). The Egyptians were visited with ten plagues (Ex. viii.–xi.); as a punishment ten women were to bake bread in one oven (Lev. xxvi. 26), while of a hundred who went forth to war ten only would remain alive (Amos v. 3). Furthermore, "a new song" was played in the Temple on an instrument of ten strings (Ps. cxliv. 9), and Jacob promised to give God a tenth of all that He might give him (Gen. xxviii. 22). Abraham bestowed a tenth of everything on the priest (Gen. xiv. 20), so that the Levites and the poor received a tithe (Num. xviii. 26; Lev. xxvii. 30–32; et al.), while according to a very ancient custom the king demanded a similar portion (I Sam. viii. 15, 17).

Ten is used also as a round number (Gen. xxxi. 7; Num. xiv. 22; Job xix. 3; I Sam. i. 8; et al.), and it often occurs in the Bible, although a large portion of its symbolic interpretations are unwarranted. The multiples of ten likewise occur frequently; but seventy (as in Num. xi. 16) is to be regarded as a multiple of seven. In general, ten is the number of completion, of perfection, of foundation, and the like.

In the Talmud and Midrash the number ten is still more important; out of a single incomplete series of sayings beginning with a definite number, twenty-six commence with ten ("Pirḳe de-Rabbenu ha-Ḳadosh," in Schönblum, "Sheloshah Sefarim Niftaḥim," pp. 39–41, Lemberg, 1877). It is found also both in the Halakah and in the Haggadah.

Talmud and Midrash.

In the regulations governing the day on which the scroll of Esther is to be read a "large" city is defined as one in which there are ten men who have no occupation, and hence are always free for divine service (Meg. i. 3; comp. Baṭlanim); and in Meg. iv. 3 nine functions are enumerated at which ten men must be present, since they form a congregation in themselves (Abot iii. 6; Meg. 23b; see Jew. Encyc. viii. 603b). Ten classes of families were distinguished in regard to racial purity (Ḳid. iv. 1), and just as many kinds of leprosy in houses (Neg. xiii. 1), while ten verses of Scripture in which God's attributes are mentioned were to be recited on New-Year's Day (R. H. iv. 6). Ezra instituted ten laws (B. Ḳ. 82a, top), and there were ten special legal regulations for Jerusalem (ib. 82b). A large number of similar laws existed. Josephus, for example, states ("B. J." vi. 9, § 3) that as a rule not less than ten men gathered around every Passover meal.

The Haggadah is even more partial to the number ten, as a reference to a few selected passages will show. The world was created by ten utterances of God, while between Adam and Noah, as well as between Noah and Abraham, there were ten generations. Ten things were created in the evening twilight of the first Friday, including the rainbow, the art of writing, the stylus, and the two tables of the Law (Abot v. 1–6). There are, moreover, ten things (the instances cited number twelve) which form a series in the order of their strength, so that one overcomes the

Haggadah.

other: rock, iron, fire, water, cloud, wind, the body (which inhales the wind), anxiety, wine, sleep, death, and alms (B. B. 11a). Ten measures of wisdom came down from heaven to earth, the land of Israel taking nine, and the rest of the world one. The same proportion is observed in the distribution of beauty between Jerusalem and the world; nine-tenths of the wealth in the world was Rome's; of poverty, Babylon's; of pride, Elam's; of bravery, Persia's; of lice, Media's; of magic, Egypt's; of immorality, Arabia's; of shamelessness (or bastards), Mesene's; of gossip, women's; of drunkenness, Ethiopia's; of sleep, slaves' (Ḳid. 49b; Ab. R. N., Recension A, xxviii., beginning; Recension B, xli.; comp. "Monatsschrift," xxii. 270–276). There are also midrashic works whose titles contain the number ten: Ten Martyrs (Jellinek, "B. H." ii. 66, vi. 19–35); The Ten Signs of the Messiah (ib. ii. 58); and The Exile (ib. iv. 133, v. 113).

Pythagorean speculation ascribed a peculiar creative power to the number ten, which is important also in Jewish mysticism. According to the "Sefer Yezirah," a work based on Pythagorean principles, beside the twenty-two letters of the alphabet stand "the ten digits, since they, as a complete decade, form the higher principle of existence which is superior to that of the letters" (Bloch, "Gesch. der Entwickelung der Kabbala," p. 23; translation of the chief passages, p. 27; comp. Epstein, "Recherches sur le Sepher Yeçira," p. 29; Lehmann, "Aberglaube und Zauberei," p. 122; and Jew. Encyc. iii. 474 et seq., s.v. Cabala [the Ten Sefirot]).

The custom of pouring out ten glasses of wine for the mourners on the day of a funeral (Sem., end) and for a bridegroom on the wedding-day belongs to the domain of folk-lore.

Bibliography: Bähr, *Symbolik des Mosaischen Cultus,* Heidelberg, 1837; *Z. D. M. G.* xxiv. 662 et seq.; Bloch, *Gesch. der Entwickelung der Kabbala,* Treves, 1894; Epstein, *Recherches sur le Sepher Yeçira,* Versailles, 1894; Lehmann, *Aberglaube und Zauberei,* Stuttgart, 1898; Pick, *Der Einfluss der Zehnzahl und der Siebenzahl auf das Judenthum,* in *Allg. Zeit. des Jud.* lviii. 29–31.
W. B.   L. B.

TEN COMMANDMENTS. See Decalogue.

TEN PLAGUES. See Plague.

TENANT. See Landlord and Tenant.

TENCZER, PAUL: Hungarian author; born at Nagy Bejom April 11, 1836; died at Budapest Feb. 6, 1905. He was educated at Keszthely and in Budapest, where he studied law. In 1861 he was one of the founders of the society for the naturalization and emancipation of Hungarian Jews; and from 1862 to 1867 he edited the "Magyar Izraelita," the organ of that society. In 1868 he was elected a member of the Diet, in which he was one of the leaders of the Radical party.

Tenczer founded the periodicals "Magyar Ujság" and "Neues Politisches Volksblatt," the latter of which he edited for eighteen years. He was prominent both in Jewish and in communal affairs in Budapest, and it was due to his efforts that tuition was made free in the public schools of the Hungarian capital.

Bibliography: *Pallas Lex.*
s.   L. V.

TENNESSEE: One of the Southern States of the American Union; admitted in 1796—the third after the incorporation of the original thirteen; seceded June 18, 1861; readmitted in 1866. A few Jews were among a number of traders who settled near the Holston River, in the present Hawkins county, in 1778; otherwise no traces of Jewish settlement during the eighteenth century are found. The first congregations organized were those of MEMPHIS and Nashville (see below). In 1920 the Jewish population of the state was 14,390.

Chattanooga: Jews settled here in 1858; but for many years divine services were held only during the holy days. About 1890 the Mizpah congregation was organized and Reform worship introduced, the officiating rabbis being successively Judah Wechsler, L. Weiss, Moses Gries, L. Rubinstein, S. H. Sonneschein, Leo Mannheimer, and Jonah Wise. In 1920 J. H. Miller was the rabbi. An Orthodox congregation, the B'nai Zion, has also been established. The societies organized for benevolent purposes are: the Hebrew Ladies' Aid Association; the Jewish Relief Society of Chattanooga; the Federation of the Sons and Daughters of Zion; Chattanooga Lodge I. O. B. B. Two of the most prominent members of the community have been Adolph Ochs and George W. Ochs, the former as editor of the "Chattanooga Times," and the latter as mayor and president of the Chamber of Commerce, the Board of Education, and the Library Association. The former is publisher and proprietor of the "New York Times," and the latter was editor of the "Philadelphia Public Ledger" from 1902-15; both brothers now reside on the Atlantic coast. Chattanooga had a population of 57,900 in 1920, including about 1,000 Jews.

Knoxville: The community of Knoxville is divided into two Orthodox congregations—Beth-El and Cheska Emunah. In 1904 a B'nai B'rith lodge was organized; a Young Men's Hebrew Association was formed in 1900. The Ladies' Hebrew Benevolent Society and the Jewish Ladies' Sewing Circle attend to the needs of the poor. The Rev. I. Winnick is the rabbi of the Cheska Emunah congregation. Knoxville has a population of 77,820, including about 700 Jews.

Nashville: In 1845 several Jewish families settled in Nashville. Additions to these resulted in the establishment in 1854 of the Congregation Magen David, with Abraham Schwab as president. Another congregation was formed at the same time under the name B'nai Jeshurun; and this in 1865 was merged in the Reform congregation Ohavai Sholom, with the Rev. Judah Wechsler as rabbi. The latter congregation, whose pulpit has been occupied in turn by H. Goldammer, L. Tintner, I. S. Moses, and I. Lewinthal (the present incumbent), is progressive and prosperous; it has a synagogue on Vine street and a cemetery with a mortuary chapel. Its membership is 225, and 150 pupils attend the Sabbath-school. A Ladies' Auxiliary Society is attached to it. The Orthodox congregation Adath Israel is fully organized, and its membership has been augmented by an influx of Russian immigrants. The following benevolent societies have been established: Maimonides Lodge I. O. B. B.; Gal-Ed Lodge, Free Sons of Israel; the Hebrew Relief Society (founded 1885), and the Standard Club (1880; a social organization). Nashville had a population of 118,342 in 1920, of whom about 3,000 were Jews.

Brownsville (population 3,062) and **Jackson** (population 18,860) both have congregations. Though the Jewish population of Brownsville is only 100, its congregation, known as Adas Israel, was established and its burial ground purchased as early as 1867. The 1905 incumbent of the rabbinate was Emil Tamm. Its synagogue was dedicated in 1882 by Dr. M. Samfield of Memphis. West Tennessee Lodge I. O. B. B. and a Ladies' Hebrew Relief Association discharge the charitable obligations of the community. Jackson, with a Jewish population of 150, has a congregation and a synagogue. A B'nai B'rith lodge was formed there in 1903. **Columbia** and **Clarksville** have small Jewish communities; and Jewish settlers are found in **Franklin, Ripley, Murfreesboro, Bristol, Pulaski,** and **Dyersburg.**

A. M. SA.

TENT (אֹהֶל): The usual home of nomads, who are accordingly described as dwelling in tents (Gen. iv. 20). As distinguished from the hut of boughs ("sukkah") it is a portable habitation of skin or cloth stretched over poles. The tent of the ancient Israelites was in all probability very similar to that of the modern Bedouins of Syria and Arabia. The covering of the tent ("yeri'ah") originally consisted of skins, later of the modern coarse tent-cloth spun of the hair of black goats (comp. Cant. i. 5); the Arabs accordingly speak of their "houses of hair" ("bait wabar," "bait sha'r"). This cloth, which is spun in long narrow strips on primitive looms by the Bedouin women, felts quickly, and is proof against the heaviest rains. The strips are sewed together to form a covering of the required size, and are stretched over three rows of three tent-poles each ("ammudim"; Judges xvi. 26). The center poles are somewhat higher than those in front and behind, and the covering of the tent consequently falls away slightly on either side, where the rows of poles, also, are frequently lower, so that the roof is somewhat arched; Isaiah accordingly compares the heavens to a tent which is spread out (Isa. xl. 22).

The covering of the tent was held in place by strong cords ("metarim," Ex. xxxv. 18, Isa. liv. 2, Jer. x. 20; "yeter," Job iv. 21), which were fastened to wooden pegs driven into the ground ("yated"; see below), whence were derived such phrases as "nasa'," with or without "yated," in the sense of breaking camp (Gen. xxxv. 16 et passim). A tent-cloth was hung from the top in such a way as to give protection against wind and sun; and a curtain suspended on the three middle poles divided the tent into two sections, one for the men and the other for the women ("heder"; Judges xv. 2; Gen. xliii. 30), since only the wealthiest had special tents for the latter (Gen. xxiv. 67, xxxi. 33). The tents of a clan or a family were grouped as a camp, a small number being pitched in a circle (comp. "tirah" [= "enclosure"] used as a term for the camp of the Israelites), while larger encampments formed long rows.

The tents were furnished with extreme simplicity. A few coarse straw mats covered a portion of the floor and served for both chairs and beds, while a hole in the ground in the men's division formed the hearth. A round piece of leather was spread on the floor as a table ("shulḥan"), and bags of goatskin ("no'd," "ḥemet") with the hair outward contained water, milk, or grain, the equipment being completed by a baking-pan, a few rough metal spoons, a hand-mill for grinding grain, and saddles for the camels.

After settling in the land of Canaan, and in proportion as they became agriculturists, the Hebrews ceased to dwell in tents, although, for religious reasons, the RECHABITES long observed the ancient into the ground at a certain distance from the tent. These pegs are of wood, about a foot long and an inch in diameter, pointed at one end, and with a hook at the other, to which the rope can be tied. The Hebrew equivalent for the expression "to pitch a tent" is, therefore, "taḳa'" (comp. Gen. xxxi. 25; Jer. vi. 3), which means "to drive in the tent-pins." In the same way "to pull out the tent-pins," as noted above, means to strike tent for a journey.

E. C.   I. BR.

TE'OMIM, HEZEKIAH (FEIWEL) BEN JONAH: Rabbi at Przemysl; lived in the seventeenth and eighteenth centuries. He was the au-

BEDOUIN TENT.
(From a photograph by Bonfils.)

mode of life; and even to the latest period the Hebrew language retained, even in cases where the primitive idea was no longer present, a number of terms originally derived from life in tents, as is shown by the phrase "halak le-oholo" = "to return home" (comp. Josh. xxii. 4 *et seq.*; Judges vii. 8, xix. 9; I Kings xii. 16), and by the frequent mention of tents in symbolic language (*e.g.*, in Isa. xxii. 23, xxxviii. 12; Ezra ix. 8; Jer. iv. 20).

The word "yated" (Ex. xxvii. 19, xxxv. 18, xxxviii. 31; Judges iv. 21, 22; Isa. xxxiii. 20, liv. 2) designates a tent-pin. Among the Bedouins today the poles which form the framework of the tent, as well as part of the tent-cloth placed upon them, are held in place by ropes fastened to pegs driven thor of "Teḳa' be-Shofar" (Breslau, 1719), containing documents concerning the litigation between the author and the community of Przemysl, which, in spite of a formal contract, had nominated for rabbi Samuel of Lemberg, formerly rabbi of Slonim.

BIBLIOGRAPHY: Steinschneider, *Cat. Bodl.* col. 845.

E. C.   I. BR.

TE'OMIM, JONAH BEN ISAIAH: Bohemian rabbi at Prague; died at Metz April 16, 1669. After having exercised the function of rabbi at Nikolsburg and in several other Bohemian communities he was called in 1660 to the rabbinate of Metz. In 1666 he was appointed rabbi of Posen, but he was prevailed upon by the community of Metz to remain in the latter city. Te'omim was the author of

"Nimuḳim," containing notes on David ben Samuel's "Ṭure Zahab" (on Ḥoshen Mishpaṭ; Cracow, 1692), and "Ḳiḳayon de-Yonah," novellæ on three Talmudical treatises (Amsterdam, 1669–70).

BIBLIOGRAPHY: Zunz, in Liebermann's *Deutsches Volkskalender*, 1853, p. 68; Carmoly, in Jost's *Annalen*, ii. 88; idem, in *Revue Orientale*, ii. 172; Steinschneider, *Cat. Bodl.* col. 1430; Abraham Cohen, *Les Rabbins de Metz*, p. 34, Paris, 1886.
E. C.   I. BR.

TE'OMIM, JONAH (ḤAYYIM) BEN JOSHUA FEIWEL: Rabbi successively at Przemysl, Zülz, and Breslau; lived in the seventeenth and eighteenth centuries; son-in-law of David Oppenheim, rabbi of Prague, and later of Hirsch ben Benjamin, rabbi of Berlin. He was the author of: "'Aleh de-Yonah," novellæ on Shulḥan 'Aruk, Ḥoshen Mishpaṭ, and including some parts of his commentary on Maimonides' "Perush ha-Mishnah"; "Ḳonṭres R. Ḥayyim Yonah," novellæ on the laws called נרמי (Jesnitz, 1723); and novellæ on Shebu'ot (*ib.* 1724).

BIBLIOGRAPHY: Steinschneider, *Cat. Bodl.* col. 1431.
E. C.   I. BR.

TE'OMIM, JOSEPH BEN MEÏR: Galician rabbi; born at Lemberg in 1727; died at Frankfort-on-the-Oder in 1793. While still young he succeeded his father in the position of preacher and rabbinical instructor in the yeshibah of Lemberg. Later he went to Berlin, where he stayed several years in the bet ha-midrash of Daniel Jafe. Then he resumed his former position at Lemberg, and in 1782 was appointed rabbi at Frankfort-on-the-Oder, where he remained until his death.

Te'omim, who was one of the foremost rabbis of his time, was a thorough student of rabbinical literature, and was not unlearned in the secular sciences. He wrote: "Peri Megadim," a twofold commentary on the Oraḥ Ḥayyim — one part being entitled "Mishbezot Zahab," containing a supercommentary on David ben Samuel's "Ṭure Zahab," and the other "Eshel Abraham," on Abraham Abele's "Magen Abraham" (Frankfort-on-the-Oder, 1753); "Porat Yosef," novellæ on Yebamot and Ketubot, with rules for halakic decisions (Zolkiev, 1756); "Ginnat Weradim," seventy rules for the comprehension of the Talmud (Frankfort-on-the-Oder, 1767); "Peri Megadim," a twofold commentary on the Yoreh De'ah—one part being entitled "Mishbezot Zahab," containing a supercommentary on David ben Samuel's "Ṭure Zahab," and the other "Sifte Da'at," on Shabbethai Kohen's "Sifte Kohen" (ש"ך; Berlin, 1772); "Tebat Gome," on the Sabbatical sections (Frankfort-on-the-Oder, 1782); "Shoshanat ha-'Amakim," a methodology of the Talmud, published together with the preceding; "No'am Megadim," commentaries on the prayers, published with the prayer-book "Hegyon Leb." Te'omim left in manuscript "Sefer ha-Maggid" (a commentary on the Pentateuch and the Hafṭarot, sermons for Sabbaths and festivals, and a twofold commentary on Pirḳe Abot) and "Em la-Binah" (a Hebrew, Aramaic, and Chaldaic lexicon; Neubauer, "Cat. Bodl. Hebr. MSS." No. 1500). In the introduction to the last-named work Te'omim mentions a great number of writings of his own, on halakot and ethics, which are no longer in existence.

BIBLIOGRAPHY: D. Cassel, in Ersch and Gruber, *Encyc.* section ii., part 31, p. 97; Steinschneider, *Cat. Bodl.* col. 1534; Neubauer, in *Ha-Maggid*, xiii. 285; Fuenn, *Keneset Yisrael*, p. 514; Buber, *Anshe Shem*, p. 95.
E. C.   I. BR.

TE'OMIM, JOSHUA FEIWEL BEN JONAH: Rabbi at Przemysl in the seventeenth and eighteenth centuries. He was the author of "Panim Masbirot," a polemical work directed against Meïr ben Isaac Eisenstadt (1715).

BIBLIOGRAPHY: Steinschneider, *Cat. Bodl.* col. 1564.
E. C.   I. BR.

TE'OMIM (ARYEH JUDAH), LÖB BEN MOSES (called also **Zunz** or **Zinz**): Rabbi and scholar of the seventeenth and eighteenth centuries; lived in Pinczow, and later in Plotzk. He was the author of the following works: "Ya'alat Ḥen" (Zolkiev, 1802), sermons on different parashiyyot; "Geṭ Meḳushshar" (Warsaw, 1812), compendium to that part of Maimonides' "Yad" which treats of divorce; "Magen ha-Elef," called also "Shem Ḥadash" (*ib.* 1817), on the regulations of the ritual codex referring to the Passover festival (to this work are appended notes on the "Maḥaẓit ha-Sheḳel" of Samuel ha-Levi Kolin); "She'elot u-Teshubot Gur Aryeh Yehudah" (Zolkiev, 1827), compendium of the four ritual codices; "Ḥiddushim" (Warsaw, 1830), treating of the sheḥiṭah and ṭerefah; "Simḥat Yom-Ṭob" (*ib.* 1841), complete commentary on the treatise Beẓah; "She'elot u-Teshubot Meshibat Nefesh" (*ib.* 1849), responsa on the ritual codices; "Ḥiddushim" (*ib.* 1859), compendium of the ritual codex Yoreh De'ah; "Birkat ha-Shir" (n.p., n.d.), a Passover Haggadah together with commentary; "Melo ha-'Omer," commentary on the Pentateuch and the Five Megillot; and "Ṭib Ḥaliẓah" and "Ṭib Ḳiddushin" (n.p., n.d.), collections of responsa on the ceremony of ḤALIẒAH as observed in modern times, and on marriage contracts.

BIBLIOGRAPHY: Fürst, *Bibl. Jud.* s.v. *Zinz*; Benjacob, *Oẓar ha-Sefarim*, pp. 94, 96, 175, 208, 227, 296, 376, 591, 592, 594, 636.
S.   S. O.

TE'OMIM, MEÏR BEN SAMUEL: Polish Talmudist of the eighteenth century; died July, 10, 1773. Meïr was a grandson of Joseph Te'omim, and was a preacher in Lemberg. He wrote: "Nofet Ẓufim" (included in his son Joseph Te'omim's "Rab Peninim"; Frankfort-on-the-Oder, 1782); "Birkat Yosef we-Eliyahu Rabba" (Zolkiev, 1750). According to his son Joseph, he wrote a work entitled "'Emeḳ Halakah," comprising explanations of a large part of the Talmud. His decisions are cited in the works of later Talmudists.

BIBLIOGRAPHY: Walden, *Shem ha-Gedolim he-Ḥadash*, i. 87; Buber, *Anshe Shem*, p. 136; Benjacob, *Oẓar ha-Sefarim*, p. 88, No. 654; p. 542, No. 59; Steinschneider, *Cat. Bodl.* col. 1717; Zedner, *Cat. Hebr. Books Brit. Mus.* No. 256.
E. C.   A. PE.

TE'OMIM-FRÄNKEL, BARUCH BEN DAVID: Rabbi at Wisnicz, Austrian Galicia, and at Leipnik, Moravia, during the first half of the nineteenth century; grandson of Aryeh Löb ben Joshua Feiwel Te'omim. He was famous as a Talmudist, and was the author of "Baruk Ṭa'am" (Lemberg, 1841), Talmudic dissertations, and of notes to the Mishnah and the Talmud, included in the Lemberg (1862) edition of the former and in the Warsaw (1859–64) edition of the latter.

BIBLIOGRAPHY: Zedner, *Cat. Hebr. Books Brit. Mus.* p. 756; Fürst, *Bibl. Jud.* i. 290; Walden, *Shem ha-Gedolim he-Ḥadash*, p. 32; Dembitzer, *Kelilat Yofi*, i. 82, note.
s. s. A. Pe.

TEPLITZ: Town in northern Bohemia, about 46 miles northwest of Prague. The earliest documentary evidence of the presence of Jews there is dated 1414; but the earliest Jewish source referring to them belongs to the end of the sixteenth century. In 1480 the Jewish community obtained from the town a burial-ground and built a synagogue. In an agreement dated Aug. 1, 1583, the Jews bound themselves to pay the town a certain sum yearly, in return for which they were permitted the unrestricted use of the baths. The Thirty Years' war caused a decrease in the number of Jews in Teplitz; in 1621 there were only 24 Jewish families there, occupying 11 houses; but in spite of this small number the old synagogue was torn down and rebuilt on a larger scale.

With the counter-reformation in Bohemia evil times came to the community in Teplitz. Those Jews who had no fixed business there were expelled (1667); this left only 8 families (34 persons); and though enough returned to bring the number up to 262 before the year expired, in 1668 they were again forced to leave the town. The Jews were by this time restricted to the Judengasse, and as a distinctive badge they were required to wear a large ruff around the neck. About this time, too, the old cemetery was closed and a new one opened. The wearing of the white ruff around the neck was abolished in 1781, in accordance with the decree of toleration issued by Emperor Joseph. Three years later, in accordance with a law relating to the Jews throughout the empire, the Teplitz Jews, whose disputes hitherto had been settled by their rabbi, were placed under the jurisdiction of the civil authorities.

After 1848, when the walls of the ghetto disappeared and the Jews obtained full liberty, the community grew appreciably. The Jews were active not only in commerce, but in manufacture, the introduction and development of which must be largely attributed to them, for they were among the founders and first builders of factories in Teplitz. Hosiery and glassware are the chief manufacturing products. In 1862 the second cemetery was closed and a new one opened. In 1883, about 400 years after the building of the first place of worship, a new basilican synagogue was erected at a cost of 150,000 kronen.

Whether the Jews of Teplitz had a rabbi previous to 1548 is doubtful, as the following clause is found among the instructions given them in that year by the lord of the manor Radislau: "The Jews of Teplitz must in the future conform to the order issued to earlier Jews, forbidding them to submit their difficulties to the rabbi in Prague, and requiring them to lay them before the elder of the Jewry and the local authorities in Teplitz." No mention is here made of a rabbi in the latter place. Probably the first rabbi was Nathan, son of Rabbi Joseph, who died in 1599, and whose tombstone was dis-

covered in the old cemetery. Other rabbis known to have officiated in Teplitz were: Jacob, son of Monasch (d. 1717); Simḥah Kohen Poppers (d. 1744); Abraham Kohen Poppers (d. 1775); Isaac Kalisch (d. 1783); Naphtali Herz Emden (d. 1796); Joseph b. Abraham (d. 1800); Solomon Strasser (d. 1820); Isaiah Levi Eidlitz (d. 1831); Zacharias Frankel (called to Dresden in 1836); David Pick (district rabbi; d. 1878); Adolf Rosenzweig (to 1887, when he was called to Berlin) and Adolf Kurrein, incumbent in 1905.

The communal institutions of Teplitz include a hebra ḳaddisha, a bikkur holim, an almshouse (founded 1834), a bride's dowry society (founded 1866), a women's society (Nashim Ẓidkoniyyot), a society for the aid of sick and necessitous women, a Tempelverein (founded 1882 for the building and decoration of the synagogue), Samel's orphan foundation, Philipp Spitz's Chanukkastiftung for clothing poor school-children at Hannukkah, Wilhelm Rindskopf's institute for the blind, a society for the support of poor wayfarers passing through Teplitz, and a hospital for residents or visitors in need of treatment at the springs (founded in 1836 by Naphtali Katz). The following table shows the growth of the Jewish population of Teplitz:

Year.	Number of Jewish Inhabitants.	Year.	Number of Jewish Inhabitants.
1414	20	1786 (47 houses)	452
1590	78	1791	403
1621	96	1792	425
1640	211	1823 (50 houses)	496
1650	231	1835	554
1660	237	1870	1,290
1667	262	1880	1,720
1674	154	1890	1,900
1702 (944 Christians)	187	1900	3,000
1724	321		

Before the European War (1914–16) the total population of Teplitz was 30,000.

BIBLIOGRAPHY: Hallwich, *Gesch. von Teplitz*, Leipsic, 1886; Rosenzweig, *Skizze zur Gesch. der Juden in Teplitz*, in *Allg. Zeit. des Jud.* 1887, pp. 13 *et seq.*
s. A. Ku.

TERAH: Father of Abraham, Nahor, and Haran (Gen. xi. 26). His original home was Ur of the Chaldees; but later he emigrated with his sons to Haran, where he died (Gen. xi. 32). According to Joshua's remarks at the assembly of the Israelites at Shechem, he was an idolater (Josh. xxiv. 2). Modern exegetes do not agree as to the etymology of the name "Terah," some identifying it with the Assyrian "turahu" (wild goat), with which the name of the Mesopotamian town Til-sha-turakhi might be compared, while others suppose it to be identical with the Syriac "tarḥa." Recently the name "Terah" has been regarded as a mutilation of "yeraḥ" (moon); in this case it would refer to a mythological person.

According to the Midrash (Gen. R. xxxviii.), Terah, in addition to being an idolater himself, made and sold idols; and during his absence he compelled Abraham to act as a merchant for him. The "Sefer ha-Yashar" (ed. Leghorn, 1876, pp. 14b *et seq.*) regards him as a great general of Nimrod, whom he accompanied on all his campaigns. Angry at Abraham for the destruction of his idols, Terah accused his son before Nimrod, who condemned him to be burned to death. Thereupon Abraham persuaded his father to emigrate to Canaan. See ABRAHAM IN APOCRYPHAL AND RABBINICAL LITERATURE.

BIBLIOGRAPHY: Hastings, *Dict. Bible*; Friedrich Delitzsch, *Prolegomena zu einem Neuen Hebr.-Aram. Wörterbuche*, p. 80, Leipsic, 1886; Nöldeke, in *Z. D. M. G.* 1886, p. 167; Winckler, *Gesch. des Volkes Israel*, ii. 24, note 1, Leipsic, 1900.

W. B.   S. O.

TERAPHIM (תרפים): Plural word of unknown derivation used in the Old Testament to denote the primitive Semitic house-gods whose cult had been handed down to historical times from the earlier period of nomadic wanderings. The translation of the term "teraphim" by the Greek versions, as well as its use in the Scriptures, gives an excellent idea of the nature of these symbols. Thus Aquila renders the word by "figures"; the Septuagint in Genesis by "images," in Ezekiel by "carved images," in Zechariah by "oracles," and in Hosea by "manifest objects" (δῆλοι). The Authorized Version often simply transcribes the word, as in Judges xvii. 5, xviii. 14 *et seq.*, and Hos. iii. 4, but frequently translates it "images," as in Gen. xxxi. 19 *et passim*. The rendering "images" occurs in I Sam. xix. 13 also, "idols" in Zech. x. 2, and "idolatry" in I Sam. xv. 23.

The form of the word in Hebrew must be regarded as a plural of excellence. Just as "Elohim" denotes "gods" and "God," the form "teraphim" is applicable to each single object as well as to the entire class (comp. I Sam. xix. 13 and Gen. xxxi. 19).

——**Biblical Data:** That teraphim were really images of human shape and of considerable size is plainly seen from I Sam. xix. 13, where Michal, the daughter of Saul, places one in David's bed in order to conceal his escape from her enraged father. It is furthermore evident that they were not too large to be easily portable, inasmuch as Gen. xxxi. 19 mentions that Rachel, without her husband's knowledge, stole the teraphim which belonged to her father, Laban, and, when she wished to conceal them, placed them among the camel's furniture and sat upon them (Gen. xxxi. 34).

The nature of the teraphim cult and its gradual decay seem also perfectly clear. It may be noted that teraphim were regarded in early times as representatives of real gods endowed with divine attributes (comp. Gen. xxxi. 30, where Laban, rebuking Jacob for Rachel's theft of the teraphim, asks, "Wherefore hast thou stolen my gods?"), and that evidently the teraphim cult was practically on a plane with YHWH worship. In Judges xvii. 5 Micah has "an house of gods" (בית אלהים) with a duly appointed priest; he makes an ephod (see below) and teraphim, which were used together with "a graven image" and "a molten image" made from silver dedicated to YHWH; the figures were evidently YHWH images. The value of the teraphim to the family and the tribe is shown by the statements that Rachel stole them from her father (Gen. xxxi. 19), and that the Danites, when they went to spy out the land of Laish, took away by force from the house of Micah not only the YHWH images just

Nature of Cult.

mentioned, but also the ephod, the teraphim, and the Levitical priest (see Judges xviii.).

In early times teraphim-worship was undoubtedly tolerated by the YHWH religion, as may be seen, for example, from I Sam. xix. 13 (the story of Michal, the daughter of Saul), where it is tacitly implied that a teraphim was a usual piece of furniture in the household of a loyal follower of YHWH. In Hos. iii. 4 and in Gen. xxxi. 19, also, teraphim are alluded to without comment, although Prof. H. P. Smith ("Samuel," p. xxxiv.) thinks he detects a touch of sarcasm in the latter passage. It is certain, however, that teraphim soon became an object of distinct condemnation in the YHWH cult.

Acceptance and Rejection.

In Gen. xxxv. 2 *et seq.* Jacob orders that the "strange gods" (אלהי הנכר), by which teraphim images were probably meant, be put away by his household and buried. The spot which was thus defiled was made a holy place by Joshua (Josh. xxiv. 20–26). Furthermore, in I Sam. xv. 23 Samuel in his rebuke to Saul is made to classify teraphim with iniquity (און) and rebellion (מרי). Josiah, the reforming king, did away with the magicians and wizards as well as with the teraphim and idols (גללים), all of which are grouped together as "abominations" (II Kings xxiii. 24). With these passages should also be compared Zech. x. 2 (R. V.): "for the teraphim have spoken vanity, and the diviners have seen a lie; and they have told false dreams."

It will appear from the above quotations that the most important function of the teraphim, at any rate after the spread of the YHWH cult over Israel, was that of divination. Evidently the images were used chiefly for oracular purposes, although nothing is known of the method of their consultation; it is probable, however, that they were used in connection with casting the sacred lot (comp. Zech. x. 2; Ezek. xxi. 26 [A. V. 21]). The mention of an ephod in connection with teraphim (Judges xvii. 5, xviii. 20) is a peculiar use of that word, which in these passages represents merely "a portable object employed or manipulated by the priest in consultation with the oracle" (comp. Moore, "Judges," p. 379, and see Judges viii. 27, which clearly describes an ephod as an object employed in divination). This use of the word seems to be quite distinct from that in the so-called P document (Ex. xxviii. 6 *et seq.*), where a high-priestly garment of the same name is referred to (see EPHOD).

Function.

Such oracles were probably consulted down to a quite late date (comp. Hos. iii. 4, Hebr.: "for the children of Israel shall abide many days without a king, and without a prince, and without a sacrifice [זבח], and without a pillar [מצבה], and without an ephod, and without teraphim"). The passage II Kings xxiii. 24, cited above, makes it evident that teraphim had survived in later Judah. The mention of teraphim in Zech. x. 2 may have been due to an archaizing tendency of the author of this section (see ZECHARIAH), and would not in itself be sufficient evidence to prove that the teraphim cult had continued into the Greek period; if, however, this passage is taken in conjunction with the statement of Josephus ("Ant." xviii. 9, § 5) that the custom of carrying house-gods on journeys into strange countries prevailed in his time in the Mesopotamian regions, it appears highly likely that the use of teraphim continued into the first Christian century and possibly even later.

It would seem, then, as remarked above, that teraphim, like the Roman Lares and Penates, originally represented house-gods, which were carried about by the primitive Semitic nomads as fetishes along with their family effects, and that

As Household Gods. these deities were in all probability worshiped at first as the most important divine objects known to the followers of this cult. Although nothing whatever is known about the origin of the teraphim cult, it may have been a survival of primitive ancestor worship; i.e., the images may have originally represented the deified ancestors of the family which revered them, and may have become later a sort of Manes oracle. They were probably not astral personifications. The cult could not have been regarded as indigenous among the Israelites, because the deities are characterized as " gods of the stranger " (A.V. "strange gods ") in Gen. xxxv. 4. In Ezek. xxi. 26 (A. V. 21) it is recorded that the King of Babylon consulted teraphim and "looked in the liver "; i.e., he made use of magical incantations as well as of the astrological rites common in Babylonia. It is not at all unlikely that the Israelites obtained the teraphim cult from their Aramean kinsmen.

E. C.   J. D. P.

——In Rabbinical Literature : The word "teraphim " is explained by the Rabbis as meaning "disgraceful things " (Yer. 'Ab. Zarah ii. 41b; Tan., Wayeze). It is rendered "zalmanaya " or "zilmanaya " (= "images ") by the Targumim of Onkelos and pseudo-Jonathan to Gen. xxxi. 19, 34, and by the Targum of Jonathan in the other parts of the Bible, except in connection with the image of Micah (Judges xvii. 5; xviii. 14, 18, 20), where it is rendered "dema'in " (= "likenesses "). The nature of the teraphim is much discussed by ancient commentators. According to Targ. pseudo-Jonathan to Gen. xxxi. 19, the teraphim were made of the head of a man, a first-born, which, after the man had been slain, was shaved and then salted and spiced. After a golden plate on which magic words were engraved had been placed under the tongue, the mummified head was mounted on the wall, and it spoke to the people. This legend is more fully developed in Pirke R. El. xxxvi., where it is said that after the head had been displayed on the wall, lighted candles were placed round it; the people then prostrated themselves before it, and it talked to them.

Ibn Ezra (on Gen. l.c.) records two definitions of "teraphim"; namely, (1) a copper dial by means of which one might ascertain the exact time, and (2) an image made by astrologers at a certain time and under the influence of certain stars, which caused it to speak. Ibn Ezra himself favored the latter interpretation, it appearing from I Sam. xix. 13, 16 that the teraphim had the shape of a man. Nahmanides (on Gen. l.c.), however, thinks that while the teraphim of Laban might have been idols, those of I Sam. l.c. were not, inasmuch as there could have

been no idols in David's house. He thinks that in general teraphim were astrological tables by means of which one might learn future events (comp. Kimhi on I Sam. l.c.). The "Sefer ha-Yashar " (section "Wayeze," pp. 46b–47a, Leghorn, 1870), after having repeated the description which Pirke R. Eliezer gives of the teraphim, declares that they were made of gold or silver, in the image of a man and at a certain moment, and that by the influence of the stars they revealed the future. It adds that the teraphim of Laban were of the latter description.

W. B.   M. Sel.

TEREBINTH. See Oak and Terebinth.

TEREFAH : Term signifying originally the flesh of a clean animal that had been torn or mortally wounded by beasts of prey, and had been rendered thereby unfit for food. In rabbinical literature the word came to be applied to the flesh of an animal that had received a fatal injury, or suffered any one of certain diseases, or was marked by some physical abnormality, but which otherwise would be "kasher " (fit and proper as food). "Terefah " in a broader sense includes also a regularly but unskilfully killed animal, in contradistinction to Nebelah, which refers to the carcass of a clean animal that has died an unnatural death or been killed irregularly (comp. Hul. iv. 2). Both flesh that is nebelah and flesh that is terefah are forbidden as food by the Mosaic law (Lev. xxii. 8).

The Talmudic rule is that when an animal is so injured that it can not live, its flesh is terefah; hence only such injury, disease, or abnormality is involved as must cause an untimely death and affect the health of the animal at the time it is slaughtered (Hul. iii. 1; 42a).

According to 'Ulla, the Mosaic law recognizes eight principal terefah signs, as follows: (1) "derusah " (violent attack by beast or bird of prey); (2) "nekubah " (perforation of a vital organ); (3) "hasurah " (natural deficiency of an organ); (4) "netulah " (loss of an organ); (5) "keru'ah "

Symptoms of Terefah. (a rent in the body); (6) "nefulah " (a fall that might cause internal injuries); (7) "pesukah " (severance or dislocation of a limb); (8) "sheburah " (fracture of a rib or other bone). In each of these classes there are a number of cases. The Mishnah gives a list of eighteen principal ones: (1) when the gullet ("weshet ") is punctured or perforated, the hole penetrating to the interior; (2) when the windpipe ("gargeret ") is split or torn across its width; (3) when the membrane ("kerum ") nearest to the brain is perforated; (4) when the heart is pierced as far as one of its ventricles; (5) when the spine is broken and the spinal cord is severed; (6) when the liver is entirely wanting; (7) when there is a perforation through the two membranes covering the lungs; (8) when the lungs lack any of their lobes; (9) when there is a hole in the maw, or (10) in the gall-bladder, or (11) in the intestines; (12) when there is a hole in the interior, or lower, stomach, or when (13) the greater part of the flesh covering the stomach is torn; (14) when there is a perforation of the omasum (המסס = "manyplies "), or (15) in the greater venter, or upper stomach, beyond the place where the two stomachs are joined; (16) when the animal has fallen off a roof; (17) when the majority of the ribs are fractured; (18) when the animal has been seized by a wolf with its forepaws or claws. A small bird is ṭerefah when a sparrow-hawk has struck its talons into it; and a larger bird, as a fowl or goose, when it has been struck by a falcon, eagle, or other large bird of prey.

Maimonides enumerates seventy indications of ṭerefah ("Yad," Sheḥiṭah, x. 9), and says: "Seventy ṭerefot are the limit, and must not be increased or diminished, even though it should be found by scientific investigation that some of the injuries are

The Seventy Ṭerefot. not dangerous to the life of the animal, or that some unenumerated conditions are dangerous to its life. Only those indications of ṭerefah may be followed which have been accepted by the Rabbis and handed down by tradition" (ib. x. 12, 13). Questions of Jewish law can not be decided by the evidence of philosophers (R. Sheshet, responsum No. 447).

The Shulḥan 'Aruk arranges the symptoms according to the various parts of the animal, describing minutely every injury, disease, or abnormality, from the head to the hind legs, internally and externally, whether a perforation, fracture, amputation, or discoloration, which might make the flesh of the animal ṭerefah; stating also when such defects are harmless. The lungs are more liable to injury than any other organ: the number and position of the lobes, the bronchial tubes, the tubercles, and any adhesion to the flesh ("sirka") must be considered. The lungs are inflated to discover any perforation. When the lungs are shrunk it is a sign of fright, and if the fright has been caused by human agency, as when an animal sees a man killing another animal, the flesh is ṭerefah. But if the fright was caused by an act of God, as by thunder or lightning, or if the animal has seen one animal kill another, the flesh is kasher. A test is made by soaking the lungs in lukewarm water for twenty-four hours: in the first case the shrinkage remains; in the second case the shrinkage disappears. Double organs, such as two livers, in an animal or fowl render it ṭerefah, as the rule is that "a superfluity is to be treated like a deficiency." When the gall is wanting, the flesh is ṭerefah; but when a part of it remains, it is kasher. A test is made by cutting the liver across and touching the incision with the tongue; if there is no bitter taste, it proves the entire absence of the gall. Two gall-bladders render the animal ṭerefah; but when there is a connecting flow between them, though they appear double, it is kasher. Some species of fowl, as doves and pigeons, have no gall-bladders, and are kasher.

A cow or an ox has twenty-two large ribs, eleven on each side; if twelve or more are fractured, it is ṭerefah. The extraction of only one rib with its vertebra renders it ṭerefah. If the spine is broken, but the spinal cord is not severed, it is kasher.

The signs of ṭerefah in derusah are explained. The lion's attack is fatal to any animal; the wolf's is not fatal to large cattle, like oxen or calves, but it is fatal to small cattle, like sheep; that of a cat or marten ("nemiyyah"; Ḥul. 52b) and a fox is fatal

only to kids, lambs, and fowls; that of a weasel is fatal only to fowls. The lion and the wolf are the

Derusah. most ferocious animals of their size; the attacks of other beasts of prey are not fatal to animals. The attacks of birds of prey are not fatal to cattle, except in the case of the hawk, which is fatal to kids and lambs when it pierces their bodies with its beak. The attacks of ordinary birds of prey are fatal only to birds of their own size, or smaller; that of the eagle is fatal to all other birds.

A fall of ten "ṭefaḥim" (handbreadths) renders the flesh of an animal ṭerefah. A shorter fall, if sudden, without a chance of adjustment on the part of the animal, might be fatal, as internal injuries are possible. Therefore special care must be taken when casting the animal for the sheḥiṭah.

In later rabbinical speech the term "ṭerefah" is applied to food rendered unfit by the mixture of meat and milk; or to things forbidden by the dietary laws; or to things to which the terms "pasul" and "asur," often interchanged, are applied. See BEDIḲAH; CARCASS; CLEAN AND UNCLEAN ANIMALS; DIETARY LAWS; KASHER; NEBELAH; PORGING; SHEḤIṬAH.

BIBLIOGRAPHY: Maimonides, Yad, Sheḥiṭah, v.-xi.; Joseph Caro, Shulḥan 'Aruk, Yoreh De'ah, 29-60; Alexander Sender Schorr, Tebu'ot Shor, Zolkiev, 1733; Benjamin Wolf Winternitz, Gebul Binyamin, Vienna, 1824; Isaac ha-Kohen, Zibḥe Kohen (Hebrew and Italian), Leghorn, 1832; Rabbinowicz, Principes Talmudiques de Schehitah et de Terepha, Paris, 1877; idem, Médecine des Thalmuds, pp. 258-262, Leipsic, 1883; Krochmal, in He-Ḥaluẓ, i. 73, ii. 87, iii. 25; Wiener, Die Jüdischen Speisegesetze, pp. 220-248, Berlin, 1895.
W. B.   J. D. E.

TERNI, DANIEL BEN MOSES DAVID: Italian rabbi, poet, and Biblical commentator of the eighteenth and nineteenth centuries; a native of Ancona. After having taught for some time at Lugo, he was called to the rabbinate of Florence. He was the author of the following works: "Se'uddat Miẓwah" (Venice 1791), consisting of sermons for holy days and some responsa; "Simḥat Miẓwah" (Florence, 1793), a dramatic poem in two parts composed on the occasion of the inauguration of a new synagogue at Florence, and mentioned in his "'Iḳḳere Dinim"; "Mattenat Yad" (ib. 1795), a treatise on charity in the form of sermons; "'Iḳḳere Dinim," called also "'Iḳḳere ha-Dat" = "ha-Rab Daniel Terni" (ib., 1803), a compendium of the laws contained in the Shulḥan 'Aruk (Oraḥ Ḥayyim and Yoreh De'ah), arranged according to ancient and later responsa; "Derek Siaḥ," casuistic sermons, and "En Ḳeẓ," a bibliographical work similar to Shabbethai Bass' "Sifte Yeshenim" (both of these works are still unpublished); and "Shem 'Olam," a commentary on the Pentateuch (a manuscript of this work was in Osias Schorr's library).

BIBLIOGRAPHY: Fuenn, Keneset Yisrael, p. 263; Fürst, Bibl. Jud. iii. 418; Nepi-Ghirondi, Toledot Gedole Yisrael, p. 79.
E. C.   M. SEL.

TERNI, MATTATHIAH NISSIM BEN JACOB ISRAEL: Italian rabbi and poet; flourished in the eighteenth and nineteenth centuries. He was rabbi at Florence, Urbino, Pesaro, and Sinigaglia. He wrote: "Sefat Emet," halakic decisions (Leghorn, 1797); "Midbar ba-'Arabah," on the marriage laws (Florence, 1807 [?]); "Midbar Mattanah," responsa, in four parts (*ib.* 1810; the appendix, in Italian, was published at Urbino). A volume of poems by him is entitled "No'am we-Ḥobelim we-Derek Emunah" (Geiger, "Zeit. Jüd. Theol." iii. 286, No. 44).

BIBLIOGRAPHY: Fürst, *Bibl. Jud.* iii. 418; Mortara, *Indice,* p. 64; Steinschneider, *Cat. Bodl.* col. 1684.
E. C.   M. SEL.

TERONGI, RAPHAEL BENITO: Martyr. He, his teacher Raphael Valls, and his sister Catalina Terongi were together publicly burned as "Judios impenitentes" at the auto da fé held in Palma, Majorca, May 6, 1691. As soon as the victims beheld the flames they tried with all their power to escape the fetters, in which effort Raphael Terongi finally succeeded, immediately flinging himself upon the pyre. Catalina implored pitifully to be saved from the flames, though she was not able to bring herself to utter the name of Jesus. According to a report of James Stanhope (who was an eye-witness of this and other autos da fé held in Palma) to his father in Madrid, the victims were, in most cases, wealthy and the owners of magnificent dwelling-houses.

BIBLIOGRAPHY: *Spain Under Charles II.* pp. 12 *et seq.*; Garan, *La Fe Triumfante,* in A. de Castro, *Judios en España,* p. 215; Kayserling, *Geschichte der Juden in Spanien,* i. 187; idem, *Ein Feiertag in Madrid,* p. 45.
S.   M. K.

TERQUEM, OLRY: French mathematician; born at Metz June 16, 1782; died at Paris May 6, 1862. In 1801 he began his studies at the Ecole Polytechnique in Paris, where he became assistant professor in mathematics in 1803. In the following year, after obtaining his degree as "docteur ès sciences," he received a call as professor of higher mathematics to the Lyceum of Mayence, then still a French city. In 1811 he became professor at the artillery school at Mayence, and went in the same capacity to Grenoble in 1814. In 1815 he returned to Paris as librarian of the artillery central depot of St. Thomas d'Aquin, which position he retained until his death. In 1842 he, together with Gerono, founded the "Nouvelles Annales de Mathématiques" (continued by Charles Brisse). He also edited, from 1855 to 1861, the "Bulletin de Bibliographie, d'Histoire et de Biographie de Mathématiques."

In 1852, when Napoleon III. visited the Musée d'Artillerie, Olry Terquem was created an officer of the Legion of Honor. His funeral, which was attended by General Lebœuf as representative of the emperor, and a dozen other generals, all his former pupils, was remarkable in that Terquem insisted on being buried according to the rites of Judaism, although no other member of his family remained true to his ancestral faith. Isidor, chief rabbi of France, officiated; but General de Bressolles as representative of the minister of war delivered the funeral oration.

Besides several handbooks on elementary mathematics and mechanics, a "Commentaire sur la Mécanique Céleste [of Laplace]," and a "Histoire d'Artillerie" (the latter two works remaining unfinished), Terquem wrote "Lettres Tsarphatiques" (nine pamphlets, Paris, 1831–37), which were first published in the "Journal de la Moselle." In these

letters he pleaded for the introduction of reforms in Judaism, especially for a Sunday Sabbath.

Terquem contributed also several treatises to the French Bible translation by S. Cahen, and a great number of articles to the "Archives Israélites."

BIBLIOGRAPHY: E. Prouhet, in *Bulletin de Bibliographie, d'Histoire et de Biographie de Mathématiques,* 1861, pp. 81–90; *Archives Israélites,* 1862, pp. 313–320; *La Grande Encyclopédie*; Fuenn, *Keneset Yisrael,* s.v. *Olry Terquem.*
                                                       S.

TERRACINO: Italian rabbinical family, of which the following members are known:

David Mordecai Terracino: Rabbi at Asti in the nineteenth century.

Hezekiah Terracino: Italian scholar of the seventeenth century; flourished in Lugo, where he probably held the position of ab bet din; a contemporary of Nathanael Trabotti. In a responsum printed in Lampronti's "Paḥad Yiẓḥaḳ" (i. 112) Hezekiah pleads total blindness as an excuse for the incomplete answer given to a question addressed to him.

Moses ben Menahem Terracino: Rabbi at Ferrara in the seventeenth century. He was the author of a responsum on the controversy at Lodi between Manasseh ha-Kohen and the Pavia brothers; also of a responsum (in the collection "Palge Mayim," p. 36) in which he retracted a decision previously given.

Solomon Terracino: Mentioned in Shabbethai Bär's responsa collection (§ 51).

BIBLIOGRAPHY: Mortara, *Indice,* p. 64; Nepi-Ghirondi, *Toledot Gedole Yisrael,* pp. 111, 237; Fürst, *Bibl. Jud.* iii. 418 and note 2.
E. C.   S. O.

TERRITORIALISTS. See ZIONISM.

TERU'AH. See SHOFAR.

TERUEL (טירול): City of Aragon. In the Middle Ages it possessed a prominent Jewish community, which enjoyed several privileges, and which paid in the fourteenth century a yearly tax of 300 sueldos. Its members were engaged in commerce and industry, especially in wool-weaving. During the persecutions of 1391 many of them were killed, while others accepted Christianity in order to save their lives. The Jews of Teruel had a statute according to which a document was legal only if it had been drawn up by the communal secretary and bore his seal. Failure to comply with these regulations entailed a fine of 20 gold gulden (Isaac b. Sheshet, Responsa, No. 304). About 1385 a delator ("malsin") appeared at Teruel; and the community asked Isaac b. Sheshet how, under existing circumstances, he should be dealt with. Among the many wool-dealers of the city were Don Solomon ibn Yahya and Don Judah ibn Yahya. Other prominent Jews living in Teruel were the scholarly Judah ben David, whom Isaac b. Sheshet commended to the community, and his contemporaries Rabbi Moses Gabbai and Isaac Lappa.

BIBLIOGRAPHY: Jacobs, *Sources,* Nos. 789, 943, 988; Rios, *Hist.* ii. 297, 378, 402; Isaac b. Sheshet, *Responsa,* Nos. 222, 225, 234 *et seq.,* 252, 347, 452.
S.   M. K.

TERUMOT: Treatise in the Mishnah, Tosefta, and Palestinian Talmud. There were two kinds of heave-offerings or gifts to the priest: one was the regular heave-offering, known also as the "great heave-offering" ("terumah gedolah"), which the Israelites were required to give to the priest from the fruits of their fields (comp. Num. xviii. 8 *et seq.*; Deut. xviii. 4); the other was the so-called "tithe heave-offering" ("terumat ma'aser"), *i.e.*, the tithe which the Levites put aside for the priests from the tithe due to them as Levites (comp. Num. xviii. 25 *et seq.*). The treatise gives a more precise definition of the rules governing both these heave-offerings, but the great heave-offering forms the chief subject of discussion. In most editions of the Mishnah this treatise is sixth in the order Zera'im. It is divided into eleven chapters, containing altogether one hundred and one paragraphs.

Ch. i.: Enumeration of five classes of persons who may not make the heave-offering (§§ 1–3). From what sacrifices the heave-offering may not be taken (§§ 4–5). Five other classes of persons who may not make the selection, though where they have done so in ignorance of the prohibition, their act is considered valid (§ 6). The selection is not to be made according to measure, weight, or number, but according to estimated value (§ 7). Different cases in which the heave-offering is considered valid, although the method by which it was selected is generally not permissible (§§ 8–10).

Ch. ii.: Further enumeration of cases in which the heave-offering is valid, although the method of procedure followed in selecting it was not legitimate, such as in selecting clean grain for unclean as a heave-offering (§ 1). Cases in which the heave-offering obtained by an unallowable method of procedure is valid only if the wrong method was used unwittingly. In this connection various methods are enumerated which, although properly not allowed,

Contents. are considered valid if they have been used unwittingly (§§ 2–3). The heave-offering may not be made from one kind for another kind, nor from imperfect fruits for perfect ones of the same kind, although perfect fruits may be given as a heave-offering for imperfect fruits of the same kind (§§ 4–6).

Ch. iii.: Circumstances under which the heave-offering must be given twice (§§ 1–2). A case in which each of two joint owners sets apart the heave-offering from the fruits belonging to them in common (§ 3). The owner may empower his servant to set apart the heave-offering (§ 4). How the heave-offering is determined (§ 5). In what order the different taxes, as the first-born tax, the heave-offering, and the tithe, are to be given (§§ 6–7). What shall be done when one makes a slip of the tongue while selecting the heave-offering, or during the consecration of the sacrifice or the taking of an oath (§ 8). Gifts and offerings of non-Jews (§ 9).

Ch. iv.: Selecting and measuring the great heave-offering. The great heave-offering should be about one-fortieth, one-fiftieth, or one-sixtieth of the whole from which it is taken, according to the generosity of the giver (§§ 1–5). The tithe heave-offering, like the tithe, is taken according to number, measure, or weight (§ 6). Concerning the mixing of heave-offerings with other fruits and the proportions of the various ingredients in regard to the question of "meduma' " (§§ 7–13).

Ch. v.: Further discussion concerning the mixing with other fruits of clean heave-offerings and of those which have become unclean.

Ch. vi.: Concerning the compensation that must be made by one who has eaten, or otherwise derived benefit from, a heave-offering (comp. Lev. xxii. 14).

Ch. vii.: Continuation of ch. vi.; cases in which only the value of what has been eaten need be paid, without the additional fifth part ("homesh"; §§ 1–4). Further regulations concerning the mixing of heave-offerings (§§ 5–7).

Ch. viii.: The same theme continued (§§ 1–3). Regarding wine, set apart for the heave-offering, which has stood uncovered; the danger of poisoning (§§ 4–7). Concerning the defilement of heave-offerings (§§ 8–11). Regarding women who are in danger of being outraged by heathen (§ 12).

Ch. ix.: What must be done in case, either wittingly or unwittingly, a heave-offering has been sown; regulations concerning the fruits from the sowing of a heave-offering.

Ch. x.: Cases in which the taste which certain foods have acquired from a heave-offering makes them unlawful; regulations regarding other cases in which lawful foods become unlawful through the taste which they have derived from unlawful foods.

Ch. xi.: Regulations concerning the use which may be made of clean heave-offerings, as well as of those which have become unclean.

The Tosefta is divided into ten chapters, and, besides additions to and amplifications of the Mishnah, contains some interesting utterances, as, for instance, the definition of the boundaries of the **Tosefta** territory belonging to the land of Israel **and** (ii. 12). The Palestinian Gemara to **Gemara.** this treatise explains and discusses the halakot of the Mishnah and contains almost no haggadic sayings. There are only a few narratives in it; from these the following has been selected:

Diocletian, in his youth, was a swineherd in Tiberias, where the young pupils from the school of Judah II. used to beat him and make fun of him. When he became emperor he determined to revenge himself on the Jews and especially on the scholars. He went to Paneas, a place at some distance from Tiberias, and from there sent a summons to Judah (ha-Nasi) II., ordering him, with the other scholars, to appear before the emperor on Sabbath evening. He directed his messenger to deliver the summons to Judah on Friday evening so that the scholars, who would not travel on the Sabbath, would have no time to make the journey, and would therefore render themselves liable to punishment for disobedience. By a miracle, however, the scholars succeeded in appearing before the emperor on Sabbath evening; and they appeased his anger by saying that they scorned only the swineherd Diocletian, but obeyed and honored the emperor. Diocletian then remarked that they should be cautious, and never insult a Roman even of lowly condition, because he might mount in rank and take revenge (46b). The same story, with a few divergencies in detail, is found in Gen. R. lxiii. 12.

w. b.   J. Z. L.

TESTAMENT. See Wills.

TESTAMENTS OF THE TWELVE PA-TRIARCHS

TESTAMENTS OF THE TWELVE PA-TRIARCHS : Title of twelve connected documents which purport to record the last words and exhortations of the twelve sons of Jacob. They also bear in several of the manuscripts subtitles indicating the virtues inculcated or the vices condemned by each of these patriarchs in turn. Thus Reuben discourses of evil motives and desires, especially as regards women; Simeon, of envy; Levi, of priesthood and pride; Judah, of courage, avarice, and fornication; Issachar, of simple-mindedness; Zebulun, of compassion and pity; Dan, of anger and falsehood; Naphtali, of natural goodness; Gad, of hatred; Asher, of the two characters of vice and virtue; Joseph, of temperance and chastity; Benjamin, of purity of heart.

In each testament the patriarch first narrates his own life, dwelling on his virtues or his sins. Next he exhorts his descendants to emulate the one and to

Contents. avoid the other. Lastly, he launches out into prophetic visions of their futures. In these apocalyptic passages the writings of Enoch are often appealed to and cited, though the citations are seldom found in the Ethiopic or Slavonic Enoch. In the biographies the writer follows the Old Testament, adding many details from Jewish tradition.

Many prophetic passages are apparently of Christian origin, and foretell the incarnation, the sanctification by water (*i.e.*, baptism), and the crucifixion of the Highest. In them Jesus is often identified with God. It is easy to detect and detach these Christian passages; and the manuscripts and versions assist one in doing so. Notably a eulogy of Paul (in which, however, his name is not mentioned), found in the Greek text of the Testament of Benjamin, is absent from the old Armenian version. Tertullian ("Adversus Marcionem," v. 1) seems to allude to this passage. If so, it was interpolated at least as early as the second century. However, Tertullian's allusion is not certain.

There is little external testimony regarding the Testaments. Besides the doubtful allusion of Tertullian (*c.* 200), a mention of them by name occurs in Origen ("Homilia XV. in Josuam," ch. vi.). There are doubtful references also in Jerome and Procopius, as well as specific mention in the "Synopsis Sacræ Scripturæ" wrongly ascribed to Athanasius, and in the "Stichometria" of Nicephorus. The Testaments are not again heard of until Matthew Paris relates in his chronicle (ed. London, 1571, p. 801), under the year 1242, that Robert Grosseteste, Bishop of Lincoln, translated them into Latin, a certain John of Basingstoke having brought them from Athens. This translation was rendered into most modern languages, as a weapon serviceable against the Jews. It was frequently printed before Grabe in 1698 edited the Greek text in his "Spicilegium."

Apart from Christian interpolations, these Testaments are Jewish documents, originally written in

Jewish Documents. Aramaic or Hebrew; and in the genizah of old Cairo, fragments of the original Semitic text have been discovered by M. Gaster, H. L. Pass, and A. Cowley. Dr. Gaster's Hebrew fragment ("Proc. Soc. Bibl. Arch." vol. xii.) answers to a part of

Naphtali; but it is probably a late Jewish paraphrase of an older Aramaic text. The other fragments are Aramaic, and closer to the Greek text. They belong together and answer to parts of Levi. Pass, assisted by J. Arendzen, published his fragment in "J. Q. R." (iii. 651-661). Cowley's awaits publication. An old Syriac fragment (noticed by Sinker) in Brit. Mus. Codex Add. 17,193 (of the year 874) is nearly identical verbally with the Aramaic fragment.

These discoveries confirm the previous conjectures of such scholars as Grabe, Kayser, Schürer, and Schnapp, and explain the many Semitisms of the Greek text. They prove that the latter is a paraphrase of an old Aramaic midrash, interpolated by generations of Christians.

The only critical edition is that of R. Sinker (Cambridge, 1869), who takes a tenth-century Cambridge manuscript as the basis of his text, adding a

Editions. collation of four more. A collation of a twelfth-century manuscript in the Vatican (No. 1238) has been published by the present writer ("J. Q. R." v., viii.), as well as a collation of the old Armenian. An old Slavonic version also exists, and has been published by Tichonrawow. An old Georgian version also exists.

The Testaments of the Twelve Patriarchs are usually included in Armenian codices of the Bible; the Vatican codex mentioned above as containing them is a Septuagint, and entitles them "Lepté Genesis" or "Parva Genesis." A new critical edition, taking account of the recovered Semitic texts, of the Greek codices in Athos, Patmos, Paris, and Rome, and of the ancient Armenian and Slavonic versions, is being prepared by Professor R. H. Charles.

BIBLIOGRAPHY : Besides the works mentioned above see the references given under APOCALYPSE and APOCRYPHA.

T.   F. C. C.

Owing in part to its Christological interpolations, and in part to the similarity of many of its teachings and utterances to those of the New Testament, the Testaments of the Twelve Patriarchs was regarded as a Christian work until by critical analysis Grabe, in his "Spicilegium Patrum" (Oxford, 1714), arrived at the conclusion that the basis of the work is Jewish, though there are many Christological interpolations. Nevertheless, the old view prevailed, and the work was ascribed to a Judæo-Christian (see, *e.g.*, Sinker, in his edition of the Testaments, Cambridge, 1869). Schnapp, however, in his "Die Testamente

The Hebrew Original and Its Haggadic Character. der Zwölf Patriarchen Untersucht" (Halle, 1884), revived Grabe's view and elaborated it, proving the spurious character of the Christian passages and also distinguishing two different Jewish sources in the main work. Schnapp's results were approved by Schürer ("Gesch." 3d ed., iii. 252-262) as far as the Jewish origin of the book is concerned, while the Armenian version brought to light by Conybeare ("J. Q. R." v. 375-378; viii. 260-268, 471-485) shows the gradual growth of Christian interpolations. New light was thrown on the book by "The Pre-Talmudic Haggadah" of Kohler (*ib.* v. 400-414), who found direct allusions to the Testaments in Sifre, Num. 12; Soṭah 7b; and Yer. Soṭah

16d, where "early writings" ("ketubim rishonim") are mentioned containing haggadic matters concerning the relations of Reuben with Bilhah and of Judah and his relations with Tamar. In the same article it was shown that the king and priest with prophetic powers described in the Testament of Levi is none other than John Hyrcanus, and that the campaigns of the sons of Jacob recounted in the Testament of Judah correspond exactly with the Maccabean wars.

The various spellings of the names in Test. Patr., Joseph, 1–9 and 10–18 led Sinker to postulate a double authorship for this section of the work, although two different tendencies are distinctly visible throughout the book, especially in the Testaments of Levi and Joseph, thus indicating two different writers, one Hasidæan and the other Maccabean. The monition to respect the priestly tribe of Levi is

Com-position. shown by closer investigation to be a mere addition to the main part of the book, which is ethical in character and may have been used in the Temple like one of the Hagiographa. The apocalyptic portion in Test. Patr., Levi, 14 seems to refer to the orgies of Alexander Jannæus (Josephus, "B. J." i. 4, § 6), but there are no allusions to Rome, thus disproving the hypothesis of Bousset, who dates the work in the time of Pompey. The original language of the Testaments of the Patriarchs was Hebrew, as is shown by the etymologies of the names (Test. Patr., Simeon, 2; Levi, 11; Judah, 1; et passim), by the Hebrew parallelism of poetry, and especially by many mistranslations of Hebrew words, such as "King Zur" and "King Tapuah" for "King of Hazor" and "King of Tappuah."

Omitting the Christian interpolations altogether, the following summary may be given of the twelve

Contents of the Book. sections in which each of the twelve sons of Jacob delivers a farewell address giving an account of such of his experiences as offer some lesson, either warning against sin that he had committed or exhorting to virtues that he had practised.

Reuben: Unchastity. Reuben relates (ch. i. 3–4) how, inflamed with passion at the sight of Bilhah, he had committed an incestuous crime in Edar near Beth-lehem (Gen. xxxv. 21–22). Stricken with sorrow and shame, he had suffered for seven months from disease of the loins, owing his recovery only to his father's prayer. He then became a life-long penitent. Seven months he fasted, abstaining from wine and meat and pleasant bread (comp. Dan. x. 3; and for Reuben's repentance see Pesiḳ. 159b; Gen. R. lxxxii. 12, lxxxiv. 18). He accordingly warns his children against looking on women with lustful eyes (comp. Matt. v. 28; Sifre, Num. 115; Ber. 12b, 14a; Ned. 20b; B. B. 57b; 'Ab. Zarah 20a, b), against being alone with a married woman (comp. Sanh. 21a) or meddling with the affairs of women (Ḳid. 70a, 80b; Ab. i. 5), and against every lustful thought (Ber. 12a; Yoma 29a), since

Testament of Reuben. it is the imagination, when man is filled with the spirit of BELIAL, which works iniquity. Ch. iv., on the seven evil spirits, seems a later interpolation. The fall of the angels in the legend of Enoch, on the other hand, is used (ch. v.–vi.a; comp. Enoch viii., xvi. 3; Jubilees vii. 21; 'Ab. Zarah 20b; Targ. Yer. to Gen. vi. 2; I Cor. xi. 10) to warn women against captivating men by their adornments of head and face. Even the longing for licentiousness ("zenut") is destructive (comp. Job xxxi. 1; Prov. vii. 26–27), to say nothing of licentious conduct. Joseph, however, was protected against lustful thought in the hour of temptation by his singleness of heart in the fear of God.

This section is followed, with no connecting-link except the word "ḳin'ah" (= "jealousy") in ch. vi.a, by a warning against any jealousy of the tribe of Levi, who was the priest that gave instruction in the Law, and the judge that offered up the sacrifices for Israel, blessed the people whom he ruled with Judah, and gave his life for them in wars visible and invisible, thus reestablishing the kingdom for all time (comp. Targ. Yer. to Deut. xxxiii. 11 with reference to John Hyrcanus).

Simeon: Envy. In the first four chapters of his Testament, Simeon dwells on the spirit of jealousy with which Satan, the "sar ha-mastemah" of the Jubilees, had filled him so that he had hated his brother Joseph and had plotted his murder, being prevented only by Judah, who had sold Joseph as a slave while Simeon was absent. The lameness of his right hand for a week showed him God's punitive justice in view of his own five months' wrath, and for two years he had repented and fasted. In like manner, he looked upon his imprisonment in Egypt by Joseph as a punishment which he indeed deserved (comp. Targ. Yer. to Gen. xxxvii. 19, xlii. 24; Gen. R. xci. 6). He accordingly warns his children against jealousy, which destroys both him that is envied and him that envies, and he exhorts them (ch. iv.–v.) to emulate Joseph, who loved his brothers, though they had hated him; and who was good to look upon, since there was no wickedness in him, nor had the evil eye any power over him (comp. Targ. Yer. to Gen. xlix. 22; Soṭah 36b). "You also," he says in conclusion (ch. vi.), "will flourish after all envy has been removed from your hearts, and your holy ones will multiply, and their branches will

Testament of Simeon. spread afar, and the seed of Canaan, Amalek, Caphtor [Cappadocia], Kittim [Macedonia], and Ham [= Egypt] will be destroyed for the triumph of Shem and the establishment of the kingdom of the God of Israel, before whom all the spirits of deceit [idolatry] will vanish forever."

The Testament closes with a warning against a war of rebellion against the Maccabean dynasty represented by the priestly tribe of Levi and by the victorious royal leader from the midst of Judah. In the concluding words the bones of Simeon are described as placed in a coffin of incorruptible wood.

Levi: The Priesthood and Pride. The Testament of Levi, which is incomplete at the beginning and at the close, contains two different accounts of his election to the priesthood, the Hasidæan version being spiritual in character, and the Maccabean political. According to the former (ch. i.–iv.), Levi, when a youth of twenty, was filled with sorrow for the iniquity and corruption of men, whereupon God answered his prayer for salvation by sending him an angel who showed him the throne of the Most High in the third heaven. He was also told that he should stand in the presence of the Lord, and serve Him, and be His son; that he should be a light of knowledge and a sun to Israel; and

Hasidæan Testament of Levi.

that he should be given understanding and counsel to instruct his sons concerning God. In another vision (ch. viii.) the seven insignia of priesthood were conferred upon him by seven angels, who anointed him with pure oil and consecrated him, since his seed was to be divided into the three kingdoms of the priests, the judges and scribes, and the guardians of the sanctuary. Thereupon, in accordance with a vision, Levi's father, Jacob, made him priest over his house, while his grandfather, Isaac (comp. Jubilees xxxi. 9-32), instructed him in all the laws concerning priesthood, sacrifice, and purification. Levi is particularly warned against (Samaritan) pollution of his seed by marrying a foreign (Philistine) or Gentile (Amorite) wife; and he accordingly married his kinswoman Milkah, who bore him three sons, among whom Kehat, the ancestor of Aaron and Moses, stood forth in his vision as "one amid the haughty of the assembly." In ch. xiii. Levi admonishes his children to walk in the way of the Law in all simplicity of heart and in the fear of God, and warns them never to cease to study it, lest they should fail to give their children knowledge which should win them honor and friends. "Perform righteousness on earth that ye may find treasures in heaven [comp. Luke xii. 21]; sow good works in your souls that ye may reap them in life." This exhortation is followed by a eulogy of wisdom, and the address closes with the words: "If a man teach these things and do them, he shall sit upon a throne with the king, as did our brother Joseph."

According to the other version (comp. Jubilees xxx. 17-23), Levi's act of vengeance upon Shechem fitted him for the priesthood (ch. v.-vii. and part of ch. viii.), for Michael, "the angel who intercedeth for the race of Israel," bestowed upon him a shield and a sword with which he should wreak vengeance on Shechem for Dinah; and though the Shechemites were circumcised, he acted in accordance with the will of God, despite his father's curse (Gen. xlix. 7), and exterminated the city of "the foolish" (comp. נבלה = "folly," Gen. xxxiv. 7; Ecclus. [Sirach] l. 26). The "three kingdoms" that were to

Maccabean Testament of Levi.

spring from Levi were, accordingly, distinct from the three classes mentioned above, being Moses, who was "faithful" (Num. xii. 7), Aaron, and John Hyrcanus, the royal priest who, like Melchizedek (Ps. cx. 4), was to manifest his prophetic power (comp. Josephus, "B. J." i. 2, § 8; Tosef., Soṭah, xiii. 5). Ch. x. and xiv.-xvii., devoted to the fearful corruption and depravity of the priesthood under Alexander Jannæus, which is mentioned also in the Psalms of Solomon, disclose the last experiences of the Maccabean writer. The Messianic prophecy in ch. xviii. seems to belong to the older Hasidæan document, and its Messiah opens the gates of paradise to the saints while he overcomes Belial with his hosts. In the closing chapter Levi bids his children, who are themselves represented as speak-

ing, to choose between the Lord and Belial, whereupon they swear allegiance to God.

Judah: Courage, Avarice, and Fornication. Judah narrates to his children (ch. i.-vii., ix.) the feats of strength which he, who was, like David, destined to be a king, had displayed in his youth. He also tells them of the swiftness, courage, and power which he had shown in his wondrous combats with all kinds of wild beasts that assailed his flock and with the Canaanitish kings of Hazor and Tappuah and their men, besides describing how he surpassed his brothers in the war with the Amorites and the sons of Esau (comp. Jubilees xxxiv. 1-9; Midr. Wayissa'u, ed. Jellinek, "B. H." iii. 1-5 and Introduction; Kohler, l.c.). A boast of immaculate youth which he made to Reuben caused him, like David (Sanh. 107a), to be ensnared by a woman (ch.

Testament of Judah.

viii. 10-14). At a feast given him by Barsua', the King of Adullam, he became drunk, and in that state he fell in love with the princess Bat Sua', who was presented to him decked with gold and pearls. He married her, but the children of the union were wicked (Gen. xxxviii. 3-10). Bat Sua' hated Tamar because she was related to Abraham, being the daughter of Shem, according to Gen. R. lxxxv. 11; Targ. Yer. to Gen. xxxviii. 6, and refused to allow her sons to marry her. Even when Tamar contrived to be united with Judah in a levirate marriage, he was again deceived by drunkenness, due to the feast he celebrated at the waters of Kezib (ch. xiii.-xvii.). Judah accordingly warns his children against excessive pride, covetousness, and licentiousness, but most of all against indulgence in wine, since it reveals all the secrets of God and leads to sin. Ch. xv. is an interpolated midrash on Gen. xxxviii. 18 (comp. Gen. R. lxxxv. 10). His monition concludes with the statement (ch. xx.) that Satan is the cause of sin, wherefore they must choose between the Lord, the Spirit of Truth, who sees each act of man written on his breast, and the Spirit of Error. The address closes (ch. xxii. 24-25) with a Messianic prophecy which emphasizes Judah's lasting claim to the resurrection of the saints, the triumph of the poor and the martyrs, and the burning of Belial and all his hosts. A denunciation of the royal custom of embalming, which was antagonistic to the doctrine of the resurrection, ends the Testament.

In sharp contrast to this Judaic or Davidic prophecy stand the accentuation of the Levitic or Maccabean royalty (ch. xxi.) and the references to its hero (ch. xxv.). These are obviously interpolations by the Maccabean reviser, and ch. xxiii. is a still later insertion.

Issachar: Simplicity. Issachar, whose name is explained at length in accordance with Gen. xxx. 14-18, represents himself to his children as one who walked all his life in simplicity (ch. iii.). Being a husbandman, he never failed to give the priest the first-fruits of his lands, sharing the residue with his father and with the poor and afflicted, so that he was greatly blessed. He spoke ill of no one, nor did he meddle in the affairs of others; he harbored no lustful thoughts in his heart and was happy with his wife and his field. He accordingly admonishes his children (ch. iv.–vii.) to walk in simplicity, and to refrain from envy and all lustful thoughts, prying into no secrets, but loving God and man, and filled with compassion for the poor and feeble. He urges them, moreover, to find contentment in husbandry and to seek the divine blessing in the fruit of the soil, for abandonment of agricultural life would, in his view, lead them in the latter days to transgression and dispersion among the Gentiles. This denunciation of mercantile pursuits, which were the chief occupations of the Jews in the Diaspora, indicates the period at which the original Testaments were written. With a glance at the Epicurean life of the Sadducees, Issachar concludes with the words: "I am 120 years old, and have known no mortal sin. Except my wife, I have known no woman, nor have I gone a-whoring with the lifting up of mine eyes; I have drunk no wine to lead me astray, nor have I desired the desire of my neighbor. Craft hath not been in my heart, nor hath falsehood come through my lips. I sighed with every one that was troubled, and I gave my bread to the poor. I ate not alone; I broke no oath; I wrought piety and truth all my days. I have loved the Lord with all my might, and I have loved every man even as my children. Do ye these things, my children, and every spirit of Belial will flee from you, and no deed of evil men will have power over you; and ye shall subdue every wild beast, having with you the God of heaven, that walketh with men in simplicity of heart." In this picture of the ideal Ḥasid, who dies "at a good old age and with his strength unabated," the passage in ch. v., which emphasizes the supremacy of Levi and Judah as priest and ruler, contains no indication of late Maccabean influence (comp. Targ. Yer. to Gen. xlix. 14–15; Gen. R. xcix. 11).

Zebulun: Compassion and Pity. Unlike the rabbinical conception of Zebulun, which is that of the merchant who supports Issachar while he devotes his life to the study of the Torah (see Targ. Yer. to Deut. xxxiii. 18), Zebulun in the Testaments Ḥasidically typifies the fisherman who supplies the household with fish and gives of his store to the stranger, the sick, the aged, and the needy that he may be blessed by God for his compassion (ch. vi.). He tells his children, moreover, that it was his deep compassion for Joseph which restrained Simeon and Gad from bloodshed, for he had joined his youngest brother in an appeal to their sympathy and had adjured them with tears not to commit the crime, thus anticipating even Reuben, who made the proposal to cast Joseph into the pit to save the young lad's life. When the other brothers took the twenty pieces of silver for which they sold Joseph and used them to buy sandals (Pirḳe R. El. xxxviii.; Targ. Yer. to Gen. xxxvii. 28, based on Amos ii. 6), Zebulun, like Reuben, refused to share in the money. Whenever he saw a person unclad he used to cover him with garments of his own, and he was accordingly blessed by God, nor did any sickness befall his house, for "as man showeth compassion on his fellow beings, so doth God show compassion on him" (Sifre, Deut. 96; Shab. 151b).

Testament of Issachar.

Testament of Zebulun.

Zebulun therefore admonishes his children to show mercy to every man, and to bear neither grudge nor malice toward any, but to love one another, taking Joseph for their model. The address closes (ch. ix.) with a warning against dissensions in Israel, since they would lead to a division of the kingdom and to dispersion among the Gentiles, and with an expression of his longing for the Messianic period, when Belial and his hosts should be trodden under foot and God alone should reign in Jerusalem as the sun of righteousness with the healing of compassion on its wings. The closing chapter expresses the hope of resurrection as forming part of the final judgment in which Zebulun, one of the twelve judges, will appear as the ruler of his tribe. The name of Levi does not occur in this Testament.

Dan: Anger and Falsehood. Dan, the black sheep among the tribes of Israel (see DAN), tells his children (ch. i.) that, under the influence of Belial, he had been filled with anger against Joseph and that, "eager to devour him as a leopard devours a kid," he had planned to kill him that he might supplant him in the heart of his father. Dan accordingly warns his children (ch. ii.–v.a) against anger, since it heeds neither parent, nor brother, nor prophet, nor righteous man, nor friend. Ch. iii. and other interpolated passages add a warning against lying which is scarcely a genuine part of the Testament. Anger may be roused by words only, yet it leads to action. Therefore his children are exhorted to refrain from anger either at spoken words or at misfortunes, lest they should be overcome by Belial and the Lord should depart from them, the lesson of the Testament being that they should flee from wrath and love God and man in order that the Lord might dwell among them and Belial be driven from them. The last sentence of the Testament is obviously a Jewish interpolation.

Testament of Dan.

Naphtali: Natural Goodness. Naphtali, who died in perfect health at the age of 132, relates to his children that he resembled Joseph since he was born on Rachel's knees. The explanation of the names of Naphtali (comp. Gen. R. lxxxix. 22; Num. R. xiv. 23; Epstein, "Mi-Ḳadmoniyyot ha-Yehudim," p. 74), Bilhah, and Zilpah are curious haggadic remnants. Swift of foot as a deer (Gen. xlix. 21; comp. Pirḳe R. El. xxxix.; Soṭah 13a), Naphtali served his father, Jacob, as a messenger; and in the father's grief at the loss of Joseph he was comforted by Naphtali, who told him of two dreams in which the future greatness of Levi, Judah, and Joseph had been revealed to him (ch. v.–vi.). The text is extremely corrupt, and must be corrected on the basis of the Hebrew "Testament of Naphtali" discovered by Gaster in the "Chronicles of Jerahmeel" and reproduced in a German translation by Schnapp, in Kautzsch, "Apocryphen," ii. 489–492. According to this document, which is decidedly better preserved than the Greek version, Naphtali speaks of the pleasant land that fell to the lot of his tribe (Deut. xxxiii. 23) and then warns his children not to become overbearing in their prosperity. The monition to observe the law of God and to refrain from such corruptions as had been prac-

Testament of Naphtali.

tised by the men of Sodom, the idolatrous nations, and the fallen angels in the days of Enoch is preceded by the lesson that, in accordance with Deut. xxxii. 8–9 (comp. Targ. Yer. *ad loc.*), each of the seventy nations worships its own guardian angel as a deity, while Abraham chose on behalf of his descendants the only one God and Creator of the world as Guide and Protector, since Michael, the guardian angel of Israel, had taught him the Hebrew language, thus enabling him to learn the true order of things and the wisdom of creation. As sun, moon, and stars change not their order, so should the children of Naphtali not change the order of things. This section is followed by the apocalyptic part, in which Maccabean elements referring to the supremacy of Levi seem again to be mingled with Hasidæan tenets.

Gad: Hatred. Gad tells his children that in his strength he had been accustomed to guard the flock at night, and to kill every wild beast that assailed it. Joseph, however, was too delicate to stay with the flock in the heat of the day and went home to his father, whom he informed that Gad and the other sons of the two concubines were eating lambs that had been torn by wild beasts and had not been slaughtered either by Judah or by Reuben according to the prescribed rule (comp. Targ. Yer. to Gen. xxxvii. 2; Pirḳe R. El. xxxviii.; Gen. R. lxxxiv. 7). This so provoked Gad that he hated Joseph, and, like Simeon, wished to kill him, being eager "to devour him as the calf devours the grass." His hatred finally brought upon him a disease of the heart which lasted for eleven months, the length of time that he entertained this feeling of enmity before he repented and his father's prayers saved him from death (ch. i.–ii. 5). He therefore warns his children against the spirit of hatred which fills the heart with poison, and allies itself with Satan and with every evil, leading to all manner of impiety and death, while love effects the salvation of man. "Love ye one another in act, and word, and thought. . . . If one sin against thee, tell him in peace, removing the poison of hate, and foster not guile in thy soul [comp. Lev. xix. 17; Matt. xviii. 15]. And if he confess and repent, forgive him [Yoma 87a; Luke xvii. 3] . . . and if he deny it, strive not with him lest he swear and thou sin doubly. . . . But give the vengeance unto God" (Deut. xxxii. 35; Rom. xii. 19). "Envy not the prosperous, for the poor man who is free from envy is rich" (ch. vi.–vii.). As its concluding words this Testament contains a totally irrelevant passage concerning Judah and Levi.

Asher: The Two Characters of Vice and Virtue. It is possible that the Testament of Asher is defective, since the only reference to his own personal experience is found in ch. v., where he says that he observed life and sought out the commandments of God, only to find that the two ways of light and darkness, of good and evil, and of truth and error must ever be kept distinct, for doublefacedness serves not God but Belial (ch. iii.). The allusions in ch. ii. to unclean animals, such as swine, which appear half clean but in reality are unclean, and the reference in ch. iv. to clean animals, such as stags and hinds, which appear unclean in a wild

Testament of Gad.

Testament of Asher.

state but are actually clean, are indicative of such concepts as are expressed in the Letter of Aristeas, §§ 153–169. The moral of the Testament may be summed up in the words: "Follow the truth with singleness of face and hate the spirits of error, . . . distinguishing the angels of the Lord and of Satan" (ch. vi.; comp. II Cor. xi. 14), and it closes with a brief apocalyptic passage predicting the exile and the restoration.

Joseph: Chastity. The Testament of Joseph presents Joseph in two different aspects. In the first part (ch. i.–x.a) he speaks as the same type of chastity in which he is presented by the rabbinic Haggadah (Targ. Yer. to Gen. xlix. 22; Soṭah 36b; Pirḳe R. El. xxxix.). In the second part (ch. x.b–xvii.) he appears as the model of brotherly love. In the former, Potiphar's wife is termed "the Egyptian"; in the latter "the Memphian." The first portion of the Testament is written in forcible poetic style; the latter, which chronologically is the earlier, is in simple prose, so that the whole is evidently the work of two different authors.

Joseph begins by declaring that his trust in God brought him rescue and exaltation through all the time that he was envied and hated, sold and slandered. It is, accordingly, the picture of a Ḥasid, the persecuted saint, that is exhibited in the first two chapters. During his stay of seven years with "the shameless woman," he proved another Daniel, even his fasting lending greater beauty to his face. He gave his food to the poor, and wept and prayed for the conversion of Potiphar's wife, even after his prayer had obtained for her, in her childless state, a son. He wished to instruct her in the way of righteousness, while she attempted to capture him by means of witchcraft (ch. iii.–vi.); and finally, when all her contrivances failed and he was cast into prison because of her slander, he sang songs of thanksgiving to God for his escape from the allurements of her shameless attitudes (ch. vii.–ix.; the last sentence is misplaced). "God loveth the chaste who endureth in his den of darkness. . . . If, therefore, ye follow after chastity and holiness in patience and humility of heart, the Lord will dwell among you, . . . and exalt you, and bless you with all good things even as He blessed me" (ch. ix.–x.).

In the second part (ch. x.b–xvii.) Joseph dwells on the fact that, lest he should put his brothers to shame, he never revealed his birthplace and his family either to the merchants, who had bought him as a slave, or to Potiphar, whose wife had fallen in love with the beautiful lad at sight of him, or to any of the eunuchs of Pharaoh, who stripped and beat him to wrest from him the confession that he was the son of a mighty man in Canaan (comp. Gen. xl. 15). "Therefore," said he to his children, "love one another, and with long-suffering hide each other's faults, for God delighteth in the unity of brethren" (ch. xvii.).

The apocalyptic passage, preserved in longer form in the Armenian version, but obviously curtailed and interpolated by Christian hands, describes the captivity and downfall of the kingdom of Joseph and the permanence of the kingdom of Judah. The reference to Levi is a Maccabean insertion.

Testament of Joseph.

Benjamin: Purity of Heart. Benjamin, who is represented both by the Testament which bears his name and by rabbinic literature as the one who clings lovingly to his brother Joseph (see Gen. R. xciv. 7), typifies affectionate regard for the righteous. The hero himself, whose name is explained in ch. i. as "the child of old age," dwells on the nobility of Joseph, but since he would not impute an evil act to his brothers, he construed the story of the coat in their favor (ch. ii.), and be-

Testament of Benjamin. sought his father to pray to God that He should not impute to them the evil they had devised against him (ch. iii.).

Benjamin accordingly admonishes his children ever to direct their mind toward the good and pure, for the good man has no "evil eye," but sympathy for all, and mercy to the poor (ch. iv.), thus having a good influence even on the evil (ch. v.). The spirit of Belial will have no power over him, nor will he look with lust upon woman. Cain, the evil brother, had to suffer for seven hundred years, but Joseph could be defiled by sin no more than is the sun by shining over dung and mire. The whole monition (ch. ii.–viii.), however, is in great disorder. The apocalyptic portion (ch. ix.–xi.), based partly upon Gen. xlix. 27 and partly upon Deut. xxxiii. 12, is so interpolated by Christian writers that any analysis of it is extremely difficult.

Charles (l.c.) has already called attention to the frequent use of the Testaments of the Twelve Patriarchs by Paul and other writers of the New Testament. I Thess. ii. 16 is a quotation

In the New Testament. of Test. Patr., Levi, 6, 10; Rom. xii. 19 of Gad, 6, 10; Rom. xii. 21 of Benjamin, 6, 3; II Cor. vii. 10 of Gad, 5, 7; and Ephes. v. 6 of Naphtali, 3, 1. As has been indicated above, the New Testament teaching of forgiveness, of love even for enemies, of chastity in thought, and of similar matters is clearly presented in these far older Essene utterances of the patriarchs Gad, Issachar, Joseph, Benjamin, and others. The dualistic psychology and cosmology, as well as the eschatology, are the same in both, and the Testaments belong to the same class of literature and age as the DIDACHE and DIDASCALIA, being Jewish works appropriated and remodeled by the Church.

BIBLIOGRAPHY: Edition by Sinker, Cambridge, 1869; translated by the same scholar on the basis of this text in the *Anti-Nicene Library*, Edinburgh, 1890. For the literature see Schürer, *Gesch.* 3d ed., iii. 252–262, and Bousset in *Zeit. für Neutestamentliche Wissenschaft*, 1900, pp. 141–209; Charles, in *Hibbert Journal*, 1905, pp. 558–573.
T.   K.

ṬET (ט): Ninth letter of the Hebrew alphabet. The signification of its name is uncertain. Its sound is that of an emphatic surd dental (palatal English "t"). It occurs only as a radical, seldom as a formative element. It sometimes interchanges with the dentals ד and ת and with the sibilant צ. As a numeral, "ṭet" (in the later period) has the value 9.
T.   I. BR.

TETRAGRAMMATON: The quadriliteral name of God, יהוה, which is thus referred to in Josephus, in the Church Fathers, in the magic papyri, and in the Palestinian Talmud (Yoma 40a, below), whence it has passed into the modern languages.

Other designations for this name, such as "Ha-Shem," "Shem ha-Meforash," and "Shem ha-Meyuḥad," have frequently been discussed by recent scholars (see bibliography in Blau, "Altjüdisches Zauberwesen," p. 128, note 1, and, on the terms, pp. 123–128). The term "Tetragrammaton" apparently arose in contradistinction to the divine names containing respectively twelve and forty-two letters and formed likewise from the letters y, h, w, h (*ib.* pp. 137–146); for only thus is the designation intelligible, since ADONAI likewise has four letters in Hebrew.

The Tetragrammaton is the ancient Israelitish name for God. According to actual count, it occurs 5,410 times in the Bible, being divided among the books as follows: Genesis 153

Statistics of Occurrences. times, Exodus 364, Leviticus 285, Numbers 387, Deuteronomy 230 (total in Torah 1,419); Joshua 170, Judges 158, Samuel 423, Kings 467, Isaiah 367, Jeremiah 555, Ezekiel 211, Minor Prophets 345 (total in Prophets 2,696); Psalms 645, Proverbs 87, Job 31, Ruth 16, Lamentations 32, Daniel 7, Ezra–Nehemiah 31, Chronicles 446 (total in Hagiographa 1,295).

In connection with אדני the Tetragrammaton is pointed with the vowels of "Elohim" (which beyond doubt was not pronounced in this combination); it occurs 310 times after אדני, and five times before it (Dalman, "Der Gottesname," etc., p. 91), 227 of these occurrences being in Ezekiel alone. The designation "Yhwh Zeba'ot," translated "Lord of Hosts," occurs 260 times, and with the addition of "God" four times more. This designation is met with as follows: Isaiah 65 times, Jeremiah 77, Minor Prophets 103 (Zechariah 52; Malachi 24), Samuel 11, Kings 4; but it does not occur, on the other hand, in the Pentateuch, in Joshua, in Judges, or in the Hagiographa. Adding these 264 occurrences and the 315 just noted to the 5,410 instances of the simple Tetragrammaton, the word "Yhwh" is found to occur 5,989 times in the Bible. There is no instance of it, however, in Canticles, Ecclesiastes, or Esther; and in Daniel it occurs 7 times (in ch. ix.)—a fact which in itself shows the late date of these books, whose authors lived at a period when the use of the Tetragrammaton was already avoided, its utterance having become restricted both in the reading of the Bible and still more in colloquial speech. For it was substituted ADONAI; and the fact that this name is found 315 times in combination with "Yhwh" and 134 times alone shows that the custom of reading the Tetragrammaton as if written "Adonai" began at a time when the text of the Biblical books was not yet scrupulously protected from minor additions. This assumption explains most of the occurrences of "Adonai" before "Yhwh"; *i.e.*, the former word indicated the pronunciation of the latter. At the time of the Chronicler this pronunciation was so generally accepted that he never wrote the name "Adonai." About 300 B.C., therefore, the word "Yhwh" was not pronounced in its original form. For several reasons Jacob ("Im Namen Gottes," p. 167) assigns the "disuse of the word 'Yhwh' and the substitution of 'Adonai' to the later decades of the Babylonian exile."

The avoidance of the original name of God both in speech and, to a certain extent, in the Bible was

Reason for Disuse.

due, according to Geiger ("Urschrift," p. 262), to a reverence which shrank from the utterance of the Sublime Name; and it may well be that such a reluctance first arose in a foreign, and hence in an "unclean" land, very possibly, therefore, in Babylonia. According to Dalman (*l.c.* pp. 66 *et seq.*), the Rabbis forbade the utterance of the Tetragrammaton, to guard against desecration of the Sacred Name; but such an ordinance could not have been effectual unless it had met with popular approval. The reasons assigned by Lagarde ("Psalterium Hieronymi," p. 155) and Halévy ("Recherches Bibliques," i. 65 *et seq.*) are untenable, and are refuted by Jacob (*l.c.* pp. 172, 174), who believes that the Divine Name was not pronounced lest it should be desecrated by the heathen. The true name of God was uttered only during worship in the Temple, in which the people were alone; and in the course of the services on the Day of Atonement the high priest pronounced the Sacred Name ten times (Tosef., Yoma, ii. 2; Yoma 39b). This was done as late as the last years of the Temple (Yer. Yoma 40a, 67). If such was the purpose, the means were ineffectual, since the pronunciation of the Tetragrammaton was known not only in Jewish, but also in non-Jewish circles centuries after the destruction of the Temple, as is clear from the interdictions against uttering it (Sanh. x. 1; Tosef., Sanh. xii. 9; Sifre Zuṭa, in Yalḳ., Gen. 711; 'Ab. Zarah 18a; Midr. Teh. to Ps. xci., end). Raba, a Babylonian amora who flourished about 350, wished to make the pronunciation of the Tetragrammaton known publicly (Ḳid. 71b); and a contemporary Palestinian scholar states that the Samaritans uttered it in taking oaths (Yer. Sanh. 28b). The members of the Babylonian academy probably knew the pronunciation as late as 1000 C.E. (Blau, *l.c.* pp. 132 *et seq.*, 138 *et seq.*). The physicians, who were half magicians, made special efforts to learn this name, which was believed to possess marvelous powers (of healing, etc.; Yer. Yoma 40a, below). The cures, or the exorcisms, of demons in the name of Jesus which are mentioned in the New Testament and the Talmud (see EXORCISM) imply that Jesus was regarded as a god and that his name was considered as efficacious as the Tetragrammaton itself, for which it was even substituted. It was in connection with magic that the Tetragrammaton

Church Fathers and Magic Papyri.

was introduced into the magic papyri and, in all probability, into the writings of the Church Fathers, these two sources containing the following forms, written in Greek letters: (1) "Iaoouee," "Iaoue," "Iabe"; (2) "Iao," "Iaho," "Iae"; (3) "Aia"; (4) "Ia." It is evident that (1) represents יהוה, (2) יהו, (3) אהיה, and (4) יה. The three forms quoted under (1) are merely three ways of writing the same word, though "Iabe" is designated as the Samaritan pronunciation. There are external and internal grounds for this assumption; for the very agreement of the Jewish, Christian, heathen, and Gnostic statements proves that they undoubtedly give the actual pronunciation (Stade's "Zeitschrift," iii. 298; Dalman,

l.c. p. 41; Deissmann, "Bibelstudien," pp. 1–20; Blau, *l.c.* p. 133). The "mystic quadriliteral name" (Clement, "Stromata," ed. Dindorf, iii. 25, 27) was well known to the Gnostics, as is shown by the fact that the third of the eight eons of one of their systems of creation was called "the unpronounced," the fourth "the invisible," and the seventh "the unnamed," terms which are merely designations of the Tetragrammaton (Blau, *l.c.* p. 127). Even the Palestinian Jews had inscribed the letters of the Name on amulets (Shab. 115b; Blau, *l.c.* pp. 93–96); and, in view of the frequency with which the appellations of foreign deities were employed in magic, it was but natural that heathen magicians should show an especial preference for this "great and holy name," knowing its pronunciation as they knew the names of their own deities.

It thus becomes possible to determine with a fair degree of certainty the historical pronunciation of the Tetragrammaton, the results agreeing with the statement of Ex. iii. 14, in which YHWH terms Himself אהיה, "I will be," a phrase which is immediately preceded by the fuller term "I will be that I will be," or, as in the English versions, "I am" and

Meaning and Etymology.

"I am that I am." The name יהוה is accordingly derived from the root הוה (= היה), and is regarded as an imperfect. This passage is decisive for the pronunciation "Yahweh"; for the etymology was undoubtedly based on the known word. The oldest exegetes, such as Onḳelos, and the Targumim of Jerusalem and pseudo-Jonathan regard "Ehyeh" and "Ehyeh asher Ehyeh" as the name of the Divinity, and accept the etymology of "hayah" = "to be" (comp. Samuel b. Meïr, commentary on Ex. iii. 14). Modern critics, some of whom, after the lapse of centuries, correct the Hebrew texts without regard to the entire change of point of view and mode of thought, are dissatisfied with this etymology; and their various hypotheses have resulted in offering the following definitions: (1) he who calls into being, or he who gives promises; (2) the creator of life; (3) he who makes events, or history; (4) the falling one, the feller, *i.e.*, the storm-god who hurls the lightning; (5) he who sends down the rain (W. R. Smith, "The Old Testament," p. 123); (6) the hurler; (7) the destroyer; (8) the breather, the weather-god (Wellhausen). All these meanings are obtained by doing violence to the Hebrew text (Herzog-Hauck, "Real-Encyc." viii. 536 *et seq.*).

Attempts have also been made to explain the Divine Name יהוה as Hittite, Persian, Egyptian, and even as Greek; but these assumptions are now absolutely set aside, since the name is at all events Semitic. The question remains, however, whether it is Israelitish or was borrowed. Friedrich Delitzsch, in discussing this question, asserts that the

Assyro-Babylonian Cuneiform Inscriptions.

Semitic tribes from whom the family of Hammurabi came, and who entered Babylon 2500 B.C., knew and worshiped the god Ya've, Ya'u (*i.e.*, YHWH, Yahu; "Babel und Bibel," 5th ed., i. 78 *et seq.*); and Zimmern (in Schrader, "K. A. T." 3d ed., pp. 465–468) reaches the conclusion that "Yahu" ór "YHWH" is found in Babylonian only as the name of a foreign deity, a view with which Delitzsch agrees in his third and final lecture on "Babel und Bibel" (pp. 39, 60, Stuttgart, 1905). Assyriologists are still divided on this point, however; and no definite conclusions have as yet been reached (comp. the voluminous literature on "Babel und Bibel").

"Yah," an abbreviated form of the Tetragrammaton, occurs 23 times: 18 times in the Psalms, twice in Exodus, and three times in Isaiah. This form is identical with the final syllable in the word "Hallelujah," which occurs 24 times in the last book of the Psalms (comp. also "be-Yah," Isa. xxvi. 4 and Ps. lxviii. 5). It is transcribed by the Greek "Ia," as "Ehyeh" is represented by "Aia," thus showing that "Yah" was the first syllable of יהוה.

Abbreviated Tetragrammaton. The form corresponding to the Greek "Iao" does not occur alone in Hebrew, but only as an element in such proper names as Jesaiah ("Yesha'yahu"), Zedekiah ("Zidkiyahu"), and Jehonathan. According to Delitzsch ("Wo Lag das Paradies?" 1881), this form was the original one, and was expanded into יהוה; but since names of divinities are slow in disappearing, it would be strange if the primitive form had not been retained once in the Bible. Franz Delitzsch thought that "Yahu" was used independently as a name of God (Herzog-Plitt, "Real-Encyc." vi. 503); but, according to Kittel, "This could have been the case only in the vernacular, since no trace of it is found in the literary language" (Herzog-Hauck, "Real-Encyc." viii. 26, 533). All the critics have failed to perceive that the name "Yao" was derived from the same source as "Yaoue," namely, from Gnosticism and magic, in which Jews, Christians, and heathen met. "Yahu" was in fact used in magic, as is clear from the "Sefer Yezirah," which shows many traces of Gnosticism; in the cosmology of this work the permutation of the letters יהו furnishes the instruments of the Creation.

With the Tetragrammaton must be included the names of God formed of twelve, forty-two, and seventy-two letters respectively, which are important factors in Jewish mysticism (Ḳid. 71a et passim).

Other Names of God. They have, according to tradition, a magical effect; for mysticism and magic are everywhere allied. These great names are closely akin to the long series of vowels in the magic papyri, and are obtained by anagrammatic combinations of the effective elements of the Tetragrammaton. The simplest way of determining these three names is to form a magic triangle, whose base is a single Tetragrammaton, and its apex the Tetragrammaton repeated thrice. The four upper lines (12 + 11 + 10 + 9) give the names with forty-two letters; and the entire figure represents the Divine Name of seventy-two letters (Blau, l.c. pp. 144 et seq.). According to the book of BAHIR (ed. Amsterdam, 1651, fol. 7a), the Sacred Name of twelve letters was a triple יהוה (Dalman, l.c. p. 39; Blau, l.c. p. 144).

In the earliest manuscripts of the Septuagint the Tetragrammaton was given in Hebrew letters, which in Greek circles were supposed to be Greek and were read πιπι (Field, "Origenis Hexaplorum Quæ Supersunt," i. 90, Oxford, 1875; Herzog-Hauck, l.c. viii. 530; Blau, l.c. p. 131). See also ADONAI; AQUILA; GNOSTICISM; JEHOVAH; NAMES OF GOD; SHEM HA-MEFORASH.

BIBLIOGRAPHY: Hamburger, R. B. T. i. 48–56, 538; Hastings, Dict. Bible, ii. 199; Herzog-Hauck, Real-Encyc. viii. 529–541; Baudissin, Studien zur Semitischen Religionsgeschichte, i. 181–254, Leipsic, 1876; S. R. Driver, Recent Theories on the Origin and Nature of the Tetragrammaton, in Studia Biblica, i. 1–20, Oxford, 1885; Dalman, Der Gottesname Adonaj und Seine Geschichte, Berlin, 1889; Deissmann, Bibelstudien, Marburg, 1895; Blau, Das Altjüdische Zauberwesen, Strasburg, 1898; M. Jastrow, Jr., in Stade's Zeitschrift, 1896, pp. 1 et seq. (on the proper names combined with YHWH); Schrader, K. A. T. 3d ed., pp. 465–468, Berlin, 1902–3; Jacob, Im Namen Gottes, Berlin, 1903. For further material, especially earlier works, see Herzog-Hauck, l.c.
T.   L. B.

TETRARCH (Greek, τετράρχης): A governor of a quarter of a province; the title of several feudal lords of Palestine and neighboring countries who were subject to Roman suzerainty. This title, which evidently implies a rank somewhat lower than that of ETHNARCH, was held by the following Jewish princes: Herod the Great before he became king, and his brother PHASAEL, both of whom received the office from Antony (Josephus, "Ant." xiv. 13, § 1; idem, "B. J." i. 12, § 5); PHERORAS, whom Augustus, at the request of Herod, appointed tetrarch of Perea (20 B.C.), a post which yielded him an income of 100 talents ("Ant." xv. 10, § 3; "B. J." i. 24, § 5); HEROD ANTIPAS, who was tetrarch of Galilee (Luke iii. 1); PHILIP, who governed Iturea and Trachonitis (ib.); and Lysanias, who ruled Abilene (ib.).

The district governed by a tetrarch was called a tetrarchy ("Ant." xx. 7, § 1); and this term was first used by Euripides, who applied it to Thessaly, attributing to it its original connotation of a quarter province, since Thessaly was divided into four districts. "Tetrarch" was employed in a similar sense with reference to Galatia; but in other countries, as well as among the Jews, it lost its primary meaning, and came to imply a ruler whose power was less than that of a king. Such tetrarchs were especially numerous in Syria (Pliny, "Historia Naturalis," v. 74), and one Sohemus of Lebanon is mentioned by Josephus ("Vita," § 11). Kings and tetrarchs furnished auxiliary troops to the army of VARUS ("Ant." xvii. 10, § 9). The Herodian tetrarchs, either from error or from mere flattery, were addressed also as kings (comp. Matt. ii. 22, xiv. 9); and it was with but little justification that AGRIPPA II. styled himself "king," since, as a matter of fact, he was but a tetrarch.

BIBLIOGRAPHY: Winer, B. R. 3d ed., s.v.; Schürer, Gesch. 3d ed., i. 423.
E. C.   S. KR.

TETUAN. See MOROCCO.

TEWELES, HEINRICH: Austrian dramatist; born at Prague Nov. 13, 1856. He made his début in 1881 with a drama entitled "Die Schauspielerin." His other works are: "Kampf um die Sprache," 1884; "Die Armen," novel, 1885; "Presse und Staat," 1886; "Eherecht," a comedy, 1886; "Schule der Frauen," comedy, 1887; "Der Ring des Polykrates," comedy, 1888; "Gesellschafterin," comedy, 1889; "Der Hundertste Geburtstag," play, 1891; "Mein Papa," farce, 1893; "Johann Strauss," play, 1894; "Demetrius," a rewritten version of Hebbel's play, 1895; "Volksfreund," sketch, 1898;

and "Beitrag zur Goethefeier in Prag," 1899. He published also the "Prager Dichterbuch," 1893.

Teweles is dramaturgist of the German Landestheater in his native city.

s. E. Ms.

TEXAS : Largest state in the American Union; admitted in 1845; seceded Feb. 1, 1861; and readmitted in 1870. Previous to its admission to the Union, Texas was an independent republic (1836–45).

Samuel Isaacs removed from the United States to Texas in 1821, with Austin's first colonists. For serving in the army of the Republic of Texas he was given 320 acres of land. When Abraham Cohen Labatt visited Texas in 1831, he found at Velasco Jacob Henry and Jacob Lyons, of England and Charleston, S. C., respectively, engaged in mercantile pursuits. Jacob Henry's will provided for the building of a hospital at Velasco. Nacogdoches seems to have been the center of immigration. Prominent settlers (1832–40) were Adolphus Sterne, who participated in the Fredonian war, subsequently acting as alcalde and official interpreter; Dr. Joseph Hertz and his brother Hyman, Simon Schloss, Albert Emanuel, Sam. Maas (who married a sister of Offenbach, the composer), and Simon Weiss. They were pioneers in mercantile enterprises, and served the government in civil and military capacities. Simon and Jacob Mussina settled in Galveston (1836), the former editing a paper and practising law. Edward J. Johnson, from Cincinnati, Ohio, was killed while fighting under Fannin at Goliad (1836), where three other Jews also fought—Benjamin H. Mordecai (killed by Indians in 1840), M. K. Moses, and Herman Ehrenberg. Notable services were rendered to Texas by Levi Charles Harby (sometimes known as Levi Myers HARBY), Isadore DYER, and Leon DYER. Michael Seeligson settled in Galveston in 1836; he was alderman of the city in 1840 and 1848, mayor in 1853, and worked untiringly for the annexation of the Republic of Texas to the United States. Henry Seeligson, his son, went to Galveston from Michigan in 1839, held several military appointments, and fought in three wars, in one of which he was highly complimented by Gen. Zachary Taylor. Prominent in the early wars, from San Jacinto (1835) to the war with Mexico (1846), were: Eugene Joseph Chiméne, Kohn (Texas spy-company), Henry Wiener, Moses Albert Levy (surgeon-general in Sam. Houston's army in the Texas-Mexican war; was present at the storming of the Alamo, Dec. 5, 1835), A. Wolf (killed in the Alamo, 1836; his name is inscribed on the Alamo monument at Austin), Dr. Isaac Lyons of Charleston (surgeon-general, 1836), and D. I. Kokernot. Michael de Young, a French Jew, settled in San Augustine in 1840, and furnished the necessary equipment to volunteers during the war with Mexico. Three years earlier Edward S. Solomon settled in the same town. Many acres of land in Texas, now under cultivation, were originally allotted to David Moses and Michael de Young for services rendered to the republic.

Jacob de Cordova (b. Spanish Town, Jamaica, 1808; d. Texas, 1868) removed to Galveston from New Orleans in 1837, and became an expert in real estate; "De Cordova's Land Agency" was known throughout the states. Upon a visit to Jamaica in 1833 he founded the "Daily Gleaner." In 1856 he published at Austin "The Texas Emigrant's and Traveler's Guide-Book," and later "Texas, Her Resources and Her Public Men " (Philadelphia, 1858). De Cordova introduced the Order of Odd Fellows into Texas. In 1847 he represented Harris county in the Texas legislature, and in 1849 he laid out the city of Waco. During 1856–58 he lectured on the resources of Texas in the large cities of the United States and in England. In 1848 his brother Phinehas (b. Philadelphia, 1819; d. 1903) joined him in the establishment of the "Texas Herald," a fortnightly. Phinehas subsequently edited in Austin the "South-Western American," a weekly (1849–52), which successfully advocated the loaning of the school-fund and the donating of a portion of the public lands to aid the building of railroads.

Emigration to Texas found an active advocate in Henry Castro (b. France, 1786; d. Mexico, 1861). In 1842 Castro entered into a contract with Sam. Houston, President of the Republic of Texas, to settle a colony west of the Medina, and Houston appointed him consul-general in France for Texas. Between 1843 and 1846 Castro sent to Texas 5,000 emigrants from the Rhenish provinces—the first organized emigration to Texas from a foreign country; considering the unsettled state of the country, it was a masterly undertaking. These emigrants settled in the towns of Castroville and Quihi (1845), Vandenburg (1846), and D'Hanis (1847). Castro county, in northwest Texas, was named in honor of this intrepid Jew, who sank $150,000 of his personal estate in the venture. Castro published pamphlets and maps in French and German to facilitate his emigration scheme.

The Jewish settlers in each district began communal life by establishing first a cemetery and then a synagogue. A cemetery was established in Houston in 1844, and a synagogue in 1854; in Galveston, 1852 and 1868 respectively; in San Antonio, 1854 and 1872; in Austin, 1866 and 1876; in Waco, 1869 and 1881; in Dallas, 1872 and 1874.

German immigration from the fifties to the seventies was followed by Russian immigration from the eighties until the year 1905; during the latter period Orthodox synagogues have been erected in all the foregoing cities. Synagogues, cemeteries, and communally active congregations exist in the following towns: Beaumont (synagogue erected 1895), Brenham (1895), Corsicana (1898), El Paso (1898), Fort Worth (Orthodox, 1892; Reform, 1904), Gainesville (1882), Hempstead (1897), Marshall (1886), Palestine (1900), Texarkana (1900), Tyler (1889), Victoria (1894).

There are cemeteries in Bonham, Brownsville, Bryan, Calvert, Cleburne, Columbus, Corpus Christi, Denison, Ennis, Greenville, Hallettsville, Henderson, Jefferson, Laredo, Lufkin, Luling, Marlin, Mexia, Mineola, Nacogdoches, Navasota, Orange, Wharton. In these towns services are held on Rosh ha-Shanah and Yom Kippur, and religious schools have been organized in most of them, largely through the influence of Jeannette Miriam Goldberg. Hebrew benevolent associations, ladies' auxiliary and general social societies, and branches of national and international Jewish organizations are widespread; a few Zionists are found in the larger cities.

The following towns in addition to those which have been mentioned have from two to ten Jewish families each: Abilene, Alto, Alvarado, Amarillo, Aquilla, Beeville, Bellville, Bremond, Caldwell, Clarksville, Columbia, Crockett, Decatur, Del Rio, Denton, Eagle Lake, Eagle Pass, Elgin, Farmersville, Giddings, Gonzales, Groesbeck, Hearne, Hillsboro, Honey Grove, Jacksonville, Kaufman, Kennedy, Kyle, Lagrange, Llano, Lockhart, Longview, McDade, McKinney, Mount Pleasant, Mount Vernon, Paris, Pittsburg, Richmond, Rio Grande City, Rockdale, Rusk, San Angelo, San Diego, Schulenburg, Sealy, Seguin, Sherman, Skidmore, Sulphur Springs, Taylor, Temple, Terrell, Uvalde, Waelder, Waxahachie, Weatherford, Weimar, Wichita Falls, Willis, Wills' Point, and Yoakum.

In the early days, before there was any Jewish communal life, intermarriage between Jews and non-Jews was not uncommon; but to-day throughout the state, although Jew and Gentile mingle freely, intermarriage does not obtain to any appreciable degree.

During the Civil war 103 Texas Jews served in the contending armies (Simon Wolf, "The Jew as Patriot, Soldier, and Citizen," p. 424), and the defense of Galveston is inseparably connected with the name of Capt. L. C. Harby (*ib.* pp. 72 *et seq.*, 116). The number of Texas Jews serving with the American forces in the Spanish-American war (1898) was: regular officers and enlisted men, 67 (state volunteers); non-commissioned officers and privates, 25. Benjamin Frenkel was surgeon on the U. S. S. "Hornet," and subsequently served at the naval station at San Juan, Porto Rico. Adjutant-General Openheimer, Texas State Militia, served as colonel of the Second Volunteer Infantry and major-general of the Texas Volunteer Guard ("Am. Jewish Year Book," 1900–1, pp. 535 *et seq.*). Colonel Openheimer is a member of the National Board for the Promotion of Rifle Practise, appointed by the secretary of war March 11, 1893.

Texas Jews in Army and Navy.

Jews are found in both houses of the Texas legislature; Jewish physicians and lawyers are to be met with in all the larger towns; and the state's second assistant attorney-general, Isaac Lovenberg, is a Jew, as was Leo N. Levi (b. Victoria, Texas, 1856; d. New York city, 1904).

In C. W. Raines's "A Bibliography of Texas" (Austin, 1896) mention is made of the following publications of interest to Jews: George M. Walton, "The Jews, Their Origin, History, and Final Destiny" (Austin, 1895); J. E. McAshen, "The Jews," in the "Texas Quarterly"; Major B. Rush Plumley, "Poems for Rosh Hashono" (Galveston, 1876–78). Mrs. Leah Cohen HARBY is the author of the "Flag-Song of Texas."

A considerable number of local and national Jewish and non-sectarian institutions have been the beneficiaries of Texas Jews; in this way the names of Rosanna Osterman, Isadore Dyer, Mrs. Tennie H. Northman, Moritz Kopperl, and Isabella Kopperl have become well known.

In 1920 Texas had a total population of 4,663,228, of whom about 32,660 were Jews. The Jewish population increased as a consequence of direct immigration from Europe through the port of Galveston. See AMERICA; DALLAS; GALVESTON; HOUSTON; SAN ANTONIO.

BIBLIOGRAPHY: Henry Cohen, *Settlement of the Jews in Texas*; idem, *The Jews in Texas*; Henry Castro, *Pioneer and Colonist*, in *Publ. Am. Jew. Hist. Soc.* Nos. 2, 4, 5; Simon Wolf, *The Jew as Patriot, Soldier, and Citizen.*
A.   H. C.

TEXEIRA. See TEIXEIRA.

THANKSGIVING. See BENEDICTIONS.

THEBEN, KOPPEL (JACOB BEN ABRAHAM MANDL): President of the Jewish community in Presburg; died at Prague Aug. 26, 1799. As "sheṭadlan" of the Hungarian Jews he gained distinction; and under Joseph II., Leopold II., and Francis I. he labored indefatigably in behalf of his coreligionists, striving to protect them from harsh regulations. On March 31, 1783, Joseph II. issued the proclamation which was the foundation of the culture of the Hungarian Jews and the beginning of a happier era. One of its provisions, however, was that the Jews should not wear beards; but Theben obtained the revocation of this clause. When Joseph II. compelled the Hungarian Jews to perform military service, Theben sought, though unsuccessfully, to have this ordinance also revoked. In these undertakings his associate was Naphtali ben Isaac Judah Rosenthal, a wealthy citizen of Moor, and in his youth a friend of Moses Mendelssohn.

In 1791, when Leopold II. was crowned at Presburg, the Hungarian Jews, led by Theben, arranged an enthusiastic celebration, during which Theben urged the king not to require the Jews to serve any longer as soldiers. On this occasion the king presented Theben with a gold medal. In the same year Theben strove to free certain Jews who had been imprisoned and tortured in Per on account of a blood accusation. Indeed, there was scarcely any important matter connected with the Jews in which the Theben community did not take an active part.

"Theben" (Hungarian, "Dévény") is the name of a place near Presburg, whence Theben's ancestors probably came.

BIBLIOGRAPHY: Ignatz Reich, *Beth-El*, 2d ed., ii. 363–381; Joshua Levinsohn, *Rabbi Ya'aḳob Koppel Theben*, Warsaw, 1899.
E. C.   A. Bü.

THEBES: Ancient and famous city of Greece; capital of Bœotia. Although there is no documentary evidence of the presence of Jews at Thebes in antiquity, it may be assumed that they resided there, since their coreligionists had lived from a very early period throughout Greece, including the neighboring cities of ATHENS and CORINTH, while in the letter of Agrippa to the emperor Caius, Bœotia is described as inhabited by Jews (Philo, " Legatio ad Caium," § 36). At the time of the First Crusade a certain Tobias of Thebes is described as bringing Messianic prophecies from Salonica to Cairo (" J. Q. R." x. 148), and in Al-Ḥarizi's " Taḥkemoni " (ed. Lagarde, p. 92) mention is made of one Michael ben Caleb of Thebes. Abraham Zuṭra (or Zuṭa) of Thebes, moreover, was the author of a commentary on the Sifra (Zunz, in Asher's ed. of Benjamin of Tudela's " Itinerary," ii. 36; Michael, " Or ha-Ḥayyim," No. 86); for the study of the Midrashim was cultivated in Thebes as well as elsewhere in the Byzantine empire.

These scanty data are insufficient to determine the size of the Jewish community in Thebes, the earliest specific information in relation to which is derived from Benjamin of Tudela (ed. Grünhut, i. 15), who describes the city as a large one with more than 2,000 Jewish families, including the most skilful manufacturers of silk and purple in all Greece. Among them were many students of the Mishnah and of the Talmud; and they belonged to the foremost scholars of their age. At the head of the community stood R. Aaron Kuti, his brother R. Moses, R. Elijah Tortono, and R. Joktan; and their equals were not to be found in any of the Greek dominions except Constantinople. Of the large and prominent community of Thebes no further data exist.

E. C.　　　　　　　　　　　　　　　　　　S. Kr.

THEF T (גנבה) **AND STOLEN GOODS.—**
The Moral Aspect : To steal is to break one of the Ten Commandments, " Thou shalt not steal "; and it is immaterial whether one steals from an Israelite or from an idolatrous Gentile, from an adult or from a child. The value of a peruṭah was regarded as the minimum value the theft of which constituted a complete transgression. But it is forbidden to steal anything, even as a joke, or with the intention of returning it or of paying for it; for by acting thus a person learns to steal in earnest (B. M. 61b; Sanh. 57a).

It is forbidden to buy a stolen article; indeed, it is a great sin; for thereby the hand of transgressors is strengthened, and the thief is led to steal more. If there were none to buy, there would be none to steal; whence the Scripture, " Whoso is partner with a thief hateth his own soul " (Prov. xxix. 24). And one should not buy from men whose employment indicates that the articles offered by them belong to their employers. In the Talmud this law is applied mainly to herdsmen. Wool or kids should not be bought from them; milk and cheese only in the wilderness, not in the settled country. However, one may buy four sheep or four fleeces from the shepherd of a small flock, and five from the shepherd of a large one, there being no presumption against these being his own. Nor should grain or fruits or wood be bought from those charged with watching such articles, unless the sellers offer their wares in public, with the baskets and scales before them; and garden stuff should be purchased only at the front gate of the garden, not at the back gate. It is, however, allowable to buy produce from a tenant on shares. Goods

**Receiver
Worse than
Thief.**

should not be bought from housewives, from servants, or from children, except those articles which such persons are in the habit of selling with the knowledge of the owner. Nor should remnants be bought from an artisan working up for his customers materials which by the custom of the country do not belong to him; and in all cases it is forbidden to buy from a person who says " Hide it " (B. Ḳ. 118b).

Criminal and Civil Liability : There is this distinction between theft and robbery: the thief takes the property of another secretly and without his knowledge, while he who takes openly by force is not a thief, but a robber. One is not punished as a thief for stealing either slaves, or documents having no intrinsic value. On the principle that where the Torah prescribes another penalty for a forbidden act stripes are not inflicted, the only punishment for theft is double restoration, and for stealing an ox or sheep, and selling or slaughtering it, fourfold and fivefold compensation (Ex. xxi. 37, xxii. 3); and on the strength of the words (*ib.* xxii. 8) " he shall pay double to his neighbor " it is held that he who steals either from a Gentile or from the Sanctuary is held only for single compensation: in other words, he is not punished at all. No compensation may be recovered from infants—not even simple restitution if the stolen article has been consumed — nor from a slave, as he has no property; but should the latter be manumitted, he is then liable for double compensation. It is, however, the duty of the court, when a boy is caught stealing, to cause a moderate whipping to be administered to him, and to a slave a sound whipping, so as to check the stealing habit. The master is not liable for what his slave steals any more than for damage arising from the latter's negligence.

**Punish-
ment
Double
Restitu-
tion.**

The verse quoted above refers to the depositary who steals deposited goods. It orders double compensation only from him whom the judges condemn. Hence this penalty can not be imposed where the thief confesses; and opinions in the Talmud go so far as to relieve him, if he confesses to the court, of all but simple restitution, even though witnesses appear against him immediately thereafter. Nor can he in any case be sold for a Hebrew servant in satisfaction of more than simple restitution (Ḳid. 18a, expounding Ex. xxii. 2). He who steals a thing from a thief before the owner has given up the hope of recovery, and before the thing has been changed in substance, is not liable to the penalty, either to the first thief or to the owner. To make him liable for double compensation there must be such a taking of possession by the thief as would in a sale give " ḳinyan " (see ALIENATION AND ACQUISITION); hence pulling the article or beast as long as it is within the owner's premises, even with delivery to a third person, is not sufficient; but lifting it, which always gives ḳinyan, completes the theft (B. Ḳ. vii. 6).

The fourfold restitution for an ox which the thief has sold or slaughtered and the fivefold restitution for a sheep or goat so disposed of are thus treated in the Mishnah (*ib.* vii. 2):

" He who has stolen, as proved by two witnesses, and has slaughtered, as proved by these or by two others, must pay fourfold or fivefold; he who has stolen and sold on the **Fourfold** Sabbath, stolen and sold for idol-worship, stolen **and Fivefold** and slaughtered on the Day of Atonement, **Restitution.** stolen his father's beast and slaughtered or sold and whose father then dies, or stolen and slaughtered and has then consecrated, pays fourfold and fivefold: he who has stolen and slaughtered for use as a medicine or as food for dogs, or has slaughtered and the carcass proves to be unsound [" ṭerefah "], or has slaughtered common food within the Temple yard, pays fourfold or fivefold."

The validity of the last two provisions is disputed. After another section dealing with the liability of plotting witnesses (see ALIBI) who have testified against the supposed thief (*ib.* vii. 4), the Mishnah proceeds:

" He who, according to two witnesses, has stolen and, according to one witness or his own admission, has slaughtered or sold pays twofold restitution. but not fourfold or fivefold; he who has stolen or slaughtered on the Sabbath, or for the purposes of idol-worship, or has stolen from his father and, his father having died, has sold and slaughtered thereafter, or has sold and consecrated and thereafter sold or slaughtered, pays double, but not fourfold or fivefold [with a disputed distinction, *ib.* vii. 5]. He who has sold all but a one-hundredth part thereof [which refers to other than horns or fleece] or has sold an article in which he himself has a joint interest, or has slaughtered in an unlawful manner, pays twofold, but not fourfold or fivefold. He who has stolen within the domain of the owner, but has sold or slaughtered outside thereof, pays fourfold or fivefold; but if he has stolen and sold or slaughtered all within the owner's dominion he is free."

The depositary who, when he has converted goods to his own use, claims that they are lost, is deemed a thief (Ex. xxii. 8); and if the deposit is an ox or a lamb, which he has sold or slaughtered, he is liable to fourfold or fivefold restitution (B. Ḳ. 106a).

In the baraita under these sections there are a number of other distinctions, especially as to the conditions and value of a stolen beast at the time of the theft and the time of the trial. The restitution, beyond the simple return of the stolen thing, is in all cases to be made in money, not in kind.

It happens sometimes that, in order to avoid disgrace, a thief voluntarily restores a stolen article without acquainting the owner of the restitution. In such a case, if he puts it back in its place and it is lost or stolen before the owner who has missed it has knowledge of its return, the repentant thief is liable for the loss (*ib.* 118a, where some nice distinctions will be found).

The Stolen Article; Title: As a general principle, when the stolen thing is given, bartered, or sold to a third person, or when, upon the death of the thief, its possession passes to his sons, the title remains in the former owner; and his rights are more fully enforced as regards goods stolen than those taken by robbery and force. However, the Talmud speaks of an " institution of the market " (*ib.* **Sale** 115a), according to which, when the **in Market** seller of the stolen goods is not a no**Overt.** torious thief, the owner should repay to the buyer the price—generally much less than the value of the goods—which the latter has paid the thief, should take the stolen thing, and should then go to law with the thief regarding the sum paid. This institution calls to mind the sale in market overt under the common law of England. But, to bring the institution into

play, the thief must have sold for money: it does not apply where he has paid a debt with the stolen thing; but it does apply where he has pawned the thing for an advance of money.

It would seem that the circumstances mentioned above, under which it is forbidden to buy goods because they are presumably stolen, would affect not only the conscience but also the title of the buyer; but the codes do not say so explicitly, referring only to purchase from a notorious thief. Certainly the words " Hide it " are an indication of theft.

If the stolen thing has been sold after the owner has lost all hope of recovery (see ROBBERY) or after it has lost its shape and name, the title passes to the buyer. It is remarked that where the stolen articles are (Hebrew) books, the presumption will hardly ever arise that the owner has lost all hope of recovery, inasmuch as the thief can not sell them to Gentiles, but only to Israelites.

When implements, books, or other articles in a house are not kept for sale, and some are stolen, and the owner finds them and recognizes them as his; or when goods are kept for sale, but the owner, after a theft, recognizes articles that were kept to be hired out, then the owner should prove by witnesses that they are his, and the buyer should swear in solemn form what he has paid for them. On repaying this amount the owner should recover his goods, but not otherwise; for, as the Mishnah (*ib.* x. 3) says, he might have sold them to a third person, from whom they were bought. This passage in the Mishnah is a basis for the " institution of the market " found, as above cited, in the Talmud.

BIBLIOGRAPHY: *B. Ḳ.* ch. vii., x., and Talmud thereon; *Yad, Genebah*; *Shulḥan 'Aruk, Ḥoshen Mishpaṭ,* §§ 248-258.

W. B.   L. N. D.

THEOCRACY (Greek, Θεοκρατία): System of state organization and government in which God is recognized as the ruler in whose name authority is exercised by His chosen agents, the Priests or the Prophets. The word in its technical meaning seems to have been first used by Josephus, to describe the peculiar nature of the Jewish government as devised under divine direction by Moses: " Our **Derived** legislator . . . ordained our govern**from** ment to be what, by a strained expres**Josephus.** sion, may be termed a theocracy, by ascribing the authority and the power to God " (" Contra Ap." ii., § 17).

The term expresses most succinctly the conception of the Old Testament historiographers, and more especially that of the books which are written from a priestly-Levitical point of view (*e.g.*, Chronicles, the Levitical code P). Basic to the notion is the relation of Israel to God as His peculiar people (comp. Ex. xix. 5), which therefore is to constitute " a kingdom of priests and an holy nation " (*ib.* xix. 6). By redeeming Israel from Egyptian bondage God has acquired this people for Himself (*ib.* xv. 16). The wonderful manifestations of divine power at the Red Sea proclaim God the Ruler forever (*ib.* xv. 18). Moses is only God's man, bringing the people's concerns before YHWH (*ib.* xviii. 19), and communicating to the people God's will. Gideon rejects the proffered crown on the plea that God alone should rule over Israel (Judges viii. 22 *et seq.*).

The desire of the people for a king is regarded as equivalent to the rejection of YHWH (I Sam. viii. 7). Even after the kingdom is established God is said to go before the king (II Sam. v. 24). Therefore, down to their least details all legal, political, and social provisions are essentially religious, as the direct outflow of God's regal and supreme will; and the Torah as God's word is the ultimate revelation of the divine King's commands, and the basic law of the nation. Even the retribution meted out to criminals and their detection are the immediate concern of God (Lev. xx. 3, 5–6, xxiv. 12; xx. 20; Num. v. 12 *et seq.*; Josh. vii. 16).

The visible king—originally not known and recognized in Israel—is seated on God's throne (I Chron. xxix. 23; comp. *ib.* xxviii. 5). His authority is

Relation Between Heavenly and Earthly Ruler.
derived from that of the real ruler, God: hence the prophet's prerogative to dethrone even the king (comp. SAMUEL; see I Sam. xv. 26, xvi. 1 *et seq.*; I Kings xi. 29, xiv. 10, xvi. 1 *et seq.*, xxi. 21). The king represents before the people the reflected majesty of God (Ps. xlv. 7). The king's enemies are God's enemies (Ps. ii. 1 *et seq.*, xxi. 10): hence the Messianic visions are organically interwoven with the restoration of the kingdom in the dynasty of David (see MESSIAH). But the rerise of this theocratic kingdom in Israel will coincide with the acknowledgment of God as the ruler over the whole earth (see 'ALENU; ROSH HA-SHANAH; SHOFAR).

It is certain that in antiquity every people felt itself to be under the direct tutelage and government of its ancestral god: all government in ancient days was theocratic; and the conception that Israel is bound to be loyal to YHWH is not exceptional. In the stories relating to the rise and fall of Saul's family and the choice of David, later antipathies and sympathies of the prophetic party come to light (see SAMUEL; SAUL). The theocratic idea, in the sense that it postulates the supreme authority of the Torah with the effect of making Israel a holy nation, is the final development of the Levitical-sacerdotal program culminating in P, and carried out under Ezra and Nehemiah, leading at the same time to the recasting of antecedent history along the lines of this sacerdotal program (see CHRONICLES).

An original theocratic republicanism of Israel can not be admitted. The tribal organization of Israel was none other than that obtaining among its cognates. The restrictions placed upon royal authority (Deut. xvii. 14–20) by the Deuteronomist reflect on the practises prevailing at court, as the strictures placed on the lips of Samuel (I Sam. viii. 6 *et seq.*) describe actual conditions that prevailed in pre-Deuteronomic times and that were, of course, condemned by the Prophets. The hereditary kingdom was probably an adopted foreign (Canaanitish) institution; the Israelitish tribes, jealous of their independence, being ruled by elders (sheiks) or judges, possibly by elective monarchs. But even these sheiks were only in so far agents of theocracy as the "oracles" of the tribal deity were consulted and obeyed. The dominance of the Law is as clearly recognized in Islam as it ever was in post-exilic

Judaism. In fact, Islam is even to-day a theocracy (comp. Juynboll, "Handleiding der Mohammedaansch Wetenschap," Leyden, 1903).

к. E. G. H.

THEODOR, JULIUS (JUDAH): German rabbi; born Dec. 28, 1849, at Schmalleningken, East Prussia. He studied philosophy and Orientalia at the University of Breslau and rabbinica at the Jewish theological seminary in the same city. After receiving from Breslau his diploma as rabbi and his Ph.D. from the University of Königsberg (1876), he became second rabbi and teacher at the religious school at Bromberg. In 1885 he was called as rabbi to Berent; and since 1888 he has occupied the rabbinate of Bojanowo, Posen. In 1890 he visited London, Oxford, and Paris for the purpose of examining the midrashic manuscripts in the libraries of those cities.

Theodor is the author of: "Zur Composition der Agadischen Homilien," in "Monatsschrift," 1879–80; "Die Midraschim zum Pentateuch und der Dreijährige Palästinische Cyclus," *ib.* 1885–87; "Der Midrasch Bereschit Rabba," *ib.* 1893–95; and "Bereschit Rabba mit Kritischem Apparate und Kommentare," parts i. and ii., Berlin, 1903, 1904.

s. F. T. H.

THEODORA: Queen of Bulgaria from 1335 to 1355; born at Tirnova la Grande, capital of the ancient kingdom of Bulgaria, of a family of Byzantine Jews, from whom she received the Greek name of Theodora, although she was called also Sarah and was termed "the beautiful Jewess." She was chosen on one occasion to present a petition to Ivan Alexander, Czar of Bulgaria, and that monarch, though he had had two wives and was the father of three children, became infatuated with her and married her after she had accepted Christianity of her own accord. He became by her the parent of three children: two sons, named Assen and Ivan Chichman, and a daughter, called Tamar or Mara (but see JEW. ENCYC. iii. 426a, *s.v.* BULGARIA).

According to Christo J. Poppof, an ecclesiastical historian of Bulgaria, the Jews of Tirnova, taking advantage of the fact that one of their number sat on the throne, and presuming on the queen's favor, set no limits to their insolence, profaning the icons, the churches, even the eucharist itself, and blaspheming all that is most sacred to Christianity; so that their evil deeds encouraged heretics and fomented popular disturbances.

By the advice of the patriarch Theodore, Ivan Alexander called a national council in 1352, which was attended by all the prelates of the country; and in the presence of the czar himself and of Queen Theodora and her children a solemn anathema was pronounced against all heretics and Jews, and their expulsion from the country was decreed. Owing to the entreaties of Theodora, however, three Jews who had been condemned to death for blasphemy were reprieved, their sentences being commuted to other punishments; but in accordance with the decree of the council, the community of Tirnova, which had long inhabited a ghetto at the foot of the citadel of Trapesitza, was dispersed, and Jews never settled again in that city. According to another account (see JEW. ENCYC. *l.c.* p. 426b), they emigrated to Nicopolis on the death of Ivan Chichman.

Theodora brought her influence to bear on her husband and secured the throne for Ivan Chichman, her own son by him, leaving for her two stepsons only the provinces of Widdin and Dobrudja, and thus exposing herself to the charge of the Bulgarian historians that in her maternal blindness she weakened the kingdom. Ivan Chichman was defeated by Sultan Murad I. about 1360; and Theodora died some years later.

BIBLIOGRAPHY: Poppof, *Etvimii, Dernier Patriarche de Tirnova et de Trapesitza*, Philippopolis, 1901; *Revue des Ecoles de l'Alliance Israélite Universelle*, July, 1901. A portrait of Theodora and her children appears in *Svornik Narodni Umutvorenia*, Sofia, 1892.

S.   M. FR.

THEODORE OF MOPSUESTIA: Christian bishop and Church father; born and educated at Antioch; died at Mopsuestia about 429; teacher of Nestorius and Theodoret, and the foremost exegete of the school of Antioch, which was represented also by Lucian, Diodorus, and several others. In that school the historical interpretation of the Old Testament, which was at variance with the allegorical hermeneutics of ORIGEN, had become the rule; and in this, the only rational and adequate exegesis, no one in antiquity was greater than Theodore, who, therefore, is in perfect harmony with modern methods of interpretation.

The early maturity of his friend Chrysostom impressed Theodore to such an extent that he, after a crisis in his life, early devoted himself to the study of the Bible, and at the age of twenty published his
Commen- commentary on the Psalms, his most
tary on the important work from a Jewish and an
Psalms. exegetical point of view. As a priest in Antioch Theodore sided with Diodorus and with Flavian, likewise a famous exegete; and he waged an active warfare against Arians, Apollinarians, and other heretics (Theodoret, "Historia Ecclesiastica," v. 39), although there is no mention of Jews in the long list of those whom he opposed. The fame which he acquired secured for him the bishopric of Mopsuestia, which he retained for the remainder of his life. After his death his works, like those of Diodorus, were declared heretical by the Fifth Ecumenical Council on the ground that he had interpreted the Psalms "in Jewish fashion."

None of the Church Fathers equaled Theodore either in accurate grammatical and historical hermeneutics or in originality of view. His commentaries are free from rhetoric and homiletics; but this very fact gives them value in the eyes of modern exegetes. He is, moreover, rigid in his interpretations, since he systematically avoids symbolisms and allegories. He is the chief authority, the "interpreter" par excellence, for the Syrian Nestorians. The boldness of his hermeneutics is astonishing; and in his criticism he is centuries ahead of his time.

Theodore was the author of numerous works, the titles of forty-one volumes by him being mentioned by Assemani; and to these works must be added several written in Syriac (Assemani, "Bibliotheca Orientalis Clementino-Vaticana," ii. 478). His chief works of Jewish interest are his commentaries on the Psalms, on Job, on Canticles, and on the
Twelve Minor Prophets, as well as
Works. his five books against the allegorists; the latter work, now lost, probably contained his principles of exegesis.

Although Theodore made the mistake, which JEROME alone avoided, of interpreting the Septuagint instead of the Hebrew, he knew that the text of the former was sometimes corrupt; and he therefore examined it critically, having recourse to the Syriac version, to Aquila, to Theodotion, and, above all, to Symmachus (Stade's "Zeitschrift," vi. 265). Diestel alleges that Theodore knew neither Syriac nor Hebrew, and consequently lacked the fundamental knowledge necessary for exegesis, but Baethgen has proved that his commentaries show a certain knowledge of Hebrew, and that he was familiar with the curt lapidary Hebrew style which becomes incomprehensible when imitated in Greek. It must be confessed, nevertheless, that his knowledge of Hebrew was faulty, and that he relied far too much on the text of the Septuagint. His brother Polychronius, who was an adherent of the same school, was far superior to him in knowledge of Hebrew; but Theodore was the more important exegete.

Theodore interpreted most of the Psalms historically, holding, however, that David's prophetic gifts enabled him to foretell future events and to identify himself with them. He carried the idea of
prophecy too far, however; for in his
Views on opinion it consisted merely in the
Prophecy. ability to foretell events, embracing the immediate as well as the far distant future. But, though he refers much (in the Psalms) to the future, he confines his references to Jewish history, alluding but seldom to Jesus, which is the more remarkable since his was the period of the wildest allegorical and typological interpretation. He considers that Jesus is referred to in only three of the Psalms, namely, viii., xlv., and cx., to which may possibly be added, on the basis of other indications, lxxxix. and cxviii.; but not in xxii. nor in lxxii., which at most, he thought, might be interpreted typically in so far as Solomon, like Jesus, was a prince of peace. For seventeen psalms he offers no historical explanation, while he holds that references to David and his time occur in nineteen, to Jeremiah in one, to the Assyrian in twenty-five, to the Chaldean in sixty-seven, and to the Maccabean period in seventeen. This feature of his commentary is of especial importance as showing the keenness and soundness of his criticism. Not less noteworthy is the courage with which he rejects the authenticity of the superscriptions to the Psalms, which, he declares, were added by ignorant scribblers who could not be too severely censured.

He absolutely denied, moreover, that the Old Testament contained any references to the Son of God or to the Trinity, while any interpretation of Zech. ix. 9, 10 as applicable to Jesus was, in his view, evidence of extreme ignorance, since this passage, like Amos ix. 10, 11 and Micah v. 2, referred rather to Zerubbabel. The Song of Solomon he regarded as a secular epithalamium; and the Book of Job he considered a mixture of fact and fiction. It was a cardinal maxim of Theodore's that the authors of the Old and New Testaments were equally endowed with the mysterious gift of the Holy Spirit (commentary on Neh. i. 1).

Three degrees of inspiration were recognized by Theodore, although he gave no clear definition of them, asserting, for example, that David had the

Views on Inspiration.

gift of the spirit (on Ps. lxxxi. 3, τῇ τοῦ πνεύματος χάριτι), yet regarding him in all other respects as a prophet. According to Theodore, Solomon had the gift of wisdom only, not that of prophecy; this view shows the influence of Jewish tradition, which accepted a similar gradation as existing in the three groups of the canonical Scriptures.

Although Baethgen has advanced the hypothesis that Theodore's works contain other traces of Talmudic tradition, such as the view advocated by him in his commentary on Ps. lv. that the son of Simon, and not the son of Onias III., built the temple at LEONTOPOLIS, no deductions can be drawn from such meager data. In his theories concerning the superscriptions in the Psalter and the Maccabean portions of that book, Theodore showed himself a decided opponent of tradition. The orthodox Church, however, could not endure the candor of his exegesis; and consequently only fragments of his commentaries have survived, namely, of that on the Psalms (part of which exists in a Syriac version), of that on the Twelve Minor Prophets, and of those on various books of the New Testament (see Baethgen's "Studies" in Stade's "Zeitschrift," v.-vii.)

BIBLIOGRAPHY: Fabricius-Harles, *Bibliotheca Græca*, x. 346–362 (list of the works of Theodore); Migne, *Patrologia Græca*, lxvi. 647–696 (incomplete collection of the fragments); Corderius, *Expositio Patrum Græcorum in Psalmos*, ii., Antwerp, 1643–46 (the catena of Theodore on the Psalms); Sieffert, *Theodorus Mopsuestenus Veteris Testamenti Sobrie Interpretandi Vindex*, Königsberg, 1827; Fritzsche, *De Theodori Mopsuesteni Commentariis in Psalmos*, etc., Halle, 1836; idem, *De Vita et Scriptis Theodori Mopsuesteni*, 1836; Water, *De Theodoro Prophetarum Interprete*, Amsterdam, 1837; Wegnern, *Theodori Antiocheni . . . Quæ Supersunt Omnia*, i., *Commentarius in Duodecim Prophet. Minores*, Berlin, 1834; L. Diestel, *Gesch. des Alten Testaments in der Alten Kirche*, pp. 129–133, Jena, 1869; E. Sachan, *Theodori Mopsuestiani Fragmenta Syriaca*, Leipsic, 1869; I. P. de Barjean, *L'Ecole Exégétique d'Antioche*, pp. 36–39, Paris, 1898; Harnack, *Dogmengeschichte*, 3d ed., ii. 78; Kihn, *Theodorus von Mopsuestia und Junilius Africanus als Exegeten*, 1880; Smith-Wace, *Dictionary of Christian Biography*, iv. 934.

T.   S. KR.

THEODOSIA. See KAFFA.

THEODOTION : One of the Greek translators of the Old Testament (see JEW. ENCYC. iii. 187, *s.v.* BIBLE TRANSLATIONS). He is the supposed author of one of the two extant Greek versions of the Book of Daniel and the apocryphal additions thereto, to a discussion of which the present article is confined. The other version is that of the Septuagint. In Church use the latter has been replaced by the former so effectively that only one manuscript of the Greek Old Testament contains the Septuagint

Used in Daniel for Septuagint.

text, viz., the Codex Chisianus, known as Codex 87 (Holmes and Parsons MS. 88), though the translation of the Seventy underlies the Syriac Hexaplar (see Swete, "The Old Testament in Greek," iii., pp. vi., xii.; he publishes both texts).

"The relation of the two extant Greek versions of

Daniel is a perplexing problem" (Swete, "Introduction to the Old Testament in Greek," p. 46). The preference for Theodotion goes back to a very early period. Origen gave the Septuagint a place in his Hexapla, but an examination of his quotations proves that in his writings he almost invariably cites according to Theodotion. Jerome (in his preface to Daniel) records the fact of the rejection of the Septuagint version in Church usage, assigning as the reason therefor that that translation is very faulty. Earlier Church fathers, Clement of Alexandria, for instance, had set the precedent; and in Hermas and in Justin clear indications are found of the extensive popularity of Theodotion's version (Swete, "Introduction," p. 47; Gwynn, in "Dictionary of Christian Biography," *s.v.* "Theodotion," iv. 97 *et seq.*).

Still it is plain that Theodotion did not translate Daniel directly from the Hebrew-Aramaic (Masoretic). For the apocryphal additions no Aramaic (or Hebrew) original may be assumed. Gaster (in "The Unknown Aramaic Original of Theodotion's Additions to Daniel," in "Proc. Soc. Bibl. Arch." 1894, xvi.) proves that the Aramaic text is itself an adaptation from the Greek of Theodotion, not its original (see, also, Schürer in Herzog-Hauck, "Real-Encyc." i. 639). Nor are other Aramaic-Hebrew accounts of the Dragon or of Susanna (Neubauer, "The Book of Tobit," 1878, p. xci.; Jellinek, "B. H." vi. 126-128) entitled to be considered as originals. The original language of the additions was Greek. Theodotion's version is an elaboration of this Greek original; and his translation of the text of Daniel also is manifestly a working over of a previous Greek rendering.

But whether this Greek version which underlies Theodotion's text is the Septuagint as contained in the Chigi manuscript or another, independent, translation, is still in doubt. Schürer (*l.c.*)

Relation to Chigi Manuscript of Septuagint.

inclines to the opinion that Theodotion used the Septuagint and corrected it and supplied its deficiencies by comparison with the Masoretic text, while in the additions he recast the Septuagint with a free hand. Gwynn, whose treatise on Theodotion in the "Dictionary of Christian Biography" presents an elaborate investigation of the matter, argues for the view that two pre-Christian versions of Daniel, both passing as Septuagint texts, were current, one of which is that preserved in the Codex Chisianus, while the other furnished the basis for Theodotion's revision, the reviser consulting where possible the standard Hebrew text.

In order to illustrate the character of Theodotion's work, a comparison of his version of the additions to Daniel with that of the Chigi manuscript is very helpful. In The Song of the Three Holy Children he and the Septuagint agree in the main. The prayer of Azarias is placed after Dan. iii. 23. In the Septuagint the text of the preceding Biblical passages is somewhat changed in order to establish a better connection for the insertion. Theodotion omits verse 22b, while in verse 23 the simple statement is made that Shadrach, Meshach, and Abednego (Septuagint has Azarias) had fallen bound into the heated furnace. Verse 24 in the Septuagint reads: "In the following manner did Ananias,

Azarias, and Mizael pray and praise the Lord when the king had commanded that they should be cast into the furnace." Theodotion's rendering is as follows (verse 24): "And they went about in the midst of the flames, praising God and blessing the Lord. Then [verse 25] Azarias stepped forth and prayed; he opened his mouth in the midst of the flames and spake." Other variants consist in transpositions of

Variants from Septuagint. verses (e.g., verses 54 and 55 occur in the reverse order in Theodotion), the omission of conjunctions, the substitution of the singular for the plural, and of the definite for the indefinite article, and the dropping of parts of verses. Analysis of these discrepancies confirms the view that Theodotion's text presents a recast of an anterior Greek version which, if not identical with, must have been similar to the one now extant in the Septuagint.

The history of Susanna presents wider divergencies, the Septuagint being briefer, and Theodotion's text exhibiting the character of an elaboration. The fact is clear that they are based on a common traditional story, while it is perhaps doubtful whether Theodotion's amplifications presuppose his use of the extant Septuagint text. The possibility that the two are parallel developments of an antecedent written account is, theoretically, certainly admissible. A few passages may illustrate the foregoing observations. Verses 12 et seq. read in the Septuagint:

"But when the morning had dawned, they set out and hurried clandestinely, each hiding before the other, who should meet her and speak to her. And behold she was walking about as was her wont. But as soon as one of the elders had arrived, the other also made his appearance, and one asked the other: 'Why art thou gone forth so early without bidding me go along?' And they confessed to each other their pains of love."

Theodotion's version is as follows:

"Yet they watched jealously from day to day to see her. And the one said to the other, 'Let us now go home; for it is dinner-time.' So when they were gone out, they parted one from the other, and, turning back again, they came to the same place. After they had asked one another the cause, they acknowledged their lust, and then appointed a time both together when they might find her alone."

The account of how they met Susanna is very elaborate in Theodotion (verses 15–28), while the Septuagint sums up the proposal and answer in two terse sentences. It must be noted that the play on the names of the respective trees occurs in both versions (verses 55 and 59).

In Bel and the Dragon Theodotion affects greater historical accuracy, giving details concerning names and dates that are not found in the Septuagint, where general statements, such as the "King of Babylon," predominate. Theodotion's Daniel is more profuse in his profession of faith, e.g., verse 25, "Thy Lord, my God, will I worship; for He is a living God," which the Septuagint omits. These traits again suggest that Theodotion's method was that of an elaborator.

T.   E. G. H.

THEOLOGY: The science that treats of God and of His relation to the world in general and to man in particular; in a less restricted sense, the didactic representation of the contents and es-

sence of a religion. Jewish theology, therefore, denotes the doctrinal representation of the contents and essence of Jewish religion, the principles on which it rests, and the fundamental truths it endeavors to express and to realize.

Orthodox, or conservative, Judaism, from the standpoint of which this article is written, regards

Judaism a Revealed Religion. the Jewish religion as a revealed religion, the teachings of which were made known by God to man by supernatural means. These supernatural, divine communications of religious truths and doctrines took place, however, only at certain times in the past; and they were made only to chosen people (the Prophets, among whom Moses was preeminent). With the cessation of prophecy they were discontinued altogether. Through these supernatural manifestations God revealed to human beings all the religious truths essential to their guidance through life and to their spiritual welfare. These religious truths it is not necessary for man to supplement with human doctrines; nor may any of them be annulled. They are mainly contained in the Holy Scriptures, written by men who were inspired by God; and in part they are among the teachings and manifestations revealed by God to Moses which were not written down, but were preserved to the nation by oral tradition. Although the source of all religious truths within Judaism is to be found in revelation, Jewish theology is not solely revealed theology: natural theology has received recognition also. It is considered a fundamental maxim among almost all Jewish theologians and religious philosophers that the teachings and religious truths contained in the Scriptures as emanating from God can not be in direct contradiction to human intellect, which is itself of divine origin. The truths, understood and accepted by the human mind, which constitute the sum of natural theology are therefore taken into consideration in the determination of revealed religious truths. And, besides, the human mind has been allotted a general right to judge of the value and importance of the

Connection with Natural Theology. divine teachings; this it could do only by using as a standard the fundamental truths recognized by itself. The theological system binding on every Orthodox, conservative Jew, and containing his confession of faith, is therefore a composition of natural and revealed theology. Revealed theology, however, is the preponderating element; for even such teachings and principles as might have been set up by human intelligence are considered, when embodied in the Holy Scriptures, as revealed by God. This theological system is not, however, simply a system of abstract truths and articles of faith in which the Jew is merely required to believe; for it contains the fundamental theological teachings and religious principles on which is based the Jewish conception of the world and of life; and it requires not only a belief in and approval of these principles, but also, as a necessary adjunct to such approval, the doing of deeds which are in keeping therewith. It imposes upon the believing Jew duties by which his life must be regulated. It must be admitted that Judaism—that is, the sum total of the rules and laws, ideas and sentiments, manners and customs, which regulate the actions, feelings, and thoughts of the Jews—is more than a mere theological system, inasmuch as many of its rules and customs are of national character. It is not easy, however, to differentiate strictly between

Connection with Jewish National Customs. the national and the theological elements in Judaism. Several national customs are also divine precepts, whose observance is recommended in the Scriptures. And, besides, there exists between the Jewish religion and its supporters, the Jewish nation, a connection so intimate that Jewish nationalism and Jewish theology also are closely allied. National customs have become formulas expressing certain theological ideas and doctrines, while, on the other hand, theological rules have come to be considered characteristics of the nation, because they have become habitual to the people. Thus, for example, the customs and habits observed in commemoration of the most important national event—the delivery from Egypt—at the same time convey an idea of God's providence and of His influence upon the history of the nation which found such glorious expression in the Exodus. On the other hand, the theological system, with its precepts and requirements, has become a national bond which keeps the Jews together as one people. Without denying the partly national character of Judaism, it may therefore be said that Judaism is a peculiar theological system which, among other purely theological doctrines and religious principles, also sets up as articles of faith the belief in the imperishability of the Jews as a nation and the hope of a revivification of their independence. It imposes also the duty of preserving the nationality of Israel by observing the prescribed customs.

The present article gives a representation of this theological system: the individual religious truths and fundamental teachings—the dogmas of the Jewish faith—will be cited and explained; and their importance for the practical religious life, as well as the moral and religious duties deduced from them, will be referred to. This imposition of moral and religious duties is characteristic of the dogmas of the Jewish religion, which, however, are not dogmas in the sense that belief in them alone insures the salvation of the soul; for mere belief in them, without action in accordance with such belief, is, according to the Jewish theological conception, of no value. The dogmas of the Jewish faith must not only be believed and acknowledged, but they also demand that one act in accordance with their logical requirements. In this sense the dogmas of the Jewish religion are not only those truths and fundamental doctrines with the denial of which Judaism would cease to be a religion, but also such teachings and articles of faith as are obligatory upon each individual. With these

The Dogmas of Judaism. doctrines and articles of faith the most enlightened spirits and the most prominent thinkers of the Jewish nation have at all times occupied themselves. This being the case, it is not to be wondered at that differences of opinion have arisen

XII.—9

with regard to details of individual points, one scholar having interpreted a particular sentence at variance with another. In all such cases where the most enlightened men of the nation have disagreed in the interpretation of a doctrine or an article of faith, the authoritative opinion of the majority is used as a basis in the following discussion (see AUTHORITY). Such views and teachings as were at all times considered obligatory on adherents of the Jewish religion are the fundamental doctrines of Judaism. Any interpretation of an article of faith which was at any time advocated by only one or a few persons is to be regarded merely as his or their individual opinion; it is not obligatory upon all followers of Judaism and will therefore not be considered here.

The fundamental dogma of the Jewish religion, without which such faith would be inconceivable, is the belief in the existence of God. This is also the fundamental principle of all other religions; but the conception of God taught by the Jewish faith is in essential points different from the conceptions voiced by other creeds. This peculiarly Jewish conception of God regards Him as the Creator of the world and of all creatures; and it bestows upon Him, therefore, the name "Ha-Bore yitbarak shemo" (The Creator whose name is glorified).

The conception of God as the Creator of the universe, which is taught in the history of the Creation (Gen. i.), finds expression in the Decalogue also (Ex.

God as Creator. xx. 11), and is often repeated in the prophetic books. "I have made the earth, and created man upon it: I, even my hands, have stretched out the heavens, and all their host have I commanded," says God through the mouth of the prophet (Isa. xlv. 12). Nehemiah says: "Thou, even thou, art Lord alone; thou hast made heaven, the heaven of heavens, with all their host, the earth, and all things that are therein, the seas, and all that is therein, and thou preservest them all" (Neh. ix. 6); and the Psalmist calls God the Creator "which made heaven, and earth, the sea, and all that therein is" (Ps. cxlvi. 6). The creation of the world by God, as the Jewish religion teaches, was a "creatio ex nihilo," since God, the Creator, merely through His will, or His word, called into existence the world out of absolute nothingness (Maimonides, "Yad," Teshubah, iii.; "Moreh Nebukim," ii. 27; Albo, "'Ikkarim," i. 12). God, as the Creator of the world, is its preserver also; and the creation is not a completed act, but a continuous activity. The laws which, with great regularity, rule the world have been instituted by God, and remain valid only through the will of God, who in this way "repeats every day the work of creation through His goodness." But "whatsoever the Lord pleased, that did he in heaven, and in earth, in the seas, and all deep places" (Ps. cxxxv. 6); and He is able to abolish the laws which govern nature. At certain times in the world's history, when it was necessary for higher purposes, He has done this, and caused events and phenomena to happen which were contrary to the usual laws of nature (see MIRACLE). All the miracles recorded by the Scriptures happened in this manner. The natural laws are nevertheless to be regarded as valid forever; for they were introduced by God in His wisdom as permanent rules for the order of nature, and He never has cause to change the plans once made by Him, nor to change the arrangements made according to these plans. Even the miracles, although taking place during a temporary suspension of natural laws, were not due to changes in the divine plans; for they were embodied in the original plan. For from the very creation of the world and the establishment of natural laws, God, in His prescience, realized that at certain times a deviation from this order would be necessary for the welfare of humanity, in order to show it that the laws of nature had no independent power, but were subject to a higher being, their Creator. It was therefore prearranged that these deviations should take place at the times decided upon. In the personificative language of the Midrash this teaching is expressed as follows: "When God ordered Moses to cleave the sea, the latter wondered, and said, 'Thou, O Lord, hast said it Thyself, and hast instituted it as a natural law, that the sea should never become dry.' Whereupon the Lord said, 'From the beginning, at the time of creation, when I decided the laws for the sea, I have stipulated that it should divide itself before Israel, and leave a dry path through its midst for that nation'" (Ex. R. xxi. 6). What has here been said concerning the phenomenal division of the water refers also to every other phenomenon which is a deviation from the natural order of things.

Even as God is recognized as the Creator and Upholder of the world, so is He regarded as its Ruler. God's rulership over the world is secured through His creatorship (Ps. xxiv. 1–2). The doctrine of recognizing in God not only the Creator of the world, but also the Arbiter of its destiny, was

God in History. revealed by God Himself upon Mt. Sinai when He declared to the Israelites that it was He who had freed them from Egyptian bondage and made them an independent nation (Ex. xx. 2). Nehemiah, after having recognized God as the Creator and Upholder of the world, enumerates His marvelous deeds, thereby acknowledging Him also as the Arbiter of its destiny (Neh. ix. 7–13). In Ps. cxxxvi. God is praised and acknowledged both as the Creator of the world and as the Author of all events. The direct result upon man of this belief in God as the Creator and Upholder of the world and as the Arbiter of its destiny, is to make him dependent upon and responsible to God who created him. According to Gen. i., God's creation of the world culminated when He created man in His own image. This resemblance of man to God refers to his spiritual qualities, which raise him above the animals, and enable him to rule the world. It also enables man to commune with God, to acknowledge Him, and to act according to His will. It therefore becomes the duty of man to exercise his God-given rulership of the world only in accordance with divine precepts. He may not follow his own inclination, but must in all things do according to the will of God. And in order to make it possible for man to do according to the divine will, God has,

through a revelation, communicated His will to man (see REVELATION).

The belief in God as the sole Creator of the world and of all living creatures necessitates also a belief in the eternity of God. He is the Cause which has called all things into existence. But He needed no outer cause for His own existence, He Himself being the cause thereof. From this it follows that no limit can be placed upon His existence, that He has existed from all eternity, and that He will continue to exist forever. "I am the first, and I am the last," says the Lord through the mouth of the prophet (Isa. xliv. 6). He is called, therefore, "the eternal God" ("Elohe ḳedem"; Deut. xxxiii.), and the Psalmist calls Him the God who "from everlasting to everlasting is God" (Ps. xc. 2). This God, teaches the Jewish religion, is no carnal being; no carnal attributes may be assigned to Him, nor do

God Incorporeal. earthly conditions apply to Him; and there exists, moreover, no other being that resembles Him. This doctrine is especially emphasized by Jewish theologians, because several Biblical expressions apparently favor a conception of God as a carnal being, and many teachers take these expressions literally. It is the nature of a carnal body that it is limited and defined by space. God, as a non-corporeal being, is not limited by space; and Solomon says, therefore, "behold, the heaven and heaven of heavens can not contain thee" (I Kings viii. 27). The sages expressed this conception thus: "God arranges the whole universe and sets its limits: but the universe has not sufficient room for Him; it can not contain Him" (Midr. Teh. to Ps. xc. 1 [ed. Buber, 195b–196a]). God is thus omnipresent. When expressions occur in the Holy Scriptures mentioning God as dwelling at a certain place, or when a house of God is spoken of, it is not to be understood that God is subject to limitations of space. For the heavens and the entire universe can not contain Him; how much less can a temple built by human hands? All such expressions are only means to convey the idea that certain places are fitted to bring human beings into such a frame of mind that they may approach God and find Him. In like manner do the Holy Scriptures warn against the attribution to God of any definite shape, and the conception of Him in any given likeness. "Ye heard the voice of the words, but saw no similitude. . . . Take ye therefore good heed unto yourselves; for ye saw no manner of similitude on the day that the Lord spake unto you in Horeb" (Deut. iv. 12, 15). All the Biblical expressions which mention God in anthropomorphic terms are to be understood figuratively. God's "hand" signifies His power; His "eye" and His "ear," His omniscience, through which He sees and hears everything. His "joy" signifies His satisfaction; His "anger," His disapprobation of human acts done against His will. All these expressions are merely metaphorical, and were selected in order to make the power of God comprehensible to human beings, who are accustomed to see every action done through a human agency. When the Bible wishes to explain anything that has taken place on earth through divine intervention, it uses the same expressions as are employed in the case of human acts. But in reality there is no comparison whatever possible between God, the absolute, spiritual being, and man, or between God's acts and man's. "To whom then will ye liken God? or what likeness will ye compare unto him? . . . To whom then will ye liken me, or shall I be equal? saith the Holy One" (Isa. xl. 18, 25). "For my thoughts are not your thoughts, neither are your ways my ways, saith the Lord" (*ib.* lv. 8; comp. Maimonides, "Moreh,"i.48; Albo,*l.c.*ii.14–17).

A further article of faith teaches the acknowledgment of God as the only God, and the belief in no gods besides Him. "I am the Lord **God Unique.** thy God, which have brought thee out of the land of Egypt, out of the house of bondage. Thou shalt have no other gods before me," says God to Israel on Mt. Sinai (Ex. xx. 2-3). Even prior to the revelation on Sinai monotheism (the belief in one God) was an inheritance of the Jewish nation. The patriarch Jacob, in his dying hour, is filled with unrest because he doubts whether his children will preserve the faith which Abraham transmitted to him. His children, who are gathered about him, declare, however, that even as he believes in one God only, so also will they believe in the only God; and they pronounce the monotheistic article of faith: "Hear, O Israel: The Lord our God is one Lord" (Deut. vi. 4; Gen. R. xcviii. 4). This confession of faith the Jew pronounces thrice daily, and even in his dying hour he breathes it (see SHEMA'). With this confession on their lips, thousands of Jews have suffered martyrdom because they would not deny the unity of God. Many later religions have derived the monotheistic belief from Judaism, without, however, preserving it in the same degree of strict purity. The Jewish religion not only teaches its adherents to believe in no other god besides the One, but it also forbids the ascription to God of any attributes which, directly or indirectly, conflict with the strict belief in His unity. To ascribe to God any positive attributes is forbidden because it might lead to a personification of the divine qualities, which would interfere with the purity of the monotheistic faith. Many of the attributes ascribed to God are explained as negative characteristics. Thus, when it is said that God has a will, it implies only that He is not constrained in His actions; it must never be understood in the sense that His will is anything apart from Himself. Nor may it be taken to mean that His will is a part of His essence, for the unity of God is absolute and indivisible. Most of the attributes ascribed to God in Holy Writ and in the prayers are to be understood not as inherent qualities, but as ways and means by which He rules the world (see MIDDOT, SHELOSH-'ESREH). The emphatic mention of these divine attributes occurs so often in the Bible and in the prayers, because they exercise a great influence upon the religious and moral life of man. And for the same reason, and that its adherents may realize that they can rely only on God, does the Jewish religion impress upon them the fact that God is omnipotent. In their belief in God's omnipotence they can say with the Psalmist: "The Lord is on my side; I will not fear: what can man do unto me?" (Ps. cxviii. 6). God,

in His omnipotence, can frustrate any plans made against them; and the fear of man need therefore never lead them astray from the path of their religion. They can proudly refuse to commit any immoral act, although demanded of them by the mightiest of the earth, even as Hananiah, Mishael, and Azariah refused the order of Nebuchadnezzar with the words: "If it be so, our God whom we serve, He is almighty, and He can deliver us and protect us" (Dan. iii. 17, Hebr.). To the many occasions on which this confidence in the omnipotence of God has protected the Jews from denying their faith, every page of their history bears witness.

God is omniscient. This is the basis of the belief in the divine providence, of which the following is a circumstantial treatment. The belief in God's **God's Om-** omniscience exercises great influence **niscience.** also on the moral and religious thoughts and acts of human beings. "Can any hide himself in secret places that I shall not see him?" says the Lord through the mouth of His prophet (Jer. xxiii. 24). All human acts are seen by God; and though they may be hidden from the eyes of human justice, they can not be hidden from Him. Therefore, no evil deed may be committed even in secret. Also the inmost emotions of the human mind are known to God, for He "knoweth the thoughts of man" (Ps. xciv. 11). Man may entertain no wicked feelings in his heart; for God "seest the reins and the heart" (Jer. xx. 12).

God is omniscient and all-kind. This faith is the foundation of Jewish OPTIMISM. The world is the best possible world that could be created (Gen. R. ix. 2), for "God saw everything that he had made, and, behold, it was very good" (Gen. i. 31). Also in His government of the world does God exercise His loving-kindness, and "all that God does is done for the good" (Ber. 60b), even when it does not so appear to human beings. This faith, together with the belief in God's justice and never-ending love, gives man courage and strength to follow the straight path to his perfection unhindered by the adversities of life, and to endure with equanimity and with faith in God all the hardships of life. "It must not be believed of God that He would pass an unjust judgment upon man" (Ber. 5b). When, therefore, man is visited by affliction, he should first submit his entire conduct and all his actions to a severe test, to see if he has not called down his sufferings upon himself through his own misconduct. But even if, after a strict examination of his life, he can find nothing which could have been the cause of his suffering, he should despair neither of himself nor of divine justice; he should regard his afflictions as the "sufferings of love" ("yissurin shel ahabah") which God, out of His loving-kindness, has visited upon him (Ber. 5a). "For whom the Lord loveth he correcteth" (Prov. iii. 12), and He inflicts sufferings upon him in order to lead him to his salvation.

The Jewish faith in the absolute unity of God necessarily implies His immutability, **God Im-** the unchangeableness of His resolu- **mutable.** tions, and the constancy of His will. This doctrine of God's immutability is often emphasized in the Scriptures: "For I am the Lord, I change not" (Mal. iii. 6); "God is not a man, that he should lie; neither the son of man, that he should repent" (Num. xxiii. 19); "And also the Strength of Israel will not lie nor repent: for he is not a man, that he should repent" (I Sam. xv. 29). It is also said with reference to His ordinances that they are everlasting and unchangeable: "He hath also stablished them for ever and ever: He hath made a decree which shall not pass" (Ps. cxlviii. 6; comp. Maimonides, "Moreh," iii. 20; Albo, *l.c.* ii. 19).

This doctrine of the immutability of God and the constancy of His will is in apparent conflict with two other important teachings of Judaism; namely, the doctrines of the power of repentance and the efficacy of prayer. These doctrines will therefore be briefly treated here; and it will be shown how Jewish theologians view this apparent contradiction. Almost all the prophets speak of the power of RE-PENTANCE to avert from man the evil which threatens him, and to procure for him the divine grace. "Let the wicked forsake his way, and the unrighteous man his thoughts: and let him return unto the Lord, and he will have mercy upon him; and to our God, for he will abundantly pardon," says the prophet Isaiah (lv. 7); and in the same spirit speak Hosea (xiv. 2), Joel (ii. 12–14), Amos (iv. 6–11), Jonah (iii. 8–10), Zephaniah (ii. 1–3), Jeremiah (iii. 22, iv. 1–2), and Ezekiel (xviii. 21–32). And in like manner speak the sages of the Mishnah and the Talmud, comparing repentance to a shield which protects man from the punishment decreed upon him (Ab. iv. 13), or to a mediator who speaks to God in man's defense and obtains for him divine grace (Shab. 32a), or to a medium which brings salvation to the world (Yoma 86a). The question arises: How can God, on account of man's repentance, change His resolve, and avert the unfavorable judgment passed upon him; and does not such action conflict with the doctrine of the immutability of His plans? The answer to this question is that God never changes His will; and when man is able, through conversion, to escape the unhappy fate which would otherwise have been his, such escape is due to the fact that it was included in God's original plan. "Have I any pleasure at all that the wicked should die? saith the Lord God: and not that he should return from his ways, and live?" (Ezek. xviii. 23, 32). Sufferings and misfortunes were preordained for man on account of his sins; but it was also preordained that they should afflict him only as long as he persisted in his ungodly life and evil ways—the cause of his sufferings. And it is preordained, also, that when man through repentance removes the original cause of his sufferings, these and his misfortunes shall leave him (comp. Albo, *l.c.* iv. 18). The sages of the Talmud expressed this as follows: "Even before the world was created repentance ["teshubah"] was called into existence" (Pes. 54a); which means that before God created the world and human beings, before He decreed any fate for man, and before He made any resolutions, He had "teshubah" in mind; ordaining that through penance, which changes man's attitude toward God, God's attitude toward man should also become more

Re-pentance.

favorable. Man's repentance, therefore, causes no change in God's will or decisions.

What has been said above in regard to the power of penance applies likewise to prayer. The belief in the power of prayer to obtain God's help and grace finds expression in the Bible, where it is said of the Patriarchs and the Prophets that they prayed; and the Biblical examples of prayers that have been answered are numerous (see PRAYER). The most conspicuous examples are the prayers of Hannah (I Sam. i. 10 *et seq.*) and Jonah (Jonah ii. 2 *et seq.*). But the efficacy of prayer does not necessitate a change in the divine plans. The only way in which to pray so that the prayer may be heard and answered is for man to turn to God with all his heart and with all his soul (comp. I Kings viii. 48–50), to repent all his sins, and to resolve henceforth to live in such a way as will be pleasing to God, from whom he solicits aid and grace. A prayer uttered in such a frame of mind and with such intention is not only a desire spoken to God, but it is an expression of the inner transformation which has taken place in the one who prays. His thoughts and his intentions have become entirely changed, and pleasing to God; and he deserves, therefore, the divine grace which has previously been withheld from him only because he lacked the sentiments to which his prayer has given expression (comp. Albo, *l.c.* iv. 18). The Talmudists express this teaching as follows: "How can a prayer help any one who is sick? If it be the divine intention that he die from his disease, no prayer can help him, since the divine resolution is unchangeable. But if it be the intention of God that he recover, why then should he pray?" The answer is: "Prayer can help man, even if the divine decree be not in his favor" (R. H. 16a). The unfavorable decree has been rendered conditionally and is to be fulfilled only if the man remains in his original frame of mind. But if he repents, and through prayer expresses the change that has taken place in him, then the decree is annulled; for thus was it preordained by God.

Power of Prayer.

Besides the belief in the efficacy of prayer, the Jewish religion teaches also another sentence regarding prayer which distinguishes it from other creeds. This doctrine is that prayer may be directed only to God; and that, besides Him, there is no other being worthy of prayer (Maimonides' commentary on Sanh. xi. 1). This doctrine is, of course, only a consequent result of the doctrine of God's omnipotence, and that He alone is the Creator and the Ruler of the world, so that He alone can grant men their desires. But in this inhibition against praying to other beings, the Jewish religion includes also the invocation of angels or aught else as mediators between God and man. The Jew needs no agent whatever when he prays to his God: "When men will approach God," says the Talmud (Yer. Ber. ix. 13a), "they need seek out no mediator, nor need they announce their arrival through a doorkeeper. God says to them, 'When ye are in need, call upon none of the angels, neither Michael nor Gabriel, but call upon Me, and I will hear ye at once, as it is written (Joel iii. 5 [A. V. ii. 32]): "Whosoever shall call on the name of the Lord shall be delivered." ' " Every man can reach his God through prayer, without any mediation; for even though God is elevated high above the world, when a man enters a house of God and utters a prayer, even in a whisper, He hears it immediately (Yer. Ber. *l.c.*). "The Lord is nigh unto all them that call upon him, to all that call upon him in truth" (Ps. cxlv. 18). He is equally near to all: to the highest as well as to the lowliest. If a prayer be uttered in the right frame of mind and with right intentions, it is efficacious whether pronounced by a Moses or by the lowliest one in Israel (comp. Ex. R. xxi. 3).

Holy Scripture mentions several instances where a prophet or a pious man prays for another; as, for example, Abraham for Abimelech, Moses for Pharaoh, etc. These prayers, although not expressive of the improved condition of those for whom they are uttered, are nevertheless heard by God, in order to show that He is the Ruler of the world and that those who believe in Him do not call upon Him in vain. "He is a prophet, and he shall pray for thee, and thou shalt live," says God to Abimelech (Gen. xx. 7). God inflicts sufferings upon unbelievers, with the intention of recalling them through the prayer of a pious one, thereby to show the unbelievers that He, the Ruler of the world, is accessible to the prayers of those that believe in Him.

As has been said above, the circumstance that man was created in the image of God imposes upon him the duty of ordering his life entirely according to the will of God; and only by doing so can he attain the highest perfection and fulfil his destiny. In order to act according to the will of God it is necessary that man should know what God wills of him. Through his God-given intellect man is enabled, in many cases, to recognize the will of God; but, in order to understand it fully, he needs a direct communication from God; that is, a divine revelation. Such a manifestation of the divine will was made even to the first human being, Adam, as well as to Noah and to the patriarchs Abraham, Isaac, and Jacob. Moses assured Israel that God would raise after him other prophets, who would make known to the people the divine will (Deut. xviii. 15-18); and he indicated to them the signs by which they might distinguish a true prophet from a false one (*ib.* xiii. 2-6, xviii. 20-22). The purpose of the true Prophets was only to enlighten the people as to the will of God, thereby bringing them to a clearer understanding of their duty: to live according to that will (Albo, *l.c.* iii. 12). The seers that arose in Israel and in Judah, and whose prophecies have been preserved in the books of the Old Testament, proved themselves true prophets through their personal characters as well as through the nature of their prophecies. The Jewish religion has, therefore, established as an important doctrine the recognition, as inspired by God, of all the prophetic utterances that have been handed down (Maimonides' commentary on Sanh. xi. 1). The times and places at which God bestows on a man the distinction of revealing Him to the people depends entirely upon His own will; but prophets must possess certain virtues and characteristics that

Divine Revelation.

make them worthy of receiving the divine communications (see PROPHETS AND PROPHECY). Those whom God found worthy of receiving such direct information regarding His will were, in a manner which seemed inexplicable and supernatural to the laity, possessed of the firm impression and the unshakable conviction that God spoke to them and apprised them of His will. They were convinced also that this impression was not a mere feeling of their souls, but that it came to them from without: from God, who revealed Himself unto them, making them His instruments through which He communicated His will to their fellow beings (see REVELATION). But in order to inspire the laity with faith in the Prophets, God considered it necessary on Mt. Sinai to let the whole Jewish people hear that He spoke to Moses, that they might believe him forever (Ex. xix. 9); and when God then revealed Himself to the entire nation He convinced them "that He could commune with a human being" (comp. Deut. v. 24). They thereupon renounced all desire to receive commands and teachings from God direct. They were convinced that Moses repeated God's words to them faithfully; and they declared themselves willing to hear all that he spoke in God's name, and to act accordingly (Deut. v. 24). God thereupon revealed to Moses all the commandments and all the statutes and judgments, which Moses communicated to the people (*ib.* 31) This revelation on Mt. Sinai is therefore the chief foundation of the Jewish faith, and guarantees the divine origin of the Law as contained in the Pentateuch. Before his death Moses wrote down the five books named after him (the Pentateuch), and gave them to the people (*ib.* xxxi. 24-26); and he commanded them to observe everything therein written, and to transmit it to their children as the teaching of God. However much the succeeding generations of Israel, after the death of Moses, fell off from God and became idolaters, there has been in each generation a group of pious men who have guarded faithfully the holy inheritance and transmitted it to their children. And through this careful transmission the teachings of Moses have been preserved unchanged through all ages. It is therefore set up as one of the fundamental dogmas of the Jewish religion that the Torah contained in the Pentateuch is identical with that which was revealed by God to Moses on Mt. Sinai (Maimonides' commentary on Sanh. xi. 1). No changes have been made therein except with regard to the characters in which it was written (Sanh. 21b).

The Torah.

The Torah contains rules and regulations which should govern the life of man and lead him to moral and religious perfection. Every rule is expressive of a fundamental ethical, moral, or religious idea. Those regulations in which human intelligence is unable to discern the fundamental idea are, through belief in their divine origin, vouchsafed the same high religious importance; and the ethical value of submission to the will of God where its purpose is not understood is even greater. In observing the Law man's good intention is the chief point (see NOMISM).

These written laws are supplemented through

oral teachings; and the interpretation of the written doctrines is entrusted to the sages and scholars, who expound them according to prescribed rules. They add to or deduct from the individual regulations; and in many instances, when it is for the good of the Law, they may annul an entire clause. In such cases, however, the whole body of scholars, or at least a majority, must agree as to the necessity and correctness of the measure (see AUTHORITY; ORAL LAW). Aside from such minor changes and occasional annulments, which are made in the spirit of the Law, and are intended to sustain the entire Torah ("Biṭṭulah shel torah zehu yissudah"; Men. 99b), the Law is to be regarded, in whole or in parts, as unchangeable and irrevocable. It is a firm article of faith in the Jewish religion that this Law will never be changed, and that no other doctrines will be given by God to man (Maimonides, *l.c.*).

Of many clauses of the Law it is expressly stated that they are meant to be eternal rules ("ḥuḳḳot 'olam"), or that they are obligatory on all generations ("le-dorot 'olam"); and there is not a single indication in the Holy Scriptures that the Law is ever to be replaced by other revealed doctrines. The new covenant of which Jeremiah speaks (xxxi. 31–33) is not to be made on the basis of a new revealed law, but on the basis of the old law, which shall take firmer root in the hearts of the believers. It was even promised to the Israelites that new prophets should arise, and they were commanded to harken to the words of these prophets (Deut. xviii. 15–18). But the new prophets can reveal no new law, and a prophet who sets up a law which conflicts with the old doctrines is a false prophet (*ib.* xiii. 1–4). And also a prophet who declares the old law to be valid for a certain period only, is a false prophet, for his statement conflicts with the teachings of Moses, the greatest of all prophets, who plainly says in many passages (Ex. xii. 14, 17 *et seq.*) that the regulations shall be obligatory forever (Maimonides, "Yad," Yesode ha-Torah, ix.; *idem*, "Moreh," ii. 39; Saadia, "Emunot we-De'ot," iii. 7–10). The words "It [the commandment] is not in heaven" (Deut. xxx. 12) are explained in the Talmud (B. M. 59b) as meaning that there is nothing left in heaven that has yet to be revealed in order to elucidate the Law. A decision or a legal question based only on such a heavenly revelation is not recognized (Maimonides, "Yad," *l.c.*). The doctrine of the unchangeableness of the Law is further emphasized by another fundamental dogma of Judaism, which declares the prophecy of Moses to surpass that of any of his predecessors or successors (Maimonides, *l.c.*). That the prophecy of Moses is different from and superior to that of any other prophet is explicitly stated in Num. xii. 8. Whether this difference was one of quality, as Maimonides thinks ("Yad," *l.c.* vii. 6; "Moreh," ii. 35), or one of degree only, as Albo (*l.c.* iii. 17) supposes, is immaterial. The fact is sufficient that the prophecy of Moses was superior to that of any other prophet. The Torah was given through Moses, of whose superior gift God Himself convinced the Israelites on Mt. Sinai. Should another prophet arise and declare

**Perma-
nence and
Sufficiency
of
the Torah.**

the Law given by God through Moses to be invalid, then he would have to be a greater prophet than Moses; this, however, is inconceivable according to the fundamental doctrine which declares Moses to be the greatest prophet of all time. Those prophets are not to be believed who declared the old covenant to be dissolved, and that they were sent by God to make a new one; for one can not be as firmly convinced of their divine authority as of that of the old covenant, which they themselves do not deny (Abraham ibn Daud, in "Emunah Ramah," ii.; comp. also Albo, *l.c.* iii. 19).

The fact that the Law was given to man, and that he was requested to observe its precepts, implies that it depends on man alone whether or not he will do so. The freedom of the human will is explicitly announced in the Bible also: "I call heaven and earth to record this day against you, that I have set before you life and death, blessing and cursing: therefore choose life, that both thou and thy seed may live: That thou mayest love the Lord thy God, and that thou mayest obey his voice, and that thou mayest cleave unto him: for he is thy life, and the length of thy days" (Deut. xxx. 19–20). The Mishnah teaches: "Everything has been foreseen by God, and yet He has given to man freedom of will" (Ab. iii. 15). Also the Talmud plainly teaches of the freedom of will: "Everything is in the hand of God, with the exception of the fear of God, and piety: these alone are dependent upon the will of man" (Ber. 33b). "When any one would keep his life clean and virtuous, he is aided; but if he chooses to keep it unclean and wicked, he is not hindered," says Simeon ben Laḳish (Shab. 104a). The teachers of post-Talmudic times all regarded the liberty of the human will as a fundamental doctrine of Judaism. Although it is difficult to reconcile this doctrine with the knowledge or prescience of God, various attempts have been made to effect such a reconciliation, in order that it might not become necessary to deny either of them (comp. Saadia, "Emunot we-De'ot," ii. 9; "Cuzari," v. 20; Maimonides, "Moreh," iii. 20; Crescas, "Or Adonai," II. i. 4; Albo, *l.c.* iv. 5). The liberty and responsibility of man justify some retribution for his acts: rewards for the observance of divine precepts and commandments, and punishment for their transgression. A just retribution presupposes God's providence and His omniscience. The belief in God's omniscience—that is, the belief that He sees and knows everything, even the secret thoughts of man, and that nothing can take place in the world otherwise than by His will—is one of the fundamental dogmas of Judaism. Moses warns Israel not to forget that all events proceed from God: "And thou say in thine heart, My power and the might of mine hand hath gotten me this wealth. But thou shalt remember the Lord thy God: for it is he that giveth thee power to get wealth" (Deut. viii. 17, 18). Isaiah promises that punishment shall be meted out to the Assyrian king because he flattered himself with the belief that he owed his glory to his own power and to his own wisdom, and did not realize that he was only God's instrument (Isa.

**Freedom of
the Will.**

**God's Prov-
idence.**

x. 12–16). Only the ungodly say, "The Lord shall not see, neither shall the God of Jacob regard it" (Ps. xciv. 7). The Psalmist reproves them, and says to them that God sees and hears everything, and that He knows the very thoughts of men, even when they are vain (*ib.* verses 8–11). And in another passage he thanks God for regarding even the lowliest and most insignificant of men and for caring for them (Ps. viii. 5, cxliv. 4). The words "Fear thy God" are, according to the Rabbis, added to commandments which depend upon the intentions of man; as if to say to him: "Fear God who knows thy thoughts" (Ḳid. 32b). That nothing takes place in the world without divine ordination is expressed by the Rabbis in the maxim that no man hurts his finger here on earth unless Heaven willed it so (Ḥul. 7b). Also the theologians and religious philosophers of the Middle Ages recognized the belief in divine providence as a fundamental doctrine of Judaism (comp. Maimonides, "Moreh," iii. 17–18; Albo, *l.c.* iv. 7–11; see also PROVIDENCE).

In close relation with the doctrine of divine providence stands the doctrine of retribution: that God rewards those who keep His commandments, and punishes those who transgress them. The doctrine of retribution is one of the fundamental teachings of Judaism, and was revealed to the Jews on Mt. Sinai when God said to them that He would visit the sins of the fathers upon the children, and show mercy to those who loved Him and kept His commandments (Ex. xx. 5–6). In many commandments the reward given for their observance is indicated (Ex. xx. 12; Deut. xxii. 6–7). This doctrine, however, contains also a difficulty; for if nothing can take place in the world without God's will, and since He rewards the pious and punishes the transgressors, how does it come to pass that so many pious suffer while the ungodly prosper? This problem, which engaged the prophets Jeremiah (xii. 1) and Habakkuk (i. 13, ii. 4), the author of Job, and the psalmist Asaph (Ps. lxxiii. 2 *et seq.*), has also in post-Biblical times held the attention of the most prominent spirits of each generation; and in Talmudic, as also in post-Talmudic, times several attempts were made to solve and explain it (comp. Ber. 7a; Albo, *l.c.* iv. 7, 12–15). Most of the solutions and explanations have been based on the following two ideas: (1) Man, with his limited intellect, is not able to determine who is in reality a pious man ("zaddiḳ gamur") or who is in reality a sinner ("rasha' gamur"). Man can mistake a pious one for a transgressor, and vice versa. Nor can man correctly determine actual good and actual evil. Much which appears evil to man proves to be productive of good; while, on the other hand, many things which are seemingly good have evil results for human beings. Short-sighted man, therefore, able to judge from appearances only, may not pretend to judge the acts of God. (2) The other idea which endeavors to reconcile the doctrine of divine retaliation with the fact that pious men suffer while transgressors prosper, is the idea of the immortality of the soul. When man dies his soul does not die with him, but returns to God who gave it to man (Eccl. xii. 7). The soul is immortal,

Divine Retribution.

and after the death of man, separated from the body, it continues its existence in another world; and in this other world does complete retaliation take place. The doctrine of the immortality of the soul and of a future life is not definitely stated in the Holy Scriptures; but it is implied in many passages, especially in the Psalms (comp. "Cuzari," i. 115; Albo, *l.c.* iv. 39–40; Wohlgemuth, "Die Unsterblichkeitslehre in der Bibel," in "Jahresbericht des Rabbinerseminars in Berlin," 1899).

Immortality of the Soul. The doctrine of the soul's immortality, and of a future life in which retribution shall take place, is set forth plainly and emphatically in post-Biblical Jewish literature—in the Mishnah and in the Talmud. "Let not thy imagination persuade thee that the grave is to be a place of refuge for thee," says the Mishnah (Ab. iv. 22); "Thou wert born against thy will, and against thy will livest thou. Against thy will shalt thou die and be compelled to account for thy life before the King of Kings, the Holy One, praised be He." In Deut. vii. 11 it is said with reference to the commandments: "which I command thee this day, to do them," and these words are explained by the Rabbis as meaning: "To-day—that is, in this world—shall man observe the commandments; but he should not expect his reward in this world, but in another" ('Ab. Zarah 3a). "Reward for good deeds should not be expected in this world" (Ḳid. 39b). By the promise of a long life for those who honor their parents (Ex. xx. 12) is meant eternal life in the hereafter. The reward and punishment for good and evil deeds respectively to be meted out in the other world, can be of a spiritual nature only, since they apply entirely to the soul. "In the future world are to be found no material pleasures; but the pious ones, with their crowns of glory, enjoy the splendor of God," says the Talmud (Ber. 17a). As the object of doctrines and commandments is to lead man to the highest degree of perfection, so also is the reward for his observance of the Law an eternal enjoyment of the presence of God and true knowledge of Him. The punishment of the transgressor consists in his being excluded from all the divine splendor. This causes the soul to experience the greatest agony and remorse for its ungodly life. Although the belief in divine retribution is a fundamental doctrine of the Jewish religion, the latter teaches at the same time that neither the expectation of a reward nor the fear of punishment should influence the mind of man in his observance of the divine precepts. Judaism sets it up as an ideal that the commandments be kept through love of God (Soṭah 31a; 'Ab. Zarah 19a; see IMMORTALITY; NOMISM).

The belief in the resurrection of the dead is closely connected with the doctrine of the immortality of the soul and of retribution in the hereafter. This belief in resurrection is conceived in various manners by Jewish theologians. Some hold that, since retribution in the world to come can fall upon the soul only, bodies will, upon the day of resurrection, rejoin their souls so that both may be rewarded or punished together for the deeds done in common (comp. Albo, *l.c.* iv. 35).

Resurrection of the Dead.

This conception is expressed also in the parable of the lame and the blind (Sanh. 91a, b). Maimonides, on the other hand, understands resurrection figuratively only, and believes it refers to the immortality of the soul, which, after death, awakens to a new life without incarnation ("Ma'amar Teḥiyyat ha-Metim," *passim*).

But no matter how differently the theologians view the doctrine of resurrection, they all firmly believe that God can quicken the dead, and that He will do it when He so chooses (Maimonides' commentary on Sanh. xi. 1). As to when, in what manner, and for what purpose resurrection will take place; who will participate therein, whether the Jewish nation alone, or even only a part thereof; and whether the resurrected dead will thenceforth live forever or die anew — all these questions can not be answered. Explanations bearing on them have been made by various teachers (Saadia, "Emunot we-De'ot," vii.), but they are all mere conjectures (comp. Albo, *l.c.* iv. 35).

The doctrine of resurrection is expressed by Daniel (xii. 2): "And many of them that sleep in the dust of the earth shall awake, some to everlasting life, and some to shame and everlasting contempt." The sages of the Talmud hold that resurrection is alluded to also in various passages of the Pentateuch (comp. Sanh. 90b), one of which is as follows: "I kill, and I make alive" (Deut. xxxii. 39). The Mishnah sets up this doctrine as an important article of faith, and holds that those who do not believe therein, or who do not believe that it is embodied in the divine teachings of Judaism, and indicated in the Law, can have no share in the world to come (Sanh. xi. 1). By the Talmud, and by the theologians and religious philosophers of medieval times also, the doctrine of resurrection was recognized as an important article of faith (comp. "Albo," *l.c.*). The supporter of the Jewish religion and of all the ethical and moral ideals therewith connected is the Jewish nation, which God chose from among all peoples (Deut. vii. 6). The selection of the Jewish nation is evidenced in the fact that God found it worthy of a direct manifestation on Mt.

The Chosen People. Sinai, that He revealed to it religious truths, and that He bestowed upon it the peculiar grace of causing prophets, who should explain these truths, to arise from its midst.

This choice of the Jewish nation was not, however, made arbitrarily by God; it was based upon special merit which the Jews possessed above other ancient peoples. Abraham, the progenitor of the Jewish nation, possessed a true knowledge of God; and he commanded his children and descendants to "keep the way of the Lord, to do justice and judgment" (Gen. xviii. 19). But of all the descendants of Abraham, the Jewish people is the only one which has kept the legacy of its progenitor (comp. "Cuzari," ii. 6).

This knowledge of God which the Jews inherited from Abraham made them more religiously inclined than other nations; it made them fit to receive revelation, and to acknowledge the value of the laws and accept them. R. Johanan expresses this as follows: "God offered the Torah to all the nations, but none could or would accept it, until He offered it to the Israelites, who were both willing and qualified to receive it" ('Ab. Zarah 2b). Israel, however, may not keep these teachings for itself alone; they were not given it for its own exclusive property. The doctrines were given to Israel only because it was the only one among the nations which was qualified to accept them and to live according to them. And through Israel's example the other nations will be led to a true knowledge of God, and to the acceptance of His teachings. In this way will be fulfilled the promise which was given to Abraham (Gen. xxii. 18), that "in thy seed shall all the nations of the earth be blessed." With the exception of such laws and precepts as are based on national events, the whole Law is intended for all of humanity, which, through observance of the divine doctrines, may acquire a true knowledge of God and of His will.

With reference to Lev. xviii. 5, the sages say that by the statutes of the Law are designated not the law for the priests or the Levites or the Israelites, but the statutes of the Law which man has to observe, and according to the regulations of which he must live (Sifra, Aḥare Mot, xiii. [ed. Weiss, p. 86b]). Israel has acted according to this principle, and has not withheld the laws of God from the nations. Most civilized nations owe their knowledge of God to these teachings. But the nations have not yet attained to a correct understanding of these doctrines, and neither in their political nor in their social lives have they reached the ideals of justice and brotherly love. The Jews, in possession of the revealed doctrines, and peculiarly gifted to comprehend the same and to realize their ideals, have been called upon, as they once taught the nations the knowledge of God, so in future to teach them other religious ideals. But this they can not do as long as they live in exile, dependent and persecuted and despised, and regarded as the reprobate sons of God. They can do this when they again attain political independence, settling in the land of their fathers, where they, in their political and social life, can realize the ideals of justice and love taught by the Jewish religion. The belief

The Messiah. that this will some time happen constitutes an article of faith in Judaism which reads as follows: "A redeemer shall arise for the Jewish nation, who shall gather the scattered Jews in the land of their fathers. There they shall form an independent Jewish state and reawaken to independent national life. Then all nations shall go often to Palestine to study the institutions of a state founded on love and justice. From Zion the peoples shall be taught how they, in their own state institutions, may realize the ideals of justice and brotherly love; and the highest religious doctrines shall go forth from Jerusalem" (comp. Isa. ii. 2-4; Mic. iv. 1-4). The mission of salvation to be accomplished through the redemption of Israel is, however, only an indirect and remote aim. The direct and first aim is to compensate the Jewish nation for all the sufferings it has endured through its years of exile. God's relations to a nation are similar to those toward an individual.

The Jewish nation lost its political independence on account of its sins and failings, and was sent into exile for that reason. This punishment, however, is not calculated to annihilate the Jewish people; for as God does not wish the death of the individual transgressor, but rather his conversion, neither does He wish the destruction of a nation which has sinned. God has promised

The Resto- the Jews that He will not cast them
ration away even while they are in the lands
of Israel. of their enemies; neither will He break His covenant with them (comp. Lev. xxvi. 44).

God has promised to redeem them when they repent of all the sins which caused the loss of their national independence. "And it shall come to pass, when all these things are come upon thee, the blessing and the curse, which I have set before thee, and thou shalt call them to mind among all the nations, whither the Lord thy God hath driven thee, And shalt return unto the Lord thy God, and shalt obey his voice according to all that I command thee this day, thou and thy children, with all thine heart, and with all thy soul; That then the Lord thy God will turn thy captivity, and have compassion upon thee, and will return and gather thee from all the nations, whither the Lord thy God hath scattered thee. If any of thine be driven out unto the utmost parts of heaven, from thence will the Lord thy God gather thee, and from thence will he fetch thee: And the Lord thy God will bring thee into the land which thy fathers possessed, and thou shalt possess it; and he will do thee good, and multiply thee above thy fathers" (Deut. xxx. 1–5). When and in which manner this redemption will take place is not explained by any reliable tradition; and the many descriptions given by various teachers are only personal conjectures. When will the redemption take place? That is a question which can not be answered. And all calculations regarding the time of the advent of the redeemer are only conjectures. But it is a traditional belief among the Jews that it may take place at any time when the people are properly prepared to receive him (Sanh. 98a). The natural consequence of this belief is the demand for good acts. The nation must uphold its national and religious endowments, and not, through ill conduct, irreligious actions, and antinational endeavors, frustrate or make difficult its redemption. When the Jewish people believe in their redemption, when they desire it with all their hearts, and when with all their actions they strive to deserve it—then the redeemer may at any time arise from among them (ib.).

BIBLIOGRAPHY: Besides the works cited throughout the article see also: Baḥya b. Joseph, *Ḥobot ha-Lebabot*; Samson Raphael Hirsch, *Nineteen Letters of Ben Uziel*, transl. by Drachman, New York, 1899; S. Schechter, *Studies in Judaism*, Philadelphia, 1896; M. Friedländer, *The Jewish Religion*, London, 1891; Morris Joseph, *Judaism as Creed and Life*, ib. 1903.

K.   J. Z. L.

THEOPHANY : Manifestation of a god to man; the sensible sign by which the presence of a divinity is revealed. If the word is taken in this sense, and the passages which merely mention the fact of a revelation without describing it are separated from those which speak of the "angel of God,"

only four theophanies will be found in the Bible. Kautzsch (in Herzog-Plitt, "Real-Encyc." xv. 538) interprets the term in a broader sense, and divides theophanies into three classes, as follows: (1) those related as historical facts; (2) those which are the subjects of prophetic vision or annunciation; and (3) those which consist in purely poetic fancy. This classification may be applied to the four theophanies. The Sinaitic revelation is historical; the passages relating to the divine inspiration of Isaiah (Isa. vi.) and of Ezekiel (Ezek. i.) represent subjects of prophetic vision; and Ps. xviii. 4–16 is poetic description.

The Sinaitic revelation is related in calm, simple language in Ex. xix. 16–25. The manifestation is ac-
The Sina- companied by thunder and lightning;
itic The- there is a fiery flame, reaching to the
ophany. sky; the loud notes of a trumpet are heard; and the whole mountain smokes and quakes. Out of the midst of the flame and the cloud a voice reveals the Ten Commandments. The account in Deut. iv. 11, 12, 33, 36 and v. 4, 19 is practically the same; and in its guarded language it strongly emphasizes the incorporeality of God. Moses in his blessing (Deut. xxxiii. 2) points to this revelation as to the source of the special election of Israel, but with this difference: with him the point of departure for the theophany is Mount Sinai and not heaven. God appears on Sinai like a shining sun and comes "accompanied by holy myriads" (comp. Sifre, Deut. 243). Likewise in the song of Deborah the manifestation is described as a storm: the earth quakes; Sinai trembles; and the clouds drop water. It is poetically elaborated in the prayer of Habakkuk (Hab. iii.); here past and future are confused. As in Deut. xxxiii. 2 and Judges v. 4, God appears from Teman and Paran. His majesty is described as a glory of light and brightness; pestilence precedes Him. The mountains tremble violently; the earth quakes; the people are sore afraid. God rides in a chariot of war, with horses—a conception found also in Isa. xix. 1, where God appears on a cloud, and in Ps. xviii. 11, where He appears on a cherub.

Isaiah and Ezekiel receive their commissions as prophets amid glorious manifestations of God. Isaiah supposedly sees God on a high and lofty
In Isaiah throne. In reality, however, he sees
and not Him but only His glorious robe,
Ezekiel. the hem and train of which fill the whole temple of heaven. Before the throne stand the seraphim, the six-winged angels. With two wings they cover their faces so as not to gaze on God; with two they cover their feet, through modesty; and with the remaining two they fly. Their occupation is the everlasting praise of God, which at the time of the revelation took the form of the thrice-repeated cry "Holy!" (Isa. vi.).

Ezekiel in his description is not so reserved as Isaiah. The divine throne appears to him as a wonderful chariot. Storm, a great cloud, ceaseless fire, and on all sides a wonderful brightness accompany the manifestation. Out of the fire four creatures become visible. They have the faces of men; each one has four wings; and the shape of their feet enables them to go to all four quarters of the earth with equal rapidity and without having to turn. These living creatures are recognized by the prophet as cherubim (Ezek. x. 20). The heavenly fire, the coals of which burn like torches, moves between them. The movement of the creatures is harmonious: wherever the spirit of God leads them they go. Beneath the living creatures are wheels ("ofannim") full of eyes. On their heads rests a firmament upon which is the throne of God. When the divine chariot moves, their wings rustle with a noise like thunder. On the throne the prophet sees the Divine Being, having the likeness of a man. His body from the loins upward is shining ("ḥashmal"); downward it is fire (in Ezek. viii. 2 the reverse is stated). In the Sinaitic revelation God descends and appears upon earth; in the prophetic vision, on the other hand, He appears in heaven, which is in keeping with the nature of the case, because the Sinaitic revelation was meant for a whole people, on the part of which an ecstatic condition can not be thought of.

Very different is the theophany of the Psalmist (Ps. xviii. 8–16). He is in great need; and at his earnest solicitation God appears to save him. Before Him the earth trembles and fire glows. He rides on a cherub on the wings of the wind. He is surrounded with clouds which are outshone by His brightness. With thunder and lightning He destroys the enemies of the singer and rescues him.

In the Psalms.

As may be seen from the descriptions of the various theophanies, the deep monotheistic spirit of the Israelites hesitates to describe the Divine Being, and confines itself generally to describing the influence of the revelation upon the minds and characters of those beholding it. See REVELATION.

BIBLIOGRAPHY: Kautzsch, in Herzog-Plitt, *Real-Encyc.* xv., *s.v.*; Hamburger, *R. B. T.* i., s.v. *Herrlichkeit Gottes.*

K. M. RI.

THEOPHILUS: High priest; son of Anan, and brother of JONATHAN, who was deposed by Vitellius in 37 C.E. in favor of Theophilus (Josephus, "Ant." xviii. 5, § 3). He officiated for about three years, when he was succeeded by Simon Cantheras. This Theophilus is probably identical with the father of the high priest Matthias, and, according to Büchler, he is likewise the same as Hananeel the Egyptian (Parah iii. 5). The name of Theophilus figures in the Seder 'Olam (Neubauer, "M. J. C." i. 167).

BIBLIOGRAPHY: Grätz, *Gesch.* 4th ed., iii. 317; Schürer, *Gesch.* 3d ed., ii. 218; Büchler, *Das Synedrion in Jerusalem*, p. 97, Vienna, 1902.

W. B. S. KR.

THEOSOPHY. See CABALA.

THERAPEUTÆ (Greek, Θεραπευταί = "Worshipers of God"): A community of Jewish ascetics settled on Lake Mareotis in the vicinity of Alexandria at the time of Philo, who alone, in his work "De Vita Contemplativa," has preserved a record of their existence. The fact that the Therapeutæ are mentioned by no other writer of the time, and that they are declared by Eusebius (3d cent.) in his "Historia Ecclesiastica" (II., ch. xvi.–xvii.) to have been Christian monks, has induced Lucius, in a special work entitled "Die Therapeuten und Ihre Stellung

in der Geschichte der Askese" (1879), to attempt to prove the Christian origin and character of the Philonean work and of the "monks and nuns" described therein, after Grätz ("Gesch." 4th ed., iii. 799) had declared it to be spurious. Lucius found many followers, among whom was Schürer ("Gesch." 3d ed., iii. 535–538). His arguments, however, have been refuted by the leading authorities on Philo, viz., Massebieau ("Revue de l'Histoire des Religions," 1887, pp. 170–198, 284–319), Wendland ("Die Therapeuten," 1896), and most thoroughly and effectively by Conybeare ("Philo About the Contemplative Life," Oxford, 1895; see also Bousset, "Religion des Judenthums im Neutestamentlichen Zeitalter," 1903, pp. 443–446). Although the life of the Therapeutæ as depicted by Philo appears rather singular and strange, its Jewish character may as little be questioned as the authenticity of the Philonic work itself. The influx of many currents of thought and religious practise produced in the Jewish diaspora many forms of religious life scarcely known to the historian: several of these helped in the shaping of the Christian Church. The name "Therapeutæ" (Θεραπευταί; 'Ικεταί is another name for these ascetics) is often used by Philo for Jewish believers or worshipers of God; and it was the official title of certain religious gilds found in inscriptions, as was also the Latin name "Cultores" = "Worshipers" (see Conybeare, *l.c.* p. 293, and METUENTES). It corresponds with the Aramean "Pulḥane di-Elaha." The members of the sect seem to have branched off from the Essene brotherhood; hence also the meaning "Physicians" given to the name "Therapeutæ" (Philo, *l.c.* § 1), just as the title "Asaiai" (= "Healers") was given to the Esaioi (see ESSENES). The Therapeutæ differed, however, from the Essenes in that they lived each in a separate cell, called "monasterium," in which they spent their time in mystic devotion and ascetic practises, and particularly in the study of the Torah ("the Law and the Prophets") and in reciting the Psalms as well as hymns composed by them. While remaining in retirement they indulged in neither meat nor drink nor any other enjoyment of the flesh.

Depicted by Philo.

Mode of Life.

Like the Essenes, they offered every morning at sunrise a prayer of thanksgiving to God for the light of day as well as for the light of the Torah, and again at sunset for the withdrawal of the sunlight and for the truth hidden within the soul. In studying the Scriptures they followed the allegorical system of interpretation, for which they used also works of their own sect. They took their meals only after sunset and attended to all their bodily necessities at night, holding that the light of day was given for study solely. Some ate only twice a week; others fasted from Sabbath to Sabbath.

On the Sabbath they left their cells and assembled in a large hall for the common study of the Law as well as for their holy communion meal. The oldest member of the community began with a benediction over the Torah and then expounded the Law while all listened in silence; the others followed in turn.

Sabbath.

After this they sat down to a common meal, which was very simple, consisting of bread and salt and herbs (hyssop); and water from a spring was their drink in place of wine. The Therapeutæ, differing in this respect from the Essenes, included women members. These, though advanced in years, were regarded as pure virgins on account of their lives of abstinence and chastity; and they seem to have been helpful in nursing and educating waifs and non-Jewish children that took refuge in such Essene communities (Philo, *l.c.* § 8). For these female members a partition was made in the assembly hall, separating them from the men by a wall three to four cubits in height, so that they might listen to the discourses on the Law without infringing the rules of modesty becoming to women (comp. the "tiḳḳun gadol" in the Temple gatherings at Sukkot; Suk. v. 2); also at meals the women sat at separate tables remote from the men. Young men, but no slaves, waited at table; and probably young women at the tables of the women. They all wore white raiments like the Essenes. After the repast, passages of Scripture were explained by the presiding officer and other speakers, with special reference to the mysteries of the Law; and each of these interpretations was followed by the singing of hymns in chorus, in which both men and women invariably joined.

Of all the festivals of the year they celebrated with especial solemnity "the night of the seventh Sabbath" (Pentecost), when they ate unleavened bread in place of the two loaves of leavened bread from the new wheat offered on Pentecost in the Temple. After this they spent the whole night until sunrise in offering up praises and in songs of thanksgiving sung in chorus by men and women; the song of Moses and Miriam at the Red Sea was thus sung. The singing itself was rendered according to the laws of musical art, which seems to have been borrowed from Egyptian temples, and was then transmitted to the Christian Church (see Conybeare, *l.c.* p. 313).

Pentecost.

Whether these nocturnal celebrations took place every seventh week or only at Passover and Pentecost (and the Feast of Sukkot), as Conybeare thinks, is not made clear in Philo's description. The probability is that the Passover night gave the first impulse to such celebration (see Wisdom xviii. 9); and the custom of rendering the song of the Red Sea chorally appears to have prompted its recitation every morning in the synagogal liturgy in a manner betraying an Essene tradition. How far back the celebration of the night preceding Shabu'ot by study and song until daybreak goes may be learned from the Zohar (Emor, iii. 93), where reference is made to the custom of "the ancient Ḥasidim who spend the whole night in the study of the Law and thus adorn Israel as a bride to be joined anew to God, her bridegroom."

In no way, however, does the Philonic description bear any trace of the Christian character attributed to it by Grätz and Lucius. See also Jew. Encyc. x. 8b, *s.v.* Philo Judæus.　　　　　　　K.

THESSALONICA. See Salonica.

THESSALY: Province of northern Greece, on the Ægean Sea. It numbered Jews among its inhabitants at a very early date, although those that now reside there speak Spanish and declare they are descendants of refugees who emigrated from Spain. There are Jewish communities at Larissa, Trikala, and Volo. None of them has a rabbi; and Hebrew studies there are in a state of decay. At Larissa and Trikala religious instruction is given in Jewish public schools established under the provincial law relating to such schools; they are supported by the government. The community of Trikala, by reason of numbering (according to the census) "not more than 1,000 members," has no special school. The Jewish students finish their education in the government higher schools; and some even enter the University of Athens.

The congregations have synagogues similar to those of every community in Turkey: one story, with colored windows, and with columns in the middle which support the dukan and candlesticks. The most beautiful of these synagogues is that at Larissa, which is very large and is situated in the center of a court in which there are several "batte midrashim"; one of these serves as a library and yeshibah, where religious studies are daily pursued. The congregation of Larissa is proud of its past grandeur. Its members speak of the famous "Yeshibat Rabbanim," which was a seat of learning at which twenty to twenty-five chief rabbis studied the Talmud and wrote religious works. Of the latter some manuscripts still exist in the old library.

Larissa, which formerly possessed a great number of rich Jews, was called "The Tree of Gold." About fifty-five years ago a riot took place, the poor Jews rising up against the rich. It became so serious that many of the wealthy Israelites emigrated, which wrecked the city's prosperity. To-day its rich Jews may be counted on the fingers; and the numerous poor ones are cared for by a charitable institution. Among the philanthropic members of the congregation should be mentioned the Matalon brothers. The Greco-Turkish war of 1897 gave the finishing stroke to this already impoverished community: besides the misfortune which the Jews shared in common with the other inhabitants in having their homes destroyed and their property stolen, they were accused by slanderers of having taken part in the plundering.

The community of **Trikala,** which is younger than that of Larissa, is more prosperous, not having suffered from the ruinous consequences of the war. This community numbered among its members the richest Greek Jew, Elia Cohn, whose fortune was estimated at from five to ten million francs.

Volo possesses the youngest Jewish community in Thessaly. It was organized toward the close of the nineteenth century by Spaniards of the province, and by other Jews who came from Janina, Chalcis, and Salonica. Since its annexation to Greece the city has become the first port in Thessaly. Most of the Jews of Volo are in easy circumstances; there are hardly any poor among them. The community is the most progressive in Greece. The Jewish youth speak Greek even in their social intercourse; and they have organized a club, called "The Future," in con nection with which instructive lectures are delivered; and work is undertaken having for its aim the building up of the community. This club was presided over by Solomon Daffas, formerly director of a school of the Alliance Israélite Universelle. The Jews of Volo have organized also a Philharmonic Society.

s.   M. C.

THEUDAS : 1. Pseudo-Messiah, who appeared during the consulate of Cuspius Fadus and succeeded in winning a large number of adherents. In proof of his Messianic mission he is said to have promised to lead his followers across the Jordan after dividing its waters simply by his word. Regarding this as indicative of open rebellion against Rome, Cuspius sent a division of cavalry against Theudas and his followers, who were almost entirely annihilated (comp. Acts v. 36). Theudas was decapitated, and his head was carried to Jerusalem as a trophy of victory.

BIBLIOGRAPHY: Josephus, *Ant.* xx. 5, § 1; Eusebius, *Hist. Eccl.* II. ii.; Schmidt, in Herzog-Plitt, *Real-Encyc.* xv. 553–557; Klein, in Schenkel, *Bibel-Lexikon*, v. 510–513; Schürer, *Gesch.* i. 566, and note 6.

2. Expounder of the Law; flourished in Rome during the Hadrianic persecutions. He aided with generous gifts of money the teachers of the Law who had suffered from these persecutions, and arranged with the Roman communities that the taxes formerly paid to the Temple in Jerusalem should be used for the schools, which otherwise would have been without any source of support (Yer. M. Ḳ. 81a).

Theudas introduced into Rome the practise of eating on the eve of Passover a lamb prepared in accordance with the custom observed in Jerusalem with regard to the sacrificial lamb (Pes. 53a, b; Ber. 19a; Beẓah 23a). According to tradition, this so enraged the Palestinian codifiers that they sent him the following message: "If you were not Theudas we would excommunicate you." In his capacity as archisynagogue it was Theudas' duty to deliver a sermon in the synagogue each Saturday. One of these sermons has been preserved, in which he emphatically asserts that it is the duty of a Jew to suffer martyrdom rather than abandon his faith (Pes. 53b; Midr. Teh. to Ps. xxviii.).

In the Talmud, Theudas is once erroneously mentioned in connection with Simeon ben Sheṭaḥ—a mistake which has been pointed out by Bacher. The oldest Mishnah teacher to mention Theudas is R. Jose.

BIBLIOGRAPHY: Brüll, *Jahrb.* viii. 27; Bacher, *Ag. Tan.* ii. 560; Vogelstein and Rieger, *Gesch. der Juden in Rom*, i. 30, 70, 108 *et seq.*, 176.
W. B.   S. O.

THIEF. See THEFT AND STOLEN GOODS.

THIENGEN. See TYPOGRAPHY.

THISTLES. See THORNS AND THISTLES.

THOMAS, EMILE (EMIL TOBIAS): German actor; born at Berlin Nov. 24, 1836. Thomas has had a most varied career. He made his début in 1852 with the company of Pitterlin, which traversed the Erzgebirge, Saxony. The plays were ultrasensational—"Der Wahnsinnige," "Die Giftmischerin,"

and "Die Grabesbraut." Thomas received no monetary compensation, being paid in food; and the arrangement lasted for three years. He then obtained engagements in Görlitz, Leipsic, Cologne, Danzig, and Breslau. In the last-named city, Dreichmann, director of the Friedrich-Wilhelmstädtische Theater, Berlin, saw the young actor and engaged him for his house. Thomas made his début there Dec. 3, 1861, as the *Baker's Boy* in "Hermann und Dorothea." So great was his success that he was made stage-manager. In this capacity he produced Offenbach's "Die Schöne Helene" (himself playing *Kalchas*) and Salingré's "Pechschulze." In 1866 Chéri Maurice engaged him for the Thalia Theater, Hamburg, where he remained until 1875, when he became manager of the Woltersdorfftheater, Berlin. Two years later he resigned and went on a starring tour which lasted a year; he then joined the Ringtheater, Vienna. After the destruction of this house in 1881, Thomas appeared at the Wallnertheater, Berlin. In 1886 he went with his wife, Betty Thomas-Damhofer, to the United States, scoring financial and artistic successes.

On his return to Germany in 1887, Thomas assumed the management of the Centraltheater, Berlin, which he renamed the "Thomas-Theater"; but his direction was most unsuccessful, and he was forced to relinquish it. Since then he has played in the principal theaters of Germany and Austria. Since 1902 he has acted at the Metropoltheater, Hamburg. His best rôles are: *Striese* in "Der Raub der Sabinerinnen"; *Kälbchen* in "1733 Thaler, 22½ Silbergroschen"; and *Geier* in "Der Flotte Bursche."

BIBLIOGRAPHY: *Das Geistige Berlin*, p. 540; Eisenberg, *Biog. Lex.*
s.   E. Ms.

THOMAS, FATHER. See DAMASCUS AFFAIR.

THOMASHEFSKI, BORIS : Judæo-German actor; born at Kiev May 30, 1866. He went to New York to seek work in 1881 and soon organized a Jewish troop which played in Turn Hall, Fourth street. Three years later he removed to Chicago, where he became a theatrical manager. In 1893 he settled in New York, and became one of the leading Yiddish actors. In 1905 he was lessee and manager of the People's Theater, in 1923 of the Thomashefski Theater, W. 44th St., both in that city.

Thomashefski plays the chief character in almost all the pieces produced at his theater, most of which are written by Latteiner. He has himself written some Judæo-German plays and published a collection of witty sayings (in "Theatre Journal," 1903–1905, i., ii.).

BIBLIOGRAPHY: *American Jewish Year Book*, 5665 (1905), p. 200; H. Hapgood, *The Spirit of the Ghetto*, pp. 139–140, New York, 1902.
A.   M. Sel.

THORN: Town of Poland formerly belonging to West Prussia, founded in 1233 by the Knights of the Teutonic Order. Jews were not permitted to dwell there under the knights; and after the Polish government took possession of the town, in 1453, they were admitted only occasionally. Several Jews were living there about the middle of the seventeenth century; and in 1749 they were allowed to open a school. In 1766 all the Jews except six were expelled; but they seem to have returned in the following years. In 1774 and 1779 the Jews were again driven out; returning, they were once more ordered to leave in 1793, when Prussia took possession of the town; and, though they succeeded in obtaining a respite, they were expelled in 1797. Many Jews settled gradually in the town when it became part of the duchy of Warsaw, after the Peace of Tilsit; according to the town records, they stole in during the French occupation. In 1823 the community numbered 52 families, comprising 248 individuals.

The first rabbi was Samuel Heilmann Leyser of Lissa, who seems to have settled in the town toward the end of the eighteenth century; he officiated without remuneration down to 1847. His successors were: Dr. Krakauer (1847–57); Dr. Engelbert (1857–62); Dr. Rahmer (1862–67); Dr. Oppenheim (1869–91); and Dr. I. Rosenberg, the later incumbent, who became rabbi in 1892. The following scholars have lived at Thorn: Ẓebi Hirsch Kalischer (d. 1875), author of "Derishat Ẓiyyon," "Emunah Ramah," and "Sefer ha-Berit 'al ha-Torah"; his son Louis Kalischer, author of "Ḳol Yehudah"; and Isaac Miesses, author of "Ẓofnat Pa'neah" and other works.

The community possesses a synagogue, built in 1847; a home for the aged, organized in 1892; a religious school, a loan society, a ḥebra ḳaddisha, and literary society. In 1921 the Jews of Thorn numbered about 1,500 in a total population of 39,419. The Jewish inhabitants of the suburbs of Podgorz and Mocker, and of several neighboring villages, are members of the Thorn congregation.

BIBLIOGRAPHY: Töppen, *Acten der Ständetage Preussens*, Leipsic, 1878–86; Wernicke, *Gesch. Thorns*; *Mittheilungen des Coppernicusvereins zu Thorn*, No. viii., Thorn, 1842.
s.　　　　　　　　　　　　　　　　　　I. R.

THORNS AND THISTLES: The desert flora of Palestine is unusually rich in thorns and thistles, containing a whole series of acanthaceous shrubs and various thistles, including Acanthus, Carduus (thistle), Centaurea Calcitrapa (star-thistle), Cirsium acarna, Linn. (horse-thistle), Cnicus benedictus, Linn. (blessed thistle), Cynara Syriaca, Linn. (cardoon), Echinops (globe-thistle), Eryngium nitraria, Noea, Notobasis Syriaca, Linn. (Syrian thistle), Ononis antiquorum, Linn. (tall rest-harrow; var. leiosperma, Post), Onopordon (down-thistle), Phæopappus scoparius, Sieb., Silybum Marianum, Linn. (milk-thistle), Tribulus terrestris, Linn. (land-caltrops), and others, some of them in many subspecies. All these plants were very troublesome to the farmer (Prov. xxiv. 31), who frequently set fire to his fields to get rid of them (Isa. x. 17), while the Prophets threatened the people with a plague of briers and thistles (Isa. v. 6; Jer. xii. 13). The tyrant is compared to the useless bramble (Judges ix. 14); and King Amaziah is likened to the thistle (II Kings xiv. 9). Instead of fruit the earth is to bring forth "thorns and thistles" (Gen. iii. 18), which must, therefore, be edible, and which are considered by the Midrash to be artichokes.

Many names for these plants are found in the Bible as well as in post-Biblical literature. Acanthaceous trees and shrubs, some of them admitting of classification, constitute the first group, which includes: אטד, Bible and Mishnah (also Assyrian, Phenician, and Aramaic) = Lycium Europæum, Linn. (not Rhamnus), box-thorn; סנה, Bible, Mishnah, and Aramaic = Rubus sanctus, Schreb., blackberry; שטה = Acacia; עוזרד, Mishnah, and תולשי, Talmud = Cratægus Azarolus, Linn., hawthorn; רימין, Mishnah, and כנרא, Talmud = Zizyphus lotus, Lam., jujube, and Zizyphus spina-Christi, Linn., Christ's-thorn; שיזפין, Mishnah, and שיסקי, Talmud = Zizyphus vulgaris, Lam., common jujube.

The second group comprises acanthaceous or prickly herbs, shrubs, and nettles: נעצוץ (?), Bible, הינה, Mishnah, and הינתא, Talmud (Assyrian, "egu" [?]) = Alhagi Maurorum, DC., alhagi; חריע and קוץ, Mishnah, מוריקא and מוריקא, Talmud = Carthamus tinctorius, Linn., safflower; דרדר, Bible, and חיזרא, Talmud = Centaurea Calcitrapa, Linn., star-thistle; חוח (?), Bible, היזמא, Mishnah and Talmud = Echinops spinosus, Linn., or Echinops viscosus, DC., echinops (?); הרחבינה = Eryngium Creticum, Lam., button-snakeroot; קינרס, כנגר = Cynara Scolymus, Linn., artichoke; עכבית = Cynara Syriaca, Boiss., and Cynara Cardunculus, Linn., cardoon (the heads of which are well described by Rashi in his commentary on Ps. lxxxiii. 14); שמיר = Paliurus aculeatus, Linck., garland-thorn; ברקנים (?), Bible = Phæopappus scoparius, Sieb., phæopappus; הדק = Solanum coagulans, Forsk., nightshade; קמש, סרפד (?), Bible, and קרצובא, Talmud = Urtica urens, Linn., nettle.

General terms, some of them applied also to thorns, are חוח, סיר, צנים, קוץ, שכים, and שית in the Bible, and עצבנית, כובא, יערא, חוח, הובאי, and קוץ in the Mishnah and Talmud.

s.　　　　　　　　　　　　　　　　　　I. Lö.

THRASHING-FLOOR. See AGRICULTURE.

THREE. See NUMBERS AND NUMERALS.

THRESHOLD: In early times the threshold had a special sanctity; and that of the Temple was a marked spot, indicating specific taboos (see I Sam. v. 4 *et seq.*; comp. Zeph. i. 9). There were special keepers (A. V. "porters") of the threshold (II. Kings xxii. 4; I Chron. ix. 22; II Chron. xxiii. 4; Jer. xxxv. 4). There is a wide-spread custom of making family sacrifices at the threshold in addition to those at the hearth. Herodotus reports this of the Egyptians (ii. 48). Trumbull suggests that there is a specific reference to the threshold in Ex. xii. 22 (LXX.), in connection with the institution of the Passover. Even to the present day it is considered unlucky to tread on the threshold. He suggests also that the word "pesaḥ," or "passover," means a "leaping over" the threshold, after it has been sanctified with the blood of the threshold-covenant. The threshold of Dagon's temple was evidently sacred in this way; and it has been suggested by Cheyne that I Kings xviii. 20–21 should be rendered "How long will ye leap over both thresholds?" (that is, worship both Baal and YHWH).

BIBLIOGRAPHY: H. Clay Trumbull, *Threshold Covenant*, Philadelphia, 1896.
J.

THRONE: 1. A royal seat, or chair of state. The king sits "upon the throne of his kingdom" (Deut. xvii. 18). Pharaoh delegated full power to

Joseph to rule over Egypt; "only in the throne will I be greater than thou" (Gen. xli. 40). The royal throne is sometimes designated as "the throne of the kings" (Jer. lii. 32). The most magnificent throne was that of SOLOMON (see JEW. ENCYC. xi. 441 et seq.; J. S. Kolbo made a model of Solomon's throne and exhibited it in New York city in 1888). The throne, like the crown, was a symbol of sovereign power and dignity. It was also the tribunal, the "throne of judgment" (Prov. xx. 8), where the king decided matters of law and disputes among his subjects. Thus "throne" is synonymous with "justice."

2. The Throne, the abode of God, known as "Kisse ha-Kabod" (the Throne of Glory), from which God manifests His majesty and glory. Micaiah "saw the Lord sitting on his throne, and all the hosts of heaven standing by him on his right hand and on his left" (I Kings xxii. 19; compare the vision of Isaiah [vi. 1] with that of Ezekiel [x. 1]). The throne of God is Heaven (Isa. lxvi. 1); in future it will be Jerusalem (Jer. iii. 17), and even the Sanctuary (Jer. xvii. 12). Thus the idea of the majestic manifestation of God gradually crystallized in the cabalistic expression "koah ha-zimzum" (the power of concentration). God's Throne is the symbol of righteousness; "justice and judgment are the habitation of thy throne" (Ps. lxxxix. 15 [A. V. 14]).

The Throne of Glory is an important feature in the Cabala. It is placed at the highest point of the universe (Ḥag. 12b); and is of the same color as the sky—purple-blue, like the "sapphire stone" which Ezekiel saw and which had previously been perceived by the Israelites (Ex. xxiv. 10; Soṭah 17a). Like the Torah, it was created before the world (Pes. 54a). R. Eliezer said that the souls of the righteous are concealed under the Throne (Shab. 152b). When Moses ascended to heaven to receive the Torah the angels objected, whereupon God told him to hold on to the Throne and defend his action (Shab. 88b). It is asserted that the likeness of Jacob is engraved on the Throne of Glory (Zohar, Wayiggash, p. 211a). For the throne of Elijah see ELIJAH'S CHAIR.

J.   J. D. E.

THUNDER: The sound that follows lightning. The proper Hebrew term for it is רעם (Ps. lxxvii. 19 et passim; Job xxvi. 14; Isa. xxix. 6), but it is often rendered in the Bible by קול, plural קולות (= "voice," "voices"), the singular being always followed by יהוה (= "the voice of YHWH"; Ps. xxx. 3; Isa. xxx. 30). In the plural, with the exception of Ex. ix. 28, where it is followed by אלהים, the word "God" is omitted but understood (ib. ix. 23 and elsewhere).

Thunder is one of the phenomena in which the presence of YHWH is manifested; and it is also one of His instruments in chastising His enemies. According to Ps. lxxvii. 18–19, it was a thunder-cloud that came between the Israelites and the Egyptians when the former were about to cross the Red Sea (comp. Ex. xiv. 20). The hail in the seventh plague of Pharaoh was accompanied by thunder (ib. ix. 23 et passim). The Law was given to the Israel-

ites from Sinai amid thunder and lightning (ib. xix. 16). In the battle between the Israelites and the Philistines in the time of Samuel, a thunder-storm decided the issue in favor of the Israelites (I Sam. vii. 10; Ecclus. [Sirach] xlvi. 17). Later, when the Israelites asked Samuel for a king he prayed to God for a thunder-storm that the petitioners might be overawed (I Sam. xii. 18). The declaration of Jeremiah (Jer. x. 13): "When he uttereth a voice there is a multitude of waters," probably refers to thunder. The most poetical description of a thunder-storm occurs in Ps. xxix. 3 et seq. Thunder following lightning is spoken of in Job xxxvii. 3–4; and in two other passages they are mentioned together (ib. xxviii. 26, xxxviii. 25). The separation of the water from the dry land at the time of the Creation (comp. Gen. i. 9) is said in Ps. civ. 7 to have been accomplished by the voice of God, which probably refers to thunder. The clattering noise of battle is likened to thunder (Job xxxix. 25). Thunder is metaphorically used to denote the power of God (ib. xxvi. 14). The goods of the unjust disappear in a noise like thunder (Ecclus. [Sirach] xl. 13). In the ritual is included a special benediction to be recited on hearing thunder (see LIGHTNING, BENEDICTION ON).

s.   M. SEL.

THURGAU. See SWITZERLAND.

TIAO KIU KIAOU. See CHINA.

TIBBON. See IBN TIBBON.

TIBERIAS: City founded by Herod Antipas in the year 26 C.E., and named in honor of the emperor Tiberius; situated on the western shore of Lake Gennesaret, near certain hot springs, in the most beautiful region of Galilee. The population of the city was very heterogeneous, thus giving rise to various stories. For example, one legend was to the effect that after the building of the city had been begun human bones were found, whence the conclusion was drawn that the site must once have been a burial-place; so that the whole city was declared unclean. The pious were accordingly forbidden to dwell there, since the merest contact with graves made one unclean for seven days (Num. xix. 16; Oh. xvii., xviii.). Herod, being determined to people the city at all hazards, was, therefore, obliged to induce beggars, adventurers, and foreigners to come there; and in some cases he had even to use violence to carry out his will. The majority of the inhabitants, nevertheless, were Jews.

Founded by Herod Antipas.

The city had its own government, with a council (βουλή) of 500 members at the head, the archon (ἄρχων) being the presiding officer. From this council was chosen a board of ten members called "the ten elders" (δέκα πρῶτοι), their chief function being the punctual levying of the taxes, for which their own means were security. There were also hyparchs and an "agronomos" at the head (comp. Pauly-Wissowa, "Real-Encyc." s.v.). Since Tiberias was the capital of Galilee, it was ruled by Herod until he was exiled to Lyons (France) in 39. It then came under Agrippa I., in whose possession

Government.

it remained until his death in 44, after which it was subject directly to Rome. It was the capital of Galilee until 61, when Nero gave it to Agrippa II., and thus detached it from Galilee, since that province did not belong to him.

When, in 66, the great revolution raged through the whole of Palestine, the inhabitants were divided into three factions: (1) the party on the side of Agrippa and the Romans; (2) the great mass of the poor, who were partizans of the rebellion; and (3) the neutrals, including the historian Justus of Tiberias, who were neither friendly to Rome nor eager for the revolution. The revolutionists, headed by Jesus ben Zappha or Zopha, archon of the city, soon gained control; but the Roman faction would not give way. When, therefore, John of Giscala lodged a complaint in the Sanhedrin at Jerusalem against Josephus, who was then at Tiberias, the council sent to the city an embassy of four men with 2,500 troops. Josephus at first sought to annul the decision of the Sanhedrin; but his efforts proved unsuccessful, and, compelling the embassy to return to Jerusalem, he subdued the revolutionary party, whereupon the Roman sympathizers appealed to Agrippa for aid, which he refused to grant. After Vespasian had conquered the greater part of Galilee, however, Tiberias voluntarily opened its gates to him, and favor was shown the inhabitants for Agrippa's sake.

Of the famous buildings in Tiberias the most prominent were the royal palace (which was stormed and destroyed in the Jewish war on **Buildings.** account of its pictures), the stadium, a synagogue ($\pi\rho o\sigma\varepsilon\upsilon\chi\acute{\eta}$), and a great assembly hall ($\mu\acute{\varepsilon}\gamma\iota\sigma\tau o\nu$ $o\emph{\i}\kappa\eta\mu\alpha$), while after the close of the war pagan temples, including the Adrianeum ('A$\delta\rho\iota\alpha\nu\varepsilon\emph{\i}o\nu$), were built there as well as in other cities. The baths of Tiberias, called "demosin" or "demosin de-Ṭebarya" ($\delta\eta\mu\acute{o}\sigma\iota\alpha$), were famous as early as the third century (Yer. Ber. ii. 5, 3; iii. 6, 3). The synagogues of the city were the Kifra (Yer. Meg. i. 1) and the Kenishta 'Attiḳta de-Serongin (Yer. Kil. ix. 5), while the "castle of Tiberias," mentioned in Yer. 'Ab. Zarah iii. 1, appears to have been the building which Josephus fortified to defend the city. A saying of Raba or of Abaye, "I know this or that halakah as well as Ben 'Azzai [a tanna of the early part of the second century] knows the streets of Tiberias" ('Er. 29a; Ḳid. 20a;

Soṭah 45a; 'Ar. 30b), shows that Jewish scholars lived in the city, at least temporarily, very soon after its foundation, although there is no mention of a definite Jewish settlement there until the second half of the second century.

After Simeon ben Yoḥai had fled from the persecutions of the Romans, and had lived in hiding for many years, thus injuring his health, he bathed in the springs of Tiberias and recovered. He seems, in his gratitude, to have declared either a part or the whole of Tiberias to be clean (Yer. Sheb. ix. 38d; Gen. R. lxxix.; Eccl. R. on x. 8; Esther R. i. 9; Shab. 35b; 'Ab. Zarah 10a; Grätz, "Gesch." iv. 208, 473). Judah ha-Nasi also resided there (R. H. 31b; comp. Rashi, s.v. "Bet She'arim"); and from the time when Johanan b. Nappaḥa settled in Tiberias (Yer. Sheb. ix. 1; Beẓah i. 1) the city became the center of scholarship, so that other academies could not compare with it. Even R. Abbahu sent his son from Cæsarea to Tiberias to study (Yer. Pes. iii. 7). It was, moreover, the last city in which a Sanhedrin held sittings (R. H. 51b; Yer. Pes. iv. 2).

During the persecutions in the reigns of the emperors Constantius and Gallus the Tiberian scholars decided to intercalate a month in the calendar for the year 353; but fear of the Romans led to the substitution of "Rakkath" (Josh. xix. 35) for "Tiberias" in the letter which conveyed the information to Raba at Maḥuza (Sanh. 12a). The sessions of the scholars were held in a grotto near Tiberias, and only by the flickering of torches was it possible to distinguish between night and day (Gen. R. xxxi.). In several places in the Talmud, e.g., in Meg. 6a, the identity of Tiberias with Rakkath is established.

Jewish School-Children at Tiberias.
(From a photograph by E. N. Adler.)

During Persecutions.

Even in the sixth century Tiberias was still the seat of religious learning; so that Bishop Simeon of Bet-Arsham urged the Christians of Palestine to seize the leaders of Judaism in Tiberias, to put them to the rack, and to compel them to command the Jewish king, Dhu Nuwas, to desist from persecuting the Christians in Najran (Assemani, "Bibliotheca Orientalis Clementino-Vaticana," i. 379).

In 614 a monk of Mt. Sinai went to Tiberias to become a Jew. He received the name of Abraham, and married a Jewess of that city (Antiochius, "Homilia Octoginta-Quarta," in Migne, "Patrologia Græca," xii. 265). In the ninth century the grammarians and Masorites Moses and Aaron ben Asher lived at Tiberias, which was then called Mu'izziyyah, in honor of the Fatimite calif Mu'izz. The system of Hebrew punctuation still in use originated in Tiberias and is accordingly called the Tiberian system (comp. Grätz, *l.c.* 3d ed., v., note 23, ii., and the remarks of Halberstam).

At the beginning of the twelfth century the Jewish community in Tiberias numbered about fifty families; and at that time the best manuscripts of the Torah were said to be found there. According to some sources the grave of Moses Maimonides is at Tiberias; but this statement is of very doubtful accuracy (see Conforte, "Ḳore ha-Dorot," p. 13a; "Sefer Yuḥasin," ed. Filipowski, p. 131b).

In the sixteenth century Joseph ben Ardut, aided by the riches of Doña Gracia and by the daily remittances of 60 aspers sent him by order of Sultan Sulaiman, undertook to rebuild the city of Tiberias,

BIBLIOGRAPHY: Robinson, *Researches,* iii. 500-525; Sepp, *Jerusalem und das Heilige Land,* ii. 188-209; *Z. D. P. V.* 1886, ix. 81-103; Kaminka, *Studien zur Geschichte Galiläas,* Berlin, 1889; Schürer, *Gesch.* 3d ed., Index, *s.v.;* Grätz, *Gesch.* iii. 269 *et seq.;* iv. 181 *et seq.;* vi. 169, 242 ix. 398; H. T. de Graaf, *De Joodsche Wetgelurden in Tiberias van 70-400 n. C.,* Gröningen, 1902; Neubauer, *G. T.* pp, 25, 35, 208 *et seq.*

E. C.   S. O.

TIBERIAS, LAKE. See CHINNERETH.

TIBERIUS JULIUS ALEXANDER. See ALEXANDER, TIBERIUS JULIUS.

TIBNI: One of the rulers of the kingdom of Israel during the interregnum between Zimri and Omri; son of Ginath. When Zimri, after a reign of seven days, had ended his life, the people of Israel were divided into two factions, one siding with Omri, and the other with Tibni. Omri's followers gained the upper hand; and, finally, Tibni having died, Omri was declared king (I Kings xvi. 21-22). From a comparison of verses 15 and 23 of the

VIEW OF TIBERIAS SHOWING THE TOMB OF RABBI MEÏR.
(From a photograph by the American Colony at Jerusalem.)

and to allow only Jews to reside there. The old superstition was revived, however, that the Jewish religion would conquer all others when Tiberias was rebuilt, whereupon the workmen refused to work and had to be forced to do so. After a year the city was completed, and Joseph wished to introduce the breeding of silkworms and the manufacture of wool (Charière, "Négociation," ii. 736; Gratiani, "De Bello Cypro," p. 492, note). The first Jewish immigrants to the new city went thither from the Pontifical States, as a result of a papal bull; and they were aided by Joseph Nasi. Their numbers and fortunes are alike unknown.

Don Joseph Nasi.

In 1837 an earthquake destroyed most of the city, while in 1865 and 1866 the ravages of the cholera forced the leaders of the community to apply to Europe for aid, appeals being printed in nearly all the Jewish weekly periodicals. Conditions have much improved, however; and since the year 1889 the community has had its own physician. The cemetery is situated on the ruins of the old city. The Jews of Tiberias number about 2,000 in a total population of 3,600.

chapter just cited, it appears that Tibni was regent over half the kingdom of Israel for a period of four years. According to the Septuagint (*ad loc.*), Tibni had a brother named Joram, who seconded him in the dispute over the throne and who died at the same time as himself, probably at the hands of Omri's party.

J.   M. SEL.

TIEN-TSIN: Commercial city of China. Its Jewish inhabitants number about 150, most of whom are Russian and Polish. They have not organized as a community and hold divine services only during the penitential season, when private halls are used and Sefer Torahs are brought from Shanghai. In 1902 J. Dietrich purchased a piece of land and presented it to the Jewish inhabitants for burial purposes. In 1904 a branch of the Anglo-Jewish Association was formed, of which Dr. M. Linscer was president. The Tien-Tsin Jews are mainly merchants and hotel-keepers.

J.   N. E. B. E.

TIETZ, HERMANN: German rabbi; born at Birnbaum, Posen, Germany, Sept. 3, 1834, and edu-

cated at the University of Berlin (Ph. D. Halle). He was rabbi in Schrimm, and since 1888 he has been a "Stiftrabbiner" and teacher in the bet ha-midrash at Inowrazlaw. He has published "Das Hohe Lied," translated in verse, and with notes according to the Midrash (Berlin, 1878), and "Megillat Eka," with a metrical translation and a Hebrew commentary, under the title "Zikron Yehudah" (Schrimm, 1881).
s.　　　　　　　　　　　　　　F. T. H.

TIFLIS. See CAUCASUS.

TIGLATH-PILESER (Hebrew, תגלת־פלאסר, and a corrupt form, תלגת־פלנסר, in I Chron. v. 6, 26; II Chron. xxviii. 20; Assyrian, "Tukulti-apil-e-šar-ra " = " my help is the son of Ešarra "): King of Assyria from 747 to 727 B.C.; designated by modern Oriental historians as Tiglath-pileser III. He first appears under the name "Pul" (II Kings xv. 19; comp. I Chron. v. 26), the proper form of which is "Pulu," as is seen in the list of Babylonian kings. When he assumed the crown over Assyria he seems to have called himself Tukulti-pal-Ešar-ra after the great ruler of the same name in the twelfth century.

Tiglath-pileser left several important inscriptions of his reign; but these were badly broken when discovered. Upon his accession he inaugurated a new policy for the government and administration of Assyria. Former kings had maintained by military force the union of the so-called empire; the new policy established a method of organization which more closely united the central and provincial sections of the government: systems of transportation and transplantation of strong but rebellious subjects minimized dangers that had wrecked other governments. This was the method pursued by Sargon at Samaria, by Sennacherib, and by other rulers down into Persian times.

Tiglath-pileser's first campaign into the west country took place in 743–742, when he entered northern Syria. While here he received tribute from Rezin of Damascus and Hiram of Tyre. A two-year siege was necessary to reduce to complete submission the plucky little city of Arpad, in 740 (comp. Isa. x. 9; II Kings xix. 13). The very next year he seems to have clashed with the interests of Azariah (Uzziah), King of Judah, far in the north (comp. II Kings xiv. 28) and to have established Assyrian sovereignty there. Either in this or in the following year Menahem (II Kings xv. 19, 20), king of northern Israel, purchased his throne of the Assyrian ruler.

Not until 734 was Tiglath-pileser's presence again required in the west. Pekah, who had secured by strategy and tragedy the throne of northern Israel, formed a league with Rezin of Damascus to withstand any further assumption of sovereignty over Israel and Syria by the power centered on the Tigris. Together they besieged Ahaz at Jerusalem, either to force him to join the anti-Assyrian coalition or to put a man of their own choice on the throne. Ahaz in desperation appealed to Tiglath-pileser for help. The Assyrian king made a dash for Damascus and laid siege to it. In the meantime he ravaged northern Israel (comp. II Kings xv. 29) and other territory all the way to Philistia. In 732 Damascus fell (comp. Isa. viii. 4; II Kings xvi. 9). At this time

XII.—10

apparently Ahaz, among a number of petty kings, appeared within Damascus before the throne of the great conqueror and paid the price of submission. Soon after this event, probably, Tiglath-pileser incited or encouraged Hoshea to slay Pekah, the unyielding king of northern Israel. Hoshea was rewarded by being put in authority over this Assyrian province; and Tiglath-pileser retired to the east. In 728 he became master of Babylon, and died the following year.
j.　　　　　　　　　　　　　　I. M. P.

TIGRIS (Hebrew, חדקל; Aramaic and Talmudic, דגלת; the modern **Dijlah**): One of the four streams mentioned in Gen. ii. 14 as watering the Garden of Eden, and described, from the standpoint of Palestine, as flowing "in front of Assyria" (R. V.). The Tigris has its source in several springs in Mount Ararat, not far from the head-waters of the Euphrates. Near one of these springs the figures of Sardanapalus and Tiglath-pileser III. are found carved in the rock. After flowing a short distance the river receives the waters of several mountain brooks from the east; and at Diarbekr it is already a fairly large stream. South of Mosul it is navigable for rafts, and at Bagdad it carries boats, while at Korna it unites with the Euphrates to form the Shaṭṭ al-'Arab, which empties into the Persian Gulf. Its chief period of rise occurs, opposite Mosul, at the time of the melting of the snow (Ecclus. [Sirach] xxiv. 25), when it devastates the surrounding country. Hence, even in antiquity it was necessary to dig transverse canals in various places to carry off the superfluous water, which is whitish in color and is famed for its potability among those who live in the vicinity and who are accustomed to it. The river contains great numbers of fish. The Tigris is referred to in only one other place in the Bible, namely, Dan. x. 4, where in the English version the name is transliterated simply "Hiddekel."

The Targum and the Talmud term it the Diglat, the earlier form of the name. In answer to the question why this river was called also Hiddekel, R. Ashi replied that it was on account of its sharpness and swiftness, the word חדקל being etymologized as a compound of חד ("sharp," "swift") and קל ("light," "quick"; Ber. 59a). Neubauer proposed to separate the name into חד or חין and דקל ("the swiftly running Diklah"). In the Talmud the water of the river is considered to be both quickening for the mind and healthful for the body on account of its lightness (ib.). It was also held to be one of the oldest rivers; and when a Jew saw its waters from the bridge Bostane he was enjoined to recite the blessing "Blessed be He who hath made the work of Creation" (ib.; Yeb. 121a).

From Bagdad to Apameia the river formed the boundary of Babylon (Ḳid. 71b).

BIBLIOGRAPHY: McClintock and Strong, Cyc. iv. 232, x. 403; Herzog-Hauck, Real-Encyc. xv. 662; Nöldeke, in Schenkel, Bibellexicon, v. 536 et seq.; Friedrich Delitzsch, Wo Lag das Paradies? Index, Leipsic, 1881; Neubauer, G. T. pp. 334–337, Paris, 1868; S. Löwisohn, Meḥḳere Ereẓ, pp. 136–137, Vienna, 1819.
s.　　　　　　　　　　　　　　S. O.

TIKTIN: A Silesian family of rabbis originating from Tiktin, a town in Poland.

Abraham ben Gedaliah Tiktin: German rabbi; born at Schwersenz, Posen; died at Breslau Dec. 27, 1820. In 1811 he was appointed rabbi at Glogau, and five years later, by a royal rescript of Sept. 5, he became chief district rabbi at Breslau, where he officiated until his death. He was the author of several works, although only one appeared in print, namely, "Petaḥ ha-Bayit" (Dyhernfurth, 1820), novellæ on the fourth part of the Shulḥan 'Aruk.

Abraham Tiktin.
(From an old print.)

At Tiktin's funeral Rabbis Jacob of Lissa, Moses Kronik, and Solomon Plessner delivered sermons, all of which were published.

s.   S. O.

Gedaliah Tiktin: German rabbi; born about 1808; died at Breslau Aug. 8, 1886. Like his father, Solomon Tiktin, whom he succeeded in the rabbinate of Breslau in 1843, Gedaliah was the champion of Orthodox Judaism. The war which had been carried on for years between the Orthodox and Reform parties, headed respectively by Solomon Tiktin and Abraham Geiger, was continued after the former's death. The Reform party endeavored to influence the German government to recognize Geiger as rabbi of Breslau; but, owing to Tiktin's personal merit, King Frederick William IV. confirmed him in office, and, later, even conferred on him the title of "Königlicher Landesrabbiner." It was not until after Geiger's death that Tiktin and Joël, Geiger's successor, came to an understanding in order to maintain peace in the Jewish community of Breslau. Even after his confirmation by the king, Tiktin had not exercised his power with regard to the slaughterers ("shoḥaṭim"), but had contented himself with abstaining for several years from eating meat.

Tiktin was known also for his charitable activity during the forty-three years of his rabbinate; and there was hardly any charitable institution of which he was not a member. In 1870 he received the decoration of the Order of the Red Eagle in recognition of services rendered by him to the sick and wounded during the Franco-German war of 1870–71. Special courtesies were paid to him by the German government on account of his weekly visits to the Jewish prisoners.

Tiktin was the author of a pamphlet entitled "Beitrag zur Bearbeitung der von Seiten der Behörde . . . Gerichteten, den Jüdischen Kultus Betreffenden Fragen" (Breslau, 1843).

BIBLIOGRAPHY: *Allg. Zeit. des Jud.* 1886, p. 554; Fürst, *Bibl. Jud.* iii. 431; *Ha-Zefirah*, xiii., No. 106.

Solomon Tiktin: German rabbi; born at Glogau; died in Breslau March 20, 1843; son of Abraham Tiktin. He was a prominent champion of Orthodox Judaism; and some idea of his anti-Reform activity may be gathered from the writings of his opponent, A. Geiger. Tiktin became rabbi at Breslau in 1824. In 1836 he prohibited the printing in Breslau of Moses Brück's "Die Reform des Judenthums." But the real war between Tiktin and the Reform party began when Geiger presented himself as a candidate for the position of second rabbi ("Rabbinatsassessor" or "dayyan") of Breslau. Geiger was invited to preach in Breslau on July 21, 1838; but Tiktin is said to have applied to the police to prevent Geiger from doing so. In 1842 Tiktin published his two pamphlets, "Darlegung des Sachverhältnisses in Seiner Hiesigen Rabbinats-Angelegenheit" and "Entgegnung auf den Bericht des Ober-Vorsteher-Collegiums der Hiesigen Israeliten-Gemeinde an die Mitglieder," in which he accused Geiger of having deliberately planned the destruction of the foundations of Judaism. Tiktin insisted that Geiger should not be present either at a divorce or at a ḥaliẓah ceremony, thus denying him recognition as a rabbinical authority.

BIBLIOGRAPHY: A. Geiger, *Nachgelassene Schriften*, i. 52 et seq.; idem, in *Der Israelit*, 1843, p. 64; E. Schreiber, *Abraham Geiger*, pp. 20 et seq., Spokane, 1892.
s.   M. SEL.

TIKTINER, JUDAH LÖB BEN SIMḤAH: Russian rabbi of the eighteenth century. He officiated as ab bet din in Zagora, and later was a resident of Wilna. Tiktiner was the author of "Shalme Simḥah" (2 vols., Wilna, 1806), containing novellæ on the halakot of Asher ben Jehiel, preceded by a presentation of various basal principles of the Talmud, as well as of various casuistic writings. The work is, however, incomplete, extending only as far as the treatise Ta'anit.

BIBLIOGRAPHY: Steinschneider, *Cat. Bodl.* col. 1373; Benjacob, *Ozar ha-Sefarim*, p. 589.
E. C.   S. O.

TIKTINER, REBECCA BAT MEÏR: Austrian authoress of the sixteenth century; flourished at Prague, where she died, apparently in 1550. She wrote two works: (1) "Meneḳet Ribḳah" (Prague, 1609; Cracow, 1618), divided into seven "gates," treating of a housewife's duties, and containing various Talmudic and Midrashic anecdotes; (2) "Simḥat Torah Lied" (Prague, n.d.), a poem for the Simḥat Torah festival.

BIBLIOGRAPHY: Hock-Kaufmann, *Die Familien Prags*, p. 153a; Zunz, *Z. G.* p. 285; Benjacob, *Ozar ha-Sefarim*, p. 325; Steinschneider, *Cat. Bodl.* cols. 562, 573, 2134–2135; Nepi-Ghirondi, *Toledot Gedole Yisrael*, p. 310; De Rossi, *Dizionario*, p. 313.
E. C.   S. O.

TIKTINSKI, ḤAYYIM JUDAH LÖB B. SAMUEL: Lithuanian Talmudist; born in Mir Oct. 13, 1823; died in Warsaw March 30, 1899. He was the second son of Samuel Tiktinski, founder of the yeshibah in Mir, who died in 1835, leaving his eleven-year-old son without any material means. Despite his very unfavorable circumstances, young Tiktinski succeeded by diligent application in passing a rabbinical examination before he was twenty, at which age he officiated as substitute for Rabbi Elihu Shik in Deretschin when the latter went on a long journey. In 1850 he was invited by Rabbi

Moses Abraham ben David of Mir to deliver lectures before the local yeshibah. By his brilliant delivery and his rejection of the pilpul he attracted many scholars; and when, in 1867, Moses Abraham died, Tiktinski was entrusted with the entire control of the yeshibah. Among his many pupils were Meïr, rabbi of Draderkewin, and Mordecai Elihu, author of "Ner le-Ma'or."

In 1876 Tiktinski's son **Samuel** delivered some of the lectures at the yeshibah; and in 1883, when Samuel died, his younger brother, **Abraham,** took his place. When, in the summer of 1898, the yeshibah was destroyed by fire for the second time, Tiktinski, in spite of illness, procured the necessary funds to rebuild it. He left no works, his contributions to the explanation of the Talmud having been destroyed in the above-mentioned fire.

Bibliography: M. L. Goldberg, *Sefer Toledot ha-Gaon Ḥayyim Judah Löb*, Warsaw, 1901.
E. C.   A. Pe.

TIMBREL or **TABRET**: Musical instrument. In the Hebrew music of Old Testament times, as indeed in Oriental music to-day, rhythm was of much greater importance, in comparison with the melody, than it is in modern Occidental music. Accordingly instruments like the drum and tambourine, which serve principally to accentuate the rhythm, played the greatest part. The most ancient means of marking rhythm was the clapping of hands, a method which is still employed. Among the instruments of percussion, the timbrel or hand-drum ("tof") is the oldest and most popular. It is very simple, consisting of a broad or narrow hoop of wood or metal over which the skin of an animal is stretched. Sometimes small, thin pieces of metal are hung upon the rim, which jingle when the timbrel is shaken, as in the modern tambourine. The instrument is held high in one hand, while the performer beats on the drumhead with the fingers and the back of the other hand. The form of the instrument is similar to that of the modern tambourine, as is also the manner of playing on it.

The Egyptians and the Assyrians possessed this instrument. The pictures of the former show it only in the hands of women; among the Assyrians it was played by men also. Among the Hebrews it was usually played by women, as an accompaniment to joyful dancing (Judges xi. 34; I Sam. xviii. 6; Jer. xxxi. 4) and to songs (Gen. xxxi. 27; Ex. xv. 20; I Sam. xviii. 6). The timbrel is an instrument which in its whole character is inappropriate for mournful occasions, being in keeping only with cheerful songs and games, such as accompany weddings (I Macc. ix. 39), popular rejoicings (*e.g.*, the reception of a victorious general; I Sam. xviii. 6 *et seq.*), banquets (Isa. v. 12), and religious festivals of a joyful and popular character (Ex. xv. 20; Ps. lxxxi. 2). It is more rarely found in the hands of men. All the prophets who speak at length of music refer to the hand-drum (I Sam. x. 5).

The tambourine apparently had no place in the Temple service, however; at least in the enumeration of the instruments of the Temple orchestra (II Chron. v. 12 *et seq.*) only the cymbals are mentioned among the instruments of percussion.
E. C.   I. Be.

TIMNATH-SERAH (in Judges ii. 9, **Timnath-heres**): Town in Mount Ephraim, situated on the northern slope of the hill of Gaash (Josh. xxiv. 30). It was given to Joshua as an inheritance, was fortified by him (*ib.* xix. 50), and served as his place of burial (*ib.* xxiv. 30). According to the "Onomasticon" of Eusebius, Timnath was an important city in the district of Diospolis (Lydda); and the grave of Joshua was shown there. On the site of the city is situated the modern town of Tibna, about ten miles north of Beth-el on the Roman road from Cæsarea to Jerusalem. Among its ruins and tombs is a grave of remarkable size and construction, which is probably the one identified in the days of Eusebius as that of Joshua. Another tradition, however, of Samaritan origin, locates the tomb farther to the northeast, in the small village of Kafr Ḥaris, which is therefore frequently regarded as the site of Timnath. The city seems to have been identical with the Thamnatha of I Macc. ix. 50, which, according to Josephus ("Ant." xiv. 11, § 2; "B. J." iv. 8, § 1), was the capital of a Jewish toparchy.

Bibliography: Guérin, *Judée*, iii. 37; idem, *Samarie*, ii. 89 *et seq.*; *Pal. Explor. Fund, Memoirs*, ii. 374 *et seq.*; idem, *Quarterly Statement*, 1879, pp. 193 *et seq.*; *Z. D. P. V.* ii. 13 *et seq.*; Schürer, *Gesch.* 3d ed., ii. 181-186.
E. C.   I. Be.

TIN. See Metals.

TIRADO, JACOB: Convert to Judaism in Amsterdam in the sixteenth century; died in Jerusalem. With several Maranos he sailed from Portugal in a vessel which was driven out of its course to Emden in East Friesland. Following the advice of Rabbi Moses Uri ha-Levi, he continued his travels with his companions to Amsterdam. After his arrival there he confessed the Jewish faith openly, and afterward, though advanced in years, underwent the rite of circumcision.

Together with Jacob Israel Belmonte and Samuel Palache, Tirado founded the Spanish-Portuguese community of Amsterdam, being its first president. Having acquired a house on the Houtgracht, he transformed it into a synagogue, which was called after him "Bet Ya'aḳob," or "Casa de Jacob," and was consecrated at the New-Year's festival, 5358 (= Sept., 1597). Annually on Yom Kippur a special prayer in his behalf is recited as an acknowledgment of his important services to the community. In his old age Tirado traveled to Jerusalem, where he died. See Moses Uri b. Joseph ha-Levi.

Bibliography: De Barrios, *Casa de Jacob*, pp. 3 *et seq.*; idem, *Relacion de los Poetas*, p. 53; D. H. de Castro, *De Synagoge der Portugeesch-Israelitische Gemeente te Amsterdam*, pp. 5, 7; Grätz, *Gesch.* ix., pp. lxxxiii. *et seq.*
S.   M. K.

TIRHAKAH (תרהקה): King of Ethiopia (*i.e.*, Nubia). When Sennacherib and his general (Rabshakeh) were besieging Lachish, Libnah, and Jerusalem, it was reported that Tirhakah was approaching with an army to assist the Palestinians against the Assyrian forces (II Kings xix. 9; Isa. xxxvii. 9).

This king, the Tarakos of Manetho (comp. "Tharaca," LXX. and Vulgate), the Tearkos of Strabo, the Tharsikes of Josephus, and the Tarḳu of the Assyrian inscriptions (written "Ta-h-ru-ḳ" in hieroglyphics with strange vocalization; the consonants suggest as emendation a transposition of the second and third consonants in the Hebrew form), was the third Pharaoh of the twenty-fifth or Ethiopian dynasty of Egypt. He was a usurper who tried later to legalize his usurpation by marriage with the widow of his predecessor, Shabataka (the Sebichos of Manetho). Assyrian reports assign his death to 668–667 B.C.; and Egyptian inscriptions state that he reigned twenty-six years (twenty or eighteen according to Manetho). Thus his ascension to the throne would fall in 694–693 B.C. (according to others, his coronation occurred in 691 and his death in 665).

Tirhakah has left in Egypt many monuments, extending from Tanis to Napata, his capital in Nubia. No line of his inscriptions speaks of the great wars which he had to wage, at least from 676. The Assyrians, accusing him of having aided their rebellious vassal, King Baal of Tyre, invaded Egypt in that year, but their army was finally annihilated. In 671, however, King Esarhaddon undertook another expedition, invaded Egypt by way of Magdali (perhaps the Biblical Migdol), defeated an army at Iskhupri, and by two further victories drove Tirhakah out of Egypt. The twenty petty rulers (nomarchs) among whom this country was distributed by the Assyrians followed a treacherous course, wavering between the Assyrians and Tirhakah, who invaded Egypt again in 669 and occupied the land. A third Assyrian army, however, was victorious at Karbanit (in the northwest of the Delta), destroyed the rebellious Saïs, Mendes, and Tanis, and pursued Tirhakah as far back as Thebes, which closed its doors to the fugitive king. The energetic Ethiopian rallied his troops for another campaign, and had already forced Thebes to surrender, when he died. His stepson and successor, Tandamani (thus the Assyrian; Tinwat-Amon in hieroglyphics; Tementhes in Polyænus, "Strategica," vii. 3), made only one more futile attempt to regain Egypt.

It will be seen from the above chronology that the monumental data can not easily be harmonized with the seemingly conflicting chronology of the Bible, which mentions Tirhakah in 701 both as king and as at war with the Assyrians. It is at present not possible to explain this discrepancy; the latest attempt at an explanation is that of Prašek ("Mitteilungen der Vorderasiatischen Gesellschaft," 1903, viii. 148), who holds that the Biblical passage concerning Tirhakah referred originally to an expedition in 691 or later, the report being misplaced in the present text.

BIBLIOGRAPHY: For the monuments of Tirhakah: Wiedemann, *Gesch. Aegyptens*, p. 590. For his ascension to the throne: Maspero, *Histoire Ancienne*, 1899, iii. 361 (with some reservations). On the cuneiform accounts: Winckler, in Schrader, *K. A. T.* 3d ed., pp. 88 *et seq.* (also *Mitteilungen der Vorderasiatischen Gesellschaft*, 1898, p. 29; *Altorientalische Forschungen*, p. 97).

E. C.   W. M. M.

TIRZAH: 1. Ancient Canaanitish capital (Josh. xii. 24), which, from the context, seems to have been situated in the northern part of the country. Possibly, therefore, it should be distinguished from the Israelitish capital of the same name (I Kings xiv. 17; xv. 21, 33), which was made a royal city by Jeroboam I. (*ib.* xiv. 17), and which remained the residence of the kings of Israel until Omri. Subse-

quently Tirzah is mentioned only as the center of the revolution of Menahem (II Kings xv. 14, 16); and even in this passage "Tirzah," on the basis of the Septuagint text, should perhaps be read "Tharseila" and be identified with the village of that name, which, according to the "Onomasticon" of Eusebius, was a Samaritan town in Bashan, corresponding to the modern Tsil.

The only information possessed concerning the royal city of Tirzah, which is praised for its beauty in Cant. vi. 4, is that it was situated in the district of Zelophehad in the tribe of Manasseh (Num. xxvi. 33, xxvii. 1, xxxvi. 11; Josh. xvii. 3); but, since neither Josephus nor the "Onomasticon" gives any details regarding it, all identifications are uncertain. Robinson considered it to be the site of the modern Talluza, the Tarlusa of the Talmud, a town about seven kilometers northeast of Nablus (Neubauer, "G. T." p. 268), while Conder, on the other hand, identified it with Tayasir, an ancient site with caverns, tombs, and other remains, nineteen kilometers northeast of Nablus. The translation of "Tirzah" by "Tir'an" in the Targum to Cant. vi. 4 has led other scholars to identify the place with the modern Al-Tirah, which lies south of Nablus, although this Tir'an may perhaps be represented rather by Tur'an, northeast of Nazareth.

2. The youngest of the five daughters of Zelophehad (Num. xxvi. 33).

E. C.   I. BE.

TISHBI, ELIJAH. See LEVITA, ELIJAH.

TISHBI, JUDAH BEN ELIJAH: Karaite scholar and liturgical poet; flourished at Belgrade in the first half of the sixteenth century; grandson of Abraham ben Judah. He copied and completed the exegetical work of his grandfather, entitled "Yesod Mikra," and was the author of liturgical poems, several of which have been inserted in the Karaite prayer-book ("Siddur ha-Kera'im," ii. 215; iii. 171, 172, 174). Judah was the copyist of the "Yehi Me'orot," on the precepts attributed to Tobiah ben Moses.

BIBLIOGRAPHY: Pinsker, *Likkute Kadmoniyyot*, p. 93; Fürst, *Gesch. des Karäert.* ii. 293.

K.   I. BR.

TISZA-ESZLAR AFFAIR: Accusation of ritual murder brought against the Jews of Tisza-Eszlar, a Hungarian town situated on the Theiss. On April 1, 1882, Esther Solymosi, a Christian peasant girl fourteen years old, servant in the home of Andreas Huri at Tisza-Eszlar, was sent on an errand from which she did not return. The search for her being fruitless, a rumor was circulated that the girl had become a victim of religious fanaticism. The agitations of the anti-Semites, whose leaders, Onody of Tisza-Eszlar and Victor von Istóczi, had in the House of Deputies proposed the expulsion of the Jews, exercised a most pernicious influence upon

Origin of the Accusation.

the country population. In the general excitement which they stirred up and which led to bloody excesses in many parts of Hungary, the suspicion that the Jews had foully dealt with the girl, in order to use her blood at the approaching Passover (April 4), found ready credence; and on May 4 the alarmed mother accused the Jews before the local judge of having killed her daughter, and urged him to hold an investigation.

On May 19 the county court of Nyireghyhaza sent the notary Bary to act as examining judge at Tisza-Eszlar. After having placed the suspected Jews under the surveillance of the police, Bary began his inquiry with Samuel, the five-year-old son of the synagogue sexton Josef Scharf. The babble of this child, from whom by means of money presents and pieces of sugar some women and girls had elicited the statement that his father had called Esther into his house and pinioned her, and that the slaughterer ("shohet") had cut off her head, was the point at issue in all the proceedings. Before Bary the boy stated that in the presence of his father and other men the slaughterer had made an incision in the girl's neck, while he himself and his brother Moriz had received the blood in a plate. The father, as well as Moriz, who was nearly fourteen years old, and the other suspected persons, denied any knowledge of the disappearance of the girl and of her conjectured murder. On May 19 Scharf and his wife were arrested; Moriz repeated his statement, and said in addition that he had never known anything about the missing girl, not even from hearsay. On the evening of that day Moriz was given in charge of Recszy, the commissary of safety, who took him to his country house in Nagy-Falu, where the court clerk, Peczely, received orders to watch over the boy's safety. Peczely, a brutish man who had served twelve years in jail for murder, connived with Recszy to make Moriz the instrument of a blood accusation. Intimidated by cruelty and threats, the boy confessed in the night that after Sabbath morning service his father had called Esther to his house under the pretext of requiring her to remove some candlesticks (an act forbidden to Jews on Saturday); that a Jewish beggar, Hermann Wollner, who lodged with them, had led the girl to the vestibule of the synagogue and felled her; and that, after having undressed her, two slaughterers, Abraham Buxbaum and Leopold Braun, had held her while another slaughterer, Solomon Schwarz, incised her neck with a large knife and emptied the blood into a pot. These three men, applicants for the vacant position of precentor and shohet, had come to Tisza-Eszlar to officiate on that particular Sabbath, and had, as the boy said, remained in the synagogue after morning service. All this, according to his confession, Moriz had observed through the keyhole of the synagogue door. During forty-five minutes that he thus stood

"Confessions" of the Scharf Children.

on watch, he saw also that after the operation a rag was tied around the neck of the girl and her body dressed again, in the presence of Samuel Lustig, Abraham Braun, Lazar Weissstein, and Adolf Jünger. The two conspirators Recszy and Peczely immediately sent for the examining judge Bary, before whom the same night Moriz repeated his account, adding that, after the perpetrators had left the scene of their crime he had locked the synagogue, and that neither the corpse nor any blood marks were to be found. With feverish zeal Bary continued his investigations in the synagogue and houses and among the graves; but nowhere could any traces of the living or dead girl be discovered. Twelve Jews were arrested on suspicion; and Moriz Scharf was given in charge of the jailer.

On June 18 there was drawn out of the River Theiss near Dada a body which the district physician declared to be that of a fourteen-year-old girl,

Synagogue at Tisza-Eszlar, with Home of Joseph Scharf.
(From a photograph.)

and which many recognized as that of Esther Solymosi. Her mother, however, emphatically denied that it was Esther's corpse, although she afterward recognized the clothes in which the body was found as those of her daughter. A committee of experts, two physicians and one surgeon, declared that the corpse was that of a girl eighteen to twenty years of age, who had met with her death but eight or ten days before. It was then buried in the Catholic cemetery of Tisza-Eszlar. The anti-Semites, among whom was the Catholic priest of the town, insinuated that the body had been smuggled in by the Jews and clothed in the garments of Esther Solymosi in order to conceal the crime of ritual murder. Several of the raftsmen who had found the body were induced by promises, threats, and cruel treatment to revoke their former testimony and to declare that they had brought the body to the river and that an unknown Jewess had furnished them with the clothes in which they had dressed it. New arrests were made; and the affair, which had now become a cause célèbre, was considerably protracted.

On July 29 formal accusations were made against fifteen persons, as follows: Solomon Schwarz, Abraham Buxbaum, Leopold Braun, and Hermann Wollner, of murder; Josef Scharf, Adolf Jünger, Abraham Braun, Samuel Lustig, Lazar Weissstein, and Emanuel Taub, of voluntary assistance in the crime; Anselm Vogel, Jankel Smilovics, David Hersko, Martin Gross, and Ignaz Klein, of abetting the crime and smuggling the body. The delay in the case was caused mainly by the illegal and arbitrary acts of Bary, who conducted his examinations without the aid of the state attorney,

Formal Accusations Made.

wrote without witnesses the minutes of the proceedings, and tortured the accused and suspected. By order of the government, Moriz Scharf was given in charge of the district bailiff, who placed him in the custody of the warden Henter; thus removed from contact with his coreligionists, he was entirely under the influence of their adversaries, and received instructions as to the testimony to be given by him at the trial.

The accused were defended by Karl Eötvös, journalist and member of the House of Deputies, with whom were associated the advocates B. Friedmann, Alexander Funtak, Max Szekely of Budapest, and Ignaz Heumann of Nyireghyhaza, the seat of the county court before which the case was tried. In a petition to Minister of Justice Pauler, Eötvös protested against the system of torture practised by Bary, Recszy, and Peczely; but this protest had little effect upon that official. The affair was so long drawn out that State Attorney Kozma of Budapest went to Nyireghyhaza in September to hasten the examination.

This dragging on of the proceedings attracted general attention. The country was greatly agitated. A number of pamphlets appealed to the passions of the people, and attempted to establish the guilt of the accused. Louis Kossuth, then living in exile at Turin, raised his powerful voice to castigate the action of the authorities and to deprecate this stirring up of medieval prejudices. The suspicion of ritual murder, he considered, was a disgrace to Hungary; to represent as a racial

Protest by Louis Kossuth. crime or as a ritual crime a murder which at the worst was an individual one was, he said, unworthy of modern civilization. This cry of indignation from the veteran patriot was strangely in contrast with the fury of persecution and prejudice which raged throughout the country and which was echoed in the House of Deputies. An interpellation addressed to the minister of justice by the deputy Ernest Mezei in Nov., 1882, called forth exciting scenes. The attorney-general Havas was then sent to Nyireghyhaza, and he found that, despite the official declaration of the examining judge, the accused had not had a single hearing. He released some prisoners; but, realizing that he was hampered by powerful influences in his endeavor to accelerate the affair, he offered his resignation, which was readily accepted.

In the middle of November the wife of Josef Scharf was set free, her husband and the other prisoners being still detained. At the request of the defending lawyers the body found in the Theiss was exhumed (Dec. 7) and reexamined by three professors of medicine at the University of Budapest—Schenthauer, Belky, and Mihalkovics. They found that the opinion of the members of the former committee of examination had no scientific basis, and later, before the court, they taxed them with

Esther's Corpse Exhumed. gross ignorance: the body was too much decayed to allow a positive judgment. The fact that the corpse was not claimed by any one, left no doubt in their opinion, however, that it was that of Esther Solymosi; and as the neck was not cut, no ritual murder could have been committed.

On June 17, 1883, the last act in this shameful affair began before the court of Nyireghyhaza. Judge Francis Korniss presided, Eduard Szeyffert acting as state attorney. Although the testimony of Moriz Scharf was the only basis of the accusation, the court held thirty sessions to examine the case in all its details; and many witnesses were heard. The glaring contradictions of the boy despite the careful training he had received, and the falsity of his accusation as exposed by a local inspection of the alleged scene of the murder made by the court in Tisza-Eszlar on July 16, resulted, as was inevitable, in the unanimous acquittal of the accused (Aug. 3). Szalay, the attorney for the widow Solymosi, in a speech full of bitter invectives, appealed against the decision; but the supreme court rejected his appeal and confirmed the verdict of the county court.

The youthful accuser whom the maneuvers of the anti-Semites had alienated from his faith and his coreligionists, and whose filial feelings they had suppressed, returned to his parents, who gladly received him. Moriz fully redeemed his past: he supported his father until the death of the latter (1905).

The verdict of acquittal and the deliverance of the prisoners, most of whom had languished fifteen

Acquittal of the Accused. months in prison, were the signal for uprisings in Presburg, Budapest, and other parts of Hungary. The spectators who thronged the court-house during the sessions, and among whom Onody, the representative of Tisza-Eszlar in the House of Deputies, was most conspicuous, conducted themselves scandalously during the proceedings: they insulted the prisoners, threatened the witnesses and lawyers for the defense, and exhibited intense passion, prejudice, and hatred.

Bibliography: *Allg. Zeit. des Jud.* 1882–83, 1884, p. 248; *Die Neuzeit,* 1882–83; *Der Blutprozess von Tisza-Eszlar,* New York, 1883; Paul Nathan, *Der Prozess von Tisza-Eszlar,* Berlin, 1892.

S.   S. Man.

TITHE (מעשר): The tenth part of anything, appropriated as tax or sacrifice.—**Biblical Data:** Tithing one's possessions was a very ancient custom, existing as early as the time of the Patriarchs. Abraham gave Melchizedek "tithes of all" (Gen. xiv. 20); and Jacob made a vow that if he should return to his father's house in safety he would acknowledge Yhwh as his Lord and would give Him a tenth of everything he possessed (*ib.* xxviii. 20–22). Later the Mosaic law made the tithe obligatory upon the Israelites. The tithe, whether of the seed of the land or of the fruit of the tree, belonged to Yhwh and consequently was holy. It was redeemable by "adding thereto the fifth part thereof." The tithe of cattle, however, was not redeemable; and if one beast was exchanged for another both became holy unto the Lord. The method of levying the tithe of cattle is indicated: they were counted singly; and every tenth one that passed under the rod became the tithe animal (Lev. xxvii. 30–33).

There is apparently a discrepancy between the Book of Numbers and that of Deuteronomy with regard to the tithe. In Num. xviii. 21–26 it is stated that "all the tenth in Israel" is given to the Levites "for an inheritance"; as they had no part in the land, the tithe was to be their principal source of sustenance. On the other hand, the Levites themselves were required to give the priests a tenth of all the tithes received by them. Deut. xiv. 22-29, however, enjoins the annual tithing of the increase of the field only; this was to be eaten before the Lord, that is to say, in the city in which the Temple was built. But if the distance to such city was so great as to render the transportation of all the tithes impracticable, the people might convert the tithe into money and spend the sum in the city on eatables, etc. ("whatsoever thy soul desireth"; *ib.* verse 26). Every third year the tithes were not to be carried to the city of the Temple, but were to be stored at home ("within thy gates"), and "the Levite, the stranger, and the fatherless, and the widow" were to "eat and be satisfied" (*ib.* verse 29). It is to be concluded that, the seventh year being a Sabbatical year and no tithing being permissible therein, the tithe of the first, second, fourth, and fifth years of every cycle of seven years had to be brought to the Temple and eaten by the landowner and his family, while the tithe of the third and sixth years was to be left at home for the poor.

The third year was called the year of tithing; and after the distribution of the tithe among the Levites and others, the landowners were required to announce solemnly before the Lord that they had observed all the laws connected therewith, concluding such declaration with a prayer for God's blessing (*ib.* xxvi. 12-15). A mourner was not allowed to eat the tithe, nor might one employ it for any unclean use, nor give it for the dead.

Samuel informed the Israelites that they would have to give a tenth of everything to the king (I Sam. viii. 15, 17). When the Israelites afterward fell into idolatry, they continued to bring their tithes to the temple of their idols; but they seem to have adopted another system of offering them (comp. Amos iv. 4, Hebr. and R. V.). King Hezekiah again imposed the tithe on his subjects; and the people of Judah brought it in abundance, apparently for the use of the Levites. Indeed, the quantity was so great that the king ordered special chambers in the Temple to be prepared for its reception (II Chron. xxxi. 6-12). The same arrangement was made later by Nehemiah (Neh. x. 39, xiii. 12).

   J.   M. SEL.

——**In Rabbinical Literature:** According to the Rabbis, the Books of Numbers and Deuteronomy are complementary to each other (comp. TITHE, BIBLICAL DATA); consequently there can be no contradiction between them. Thus there were three kinds of tithes: (1) that given to the Levites as stated in Num. xviii. 21 *et seq.*, and termed "the first tithe" ("ma'aser rishon"); (2) the tithe which was to be taken to Jerusalem and there consumed by the landowner and his family, and which was termed "the second tithe" ("ma'aser sheni"), it being taken from what remained after the first tithe had been appropriated; and (3) that given to the poor ("ma-'aser 'ani"). Therefore two tithes were to be taken every year except in the seventh year: Nos. 1 and 2 in the first, second, fourth, and fifth years; Nos. 1 and 3 in the third and sixth years.

The Rabbis inferred from Deut. xiv. 22 that each tithe was to be taken of every year's produce separately, whether of crops, of cattle, or of anything else subject to tithing (Sifre, Deut. 105; Ter. i. 5; R. H. 8a, 12b). Also they fixed a par-

The Tithing Year. ticular day to mark the beginning of the year for tithing. The first of Elul according to R. Meïr, or the first of Tishri according to R. Eleazar and R. Simeon, is the new year for the tithing of cattle; the first of Tishri, for the produce of the land; the first of Shebaṭ according to the school of Shammai, or the fifteenth of Shebaṭ according to the school of Hillel, for the fruit of the trees (R. H. i. 1). The removal of the tithes and the recitation of the confession (comp. Deut. xxvi. 12 *et seq.*) must take place on the eve of the Passover festival of the fourth and seventh years of every cycle of seven years. Although the removal is mentioned only with regard to the tithe of the poor, the Rabbis concluded that the other two tithes must also be cleared away at the same time (Sifre, Deut. 109). The Rabbis fixed the following rules by which one might distinguish tithable produce: it must be eatable, the property of an individual, and the product of the soil. Fruit must be ripe enough to be eaten; when one eats untithed fruit in an immature state, he is not guilty of having transgressed the Law (Ma'as. i. 1 *et seq.*). As appears from the Bible, the law of tithing was originally to be applied in Palestine only; the Prophets, however, ordained that tithing should be observed in Babylonia also, it being near Palestine. The earlier rabbis applied the law of tithing to Egypt and to the lands of Ammon and Moab (Yad. iv. 3); and the scribes seem to have instituted tithes in Syria (Dem. vi. 11; comp. Shulḥan 'Aruk, Yoreh De'ah, 331, 1 *et seq.*).

The Rabbis emphasize in more than one instance the importance of tithes. Tithing is one of the three things through the merit of which the world was created (Gen. R. i. 6), and by virtue of which the Israelites obtain from God their desire (Pesiḳ. xi. 96b; Tan., Re'eh). Through the merit of tithes, also,

Merit of the Tithe. the Israelites after death escape the punishment which the wicked suffer for twelve months in hell (Pesiḳ. xi. 97b-98a; Midr. Mishle xxxi.). The Patriarchs observed the law of tithing, concerning which statement there are two different accounts: (1) Abraham offered the first tithe, Isaac brought the heave-offering for the priests ("terumah gedolah"), and Jacob brought the second tithe (Pesiḳ. R. 25 [ed. Friedmann, p. 127b]); (2) Abraham presented the heave-offering, Isaac offered the second tithe, and Jacob brought the first one (Pesiḳ. xi. 98a; comp. Gen. R. lxiv. 6; Num. R. xii. 13; Pirḳe R. El. xxvii., xxxiii.). He who partakes of fruit which has not been tithed is like one who eats carrion; and Judah ha-Nasi's opinion is that one who eats fruit of which the tithe for the poor has not been appropriated is deserving of death (Pesiḳ. xi. 99a, b). One of the interpretations of Prov. xxx. 4 is that he who fulfils the duty of tithing causes rain to fall, and that he who fails therein causes drought (Yalḳ., Prov. 962). Non-fulfilment of the law of tithing brings hurricanes (Midr. Teh. to Ps. xviii.).

The tithe for the poor gave rise to the tithing

of one's earnings, with the object of distributing among the needy the sum so appropriated. This is inferred in Sifre (quoted in Tos. to Ta'an. 9a) from Deut. xiv. 22, and is therefore considered as an obligation imposed by the Mosaic law ("Ṭure Zahab" to Shulḥan 'Aruk, Yoreh De'ah, 249, 1; comp. Isaiah Horwitz, "Shene Luḥot ha-Berit," and Joseph Hahn, "Yosef Omeẓ," p. 176, Frankfort-on-the-Main, 1723). Joel Sirkes in his "Bayit Ḥadash" (to Shulḥan 'Aruk, l.c.), however, thinks that tithing one's earnings is simply a custom and is not obligatory either under the Mosaic or under the rabbinical law. The whole of the tithe must be given to the poor; and no part of it may be appropriated to any other religious purpose (Shulḥan 'Aruk, l.c., Isserles' gloss).

W. B.   M. Sel.

——**Critical View:** There are evidently two conflicting sources with regard to tithes. D mentions

That the tithe spoken of in D, and which is termed by the Rabbis "the second tithe" (see Tithe in Rabbinical Literature), is more ancient has been concluded by W. R. Smith ("Rel. of Sem." 2d ed., pp. 245 *et seq.*), who, moreover, thinks that in earlier times the tribute was not a fixed amount, but that it took the form of first-fruits, and that at a later period a tithe was fixed to provide the public banquets at sacred festivals. Subsequently the tithe became the prerogative of the king (I Sam. viii. 15, 17); but from the Book of Amos (iv. 4) it appears that in the time of that prophet the Israelites paid tithes for the use of their sanctuaries in the Northern Kingdom, as, similarly, in the Persian period the tithes were converted to the use of the Temple of Yhwh (Mal. iii. 8–10). Those instituted by Nehemiah for payment to the Levites were a development of the heave-offering ("terumah")

TITLE-PAGE OF TRACTATE MENAḤOT, PRINTED BY DANIEL BOMBERG, VENICE, 1522.
(From the Sulzberger collection in the Jewish Theological Seminary of America, New York.)

only the tithes of corn, wine, and olive-oil, which were to be levied every year and to be eaten by the landowner in the Holy City in the first, second, fourth, and fifth years of every Sabbatical cycle, while in the third and sixth years they were to be distributed among the Levites, strangers, orphans, and widows (Deut. xii. 16, xiv. 22 *et seq.*). P, on the other hand, destines this tithe for the Levites (Num. xviii. 21 *et seq.*); and, in a probably late addition (Lev. xxvii. 30–33), tithing is extended to the fruit of the trees and to cattle also. It is true that in D the Levites, too, have a share in the tithe (Deut. xii. 18; comp. xiv. 27); but the owner's invitation to the Levite to partake thereof seems to have been voluntary. It may be noticed that in the priestly part of the Book of Ezekiel (xliv. 15 *et seq.*) there is no mention whatever of a tithe appointed for the Levites. Nehemiah instituted such a tithe; and he directed that the Levites should give a tithe of their portions to the priests (see Tithe, Biblical Data). Hence it may be concluded that the passages in Numbers and Leviticus regarding tithes were written under the influence of the Book of Nehemiah.

given to the priests. Not only do the terms "terumah" and "ma'aser" often occur together in the Old Testament, but it is stated in Neh. x. 37 *et seq.* that the Levites were required to collect their tithes under the supervision of a priest. R. Eleazar b. Azariah held that the first tithe might also be paid to the priest (Yeb. 86b).

Comparing verse 30 with verse 32 of Lev. xxvii., it may be concluded that the tithe of cattle was to go to the priests or the Levites. This was the opinion of Philo ("De Prœmiis Sacerdotum," § 2 [ed. Mangey, ii. 234]); but the Rabbis refer the whole passage to the second tithe (Sifre, Deut. 63; Ḥag. i. 4; Men. vii. 5).

J.   M. Sel.

TITLE-PAGE: Hebrew incunabula, like manuscripts, were mostly provided with colophons, which served as title-pages. The title of the Soncino edition of Berakot, 1483, is given in the printer's colophon. The title-page of Ibn Gabirol's (or Jedaiah Bedersi's?) "Mibḥar ha-Peninim" (Soncino, 1484) is preceded by a short preface. In Naḥmanides' commentary on the Pentateuch (Lisbon, 1489) the title, "Ḥiddushe Torah," precedes the preface. In

TITLE-PAGE OF "SEFER NIẒẒAḤON," ALTDORF, 1644.
(From the Sulzberger collection in the Jewish Theological Seminary of America, New York.)

"Seder ha-Taḥanunim Asher Nahagu Bene Roma" (= The Order of Devotions According to the Custom of Rome) the title is given in the colophon (Soncino, 1487). In David Ḳimḥi's "Sefer ha-Shorashim" (Naples, 1491) the title, on the first page, is surrounded by a wood-engraving.

In the early sixteenth century the colophon still predominated. The title of the "Sefer Minhag Abot," the condensed liturgical code of Zedekiah b. Abraham's "Shibbole ha-Leḳeṭ," appears in the colophon (Mantua, 1514). About this period the titles of books began to appear on the first page, next to the cover. In the first complete Babylonian Talmud, which was printed by Bomberg in Venice, 1520–23, the title on the first page occupies a narrow space of five lines, a little above the center, and, translated, reads: "Masseket Niddah, with Commentaries of Rashi, Tosafot, Extracts of Decisions in Tosafot, Commentary on the Mishnah by Maimonides, Commentary and Decisions by Asheri. Printed by Daniel Bomberg, in the year 5280, in Venice." Soon, however, the titles began to occupy the entire page, some being bordered with ornamental wood- or metal - engravings of flowers, or of Moses, Aaron, David, and Solomon, or of angels, deer, and lions. The original engravings were sometimes used by non-Jewish artists, which accounts for the non-Jewish character of some of the title-pages. The borders included the printer's device and marks. The printers at Prague in the sixteenth century decorated their title-pages in the style of an illuminated manuscript. As a popular title-page design, the entrance to the Temple, above which was inscribed "This gate of the Lord, into which the righteous shall enter" (Ps. cxviii. 20), with the pillars of Jachin and Boaz, occupied high rank. The Amsterdam, 1666, "Tiḳḳun," for night reading, has an engraved title-page with a representation of Shabbethai Ẓebi and his disciples. Isaac Aboab's "Menorat ha-Ma'or" (Amsterdam, 1722) has a

Decorations. very elaborately engraved title-page. Maimonides' "Sefer ha -.Miẓwot" (with Judæo-German translation by J. Landau, Prague, 1798) has the entire first title-page, including the title and inscription of the book, engraved, and contains the figures of David and Solomon, the Levites' musical instruments, the Ark, and the candlestick.

Frequently two title-pages were used, the first being ornamented and giving the name and contents of the book in general terms, the second giving a fuller description in plain type. The Amsterdam, 1679, edition of the Bible, which has a Judæo-German translation, has a second engraved title-page. Often the title-page was artistically very attractive; the largest types were used for the title. The Talmud published by Schapira in Slobuta (1817–22) gives the titles of the treatises and the special commentaries (not printed in former editions) and the name of Slobuta in red. In the second Slobuta edition, 1834–36 (only Berakot, Shabbat, and 'Erubin being published), there were two title-pages, some lines being in red and some in black; the Wilna-Grodno edition (1832–52) followed this style. The

Title-Page of "Shefa' Ṭal," Hanau, 1612.
(From the Sulzberger collection in the Jewish Theological Seminary of America, New York.)

matter on the title-page is sometimes spaced and sometimes crowded. The Venice Abudarham of 1566 has the author's preface of eighteen lines on the title-page. Joshua Falk Cohen's "Abne Yehoshua'," the first rabbinical work published in America (New York, 1860), has the description of the contents, on the title-page, set in the form of a triangle. A number of modern books use vowel-points on the title-page.

Some title-pages misrepresent the contents of the book. The title-page of the Bomberg Pentateuch,

TITLE-PAGE OF BIBLE, AMSTERDAM, 1679.

(From the Sulzberger collection in the Jewish Theological Seminary of America, New York.)

Venice, 1524, calls for Ibn Ezra's commentary on the Five Rolls, which, however, is not in the book. The same thing occurred in the case of Isaac Abravanel's commentary on the Megillot (Venice, 1573). Judah ha-Levi's "Cuzari," with translation and commentary by David Cassel (Leipsic, 1853), has a second title-page, dated 1841, which states that part of the commentary was written conjointly by H. Jolowicz and D. Cassel. Moses Hayyim Luzzatto's "Migdal 'Oz" (*ib.* 1854) mentions "F. Delitzschii prolegomena" in the title-page, but the latter is not included in the book.

Some old works were supplied with new title-pages. Elijah Levita's "Sefer ha-Tishbi" (Isny, 1541) was given a new title-page and preface at

TITLE-PAGE FROM A SHABBETHAIAN "TIKKUN,"
AMSTERDAM, c. 1666.
(From the Sulzberger collection in the Jewish Theological Seminary of America,
New York.)

Basel in 1557. The title-page bearing the imprint of Frankfort-on-the-Oder, 1595, covers the edition of Wittenberg, 1587, by Crots. The "Yosippon," with the title-page of Leipsic, 1710, is the old edition of Gotha, 1707. The commentary of Abravanel on the Early Prophets with the title-page of

Frankfort-on-the-Main, 1736, is the Leipsic edition of 1686. This device of changing the title-page was probably due to the bookseller's desire to mislead the purchaser; or perhaps the old title-pages were missing and were replaced by a second printer. Still it is difficult to explain why one edition of a certain date and place should have various title-pages, as in the case of Ibn Shu-'aib's "Kol Bokim," a commentary on Lamentations (Venice, 1589), and Hayyim Abraham Ostrosa's "Sefer Ben le-Abraham" (Salonica, 1826), some copies of which read "Sefer Ben Abraham," omitting the "le"; per-

Title-Page from a Miniature Siddur,
Amsterdam, 1728.
(From the Sulzberger collection in the Jewish
Theological Seminary of America, New York.)

haps the printer dropped that letter from the form before he had finished the edition.

Some of the errors in the title-pages affect the name of the author. In Moses b. Elijah Galina's "Hokmat ha-Parzuf" (Amsterdam, 1658) the name reads "Elijah ben Moses." In Elijah Alfandari's "Seder Eliyahu Rabbah," responsa (Constantinople, 1719), the name "Shabbethai" on the title-page is an error. Mistakes in dates of publica-

Errors in Names and Titles. tion, especially in acrostics, are numerous. Sometimes the date on the title-page is different from that in the colophon, or the two title-pages disagree. For example, the Amsterdam, 1705, edition of the Bible has a second title-page dated 1700–3. Elijah b. Joseph Trillinger's "Mishnat R. Eli'ezer" (Frankfort-on-the-Oder, 1707) gives the correct date in the colophon, but on the title-page of the first volume the date 1655 is given in acrostic. On some title-pages the dates are incorrectly given, as in the Tur Hoshen Mishpat of Venice, 1567, in which the date given is 5027, instead of 5327. A similar mistake occurred in Joseph b. Hayyim Jabez's commentary on the Psalms (Salonica, 1571), in which the words "Shelosh Me'ot" (= "three hundred") are omitted.

BIBLIOGRAPHY: De Vinne, *Title-Pages as Seen by a Printer*, New York, 1901.
J.   J. D. E.

TITLES OF HEBREW BOOKS: In Hebrew literature, books, with few exceptions, are recognized by their titles independently of their authors' names. Citations from and references to the "Pene Yehoshua'," or "Sha'agat Aryeh," are often made by students who neither know nor care to know the name of the author. Hence the bibliographer's first aim is the listing of Hebrew books by their titles rather than by the names of their authors.

The titles of the Biblical books are said to have been decided by the Great Assembly, headed by Ezra. "Torah," "Nebi'im," and "Ketubim" (Pentateuch,

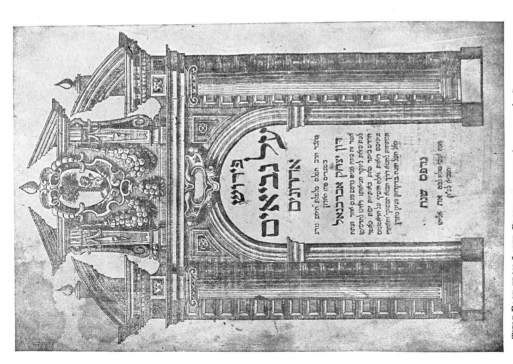

TITLE-PAGE FROM LATER PROPHETS, WITH ABRAVANEL'S COMMENTARY,
AMSTERDAM, 1641.
(From the Sulzberger collection in the Jewish Theological Seminary of America, New York.)

TITLE-PAGE FROM BIBLE, WILNA, 1865.
(From the Sulzberger collection in the Jewish Theological Seminary of America, New York.)

Prophets, and Hagiographa) were the titles given to the principal divisions. The Torah was subdivided into five "fifths," entitled "Ḥamishshah Ḥumshe Torah" (Ḥag. 14a). The Book of Exodus was called "Ḥomesh Sheni" (Second Fifth), and Numbers, "Ḥomesh ha-Peḳudim" (Fifth of the Numbered; Soṭah 36b). The Minor Prophets were known as the "Shenem 'Asar" (The Twelve), and Chronicles as "Dibre ha-Yamim" (The Events of the Days; B. B. 14a).

In a later period the five "books of Moses" received respectively the titles "Bereshit," "Shemot," "Wayiḳra," "Bemidbar," and "Debarim," these being merely the first important words in **Biblical** the five books; while the separate **Titles.** sections of the Talmud and the different midrashic works became known by titles indicating either their contents or the general nature of their relation to the Law. The Mishnah and Gemara together form the Talmud, *i.e.*, the "Study," "Teaching."

In the geonic period, besides the collections of responsa and codes called "Halakot Pesuḳot," or "Halakot Gedolot" (halakic decisions credited to Judah Gaon), there were Saadia Gaon's "Sefer ha-Emunot we ha-De'ot" (Book of Creeds and Opinions), Hai Gaon's "Miḳḳaḥ u-Mimkar" (Buying and Selling), and Amram Gaon's "Seder," or "Siddur." The title "Reumah" is curious for a work on "sheḥiṭah" by Nahshon Gaon; but this is explained by Reifmann to be a misprint, the proper title being "Re'u Mah" (See What), the two words beginning the text.

Immediately after the geonic period the works of legal authorities were known by their authors' names—Alfasi, RaMBaM (Maimonides), Mordecai, Asheri. The commentators Rashi, Ibn Ezra, RaSHBaM, Abravanel, and others gave no other title than "Perush" (exposition, commentary) to their works. Later, the titles of the books again took the place of the authors' names, and references were made to the "Ba'al ha-Ṭurim," the "Ba'al ha-Lebushim," the "Bet Yosef," and the "Shulḥan 'Aruk"; among the few exceptions in later times were the works of Wilna Gaon and R. Akiba Eger. Cabalistic books bear fanciful and highly poetical titles: "Zohar" (Brightness), formerly known as the "Midrash of R. Simeon b. Yoḥai"; "Bahir" (Shining); "Ra'ya Mehemna" (True Shepherd); "Sifra di-Ẓeni'uta" (Book of Secrets); "Libnat ha-Sappir" (Sapphire Paving); "Ginnat Bitan" (Garden of the Palace); "Bat Melek" (Daughter of the **Cabalistic** King); "'Eẓ Ḥayyim" (Tree of Life). **Books.** General titles were given to certain classes of literature, such as "Tosafot" (additions or glosses to the Talmud, chiefly by French rabbis), "Posḳim" (decisions), "Ḥiddushim" (novellæ on halakic subjects), and "Derushim" (notes on haggadic expositions). The "She'elot u-Teshubot" (responsa) bear sometimes the name of the author, sometimes a special title. In modern times "Bi'ur" (explanation) has replaced the title "Perush."

Most Hebrew titles are catchwords or familiar Biblical phrases; some have reference to the name of the author; for example, "Zera' Abraham" or "Zera' Yiẓḥaḳ" (Seed of Abraham, or Isaac). "Helel ben Shaḥar" ("Lucifer, son of the morning"; Isa. xiv. 12) is appropriated by an author whose first name is Hillel. "Derek Oniyyah" ("the way of a ship"; Prov. xxx. 19) is due to the surname of the author being "Schiff" (ship). One author by the name of Cohen made the titles of all his works refer to that name, all beginning with a "waw": "We-Shab ha-Kohen" ("And the priest shall come again,"; Lev. xiv. 39); "We-He'erik Oto ha-Kohen" ("and the priest shall value him"; Lev. xxvii. 8); "We-Hish-shab-Lo ha-Kohen" ("And the priest shall reckon unto him"; Lev. xxvii. 18, Hebr.). Samuel Jaffe chose as titles for his works Biblical phrases beginning with his name; thus, "Yefeh 'Enayim" (Beautiful Eyes), "Yefeh Ḳol" (Beautiful Voice), etc. "Elef ha-Magen" ("a thousand bucklers"; Cant. iv. 4) is the title of a work by Moses Galante containing a thousand responsa. The title of one of Azulai's books is "Debash le-Fi" (Honey to My Mouth), "DeBaSh" being the abbreviation of "David ben Sarah." Lipschütz's "Tif'eret Yisrael" contains references to his own name and to the numerical **Special** values of the names of his father, chil- **Ex-** dren, and grandchildren (see his intro- **pedients.** duction to Ṭohorot). Most of the Biblical phrases used as titles have no relation to the names of the authors of the works, as in the case of "Ba-Urim Kabbedu Yhwh" ("Glorify ye the Lord in the fires"; Isa. xxiv. 15), the title of a commentary on Rashi on the Pentateuch.

Some authors found titles in the nomenclature of the Tabernacle—its accessories, the vestments of the priests, the various ingredients of the incense—and the names of flowers, fruits, wines, and oils. Mordecai Jaffe is the author of the "Lebushim" (Garments), divided into "Lebush Tekelet" (Blue Apparel), "Ḥur" (White), "Buẓ we-Argaman" (Linen and Purple), "'Aṭeret Zahab" (Crown of Gold), "'Ir Shushan" ("the city of Shushan"; based on Esth. viii. 15). It made little difference whether the title had or had not any bearing on the contents of the book so long as it appealed to the fancy of the author. Abraham Jacob Paperna, in criticizing this method, said that if the custom of choosing Biblical phrases at random were continued, it would soon be possible to read the whole Bible by collecting and arranging Hebrew book-titles. According to a popular belief, the Messiah will appear when that has been done ("Ḳanḳan Ḥadash Male Yashan," p. 24, Wilna, 1867). Authors borrowed also Talmudical phrases, such as the one just quoted, which means "A New Vessel Full of Old [Wine]" (Ab. iv. 20), and "Emat Mafgia' 'al Ari" (The Lion's Fear of the Gnat; see Shab. 77b), the title of a counter-criticism by Benamozegh of Leon of Modena's "Ari Nohem" (The Howling Lion), an attack upon the Zohar.

The relation of a commentary to a text is sometimes indicated by a similarity in titles; Maimonides' "Mishneh Torah" was followed **Self-** by Caro's commentary "Kesef Mish- **Flattery in** neh" (Double Money), De Boton's **Titles.** "Leḥem Mishneh" (Double Bread), and Judah Rosanes' "Mishneh le-Melek" (Vice-King). Caro's Shulḥan 'Aruk (Table Prepared) is covered by Isserles' "Mappah" (Table-

TITLE-PAGE IMITATING VIGNETTES IN HEBREW MANUSCRIPTS.
(From Günzburg's "Ornamentation des Anciens Manuscripts," St. Petersburg, 1904.)

cloth), annotations. Caro himself annotated his "Bet Yosef" (House of Joseph) in his "Bedeḳ ha-Bayit" (Breach in the House). In his eagerness to embellish his work with a beautiful Biblical phrase an author rarely hesitated, on the score of modesty, to select such a title as "Zeh Yenaḥamenu" (He [This] Shall Comfort Us) or "Matoḳ mi-Debash" (Sweeter than Honey). Highly extravagant titles, especially when referring to nobles or kings, sometimes aroused the suspicion of a government. This

Eulogistic Titles. was so in the case of Yom-Ṭob Lipmann Heller's commentaries on Asheri which he entitled "Ma'adanne Melek" (Royal Dainties) and "Leḥem Ḥamudot" (Pleasant Bread [from the King's Table]; see Dan. x. 3; the Prague, 1628, edition), the author being accused of treasonable pretensions. Consequently the publishers of the edition of Fürth, 1745, were compelled to change the titles to "Ma'adanne Yom-Ṭob" (Dainties of Yom-Ṭob) and "Dibre Ḥamudot" (Pleasant Words).

On the other hand, some authors took pains to select titles that would indicate the nature of the contents of their books, as in the works "Agur" (Gatherer); "Kol Bo" (All in It), collections of liturgical minhagim; "Keneset ha-Gedolah" (Great Assembly), a digest of all the responsa in the order of the Ṭurim; "Torat ha-Kena'ot" (Law of Jealousies), rules for polemics; and "Shebeṭ le-Gew Kesilim" (Rod for the Fool's Back), the last-named being a severely censorious work. Perhaps the most appropriate titles are those used in memorial and eulogistic works. The Talmudical treatise "Ebel Rabbati" (Great Mourning) later received the euphemistic title "Semaḥot" (Joys). The modern manual for mourners is similarly called "Sefer ha-Ḥayyim" (Book of the Living). The book of recitations and prayers in commemoration of Simeon b. Yoḥai is called "Hillula Rabbah" (Grand Celebration). Others have such titles as "Allon Bakut" (Gen. xxxv. 8), "Ebel Kabed" (Grievous Mourning), "Ebel Mosheh" (Mourning for Moses), "Misped Mar" (Bitter Wailing), "Ḳol Nehi" (Voice of Lamentation), "Ḳol Bokim" (Voice of Crying), "'Emeḳ ha-Baka" (Valley of Baca; see Ps. lxxxiv. 6). Some books have two Hebrew titles, and others have one in Hebrew and one in another language, references being made to either.

The repetition of the same title by various authors is a source of annoyance and confusion to the bibliographer. Benjacob, in his "Oẓar ha-Sefarim" (up to 1863), records no less than 27 books entitled "'Eẓ Ḥayyim"; 20 entitled "Shir Yedidut"; 16 entitled "Ẓofnat Pa'aneaḥ"; 15 entitled "Leshon Limmudim"; 14 each entitled "Keter Torah," "Leḳaḥ Ṭob," "Ma'amar Mordekai," "Meḳor Ḥayyim," "Sefat Emet"; 13 each called "Ḥesheḳ Shelomoh," "Safah Berurah"; 12 each entitled "Eben Boḥan," "Dereḳ Ḥayyim," "Miḳweh Yisrael"; and there are twenty other titles each of which is used for from 8 to 12 books.

BIBLIOGRAPHY: Delmedigo, Beḥinat ha-Dat, ed. Reggio, p. 132, Vienna, 1833; I. D'Israeli, Curiosities of Literature, p. 104; Reifmann, in Ha-Shaḥar, ii. 342; S. Schechter, Studies in Judaism, xi.; A. Berliner, Hebräische Büchertitel, Frankfort-on-the-Main, 1905.
J.   J. D. E.

TITLES OF HONOR: Words and phrases applied to persons to distinguish their noble birth, or their official or social rank and station, or as marks of acknowledgment of their learning and piety.

——**Biblical Data:** The title "adon" = "lord" was given to the owner of property and slaves; also to the person to whom homage was paid as a guest of honor (Gen. xviii. 3) or who has done an act of kindness (ib. xix. 18). Abraham was entitled "lord" and "nesi elohim" = "mighty prince" (ib. xxiii. 6), also "prophet" (ib. xx. 7). The representative of the people was a "melek" = "leader," or in some cases "king." Next in rank was the "aluf" = "duke" or "chieftain." Each of the dukes of Esau was the ruler of a family or clan (ib. xxxvi. 15), and was probably subject to the head of the whole tribe. The king appointed a viceroy

Origin. termed "mishneh" = "second." Joseph was mishneh to Pharaoh, with the title "abrek" = "bow the knees" (ib. xli. 43), denoting the reverence due to his dignity; though according to the Talmud "ab-rek" (אב רך) is a compound word whose two elements signify respectively "father" (in wisdom) and "young" (in years), the whole denoting "young father" in the sense of "Jupiter" = "Ju" + "pater" (Levinsohn, "Shorashe Lebanon," s.v. אברך). Pharaoh renamed Joseph "Zaphnath-paaneah" = "the revealer of secrets."

Moses as a spiritual leader was recognized by the titles "ish ha-Elohim" = "the man of God" (Deut. xxxiii. 1) and "'ebed YHWH" = "the servant of the Lord" (ib. xxxiv. 5). These titles were applied to other prophets also (I Sam. ii. 27; Isa. xlii. 19).

The civil administration was conducted by judges who had the title of "prince," "ruler" ("sar," "sarim") over certain divisions of the people, comprising thousands, hundreds, fifties, and tens (Ex. xviii. 21). In a later period the judges ("shofeṭim") became the real rulers of the Israelites, till, like the Gentiles, the latter adopted a king. In Moses' time these were called also the "zeḳenim" = "elders" and the "nesi'im" = "rulers" (Lev. iv. 22) of the congregation.

The title of birth, "bekor," assigned to the first-born son in every family, carried with it special privileges of inheritance. The title "kohanim" = "priests," applied to all descendants of Aaron, and that of "Lewiyim" = "Levites," to the rest of the tribe of Levi, carried with them privileges with regard to tithes and certain duties in

Titles of Birth and Nobility. connection with the administration of religious services in the Temple; thus the senior priest was called "kohen mashiaḥ" = "the anointed priest" or "kohen gadol" = "the high priest." The prophet ("nabi") bore also the titles "ro'eh" and "ḥozeh" = "seer" (I Sam. ix. 9; II Kings xvii. 13).

Titles of nobility not connected with the tribe of Levi, but recognized by the people or conferred by the king as distinctions of ancient and noble stock, high descent, and gentility, were the following: "azil," "ḥor" = "freeman"; and "nasik," "rozen," or "razon" (Prov. xiv. 28) = "prince." Titles of civil officers chosen by the people were: "aluf," "nasi," "nagid," "ḳazin," and "rosh" = "chief." Titles of officers connected with the royal palace were: "abi ha-melek" (the father of the king, *i.e.*, prime minister); "saris" (eunuch, chamberlain, the king's friend; I Kings iv. 57); "rab ha-ṭabbaḥim" (executioner); "yoresh 'eẓer" (crown prince); "mishneh" (viceroy); "shalish" (third in rank, chief of staff); "nizẓab" or "nezib" (tribal governor; I Kings iv. 7); "peḥah," "sagan" (lieutenant and deputy; Jer. li. 23); "abir," "addir" (knight and hero); "kereti" and "peleti" (royal couriers and headsmen forming the body-guard of David); "seren" (satrap of the Philistines); "ṭifsar" (a military prefect); "partam," "'aḥashdarpan" (satrap under the Persian government); "sarek" (overseer; Dan. vi. 3); "rab," "rabreban" (chief, chieftain); "mazkir" (recorder). During the Exile the Persian king gave his courtiers titles: thus Daniel was renamed "Belteshazzar" (*ib.* i. 7), and Nehemiah "Tirshatha" (Neh. viii. 9). For later titles see Exilarch, Gabbai, Gaon, Nasi, Parnas, Rabbi, etc.

J.   J. D. E.

——**In Rabbinical Literature:** The Rabbis lay stress on the distinction due to "yiḥus" and "zekut abot" (see Patriarchs). A descendant of a noble family is a "yaḥsan" (well-born; comp. "gentle" in "gentleman"). The destruction of Jerusalem is ascribed to the lack of distinction between the nobles and the common people: "As with the people, so with the priest; as with the servant, so with the master" (Isa. xxiv. 2; Shab. 119b). With the exception of Simeon ha-Ẓaddiḳ (= "the just") the members of the Great Assembly and of the Sanhedrin were not referred to by any title (Ab. i. 2). The Biblical title "nasi" for the president of the community and "ab bet din" (father of the court of law) for the chief justice existed at an early period in the Palestinian academies. The title "rabban" (general master of the community) was given to Johanan b. Zakkai and to Gamaliel the Elder. The title "rabbi," designating an individual master, was only less honorable than "rabban." In the Babylonian schools "rab" was used instead. The title "rabbi" without the proper name was used to designate Judah ha-Nasi I. The scholars mentioned in the Mishnah, known as Tannaim, except those of the early period, have the title "rabbi" prefixed to their names, as have also the Palestinian amoraim, the Babylonian amoraim bearing that of "rab" (see Amoraim). The later Talmudists bear the title Mar (master). Ḥaber ("colleague") and Ḥakam were titles used in Palestine. Abba was used in Babylon, as was the title "resh galuta" (Exilarch), or "rosh ha-keneset" (head of the synagogue). Resh Kallah denoted the president of the students who assembled in the months of Adar and Elul. Parnas was the title of the administrator of the community; Gabbai, that of the public almoner, the collector and distributer of charities (Ned. 65b). The Ḥazzan in the mishnaic period was the sexton of the synagogue; in later times he was the reader of prayers; while the sexton or beadle was known as the "shammash." A teacher was called "melammed," and his assistant "resh dukana" (B. B. 21a). The latter taught the class of younger

XII.—11

Aris-
tocracy.

Communal
and
Religious
Titles.

children stationed on a platform; hence the name Dukan.

Honorific phrases used as epithets were assigned to the great rabbis in the Talmudic period by their disciples and admirers. R. Johanan b. Zakkai was called "the light of Israel, the right pillar, the mighty hammer" (Ber. 28b). Jose the priest, a disciple of Johanan b. Zakkai, was styled "ḥasid" = "pious" (Ab. ii. 11); there was also a R. Simeon Ḥasida (Suk. 52b). R. Eleazar called R. Asi "mofet ha-dor" = "the wonder of the generation" (Ḥul. 103b). Metaphorical terms were similarly used: R. Eleazar b. Simeon was "a lion the son of a lion" (B. M. 84b); R. Ḥiyya b. Abin was exalted as "the lion of society" (Shab. 111); Samuel was known as "the lion of Babylon" (*ib.* 53a); R. Akiba, as "oẓar balum" = "a treasure of knowledge" (Giṭ. 67a); R. Meïr (whose real name was Me'ashah) was so called because he enlightened the eyes of the wise in the Halakah ('Er. 13b); R. Menaḥem b. Simeon, "the son of the holy" ('Ab. Zarah 50a); R. Eleazar, "the best scholar" (Ker. 13b); R. Joseph, a "sharp knife" (Yeb. 122a), meaning that he was keen and logical in reasoning. The last-mentioned title was given also to Raba, Joseph's son (Ḥul. 77a). R. Joseph was styled "Sinai," and Rabbah "'oḳer harim" = "mountain-razer" (Hor. 14a). The former title describes the traditional and logical scholar; the latter, the pilpulist who depends on technical argumentation.

In the geonic period the title Gaon replaced "nasi" as referring to the president of the community. The principal of the academies of Sura and Pumbedita were known as "rosh yeshibah" or "resh metibta." The principal teachers were the "resh sidra" and the "resh kallah." The title "nagid" was conferred on R. Samuel (1027-55), the author of "Mebo ha-Talmud," and later replaced the title "gaon" in Egypt (see Egypt). The title "dayyan" (judge) appears to have been first used in the eleventh century, in Spain (see Bahya, Joseph ibn Paḳuda). In France and Germany the title "parnas" was revived, "manhig" (leader) being applied to the same official. The title Gabbai for the receiver of the taxes and contributions of the congregation was revived among the Sephardim; he ranked next to the parnas. The title "rabbenu" (our master) was given to Gershom, Tam, Hananeel, and Nissim.

The title Morenu ("our teacher") as a rabbinical degree introduced by R. Meïr ha-Levi of Vienna, was first conferred on R. Shalom and R. Jacob Mölln at the end of the fourteenth century. The titles "darshan" and Maggid were given to preachers.

Among the titles conferred on eminent Jews by governments in various countries were the following: In England during the twelfth and thirteenth centuries Bishop of the Jews, or "episcopus Judæorum," and Presbyter Judæorum, equivalent to the title "rabbi" or "ab bet din." In Germany the rabbi was sometimes called Hochmeister, "Judenmeister," or "Judenbischoff"; the learned Jew, "gelehrte Jude." "Court Jew" ("Hofjude") was equivalent to Shetadlan (שתדלן), the title of the attorney and representative of the Jews in their re-

Titles in
the Middle
Ages.

lations with the government in Poland and later in Russia.

King Matthias of Hungary created the offices of "princeps Judæorum," "supremus Judæorum," and "præfectus Judæorum," held by members of the MENDEL family (1482–1539), who were respon-

Government Titles. sible for the Jewish taxes and were clothed with special jurisdiction over the Jews. Other government officials were "doctor Judæorum" and "magister Judæorum," whom the emperor appointed to settle all disputes between the Jews (Jost, "Gesch. der Israeliten," vi. 54, Berlin, 1826). Rabbi Leon of Mantua in the fifteenth century received the title of Messer ("maestre"), usually given to physicians. The Turkish government confers the title "ḥakam bashi" on the chief rabbi of the Sephardim; it thus also occurs in Egypt.

In the sixteenth century the title "maran" (our lord) was applied to Joseph Caro of Safed, author of the Shulḥan 'Aruk; and for a long time thereafter it was not given to any other person. The title "gaon" was revived in honor of ELIJAH B. SOLOMON of Wilna (1720–97); and since it has been misapplied to ordinary rabbis, the gaon of Wilna is described also as "gaon amitti" = "the genuine gaon." The title "ḥarif," from the Talmudic title "sakkina ḥarifa" (sharp knife), was revived in the eighteenth century. The title BAḤUR dates back perhaps to the fourteenth century. It was used later in combination with an adjective, as "baḥur heḥashub" (the honored or worthy youth); and "yeshibah baḥur" designated the student in the yeshibah. The title "'illuy" (par excellence) described the young Talmudic genius.

The Ḥasidim came into existence in the time of Elijah Wilna. Their rabbis are variously styled "ẓaddiḳ" (righteous), "ba'al mofet" (wonder-master), "ba'al shem" (renowned master), and in Judæo-German "Rebbe" or "guter Yid."

In modern times the principal rabbi is known as "rab ha-galil" (district rabbi) and "rab ha-kolel" (equivalent to "chief rabbi" and "grand rabbin");

Modern Titles. also as "rabbi" and "dayyan," with "ab bet din" connoting the president of the religious and civil court. A new title, "zeḳan ha-rabbanim" (elder rabbi), was conferred by the United Orthodox Rabbis of America, at their convention in Philadelphia in 1903, on R. Jacob David RIDBAZ.

The German titles are "Rabbiner," "Rabbinats Assessor" (dayyan), and "Rabbinats Verweser." The title "reverend," conferred by the chief rabbi of England upon a Hebrew teacher, was criticized on the ground that "it ranks among the most mischievous and un-Jewish innovations peculiar to latter-day Anglo-Judaism" ("Jew. Chron." Jan. 3, 1902).

During the nineteenth century all Jewish titles were used in great profusion and indiscriminately. The title "gaon" was applied to nearly every rabbi, and some were addressed as "ha-ga'on ha-gadol" (the great gaon), "ha-ga'on ha-mefursam" (the well-known gaon), and, as if to out-Herod Herod, "ga'on ha-Ge'onim" (the gaon of the Geonim); also as "ha-ma'or ha-gadol" (the greater light), "me'or ha-

Golah" (the light of the Exile), and "rabban shel kol bene ha-Golah" (the master of all the members

Abuse of Titles. of the Exile). The titles "ḥarif," "baḳi" (familiar with the Law), and "muṭlag" (extraordinary) were common ones for the ordinary learned layman. The abuse of titles has been the subject of biting criticism, sarcasm, and even ridicule by the Maskilim, especially by Isaac ERTER and Leon GORDON.

As to the moral right to address one by an unmerited title, R. Samuel di MEDINA (1505–89) rules against it, though he permits such titles as are customary (Rashdam, "Eben ha-'Ezer," No. 65). Ḥayyim Hezekiah Medini, in his "Sedeh Ḥemed" (i., letter ה, § 140; ק, § 157, Warsaw, 1896), reviews the decisions in the responsa collections on this question, and comes to the conclusion that since the title "gaon" has become a common rabbinical one it would be a breach of etiquette to omit it in addressing a rabbi of some authority and repute.

Some authors in compiling their responsa are careful to remove personal titles from their correspondence. R. Akiba EGER in his testament ordered his executors to erase before publication all titles except "rabbi" in the numerous letters addressed to him on matters of casuistry.

Joel Höschel ("'Aṭeret Yeshu'ah," Wilna, 1799) and Jehiel HEILPRIN ("'Erke ha-Kinnuyim," Dyhernfurth, 1806) give lists of epithets of Biblical personages. Certain Hebrew letter-writers also contain various forms of titles; in particular that of Joseph Rakower, "Leshon Naḳi" (Prague, 1704, and often reprinted), should be mentioned. The only special work known on the subject of this article is one in manuscript by Jehiel Mendelssohn (d. 1904).

J.   J. D. E.

TITUS (full name, **Titus Flavius Sabinus Vespasianus**): Emperor of Rome from 79 to 81; born in 39 or 41; died Sept. 13, 81; son of VESPASIAN, the conqueror of Jerusalem. He was educated at the courts of Claudius and Nero. Titus served first in Germany and later in Britain under his father, whom he subsequently assisted greatly in Judea by suppressing the rebellion of the Jews.

While Vespasian was operating in Galilee, the news of the death of Nero (June 9, 68) was received; and Titus, accompanied by AGRIPPA II., was sent to Rome to swear allegiance to Nero's successor. Galba was murdered in the meantime, however; and Titus hastened back to Judea, where the Egyptian and Syrian troops proclaimed Vespasian emperor, an occurrence which Josephus declares he had predicted in the presence of Titus himself (Josephus, "B. J."

In Judea. iii. 8, § 9; comp. Suidas, s.v. Ἰώσηπος; in Dion Cassius, lxvi. 1, Titus is not mentioned). It was Titus, moreover, who, under the leadership of his father, reduced the cities of Jotapata, Taricheæ, and Giscala, where he displayed, on the one hand, great courage and contempt of death, and, on the other, bitter cruelty toward the conquered; when, therefore, Vespasian went to Rome as emperor, Titus was left to prosecute the Jewish war.

With a considerable force he left Cæsarea and

reached the walls of Jerusalem a few days before the Passover festival of the year 70. Omitting the details of this memorable war, only those events which concern Titus personally need be mentioned here. Together with 600 horsemen he rode ahead of his main army to reconnoiter the surrounding country, and had ventured so far in advance that only his valor saved him from capture in a Jewish attack ("B. J." v. 2, § 2). He endeavored at first to per-

Coin of Titus Struck in Palestine, with Inscription, "Ivdæa Devicta."
(After Madden, " History of Jewish Coinage.")

suade the Jews to submit by making promises to them (Dion Cassius, lxvi. 4); and Josephus was sent to them several times with messages to that effect. They refused all overtures, however; and battering-rams were then set in action, and the beleaguerment of Jerusalem began. The Jews often **Besieges** destroyed these siege-works, and dur- **Jerusalem.** ing one of their sorties Titus himself was so severely wounded in the left shoulder by a stone that his hand remained weak ever afterward (Dion Cassius, l.c. § 5; Josephus in "B. J." v. 6, § 2 relates a similar occurrence, although he does not mention the wounding of Titus). According to Dion Cassius, the Romans refused to attack the Temple on account of their respect for its sanctity; and Titus had to force them to do so. Josephus, on the other hand, differs on this point also,

Coin of Titus, with Inscription "Ivdaea Navalis."
(After Madden, " History of Jewish Coinage.")

stating instead that Titus first held a council of war with his commanding officers, among them TIBE-RIUS JULIUS ALEXANDER, and that certain generals advised the destruction of the Temple. He himself, however, wished to spare it ("B. J." vi. 4, § 3), and gave orders to extinguish the fire which had begun to consume the cloisters, apparently displaying this mildness either on account of BERENICE or to show his friendship for Agrippa. Against this stands the narrative of the monk Sulpicius, who is said to have drawn his information from Tacitus; and, follow-

ing this authority, Jacob Bernays (" Programm des Jüdisch-Theologischen Seminars in Breslau," 1861, p. 48) charges Josephus with untruthfulness; Grätz, however (" Gesch." iii. 539), is inclined to believe in the veracity of Josephus' statement.

On the following day (the tenth of Ab, 70) the Jews made a desperate sortie, and one of the Roman soldiers, weary of fighting, threw a burning piece of wood into the Temple. In vain did Titus give orders to extinguish the flames; his voice was drowned in the uproar. Titus himself, impelled by curiosity, entered the Sanctuary, but the smoke forced him to withdraw; and thus the destruction **Burning of** of the Temple of Jerusalem became **the** associated with his name. On the **Temple.** ruins of the Sanctuary Titus was proclaimed emperor by his soldiers ("B. J." vi. 6, § 1; Dion Cassius, l.c. § 7; Suetonius, "Titus," v.), although both he and his father refused the epithet "Judaicus," because the word might suggest an inclination toward the Jewish religion (see, however, Joël, "Blicke in die Religionsgeschichte," ii. 46).

Even Josephus was able to point to only scanty traces of mildness in the life of Titus, while, on the other hand, cruelties are recorded which must be attributed to personal hatred on his part, and not to the unavoidable harshness of war. In Cæsarea in Palestine, in Cæsarea Philippi, and in Berytus he forced the captive Jews to fight against wild animals and also against one another; and many thousands more were slain to please the revengeful Syrians and Greeks. It was in Rome, however, that he celebrated his triumphs, together with his father and his brother Domitian; there 700 Jews of splendid physique and the leaders of the Zealots, John of Giscala and Simon bar Giora, helped to grace his procession. Two triumphal arches were erected in his honor. Of these, one no longer **Arches of** exists, and is remembered only on ac- **Titus.** count of the inscription which it bore ("C. I. L." vi. 444), but the other, a beautiful structure, still stands in Rome, and on it may be seen representations of the captured vessels of the Temple. See TITUS, ARCH OF.

The Jews hated Titus on account of his share in the destruction of the Temple; and the Rabbis accordingly termed him "Titus the miscreant," thus contrasting sharply with the statements of the classical writers, who regarded him as an ornament of the human race. It may be proved, however, that he was anything but upright while he was crown prince; indeed, he was cruel, licentious, and ambitious, and was even suspected of having sought to poison his father. Only during the latter part of his reign did he display praiseworthy qualities. A significant saying of frequent recurrence in rabbinic sources is to the effect that he was honored in Rome as the conqueror of the barbarians (νικητὴς βαρβάρων; Gen. R. x.; Lev. R. xxii. 3; Lam. R., Introduction, No. 23, etc.), thus showing that the Jews were regarded as an inferior and barbarous nation. All the other accounts of Titus in rabbinical literature are purely legendary, and their utter unreliability is shown by the fact that he is called the nephew instead of the son of Vespasian, a view which was repeated in medieval chronicles (Neubauer, "M. J. C." i. 50, 70). In the Holy of Holies, moreover, he was said to have pierced the veil of the Ark, to have had intercourse with two courtezans (a rem

Rabbinical iniscence of his relations with Bere

Legends. nice), and to have defiled the Torah (*ib.*; Giṭ. 56b); in short, to have blasphemed God. That he packed the sacred vessels in a basket and took them on board his ship was also stated in rabbinical tradition. As he stepped from his bath—so runs a legend—a drink was handed to him, when suddenly a gnat (יתוש) stung him in the nose, and thus caused his death (Ab. R. N., Recension B, vii.; it is noteworthy that this form of retribution also figures in Arabic legends, which often confuse Titus with Nebuchadnezzar, who likewise destroyed the Temple; "R. E. J." lxix. 212). This has been interpreted as implying that Titus became melancholy and insane in his declining years (Hamburger, "R. B. T." *s.v.*); but such an explanation seems inadmissible. Despite the Jewish hatred of Titus, many Jews as well as Christians have borne his name (in the New Testament, Titus i. 4; Gal. ii. 3; II Cor. ii. 13, and elsewhere; for the Jews, see Krauss, "Lehnwörter," ii. 262); and in later times four prominent Jewish families of Italy have traced their descent from prisoners taken by him (see ROME).

The medieval Jews invented numerous legends concerning Titus; thus, according to "Yosippon" and Benjamin of Tudela, the Roman consuls (*i.e.*, senators) blamed him for taking three years instead of two to conquer Jerusalem. Benjamin claims also to have seen the supposed palace of Titus at Rome; and, according to Abraham ibn Daud ("Sefer ha-Ḳabbalah," ed. Prague, 1795, p. 40b), Titus put to death the high priest Ishmael b. Elisha and R. Simeon b. Gamaliel, although only the latter was actually executed. The names of hosts of other patriots and martyrs who lost their lives through Titus are unknown.

BIBLIOGRAPHY: Grätz, *Gesch.* 4th ed., iii. 494, 532, 539, *et passim*; Schürer, *Gesch.* 3d ed., i. 610–637 *et passim*; Vogelstein and Rieger, *Gesch. der Juden in Rom*, i. 22–25, 91. For the Jewish legends, see I. Lévi in *R. E. J.* xv. 62–69.

J.   S. KR.

TITUS, ARCH OF: A triumphal arch erected at Rome in honor of the emperor Titus and in celebration of his victory over the Jews. It rises on the prominent part of the Via Sacra, about 20 yards above the Tiber. One of its faces fronts the Colosseum; the other, the Forum. Under the pontificate of Pius VII. the arch was restored in its lateral portions, which had become injured by time. The structure consists of a single arcade adorned with sculptured crowns and tympans. On the right and on the left are two united columns of a composite order with rich entablature, and an elevated attic. Three bas-reliefs adorn the passage of

Arch of Titus at Rome.
(From a photograph.)

the arcade. One, on the Colosseum side, shows Titus, crowned by Victory, standing upright in a car drawn by four horses and conducted by a female personifying the city of Rome. The second represents Roman soldiers without weapons, crowned with laurels, and carrying the spoils of the Temple of Jerusalem. These spoils are: two tablets fastened on staffs, the seven-branched candle-stick, and the golden table upon which are leaning the sacred trumpets. The third bas-relief, under the vault, exhibits Titus sitting on an eagle, as he appears on the medals struck to consecrate his apotheosis.

A tradition, which still prevails in Rome, says that formerly no Jew ever passed under this arch, and that, in order to go from the Colosseum to the Capitol, the inhabitants of the ghetto opened a way between the arch and the Palatine.

BIBLIOGRAPHY: Philippi, *Ueber die Römischen Triumphalreliefs*, pl. ii., iii., Leipsic, 1872; Reinach, *L'Arc de Titus*, in *R. E. J.* xx., lxv.; Reland, *De Spoliis Templi Hierosolymitani in Arcu Titiano*. See, also, T. Reinach, *ib.* xx.; Appendix, lxv.–xci.; B. Wolff-Beckh, *Kaiser Titus und der Jüdische Krieg*, in *Neue Jahrbücher für das Klassische Alterthum*, 1903, vi. (also published separately, Berlin, 1904).

J. JR.   I. BE.

ṬOB 'ELEM, JOSEPH. See BONFILS, JOSEPH B. SAMUEL.

ṬOB LE-HODOT. See MIZMOR SHIR LE-YOM HA-SHABBAT.

TOBACCO (טוטון, טאבאקן): The use of tobacco for smoking and in the form of snuff is common among Jews, who in some countries control to a large extent the manufacture and sale of the product. It is asserted that a Jew named Luis de Terres, who accompanied Columbus on his expedition in 1492, settled in Cuba, learned the use of tobacco, and introduced it into Europe. From this time Jews have

("Keneset ha-Gedolah," to Oraḥ Ḥayyim, 551, 21). He points out the inconsistency of those authorities who permit smoking on holy days because it is a "necessity," a "means of sustaining life," and who allow it on fast-days because smoke has no "substance" like food. In Benveniste's opinion smoking

SPOILS OF THE TEMPLE, PICTURED ON THE ARCH OF TITUS.
(After Bartoli's "Admiranda.")

been connected with the trade in tobacco, one of the most important in early American history (M. J. Kohler, in "Publ. Am. Jew. Hist. Soc." x. 52). The introduction of tobacco into Europe encountered the resolute opposition of the clergy, who characterized tobacco-smoking as "offering incense to Satan." The Rabbis, however, discussed the use of tobacco not from a moral, but from a legal standpoint—concerning its prohibition on Sabbaths, holy days, and **In Jewish** fast-days, and as to whether smoking **Law.** requires a special benediction. As a subject of controversy it appears first in the "Keneset ha-Gedolah" of R. Ḥayyim Benveniste (1603–73) and the "Magen Abraham" of Abraham Gombiner (1635–83), which fact tends to show that during the seventeenth century the practise of tobacco-smoking spread rapidly among the Jews of all nations.

Gombiner describes the "drinking of tabak through a pipe by drawing the smoke into the mouth and discharging it." The rabbi is in doubt whether or not one must pronounce a benediction before inhaling the smoke, since it is a means of refreshment. As an argument against pronouncing a blessing he observes that there is no "substance" in the benefit derived ("Magen Abraham," to Shulḥan 'Aruk, Oraḥ Ḥayyim, 210, 9). He prohibits smoking tobacco "through the mouth" on Passover, as he was informed that the tobacco was soaked in beer, which is "ḥameẓ" (ib. 343). Benveniste expresses himself very forcibly against smoking "ṭuṭun" (tobacco) on the Ninth of Ab; and he even **excommunicated** one who smoked on that day

should be prohibited on holy days; he quotes the venerable R. Joseph Escapa as coinciding in this view, though he thought it unwise to enforce a generally accepted law.

Table of Showbread, Pictured on the Arch of Titus.
(After Reland, "De Spoliis Templi," 1716.)

The Jews of Turkey at that time must have been very much addicted to the habit, for Benveniste pictures them as inveterate smokers, impatient for the close of Sabbath, when they might resume smoking, and as watching for the appearance of the three stars which indicate the end of the day; some began smoking even before "Habdalah." "They lingered in the streets and public houses, every man with a censer in his hand, inhaling the smoke and discharging it in fantastic diffusion,"

Tobacco-Lovers. until "a thick cloud of incense went up" (comp. Ezek. viii. 11). He declares that the Name of God is desecrated when the Gentiles observe Jews smoking on their fast-days, while Mohammedans refrain from smoking on theirs ("Keneset ha-Gedolah," *ib.* 567 [ed. Constantinople, 1729, pp. 101 *et seq.*]). Some Jews, unable to abstain from tobacco even for one day, filled a hooka with smoke on Friday and inhaled it on the Sabbath. Others would visit Mohammedan neighbors for the sake of the tobacco smoke in their houses. This practise was eventually prohibited on the ground that it would make Judaism ridiculous in the eyes of the Gentiles (Alkalai, "Zekor le-Abraham," i. 142-143, Salonica, 1798).

The Turkish narghile, in which the smoke passes through water, early became popular; Benveniste rules that the "tumbak" (cake of tobacco, over which a burning coal is placed at the other end of the narghile) extinguishes the fire, which is forbidden even on holy days. Gombiner prohibits tumbak because it is like "mugmar" (spice for burning), mentioned in the Talmud, which likewise is prohibited. This, however, is disputed by R. Mordecai ha-Levi in his "Darke No'am" (No. 9, Venice, 1698), who permits the use of the narghile on holy days (see "Be'er Heteb," to Shulḥan 'Aruk, Oraḥ Ḥayyim, 514, 1). The controversy finally ended in a victory for those rabbis who permitted the use of tobacco on holy days and fast-days, except of course on Yom Kippur, which is like Sabbath; still, some Jews still abstain from smoking on the Ninth of Ab.

In spite of some objections, snuff-taking was permitted at any time—Sabbaths, holy days, fast-days, and Yom Kippur ("Leḳeṭ ha-**Snuff.** Ḳemaḥ," p. 51b, Amsterdam, 1707). Jacob Ḥaziz (1620-74) quotes a responsum of Isaiah Pinto permitting the use of snuff on Sabbaths, even though it cures catarrh; for everybody, even healthy people, snuff, and it can not therefore be considered a drug ("Halakot Ḳeṭannot," No. 101).

It appears that women used tobacco almost as much as men (see Elijah of Lublin, "Yad Eliyahu," responsum No. 65, Amsterdam, 1712). Jewish women in the Orient mostly used the narghile, while in Russia old women used snuff; others smoked cigarettes, like men. So prevalent was the habit of smoking that it was practised even in the bet hamidrash. A strong effort, however, was made to prohibit smoking and snuffing in places of worship ("Paḥad Yizḥaḳ," ṭ, p. 62a). In some batte midrashot prohibitory notices were posted in front of the doors ("Ha-Maggid," 1859, vol. iii., No. 16).

In countries where the government had a monopoly of the tobacco trade, manufacturing and trading privileges were assigned to Jewish merchants at a fixed price per annum for a number of years. The question was raised whether the contractor had a prior right to the next contract as against the claims of a new competitor. Lampronti decided that con-

tracts were open to competition, inasmuch as the matter depended on the laws and regulations of the government ("Paḥad Yizḥaḳ," א, p. 90a). Russian Jews have invented some practical cigarette-making machines for which they have obtained patents.

A remarkable book is Raphael Kohen's "Ḥuṭ ha-Meshullash" (Odessa, 1874), which deals with the question of cigar-smoking on Sabbaths, and which finally reaches the conclusion that it is permissible on the ground that it affords "'oneg shabbat" (delight and enjoyment). Not daring to publish his name, the author issued his book under a pseudonym. His discussion was not considered a serious one; nevertheless it is of a kind unusual in Hebrew literature.

There are several Hebrew poems for and against smoking. Solomon Wilder of Amsterdam composed one in acceptance of a tobacco-pipe as a birthday present ("Ha-Karmel," 1862, vol. ii., No. 20). Another poem characterizes the cigar and cigarette as "the two tails of these smoking firebrands" (Isa. vii. 4; see "Ha-Boḳer Or," i. 123).

BIBLIOGRAPHY: *Ha-Maggid*, viii., No. 37; *Ha-Ẓefirah*, i., No. 8; *Keneset ha-Gedolah*, iii., end; A. K. Kaufman, *Räuchert un Shikkert*, Warsaw, 1900; Löw, *Lebensalter*, p. 351; Abrahams, *Jewish Life in the Middle Ages*, p. 139; Steinschneider, in *Die Deborah* (1894), vol. xl., No. 1.
J. J. D. E.

TOBIA BEN MOSES HA-ABEL (surnamed also **Ha-'Obed** = "the worshiper," **Ha-Baḳi** = "the erudite," **Ha-Maskil** = "the teacher," and **Ha-Ma'tiḳ** = "the translator"): Karaite scholar, Biblical commentator, liturgical poet, and translator; flourished at Constantinople in the eleventh and twelfth centuries. Fürst ("Gesch. des Karäert." ii. 198 *et seq.*) conjectures Tobia's dates to have been about 1070 to 1140; but it will be seen later that he was born earlier (see also Steinschneider, "Hebr. Uebers." p. 457). Tobia's last three surnames indicate the range of his erudition and literary **Epoch and** activity; indeed, his works them-**At-** selves show his thorough knowledge **tainments.** of rabbinics, philosophy, and theology. He moreover went to Jerusalem, where he studied for some time under Jeshua b. Judah, and where he became acquainted with the Arabic writings of the latter as well as with those of Joseph b. Abraham ha-Ro'eh, afterward translating into Hebrew many of the works of both. In one of his books, entitled "Yehi Me'orot," Tobia declares that he was a propagandist of Karaism, owing to which he suffered many persecutions from his own family as well as from his opponents. But, he says, when one is fully convinced of the truth he must regard neither family nor his own life. It would thus appear that Tobia was of a Rabbinite family and that through studying Karaite works he became an adherent of Karaism, in consequence of which his family turned against him. Possibly the writings of no other scholar were the subject of so much dispute as those of Tobia ben Moses. The following is a list of them as may be gathered from various sources:

(1) "Yehi Me'orot," a work on the commandments, so called after the opening sentence; it is called also "Sefer ha-Miẓwot." Firkovich ascribed it to Judah Hadassi; but Aaron b. Joseph in

his "Mibḥar" (on Emor) and Elijah Bashyaẓi in his "Adderet Eliyahu" clearly show Tobia to have been its author. The earliest Rabbinite authority quoted therein is Hai b. David, whose anti-Karaite work with regard to the Rabbinite calendar is repeated; then comes Saadia, many of whose anti-Karaite passages are repeated and refuted; and of Saadia's successors may be mentioned Tobiah b. Eliezer ("Leḳaḥ Ṭob"). It may be concluded from

Works.

the latter's work that Tobia wrote the "Yehi Me'orot" not earlier than 1100.

(2) "Zot ha-Torah," commentary on the Pentateuch, a manuscript of which was found in the library of Eupatoria (Kozlov), but was lost during the Crimean war of 1853–56.

Another important work by Tobia was (3) "Ozar Neḥmad," described by Simḥah Luzki ("Oraḥ Ẓaddiḳim," p. 22b) as in two parts, the first treating of lawful and forbidden foods, and the second of the laws regarding cleanness and uncleanness. In reality this work deals with all the laws contained in Leviticus, as appears from Bashyaẓi (*l.c.* pp. 41d, 43b). The author quotes all the Karaite Biblical commentators; and he particularly refutes the doctrines of MESHWI AL-'UKBARI, or Moses of Baalbek, whom he declares to have embraced Christianity toward the end of his life. The main authority upon whom the work is based is David b. Boaz ha-Nasi. Besides Simḥah Luzki (*l.c.*), who asserts that the "Ozar Neḥmad" was the work of Tobia, Delmedigo ("Nobelot Ḥokmah," p. 56a, Basel, 1631) and Aaron b. Joseph (in his "Sefer ha-Miẓwot," quoted by Mordecai b. Nissan in his "Dod Mordekai") ascribe it to him. Pinsker ("Liḳḳuṭe Ḳadmoniyyot," Appendix, pp. 93–94), however, thinks that the work belongs to Jeshua b. Judah, as is indicated by Bashyaẓi (*l.c.*), and that as Tobia translated this work from Arabic into Hebrew, Luzki mistook him for its author. It must be said, however, that Luzki distinguishes between the "Ozar Neḥmad" of Tobia and Jeshua's work which bears the same title and which was actually translated by Tobia.

Other works by Tobia were: (4) "Teshubat ha-'Iḳḳar" (Eupatoria, 1834), which, according to Fürst (*l.c.*), is a compendium of Jeshua's "Kitab al-'Arayot" (but see Steinschneider, *l.c.* p. 943). In the introduction the author speaks of the four kinds of intellect ("da'at"), termed in Hebrew "sekel," "ḥokmah," "tushiyyah," and "binah"; he then gives the rules for exegesis, the thirteen hermeneutic rules ("middot") of R. Ishmael, and the twelve of the Greeks. (5) Religio-philosophical questions ("she'elot") addressed to his teacher Jeshua b. Judah in Jerusalem (see Judah Hadassi, "Eshkol ha-Kofer," p. 76a). (6) Addition ("tosafah") to Joseph ha-Ro'eh's "Kitab al-Manṣuri," which he translated into Hebrew under the title "Maḥkimat Peti."

Tobia's surname "Ha-Ma'tiḳ" shows his great activity in translating. Steinschneider (*l.c.* p. 457) supposes that this activity began about the middle

Translations.

of the eleventh century; Tobia would then be the first known translator from Arabic into Hebrew. Fürst enumerates the following thirteen works of Joseph ha-Ro'eh and five of Jeshua b. Judah which were translated by Tobia: (1) "Kitab al-Ṣiḥ-

ḥah"; (2) "Kitab al-Shira‘"; (3) "Kitab al-'Arayot"; (4) "Kitab al-Tauḥid," which Steinschneider supposes to be a mistake for "al-Tamyiz"; (5) "Kitab al-Siraj" under the Hebrew title "Sefer ha-Ma'or" or "Sefer ha-Me'orot" or "Sefer ha-Urim"; (6) a work on "Abib" written against Saadia; (7) one on feasts under the Hebrew title "Sefer ha-Mo'adim"; (8) "Kitab al-Manṣuri" under the Hebrew title "Maḥkimat Peti" (see above); (9) "Kitab al-Rudd 'Ala Abi Ghalib Thabit"; (10) "Aḥwal al-Fa'il"; (11) "Zidduḳ ha-Din"; (12) "Al-Muḥtawi," in Hebrew "Sefer ha-Ne'imot" or "Zikron ha-Datot"; (13) "Masa'il wa-Jawa'ib," in Hebrew "She'elot u-Teshubot." Jeshua's works translated by Tobia were: (1) the first part of his religious philosophy, under the Hebrew title "Marpe ha-'Eẓem"; (2) "Meshibat Nefesh"; (3) "Ozar Neḥmad"; (4) a work on speculation under the Hebrew title "Sefer ha-Ra'yon"; (5) Jeshua's completion of Joseph's "Al-Muḥtawi." Fürst, however, omits mention of (6) Jeshua's commentary on the Decalogue translated by Tobia under the title "Pitron 'Aseret ha-Debarim" (see P. Frankl in "Monatsschrift," xxix. 472).

The "Ḥazanya" (old Karaite ritual) contains two piyyuṭim by Tobia: one beginning "Elohenu mi-kol ummah ahabtanu," arranged in alphabetical order, and signed "Tobia b. Moses Ḥazaḳ"; the other beginning "Esh'alah me-El," and being an acrostic on "Tobia b. Moses ha-'Obed." The "Siddur ha-Ḳara'im" (iv. 88) also contains a piyyuṭ by Tobia. It may be added that Firkovich, in a note to Gottlober's "Biḳḳoret le-Toledot ha-Ḳara'im" (p. 169), distinguishes between Tobia ha-Baḳi, the author of "Zot ha-Torah" and of a metrical piyyuṭ beginning "Ṭahor 'en sefatai tiftaḥ," and Tobia ha-'Obed, the former having lived about a century earlier than the latter. Firkovich thinks that Tobia ha-'Obed was a descendant of Tobia ha-Baḳi and was the author of "Zot ha-Ḥayyah," a work on clean and unclean animals. Still, Firkovich, in a letter to Pinsker ("Liḳḳuṭe Ḳadmoniyyot," Appendix, p. 94, note 1), contradicts himself in this matter.

BIBLIOGRAPHY: Fürst, *Gesch. des Karäert.* ii. 198–207; Gottlober, *Biḳḳoret le-Toledot ha-Ḳara'im,* pp. 169–170; S. Pinsker, *Liḳḳuṭe Ḳadmoniyyot,* p. 219, Appendix, pp. 93 *et seq.,* 139; Steinschneider, *Hebr. Uebers.* pp. 154 *et seq.,* 940 *et seq.*
E. C.   M. SEL.

TOBIADS: Jewish party in the Maccabean period. A combination of the statements of Josephus ("Ant." xii. 4, §§ 1–11) and of II Macc. iii. 11 yields an interesting family history, which, however, requires critical examination.

During the reign of the Egyptian king Ptolemy and his wife Cleopatra, the high priest Onias, who was feeble-minded and extremely miserly, refused to pay the Jewish tribute of twenty talents which his father, Simon the Just, had always given from his own means. In his anger the king sent Athenion as a special envoy to Jerusalem, threatening to seize the land of the Jews and to hold it by force of arms if the money was not forthcoming. Although the high priest disregarded this threat, the people were greatly excited, whereupon Onias' nephew Joseph, a son of Tobias and a man greatly beloved and respected for his wisdom and piety, reproached his uncle for bringing disaster upon the people, declaring, moreover, that Onias ruled the Jews and held the high-priestly office solely for the sake of gain. He told him, furthermore, that he ought at all events to go to the king and petition him to remit the tribute-money, or at least a part of it. Onias, on the other hand, replied that he did not wish to rule, and expressed himself as willing to resign the high-priesthood, although he refused to petition the king. He permitted Joseph, however, to go to Ptolemy, and also to speak to the people. Joseph quieted the Jews, and received the envoy hospitably in his own house, besides giving him costly presents, so that, when Athenion returned to Alexandria, he informed the king of the coming of Joseph, whom he styled the ruler ($\pi\rho o\sigma\tau\acute{a}\tau\eta\varsigma$) of the people. Shortly afterward Joseph started on his journey, having first raised a loan of about 20,000 drachmæ in Samaria, although he was obliged to submit to the jeers of prominent men of Syria and Phenicia, who were visiting Alexandria in order to farm the taxes, and who derided him on account of his insignificant appearance.

Not finding Ptolemy at Alexandria, Joseph went to meet him at Memphis, where the king graciously granted him a seat in his own chariot, together with the queen and Athenion. His cleverness won for him the monarch's friendship; and by his offer of 16,000 talents against the 8,000 bid by his **Relations** opponents he secured the contract **with Alex-** for farming the taxes, the king and **andria.** queen becoming his sureties, since he did not have sufficient ready money. He left Alexandria with 500 talents and 2,000 soldiers, and by punishing all who opposed him in Ashkelon and Scythopolis and confiscating their estates, he made himself feared through all the cities of Syria and Phenicia, while the great fortune which his extortions won was held secure by his continual presents to the king, queen, and courtiers, so that he retained his office of tax-farmer until his death, twenty-two years later. By his first wife Joseph had seven sons. At Alexandria he became infatuated with a dancer, for whom his brother Solymius, who lived in the city, substituted his own daughter, the child of this union being Hyrcanus, who was his father's favorite son and consequently the object of his brothers' enmity.

On the birth of a prince, Joseph feeling too old to visit Alexandria and his other sons likewise declining to go, sent Hyrcanus to bear his congratulations to the court. Arion, Joseph's representative in Alexandria, however, refused to allow Hyrcanus money, and the latter accordingly put him in chains, not only escaping punishment from the king, but even winning both his favor and that of the courtiers, whose aid his brothers had secretly invoked against him. Although the king sent letters recommending him warmly to his father, his brothers, and the officials of Cœle-Syria, the other sons of Joseph met him with armed resistance. He defeated them, however, and killed two of them; but, being unable to remain in Jerusalem, he crossed the Jordan, and in the vicinity of Heshbon built the castle of Tyre, carrying on war with the Arabs, and ruling the district east of the Jordan during the entire seven years of Seleucus IV. The following statement is made by Josephus ("Ant." xii. 4, § 10): "And Hyrcanus' father, Joseph, died. He was a good man, and of great magnanimity, and brought the Jews out of a state of poverty and meanness to one that was more splendid. He retained the farming of the taxes of Syria, and Phenicia, and Samaria twenty-two years. His uncle, Onias, also died, and left the high-priesthood to his son Simon." This statement of Josephus is followed by the correspondence between Onias and King Areus of Sparta, and by an account of the Jewish disturbances due to feuds after the death of Joseph, when the Tobiads became involved in a civil war. The majority of the people, as well as Simeon the high priest, however, sided with the elder brother, and Hyrcanus did not return to Jerusalem, but continued his warfare against the Arabs. Both for his own comfort, and also as a safeguard against attacks by his brothers, he built the castle of Tyre and various other strongholds, ruling there until the death of Seleucus IV. Ptolemy Epiphanes also died, leaving two young sons; but when Hyrcanus saw that Antiochus Epiphanes, the new king of Syria, possessed great power, and when he realized that he would be unable to vindicate himself for his murderous attacks upon the Arabs, he committed suicide, and his property was seized by Antiochus.

It is clear, therefore, that there are here two accounts, both legendary, the hero of the one being Joseph, and of the other, Hyrcanus. **The Two** The history of the earlier years of the **Accounts.** father closely resembles that of the son; in both cases the ambitious youth is opposed by the miserly parent, and in both cases the youth succeeds in putting his competitors to shame before the royal court. The narrative is suspicious in many respects. Onias angers the king, but Joseph travels to the court both to assuage the king's anger and to farm the taxes, while the sanguinary battle between Hyrcanus and his brothers is also obscure. The most serious difficulty, however, is the chronology. An old interpolator of Josephus advanced the opinion that the king mentioned in the story was Ptolemy III.; but this monarch was not the consort of Cleopatra, nor was his immediate successor Seleucus IV. The only ruler to whom the narrative can properly refer is Ptolemy V., Epiphanes (205–182), who in 193 married Cleopatra, the daughter of Antiochus III. In that case, however, Joseph could not have farmed the Egyptian taxes, since Cœle-Syria was then under Syrian, and not under Egyptian, suzerainty, while the assertion that the two powers had divided the revenues of the country is merely an attempt on the part of Josephus to evade the difficulty. Nor was the period between Ptolemy V.'s marriage (193) and his death (182) sufficiently long to agree with the statement concerning the length of time during which Joseph farmed the taxes (twenty-two years), and still less could Hyrcanus have reached manhood in so short a space. Büchler, therefore, finds himself compelled to place Joseph's term of office between 219 and 199, although this stultifies the statement of Josephus regarding a division of the taxes.

Wellhausen accordingly denies both the historicity and the value of the narrative, although he thinks

Modern Views.

that the portion dealing with the period of Seleucus IV. and Antiochus IV. may be trustworthy, and he regards the suicide of Hyrcanus as probable, since the latter supported the Ptolemies against the new régime of the Syrians, and might consequently fear the revenge of Antiochus IV. II Macc. iii. 11 mentions money deposited by Hyrcanus, the son of Tobias, "a man of great dignity," taking it for granted that a friendship existed between Onias and Hyrcanus, a supposition which is very reasonable, since only the other Tobiads, the brothers of Hyrcanus, were involved in quarrels with the legitimate high priest. That Hyrcanus is called the son of Tobias, and not of Joseph, is due, Wellhausen holds, to mere abbreviation, and does not imply any divergency in the two accounts.

Willreich distinguishes a threefold tradition concerning the Tobiads, the first being that of the pseudo-Hecatæus (according to Willreich's interpretation), which represents Onias as a worthy man, and attributes to the Tobiads all the misfortunes which befell the Jews. The account of Josephus, on the other hand, which represents Onias as a weakling and the Tobiads as the promoters of Israel's welfare, is drawn from Samaritan sources. With this theory Büchler also agrees, thus explaining why Joseph sought aid in Samaria, and why the account fails to express disapproval of the non-Jewish conduct of Joseph, who ate at the court of an Egyptian king and had dealings with Gentiles. Willreich likewise brings the Tobiads into association both with Tobiah, the servant mentioned by Nehemiah as an Ammonite (ii. 19), who consequently came from the east-Jordanic district, and with the Tubieni (II Macc. xii. 17), who were the enemies of the Jews (comp. I Macc. v. 13). Although Willreich does not absolutely deny the historicity of the narrative, since the castle of Hyrcanus has been discovered in modern times (Schürer, "Gesch." 3d ed., ii. 49), he incorrectly regards Joseph and Hyrcanus as mere names, representing in part Jason and Menelaus, although such a view is quite untenable. The third form of the tradition is that of Jason of Cyrene, on which the second Book of the Maccabees is based; and Schlatter is even of the opinion that Josephus himself drew his account of the Tobiads from this same source.

Büchler's researches have probably established the historicity of the account of the Tobiads, thus furnishing a valuable contribution to the history of the period preceding the Maccabean revolt. The author of the first Book of the Maccabees makes no mention of these events because they added little credit to the fame of the Jews. The quarrels were factional ones, the issue being whether the old and popular government of the Ptolemies should continue, or whether the Jews should deliver themselves over to the Syrian kings and their Hellenization. When Jason and Menelaus struggled for the dominant power in Jerusalem, which was, according to Büchler, political office (the προστασία mentioned in the account of the Tobiads), and no longer the high-priesthood, the sons of Tobias (οἱ Τωβίου παῖδες) took

sides with Menelaus (Josephus, "Ant." xii. 5, § 1; "B. J." i. 1, § 1); and Büchler justly regards the struggle between the Tobiads and the Oniads as a contest between Ptolemæan and Seleucid supremacy in Jerusalem. According to the same scholar, moreover, Menelaus and Jason themselves were Tobiads, although this is denied by Schürer. All scholars are agreed that many points of the Tobiad problem still await solution; and it is also a moot point whether a number of passages in Ecclesiasticus (Sirach) and one in the Assumptio Mosis (v. 3-6) refer to the Tobiads.

BIBLIOGRAPHY: Willreich, *Juden und Griechen vor der Makkabäischen Erhebung*, pp. 64-107, Göttingen, 1895; Wellhausen, *I. J. G.* 4th ed., pp. 243-246; Büchler, *Tobiaden und Oniaden*, Vienna, 1899; Schlatter, in *Theologische Studien und Kritiken*, 1891; Grätz, in *Monatsschrift*, 1872; Schürer, *Gesch.* 3d ed., i. 195.

J.   S. KR.

TOBIAH BEN ELIEZER: Talmudist and poet of the eleventh century; author of the "Leḳaḥ Ṭob" or "Pesiḳta Zuṭarta," a midrashic commentary on the Pentateuch and the Five Megillot. Zunz ("G. V." pp. 293 *et seq.*) inferred from Tobiah's reference to his father as "the great" and from his mention of the massacre in Mayence in 1096, that he was a native of Mayence and a son of ELIEZER B. ISAAC HA-GADOL, who is thought by Conforte ("Ḳore ha-Dorot," p. 8b) to have been one of Rashi's teachers. But as in the course of his work Tobiah often attacks the Karaites and, besides, manifests a thorough knowledge of Mohammedan customs, Rapoport, in his biography of Ḳalir, note 33 (in "Bikkure ha-'Ittim," x. 122-123), concluded that toward the end of his life Tobiah settled in Palestine. As to Tobiah's birthplace, it has been proved by Solomon Buber that he was a native of Castoria in Bulgaria, as is testified to by Tobiah's countryman Judah Leon Mosconi in his supercommentary on Ibn Ezra's commentary on the Pentateuch. According to him, the

A Bulgarian.

author of the commentary on the Pentateuch mentioned by Ibn Ezra in the preface to his own work was a certain Meïr of Castoria, a pupil of Tobiah b. Eliezer. On the other hand, in his commentary on Ecclesiastes, Tobiah mentions a R. Samson as his teacher; and Buber supposes that he may be identical with the Samson quoted by Rashi in his commentary on Isa. lviii. 14 and Amos vi. 3. It is also to be concluded from various dates given by Tobiah in the course of his work that he wrote it in 1097 and revised it in 1107 or 1108.

Tobiah himself entitled his work "Leḳaḥ Ṭob" in allusion to his name Tobiah; and it is so cited by the earlier rabbis, *e.g.*, IBN EZRA (*l.c.*), Asheri in "Hilkot Tefillin," Zedekiah b. Abraham in "Shibbole ha-Leḳeṭ" (§ 118), and many others. Since the middle of the sixteenth century, however, it has been most often referred to as "Pesiḳta Zuṭarta" (= "the Lesser Pesiḳta") in distinction to the "Pesiḳta Rabbati" (= "the Greater Pesiḳta"). This second title was due to the fact that the editors of the part relating to Leviticus, Numbers, and Deuteronomy (Venice, 1546), found no title in the manuscript, but noted that every verse was headed פס (= "piska"), and took it for granted that it was entitled "Pesiḳta." Consequently the rimed title which, Zunz (*l.c.*) thinks, was composed by the press-corrector Johanan Treves begins פסיקתא זוטרתא או רבתא (="Pesiḳta, be it small or great"). In the colophon the editors call it "Pesiḳta Zuṭarta." It was owing to the latter title that the "Leḳaḥ Ṭob" was confused with the Pesiḳta Rabbati by Gedaliah ibn Yaḥya ("Shalshelet ha-Ḳabbalah," p. 24b, Amsterdam, 1697), by Heilprin ("Seder ha-Dorot," i.), by Azariah dei Rossi ("Me'or 'Enayim," ch. xix.), and by others. The "Leḳaḥ Ṭob" is in reality half commentary and half hagga-dah, covering the whole Pentateuch and the Five Megillot. Every weekly lesson is introduced by a Biblical verse containing the word "ṭob." Moreover, in the text he very often says, "I, Tobiah b. Eliezer" or "Tobiah said." It is true that in the Jerusalem manuscript there occurs very often the expression "our teacher Tobiah b. Eliezer," from which it might be assumed that the "Leḳaḥ Ṭob" was written by Tobiah's pupils; but from a closer examination of the text, and to judge from the Florence manu-script, it is evident that the expression in question is merely a copyist's mistake.

As has been said above, the "Leḳaḥ Ṭob" is both a simple commentary ("peshaṭ"), giving the gram-matical meaning of the words, and very often a hag-gadic commentary also. But in many instances Tobiah declares that the standard interpretation is the simple one. Even in his haggadic interpre-tation, which he derives from the Tal-mud and from the pre-Talmudic and post-Talmudic literatures, Tobiah manifests his love of good style. He endeavors to arrange the various midrashim in perfect order and to edit them in few words and clear language. He therefore shortens the mid-rashic passages, and, instead of the Aramaic in which those passages were written, renders them into good Hebrew, omitting also the foreign words which oc-cur in the midrashim. In the parts of the Penta-teuch which deal with the commandments he inserts many halakot, apparently taken from various hala-kic collections, particularly from Aḥai Gaon's "She'eltot." The Talmudic passages which he cites in connection with the halakot he often interprets according to his own judgment and differently from Rashi.

Throughout the whole commentary Tobiah shows his thorough knowledge of Hebrew grammar and his acquaintance with the works of the earlier gram-marians. Incidentally it may be remarked that he seems to have held the opinion that the He-brew roots are not necessarily triliteral. In certain places he interprets a Biblical word as though it were a mishnaic or Talmudic one. He considers there is not a letter too many or too few in the whole Pentateuch; and he bases many of his hag-gadic interpretations on the "ḳeri" and "ketib." One of the main features of his commentary is the allegorical interpretation of all the Biblical pas-sages which speak of God as a corpo-real being. He likewise considers that the expressions in R. Ishmael's "He-kalot" must be taken figuratively (see "Leḳaḥ Ṭob" on Deut. iv. 12). In many places he refutes assertions of the Karaites, though he does not expressly name their authors.

The "Leḳaḥ Ṭob."

Character-istics and Sources.

Like many other Biblical commentators, he trans-lates certain words into the language of the country ("la'az") in which he is living, namely, Greek.

Tobiah seldom mentions the sources for his com-mentary; but they are found to be as follows: Tar-gum of Onḳelos; Baraita of R. Ishmael; Baraita of R. Eliezer ben Jose ha-Gelili; Sifra; Sifre; Mekilta; Seder 'Olam; "Sefer Yeẓirah"; both Talmudim; Genesis Rabbah; a midrash on the blessing of Jacob (Jellinek, "B. H." iii. 73 et seq.); Leviticus Rabbah; midrash on the Five Megillot; Tanḥuma; Yelam-medenu; Pirḳe de-Rabbi Eli'ezer; Baraita di-Meleket ha-Mishkan; Agadat Mashiaḥ; "Hekalot" of R. Ishmael; "Sefer ha-Yashar"; Midrash Abkir; Midrash Hashkem; and many other midrashim. It seems that he utilized the "She'eltot" of R. Aḥai, the "Halakot Gedolot," and the "Yosippon." He quotes also Eleazar ha-Ḳalir, Saadia, Hai Gaon, Shab-bethai Donnolo, Ben Asher, Ben Naphtali, and his teacher R. Samson, while he cites passages from Menahem b. Saruḳ and Moses ha-Darshan without mentioning their names. Tobiah is in turn quoted by those of Rashi's pupils who redacted the "Liḳ-ḳuṭe ha-Pardes," and by the following: Menahem b. Solomon in his "Sekel Ṭob"; Jacob Tam in his "Sefer ha-Yashar"; RaSHBaM in his commentary on the Pentateuch; Ibn Ezra (see above); Tobiah b. Moses the Karaite in his "Yehi Me'orot"; Isaac b. Abba Mari in his "Sefer ha-'Iṭṭur"; Isaac b. Moses in his "Or Zarua'"; Zedekiah b. Abraham (see above); Judah b. Eliezer in his "Minḥat Yehudah"; Eliezer b. Nathan in his piyyuṭ "Lel Shimmurim"; and numerous later Biblical commentators, hala-kists, and casuists. It will thus be seen that the "Leḳaḥ Ṭob" was considered as an authority by the German, French, and Italian, but not by the earlier Spanish, scholars. Of the latter Ibn Ezra alone men-tions it, disparagingly. But later Spanish authori-ties who, after the expulsion, settled in the East considered the "Leḳaḥ Ṭob" as the chief source for their works.

As has been said above, only that part of Tobiah's work covering Leviticus, Numbers, and Deute-ronomy was edited in Venice, 1546. The same part was afterward reedited with a Latin trans-lation under the title "Pesiḳta" by Ugolino in his "Thesaurus Antiquitatum Sacrarum" (xv.-xvi.); and was subsequently republished by Aaron Moses Padua under the title "Midrash Leḳaḥ Ṭob" (Wilna, 1880), with a short commentary or "bi'ur." Four years later the part comprising Genesis and Exodus was published, also under the title "Midrash Leḳaḥ Ṭob," by Solomon Buber (Wilna, 1884), who added a long introduction and copious notes. The part covering the Five Megillot is not yet printed; but extracts were published by Jellinek in 1855. The commentary on Lamentations was edited by Nacht ("Tobiah b. Eliezer's Commentar zu Threni," Frank-fort-on-the-Main, 1895), and that on Ruth by Bam-berger (Mayence, 1887).

Tobiah is known as a Hebrew poet through four poems of his which are still extant. One is an in-troduction to his commentary on Genesis, another is an epilogue to the same, both being acrostics on "Tobiah bar Eliezer Ḥazaḳ"; a third is a short acrostic on "Tobiah," forming an epilogue to Leviticus; and the remaining one is a "seliḥah" beginning "Ehyeh asher Ehyeh," the verses being arranged in alphabetical order, and signed "Tobiah b. Eliezer Ḥazaḳ." The last-cited poem has been published by Buber at the end of his introduction to the "Leḳaḥ Ṭob."

BIBLIOGRAPHY: Azulai, *Shem ha-Gedolim*, i.; Brüll's *Jahrb.* v. 132 *et seq.*; *Midr. Leḳaḥ Ṭob*, ed. Buber, Introduction; *Ha-Maggid*, xxxix., Nos. 36–37; Steinschneider, *Cat. Bodl.* col. 2674; Winter and Wünsche, *Jüdische Literatur*, ii. 270 *et seq.*; Zunz, *G. V.* pp. 293 *et seq.*; Kaufmann, *Eine Unbekannte Messianische Bewegung Unter den Juden*, in *Jahrbuch für Jüdische Geschichte und Literatur*, i. 148 *et seq.*, Berlin, 1898.
S. M. SEL.

TOBIAH BEN ELIJAH OF VIENNE (BURGUNDY) (called also **Tobias of Burgundy** or simply **R. Tobias**): French tosafist of the thirteenth century. He was a younger contemporary, and perhaps also a pupil, of Isaac ben Abraham of Dampierre, at whose funeral he was present in 1210. Authors of the thirteenth and fourteenth centuries speak of Tobiah as a very prominent teacher of the Law: and he is known also as a Bible commentator and liturgical poet. It seems that he wrote a highly important casuistic work, from which the many decisions quoted in his name were taken. His pupil Abraham ben Ephraim often refers, in his "Sefer ha-Miẓwot," to Tobiah as an authority.

Tobiah is quoted in the Tosafot (B. Ḳ. 69b), several times in "Mordekai," in the "Shibbole ha-Leḳeṭ," and in "Tashbeẓ." His religious poetry, inspired by the persecutions of his coreligionists, consists of "seliḥot," included in a Burgundian Maḥzor. They are impressive in style, and show mastery of form. It appears from a passage in a Cambridge manuscript that Jehiel of Paris visited Tobiah on his journey to Palestine in 1260.

BIBLIOGRAPHY: Zunz, *Z. G.* p. 56; idem, *Literaturgesch.* p. 303; Gross, *Gallia Judaica*, p. 192.
E. C. A. PE.

TOBIAS, EMIL. See THOMAS, EMILE.

TOBIT, BOOK OF: A late Jewish work, never received into the Jewish canon, and included in the Apocrypha by Protestants, although it was pronounced canonical by the Council of Carthage (397) and the Council of Trent (1546). It takes its name from the central figure, called Τωβείτ (Τωβίτ, Τωβείθ) in Greek, and Ṭobi (טובי) in a late Hebrew manuscript.

The story of the book is as follows: Tobit, a pious man of the tribe of Naphtali, who remained faithful to Jerusalem when his tribe fell away to Jeroboam's cult of the bull, was carried captive to Nineveh in the time of Enemessar (Shalmaneser), King of Assyria. There, together with his wife, Anna, and his son Tobias, he gave alms to the needy, and buried the outcast bodies of the slain, keeping himself pure, moreover, from the food of the Gentiles. He was in favor with the king, however, and so prosperous that he was able to deposit ten talents of silver in trust with a friend in Media. With **Outline of the Story.** the accession of Sennacherib (the successor of Enemessar) the situation changed. Accused of burying the dead slain by the king, he had to flee, and his property was confiscated; but when Sarchedonus (Esar-

haddon) came to the throne Tobit was allowed to return to Nineveh at the intercession of his nephew Achiacharus (AḤIḲAR), the king's chancellor. Here he continued his works of mercy; but, accidentally losing his eyesight, he fell into great poverty, so that in his dire distress he prayed that he might die. On that same day a similar prayer was offered by Sarah, the daughter of Raguel of Ecbatana (in Media), in despair because she had been married to seven husbands who had each been slain by a demon on the wedding night. The same day Tobit, remembering his deposit of money in Media, determined to send his son for it. A companion and guide (who turns out to be the angel Raphael) being found for him, the two proceeded on their journey. At the river Tigris, Tobit caught a fish and was instructed by his companion to preserve its heart, liver, and gall. Conducted to Raguel's house, he asked Sarah's hand in marriage, drove away the demon by burning the heart and liver of the fish in the bridal chamber, sent Raphael (whose assumed name was Azarias) for the money, and returned, with him and Sarah, to Nineveh, where Tobit's eyesight was restored by smearing his eyes with the fish's gall. Father, mother, and son reached a good old age (Tobias living to rejoice over the destruction of Nineveh), and died in peace. This brief outline does not do justice to the artistic construction of the story, or to the fine touches in its descriptions of family life, social customs, and individual experiences. It may be reckoned among the most delightful of short stories.

The text exists in Greek, Latin, Syriac, and Judæo-Aramaic, besides two late Hebrew translations. Of the Greek there are three versions: one given in the Vatican and Alexandrian manuscripts of the Septuagint; one in the Sinaitic; and one in Codices 44, 106, 107 of Holmes and Parsons. Of the Latin there are two recensions: the Old Latin, which agrees substantially with the Sinaitic Septuagint; and the Vulgate, made by Jerome from an Aramaic text, which often agrees with it, although it presents many divergencies. The Syriac follows the Vatican in general, although it is by no means literal, while Codices 44, 106, 107 agree **Text and** sometimes with this text, sometimes **Original** with that of the Sinaitic. The Ara- **Language.** maic text (published by Neubauer) also represents the Sinaitic recension in a general way, but is late, and can scarcely be considered the descendant of Jerome's original. The Hebrew copies are late and of no authority. The two chief Greek recensions are the earliest sources for the text of Tobit, though suggestions may be gained from the Latin and the Syriac. Of the Greek forms the Vatican is the shortest (except in ch. iv.); its style is rough and often incorrect, and it has many errors, frequently clerical in nature. The Sinaitic text is diffuse, but frequently gives the better readings. Both of them may depend on an earlier form which has been corrupted in the Vatican and expanded in the Sinaitic, although the question is a difficult one. Equally problematical is the determination of the original language of the book. The forms of the proper names, and such an expression as χάριν καὶ μορφήν (i. 13), which suggests חן וחסד

(Esth. ii. 17), may be held to point to Hebrew, as may also the type of piety portrayed, although it must be noted that there is no mention in early times of a Hebrew text, which Jerome would doubtless have used had he known of its existence. The Sinaitic forms "Ather" for "Asur" (xiv. 4) and "Athoureias" for "Asureias" (xiv. 15), on the other hand, are Aramaic. The excellent Greek style of the Sinaitic may suggest a Greek original. In view of the conflicting character of the data, it is best to reserve opinion as to the original language; the text appears to have suffered a number of revisions and misreadings.

The picture of religious life given in Tobit (especially the devotion to ritual details) indicates a post-Ezran date for the book. The special significance attached to almsgiving (iv. 10; xii. 8, 9) is identical with the idea in Ecclus. (Sirach) iii. 30 (comp. also Prov. x. 2), and the injunction in iv. 17, "Pour out thy bread on the burial of the just, but give nothing to the wicked," is repeated in import in Ecclus. (Sirach) xii. 4–5. The prediction in xiv. 5 implies a period after the building of the Second Temple, and, apparently, before the commencement of Herod's Temple. The prominence given to the duty of burying the outcast slain (the survival of a very ancient conception) seems to point to a time when the Jews were slaughtered by foreign enemies, as, for example, by Antiochus or by **Time and** Hadrian. The necessity of marrying **Place.** within the kin was recognized during a long period and does not define the date precisely. Polycarp's saying ("Ad Phil." x.), "Almsgiving delivers from death," does not prove that he was acquainted with Tobit, since Prov. x. 2 may have been so understood by him. There is no Messianic hope expressed in the book. The more probable view is that it was composed between 200 and 50 B.C. If the original language was Hebrew, the place was Palestine; if Greek, it was Egypt; but this point, too, must be left undecided.

The reference in xiv. 10 to Achiacharus introduces new perplexities into the question of the origin of the book (see AHIKAR). Here it need only be remarked that the reference is merely an illustration, showing acquaintance with an Ahikar story; the allusion is scarcely organically connected with the story of Tobit.

The original form of the book may have told simply how a pious man, doing his duty, came safe out of trouble. The episode of Sarah and ASMODEUS appears to be a separate story, here skilfully combined with the other. The advisory discourses in iv. (much shortened in the Sinaitic text) and xii. look like the insertions of an editor. For the ethical tone see especially iv. 15, 16, and for the religious ideas, xii. 8. The book is to be compared with Proverbs, Ecclesiasticus (Sirach), Daniel, and Ecclesiastes.

BIBLIOGRAPHY: Swete, *The Old Testament in Greek* (texts of the Vatican, Alexandrian, and Sinaitic codices); Fritzsche, in *Handbuch zu den Apokryphen*; Neubauer, *The Book of Tobit* (Old Latin, Aramaic, and modern Hebrew texts); Schürer, in Herzog-Hauck, *Real-Encyc.* i.; Robertson Smith, in *Encyc. Brit.*; Erbt, in Cheyne and Black, *Encyc. Bibl.*; Marshall, in Hastings, *Dict. Bible*; Schenkel, *Bibel-Lexikon*; Schürer, *Gesch.* 3d ed., iii.; Andrée, *Les Apocryphes de l'Ancien Testament*; Nöldeke, in *Monatsberichte der Berliner Akademie der Wissenschaften*, 1879; Kohut, in Geiger's *Jüd. Zeit.*; Grätz, *Gesch.* iv.; Plath, in *Theologische Studien und Kritiken*, 1901; Israel Lévi, in *R. E. J.* 1902; Abrahams, in *J. Q. R.* i.; Bissell, *The Apocrypha of the Old Testament* (Lange series); Fuller, in Wace, *Apocrypha*.

T.

TOCKELS, MORDECAI BEN ABRAHAM (called also **Mordecai Lisser**): German Talmudist; born at Lissa; died in Berlin June 12, 1743. As a poor young man he went to Berlin, where he was adopted by a Frau Tockels, whose name he adopted in gratitude for her kindness. Tockels' first wife was the daughter of the chief of the Vienna exiles, Abraham ben Model Ries; his second, a daughter of the equally prominent Wolf ben Meshullam Salman. In 1723 Tockels was appointed dayyan; and in 1726 he was made assistant rabbi ("rosh bet din") under Chief Rabbi Michael Ḥasid. In 1729 he was chosen director of the ḥebra ḳaddisha, which office he held until his death.

Tockels was the author of "Torat Ḥayyim we-Aḥabat Ḥesed," which was edited by his brother-in-law Abraham ben Meïr (Berlin, 1750, 1829).

BIBLIOGRAPHY: Zedner, *Cat. Hebr. Books Brit. Mus.* p. 439, s.v. *Lisser*; Landshuth, *Toledot Anshe Shem*, p. 20.
E. C.   A. PE.

TODESCO, HERMANN: Austrian financier and philanthropist; born at Presburg 1792; died there Nov. 23, 1844. At first engaging in the silk trade, he later won fame and wealth in the cotton business; and he established in Marienthal, near Vienna, one of the first cotton-mills worked by machinery. In 1835 he bought the state domain of Legnaro. near Padua, where he established a cotton-mill which became one of the most important of its kind in Europe.

Todesco's main activity, however, lay in philanthropy. At an expense of 25,000 gulden he established a primary and infant school in his native town in 1843, and its inaugural ceremonies, on May 7 of the following year, were attended by the archduchess Maria Dorothea. Todesco was also one of the principal founders of the Jewish hospital at Baden, near Vienna.

After his death his son **Eduard** became the head of the banking firm of Hermann Todesco's Sons, and was raised to the Austrian nobility in 1869. Among his philanthropies special mention may be made of his gift of 100,000 gulden in 1854, of which three-fifths went to the Erzherzog Albrecht Vorschussfund für Unbemittelte K. K. Offiziere, and the remainder was devoted to the establishment of a Speise-Anstalt für Arme Israelitische Studenten. His daughter was married in 1864 to Baron Henry de Worms (later Lord PIRBRIGHT).

Hermann's other son, **Moritz Ritter von Todesco,** who was an associate of the firm, died July 17, 1873, at the age of fifty-seven. Eduard's son **Hermann** (born 1850) died at Baszon, Veszprim, Hungary, June, 1876.

BIBLIOGRAPHY: *Neuer Nekrolog der Deutschen*, ii. 755, Weimar, 1844; *Wiener Zeitung*, 1845, No. 17; Wurzbach, *Biographisches Lexikon*.
S.

TODROS OF BEAUCAIRE: 1 (called **Ha-Ḳaẓin**). One of the chief poets of the second half of the thirteenth century; resided in Montpellier. In 1277 he was one of the five representatives of the

Jewish community to which James II. of Aragon granted a synagogue for a long term of years in consideration of the payment of five Melgorian sous annually by the Jews of the city. Abraham Bedersi, who esteemed Todros highly, and considered him, together with Kalonymus ben Meïr of Arles and Kalonymus ben Todros of Narbonne, as one of the greatest men of his period, complained to him in bitter terms of the evil days in which they lived and, of the low opinion held of poetry. Abraham also replied in verse to a poem which Todros addressed to him and which when read from left to right has an entirely different sense from that which it has when read from right to left.

BIBLIOGRAPHY: Renan-Neubauer, *Les Rabbins Français*, pp. 712, 716; *R. E. J.* xix. 265, 273.

2. Rabbinical scholar of Montpellier at the beginning of the fourteenth century. He was one of the most devoted adherents of Abba Mari of Lunel during the period of religious polemics between 1303 and 1306, bitterly opposing all who studied science or philosophy. Despite the presence of Don Crescas Vidal of Perpignan, who was at Montpellier at the time, the fanaticism of Todros drove him to protest violently against the author (probably Moses ibn Tibbon) of a commentary on the Pentateuch which explained as allegories events recorded in the first five books of the Bible. Like Abba Mari, he did not hesitate to disregard the opposition of Jacob ben Machir, and to read publicly in the synagogue of Montpellier the letter addressed by fifteen rabbis of Barcelona, headed by Solomon ben Adret, to the Jewish community, in which the sentence of excommunication was pronounced against all who should devote themselves to the study of philosophy under the age of thirty. This rabbi is identified by Zunz and Gross with Todros ha-Ḳazin of Beaucaire.

BIBLIOGRAPHY: Gross, *Gallia Judaica*, p. 329; Abba Mari, *Minḥat Ḳena'ot*, ed. Presburg, pp. 48, 61, 63; Renan-Neubauer, *Les Rabbins Français*, pp. 659, 663; Zunz, *Z. G.* p. 476.
S. S. K.

TODROS (or TAUROS) OF CAVAILLON: French physician of the latter part of the fourteenth century, who flourished, according to Carmoly, about 1375. He was the author of a treatise entitled "Sha'are ha-Harkabot" (MSS. Paris, No. 1191, 1; Cat. p. 219), a sort of pharmacopœia, written partly in Hebrew and partly in Latin. Carmoly states that Todros was appointed rabbi of Cavaillon by the "elders of the community," but gives no proof of his assertion. Todros is probably identical with the Maestro Toros de Cavaillon who was one of the five "baylons" or directors of the Jewish community of Avignon in 1440. See also TODROS BEN MOSES YOM-ṬOB.

BIBLIOGRAPHY: Carmoly, *Histoire des Médecins*, p. 108; Brüll, *Jahrb.* ix. 83; Gross, *Gallia Judaica*, p. 539; Renan-Neubauer, *Les Ecrivains Juifs Français*, p. 379; *R. E. J.* i. 273; Steinschneider, *Hebr. Uebers.* p. 783.
S. S. K.

TODROS BEN ISAAC: Talmudist; lived in Italy or in southern France in the latter part of the thirteenth century and the early part of the fourteenth. He was the author of novellæ on the Talmud treatise Nazir, which are still extant in manuscript (Neubauer, "Cat. Bodl. Hebr. MSS." No. 447). To-

dros concludes his work by saying that he composed it in 1322, a year in which the Jews were undergoing many persecutions. After the massacre of the lepers (see JEW. ENCYC. v. 462 *et seq.*), followed by the outbreak of the PASTOUREAUX, the Talmud was burned, and the Roman emperor projected still other persecutions. According to Grätz, this Roman emperor was Frederick, the rival of Louis of Bavaria and an enemy of the Jews; and he also advances the theory that an allusion to the persecution mentioned by Todros is contained in an elegy which a certain Joab wrote on the burning of the Talmud and which is found in an Oxford manuscript (Neubauer, "Cat. Bodl. Hebr. MSS." No. 1061; comp. idem in "Monatsschrift," 1872, p. 376).

BIBLIOGRAPHY: Grätz, in *Monatsschrift*, 1886, p. 8; *idem*, in *J. Q. R.* ii. 104.
E. C. I. BR.

TODROS BEN KALONYMUS: French scholar and liturgical poet; lived at Narbonne in the first half of the twelfth century; son of Kalonymus the Great, who flourished at Narbonne in the eleventh century, and reached the age of eighty years, being renowned for his learning and the services which he rendered to his coreligionists. A war of succession between the city of Narbonne and the Count of Toulouse, which lasted nearly ten years, entailed much suffering on the Jews, then numbering about two thousand; and Todros gave his family in bondage for the special taxes which were imposed upon the Jews to meet the expenses of the war. He was the author of "Azharot," or liturgical poems. He had a son, **Kalonymus Nasi,** as well as a nephew, **Todros ben Moses,** who flourished at Narbonne about the middle of the twelfth century, and is probably identical with the Todros b. Moses who, together with other rabbis of Narbonne, signed a responsum written about 1150.

BIBLIOGRAPHY: Gross, *Gallia Judaica*, pp. 406-407.
D. S. MAN.

TODROS BEN MESHULLAM BEN DAVID (called also **Todros Todrosi**): Provençal translator; born at Arles in the early part of the fourteenth century. Of his life no details are known except that in 1337 he lived at Trinquetaille, where he completed his translation of Aristotle's "Rhetoric." Many hypotheses have been put forth to explain why Todros, in signing this translation, added to his name the words "mi-zera' ha-Yehudim" (= "of the seed of the Jews"), and affixed to the date "ḥeshbon ha-Yisra'elim" (= "chronology of the Israelites"), although it is possible that he feared that he might be confused with a relative of the same name who had embraced Christianity.

Todros made himself known by his Hebrew translations of Arabic philosophical works, these versions being as follows: (1) "'En Mishpaṭ ha-Derushim," a selection of philosophical aphorisms by Alfarabi (Neubauer, "Cat. Bodl. Hebr. MSS." No. 1339, 2; also in many other libraries), which Todros translated when he was only twenty years of age; (2) "Hazzalat ha-Nefesh," a rendering of the physical and metaphysical sections of Avicenna's "Kitab al-Najah" (Cod. Paris, 1023, 4); (3) "Bi'ur," the Middle Commentary of Averroes on Aristotle's "Rhetoric" (*ib.* 932, 4; 933, 3; also in many other libraries); (4) "Bi'ur Sefer ha-Shir," the Middle Commentary of Averroes on Aristotle's "Poetics" (in many libraries); (5) the following three treatises of Averroes: refutation of Avicenna's system, which divided all things into the two categories of those whose existence is only possible of themselves while necessary as a result of the causes from which they proceed, and those whose existence is necessary of themselves; an essay on this system; and "Ma'amar be-Da'at ha-Ḳiddum," a treatise on the problem whether God knows the details concerning His creatures before they are created, and whether His creatures exist potentially before they are actually formed (in many libraries); (6) "Ma'amar be-Sekel ha-Hayulani," a fragment of the treatise of Averroes on the hylic intellect (Cod. Paris, 989, 2; 1023, 5).

Bibliography: Carmoly, *Biographie des Israélites de France,* p. 91; Gross, in *Monatsschrift,* 1880, p. 61; Steinschneider, *Hebr. Uebers.* pp. 62, 182, 197, 285, 294; idem, *Cat. Bodl.* cols. 2680–2683; Renan, *Averroes et Averroisme,* pp. 69–70.
J.   I. Br.

TODROS BEN MOSES YOM-ṬOB (or **BONDIA**): French physician; flourished at Cavaillon in the second half of the fourteenth century; identified by Steinschneider with Todros of Cavaillon. In 1394 he prepared a Hebrew translation of a Latin treatise on fever by Johanan ibn Masuyah with a commentary by Peter of Spain. He likewise translated other works, the most important being the treatise of Arnold of Villeneuve on digestive and purgative medicines.

Bibliography: Renan-Neubauer, *Les Ecrivains Juifs Français,* p. 726; Steinschneider, *Hebr. Uebers.* p. 791.
S.   S. K.

ṬOHOROT ("Purifications"): **1.** Name of the sixth and last order in the Mishnah and the Tosefta. "Ṭohorot" is a euphemism for uncleanness, all the treatises of this order dealing with the laws governing impurity. The order comprises twelve treatises, which, arranged according to the number of their chapters, are as follows: Kelim (30 chapters), Ohalot (18), Nega'im (14), Parah (12), Ṭohorot (10), Miḳwa'ot (10), Niddah (10), Makshirin (6), Zabim (5), Ṭebul Yom (4), Yadayim (4), 'Uḳzin (3).

2. Treatise in the Mishnah and in the Tosefta, treating especially of the lesser degrees of uncleanness the effects of which last until sunset only. In most editions of the Mishnah it is the fifth treatise in the order Ṭohorot. It is divided into ten chapters, comprising ninety-six paragraphs in all. The contents may be summarized as follows:

Ch. i.: The thirteen regulations concerning the Nebelah of a bird, *i.e.,* a fowl not ritually slaughtered; what quantity of such fowl causes uncleanness as nebelah, and what quantity uncleanness merely as other unclean foods; which parts are not included to make up the minimum required quantity; from which moment a head of cattle not ritually slaughtered acquires a lesser degree of uncleanness, *i.e.,* that of ordinary foods, and when the higher degree of impurity, that of the nebelah; which parts are included in order to make up the minimum quantity for the lesser degree, but not for the higher degree (§§ 1–4); the mixing of different unclean foods to make up the required quantity—the size

of an egg; cases in which, when the parts possess different degrees of impurity, the entire quantity

<table>
<tr><td>Contents:</td><td>becomes unclean either in the lesser or in the higher degree (§§ 5–6); parts</td></tr>
<tr><td>Ch. i.-iv.</td><td>of a mass of dough or a loaf of bread connected with or touching each</td></tr>
</table>

other; how the uncleanness of one part affects the others (§§ 7–9).

Ch. ii.: How foods become impure when touched by an unclean person (§ 1); how a person becomes unclean through partaking of impure food (§ 2); difference between foods not sanctified, those constituting "terumah" (see Heave-Offering), and other sanctified foods, as regards their becoming unclean in the various degrees (§§ 3–8).

Ch. iii.: Impurity of beverages when in a liquid state, and when they have solidified; which drinks acquire the same degree of uncleanness in the liquid as in the solid state (§§ 1–3); how unclean foods become clean by a change of the prescribed quantity (§ 4); the degree of uncleanness of a thing is judged from the condition in which it is found (§ 5); doubtful cases of uncleanness, when it is not known whether the unclean parts have been touched by the person in question; the difference between reasoning and unreasoning beings in such cases; cases in which it is doubtful whether an animal has transferred impurity from unclean drinks to foods (§§ 6–8).

Ch. iv.: Doubtful cases of impurity (§§ 1–4); six cases in which terumah is burned because of suspected impurity (§§ 5–6); doubtful cases of impurity in which the sages declared the object to be clean; other doubtful cases in which the sages declared the object to be permissible (§§ 7–12).

Ch. v.: Regulations concerning various cases of doubtful impurity.

Ch. vi.: Difference between private domain ("reshut ha-yaḥid") and public domain ("reshut ha-rabbim") with reference to cases of

<table>
<tr><td></td><td>doubtful impurity: in the former in</td></tr>
<tr><td>Ch. v.-x.</td><td>all doubtful cases objects are to be</td></tr>
</table>

declared unclean; in the latter, clean (§§ 1–5); different localities which are considered private domain with reference to the Sabbath, but public domain with regard to cases of doubtful impurity (§§ 6–10).

Ch. vii.: Various cases in which a thing is rendered unclean by being touched by a person ignorant of the law ("'am ha-areẓ"): as such a person does not observe the laws of cleanliness, his touch is necessarily unclean. Cases in which one must suspect an 'am ha-areẓ of having touched foods and drinks, although he, personally, may have had nothing to do with them. If, for example, the wife of an 'am ha-areẓ is seen to attend to the fire in a stove on which a pot containing terumah is standing, it must be assumed that she, although attending to the fire only, has touched the food also; women being generally curious to find out what their neighbors are cooking, she would most likely remove the cover of the pot in order to discover the contents.

Ch. viii.: Further regulations concerning precautions to be taken by one conversant with the Law ("ḥaber") in order to protect himself against uncleanness caused by the touch of an 'am ha-areẓ

(§§ 1-5); what is to be considered fit for human food, thus forming a basis for the regulations concerning the impurity of foods (§ 6); further regulations concerning the impurity of beverages (§§ 7-9).

Ch. ix.-x.: Concerning olives and the pressing of oil; how they can be rendered unclean. Other regulations concerning cleanness and uncleanness, with special reference to wine-presses.

The Tosefta to this treatise is divided into eleven chapters, and contains many passages elucidating the mishnaic treatise.

W. B.　　　　　　　　　　　　　J. Z. L.

TOKAHAH ("admonition," "malediction"): The term used to connote the prediction by Moses of due punishment in case of disobedience of the divine law on the part of the children of Israel. It was first pronounced in Lev. xxvi., and repeated in Deut. xxviii., the blessings for obedience to the Law being cited first in both passages. According to the Midrash (Deut. R. i. 4), R. Aḥa b. Ḥanina declared that the tokaḥah should, strictly speaking, have been pronounced by Balaam and the blessings by Moses, but this order had been reversed that the Gentiles might learn the blessings through their prophet Balaam, and that the children of Israel might not question the motive of the tokaḥah when given by their friend Moses. The Mishnah terms the tokaḥah "ḳelalot" (= "curses"), in contradistinction to "berakot" (= "blessings"), both being read together on public fast-days, and the whole chapter being assigned to one person (Meg. iii. 6). R. Ḥiyya b. Gammada quoted the verse "Despise not the chastening of the Lord; neither be weary of his correction" (Prov. iii. 11) as a reason for insisting that the reading be continuous and not in sections, while R. Jose b. Abin interpreted it as implying that the portions read in public must be so arranged that each passage should begin and end with a cheerful verse (Yer. ib.).

Later custom, however, forbade any subdivision of either version of the tokaḥah (Shulḥan 'Aruk, Oraḥ Ḥayyim, 428, 6). The order of reading the sidra "Beḥuḳḳotai" for the third person called up to the Law is Lev. xxvi. 10-46, and that of "Ki Tabo," for the sixth, is Deut. xxviii. 7-69, both these sections beginning and ending with "good" verses, with the tokaḥah between them. The Ashkenazim do not call up by name the person to whom the tokaḥah is assigned at the public reading in the synagogue; the Sephardim do, although they permit him to read the tokaḥah by himself instead of through the "ba'al ḳore," or public reader. In some congregations the passage was assigned to an "'am ha-arez," who did not understand the meaning of the text; hence the reading of the tokaḥah became a sort of reproach, so that many declined to read it when called up to do so. To remedy this disrespect for a portion of the Torah, the ḥakam or rabbi then volunteered to read the passage. In Yiddish parlance, "to lay the tokaḥah on him" means to curse one with all the contents of the tokaḥah.

W. B.　　　　　　　　　　　　　J. D. E.

TOLA: 1. A son of Issachar who had journeyed to Egypt with Jacob (Gen. xlvi. 13). In the census of the people made by Moses and the high priest Eleazar after the plague the Tolaites appear as a tribe (Num. xxvi. 23), and during the reign of David they could put 22,600 warriors in the field (I Chron. vii. 2).

2. The son of PUAH. He became judge in Israel after the death of Abimelech. He dwelt in Shamir in the plateau of Ephraim, apparently residing in the extreme northern portion near the borders of Issachar. He was judge for twenty-three years, and was buried in his native city of Shamir (Judges x. 1-2).

E. G. H.　　　　　　　　　　　　S. O.

TOLEDANO (or **DE TOLEDO**): A family taking its name from Toledo, the city in which it originated, and including printers, Talmudic scholars, rabbis, and diplomats in Turkey, Africa, Holland, and England, being still represented in Salonica, Jerusalem, Tiberias, and elsewhere. Its most important members are as follows:

Aaron de Toledo: Author of religious lectures which appeared at Salonica in 1795 under the title "Dibre Ḥefeẓ."

BIBLIOGRAPHY: Conforte, Kore ha-Dorot, p. 46a; Zedner, Cat. Hebr. Books Brit. Mus. p. 759.

Abraham Toledano: Rabbi in Salonica about 1640; a contemporary of Shabbethai Jonah, with whom he corresponded.

Abraham de Toledo: Author of "Coplas de Joseph ha-Ẓaddiḳ." This work was written in Judæo-Spanish and published at Constantinople in 1732.

Daniel Toledano: Born at Miquenes; a friend of R. Jacob Sasportas. He was thoroughly versed in the Talmud, possessed a considerable knowledge of statesmanship, and acted as councilor to Sultan Muley Ismail.

BIBLIOGRAPHY: Grätz, Gesch. x. 259.

Eliezer Toledano: A scholar who went from Toledo to Lisbon, where he established a printing-house from which he issued the following works between 1489 and 1492: an edition of the Pentateuch with the commentary of Naḥmanides, David Abudarham's work on the ritual, Isaiah and Jeremiah with the commentary of Ḳimḥi, Proverbs with the commentary "Ḳab we-Naḳi," and the "Halikot 'Olam," but neither the "Ṭur Oraḥ Ḥayyim" nor any treatise on the Talmud was issued from his press, despite statements to the contrary. Don Judah Gedaliah (not Yaḥya), who was employed in Eliezer Toledano's printing-office, later established a press at Salonica (not Constantinople) with type brought from Lisbon.

BIBLIOGRAPHY: Ersch and Gruber, Encyc. section ii., part 28, p. 37; Kayserling, Gesch. der Juden in Portugal, p. 89; Nehama, Miktebe Dodim, p. 162; see also JEW. ENCYC. viii. 107.

Eliezer de Toledo: Rabbi at Costa, where he died in 1848. He was the author of the collection of responsa entitled "Mishnat R. Eli'ezer" (2 vols., Salonica, 1853).

BIBLIOGRAPHY: Jellinek, Ḳonṭres ha-Maspid, p. 7.

Ḥabib Toledano: Son of Eliezer, and brother of Abraham and Jonah Toledano; born at Miquenes, where he suffered great hardships throughout his life. He was the author of the "Derek Emunah," a commentary on the Passover Haggadah, which was published, together with the commentaries of Rashi, Samuel ben Meïr, and Yom-Ṭob Ishbili, under the title "Peh Yesharim" (Leghorn, 1838), while his apologetic work, "Terumat ha-Ḳodesh" (*ib.* 1866), is chiefly devoted to a criticism of Reggio.

Bibliography: Nepi-Ghirondi, *Toledot Gedole Yisrael*, pp. 112, 114, which also contains Ḥabib Toledano's genealogical tree of his family; Steinschneider, *Hebr. Bibl.* xiii. 54.

Ḥayyim Toledano: Brother of Joseph Toledano. About 1700 he was appointed ambassador to Holland and England by Sultan Muley Ismail of Morocco.

Bibliography: Grätz, *Gesch.* x. 260.

Ḥayyim de Toledo: Lived at Salonica, where he published his "Ḥayyim Medabber," a collection of commentaries on legal codes and rulings (Salonica, 1818).

Isaac Toledano: A contemporary of Elijah Mizraḥi and Tam Yaḥya; lived at Brusa about 1530.

Bibliography: Zunz, *Z. G.* p. 440.

Isaac Toledano: Rabbi at Salonica; died there in Nov., 1683. He was the teacher of R. Joseph David, who delivered a funeral oration in his honor.

Isaac ben Joseph Toledano: Rabbi in Salonica; died Aug., 1713.

Jacob Toledano: Correspondent of Elijah Mizraḥi; lived at Salonica about 1510. Another **Jacob Toledano**—possibly the one that sent to Azulai the manuscript treatises which the latter printed at Leghorn in 1805—was dayyan, together with his brother Ḥayyim, at Miquenes in 1748.

Bibliography: Zunz, *Z. G.* p. 441; Steinschneider, *Verzeichnis der Hebräischen Handschriften der Königlichen Bibliothek in Berlin*, Nos. 56, 66; the latter work also mentions other members of the Toledano family, chiefly those living at Miquenes.

Joseph Toledano: Son of Daniel, and brother of the ambassador Ḥayyim Toledano. Muley Ismail, the Sultan of Morocco, who had received valuable assistance from Joseph on his accession to the throne of Muley Mohammed, sent him to The Hague to conclude treaties of reciprocity regarding peace, navigation, and commerce.

Interior of the Church of St. Maria la Blanca, Toledo, Formerly a Synagogue.
(From a photograph.)

Bibliography: De Barrios, *Historia Universal Judayca*, pp. 9 *et seq.*, 23; Manasseh ben Israel, *Spes Israelis*, Hebr. transl., p. 56b; Koenen, *Geschiedenis der Joden in Nederland*, p. 209; Isaac da Costa, *Israel und die Völker*, German transl. by Mann, p. 276.

Moses de Toledo: A resident of Jerusalem, and the author of the "Ḥazozerot Mosheh; La Trompeta de Mose de Toledo, Dividida en Siète Voces, con los Dinim de la Tephilla y Casa de la Oracion" (Venice, 1643), which is probably identical with the "Advertencias Devotas" (Frankfort-on-the-Main, 1641) generally attributed to him.

Bibliography: Wolf, *Bibl. Hebr.* iii. 821; Fürst, *Bibl. Jud.* iii. 434; Kayserling, *Bibl. Esp.-Port.-Jud.* p. 106.

Moses ben Daniel Toledano: A native of Miquenes; author of "Meleket ha-Ḳodesh," a commentary on Rashi, published by Jacob Toledano (Leghorn, 1803).

Solomon Toledano: Son of Isaac Toledano; died of the plague at Salonica in April, 1697.

Bibliography: Jellinek, *Ḳonṭres ha-Maspid*, pp. 26, 41.

J. M. K.

TOLEDO: Metropolitan city of Gothic and Moorish Spain, and capital of Old Castile. Jews must have been established there as early as the sixth century; for the third Toledo Council (589) inserted in its canon provisions against the intermarriage of Jews and Christians, and against Jews holding public office or possessing Christian servants. The eighth Toledo Council (652) confirmed the anti-Jewish legislation of the laws of King Sisenand (Scherer, "Rechtsverhältnisse der Juden," pp. 22–25), while the ninth council (654) ordered baptized Jews to observe Christian as well as Jewish feasts (Aguirre, "Collectio Maxima Conciliorum Hispaniæ," ii. 567). Similarly in 681 the twelfth Toledo Council confirmed the Erwicz decrees against Jewish converts to Christianity (Aguirre, *l.c.* pp. 682–686), and in 693 the sixteenth Toledo Council confirmed the other anti-Jewish laws. It is not surprising, therefore, that the Jews are reported to have assisted the Arabs in the conquest of Toledo (715). During the Arabic period of the city's history little is known of the position of its Jews. Probably it was very advantageous, and the Jews doubtless thoroughly as-

INTERIOR OF "EL TRANSITO," TOLEDO, FORMERLY A SYNAGOGUE.

(From a photograph.)

similated themselves with the general population in language and customs, inasmuch as the minutes of the congregation were kept in Arabic down to the end of the thirteenth century (Asher b. Jehiel, Responsa, No. 56; Solomon ben Adret, Responsa, iii. 427).

Several Jewish authors who wrote in Arabic were born and probably educated at Toledo, even after its conquest by the Christians, not to speak of Judah ha-Levi and Abraham ibn Ezra, who were born in Toledo but educated at Cordova. Other Jewish writers in Arabic were: Abraham ibn al-Fakhkhar the poet (b. in Toledo; d. there 1231 or 1239); Israel of Toledo (Zunz, "Z. G." pp. 427-428); Israel Israeli ben Joseph, who as late as the second half of the fourteenth century wrote on the ritual (*idem*, "Ritus," p. 30). It is not surprising, therefore, that Toledo should have been the center of European activity in translation from Arabic into Hebrew, Latin, and Castilian, as will be seen later.

When Alfonso X. took Toledo from the Arabs he recognized the position of the Jews by granting them full equality with the Christians; but friction soon arose between the members of the two faiths. Al-

Details of Interior Ornamentation on Wall of "El Transito," Toledo.
(From a photograph.)

fasi refers to persecutions in Toledo in 1090 (responsum No. 217); and there was a massacre of the Jews in 1108, in which Solomon ibn Farissol was murdered (Rios, "Hist." i. 189, 297). The equality of the Jews with the Christians was short-lived; for in 1118 a local decree was passed prohibiting any Jew, or any convert, from exercising jurisdiction over a Christian. It would appear that the "nasi," or chief justice, of the Toledo Jews, who is mentioned about this time, had previously had the right to hale Christians before his court. In 1147 Judah b. Joseph ibn Ezra, probably a relative of the poet and exegete, was nasi at Toledo, and at the same time court chamberlain. In the same year many Jewish

exiles, driven out of Arabic Spain by the persecution of the Almohades, took refuge in Toledo. The Jews held important positions at court there, possibly owing to the influence of Fermosa, the Jewish mistress of Alfonso VIII. Thus Ḥayyuj Alfata became the royal physician. This favoritism appears to have led to a riot in Toledo in 1178, in which Fermosa was killed (Lindo, "History of the Jews of Spain and Portugal," p. 71). It is possible that at the same time Judah and Samuel Alnaqua suffered martyrdom (Zunz, "Z. G." p. 434).

At the beginning of the thirteenth century the Shushans, the Al-Fakhkhars, and the Alnaquas were among the chief Jewish families of Toledo, Samuel ibn Shushan being nasi about 1204. His son Joseph built a synagogue which attracted the attention of Abraham ben Nathan of Lunel ("Ha-Manhig," § 22), who settled in Toledo before 1205. During the troubles brought upon Castile by the men of "Ultrapuertos" in 1211-12 Toledo suffered a riot (Rios, *l.c.* pp. 347-349); and this appears to have brought the position of the Jews more closely to the attention of the authorities. In 1219 the Jewish inhabitants became more strictly subject to the jurisdiction of the Archbishop of Toledo, who imposed upon every Jew over twenty years old an annual poll-tax of one-sixth of a gold mark; and any dispute about age was to be settled by a jury of six elders (Jacobs, "Sources," No. 1265), who were probably supervised by the nasi, at that time Solomon ben Joseph ibn Shushan. In the same year papal authority also interfered with the affairs of the Toledo Jews, ordering them to pay tithes on houses bought by them from Christians, as otherwise the Church would be a considerable loser (Jacobs, *l.c.* No. 1273).

Under Alfonso X., the Wise, Toledo rose in importance as a center of Jewish activity in translation from

HOUSE OF SAMUEL HA-LEVI AT TOLEDO, FOURTEENTH CENTURY.

(From a photograph.)

the Arabic into Hebrew, and less often into Latin and Spanish. Similar activity had occurred previously; but the Jewish translators either were not born in

School of Transla-tors Under Alfonso X.

Toledo (as Johannes Hispanensis, who only settled there, and Samuel ibn Tibbon) or flourished mainly elsewhere (as Judah ben Solomon ha-Kohen ibn Matḳah, who was born in Toledo, but passed the greater part of his life in Italy). However this may be, the number of Jewish translators increased under the patronage of the king. Don Zag ibn Sid was the chief compiler of the ALFONSINE TABLES; and Judah Moses Cohen also translated works on astronomy from Arabic into Spanish, as did Abraham of Toledo and Samuel ha-Levi Abulafia. In medicine Abraham Alfaquin was active, as were also Ḥayyim Israel and Judah Cohen. Todros ha-Levi was another translator of the same period and the same place. It is probable also that the Spanish translation of "Kalilah wa-Dimnah" was executed at Toledo about this time.

It was likewise at this period (1260) that the Jews of Toledo obtained permission from Alfonso to build the largest and most beautiful synagogue in Spain, though a bull of Innocent IV. expressly forbade the erection of any new synagogue, especially any building higher than or in any way superior to the surrounding churches or houses. After the expulsion this synagogue became the Church of St. Maria la Blanca; and it still (1905) survives as a national monument. Its numerous pillars and arches render it one of the most characteristic buildings of the Moorish type in Spain; and during the nineteenth century its ornamentation formed the model for numerous synagogues in other countries (see SYNAGOGUE ARCHITECTURE).

The favorable condition of the Jews of Toledo during Alfonso's reign is indicated by the large proportion of the poll-tax for Castile paid by them in 1290—namely, 1,062,902 maravedis out of the total of 2,594,014, the amount of their "servicio" not being given for that year. In addition to this payment, they had to pay tribute to the archbishop in the following year (1291; Jacobs, l.c. No. 1282); and there are occasional indications of friction between the royal officers and the episcopal dignitaries as to the exact limitation of their taxation rights over the Jews.

It was toward the beginning of the fourteenth century (probably about 1305) that the Jews of Toledo, on the recommendation of Solomon ben Adret,

chose as their spiritual leader Asher ben Jehiel (d. 1328), perhaps the greatest halakist of his time in

Asherites.

Germany. His influence, like that of his two sons (Jacob, author of the "Ṭur," and Judah, who succeeded his father in 1328), was directed against the more rationalistic and philosophical tendencies of Jewish Spain; and the family of the Asherites, of which the pedigree given by Zunz ("Z. G." p. 422) is here reproduced, thenceforth ruled spiritual matters in Toledo. In the great controversy between the Maimonists and anti-Maimonists, the Jews of Toledo—e.g., Meïr ben Abraham, Jacob Crisp, Jonathan Ashkenazi, Samson b. Meïr, Meïr b. Joseph, and Solomon b. Moses Abudarham—supported the traditional side (Perles, "R. Salomo b. Abraham b. Adereth," 1863, pp. 10, 45, 48).

In the middle of the fourteenth century there rose into prominence in Toledo, Samuel ha-Levi Abulafia, who appears to have acted as a kind of treasurer and general adviser to Pedro the Cruel. It was on his advice that the king established Maria de Padilla, his mistress, at Toledo; and in the struggles between Pedro and his brother Henry de Trastamara this fact was cited by the adherents of the latter as an explanation of their opposition to Samuel Abulafia. On May 7, 1355, an attack was made on the "alcana," or smaller Jewry, of Toledo by Henry de Trastamara, in which no fewer than 1,200 Jews were killed or wounded (Rios, l.c. ii. 224). Notwithstanding this, Samuel Abulafia's influence and riches grew apace; and, in addition to a magnificent private mansion, he obtained permission to build another synagogue, inscriptions in which still recall his munificence. After the expulsion the synagogue was turned into a church and became known as "El Transito"; but in the year 1888 it was converted into a national monument, and the interior decorations, which are in the finest Moorish style, were cleansed and restored. While not presenting so striking an interior as St. Maria la Blanca, the friezes on the walls and the interior lighting by narrow windows near the roof make it remarkable, and have led to imitation in many modern synagogues (see SYNAGOGUE ARCHITECTURE). In the very year (1360) in which the synagogue was built Samuel Abulafia lost his influence with Pedro and was seized and forced to leave Toledo.

Notwithstanding the influence of the Asherites, the increasing stringency of the Castilian laws against the Jews and the great inducements held out

Old Juderia of Toledo, from the Plaza de Barrio Narevo.
(From a photograph by Dr. William Popper.)

to them to accept baptism led to a large number of conversions, either forced or voluntary, at Toledo. The converts ("conversos") were freed from the anti-Jewish legislation of the Cortes, and had at the same time relations with and support from their former brethren in faith; and their political and social influence was increased. This condition of things was strongly opposed by the ecclesiastics of Toledo; and the complaints and bickerings between the two parties led to a violent outbreak against the conversos, lasting three weeks (July 19 to Aug. 9, 1367), during which no fewer than 1,600 houses were burned and a considerable number of conversos lost their lives (Rios, *l.c.* iii. 149; for the details see JEW. ENCYC. viii. 319, *s.v.* MARANOS). Notwithstanding, or perhaps in consequence of, this, a tribute of no less than 20,000 doubloons was extorted from the Jews of Toledo by the king (June 6, 1369). Friction continued to exist between the ecclesiastical authorities and the Jews. Thus a quarrel arose between the monastery of St. Ursula and the Toledo

Asher and Israel b. Joseph Alnaqua. Four years later, inhabitants of the neighboring villages of Carlo and Santa were summoned before the Archbishop of Toledo to account for their action on the day of the riots (*ib.* No. 1317).

This was practically the ruin of the Toledo Jewry. Only a few years later Henry III. threatened the Jews with slavery if they did not pay all their taxes (*ib.* No. 1300); and the next year John II. withdrew civil jurisdiction from them and entrusted it to the alcaldes. Ferrer visited the city for a fortnight in May, 1411, with the result that, as stated above, the synagogue was turned into the Church of St. Maria la Blanca. In truth, the majority of the survivors of the massacre of 1391 had saved their lives by becoming converted; so that very few true believers still remained in the city, and the history for the following century deals mainly with the conversos. These were deprived in 1419 of all opportunity to hold public office (*ib.* No. 1264); and on June 15, 1449, thirteen of them were turned out of

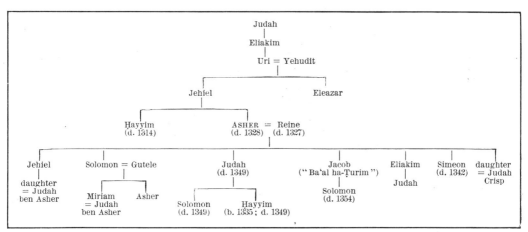

ASHERITES AT TOLEDO.

aljama with regard to certain rights connected with the Jewish abattoirs (Jacobs, *l.c.* No. 1291). Nevertheless, Archbishop Pedro, on May 17, 1388, appointed his own physician, Ḥayyim, as judge of the Jews throughout the whole archbishopric during the absence of Rabbi Don Zulema al-Fakhkhar (Rios, *l.c.* p. 257). The king, however, claimed the right of confirmation for this office (Jacobs, *l.c.* No. 1294).

In the terrible massacres of 1391, induced by the violent exhortations of Vicente FERRER, the city was the scene of one of the most appalling outbreaks. Hitherto the nobles of Toledo had on the whole done their part in protecting the Jews; but when the agitation reached that city (Aug. 5) they were found among the most violent in the onslaught on the larger Jewry. This had resisted the attacks of Henry II.; but it was now entered by the rioters at different gates, almost all the Jews being put to death, and their houses and synagogues sacked. Many of the latter edifices were torn down. Among the victims of the riots were Chief Rabbi Judah b.

office as "suspects in faith," among them being members of the Lunez, Lopez, Gonzalez, Herrera, and Cota families, afterward distinguished among the Maranos, whose very name is supposed to have originated in Toledo at this time (Rios, *l.c.* iii. 123). The conversos did not yield their positions without a struggle. There was even another riot in 1467, in which they appear to have got the better of their oppressors; for in the same year they were forbidden to bear arms thenceforth, and in the following year their exclusion from public office was confirmed by Ferdinand IV. (Jacobs, *l.c.* No. 1322).

The few writers whose birth or activity connects them with Toledo after 1391 are mainly converts, as Martin of Toledo, the mathematician; Juan de España and Rodrigo Cota, the poets; and Alfonso de Spina, the controversialist, who was the first to suggest the expulsion of the Jews. A further indication of the low condition to which the Jews of Toledo had fallen is the fact that they were able to pay only 2,600 maravedis for their servicio to the archbishop (1474). Though freed from taxes upon inheritance throughout Castile, at Toledo the Jews had to pay on succeeding to the property of their fathers.

Though the Inquisition was first introduced at Seville, in Jan. 6, 1481, the largest number of autos da fé in Spain during the existence of the Jews there were held at Toledo. In 1484 many Jews were reconciled by the Inquisition (*ib.* No. 1260). An auto

Introduction of the Inquisition. da fé was held on Dec. 10, 1486, at which no fewer than 1,640 were absolved or reconciled, and others on Jan. 15, March 15, and May 7 in the following year, when 822 were reconciled. In 1488 two autos were held, on May 24 and July 30, respectively, at the former of which 21, and at the latter 16, Jews were burned, 400 others being punished later. The tragedy of La GUARDIA was immediately connected with the Jewry of Toledo; and a representation of the punishment of the victims is still extant in one of the cloisters of the cathedral. The affair is said to have had a determining influence in connection with the expulsion which took place two years later.

Toledo was practically the center of the Spanish Jewry in Christian Spain. Besides the writers already mentioned, both Judah ha-Levi and Abraham ibn Ezra were born at Toledo, though both left it early for Cordova; Abraham ibn Daud was a Toledan; Judah al-Ḥarizi was born and passed most of his life in the city. Among the payyeṭanim of Toledo may be mentioned Joseph b. Israel, Jacob b. Eleazar, and Mar Isaac b. Jacob. Of secular poets may be mentioned Judah ibn Shabbethai and Jehiel b. Asher. Besides, the astronomer Israel Israeli the Younger deserves notice, as well as Joseph Naḥmias and Abraham ibn Zarzal, though the last-named was more of an astrologer, Toledo being a center for the magic arts generally. It is said that Michael Scott learned his magic from a Toledo Jew named Andreas, who translated works on magic from the Arabic. Judah ibn Balaam the grammarian, Judah ben Shabbethai the satirist, and the cabalists Shem-Ṭob ben Jacob, Joseph ibn Waḳḳar, and Joseph ben Judah lived there; and Jonah Gerondi, Todros Abulafia, Moses Narboni, Solomon Zarfati, and Azariah ben Joseph (Bonafos Astruc) were among the vis-

itors to the city. After the arrival of Asher b. Jehiel, Toledo was distinguished as a center of Talmudic study also. Jeroham b. Meshullam lived

Rabbis and Scholars. there, as did Aaron ben Joseph ha-Levi Toledo (for a short time about 1291); Menahem b. Aaron was an authority on the ritual there about 1374; Samuel Sevillo and Joshua Levi b. Joseph learned the Talmud at Toledo; Meïr Cohen, the casuist, lived there, and Isaac, the father of Joseph Caro, was born there; while the name of the first printer in Portugal, Eleazar Toledo, indicates his connection with the Spanish city.

At one time the whole of the southwest portion of the city was inhabited by Jews, and there were two Jewish quarters—the Alcana, or smaller Jewry, and the Juderia itself, in which both the still extant synagogues were located. The Jewish quarters were surrounded by a wall after the Catholic monarchs at the Cortes of Toledo in 1480 had ordered that all Jews should be separated into special "barrios."

Tombstones of the old Toledo Jewry are still in existence; and the inscriptions on them have been published by Luzzatto under the title "Abne Zikkaron."

"El Transito," Formerly a Synagogue.
(From a photograph by Dr. William Popper.)

BIBLIOGRAPHY: Zunz, *Z. G.* pp. 404–441; Jacobs, *Sources*, pp. 69–78, 209, 210, 248b; Rios, *Toledo Pintoresca*, Toledo, 1848.

E. C.   J.

TOLEDO, OHIO. See OHIO.

TOLEDOT YESHU'. See JESUS IN JEWISH LEGEND.

TOLERANZPATENT. See JOSEPH II.

TOLL. See LEIBZOLL.

TOMASHOV, JACOB B. SIMEON: Polish rabbi of the seventeenth century. His father is styled "ha-Ḳadosh," a term generally given to a martyr, so that Simeon may have been martyred during the massacres instigated by CHMIELNICKI. Jacob was probably rabbi at Nemirov, where his wife and three sons were murdered in 1648. He then resolved to emigrate to Palestine, but seems to have remained for several years in Venice, where he published his "Ohel Ya'aḳob" (1667), a homily on that part of the Pentateuch which deals with the 'Aḳedah. He left a work, as yet unpublished, entitled "Toledot Ya'aḳob," which contains homilies on the Pentateuch, the preceding work probably being a part of it.

BIBLIOGRAPHY: Benjacob, *Oẓar ha-Sefarim*, p. 19, No. 374; Nepi-Ghirondi, *Toledot Gedole Yisrael*, p. 182; Steinschneider, *Cat. Bodl.* col. 1256.

s.   M. SEL.

TOMBS: From the earliest times the Hebrews practised burial of the dead (קבר, whence "ḳeber" = "tomb"), so that cremation, which was customary among the Moabites and Edomites, was regarded by the Jewish prophets as sinful and inhuman (Amos ii. 1), and was used only as an additional punishment in the case of criminals (Josh. vii. 25; but see I Sam. xxxi. 12). The most primitive mode of burial seems to have been either to throw the corpse into a pit or to pile stones over it wherever it happened to be at the time of death, an analogy

passage, which refers to Joab, shows that this custom was not restricted to the burial of kings and prophets, as Winer ("B. R." i. 444) has **Single** supposed. The custom of interring **Tombs.** Jewish kings in their castles, close to the Temple wall, is severely condemned by the prophet (Ezek. xliii. 7-9), this criticism showing that graves were considered unclean, and were therefore not to be made near human habitations (Num. xix. 16). Graves were, accordingly, outside the cities (Luke vii. 12; John xi. 30), or, according to rabbinical precepts, fifty ells from the town (B. B. ii. 9). A special field thus came to be set apart for the dead, but the simple methods of burial observed by the Jews prevented any development of a necropolis resembling the Greek or the modern Italian type. Special care was taken to keep lepers separated from

FAÇADE OF THE CHURCH OF ST. MARIA LA BLANCA AT TOLEDO, FORMERLY A SYNAGOGUE.
(From Amador de los Rios, " Monumentos.")

being found in the Mosaic law that the blood of animals which had been killed must be covered with dust on the place where it had been poured out (Lev. xvii. 13). According to Josh. vii. 26, the remains of Achan were buried under a heap of stones in the valley of Achor, and the corpse of a conquered king was similarly interred (*ib.* viii. 29), while Absalom's body was thrown into a pit in the forest, and covered with stones (II Sam. xviii. 17). Adam and Eve are said to have been taught interment by seeing a raven bury its young in the sand (Pirḳe R. El. xxi.), and even Moses interred an Egyptian in the very place where he had killed him (Ex. ii. 12).

Single burial was customary in ancient times, as is still the case among many peoples and in many lands. The most natural method was to bury one's dead near the house on one's own land, as is clear from I Sam. xxv. 1 and I Kings ii. 34, while the latter

others in death as well as in life, and the body of a leprous king was accordingly buried in the open field (II Chron. xxvi. 23). The graves of the common people were likewise kept separate from those of the wealthy and prominent (II Kings xxiii. 6; Jer. xxvi. 23).

The tomb is to the dead what the house is to the living, so that the grave is termed a "house" (Isa. xiv. 18), or the "long home" (Eccl. xii. 5), while in Job xxx. 23 it is called "the house appointed for all living." The terrors associated with it are expressed by the terms "pit" (Isa. xiv. 19, xxxviii. 18), or "pit of destruction" (Ps. lv. 24), while the appropriate metaphor "silence" (*ib.* xciv. 17, cxv. 17) is still in current use among the Jews. The powers of death are implied by the words "hell" ("sheol") and "destruction" ("abaddon"; Prov. xv. 11; Job xxvi. 6). The later Jewish terms, on the other hand, contain no allusion to the horror of death, the cemetery being called simply the "house of graves" (בית הקברות), or the "house of eternity" (בית עלמין; see Eccl. xii. 5), or even, in a euphemistic sense, the "house of life" (בית החיים).

The wealthy and prominent followed the custom of the neighboring country of Egypt, and prepared their tombs in their own lifetime, often on an elaborate scale, as is evident from the allusions to Jacob (Gen. xlix. 29, 30; l. 5, 13), Asa (II Chron. xvi. 14), Shebna (Isa. xxii. 16), and Joseph of **Family** Arimathea (Matt. xxvii. 60), the refer-**Sepulchers.** ence in all these instances being to family sepulchers, which were the rule. This is confirmed by such phrases, frequently used in mentioning the Patriarchs and David, as "gathered

stances of prominent men who were interred there. This custom has increased in the course of time to such an extent that many Jews make a point of spending their last days in Palestine so as to be buried there.

Desecration of a tomb was regarded as a grievous sin, and in ancient times the sanctity of the grave was evidenced by the fact that it was **Desecra-** chosen as a place of worship, thus ex-**tion and** plaining the circumstance that a sacred **Conse-** stone ("maẓẓebah") was set on Rachel's **cration.** grave, and that sacred trees or stones always stood near the tombs of the righteous. The ancient Bedouin custom of placing the graves of their ancestors and of men of superior

TRADITIONAL TOMBS OF THE KINGS, NEAR JERUSALEM.
(From a photograph by Bonfils.)

unto his fathers," "slept with his fathers," or "gathered unto his people." Not only was this true of kings and men of prominence (II Kings ix. 28; II Chron. xxxii. 33, xxxv. 24; I Macc. ii. 70, ix. 19, xiii. 25), but the custom was a general one (Gen. xxiii. 20; Judges viii. 32; II Sam. ii. 32; I Kings xiii. 22; Tobit xiv. 10), and it was the natural desire of those who died away from home to be buried in the family grave (Gen. xlvii. 29; II Sam. xix. 38; I Kings xiii. 22, 31; Neh. ii. 3). One who could not hope to be interred thus was at least eager to rest in his native country (II Macc. v. 10) and in holy ground (Josephus, "Ant." x. 4, § 3). From the Talmudic period to the present time it has been the desire of all pious Jews to be buried in the sacred soil of Palestine; and the Talmud itself enumerates in-

sanctity on high mountain peaks was imitated by the Israelites, who located the tomb of Aaron on Mount Hor. The mountain summit thus became a place of worship of the divinity, and may, by a slight extension of the term, be designated as taboo, since it was partly holy and partly unclean. Traces of such places of worship can still be found in Palestine, and the Mohammedans in like manner use high places as burial-grounds. "In this respect the usage corresponds precisely to what we find to-day. The 'maḳam' is the place of the saint. It is preferably on a hilltop, but may simply be a tomb of a saint in a rude enclosure under the open heavens, or the tomb may be in a little building, usually with a dome, called a 'ḳubbah'" (Curtiss, "Primitive Semitic Religion To-Day," p. 143, London,

1902; see illustration annexed to p. 178: "Grave of Holy Man near Medeba ").

No stranger might be interred in a family sepulcher (Matt. xxvii. 60); and the Nabatæan inscriptions contain curses against those who desecrate the family tombs (Neubauer, in "Studia Biblica," i. 212), a similar inscription being found on the sarcophagus of Eshmunazar, King of Sidon. Freedmen, however, were buried in the family tombs of their former masters. Violation of the tomb was punishable by fines (Schürer, "Gesch." 3d ed., iii. 54).

The preference for family sepulchers resulted in the development of a monumental style of tomb in

Interment in the rocks of the hills was suggested to the Phenicians by the natural conformation of the country, which contained caves everywhere that required artificial agencies only for the final touch. These cave-tombs were often situated at heights which seemed almost inaccessible; and where no natural caverns were formed in the walls of the rock, rectangular and roomy caves were artificially made by hewing excavations into the stone from above, while occasionally subterranean chambers were cut with lofty walls in which the graves were made. According to a Palestinian explorer, "the Phenician sepulchral chambers at Sidon and at Tyre

ANCIENT TOMBS OUTSIDE THE CITY WALLS OF JERUSALEM.
(From a photograph by Bonfils.)

Palestine as elsewhere. Although such structures afforded ample opportunity for a display of pomp and for the employment of sculpture and painting, as is shown by Egypt, the Jews did not bend their energies in that direction. Despite their insignificant appearance, however, these tombs are the very ones which testify to the activity of the former inhabitants of the country, since the graves, hewn into the solid rock, have shown themselves proof against decay. Few of these tombs reflected any architectural credit on the Jews, since they were mere feeble imitations of the work of the Phenicians and developed no originality of their own.

Rock-Tombs.

consist for the most part of quadrangular vaults with three half-arched niches, one facing the entrance, and the other two on the sides. The Jewish tombs, on the other hand, are low, oblong chambers with many rows of partitions, so that the corpses are separated only by a small stone ridge. The Phenician structures apparently contained sarcophagi, while the plan of the Jewish tombs shows that they were intended for corpses wrapped in cloth " (Van de Velde, "Reise Durch Syrien und Palästina," German transl. by K. Göbel, i. 235, Leipsic, 1855).

According to the results thus far obtained, three different types of Palestinian tombs may be distinguished: (I.) Tombs hewn in the rock, which are the most numerous, since the soft limestone of the Palestinian hills favored their construction. A characteristic feature of these tombs is the preference for entire walls instead of pillars (Renan, "Mission de Phénicie," p. 822). These Jewish sepulchers are simple, having nothing in common with the Egyptian pyramids. They are entirely unadorned with paintings; and only those of a comparatively recent period contain inscriptions. Of this type of tombs three varieties may be distinguished: (1) Single chambers without doors or other means of closing them and with but one grave, hewn vertically into the ground. (2) Single chambers with several graves, which might be either (*a*) shelf-graves, in which the corpses were laid on stone shelves which ran along the sides of the rock and which were often hewn breadthwise into it, so that a sort of overhanging vault ("arcosolia") was formed; or (*b*) thrust-graves, quadrangular galleries, which were cut lengthwise into the cliff, and into which the bodies were thrust horizontally. These galleries, or niches, which were called "kok" (plural, "kokim") by the Rabbis, had a length of about 1.8 meter, a width of 0.45 meter, and a height of 0.45 meter, and may be regarded as the specifically Jewish type of grave. (3) Tombs of large size with connecting chambers, which, if not located in a natural cave about the level of the ground, were reached by small stairways hewn into the rock. Tombs entered by vertical shafts, like those constructed by the Egyptians, have not thus far been discovered in Palestine.

(II.) Artificial tombs, which are of later date and occur less frequently. They may be compared with the modern Egyptian graves, which consist of "an oblong vault, having an arched roof, . . . made large enough to contain four or more bodies. Over the vault is constructed an oblong monument (called 'tarkeebeh') of stone or brick, with a stela or upright stone ('shahid') at the head and foot" (Lane, "Manners and Customs of the Modern Egyptians," ii. 302, London, 1846; 5th ed. ii. 265).

(III.) Sarcophagi, which were anthropoid in shape among the Phenicians, but which consisted in their Hebrew type simply of troughs, cut to the length of the body and hewn vertically in the walls. They

Interior View of the Traditional Tombs of the Judges, Showing Arrangement of Vaults.
(From the "Journal of Biblical Literature.")

were, therefore, virtually shelf-graves, although they also bore a certain resemblance to the vertical tombs.

The two types chiefly known to the Rabbis were thrust-graves ("kokim") and vertical graves ("ḳebarot"), neither of which might be constructed on a festival, although it was permitted to dedicate the former if the communal interests required it (M. Ḳ. i. 6). A tannaitic and an amoraic saying state that kokim were dug, while ḳebarot were built. Thrust-graves were so little known among the Jews of the later period that Maimonides did not mention them in his codification of the passages bearing on the subject, alluding only to the earth-grave ("ḳeber"). A section of the Mishnah, however, clearly explains the construction of a family tomb (B. B. vi. 8).

In case one sold a place of burial to an associate, or obtained one from him, he might make the inner room four ells broad and six ells long, the height of the cave being given in Tosef., B. B. vi. 22 as four ells. In this room, moreover, he might construct eight cavities, three in either side wall, and two in the narrow wall facing the entrance. Each cavity was four ells in length, seven in height, and six in width (the Tosef., however, made the height seven "ṭefaḥim," or handbreadths, an extra ṭefaḥ being added for the arched cover of the sarcophagus).

According to R. Simeon, "the inner room of the cave is six ells broad and eight ells long, and it contains thirteen cavities, four on the right, four on the left, three opposite the entrance, and one on each side of it." The owner of the ground on which the tomb was situated was required to grant a frontage of six ells square, so as to admit the bier and its bearers. The purchaser of the vault might from its interior open an additional one to the right and one to the left of the original tomb. In the opinion of R. Simeon, however, the purchaser might open an additional vault on each of the four sides, while R. Simeon b. Gamaliel regarded this as dependent on the formation of the rock (see Samuel b. Meïr's commentary *ad loc.*, and the plan given in all editions of the Talmud).

As the honor of the dead was carefully guarded, the Talmud entered into a discussion of R. Simeon's scheme of construction, which allowed two graves at the entrance since visitors to the tomb would necessarily have to step on them. To the suggestion that they might project from the wall like bolts from a door, the retort was given that not even an ass (or, according to Yer., not even a dog) would be buried in such a fashion. They could, therefore, be located only in the corners of the cave opposite

Forms of Tombstones from the Old Cemetery at
Frankfort-on-the-Main.
(From Horovitz, "Inschriften.")

the entrance, and must have been sunk deep in the wall, otherwise they would have touched each other (B. B. 101b). The Palestinian source, however, presupposes a special construction of the cave itself, and considers it allowable to have two cavities, one above the other, provided the cave was protected against trampling (Yer. B. B. 15c).

A field in which such graves were located was subject to special laws. Trees might not be planted upon it, nor might seed be sown in it. **Laws About** In Oh. xviii. 4 the corrupt form שדה **Tombs.** בוכין appears, which was erroneously derived in M. Ḳ. 5b from "baka," since it was the scene of wailing and lamentation over the dead. Tosef., Oh. xvii. 1, however, has the better reading שדה כוכים, with the correct interpretation: "A kokim field is one in which the earth has been dug up and cavities excavated at the sides." Such niches were known to all ancient Semitic races; the Nabatæans called them "goḥ," and the Palmyrenes "gamchin" (Krauss, "Lehnwörter," ii. 282; I. Löw, ib.). The pious will rise from the dead by means of these niches (Targ. Cant. viii. 5), which in other passages are described as cavities ("meḥilot"; Ket. 111a).

Outside of Palestine the custom of interring bodies in galleries was continued in the CATACOMBS; but among the Jews the single grave became more common, as was also the case in Babylonia, where the soil was sandy. Later information concerning the subject is found in a responsum by Naṭronai, gaon of Sura, who was asked whether the face of a corpse laid in a cavity should remain exposed, or whether it should be covered with earth (Kohut, "Aruch Completum," iv. 210). The Jewish graves in Carthage have the exact measurements of the rabbinical kokim.

Many natural graves have been preserved in Palestine. Van de Velde (l.c. i. 136) saw at the ancient Canaanitish town of Hazor a vault, called "ḳabur,"

or grave-cellar, which he declared must have a very large subterranean chamber, though the entrance was filled up.

Among the famous graves which have been partly preserved, and more or less accurately identified, may be mentioned the tombs of David, John Hyrcanus, Alexander Jannæus, Herod, and **Famous** most of the tombs of the kings; also **Graves.** the tomb-chambers of Helena of Adiabene, and the tomb of St. James with the very ancient inscription "Bene Ḥezir." All of these graves, which are of the kokim type, are at Jerusalem.

No less renowned are the tombs of the patriarchs at Hebron, Joshua's tomb at Thamna, the tomb of the Maccabees at Modein, and the grave of Archelaus at Bethlehem, while Jewish legends know also numerous other graves of prophets and rabbis in Palestine and Babylonia (see Luncz, "Jerusalem," i. 71 et seq., where about 300 are mentioned), which still receive great honor, even from Mohammedans. That so few tombs have been preserved is due, ac-

Tombstone of the Sixteenth Century.
(In the Museo Civico, Bologna, Italy.)

cording to the Jewish traveler Benjamin of Tudela, to the fact that "the graves of the Jews are situated about three miles from Jerusalem. In ancient times the dead were buried in caves, and each grave was marked with the year of death ["ta'rikh," which, however, can hold good only of the medieval period], but the Christians destroyed the graves, and used the stones for building-material " (" J. Q. R." vii. 128). It is clear, therefore, that the same fate was then befalling the Jewish monuments which is still annihilating them, like all other antiquities of the Holy Land.

In ancient times the graves had but one enemy, the ravenous jackal (Pliny, "Hist. Nat." viii. 44), and the tombs were, therefore, closed by means of doors, or by large stones (Matt. xxvii. 60, xxviii. 2; John xi. 38), which in the Talmud is often expressed by the phrase סתם הגולל ("he closed the

The mishnaic saying (M. Ḳ. i. 1), " The graves should be marked [מצײנין] at the festival," probably referred originally to the tombstones, since the Talmud itself bases the passage on the Biblical ציון (M. Ḳ. 5a). It is generally regarded, however, as an allusion to the whitening of the graves after the rainy season (Ma'as. Sh. v. 1; B. Ḳ. 69a, where the reason is given "that the bones are white "), which was done to protect against defilement the numerous pilgrims who traversed the roads at the Passover festival (see Josephus, "Ant." xviii. 2, § 3; Matt. xxiii. 27). R. Bannaah was especially praised for

INSCRIPTION ON THE TOMBSTONE OF SAMUEL BEN SHEALTIEL, DATED MONZON, PALENCIA, 4857 (1096).
(From the " Boletin de la Real Academia de la Historia," Madrid.)

top-stone "; see Kohut, "Aruch Completum," ii. 281; Jastrow, "Dict." p. 222), "golel" being frequently used in combination with "dofeḳ"
Protection (Jastrow, *l.c.* p. 287), which signifies a
of Graves. low estrade of stone enveloping the grave on all sides, and probably used to support the stone cover. In addition to closing the grave with a stone, it was occasionally sealed (Krauss, "Leben Jesu," p. 262, Berlin, 1902).

These stone covers, however, must not be confounded with the tombstones erected on graves in honor of the dead. The Sephardic Jews lay these tombstones flat on the graves; but since these monuments are erected to be seen, the upright position, preferred by the German Jews, is the more normal one. In Biblical Hebrew the tombstones are called ציון (II Kings xxiii. 17; Jer. xxxi. 21; Ezek. xxxix. 15), while the Rabbis termed them נפש. The grave-stone was erected at the expense of the estate of the deceased (Sheḳ. ii. 5), although it was not necessary to set up a monument in memory of the righteous, since their own deeds (their teachings) were a memorial of them (Yer. Sheḳ. 47a; Gen. R. lxxxii.).

thus marking caves (tombs), including that of Abraham (B. B. 58a), while Simeon ben Laḳish is likewise said to have marked the burial-place of R. Ḥiyya (B. M. 85b), and to have cast himself in prayer, for the propitiation of the great, on the graves of the pious (*ib.*), of the Shammaites (Ḥag. 22b), of the justified (*ib.* 16b), and of the wronged (Yoma 87a). In the Middle Ages Jonah Gerondi wished to offer an apology on the grave of Maimonides (Grätz, "Gesch." 3d ed., vii. 98).

The custom of making pilgrimages to famous tombs, and of praying at the graves of parents and ancestors, is still maintained among
Pilgrim- all classes of Jews. Even in the Bib-
ages. lical period the belief was current that interment beside a great man might work miracles (II Kings xiii. 21). See PILGRIMAGES.

Judicial procedure required two forms of burial, one for criminals who had been beheaded or hanged, and the other for those who had been stoned or burned (Sanh. 46a), while interment among convicts was the utmost disgrace (Yeb. 32b). The tombs of Gentiles were entirely different from those of Jews

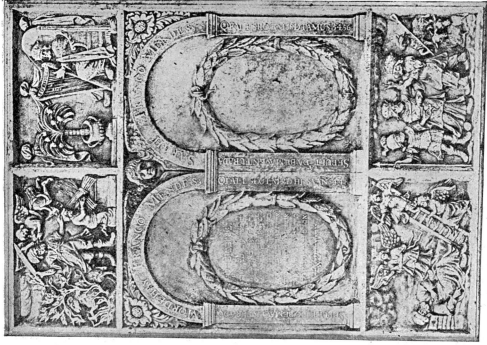

DOUBLE TOMBSTONE FROM THE CEMETERY AT AMSTERDAM, DEPICTING BIBLICAL INCIDENTS.

(From Castro, " Keur van Grafsteenen.")

ORNAMENTAL TOMBSTONES FROM THE CEMETERY AT AMSTERDAM.

(From Castro, " Keur van Grafsteenen.")

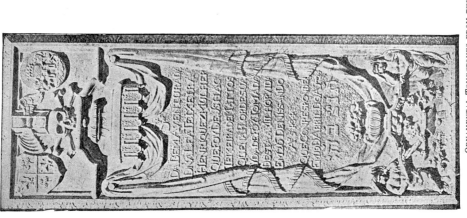

(*ib.* 61a). Special caves were used for the interment of the pious ("ḥasidim") and of the members of the Sanhedrin ("dayyanim"; M. Ḳ. 17a), as well as for still-born children ("nefalim"; Ket. 20b). In the ancient cemetery of Prague the Nefel-Platz is still to be seen: different legends are, however, attached to it, and its origin can not, therefore, be determined. Even at the present time all Jewish communities invariably bury suicides in a separate part of the cemetery. Abba Saul was buried at his father's feet (Sem. xii.), thus reviving in a certain measure the use of family tombs.

TOMBSTONES (Hebr. מצבה, pl. מצבות): The custom of marking a grave by a stone which bore an inscription describing the qualities of the deceased and giving his age and the date of his death was foreign to the ancient Hebrews. Stones were indeed used to mark the sites of graves, such as the pillar ("maẓẓebah") placed by Jacob on the tomb of Rachel (Gen. xxxv. 20), and the sign ("ẓiyyun") set up according to Ezekiel (xxxix. 16); but they were not intended as monuments and bore no inscriptions. Even in the geonic period the custom seems to have been unknown to the Jews of the East, and it can not,

CEMETERY AT ROME.
(From a photograph.)

Every one who beholds a Jewish grave is required to repeat the following prayer: "Blessed be He who begat thee in righteousness, who nurtured thee in righteousness, who letteth thee rest in righteousness, and who will resurrect thee in righteousness. . . . Blessed be He who giveth life to the dead" (Ber. 58b). For other expressions of the religious sentiments of the Jews as displayed in their tombs, see BURIAL; BURIAL SOCIETY; CREMATION; FUNERAL RITES; MOURNING.

BIBLIOGRAPHY: Nicolai, *De Sepulcris Hebraicis*, in Ugolino, *Thesaurus*, xxxiii.; Winer, *B. R.* i. 443; Nicoll, in Hastings, *Dict. Bible*, iv. 454; Stade, *Gesch. des Volkes Israel*, i. 14–15; Hamburger, *R. B. T.* i. 476; Kinzler, *Die Biblischen Altertümer*, p. 345, Calw and Stuttgart, 1884; Rosenmüller, *Arch.* ii. 2; Benzinger, *Arch.* pp. 163 *et seq.*
J.   S. KR.

therefore, have been current in Talmudic times. The stone termed "golel" in the Mishnah (Oh. ii. 1), which, according to Hai Gaon, was laid up on the side-walls (dofeḳin), served only to protect the grave from jackals, while that called "ẓiyyun" was merely a mark to warn passers-by against Levitical impurity. Graves in Palestine were not devoid of monumental ornamentations, however, for "nefashot," or stone buildings in the shape of houses or cupolas, were erected, in Phenician fashion, over them ('Er. v. 1; Sheḳ. ii. 5). On the tomb of his father and brothers at Modin, Simon Maccabeus erected a monument consisting of seven pyramids on which were carved armor and

None in Palestine in Biblical or Talmudic Times.

ships (I Macc. xiii. 27–29). Such monuments became the fashion in the first centuries of the common era, while the rivalries which arose between families, and the love of ostentation, led to the spending of great sums for the adornment of graves. To put an end to this extravagance Simeon ben Gamaliel declared that the pious were remembered by their words, and that it was an insult to their memory to put monuments on their graves as though they would have been forgotten without them (Yer. Shek. ii. 7, 47a). It was only outside Palestine that some Jews, adopting the custom of the Greeks and the Romans, began to use tombstones with inscriptions commemorating the status of the deceased. These epitaphs were written in Greek or Latin in the first centuries of the common era, and began with the name of the deceased or with the introductory phrase 'Ενθάδε καῖται (κεῖται) or "Hic jacet" (= "Here lies"), while eulogies recalling Biblical verses and idioms were used as final formulas, as, for instance, Isa. lvii. 2 or Ps. iv. 9. The stones were adorned with a variety of symbols in addition to the epitaphs themselves, the most common being a seven-

Section of the Old Chatham Square Cemetery, New York.
(From a photograph.)

branched candlestick (in allusion to Prov. xx. 27, "The spirit of man is the candle of the Lord"), a fruit from which sprang an ear of grain (probably an allusion to the resurrection of the dead), an oil-vessel, a palm-branch, or a curved horn representing the SHOFAR which will be blown by the Messiah to announce the resurrection of the dead. Except for the presence of these symbols, the Jewish tombstones of the first centuries of the common era could not be distinguished from those of the Christians. Later gravestones, however, bore, in addition to the Greek or Latin inscription, the Hebrew formula שלום על ישראל, as does the tombstone of Nar-

bonne of 688; or else they had a Hebrew translation of the Greek or Latin inscription, as does that of Tortosa.

It can not be determined with certainty when the custom of inscribing Hebrew epitaphs **Earliest in** on tombstones first became general **Europe.** among the Jews in Europe. The oldest example known is a gravestone of Brindisi dated 832. It is true that Jacob Mölln (MaHaRIL) asserts that in his lifetime a gravestone was discovered in the cemetery of Mayence bearing a Hebrew epitaph which was eleven hundred years old, but as he does not state that he himself deciphered the inscription, no credence can be given to his assertion ("Likkuṭe Maharil," ed. Warsaw, p. 86b). A characteristic feature of the epitaphs of the early Middle Ages was the simplicity of their style. They usually began with the words הציון הזה, האבן הזאת, or המצבה הזאת, and closed with one of the usual eulogies (see INVOCATION).

In the later medieval period epitaphs became more detailed and bombastic, and in some German cemeteries various emblems representing the profession of the deceased were added to the inscriptions. Thus, for instance, a tailor had a pair of shears on his tombstone; a musician, a violin or a harp; a goldsmith, a crown and two chains; a physician, a lion holding a sword; and an apothecary, a mortar. In some places in Germany the tombstones bore the emblems of the houses in which the deceased had lived, thus showing figures of dragons, bears, lions, or stars. The tombs of kohanim are distinguished by two open hands as placed during the priestly benediction, while a Levite's gravestone often bears a ewer. Names, especially those derived from plants or from animal life, are frequently represented pictorially; and reliefs of the whole human body are found.

The form of the tombstone was generally very simple; and the material varied considerably in different countries. In Frankfort-on-the-

Inscriptions. Main gravestones were generally made of red sandstone, rarely of white sandstone or granite. The Ashkenazim usually placed the tombstones upright, while the Sephardim laid them horizontally on the graves.

The custom of carving Hebrew inscriptions on gravestones seems to have developed much later in the East than in Europe, since there is no mention of it in geonic literature. Although Benjamin of Tudela attributes the dearth of very ancient tombstones in Palestine to the fact that the Christians destroyed the Jewish graves and used the stones for building-material, this is a mere supposition, and there is no proof whatever that the use of tombstones with Hebrew inscriptions became general in Palestine much earlier than the twelfth century. It is true, on the other hand, that both in the lifetime of Benjamin of Tudela and for several centuries afterward Jewish graves were often destroyed and the stones were used for building purposes in Christian and Mohammedan countries alike. Thus, when the Jews were banished from Fürth, the gravestones of the community were used to erect walls around the city; and David ibn Abi Zimra (sixteenth century) relates that in his lifetime the Egyptian Mohammedans used to steal Jewish tombstones and resell them to Jews after having obliterated the inscriptions. To put an end to this traffic, the local rabbis allowed their congregations to use only newly quarried stones for monuments to the dead (Radbaz, i. 741, quoted by Abrahams, "Jewish Life in the Middle Ages," p. 78). Although tombstones became customary, they were not obligatory (Shulḥan 'Aruk, Yoreh De'ah, 364), and every Jewish cemetery contains some graves without them. The stone was seldom set up before the expiration of a year after the date of death, since the departed soul required that lapse of time before it could be purified. Inscriptions are generally dated according to the era of creation; and the year is preceded by the day of the month, or the Sabbatical section, or both. In some cases the numerical value of a Scriptural phrase is used to mark the date, and there are also instances in which the Christian date is given side by side with the year of creation.

Cemetery of the White Jews of Cochin.

(From a photograph.)

The following are specimens of Hebrew inscriptions found on the tombstones of prominent men. The gravestone of Elijah Levita reads: הלא אבן

מקיר תזעק ‖ ותהמה לכל עובר ‖ עלי זאת הקבורה ‖ עלי
רבן אשר נלקח ‖ ועלה בשמים ‖ אליהו בסערה ‖ הלא
הוא זה אשר האיר ‖ בדקדוק אפלתו ‖ ושם אותו לאורה
שנת ש״ט שבט עלה בסופו ‖ ונפשו צרורה בצרור החיים.

"The stone crieth from the wall, and mourneth before every passer-by over the grave—over our rabbi who hath departed and ascended into heaven. Elijah is gone to the Lord in a whirlwind [comp. II Kings ii. 11]—he who shed light on the darkness of grammar and turned it into light. He ascended Shebaṭ toward the end, in the year 309 [= 1549], and his soul is bound up in the bundle of life."

The following epitaph is found on the tombstone of Leon of Modena: ארבע אמות

קרקע בחצר זה אנב
קנין סודר מימות
עולם הקנו ממעל
ליהודה אריה ממודינה בזה נסתר ונעלם.

"Four yards of ground in this graveyard, 'by purchase by kerchief,' were from eternity transferred from above to Judah Aryeh of Modena. In these he hid himself and disappeared."

Manasseh ben Israel's tombstone bears the words: לא מת הרב עוד לא כבה נרו ‖ הנה עודנו חי במרומי
ערץ ‖ ובעד עטו גם עדן מדברו ‖ נצח יהיה זכרו
כימי הארץ.

"The rabbi did not die; his light is not yet extinguished; he liveth still in the heights of the Terrible.

Examples of Inscription. By his pen and the sweetness of his speech his remembrance will be eternal like the days of the earth."

On the tombstone of Joseph Delmedigo is found the following inscription: שאו בכי יללה וקינה וספדו
באבילות ובאניה ומרורים שאו כלענה ‖ כי נפל שר
וגדול במחנה אשר היה עטרה לחכמי מורשה ותכונה ‖
נאבדה החכמה ונסתרה התבונה הנמצא כזה בכל עבר
ופינה ‖ ימה וקדמה נגבה וצפונה אשר רוח אלהים בקרבו
נתנה ‖ חכמתו בחיץ תרונה נשמתו תחת כנפי השכינה
היא גנוזה וטמונה ‖ מהרו וספדו אוי והוי על נבר על
נאון ישראל אשר בין הגזירה עבר ‖ כי הוא זה יוסף
המשביר בר אשר שמעו הולך בכל עבר מפרק הרים
וסלעים שבר ‖ ולא נעלם ממנו כל דבר בלשון מדברת
גדולות ספרים חבר ‖ ספר נובלות החכמה נכבדות
בהם מדבר ‖ בתכונה כפשוטה ועיבור ‖ לעשות ספרים
הרבה נמר וסבר ובכל שבע חכמות היה כנובר גבר לא
הניח דבר קטן וגדול הכל אסף וצבר.

"Take up weeping, wailing, and lamenting, howl in mourning and desolation, suffer bitterness like wormwood, for a chief

and a great man is fallen in the camp, one who was the crown of the inherited [sciences, *i.e.*, Jewish learning] and astronomy. Wisdom was lost [with him] and understanding disappeared. Is there one like him in clime or country—west, east, south, north—to whom the spirit of God hath been given ? His wisdom singeth in the streets, while his soul, under the wings of the Shekinah, is hidden and preserved. Hasten, break out in lamentations and howlings over the man, the pride of Israel who hath passed away [the phrase בין הגזירה is merely a rhetorical figure in imitation of Gen. xv. 17]. For he is the Joseph who sold corn [*i.e.*, propagated learning ; comp. Gen. xlii. 6], whose reputation spread everywhere, who tore up mountains and broke rocks. Nothing was hidden from him. In a tongue that speaketh proud things he composed works. In the 'Noblot Ḥokmah ' he creditably speaketh of astronomy and ''ibbur.' To compose many works was his intention and desire. In all the seven sciences he was very efficient. He omitted nothing, small or great ; he collected and thesaurized everything."

Some prominent men composed for themselves the epitaphs which they wished to be put on their tombstones, such as the one found on the gravestone of Jonathan Eybeschütz, which reads as follows:

יראו כל עובר החרות על הלוחות || האיש אשר עמד
לנס והיה כשושן פורחת || ושב אל עפר ומראהו מאיש
נשחת || נא שימו על לב לשוב בתשובה ניצחת || תפלה
תרבו בעדו לאלקי הרוחות || נפשו אליו יאסוף ובל
תהיה נדחת || זכות מעשיכם יגונו כי נפשות ישראל
אחת !! למדו מוסר לשנוא כבוד ומגדולה תהי נפשיכם
בורחת.

" Every passer-by should see what is engraved on these tables.

THE CEMETERY AT TUNIS.
(From a photograph in the possession of Dr. Maurice Fishberg, New York.)

The tombstone of Moses Ḥagiz bears the epitaph :

עובר פנה אלי קרא נאות || תחתי אנוש הכין מעון ביתו ||
אתמול בהוד זרח מאור פניו || יורה גדולתו ומלכותו ||
נושי אדמה כתרו היום הדרת גויתו ותפארתו || אילו
[read : אין לו] דמות הגוף ואינו גוף לא נערוך אליו ||
לך רק פקח עין ודע כי עוד תפול תמונתו [תמונתך ?]
כמו נפל במכמרתו || יום אחרון שור כי חכם לב יביט
לסוף דבר בקדמותו.

" Passer-by, turn toward me, read something beseeming : Underneath me a man prepared his dwelling-place. Yesterday the light of his face shone majestically, showing his greatness and sovereignty ; to-day clods of earth encompass the beauty of his body and its brilliancy. It hath neither bodily form nor substance ; we can compare naught unto it. It behooveth thee only to keep thine eyes open ; know that, like him, as a stillborn child thou wilt fall in its [death's] trap. Beware of the last day, for the wise man foreseeth the end from the beginning."

The man who stood as a model, who flourished like a lily, returned to dust, and his visage became marred more than any man's. Pray, take it to heart to repent sincerely and to offer for him many prayers to the Lord of spirits that He should gather to Him his soul, and not cast it away. The merit of your deeds will be a protection, for all the souls of Israel are one. Learn to despise honors and to flee from greatness."

See, also, the articles BURIAL, CEMETERY, and PALEOGRAPHY.

BIBLIOGRAPHY : Perles, *Die Leichenfeierlichkeiten des Nach-biblischen Judenthums,* in *Monatsschrift,* 1860 ; Geiger, *Zeitschrift für die Gesch. der Juden in Deutschland,* iii. 211 *et seq.*: Bender, *Beliefs, Rites, and Customs of the Jews Connected with Death, Burial, and Mourning,* in *J. Q. R.* 1894, 1895 ; S. Rapoport, *Gal 'Ed,* Introduction ; Horowitz, *Inschriften des Alten Friedhofs,* Introduction, Frankfort-on-the-Main, 1901 ; Schuchostov, *Maẓẓebat Ḳodesh,* Introduction, Lemberg, 1863-69.
J.   I. BR.

The shape of Jewish tombstones varies, as a rule, according to the country in which they are found, though occasionally the Jews carry with them to other countries the practise of their native land. No very careful examination of the development of Jewish tombstones has hitherto been made; but it appears probable that in the earlier instances the grave of an important personage was covered by a stone in the shape of a sarcophagus, at the end of which a description of the person interred beneath it was incised. This is clearly shown in the collection of tombstones in the old Sarajevo cemetery (see JEW. ENCYC. xi. 60) and in the **Sar-** tomb of Isaac ben Sheshet (*ib.* vi. **cophagus** 632). A further development of **Model.** this method is found in the tomb of Joseph Delmedigo at Prague (*ib.* iv. 509), with which may be compared the tombs of Judah Löw ben Bezaleel (*ib.* vii. 354) and Mordecai Meisel (*ib.* viii. 442). All these have ornamental and decorated panels of stone, corresponding, as it were, to the head and foot of an old-fashioned bedstead. From this type the shape of tombstones appears to have developed in two different directions, adopted by the Sephardim and Ashkenazim respectively. The Sephardim, who, at Amsterdam, for example (*ib.* i. 544, iii. 435), used the sarcophagus form without end-pieces, gradually lowered the sarcophagus till it was almost level with the ground, as can be seen in the Beth Ḥolim burial-ground at London (*ib.* viii. 158); the top was rounded, and on this the inscription was engraved. In Amsterdam this rounding was found inconvenient for the somewhat elaborate coats of arms carved upon tombstones, and the top was made perfectly flat, and practically rested on the ground, so that as the graveyard became filled up it was almost entirely paved with tombstones, as at Altona (*ib.* i. 475) and at Tunis. In Cochin occur sarcophagus tombstones on which the inscriptions still retain their original position at the end (see illustration on p. 192). In Italy the sarcophagus form appears to have been retained only as regards the lid, which formed the whole of the tombstone (*ib.* x. 61).

With the Ashkenazim, on the other hand, the footpiece, possibly for economy's sake, was detached from the sarcophagus, and the inscription was incised upon it, apparently on the outside of the grave, as in the case of the Brody cemetery (*ib.* iii. 640), where obviously the inscriptions which abut

Vault of Friedlander Family at Saint Petersburg, Russia.
(From a photograph.)

on the path must be at the ends of the graves, since the latter would otherwise be under the path. Afterward the inscription was cut on the interior of the upright stone, *i.e.*, the portion facing the tomb itself.

The earliest form seems to have been a plain, square, somewhat thick stone, as at Mayence, with which may be compared the Seville tombstone illustrated in JEW. ENCYC. xi. 208. This square form is found also in the old cemetery at Worms (see page 562). At Erlangen each grave was marked by a perfectly square block of stone, as can be seen in the article BURIAL (*ib.* iii. 434). The first attempt at ornament seems to have been to make the top of the stone come to a point, as is seen in many of the tombstones in the old Prague cemetery (*ib.* x. 165). The headstone was shaped at the top, and the inscription was inserted over the head of the corpse and facing the grave itself. A further process was to make a kind of margin for the inscription, which took various forms according to the outline of the stone itself (see illustration on p. 187). Excellent examples of all these types can be seen in the illustration of the Endingen cemetery (*ib.* iii. 639). In the later forms of the sarcophagus tombs of Prague these borders and outlines became very elaborate, as can be seen from the tombstone of Judah Löw (*ib.* vii. 354). Florence uses round pillars instead of the sarcophagus model.

In western Europe and America, Jewish tombstones have become exactly similar to those of the surrounding population. Thus, in the United States the stone put over Moses Seixas is a plain square slab of the old-fashioned type (*ib.* xi. 161); that over Judah Touro is a short obelisk (*ib.* ix. 295), while the monument over the grave **Modern** of Uriah Levy is in its way quite a **Forms.** work of art, and has distinct reference to his naval career (*ib.* viii. 65). In the richer Jewish families the gravestone has already been replaced by a family vault of a somewhat elaborate character. Reference to the following illustrations in THE JEWISH ENCYCLOPEDIA (volume and page are given) will show the variety in the shape of tombstones:

Altona.. i. 475
Amsterdam... i. 544
Brody... iii. 640
Delmedigo, Joseph.................................. iv. 509

xix. 6, 11, 12, 13, 14) and once in II Kings (xxiii. 10) to designate a place in one of the valleys just outside the walls of Jerusalem. The meaning of the word is much in dispute. W. Robertson Smith ("Rel. of Sem." p. 227, note) connects it with an Aramaic loan-word which means "fireplaces." The formation of the word is similar to that of "Molech" and "Ashtoreth." The passage in Kings locates the place in the valley of the son of Hinnom. Now there are three valleys in Jerusalem which converge

VAULTS OF ARNHEIM AND ZORKOWSKI FAMILIES, SALEM FIELDS CEMETERY, NEW YORK.
(From a photograph.)

BIBLIOGRAPHY: Admirable examples of old tombstones are given in H. de Castro, *Keur van Grafsteenen*, Leyden, 1883, and in L. Jerabek, *Der Alte Prager Juden-Friedhof*, 1903.

J.

TOPAZ. See GEMS.

TOPEKA. See KANSAS.

TOPHET (תפת; תפתה, Isa. xxx. 33): Old Testament term used chiefly by Jeremiah (vii. 31, 32;

just below the pool of Siloam: Kidron from the east side of the city; Wady al-Rababi from the southwest; and the Tyropœon extending from the Jaffa gate to Siloam. There is no consensus of opinion as to which of these valleys represents the ancient Tophet. There is, however, agreement that the convergence of the three valleys marks a part of Tophet. It is also very generally agreed that Tophet did not extend up the valley of the Kidron on the east side of Jerusalem. It is to be connected, then, either with the Tyropœon depression or, preferably, with the great valley marking the southwest border of the city.

Tophet as described especially in Jer. vii. 31, 32 was dedicated to the horrible rites of human sacrifice, of the immolation of children to Baal and other abominable idols. Josiah takes especial pains (II Kings xxiii. 10) to defile this despicable spot and thus to put a stop to the atrocious sacrifices of human life which had been made by at least two kings of Judah. Jeremiah's references to Tophet characterize it and at the same time specify that the punishment which threatens rebellious Judah shall so revolutionize and reverse current wrongs as to fill this valley with the corpses of those who shall be slain in the impending calamities. Tophet shall henceforth be called "the valley of slaughter" (Jer. vii. 32). After the overthrow of Jerusalem in 586 B.C., and down to New Testament times, incidental references to Tophet or Gehenna (גיא בן הנם) indicate that it was a kind of perpetually burning rubbish-heap, where the refuse of Jerusalem was consumed.

E. G. H.   I. M. P.

TORAH (Hebrew, תורה; Aramaic, אורייתא; Greek, Νόμος): Name applied to the five books of Moses, GENESIS, EXODUS, LEVITICUS, NUMBERS, and DEUTERONOMY. The contents of the Torah as a whole are discussed, from the point of view of modern Biblical criticism, under PENTATEUCH, where a table gives the various sources; while its importance as a center of crystallization for the Hebrew canon is treated under BIBLE CANON. The present article, therefore, is limited to the history of the Pentateuch in post-Biblical Judaism.

The Torah receives its title from its contents, the name itself connoting "doctrine." The Hellenistic Jews, however, translated it by νόμος = "law" (e.g., LXX., prologue to Ecclus. [Sirach], Philo, Josephus, and the New Testament), whence came the term "law-book"; this gave rise to the erroneous impression that the Jewish religion is purely nomistic, so that it is still frequently designated as the religion of law. In reality, however, the Torah contains teachings as well as laws, even the latter being given in ethical form and contained in historical narratives of an ethical character.

In the books of the Bible the following names of the Pentateuch occur: ספר תורת יהוה in II Chron. xvii. 9, Neh. ix. 3, and, with the added

Name. epithet ביד משה, II Chron. xxxiv. 14; while תורת יהוה alone, without ספר, is found in II Kings x. 31, I Chron. xxii. 11, and II Chron. xii. 1, xxxi. 3, 4, and xxxv. 26. Sometimes אלהים, or a word of similar meaning, is added, as ספר תורת אלהים, Josh. xxiv. 26, Neh. viii. 18 (without ספר, ib. x. 29). Another designation is ספר תורת משה, Josh. viii. 31, xxiii. 6; II Kings xiv. 6; Neh. viii. 1; or תורת משה, I Kings ii. 3; II Kings xxiii. 25; Mal. iii. 22 (A. V. iv. 4), with the addition of עבדי; Ezra iii. 2 (with the addition of איש האלהים), vii. 6; ספר משה, II Chron. xxv. 4 (preceded by בתורה), xxxv. 12. The oldest name doubtless is ספר התורה (Deut. i. 5; xxxi. 9, 11, 24; xxxii. 46; Neh. viii. 2), sometimes shortened to התורה (Deut. i. 5; xxxi. 9, 11, 24; xxxii. 46; Neh. viii. 2), or to הספר (Neh. viii. 5), or to תורה (Deut. xxxiii. 4). The last two names occur with great frequency in Jewish tradition, where the Torah becomes a living creature. The expression "the five books," which is the origin of the term "Pentateuch," occurs only in Jewish tradition, which has also been the source for "Genesis," etc., as the

names of the books of the Pentateuch (see Blau, "Zur Einleitung in die Heilige Schrift," pp. 40–43).

According to all critics, regardless of the schools to which they belong, the Torah forms a single work, which is represented, even at the present day, by the synagogal SCROLL OF THE LAW; nor does history know of any other Torah scroll. The five-

Quinary   fold division of the Pentateuch was
Division of   due to purely external causes, and not
the Torah.   to a diversity of content; for in volume the Torah forms more than a fourth of all the books of the Bible, and contains, in round numbers, 300,000 letters of the 1,100,000 in the entire Bible. A work of such compass far exceeded the normal size of an individual scroll among the Jews; and the Torah accordingly became a Pentateuch, thus being analogous to the Homeric poems, which originally formed a single epic, but which were later split into twenty-four parts each. Like them, moreover, the Pentateuch was divided according to the sense and with an admirable knowledge of the subject (Blau, "Althebräisches Buchwesen," pp. 47–49), while subdivisions were also made into the so-called open and closed "parashiyyot," whose exact interrelation is

            not yet clear. There are in all 669
Division   sections, 290 open and 379 closed.
into   Another class of parashiyyot divides
Sections.   the weekly lessons, now called "sidrot," into seven parts. The Torah also falls, on the basis of the lessons for the Sabbath, into 54 sidrot according to the annual cycle, and into 155 according to the triennial cycle. The former division, which is now used almost universally, is the Babylonian; and the latter, which has recently been introduced into some Reform congregations, is the Palestinian. The latter class of sidrot, however, has no external marks of division in the scrolls of the synagogue; while the divisions in the former, like the parashiyyot, are indicated by blank spaces of varying length (see SIDRA). This probably implies a greater antiquity for the sections which are thus designated, although the divisions into 5,845 verses, which seem to be still older, have no outward marks. The system of chapters was introduced into the editions of the Hebrew Bible, and hence into the Torah, from the Vulgate. This mode of division is not known to the Masorah, though it was incorporated in the final Masoretic notes, for individual books of the Pentateuch. It is given in modern editions of the Hebrew Bible simply on the basis of the stereotyped editions of the English Bible Society, which followed earlier examples.

The external form of the Torah is discussed in such articles as MANUSCRIPTS, SCROLL OF THE LAW, and MANTLE OF THE LAW; but so numerous are the assertions of tradition concerning its contents and its value that the repetition of even a very small part of them would far exceed the limits of this article. Every page of the Talmud and Midrash is filled with citations from the Pentateuch and with the most fulsome praise of it, united with superhuman love and divine respect therefor. In the five volumes of Bacher's work on the Haggadah, the Torah and its study form a special rubric in the account of each "sofer," or scholar of the Law. In all probability there never was another people, except possibly the Brahmans, that surrounded its holy writings with such respect, transmitted them through the centuries with such self-sacrifice, and preserved them with so little change for more than 2,000 years. The very letters of the Torah were believed to have come from God Himself (B. B. 15a), and were counted carefully, the word "soferim" denoting, according to the Talmud (Ḳid. 30a), "the counters of the letters." A special class of scholars devoted all their lives to the careful preservation of the text ("Masorah"), the only analogy in the literature of the world being found in India, where the Vedas were accurately preserved by similar means.

The Torah is older than the world, for it existed either 947 generations (Zeb. 116a, and parallels) or 2,000 years (Gen. R. viii., and parallels; Weber, "Jüdische Theologie," p. 15) before the Creation. The original Pentateuch, therefore, like everything celestial, consisted of fire, being written in black letters of flame upon a white ground of fire (Yer. Sheḳ. 49a, and parallels; Blau, "Althebräisches Buchwesen," p. 156). God held counsel with it at the creation of the world, since it was wisdom itself (Tan., Bereshit, *passim*), and it was God's first revelation, in which He Himself took part. It was given in completeness for all time and for all mankind, so that no further revelation can be expected. It was given in the languages of all peoples; for the voice of the divine revelation was seventyfold (Weber, *l.c.* pp. 16–20; Blau, "Zur Einleitung in die Heilige Schrift," pp. 84–100). It shines forever, and was transcribed by the scribes of the seventy peoples (Bacher, "Ag. Tan." ii. 203, 416), while everything found in the Prophets and the Hagiographa was already contained in the Torah (Ta'an. 9a), so

Preexist- that, if the Israelites had not sinned,
ence of only the five books of Moses would
the Torah. have been given them (Ned. 22b). As a matter of fact, the Prophets and the Hagiographa will be abrogated; but the Torah will remain forever (Yer. Meg. 70d). Every letter of it is a living creature. When Solomon took many wives, Deuteronomy threw himself before God and complained that Solomon wished to remove from the Pentateuch the yod of the word ירבה (Deut. xvii. 17), with which the prohibition of polygamy was spoken; and God replied: "Solomon and a thousand like him shall perish, but not one letter of the Torah shall be destroyed" (Lev. R. xix.; Yer. Sanh. 20c; Cant. R. 5, 11; comp. Bacher, *l.c.* ii. 123, note 5). The single letters were hypostatized, and were active even at the creation of the world (Bacher, *l.c.* i. 347), an idea which is probably derived from Gnostic speculation. The whole world is said to be only $\frac{1}{3200}$ of the Torah ('Er. 21a).

Israel received this treasure only through suffering (Ber. 5a, and parallels), for the book and the sword came together from heaven, and Israel was obliged to choose between them (Sifre, Deut. 40, end; Bacher, *l.c.* ii. 402, note 5); and whosoever denies the heavenly origin of the Torah will lose the future life (Sanh. x. 1). This high esteem finds its

expression in the rule that a copy of the Pentateuch is unlimited in value, and in the ordinance that the inhabitants of a city might oblige one another to procure scrolls of the Law (Tosef., B. M. iii. 24, xi. 23). The pious bequeathed a copy of the Torah to the synagogue (*ib.* B. Ḳ. ii. 3); and it was the duty of each one to make one for himself, while the honor paid the Bible greatly influenced the distribution of copies and led to the foundation of libraries (Blau, "Althebräisches Buchwesen," pp. 84–97).

The highest ideal of young and old and of small and great was the study of the Law, thus forming a basis for that indomitable eagerness of the Jewish people for education and that unquenchable thirst for knowledge which still characterize them. "As the child must satisfy its hunger day by day, so must the grown man busy himself with the Torah each hour" (Yer. Ber. ch. ix.). The mishnah (Pe'ah i.) incorporated in the daily prayer declares that the study of the Law transcends all things, being greater than the rescue of human life, than the building of the Temple, and than the honor of father and mother (Meg. 16b). It is of more value than the offering of daily sacrifice ('Er. 63b); a single day devoted to the Torah outweighs 1,000 sacrifices (Shab. 30a; comp. Men. 100a); while the fable of the Fish and the Fox, in which the latter seeks to entice the former to dry land, declares Israel can live only in the Law as fish can live only in the ocean. Whoever separates himself from the Torah dies forth-

Study of with ('Ab. Zarah 3b); for fire con-
the Torah. sumes him, and he falls into hell (B. B. 79a); while God weeps over one who might have occupied himself with it but neglected to do so (Ḥag. 5b). The study must be unselfish: "One should study the Torah with self-denial, even at the sacrifice of one's life; and in the very hour before death one should devote himself to this duty" (Soṭah 21b; Ber. 63b; Shab. 83b). "Whoever uses the crown of the Torah shall be destroyed" (Ned. 62a). All, even the lepers and the unclean, were required to study the Law (Ber. 22a), while it was the duty of every one to read the entire weekly lesson twice (Ber. 8a); and the oldest benediction was the one spoken over the Torah (*ib.* 11b). Prophylactic power also is ascribed to it: it gives protection against suffering (*ib.* 5a), against sickness ('Er. 54b), and against oppression in the Messianic time (Sanh. 98b); so that it may be said that "the Torah protects all the world" (Sanh. 99b; comp. Ber. 31a). The following sayings may be cited as particularly instructive in this respect: "A Gentile who studies the Torah is as great as the high priest" (B. Ḳ. 38a). "The practise of all the laws of the Pentateuch is worth less than the study of the scriptures of it" (Yer. Pe'ah i.), a conclusive refutation of the current view of the NOMISM of the Jewish faith. After these citations it becomes readily intelligible that, according to the Talmudic view, "God Himself sits and studies the Torah" ('Ab. Zarah 3b).

The spirit of criticism naturally developed from this devotion to the Pentateuch, in spite of faith and reverence. The very existence of the doctrine that the Law was of heavenly origin, and that whosoever

denied this dogma had no share in the life to come (Sanh. x.), shows that there was a school which
assumed a critical attitude toward the

Criticism of the Torah Among Jews. Torah. There is much evidence in proof of this; but here only the history of criticism within the orthodox synagogue will be discussed. It was a moot point whether the Law was given all at once or in smaller rolls at different times (Giṭ. 60a); and the further question was discussed, whether Moses or Joshua wrote the last eight verses of the Pentateuch (B. B. 14b–15a). It was definitely affirmed, on the other hand (*ib.*), that Moses composed the sections concerning Balaam (Num. xxii.–xxiv.), thus closing all discussions on that score. Many tacit doubts are scattered through the Talmud and Midrash, in addition to those which Einstein has collected. In the post-Talmudic period, in like manner, there was no lack of critics, some of them recognized as such again only in recent times, although Abraham ibn Ezra, who was joined by Spinoza, has long been recognized as belonging to this class.

The composition of the Torah should be discussed on the basis of the old Semitic concepts, which planned a work of literature practi-

Composition. cally rather than systematically. Repetitions, therefore, should not be eliminated, since things which are good and noble may and should be brought to remembrance many times. From the point of view of effective emphasis, moreover, a change of context may develop a new and independent application of a given doctrine, especially if it be repeated in other words. Thus tradition (The Thirty-two Rules of Eliezer b. Jose ha-Gelili) took "the repeated doctrine" as its rule of interpretation, and left large numbers of repetitions (parallel passages) in its collections of oral teachings. The framework of the Pentateuch is historical narrative bound together by the thread of chronology. There is no rigid adherence to the latter principle, however; and the Talmud itself accordingly postulates the rule: "There is no earlier and no later in the Torah" (Pes. 6b *et passim*). From a Masoretic point of view, the Mosaic code contains the history of a period of about 2,300 years. As has already been noted in regard to the names of the individual books, the Talmud and the Masorah divided the Torah into smaller units according to its contents, so that Genesis includes the story of Creation and of the Patriarchs, Exodus the account of the departure from Egypt, the revelation, and so on.

The style of the Pentateuch, in keeping with its content, differs widely from the diction of the Prophets and the Psalms. It is less lofty, although it is not lacking in dramatic force, and it is concrete rather than abstract. Most of the laws are formulated in the second person as a direct address, the Decalogue being the best example. In certain cases, however, the nature of the subject requires the third person; but the Torah reverts as quickly as possible to the second as being the more effective form of address (comp., for example, Deut. xix. 11–21). In the Pentateuch, temporal depiction is the usual method. The process of creation, rather than the universe as a whole, is described; and the account brings the world visibly into being in six main parts. In the creation of man, of plants, and of paradise God is seen at work, and the same process of coming into being may be traced in the ark of Noah and similar descriptions. A

Style. remarkable example of word-painting is the account of the consecration of Aaron and his sons to the high-priesthood (Lev. viii.). Here the reader watches while Moses washes the candidates, dresses them, etc. ("Magyar-Zsidó Szemle," ix. 565 *et seq.*). Naïve simplicity is a characteristic trait of Pentateuchal style, which understands also the art of silence. Thus, as in all great products of world-literature, feminine beauty is not described in detail; for Sarah, Rachel, and other heroines are merely said to be beautiful, while the completion of the picture is left to the imagination of the reader.

The contents of the Torah fall into two main parts: historical and legal. The latter commences with Ex. xii.; so that the Tannaim maintained that the Law actually began there, proceeding on the correct principle that the word "Torah" could be applied only to teachings which regulated the life of man, either leading him to perform certain acts (commands = מצות עשה) or restraining him from them (prohibitions = מצות לא תעשה). The Talmud enumerates a total of 613 rules, 248 being commands and 365 prohibitions (see Jew. Encyc.

Laws of the Torah. iv. 181, *s.v.* Commandments, The 613). In the post-Talmudic period many works were written on these 613 "miẓwot," some even by Maimonides. The legal parts of the Pentateuch include all the relations of human life, although these are discussed with greater detail in the Talmud (see Talmudic Laws). The Torah recognizes no subdivisions of the commandments; for all alike are the ordinances of God, and a distinction may be drawn only according to modern ideas, as when Driver (in Hastings, "Dict. Bible," iii. 66) proposes a triple division, into juridical, ceremonial, and moral "torot."

Montefiore was correct when, in laying emphasis on the ethical aspect of the Biblical concept of God, he declared that even the law of the Bible was permeated with morality, propounding his view in the following words ("Hibbert Lectures," p. 64): "Most original and characteristic was the moral influence of Jahveh in the domain of law. Jahveh, to the Israelite, was emphatically the God of the right. . . . From the earliest times onward, Jahveh's sanctuary was the depository of law, and the priest was His spokesman." The most prominent characteristic of the Pentateuchal law, as compared with the laws of ancient peoples and of medieval Europe, is mildness, a feature which is still further developed in the Talmud. The Torah is justly regarded as the source of humane law. Although

Penal Law. such phrases occur as "that soul shall be cut off from his people" or "so shalt thou put the evil away from the midst of thee," it would be incorrect to take them literally, or to deduce from them certain theories of penal law, as Förster has recently done. On the contrary, these expressions prove that the Mosaic law was not a legal code in the strict sense of the term, but an ethical work. Although the Talmudists made it a penal code, instinctively reading that character into it, the penal law of the Torah is something theoretical which was never put into practise. This view is supported by the fact that a commandment is stated sometimes without the threat of any penalty whatever for its violation, and sometimes with the assignment even of death as a punishment for its transgression. In like manner, tradition frequently substitutes such a phrase as "he forfeited his life" for "transgression worthy of death."

On the other hand, the civil law of the Torah, which is more developed and bears a practical character, probably accords more closely
Civil Law. with ancient Jewish legal procedure. It reflects the conditions of an agricultural state, since most of the laws relate to farming and cognate matters. There was no Hebrew word for "store," although "just measure" was mentioned. It must be borne in mind, however, that to satisfy the more advanced conditions of later times, the Talmudists both supplemented the Mosaic law and by means of analogy and similar expedients interpolated into the Torah much which it did not contain originally.

From the earliest times the Synagogue has proclaimed the divine origin of the Pentateuch, and has held that Moses wrote it down from dictation, while the religions based on Judaism have until very recently held the same view. Biblical criticism, however, denies the Mosaic authorship and ascribes only a portion of varying extent to so ancient an origin. A history of criticism in regard to this point is given by Winer ("B. R." ii. 419 et seq.) and by Driver (in Hastings, "Dict. Bible," iii. 66), while Montefiore expresses himself as follows (l.c.):

"The Torah—or teaching—of the priests, half judicial, half pædagogic, was a deep moral influence; and there was no element in the religion which was at once more genuinely Hebrew and more closely identified with the national God. There is good reason to believe that this priestly Torah is the one religious institution which can be correctly attributed to Moses. . . . Though Moses was not the author of the written law, he was unquestionably the founder of that oral teaching, or Torah, which preceded and became the basis of the codes of the Pentateuch."

The legal parts of the Torah are found in Ex. xx.-xxiii., xxv.-xxxi., xxxiv.-xxxv.; Lev. i.-viii., xi.-xxv., xxvii.; Num. v.-x., xviii., xix., xxvii.-xxx., these laws being repeated in Deut. iv. et seq.

BIBLIOGRAPHY: Bacher, *Ag. Tan.*; idem, *Ag. Pal. Amor.* Index, s.v. *Tora* and *Studium der Lehre*; Baumgartner, *Les Etudes Isagogiques chez les Juifs*, Geneva, 1886; Blau, *Zur Einleitung in die Heilige Schrift*, Strasburg, 1894; idem, *Studien zum Althebräischen Buchwesen und zur Biblischen Litteraturgeschichte*, Strasburg, 1902; Büchler, *The Triennial Reading of the Law and Prophets*, in *J. Q. R.* vi. 1-73; Eisenstadt, *Ueber Bibelkritik in der Talmudischen Litteratur*, Frankfort-on-the-Main, 1894; Förster, *Das Mosaische Strafrecht in Seiner Geschichtlichen Entwickelung*, Leipsic, 1900; Hamburger, *R. B. T.* supplementary vol. iii. 60-75; Hastings, *Dict. Bible*, iii. 64-73; JEW. ENCYC. vii. 633-638; Michaelis-Saalschütz, *Mosaisches Recht*, Berlin, 1842-46; Herzog-Hauck, *Real-Encyc.* xiii. 486-502; Weber, *Jüdische Theologie*, pp. 14-34, and Index, Leipsic, 1897; Winer, *B. R.* 3d ed., i. 415-422. For the criticism of the Torah compare the text-books of the history of Judaism and of Old Testament theology. See also PENTATEUCH.
J.   L. B.

TORAT KOHANIM (THE SIFRA). See MIDRASH HAGGADAH.

TORDESILLAS: Spanish city near Valladolid, with a Jewish community, which was visited by Vicente Ferrer toward the end of 1411 for propagandic purposes. He advised the Jews of the city to change their abode for the narrow ghetto of Valladolid, but his counsel was disregarded. In 1474 the number of Jews in Tordesillas was still so great that they paid 900 maravedis in taxes. Tordesillas was the birthplace of Moses ha-Kohen de TORDESILLAS.

BIBLIOGRAPHY: Rios, *Hist.* ii. 428 et seq., iii. 594.
J.   M. K.

TORDESILLAS, MOSES HA-KOHEN DE: Spanish controversialist, who was called upon to suffer for his faith, an attempt being made to convert him to Christianity by force. Despite cruel persecution, he remained true to his convictions, although he was robbed of all his possessions and reduced to poverty. Before long he was chosen rabbi by the community of Avila, where he was compelled to carry on a religious debate, about 1372, with the convert JOHN OF VALLADOLID in the presence of Christians and Mohammedans. It was an easy task for Moses ha-Kohen, who was acquainted with the Christian sources, to refute in four debates the arguments of his opponent, who tried to prove the Christian dogmas from the Scriptures. Soon afterward he was obliged to enter upon a new contest with a disciple of the convert ABNER OF BURGOS, with whose writings, especially with his "Mostrador de Jeosticia," Moses was thoroughly acquainted. In 1374, at the desire of the members of his community, he wrote, in the form of a dialogue between a Jew and a Christian, the main substance of his debates, which treated of the Trinity, of the virginity of Mary, of sacrifice, of the alleged new teachings of Jesus and of the New Testament, of the seven weeks of Daniel, and of similar matters. His book, which is divided into seventeen chapters, dealing with 125 passages emphasized by Christian controversialists, is entitled "'Ezer ha-Emunah" (The Support of Faith). It was sent by its author to David ibn Ya'ish at Toledo, and manuscripts of it are found at Oxford, Berlin, Parma, Breslau, and elsewhere.

BIBLIOGRAPHY: De Rossi-Hamberger, *Hist. Wörterb.* pp. 317 et seq.; Grätz, *Gesch.* 3d ed., viii. 20-21; Neubauer, *Jewish Interpretations of the Fifty-third Chapter of Isaiah*, p. 10; Steinschneider, *Verzeichnis der Hebräischen Handschriften der Königlichen Bibliothek zu Berlin*, p. 51; idem, *Hebr. Bibl.* ii. 85, note 10.
J.   M. K.

TORONTO: Canadian city; capital of the province of Ontario. Toronto possesses four regularly organized Jewish congregations, the oldest being the Holy Blossom congregation, which had its beginnings in 1845, though it was not formally organized until 1852. Its first synagogue was in Richmond street, the building being dedicated in 1857; later the congregation moved to its present home in Bond street. Attached to it is a large and well-organized Sabbath-school. The Goel Tsedek congregation, founded in 1880, has a synagogue in Elm street; the Shomerei Shabbas, an Austrian congregation organized in 1891, worships in Chestnut street; and the Chevra Tillim congregation, organized in 1895, is at Richmond and York streets. In addition to these there are a number of minor congregations, formed in recent years, but acquiring a large membership and steadily growing in importance.

The Jewish communal institutions of Toronto include organizations of a philanthropic, educational, religious, and literary character. Among these are the Jewish Benevolent Society, the Ladies' Montefiore Aid Society, the Ḥebra Ḳaddisha, the Toronto Hebrew Ladies' Aid Society, the Ḥebra Linous Hatsedek, the Austrian Hebrew Ladies' Aid Society, a branch of the Anglo-Jewish Association, the Toronto branch of the Council of Jewish Women, the Young Men's Hebrew Association, the Jewish Literary Society, the Talmud Torah, the Toronto Hebrew Benevolent Society, the Jewish Shelter Society, the Judean Club, several lodges, and four Zionist organizations—the Agudath Zion, Toronto Daughters of Zion, B'nai Zion Association, and Ahavath Zion Society.

Toronto had a population of 519,290 in 1921, of whom about 35,000 were Jews.

A.   C. I. DE S.

TORQUEMADA, TOMAS DE. See AUTO DA FÉ; INQUISITION.

TORRE, LELIO (HILLEL) DELLA: Italian rabbi and educator; born in Cuneo, Piedmont, Jan. 11, 1805; died in Padua July 9, 1871. His father, Solomon Jehiel Raphael ha-Kohen, died in 1807; and Lelio was brought up by his uncle Sabbatai Elhanan Treves, a rabbi in Piedmont. From 1823 to 1829 he acted as tutor in Hebrew and in Biblical exegesis in the Collegio Colonna e Finzi founded in Turin by the Jewish community; and in 1827 he was appointed assistant rabbi. When the rabbinical college was founded in Padua in 1829, Della Torre was appointed professor of Talmud, homiletics, and pastoral theology, which position he held until his death; in 1869 he occupied for several months, during a vacancy, the rabbinical chair of Padua. Cuneo, his native town, honored him by engraving his name on a bronze tablet among those of the most illustrious citizens of Italy.

Besides his thorough familiarity with all branches of Hebrew literature and Jewish history, Della Torre was master of several ancient and modern languages, writing Hebrew, Italian, and French with equal facility. He wrote numerous Hebrew poems, most of which were included in his collection " Ṭal Yaldut," which, together with a supplement of later compositions entitled " Egle Ṭal," appeared in Padua in 1868. He was the author also of various articles in Hebrew periodicals, treating mostly of subjects relating to the science of Judaism and written in pure classical Hebrew. They may be found in " Kerem Ḥemed " (iv. 9), in the new " Bikkure ha-'Ittim," in " Oẓar Neḥmad " (i.), and in various volumes of " Kokebe Yiẓḥaḳ." Of his published works the following may be mentioned: " Cinque Discorsi," Padua, 1834; " Della Condizione Degli Ebrei Sotto l'Impero Germanico nel Medio Evo," ib. 1842; " I Salmi Volgarizzati sul Testo Massoretico ed Illustrati con Argomenti e Note. Parte Prima, Testo, Traduzione ed Argomenti," Vienna, 1845; " Preghiere degl' Israeliti. Traduzione dall' Ebraico," ib. 1846; " Orazioni per Ordinazioni Rabbiniche," Ven-

ice, 1852; " Poésies Hébraïques," Padua, 1869; " Iscrizioni Sepolcrali," ib. 1870; and " Pensieri sulle Lezioni Sabbatiche del Pentateucho," ib. 1872. His " Orazioni Postume" (Padua, 1879, pp. 189-202) contains an autobiographical sketch and a complete list of his works.

BIBLIOGRAPHY: Oẓar ha-Sifrut, iii. 91-92; S. Jona, in Corriere Israelitico, 1872.

S.   P. WI.

TORT (Hebrew, נזיקין; Latin, " delictum "): Any wrongful act, neglect, or default whereby legal damage is caused to the person, property, or reputation of another. Liability arises either from contract or from tort. Direct and wilful tort is TRESPASS. Trespass on the person is ASSAULT AND BATTERY. Other torts arise from lack of skill or care (see ACCIDENT; BAILMENTS [sometimes deemed liabilities from contract]; FAULT; FRAUD AND MISTAKE; GORING OX). Among the torts not elsewhere treated are:

Mesne Profits: The income derived from land unlawfully held by the possessor, for which he is answerable to the true owner when the latter recovers the land from him by the judgment of a court. The Talmud speaks of the possessor of land without right as the " robber of the land " (in English law, " disseizor "); and he, or even a third person who takes fruits or branches from land thus withheld from the true owner, is considered as morally guilty of robbery (see the prohibition of an Israelite using, in the ritual thyrsus on the Feast of Booths, a palm-branch or citron taken from land held by a disseizor [Suk. iv. 1, 2]). The liability to pay mesne profits is implied and rather distantly indicated in the Mishnah (Giṭ. v. 2). Assuming that he who sells land with warranty is liable not only for the price of the land which he receives, but also for the mesne profits which the purchaser will have to pay after eviction to the true owner, it is here taught that from motives of public policy the warranty inserted in the deed of sale, though in the nature of a bond, is to be levied, as far as it secures the purchaser against this liability, only upon " free property," not on " subjected property," i.e., on lands which in the meanwhile have been given away, sold, or encumbered (for the distinction see DEED). The Gemara (B. M. 14a, b) discusses this matter fully in the light of the warranty, the liability of the unlawful possessor being taken for granted (see Maimonides, " Yad," Gezelah, ch. xiv.).

Depasturing: A liability for full damages is imposed by Ex. xxii. 4 (Hebr.). " If a man pastures on field or vineyard and sends his cattle to pasture in the field of another, he shall make it good with the best of his field and the best of his vineyard." When he pastures thus purposely, it is really a trespass; but the liability for " foot or tooth " is often as full when beasts go of themselves into the domain of another. Accidental injuries of this kind have been referred to under ACCIDENT. But when a beast eats the neighbor's produce, is the owner liable for the harm done, or only for his profit by its eating? In the case put in Scripture he is of course bound for the former. Other cases are thus put by

Maimonides ("Yad," Nizḳe Mamon, iii. 6-12), who draws from B. Ḳ. 14-27 *passim*:

When, from necessity, a beast eats something not its usual food, *e.g.*, when an ass eats vetches or fish, the owner pays full damage, if the occurrence took place on the grounds of the injured party; but if on the highway, he pays only the amount which he has profited. Where **Wilful and** a beast of prey enters the grounds **Ac-** of the injured party and tears or de- **cidental.** vours a domestic animal, the owner of the beast is liable for full damage, because it is its nature to act in the manner as it did: but if a dog should trespass and eat lambs or a cat eat grown hens, only half damage is due; for this is unusual. When an ass, finding bread in a basket, eats the bread and breaks the basket, the owner pays full damage for both. Where a beast, whether walking or standing, eats grass from the middle of a square, the owner pays what he profits: where it eats from the side he pays full damage. For what it eats out of the door of a shop, its owner is required to pay the equivalent of what he has profited thereby; from the interior of the shop, full damage. If, walking along the road, a beast eats off the back of another beast, only the saving in fodder is paid for; if it jumps out of its place, full damage is due. If one's beast glides or stumbles into another's garden and eats, etc., the owner owes only for what he profits, even if the beast goes from bed to bed, or stays in the garden all day; but if it walks into the garden in the regular way, there is liability for full damage. So, also, if it is pushed into the garden by a companion; for the owner should lead his herd in single file.

Unintentional Injury: Though "a man is always forewarned," that is, liable for his actions, asleep or awake, intentional or unintentional (see ASSAULT AND BATTERY, and authorities there cited), there is a broad exception to the rule; viz., when the mischief is done on the ground of the injuring party. For what a man does within his own domain, he is liable in damages only if it was done wilfully; but he is not liable if done either unconsciously or under compulsion. Where a man climbs a ladder, and a rung falls out under him and strikes another, he is liable if the rung was not strong enough or not well set; but if it was strong and well set, the harm done is regarded as providential, and he goes clear, even if it happened within the domain of the injured party; while on his own ground he would go clear in either case ("Yad," Ḥobel, iv. 3, 4, based on B. Ḳ. 28).

Betrayal: The man of violence ("annas," generally denoting an arbitrary or cruel official of the Gentile kingdom) is often mentioned in the Talmud and the codes. The most odious among torts was that of betraying the person or property of a fellow Israelite into the hands of the annas (see B. Ḳ. 5a, 114a; "Yad," Ḥobel, viii.; Shulḥan 'Aruḳ, Ḥoshen Mishpaṭ, 328). In the 'Aruk it is put thus: "He who [by informing] delivers up property into the hands of an annas, whether Gentile or Jew, is bound to make good, from the best part of his estate, whatever the annas has taken, though he has not handled the thing at all, but has only shown the

way; and if he dies, the damage done is levied from his estate in the hands of his heirs." The informer is excused if he has given informa- **Informers.** tion under bodily duress; but if he has handled the property himself, he is liable even then; for a man has no right to save himself at the cost of another. Further on, a religious sanction is given to this civil liability: "He who delivers up an Israelite, either in his body or in his property, to the Gentile has no share in the world to come." And on the strength of a case reported in B. B. 116a it is also said that it is not only permissible but meritorious to kill an informer in order to put a stop to his villainous trade.

Slander and Insult: It has been shown under ASSAULT AND BATTERY that the insult or humiliation incidental to an assault is to be paid for separately; but in the case of an insult when there is no assault, even when one spits at another and does not reach his body but only his garment, there is no ground for recovery (B. Ḳ. 91a). And in the same connection a Palestinian amora is quoted: "The tradition goes [זאת אומרת], 'He who shames another by words is free from everything.'" But the Jerusalem Talmud (B. Ḳ. 6c) makes an exception in favor of the "elder," meaning a rabbi. Thus: "He who puts an elder to shame pays him the price of his shame. One Meshullam affronted R. Judah ben Ḥanina: the matter came before R. Simeon ben Laḳish; and he fined Meshullam a litra **Elder** of gold." This precedent was carried **"Put to** into the Halakah; and all the Geonim **Shame."** followed it. They applied it to every scholar (תלמיד חכם), and thus the rule appears in the code of Maimonides ("Yad," Ḥobel, iii. 5), where the penalty is put at 35 denarii of gold (the weight of 8¾ shekels of gold); but he adds that in Spain many of the scholars waive their privilege. While others than scholars have no civil remedy for insult or slander, the act of "blanching a man's face in public" or that of "attaching a nickname to one's neighbor" is, as has been seen in ONA'AH, among the unpardonable sins punished in the future world. It is also found (Ket. 46a) that the sin of "bringing out an evil report" (slander) is fully recognized, on the strength of the text "Thou shalt not go up and down as a tale-bearer among the people" (Lev. xix. 16); but there is no civil remedy for the wrong done.

E. C.   L. N. D.

TORTOISE: Rendering in the Authorized Version of the Hebrew word "ẓab" (Lev. xi. 29; see LIZARD). Some commentators assume "gallim" in Hos. xii. 12 to mean "tortoises," a view which has the support of the Septuagint, the Peshiṭta, and old Arabic versions. Two species of land tortoise, *Testudo græca* and *Testudo leithii*, and several of the aquatic tortoises have been found in Palestine. Of the latter the *Emys caspica* is the most numerous.

The Talmud uses "ẓab" and also "zabuni" to denote the toad (Ṭoh. v. i). In Ber. 33a it is said that the water-snake is the issue of the toad and the snake. The tortoise is assumed to be intended in כילתא and כילי in Nid. 17a and Gen. R. lvii. 2.

BIBLIOGRAPHY: Tristram, *Nat. Hist.* p. 255; Lewysohn, *Z. T.* p. 232.

E. G. H.   I. M. C.

TORTOSA: City in Catalonia where Jews lived and owned land as early as the Roman period. This Jewish community was one of the richest in the country in the thirteenth and fourteenth centuries, and had certain ancient privileges which were confirmed from time to time until 1328. In 1262 the "bayle" of Tortosa and farmer of the royal taxes was Astruc Jacob Xixen or Xuxen (Shushan). The Jews of the city owed him 9,000 sueldos, and on their refusal to pay, the king, with whom he stood in special favor, and who had granted him privileges for life, gave him the right of distrainer.

The Jews of Tortosa were always ready, however, to make sacrifices if it was for the good of the country. When James II. was in need of money for conquering the county of Urgel, which also contained Jewish communities, the Jews of Tortosa, together with those of Barcelona, Gerona, Valencia, and Lerida, furnished him with 115,000 livres; and when Alfonso, the son and successor of James, was fitting out a fleet in 1323 for the conquest of Cerdeña, the Jewish community of Tortosa contributed and manned two ships, being exempted from all taxes for several years in recognition of their services.

The chief occupations of the Jews of this city were farming, viniculture, commerce, and manufacturing. In 1220 the brothers Astruc of Tortosa possessed lands upon the island of Majorca. They owned large establishments for dyeing linen and cotton, and sold their wares in a special market-place. They were allowed to take an annual interest of four dinars per livre, but were subject to heavy special taxes, since they were obliged to pay the state 4,000 sueldos in 1284 alone, as table-moneys ("cenas"), in addition to the municipal assessments on their houses and lands. On its own responsibility the Jewish community in Tortosa ordained that, to be valid, all marriages must be performed before authorized persons of the community and in the presence of ten grown men, and that any woman of Tortosa could contract a new marriage without a previous ritualistic divorce, unless married in this fashion. The year of terror, 1391, was eventful for the Jews in Tortosa as well as in other cities. The community, previously so wealthy, could no longer pay its taxes, and there, as elsewhere, many accepted baptism; many Maranos fell victims to the Inquisition in Tortosa.

Tortosa was either the birthplace or the residence of several Jewish scholars. Menahem ben Saruḳ, the earliest Hebrew lexicographer; Shem-Ṭob ben Isaac and his son Abraham, both Hebrew translators; and the physician and philosopher Jacob Mantino were born there; there, too, lived Isaac Maimon and Abraham b. Alfual, who carried on a correspondence with Isaac ben Sheshet; and also the modern Hebrew satiric poet Solomon ben Reuben Bonfed, rabbi and delegate of the community at the disputation of Tortosa.

BIBLIOGRAPHY: Belaguer, *Historia de Cataluña*, vi. 12; *Boletin Acad. Hist.*, lii. 508; Isaac b. Sheshet, *Responsa*, Nos. 361 *et seq.*, 399; Jacobs, *Sources*, Nos. 201, 253, 806, 830, 834; Rios, *Hist.* ii. 71, 155.

s. M. K.

TORTSCHINER, LÖB B. ABRAHAM. See CORDOVERO, ARYEH LÖB.

TOSAFOT ("additions"): Critical and explanatory glosses on the Talmud, printed, in almost all editions, on the outer margin and opposite Rashi's notes. The authors of the Tosafot are known as **Tosafists** ("ba'ale ha-tosafot"). For what reason these glosses are called "tosafot" is a matter of dispute among modern scholars. Many of them, including Graetz, think the glosses are so called as additions to Rashi's commentary on the Talmud. In fact, the period of the Tosafot began immediately after Rashi had written his commentary; the first tosafists were Rashi's sons-in-law and grandsons, and the Tosafot consist mainly of strictures on Rashi's commentary. Others, especially Weiss, object that many tosafot, particularly those of Isaiah di Trani, have no reference to Rashi. Weiss, followed by other scholars, asserts that "tosafot" means "additions" to the Talmud, that is to say, they are an extension and development of the Talmud. For just as the Gemara is a critical and analytical commentary on the Mishnah, so are the Tosafot critical and analytical glosses on those two parts of the Talmud. Further, the term "tosafot" was not applied for the first time to the glosses of Rashi's continuators, but to the Tosefta, the additions to the Mishnah compiled by Judah ha-Nasi I. "Tosefta" is a Babylonian term, which in Palestinian writings is replaced by "tosafot" (see Yer. Pe'ah ii. 17a; Lev. R. xxx. 2; Cant. R. vi. 9; Eccl. R. v. 8). The Tosafot resemble the Gemara in other respects also, for just as the latter is the work of different schools carried on through a long period, so the former were written at different times and by different schools, and gathered later into one body.

Up to and including Rashi, the Talmudic commentators occupied themselves only with the plain meaning ("peshaṭ") of the text; but after the beginning of the twelfth century the spirit of criticism took possession of the teachers of the Talmud. Thus some of Rashi's continuators, as his sons-in-law and his grandson Samuel ben Meïr (RaSHBaM), while they wrote commentaries on the Talmud after the manner of Rashi's, wrote also glosses on it in a style peculiar to themselves. The chief characteristic of the Tosafot is that they evidence no recognition of any authority, so that, in spite of the great respect in which Rashi was held by the Tosafists, the latter freely corrected him. Besides, the Tosafot do not constitute a continuous commentary, but, like the "Dissensiones" to the Roman code of the first quarter of the twelfth century, deal only with the difficult passages of the Talmudic text. Single sentences are explained by quotations which are taken from other Talmudic treatises and which seem at first glance to have no connection with the sentences in question. On the other hand, sentences which seem to be related and interdependent are separated and embodied in different treatises. It must be added that the Tosafot can be understood only by those who are well advanced in the study of the Talmud, for the most entangled discussions are treated as though they were simple. Glosses explaining the meaning of a word or containing a grammatical observation are very rare.

The Tosafot may be considered from the point of view of a methodology of the Talmud. The rules are certainly not gathered together in one series, as they are, for instance, in Maimonides' introduction to the Mishnah; they are scattered in various parts, and their number is quite considerable. Neither are they stated in fixed terms; a generally accepted rule is followed by "This is the way of the Talmud" or "The Talmud usually declares." Sometimes the negative expression is found, "This is not the way of the Talmud." A frequently recurring rule is indicated by some such formula as "We find many like this." It must be borne in mind that what has been said hitherto concerns the general features of the Tosafot, and does not conflict with the fact that the writings of different tosafists differ in style and method. With regard to method, it should be said that the Tosafot of Touques (see below) concern particularly the casuistic interpretation of the traditional law, but do not touch halakic decisions.

The chief home of tosafot literature was incontestably France, for it began with Rashi's pupils, and was continued mainly by the heads of the French schools. It is true that, practically, tosafot began to be written in Germany at the same time as in France, but the French tosafists always predominated numerically. The first tosafot recorded are those written by Rashi's two sons-in-law, Meïr b. Samuel of Ramerupt (RaM) and Judah ben Nathan (RIBaN), and by a certain R. Joseph (Jacob Tam, "Sefer ha-Yashar," No. 252; "Haggahot Mordekai," Sanh., No. 696; see below). But their tosafot not being otherwise known, the actual father of the tosafot in France was undoubtedly JACOB B. MEÏR TAM, whose style was adopted by his successors. He wrote a great number of tosafot, many of which are to be found in his "Sefer ha-Yashar"; but not all, as many passages that are cited in the edited tosafot are not found in the work just mentioned. In Germany, at the same time, there flourished ISAAC BEN ASHER HA-LEVI (RIBA), leader of the German tosafists, who wrote numerous tosafot, which are mentioned by Abraham b. David ("Temim De'im," Nos. 158, 207–209), and which are very often cited in the edited tosafot (e.g., to Soṭah 17b). But Isaac ben Asher's tosafot were revised by his pupils, who, according to Jacob Tam ("Sefer ha-Yashar," No. 282), sometimes ascribed to their teacher opinions which were not his. Zedekiah b. Abraham ("Shibbole ha-Leḳeṭ," i., No. 225), however, refutes Jacob Tam's assertion.

The most prominent tosafist immediately after Jacob Tam was his pupil and relative ISAAC BEN SAMUEL HA-ZAḲEN (RI) of Dampierre, whose tosafot form a part of the **Tosafot Yeshanim** (see below). Isaac was succeeded by his pupil SAMSON BEN ABRAHAM OF SENS (d. about 1235), who, besides enriching the literature with his own compositions, revised those of his predecessors, especially his teacher's, and compiled them into the group known as the **Tosafot of Sens** (תוספות שאנץ). Samson's fellow pupil JUDAH B. ISAAC OF PARIS (Sir Leon) was also very active; he wrote tosafot to several Talmudic treatises, of which those to Berakot were published at Warsaw (1863); some of those to 'Abo-

Mostly of French Origin.

dah Zarah are extant in manuscript. Among the many French tosafists deserving special mention was SAMUEL B. SOLOMON OF FALAISE (Sir Morel), who, owing to the destruction of the Talmud in France in his time, relied for the text entirely upon his memory (Meïr of Rothenburg, Responsa, No. 250).

The edited tosafot owe their existence particularly to Samson of Sens and to the following French tosafists of the thirteenth century: (1) MOSES OF EVREUX, (2) ELIEZER OF TOUQUES, and (3) PEREZ BEN ELIJAH OF CORBEIL.

(1) Moses of Evreux, one of the most prolific tosafists, furnished glosses to the whole Talmud; they form a distinct group known as the **Schools of Tosafot of Evreux** (תוספות איבורא or תוספות איירא). It may be presumed that the "Tosafot of R. Moses" mentioned by Mordecai b. Hillel ("Mordecai," on Sanh., No. 937) are identical with the tosafot just mentioned. According to Joseph Colon (Responsa, No. 52) and Elijah Mizraḥi ("Mayim 'Amuḳḳim," i., No. 37), Moses wrote his glosses on the margin of Isaac Alfasi's "Halakot," probably at the time of the burning of the Talmud.

Schools of Tosafists.

(2) Eliezer of Touques, of the second half of the thirteenth century, made a compendium of the Tosafot of Sens and of Evreux; this compendium is called the **Tosafot of Touques** (תוספות טוך), and forms the basis of the edited tosafot. Eliezer's own glosses, written on the margin, are known as the **Tosafot Gillayon** or **Gilyon Tosafot**. It must be premised, however, that the Tosafot of Touques did not remain untouched; they were revised afterward and supplemented by the glosses of later tosafists. Gershon Soncino, who printed these tosafot, declares that his ancestor Moses of Fürth, who lived in the middle of the fifteenth century, was a descendant in the fifth generation of Moses of Speyer, who is mentioned in the Tosafot of Touques. It is supposed that the last redactor of these tosafot was a pupil of Samson of Chinon.

(3) Perez ben Elijah of Corbeil was one of the most active of the later tosafists. Besides supplying tosafot to several treatises, which are quoted by many old authorities and are included among the edited tosafot (and many of which were seen in manuscript by Azulai), he revised those of his predecessors. His pupils were not less active; their additions are known as the **Tosafot of Perez b. Elijah's Pupils.**

It has been said that the first German tosafist, Isaac b. Asher ha-Levi, was the head of a school, and that his pupils, besides composing tosafot of their own, revised his. In the thirteenth century the German schools were represented by BARUCH BEN ISAAC, in Regensburg, and later by MEÏR OF ROTHENBURG; the Italian school was represented by ISAIAH DI TRANI. If the tosafot of ASHER B. JEHIEL (d. 1328) are to be included, the tosafistic period extended through more than two centuries. When the fanaticism of the French monasteries and the bigotry of Louis IX. brought about the destruction of the Talmud, the writing of tosafot in France soon ceased.

Other bodies of tosafot are:

French Tosafot: Mentioned in the novellæ on Tamid ascribed to Abraham b. David. Zunz ("Z.

G." p. 57) thinks that the Tosafot of Sens may be referred to under this title; but the fact that Abraham b. David was much earlier than Samson of Sens leads to the supposition that the glosses indicated are those of previous tosafists, as Jacob Tam, Isaac b. Asher ha-Levi, and Isaac b. Samuel ha-Zaḳen and his son.

Pisḳe Tosafot ("Decisions of the Tosafot"): Collection of halakic decisions gathered from the edited tosafot to thirty-six treatises—Nazir and Me'ilah being excepted—and generally printed in the margin of the Tosafot; in the later editions of the Talmud, after the text. These decisions number 5,931; of these 2,009 belong to the treatise Berakot and the order Mo'ed; 1,398 to Niddah and the order Nashim; 1,503 to Neziḳin; and 1,021 to Ḳodashim. The decisions contained in the tosafot to Shabbat, Pesaḥim, Giṭṭin, Ketubot, Baba Ḳamma, Baba Meẓi'a, Baba Batra, and Ḥullin number fully one-half of those recognized as authoritative. The compiler of these decisions can not be identified with certainty; Asher b. Jehiel, his son Jacob b. Asher, and Ezekiel, uncle of Eliezer of Touques, are given by different authorities. Jacob Nordhausen, also, is known to have compiled tosafot decisions; in fact, references to two groups of "Pisḳe Tosafot" are found in the works of the later casuists.

Spanish Tosafot: This term is used by Joseph Colon (Responsa, No. 72) and by Jacob Baruch Landau ("Agur," § 327), and may apply to Talmudic novellæ by Spanish authors. Jeshuah b. Joseph ha-Levi, for instance ("Halikot 'Olam," § 327), applies the term "tosafot" to the novellæ of Isaac ben Sheshet.

The Edited Tosafot (called also **Our Tosafot**): The tosafot which have been published with the text of the Talmud ever since its earliest edition (see TALMUD, EDITIONS OF). They extend to thirty-eight treatises of the Babylonian Talmud. Most of the treatises are covered by the Tosafot of Touques, some by the Tosafot of Sens; many are provided with the tosafot of various authors, revised by Perez b. Elijah's school. The authorship of the tosafot to seventeen treatises only can be established with certainty: Berakot, Moses of Evreux; Shabbat, 'Erubin, and Menaḥot, the Tosafot of Sens; Beẓah, Nedarim, Nazir, Sanhedrin, Makkot, and Me'ilah, Perez b. Elijah's school (many written by Perez himself); Yoma, Meïr of Rothenburg; Giṭṭin, Baba Ḳamma, and Ḥullin, the Tosafot of Touques; Soṭah, Samuel of Evreux; 'Abodah Zarah, Samuel of Falaise; Zebaḥim, Baruch b. Isaac of Worms. The tosafot to Mo'ed Ḳaṭon were written by a pupil of a certain R. Isaac; the author of the tosafot to Ḥagigah wrote tosafot to other treatises also. Those to Ta'anit belong to the post-tosafot period, and differ in style from those to other treatises.

Tosafot Alfasi: Quoted by Joseph Colon (Responsa, Nos. 5, 31) and Judah Minz (Responsa, No. 10). The term may designate either the tosafot of Samuel b. Meïr and Moses of Evreux, or glosses to Alfasi's "Halakot."

Tosafot of Gornish (גורניש, גורניין, גורנים): Mentioned by Joseph Solomon Delmedigo ("Nobelot Ḥokmah," Preface) and Solomon Algazi ("Gufe

Halakot," No. 195), the latter quoting these tosafot to Baba Ḳamma. But as the same quotation is made by Bezaleel Ashkenazi ("Shiṭṭah Meḳubbeẓet," to Baba Ḳamma) and ascribed to a pupil of Perez ben Elijah, Azulai ("Shem ha-Gedolim," ii.) concludes that these tosafot originated in Perez b. Elijah's school. Still, Mordecai b. Hillel ("Mordekai," B. B. on No. 886) mentions a R. Judah of Gornish, and Abraham ibn Akra ("Meharere Nemerim," Venice, 1599) reproduces Talmudic novellæ by "M. of Gornish" (Embden gives "Meïr of Gornish" in the Latin translation of the catalogue of the Oppenheim Library, No. 667). Manuscript No. 7 of the Günzburg collection bears the superscription "Tosafot of Gornish to Yebamot," and in these tosafot French and German rabbis are quoted. Manuscript No. 603 of the same collection contains also the Tosafot of Gornish and novellæ by Judah Minz, and fragments of Gornish tosafot are found in manuscripts in other libraries.

Different theories have been advanced with regard to the name "Gornish." According to Schechter ("Jew. Chron." May 4, 1888), it is a corruption of "Mayence," while H. Adler thinks it a corruption of נוראיץ (the English "Norwich"; see Neubauer in "R. E. J." xvii. 156, and Gross, "Gallia Judaica," pp. 136 et seq.). Gross (l.c.) thinks that Gornish may be identical with Gournay, in France, and that "M. of Gornish," apparently the author of the Tosafot of Gornish, may be Moses of Gornish and identical with the Moses of גריינץ mentioned in the Tosafot of Sens (to Pesaḥim). It may be added that in the supplement to Zacuto's "Yuḥasin" (p. 164a, Cracow, 1581) a David of "Durnish" occurs.

Tosafot Ḥiẓoniyyot ("Exterior" or "Uncanonical Tosafot"): Tosafot which are neither of Sens nor of Touques. They are so called by Bezaleel Ashkenazi; he included many fragments of them in his "Shiṭṭah Meḳubbeẓet," to Baba Meẓi'a, Nazir, etc.

Tosafot Shiṭṭah (or **Shiṭṭah**): Name sometimes applied to the recensions of Perez b. Elijah or to the tosafot of Jehiel of Paris (Bezaleel Ashkenazi, l.c.; notes to "Sha'are Dura," § 57; and many other authorities).

Tosafot Yeshanim ("Old Tosafot"): This group comprises four smaller ones: (1) the general tosafot of Sens, including those appearing among the edited tosafot; (2) the earlier unedited tosafot (for example, those to Ḳiddushin by Isaac b. Samuel ha-Zaḳen of Dampierre, and those to 'Abodah Zarah by his son Elhanan b. Isaac); (3) a collection of old tosafot published by Joseph Jessel b. Wolf ha-Levi in "Sugyot ha-Shas" (Berlin, 1736); (4) various tosafot found in ancient manuscripts, as the tosafot to Ḥullin written in 1360, the manuscript of which is in the Munich Library (No. 236). In the collection published by Joseph Jessel b. Wolf ha-Levi (No. 3), besides the old tosafot to Yoma by Moses of Coucy (comp., however, Israel Isserlein, "Terumat ha-Deshen," No. 94, who declares they belong to the Tosafot of Sens), there are single tosafot to sixteen treatises—Shabbat, Rosh ha-Shanah, Megillah, Giṭṭin, Baba Meẓi'a, Menaḥot, Bekorot, 'Erubin, Beẓah, Ketubot, Ḳiddushin, Nazir, Baba Batra, Horayot, Keritot, and Niddah. In the recent Wilna

Talmud edited by Romm the old tosafot to several treatises are printed.

The Tosafot quote principally Rashi (very often under the designation "ḳonṭres" [= "commentarius"?]), most of the tosafists, many of the ancient authorities (as Kalonymus of Lucca, Nathan b. Jehiel, and R. Hananeel), some contemporary scholars (as Abraham b. David of Posquières, Maimonides, Abraham ibn Ezra, and others), and about 130 German and French Talmudists of the twelfth and thirteenth centuries. Many of the last-named are known as authors of general Talmudic works, as, for instance, Eliezer b. Nathan of Mayence, Judah of Corbeil, and Jacob of Coucy; but many of them are known only through their being quoted in the Tosafot, as in the case of an Eliezer of Sens, a Jacob of Orleans, and many Abrahams and Isaacs. Some are even mentioned but once, as Eliezer of פְּלִירָא (Tos. B. B. 79b), Ephraim b. David (supposed contemporary of Judah Sir Leon; Tos. 'Ab. Zarah 39a), and one Hezekiah (Tos. B. B. 44b). A commentary on the Pentateuch entitled "Da'at Zeḳenim" (Leghorn, 1783) is attributed to the Tosafists. In form this commentary follows the style of the Tosafot; Rashi is often discussed, and sometimes corrected.

Of the great number of tosafists only forty-four are known by name. The following is an alphabetical list of them; many, however, are known only through citations:

A(HaRA): Quoted in the edited tosafot to M. Ḳ. 14b, 19a, 20b, 21a et seq.

Abigdor b. Elijah ha-Kohen: Flourished in the middle of the thirteenth century; his tosafot are mentioned in the edited tosafot to Ket. 63b.

Asher b. Jehiel: His tosafot, entitled "Tosefot ha-Rosh" or "Tosefe Tosafot," appeared in various epochs and works. Many of them were inserted by Bezaleel Ashkenazi in his "Shiṭṭah Meḳubbeẓet"; those to Yebamot and Ketubot appeared separately at Leghorn, 1776; to Soṭah, partly at Prague, 1725, and partly in Jacob Faitusi's "Mar'eh ha-Ofannim" (Leghorn, 1810); to Megillah and Shebu'ot, in Elijah Borgel's "Migdanot Natan" (ib. 1785); and to Ḳiddushin, in the "Ma'aseh Roḳem" (Pisa, 1806). They are included in Romm's recent edition of the Talmud.

Baruch b. Isaac (see above and JEW. ENCYC. ii. 559).

Eleazar b. Judah of Worms: Author of tosafot to Baba Ḳamma, extracts from which are found in Bezaleel Ashkenazi's "Shiṭṭah Meḳubbeẓet."

Elhanan b. Isaac: Flourished at the end of the twelfth century; his tosafot are mentioned by Abraham b. David in his "Temim De'im" and in the edited tosafot to B. M. 11b and Sheb. 28a. His tosafot to Nedarim are referred to by Joseph Colon (Responsa, No. 52); those to Megillah, in Isaiah di Trani's "Ha-Makria'" (No. 31, p. 19d); those to 'Abodah Zarah, in "Mordekai" (No. 1364).

Eliezer b. Joel ha-Levi (רָאבִי"ה): Flourished in the beginning of the thirteenth century; author of tosafot to several treatises (comp. Michael, "Or ha-Ḥayyim," No. 427).

Eliezer ben Samuel of Metz (Re'EM): Au-

thor of tosafot to several treatises, of which those to Ḥullin were seen by Azulai.

Eliezer of Toul: French tosafist of the beginning of the thirteenth century, whose tosafot are mentioned by Zedekiah Anaw in his "Shibbole ha-Leḳeṭ."

Eliezer of Touques (see above and JEW. ENCYC. v. 120).

Elijah ben Menahem: His tosafot are mentioned in "Haggahot Maimuniyyot," Ḳinnim, No. 20.

I (RI, probably R. Isaac, but not to be confused with Isaac b. Samuel ha-Zaḳen, who occurs most often as RI): His tosafot, in which the older RI is quoted, are mentioned by Samson b. Zadok ("Tashbeẓ," § 336).

Isaac ben Abraham (RIBA or **RIẒBA),** surnamed **ha-Baḥur** ("the younger," in distinction from his teacher Isaac b. Samuel ha-Zaḳen): Brother of Samson ben Abraham of Sens. Like his brother, Isaac lived as a youth at Troyes, where he attended the lectures of Jacob Tam ("Temim De'im," No. 87), and afterward at Sens (ib.; "Haggahot Maimuniyyot," Ishut, No. 6). After the death of Isaac ben Samuel, Isaac ben Abraham succeeded him as head of the school of Dampierre, after which place he is often called ("Or Zarua'," i. 225a). Isaac ben Abraham was one of the French rabbis to whom Meïr ben Todros Abulafia addressed his letter against Maimonides' theory of resurrection. He died at Dampierre prior to 1210, not long before his brother Samson emigrated to Palestine ("Semaḳ," No. 31; "Mordekai" on Ketubot, No. 357). As he is mentioned often in the edited tosafot (Shab. 3a, passim; Yoma 20a; et al.) and by many other authorities ("Or Zarua'," i. 26b; "Shibbole ha-Leḳeṭ," i., No. 231), it may be concluded that he wrote tosafot to several Talmudic treatises. Those to Bekorot were in the possession of Ḥayyim Michael of Hamburg. Isaac ben Abraham is frequently mentioned as a Biblical commentator ("Da'at Zeḳenim," 3a, 48b, 49b, Leghorn, 1783; "Minḥat Yehudah," 3a, 13a), and his ritual decisions and responsa are often quoted ("Or Zarua'," i. 13b et passim; Meïr of Rothenburg, Responsa, No. 176; et al.).

Isaac ben Abraham ha-Baḥur may be identical with the liturgical poet Isaac b. Abraham who wrote a hymn beginning "Yeshabbeḥuneka be-ḳol miflal," for Simḥat Torah or for the Sabbath after it, and a seliḥah for Yom Kippur beginning "Hen yom ba la-Adonai" (comp. Zunz, "Literaturgesch." p. 335).

Isaac b. Asher ha-Levi (see above and JEW. ENCYC. vi. 620).

Isaac ben Jacob ha-Laban: Pupil of Jacob Tam and one of the earlier tosafists ("ba'ale tosafot yeshanim"). He was the author of a commentary on Ketubot quoted by Isaac Or Zarua' (see Judah Minz, Responsa, No. 10). He is quoted very often in the edited tosafot (Yeb. 5b; B. Ḳ. 72a; et al.).

Isaac ben Meïr (RIBaM) of Ramerupt: Grandson of Rashi, and brother of Samuel b. Meïr (RaSHBaM) and Jacob Tam; died before his father, leaving four children (Jacob Tam, "Sefer ha-Yashar," No. 616, p. 72b, Vienna, 1811). Although he died young, Isaac wrote tosafot, mentioned by Eliezer b. Joel ha-Levi ("Abi ha-'Ezri," § 417), to several treatises of the Talmud. Isaac himself is often quoted in the edited tosafot (Shab. 138a; Ket. 29b *et passim*).

Isaac ben Mordecai of Regensburg (RI-BaM): Flourished in the twelfth century; pupil of Isaac b. Asher ha-Levi. He corresponded with Jacob Tam and was a fellow pupil of Moses b. Joel and Ephraim b. Isaac. His tosafot are quoted by Eliezer b. Joel ha-Levi (*l.c.* § 420) and Meïr of Rothenburg ("Semahot," § 73; "Haggahot Maimuniyyot," Abelot, p. 294a). He is often quoted also in the edited tosafot (Ket. 55a; B. Ḳ. 22b *et passim*).

Isaac ben Reuben: His tosafot are mentioned in the "Shiṭṭah Meḳubbeẓet," Ketubot, 43a. He may be identical with the Isaac b. Reuben who made a comment on Rashi to B. Ḳ. 32d.

Isaac b. Samuel ha-Zaḳen (see above and JEW. ENCYC. vi. 631).

Isaiah di Trani (RID): Italian tosafist of the first half of the thirteenth century. The greater part of his tosafot were published under the title "Tosefot R. Yesha'yahu" (Lemberg, 1861–69); and many were inserted by Bezaleel Ashkenazi in his "Shiṭṭah Meḳubbeẓet."

Israel of Bamberg: Lived in the middle of the thirteenth century; mentioned as an author of tosafot in "Mordekai" (to 'Ab. Zarah, Nos. 1244, 1279, 1295, 1356) and "Haggahot Mordekai" (to Shab. xiv.). Extracts from the tosafot of Israel's pupils were reproduced by Bezaleel Ashkenazi (*l.c.*).

J. Cohen: Supposedly a contemporary of Meïr b. Baruch of Rothenburg, and perhaps identical with Judah ha-Kohen, Meïr's relative. In the extracts from his tosafot to Baba Ḳamma, inserted in the "Shiṭṭah Meḳubbeẓet," he quotes, among many other authorities, his still living teacher, the Kohen whom Zunz ("Z. G." p. 42) supposes to be identical with Abigdor b. Elijah ha-Kohen. From the "Shiṭṭah Meḳubbeẓet" to Baba Meẓi'a it is seen that J. Cohen wrote tosafot to the same treatise.

Jacob of Chinon: Lived in the thirteenth century; pupil of Isaac ben Abraham, author of a "Shiṭṭah" ("Mordekai," on Sanh., No. 928). He himself is quoted in the edited tosafot (Ber. 12a; Nazir 53a; *et al.*).

Jacob ben Isaac ha-Levi (Jabez): Flourished at Speyer about 1130; a pupil of Kalonymus b. Isaac the Elder (Eliezer b. Nathan, "Eben ha-'Ezer," p. 13c, Prague, 1610). He was the author of tosafot ("Haggahot Maimuniyyot," Ḳinnim, No. 16) and of decisions ("pesaḳim"; "Mordekai," Ḥul., No. 1183). He is quoted also in the edited tosafot (to Ḳin. 23a).

Jacob ben Meïr Tam (see above and JEW. ENCYC. vii. 36).

Jehiel ben Joseph of Paris (d. 1286): His tosafot are quoted as authoritative by Perez b. Elijah (glosses to "'Ammude Golah," p. 50a, Cremona, 1556), in "Kol Bo" (No. 114), and in "Mordekai" (Ḥul., No. 924). He is frequently quoted also in the edited tosafot.

Joseph (or **Yehosef**): Flourished, according to Zunz ("Z. G." p. 33), about 1150. Zunz identifies this Joseph with the pupil of Samuel b. Meïr whose glosses are quoted in the edited tosafot (to Ket. 70a), and thinks he may be identical with the Joseph of Orleans often cited in the edited tosafot (Shab.

12a *et passim*). If so, he must be identified, according to Gross ("Gallia Judaica," p. 34), with JOSEPH BEN ISAAC BEKOR SHOR. Weiss, however, suggests that this Joseph might have been either Joseph Bonfils, Jacob Tam's teacher, or Joseph b. Isaac of Troyes, one of Rashi's pupils. Thus it seems that in any case the tosafist mentioned in the "Sefer ha-Yashar" must be distinguished from the one mentioned in Tos. Ket. 70a, as the latter was a pupil of R. Samuel.

Joseph Porat: Many fragments of his tosafot to Shabbat are included in the edited tosafot.

Judah b. Isaac of Paris (see above and JEW. ENCYC. vii. 344).

Judah ben Nathan (RIBaN): Son-in-law and pupil of Rashi, and to a great extent his continuator. It was Judah who completed Rashi's commentary on Makkot (from 19b to the end) and who wrote the commentary on Nazir which is erroneously attributed to Rashi. He wrote, besides, independent commentaries on 'Erubin, Shabbat, Yebamot (Eliezer b. Joel ha-Levi, "Abi ha-'Ezri," §§ 183, 385, 397, 408), and Pesaḥim ("Semag," prohibition No. 79). Finally, Halberstam manuscript No. 323 contains a fragment of Judah's commentary on Nedarim. It is generally considered that Judah b. Nathan wrote tosafot to several treatises of the Talmud, and he is mentioned as a tosafist in "Haggahot Mordekai" (Sanh., No. 696). He is often quoted in the edited tosafot.

Levi: His tosafot are quoted in the "Mordekai" (B. M. iv., end).

Meïr b. Baruch of Rothenburg (see above and JEW. ENCYC. viii. 437).

Meïr b. Samuel of Ramerupt: His tosafot are mentioned by his son Jacob Tam ("Sefer ha-Yashar," No. 252) and often in the edited tosafot.

Moses b. Jacob of Coucy: Author of Old Tosafot to Yoma and of some published in the collection "Sugyot ha-Shas" (Berlin, 1736).

Moses b. Meïr of Ferrara: Flourished in the thirteenth century; probably a pupil of Judah b. Isaac of Paris. His tosafot were used by the compiler of the "Haggahot Maimuniyyot" (see JEW. ENCYC. ix. 86).

Moses b. Yom-Ṭob of Evreux (see above and JEW. ENCYC. ix. 65).

Perez ben Elijah of Corbeil (see above and JEW. ENCYC. ix. 600).

Samson b. Abraham of Sens (see above and JEW. ENCYC. xi. 375).

Samson b. Isaac of Chinon: Flourished in the thirteenth and fourteenth centuries; author of the "Sefer Keritut." In this work (i. 7, § 1; v. 3, §§ 120, 148) Samson refers to his glosses on 'Erubin and 'Abodah Zarah; he appears to have written glosses on other Talmudic treatises also.

Samuel of Evreux: Author of tosafot to several treatises; those to Soṭah are among the edited tosafot (see JEW. ENCYC. xi. 16).

Samuel ben Meïr (RaSHBaM): Author of tosafot to Alfasi; under his supervision his pupils prepared tosafot to several treatises ("Sefer ha-Yashar," p. 85d).

Samuel b. Naṭronai (RaSHBaṬ): German Talmudist of the end of the twelfth century; author of tosafot to 'Abodah Zarah (see "Kerem Ḥemed," vii. 50).

Samuel b. Solomon of Falaise (see above and Jew. Encyc. xi. 28).

Simḥah b. Samuel of Speyer: Flourished in the thirteenth century; his tosafot are mentioned by Meïr of Rothenburg (Responsa, iv., No. 154).

Bibliography: Azulai, *Shem ha-Gedolim*, ii.; Benjacob, *Oẓar ha-Sefarim*, pp. 621 *et seq.*; Buchholz, in *Monatsschrift*, xxxviii. 342, 398, 450, 559; Grätz, *Gesch.* 3d ed., vi. 143-144, 210; vii. 108-110; Karpeles, *Gesch. der Jüdischen Literatur*, i. 574 *et seq.*; Weiss, *Dor*, iv. 336-352; idem, *Toledot Rabbenu Tam*, pp. 2-4; Winter and Wünsche, *Jüdische Literatur*, ii. 465 *et seq.*; Zunz (the chief source for this article), *Z. G.* pp. 29 *et seq.*

J.   M. Sel.

TOSEFTA (lit. "extensions"; "additions"): Name of a collection of baraitot which treat in a more complete form than does the Mishnah the subject of traditional law. In tannaitic literature old halakot are often amplified by explanatory notes and additions. Such additions were made by R. Akiba ('Eduy. ii. 1, viii. 1; Kil. i. 3; 'Orlah iii. 7), R. Eliezer ben Zadok (Tosef., Men. x. 23), R. Simeon (Sifra, Wayiḳra, Ḥobah, vii. [ed. Weiss, p. 21b]), R. Judah (Shab. 75b; 'Ab. Zarah 43a), R. Jose (Tosef., Kelim, B. Ḳ. vii. 4), and other tannaim. The explanatory notes are introduced with the word "Hosif" ("He has added" or "He has extended"). A sentence thus elucidated and completed was called a tosefta, this term being used not for the additional notes only, but for the entire aphorism in its completed form. This meaning is plainly seen in Yer. Shab. viii. 11a (comp. also Pesiḳ. R. 14; Eccl. R. viii. 1), where it is stated that R. Abbahu was greatly pleased over the discovery of an ancient tosefta, which, as a matter of fact, was an old tannaitic maxim with added explanatory matter.

The work known by the name "Tosefta" consists of a collection of such elucidated maxims, giving the traditional sayings in a remarkably complete form, whereas the Mishnah gives **Contents.** them in a condensed form only. The title of this collection, תוספתא, is really a plural word, and ought to be pronounced "Tosefata," as is apparent from the Hebrew form (תוספות, which is used for the Aramaic תוספתא; Eccl. R. v. 8). Erroneously, however, the singular form "Tosefta" has been adopted. A compilation entitled "Tosefta" is often mentioned in Talmudic-midrashic literature; and most authoritative critics regard it as identical with the extant Tosefta, of which this article treats. From R. Johanan's allusions to the Tosefta (Sanh. 86b) nothing can be adduced against the theory of the identity of the extant Tosefta with the work to which he refers; and his words in no way indicate, as Brüll has interpreted them, that R. Nehemiah was the author of the Tosefta (see below). Moreover, the Babylonian Talmud refers to a Tosefta which is certainly identical with the work here treated. Thus Yoma 70a correctly cites a saying by R. Akiba as being contained in the Tosefta (Tosef., Yoma, iii. 19, textus receptus).

Scholastic tradition regards the tanna Ḥiyya bar Abba as the author of the Tosefta, this belief being based on the circumstance that the schools of the Amoraim regarded as authoritative only those tan-

naitic traditions which had their origin in the collections of R. Ḥiyya or R. Hoshaiah; and inasmuch as only one Tosefta from the **Attributed** period of the Amoraim had been pre- **to Ḥiyya** served, there was justification for the **bar Abba.** belief that only the authentic (and therefore the most commonly used) collection had been saved in the vicissitudes of the ages. On a closer view of the matter, however, this circumstance can not be accepted as proof of Ḥiyya's authorship; for since the collection of Hoshaiah was also considered authoritative, there are equal grounds for supposing either that the latter was the sole author of the Tosefta, or that he and Ḥiyya edited the work in collaboration. Inasmuch, however, as Ḥiyya himself is mentioned in the Tosefta (Neg. viii. 6), the final redaction of the work must be attributed to a later hand.

To define the purpose of the work presents as many difficulties as does its authorship. Formerly the Tosefta was generally regarded as a sort of commentary on the Mishnah, this belief being fostered by a false interpretation of its title as "supplements." But even disregarding the fact that the correct definition of the word "Tosefta" as given above stamps the work as independent of the Mishnah, a cursory examination of its contents will show that it can not be regarded as a commentary. It does not discuss the passages in the Mishnah in a commentarial manner, and, to judge by its contents, it might be regarded either as a continuation of the Mishnah or as a work of equal rank therewith; for it cites the mishnaic passages in almost the same terms as the Mishnah itself. The latter circumstance, also, precludes the possibility of regarding the Tosefta as a commentary, inasmuch as it contains additions and supplements to the Mishnah; for in a mere supplement there would be no room for al- **Relation to** most verbatim repetitions of sentences **Talmudic** contained in the Mishnah itself. To **Baraitot.** this succeeds the question of the relation of the Tosefta to the baraitot cited in Talmudic discussions; for several such baraitot are contained literally in the Tosefta, while others are paraphrased, although the redaction of the parallel passages differs in respect to important points.

The question which thus presents itself is whether the Talmudic baraitot are mere citations from the Tosefta, or whether they originally constituted an independent collection. In the first case it would be difficult to explain the reason for the redactorial differences in the parallel passages. In the second, on the other hand, it would be necessary to take for granted not only the existence of an earlier Tosefta, but also that this, and not the one now extant, was the authentic one. For, as stated above, the Amoraim made use of authentic sources only; and those baraitot that are cited in the Talmud but are not contained in the extant Tosefta must necessarily have been taken from an earlier work. This would disprove the identity of the existing Tosefta with the work mentioned in Talmudic literature. All these questions show how difficult it is to determine the origin, the nature, and the importance of the Tosefta. The solution of the problem has been attempted by various scholars at various periods; and of these attempts those made by Sherira, Maimonides, Me'iri, and Frankel were the most important because they alone rest on critical investigations of historical sources. But even these investigators failed to solve the problem in a manner wholly satisfactory. Frankel's theory, although deficient in so far as it leaves some points unexplained and others not accurately defined, comes nearer the truth than any other. When these deficiencies are supplied and some points modified, a correct conception of the origin and nature of the Tosefta may be formed.

Any investigation to determine the status of the Tosefta must be directed to the following points: the origin and scope of the work; its redaction; its relation to the Mishnah; and its relation to the baraitot cited in the Talmud. Information bearing on the first point is derived from a literary-historical notice by R. Johanan (Sanh. 86a), which, after eliminating material unnecessary for this question, runs as follows: "Those mishnaic sentences that are cited without mention of the author's name (סתם) belong to R. Meïr; the sentences in the Tosefta cited without the name of the author are R. Nehemiah's; all, however, are given in the spirit and according to the method of R. Akiba." This utterance of R. Johanan's implies, therefore, that as the Mishnah had three successive redactors (Akiba, Meïr, and Judah ha-Nasi I.), so must also the redactors of the Tosefta be supposed to have been three in number, namely, Akiba, Nehemiah, and a third, unknown redactor. The origin of the Tosefta can therefore be traced back to Akiba, who laid the foundation of this work as well as of the Mishnah, in both of which he used a peculiar redactorial system of his own. Thus in the Mishnah he gave only the fundamental principles in condensed form, in order to furnish a handbook of traditions as an aid to the memory. In the Tosefta, however, he gave the traditional sentences in their complete form, supplementing them with explanatory notes; he gave also various cases, which in the Mishnah were represented by a single statement. These two collections, compiled according to different methods, were intended to supplement each other; and it was Akiba's aim through them to preserve the traditional teachings in their entirety and in a systematic way, as well as to promote a knowledge of them. Meïr and Nehemiah, both pupils of Akiba, endeavored to accomplish the object had in view by their master; but each restricted himself to one of Akiba's methods. Meïr chose the method of condensation, and compiled a work in which he included much of the material from Akiba's Tosefta, and which combined many of the more important features in both of Akiba's collections. Nehemiah followed the same plan of combining both of Akiba's collections in one work; but in doing so he chose the casuistic method. In this way originated two collective works —Meïr's Mishnah, edited according to the system used by Akiba in his edition of that work, and Nehemiah's Tosefta, edited according to the method followed by Akiba in his Tosefta edition.

The relation of Meïr's Mishnah to Nehemiah's

Critical Problems.

Relations to Mishnah of R. Meïr.

Tosefta was not, however, the same as that which existed between Akiba's collections of the same names. The former were not two collections mutually dependent on and supplementing each other: they were rather two independent works, both of which aimed at the preservation and proper arrangement of traditional maxims. The difference between them consisted only in the different methods employed in their compilation. Meïr's Mishnah contained the traditional maxims in condensed form, while Nehemiah's Tosefta cited them in their complete form and provided them with explanatory and supplementary notes. The methods evolved by Akiba and used by Meïr and Nehemiah were adopted also by later compilers in their endeavors to preserve and transmit traditional doctrines. Judah ha-Nasi I., whose Mishnah compilation was based on that of Meïr, followed the latter's method of redaction; while the redactor of the Tosefta now extant followed the method used by Nehemiah, whose Tosefta constituted the basis for his work. The relation between the Mishnah of Judah ha-Nasi and the Tosefta which has been preserved corresponds with that which existed between Meïr's Mishnah and Nehemiah's Tosefta. They are independent works which seek to accomplish by different means a similar purpose. There is, of course, a certain homogeneity between the two works, inasmuch as the Tosefta treats and elucidates the corresponding passages in the Mishnah; but the purpose of the redactor of the Tosefta was to produce an independent collection, and not merely additions to and explanations of another compilation.

Who was the redactor of the extant Tosefta? As has already been proved, the scholastic tradition attributing its authorship to R. Ḥiyya is unreliable, since the circumstance that Ḥiyya himself is mentioned in the Tosefta eliminates the possibility of his being its author; and that Ḥiyya and Hoshaiah edited the work in collaboration is most unlikely. The Jerusalem Talmud often refers to dissensions between these two amoraim; and if the Tosefta should be considered the product of their combined efforts, it would be natural to ask whose authority was accepted as decisive in cases where the redactors disagreed. How, indeed, could a decision have been possible in a case where the difference of opinion related to a halakic tradition? To regard Hoshaiah as sole redactor of the Tosefta is not possible either; for in many questions on which, according to the Jerusalem Talmud, he and Ḥiyya disagreed, the opinion of the latter has been given general validity (comp. Frankel, "Mebo," p. 25a). Only one surmise is possible; namely, that Ḥiyya and Hoshaiah, independently of each other and perhaps with quite different objects in view, were engaged in the compilation of baraitot, as were also their contemporaries Levi, Bar Ḳappara, and Samuel. The collections of Ḥiyya and Hoshaiah differed from the others in that these two compilers took Nehemiah's Tosefta as a basis for their collections. Each of them thus compiled an extended Tosefta enriched with new elements; and these two Toseftot differed in various important respects. A later redactor, whose name has not been ascertained, combined

Authorship.

these two Toseftot into one work, to which he added some maxims taken from the collections of Levi, Bar Ḳappara, and Samuel; and in this manner originated the Tosefta in the form in which it is now extant. This final redactor considered Ḥiyya's opinions authoritative; and in all points where Hoshaiah's Tosefta differed from Ḥiyya's the latter's opinions alone were given validity.

The preference thus given to Ḥiyya's work, however, must not be ascribed to any views held by the schools of the Amoraim, but to the personal convictions of the final redactor. In the schools both Toseftot were considered authoritative, and baraitot cited from either were regarded as authentic. This view also explains the relation of the existing Tosefta to the Talmudic baraitot, which latter could have been taken only from one of these authentic Toseftot. Such baraitot as are given verbatim in the existing Tosefta are either citations from Ḥiyya's work or baraitot which were given alike in both Toseftot; while those baraitot which, either essentially or verbally, differ from the parallel passages in the present Tosefta were taken from the Tosefta of Hoshaiah, the reason for the divergence being that the final redactor of the existing Tosefta preferred the opinion of Ḥiyya.

Like the Mishnah, the Tosefta is divided into six orders ("sedarim"), the names of which correspond to those of the mishnaic orders; namely, (1) Zera'im, (2) Mo'ed, (3) Nashim, (4) Neziḳin or **Division.** Yeshu'ot, (5) Ḳodashim, and (6) Ṭohorot. The orders are subdivided into treatises, which, with a few exceptions, bear the same names as those of the Mishnah. Four treatises are missing from the Tosefta, namely, Abot in the order Neziḳin, and Ḳinnim, Middot, and Tamid in the order Ḳodashim. The number of treatises in the Tosefta is thus fifty-nine; but the treatise Kelim in this work is divided into three parts, namely, Baba Ḳamma, Baba Meẓi'a, and Baba Batra. If these three "babot" were regarded as three different treatises the total number would be sixty-one. The treatises are divided into chapters ("peraḳim"), which again are divided into paragraphs; but the division into chapters is not the same in the different manuscripts. According to the Erfurt manuscript, the total number of chapters is 428; according to the Vienna manuscript and the older Tosefta editions, 421.

The Tosefta appeared first as an addendum to Isaac Alfasi's "Halakot" (Venice, 1521), and has since been appended to all editions of that work. The best edition of the Tosefta is that published by M. S. Zuckermandl (Pasewalk, 1880), who made use of the Erfurt manuscript. Zuckermandl published also a supplement (Treves, 1882) containing a summary of the work, an index, and a glossary. A Latin translation of thirty-one Tosefta treatises was published by Ugolino in his "Thesaurus Antiquitatum Sacrarum" (vols. xvii.-xx., Venice, 1755-57).

The Tosefta has been the subject of many commentaries. The Wilna edition of the Talmud, for example, which contains the Tosefta in addition to Alfasi's "Halakot," reprints the following two commentaries: (1) "Tana Tosefa'ah," by Samuel Abigdor b. Abraham, a work in two parts, part i., entitled

XII.—14

"Minḥat Bikkurim," being the main commentary, while part ii., entitled "Miẓpeh Shemu'el," contains an index to the Tosefta passages **Texts and** cited in the Talmud and in the Mid- **Com-** rashim. (2) "Ḥasde Dawid," explan- **mentaries.** atory notes by David Pardo. In addition to these two commentaries, which cover the entire Tosefta, the same Talmud edition contains the following commentaries on single treatises: "Magen Abraham," by Abraham Abali of Kalisz, on the order Neziḳin; a commentary by Elijah Gaon of Wilna on the order Ṭohorot; and Jacob Kahana of Wilna's "Mare de-Matnita," on the treatise 'Erubin. M. Friedmann wrote a commentary on the order Mo'ed, which he published under the title "Tekelet Mordekai," appending it to his edition of the Tosefta (part i., containing the treatises Shabbat and 'Erubin, Paks, 1898; part ii., Pesaḥim, Sheḳalim, Yoma, and Sukkah, ib. 1900). Medieval authors mention two Toseftot to Berakot (see Brüll in "Ha-Maggid," xiii. 127), but it is not clear to which works they applied the name "Tosettot."

BIBLIOGRAPHY: Letter of Sherira Gaon, in Neubauer, *M. J. C.* i. 13-15; Maimonides, *Einleitung in die Mischnah*; Meïri, in his commentary on *Abot*, ed. Stern, Vienna, 1854; Frankel, *Hodegetica in Mischnam*, pp. 304-307, Leipsic, 1859; J. Oppenheim, *Toledot ha-Mishnah*, in *Bet Talmud*, ii. 237-245, 348-353; J. H. Dünner, *Die Theorien über Wesen und Ursprung der Tosefta Kritisch Dargestellt*, Amsterdam, 1874; D. Hoffmann, *Mischnah und Tosefta*, in Berliner's *Magazin*, 1882, pp. 153-163; M. S. Zuckermandl, *Die Erfurter Handschrift der Tosefta*, Berlin, 1876; idem, *Der Wiener Tosefta Codex*, Magdeburg, 1877; idem, *Tosefta Varianten*, Treves, 1881; N. Brüll, *Begriff und Ursprung der Tosefta*, in *Jubelschrift zum Neunzigsten Geburtstag des Dr. L. Zunz*, pp. 92-110, Berlin, 1884.

W. B.　　　　　　　　　　　　　　　　　J. Z. L.

TÖTBRIEF: Term applied in Germany to the edicts issued by the kings and emperors, to the papal bulls, and to the edicts of various ecclesiastical authorities, by which the Christians were exempted from paying their debts to Jews. The Tötbrief might deprive the creditor either of the interest due on the money loaned or of both principal and interest. The first Tötbrief known was that of Louis VII. of France, who, at the instigation of Peter Venerabilis, Abbot of Cluny, issued in 1146 a decree exempting all Crusaders from payment of their debts to the Jews, in accordance with the papal enactment of Eugenius III. in the preceding year. Later, in 1180, Philip Augustus relieved all Christians from their liabilities to their Jewish creditors on condition of their paying to him the fifth part of their debts. Louis VIII. annulled, in 1223, all debts due to Jews by Christians that had been outstanding for five years or more, and canceled the interest on debts less than five years old.

In Germany, in the fourteenth century, such cancelations were common. The first case in which Jews were deprived of the interest due to them was in 1299, when King Albert diverted such interest payments to the Monastery of Eberbach. After the time of Henry VII. and Louis the Bavarian cancelations of the whole debt, principal and interest, were very frequent. The former exempted (1312) Conrad of Weinsberg from the payment of such debts; while the latter relieved (1315) the city of Esslingen from its debts to the Jews of Ueberlingen as well as to other Jews who had settled in cities hostile to him. In 1316 Louis issued a similar edict in favor of the inhabitants of Heilbronn; in 1323, in favor of the Abbey of Fulda; in 1326, in favor of a number of noblemen who owed money to Jews of Alsace; in 1332, in favor of the Abbey of Bamberg. These exemptions were even more numerous in the third and fourth decades of the fourteenth century, when, during the persecutions, the emperors canceled the claims of Jews both living and dead.

All these were single instances of the cancelation of debts due to Jews; only under King Wenzel, toward the end of the fourteenth century, did the Tötbrief assume seriously comprehensive proportions. On June 12, 1385, the king concluded a treaty with the representatives of all the Swabian towns, who agreed that their municipalities should pay the king 40,000 gulden in return for a "privilege," consisting of eight articles, by which their debts to Jews were either entirely or partially canceled, and through which the Jews finally lost all their claims. For, while many Jews who had the means recovered part of the money due to them by paying a certain sum to the city authorities, King Wenceslaus, in order to check this, issued a second edict (1390), commanding the Jews to abandon all claim to debts due from Christians. It must be said, however, that the Tötbrief of 1390 did not apply throughout the whole German empire, but only to its southwestern part, as Bavaria, Würzburg, and other provinces. In Spain the same sort of edict was called a "moratoria" (see Jacobs, "Sources," pp. xxiv., xxv., Nos. 97, 100–103; p. xliii., No. xlv.).

BIBLIOGRAPHY: Grätz, *Gesch.* 3d ed., vi. 148 *et seq.*, vii. 23, viii. 50 *et seq.*; Nübling, *Die Judengemeinden in Deutschland*, pp. 134, 374, 391, 402; Stobbe, *Die Juden in Deutschland*, pp. 131 *et seq.*, 249 *et seq.*

J.   M. Sel.

TOTEMISM: A primitive social system in which members of a clan reckoned kinship through their mothers, and worshiped some animal or plant which they regarded as their ancestor and the image of which they bore tattooed on their persons. It was suggested by J. S. Maclennan (in "The Fortnightly Review," 1870, i. 207) that this system existed among the early Hebrews; and his view was taken up by Robertson Smith (in "The Journal of Philology," 1880), who based his theories upon the researches of J. G. Frazer on totemism. Robertson Smith later connected this view with his theory of sacrifice, which he regarded as originally a method of restoring the blood covenant between the members of a clan and its totem. The following are the chief arguments in favor of the existence of totem clans among the ancient Israelites:

I. Animal and Plant Names: A considerable number of persons and places in the Old Testament have names derived from animals or plants. Jacobs ("Studies in Biblical Archæology," pp. 94–103) has given a list of over 160 such names, including Oreb (the raven) and Zeeb (the wolf), princes of the Midianites; Caleb (the dog), Tola (the worm), Shual (the fox), Zimri (the chamois), Jonah (the dove), Huldah (the weasel), Jael (the ibex), Nahash (the serpent), Kezia (the cassia), Shaphan (the rock-badger), Ajalon (the great stag), and Zeboim (the hyena). Many of these, however, are personal names; but among the Israelitish tribes mentioned in Num. xxvi. are the

Shualites, or fox clan of Asher; the Shuphamites, or serpent clan of Benjamin; the Bachrites, or camel clan; and the Arelites, or lion clan of Gad. Other tribes having similar names are the Zimrites, or hornet clan, and the Calebites, or dog tribe. In the genealogy of the Horites (Gen. xxxvi.) several animal names occur, such as Shobal (the young lion), Zibeon (the hyena), Anah (the wild ass), Dishan (the gazel), Akan (the roe), Aiah (the kite), Aran (the ass), and Cheran (the lamb). The occurrence of such a large number of animal names in one set of clan names suggests the possibility that the Horites, who were nomads, were organized on the totem-clan system.

II. Exogamy is the system under which any member of a clan may not marry within his own clan, but must marry a member of a kindred clan. Smith deduces the existence of such clans among the Horites from the mention of Anah clans and Dishan clans in the list. He also draws attention to Shimeis among the Levites, Reubenites, and Benjamites. Female descent is the only means of tracing kinship in exogamous clans; and Smith sees a survival of this in the case of the marriage of Abraham and Sarah, who were not of the same mother, while Abimelech appealed to his mother's clan as being of his flesh (Judges viii. 19), and Naomi told Ruth to return to her mother's house (Ruth i. 8).

III. Ancestor and Animal Worship: Smith attributes the friendship between David and Nahash, King of the Ammonites, to the fact that they were both members of a serpent clan spread throughout Canaan. That animals were worshiped among the Hebrews is well known, as is shown by the legends of the golden calf and the brazen serpent. The second commandment prohibits this. Smith draws attention to the case of animal worship in Ezek. viii. 7–11, where Ezekiel sees "every form of creeping things, and abominable beasts, and all the idols of the house of Israel, portrayed upon the wall round about," and in the midst of them stood Jaazaniah ben Shaphan (the rock-badger), "with every man his censer in his hand, and a thick cloud of incense went up." Here there is animal worship connected with the name of a person who appears to be connected with an unclean beast, the "shaphan." See also Ancestor Worship.

IV. Forbidden Food: Members of a totem clan did not eat the totem animal. As such totems gradually spread throughout the nation, a list of forbidden animals would arise which might be analogous to the list of forbidden animals given in Lev. xi. and Deut. xv. Jacobs, however, has shown that in the list of animal names given by him forty-three are clean as against forty-two unclean.

V. Tattooing and Clan Crests: A totem is tattooed on the skin of the totem worshiper; and there is evidence in Lev. xix. 28 that the Israelites were forbidden to make tattoo-marks, while an allusion to this practise may be contained in Isa. xliv. 5 and in Ezek. ix. 4. The mark of Cain may perhaps have been a tattoo-mark. In none of these instances, however, are there indications that the tattoo-marks were in an animal form or connected with animal worship. The tribes of Israel when on the march had standards (Num. i. 52, ii. 2 *et seq.*); and rabbinic literature gives details of the crests (see FLAG), which

Absence of Historic Connection.

were derived from the blessings of Jacob (Gen. xlix.) and Moses (Deut. xxxiii.). In these most of the tribes are compared to an animal: Judah to a lion; Issachar to an ass; Dan to a serpent; etc. In Moses' blessing, however, Dan is compared to a lion's whelp, which seems to show that the tribes were not arranged on a totemic system.

VI. Blood Feud: The practical side of the totem system insured the existence of relatives scattered throughout a tribe, who would guarantee the taking up of the blood feud in case one of the members of the totem clan was injured or killed. The existence of the blood feud can be recognized in Israel (see GO'EL), but there is no evidence of a connection with totemism. Altogether, while traces and survivals are found of institutions similar to those of the totem clan, there is not sufficient evidence to show that it existed in Israel during historic times, though it is possible that some such system was found among the Edomites.

BIBLIOGRAPHY: W. Robertson Smith, *Animal Worship and Animal Tribes Among the Ancient Arabs and in the Old Testament*, in *Journal of Philology*, ix. 75-100; Jacobs, *Studies in Biblical Archæology*, pp. 64-103; J. S. Cook, in *J. Q. R.* 1903; Zlapetal, *Totemismus im Alten Testamente*, Freiburg, 1903; I. Lévi, *La Famille chez les Anciens Hébreux*, Paris, 1903; S. Reinach, *Cultes, Mythes et Religions*, Paris, 1904.
J.

TOUL (Hebr. טול, טולא; "Or Zarua'," i. 131b; "Mordekai" on B. Ḳ. x., No.193): Capital of an arrondissement in the department of Meurthe-et-Moselle, France, with a Jewish population dating from the thirteenth century. Among the scholars who were once residents of this city may be mentioned R. Eliezer of Toul, the author of tosafot; and his brother Abraham, a pupil of Rabbi Isaac the Elder of Dampierre and identical, according to Gross, with Abraham of טוך (read טול), one of the scholars to whom Meïr ben Todros Abulafia of Toledo addressed his epistle assailing the doctrine of the resurrection as set forth by Maimonides.

In 1708 the Bishop of Toul petitioned the French government to expel from Nancy the Jewish bankers Samuel and Solomon Levy, Jacob Schwob, Isaiah Lambert, and Moses Alcan, but his efforts were unsuccessful. In 1721, 180 Jewish families, many of them residents of Toul, were permitted by Duke Leopold to remain on his estates without molestation in their religion and commerce. Leon Cohen, one of the leading members of the community of this city, took part in the General Assembly convoked at Paris by Napoleon in 1806. The community of Toul is governed by the Jewish consistory of Nancy, and at present contains forty or fifty Jewish families.

BIBLIOGRAPHY: Gross, *Gallia Judaica*, pp. 211-212; idem, *Monatsschrift*, 1885, p. 519; *R. E. J.* xxxiv. 108; Zunz, *Z. G.* p. 39.
S.   S. K.

TOULON (Hebr. טולון): Capital of an arrondissement in the department of the Var, France. Like most of the principal cities of Provence, Toulon contained a Jewish community in medieval times;

and under the counts of Provence the Jews of the city fared like those of many other communities, being sometimes oppressed and sometimes treated with kindness. When the Black Death raged throughout France in 1348, the Jews of Toulon were accused of having poisoned the neighboring springs and wells, and forty were killed in a single night. Noteworthy among the scholars of the city were: Berechiah ben Azariah of טולן or טולן (Rabbinovicz, "Diḳduḳe Soferim," xi. 17), to whom belonged the Codex Vat. 120, dating from the fourteenth century and containing a number of treatises of the Talmud; and Astruc of Toulon, one of the publishers of the first edition of Jehiel ben Jekuthiel's "Bet Middot."

At the present time the Jewish community of the city forms a part of the consistorial circumscription of Marseilles, and numbers about thirty families.

BIBLIOGRAPHY: Gross, *Gallia Judaica*, p. 213; Papon, *Histoire Générale de Provence*, iii. 190; Steinschneider, *Cat. Bodl.* col. 1278; Steinschneider, *Hebr. Bibl.* xiii. 84.
S.   S. K.

TOULOUSE (Hebr. טולוזה, טולישה): Capital of the department of Haute-Garonne, France, where a large number of Jews lived as early as the beginning of the eighth century. In conformity with an old custom, and in punishment for some fancied crime, one of their number, generally the most respected old man of the community, was obliged to appear every Good Friday at the door of the cathedral to have his ears boxed in public. They vainly addressed a petition to King Charles the Bald in 850 to have this custom abolished; but it continued until the beginning of the twelfth century, when it was replaced by an annual tax payable to the monks of St. Sernin between All Saints' Day and the feast of St. Sernin, and by a yearly contribution of 44 pounds of wax, to be delivered on Good Friday at the Cathedral of St. Stephen.

In the thirteenth century the counts of Toulouse were favorably disposed toward the Jews on all occasions, and granted them the right of acquiring real estate without paying rent. Many estates were held by two prominent Jewish families, one represented by Espagnol and his sons Solomon and Provençal, and the other by Alacer (Eliezer) and his sons Abraham and Belid. In 1242 Raymond VII. granted the Jews the right of freely disposing of their property, and of selling, mortgaging, or leasing their farms, estates, and seigniories on condition of paying a tax of 12 Toulouse deniers on each pound of the sale price and 6 deniers on each pound of the rent; but in 1290 King Philip the Fair took action against those Jews who had surreptitiously obtained letters of exemption from the taxes imposed upon them. In the district of the seneschal of Carcassonne a special judge was appointed to take charge of the cases in which Jews were interested; but in Toulouse the Jews were tried before the same judges as the Christians. Philip the Fair confirmed this arrangement in 1304 by decreeing that the regular judges should handle all Jewish cases, whether civil or criminal. Several Jews who were arrested in 1306 accepted baptism rather than leave the city, but Solomon ibn Verga goes too far when he says that the whole community was converted.

The total amount confiscated by the king in the seneschalate of Toulouse was 75,264 pounds Tours currency.

Returning to Toulouse in 1315, the Jews were soon subjected to a tax of 2,000 pounds. In 1321 the PASTOUREAUX massacred many Jews, and forced the remainder to accept baptism, thus annihilating the community.

As early as the eleventh century the Jews of Toulouse possessed a synagogue, which was under the direction of R. Judah b. Moses ha-Darshan, who later went to Narbonne. He is called רשא דונזילה in "R. E. J." x. 102, which, according to a happy conjecture of Gross ("Gallia Judaica," p. 215), must be read דרשן דטולוזה. This synagogue was situated on the present Place des Carmes, but it was confiscated by Philip the Fair in 1306, and sold in 1310.

From the time of the massacre by the Pastoureaux there was no Jewish community at Toulouse until the beginning of the nineteenth century. At the present time it contains between fifty and sixty families, who are subject to the Jewish consistory of Bayonne.

BIBLIOGRAPHY: *Vita Sancti Theodardi,* in *Acta Sanctorum, Mensis Mai,* i. 142; *Arch. Isr.* 1861, p. 449; Bédarride, *Les Juifs en France,* pp. 89–90, 227; Catel, *Mémoirs,* pp. 237, 520, 890; Depping, *Les Juifs dans le Moyen Age,* pp. 47, 145, 160; Dom Vaissète, *Histoire Générale de Languedoc,* ii. 151, iii. 55; Gross, *Gallia Judaica,* pp. 213–215; Joseph ha-Kohen, *'Emek ha-Baka* (translated by Sée), pp. 69, 71, 72, 235; *Ordonnances des Rois de France,* i. 397, 443; Saige, *Les Juifs du Languedoc,* pp. 11, 14 *et seq.;* Solomon ibn Verga, *Shebet Yehudah,* pp. 6, 45.
S.   S. K.

TOURO, JUDAH: American philanthropist; born at Newport, R. I., June 16, 1775; died at New Orleans, La., Jan. 13, 1854; son of Rev. Isaac Touro and Reyna Hays. His father was of Portuguese origin and had settled in Jamaica, but went to Newport about 1760 to serve as minister of the Jewish congregation there. During his residence in the town he became a close friend of Ezra Stiles.

Judah Touro.

Shortly after the outbreak of the American Revolution, Newport was taken by the British, and the Jewish patriot citizens consequently left. The synagogue was closed, and its members scattered throughout the other colonies. The father of Judah went to Kingston, Jamaica, where he died Dec. 8, 1783; thereupon the mother returned to the United States with her children, making her home with her brother, Moses Michael Hays, who had become an eminent merchant of Boston. She died in 1787; and young Touro was reared and educated by his uncle, in whose counting-house he was later employed. At the age of twenty-two he was sent as supercargo with a valuable shipment to the Mediterranean; and the results of the trip showed his remarkable business ability.

A few years later (1802) he went to the French territory of Louisiana, settling at New Orleans, then a small town of about 10,000 inhabitants. There he opened a store, and soon built up a thriving trade in New England products. Later he became the owner of many ships and of valuable real estate, until he was numbered among the most prominent merchants of the place. After the territory had become part of the United States, Touro repeatedly exhibited his public spirit. During the defense of New Orleans by Andrew Jackson he entered the ranks as a common soldier, and was severely wounded on Jan. 1, 1815, being given up for dead; but he was saved by the bravery and care of his friend Rezin Davis Shepherd, a young Virginian merchant, who had settled in the same city. Their friendship continued throughout their lives; and both of them amassed great fortunes.

Settles in New Orleans.

Touro's name will always be numbered among the foremost in the annals of American philanthropy. His charities knew neither race nor creed, and his public spirit was no less noteworthy.

To Amos Lawrence and Judah Touro belongs the credit of supplying the funds for completing the Bunker Hill Monument, each subscribing $10,000 for the purpose. In 1843 the completion of the monument was celebrated by a banquet in Faneuil Hall, Boston, at which the generosity of the two donors was publicly acknowledged. A resolution was also adopted by the directors to the effect that John Quincy Adams, Daniel Webster, Joseph Story, Edward Everett, and Franklin Dexter be appointed a committee to prepare an inscription for a tablet which was to be placed on the monument and which was partly to record the liberality of Lawrence and Touro.

Another object of his generosity was his native city of Newport. In 1842 he improved the enclosures of the old Jewish cemetery immortalized by Longfellow; and it was his money which purchased the Old Stone Mill supposed to have been built by the Norsemen, Touro's desire being that the historic landmark and the surrounding grounds might be saved for the town.

Benefactions to Newport.

The grounds in which the mill is situated are still known as Touro Park.

In him the poor of New Orleans had a constant friend and benefactor, and many incidents of his charity are recorded. A noteworthy case was that of a Universalist congregation whose church was sold at auction under foreclosure of a mortgage and was bought by Touro, who returned it to the worshipers. Its minister, the Rev. Theodore Clapp, became Touro's friend; and in his memoirs he gives a most appreciative account of the benefactor of his church.

Though he gave liberally to charitable objects during his entire life, the provisions of the will of Touro, who died unmarried, disposed of over half a million dollars in charity, an enormous sum in those days. These provisions were published throughout

Touro's Will.

the United States and even in the journals and periodicals of many European countries. Among the larger bequests were $80,000 for founding the New Orleans Almshouse, liberal endowments for nearly all the Jewish congregations of the country, bequests to the Massachusetts Female Hospital, the Female Asylum, and the Boys' Asylum of Boston, and one for the preservation of the old cemetery at Newport, and for the payment of the salary of the minister of the old synagogue in that city. A large sum was also left in trust to Sir Moses Montefiore for almshouses in JERUSALEM. In addition to these, there were private bequests, including one to the Rev. Theodore Clapp already mentioned; while the entire residuary estate was left by Touro to his friend Shepherd. His body was taken to Newport, and lies in the old Jewish cemetery. The funeral is stated "not to have been equaled since the reinterment of Commodore Perry in 1826." At a later date a public meeting was held at Boston to express regret at his death. On his tombstone, which may still be seen, are inscribed the appropriate words: "The last of his name, he inscribed it in the Book of Philanthropy to be remembered forever."

A few years after his death a public movement was inaugurated by the citizens of New Orleans to erect a monument to his memory; but opposition to this tribute came from a number of Jewish rabbis throughout the country, who claimed that Judaism forbade the erection of any graven image, and that a statue came within the scope of prohibition. This led to an interesting theological controversy, much of which has been preserved in Benjamin's "Drei Jahre in Amerika"; but the outbreak of the Civil war put a sudden end to the matter. The story of Touro's life has been woven into Wassermann's German novel "Judah Touro" (Leipsic, 1871).

BIBLIOGRAPHY: Walker, *Judah Touro*, in Hunt, *Lives of American Merchants*, ii. 440–467, New York, 1858; Appleton's *Cyclopedia of American Biography*, vi. 144, *ib.* 1894; Denison, *The Israelites of Rhode Island*, in *Narragansett Historical Register*, iv. 308–312; Warren, *History of Bunker Hill Monument*, pp. 283, 311–312, 330; Clapp, *Autobiographical Sketches and Recollections During a Thirty-five Years' Residence in New Orleans*, 3d ed., pp. 94–104, Boston, 1858; Daly, *The Settlement of the Jews in North America*, New York, 1893; Wolf, *The American Jew as Patriot, Soldier, and Citizen*, pp. 63–64, 71, 440; Benjamin II., *Drei Jahre in Amerika*, pp. 365–381, Hanover, 1862; Mendes, *The Jewish Cemetery at Newport*, in *Rhode Island Historical Magazine*, vi. 103; *National Cyclopedia of American Biography*, vi. 361, New York, 1901; Abraham, in *Publ. Am. Jew. Hist. Soc.* iii. 98–100; Phillips, *ib.* vi. 139; Frankland, *Fragments of History*, in *American Jews' Annual*, 1889–95, p. 30.

J. L. Hü.

TOURS (Hebr. טורש, "Mordekai" on M. Ḳ. No. 921; or תורש, "Yosippon," ed. Venice, p. 6b): Capital of the department of Indre-et-Loire, France. Since the first half of the sixth century Jews have lived either in the city or in its environs, especially in Civray. About the year 580 a Jewish tax-gatherer of Tours named Amantius, together with his three attendants, one Jew and two Christians, was attacked by a certain Injuriosus, stripped, murdered, and thrown into a well. At the close of the eleventh century Philip I. of France made over to his wife, Bertrade, half the revenues from the Jews of Tours, while in 1119 and 1143 Louis VI. and his son, Louis VII., presented this income as an offering to the Abbey of Saint Martin. In 1141 the Jews were obliged to give the king at Easter the sum of thirty sous, together with half a pound of pepper and other gifts in kind; and at Christmas they were forced to give half a pound of pepper, two loaves of bread, a pitcher of wine, and a certain quantity of meat. At the end of the twelfth century they were compelled to pay 30 sous annually to Richard, King of England and Count of Tours, and to the Abbey of Saint Martin. After the year 1202 the kings of France collected the revenues of the Jews, which amounted to 120 livres in 1234, but which increased to 1,024 livres and 5 denarii in 1298, and reached the sum of 2,077 livres, 9 denarii in the following year. In 1306 the Jews were expelled from Tours; but they returned in 1315, and were molested four years later by a band of rogues who pretended to have a commission from the king to extort money from them. Then came the charge of poisoning the wells, and in 1321 they were again driven from Tours, Amboise, Loches, and Chinon.

The Jews of Tours had their own ghetto, which was called "la Juiverie" and was situated in the parish of Saint-Pierre du Boile in the Rue des Maures, called the Rue des Morts or de la Juiverie in the eighteenth century. In 1306 Philip the Fair presented the Jewish quarter to the archbishop and his clergy.

The cemetery was in the parish of Saint Vincent, in front of the "old garden"; it extended from the vineyards of Saint Vincent to the Rue de la Chèvre, and from the vineyards of the vestry of Saint Julian to the street which ran in front of the "old garden." In the thirteenth century certain disputes arose between the Jews of Tours and the archbishop, Pierre de Lamballe, but in 1255 the latter guaranteed them perpetual possession of their cemetery and of a house and the vineyards attached, reserving for himself only the right of jurisdiction and a rent of five gold oboles of the value of 25 sous, payable annually at Christmas. In case of non-payment the Jews were liable to a fine of 7½ sous, and they were forbidden to till the ground until they should have discharged their debt. In return, the archbishop, in guaranteeing the peaceable possession of the cemetery, granted also the right to inter therein the bodies of their coreligionists without regard to the place of death, while in the house attached to the graveyard they were permitted to place a guardian exempt from service to the archbishop and from the payment of any rental. This agreement was ratified in 1305 by Archbishop Renaud, the successor of Pierre de Lamballe; but in the following year the cemetery was confiscated, together with the other property of the Jews, and it disappeared completely in 1359-60.

The most noteworthy scholars of the city were: Solomon of Tours, the correspondent of Rashi, who called him his "dear friend"; David of Tours; and Joseph ben Elijah, brother of Perez of Corbeil (Zunz, "Z. G." p. 41). At present there are about twenty Jewish families in the city.

BIBLIOGRAPHY: Boutaric, *Actes du Parlement*, ii., No. 5713; Giraudet, *Histoire de la Ville de Tours*, i. 127, 138; Gross, *Gallia Judaica*, pp. 217-218; Lelogeais, *Histoire des Rues de Tours*, p. 81; *R. E. J.* xv. 247, 254; xvii. 210-234; xviii. 262-270; Venantius Fortunatus, *Vita Sancti Germani*.

s.   S. K.

TOWER (Hebr. מִגְדָּל): A building of strength or magnificence (Isa. ii. 15; Cant. iv. 4, vii. 4), and, with a more limited connotation, a watch-tower in a garden or vineyard or in a fortification. It was customary to erect watch-towers in the vineyards for the guards (Isa. v. 2), and such round and tapering structures may still be seen in the vineyards of Judea. Similar towers were built for the protection of the flocks by the shepherd, in the enclosures in which the animals were placed for the night (comp. the term "tower of the flock," Gen. xxxv. 21; Micah iv. 8), and it is expressly stated that Uzziah built such structures in the desert for his enormous herds (II Chron. xxvi. 10). Around these towers dwellings for shepherds and peasants doubtless developed gradually, thus often forming the nuclei of permanent settlements.

Towers for defense were erected chiefly on the walls of fortified cities, the walls themselves being strengthened by bastions (Neh. iii. 1), and the angles and gates being likewise protected by strong towers (II Kings ix. 17). Thus the walls of the city of Jerusalem were abundantly provided with towers in antiquity, and the ancient tower of Phasael (the so-called "tower of David") in the modern citadel is an excellent specimen of this mode of defense, its substructure being of massive rubblework, and the ancient portion of the tower erected upon it being built of immense square stones (for illustration see JEW. ENCYC. vii. 142). The citadel forming the center of a fortified city was also termed "migdol" (Judges viii. 9, ix. 46). It was usually erected at the highest point of the city, and formed the last place of refuge in case the town was besieged and its walls stormed (Judges ix. 46).

E. G. H.   I. BE.

TOY, CRAWFORD HOWELL: American Christian Orientalist; born at Norfolk, Va., March 23, 1836. He was educated at the University of Virginia, and studied Orientalia at the University of Berlin (1866-68). On his return from Europe he was appointed professor of Hebrew at the Southern Baptist Theological Seminary, Greenville, S. C., and in 1880 became Hancock professor of Hebrew and Oriental languages at Harvard University. He is the author of "The Religion of Israel" (1882), and "Judaism and Christianity" (Boston, 1890), a careful and sympathetic study of the relation between the

two religions. He edited the Hebrew text and the English translation of Ezekiel for the Polychrome Bible in 1899, and published a commentary on Proverbs in the "International Critical Series" in the same year. Toy was editor of the Hellenistic department of THE JEWISH ENCYCLOPEDIA since its inception. He died May 12, 1919.

BIBLIOGRAPHY: *Who's Who in America*, 1905.

J.

TRABOT (TRABOTTI): Family of Italian scholars of the fifteenth, sixteenth, and seventeenth centuries, which immigrated to Italy from France, so that several of its members bore the additional name "Zarfati." The most important representatives of the family are as follows:

Azriel Trabot: 1. Scholar of the sixteenth century; probably a member of the rabbinical college in Rome. Nothing is known of his literary activity. **2.** Rabbi at Florence and Ascoli in the sixteenth century; son of Jehiel Trabot (1). A responsum by him, dated 1567, is extant in manuscript. **3.** Rabbi of Ascoli at the beginning of the seventeenth century; son of Jehiel Trabot (2). He was the author of some responsa, extant in manuscript, and of a list of rabbis (reprinted in "R. E. J." iv. 208-225) from Rabina and R. Ashi to R. Nissim the Younger.

Jehiel Trabot: 1. Rabbi at Pesaro during the earlier part of the sixteenth century; son of Azriel Trabot (1). On the maternal side Jehiel was a grandson of Joseph Colon, whose name he bore in addition to his own. He is mentioned in Jacob Alpron's collection of responsa entitled "Nahalat Ya'akob," and responsa signed by him in 1519 and 1520 are extant in manuscript. **2.** Rabbi of Ferrara and Pesaro; died after 1590; son of Azriel Trabot (2). He was the author of certain responsa divided according to the ritual codes; they have been preserved in manuscript.

Levi Trabot: One of the earliest members of the family. He flourished in the first half of the fifteenth century, and emigrated from France to Italy, whence he went to Jerusalem, so that his son Nathaniel called him אִישׁ יְרוּשָׁלַם. Like several other members of the family, he bore the name "Zarfati." Codex Turin No. 65 contains two poems by another Levi Trabot, written in honor of the presentation of scrolls of the Law to the synagogue in Mantua, one being composed in 1581, and the other in 1596.

Menahem ben Perez Trabot: Rabbi at Ferrara in the latter part of the fifteenth and the beginning of the sixteenth century. Responsa by him are still extant in manuscript.

Nethaneel ben Benjamin ben Azriel Trabot: Rabbi of Modena; born about 1576; died Dec. 22, 1653; uncle of Solomon Graciano. He was one of the greatest and most respected of Italian rabbis. Of his works the following have been preserved: a ritual decision at the beginning of the collection of responsa entitled "Kenaf Renanim"; a responsum in the "Pahad Yizhak" of Lampronti (i. 111b-112a); and a responsum in the "Debar Shemu'el" of Samuel Aboab (No. 19). His great learning is mentioned in the collection entitled "Be'er 'Esek" (No. 53); and his so-called "Testament" has been reprinted by Mortara in Berliner's "Magazin" (xiv. 11-22). Mention should also be made of a responsum treating of the reformation of synagogal music, addressed to Samuel Norzi, and reprinted in the "Monatsschrift," xxxix. 350–357. Four elegies on his death were reprinted in "R. E. J" xxxv. 256–263.

Nethaneel ben Levi ha-Naḳdan Trabot : Calligrapher and punctuator; flourished in the sixteenth century. A copy of the Masorah entitled "Patshegen" (Codex de Rossi No. 7), and a manuscript of the Pentateuch (Codex Ambrosianus No. 35) are still preserved as specimens of his work. He was also known as a liturgical poet, being the author of two Habdalot (Codex de Rossi No. 1050). He likewise composed an elegy in twenty-six stanzas.

E. C.   S. O.

Perez Trabot : Hebrew lexicographer; lived in Italy at the close of the fourteenth and the beginning of the fifteenth century. He calls himself either "Zarfati" or "Katelani," thus showing that he had emigrated, probably after the expulsion of the Jews from France in 1395, to Catalonia, and thence to Italy. He was the author of a work entitled "Maḳre Dardeḳe," containing a Hebrew-French or a Hebrew-Catalan vocabulary (Naples, 1488), and in his introduction to this work he speaks of the banishment of the Jews from France.

BIBLIOGRAPHY: Neubauer, in *R. E. J.* ix. 316; Schwab, *ib.* xvi. 253; Perles, *Beiträge zur Gesch. der Hebräischen und Aramäischen Sprachstudien,* pp. 111 *et seq.*; Renan, *Les Ecrivains Juifs Français,* pp. 576 *et seq.*

E. C.   I. Br.

Perez Jehiel ben Nethaneel Trabot : Liturgical poet of the sixteenth century. He was the author of three elegies beginning (1) אבן מקיר תזעק; (2) איכה ישבה; and (3) אני ישן.

The following members of the Trabot family are also mentioned: **Abraham Trabot,** who wrote Codex Turin No. 17 as far as Numbers, and dated the colophon on the 2d of Ḥeshwan (Nov.), 1664; **Beraḥiel ben Hezekiah Trabot,** author of a small maḥzor completed at Florence on the 7th of Nisan (March 9), 1490 (Codex Modena No. 6); **Ḥayyim ben Raphael Trabot,** whose signature appears in a Florentine codex (Plut. I., No. 30) of 1462; **Jacob ben Aaron Trabot,** the author of marginal glosses in Codex Turin A. xiii. 3; **Judah Trabot of Nizza,** the author of a commentary on the "Tempio" of Rieti (Codex Turin A. v. 27); **Menahem ben Nethaneel Raphael Trabot,** who purchased Codex Turin A. vii. 18 on July 22, 1472; **Perez ben Menahem Trabot,** rabbi at Ferrara in the sixteenth century (Lampronti, "Paḥad Yiẓḥaḳ," iv. 22); **Phinehas ben R. Menahem Trabot,** rabbi of Ferrara in the sixteenth century (*ib.,* s.v. חליצה); **Raphael Trabot,** who sent Abraham of Perugia an account of a journey to Jerusalem, dated the 28th of Ab (Aug. 21), 1523 (Cod. Florent., Plut. II., No. 35); **Solomon Trabot,** said to have been the father of Joseph Colon (Codex Parma No. 1420; Codex No. 2 of the Foa collection); and **Solomon (da Trevoux) Trabot,** rabbi of Savigliano in the fifteenth century (Steinschneider, "Hebr. Bibl." xii. 117).

BIBLIOGRAPHY: Kaufmann, in *R. E. J.* iv. 208–225, xxxv. 256–263; Mortara, in Berliner's *Magazin,* xiv. 11–24; Azulai, *Shem ha-Gedolim,* i. 43a, 74b–75a; Gedaliah ibn Yaḥya, *Shalshelet ha-Kabbalah,* ed. Amsterdam, pp. 48b, 50a, 52–53; Nepi-Ghirondi, *Toledot Gedole Yisrael,* pp. 34, 210, 271, 296; Fuenn, *Keneset Yisrael,* p. 525a; Steinschneider, *Hebr. Bibl.* xii. 117, xv. 104; *Kerem Ḥemed,* ii. 152–153; Conforte, *Ḳore ha-Dorot,* ed. Cassel, p. 50a; Steinschneider, *Cat. Bodl.* cols. 2052–2053; Kaufmann, in *Monatsschrift,* xxxix. 350–357; Mortara, *Indice,* pp. 65–66; *Mosè,* v. 155; vi. 52, 264, 338; Zunz, *Literaturgesch.* pp. 507, 588.

E. C.   S. O.

TRACHTENBERG, HERMAN : Russian jurist; born in Jitomir 1839; died there 1895. He studied law at the University of St. Petersburg, and at the end of his course entered the government service. For meritorious work he was granted the Order of Stanislaus of the third degree and that of Vladimir of the fourth degree, thus gaining the rights and privileges of a hereditary citizen. He was noted for his compilations of briefs on criminal cases. At the end of the seventies he was accorded the rare honor of being elected honorary justice of the peace for the district of St. Petersburg.

Trachtenberg always took an active interest in the affairs of the Jewish community of St. Petersburg, and in 1891 devoted much time and energy to the case of the Starodub Jews, who were victims of the anti-Jewish riots.

BIBLIOGRAPHY: *Khronika Voskhoda,* 1895, No. 34.

H. R.   J. G. L.

TRADE. See COMMERCE.

TRADE-UNIONISM.—In England : Excepting in Holland, the creation of a Jewish proletariat has everywhere followed immigration from the east-European centers, where the massing of population gradually led to the formation of a Jewish laboring class. The first union in which mainly Jews were interested, the tailors' union, was founded in 1872. Prior to that date, and for some years after, the Jews had no specific reason for being interested in labor organization. Excepting two, such crafts as the earlier settlers followed called for individual rather than organized effort. These two exceptions

In Diamond and Cigar Trades.

were the various branches of the diamond and cigar trades, both of Dutch origin. Diamond-polishing was early subdivided into four branches; and the introduction of steam fostered the natural tendency in this trade toward factory methods. But few men were engaged in the trade at the time of the discovery of the South-African diamond-fields, and the labor system in vogue among them maintained a certain form of mastership for one in every three of the mill-hands.

The cigar industry, owing to heavy duties and licenses, was at an early date forced to follow the factory system, although there was little if any machinery employed in the work, and the subdivision of labor was of the simplest kind. This trade, however, was one of the first to adopt the trade-union principle, and the Jews entered this organization, still one of the strongest in existence, in large numbers; only recently, owing to the combination in some cases of cigar- and cigarette-making, and to the use of Yiddish, have Jews found it necessary to form a specific Jewish union in that trade.

The formation of a Jewish artisan class, particularly in East London, after 1881, together with the introduction of machinery, created possibilities of Jewish labor combination, and the history of some of the strongest organizations begins with 1882. The immigrants introduced into England the manufacture of cheap clothing (displacing the historic Jewish trade in old clothes), mantle-making, and ladies' tailoring, and developed the fur and rubber trades, both of which are practically in Jewish hands. The evidence presented to the Royal Commission on Alien Immigration, 1902–3, before which the founders of various trades appeared, contains much interesting information on these points. There were at all times certain rough divisions in the various branches of the "needle industries," but the introduction of the steam-driven sewing-, cutting-, and braiding-machines changed the form of the industry from what had been largely home work to factory labor of a highly specialized kind. The Jews were directly responsible for this. One of their advocates before the Royal Commission on Alien Immigration said that "they utilized the sewing-machine as a scientific instrument of production." This subdivision presented the possibility of the middleman turning "sweater," and forcing down the price of labor by introducing the "greener," the craftless immigrant who could learn one or another branch of the trade, according to the degree of skill required, in from six weeks to eighteen months. The same principles applied to the leather and cabinet-making trades; but owing to the existence of the factory form of labor prior to the introduction of specialized machinery the general trade-unions in both cases proved sufficiently powerful to be able to absorb the special Jewish unions soon after their formation. Jewish unions or Jewish unionists, as such, are not nowadays found engaging in strikes. The needle industries, however, became more strongly Jewish, and in 1889 the masters confronted the organizations of their employees by forming their own union, the Jewish Masters' Society. Jewish labor combination followed logically upon the sweater, the greener, and the demand for cheap clothing. Indeed, the creative cause and the condition of Jewish labor are well told in the following demands made in the 1889 strike, in which fully 10,000 Jews participated:

In the Clothing Industries.

(1) That the hours of work shall be reduced to twelve, with one hour for dinner and a half-hour for tea.

(2) That meals shall be taken outside the factory premises.

(3) That government contractors shall pay wages at trade-union rates.

(4) That government contractors and sweaters shall not give out work to be done at home at night after working hours.

This strike lasted six weeks, and it seems to have been to the ultimate disadvantage of the Jewish working classes. The history of the movement from that day represents a series of attempts to organize or reorganize, the effort being unquestionably hampered by the fact that the union is estranged from the general trade-unions by the use of Yiddish in all meetings and by the existence of marked socialistic and anarchistic tendencies among the leaders. Of late, however, these have exhibited a well-defined Zionist attitude. In the nineties there were a number of strikes; and in several cases these resulted in shorter hours and better wages. The strikers also made a considerable point of their desire to observe the Sabbath and the Jewish holy days; and in this

The First Strike.

way they gained the support of the rabbinate. It can not, however, be said that at any time a serious attempt was made to enforce this observance, and it would appear that the pleas of the strikers were more political than religious in purpose.

With the growth of immigration there came an increase in the number of the trades in which the Jews were interested, and a corresponding growth in the strength of the trade-union organizations formed. The movement spread to Birmingham, Leeds, Manchester, and other manufacturing cities. Inter-Jewish conferences were held, an attempt was made to bring the Jewish labor movement as a whole under one organization, and the representatives of the Jewish unions were recognized and took part in the general trade-union conferences held from time to time. Of all these unions only one has so far become conspicuous—that of the Jewish bakers, who have not only fought their masters for sanitary bakehouses, better wages, and shorter hours, but have aided their masters in the fight against the general trade-union of bakers, which endeavored to compel the Jews to obey a law several hundred years old prohibiting the baking of bread in London on Sundays, a restriction that was apparently ignored when Parliament enacted the Sunday exemption clauses for Jews in the Factory Acts.

The strength of the movement has differed at various times; to-day (1905) it is weaker than it was ten years ago. It has had its organs and its recognized leaders; but it is contended that a Jew does not make a good unionist, "because one ruling passion never leaves him—his desire to rise from his low position and be a master." Lewis Lyons, who has been particularly active in the creation of the specifically Jewish unions, told the above-mentioned commission that "Jewish trade-unions fluctuate in consequence of excessive immigration, and that the labor leaders have from time to time the utmost difficulty in maintaining a solid and disciplined organization." On the other hand, statistics show that in the tailoring trade proportionately more Jews than non-Jews are united.

Weakness of the Movement.

There are no accurate statistics as to the number of Jews in the various Jewish and general unions in England; and the following is merely a list of the number of organizations existing in London between 1882 and 1902: tailors, 31 unions; butchers, 1; bakers, 1; cigar-makers, 1; iron and tin-plate workers, 1; compositors, 1; brush-makers, 1; house-painters, 1; card-box makers, 1. Of these 39 unions, 6 were dissolved and 3 were merged in other organizations. A furriers' and a costermongers' union have been founded since 1902, bringing the present total up to 32. There are, in addition, Jewish tailors' unions in Birmingham (1), Leeds (2, with 1,300 members), Manchester (3), and Sheffield (1). Tailors' organizations probably exist also in Bradford, Bristol, Glasgow, Hull, and Reading.

The chief organs of the Jewish trade-union movement have been: "Der Polischer Jüdel" (1882), "Die Zukunft" (1884), "Die Neue Welt" (1900–1). News items are also given in "Reynolds's Newspaper."

BIBLIOGRAPHY: Georg Halpern, *Die Jüdischen Arbeiter in London*, in *Münchener Volkswirtschaftliche Studien*, Stuttgart and Berlin, 1903; John Dycke, *The Jewish Immigrant*, in *Contemporary Review*, vol. lxxv. (1899); *Report of the Select Committee of the House of Lords on the Sweating System, 1889–90*; *Wages in Jewish Tailoring Workshops in Leeds and Manchester*, in *Labor Gazette*, vol. i., No. 1 (1893); Henri Dagan, *Le Prolétariat Juif*, in *La Revue Blanche*, Oct., 1901; D. F. Schloss, *The Jew as Workman*, in *Nineteenth Century*, Jan., 1891; *Report of the Royal Commission on Alien Immigration*, London, 1903; *Jew. Chron.* (Labor Column), passim; *Jewish Year Book*, 1902-5.

J.　　　　　　　　　　　　　　　　　J. DE H.

——In the United States : It is only in the United States and in England that Jews find the opportunity to enter non-Jewish trade-unions in large numbers. In these countries Jewish workers, like others, enter the unions of their various crafts. From their ranks have risen such trade-union leaders as Samuel Gompers (for more than twenty years president of the American Federation of Labor), Joseph Barondess, and Henry White. Jews have shown a special preference for the clothing trades. According to official reports, three-fourths of the workmen in these trades in New York are Jews. In these industries, therefore, the unions are practically Jewish organizations.

The first attempts at organization among Jewish workmen antedate the main influx of Jewish immigration into England and America. The first union of Jewish tailors in New York was **The Be-** organized in 1877. It had an ephem-**ginnings.** eral existence. When, in the eighties, Jews began to arrive in large numbers, the need of organization was soon realized. Several unions came into existence, and strikes were declared which met with varying degrees of success. About the time of the eleventh census (1890) New York city had become the center for the manufacture of women's ready-made clothing. The year 1890 witnessed the first great strike of Jewish workmen: the cloak-makers struck in all factories and sweat-shops, and after enduring great suffering for eight weeks they won the strike. Wages were raised to such an extent that the workers were able to earn during the busy season from $25 to $30 a week.

The first success cemented the union. In the winter of 1892 another general strike was declared with the object of maintaining the advantages which had been gained by the previous movement; and although this time the employers formed an association and firmly withstood for a while the demands of the strikers, they at length gave way. The union then demanded from the employers the payment of an indemnity for the losses incurred through the strike. The employers regarded this demand as extortion; they paid, but instituted a criminal prosecution against the secretary of the union, Joseph Barondess. He was indicted, found guilty, and sentenced by the trial court. The Supreme Court of the State of New York reversed the sentence, holding that in the absence of intent to appropriate the money to his own use the defendant, who merely acted as the representative of his union, was not guilty of extortion. The decision of the Supreme Court was reversed by the New York Court of Appeals, which affirmed the sentence of the trial court. The defendant, however, was soon pardoned by the governor.

Litigation had exhausted the resources of the union, and when the general depression of business began the union was soon broken up. With the **Varying** restoration of business prosperity in **Fortune.** 1897 it was revived, and has since had a continuous existence, its paying membership reaching at one time 15,000; but at other times its membership has sunk very close to the zero point.

The history of other Jewish unions is similar to that of the Cloak-Makers' Union, which under normal conditions has the largest membership. The weakness of all Jewish unions in the tailoring trades is the fluctuating character of their membership. Prof. John R. Commons, in his report on "Immigration and Its Economic Effects," prepared for the Industrial Commission, speaks as follows regarding the character of Jewish trade-unions in the United States:

"The Jew's conception of a labor organization is that of a tradesman rather than that of a workman. In the clothing manufacture, whenever any real abuse arises among the Jewish workmen, they all come together and form a giant union and at once engage in a strike. They bring in 95 per cent of the trade. They are energetic and determined. They demand the entire and complete elimination of the abuse. The demand is almost always unanimous, and is made with enthusiasm and bitterness. They stay out a long time, even under the greatest of suffering. During a strike large numbers of them are to be found with almost nothing to live upon and their families suffering, still insisting, on the streets and in their halls, that their great cause must be won. But when once the strike is settled, either in favor of or against the cause, they are contented, and that usually ends the union, since they do not see any practical use for a union when there is no cause to fight for. Consequently the membership of a Jewish union is wholly uncertain. The secretary's books will show 60,000 members in one month and not 5,000 within three months later. If perchance a local branch has a steady thousand members from year to year, and if they are indeed paying members, it is likely that they are not the same members as in the year before."

The instability of the Jewish unions has been ascribed to the character of the Jew, who has an inborn desire to be "his own boss"; the ambition of the Jewish worker is to rise above the working class, rather than to improve his own condition simultaneously with that of his class; hence the sweating system, with its numerous contractors and subcontractors. The clothing trade in its beginnings requiring little capital, the development of the clothing industry in New York within recent years has been **Sweating.** marked, in contrast with the general trend of the time, by a tendency toward small-scale production. The scattering of employees in numerous small shops is unfavorable to organization. Another cause which has interfered with the progress of organization in trades followed largely by Jews is the influence of Socialist agitation among Jewish workers. More than one Jewish trade-union has been wrecked by dissensions between divergent schools of Socialism.

One of the oldest and strongest Jewish trade-unions is the organization of compositors of Jewish newspapers and printing-offices, the Hebrew-American Typographical Union, which is affiliated with the International Typographical Union. The Jewish unions of New York are combined in a central body, known as The United Hebrew Trades. This federation comprises the unions of those working in the clothing trades, of compositors, of employees of the

Jewish theaters, and a few minor unions. Some of these unions are affiliated with the American Federation of Labor.

BIBLIOGRAPHY: *Report of the Industrial Commission on Immigration*, 1901, vol. xv.; Georg Halpern, *Die Jüdischen Arbeiter in London*, in *Münchener Volkswirtschaftliche Studien*, Stuttgart and Berlin, 1903; *Report of the Chief Labor Correspondent of the Board of Trade on Trade-Unions*, in the *Annual*, 1892 *et seq.*

A.   I. A. H.

TRADITIONELLE JUDENTHUM, DAS.
See PERIODICALS.

TRADITIONS: Doctrines and sayings transmitted from father to son by word of mouth, and thus preserved among the people. Such traditions constitute a large part of Jewish oral teachings (see ORAL LAW); and many halakic doctrines seek to trace their descent from Moses on Mount Sinai (see SINAITIC COMMANDMENTS). There are other traditions, however, which refer to national and historical events, rather than to halakic problems. Of these haggadot, scattered through Talmudic and midrashic literature, the following two may be cited as examples: (1) Soṭah 10b: " We have received the tradition from our fathers that Amoz, the father of the prophet Isaiah, and Amaziah, the king of Judah, were brothers "; and (2) Yer. B. B. 15c: " It is a haggadic tradition that the space occupied by the Holy of Holies in the Temple was not included in the stipulated measurement of the latter."

The Hebrew designations for tradition are "Masoret " (מסורת) and "Ḳabbalah " (קבלה), while halakic tradition is designated also as "Halakah " (הלכה).

s.   J. Z. L.

TRAJAN: Roman emperor from 98 to 117. Like Vespasian, Titus, and Hadrian, he is frequently mentioned by Jewish writers; and he exercised a profound influence upon the history of the Jews throughout the Babylonia, Palestine, and Hellenistic Diaspora. His ambition led him to the farthest eastern boundaries of the Roman empire, where he warred against the Parthians, although in the meantime the Jews arose in Egypt and in Cyrene "as though carried away by some wild and riotous spirit " Eusebius, "Hist. Eccl." iv. 2). The insurrection at Alexandria is mentioned in a papyrus fragment in the Louvre, which refers to a suit brought before the emperor by an Alexandrian and a Jew, although the ruler there designated may be HADRIAN, Trajan's successor (see T. Reinach in "R. E. J." xxxvii. 218).

The task of subduing the Jews in Egypt and Cyrene was entrusted by Trajan to Marcius Turbo, with whom the emperor is confused in rabbinical sources, which frequently write the name Trajan "Tarkinos " (Krauss, in "R. E. J." xxx. 206, xxxi. 47; *idem*, "Lehnwörter," ii. 273). Cyprus also was the scene of a violent Jewish uprising, which seems likewise to have been quelled by Turbo. In the same year (116), or possibly a year later, when Trajan thought the Parthians subdued, the Jews of Mesopotamia, mindful of the treatment which their Palestinian brethren had received at the hands of the Romans, and of their own sufferings, especially at Nisibis and Adiabene, during the four years of Trajan's campaign, arose in rebellion, determined to expel the Romans from their country. Trajan there-

upon ordered the Mauritanian prince Lusius QUIETUS to proceed against the Jews, and gave him strict orders to purge the provinces of them, his rigid obedience to this order winning for the legate the governorship of Palestine (Eusebius, " Hist. Eccl." iv. 2; *idem*, "Chronikon," ed. Schoene, ii. 164; Orosius, vii. 12; Dion Cassius, lxviii. 32).

In the meantime, however, rebellion had again broken out in Judea; and it is highly probable that the Palestinian Jews also rendered assistance to their oppressed brethren elsewhere, especially in Egypt, this fact possibly furnishing an explanation of Trajan's expedition to Egypt (Esther R. proem, § 3). The rabbinical legend gives the following reason for the revolution: The emperor's wife (the governor's wife is probably meant) bore a child on the 9th of Ab, when the Jews were lamenting, and it died on the Feast of Ḥanukkah, when the Jews illuminated their houses; and in revenge for these fancied insults the wife urged her husband to punish the Jews (*ib.*). No such legend, however, is needed to explain the Jewish rebellion against the Roman government, for during the reign of Trajan the Christian descendants of David, who were relatives of Jesus, were persecuted; and Schlatter rightly infers that the patriarchal family likewise died for its faith, since it was supposed to be Davidic. The Palestinian revolt appears to have been organized by two brothers, PAPPUS and Luliani, and rabbinical sources expressly allude to Trajan's proceedings against the pair (Sifra, Emor, viii. 9, and parallels; see also Kohut, " Aruch Completum," iv. 74), whom he is said to have sentenced to death in Laodicea, although he afterward ordered them taken to Rome, where they were executed. Here again the rabbinical sources confuse Trajan with his governor, Lusius Quietus, who was later deposed and executed by Hadrian. The marvelous escape of Pappus and Luliani was celebrated by a semifestival called " Trajan's Day," which fell, according to the Meg. Ta'an., on the 12th of Adar (see Ratner in Sokolow, " Sefer ha-Yobel," p. 507), although it is more probable that this day really commemorated the success of the Jewish forces against the Roman army. Denarii of Trajan are mentioned in the Talmud ('Ab. Zarah 52b); and it is also noteworthy that, according to the inscriptions of this emperor, he constructed a road from the Syrian border to the Red Sea. The unrest which marked the end of his reign was not allayed until his successor Hadrian became emperor.

BIBLIOGRAPHY: Grätz, *Gesch.* 3d ed., iv. 112–117; Schürer, *Gesch.* 3d ed., i. 661–668; Schlatter, *Die Tage Trajans und Hadrians*, p. 88, Gütersloh, 1897.

s.   S. KR.

TRANI: Family of scholars, members of which were prominent in Spain and the Levant.

Aaron di Trani: Spanish tosafist; born in Castile; descendant of a family which produced several eminent Talmudists. He received his education under the direction of R. Joseph Alfasi. At an early age he removed to Italy, whence he went, in 1502, to Adrianople. There he made the acquaintance of Joseph Caro, who had gone thither to publish his " Bet Yosef." As a Talmudist, Trani was very highly esteemed by his contemporaries. He ranks among the representatives of pilpul, not only on account of his preference for the Tosafists, but also by virtue of the fact that his nephew and pupil Moses di TRANI, in conjunction with the son of Joseph Caro, introduced pilpul into the schools of Palestine. It may, however, be assumed that Aaron Trani's pilpul did not go to extremes, else Joseph Caro would not have spoken of him so highly. The few notes concerning him which may be found in the works of others were collected by Michael in his "Or ha-Ḥayyim."

J. SR. L. G.

Isaiah (ben Elijah) di Trani (the Younger): See JEW. ENCYC. vi. 644.

Isaiah (ben Mali) di Trani (the Elder; RID): See JEW. ENCYC. vi. 644.

Joseph di Trani: Scholar of the fifteenth and sixteenth centuries; uncle of Moses di Trani. Expelled, with his brother, from the city of his birth in 1502, he settled in Salonica.

Joseph di Trani (the Elder): Talmudist of the latter part of the sixteenth century; lived in Greece. By contemporary scholars he was called ט״מהרימ, and regarded as one of the foremost Talmudists of his time. He was the author of "She'elot u-Teshubot," a work in three parts: part i. comprises 152 responsa, together with a general index (Constantinople, 1641); part ii. consists of 111 responsa in the order of the first three parts of the ritual codex (Venice, 1645); part iii. contains responsa to the fourth part of the ritual codex, together with novellæ to the treatise Ḳiddushin, and supercommentaries on RaN's and Alfasi's commentaries on the treatises Ketubot and Ḳiddushin (ib. 1645). The entire work appeared in Fürth in 1764. Joseph also published novellæ to the treatises Shabbat, Ketubot, and Ḳiddushin (Sudzilkov, 1802), and the responsa which were embodied in Alfandari's "Maggid me-Reshit" (Constantinople, 1710). He left several commentaries in manuscript—on Alfasi, on Maimonides' "Yad," and on R. Nathan's "'Aruk."

Joseph (ben Moses ben Joseph) di Trani (the Younger): Talmudist; born at Safed 1573; died at Constantinople 1644. He early showed a marked predilection for Talmudic studies, and upon the death of his father (1585) he was sent to Egypt, where he continued them under his uncle Solomon di Trani. When the latter, in 1587, fell a victim to the plague, Joseph returned to Safed, where he became a pupil of Solomon Sagi. There he remained until 1609, when he received a call to a rabbinate in Constantinople, where he officiated until his death. He is reported to have founded several benevolent institutions in Constantinople. Of his works the only one known is "Zofenat Pa'neaḥ" (Venice, 1653; Frankfort-on-the-Oder, 1694), a collection of sermons on the weekly lessons and the festivals.

Moses ben Joseph di Trani (the Elder; called ט׳המבי׳): Talmudist; born at Salonica 1505; died in Jerusalem 1585. His father had fled to Salonica from Apulia three years prior to his birth. While still a boy Moses was sent to Adrianople to pursue the study of the Talmud under the supervision of his uncle Aaron. At the age of sixteen he went to Safed and completed his studies under Jacob Berab. In 1525 he was appointed rabbi at Safed; he held this office until 1535, when he removed to Jerusalem.

Moses di Trani was the author of: "Ḳiryat Sefer" (Venice, 1551), commentary on the Bible, the Talmud, and difficult passages in the commentaries of Maimonides; "Sefer ha-Teḥiyyah weha-Pedut" (Mantua, 1556; Wilna, 1799; Sudzilkov, 1834; Warsaw, 1841), commentary and notes on ch. vii. and viii. of Saadia Gaon's "Emunot we-De'ot"; "Bet Elohim" (Venice, 1576), a moral and philosophical work on prayer, atonement, and the fundamental principles of faith; "She'elot u-Teshubot" (vol. i., ib. 1629; vol. ii., ib. 1630), a collection of 841 responsa, with an index.

Moses ben Joseph di Trani (the Younger): Flourished during the first half of the seventeenth century. He published the commentaries of his father, and wrote some sermons, which appeared in the "Zofenat Pa'neaḥ" (Venice, 1653).

Solomon di Trani: Son of Moses ben Joseph the Elder, and brother of Joseph di Trani the Elder; flourished in Egypt, where he died from the plague in 1587. He wrote a preface to the works of his father, in which is contained much information bearing on the Trani family. He is also the reputed author of "Marbiz Torah be-Yisrael," a collection of sermons, still extant in manuscript.

BIBLIOGRAPHY: Zunz, Z. G. pp. 58, 229–230; idem, Literatur-gesch. p. 363; Azulai, Shem ha-Gedolim; Conforte, Ḳore ha-Dorot (ed. Cassel); Jost, Gesch. der Juden, viii. 456, note; Güdemann, Gesch. ii. 189 et seq.; Bass, Sifte Yeshenim, i. 49a, 68a; Berliner, Peleṭat Soferim, p. 13; idem, in his Magazin, i. 45, 54; Fuenn, Keneset Yisrael; Benjacob, Ozar ha-Sefarim; Steinschneider, Cat. Bodl. cols. 1392, 1536, 2006–2007; De Rossi, Dizionario, p. 319; Ibn Yaḥya, Shal-shelet ha-Ḳabbalah, ed. Amsterdam, p. 51a.
E. C. S. O.

TRANSFER. See ALIENATION AND ACQUISITION.

TRANSLATIONS.—Into Hebrew: After the early victories of the Mohammedans and the consequent spread of Arabic civilization, the Jews of the Eastern countries became familiar with and adopted to a large extent the Arabic language; so much so that rabbis and scholars, if they desired to be understood by the masses, were compelled to write their works in that language. After the center of Jewish learning shifted from the Orient to Spain and southern France, some of these works, especially those dealing with the Halakah and Hebrew grammar, were translated from Arabic into Hebrew. In the lists of translations in this article the title of the translation is, as a rule, given in parentheses, with the date and place of publication of the first edition.

The oldest Hebrew translations from Arabic date from the eleventh century. In 1078 Isaac ben Reuben Albargeloni rendered into Hebrew, under the title "Ha-Miḳḳaḥ weha-Mimkar," Hai Gaon's treatise on purchase (Venice, 1602), also Ibn
From Janaḥ's lexicon "Kitab al-Uṣul" ("Se-
Arabic. fer ha-Shorashim"). About the same time, perhaps a little earlier, some Karaite writings were translated into Hebrew by Moses ben Tobia. At the beginning of the twelfth century Moses ben Samuel ha-Kohen ibn Gikatilla translated the two principal works of Ḥayyuj, the treatises on "Verbs Containing Weak Letters" and "Verbs Containing Double Letters" (edited with an English translation by John W. Nutt, London and

Berlin, 1870). From the first half of the twelfth century there are a translation, or rather a paraphrase, of Saadia's "Emunot we-De'ot," and a translation of his commentary on the "Sefer Yeẓirah," both by Moses ben Joseph of Lucena. Toward the middle of the same century Ibn Ezra translated Ḥayyuj's grammatical works, two works on the astrology of Mashallah ("She'elot" and "Kadrut"), and a treatise on geomancy ("Sefer ha-Goralot"). About the same time Judah ben Isaac ibn Ghayyat translated a casuistical dissertation on a part of Shebu'ot.

All these translations are said by Judah ibn Tibbon, in the introduction to the "Ḥobot ha-Lebabot," to be defective in character, their imperfections being due either to a less than thorough knowledge of Arabic or Hebrew on the part of the translators, or to the fact that the latter give their own opinions instead of those of the authors. A similar view is expressed by Judah ben Barzillai, in his commentary on the "Sefer Yeẓirah," with regard to Moses ben Joseph's translation of Saadia's commentary on that work, the Hebrew of which he declares to be unintelligible.

A new era in regard to methods of translation began with Judah IBN TIBBON, "the father of translators." At the request of Meshullam **The Ibn** ben Jacob and his son Asher, Judah **Tibbons.** translated, in 1161, the first treatise of Baḥya ben Joseph ibn Paḳuda's ethical work "Kitab al-Hidayah ila Fara'iḍ al-Ḳulub." After its completion Joseph Ḳimḥi translated the remaining nine treatises and then the first one also. However, at the request of Abraham ben David of Posquières, Judah completed, under the title "Ḥobot ha-Lebabot" (Naples, 1489), the translation of the whole work, his version gradually superseding that by Ḳimḥi, of which only a small fragment has been preserved (published by Jellinek in Benjacob's edition of the "Ḥobot ha-Lebabot," Leipsic, 1846). The translation of Baḥya's work was followed by translations of Ibn Gabirol's "Kitab Iṣlaḥ al-Akhlaḳ" ("Tiḳḳun Middot ha-Nefesh," Constantinople, 1550), Judah ha-Levi's "Kitab al-Ḥujjah" ("Sefer ha-Kuzari," Fano, 1506), Ibn Janaḥ's "Kitab al-Luma'" ("Sefer ha-Riḳmah," ed. B. Goldberg, Frankfort-on-the-Main, 1856) and "Kitab al-Uṣul" ("Sefer ha-Shorashim," ed. W. Bacher, Berlin, 1896), and Saadia's "Kitab al-Amanat wal-I'tiḳadat" ("Sefer ha-Emunot weha-De'ot," Constantinople, 1562). To Judah ibn Tibbon is attributed also, although on very slight grounds, the translation of the collection of maxims "Mibḥar ha-Peninim," usually ascribed to Ibn Gabirol, and of Aristotle's "Posterior Analytics." In all these translations Judah endeavored to render faithfully the very words of the authors—by no means an easy task, considering the richness of the Arabic vocabulary and the poverty of the Hebrew.

In order to reproduce the abstract ideas found in the philosophical writings new word-forms and technical terms had to be established. These word-forms and technical terms were naturally modeled after those of the Arabic, which, in their turn, were literal translations from the Greek. It is not surprising, therefore, that in the Hebrew versions of the philosophical writings there are many expressions which are unintelligible to those unacquainted with the Arabic terminology; but this can not be imputed as a fault to the translator, who could not find in Hebrew words adequate to the expression of abstract ideas, Hebrew being essentially the language of a people of concrete ideas. Judah's work is nevertheless far from being above criticism; it contains many faults which are due either to the translator's limited knowledge of Hebrew or to his misunderstanding of the original. Desiring to be faithful to the latter, Judah, like all the translators who took him as their guide, invariably rendered each Arabic word into an equivalent in Hebrew, without considering that a literal translation is not always possible and that some sentences must necessarily be recast in order to make them intelligible to a reader who is a stranger to Arabic constructions.

Literal Method of Translation.

Another grave defect in Judah's method of translation, and one which gave rise to many errors and misunderstandings, was that he always used the same Hebrew word as an equivalent for a given Arabic word, regardless of the variations of meaning attached to the latter. Thus, for instance, he always uses the Hebrew verb עמד ("to stand") for the Arabic וקף, although, according to the preposition by which the latter is followed, it may also mean "to read," "to study," etc. Yet, notwithstanding numerous faults, Judah's translations were recognized as standards and accepted as models by all the Hebrew translators of Arabic in the Middle Ages. Thus his version of the "Cuzari" superseded that made a little later by Judah ibn Cardinal, as his rendering of the "Kitab al-Uṣul" superseded those made by Isaac ha-Levi and Isaac ben Judah Albargeloni.

The thirteenth century was especially rich in Hebrew translations from the Arabic, and those of Samuel IBN TIBBON, the son of Judah, were prominent among them. An enthusiastic admirer of Maimonides, Samuel began by translating several of his works, the most important among which was the "Dalalat al-Ḥa'irin," which he finished in 1190 under the title "Moreh Nebukim." Samuel clung more tenaciously than his father to the **Translation of Maimonides.** letter of the Arabic text; he even introduced Arabic words into his translations, and, by analogy with the Arabic, gave to certain Hebrew words meanings different from the accepted ones. This system of translation could but impair the intelligibility of a text difficult in itself; and thus the "Moreh" abounds in passages which are enigmatic to those who do not possess a profound knowledge of Arabic. Samuel's translation was, indeed, approved by Maimonides himself, to whom it had been sent for revision; but in such a case Maimonides was the person least qualified to judge, since, as the author of the original and an expert in Arabic, he naturally had no difficulty in reading the Hebrew version. This at least must have been the opinion of the poet Judah al-Ḥarizi, who, at the beginning of the thirteenth century, made a new translation of Maimonides' work and accused Samuel ibn Tibbon of having intentionally obscured the text. Al-Ḥarizi was not successful in his attempt to supersede Samuel's translation with his own, for the former was found by some critics to be more faithful to the original. Thus Shem-Ṭob ibn Falaquera, passing judgment upon both translations, says: "In Ibn Tibbon's translation the errors are few, and if the learned translator had had time he certainly would have corrected them; but in Al-Ḥarizi's, mistakes are numerous and words are often given wrong meanings."

In addition to the "Moreh," Samuel translated the following works of Maimonides: a treatise on resurrection ("Iggeret," or "Ma'amar Teḥiyyat ha-Metim "); the Mishnah commentary on Pirḳe Abot, with the psychological introduction ("Shemonah Peraḳim "); the "Thirteen Articles of Faith " ("Shelosh 'Esreh 'Iḳḳarim "); a letter addressed to Joseph ibn 'Aknin. Samuel did not confine his activity to Jewish writings, but translated works written by Arabs and bearing on philosophy and medicine. Among these were: Yaḥya ibn Baṭriḳ's Arabic translation of Aristotle's "Meteora " ("Otot ha-Shamayim," or "Otot 'Elyonot "), three small treatises of Averroes ("Sheloshah Ma'amarim "), and Ali ibn Riḍwan's commentary on the "Ars Parva " of Galen.

No less prominent in the field of translation was the above-mentioned poet Judah al-Ḥarizi. In addition to the "Dalalat al-Ḥa'irin," he translated Maimonides' treatise on resurrection (already rendered into Hebrew by Samuel ibn Tibbon) and his Mishnah commentary on Ze-ra'im, Ḥariri of Busrah's "Maḳamat " ("Maḥberot Itiel "), Ali ibn Riḍwan's ethical epistle, Galen's essay against hasty interment, a treatise on the soul ("Sefer ha-Nefesh ") also attributed to Galen, an originally Greek work on the "Dicta of the Philosophers " ("Mussare ha-Filosofim "), and an anonymous treatise on geomancy ("Sefer ha-Goralot ").

Judah al-Ḥarizi.

A prolific translator, whose style, although less poetic, was more clear than that of his contemporary Al-Ḥarizi, was Abraham ben Samuel Ḥasdai. Among his translations are the following: the pseudo-Aristotelian "Kitab al-Tuffaḥah " ("Sefer ha-Tappuaḥ," Venice, 1519; frequently reprinted); Ghazali's ethical work "Mizan al-'Amal " ("Mozene Ẓedeḳ," in which the translator replaced the quotations from the Koran and the Sunnah with their equivalents from Bible and Talmud; ed. Goldenthal, Leipsic, 1839); Isaac Israeli's "Kitab al-Istiḳsat " ("Sefer ha-Yesodot "); Maimonides' "Sefer ha-Miẓwot," with his letter to the Yemenite Jews ("Iggeret Teman "); and a romance presenting incidents in the life of Buddha ("Ben ha-Melek weha-Nazir," Constantinople, 1518). About the same time as the last-named work a famous book of fables was translated, under the title "Sefer Kalilah wa-Dimnah," by the grammarian Jacob ben Eleazar.

From about 1230 to 1300 the most important Arabic works on philosophy, medicine, astronomy, mathematics, and other branches of learning were translated. The leading translators of that period were Jacob ANATOLIO (son-in-law of Samuel ibn Tibbon), Moses IBN TIBBON, Jacob ben Machir IBN

TIBBON, the Italian physician Nathan ha-ME'ATI, and Zerahiah ben Isaac ben Shealtiel GRACIAN. Anatolio translated the "Almagest " of Ptolemy ("Ḥibbur ha-Gadol ha-Niḳra al-Majesti "), the "Elements of Astronomy " by Al-Fargani, a treatise on syllogisms by Al-Farabi ("Sefer Heḳḳesh ha-Ḳaẓer "), and the first five books of Averroes' Middle Commentary on Aristotle's "Logic," consisting of the Introduction of Porphyry and the four books of Aristotle on the "Categories," "Interpretation," "Syllogisms," and "Demonstration."

Moses ibn Tibbon, like his father, began his career as a translator with several works of Maimonides, including the treatise on hygiene ("Miktab," or "Ma'amar be-Hanhagat ha-Beri'ut "), a mishnaic commentary (probably on Zera'im), the "Book of Precepts " ("Sefer ha-Miẓwot," Constantinople, c. 1516), the treatise on logic ("Millot ha-Higgayon," Venice, 1552), the treatise on poisons ("Ha-Ma'amar ha-Nikbad," or "Ha-Ma'amar be-Ṭeri'ak "), and the commentary on Hippocrates' "Aphorisms." Moses' other translations are: Averroes' commentaries on Aristotle's "Physica Auscultatio " ("Kiẓẓure ibn Roshd 'al Shema' Ṭib'i," Riva di Trento, 1559); "De Cœlo et Mundo " ("Kelale ha-Shamayim weha-'Olam "); "De Generatione et Corruptione " ("Sefer ha-Hawayah weha-Hefsed "); "Meteora " ("Sefer Ototha-'Elyonot "); "De Anima " ("Kelale Sefer ha-Nefesh "); the Middle Commentary on the last-named work ("Bi'ur Sefer ha-Nefesh "); "Parva Naturalia " ("Ha-Ḥush weha-Muḥash "); "Metaphysica " ("Mah she-Aḥar ha-Ṭeba' "); a commentary on Avicenna's "Arjuzah " ("Bi'ur Arguza "); Avicenna's "Small Canon " ("Ha-Seder ha-Ḳaṭan "); Batalyusi's "Al-Ḥada'iḳ " ("Ha-'Agullot ha-Ra'yoniyyot," ed. Kaufmann, Leipsic, 1880); Al-Ḥassar's treatise on arithmetic ("Sefer ha-Ḥeshbon "); Euclid's "Elements " ("Shorashim," or "Yesodot "); Al-Farabi's "Book of the Principles " ("Hathalot ha-Nimẓa'ot ha-Ṭib'iyyim," ed. Filipowski, Leipsic, 1849); Geminus' introduction to the "Almagest " ("Ḥokmat ha-Kokabim," or "Ḥokmat ha-Tekunah "); Ibn al-Yazzar's "Viaticum " ("Ẓedat ha-Derakim "); Ḥunain's introduction to medical science ("Mabo el-Meleket ha-Refu'ah "); Razi's works on the division of maladies ("Ha-Hilluḳ weha-Ḥilluf ") and on the antidotes; Ḥunain's translation of Themistius' commentary on the treatise "Lamda " ("Perush Ma'amar ha-Nirsham be-Ot Lamed ") and of the Aristotelian physical questions ("She'elot Ṭib'iyyot "); Kosta ben Luka's translation of the "Sphærica " of Theodosius Tripolitanus ("Sefer Teodosiyus be-Kadur "); and Ibn Aflaḥ's astronomical work "Kitab Ilahiyah."

Jacob ben Machir ibn Tibbon translated: the "Elements " of Euclid; the treatise of Kosta ben Luka on the armillary sphere; the "Data " of Euclid ("Sefer ha-Mattanot ") according to the Arabic translation of Isḥaḳ ben Ḥunain; the treatise of Autolycus on the sphere in movement ("Ma'amar Ṭalḳus "); three treatises on the sphere by Menelaus of Alexandria; Abu 'Ali ibn Ḥasan ibn al-Haitham's astronomical work ("Ma'amar bi-Tekunah," or "Sefer 'al Tekunah "); Abu al-Ḳasim Aḥmad ibn al-Ṣaffar's treatise on the use of the astrolabe; Abu

(margin) Arabic Philosophy and Science.

Mohammed Jabar ibn Aflaḥ's compendium of the "Almagest"; Abu Isḥaḳ ben al-Zarḳalah's astronomical work ("Iggeret ha-Ma'aseh be-Luaḥ ha-Niḳra Sofiḥah"); the preface to Abraham bar Ḥiyya's astronomical work; an extract from the "Almagest" on the arc of a circle; Averroes' compendium of the "Organon" ("Ḳiẓẓur mi-Kol Meleket Higgayon," Riva di Trento, 1559); Averroes' paraphrase of books xi.–xix. of Aristotle's history of animals; Ghazali's "Mizan al-'Uyun," in which are refuted the philosophical ideas antagonistic to religion ("Mozene ha-'Iyyunim").

Nathan ha-Me'ati, called the "Prince of Translators" and the "Italian Tibbonide," translated the following medical works: 'Ammar ben 'Ali al-Mauṣuli's "Al-Muntaḥib fi 'Ilaj al-'Ain," on the treatment of the eye; the "Canon" of Avicenna; the aphorisms of Hippocrates, with Galen's commentary; the aphorisms of Maimonides, and a selection from various authors, chiefly from Galen ("Pirḳe Mosheh," Lemberg, 1804). Many anonymous

Thirteenth-Century Activity. translations are attributed to Nathan ha-Me'ati: Razi's treatise on bleeding ("Ma'amar be-Haḳḳazah"); Zahrawi's "Kitab al-Taṣrif" (Hebrew title, "Zeruf"); Ibn Zuhr's "Kitab al-Aghdhiyah" ("Sefer ha-Mezonot"); an anonymous work on the causes of eclipses ("Ma'amar 'al Libbot Liḳḳut ha-Me'orot"). A translation of Galen's commentary on Hippocrates' work "On Airs, Waters, and Places," begun by Nathan, was completed in 1299 by his son Solomon, whose son Samuel in turn concluded the translation of an extract from Galen's commentary on Hippocrates' work "On Regimen in Acute Diseases," and the translation of a medical work by Ibn Zuhr.

Zerahiah ben Isaac ben Shealtiel Gracian translated: Aristotle's "Physics" ("Sefer ha-Ṭeba'"), "Metaphysics" ("Mah she-Aḥar ha-Ṭeba'"), "De Cœlo et Mundo" ("Ha-Shamayim weha-'Olam"), "De Anima" ("Sefer ha-Nefesh"), and "De Causis" ("Ha-Bi'ur ha-Ṭob ha-Gamur"); Averroes' Middle Commentaries on Aristotle's "Physics," "Metaphysics," and "De Cœlo et Mundo," with the commentary of Themistius on the last-named work; the first two books of Avicenna's "Canon"; Al-Farabi's "Risalah fi Mahiyyat al-Nafs" ("Ma'amar be-Mahut ha-Nefesh"); a medical work of Galen from the Arabic of Ḥunain ibn Isḥaḳ ("Sefer ha-Hola'im weha-Miḳrim"); three chapters of Galen's Καταγενή, with the same title in Hebrew characters; Maimonides' treatise on sexual intercourse; the "Aphorisms" of Maimonides.

The other translations of the second half of the thirteenth century were by:

Albalag, Isaac: Ghazali's "Maḳaṣid al-Falasifah"; Elijah Cohen's "Maḳamah" (similar to the "Assemblies" of Ḥariri), under the title "Megillat ha-'Ofer."

Almoli, Nethaneel: Maimonides' commentary on Ḳodashim.

Ḥayyim ibn Vives: Farewell letter of Ibn Sa'igh to 'Ali ben 'Abd al-'Aziz ibn al-Imam of Granada.

Jacob ben Moses ibn 'Abbasi: Maimonides' commentary on Nashim.

Joseph al-Fawwal: Maimonides' Mishnah commentary on Mo'ed.

Ma'arabi, Nahum: Maimonides' "Iggeret Teman" ("Petaḥ Tiḳwah"); Isaac Israeli's, or Jacob ben Nissim's, commentary on the "Sefer Yeẓirah"; Joseph ibn Zaddiḳ's "Microcosmos" ("Ha-'Olam ha-Ḳaṭan"); Saadia's commentary on the thirteen hermeneutic rules of R. Ishmael ("Shelosh-'Esreh Middot").

Shem-Ṭob ibn Falaquera: Ibn Gabirol's "Meḳor Ḥayyim."

Shem-Ṭob ben Isaac: Averroes' Middle Commentary on "De Anima"; Razi's "Al-Manṣuri"; Zahrawi's "Al-Taṣrif."

Solomon ibn Ayyub: Averroes' "De Cœlo et Mundo"; Avicenna's "Arjuza"; Ibn Janaḥ's "Kitab al-Taswiyah"; Maimonides' "Kitab al-Fara'iḍ."

Solomon ibn Ya'aḳub: Maimonides' commentary on Neziḳin.

A great number of Arabic works on mathematics, medicine, astronomy, and philosophy, especially by Averroes, were translated during the fourteenth century. The leading translator in the first twenty years of that century was KALONYMUS BEN KALONYMUS BEN MEÏR (Maestro Calo), who rendered the following Arabic works into Hebrew:

Al-Farabi's treatise on the intellect ("Ma'amar be-Sekel weha-Muskal").

Al-Farabi's division of the sciences ("Ma'amar be-Mispar ha-Ḥokmot").

Al-Farabi's treatise on the method of studying philosophy ("Iggeret be-Siddur Ḳeri'at ha-Ḥokmot").

Al-Kindi's treatises on nativities ("Iggeret be-Ḳiẓẓur ha-Ma'amar be-Moladot") and on the influence of the heavenly bodies on rain ("Iggeret be-'Illot").

Al-Kindi's treatise on humidity and rain ("Iggeret be-Laḥit ube-Maṭar").

'Ali Ibn Riḍwan's "Kitab al-'Imad fi Uṣul al-Ṭibb" ("Ha-'Ammad be-Shoroshe ha-Refu'ah").

Archimedes' treatise on the sphere and the cylinder, from the version of Kosta ben Luka.

Averroes' commentaries on the "Topics" ("Bi'ur Sefer Ṭobiḳi") and on "Sophisms" ("Bi'ur Sufisṭiḳa").

Averroes' Great Commentary on the "Second Analytics" ("Bi'ur Sefer ha-Mofet").

Averroes' Middle Commentaries on "Physics"; on "De Generatione et Corruptione" ("Sefer ha-Hawayah weha-Hefsed"); on "Meteora" ("Otot ha-Shamayim").

Translations of Averroes. Averroes' Middle Commentary on the "Metaphysics" ("Sefer Mah she-Aḥar ha-Ṭeba'").

Averroes' dissertations on the first book of the "First Analytics."

Commentary on the Καρπός of Ptolemy, from the Arabic version of Abu Ja'far Aḥmad ben Yusuf ben Ibrahim ("Sefer ha-Peri ha-Niḳra Me'ah Dibburim").

Galen's treatise on clysters and colic, from the version of Ḥunain ibn Isḥaḳ ("Sefer Galyanus be-Ḥaḳna ube-Kulga").

Galen's essay on bleeding ("Sefer Galyanus be-Haḳḳazah").

Nichomæus of Gerasa's treatise on arithmetic, with a commentary of Abu Sulaiman Rabiya ibn Yaḥya.

Ptolemy's treatise on the planets ("Be-'Inyane ha-Kokabim ha-Nebukim").

Thabet ibn Kurrah's work on geometry, "Fi al-Shakl al-Kuṭṭa" ("Sefer ha-Temunah ha-Ḥittukit").

Treatise on the triangle by Abu Sa'adan.

Treatise on mathematical propositions ("Sefer Meshalim be-Tishboret").

Treatise on Euclid's five geometrical bodies in relation to the theory of Apollonius, and the commentary of Simplicius.

Treatise on cylinders and cones ("Ma'amar be-Iẓṭawwonot ube-Ḥiddudim").

Treatise on plants, attributed to Aristotle, with Averroes' commentary ("Sefer ha-Zemaḥim").

Treatise on animals ("Iggeret Ba'ale Ḥayyim"), from the twenty-first treatise of the encyclopedia of the Brethren of Sincerity (Mantua, 1557).

Another important translator from the Arabic, and of the same period, was Samuel ben Judah (Bonjudas) Males. His translations include:

Abu Abdallah Mohammed ibn Mu'ad of Seville on the eclipse of the sun, July 3, 1097, and on the dawn ("Iggeret be-'Ammud ha-Shaḥar").

Abu Isḥaḳ al-Zarḳalah on the movement of the fixed stars ("Ma'amar be-Tenu'at ha-Kokabim ha-Ḳayyamim").

Abu Mohammed Jabbar ibn Aflaḥ's compendium of the "Almagest."

Alexander of Aphrodisias on the intellect ("Ma'amar Aleksander al-Firduzi").

Averroes' Middle Commentary on Aristotle's "Nichomachean Ethics."

Averroes' commentary on Plato's "Republic."

Averroes' Short Commentary on the "Organon"; on geometrical bodies (books xxx. and xxxi. of Euclid), a supplement to the translation of Kalonymus ben Kalonymus; commentary on the "Almagest," i.-iii.

Dissertations on some obscure passages of Averroes' commentary on the "Organon," by Abu al-Ḳasim ibn Idris, Abu al-Ḥajjaj ibn Ṭalmus, Abu al-'Abbas Aḥmad ben Ḳasim, and 'Abd al-Raḥman ben Tahir.

Other Arabic works were translated in the fourteenth century by:

Ibn Vives al-Lorqui: Various books of the "Short Canon" of Avicenna.

Isaac ben Joseph ibn Pulgar: Ghazali's "Maḳaṣid al-Falasifah" ("Kawwanot ha-Filosufim").

Isaac ben Nathan of Cordova: Maimonides' "Maḳalah fi al-Tauḥid" ("Ma'amar ha-Yiḥud"), Tabrizi's commentary on Maimonides' twenty-five premises, and probably Joseph ibn 'Aknin's metaphysical essay.

Joseph ben Abraham ibn Waḳḳar: A medical work ("Sefer Refu'ot") and Zahrawi's "Kitab al-Taṣrif."

Moses ben Samuel ben Asher: Averroes' commentary on "Logic."

Moses ben Solomon of Beaucaire: Averroes' Great Commentary on the "Metaphysics."

Nathan Judah ben Solomon: Ibn Abi Ṣalt Umayya's medical work ("Kelal Ḳazer weha-Sammim ha-Nifradim") and Ghazali's "Maḳaṣid" ("Kawwanot ha-Filosufim").

Nethaneel ben Meshullam (or Menahem ben Nethaneel): Judah ibn Balaam's treatise on the Hebrew accents ("Horayyat ha-Ḳore").

Samuel Motot: Abraham ibn Daud's "Al-'Aḳidah al-Rafi'ah" ("Emunah Ramah"; the same work was translated, under the title "Emunah Nisa'ah," by Solomon Labi). Samuel Motot translated also passages from pseudo-Ibn Ezra ("Sefer ha-'Aẓamim").

Shem-Ṭob Ardotial: Isaac Israeli's ritual work ("Miẓwot Zemaniyyot").

Samson ben Solomon: The compendium of Galen's writings by the Alexandrians ("Ha-Ḳibbuẓim le-Aleksandriyim").

Solomon Dapiera: Moses ben Tobi's commentary on the didactic poem "Al-Saba'niyyah" ("Batte ha-Nefesh").

Solomon ibn Patir: Ibn Haitham's astronomical work "Ḳaul fi Hi'at al-'Alam."

Todros Todrosi: Averroes' Middle Commentaries on the "Poetics" and "Rhetoric," the three essays **Aristotelian** against Avicenna, the treatise on the intellect, **Com-** Avicenna's "Naja," and Al-Farabi's philo- **mentaries.** sophical questions, "'Uyun al Masa'il" ("'En Mishpaṭ ha-Derushim").

————Averroes' treatise against Ghazali's "Tahafut al-Falasifah" ("Happalat ha-Happalah").

————Ghazali's answers to philosophical questions ("Ma'amar bi-Teshubot She'elot Nish'al Mehem").

————Pseudo-Ibn Ezra's "Sefer ha-'Aẓamim," and Joseph ibn Waḳḳar's and Solomon ibn Ya'ish's supercommentaries on Ibn Ezra's commentary on the Pentateuch.

With the fourteenth century the era of translations from the Arabic was practically closed, only a few works being translated during the fifteenth and sixteenth centuries. These were:

Ḥayyim ibn Musa: A medical work of Al-Jazzar.

Isaac ben Joseph Alfasi: Ghazali's "Mishkat al-Anwar" ("Mashkit ha-Orot we-Pardes ha-Niẓanim").

Maẓliaḥ of Galilee and Solomon Ma'arabi: Isaac Alfasi's rules relating to the treatise Ketubot.

Moses Galina: An astronomical treatise of Omar ibn Mohammed Meṣuman ("Sefer Mezuḳḳaḳ"). Moses Galina translated also a work on astrology ("Mishpaṭ ha-Mabbaṭim") and one on geomancy ("Sefer ha-Goralot").

Moses ben Joseph Aruvas: The pseudepigraphic work known as the Aristotelian "Theology."

Saadia ben David al-Adeni: Ghazali's "Zakat al-Nufus." (Saadia declared this to be his own work.)

Tanḥum Moses of Beaucaire: Hippocrates' "Prognostics" ("Panim le-Panim").

Zerahiah ha-Levi Saladin: Ghazali's "Tahafut al-Falasifah" ("Mappalat ha-Pilusufim").

Several translations from the Arabic were made in the second half of the nineteenth century: Reck-

endorf translated the Koran (Leipsic, 1857); Joseph Derenbourg translated Maimonides' commentary on Seder Ṭohorot (Berlin, 1887–89); fragments of Saadia's commentaries on Proverbs, Isaiah, and Job were translated by Derenbourg, Meyer Lambert, and Wilhelm Bacher; Isaac Broydé translated Baḥya's "Ma'ani al-Nafs" ("Torot ha-Nefesh," Paris, 1896).

The following are among the numerous works translated anonymously by Jewish authors:

Sahl ibn Bishr, astrological work, under the title "Kelalim"; four works attributed to Isaac Israeli: (1) "Kitab al-Adwiyat al-Mufridah wal-Aghdhiyah," on diet ("Sefer **Anonymous** Meḥubbar mi-Ma'amar ha-Rishonim be-Ṭeba' **Transla-** ha-Mezonot we-Koḥatam"); (2) "Kitab al- **tions.** Bul" ("Sefer Meḥubbar mi-Ma'amar ha-Rishonim be-Yedi'at ha-Sheten"); (3) "Kitab al-Ḥummayat"; (4) "Aphorisms" ("Musar ha-Rofe'im"); Saadia's "Emunot"; Hai Gaon's treatise on oaths ("Mishpeṭe Shebu'ot"); Responsa of the Geonim (Naṭronai, Saadia, Sherira, Hai); Japheth ben Ali's commentary on the Pentateuch; Joshua's "Teshubot ha-'Iḳḳarim" and Bereshit Rabbah; Judah ibn Baalam's works on homonyms ("Kitab al-Tajnis"), on the particle ("Otot ha-'Inyanim"), and on "Verba Denominativa," "Al-Af'al al-Mushtaḳḳah min al-Asma'" ("Ha-Po'alim Shehem me-Gizrot ha-Shemot"); Moses ibn Ezra's "Kitab al-Ḥada'iḳ fi Ma'ani al-Mujaz wal-Ḥaḳiḳah" ("Arugat ha-Bosem"); Joseph ibn Zaddiḳ's "Microcosm" ("'Olam Ḳaṭan"); Maimonides' treatises on the calendar ("Sefer ha-'Ibbur"), on happiness, "Maḳalah fi al-Sa'adah" ("Pirḳe ha-Haẓlaḥah"), and on forced conversions ("Iggeret ha-Shemad"), responsa on hemorrhoids, "Fi al-Bawasir" ("Ha-Ma'amar be-Refu'at ha-Ṭeharim"), on sexual intercourse, "Fi al-Jama'ah" ("Ma'amar ha-Mishgal"), and on poisons, "Al-Sumum wal-Mutaḥarriz min al-Adwiyah al-Ḳitalah," and the commentary on Hippocrates' "Aphorisms"; Joseph ibn 'Aḳnin's "Maḳalah fi Ṭibb al-Nafs" ("Marpe le-Nefesh"); Abraham Maimonides' "Kifayah"; Moses Abulafia's theological work "Ma'amar Elohi"; Joseph ibn Naḥmias' astronomical work "Nur al-'Alam" ("Or 'Olam"); Joseph ibn Waḳḳar's work on the Sefirot.

The oldest known Hebrew translation from the Latin belongs to the thirteenth century. About 1250 Solomon ben Moses Melgueiri translated the treatise known as "De Somno et Vigilia" and attributed to Aristotle ("Ha-Shanah weha-Yeḳiẓah"); Averroes' commentary on the third book of Aristotle's "Metaphysics"; Avicenna's "De Cœlo et Mundo"; and Matthæus Platearius' "De Simplici Medicina." About the same time Berechiah ben Naṭronai Krespia ha-Naḳdan gave a Hebrew version of Adelard of Bath's "Quæstiones Naturales," and of a "Lapidary" containing a description of sixty-three kinds of stones. Toward the end of the same century Samuel ben Jacob of Capua rendered into Hebrew, under the general title "Meha-'Eẓah weha-Ṭeba'im," the Latin version "De Medicamentarum Purgationum Delectio," or "Castigatione," of a work of Mesue the Elder. About the same time Hillel ben Samuel translated the Latin version of Hippocrates' "Aphorisms" by Constantinus Africanus, and "Chirurgia Burni."

The fourteenth century, an age of translations from the Arabic, was equally fertile in translations from the Latin. About 1305 Estori Farḥi translated, under the title "Targum Sefer Refu'ot," Armengaud Blaise's "De Remediis," and, under the title "Sefer **From the** ha-Kibbusim," an anonymous work on **Latin.** purgatives that had been rendered into Latin from the Arabic by Elijah ben Judah. In 1320 Hezekiah ben Ḥalafta gave a Hebrew version of Petrus Hispanus' treatise on logic ("Higgayon"). About the same time Samuel ben Benveniste translated, under the title "Menaḥem Meshib Nafshi," Boethius' "De Consolatione Philosophiæ." In 1327 Israel Caslari translated, under the title "Ma'amar be-Hanhagat ha-Beri'ut," Arnaud de Villeneuve's "Regimen Sanitatis."

More important than the above translations from the Latin were those made by Leone Romano, who, toward the middle of the same century, rendered into Hebrew the following works: Ægidius, "De Esse et Essentia" ("Ma'amar ha-Nimẓa weha-Meẓi'ut"); his treatises on the faculties of the soul ("Ma'amar Hebdale Koḥot ha-Nefesh we-Ḥilluḳehem"), and on syllogisms ("Ma'amar ha-Hawayah ha-Heḳḳeshiyyah"); his commentary on the third book of Aristotle's "De Anima"; and extracts from the commentary on Aristotle's "De Demonstratione"; Albertus Magnus' commentary on the third book of Aristotle's "De Anima," and various extracts from Albertus Magnus' works; Alexander the Minarite's glosses to Aristotle's "Metaphysics"; extracts from Angelo de Camerino's works; the "Liber de Causis" ascribed to Aristotle; Thomas Aquinas' "Treatise on Ideas," and extracts from his "Contra Gentiles" ("Neged ha-Ummot"); Averroes' "De Substantia Orbis" ("'Eẓem ha-Shamayim"); Boethius' "De Unitate et Uno" ("Ma'amar ha-Eḥad weha-Aḥadut"). Other translations from the Latin were as follows: Johannes Paulinus' treatise on the medical virtues of the skin of the serpent ("Ma'amar bi-Segullot 'Or ha-Naḥash"), by David ibn Bilia; Francesco dei Cenneli's, Gentile da Foligno's, and John of Burgundy's "Consilia" ("'Eẓah"), by Joshua of Bologna; Arnaud de Villeneuve's treatise "De Vinis" ("Ha-Dibbur be-Yenot"), and Bernard of Gordon's and Gilbert's treatises on fevers, both translated by Judah Nathan ("En Bongodas" and "Bonjues"); Bernard de Gordon's "Lilium Medicinæ" ("Peraḥ ha-Refu'ot"), by Moses ben Samuel of Roccambra (John of Avignon) and by Jekuthiel ben Solomon of Narbonne ("Shoshan ha-Refu'ah"); Leon's "Historia de Prœliis" ("Toledot Aleksander"), by Immanuel ben Jacob Bonfils; Bernard Alberti's "Materia Medica" ("Mebo ha-Melek"), Arnaud de Villeneuve's "Medicationis Parabolæ" and his work on digestion and purgatives, the commentary of Gerard de Solo on the ninth book of Razi's "Al-Manẓuri," and Petrus Hispanus' treatise on logic, all by Abraham Abigdor (Bonet) ben Meshullam ben Solomon; Gerard de Solo's commentary on the ninth book ("Pathology") of Razi and his manual of medicine ("Meyashsher ha-Matḥilim"), a chapter on the relation between astronomy and medicine attributed to Hippocrates, and Bernard de Gordon's "Lilium Medicinæ" and "Prognostic," all by Leon Joseph of Carcassonne; Arnold de Villeneuve's "Digestiva," by Todros ben Moses Yom-Ṭob; Arnold de Villeneuve's "De Judiciis Astronomiæ" ("Panim la-Mishpaṭ") and Sacrobosco's "Sphæra Mundi" ("Moreh ha-Ofannim"), by Solomon ben Abraham Abigdor (the first work was translated by him at the age of fifteen); Arnold de Villeneuve's "Tabula Super Vita Brevis," by Bonenfante of Milhaud; Ibn Rijal's astronomical work from the Latin version of Ægidius or of Petro de Regio ("Mishpaṭe ha-Kokabim"), by Solomon ben David Davin.

The fifteenth century was for the Hebrew translations from the Latin what the fourteenth was for those from the Arabic; it was the richer in literary productions, but with it the era of translations closed. The most important of the translated works in that century were:

Abraham ben Joseph ben Naḥmias: Thomas Aquinas' commentary on Aristotle's "Metaphysics."

Abraham Solomon Catalan: Albertus Magnus' "Philosophica Pauperum" ("Ḳizẓur ha-Filosofia ha-Ṭib'it"), and Marsilius' "Questions" on the "Isagoge" of Porphyry, on the "Categories," and on hermeneutics.

Abu al-Khair: Albubather's "Liber de Nativitatibus" ("Sefer ha-Moladot") and Rajil's astronomical work "Completus."

Asher ben Moses Valabrega: Guy de Chauliac's "Chirurgia Parva."

Azariah ben Joseph ben Abba Mari: Boethius' "De Consolatione Philosophiæ," the twenty-eighth book of **Medieval** Zahrawi's "Liber Practicæ" (after the Latin **Science and** of Simon of Genoa), the second book of De **Philosophy.** "Simplicia" of Dioscorides, and Gerard de Sabbionetta's astronomical work "Theorica."

Baruch ben Isaac ibn Ya'ish: Aristotle's "Metaphysics" and the tales, "Gesta Romanorum" ("Sefer Ḥanok"), of Petrus Alfonsi.

Benjamin ben Isaac of Carcassonne: Juan de Burgundia's treatise on the spread of the plague ("Be-'Ippush ha-Awwir weha-Deber," or "'Ezer Eloah").

David ben Jacob Meïr: John of Gmünd's astronomical work.

David ibn Shoshan ben Samuel of Avignon: Thomas Bicot's "Textus Abbreviatus Aristotelis, Super VIII. Libros Physicæ et Tota Naturalis Philosophia" ("Toledot Adam").

Elijah ben Joseph Ḥabillo: Thomas Aquinas' "Quæstiones Disputatæ," "Quæstio de Anima," "De Anima Facultatibus" ("Ma'amar be-Koḥot ha-Nefesh," published by Jellinek in "Philosophie und Kabbalah," Leipsic, 1854), and "De Universalibus"; Questions on Thomas Aquinas' treatise on "Being and Quality" ("She'elot Ma'amar be-Nimẓa ube-Mahut"); Occam's "Summa Totius Logices" and "Quæstiones Philosophicæ"; Aristotle's "De Causa"; and Vincenz de Beauvais's "De Universalibus."

Ephraim Mizraḥi: Georg Purbach's astronomical work "Theorica" ("Ṭe'oriḳa ha-Niḳra Mahalak ha-Kokabim").

Isaac Cabret (or Cabrit): John Sancto Amanelo's "Expositio in Antidotarium Nicolai."

Joseph ben Benveniste: Joshua ben Joseph ibn Vives al-Lorqui's treatise on the effects of nourishment, and on the simple and compound medicaments ("Gerem ha-Ma'alot").

Judah Shalom (Astruc) ben Samuel: Petrus Hispanus' "Parva Logica" and his commentary on Hippocrates' "Aphorisms."

Meïr Alguadez: Aristotle's "Ethics" and "Economics."

Mordecai Finzi: The Alfonsine Tables.

Moses ben Abraham of Nîmes: The Alfonsine Tables.

Moses ben Maẓliaḥ: Serapion's "Simplicia," from the Latin of Gerard de Cremona.

Phinehas ben Ẓebi ben Nethaneel: Raimundus Lullus' "Ars Brevis."

Solomon ben Moses Shalom: Antonius Guainerius' "De Febribus" ("Kelal meha-Ḳaddaḥut") and Bartolomeo Montagnana's "Consilium" ("Meha-'Ezah").

Thaddeus: Treatise on fevers ("Kelal Ḳaẓer 'al Minhag ha-Ḳaddaḥut").

After the sixteenth century Hebrew translations from the Latin became very scarce. The few works translated included: a treatise on eclipses of the sun and moon ("Ma'amar Nikbad be-Liḳḳuyot Shamshiyyot we-Yeraḥiyyot"), by Moses ben Abraham Sahlun; Albertus' (Magnus ?) "Questions and Answers on the Six Natural Things Required by the Body According to the Science of Medicine," by Moses ibn Ḥabib; an ethical work ("Ẓemaḥ Ẓaddiḳ," Venice, 1600), by Leon de Modena; Thomas Aquinas' "Summa Theologiæ Contra Gentiles," by Joseph Ẓahalon; the letters of Seneca, by Judah Leon ben Eliezer Brieli (published in "Kerem Ḥemed," ii. 119 et seq.); Spinoza's "Ethics," by Solomon Rubin ("Ḥeḳer Eloah"); the thirteenth chapter of Tacitus' history, by Solomon Mandelkern.

During the sixteenth and seventeenth centuries very few works of any kind were translated into Hebrew; but with the Haskalah movement in Rus-

Modern Times.

sia and Galicia the works of prominent European writers began to be rendered into that language. The following is a list of them, given under the heading of the language from which the translations were made:

English. Aguilar, Grace: "Vale of Cedars" ("'Emeḳ ha-Arazim," by Abraham Shalom Friedberg, Warsaw, 1875).

Bunyan: "Pilgrim's Progress" (transl. by S. Hoga, London, 1845).

Byron: "Hebrew Melodies" ("Shire Yeshurun," by Solomon Mandelkern, Leipsic, 1890).

Cumberland, Richard: "The Jew" ("Ish Yehudi," by Joseph Brill, Wilna, 1878).

Defoe, Daniel: "Robinson Crusoe" ("Kur 'Oni," by Isaac Moses Rumseh, Wilna, 1861).

Disraeli, Benjamin: "David Alroy" ("Ḥoṭer mi-Geza' Yishai," by Abraham Abel Rekowski, Warsaw, 1880); "Tancred" ("Nes la-Goyim," by Judah Löb Levin, ib. 1883).

Eliot, George: "Daniel Deronda" (transl. by David Frischman, Warsaw, 1894).

Longfellow: "Excelsior" (transl. by Henry Gersoni, New York, 1871).

Milton: "Paradise Lost" ("Wa-Yegaresh ha-Adam," by Isaac Edward Salkinson; also under the title "Toledot Adam we-Ḥawwah," by Samuel Raffalowich, Jerusalem, 1892).

Mocatta, F. D.: "The Jews in Spain" ("Ha-Yehudim bi-Sefarad," by Israel Be'er Franklin, Jerusalem, 1876); "The Jews in Spain and Portugal, and the Inquisition" (transl. by Isaac Hirsch Barth, Cracow, 1888).

Shakespeare: "Othello" and "Romeo and Juliet" ("Itiel" and "Rom we-Ya'el," by Isaac Edward Salkinson, Vienna, 1874 and 1878).

Spencer, Herbert: "Education, Intellectual, Moral, and Physical" ("Sefer ha-Ḥinnuk," by Judah Löb Davidovich, Warsaw, 1894).

Zangwill, Israel: "Ghetto Tragedies" ("Maḥazot ha-Geṭṭo," by S. L. Gordon, Warsaw, 1896).

French. Bernardin de Saint Pierre: "Harmonie de la Nature" ("Sulam ha-Ṭeba'," by Joseph Herzberg, Wilna, 1850).

Carnot, Hippolyte: "Histoire de la Révolution Française" ("Ha-Mahpekah ha-Ẕarfatit," by Ludvipol, Warsaw, 1898).

Daudet, Alphonse: A short novel transl. by Abraham Shalom Friedberg, in "Me-Sifrut ha-'Ammim."

Florian, Jean Pierre Claris de: "Numa Pompilius" ("Eli'ezer we-Naftali" [?], by Aaron Margolis, Warsaw, 1864; also by Isaac Troller, Wilna, 1867).

Halévy, Ludovic: A short novel transl. by Abraham Shalom Friedberg, in "Me-Sifrut ha-'Ammim."

Hugo, Victor: "L'Ane" ("Ha-Ḥamor weha-Filosof," by Wolfgang Gronich, Vienna, 1881); "La Guerre Civile" ("Milḥemet 'ben Aḥim," by J. Lewner, Warsaw, 1896); "Le Dernier Jour de la Vie d'un Condamne" (transl. by Safran, ib. 1898).

Kahn, Zadoc: "L'Esclavage Selon la Bible et le Talmud."

Maspero: "Histoire des Anciens Peuples de l'Orient" (transl. by Ludvipol and Joseph Halévy, Warsaw, 1898).

Massé, Victor: "Histoire d'une Miette" ("Toledot Pas Leḥem," by Abraham Jacob Tiktin, Warsaw, 1882); "Une Episode de la Révolution Française" (transl. by Moses Weissberg, ib. 1884).

Maupassant, Guy de: "Selections" ("Ketabim Nibḥarim," 7 vols., Warsaw, 1904–5, by N. Slouschz).

Mickiewicz, Adam: "Le Livre de la Nation Polonaise et les Pelerins Polonais" ("Sefer 'Am Polonim we-Gere Polonim," by Moses Ezekiel Ascarelli, Paris, 1881).

Racine: "Esther" (transl. by Joseph Haltren and Solomon J. Rapoport) and "Athalie" (transl. by Meïr ha-Levi Letteris, Prague, 1843).

Scribe: "La Juive" ("Raḥel ha-Yehudiyyah," by Süsmann Marik, Warsaw, 1886).

Sue, Eugène: "Les Mystères de Paris" ("Mistere Pariz," by Kalman Schulman, Wilna, 1857–76); "Le Juif Errant" ("Ha-Ẕofeh be-Ereẓ Nod," by Simḥah Posner, Warsaw, 1856–1873); "Les Sept Péchés Capitana" ("Sheba' Ḥaṭṭa'ot She'ol," by Lasar Schapira, in "Meged Yeraḥim").

Verne, Jules: "Vingt Mille Lieues sous les Mers" ("Be-Meẓulot Yam," by Isaac Wolf Sperling); "Voyage au Centre de la Terre" ("Be-Beṭen ha-Adamah," idem).

Zola: Three short stories translated by S. Sluschtsch. Warsaw, 1898.

Z——ski, L.: Novel, published by the "Archives Israélites," depicting Jewish life in Russia ("Ḥatan Damim," by Abraham Jacob Bruck, Lemberg, 1878).

German. Andersen: "Märchen und Erzählungen" (transl. by D. Frischmann, Warsaw, 1897).

Bernstein: "Aus dem Reiche der Natur" ("Yedi'at ha-Ṭeba'," by D. Frischmann, ib. 1882–85); "Brahmanische Weisheit" ("Mishle Brakman," by Schorr, Lemberg, 1867).

Börne, Ludwig: "Briefe aus Paris" (transl. by S. J. E. Triwasch, Warsaw, 1897).

Campe: "Theophron" ("Musar Haskel," by Baruch Schönfeld, Prague, 1831; transl. also by Arnopolsky, Odessa, 1863); on sea-voyages ("Massa'ot ha-Yam," by Elias Levi, Zolkiev, 1818); "Sittenbüchlein" (transl. by David Zamoscz, Breslau, 1818); "Die Entdeckung Amerika's" ("Meẕi'at Ameriḳa," by Moses Mendelsohn, Altona, 1807; transl. also by David Zamoscz, Breslau, 1824); "Robinson der Jüngere" (transl. by David Zamoscz, ib. 1824).

Cassel, David: "Geschichte und Literatur der Juden" (transl. by D. Radner, Warsaw, 1880).

Eckhard: German transl. of Philo's "Legatio ad Caium" ("Malakut Filon ha-Yehudi," by Marcus Aaron Günzburg, Warsaw, 1837).

Ellenberger, Henri: "Die Leiden und Verfolgungen der Juden" ("Ẕal we-Or," by Hermann Horowitz, Presburg, 1882).

Francolm: "Die Juden und die Kreuzfahrer" ("Ha-Yehudim be-Angliya," by Miriam Mosessohn).

Goethe: "Faust" ("Ben Abuyah," by Meïr ha-Levi Letteris, Vienna, 1860); "Hermann und Dorothea" ("Ha-Ẕedeḳ," by Marcus Rothenburg, Warsaw, 1857).

Grätz, Heinrich: "Geschichte der Juden" ("Dibre ha-Yamim li-Bene Yisrael," by S. P. Rabbinowitz, Warsaw, 1890).

Güdemann: "Geschichte des Erziehungswesens" ("Ha-Torah weha-Ḥayyim ba-Arazot ha-Ma'arab li-Yeme ha-Benayim," by Abraham Shalom Friedberg, ib. 1893–95).

Gustavsohn: "Sammlung von Jugenderzählungen" (transl. by N. Pius, Warsaw, 1896–98); "Die Drei Brüder" ("Shelashot Aḥim "); "Der Hirt und die Königstochter" ("Ha-Ro'eh we-Bat ha-Melek "); "Der Schlaflose König" (the last three transl. by J. Lewner, Warsaw, 1896–98).

Heine, Heinrich: "Judah ha-Levi," a poem (transl. by Solomon Luria, Warsaw, 1886).

Heise, Paul: "Sulamit" (transl. by S. Gordon, ib. 1896).

Herzberg, Frankel: "Die Vergeltung" ("Ha-Gemul," by P. Slonimsky, Odessa, 1867).

Herzl, Theodor: "Der Judenstaat" ("Medinat ha-Yehudim," by Michel Berkovitz, Warsaw, 1896); "Das Neue Ghetto" ("Ha-Geṭṭo he-Ḥadash," by Reuben Brainin, ib. 1898).

Hoffmann, Fr.: "Königssohn" ("Ben ha-Melek," by Moses Samuel Sperling, Warsaw, 1876); "Unredliches Gut" ("Naḥa-lah Mebohelet," by Manus Manassewitz, Wilna, 1887).

Honigmann: "Die Erbschaft" ("Ha-Yerushshah," by Samuel Joseph Fuenn, Wilna, 1884).

Jellinek, A.: "Der Jüdische Stamm in Nichtjüdischen Sprüchwörtern" (transl. by Elimelech Wechsler, in "Ha-Asif," vol. iii.).

Josephus: "Jüdische Alterthümer" ("Ḳadmoniyyot ha-Yehudim," by Kalman Schulman, Wilna, 1864); "Kriege" ("Milḥamot ha-Yehudim," idem, ib. 1884).

Kayserling: "Biographische Skizze des Menasseh ben Israel" ("Toledot Manasseh ben Yisrael," by Joseph Lasar Epstein, in "Ha-Karmel," iii.).

Klopstock, G.: "Der Tod Adams" ("Mot Adam," by Menahem M. Litinsky, Prague, 1817).

Kohn, S.: "Der Retter" ("Podeh we-Maẓẓil," by Lasar Isaac Schapira, Warsaw, 1866).

Kompert, L.: "Zwei Trümmer" ("Shete Ḥarabot," by Süsmann Marik, St. Petersburg, 1880; transl. also by Wolf Jawetz, Warsaw, 1887).

Kotzebue: "Der Schatz" ("Ha-Oẓer," by David Rosenhand, Warsaw, 1845); "Der Arme Poet" ("Ha-Meshorer ha-'Ani," by Isidor Brüstiger, Lemberg, 1884).

Lazarus, M.: "Der Prophet Jeremiah" (transl. by Reuben Brainin, Warsaw, 1896).

Lehmann, M.: "Der Graf und Jude" (transl. by Joseph Löb Petuchowsky, in "Ha-Lebanon," 1872; also by Samuel Joseph Fuenn, under the title "Ha-Ḥilluf," Wilna, 1873); "Das Licht der Diaspora" ("Ma'or ha-Golah," by Joseph Löb Petuchowsky, ib. 1890); "Bostanai" (transl. by Samuel Joseph Fuenn, ib. 1872).

Lessing, Gotthold Ephraim: "Nathan der Weise" ("Nathan he-Ḥakam," by S. Bacher, Vienna, 1866; transl. also by A. B. Gottlober, who rendered the Hebrew in the same meter as the original, ib. 1874); "Philotas" ("Abinadab," by J. Falkovich, Odessa, 1868); "Die Juden" ("Ha-Yehdim," by Jacob Kohn, Warsaw, 1875; also in verse by Hirsh Teller, Vienna, 1881); "Der Freigeist" ("Ḥonen we-Noten," by D. Kohn); "Miss

Sara Sampson" ("Sarah Bat Shimshon," by Israel Frenkel, Warsaw, 1887); "Fabeln" ("Lessing we-Sippuraw," by Moses Reicherson, New York, 1902).

Lippert, Julius: "Kulturgeschichte" ("Toledot Hashlamat ha-Adam," by David Frischmann, Warsaw, 1894–1901).

Maier: "Die Zerstörung von Betar" ("Harisut Beter," by Kalman Schulman, Wilna, 1858); "Elisha ben Abuyah" (in "Safah Berurah," idem, ib. 1847).

Manes: "Gesammelte Schriften" (transl. by Joseph Kuttner, Vienna, 1865).

Meisel: "Die Meiselgasse" (transl. by J. Lewner, Warsaw, 1897).

Mendelssohn, Moses: "Jerusalem" (transl. by A. B. Gottlober, Jitomir, 1867; also by Vladimir Federow, Vienna, 1876); "Die Sache Gottes" ("Ma'amar 'al ha-Hashgaḥah," by Samuel Joseph Fuenn, Wilna, 1872); "Phädon" (transl. by Isaiah Beer-Bing, Berlin, 1786).

Mosenthal: "Deborah" (transl. by David Radner, Warsaw, 1880).

Philippson, Ludwig: "Israelitische Religionslehre" ("Yesod ha-Dat ha-Yisraelit," by Isaac Beer Epstein, Königsberg, 1849); "Miriam die Hasmonäerin" ("Miryam ha-Ḥashmonit," by Joseph Lasar Epstein, Wilna, 1863); "Spanien und Jerusalem" ("Sefarad we-Yerushalayim," by Phöbus Dicker, in "Ha-Asif," vol. iii.); "Die Marranen" ("Nidḥe Yisrael," by Abraham Abel Rakowsky, Warsaw, 1875); "Jacob Tirado" ("Ya'aḳob Ṭirado," by Samuel Joseph Fuenn, Wilna, 1874); "Der Flüchtling aus Jerusalem" ("Ha-Paliṭ," by Miriam Mosessohn); "'Ezra ha-Sofer" (epic poem, transl. by Solomon Mandelkern, Vienna, 1886); "Das Martyrerthum" ("Ḳiddush ha-Shem," by Zupnik, Brody, 1867; "Jojachin" (transl. by S. Bacher, Vienna, 1859).

Reckendorf: "Geheimnisse der Juden" ("Zikronot le-Bet Dawid," by A. S. Friedberg, Warsaw, 1893–95; under the title "Mistere ha-Yehudim," the first volume was translated by Abraham Kaplan).

Reclam: "Gesundheitschlüssel" ("Netib Ḥayyim," by A. Schapira, Warsaw, 1887).

Samter: "Rabbi von Liegnitz" ("Rab le-Hoshia'," by Abraham Shalom Friedberg, Warsaw, 1886).

Samuely: "Aus dem Finsteren" (transl. by A. Mirsky, in "Keneset Yisrael," vol. iii.).

Schiller: "Spaziergang Unter den Linden" (transl. by Kalman Schulman, in "Safah Berurah," Wilna, 1847); "Philosophische Briefe" (transl. by Solomon Rubin, Lemberg, 1851); "Die Zerstörung Troja's" ("Harisat Ṭroya," in verse, by Micah Lebensohn, Wilna, 1851); "Die Sendung Moses" ("Dibre Emet," by Elias Levin, ib. 1866); "Die Braut von Messina" ("Medanim ben Aḥim," by Jacob Levin, Brody, 1868); "Die Räuber" ("Ha-Shodedim," by Moses Schulbaum, Lemberg, 1871); "Wilhelm Tell" (transl. by David Radner, Wilna, 1878); "Don Carlos" (by the same, ib. 1879); "Marie Stuart" (transl. by Solomon Kovner, ib. 1879); "Turandot" ("Tirẓah," by Osias Atlas, Przemysl, 1879); "Fiesco" ("Ḳesher Fiesko," by Samuel Apfel, Drohobicz, 1889); "Resignation" ("Amarti Yesh Tiḳwah," by Neumanowitz, Warsaw, 1888). Meïr ha-Levi Letteris translated a number of pieces in "Ayyelet ha-Shaḥar," Vienna, 1860.

Schleiden, M.: "Die Bedeutung der Juden" ("Mif'alot ha-Yehudim," by Arie Geronim Gordon, Wilna, 1882).

Schumacher, P.: "Berenika" (transl. by David Frischmann, Warsaw, 1895).

Steinschneider, Moritz: "Die Jüdische Literatur" ("Sifrut Yisrael," by Malter, Warsaw, 1899).

Tugendhold, W.: "Der Denunciat" ("Ha-Moser," or "Aḥarit Resha'," Breslau, 1847).

Weisel, L.: "Die Goldene Strasse" ("Reḥob ha-Zahab," by J. Lewner, Warsaw, 1897); "Die Falsche Beschuldigung" ("'Alilot Shaw," by Moses Samuel Sperling, Warsaw, 1878).

Wertheimer, Ritter von: "Jüdische Lehre und Jüdisches Leben" ("Emet we-Mishpaṭ," by Zupnik, Drohobicz, 1883).

Zschokke: "Das Abenteuer der Neujahrsnacht" ("Lel Shimmurim," by Isidor Margolis, Wilna, 1878).

Italian. Dante: "Divina Commedia" ("Mar'ot Elohim," by Saul Farmiggini, Triest, 1869).

Luzzatto, Simeon: "Discorso Circa il Stato Degli Hebrei, ch. xiii." (transl. by Isaac Reggio, in "Iggeret Yashar," vol. i.).

Marfei: "Merope," a tragedy (transl. by Samuel Aaron Romanelli, Rome, 1903).

Metastasio: "Isacco" ("Aḳedat Yiẓḥaḳ," by Elijah Bardach, Vienna, 1833); a poem ("Teshu'at Yisrael bi-Yede Yehudit," by Franco-Mendez, Rödelheim, 1804).

Polish. Kozlowski: "Estherka," a drama ("Ma'aseh Ester," by Israel Frankel, Warsaw, 1889).

Orzhesko: "Okanski" and "Mirtala" (transl. by Abraham Abel Rakowsky, Warsaw, 1886 and 1888).

Paulicki: On popular medicine ("Marpe le- 'Am," by Bezaleel Judah Eliasberg, Wilna, 1834, 1842; Jitomir, 1886).

Rinaldo Rinaldini: novel ("Lahaḳat Shodedim," by Ḥayyim Goldstein, Warsaw, 1859).

Russian. Bogron: "Poimannik" ("Ha-Nilkad be-Sheḥitot Anshe Resha'," by Isaac Andres, Warsaw, 1877).

Frug: Poems ("Kol Shire Frug," by Jacob Kaplan, Warsaw, 1898).

Harkavy: "Judah ha-Levi" (transl. by Abraham Shalom Friedberg, in "Keneset Yisrael," vol. ii., 1886).

Hufeland: "Enchiridion Medicon" ("Darke ha-Refu'ot," by Jacob Frohnberg, Jitomir, 1869).

Krilov: Fables ("Tiḳḳun Meshalim," by Moses Reicherson, Wilna, 1860).

Lewanda: "Genev i Milost Magnata" ("'Ir u-Benalot," by Samuel Löw Citron, in "Keneset Yisrael," 1886); "Abraham Yosefovich" ("Abraham ben Yosef," idem).

Rabbinovich, Osip: "Shtrafnoi" ("Ben 'Onesh," by Kanelsky, Odessa, 1865).

Turgenef: Short story transl. by Abraham Shalom Friedberg, in "Me-Sifrut ha-'Ammim."

Spanish. Cervantes: "Don Quixote" ("Abino'am ha-Gelili," by I. Fraenkel, Lemberg, 1871).

Crescas, Ḥasdai: "Tratado" ("Biṭṭul 'Iḳre Dat ha-Noẓarim," by Joseph ibn Shem-Ṭob, published by Ephraim Deinard, Kearny, N. J., 1894).

Escudero, Lorenzo (Abraham Peregrino): "Fortalezza del Judaismo y Confusion del Estraño" ("Ẓeriaḥ Bet El," by Marco Luzzatto of Triest [in manuscript]).

Morteira, Saul: "Tractado de la Verdad de la Ley" ("Torat Mosheh," by Isaac Gomez de Gosa [in manuscript]).

——**From the Hebrew:** Aside from the Arabic versions of the Bible, the Talmud, and the prayers (with which this article is not concerned), only three Arabic translations from the Hebrew **Into Arabic.** are extant: the travels of Eldad ha-Dani, by an anonymous translator; the Yosippon ("Yusuf ibn Karyun"), by Zechariah ibn Sa'id; and Isaac ibn Crispin's "Sefer ha-Musar" ("Maḥasin al-Adab"), by Joseph ibn Ḥasan, which is supposed by Steinschneider to have been itself an adaptation from the Arabic. Through the Hebrew versions of the Arabic scientific works the treasures of the East and of ancient Greece were opened to the West. Indeed, with the exception of a small number of Latin translations made directly from the Arabic, mostly with the assistance of Jewish interpreters, all the works from which the Latin world learned mathematics, astronomy, medicine, philosophy, and other sciences were translated from the Hebrew versions made from the Arabic. Although it is possible that some among the Latin translations of the twelfth century were made from the Hebrew, the oldest known dates only from the thirteenth century. About 1260 John of Capua translated, under the title "Directorium Vitæ Humanæ" (published by J. Derenbourg, Paris, 1887), Joel's Hebrew version of the "Kalilah wa-Dimnah." He translated also Maimonides' work on the dietary laws and Ibn Zuhr's medical work "Al-Taisir." Toward the end of the same century Armengaud Blasius translated Jacob ben Machir ibn Tibbon's treatise on the quadrant invented by the latter, under the title "Quadrans Novus" or "Quadrans Judaicus."

During the fourteenth century only a few works were translated from the Hebrew into Latin. Among these were the anonymous "Sefer ha-Ḥinnuk," on the precepts, and Abner of Burgos' "Iggeret ha-Gezerah." During the fifteenth century Latin literature was enriched with many valuable works from the Hebrew. About 1486 Elijah Delmedigo made the following translations: "Quæstiones Tres: i. De

Primo Motore; ii. De Mundi Efficientia; iii. De Esse Essentia et Uno" (Venice, 1501); "Averrois Quæs-tio in Libro Priorum" ("Analytics," Venice, 1497); Averroes' commentary on Plato's "Republic" (" De Regimine Civitatis"); "Averrois Commentatio [Summa] in Meteora Aristotelis," with **Into Latin.** fragments from Averroes' Middle Commentary (*ib.* 1488); "Averrois Commentatio [Media] in Metaph. Aristotelis," i.-vii. (*ib.* 1560); Averroes' proem to the Large Commentary on Aristotle's "Metaphysics," xii.; Averroes' "De Substantia Orbis"; "Sperma." Delmedigo's protector, Pico de Mirandola, translated at the same time the commentary of Menahem Recanati on the Pentateuch, the "Ḥokmat ha-Nefesh" ("Scientia Animæ") of Eleazar of Worms, and the "Sefer ha-Ma'alot" of Shem-Ṭob Falaquera. The teacher of Pico de Mirandola, Flavius Mithridates, translated thirty-eight fragments of various cabalistic works, Maimonides' epistle on resurrection, Levi ben Gershon's commentary on Canticles, and Judah's "Ma'amar ha-Hawwayah ha-Heḳḳeshiyyah" ("Sermo de Generatione Syllogismorum Simplicium et Compositorum in Omni Figura").

Very important contributions to Latin literature from the Jewish mystical writings were made at the end of the fifteenth century and at the beginning of the sixteenth by Cardinal Ægidius de Viterbo, who translated the Zohar, "Ginnat Egoz," "Sefer Razi'el," "Ma'areket Elahut," "'Eser Sefirot," and other cabalistic works. Among the translations of purely scientific works made in the sixteenth century, the most noteworthy are those of Abraham de Balmes, Kalonymus ben Judah (Maestro Calo), Jacob Mantino, and Moses Alatino. Abraham de Balmes translated Ibn Haitham's astronomical work ("Liber de Mundo") from the Hebrew version of Jacob ben Machir ibn Tibbon, and the "farewell letter" of the Arabic philosopher Ibn Baga or Avempace ("Epistolæ Expeditionis"). Kalonymus ben Judah translated Zerahiah ha-Levi's Hebrew version of Ghazali's "Tahafut al-Falasifah" ("Destructio," Venice, 1527), Samuel ibn Tibbon's Hebrew version of Averroes' treatise on the intellect ("De Conversione Intellectus," *ib.*), and Moses ibn Tibbon's Hebrew version of Alpetragius' treatise on astronomy (Venice, 1531). The translations of Jacob Mantino were: "Paraphrasis Averrois de Partibus et Generatione Animalium," with the commentary of Levi ben Gershon; Averroes' compendium of Aristotle's "Metaphysics"; the Middle Commentary on Aristotle's "Isagoge"; books i.-iv. of "Topics" and "Poetics" (Venice, 1550); a commentary on Plato's "Republic"; proem to the Large Commentary on the third book of Aristotle's treatise on the soul; proem to book xii. of Aristotle's "Metaphysics"; the Middle Commentary on Aristotle's "Physics"; Averroes' medical work "Colliget"; the first book of Avicenna's "Canon"; Maimonides' "Shemonah Peraḳim." Moses Alatino translated Moses ibn Tibbon's Hebrew version of Themistius' paraphrase of the four books of Aristotle's "De Cœlo" (Venice, 1574); Avicenna's "Canon"; Nathan ha-Me'ati's Hebrew version of Galen's commentary on a work of Hippocrates ("De Aëre, Aquis et Locis"). Among other works trans-

lated into Latin in the sixteenth century were: Ezobi's "Ḳa'arat Kesef" (by Reuchlin, Tübingen, 1512-14, and Jean Mercier, Paris, 1561); Levita's "Tishbi" (by Paul Fagius, 1541, who translated also the "Alfabeta de Ben Sira" and the "Sefer Amanah"); Benjamin of Tudela's travels (by Arias Montanas); the travels of Eldad ha-Dani (by G. Genebrard, Paris, 1584); Levita's grammatical works and Maimonides' treatise on logic (by Sebastian Münster, Basel, 1524 *et seq.*, who translated also the Yosippon, 1529-41); and a list of the 613 commandments from "SeMaG" (1533).

With the close of the sixteenth century the era of Latin translations, from the Hebrew, of Arabic scientific works ended, and the Jews ceased to serve as intermediaries between the civilizations of the East and the West. The work dropped by them was taken up by Christians, who had acquired from Jews their knowledge of Hebrew and other Oriental languages, and who made Latin translations of many Jewish writings of the Middle Ages. Foremost among these translators, in the first half of the seventeenth century, were the Buxtorfs; the elder Buxtorf translated the Biblical concordance, "Me'ir Netib," of Isaac Nathan ben Kalonymus and the "Iggeret Shelomim" ("Institutio Epistolaris Hebraica, sive de Conscribendis Epistolis Liber, cum Epistolarum Hebraicarum Centuria," Basel, 1610); the younger Buxtorf, Johannes, translated Maimonides' "Moreh Nebukim" ("Doctor Perplexorum," Basel, 1629) and Judah ha-Levi's "Cuzari" ("Liber Cosri," *ib.* 1660). Among the other Jewish works translated in the same century the most noteworthy were: Lipman-Mühlhausen's "Sefer ha-Niẓẓahon" (by John Heinrich Blendinger, Altdorf, 1645); the disputations of R. Jehiel and of Naḥmanides; Isaac Troki's "Ḥizzuḳ Emunah"; the "Toledot Yeshu"; the "travels" of R. Pethahiah and the "Megillat Wenz" (by Wagenseil); Cordovero's "Pardes Rimmonim" ("De Sanctissima Trinitate Contra Judæos," by Joseph Ciantes, Rome, 1664); Leon de Modena's dialogue on the subject of gambling (by August Pfeifer, Wittenberg, 1665; also by Thomas Hyde, Oxford, 1698, who translated Farissol's "Iggeret Orḥot 'Olam," under the title "Tractatus Itinerum Mundi," *ib.* 1691); the commentaries of Abravanel and others on Joshua; Moses Ḳimḥi's "Introductio ad Scientiam"; Joseph Yaḥya's commentary on Daniel; "Itinerarum Benjaminis of Tudela" (by Constantin l'Empereur); the "Alphabet of Ben Sira," "Megillat Antiochus," "Otiot de Rabbi 'Aḳiba," a part of Eldad ha-Dani's mythical travels, and Azariah dei Rossi's "Me'or 'Enayim" (all by Bartolocci in his "Bibliotheca Magna Rabbinica"); Abravanel's commentary on Daniel (by Hottinger); the "Idra Rabbah," the "Idra Zuṭa," the "Sifra de-Ẓeni'uta," the cabalistic essays of Naphtali Herz and Jacob Elhanan, the "Sha'ar ha-Shamayim" of Abraham Cohen de Herrera, and several of the writings of Isaac Luria (by Knorr von Rosenroth in his "Kabbala Denudata," Sulzbach, 1677-78); Maimonides' hilkot "'Abodat Yom ha-Kippurim," "Ḥamez u-Maẓẓah," "Ḳiddush ha-Ḥodesh," "Ta'aniyot," "Seder ha-'Abodah," and "Seder ha-Ḳorbonot" (by Ludwig

Christian Translators into Latin.

Compiegne de Weil, who translated also Abraham Yagel's catechism, "Leḳaḥ Ṭob"); the first part of Gans's "Zemaḥ Ṭob" (by Wilhelm Varot and also by Voisin); Zacuto's "Sefer ha-Yuḥasin," various parts of Maimonides' "Mishneh Torah," and part of the account of the travels of the Karaite Samuel ben David; Maimonides' "Yad," Talmud Torah and Teshubah (by Robertus Claverius).

Among the Latin translations of the eighteenth century the most noteworthy are: part of Maimonides' "Mishneh Torah" and extracts from the rabbinical commentaries on Psalms (by Heinrich Jacob Bashuysen, Hanover, 1705; Hanau, 1712); the "Sefer ha-Tappuaḥ" ("Biga Dissertationum," Giessen, 1706); Rashi's commentary on the Bible and the "Yosippon" (by John Frederick Breithaupt, Gotha, 1707, 1710); the Karaite Mordecai ben Nissim's "Dod Mordekai" ("Notitia Karæorum ex Tractate Mardochai," by Wolf, who translated also various fragments of Jewish writings in his "Bibliotheca Hebræa"); selections from the commentaries of Rashi, Abravanel, Ibn Ezra, and Isaiah di Trani on Joshua, and Moses Naḳdan's "Sha'ar ha-Neginot" ("Porta Accentuum," by John Georg Abicht); a part of Elijah Levita's "Shibre Luḥot" (by Nagel, Altdorf, 1758–71); portions of the "Taḥkemoni" (by Ure); Jedaiah Bedersi's "Beḥinat 'Olam" (by Uchtmann); the "Seder 'Olam Rabbah" (by Eduard Maier).

The following is a list of the works which have been translated from Hebrew into modern languages:

English. Aristotle, Pseudo-: "Sefer ha-Tappuaḥ," on the immortality of the soul (by Isidor Kalisch, Detroit, 1882).

Bedersi: "Beḥinat ha-'Olam" (by Tobias Goodman).

Benjamin of Tudela: "Massa'ot" (by Asher, London, 1840).

Ḥayyuj, Judah: "Two Treatises on Verbs Containing Treble and Double Letters," and the "Treatise on Punctuation" (by John W. Nutt, London and Berlin, 1870).

Joseph ha-Kohen: "Dibre ha-Yamim" (by Bialloblotzky, London, 1834–36).

Judah al-Ḥarizi: Portions of the "Taḥkemoni" (by F. de Sola Mendes, in "Jew. Chron." London, 1873).

Judah ha-Levi: Poems (by M. Breslau, in "Ginze Oxford," London, 1851; Edward G. King, in "Jew. Quart. Rev." vii. 464; Joseph Jacobs, in "Jewish Ideals"; Emma Lazarus, "Songs of a Semite," New York, 1882; Lady Magnus, "Jewish Portraits," London, 1897; A. Lucas, in "Jewish Year Book," London, 1898; Nina Davis, "Songs of an Exile," Philadelphia, 1901).

Levinsohn: "Efes Damim" (by Loewe, London, 1840).

Levita, Elijah: "Massoret ha-Massorah" (by Ch. D. Ginsburg, London, 1887).

Maimonides: "Moreh Nebukim" (by Michael Friedländer, London); parts of the "Mishneh Torah" (by H. Bernard and E. Solowcyczik, ib. 1863).

Mapu, Abraham: "Ahabat Ziyyon" (by Frank-Jaffe, London, 1887).

Nieto, David: "Maṭṭeh Dan" (by Loewe, London, 1842).

Pethahiah of Regensburg: "Massa'ot" (by Benisch, London, 1856).

Romanelli: "Massa' ba-Arab" (by Schiller-Szinessy, Cambridge, 1887).

Schwarz: "Dibre Yosef," geography of Palestine (by Isaac Leeser, Philadelphia, 1850).

Troki, Abraham: "Ḥizzuḳ Emunah" ("Faith Strengthened," by M. Mocatta, London, 1851).

"Yashar, Sefer ha-" (by Mordecai Noah, New York, 1840).

"Yezirah, Sefer" (by Isidor Kalisch, 1877).

Yosippon: Parts (by Gaster, in "Jerahmeel," London, 1899).

French. Abraham ibn Ezra: "Ma'adanne Melek" ("Délices Royales, ou le Jeu des Echecs," by Hollaenderski, Paris, 1864).

Alfonsi, Petrus: "Sefer Ḥanok," tales (by Picques).

Bedersi, Jedaiah ben Abraham: "Beḥinat ha-'Olam" (by Philippe Aquinas and Michel Beer).

Benjamin of Tudela: "Massa'ot" (by Jean Philippe Boratier, Paris, 1734).

Bilia, David ben Yom-Ṭob ibn: "Yesodot ha-Maskil" (by S. Klein, Metz, 1849).

Caro, Joseph: Shulḥan 'Aruk (extracts from the first and second parts under the title "Rituel du udaïsme," by Pavly and Neviasky, Orleans, 1896–1901).

Eldad ha-Dani (transl. by Carmoly, Brussels, 1834).

Joseph ha-Kohen: "'Emeḳ ha-Baka" ("Vallée des Pleurs," by Julian Sée, Paris, 1881).

Judah al-Ḥarizi: "Taḥkemoni" (by Carmoly, Brussels, 1843–1844; parts were translated by Sylvestre de Sacy).

Maimonides: Treatise on poisons ("Traité de Poisons," by I. M. Rabbinowicz, Paris, 1865); "Moreh Nebukim" ("Guide des Égarés," by S. Munk, Paris, 1856).

Modena, Leon of: Dialogue on the subject of gambling ("Le Joueur Converti," by Carmoly).

Pethahiah of Regensburg: "Sibbub Rab Petaḥyah" (by Carmoly, who translated also, under the title "Itinéraires de la Terre Sainte," accounts, by various writers, of travels in Palestine).

German. Aboab, Isaac: "Menorat ha-Ma'or" (by Jacob Raphael Fürstenthal, Breslau, 1844).

Abraham ibn Daud: "Emunah Ramah" (by S. Weil, Frankfort-on-the-Main, 1882).

Abraham ibn Ezra: "Yesod Mora" (by Michael Creizenach, Mayence, 1840).

Albo, Joseph: "Sefer ha-'Iḳḳarim" (by W. Schlessinger, Frankfort-on-the-Main, 1844).

Aristotle, Pseudo-: "Sefer ha-Tappuaḥ" (by J. Musen, Lemberg, 1873).

Baḥya ben Joseph: "Ḥobot ha-Lebabot" (by Fürstenthal, Breslau, 1835, and by Baumgarten and Stern, Vienna, 1854).

Bedersi, Jedaiah: "Baḳḳashat ha-Memim" (by Benjamin Wolf Prerau, Brünn, 1799); "Beḥinat 'Olam" (by Isaac Auerbach, Hirsh ben Meïr, Joel ben Joseph Faust, Simson Hamburger, Auerbach, J. Levy, Joseph Hirshfeld, Stern [in verse], and Judah Kron).

Benjamin of Tudela: "Massa'ot" (by Mordecai Drucker, Amsterdam, 1691).

Carmoly: "Maimonides und Seine Zeitgenossen" (Frankfort-on-the-Main, 1840).

Caro, Joseph: Shulḥan 'Aruk (by H. Löwe, Vienna, 1896, and by Fr. Lederer, 1897–1901).

Crescas, Ḥasdai: The fifth chapter of the "Or Adonai" (by Philip Bloch, 1879).

Duran, Profiat: "Al Tehi ka-Aboteka" (by Geiger, in "Wiss. Zeit. Jüd. Theol." iv.).

Eldad ha-Dani (Dessau, 1700; Jessnitz, 1723; and in Eisenmenger's "Entdecktes Judenthum," ii. 527).

Ephraim of Bonn: The persecutions by the Crusaders (by S. Baer, Berlin, 1892).

Francis, Immanuel: "Meteḳ Sefatayim" ("Die Hebräische Verskunst," by Martin Hartmann, Berlin, 1894).

Ḥasdai, Abraham: "Ben ha-Melek weha-Nazir" ("Prinz und Dervisch," by Wolf Alois Meisel, Stettin, 1847).

Isaac Israeli: "Sefer ha-Yesodot" (by S. Fried, Frankfort-on-the-Main, 1900).

Joseph ha-Kohen: "'Emeḳ ha-Baka" (by Wiener, Leipsic, 1858).

Judah al-Ḥarizi: "Taḥkemoni" (by Kämpf, Berlin, 1845); "Mussare ha-Filosufim" (by J. Löwenthal).

Judah ha-Levi: "Cuzari" (by D. Cassel and Jelowicz, Leipsic, 1841); poems (by Zunz, Geiger, Kämpf, Sachs, Steinschneider, Heller, and Sulzbach).

Kalonymus ben Kalonymus: "Eben Boḥan" (by Moses Eisenstadt, or, according to Zedner, by Katzenellenbogen, Sulzbach, 1705; in condensed prose by W. Meisel, Budapest, 1878).

Lebensohn, Micah Joseph: "Shire Bat Ziyyon" ("Gesänge Zion's," by Joshua Steinberg, Wilna, 1869).

Levinsohn: "Efes Damim" (by Albert Katz, Berlin, 1884).

Levita, Elijah: "Massoret ha-Massorah" (by Mayer Gottlieb, 1772).

Maimonides: "Moreh Nebukim" (the first part by Fürstenthal, Krotoschin, 1839; the second, by M. Stein, Vienna, 1864; the third, by Scheyer, Frankfort-on-the-Main, 1838); "Millat ha-Higgayon" (by M. S. Neumann, Vienna, 1822; by Heilberg, Breslau, 1828); Introduction to the Mishnah ("Das Jüdische Traditionswesen," by Fürstenthal, Breslau, 1844); treatise on poisons ("Gifte und Ihre Heilungen," by M. Steinschneider, Berlin, 1873); essays on hygiene (by D. Winternitz, 1843).

Mapu, Abraham: "Ahabat Ziyyon" ("Tamar," by S. Mandelkern, Leipsic, 1885).

Mendelssohn, Moses: "Sefer ha-Nefesh" (by David Friedländer, Berlin, 1887).

Modena, Leon of: Dialogue on gambling (by Friedrich Albert Christiani, 1638); the abridged commentary on the Passover Haggadah of Isaac Abravanel, entitled "Zeli Esh" (Fürth, 1804).

Rashi: Commentary on the Pentateuch (Prague, 1833-38).

Rosenfeld: "Tenubot Sadeh," poems and epigrams (by Fürstenthal, Breslau, 1842).

Saadia: "Emunot we-De'ot" (by Julius Fürst, Leipsic, 1845; the introduction and first chapter, by Philip Bloch, 1879).

Schweitzer: "Mazkeret Ahabah" (metrically translated by Fürstenthal, Breslau, 1841).

Verga, Solomon: "Shebeṭ Yehudah" (by Wiener, Hanover, 1856).

Wiener: "Gezerat Ostraik" (by Jehiel Michael Moroweyczyk, Cracow, 1852).

Italian. Baḥya: "Tokaḥah" (by Deborah Ascarelli, Venice, 1601).

Bedersi, Jedaiah: "Beḥinat 'Olam" (in "Antologia Israelitica," 1880).

Judah al-Ḥarizi: "Mishle Ḥakamim" ("Motti di Diversi Saggi," by Simon Massarani).

Judah ha-Levi: "Canzoniere Sacra di Giuda Levita" (by S. de Benedetti, Pisa, 1871).

Luzzatto, S. D.: "Derek Ereẓ" ("Il Falso Progresso," by Pontremoli, Padua, 1879).

Maimonides: "Moreh Nebukim" (by Jedidiah Moses of Recanati, 1580, and by D. J. Maroni, 1870).

Mizraḥi, Elijah: Part of the "Sefer ha-Mispar" (by M. Steinschneider, Rome, 1866).

Modena, Leon of: The abridged commentary of Abravanel on the Passover Haggadah, entitled "Zeli Esh."

Moses: "Vita e Morte de Mose" (by Benedetti de Salvatore).

Rieti, Moses: The second part of the "Miḳdash Me'aṭ," entitled "Me'on ha-Sho'alim" (by Deborah Ascarelli, Venice, 1601).

Solomon: "Clavis Solomonis" (by Abraham Colorni).

Russian. Abramovich: "Ha-Abot weha-Banim" ("Otzy i Dyeti," by Leo Bienstok, St. Petersburg, 1867).

Brandstädter: "Mordekai Kizwiz" (in "Yevreiskaya Biblioteka").

Eichhorn: "Ha-Ḳerab" (by Osip Rabbinovich, 1847).

Joshua ben David of Samoscz: "Ẓuḳ ha-'Ittim" ("Byedstoiya Vremion," by Moses Berlin).

Nathan Nata of Hanover: "Yewen Meẓulah" (by S. Mandelkern, St. Petersburg, 1878).

Rosensohn: "Shelom Aḥim," on the catholicity of the Mosaic religion (transl. Wilna, 1876).

Spanish. Abner of Burgos: "Moreh Ẓedeḳ" ("El Mostador de Justicia"); "Milḥamot Adonai" ("Las Batallas de Dios").

Alguadez, Meïr: Prescriptions for various diseases (by Joseph ha-Kohen).

Baḥya ben Joseph ibn Paḳuda: "Ḥobot ha-Lebabot" (by Joseph Pardo, Amsterdam, 1610).

Elijah de Vidas: Several sections of the "Reshit Ḥoḳmah" (by David Cohen Lara, under the title "Tratado del Temur Divino," Amsterdam, 1633).

"Ḥinnuḳ, Sefer ha-": Anonymous work on the precepts, of the thirteenth century.

Jonah Gerondi: Ethical work (by Joseph Shalom Gallego, or Galigo, under the title "Sendroe [Sendero] de Vidas," Amsterdam, 1640).

Judah ha-Levi: "Cuzari" (by Jacob Abendana).

Maimonides: ("Tratado de los Articulos de la Ley Divina," by David Cohen de Lara, Amsterdam, 1652); commentary on the Mishnah (by Jacob Abendana).

For other translations from and into the Hebrew see BIBLE TRANSLATIONS; MAḤZOR; TALMUD.

J.   I. BR.

TRANSLITERATION.—Into Hebrew: The Greek and Latin words which entered into the language of the Hebrews are transcribed in the Talmud, Midrash, and Targum according to purely phonetic principles, their etymologies being entirely disregarded. Besides the lack in Hebrew of that rich system of vocalization which characterizes the Latin, and especially the Greek, the alphabets of these languages include characters which are not represented in the Hebrew, and therefore their transliteration is attended with many complications; sometimes it is even very difficult to detect the root of the transcribed word. The Hebrew consonants represent the following Greek and Latin equivalents: ב = β or "b," π or "p," φ or "f"; ג = γ or "g" and sometimes also κ; ד = δ or "d"; ו = the Latin "v"

and sometimes also β or "b"; ז = ζ or "z" and sometimes also σ; ח = χ; ט = θ and also τ or "t"; י = the Latin "j"; כ = χ and sometimes also κ; ל = λ or "l"; מ = μ or "m"; נ = ν or "n"; ע has no equivalent either in Greek or in Latin; פ = π or "p" and φ or "f"; צ = σ; ק = κ or "k" and the Latin "q"; ר = ρ or "r"; ש = σ; ת = θ. The Greek double letters ξ and ψ are respectively represented by קם or כם, and by פם. The nasal sounds γγ, γκ, γχ are reproduced in a manner analogous to the Latin, Syriac, Arabic, etc., as, for instance, אנגלא for ἄγγελος, אננקי for ἀνάγκη, קונכי for κόγχη. The Latin and Greek vowels are transcribed as follows: a by א, sometimes by ע or ה; ε or "e" by א, sometimes by ע or י; ι by א, אי, or י; o by א, או, or ו; η by אי or י, less frequently by ה; ω by אי or ו; αι (Latin "æ") by אי or י; ει by י; οι by א or י; αυ by אי, אב, or אב; ευ by אי, אוי, or אי, ου (Latin "u") by אי or ו. The hiatus is always neglected, while both the spiritus asper and the spiritus lenis are scrupulously represented, the former by ה and the latter by א. The aspirated ῥ is indicated by רה or הר; even internal aspiration occurs, as, for instance, סנהדרין for συνέδριον. However, the vowels are not always kept intact, but are often interchanged contrary to the rule. Syllables are frequently elided by apocope, apheresis, and especially syncope.

With the adoption of the Arabic language by the Jews residing in Moslem countries, the Jewish writers treating of subjects pertaining to religion and Judaism were forced in some degree to conform to the culture of the people for whom they wrote, the great mass of whom, though speaking Arabic as their mother tongue, were not able to read it. Jewish authors, or at least those among them whose works were destined for the common people, were therefore compelled to transliterate their Arabic into Hebrew characters. The system of transliteration generally adopted by them was as follows: For each Arabic letter the corresponding Hebrew was given. The letters, ث خ ذ ض ظ غ, which have no equivalents in Hebrew, were represented by תכדצטע, with dots above or below the letters except in the case of the ג, which, when dotted, corresponds to ج and not to خ. In some writings both ض and ظ are rendered by a dotted צ. In vocalized texts the vowel-points are reproduced either by the same signs as are used in the Arabic or by the vowel letters ואי; the "hamza," the "waslah," and the "tashdid" are always rendered by the same signs as in the Arabic. Indeed, the transliteration into Hebrew from the Arabic is the most simple and the easiest, since, with the exception of the six letters mentioned, which are always transcribed in the same way, the pronunciation of each Arabic letter finds an exact equivalent in Hebrew. Far more complicated is the system of transliteration from the Persian, which includes four additional characters that have no equivalents either in Arabic or in Hebrew; even the purely Arabic characters have not always the same sound in both languages, and their transcription in Hebrew is variable. Thus in the older Judæo-Persian literary productions the system of transliteration is different from that used in more recent writings in Bokhara. In the former ב is frequently written with dagesh when it designates "b" and without dagesh when it stands for "w"; ג with or without dagesh corresponds to the Persian ژ; ج corresponds to غ ج چ‎ and also to ج‎; ד represents the ذ, and sometimes also the ض; ב with or without dagesh represents ك and خ; ם = ص; פ with rafeh = ف, without it ب. In the vocalized texts the long "ā" is indicated by the vowel letter א or by ḳameẓ; short "ă" or "ĕ" is designated either by shewa or by א; short "ŭ" is designated by the vowel letter ו; short "ĭ" by the vowel letter י. In the modern writings four forms of ג are used: (1) ג for ج; (2) ג for the غ; (3) ג for ژ; and (4) ג for چ.

The use of Hebrew characters for foreign words or sentences was introduced into France in the tenth century. Some Biblical or Talmudical commentators, in order to convey to the reader the exact meaning of a word or sentence not easily explained in Hebrew, accompanied the Hebrew word or sentence with an equivalent in the vernacular. With the exception of the following letters, the method of transliteration adopted by these commentators is the same as that used in the Talmud for the Latin consonants: "c" before "a," "o," "u," or in combination with "h" is represented by ק, and before "e," "i," "y," or when it is provided with a cedilla ("ç"), by צ; "g" before "a," "o," "u" is reproduced by ג, and before "e," "i," "y," by ז; double "s" is represented by צ; "j" by a single or double י, and sometimes also by ג, as, for instance, ניטיר (= "jeter"); "gn" is rendered by a single or double י, and also by ג; "n" is often eliminated in the transliteration, as, for instance, אפנט (= "enfant"), and מ is often rendered by ג, as, for instance, נון (= "nom"); "h" is rendered by א or י; "x" and "z" by ש or צ; "v" is rendered by ב or ו. The system of transliteration of the simple vowels "a," "e," "i," "o," "u," "y" is the same as that used in the Talmud for the Latin, their pronunciation being identical in both languages: "a" = א; "o" and "u" = ו; and "e," "i," "y" = י. The accentuated "e" is sometimes rendered by a double י, and the mute "e" at the end of a word by א or ה or by both. As to the diphthongs, "ai," "ei," "ie" are represented by a single or double י, with or without א; e.g., אליינא (= "haleine"), ביין (= "bien"); "oi," "aui," "aeu," and "eui" are reproduced by a single or double י preceded by ו, as, for instance, פויילא (= "feuille"), אויברא (= "œuvre"); "au" and "eau" are rendered by א or ו or by both; "eu" and "ou" almost always by ו.

With the single exception of "a," which is sometimes rendered by ה instead of א, the simple vowels are transliterated in Judæo-Spanish, or Ladino, in the same way as in French. The Spanish diphthongs, being very limited in number, and each of the vowels being pronounced, present no difficulty; thus "ei," "ey," and "ie" are always rendered by a double י, while "io," "ya," and "yo" are reproduced by either a double or a single י; "ia" is reproduced by a single י, followed by א or ה or both. Great confusion reigns in the transliteration of the consonants,

many of which are indifferently reproduced by various Hebrew letters, while the same Hebrew letter may represent many Spanish. Thus the soft "c" is indifferently represented by ז, ם, צ, and ש; "f" and "g" are rendered by ח, e.g., חואי (= "fue"), חינירא (= "genero"); "h" by ג (especially before "æ"), פ, and א, and when occurring at the beginning or in the middle of a word it is frequently omitted; "j" by ג, ח, ז, ש, and sometimes also by י; "ll" and "ñ" by double י; "m" and "n" often interchange in the transliteration, as, for instance, קאנפי (= "campe"), מום (= "nos"). Metathesis of "d" before "r" takes place in the transliteration, as, for instance, וירדי (= "verde"), אקורדראר (= "accordar"); or of "r" before "e," as, for instance, מאדרה (= "tarde"); "q" preceding "i" is rendered by קי; "s" = ם, ש, and ז; "x" = ש; "z" = ם or ז. The other consonants are represented by the same Hebrew letters as their equivalents in Latin or French. The following first two verses of the Bible in Ladino and in Spanish may serve as an illustration of the method of transliteration: אין פרינסיפיו קריאו איל דיו לוש סיילוש אי לה טיירה אי לה טיירה אירה ואגואה אי וואזיאה אי אישקורידד שוברי פאסיש די אבישמו אי ויינטו דיאיל דיו אישמוניינשי שוברא פאסיש די לאש אגואש = "En principio crio el Dios los cielos y la tierra. Y la tierra era vagua y vacia y escuridad sobre faces del abysmo, y viento del Dio esmoniense sobre faces de las aguas."

The transliteration of Italian into Hebrew differed but little from that of French and Spanish. The soft "c" was represented by ז, ם, צ, while the hard "c," "ch," and "cch" were rendered by ק; "g" before "e," "i," "l," or "n," and "gg" were rendered by a single or double י, as, for instance, יודיצי (= "giudice"), יורנו (= "giorno"), פרמייו (= "formaggio"); "gu" and "qu" were generally reproduced by גו; "s," "ss," and "sc" were rendered by ז, ם, and ש; when the "c" following the "s" was a hard one they were rendered by קם or קש. In some cases the "t" was rendered by צ, as, for instance, סטולטיציאה (= "stoltitia"); "z" and "zz" were reproduced by ז, צ, and ש, and in some cases also by ט. The vowels were rendered in the same way as in French, with the exception of the "o," which in Italian was represented by א or או instead of ו. The diphthong "ia" was rendered by a single or double י followed by אה or by א alone; "ie" was represented by a single or double י; "au" and "ao" by או; "ae" by a double י; the vowels which are not pronounced were left out altogether, as, for instance, צוטיל (= "ciottolo"). As an illustration of the Italian method of transliteration the following verse of the "Me'on ha-Sho'alim" of Moses Rieti may serve, which was translated into Italian by Deborah Ascarelli, and incorporated in Hebrew characters in the Roman Maḥzor: או טימפיו דאראטורי וילייא אינפינינטה די קי צירקא פיטא גראצייא אי פאווארי טוא פונטי ביניטיטו ספאנדוויטה = "O tempio dóratori, voglia infinita, di chi cerco pieta grazia e favore, tuo fonte benedetto spanda vita."

Judging from the Anglo-Jewish contracts of the thirteenth century published by the Anglo-Jewish Historical Exhibition, the method of transliteration into Hebrew from the English differed from the French or Italian only in those consonants and vowels which have a special pronunciation. The soft "c" was represented by צ or שׂ; "ch" by ק or צ; "j" and the soft "g" by a single or double י; "s" or "ss" by שׂ, צ, or ז; "th" by ז, זט, or טה, followed by שׂ or צ; "v" by וו or בו. כ sometimes stands for ק; ת for ט; ב (rafeh) for ו; and נ for מ. The simple vowels were transcribed in the same way as the French; as to the diphthongs, "ai" and "ay" were rendered by double י; "au" and "ou" by ו, ואו, or א; "ea" and "ee" by a single י; "ei" by a single or double ו; "ia," "ie," and "ey" by a double or single י followed by א or ה or both; "oi" and "oy" by יו; "ew" by י or by ו. In the transliteration of the numerous English words which entered the Judæo-German in the English-speaking countries, the pronunciation was faithfully preserved. The hard "c," "ch," and "q" are represented by ק, while the soft "c" is rendered by צ; the "f" and "p" are both rendered by פ, with the only difference that for the former the פ is rafeh, while for the latter it is with a dagesh; the soft "g" is represented by שׁ; the "j" by דׁ; "s" or "ss" by ס; "t" by ט, and before "ion" by שׂ; "th" by דה; "v" by ב (rafeh) or ו; "w" by וו or אוּ. According to the English pronunciation, the "a" is represented by א or יי; the "e" by ע or י; the "i" by י or איי; the "o" by ו; the "u" by ו or א. In the transliteration of the diphthongs the vowels that are not pronounced are left out altogether.

Up to the beginning of the nineteenth century the transliteration of the German words which form the bulk of the jargon called Judæo-German differed little from that current in the other Western dialects; the only deviation in the transcription of the vowels was the use of the א to represent both "a" and "o," whereas the latter was rendered in Spanish and French by ו. At the beginning of the nineteenth century the transliteration of the German underwent many changes. א became silent at the end of words after vowels, and at the beginning before ו and י. "E" was represented by ע instead of by י; "aj" and "ej" by יי; "ö" and "ü" by וי; "ä," "au," "eu" by ווי; "ei" by יי or איי; "au" by וו or אוו. Of the consonants the following may be mentioned: "ch" was represented by כ (rafeh), but when followed by "s," by ק; "sch" and "ss" by שׂ; soft "s" by ז; "s" before "t" or "p" by שׂ; "f" and "v" by ב (rafeh) and ו. In modern times "v" is rendered by ו and not by ב, and "w" by וו, so that only one letter occurs with rafeh, namely, פ for "f." In printed books פ stands generally for "p," while פ is "f."

——From Hebrew: From the time of Origen (c. 185–254), who in his Hexapla transliterated the text of the Pentateuch into Greek characters, to the middle of the nineteenth century no attempt was made to elaborate a scientific system of transcription of Hebrew in foreign characters, and every one followed his own caprice. In 1854 Bargès published the Book of Ruth with a French transliteration of the text. In his system, which was followed by nearly all the French Orientalists, the letters בנדכפת, according as they have or have not dagesh, are represented by their equivalent French letters with or without "h." Thus ב = "b," ב = "bh," ג

= "g," ג = "gh," ד = "d," ד = "dh," כ = "k," כ = "kh," פ = "p," פ = "ph." Both ה and ח are represented by "h," the former pronounced with a slight aspiration, and the latter with a hard one. ע is represented by a capital "H"; צ by "ts" or "s"; ק by "q"; שׁ by "sch." The following may serve as an illustration of Bargès' method of transliterating both the Hebrew consonants and vowels: "Va-iehi b-îmé schephot hasch-schôphetim va-iehi ra Habh bâ'arets. Va-ielekh isch mib-bet Lehem iehoudhah la-ghour bi-sedhé Mo'ab hou ve-ischt-o ou-schene bhanâ-v," which reads in Hebrew: וַיְהִי בִּימֵי שְׁפוֹט הַשֹּׁפְטִים וַיְהִי רָעָב בָּאָרֶץ וַיֵּלֶךְ אִישׁ מִבֵּית לֶחֶם יְהוּדָה לָגוּר בִּשְׂדֵי מוֹאָב הוּא וְאִשְׁתּוֹ וּשְׁנֵי בָנָיו.

A more rational system of transliteration was suggested by the Royal Asiatic Society for Great Britain and Ireland, which transcribes the Hebrew alphabet as follows: א = "'"; בּ = "b"; ב = "b̲"; ג = "g"; ג = "g̲"; ד = "d"; ד = "d̲"; ה = "h"; ח = "h̲" or "hh"; ו = "v"; ז = "z"; ח = "h"; ט = "ṭ"; י = "y"; כּ = "k"; כ = "k̲"; ל = "l"; מ = "m"; נ = "n"; ס = "s̲"; ע = "'"; פ = "p"; פ = "f"; צ = "ṣ"; ק = "q"; ר = "r"; שׂ = "s̠"; שׁ = "s"; ת = "t̲"; ת = "t." The long vowels are represented by "ā," "ē," "ī," "ō," "ū"; the short by "a," "e," "i," "o," "u"; the three vowels with the ḥaṭaf by "a̭," "ḙ," "o̭"; the dagesh forte by doubling the letter. As an illustration of the latest system of transliteration adopted by German scholars the following passage of Jeremiah published by Wilhelm Erbt (Göttingen, 1902) may serve: "Pittitani, Jahvé, wa'eppat ha-zaqtani wattukal, hajiti lishóq kol-hajjom kulló lo'eg-li ki-middé 'adabbèr 'ez'aq: ḥamàs wašod 'eqrá'. Ki-hajâ debar-jahwe li leḥerpa ul-qelés Kol-hajjom. We 'amarti: lo-'ezkerennu, we lo 'adabber 'od bišmó, wehaja belibbi ke'eš bo'eret 'aṣur be'aṣmotái, wenil'éti kalkél, welo 'ukal." = פִּתִּיתַנִי יְהֹוָה וָאֶפָּת חֲזַקְתַּנִי וַתּוּכָל הָיִיתִי לִשְׂחוֹק כָּל־הַיּוֹם כֻּלֹּה לֹעֵג לִי :כִּי־מִדֵּי אֲדַבֵּר אֶזְעָק חָמָס וָשֹׁד אֶקְרָא כִּי־הָיָה דְבַר־יְהֹוָה לִי לְחֶרְפָּה וּלְקֶלֶס כָּל־הַיּוֹם :וָאָמַרְתִּי לֹא־אֶזְכְּרֶנּוּ וְלֹא־אֲדַבֵּר עוֹד בִּשְׁמוֹ וְהָיָה בְלִבִּי כְּאֵשׁ בֹּעֶרֶת עָצֻר בְּעַצְמֹתַי וְנִלְאֵיתִי כַּלְכֵל וְלֹא אוּכָל.

In regard to the system of transliteration followed in THE JEWISH ENCYCLOPEDIA, see p. vii. of this volume.

s.   I. BR.

TRANSMIGRATION OF SOULS (termed also **Metempsychosis**): The passing of souls into successive bodily forms, either human or animal. According to Pythagoras, who probably learned the doctrine in Egypt, the rational mind (φρήν), after having been freed from the chains of the body, assumes an ethereal vehicle, and passes into the region of the dead, where it remains till it is sent back to this world to inhabit some other body, human or animal. After undergoing successive purgations, and when it is sufficiently purified, it is received among the gods, and returns to the eternal source from which it first proceeded. This doctrine was foreign to Judaism until about the eighth century, when, under the influence of the Mohammedan mystics, it was adopted by the Karaites and other Jewish dissenters. It is first mentioned in Jewish literature by Saadia, who protested against this belief, which at his time was shared by the Yudghanites, or whomsoever he contemptuously designated as "so-called Jews" (ממיש נקראים יהודים; see Schmiedl, "Studien," p. 166; *idem*, in "Monatsschrift," x. 177; Rapoport, in "Bikkure ha-'Ittim," ix. 23; *idem*, introduction to Abraham bar Ḥiyya's "Hegyon ha-Nefesh," p. lii.; Jellinek, in "Orient, Lit." 1851, p. 410; Fürst, "Gesch. des Karäert." i.

Doctrine Refuted by Saadia.
81). According to Saadia, the reasons given by the adherents of metempsychosis for their belief are partly intellectual and partly Scriptural. The former are as follows: (1) Observation shows that many men possess attributes of animals, as, for instance, the gentleness of a lamb, the rage of a wild beast, the gluttony of a dog, the lightness of a bird, etc. These peculiarities, they assert, prove that their possessors have in part the souls of the respective animals. (2) It would be contrary to the justice of God to inflict pain upon children in punishment for sins committed by their souls in a previous state. The Scriptural reasons are conclusions drawn from certain Biblical verses, such as: "Neither with you only do I make this covenant and this oath; but with him that standeth here with us this day before the Lord our God, and also with him that is not here with us this day" (Deut. xxix. 14, 15); "Blessed be the man that walketh not in the counsel of the ungodly," etc. (Ps. i. 1). Both sets of reasons are refuted by Saadia, who says that he would not consider it worth while to show the foolishness and the low-mindedness of the believers in metempsychosis, were he not afraid lest they might exercise a pernicious influence upon others ("Emunot we-De'ot," vi.).

Influence of Cabala.
The doctrine counted so few adherents among the Jews that, with the exception of Abraham ibn Daud ("Emunah Ramah," i. 7), no Jewish philosopher until Ḥasdai Crescas even deemed it necessary to refute it. Only with the spread of the Cabala did it begin to take root in Judaism, and then it gained believers even among men who were little inclined toward mysticism. Thus one sees a man like Judah ben Asher (Asheri) discussing the doctrine in a letter to his father, and endeavoring to place it upon a philosophical basis ("Ṭa'am Zeḳenim," vii.). The cabalists eagerly adopted the doctrine on account of the vast field it offered to mystic speculations. Moreover, it was almost a necessary corollary of their psychological system. The absolute condition of the soul is, according to them, its return, after developing all those perfections the germs of which are eternally implanted in it, to the Infinite Source from which it emanated. Another term of life must therefore be vouchsafed to those souls which have not fulfilled their destiny here below and have not been sufficiently purified for the state of reunion with the Primordial Cause. Hence if the soul, on its first assumption of a human body and sojourn on earth, fails to acquire that experience for which it descended from heaven, and becomes contaminated by

that which is polluting, it must reinhabit a body till it is able to ascend in a purified state through repeated trials. This is the theory of the Zohar, which says: "All souls are subject to transmigration; and men do not know the ways of the Holy One, blessed be He! They do not know that they are brought before the tribunal both before they enter into this world and after they leave it; they are ignorant of the many transmigrations and secret probations which they have to undergo, and of the number of souls and spirits which enter into this world and which do not return to the palace of the Heavenly King. Men do not know how the souls revolve like a stone which is thrown from a sling. But the time is at hand when these mysteries will be disclosed" (Zohar, ii. 99b). Like Origen and other Church Fathers, the cabalists used as their main argument in favor of the doctrine of metempsychosis the justice of God. But for the belief in metempsychosis, they maintained, the question why God often permits the wicked to lead a happy life while many righteous are miserable, would be unanswerable. Then, too, the infliction of pain upon children would be an act of cruelty unless it is imposed in punishment for sin committed by the soul in a previous state.

Opposition to the View.
Although raised by the Cabala to the rank of a dogma, the doctrine of metempsychosis still found great opposition among the leaders of Judaism in the fourteenth and fifteenth centuries. In his "Iggeret Hitnaẓẓelut," addressed to Solomon ben Adret in defense of philosophy, Jedaiah Bedersi praises the philosophers for having opposed the belief in metempsychosis. Ḥasdai Crescas ("Or Adonai," iv. 7), and after him his pupil Joseph Albo ("Iḳḳarim," iv. 29), attacked this belief on philosophical grounds, considering it to be a heathen superstition, opposed to the spirit of Judaism. The opposition, however, gradually ceased; and the belief began to be shared even by men who were imbued with Aristotelian philosophy. Thus Isaac Abravanel sees in the commandment of the levirate a proof of the doctrine of metempsychosis, for which he gives the following reasons: (1) God in His mercy willed that another trial should be given to the soul which, having yielded to the sanguine temperament of the body, had committed a capital sin, such as murder, adultery, etc.; (2) it is only just that when a man dies young a chance should be given to his soul to execute in another body the good deeds which it had not time to perform in the first body; (3) the soul of the wicked sometimes passes into another body in order to receive its deserved punishment here below instead of in the other world, where it would be much more severe (commentary on Deut. xxv. 5). These arguments were wittily refuted by the skeptical Leon of Modena in his pamphlet against metempsychosis, entitled "Ben Dawid." He says: "It is not God, but the planets, that determine the temperament of the body; why then subject the soul to the risk of entering into a body with a temperament as bad as, if not worse than, that of the one it has left? Would it not be more in keeping with God's mercy to take into consideration the weakness of the body and to pardon

the soul at once? To send the soul of a man who died young into another body would be to make it run the risk of losing the advantages it had acquired in its former body. Why send the soul of the wicked to another body in order to punish it here below? Was there anything to prevent God from punishing it while it was in its first body?"

Upon the doctrine of metempsychosis was based the psychological system of the practical Cabala, inaugurated by the cabalists of the school of Luria. According to them, all the souls destined for the human race were created together with the various organs of Adam. As there are superior and inferior organs, so there are superior and inferior souls, according to the organs with which they are respectively coupled. Thus there are souls of the brain, of the eye, of the head, etc. Each human soul is a spark ("niẓaẓ") from Adam. The first sin of the first man caused confusion among the various classes of souls; so that even the purest soul received an admixture of evil. This state of confusion, which gives a continual impulse toward evil, will cease with the arrival of the Messiah, who will establish the moral system of the world on a new basis. Until that time man's soul, because of its deficiencies, can not return to its source, and has to wander not only through the bodies of men, but even through inanimate things. If a man's good deeds outweigh his evil ones, his soul passes into a human body; otherwise, into that of an animal. Incest causes the soul to pass into the body of an unclean animal; adultery, into that of an ass; pride in a leader of a community, into that of a bee; forgery of amulets, into that of a cat; cruelty toward the poor, into that of a crow; denunciation, into that of a barking cur; causing a Jew to eat unclean flesh, into a leaf of a tree which endures great suffering when shaken by the wind; neglect to wash the hands before meals, into a river.

The main difference between the passing of the soul into a human body and its transmigration into an animal or an inanimate object consists in the fact that in the former case the soul ignores its transmigration, while in the latter it is fully aware of its degradation, and suffers cruelly therefrom. With regard to the transmigration of the soul into a crow Moses Galante, rabbi at Safed, relates that once he accompanied Isaac Luria to 'Ain Zaitun to pray at the tomb of Judah ben Ilai. On approaching the place he noticed on an olive-tree which grew near the tomb a crow which croaked incessantly. "Were you acquainted," asked Luria, "with Shabbethai, the tax-farmer of Safed?" "I knew him," answered Galante: "he was a very bad man and displayed great cruelty toward the poor, who were not able to pay the taxes." "This crow," said Luria, "contains his soul" ("Shibḥe ha-Ari," p. 29).

A quite new development of the doctrine of metempsychosis was the theory of the impregnation of souls, propounded by the cabalists of the Luria school. According to this theory, a purified soul that has neglected some religious duties on earth must return to the earthly life and unite with the soul of a living man, in order to make

The School of Luria.

Impregnation of Souls.

good such neglect. Further, the soul of a man freed from sin appears again on earth to support a weak soul unequal to its task. Thus, for instance, the soul of Samuel was supported by those of Moses and Aaron; the soul of Phinehas, by those of Nadab and Abihu. However, this union, which may extend to three souls at one time, can take place only between souls of a homogeneous character, that is, between those which are sparks from the same Adamite organs. As the impregnated soul comes either to make good a neglect or to support a weak soul, it enters into the body only after the man has completed his thirteenth year, when he reaches the age of religious duty and responsibility.

The dispersion of Israel has for its purpose the salvation of man; and the purified souls of Israelites unite with the souls of other races in order to free them from demoniacal influences. Each man, according to the practical Cabala, bears on his forehead a mark by which one may recognize the nature of the soul: to which degree and class it belongs; the relation existing between it and the superior world; the transmigrations it has already accomplished; the means by which it may contribute to the establishment of the new moral system of the world; how it may be freed from demoniacal influences; and to which soul it should be united in order to become purified. He who wishes to ascertain to which of the four worlds his soul belongs must close his eyes and fix his thought on the four letters of the Ineffable Name. If the color he then beholds is a very bright, sparkling white, his soul has proceeded from the world of emanation (עולם האצילות); if an ordinary white, from that of creative ideas (עולם הבריאה); if red, from that of creative formation (עולם היצירה); and if green, from that of creative matter (עולם העשיה).

The cabalists of the Luria school pretended to know the origins and transmigrations of all the souls of the human race since Adam; and in their works accounts are given concerning Biblical personages and the great teachers of Judaism. Thus, for instance, the soul of Aaron is said to have been derived from the good part of that of Cain. It entered into the body of the high priest Eli, who, in expiation of the sin committed by Aaron in making the golden calf—a sin punishable with lapidation— broke his neck in falling from his seat. From Eli it transmigrated into the body of Ezra; and it then became purified. The name "Adam" contains the initials of David and Messiah, into whose bodies the soul of the first man successively entered. The name "Laban" contains the initials of Balaam and Nabal, who successively received Laban's soul. Jacob's soul passed into Mordecai; and because the former had sinned in prostrating himself before Esau, Mordecai obstinately refused to prostrate himself before Haman, even at the risk of endangering the safety of the Persian Jews. Interesting is the account given in the "Sefer ha-Gilgulim" of the souls of some contemporaries of Isaac Luria. The soul of Isaac de Lattes is said there to have been a spark from that of a pious man of the olden times (צדיק קדמון); that of Joseph Vital, one from the soul of Ezra; that of Moses Minz, one from the soul

Special Instances.

of Seth, the son of Adam. To the soul of Moses Alshech was united that of the amora Samuel ben Naḥmani; hence the former's talent for preaching. Both Moses Cordovero and Elijah de Vidas partook of the soul of Zechariah ben Jehoiada; hence the great friendship that existed between them. Because of some sin his soul had committed in a previous state Moses Vital was unable to acquire a perfect knowledge of the Cabala. The soul of Joseph Delpino entered into a black dog. Ḥayyim Vital possessed, according to Isaac Luria, a soul which had not been soiled by Adam's sin. Luria himself possessed the soul of Moses, which had previously been in the bodies of Simeon ben Yoḥai and Hamnuna Saba.

Generally the souls of men transmigrate into the bodies of men, and those of women into the bodies of women; but there are exceptions. The soul of Judah, the son of Jacob, was in part that of a woman; while Tamar had the soul of a man. Tamar's soul passed into Ruth; and therefore the latter could not bear children until God had imparted to her sparks from a female soul. The transmigration of a man's soul into the body of a woman is considered by some cabalists to be a punishment for the commission of heinous sins, as when a man refuses to give alms or to communicate his wisdom to others.

The theory of impregnation gave birth to the superstitious belief in "dibbuḳ" or "gilgul," which prevailed, and still prevails, among the Oriental Jews and those of eastern Europe. This belief assumes that there are souls which are condemned to wander for a time in this world, where they are tormented by evil spirits which watch and accompany them everywhere. To escape their tormentors such souls sometimes take refuge in the bodies of living pious men and women, over whom the evil spirits have no power. The person to whom such a soul clings endures great suffering and loses his own individuality; he acts as though he were quite another man, and loses all moral sense.

Gilgul. He can be cured only by a miracle-working rabbi ("ba'al shem") who is able to cast out the soul from his body by exorcisms and amulets. The usual exorcism in such cases consisted in the rabbi's reciting, in the presence of ten men (see MINYAN), the 91st Psalm, and adjuring the soul in the name of God to leave the body of the afflicted one. In case of refusal on the part of the soul to yield to this simple injunction, the ban and the blowing of the shofar are resorted to. In order that it may cause the least possible amount of damage to the body, the soul is always directed to pass out through the small toe.

The belief that migrant souls seek refuge in the bodies of living persons became more and more deeply rooted; and regular methods for expelling them are given in the cabalistic works of the seventeenth century. This superstition is still widely spread, especially in Ḥasidic circles. Curtiss relates ("Primitive Semitic Religions of To-Day," p. 152) that a few years ago a woman was exorcised in Palestine, and that the spirit when questioned replied that it was the soul of a Jew who had been murdered in Nablus twelve years before. The migrant soul was generally believed to belong to a wicked

or murdered person; but it may happen that that of a righteous man is condemned, for a slight offense committed by it, to wander for a while in this world. Such a soul is, however, free from demoniacal influences, and it enters the body of a living person not to avoid evil spirits (who have no power over it), but to atone for the fault it has committed. As soon as this has been accomplished it leaves the body of its own free will. Ḥayyim Vital records that while sojourning at Damascus in 1699 he was called upon to entertain himself with the soul of a pious man which had entered the body of the daughter of Raphael Anaw. The soul informed him that it was exiled from heaven for having slighted the virtue of repentance. For a time it dwelt in a fish, but this fish was caught and sold to Raphael for the Sabbath meal; the soul then entered the body of the daughter of the house. In proclaiming before Vital the great importance of repentance it became free to return to its heavenly abode ("Shibḥe Ḥayyim Wiṭal," ed. Lemberg, p. 11). Narratives of this sort abound in the cabalistic writings of the seventeenth and eighteenth centuries, and many of them are reproduced in the "Nishmat Ḥayyim" of Manasseh ben Israel, who showed himself a firm believer in all kinds of gilgulim and dibbuḳim. He even went so far as to endeavor to demonstrate that references to them are to be found in the Bible. It is noteworthy that most of the cases of exorcism occurred at Safed or in its neighborhood; that is, in localities where mysticism was flourishing. A curious case is cited by Moses Prager in his "Zera' Ḳodesh": it is interesting from the fact that David Oppenheim, the collector of Hebrew books and manuscripts, who was the rabbi of Nikolsburg, Moravia, was one of the signatories of the narrative. See DIBBUḲIM.

BIBLIOGRAPHY: Azariah da Fano, *Gilgule Neshamot*, passim; Manasseh ben Israel, *Nishmat Ḥayyim*, part iii., ch. xiv.; part iv., ch. xx.; Luria, *Sefer ha-Gilgulim*, passim; *Shebaḥe ha-Ari*, passim; Israel Saruk, *Shibḥe Ḥayyim Wiṭal*, passim; Abraham Shalom Ḥai, *Sefer Nifla'im Ma'aseka*, p. 18; Ginsburg, *The Kabbalah*, p. 42; Karppe, *Etude sur l'Origine du Zohar*, pp. 320 et seq., Paris, 1902; P. Rudermann, *Uebersicht über die Idee der Seelenwanderung*, Warsaw, 1878; S. Rubin, *Gilgul Neshamot*, Cracow, 1898; Alexander W. M. Menz, *Demonic Possession in the New Testament*, Edinburgh, 1902; Güdemann, *Gesch.* i. 202, 205, 216.
K.   I. Br.

TRANSVAAL. See SOUTH AFRICA.

TRANSYLVANIA (Hungarian, **Erdély**; German, **Siebenbürgen**): A district which has formed a part of Hungary since 1867. According to one tradition, the first Jewish settlers of this region were subjects of the Persian king Xerxes, who fled thither after the battle of Salamis; while another tradition states that they were colonized there by the Dacian king Decebulus. It is certain, at all events, that Jews lived in Transylvania soon after the country had become a part of Dacia during the Roman period. The earliest mention of them in historical sources, however, is in 1578, when it was decreed in Art. xxii. of the regulations passed by the national assembly at Kolozsvar that "Greeks and likewise Jews might not engage in trade, except in places especially assigned them for residence." This "locus depositionis" in which Jews were allowed to live was Gyulafehérvár (Karlsburg, formerly called Weissenburg, Alba Julia, and Alba Carolina), a frontier town, where the Turkish trade passed through Jewish hands. In 1623 the grand duke Gabriel Bethlen granted the Jews the privilege of settling in fortified cities, of carrying on commerce throughout the country, and of unrestricted observance of religion. This privilege, although made a law by the national assembly in 1627, was of short duration. The ordinances passed by the national assembly in 1650 provided that the Jews should be restricted commercially, and should be forced, like the Greeks, to wear distinctive articles of clothing and badges; and the intolerant grand duke George Rakoczy II. deprived them of the right of residence in fortified towns. These provisions, however, were never carried out. While the emperor Joseph II., in his patent of 1781, appointed Gyulafehérvár as a residence for the Jews, and while the same provision was made by the government as late as 1845, the Jews have always lived in various parts of the country, although their numbers may have been small. The religious congregation and the only community officially recognized, however, were at Gyulafehérvár, where there was a bet din as early as 1591. The first rabbi whose name is known was Joseph Reisz Auerbach (1742-50), who was succeeded by Solomon Selig b. Saul ha-Kohen (1754-58), Johanan b. Isaac of Belgrade (until 1760), Benjamin Zeeb Wolf of Cracow (until 1777), Moses b. Samuel ha-Levi Margolioth (1778-1817), Menahem b. Joshua Mendel (1818-23), Ezekiel b. Joseph Panet (1823-45), and Abraham Friedmann (1845-79), all of whom held the title of district rabbi.

The Sabbatarians (Sambatianer) are important factors in the history of the Jews in Transylvania. This sect originated among the Christians, under the influence of the Reformation, and was founded in 1588 by Andreas Eössy, whose followers regarded the Jews as the chosen people and held their belief to be the only true faith. They observed the Jewish dietary laws, kept the Jewish feasts, and were especially strict in their observance of the Sabbath. The persecutions of the princes Gabriel Bethlen and George Rakoczy I. alienated the Sabbatarians until they approached Judaism so closely that the only congregation surviving the persecution, and still existing in Bözöd-Ujfalu, officially adopted Judaism with the permission of Baron Eötvös, minister of religion. Before the European War (1914-16) the Jewish population of Transylvania was about 65,000. In 1918, Transylvania became part of Roumania.

BIBLIOGRAPHY: S. Kohn, *A Szombatosok, Történetük, Dogmatikájuk, és Irodalmuk*, Budapest, 1888; H. Hazai, *Munkálatok a Szombatosokról*, ib. 1903; Eisler, *Ar Erdélyi Zsidók Multjából*, Klausenburg, 1901.

s.　　　　　　　　　　　　　　　　　　L. V.

TRASTEVERE. See Rome.

TRAUBE, LUDWIG: German physician and medical author; born at Ratibor, Prussian Silesia, Jan. 18, 1818; died at Berlin April 11, 1876; elder brother of Moritz Traube. He studied at the gymnasium of his native town and the universities of Breslau, Berlin (M.D. 1841), and Vienna. After a postgraduate course at Vienna University he established himself as a physician in the city of Berlin in 1842. In 1843 he opened a private seminary course

on auscultation and percussion, which he continued for a year; in 1844 he commenced his experiments on animals, especially in regard to affections of the lungs through cutting of the nervus vagus, in which experiments he followed the work of Longet. The results of his labors were: "Die Ursachen und die Beschaffenheit Derjenigen Veränderungen, Welche das Lungenparenchym nach Durchschneidung der Nervi Vagi Erleidet" and "Beitrag zur Lehre von den Erstickungserscheinungen am Respirations-Apparat," published in 1846 and 1847 respectively in "Beiträge zur Experimentellen Pathologie."

Traube became privat-docent at Berlin University and assistant to Schoenlein at the Charité Hospital in 1848, and was appointed chief physician of a department of the same institution and assistant professor in 1857. In 1862 he was appointed professor at the Prussian institution for army surgeons (Friedrich Wilhelms-Institut zur Ausbildung von Militärärzten); in 1866 he received the title of "Geheimer Medizinalrath"; and in 1872 he became professor at the university.

Through the above-mentioned essays Traube became one of the leading German specialists in experimental pathology, in which field he remained prominent up to his death. His fame as a clinician, too, was great, he being one of the best teachers at his university. Traube was also one of the leading practitioners of Europe. Many of his essays were epoch-making. To these belong his monographs on digitalis, fever, thermometry in medicine, diseases of the lungs, heart, and kidneys ("Ueber den Zusammenhang von Herz- und Nierenkrankheiten," Berlin, 1856), and above all his works on experimental pathology. His essays were originally published in the "Charité Annalen," "Verhandlungen der Berliner Medizinischen Gesellschaft," and other medical journals. He collected them later and published them in "Gesammelte Beiträge zur Pathologie und Therapie" (vol. i., Berlin, 1871, contains his experimental essays; vol. ii., *ib.* 1871, his clinical experiments; vol. iii., *ib.* 1878, published after his death by his nephew Albert Fränkel, contains his diary, and minor scientific works). In 1867 Traube published "Die Symptome der Krankheiten des Respirations- und Circulationsapparates" (not complete).

In 1878 a monument was erected to the memory of Traube in the second court of the Charité.

BIBLIOGRAPHY: Pagel, *Biog. Lex.* Vienna, 1901; *Meyers Konversations-Lexikon*; *Brockhaus Konversations-Lexikon*; Leyden, *Gedächtnissrede auf Ludwig Traube*, Berlin, 1876; Freund, *Gedächtnissrede auf Ludwig Traube*, Breslau, 1876.

s.　　　　　　　　　　　　　　　　　F. T. H.

TRAUBEL, HORACE: American editor; born at Camden, N. J., Dec. 19, 1858; educated in the public schools of his native town. In 1892 he was appointed, jointly with Richard Maurice Buckle and Thomas B. Harned, literary executor of Walt Whitman; he has contributed to the periodical press a number of essays on that poet. In 1886 he founded the Contemporary Club in Philadelphia. Among the publications which Traubel has edited are: "The Conservator" (Philadelphia; from 1890 to 1905); "The Dollar or the Man," and "Cartoons of Homer Davenport" (1900). In conjunction with his coexecutors he edited a memorial volume on Walt Whitman. Traubel was editor-in-chief of "The Artsman," a publication founded in Philadelphia in 1903. He was also secretary of the International Walt Whitman Fellowship. He died Sept. 7, 1919.

A.   F. H. V.

TRAVELERS : Jews early became accustomed to wandering, either by compulsion, as in the Exile and in the Diaspora, or through natural dispersion. The spreading out of the Jewish race in the first and second centuries indicated a willingness to change homes rarely found in other classes under the Roman empire, owing to the local nature of their cults. After the destruction of the Temple there was nothing to prevent Jews worshiping in any part of the habitable globe. Jews were found as far north as the Black Sea and as far west as Spain, and the intercourse between Palestine and Babylonia was continued, as is shown by the cases of Hillel, Akiba, and Rab. Communications between Palestine and Rome were frequent; and the example of Saul of Tarsus shows the wide extent of country that an individual without any means could cover in the course of a few years (see Harnack, "Ausbreitung des Christenthums," Berlin, 1904). With the spread of Islam, Jewish traders became the chief intermediaries between Moslem and Christian lands; and two routes between Spain and China are recorded as traversed by Jewish traders known as "Radanites," who are described in the "Book of Ways," written about 817 by Ibn Khordadhbeh (see Commerce). Other Jewish trade-routes ran from Byzantium to Prague, and possibly extended farther north. A Jew named Isaac accompanied an embassy of Charlemagne's from Aix-la-Chapelle to Bagdad in 802. It is said that Jacob ibn Tarik was sent in the ninth century from Bagdad as far as Ceylon to obtain astronomical books from the Indians; and according to Abraham ibn Ezra a Jewish traveler brought from India the so-called Arabic numerals (see "Fables of Bidpai," ed. Jacobs, p. xxiv.). His name is given also as "Joseph of Spain" (Weissenbron, "Zur Gesch. der Jetzigen Ziffern," 1892, pp. 74-78).

The travels of Eldad ha-Dani are stated to have extended from Babylonia to Spain, but their authenticity is somewhat doubtful. The travels of Abraham ibn Ezra between 1140 and 1168 extended as far as Palestine on the one side, and to England on the other. The same century was distinguished by two important travelers. Benjamin of Tudela started from Saragossa in 1160 and went at least as far as Bagdad, returning to Spain about 1171. It is doubtful whether his accounts of countries east of Bagdad are derived from personal knowledge or from hearsay. About the same time Pethahiah of Regensburg traveled from Prague to Poland and South Russia, to Bagdad, to Jerusalem, and back to Greece and Bohemia. In 1210 a band of over 300 rabbis from France and England made a pilgrimage to the Holy Land, following the example of Judah ha-Levi in 1140 and starting the practise of pilgrimages, a list of which will be found under Pilgrimage. Estori Farḥi was perhaps the most important of their followers; after the expulsion of Jews from France in 1306 he wandered in Spain, Egypt, and

Palestine, over which he traveled very thoroughly for seven years for geographical purposes.

Jews were intimately connected with the important extension of geographical knowledge in the fifteenth century—theoretically through the school of Majorca map-makers to which belonged Cresques lo Juheu and Mecia, and practically through a number of travelers like Affonso de Bayba, Abraham of Bega, and Joseph of Lamejo, who accompanied Pedro de Covilham on the discovery of the land-route to the East Indies, and Gaspar da Gama, who had gone from Poland to Goa, where he met Vasco da Gama (Jacobs, "Story of Geographical Discovery," p. 89, New York, 1904). Jews accompanied Columbus on his first voyage to America (see America, Discovery of).

Part in Geographical Discovery.

Pilgrimages like those of Meshullam b. Menahem of Volterra and Obadiah Bertinoro to the Holy Land and back became too frequent to deserve special mention; David Reubeni's travels were in the opposite direction. A certain Jew named Jehonadab of Morocco, mentioned by André Thevet as having acquired twenty-eight languages from personal intercourse with those who spoke them, was probably well acquainted with North Africa. Antonio de Montesinos appears to have traveled widely in South America; he claimed to have discovered there the Lost Ten Tribes about 1642. Moses Pereira de Pavia traveled from Holland to Cochin and described the Jews there (1687), while Teixeira's descriptions of his travels in the Philippines, China, and parts of America are of considerable interest. In the eighteenth century few names of travelers occur, apart from those of pilgrims to Palestine and wanderers through Europe, though Samuel Romanelli of Mantua, who lived in Berlin in 1791, described his travels from Gibraltar to Algiers and Morocco, giving many interesting details. In the nineteenth century Jews took a large share in travel in unknown parts. Mention may be made of Joseph Wolf and his travels to Bokhara; of Nathaniel Isaacs, who was one of the earliest to explore Zululand and Natal; and of C. S. Pollack, one of the earliest settlers in New Zealand, of which he wrote an account ("Residence in New Zealand," 2 vols., London, 1831-37). W. G. Palgrave gave an interesting account of his journeys in central Arabia; Arminius Vámbéry of his in central Asia; Captain Binger discovered the bend of the Niger; and Captain Foa wandered from South to North Africa. Emin Pasha and Louis A. Lucas are also to be mentioned as having added to the knowledge of darkest Africa. On Polar expeditions Bessels, Israel, and Angelo Heilprin have done service.

Among modern travelers who have devoted their attention particularly to the condition of Jews in various lands have been: Benjamin II., who wandered over all the continents except Australia; Jacob Saphir, who was especially interested in the Jews of Yemen; J. Halévy, who visited the Falashas; and J. Rinmann, who traveled among the Jews of India. Chorny's travels among the Jews of the Caucasus and Deinard's among those of the Crimea should be mentioned. To these should be added E. N. Adler, who has visited most of the outlying colonies of Jews in Africa, Asia, and America ("Jews of Many Lands," Philadelphia, 1905).

BIBLIOGRAPHY: Zunz, *Literatur der Juden*, in *G. S.* i. 146–216.
s.   J.

TRAVNIK: Town of Bosnia. The first Jews settled there at the beginning of the nineteenth century, during the reign of the sultan 'Abd al-Majid, most of them being Sephardim from Sarajevo. The first to come were the army purveyor Abraham Eskenasi, the Ottoman army surgeon Isaac Salom (descendants of both of whom are now living at Sarajevo), and the rabbi Isaac Attias. About this time Moses Amar, a Jew from Belgrade, whose descendants still live in that city, was employed by the Ottoman government as collector of taxes at Travnik. His successors down to the time of the occupation (1878) were the following Jews: Judah Montilijo, R. Salom, T. Levi, D. Salom, and M. I. Salom. The Ottoman government treated them liberally, allowing them to close the tax-office on Jewish feast-days and on Saturdays—a fact which indicates the influence and respect which the Jews enjoyed.

The Jews of Travnik have always been conservative. About 1840, when their number had increased, they built a wooden chapel, which was replaced by a massive temple in 1863, the leading Jews of the community helping in its construction by personally carrying stone and brick. A schoolhouse was erected in 1877, but both these edifices were burned in the conflagration of Sept. 3, 1903. The acting rabbi, Isaac Attias, who has already been mentioned, was succeeded by Abraham Abinon, who officiated for twenty-six years, when he was called to SARAJEVO as chief rabbi of the Sephardim in Bosnia-Herzegovina. The Jews of Travnik have never been subjected to any persecutions or restrictions on account of their religion, and have always lived peaceably with the followers of other creeds. In 1903, out of a total population of 6,626, there were 426 Jews in the town, comprising in a single community sixty-five Sephardic and twenty-four Ashkenazic families, the latter having come after 1878.

J.   S. WE.

TREASON.—Biblical Data: In the strictest sense there is no record in the Bible of an attempt to betray one's country, nor is there any mention of an unsuccessful attempt at regicide, which is high treason; but there are numerous instances of successful attempts to overthrow the government by killing its head. Abimelech, the son of Jerubbaal, slew his half-brothers, the seventy sons of Gideon, and proclaimed himself ruler of Israel (Judges ix. 1–5). Athaliah annihilated all those of royal blood and made herself Queen of Judah (II Kings xi. 1).

Saul evidently considered David's action as treasonable and deserving of death (I Sam. xx. 31), and he executed Abimelech and his family of priests for aiding David (I Sam. xxii. 11–18), though Samuel, by God's command, had already anointed David as Saul's successor. Nevertheless, David killed the Amalekite who assisted Saul in committing suicide, "for stretching forth his hand to destroy the Lord's anointed" (II Sam. i. 14). Baanah and Rechab, two captains, killed Ish-bosheth, the son of Saul, in the expectation of being rewarded by David; but the latter charged them with treason and executed them (II Sam. iv. 2–12). Joab killed Absalom for having attempted to overthrow the government and to depose his father, David, in the kingship (II Sam. xviii. 14). Shimei, the son of Gera, was guilty of treason in insulting and cursing David (II Sam. xvi. 5–8). When Shimei begged David's forgiveness, the latter pardoned him (II Sam. xix. 21), but King Solomon found a pretext to avenge his father (I Kings ii. 46). Sheba, the son of Bichri, raised the standard of rebellion against David, and was killed by those he had misled (II Sam. xx. 22). Adonijah was found guilty of treason, and was finally executed (I Kings i. 5, ii. 25).

Zimri, a captain in the army of Elah, the son of Baasha, killed his king, and after a reign of seven days, fearing capture, committed suicide (I Kings xvi. 9–18). His action became proverbial, and was recalled in Jezebel's remark, "Zimri, . . . who slew his master" (II Kings ix. 31). Pekahiah, the son of Menahem, King of Israel, was killed by his captain Pekah, the son of Remaliah, who succeeded him. In return, Hoshea, the son of Elah, conspired against Pekah, killing and replacing him (II Kings xv. 25, 30). Ishmael killed Ahikam's son Gedaliah, whom the king of Babylon had appointed governor (II Kings xxv. 25).

——In Rabbinical Literature: The Rabbis find the penalty of death for disobedience to the king in Josh. i. 18 (see Sanh. 49a). A Jewish king may inflict death upon those guilty of revolt. Even if the king orders one of his subjects to go to a certain place, or forbids him to leave his own house, he must obey or become liable to capital punishment. The king also has the right to kill one who insults or disgraces him, as in the case of Shimei ben Gera. Death for treason is by the sword only. The king may also punish the offender otherwise, but he may not confiscate his property, as this would be robbery (Maimonides, "Yad," Melakim, iii. 8). David ben Solomon ibn Abi Zimra defines a king as one chosen by a prophet or elected by the people, but not a self-appointed ruler who has acquired his kingdom by usurpation. No one can be guilty as a "mored be-malkut" in the case of such a king (commentary on the "Yad," *ad loc.*, ed. Wilna, 1900). R. Joseph partly justifies David's action against Uriah by the latter's reference to "my lord Joab, and the servants of my lord" (II Sam. xi. 11), which placed Joab on equal terms with the king, an offense which amounted to treason (Shab. 56a). Others are of the opinion that Uriah deserved death because he disobeyed David's command to go home (Tos. *ad loc.*, s.v. ואמר). David adjudged Nabal guilty of disrespect to the king; but Abigail pleaded that Saul was still living and that David was not yet recognized generally as king: David admitted the force of her argument (I Sam. xxv. 33; Meg. 14b). Amasa was guilty of disobedience when he "tarried longer than the set time which he [David] had appointed him," and thereby earned his death at the hands of Joab (II Sam. xx. 5, 10; Sanh. 49a).

J.   J. D. E.

TREASURE-TROVE. See FINDER OF PROP-
ERTY.

**TREBINO (TREMINO) DE SOBRE-
MONTE, TOMAS:** Martyr; burned at the stake
at Mexico, or Lima, April 11, 1649. He had previously been reconciled by the Inquisition; but in
1642, during the trial of Gabriel de Granada, information was brought against him and his wife, Maria
Gomez. He appears to have been thrown into the
dungeon of the Inquisition at that time, and kept in
imprisonment till his death, possibly in order that
the Inquisitor might obtain possession of his fortune;
for when burning he taunted the officials with using
up wood which had cost them nothing, because it
had been bought with his money. Out of a group of
109 prisoners, Trebino de Sobremonte was the only
one to be burned alive. He died without uttering
a groan, mocking "the pope and his hirelings," as
he called them, and taunting his tormentors with his
last breath. De Barrios, the Spanish-Jewish historian, who visited Cayenne in 1660, dedicated two
sonnets to him.

BIBLIOGRAPHY: Obrégon, *Mexico Viejo*, vol. ii.; C. Adler, in
Publ. Am. Jew. Hist. Soc. vii., pp. vi. 5, 59, 60, 65; G. A.
Kohut, *ib.* iv. 124, 161–162; xi. 164.
A.   J.

**TREBITSCH, ABRAHAM BEN REUBEN
ḤAYYAṬ:** Austrian scholar; born at Trebitsch,
Moravia, about 1760; died at Nikolsburg in the first
half of the nineteenth century. He attended the
yeshibah of Löb Fischels at Prague in 1775 ("Ḳorot
ha-'Ittim," p. 24a), and then settled in Nikolsburg,
where he became secretary to the "Landesrabbiner."
He was the author of "Ḳorot ha-'Ittim," a history of
the European monarchs, including the emperors of
Austria, from 1741 to 1801 (part i., Brünn, 1801;
with additions, under the title "Ḳorot Nosafot," up
to the year 1830, by Jacob Bodek, Lemberg, 1841).
It deals especially with the history and literature of
the Jews in the Austrian states. Trebitsch's work
is a continuation of Menahem Mann ben Solomon
ha-Levi's "She'erit Yisrael," which traces the history
down to the year 1740 (see JEW. ENCYC. i. 490, *s.v.*
AMELANDER).

Trebitsch, with Hirsch Menaḳḳer, was the author
of "Ruaḥ Ḥayyim," a story of the exorcising of an
evil spirit that possessed a young man (published in
Hebrew and Yiddish, Nikolsburg, 1785; Frankfort-
on-the-Oder, 1794).

BIBLIOGRAPHY: Benjacob, *Oẓar ha-Sefarim*, p. 527, No. 327;
Fürst, *Bibl. Jud.* iii. 442; Zedner, *Cat. Hebr. Books Brit.
Mus.* p. 176.
D.   S. MAN.

**TREBITSCH, NEHEMIAH (MENAHEM
NAHUM):** Austrian rabbi; born at Prague Aug.
14, 1779; died there July 4, 1842. He was a son
of Selig Trebitsch, ḥazzan at the Altneuschule, and
he received a thorough Talmudical training at the
yeshibah of Jacob Günsberg. Upon the recommendation of the "Landesrabbiner" Mordecai Benet
(Marcus Benedict), Trebitsch became rabbi of Prossnitz in 1826.

On May 13, 1832, the government confirmed the
election of Trebitsch as "Landesrabbiner" of Moravia,
in succession to Mordecai Benet, and granted him a
salary of 600 florins; he was the last Moravian

"Landesrabbiner" of the old school. In Sept., 1833,
the provincial government issued a decree conferring
upon the chief rabbi the power of proposing candidates for the various rabbinates of the province, and
of making an appointment when the congregation
failed to inform him of a vacancy or rejected the
candidate proposed by the "Landesrabbiner." This
decree, for which Trebitsch was declared by his opponents to be responsible, brought him into conflict with the congregations of Gewitsch, Weisskirchen, Prossnitz, and Loschitz; and five years later
(May 23, 1838) another decree canceled the chief
rabbi's privilege of proposing candidates. Abraham
Neuda, rabbi of Loschitz, whom Trebitsch refused
to confirm on account of liberal tendencies, was reinstated after having passed a successful examination before a committee of which Trebitsch was a
member. This defeat, and the censure of the government for his opposition to the use of the German
language among the Jews greatly affected Trebitsch, who died while on a journey to Carlsbad.

Trebitsch wrote: "Shelom Yerushalayim," glosses
on Seder Mo'ed of the Palestinian Talmud, with the
text and David Fränkel's commentary (Vienna,
1821); "Ḳobeẓ 'al Yad," notes on Maimonides'
"Yad ha-Ḥazaḳah," part i., with text (*ib.* 1835).

BIBLIOGRAPHY: *Ḳol Neḥi*, a funeral sermon (Hebr. and German), Prague, 1842; L. Löw, *Das Mährische Landesrab-
binat*, in *Gesammelte Schriften*, ii. 195–212.
S.   S. MAN.

TREE OF LIFE.—Biblical Data: According
to Gen. ii. 9, there stood in the midst of the Garden
of Eden a "tree of life," apparently by the side of
the "tree of knowledge of good and evil." Although
Gen. iii. 3 seems to presuppose but one tree there,
Gen. iii. 22 asserts that, after the primitive pair
had eaten of the tree of knowledge, they were expelled from Eden lest they should put forth their
hands and take of the tree of life and live forever.
The view of the writer was that Eden contained a
tree the magical power of the fruit of which conferred immortality upon him who partook of it,
though YHWH prohibited mortals from partaking
of this fruit.

A tradition of this tree lingered long in Israel. In
Prov. iii. 16–18 the poet says of wisdom, "Length
of days is in her right hand; . . . She is a tree of
life to them that lay hold upon her," a passage
which clearly alludes to the primitive conception of
a life-prolonging tree. Again, Prov. xi. 30 reads,
"The fruit of the righteous is a tree of life"; and
Prov. xiii. 12, "Hope deferred maketh the heart sick:
but when the desire cometh, it is a tree of life." In
Prov. xv. 4 it is said, "A wholesome tongue is a tree
of life." In the last three references the thought
may not be so literal as in the first, but the use of
the tree of life in this gnomic poetry
is evidence that the tradition lived.
In Ezek. xlvii. 12 also there seems to
be an allusion to the tree of life. In
describing the river which would flow
out from Jerusalem to the Dead Sea the prophet
says, "And by the river upon the bank thereof, on
this side and on that side, shall grow all trees for
meat, whose leaf shall not fade, neither shall the
fruit thereof be consumed: it shall bring forth new

*Referred to
in
Proverbs.*

fruit according to his months." In the New Testament, where this passage is quoted (Rev. xxii. 2), the tree is described as the tree of life.

In the extracanonical literature there are two or three additional references. The Ethiopic Book of Enoch (xxiv. 4) describes the tree of life as having "a fragrance beyond all fragrance; its leaves and bloom and wood wither not forever; its fruit is beautiful and resembles the dates of a palm." The Slavonic Book of Enoch (viii. 3) says, "In the midst there is the tree of life . . . and this tree can not be described for its excellence and sweet odor." IV Esd. viii. 52, in describing the future, says, "Unto you is paradise opened, the tree of life is planted," etc.

——**Critical View:** Budde ("Urgeschichte," pp. 46 et seq.) showed that in the original narrative of Gen. ii.–iii. there was but one tree. This, he thought, was the tree of knowledge, and he accordingly eliminated the tree of life. Barton, however, has shown ("Semitic Origins," pp. 93 et seq.) that in primitive Semitic life the especially sacred tree was the date-palm, and that, because of its bisexual nature and because of a belief that man came to self-realization through sexual relations, it was regarded as both the tree of knowledge and the tree of life. The differentiation which divided these functions between two trees came in at a later time, when knowledge of the origin had become in part obscured. That this is the source of the idea of the tree of life among the Hebrews is rendered probable by the following considerations: (1) the Temple of Solomon, which was evidently intended to imitate a garden (comp. Bevan, in "Jour. of Theol. Studies," iv. 502 et seq.), was carved with cherubim, palm-trees, and flowers (I Kings vi. 29-32); (2) a recollection of the real origin of the tree of life crops out in Ethiopic Enoch, xxiv. 4; (3) the tradition came to the Hebrews by way of Babylonia (comp. PARADISE, CRITICAL VIEW), and in Babylonia not only was the palm the sacred tree of a sacred garden (comp. Barton, l.c. p. 107), but in the literature its name is sometimes written with the determinative for deity (idem, "Documents from the Archives of Telloh," 1905, plate 25). For a similar Babylonian conception of a food of life see PARADISE, CRITICAL VIEW. In Hebrew literature this idea first appears in its literal form in Genesis, is used as a literary metaphor in Proverbs, and in Ezekiel and the apocalypses becomes a part of the picture of the heavenly paradise.

BIBLIOGRAPHY: Budde, Urgeschichte, pp. 46–88, Giessen, 1883; Toy, Proverbs, in International Critical Com. 1899, pp. 69, 70; Barton, Sketch of Semitic Origins, pp. 90-98, New York, 1902.

E. G. H.   G. A. B.

TREE-WORSHIP: Trees have been objects of worship in all parts of the world (comp. Mannhardt, "Wald- und Feldkulte," Berlin, 1875). They were worshiped among the Semites (comp. Wellhausen, "Reste Arab. Heidentums," 2d ed., 1897, pp. 101 et seq.; W. R. Smith, "Rel. of Sem." 2d ed., 1894, pp. 185 et seq.; Barton, "Sketch of Semitic Origins," pp. 87 et seq.), and the Hebrews were no exception to this. The tree that was generally regarded as sacred in Palestine was the oak, or the terebinth, which in hot countries, especially the more southerly of those

about the Mediterranean, takes the place of the oak. It is called "allon," which possibly meant "divine tree" (from אֵל), though another etymology is perhaps more probable. This was not the only sacred tree; for traces of the worship of the palm-tree survive (comp. TREE OF LIFE), and Abraham planted an "eshel" (tamarisk) by the sacred wells at Beer-sheba and called on the name of God there (Gen. xxi. 33). Tamarisks existed also at Ramah in the time of Saul and at Jabesh in Gilead (I Sam. xxii. 6, xxxi. 13, Hebr.). It was the terebinth, however, which was generally worshiped, and the worship of which was denounced by the Prophets.

The worship of this tree is connected with the earliest traditions. At Shechem, YHWH is said to have appeared to Abraham at the terebinth (R. V. margin) of Moreh, when he first entered the land (Gen. xii. 6 et seq.). Under this tree Jacob buried the foreign gods of his followers (Gen. xxxv. 4); and Joshua set up a "mazzebah" under **The Sacred** the terebinth which was in the sanc-**Terebinth.** tuary of YHWH (Josh. xxiv. 26). Perhaps it was this tree to which allusion is made in Judges ix. 37. Near Beth-el there was another of these sacred terebinths (Eng. versions, "oak"; Gen. xxxv. 8). At Hebron, Abraham built an altar under one; there he dwelt, and there YHWH

Sacred Terebinth on Jabal Ausha', Palestine.
(From a photograph.)

appeared to him (Gen. xii. 18, xiv. 18, xviii. 1 et seq.). A descendant of this tree (see illustration s.v. ABRAHAM'S OAK) is still pointed out at Hebron, and is venerated by the Russo-Greek pilgrims who visit Palestine every year: it has probably maintained its sacred character through all the intervening centuries. At Ophra a sacred terebinth (A. V. "oak") existed in the time of Gideon (Judges vi. 11, 19). The wide-spread existence of this tree is evidenced by the names derived from it—as Elim (Ex. xv. 27), Elon (Judges xii. 11), and Elath (II Kings xiv. 22). The extent of its worship is indicated also by the denunciations of the Prophets. A favorite phrase of theirs in describing idolatrous practises was "upon every high hill and under every green tree" (Deut. xii. 2; Jer. ii. 20). Some times the name of the terebinth is combined with this phrase (comp. Isa. lvii. 5 and Ezek. vi. 13, R. V. margin), showing that it was to this tree the Prophets referred.

The sacred character of many of these trees has survived to the present time. There is, for example, one on Jabal Ausha', and others are at 'Ain Yajuz and Suf (comp. Barton in "Biblical World," 1904, xxiv. 170, 174; *idem*, "A Year's Wandering in Bible Lands," 1904, p. 162). The one at Suf is thickly hung with rags. In southern Gilead to-day the limbs of the ordinary terebinth are cut for fire-wood, so that the tops of the trees are kept small and are much misshapen. The sacred ones, on the contrary, are left intact and cast a fine shade. Perhaps this was the case in ancient times also. If so, it would explain the phrase "green tree" as applied to those which were sacred.

Other trees besides those mentioned may have had a sacred character, as is suggested by the fact that David once received an oracle through the mulberry- or balsam-tree ("baka"; comp. II Sam. v. 24); but nearly all trace of such a character has disappeared. As has been pointed out, the Prophets were unable completely to suppress tree-worship, which has survived in Palestine through all religious changes to the present day.

BIBLIOGRAPHY: In addition to the works mentioned, see Baudissin, *Studien*, vol. ii.; Jacobs, *Studies in Biblical Archæology*, pp. 68–74.

E. C.   G. A. B.

TREES, LAWS CONCERNING: Cutting down fruit-bearing and useful trees is forbidden by the Mosaic law. In time of war the fruit-trees about a besieged city may not be injured or used to build defenses; for war is waged against foes, and not against the life-preserving works of nature (Deut. xx. 19–20). The Rabbis regard this as an admonition against any kind of waste or wilful destruction. The prohibition is technically known as "bal tashḥit" (thou shalt not destroy; Shab. 129a). Some authorities, however, permit the cutting down of fruit-trees when the site is needed for a dwelling ("Ṭure Zahab," to Shulḥan 'Aruk, Yoreh De'ah, 117, 6).

A tree which extends into the public road may be cut to allow a camel and its rider to pass beneath (B. B. ii. 14). Trees were often used to mark the boundary between fields belonging to different owners. The fruit of a tree belongs to the owner of the land in which the tree is planted, though the branches extend over other property. If the trunk of the tree is in two properties, the two owners become partners in the tree and divide the fruit (B. M. 107a; "Yad," Shekenim, vi. 9). One who purchases three trees in one field may claim the right to as much ground around the trees as is necessary for the gatherer and his basket (B. B. 82b); one who purchases less than three trees has no claim to ground. An adjacent owner can not object because the roots of a tree are in his ground. He may, however, cut the roots when they are in the way of his plow or if they enter his well. When there is no fence between two separately owned fields, one must not plant trees nearer than 4 ells from his neighbor's boundary-line (B. B. 26a). Enough space must be left on either side of a river to allow a rower room to run his boat ashore (Shulḥan 'Aruk, Ḥoshen Mishpat, 155).

W. B.   J. D. E.

TREMELLIUS, JOHN IMMANUEL: Italian Hebraist; born at Ferrara 1510; died at Sedan Oct. 9, 1580. He was educated at the University of Padua. He was converted about 1540 to the Catholic faith through Cardinal Pole, but embraced Protestantism in the following year, and went to Strasburg to teach Hebrew. Owing to the wars of the Reformation in Germany he was compelled to seek asylum in England, where he resided at Lambeth Palace with Archbishop Cranmer in 1547. In 1549 he succeeded Paul Fagius as regius professor of Hebrew at Cambridge. On the death of Edward VI. he revisited Germany, and, after some vicissitudes, became professor of Old Testament at Heidelberg (1561). He ultimately found refuge at the College of Sedan, where he died. His chief literary work was a Latin translation of the Bible from the Hebrew and Syriac. The five parts relating to the Old Testament were published at Frankfort-on-the-Main between 1575 and 1579, in London in 1580, and in numerous later editions. Tremellius also translated into Hebrew Calvin's "Catechism" (Paris, 1551), and wrote a "Chaldaic" and Syriac grammar (Paris, 1569).

BIBLIOGRAPHY: *Dictionary of National Biography*.

T.   J.

TRÉNEL, ISAAC: French rabbi; born at Metz Dec. 28, 1822; died at Paris in 1890. He studied at Marmoutier under his uncle Jacob Haguenauer, a famous Talmudist, and later at Merzig, Prussia, under the Talmudist Moïse Lévy, known also as R. Mochè Merzig. After completing his studies at the rabbinical school of Metz, Trénel was appointed rabbi at Besançon; he resigned that office soon after, however, and went to Paris, where he was for a time secretary of the Comité de Bienfaisance Israélite. After some years he was appointed assistant to the chief rabbi of Paris, and in 1856 director of the Ecole Centrale Rabbinique, which was transferred to Paris in 1859; he retained the latter office until his death. He was the author of a Hebrew-French dictionary, compiled in collaboration with N. Sander (Paris, 1859), and of a study on the life of Hillel the Elder, published in the report of the Séminaire Israélite (*ib.* 1867).

S.   I. L.

TRENT (German, **Trient**): Oldest city of the Tyrol; a sovereign bishopric from 1027 to 1803. During the first half of the fourteenth century a small number of Jews, probably from Italy, settled in the episcopal see. During the first decades their history differed in no wise from that of the Jews living in the rest of the TYROL; but by the beginning of the fifteenth century there existed for the Jews of Trent special ordinances similar to those in force in Bozen, as is proved by an order promulgated by Bishop Ulrich III. of Brixen in 1403. The Jews as prominent business men showed themselves of service to the bishops, and accordingly stood high in favor with them. Thus Bishop Alexander of Masovia (1423–44) on one occasion gave a decision in favor of the Jew Isaac against Peter von Rido (Sept. 3, 1440). The Jewish physician Tobias, who later (1475) died a martyr for his faith, was likewise very popular among the Christians.

The Jews owned houses, estates, and a separate Jewish school, and in general lived on the best of terms with their Christian fellow citizens, until the fanaticism of a priest caused untold disaster to descend upon the small but prosperous community. Bernardinus of Feltre, the indirect and probably the direct instigator of the murder of Simon of Trent, brought about the notorious ritual-murder proceedings of 1475 (see SIMON OF TRENT). The community was dissolved; its rich members were put to death after the confiscation of their property by order of Bishop Hinderbach; and the surviving members were expelled. Sixtus IV., seriously ill at the time, in the bull "Facit nos pietas," dated June 20, 1478, sanctioned these proceedings in spite of the efforts made by the Bishop of Ventimiglia, who showed that the charges which had been brought were a mere tissue of lies. For centuries from that time no Jews dwelt in Trent; and as late as Oct. 20, 1638, the proceedings of 1475 were cited by the prince bishop Karl Emanuel of Madruzzo as ground for forbidding the settlement of Jews in the town. On the same occasion a law was promulgated to the effect that Jews when traveling might not pass through the precincts of Trent in closed wagons or sedan-chairs, and that they must wear on the breast a badge the size of a thaler. The penalty for violating this law was to be a long imprisonment or heavy fine. In 1725 and again in 1731 it was ordered that Jews wear hats covered with red or yellow cloth. A few Jews were allowed to stay in Trent when provided with special letters of protection from the emperor, but only for a few days. Such a safe-conduct was granted, for example, by Emperor Maximilian to the Jew Emanuel, son of Samson, on March 1, 1516.

In recent times several Jewish merchants have settled in Trent; but they have no opportunities for holding religious services, and, like all the Jews in the Tyrol, they belong to the community of HOHENEMS.

J.　　　　　　　　　　　　　　　　　　　　A. TÄ.

TRESPASS : Injury done directly, in most cases purposely, to the person or property of another. Trespass on the person has been discussed under the head of ASSAULT AND BATTERY: it remains to speak of the Talmudic law of trespass on property.

According to the Mishnah (B. K. ii. 6), "a man is always forewarned." That is, like the master of the forewarned ox (see GORING OX), he is always liable for the whole damage arising from his direct act; and the words are added: "whether awake or asleep, whether acting of purpose or from ignorance."

The Scripture prescribes punishment for only one typical case ("ab") of trespass on property (Lev. xxiv. 8, Hebr.): "And he who kills a domestic animal shall make it good, life for life"; and (ib. verse 21): "And he who smites a beast shall make it good." This is extended by the oral law to all cases of direct harm done to property; but the above-quoted section of the Mishnah also singles out as a case, "whether

XII.—16

he has blinded one's eye, or has broken his vessel, he pays full damage." In other places the Mishnah or Baraita speaks of tearing a person's clothes, or destroying his crops or plants, or killing his beast. Only one exception is made: viz., when the trespass constitutes otherwise a death-deserving, sinful act, there is no liability to make the damage good in money (see the case of the burglar in Sanh. viii. 6).

Trespass on Property.

Not only is sleep or ignorance no defense against the charge of trespass, but unwillingness or acting under compulsion (אנוס) does not free from liability —for instance, where one stumbles or falls from the roof and in so doing hurts a person or breaks a thing—unless the hurtful movement was made under irresistible force and was not caused by lack of care (B. K. 26–28). This is illustrated in the Mishnah (B. K. iii. 4–5) thus:

" When two potters [men carrying earthenware] are walking one behind the other, and the first stumbles and falls, and the second stumbles over him, the first is liable for the damage done to the other. Or when one goes along with his jar or barrel, and the other with his joist [meaning side by side], and the jar of the one is broken against the joist of the other, the latter goes clear; for each had the right to go where he went. If the man with the joist walked in front and the jar or barrel was broken against it, the man with the joist goes clear; but if he stood still, unless he told the man with the barrel to stand still also, he is liable. If the man with the barrel walked in front, and the other man behind him, and the barrel was broken by the joist, [the bearer of the latter] is liable; but if the man with the barrel suddenly stands still, without telling the man behind him to stop, the latter goes free. And the same results will follow where one carries a burning lamp and another a bundle of flax."

But when the injurious act is committed on the grounds of the injuring party, he who commits it is liable only for what he does wilfully, not for what he does unwittingly or involuntarily; such at least is the opinion of Maimonides, taken from post-Talmudic authorities, though based upon hints and analogies in the Mishnah and the Baraita.

The trespasser is responsible not only for what he does with his hand or other parts of his body, or with a weapon or implement which he wields, but also for any injury which he does by throwing or shooting or by spitting. But if he casts anything on the ground (even his saliva) and injury arises therefrom afterward (e.g., where it causes a man or a beast to stumble), it is not a trespass, but is in the nature of a pit (see JEW. ENCYC. i. 160b, s.v. ACCIDENT).

Extent of Trespass.

Where one strikes iron with a hammer so that sparks issue therefrom, by which a neighbor's house or goods are burned or otherwise damaged, it is deemed a trespass, for which the wielder of the hammer is liable. When one pushes his neighbor's beast into the water, or prevents it from leaving the water, and it is drowned, or when he locks it in a circumscribed place, where it dies from heat or from lack of air, he is liable; and thus in similar cases of death indirectly inflicted.

Where an injury does not affect the neighbor's property in the body and can not be seen—where the shape of the thing is not changed, yet the thing itself is diminished in value—it is held (Giṭ. 53b) that under the letter of the Torah there is no liability for damage; but there is a rabbinical ordinance to the effect that the person causing the diminution in value must make it good. This would happen where things Levitically clean were defiled by the act of one not the owner; or where "wine of a heathen libation" (יין נסך) was mixed with another man's wine, rendering its use unlawful; or in like cases where food or drink has by the trespasser's act been made a thing forbidden under the Jewish dietary, Levitical, or other religious laws.

Where one man orders or procures another to commit a trespass, and the agent does so, both principal and agent are liable for the damage done. Where the construction of a house, or of a similar thing in which several work together, causes an injury, if those doing the several parts of the work are associated as partners therein, all are liable; but if they work as employees, each for his own wages, only the one who actually causes the injury is liable.

Trespass Through Agent.

This case is also put: Five men have each put a burden on a beast, and it walks along; a sixth puts a further burden on it, and it stops and dies; the sixth alone is liable. If, however, the beast had stopped before the additional weight was laid on it, the sixth man goes free; but if there is doubt as to the facts, all six are liable, and the damage is divided among them; and generally, when two or more jointly have killed an animal or broken an implement, the damage is paid by them in equal parts.

All damages to property are paid in money, and are ascertained by subtracting the value of the dead beast or of the wreckage from the worth of the beast or other article before the trespass was committed. See ROBBERY.

BIBLIOGRAPHY: Maimonides, Yad, Ḥobel u-Mazziḳ, vii. 7; Shulḥan 'Aruk, Ḥoshen Mishpaṭ, 400-419, passim.

E. C.   L. N. D.

TRESPASS-OFFERINGS. See SACRIFICE.

TREUE ZIONSWÄCHTER, DER. See PERIODICALS.

TREUENBURG or TREUENFELD, JACOB. See BASSEVI, JACOB; COAT OF ARMS.

TREVES (ancient, **Augusta Treverorum;** German, **Trier**): City of Rhenish Prussia, formerly an electorate comprising upper and lower bishoprics with Treves and Coblenz as capitals (see JEW. ENCYC. iv. 133). In all probability Jews lived in the city in the early centuries of the common era, for Treves was the central point connecting Gaul and Rome. There is no specific mention of them, however, before 1066, when Archbishop Eberhard (1047–66) menaced them with expulsion unless they should accept baptism before Easter; but this threat was ineffective, for he was murdered on Feb. 12, 1066, by a priest named Christian, who had been instigated, it was alleged, by the Jews. Thirty years later (June, 1096) the pillaging bands of Emikos advanced upon Treves. Several Jews committed suicide, while the remainder sought refuge in the palace of Archbishop Egilbert, who endeavored to persuade them to accept baptism, although those who were converted obtained the permission of Emperor Henry IV. in the following year to return

to Judaism (see Grätz, "Gesch." vi. 102 et seq.; Salfeld, "Martyrologium," pp. 3, 19 [Hebrew part], and pp. 98, 140 et seq. [German part], where a list of the names of the martyrs is given). The other communities of Treves, including those at Berncastel, Cochem, and Wittlich, were almost totally destroyed by the Crusaders. During the archbishopric of Bruno of Treves early in the twelfth century (1102–1124), one of the residents of the city was a Jew named Joshua, who later embraced Christianity, and who enjoyed a reputation as a physician, mathematician, astronomer, and student of Hebrew literature. Abrion, the Jew of Treves, who was unusually well versed in German, seems to have been a contemporary of Joshua (Goethe, "Reineke Fuchs," ii.).

In 1262 the Jews were expelled from Treves by Archbishop Heinrich of Vinstingen, who invited Lombards to take their places, although the latter proved to be even more usurious than the Jews. The elector Baldwin of Treves employed Jewish financial agents, among them Muskin (1323–36); Jacob Daniel (until 1341), a banker who had a Hebrew chancellery and who, like his chief manager, bore the title of "Judæorum dominus"; and Michael, Jacob's son-in-law, who was in the electoral service until 1349. The Jews of Treves suffered much during the ARMLEDER PERSECUTIONS in 1336, when their houses were pillaged (Salfeld, l.c. p. 239, note 1); but three years later they were permitted to remain in Treves in consideration of an annual tax of 100 pounds heller, half this sum being paid in May and half on St. Martin's Day. At Coblenz on March 17, 1345, two Jews of Treves farmed the archiepiscopal "Rheinzoll" of 15 tournois for three years at 655 livres gros tournois annually.

First Expulsion, 1262.

At the time of the Black Death the Jews of Treves were persecuted, like those of the entire Moselle valley (Salfeld, l.c. pp. 69, 78, 80, 84 [Hebrew part]; pp. 246 et seq., 268, 276, 286 [German part]). On Oct. 9, 1354, Archbishop Boemund II. engaged the Jew Symon as his physician in ordinary, and Emperor Charles V., in a document dated Metz, Dec. 13, 1356, granted the elector the right of admitting Jews. On Sept. 30, 1362, an agreement was made between Archbishop Cuno of Falkenstein and the city of Treves by which the latter pledged itself to protect the Jews of the archbishopric like any other citizens, although the number of families permitted to reside there was limited to fifty; and they were ordered to pay an annual tax of 100 livres noir tournois in two instalments, at St. John's Day and at Christmas, while in case twenty-five families or fewer lived there, they were to pay 50 livres. On Aug. 24, 1405, King Ruprecht waived his claim to the OPFERPFENNIG which had not been collected from the Jews of Treves for several years, although he ordered them for the future to pay it annually (Stern, "König Ruprecht von der Pfalz," p. 31, Kiel, 1898).

The Jews of Treves anciently lived in a district ("Vicus Judæorum," mentioned in a document of Sept. 21, 1284) represented by the modern Judenplatz; the main street of residence was the Judenmauergasse (Jüdemergasse) near the Jewish cemetery. This

The Jewry.

Jewish quarter is mentioned in documents of 1330, 1346, and 1350; the synagogue ("scola") in one of 1235; the cemetery, of 1240; the "Spylhus," or dancing-hall, which was used for marriages (see Güdemann, "Gesch." iii. 138 *et seq.*), of 1315; the hospital, of Oct. 12, 1422; and a "Judenporte" in Simeonsgasse, of 1460. At the head of the Treves community, whose members appear as owners of real estate as early as 1229 and Feb. 19, 1235, was a BISHOP OF THE JEWS ("episcopus," "magistratus Judæorum" [1307]), who was required to loan the archbishop 10 marks yearly without interest, receiving in return a cow, an aam of wine, two bushels of wheat, and a discarded cloak. Each Christmas and Easter the Jews gave six pounds of pepper to the archbishop and two to the chamberlain, besides furnishing silk and girdles for new garments for the former. For their cemetery they had to pay six denarii to the cathedral on St. Stephen's Day (Dec. 26 or Aug. 3).

In 1418 Archbishop Otto von Ziegenheim banished the Jews from the entire electorate of Treves; and almost seventy years elapsed before the Jew Ytzinger was admitted (1486) as a veterinary surgeon into Vallendar, south of Coblenz, where other Jews were afterward allowed to settle (July 19 and Oct. 7, 1499) for a period of five years, on payment of an annual tax of 35 gulden. In the beginning of the sixteenth century Jews were again permitted to live in the archbishopric of Treves, and in a document dated at Cochem, Feb. 1, 1555, Archbishop Johann of Isenburg granted them the privilege, renewed in 1679, of appointing a rabbi, although they were obliged to submit to additional taxation. On July 1, 1561, however, Archbishop Johann von der Leyen notified the Jews that they must leave the archbishopric within five months, though twenty-three families were permitted to remain for another period of five years from Dec. 1, 1561; while Jacob III. and Johann VII. of Schoeneberg ordered the Jews to leave Treves in 1580 and the following years, their complete expulsion occurring on Oct. 28, 1589. After a few years, however, the electors of Treves granted special commercial privileges to some Hebrew merchants, headed by the silk manufacturer MAGINO, and as early as 1593–94 Jews were again residing in the episcopal city, although, according to the statute-books, they were compelled to wear the yellow BADGE on their garments. On Jan. 15, 1618, Archbishop and Elector Lothar von Metternich promulgated a special ordinance for the Jews, which was reissued on Feb. 14, 1624; and in 1663 the electoral court chancery enacted that those Jews of Treves who were under the archbishop's protection should be permitted to use wells and pastures and to gather firewood anywhere.

The 15th of Elul, 5435 (= 1675), marked the beginning of a persecution of the Jews in Treves which lasted until Purim of the same year; and by order of the physician Tewle, who was the head of the Jewish congregation, and who began the Treves memorbook in 1664, this day was appointed a general fast for the community in memory of this event. At Treves, as elsewhere, the Jews suffered at times from the pranks of Catholic students, as in 1666, 1687,

Second Expulsion, 1418.

1707, and 1723. In 1681 Archbishop Johann Hugo issued a new Jewish ordinance, and in 1696 the Jews were forbidden to acquire real estate. A law relating to the Jews, promulgated by Elector Franz Ludwig in 1723, remained in force until the end of the electorate, although the archbishopric was secularized in 1803.

The city of Treves was taken by the French on Aug. 10, 1794; by a law enacted on the 29th of Fructidor, year 5 (= Sept. 15, 1797), the LEIBZOLL was abolished (see Hansen, "Treviris, oder Trierisches Archiv für Vaterlandskunde," ii. 37, No. 217, Treves, 1841); and the French invasion brought also civic equality to the Jews. Treves then became a consistorial diocese, like Bonn and Krefeld. On Sept. 9 and 10, 1859, the new synagogue of Treves was dedicated. At present the community numbers about 1,000, and maintains several benevolent societies, as well as a Society for Jewish History and Literature. A separate Orthodox congregation also exists.

Under the French.

Among the rabbis and scientists of Treves the following may be mentioned: David Tewle b. Isaac Wallich, communal leader and physician (exiled from Fulda; died Oct. 5, 1691; see Kaufmann, "Vertreibung der Juden aus Wien," pp. 225 [note 3], 226 [note 1]; Löwenstein, "Gesch. der Juden in der Kurpfalz," p. 6, note 2; also mentioned in Gershon Ashkenazi's Responsa, Nos. 13, 21, 84, 89, and in the preface); R. Joseph Israel b. Abraham Worms (died in Bingen Sept. 9, 1684); his son R. Isaac Aaron Worms (died in Metz July 25, 1722; see Löwenstein, *l.c.* p. 99 and note 1; Gershon Ashkenazi's Responsa, No. 18; Cahen, "Le Rabbinat de Metz," in "R. E. J." 1886, pp. 48 *et seq.*); Moses Meïr Grotwohl (died 1691; see Löwenstein, *l.c.* p. 86, note 2; Jair Hayyim Bacharach's Responsa, p. 234b; Jacob Reischer's Responsa, i. 110; Freudenthal, "Aus der Heimat Mendelssohns," p. 287); Moses Lewow (see Friedberg, "Luḥot Zikkaron," 2d ed., 1904, p. 78; Lewinstein, "Dor Dor we-Dorshaw," p. 95, No. 628); R. Moses b. R. Heshel (died 1st of Ab, 1788); R. Moses Shaḥ (or Moses Trier b. R. Eliezer = R. Moses Levy, died Nisan, 1840; see Löwenstein in "Blätter für Jüdische Gesch. und Literatur," iii. 98); Joseph KAHN; Dr. I. Holländer (died Dec. 8, 1880); Dr. M. S. Zuckermandel (in 1905 "Stiftsrabbiner" in Breslau); and the then chief rabbi, Dr. Bassfreund.

Rabbis and Scholars.

BIBLIOGRAPHY: Ehrmann, in *Israelit*, 1881, Nos. 34 *et seq.*; G. Liebe, in *Westdeutsche Zeitschrift für Gesch. und Kunst*, xii. 321 *et seq.*; A. Schoop, *ib.*, supplementary vol. i. 144 *et seq.*; Schömann, in *Jahresbericht der Gesellschaft für Nützliche Forschung zu Trier*, 1854, p. 40; 1859–60, p. 2 (Hebrew epitaphs of 1346); Lewin, *Das Trierer Memorbuch*, in Rahmer's *Jüd. Lit.-Blatt*, 1881, Nos. 40–41, p. 159; Aronius, *Regesten*, Nos. 2, 160, 176, 180, 189, 222, 352, 475, 499, 581, *et passim*; Joseph ha-Kohen, *'Emeḳ ha-Baka*, ed. Wiener, pp. 17, 158, note 62, p. 162, note 80 (on the murder of R. Simeon of Treves); Lamprecht, *Deutsches Wirtschaftsleben im Mittelalter*, 1886, 1, 2, 1446 *et seq.*, 1472 *et seq.*; comp. also Lewinsky in Brann's *Monatsschrift*, 1904, p. 457; Hecht, *ib.* 1858, pp. 179 *et seq.*; 1861, pp. 358 *et seq.*; Güdemann, *Gesch.* i. 224; Kohut, *Gesch. der Deutschen Juden*, pp. 186, 188, *et passim*; Statistisches Jahrbuch des Deutsch-Israelitischen Gemeindebundes, 1903, p. 85.
D. A. LEW.

TREVES: Family which derived its name from the Prussian city of Treves, famous for its prominent men. No other family can boast such a continuous line of scholars as this one, branches of which have been known under the names **Treves, Tribas, Dreifuss, Trefouse,** and **Drifzan.** There exist, however, no means of tracing the connection of these various branches, which even as early as the fourteenth and fifteenth centuries were already scattered over Germany, Italy, southern France, Greece, Poland, and Russia.

BIBLIOGRAPHY: *Ḳobeẓ 'al Yad*, iii. 14, 15; Steinschneider, *Hebr. Bibl.* iv. 152; *Zeitschrift für Gesch. der Juden in Deutschland*, i. 311; Gross, *Gallia Judaica*, p. 242; A. Epstein, in *Monatsschrift*, xlvi. 159-160, notes 2-6.
s.   S. O.

The subjoined chart is that of the Italian branch, which is the only one of which a genealogy can be given.

BIBLIOGRAPHY: Mortara, *Indice*, p. 66; Zunz, *Ritus*, p. 32, note b; Steinschneider, *Cat. Bodl.* col. 711; Benjacob, *Oẓar ha-Sefarim*, p. 87; Azulai, *Shem ha-Gedolim*, ii. 20; Brüll's *Jahrb.* i. 109-111.

Aryeh Löb ben Naphtali Treves: Russo-Polish scholar; born 1848; died 1873; lived in Augustovo. He was a valued collaborator on the journal "Ha-Maggid," to which he contributed articles over the signature "Ṭure Eben."

BIBLIOGRAPHY: Brüll's *Jahrb.* i. 121; *Ha-Maggid*, 1873, p. 60.

Dob Bär ben Judah Treves: Scholar of the eighteenth century; died 21st of Tishri (Oct. 17), 1803. Prior to 1760 he officiated as rabbi in Hungary, and from that year to 1790 as rabbinical judge in Wilna. He was the author of "Rebid ha-Zahab" (Grodno, 1797), a commentary on the Pentateuch, in which, through cabalistic explanations, he en-

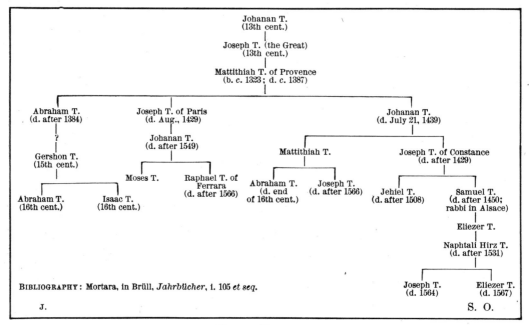

TREVES PEDIGREE.

Abraham b. Gershon Treves (called also **Ẓarfati**): French cabalist; flourished about 1572. He was the author of the following works: (1) commentary on the "Ma'areket ha-Elahut" of R. Perez; (2) glosses to the "Sefer Yeẓirah" and to the commentaries of Moses Botarel, Naḥmani, and Abraham b. David; (3) glosses to the "Sha'are Orah."

BIBLIOGRAPHY: Nepi-Ghirondi, *Toledot Gedole Yisrael*, p. 8; Fürst, *Bibl. Jud.* iii. 444; Brüll's *Jahrb.* i. 113-114.
s.   F. T. H.

Abraham ben Solomon Treves (called also **Ẓarfati**): Scholar of the sixteenth century. He emigrated from Italy to Turkey, where he officiated as rabbi of German and Portuguese congregations in Adrianople and various other cities. He favored the Sephardic ritual, and corresponded with David Cohen and Elijah Mizraḥi. From one of his letters to Joseph Caro ("Abḳat Roḳel," No. 34) it appears that he was a physician also. He was the first scholar to quote the "Kol Bo," and was the author of "Birkat Abraham," a work on the ritual.

deavored to establish a connection between the written and the oral law. He wrote also "Shir Ḥadash" (Wilna, 1800), a commentary on the Song of Solomon.

BIBLIOGRAPHY: Steinschneider, *Cat. Bodl.* cols. 893-894; Benjacob, *Oẓar ha-Sefarim*, pp. 543, 575; Fuenn, *Ḳiryah Ne'emanah*, p. 200; Brüll's *Jahrb.* i. 121.

Eliezer ben Naphtali Hirz Treves (known also as **Eliezer Frankfurt**): German rabbi; born 1495; died 1567. He officiated as rabbi in Frankfort-on-the-Main. He was an adherent of Asher LEMMLEIN, a pseudo-Messiah who appeared in the sixteenth century, and attributed the non-fulfilment of Lemmlein's prophecy concerning the Messiah to circumstances other than fraud.

Eliezer held the Frankfort rabbinate for twenty-two years; and during a ritualistic controversy which took place in 1550 he was called upon to render a decision. In 1558 he was a member of a committee appointed by Emperor Ferdinand I. to organize a system for registering the votes of the Jews of Prague. In 1561 he went for a time to Cracow, where he copied Solomon Molko's commentaries. He was an enthusiastic collector of manuscripts, from which he prepared certain treatises. There are extant several decisions signed by Eliezer, pertaining to the community of Frankfort-on-the-Main, and extending over the period 1556–66 with the exception of the time spent by him in Cracow.

BIBLIOGRAPHY: Gans, *Ẓemaḥ Dawid*, p. 40b; Moses Isserles, *Responsa*, No. 58; Wolf, in Steinschneider, *Hebr. Bibl.* 1861, p. 151; Grätz, *Gesch.* ix. 364; Zunz, *Z. G.* p. 233 and note d; Gedalia ibn Yaḥya, *Shalshelet ha-Ḳabbalah*, ed. Amsterdam, p. 51a; De Rossi, *Dizionario*, p. 520; Steinschneider, *Cat. Bodl.* col. 967; Brüll's *Jahrb.* i. 105-106.

Eliezer ben Samuel Treves (surnamed **Ashkenazi**): Polish scholar of the sixteenth and seventeenth centuries; officiated as rabbi in Opatow. He wrote several Talmudic commentaries, of which, however, only one was published; namely, that on the treatise Ḥullin, entitled "Dammeseḳ Eli'ezer" (Lublin, 1646). In the same year he published a collection of daily prayers under the title "Siaḥ ha-Sadeh." He was the author also of a treatise on the writing of names in bills of divorce; and on a journey through Belgrade he gave a copy of that work to Rabbi Simḥah ha-Kohen Portrapa, who happened to be there at that time, and who later embodied it in a work published by himself. In 1648 Eliezer approved Jacob Chentschin's commentary on the Masorah.

BIBLIOGRAPHY: Azulai, *Shem ha-Gedolim*, i. 23b; Steinschneider, *Cat. Bodl.* col. 964; Bass, *Sifte Yeshenim*, p. 75b, No. 106; Benjacob, *Oẓar ha-Sefarim*, p. 175; Brüll's *Jahrb.* i. 117, 118.

S. O.

Emilio Treves: Italian writer; born at Triest Dec. 31, 1834. He was educated in his native town, and when quite young entered the printing-office of the "Oesterreicher Lloyd" in that city. He contributed to the "Raccolta dei Classici," a work issued from that press and edited by Anton Racheli. At the same time Treves wrote anonymously for "L'Anelo," a journal prohibited by the Austrian government. When his association with "L'Anelo" was discovered he went to Paris, where he was correspondent for the "Crepusculo" of Milan. Two years later he went for a short time to Turin, and then became manager of a printing establishment at Fiume. When this house failed Treves followed the vocation of a teacher in Udine.

In 1858 he settled in Milan and became translator for the official journal "Gazzetta di Milano," at the same time contributing to the "Italia Musicale" and "Uomo di Pietra." In the war of 1859 he served in Garibaldi's legion, and after peace was declared resumed his connection with the "Gazzetta." In 1862 he founded the "Museo di Famiglia," and in 1865 the "Biblioteca Utile," comprising examples of Italian literature as well as various works translated from other languages into Italian. In 1869 he resigned his position on the "Gazzetta di Milano" and founded the "Corriere de Milano," which he sold in 1871. In the latter year he entered into partnership with his brother Giuseppe, and in 1874 the two founded in Milan the "Illustrazione Italiana," which proved very successful.

Treves has written many articles for various journals and publications, and is the author also of several dramas, *e.g.*, "Richezza e Miserie," Triest, 1847,

which was well received, and "Il Duca d'Enghien," *ib.* 1850.

BIBLIOGRAPHY: P. Wurzbach, *Biographisches Lexicon des Kaiserthums Oesterreich*, Vienna, 1882.

Gershon Treves: Scholar of the fifteenth century. He was of German descent and resided in Avignon. Upon the death of Joseph Colon, his father-in-law, he arranged the latter's collection of responsa, Nos. 13, 14, 98, and 102 of which contain letters addressed to himself. During a controversy between the rabbi of Padua and Lewa Landau, Treves was drawn into the dispute (see Moses Minz, Responsa, No. 98).

BIBLIOGRAPHY: Colon, *Responsa*, No. 102; Brüll's *Jahrb.* i. 100.

Giuseppe Treves: Brother of Emilio Treves, and with him cofounder in 1874 of the "Illustrazione Italiana."

S.   F. T. H.

Ḥayyim Treves (known also as **Ḥayyim Schwarz**): Scholar of the sixteenth century; rabbi of the former provinces of Cologne and Jülich. In 1577 he resided in Königswinter, and from 1585 to 1595 in Ahrweiler. His son-in-law was Isaac ben Ḥayyim of Ahrweiler. Treves in deciding a certain question was said to have attacked Christianity; and his son-in-law, together with other contemporary scholars, was compelled to give testimony in the matter.

BIBLIOGRAPHY: Auerbach, *Berit Abraham*, p. 23a; Brüll's *Jahrb.* i. 106-107.

Isaac Treves: Son of Shneor Treves of Frankfort-on-the-Main. He was rabbi of Kopytzk; but no details of his life are known.

Isaac ben Gershon Treves: Venetian scholar of the sixteenth century. He was employed as a corrector of the press on several rabbinic Bible editions which appeared at Venice in 1508, and later on Issachar ibn Susan's "'Ibbur ha-Shanim" (Venice, 1579), a work treating of the Hebrew calendar. Isaac was the author of an introduction to Eliezer Ashkenazi's "Ma'ase Adonai," of an index to Elijah de Vidas' "Reshit Ḥokmah," and of additions to Solomon al-Ḳabiẓ's commentary on the Book of Esther.

BIBLIOGRAPHY: Steinschneider, *Cat. Bodl.* cols. 585, 2912; Nepi-Ghirondi, *Toledot Gedole Yisrael*, p. 182; Zedner, *Cat. Hebr. Books Brit. Mus.* p. 365; Brüll's *Jahrb.* i. 114.

S.   S. O.

Isaac and Jacob Treves: Two Austrian philanthropists who in 1828 donated a fund of 2,100 florins to the Sick Soldiers' Home in Vienna (Militär-Invalidenhaus).

S.   F. T. H.

Israel Hezekiah Treves: Ḥazzan at the Italian synagogue in Padua in the eighteenth century, and, on the death of its rabbi in 1782, rabbinical judge there. He was a pupil of the poet Moses Ḥayyim Luzzatto, who introduced him to the mysteries of Cabala.

BIBLIOGRAPHY: Almanzi, in *Kerem Ḥemed*, iii. 374; Carmoly, in *Revue Orientale*, ii. 182; Nepi-Ghirondi, *Toledot Gedole Yisrael*, p. 204; Grätz, *Gesch.* x. 338; Brüll's *Jahrb.* i. 116.

Jacob Treves (called also **Jacob Brisker**, after his native town, Brest, in Russia): Scholar of the seventeenth century; son of the martyr Moses Abraham Treves (Ashkenazi); lived in Frankfort-on-the-Main. In 1680 he wrote an addendum to Shabbethai Bass' supercommentary on Rashi's commentary on the Pentateuch (Frankfort-on-the-Main, 1712).

BIBLIOGRAPHY: Steinschneider, *Cat. Bodl.* col. 2230; Benjacob, *Oẓar ha-Sefarim,* p. 609; *Sifte Yeshenim,* Introduction; Brüll's *Jahrb.* i. 119.

Jehiel ben David Treves: German scholar of the seventeenth and eighteenth centuries; rabbi of Gailingen. He was the author of important notes to Rashi and to the tosafot of the treatise Beẓah (Offenbach, 1717).

BIBLIOGRAPHY: Wolf, *Bibl. Hebr.* ii. 910; Brüll's *Jahrb.* i. 117.

Jehiel ben Simeon Sofer Treves (Ashkenazi): Russian rabbi of the eighteenth century; officiated in Tikoczin, Russia. Nothing is known concerning his career; but his "Be'er Ḥeṭeb," a compendium of the Shulḥan 'Aruk, has won the approval of the casuists, and is regarded as a standard work on Jewish law. Certain eminent Talmudists, however (Jacob Reischer and Raphael Meisels, for example), have pointed out the author's imprudence in attacking Moses Isserles in an unjustifiable manner ("Shebut Ya'aḳob," iii., No. 41; introduction to the "Tosefet Shabbat").

BIBLIOGRAPHY: Steinschneider, *Cat. Bodl.* col. 1242; Azulai, *Shem ha-Gedolim,* ii. 12; Benjacob, *Oẓar ha-Sefarim,* p. 64; Brüll's *Jahrb.* i. 119–120.

s. S. O.

Johanan ben Mattithiah Treves: Chief rabbi of France from about 1385 to 1394; died in Italy July 21, 1439. After having received his rabbinical diploma from his father, who was chief rabbi of France, he married the daughter of the rich and influential Manessier de Vesoul, and filled the position of rabbi in a provincial town. On the death of his father he returned to Paris and was appointed, by agreement of Charles VI. with the community, to the chief rabbinate.

During the last years of his incumbency he suffered much persecution at the hands of Isaiah ben Abba Mari (called also "Astruc of Savoy"), a former pupil of his father. Being well versed in rabbinical literature, Isaiah arrogated to himself, with the approbation of Meïr ben Baruch of Vienna, the right to ordain French rabbis, and endeavored by all possible means to undermine Johanan's authority. The latter applied for aid to Ḥasdai Crescas and Isaac ben Sheshet, who pronounced themselves in favor of the persecuted rabbi, blaming both Isaiah and his supporter Meïr ben Baruch ("She'elot u-Teshubot Ribash," No. 270). The quarrels, however, ceased only with the expulsion of the Jews from France in 1394. Johanan then settled in Italy, where he remained until his death.

Johanan was one of the most eminent rabbinical authorities of his time; and his halakic decisions were often cited ("Sha'are Dura," see Neubauer, "Cat. Bodl. Hebr. MSS." No. 690). From Italy he carried on a scientific correspondence with Jacob Mölln (MaHaRIL). A responsum of his on the prayers of orphans for their deceased parents, and a letter addressed to the community of Padua, are still extant in manuscript in the Florence Library

(Bisconi, "Bibliothecæ Hebraicæ Florentinæ Catalogus," p. 426).

BIBLIOGRAPHY: Rieti, *Miḳdash Me'aṭ,* p. 104; Lebrecht, *Handschriften und die Ersten Ausgaben des Talmuds,* p. 57, note 2; Carmoly, in *Arch. Isr.* 1856, p. 262; Brüll's *Jahrb.* i. 95 *et seq.*; Gross, *Gallia Judaica,* p. 534.

G. I. Br.

Joseph ben Hirz Treves: German scholar; born in 1490. Together with his brother Eliezer he published his father's commentary on the prayer-book, to which he added an introduction and glosses. He took part in the publication of the mystagogic Midrash on Ruth, which appeared under the title "Tappuḥe Zahab," or "Yesod Shirim" (Thingen, 1560; Cracow, 1569).

BIBLIOGRAPHY: Brüll's *Jahrb.* i. 104–105 and note 76.

Joseph ben Johanan Treves I. (surnamed **ha-Gadol** = "the Great"): First bearer of the name of Treves. He flourished in the fourteenth century, and, according to Zunz ("Z. G." p. 173), was rabbi in Paris. Brüll, however ("Jahrb." i. 90), refers to him as rabbi of Marseilles about 1343. His wife was well versed in Jewish literature, and explained several Talmudical passages; and when later she with her sons took up her residence in Paris the whole family was exempted from wearing the Jewish badge.

BIBLIOGRAPHY: Zunz, *Z. G.* p. 173; Grätz, *Gesch.* viii. 8–9; Isaac ben Sheshet, *Responsa,* No. 271; Isaac de Lattes, *Responsa,* p. 88, Vienna, 1860; Carmoly, in *Revue Orientale,* ii. 114; Brüll's *Jahrb.* i. 90–91.

Joseph ben Lipmann Eliezer Treves (surnamed **Ashkenazi**): Rabbi of the seventeenth century; officiated in Prossnitz, Moravia. He edited a brief abstract of Jacob Weil's "Hilkot Sheḥiṭah" (Amsterdam, 1660), and wrote an elegiac poem ("ḳinah") on the destruction of Kremsir by the Swedes in 1643 and on the devastations which took place in Poland and Lithuania. The poem appeared in 1648.

BIBLIOGRAPHY: Zunz, *Literaturgesch.* p. 435; Steinschneider, *Cat. Bodl.* col. 1456.

Joseph ben Mattithiah Treves: Brother of Johanan Treves; scholar and liturgical poet of the fifteenth century; died on the Ninth of Ab, 1429. At an early age he emigrated to Italy, and there wrote the following liturgical poems: a yoẓer for the Sabbath preceding New-Year; "Silluḳ," consisting of three parts and containing exhortations to repentance; and "Tokaḥah," a prayer written in the form of a dialogue between the living and the dead. In Italy he had copies made of several writings, of which one, of the "Sefer ha-Nayyar," written in 1392, is still extant.

BIBLIOGRAPHY: Zunz, *Literaturgesch.* p. 370; idem, *Ritus,* p. 31; Brüll's *Jahrb.* i. 99.

Joseph ben Mattithiah Treves: Rabbi of Savigliano, Italy, in the sixteenth century. In the divorce proceedings instituted by the physician Joseph Tamari of Venice against his son-in-law Samuel Venturozzo of Perugia, Joseph sided with the latter. Of his writings only a responsum has appeared in print (in Lampronti's "Paḥad Yiẓḥaḳ," i. 105a). A commentary by him on the first chapter of Genesis, and a treatise of his on the Talmudic proverb "An old man in the house is a burden; an old woman, a treasure" ('Ar. 19a), are extant in manuscript.

BIBLIOGRAPHY: Nepi-Ghirondi, *Toledot Gedole Yisrael*, p. 161; Mortara, *Indice*, s.v. *Treves*; Zunz, *Ha-Palit*, pp. 22-23.

Levi ben Jacob Treves (surnamed **Ẓarfati**): French scholar of the sixteenth century. He was the first who declared it permissible at the reading from the Law to call up before any Cohen who might be present an Israelite who paid for the privilege. In the course of time this seems to have become customary in several places; for even in the eighteenth century German casuists protested vigorously against it. Levi is probably identical with the Levi ben Jacob who copied Abravanel's commentary on Isaiah, and who, at an advanced age, emigrated to Jerusalem.

BIBLIOGRAPHY: Ibn Yahya, *Shalshelet ha-Ḳabbalah*, ed. Amsterdam, p. 48b; Hayyim Benveniste, *Keneset ha-Gedolah* on *Shulḥan 'Aruk, Oraḥ Ḥayyim*, No. 135; Ezekiel Katzenellenbogen, *Keneset Yeḥezkel*, No. 7; Steinschneider, *Hebr. Bibl.* 1871, p. 135; Brüll's *Jahrb.* i. 115.

Mattithiah ben Joseph Treves (called **the Provençal**): French scholar; chief rabbi of Paris; born there about 1325; died about 1387. He was educated by his father, and later studied under Nissim ben Reuben and Perez Cohen ben Isaac. He lived in various Spanish cities until 1361, when he returned to Paris; and, as at that time there were only a few scholars in France, he founded a seminary in the French capital. Through the intercession of his brother-in-law, Procurator Manessier de Vesoul, Charles V. in 1363 appointed him chief rabbi of Paris.

Mattithiah collected books, and also engaged in literary pursuits. A responsum signed by him is extant in the Paris Library (Codex 676, No. 5). He was the author of a work on Talmudic methodology, fragments of which have been preserved in Joseph ibn Verga's "She'erit Yosef" (ed. Mantua, pp. 3b, 4a). He is said to have been styled "Ha-Parnas," and to have composed several liturgical poems, among which were one for the eve of the Day of Atonement, and one—a penitential prayer in twenty stanzas—treating of the Ten Martyrs. He is the alleged author of a work entitled "Eben Boḥan." A manuscript copy of the Talmud, now in the Royal Library, Munich, and which was made by a German copyist for Benjamin Josiphiah, was at one time in the possession of Mattithiah.

BIBLIOGRAPHY: Gross, *Gallia Judaica*, pp. 532-534; Judah ibn Verga, *Shebet Yehudah*, ed. Amsterdam, p. 50; Zunz, *Literaturgesch.* p. 368; Ibn Yahya, *Shalshelet ha-Ḳabbalah*, ed. Zolkiev, p. 48a; Bass, *Sifte Yeshenim*, x., No. 9; Heilprin, *Seder ha-Dorot*, ii. 327; Dukes, in *Ḳobeẓ*, Introduction, p. 6; Rabbinovicz, *Diḳduḳe Soferim*, i., Introduction, pp. 27-35; Brüll's *Jahrb.* i. 91 *et seq.*

Menahem ben Abraham Treves (Dreifuss): Rabbi in Sulzburg; died 1857. He was the author of "Oraḥ Mesharim" (Mühlhausen, 1858; 2d ed., Mayence, 1878), treating of the dogmas of faith.

BIBLIOGRAPHY: Zedner, *Cat. Hebr. Books Brit. Mus.* p. 761; Benjacob, *Oẓar ha-Sefarim*, p. 50; Zeitlin, *Bibl. Post-Mendels.* p. 398; Brüll's *Jahrb.* i. 122.

s. S. O.

Michael Treves: Italian engineer of the nineteenth century; lived in Venice. He is the author of "Sulla Perforazione Meccanica delle Ferriere ed in

Particolare sul Gigantesco Traforo delle Alpi Cozie dette del Montcenisio," Venice, 1864; "Di Alcuni Errori Economici . . . della Veneta Industria Vetraria," *ib.* 1864; "Pensieri sull' Avvenire del Commercio e dell' Industria in Italia," *ib.* 1864; "Lezioni Popolari Presso l'Ateneo Veneto," etc., *ib.* 1865.

BIBLIOGRAPHY: Fürst, *Bibl. Jud.* iii. 444; Wurzbach, *Biographisches Lexicon des Kaiserthums Oesterreich*, Vienna, 1882.

s. F. T. H.

Mordecai Treves: Italian scholar of the fourteenth century. He was the author of a historical work treating of the seliḥah poets, in the introduction to which he tells of the persecutions of 1349. He mentions a town named Heila (היילא), where Mar Zuṭra was buried, and which contained large institutions of learning. From this, as well as from the circumstance that Treves confuses the names of the seliḥah poets, Zunz deduces that he failed to consult historical sources.

BIBLIOGRAPHY: Zunz, *Literaturgesch.* pp. 625-627; Brüll's *Jahrb.* i. 115.

Moses ben Jacob Treves: Venetian rabbi and scholar of the seventeenth century. His father was a friend of David de Pomis. From 1648 he maintained a regular correspondence with Samuel Aboab. In 1661 he wrote a poem in honor of Yom-Ṭob Valvason, the founder of a bet ha-midrash in Venice; this poem was published in "Hed Urim" (Venice, 1661). In 1668 he was a member of the rabbinical committee of Venice before which the itinerant prophet Nathan of Gaza was arraigned. In 1670 he sanctioned the publication of Solomon Rocca's "Kawwanat Shelomoh," a cabalistic commentary on the prayers.

BIBLIOGRAPHY: *Debar Shemu'el*, No. 375; Emden, *Torat ha-Kena'ot*, ed. Lemberg, No. 67; Nepi-Ghirondi, *Toledot Gedole Yisrael*, p. 245; Mortara, *Indice*, p. 66; Zedner, *Cat. Hebr. Books Brit. Mus.* p. 786; Brüll's *Jahrb.* i. 115-116.

Naphtali Hirz Treves: Younger brother of Eliezer ben Samuel Treves (Ashkenazi). He held an important rabbinate in Poland, but no details of his life and literary activity are known.

Naphtali Hirz ben Eliezer Treves: Cabalist and scholar of the sixteenth century; officiated as ḥazzan in Frankfort-on-the-Main. He was the author of "Perush" (1560), a famous cabalistic commentary on the prayer-book; and probably also of "Naftule Elohim" (Heddernheim, 1546), an index to Baḥya ben Asher's commentary on the Pentateuch. The preface to the "Naftule Elohim" consists partly of the result of private studies and partly of quotations from other cabalistic works. Treves wrote, too, a supercommentary on Rashi, which is still extant. Naphtali Hirz engaged in disputations with Christian scholars; and he made comments on the pronunciation of German. He is especially important for his accounts of Jewish customs and ceremonies.

BIBLIOGRAPHY: Steinschneider, *Cat. Bodl.* cols. 2028-2030; Nepi-Ghirondi, *Toledot Gedole Yisrael*, p. 94; Conforte, *Ḳore ha-Dorot*, p. 27a; Jost's *Annalen*, ii. 162; Zunz, *Z. G.* p. 190; Gans, *Zemah Dawid*, p. 406, Frankfort-on-the-Main, 1692; Azulai, *Shem ha-Gedolim*, ii. 92a; Zunz, in Steinschneider, *Hebr. Bibl.* x. 134; Brüll's *Jahrb.* i. 101-104.

Raphael ben Baruch Treves: Italian scholar of the seventeenth century. He was the author of a commentary on the Song of Solomon, which, together with some of his Talmudic decisions, was printed in Constantinople in 1743. This commentary is written in the style used by the philosophers of the early Middle Ages, and follows the methods known as "PaRDeS" (the initials of "Peshaṭ," "Remez," "Derash," and "Sod"). Raphael affixed his approbation to Elijah ha-Kohen's "Shebeṭ Musar" (Smyrna, 1667).

Raphael ben Baruch must not be confounded with the Raphael Treves who, in the beginning of the eighteenth century, owned a printing establishment in Constantinople, from which R. Nissim's novellæ to Giṭṭin were issued.

BIBLIOGRAPHY: Zedner, *Cat. Hebr. Books Brit. Mus.* p. 761; Azulai, *Shem ha-Gedolim*, ii. 29a; Benjacob, *Oẓar ha-Sefarim*, p. 108; Steinschneider, *Cat. Bodl.* col. 3024; idem, *Jüdische Typographie*, in Ersch and Gruber, *Encyc.* section ii., part 28, p. 63b; Brüll's *Jahrb.* i. 117.

Raphael Joseph ben Johanan Treves: Rabbi of Ferrara in the sixteenth century. Of his works only two responsa are extant, one treating of the legality of the levirate marriage, and the other of the permissibility of business partnerships between Jews and Christians when the latter attend to business on Saturdays and Jewish holy days. Treves is especially known as a corrector of the press in Foa's printing establishment at Sabbionetta. He wrote encomiums on Maimonides' "Moreh," and Meïr Me'iri's "Yaïr Natib," which appeared in 1553; and he supplied marginal glosses to Abraham ben Isaac ha-Levi's commentary on the Song of Solomon (1558).

In the Tamari-Venturozzo case Treves played a double rôle, for after having signed the sentence of excommunication against Samuel (1566), he appeared as a witness for the latter.

BIBLIOGRAPHY: Nepi-Ghirondi, *Toledot Gedole Yisrael*, p. 307; Lampronti, *Paḥad Yiẓḥak*, iii., part 2, pp. 21–23; Steinschneider, *Cat. Bodl.* col. 2129; *Mosè*, v. 125, 231, 232; vi. 268; Brüll's *Jahrb.* i. 113.
s.   S. O.

Sabbato Graziado Treves: Austrian rabbi; born at Vercelli in Piedmont about 1780; died at Turin June 25, 1856. Instructed by his father, who was a rabbi, he himself became, about 1800, a rabbi in Asti, where he remained until 1820, when he became chief rabbi at Turin. This office he held until 1833, when he was called to Triest, where he officiated during the remainder of his life.

s.   F. T. H.

Samuel ben Eliezer Treves (surnamed **Ashkenazi**): Rabbi of Opatow in the sixteenth and seventeenth centuries. He was the author of novellæ ("ḥiddushim") on the treatises Ketubot and Ḳiddushia (Prossnitz, 1600–2), consisting of abstracts of the works of Joseph ibn Leb, Samuel di Medina, and Solomon Cohen. He appears to have settled permanently in Moravia toward the close of his life.

BIBLIOGRAPHY: Benjacob, *Oẓar ha-Sefarim*, p. 183; Steinschneider, *Cat. Bodl.* col. 2424; idem, *Jüdische Typographie*, in Ersch and Gruber, *Encyc.* ii. 55; Wolf, *Bibl. Hebr.* i. 1089; Brüll's *Jahrb.* i. 118, note 167.

Samuel Isaac Treves: Italian scholar of the eighteenth century. He published a work entitled "Ḥuṭ ha-Meshullash" (Leghorn, 1876), and consisting of songs, elegies, and lyric poems.

BIBLIOGRAPHY: Zeitlin, *Bibl. Post-Mendels.* p. 398.

Shneor ben Joseph Joel Treves: Rabbi of Frankfort-on-the-Main in the seventeenth century. He was the author of a Biblical commentary entitled "Ḥibbur," which was known in Russia in the eighteenth century. With him originated the often-mentioned custom followed by the Treves family of not partaking of a meal in the tabernacle on the eve preceding Shemini 'Aẓeret.

BIBLIOGRAPHY: Fuenn, *Ḳiryah Ne'emanah*, pp. 172, 200, 284, 287; Brüll's *Jahrb.* i. 119; Epstein, in *Monatsschrift*, xlvi. 159–160.

Simeon Treves: Son of Shneor ben Joseph Joel Treves. He was secretary to the community of Frankfort-on-the-Main.

s.   S. O.

Virginia Treves (née **Tedeschi**): Italian author; born at Verona; wife of Giuseppe Treves. She contributed to the "Illustrazione Italiana" under the nom de plume "Cordelia," and was the author of "Il Regno della Donna" (Milan, 1879) and "Prime Battaglie" (*ib.* 1881).

BIBLIOGRAPHY: Wurzbach, *Biographisches Lexicon des Kaiserthums Oesterreich*, Vienna, 1882.
s.   F. T. H.

Ẓebi Hirsch Treves: Scholar in Wilna; son of Zeeb Wolf Treves.

Zeeb Wolf ben Jacob Treves: Scholar of the eighteenth century. He lived in Wilna; and his signature appears attached to rabbinical decisions of the period.

BIBLIOGRAPHY: Fuenn, *Ḳiryah Ne'emanah*, pp. 122, 196; Brüll's *Jahrb.* i. 121.
s.   S. O.

TRÉVOUX (Hebrew, טרבוט): Principal town of the arrondissement of the same name in the department of Ain, France. Henry of Villars, Archbishop of Lyons and seignior of Trévoux, stipulated in the charter which he gave to the latter town in 1300 that no Jew should be allowed to settle in it. A certain number of Jews nevertheless obtained permission to establish themselves there on payment of a yearly tax of 15 livres. The Jews who were expelled from Lyons in 1420 sought refuge at Trévoux, where they engaged in making gold and silver wire. In 1425 they were obliged to contribute largely to the forced loan which the city had to make to the Duchess of Bourbon, who had succeeded to the seignioralty of Trévoux.

The other inhabitants of the town, who were jealous of the Jews, especially of their commercial prosperity, accused them in 1429 of having in their possession Hebrew books containing blasphemies against the Christian religion. At the instance of the archbishop the Duchess of Bourbon ordered an investigation, which she entrusted to Jean Namy, appellate judge of Beaujolais; Jean Châlon, licentiate in law; and Ayme, a baptized Jew of Chambéry, who was commissioned to inspect the Hebrew books and to translate the reprehensible passages. The books were thereupon seized and burned, and the Jews, after being sentenced to pay various fines, were expelled from the city (see CHAMBÉRY). Three years later a few of them returned; but they were again driven out in 1467; and there was another expulsion in 1488. A certain number of these Jews subsequently took the name "Trabot" or "Traboto," indicating their native place. Steinschneider ("Cat. Bodl." col. 2052) has given a list, which has been completed by Berliner (see his "Magazin," ii. 16, 96).

BIBLIOGRAPHY: Bédarride, Les Juifs en France, etc., p. 316; Depping, Les Juifs dans le Moyen Age, p. 195; Gross, Gallia Judaica, pp. 219-223; Jolibois, Histoire de la Ville et du Canton de Trévoux, pp. 12 et seq., Lyons, 1853; R. E. J. x. 33-59.
s.   S. K.

TRIAL. See PROCEDURE IN CIVIL CAUSES.

TRIBES, LOST TEN : According to the Bible, Tiglath-pileser (II Kings xv. 29) or Shalmaneser (ib. xvii. 6, xviii. 11), after the defeat of Israel, transported the majority of the inhabitants of the Northern Kingdom to Assyria, and placed them in Halah and Habor, on the stream of Gozan, and in the towns of Media. In their stead a mixed multitude was transported to the plains and mountains of Israel. As a large number of prophecies relate to the return of "Israel" to the Holy Land, believers in the literal inspiration of the Scriptures have always labored under a difficulty in regard to the continued existence of the tribes of Israel, with the exception of those of Judah and Levi (or Benjamin), which returned with Ezra and Nehemiah. If the Ten Tribes have disappeared, the literal fulfilment of the prophecies would be impossible; if they have not disappeared, obviously they must exist under a different name. The numerous attempts at identification that have been made constitute some of the most remarkable curiosities of literature.

Japanese Types, Showing Jewish Features.
(According to McLeod, "Epitome of the Ancient History of Japan," Tokyo, 1879.)

In the Apocrypha it is presumed that the Ten Tribes still exist as tribes. Thus Tobit is stated to be of the tribe of Naphtali, and the Testaments of the Twelve Patriarchs assume their continuous existence. In the Fourth Book of Ezra (xiii. 39-45) it is declared that the Ten Tribes were carried by Hosea, king in the time of Shalmaneser, to the Euphrates, at the narrow passages of the river, whence they went on for a journey of a year and a half to a place called Arzareth. Schiller-Szinessy pointed out that "Arzareth" is merely a contraction of "erez aḥeret," the "other land" into which the Lord says He "will cast them [the people] as this day"; see Deut. xxix. 27, which verse is referred by R. Akiba to the Lost Ten Tribes (Sanh. x. 4; comp. "Journal of Philology," iii. 114).

According to haggadic tradition, the Ten Tribes were divided into three groups, one on this side of the River Sambation, another on the opposite side, and the third in the neighborhood of Daphne, near Antioch (Lam. R. v. 2). This was based on the Targum of pseudo-Jonathan to Ex. xxxiv. 10; but the course of the River Sambation is differently given, according to the prepossessions of the various writers (see SAMBATION). Akiba, indeed, because he was a believer in the Messianic claims of Bar Kokba, and trusted in the immediate fulfilment of such passages as Isa. xi. 11, Jer. xxi. 7, Ezek. xxxvii. 15, without the restoration of Israel, distinctly expressed the opinion that the Ten Tribes would never return (Sanh. x. 3). In the ninth century ELDAD BEN MAHLI HA-DANI came forward, claiming to give specific details of the contemporary existence of the Ten Tribes and of their location at that time. Dan, Naphtali, Gad, and Asher were in Havilah; Zebulun and Reuben in the mountains of Paran; Ephraim and half of Manasseh in South Arabia; Simeon and the other half of Manasseh in the land of the Chazars (?). According to him, therefore, the Ten Tribes were settled in parts of southern Arabia, or perhaps Abyssinia, in conformity with the identification of Havilah. The connection of this view with that of the Jewish origin of Islam is obvious; and David Reubeni revived the view in stating that he was related to the king of the tribes of Reuben situated in Khaibar in North Arabia.

According to Abraham Farissol, the remaining tribes were in the desert, on the way to Mecca, near the Red Sea; but he himself identifies the River Ganges with the River Gozan, and assumes that the Beni-Israel of India are the descendants of the Lost Ten Tribes. The Ganges, thus identified by him with the River Sambation, divides the Indians from the Jews. The confusion between Ethiopia and Farther India which existed in the minds of the ancients and medieval geographers caused some writers to place the Lost Ten Tribes in Abyssinia. Abraham Yagel, in the sixteenth century, did so, basing his conclusions on the accounts of David Reubeni and Eldad ha-Dani. It is probable that some of the reports of the FALASHAS led to this identification. According to Yagel, messengers were sent to these colonists in the time of Pope Clement VII., some of whom died, while the rest **Arabia,** brought back tidings of the greatness of **India, and** the tribes and their very wide terri- **Abyssinia.** tories. Yagel quotes a Christian traveler, Vincent of Milan, who was a prisoner in the hands of the Turks for twenty-five years, and who went as far as Fez, and thence to India, where he found the River Sambation, and a number of Jews dressed in silk and purple. They were ruled by seven kings, and upon being asked to pay tribute to the sultan Salim they declared they had never paid tribute to any sultan or king. It is just possible that this may have some reference to the "Sâsanam" of the Jews of COCHIN. It is further stated that in 1630 a Jew of Salonica traveled to Ethiopia, to the land of Sambation, and that in 1646 one Baruch, traveling in Persia, claimed to have met a man named Malkiel of the tribe of Naphtali, and brought back a letter from the king of the children of Moses; this letter was seen by Azulai. It was afterward reprinted in Jacob Saphir's book of travels ("Eben Sappir," i. 98). Moses EDREHI wrote a separate work on the subject. So much interest was taken in this account that in 1831 a certain Baruch ben Samuel of Pinsk was sent to search for the children of Moses in Yemen. He traveled fifteen days in the wilderness, and declared he met Danites feeding flocks of sheep. So, too, in 1854 a certain Amram Ma'arabi set out from Safed in search of the Ten Tribes; and he was followed in 1857 by David Ashkenazi, who crossed over through Suakin to make inquiries about the Jews of Abyssinia.

In 1835 Asahel Grant, an American physician, was appointed by the American Board of Foreign Missions to pursue his calling among the Nestorians of Mesopotamia. He found among them a tradition that they were descendants of the Lost Ten Tribes, a tradition which had already **Nestorians** been gathered by Smith and White **and Devil-** during their earlier mission ("Re-**Worship-** searches in Armenia," vol. ii.). He **ers.** found also among the Jews of the neighborhood of Urumiah recognition of this tradition, which he considered to be confirmed by the following facts: they dwelt in the neighborhood to which the Israelites were originally deported, while Josephus declared that the Ten Tribes lived beyond the Euphrates up to his time ("Ant." xi. 5, § 3), and his statement is confirmed by Jerome ("Opera," vi. 780); their language is a branch of the Aramaic; they still offer sacrifices and first-fruits like the ancient Israelites, and they prepare for the Sabbath on the preceding evening; they have Jewish names and Jewish features. Other similarities of custom are recorded by Grant ("The Nestorians, or the Lost Tribes," New York, 1845). Grant was of the opinion also that the Yezidis, or devil-worshipers, of the same region were likewise descended from the Ten Tribes, as they observed the rite of circumcision, offered sacrifices, including that of the paschal lamb on the 24th of Nisan, and also abstained from forbidden food (ib. pp. 363-372).

According to their native traditions, the Afghans also are to be identified with the Lost Ten Tribes. They declare that Nebuchadnezzar banished them into the mountains of Ghur, whence they maintained correspondence with the Arabian Jews. When some of the latter were converted by Mohammed, one **Afghans.** Khalid wrote to the Afghans and invited them to embrace Islam. Several Afghan nobles went to Arabia under one Ḳais, who claimed to trace his descent through forty-seven generations from Saul. He was accordingly greeted by Mohammed by the title of "malik," in deference to this illustrious descent. Ḳais is reported to have died at the age of eighty-seven, in

662; and all the modern chiefs of Afghanistan claim to be descended from him (Malcolm, "History of Persia," ii. 596, London, 1815). The Afghans still call themselves "Beni-Israel," and are declared to have a markedly Jewish appearance. Their claim to Israelitish descent is allowed by most Mohammedan writers. G. Moore, in his "Lost Tribes" (pp. 143-160, London, 1861), also identified the Afghans with the Ten Tribes.

In order to avoid the disabilities imposed upon Rabbinite Jews, the Karaites of Russia attempted to prove that they were guiltless of the execution of **Karaites** Jesus because they were descended **and the** from the Lost Ten Tribes and had **Caucasus.** been settled in the Crimea since the time of Shalmaneser (seventh century B.C.). In particular Abraham FIRKOVICH edited a number of forgeries of inscriptions on tombstones and manuscripts to prove the early date of their settlement in the Crimea. The argument was effective with the Russian government in 1795, when they were exempted from the double taxation imposed upon the Rabbinites, and in 1828, when it obtained for them exemption from military service. From the similar traditions among the Jews of the Caucasus, according to Chorny ("Sefer ha-Massa'ot," p. 585, St. Petersburg, 1884), the Jews of Derbent declared that the Daghestan Jews were those who were carried away by the Assyrians, and that some of them had ultimately migrated to Bokhara, and even as far as China. It is, of course, only natural that the outlying colonies in China, in India, and even in the Sahara should have been at one time or another identified as remnants of the Lost Ten Tribes.

G. Moore, indeed, attempts to prove that the highclass Hindus, including all the Buddhists, are descendants of the Sacæ, or Scythians, who, again, were the Lost Ten Tribes. He transcribes many of the Indian inscriptions into Hebrew of a wonderful kind to prove this contention. Buddhism, according to him, is a fraudulent development of Old Testament doctrines brought to India by the Ten Tribes. The Kareens of Burma, because of their Jewish appearance, their name for God ("Ywwah"), and their use of bones of fowls for divination purposes, are also identified by him and by Mason as descendants of the Lost Tribes.

The identification of the Sacæ, or Scythians, with the Ten Tribes because they appear in history at the same time, and very nearly in the same place, as the Israelites removed by Shalmaneser, is one of the chief supports of the theory which identifies the English people, and indeed the whole Teu-**Anglo-** tonic race, with the Ten Tribes. Dan **Israelism.** is identified sometimes with Denmark, and sometimes with the Tuatha da Danaun of Irish tradition; but the main argument advanced is that the English satisfy the conditions of the Prophets regarding Israel in so far as they live in a far-off isle, speak in a strange tongue, have colonies throughout the world, and yet worship the true God. For further discussion of the argument and the history of its development see ANGLO-ISRAELISM.

One of the most curious offshoots of the theory is

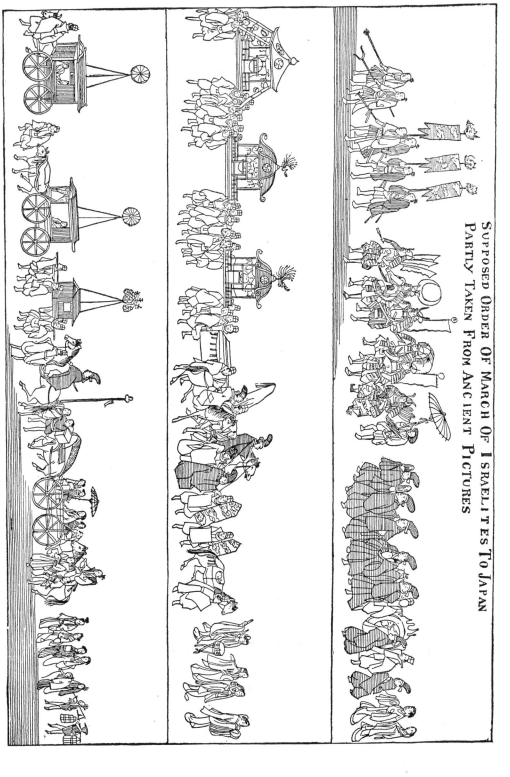

SUPPOSED ORDER OF MARCH OF ISRAELITES TO JAPAN
PARTLY TAKEN FROM ANCIENT PICTURES

(From McLeod's "Epitome of the Ancient History of Japan," Tokyo, 1879.)

that which identifies the Shindai, or holy class, of Japan as the descendants of the Lost Ten Tribes. This is advocated by N. McLeod in his "Epitome of the Ancient History of Japan" (3d ed., Tokyo, 1879). He calls attention to a point of agreement between the two, namely, the fact

Japan. that the first known king of Japan was Osee, 730 B.C., and the last king of Israel was Hosea, who died 722 B.C. In addition to this, McLeod points out that the Shinto temple is divided into a holy and a most holy place. The priests wear a linen dress, bonnet, and breeches, like the Jewish priests of old, and the ancient Temple instruments are used in the Shinto temple. The Japanese worship their ancestors, as the old Israelites did; and in addition to this McLeod points out the Jewish appearance of some Japanese, and supplements his "Epitome" with a volume of illustrations depicting among other things the supposed rafts on which the Israelites crossed, via Saghalien, to Japan, and their supposed order of march. Still further removed is the suggestion of some writers that the Australians are the Lost Tribes because they practise circumcision ("Allg. Zeit. des Jud." 1842, No. 6).

Quite recently the Masai of British East Africa have been identified owing to similarity of custom (M. Merker, "Die Masai," Berlin, 1904).

Immediately after the discovery of Central and South America the legend of the Lost Tribes began to be referred to the aboriginal inhabitants.

America. Garcia, in his "Origen de los Medianos" (1607, pp. 79–128), declares that the Tribes passed over the "Strait of Aninai," *i.e.*, Bering Strait, and went by that way to Mexico and South America. He deduces their identity from the common cowardice and want of charity of the Israelites and Indians. Both of these peoples, according to him, bury their dead on the hills, give kisses on the cheek as a sign of peace, tear their clothes as a sign of mourning, and dance as a sign of triumph. Garcia claimed to have found many Hebrew terms in the American language.

According to Manasseh ben Israel, Antonio Montesinos deposed in 1644 before the bet din of Amsterdam that while traveling in Peru he had met with a number of the natives who recited the "Shema'" in Hebrew, and who informed him through an interpreter that they were Israelites descended from Reuben, and that the tribe of Joseph dwelt in the midst of the sea. He supported their statements by tracing Jewish customs among other inhabitants of Central and South America. The Indians of Yucatan and the Mexicans rent their garments in mourning and kept perpetual fires upon their altars, as did also the Peruvians. The Mexicans kept the jubilee, while the Indians of Peru and Guatemala observed the custom of levirate marriage. Manasseh ben Israel therefore concluded that the aboriginal inhabitants of America were the Lost Ten Tribes, and as he was of the opinion that the Messiah would come when the whole world was inhabited by the descendants of Israel, he directed his efforts to obtaining admission for the Jews to the British Islands, from which they were at that time excluded (see MANASSEH BEN ISRAEL). The Mexican

theory was later taken up by Viscount Kingsborough, who devoted his life and fortune to proving the thesis that the Mexicans were descended from the Lost Ten Tribes, and published a magnificent and expensive work on the subject ("Antiquities of Mexico," 9 vols., 1837–45). Kingsborough's chief arguments are that Mexicans and Israelites believe in both devils and angels, as well as in miracles, and use the blood of the sacrifice in the same way, namely, by pouring it on the ground; also that the high priest of Peru is the only one allowed to enter the inner, most holy part of the temple, and that the Peruvians anointed the Ark, as did the Israelites. He also finds many similarities in the myths and legends. Thus certain Mexican heroes are said to have wrestled with Quetzalcohuatl, like Jacob with the angel ("Antiquities of Mexico," vol. vii.).

Manasseh b. Israel's views were taken up by T. Thorowgood in his "Jewes in America" (London, 1650), and he was followed by the "Apostle" Eliot

North-American Indians. in a publication ten years later; and their views, referring now to the North-American Indians instead of the Mexicans or Peruvians, were adopted by Cotton Mather, Roger Williams, and even William Penn. S. Sewall also gave expression, in 1697, to the same views in a special publication.

Charles Beatty, in his "Journal of a Two-Months' Tour" (London, 1678), declared that he had found among the Delaware Indians traces of Israelitish origin; and J. Adair, in his "History of the American Indians" (London, 1775), devotes a considerable amount of attention to the same view, which he accepts. Adair was followed by Jonathan Edwards. A special work was written by E. Boudinot ("A Star in the West," Trenton, N. J., 1816); and he was followed by Ethan Smith in 1825, and by Israel Worsley ("View of the American Indians, Showing Them to Be Descendants of the Lost Tribes of Israel," London, 1828). Mordecai M. Noah accepted the Israelitish origin of the Indians (1837) in a pamphlet republished in Marryat's "Diary in America" (vol. ii.). J. B. Finlay claimed to have found traces among the Wyandottes in 1840, and the view was even considered by George Catlin in his "Manners . . . of the North American Indians" (London, 1841). Discoveries of alleged Hebrew tablets, as at Pittsfield, Mass., 1815, and Newark, Ohio, about 1860, have given fresh vigor to the theory. Altogether, with the exception of the Anglo-Israelite craze, a larger amount of literature has been written on this identification than on any other.

It was doubtless owing to this belief in the identity of the Lost Ten Tribes with the American Indians that Joseph Smith was led to adopt a somewhat similar view in his celebrated "Book of Mormon."

The Mormons. According to him, America was colonized by two sets of people—one being the Jaredites, who came over after the dispersion from the Tower of Babel; the other a group of sixteen, who came from Jerusalem about 600 B.C. Their chief families were destroyed about the fourth century B.C., and descendants of the remainder are the North-American Indians.

BIBLIOGRAPHY: Manasseh b. Israel, *Hope of Israel*, ed. Wolf, pp. 24–28, London, 1901; Eisenmenger, *Entdecktes Judenthum*, ii. 515–573; A. Neubauer, *Where Are the Ten Tribes?* in *J. Q. R.* i. 14–28, 95–114, 185–201, 408–423; A. F. Hyamson, *The Lost Tribes and the Influence of the Search for Them on the Return of the Jews to England*, in *J. Q. R.* xv.; M. Lewin, *Wo Sind die Stämme Israels zu Suchen?* Presburg, 1901; Bancroft, *Native Races of the Pacific*, v. 78–102; Justin Winsor, *Narrative and Critical History of America*, i. 115–116; Mallory, *Israelite and Indian*, New York, 1889.

E. C.   J.

TRIBES, THE TWELVE: The individual tribes having been treated under their respective captions, it is proposed to discuss in the present article the theories concerning the nature, number, and origin of the tribes of Israel. The uncritical or precritical theory accepts as data of personal histories the Biblical accounts of the Patriarchs' lives. Accordingly, the tribes are regarded as having been formed in the main by the natural increase of the offspring of Jacob. The descendants of each of his sons are believed to have held together and thus constituted a social entity, though foreign wives and slaves were at times admitted and their offspring absorbed. The difficulties which have led to the rejection of this theory by most Biblical scholars are of a twofold nature. In the first place, such natural origin could by no means account for the numbers given in the Biblical books as the census of the various tribes. Anthropology furnishes no other example of a nation having arisen by natural descent from one ancestral family. In the second place, the study and comparison of the various (and only in one instance perfectly concordant) lists

The Lists. of the tribes, as preserved in the Biblical records, suggests that considerations other than the fact of common descent underlie the different groupings and discordant order of these tribal tables, and the common origin is thus shown to be only theoretical. The tribes are arranged in twenty different orders, only one of which (Num. ii., vii., x. 14–29) recurs.

Various principles are readily detected to be worked out in the tables. (1) A certain number of tribal lists (*e.g.*, those in Gen. xxix.-xxxv., xlvi., xlix.; Ex. i.; Num. i., ii., vii., x., xiii., xxvi.; I Chron. ii., xxvii.) trace descent from Jacob, but through his various wives and concubines, grouping those always together that have a common mother, thus: (*a*) tribes of Leah: Reuben, Simeon, Levi, Judah, Issachar, Zebulun; (*b*) tribes of Zilpah (Leah's slave): Gad, Asher; (*c*) tribes of Rachel: Joseph, Benjamin; (*d*) tribes of Bilhah (Rachel's slave): Dan and Naphtali. (2) Other lists are arranged according to geographical position (Num. xxxiv.; Deut. xxxiii.; Josh. xiii.; Judges v.; I Chron. ii. 3–viii.). (3) Tradition concerning both affinity and geographical position (Deut. xxvii.). But even here the relative importance of the tribes decides whether they are to receive a blessing or a curse. Ezekiel's list (Ezek. xlviii.) reflects the prophet's ideal conceptions. It is thus plain that the records do not give simple and indubitable facts, but disclose certain theories and reflect certain postpatriarchal conditions.

As anthropology presents no warrant for assuming that nations are formed through natural descent from one ancestor, so the process of a tribe's origin must be the reverse of that underlying the presentation of Biblical patriarchal tradition. Tribes result from combinations of various septs or clans. The tribe (Hebr. "maṭṭeh" or "shebeṭ") was a confederation of "mishpaḥot" (R. V. "families") and septs; and these again were composed of various households ("battim" or "batte abot"). Community of worship is the characteristic and constitutive element of this ascending and enlarging order of tribal society (comp. I Sam. xx. 6). The names of the tribes probably represent, therefore, former eponymous deities whose "sons"—even in a physical sense—the members of the tribe felt themselves to be. The tribal denominations therefore do not represent historical and personal progenitors, but mythical figures, former divinities, or heroes.

This is the theory now held by most of the modern scholars, modified by the recognition that many

Modern View. of the subclans' names point to localities—the numen of the place being believed to be the father of the inhabitants. This fact suggests a similar original meaning of the names of some of Jacob's sons (*e.g.*, Asher, Benjamin [the southern]); and it is evident that in the patriarchal cycles later history is projected into earlier centuries, so that tribal rankings as expressed in patriarchal family events correspond to subsequent historical relations. For example, Joseph and Judah typify two distinct lines of descent, Judah in all likelihood being a non-Israelitish mixed tribe. In the quarrels of Leah and Rachel are mirrored the struggles for the hegemony waged by these two sets of tribes.

That some of these tribes are descended through a concubine, the bondwoman of a legitimate wife, expresses the historical fact that they were deemed to be of less pure blood or of less importance than others, and were held to a certain extent in vassalage by the more powerful tribes. In like manner later territorial relations are worked out in the tribal genealogies, which accounts for the omission of some of the tribes (*e.g.*, Simeon and Levi) from the lists or from the blessings (Deut. xxxiii., for instance).

The historical kernel involved in all the tribal catalogues and the patriarchal legends would appear to be this: In the Sinaitic Peninsula a number of pastoral tribes had for centuries been pasturing their flocks; and at times, when food was scarce, were driven to take refuge in Egypt, in the border district of which country some (*e.g.*, Joseph) of their number found settled habitations. These tribes were loosely conscious of their common religious affinity, regarding as their progenitor Israel, whose sons they were called ("Beni Israel"). This loose consciousness gave way to a deeper national sense of unity under Moses, though in the conquest of Palestine the tribes still acted without coher-

Historical Kernel. ence. Judah seems to have stood aloof from the tribe of Joseph and its vassals, and to have joined its fortunes with theirs only after the Joseph group had finally gained a foothold across the Jordan. Geographical considerations after this replaced the traditional memories of relations that prevailed in the trans-Jordanic districts, Judah and Benjamin in the south gaining for a time the ascendency over Joseph in the north.

With the establishment of the kingdom and the later division of the realm the force of tribal association gradually waned. In fact, the premonarchical period of tribal dissensions and intertribal feuds had reduced many of the tribes to a state of weakness which resulted in their absorption by their stronger and more numerous neighbors. This process of tribal disintegration was accelerated by the Syrian and Assyrian wars leading up to deportation and exile, the "ten" tribes constituting the Northern Kingdom being "lost" through natural decimation in consequence of war and famine at home and through absorption by the "people of the land," the Syrians north of them and the colonists settled in their territory by the Assyrian conquerors.

The artificiality of the number twelve is apparent. The subdivisions of Joseph (Ephraim and Manasseh) intrude into the duodecimal notation, while, on the other hand, omissions as frequently reduce the number. Manasseh at times is treated as two, which again interferes with the theory. That twelve is a favorite conventional number, even in connection with non-Jacobean tribes, appears from Gen. xvii. 20; xxii. 20–24; xxv. 13–16; xxxvi. 15–19, 40–43. It probably is of mythological character, having some connection with the twelve months of the year and the twelve signs of the zodiac. According to B. Luther (in Stade's "Zeitschrift" [1901], xxi.), this number recalls the twelve departments into which Solomon divided the land of Israel, which division, however, attests the sacred nature of the number, twelve being used as a round figure. Other reckonings, as ten and eleven, are indicated in II Sam. xix. 43; I Kings xi. 31.

BIBLIOGRAPHY: G. B. Gray, *The Lists of the Twelve Tribes*, in *Expositor*, March, 1902; Charles, *Book of Jubilees*, 1902, pp. 170 *et seq.*; Wellhausen, *I. J. G.* pp. 11–13; idem, *Prolegomena*, etc., 4th ed., pp. 322–329; Stade, *Gesch. des Volkes Israel*, 3d ed., i. 519 *et seq.*; Stade's *Zeitschrift*, i.; Steuernagel, *Die Einwanderung der Israelitischen Stämme in Kanaan*, 1901; Gunkel, *Genesis*, 2d ed., p. 285; C. Matthes, *Israels Nederzetting in Kanaan*, in *Theologisch Tijdschrift* (1902), xxxvi.

E. G. H.

TRIENNIAL CYCLE: A cycle of three years, in the course of which the whole Law is read on Sabbaths and festivals. This was the practise in Palestine, whereas in Babylonia the entire Pentateuch was read in the synagogue in the course of a single year (Meg. 29b). The modern practise follows the Babylonian; but as late as 1170 Benjamin of Tudela mentioned Egyptian congregations that took three years to read the Torah ("Itinerary," ed. Asher, p. 98). The reading of the Law in the synagogue can be traced to at least about the second century B.C., when the grandson of Sirach refers to it in his preface as an Egyptian practise; it must, therefore, have existed even earlier in Palestine. It has been suggested that the reading of the Law was due to a desire to controvert the views of the Samaritans with regard to the various festivals, for which reason arrangements were made to have the passages of the Pentateuch relating to those festivals read and expounded on the feast-days themselves.

The Masoretic divisions known as "sedarim" and variously indicated in the text, number 154 in the Pentateuch, and probably correspond, therefore, to the Sabbath lessons of the triennial system,

as was first surmised by Rapoport ("Halikot Ḳedem," p. 11). The number varies, however, so that Menahem Me'iri reckoned 161 divisions, corresponding to the greatest number of Sabbaths possible in three years; the Yemen grammars and scrolls of the Pentateuch enumerate 167 (see SIDRA); and the tractate Soferim (xvi. 10) gives the number as 175 (comp. Yer. Shab. i. 1). It is possible that this last division corresponds to a further development by which the whole of the Pentateuch was read twice in seven years, or once in three and a half years. The minimum seder for a Sabbath portion when seven persons are called up to the Law (see 'ALIYAH) should consist of twenty-one verses, since no one should read less than three verses (Meg. iv. 4). Some sedarim have less than twenty-one verses, however, as, for example, Ex. xxx. 1–8.

If the 154 sedarim are divided into three portions corresponding to the three years, the second would commence at Ex. xii. and the third at **Divisions** Num. vi. 22, a passage treating of the **and Begin-** priestly blessing and the gifts of the **ning of** twelve tribal chiefs after the erection **the Cycle.** of the Tabernacle. Tradition assumes that the events described in Num. vi. took place on the 1st of Nisan, and it would follow that Gen. i. and Ex. xi. would also be read on the first Sabbath of that month, while Deut. xxxiv., the last portion of the Pentateuch, would be read in Adar. Accordingly, it is found that the death of Moses is traditionally assigned to the 7th of Adar, about which date Deut. xxxiv. would be read.

A. Büchler has restored the order of the sedarim on the assumption that the reading of the Law was commenced on the 1st of Nisan and continued for three years, and he has found that Genesis would be begun on the 1st of Nisan, Deuteronomy on the 1st of Elul, Leviticus on the 1st of Tishri, and Exodus and Numbers on the 15th of Shebaṭ, the four New-Years given in the Mishnah (R. H. i. 1). Nisan has always been regarded as the ecclesiastical New-Year. This arrangement would account for many traditions giving definite dates to Pentateuchal occurrences, the dates being, strictly speaking, those of the Sabbaths on which the lessons recording the occurrences are read. Thus, it is declared that the exodus from Egypt took place on Thursday, the 15th of Nisan ("Seder 'Olam," x.), and the passage relating to the Exodus was read on that day. The slaying of the Passover lamb is said to have occurred on the 10th of Nisan, and is described in Ex. xii. 21, the passage read in the triennial cycle on the second Sabbath of Nisan, which would be the 10th where the 15th fell on Thursday. This likewise explains the tradition that the Israelites encamped at Rameses on a Sabbath, the 17th of Nisan, on which Ex. xii. 37 would be read in the triennial cycle. The tradition that Rachel was remembered on New-Year's Day (R. H. 10b) is due to the fact that in the first year of the cycle the sidra Gen. xxx. 22, beginning, "And God remembered Rachel," would be read on Rosh ha-Shanah. As the reading of Deut. xxxiv. would occur on the 7th of Adar, there would be four remaining Sabbaths to be filled in before the new triennial cycle, which began with Nisan. Four special Sabbaths, Sheḳalim, Zakor, Parah, and Ha-

Ḥodesh, still occur in Adar. Including these and the festival parashiyyot, and possibly also the special sedarim for Ḥanukkah and Purim, eleven extra divisions would be obtained, making up the 166 or 167 of the Yemen Bible.

The triennial cycle seems to have been established in New Testament times. John vi. 4 contains an allusion to the Passover, and vii. 2 to the Feast of Tabernacles, while in vi. 59, between the two, reference is made to a sermon delivered in the synagogue at Capernaum. This would be appropriate for a discourse on the text for the first or eighth of the month Iyyar (*i.e.*, between Passover and Tabernacles), which, in the triennial cycle, dealt with Ex. vi. 1–xvii.1, where the account of the manna is given. So, too, at the season of Pentecost the cycle of readings in the first year would reach Gen. xi., which deals with the story of Babel and the confusion of tongues, so that in Acts ii. Pentecost is associated with the gift of the spirit which led to a confusion of tongues. Similarly, the Decalogue was read on Pentecost in the second year of the cycle, whence came, according to Büchler, the traditional association of the giving of the Law with Pentecost. Ex. xxxiv., which contains a second Decalogue, is accordingly read on the 29th of Ab, or 80 days after Pentecost, allowing exactly forty days before and after the sin of the golden calf. So too Deut. v., containing a third Decalogue, began on the same day, the 29th of Ab. The above diagram shows the arrangement and the connection of the various dates with the successive sedarim, the three concentric rings showing the three cycles, and the twelve radii separating the months of the Jewish year indicated in the inner circle.

In addition to this division of the Pentateuch into a triennial reading, E. G. King has proposed an ar-

Connections Between Readings and Festivals.

rangement of the Psalms on the same system, thus accounting for their lection in a triennial cycle which varied between 147 and 150 Sabbaths; and he also shows the agreement of the five divisions or books of the Psalms, now fixed by the doxologies, with the five divisions of the Pentateuch, the first and third books of both the Psalter and the Pentateuch ending in the month Shebaṭ. Ps. lxxii. 19 would be read on the same day as Ex. xl. 34, the two passages throwing light on each other. The Asaph Psalms (lxxiii.–lxxxiii.) would begin, on this principle, on the Feast of "Asif" in the seventh month, just when, in the first year of the Pentateuchal cycle, Gen. xxx. *et seq.* would be read, dealing with the birth of Joseph, whose name is there derived from the root "asaf."

The Triennial Cycle of the Psalms.

A still more remarkable coincidence is the fact that Ps. c. would come just at the time in Adar when, according to tradition, the death of Moses occurred, and when Deut. xxxiii. would be read; hence, it is suggested, originated the heading of Ps. xc., "A prayer of Moses, the man of God." The Pilgrim Psalms (cxx.–cxxxiv.) would be read, in this system, during the fifteen Sabbaths from the 1st of Elul to Ḥanukkah, the very time when a constant procession of pilgrims was bringing the first-fruits to the Temple. Many other associations of appropriate Psalms with the festivals which they illustrate have been pointed out.

Besides these examples Büchler gives the following sections of the Pentateuch read on various Sabbaths in the different years of the cycle, basing his identification on certain haggadic associations of the Sabbaths with the events to which they refer. In the first year the four sedarim of Nisan appear to be Gen. i. 1–ii. 3, ii. 4–iii. 21, iii. 22–iv. 26, and v. 1–vi. 8. The second Sabbath of Iyyar was probably devoted to Gen. vi. 9–vii. 24 (comp. vii. 1). In the

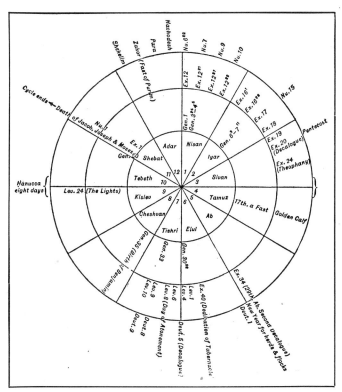

Diagram Showing Arrangement of Readings from the Law During the Triennial Cycle. The Readings are Represented by Concentric Circles; Hebrew Months are Indicated by Radii.

(From the "Journal of Theological Studies.")

second year the readings on the Sabbaths of Nisan deal with Ex. xii., xiii., xiv., and xv., ch. xiv. concurring with the Passover; and it is for this reason that the Haggadah states that Adam taught his sons to bring a Passover offering, since the passage Gen. iii. was read during the Passover week in the cycle of the first year. In Iyyar of the second year the readings included Ex. xvi. 1, xxviii., xvii. 1, xviii. 1, and xix. 6, there being usually five Sabbaths in that month. Two of the portions for Siwan are also identified as Ex. xx. 1, xxii. 4; at the end of Elul Lev. i. was read; while on the first days of Tishri *ib.* iv. 1, v. 1, and vi. 12 were the readings, and on the 10th (Yom Kippur) *ib.* viii. 1 and x. 7.

In the third cycle, besides the account of the death of Moses already referred to as being read on the 7th of Adar, or the 7th of Shebaṭ, in Nisan the four pericopes were Num. vi. 22, vi. 48, viii. 1, and ix. 1, while the third Sabbath of Iyyar was devoted to the reading of Num. xv. 1, and the 3d of Ab to that of *ib.* xxxvi. Some of these passages were retained for the festival readings, even after the annual cycle had been introduced.

Besides the readings from the Law the readings from the Prophets were also arranged in a triennial cycle. These appear to have been originally a few selected verses intended to strengthen the passage from the Law read previously,

Ḥafṭarot. and so connect it with the following discourse of the preacher, which took for its text the last verse of the hafṭarah. Thus there is evidence that Isa. lii. 3–5 was at one time regarded as a complete hafṭarah to Gen. xxxix. 1. Even one-verse hafṭarot are known, as Ezek. xlv. 17 and Isa. lxvi. 23, read on New Moons. A list of the earlier hafṭarot suitable for the festivals is given in Meg. 31a. Evidence of two hafṭarot for one festival is shown in the case of Passover, for which Josh. v. 10 and Josh. iii. are mentioned. This

can easily be explained by the existence of a triennial cycle, especially as Num. ix. 2–3 was the reading for the first day of Passover, and corresponds exactly to Josh. v. 20. In the case of the New-Year it has been possible to determine the hafṭarot for the three cycles: I Sam. ii. 21, Jer. xxxi. 19, and, for the third year, Joel ii. 1, corresponding to the reading Deut. v., which formed the Pentateuchal lesson. For Ḥanukkah, the Torah seder of which treats of lamps (Num. viii. 1–2), the hafṭarot Zech. iv. 2 and I Kings vii. 49 were selected as being suitable passages. A third hafṭarah is also found (I Kings xviii. 31), completing the triennial arrangement.

The Karaites adopted some of the triennial hafṭarot in their reading of the Law. The hafṭarot of the first year of the cycle can often be identified by this fact. Of the twenty-nine sedarim of the Book of Exodus eighteen were taken from Isaiah, three from Jeremiah, four from the Minor Prophets, three from the historical works, and one from Ezekiel, whose words, for some reason, seem on the whole to have been eschewed by those who selected the prophetic readings. A certain confusion seems to have arisen among the hafṭarot, owing to the fact that among some congregations the reading of the Pentateuchal portions was begun on the 1st of Elul (also regarded as a New-Year).

In the Masoretic text of the Prophets occur a number of divisions marked as sedarim which correspond to smaller divisions in the Torah. Among these may be mentioned:

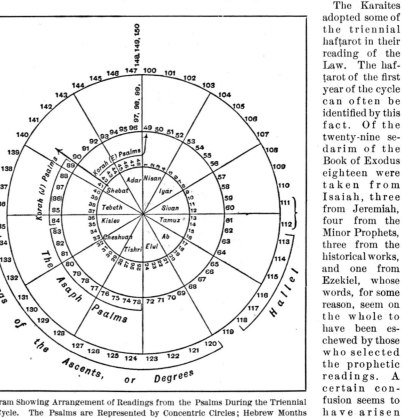

Diagram Showing Arrangement of Readings from the Psalms During the Triennial Cycle. The Psalms are Represented by Concentric Circles; Hebrew Months are Indicated by Radii.

(From the "Journal of Theological Studies.")

I Kings vi. 11-13 corresponding to Ex. xxv.

Ezek. xii. 20	"	"	Lev. xxvi. 3 or 4 ?
I Sam. vi. 14	"	"	Num. iv. 17
Josh. xvii. 4	"	"	Num. xxvi. 52
Jer. ix. 22-24	"	"	Deut. viii.
II Kings xiii. 23	"	"	Deut. x.
Judges ii. 7	"	"	Deut. xxxi. 14

The present arrangement of hafṭarot seems to have been introduced into Babylonia by Rab. especially

SIDROT
(THE LAW)

First year cycle begins in Nisan with Genesis 1: 1.

Sidrot for Holy Days given on outer margin, vary for each year of the cycle.

Asterisks indicate slight changes in annual cycle.

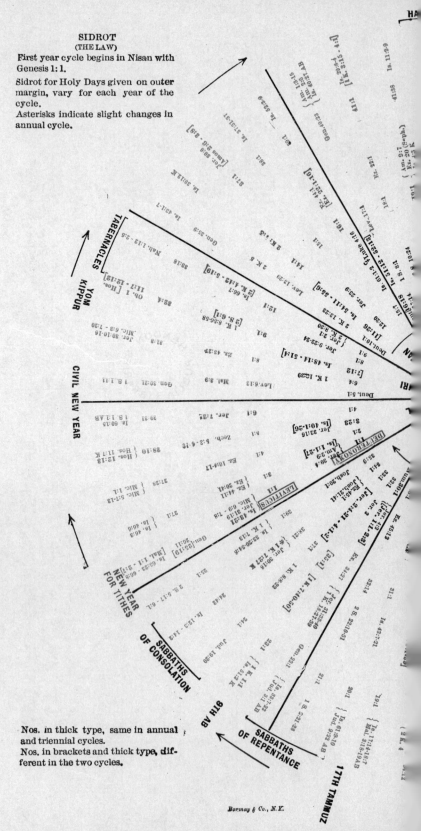

Nos. in thick type, same in annual and triennial cycles.

Nos. in brackets and thick type, different in the two cycles.

Bormay & Co., N.Y.

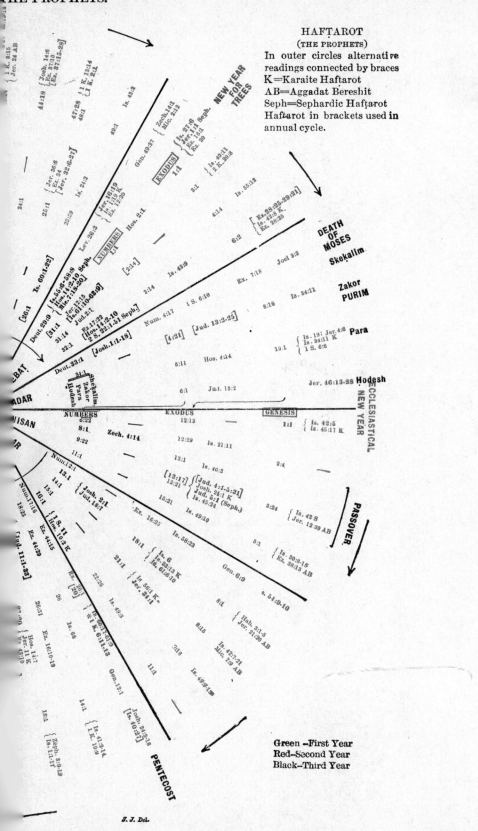

HAFTAROT
(THE PROPHETS)
In outer circles alternative
readings connected by braces
K=Karaite Haftarot
AB=Aggadat Bereshit
Seph=Sephardic Haftarot
Haftarot in brackets used in
annual cycle.

Green –First Year
Red–Second Year
Black–Third Year

J. J. Del.

those for the three Sabbaths of repentance preceding the Ninth of Ab, and the three consolatory ones succeeding it. Büchler has traced the prophetic portions of these three latter Sabbaths for each of the three years of the cycle as follows:

I. Isa. xl. 1, li. 12, liv. 11.
II. Isa. xlix. 14, lx. 1, lxi. 10.
III. Isa. liv. 1, Zech. ii. 14, ix. 9.

He finds traces of the triennial cycle also in the prophetic portions for the four supplementary Sabbaths, Sheḳalim, Zakor, Parah, and Ḥodesh. For Sheḳalim hafṭarot are found from (a) II Kings xii., (b) Ezek. xlv. onward (among the Karaites), and (c) I Kings iv. 20 onward. It is tolerably clear that these were the hafṭarot of the three different years of the cycle when that particular Sabbath came round. It is possible that when the arrangement of the calendar and of the reading of the Law was first made these four supplementary Sabbaths were intended to fill out the time between the 7th of Adar, when the account of the death of Moses in Deut. xxxiv. was read, and the first Sabbath in Nisan, when the cycle began. Traces of the cycle are also found in the hafṭarot for the festivals. Thus, on the first day of Passover, Ex. xii. 29 was read, approximately in its due place in the cycle in the second year; and corresponding to this Josh. v. 10 was read in the Prophets, whereas there are also traces of Num. ix. 22 being read on that day, as would occur in the third year of the cycle, when Josh. iii. was read as the hafṭarah. The passage for the second day of Passover, Num. ix. 1 et seq., which was introduced by the Babylonians, has attached to it II Kings xxiii. 21 as the hafṭarah, and would correspond to the section in the first year's cycle. On Pentecost, Ex. xix. was read in the second year, while Gen. xi. 15 was read for the first year of the cycle. So, too, on New-Year, Gen. xxx. 22 was read in the first year, Lev. iv. in the second, and Deut. v. in the third, the corresponding hafṭarot being Jer. xxxi. 19, I Sam. ii., and Joel ii. For the Sukkot of the first year for the sidra of Gen. xxxii., the hafṭarah was Zech. xiv. 16-19; for that of the second year, Lev. ix. 10, the hafṭarah was I Kings viii. 8; and for that of the third year, Deut. viii. 9, the hafṭarah was Isa. iv. 6 (among the Karaites).

In the accompanying diagram the sidrot of the Law for the Sabbaths of the three years of the cycle are indicated, as well as the hafṭarot which accompany them. Sometimes these have alternatives, and in several cases, as for Gen. xl. 23, xliii. 14, Ex. i. 1, xxvii. 20, and Lev. xix. 1, three hafṭarot are given for the sidra, pointing in all probability to the hafṭarot reading during the triennial cycle. In this enlarged form the connection of the beginning of the reading of the books with the various sacred New-Years, those of Nisan, of Elul (for tithes), and of Shebaṭ (for trees), comes out most clearly and convincingly. The manner in which the present-day reading of the Law and the Prophets has been derived from the triennial cycle is shown clearly by the diagram. It would appear that at the beginning of the cycle all the sidrot of the month were read together; but this was soon given up, as obviously it would result in the whole of the Law being read in three-quarters of a year or less.

XII.—17

There are indications of the application of the triennial cycle to the Psalms also. The Aggadat Bereshit treats twenty-eight sedarim of Genesis uniformly in three sections, one devoted to a passage in Genesis, the next to a corresponding prophetic passage (hafṭarah), and the third to a passage from the Psalms, generally cognate with either the Law or the Prophets. It may be added that in Luke xxiv. 44 a threefold division is made of "the Law of Moses and the Prophets and the Psalms."

The transition from the triennial to the annual reading of the Law and the transference of the beginning of the cycle to the month of Tishri are attributed by Büchler to the influence of Rab, and may have been due to the smallness of the sedarim under the old system, and to the fact that people were thus reminded of the chief festivals only once in three years. It was then arranged that Deut. xxviii. should fall before the New-Year, and that the beginning of the cycle should come immediately after the Feast of Tabernacles. This arrangement has been retained by the Karaites and by modern congregations, leaving only slight traces of the triennial cycle in the four special Sabbaths and in some of the passages read upon the festivals, which are frequently sections of the triennial cycle, and not of the annual one. It would further be of interest to consult the earlier lectionaries of the Church (which has borrowed its first and second lessons from the Jewish custom) to see how far they agree with the results already obtained for the triennial cycle. The Church father Chrysostom about 175 C.E. declared that it was customary to begin reading from Genesis during Lent, that is, in Nisan, thus showing that to the end of the second century the Church followed the Synagogue in commencing the reading of the Law at the beginning of the Jewish ecclesiastical New-Year. See also PARASHIYYOT; SIDRA.

BIBLIOGRAPHY: Büchler, in J. Q. R. v. 420-468, vi. 1-73; E. N. Adler, ib. viii. 528-529; E. G. King, Journal of Theological Studies, Jan., 1904; I. Abrahams, in J. Q. R. xvi. 579-583.
　　　　　　　　　　　　　　　　　　　　　　　　　　　J.

TRIER, ERNST JOHANNES: Danish educator; born in Copenhagen Jan. 23, 1837; died at Vallekilde Dec. 29, 1893. He was graduated from the University of Copenhagen (B.D. 1863), officiated for some time as teacher at Blaagaards Seminary, and took part in the war with Germany (1864). In 1865 he became an ardent adherent of Grundtvig, at whose initiative he founded (1866) at Vallekilde a high school which soon grew to be the foremost school of its kind in Denmark. It offers not only the ordinary high-school curriculum of studies, but also courses in navigation and in various branches of trade. It was the first Danish school in which the Swedish system of gymnastics was introduced.

Of Trier's memoirs, entitled "Fem og Tyve Aars Skolevirksomhed i Vallekilde," only two volumes appeared (Copenhagen, 1890, 1894), his untimely death—brought on by overstudy—preventing him from completing the work. Trier was a convert to Christianity.

BIBLIOGRAPHY: C. F. Bricka, Dansk Biografisk Lexicon.
　　s.　　　　　　　　　　　　　　　　　　　　　　　　F. C.

TRIER, FREDERIK JACOB: Danish physician; born in Copenhagen June 14, 1831; died there May 17, 1898. He studied at the Metropolitan School and at the University of Copenhagen (M.D. 1860). In the following year he published several clinical essays (of which " Ulcus Duodeni " was the most noteworthy), and became editor of " Ugeskrift for Læger," a medical journal, a position which he held until 1874. He was also for some years coeditor of " Nordisk Medicinsk Arkiv," to which he contributed valuable medical papers. In 1881 his alma mater conferred upon him the title of professor. From 1874 till his death Trier was resident physician of the clinical division of the Communal Hospital of Copenhagen, and he was president of the medical section of the International Congress of Physicians, held at Copenhagen in 1884. He was a member of the medical board of revisers of the " Pharmacopea Danica " (1889).

BIBLIOGRAPHY: Caröe and Selmer, *Den Danske Lægestand*, 6th ed.; C. F. Bricka, *Dansk Biografisk Lexicon*.
s. F. C.

TRIER, HERMAN: Danish educator, writer, and politician; born in Copenhagen May 10, 1845. He received his early education at the Von Westenske Institut, later attending the University of Copenhagen, where he studied jurisprudence for a few years. In 1864 he took up the study of pedagogics, in which field he has won international fame. In 1876 Trier began publishing a series of " Kultur-Historiske Personligheder," containing biographies and character studies of different authors. In the same year appeared his first work on pedagogics, " Pædagogikken som Videnskab," which endeavored to establish for pedagogics a place among the abstract sciences.

Since 1879 Trier, together with School-Inspector P. Voss of Christiania, has published " Vor Ungdom," a periodical devoted to pedagogics. From 1892 to 1893 he published " Pædagogiske Tids- og Stridssporgsmaal," and in 1901 a valuable addition to the knowledge of the medieval history of Copenhagen, entitled " Gaarden No. 8 Amagertorv." In 1884 he was elected a member of the Danish Folkething (House of Commons) for the first district of Copenhagen, and in 1898 he became a member of the board of aldermen of that city.

s. F. C.

TRIER, SALOMON MEYER: Danish pharmacist; born in Copenhagen in 1804; died there in Dec., 1888. He was graduated from the Copenhagen College of Pharmacy in 1826, and was from 1830 to 1856 the owner of a pharmacy in Lyngby, Zealand. From 1844 to 1866 Trier published " Archiv for Pharmacy," and in 1868 he assisted in compiling the " Pharmacopea Danica," which is still in use in Denmark and Norway.

s. F. C.

TRIER, SELIGMANN MEYER: Danish physician; born in Copenhagen June 7, 1800; died there Dec. 20, 1863. He was the son of poor parents, who destined him for a mercantile career. His unusual brightness, however, attracted the attention of the family's physician, Professor Herholdt, who took an interest in him and sent him to the University of Copenhagen, where he studied medicine. He graduated in 1823, and in 1825 was appointed physician for the Jewish poor, and shortly after assistant physician at the Royal Frederik's Hospital in Copenhagen. In 1827 he obtained the degree of doctor of medicine from his alma mater. In 1828 Trier's attention was called to the French physician Laënnec's great discoveries in the field of pathological anatomy, and to his invention of the stethoscope for examination of the thorax. Trier devoted some time to the intimate study of these discoveries, and published in 1830 his " Anvisning til at Kjende Lunge og Hjærtesygdomme ved Perkussion og Middelbar Avskultation." This work was translated into Swedish (Stockholm, 1831) by Elliot, and it was for a long time the only authentic Danish manual on stethoscopy. From 1831 to 1832 Trier was coeditor of " Samlinger til Kundskab om Kolera," an instructive work on the symptoms and treatment of Asiatic cholera. In 1836 he was appointed a member of the Copenhagen board of health, an appointment which, on account of his religion, caused a great deal of comment. In 1842, on the death of Prof. O. Bang, Trier became physician-in-chief of the Royal Frederik's Hospital, a position he held for eighteen years. From 1848 to 1853 he assisted in the publication of " Hospitals-Meddelelser," a medical journal of prominence. In 1847 his alma mater conferred upon him the title of professor, and in 1857 King Frederick VII. honored him with the title of " Etatsraad." Trier was a member of the board of revisers of the " Pharmacopea Danica " (1863).

BIBLIOGRAPHY: C. F. Bricka, *Dansk Biografisk Lexicon*; Smith and Bladt, *Den Danske Lægestand*, 4th ed.; Erslew, *Forfatter-Lexicon*; *Illustreret Tidende*, v. 222.
s. F. C.

TRIESCH: City in Moravia. Its Jewish congregation was most probably founded by exiles from IGLAU shortly after 1426. In the latter city the Jews of Triesch transacted their business during the day, spending the night beyond the city limits, and returning home for the Sabbath. They dealt chiefly in wool, which they sold to the cloth-makers in Iglau. Joseph ben Moses, a disciple of Israel Isserlein of Marburg, mentions in his " Leket Yosher " (ed. J. Freimann, Berlin, 1904) a rabbinical scholar named Isaac of Triesch (1469). It may be, too, that Isaac of טריש, mentioned in the letter of JONATHAN LEVI ZION to the congregation of Frankfort-on-the-Main (1509) as having assisted him in his efforts to obtain from Emperor Maximilian the repeal of the confiscation of Hebrew books (see PFEFFERKORN), was from Triesch, which the Jews called " Trieschet " or " Tritsch," and not from Triest (" Monatsschrift," 1900, p. 125). The grant of freedom of residence to the Jews of Austria in 1848 reduced the congregation of Triesch considerably; and the national fanaticism of the Czech population deprived the Triesch Jews of their former position in the commercial life of the town. On the other hand, Jews became prominent manufacturers of cloth, furniture, and matches.

Of the rabbis of the city the following are known: Mordecai Bet ha-Levi, a prolific cabalistic author whose numerous manuscripts were destroyed in the great conflagration of 1824. He composed for the

Seventh of Adar a special service which is still in use. Eleazar Löw, author of "Shemen Roḳeaḥ," was rabbi in Triesch about 1800 to 1810 and, after having officiated meanwhile at Ronsperg, again from 1812 to 1820. He was a prolific author, and took an active part in the controversy on the Hamburg Tempel. Before his second term of office Moses Schreiber urged the candidacy of his own father-in-law, Akiba Eger. Löw was succeeded by Moses Friedenthal, Joseph Frankfurter, B. Friedmann (later in Grätz), and Dr. M. L. Stern, the present (1905) incumbent, who has held office since 1885. Moses Joseph Spiro was a native of Triesch.

The congregation of Battelau belongs to the district of Triesch. The Jews of Triesch number about 300 in a total population of 5,000. The congregation has numerous well-endowed foundations.

D. M. L. S.

TRIESCH, FRIEDRICH GUSTAV (pseudonyms, **Alex Hartmann, Paul Richter, H. Martin**): Austrian dramatist; born at Vienna June 16, 1845. Triesch studied sculpture for a time at the Akademie der Bildenden Künste, Vienna, but soon turned to literature. Lack of means forced him to follow mercantile pursuits for a short period, but the success of his second piece, the farce "Lachende Erben" (1867), caused him to devote all his time to playwriting. In 1868, in the prize competition of the Hofburgtheater, Vienna, he obtained honorable mention and a production for his comedy "Im XIX. Jahrhundert," and in 1877 two of his plays, "Höhere Gesichtspunkte" and "Die Wochenchronik," were similarly honored. In 1879 his comedy "Neue Verträge" won the first prize offered by the Munich Hoftheater; and in 1892 his drama "Ottilie" won the first prize in the competition instituted by the Litterarisches Vermittlungsbureau of Hamburg, there being 383 competitors.

Triesch is also the author of numerous poems and short stories and of the following plays: "Amalie Welden," comedy, 1865; "Mädchenherzen," drama, 1873; "Träume Sind Schäume," comedy, 1873; "Vorsicht," comedy, 1876; "Reine Liebe," comedy, 1877; "Anwalt," drama, 1881; "Hexenmeister," comedy, 1884; "Nixe," comedy, 1887; "Hand in Hand," 1890; "Factotum Flitsch," farce, 1892; "Liquidator," farce, 1896; "Ihr System," farce, 1898; "Endlich Allein," comedy, 1900.

Bibliography: *Das Geistige Wien,* i. 586-587.

S. E. Ms.

TRIEST: A commercial seaport, at the head of the Adriatic; formerly ethnographically Italian, but politically Austrian; ceded to Italy by treaty of St. Germain (1919). Although no consecutive history of the Jews of Triest has ever been written, much information concerning them may be gleaned from unpublished documents preserved in the municipal records. The city was originally an insignificant town, and first gained importance after it placed itself under Austrian control in 1832. Even before that time, however, a small colony of Jews had settled there, and one of them, the city banker, was permitted to reside in the great square of the city. It appears, moreover, that certain banking establishments existed at Triest under the management of Jews from various parts of Italy, although the earliest Jewish inhabitants of the city seem to have been Germans, since the Ashkenazic ritual was adopted in the first synagogue. This building was situated in the most ancient portion of the ghetto at the head of the Via dei Capitelli, where the structure traditionally regarded as the synagogue was still in existence thirty years ago. Strictly speaking, however, it has been many years since there has been a ghetto at Triest, as the Jews have always enjoyed exceptional favor there, being allowed to live in any part of the city and being exempt from wearing the Badge. With the growth of Triest the center of the Jewish quarter changed to what is now the Piazza delle Scuole Ebraiche, where an Ashkenazic synagogue was erected. This edifice, together with all the ancient records, was destroyed in a conflagration, and was subsequently rebuilt. A new synagogue, with the German ritual, was erected about 1787 to meet the requirements of the rapid growth of the community. This building, a magnificent structure for its time, is still standing. The first floor is now used as a synagogue by the Jews who have immigrated to Triest from Dalmatia and the East; they adopt the Sephardic ritual. A number of years later a synagogue was built especially for the Sephardim in a central part of the city on the site of an ancient cemetery in the Via del Monte, near the Talmud Torah (to which is annexed a Jewish public school) and the Jewish hospital. The oldest gravestones in this cemetery are between 140 and 150 years old, showing that the Jews must formerly have possessed another burial-place. A new cemetery, later enlarged, was opened about seventy-five years ago on a site allotted by the municipal government at some distance from the city and in the vicinity of the other cemeteries. Triest likewise has an orphan asylum, a convalescent home for aged invalids, and

Institutions. many charitable societies, the principal one being the wealthy Fraternità della Misericordia, while the Beneficenza Israelitica also disburses large sums of money. The community has later acquired a site for a new temple, the plans for which were in process of preparation in 1905.

The Jewish population of Triest has recently been increased by a large number of German and Hungarian families, attracted thither by commercial interests. Among the noted Jewish families of the city are the Parentes, Morpurgos, Hirschels, Salems, and Minerbis. Aaron Parente was president of the chamber of commerce of Triest, and was succeeded by his son Solomon, while Baron Elio Morpurgo and his son Mario have been presidents of the Austrian Lloyd. Caliman de Minerbi has been vice-podestà, and the Hirschel family was received at court at a time when the Jews of other cities were persecuted and despised. Jews controlled the principal banks and commercial institutions and the chief insurance companies. The rabbinate of Triest has included such noted men as Formiggini, Levi, Treves, Castiglione, and Marco Tedeschi. The city ranks high in the history of Jewish literature as the birthplace of Samuel David Luzzatto and his cousin, the poetess Rahel Morpurgo; of Giuseppe Lazzaro Morpurgo, an economist and Hebrew poet; of Saul Formiggini, who translated Dante's "Inferno" into Hebrew; of Samuel Vita Zelman, poet and author of the "Yelid Kinnor,"; of Moses Tedeschi, rabbi and author of "Ho'il Mosheh" (a commentary on the entire Bible), of a dictionary of synonyms, and of other works; and of Aaron Romanini and Vittorio Castiglione, Hebrew poets of high reputation, the latter being also the author of a number of literary, philosophical, and pedagogic works in Hebrew and Italian, and later the chief rabbi of Rome. The population of Triest in 1921 was 238,655, including 7,000 Jews.

s.   V. C.

TRIESTE, GABRIEL: Italian merchant and philanthropist; born Dec. 24, 1784; died at Padua March 9, 1860. He was president of the Jewish community in Padua. Of his many benevolent foundations two call for special mention; viz., that of 24,000 Austrian lire for the promotion of art among young Jewish artists, and his prize of 1,000 gulden, in 1850, for the publication of a history of the Jews. Trieste translated Troki's "Ḥizzuḳ Emunah."

BIBLIOGRAPHY: Joseph Wertheimer, in *Jahrbuch für Israeliten*, Vienna, 1861; Wurzbach, *Biographisches Lexikon*, s.v.; Fürst, *Bibl. Jua.* s.v.

S.

TRILLINGER, ELIEZER BEN JOSEPH YOSPA (called also **Eliezer Nin of Nikolsburg**): Austrian rabbi; lived in the latter half of the seventeenth and at the beginning of the eighteenth century; died at Wilna. The name "Trillinger" is probably derived from "Wassertrüdingen," called by the Jews "Wassertrilling" or "Trilling." Trillinger was active in several congregations. At an advanced age he set out for Palestine, but on his way he fell ill at Wilna and, as stated above, died there. He was the author of "Mishnat Rabbi Eli-'ezer," derashot on the Pentateuch, published by his son Joseph Yospa at Frankfort-on-the-Oder in 1707 (not 1717, as erroneously stated by some bibliographical authors).

BIBLIOGRAPHY: Azulai, *Shem ha-Gedolim*, i. 18b, No. 198; ii. 62b, No. 249; Benjacob, *Ozar ha-Sefarim*, p. 385, No. 2535; Fürst, *Bibl. Jud.* iii. 447; Michael, *Or ha-Ḥayyim*, No. 429; Zedner, *Cat. Hebr. Books Brit. Mus.* p. 222.

D.   S. MAN.

TRINITY: The fundamental dogma of Christianity; the concept of the union in one God of Father, Son, and Holy Spirit as three infinite persons. It was the Nicene Council and even more especially the Athanasian Creed that first gave the dogma its definite formulation: "And the Catholick Faith is this: That we worship one God in Trinity, and Trinity in Unity; Neither confounding the Persons; nor dividing the Substance." Equalization of the Son with the Father marks an innovation in the Pauline theology: "Yet to us there is one God, the Father, of whom are all things, and we unto him; and one Lord, Jesus Christ, through whom are all things, and we through him" (I Cor. viii. 6, R. V.), while in another passage the Holy Ghost is added (ib. xii. 3; comp. Titus ii. 13), thus rapidly developing the concept of the Trinity (II Cor. xiii. 14). Although the Judæo-Christian sect of the EBIONITES protested against this apotheosis of Jesus

("Clementine Homilies," xvi. 15), the great mass of Gentile Christians accepted it.

The Holy Ghost as the third person of the Trinity could originate only on Gentile soil, since it was based on a linguistic error. The "Gospel According to the Hebrews," which was once held **The Holy** in high esteem, especially in Ebionitic **Ghost.** circles, still regards the term "mother" as equivalent to "Holy Ghost" (Origen, Commentary on John ii. 12; see Preuschen, "Antilegomena," p. 4, Giessen, 1901; Henneke, "Neutestamentliche Apokryphen," p. 19, Tübingen, 1904), since in Aramaic, the language of this Gospel and possibly the original dialect of all the Gospels, the noun "ruḥa" (spirit) is feminine (comp. the Gnostic statement ἐντεῦθεν πάλιν ἀναδεχθῆναι μητέρα καὶ υἱόν; Irenæus, "Adversus Hæreses," i. 271). The OPHITES, furthermore, actually taught a trinity of father, son, and mother (Hilgenfeld, "Ketzergeschichte," p. 255); and the fact that the Church father Hippolytus found among the Ophites the Assyrian doctrine of the trinity of the soul (Hilgenfeld, l.c. p. 259) justifies the assumption of a kinship of the dogma of the Trinity with older concepts. The MANDÆANS also believe ruḥa to be the mother of the Messiah, though they regard them both as demons (Brandt, "Die Mandäische Religion," p. 124, Leipsic, 1889). The original trinity must, therefore, have included a feminine being, since thus alone could the concept of ruḥa have been obtained, and only after this form of trinity had been accepted in Judæo-Christian circles could the Greek τὸ πνεῦμα be regarded as a person, although it then became masculine instead of feminine. Philo's doctrine of the Logos is connected with this belief. God, who created His son in His own image (Gen. ii. 7), thereby made Himself triform, so that He Himself and the biform first Adam (= Logos = Jesus) constituted the first trinity.

The controversies between the Christians and the Jews concerning the Trinity centered for the most part about the problem whether the writers of the Old Testament bore witness to it or not, the Jews naturally rejecting every proof brought forward by their opponents. The latter based their arguments on the Trisagion in Isa. vi. 3, a proof which had been frequently offered since Eusebius and Gregory of Nazianzus. The convert Jacob **Jewish** Perez of Valentia (d. 1491) even found **Objections.** an allusion to the Trinity in the word "Elohim," and Luther saw distinct traces of the doctrine in Gen. i. 1, 26; iii. 21; xi. 7, 8, 9; Num. vi. 22; II Sam. xxiii. 2; and Dan. vii. 13. The Jewish polemics against this doctrine date almost from its very conception. Even in the Talmud, R. Simlai (3d cent.) declared, in refutation of the "heretics," "The three words 'El,' 'Elohim,' and 'YHWH' (Josh. xxii. 22) connote one and the same person, as one might say, 'King, Emperor, Augustus'" (Yer. Ber. ix. 12d), while elsewhere he substitutes the phrase "as if one should say, 'master, builder, and architect'" (ib. 13a). There are, however, no other allusions to the Trinity in Talmudic literature, as has been rightly pointed out by Herford ("Christianity in Talmud and Midrash," p. 395, London, 1903), since the polemics of the rabbis of that period

were directed chiefly against dualism (שתי רשויות).
Another polemic, which is noteworthy for its antiquity and its protagonists, was the disputation between Pope Sylvester I. (314–335) and the Jew Noah
(Migne, "Patrologia Græca," viii. 814).

In the Middle Ages the nature of the Trinity was
discussed in every one of the numerous disputations
between Christians and Jews, the polemic of Abraham Roman (in his "Sela' ha-Maḥaloḳet," printed in
the "Milḥemet Ḥobah," Constantinople, 1710) being
especially bitter; while in his well-known disputation Naḥmanides wrote as follows:

"Fra Pablo asked me in Gerona whether I believed in the
Trinity [שלוש]. I said to him, 'What is the Trinity? Do three
great human bodies constitute the Divinity?' 'No!' 'Or are
there three ethereal bodies, such as the souls, or are there three
angels?' 'No!' 'Or is an object composed of three kinds of
matter, as bodies are composed of the four elements?' 'No!'
'What then is the Trinity?' He said: 'Wisdom, will, and
power' [comp. the definition of Thomas Aquinas cited above].
Then I said: 'I also acknowledge that God is wise and not foolish, that He has a will unchangeable, and that He is mighty
and not weak. But the term "Trinity" is decidedly erroneous;
for wisdom is not accidental in the Creator, since He and His
wisdom are one, He and His will are one, He and His power are
one, so that wisdom, will, and power are one. Moreover, even
were these things accidental in Him, that which is called God
would not be three beings, but one being with these three accidental attributes.' Our lord the king here quoted an analogy
which the erring ones had taught him, saying that there are also
three things in wine, namely, color, taste, and bouquet, yet it is
still one thing. This is a decided error; for the redness, the
taste, and the bouquet of the wine are distinct essences, each of
them potentially self-existent; for there are red, white, and
other colors, and the same statement holds true with regard to
taste and bouquet. The redness, the taste, and the bouquet,
moreover, are not the wine itself, but the thing which fills the
vessel, and which is, therefore, a body with the three accidents.
Following this course of argument, there would be four, since
the enumeration should include God, His wisdom, His will, and
His power, and these are four. You would even have to speak
of five things; for He lives, and His life is a part of Him just as
much as His wisdom. Thus the definition of God would be
'living, wise, endowed with will, and mighty'; the Divinity
would therefore be fivefold in nature. All this, however, is an
evident error. Then Fra Pablo arose and said that he believed
in the unity, which, none the less, included the Trinity, although
this was an exceedingly deep mystery, which even the angels
and the princes of heaven could not comprehend. I arose and
said: 'It is evident that a person does not believe what he does
not know; therefore the angels do not believe in the Trinity.'
His colleagues then bade him be silent" ("Milḥemet Ḥobah,"
p. 13a).

The boldness of the Christian exegetes, who converted even the "Shema'," the solemn confession of
the Divine Unity, into a proof of the Trinity (Maimonides, in "Teḥiyyat ha-Metim," beginning), furnishes an explanation of the bitterness of the Jewish
apologists. Joseph Ḳimḥi assailed the doctrine of
the Trinity first of all ("Milḥemet Ḥobah," p. 19a),
refuting with weighty arguments the favorite proof
based on Gen. xviii. 1–2, where YHWH is described
as first appearing alone to Abraham, who later beholds two persons (comp. Abraham ibn Ezra's commentary, ad loc.). Simeon ben Ẓemaḥ Duran, who
also refuted the Trinitarian proofs, added: "The
dogma itself is manifestly false, as I have shown by
philosophic deduction; and my present statements
are made only with reference to their [the Christians'] assertions, while the monk Nestor accepted
Judaism for the very reason that he had refuted them"
("Milḥemet Ḥobah," p. 48b). Noteworthy among
modern polemics against the Trinity is Joshua
Segre's critique ("Zeit. für Hebr. Bibl." viii. 22).

The Cabala, on the other hand, especially the
Zohar, its fundamental work, was far less hostile to
the dogma of the Trinity, since by its speculations
regarding the father, the son, and the
In the spirit it evolved a new trinity, and
Zohar. thus became dangerous to Judaism.
Such terms as "maṭrona," "body,"
"spirit," occur frequently (e.g., "Tazria'," ed. Polna,
iii. 43b); so that Christians and converts like Knorr
von Rosenroth, REUCHLIN, and RITTANGEL found
in the Zohar a confirmation of Christianity and especially of the dogma of the Trinity (Jellinek, "Die
Kabbala," p. 250, Leipsic, 1844 [transl. of Franck's
"La Kabbale," Paris, 1843]). Reuchlin sought on
the basis of the Cabala the words "Father, Son, and
Holy Ghost" in the second word of the Pentateuch,
as well as in Ps. cxviii. 22 (ib. p. 10), while Johann
Kemper, a convert, left in manuscript a work entitled "Maṭṭeh Mosheh," which treats in its third section of the harmony of the Zohar with the doctrine
of the Trinity (Zettersteen, "Verzeichniss der Hebräischen und Aramäischen Handschriften zu Upsala," p. 16, Lund, 1900). The study of the Cabala
led the Frankists to adopt Christianity; but the Jews
have always regarded the doctrine of the Trinity
as one irreconcilable with the spirit of the Jewish
religion and with monotheism. See CHRISTIANITY
IN ITS RELATION TO JUDAISM; POLEMICS.

BIBLIOGRAPHY: F. C. Bauer, Die Christliche Lehre von der
Dreieinigkeit, etc., 3 vols., Tübingen, 1841–43; H. Usener,
Die Dreiheit, in Rheinisches Museum für Klassische Phi-
lologie, lviii. 1–47.
K.   S. KR.

TRINQUETAILLE (Hebrew, טרנקאטאלייש or
טרנקטליש): Suburb of Arles, France, on the right
bank of the Rhone. Its Jewish community was of
much importance in the Middle Ages. Favorably
received by the lords of Baux, the Jews lived peace-
fully at Trinquetaille until 1300, when the town
was incorporated with Arles, the two communities
being likewise united. In 1349, however, the "baylons" of Arles were obliged to request the provost
to authorize them to separate from the Jews of
Trinquetaille, who "refused to share in the communal expenses." A reference to the place occurs in
Isaac ben Jacob Lattes, "Sha'are Ẓiyyon," pp. 72,
75 (see "R. E. J." ix. 222).

In the thirteenth and fourteenth centuries Trinquetaille was the home of many scholars, including
the following: Meïr ben Isaac, author of the "Sefer
ha-'Ezer," in which he defended Alfasi against the
attacks of Zerahiah ben Isaac ha-Levi Gerondi; Nathan ben Meïr, author of a commentary on the Pentateuch and of the "Sha'are Tefisah," on illegal seizures; and TODROS BEN MESHULLAM BEN DAVID
(Todros Todrosi).

BIBLIOGRAPHY: Carmoly, Biographie des Israélites de France,
p. 91; Gross, Gallia Judaica, pp. 246–248; idem, in Monatsschrift, 1878, p. 379; 1880, p. 61; Munk, Mélanges, pp. 358,
438; Renan-Neubauer, Les Rabbins Français, p. 515; idem,
Les Ecrivains Juifs Français, pp. 570–573; Renan, Aver-
roès, pp. 69, 70, 191; R. E. J. xli. 64; Steinschneider, Hebr.
Uebers. pp. 62, 182, 285, 294; idem, Hebr. Bibl. x. 54, xiii. 17.
S.   S. K.

TRIPOLI (ancient **Oea**): Seaport on the northern coast of Africa; capital of the Turkish vilayet
of the same name. Local tradition states that
under the Fatimite dynasty in Egypt, Jews from the

oasis of Pessato established the most ancient community in Tripoli. Benjamin of Tudela, on the other hand, who traveled through northern Africa in the latter part of the twelfth century and visited Tunis and Alexandria, makes no mention of Tripoli. When the Jews were exiled from Spain in 1492, they avoided Tripoli, which was then a part of the dominions of Ferdinand the Catholic; nor did they settle there until it passed into the hands of Sultan Sulaiman the Magnificent in 1551. The surnames of the Jewish families of Tripoli show that Spanish Jews never resided in the city in considerable numbers; for instead of bearing names like "Toledo," "Carmona," and "Tarragone," they are called "Arbib," "Hasan," "Halefi," "Racah," "Tayar," "Tamam," etc. Moreover, the traveler Benjamin II. drew particular attention to the fact that the family of Sylva was descended from Spanish Maranos who had come to the city at some unknown period. In 1667 Miguel Cardoso, one of the most ardent disciples of Shabbethai Zebi, endeavored to establish a Shabbethaian sect at Tripoli, but was forced by the Jews to leave the city.

Early History.

In 1705 the Bey of Tunis made war upon Halil Pasha, governor of Tripoli, and threatened to put the inhabitants to the sword; but his camp was ravaged by an epidemic, and he was forced to retreat. In memory of this event the local rabbis instituted a yearly festival on the 24th of Ṭebet, called "Purim Sherif," or "Purim Kidebuni." Eighty-seven years later a corsair named Borghel attacked Ali Pasha Karamanli, the governor, and committed many atrocities in the city, burning at the stake the son of Abraham Ḥalfon, the caid of the Tripolitan Jews. At the end of two years, however, Karamanli succeeded in expelling the invaders; and in commemoration of this deliverance the Jews

Special Purims.

established the Purim Borghel, which falls on the 29th of Ṭebet. See PURIMS, SPECIAL.

When Benjamin II. visited Tripoli in 1850, he found there about 1,000 Jewish families, with eight synagogues and several Talmudic schools, while the spiritual interests of the community were in the keeping of four rabbis.

Tripoli has produced a number of rabbinical authors, the most important being the following: Simeon b. Labi, who flourished about 1509 and was the head of a local Talmudic school, besides being the author of a cabalistic commentary on Genesis entitled "Ketem Paz" and of a hymn on Simeon b. Yoḥai; Abraham Ḥalfon, who flourished in the latter part of the eighteenth century and wrote "Ḥayye Abraham" (Leghorn, 1826), on the ritual laws of the Bible and the Talmud, in addition to a manuscript diary, still extant; Moses Serussi, who flourished in the second half of the nineteenth century and wrote the "Wa-Yasheb Mosheh"; and Ḥayyim Cohen, author of "Millot ha-Melek," "Leb Shomea'," "Zokrenu le-Ḥayyim," "'Ereb Pesaḥ," "Allon Bakut," "Perush al-Seliḥot," "Na'awah Ḳodesh," "Torat Ḥayyim," "Perush Hosha'anot," and "Miḳra Ḳodesh."

Interior of a Bet Ha-Midrash at Tripoli
(From a painting by Israel Gentz.)

The administration of the community, which pays an annual tax of 4,890 francs for exemption from military service, is in the hands of a chief rabbi ("ḥakam bashi"), who is assisted by four judges. Since 1840 the following chief rabbis have officiated at Tripoli: Jacob Memun (d. 1849), Shalom Tito, Moses Arbib, Elijah Hazan (1874–88; appointed by a firman of the sultan Aziz and decorated with the Order of the Medjidie), Ezekiel Sasson (1897), David Ḳimḥi (1897–1902), and the present incumbent, Shabbethai Levi. The Jews of Tripoli, who are characterized by many superstitious beliefs, now (1911) number 12,000 in a total population of 29,761. They

Rabbis and Scholars.

have many representatives in various mechanical and mercantile pursuits. They possess eighteen synagogues, eleven yeshibot, a society for the relief of the sick; also two schools maintained by the Alliance Israélite Universelle.

A number of towns in the vicinity of Tripoli contain a considerable Jewish population, e.g., **Amrum,** 1,000; **Derne** or **Derna,** 150; **Garian,** 300; **Homs,** 300; **Messilata,** 350; **Misserato, Idir,** and **Maatin,** 400; **Tajoorah,** 200; **Yiffren** or **Jebel,** 1,000; **Zanzbur,** 60; **Zawiel,** 450; and **Ziliten,** 450.

BIBLIOGRAPHY: Dezobry, *Dictionnaire d'Histoire et de Géographie*; Benjamin II., *Mas'e Yisrael,* p. 166; Franco, *Histoire des Israélites de l'Empire Ottoman,* p. 121; Hazan, *Ha-Ma'alot li-Shelomoh,* pp. 38, 116; Azulai, *Shem ha-Gedolim,* s.v. *Simeon b. Labi; Bulletin de l'Alliance Israélite Universelle,* 1885, 1889, 1890, 1903; *Revue des Ecoles de l'Alliance Israélite Universelle,* pp. 81, 153, 358, 421, 428; *R. E. J.* xx. 78 et seq.

s.　　　　　　　　　　　　　　　　　M. Fr.

TRISTRAM, HENRY BAKER: English clergyman, Biblical scholar, and traveler in Palestine; born May 11, 1822, at Eglingham, Northumberland. He was educated at Durham School and Oxford University, and took orders in 1845; but sickness compelled him to live abroad. He explored the northern Sahara, and in 1858 paid his first visit to Palestine. In 1863 and in 1872 he again visited Palestine and spent a great deal of time there in making scientific observations and identifying Scripture localities. In 1873 he made a similar tour into Moab. In 1879 he declined the offer of the Anglican bishopric of Jerusalem, made to him by the Earl of Beaconsfield. In 1881 he journeyed extensively in Palestine, the Lebanon, Mesopotamia, and Armenia. In 1873 he became canon residentiary of Durham.

Among Tristram's many publications those dealing with the Holy Land are: " The Land of Israel, a Journal of Travels with Reference to Its Physical History," London, 1865 (many editions); "The Natural History of the Bible " (*ib.* 1867); " Land of Moab " (*ib.* 1874); "Pathways of Palestine " (*ib.* 1882); " The Fauna and Flora of Palestine " (*ib.* 1884); and " Eastern Customs in Bible Lands " (*ib.* 1894). He died in 1906.

BIBLIOGRAPHY· *Men and Women of the Time,* 1899; *Who's Who,* 1902.

J.　　　　　　　　　　　　　　　　　A. M. F.

TRIWOSCH, JOSEPH ELIJAH: Russian Hebrew writer and poet; born at Wilna Jan. 18, 1856; settled at Grodno as a teacher of Hebrew and Russian. His literary activity began in 1873, in which year he published in " Ha-Lebanon " his first articles. Since then he has contributed to most of the Hebrew literary periodicals. With the exception of his " Dor Tahapukot " (Warsaw, 1881), which describes the activity of the Russian Social-Democrats, all his novels, representing Jewish life in Russia, have been published in various periodicals. They are as follows: "Toḥelet Niḳzabah," in "Ha-Shaḥar," viii., No. 12; "Bi-Meḳom Ẓawwa'ah," in "Ha-Karmel," iv.; "Ha-Liṭo'i," in "Ha-Shaḥar," x., No. 12; "'Al Shete ha-Se'ippim," in "Ha-Asif," ii. 577-629. Many of his poems likewise have been published in " Ha-Shaḥar " and in other periodicals.

BIBLIOGRAPHY: Sokolow, *Sefer Zikkaron,* p. 46; Zeitlin, *Bibl. Post-Mendels.* p. 398.

H·R·　　　　　　　　　　　　　　　　M. Sel.

TROKI: District city in the government of Wilna, Poland. It was an important Jewish center in the fourteenth, fifteenth, and sixteenth centuries; and there is a tradition, quoted by Firkovich, that 330 out of the 483 Karaite families which Grand Duke Witold of Lithuania brought from the Crimea after his war with the Tatars, were settled in the new city of Troki, which was built expressly for them. The provisions of Witold's charter of 1388 to the Jews of Lithuania applied to those of Troki also. In describing Troki as it appeared in 1414 Gilbert de Lannua of Burgundy says: " In this city there live Germans, Lithuanians, Russians, and a great number of Jews, each of these peoples using its own language."

Casimir IV. granted the Magdeburg Rights to the Karaites of Troki in 1441. The latter were to be subject to the jurisdiction of their own elder; and he in turn was to be responsible directly to the king or to judges appointed by the latter. Neither the waywode nor the starost was to interfere in local matters concerning only the Karaites. Lawsuits between Karaites and Christians were to be decided by a tribunal composed of the Karaite elder and the waywode. These privileges were confirmed by Alexander Jagellon in 1492.

Toward the end of the fifteenth century the autonomy of the Jewish community in Troki was still further strengthened by a royal order (1485) directing a separate levy and collection of taxes for its members. Individual Jews gained in influence through their growing commercial enterprises, as is shown by a series of contemporary documents.

Fourteenth, Fifteenth, and Sixteenth Centuries. Thus in 1484 the customs duties of Novogrudok were leased to the Troki Jews Ilia Moiseyevich, Rubim Sakovich, Avram Danilovich, and Eska Shelemovich; in 1486 those of Jitomir, Putivl, Kiev, and Vyshegorod were leased to Simsa Kravchik, Sadka, Shamak Danilovich, and Rizhka, Jews of Kiev and Troki; and in 1489 those of Troki were leased to the Jew Mikhail Danilovich, of whom mention occurs in a document of 1495 also.

At the beginning of the sixteenth century the prosperity of the Troki Jews had declined considerably, and they petitioned King Sigismund for relief. In response the king issued the following decree, dated July, 1507: "In view of the impoverished condition of the Jews of Troki, and desiring to help them to regain the prosperity which they enjoyed under King Casimir, King Sigismund confirms to them their ancient privileges." Suits between Jews were to be decided by the Jewish elder appointed by the waywode of Troki with the king's consent. Suits of Jews against "Lithuanians, Russians, and others" were placed under the jurisdiction of the waywode or his vicegerent. The Jews of Troki were to pay taxes once a year on equal terms with the other citizens; and no other taxes were to be levied upon them. In emergencies, following an ancient practise, they were to contribute according to their means, in common with the other citizens of Troki—Lithuanians, Russians, and Tatars—living in the Jewish portion of the town. They were

Decree of 1507.

further permitted to pasture their cattle and to gather hay on the meadows which Jews had used from olden times. They were exempted from all customs duties; and they were further permitted to travel unrestrictedly on the highways and rivers. They were also exempted from field-work and similar tasks connected with the royal castle in Troki.

In 1514 the Troki Jews again petitioned the king for the confirmation of their ancient privileges; and in 1516 Sigismund ordered, "in response to the petition of the inhabitants of Troki of the Roman, Greek-Catholic, and Jewish religions, in consequence of the great impoverishment of the city," that semi-annual fairs be held at Troki, and that all merchants traveling from Kovno to Wilna, or vice versa, pass through Troki. In March, 1521, the Jewish elder of Troki, Mordecai Yeskovich, complained to the king that the waywode of Troki had quartered his servants in the Jewish houses contrary to previous usage, which permitted the quartering of officers and nobles in houses of the Jews only during the king's sojourn in the city. The king's decision was favorable to the petitioners. In 1522 mention is made of the Jews of Troki as sharing the privileges granted to the Jews of Lithuania, and in 1529 as having paid their share of the tax of 1,000 kop groschen levied on all the Jews of Lithuania. A document of 1540 confirms the Troki Jew Batko Agrianovich in the possession of lands and of two lakes formerly belonging to Boyar Yuri Stanislavovich. The Troki Jews are mentioned in 1551 as being exempt from the payment of the SEREBSZCZYZNA; also in documents of 1552 and 1555. From a document of 1562 it appears that the salt monopoly of Troki was leased in that year to the Jew Yesko Mordukhayevich; and from one of 1563 it is evident that the Jews of Troki paid a tax of 376 kop groschen imposed on the Jews of Lithuania. Important properties were at this time held by Jews of Troki, as is evidenced by a document of 1568, wherein the king confirms the Jew Zakharias Moizeshovich in the possession of one of the castle properties, and by another of 1569, which refers to the sale of the "Jewish castle" held by the Jew Ogron Mordukhayevich. The castle property included fields, forests, pastures, swamps, etc., as is indicated by the bill of sale, which was signed by Ogron in Hebrew letters.

Stephen Bathori included the Jews of Troki in the confirmation of ancient privileges granted to the Jews of Lithuania in 1576. In

Under Stephen Bathori.
1578 he reminded them of their arrears of taxes; and in 1579 he decreed that the taxes imposed upon them should not exceed in amount those levied in the preceding reigns, and confirmed the privileges granted them by Sigismund in 1507. In 1579 Bathori found it necessary to adjust a suit originating in the commercial rivalry between the Christians, Jews, and Tatars of Troki and the Christian burghers of Kovno. In 1582 the Jewish burghers of Troki, represented by their elder Alexander Isakovich, made complaint to King Stephen Bathori against the waywode Stephen Koributovich, who had quartered his servants in Jewish houses during the king's absence from the town. The complaint

was sustained. In 1585 the Jews together with the Christians of Troki are mentioned in a lawsuit against the farmer of the customs duties, who had seized merchandise belonging to them. The difficulty seemingly arose in the abuse by the citizens of Troki of an old privilege exempting them from the payment of customs duties. Four years later the Jews of Troki, through their elder Aaron Sholomovich, complained to King Sigismund that the burghers of Kovno prohibited them from trading freely in that city and confiscated their wares contrary to privileges granted to the Jews by the Polish kings and Lithuanian grand dukes. In response to this petition the king directed (March 28, 1589) that the rights of the Jews of Troki be respected. In 1619 reference is made in a legal document to the Jew Samuel Yakhimovich of Troki.

In 1897 Troki had a total population of 2,390, of whom 818 were Rabbinites and 424 were Karaites. The Karaites, who enjoy full civic rights, are as a rule friendly to their Rabbinite neighbors, but live separate from them. Considerable antagonism arose between these two classes in the reign of Nicholas I., largely through the action of Firkovich. A law was passed prohibiting Rabbinites from residing in Troki; but this was repealed in the sixth decade of the nineteenth century. The Karaites still use their ancient Tatar dialect; but in their religious services according to the Sephardic ritual they employ Hebrew. In olden times the Karaites were granted 250 deciatines of land, which they are now permitted to use for farming purposes. Most of them are market-gardeners and truckers, and lease their meadows to the peasants. They are engaged also in retail trade and in handicrafts. The young Karaites, desiring broader opportunities, leave their native town to seek their fortunes elsewhere. Some of them enter the liberal professions or become government officials; and not a few have achieved notable success as merchants and manufacturers. Most of them remember their native town and contribute generously toward its communal needs. Large numbers return to Troki for the fall holy days. The evening after Yom Kippur is celebrated with great gaiety. A Karaite ḥakam was formerly stationed at Troki; but now there is only one for all the Russian Karaites: he resides at Eupatoria. The Karaites of Troki have their own shoḥeṭ; but they employ the Rabbinite mohel. Troki has one Karaite school, in which religious instruction is given to the children. The Rabbinites are for the most part merchants of small means. There are no very important industries in the place.

Present Day.

The Troki Karaites.

Some of the early Karaite settlers in Troki emigrated to Lutsk in Volhynia and to Halicz in Galicia, and established Karaite communities in those towns. See JEW. ENCYC. vii. 438, s.v. KARAITES.

BIBLIOGRAPHY: *Regesty i Nadpisi*, s.v.; *Russko-Yevreiski Arkhiv*, vols. i. and ii., s.v.; *Khronika Voskhoda*, 1900; *Entziklopedicheski Slovar*, xiv. 431–432; Harkavy, *Altjüdische Denkmäler aus der Krim*, 1876.

H. R.   J. G. L.

The Karaite community of Troki produced several important scholars, among them being the following: Isaac ben Abraham Troki (16th cent.), author of the apologetic work "Ḥizzuḳ Emunah"; Zerah Troki (17th cent.), for whom Joseph Solomon Delmedigo wrote his "Elim"; Ezra Troki (d. 1666), who was a relative and pupil of the above-mentioned Zerah, and studied medicine under Delmedigo, later becoming physician to King John Casimir of Poland; Abraham b. Samuel (second half

Scholars. of 17th cent.), a judge of the Karaites of Troki, and reputed to have been a favorite of King John Sobieski. At that time Troki was recognized as the seat of authority for the Karaites of the surrounding towns of Posvol, Birzhi, Seltz, Shat, Zermer, Neustadt, and others; but the number of Karaites in Troki was apparently very small. In a decision of the Lithuanian council, or "wa'ad," dated Zabludowo, 9th of Adar (March 7), 1664, and relating to the adjustment of the rates of taxation (a matter in which the Karaites seem to have been dependent on the Rabbinites), the authority of the Karaites of Troki was recognized on the condition that at the end of two years Troki should be found to have not less than ten Karaite "ba'ale battim," or heads of families. This amply disproves Firkovich's statement that prior to the pestilence of 1710, in which almost all of them perished, Troki had 500 Karaite families. Since then Troki has been of little importance among the Karaites; and its name is seldom seen in the lists of subscribers to Karaite works. Gabriel Firkovich, son-in-law of Abraham Firkovich, was probably the last Karaite of Troki to attain any prominence.

The Rabbinite community of Troki is likewise of little importance. Rabbi Ẓebi Hirsch, father of Samuel Salant of Jerusalem, was rabbi of Troki in the first half of the nineteenth century, and Benjamin Friedman, later rabbi of Antokol, a suburb of Wilna, occupied the Troki rabbinate from 1865 to 1870.

Bibliography: Firkovich, *Abne Zikkaron*, pp. 251-254, Wilna, 1871; Fürst, *Gesch. des Karäert.* iii. 42, Leipsic, 1869; Maggid, *Zur Geschichte und Genealogie der Günzburge*, pp. 207-210, St. Petersburg, 1899.

H. R. P. Wi.

TROKI: Karaite family deriving its name from the city of Troki, in the government of Wilna, Russia. The more important members of the family are:

Abraham ben Aaron Ḥazzan Troki: Karaite liturgical poet; lived at Troki in the sixteenth century. A liturgical poem of his, beginning with the words אשורך לאדון עולם במורא, for the Sabbatical section "Beshallah," has been inserted in the Karaite Siddur (i. 315). It is possible that the numerous liturgical poems found there under the name "Abraham" without any other indication may also have been composed by Troki.

Bibliography: Fürst, *Gesch. des Karäert.* iii. 37; Gottlober, *Bikkoret le-Toledot ha-Kara'im*, p. 151, Wilna, 1865.

Abraham ben Josiah ha-Shofeṭ Troki: Karaite physician and scholar; born at Troki; died Dec., 1688. He was physician to John III., Sobieski, and later to Grand Duke Sigismund II. Troki was the author of two medical works: one, in Hebrew, entitled "Oẓar ha-'Am," and the other, in Latin, still extant in manuscript (St. Petersburg Cat., No. 732). According to Abraham Firkovich, Troki wrote also a work in seven sections entitled "Masa ha-'Am,"

which, after having translated it into Latin, he sold to the Dominican friars at Wilna. Simḥah Luzki mentions two other works by Troki, "Bet Abraham" and "Pas Yeda," both of which dealt with scientific subjects.

Bibliography: Fürst, *Gesch. des Karäert.* iii. 94; Gottlober, *Bikkoret le-Toledot ha-Kara'im*, p. 151; Simḥah Luzki, *Oraḥ Ẓaddiḳim*, s.v. ב and פ; Fuenn, *Keneset Yisrael*, p. 29; Neubauer, *Aus der Petersburger Bibliothek*, p. 72.

S. I. Br.

Isaac ben Abraham Troki: Karaite polemical writer; born at Troki 1533; died in the same city 1594. He was instructed in Bible and Hebrew literature by the Karaite scholar Zephaniah ben Mordecai, and in Latin and Polish literatures by Christian teachers. Moving in Christian circles, Troki was often called upon to take part in religious controversies; and this prompted him to study religious philosophy and Christian theology and to acquaint himself with the tenets of the various Christian sects. In the course of his studies he became interested in the anti-Christian and anti-Jewish writings of his contemporaries and compatriots Nicholas Paruta, Martin Czechowic, and Simon Budni. To refute the arguments of the writers against the Jewish religion and to show the superiority of Judaism, Troki wrote his epoch-making "Ḥizzuḳ Emunah."

This work is in two volumes, containing ninety-nine chapters in all. The author begins by demonstrating that Jesus was not the Messiah predicted by

His "Ḥizzuḳ Emunah." the Prophets. "This," he says, "is evident (1) from his pedigree, (2) from his acts, (3) from the period in which he lived, and (4) from the fact that during his lifetime the promises that related to the advent of the expected Messiah were not fulfilled." His arguments on these points are as follows: (1) Jesus' pedigree: Without discussing the question of the relationship of Joseph to David, which is more than doubtful, one may ask, What has Jesus to do with Joseph, who was not his father? (2) His acts: According to Matt. x. 34, Jesus said, "Think not that I am come to make peace on earth: I came not to send peace, but a sword. For I am come to set a man at variance against his father, and the daughter against her mother, and the daughter-in-law against her mother-in-law." On the other hand, Holy Writ attributes to the true and expected Messiah actions contrary to those of Jesus. (3) The period of his existence: It is evident that Jesus did not come at the time foretold by the Prophets; for they predicted the advent of the Messiah in the "last days" (Isa. ii. 2). (4) The fulfilment of the Messianic promises: All the Prophets predicted that at the advent of the Messiah peace and justice would reign in the world, not only among men, but even among the animals; yet there is not one sincere Christian who would claim that this has been fulfilled.

Among Troki's objections to the divinity of Jesus the following may be mentioned: The Christian who opposes Judaism must believe that the Jews tormented and crucified Jesus either with his consent or against his will. If with his consent, then the Jews had ample sanction for what they did. Besides, if Jesus was really willing to meet such a fate, what cause was there for complaint and afflic-

tion? And why did he pray in the manner related in Matt. xxvi. 39? On the other hand, if it be assumed that the crucifixion was against
Arguments. his will, how then can he be regarded as God—he, who was unable to resist the power of those who brought him to the cross? How could one who had not the power to save his own life be held as the Savior of all mankind ("Ḥizzuḳ Emunah," ch. xlvii.). In the last chapter Troki quotes Rev. xxii. 18, and asks how Christians could consistently make changes of so glaring a nature; for the change of the Sabbath from the seventh to the first day of the week was not authorized by Jesus or by any of his disciples. Moreover, partaking of the blood and flesh of a strangled beast is a palpable infringement of the dictates of the Apostles.

Troki died before completing his work, the index and preface to which were made by his pupil Joseph ben Mordecai Malinovski Troki. The "Ḥizzuḳ Emunah" remained for many years in manuscript, and the text underwent many changes at the hands of the copyists. One rabbi went so far as to substitute for many of Troki's philosophical arguments Talmudical sayings. The work was first published, with a Latin translation, by Wagenseil in his "Tela Ignea Satanæ" (Freiberg, 1681), and was reprinted in Amsterdam (1705), Jerusalem (1845), and Leipsic (1857). It was also translated into Judæo-German (Amsterdam, 1717), into English by Mocatta (London, 1851), into German by David Deutsch (Sohran, 1865, 2d ed. 1873, with the Hebrew text) and into Spanish, the last-mentioned translation being extant in manuscript. Through its Latin translation the "Ḥizzuḳ Emunah" became the object of passionate debates in Christian circles; and its arguments against Christianity were used by all freethinkers.
Editions and Translations. Voltaire gives the following appreciation of it: "Il a rassemblé toutes les difficultés que les incrédules ont prodiguées depuis. Enfin les incrédules les plus determinés n'ont presque rien allegué qui ne soit dans le Rempart de la Foi du rabbin Isaac" ("Mélanges," iii. 344).

Simḥah Luzki mentions two other works by Troki; namely, a treatise on the new moon, according to the "Gan 'Eden" of Aaron the Younger, and a work, in the form of questions and answers, on the slaughtering of animals, also according to the "Gan 'Eden." Troki composed also liturgical poems, some of which have been inserted in the Karaite Siddur.

BIBLIOGRAPHY: Fürst, Gesch. des Karäert. iii. 30 et seq.; Neubauer, Aus der Petersburger Bibliothek, p. 64; Geiger, Nachgelassene Schriften, pp. 178–224, Berlin, 1876; Gottlober, Bikkoret le-Toledot ha-Kara'im, p. 184; Grätz, Gesch. ix. 490; Fuenn, Keneset Yisrael, p. 614.
J.
I. Br.

Joseph ben Mordecai Malinovski Troki: Karaite scholar; lived at Troki in the sixteenth century; pupil of Isaac ben Abraham Troki, to whose "Ḥizzuḳ Emunah" he wrote the preface and the index. Joseph Troki was the author of: "Ha-Elef Leka" (Amsterdam, c. 1626), a prayer consisting of 1,000 words, each beginning with the letter ה; "Ḳizzur 'Inyan Sheḥiṭah" (Vienna, 1830), on the laws concerning the slaughtering of animals according to Elijah Bashyaẓi, published together with the

"Dod Mordekai" of Mordecai ben Nissim. Simḥah Luzki attributes also to Troki: "Sefer Minhagim," on the ritual customs of the Karaites; "Perush 'al Haḳdamat Aẓulah," a commentary on the prayer "Aẓulah"; a commentary on the ten Karaite articles of faith; and "Perush 'al 'Inyan ha-'Arayot," on the laws of incest according to Elijah Bashyaẓi.

BIBLIOGRAPHY: Fürst, Gesch. des Karäert. iii. 37; idem, Bibl. Jud. iii. 448; Simḥah Moses Luzki, Oraḥ Ẓaddiḳim, s.v. ד; Steinschneider, Cat. Bodl. col. 1509.

Solomon ben Aaron Troki: Karaite scholar; lived at Troki in the seventeenth and eighteenth centuries. He was a relative of Mordecai ben Nissim, author of the "Dod Mordekai," whom he surpassed in knowledge both of rabbinical literature and of secular science, of which latter he made use in his writings. Troki was the author of: "Migdal 'Oz," a polemical work, in seven chapters, against Christianity; "Rak we-Ṭob," a controversy between Karaites and Rabbinites, in the form of questions and answers; "Leḥem Se'orim," in two volumes, each containing five chapters, on the differences between the Karaites and the Rabbinites; "Appiryon," a religious code in two volumes, the first, entitled "Reḥaba'am ben Shelomoh," giving the Karaite view of the Mosaic precepts, and the second, entitled "Yarabe'am ben Nebaṭ," refuting the Christian dogmas. Troki displayed in the last-named work, which is extant in manuscript (St. Petersburg Cat., Nos. 754, 755), a wide knowledge of rabbinical literature. He enumerates the Lithuanian scholars of his time and gives a list of the Karaite works in the possession of Joseph Delmedigo. One chapter is devoted to pedagogy and the religious customs of Karaites in Poland. Troki was the author of another work, also bearing the title "Appiryon," in which he answers in concise form the questions of the minister of the government of Sweden as to the origin of Karaism and as to the points in which it differs from Rabbinism. It is divided into twenty-four short chapters, in which all the ceremonial laws of the Karaites are passed in review. The "Appiryon" has been published by Neubauer in his "Aus der Petersburger Bibliothek" (p. 79, Leipsic, 1866).

BIBLIOGRAPHY: Fürst, Gesch. des Karäert. iii. 80 et seq.; Gottlober, Bikkoret le-Toledot ha-Kara'im, p. 201.

Zerah ben Nathan Troki: Karaite scholar; born at Troki 1580. He addressed to Joseph Delmedigo twelve questions on mathematics, astronomy, angelology, Cabala, etc. The answers to these questions, together with seventy mathematical paradoxes, form the subject of Delmedigo's "Elim," which work the Karaites attribute to Troki. Troki's letters to Joseph Delmedigo and to Meïr of Metz, with whom the Karaite scholar became acquainted, were published by Abraham Geiger under the title "Miktab Aḥuz" in his "Melo Chofnajim." Troki composed several liturgical poems, two of which have been inserted in the Karaite Siddur (i. 402; iv., end).

BIBLIOGRAPHY: Fürst, Gesch. des Karäert. iii. 28; Gottlober, Bikkoret le-Toledot ha-Kara'im, p. 165; Geiger, Melo Ḥofnayim, Introduction, p. xxxvii.
S.
I. Br.

TROP: Judæo-German term for tropes, the short musical cadences, called "distinctions" in the

Church plain-song, which are the traditional vocal interpretation of the accents in the CANTILLATION of the Hebrew Scriptures. See also ACCENTS IN HEBREW.

F. L. C.

TROY, N. Y.: City and the capital of Rensselaer county in the state of New York; situated on the east bank of the Hudson River six miles above Albany. Although it was settled in 1787, no authentic record is found of a Jewish inhabitant until about 1842, when Emanuel Marks of Albany, a merchant, retired in 1905, established business relations with some of the people of Troy and, being pleased with their public spirit and progressiveness, settled in that city. He was followed in 1843 by Herman Levy and family, and in 1845 by Charles Wolf.

In Sept., 1851, Emanuel Gratz, who also had settled in Troy, undertook the task of organizing a congregation. He rented two rooms, one for men and one for women, in the old Wotkyns Block on Congress street, and engaged a certain Königsberg as cantor for the holy days, thereafter officiating himself. In 1853, the membership having increased to eighteen, he organized a permanent congregation under the name "Anshe Chased." A hall was hired in Wotkyns Block and furnished in the Orthodox style. In 1855 dissensions arose among the members, and many withdrew, leaving in the old congregation but eight members, not sufficient for a quorum. The seceding members organized a congregation of their own.

In 1857 Aaron Ksensky made Troy his home, and became active in Jewish matters. Seeing the uselessness of two congregations, he at once took steps to reunite them. At a meeting, lasting almost an entire day, harmony was restored, and a congregation was organized under the name "Berith Shalom" (Covenant of Peace). This congregation in 1870 erected on the corner of Third and Division streets a synagogue which is known as the Third Street Temple. About this time some members adhering to the Orthodox doctrine withdrew and formed a congregation known as "Beth Israel Bickur Cholim"; they held their services in a hall at No. 8 State street. In 1873 another Orthodox congregation came into existence under the name "Sharah Tephilah": it has erected a synagogue on Division street.

The following orders have lodges in Troy: B'nai B'rith, Free Sons of Israel, Kether shel Barzel, B'rith Abraham, and Sons of Benjamin. The following Jewish charitable organizations exist in the community: Sisterhood of the Third Street Temple, the Hebrew Shelter Society, the Ladies' Hebrew Aid Society, and the Ladies' Hebrew Benevolent Society. Troy has a Jewish population of 3,000.

J. L. LOE.

TROYES (Hebrew, טרוייש or טרויץ): Capital of the department of Aube, France. It contained a Jewish population as early as the tenth century, as is clear from a responsum addressed to the community of Troyes about the year 1000 by Judah ben Meïr ("Sire Léontin") and Eliezer ben Judah (or, more probably, Eliezer the Great, pupil of R. Gershom). Another "teshubah," sent to the same community by Joseph ben Samuel Bonfils of Limoges in the early part of the eleventh century, shows that at that time the Jews of Troyes, with the sanction of the counts of Champagne, who regarded them as an important source of revenue, owned vineyards and other real estate. At the end of the twelfth century and at the beginning of the thirteenth the counts of Champagne and the King of France entered into an agreement by which the contracting parties bound themselves to surrender to each other all Jews who should quit the domains of the one and settle in the territories of the other. In 1204 all rights over the Jews who settled in Ervy were waived by the Seigneur d'Ervy in favor of Countess Blanche of Troyes; and in 1222 Thibaud, Count of Champagne, acknowledged the receipt for 160 livres given by the Jews of the city to Jacob, "Master of the Jews of Troyes."

In March, 1288, the Jewish inhabitants of Troyes were accused of a ritual murder; and on April 24 of the same year the tribunal of the Inquisition condemned to the stake thirteen Jews, whose names, according to the elegy of Jacob ben Judah on the auto da fé, were as follows: Isaac Châtelain, with his wife, two sons, and daughter-in-law, Samson Ḳadmon, Solomon or Salamin ben Vivant, Baruch d'Avirey or Baruch Ṭob 'Elem (Bonfils), Simeon of Châtillon, Jonah or "le Beau Colon," Isaac Cohen, Ḥayyim of Brinon (department of Yonne) or "le Maître de Brinon," and Ḥayyim of Chaource (department of Aube). In 1298 Vivant of Troyes was one of the Jews subsidized by the treasury as an administrator for the Jews of France.

The Jewish revenues from the bailiwick of Troyes indicate that at this time the Jews were very numerous throughout the country; for in 1301 their total income amounted to 1,000 livres. Prosperity reigned among them; and the seigniors of the country and the ecclesiastical dignitaries when financially embarrassed applied to them for assistance. The Jews were expelled from Troyes in 1306, but returned in great numbers in 1315. The "Document sur les Juifs du Barrois" contains the names of some who settled at Troyes during the years 1321 to 1323: Maistre Deuaye, Bonjuyf son of Bonjuyf, Bonne Vie and Domim his son, Terine, and Haquinet. In 1379 the family of Isaac Lyon of Troyes obtained as a special favor permission to reside in Burgundy. Toward the close of the fourteenth century Abraham of Treves, son of Mattithiah, and Johanan of Treves lived at Troyes. At the present time the Jewish community contains about forty families.

A Hebrew school of great importance, directed by the highest rabbinical authorities and attended by numerous students from various lands, especially Germany and France, flourished at Troyes in the twelfth century. Several synods whose ordinances were adopted in foreign countries assembled at Troyes about 1160.

Among the most noted scholars of the city were RASHI and his chief disciples, Simḥah of Vitry, Judah ben Nathan (ריב״ן), Joseph ben Simeon Ḳara, Shemaiah and Judah ben Abraham, Samuel ben Meïr (RaSHBaM), Jacob ben Meïr (R. Tam), Joseph ben Moses, Isaac ben Hoshaiah ha-Levi, and Simeon the Tosafist (11th and 12th cents.), as well as Joseph

Ḥazzan ben Judah, and Menahem and his disciple Judah ben Eliezer (13th cent.). Troyes is mentioned in "Mordekai" on Giṭ. ix., No. 446. The "Seder Troyes" (Troyes ritual) has been edited by Max Weiss in the "Festschrift" published in honor of Moses Bloch (Budapest, 1905).

BIBLIOGRAPHY: Carré, Histoire Populaire de Troyes, p. 90; M. A. Gerson, Essai sur les Juifs de la Bourgogne, p. 42, Dijon, 1893; Gross, Gallia Judaica, pp. 223–243; Bibliothèque de l'Ecole de Chartes, 1849, p. 414; Laloue, Cartulaire de l'Abbaye de Saint-Loup de Troyes; Renan-Neubauer, Les Rabbins Français, p. 475; R. E. J. ii. 199; iii. 16, 212; xv. 240–259; xix. 252; xlix. 231; Simonnet, Juifs et Lombards, in Mémoires de l'Académie des Sciences et Belles-Lettres de Dijon, 1865, p. 194.

S.

S. K.

TRUMBULL, HENRY CLAY: American Christian Orientalist; born at Stonington, Conn., June 8, 1830; died at Philadelphia Dec. 8, 1903. He was educated at Williston Seminary, Mass., and took up Sunday-school work, becoming in 1858 state missionary of the American Sunday-School Association, and in 1865 the New England secretary of the American Sunday-School Union. In 1875 he took charge of the "Sunday School Times," which he made an organ of considerable influence, even in scholarly circles. In 1881 ill health caused him to travel. He visited Egypt, Arabia, and Syria, and during the journey he identified the site of Kadesh-barnea, on which he wrote a monograph (Philadelphia, 1884). He wrote also "Studies in Oriental Social Life" (1894), dealing especially with the aspects which threw light upon Biblical archeology; and two works of considerable influence; namely, "The Blood Covenant" (New York, 1885), in which he laid down the theory, afterward developed by W. R. Smith, that sacrifice was a blood covenant; and "The Threshold Covenant" (1896; see THRESHOLD).

BIBLIOGRAPHY: Nat. Cyc. of American Biography, vol. ix.

A.

J.

TRUMPET ("ḥaẓoẓerah"): In Shab. 36a (comp. Suk. 34a) it is noted that since the destruction of the Temple the names for the shofar and the trumpet had been confused. The same complaint may be made against the Septuagint, which generally renders the Hebrew "shofar" by σάλπιγξ, properly applicable only to the ḥaẓoẓerah, and against the English versions, which render it by "trumpet" or, still more incorrectly, by "cornet." In the Hebrew text the distinction between SHOFAR and trumpet is well maintained, as may be seen from such passages as Ps. xcviii. 6 and I Chron. xv. 28, where "shofar" and "ḥaẓoẓerah" are mentioned side by side.

In Num. x. 1 et seq. two trumpets of beaten silver are ordered to be made, and, according to II Chron. v. 12, the number was increased in Solomon's Temple to 120; while, judging from the representation on the Arch of Titus, in the Herodian Temple the number was reduced to the original two. Besides the shofar, the trumpet is the only musical instrument of the Old Testament concerning whose shape there is absolute certainty, there being extant a detailed description of it in Josephus and representations on the Arch of Titus and on a Bar Kokba coin. According to Josephus ("Ant." iii. 12, § 6), the trumpet was nearly a yard long and a little wider than a flute, with a slight expansion near the mouthpiece to catch the breath, and terminated in a

bell. This description tallies better with the representation on the Bar Kokba coin than with that of the two trumpets leaning against the table of showbread on the Arch of Titus.

The trumpet, like the shofar, was not so much an instrument of music as one of "teru'ah" (noise), that is, of alarm and for signaling. Its primary use was to give signals to the people and their chiefs to assemble and to break camp (Num. x. 5 et seq., 9, where the manner of blowing is specified so as to indicate the different signals intended); also generally to announce an important event and to aid in the joyous shouting of the people on festive occasions (II Kings xi. 14; Hos. v. 8; Ps. xcviii. 6, cl. 3). But its chief use, at least in later times, was religious; and it was therefore almost exclusively a priestly instrument (Num. x. 8, xxxi. 6; II Chron. xiii. 12, 14). It was sounded on New Moons; at the daily offerings; and during the pauses in the singing of the Psalms, when the people fell down and worshiped (Num. x. 10; II Chron. xxix. 26–28; Tamid vii. 3; comp. Ecclus. [Sirach] l. 16 et seq.; I Macc. iv. 40, v. 33). Altogether from twenty-one to forty-eight trumpet-blasts are said to have been sounded daily in the Temple (Suk. 53b). The sound of the trumpet also accompanied the joyous ceremony of water-drawing on the Feast of Tabernacles (ib. 51b); and a blast of trumpets announced the beginning and close of the Sabbath (ib. 53b; Shab. 35b). As the shofar was the instrument par excellence of New-Year's Day, so was the trumpet that of solemn fast-days (R. H. 26b; Ta'an. 15b, 16b).

From Neh. xii. 41 and I Chron. xv. 24 it has been inferred that there were seven trumpets in the Temple orchestra (comp. Stade's "Zeitschrift," 1899, p. 329).

BIBLIOGRAPHY: Adler and Casanowicz, Biblical Antiquities, in Report of the U. S. National Museum for 1896, p. 977; Brown, Musical Instruments and Their Names, New York, 1880; H. Grossmann, Musik und Musik-Instrumente im Alten Testament, Giessen, 1903; Pfeiffer, Die Musik der Alten Hebräer, 1779; Psalms, in S. B. O. T. (Eng. ed.) p. 220; Johann Weiss, Die Musikalischen Instrumente in den Heiligen Schriften Alten Testaments, Gratz, 1895.

A.

I. M. C.

TRUMPETS, FEAST OF. See NEW-YEAR.

TRUSTS AND TRUSTEES: It has been shown under GUARDIAN AND WARD and under COMMUNITY how the Jewish law took notice of the various powers and duties of those to whom the property of orphan children or of the community was entrusted for management. But a fiduciary relation might also be sustained toward other parties, as, for instance, a betrothed or married woman; and then the trustee was known as שליש (lit. "a third man"). There is, however, no wide development of the law of trusts, such as is found in modern, especially Anglo-American, law.

The Mishnah (Ket. v. 8) puts the case of a husband who maintains his wife in food and clothing through a trustee, and prescribes the least amount of food, raiment, and pin-money which he must furnish annually. A much more important passage for this purpose, however, is Ket. vi. 7, which presents a case like that of a trust for the separate use of a married woman under the English equity system:

. "When one puts money in the hands of a trustee for his daughter and she says, ' I have full confidence in my husband,' the trustee should nevertheless carry out the trust placed in him [that is, he should disregard her wish and invest the money in land for the daughter's use]. Such is the opinion of R. Meïr; while R. Jose says, even if the field has been already bought and she is willing to sell it, it is sold right then. When does this apply ? In the case of an adult woman ; but the wishes of an infant amount to nothing."

In the Talmud (Ket. 69b), on the basis of a baraita, the position of the sages is thus explained : A betrothed damsel may not, according to R. Meïr, turn the trust fund over to her betrothed. R. Jose says she may. Both, however, agree that, when actually married, the wife, if of age, may turn the fund over to her husband. Later authorities (see Bertinoro ad loc.) hold that the Halakah is with R. Meïr.

In Giṭ. 64a a trustee (שליש) is entrusted by the husband with a bill of divorcement, and a dispute arises between the husband and the trustee as to whether the bill was merely deposited with the latter, or was given to him for delivery to the wife, to dissolve the marriage bond. Two amoraim differ on the point whether the husband or the trustee should be credited in his assertion in such a case ; but the question is broadened to apply to the more frequent case in which a bond or deed for money or property is deposited with a trustee for both parties to the instrument. The conclusion arrived at is that the word of the trustee must be taken, without any oath, against the assertion of either of the parties who appointed him ; for by making him their trustee they have vouched for his truthfulness. It is so ruled in the codes ; e.g., in Maimonides, "Yad," Malweh, xv. 8 ; Shulḥan 'Aruk, Ḥoshen Mishpaṭ, 56, 1.

E. C. L. N. D.

TRYPHON : 1. Son of Theudion ; one of the four envoys sent by the Jews in 45 C.E. to petition Emperor Claudius that the high-priestly vestments might remain in the possession of the Jews (Josephus, "Ant." xx. 1, §§ 1-2 ; see also DOROTHEUS).

2. See ṬARFON.

S. S. KR.

TSCHERNIGOFF. See CHERNIGOV.

TUBAL-CAIN : Brother of Jabal and Jubal, sons of Lamech, who appear to have been the originators of several industries and arts. The correctness of the Masoretic text (לטש כל־חרש נחשת וברזל) of Gen. iv. 21-22, describing Tubal-cain, is in dispute. Holzinger and Gunkel maintain that לטש was a marginal gloss to חרש, and that, as in verses 20 and 21, there stood before כל originally הוא היה אבי. This would give Tubal-cain a position in metal industries comparable with those of his brothers in their lines. The Septuagint, however, omits any equivalent of קין. This fact is noted by Dillmann, Wellhausen, and others, who think that "Tubal" originally stood alone, and קין, being a later addition, was translated " smith."

Tubal is identified (by Dillmann, Schrader, and Delitzsch) with the Assyrian Tobal, a people living southeast of the Black Sea, and known in later history as the Aryan people, the Tibareni, with whom Phenicia (Ezek. xxvii. 13) traded for articles of bronze (A. V. "brass"). This fact would seem to point to the correctness of the view that "Tubal" originally stood alone and that the bearer of that name was the progenitor of a people whose chief industry was the production of vessels, instruments, and other objects of bronze and iron.

E. G. H. I. M. P.

As stated above, the Septuagint text calls the inventor "Tobel" ("Tubal"). An apocryphal tradition adds " Ḳainan " to the name (" The Book of the Bee," ed. Budge, ch. xix.). This variance of tradition continues in later times. Philo of Byblus (in Eusebius, " Præparatio Evangelica," i. 10) names two brothers as the inventors, one of whom was called " Chrysor " (χρυσώς, perhaps from חרש). These brothers discovered enchantment and sorcery as well as the art of working in iron (comp. חרש and לחש ; also נחש and נחשת), and invented rafts and various fishing-implements.

E. G. H. S. KR.

TUBERCULOSIS. See CONSUMPTION.

TUCHMANN, JULES : French folklorist; born in Paris March 23, 1830 ; died there Feb. 28, 1901. Privately educated, he devoted his whole life to investigating the traces of supernaturalism in traditional beliefs. The results of some of his investigations appeared in a remarkable series of articles on " The Evil Eye " (" La Fascination ") which ran through the whole ten volumes of the folk-lore journal " Melusine." While nominally devoted to this subject, however, the monograph deals with all kindred topics, as, for example, witches and witchcraft, folk-medicine, etc. It is perhaps the most thorough investigation of any single branch of folklore.

BIBLIOGRAPHY : Melusine, x. 8, April, 1901.

S. J.

TUDELA (טודילה, חתילא ; ancient **Tutela**): The oldest and most important Jewish community in the former kingdom of Navarre. When Alfonso the Valiant captured the city from the Moors in 1114 it contained a large number of Jews. As they were mentioned after the Moors and the Christians in the " fuero " granted them in 1115 by the conqueror, and suspecting that their safety was threatened, the Jews decided to emigrate ; and only at the special request of Alfonso and on his promise that they should be granted municipal rights similar to those of Najera, did they consent to remain. As they continued to suffer much from the hatred of the Christians, they declared to the king that they would be obliged to leave the city if these abuses were not checked ; whereupon Sancho the Wise in 1170 confirmed all the rights which Alfonso had granted them. For their greater security he even assigned to them the fortress as a residence and freed them from the tax on merchandise (" lezta "). He permitted them freely to sell their houses located in their former Juderia, and allowed them to establish a cemetery outside the city. He also showed tolerance in his regulation of their legal status (comp. Kayserling, "Gesch. der Juden in Spanien," i. 197).

Jewish Body-Physicians. Like his grandfather, who had for his body-physicians the Jews Don Joseph and Don Moses Aben Samuel, Sancho also had a Jewish physician, named Solomon, to whom he not only granted baronial rights in the whole kingdom, but also gave farm- and vine-lands in two villages near Tudela. Further, in 1193, a few months before his death, he granted Solomon also proprietary rights in the bath located in front of the Albazares gate.

In Feb., 1235, Tudela was the scene of a rebellion against the government, when many Jews were wounded and several were sacrificed to the rage of the populace. Peace was restored only through a treaty between King Theobald I. and the city council (Kayserling, *l.c.* pp. 200 *et seq.*). The shepherd persecutions of 1321 really began in Tudela. About 30,000 rapacious murderers fell upon the Jews in Tudela, killing many of them. When, some time later, 500 (or, according to other accounts, 300) made another attempt to surprise the Jews, they were overcome by a knight who lay in wait for them. Out of gratitude to Providence for their escape from this danger the wealthier Jews endeavored to alleviate the condition of their coreligionists who had suffered from the persecutions. They collected grain and oil in storehouses, and supported poor Jews therefrom for a period of three years. In the great persecution of 1328, during which 6,000 Jews perished in Navarre, those of Tudela did not escape.

The Jews of Tudela followed the most varying occupations; they traded in grain, wool, cloth, and other wares. There were among them tanners, who were obliged to pay 35 sueldos a year to the king for the use of their tannery, which
Special Market-Place. was situated on the Ebro; and the Jewish shoemakers and gold- and silver-workers had their shops in a special market-place, for which in the year 1269 they paid to Theobald II. 1,365 sueldos. They had also their own "motalafia," or gagers' bureau, where their weights and measures were subjected to official inspection. They engaged in money-lending also, while some of them—D. Joseph and D. Ezmel de Ablitas, for example—had large commercial houses. The farming of the taxes likewise was in their hands. Solomon and Jacob Baco and Ezmel Falaquera were tax-farmers, and Nathan Gabai was chief farmer of the taxes.

As in the other cities of Spain, in Tudela the Jews lived in a separate quarter ("Juderia"), which was located in the fortified part of the city, where were also the large synagogue (repaired in 1401) and several smaller ones. They had their own magistrates, comprising two presidents and twenty representatives ("regidoros"), who drew up new statutes, inflicted penalties, excluded from membership in the community, and pronounced the ban. In 1359 the Jews of Tudela petitioned D. Luis, brother and representative of King Charles II., that they might be allowed to punish those Jews who violated their religious regulations. In a statute drawn up in March, 1363, by the representatives of the community it was decided to deal energetically with denunciators and slanderers. This statute was publicly read in all the synagogues on the Day of Atonement; and in 1400 it was renewed for a period of forty years (the statute is given in Kayserling, *l.c.* pp. 206 *et seq.*). The Jews of Tudela, whose 500 families had by 1363 diminished to 270, were greatly oppressed by the taxes imposed on them by the king. These in 1346 and the following years had amounted to 2,000 livres annually, and in 1375 to 3,382 livres; in addition, the Jews had to pay subsidies from time to time. In consequence of the war with Castile and owing to the ravages of the plague in 1379 and 1380, the community continued to decrease in numbers till in 1386 there were scarcely 200 Jewish families in the city, and these were so poor that the taxes could not be collected from them.

In 1498 King John, urged by the sovereigns of Castile, issued an edict to the effect that all Jews must either be baptized or leave the
Baptism or Exile. country. In Tudela 180 families received baptism, many of them emigrating a few years later to France. The Maranos, or secret Jews, were subjected to scorn, their names being published in a great roll called "La Manta" and exposed in the nave of the cathedral at Tudela.

Tudela was the birthplace or residence of several Jewish scholars, the most famous of whom was the traveler known as BENJAMIN OF TUDELA, the account of whose travels was translated into several languages. The cabalist Abraham Abulafia passed his youth in Tudela; and Ḥayyim ben Samuel, author of the "Ẓeror ha-Ḥayyim," Shem-Ṭob ben Isaac Shaprut, the philosopher and apologist, and several members of the learned MINIR family were born in the city. The following rabbis of Tudela are known: Joel ibn Shu'aib, author of sermons and Bible commentaries; Ḥasdai ben Solomon, a contemporary of Isaac ben Sheshet; and R. Astruc.

BIBLIOGRAPHY: José Yanguas y Miranda, *Historia de Navarra*, San Sebastian, 1832; idem, *Diccionario de Antigüedades de Navarra*, Pamplona, 1842; Rios, *Hist.* ii. 28, 50, 173, 291, 453; iii. 191, 328; Kayserling, *Gesch. der Juden in Spanien*, i.; Jacobs, *Sources*, Nos. 1569, 1619, 1629, 1651, 1659.

S.   M. K.

TUGENDHOLD, JACOB: Russian educator and author; born in Breslau 1791; died at Warsaw April 20, 1871. Realizing that education was one of the best means for improving the condition of the Jews in Poland and Lithuania, he founded at Warsaw in 1819 a school for Jewish children, where the instruction was given according to the most modern principles of pedagogy and was not limited to purely Jewish subjects. In carrying out this plan Tugendhold had to overcome many obstacles which the conservative "melammedim" put in his way. In 1820 he was appointed by the Russian government censor of all the Jewish publications that appeared in Warsaw; and when the rabbinical school was established in that city, in 1853, Tugendhold was made director of the institution, which post he held until the school was closed in 1862.

Tugendhold was active not only as an educator but also as a communal worker. It was due to him that the Warsaw Home for Aged and Invalid Jews was built; and he was instrumental also in establishing a number of other benevolent institutions in that city. For a number of years he served as president of the Warsaw ḳahal.

Tugendhold's literary works include the following: "Book of Errors" (in Polish, Warsaw, 1830), a work, written with the assistance of Dr. Stern, which points out more than 900 errors in L. Chiarini's work on the Hebrew language; an answer to the work "Sposob na Zydow" (*ib.* 1831); "Obrana Izraelitow" (*ib.* 1831), a translation into Polish of Manasseh ben Israel's "Vindiciæ Judæorum," a defense against the blood accusation; "Fedon," a translation of Moses Mendelssohn's "Phädon"; "Ben Yaḳḳir" (*ib.* 1824), a text-book on the fundamental principles of the Jewish faith; "Pierwsza Wskrzeszona Mysl o Jstniemu Boga" (*ib.* 1840),.a translation into Polish of Solomon Cohen's poem "Haẓẓalat Abram me-Ur Kasdim"; "Ḳoshṭ Imre Emet we-Shalom" (Polish title, "Wskasawki Prawdy"; *ib.* 1844), a collection of passages from ancient and modern Jewish writings, showing Judaism in its relation to other religions; "Beḥinat 'Olam," a translation of Bedersi's work on the vanity and instability of all that is worldly.

Tugendhold wrote also "Marnot" (*ib.* 1851), a drama in three parts, and contributed extensively to many Polish and German periodicals of his time.

BIBLIOGRAPHY: Zeitlin, in *Maggid Mishneh*, 1872, pp. 59–61; idem, *Bibl. Post-Mendels.* p. 400; *Den*, 1872, No. 21.
s.   J. Go.

TUGENDHOLD, WOLF: Russian educator and author; brother of Jacob Tugendhold. He was teacher in the rabbinical school of Wilna and also censor of all the Jewish publications that appeared in that city. Of his writings the following are the most important: "Der Denunciant," a story of Jewish life in Poland based partly upon his brother's drama; "Stimmen der Feiernden Menge" (Warsaw, 1841), a translation of Lebensohn's "Ḳol Hamon Hogeg," which was made on the occasion of the celebration of the betrothal of the heir to the Russian throne; and a eulogy on the life and works of the Hebrew writer M. A. Günzberg.

BIBLIOGRAPHY: Zeitlin, in *Maggid Mishneh*, 1845; idem, *Bibl. Post-Mendels.* pp. 26, 193, 352.
s.   J. Go.

TULL, EDMUND: Hungarian artist; born at Szekesfejervar 1870. He was educated at Budapest, Milan, and Paris, being in the last-named city a pupil of J. P. Laurens and of B. Constant. His first work, "The Cathedral of Notre Dame," attracted attention at the exposition in Budapest in 1896, while his etchings are especially valued in London and Vienna. His best-known works are: "Peasant Mowing," "A Lane in Dort," and "The Island of Capri," in the historical art museum of Budapest; and "The Smithy," owned by Archduchess Isabella.
s.   L. V.

TUNIS: Formerly one of the Barbary States of North Africa, but since 1881 a dependency of France; situated between latitude 31° and 37° north, and longitude 8° and 11° east, and bounded north and northeast by the Mediterranean, southeast by Tripoli, south and southwest by the desert of Sahara, and west by Algeria. A tradition is current among the descendants of the first Jewish settlers, traces of whom are still to be found among the nomadic Mussulman tribes of Drid, Henansha, and Khumir, that their ancestors settled in that part of North Africa long before the destruction of the First Temple. Though this is unfounded, the presence of Jews there at the appearance of Christianity is at-

tested by the Jewish monument found by Prudhomme at Ḥammam al-Laṭif in 1883 (see "Mémoires de l'Académie des Inscriptions et Belles-Lettres," 1883; "Revue Archéologique," March and April, 1883; "R. E. J." 1886).

In Roman Times. After the dissolution of the Jewish state a great number of Jews was sent by Titus to Mauritania, and many of them settled in Tunis. These settlers were engaged in agriculture, cattle-raising, and trades. They were divided into clans, or tribes, governed by their respective heads, and had to pay the Romans a capitation-tax of 2

Tunisian Jewess.
(From a photograph.)

shekels. Under the dominion of the Romans and (after 429) of the fairly tolerant Vandals, the Jewish inhabitants of Tunis increased and prospered to such a degree that African Church councils deemed it necessary to enact restrictive laws against them. After the overthrow of the Vandals by Belisarius (534), Justinian issued his edict of persecution, in which the Jews were classed with the Arians and heathens ("Novellæ," xxxvii.).

In the seventh century the Jewish population was

largely augmented by Spanish immigrants, who, fleeing from the persecutions of the Visigothic king Sisebut and his successors, escaped to Mauritania and settled in the Byzantine cities. These settlers, according to the Arabic historians, mingled with the Berber population and converted many powerful tribes, which continued to profess Judaism until the reign of the founder of the Idriside dynasty. Al-Ḳairuwani relates that at the time of the conquest of Hippo Zaritus (Bizerta) by Ḥasan in 698 the governor of that district was a Jew. When Tunis came under the dominion of the Arabs, or of the Arabian califate of Bagdad, another influx of Arab Jews into Tunis took place. Like all other Jews in Mohammedan countries, those of Tunis were subject to the ordinance of OMAR.

In 788, when Imam Idris proclaimed Mauritania's independence of the califate of Bagdad, the Tunisian Jews joined his army under the leadership of their chief, Benjamin ben Joshaphat ben Abiezer. They soon withdrew, however; primarily, because they were loath to fight against their coreligionists of other parts of Mauritania, who remained faithful to the califate of Bagdad; and secondarily, because of some indignities committed by Idris against Jewesses. The victorious Idris avenged this defection by attacking the Jews in their cities. After an unsuccessful resistance peace was concluded, according to the terms of which the Jews were required to pay a capitation-tax and to provide a certain number of virgins annually for Idris' harem. The Jewish tribe 'Ubaid Allah preferred to migrate to the East rather than to submit to Idris; according to a tradition, the Jews of the island of Gerba are the descendants of that tribe. In 793 Imam Idris was poisoned at the command of Harun al-Rashid (it is said, by the governor's physician Shamma, probably a Jew), and about 800 the Aghlabite dynasty was established. Under the rule of this dynasty, which lasted until 909, the situation of the Jews in Tunis was very favorable. As of old, Bizerta had a Jewish governor, and the political influence of the Jews made itself felt in the administration of the country. Especially prosperous at that time was the community of KAIRWAN, which was established soon after the foundation of that city by 'Uḳba ibn Nafi', in the year 670.

Under Islam.

A period of reaction set in with the accession of the Zirite Al-Mu'izz (1016–62), who persecuted all heterodox sects, as well as the Jews. The persecution was especially detrimental to the prosperity of the Kairwan community, and members thereof began to emigrate to the city of Tunis, which speedily gained in population and in commercial importance.

The accession of the Almohade dynasty to the throne of the Maghreb provinces in 1146 proved very disastrous to the Jews of Tunis. In pursuance of a fanciful belief, of which there is no trace in Moslem tradition, the first Almohade, 'Abd al-Mu'min, claimed that Mohammed had permitted the Jews free exercise of their religion for only five hundred years, and had declared that if, after that period, the Messiah had not come, they were to be forced to embrace Islam. Accordingly Jews as well as Christians were compelled either to embrace Islam or to leave the country. 'Abd al-Mu'min's successors pursued the same course, and their severe measures resulted either in emigration or in forcible conversions. Soon becoming suspicious of the sincerity of the new converts, the Almohades compelled them to wear a special garb, with a yellow cloth for a head-covering.

The intellectual status of the Tunisian Jews at that time was on a level with their political situation. Mai-

Interior of the Great Synagogue at Tunis.
(From a photograph.)

monides, who, while on his way to Egypt, sojourned some time in the island of Gerba and other localities, expressed himself, in a letter addressed to his son, in the following terms:

Maimonides' Opinion.

"Beware of the inhabitants of the West, of the country called Gerba, of the Barbary States. The intellect of these people is very dull and heavy. As a rule, beware always of the inhabitants of Africa, from Tunis to Alexandria; and also of those who inhabit the Barbary coasts. In my opinion they are more ignorant than the rest of mankind, though they be attached to the belief in God. Heaven is my witness that they can be compared only to the Karaites, who possess no oral law. They evince no lucidity of spirit in their study of the Pentateuch, the Prophets, and the Talmud; not even when they discuss the haggadot and the laws, although there are among them rabbis and dayyanim. With regard to impure women they have the same beliefs and customs as the Bene Meos, a Mussulman tribe which inhabits the same country. They do not look upon the impure woman, and turn their eyes neither to her figure nor to her garments. Nor do they speak to her; and they even scruple to tread on the ground touched by her feet. They do not eat the hinder part of slaughtered animals. In short, there is much to say about their ways and customs."

The Jews of Tunis at that time scrupulously observed most of the festivals, but did not celebrate the second days; they entirely ignored the festival of Purim, although they observed that of Ḥanukkah. According to their statutes, a man who had lost two wives could marry only a widow; on the other hand, if a woman lost two husbands she was called a "husband-killer" and was not allowed to remarry. This prohibition included also a woman who had been twice divorced. Male twins were always named Perez and Zerah; female twins, Sarah and Rebekah; a male and female, Isaac and Rebekah.

Under the Ḥafṣite dynasty, which was established in 1236, the condition of the Jews greatly improved. Besides Kairwan, there were at that time important communities in Mehdia, Kalaa, the island of Gerba, and the city of Tunis. Considered at first as foreigners, the Jews were not permitted to settle in the interior of the last-named city, but had to live in a building called "Funduḳ"; later, however, a wealthy and humane Mussulman, Sidi Mahrez, who in 1159 had rendered great services to the first Almohade, 'Abd al-Mu'min, obtained for them the right to settle in a special quarter of the city proper. This quarter, called the "Hira," constituted until 1857 the ghetto of Tunis; it was closed at night. In 1270, in consequence of the defeat of Saint Louis of France, who had undertaken a crusade against Tunis, the cities of Kairwan and Ḥammat were declared holy; and the Jews were required either to leave them or to embrace Islam. From that year until the conquest of Tunis by France (1857), Jews and Christians were forbidden to pass a night in either of these cities; and only by special permission of the governor were they allowed to enter them during the day.

Under the Ḥafṣites.

That the Jews of Tunis, during the fourteenth and fifteenth centuries, were treated more cruelly than those of the other Barbary States may be surmised from the fact that, while refugees from Spain and Portugal flocked to Algeria and Morocco, only a few chose to settle in Tunis. Indeed, the Tunisian Jews had no rabbis or scholars worthy of mention, and had to consult those of Algeria or Morocco on the most ordinary religious questions. Their communal affairs were directed by a council, nominated by the government, the functions of which consisted in the administration of justice among the Jews, and, more especially, in the collection of the Jewish taxes. Three kinds of taxes were imposed upon the Tuni-

Taxation.

Tunisian Jewess.
(From a photograph.)

XII.—18

sian Jews: (1) a communal tax, to which every member contributed according to his means; (2) a personal or capitation tax; and (3) a general tax, which was levied upon the Mohammedans also. In addition to these, every Jewish tradesman and industrial had to pay an annual tax to the gild to which

Tunisian Jewesses.
(From a photograph.)

his trade or industry belonged. In spite of all these exactions, however, the commerce of the country was in Jewish hands, and even the government was compelled to have recourse to Jewish merchants for the exploitation of the various monopolies; after the

Jewish Girls of Tunis.
(From a photograph.)

thirteenth century it adopted the policy of entrusting to a Jew the post of receiver of taxes. This functionary, who bore the title of "caid," served also as an intermediary between the government and the Jews, and his authority within the Jewish community was supreme. The members of the council of elders, as well as the rabbis, were nominated at his recommendation, and no rabbinical decision was valid unless approved by him.

During the Spanish occupation of the Tunisian coasts (1535-74) the Jewish communities of Bizerta, Susa, Sfax, and other seaports suffered greatly at the hands of the conquerors; while under the subsequent Turkish rule the Jews of Tunis enjoyed a fair amount of security, being practically guaranteed the free exercise of their religion, and liberty to administer their own affairs. They were, however, always exposed to the caprices of princes and to outbursts of popular fanaticism. Petty officials were allowed to impose upon them the most difficult drudgery without compensation. They were obliged to wear a special costume, consisting of a blue frock without collar or ordinary sleeves (loose linen sleeves being substituted), wide linen drawers, black slippers, and a small black skull-cap; stockings might be worn in winter only. They might ride only on asses or mules, and were not permitted to use a saddle.

Under the Spaniards.

From the beginning of the eighteenth century the political status of the Jews in Tunis steadily improved. This was due to the ever-increasing influence of the political agents of the European powers, who, while seeking to ameliorate the condition of the Christian residents, had to plead also the cause of the Jews, whom Moslem legislation classed with Christians. Joseph Azulai, who visited Tunis in 1772, described in glowing terms the influence at court of the caid Solomon Nataf. Forty-two years later the United States consul to Tunis, Mordecai M. Noah, gave the following account of the situation of the Tunisian Jews:

"With all the apparent oppression, the Jews are the leading men; they are in Barbary the principal mechanics, they are at the head of the custom-house, they farm the revenues; the exportation of various articles, and the monopoly of various merchandise, are secured to them by purchase, they control the mint and regulate the coinage of money, they keep the bey's jewels and valuable articles, and are his treasurers, secretaries, and interpreters; the little known of arts, science, and medicine is confined to the Jews. . . . If a Jew commits a crime, if the punishment affects his life, these people, so national, always purchase his pardon; the disgrace of one affects the whole community; they are ever in the presence of the bey, every minister has two or three Jewish agents, and when they unite to attain an object, it cannot be prevented. These people, then, whatever may be said of their oppression, possess a very con-

trolling influence, their friendship is worthy of being preserved by public functionaries, and their opposition is to be dreaded" ("Travels in Europe and Africa," p. 308, New York, 1819).

During the long reign of Aḥmad Bey the Jews enjoyed a period of great prosperity. His successor, Mohammed Bey, inaugurated his reign in 1855 by abolishing the drudgeries formerly imposed upon the Jews; the caid Joseph Scemama, with whom the bey was on very intimate terms, probably used his influence in behalf of his coreligionists. In the same year, however, Mohammed Bey, being very religious, caused the execution of a Jew named Batto Sfoz on a charge of blasphemy. This execution aroused both Jews and Christians, and a deputation was sent to Napoleon III., asking him to interfere in their behalf. After two years of diplomatic negotiations a man-of-war was sent to enforce the demands of the French government. Mohammed Bey yielded, and issued a constitution, according to which all Tunisians, without distinction of creed, were to enjoy equal rights. The following articles of this constitution were of special interest to the Jews: (§ 4) "No manner of duress will be imposed upon our Jewish subjects forcing them to change their faith, and they will not be hindered in the free observance

Moham-med Bey.

Interior of the Great Synagogue at Tunis, Showing Ark of the Law.
(From a photograph.)

of their religious rites. Their synagogues will be respected, and protected from insult." (§ 6) "When a criminal court is to pronounce the penalty incurred by a Jew, Jewish assessors shall be attached to the said court." The constitution was abrogated in 1864 in consequence of a revolution, which entailed great suffering on several Jewish communities, especially on that of Sfax; but the constant fear of foreign interference rendered the government very circumspect in its treatment of the Jews. Since 1881 Tunis has been a dependency of France; and the Jews now enjoy the same rights as their Mohammedan fellow citizens.

A great number of the Jewish population of the regency, which numbers about 47,640 souls, is found in the city of Tunis (19,030 in a total population of 171,672). The Jews of that city are divided into two distinct communities: (1) the Tunsi, which comprises the descendants of the first settlers, and (2) the Grana (from "Granada"), which includes the descendants of the Spanish and Portuguese exiles, and of Jews of Leghorn ("Gorneyim")

Population and Organization.

who settled there during the seventeenth and eighteenth centuries. At first, owing probably to their small numbers, the Spanish and Portuguese exiles mixed with the old settlers; but toward the end of the sixteenth century they formed a separate congregation under the name "Ḳehal Gerush," and worshiped in a reserved place in the Great Synagogue. The new congregation was greatly augmented by the arrival of Italian, or Leghorn, Jews, and by the middle of the seventeenth century it had its own synagogue and its own rabbis. The two congregations, however, were united in so far as both were under the jurisdiction of the caid, both contributing to the communal revenues derived from taxation on articles of consumption, more especially on meat and Passover bread. A complete separation of the two congregations took place at the end of the seventeenth century, when the Leghorn Jews established butchershops of their own, refusing to pay the high tax on meat. This naturally provoked bad feelings on the part of the Tunsi congregation, which now had to bear the whole burden of this tax. At last, in 1741, the two congregations entered into an agreement according to which the Tunsi was to pay two-thirds

Jews of Tunis in Native Costume.
(From a photograph.)

of the taxes and the Grana the remaining third. The Grana congregation remained under the authority of the caid until 1824, when Ḥusain Bey officially recognized its autonomy.

The intellectual condition of the Tunisian Jews kept pace with their political progress. Even in the seventeenth century there were prominent rabbis and scholars in the city of Tunis and in Gerba. In the middle of that century a descend-
Rabbis and ant of Ẓemaḥ Duran settled at Tunis
Scholars. and established a Talmud Torah which produced many Talmudic scholars. Isaac Lombroso, who officiated as chief rabbi of Tunis from about 1710 to 1752, was the author of a commentary, entitled "Zera' Yiẓḥaḳ," on different sections of the Talmud; this work, which appeared posthumously in 1768, is the only Hebrew book which has as yet been published in Tunis. Lombroso's successor as chief rabbi was Mas'ud Raphael Alfasi, who, conjointly with his sons Ḥayyim and Solomon, published the "Mishḥa de-Rabuta" in Joseph Caro's Shulḥan 'Aruk (Leghorn, 1805). Among other rabbis of the eighteenth century were Nathan ben Abraham Burgel, author of "Ḥoḳ Natan," novellæ and explanations on the mishnaic order Ḳodashim and the treatise Horayot, etc.; and Elijah Ḥai Vita Burgel, author of "Migdanot Natan," novellæ on various Talmudic treatises. The most prominent rabbis of the nineteenth century were: Joseph Burgel, author of "Zera' de-Yosef," on the Tosafot; Isaac Ṭayyib, author of "'Erek ha-Shulḥan," on the Shulḥan 'Aruk, "Ḥuḳḳot ha-Pesaḥ," on the laws of Passover, and "Wawe ha-'Ammudim," on the "Sefer Yere'im" of Eliezer of Metz; Judah Nijar, author of "Ohole Yehudah," on the Sifre, "Shebut Yehudah," on the Mekilta, "Alfe Yehudah," on the treatise Shebu-'ot, "Mo'ade Adonai," on the Semag, and "Simḥat Yehudah," on the small Talmudic treatises; Joshua Bases; Nathan Burgel; Samuel Sefag; Aaron ha-Kohen Mogadar; Abraham ha-Kohen Tanuji; Samuel Sefag; Abraham Ḥajjaj; Moses Faitusi; Nissim Marik; and Ḥai Bismut. The Tunisian rabbis possess full judicial power in all civil and commercial matters, and even in criminal cases if the crime committed is not one that calls for capital punishment. The community of Tunis possesses twenty-seven synagogues, among which the Great Synagogue of the Tunsi congregation, and that of the Portuguese, are very large. The Jewish inhabitants of Tunis include some financiers and a number of persons following liberal professions, but they are mostly engaged in commerce,

in petty traffic, and especially in brokerage. There is also a considerable number of persons who follow various handicrafts.

The other communities of the regency of Tunis are: **Bizerta,** with a Jewish population of about 600 persons; **Gabès,** with 500 Jews; **Gerba,** having 4,500 Jews and six synagogues; **Go-** **Other Com-** letta, 400 Jews and one synagogue; **munities. Keff,** with 450 Jews, one synagogue; **Mehdia,** 100 Jews; **Monastir,** containing 500 Jews and one synagogue; **Nabel,** having 1,500 Jews; **Porta Farina,** 1,500 Jews; **Ras el-Jabel,** with 600 Jews and two synagogues; **Soliman,** 700 Jews; and **Susa,** with a Jewish population of 600 souls. Schools for children were established by the Alliance Israélite Universelle at Tunis, Mehdia, Susa, and several other places; special schools for Jews were established by the government

brated with great pomp, and the rabbis proclaim publicly full absolution from all sins. Passover cakes, as made in other countries, are wholly unknown to the Tunsi, but they use a peculiar method of their own in fashioning the unleavened dough into sticks, by joining the ends of which the cakes are made in the form of rings.

The Tunsi pronounce Hebrew largely according to the phonetic rules of Arabic. No distinction is made between the long and short vowels; the "ḳameẓ" is always pronounced as "ā." The pronunciation of the "ẓere" resembles more the "ḥiriḳ," while that of the "segol" approaches the "pataḥ." The פ and the ב are often confounded in pronunciation. No distinction is made between the "shewa" quiescent and the "shewa" mobile. Very peculiar is their custom of separating the Sabbatical sections "Maṭṭot u-Mas'e" at times when elsewhere they are

JEWISH CEMETERY AT TUNIS.
(From a photograph in the possession of Dr. Maurice Fishberg, New York.)

at Sfax and Gabès. The superior hygienic conditions prevailing among the Jews of Tunis, in comparison with the other nationalities, caused great surprise to the French military physicians Testivint and Reinlinger. Instituting an inquiry into the number of deaths caused by tuberculosis among the various races of the regency, they found that from 1894 to 1900 the death-rate among the Mussulmans was 11.30 per 1,000 inhabitants; among the Europeans, 5.13; and among the Jews only 0.75 ("Revue d'Hygiène," xxii., No. 11).

The Tunsi preserve many peculiar religious customs which are not followed elsewhere. **Religious** Their ritual, especially for the divine **Customs.** service on festivals, differs from the Sephardic as well as from the Ashkenazic. Some of the prayers are in Arabic. The first of every month the Yom Kippur Ḳaṭan is cele-

read together, and vice versa. Contrary to the Masorah, the section Mishpaṭim is subdivided by the Tunsi into two sections, the first bearing the title of "Mishpaṭim," and the second that of "Im Kesef." Likewise another order is adopted in reading the Hafṭarot. With regard to the examination of the lungs of slaughtered animals ("bediḳah"), the Tunsi do not follow the regulations of Joseph Caro, but an older authority, whose prescriptions are less rigid.

Brides of twelve or thirteen are not uncommon among the Tunsi. The marriage ceremony is performed by a rabbi, and usually takes place in the synagogue. The bride and bridegroom are seated on chairs placed on a table, and a ṭallit covers the heads of both. Two witnesses stand one on each side, while the officiating rabbi takes his position in front of the table, with the prayer-book in one hand and the cup of blessing in the other. It is customary among the Tunsi women to appear every Friday in the cemetery with a small earthen jar containing slaked lime, and a brush, with which they clean and whitewash the tombstones of their relatives and friends. The cemetery is usually outside the city walls, and, not being enclosed, is frequently entered by animals; the tombs, which are built of brick and mortar, are flat, and not more than six inches above the ground. See CARTHAGE.

BIBLIOGRAPHY: L. Addison, *The Present State of the Jews in the Barbary States*, 1675; Morgan, *Istoria degli Stati d'Algeri, Tunisi, Tripoli, e Morocco*, London, 1784; Marcus Fischer, *Toledot Yeshurun*, Prague, 1817; D. Cazès, *Essai sur l'Histoire des Israélites de Tunisie*, Paris, 1888; E. Mercier, *Histoire de l'Afrique Septentrionale*, i. 167, Paris, 1888; Grätz, *Gesch.* v. 236 *et seq.*: vi. 6, 9 *et seq.*; Eliezer Ashkenazi, in *Ha-Lebanon*, ii. 181 *et seq.*, iii. 6 *et seq.*, iv. 75 *et seq.*, v. 236 *et seq.*, vi. 85 *et seq.*; Freund, *Vom Tunesischen Judenthum*, in *Yeshurun*, iv. 592; Cognat, *Israélites à Tunis*, in *Tour du Monde*, 1893, ii. 98.

J.   I. BR.

TUR, NAPHTALI WOLF: Russian Hebraist; born at Wilna; died there May 29, 1885 (according to Zeitlin, June 8, 1884). Tur settled in Warsaw, where he taught Hebrew and several modern languages. He was a talented poet; but, owing to his untimely death, most of his productions remain unpublished. Of those which have been printed may be mentioned: "Ha-Yobel" (in "Ha-Asif," i. 1–10), a long poem in honor of Sir Moses Montefiore's centenary; "Geberet ha-Heshbon"; and "El ha-Ishshah" (*ib.* ii. 556–561). Several of his poems are published in Gottlober's "Ha-Boker Or."

BIBLIOGRAPHY: *Ha-Asif*, ii. 763; Zeitlin, *Bibl. Post-Mendels.* p. 400.

S.   M. SEL.

TURIM. See JACOB BEN ASHER.

TURIN: Italian city on the River Po; formerly capital of the duchy of Savoy, and later of the kingdom of Sardinia; now the chief city of the province of the same name. Jews were admitted to Turin in 1424, probably because they loaned money at a lower rate of interest than the Christians. The first Jew to settle with his family in the city in that year was Elia Alamandi. A statute of Amadeus VIII., dated June 17, 1430, obliged the Jews of the duchy to wear a badge of red cloth on the shoulder, forbade them to live among Christians, and prohibited them from building new synagogues, besides imposing other restrictions. The Jews were now compelled to live in the Via San Tommaso, near the so-called "Gamelotto." About this time originated the treaty or agreement between the duke of Savoy and the Hebrews. It was made for ten years only, but was renewable; it guaranteed to the Jews freedom of residence in Turin, and regulated their rights and privileges. Amadeus, besides, promulgated a special decree forbidding Christians to kill, wound, or flog the Hebrew residents, or to disturb them in their religious worship or festivals.

The reign of Emmanuel Philibert (1553–80) fell in a disastrous period for all the Italian Jews. Those of Piedmont alternately received concessions and suffered persecutions, according to the duke's need of money. On July 19, 1560, Emmanuel Philibert decreed the expulsion of all Jews from his dominions; but their own entreaties and the intercession made in their behalf by the Duchess Margherita secured for them a respite of four months. One of the duke's councilors, Negron de Negri of Genoa, urged his master to renew the decree of expulsion and to insist upon the departure of the Jews within ten days. Fortunately, however, the **Under Emanuel Philibert.** kindly intervention of an official at the ducal tribunal obtained the revocation of the decree; and the duke made an agreement with the Jews under which they were still permitted to inhabit Piedmont. Very soon after, however (Oct., 1566), Emmanuel Philibert again issued a decree ordering the departure of the Jews from his domains within a space of fifteen days unless they paid down 40,000 gold florins. The Jews at once quitted his dominions, but on the payment of half the sum demanded they were permitted to return. They then executed a new agreement under which they pledged themselves to pay a yearly tax of 1,500 gold florins. By another decree (Sept. 4, 1572) Emmanuel Philibert, at the request of Vitale Sacerdoti, introduced some favorable alterations into the statutes of Amadeus VIII. Among other things, the Jews were permitted to enjoy the right of "hazakah" and of owning real estate. Simon, a brother of Sacerdoti, was sent by the duke in the same year to Constantinople to propose the establishment of a consulate there. Emmanuel Philibert furthermore granted the Jews the right of assembling once a year (for religious purposes), and of owning a special piece of land as a cemetery.

At Philibert's death his son, Charles Emmanuel I., ascended the throne (1580–1630). Cardinal Borromeo of Milan urged him to expel the Hebrews again from his dominions. He yielded, however, to the entreaties of the latter, and made a new contract with them, allowing them to remain in the country on certain conditions. He also confirmed the privileges granted them by his father, and placed them under the jurisdiction of a specially appointed judge called the "conservatore." The first "conservatore" was the senator Gasparo Tesauro, Marquis of Fossiano. Charles Emmanuel also repealed the obligation, imposed on the Jews in 1560, of paying a yearly sum of 25 scudi to the students of the university on St. Catherine's Day. He twice renewed the decree forbidding Christians to molest the Jews or to offend them by disturbing their religious functions (Dec. 15, 1603, and Oct. 20, 1610). In the first instance he also agreed, on condition of a donation of 60,000 scudi payable in twelve years beginning with 1604, that the Jews should engage unmolestedly in trade and commerce, and should not be more heavily taxed than other citizens. Further, he allowed them to lend on pledges, which had been forbidden them by Amadeus VIII.

This was, however, regulated by special laws. The tribunals were required **In the Seventeenth Century.** to recognize the trustworthiness of the books in which the Jews entered their contracts. Permission was further granted the Jews to meet twice a year to elect their leaders and to arrange for the payment of the tribute due the state. In order to raise this tribute the Jewish community was allowed to tax all Hebrews who came to reside within the limits of the state.

Physicians and surgeons were allowed to follow their professions, subject, however, to the consent of the Archbishop of Turin. Finally, he granted a full pardon for all crimes, offenses, and infractions of the law committed up to the day of publication of the decree on condition of the payment of 2,000 ducats volunteered by certain members of the community, namely, G. Lattes, M. Jarach, C. and S. Melle, and S. Brisa, who were afterward exempted from wearing the distinctive badge. In Aug., 1612, a Jew named Leone Segre was murdered in the enclosure of the ghetto. The Jews accused of this deed were liberated on the payment of 50,000 "ducantoni." In 1614 all sentences then being served were remitted in consequence of the payment of 18,000 "ducantoni."

In 1618 the Jewish community of Piedmont was united with that of the city and territory of Nizza. In 1626 the residence of the Jews was changed, and the district at that time called "San Giovanni di Dio" was assigned to them. In 1640 Victor Amadeus I., at the request of M. Treves, L. Lattes, and A. Levi, confirmed all the rights and privileges granted to the Jews by his predecessors. At the instance

The Synagogue at Turin, Italy.
(From a photograph.)

of the Jewish community, which presented him with 3,300 lire, these privileges were further confirmed by the Senate on the occasion of the marriage of Charles Emmanuel II. in 1662. In 1680, by an order of the regent, Madama Reale, dated Aug. 12, 1679, the site of the ghetto was again changed, this time to the quarter of Beatus Amadeus; and here the Jews continued to dwell until 1828, in which year certain wealthy families obtained leave to reside beyond the ghetto limits. In 1706 the Jewish cemetery situated near the arsenal was destroyed by the chances of war, and the Jews obtained leave to bury their dead in San Giovanni di Dio, abandoned in 1680 (in 1782 this cemetery became part of the Vanchiglia district, near the River Po; and at length, in 1854, it was incorporated with the common cemetery).

The condition of the Jews of Piedmont was no better during the eighteenth century, owing to the intolerant spirit shown by the papal government. Indeed, their legal status became in some respects considerably worse. For instance, Victor Amadeus II. wished to deprive them of the **In the** power of acquiring landed property. **Eighteenth** He therefore enforced the constitu- **Century.** tions of the years 1723, 1729, and 1770, which, like so many of the ducal laws, were hostile to the interests of the Jews. A certain Luigi Pisani of Jerusalem, formerly a rabbi, but later converted to Christianity, preached a sermon to the Jews of Turin on Feb. 7, 1715, in the church of San Francesco di Paola, to demonstrate to them "the blindness, error, and falseness which enveloped them." In 1780 there were about 1,500 Jews in Turin.

The first indications of the approach of better times for the Jews came with the French Revolution; but the provisional Austro-Russian-Piedmontese government (May, 1799) demanded a stricter observance of all the laws and regulations than had been exacted of the Jews before the Revolution, and subjected the entire community to heavy penalties for the slightest infraction. On the return of French domination, the Jews of Turin obtained from the imperial government equality with their French coreligionists; but upon the restoration the old restrictions soon came into force again. Jewish students were expelled from the schools; and the proprietary classes were allowed five years in which to sell their possessions. At length, by a decree dated March 6, 1816, Victor Emmanuel I. finally exempted the Jews from wearing a distinctive badge, and gave them full liberty to engage in trade, commerce, and the useful arts. They were still excluded, however, from the universities, from municipal offices, and from the administration of works of charity. But better times were approaching. In 1848 a pamphlet, entitled "Dell' Emancipazione

Civile degl' Israeliti," by the Marquis Massimo d'Azeglio of Turin, later minister of the kingdom of
Sardinia, appeared in Florence, and
Eman- was followed by the statute of March
cipation. 4 of that year. On July 19, 1848, a
law was passed declaring the equality of Jews with other citizens.

The following rabbis of note were natives of Turin: sixteenth century: Nethaneel ben Shabbethai ha-Dani; seventeenth century: Joseph Calvo, Daniel ben Joseph Calvo, and Joseph ben Michael Ravenna; eighteenth century: Joshua Colon, Isaac Formiggini, Abraham Sanson ben Jacob ha-Levi Fubini, Michel Solomon Jonah, Gabriel Pontremoli, Jacob ben Joshua Benzion Segre, Abraham ben Judah Segre, Daniel Valabrega; nineteenth century: Abraham de Cologna, Felice Bachi, Elijah Aaron Lattes, Samuel Solomon Olper, Isaiah Foâ Lelio della Torre, Sabbato Graziadio Treves, Giuseppe Lattes, Samuel Ghiron, G. Foa, and G. Bolaffio.

The Jews of Turin in 1921 numbered 5,100.

BIBLIOGRAPHY: M. Finzi, in *Rivista Israelitica*, i. 226 *et seq.*;
Mortara, *Indice*, passim; G. Sacerdoti, in *Vessillo Israelitico*,
1901, pp. 245 *et seq.*; Volino, *Condizioni Giuridiche Degli
Israeliti in Piemonte Prima dell' Emancipazione*, Turin,
1904; Joseph ha-Kohen, '*Emek ha-Baka*, ed. Wiener, pp. 102,
105, 126; *R. E. J.* v. 231.
s.   U. C.

TURKEY: Empire of southeastern Europe and western Asia. For present purposes Turkey is taken to mean that part of Europe which is directly under Ottoman rule, Asia Minor, the islands of the Archipelago, and Mesopotamia. SYRIA and PALESTINE, although under the direct administration of the Porte, and ARABIA are considered as distinct countries, and have been so treated in THE JEWISH ENCYCLOPEDIA.

Jews have lived in Turkey from very early times. Tradition says that there was a colony of them in Thessaly at the time of Alexander the Great; and later they are found scattered throughout the eastern Roman empire (see ADRIANOPLE; BYZANTINE EMPIRE). The first Jewish colony in Turkey proper was at BRUSA, the original Ottoman capital. According to one tradition, when Sultan Urkhan conquered the city (1326) he drove out its former inhabitants and repeopled it with Jews from Damascus and the Byzantine empire. These Jews received a firman permitting them to build a synagogue; and
this edifice still exists, being the old-
Early est in Turkey. The Jews lived in a
History. separate quarter called "Yahudi Mahalessi." Outside of Brusa they were allowed to live in any part of the country; and on payment of the "kharaj," the capitation-tax required of all non-Moslem subjects (see below), they might own land and houses in the city or country.

Under Sultan Murad I. (1360–89) the Turks crossed over into Europe, and the Jews of Thrace and Thessaly came under Ottoman dominion. The change was a welcome one to them, as their new Moslem rulers treated them with much more toleration and justice than they had received from the Christian Byzantines. The Jews even asked their cobelievers from Brusa to come over and teach them Turkish, that they might the quicker adapt themselves to the new conditions. The Jewish community of

Adrianople began to flourish, and its yeshibah attracted pupils not only from all parts of Turkey,
but also from Hungary, Poland, and
Fourteenth Russia. The grand rabbi at Adria-
and nople administered all the communities
Fifteenth of Rumelia. About fifty years after
Centuries. the conquest of Adrianople a converted
Jewish Moslem, Torlak Kiamal by name, took part in an insurrection of dervishes and preached communistic doctrines, for which he was hanged by Sultan Mohammed I. (1413–21).

Sultan Murad II. (1421–51) was favorably inclined toward the Jews; and with his reign began for them a period of prosperity which lasted for two centuries and which is unequaled in their history in any other country. Jews held influential positions at court; they engaged unrestrictedly in trade and commerce; they dressed and lived as they pleased; and they traveled at their pleasure in all parts of the country. Murad II. had a Jewish body-physician, Isḥak Pasha, entitled "ḥakim bashi" (physician-in-chief), to whom the ruler granted a special firman exempting his family and descendants from all taxes. This was the beginning of a long line of Jewish physicians who obtained power and influence at court. The same sultan created also an army corps of non-Moslems called "gharibah" (= "strangers"); and to this Jews also were admitted when they were unable to pay the kharaj.

Murad's successor, Mohammed the Conqueror (1451–81), issued three days after the conquest of Constantinople a proclamation inviting all former inhabitants to return to the city without fear. Jews were allowed to live freely in the new capital as well as in the other cities of the empire. Permission was granted them to build synagogues and schools and to engage in trade and commerce without restrictions of any kind. The sultan invited Jews from the Morea to settle in Constantinople; and he employed Jewish soldiers. His minister of finance ("defter-dar") was a Jewish physician named Ya'ḳub, and his body-physician was also a Jew, Moses Hamon, of Portuguese origin. The latter likewise received a firman from the sultan exempting his family and descendants from taxes.

It was in this reign that the office of ḥakam bashi of Constantinople came to have so much importance.
Moses CAPSALI was the first to fill the
Office position, being appointed thereto by
of Ḥakam the sultan. He took his place in the
Bashi. Turkish divan, or state council, beside
the mufti, or chief of the Ulema, and above the Greek patriarch. He was the official representative of the Jews before the Turkish government: he apportioned and collected their taxes, appointed rabbis, acted as judge, and administered the affairs of the Jewish communities generally. After Capsali the Jews themselves elected their chief rabbi, the government ratifying their choice as a mere matter of form.

Another celebrated rabbi who lived during the reign of Mohammed the Great was Mordecai b. Eliezer COMTINO. Karaites as well as Rabbinites studied under him. The former, although having been the most influential element among the Jews during the Byzantine empire, had now fallen into such a state of ignorance that for a full century they had produced no author of repute and had been obliged to turn to the Rabbinites for instruction. They were stirred to new life, however, by the increase in their numbers through immigration from Poland and the Crimea, and by contact with the Rabbinites; and they used their new energy in disagreeing among themselves, notably in regard to a reform in connection with the Sabbath light and about the old question of the calendar (see KARAITES). Certain Rabbinites, therefore, particularly Gedaliah ibn Yaḥya, thought the proper time had come to effect a reconciliation between the two parties. Mordecai Comtino spoke with respect of the Karaites; and the Karaites and Rabbinites who studied under him acquired tolerance as well as knowledge. The Rabbinite teachers Enoch Saporta, Eliezer Capsali, and Elijah ha-Levi made their Karaite pupils promise not to speak disrespectfully of the Talmudic authorities, and to observe the Rabbinite festivals. On the other hand, the grand rabbi, Moses Capsali, was strongly opposed to any affiliation of the two parties, holding that Karaites ought not to be instructed in the Talmud, since they rejected it. His successor, Elijah Mizraḥi, was more tolerant, and used all his influence to preserve friendly relations. The Karaite community, however, became more and more isolated. Many of its members went to the Crimea; and those who were left lived in a separate quarter walled off from the rest of the Jews.

Comtino and the Karaites.

The condition of the Jews in Turkey about the middle of the fifteenth century was so prosperous and in such contrast to the hardships endured by their fellow Israelites in Germany and Europe generally that Isaac Ẓarfati, a Jew who had settled in Turkey, was moved to send a circular letter to the Jewish communities in Germany and Hungary inviting their members to emigrate to Turkey. The letter is preserved in the Bibliothèque Nationale at Paris (Ancien Fonds, No. 291). It gives a glowing description of the lot of Jews in Turkey (for its date see Grätz, "Gesch." viii., note 6). Ẓarfati says:

Isaac Ẓarfati's Letter.

"Turkey is a land in which nothing is lacking. If you wish, all can go well with you. Through Turkey you can safely reach the Holy Land. Is it not better to live under Moslems than under Christians? Here you may wear the finest stuffs. Here every one may sit under his own vine and fig-tree. In Christendom, however, you may not venture to dress your children in red or blue without exposing them to the danger of being beaten blue or flayed red."

This letter caused an influx into Turkey of Ashkenazic Jews, who soon became amalgamated with the earlier Jewish inhabitants.

The greatest influx of Jews into Turkey, however, occurred during the reign of Mohammed's successor, Bayazid II. (1481–1512), after the expulsion of the Jews from Spain and Portugal. That ruler recognized the advantage to his country of this accession of wealth and industry, and made the Spanish fugitives welcome, issuing orders to his provincial governors to receive them hospitably. The sultan is said to have exclaimed

Effects of Expulsion from Spain.

thus at the Spanish monarch's stupidity: "Ye call Ferdinand a wise king—he who makes his land poor and ours rich!" The Jews supplied a want in the Turkish empire. The Turks were good soldiers, but were unsuccessful as business men; and accordingly they left commercial occupations to other nationalities. They distrusted their Christian subjects, however, on account of their sympathies with foreign powers; hence the Jews, who had no such sympathies, soon became the business agents of the country. Coming as they did from the persecutions of Europe, Mohammedan Turkey seemed to them a haven of refuge. The poet Samuel Usque compared it to the Red Sea, which the Lord divided for His people, and in the broad waters of which He drowned their troubles. The native Turkish Jews helped their persecuted brethren; and Moses Capsali levied a tax on the community of Constantinople, the proceeds of which were applied toward freeing Spanish prisoners.

The Spanish Jews settled chiefly in Constantinople, Salonica, Adrianople, Nicopolis, Jerusalem, Safed, Damascus, and Egypt, and in Brusa, Tokat, and Amasia in Asia Minor. Smyrna was not settled by them until later. The Jewish population at Jerusalem increased from 70 families in 1488 to 1,500 at the beginning of the sixteenth century. That of Safed increased from 300 to 2,000 families and almost surpassed Jerusalem in importance. Damascus had a Sephardic congregation of 500 families. Constantinople had a Jewish community of 30,000 individuals with forty-four synagogues. Bayazid allowed the Jews to live on the banks of the Golden Horn. Egypt, especially Cairo, received a large number of the exiles, who soon outnumbered the native Jews (see EGYPT). The chief center of the Sephardic Jews, however, was Salonica, which became almost a Spanish-Jewish city owing to the fact that the Spanish Jews soon outnumbered their coreligionists of other nationalities and even the original native inhabitants. Spanish became the ruling tongue; and its purity was maintained for about a century.

Sixteenth Century.

The Jews introduced various arts and industries into the country. They instructed the Turks in the art of making powder, cannon, and other implements of war, and thus became instruments of destruction directed against their former persecutors. They distinguished themselves also as physicians and were used as interpreters and diplomatic agents. Salim I. (1512–20), the successor of Bayazid II., employed a Jewish physician, Joseph HAMON. This ruler also was kind to the Jews; and after the conquest of Egypt (1517) he appointed Abraham de CASTRO to the position of master of the mint in that country. Salim changed the administrative system of the Jews in Egypt, and abolished the office of nagid. It is interesting to note that the Turkish Jews were in favor of the conquest of Egypt, whereas the orthodox Moslems opposed it.

Sulaiman the Magnificent (1520–66), like his predecessor Salim II., had a Jewish body-physician, Moses Hamon II., who accompanied his royal master on his campaigns. Turkey at this time was at the high-water mark of its power and influence and was feared and respected by the great powers of

Europe. Its Jews were correspondingly prosperous. They held positions of trust and honor, took part in diplomatic negotiations, and had so much

Under Sulaiman the Magnificent.
influence at court that foreign Christian ambassadors were frequently compelled to obtain favors through them. Commerce was largely in their hands; and they rivaled Venice in maritime trade. In Constantinople they owned beautiful houses and gardens on the shores of the Bosporus. In 1551 Nicolo Nicolai, chamberlain to the King of France, who accompanied the French ambassador to Constantinople, described the Jews in Turkey as follows:

" There are so many Jews throughout Turkey, and in Greece especially, that it is a great marvel and downright incredible. They increase daily through the commerce, money-changing, and peddling which they carry on almost everywhere on land and on water; so that it may be said truly that the greater part of the commerce of the whole Orient is in their hands. In Constantinople they have the largest bazars and stores, with the best and most expensive wares of all kinds. In addition, one meets among them many skilled artists and mechanicians, especially among the Maranos, who some years ago were driven out of Spain and Portugal. These, with great harm and injury to

Nicolo Nicolai's Account.
Christendom, have taught the Turks to make implements of war. . . . The said Jews have also established a printing-press, which is a wonderful thing to the Turks. They print books in Latin, Greek, Italian, Syriac, and Hebrew; but in Turkish and Arabic they are not allowed to print. Besides, they know most languages; so that they are employed as interpreters " (" Viaggi nella Turchia," pp. 142-143, Venice, 1580).

Nicolai also mentions Hamon as " a person of great honor, great activity, great renown, and great wealth."

If one recalls the warlike activity of the Turks at this time, when they were laying siege to Vienna and threatening to overrun Europe, the full significance of Nicolai's allusion to the manufacture of implements of war is evident. The Jews also had a more direct influence on the making of war and of peace through the diplomatic negotiations in which they took part. Moses Hamon influenced the sultan in favor of Donna Gracia MENDESIA; and the ruler sent an imperial messenger to Venice demanding that the authorities set her at liberty and allow her to proceed to Turkey. She and her nephew Don Joseph NASI at once took a prominent part in Jewish affairs in Turkey. Joseph, through his wide business connections among his fellow Maranos in the capitals of Europe, was able to furnish the sultan with confidential information as to what was taking place at the foreign courts; and he soon became a favorite counselor. The sultan was induced to take an interest in the fate of the Turkish Jewish prisoners at Ancona; and he wrote a haughty letter to Paul IV. demanding their release. In revenge for the fate of the other Jews at Ancona, the Turkish Jews, led by Donna Gracia and Joseph, endeavored to place an effective boycott upon the port of that city, and to transfer its trade to Ferrara; but the scheme fell through owing to lack of unity among its promoters. Joseph's influence at court was further strengthened by the fact that he openly supported the claims of Sulaiman's son Salim to the throne at a time when the succession was doubtful. He thus won that prince's lasting favor, of which all

the later intrigues of the French and the Venetian envoys were unable to deprive him.

Sulaiman instituted for the benefit of the Jews the office of " ḳiahya " or KAHIYA (קהייא). It was

Office of Kahiya.
the duty of this official to represent them at court and to defend them against injustice and oppression. The first incumbent of the office, appointed by the sultan himself, was Shealtiel. There was the more need for such a defender, since the Jews in the Turkish empire were continually being harassed by their Christian neighbors. In Amasia, in Asia Minor, the old accusation of ritual murder was revived; and several Jews were slain. Later, when their innocence had been established, the cadi in anger put to death some of the Greeks who had made the accusation. Another instance of the kind led Sulaiman to enact a law under which all future blood accusations should be tried before the sultan himself.

Sulaiman conferred the city of Tiberias and its environs upon his favorite Joseph Nasi; and the latter at one time planned the foundation of a Jewish colony in Palestine. The walls of Tiberias were rebuilt, and Joseph invited Jews from Europe, even providing ships for their transportation. It is not known how many responded to the call; but the scheme of a Jewish colony in Tiberias was not realized, and Joseph appears to have transferred his interest elsewhere.

At the accession of Salim II. (1566) Joseph was created Duke of Naxos and of the Cyclades Islands; but he continued to reside at Constantinople, appointing as his vicegerent for the islands a Spanish nobleman named Coronello. Thus in less than 100 years after the Jews had been driven out of Spain a nobleman of that realm was in Jewish employ. In

French Ships Seized by Joseph Nasi.
the year following Salim's accession an Austrian embassy was commissioned to call on Joseph Nasi and offer him a fixed salary to secure his good graces. In the next year he received a firman from the sultan empowering him to seize the cargoes of French ships in Turkish waters, to the amount of the debt which the French government had long owed to the Mendesia family and which both Sulaiman and Salim had unsuccessfully tried to collect for him. In 1569 he finally succeeded in reimbursing himself from cargoes seized in the port of Alexandria, France complaining and protesting in vain. Not more successful were the efforts of the French ambassador to undermine Joseph's position at the Turkish court (see NASI, JOSEPH). A few years later Joseph succeeded in influencing the sultan to make war against Venice because of Cyprus. Joseph's influence with the sultan was known to be such that even Christian rulers applied directly to him. Emperor Ferdinand of Austria addressed a letter to him, as did also William of Orange, the latter trying to induce him to declare war on Spain. This move, although favored by Don Joseph, was opposed by the grand vizier Mohammed Sokolli, who had long been his enemy. Joseph's influence ceased at the death of Salim, when the rule of the grand viziers, beginning with Sokolli, commenced.

Joseph Nasi's place was taken by another Jew, Solomon Ashkenazi, who, although remaining more in the background, and working through the grand viziers instead of coming directly in contact with the sultan, was even more influential than Joseph. Ashkenazi's name is frequently mentioned in the diplomatic correspondence of the time between the Porte and the other European courts. The war with Venice which had been begun by one Jew was terminated by another. Ashkenazi, who had been working in behalf of peace while hostilities were still in progress, was delegated by the Porte to arrange terms of peace and was sent to Venice for that purpose. The Venetians, distasteful as it was to them, were obliged to receive the Jew with all the honors due the ambassador of so powerful a nation as Turkey. Ashkenazi was influential also in causing the choice of a king of Poland to fall on Henry of Anjou. He was likewise entrusted with the negotiations for a peace between Spain and Turkey.

All the favor shown to individual Jews, however, did not affect the lot of the community as a whole, whose fate depended on the caprice of a despotic ruler. Sultan Murad III., for instance, on one occasion ordered the execution of all the **Sumptuary** Jews in the empire merely because he **Laws.** was annoyed by the luxury which they displayed in their clothing. It was only after the intervention of Solomon Ashkenazi and other influential Jews with the grand vizier, seconded by the payment of a large sum of money, that the order was changed into a law restricting dress. Thereafter Jews were required to wear a kind of cap instead of a turban, and to refrain from using silk in making their garments.

Certain Jewesses became prominent about this time as physicians and intriguers. Esther Kiera was especially famous as the favorite of the Venetian sultana Baffa, wife of Murad III. and mother of Mohammed III. Turkish women of the harem have always exercised more influence than is commonly attributed to them; and the Jewesses who were made welcome there in various capacities frequently acted as go-betweens, and indirectly influenced the actions of prominent men. Esther Kiera, through her position as an intimate of the sultana Baffa, became all-important in the diplomatic intrigues of the time; and she carried on a traffic in army posts. She acquired great wealth, much of which was spent in helping her poor coreligionists and in furthering their literary efforts. Greed, however, appears to have overmastered her discretion; and she met a tragic end. The Mendesia family produced two women, Gracia Mendesia and her daughter Reyna Nasi, wife of Joseph Nasi, who did much for the Jews of Turkey. Another Jewess of importance was the widow of Solomon Ashkenazi. She succeeded in curing the young sultan Ahmad I. of the smallpox, after all other doctors had failed. A contemporary of Esther Kiera in 1599 wrote a letter which accompanied a present from the sultan's mother to the Queen of England. A translation of it may be found in Kayserling, "Die Jüdischen Frauen," pp. 91-92.

The prosperity enjoyed by the Jews of Turkey in the sixteenth century led them to entertain hopes of the Messiah, and cabalistic doctrines spread rapidly. Especially prominent in promoting them were Judah Hayyat, Baruch of Benevento, Abraham b. Eliezer ha-Levi of Adrianople, Meïr ibn Gabbai, and David ibn Abi Zimra (Franco, "Histoire des Israélites de l'Empire Ottoman," p. 52). In the early part of the century the appearance of that eccentric adventurer David Reubeni, who claimed to be an ambassador from an independent Jewish king in Arabia, sent to seek aid against the Turks, aroused hopes throughout the Jewish world that he was the precursor of the Messiah. Influenced by him, Solomon Molko of Portugal began to have visions, and was moved in one of them to go to Turkey. In Salonica, one of the chief seats of the Cabala in the empire, he fell in with the aged cabalist Joseph Taitazak; and **Messianic** in Adrianople he inspired the young **Hopes.** Joseph Caro with cabalistic visions. Molko went also to Palestine and remained for some time in Safed, at that time a veritable nest of cabalism. He proclaimed that the Messianic period would begin in 1540 (5300 A.M.). After Molko's death (1532) the Jews of Safed still clung to their hope of the Messiah; and, in order to prepare the way for him, they attempted to introduce unity into Judaism by organizing a recognized Jewish tribunal or Sanhedrin. The plan, however, came to nothing, owing to the personal rivalry of the two leaders of the Safed and Jerusalem communities respectively, Jacob Berab and Levi b. Jacob Habib.

After Berab's death Joseph Caro became the leading rabbi in Safed, having come to Palestine filled with the idea that he was destined to take a prominent part in preparing the way for the Messiah. He, like Molko, saw visions and dreamed dreams. But the visions and religious ecstasies of Molko and Caro were as nothing compared with the extravagances of the cabalistic leaders who succeeded them. In the last three decades of the sixteenth century Safed and all Galilee became the scene of excesses of religious demoniacs, conjurers, and miracle-workers; and cabalistic notions spread thence throughout Turkey and into Europe. This movement derived its impulse principally from two men, Isaac Luria and his disciple Hayyim Vital. The former communed with departed spirits, talked with animals and angels, and developed a peculiar theory concerning the origin and quality of souls and their migrations. The Zohar was placed on a level with the Talmud and the Bible.

The prosperous condition of the Jews in Turkey during this period was not a deep-rooted one. It did not rest on fixed laws or conditions, but depended wholly on the caprice of individual rulers. Furthermore, the standard of civilization throughout Turkey was very low, and the masses were illiterate. In addition there was no unity among the Jews themselves. They had come to Turkey from many lands, bringing with them their own customs and opinions, to which they clung tenaciously, and had founded separate congregations. And with the waning of Turkish power even their superficial prosperity vanished. Ahmad I., who came to the throne in the early years of the seventeenth century, was, it is true, favorably disposed toward the Jews, having been cured of smallpox by a Jewess (see above); and he imprisoned certain Jesuits for trying to convert them.

Seventeenth Century. But under Murad IV. (1623–40) the Jews of Jerusalem were persecuted by an Arab who had purchased the governorship of that city from the governor of the province; and in the time of Ibrahim I. (1640–49) there was a massacre of Ashkenazic Jews who were expecting the Messiah in the year 1648, and who had probably provoked the Moslems by their demonstrations and meetings. The war with Venice in the first year of this sultan's reign interrupted commerce and caused many Jews to remove to Smyrna, where they could carry on their trade undisturbed. In 1660, under Mohammed IV. (1649–87), Safed was destroyed by the Arabs; in the same year there was a fire in Constantinople in which the Jews suffered severe loss. Under the same sultan Jews from Frankfort-on-the-Main settled in Constantinople; but the colony did not prosper. It was also during this reign that the pseudo-Messiah SHABBETHAI ZEBI caused such an upheaval in Judaism. It is characteristic of the Turkish attitude toward the Jews, and in striking contrast with the attitude of European powers, that no steps were taken to punish the Jews who took part in the agitation. Shabbethai Zebi was one of the few pseudo-Messiahs who have left sects behind them. The chief seat of his followers is at Salonica.

The Dönmeh. They are called "Dönmeh" (a Turkish word signifying "apostates") or "Ma'aminim." There are three subsects, whose devotions are separate and secret. The first is that of the Ismirlis or Smyrnians, who shave their chins; the second is composed of the followers of Jacob Querido, a reputed son of Shabbethai, who shave their heads, but not their chins; and the third, the members of which shave neither the chin nor the head, consists of followers of Othman Baba, who in the eighteenth century tried to reconcile the first two sects. The Dönmeh resemble the Moslems and outwardly practise their customs, even going to the mosques on Fridays. Their own meeting-houses, or "kals," are secret, and connect with their dwelling-houses by interior passages. They are very respectable and prosperous, and are said to have no poor among them (see DÖNMEH; J. T. Bent, "A Peculiar People," in "Longman's Magazine," xi. 24–36).

Michel Febre, a Capuchin monk who lived in Turkey for eighteen years and who published an account of his experiences there and in other lands, has given a description of the Jews in Turkey in the middle of the seventeenth century. He says ("Théâtre de la Turquie," in "R. E. J." xx. 97 et seq.):

Michel Febre's Description. "There are two classes of Jews in Turkey, viz., natives, or original inhabitants of the country, and strangers, so called because their ancestors came from Spain and Portugal. The former, like the Christians, wear colored turbans, and are only to be distinguished from them by their shoes, which are black or violet, while those of the Christians are red or yellow. The second class wear a ridiculous head-dress, like a brimless Spanish hat. They have separate cemeteries and do not agree with Jews of the other class on certain tenets of religion. Both classes are found in large numbers in most of the cities belonging to the grand seignior, especially in commercial towns such as Smyrna, Aleppo, Cairo,

Thessalonica, etc. They are mainly occupied as bankers, money changers, and usurers; in buying old things and, after mending them, selling them as new; as employees in the custom-houses, as intermediaries in bargains, and as doctors, chemists, and interpreters. . . . They are so skilful and industrious that they make themselves useful to every one; and there will not be found any family of importance among the Turks and the foreign merchants which has not in its employ a Jew, either to estimate merchandise and to judge of its value, to act as interpreter, or to give advice on everything that takes place."

Febre also comments on the filth which he noticed in the Jewish houses.

The history of the Jews in Turkey in the eighteenth century is principally a very brief chronicle of misfortunes. One name stands out

Eighteenth Century. against the dark background—that of Daniel de FONSECA, who was chief court physician and played a certain political rôle. He is mentioned by Voltaire, who speaks of him as an acquaintance whom he esteemed highly. Fonseca was concerned in the negotiations with Charles XII. of Sweden.

In 1702 a law was passed forbidding Jews to wear yellow slippers and ordaining that in future they should wear only black coverings for the feet and head. In 1728 the Jews living near the Baluk Bazar, or fish-market, were obliged to sell their houses to Moslems and to move away so as not to defile the neighboring mosque by their presence. In 1756 one of the most terrible fires that Constantinople has ever experienced broke out in the Jewish quarter and devastated the city; in the following year the sumptuary laws against the Jews were renewed; and in the next year an earthquake destroyed 2,000 Jewish houses in Safed.

In the beginning of the eighteenth century a colony of Turkish Jews settled in Vienna. Their position was established in the Treaty of

Turkish Colony at Vienna. Passarowitz (1718) between Turkey and the German empire, which made it possible for the inhabitants of one country to live in and to receive the protection of the government of the other, and vice versa. Many Turkish Jews took advantage of this treaty to live in Vienna, which was forbidden to native Austrian Jews. Consequently the latter obtained passports allowing them to live in Vienna as Turkish subjects (see AUSTRIA).

The destruction of the janizaries in the early part of the nineteenth century (1826) was a great boon to the Jews; for this lawless corps of soldiery had long been such a terror to them that

The Janizaries. the word "janissaro" was (and still is) used by Jewish mothers to frighten their disobedient children. The word "janizary" (Turkish, "yenicheri") was applied to soldiers recruited from Christians who as children had been taken away from their parents and brought up in the Mohammedan faith. The corps was first instituted in the middle of the fourteenth century. No Jews appear ever to have been forced into this service; but they suffered most from the excesses of this unruly military body. Nearly every great fire in Constantinople started in the Jewish quarter, being lighted by greedy janizaries, who then pretended to help to quench the flames, while in reality they plundered the houses. The rabbinical responsa from the sixteenth to the nineteenth century are full of cases submitted to Jewish tribunals concerning the outrages, assassinations, and robberies of which the Jews were victims at the hands of these soldiers, both in Constantinople and in the provinces. Nevertheless certain wealthy Jews, under imperial authorization, held the position of banker to this corps. They were called "ojak baziriani," "sarraf bashi," "ojak ṣarrafi," or "shapchi bashi." The best-known Jews who occupied this post were Judah Rosanes, Meïr Ajiman, Jacob Ajiman, and Baruch Ajiman, in the eighteenth century, and Isaiah Ajiman and Behor Carmona, at the beginning of the nineteenth century. The Jews of the lowest classes at times fraternized with the janizaries in their drunken debauches; and on the day of their destruction many janizaries sought refuge in Jewish houses.

The low grade of civilization existing throughout Turkey since the beginning of the wars with Russia in the eighteenth century seriously affected the status of the Jews, who were in a miserable condition until toward the end of the nineteenth century, when the fruit of the labor expended by the Alliance Israélite Universelle for their enlightenment began to be visible. The masses are still very ignorant; and in the large cities they live in cramped, **In the** dirty quarters. Their sufferings are **Nineteenth** due not to the legal discriminations **Century.** against them, but to the general economic condition of the country and to the poverty and ignorance caused by the despotic rule of centuries. The attitude of the government is uniformly kind; and prompt punishment follows attacks on the Jews. Thus reparative acts on the part of the government followed the events that caused the Damascus Affair in 1840; the abduction of a Jewish girl at Haifa in 1864; the extortions of the governors of Bagdad, Larissa, and Salonica in 1866; the troubles in Janina in 1872; and those in Smyrna in 1873. In 1875, through the intervention of the Alliance, the Jews in the region of Diarbekr were protected from molestation by surrounding Kurds. In the same year in Khania the Alliance brought about the appointment of a representative of the Jews in the general council of the island; and again in 1882 the threatened electoral rights of the Jews were safeguarded. In 1883 the sultan publicly expressed his sympathy for the fate of the Jews of other countries and declared his satisfaction at the presence of Jewish officials in the Ottoman administration. That same year, when a fire devastated the Jewish quarter at Haskeui, in Constantinople, the sultan subscribed £T1,000 for the relief of those who had been left homeless, and placed certain barracks at their disposal. In 1887 the minister plenipotentiary from the United States to Turkey was a Jew, Oscar S. Straus. When Straus was replaced by Solomon Hirsch, the grand vizier in his address of welcome to the latter said (see "Allg. Zeit. des Jud." Aug. 15, 1889): "I can not conceal the satisfaction it gives me to see that for a second time your country has called a son of Israel to this eminent position. We have learned to know and esteem your coreligionists in our country, which they serve with distinction." Straus was again minister from 1897 to 1900. The Jews have been loyal supporters of the government. In the war of 1885, although not admitted to the army, they gave pecuniary and other aid. In Adrianople 150 wagons were placed by them at the disposal of the government for the transportation of ammunition; and in the war of 1897 the Jews of Constantinople contributed 50,000 piasters to the army fund.

On the failure, in 1866, of a Belgian firm, Baron de Hirsch acquired from the sultan concessions for the construction of railways in Turkey; and it was owing to his enterprise that the important line connecting Constantinople with the rest of Europe was carried through.

The Turkish government discriminates against foreign Jews visiting Palestine; and they are not allowed to stay in the Holy Land longer than three months. The question of Jewish immigration to Turkey came to the front in 1882, when the good offices of the United States were invoked in obtaining permission for Russian Jews to settle in Turkey. In 1885 the Lubrowsky brothers, two American citizens, were expelled from Safed because they were Jews. The United States government at once protested; but no permanent settlement of the question was arrived at. In 1888 the Porte declared that foreign Jews could not remain in Palestine longer than three months, whereupon the governments of the United States, Great Britain, and France sent notes protesting against such discrimination against creed and race. The Turkish government then announced that the restriction applied only to Jews arriving in Palestine in numbers, the political effects of colonization there being feared. Various protests have since been made at different times and by different governments, but the rule remains in force, and foreign Jews are not allowed to remain in the Holy Land longer than three months.

In 1895 the further question arose whether foreign Jews might hold real estate in Jerusalem, and the Porte decided it in the negative.

On the subject of Zionism, Dr. Theodor Herzl had several long interviews with the sultan in May, 1901 (see also Zionism).

Accusations of ritual murder were frequent during the nineteenth century, hardly an interval of more than two or three years passing **Blood Ac-** in which a disturbance on that score **cusations.** was not created in some part of the country. So late as 1903 there was a serious outbreak in Smyrna. The Ottoman government has always been quick to punish the guilty. The law made in the sixteenth century by Sulaiman the Magnificent in this connection has already been noticed. In 1633 a plot to injure certain Jews by the same accusation was discovered by the grand vizier, and the offenders were summarily punished by the sultan. In 1840 an outbreak in Damascus (see Damascus Affair) caused so serious a massacre of the Jewish inhabitants that the attention of the outside world was attracted to the sufferings of the Jews. A committee composed of Moses Montefiore, Isaac Adolphe Crémieux, and Salomon Munk journeyed to the Orient and insisted on reparation to the injured. This event, by revealing to the Western world the miserable condition of the Jews in Turkey, led to the foundation of the Alliance Israé-

TURKISH JEWS OF THE SIXTEENTH CENTURY.
(From Nicolo Nicolai's "Viaggi nella Turchia," Venice, 1580.)

LITE UNIVERSELLE. This society, through its schools—especially its manual-training and agricultural schools, which prepare their pupils for occupations other than those connected with the handling of money—has done much and is doing more to elevate the Turkish Jews. The names of the Hirsch and Rothschild families as well as that of Sir Moses Montefiore will be forever associated with the work of improving the condition of the Jews in Turkey. With influence and money and through philanthropic foundations they have ably seconded the work of the Alliance. At different times cholera, fire, and famine have reduced the Turkish Jews to the utmost misery, which their Western coreligionists have done their best to alleviate. The Jews in Asia Minor were affected also by the Armenian troubles in the latter part of the nineteenth century; and a rabbi was killed in Keui Sanjak on the Little Zab.

The flourishing period of Jewish literature in Turkey was in the fifteenth and sixteenth centuries, after the arrival of the Spanish exiles,

Literature. though before this time, also, the Turkish Jewry had not been without its literary and scientific men. Printing-presses and Talmud schools were established; and an active correspondence with Europe was maintained. Moses Capsali and his successor, Elijah Mizrahi, were both Talmudists of high rank. The latter was noted also as a mathematician for his commentary on Euclid's "Elements," as well as for his independent work "Sefer Ha-Mispar." Mordecai Comtino wrote a Bible commentary entitled "Keter Torah," and commentaries on the mathematical and grammatical works of Ibn Ezra and others, and on the logical works of Aristotle and Maimonides. Elijah Capsali, in Candia, a nephew of the hakam bashi, wrote in Hebrew a history of the Turkish dynasties (1523), and his correspondence, entitled "Sefer No'am," is of historical value concerning the disputes between Italian, Greek, and Turkish rabbis. Another contributor to historical literature was Samuel Shullam from Spain, who edited Abraham Zacuto's "Yuhasin" (1566) and wrote a continuation of Abu al-Faraj's "Historia Dynastiarum." Solomon Algazi wrote a compendium of chronology; and Perahyah and Daniel Cohen (father and son) in Salonica, and Issachar ibn Susan in Safed, published mathematical and astronomical works. Karaite literature was represented by Elijah Bashyazi and Caleb b. Elijah Afendopolo.

Especially eminent as Talmudic authorities were Levi b. Habib (son of Jacob b. Habib of Salonica, author of "'En Ya'akob") and Jacob Berab, the dispute between whom, noticed above, causing the leading rabbinical writers to take sides with one or the other. Moses Alashkar, the synagogal poet, defended Habib, while Moses b. Joseph Trani, the ethical and homiletic writer, took up the cudgels in behalf of Berab. Trani wrote a collection of ethical treatises entitled "Bet Elohim," and a commentary on Maimonides' "Mishneh Torah." His son, Joseph Trani, was also prominent in this field. Other Talmudic scholars were: David ibn Abi Zimra, who wrote exegetic, cabalistic, and methodological works; Samuel Sedillo of Egypt; and his namesake in Safed, who

wrote a commentary on the Palestinian Talmud. Collections of responsa were made by David ha-Kohen,

Talmudists. David b. Solomon Vital, Samuel of Medina, Joseph b. David ibn Leb, Joseph Taitazak, Eliezer Shim'oni, Elijah ibn Hayyim, Isaac Adarbi, Solomon b. Abraham ha-Kohen, Solomon Levi, Jacob b. Abraham Castro, Joseph ibn Ezra, Joseph Pardo, Abraham di Boton, Mordecai Kala'i, Hayyim Shabbethai, Elijah Alfandari, Elijah ha-Kohen, Benjamin b. Metalia, and Bezaleel Ashkenazi of Egypt.

Commentaries on different books of the Old Testament were written by Jacob Berab, David ibn Abi Zimra, Joseph Taitazak, Isaac b. Solomon ha-Kohen, Joseph Zarfati, Moses Najara, Meïr Arama, Samuel Laniado, Moses Alshech, and Samuel Valerio. Moses b. Elijah Pobian published a translation of the Bible into modern Greek (1576); and a Persian translation was made by Jacob Tawus, who appears to have been brought from Persia to Constantinople by Moses Hamon. Moses Almosnino, a celebrated preacher in Salonica, wrote articles on philosophy and astronomy, a commentary on the Bible, a collection of sermons, and a description of Constantinople entitled "Extremos y Grandezas de Constantinople." Poetry, also, flourished. The most important Hebrew poet of Turkey and of the century was Israel b. Moses Najara of Damascus, who is represented in the ritual of Jewish congregations everywhere.

The more distinguished cabalistic writers were: Moses Cordovero, Solomon Alkabiz, Moses Galante and his sons, Elijah di Vidas, Moses Alshech, Moses

Cabalistic Writers. Basula, and, most celebrated of all, Isaac Luria and Hayyim Vital. The leading representative of the Halakah was Joseph CARO, whose Shulhan 'Aruk, the only really great work published on Turkish soil, marked an epoch in the history of Judaism.

Jewish literature in Turkey declined somewhat after the sixteenth century. The best-known writers of the seventeenth were Joseph Delmedigo, Joseph Cattawi, and Solomon Ayllon; of the eighteenth, Jacob Culi, Abraham of Toledo, and Jacob Vitas, who wrote in Judæo-Spanish. A large number of Talmudic works appeared in the eighteenth century (see Franco, *l.c.* pp. 124 *et seq.*). Many rabbinical works in Hebrew were published during the nineteenth century also; but the Judæo-Spanish literature underwent a change, becoming more popular in style and including translations of novels, biographies of eminent men, histories, scientific works, etc. (see list in Franco, *l.c.* pp. 270 *et seq.*). A certain amount of Hebrew literature has been published in Turkey by Protestant missionary societies (Franco, *l.c.* p. 276).

The only important Jewish writer in Turkish was Haji Ishak Effendi, who became converted to Islam and was in the service of the Ottoman government as professor of mathematics and interpreter.

The total number of Jews in Turkey, including Syria, Palestine, and Tripoli, is estimated at 463,688 ("Bulletin de l'Alliance Israélite Universelle," 1904, p. 168). Of these, 188,896 (including the Jews of Constantinople) are in Europe. The accompanying table No. I. (compiled from Cuinet, "La

Turquie d'Asie," Paris, 1892) shows the distribution of Jews in Asiatic Turkey, Syria, and Palestine, according to vilayets, sanjaks, and mutessarifats or mutessarifliks. Table No.

Distribution of Jews.
II. shows the Jewish population according to cities, and the schools of the Alliance Israélite Universelle. Where the two tables do not agree the figures in No. II. should be given the preference, as the figures are based on estimates ("Bulletin de l'Alliance," 1904, p. 164). The total Jewish population of European Turkey estimated 1922 was 80,000, and Asiatic Turkey, 70,000. The tables that follow date from pre-World War times.

TABLE No. I.

Vilayet.	Sanjak.	Jewish Population.	Vilayet.	Sanjak.	Jewish Population.
Adana ...	....	No Jews.	Diarbekr.	Arghana ...	405
				Diarbekr...	284
Aleppo...	Aleppo.....	19,265		Mardin.....	580
	Marash.....	368	Erzerum..	Erzerum....	6
	Urfa........	367	Konia....	Adalia	424
Angora ..	Angora	6		Burbur	45
	Cæsarea.			H a m i d - Abad.	20
	Kir Shehr.				
	Yuzgat	478		Konia	70
Bagdad ..	Bagdad	52,200		Nigdeh	41
	Hillah......	500	Mamou- ret ul- Aziz.	....	No Jews.
	Kerbela	800			
Bassora ..	Amara	950			
	Bassora ...	2,050	Mosul....	Mosul......	6,000
	Muntefilk ..		Sivas	....	No Jews.
	Nejd	1,500			
Beirut ...	Acre.......	20,637	Smyrna...	Aidin	2,024
	Balka	297		Denizli.	
	Beirut	3,100		Menteche ..	423
	Latakia.			Sarukhan ..	1,939
	Tripoli	1,102		Smyrna....	18,130
Bitlis.....	....	No Jews.	Syria	Hamah.	
				Hauran.	
Brusa....	Brusa......	2,701		Ma'an.	
	Ertoghrul ..	53		S h a m - i - Sherif (Damascus).	5,380
	Kara Hissar Sahib.				
	Karassi.....	501	T r e b i - zond.	G u m u s h - Khana.	40
	Kutaya.....	100			
Castamu- ni.	Bolu.			Lazistan ...	40
	Castamuni .	8		Samsun	250
	Kangheri.			Trebizond..	110
	Sinope	9	Van......	....	360
Constanti- nople.	(Asiatic) ...	5,670		Bigha (cap. Lardanelles).	2,062
Crete.....	Candia.....	52		Ismid......	2,500
	Khania	525		Jerusalem..	39,866
	Lassethi	38		Zor........	50
	Rethymo...	31			

TABLE No. II.
(Asterisks denote cities that have Alliance schools.)

TURKEY IN EUROPE. City.	Jewish Population.	No. of Pupils in Alliance Schools.			
		Primary.		Apprentice.	
		Boys.	Girls.	Boys.	Girls.
*Adrianople	17,000	355	558	33	19
Avlono	50				
Baba-Eski..........	40				
Camanova..........	70				
Caraferia	500				
Castoria	1,600				
Caterina	80				
Cavalla	2,000				
*Constantinople.....	65,000	1,338	1,861	45	66
Dedeagatch	200				
*Demotika..........	906		159		
Djumbala..........	175				
Doiran	75				
Drama	380				
Eskiji..............	185				
Gallipoli...........	1,200				

TABLE No. II.—*Continued.*
(Asterisks denote cities that have Alliance schools.)

TURKEY IN EUROPE. City.	Jewish Population.	No. of Pupils in Alliance Schools.			
		Primary.		Apprentice.	
		Boys.	Girls.	Boys.	Girls.
Gumuljina	1,200				
Istip..............	500				
*Janina............	4,000				
Kirjali............	50				
*Kirklisseh	1,000			3	
Loule Burgas......	350				
*Monastir	6,000	172	185		
Mustapha Pasha...	1,700				
Nevrokop..........	110				
Ouzun Köpri.......	200				
Preveza...........	200				
Prichtina	300				
*Rodosto...........	2,100				
*Salonica...........	75,000	806	724	50	300
*Serres	2,000		150		
*Silivri	1,200				
Souffli	25				
Strumnitza	650				
Tchorlu	900				
*Uskub	1,700	136			
Yenibazar	130				
Yenije Vardar	60				
Yevgueli	60				
Totals...........	188,896	2,807	3,328	131	385
TURKEY IN ASIA. City.					
Archipelago :					
*Chios.............	350	48		3	
Cos	103				
Mitylene.........	100				
*Rhodes	4,000	157	121	5	
Tenedos..........	4				
Asia Minor :					
Adalia............	203				
Adil Djevas......	74				
Adramit..........	20				
*Aidin.............	3,500	241			
Aintab...........	857				
Ak-Issar	427				
Akra.............	300				
Alashehir.........	339				
*Aleppo...........	10,000	267	300	10	5
Alexandretta.....	42				
Amadia	1,900				
Angora	800				
Antioch..........	266				
Ardjesh..........	60				
Arghana	405				
Bahkesser	75				
Baindir..........	100				
Bairamitch	170				
Bazdoghan	14				
Biridjick.........	45				
Boudroun	45				
*Brusa...........	3,502	336	128	18	9
*Cassaba.........	1,150	85			
Castamuni.......	8				
*Dardanelles......	2,900	161	172		
Deirmendjik.....	30				
Denizli	50				
Diarbekr.........	280				
Elbab-Djebul	38				
Elback	1,600				
Endemish	310				
Erdeck	500				
Ertoghrul	53				
Erzerum	6				
Eski Shehir......	100				
Ghevas	300				
Ghevash.........	59				
Hamid Abad.....	20				
Hehkiari.........	4,000				
Hermasti ...?.....	80				
Isineh	100				
Ismid	2,500				
Kardighan	68				
Kilis	747				
Konia............	70				
Kutaya...........	100				
Lampsaki........	17				
Lazistan	40				
*Magnesia	1,700	191	108	7	2
Makri............	300				
Marash	211				
Mardin...........	580				

TABLE No. II.—*Continued.*

(Asterisks denote cities that have Alliance schools.)

TURKEY IN ASIA. City.	Jewish Popu- lation.	Primary. Boys.	Girls.	Apprentice. Boys.	Girls.
Mazileh..........	150				
Mehalitch........	200				
Melas	600				
Menemen........	287				
Moks	72				
Mondamia.......	50				
Nazili...........	400				
Nigdeh	41				
Pergamus........	600				
Perghri..........	87				
Phocea	150				
Salikh (and envi- rons)	305				
Samsun..........	250				
Scala Nova.......	188				
Shemdinan	200				
Shitak...........	80				
Sinope...........	9				
*Smyrna.........	25,500	262	291	32	30
Tchal...........	200				
Tchesmeh	190				
Thyra	1,450				
Tokat	400				
Trebizond	110				
Urfa.............	367				
Van.............	500				
Vourla	458				
Crete:					
Candia..........	52				
Khania	525				
Lassethi	38				
Rethymo.........	31				
Mesopotamia:					
Ali Gharbi.......	250				
Amara	1,000				
Ana	1,000				
Arbela	1,500				
Azer	100				
*Bagdad.........	40,000	404	170	14	27
Bakouba	650				
*Bassora.........	1,500	155			
Charban	120				
Chatra	150				
Divanieh	75				
Djelaa	150				
Faloudja........	60				
Halabdja	150				
Hanakin.........	1,200				
Hay	250				
Hillah	1,500				
Hindieh	200				
Hit	60				
Kerbela Nedjef ..	70				
Kerkouk.........	2,000				
Keuy Sanjak.....	250				
Kezrabat........	200				
Kiffel...........	250				
Koufri..........	1,000				
Kout Azizieh.....	200				
Mendeli.........	400				
Mosul	2,000				
Mousseyb........	200				
Nasrieh	200				
Revenduss.......	200				
Saklaweh........	50				
Samara..........	250				
Semawa	50				
Suleimanieh	2,000				
Palestine and Syria:					
Abedit	150				
Acre	93				
*Beirut	3,000	280	198	19	6
Chefar-Am.......	19				
*Damascus........	10,000	214	264	19	8
Gaza............	110				
*Haifa...........	1,260	175	115	9	
Hebron	1,130				
*Jaffa...........	3,500	188		10	
*Jerusalem........	40,000	321			
Pekiim	100				
Ramleh..........	80				
*Safed	6,870	90	274	12	
*Saida (and envi- rons)	610		110		
*Tiberias	5,720	140	290	8	
Totals	210,983	3,715	2,431	166	87

Besides these schools, the Alliance has charge of the following: the Talmud Torahs of Adrianople and Damascus, numbering respectively 1,082 and 771 pupils; the Talmud Torah of Smyrna; the schools Revka-Nurial and Aaron Saleh, numbering 500 pupils, in Bagdad; and the common school in Smyrna, numbering 255 pupils. The Alliance has also agricultural schools, which, together with the industrial ones, offer the most hopeful outlook for the Jews of Turkey.

The Sephardim have held themselves more aloof from the original Jewish inhabitants of the country, and have preserved many of the customs which they brought with them from Spain. The chief seat of the Sephardic Jews is at Salonica; but they predominate in the other cities of western Turkey. Besides these Jews of foreign descent there are the original Jewish inhabitants of the country, called in Palestine "Musta'ribin," and also the "Maghrabin," or Jews of northern Africa. In the eastern part of the Turkish empire, in the vilayets of Van and Mosul, are Jews who are said to be descendants of the Assyrian captives and of those brought back from Palestine by the Armenian king Tigranes III. They are hardly distinguishable from the other inhabitants of the country except by the long curls that they wear hanging over the temples (Cuinet, *l.c.* ii. 654). Of the 5,000 Jews in the vilayet of Van, only 360 adhere to their ancient faith, the rest having adopted the religion of the Armenians.

Characteristics.

The language spoken by the Jews in Turkey is mainly a mixture of Spanish and Hebrew, in which the former is the predominating element. The Ashkenazic Jews speak a Judæo-German jargon. For about a century after their arrival in Turkey the Spanish exiles preserved their mother tongue in its original purity. Gonsalvo de Illescas, a Spanish writer of the sixteenth century, says that he met Jews in Salonica who spoke Castilian with as pure an accent as his own. In later years, however, through the intermixture of words from Hebrew and other tongues, the language degenerated into a jargon (see JUDÆO-SPANISH). For some unknown reason, contrary to their practise in most lands, the Jews have been slow to learn the official language of the country, which is Turkish. Even in the schools founded by the Alliance a knowledge of French was at first held to be more important. Of late years, however, the Jews have become alive to the fact that through their ignorance of the official language they have been crowded out of governmental positions by Greeks and Armenians; and an earnest effort is being made to spread the knowledge of Turkish. The Jews do not appear to have the same antipathy to Arabic; and in Aleppo, Syria, and Mesopotamia, or south of the linguistic line dividing Turkish and Arabic, the Jews ordinarily speak the latter, although Hebrew also is used. In the vilayet of Van the Jews use an Aramaic dialect. The Jews are called "Yahudi" by the Turks, or, with more respect, "Musavi" = "descendants of Moses." A term of contempt which is very commonly applied to them is "tchifut" = "mean," "avaricious."

Language.

The Jews have in the main been well treated by

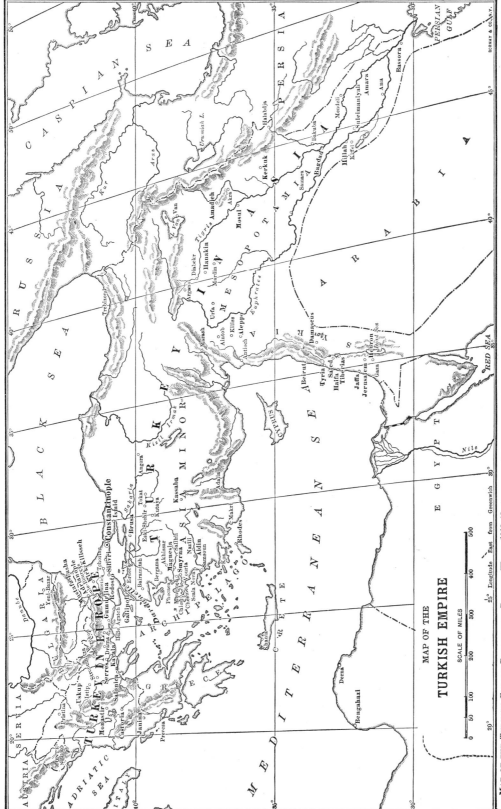

MAP OF THE
TURKISH EMPIRE

SCALE OF MILES

BORMAY & CO., N.Y.

XII.—19

MAP OF THE TURKISH EMPIRE BEFORE THE BALKAN WARS, 1912–13, SHOWING PLACES WHERE JEWS RESIDE. TOWNS HAVING MORE THAN 1,000 JEWS ARE PRINTED IN HEAVY TYPE.

the Turkish government; and, as compared with their coreligionists in European countries generally, have been subjected to few restrictions as regards dress and residence. To-day they enjoy the same privileges as all "rayahs," i.e., non-Moslem subjects, whose official position was established in the laws of the "tanzimet" (reform). These were contained in the ḥaṭṭi-sherif of Gul-Haneh of 1839 and the ḥaṭṭi-humayun of 1856, both issued by the sultan Abd-ul-Mejid. The former placed rayahs and Moslems on an equal footing, guaranteeing them inviolability of person and property. This edict was confirmed and the privileges granted to non-Moslems were increased by the ḥaṭṭi-humayun, which assured to all subjects of the sultan, irrespective of creed, the following rights: (1) security of life, honor, and property; (2) civil equality; (3) admission to civil and military service; (4) liberty of religious worship and public instruction; (5) equal taxation; (6) equality on the witness-stand; (7) special and mixed courts; and (8) representation in provincial and communal councils and in the supreme councils of justice. This edict also admits the principle of exemption from military service among non-Moslems on the payment of a fixed tax; and this is the system at present in vogue, non-Moslems not being admitted to the army and paying instead a tax known as "bedel-i-askerieh" (see below).

After the DAMASCUS AFFAIR in 1840 the sultan issued a special firman defining the position of the Jews and protecting them from calumnious accusations. Sultan Abd-ul-Aziz issued a similar firman in 1866 for a similar cause (Franco, "Histoire des Israélites de l'Empire Ottoman," p. 222).

The constitution of 1876 proclaimed the equality of all Ottomans before the law, and admitted them to public office. Thus in the national assembly of 1877 three of the deputies were Jews; there were two Jews in the senate, and two in the council of state; and the secretary of the council was also a Jew. This parliament, however, was adjourned sine die before the world was able to discover what a Turkish parliament could accomplish.

At the time of the Armenian troubles more reforms and privileges were granted to the sultan's non-Moslem subjects, without, however, materially affecting their position. It is not from the nature of the laws but from the method of their execution that the Jews in Turkey suffer; and in this particular they fare no worse than all the other classes of the population.

As regards taxation, it may be remarked that originally the kharaj (see above) was a ransom exacted according to Mohammedan law from conquered peoples who refused to accept Islam and hence were liable to death. Later it came to be regarded as a compensation for exemption from military service. The Jews of Brusa were the first to pay the tax. The tax-paying Jews were distributed into three classes according to property: those of the first class paid 40 drams of silver; those of the second, 20; and those of the third, 10 (a dram at that time was worth a little over 5 cents). The "ḥakam bashi," or chief rabbi, the "millet-cha'ush," or secular agent of the

Legal Status of the Jews.

Taxation.

community, the "ḥakam cha'ush," or rabbinical representative, the officiating ministers, teachers, the public slaughterer, and a few families specially favored by the state, were exempt from the tax. It was collected by the millet-cha'ush; and as it was discovered that the statistical lists were not trustworthy, owing to the fact that the rich Jews sometimes paid the tax for the poor, the Jewish tax-gatherers were required to take an oath on a scroll of the Law before delivering the taxes collected by them.

At the end of the sixteenth century the signification of the term ".kharaj" was extended to include twelve different taxes; so that to be exempt from the kharaj was to be exempt from all taxes. The twelve taxes, paid by Jews and Christians alike, were the following: (1) "saliane," or annual levy; (2) "ordu-akchesi," or army-tax; (3) "resim-kismet," or heritage-tax; (4) "cherahor-akchesi," or imperial pasturage-tax; (5) "ḳaza-akchesi," or tax for maintaining the residence of the governor; (6) "ḳassab-akchesi," or meat-tax; (7) "chair-akchesi," or bird-tax; (8) "rab-akchesi," a tax payable by the community collectively; (9) "bedel-kharaj," or "bashi-kharaj," tax for exemption from military service; (10) "jelb-akchesi," tax for the support of the imperial flocks; (11) tax for the support of the imperial couriers; and (12) tax to supply the sultan with furs. Besides these levies the kharaj included certain services to the number of seven, exemption from which might be purchased. These were: work on the fortifications, public buildings, roads, etc.; sentry duty, etc.; and the quartering of new recruits. The promulgation of the ḥaṭṭi-sherif of 1839 abolished the kharaj in principle, although the tax survived in fact as compensation for non-performance of military duty, until the issue of the ḥaṭṭi-humayun. The admission of rayahs into the army as ordained by this edict presented so many difficulties that a new device was invented: every rayah purchased exemption from military duty by paying the bedel-i-askerieh (see above) instead of the old kharaj. The rayahs of Constantinople—Jews and Christians alike—were exempt from this tax. In the provinces the tax was collected by the "mukhtar," or collector for the rabbinate.

In its turn the bedel was modified; and to-day the rayahs throughout the empire (Constantinople excepted) pay in place of the old kharaj two annual taxes, namely: (1) the "bedel-i-askerieh," which amounts to about $1.68 for every male between the years of twenty and sixty; and (2) the "darbieh," or "yol-parasi" (road-tax), which averages about 76 cents for every male between the same years. In addition the Jews pay communal taxes.

In the year 1864 the Jews of Constantinople, at the request of the government, drew up a constitution which was approved by Sultan Abd-ul-Aziz May 5, 1865. This provided for three councils: (1) a "mejlis-'umumi," or national assembly, to be composed of eighty members; (2) a "mejlis-jismani," or temporal council, of seven lay members; and (3) a "mejlis-ruḥani," or spiritual

Amplification of the Term "Kharaj."

Present Administration.

council, of nine rabbis. The grand rabbi at Constantinople has no authority over the other grand rabbis of the empire, merely representing them before the Porte and transmitting to them communications from the government. It should be stated that beginning with the reign of Sultan Maḥmud II. (1808–39) the spiritual chief chosen by the Jews has received the imperial sanction before entering upon his duties. The first rabbi to be elected in this way was Abraham Levy (1835), who was installed in office with much pomp and ceremony. His successor, Samuel Ḥayyim, was removed by the government after a year of office because he was a foreigner. Since that time there have been five ḥakam bashis (see CONSTANTINOPLE). The present chief rabbi, Moses ha-Levi, bears the title "ḳaimaḳam" (= "locum tenens").

The judicial authority is in the hands of a bet din of three members, who adjudicate civil and religious cases, but may not pronounce sentence of capital punishment. In the provinces the rabbi or a member of the bet din represents the community before the governor of the province. There are ḥakam bashis also at Adrianople and Salonica in Europe and at Aleppo, Bagdad, Beirut, Jerusalem, and Smyrna in Asia. See ARABIA ; BULGARIA ; EGYPT; PALESTINE; RUMANIA; SERVIA; SYRIA; and special articles on the cities of these countries and of Turkey.

BIBLIOGRAPHY : R. Andree, *Zur Volkskunde der Juden*, Bielefeld and Leipsic, 1881 ; P. Baudin, *Les Israélites de Constantinople* ; *Bulletin de l'Alliance Israélite*, passim ; V. Cuinet, *La Turquie d'Asie*, Paris, 1892 ; idem, *Syrie, Liban et Palestine*, Paris, 1896–1901 ; Pulido Fernandez, *Los Israelitas Españoles*, Madrid, 1904 ; M. Franco, *Essai sur l'Histoire des Israélites de l'Empire Ottoman*, Paris, 1897 ; Frankl, *The Jews in the East*, transl. by P. Beaton, London, 1859 ; L. M. G. Garnett, *The Women of Turkey*, ib. 1893 ; Grätz, *Gesch.* Index ; J. von Hammer-Purgstall, *Gesch. des Osmanischen Reiches*, passim ; M. A. Levy, *Don Joseph Nasi*, Breslau, 1859 ; I. Loeb, *La Situation des Israélites en Turquie*, Paris, 1877 ; Nicolo Nicolai, *Viaggi nella Turchia*, Venice, 1850.
J.   **M. W. M.**

TURTELTAUB, WILHELM : Austrian physician and poet; born at Rzeszow, Galicia, March 25, 1816. At the age of twelve he wrote a comedy in imitation of Kotzebue's "Sorgen Ohne Noth." In 1830 he entered the University of Vienna to study medicine (M.D. 1840), collaborating at the same time on the "Zuschauer," "Wanderer," and "Sammler." From 1841 he practised his profession in his native town. In 1835 his first work, "Wiener Fresko-Skizzen," was published; and his one-act comedy "Der Nachtwandler bei Tage" was produced with success at the Leopoldstädter Theater. At this time he made the acquaintance of Saphir, who induced him to contribute to his periodical "Der Humorist." In 1837 his "Nur Eine Löst den Zauberspruch" was played in Vienna and various other cities of Austria, and in Germany also. His "Der Abenteuerer" and "Der Jugendfreund" were produced at the Hofburg Theater, Vienna. In 1859 Turteltaub edited the "Wiener Volksbühne."

BIBLIOGRAPHY : *Der Jüdische Plutarch* ; Wurzbach, *Biographisches Lexikon*.
                 S.

TURTLE-DOVE. See DOVE.

TUS, JACOB. See TAWUS.

TUSHIYYAH (lit. "sound knowledge "): Publishing establishment founded in Warsaw in 1896, which, though a private enterprise, is in reality a Hebrew publication society striving to further the development and spread of Neo-Hebrew literature. Its founder, BEN-AVIGDOR, who was also one of the founders of the older and similar concern, the AḤIASAF, was its first editor, and M. Balascher was his associate in the business management. In 1905 the editors were Ben-Avigdor and S. L. Gordon (born in Lida, government of Wilna, 1866). The Tushiyyah's program is given in its subtitle: "The editing of good and useful books in the Hebrew language for the spread of knowledge and for the teaching of morality and civilization among Jewish youth; also scientific books in all branches of literature." It has published, either in the original or in translations, numerous novels, biographies, poems, and historical and miscellaneous works, and has contributed much to the revival of Hebrew literature in its latest phases. It has provided Hebrew teachers with the most popular text-books for the elementary teaching of Hebrew according to modern methods, and has also done much to encourage talented Hebrew writers. Among the authors whose works have been published by the Tushiyyah are: Frischman, Bernfeld, Brainin, Ludvipol, Slouschz, Taviov, Berdyczewski, and Rabinowitz.

BIBLIOGRAPHY : Lippe, *Bibliographisches Lexicon*, ii. 32, 379–384, Vienna, 1899 ; *R. E. J.* 1902, *passim*.
H. R.   **P. Wi.**

TYCHSEN, OLAUS GERHARD : Christian Hebraist and Orientalist; born at Tondern in Sleswick, Denmark, Dec. 14, 1734; died at Rostock, Germany, Dec. 30, 1815. He studied rabbinics at the University of Halle, and journeyed through Germany and Denmark in the years 1759 and 1760 on a fruitless mission for the conversion of the Jews, giving rise to an unseemly altercation by a conversionist sermon in the Altona synagogue. In the latter year he was called to the newly founded University of Bützow, Mecklenburg, and remained there as professor of Oriental languages till the university ceased to exist (1789), when he became chief librarian and director of the museum at Rostock. Besides many works on Arabic and Syriac archeology and philology, he published "Bützowische Nebenstunden " (6 vols., Wismar, 1766–69), containing a large amount of material regarding the text of the Old Testament, derived mainly from Jewish commentators like Rashi and from the older versions, as the Septuagint and Targum. He claimed the ability to speak "the Talmudic language," and in a special monograph denied the authenticity of the Maccabean and other Jewish coins.

BIBLIOGRAPHY : Hartmann, *Oluf Gerhard Tychsen*, Bremen, 1818–20 ; *Brockhaus Konversations-Lexikon* ; McClintock and Strong, *Cyc.* s.v.
T.   **J.**

TYPES, ANTHROPOLOGICAL : Correlated norms of racial qualities. Individuals who present an interrelation between the color of the hair and that of the eyes are considered typical representatives of their race. In the blond races fair hair is generally accompanied by blue eyes; in brunette races brown or black hair is generally accompanied by dark eyes. The former are considered anthropologically blond types; the latter, brunette types. Individuals who do not exhibit such an interrelation of the color of the hair and eyes, having dark hair with blue eyes and vice versa, are called mixed types. Owing to the preponderance of dark hair and eyes among the Jews (see EYE; HAIR), anthropologists have counted them among the races of a brunette type.

From extensive investigations of the color of the hair and eyes of the school-children in Germany, Virchow has shown that the Jews have not maintained their type in as pure a state as has been generally supposed. Of 75,377 Jewish children examined, only 46.83 per cent were brunettes having both dark hair and dark eyes; 11.17 per cent were blonds having light hair and light-colored eyes; and 42 per cent were of the mixed type having either dark hair with fair eyes, or vice versa. In Austria, according to Schimmer, 32 to 47 per cent (according to the province) of the Jewish children are pure brunettes, and 8 to 14 per cent are pure blonds. In Bulgaria, Wateff has found that only 49.57 per cent of Jewish children are brunettes, while 8.71 are blonds and 41.72 are of mixed type; and even in North Africa, where the dark type predominates among the Jews, 76.40 per cent are brunettes, 4.62 per cent are blonds, and 18.98 per cent are of mixed type.

TYPES OF PIGMENTATION IN JEWS OF VARIOUS COUNTRIES.

Nativity.	Type (per cent).			Number Observed.	Observer.
	Brunette.	Blond.	Mixed.		
Galician Jews:					
Men in New York.....	43.93	13.12	42.95	305	Fishberg.
Women in New York.	50.82	16.39	32.79	122	Fishberg.
Polish:					
Men in New York.....	53.65	9.52	36.83	315	Fishberg.
Women in New York.	50.00	5.36	44.64	56	Fishberg.
Men in Poland........	57.92	0.55	41.53	183	Elkind.
Women in Poland	58.50	8.50	33.00	118	Elkind.
Lithuanian and White-Russian:					
Men in New York.....	53.09	8.73	38.18	275	Fishberg.
Women in New York..	53.00	12.00	35.00	100	Fishberg.
Men in Lithuania.....	63.06	10.19	26.75	314	Yakowenko, Talko-Hryncewicz.
Women in Lithuania..	74.00	6.00	20.00	100	Yakowenko.
Little-Russian:					
Men in New York.....	49.31	7.31	43.38	219	Fishberg.
Women in New York..	55.41	8.11	36.49	74	Fishberg.
Men in Little Russia..	51.30	16.20	34.00	869	Talko - Hryncewicz.
Women in Little Russia.	68.60	6.90	24.30	799	Talko - Hryncewicz.
Rumanian:					
Men in New York.....	46.67	10.66	42.67	150	Fishberg.
Women in New York..	50.00	13.64	36.36	44	Fishberg.
Hungarian:					
Men in New York.....	45.71	12.14	42.15	140	Fishberg.
Women in New York..	61.54	5.13	33.33	39	Fishberg.
United States:					
Men in New York.....	50.81	8.87	40.32	124	Fishberg.

Among Jewish adults anthropological investigation has shown that the brunette type is not in the majority. From the accompanying table it will be observed that the percentage of brunettes is only 43 among the Galician Jews, while it reaches as high as 74 per cent among Lithuanian Jewesses. Blonds

are very rare among the Jews of Russian Poland; but among other classes they are encountered quite often. Among the Little-Russian Jews the proportion reaches 16 per cent. The mixed types are everywhere found in the proportion of from 30 to 40 per cent of all the individuals examined.

The origin of the blond and mixed types among the Jews has been a favorite topic of discussion for many anthropologists. Some have maintained that **Origin of** they are the product of intermixture **Blond** with the indigenous peoples of the **and Mixed** European countries in which the Jews **Types.** have lived; others show that even among Jews who do not live among blond races, as, for instance, those of Syria, Tunis, Morocco, and Algiers, many blonds are met with. It is also shown that if intermixture with northern European races were the origin of the blond Jews, the countries whose non-Jewish populations present the largest percentage of blonds, as Prussia, Lithuania, etc., should have the largest proportion of Jewish blonds also. On the other hand, in the south and the east of Europe, where the Gentiles are darker, more Jewish brunettes and fewer blonds should be found. That this is not the case is shown by the following figures, taken from Virchow's census of the color of the hair and eyes of school-children in Germany:

Province.	Per Cent of Blonds.		Per Cent of Brunettes.	
	Jews.	Christians.	Jews.	Christians.
Prussia	11.23	39.75	43.34	14.05
Hesse................	11.17	31.53	41.50	13.22
Baden	10.32	24.34	41.95	21.18
Bavaria	10.38	20.36	39.45	21.10
Alsace-Lorraine......	13.51	18.44	34.59	25.21

These figures show in a striking manner that in the provinces of Germany where the percentage of brunettes is smallest among the Christian population—in Prussia, for instance, only 14.05 per cent—the Jews have 42.34 per cent of brunettes; while in Alsace-Lorraine and Bavaria, where the Christians show 25.21 and 21.1 per cent of brunettes respectively, the Jews have only 34.59 and 39.45 per cent respectively of such. This is further confirmed by the following figures (from the works of Virchow and Schimmer) showing the distribution of Jewish pure blond and brunette types in Germany and Austria:

Province.	Germany (Virchow).		Province.	Austria (Schimmer).	
	Pure Blonds.	Pure Brunettes.		Pure Blonds.	Pure Brunettes.
Silesia............	8.20	49.53	Bohemia	8.29	46.87
Pomerania.......	8.85	50.58	Lower Austria...	8.69	46.16
Brandenburg......	9.64	47.39	Moravia..........	9.86	43.15
East and West Prussia	11.61	43.04	Bukowina.......	13.55	35.21
Posen............	12.39	39.22	Galicia	13.97	32.91

It is evident from these figures that the farther one goes south and east in Europe, the smaller is the percentage of brunettes encountered among the Jews and the larger the percentage of blonds. With the non-Jewish population the reverse is the fact. Most of the blonds are found in Prussia, Pomerania, Sleswick-Holstein, Hanover, Westphalia, etc., while farther east, reaching to Posen, Silesia, Bohemia, Moravia, Upper and Lower Aus-

Distribution of Blonds. tria, Bukowina, and Galicia, the percentage of pure blonds decreases and that of brunettes increases. It is also noteworthy, as has been pointed out by Virchow, that in localities where, owing to religious and social prejudices, the Jews have lived for centuries in strict isolation from other races, and presumably have not intermarried with their Gentile neighbors, the proportion of blond types is larger than in the Prussian provinces, where they have not been socially isolated, but, on the contrary, have entered into general social intercourse with the non-Jewish inhabitants. Here the largest proportion of

served that the Jews with fair eyes measure on the average 1.644 meters, and those with dark eyes 1.617 meters only. But all these conclusions are based on a small number of cases, and other investigations tend to disprove them. In Baden, Otto Ammon found no relation between blond hair, blue eyes, and dolichocephalism, while in Poland, Elkind noticed that Jews with dark hair and eyes were taller than those with fair hair and light eyes, which phenomena are the reverse of those in the so-called Aryan type. Similar results were obtained by Fishberg in his observations of the immigrant Jews in New York. The darker Jews had practically the same head-form (cephalic index 81.97) as the blond-haired (82.35). The same was the case with tall Jews as compared with those of short stature: the craniometrical lines were about the same. Indeed, Jews with fair hair and eyes were taller than those with dark hair and eyes.

Fishberg concludes from all the statistics gathered

COMPOSITE PORTRAITS OF TEN BOYS OF THE JEWS' FREE SCHOOL, LONDON.
A is the composite portrait of five boys, B of another five, and C a composite of A and B.
(From the "Journal of the Anthropological Institute.")

brunettes is found among the German and Austrian Jews. But it must be mentioned that in Algiers, Tunis, and Morocco, where the indigenous population is of a dark type, the Jews also are darker.

It has been suggested that the blond type among the Jews is due to intermixture with the so-called Aryan, or north-European, races, in proof of which the following argument has been advanced: The Aryan type is known to consist in the combination of blond hair, blue eyes, tall stature, and dolichocephalism or long-headedness. Among the Galician Jews, Majer and Kopernicki found that while among the brunette Jews 6.2 per cent are dolichocephalic, 20 per cent of the blond Jews of the same section are so. This has been repeatedly cited as evidencing a relation between blondness and long-headedness among the Jews in Galicia, and is thought to be due to Teutonic intermixture. In Odessa, Pantukhof ("Proc. Russian Anthropological Society," pp. 26–30, St. Petersburg, 1889) has found that the Jews who have dark hair and eyes are of short stature, while those who have fair eyes and hair are taller. In Caucasia the same author has ob-

by him that the ideal Aryan type is not to be observed among the Jews. On the contrary, the rule appears to be that tall persons have darker hair and eyes, and that a smaller percentage of them are dolichocephalic; while Jews of short stature are of fairer complexion and include a larger percentage of dolichocephalic persons. This tends to exclude the hypothesis that Aryan influence is the cause of the Jewish blond type; but it tends to confirm the theory of admixture from the Slavonian type.

BIBLIOGRAPHY: M. Fishberg, *Materials for the Physical Anthropology of the Eastern European Jews*, in *Annals of the New York Academy of Sciences*, 1905; S. Wateff, *Anthropologische Beobachtungen der Farbe der Augen, der Haare und der Haut bei den Schulkindern von den Türken, Pomaken, Tataren, Armenier, Griechen und Juden in Bulgarien*, in *Correspondenzblatt der Deutschen Gesellschaft für Anthropologie*, 1903, xxxiv., Nos. 7, 8. See also EYE and HAIR.
J.   M. Fi.

What is popularly known as "the Jewish type" is not a correlation of definite anthropological measures or characteristics, but consists principally in a peculiar expression of face, which is immediately and unmistakably recognized as "Jewish" in a large number of cases of persons of the Jewish race. It has been observed that children in New York, Gentile as well as Jewish, can unerringly distinguish between Jew and Gentile, whether juvenile or adult. The negroes of the Gold Coast are said to differentiate the two types of Europeans with equal exactitude, saying "here come two whites and a Jew," instead of "here come three whites" (Andree, "Zur Volkskunde der Juden," p. 38). Yet when taken together in large numbers, a considerable proportion of Jews fail to betray their racial provenience. In collective photographs of Jewish school-children and inmates of institutions it has been found that while about 53 per cent of the subjects can be more or less certainly identified as Jews by their facial expression, the remaining 47 per cent fail to show any distinctive feature which would definitely mark them as Semites, though if compared with Gentiles of the same class they could probably be differentiated. It has also been remarked that persons who do not have the Jewish expression in their youth acquire it more and more as they grow from middle to old age. Although Jewesses appear to be more variable in appearance than Jews, they seem to show the type in its greatest purity when they actually are Jewish in features.

The precise nature of this Jewishness is very difficult to determine with any degree of certainty or accuracy. Evidently it is not in any **Expression.** one feature, for whenever any single trait, such as the shape of the nose or the brilliancy of the eyes, is assumed to be characteristic, the very next example is liable to disprove the validity of the test. The sole attempt to obtain any scientific discrimination of the Jewish expression was made by F. Galton and Joseph Jacobs in 1885, by means of composite portraiture. In their experiments Jewish boys of the Jewish Free School, London, were selected as being typically Jewish in appearance, and full-face and profile photographs were first taken on a uniform scale, and then superimposed on a single plate, so that the eyes and mouth in each case fell upon the same spots on the plate. By this means all the varying traits and features blurred out, while the common characteristics were emphasized and became stronger. The results were given in "The Photographic News," April, 1885, and in "The Journal of the Anthropological Institute," 1885. The full-face composite here given is made up of (a) that of five Jewish lads, (b) that of another five, and (c) one of (a) and (b), thus giving the summary of the characteristic features of ten typically Jewish boys. The result is remarkably Jewish in appearance, and it will be found that this character is given by the eyebrows, eyes, nose, and lips, while the position and contour of the cheek-bone also serve to determine it. The eyebrows are generally well-defined, somewhat bushy toward the nose, and **Composite** tapering off toward the extremities. **Portraits.** The eyes themselves are generally brilliant, both lids are heavy and bulging, and it seems to be the main characteristic of the Jewish eye that the upper lid covers a larger proportion of the pupil than among other persons. This **may** serve to give a sort of nervous, furtive look to

the eyes, which, when the pupils are small and set close together with semistrabismus, gives keenness to some Jewish eyes. The lymph-sac beneath the eye is generally fuller and more prominent than among non-Jews. The high cheek-bone gives as a rule the hollow cheek that adds to the Jewish expression, while the nose in full face can be discerned only by the flexibility of the nostrils, the chief Jewish characteristic of this organ (see NOSE). The upper lip is generally short, and the lower projects, giving a somewhat sensual appearance to the face. The chin almost invariably recedes from the lip, leaving an indentation beneath it in the great majority of instances. The ears of many Jewish persons project, and in boys increase the impression of Jewishness.

With growth, as already noted, the Jewish expression becomes even more marked. In males this may be due to the appearance of the mustache and beard, and it is frequently found that **Adults.** the mustache is somewhat sparse, a rather bare portion intervening between the tuft under the nostril and the mustache proper. The beard is in some cases comparatively thick and in others luxuriant, curling, and parting naturally. It is to be observed that some Jewish faces have almost all of these stigmata. The miniature of Spinoza (JEW. ENCYC. xi. 512) shows the brilliant and sensitive eye, the conspicuous nostril, and the thick underlip. That of Benfey (ib. iii. 16) has the projecting ears, the thick underlip, and the conspicuous alæ of the nose, while the lymph-sac is well developed and the pupil of the eye is nearly half hidden by the upper lid. The same characteristic will be seen in the portrait of Moses Berlin (ib. iii. 80), which has, in addition, the marked eyebrows and the curved nostril.

Besides all these details, there is something in the whole formation of the face which is generally found in the Jewish type. As a rule, the face is oval in shape, especially in the best type of Jewesses, and if regarded in profile, it is distinctly convex, the nose being, as it were, an appendix to the ellipsoid. It is rare indeed that a Jew is found with a prognathous jaw.

Notwithstanding the similarity of expression found in large measure among all Jews, there are a number of distinctions which enable a close observer to distinguish between various subtypes of the Jew. Close attention to Talmudic study, combined with the peculiar work of the sweat-shop, produced in eastern Europe what is known as "the ghetto bend." The need for wearing phylacteries on the forehead while the head is covered has led in many instances to the hat being worn upon the back of the head. These two characteristics often enable observers to identify Jews from eastern Europe, even before their faces are seen. Among them, too, it has been claimed, various subdivisions can be discerned, consisting mainly in differences in the projection of the cheek-bones, the formation of the eyelids, and the thickness of the lips. It has even been held by those who believe in a strong admixture from surrounding nations that there is a Slavonic, Mongoloid, and Armenioid type of the Jew, due to admixture of Slavic, Tatar, or Armenian blood. Luschan indeed professes to regard

THE JEWISH TYPE.

Composite Portrait of ten Jewish Lads, New York.

(A=composite of a^1 a^2 a^3 a^4 a^5.   B=composite of b^1 b^2 b^3 b^4 b^5.   C=co-composite of A and B.)

the last-named as the original source of the Jewish race.

Numbers of Jews are found, on the other hand, who possess none of the characteristics here noted, and yet are recognizable as Jews. This is especially true of the Little-Russians, who apparently resemble their Gentile neighbors in every facial characteristic, but are differentiated from them by some subtile nuance which distinguishes them as Semites. It is seemingly some social quality which stamps their features as distinctly Jewish. This is confirmed by the interesting fact that Jews who mix much with the outer world seem to lose their Jewish quality. This was the case with Karl MARX, HALÉVY the musician (MEYERBEER was remarkably Jewish), Sir Julian GOLDSMID, Sir John SIMON (in whom there was a mixture of Gentile blood), Sir David SALOMONS, and RUBINSTEIN. Two illustrious living Italians, LOMBROSO and LUZZATTI, would scarcely be taken for Jews; and even the late Theodor HERZL was not distinctively Jewish, all observers drawing attention to his resemblance to the Assyrian rather than to the Jewish type.

BIBLIOGRAPHY: Jacobs, *Jewish Statistics*, pp. xxxii.-xxxiv.

             J.

TYPOGRAPHY: The art of printing. The invention of printing was welcomed by the Jews as "the art of writing with many pens." From the time of the earlier printers reference is made to their craft as "holy work" ("'Abodat ha-Ḳodesh"). It may here be treated under the two headings of history and characteristics.

I. History: The history of Hebrew printing is divided into five stages, of which only a sketch can be attempted in this place, many of the details being

Jews made use of the art for Hebrew printing, as the conditions in Germany did not admit of their doing so there; and all the Hebrew printing of the fifteenth century was done in the Italian and Iberian peninsulas, where about 100 works were produced before 1500. Hebrew printing began in Italy;

Incunabula. and apart from **Reggio di Calabria,** where the first printed book was produced in 1475, and **Rome,** where possibly the earliest Hebrew press was set up, printing was centered about **Mantua,** where it began in 1477. In the same year **Ferrara** and **Bologna** started printing. The chief printer family of Italy was that of the SONCINOS, which besides working at Mantua printed at **Casale-Maggiore, Soncino, Brescia, Naples,** and **Barca.** Bible, Talmud, and ritual, halakic, and ethical works naturally formed the chief subjects of printing in these early days. In Spain, Hebrew printing began at **Guadalajara** in 1482, went three years later to **Ixar,** and finished at **Zamora,** while in Portugal it began at **Faro** in 1487, went to **Lisbon** in 1489, and finished at **Leiria** in 1792. The total number of books printed in Spain and Portugal amounted to only 17. The early types were rough in form; but the presswork for the most part was excellent, and the ink and paper were of very enduring quality. Owing to the work of the censor and the persecution of the Jews, the early productions of the Hebrew presses of Italy and the Iberian Peninsula are extremely rare, one-fifth of them being unique (for further particulars see INCUNABULA).

II. (1500–42): This period is distinguished by the spread of Jewish presses to the Turkish and Holy Roman empires. In **Constantinople,** Hebrew print-

FROM THE TRACTATE BABA MEẒI'A, SONCINO, 1515.

already treated under the names of prominent printers or presses. The five stages of Hebrew typography are as follows: I., 1475–1500, incunabula in southern Europe; II., 1500–42, spread to north and east; III., 1542–1627, supremacy of Venice; IV., 1627–1732, hegemony of Amsterdam; V., 1732–1900, modern period, in which Frankfort, Vienna, and, more recently, Wilna and Warsaw have come to the front. For the most part Hebrew printing has been done by Jews, but the printing of Bibles has been undertaken also by Christian typographers, especially at the university towns of Europe. These productions, for lack of space, are for the most part to be neglected in the following sketch.

I. (1475–1500): It was twenty years before the

ing was introduced by David Naḥmias and his son Samuel about 1503; and they were joined in the year 1530 by Gershon Soncino, whose work was taken up after his death by his son Eleazar (see CONSTANTINOPLE—TYPOGRAPHY). Gershon Soncino put into type the first Karaite work printed (Bashyaẓi's "Adderet Eliyahu") in 1531. In **Salonica,** Don Judah Gedaliah printed about 30 Hebrew works from 1500 onward, mainly Bibles, and Gershon Soncino, the

Second Period. Wandering Jew of early Hebrew typography, joined his kinsman Moses Soncino, who had already produced 3 works there (1526–27); Gershon printed the Aragon Maḥzor (1529) and Ḳimḥi's "Shorashim" (1533). The prints of both these Turkish cities were not of a very high order. The works selected, however, were important for their rarity and literary character. The type of Salonica imitates the Spanish Rashi type.

Turning to Germany, the first Jewish press was set up in **Prague** by Gershon ben Solomon Cohen, who founded in that city a family of Hebrew printers, known commonly as "the Gersonides." He

burg and Ulm, and finally settled in 1546 at **Heddernheim**, where he published a few works. At Augsburg, 1544, the convert Paulus Emilius printed a Judæo-German Pentateuch. Three works of this period are known to have been printed at **Cracow**, the first of them, in 1534, a commentary of Israel Isserlein on "Sha'are Durah" with elaborately decorated title-page.

FROM TRACTATE 'ERUBIN, PRINTED BY BOMBERG, VENICE, 1521.

began printing in 1513 with a prayer-book, and during the period under review confined himself almost exclusively to this class of publications, with which he supplied Jewish Germany and Poland. He was joined about 1518 by Ḥayyim ben David Schwartz, who played in northern Europe the same wandering rôle the Soncinos assumed in the south. From 1514 to 1526 he worked at Prague, but in 1530

Other towns of Germany also printed Hebrew works during this period, but they were mainly portions of the Biblical books, mostly editions of the Psalms, produced by Christian printers for Christian professors, as at **Cologne** (1518), **Wittenberg** (1521 onward), **Mayence** (1523), **Worms** (1529), and **Leipsic** (1538). To these should be added Thomas Anshelm's edition of the Psalms at **Tü-**

FROM THE FIRST ILLUSTRATED PRINTED HAGGADAH, PRAGUE, 1526.

he was found at **Oels** in Silesia, printing a Pentateuch with the Megillot and Hafṭarot. He transferred his activity to the southwest at **Augsburg,** where in 1533 he published Rashi on the Pentateuch and Megillot, the next year a Haggadah, in 1536 a letter-writer and German prayer-book, and in 1540 an edition of the Ṭurim, followed by rimed Judæo-German versions of Kings (1543) and Samuel (1544). In 1544 he moved to **Ichenhausen,** between Augs-

bingen in 1512. It was followed by his edition of Ḳimḥi's grammar at **Hagenau,** 1519. With these may be mentioned the **Paris** printers of the sixteenth century (from 1508 onward), who produced grammars and Bibles (see Paris).

Returning to the earlier home of Hebrew printing, a considerable number of towns in Italy had Hebrew presses early in the sixteenth century, mainly through the activity of Gershon Soncino,

From "Seder Tefillot," Verona,
1648.

From "Koh Tebareku,"
Leghorn, 1653.

From "Seder Tefillot," Amsterdam,
1739.

From "Tefillot Ma'ariv," Sulzbach, 1736.

From Pentateuch, Constantinople or Salonica, 1516.

SPECIMENS OF SMALL FORMAT.

who is found in **Fano** (1515), **Pesaro** (1517), **Ortona** (1519), and **Rimini** (1521); other presses were temporarily worked in **Trino, Genoa,** and Rome, the last under Elijah LEVITA. In Bologna nine works were produced between 1537 and 1541, main-

From the "Wikkuaḥ" Printed by Sebastian Münster, Basel, 1539.

ly prayer-books and responsa. Above all, this period is distinguished in Italy by the foundation and continuance of the Venetian press under the guidance of Daniel BOMBERG, a Dutchman from Antwerp. His thirty-five years' ac-

Daniel Bomberg. tivity from 1515 to 1549 was in a measure epoch-making for Hebrew typography. His productions shared in all the excellence of the Venice press, and included the first rabbinic Bible in 1517, the first complete edition of the Babylonian Talmud in 1520 (its pagination is followed at the present day), a large number of editions of the Bible in whole or part, several grammatical, lexicographic, and midrashic works, seven commentaries on the Pentateuch, six responsa collections, philosophical and ethical writings, and several rituals, including a Tefillah and a Maḥzor according to the Spanish rite, one according to the Greek rite (Maḥzor Romania), and a Karaite one. Finally, reference should be made to the university press of **Basel,** where the Frobens produced Hebrew works in a remarkably clear type, with the letters slanting to the left, somewhat after the manner of the early Mantua editions. Froben began in 1516 with an edition of the Psalms, and produced many of the works of Elijah Levita and Sebastian MÜNSTER. Altogether Schwab (in "Incunables Orientaux," pp. 49–128) enumerates about 430 works produced between 1500 and 1540. Allowing for omissions by him, not more than 600 works were produced between 1475 and 1540.

III. (1542–1627): The third period is distinguished by the activity of the censor, which lasted for two centuries or more in southern and eastern Europe. The principle of regulating the books to be read by the faithful, and even by the unfaithful, was inaugurated by the Roman Curia in 1542, though the first carrying out of it was with the burning of the Talmud in 1554. But even previous to that date Jews had taken precautions to remove all cause of offense. About 1542 Meïr Katzenellenbogen censored the seliḥot of the German rite, and Schwartz

adopted his changes in the edition which he published at Heddernheim in 1546.

Resuming the history of the Italian presses, that of **Venice** first engages attention. Bomberg was not allowed to have a monopoly of Hebrew

Third Period. Supremacy of Venice. printing, which had been found to be exceptionally profitable. Other Christians came into the field, especially Marco Antonio Giustiniani, who produced twenty-five works between 1545 and 1552. Another competitor arose in the person of Aloisio BRAGADINI, who began printing in 1550. In the competition both parties appealed to Rome; and their disputes brought about the burning of the Talmud in 1554 at Ferrara, and the strict enforcement of the censorship, even in Venice, the presses of which stopped printing Hebrew books for eight years. Similar competition appears to have taken place with regard to the Hebrew typesetters whom these Christian printers were obliged to employ. Cornelius ADELKIND and his son, German Jews of

From Pentateuch, Sabbionetta, 1557.

Padua, first worked with Bomberg, and then were taken over by Farri (1544), and they appear to have also worked for both Bragadini and Giustiniani. There was a whole body of learned press-revisers. Among them should be mentioned Jacob b. Ḥayyim, the editor of the rabbinic Bible, and Meïr Katzenellenbogen, who helped to edit Maimonides' "Yad" (1550). When Venice ceased for a time to issue Hebrew books, printing was taken up in **Ferrara** (1551–1557) by Abraham Usque, who printed the "Consolaçam" of his brother Samuel Usque (1553). In **Sabbionetta** (1551–59) Tobias Foa printed about

Reverting to Venice, printing was resumed in 1564 by Giovanni de Gara, who took up the work of Bomberg, and between 1564 and 1569 produced more than 100 different works, making use of Christian as well as Jewish typesetters, among the latter being Leon of Modena in the years 1595–1601. Besides Gara there were Grippo, Georgio de Cavalli,

FROM A SELIḤAH, HEDDERNHEIM, 1546.

twenty works, among them a very correct edition of the Targum on the Pentateuch, employing the ubiquitous Adelkind to print a fine edition of the "Moreh" and an edition of the Talmud in parts, only one of which is extant. The Sabbionetta types are said to have gone back to Venice when the Bragadinis resumed work. In **Cremona** a Hebrew press was set up in 1556 by Vincentio Conti, who issued altogether forty-two works up to 1560, including

and the Zanetti family, but none of them could compete with the activity of the Bragadinis, which was resumed about the same time. They made use of Samuel Archevolti and Leon of Modena among their typesetters. It is worthy of mention that several important works appeared at Venice from printing establishments which can not be identified, including the editio princeps of the Shulḥan 'Aruk (1565). A few works were printed at Rome (1546–81) by

FROM THE HUTTER BIBLE, HAMBURG, 1587, SHOWING HOLLOW SERVILE LETTERS.

the first edition of the Zohar, 2,000 copies of which were saved with difficulty from the fires of the Inquisition. His first edition of Menahem Zioni's commentary was not so fortunate; notwithstanding that it had received the license of the censor, it was burnt. About thirty-three works were produced during this period at **Riva di Trento** by Joseph Ottolenghi under the auspices of Cardinal Madruz, whose titular hat appears upon the title-pages of the volumes.

Antonio Bladao and Francesco Zanetti, and a couple of works in **Verona** by Francesco delle Donne.

The greatest activity in Italy outside Venice was that carried on at Mantua by the Rufenellis, who employed Joseph Ashkenazi and Meïr Sofer, both from Padua, as their chief typesetters. Their activity was followed by that of Ephraim b. David of Padua and Moses b. Katriel of Prague, both working in the last decade of the sixteenth century, the latter for the publishers Norzi brothers. Altogether

Zunz enumerates seventy-three works produced at Mantua during the third period, including a "Sefer Yeẓirah," "Tanḥuma," Aboab's "Menorat ha-Ma'or," and an edition of Abot in Italian.

During this period the Hebrew press of **Basel** received new light in the advent from Italy of Israel b. Daniel Sifroni, one of those wandering master workmen who, like Soncino and Schwartz, characterized the early history of Hebrew printing. Through his workmanship a number of important works were produced by Froben of Basel between 1578 and 1584, including a Babylonian Talmud, Isaac Nathan's Concordance, and the "'Ir Gibborim,"

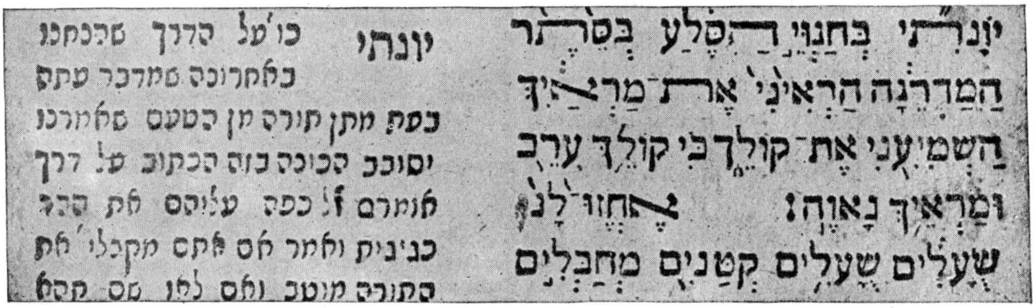

Froben and Waldkirch.

יונתי בחגוי הסלע בסתר המדרגה הראיני את מראיך השמיעני את קולך כי קולך ערב ומראיך נאוה: אחזו לנו שעלים שעלים קטנים מחבלים

FROM A COMMENTARY ON SONG OF SONGS, SAFED, 1578.

whose publisher in Prague, finding that he could not have printing done as well there as by Sifroni, sent it to the latter in Basel. In the year 1583–84 Sifroni was working for Froben at **Freiburg-im-Breisgau,** where he printed several Judæo-German works, including the Five Megillot with glossary in red ink; he printed also an edition of Benjamin of Tudela's "Travels." Froben's success, like that of Bomberg, induced other Christian printers to join in competition, as Guarin (for whom Sifroni also worked), Beber, and especially Conrad Waldkirch, who from 1598 on published a Great Tefillah, an 'Aruk, an Alfasi in octavo, and "Synagogue Music and Songs" by Elijah b. Moses Loans, who was for a time Waldkirch's corrector for the press. Mordecai b. Jacob of Prossnitz, who, as shown below, had had a large printing experience in the east of Europe, also assisted Waldkirch in 1622. After his departure the Basel Hebrew prints became scarcer, and were confined mainly to the productions of the Buxtorfs, while only sporadic Hebrew works were produced at **Altdorf, Bern,** and **Zurich** (where, however, one of the finest specimens of Hebrew printing had been produced in the Judæo-German "Yosippon" of 1546). Reference may be here made to prints of Paulus Fagius at **Constance** in 1643–44, mainly with Judæo-German or Latin translations. Altogether the total number of Hebrew works produced in Switzerland was not more than fifty.

The history of the Hebrew press in Denmark deserves treatment in fuller detail, as it has been recently investigated by Simonsen. In 1598 Heinrich Waldkirch imported some inferior Hebrew type to **Copenhagen** from Wittenberg; but nothing of importance was printed during the following three decades. In 1631 Solomon Sartor published some excerpts from the Bible; and in 1663 Henrik Göde printed similar extracts. In 1734 Marius Fogh (who later became city magistrate of Odense) published an edition of Isaac Abravanel's commentary on Gen. xlix. This work, which bore the imprint of the Copenhagen publishing-house of I. C. Rothe, was for sale as late as 1893. Christian Nold's concordance of the Bible appeared in 1679 from the press of Corfitz Luft in Copenhagen, and the solid quarto volume, containing 1,210 pages, gives evidence of the author's diligence, as well as of the printer's skill and care. A Lutheran pastor, Lauritz Petersen, in **Nyköbing** on the island of Falster, published in 1640 a new Hebrew versification of the Song of Solomon, intended as a wedding-present for the son of King Christian IV. and his bride Magdalena Sibylla. This work, which was entitled "Canticum Canticorum Salomonis," consisted of Hebrew verse with Danish translation, and with various melodies added; it was printed by Melchior Martzau. Samuel ben Isaac of Schwerin published in 1787 some Talmudic annotations entitled "Minḥat Shemu'el," printed by the Copenhagen firm of Thiele, but showing evidence of lack of skill.

To revert to Switzerland, Fagius printed a number of Biblical, grammatical, and polemical works at

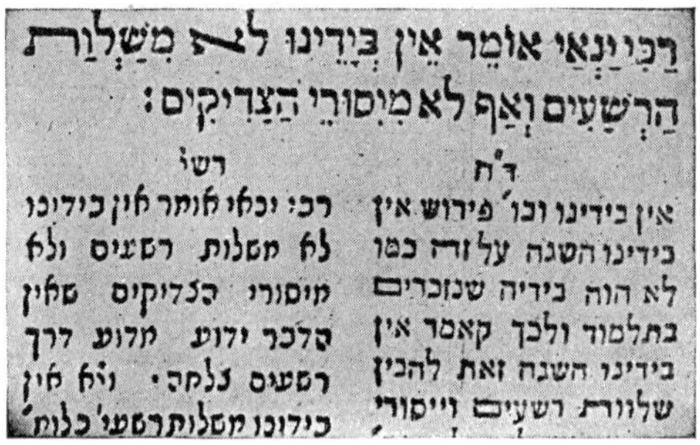

רבי ינאי אומר אין בידינו לא משלות הרשעים ואף לא מיסורי הצדיקים:

From a Commentary on Pirḳe Abot, Cracow, 1589.

Isny, with the help of Elijah Levita, who produced there the "Tishbi," "Meturgeman," and "Baḥur," besides a German translation of the "Sefer ha-Middot" in 1542, which is now very rare. Another Christian printer who is mentioned throughout this period is Hans Jacob Hene, who produced about thirty Jewish works in Hebrew at **Hanau** (1610–30). He ca-

Fagius and Hene.

tered more to the students of the Talmud and Halakah, producing three responsa collections, three commentaries on the Talmud, the Ṭur and Shulḥan 'Aruk, and three somewhat similar codes, as well as a number of Judæo-German folk editions like the "Zuchtspiegel" or the "Brandspiegel" (1626), and the "Weiberbuch" of Benjamin Aaron Solnik. Among his typesetters were a couple of the Ulmas, of the Günzburg family, and Mordecai b. Jacob Prossnitz, who has already been mentioned. Hene's type is distinguished by its clearness, and by the peculiar form of the "shin" in the so-called "Weiberdeutsch." Other isolated appearances of Hebrew works at **Tannhausen** (1594), **Thiengen** (1660), and **Hergerswiese** did not add much to German Jewish typography in this period.

Meantime, in eastern Europe, the Gersonides continued their activity at **Prague,** especially in the printing of ritual works; but they suffered from the competition of the Bak family, who introduced from Italy certain improvements from the year 1605 on-

trade from 1556 onward, when an edition of the tractate Shebu'ot appeared in the former city. Its printers were mainly of the Jaffe family; Kalonymus Abraham (1562–1600) was followed by his son Ẓebi (1602 onward), who made use of the services of the above-mentioned Mordecai b. Jacob of Prossnitz. The prints of the Jaffes were mainly productions of local rabbis and Judæo-German works. During the plague which ravaged Lublin in 1592 Kalonymus Jaffe moved his printing establishment to **Bistrovich,** whence he issued a Haggadah with Abravanel's commentary.

It should perhaps be added that at **Antwerp** and **Leyden** in this period Biblical works by Christian printers appeared, at the former place by the celebrated Christopher Plantin, who got his type from Bomberg's workshop.

IV. (1627–1732): This period is opened and dominated by the foundation of the press at **Amsterdam,** the rich and cultured Maranos of the Dutch capital devoting their wealth, commercial connec-

FROM "KEHILLOT YA'AḲOB," VENICE, 1599.

ward. Among the typesetters at Prague in this period was the Jewess Gütel (daughter of Löb Setzer), who set up a work in 1627. At Prague almost for the first time is found the practise of rabbis issuing their responsa from the local presses. The decoration employed by the Prague press of this period was often somewhat elaborate. Besides the illustrated Haggadah of 1526, the title-page of the Ṭur of 1540 is quite elaborate and includes the arms of Prague.

In **Cracow** Isaac ben Aaron of Prossnitz revived the Hebrew press in 1569, and produced a number of Talmudic and cabalistic works from that time to his death in 1614, when his sons succeeded to his business. He was assisted by Samuel Bohn, who brought from Venice the Italian methods and title-page designs, which were used up to

Cracow and Lublin.　about 1580. He produced, besides the Jerusalem and Babylonian Talmuds, two editions of the Midrash Rabbot, the "Yalḳuṭ Shim'oni" (1596), and several works of Moses Isserles and Solomon Luria, besides the "Yuḥasin," "Shalshelet ha-Ḳabbalah," and "Yosippon." Isaac b. Aaron for a time ran a press in his native city of **Prossnitz,** where from 1602 to 1605 he published four works.

Lublin competed with Cracow for the eastern

tions, and independent position to the material development of Hebrew literature in book form. For nearly a century after its foundation Amsterdam supplied the whole of Teutonic Europe with Hebrew books; and the term "Defus Amsterdam" was used to denote type of special excellence even though cast elsewhere, just as the term "Italic" was applied to certain type cast not only in Italy but in other countries. The first two presses were set up in the year 1627, one under Daniel de Fonseca, the other under Manasseh ben Israel, who in the following twenty years printed more than sixty works, many of them his own, with an excellent edition of the

Fourth Period. Hegemony of Amsterdam.　Mishnah without vowels, and, characteristically enough, a reprint of Almoli's "Pitron Ḥalomot" (1637). The work in later times was mainly done by his two sons, Ḥayyim and Samuel. Toward the latter part of Manasseh ben Israel's career as a printer an important competitor arose in the person of Immanuel Benveniste, who in the twenty years 1641–60 produced prayer-books, a Midrash Rabbah, an Alfasi, and the Shulḥan 'Aruk, mostly decorated with elaborate titles supported by columns, which became the model for all Europe. He was followed by the firm of Gumpel & Levi (1648–60). Particular interest attaches to the name of URI PHOEBUS HA-LEVI, an apprentice of Benveniste's who was in business in Amsterdam on his own account from 1658 to 1689. He was the medium through which the Amsterdam methods of printing were transferred to Zolkiev between 1692 and 1695. His productions, though in the Amsterdam style, were generally of a less costly and elegant nature, and he appears to have printed prayer-books, Maḥzors, calendars, and Judæo-German works for the popular market. Just as Uri Phoebus worked for the German Jews, so Athias contemporaneously published ritual works for the Spanish Jews, who demanded

uprisings in 1648–56 were employed by Christian printers of that city, as Albertus Magnus, Christoph von Ganghel, the Steen brothers, and Bostius, the last-named of whom produced the great Mishnah of Surenhusius (1698–1703). A most curious phenomenon is presented by Moses ben Abraham, a Christian of Nikolsburg, who was converted to Judaism, and who printed several works between 1690 and 1694. Abraham, the son of another proselyte named Jacob, was an engraver who helped to decorate the Passover Haggadah of 1695, printed by Kosman Emrich, who produced several important works between 1692 and 1714.

FROM A PASSOVER HAGGADAH, AMSTERDAM, 1695.

usually a much higher grade of printing, paper, and binding than did their poorer German coreligionists (1660–83). Athias' editions of the Bible, and especially of the Pentateuch, for which he had Leusden's help, are especially fine; and the edition of Maimonides' " Yad " which his son and successor, Immanuel, published in 1703, is a noteworthy piece of printing. A third member of the Athias family printed in Amsterdam as late as 1739–40.

The Sephardic community of Amsterdam had also the services of Abraham de Castro Tartas (1663–95), who had learned his business under the Ben Israels. He printed, chiefly, works in Spanish and Portuguese, and in the decoration of his titles was fond of using scenes from the life of David. A number of Poles who fled to Amsterdam from the Cossack

Less important presses at the beginning of this period were erected in Amsterdam by Moses Coutinho, Isaac de Cordova, Moses Dias, and the firm of Soto & Brando. Members of the Maarssen family are also to be reckoned among the more productive Hebrew printers of Amsterdam. Jacob, Joseph, David, and Mahrim Maarssen produced many works between 1695 and 1740, among them reproductions of cursive writing. The last-named settled later at Frankfort-on-the-Main.

The Proopses. By this time the Hebrew press at Amsterdam had become entirely dominated by mercantile considerations, and was represented by the publishing- and printing-houses of Solomon ben Joseph Proops, whose printed catalogue " Appiryon Shelomoh," 1730

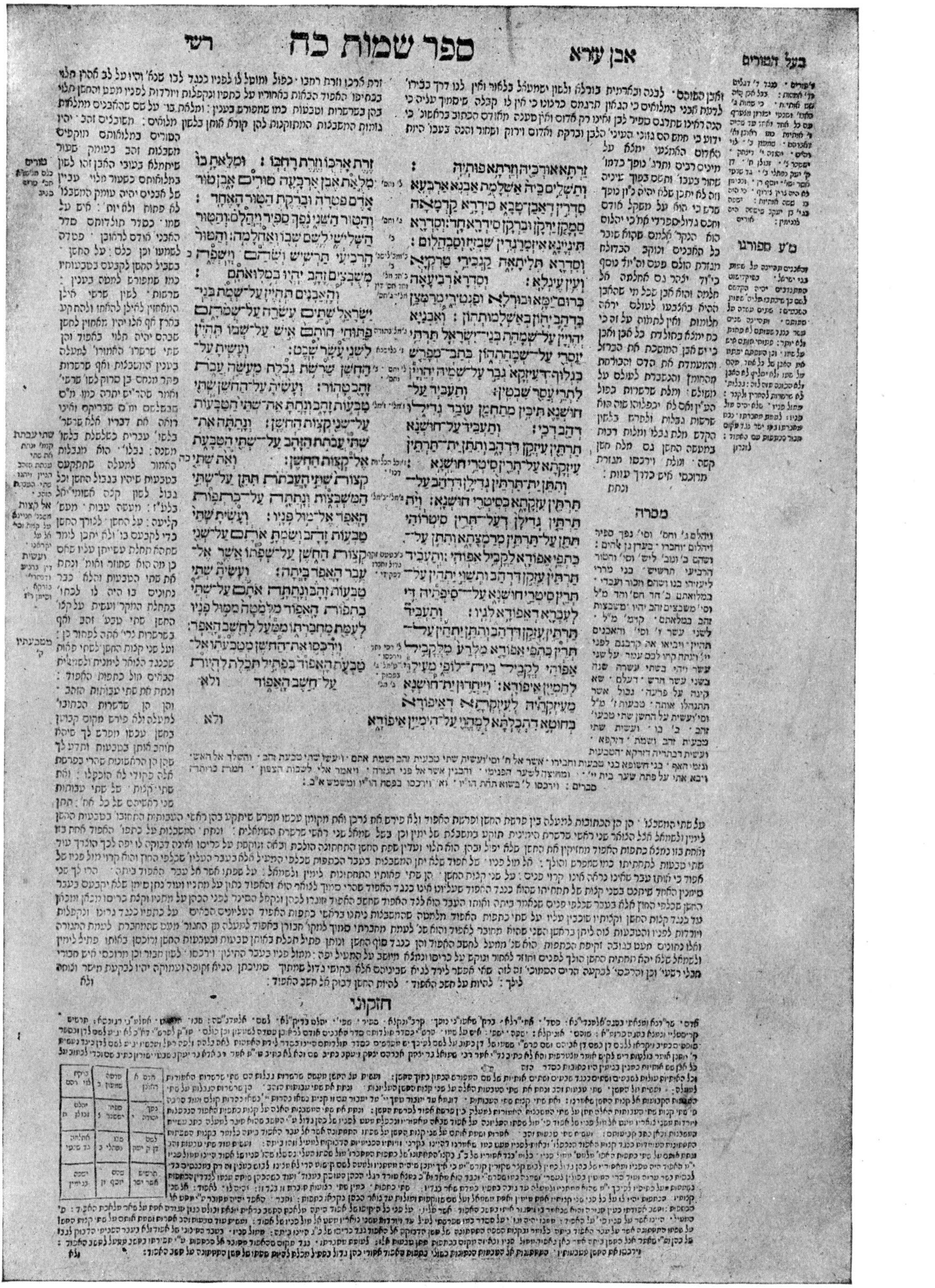

ספר שמות כח

רשי · אבן עזרא · בעל הטורים

זרת ארכו וזרת רחבו: ומלאת בו מלאת אבן ארבעה טורים אבן טור אדם פטדה וברקת הטור האחד: והטור השני נפך ספיר ויהלם: והטור השלישי לשם שבו ואחלמה: והטור הרביעי תרשיש ושהם וישפה משבצים זהב יהיו במלואתם: והאבנים תהיין על שמת בני ישראל שתים עשרה על שמתם פתוחי חותם איש על שמו תהיין לשני עשר שבט: ועשית על החשן שרשת גבלת מעשה עבת זהב טהור: ועשית על החשן שתי טבעות זהב ונתת את שתי הטבעות על שני קצות החשן: ונתתה את שתי עבתת הזהב על שתי הטבעת אל קצות החשן: ואת שתי קצות שתי העבתת תתן על שתי המשבצות ונתתה על כתפות האפד אל מול פניו: ועשית שתי טבעות זהב ושמת אתם על שני קצות החשן על שפתו אשר אל עבר האפד ביתה: ועשית שתי טבעות זהב ונתתה אתם על שתי כתפות האפוד מלמטה ממול פניו לעמת מחברתו ממעל לחשב האפד: וירכסו את החשן מטבעתו אל טבעת האפוד בפתיל תכלת להיות על חשב האפוד ולא

זרתא אורכיה וזרתא פותיה: ותשלים ביה אשלמות אבנא ארבעא סדרין דאבן טבא סדרא קדמאה סמקן ירקן וברקן סדרא חד: וסדרא תנינא איזמרגדין שבזיז וסבהלום: וסדרא תליתאה קנכירי טרקיא ועין עגלא: וסדרא רביעאה כרום ימא ובורלא ופנתירי מרמצן בדהב יהון באשלמותהון: ואבניא יהויין על שמהת בני ישראל תרתי עסרי על שמהתהון כתב מפרש כגלוף דעיזקא גבר על שמיה יהוין לתרי עסר שבטין: ותעביד על חושנא תיכין מתחמן עובד גדילו דהב דכי: ותעביד על חושנא תרתין עיזקן דדהב ותתן ית תרתין עיזקתא על תרין סיטרי חושנא: ותתן ית תרתין גדילן דדהב על תרתין עזקתא בסיטרי חושנא: וית תרתין גדילן דעל תרין סיטרוהי תתן על תרתין מרמצתא ותתן על כתפי אפודא לקביל אפוהי: ותעביד תרתין עזקן דדהב ותשוי יתהין על תרין סיטרי חושנא על ספיה די לעברא דאפודא לגיו: ותעביד תרתין עזקן דדהב ותתן יתהין על תרין כתפי אפודא מלרע מלקביל אפוהי לקביל בית לופי מעילוי להמיין אפודא: ויחדון ית חושנא מעזקתיה לעיזקתא דאפודא בחוטא דתכלתא למהוי על המיין אפודא

מ״ע ספורנו

מסרה

חזקוני

Page from the "Miḳra'ot Gedolot," Amsterdam, 1724.

(the first known of its kind), shows works published by him to be mainly rituals and a few responsa, two editions of the "'En Ya'aḳob," the "Ḥobot ha-Lebabot," and the "Menorat ha-Ma'or," two editions of the Zohar (1715), and the Judæo-German "Ma'asehbuch." Proops was evidently adapting himself to the popular taste from 1697 onward. The house established by him continued to exist down to the middle of the nineteenth century, Joseph and Jacob and Abraham being members thereof from 1734 until about 1780. They were followed by Solomon ben Abraham Proops in 1799, while a David ben Jacob Proops, the last of the family, died in 1849, and his widow sold the business to I. Levisson.

Mention should be made here of the two Ashkenazic Dayyanim of Amsterdam, who added printing to their juridical accomplishments, Joseph Dayyan from 1719 to 1737, and Moses Frankfurter from 1720 to 1743; the latter produced between the years 1724 and 1728 the best-known edition of the rabbinic Bible. The only other Amsterdam printer whom it is necessary to mention is Solomon London (c. 1721), on account of his later connection with Frankfort-on-the-Main.

Resuming the history of the **Prague** press during

two works there in poor style in 1691. He was followed in 1712 by Israel ben Meïr of Prague, who sold out to Hirsch ben Ḥayyim of Fürth. Among the 150 productions of these presses may be mentioned a list of post-offices, markets, and fairs compiled by the printer Hirsch ben Ḥayyim and printed in 1724.

In Prague itself the Baks found a serious competitor in Moses Cohen Ẓedeḳ, founder of the Katz family of typographers; this competition lasted for nearly a century, the two houses combining in 1784 as the firm of Bak & Katz.

Cracow during this period is distinguished by the new press of Menaḥem (Nahum) Meisels, which continued for about forty years from 1631 onward, producing a considerable number of Talmudic and cabalistic works, including such productions of the local rabbis, as the "Ḥiddushe Agadot" of Samuel Edels; this was put up in type by Judah Cohen of Prague, and corrected by Isaac of Brisk. The year 1648, so fatal to the Jews of Slavonic lands, was epoch-making for both Cracow and Lublin. At the latter place a few works appeared from 1665 onward, mainly from the press of Samuel Kalmanka (1673-83) of the Jaffe family.

FROM BACHARACH'S "ḤAWWOT YAÏR," FRANKFORT-ON-THE-MAIN, 1699.

this period, the Bak family continued its activity, especially in printing a number of Judæo-German works, mostly without supplying the place or the date of publication. Many local folk-songs in German now exist only in these productions. One of the productions of this firm, a Maḥzor, the first

From a Pentateuch, Amsterdam, 1726.

volume of which appeared in Prague in 1679, was finished in **Wekelsdorf** by the production of the second volume in 1680.

Another offshoot of the Prague press was that of **Wilhermsdorf**, which was founded in 1669 in order to take advantage of the paper-mills erected there by Count von Hohenlohe. The first printer there was Isaac Cohen, one of the Gersonides who printed

This period is especially distinguished by the rise of the Jewish Hebrew press in Germany, chiefly in five centers: (1) Frankfort-on-the-Main, (2) Sulzbach, (3) Dessau, (4) Hamburg, and (5) Dyhernfurth. For various reasons presses were erected also in the vicinity of each of these centers.

Germany. In **Frankfort-on-the-Main** the municipal law prohibited any Jew from erecting a printing-press, so that, notwithstanding its large and wealthy Jewish population, the earliest Hebrew productions of this city came from Christian printers, especially Christian Wüst, who produced a Bible in 1677, and an edition of the "Ḥawwot Yaïr" in 1699. Then came the press of Blasius Ilsner, who began printing Hebrew in 1682, and produced the "Kuhbuch" of Moses Wallich in 1687, in which year he produced also part of a German Pentateuch as well as a standard edition of the Yalḳuṭ. This last was published by the bookseller Seligmann Reis. Besides other Christian printers like Andreas and Nicholas Weinmann, Johann Koelner produced a number of Hebrew works during the twenty years 1708-27, including the continuation of an edition of the Talmud begun at Amsterdam and finished at Frankfort-on-the-Main (1720-23); it is probable that the type was brought from Amsterdam. An attempt of Koelner to produce 1,700 copies of an Alfasi by means of a lottery failed, though an edition was produced in Amsterdam four years later. Many of the typesetters of Amsterdam and Frankfort about this period frequently alternated their residence and activity between the two cities. In 1727 few Hebrew books were produced at Frankfort-on-the-Main. In connection with the Frankfort book market a number of presses in the neighborhood turned out Hebrew books, in **Hanau** as early as 1674. The book entitled "Tam we-Yashar" was printed there, with Frankfort as its place of publication. From 1708 onward Bashuysen produced a series of books, including Abravanel on the Pentateuch (1710), which was issued by Reis of Frankfort. Among his workmen were David Baer of Zolkiev, who had worked at Amsterdam, and Menahem Maneli of Wilmersdorf. Bashuysen sold his rights to Bousang (1713), who continued producing Hebrew works till 1725.

Homburg was also one of the feeding-presses for Frankfort, from 1711 to 1750. Its press was pos-

these first productions till the "Kabbala Denudata" was finished in 1684, when Knorr determined to have an edition of the Zohar printed at Sulzbach, and for that purpose had one Moses Bloch cut Hebrew letters, with which the Zohar was printed in a rather elementary fashion. This attracted attention to Sulzbach as a printing-place; and an imperfect edition of the Talmud was printed in 1694 by Bloch and his son (the latter succeeded Bloch). The competition of the Amsterdam edition of 1697–99 prevented its completion. One of the most curious productions of the Sulzbach press was a Purim parody, which was issued anonymously in 1695. Bloch was followed by Aaron Frankel, son of one of the exiles of Vienna, and founder of the Frankel-Arnstein family, having worked at the office of Bloch as early as 1685. He set up his press in 1699, his first production being a Maḥzor and part of the Talmud; and his son Meshullam carried on the press for forty years from 1724 to 1767. One hundred and fourteen productions of the Sulzbach press have been enumerated up to 1732.

Fürth also commenced in this period its remarka-

FROM A "SHE'ELOT U-TESHUBOT" OF EYBESCHÜTZ, CARLSRUHE, 1773.

sessed from 1737 on by Aaron of Dessau, an inhabitant of the Frankfort Judengasse, who produced among other works two editions of the "Ḥiddushim" of Maharam Schiff (1745). Seligmann Reis, who had learned printing in Amsterdam, started another press in **Offenbach** (1714–20), mostly for Judæo-German pamphlets, including a few romances like the "Artus Hoof," "Floris and Blanchefleur," and "The Seven Wise Masters." In opposition to Reis was Israel Moses, working under the Christian printer De Launoy from 1719 to 1724 and for himself till as late as 1743.

The history of the **Sulzbach** Hebrew press is somewhat remarkable. On May 12, 1664, one Abraham Lichtenthaler received permission to found a printing-press at Sulzbach. He began to print in 1667 Knorr von Rosenroth's "Kabbala De-

Sulzbach. nudata," a work which was for the Christian world the chief source of information as to the Cabala. This appears to have attracted to Sulzbach Isaac Cohen Gersonides, who produced in the year 1669 a couple of Judæo-German works, "Leb Ṭob" and "Shebeṭ Yehudah," from the press of Lichtenthaler. Nothing followed

ble activity as a producer of Hebrew works, more distinguished perhaps for quantity than quality. Beginning in 1691 just as the Wilmersdorf press gave up, Joseph Shneior established a press at Fürth, which produced about thirty works during the next

Fürth and eight years. Most of his typesetters **Hamburg.** had come from Prague. An opposition press was set up later (1694, 1699) by Ẓebi Hirsch ha-Levi and his son-in-law Mordecai Model. This was one of the presses which had as a typesetter a woman, Reichel, daughter of Isaac Jutels of Wilmersdorf. The former press was continued in 1712 by Samuel Bonfed, son of Joseph Shneior, together with Abraham Bing (1722–24); the firm lasted till 1730.

Similar presses were founded at **Dessau** by Moses Bonem (1696), and at **Köthen** in 1707–18 by Israel ben Abraham, the proselyte, who had previously worked at Amsterdam, Offenbach, and Neuwied. Israel then transferred his press to **Jessnitz,** where he worked till about 1726, at which date he removed it to **Wandsbeck,** near Hamburg, staying there till 1733, when he wandered to **Neuwied** and back to Jessnitz (1739–44) together with his sons Abraham and Tobias. Another proselyte, Moses ben Abraham, had printed Hebrew in **Halle** (1709–14).

The earliest production of the Hebrew press of **Hamburg** was a remarkable edition of a Hebrew Bible, set up by a Christian, Elias Hutter, and having the servile letters distinguished by hollow type, so as to bring out more clearly the radical letters. Hutter was followed by two Christians: (1) George Ravelin, who printed a Pentateuch with Targum and Haftarot in 1663; and (2) Thomas Rose, who from 1686 to 1715 printed several Jewish books and who was succeeded by his son Johann Rose up to 1721. In the neighboring city of **Altona** Samuel Poppart of Coblenz started printing in 1720, mainly ritual matters; and he was followed by Ephraim Heksher in 1732 and Aaron Cohen of Berlin in 1735.

Finally more to the east Shabbethai Bass established at **Dyhernfurth** in 1689 a printing-press especially devoted to meeting the wants of the Breslau book market, which had hitherto been dependent upon Amsterdam or Prague. For the varying history of his press, which lasted till 1713, see his biography (JEW. ENCYC. ii. 583). It was sold by Shabbethai's son Joseph to his son-in-law Issachar Cohen for 5,000 thalers, who carried it on till 1729, when he died, his wife then continuing the business.

Dyhern-
furth.

Hebrew works were early printed at **Frankfort-on-the-Oder**, by two Christians, Hartmann Brothers, from 1595 to 1596, who produced Bibles, and Eichhorn, who printed the "Musar Haskel" of Hai Gaon in 1597. Their work was continued in the next century by Professor Beckmann in 1681, and Michael Gottschek, who produced, at the cost of Baermann Halberstade, an edition of the Babylonian Talmud in 1698 to supply the loss of the Talmuds during the Cossack outbreaks. A second edition of this Talmud was produced by Gottschek in company with Jablonski at Berlin, who had purchased a Hebrew set of types in 1697. They began work in 1699, and produced a Pentateuch with a Rashbam in 1705, and the aforesaid Talmud in 1715–21. One of his chief typesetters was Baruch Buchbinder, who afterward printed in Prausnitz. Other Hebrew books were produced by Nathan Neumark (1720–26), in whose employ Aaron Cohen, afterward at Altona, learned to set type.

In this period a beginning of Hebrew typography was made also in the British Isles, by Samuel Clarke at OXFORD about 1667, and by Thomas Ilive (1714–1718) in LONDON, both Christian printers.

To return to the south of Europe: the **Venice** press was carried on by a succession of the Bragadinis:

Aloisio II. (1625–28), Geralamo (1655–64), and Aloisio III. (1697–1710). Among the Jewish setters or correctors for the press employed by the Bragadinis may be mentioned Leo de Modena, Moses Zacuto, Menahem Ḥabib, Moses Ḥayyim of Jerusalem, and Solomon Altaras. The chief competitor of the Bragadinis was Vendramini, from 1631 onward; but the opposition of Amsterdam reduced the activity of the Venetian press toward the end of the seventeenth century, while **Leghorn** began to cater to the printing of the Oriental Jews about 1650, when Jedidiah Gabbai produced the "azharot" of Solomon ibn Gabirol. His chief production was a Yalḳuṭ in 1660, after which he removed to **Florence** and finally settled in Smyrna, where his son Abraham printed from 1659 to 1680 with the aid of Samuel Valenci from Venice. Abraham's productions include a few Ladino works in Hebrew characters, among the earliest of the kind. In Constantinople a family of printers named Franco—Solomon (1639), Abraham (1641–83), and Abraham (1709–20)—produced a number of casuistic works. Among their typesetters was Solomon of Zatanof (1648), who had escaped the Cossack outbreaks. The pause from 1683 to 1710 was broken by two Poles from Amsterdam, Jonah of Lemberg and Naphtali of Wilna. Jonah of Lemberg printed a few of his works at **Ortakeui,** near Constantinople, and finally settled at Smyrna.

With the year 1732 the detailed history of Hebrew typography must cease. It would be impossible to follow in minute detail the spread of Hebrew presses throughout the world during the last 160 years. The date 1732 is also epoch-making in the history of Hebrew bibliography, as up to that date the great work of Johann Christoph WOLF, amplified and

From "Sefer Ḥoḳmat ha-Mishkan," Leghorn, 1772.

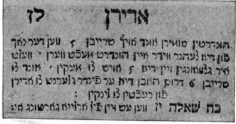

From Moses Eidlitz's "Meleket ha-Ḥeshbon," Prague, 1775.

corrected by Steinschneider in his "Bodleian Catalogue," gives a complete account of the personnel of the Hebrew press, both Jewish and Christian. The list of these printers given by Steinschneider is of

(ק׳ קַבֵּל בְּרַחֲמִים וּבְרָצוֹן אֶת תְּפִלָּתֵנוּ :)

תִּתְקַבֵּל צְלוֹתְהוֹן וּבָעוּתְהוֹן דְּכָל יִשְׂרָאֵל קֳדָם אֲבוּהוֹן
דִּי בִשְׁמַיָּא וְאִמְרוּ אָמֵן : יְהִי שֵׁם יְיָ מְבֹרָךְ מֵעַתָּה וְעַד עוֹלָם :
יְהֵא שְׁלָמָא רַבָּא מִן־שְׁמַיָּא וְחַיִּים עָלֵינוּ וְעַל־כָּל־
יִשְׂרָאֵל וְאִמְרוּ אָמֵן : ק׳ עֶזְרִי מֵעִם יְיָ עֹשֵׂה שָׁמַיִם וָאָרֶץ :
עֹשֶׂה שָׁלוֹם בִּמְרוֹמָיו הוּא יַעֲשֶׂה שָׁלוֹם עָלֵינוּ וְעַל כָּל יִשְׂרָאֵל

FROM "SIDDUR HEGYON LEB," KÖNIGSBERG, 1845.

חַלְּצֵנִי יְיָ מֵאָדָם רָע מֵאִישׁ חֲמָסִים תִּנְצְרֵנִי : אֲשֶׁר חָשְׁבוּ רָעוֹת בְּלֵב | כָּל־יוֹם
יָגוּרוּ מִלְחָמוֹת : שָׁנְנוּ לְשׁוֹנָם כְּמוֹ נָחָשׁ | חֲמַת עַכְשׁוּב תַּחַת שְׂפָתֵימוֹ
סֶלָה : שָׁמְרֵנִי יְיָ מִידֵי רָשָׁע | מֵאִישׁ חֲמָסִים תִּנְצְרֵנִי | וַאֲשֶׁר חָשְׁבוּ לִדְחוֹת
פְּעָמָי : טָמְנוּ גֵאִים פַּח לִי וַחֲבָלִים פָּרְשׂוּ רֶשֶׁת לְיַד מַעְגָּל | מֹקְשִׁים שָׁתוּ לִי
סֶלָה : אָמַרְתִּי לַיְיָ אֵלִי אָתָּה | הַאֲזִינָה יְיָ קוֹל תַּחֲנוּנָי : יְיָ אֲדֹנָי עֹז
יְשׁוּעָתִי וְסַכֹּתָה לְרֹאשִׁי בְּיוֹם נָשֶׁק : אַל־תִּתֵּן יְיָ מַאֲוַיֵּי רָשָׁע | זְמָמוֹ אַל־תָּפֵק
יָרוּמוּ סֶלָה : רֹאשׁ מְסִבָּי | עֲמַל שְׂפָתֵימוֹ יְכַסֵּימוֹ : יִמּוֹטוּ עֲלֵיהֶם גֶּחָלִים בָּאֵשׁ

FROM A KARAITE "SIDDUR," VIENNA, 1851.

FROM PENTATEUCH, VIENNA, 1859.

considerable importance, both for identifying unknown or imperfect works of the earlier period, and
as affording information of persons learned in
Hebrew lore who utilized it only as typesetters or
correctors for the press. Many, if not most, of the
more distinguished families of recent date have been
connected with these masters of printing, whose
names are thus of importance for pedigree purposes
(see PEDIGREE). For these reasons Steinschneider's
list is here reprinted in shortened form.

LIST OF PRINTERS TO 1732.

Name.	Place.	Date.
Aaron........................	Amsterdam....	1703, 6
Aaron b. Aaron Kohen..........	Amsterdam....	1697
Aaron b. Abraham..............	Hanau........	1722
Aaron da Costa Abendana b. Samuel.	Amsterdam....	1726, 30
Aaron (Hezekiah) Credo........	Amsterdam....	1726
Aaron b. (Hayyim) David Levi...	Zolkiev........	1716, 18, 21, 47
Aaron b. David Witmund.......	Amsterdam....	1659-64
Aaron b. Elijah Kohen of Hamburg.	Hamburg.....	1714-15, 32
	Offenbach.....	1716
	Sulzbach......	1717
	Frankfort - on - the-Oder.	1719
	Jessnitz......	1724
	Berlin........	1724-26
	Wandsbeck ...	1726
	Altona........	1735
Aaron (Shneor Zalman) b. Gabriel	Amsterdam....	1721
Aaron Hamon..................	Constantinople	1723
Aaron b. Isaac (Drucker) b. Aaron	Prossnitz......	1608-9, 10-12, 12-13, 13-19
Aaron b. Isaac Sofer...........	Amsterdam....	1713
Aaron b. Jacob Levi...........	Dyhernfurth..	1689
Aaron b. Jacob Senior..........	Amsterdam....	1659
Aaron Jaffe b. Israel	....	1702
Aaron Leon...................	Constantinople	1576-77
Aaron b. Manasseh Ephraim......	Amsterdam....	1661
Aaron b. Meïr................	Prague........	1705-13
Aaron b. Moses Krumenau......	Cracow	1608-9, 10-12, 17-18
Aaron Rodrigues-Mendes........	Amsterdam....	1728, 30
Aaron b. Selig of Glogau........	Berlin........	1709
	Dyhernfurth..	1713
	Berlin........	1717
	Amsterdam....	1726
Aaron b. Shabbethai...........	Amsterdam....	1723-24
Aaron b. Uri Lipmann..........	....	1700-17
Abba b. Solomon..............	Basel.........	1609
Abba-Mari of Vienna...........	Prague........	1623
Abbele b. Judah	Prague........	1706, 10
Abigdor b. Eliezer Ashkenazi	Constantinople	1547
Abigdor b. Eliezer Kohen.......	Prague........	1614
Abigdor b. (Israel) Joseph	Cracow	1638-40, 43, 48
Abigdor b. Samuel b. Moses Ezra.	Cracow	1619
Abraham......................	Amsterdam....	1708
Abraham b. Aaron	Prague........	1674 (?)
Abraham b. Abigdor	....	1530
Abraham Aboab, Sr............	Venice........	1590
Abraham Aboab, Jr............	Venice........	1655, 57, 59, 60, 69
Abraham b. Abraham	Adrianople (?)	
Abraham Abudiente............	Constantinople	1654
Abraham ibn Akra.............	Salonica......	1595
	Venice........	1599
Abraham b. Alexander..........	Venice........	1606
Abraham Algazi b. Simeon.......	Constantinople	1711
Abraham Algazi b. Solomon......	Smyrna.......	1659
Abraham Alkabiẓi	Constantinople	1516
Abraham Alḳaras..............	Damascus.....	1605-6
Abraham Altschul b. Jacob.......	Frankfort - on - the-Oder.	1697-99
Abraham Amnon b. Jacob Israel..	Leghorn	1653-54
Abraham Arama b. Isaac........	Salonica......	1520
Abraham ibn Ashkara Ẓarfati b. Samuel.	Pesaro........	1511
Abraham Bassa of Jerusalem....	Amsterdam....	1722
Abraham Benveniste b. Aaron....	Venice........	1546
Abraham b. Bezalel of Posen.....	Lublin........	1622-26, 30, 33-34, 45, 46
Abraham di Boton b. Aaron......	Smyrna	1600, 71, 74
Abraham (Hezekiah) Brandon ibn Yaḳḳar.	Amsterdam	(d. 1725)
Abraham Breit b. Moses.........	Amsterdam....	1650

Name.	Place.	Date.
Abraham Broda b. Elijah of Prague.	Sulzbach......	1715
	Wilmersdorf ..	1716
Abraham Cassel................	Strasburg	1521
Abraham ("Senior") Coronel....	Amsterdam....	1661, 67
Abraham Dandosa..............	Constantinople	1513
Abraham b. David Gojetein......	Cracow	1586, 93
	Prague........	1608
Abraham b. David Naḥman......	Salonica......	1709, 13, 24, 29
	Constantinople	1711
Abraham b. David Posner........	Wilmersdorf ..	1685
Abraham b. Dob (Baer) of Lissa..	Amsterdam....	1701
Abraham Dorheim b. Moses Dorheim.	Frankfort - on - the-Main.	1719
Abraham b. Eliezer Braunschweig	Hanau........	1610, 17
	Basel	1618-19
Abraham b. Eliezer Kohen.......	Cracow	1589
Abraham b. Eliezer Kohen.......	Wilmersdorf ..	1685-90, 1712-23
	Sulzbach......	1691-1712
Abraham b. Eliezer Rödelsheim..	Cracow	1600
Abraham ibn Ezra	Salonica......	1721
Abraham Facon (?).............	Naples........	1492
Abraham Faraji b. Meïr.........	Salonica......	1593-94
Abraham de Fonseca...........	Amsterdam....	1627
Abraham ben (ibn) Garton b. Isaac.	Reggio........	1475
Abraham Gedaliah..............	Leghorn	1650-57
Abraham Ger..................	Salonica......	1651-55
Abraham Ḥaber-Ṭob b. Solomon..	Venice........	1595, 99, 1614, 17-19, 24, 32-34, 37, 40, 42, 43
	Leghorn	1650-57
Abraham Ḥavez................	Amsterdam....	1724
Abraham b. Ḥayyim............	Pesaro........	1477
	Ferrara.......	1479
	Bologna.......	1482
	Soncino	1488
Abraham Ḥayyim of Fano........	Ferrara.......	1693
Abraham Ḥayyon b. Solomon b. Abraham.	Constantinople	1578-79
Abraham Hurwitz b. Isaiah......	Amsterdam....	1728, 29
Abraham Hurwitz b. Judah (Löb) Deborles Levi.		
Abraham b. Isaac Ashkenazi.....	Safed	1577-79, 87
Abraham b. Isaac b. David......	Ixar..........	1490
Abraham b. Israel.............	Cracow	1617, 18
Abraham b. Israel Menahem	Lublin	1578
	Offenbach.....	1729
Abraham b. Israel b. Moses.......	Neuwied	1735-37
	Jessnitz.......	1739-40
Abraham b. Issachar Kohen (Kaz) Gersoni of Prague.	Wilmersdorf ..	1679, 82
	Sulzbach......	1684
	Prague........	1686, 88, 90-93
Abraham b. Jacob..............	Hanau........	1726
Abraham b. Jacob Levi..........	Amsterdam....	1726, 30
Abraham (Israel) b. Jacob (Koppel) of Vienna.	Frankfort - on - the-Oder.	1705, 9, 11-12
Abraham Jedidiah de Cologna.		
Abraham b. Jekuthiel..........	Hanau........	1715, 47
Abraham b. Jekuthiel Kohen.....	Hanau........	1611-14, 23-30
Abraham b. Joseph.............	Lublin	1571-72
Abraham b. Joseph.............	Hamburg	1690
Abraham b. Joseph Manasseh...	Constantinople	1732
Abraham b. Joshua Sezze........	Venice	1696
Abraham b. Joshua of Worms....	Amsterdam....	1643-48, 45-46
Abraham b. Judah	Frankfort - on - the-Oder.	1697-99
Abraham b. Judah (Loeb)........	Constantinople	1710, 12, 16-20, 26-27, 37
Abraham b. Judah b. Nisan.		
Abraham b. Kalonymus Reumold.	Prague........	1614, 17-19, 21-24, 25
Abraham Ḳara.................	Salonica......	1587
	Venice........	1589
	Mantua	1589-90
Abraham Landau b. Jacob	Naples	1491-92
Abraham Laniado..............	Venice........	1603
Abraham (Kohen) de Lara........	Amsterdam....	1691
Abraham Lichtenthaler	Sulzbach......	1697
Abraham Luria................	Jessnitz.......	1723
Abraham Mendes-Lindo	Amsterdam....	1725
Abraham b. Meshullam of Modena.	Mantua	1558-60
Abraham Molko b. Joseph........	Salonica......	1709
Abraham b. Mordecai Kohen.....	Amsterdam....	1661
Abraham b. Moses (Schedel)....	Prague........	1602-4
Abraham b. Moses Goslar.......	Wandsbeck ...	1733
Abraham b. Moses Kohen........	Bologna.......	1538
Abraham b. Moses Nathan.......	Amsterdam....	1700

Name.	Place.	Date.
Abraham b. Naḥman Kohen	Lublin	1635
Abraham b. Nathan	Amsterdam	1652
Abraham ibn Nathan b. Ḥayyim of Salonica.	Constantinople	1716, 17, 18, 19
Abraham Netto b. Joseph	Venice	1622
Abraham (Ḥai) Ortona b. David.	Verona	1652
Abraham ibn Paredes	Constantinople	1522
Abraham Pereira b. Elijah	Constantinople	1642–43
Abraham Perls	Amsterdam	1678
Abraham Pescarol b. Kalonymus.	Venice, Cremona.	1544, 65
Abraham ibn Phorni	Venice	1565
Abraham Porto	Venice	1563, 64, 65, 66, 74, 84, 88, 89
Abraham Porto b. Jehiel	Verona	1594
Abraham b. Reuben Abi Saglo	Venice	1606
Abraham Reyna	Constantinople	1560
Abraham Rosanes b. Meïr	Constantinople	1711, 19–20
Abraham Sacchi	Venice	1586
Abraham b. Solomon Levi	Hamburg	1706–7
Abraham b. Samuel b. David Levi.		1692
Abraham b. Samuel Kohen	Constantinople	1561
Abraham b. Selig of Glogau	Berlin	1711–12
	Offenbach	1721
	Wilmersdorf	1726
	Dyhernfurth	1726
	Wandsbeck	1733
	Homburg	1738–41
Abraham Selzer b. Aaron of Minsk	Frankfort-on-the-Oder.	1702
Abraham b. Shalom	Prague	1608
Abraham Shalom b. Isaac	Salonica	1717
Abraham ibn Shangi b. Ephraim.	Constantinople	1534
Abraham b. Shemariah	Constantinople	1539–40
Abraham Shoshan	Constantinople	
Abraham de Silva b. Solomon	Venice	1672, 78, 1728
	Amsterdam	1728
Abraham b. Simeon Friedburg	Prague	1713
Abraham b. Simeon Kolin	Prague	1697
Abraham Sonina	Constantinople	1717
Abraham Talmid Sefardi	Naples	1492
Abraham Uzziel b. Baruch	Venice	1655–56
Abraham von Werd	Fürth	1699
Abraham ibn Ya'ish b. Joseph	Constantinople	1505, 9
	Salonica	1520
Abraham ibn Yaḳḳar b. Jacob Hananiah.	Venice	1718
Abraham Yerushalmi (b. Yom-Ṭob ?)	Constantinople	1512
Abraham Ẓalaḥ b. Shabbethai	Venice	1599–1606
Abraham Ẓarfati	Amsterdam	1626–27
Abraham b. Ẓebi	Lublin	1637
Abraham b. Ẓebi	Verona	1649 (?)
Abraham (Ḥayyim) b. Ẓebi (Hirsch)	Amsterdam	1725–32
Abraham b. Ẓebi of Cracow	Amsterdam	1641, 43
	Cracow	1663
Abraham b. Ẓebi (Hirsch) Kohen	Frankfort-on-the-Oder.	1697–99
Abraham b. Zeeb (Wolf) Levi	Amsterdam	1688, 1706
Adelkind (Brothers)	Venice	1519, 21, 22, 22, 24
Adelkind (Cornelius b. Baruch)	Venice	1524, 24–25, 27, 28–29, 44, 45, 45, 46, 46–48, 48–49, 50–52, 52
	Sabbionetta	1553–54
Adelkind (Daniel b. Cornelio)	Venice	1549–52
Akiba b. Uri (Phoebus)	Berlin	1713
Alexander b. Ezekiel	Prague	1618–20
Alexander b. Ḥayyim Ashkenazi.	Prague	1616–17
Alexander (Süsskind) b. Kalonymus.	Amsterdam	1700, 2, 4
Alexander (Sender) b. Meïr Kassewitz.	Prague	1718–19
Antunes (Antones ?), Aaron	Amsterdam	1717–21 (25?)
Aryeh (Loeb) b. Gershon Wiener.	Frankfort-on-the-Oder.	1727
Aryeh (Judah Loeb) Krochmal b. Menahem.		
Aryeh (Judah) Sabibi b. David.		
Aryeh (Loeb) b. Saul b. Joshua	Amsterdam	1711
Aryeh Sofer b. Ḥayyim	Berlin	1706
Aryeh b. Solomon Ḥayyim	Bologna	1537–40
Aryeh (Loeb) b. Solomon Kohen	Zolkiev	1709
Aryeh (Judah Loeb) Te'omim b. Aaron.	Frankfort-on-the-Main (?).	1710
Aryeh (Loeb) b. Zeeb (Wolf) Levi.	Amsterdam	1686, 99
Asher (Anschel)		1700

Name.	Place.	Date.
Asher (Anschel) Altschüler b. Naphtali Herzel.	Prossnitz	1603
	Prague	1604, 11–17, 18, 20–21, 22–23
Asher (Anschel) b. Eliezer	Amsterdam	1663–85, 86, 1692–1703, 5, 13
Asher (Anschel) b. Elijah	Amsterdam	1698
Asher (Anschel) b. Gershon Kohen	Prague	1609–10
Asher (Selig) Hurwitz b. Isaac Levi.	Lublin	1624
Asher (Selig) b. Isaac of Dubno.	Sulzbach	1702
Asher (Selig) b. Isaac Kohen	Berlin	1703
Asher (Anschel) b. Meïr Prostitz.	Amsterdam	1708
Asher Minz b. Perez	Naples	1491
Asher (Anschel) b. Moses	Cracow	1643
Asher Parentio (Parenz) b. Jacob.	Venice	1579–95
Asher Tiktin b. Menahem	Cracow	1598
Astruc de Toulon b. Jacob	Constantinople	1510–30
Athias, Abraham b. Raphael Hezekiah.	Amsterdam	1728–41
Athias, Immanuel b. Joseph	Amsterdam	1700–9
Athias, Joseph b. Abraham	Amsterdam	1658–85
Azariah	Bologna	1537–38
Azariah Talmid	Venice	1648
Azriel b. Joseph (b. Jacob Gunzenhäuser) Ashkenazi.	Naples	1491, 92
Azriel b. Moses	Hanau	1716
	Fürth	1726
Azriel b. Moses Schedel		1602–9, 13
Azriel Peraḥyah Kohen	Amsterdam	1703
Azriel ben Solomon Diena	Sabbionetta (?)	1550–51
Baer (b. Meshullam Zalman Mirls ?) of Posen.	Berlin	1716–17
Baerle Rappa	Frankfort-on-the-Main.	1713
Baermann b. Judah Lima Levi of Essen.		1697–99, 1721
Bak (Israel b. Joseph b. Judah).	Prague	1686, 89, 90, 91, 95
Bak (Jacob [II.] b. Judah)	Lublin	1648, 73–96
	Prague	1680
Bak (Joseph [I.] b. Jacob)	Prague	1623, 23–24, 24, 29, 57–60, 62
Bak (Joseph [II.] b. Judah)	Prague	1673–96, 79, 84, 86
Bak (Judah [I.] b. Jacob)	Prague	1620–60, 61–69
Bak (Judah [II.] b. Moses b. Jacob)	Prague	1705, 6, 8, 13–20
Bak (Moses [I.] b. Jacob b. Judah)	Prague	1686, 97, 1716
Bak (Moses ben Judah)	Prague	1697
Bak (Yom-Ṭob Lipman b. Moses b. Jacob).	Prague	1713–18, 25
	Fürth	1723–24
	Venice	1598, 99
Bak, Jacob (I.) b. Gershon Wahl.	Prague	1605, 7, 9, 12–15
Baruch	Pesaro	1517
Baruch Bloch b. Jacob	Cracow	1609
Baruch Buchbinder of Wilna	Berol	1708–9
	Prossnitz	1711
	Berlin	1712–15, 17
Baruch b. Eliezer Kohen	Venice	1579
Baruch of Frankfort-on-the-Oder.	Frankfort-on-the-Oder.	1705
Baruch b. Joseph b. Baruch	Leghorn	1657
Baruch of Korez	Cracow	1637
Baruch b. Lipmann Wiener	Amsterdam	1726–27
Baruch (Bendet) b. Nathan	Fürth	1727–38
	Sulzbach	1729
Baruch b. Simḥah Kalman	Venice	1583
Baruch b. Simḥah Levi	Amsterdam	1670, 74
Baruch b. Solomon	Lublin	1639
Baruch Uzziel	Ferrara	1551, 56
Baschwitz (Meïr b. Ẓebi Hirsch).	Jessnitz	1731–32
	Berlin	1736
Baschwitz (Ẓebi Hirsch b. Meïr).	Berlin	1701, 3, 9
	Frankfort-on-the-Oder.	1708
	Dyhernfurth	1719, 20
	Hanau (?)	1722
Bat-Sheba (Abraham Joseph)	Salonica	1592–1605
Bat-Sheba (Abraham b. Mattathiah).	Verona	1594
	Salonica	1605, 5–6
Bat-Sheba (Mattithiah)	Salonica	
Bella Hurwitz Levi	Prague.	
Benjamin (Benusch)	Lemberg (?)	1728
Benjamin (Wolf) b. Aaron Eliezer Worms of Durlach.	Frankfort-on-the-Main.	1712–16
Benjamin b. Aaron Polacco	Venice	1719, 21
	Mantua	1724, 27
	Venice	1728, 29, 30, 44, 53
Benjamin b. Abraham	Cracow	1638–39, 40

Name.	Place.	Date.
Benjamin (Samuel) b. Abraham..	Lublin........	1574–75, 76
Benjamin (Wolf) b. Abraham Kohen Hinfeld.	Wilmersdorf..	1677
Benjamin (Wolf) b. Asher (Anschel).	Amsterdam....	1692, 95–96, 97, 1703
Benjamin Diaz Patto b. Jacob....	Amsterdam....	1645
Benjamin (Zeeb Wolf) b. Elijah..	Frankfort-on-the-Oder.	1680, 97–99
Benjamin b. Elijah Levi..........	Offenbach.	
Benjamin Galmidi	Amsterdam....	1631–33
Benjamin (Kohen) Gersoni......	Prague........	1624
Benjamin (Shneor) Godinez......	Amsterdam....	1687–88
Benjamin (Zeeb Wolf) b. Jacob of Ofen.	Prague........	1689
Benjamin b. Jehiel (Michael) of Kalisz.	Amsterdam....	1702
Benjamin b. Jekuthiel............	Hanau........	1624
Benjamin di Jonak...............	Amsterdam....	1708–10
Benjamin b. Joseph d'Arignano..	Rome.........	1546
Benjamin b. Joseph of Berlin....	Berlin........	1711–12, 17
Benjamin (Wolf) b. Moses Dayyan Frankfurter.	Amsterdam....	1722, 23, 24, 26, 27, 30
Benjamin b. Moses b. Mattithiah b. Benjamin.	Venice........	1614
Benjamin b. Naphtali Moses......	Offenbach	1716
Benjamin (Saul) de Rubeis.......	Ferrara	1554
Benjamin b. Solomon Cantoris....	Lublin........	1624, 37
	Cracow	1646
Benjamin (Zeeb) b. Solomon Kohen of Zolkiev.	Berlin........	1712
Benjamin Wolf b. Joseph Isaac...	Amsterdam....	1725–29
Benjamin Wolf of Lemberg......	Prague........	1614
Benveniste, or Benbeniste (Immanuel).	Amsterdam....	1641–59
Benzion Zarfati (Gallus)........	Venice........	1606–7
Bezaleel b. Abraham............	Lublin........	1614
Bing (Abraham b. Isaac).........	Fürth........	1722–24
Bloch (Moses b. Uri Schraga)....	Sulzbach......	1684–93
Bonfed, Shneor b. Joseph b. Zalman Shneor.	Fürth	1722–24, 25–28, 29
Caleb Hazzan b. Joseph	Smyrna	1730
Caleb b. Judah Magia'...........	Constantinople	1726–37
Canpillas (Yom-Tob b. Moses)....	Constantinople	1711
	Salonica......	1713–24, 29
Castro- (Crasto-) Tartas (David b. Abraham).	Amsterdam....	1660–95
Castro-Tartas (Jacob b. Abraham).	Amsterdam....	1664–65, 69
Christfels, Phil. Ernest (Mordecai b. Moses of Illenfeld).	Wilmersdorf..	1713
Cividal Brothers................	Venice........	1675
Conat (Abraham b. Solomon).....	Mantua	1476
Conat (Estellina).		
Concio (Conzio?), Abraham b. Joseph.	Chieri........	1627–28
Cordova (Abraham b. Jacob).....	Amsterdam....	1700–5, 6, 8
Cordova (Isaac Hezekiah b. Jacob Hayyim).	Amsterdam:...	1688–1726
	Hamburg	1710–14
Cordova (Jacob Hayyim b. Moses Raphael).	Amsterdam....	1662–64, 64, 65, 66, 67–69, 75, 78, 81
	Wilmersdorf..	1683, 92–93, 98–99, 1701–3, 14
Cordova (Moses b. Isaac de)..,...	Amsterdam....	1641–42
Daniel Pereira b. Abraham.......	Amsterdam....	1729, 31
David b. Aaron Judah Levi of Pinsk.	Amsterdam....	1685
David Aboab b. Samuel..........	Venice........	1702
David b. Abraham (Azubib? Asovev?).	Salonica......	1578–86 (87?)
David Abravanel-Dormido........	Amsterdam....	1642
David Altaras b. Solomon........	Venice	1675–1718
David Bueno....................	Leghorn.	
David Bueno b. Raphael Hayyim.	Venice........	1704–5, 6, 7, 7–8, 16, 20–21, 32
David de Cazeres................	Amsterdam....	1661
David b. Elasah Levi............	....	1489
David b. Eliezer Levi of Darlipstadt	Amsterdam....	1723, 28, 30, 33
David b. Elijah (Casti)...........	Constantinople	1574, 75, 86
David b. Elijah b. David.........	Salonica......	1713–21, 29
David Fernandez (b. David)......	Amsterdam....	1715, 26
David Ginz b. Solomon..........	Offenbach	1717
David Grünhut.................		1712
David b. Hayyim Hazzan........	Smyrna	1729–41
David b. Isaac Kohen...........	Amsterdam....	1644
David b. Isaac of Ottensoss......	Fürth........	1727
David b. Issachar (Dob Baer of Zolkiev).	Zolkiev	1694, 96
	Berlin........	1699, 1701, 3, 12
	Amsterdam....	1700, 1, 5
	Hanau........	1710
	Zolkiev.......	1721
David Jonah Jonathan...........	Oels.........	1530
David Jonah Joseph Muskatels...	Prague........	1705–6

Name.	Place.	Date.
David Jonah b. Shabbethai Jonah.	Salonica.......	1653
David b. Judah (Loeb) of Cracow.	Lublin.	
David Kohen....................	Constantinople	1509
David de Lida b. Pethahiah b. David.	Frankfort-on-the-Main.	1727
David of Maarsen	Amsterdam....	1715
David Maza b. Aaron............	Mantua	1612
	Salonica.......	1614
David b. Menahem Kohen........	Hanau........	1626–28
David b. Moses of Rheindorf......	Frankfort-on-the-Main.	1692
David Nördlingen................	Cremona......	1565
David Nuñez-Torres	Amsterdam....	1697–99 1700–5
David Peppe b. Abraham.........	Venice........	1663
David Pizzighetton b. Eliezer Levi.	Venice........	1524
David Portaleone b. Moses........	Mantua	1623
David Portero...................	Pesaro	1511
David Provençal b. Abraham.....	Venice........	1565
David (Naphtali) di Rieti b. Hananiah.	Mantua.	
David de la Rocca...............	Venice........	1601–2
David b. Samuel Kohen..........	Amsterdam....	1726, 32
David b. Shemaiah Saugers.......	Frankfort-on-the-Main.	1700
David de Silva b. Hezekiah.......	Amsterdam....	1706, 26
David (Israel) del Soto...........	Amsterdam....	1642
David b. Uri (Phoebus)..........	Amsterdam....	1664, 66
	Zolkiev	1705–15 (?)
David Valensi...................	Leghorn	1650–57
David ibn Yahya b. Joseph.......	Constantinople	1509
David b. Yom-Tob Deuz.........	Amsterdam....	1649–53
Eleazar (Enoch) Altschul........	Prague........	1686, 1705–6
Eleazar b. David................	Cracow	1596
Eleazar b. Isaac Levi............	Frankfort-on-the-Oder.	1686
Eleazar b. Moses Kohen..........	Amsterdam....	1693
Eleazar b. Shabbethai Balgid.....	Venice........	1586–87
Eleazar Sussmann b. Isaac.......	Amsterdam....	1733
Elhanan (Jacob) Archevolti b. Samuel.	Venice........	1602
Elhanan b. Naphtali.............	Amsterdam....	1628
Eliakim (Goetz) b. Israel.........	Homburg	1724
Eliakim b. Jacob................	Amsterdam....	1685–1705
Eliakim (Goetz) b. Mordecai.		
Eliezer (Leser) b. Abraham	Jessnitz......	1724–26
Eliezer (ibn) Alantansi b. Abraham.	Ixar	1487–90
Eliezer b. Benjamin of Prossnitz.	Cracow	1591
	Prossnitz	1602
Eliezer of Braunschweig.........	Sabbionetta...	1567
Eliezer Darli...................	Salonica......	1522
Eliezer (Lasi) b. David Emrich...	Amsterdam....	1692
Eliezer (Leser) Floersheim.......	Frankfort-on-the-Main.	1707, 8, 9
Eliezer b. Hayyim...............	Prague........	1610
	Hanau........	1614, 15
Eliezer Hayyut b. Isaac..........	Frankfort-on-the-Oder.	1732
Eliezer b. Isaac Ashkenazi.......	Constantinople	1575–76, 86
	Safed	1577–79, 87
Eliezer b. Isaac Jacob of Lublin..	Lublin........	1646
Eliezer b. Isaac b. Naphtali......	Wilmersdorf..	1727
Eliezer b. Isaac of Prague.......	Lublin........	1556–73
Eliezer (Hayyim) b. Isaiah Nizza.	Venice........	1657
Eliezer (Leser) b. Israel Levi....	Amsterdam....	1726, 33
Eliezer d'Italia.................	Mantua	1612
Eliezer b. Jacob.................	Constantinople	1670–71
Eliezer b. Joseph of Lisk.........	Wilmersdorf..	1673–75, 77
	Frankfort-on-the-Oder.	1680–81
Eliezer b. Joshua Nehemiah......	Wandsbeck ...	1732
Eliezer Kohen..................	Cracow.......	1593–94
Eliezer Liebermann b. Alexander Bingen.	Hanau	1715
Eliezer Liebermann b. Yiftah Levi.	Amsterdam....	1710
Eliezer Lipmann b. Issachar Kohen Hannover.	Amsterdam....	1682
	Frankfort-on-the-Oder.	1683
Eliezer b. Meshullam............	Lublin	1567
	Prague........	1578
Eliezer b. Meshullam of Lublin...	Prague........	1601
Eliezer b. Mordecai Reckendorf..	Offenbach	1716
Eliezer Provençal b. Abraham b. David.	Mantua	1596
Eliezer b. Samuel...............	Soncino	1490
Eliezer (Leser) Shuk.............	Frankfort-on-the-Main.	1690–1700
Eliezer ibn Shoshan b. David.		
Eliezer Supino.................	Venice........	1718
Eliezer Todros.................	Salonica.......	1532–33
Eliezer Toledano...............	Lisbon	1489–92

Name.	Place.	Date.
Eliezer Treves b. Naphtali Hirz...	Zurich	1558
	Thiengen	1560
Eliezer Ẓarfati b. Elijah.		
Elijah Aboab	Amsterdam	1644-45
Elijah b. Abraham (Israel) b. Jacob Levi.	Frankfort-on-the-Oder.	1711-12
Elijah b. Azriel Wilna	Amsterdam	1690
	Frankfort-on-the-Main.	1704-18
	Homburg	1738
Elijah Belin b. Moses (Joseph)	Hamburg	1663
Elijah Galmidi	Constantinople	1574
Elijah (Menahem) Ḥalfan b. Abba Mari.	Venice	1551
Elijah b. Isaac Schleifer	Prague	1612
Elijah b. Joseph Frankfort	Verona	1649
Elijah b. Joseph of Samoscz	Amsterdam	1697
Elijah b. Judah Ulma	Hanau	1611-14
	Basel	1622
	Hanau	1623-30
Elijah (Judah de) Leon b. Michael.	Amsterdam	1659, 66
Elijah Levi b. Benjamin	Constantinople	1503, 9
Elijah Levita	Venice	1525, 29, 32, 38, 45, 46, 47, 48
Elijah b. Moses b. Abraham Abinu	Frankfort-on-the-Oder.	1704-8
Elijah Rabbah b. Menahem	Venice	1604-5
Elijah Ricco	Salonica	1529
Elijah b. Simeon Oettingen	Fürth	1692
Elijah Velosinos	Amsterdam	1664
Elijah Zünzburger b. Seligman (Selikmann) b. Moses Simeon Ulma.	Hanau	1615-17
Elijah Zur b. Samuel Ẓuri	Constantinople	1537
Elimelech b. David Melammed of Cracow.	Berlin	1705
Elishama Sifroni b. Israel	Mantua	1593
	Venice	1596, 1601
	Mantua	1612
Ella (bat Moses ben Abraham ?).	Frankfort-on-the-Oder.	1699-1700
Ella bat Ḥayyim	Lublin	1556
Enoch	Prague	1602
Enoch b. Issachar (Baermann) Levi.	Berlin	1709
	Frankfort-on-the-Oder.	1712
Ephraim Bueno (ben Joseph)	Amsterdam	1626-28, 30, 48, 50, 52, 61-64
Ephraim b. David Patavinus	Mantua	1589-90
Ephraim b. Isaac	Mantua	1563
Ephraim b. Jonah of Tarli	Frankfort-on-the-Main.	1681
Ephraim Kohen	Adrianople	1555
Ephraim Melli b. Mordecai	Mantua	1676
Ephraim b. Pesach of Miedzyboz.	Lublin (?)	1673
Ephraim (Zalman) b. Solomon Reinbach (Rheinbach ?) of Lissa.	Amsterdam	1699
Esther, widow of Elijah Ḥandali.	Constantinople	1566
Ezekiel b. Jacob.	Amsterdam	1695
Ezekiel (Moses) b. Jacob	Prague	1590
Ezekiel b. Moses Gabbai	Cracow	1587-88, 93-94
Ezra Alchadib b. Solomon	Venice	1608-9
Ezra b. Mordecai Kohen	Dyhernfurth	1712, 13, 15, 19, 20, 26
Foa (Nathaniel)	Amsterdam	1702-15
Foa (Tobia b. Eliezer)	Sabbionetta	1551-59
Fonseca (Daniel de)	Amsterdam	1627
Franco (Abraham b. Solomon)	Constantinople	1640-83
Franco (Solomon)	Constantinople	1638-40
Frosch, Christian, of Augsburg	Frankfort-on-the-Main.	1711
Fundam (Isaac)	Amsterdam	1723-24
Gabbai (Abraham b. Jedidiah)	Smyrna	1657-75
	Constantinople	1662
Gabbai (Isaac)	Venice	1597
Gabbai (Jedidiah b. Isaac)	Leghorn	1650-57
Gabriel Levi of Vratislavia	Frankfort-on-the-Oder.	1725
Gabriel Strassburg b. Aaron	Soncino	1484
Gad Conian b. Israel	Constantinople	1719, 20
Gamaliel b. Eliakim (Götz) of Lissa.	Hamburg	1687
Gedaliah (Don Judah)	Lisbon. Salonica	1515-35
Gedaliah Cordovero b. Moses	Venice	1587, 88
Gedaliah b. Solomon Lipschütz	Venice	1616
Gela (Gella)	Halle	1709-10
Gershon Ashkenazi	Cracow	1646-47
Gershon b. Ḥayyim David Levi	Zolkiev	1730
Gershon Ḥefez b. Kalonymus	Venice	1627
Gershon Poper (or Popper)	Prague	1610, 11

Name.	Place.	Date.
Gershon Wiener b. Naphtali Hirsch	Frankfort-on-the-Oder.	1690, 96, 98, 1700, 2, 3, 5, 7, 8, 14, 17, 21, 24
	Berlin	1702, 3, 9
Gumpel Kohen b. Jacob Hannover	Amsterdam	1712
Gumprich b. Abraham	Amsterdam	1717, 21, 25, 26, 27, 28
Gütel bat Judah Loeb b. Alexander Kohen.	Prague	1627
Haehndel (Elhanan) b. Ḥayyim Drucker.	Amsterdam	1711, 13
Halicz (Johannes)	Cracow	1538-39
Halicz (Paul)	Cracow	1540
Halicz (Samuel b. Ḥayyim)	Cracow	1534
Hananiah b. Eliezer ha-Shimeoni Sustin.	Constantinople	1513
Hananiah Finzi	Venice	1587
Hananiah b. Jacob Saul	Salonica	1719
Hananiah ibn Yaḳḳar	Constantinople	1573, 78
Hananiah Marun	Mantua	1623-24
Hananiah ibn Sikri (Saccari ?) b. Isaiah.	Amsterdam	1715
Ḥayyim b. Abraham	Constantinople	1719
Ḥayyim Alfandari	Constantinople	1717
	Ortakeui	1719
Ḥayyim Alscheich b. Moses	Venice	1601, 3, 5, 7
Ḥayyim Alton b. Moses	Venice	1522-23, 27
Ḥayyim Altschul b. Mordecai (Gumpel) of Prague.	Dessau	1696-99
	Dyhernfurth	1703
	Amsterdam	1708, 9, 10, 10-12, 17-18, 21, 23, 24, 26, 32
Ḥayyim Casino	Constantinople	1719
Ḥayyim Cesarini (Casirino) b. Shabbethai.	Constantinople	1519
Ḥayyim b. David Kohen	Constantinople	1537
	Venice	1546
Ḥayyim b. Ephraim (Gumprecht) of Dessau.	Berlin	1712, 17
	Köthen	1717
	Jessnitz	1719
	Berlin	1724 (?)
	Prague	1728(and 35)
	Sulzbach	1729
Ḥayyim (Jedidiah) ibn Ezra	Salonica	1721
Ḥayyim Gatigno b. Samuel	Cremona	1519
Ḥayyim b. Ḥayyim	Wilmersdorf	1713, 17, 19
Ḥayyim Ḥazzan b. David Ḥazzan	Constantinople	1717
Ḥayyim b. Isaac b. Ḥayyim	Lublin	1556-67
Ḥayyim b. Isaac Levi Ashkenazi.	Naples	1486
Ḥayyim b. Israel	Amsterdam	1709
Ḥayyim b. Issachar b. Israel	Prague	1623-24
Ḥayyim b. Jacob Drucker	Amsterdam	1680-1724
Ḥayyim b. Jacob of Hamelburg	Amsterdam	1670
Ḥayyim b. Jacob (Gel Jäkels) Kohen.	Prague	1603-4
Ḥayyim (Mordecai) b. Joseph		1477
Ḥayyim b. Joseph Kohen	Prague	1691, 1705-6
Ḥayyim b. Judah	Lublin	1648
	Prague	1657, 62-63, 75
Ḥayyim b. Judah (Loeb)	Prague	1689, 91, 94, 96, 97, 1705-6
Ḥayyim b. Judah (Loeb)	Amsterdam	1695
Ḥayyim b. Ḳatriel of Cracow	Prague	1686
	Dyhernfurth	1689, 90, 91, 93, 96, 99
	Berlin	1703-5, 9, 14, 17
	Frankfort-on-the-Oder.	1717
Ḥayyim Katschigi b. Jacob	Constantinople	1732
Ḥayyim Ḳimḥi b. Jacob	Constantinople	1714
Ḥayyim Lubliner	Amsterdam	1702
Ḥayyim (Shalom) Ma'ali Kohen b. Benjamin.	Constantinople	1719-20
Ḥayyim b. Moses Menahem (Man) Danziger Danzig.	Amsterdam	1725-26, 26, 39-40
Ḥayyim (Selig) b. Nathaniel		1697
Ḥayyim b. Samuel Ashkenazi	Constantinople	1561-62
Ḥayyim ibn Saruḳ	Venice	1566, 74
Ḥayyim b. Simḥah Ashkenazi Levi	Basel	1609
Ḥayyim b. Solomon Austerlitz	Prague	1601
Ḥayyim Ṭawil b. Moses	Constantinople	1715-18
Ḥayyim b. Ẓebi (Hirsch) Kohen of Kalisz.	Dyhernfurth	1709, 13, 15
	Hanau	1710
Ḥayyim b. Zeeb (Wolf) Levi	Amsterdam	1674-76, 85
Hene (Coelius) of Basel	Prague	1624
Hezekiah Fano	Venice	1574-75
Hezekiah Montro	Venice	1477
Hirsch (Ẓebi) b. Ḥayyim	Wilmersdorf	1712-38
	Fürth	1739-49
Hirz, Gener Eliezer Vindob	Amsterdam	1712

Name.	Place.	Date.
Hirz Levi Rofe	Amsterdam....	1721, 25, 26, 27–68
Ḥiyya Meïr b. David	Venice	1519–22
Ḥiyya Pisa	Venice	1574
Hosea Cividal b. Raphael	Venice	1593–94
Immanuel	Zamora	1492
Immanuel ibn Atthar ('Aṭṭar)	Amsterdam....	1686
Immanuel b. Gabriel Gallichi	Mantua	1558–60
Immanuel Henriquez b. Joshua	Amsterdam....	1730, 32
Isaac	Lublin	1680
Isaac b. Aaron	Prague	1605
Isaac b. Aaron of Prostitz	Cracow	1569–1612
	Prossnitz	1602–5
Isaac b. Aaron Samuel	Prague	1610
Isaac b. Abigdor Levi	Rome	1518
Isaac Aboab	Venice	1590
Isaac Aboab b. David	Amsterdam....	1626–27
Isaac Aboab b. Mattithiah.		
Isaac b. Abraham	Lublin	1574–76
Isaac b. Abraham Ashkenazi	Lublin	1597
Isaac b. Abraham Ashkenazi	Damascus	1606
Isaac b. Abraham Kohen of Meseritz.	Lublin	1646
Isaac Alfandari b. Abraham	Constantinople	1711, 16–20
Isaac Alnaqua	Venice	1648
Isaac b. Aryeh (Loeb) Dayyan b. Isaac.	Amsterdam....	1727
Isaac b. Asher (Ensel = Anschel) of Nerol.	Wandsbeck....	1732
Isaac Bassan b. Samuel	Venice	1560
Isaac Benveniste b. Joseph	Hamburg	1710–11
	Amsterdam....	1715
Isaac Bingen b. Samuel	Lublin	1646
	Venice	1654
Isaac (Eisak) Bresnitz Levi	Prague	1623
Isaac Bueno de Mesquita b. Joseph.	Amsterdam....	1718
Isaac Cansino	Amsterdam....	1685
Isaac Cavallino b. Eliezer Patavini of Mantua.	Venice	1624
Isaac Diaz b. Abraham	Amsterdam....	1719
Isaac (Eisak) b. Elia of Rogasen.	Frankfort-on-the-Oder.	1725, 29
Isaac (Eisak) b. Elia of Tarli	Frankfort-on-the-Oder.	1717
Isaac b. Eliakim of Bingen	Amsterdam....	1643–44
Isaac (Eisak) Eliezer (Lipman)	Hamburg	1690
Isaac (Eisak) Eliezer b. Isaac of Prague.	Lublin	1567–68, 70–73
Isaac (Jacob) b. Eliezer of Prostitz	Lublin	1616, 26, 39, 46
Isaac (Eisak) b. Elijah of Berlin	Amsterdam....	1706
Isaac b. Elijah of Brzesc	Cracow	1631
Isaac (Meïr) Fraenkel Teomim	Amsterdam....	1676–78
Isaac Gakil	Salonica	1594
Isaac Gershon	Venice	1587–1615
Isaac Gershon	Berlin	1706
Isaac b. Gershon of Torbin	Cracow	1628
Isaac b. Ḥayyim of Cracow	Cracow (?)	
	Lublin (?)	16–
	Prague (?)	
Isaac b. Ḥayyim of Cracow	Wandsbeck	1727–30
	Berlin	1733
	Amsterdam....	1739
	Dessau	1742
Isaac b. Ḥayyim Ḥazzan	Constantinople	1550
Isaac b. Ḥayyim b. Isaac Kohen b. Simson.	Prague	1655
	Frankfort-on-the-Main.	1687
Isaac Ḥazzan b. Joseph	Venice	1567
Isaac R. Hoeschels (i.e., b. Joshua)	Cracow	1571
Isaac Hurwitz Levi b. Meshullam.	Frankfort-on-the-Oder.	1677, 80
	Prague	1688–94, 95
	Frankfort-on-the-Oder.	1697–99
	Prague	1705–6, 10
Isaac Hurwitz Levi b. Moses Ḥayyim.	Hamburg	1700–1
Isaac b. Isaiah Jehiel	Constantinople	1654
Isaac Israel	Cracow	1596
Isaac b. Jacob b. Isaac	Venice	1695, 96, 1700, 2, 5, 6
Isaac Jafe b. Israel	Berlin	1717
Isaac Jafe b. Samuel	Venice	1597–1606
Isaac Jare b. David	Mantua	1718–23
Isaac Jeshurun	Smyrna	1659
Isaac (Eisak) b. Jonathan of Posen	Lublin	1595
Isaac (Eisak) b. Joseph (b. Isaac b. Isaiah)	Jessnitz	1724, 26
	Dyhernfurth.	1725
	Wandsbeck	1727–32
Isaac (Selig) b. Judah Budin	Dyhernfurth.	1692
	Zolkiev.	1693
Isaac b. Judah (Loeb) Jüdels Kohen.	Wilmersdorf.	1670–90
	Sulzbach.	
Isaac b. Judah Kohen (Kaz)	Prague	1648

Name.	Place.	Date.
Isaac b. Judah Kohen Wahl of Janospol.	Amsterdam....	1685–87
Isaac b. Kalonymus of Bilgoraj	Jessnitz	1720
Isaac (Eisak) b. Kalonymus Kohen	Dyhernfurth	1725–26, 27
Isaac Kaspota	Constantinople	1505, 9
Isaac Katzenellenbogen b. Abraham.	Amsterdam....	1686
Isaac (Kohen) de Lara b. Abraham	Amsterdam....	1699–1704
Isaac (Joshua) de Lattes	Rome	1546
Isaac Leon	Venice	1605
	Constantinople	1618
	Venice	1630
Isaac ha-Levi b. Jacob	Venice	1635, 52
Isaac Luria b. Moses	Venice	1712
Isaac Mahler	Prague	1700
Isaac Marquez di Paz	Amsterdam....	1706
Isaac Masia	Tannhausen..	1594
Isaac b. Meïr Ashkenazi	Amsterdam....	1695
Isaac b. Menahem	Cracow	1534
Isaac (Eisak) b. Menahem (Ẓoref)	Cracow	1638–40, 48
	Lublin.	
Isaac b. Meshullam Posen	Cracow (Novidvor).	1591
Isaac Montalto b. Elijah	Amsterdam....	1637
Isaac b. Moses Eckendorf	Basel	1599
Isaac (Eisak) b. Moses Grillingen.	Wilmersdorf..	1732
	Fürth	1738–45
Isaac (Eisak) b. Naphtali Didenhofen.	Wilmersdorf..	1726
Isaac b. Naphtali (Hirz) Kohen	Amsterdam....	1710, 23–24, 32
Isaac Nehemiah	Amsterdam....	1627
Isaac Norzi b. Samuel	Mantua	1593
Isaac Nuñez b. David	Amsterdam....	1664
Isaac Pacifico b. Asher	Venice	1712–15
Isaac (Lopez) Pereira b. Moses	Amsterdam....	1726, 29
Isaac della Pinia b. Abraham	Amsterdam....	1712
Isaac Rabbino b. Abraham	Mantua	1718
Isaac Sasportas b. Jacob	Amsterdam....	1685
Isaac b. Selig	Frankfort-on-the-Oder.	1725, 27, 29
Isaac Simeon b. Judah (Loeb) of Hechingen.	Frankfort-on-the-Main.	1697
Isaac b. Simeon Samuel Levi	Hanau	1610, 11–14, 23
Isaac b. Solomon (Gumi ?)	Constantinople	1511
Isaac b. Solomon (Zalman)	Dyhernfurth..	1695, 96
	Frankfort-on-the-Oder.	1698, 1708, 13, 17, 18, 26
Isaac b. Solomon b. Israel	Wilmersdorf.	1730
Isaac Spira b. Nathan	Lublin	1597
Isaac Sullam (Salem ?) b. Joseph	Mantua	1563, 65
	Venice	1568, 1687
Isaac Tausk b. Selig	Prague	1703, 6, 10, 18–19, 25, 28, 35–36
Isaac Treves b. Gershon	Venice	1568, 78, 83, 85
Isaac Tschelebi b. Elia Polichrono	Venice	1630
Isaac (Elijah) b. Uri Kohen	Prague	1621
Isaac (Eisak) b. Ẓebi (Hirsch) Levi of Kalisz.	Jessnitz.	
Isaiah Anaw	Basel	1610
Isaiah Ashkenazi	Constantinople	1719
Isaiah b. Isaac b. Isaiah of Woidislaw.	Frankfort-on-the-Oder.	1717
	Köthen	1717
	Jessnitz	1719–20
Isaiah b. Meïr Bunzlau	Cracow	1594
Isaiah b. Moses of Sniatyn	Constantinople	1711
Isaiah Parnas b. Elasar (Eliezer)	Venice	1529, 31–32
Isaiah di Trani b. Joseph	Constantinople	1641
Ishmael Marono	Venice	1601
Israel b. Abraham	Köthen	1717
	Jessnitz	1719–26
	Wandsbeck	1726–33
Israel Altschul b. Solomon	Jessnitz	1739–44
	Prague	1613, 20
Israel Ashkenazi	Pisaur.	
Israel b. Eliakim (Goetz)	Venice	1704–5
Israel b. Ḥayyim Bunzlau	Amsterdam....	1688
Israel b. Jedidiah of Leipnik	Lublin	1619
Israel Kohen b. Joseph	Lublin	1556, 66
Israel b. Meïr	Wilmersdorf .	1712
Israel b. Moses	Dessau	1696
	Frankfort-on-the-Oder.	1700
	Dessau.	1704
Israel b. Moses b. Abraham	Offenbach	1719–33
	Homburg	1734
	Neuwied	1735–36
	Offenbach	1737–38
	Jessnitz	1739
Israel b. Moses b. Abraham Abinu	Amsterdam....	1694
Israel b. Moses of Berlin	Berlin	1727

Name.	Place.	Date.
Israel Sifroni b. Daniel	Sabbionetta.	
	Basel	1578–81, 83
	Freiburg	1583–84
	Venice	1588, 1604
Israel Zarfati of Milhau	Constantinople	1518
Issachar (Baer) b. Aaron b. Isaac Drucker.	Cracow	1619
Issachar (Baer) b. Abraham of Kalisz.	Dessau	1704
Issachar (Baer) b. Eliezer of Minden.	Amsterdam	1685, 88, 92–1703, 11
Issachar (Dob Baer) b. Gershon Wiener.	Frankfort-on-the-Oder.	1727–72
Issachar (Baer) Hazzan.	Prague	1609–10
Issachar (Dob Baer) b. Isaac.	Lublin	1680–81
Issachar (Baer) b. Issachar Kohen	Fürth	1691
	Prague	1692, 95, 1718–19
Issachar (Dob Baer) b. Judah (Loeb).	Amsterdam	1725–26, 27, 30, 33
Issachar (Baer) b. Nathan Kohen.	Dyhernfurth	1718–33
Issachar Perlhefter.	Prague	1687
Issachar b. (Abi Esri) Selke.	Frankfort-on-the-Oder.	1697–99, 1703, 11
	Berlin	1712, 14–15, 17
	Prague	1718–20
	Frankfort-on-the-Oder.	1727, 29
Jabez (Solomon b. Isaac b. Joseph b. Hayyim).	Adrianople	1544
	Salonica	1555
	Constantinople	1559–67, 73–75
Jabez Joseph b. Isaac.	Adrianople	1554
	Salonica	1563–72, 73–75, 76–84
Jacob b. Aaron Ashkenazi.	Venice	1704
Jacob (Koppel) b. (Hayyim?).	Offenbach	1718
Jacob b. Abigdor Levi.	Rome	1518
	Tridini	1525
Jacob Aboab b. Abraham.	Venice	1669, 82, 83
Jacob Aboab b. Joseph.	Venice	1708, 11
Jacob b. Abraham.	Venice	1665–72
Jacob b. Abraham Ashkenazi.	Damascus	1606
Jacob b. Abraham Ashkenazi of Ziwatow.	Constantinople	1648, 52, 54
Jacob b. Abraham Ger.	Amsterdam	1708-9, 9, 12, 13, 15, 21, 22, 25, 28, 30
Jacob b. Abraham Israel Ger.	Amsterdam	1664
Jacob b. Abraham of Jerusalem.	Constantinople	1719–20
Jacob b. Abraham of Leipnik.	Cracow	1618
	Lublin	1627, 33–35
Jacob b. Abraham of Lublin.	Lublin	1618–20, 22–27, 33 (35?)
Jacob b. Abraham Moses.	Amsterdam	1661
Jacob b. Abraham Polak.	Basel	1598, 99, 1600, 3
Jacob b. Abraham of Rowno.	Berlin	1726
Jacob b. Abraham Tininger.	Basel	1599
Jacob Alfandari b. Hayyim.	Constantinople	1670–71
Jacob Alvarez-Soto.	Amsterdam	1708–10
Jacob (Alnis?)	Venice	1621
Jacob Auerbach b. Isaac Reis of Vienna.	Sulzbach	1716–17
Jacob Baruch b. Samuel Baruch.	Venice	1656
Jacob Basch.	Prague	1627
Jacob Bassan b. Abraham.	Amsterdam	1725
Jacob Bibas.	Constantinople	1715–16
Jacob Broda.	Giessen	1714
Jacob Carillo.	Amsterdam	1644
Jacob Castelo.	Amsterdam	1661–64
Jacob b. David (Gutrath).	Lublin	1556, 59, 67, 68, 78
Jacob b. Eliakim Ashkenazi.	Lublin	1574–76
Jacob (Zebi) b. Eliezer.	Dessau	1698
	Berlin	1699
Jacob b. Eliezer Levi.	Venice	1566
Jacob b. Enoch b. Abraham b. Moses Melammed.	Jessnitz	1720
Jacob Florentin.	Salonica	1724
Jacob (Hai) Florez b. Abraham.	Leghorn	1650
	Venice	1651
Jacob Gabbai.	Constantinople	1640–43
Jacob of Haag.	Amsterdam	1728, 30
Jacob Haber Tob.	Mantua	1718–23
Jacob ibn Hason.	Salonica	1732
Jacob b. Hayyim.	Venice	1520
Jacob b. Hayyim.	Constantinople	1711
Jacob b. Hayyim b. Jacob Erbich.	Amsterdam	1700–26, 32
Jacob Hazkuni b. Abraham.	Amsterdam	1694, 1726
Jacob b. Hillel of Lublin.	Prague	1675
Jacob b. Isaac Gomez.	Verona	1650

Name.	Place.	Date.
Jacob b. Isaac Levi	Venice	1678, 82, 90, 90–91, 96
Jacob b. Isaac Levi	Amsterdam	1688
Jacob Israel	Mayence (?)	1584
Jacob b. Issachar (Dob) Cantor.	Zolkiev	1718
Jacob Jeshurun.	Amsterdam	1660
Jacob b. Joel Levi.	Amsterdam	1701
Jacob b. Joseph.		
Jacob (Hai) b. Joseph (Hai) Kohen.	Venice	1693, 96, 98, 1702, 4, 5, 12–15
Jacob b. Judah Noah Kohen Norden.	Amsterdam	1640
Jacob b. Judah Shneor.	Amsterdam	1683
Jacob (Koppel) Kohen.	Amsterdam	1715
	Offenbach	1718
Jacob Kohen della Man.	Venice	1616
Jacob Kulli.	Constantinople	1719, 27, 28, 31
Jacob Landau.	Naples	1487
Jacob (Koppel) Levi.	Sulzbach	1700
Jacob Levi of Tarascon.	Mantua	Ante 1480
Jacob Lubemila.	Amsterdam	1728
Jacob Luzzat b. Isaac.	Cracow	1569
Jacob Marcaria.	Riva di Trento	1558–62
Jacob b. Meïr.	Lublin	1598–99
Jacob b. Meïr Hölischau.	Cracow	1608, 17
Jacob Mendez da Costa.	Wandsbeck	1733
Jacob de Meza.	Amsterdam	1705
Jacob b. Mordecai.	Amsterdam	1708
Jacob b. Mordecai b. Jacob.	Prague	1597
Jacob b. Moses.	Amsterdam	1696
Jacob (Zebi) b. Moses.	Wilmersdorf	1688-90,1712-17, 19–22, 26–38
	Fürth	1691-97,1724-26, 38
	Sulzbach	1699–1712, 29
Jacob b. Moses Bohemus.	Lublin	1556, 59, 66
Jacob b. Moses Drucker.	Amsterdam	1690
Jacob b. Moses Kohen.	Hanau	1710–11
Jacob (Eliezer) b. Moses Lesers of Wilna.	Cracow	1640
Jacob b. Moses Levi.	Amsterdam	1690, 95, 97, 99, 1702–3, 4, 6, 5–10, 11–12,14,15, 21,28, 30, 39
Jacob b. Moses Levi Josbel.	Venice	1643, 47–48, 57, 61, 67
Jacob b. Moses-Loeb Pizker.	Prague	1609
Jacob b. Moses of Posen.	Dessau	1698
Jacob b. Naphtali.	Cracow	1576–81?
Jacob b. Naphtali.	Fürth	1723
	Wilmersdorf.	1728–29, 30
	Sulzbach	1750
	Fürth	1757, 69
Jacob b. Naphtali (Hirsch).	Amsterdam	1683
	Dyhernfurth	1691, 93
Jacob b. Naphtali Kohen of Gazolo	Sabbionetta.	1551
	Mantua	1556, 57–60, 60–62
Jacob (Koppel) b. Naphtali (Hirsch) Pas.	Amsterdam	1726, 30
Jacob ibn Phorna b. David	Constantinople	1710, 11, 13, 14
Jacob (Jokew) b. Phinehas Selig.	Jessnitz	1722–26
Jacob (Israel) de la Pinia.	Amsterdam	1664, 69
Jacob Rewah.	Constantinople	1718
Jacob Rodriguez Guadeloupe b. Abraham.	Amsterdam	1663–64, 69, 69
Jacob Sagdun.	Venice	1648
Jacob b. Samuel.	Amsterdam	1713
Jacob b. Samuel (Sanwel).	Fürth	1722
Jacob b. Samuel of Lemberg.	Amsterdam	1697
Jacob Saraval b. Joshua Nehemiah	Venice	1640, 45
Jacob Sasportas.	Amsterdam	1651, 53
Jacob (Israel) Shalom b. Samuel.	Venice	1709
Jacob Sibuyah	Smyrna	1730, 58
Jacob b. Solomon.	Amsterdam	1732
Jacob Stabnitz Levi.	Prague	1607
Jacob Sullam.	Venice	1614
Jacob Tabuh.	Smyrna	1731
Jacob Treves b. Mattathias of Worms.	Prague	1614–15
Jacob b. Uzziel Solomon.	Salonica	1709
Jacob Wimpfen b. Eliezer Wimpfen.	Amsterdam	1689
Jacob ibn Yakkar	Constantinople	1511
Jacob b. Zebi.	Wilmersdorf.	1689–90
Jacob b. Zebi.	Lublin	1637
	Amsterdam	1641, 43
	Verona	1649
	Constantinople	1654
	Cracow	1670
Jacob b. Zebi of Fürth.	Sulzbach	1715

Name.	Place.	Date.	Name.	Place.	Date.
Jaffe (Ḥayyim b. Kolonymus)....	Lublin........	1572–96	Joseph (ibn) Alzaig, the elder....	Constantinople	1643
Jaffe (Joseph [I.] b. Kalonymus) .	Lublin........	1572–75	Joseph Alzaig b. Isaac, the young-	Constantinople	1511
Jaffe (Joseph [II.] b. Ẓebi Hirsch	Lublin........	1633	er.		
Ḳalmanḳes).			Joseph Amaragi b. Moses.........	Salonica.......	1653
Jaffe (Kalonymus [I.])..........	Lublin........	1556–97	Joseph b. Asher of Prague........	Prague.......	1674–75
	Bistrowitz	1592	Joseph Askaloni b. Isaac.........	Belvedere	1593-94, 97-
Jaffe (Kalonymus [II.] b. Ẓebi	Lublin........	1635–46		(Kuru Ches-	98
Hirsch Ḳalmanḳes).				me).	
Jaffe (Ẓebi b. [Abraham Ḳalman-	Lublin........	1577, 78, 96,	Joseph b. Benjamin Ḥayyim Levi.	Verona........	1650
ḳes] Kalonymus).		1604–28, 48	Joseph Bibas...................	Constantinople	1505–22
Jaffe, Sarah, daughter of Kalony-	Lublin........	1665	Joseph Caravita b. Abraham......	Bologna.......	1482
mus (II.).			Joseph (Simel) Cividal b. Asher..	Venice........	1665
Jaffe (Solomon or Zalman b. Jacob	Lublin........	1665–85	Joseph Crasnik of Rakow........	Prague........	1732
Ḳalmanḳes) of Torbin.			Joseph di Crasto................	Salonica.......	1522
Jedidiah Kohen b. Aryeh Judah	Constantinople	1732	Joseph ibn Danan b. Jacob......	Venice........	1615, 17–19
Loeb.			Joseph b. Daniel................	Cracow	1587–88
Jehiel (Michael b. Judah Loeb of	Zolkiev........	1718	Joseph b. Eliakim b. Naphtali....	Venice........	1606
Zolkiev).			Joseph b. Eliezer Ḥalfan........	Basel........	1602
Jehiel (Michael) b. Abraham Zal-	Wilmersdorf..	1670	Joseph b. Eliezer Ḥazzan of Posen	Basel........	1602
man Shammash.	Prague........	1674, 78	Joseph Elkeser b. Benjamin	Berlin (?).....	1699–1700
	Weckelsdorf ..	1686, 89, 92	Joseph b. Ephraim (Hungarus)...	Lublin	1577
Jehiel b. Asher Kohen...........	Cracow	1583	Joseph Epstein b. Benjamin Zeeb	Berlin........	1713
Jehiel Ashkenazi................	Constantinople	1546–47	Wolf Levi.		
Jehiel (Michael) b. Baruch.......	Prague........	1675	Joseph Esobi b. Judah b. Solomon	Venice.........	1621
Jehiel Elia Rafael...............	Pisaur	1509–18	Joseph Falcon b. Solomon Zalman	Constantinople	1710
Jehiel b. Jedidiah...............	Cracow	1587	Joseph Franco Serrano...........	Amsterdam....	1680, 83
Jehiel b. Jekuthiel Kohen Rapa..	Venice........	1544–47	Joseph Fürst....................	Hamburg	1716, 18
Jehiel Luria Ashkenazi..........	Venice........	1601	Joseph Gabbai..................	Constantinople	1512
Jehiel (Fishel) b. Menahem Levi	Smyrna	1730–31	Joseph b. Gershon of Torbin.....	Lublin........	1627, 30
Ashkenazi.	Constantinople	1734, 36	Joseph (Iseppo) Goa............	Padua........	1640
Jehiel de Monteles b. Solomon....	Venice........	1585	Joseph ibn Ḥasan b. Solomon....	Salonica.......	1732
Jehiel b. Solomon of Verona.....	Bologna.......	1537–40	Joseph b. Ḥayyim Gumpels.......	Frankfort-on-	1677, 80, 86
Jehiel (Michael) Stern Kohen b.	Frankfort-on-	1713		the-Oder.	
Wolf.	the-Main.			Prague........	1691–92, 94–
	Hanau........	1715			95, 1700–1
Jehiel Teshubah	Venice........	1640	Joseph b. Ḥayyim Ḳaddish.......	Frankfort-on-	1688
Jehiel Treves b. David of Galingen	Offenbach.....	1717		the-Main.	
Jehiel b. Ẓebi Hirsch............	Amsterdam....	1703, 9	Joseph Ḥazzan..................	Venice........	1566, 67
Jekuthiel b. Asher..............	Salonica.......	1587	Joseph b. Immanuel Kohen.......	Salonica.......	1517
Jekuthiel Blitz.................	Amsterdam....	1659, 60, 61	Joseph b. Isaac b. Isaiah Woidi-	Dyhernfurth ..	1696, 97,
Jekuthiel b. David..............	Prague........	1597–1618	slaw.		1700, 3, 4–5,
Jekuthiel b. Isaac Dan	Prague........	1512, 15, 18			13, 16, 18,
Jekuthiel (Süsskind) b. Isaac of	Frankfort-on-	1726			20
Pinczow.	the-Main.		Joseph b. Isaac b. Jehiel.........	Venice........	1544
	Offenbach.....	1714–26	Joseph b. Isaac Kohen...........	Constantinople	1547
Jekuthiel (Zalman) b. Katriel of	Constantinople	1654		(?)	
Satanow.			Joseph b. Israel................	Constantinople	1518
Jekuthiel b. Moses Kohen.......	Frankfort-on-	1702	Joseph b. Israel (b.?) Hirsch.....	Prague........	1691
	the-Oder.		Joseph b. Issachar Baer..........	Prague........	1616, 21
Jeremiah (Aryeh Loeb) b. Samuel	Fürth	1694, 98,	Joseph ibn Jacob...............	Lublin	1618–20
		1722	Joseph ibn Jacob Ashkenazi......	Naples	1487–90
Jeroham b. Menahem of Slonim..	Amsterdam....	1697	Joseph ibn Jacob Braunschweig...	Basel........	1609
Jesse Almoli....................	Smyrna	1660	Joseph b. Jacob Kohen..........	Venice........	1657, 59–60,
Joab b. Baruch of Piatelli (?).....	Venice........	1665			61, 75, 85,
Joel b. Aaron of Fürth..........	Fürth	1692–93			1709, 12–15
Joel b. Aaron Levi..............	Lublin........	1598–99	Joseph ibn Jaḳḳar..............	Schenhausen..	1544
Joel b. Phoebus................	Wandsbeck ..	1727	Joseph b. Jekuthiel Zalman	Berlin........	1715
Johanan b. Aaron Isaac..........	Amsterdam....	1713	Joseph (Jospe) b. Joseph But Levi	Prague.	
Johanan Durante...............	Venice........	1578	Joseph b. Joshua (Hoeschel) Ko-	Offenbach.....	1721
Johanan of Meseritz............	Frankfort-on-	1697–99	hen.		
	the-Oder.		Joseph (Jospe) b. Judah.........	Lublin........	1598–99
Johanan Treves................	Venice........	1545	Joseph Ḳabiẓi b. Ayyid.........	Constantinople	1515
Jonah Abravanel	Amsterdam....	1628, 30, 48,	Joseph Khalfon.................	Lisbon........	1491
		50, 52	Joseph Kohen..................	Constantinople	1509
Jonah b. Isaac of Strim.........	Wandsbeck....	1731	Joseph b. Kutiel................	Dessau........	1698
Jonah b. Jacob Ashkenazi........	Constantinople	1712–42	Joseph de Leon b. Solomon Israel.	Venice........	1690–91, 93,
	Ortakiewai....	1717–19			94
	Amsterdam....	1721	Joseph b. Manasseh b. Israel......	Amsterdam....	1646–47, 47,
	Smyrna.......	1729–41			48
Jonah b. Judah of Prague.......	Prague........	1608, 10	Joseph (Solomon) b. Mendel Plotz-	Cracow	1642–44
Jonah (Ḳlavi ?)	Venice........	1666	kers.		
Jonah b. Moses Polak...........	Amsterdam....	1727, 29, 30,	Joseph b. Meshullam Phoebus	Frankfort-on-	1701–2
		32, 33, 39	Ḥazzan.	the-Oder.	
Joseph (?).....................	Venice........	1592	Joseph Meṭaṭron................	Salonica.	
Joseph (Jekuthiel Kofman Wahl).	Prague	1587, 92	Joseph b. Michael Nehemiah......	Hamburg	1711
Joseph (Venturin b. David)	Venice........	1651, 52, 53,	Joseph Molcho..................	Venice........	1589
		54, 55, 56,	Joseph b. Mordecai Gershon......	Cracow	1571
		57, 59, 60,	Joseph b. Mordecai Kohen........	Amsterdam....	1708
		62, 63, 64,	Joseph b. Moses Levi of Hamburg.	Amsterdam....	1692–93, 99,
		65, 75			1702, 3–6,
Joseph (Maestro)		1477			11, 14, 16,
Joseph b. Abraham.............	Prague........	1728			18–19, 26,
	Sulzbach......	1729			30
	Amsterdam....	1732	Joseph b. Moses Reviẓi (Rachiẓi ?)	Venice........	1528–29
Joseph b. Abraham Benjamin	Amsterdam....	1727	Joseph Mubḥar Sefardi..........	Constantinople	1509
Zeeb.			Joseph b. Naphtali (Treves ?)....	Zurich........	1558
Joseph b. Abraham of Jerusalem.	Amsterdam....	1712		Thiengen......	1560
Joseph b. Alexander Süsskind....	Amsterdam....	1677	Joseph b. Naphtali of Konskawola	Amsterdam....	1648
Joseph Algazi..................	Smyrna.......	1671, 83	Joseph b. Nathan................	Fürth	1726
Joseph al-Ḳala'i	Constantinople	1711	Joseph Nissim..................	Ferrara	1693
Joseph Alnaqua b. Abraham......	Salonica.......	1520	Joseph de Noves b. Judah b. Sam-	Venice........	1605
	Constantinople	1522	uel.		
Joseph (Joseph) Alvalensi b. Abra-	Venice........	1676, 78	Joseph Oberlaender.............	Venice........	1701
ham.			Joseph Ottolengo................	Riva di Trenta	1558–60
			Joseph Pardo	Venice........	1597–1606
			Joseph (Solomon) Pinia..........	Leghorn	1657

Name.	Place.	Date.
Joseph ibn Piso	Naples	1492
Joseph Porjes b. Judah Loeb	Amsterdam	1709
Joseph Samega	Venice	1587
Joseph (b.?) (Moses) b. Samson	Venice	1598
Joseph b. Samuel Levi	Constantinople	1546–47
Joseph ibn Saruk b. Ḥayyim	Venice	1591, 1607-8
Joseph Sason	Constantinople	1726
Joseph Sason b. Aaron of Gallipoli.	Venice	1618
Joseph Sason b. Jacob	Venice	1584, 98–1600
Joseph b. Shabbethai Bass	Dyhernfurth	1707–18
Joseph Shallit		1550–73
Joseph ibn Shoshan	Constantinople	1520–22
Joseph Sid b. Isaac	Salonica	1529, 35
Joseph b. Simeon	Amsterdam	1717
Joseph (Dob Baer) b. Solomon	Dyhernfurth	1713, 15, 17, 19
Joseph b. Solomon b. Isaiah Nizza	Venice	1711, 12
Joseph (Sofer) b. Solomon Levi	Cracow	1597–98
Joseph (Ḥayyim) Strasburg b. Aaron.	Bologna	1482
Joseph (Jospe) Trier Kohen	Frankfort-on-the-Main.	1690–1715
Joseph Trillinger b. Eliezer		1707
Joseph Wehle b. Solomon	Amsterdam	1685–87
	Zolkiev	1693–96
	Berlin	1699, 1700, 17
Joseph of Witzenhausen	Amsterdam	1644, 47–48, 68–70, 73, 76, 79–86
Joseph ibn Yaḥyah b. Tam	Constantinople	1542, 43
Joseph b. Zalman Shneor	Fürth	1691–92, 98
Joseph b. (Solomon) Zalman of Wilna.	Amsterdam	1726, 27, 29
Joseph Ẓarfati	Amsterdam	1693, 1702
Joseph Ẓarfati b. Judah of Ẓafat	Lublin	1613
Joseph Ẓarfati b. Samuel	Venice	1525
Joseph (Josbel) b. Ẓebi	Offenbach	1716–19
Joshua (Elhanan) b. Abraham Joseph.	Venice	1730
Joshua Falk of Lissa	Frankfort-on-the-Oder.	1697–99
Joshua b. Israel	Lublin	1619–28
Joshua (Gershon) Levi	Mantua	1672
Joshua b. Meïr Levi of Schwersenz.	Wilmersdorf	1727
Joshua b. Michael of Sezze	Mantua	1718–32
Joshua da Silva	Amsterdam	1666–67
Joshua Sin (?).		
Joshua (Hoeschel) b. Solomon Kohen.	Offenbach	1719
Joshua Sonina	Constantinople	1717, 19
Joshua (Falk) b. Zalman of Wiscnowicz.	Constantinople	1710–11
Joshua Ẓarfati (Gallus)	Amsterdam	1658–59, 66
Josiah b. Abigdor of Kalisz	Berlin	1699, 1700
Josiah Mizraḥi	Constantinople	1711
Judah (Loeb) b. Aaron of Prague	Prague	1691, 95, 1700, 1, 7, 10
Judah (Loeb) b. Abraham	Cracow	1642–44
Judah Abudienti	Amsterdam	1675
Judah Albelda b. Moses	Venice	1600-1, 2
Judah b. Alexander Kohen	Prague	1602, 3–4, 5, 6, 9–10, 10, 11, 13, 14, 35, 48
	Lublin	1630, 39
	Cracow	1631
Judah b. Alexander Levi of Worms.	Frankfort-on-the-Main.	1697
Judah (Loeb) b. Asher Anschel Abigdor.	Prague	1669
	Cracow	1670
Judah (Loeb) b. Baruch Wahl	Dyhernfurth	1725
Judah Bassan b. Samuel	Verona	1650
Judah b. Benjamin Zeeb	Prague	1688
	Frankfort-on-the-Oder.	1691
Judah of Berlin	Amsterdam	1682
Judah Briel	Mantua	1672, 94–95
Judah (Lewa) b. David	Prague	1615
Judah b. David b. Judah	Cracow	1644
Judah b. David (Isaac Saekel) Levi of Fürth.	Berlin	1709
Judah b. David Reuben	Venice	1661
Judah b. Eleazar Lubemila		1603
Judah (Selig) b. Eliezer Lipman Kohen of Zolkiev.	Zolkiev	1721, 33
Judah (Loeb) Ginzburg.		
Judah b. Hananiah Castoriano	Constantinople	1732
Judah Ḥazzan	Smyrna	1730
Judah (Loeb) Hurwitz Levi of Prague.	Sulzbach	1688
Judah b. Isaac	Prague	1660, 62
Judah (Loeb) b. Isaac Brzesc	Amsterdam	1713
Judah (Loeb) b. Isaac Joel	Amsterdam	1712

Name.	Place.	Date.
Judah (Loeb) b. Isaac Jüdels Kohen (Kaẓ).		1619-20, 20, 22, 23, 24, 28
Judah b. Isaac Levi	Mantua	1623
Judah b. Isaac Levi Ashkenazi	Venice	1544–47, 48
	Mantua	1561
Judah (Loeb) b. Isaac of Tikotin	Lublin	1619
Judah b. Israel Samuel Kohen	Prossnitz	1603
Judah b. Issachar Kohen	Wilmersdorf	1673–75
Judah (Loeb) b. Jacob of Prostitz	Lublin	1602–5, 9, 11, 13, 14, 19
Judah (Loeb) b. Jacob Wandsbeck of Krotoschin.	Hamburg	1686, 88, 90
Judah (Loeb) b. Joel b. Eliezer		1724
Judah (Loeb) b. Joel Levi	Amsterdam	1698
Judah b. (Joseph) Josbel Wetzlar	Offenbach	1720
Judah (Loeb) b. Joseph	Wilmersdorf	1671, 73–74, 80, 81–82, 85–86, 88–90
Judah (Loeb) b. Joseph	Cracow	1592, 94, 99
Judah (Loeb) b. Joseph	Berlin	1699–1700
Judah b. Joseph Levi	Constantinople	1716
Judah b. Joseph Obadiah	Constantinople	1666
Judah (Aryeh Loeb) b. Joseph Samuel.	Frankfort-on-the-Main.	1713
Judah (Loeb) b. Judah Joseph	Amsterdam	1700
Judah (Loeb) b. Judah Kohen	Lublin	1626–35
Judah Karo b. Joseph	Salonica	1597
Judah (Loeb) Klesmer b. Wolf	Berlin	1701, 7
Judah (Loeb) b. Ẓebi of Janow	Jessnitz	1722–23
Judah Lapapa b. Isaac	Smyrna	1674
Judah Luria b. Johanan	Amsterdam	1700–10
Judah (Aryeh Loeb) of Lublin	Cracow	1571
Judah (Aryeh Loeb) Maeler b. Joseph.	Amsterdam	1663
Judah di Medina b. Moses Sustin.	Salonica	1614
Judah (Loeb) b. Meïr	Hamburg	1687
Judah (Loeb) b. Menahem	Dyhernfurth	1719
Judah (Loeb) b. Menahem Nahum Kaẓ.	Prague	1686
Judah di Modena		1595–1648
Judah (Loeb) b. Mordecai Gumpel	Amsterdam	1631–32, 37, 40, 42, 43–46, 53, 58, 61–64
Judah (Loeb) b. Mordecai b. Judah.	Dyhernfurth	1719
Judah (Saltaro) b. Moses de Fano.	Venice	1602
Judah (Loeb) b. Moses Jacob of Leipnik.	Prague	1608, 13, 18, 24
Judah (Loeb) b. Moses Schedel	Prague	1602, 3, 4, 5, 6–7, 8, 9, 13
Judah (Aryeh Loeb) b. Naphtali (Hirsch).	Amsterdam	1690
Judah b. Nathan of Cracow	Cremona	1565
Judah (Loeb) Nikolsburg		1700 (?)
Judah Perez	Venice	1706–11
Judah Pesaro	Pesaro	1505
Judah Rosanes	Constantinople	1719
Judah (Loeb) b. Sara	Amsterdam	1701
Judah Sason b. Joseph	Constantinople	1514, 15, 16
Judah (Loeb) Schnapper	Frankfort-on-the-Main.	1710
Judah (Gur Aryeh) b. Shalom	Naples	1492
Judah Shamu	Venice	1665
Judah b. Simḥah	Cracow	1592–93
Judah (Loeb Rofe) b. Simeon	Frankfort-on-the-Main.	1677
Judah b. Solomon Kohen Lipschütz.	Lublin	1622 (17–?)
Judah ibn Ya'ish	Venice	1705
Kalonymus b. Isaac b. Isaiah of Woidislaw.	Prossnitz	1711
	Dyhernfurth	1712, 13, 15, 19, 20, 26
	Frankfort-on-the-Oder.	1717
Kalonymus b. Isaac of Zloczow	Dyhernfurth	1703
Kalonymus (Kalman) b. Judah Ashkenazi.	Constantinople	1719, 20
Kalonymus (Kalman) b. Judah (Loeb) Kalisch.	Amsterdam	1721
Kalonymus b. Ẓebi (Hirsch) Kohen b. Kalonymus.	Dyhernfurth	1703, 5, 7, 12–13, 19
Katriel b. Jekuthiel Zalman of Satanow.	Constantinople	1648
Katriel b. Ẓebi Szidlower	Cracow	1638–39, 42
	Lublin	1645
	Cracow	1666, 70
Kaẓ	Prague	1682, 85, 89, 92–95, 98–1700, 2, 6
Kaẓ	Prague	1687–1726,35
Kaẓ (Aaron b. Israel)	Frankfort-on-the-Oder.	1677, 80
	Prague	1695

Name.	Place.	Date.	Name.	Place.	Date.
Kaẓ (Bezaleel b. Mordecai)	Prague	1569, 78, 85–90 (92?)	Meïr Oppenheim b. Abraham b. Baer.	Frankfort-on-the-Main.	1697
Kaẓ (David b. Aaron b. Israel)	Prague	1701, 3, 8	Meïr Parenz	Venice	1545–75
Kaẓ (Geronim b. Solomon)	Prague	1526	Meïr b. Pethahiah	Lublin	1643
Kaẓ (Gershon [II.] Israel)	Prague	1569	Meïr Rofe b. Ḥiyya Rofe	Venice	1657
Kaẓ (Gershon [III.] b. Joseph Bezaleel).	Prague	1586, 89, 95–96, 1600, 8, 9, 10	Meïr ibn Schangi	Constantinople	1586
			Meïr b. Selig of Kalisch	Halle	1710
Kaẓ (Israel b. Judah [Loeb])	Prague	1652 (?)	Meïr b. Shalom	Lublin	1568
Kaẓ (Judah b. Gershon)	Prague	1541	Meïr b. Solomon	Lublin	1681
Kaẓ (Judah b. Jacob)	Prague	1624	Meïr b. Wolf Schwab	Amsterdam	1722–24
Kaẓ (Mordecai b. Gershon)	Prague	1529–90	Meïr (ibn) Yaḥya b. Joseph	Fano	1506
Kaẓ (Mordecai [II.] b. Gershon)	Prague	1608, 20, 23, 24	Meïr b. Zechariah	Venice	1639–61
Kaẓ (Moses b. Gershon)	Prague	1533–34, 35, 36, 40, 41, 49–50, 56	Meisel(s) (Judah Loeb b. Simḥah Bonem).	Lublin	1648
				Cracow	1663–70
			Meisels (Menahem)	Lublin	1623–27
				Cracow	1631–59
Kaẓ (Moses [II.] b. Joseph Bezaleel).	Prague	1592–94, 99–1635, 47 (?), 48 (?)	Meisels (Tchernah bat Menahem).	Cracow	1638–39, 46
			Menahem b. Aaron Polacco	Venice	1704–5, 8, 11, 12, 19, 28, 30, 60
Kaẓ (Pesaḥ b. Mordecai)	Prague	1556–69	Menahem b. Abraham Kohen	Venice	1648
Kaẓ (Samuel b. Mordecai)	Prague	1569, 78	Menahem (Mannes) b. Abraham Kohen of Glogau.	Frankfort-on-the-Main.	1694
Kaẓ (Solomon [I.] b. Gershon)	Prague	1529, 30, 33–34, 35, 36, 40			
			Menahem b. Abraham of Modena.	Bologna	1537–40
Kaẓ (Solomon [III.] b. Gershon)		1608	Menahem Azariah	Venice	1589
Kaẓ (Solomon [II.] b. Mordecai).	Prague	1569, 80–81, 85–89, 90, 92–94	Menahem (Mendel) b. Bezaleel of Lublin.	Lublin	1665, 72, 80–81
Kaẓ Gershon (I.)	Prague	1515, 18, 22, 26, 29, 30, 41	Menahem (Mendel) Bloch b. Moses	Frankfort-on-the-Main.	1713
			Menahem Crispin	Salonica	1709
Klessner (Georg) of Leipsic	Jessnitz	1720	Menahem Dayyan	Constantinople	1525
Koffman b. Asher of Lublin	Constantinople	1711	Menahem (Man) b. Eliezer	Amsterdam	1699
Kosmann Emrich b. Elijah Cleve	Amsterdam	1688–89, 92–97	Menahem (Jacob) b. Eliezer Judah Ashkenazi.	Venice	1606
Lemberger (Abraham b. Simeon Heide).	Prague	1610, 12, 13–28	Menahem (Mandel) Grünhut b. David.	Hanau	1717
Leon-Templo (Isaac b. Solomon Judah).	Amsterdam	1726	Menahem (Mendel) b. (Bär) Hirschel.	Prague	1689–90, 92, 1701
Leon-Templo (Solomon)	Amsterdam	1726–27, 30, 31		Berlin	1703
				Prague	1714, 20, 28,
Leon-Templo (Solomon Judah Raphael b. Jacob).	Amsterdam	1697–99, 1703	Menahem (Man) b. Isaac (Jacob) of Prague.	Prague	1668
Levi	Venice	1602		Wilmersdorf	1671, 73–74, 80, 81
Levi Laniado (and Isaac Laniado).	Venice	1657		Sulzbach	1684–88
Levi b. Süsschen	Amsterdam	1701		Dyhernfurth	1689–90, 93
Levi Tilio	Constantinople	1652	Menahem Mendel b. Isaac Levi	Cracow	1587–88
Licht (Johann)	Hamburg	1715	Menahem (Mendel) b. Israel Kohen Jaroslaw of Lemberg.	Amsterdam	1690
Lima b. Naphtali of Fürth	Amsterdam	1711			
Lipmann b. Abraham	Frankfort-on-the-Main.	1688	Menahem b. Jacob of Cracow	Venice	1712
			Menahem (Man) b. Jacob Jekuthiel.	Wandsbeck	1732
Mahalalel b. Menahem Isaac Levi	Mantua	1713, 24		Altona	1735
Mahrim b. (Moses) Jacob Maarssen.	Amsterdam	1710, 15, 20	Menahem b. (Noah) Jacob Kohen of Norden.	Amsterdam	1649, 76
			Menahem Jaffe b. Isaac	Venice	1631
Mahrim b. Jacob b. Moses Levi	Amsterdam	1726–29, 30, 35, 39–40, 46		Constantinople	1648
				Venice	1657
Manasseh b. Israel	Amsterdam	1626–40	Menahem (Manusch) b. Judah	Hanau	1712
Manasseh (Jacob) b. Judah Levi of Lubemil.	Cracow	1590		Sulzbach	1716–17
				Fürth	1723–26
Manasseh Kazin b. Solomon	Venice	1599–1600		Offenbach	1729
Margalita (Aaron)	Halle	1711		Homburg	1734
Masus b. Alexander	Amsterdam	1730	Menahem b. Meïr Wilna	Amsterdam	1663, 69
Meïr	Verona	1647	Menahem Mendel Korchman b. Samuel Kohen.	Frankfort-on-the-Oder.	1701–2
Meïr b. Asher	Venice	1565, 74			
Meïr b. David	Prague	1512, 15, 18, 22, 26, 29	Menahem b. Moses Israel	Prague	1549–50
				Ferrara	1555
Meïr b. David b. Benjamin	Hamburg	1715, 20	Menahem (Mendel) b. Nathan Eisenstadt.	Prague	1705
Meïr b. David of Kulk	Lublin	1627	Menahem de Rossi b. Azariah	Mantua	1565
	Cracow	1642–44	Menahem b. Samuel Esra		1614
Meïr b. Eliezer Lipman Kaẓ (Kohen).	Prossnitz	1711	Menahem (Man) b. Solomon Levi.	Amsterdam	1724–27, 32, 33, 38–39
	Frankfort-on-the-Oder.	1717	Menahem Stummer Kohen	Prague	1686–90
	Dyhernfurth	1718–20	Menahem Trinki b. David	Venice	1622
Meïr b. Ephraim	Mantua	1557–60, 63–87	Menahem (Manle b. Judah Loeb) of Wilmersdorf.	Dyhernfurth	1690–91
				Sulzbach	1701
Meïr Epstein b. Jacob Levi	Prague	1515, 18, 22		Hanau	1710–12
Meïr Friedburg	Hanau	1719		Wilmersdorf	1713–14
Meïr Gans b. Menahem	Prague	1647 (?)		Berlin	1716–17
Meïr (Menahem) Ḥabib b. Joseph.	Venice	1657		Frankfort-on-the-Oder.	1717
Meïr Heilbronn (Heilpron) b. Moses.	Cremona	1557–58	Meshullam (Phoebus) b. Aaron Ḥayyaṭ.	Frankfort-on-the-Oder.	1703, 12, 25, 29
	Mantua	1563			
Meïr b. Isaac of Loktsch	Sulzbach	1702	Meshullam (Zalman) b. Aaron b. Uri.	Sulzbach	1716–17, 22, 67 (?)
Meïr b. Jacob Koppel	Hamburg	1711			
Meïr b. Joseph (Jospe) Kohen of Hamburg.	Offenbach	1717	Meshullam (Zalman) b. Abraham Berech Pinkerle.	Amsterdam	1683, 84–85, 85
Meïr b. Manasseh Nikolsburg	Prague	1680		Venice	1700, 4
Meïr b. Melli	Venice	1617–19	Meshullam Ashkenazi	Venice	1685
Meïr b. Mordecai Levi	Lublin	1568	Meshullam Bassan	Venice	1587
Meïr b. Naphtali Kossowitz	Prague	1691	Meshullam Cusi	Piove di Sacco	1475
	Frankfort-on-the-Oder.	1698	Meshullam Cusi Levi	Venice	1614
	Prague	1709, 13, 14, 28, 35–36	Meshullam (Phoebus) b. Elijah	Frankfort-on-the-Oder.	1709, 11–12, 29, 32
Meïr Oettingen	Offenbach	1722	Meshullam Gentile b. Moses	Mantua	1675

Name.	Place.	Date.
Meshullam (Phoebus Zalman) Hurwitz.	Frankfort-on-the-Oder.	1703, 5, 8, 11–12, 13, 29
Meshullam Hurwitz Levi.........	Prague........	1647, 48, 63
	Wilmersdorf..	1671, 73
	Frankfort-on-the-Oder.	1677
	Sulzbach......	1695–96 (?)
Meshullam (Phoebus) b. Isaac....	Amsterdam....	1715
Meshullam (Kofman) b. Shemaiah.	Venice........	1545–46, 49, 52
Meshullam b. Solomon........	Lublin........	1556, 59, 66
Meshullam Sullam (Salem?) b. Isaac.	Mantua........	1589–90
Michael b. Abraham.............	Berlin........	1699–1700
Michael Diaz Mocatto	Leghorn.......	1650–52, 55–57
Michael G'acon (?).............	Constantinople	1732
Michael Hanau b. Solomon.......	Frankfort-on-the-Main.	1717, 20
Michael b. Hayyim Talmesingen.	Fürth.........	1727
Michael b. Yom-Ṭob Kohen	Salonica......	1732
Mordecai	Verona.......	1647
Mordecai b. Abraham of Posen...	Offenbach.....	1718
Mordecai b. Abraham Teimer of Zolkiev.	Dyhernfurth ..	1715
Mordecai Alfandari b. Shabbethai.	Amsterdam....	1717–18, 20
Mordecai of Ansbach...........	Constantinople	1719, 23
Mordecai ibn 'Atthar b. Reuben..	Fürth.........	1692–93, 1701
Mordecai Azulai b. Moses........	Amsterdam....	1721
Mordecai b. Baruch of Tivoli.	Amsterdam....	1693, 97
Mordecai b. Benjamin Zeeb of Cracow.	Venice........	1585
	Prague........	1657
	Cracow	1670
Mordecai b. David.............	Prague........	1512
Mordecai (Gumpel) b. Eleazar Hendels.		
Mordecai Gener Baermann Halberstadt.	Amsterdam....	1712
Mordecai b. Jacob of Prostitz	Lublin	1596, 1602–5
	Prague........	1608, 9
	Hanau.......	1610
	Basel	1622
	Hanau.......	1623–25
Mordecai (Baer) Jakerl.........	Prague........	1705
Mordecai b. Jehiel Michael Slawatich.	Frankfort-on-the-Oder.	1690
Mordecai b. Joseph Judah Wahl..	Basel	1611–12
Mordecai (Gumpel) b. Judah Loeb (b. Mordecai) Polak.	Amsterdam....	1648–50, 50–51, 53, 56, 58, 60–64, 66, 67, 70–71, 83, 89
Mordecai b. Moses Levi..........	Basel	1580
Mordecai b. Moses Menahem Nahum.	Berlin........	1703
	Prague........	1705–6, 9–10
Mordecai b. Naphtali............	Basel	1612
Mordecai b. Naphtali Hirz........	Fürth........	1692
	Amsterdam....	1702
Mordecai b. Reuben Basla.......	Soncino.......	1489
Mordecai Saul b. Samuel Saul....	Venice........	1607
Mordecai b. Shabbethai.........	Basel	1598, 1618–19
Mordecai b. Simḥah.............	Venice.......	1576
Mordecai Sofer of Prague	Prague........	1512
Mordecai b. Solomon.............	Amsterdam....	1732
Moses (b....?).................	Lublin	1646
Moses (Moses b. Moses?)........	Cracow	1586, 92–93
Moses b. (Aaron?) of Zolkiev....	Zolkiev.......	1718
Moses b. Aaron Ashkenazi	Constantinople	1652
Moses b. Aaron Kohen of Witmund.	Amsterdam....	1727
Moses b. Aaron of Worms.......	Amsterdam....	1650, 53, 56–57, 58, 61–63, 64–66, 70–71, 80
Moses b. Abraham Abinu.........	Amsterdam....	1686, 87, 90–94
	Halle.........	1709–14
Moses b. Abraham Kohen........	Wilmersdorf..	1721–23, 27–28, 30, 32
Moses b. Abraham of Leipnik	Lublin	1619
Moses b. Abraham Nathan	Lublin	1636 (?)
Moses Abulafia.................	Venice.......	1587
Moses b. Alexander Levi.........	Basel	1610
Moses Alfalas..................	Venice.......	1598–1600
Moses Altaras..................	Venice.......	1619
Moses (Nathaniel) Altschul b. Aaron Freund of Prague.	Frankfort-on-the-Oder.	1697–99
Moses Amarillo b. Solomon.......	Salonica......	1719, 22
Moses (Isaac) b. Assher.........	Prague........	1668, 1673–75
Moses b. Asher Kohen of Halle...	Jessnitz.......	1725
Moses (Simeon) Basilia b. Shabbethai.	Verona.......	1652
Moses Belmonte................	Amsterdam....	1644–45
Moses Benveniste...............	Venice.......	1647
Moses Ben-Ẓion................	Mantua.......	1667

Name.	Place.	Date.
Moses (ibn Yakkar) Brandon.....	Amsterdam....	1708–10
Moses Carillo..................	Smyrna.......	1659
Moses Corcos..................	Venice.......	1606 (?)
Moses b. Daniel of Rohatyn	Zolkiev.......	1693
Moses b. David.................	Amsterdam....	1723
Moses Diaz b. Isaac.............	Venice.......	1706–13(15?)
Moses Dorheim	Frankfort-on-the-Main.	1719, 23
Moses b. Eliezer................	Venice.......	1614
Moses b. Eliezer................	Cracow	1640
Moses b. Eliezer of Wilna........	Lublin	1622
Moses b. Ezra..................	Cracow	1571
Moses b. Facilino b. Samuel........	Constantinople	1516
Moses Falcon b. Samuel.........	Salonica......	1719–29, 32
Moses Frankfurter..............	Amsterdam....	1721
Moses Gabbai	Venice.......	1578
Moses Gabbai	Salonica......	1658
Moses Gifrut...................	Smyrna.......	1730, 58, 64
Moses Gomez Mesquita b. Isaac...	Amsterdam....	1707–8
Moses Ḥabib	Naples........	1488
Moses Ḥagiz...................	Venice.......	1703–4
	Amsterdam....	1708–14
	Wandsbeck...	1726–33
Moses b. Ḥalifah Sa'adia	Venice.......	1711
Moses b. Ḥalimi b. Solomon........	Constantinople	1518
Moses b. Hamon b. Joseph........	Constantinople	1515, 16, 46
Moses Hausen b. Joseph Moses...	Sulzbach......	1684–85, 88
	Fürth.........	1701
Moses (David) Hausen b. Zalman.	Venice.......	1704–5
Moses (David Tebele) b. Ḥayyim Koethen.	Wandsbeck ...	1723
Moses b. Ḥayyim of Tikotin......	Offenbach.....	1722
Moses Heilprin b. Phinehas.......	Amsterdam....	1650, 62
Moses Hock b. Isaac.............	Prague........	1694
	Frankfort-on-the-Oder.	1698
	Berlin........	1699–1701
	Prague........	1710, 18–20
Moses b. Isaac..................	Naples	1492
Moses b. Isaac..................	Constantinople	1716–17, 19
	Salonica.......	1719, 31
Moses b. Isaiah b. Isaac.........	Cracow	1604
Moses b. Israel (Isser) Lasar Cracow.	Lublin	1636
	Cracow	1646
Moses b. Issachar (Baermann) Wink.	Amsterdam....	1725–26, 26–27, 30, 32–33, 39–40
Moses b. Jacob Gelhaar of Prague	Prague........	1609–10, 13, 14, 16(17?), 20, 23
Moses b. Jacob Maarsen Levi of Amsterdam.	Altona........	1728
	Hamburg.....	1741
	Rödelheim....	1753
	Frankfort-on-the-Main.	1756
	Metz.........	1764
Moses b. Jacob of Slutzk.........	Jessnitz.......	1724
Moses Jaffe....................	Venice.......	1645
Moses b. Jonah Gamburg.........	Frankfort-on-the-Main.	1722–28
Moses b. Joseph................	Lublin	1642, 48
Moses b. Joseph................	Amsterdam....	1695
Moses b. Joseph Aryeh..........	Venice.......	1606
Moses b. Joseph (b. Isaac Isaiah of Woidislaw).	Prossnitz......	1711
	Dyhernfurth ..	1719
	Jessnitz.......	1720–26
	Dyhernfurth ..	1726
	Wandsbeck ...	1727, 28
Moses b. Joseph Emden..........	Amsterdam....	1698
Moses b. Judah (Loeb) Cleve.....	Jessnitz.......	1722
Moses b. Judah of Emden........	Amsterdam....	1718
Moses (Menahem Nahum) b. Judah (Loeb) Kaz.	Lublin	1648
	Prague........	1657, 60, 62, 74–75, 78
	Weckelsdorf..	1682, 86, 90,
	Fürth	1691–92, 94, 97
	Prague........	1705–6 (?)
Moses Kala'i b. Mattithiah b. Samuel.	Venice.......	1599–1600
Moses Kalaẓ (Khallaẓ)...........	Constantinople	1536–37
Moses b. Kalman Speier.........	Frankfort-on-the-Main.	1721
Moses Levi Ashkenazi of Modena.	Constantinople	1509
Moses Levi Ḥazzan..............	Venice.......	1598
Moses Levi Muja................	Venice.......	1675–78
Moses Maḥbub b. Maimon........	Constantinople	1520–22, 42
Moses Maguro b. Daniel	Venice.......	1693, 94, 96
Moses di Medina b. Samuel.......	Salonica......	1593–1615
Moses di Medina b. Shemaiah.....	Mantua.......	1648
Moses (Yom-Ṭob Lipmann) b. Menahem (Man) b. Isaac Jacob.	Dyhernfurth ..	1693
	Sulzbach......	1688
Moses Mendez Coutinho b. Abraham.	Amsterdam....	1695, 99–1711
Moses b. Meshullam (Zalman)	....	1727
Moses ibn Minir................	Venice.......	1593

Name.	Place.	Date.
Moses Minz Levi b. Asher........	Amsterdam....	1713
Moses Minz Levi b. Isaac Menahem b. Moses.	Venice	1601
Moses (Hezekiah) b. Mocatta.....	Amsterdam....	1708
Moses b. Moses	Cracow	1594, 96, 99
Moses b. Moses....................	Wilmersdorf..	1726–28
Moses b. Moses Meïr Kohen.......	Lublin	1591
Moses b. Nathan Hamelburg......	Amsterdam....	1644, 49
Moses (Raphael) Ottolenghi b. Samuel David.	Amsterdam....	1712
Moses Parnas b. Eleazar.........	Constantinople	1546–47, 47–50, 54
Moses Pereira	Amsterdam....	1688
Moses Phorno	Smyrna	1731
Moses Pinto Delgado.............	Amsterdam....	1644
Moses Poki......................	Constantinople	1581
Moses (Aryeh) Posen	Berlin........	1715
Moses Principal.................	Venice	1617
Moses Sachs b. Simeon of Posen..	Frankfort - on - the-Oder.	1705
Moses Saertels...................	Prague........	1606, 11
Moses b. Samuel (Sanvel)........	Hamburg	1690
Moses b. Samuel Kohen of Brzesc.	Amsterdam....	1709
Moses b. Saul Pauer.............	Lublin	1571–72
Moses Schedel...................	Prague........	1585–1605
Moses Selimi....................	Constantinople	1522
Moses Shabbethai b. Ḥayyim Sabbata.	Salonica......	1651
Moses b. Shabbethai of Loktsch...	Prague........	1590
Moses b. Shneor (Zalman) Kohen.	Amsterdam....	1707
	Berlin........	1715
Moses ibn Shoshan...............	Sabbionetta...	1554–55
Moses Simeon....................	Salonica......	1621
Moses b. Simeon.................	Amsterdam....	1687
Moses b. Simeon (b.) Anschel Herzel's.	Wilmersdorf..	1671–73
	Prague........	1686
Moses b. Simḥah Bonem	Dessau........	1696–1701, 4
	Jessnitz.......	1720
Moses Solomon...................	Cracow	1642
Moses b. Solomon Ashkenazi.....	Venice	1713
Moses b. Solomon Levi...........	Amsterdam....	1669
Moses Spira b. Jacob.............	Frankfort - on - the-Main.	1719
Moses Taranto...................	Smyrna	1730
Moses Ṭarfon	Venice	1606
Moses Tausk b. Phinehas Shoḥeṭ .	Dyhernfurth ..	1696, 97
	Berlin........	1699, 1705, 9, 14–15, 17
	Frankfort - on - the-Oder.	1724–25, 33
Moses Trinco Levi of Morea......	Venice	1620
Moses Utiz b. Eliezer............	Prague........	1610, 12
Moses (Ḥai) Venturin b. Joseph.	Venice	1707
Moses of Vienna	Prague........	1623
Moses Waag.....................	Frankfort - on - the-Main.	1711–12
Moses Weisswasser b. Katriel....	Mantua........	1589, 93
	Prague........	1595–97
	Cracow	1598
	Prague........	1605–6, 9, 10, 14, 18, 21–22
Moses Welsch....................	Frankfort - on - the-Main.	1704
Moses b. Zachariah Kohen Corfu..	Venice	1546, 49, 51, 53, 76
Moses Zacuto....................	Venice	1648–72
	Mantua........	1673–95
Moses (Ḥayyim) Zalach..........	Venice	1665
Moses Ẕarfati di Gerona..........	Amsterdam....	1726
Moses b. Ẕebi....................	Dyhernfurth ..	1690–91
Moses b. Ẕebi Kalonymus of Halberstadt.	Amsterdam....	1712
Moses b. Zerah Ashkenazi........	Constantinople	1726
Naḥman b. Jacob of Lublin.......	Lublin	1648 (?)
Naḥman b. Jehiel of Dessau......	Jessnitz.......	1724
Naḥmias (David ibn)	Constantinople	1503–11
Naḥmias (Samuel b. David)......	Constantinople	1503–11, 11–22
Nahum Kohen....................	Amsterdam....	1669
Naphtali (?).....................	Lublin	1648
Naphtali b. Aaron Ashkenazi.....	Venice	1704–5
Naphtali Altschul b. Tobiah.....	Cracow	1593–94, 98
Naphtali (Herzel) Altschüler b. (Jacob) Ascher Anschel b. Naphtali Herzel.	Prague........	1629, 49
Naphtali Ashkenazi b. Joseph....	Salonica.......	1596–97
	Venice	1601–2
Naphtali (Hirsch) b. Azriel Wilna.	Constantinople	1510–11
Naphtali (Hirsch) b. Jacob.......	Amsterdam....	1683–85
Naphtali (Ẕebi) b. Jacob........	Venice	1649
Naphtali (Ẕebi) b. Jacob Levi of Gnesen.	Berlin........	1715
Naphtali (Hirz) b. Judah Lima of Essen.	Sulzbach......	1615–17

Name.	Place.	Date.
Naphtali (Hirsch) b. Moses of Gojetein.	Prague........	1595
Naphtali (Zebi Hirsch) b. Moses Tobiah (Gutmann).	Cracow	1625
Naphtali (Hirsch) Pappenheim...	Amsterdam....	1650, 56, 56–57, 58
Naphtali b. Samuel Heida........	Prague........	1675, 82, 86
Naphtali Schwarz................	Lublin	1568
Naphtali (Hirz) b. Simson Langlos	Frankfort - on - the-Oder.	1692
Nathan Auerbach b. Moses of Wisnicz.	Wilmersdorf ..	1726–27
	Altona........	1732
Nathan b. David Levi............	Lublin	1614
Nathan b. Gershon Ashkenazi....	Frankfort - on - the-Main.	1699
Nathan Gota (Gutta ?) b. Isaac b. Abraham.	Venice	1629–30
Nathan b. Isaac Friedburg........	Cracow	1593
Nathan (Feitel) b. Judah.........	Amsterdam....	1700–10
Nathan Michelbach b. Eliezer....	Basel.........	1612
Nathan (Pheibel) b. Moses........	Frankfort - on - the-Oder.	1702
Nathan b. Moses Petlitzer........	Cracow	1569–71
Nathan de Salo..................	Ferrara	1477
Naṭhan b. Samuel................	Amsterdam....	1726
Nathan (Nata) b. Samuel.........	Fürth	1722–27
Nathan (Nata) b. Simeon of Posen.	Lublin	1623–27
Nathan b. Solomon Ashkenazi....	Venice	1605
Nathanael Ḥalfan b. Perez.......	Trini.........	1525
Nathanael b. Judah..............	Lublin	1623–27
Nathanael b. Levi of Jerusalem...	Naples........	1487–92
Nehemiah b. Abraham............	Amsterdam....	1721–27 (26?)
Neumark (Nathan b. Loeb).......	Berlin........	1719–26
Neumark, Moses (or Judah Loeb)..	Berlin........	1699–1703(?)
Nicolai (Christian)..............	Frankfort - on - the-Main.	1699
Nissim b. Azriel.................	Hanau	1712
Nissim Ḥalfan b. Abba-Mari.....	Venice	1545
Nissim b. Ḥayyim Ashkenazi	Constantinople	1732
Nissim (David) b. Moses..........	Venice	1719
Nissim ibn Shoshan..............		1 5 9 7, 99, 1601, 3–4, 5
Nissim Vileisit..................	Constantinople	1643
Noah Casirino...................	Mantua........	1653
Noah b. Hezekiah................	Prague........	1675
Noah b. Samuel..................	Lublin	1623–27
Obadiah Maron and Jehiel d'Italia	Mantua........	1672
Obadiah Sabbakh................	Constantinople	1578
Obadiah b. Zachariah............	Venice	1549
Paulus of Prague................	Helmstadt....	1580
Pelta (= Paltai) of Meseritz.....	Frankfort - on - the-Oder.	1697–99
Perugia (Joshua b. Judah Samuel)	Mantua........	1648
Perugia (Judah Samuel).........	Mantua........	1622–26
Perugia (Judah Samuel).........	Mantua........	1657, 59, 61, 62, 64
Perugia, Louis of (?).............	Mantua........	1667–72, 95, 99
Pethahiah (Moses) b. Joseph of Ofen	Prague........	1586, 90–92
Phinehas b. Eliakim.............	Amsterdam....	1706, 10
Phinehas Heilpron b. Judah of Neuersdorf.	Basel.........	1602
Phoebus b. Menahem b. Phoebus .	Offenbach.....	1723
Pinne bat Wolf..................	Berlin........	1717
Polychron b. Isaac...............	Constantinople	1726–37
Proops (Solomon)................	Amsterdam....	1704–34
Proops' Heirs	Amsterdam....	1734–1849
Pugil (Johann Kaspar)...........	Frankfort - on - the-Main.	1704
Raḥamim Ḥalfon................	Venice	1711
Raphael	Hague	1518–19
Raphael Abbas b. Joshua.........	Amsterdam....	1709
Raphael Altschul b. Mordecai Gumpel of Prague.	Fürth	1691–92
Raphael Ḥayyim Supino (Sopino ?)	Leghorn.......	1651–52
Raphael (Ḥayyim) d'Italia........	Mantua........	1724
Raphael b. Moses b. Isaac Judah..	Cracow	1667, 70
Raphael di Palasios b. Joshua....	Amsterdam....	1714–16
Raphael b. Solomon of Lithuania..		1692
Raphael b. Samuel...............	Frankfort - on - the-Oder.	1683
Raphael de Silva b. Solomon......	Venice	1656
Raphael Talmi b. Immanuel of Forli.	Bologna.......	1537–40
Raphael Treves..................	Constantinople	1711
Rebecca bat Isaac b. Judah Jüdels	Wilmersdorf ..	1677
Reichel bat Isaac b. Judah Jüdels.	Wilmersdorf ..	1677, 79, 80, 8.
	Sulzbach......	1691
	Fürth	1692–99, 1701
Reis (Hirz b. Seligmann)........	Offenbach.....	1715
Reis (Isaac Eisak b. Hirz)........	Frankfort - on - the-Main.	1687
Reis (Seligmann b. Hirz).........	Frankfort - on - the-Main.	1687, 1706–11
	Homburg	1711–12
	Offenbach	1714–19, 21

Name.	Place.	Date.
Reuben b. Eliakim of Mayence....	Amsterdam....	1644, 46–47, 47–53, 56, 58, 61–63, 70–71, 78
Reuben Fürst (Ferst) b. Nethaneel	Berlin.........	1706
Reuben b. Isaac Levi Breidenbach (Breitenbach).	Frankfort-on-the-Oder.	1725, 29
Reyna (Donna)...................	Constantinople	1593–94
	Kuru Tchesh-me.	1597–98
Roizel (wife of Fishel)..........	Cracow.......	1586
Saadia b. Abigdor b. Eliezer Kohen	Prague........	1614
Saadia Angel b. Samuel..........	Salonica.......	1720–21, 29, 32
Saadia b. David.................	Venice........	1623
Saadia Kohen b. Zalman..........	Leghorn	1655
Samson b. Aaron Isaac...........	Lublin........	1636?
Samson Ḥabillo.................	Venice........	1654
Samson Hanau b. Solomon.......	Homburg	1724–25
Samson Melli b. Mordecai.......	Mantua.......	1676
Samson b. Moses................	Lublin	1618–20, 23–27
Samson Sanguine b. Michael......	Verona	1650
Samson Tarnigrod b. Ḥayyim....	Frankfort-on-the-Oder.	1691
Samuel b. . . .? (of the family of Isaiah b. Samuel Levi).	Lublin........	1646
Samuel Abravanel Soeyro.........	Amsterdam....	1650–52
Samuel Amato..................	Constantinople	1728
Samuel Archevolti..............	Venice........	1564–1602
Samuel b. Aryeh (Loeb) Levi of Posen.	Amsterdam....	1707, 7–8, 8, 15
Samuel b. Asher Levi............	Prague........	1512
Samuel ibn Ashkara Zarfati.......	Ferrara........	1551–52
Samuel Baruch and Jacob Baruch	Venice........	1656
Samuel Bergel b. Judah Reutling.	Sulzbach......	1712
Samuel Bloch b. Jacob	Zolkiev.......	1695
Samuel Caleb....................	Salonica.......	1597
Samuel di Campos...............	Amsterdam....	1685
Samuel Cases b. Moses...........	Mantua.......	1559
Samuel di Cazeres..............	Amsterdam....	1659
Samuel b. David Gumpel.........	Prague........	1515, 18
Samuel ibn Deisus..............	Venice........	1596, 97, 98
Samuel Dresle...................	Cracow.......	1631 (?), 39–40, 1737
	Berlin........	1712
Samuel (Sanwel) b. Eliakim b. Meïr.	Frankfort-on-the-Main.	1714
Samuel b. Elkanah..............	Fürth........	1724, 25, 26
Samuel Fürth (same as preceding?)	Hanau	1719
Samuel (Don) G'acon............	Faro	1487
Samuel Ḥabillo.................	Venice........	1643
Samuel Ḥagiz..................	Venice........	1596–98
Samuel b. Ḥayyim..............	Homburg......	1712
Samuel Ḥazzan.................	Venice........	1648
Samuel Heidah b. Joseph of Hamburg	Berlin........	1706
Samuel b. Hezekiah Levi.........	Naples........	1492
Samuel Hurwitz b. Meshullam (Zalman) b. Joseph Levi of Prague.	Wilmersdorf... Frankfort-on-the-Oder.	1670, 73–74 1677, 80, 86, 89, 91–1701, 5, 11, 13
Samuel b. Isaac Boehm..........	Cremona.....	1556
	Padua........	1562
	Venice........	1565–67
	Cracow.......	1569–81
Samuel (Sanwel) b. Jacob (of Lissa).	Hamburg......	1686, 87, 88, 90
	Fürth.........	1691–92, 93–94
Samuel b. Jacob Levi Brandeis...	Wilmersdorf...	1716
Samuel (Sanwel) b. Jacob Poppicz	Wilmersdorf...	1673–74
	Lublin........	1599
Samuel b. Jerahmeel.............	Wilmersdorf...	1729
Samuel (Ẓebi Hirsch) b. Joel Sirks	Cracow.......	1631–40
Samuel b. Jonah (Askeri ?) of Salonica.	Amsterdam....	1728
Samuel b. Joseph...............	Amsterdam....	1681–82
Samuel b. Judah.		
Samuel b. Judah Shammash......	Amsterdam....	1713
Samuel Katzenellenbogen........	Venice........	1563
Samuel Kolodro................	Leiria........	1492
Samuel Kusin b. Levi...........	Venice........	1636–37
Samuel Laṭif...................	Naples........	1490
	Mantua.......	1513–14
Samuel Levi....................	Cracow.......	1613(?)
Samuel Levi ibn Ḥakim.........	Constantinople	1546–47, 47–48
Samuel Magreso................	Constantinople	1717
Samuel Mantino b. Jacob........	Venice........	1546
Samuel Marquez b. Solomon......	Amsterdam....	1709, 14–16
Samuel di Medina b. Shemaiah...	Venice........	1647
	Mantua.......	1648
Samuel Meisel..................	Prague........	1614–15
Samuel b. Michael..............	Venice........	1721
Samuel b. Mordecai Ashkenazi of Przemysl.	Cracow.......	1612

Name.	Place.	Date.
Samuel (Joseph) b. Mordecai Grasmark.	Cracow........	1595–96, 1601–6
Samuel b. Moses Frankfurter.....	Amsterdam....	1731
Samuel b. Moses Levi............	Salonica.......	1563
Samuel b. Moses Levi............	Amsterdam....	1648–51, 52
Samuel b. Moses Sedjelmessa....	Salonica.......	1709, 13, 22
Samuel b. Musa................	Zamora.......	1492
Samuel Norzi b. Isaac...........	Mantua.......	1589–90
Samuel b. Peraḥyah.............	....	1565–84
Samuel Pinto..................	Amsterdam....	1666–67
Samuel Poppert................	Altona........	1727–30
Samuel Rikomin................	Constantinople	1511–13
Samuel Rodrigues-Mendes.......	Amsterdam....	1726
Samuel Rosa b. Isaac Baruch.....	Amsterdam....	1664–66
Samuel b. Samuel de Roma......	Naples	1486
Samuel Schwab b. Joseph of Günzburg.	Amsterdam....	1713, 26, 33–39
Samuel Shalom Sedjelmessi of Lepanto.	Venice........	1596
Samuel Teixeira...............	Amsterdam....	1678, 82, 85–87, 88, 95, 1723, 26
Samuel Valensi.................	Smyrna.......	1657–59
Samuel (Oppenheim) of Vienna...	....	1699
Samuel Zarfati.................	Rome	1547
Samuel b. Zeeb Wolf b. Ephraim Fischel of Lemberg.	Amsterdam....	1697, 98
Sarah bat Jacob................	Prague........	1605–15
Saul Belgrad b. Joseph of Udine..	Venice........	1606, 17
Saul b. Benjamin b. Isaac.......		1645
Saul of Frankfort-on-the-Oder....	Frankfort-on-the-Oder.	1712
Saul (Simeon) b. Judah Levi.....	Lublin........	1611–21, 27
Schwarz (Ḥayyim b. David).....	Prague........	1515, 18, 22, 26
	Oels..........	1530
	Augsburg.....	1533–43
	Ichenhausen..	1544–45
	Heddernheim..	1546
Selig b. Abraham Levi...........	Amsterdam....	1697
Selig (Abi 'Ezri) b. Solomon of Venice.	Dyhernfurth .. Frankfort-on-the-Oder.	1692–96 1697–99, 1701, 5
	Berlin........	1705, 9
	Frankfort-on-the-Oder.	1712, 13, 25, 29, 34
Seligmann Ulma b. Moses Simeon.	Hanau	1610–15, 16
Shabbethai (?).................	Venice........	1675
Shabbethai Bass...............	Amsterdam....	1679, 80, 82
	Dyhernfurth..	1689–1718
Shabbethai b. Mordecai of Posen	Basel	1599
Shalom b. David Moses..........	Prague........	1608
Shalom Galliago b. Joseph of Salonica.	Amsterdam....	1627
Shalom b. Gershon of Horodlo....	Lublin........	1604–5
Shalom (Schechna) b. Nahum Kaidanower.	Wilmersdorf.. Jessnitz......	1716 1721
Shalom (Mann) Stoks...........	Offenbach.....	1718
Shemariah b. Ahron............	Cracow.......	1589, 98
Shemariah b. Jacob of Grodno....	Amsterdam....	1711
Shem-Ṭob.....................	Salonica.......	1526–27
Shem-Ṭob ibn Minir............	Constantinople	1569
Shem-Ṭob ibn Polkar b. Moses....	Constantinople	1511
Shneor Falcon b. Judah	Constantinople	1560
	Venice........	1567
Shneor (Zalman) b. Israel Baruch Biechower.	Amsterdam....	1685–87
Shneor (Zalman) b. Jonathan Kohen of Posen.	Amsterdam....	1698, 1701, 7
Simeon Almosnino..............	Venice	1587–88
Simeon Altschul b. Asher Anschel Herzels.	Prague	1629
Simeon Altschüler b. Judah (Loeb)	Prague	1701
Simeon (Wolf) b. Asher Kohen Ashkenazi of Frankfort.	Cracow.......	1646–47
Simeon Blansa Ashkenazi.......	Venice	1696
Simeon (Wolf) Brandeis b. Jacob.	Frankfort-on-the-Oder.	1693
Simeon Coflo (Copio?)...........	Venice	1592
Simeon b. Isaac Cracow	Cracow.......	1574
Simeon b. Judah Joseph.........	Amsterdam....	1700
Simeon (Isaac) Kohen...........	Cracow.......	1584
Simeon Labi...................	Venice........	1648
Simeon Levi...................	Cremona	1565
Simeon (or Wolf) Menz b. Abraham.	Frankfort-on-the-Main.	1709–13
	Offenbach.....	1719
Simeon b. Naphtali Hirz........	Amsterdam....	1708, 11–15
Simeon Raner of Danzig.........	Amsterdam....	1685
Simeon Rodeti.................	Smyrna.......	1660
Simeon Treves	Frankfort-on-the-Main.	1719
Simeon Witzenhausen b. Joseph..	Amsterdam....	1679
	Frankfort-on-the-Main.	1680–84, 91

Name.	Place.	Date.
Simḥah b. Isaac	Cracow	1588, 97–98
	Basel	1602, 8
Sinai Ḳimḥi b. Ḥayyim	Constantinople	1717
Solomon	Amsterdam	1662
Solomòn (b. . . ?)	Salonica	1621
Solomon (Zalman) b. Aaron Isaac (Säkel) of Norden.	Hamburg	1692
Solomon b. Aaron Levi of Cracow.	Cracow	1648
Solomon Abrabalia (Abravalia)	Salonica	1520
Solomon b. Abraham	Mantua	1561
Solomon b. Abraham of Moravia	Lublin	1571
Solomon ibn Alḳabiẓ b. Moses Levi	Guadalajara	1482
Solomon Altaras	Venice	1685
Solomon Altaras b. David	Venice	1712, 18, 19, 30
Solomon Aptrod b. David	Frankfort-on-the-Main.	1722–30
Solomon (Zalman) Ashkenazi.	Amsterdam	1730
Solomon Barzillai b. Moses	Mantua	1565
Solomon (Zalman) b. Bonfet (Bonfed) Shneor.	Fürth	1729, 30
Solomon Bueno b. Jacob	Cremona	1576
Solomon Cavaliero (or Cavallero).	Salonica	1532–33
Solomon b. David	Venice	1600
Solomon Dels b. Simeon	Frankfort-on-the-Main.	1697
Solomon b. Eliezer Kohen	Lublin	1635
Solomon b. Ephraim Kohen	Amsterdam	1708
Solomon ibn Ezra b. Moses	Smyrna	1657–74
Solomon (Zalman) Fürth	Wilmersdorf	1673–74
Solomon Gabbai	Constantinople	1662
Solomon (Ḥayyim) Ḥaber-Ṭob.	Venice	1599
Solomon b. Hähnle Naske	Prague	1620
Solomon (Zalman) Hanau	Frankfort-on-the-Main.	1692–1714, (17?)
Solomon b. Isaac Kohen Ashkenazi	Salonica	1597
Solomon b. Isaac of Lisbon	Rome	1546
Solomon b. Isaiah Nizza	Venice	1684
Solomon b. Israel of Dubno	Amsterdam	1719
Solomon b. Jacob Judah of Norden (?).	Amsterdam	1640, 42
Solomon Jonah	Venice	1666
Solomon b. Joseph Kohen	Prague	1598
Solomon (Zalman) b. Joshua Ashkenazi.	Prague	1598
Solomon b. Judah Loeb	Prague	1725
Solomon (Zalman) b. Judah Loeb.	Wilmersdorf	1688–89
Solomon (Zalman) b. Kalman Kohen.	Frankfort-on-the-Main.	1699–1700
Solomon ibn Ḳoryaṭ	Leghorn	1650
Solomon (Zalman) of Lemberg	Venice	1716
Solomon London	Amsterdam	1709–14
	Frankfort-on-the-Main.	1714–25
	Offenbach and Hanau.	1716–20
	Amsterdam	1731–35
Solomon Luria	Venice	1607
Solomon Luzzatto b. Abraham	Venice	1567
Solomon Mar David	Venice	1599
Solomon b. Mazzal-Ṭob	Constantinople	1513–49
Solomon (Zalman) b. Mattithiah.	Berlin	1705, 6, 8, 13, 15
Solomon b. Meïr	Cracow	1587–88
Solomon (Zalman) b. Meïr Levi of Schwersenz.	Jessnitz	1720–23
Solomon b. Mordecai	Constantinople	1710
Solomon (Zalman) b. Mordecai	Frankfort-on-the-Oder.	1708
	Amsterdam	1717–18
Solomon b. Moses Abraham	Prague	1713 (?)
Solomon b. Moses Ashkenazi	Dyhernfurth	1712
Solomon (Zalman) b. Moses Frankfurter.	Amsterdam	1722, 24, 26, 33
Solomon b. Moses Ḥazzan	Venice	1711
Solomon b. Moses Levi	Amsterdam	1663, 76
Solomon ibn Mubḥar	Constantinople	1642–43
Solomon ibn Naḥmias b. David	Venice	1599
Solomon Nissim	Venice	1667
Solomon Norzi b. Samuel	Mantua	1593
Solomon Oliveyra	Amsterdam	1680, 86
Solomon b. Perez Bonfoi Zarfati.	Soncino	1484
	Naples	1490, 92
Solomon b. Samuel Levi	Prague	1512, 15, 22
Solomon (Zalman) b. Samuel Steina-Kopf of Prague.	Sulzbach	1685
Solomon (Hai) Saraval b. Nehemiah.	Venice	1667
Solomon ibn Shoshan b. Samuel	Salonica	1580, 82
Solomon Ṭobyana	Amsterdam	1685
Solomon b. Todros	Amsterdam	1662 (?)
Solomon Trani b. Moses	Venice	1629–30
Solomon Usque	Constantinople	1561
Solomon (Don) Walid b. Judah.	Venice	1521
Solomon Wehle b. Moses	Zolkiev	1702–4
Solomon ibn Yaḳḳar	Constantinople	1522
Solomon Yerushalmi b. Menahem.	Salonica	1551
	Sabbionetta	1554
Solomon Zalmati b. Maimon	Ixar	1490
Solomon b. Ẓebi Lokatscher	Dyhernfurth	1700, 2
	Berlin	1703
Soncino (Moses b. . . ?)	Salonica	1526–27
Soncino, Eliezer b. Gershon	Constantinople	1534–47
Soncino, Gershon b. Moses	Soncino	1488–90
	Brescia	1491–94
	Barco	1496–97
	Fano	1503, 5–6
	Pesaro	1507–20
	Fano	1516
	Ortona	1518, 19
	Rimini	1521–26
	Constantinople	1530–33
	Salonica	1532–33
Soncino, Israel Nathan b. Samuel b. Moses.	Soncino	1483
	Casal Maggiore	1486
Soncino, Joshua Solomon b. Israel Nathan.	Soncino	1483–88
	Naples	1490–92
Soncino, Solomon b. Moses	Soncino	1490
Tobiah b. Abraham Kohen	Wilmersdorf	1714, 16–18, 21, 29–30
	Sulzbach	1741
	Fürth	1745
Uri (Phoebus) b. Aaron Witmund Levi.	Amsterdam	1645–48, 56, 58–89
	Zolkiev	1692–95
Uri (Phoebus) b. Abraham Bärmes	Amsterdam	1670–80, 82, 86
Uri b. Abraham Kohen	Amsterdam	1698
Uri (Phoebus) b. Joseph	Amsterdam	1723, 24, 26, 27
Uri b. Moses	Amsterdam	1650
Uri (Shragga Phoebus) b. Solomon (Zalman).	Cracow	1638–40, 43, 48
Usque (Abraham)	Ferrara	1553–57
Veile bat Moses Schlenker of Fürth	Wilmersdorf	1727
Vittoria Eliano	Cremona	1557, 58, 58–60
	Venice	1564, 65, 66, 67
	Rome	1578, 81
Weglin (Sebald)	Frankfort-on-the-Main.	1709
Yaḥya b. Abraham ibn Ḥama Fas.	Venice	1574
Yom-Ṭob b. Michael Kohen	Salonica	1717
Yom-Ṭob Modigliano b. Samuel.	Salonica	1723
Yom-Ṭob Zikri b. Rafael	Constantinople	1519
Yom-Ṭob Zarfati b. Perez	Naples	1489
Zachariah	Venice	1667
Zadok b. Abraham of Meseritz.	Frankfort-on-the-Oder.	1697–99, 1702, 5–8, 11–13, 13, 20, 24, 25
Ẓebi (Hirsch) b. Aaron Ḥayyat	Frankfort-on-the-Oder.	1714
Ẓebi (Hirsch) b. (Jacob) Abraham	Cracow	1642–43
Ẓebi (Hirsch) b. Abraham of Wronek.	Amsterdam	1700–1
Ẓebi (Hirsch) b. Elijah b. Baer Lübeck.	Prague	1691–92
	Dessau	1696
	Frankfort-on-the-Oder.	1697–99
	Berlin	1699, 1700
	Prague	1705–6, 25
Ẓebi (Hirsch) b. Falk Kohen Kümmelbrod.	Fürth	1692
Ẓebi (Hirsch) b. Gershon	Amsterdam	1700–5, 10, 11, 14
Ẓebi (Hirsch) b. Isaac Levi	Amsterdam	1717–18, 23, 26, 28, 30, 33, 38–39
Ẓebi b. Isaac of Ostrog	Cracow	1576–77
Ẓebi b. Isaac of Posen	Lublin	1622
Ẓebi b. Jacob	Lublin	1685
Ẓebi (Hirsch) b. Joseph Levi	Fürth	1691–94, 99, 1701
Ẓebi (Hirsch) b. Josiah Crasnik	Lublin	1627
Ẓebi (Hirsch) b. Kalonymus Kohen of Kalisz.	Dyhernfurth	1691, 96
	Frankfort-on-the-Oder.	1697–99
	Dyhernfurth	1700–1
Ẓebi Levi Ḥazzan	Venice	1598
Ẓebi (Hirsch) Liberls Sofer	Prague	1707
Ẓebi (Hirsch) b. Meïr of Janow	Jessnitz	1720, 21, 22
Ẓebi (Hirsch) b. Meïr of Kossowitz	Prague	1713
Ẓebi (Hirsch) Minz Levi b. Asher.	Amsterdam	1725–26, 26
Ẓebi b. Moses	Lublin	1622
Ẓebi (Hirsch) b. Moses Frankfort.	Amsterdam	1701
Ẓebi b. Shalom	Cracow	1642–44
Ẓebi (Hirsch) b. Tobiah	Lublin	1623–27

Name.	Place.	Date.
Zeeb (Wolf) b. Aryeh (Loeb) b. Isaac.	Amsterdam....	1724
Zeeb (Wolf) b. Isaac Josels.......	Cracow	1638–39
Zeeb (Wolf) b. Levi................	Amsterdam....	1685–87
Zeeb (Wolf) b. Meshullam........	Berlin.........	1702–3, 12, 16–17
Zeeb (Wolf) b. Mordecai..........	Cracow	1638–40, 43, 48
Zeeb (Wolf) b. Samuel...........	Amsterdam....	1698

LIST OF CHRISTIAN PRINTERS.

Name.	Place.	Date.
Alberti (Idzardus)................	Franeker......	1642
Albrizzi (Hier.)..................	Venice	1707 (?)
Ambrosini (Christoforo)	Venice	1667, 71–74
Andreae (Jo. Ph.)................	Frankfort - on - the-Main.	1716
Andreae (Matth.).................	Frankfort - on - the-Oder.	1707–12
Andreae (St.)....................	Heidelberg	1586
Anshelm (Thom.).................	Tübingen	1512–14
	Hagenau......	1518–19
Bakenhoffer (Jo. Phil.).........	Copenhagen ..	1696
Baron (Jo. Zach.)................	Leyden	1658
Baroni (Andera).................	Venice	1692
Bashuysen (H. J. P.)............	Hanau........	1709–12
Bauernfeld (Jac.)................	Jena..........	1678
Beausang (Jo. Jac.).............	Hanau........	1715–19
Bebel............................	Basel	1534–95
Beckmann (Joh. Christ.)........	Frankfort - on - the-Oder.	1677
Blaak (Laur.)...................	Amsterdam ...	1676–78
Bladao (Maestro Anton. B. de Asula).	Rome	1524, 46–47
Blaise (Thom.)..................	Paris.........	1622
Blaue (Wilh.)...................	Amsterdam....	1676–78
Bomberg (Daniel)...............	Venice	1516–48
Bona (Domenico)................	Venice	1678
Boom, Baum (Joh.).............	Amsterdam....	1705
Borstius (Gerhard and Jacob)....	Amsterdam....	1698–1703
Bragadina.......................	Venice	1664
Bragadini (Aluise, Aloyse).......	Venice	1550–53, 63 (?)–75
Bragadini (Aluise [II.], Aloyse)..	Venice	1624–30, 39–50
Bragadini (Aluise [III.]).........	Venice	1697–98, 1710
Bragadini, Bragadino............	Venice	1550–1800
Bragadini (Giacomo, Jacob)......	Venice	1639–50
Bragadini (Girolamo, Gerolimo, Hieronym.).	Venice	1639–50, 55–64, 67
Bragadini (Juan, Zuan, Giovan., Johann.).	Venice	1579–1614 (15?)
Bragadini (Lorenzo, Laurent.)....	Venice	1615–30, 39–50
Bragadini (Nicol.)...............	Venice	1639–50
Bragadini (Pietro)..............	Venice	1614–30, 39–49
Bragadini (Vicenzo [I.], Vincent.)	Venice	1639–49
Bragadini (Vicenzio [II.]).......	Venice	1697–98
Brand (Justin.).................	Leipsic........	1683–86
Brandenburger..................	Leipsic........	1712
Brandmüller (Jo.)...............	Basel	1691
Breitkopf (Bernh. Christ.).......	Leipsic........	1725
Brion (Anton)..................	Riva..........	1557–58
Brocario (Bul. de)..............	Complutum...	1514–17
Brucello (Franc.)...............	Venice	1544
Cajon	Venice	1613–22, 22–41
Calleoni, Caleoni (Anton)........	Venice	1642–57
Caphallon.......................	Paris	1533
Cavalli, Caballi (Zorzo).........	Venice	1565–68
Christiani (Wilm.)..............	Leyden ...	1633
Clugus (Jos.)...................	Wittenberg....	1525, 29
Collegium Italorum..............	Paris	1539
Commelius.......................	Heidelberg....	1599–1616
Conti (Vicenz., Vincent.)........	Cremona.....	1556–61, 65–66, 67
	Sabbionetta...	1567
Cramosius (Sebast.).............	Paris	1632
Cratander (Andr.)...............	Basel	1531
Crati (Zach.)...................	Wittenberg...	1586–87
Crato (Jo.).....................	Wittenberg ..	1563–76, 82
Crivellari (Gaspar).............	Padua	1622–23
Crivellari (Giulio, Julius)........	Padua	1640
Decker (Ge.)...................	Basel	1660
Donne (Francesco delle).........	Verona	1594–95
Doriguzzi (Zuane, Giov.)........	Venice	1670, 85
Draconi (Christoph.)............	Cremona......	1576
Dreunen (Meinardus)	Utrecht.......	1665

Name.	Place.	Date.
Eichhorn.....................	Frankfort - on - the-Oder.	1597
Ellinger (J. G.)..............	Leipsic	1672
Elzevir......................	Leyden	1630–34
Episcopus (Nicol.)............	Basel	1536, 37, 47–48, 56, 63
Erpeniana....................	Leyden	1621
Facciotto or Fazot de Montecchio (Giov., Giac).	Rome	1518
Fagius (Paul.)...............	Isny..........	1541–42
	Constantinople	1543–44
Farri (Messer Zuane or Giovanni)	Venice	1544
Filippon(o), Filipponi (Filotarsi).	Mantua........	1563–64, 68
Filippono (Francesco)...........	Mantua........	1561–63
Filoni.......................	Ferrara.......	1693
Froben......................	Hamburg	1596
Froben (Ambros.).............	Basel	1578–81
	Freiburg......	1583–84
Froben (Hieron.).............	Basel	1531, 36–63
Froben (Jo. [I.]).............	Basel	1516–27 (32)
Fuldius (Mart.)..............	Leipsic	1712
Fyner (Conrad)..............	Esslingen.....	1475, 77
Ganghel (Christoph. van)......	Amsterdam....	1683
Gara, Garra (di, dei)..........	Venice	1564–1609 (10)
Gardoni (Alessandro).........	Venice	1577–78
Giustiniani, Justiniani (Bern)...	Venice	1593
Giustiniani, Justiniani (Marco Antonio).	Venice	1545–52
Goebelius....................	Augsburg.....	1680–83
Gottschalk (Mich.)...........	Frankfort - on - the-Oder.	1693–1734
Gourmont (Aegid.)...........	Paris.........	1520–29
Gross (Jo. Ad.)...............	Hanau........	1714–15
Gruler (Peter)...............	Tannhausen...	1594
Grunbergius (J.).............	Wittenberg....	1521
Grymm (Sigismund), Medicus...	Augsburg.....	1520
Gryphius (Franc.)............	Paris.........	1532
Gryphius (Sebast.)...........	Lyons........	1528–30
Grypho (Giov., Joh.)..........	Venice	1564–67
Guarin (Thom.)..............	Basel.........	1583
Gyselaar, Gijselaar (Joh.).....	Franeker......	1690
Halma (Fr.).................	Amsterdam....	1701
Hamm (Gn. Wolfg.)..........	Helmstedt.....	1702–3
Harper (Thom.)..............	London........	1643
Hartmann (Joach. and Frid.)....	Frankfort - on - the-Oder.	1595–96
Hayes (Jo.).................	Cambridge....	1685
Heinscheit, Henscheid (Anton)...	Frankfort - on - the-Main.	1711–19
Henckel (Mart.).............	Wittenberg....	1609
Hene (Hans, Jacob)...........	Hanau........	1610–14
Hering (Joh.)...............	Frankfort - on - the-Oder.	1727
Hofer (? Joh.)...............		1625
Hoogenhuysen (Cornel.).......	Amsterdam....	1711
Hutter (Elias)...............	Hamburg......	1586–87
	Nuremberg....	1599–1602
Ilive (Thom.)................	London........	1714–17
Ilsnerus (Blasius)............	Frankfort - on - the-Main.	1682
Imberti (Zuane, Giov., Joh.)......	Venice	1651–56
Isingrinius (Mich.)...........	Basel.........	1534–35
Jablonski (Dan. Ern.).........	Berlin........	1697
Jaeger (Gottfr.).............	Lübeck........	1650
Jaeger (Heredes Jos.).........	Güstrow	1634
Jansson (Ant.)..............	Leipsic........	1683
Jansson (Joh.)..............	Amsterdam....	1633
Jay (Mich.).................	Paris.........	1628–45
Juilleron (Nicol.)............	Lyons........	1622
Justinianus (Aug.)...........	Paris.........	
Juvenis (Martin).............	Paris.........	1552–54, 59, 63, 68, 69, 74
Kelner (G.).................	Wittenberg....	1615
Kilius (Nic.).................	Rostock	1637
Kirchner (Christ.)...........	Leipsic........	1657
Knebel (Jo. Henr.)...........	Berlin........	1699
Koelner (Joh.)..............	Frankfort - on - the-Main.	1708–27
Koenig (Joh.)...............	Basel.........	1662, 75
Koenig (Lud.)...............	Basel.........	1618–32, 48
Kopmeier...................	Augsburg.....	1680–83
Kurzius (Joh.) of Gross-Glogau..	Cracow.......	1539
Lacquehay (Joh.)............	Paris.........	1629
Launoy (Bonaventura de)......	Offenbach.....	1719–24
Laurentius (Henr.)..........	Amsterdam....	1630–32, 34–35
Lotther (Melchior)..........	Leipsic........	1533
Luchtmans (Jord.)..........	Leyden........	1685
Lucius (Jac.)...............	Helmstedt.....	1580
	Hamburg......	1587
Madruz (Christofolo)........	Riva.	
Magnus (Albertus)..........	Amsterdam....	1687–88
Maire (Joh.)................	Leyden	1621, 22, 37, 50
Martinelli (Giov., Jos.)..........	Venice	1636–42, 56

Name.	Place.	Date.
Martzan (Melchior)...............	Copenhagen...	1640
Meyer (Henr.)....................	Altdorf.......	1680
Moeller (Reinhart Eustachius)....	Frankfort - on - the-Main.	1725
Morellus (Guilelmus).............	Paris.........	1559–63
Moresini, Morosini	Venice........	1660–65
Morrhius (Gerardus)	Paris.........	1531
Nisselius (Jo. Ge.)..............	Leyden........	1656, 62
Oeglin (Erhard)..................	Augsburg.....	1514
Oporini (Jos.)...................	Basel.........	1567
Orphanotropheum (Waisenhaus)..	Halle.........	1710–19
Paddenburg (Gysbert of)........	Utrecht.......	1714
Panzoni (Alb.)..................	Mantua.......	1730
Paoli, Pauli (Giov., Joh.)........	Venice........	1708–12, 15
Pasquato (Laur.)................	Padua........	1562, 67
Pauli (Joh.)....................	Upsala........	1652–60
Pauli (Nic. Justinian.)...........	Genoa........	1516
Petrus (Henr.)..................	Basel.........	1530–57
Pieters (Jac.)..................	Amsterdam....	1643
Pillehotte (Ant.)...............	Lyons........	1622
Plantinus (Christoph.)...........	Antwerp.....	1566–89
Portevecchio (Piero del).........	Padua........	1562, 67
Presigno (Comin[o]).............	Venice.......	1593–96
Procurator (Federigo Contarino)..	Venice.......	1659–67
Propaganda Fide................	Rome........	1683
Quirino (Carlo).................	Venice.......	1549
Radaeus (Aegid.)...............	Franeker.....	1597
Raphelengius (Franc.)...........	Leyden........	1590–1615, 21–22
Ravestein (Nic.)................	Amsterdam....	1638, 48
Rebenlin (Georf)................	Hamburg.....	1663–68
Rehte (Dav. Fred.)..............	Gedani........	1675
Reuther (Barth.)................	Kiel..........	1709
Rhamba (Joh.)..................	Leipsic.......	1564
Rizzini (Anton.)................	Venice.......	1657–59, 60
Rose (Joh., son of Thom.)........	Hamburg.....	1709, 11, 15–21
Rose (Thom.)...................	Hamburg.....	1686–1709
Rossi (Francesco de)............	Verona.......	1646–52
Rouviere (Petr. de la)...........	Geneva.......	1609–18
Roycroft (Thom.)...............	London.......	1651, 53–57
Rufinelli (Giacomo, Jac.)........	Mantua.......	1560–90
Rufinelli, Rufinello (Messer Venturin).	Mantua.......	1556–59
Rufinelli (Tommas., Thom.)......	Mantua.......	1593
Rüh(e)l (Joh. and Conr.)	Wittenberg...	1586–87
Sartorius......................	Copenhagen...	1631
Saxo (Joh.)....................	Hamburg.....	1586–87
Schadaeus (El.)................	Strasburg.....	1591
Schaefer (Petr.)...............	Worms.......	1529
Schall (Andr.).................	Gotha........	1707, 10
Schoennerstaedt (Joh. Henr.)....	Altdorf.......	1674
Schurmann (Stephan)...........	Tannhausen...	1593–94
Selfisch (Heredes Sam.)..........	Wittenberg...	1615
Soter (Jac.)....................	Cologne......	1563
Soter (Joh.)....................	Solingen......	1538
Spoor (Jo. Frid.)...............	Strasburg.....	1670
Stark (Seb. Gott.)..............	Berlin........	1710
Steen (Caspar).................	Amsterdam...	1692–1703
Stephanus (Carol.).............	Paris.........	1556–59
Stephanus (Rob.)...............	Paris.........	1528, 39–46
	Geneva........	1554, 56
Stephanus (Rob.)..............	Paris.........	1563–66
Thymii (Jo. Heredes)...........	Frankfort - on - the-Oder.	1630
Vaesberge (Jo.)................	Utrecht.......	1657
Vedelago (Domenigo)...........	Venice.......	1662–64, 63, 65, 74–82
Vendramini, Vendramin	Venice.......	1630–41
Vendramini....................	Venice.......	1642–1705, 1651, 53, 55
Vieceri (Francesco).............	Venice.......	1643–54
Vignon (Eust.).................	Geneva.......	1578
Vitray (Ant.)..................	Paris.........	1628–45
Voliet, Vogliet (? Jakob)........	Basel........	1583
Waldkirch (Conr.)..	Basel........	1598–1612
Water (Gül. van de)...........	Amsterdam...	1701
Water (Jo. van de).............	Utrecht.......	1683–88
Weimmann (Nic.)..............	Frankfort - on - the-Main.	1709
Wellens (Jo.)..................	Franeker.....	1663
Wernerianis...................	Upsala.......	1727
Wittigau (Jo.).................	Leipsic.......	1661
Wust (Jo.)....................	Frankfort - on - the-Main.	1694–1707
Zanetti, Gianetti, Zanetius (Christofolo).	Venice.......	1564–66
Zanetti (Daniel)...............	....	1596, 97–1606
Zanetti (Francesco)............	Rome........	1578, 80–81
Zanetti (Matteo)...............	Venice.......	1593–96
Zanetti, Zanetto (Zuan, Giov., Jo.)	Venice.......	1606–9
Zeitler (Frid.) and H. G. Mussel..	Magdeburg...	1700
Ziletti (Giordano, Jordanus)....	Venice.......	1571–72
Zschauer (Jo. Andr.)...........	Leipsic.......	1696
Zyll (Gilb.)....................	Utrecht.......	1656

V. (1732–1900): From 1732 many of the presses already referred to have continued their activity down to the present day. That of **Leghorn,** for example, began a new life in 1740 in the workshop of Abraham Meldola; and he was followed by a number of Hebrew printers, who found a market for their products in the Levant and the Barbary States, so much so that Christian printers like Carlo Gorgio (1779) and Giovanni Falerno (1779) found it worth while to compete in producing ritual and cabalistic works for the southern markets. This period also saw the beginning of the remarkable activity of Wolf Heidenheim at **Rödelheim,** producing the well-known editions of the ritual. These, while originally intended for the Frankfort market, have been used by Ashkenazic congregations throughout the world; and the Tefillah had run to as many as 128 editions by 1902 ("Zeit. für Hebr. Bibl." v. 99). This period was likewise marked by the inauguration of Hebrew printing at **Carlsruhe,** at first under the egis of Christian printers beginning with Johann Herald in 1755, and later under Wilhelm Lotter from 1766. It was not till 1782 that Hirsch Wormser and his brother-in-law were allowed to start a printing-press, chiefly for ritual works. They were followed in 1814 by David Marx. Altogether about 61 Hebrew prints from this press are known.

But the period is especially noteworthy for the rise and development of Hebrew printing in the lands where most persons lived who were acquainted with Hebrew. It is somewhat difficult to account for the fact that there was absolutely no Hebrew printing in the districts now constituting Russian Poland and the Pale of Settlement till past the middle of the eighteenth century, though they have for the past 200 years contained the largest number of Jews and the greatest number of those acquainted with Hebrew. In the old Polish kingdom the Council of the Four Lands kept a somewhat rigid control over the production of Hebrew books, **Russia.** to which it secured a kind of copyright by threatening excommunication for anybody reprinting works having its approbation. The Cossack outrages of 1648 had destroyed the chance of any independent printing in these countries, and the markets were mainly supplied by Prague, Cracow, Lublin, and later Frankfort-on-the-Oder. It was not till after the troublous period of the three partitions (1772–95) that local presses began to be established in Russia. Mention may here perhaps be made of the printing of the Karaite Tefillah (1784) at **Eupatoria** (not yet, however, within the precincts of the Russian empire), followed by that of the Krimchaks in the next year, and reference may also be made to two or three works printed at **Olexnitz** (1760–67) in connection with the beginnings of Ḥasidism. Soon after this, printing had begun in **Koretz** (1777), and was followed at **Neuhof** (Novy Dvor) near Warsaw (1782), at **Polonnoye** (1783–91), at **Shklov** (1783), and at **Poretzk** (1786–91). Lithuania for the first time obtained a printing-press of its own by the privilege granted by King Stanislaus Augustus to Baruch Romm, who established a printing-office at **Grodno** in 1789. After the settlement at the third partition under Catherine II., a considerable number of Russian printing-offices sprang up, which will be found in the list on pages 328 and 330. They continued to increase during the nineteenth century till Nicholas I. in 1845 passed a law restricting all Hebrew printing to two establishments, one at **Wilna**, the other at **Slavuta**. **Königsberg, Johannisberg, Lyck, Memel, Eydtkuhnen**, and other cities of East Prussia supplied the Russian requirements. This practically gave a monopoly of the Russian market to the firm of Romm, which had moved from Grodno to Wilna in 1799. But it maintained connection with Grodno, producing in 1835 a well-known edition of the Talmud which bears the imprint "Wilna and

the business was bought by De la Torre. The monopoly being given up, J. Schlesinger assumed the work; he devoted himself especially to rituals also for the outlying colonies of Jews, producing a Siddur for the Yemen Jews, a Maḥzor for the Algerian Jews, and other rituals for northern Africa; the Catalonian and Aragonian congregations of Salonica also had their rituals printed at Vienna. Other Austrian and Hungarian presses were at **Lemberg, Cracow** (Joseph Fischer), **Presburg** (Alkalai), **Paks, Przemysl, Lublin**, etc.   J.

Mention has already been made of the beginnings of Oriental typography in the city of **Con-**

FROM THE HEIDENHEIM MAḤZOR, RÖDELHEIM, 1832.

Grodno." The Romms down to the present day continue to be the most extensive Hebrew printers in Russia; but of recent years the Warsaw publishing firms "Tushiyyah" and "Aḥiasaf" produce perhaps even to a larger extent than the Wilna firm.

Mention may be made here of the Austrian presses in the nineteenth century, which have been very productive, especially those of **Vienna, Austria.** where Anton von SCHMID obtained from 1800 onward the monopoly for the Austrian empire, and as a consequence produced about 250 Hebrew works, including a reprint of the Mendelssohn Bible and many Jewish prayer-books, besides the periodical "Bikkure ha-'Ittim." He was succeeded by his son, from whom

stantinople. Toward the end of the sixteenth century Donna Reyna Mendesia founded what might be called a private printing-press at **Belvedere** or **Kuru Chesme** (1593). The next century the Franco family, probably from Venice, also established a printing-press there, and was followed by Joseph b. Jacob of Solowitz (near Lemberg), who established at Constantinople in 1717 a press which existed to the end of the century. He was followed by a Jewish printer from **Oriental.** Venice, Isaac de Castro (1764–1845), who settled at Constantinople in 1806; his press is carried on by his son Elia de Castro, who is still the official printer of the Ottoman empire. Both the English and the Scotch missions to the Jews published Hebrew works at Constantinople.

Together with Constantinople should be mentioned **Salonica,** where Judah Gedaliah began printing in 1512, and was followed by Solomon Jabez (1516) and Abraham Bat-Sheba (1592). Hebrew printing

From Ḥayyim Vital's "Sha'are Ḳedushshah," Aleppo, 1866.

was also conducted here by a convert, Abraham ha-Ger. In the eighteenth century the firms of Naḥman (1709–89), Miranda (1730), Falcon (1735), and Ḳala'i (1764) supplied the Orient with ritual and halakic works. But all these firms were outlived by an

Griffith, the printer of the English Mission, and B. Tatiḳian, an Armenian, also printed Hebrew works at Smyrna. A single work was printed at **Cairo** in 1740. Hebrew printing has also been undertaken at **Alexandria** since 1875 by one Faraj Ḥayyim Mizraḥi.

Israel Bak, who had reestablished the Safed Hebrew press, and was probably connected with the Bak family of Prague, moved to **Jerusalem** in 1841 and printed there for nearly forty years, up to 1878. Quite a number of presses **Jerusalem.** which deserve enumeration have been set up in the Holy City; viz., those of Israel Bak (1841) and his son Nisan; Joel Moses Solomon (1863); Elijah Moses Ḥai Sassoon (1864); Israel Dob FRUMKIN (1871), the editor of the journal "Ḥabaẓẓelet"; Isaac Goscinny (1876); Elhanan Tenenbaum (1879-90); Isaac b. Jacob Hirschensohn (1880) and his successors; Samuel Levi Zuckermann (1882); Moses Perez (1884); Abraham Moses LUNCZ (1885), known for his annual publications "Luaḥ Ereẓ Yisrael" and "Yerushalayim"; Eliezer ben Judah, called Perlemann, director of the journal

FROM "SEFER HA-'IBBUR," PRINTED BY FILIPOWSKI, LONDON, 1853.

Amsterdam printer, Bezaleel ha-Levi, who settled at Salonica in 1741, and in whose name the publication of Hebrew and Ladino books and periodicals still continues. The Jabez family printed at **Adrianople** before establishing its press at Salonica; the Hebrew printing annals of this town had a lapse until 1888, when a literary society entitled Doreshe Haskalah published some Hebrew pamphlets, and the official printing-press of the vilayet printed some Hebrew books.

From Salonica printing passed to **Safed** in Palestine, where Abraham Ashkenazi established in 1588 a branch of his brother Eleazar's Salonica house. According to some, the Shulḥan 'Aruk was first printed there. In the nineteenth century a member of the Bak family printed at Safed (1831–41), and from 1864 to 1884 Israel Dob Beer also printed there. So too at **Damascus** one of the Bat-Shebas brought a press from Constantinople in 1706 and printed for a time. In **Smyrna** Hebrew printing began in 1660 with Abraham b. Jedidiah Gabbai; and no less than thirteen other establishments have from time to time been founded. One of them, that of Jonah Ashkenazi, lasted from 1731 to 1863. E.

"Hashḳafah," originally "Ha-Ẓebi"; J. Nahum Lewi (1887); Adelmann and Meyuḥas (1887); M. Lilienthal (1895); Meir Blumenthal (1897); Sonnenfeld & Blumenthal (1897); Loeb Kahana (1899); A. M. Goldberg (1901); and Moses A. Azriel (1901).

One of the Jerusalem printers, Elijah Sassoon, moved his establishment to **Aleppo** in 1866. About the same time printing began in **Bagdad** under Mordecai & Co., who recently have had the competition of Judah Moses Joshua and Solomon Bekor Ḥussain. At **Beirut** the firm of Selim Mann started printing in 1902. Reverting to the countries formerly under Turkish rule, it may be mentioned that Hebrew and Ladino books have been printed at **Belgrade** since 1814 at the national printing establishment by members of the Alḳala'i family. Later Jewish printing-houses are those of Eleazar Rakowitz and Samuel Horowitz (1881). In **Sarajevo** Hebrew printing began in 1875; and another firm, that of Daniel Kashon, started in 1898. At **Sofia** there have been no less than four printing-presses since 1893, the last that of Joseph Pason (1901), probably from Constantinople. Also at **Rustchuk,** since 1894, members of the Alḳala'i family have

ביצד הרגל פרק שני בבא קמא

שיבולת ושיבולת ר' יוחנן אמר נעשה כזורק את
החץ ממקום למקום א"ר יצחק בר טבליי מתניתא
(א) מסייע לר"ש לקיש **היה גדי כפות לו
ועבד סמוך לו ונשרף עמו חייב עבד כפות לו
וגדי סמוך לו פטור אם אומר את שאין כזורק
את החץ ממקום למקום על שיבולת הראשונה
נתחייב מיתה מיכן והילך תשלומין ׃ א"ר יוסי
ואת שמע מינה *שורו ׃ שהדליק את הגדיש
בשבת חייב והוא שהדליק את הגדיש בשבת
פטור

FROM JERUSALEM TALMUD, JITOMIR, 1865.

גן עניין שבת עדן לד

לטלטל אסור לנמות בריח אף אם הוא על כרתו
אפשר שיהיה בלי שינמה בריח ׃ והחכמים אסרו
הצום בשבת משום שהכתוב אומר אכלוהו
היום ׃ ומקצתם התירו הצום בשבת ואמרו כי
מאמר אכלוהו היום הוא רשות ולא חובה ׃
והאמת כי הצום יאסר בשבת משום שאסרו
וקראת לשבת עונג והעונג הוא באכילה
ושתיה כמו שיתבאר על כן אין ראוי לנדור
נדר להתענות ואפילו שלא עיין את השבת

אשר ברא אלהים לעשות שזה היום נברא
לעצמו ושבחו והבדילו משאר הימים היותו
אות לישראל עמו ומעיר להטיב העיון בהקירת
מופתי השכל לחדוש העולם להורות על קיום
המחדש הוא האל ית' שמו כאשר אמר כי
אות היא ביני וביניכם לדורותיכם לדעת כי
אני ה' מקדשכם ׃ ובאר בשני מקומות איך
יהיה יום שבת אות לידיעתו ית' כאשר אמר
בעשרת הדברים ביום המעמד כי ששת ימים

FROM "SEFER GAN 'EDEN," GUZLOW, 1866.

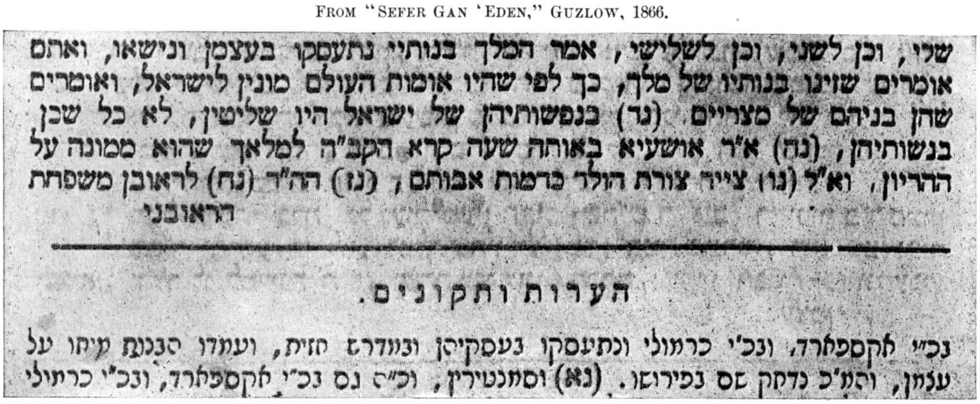

שלי, וכן לשני, וכן לשלישי, אמר המלך בנותיי נתעסקו בעצמן ונישאו, ואתם
אומרים שזינו בנותיו של מלך, כך לפי שהיו אומות העולם מונין לישראל, ואומרים
שהן בניהם של מצריים (נד) בנפשותיהן של ישראל היו שליטין, לא כל שכן
בנשותיהן, (נה) א"ר אושעיא באותה שעה קרא הקב"ה למלאך שהוא ממונה על
ההריון, וא"ל (נו) צייר צורת הולד כדמות אבותם, (נז) הה"ד (נח) לראובן משפחת
הראובני

הערות ותקונים.

נכ"י אקספארד, ונכ"י כרמולי ונתעסקו בעסקיהן ובמדרש חזית, ועמדו הבנות מיחו על
עצמן, והמ"כ נדחק שם בפירושו. (נא) וסמנטירין, וכ"ה גם נכ"י אקספארד, ונכ"י כרמולי

FROM BUBER'S PESIḲTA, LYCK, 1868.

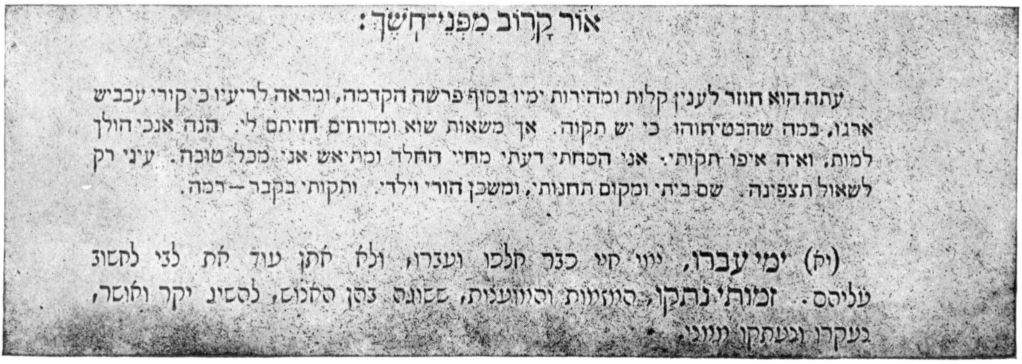

אוֹר קָרוֹב מִפְּנֵי־חֹשֶׁךְ׃

עתה הוא חוזר לענין קלות ומהירות ימיו בסוף פרשה הקדמה, ומראה לריעיו כי קורי עכביש
ארגו, במה שהבטיחוהו כי יש תקוה. אך משאות שוא ומדוחים חזיתם לי. הנה אנכי הולך
למות, ואיה איפו תקותי׃ אני הסחתי דעתי מחיי החלד ומתיאש אני מכל טובה. עיני רק
לשאול תצפינה. שם ביתי ומקום תחנותי, ומשכן הורי וילדי. ותקותי בקבר—רמה.

(יא) ימי עברו, ימי חיי כבר חלפו ועברו, ולא יתן עוד את לבי לחשוב
עליהם. זמותי נתקו, המזמות והיועצות, שבונה בהן האנוש, להשיג יקר ואוצר,
נעקרו ונעתקו ממני.

FROM SZOLD'S COMMENTARY ON JOB, BALTIMORE, 1886.

printed, while at **Philippopolis** the Pardo Brothers started their press in 1898 before moving it to Safed. Altogether in the Levant about eighteen cities have had 121 Hebrew printing establishments between 1504 and 1905. Their productions have been mainly rituals, responsa of local rabbis, and Cabala; the type has been mostly Rashi, and the result has not been very artistic.

J.   M. FR.

In the English-speaking lands Hebrew printing proceeded slowly among the Jews. In England, for example, after a few Hebrew books had been printed by Christian printers the ALEXANDERS began their series of prayer-books about 1770, which have continued to be reissued down to the present day; they were succeeded by the VALENTINES. The firm of Wertheimer, Lea & Co. printed most of the Jewish Hebrew productions of England till recently, including the first edition of the popular authorized prayer-book, of which 100,000 copies have been issued. The Clarendon Press, however, has during the last thirty years printed many works on rabbinic subjects, and

England and the United States.

From Rabinowicz's "Catalogue Merzbacher," Munich, 1888.

has been followed by the Pitt Press of Cambridge, which issued especially the Mishnah edition by W. H. Lowe and the "Pirḳe Abot" of C. Taylor.

In the British colonies only sporadic works have been published at **Bombay** and **Aden,** where the Yemen Jews have recently been printing a few of their manuscripts in oblong format. The use of Hebrew type in the Australian and African colonies appears to be confined to newspapers. The same applies to the French colonies in North Africa, though various productions have appeared at **Algiers, Tunis,** and **Oran.**

In the **United States** Hebrew printing was even later in appearance. Apart from a reprint at Philadelphia in 1814 of Athias' unpointed Bible, and Leeser's reprint of the Van der Hooght Bible in 1849, the first Hebrew book printed in America was "Abne Yehoshua'," by Joshua Falk, at **New York** in 1860. The chief production of the Hebrew press of the United States hitherto has been the commentary on Job by B. Szold, printed by I. Friedenwald at **Baltimore;** but since the emigration from Russia and Rumania large numbers of occasional works have been produced at New York, Philadelphia, and **Chicago.** In the first-named city the productions of the press of A. H. Rosenberg are voluminous.

A great deal of very good Hebrew printing, however, is done by non-Jewish printers, and often at

From "Zimrot Yisrael," Aden, 1891.

university presses, where the Christian theologians who devote their attention to rabbinics print their

[עדיות פרק ד' הל' ז—פרק ה' הל' ב]

טופח ר' יהודה אומ' מסוס בית הלל טופח ומטפיח" ‪ ‬ ‪ן‬ האשה "מתקדם בדינר
ובשוה דינר כדברי בית שמיי ובית הלל אומרין בפרוטה ‪ ‬ ובשוה פרוטה וכמה
היא פרוטה אחד משמונה באסר האיטלקי בית שמיי אומ' פוטר הוא אדם את
אשתו בגט ישן ובית הלל אוסרין ואי זה הוא "ישן כל שנתיחד עמה מאחר שכתבו לה "
‪ה‬ המגרש את אשתו ולנה עמה בפונדקי בית שמיי אומרי' אינה נריכה ממנו גט
שיני ובית הלל אומרי' נריכה ממנו גט שני אמתי בזמן שנתגרסה מן "האֵרוסֵין ס

From W. H. Lowe's "The Mishna," Cambridge, 1883.

וּמַה הוֹעִיל בְּאִישׁ אַחֵר[8] לְבִבוֹ ‪ ‬ ‪ ‬ לְבַל יָתוּר וְתַאֲוָתוֹ נְכֵחוֹ
וְהַשְׁלִים אֲשֶׁר יַשְׁלִים לְדֵעוֹ ‪ ‬ וְהַמֹּשֵׁל אֲשֶׁר יִמְשֹׁל בְּרוּחוֹ[9]
וְהַגִּבּוֹר אֲשֶׁר יֵלֵךְ בְּמוֹ אֵשׁ ‪ ‬ ‪ ‬ וְלֹא יִירָא יְקוֹד כִּבְשָׁן וּפִיחוֹ
וְהַמַּשְׂכִּיל אֲשֶׁר יִתְעַל בְּשִׂכְלוֹ ‪ ‬ ‪ ‬ וְהֶחָלָשׁ אֲשֶׁר יָעוֹז בְּכֹחוֹ[10]

[1] ר"ל: אד יעלה מן הקרבים וממנו יתהוו הדמעות אשר יצאו אח"כ דרך עיניו החוצה, כי גדל
הכאב מאד על הפרדו מעל רעהו.

[2] ר"ל: הלבות ינקו את שדי הידידות; במקום: מאת, יש בכ"י תקון: מאד, ואיני יודע מה
הביא את המתקן לדבר זה, להגיה במקום שאין הברה תקון, ואם קבלה היא נקבל.

From the "Steinschneider Festschrift," Leipsic, 1896.

בכך כי מילתא דתליא בחושבן היא והמבין יחשוב לעצמו והיינו דבר מועט יש ולא
נתנו בו חכמים שיעור, ובירושלמי רל) גרסינן נמי הכי בהאי ענינא ר' שמואל ב-
נחמיני בשם ר' יונתן מחצר המשכן למדו דהוי לה אורך ק' אמה ורוחב נ' אמה זימנין
ק' אמה הויין בתבריתא המשה אלפין אמין, שבעים על שבעין בתבריתא הויין חמש

עתים לבינה

הריטב"א שם ותבין, רכו) נ"ז ע"ב, ועיין ירושלמי שם דר"מ ורבנן תרויהו דרשו לה מקרא זה
דמקיר העיר וחוצה ועיין בחי' הריטב"א שם שהביא ירושלמי זה בשיבוש יעוש"ה, ובירושלמי איתא

From Schorr's "Sefer Ha-'Ittim," Cracow, 1902.

להודיע לכל שאינן את כולם כדי כלום וכן הוא
אומ' וכל דיירי ארעא כלא חשיבן (דניאל ד' ל"ב)
לך נאמר והנני משחיתם את הארץ (מב).

יד) עשה לך תבת. מושלין אותו משל
לספן שהיה בתוך
הים ובאו עליו נחשולין הרבה וידע שספינתו טובעת.

שנית ידו (ישעיה י"א י"א) (מז).

שלש מאות אמות ארך התיבה. כיצד
עשה אותה ר' יהודה אומ' שלש
מאות ושלשים קילין היו בה כל קילה עשר אמות
על עשר אמות. ושני פלטיאות שלארבע ארבע
אמות קילה מכאן וקילה מכאן ושני אמות לצדדין.
הא כיצד רוחב התיבה חמשים אמה וארבעה קילין

(מב) עי' ב"ר פל"ד ס"א והנוֹסחא כאן קרובה יותר להסגנון בויקרא רבה פ"א ס"א. ע"ש. (מג) צ"ע. (מד) עי' סנהדרין ק"ח
ע"ב ובערוך ערך אדר ובינה מין ע"ב. וע"ע ב"ר פל"א ס"ח על מאמר ר' נתן ובכתה"מ מכריגא (ת' מבליגא). ובכי"ק
אדארא (ת' אדארא). (מה) עי' לקמן בהערות אות מ"ח. (מו) נראה שצ"ל סוד גאו:ו:ת ובכ"עדוך ערך חמש ע"ש וע'
פדרי פכ"ג. (מז) עי' פדר"א פמ"ח ובביאור רד"ל שם.

From Schechter's "Midrash Ha-Gadol," Vienna, 1902.

lucubrations. In addition, presses that make a special business of Oriental printing, like those of Drugulin of Leipsic and Brill of Leyden, also produce Hebrew works, the former having printed the well-known Polychrome Bible edited by Professor Haupt and published at Baltimore. By a special process the various sources of the Biblical books in this edition are distinguished by different colors, not of the type, but of the paper upon which the sections are printed. The various Bible societies have also produced some fine specimens of Hebrew printing, the chief being the so-called Letteris Bible, having the Authorized Version at the side, printed at Vienna; and the Ginsburg Bible, printed by the court printer Karl Fromme in Vienna. The Masorah, also edited by Ginsburg, is another fine piece of Hebrew printing by Fromme; while one of the best Hebrew prints is the fifth edition of the translation into Hebrew of the New Testament, by Franz Delitzsch, printed by Trowitsch & Co. of Berlin.

The following is a list (extending from the introduction of printing to the present day) of towns at which Hebrew presses are known to have existed; those places in which only Christian printers have been concerned, mainly in issuing Biblical editions, are set in italics. As far as possible, dates have been given for the first publication of Hebrew at the different localities. Where this was effected by Christian printers the date is marked with an asterisk. The letters "J. E." within parentheses following the names of towns indicate that special articles are given in THE JEWISH ENCYCLOPEDIA upon the typography of such towns. In a number of instances special monographs have been written upon the typography of various places, and these are cited together with their references. The remaining towns are mentioned by Steinschneider in his "Jüdische Typographie," in Ersch and Gruber, "Encyc." (section ii., part 28, pp. 21–94), or by Zedner and Harkavy. In a few instances the entries from Zedner may refer to publication rather than to printing.

HEBREW PRESSES.

Aden............ 189–
Adrianople...... 1554–55
Aix............. 1855
Alcala (Complutum)...... 1514
Aleppo.......... 1866
Alexandria (No-Ammon)...... 1875
Algiers.......... 1855
Altdorf....... 1674
Altona.......... 1727 et seq.
  Grunwald, *Hamburgs Deutsche Juden*; Steinschneider, *Zeitschrift für Gesch. der Juden in Deutschland*, i. 1–5.
Amsterdam...... 1627 et seq.
Andover, Mass.
Antwerp....... 1566–90
Augsburg....... 1514–43
  Steinschneider, *Zeitschrift für Geschichte der Juden in Deutschland*, i. 1–5.
Avignon........ 1765
Bagdad....... 1657, 1867
Baltimore.
Bamberg........ 1837
Barco.......... 1496–97
Basel.......... 1516

Bath 1803
Beirut 1839, 1902
Belgrade........ 1841
Berdychev...... 1798
Bergamo........ 1599
Berlin.......... *1699
Bern .... 1555 ?
Bistrovitz...... 1592
Blizurka........ 1806–7
Boguslav....... 1809–
Bologna........ 1482–83
Bombay 1856
Bonn.......... 1537–41
Boston.......... *1735
Bremen......... 1673
Brescia........ 1491–94
Breslau......... 1719
  Brann, *Volkskalender*, 1890.
Breznitza.
Brilon 1862
Brody.
Brooklyn........ 1893
Brünn 1799
Brunswick...... 1838
Brussels........ 1841
Bucharest...... 1860
Budapest....... 1823
Buenos Ayres ... 1891
Byelaya Tserkov 1817–

Byelostok....... 1805–
Cairo........... 1740
Calcutta........ 1844
Cambridge..... *1685
Carlsruhe...... 1755–
  Biberfeld, *Zeitschrift für Hebr. Bibl.* i., ii.
Carpentras.
Casal-Maggiore.. 1486
Cassel.......... 1807
Chicago.
Chieri.......... 1627–29
Cincinnati...... 1857
Cleveland.
Cleves 1770
Cologne........ 1518, 53–63
Colomea.
Constance...... 1543–44
Constantinople (J. E.)...... 1503–86
Copenhagen.... 1628
Corfu........... 1829
Cöthen......... 1703
  Freudenthal, *Aus der Heimat Moses Mendelssohns*.
Cracow (J. E.).. 1530–1670
Cremona........ 1556–60
  De Rossi, *Annali Typographici*, 1808.
Czernowitz...... 1856
Damascus....... 1605–6
Danzig......... 1849
Darmstadt...... 1822
Dessau (J. E.)... 1696
  Freudenthal, *Aus der Heimat Moses Mendelssohns*.
Dorpat.......... 1804
Drogobuzh.
Dubno.......... 1794
Dubrovna....... 1802–4
Dyhernfurth (J. E.)........... 1689
  Brann, in *Monatsschrift*, 1896.
Edinburgh....... 1857
Erlangen........ 1593
Esslingen........ 1475
Eupatoria....... 1734
Eydtkuhnen.
Fano........... 1503–16
Faro (J. E.)..... 1487
Ferrara (J. E.).. 1477
  De Rossi, *De Typographia Hebræo-Ferrariensi*, Parma, 1780.
Florence........ 1736
Franeker....... 1597–1681
Frankfort-on-the-Main (J. E.)... 1512
Frankfort-on-the-Oder (J. E.) ... 1551(?),1677–
Freiburg........ 1583–84
Fürth........... 1691–1730
  Steinschneider, *Hebr. Bibl.* xviii. 114 et seq.
Galatz........... *
Geismar......... 1649
Geneva......... 1554
Genoa.......... 1516
Giessen......... 1705, 14
Glogau.......... 1840
Görtz........... 1852
Gotha.......... 1702
Göttingen...... 1742
Grodno.......... 1788–
Gröningen...... 1676
Grubeschov...... 1817–
Guadalajara..... 1482
Güstrow........ 1634
Hagenau........ 1515
Hague........... 1779–
Halberstadt...... 1859

Halle........... 1700–19
  Freudenthal, *Aus der Heimat Moses Mendelssohns*.
Hamburg 1587–
  Grunwald, *Hamburgs Deutsche Juden*, pp. 153.
Hanau.......... { 1610–30 { 1708–25
Hanover........ 1840
Heddernheim ... 1546
Heidelberg...... 1586
Helmstedt.
Hergeswiese ?
Homburg........ 1711–50
Hrubieszow..... 1819
Husiatyn.
Ichenhausen..... 1544
  Steinschneider, *Hebr. Bibl.* xii. 125, Suppl.; idem, *Cat. Bodl.* No. 361.
Inowrazlaw.
Isny............. 1541–42
Ixar............. 1485–95
Jassy............ 1843
Jastowitz *1898
Jena............ 1675
Jerusalem....... 1846
Jessnitz........ 1719–26
  Freudenthal, *Aus der Heimat Moses Mendelssohns*.
Johannesburg.. *1897
Johannisberg.... 1855
Jozefov......... 1826
Kale............ 1734
Kalios.......... 1809–10
Kearny (N. J.) .. 1904
Kiel............ 1709
Kishinef........ 1883
Kones.......... 1797–
Königsberg...... 1759
Kopust......... 1818
Koretz.......... 1776–
Koslov (see Eupatoria).
Kremenetz...... 1805–
Krotoschin...... 1837
Kupil........... 1796
Kuru Chesme ... 1597
Ladie........... 1805
Laszow......... 1815
Leghorn........ 1650–
Leipsic......... 1538–
Leiria.......... 1492–94
Lemberg........ 1810
Leyden......... 1528–1756
Libau.......... *1879
Lisbon.......... 1489–92
Lissa........... 1824
  Lewin, *Geschichte der Juden in Lissa*, pp. 153–154, Pinne, 1904.
London (J. E.)..*1711–
Lübeck......... 1650
Lublin (J. E.)... 1550, 56–74
  Friedberg, *Zur Geschichte der Hebräischen Typographie in Lublin*, Cracow, 1890.
Lunéville....... 1798–
Lyck........... 1859
Lyons.......... 1526
Madras........ 1819
Madrid.
Magdeburg..... 1607
Mannheim...... 1856
Mantua (J. E.). { 1476–80 { 1513–14 { 1580–1699
  Zunz, *Z. G.* pp. 249–260.
Marburg.
Mayence........ 1523–
Mecklenburg.... 1724

לָחֶם שְׁעָרִים מָגֵן אִם יֵרָאֶה וָרֹמַח בְּאַרְבָּעִים אֶלֶף בְּיִשְׂרָאֵל: ט לִבִּי לְחוֹקְקֵי יִשְׂרָאֵל הַמִּתְנַדְּבִים בָּעָם בָּרְכוּ יְהוָה: י רֹכְבֵי אֲתֹנוֹת צְחֹרוֹת יֹשְׁבֵי עַל מִדִּין וְהֹלְכֵי עַל דֶּרֶךְ שִׂיחוּ:

רִישֵׁי מַשִׁרְיָן בְּחַמְשִׁין אַלְפִין אַחֲדֵי סַיְפִין כְּשִׁתִּין אַלְפִין אַחֲדֵי רוּמְחִין בְּשַׁבְעִין אַלְפִין אַחֲדֵי תְּרִיסִין בִּתְמָן אַלְפִין מְמַצֵּי גִירַיָא כַּר מַתְשַׁע מְאָה לְתֵיכִין דְּכָרְזֵלָא דַּהֲוֹ עִמֵּיהּ וּרְתִיכוֹהִי כָּל אִלֵּין אַלְפַיָא וְכָל אִלֵּין מַשִׁרְיָתָא לָא יְכִילוּ

ת"א לחוקקי ישראל . זהר ויקהל . רוכבי אתונות . עירובין נג :

לְמַיבָּם קֳדָם בָּרָק וְנָקָם בָּרָק יַת שָׂרָא דְּעַמֵיהּ: ט אֲמַרַת דְּבוֹרָה בִּנְבוּאָה אֲנָא שְׁלִיחָא לְשַׁבְּחָא לְסַפְרֵי יִשְׂרָאֵל דְּכַד הֲוַת עָקְתָא הַהִיא לָא פַּסְקוּ מִלְּמִדְרַשׁ בְּאוֹרָיְתָא וְכַד יַצֵּי לְהוֹן דַּיְתְבִין בְּבָתֵּי כְנִשְׁתָּא בְּרֵישׁ גְּלֵי וּמְאַלְּפִין יַת עַמָּא פִּתְגָּמֵי אוֹרָיְתָא וּמְבָרְכִין וּמוֹדִין קֳדָם יְיָ : י בַּהֲווֹ מְבַטְלִין עִסְקֵיהוֹן רְכִיבִין עַל אַתָּנָן וְחַשְׁמִיַן בְּכָל מִינֵי צִיּוּרִין וּמְהַלְּכִין בְּכָל תְּחוּם אַרְעָא דְיִשְׂרָאֵל וּמִתְחַבְּרִין לְמֵתַּב עַל דִּינָא דַּהֲוֹ אָזְלִין בְּאוֹרְחָתְהוֹן וּמִשְׁתָּעֵין עַל גְּבוּרָן דְּאִתְעֲבִידָא לְהוֹן בְּאַרְעָא דְיִשְׂרָאֵל:

רד"ק

נקודה בסגול חת"ו... שם כמו מלחמה והוא במשקל חפץ עקב חצר אלא שוה בסגול שלא כמנהג:(ט) לבי לחוקקי ישראל. גדולי ישראל ושופטי ומנהיגי שהתגברו בעם לצאת למלחמה לבי ורצוני אליהם ואומרת אליהם ברכו השם שחזכינ... אויביכם לפניכם ותקראו תגדולים חוקקים שמשימים החקים בעם . ויש לפרש חוקקי ישראל סופריו וחכמיו אומרים להם שיברכו ה" על תתשועה הזאת ופי" המתנדבים בעם לבער לחם תורה ומצוה : (י) צחורות. לבנות כמו וצמר צחר רל"ה הסתחרות רוכבי האתונות חשובות ומובות שלא היו יכולין ללכת מפני האויב עתה שיחו וזמרו לאלהים ה'/ וכן יושבי על מדין והוא שם מקום הנזכר בספר יהושע מדין ומכבה או הוא שם על דרך ירוד אצלם חיו יראים ללכת באותו הדרך מפני האויב ועתה

מנחת שי

רש"י

עליהם וכולם המים המקום במלחמת הכוכבים ונחל קישון גרפם: שערים. כמו כי ימצא בקרבך באחד שעריך : טיירות. (מ) אני לרבי . אני לדבורה לחוקקי ישראל לאזר מת חכמי ישראל שהתנדבו בעם לומר ברכו את ה' ושובו אליו : (י) רוכבי אתונות צחורות. עתה שיברכו מענתה על מתוניות לבנות החשובות מבלי יראה ולאחנת על"ג ואותן שיושבין על מדין בלשון דיינים שהיו יראים לעשות משפט בפרהסיא וכן תרגם יונתן דהוו מתחברין למיתב על דינא ואותן שהולכין רגלי על דרך . שיחו וספרו את התשועה הזאת אשר מקול המחצצים חתכם אורבים ליסטים ומוכסין שיושבין

רלב"ג

נגדודים במערכות לארוב בעברי המים שם יתנו עתה רוכבי המים על דרך האחניות והולכי

מצודת דוד

ובזמן ורומח : (מ) לבי לחוקקי וגו' . ר"ל לא גם השמח ולחין כ"א מענוצק הלב מדבר לחוקקי ישראל המתנדבים להלחם שהם ובכרו לה' על שנתן בלבם להתנדב : (י) רוכבי . כן סמריה הכוכבים על אתונות צבות לניד פגדולה כן התנוצם וישבי וו כמשא ...

מצודת ציון

מלשון מלחמה: שערים. (מ) לחוקקי. סגדולים וקולי... ממוקקים כי הם משימים מחוקים : (י) אתונות. נקבות ... צחורות. לבנות כמו ... ומו לאמר למור (יחזקאל ל"ח): מדין . מלשון דין:

קן סמוכים סכולנים בדרך . כולבם שיחו ודברו מהלום ס'.

משלי חכמים

גימטראפפין אצֶדָ... און דר פאקטער הם אם אים גיהאלפין. שפירט עם ... איצט שטארקער די טובה ווס דר פאקטער הם אם אים גיקאהן און עֶר דאנקט אים דעם פאקטער אונ קשט אים פר די טובה. זא זעלבינע איז דר ... דיא צדיקים אפילו זיי ווייסט אז נאם קון פאהן און אז זיי ווֶעלין זין אין אצֶדָה זיין און זיי נאם העלפין . פון דעסטוועגין ... פאהן גינים זיין און די אצֶדָה או גרוס . ווי די שמחה איו אז זיי זֶענען פאקט אפילו אין די אצֶדָה אונ נאם הם גיהאלפין פון דיא אצֶדָה. דֶריבֶּער אפילו אין דבורה און בָּרָק זַנֶין גֶעוֶען וֶקער אוֹיף די הילף פון נאם . פון דעם וֶעגין האבין זיי נים נעוונֶען ביז דיא הילף איז נֶעקוֶמֶען אין נאנצין :

פירוש ע"ט

הֵינֶם אַז זֵיי הָאבְּן תְּשׁוּבָה גְטוֹן מֶגֶן אִם יֵרָאֶה וָרֹמַח אִיז רֶען אֵין פָאנְצֶר גְנוּגֶן גֶוֶוֹ... צוּוֵישֶׁן דִי יִשְׂרָאֵל אוֹדֶר אֵין שְׁפֵּיז צוּ מִלְחָמָה דֶעם אַלְמֶן דֶר מִיטאקֶענֶן דִי פַּערְצִינ טוֹיזֶנְט מָאן עֶלְצְמֵי פוּן דֶעם חַיִל פוּן סִיסְרָא וֶוֹם זֶענֶן גְקוּמֶן אוֹיף דִי יִשְׂרָאֵל דֶען הקב"ה הָאט זֵיי אַלֵיר טֵיטְלָם מִיט דִי שְׁטֶערֶן אוּנ דֶער טֵיךְ קִישׁוֹן הָם זֵיי דֶר טְרֶענְקְט אוּנ אוּם גֶקערְט פוּן דֶער וֶועלְט: (מ) לִבִּי לְחוֹקְקֵי יִשְׂרָאֵל מֵיין הַאְרְץ טְרָאנֶם מִיךְ לֵיבּ צוּ הָאבְּן קְרֵיצְלָ פוּן דִיא יִשְׂרָאֵל סוֹחֲרִים אוּנ שָׂרִים וֶוֹם מֶענְן הַיְנֶם רֵימֶן הַיְנֶם בְּרֵימֶן אוֹיף וֵוֹיסֵי אֵיזְלוֹנְ... פַר דִי עָכוּ"ם מוֹרֵא אוֹיף דִי מִדְיָן בְּנְיָנִים וֶוֹם מֶעט הַיְנֶם זִיצֶן בְּפַּרְהֶסְיָא אוֹיף דִי דִין אֵין גֵייֶן אוֹיף דִיא וֶועגִן אֵיר

II. Characteristics: There are in all four chief forms in which Hebrew letters are printed: the square; the Rashi; the Weiberteutsch, so called because it was used for the "Ze'enah u-Re'enah" read by women; and finally the cursive, imitating the handwriting used for business and other correspondence. The first three appeared **Form of Letters.** as early as the beginning of Hebrew typography (see INCUNABULA); the fourth, only in the eighteenth century, mainly in books on business training, writing-books in this character being produced at Amsterdam in 1715.

One of the characteristics of Hebrew printing from its beginning was the different sizes in which the characters were printed, the Ṭur of Piove di Sacco, 1475, already showing three forms. This is attributed to the commentatorial character of rabbinic literature, the commentary naturally being printed in a smaller type than the text, and the supercommentary in a still smaller one, and the index to both in a yet more minute type. Such a difference of types soon led to the arrangement by which the text was printed in the center, with the commentaries in concentric arrangement around it. This plan has been employed with increasing elaboration; and in the last rabbinic Bible printed by the firm of Schrifgiesser at Warsaw no less than thirty-two commentaries are included, many of which are on a single page. In the beginning this arrangement simply followed that of the ordinary medieval manuscripts in which commentaries occurred. To fill spaces that would otherwise remain empty recourse was had to the use of letters of greater width, the so-called "littere dilatibiles"; but in early prints the first letter of the following word was often inserted instead. Sheet-marks and pagination were only gradually introduced; they were almost invariably in Hebrew letters printed on the recto only; each second page was numbered, the reference to the two sides (pages) of the sheet being by alef, bet, nowadays represented by a, b; *e.g.*, B. Ḳ. 10b; R. H. 17a (Isaiah Berlin tried to introduce the full point and colon, but without much success). The pagination of the Talmud was established by Bomberg, the arrangement of whose pages has been followed in all subsequent editions. Vowel-points and accents occur for the most part only in Bibles and prayer-books, and divisions of chapter and verse in the Bible only rarely till later times.

The paper of the early prints is generally good; that of the eighteenth century usually the opposite; the issues of Fürth, Cracow, and Rödel**Paper and Format.** heim are generally distinguished by their foxy paper. White paper was generally used, but the Oppenheimer collection contained fifty-seven volumes on blue, seven on green, two on yellow, and a Haggadah on red paper. Rubrics are printed in red in a work issued at Freiburg in 1584. Amsterdam printers sometimes print red on white; Deinard at Newark on varicolored paper. Large-paper editions occur rather frequently, and parchment was used for special copies, the Oppenheimer collection having fifty-one of these, and many of the copies of the Bologna Tefillah of 1537 being printed on that material, though one on excellent paper is to be found in the Sulzberger collection at New York. All kinds of format occur from the earliest times, but the folio and quarto were chiefly used, the octavo and duodecimo being employed mainly in prayer-books. In the Oppenheimer collection the proportions of the various sizes were as follows:

Folio 1,005   Octavo 901
Quarto 1,240   Duodecimo 330

Strange to say, one of the most bulky of Hebrew books was also one of the earliest, Avicenna's "Canon," with 826 folio pages; this, however, is now far exceeded by the Babli with its 2,947 pages in one volume (Berdychev, 1894).

The Leghorn prints were at times in oblong form, while the recent Aden productions are of the same form, but with the longer side at the back. For variations of the TITLE-PAGES see JEW. ENCYC. xii. 154, and for ornamentations see the article PRINTERS' MARKS. To those mentioned in the latter article the following may be added: Ashkenazi (Safed, 1587), lion with two tails; Bat-Sheba (Salonica), half lion, half eagle; Mayer ben Jacob (Venice), elephant; Conti (Cremona), shield, angel, eagle; Abraham b. David (Talmud Torah, Salonica, 1719), three crowns; Koelner (Frankfort-on-the-Main), imperial eagle; De Lannoy (Offenbach), nest of bird with flowers; Aaron Lipman (Sulzbach), tree, crab, fish, and serpent; Shabbethai Bass (Dyhernfurth), two bars of music.

The place and date of printing, as also the name of the printer, were generally expressed in COLOPHONS, but in later times were also placed on the title-page. The day of the week is often indicated by references to Biblical texts, having in view the lucky character of Tuesday as a beginning day (see WEEK). The date is also often made known by a text (see CHRONOGRAM). The omission of letters in these dates often leads to confusion (Zunz, "Datenbestimmungen," in "G. S." i.); and the place of publication does not always coincide with that of printing. Even the place of printing has sometimes to be checked, as frequently German printers attempted to claim the style and authority of Amsterdam, and those of Fürth passed themselves off as coming from Sulzbach. The place of printing was sometimes omitted in order to evade the censor.

Information is often given in these colophons as to the size of the office and the number of persons engaged therein and the character of their work. In the larger offices there would be a **master printer** ("ba'al madpis"), who was sometimes identical with the **proprietor** of the office ("ba'al ha-defus"). The actual **printer** was called "madpis," or sometimes "mehokek." The master printer was occasionally assisted by a **manager** or factor ("mizib 'al ha-defus"). Besides these there was a **compositor** ("mezaref" or "mesadder"), first mentioned in the "Leshon Limmudim" of Constantinople (1542). Many of these compositors were Christians, as in the workshop of Juan di Gara, or at Frankfort-on-the-Main, or sometimes even proselytes to Judaism (see above). Finally, good **proof-readers** or correctors for the press were always indispensable. They were called "maggihim." Notwithstanding their help, a list of errata was often necessary, one of the earliest occurring in a German Maḥzor produced at Salonica in 1563.

From the Letteris Bible, Vienna, 1892.

Colophon and Title-Page. The idea of representing the title-page of a book as a door with portals appears to have attracted Jewish as well as other printers. The fashion appears to have been started at Venice about 1521, whence it spread to Constantinople. Bomberg used two pillars in his "Miklol" of 1545, and this was imitated at Cracow and Lublin. These pillars are often supported by, or support, figures, draped or undraped, as in the "Toẓe'ot Ḥayyim" of Cracow (c. 1593). A Maḥzor of Cracow (1619) has a flying angel of death, while the Pirḳe R. Eliezer of Constantinople (1640) has a centaur and siren. The tree with the shield of David supported by two lions appears first in the Sabbionetta prints, and is imitated by other symbolic figures, as the eagle in the Amsterdam Seliḥot of 1677. These decorations of the title-page led later to illustrations within the work itself, the first of these being in the "Mashal ha-Ḳadmoni," Soncino, 1491. The "Yosippon" and other works of a historical character were favorite receptacles for rather crude illustrations of this kind, as were also the Passover Haggadot, in which even maps of the Holy Land were printed (see HAGGADAH).

Up to the nineteenth century all work was naturally hand-work, and printing was comparatively slow. It took nearly a whole year for the Soncinos to print off 638 folio pages, while sixty years later Giustiniani printed 190 pages of Maimonides' letters in seven days.

For the injury done to the correctness of the text by the censors before and even after printing, see CENSORSHIP OF HEBREW BOOKS. The existence of censors in Italy, Germany, and Poland rendered the works printed previous to 1554 (the date of the Ferrara conference on this subject) of especial value for the text, though care was taken by the Jews themselves before that date not to offend Christian prejudices too much by printing the more out-spoken passages. In a measure Jews had their own censorship in the form of APPROBATIONS ("haskamot"), without which in the seventeenth and eighteenth centuries no book was considered altogether respectable. These approbations were sometimes accompanied by special privileges, as when the rabbis of Venice issued a decree against any one buying a certain book except from the printer; and the parnasim of Amsterdam had the right of inflicting a fine for the infringement of the copyright of any one whom they favored. In the case of the Frankfort Talmud imperial permission was found necessary to produce it.

Of the cost of printing in early times little is known. The "Yezer Ṭob" of Venice (1597–1606) cost a thousand florins to print, while the thirty-six pages of the "Zore la Nefash" (?) of Venice (1619) cost as much as twenty-five ducats. Joseph Witzenhausen got four thalers a sheet for the Judæo-German translation of the Bible published by Athias. In the early days 300 copies of a work were sufficient. This number of the Psalms with Ḳimḥi (1477) was printed; so, too, of the "Yafeḳ Raẓon," while of the "Torat Ḥesed" only 200 came into existence. For the methods adopted in selling books see the article BOOK-TRADE.

Hebrew Upper and Lower Cases.

(From Theodore L. De Vinne's "Modern Methods of Book Composition," New York, 1904.)

shows that generally adopted. The characters and points most used are in the lower case; accents, broad or extended letters, and letters with points are in the upper case.

The difficulty of Hebrew printing for persons not accustomed to the language consists in the great similarity of some of the letters, as "he," "ḥet," and "taw," "dalet" and "resh," "shin" and "sin," and other letters only distinguished by a dot, representing the dagesh. Final "pe" and final "ẓade" also are sometimes confounded, while their hair-lines often tend to break off during press-work. The contrast of the shaded portions of the letters with the hair-lines is perhaps the most marked type-founder's characteristic of Hebrew as compared with Roman type, in which hair-lines are avoided as much as possible. The actual forms of the letters have changed little since the first appearance of matrices in Italy in the fifteenth century. The tendency is rather toward making the letters smaller in size and squarer. Some of the most beautiful type of this kind is that of Filipowski. It is said that compositors unfamiliar with Hebrew tend to set type more accurately, though more slowly, owing to the extra care they devote to following copy. Few ordinary printing establishments have Hebrew type, and on the rare occasions when it is necessary to use it it is customary to borrow it from an establishment with a more varied outfit of types, or to have the type set up in such an establishment, the whole matter cast, and transferred bodily as a single type into the text. Christian printers handle only the square letter, Rashi and cursive always being set up by Jewish typesetters.

Turning to the technical side of Hebrew printing, it has to be remarked that in the justification of Hebrew, wide spacing is to be preferred, and that the vowels and accents have to be justified in a separate line after the consonants have been set up. The wide spacing is rendered necessary by the fact that hyphens can not be used in ordinary Hebrew printing, though in modern works this use is creeping in. To fill out spaces, as mentioned above, the extended letters, "alef," "he," "ḥet," "lamed," "mem," and "taw," are used.

Technique of Hebrew Printing.

In ordinary Hebrew printing "the compositor begins as he does with English, by setting the characters at the left hand of his copy, turning the nicks of his type inward to face the composing-rule. When the line has been spaced and justified . . . it is turned in the stick" (De Vinne, "Modern Methods of Book Composition," p. 245, New York, 1904). The arrangement of cases for Hebrew varies in different offices, but the accompanying illustration

With regard to the works which have been turned out by Hebrew printers during the last 450 years, it would be interesting to determine approximately their number and character. During the first quarter of the century in which incunabula were produced (1475–1500) 100 Hebrew works were issued, at the rate of four per annum. During the next forty years (1500–40) about 440 were issued (M. Schwab, in "Les Incunables Orientaux," enumerates 430 up to this period) averaging eleven per annum. During the next two periods from 1540 to 1732 a rough estimate would give the number of works at 6,605; namely, Bibles,

Productivity of Hebrew Presses.

710; Targum, 70; Talmud, 590; ritual, 1,000; anonymous, 350; Judæo-German, 385; and works of specific authors, 3,500—an average of about thirty-three works issued per annum. During the 160 years since the last-mentioned date the production has rapidly increased, but it is difficult to determine the exact numbers. Some indication can be obtained by the gradually increased number of Hebrew works mentioned in the various sources as follows:

Bibliographer.	Date.	Hebrew Books.
1. Shabbethai Bass	1680	2,200
2. Bartolocci	1693	1,943
3. J. C. Wolf	1733	2,832
4. Azulai	1790	3,527
5. Oppenheimer	1826	4,221
6. Steinschneider, "Hebr. Bibl."	1858–82	2,004
7. Steinschneider	1860	5,232
8. Fürst	1863	9,360
9. Zedner	1867	5,220
10. Benjacob (including manuscripts and references)	1880	14,978 really about 6,500
11. Lippe (vols. i. and ii.)	1880–89	1,210
12. Van Straalen	1894	11,100
13. Zeitlin	1895	3,643
14. Lippe (vol. iii., addenda)	1899	878
15. Wiener (to "ṭet")	1904	4,575

Wiener's list promises to run to 17,000. If one may judge from the numbers given by him, and take account of the fact that the average recorded by Steinschneider between 1860 and 1880, about 100 per annum, is at best only a minimum, having been recently largely increased, there **Number of Hebrew Works.** can be no doubt that 20,000 volumes have been produced during the last period. This is confirmed by the fact that the Asiatic Museum of St. Petersburg, containing the largest Hebrew collection in the world, has no less than 30,000 volumes, of which

Classes.	Zedner.	Chazanowicz.
1. Bibles	1,260	
2. Bible Commentaries	510	794
3. Talmud	730	
4. Talmud Commentaries	700	202
5. Methodology	....	272
6. Codes	1,260	447
7. Code Commentaries	....	386
8. Novellæ	520	644
9. Responsa	....	512
10. Liturgy	1,200	881
11. Midrash and Yalḳuṭ	150	389
12. Sermons	450	587
13. Cabala	460	533
14. Grammar and Dictionaries	450	588
15. History, Archeology, and Memoirs.	320	1,231
16. Geography and Travels in Palestine	....	292
17. Poetry, Criticism	770	585
18. Science	180	260
19. Theology and Polemics	690	449
20. Ethics	....	430
21. Educational	....	265
22. Fiction	....	510
23. Periodicals, Newspapers, Catalogues	....	648
24. Yiddish	....	900

5,000 are written in Judæo-German and Yiddish. The Jerusalem National Library (founded by Chazanowicz) in 1902 had 22,233 volumes, 10,900 of them Hebrew ("Ha-Meliẓ," 1902, No. 259). The British Museum in 1867 had nearly the same number. It would be of interest to compare the classes under

which these various works are included, with the relative number of volumes contained in these two collections (see preceding table).

It would be still more interesting to determine the actual works and editions of them which go to make up the 20,000 or so separate works which have been produced by the Hebrew presses up to the end of the nineteenth century. Unfortunately Hebrew bibliography is not in such a state that this could be done with any approach to accuracy, but a considerable number of subject lists have been made from which a close approximation can be given for the various branches. The sources from which lists are derived vary in thoroughness, mainly according to their date. Information from Reland, or the old Oppenheim catalogue of 1826, naturally does not vie with points ascertained from Steinschneider or S. Wiener, but such as it is, the following list will serve both as an indication of the topics treated of in Hebrew literature and as a guide to the sources in which the fullest account at present known is given. Occasionally the lists include sections of works which should not strictly be counted, as this leads to duplication, and besides some of the entries include also manuscripts. On the other hand, these items probably do not more than compensate for the omissions in the older lists. In some few instances no actual enumeration is accessible, and in these cases the number given by the Chazanowicz collection has been repeated as being the closest approximation that can now be offered. Altogether about 15,380 works are thus accounted for out of the 18,000 or 20,000 Hebrew works and editions that have been produced.

Subject.	No.	Source.
I. Bibles	......	British Museum Catalogue.
Polyglot	220	
Complete	175	
Yiddish	3	
Pentateuch	177	
Prophets	6	
Hagiographa	13	
Pentateuch Parts.	15	
Megillot Parts	10	
Psalms	44	
Prophets, additional.	11	
Apocrypha	12	
II. Bible Commentaries	......	Reland, "Analecta Rabbinica."
Complete Bible	11	
Pentateuch	214	
Prophets	39	
Hagiographa	62	
Supercommentaries.	65	
Megillot	106	
Miscellaneous	145	
Targum	10	
III. Talmud	172	Zedner and Van Straalen.
IV. Talmud Commentaries on Separate Tractates.	196	Jellinek, "Ḳonṭres."
V. Methodology.		
Indexes	90	Jellinek, "Ḳonṭres."
Hermeneutics	237	Jellinek, "Ḳonṭres."
VI. Codes	310	Steinschneider, "Cat. Bodl."
VII. Code Commentaries	185	Steinschneider, "Cat. Bodl."
Maimonides	207	Jellinek, "Ḳonṭres ha-Rambam."
On the 613 Commandments.	171	Jellinek, "Ḳonṭres Taryag."
VIII. Novellæ	298	Benjacob, s.v. "Ḥiddushim."
Poskim	347	Oppenheim.
Names	93	Jellinek, "Ḳonṭres Mazkir."
IX. Responsa	611	Merzbacher, "Ohel Abraham," 1888.

Subject.	No.	Source.
X. Liturgy............	1,544	Zedner and Van Straalen.
Teḥinnot.........	123	Oppenheim.
Seliḥot...........	97	Oppenheim.
Haggadah.......	898	S. Wiener, "Oster-Hagga-dah," St. Petersburg, 1902.
XI. Midrash..........	213	Jellinek, "Ḳonṭres Mid-rash."
XII. Sermons..........	587	Chazanowicz.
Burial...........	123	Jellinek, "Ḳonṭres ha-Mas-ped."
XIII. Cabala............	104	Bartolocci.
XIV. Grammar and Dic-tionaries.	588	Chazanowicz.
Lexicons........	59	Wolf.
Grammar.......	424	Steinschneider, "Bibl. Hand."
XV. History, Archeol-ogy, and Mem-oirs.		
History..........	317	Steinschneider, "Ge-schichts-Litteratur der Juden," 1905.
Tombstone In-scriptions.	21	Jew. Encyc. iii.641-642, s.v. "Cemeteries."
Taḳḳanot........	17	Steinschneider, "Hebr. Bibl." vi. 16.
XVI. Geography.........	118	Zunz, "G. S."
Palestine........	154	Steinschneider, in Luncz's "Luaḥ," 1872.
XVII. Poetry, Criticism...	585	Chazanowicz.
Occasional Poetry	207	Benjacob, s.v. "Shirim."
Letters..........	142	Benjacob, s.v. "Iggerot."
Tales............	150	Benjacob, s.v. "Ma'assim."
Rhetoric........	56	Oppenheim.
Purim and Paro-dies.	28	Steinschneider, in "Monats-schrift," 1903.
Purim Parodies...	57	Steinschneider, in "Letter-bode."
Drama, Original..	52	Berliner, "Yesod 'Olam," p. xlii.
XVIII. Science.............	260	Chazanowicz.
Mathematics......	271	Steinschneider, "Mathema-tik bei den Juden" (to 1650).
Medicine........	46	Benjacob, s.v. "Refu'ah."
Astronomy......	80	Bartolocci.
Chronology	27	Bartolocci.
Calendar........	77	Zeitlin, in Gurland's "Lu-aḥ," 1882.
XIX. Theology and Po-lemics.	449	Chazanowicz.
Anti-Christian Po-lemics.	182	De Rossi, "Bibliotheca Ju-daica Anti-Christiana."
Future Life......	44	E. Abbot, "Literature of Future Life," 1891.
Karaitica........	51	Deinard (MS. list).
Hasidica	307	
XX. Ethics...........	34	Stein, "Ethik des Talmuds."
Wills, Ethical....	60	Abrahams, in "J. Q. R." 481, 4.
Philosophy.......	76	Oppenheim.
Proverbs.........	184	Bernstein, "Livres Parémi-ologiques," Warsaw, 1900.
XXI. Educational.......	265	Chazanowicz.
XXII. Fiction...........	510	Chazanowicz.
XXIII. Periodicals.		
Hebrew.........	199	
Yiddish.........	191	
Ladino.........	53	
Almanacs.......	58	Benjacob, s.v. "Luḥot."
Catalogues	46	Zedner.
XXIV. Yiddish..........	311	Wiener, "Yiddish Litera-ture," p. 99.
Judæo-German ..	385	Steinschneider, "Sera-peum," 1848.
XXV. Ladino...........	164	Kayserling, "Bibl. Esp.-Port.-Jud."
XXVI. Translations, Mod-ern.	152	Jew. Encyc. s.v.

Where Printed.	Date.	Title.	Jew. Encyc.
			v. P.
Alcala.........	1514	Bible Polyglot	iii. 159
Altdorf.........	1644	Title-page of "Sefer Niẓẓa-ḥon"................	xii. 153
Amsterdam	1666	Title-page of Shabbethaian "Tikkun"	xii. 156
Amsterdam....	1679	Title-page of Bible.........	xii. 155
Amsterdam....	1701	"Sefer Raziel"............	x. 336
Amsterdam....	1726	Picart, title-page of Penta-teuch	x. 29
Amsterdam	1787	"Me'ah Berakot"...........	iii. 8
Amsterdam	....	Title-page of miniature Sid-dur	xii. 156
Amsterdam....	....	Title-page of Bible	xii. 157
Basel	1534	Münster Bible.............	ix. 113
Berlin..........	1702	Jacob b. Asher, Ṭur Oraḥ Ḥayyim............	v. 151
Bologna........	1477	Psalms with Ḳimḥi.........	iii. 155
Bologna........	1482	Psalms with Pentateuch....	iii. 157
Bologna........	1538	"Tefillot Latini"...........	iii. 299
Brescia	1491	Immanuel b. Solomon, "Me-ḥabberot "................	vi. 565
Brescia	1494	Bible......................	iii. 158
Budapest.......	1903	Karaite Siddur.............	x. 179
Constantinople.	1512	Midrash Tillim.............	iv. 241
Constantinople.	1517	Moses ibn Tibbon, transla-tion of Maimonides' "Sefer ha-Mizwot"................	vi. 547
Constantinople.	1520	Baḥya b. Asher, "Kad ha-Kemah"................	iv. 243
Constantinople.	1532	Elijah Mizraḥi, "Mispar," Soncino	v. 45
Constantinople.	1620	Midrash Eleh Ezkerah......	viii. 577
Cracow	1571	Maḥzor (Judæo-German)....	iv. 330
Cracow	....	Printer's mark of Isaac b. Aaron of Prossnitz........	x. 200
Dyhernfurth....	1771	Periodicals...............	ix. 605
Fano...........	1503	Hai Gaon, "Musar Haskel".	v. 340
Fano...........	1506	Judah ha-Levi, "Cuzari"...	vii. 349
Fano...........	1516	Jacob b. Asher, "Arba' Ṭu-rim"................	iii. 643
Faro...........	1487	Pentateuch................	v. 345
Ferrara........	1555	Ḥasdai Crescas,"Or Adonai"	v. 371
Genoa..........	1612	Title-page of "Shefa'Ṭal"...	xii. 154
Guadalajara....	1482	David Ḳimḥi's Commentary on the Prophets........	vi. 103
Homberg - vor - der-Höhe..	1737	Schiff, "Ḥiddushe Halakot "	xi. 99
Isny...........	1541	Elijah Levita, "Tishbi"...	viii. 47
Ixar...........	1485	Jacob b. Asher, Oraḥ Ḥay-yim................	vii. 13
Lisbon.	1489	Abudarham................	viii. 105
Lisbon.	1489	Naḥmanides, Commentary on the Pentateuch...........	ix. 89
London	1813	Almanac..................	i. 428
Lublin.........	1590	Mordecai Jaffe, "Lebushim "	vii. 59
Lyck...........	1865	Periodicals................	ix. 610
Mantua........	1475	"Yosippon"................	vii. 261
Mantua........	1476	Jacob b. Asher, Ṭur Oraḥ Ḥayyim................	iv. 205
Mantua........	Before 1480	Levi b. Gershon, Commen-tary................	iv. 173
Mantua........	Before 1480	Levi b. Gershon, Commen-tary on the Pentateuch....	viii. 27
Mantua........	1561	"Tefillot Vulgar ".........	iv. 172
Naples.........	1487	Ḳimḥi, Commentary........	x. 247
Naples.........	1488	Abraham ibn Ezra, Commen-tary on the Pentateuch....	vi. 523
Naples.........	1489	Baḥya's "Ḥobot ha-Leba-bot"................	ii. 449
Naples.........	1489	Kalonymus, "Eben Boḥan".	vii. 427
New York......	1899	Periodicals	ix. 609
Paris	1543	Stephanus Bible............	ix. 538
Paris	1807	Sanhedrin Prayers.........	xi. 47
Pesaro.........	1512	Soncino, "Sefer Yehoshua"	iii. 321
Piove di Sacco..	1475	Jacob b. Asher, "Arba' Ṭu-rim "................	vii. 29
Prague	1525	Maḥzor	viii. 267
Prague	1526	Haggadah.................	vi. 147
Prague	1526	Haggadah.................	x. 167
Reggio	1475	Rashi, Commentary on the Bible................	x. 329
Rödelheim	1868	Siddur....................	x. 177
Rome..........	1480	"Aruk"..................	ix. 181
Rome..........	1480	"Moreh Nebukim ".........	ix. 79
Rome..........	1480	"Semag "..................	ix. 69
Sabbionetta....	1559	Talmud...................	xii. 21
Salonica.......	1522	Isaac Arama, "Aḳedat Yiẓ-ḥaḳ "................	v. 581
Soncino........	1484	Solomon ibn Gabirol, "Mib-ḥar ha-Peninim".........	vi. 531
Soncino........	1485	"Iḳḳarim"...............	xi. 465
Soncino........	1485	Maḥzor	viii. 265

In addition to the examples of Hebrew printing which are given as illustrations in the present article (all of them being derived from the Sulzberger collection in the Jewish Theological Seminary of America in New York city), the volumes of THE JEWISH ENCYCLOPEDIA contain a larger number of reproductions of Hebrew typography than have ever yet been brought together, a list of which, in order of place of publication, may fitly conclude this account.

Where Printed.	Date.	Title.	Jew. Encyc.
			v.　p.
Soncino........	Before 1500	Title-page of an unknown edition of the Talmud.....	xii.　13
Venice.........	1517	Bomberg Bible..............	iii. 160
Venice.........	1520	Bomberg Talmud..........	xii.　17
Venice.........	1522	Title-page of Bomberg Talmud.....................	xii. 152
Venice.........	1526	Bomberg Talmud	iii. 301
Venice.........	1564	Gershon b. Solomon, "Sefer Sha'ar ha-Shamayim "....	iii. 645
Venice.........	1547	Caro, Shulḥan 'Aruk........	iii. 587
Venice.........	1694	"She'elot u-Teshubot ".......	xi. 655
Venice.........	....	Title-page of Ritual........	xii. 414
Vienna.........	1901	Periodicals.................	ix. 615
Wilna..........	1865	Title-page of Bible.........	xii. 157
Wilna..........	1880	Shulḥan 'Aruk	xii. 529
Wilna..........	1884	Romm Talmud.............	xii.　22
Zurich	1546	" Yosippon " (Judæo-German)	vii. 263

BIBLIOGRAPHY: Cassel and Steinschneider, *Jüdische Typographie*, in Ersch and Gruber, *Encyc.* section ii., part 28, pp. 21-94, on which the above account is founded; De Rossi, *Annales Hebræo - Typographici*, Parma, 1795; Schwab, *Les Incunables Orientaux*, Paris, 1883; Harkavy, in *Cat. of Book Exposition*, part viii. (in Russian), St. Petersburg, 1894; Simonsen, *Hebraisk Bogtryk*, Copenhagen, 1901; Theodore L. De Vinne, *Modern Methods of Book Composition*, p. 246, New York, 1904; Ebrard, *Ausstellung Hebräischer Buchdrucke*, 2d ed., Frankfort-on-the-Main, 1902; Steinschneider, *Cat. Bodl.* cols. 2813-3103.

J.

TYRE: Principal city of Phenicia. By "the strong city Tyre," mentioned in Josh. xix. 29 and II Sam. xxiv. 7 as marking the frontier of Israel (Asher), is evidently meant not the main city, but an outpost in the mountains protecting the road to it and to the coast (the Septuagint furnishes in Joshua an interesting variant, making that point a "fountain" in place of a "city ").

Tyre is first heard of under King Hiram, who furnished to his friends David (II Sam. v. 11) and Solomon (I Kings v. 1), for their building operations, wood from Mount Lebanon and skilled working men

　　　　　　　　("Sidonians," *ib.* v. 6), for which aid
Under　　he received not only payment in grain
King Hi-　(*ib.* v. 11), but also land concessions
ram.　　in Galilee (*ib.* ix. 11). Solomon's chief
　　　　　　　　architect, Hiram, also, was a Tyrian
(*ib.* vii. 13=II Chron. iv. 11). Tyrian ships in Solomon's service sailed even from the ports on the Red Sea (*ib.* ix. 27-28).

Tyre became immensely rich (Zech. ix. 3) by her commerce (Isa. xxiii. 2-3; comp. the elaborate description in Ezek. xxvii.); and the curses of the Prophets refer especially to its flourishing slave-trade (Amos i. 9; Joel iii. 4). Tyrian merchants—if the term "Tyrians" did not include all Phenicians at that period—furnished the timber for Ezra's Temple also (Ezra iii. 7), and "brought fish and all manner of ware" to Jerusalem (Neh. xiii. 16).

Ps. xlv. 2, lxxxiii. 7, and lxxxvii. 4 treat the city as representative of all Phenicia; elsewhere, however, the Tyrians and the Zidonians are identified in a way which seems to indicate that "Zidonians" was the earlier name for the Phenicians (comp. I Kings v. 6; Judges xviii. 7; Isa. xxiii. 2; and the Homeric use). "Ethbaal king of the Zidonians," the father of Jezebel (I Kings xvi. 31), is identical with Ithobalos of Tyre (Josephus, "Ant." viii. 13, § 2), who, however, may have possessed both cities. This earlier usage dates from a time when Zidon was preponder-

ating among the Phenician cities (comp. the reference in Gen. x. 15 to Sidon, the first-born of Canaan; Tyre is not even mentioned in verse 18 of the same chapter).

Zidon always claimed that Tyre was merely a later colony. However, the Egyptian inscriptions of the eighteenth and nineteenth dynasties, which hardly mention Zidon, seem to show that even then Tyre ("Ṣa-ru," "Ṣa-ra") predominated (W. M. Müller, "Asien und Europa," p. 185), although in the El-Amarna tablets (ed. Winckler, Nos. 149-156) King Abimilki of "Ṣurri" seems to have been inferior to his adversary, Zimrida of Ziduna. This predomi-

　　　　　　　　nance of Tyre is shown also in the
Its Pre-　fact that the greatest Phenician col-
dominance. ony, Carthage, claimed to have been
　　　　　　　　founded from Tyre (probably much
before the problematic date assumed by the Greeks, *i.e.*, 826 or 814 B.C.). (Isa. xxiii. 1, 6, 10 does not necessarily imply Tyrian colonization of Tarshish, but only flourishing intercourse with that remote country.)

Josephus (*l.c.*) gives a list of ten Tyrian kings from 969 (Hiram!) to 774 (for some kings of Ṣurru in later Assyrian time see Delitzsch, "Wo Lag das Paradies?" p. 284). The long siege by the Assyrians, reported by the local historian Menander (in Josephus, *l.c.* ix. 14) to have taken place under Shalmaneser (IV.), is by modern critics considered as a confusion of several Assyrian attacks under Sennacherib, Esarhaddon, and especially Assurbanipal (see Winckler, "Altorientalische Forschungen," 2d ed., ii. 65). Finally, Tyre submitted to Assyria, but kept always her own kings (comp. Jer. xxv. 22, xxvii. 3; Ezek. xxviii. 2), as also under Persian rule. A naval battle against the Egyptian king Apries (Herodotus, ii. 161) seems to indicate that this independence sought to main-

　　　　　　　　　　tain itself against the two rivals
Stormed by Egypt and Babylonia, but Nebuchad-
Alexander nezzar (comp. Ezek. xxvi. 7) obtained,
the Great. after a siege of thirteen years, a certain
　　　　　　　　　　submission in 574 B.C. Alexander the
Great (332) first stormed the island-city after building a large dam across the shallow strait; and he sold 30,000 inhabitants as slaves.

Nevertheless, the city soon regained great importance. It enjoyed a certain liberty until Augustus, and under the Romans was the most populous of the Phenician cities (frequently mentioned in the New Testament). During the Crusades it was important owing both to its unusually strong fortifications and to its factories of glass, sugar, etc. The Christians under Baldwin II. took it in 1124 and held it to 1291 (Frederick Barbarossa was buried in the cathedral in 1190). The place degenerated afterward into a miserable village, especially after the Shi'itic sect of the Matawilah had taken possession of it; now Ṣûr has from 5,000 to 6,000 inhabitants.

The name seems to have meant "rock"; the Greek form "Tyros" suggests to some Semitists the preservation of the earlier "ẓ" for "ṣ." The earlier Latin form was "Sar(r)a." Now a peninsula by the accretion of sand to Alexander's dam, the city was originally an island (Ezek. xxvii. 3, 4) of limited space (how much of its former area has now been submersed by the sea is a subject of dispute), so that the large population was crowded together in very high houses. Nevertheless it contained a large and magnificent temple of Mel-

Its Temple. ḳart (comp. II Macc. iv. 18 on games held every fifth year in honor of Hercules). The local female divinity was Astarte. On the mainland was a considerable city, Palætyrus, which seems to have had the earlier name "Usû" (so El-Amarna tablets; comp. "Oṭu" in the hieroglyphics, Assyrian, "Usu"; Talmudic, "Usha," which, however, may be another city); from this place, before the Roman time, Tyre was provided with water. The island had two harbors: one to the north; the other, now sanded, to the south. Strabo (xvi. 223) reports that the purple-factories filled the island with an unpleasant smell from the crushed shells of which the purple was made.

BIBLIOGRAPHY: R. Pietschmann, *Gesch. der Phönizier*, pp. 61 *et seq.*, Leipsic, 1889; F. Jeremias, *Tyrus bis zur Zeit Nebukadnezars*; Winckler, *Altorientalische Forschungen*, ii. 65; Prašek, *Forschungen zur Geschichte des Altertums*, ii. 21. See also PHENICIA.

E. G. H.   W. M. M.

TYRIA or TIREH: City of Asia Minor, sixty miles from Smyrna. Its Jewish community is of ancient date, the earliest members having arrived at Tyria before the Spanish expulsion; but catastrophes have reduced the Jewish population to insignificant proportions. Since 1825 the laws of the community have been modeled on those of Smyrna; and from the same year until 1882 the community obtained its revenue by means of assessments, although its income is now derived from the salt-tax, poll-tax, gifts, and rents. Most of the Jews of Tyria, who came originally from Constantinople, Brusa, Salonica, and Smyrna, and who speak Turkish, Greek, and Judæo-Spanish, live in a narrow ghetto, while some of them have their residences among adherents of other creeds. The community possesses three synagogues, the latest of which was erected in 1887; and there are a number of benevolent societies, including one for the burial of the poor. The cemetery contains a number of ancient gravestones, one of the oldest being that of Jehiel Caro, who died in 1488. The Talmud Torah at Tyria was converted in 1895 into a school controlled by the Alliance Israélite Universelle.

The list of the chief rabbis of the city includes Ḥayyim Benveniste (author of the "Keneset ha-Gedolah" and later rabbi at Smyrna), Benjamin Lapapa (whose wife died in 1694), Ḥayyim Danon, David Garguir, Ḥayyim Isaac Jaffe, Isaac Aria, Moses Capeluto, Abraham Sasson, Moses bar Siman Ṭob, Ḥayyim Beja, and the present (1905) rabbi, Nissim Joseph Lahana. It is noteworthy, however, that in the series of "haskhabot" recited on the eve of Yom Kippur for the repose of the souls of rabbis the name of Rabbi Lapapa is preceded by the names of Mattathias ben Rey, Joseph Galante, Issachar Abulafia, Solomon Mutevili, and Israel Obadiah, the last-named being followed by Abraham Sasson, although no fixed order and no definite dates are assigned them. The rabbi and physician Moses Abbas and Rabbi Elisha Gallico, both of them predecessors of the rabbis mentioned above, are also noteworthy.

The Jews of Tyria number about 1,600 in a total population of 20,000. In commerce and in industry they have displayed much activity, exporting raisins, cereals, silk, and cotton, and importing merchandise from Europe, while nearly every trade numbers Jews among its craftsmen. The government service likewise is open to Jews. Ḥayyim Jeremiah Danon, who built a Talmud Torah in 1837 and an asylum for the poor in the following year, held a governmental appointment as cashier from 1828 to 1845; while Behor Danon was municipal physician from 1895 to 1904. Formerly the government tithes were collected by Jews.

D.   A. GA.

TYRNAU or TERNAVA (Hungarian, **Nagy-Szombath**): Manufacturing town of western Hungary. It was the scene of two martyrdoms of Jews: the first, in 1494, when fourteen men and two women gave up their innocent lives, as a manuscript dirge of the Cracow community recounts; the second, when the revenge and hatred of the citizens of Tyrnau were aroused against the Jews at the time that the inroads of the Turks terrified Hungary. The burning of the Jews at PÖSING in 1529 was followed by similar acts in the communities near Tyrnau. Still, the latter city did not succeed until ten years later in getting rid of the Jews within its limits. In 1536 a three-year-old boy of Tyrnau was found dead, whereupon the citizens, who were intriguing against the Jews, accused them of having murdered the child. King Ferdinand I. tried in vain to pacify the angry citizens: the Jews that were suspected were executed; and on the request of the city authorities Ferdinand banished (Feb. 19, 1539) forever the remaining ones (this decree was confirmed by Leopold I. in 1686). Jews were strictly forbidden to set foot within the city or the territory belonging to it; and those who even unwittingly violated the order were severely punished.

In 1717, when a subject of Count Kaunitz was punished, the count, wishing to put an end once for all to these proceedings of the city, did his utmost to secure the annulment of the charter of Ferdinand I.; but he succeeded only so far as to bring about the execution of an agreement between the city of Tyrnau and the Jews, the latter being represented by Simeon Michel, an ancestor of the German poet Heinrich Heine. Under this agreement the Jews renounced all claims that might be brought either by themselves or by their landlords against the city on account of their former imprisonment, while the city promised to allow Jews to pass through Tyrnau on payment of a certain toll. Though the agreement was supposed to be made for all time, Maria Theresa annulled it, and the Jews were again excluded from Tyrnau.

King Joseph II. allowed them to settle in the city (March 31, 1783); and from that time the once famous Jewish community of Tyrnau again began to flourish. See ISAAC TYRNAU.

BIBLIOGRAPHY: Kohn, *Die Gesch. der Juden in Ungarn*, i. 441; Schudt, *Jüdische Merckwürdigkeiten*, i.; Alex. Büchler, in *Egyenlőség*, xvi., No. 6; idem, *History of the Jews in Budapest* (in Hungarian), pp. 95–97; David Kaufmann, *Aus Heinrich Heine's Ahnensaal*, p. 220.

S.   A. Bü.

TYROL: Crownland of Austria. The earliest documents referring to its Jews date from the beginning of the fourteenth century. The statement, found in the "Privilegium Ecclesiæ S. Stephani" in Rendena (Hormayr, "Gesch. Tirols," 1808, document 231), according to which Charlemagne overcame certain Jewish owners of castles in 800, can not be credited. In the fourteenth century Jews settled at Bozen, Meran, Riva, Rovereto, and in the episcopal cities of Brixen and Trent, as merchants, money-lenders, and mint- and tax-farmers. Isaac, "Judeus de Luncz (Lienz)" is mentioned (Aug. 16, 1308) as farmer of the mint at Meran. In 1318 the Jew Nikolaus of Bozen received in fief from King Heinrich of Carinthia a house and garden in that city. According to the accounts of the monk Goswin and others, the Jews of Tyrol were bitterly persecuted in the fourteenth century at the time of the Black Death, when they were accused of poisoning the wells.

There were no general statutes for the Jews of Tyrol; but to individuals a number of grants of privileges were made, many being quite important; noteworthy among them was the liberal decree, containing twenty-seven clauses, issued at Martinmas, 1403, by Bishop Ulrich III. of Brixen, in favor of the Jews Isaac, son of Gansmann, and his brother-in-law Samuel. Still more liberal was the decree, granted May 1, 1431, by Duke Frederick With the Empty Pocket, to the Jews Mendlein, Simeon, and Rubein. Frederick's son Sigmund had the Jew Seligman in his employ as surgeon. Sigmund's reign was marked by the imposition of the first Jews' tax in Tyrol and by the notorious trial for ritual murder on account of SIMON OF TRENT. A similar occurrence is connected with the names of Anderle of Rinn near INNSBRUCK, and of Ursula of Lienz.

In 1475, while the events at Trent were still fresh in memory, twenty-one peasants of Lienz testified that on Good Friday, 1442, Ursula, the four-year-old daughter of Thomas Pöck of Lienz, had been murdered for ritual purposes by the few Jews of that city; and in consequence of this testimony the alleged murderers, two Jews, two Jewesses, and their accomplice, a Christian woman, were executed after a short trial and excruciating tortures. On Jan. 22, 1520, the Landtag issued a decree expelling all Jews from Tyrol. Soon after, however, Jews were again living at Bozen, Riva, and Nori; but they were forbidden to peddle, and were required to wear a badge and to pay a personal tax. This tax was reduced in 1573, on the complaint of one Abraham, spokesman for the Jews of Tyrol. Jews first settled at INNSBRUCK in 1578.

In the seventeenth century important privileges were granted to several Jews of Tyrol, especially to the descendants of Solomon of Bassano. In consequence of the attempt of Maria Theresa to expel all Jews from Tyrol in 1748, their numbers decreased so rapidly that by the end of the eighteenth century only eight Jewish families, tolerated under Joseph II., were living at Innsbruck and Bozen. While Tyrol was under Bavarian rule (1806-14) the edict issued by the king in 1813 granted to the Jews an assured legal status. The ancient rights of the Jews of Tyrol were confirmed by Austria in 1817, when Tyrol was again taken by that country, though the laws prohibiting the acquisition of real estate and the holding of public offices, as well as those against new settlers, remained in force. Still, there was a Jewish postmaster at Bozen at the end of the eighteenth century; Jews acted as purveyors to the Austrian army in the Napoleonic wars; and they took an especially prominent part in supporting the revolt of Andreas Hofer in Tyrol in 1809.

There is no legally recognized Jewish community in Tyrol, its Jews being subject to the community at Hohenems (Vorarlberg) in virtue of the law of 1890. Several Jews of Hohenems, as Schwarz of Bozen, have achieved distinction in industrial undertakings, notably in the building of railroads, and as brewers and bankers. In 1905 Jews were living in Tyrol only at INNSBRUCK, Bozen, Meran, and TRENT.

BIBLIOGRAPHY: Tänzer, *Gesch. der Juden in Tirol und Vorarlberg*, 1903, vol. i.; Scherer, *Rechtsverhältnisse der Juden in den Deutsch-Oesterreichischen Ländern*, pp. 572 et seq., Leipsic, 1901.

s.   A. TÄ.

U

U-BA LE-ZIYYON ("And the Redeemer shall come to Zion"; Isa. lix. 20): Opening words of the closing prayer of the daily morning service, before which one should not leave the synagogue (Shulḥan 'Aruk, Oraḥ Ḥayyim, 132). The prayer consists of a series of texts, in which are included the ḲEDUSH-SHAH following the lesson, with its Aramaic paraphrase (comp. Soṭah 49a), and two brief, ancient prayers embodying an aspiration for enlightenment through that and other studies. It is always preceded immediately or closely by ASHRE (Ps. cxlv.; Ps. xx. intervening on ordinary week-days), and it is repeated in such association before the afternoon prayer on Sabbaths and festivals, and before NE'I-LAH on the Day of Atonement.

"U-Ba le-Ziyyon" is not chanted at length; the greater portion is read in an undertone after the ḥazzan has intoned the introductory lines. The

U-BA LE-ZIYYON

mf Adagio molto tranquillo.

U - ba   le - Ziy - yon   go - 'el,   u - le - sha - be......

fe - sha' be - Ya - 'a - kob....... ne - 'um A - do - - nai.

Wa - a - ni,.... zot be - ri - ti o - tam, a - mar A -

do - - - - nai: ru - ḥi a - sher 'a - le - - - ka, u - de -

ba - rai a - sher sam - ti be - fi - - - ka, lo ya -

mu - - shu mi - pi - - - ka, u - mi - pi zar - 'a -

ka, u - mi - pi.... ze - ra' zar - 'a - ka, a - mar..... A -

do - - nai, me - 'at - tah we - 'ad 'o - lam.

chant for these, in the ritual of the Ashkenazim, is founded on the prayer-motive of the Sabbath afternoon service (see MUSIC, SYNAGOGAL); but in the tradition of the Sephardim there is employed a special chant, of which a variant is used for Ps. xvi., recited shortly afterward, at the expiration of Sabbath. It is this melody which is here transcribed. In the frequent repetition of a short phrase, and the modification of it to fit the text, it reproduces the chief peculiarity of the worship-music traceable to a Spanish source earlier than 1492.

A.   F. L. C.

UÇEDA, SAMUEL BEN ISRAEL DE: Palestinian commentator and preacher; born at Safed in the first quarter of the sixteenth century. His name, Uçeda, originally was derived from the town of that name in the archbishopric of Toledo. He was a pupil of Isaac Luria and Ḥayyim Vital, with whom he studied Cabala, and became rabbi and preacher in Safed and, later, in Constantinople. Samuel was the author of the following works: "Iggeret Shemu'el," commentary and supercommentary on the Book of Ruth (published in 1557; together with the text and the commentary of Rashi,

Kuru Chesme, 1597; Amsterdam, 1712; Zolkiev, 1800); "Leḥem Dim'ah," commentary on Lamentations, with the text and the commentary of Rashi (Venice, 1600; Amsterdam, 1710, 1715); "Midrash Shemu'el" (Venice, 1579, 1585, 1597; Cracow, 1594; Frankfort-on-the-Main, 1713). The last-named work was his chief one, and consisted of a detailed commentary on the Pirḳe Abot, with reference to the commentaries (at that time in manuscript) of Jonah Gerondi, Meïr Abulafia, Samuel ben Meïr, Menahem Me'iri, Samuel ibn Sid, Joseph ibn Naḥmias, Baruch ibn Melek, Joseph ibn Susan, Moses Almosnino, and others, most of which have since been printed.

BIBLIOGRAPHY: Conforte, *Kore ha-Dorot*, pp. 42a, 48a; Azulai, *Shem ha-Gedolim*, i. 172; De Rossi-Hamberger, *Hist. Wörterb.* p. 254; Steinschneider, *Cat. Bodl.* p. 2494; Fürst, *Bibl. Jud.* iii. 44.
W. B.   M. K.

UFHAUSEN, SOLOMON ZEBI HIRSCH. See BRENZ, SAMUEL FRIEDRICH.

UGOLINO, BLAISIO: Italian polyhistor; born at Venice about 1700. He is stated to have been a Jewish convert, and was certainly well acquainted with Talmudic literature. He is known for the huge collection of treatises on Jewish antiquities, written in Latin, which he brought together in his "Thesaurus Antiquitatum Sacrarum" (34 vols., Venice, 1744–69). In this work he reprinted most of the seventeenth-century treatises on Jewish antiquities by Bochart, Bonfrère, Buxtorf, Carpzov, Cellarius, Clavering, Deyling, Goodwin, Hottinger, Huet, Lowth, Opitz, Pfeiffer, Prideaux, Reland, Rhenferd, Saubertius, Selden, Sigonius, Spencer, Trigland, Van Til, Wagenseil, and Witsius, besides obtaining fresh contributors, and translating much himself from the Midrashim. The subjects treated are as follows: (a) Festivals, i. (b) General antiquities, ii.–iv. (c) Geography, v.–vi. (d) Priests and temple, vii.–xiii. (e) Midrashim, xiv.–xvii. (f) Talmud, xvii.–xx. (g) Ritual and synagogue, xxi. (h) Sects and proselytes, xxii. (i) Gentile deities, xxiii. (j) Jewish law, xxiv.–xxvii. (k) Numismatics, xxviii. (l) Costume, marriage, and medicine, xxix.–xxx. (m) Poetry and music, xxxi.–xxxii. (n) Death and burial, xxxiii. Biblical, Hebrew, author, and subject indexes are contained in vol. xxxiv.

Ugolino himself translated the treatises Menaḥot and Zebaḥim (vol. xix.); Pesaḥim, Sheḳalim, Yoma, Sukkah, Rosh ha-Shanah, Ta'anit, Megillah, Ḥagigah, Beẓah, Mo'ed Ḳaṭan, Ma'aserot, Ma'aser Sheni, Ḥallah, Orlah, and Bikkurim (vols. xvii.–xviii.); Sifra, Sifre, and Tosefta (vols. xvii.–xix.); besides a part of Maimonides' "Yad" and of Abraham Portaleone's "Shilṭe ha-Gibborim."

BIBLIOGRAPHY: McClintock and Strong, Cyc.; Steinschneider, Cat. Bodl. s.v.
T. J.

UJHELY (SATORALJA-UJHELY): City in the county of Zemplin, Hungary. Documents in its archives show that in 1734 Jews were living at Ujhely and that they were allowed to acquire real estate. It is evident that the community was then increasing; for ten years later the Jews possessed a school which in 1829 received a bequest of 260,000 gulden from Martin Raphael Kästenbaum, and which was thenceforth known by his name. The oldest tombstone bears date of 1760, although the ḥebra ḳaddisha, with which was connected a hospital, was not established until 1772, its founder being an itinerant rabbi named Naphtali Hirsch. The first ḥebra-book has a drawing on its title-page representing the last rites.

A synagogue was built at Ujhely in 1790; and when it was demolished in 1887, to be replaced by a new house of worship, it was found to have eight subterranean chambers, which probably served as dungeons. The oldest document of the community is dated 1831, during the rabbinate of Moses Teitelbaum, of whom the story is told that Louis Kossuth, afterward leader of the Hungarian Revolution, when suffering from an infantile sickness, was brought to him, and that the rabbi blessed the child and, referring to the word "ḳosheṭ" in Ps. lx. 6 (A.V. 4), prophesied his future greatness. Teitelbaum died in 1841, and was succeeded by his son Leopold, who, however, soon went to Marmaros-Sziget. Jeremiah Löw was then appointed rabbi of Ujhely. Löw, who was one of the leaders of the Orthodox party, was succeeded by the present chief rabbi, Koloman Weisz, and the preacher Isidor Goldberger. Michael HEILPRIN, who acted as secretary

to Minister Szemere in 1848, was, prior to the Revolution, a teacher in the Jewish school of Ujhely.

The Jews of the city number 4,500 in a total population of 13,000.

BIBLIOGRAPHY: Albert Székely, Ujhelyi Zsidók Története, in Magyarország Vármegyéi és Városai (in manuscript).
D. L. V.

'UKBA, MAR: Exilarch at Bagdad in the first half of the tenth century; the second exilarch to die in banishment. When KOHEN ẒEDEḲ II. was appointed gaon of Pumbedita he became involved in a controversy with Mar 'Uḳba over the revenues from Khorasan; and the calif Al-Muḳtadir (908–932) was induced by Ẓedeḳ's friends to depose Mar 'Uḳba. Soon afterward (917) the latter left Bagdad for Karmisin (Kermanshah), but when the young calif went for the summer to his palace at Safran, Mar 'Uḳba devised a scheme to win the royal favor by meeting Al-Muḳtadir's secretary daily in his gardens and greeting him with the recitation of beautiful verses. These pleased the calif's secretary so much that he wrote them down and showed them to his master, who in his turn was so delighted that he sent for Mar 'Uḳba, entered into conversation with him, and asked him to express a wish, whereupon the gaon requested that he might be reinstated. The calif granted this wish, and Mar 'Uḳba soon returned to Bagdad as exilarch. Kohen Ẓedeḳ and his friends, however, again succeeded in securing his deposition and banishment from the country, whereupon he went to Africa, and was received with high honors at Kairwan as a descendant of the royal house. A sort of throne ("bimah") was built for him in the synagogue, near the Ark of the Law, and he was always the third to read the "parashah," the scroll of the Law being brought to him in his seat.

BIBLIOGRAPHY: Neubauer, M. J. C. ii. 78–79; Grätz, Gesch. v. 246–248, note 12; Halevi, Dorot ha-Rishonim, iii. 25 et seq.; Weiss, Dor, iv. 134 et seq.
E. C. S. O.

UKRAINE. See RUSSIA.

'UKZIN ("Stalks of Plants"): Name of a treatise of the Mishnah and the Tosefta, dealing chiefly with the conveyance of ritual impurity by means of the roots, stalks, and hulls of plants. In the Mishnah it is the twelfth and last treatise of the order Ṭohorot; and it is also the last of the whole Mishnah. Maimonides says: "This treatise has been placed at the end because the impurity of stalks is not explained in the Bible, and depends solely on the judgment of the Rabbis." It is divided into three chapters, containing twenty-seven paragraphs in all. Its contents may be summarized as follows:

Ch. i.: Difference between roots, stalks, and hulls in regard to impurity; wet roots become unclean sooner than dry ones (§§ 1–2); size of unclean stalks; certain roots that convey no impurity (§§ 3–4); stalks that have been cut from the fruit are clean; a stalk of figs (fresh or dried), or any pods, carobs, gourds, or other portion of a plant, conveys impurity if when taken together with the body of the plant it is as large as an egg (§§ 5–6).

Ch. ii.: Olives preserved with their leaves in liquor receive no impurity; kernels of fruit receive impurity (§§ 1–2); pomegranates and melons that have been partly crushed so that the remnant is smaller than an egg can not become unclean; all husks receive impurity. Rabbi Judah says: "An onion has three skins; the outermost never receives impurity; the innermost always receives impurity; the middle one receives impurity when whole. but not when honeycombed" (§§ 3–4). What parts of garments and plants convey impurity (§§ 5–8); plants growing in the earth can not be unclean; laws relating to plants growing in vases (§§ 9–10).

Ch. iii.: Certain objects can become unclean only after they have once been wet (§§ 1–3); under what conditions dills, spices, pepper, unripe fruit, fish, milk, and honeycombs receive impurity (§§ 4–11). The Mishnah concludes with the following paragraphs (§ 12) which are later additions: "Rabbi Joshua ben Levi says, 'The Holy One, blessed be He! will cause every righteous man to inherit 310 worlds, as it is said: "To make those that love me inherit substance; and their treasuries I will fill [Prov. viii. 21, Hebr.; numerically the letters in the word יש (= "substance") amount to 310]."' Rabbi Simeon ben Ḥalafta says, 'The Holy One, blessed be He! found no other vessel capable of containing so much blessing for Israel as peace, as it is said: "The Lord will give strength unto his people; the Lord will bless his people with peace [Ps. xxix. 11]."'"

In the Tosefta likewise, 'Uḳzin is the last treatise. It is divided into three chapters, containing forty-two paragraphs in all. It includes no haggadic sayings. 'Uḳzin has no Gemara.

E. C.   S. Led.

ULAM. See Temple in Rabbinical Literature.

ULAMO, JACOB DANIEL. See Olmo.

ULIF, GERSHON ASHKENAZI. See Ashkenazi, Gershon.

ULLA (עולא; called **Rab 'Ula** in Ket. 65b and Ḳid. 31a): One of the leading halakic amoraim in Palestine during the latter part of the third and in the beginning of the fourth century. In his youth he studied under R. Eleazar II. (Tos. to Ḥul. 34a, s.v. "Man Ḥabraya"); and he transmitted nine of his teacher's halakic sayings, seven of which are contained in B. Ḳ. 11, end, one in 'Er. 21b, and one in Ket. 74a. He was greatly respected for his learning; and during his visits to Babylonia he seems to have been invited frequently by the "resh galuta" to deliver halakic lectures (Ket. 65b; Ḳid. 31a; Shab. 157b). He traveled repeatedly to Babylonia; and on one of his journeys he was in danger of assassination by one of his companions, saving his life only by condoning the murder of another (Ned. 22a).

Ulla rendered important decisions regarding the benedictions and the calculation of the new moon, and was accustomed to promulgate his rulings in Babylonia when he went thither (Ber. 38b; R. H. 22b; Pes. 53b, 104b). He was very strict in his interpretation of religious laws (Shab. 147a, 157b); and on one occasion, when he heard R. Huna use an expression which he did not approve, he retorted, "As vinegar to the teeth, and as smoke to the eyes, so are the words of R. Huna," applying to him the first half of Prov. x. 26 (Ḳid. 45b). Only in the presence

of R. Naḥman did Ulla hesitate to pronounce his opinions, generally waiting until the former had departed (Giṭ. 11b, 12a); although he frequently sought Naḥman's company (Ket. 53a). Of his contemporaries with whom he engaged in controversies may be mentioned, besides R. Naḥman, R. Abba (B. M. 11a), Abimi bar Papa, Ḥiyya bar Ammi (Ket. 53a), and R. Judah (Ḥul. 68b, 70a); but his personal friend, with whom he associated most frequently, was Rabbah bar bar Ḥana (Tosef., Ḥul. xxxiv. 1).

In addition to the sayings of his teacher Eleazar, Ulla transmitted those of R. Hoshaiah (Ḥul. 76a), Joshua ben Levi (ib. 122a), R. Johanan ('Er. 67b), Rab (Shab. 143b), and Simeon ben Laḳish (Ḥag. 8b), while his own sayings were transmitted by R. Aḥa bar Adda (B. M. 117b), Hamnuna (Shab. 10b), Ḥiyya bar Abba (Ḥag. 25b), Ḥiyya bar Ami (Ber. 8a), Raba bar Ḥinena (Men. 30b), R. Ḥisda (Ber. 38b), Judah bar Ammi (M. Ḳ. 5b), and Joshua bar Abba (ib. 5b). Raba appears to have been his only son (Shab. 83b).

Ulla died in Babylonia, before his teacher R. Eleazar; but his remains were taken to Palestine for burial (Ket. 111a).

Bibliography: Heilprin, Seder ha-Dorot, pp. 229–230; Bacher, Ag. Bab. Amor., pp. 93–97.
E. C.   S. O.

ULLMANN, ALEXANDER DE ERÉNY: Hungarian deputy and political economist; born at Budapest Feb. 18, 1850; died there 1897; son of **Karl Ullmann** (b. 1809; d. 1880), founder of the first Hungarian insurance company, and vice-president of the Bank of Commerce at Pest. Ullmann was educated in Budapest and Vienna (LL.D. 1872), and was admitted to the bar in 1873. On the death of his father the family was elevated to the Hungarian nobility. From 1884 to 1892 Ullmann represented the electoral district of Also-Arpas in the Hungarian Parliament.

In addition to numerous juridical and economic essays in the "Pester Lloyd," "Ellenör," and "Neuzeit," Ullmann wrote the following works: "A Részvényes Kereseti Jogáról" (Budapest, 1877), on the right of stockholders to institute legal proceedings; "A Kényszcregyezség Kérdéséhez" (ib. 1879), on compulsory settlements; "Az Ipartörvény Reviziója" (ib. 1880), on the revision of the industrial laws; "A Magyar Kereskedelmi és Iparkamarák Reformja" (ib. 1882), on the reform of the Hungarian board of trade and commerce; and "Zsidó Felekezeti Ügyek Rendezése" (ib. 1888), on the legal regulation of Jewish affairs.

Bibliography: Sturm, Ozsrággülési Almanach, 1887.
S.   L. V.

ULLMANN, SHALOM: Hungarian Talmudist; flourished in the beginning of the nineteenth century; officiated as rabbi in Fürth, and later at Boldogasszony (Frankirchen), a small place in the county of Wieselburg. He was the author of "Dibre Rash" (1826), a work containing notes on various Talmudic treatises.

S.   A. Ke.

ULM: City and district of Württemberg. As in many other German cities, there is in Ulm a legend that Jews lived there before the Christian era;

but the first historical evidence of a Jewish settlement is a tombstone dated 1243 and erected in memory of Huknah, daughter of R. Solomon ha-Levi. The next oldest record is a declaration, issued by the city council of Ulm in 1274, which terms the Jewish community a privileged "Darleihergenossenschaft" (loan society), fully authorized to dispose of unredeemed pledges. By the aid of a Jew the Bavarians, who in the fourteenth century

Thirteenth and Fourteenth Centuries. were at war with Austria, succeeded in reducing the city (April 20, 1316); and eight years later (Nov. 10, 1324) Louis the Bavarian pledged to the counts of Öttingen the state taxes payable by the Jews of Ulm. In like manner Charles IV. pawned the Jewish taxes of Ulm to Albrecht of Rechberg; and the Jews of the city thus found themselves compelled to collect part of their taxes from their coreligionists of Schelklingen and Ehingen. The Jews of the latter place, however, complained of this procedure; and on Aug. 1, 1348, the Jews of Ulm were officially reprimanded. The imperial prefects of Swabia finally took them under their protection on condition that they paid their "Schutzgeld" (protection-money) promptly. The other fees which they gave for protection went to the city treasury of Ulm, and were used to defray the cost of new fortifications.

About this time the Jews of Ulm were accused of poisoning the wells, and were persecuted by mobs, while the city council, on being called to account by Count Helfenstein, declared itself powerless to check the rabble. The property of the victims was attached by the city authorities; and on

Accused of Well-Poisoning. this occasion a letter from the Jewish community of Jerusalem, informing the Jews of Ulm of the crucifixion of Jesus, is said to have been found (Nübling, "Die Judengemeinden des Mittelalters," p. 300, Ulm, 1896). On the career of the "Grossjuden" Jäcklin, who was an important figure in Ulm during the latter half of the fourteenth century, see JEW. ENCYC. vii. 19.

The Jews of Ulm suffered much during the warfare between their city and the kingdom of Württemberg; for when Eberhard III., the Mild (1388–1417) ascended the throne of Württemberg he asked the assistance of the empire in enforcing the laws which had been introduced to liquidate the Jewish debt. His request was granted; and Borziwoy of Swynar was appointed prefect. The Jews of Ulm realized that, so far as they were concerned, the intention was to annul their outstanding claims in order to defray the cost of the war and to cover the so-called "Judenbrände" (riots against the Jews) of the Swabian Bund in the county of Württemberg; consequently they either took their promissory notes to places of safety or else openly resisted these demands, and delayed payment. Consequently the proposed liquidation was postponed until Aug. 11, 1392, when Wenceslaus issued an edict containing the following four clauses:

(1) The city of Ulm is granted the privilege of admitting Jews and Jewesses.

(2) One-half of the Jewish taxes is to be paid to the city, and the OPFERPFENNIG is to be paid during the week preceding Christmas.

(3) Jurisdiction in loan proceedings is vested solely in the supreme court of Ulm.

(4) For a period of ten years a large sum of money is to be paid the city by all the citizens of Ulm as well as by the Jews.

There are no records extant showing the size of the Jewish community of Ulm at this period; but the frequency of the family names "Ulma" and "Ullmann" points to a numerous congregation. That

Importance in Spiritual Affairs. it took high rank in spiritual affairs is evidenced by the fact that it possessed a yeshibah, over which R. Simelin presided. In addition to Simelin, there were three other rabbis in Ulm; namely, Seligmann, Lafen, and Gershon. Simelin violated a regulation, issued by the community of Nuremberg, to which he had himself subscribed; and the result was a controversy which involved the entire congregation. Simelin and the leaders of the community finally brought the matter before Jacob Weil for adjudication; and the latter decided that Simelin should make a public retraction of his utterances in three different communities, or suffer the penalty of excommunication.

Nothing further is known of the spiritual life of the Jews of Ulm at this period; but their social condition steadily deteriorated. The following regulations (dated Nov. 24, 1395) from the so-called "Red Book" are extant:

(1) The Jews must weigh on "sworn money-scales" ("Geldwage") everything which they buy or sell.

(2) From Palm Saturday until Easter Wednesday, as well as on Corpus Christi Day, all Jews must remain within the Jewish quarter; transgressions of this ordinance will be punishable with a fine of five pounds heller.

"Red Book" Regulations. (3) Any discourtesy shown a Jew by a Christian will be punished twice as severely as if shown to another Christian.

(4) A Jew may not lend money on a pledge unless he knows the debtor well.

(5) No Jew may have a Christian servant in his house.

(6) No inhabitants of Ulm other than Jews may engage in pawnbroking.

As a result of a complaint lodged by the goldsmiths' gild the following restrictions were imposed by the city council of Ulm: (1) No Jew may melt gold, silver, or other precious metals without the knowledge of the gild. (2) Jews may neither buy nor sell silver bullion in the city. (3) They are permitted to trade only in pearls, gems, and undamaged wares in gold and silver. On Sept. 30, 1421, the following laws were promulgated: (1) Christians may not be employed by Jews; (2) cattle purchased by Jews in the market, or meat sold by them, may be examined only by Christian butchers, and animals may be slaughtered only in the courtyard of the synagogue; (3) Jews are forbidden to touch provisions while purchasing them in the market.

On May 15, 1422, the Jews of Ulm were prohibited from advancing loans on wool or cotton. In the middle of the fifteenth century they were accused of the ritual murder of a Swiss boy named Ludwig of Bruck at Ravensburg, near Ulm, in 1428. Until the end of this century nothing further is known concerning the Jewish community; but under Maximilian I. the city council complained to the emperor of the residence of Jews in the city, and received from him a so-called "Freiheitsbrief" authorizing their expulsion under the following conditions: (1)

The Jews were to be given the shortest time possible in which to dispose of their movable property. (2) The proceeds of the sale

Expulsion in the Fifteenth Century.
of the synagogue, cemetery, hospital, bath, dwelling-houses, and the like, together with their appurtenances, were to accrue to Wolf of Asch, the prefect of Geislingen. (3) All former privileges were to be annulled. (4) After the date of the expulsion every Jew remaining in the city was to be outlawed. This manifesto was published on Aug. 6, 1499; and after four days the imperial treasury sold to the city of Ulm for 5,000 gulden the real estate belonging to the Jews, the date of the expulsion being set for five months later. No Jews were again admitted to any town in the district of Ulm until 1526, when one was allowed to settle in Albeck, on condition that he charged interest at the rate of 1, and not 2, heller per gulden. In a short time this Jew succeeded in bringing coreligionists to the district, and the council of Ulm again complained to the emperor; whereupon, on July 18, 1541, Charles V. issued a "Freiheitsrecht" from Regensburg, containing the following clause: "This Jew is not permitted to borrow money. If he does so, he is liable to a fine of 10 marks in gold; and the money, together with interest, shall go to the city of Ulm." Further, a debtor was forbidden to waive his rights under the "Freiheitsbrief" in favor of his creditor; this rendered it impossible for the Jews to remain in the city. A second "Freiheitsbrief"

Jews Again in Ulm in the Sixteenth Century.
was issued by Ferdinand I. (Vienna, March 28, 1561); and throughout the seventeenth century Jews were found in the district of Ulm only during the Diets, as imperial or princely envoys, or when traveling with safe-conducts, although occasionally they sojourned for some time in the city, and even had their own slaughter-houses.

During the eighteenth century the condition of the Jews improved slightly. On Jan. 19, 1712, the council permitted them to attend the horse-markets on payment of 10 kreutzer per diem; but they were forbidden to peddle leather. In the middle of the eighteenth century, however (May 20, 1750), they received permission to attend all the fairs and to deal in wares of any kind. They were charged 1 gulden a day for the privilege of staying in Ulm; and their safe-conducts cost 3 kreutzer per hour. At the outbreak of the French war several Jews

Eighteenth and Nineteenth Centuries.
went to Ulm, among them being the army contractors Kaulla of Hechingen, and Gumberz, manager of the Stadt-theater in Ulm. When the condition of the Jews in Württemberg was regulated (1827) and civic equality was granted to them, the Diet of Ulm lodged an unavailing protest. Soon afterward the special taxes levied on Jews for protection and the like were repealed.

On Feb. 3, 1845, the Jews of Ulm organized divine services, Simon Einstein of Laupheim being chosen ḥazzan. In 1853 a Jewish cemetery was opened; on Sept. 12, 1873, a new synagogue was dedicated; and in 1888 Solomon Fried of Ratibor was called as rabbi. The Jews of Ulm in 1919

numbered about 1,000 in a total population of about 56,020. They support four charitable organizations.

BIBLIOGRAPHY: Depping, *Juden im Mittelalter,* Stuttgart, 1834; Haid, *Ulm und Sein Gebiet,* Ulm, 1786; Hassler, *Die Ulmer Judengrabsteine,* ib. 1868; Nübling, *Die Judengemeinden des Mittelalters,* ib. 1896 (strongly prejudiced against the Jews); Pressel, *Gesch. der Juden in Ulm,* ib. 1873; idem, *Ulmisches Urkundenbuch,* i., Stuttgart, 1873; Schultes, *Chronik von Ulm,* Ulm, 1881; Veesenmeyer, *Etwas über den Ehemaligen Aufenthalt der Juden in Ulm,* in *Programm des Ulmer Gymnasiums, 1797;* Salfeld, *Martyrologium,* s.v.; Kohut, *Gesch. der Deutschen Juden,* s.v.
D.   S. O.

ULMANN, ALBERT : American banker and author; born in New York city July 2, 1861; educated in the public schools and at the College of the City of New York. In 1900 he became a member of the New York Stock Exchange firm of J. H. Sulzbacher. He is one of the founders and governors of the Judæans, and has been interested in the history of New York and of the Jews in that city. He has contributed to the "New York Times Saturday Review," to the "Saturday Evening Post," and to other journals, and is the author of: "Frederick Struther's Romance" (New York, 1889); "Chaperoned" (*ib.* 1894); "A Landmark History of New York" (*ib.* 1901); and "New York's Historical Sites, Landmarks, Monuments, and Tablets" (*ib.* 1902).

BIBLIOGRAPHY: *The American Jewish Year Book,* 1904–5; *Who's Who in America,* 1903–5; *Who's Who in New York City and State,* 1905.
A.   F. T. H.

ULMANN, BENJAMIN : French historical painter; born at Blotzheim, Alsace, May 24, 1829; died at Paris Feb. 24, 1884. He studied at the Ecole des Beaux-Arts under Drölling and Picot, and in 1859 won the Prix de Rome.

Of his paintings may be mentioned: "Sylla at the House of Marius" (1866; now in the Luxembourg Museum); "Patroclus and Amphidamas" (in the art gallery at Mans); "Junius Brutus" (in the museum at Melun); "Remorse"; "The Gitanos of Granada"; "The Bell-Ringers of Nuremberg" and "The Lorelei" (exhibited at the Paris Salon, 1872); "A Defeat"; "The Hour of Wailing"; and "The Deliverer of the Fatherland." At the Paris Salons of 1859 and 1872 Ulmann's exhibits won medals of the second and third class. In 1872 he was decorated with the cross of the Legion of Honor.

BIBLIOGRAPHY: Hans Wolfgang Singer, *Allgemeines Künstler-Lexicon,* Frankfort-on-the-Main, 1898; Clement and Hutton, *Artists of the Nineteenth Century and Their Works,* Boston, 1880; *La Grande Encyclopédie.*
S.   F. C.

ULMANN, SALOMON : French rabbi; born at Zabern, Alsace, Feb. 25, 1806; died at Paris May 5, 1865. He commenced his rabbinical studies at Strasburg under Moïse Bloch (better known as Rabbi Mosche Utenheim), and was the first pupil enrolled at the initial competitive examination of candidates for the Ecole Centrale Rabbinique, inaugurated in July, 1830. He was also the first in his class at this institution to receive the diploma of chief rabbi. In 1834 he was appointed rabbi of Lauterbourg, Alsace; in 1844 he became chief rabbi of Nancy, in Lorraine; and in 1853 he succeeded Marchand Ennery as chief rabbi of the Central Consistory of the Israelites of France.

Ulmann published a limited number of sermons and pastoral letters, and was the author also of

"Catéchisme, ou Eléments d'Instruction Religieuse et Morale à l'Usage des Jeunes Israélites" (Strasburg, 1845; 3d ed., Paris, 1871), which is considered a classic.

The most important act in Ulmann's rabbinical career was the organization of the Central Conference of the Chief Rabbis of France, over whose deliberations he presided at Paris in May, 1856. In that year Ulmann addressed a "Pastoral Letter to the Faithful of the Jewish Religion," in which he set forth the result of the deliberations of the conference, which were as follows: (1) revision and abbreviation of the piyyuṭim; (2) the introduction of a regular system of preaching; (3) the introduction of the organ into synagogues; (4) the organization of religious instruction; (5) the institution of the rite of confirmation for the Jewish youth of both sexes; (6) a resolution for the transfer of the Ecole Centrale Rabbinique from Metz to Paris.

BIBLIOGRAPHY: *Archives Israélites* and *Univers Israélite*, May, 1865.
s. J. Ka.

UMAN. See Haidamacks.

UNCLEANNESS. See Ablution.

UNGARISCH-JÜDISCHE WOCHENSCHRIFT. See Periodicals.

UNGARISCHE ISRAELIT, DER. See Periodicals.

UNGER, EPHRAIM SOLOMON: German educator and writer; born at Coswig-on-the-Elbe March 8, 1789; died Nov. 1, 1870. He studied philosophy, mathematics, and natural science at the University of Erfurt, and from 1810 to 1816 was privat-docent in mathematics and philosophy at the same institution. In 1820 he founded, together with his brother David, a school for mathematics and modern languages, which fourteen years later was transformed into a real-school. The school board offered him the directorship on condition that he embraced Christianity, but he refused to do so. He retained, however, the position of "Oberlehrer" until 1862, in which year he was pensioned.

Unger was for many years a member of the city council of Erfurt. He was made an honorary citizen; and the King of Prussia conferred upon him the title of professor and decorated him with the Order of the Red Eagle in recognition of his services. Through his efforts the Jewish congregation of Erfurt was incorporated in 1812; and for many years he was its first overseer. Of his works the following may be mentioned: "Handbuch der Mathematischen Analysis," 4 vols. (Gotha, 1824–27); "Abriss der Geschichte der Zahlenlehre von Pythagoras bis Diophant"; and "Die Bedeutung der Zwei Bücher des Apollonius von den Berechnungen für die Geometrische Analysis."
s. W. Sa.

UNGER, JOACHIM JACOB: Austrian rabbi; born at Homona, Hungary, Nov. 25, 1826; studied at the University of Berlin (Ph.D. 1859), and was appointed rabbi of Iglau, Moravia, in 1860. He is the author of several works, of which the following may be mentioned: "Hebräische Philologie und

Biblische Exegese," in "Mannheimer-Album," Vienna, 1864; "Bemerkungen über die Phönicischen Opfertafeln von Marseille und Carthago," in "Zeitschrift der Deutschen Morgenländischen Gesellschaft," xxiv.; "Die Judenfrage in Preussen," in "Neuzeit," 1874; "Patriotische Casual-Reden," Iglau, 1881 (2d ed. Prague, 1899); "Dichtungen," *ib.* 1885; "Fest- und Sabbath-Predigten," Prague and Breslau, 1903. He died in November, 1912.

BIBLIOGRAPHY: Lippe, *Biog. Lex.* pp. 505-507, Vienna, 1881; Zeitlin, *Bibl. Post-Mendels.*, p. 401.
s. F. T. H.

UNGER, JOSEPH: Austrian jurist and statesman; born in Vienna July 2, 1828. Having studied law at the university of his native city, he in 1850 was appointed assistant librarian, and in 1852 privat-docent, at his alma mater. The following year he was called to Prague as assistant professor at the university, and in 1855 to Vienna in a similar capacity. In 1857 he was appointed professor of jurisprudence at the latter institution. In 1867 he was successively elected a member of the Austrian Landtag and of the Reichsrath; but on account of ill health he had to resign in the following year. Appointed in 1869 by the Emperor of Austria a life-member of the House of Lords, he soon became the whip of the Liberal Party. Two years later he became minister (without portfolio) in Prince Auersperg's cabinet, but resigned upon the prime minister's defeat in 1879. In 1881 he was appointed president of the Reichsgericht (Supreme Court of Administration). Unger was a convert to Christianity.

Of Unger's works the following may be mentioned: "Die Ehe in Ihrer Welthistorischen Entwicklung" (Vienna, 1850); "Ueber Wissenschaftliche Behandlung des Oesterreichischen Gemeinen Privatrechtes" (*ib.* 1853); "Der Entwurf eines Bürgerlichen Gesetzbuches für das Königreich Sachsen" (*ib.* 1853); "System des Oesterreichischen Allgemeinen Privatrechts" (Leipsic, 1856–64; vols. i. and ii., 5th ed., 1892; vol. vi., 1894), a standard work on Austrian law, which established Unger's reputation; "Die Rechtliche Natur der Inhaberpapiere" (Vienna, 1857); "Der Revidierte Entwurf eines Bürgerlichen Gesetzbuches für das Königreich Sachsen" (*ib.* 1861); "Zur Lösung der Ungarischen Frage" (*ib.* 1861; written in collaboration with Fischhof, and published anonymously), a work advocating a dual monarchy for Austria and Hungary, its appearance marking Unger's entry upon a political career; "Die Verlassenschaftsabhandlung in Oesterreich" (*ib.* 1865); "Zur Reform der Wiener Universität" (*ib.* 1865); "Die Verträge zu Gunsten Dritter" (Jena, 1869); "Schuldübernahme" (Vienna, 1889); "Handeln auf Eigene Gefahr" (Jena, 1891); and "Handeln auf Fremde Gefahr" (*ib.* 1894).

BIBLIOGRAPHY: *Brockhaus Konversations-Lexikon*; *Meyers Konversations-Lexikon*.
s. F. T. H.

UNGER, MANASSE: German art critic; born in Coswig-on-the-Elbe March 14, 1802; died at Berlin May 17, 1868. When he was only four years of age his parents moved to Erfurt, where he received his first instruction in the art of sketching, and where he also devoted himself to the study of mathematics and architecture, later passing the state examination for architects in Berlin. In spite of this training, however, he decided to pursue an artist's career. Supported by a government scholarship, he traveled through Italy, visiting Venice (1844), Florence, and Rome (1845), and returning in 1846 to Berlin, where he resided until his death. During the Revolution of 1848 Unger was elected captain of the artists' corps which protected the museums. In 1852 he traveled through France, Belgium, and Holland, in which last-named country he discovered Rubens' "Sacrifice of Abraham."

Unger produced no paintings of importance, only a few portraits painted by him being in existence; but his knowledge of the technique and individuality of many a great painter made it possible for him to restore old paintings and to become an art critic of note. He was the author of "Das Wesen der Malerei," Leipsic, 1851; "Kritische Forschungen im Gebiete der Malerei Alter und Neuer Zeit," Berlin, 1868; and "Künstler und Fürst," an epos, published posthumously, Berlin, 1875. After the death of his parents Unger joined the Protestant Church.

BIBLIOGRAPHY: Albert Pick, Ueber den Erfurter Maler und Kunstgelehrten Manasse Unger, Erfurt, 1890.
s.
F. T. H.

UNICORN : Rendering in the Authorized Version of the Hebrew רים or ראם, following the Septuagint and the Vulgate. Aquila and Saadia, on Job xxxix. 9, read "rhinoceros"; Bochart ("Hierozoicon") and others, "oryx," or "white antelope"; Revised Version, "wild ox" (margin, "ox-antelope"). The allusions to the "re'em" as a wild, untamable animal of great strength and agility, with mighty horns (Job xxxix. 9–12; Ps. xxii. 21, xxix. 6; Num. xxiii. 22, xxiv. 8; Deut. xxxiii. 17; comp. Ps. xcii. 11), best fit the aurochs (Bos primigenius). This view is supported by the Assyrian "rimu," which is often used as a metaphor of strength, and is depicted as a powerful, fierce, wild, or mountain bull with large horns. The term evidently denotes from its connection some animal of the bovine or antelope class, perhaps the oryx (so LXX.). The oryx, as well as the wild bull and ox, is common in Palestine and Syria; and aurochs' teeth were found by Tristram on the flooring of an ancient cave in the Lebanon.

The Talmud has for "re'em" אורזילא or ארזילא, which etymologically recalls the Arabic "ghazal" (= "gazel"), but is said to be the name of an animal of such size that it could not enter the ark of Noah, but had to be fastened thereto by its horn (Zeb. 113b; comp. B. B. 74b; Shab. 107b; Yalḳuṭ Shim'oni, ii. 97d, where it is said that the re'em touches the clouds). If the Talmud intended the urzila for the unicorn, it can not be identical with the one-horned ox which Adam is said to have offered as sacrifice (Ḥul. 60a and parallels), because the urzila is classed among the animals of the field that may not be offered for that purpose. The Tosefta on the passage in Zebaḥim explains the urzila as the buffalo.

Again, in Ḥul. 59b is mentioned an animal called קרש (perhaps shortened from "monoceros" or "rhinoceros"), which, "though it has only one horn, is allowed as food," and is then explained as the

"hart of the forest 'Ilai" (טביא דבי עלאי; comp. B. B. 16b). The Talmud apparently thinks here of the antelope oryx, the mode of depicting which on Persian monuments gave rise to the belief by the ancients (comp. Pliny, "Historia Naturalis," viii. 21, 30) in the existence of the unicorn (comp. "S. B. O. T.," Psalms [Eng. transl.], p. 173). In Arabic likewise "re'em" is applied to the leucoryx. The aurochs is mentioned in the Talmud under the name שור הבר (= "ox of the plain"), in explanation of תורבלא, the rendering of תאו (Deut. xiv. 5) by the Targum, which Rashi (Ḥul. 80a) explains as the "ox of the Lebanon." It is classed among cattle (Kil. viii. 6), and is caught with slings (B. Ḳ. 117a; comp. Isa. li. 20).

BIBLIOGRAPHY: Tristram, Nat. Hist. p. 146; Lewysohn, Z. T. pp. 114, 126, 149; C. Cohen, Gesch. des Einhorns, Berlin, 1896.
E. G. H.
I. M. C.

UNION OF AMERICAN HEBREW CONGREGATIONS, THE : Association of American Jewish congregations composed chiefly of the Reform element, and established largely through the persistent efforts, extending for a period of over twenty years, of Isaac M. WISE. The initiative was taken by Moritz Loth, president of Wise's congregation in Cincinnati, who, in his annual message of Oct. 10, 1872, recommended the appointment of a committee to act with committees from other local congregations for the purpose of calling a convention for organization. The five Cincinnati congregations joined in a call, issued on March 30, 1873, in pursuance of which delegates from thirty-four congregations met in that city on July 8, 1873. "The Union of American Hebrew Congregations" was the official title adopted; and under that name the organization was subsequently incorporated pursuant to the laws of Ohio.

The objects of the organization are set forth in section 2 of the constitution:

A.—To establish and maintain institutions for instruction in the higher branches of Hebrew literature and Jewish theology, with the necessary preparatory schools in such cities of those States as may hereafter be designated.

B.—To provide means for the relief of Jews from political oppression and unjust discrimination, and for rendering them aid for their intellectual elevation.

C.—To promote religious instruction and encourage the study of the Scriptures and of the tenets and history of Judaism.

All this, however, without interfering in any manner whatsoever with the worship, the schools, or any other of the congregational institutions.

Under provision (A) the Hebrew Union College was called into existence by the first council, which met in Cleveland in July, 1874 (see HEBREW UNION COLLEGE). Under (B) a Board of Delegates on Civil Rights has been created with its seat in Washington, D. C., Simon Wolf being its chairman. The objects provided for by (C) have been entrusted to a Board of Managers on Synagogue and (Sabbath) School Extension, which body has charge of the work formerly carried on by the Hebrew Sabbath-School Union of America, which went out of existence in Jan., 1905.

The presidents of the union have been Moritz Loth (1873–89); Julius Freiberg (1889–1903); and Samuel Woolner (in 1903), followed by C. M. Shohl; and Lipman Levy was the first secretary, followed by G. Zepin. The legislative body of the union, and its highest authority, is a council which meets biennially, the members of which are elected by the constituent congregations. In electing these representatives there is no restriction as to sex. During the intervals between the meetings of the council the union is governed by an executive board of thirty members elected by the council. This executive board in turn elects the Board of Governors of the Hebrew Union College, the Board of Delegates on Civil Rights, and the Board of Managers on Synagogue and (Sabbath) School Extension. At present (1923) the union is composed of 267 congregations with an aggregate contributing membership of about 20,000.

BIBLIOGRAPHY: *31 Annual Reports of The Union of American Hebrew Congregations*; seventy-one volumes of manuscript correspondence collected by Lipman Levy, secretary of The Union of American Hebrew Congregations; *The American Israelite*, 1854-1905; *Die Deborah*, 1855-1900; D. Philipson and L. Grossman, *Life and Writings of Isaac M. Wise*, Cincinnati, 1900; Isaac M. Wise, *Reminiscences*, ib. 1901.
J. L. WI.

UNION ISRAÉLITE. See PERIODICALS.

UNION OF JEWISH LITERARY SOCIETIES: An association of societies founded in 1902 in London, England, for the diffusion of Jewish literature, history, and sociology, and for the coordination of the work of Jewish literary societies. The organization grew out of a conference of Jewish literary societies convened by the North London Jewish Literary and Social Union, chief among whose objects was the study of Jewish literature, history, and sociology. Its first president was Israel Abrahams.

The union has constituent societies in many districts of the British empire. Each reserves its complete local independence, and is in no way controlled by the central organization. The union, however, renders assistance to the constituent societies in many ways. It has published a directory of Anglo-Jewish lecturers, with a supplementary list of Jewish litterateurs resident abroad who have placed papers prepared by them at its disposal. It also provides literary material and guidance for members of the constituent societies desirous of preparing lectures, and it has arranged a number of illustrated lectures for their use.

An important feature of the work of the union is its publications. In addition to a number of pamphlets, it issues yearly, in time for the annual conference of constituent societies held in the month of June, the "Jewish Literary Annual," which, besides supplying a record of the work of the union and its constituent societies during the previous year, contains the installation address of the retiring president and a selection of the papers read before the constituent societies during the preceding twelve months. Another feature is a bibliography of books, essays, etc., of Jewish interest published in English during the year.

The union has been instrumental in introducing the Jewish Chautauqua movement into England. It has also arranged with considerable success summer gatherings at English seaside resorts.
J. A. M. H.

UNITARIANISM: A denomination of the Christian Church which rejects the doctrine of the Trinity. One of the Protestant sects that developed out of the Reformation, it is found under various names, first in Poland in the second half of the sixteenth century, and a little later in Transylvania, where it still flourishes, although its modern center of gravity is England and the other English-speaking countries, notably the United States. Exclusion from Protestant synods crystallized the Unitarians into a separate church in 1565. Among its prominent exponents may be mentioned the elder and the younger Socinus, who formulated its first theology; Francis David, its first martyr; and Joseph Priestley, the English discoverer of oxygen. It also claims Milton, Locke, and Newton, and it owes much to James Martineau, who rationalized the crudities of Priestley's theology, while Emerson gave it its transcendental touch and the writings of Channing and Theodore Parker furthered its propaganda.

From its inception this sect has been divided into conservative and radical wings. In the former school the divinity of Jesus is rejected, but the miracles ascribed to him are accepted, and some regard him as preexistent and superangelic. Socinus insisted on his worship. In the new, or radical, wing of Unitarianism, Jesus is still sublimated above all humanity, while the cross, the symbol of the whole of Christianity, is accepted metaphorically as expressed in poetry and hymnal. The LORD'S SUPPER is observed as a commemoration, thus uniting Unitarianism with the whole Church. For about fifteen centuries, accordingly, Unitarianism has been historically linked with Christianity, from which it has never entirely broken away. The Apostles, the Church Fathers, and the Holy Roman Empire are its remote progenitors. More specifically, its progressive steps may be traced from the Arian movement through Calvinism, Socinianism, Arminianism, Presbyterianism, and Congregationalism, the Hicksite Quakers and the Universalists occupying parallel places. Unitarianism has, therefore, been a development out of Trinitarianism. Gradually the Holy Ghost was rarefied into an "influence," and the Son of God was explained away as a figure of speech. The preponderating influence of the parent faith, however, still abides, and the Unitarians do not look upon the character of Jesus in the cold light of history.
K. M. H. H.

UNITED STATES: A federal republic of North America. The history and condition of the Jews in this territory—apart from Russia and Austria the largest concourse of Israelites under one government in the world—is treated, for convenience, under the following rubrics:

1. Successive Waves of Immigration.
2. Separate Cities and States (in order of settlement or population)—New York, Newport, New England, Maryland, Pennsylvania, Georgia, South Carolina, North Carolina, Virginia, West Virginia, Louisiana, Kentucky, Tennessee, Alabama, Mississippi, Florida, Texas, Michigan, Wisconsin, Ohio, Illinois, Missouri, Kansas, Nebraska, Iowa, California, Oregon, Utah, Colorado, Montana, Washington, Idaho, North Dakota, and South Dakota.
3. Jews in Their Relation to the Federal Government.
4. Education.
5. Philanthropy.
6. Religious Development.
7. Military, Naval, and State Service.

1. Successive Waves of Immigration: Persecution is the principal factor affecting Jewish immigration to the United States. The adventurous pioneer, seeking new lands from the desire to conquer obstacles and live a life untrammeled by the conventions of society, is less frequently found among the leaders of Jewish settlement in this country than the hardened victim of persecution—broken in almost everything but spirit and energy—in search of the opportunity merely to live in unmolested exercise of his faith. The effects of the events of European history upon American development might be written almost entirely from the annals of Jewish immigration. The first explorers and settlers of America came from Spain and Portugal; and Jews naturally followed in their wake when the Inquisition made further residence in those countries an impossibility. Naturally, also, following the lines of least resistance, the Jews went to those places where the languages were spoken with which they were familiar. Therefore the first traces of Jews are found in South and Central America and Mexico, whence they spread to the West Indies; and the changes in the map of Europe which are reflected in America during the seventeenth and eighteenth centuries caused the first settlements in the territory which is now the United States.

First Settlers from Spain and Portugal.

The tolerance of Holland (practically the only Jewish refuge in Europe in the sixteenth and seventeenth centuries) was extended to her dominions in the New World, and resulted in laying the foundation of what has developed into the great New York community. By way of gratitude for the favors shown them, Jews effectively aided the Dutch in their resistance to foreign encroachment, especially in South America. From Spain, Portugal, and Holland, then, came most of the first settlers; and though the large majority were of Sephardic stock, a few Germans are also to be found among them. England, where until the beginning of the eighteenth century but few Jews dwelt, contributed but a small number to the effective settlements she was making on the seaboard of the mainland. Though the colony of Georgia had Jewish immigrants in large numbers from 1733 on, they came in ships from England only because passage to the New World could be procured most readily from that country.

The large numbers of Germans who sought refuge from persecution in the freer air of Pennsylvania, during the eighteenth century, attracted Jews as well. They settled not only in the coast towns, but made their way into the interior, and before the close of the century they were to be found among those engaged in developing the western parts of the state. Similarly, the unhappy fate of

The German Element.

Poland, dating from 1772, caused that state to send forth its quota of Jews to the United States, and the contribution of that country would be notable if only for the commanding figure of Haym SALOMON. The Napoleonic wars and the distress which they wrought, especially upon the South German principalities, once again caused a tide of German immigration to set toward the United States. The Jews joined this migratory movement beginning toward the end of the first quarter of the nineteenth century, and increased in numbers rapidly by reason of the events of 1848. From that time until 1870, when this phase of immigration lost its strength, they came in a steady stream, so that the Jewish population of the United States was quadrupled within the twenty years between 1850 and 1870.

But none of the early migratory movements assumed the significance and volume of that from Russia and neighboring countries. This emigration, mainly from Russian Poland, began as far back as 1821, but did not become especially noteworthy until after the German immigration fell off in 1870. Though nearly 50,000 Russian, Polish, Galician, and Rumanian Jews came to the United States during the succeeding decade, it was not until the anti-Jewish uprisings in Russia, of the early eighties, that the emigration assumed extraordinary proportions. From Russia alone the emigration rose from an annual average of 4,100 in the decade 1871–80 to an annual average of 20,700 in the decade 1881–90.

Russian Immigration. Additional measures of persecution in Russia in the early nineties and continuing to the present time have resulted in large increases in the emigration, England and the United States being the principal lands of refuge. The Rumanian persecutions, beginning in 1900, also caused large numbers of Jews to seek refuge in the latter country. The total Jewish immigration to the United States, through the three main ports of entry, New York, Philadelphia, and Baltimore, from 1881 to Oct. 1, 1905, is stated to have been 996,908, although it is by no means certain that this number does not include Christians from Russia and Austria (see statistical section of this article for details).

In considering the separate states of the Union in detail, the varying records of their Jewish inhabitants may be sketched in outline, reference being made for further particulars to the special articles devoted to each state in THE JEWISH ENCYCLOPEDIA.

2. Separate Cities and States: As the Jews of the United States were destined to become more numerous, and consequently of more significance, in the state of **New York** than elsewhere, it were fitting on this account to begin this summary with the account of their settlement and development there. But there is a historical reason as well: the earliest documentary evidence concerning the Jews in this country relates to New York. Jewish connection with the Dutch colony of New Netherlands antedated by many years the beginnings of the migratory movement, for among the influential stockholders of the Dutch West India Company, founded in 1620, were a number of Jews. Their influence upon the fortunes of this company from that time on was of considerable importance. It would appear that Jews were on the muster-rolls of soldiers and sailors sent out to the colony of New Amsterdam in 1652, and that they had engaged to serve for the term of one year. Their identity, however, has been lost.

The first known Jewish settler in New Amsterdam was Jacob BARSIMSON, who arrived on July 8, 1654, in the ship "Pear Tree." He was followed in September of the same year by a party of twenty-three who had taken passage in the

First Settlement. bark "Saint Catarina." They probably came from BRAZIL, by way of Cuba and Jamaica, having been driven out when that country capitulated in 1654. The first authentic record of their arrival is obtained from the legal proceedings instituted against them, by the officers of the vessel, to procure the passage-money for which they had made themselves jointly liable. Some were unable to pay, and two were imprisoned in consequence. Others arrived while these proceedings were pending, much to the displeasure of Peter Stuyvesant, the Dutch governor of New Netherlands, who ordered them to leave the colony, and wrote to the directors of the Dutch West India Company asking authority for their exclusion. The directors overruled Stuyvesant, and under date of April 26, 1655, instructed him that his attitude "was unreasonable and unfair, especially because of the considerable loss sustained by the Jews in the taking of Brazil, and also because of the large amount of capital which they have invested in the shares of the company." They directed that "they [the Jews] shall have permission to sail to and trade in New Netherlands and to live and remain there." Stuyvesant carried out his instructions with no good grace, evaded them whenever possible, and put many obstacles in the way of these early settlers. Further appeals to the directors of the company followed, resulting in the issuance of a reproof to Stuyvesant in March, 1656; the instructions to him directed that the Jews should be permitted to enjoy all the civil and political rights in New Netherlands that were accorded them in Amsterdam, and they were to be allowed to hold real estate and to trade. But they were not to be employed in the public service, nor allowed to open retail shops. This provision against engaging in retail trade had a marked effect upon their own future, as well as upon that of the colony. It resulted in their engaging in foreign intercolonial trade, for which, because of their connections, they were peculiarly fitted. The part the Jews played as importers and exporters, and in the general field of colonial commerce, is accordingly one of great significance.

The most prominent figure among these pioneers of the New Amsterdam colony was Asser LEVY; and it was due to his determined efforts that many of the political rights which the Jews en-

Asser Levy. joyed at this time were granted. In 1655, among others, he sought enlistment in the militia; this was refused, and instead, he, with other Jews, was ordered to pay a tax because of their exemption. He declined to do this, and on Nov. 5, 1655, petitioned for leave to stand guard like other burghers of New Amsterdam. The petition being rejected, he appealed to the higher authorities, and in 1657 suc-

ceeded in obtaining certain burgher rights, and was permitted to perform guard duty like other citizens. He was the first Jew to own land in what are now known as Albany and New York city. His name figures constantly in the court records, and the litigation almost invariably resulted favorably to him. He appears to have amassed considerable wealth, and to have obtained the respect and esteem of the leading men of the town. Another of the prominent early settlers was Abraham de LUCENA, who, with several others, in 1655 applied for permission to purchase a site for a burial-ground. This was denied at the time, on the ground that there was no need for it, but was granted a year later. In June, 1658, the burgomasters declined to permit judgment in civil actions to be taken against Jacob Barsimson, holding that "though defendant is absent, yet no default is entered against him, as he was summoned on his Sabbath." This unusual instance of religious toleration foreshadowed a New York statute of two centuries later, which renders it a misdemeanor maliciously to serve any one with process on his Sabbath, or with process returnable on that day. When, in Oct., 1660, Asser Levy and Moses de Lucena were licensed as butchers, they were sworn "agreeably to the oath of the Jews" and were not to be compelled to kill any hogs.

Upon the capture of the colony by the English in 1664, the rights hitherto enjoyed by the Jews were not interfered with, and for twenty years they appear to have lived much as before

Under English Rule. the British occupation, though with slight increase in their numbers. In 1672 Rabba Couty attained prominence by his appeal to the King's Council, in England, from a decree passed against him by the courts of Jamaica, as a result of which one of his ships had been seized and declared forfeited. His appeal was successful and resulted in establishing the rights of Jews as British subjects, and his appears to be the first case in which a colonial grant of naturalization was recognized as valid.

In 1685 the application of Saul Brown to trade at retail was denied, as was also that of the Jews for liberty to exercise their religion publicly. That they did so privately in some definite place of worship would appear from the fact that a map of New York, dated 1695, shows the location of a Jews' synagogue in Beaver street, also that Saul Brown was the minister, and that the congregation comprised twenty families. Five years later the site of the synagogue was so well known that in a conveyance of property the premises were referred to as a landmark. In 1710 the minister of the congregation, Abraham de Lucena, was granted exemption from civil and military service by reason of his ministerial functions, and reference is made to the enjoyment of the same privileges by his predecessors. The minutes of the Congregation Shearith Israel of New

Shearith Israel. York begin in 1729, when it was located in Mill street, and refer to records dating back as far as 1706. This congregation established on Mill street, in 1730, on a lot purchased two years before, the first synagogue in the United States. It would thus appear that the religious rights of these early Jewish settlers had been secured in the beginning of the eighteenth century, and that they enjoyed also many political rights. An act passed by the General Assembly of New York on Nov. 15, 1727, provided that when the oath of abjuration was to be taken by any British subject professing the Jewish religion, the words "upon the true faith of a Christian" might be omitted. Three days later an act was passed naturalizing one Daniel Nuñez de Costa. A bitter political controversy of the year 1737 resulted in the decision by the General Assembly that Jews should not be allowed to vote for members of that body.

In 1740 Parliament passed a general act permitting foreign Jews to be naturalized in the colonies. Previous to this date, however, the New York Colonial Assembly had passed numerous special acts of naturalization, some of which were applicable to individuals only; others, more general in character, under which Jews could be naturalized without taking oath "upon the true faith of a Christian," were also put upon the statute-book. Between this time and the Revolutionary war the Jewish community in this colony increased by slow stages, the principal immigrants coming from Spain, Portugal, and the West Indies.

During the French and Indian war Jacob Franks was the royal agent, in association with a British syndicate, for provisioning the British forces in America; his dealings with the crown during this period exceeded £750,000 in value.

Before and during the Revolutionary war the Jews had representatives of their faith upon both sides of the controversy, though the majority joined the colonial side. On the Non-Importation Agreement of 1769 the names of not less than five Jews are found; this is also the case with respect to other agreements of a similar nature. The outbreak of the Revolutionary war dissolved the congregation in New York; and upon the eve of the British occupancy of the town the majority of the congregation, headed by Gershom Mendes SEIXAS, took all the belongings of the synagogue and removed to Philadelphia, where they established the first regular congregation, the Mickvé Israel, in 1782. The small number who remained in New York occasionally held services in the synagogue. At the close of the war most of the Jews who had gone to Philadelphia returned to New York, which was rapidly becoming one of the most important commercial cities of the country. From this time on the community grew slowly, so that by 1812 it is estimated there were not more than 500 Jews in New York. However, a number of Jewish soldiers participated in the War of 1812, and the prosperity of the community was ever on the increase. The great tide of emigration from Germany that set in toward the beginning of the first quarter of the nineteenth century brought with it many Jews. They were in sufficient numbers by 1825 to establish the first German Jewish congregation. During the next forty years the German congregations increased rapidly, so that by 1850 no less than ten had been organized. Charitable and relief organizations were established; and a considerable number of Jews took part in the Mexican war and entered the public service. The

large influx which followed in the late forties and early fifties laid the foundation for the great community which afterward developed. Previous to 1881 the emigrants came for the most part from Germany, Bavaria, and Poland. Since the latter date Russia, Rumania, and Galicia have furnished the greatest numbers. In the year 1920 the Jewish population of the state of New York is estimated at 1,701,260. Jews are now represented in New York City in every walk of life, political, professional, commercial and industrial. See NEW YORK.

Though most of the earlier emigrants settled in New York city, a few wandered beyond its limits, some even as far as the confines of what now constitutes the state of PENNSYLVANIA. In 1661, when Albany was but a trading-post, Asser Levy, as noted above, owned real estate there, but between that date and the early years of the nineteenth century there are no records of any settlers in that town. They were not there in sufficient numbers to form a congregation until 1838, and they had no rabbi until 1846. The present Jewish population is estimated at about 7,000.

Up-State Settlements.

Buffalo attained prominence in 1825 through the scheme of Mordecai M. Noah to establish ARARAT as a city of refuge for the Jews. The corner-stone of the projected city was laid in one of the churches of Buffalo in that year; but, as is well known, this scheme attracted no settlers, and the first religious organization was not established until 1847. The number of Jews there increased gradually from that time, and many members of the Jewish community have held distinguished political office. The Jewish population in 1918 was estimated at 20,000.

The first settlement of Jews in **Syracuse** probably antedates 1839, and a permanent religious organization was established in 1846. At the present time the number of Jews is estimated at 12,000. There are Jewish communities in at least fifty-two of the cities of the state of New York, and most of them have been established within the past twenty years.

Next in historical importance to the settlement of New York city is that of **Rhode Island**, at **Newport**. Established by Roger Williams upon a basis of toleration for persons of all shades of religious belief, the Jews were among the first settlers. Though the earliest authentic reference to Jews at Newport bears the date 1658, no doubt a few stragglers arrived as early as 1655. Fifteen Jewish families arrived in 1658, bringing with them the first degrees of masonry. They established a congregation almost immediately, and in 1684 had their rights to settle confirmed by the General Assembly. There is record of the purchase of a burial-place in Feb., 1677. Between 1740 and 1760 a number of enterprising Portuguese Jewish settlers from Spain, Portugal, and the West Indies arrived, and by their activity established Newport as the seat of the most extensive trade of the country. The most prominent of the settlers during this period were the LOPEZ, RIVERA, Pollock, HART, and HAYS families. Aaron LOPEZ was one of the leading merchants of his time, and owned as many as thirty vessels. With the advent of Jacob Rodriguez Rivera, a native of Portugal, in 1745, the

To the President of the United States of America.

Sir

Permit the children of the Stock of Abraham to approach you with the most cordial affection and esteem for your person & merits — And to join with our fellow Citizens in welcoming you to NewPort.

With pleasure we reflect on those days — those days of difficulty, & danger when the God of Israel, who delivered David from the peril of the Sword — shielded Your head in the day of battle: — And we rejoice to think, that the same Spirit, who rested in the Bosom of the greatly beloved Daniel enabling him to preside over the Provinces of the Babylonish Empire, rests and ever will rest upon you, enabling you to discharge the arduous duties of Chief Magistrate in these States.

Deprived as we heretofore have been of the invaluable rights of free Citizens, we now (with a deep sense of gratitude to the Almighty disposer of all events) behold a Government, erected by the Majesty of the People. — a Government, which to bigotry gives no Sanction, to persecution no assistance — but generously affording to All liberty of conscience, and immunities of Citizenship: — deeming every one, of whatever Nation, tongue, or language equal parts of the great governmental Machine: — This so ample and extensive Federal Union whose basis is Philanthropy, Mutual Confidence and Publick Virtue, we cannot but acknowledge to be the Work of the Great God, who ruleth in the Armies of Heaven, and among the Inhabitants of the Earth, doing whatsoever seemeth him good.

For all the Blessings of civil and religious liberty, which we enjoy under an equal and benign administration, we desire to send up our thanks to the Antient of Days, the great preserver of Men — beseeching him, that the Angel who conducted our forefathers through the Wilderness into the promised land, may graciously conduct you through all the difficulties and dangers of this mortal life: — And, when like Joshua full of days and full of honour, you are gathered to your Fathers, may you be admitted into the Heavenly Paradise to partake of the water of life, and the tree of immortality.

Done and Signed by Order of the Hebrew Congregation in NewPort Rhode Island August 17th 1790 —

Moses Seixas Warden.

manufacture of spermaceti was introduced in America. In 1762 the erection of a synagogue was begun,

Aaron Lopez.

and was completed and dedicated in the following year. From 1760 until the outbreak of the Revolution the Rev. Isaac Touro, who had come from Jamaica, was the rabbi of the congregation. In 1763 there were between 60 and 70 Jewish families in Newport. The first Jewish sermon which was preached in America, and which has been published, was delivered in the Newport synagogue on May 28, 1773, by Rabbi Ḥayyim Isaac CARREGAL. This was delivered in Spanish, and was afterward translated into English. Carregal was a most interesting personality; he appears to have come from Palestine, and was on terms of intimacy with Ezra Stiles, the president of Yale College. The first Jewish club in America was formed in 1761 at Newport, with a membership limited to nine persons. Just before the outbreak of the Revolutionary war the Jewish population of Newport must have numbered nearly 1,000 souls. The war dispersed the community, which never regained its importance. The Jews for the most part espoused the colonial cause, and lost the greater part of their property when the town was captured by the British. In 1790 the congregation presented an address to Washington on the occasion of his visit to the city. The letter of welcome is still preserved and is reproduced here by courtesy of the owner, Mr. Frederick Phillips, New York. Abraham Touro bequeathed a fund to the city of Newport to maintain the synagogue as well as the cemetery; this fund is still in existence, though no representatives of the original families now live in the city. The present Jewish population is about 200. There are Jewish settlements likewise in **Providence, Woonsocket,** and **Pawtucket.** The entire Jewish population of the state is estimated at 21,450.

In Other Parts of New England there were probably occasional stray settlers in the seventeenth and eighteenth centuries, but the intolerance of the Puritans rendered impossible the establishment of any religious communities. An interesting personality is that of Judah Monis, who became a convert to Christianity and filled the chair of Hebrew in Harvard College from 1722 until his death in 1764.

Mention is found of a Jew in **Connecticut** under date of Nov. 9, 1659, and of another in 1670. The first Jewish family to settle in **New Haven** came in 1772, though a few individuals who had become converts to Christianity dwelt there a few years before. The first congregation was established about 1840, the congregants being members of about twenty Bavarian families. From that date on the community increased by slow stages, and there are at the present time (1923) in New Haven about 20,000 Jewish inhabitants. There are Jewish settlements also in **Bridgeport, Ansonia, Derby, Waterbury, New London,** and **Hartford.** In the last-mentioned city there are about 16,000 Jewish inhabitants, the first congregation having been established in 1843. Since 1891 a number of Jewish farmers have been settled in various parts of the state. The total Jewish population of the state is about 71,870.

The earliest mention of a Jew in **Massachusetts** bears the date May 3, 1649, and there are references to Jews among the inhabitants of Boston in 1695 and 1702; but they can be regarded only as stragglers, as no settlers made their homes in Massachusetts until the Revolutionary war drove the Jews from Newport. In 1777 Aaron Lopez and Jacob Rivera, with fifty-nine others, went from Newport to **Leicester,** and established themselves there; but this settlement did not survive the close of the war. A number of Jews, including the Hays family, settled at **Boston** before 1800. Of these Moses Michael HAYS was the most important. In 1830 a number of Algerian Jews went to Boston, but they soon disappeared. The history of the present community begins with the year 1840, when the first congregation was established.

The Jewish immigrants to **Vermont** and **New Hampshire** have never been very numerous, though there are congregations in **Burlington,** Vt., and in **Manchester, Portsmouth,** and **Nashua,** N. H. The number of Jews at the present time (1923) in these two states is estimated at 6,630. Little of importance can be said about the communal life of the Jews in New England, and their numbers increased but slowly until after the beginning of the great Russian emigration in 1882, when the overflow from New York as well as the emigration through Canada commenced to stream into New England. It is estimated that the number of Jews now inhabiting the New England States is about 305,840, of whom 199,300 reside in Massachusetts alone.

The opening up of the West and the resulting unprofitable nature of farming in New England drew away from this part of the United States many thrifty farmers, who abandoned their unfruitful fields for the more attractive opportunities in the Western States. Of interest in connection with this shifting of the population is the fact that many of these abandoned farms, especially in Connecticut, have been taken up by Russian Jews, who, principally as dairy farmers, have added a new and useful element to the agricultural community.

It would seem that only a few Jews found their way to **Maryland** during the first half of the seventeenth century, and that the first settlers of this colony came as individuals, and not in considerable numbers at any time, as was the case in New York, Newport, Savannah, and Charleston. To judge by the names alone it would appear that a few Jews were resident in Maryland from the earliest days of the colony. The most prominent figure, who was unquestionably a Jew, was a Dr. Jacob LUMBROZO,

Jacob Lumbrozo.

who had arrived Jan. 24, 1656, and who, in 1658, was tried for blasphemy, but was released by reason of the general amnesty granted in honor of the accession of Richard Cromwell (March 3, 1658). Letters of denization were issued to Lumbrozo Sept. 10, 1663. Besides practising medicine, he also owned a plantation, engaged in trade with the Indians, and had active intercourse with London merchants. He was one of the earliest medical practitioners in the colony, and his career casts much light upon the history and nature of religious tolerance in Maryland. By the strength of his personality he was able to disregard nearly all the laws which would have rendered his residence in the colony impossible, and he seems to have observed his faith even though this, under the laws, was forbidden. The unfavorable environment rendered the admittance of Jews to Maryland difficult, and until the Constitution of 1776 established the religious rights of all, few Jews settled in the colony. Beginning with the year 1797, by which time a considerable number of Jews had arrived there, the history of the Jews of Maryland is of special interest. By the terms of the Constitution of 1776 none could hold office in the state who was not a subscriber to the Christian religion. In the year just mentioned Solomon ETTING and Barnard GRATZ, and others, presented a petition to the General Assembly at Annapolis asking to be placed upon the same footing with other citizens. This was the beginning of an agitation, lasting for a generation, to establish the civil and polit-

Jacob I. Cohen and the Struggle for Religious Liberty. ical rights of the Jews. As this first effort failed it was renewed at almost every session of the Assembly until 1818. During the succeeding seven years the Cohen family, which had come to Baltimore in 1803 from Richmond, Va., took an important part in the attempt to establish their rights as citizens. The most active member of the family in this struggle was Jacob I. COHEN, who was ably assisted by Solomon Etting. Their persistent efforts met with success in 1825, when an Act of Assembly was passed removing the disabilities of the Jews; and in 1826 both of the above-named were elected members of the city council.

At the outbreak of the Civil war Maryland, although remaining in the Union, numbered among her citizens a large body of sympathizers with the Confederate cause. Owing to the pronounced anti-slavery attitude assumed by Rabbi David EINHORN, the conflict of opinion was especially severe among the Jews. For the most part the history of Maryland is the history of **Baltimore,** where Jews had settled in small numbers prior to the Revolution. The most prominent of these settlers was Benjamin LEVY, who, in addition to being a prominent merchant, had the distinction of being appointed one of the committee to arrange the celebration in Baltimore of the adoption of the Declaration of Independence. The first cemetery was procured as early as 1786, and the beginnings of communal organization date from 1826, although the congregation was not regularly organized until 1838. The Jews of the city have participated to a considerable extent in the civic life of the town and state, and have taken some part in national affairs. A number have been members of the Assembly, and in the year 1905 Isidor RAYNER was a United States senator. The Jewish population of Baltimore in 1918 was estimated at 60,000, and that of the twenty-three counties, including towns, outside of Baltimore, at 5,330, making 65,330 the total Jewish population of the state.

It is of record that Jews from New Amsterdam traded along the Delaware River as early as 1655. There were probably some settlers in the southeastern portion of the territory of which William Penn took possession in 1681. A very considerable number of the early **Pennsylvania** colonists were Ger-

man Jews. The first Jewish resident of PHILADELPHIA was Jonas Aaron, who was living there in 1703. Another early pioneer and one of considerable prominence was Isaac Miranda. He was the first to settle at LANCASTER, at which place, as also at Shaefferstown, there was an early Jewish immigration. Miranda became a convert to Christianity and held several state offices. A number of Jews settled in Philadelphia in the first half of the eighteenth century, and became prominent in the life of the city. Among these were David Franks, Joseph Marks, and Sampson Levy. The Non-Importation Resolutions of 1765 contained the signatures of eight Jews, an indication of the importance of the Jewish community at this time. As early as 1747 a number of persons held religious services in a

Philadelphia. small house in Sterling alley, and afterward in Cherry alley—between Third and Fourth streets. They were mostly German and Polish Jews; and their differences as to the liturgy to be followed prevented, at the time, the formation of any regular congregation. Attempts, indeed, were made in 1761 and 1773 to form one, but none was established until the influx of Jews from New York during the Revolutionary war, with the arrival of Gershom Mendes Seixas, gave the community sufficient strength to carry out this cherished object. A lot was purchased and a synagogue erected, the dedication occurring in Sept., 1782. A number of Philadelphia Jews served in the army of the Revolution; and the inestimable services rendered by Haym SALOMON to Robert Morris in the finances of the Revolution make his name stand out as the most prominent character in American Jewry. The Congregation Mickvé Israel adopted the Sephardic ritual, and the most important minister of the congregation after Seixas was Isaac LEESER, who arrived in 1829. He was the leading Jewish minister of his time, and few others have left such an impress upon American Jewish affairs as he. As minister, teacher, organizer, translator of the Bible, editor, and publisher he was a man of indefatigable energy and rare ability. Prominent also were members of the PHILLIPS family, chief among whom were Zalegman Phillips and Henry M. Phillips. The latter was one of the leading lawyers of Philadelphia, a politician of importance, and a member of the 35th

Mickvé Israel and Rodeph Shalom. Congress. Leeser's successor as minister of the Mickvé Israel congregation was Sabato MORAIS, a native of Leghorn, Italy, who, from 1851 until his death in 1897, was a leading figure in American Jewish affairs. It was due to his efforts that a Jewish Theological Seminary was established in New York.

The first German congregation was the Rodeph Shalom, which was organized in 1802, but which probably had meetings at an earlier date. The most prominent of its rabbis was Marcus JASTROW, who was succeeded by the present incumbent, Henry Berkowitz. The best-known cantor of this congregation was Jacob Frankel. During the Civil war he acted as chaplain of hospitals under the United States government. The first leading Reform minister installed in Philadelphia was

Samuel Hirsch. Many other congregations have been formed, especially since 1882, when the Russian emigration brought large numbers to the city. Next in importance to the settlement at Philadelphia was that at **Lancaster,** where Jews were to be found in 1730, before the town and county were organized. Joseph Simon was the best known of the first arrivals. Meyer Hart and Michael Hart were among the earlier settlers at **Easton,** where they arrived previous to the Revolutionary war. A synagogue was established there in 1839. **Shaefferstown** had a few Jewish settlers at an early date, and a synagogue and cemetery in 1732. For a considerable number of years preceding the Revolutionary war a number of Jews of Pennsylvania were engaged in the exploitation and sale of western Pennsylvania lands. Among the more prominent of these were Jacob and David FRANKS, Barnard and Michael GRATZ, Joseph Simon, and Levy Andrew Levy.

There is an important Jewish settlement in **Pittsburg,** where Jews arrived in considerable numbers as early as 1830, organizing a congregation in 1846; in **Harrisburg,** where a congregation was established in 1851; and in **Wilkesbarre, Scranton,** and **Reading.** As elsewhere, the Russian emigration of 1882 largely increased the number of Jews in Pennsylvania, and communities are now to be found in at least fifty towns of the state. The present (1923) Jewish population of Pennsylvania is estimated at 340,740, of whom about 200,000 live in Philadelphia.

The Jewish settlement in **Georgia** dates almost from the very foundation of the colony; and the early history of Georgia is practically the history of the growth and development of **Savannah,** Jewish life centering in that city. It would appear that a movement was set on foot in London to settle some Jews in the colony even before Oglethorpe, in June, 1733, led his first band of followers to the point which soon after became the city of Savannah. The second vessel which reached the colony from England (on July 11, 1733) had among its passengers no less than forty Jewish emigrants. Though their arrival was unexpected, the liberal-minded governor welcomed them gladly, notwithstanding that he was aware that the trustees of the colony in England had expressed some opposition to permitting Jews to settle there. These first settlers were all of Spanish and Portuguese extraction, though within a year of their arrival others, who were apparently German Jews, also took up their residence there. These two bands of settlers received equally liberal treatment from Oglethorpe, and were the progenitors of one of the most important communities of Jews in the United States. Many of their descendants are still living in various parts of the country. The first male white child born in the colony was a Jew, Isaac Minis.

Among the first immigrants was Dr. Nuñez, who was made welcome because of his medical knowledge, and because he, with a number of others, brought sufficient wealth to the colony to enable the immigrants to take up large tracts of land. A congregation was organized as early as 1734. Three years later Abraham de Lyon, who had been a "vineron" in Portugal, introduced the culture of grapes. The cultivation and manufacture of silk and the pursuit of agriculture and of commerce were the chief occupations of these early settlers. A dispute with the trustees of the colony respecting the introduction of slaves caused an extensive emigration to South Carolina in 1741, and resulted in the dissolution of the congregation. But in 1751 a number of Jews returned to Georgia, and in the same year the trustees sent over Joseph Ottolenghi to superintend the somewhat extensive silk-industry in the colony. Ottolenghi soon attained prominence in the political life of his associates, and was elected a member of the Assembly in 1761 and in succeeding years. There seems to have been little if any distinction made socially between the Jews and the other settlers, and educational and philanthropic institutions seem to have been supported by all alike.

Though the Jews participated prominently in the events leading up to the Revolution, it would appear that even in the midst of absorbing political discussions they were able, in 1774, to start another congregation. They were not all, however, to be found on the colonial side during the war, for Mordecai SHEFTALL, Levi Sheftall, Philip Jacob Cohen, Philip MINIS, and Sheftall Sheftall were in the first days of the Revolution disqualified by the authorities from holding any office of trust in the province because of the pronounced revolutionary ideas which they advocated. The community was dispersed during the Revolution, but many Jews returned immediately after the close of the war. In 1787 the congregation was reestablished, largely owing to the energy of Mordecai Sheftall, and it was incorporated on Nov. 30, 1790, under the name of Mickvé Israel of Savannah. The charter, with the minutes of the congregation of that date, still exists. Under date of May 6, 1789, Levi Sheftall, in behalf of the Hebrew congregation of Savannah, presented an address to Washington on the occasion of his election to the presidency, to which Washington made a gracious reply. The community does not seem to have prospered in the last days of the eighteenth and the beginning of the nineteenth century, but in 1820 began to increase in importance; and on the occasion of the consecration of a new synagogue in July, 1820, Dr. Jacob de la Motta delivered an address which was printed, and which is still a document of great value to American Jewish history. The synagogue was destroyed by fire in 1829, but was replaced by a substantial brick structure ten years later, and was consecrated in Feb., 1841, by Isaac Leeser. In 1878 the old synagogue, having been outgrown, was closed, and a new edifice was consecrated on the same day. The community has prospered materially within the past twenty-five years, and a number of its members have held important political office. Herman Meyers has held the office of mayor of the city of Savannah for a number of years.

After Savannah, **Augusta** appears to have been the next town in the state in which Jews settled. In 1825 one Florence, accompanied by his wife, was the first arrival. Other families came the following year

In the Revolution.

from Charleston, though a congregation was not organized until 1846. **Atlanta, Columbus,** and **Macon** have quite extensive communities, and congregations are to be found in Augusta, **Albany, Athens, Brunswick,** and **Rome.** They were all established after 1850, and most of them within the past twenty-five years. At Atlanta there is a home for orphans founded and managed by the Independent Order of B'nai B'rith. The community at Savannah still continues to be the most important, and numbers about 5,000. The total Jewish population of the state is estimated at 23,240.

The liberal charter which John Locke drew up in 1669 for the governance of the **Carolinas** should have operated to attract Jews thither at an early date, since "Jews, heathen, and dissenters" were by the terms of Locke's charter granted full liberty of conscience. Though political changes modified Locke's original plans considerably, the spirit of tolerance was always retained. Nevertheless no Jews in any numbers appear to have come to **South Carolina** until the exodus from Georgia in 1740–1771, already referred to. However, one Simon Valentine is mentioned as living in **Charleston** in 1698, and probably arrived there three years earlier. A few others followed him, for in 1703 a protest was raised against "Jew strangers" voting in an election for members of the Assembly. In 1748 some prominent London Jews set on foot a scheme for the acquisition of a tract of 200,000 acres of land in South Carolina. Nothing came of this, however, though on Nov. 27, 1755, Joseph SALVADOR purchased 100,000 acres of land near Fort Ninety-six for £2,000. Twenty years later Joseph Salvador sold 60,000 acres of land for £3,000 to thirteen London Sephardic Jews. This land was known as the "Jews' Lands." Another of the SALVADORS (FRANCIS, the nephew of Joseph) purchased extensive tracts of land in the same vicinity in 1773–74. Moses Lindo, likewise a London Jew, who arrived in 1756, became actively engaged in indigo manufacture, spending large sums in its development, and making this one of the principal industries of the state. During the Revolutionary war the Jews of South Carolina were to be found on both sides; and the most eminent of the revolutionists was Francis Salvador, who was elected a member of the First and Second Provincial Congresses which met 1775–76, **Jewish** the most important political office **Company.** held by any Jew during the Revolution. Two-thirds of a company of militia commanded by Richard Lushington was made up of Charleston Jews. After the fall of Charleston in 1780 the majority of Jews left that city, but most of them returned at the close of the war. The Sephardic Jews established a congregation in 1750, and the Jews of German descent another shortly thereafter. In 1791, when the Sephardic congregation was incorporated, the total number of Jews in Charleston is estimated to have been 400. At the opening of the nineteenth century the Charleston Jews formed the most important community in the United States. A number of its members held important political office, and Mayer Moses was a member of the legislature in 1810. About this time it was due to the Jews that free-

masonry was introduced into the state. A large number of Jews from New York went to Charleston at the close of the Revolutionary war and remained there until the commencement of the Civil war. The Jews of South Carolina participated in the War of 1812 and in the Mexican war, and were in considerable numbers on the Confederate side during the Civil war. Many South Carolina Jews moved north during the reconstruction period.

A congregation was organized at **Columbia** in 1822. Communities also exist at **Darlington, Florence, Orangeburg,** and **Sumter.** The first Reform movement in any congregation in America was instituted at Charleston in 1824 and another in 1840 (see below). The total number of Jews in the state at the present time (1923) is estimated at 5,060.

The first settlers in **North Carolina** seem to have come to **Wilmington** before the end of the eighteenth century, and appear to have been an offshoot of the Charleston community. In 1808 an attempt was made to expel a member of the General Assembly because of his Jewish faith. The community grew slowly, so that in 1826 it was estimated that there were but 400 Jews in the state. No considerable augmentation of their numbers occurred until after the immigration of 1848. Wilmington continues to be the leading community; a congregation was established there in 1867. There are small communities in about ten other cities. The total Jewish population of the state in 1923 was estimated at 5,140.

To judge by names alone it would appear that a few Jews wandered into **Virginia** as early as 1624. A small number seem also to have been there before the end of the seventeenth century, but for nearly 100 years no traces of Jewish settlement are found. At least one Jewish soldier—possibly two —served in Virginia regiments under Washington in his expedition across the Alleghany Mountains in 1754. It is probable that Jews drifted into the colony from Baltimore and other points in Maryland at an early date. By 1785 **Richmond** had a Jewish community of about a dozen families of Spanish-Portuguese descent, which organized a Sephardic congregation in 1791. This congregation remained in existence until 1898. The migration of German Jews to Richmond began early in the nineteenth century; and in 1829 they were in sufficient numbers to organize a congregation. In 1870, when the public-school system was established in Richmond, the first sessions were held in the rooms of the German Jewish congregation. Over one hundred Virginian Jews saw military service during the Civil war. The Richmond community has achieved prosperity, and in 1920 numbered about 4,000 Jews. An important community is established also at **Norfolk.** Nearly twenty other congregations exist in the remaining towns of the state, and there are similar organizations in about six towns of **West Virginia.** The Jewish population of the entire state of Virginia was estimated at 16,020 in 1920, and that of West Virginia about 5,440.

The most prominent early figure in the history of the Jews in **Louisiana** is Judah TOURO, who went to **New Orleans** about 1801. The community increased but slowly during the first half of the nineteenth century, but has grown rapidly since that time. The first congregation was established about 1830, and since that date, and especially during the last twenty years, a number of additional congregations have been formed and important charitable organizations established. Martin Behrman was mayor of New Orleans in 1905. About twenty towns now have Jewish communities with an estimated population of 13,020.

The Western wave of migration which took place in the early years of the nineteenth century carried with it a considerable number of Jews to **Kentucky.** Among these was one Salamon from Philadelphia, who established himself at **Harrodsburg** about 1808. In 1816 he was made cashier of the Bank of the United States at Lexington. Shortly after the War of 1812 the Jews began to go to **Louisville,** where the most important community of the state is still located. The first congregation there was chartered in 1842, and a synagogue was built in 1850. Another congregation was organized in 1856, and since the Russian emigration, beginning in 1881, a number of others have been established. In 1901 Louisville had six congregations and numerous philanthropic and educational institutions. There are other communities in at least half a dozen other towns in the state. The total Jewish population in 1920 was estimated at 13,620.

A few Jews were among the traders who settled in **Tennessee,** near the Holston River, in 1778, but they were mere stragglers and made no permanent settlement. About 1845 some Jews began to arrive in **Memphis,** where they had been preceded by Joseph J. Andrews. In 1853 a congregation was organized, and an Orthodox congregation in 1862. At **Nashville** a congregation was established in 1854. Jews have been prominent also in **Chattanooga;** in the years 1894 to 1898 George W. Ochs was mayor of the city. There are several communities in other towns of the state; the total Jewish population is estimated at 14,390.

Of the remaining states of the southern group east of the Mississippi River the principal Jewish settlements have been made in **Alabama** and **Mississippi.** An occasional Jew made his way into the territory which is now Alabama during the early part of the eighteenth century. One Pallachio became prominent in 1776. Abraham Mordecai came from Pennsylvania and settled in Montgomery county in 1785; he established trading-posts, and dealt extensively with the Indians, and in Oct., 1802, with the aid of two Jews, Lyons and Barnett, who had come from Georgia, he erected the first cotton-gin in the state. Of the other early settlers Philip PHILLIPS was the most prominent. He moved to **Mobile** about 1835, from Charleston, and held prominent political office; in 1853 he was elected to Congress. He afterward resided in Washington, and became known as a leading attorney there. The first congregation in Mobile was formed in 1841, where the largest community of the state is still to be found. A number of other congregations were established about the middle of the century, notably at **Montgomery.** About six other towns have Jewish communities. The present Jewish population is estimated at 11,150.

XII.—23

It is likely that there were a few Jews in the **Natchez** district of **Mississippi** before the close of the eighteenth century, but no congregation was organized until that of Natchez was established in 1843. No other congregation was organized before 1850. The present Jewish population of this state does not exceed 4,000.

Florida has a Jewish population of about 6,940, and the earliest congregation was established at **Pensacola,** in 1874.

Of the Western States of the southern group none has such Jewish interests as **Texas,** and with the early development of no states other than Georgia and California have Jews been so intimately associated. They were among the first of **Austin's** colonists in 1821, when Texas was still a part of Mexico; and Samuel Isaacs, who served in the Army of the Republic of Texas, received 320 acres of land in Fort Bend county for his services. Many of the earlier settlers came from England. When Abraham C. Labatt arrived in **Velasco** in 1831 he found that several other Jews had preceded him. Between 1832 and 1840 quite a number of Jews settled in the Nacogdoches district, serving the government in civil and military capacities. An unusually large number of Jews were attracted by the stirring events which preceded the annexation of Texas to the Union, and many took part in the military expeditions. Several were with Sam Houston's army in the Mexican war, and were present at the storming of the Alamo in Dec., 1835. A number received land and property for services rendered to the short-lived republic. Jacob de CORDOVA, a native of Jamaica, came to Galveston from New Orleans in 1837, and during the next thirty years was prominently identified with the development of the country. The real-estate operations in which he engaged in the early days became known far and wide. He published a news-

Jacob de Cordova.

paper, introduced the Order of Odd Fellows, was elected to the legislature from Harris county in 1847, and in 1849 laid out the city of Waco. Another of the prominent early pioneers was Henry Castro, a native of France, who had seen service in the French army and had gone to the United States in 1827. He lived for a time in Rhode Island, but went to Texas about 1840. In 1842 he made a contract with Sam Houston to settle a colony west of the Medina. Between 1843 and 1846 he sent 5,000 emigrants from the Rhenish provinces to Texas—a remarkably organized emigration for that early period. **Castroville** and Castro county, in northwest Texas, serve to perpetuate his name. On the admission of Texas into the Union David S. Kauffman, a Jew, was elected a member of Congress and served until his death in 1851. The first congregation was established at **Houston** as early as 1854, and others followed in **Galveston** and **San Antonio** shortly thereafter. Other important communities are at **Dallas** and **Waco.** Capt. L. C. Harby played a prominent part in the defense of Galveston during the Civil war. There are at present at least twelve other congregations within the state, whose Jewish population now numbers about 32,660.

Though no congregation was established in **Michigan** until 1850, a number of individual Jews played a prominent part in the settlement and early history of the territory as Indian traders. The principal settlement has been at **Detroit,** where the first arrivals were from Germany. Since 1882 there has been a large influx of Russians, who have grown to be an important element of the community. In 1883 a colony of Russian Jews was established near **Bad Axe,** which met with some success. Eleven towns have regularly organized congregations, and there are small communities in many other towns. After Detroit, the principal settlements are at **Grand Rapids, Kalamazoo, Bay City,** and **Alpina.** It is estimated that the Jewish population of the state numbers 71,360.

The first Jewish settler in the territory now comprised within the state of **Wisconsin** was Jacob Franks, who went to Green Bay from Canada as early as 1792, and who two years later was granted by the Indians a tract of land on Devil River, about four miles from Fox River. He carried on an extensive trade with the Indians. In 1805 he was known far and wide among them, and established a high reputation for integrity, fair dealing, and hospitality; he erected the first saw- and gristmill ever put up in that region, and returned to Canada in the same year. Other traders followed in his wake, but none came in sufficient numbers to establish any congregation until shortly before the middle of the nineteenth century. The principal settlement was made in **Milwaukee,** where a congregation was organized in 1855. In 1900 there were congregations in ten other cities, and in 1923 the total Jewish population of the state was estimated at 30,100.

The important community of CINCINNATI, in **Ohio,** is the oldest west of the Alleghany Mountains. From the middle of the nineteenth century its Jewish community has played a significant part in Jewish affairs in the United States. The Jewish pioneer of the Ohio Valley was Joseph Jonas, who went to Cincinnati from England in March, 1817. He attracted others from his native country a few years thereafter, and in 1819 they held the first Jewish service in the western portion of the United States. Previous to 1830 considerable additions to the community came from England, and in 1824 the first congregation was formed. Beginning with 1830, a large number of German Jews made their way to Cincinnati, and the first synagogue was erected in 1836. The community was of significance as early as 1850, and contained capable and public-spirited members. Isaac M. WISE, who went to Cincinnati in 1854, and Max LILIENTHAL, who arrived in 1855, helped materially to enable Cincinnati to impress indelibly its individuality upon Judaism in America. These two men aided in making Cincinnati a center of Jewish culture, and assisted in the development of a number of movements that were national in scope. Cincinnati is the seat of the Union of American Hebrew Congregations, the Central Conference of the Reform Rabbis of American Judaism, and the Hebrew Union College, and its graduates occupy many pulpits throughout the country. The Jews of Cincinnati have always shown great public spirit and have filled many local positions of trust, as well as state, judicial, and governmental offices. In the year

1905 Julius Fleischman was the mayor of the city. Next in importance to Cincinnati is the community of **Cleveland,** where Jews settled as early as 1837, and established a congregation in 1839. The history of the Jews in Ohio during the first half of the nineteenth century is confined to the cities just mentioned. After that date congregations grew up throughout the state. There are at the present time congregations in twenty other towns. About 1,000 Jews of Ohio saw service during the Civil war a number only exceeded by the contingent from New York. The Jewish population of Ohio was estimated in 1920 at 177,690.

The largest community of Jews in America, outside of New York and Philadelphia, is to be found in **Chicago.** It is probable that there were Jewish settlers in the **Illinois** territory when that country was still under French control. John Hays seems to have been the earliest Jewish pioneer, and he held the office of sheriff of St. Clair county from 1798 to 1818, and was appointed collector of internal revenue for the territory by President Madison in 1814, but no Jews appear to have followed in his footsteps until twenty years later. Considerable numbers of Jews found their way to the rising city Chicago previous to 1850, and the first congregation was organized in 1847. In 1842 a Jewish Colonization Society of New York sent Henry Meyer to select a tract in the vicinity of Chicago for a Jewish colony. He succeeded in attracting a considerable number of settlers, though only a few became farmers, the remainder removing for the most part to Chicago. After Chicago the next town to be settled by Jews was **Peoria,** and after the middle of the nineteenth century they settled in considerable numbers in most of the important towns in the state. Through the endeavors of B. Felsenthal, who went to Chicago in 1858, the Reform Congregation Sinai was established in 1861. He played an important part in the history of the development of the community. After the great fire of 1871 the community grew rapidly, and it has become one of the most prosperous in the country, its members being actively interested in the political life of the city and state. There are over fifty Jewish congregations in the city, and the population is estimated at 225,000. Some of the most important manufactories of the state are controlled by Jews. Samuel ALTSCHULER of Aurora was a Democratic nominee for governor in 1900. The Jewish community of Chicago has many notable educational establishments and relief institutions, and has furnished distinguished members to the legal profession, as well as renowned architects and musicians. Among its prominent rabbis, besides B. Felsenthal, have been Liebmann Adler and Emil G. Hirsch. The Jewish population of the state is estimated at 257,600.

In the southern and northwestern group of states **Missouri** stands out in special prominence. Between Chicago and San Francisco there is no city in which Jews have settled where they have formed so prosperous a community as in **St. Louis.** The pioneer Jewish settler in the state was Wolf Bloch, a native of Bohemia, who is reported to have reached St. Louis as early as 1816. A few others followed shortly thereafter, but their identity has been lost. They were not in sufficient numbers to hold services until 1836, and in the following year the first congregation was established. Two other congregations were organized before 1870. During the Civil war Isidore Bush attained prominence as a delegate on the "Unconditional Union Ticket" to the convention which decided that Missouri should remain in the Union. St. Louis harbored a number of refugees from Chicago after the fire of 1871, and since that time has grown rapidly in numbers and wealth. Representatives of the community have attained distinction politically and commercially. Moses N. Sale has been judge of the circuit court, and Nathan Frank was elected to the Fifty-first Congress. Next in importance to the community of St. Louis, whose numbers aggregate about 60,000, is that of **Kansas City**. The Jewish residents of the city number about 12,000. At **St. Joseph** Jews began to settle as early as 1850, and a congregation was organized nine years later. The Jewish population numbers 3,300. There are congregations in eight other cities of the state, whose Jewish population, however, is estimated at 82,570.

The first Jewish congregation in **Kansas** was established at **Leavenworth** in 1859; another was organized at **Kansas City** in 1870. Jews to the number of 3,000 were estimated as in the state in 1905 but in 1920 the number increased to 9,590.

The first Jewish settlement made in **Nebraska** was on the site of the present city of **Omaha** in 1856, but it was not until ten years later that the first congregation was organized. There is also a congregation at **Lincoln,** and communities in several smaller cities. The great bulk of the 14,020 Jews of the state live in Omaha.

Jews are recorded as having lived in the river towns of **Iowa,** especially at **Dubuque** and **McGregor,** as early as 1847–48. These were the main shipping- and stopping-points for the far West, and attracted settlers on this account. As the population moved westward small Jewish communities also found their way to **Davenport, Burlington,** and **Keokuk.** The first congregation was established at **Davenport** in 1861, another at **Keokuk** in 1863, and that at **Des Moines** in 1873. The largest Jewish community is in the last-named city. There are Jewish communities in eleven other towns of the state, whose total Jewish population is estimated at 16,230.

The gold discoveries of 1849 on the Pacific Coast proved not less attractive to some Jews than to other adventurous spirits, and to such an extent that as early as 1850 two congregations were organized in **San Francisco.** A striking characteristic of **California** Jewish migration is the cosmopolitan nature of its early Jewish population. Every country, even Australia, was represented among these pioneers. Another significant feature of the early settlement in California was the number of congregations which were organized in the fifties, when the gold fever was at its height, and which soon dwindled to insignificance, and during the course of the next ten or fifteen years passed out of existence. Noteworthy also is the high character of these early settlers, and the leading part they played

in consequence in the political as well as the commercial development of this new country. Among the most distinguished was Solomon HEYDENFELDT, who had gained prominence in Alabama before he came to California, where he attained the rare distinction of being elected chief justice of the state, a position which he held until his resignation in 1857. Subsequently he took a leading part in the politics of the state. Henry A. Lyons was one of the first three justices of the Supreme Court of California. A number of other Jews have occupied prominent political office; in the commercial world the Jews have been among the pioneers in the development of the state. Some of the leading Jewish bankers of New York came from San Francisco, where Jews are still a decided power in financial and commercial undertakings. Nor have they failed to develop on cultural lines; and the name of PEIXOTTO is one of distinction in art and scholarship. Emma WOLF is a distinguished authoress. M. H. De Young is proprietor of the "San Francisco Chronicle," and Max C. Sloss is prominent as one of the judges of the Superior Court of San Francisco. Julius Kahn represents the San Francisco district in Congress.

The two congregations already mentioned grew rapidly. In the year 1905 there were fourteen congregations in all, and the Jewish population of the city was estimated at 17,000; in 1920 at 30,000. There are other congregations at **Sacramento, Los Angeles,** and many other towns, making up a Jewish population for the state of 71,400.

The overflow from California made its way into **Oregon,** where Jews were to be found as early as 1850; the first congregation was established in **Portland** in 1858. As in California, they played a prominent part from the very beginning in municipal and state politics. Solomon HIRSCH was in 1889 appointed minister to Turkey by President Harrison, he having previously made himself one of the Republican leaders of the state. Joseph SIMON has the distinction of having been one of the few Jews who represented a state in the United States Senate (1898–1903). Others, notably D. Solis Cohen, have been active in local politics. There are small communities in various towns of the state, whose Jewish population numbers 18,260.

Jews first settled in **Utah** in 1860, but there is no record of religious services before 1866. The first congregation was established in **Salt Lake City** in 1880. A few Jews have held important political office. The number of Jews in the population was estimated at 3,940 in 1920.

It would appear that there were a considerable number of Jews among the first settlers of **Colorado.** The principal community is that of **Denver,** where the congregation was established in 1874. One of the prominent philanthropic institutions of the city is the National Jewish Hospital for Consumptives, founded in 1890. **Leadville** is said to have established its congregation in 1864. Five other cities in Colorado have Jewish congregations, and the Jewish population of the state numbered 15,380 in 1920.

The states of **Montana, Washington, Idaho,** and **North** and **South Dakota** have not failed to attract Jewish settlers, though for the most part they did not arrive previous to the Russian immigration.

Jews have penetrated into every state and all the territories of the Union, so that at this time practically no settlement of any significance in any part of the United States is without its Jewish community, small though it may be. Certain phases in the development of the Jewish communities throughout the United States have been common to all. The high holy days have always brought them together, often from far distant points,

Character- for religious worship. These occa-
istics of sional meetings soon resulted, when
Congrega- the communities grew greater, in the
tions. organization of congregations, which was often preceded, sometimes followed, by the purchase of a place of burial. As the communities grew the need for care of the sick and poverty-stricken resulted in the establishment of philanthropic institutions of various kinds. These were followed by the creation of various social organizations, many of which had beneficial features; and closely following in the wake of this development came the establishment, as prosperity became more enduring, of educational institutions; and practically no organized congregation ever failed to care for religious instruction.

3. Relation to the Federal Government: The DAMASCUS AFFAIR of 1840 marks the real beginning of the diplomatic or international phase in the history of American Jews, though a reference to the services which Mordecai M. NOAH rendered his country as consul at Tunis (1813–16) should not be omitted. The persecutions and tortures to which some of the most prominent Jews of Damascus had been subjected were reported to the Department of State at Washington by the United States consul at Damascus. Immediate instructions, under date of Aug. 14, 1840, were thereupon issued to John Gliddon, the United States consul at Alexandria, Egypt, by Secretary John Forsyth, in which he directed that all good offices and efforts be employed to display the active sympathy of the United States in the attempts that the governments of Europe were making to mitigate the horrors of these persecutions. Three days later David Porter, the United States minister to Turkey, was instructed by Forsyth to do everything in his power at the Porte to alleviate the condition of the unfortunates. In both these communications the reasons for the intervention of the United States are based upon sentiments of justice and humanity, no American citizens being involved; in the communication to Minister Porter stress was laid upon the peculiar propriety and right of the intervention of the United States, because its political and civil institutions make no distinction in favor of individuals by reason of race or creed, but treat all with absolute equality.

Though it would appear that this action of the United States was taken without the solicitation of any Jews of this country, measures

Damascus were already on foot to display the feel-
Affair. ing of the Jews at this time. Public meetings were held in August and September, 1840, in New York, Philadelphia, and Richmond, participated in by both Christians and Jews,

at which resolutions were passed asking the United States to intervene to procure justice for the accused and the mitigation of their hardships. Among the leaders who were instrumental in calling these meetings were Jacob Ezekiel of Richmond, J. B. Kurscheedt and Theodore J. Seixas of New York, and Isaac Leeser and John Moss of Philadelphia. Considerable correspondence passed between these leaders and the Department of State, in which the humanitarian attitude of the government and the nature of its intervention are fully disclosed ("Publ. Am. Jew. Hist. Soc." No. 8, p. 141; No. 9, p. 155; No. 10, p. 119).

Ten years later the Jews of this country were concerned in the diplomatic relations with Switzerland. Almost simultaneously the negotiations assumed two phases: (*a*) respecting the ratification of a treaty in which lurked the possibility that American citizens who were not Christians might be discriminated against, and (*b*) concerning the actual discrimination in Switzerland against American citizens, on the ground that they belonged to the Jewish faith.

In Nov., 1850, A. Dudley Mann, the American representative, negotiated a treaty with the Swiss Confederation, which was transmitted to the Senate on Feb. 13, 1851, by President Fillmore. At the same time the president sent a message in which he took exception to a part of the first article of the treaty, which specifically provided that Christians alone were to be entitled to the privileges guaranteed. An agitation against the ratification of the treaty was started by the Jews as soon as its existence was learned of, and Daniel Webster, then secretary of state, and Senator Henry Clay at once (Feb., 1851) went on record as opposed to the objectionable

clause of the treaty. The principal
Swiss Dis- agents in stirring up the opposition
abilities. were Isaac LEESER, David EINHORN, J. M. Cardozo of Charleston, S. C., and Capt. Jonas P. LEVY of New York. A movement was set on foot in this country shortly thereafter (1852–53) to procure religious toleration abroad for American citizens generally; this was quite distinct from any movement started by the Jews, but greatly aided the latter. As a result of this combined opposition the Senate declined to ratify the treaty. Senator Lewis Cass of Michigan figured largely in the opposition to it. He corresponded with Rev. Isaac Leeser and Captain Levy respecting it, delivered several notable speeches in the Senate against it in 1854, and presented a petition on April 19, 1854, which had been signed by Jews of the United States at the instance of a committee of New York Jews, of which Alexander J. Kursheedt was chairman. As a result the treaty was amended by the Senate, and in its amended form was ratified and proclaimed Nov. 9, 1855. But the amendment, though less objectionable in phraseology, retained the same connotation and rendered it possible, under its terms, for the Swiss cantons to discriminate against Jews in the manner they had adopted in 1851. Though unsuccessful in preventing the ratification of the treaty, the agitation against it did not cease. Notwithstanding the treaty was proclaimed at the end of 1855, it would appear that this was not generally known until 1857. Attention

was drawn to it by the fact that one A. H. Gootman, an American citizen and a Jew, had received notice in 1856 to leave Chaux-de-Fonds, in Neuchâtel, where he had transacted business for five years. Public meetings of protest were held during the year 1857, in Pittsburg, Indianapolis, Easton, Pa., Charleston, Baltimore, and elsewhere, and a vigorous opposition was voiced by Isaac M. WISE in his paper, "The Israelite," by David Einhorn in "Sinai," and by Isaac Leeser in "The Occident." A convention of Jews met in Baltimore in October, and a delegation appointed by this convention waited on President Buchanan in the same month to protest against the treaty and request its abrogation; the president promised to take steps to accede to their request so far as lay in his power. Numerous memorials were also transmitted to the president and the Senate. That this agitation attracted general attention is manifested by the fact that the newspapers throughout the country expressed vigorous opinions against the treaty.

Though sporadic efforts to procure an alteration in the treaty and the establishment of the rights not only of American Jews but of the Jews of all nations in Switzerland continued to be made in the United States, the principal scene of negotiations shifted to the former country, and the principal actor was Theodore Fay, the American minister. Beginning in Aug., 1853 ("U. S. Ex. Doc." xii. 3), when an American citizen, the same Gootman referred to above, received orders from the authorities of Chaux-de-Fonds, canton of Neuchâtel, to leave that canton on the ground that he was a Jew, Fay, though at first disinclined to take any very energetic stand, finally became much interested in the subject of Swiss discrimination against Jews and kept up an active agitation until his recall in 1860. He succeeded in procuring permission for Gootman to remain, but only as an act of grace, not by right. The obstacle Fay had to attempt to overcome lay in the nature of the Swiss Confederation, which left to the cantons the regulation of the rights of domicil, the Federal Council having no control over the cantons in this respect. Fay was ably supported in his contentions by the secretaries of state Marcy and Lewis Cass, especially the latter. In the course of his negotiations Fay made an elaborate study of the Jewish question as it affected Switzerland, and in June, 1859, transmitted what he called his "Israelite Note" to the Federal Council. This is an extensive treatise explaining the American contention with much force, and embodying besides a general defense of the Jews. It was translated into German and French, was offered for sale by the Federal Council, received much notice in the Swiss newspapers, and caused the restrictions against Jews to be abolished in several cantons. In 1860 the executive committee of the Board of Delegates of American Israelites, of which Myer S. Isaacs was secretary, took steps to continue the agitation in America. Henry I. Hart, the president of the above-mentioned board, took up the matter with Secretary Seward shortly after he assumed office in 1861, and the secretary issued specific instructions to the new minister to Switzerland, Fogg, to be no less active in his endeavor to establish the rights of American

Jews than was his predecessor. The restrictions in the cantons were gradually abolished, and full civil rights were finally guaranteed to all Jews by the new Swiss Constitution of 1874. It may be added, however, that the treaty of 1855 is still in force (1905; "Publ. Am. Jew. Hist. Soc." No. 11, pp. 7 et seq.).

In 1867 Myer S. Isaacs, on behalf of the Board of Delegates of American Israelites, endeavored unsuccessfully to have the government take some steps to alleviate the condition of the Jews in Servia. In 1882 Gen. Lew Wallace, United States **Servia and** minister to Turkey, moved by the **Palestine.** hardships suffered by Russian refugees whom he found starving in the streets of Constantinople, called at the Foreign Office and received a communication from the minister of foreign affairs in which the statement was made that Jews would be made welcome anywhere in Turkey except in Palestine. In 1884 he took vigorous action against the threatened expulsion from Jerusalem of sundry naturalized American Jews. In 1887 and 1888 attempts were made by the Turkish government to limit the sojourn of American Jews in Jerusalem to one month—later extended to three months. This was earnestly opposed by the American minister, Oscar S. Straus, ably supported by Secretary Bayard, who contended that the United States, by reason of its Constitution, could not recognize any distinction between American citizens in respect to their religion. By his exertions Straus successfully halted any steps to expel American citizens who happened to be Jews ("U. S. For. Rel." 1887, 1888, 1889). Secretaries Blaine, Gresham, and Hay repeatedly took a similar stand, and it would appear that rights of American citizens who are Jews have been carefully guarded in Turkey ("U. S. For. Rel." 1894, 1898, 1901).

In 1863 atrocities perpetrated upon the Jews of Morocco led the Board of Delegates to ask the intervention of the United States. Secretary Seward instructed the United States consul at Tangier to use his good offices to further the mission of Sir Moses Montefiore, basing his act on the ground of common humanity. For two years the consul exerted himself to carry out his instructions and met with some slight success. In 1878 the Board of Delegates renewed its endeavors to have the government use its good offices in Morocco, and the consul at Tangier, F. A. Matthews, took earnest steps to alleviate the condition of the Jews whenever the opportunity arose during this and succeeding years. Adolph Sanger, on behalf of the Board of Delegates, in 1880 sent out an agent, L. A. Cohen, to Morocco to report on conditions there. In March, 1881, the United States minister at Madrid, Lucius Fairchild, proceeded to Morocco to investigate the condition of the Jews. He made a sympathetic and valuable report to the secretary of state, Blaine, in which he displayed an acute interest in the unfortunate conditions in that country, and did his utmost to alleviate them.

Rumanian conditions, which have so vitally interested the United States, first had attention drawn to them by the Board of Delegates in June, 1867, when the good offices of the United States in behalf of the persecuted Jews of Rumania were requested. In

1870 B. F. Peixotto of New York was appointed consul-general to Rumania, and during the six years that he held office he exerted himself

Rumanian Disabilities. to bring about an improvement in the condition of the Jews. In 1878 John A. Kasson, minister of the United States to Austria, in a despatch to the Department of State proposed as a condition preliminary to the recognition of Rumanian independence that the United States join with the European powers in exacting from Rumania, at the Congress of Berlin, the recognition of the equal civil, commercial, and religious rights of all classes of her population, as also equal rights and protection under the treaty and under Rumanian laws, irrespective of race or religious belief. In opening negotiations with Rumania in the following year, the recognition by that country of the rights of sojourn and trade of all classes of Americans irrespective of race or creed was strongly emphasized, as it was by Kasson about the same time with respect to Servia. The continued persecutions of the Jews of Rumania, her violations of the provisions of the Treaty of Berlin, and the greatly increased proportions which the Rumanian emigration to the United States assumed in consequence, as also the failure to conclude a naturalization convention between the two countries, because Rumania would not recognize the rights of American citizens who were Jews, moved Secretary of State John Hay to address on Aug. 11, 1902, identical instructions to the representatives of the United States in Russia, France, Germany, Great Britain, Italy, and Turkey upon the subject of Rumania's attitude. In this note he drew attention to the consequences to the United States of the continued persecutions in Rumania—namely, the unnatural increase of immigration from that country—and upon this based his right to remonstrate to the signatories to the Treaty of Berlin against the acts of the Rumanian government. Further, he sustained the right of the United States to ask the above-mentioned powers to intervene upon the strongest grounds of humanity. Acting upon the forcible instructions, the representatives of the United States presented this note to the government to which each was accredited. But beyond the abolition of the Oath More Judaico (1904) and some slight diminution of the harshness of the persecution, little has been accomplished, and Rumania continued almost unrestrictedly to violate the treaty which established her as an independent nation. In 1905 Congress made provision for an American legation at Bucharest.

The diplomatic correspondence between Russia and the United States involving Jews is of considerable bulk. It relates for the most part to the failure of Russia to recognize the validity of American pass-

Russian Passports. ports where Jews are involved, which is the principal cause of difference between the United States and Russia. Russia has constantly violated the provisions of her treaty of 1832 with the United States, which gives to the citizens of the two countries unrestricted rights of sojourn, travel, and protection. Until the persecutions in Russia assumed acute form, beginning with 1880, the correspondence be-

tween the two countries was not of importance, though occasional earlier instances of discrimination by Russia against American citizens who were Jews had been vigorously protested against by the United States authorities. For the past twenty-five years the record is one of unceasing effort on the part of the United States to establish the rights of American citizens who are Jews, and of continued declination of Russia to live up to her treaty stipulations. The threatened expulsion from St. Petersburg of an American citizen named Pinkos, in 1880, was the occasion for the presentation of energetic notes of remonstrance by John W. Foster, the American minister to Russia. He acted not alone of his own responsibility, but was the recipient of specific instructions from the secretary of state, William M. Evarts. In the course of one of Evarts' letters of instruction the attitude assumed by the United States was clearly set forth in the following terms: "In the view of this government the religion professed by one of its citizens has no relation to that citizen's right to the protection of the United States" ("Am. Jewish Year Book," 1904–5, p. 287). The first protests of Foster and Evarts, inasmuch as they brought forth no satisfactory replies, were succeeded by others of the same tenor, in one of which Evarts stated "that we ask treaty treatment for our aggrieved citizens, not because they are Jews, but because they are Americans" (*ib.* p. 290). All the answers of the Russian Foreign Office are based on the claim that the proscriptive laws against the Jews were in existence prior to the treaty of 1832, that they, therefore, must be assumed under the treaty, and, furthermore, that the Jewish question in Russia was complicated by economic and other difficulties. These views were answered in the able despatch of James Blaine, secretary of state, of July 29, 1881. This despatch covers in considerable detail the whole of the American contention, and is so forcibly put that subsequent consideration of the same subject by the Department of State has been unable to add much to it ("For. Rel. U. S." 1881, p. 1030). As continued remonstrances during subsequent years led to no results, in 1893 the Department of State took the stand that it could not acquiesce in the action of Russian consuls in asking the religion of American citizens desiring to travel in Russia before granting a visé to their passports, and refusing Jews. The government regarded this as the "assumption of a religious inquisitorial function within our own borders, by a foreign agency, in a manner . . . repugnant to the national sense." In 1895 this view was forcibly presented to the Russian government by the American minister, Clifton R. Breckenridge, and in July of that year the Department of State took the attitude that a "continuance in such a course, after our views have been clearly but considerately made known, may trench upon the just limits of consideration" (*ib.* pp. 295, 297). But in spite of the presentation of the American contention in every possible light and with all possible emphasis, Russia stubbornly refused to live up to her treaty obligations.

In April, 1902, at the instance of Henry M. Goldfogle, a member of Congress from New York, the House of Representatives passed a resolution calling upon the secretary of state to inform the House "whether American citizens of the Jewish religious faith holding passports issued by this government are barred or excluded from entering the territory of the Empire of Russia," and what action concerning the matter had been taken by the government. A few days later Secretary Hay replied, stating in brief what efforts had been made by the United States for the protection of American citizens in Russia, and added that though "begun many years ago . . . [they] have not been attended with encouraging success" (*ib.* pp. 301, 302).

In Jan., 1904, Goldfogle introduced another resolution, requesting the president to resume negotiations with Russia looking to the recognition of the validity of American passports irrespective of the religion of the holder. This resolution gave rise to notable addresses on the part of a number of members of the House, and was passed, in substance, in April of that year (*ib.* pp. 304, 305). In consequence of this resolution the question of American passports was taken up anew by the Department of State during the summer of 1904. The Russian reply made at that time was to the effect that a commission had been created in 1903 to consider the revision of the passport regulations, and that the desires of the United States would be brought to the attention of that commission. In his annual message, Dec., 1904, President Roosevelt wrote vigorously against the Russian attitude, characterizing it as "unjust and irritating toward us." In Feb., 1905, a committee of members of the House of Representatives was formed, with Wachter of Maryland as chairman, to urge further action by the Department of State; but nothing significant was accomplished.

The massacres at KISHINEF in April, 1903, aroused indignation throughout the United States. Though in response to a cable of inquiry sent by
Kishinef Petition. Secretary Hay to Ambassador McCormick at St. Petersburg, asking if relief could be sent to the sufferers, the ambassador stated that he was informed officially that there was no distress or want in southwestern Russia, nevertheless mass-meetings were held in almost every city of importance, and the comments in the newspapers portrayed the feelings of horror of the American people. A practical turn was given by the collection of considerable sums to alleviate the misery of the unfortunates. In the hope that if the attention of the czar were directly brought to the plight of the Jews in his dominions their condition might be alleviated, the Independent Order of B'nai B'rith took measures to prepare a petition for transmittal to him. On June 15, 1903, a committee of the order waited upon Secretary Hay and President Roosevelt, and presented a tentative draft of the petition. This having met with their approval, it was then circulated throughout the United States, and over 12,500 signatures of Christians and Jews in all walks of life were appended to it. On July 15 the American representative at St. Petersburg was instructed to ask an audience of the minister of foreign affairs in order to find out whether the petition, which was given in full in the despatch, would be received by the

minister to be put before the czar. The minister declined to receive it, and the bound copy with the signatures was placed by Secretary Hay in the archives of the Department of State in Oct., 1903. Though the petition did not reach its destination, its words attained world-wide publicity, and its object was in a measure accomplished in this way (Adler, "Voice of America on Kishineff," 1904).

Throughout the history of the United States the government has insisted with great force upon the equal treatment of all American citizens in foreign countries, irrespective of race or creed. Further, it never has failed to intercede with foreign governments on humanitarian grounds, in behalf of the Jews who were being persecuted or of those to whom life was rendered precarious by inhuman proscriptive laws. Many Jews have held diplomatic posts, among the chief being Mordecai M. NOAH, consul to Tunis, 1813–16; Edwin de LEON, consul-general to Egypt, 1854; August Belmont, secretary of legation at The Hague, 1853–55, and minister resident, 1855–58; Oscar S. STRAUS, minister to Turkey, 1887–89, 1897–1900; Solomon HIRSCH, minister to Turkey, 1889–92; B. F. PEIXOTTO, consul to Bucharest, 1870–76; Simon WOLF, consul-general to Egypt, 1881; Max JUDD, consul-general to Vienna, 1893–97; and Lewis Einstein, third secretary of embassy at Paris, 1903, and London, 1905; Henry Morgenthau, ambassador to Turkey, 1913–16.

4. Education: Early in the history of the first Jewish congregation in New York there was attached to the synagogue a school in which secular as well as Hebrew branches were taught. It was one of the earliest general schools in America; poor children received instruction gratis. Religious instruction was established in connection with most of the early synagogues. For ordinary secular education the Jews resorted, in large measure, to the schools and colleges. There was a Jewish matriculate at the University of Pennsylvania, for instance, as early as 1772. The older communities, however, before the general establishment of the public-school system, frequently provided regular instruction in the secular branches. These schools ordinarily were adjuncts of the religious schools maintained by the congregations. In Philadelphia as early as 1838 a general Sunday-school, quite irrespective of congregational organization, was established, largely through the instrumentality of Rebecca GRATZ, who was its superintendent and president until 1864. This was the beginning of a movement, which has spread throughout the country, for the organization of educational work along lines quite independent of congregational activities.

A similar school was organized in Charleston, S. C., in the same year; in the following year, one in Richmond, Va.; in 1845 this movement spread to New York, being taken up first by the Emanu-El Society, although the Shearith Israel congregation had started a Hebrew-school system as early as 1808. In 1848 the Hebrew Education Society was founded at Philadelphia—originally a school for general instruction in the ordinary branches up to and through the grammar-school grade, together with instruction in Hebrew and in the Jewish religion. In 1864 the Hebrew Free School Association was incorporated in New York; and throughout various states of the Union a movement gradually spread for the organization of free religious schools which would bring into a common-school system children

Free Schools. from the various congregations in each city. These were largely intended to supersede the private institutions that had hitherto existed. They were, in the main, carried on by volunteer teachers; and their distinguishing feature was that the instruction was usually conducted by native-born persons and in the English language, as against the German teaching in the congregational schools.

The whole trend of this educational work was toward the unification of the community and the broadening of the interests of the individual members, with a tendency to overcome the narrowness of the congregational life that had prevailed. Within the last decade or so there has been a decided reaction; and religious schools and Sabbath-schools have been highly organized in connection with individual congregations. Particular stress is laid upon them by the congregations, which derive from them much of their communal strength. While many of the Hebrew education societies and schools continue in existence, they do not develop or flourish as might be expected; in fact, since 1882 they have largely taken upon themselves an entirely new function. With the sudden arrival in the United States of a large number of Russian Jews having no knowledge of the English language, and in many cases without any particular handicraft, there devolved upon the American Jewish community the necessity of providing, first, day- and night-schools for teaching English to the new arrivals, and, second, manual-training and technical schools.

Technical Schools. These have been established in New York, Philadelphia, Chicago, and other cities, more or less with the aid of the Baron de Hirsch Fund. The most noteworthy of these educational institutions called into existence since the Russian immigration began is the Educational Alliance of New York.

Until recently provision for higher education on specifically Jewish lines was not found practicable, though as early as 1840 the versatile and suggestive Mordecai M. Noah urged the formation of a Jewish college in the United States. His project met with no response. Nor was I. M. Wise more successful when in 1855 he endeavored to establish a theological college in Cincinnati under the name of "Zion Collegiate Institute." In 1867 the scholarly and enterprising Isaac Leeser, however, established Maimonides College at Philadelphia. It was intended that general collegiate instruction should be provided there, though naturally the Jewish branches were to be given particular attention. A certain measure of cooperation with the University of Pennsylvania was planned, and the idea held in mind was that the college should serve as the capstone to the scheme of education builded by the Hebrew Education Society. The college was, however, much ahead of the times, and after a few years of languishing life passed out of existence. Not until nearly twenty years thereafter was the first institution for the training of rabbis and teachers founded. This was

the Hebrew Union College of Cincinnati, established in 1875 by the Union of American Hebrew Congregations, an organization created at that time for the purpose, and mainly at the instance of I. M. Wise. The existence of the college has been continuous, and, though theoretically without partizan bias, it is practically the representative of the Reform wing in America. Graduates from this institution are to be found in charge of congregations in nearly every city of importance in the country. Rev. Dr. K. Kohler is president since 1905, and there is a faculty of ten professors and several instructors. In 1886 there was established in New York

Theological Institutions. the Jewish Theological Seminary, also for the training of rabbis and teachers, and representing the Orthodox wing of the community. The reorganization which this institution underwent in 1901–2 resulted in the calling of Dr. S. Schechter (d. 1915) to its presidency. At the same time it was richly endowed, and in 1903 took possession of a new building, the gift of Jacob H. Schiff. Its library, largely the gift of Judge Mayer Sulzberger, contains one of the greatest collections of Hebraica. In 1893, through a trust vested by Hyman Gratz in the Mickvè Israel congregation, Gratz College was founded in Philadelphia, which is devoted to the preparation of teachers for Jewish schools, practically occupying the place of a normal school. The largest sum ever made available for the promotion of Semitic investigation is that bequeathed in 1905 by Moses A. Dropsie of Philadelphia for the establishment of a Jewish college along broad lines, for instruction "in the Hebrew and cognate languages and their respective literatures, and in the rabbinical learning and literature." The amount of this bequest is about $800,000.

Throughout the United States there have been established in connection with the various congregations, and also independently, Young Men's Hebrew Associations and other societies which are to a certain extent educational in their character. They usually maintain small libraries and provide lecture-courses on secular and religious topics. In 1893 there was founded the Jewish Chautauqua Society, which has branches all over the country and bears the same relation to the regular schools and colleges as does the University Extension movement, as interpreted in America, to regular colleges for university work. The Council of Jewish Women has engaged to a considerable extent in educational work among its own members. In 1886 the Reform wing of American Jewry organized at Cincinnati a Hebrew Sabbath-School Union for the purpose of promoting uniformity and approved methods in Sabbath-school instruction. In 1900 there were in the United States 415 Jewish educational organizations, 291 of which were religious schools attached to congregations, with 1,127 teachers and an attendance of about 25,000 pupils. There were also 27 Jewish free schools, chiefly in large cities, with about 11,000 pupils and 142 teachers.

Three societies have been organized in the United States to issue Jewish publications—the first, in Philadelphia in 1845; the second, in New York in 1873; and the third, in Philadelphia in 1888. This last is a flourishing organization, and has issued many instructive and important works. Among the educational activities should also be mentioned the American Jewish Historical Society, organized in 1892, which in its twelve volumes of publications has made notable contributions to American Jewish history. Associated with many of the schools are circulating and reference libraries—notably the Leeser Library of the Hebrew Education Society of Philadelphia—and there are several independent ones, the largest of which is the Aguilar Library in New York, founded in 1886. The Maimonides Library of the Independent Order B'nai B'rith in New York was organized in 1851. The last two are now merged in the New York Public Library, which itself contains the largest collection of Judaica and modern Hebraica in the country. The Order B'nai B'rith and many other orders and lodges did pioneer work in the education of their members and included lectures among the educational features. The various Zionist societies throughout the country make educational work along Jewish lines one of their principal activities.

Publication Societies and Libraries.

5. Philanthropy: The measure of the American Jewry's philanthropic activity is full to overflowing. From the beginning of direct aid of individual to individual, philanthropy has progressed until it now devotes a large part of its endeavor to preventive work—the higher philanthropy—along the most approved scientific lines. In this the Jewish organizations have often been the pioneers. Dating from the days of the first arrivals, the ideal constantly maintained has been that none of the Jewish poor should become a charge upon the general community.

The simple charity of the first settlers was soon superseded by the dispensing of collective funds through the congregations. But this did not take the place of the "personal service" of our time, since the care of a needy family by one more favorably situated is one of the commonest phenomena of the earlier days. Soon, as the population increased and its needs outgrew individual or even congregational generosity, societies with specific objects were started. Some were established for the visitation of the sick and the burial of the dead; some, under congregational direction, for general charitable purposes; others for the distribution of unleavened bread at Passover. Gradually hospitals for the care of the sick, asylums for orphans, and homes for the aged were established. At first a large measure of volunteer work lightened the burden of the community, but this, though never entirely superseded, has had to give way to professional and trained service. Similarly, the small societies of the early days found it advantageous to cooperate, resulting in the formation of the United Hebrew Charities, which took general charge of all philanthropic work except that of hospitals and orphan asylums. In recent times the problem has become so complex that in a number of cities all of the charitable organizations have been federated, and the funds collected from all sources distributed pro rata to the various constituent organizations. The first Jewish hospital, the Mount Sinai, was established in 1852 in New York, and the Independent Order B'nai B'rith Home for the Aged and Infirm in 1848 at the same place. The first orphan asylum was that of New Orleans, established in 1855, though one had been projected in New York as early as 1829.

The Russian immigration, which has brought so many perplexing philanthropic and educational problems to the surface, has made itself felt in a particular degree on account of the necessity for the development of cooperative scientific philanthropic methods. The federated associations referred to have been found necessary because of the increasing inadequacy of the simpler methods of the earlier days to cope with the new conditions, and because of the fact that relief, to be effective, must be administered not only from the standpoint of the poor, but with a view to the promotion of the best interests of the community at large. Trained experts in this work have been developed, and in the larger cities the more extensive systems of relief are under their direction, though they in turn are controlled by volunteer boards of trustees. Out of the conditions just noted has developed the National Conference of Jewish Charities of the United States, organized at Cincinnati in 1899, with thirty-eight relief organizations composing its membership, distributed throughout the country. Its seat is at Cincinnati, and the objects it furthers are the discussion of the problems of charity and the promotion of reforms in administration, with a view of accomplishing uniformity of action and cooperation. Annual conferences for the reading and discussion of papers are held. The more or less mechanical methods by which relief must be distributed on the large scale now found necessary, with the element of personal sympathy largely eliminated, have, however, caused a reaction. In recent times societies, largely congregational, have been organized, whose object is the promotion of personal service in looking after the welfare of the unfortunate. See SISTERHOODS.

The numerous fraternal orders, of which the B'nai B'rith (1843), the Free Sons of Israel (1849), the B'rith Abraham (1859), and the Sons of Benjamin (1877) are the most important, do a large measure of charitable and beneficial work.

The inability of the Jews of the United States to bear the tremendous strain put upon their resources by the Russian immigration, prompted Baron de Hirsch in 1890 to come to their aid and to establish the Baron de HIRSCH FUND ($2,400,000 originally; since grown to $3,300,000), to be administered by a board of trustees named by him. Its annual income, amounting to about $125,000, is expended in looking after the reception of immigrants, the promotion of English and mechanical education, and, through the Jewish Agicultural and Industrial Aid Society (1899), the encouragement of farming and the transfer of industries to rural communities. The last-mentioned branch of the Fund and its related organization, the Industrial Removal Office, receive large subventions also from the JEWISH COLONIZATION ASSOCIATION. A town and agricultural colony were founded at Woodbine, N. J., in 1891, followed by an agricultural and industrial school at the same place in 1894. Other colo-

Baron de Hirsch Fund.

nies under the same direction have been established at Alliance, Carmel, and Rosenhayn in the same state. In the year 1905 the total number of colonies in New Jersey was about 2,500, but not more than half of the adults were engaged in farming and its related work. Industrial establishments have been introduced, and a large part of the several communities is employed in them. Other colonists have been aided in removing to New England, particularly to Connecticut, where about 600 persons are now engaged in agricultural pursuits, mainly dairy-farming. Efforts at the establishment of agricultural colonies in various other parts of the country have been made, but they have almost invariably been ultimate failures (see AGRICULTURAL COLONIES IN THE UNITED STATES).

The National Farm School, established through the instrumentality of Dr. Joseph Krauskopf in 1896, at Doylestown, Pa., aims to train boys for agricultural careers, and has met with some measure of success. Its pupils number about forty. There are two charitable organizations with a national field of activity, the ALLIANCE ISRAÉLITE UNIVERSELLE, which has had branches in the United States since 1868 (eight in 1905), and the Jewish Hospital for Consumptives at Denver, Colo., founded in 1890. A noteworthy charity is that instituted in New York in 1890 by Nathan Straus for the distribution to the poor, at nominal cost, of milk carefully prepared in accordance with the most scientific hygienic principles. Similar institutions have been aided by him in Philadelphia and Chicago. Statistical reports show a large reduction in infant mortality as a result of this efficient remedial measure.

6. Religious Development: As elsewhere, the religious life of the Jews in the United States has been centered for the most part about the congregations. The lack of theological seminaries until a comparatively late period necessitated that religious leaders should be brought from abroad. England, Germany, and to some extent Holland supplied the incumbents for pulpits in the earlier days. Naturally Germany furnished the large majority between 1840 and 1881, since which time, as in so much else, Russia has been predominant. Sephardim were at first in the majority, and organized the four earliest congregations in the country; namely, those of New York, Newport, Savannah, and Philadelphia. As early as 1766 a translation of the prayers into English by Isaac PINTO — probably the first English-Hebrew prayer-book ever issued—was published in New York.

In Jamaica and in Canada there have always been more or less direct relations with England; but in the United States the entire religious life of the Jews has been especially characterized by the absence of dependence upon any European authority, as well as by the absence of any central authority in America. Congregational autonomy has been emphasized, and is perhaps the most striking characteristic of American Jewish religious development.

Prior to 1825 all the congregations followed the Orthodox ritual. In that year, however, a movement for ceremonial reform began in Charleston, whose congregation was made up almost exclusively of Sephardim. Meeting with some success at first, the movement soon languished, only to be revived upon a more enduring basis in 1840. The Reform movement made no headway until about the middle of the nineteenth century, when Isaac M. Wise at Albany gave it considerable standing. But little was accomplished, however, until the arrival in the United States of David Einhorn and, later, Samuel Hirsch. Under the influence of these men and of other rabbis —principally from Germany—the trend toward alterations in the liturgy and ritual set in very strongly about 1860. In 1869 attempts were made to formulate the principles of Reform Judaism, followed by others in 1871 and 1885. But the large amount of autonomy common to all congregations and the absence of any generally recognized authoritative head have rendered any acceptance of a program by all congregations impossible. As a consequence the Reform movement varies from the extremes of Sunday services only, on the one hand, to a conservatism that lends its support to an Orthodox seminary, on the other. The reaction against excessive radical tendencies attained force about 1880, resulting in the formation of an intermediate or distinctly conservative group. This wing has grown in importance and has been largely instrumental, in cooperation with the outspokenly Orthodox, in the reorganization of the Jewish Theological Seminary on a firm basis. One of the results of Reform was the introduction of changes in the prayer-ritual, culminating in the adoption by most congregations of a Union Prayer-Book in 1895. This is not used universally, and individual idiosyncrasy still shows a decided preference for other forms.

Reform Movement Begun in Charleston.

An outgrowth of certain phases of the trend toward extreme liberalism was the society for Ethical Culture, founded in New York by Prof. Felix ADLER in 1876, and still claiming numerous adherents (see ETHICAL CULTURE, SOCIETY FOR).

The Reform movement has not failed to arouse a vigorous opposition from the representatives of the Orthodox rite; chief among them, in the days of the inception of Reform, was Isaac LEESER, to whom Sabato MORAIS proved an able successor. In the main, holding that its principles, having been tried by time, needed no defense, the representatives of Orthodoxy have supported their views with an intelligent perception of the needs of the new environment and conditions. The Orthodox seminary already referred to is to some extent the outgrowth of a desire effectively to counteract the inroads of Reform, as also to render a service in fitting the ancient forms to American conditions. The influx of Russian Jews during the past twenty-five years has given to the Orthodox greatly increased strength, for the Reform movement has made but slight impression upon the Russian mind as yet.

Indicative of a recognition that congregational autonomy is not free from a tendency to develop into a characterless individualism are the formation of the Union of American Hebrew (Reform) Congregations in 1873, and, more recently (1889), the establishment of the Central Conference of American Rabbis. A recent development has been an agitation for the calling of an American Jewish synod. As a means of strengthening Orthodox Judaism a Union of Orthodox Jewish Congregations in the United States and Canada was formed in 1898, followed by the creation of a similar organization, representing Russian Orthodoxy, in 1901. A Society of American Cantors was established in 1894. For further details see AMERICA, JUDAISM IN, and REFORM JUDAISM.

7. Military, Naval, and State Service: From the Dutch settlements in Brazil and other parts of South America the services rendered by the Jews to the states of their adoption or nativity have been largely in excess of their proportionate share. It is likely that a few of the more adventurous pioneers engaged in conflicts with the Indians, and, as already mentioned, ASSER LEVY, as early as 1655, claimed, on behalf of himself and his associates, the right to serve in Stuyvesant's expedition against the Swedes on the Delaware, instead of paying a tax for exemption from military service. An occasional Jewish name appears in the rosters of those serving in the colonial expeditions against the French and Indians, and one or perhaps two Jews were with Washington on his expedition across the Alleghanies in 1754, and were among the recipients of grants of land for their services.

At the outbreak of the Revolutionary movement and before the formation of strong parties was brought about, the Jews were almost to a man supporters of the colonial contentions. Though numbering only a bare 2,000 in a total population of 2,000,-000, they had developed large commercial interests in Newport, Philadelphia, Charleston, Savannah, and New York. None the less, in all these cities they were ardent supporters of the various measures of non-importation designed to frustrate the British acts, and this in the face of the fact that they were greatly engaged in intercolonial and English trade and in some places, as in Philadelphia and Newport, were the largest ship-owners. At least eight Philadelphia Jews were among the signers of the non-importation resolutions adopted in that city in 1765, and five subscribed to those of New York in 1769. When war actually broke out Jewish names occurred on the first rosters. Though no complete figures have been compiled, it is probable that not less than 100 officers and men served at one time or another in the Revolutionary war. Noteworthy in this connection are the forty Jews among the sixty men who composed Capt. Richard Lushington's company of Charleston. Twenty-four officers have been counted, among the most distinguished being Lieut.-Col. David S. FRANKS, Lieut. Isaac FRANKS (lieutenant-colonel of Pennsylvania militia, 1794), and Major Benjamin NONES. The slight increase in the Jewish population between the close of the Revolutionary war and the outbreak of the War of 1812, and the divided sentiments which prevailed during the latter war, render it likely that less than fifty Jews participated in it, and none appears to have gained special distinction. In the Mexican war about sixty Jews saw service, the most prominent being Major and Surgeon David de LEON, who twice received the thanks of Congress for gallantry, and who as surgeon-general of the Confederate armies organized their medical departments.

The effect of the increase of the Jewish popula-

Monument Erected in Memory of the Jewish Soldiers Who Died in the Civil War, Cypress Hill Cemetery, Brooklyn, New York.
(From a photograph.)

tion between 1848 and 1860 is shown in the military records of the Civil war. Between 7,000 and 8,000 Jews, in all ranks, saw service on both sides of this terrible conflict, some with rare distinction. Included in this number are 9 generals, 18 colonels, 8 lieutenant-colonels, 40 majors, 205 captains, 325 lieutenants, 48 adjutants, etc., and 25 surgeons. In the recent Spanish-American war (1898) Jews formed a far greater proportion of the forces, and served with distinction. The numbers engaged were as follows: Officers: army, 32; navy, 27; non-commissioned officers and men: army, 2,450; navy, 42.

A considerable number of Jews have always been found in the regular army and navy. As officers the following have been conspicuous: Major Alfred MORDECAI (1804–87), expert on ordnance and explosives ; Commodore Uriah P. LEVY (1792–1862), secured the abolition of corporal punishment in the navy; Capt. Levi M. HARBY (1793–1870); Capt. Adolph MARIX (1848); Col. Charles H. LAUCHHEIMER (1859); and Capt. E. L. ZALINSKI (retired 1894).

From the days when Georgia was a colony and a Jew occupied the governor's chair, and from those when Haym SALOMON not only sustained the weak credit of the Congress of the Revolution but out of his private purse supported some of the most prominent of the leaders of the time when, without his aid, the country would have been deprived of their services, down to the appointment in 1902 by President Roosevelt of Oscar S. STRAUS to the position of successor to the late President Harrison as member of the Permanent Court of Arbitration at The Hague, there has been a full record of service.

Though five Jews have been elected to the Senate (David L. YULEE [1845–61]; Judah P. BENJAMIN [1852–61]; Benjamin F. JONAS [1879–85]; Joseph SIMON [1897–1903]; and Isidor RAYNER [1905]), it is a noteworthy fact that none of these has ever held a position of leadership in the Jewish community, and their selection has been made irrespective of any support from specifically Jewish sources. Nor has any, with the exception of Judah P. Benjamin, attained a position of leadership among his colleagues in the Senate. Benjamin's services to the Confederacy as secretary of state after his resignation from the Senate, and his subsequent career in England stamp him as the foremost Jew of American birth. The House of Representatives has had about forty Jewish members, of whom four are serving at the present time. Henry M. GOLDFOGLE, representing a constituency made up largely of Jews, has displayed an intelligent activity in promoting measures of specifically Jewish interest, and has taken a prominent part in the endeavor to compel Russia to recognize American passports held by Jews. In 1904, moreover, both political parties adopted declarations in their platforms, pronouncing in favor of the institution of measures to insure the equal treatment and protection of all American citizens sojourning or traveling in foreign countries; and in his message to Congress of Dec., 1904, President Roosevelt spoke vigorously against the Russian attitude as affecting American Jewish citizens. Of Jews who have served their communities in the lesser offices, ranging from that of city alderman or councilman to the higher state positions, the numbers are so great that no ac-

count is possible here. Yet space must be allowed for the mention of Judge Mayer SULZBERGER of Philadelphia, conspicuous among American Jews not only by reason of his exceptional learning, but also because of his activity in all fields of Jewish activity.

Especially noteworthy also is the fact that the first statue presented to the United States, thereby originating Statuary Hall in the Capitol at Washington, was the gift, in 1838, of a Jew, Lieutenant, later Commodore, Uriah P. LEVY. The statue is one of Thomas Jefferson, in bronze, and was executed by the French Jewish sculptor David d'Angers.

8. Civil and Political Rights: It was within the bounds of what soon became the United States that Jews for the first time in modern history were put upon a plane of absolute equality with other races. Rhode Island, founded by Roger Williams as a refuge for the persecuted of all forms of religious beliefs, welcomed the Jews not less than others. For that reason the Jewish community in that colony attained prominence at an early date, and contributed largely to its development along commercial lines. New York, South Carolina, Pennsylvania, and Georgia gave the Jews a generous welcome as well, and attracted in consequence considerable Jewish communities at an early period of their respective histories. The unfavorable environment of Puritan New England, which actuated Roger Williams to establish his colony as a protest against the illiberal views which predominated in the adjoining colonies, rendered the establishment of any sort of Jewish community in their midst an impossibility. This was all the more remarkable since the earlier forms of government and laws were fashioned in a manner upon Old Testament lines. This was particularly the case in Massachusetts (whose first criminal code [1641] gave chapter and verse from the Bible as its authority), as also in Connecticut. The records of the colony of New Haven, founded in 1638, have a distinctly Old Testament character, and Biblical precedent is quoted for almost every governmental act. One can form some opinion of the measure of Old Testament influence when one considers that in the code of colony laws adopted in New Haven in 1656 there are 107 references to the Old Testament to 29 to the New, and of the latter 5 are of an ecclesiastical character.

But Jews as individuals contributed little or nothing to direct the trend of the colonial legislation of this early period. The few who arrived previous to the birth of liberal ideas during the period of the Revolution were contented to be allowed the rare opportunity of living in unmolested exercise of their religion, and made no contest for political rights, though an occasional bold character, such as Asser LEVY and Rabba Couty, helped much to make it known that the heavens would not fall if a Jew were accorded certain political privileges. The participation of Jews in the control of the Dutch West India Company caused the extension of liberal political ideas to the colony of New Amsterdam, and they do not appear to have been seriously curtailed after the English occupation. Jews were naturalized occasionally in most of the colonies elsewhere than in New England; and in New York they appear to have voted for state officials before 1737 (see page 348). Under the Parliamentary Act of 1740 foreigners who had been resident in the

Naturalization Act of 1740.

British colonies for a period of seven years could be naturalized without taking the sacrament, merely an oath of fidelity taken upon the Old Testament being required. Before 1762 there is record that thirty-five Jews availed themselves of this privilege, and after that date many others must have taken the oath. Georgia, Rhode Island, and South Carolina placed no obstacles in the way of a Jew holding any office, though in most of the other colonies Jews were barred because of the necessity, on the assumption of office, of taking an oath either "upon the true faith of a Christian" or declaring a belief in the divine inspiration of the New Testament. Similarly, in the more illiberal colonies the right of suffrage was restricted to Christians, though it is likely that the restrictions were not severely enforced.

Though the constitutions established during the Revolutionary period fixed no religious qualifications for the suffrage, except that of New Hampshire, they were far more stringent where the matter of holding office was concerned. All but Rhode Island, New York, and South Carolina restricted office-holders to those professing the Christian religion, and this too in spite of the fact that the preambles to most of the constitutions proclaimed emphatically the rights to which man was by nature entitled. To men of logical mind, like Jefferson and Madison, this inconsistency was always a thorn in the flesh, and in their own state, Virginia, they soon began an agitation that culminated in 1785 in the passage of the Religious Freedom Act. This liberal movement was responsible for the guaranties embodied in the ordinance of 1787, which effectively insured for all time the fullest degree of civil and religious liberty in the territory northwest of the Ohio River. Within a few months the same idea was written in the Constitution, which provides that "no religious test shall ever be required as a qualification to any public office or public trust under the United States"; this clause, strengthened by the first amendment, "Congress shall make no law respecting an establishment of religion, or prohibiting the free exercise thereof," fixed the federal law and established the absolute equality of citizens of all creeds in all the

Principle of Religious Liberty.

territory over which the United States had control. Though there is no evidence that Jews had any direct hand in placing this fitting capstone to the constitutional structure, the influence exerted by the example of so commanding a figure as Haym SALOMON, and the services rendered the United States by the Jewish soldiers in the field, probably played their part. In this connection may be mentioned the petition which Gershom Mendes Seixas, Simon Nathan Asher Myers, Barnard Gratz, and Haym Salomon, the mahamad of the Mickvé Israel synagogue of Philadelphia, on Dec. 23, 1783, sent to the Council of Censors of Pennsylvania praying for the removal of the declaration of belief in the divine inspiration of both the Old and the New Testament as a qualification for member-

ship in the Pennsylvania assembly; and the letter which Jonas Phillips addressed to the Federal Convention, Sept. 7, 1787, requesting that it abolish the same qualification ("Publ. Am. Jew. Hist. Soc." No. 2, p. 107). Before the close of the century there was great advance in conforming the state constitutions to the more liberal federal constitution. The spread of democratic ideas, started by the election of Jefferson to the presidency, which was characteristic of the first quarter of the nineteenth century, broke down the barriers of intolerance everywhere but in Maryland, and that state gave way just as the period was brought to a close. The effective work accomplished by the COHEN and ETTING families in pushing through the "Jew Bill" after more than twenty-five years of agitation has already been referred to and can be found treated in detail in the article MARYLAND. It is the only instance in American history where the establishment of a fundamental constitutional principle can be credited directly to the specific labors of individual Jews.

There have been numerous instances in which Jews have come in conflict with the universal Sunday laws. In practically all cases the right of the state to enact Sunday laws as police regulations has

Sunday Laws.

been sustained. The statutory laws of New York and Indiana exempt one who observes some day of the week other than the first day and refrains from labor thereon, from suffering prosecution under the Sunday laws ("Publ. Am. Jew. Hist. Soc." No. 11, p. 101). In 1901 S. H. BOROFSKY, a member of the Massachusetts House of Representatives, introduced a bill exempting persons who observed the seventh day as Sabbath from any penalty for laboring on the first day. The bill passed the House, but was defeated in the Senate. That the Sunday laws in many cases inflict direct hardship upon large sections of the Jewish community can not be denied, and any interpretation of them except as police regulations would undoubtedly be construed as infringements upon the religious liberty of the individual. A solution of the difficulty might be found in the general adoption of the New York and Indiana statutes, but there is as yet no indication of any movement to bring this about. In cases where Jews are interested parties or witnesses, objection has at times been raised against going to trial or giving testimony on the seventh day of the week. Occasionally a postponement has been allowed or a witness excused, but the prevailing attitude of the courts has been that where duties to one's religion and to the state come in conflict the latter must prevail. The fact that there has been a general tendency on the part of even the higher courts to maintain that this is a Christian country, and that legislation which is in conflict with the doctrines of Christianity can not be allowed to prevail, has not failed to arouse decided opposition in many Jewish quarters.

9. Science, Art, Literature, and the Learned Professions: Jews have been members of all the learned professions—principally the legal and medical—and they have contributed notably to the advancement of nearly all the sciences and of the fine arts. Many eminent physicians, medical writers, and professors in medical schools are Jews. There has been at least one distinguished Hebrew sculptor, Moses Ezekiel, and there are several others of rank, among whom Ephraim Keyser and Katherine M. Cohen should be mentioned. Louis Loeb is one of the leading painters of the country, and has done illustrating of a high order; the Rosen-

Jews Eminent in All Departments.
thals of Philadelphia, father and son, are distinguished as etchers and engravers. Among other artists of note are Toby Rosenthal, L. Dessar, E. C. Peixotto, Henry Mosler, and Albert E. Sterner; Leo Mielziner is both sculptor and portrait-painter. As caricaturists Henry Meyer and F. Opper have made their mark. Bernard Berenson is one of the foremost living art-critics, and Charles Waldstein is one of the leading authorities on ancient art. Jews are also found as inventors, e.g., Emil Berliner, inventor of the telephone-transmitter, and Louis E. and Max Levy, inventors of photoengraving processes; as architects, such as Dankmar Adler of Chicago, and Arnold W. Brunner of New York; and as engineers, the most distinguished of whom is Mendes Cohen of Baltimore, one of the pioneer railroad-builders of the country, and at one time president of the American Society of Civil Engineers.

Many Jews hold professorships in colleges: M. Bloomfield and J. H. Hollander at Johns Hopkins; Franz Boas, Richard Gottheil, and E. R. A. Seligman at Columbia; Morris Loeb at the University of New York; Morris Jastrow (d. 1921) and Leo S. Rowe at the University of Pennsylvania; Joseph Jastrow at the University of Wisconsin; Charles Gross at Harvard; Ernst Freund at the University of Chicago; Jacques Loeb (d. 1924) at the University of California; Isador Loeb at the University of Missouri; while a much larger number are assistant professors or instructors. Simon Flexner is one of the leading pathologists, and is director of the Rockefeller Institute of Medical Research; and Franz Boas is eminent as an anthropologist.

The most distinguished Jewish writer of poetry in the United States was Emma Lazarus; Michael Heilprin gained eminence as an editor and writer, as have Louis Heilprin as an encyclopedist, Angelo Heilprin as a geologist, and Fabian Franklin as a mathematician; A. Cahan, Ezra S. Brudno, Annie Nathan Mayer, Mary Moss (d. 1914) and Emma Wolf are successful novelists; and Morris Rosenfeld is a gifted Yiddish poet. Martha Wolfenstein has written Jewish tales of rare literary charm.

Of Jewish periodicals and newspapers published in the United States the number has been legion (see Periodicals). The wide distribution of the Jewish community and the marked division into the Orthodox and Reform camps have rendered impossible the establishment of one central organ for the Jews of the country, as in England. Weekly newspapers, largely of local interest, though containing much readable material upon general Jewish

Newspapers.
affairs, and making some pretense to produce articles of literary quality, are published in all the large cities. The first Jewish periodical published in the United States was "The Jew," issued at New York in 1823-

1825; and unquestionably the most significant was the "Occident," published at Philadelphia by Isaac Leeser from 1843 to 69 (the last volume edited by Mayer Sulzberger).

Among the more important weeklies are "The American Israelite," Cincinnati, 1854; "The Jewish Messenger," New York, 1857–1902; "The Hebrew," San Francisco, 1863; "The American Hebrew," New York, 1879; "The Jewish Exponent," Philadelphia, 1887; "The Reform Advocate," Chicago, 1891; and "The Jewish Comment," Baltimore, 1895. At the present time three Jewish monthlies are issued: "The Menorah" (1886), organ of the B'nai B'rith and the Jewish Chautauqua; "The Maccabean" (1901), the Zionist organ; and "The New Era Literary Magazine" (1903); all published at New York. The United Hebrew Charities of New York also publishes a magazine, "Jewish Charity," devoted to sociological work, and there are numerous publications of a similar nature issued by other philanthropic organizations.

Several periodicals have been published in German, and, since the Russian immigration, a number in Hebrew. All of these have been organs representing specifically Jewish religious and literary interests. In this respect they have differed from the multitudinous issues of the Yiddish press which have seen the light since 1882, and which, though reflecting Jewish conditions, have in only a few instances had any religious cast; they have been more literary and scientific than religious.

In music the Jews have a reputable position; Fanny Bloomfield-Zeisler is one of the greatest of living pianists; Mischa Elman, Efrem Zimbalist, and Jascha Heifetz are among the noted violinists.

Music and the Stage.
Jews are prominent also as actors and as dramatic authors. Among actors may be mentioned Aaron J. Phillips, first appeared in New York at the Park Theater in 1815 as a successful comedian; Emanuel Judah, who first appeared in 1823; and Moses S. Phillips, who acted at the Park Theater in 1827. Mordecai M. Noah, best known as diplomat, was also a dramatic author of fame. Others were Samuel B. H. Judah (born in New York in 1790) and Jonas B. Phillips; and at the present time David Belasco is a most successful playwright. The control of theatrical productions in this country is mainly in the hands of the Jews at the present time. The introduction of opera into the United States was due largely to Lorenzo da Ponte. Alfred Hertz conducted at the Metropolitan Opera House, which was under the direction of Heinrich Conried.

10. Commerce and Industry: In commerce Jews were notably important in the eighteenth century. In the early colonial period, more especially in Pennsylvania and in New York, many of the Jews traded with the Indians. The fact that the earliest settlers were men of means, and were Spanish and Portuguese Jews who had relatives and friends settled throughout the Levant, gave them specially favorable opportunities for trading. Some were extensive ship-owners, as Aaron Lopez of Newport, who before the Revolutionary war had a fleet of thirty vessels; and David and Moses Franks of Philadelphia. Jews very early traded between the West India Islands and the North-American colonies, as well as with Amsterdam, Venice, etc.

The Jewish immigrants who arrived in America during the nineteenth century were in the main poor people who commenced trading in a small way, usually by peddling, which, before the existence of railroads, was a favorite method of carrying merchandise into the country districts. By industry and frugality they laid the foundations of a considerable number of moderate fortunes. The Jews of New York became an integral part of that great trading community.

The organization out of which grew the Stock Exchange of New York originated in an agreement in 1792 to buy and sell only on a definite commission; and to this document were attached the signatures of four Jews. Since then Jews have **Jews Act-** been very active in the Stock Ex- **ive in** change and in banking circles, both **Financial** in New York and elsewhere. The **Circles.** great-grandson of Haym Salomon, William, is a factor of consequence in New York financial circles. Jacob H. Schiff (d. 1920) and James Speyer are counted among the leading financiers of the country. The Jews have also taken an important part in controlling the cotton trade, and in large measure the clothing trade has been throughout its history in their hands (see below). They are likewise very prominent in the manufacture of cloaks and shirts, and more recently of cigars and jewelry.

11. Social Condition: The social organization of the Jews resident in America has differed little from that in other countries. In the early colonial period the wealthier Hebrews seem to have taken part with their Christian fellow citizens in the organization of dancing assemblies and other social functions, and clubs. Nevertheless, in the main, and without any compulsion, Jews preferred to live in close proximity to one another, a peculiarity which still prevails.

At the time when little toleration was shown in other countries, there were in America many interchanges of mutual good-will between Christians and Jews. Rabbi Ḥayyim Isaac Carregal was one of the close friends of Ezra Stiles, president of Yale College; and as early as 1711 the Jews of New York made a contribution of £3.12s. for the building of a steeple on Trinity Church. **Jews and** Gershom Mendes Seixas, minister of **Christians** the Shearith Israel congregation, New **Cooperate.** York, was a trustee of Columbia College (1784–1815), although this organization was under the Episcopal Church; and the Episcopal bishop of New York occasionally attended service in the synagogue. After 1848 there arrived a large number of Jews who could not speak the English language, and to them a certain odium attached on this account; but this seems gradually to have worn off. The general American public exhibited great sympathy for the Jews in 1840 at the time of the Damascus murders, in 1853-57 at the time of the Swiss troubles, and again in 1882, 1903, and 1905 on the occasion of the persecutions in Russia. Hermann Ahlwardt, on his visit to America in 1895,

found the soil an unfavorable one for his anti-Semitic propaganda, and when he projected it was protected from violence by Jewish policemen.

Though there is nothing corresponding to the anti-Semitic movements of continental Europe, an undoubted and extensive social prejudice against the Jews exists, which manifests itself in numerous petty though not insignificant ways, mainly in the Eastern States, where their numbers are greatest. It has assumed the form of excluding Jewish children from certain private schools, and their elders from clubs and some hotels.

Very early the Jews in America began to form social organizations. A club was started in Newport as early as 1769; and social clubs—some comprising many members and possessed **Hebrew** of magnificent properties—have been **Clubs.** established in many sections of the country. The development of Hebrew social clubs has been larger in the United States than elsewhere. American Jews have also been especially given to the forming of secret orders, which, while they had primarily an educational and charitable purpose, had much social influence, and tended powerfully toward the continued association of Jews with one another when the hold of the synagogue upon them relaxed. These were supplemented later by the formation of Young Men's Hebrew Associations, which, like the orders, partake to some extent of the nature of social organizations.

A.   H. F.

12. Russian Immigration: Individual Russian and Polish Jews, especially the latter, emigrated to the United States at the time of the American Revolution, among whom was Haym Salomon, one of the noblest examples of devotion to American liberty and a friend of Kosciusko. The Russian ukase of 1827 drafting Jewish boys at the age of twelve to military service (see JEW. ENCYC. iii. 549b, *s.v.* CANTONISTS), and that of 1845 extending the conscription to Russian Poland were the starting-points of emigration to England and thence to America. The epoch-making period of 1848 and the revolt in Poland in 1863 were factors in increasing the emigration of Jews from Russia. But the Russo-Jewish emigration en masse did not begin till 1881. Prior to that date it had been restricted almost entirely to the provinces lying about the Niemen and the Düna, and the emigrants were voluntary ones who desired to better their economic condition and to tempt fortune elsewhere.

With the anti-Jewish riots of April 27, 1881, at Yelizavetgrad, and the later riots in Kiev and other cities of South Russia, Jewish emigra- **Emigra-** tion to the United States assumed an **tion.** entirely different character, and received an impetus so remarkable as to create a new epoch in American Jewish history. The first group of the new class of immigrants, consisting of about 250 members of the Am 'Olam Society ("Eternal People"), arrived in New York city July 29, 1881; the third and last group of the same society arrived May 30, 1882, and was followed by streams of Russo-Jewish refugees. The immigration largely increased from 1892, and still more from 1901 (see MIGRATION).

The forced emigration of the Russian Jews owing to their persecution by the Russian government evoked loud protests from prominent men in the United States, and much sympathy was expressed for the refugees. The most important meeting, convened by ex-President U. S. Grant and seventy others, was held Feb. 1, 1882, at Chickering Hall, New York, and was presided over by the mayor, William R. Grace. In Philadelphia a similar meeting was held a fortnight later (Feb. 15) under the presidency of Mayor Samuel King; and through the efforts of Drexel, the banker, a fund of $25,000 for the relief of the refugees was collected. Indeed, funds in aid of the Russian Jews were raised in all the principal cities of America. The Hebrew Immigrants Aid Society of the United States collected in 1882 about $300,000, of which the Alliance Israélite Universelle of Paris contributed $40,000, the General Committee of Paris $20,000, the Berlin Committee $35,000, the Mansion House Committee of London $40,000, and the New York Russian Relief Fund (Jacob H. Schiff, treasurer) $57,000. Altogether the last-named fund amounted to about $70,000. In 1883 about $60,000 more was collected, for the immediate relief of the Russian immigrants, and temporary quarters were built on Ward's Island and at Greenpoint, L. I. About 3,000 immigrants were temporarily housed and maintained there until they found employment.

Michael HEILPRIN induced the various committees to colonize the immigrants; but nearly all such undertakings proved unsuccessful. The Jewish Agricultural and Industrial Aid Society, however, reports for 1904 some improvement in this respect ("American Hebrew," March 17, 1905; see also JEW. ENCYC. i. 256 et seq., s.v. AGRICULTUR-

Agricultural Colonies. AL COLONIES IN THE UNITED STATES). This society is endeavoring to extend its work by starting small agricultural settlements at different points. Many farms in Connecticut and Massachusetts have passed into Jewish hands, and the number of Jewish farmers in the United States is now estimated at 12,000. Altogether the various committees and societies assisted probably 5 per cent of the total Jewish immigrants. Of the remainder, some were dependent on relatives and friends; but a great majority, independent of any assistance, worked out their own destiny as did their countrymen who preceded them.

The Hebrew Immigrants Aid Society of New York helps to find the relatives and friends of Jewish immigrants, and pleads for the discharge of detained immigrants. The society engages lawyers to defend cases of deportation. From Sept. 1, 1902, to Aug. 1, 1904, it appealed 217 cases, 128 of which were sustained and 89 dismissed. The cost of the appeals amounted to $1,305.78. The total income of the society for that period was $6,029.29.

The Jewish pioneers from Russia and Poland became glaziers, cigar-makers, pedlers, **Development of Industry.** small shopkeepers, and proprietors of supply stores for pedlers. In the fifties there were about a dozen Russian Jews in New York engaged in various trades, as tobacco, jewelry, passementerie, millinery, hats and caps, and general dry-goods. During

the sixties there were Russo-Jewish manufacturers of hoop-skirts, cloaks, and clothing. A few Russian Jews were among the California pioneers, and achieved their successes not as miners, but as merchants. Others drifted to the South, especially to Charleston and New Orleans, where they prospered as business men, cotton-planters, and even as slave-owners. Some became importers and exporters of merchandise. Abraham Raffel, a native of Suwalki, exported agricultural machinery and windmills to Moscow in 1862. Moses Gardner, a native of Sherki (b. 1815; d. 1903 in New York), imported linen crashes and furs from Russia, making annual trips to St. Petersburg, Moscow, and Nijni-Novgorod for that purpose. Solomon Silberstein, a native of Grodno, arrived in New York in 1849, went to California in 1850, and prior to 1867 was engaged in the

Name of Union.	Total Membership.	Russian Jews.	Approximate Percentage of Russian Jews.
Amalgamated Waiters' Union, No. 1, of N. Y.	200	50	25
Bakers' Union (Brooklyn and Harlem).	500	200	40
Bill-Posters' and Ushers' Union	50	45	90
Boys' Waist Makers' Union	200	60	30
Brotherhood of Tailors, U. G. W. of A.			
Pants Makers' Union, U. G. W. of A.			
Vest Makers' Union			
Knee-Pants Makers' Union, U. G.W. of A.			
Sailor Jacket Makers' Union, U. G. W. of A.	10,000	9,000	90
Children's Jacket Makers' Union, U. G. W. of A.			
Washable Stuff Sailor Suit Makers' Union.			
Second-Hand Clothing Tailors' Union			
Choristers' Union	50	25	50
Cigarette Makers' Union, Flat			
Cigarette Makers' Union, Paper	500	475	95
Cigarette Makers' Union, Progressive Rolled (60 per cent girls)			
Clipping Sorters' Union (girls)	300	150	50
Cloak and Suit Tailors' Union	6,000	3,000	50
Cutters' Union	*		
East Side Barbers' Union	*		
Hebrew Actors' Protective Union	70	35	50
Infant Shoemakers' Union	*		
Knitters' Union, New York	200	170	85
"　　"　Brooklyn			
Ladies' Waist Makers' Union	500	475	95
Ladies' Wrapper Makers' Union	300	270	90
Mineral-Water Bottlers' and Drivers' Union.	*		
Mattress Makers' Union	250	125	50
Paper Box Makers' Union	500	375	75
Purse and Bag Makers' Union	300	255	85
Shirt Makers' Union	300	270	90
Suspender Makers, L. 9560 A. F. of L.	500	400	80
"　Trimming Operators' Union			
Theatrical Musical Union (about 1,000 Jews)	*		
Trunk Makers' Union	*		
Typographical Union	150	112	75
Variety Actors' Union	100	90	90
Totals	20,970	15,582	

* Joined non-Jewish unions.

importation of furs from Alaska, then a Russian possession. Silberstein even ventured across Bering Strait to Kamchatka and Vladivostok to import merchandise to California. His business increased to such an extent that he chartered a special vessel to transport his goods; and it may be added that he gave orders to the captain not to begin the voyage on a Sabbath-day. Russian Jews were largely interested in the Alaskan Fur Company.

Reuben Isaacs, a native of Suwalki, arrived in New York in 1849 and went to California in 1850. From 1868 he was engaged with his brother Israel in the exportation of kerosene oil to Japan. Later, under the firm name "R. Isaacs & Bro.," they opened a branch at Yokohama and Kobé, Japan, and, as "The American Commercial Co.," they established another at Manila, Philippine Islands. In 1905 there were several American-Russian Jews doing business with Japan.

Up to the eighties the Russian Jews were principally pedlers, shopkeepers, and manufacturers, but with the Jewish persecution in Russia many skilled

Penal Institutions.	Total Prisoners.	Total Jews.	Russian and Polish Jews.
Albany Penitentiary............	700	4	1
Auburn "	1,100	36	8
Blackwells Island Almshouse...	2,170	7	3
Blackwells Island Workhouse...	1,100	11	..
Clinton Prison	900	25	13
Elmira Reformatory............	1,450	99	18
Kings County Prison..........	800	3	3
Sing Sing Prison..............	1,600	72	26
Totals....................	9,820	257	72

Dr. Radin gives the following figures for the New York city prisons for the years 1902, 1903, and 1904:

Penal Institutions.	1902.			1903.			1904.		
	Total Prisoners.	Total Jews.	Russian Jews.	Total Prisoners.	Total Jews.	Russian Jews.	Total Prisoners.	Total Jews.	Russian Jews.
Blackwells Island Workhouse......	1,930	55	......	1,800	48				
[Blackwells Island Workhouse during the year]....................	[17,745]	[465]	......	[19,963]	[767]	......	[19,520]	[1,036]	about 600
Brooklyn Disciplinary Training School................	225	19	......	240–250	16–20		275	21	3
City Penitentiary..................	630	47	about 2/3	580–620	45–50	about 2/3	746	52	22
House of Refuge..................	850–900	227	......	850–950	210–250	......	850	253	92
Tombs............................	430–450	30–35	......	450–500	30–40	......	1,380	153	60

laborers were forced to emigrate to America. These were later organized into various unions; and many affiliated with the **United Hebrew Trades** of the state of New York, organized in 1889 by Morris Hillquit and Joseph Barondess. The skilled Jewish laborers in New York city in 1905 numbered over 75,000, of whom two-thirds were Russian Jews. The United Hebrew Trades represented about 25,000, but in times of strikes they increased to 50,000. Abraham Lippman, secretary of the United Hebrew Trades, has furnished the table given on page 368, showing the various unions, their average memberships, and the number of Russo-Jewish members in Jan., 1905.

Russo-Jewish skilled laborers are found elsewhere than in New York. In the silk-factories of New Jersey, in the machine-shops of Connecticut, and in the jewelry-factories of Rhode Island they are to be seen side by side with the best non-Jewish working men

Russian Jews have also helped to develop the real-estate market in the principal centers of the United States. In the city of New York they are among the largest operators; and they have built up Brownsville, a suburb of Brooklyn, and a considerable part of the Bronx on the Harlem River. Russo-Jewish activity in every line of industry extends to all cities of the Union, but more particularly to New York, Philadelphia, Baltimore, Boston, Chicago, Pittsburg, and St. Louis.

Criminal statistics show a low percentage of crime among the Russian Jews as compared with the general population. The report of Dr. A. M. Radin, visiting chaplain of New York state prisons, for the year 1903 presents the following details concerning the Jewish prisoners:

The large percentage of Jewish boys in the House of Refuge on Randalls Island is accounted for by the existence of special sectarian protectories, which care for a large number of boys, while the Jews have no separate house of refuge. These statistics, from the densest and most crowded Jewish population in the Union, are the best evidence of the moral and law-abiding character of the Jews in general and of the Russo-Jewish immigrants in particular. Where the Jews are not so thickly congregated few if any are to be found in the prisons: in each of three of the penal institutions of the upper part of the state of New York, namely, the Syracuse Penitentiary, the Monroe County Penitentiary at Rochester, and the Erie County Penitentiary at Buffalo, there was in 1903 only one Jew.

The Russian Jews, even those who have neglected or have had no opportunity to study in Russia, learn the English language as soon as they **Education.** arrive in America; and some study the higher branches of English literature. Their children almost without exception attend the public schools; and many avail themselves of the education afforded in the high schools, the City College, and the Normal College, as well as the universities. More than 60 per cent of the students in these colleges are Russo-Jewish immigrants or the children of Russian Jews. The majority of the parents are poor; but they pinch themselves to keep their children in college rather than let them contribute to the support of the family.

Among the Russian Jews in New York city there were in 1905 about 400 physicians, 1,000 druggists, 300 dentists, 400 lawyers, and 25 architects, besides many in other professions, particularly musicians and composers of popular music. Biographies of the more prominent professional men will be found in the "American Jewish Year Book for 5665." Also many Russian Jews are clerks in the city departmental offices; and a large number are teachers in the public schools.

Since about 1885 the Russian Jews in America have created an amount of literature in Yiddish exceeding the productions of the same kind that have been published in Russia and elsewhere during the same period (see L. Wiener, "A History of Yiddish Literature in the Nineteenth Century," New York, 1899). Six daily Yiddish newspapers were printed in the city of New York (circulation exceeding 100,000 copies), which informed the Jewish immigrants of the general topics of the day and served by their advertisements as aids in securing employment. They served also to help the immigrants in the

Yiddish Press. reading of newspapers in English. There were, besides, the Hebrew weekly "Ha-Leom" and other Yiddish and Hebrew periodicals. The Yiddish and Hebrew press is almost exclusively in the hands of Russian Jews, who are well represented also among the reporters and journalists of the secular press (see Drachman, "Neo-Hebraic Literature in America," in "Seventh Report of Jewish Theological Seminary Association," New York, 1900).

Russo-Jewish educational work in the city of New York is conducted by **The Educational Alliance,** of which David BLAUSTEIN was superintendent and Adolph M. Radin and Harris Masliansky were lecturers. Others held special classes in various branches of science and literature. Russian Jews are devoted frequenters of the public libraries, reading the best selected literature and but little fiction. Their principal literary societies are the OHOLE SHEM ASSOCIATION and Mefize Sefat Eber. Among earlier literary societies were Doreshe Sefat Eber, founded in 1880 (issued "Ha-Me'assef," No. i., 1881); the Hebrew Literary Society of Chicago (issued "Keren Or," 2 Nos., Chicago, 1889); Mefize Sifrut Yisrael be-Amerika (issued "Ner ha-Ma'arabi," New York, 1895-97); and the Russian American Hebrew Association, organized by Dr. A. Radin in 1890.

The first Russo-Jewish congregation, the Beth Hamidrash Hagodal, was organized in New York in 1852. There are now more than 300 large and small congregations and hebras; also orders, lodges, and benevolent and charitable societies and institutions, foremost among which are the Beth Israel Hospital and the Gemiluth Ḥasadim Association. With regard to the synagogues it should be noted that the Russian Jew does not adopt Reform customs, but is strictly Orthodox. Short biographical sketches of their rabbis and cantors will be found in the "American Jewish Year Book for 5664."

The Russian Jew is quickly adapting himself to American life. According to Dr. M. Fishberg, Russo-Jewish immigrants improve in stature, chest-development, and muscular strength after their arrival. Their descendants, he says, are improving physically, morally, and intellectually under the favorable influence of American conditions. When called upon the Russian Jews in America do not

hesitate to fight for the country which has given them freedom. During the war with Spain and also in the World War, 1914-18, the number of Russian Jews who enrolled as volunteers in the United States army was greater in proportion to their population than that of other foreigners. The regular army also has a goodly number of Russian Jews in its ranks; and their bravery, energy, and power of endurance have frequently been praised by their officers.

See also AGRICULTURAL COLONIES IN THE UNITED STATES; DRAMA, YIDDISH; MIGRATION; NEW YORK; RUSSIA, EMIGRATION (where statistics are given).

BIBLIOGRAPHY: History and Data: G. M. Price, *Russki Yevrei v Amerikye* (a review of events from 1881 to 1891), St. Petersburg, 1893; Edward A. Steiner, in *The Outlook* (Sept. and Dec., 1902), lxxii. 528; Eisenstein, in *Publ. Am. Jew. Hist. Soc.* No. 9; Maurice Fishberg, in *American Monthly Review of Reviews* (1902), xxvi. 315; A. Cahan, in *Atlantic Monthly* (July and Dec., 1898), lxxx.

Immigration: A. J. L. Hurwitz, *Rumania wa-Amerika*, p. 47, Berlin, 1874; *Reports of Hebrew Emigrant Aid Society*, New York, 1882 and 1883; B. F. Peixotto, *What Shall We Do with Our Immigration?* New York, 1887; H. S. Morais, *The Jews of Philadelphia*, pp. 206-208, Philadelphia, 1894; Eisenstein, in *Ha-Modia' le Hadashim*, pp. 21-229, New York, 1901; L. E. Levy, *Russian Jewish Refugees in America*, Philadelphia, 1895 (reprint from Simon Wolf, *The American Jew as Patriot, Soldier, and Citizen*, pp. 544-564).

Colonization: Menken, *Report on the First Russian Jewish Colony in the United States*, New York, 1882 (published by the Hebrew Emigrant Aid Society); Goldman, *Colmization of Russian Refugees in the West*, 1882 (published by the same society); *Inaugural Report of Jewish Alliance of America*, Philadelphia, 1891; William Stainsby, *The Jewish Colonies of South Jersey*, Camden, N. J., 1901; *The American Hebrew*, April 10, 1903, and March 17, 1905 (on the work of the Removal Office); *The Reform Advocate*, March 21 and April 4, 1903.

Sanitation: Maurice Fishberg, *Health and Sanitation of the Immigrant Jewish Population of New York*, 1893 (reprint from *Menorah*, Aug. and Sept., 1902).

Criminality: Adolph M. Radin, *Report of Visiting Chaplain*, 1893; idem, *Asire oni u-Barzel* (in Hebrew and Judæo-German), New York, 1893; Israel Davidson, in *Jewish Charity*, Nov., 1903, and Jan., 1904.

Descriptive: Eisenstein, in *Ha-Asif* (1886), ii. 214-219; M. Weinberger, *Ha-Yehudim weha-Yehadut be-Newyork*, New York, 1887; Adolphe Danziger . . . . *New York Ghetto*, in *Jew. Chron.* Aug. 9, 23, 30, and Sept. 6, 1901; A. H. Ford, in *Pearson's Magazine*, Sept., 1903; H. Hapgood, *The Spirit of the Ghetto*, New York, 1902; Ezra S. Brudno, in *The World's Work*, vii. 4471, 4555; M. J. McKenna, *Our Brethren of the Tenement and the Ghetto*, New York, 1899; Katherine Kaufman, *In the New York Ghetto*, in *Munsey's Magazine* (1900), xxiii. 608-619; S. Rubinow, *Economic Conditions of the Russian Jews in New York*, in *Voskhod*, 1905, No. 1, xxv. 121-146 (Russian); A. Tiraspolski, *Jewish Immigrants in the United States*, in *Voskhod*, ib. No. 2, pp. 86-98; M. Z. Raisin, in *Ha-Shiloah*, vols. iv., v., vi., vii.

Fiction: N. Bernstein, *In the Gates of Israel*, New York, 1902; Abraham Cahan, *The Imported Bridegroom, and Other Stories of the New York Ghetto*, Boston and New York, 1898; idem, *Yekl, a Tale of the New York Ghetto*, 1899; Bruno Lessing, *Children of Men*, New York, 1903; Ezra S. Brudno, *The Fugitive*, New York, 1904.

H. R.   J. D. E.

13. Statistics: The growth of the Jewish population in the United States during the nineteenth century has been quite extraordinary. At the beginning of the century it probably did not number more than 2,000 (800 in Charleston, 500 in New York, 150 in Philadelphia, and the remainder scattered throughout the rest of the original states). The population received accretions, mainly from England and Germany, up to 1848, when the number had increased to 50,000. Then from the Teutonic lands there occurred a great immigration due to the failure of the Revolution of 1848, and up to 1881 the immigrants probably numbered over 100,000; then the population was estimated at 230,257. During the forty-one years 1881-1922 very nearly 2,208,816 Jewish immigrants reached the United States, as follows:

Years.	New York.	Philadelphia.	Baltimore.	Totals.
1881–84......	....	....	....	62,022
1885–98......	404,101	36,390	18,677	459,168
1899........	29,088	1,649	1,463	32,200
1900........	53,687	3,870	2,439	59,996
1901........	37,952	2,253	1,343	41,548
1902........	54,594	2,475	1,566	58,635
1903........	60,815	3,357	2,993	67,165
1904........	89,442	5,310	6,606	101,358
1905........	100,338	9,392	5,086	114,816
1906–22.....	....	....	....	1,211,808
Totals....	830,017	64,696	40,173	2,208,716

Against the extraordinary immigration must be counted a certain amount of emigration, including about one per cent who are deported, and a large number of Russian Jews who suffer from nostalgia ("American Hebrew," May 15, 1904), but no complete figures are ascertainable with regard to the numbers thus returning. On the other hand, a considerable number of Jews, especially from England and Germany, travel above the steerage class; and the statistics above given do not include persons who went through Canada. Allowing for the natural increase, the Jewish population at present is 3,600,350. The original 250,000 who were in the United States in 1877 would by natural increase have reached 400,000 by this time, and the 1,000,000 immigrants that have poured in since then must have increased at least 200,000 if they are reckoned on a mean population of 400,000 immigrants during the last twenty-five years. The movement of population within the thirty years, 1877–1905, may be estimated as follows:

	Native (1877).	Immigrant (1881–1905).	Totals.
Numbers enumerated....	250,000	1,000,000	1,250,000
Deaths..................	100,000	150,000	250,000
Births..................	250,000	350,000	600,000
Increase	150,000	200,000	350,000
Total..................	400,000	1,200,000	1,600,000
Born in America.........	350,000	300,000	650,000

The above is quite a conservative estimate. For example, the increase on the immigration reckoned at 1.02 per annum upon a mean population of 400,000 would by geometrical progression for twenty-five years reach 1.66 (= 1.02 raised to the 25th power). This would imply an increase of 266,000 rather than 200,000. Similarly, applying an increase rate of 1.02 to the 250,000 original inhabitants of 1877, it would increase to 1.78 (1.02 to the 28th power) during the twenty-eight intervening years, and would show an increase in numbers of nearly 200,000 instead of the 150,000 estimated. If these figures were adopted, the total number for the United States in the year 1905 would be 1,700,000, of whom 750,000 would have been born in the country.

The Jews are spread unequally throughout the United States. On the whole, their relative density of population corresponds to that of the population in general except as regards the North Atlantic States. A large proportion of them have landed on the Atlantic coast, and have for various reasons remained in the Eastern States. It is, however, a mistake to think that all immigrants remain in the cities at which they land.

Distribution. Apart from the exertions of institutions like the Agricultural Aid and Removal Society, many immigrants of their own accord move inland. It is on record, for example, that of the 830,017 who reached New York during the years 1885–1905, 227,523 left the city during the year in which they arrived. The following table represents the distribution of Jews according to states, with towns of 100 or more Jews in each state, the population, so far as can be ascertained, according to the estimate of 1877 and that made in 1905 and 1920 for the various states considered in this work. All are estimates, and are therefore likely to be somewhat above the reality, but each is incomplete, and it is probable that the incompleteness counterbalances the overestimation. In a few instances names of towns and agricultural colonies in which Jews settled but no longer reside are given in parentheses:

	1877.	1905.	1920.
Alabama	2,045	7,000	11,050
Anniston	....	100	220
Bessemer	....	100	110
Birmingham	20	1,400	3,500
Claiborne	....	....	....
Demopolis	....	124	107
Eufaula	....	56	110
Mobile	36	....	2,200
Montgomery	600	1,000	1,650
Selma	200	250	340
Alaska	....	....	500
Arizona	48	....	1,050
Douglas	....	....	100
Phoenix	....	....	150
Arkansas	1,466	3,085	5,150
Fort Smith...........	66	179	300
Helena	180	120	250
Hot Spring...........	....	150	309
Jonesboro	....	125	100
Little Rock..........	....	1,000	1,500
Pine Bluff...........	250	425	400
Texarkana	44	175	200
California	18,580	28,000	71,400
Berkeley	....	....	300
Fresno	....	....	400
Los Angeles..........	....	2,000	18,000
Oakland	43	....	5,000
Pasadena	227	....	350
Sacramento	....	450	900
San Bernardino	133	50	250
San Diego	....	110	600
San Francisco	16,000	17,000	30,000
San Jose	265	350	200
Stockton	200	325	1,000
Colorado	422	5,800	15,380
Boulder	....	....	100
Colorado Springs.....	....	75	660
Cripple Creek........	....	150	....
Denver	260	4,000	11,000
Pueblo	....	300	1,000
Trinidad	....	150	250
Connecticut	1,492	8,500	71,870
Ansonia	....	320	150
Bridgeport	....	....	12,000
Colchester	....	200	480
Danbury	....	....	300
Derby	....	....	250
Hartford	....	2,000	16,000
Meriden	....	....	1,000
Middletown	....	....	128
New Britain	....	200	2,500
New Haven	1,000	5,500	18,000
New London	....	400	1,000
Norwich	....	125	1,500

	1877.	1905.	1920.		1877.	1905.	1920.
South Norwalk	....	....	100	**Kentucky**	3,602	12,000	13,620
Stamford	....	....	1,500	Covington	....	....	350
Torrington	....	....	168	Henderson	....	189	275
Wallingford	....	....	200	Lexington	....	125	385
Waterbury	68	400	6,000	Louisville	2,500	7,000	9,000
Willimantic	....	....	250	Newport	....	....	300
				Owensboro	213	155	230
Delaware	585	1,500	4,010	Paducah	203	234	250
Wilmington	85	1,109	3,500				
				Louisiana	7,538	12,000	13,020
Dist. of Columbia	1,508	3,500	10,950	Alexandria	206	600	450
Washington	1,375	....	10,000	Baton Rouge	94	....	165
				Donaldsonville	179	....	100
Florida	772	3,000	6,940	Lake Charles	....	....	286
Jacksonville	130	312	2,000	Monroe	128	200	350
Key West	50	158	200	Morgan City	....	35	220
Miami	....	....	175	New Iberia	....	....	105
Pensacola	60	250	1,000	New Orleans	5,000	5,000	8,000
Tampa	30	200	1,000	Shreveport	900	700	1,500
Georgia	2,704	7,000	23,240	**Maine**	500	5,000	7,590
Albany	100	200	265	Auburn	....	100	300
Athens	110	120	340	Bangor	....	215	1,000
Atlanta	525	2,000	10,000	Bath	....	....	93
Augusta	....	125	2,500	Lewiston	85	100	275
Brunswick	....	200	138	Old Town	....	....	194
Columbus	275	335	300	Portland	....	....	2,500
Macon	350	500	550	Rockland	....	....	150
Rome	46	100	250				
Savannah	603	1,500	5,000	**Maryland**	10,337	26,500	65,330
				Annapolis	....	....	240
Idaho	85	300	1,160	Baltimore	10,000	25,000	60,000
Boise	....	102	200	Cumberland	140	165	600
				Frederick	....	....	144
Illinois	12,625	100,000	257,600	Hagerstown	42	209	250
Aurora	....	....	300				
Bloomington	115	141	275	**Massachusetts**	8,500	60,000	199,300
Cairo	57	....	375	Attleboro	....	....	530
Chicago	10,000	80,000	225,000	Beverly	....	....	550
Danville	....	....	625	Boston	7,000	45,000	77,500
Decatur	....	....	200	Brockton	....	300	1,500
East St. Louis	....	....	1,000	Cambridge	....	....	8,000
Elgin	....	....	500	Chelsea	....	2,000	13,000
Joliet	....	100	1,100	Clinton	....	....	185
Maywood	....	....	700	Everett	....	....	500
Moline	13	24	....	Fall River	....	1,500	7,500
Peoria	400	2,000	1,750	Fitchburg	....	....	528
Pontiac	27	40	....	Gardner	....	....	146
Quincy	500	126	400	Gloucester	....	....	243
Rockford	....	....	900	Haverhill	....	200	3,500
Rock Island	....	200	412	Holyoke	....	350	1,000
Springfield	150	350	700	Lawrence	....	600	2,000
Waukegan	....	....	400	Leominster	....	....	210
				Lexington	....	....	540
Indiana	3,381	25,000	26,780	Lowell	....	800	6,000
Evansville	375	800	1,500	Lynn	....	....	7,500
Fort Wayne	275	500	1,650	Malden	....	600	9,000
Gary	....	....	1,200	Medway	....	....	250
Hammond	....	....	600	Melrose	....	....	200
Indianapolis	....	2,300	10,000	New Bedford	....	1,000	3,500
Indiana Harbor	....	....	650	Newton	....	....	400
Kokomo	....	51	130	North Adams	....	....	500
Lafayette	225	200	300	Northampton	....	....	400
Ligonier	....	151	100	Peabody	....	....	750
Logansport	66	87	190	Pittsfield	....	350	1,500
Marion	....	100	400	Plymouth	....	....	510
Michigan City	....	....	450	Quincy	....	....	1,250
Muncie	....	132	200	Revere	....	300	6,000
Peru	65	73	100	Salem	....	300	1,500
South Bend	....	....	2,000	Somerville	....	....	2,000
Terre Haute	100	....	500	South Framingham	....	....	500
Wabash	....	147	150	Springfield	....	300	6,000
				Taunton	....	....	750
Iowa	1,245	5,000	16,230	Waltham	....	....	300
Burlington	121	100	225	Winthrop	....	....	1,500
Cedar Rapids	....	....	700	Worcester	....	1,000	10,000
Council Bluffs	....	....	1,000				
Davenport	204	204	600	**Michigan**	3,233	16,000	71,360
Des Moines	260	500	3,200	Ann Arbor	....	....	300
Dubuque	55	400	450	Bay City	153	....	1,000
Fort Dodge	....	....	155	Benton Harbor	....	....	580
Keokuk	152	66	143	Calumet	....	....	110
Mason City	....	....	260	Crystal Falls	....	....	165
Muscatine	....	....	429	Detroit	2,000	8,000	50,000
Ottumwa	....	....	412	Flint	....	....	385
Sioux City	48	420	2,500	Grand Rapids	201	....	1,000
Waterloo	....	....	325	Houghton	....	....	165
				Iron River	....	....	100
Kansas	819	3,000	9,590	Jackson	141	....	300
Hutchinson	....	....	200	Kalamazoo	217	275	900
Kansas City	....	....	3,500	Lansing	....	....	450
Leavenworth	455	....	600	Muskegon	....	....	300
Topeka	....	117	1,000	Port Huron	....	60	500
Wichita	....	....	300	Saginaw	52	....	1,000
				Sault Ste. Marie	....	....	206

	1877.	1905.	1920.
Minnesota	**414**	**13,000**	**33,550**
Duluth		1,000	2,300
Eveleth			110
Hibbing			165
Mankato			115
Minneapolis	172	5,000	15,000
St. Paul	225	3,500	10,000
Virginia			250
Mississippi	**2,262**	**3,000**	**3,990**
Clarksdale			220
Greenville			350
Hattiesburg			125
Jackson	88	100	126
Meridian	160	338	400
Natchez	220	450	261
Vicksburg	520	659	532
Missouri	**7,380**	**50,000**	**82,570**
Columbia			175
Jefferson City			155
Joplin			250
Kansas City	240	5,500	12,000
St. Joseph	325	1,200	3,300
St. Louis	6,200	40,000	60,000
Sedalia			178
Springfield			165
Montana	**131**	**2,500**	**2,520**
Billings			260
Butte		250	1,000
Helena	112		347
Nebraska	**222**	**3,800**	**14,020**
Fremont			100
Lincoln		225	1,200
Omaha	66	3,300	10,000
Nevada	**780**	**300**	**510**
New Hampshire	**150**	**1,000**	**3,370**
Berlin			117
Concord			158
Manchester			600
Nashua		160	350
Portsmouth	29	400	550
New Jersey	**5,593**	**40,000**	**163,180**
Alliance		512	
Asbury Park			1,250
Atlantic City		800	4,000
Bayonne		1,200	10,000
Bloomfield			1,000
Camden	29	500	2,000
Carmel		471	450
Carteret			150
Dover			300
Elizabeth		1,200	5,000
Englewood			100
Hackensack			200
Harrison			1,000
Hoboken	600	1,000	5,000
Jersey City	450	6,000	12,500
Keyport			166
Lakewood			375
Long Branch	35		1,300
Millville			170
Morristown			140
Newark	3,500	20,000	55,000
New Brunswick	173	400	3,000
Norma			100
Orange			210
Passaic	37	2,000	6,000
Paterson	427	6,000	15,000
Perth Amboy			5,000
Plainfield		200	1,500
Red Bank			500
Rosenhayn		294	300
Somerville			250
Trenton	50	1,500	7,000
Union Hill			400
Weehawken			134
West Hoboken			350
West New York			1,500
Woodbine		2,000	1,900
New Mexico	**180**	**800**	**880**
Albuquerque		165	220
New York	**80,565**	**820,000**	**1,701,260**
Albany	2,000	4,000	7,000
Amsterdam		250	300
Auburn			250

	1877.	1905.	1920.
Batavia			141
Binghamton		250	1,500
Buffalo	775	7,000	20,000
Cohoes			200
Dunkirk			164
Ellenville			330
Elmira	300	1,500	1,200
Glen Cove			281
Glens Falls	27		500
Gloversville			650
Haverstraw			220
Hudson			450
Hunter			200
Ithaca	55	100	221
Jamestown			125
Kingston	68	600	800
Lindenhurst			200
Middletown			153
Mt. Vernon			3,000
Newburgh	158	500	400
New Rochelle			3,000
New York, (Greater).			1,500,000
Niagara Falls			300
Olean			150
Ossining			114
Parksville			425
Patchogue			500
Peekskill			500
Plattsburg			205
Port Chester		300	1,000
Port Jervis			150
Poughkeepsie		75	1,600
Rochester	1,175	5,000	20,000
Rome			250
Schenectady		550	3,500
Syracuse		5,000	12,000
Tarrytown			400
Troy	500	3,000	3,000
Tupper Lake			150
Utica			1,600
Watertown			230
White Plains			400
Yonkers			5,000
North Carolina	**820**	**6,000**	**5,140**
Asheville		100	250
Charlotte			350
Durham			500
Goldsboro	147	125	165
Greensboro			187
Raleigh	78	28	120
Wilmington	200	1,500	400
Winston-Salem			116
North Dakota	**9**		**1,590**
Fargo			600
Grand Forks			126
Ohio	**14,581**	**50,000**	**177,690**
Akron		1,000	2,000
Alliance			100
Bellaire	64	140	440
Canton	96	600	1,000
Cincinnati	8,000	17,500	25,000
Cleveland	3,500	25,000	100,000
Columbus	420	1,500	9,000
Dayton	500	1,200	4,000
East Liverpool			300
Elyria			148
Hamilton	110		260
Lancaster			107
Lima		143	300
Lorain			300
Marion		60	100
Massillon			138
Middletown			225
Portsmouth	84	96	128
Sandusky			143
Springfield	148	300	400
Steubenville			400
Toledo	350		7,500
Youngstown	140		5,000
Zanesville			250
Oklahoma			**5,490**
Ardmore			150
Chickasha			125
Muskogee			225
Oklahoma City		70	1,000
Tulsa			500
Oregon	**868**	**6,000**	**18,260**
Portland	525	4,000	8,000

	1877.	1905.	1920.
Pennsylvania	18,097?	115,000	340,740
Aliquippa	....	....	300
Allentown	....	....	1,200
Altoona	....	1,200	1,000
Beaver Falls	....	....	121
Braddock	....	350	1,600
Bradford	....	....	560
Butler	....	....	150
California	....	....	117
Carbondale	....	....	1,000
Carnegie	....	....	320
Chester	....	....	1,000
Coatesville	....	....	300
Connellsville	....	....	383
Danville	....	....	104
Dickson City	....	....	174
Dubois	....	....	186
Dunmore	....	....	109
Duquesne	....	....	350
Easton	255	....	800
Erie	....	....	1,500
Exeter Boro	....	....	198
Farrell	....	....	550
Glassport	....	....	120
Greensburg	....	....	130
Harrisburg	158	550	4,000
Hazleton	....	....	950
Homestead	....	....	650
Johnstown	....	100	400
Kittanning	....	....	145
Lancaster	115	1,000	1,400
Lebanon	....	....	100
McKeesport	....	....	3,000
Mahonoy City	....	....	244
Mt. Carmel	....	....	550
Nanticoke	....	....	150
New Castle	....	....	610
New Kensington	....	....	375
Norristown	....	....	220
Oil City	....	....	380
Old Forge	....	....	263
Olyphant	....	....	280
Philadelphia	12,000	75,000	200,000
Phoenixville	....	....	220
Pittsburgh	2,000	15,000	60,000
Pittston	....	....	320
Pottstown	....	....	328
Pottsville	....	....	400
Punxsutawney	....	....	275
Reading	142	800	1,750
Scranton	245	5,000	7,500
Shamokin	....	....	235
Sharon	....	....	500
Shenandoah	....	....	550
South Bethlehem	....	....	1,300
Steelton	....	....	250
Sunbury	....	....	150
Titusville	....	....	205
Uniontown	....	....	600
Washington	....	....	400
Wilkes-Barre	250	1,800	3,000
Williamsport	....	215	350
York	....	....	700
Rhode Island	1,000	1,500	21,450
Bristol	....	....	300
Central Falls	....	....	250
Newport	....	200	500
Pawtucket	....	200	500
Providence	....	....	15,000
Westerley	....	....	212
Woonsocket	....	175	900
South Carolina	1,415	2,500	5,060
Charleston	700	800	1,900
Columbia	57	....	281
Spartanburg	....	....	120
Sumter	89	175	300
South Dakota	10	250	1,310
Aberdeen	....	....	150
Sioux Falls	....	....	200

	1877.	1905.	1920.
Tennessee	3,751	7,000	14,390
Bristol	....	....	125
Chattanooga	178	300	1,400
Jackson	....	....	160
Knoxville	67	250	350
Memphis	2,100	2,500	7,000
Nashville	1,085	....	3,000
Texas	3,300	17,500	32,660
Austin	....	225	300
Beaumont	....	....	400
Brenham	....	....	150
Corpus Christi	....	....	110
Corsicana	90	380	200
Dallas	260	1,200	8,000
El Paso	....	350	1,800
Ft. Worth	116	....	2,250
Galveston	1,000	1,000	1,100
Houston	461	2,500	5,000
Marshall	....	....	135
San Antonio	302	800	3,000
Texarkana	....	....	150
Tyler	....	225	350
Victoria	85	120	120
Waco	158	....	1,500
Utah	258	1,000	3,940
Ogden	....	....	125
Salt Lake City	180	....	2,500
Vermont	120	700	2,260
Burlington	....	450	850
Montpelier	....	....	100
Rutland	....	....	134
Virginia	2,506	15,000	16,020
Danville	....	....	150
Harrisburg	....	....	102
Lynchburg	....	140	300
Newport News	....	500	2,000
Norfolk	500	1,200	5,000
Petersburg	163	....	400
Portsmouth	....	....	1,000
Richmond	1,200	2,500	4,000
Roanoke	....	....	300
Washington	145	2,800	10,030
Bellingham	....	....	250
Everett	....	....	150
Seattle	56	....	5,000
Spokane	....	....	1,100
Tacoma	....	150	900
West Virginia	511	1,500	5,440
Bluefield	....	....	152
Charleston	92	142	1,000
Clarksburg	....	....	245
Huntington	....	71	310
Morgantown	....	....	120
Wheeling	300	400	1,000
Wisconsin	2,559	15,000	30,100
Appleton	143	162	140
Beloit	....	....	167
Eau Claire	....	....	183
Fond du Lac	....	....	125
Green Bay	....	....	300
Hurley	....	....	300
Kenosha	....	....	200
La Crosse	106	....	235
Madison	....	60	250
Manitowoc	....	....	130
Marinette	....	....	275
Milwaukee	2,075	8,000	20,000
Oshkosh	....	....	100
Racine	....	....	400
Sheboygan	....	....	852
Stevens Point	....	....	100
Superior	....	....	800
Wyoming	40	....	560
Cheyenne	....	....	118

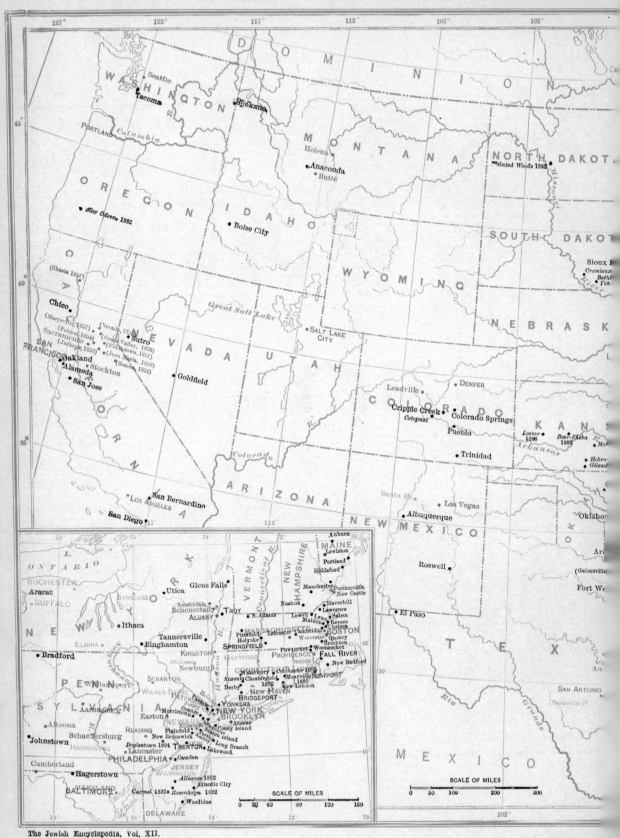

INSET: Enlarged Map of North Atlantic States.

Settlements during 1654-1800 indicated in Red; 1801-1848 in Brown;

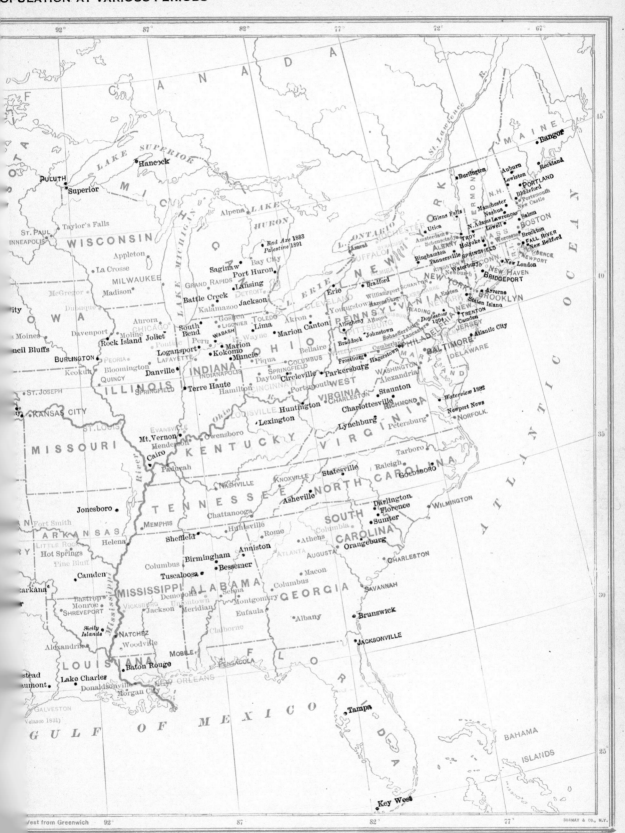

Copyright, 1905 and 1925, by Funk & Wagnalls Company, New York & London.

The relative importance of the different communities is designated by the
size of the type in which their names are printed; colonies in italics; com-

The accompanying map gives most of this information in graphic form, indicating the relative importance of towns by the size of the characters in which their names are printed, and indicating those towns in which Jews were settled before 1800 in red; those between 1801 and 1848 in purple; those from 1848 to 1881 in green; and the remainder in black.

It will be of interest to note the distribution of Jews in 1920 in the various geographical divisions:

Geographical Divisions.	Jew. Pop.	Gen. Pop.
New England........................	305,840	7,400,909
Middle Atlantic.....................	2,205,180	22,261,144
East No. Central....................	563,530	21,475,543
West No. Central...................	158,860	12,544,249
South Atlantic......................	142,130	13,989,272
East So. Central....................	43,150	8,893,307
West So. Central...................	56,320	10,242,224
Mountain	26,100	3,336,101
Pacific	99,690	5,566,871
Total	3,600,800	105,709,620

The predominant industry of the Russian Jews in the United States is tailoring, and Jews in general have been more intimately connected with the clothing trade than with any other occupation in the Union. The history of this connection has been recently investigated by J. E. Pope ("The Clothing Industry in New York," Columbia, Mo., 1905). Up to about 1840 the working classes mainly depended for their every-day clothing either on homespun goods or on renovated second-hand garments. The trade in the latter was mainly in the hands of the Jews, and this led to a connection with the clothing trade, just at the time when the sewing-machine made the ready-made trade possible.

Clothing Trade.

The Jews not alone made clothing, but it was they who first developed a system of distributing ready-made clothing, and it was due to them that clothes which were sold in the general stores up to about 1840 were deposited and distributed in clothing stores almost entirely manipulated by Jews from that time onward. Outside of the jewelry trade the clothing trade was almost the sole occupation of the Jews up to 1860, and many merchants and firms that afterward branched out as general merchants, as the Seligmans, Wormsers, and Seasongoods, began in the clothing industry, but were diverted from it by the Civil war, which suddenly broke off the large trade with the South. Several of the Jewish tailoring establishments endeavored to replace this business by supplying uniforms for the Federal soldiers, but other firms had to divert their attention to new lines of industry. On the cessation of hostilities very large demands for clothing arose from the million and a half men suddenly released from their uniforms, and these were mainly supplied by Jewish tailors, who about this time appear to have introduced the contract system, letting out to subcontractors in the rural districts contracts for large consignments of clothing to be delivered at the great centers, and thence distributed throughout the country. In this development of the tailoring industry, which lasted from about 1865 to 1880, Jews became mainly the large contractors and distributors, but the actual work was done apart from the great centers of Jewish activity.

The next stage seems to have restored the industry to the urban districts by bringing the actual work of construction inside factories. This also was the direct work of Jews. A certain number of English Jews who had learned the tailoring business went to Boston in the seventies, and removed to New York in the early part of the eighties, introducing what is known as "the Boston system," by which division of labor was widely extended in the tailoring trade. "Teams" of workmen turned out a single article at a much greater pace, and a single part of the work was learned more easily by newcomers. Russo-Jewish immigrants who arrived in large numbers at this time (1881 onward) had been incapacitated by their physique for any heavy work, and in some cases had begun the contract system of tailoring either in England or in Russia; they were, therefore, ready to take up tailoring work in the "sweat-shops" as almost the sole means by which they could obtain a livelihood immediately on arrival. Their participation in the trade became greater and greater, till in New York, the center of it, they were predominant. In 1888, of 241 clothing manufacturers in New York city 234 were Jews. Whereas previous to 1880 the imports of ready-made clothing from Germany had been about 12,000,000 marks a year, this was reduced by 1894 to less than 2,000,000. On the other hand, the clothing industry in 1880 turned out in the five chief centers goods to the amount of $157,513,528, and in 1900 $311,146,858, an increase of 97.22 per cent. By 1900 there were 8,266 clothing establishments in New York city, employing 90,950 workmen, with a capital of $78,387,849 and an annual product of $239,879,414 (Twelfth Census, viii. 622). According to Professor Pope, "to the Jews more than to any other people belongs the credit for the magnificent development which the clothing industry has attained" (*ib*. p. 293).

The social condition of the American Jews, including those of recent arrival, is eminently satisfactory. Notwithstanding the fact that the Jewish immigrant arrives with an average fortune of only $15, nothing is more remarkable than the speed with which he makes himself self-supporting. Even those who find it necessary to apply on their arrival to the charitable institutions for some slight assistance, soon get on without it. Of 1,000 applicants who thus applied to the United Hebrew Charities of New York in Oct., 1894, 602 never applied again, and five years later only 67 families still remained on the books, to be reduced to 23 in Oct., 1904 (Bernheimer, "Russian Jew," p. 66, Philadelphia, 1905). It is quite a mistake to think that the Jewish workman accepts much lower wages than his fellow workmen in the same industry. It is true that during the first rush into the clothing industries in the eighties the early comers were content to take almost starvation wages, but by the end of the century Jewish laborers working in men's clothing factories were getting $11.36 per week as against $9.82 for American working men in general, while Jewish women working on women's clothing were getting $5.86 as against $5.46. While their wages are comparatively high, however, their rents are increased by their tendency to crowd together, so that the real conditions are probably not so favorable.

Social Condition.

Thus in Boston it has been observed that 39.65 per cent of the Russian Jews dwell in "poor and bad tenements," whereas the Irish have only 27.15 per cent of this class, though the Italians have 56.23 per cent. So, too, in New York, of 1,795 Russo-Jewish families investigated by the Federation of Charities, 1,001 had dark rooms, and only 158 had baths. Also in Philadelphia, in a Jewish population of 688 the average number of persons to a room was 1.39, while in three Chicago districts the average was 1.26 persons per room ("Tenement Conditions in Chicago," p. 64). The average number of persons to a Jewish house in Philadelphia was 9.17, as against 5.4 for the general population; of 75 houses, only 8 had bathtubs. Similarly in Chicago, only 3.73 per cent of a population of 10,452 Jews had bathtubs. It should, however, be added that the Russian Jew uses the public baths, of which there are large numbers in the Jewish quarters.

Regarding persons higher in the social scale, it is obviously difficult to obtain definite information. A careful estimate, however, was made in 1888 of the annual turnover of different classes of manufactures in New York, a list of which may be subjoined as indicating the chief lines of commerce in which Jews are engaged (figures in parentheses give the number of employees):

Manufacturers of clothing	$55,000,000
Jobbers of jewelry	30,000,000
Wholesale butchers (6,000)	25,000,000
Dealers in wines, spirits, and beer	25,000,000
Jobbers of leaf tobacco	15,000,000
Manufacturers of cigars (8,000)	15,000,000
Manufacturers of cloaks	15,000,000
Importers of diamonds	12,000,000
Dealers in leather and hides	12,000,000
Manufacturers of overshirts	10,000,000
Importers of watches	6,000,000
Dealers in artificial flowers and feathers	6,000,000
Importers and jobbers of furs	5,000,000
Manufacturers of undergarments	5,000,000
Lace and embroidery importers	4,000,000
Manufacturers of white shirts	3,000,000
Manufacturers of hats	3,000,000
Manufacturers of caps	2,000,000
	$248,000,000

Besides this, it was reckoned that the Jews of New York at that time had $150,000,000 worth of real estate, and that the Jewish bankers of the city had a capital of $100,000,000. These figures would have to be considerably increased, probably quadrupled, after the lapse of twenty years. As is pointed out above, the turnover of the clothing trade alone in New York was equal in 1900 to the total amount of the Jewish industrial output in 1888, while one Jewish banking-house, Kuhn, Loeb & Co., issued $1,360,000,000 worth of bonds during the five years 1900 to 1905, and represents financially railway companies controlling 22,200 miles of railroad and over $1,300,000,000 stock.

In a list of 4,000 millionaires given by the "World Almanac," New York, the Jewish names numbered 114, somewhat over their proportion compared with their percentage in population, but somewhat under their proportion if the fact be taken into consideration that they are mostly residents of cities, where alone the very wealthy are to be found. The generally satisfactory condition of the immigrants within a few years after their arrival is perhaps best indicated by the fact that the twelve great Jewish charities of New York altogether dispense only $1,143,545 annually in a population of over 750,000, about $1.50 per head. Again, in Chicago only $150,000 per annum is spent in charity upon a population of at least 75,000, about $2 per head.

It is, of course, impossible to give the full score of Jewish philanthropy in the United States, but a rough estimate may be derived from **Charity.** the expenditures of the chief federations for charity found in several of the main centers of the Jewish population. To this may be added the expenditure of the twelve largest Jewish institutions of New York:

New York (twelve largest institutions)	$1,143,545
Philadelphia Federation	119,700
Cincinnati Federation	29,622
St. Louis Federation	43,108
Chicago Federation	148,000
Boston Federation	39,000
Detroit Federation	6,662
Kansas City Federation	4,508
Cleveland Federation	41,350

In addition to these sums, donations by Jews were reported for the year 1904 to the amount of $3,049,124, making a total of more than $5,000,000; or about $3 per head for charity and education.

It is also of interest to indicate the causes which led 10,015 applicants to appeal to the United Hebrew Charities of New York during the year 1904-5:

Sickness	3,229	Transportation	360
No male support	2,050	Release baggage or	
Lack of work	1,641	family	12
Insufficient earnings	781	Lack of tools	43
Physical defects	178	Shiftlessness	63
Old age	471	No cause	252
Insanity of wage-earner	86	Cause unknown	261
Intemperance of wage-earner	40	All other causes	504
Imprisonment of wage-earner	44	Total	10,015

The number of persons who are being punished for their crimes in the United States **Destitutes,** has not been ascertained; but the **Defectives,** numbers of Jewish aliens who are in **and Delin-** various institutions, as given in the **quents.** report of the commissioner-general of immigration for the year ending June 30, 1904, are as follows:

	Charitable.		Insane.		Penal.		All.	
	No.	Per Cent.	No.	Per Cent.	No.	Per Cent.	No.	Per Cent.
Hebrews	1,274	8.2	932	5	559	6.5	2,765	6.2

Considering that the Jewish immigrants are fully 10 per cent of the total volume of immigration to the United States, this is an excellent showing, and considering that 1,000,000 have arrived in the last twenty-five years, the smallness of the numbers is still more remarkable.

It should be observed that of the 559 Jews (484 males, 75 females) found in penal institutions, 170 were imprisoned for graver offenses, and 389 for minor offenses, whereas of the total number of immigrant prisoners, 4,124 were for graver as against 5,701 for minor offenses, Jews, as is well known, not being addicted to crimes of violence. Similarly, of the criminals reported to the Board of Magistrates of the City of New York for the year 1898, those from Russia formed 8.2 per cent of the total number, whereas their proportion of the population was 11.2. In Philadelphia the Jewish inmates of the prisons were found in 1904 to be 2.7 per cent, whereas the percentage of Jews in the population was 7.7.

Synagogues and Institutions.

In some of the early censuses of the United States details of places of worship were given for the different sects, and from these the following table was taken (excepting the last line, which is from the returns made to W. B. Hackenburg):

Census.	Synagogues.	Accommodation.	Property.
1850..............	36	18,371	$ 418,000
1860..............	77	34,412	1,135,300
1870..............	152	73,265	5,155,234
1877..............	278	12,546*	6,648,730

* This enumeration is of membership, not of accommodation.

In 1905 the real property held by synagogues and Jewish charitable institutions in New York city, and which was exempted from taxation, was valued at $13,558,100.

For the present condition of affairs the following data are given in the " American Jewish Year Book," 5662:

Congregations.......................................	850
Income of 431..	$1,233,127
Reform congregations (C. C. A. R.)..................	86
Schools..	421
Pupils...	38,694
Educational institutions and libraries...............	78
Colleges for Hebrew studies..................	3
Agricultural schools.........................	2
Technical, industrial, or trade schools........	13
Societies conducting industrial classes........	16
Societies conducting evening classes..........	9
Kindergartens...............................	11
Kitchengardens..............................	2
Training schools for nurses..................	3
Libraries....................................	19
Income of 20..	$160,456
Charitable institutions..............................	500
Income of 243.......................................	$1,808,663
Young Men's Hebrew Associations....................	23
Income of 10..	$29,828
Social clubs...	117
Income of 33..	$307,412
Other clubs...	66
Mutual benefit associations.........................	63
Income of 33..	$36,784
Loan associations...................................	22
Others..	52
Zionist societies....................................	124
Sections of Council of Jewish Women...............	49
Lodges...	954

These results were reported from 503 places in thirty-seven out of the forty-seven states. There are now in the United States about 1,000 synagogues, to which may be added 314 houses of prayer used in the East Side of New York (" Federation," March, 1904), making a total of 1,314, of which about 100 use the so-called Reform ritual. Notwithstanding this comparatively large number of synagogues, certain districts of New York have 80 per cent of their Jewish inhabitants unaffiliated with any place of worship, though in Brooklyn the proportion has sunk to 33.8 per cent (" Federation," Oct., 1905).

It is interesting to note the growth of the lodge system, of which the details given in the statistical publication of the American Hebrew Congregations of 1880 may be compared with those given in the " American Jewish Year Book," 5662:

		Grand Lodges.	Lodges.	Members.
B'nai B'rith........................	1880	7	302	22,814
	1900	..	317	
Independent Order Free Sons of Israel	1880	2	86	8,604
	1900	..	109	
Order Kesher Shel Barzel...........	1800	5	170	10,000
	1900	..	70	
Improved Order Free Sons of Israel.	1800	1	44	2,479
Independent Order Sons of Benjamin	1900	..	188	
Order B'rith Abraham..............	....	..	270	

Miscellaneous: In 1880 there were fifteen Jewish periodicals published in the United States; in 1904 there were eighty-two, as well as thirteen yearbooks or occasional publications. Of the 14,443 persons mentioned in " Who's Who in America," 169 were of Jewish race, about the proper proportion of the native Jews.

Investigation has established that the fertility of the Jews in the United States is greater than that of other creeds and nationalities. Thus it was found by an investigation in New York that whereas the average number of children in Protestant families was 1.85 and in Roman Catholic 2.03, in Jewish families it was 2.54 (" Federation," New York, June, 1903, p. 34). Against all other experience, it was found that Jewish families with domestics have a higher average of children than those without servants. This had been previously observed by J. S. Billings (" Vital Statistics of the Jews of the United States," p. 17). In one particular ward of New York the Jewish families were superior in fecundity to all others, with an average of 2.9. There is clearly no race suicide among Jews.

Besides being very fecund, their marriage-rate is excessively high, because of the large proportion of nubile persons arriving in the United States, yet there is great inequality of the sexes owing to the fact that between the years 1884 and 1905 342,300 men have arrived, as compared with 221,247 women. It is said that intermarriage is occurring in order to supply the deficiency; yet of 9,668 New York Jewish families investigated by the Federation of Churches intermarriage was reported in the case of only 78, less than one per cent.

Some remarkable results have been reached as to the low death-rate of the Jews in the United States.

Death-Rate.

In 1890 J. S. Billings investigated the death-rate of nearly 12,000 Jews, and found it as low as 7.11—in the Eastern States 6.29. In 1895 the death-rate of Russian Jews in Boston was only 6.09. These rates probably refer either to the well-nourished families investigated by Dr. Billings, or to the vigorous immigrants of the most viable ages—between twenty-five and forty-five—among whom in an ordinary population the death-rate would be even less. This is confirmed by the fact that while Russian Jews at Boston in 1895 had a death-rate of only 6.09, their children died on an average at the rate of 15.95. This is about the normal death-rate in the most congested districts, and it would be safe to take the average death-rate of the Jews of the United States at 14, that for the whole population. In the year 1900 the death-rate of the ninth ward in Chicago (an almost entirely Jewish ward) was only 11.99.

It has been observed that American Jews, even when immigrants, are taller than the average of the Jewish population of the countries whence they come, the average for New York city being 164.5 cm. as against 162.0 cm. for Russia and Galicia (see STATURE).

BIBLIOGRAPHY: *Statistics of the Jews of the United States*, New York, 1880; *Annual Reports of the Commissioner-General of Immigration*, Washington, 1902–4; *American Jewish Year Book*, 1900–5; *Annual Reports of United Hebrew Charities*, New York, 1885–1905; W. Laidlaw, in *Jewish Charity*, May, 1905; J. Markens, *Hebrews in America*, New York, 1888; J. S. Billings, *Vital Statistics of the Jewish Race in the United States*, in *Eleventh Census Bulletin*, No. 19, 1890; Bernheimer, *The Russian Jew*, Philadelphia, 1905; F. A. Bushee, *Ethnic Factors in the Population of Boston*, New York, 1903; *Hull House Maps and Papers*, Boston, 1895; T. J. Jones, *Sociology of a New York City Block*, New York, 1904; *Jewish Colonies of New Jersey*, Camden, 1901; M. H. Willett, *Employment of Women in the Clothing Trade*, New York, 1902; R. A. Woods, *The City Wilderness*, Boston, 1898; idem, *Americans in Process*, Boston, 1902; M. Fishberg, *Materials for the Anthropology of Western Jews*, New York, 1905.
J.

UNITED STATES OF COLOMBIA. See SOUTH AND CENTRAL AMERICA.

UNITED SYNAGOGUE: A body first composed of sixteen synagogues in London, England, constituted in 1870 by Act of Parliament (33 and 34 Victoria, cap. 116). Originally the "city" synagogues, as the Jewish places of worship within the borders of the city of London were called, were independent of one another, and each one had its own chief rabbi and charity organization. This led to considerable duplication of charity. In 1802 Solomon Herschell was appointed chief rabbi of the Great and Hambro' synagogues; and shortly after his accession to office he induced the three German congregations to come to an agreement for charitable purposes. This agreement continued in force until the year 1834, when a new compact was made and the scope of action was enlarged. The Great Synagogue agreed to contribute one-half, and the Hambro' and New synagogues one-quarter each, toward general and communal expenditure, both charitable and religious.

The migration of Jews westward, however, made the continued force of this agreement impracticable; and the late Chief Rabbi N. M. Adler suggested an amalgamation of the three synagogues and the Central and Bayswater synagogues in the western part of London. The project was taken up by Lionel L. Cohen, who energetically championed it; and a union was agreed to April 19, 1868. The consolidation was further strengthened and legalized by the passing of an "Act for Confirming a Scheme for the Charity Commissioners for the Jewish United Synagogues," which received the royal assent July 14, 1870. The Borough Synagogue, in the south of London, entered the union in 1873; and the North London Synagogue in 1878. The other nine synagogues have been built under the auspices of the United Synagogue. The first secretary of the United Synagogue was Dr. A. Asher. Subsequently another act was passed for the definition of the rights of the chief rabbi and the bet din and of the powers of the chief rabbi.

Each constituent synagogue controls its own surplus (if any), and pays 40 per cent of its income from seat rentals for communal purposes. In 1904 a scheme providing for "Associate Synagogues" was adopted, of which there are nine, whereby synagogues in poorer neighborhoods might enter the union without assuming all the burdens of the fully constituent synagogues. The first synagogue to enter on such terms was the South-East London Synagogue.

The United Synagogue is governed by a council constituted of: (*a*) life-members and certain officials; (*b*) the wardens of the constituent synagogues for the time being; (*c*) a certain number of representatives according to the number of members of the constituent synagogues, one in each case being the financial representative who acts as treasurer. The total number of members of the council is 150. Lionel de Rothschild is (1923) the president.
J.   I. L. B.

UNIVERS ISRAÉLITE, L'. See PERIODICALS.

UNIVERSITIES: Places of higher and liberal learning, so called from the Latin word "universitas," signifying an association or a corporation. There are traditions of the connection of Jews with the medieval universities of Salerno and Montpellier (see MEDICINE) and with that of OXFORD. No Jewish names are connected with the development either of the southern (Bologna) or the northern (Paris) type of university from the twelfth century onward. A degree or right to teach seems to have been regarded as a feudal tenure; and the acceptance of a degree was always accompanied by payment of homage to the rector or councilor. Such homage involved the recital of Christian formulas, which Jews could not recite. Besides this the twenty-fourth canon of the Council of Basel (1434) distinctly prevented Jews from taking any academic degree.

A distinction, however, is to be made between the faculties of theology, philosophy, and law and that of medicine. Jews would naturally **Medical** not study in the first of these, and **Degrees.** they could scarcely work at medieval law, which was as much canonical as civil, while the philosophical faculty was mainly a development of the Christian metaphysics of Thomas Aquinas. But Jews appear to have studied, and even to have taught, in the medical faculty; thus, Elijah Delmedigo was professor of medicine at Padua at the end of the fifteenth century. As late as 1700 the universities of Rostock and Wittenberg counseled the Christians against employing Jewish physicians, who probably practised without taking a degree. Most of the Jewish doctors whose academic training can be traced received such training at Padua.

With the revival of learning, scholars of Jewish birth, mainly those who accepted baptism, were utilized for the chairs of Hebrew in the various universities, as in the case of TREMELLIUS at Cambridge, etc. This practise was continued almost down to the present time, and spread to the whole circuit of the Semitic languages, in which Jews, from their proficiency in Hebrew, have a large opportunity.

In Holland rigid restrictions on university training do not seem to have existed, though there were few names of Jewish students recorded till the nineteenth century. So, too, in Austria, the toleration edict of Joseph II. plainly declared that there was no express law against the admittance of Jews into the Austrian universities; but the fact of its being thus mentioned is sufficient to indicate that the admission had either not taken place or was extremely rare. In France the Revolution opened the higher schools of learning to the Jews; but in England they shared the disabilities of all dissenters, and were prevented from taking degrees. Thus, Professor Sylvester, though second wrangler in the mathematical tripos at the University of Cambridge in 1837, did not obtain a degree there till 1872, after the passing of the University Test Act (1871), which was partly caused by the attainment of the senior wranglership by Numa HARTOG in 1869.

The Jews of the various German states were mostly debarred from participation in university education till the nineteenth century, though exceptions were occasionally made for Jewish medical students. In Prussia the first Jewish student at a **Germany.** university was Tobias Cohen, whom the Grand Elector allowed to study medicine at Frankfort-on-the-Oder in 1675. After the Mendelssohnian period many Jewish students began to attend the universities, but soon found that any university career was closed to them unless they were willing to submit to baptism. The Prussian government has always regarded the universities as especially connected with the cultural side of the state organization and, therefore, as bound up with the interests of the Protestant Church. Hence, from the times of Ganz and Benfey down to those of Kronecker and Hirschfeld, the majority of capable students who desired to pursue a university career found it necessary to become baptized. In Austria a very similar state of affairs existed, as is shown by the cases of Mussafia and Büdinger. In the sixties and seventies no discrimination took place, but with the rise of anti-Semitism Jewish students suffered various disabilities which caused them to form special clubs (see ZIONISM).

Notwithstanding these quasi-disabilities, Jewish students have thronged to the universities in exceptional numbers, as can be seen from the accompanying statistics. A comparison with the other creeds may perhaps best be made in Prussia, where the Protestants had 8.37, the Catholics 6.61, and the Jews 54.75 per 10,000 attending the universities in 1902-3. In Austria the proportion of Jewish among other students indicates the same condition:

NUMBER OF STUDENTS OF DIFFERENT FAITHS AT THE AUSTRIAN UNIVERSITIES IN 1902.

	Number.	Per Cent.
Catholic	26,359	75.7
Greek	1,466	4.4
Protestant	1,225	3.3
Jewish	5,779	16.6
Totals	34,829	100.0

That the proportion in Prussia has not considerably increased during the last few years is borne out by the detailed list of students attending the Prussian universities:

NUMBER OF CHRISTIAN AND JEWISH STUDENTS IN THE PRUSSIAN UNIVERSITIES.

University.	1886-87.		1899-1900.	
	Christians.	Jews.	Christians.	Jews.
Berlin	3,975	880	4,441	1,031
Bonn	1,177	41	1,889	55
Breslau	1,096	222	1,380	212
Göttingen	1,004	17	1,238	22
Greifswalde	986	15	768	12
Halle	1,459	28	1,433	22
Kiel	508	14	822	18
Königsberg	740	74	721	70
Marburg	896	22	1,079	23
Academy at Münster	483	....	603	....
Lyceum Hosianum in Braunsberg	21	....	46	....
Totals	12,345	1,313	14,420	1,465

The numbers of Jews attending the Austrian universities may also be given here:

JEWISH STUDENTS AT THE AUSTRIAN UNIVERSITIES DURING THE SUMMER OF 1902.

Vienna	1,423		Lemberg	453
Graz	36		Cracow	190
Innsbruck	2		Czernowitz	207
Prague (German)	348			
Prague (Bohemian)	70		Total	2,729

There are special conditions which would seem to prevent any large attendance of Jewish students at the Russian universities, their percentages being limited to 3 per cent of the whole body of students at Odessa and St. Petersburg, and 5 per cent in the Pale. Notwithstanding this, the history of the last twenty years shows that these proportions were largely exceeded, as can be seen from the following table:

PERCENTAGE OF JEWISH STUDENTS TO TOTAL NUMBER (RUSSIA).

University.	1880.	1899.
St. Petersburg	4.4	4.4
Moscow	5.2	3.5
Cracow	5.9	23.2
Odessa	11.9	27.5
Kasan	1.0	8.9
Kiev	15.2	17.9
Dorpat	4.2	15.8
Warsaw	11.6	16.8
Tomsk	....	5.4
	6.8	10.9

To the above details it may be added that at Columbia University, New York, in 1903, out of 900 students whose creeds were investigated, 6.9 per cent declared themselves Jews, whereas no less than 1,900 students out of the 2,100 of the College of the City of New York in 1903 were Jewish, and at the Normal College of that city 75 per cent of its students were Jewish.

For Prussia elaborate details are given by Thon and Ruppin, showing a distinct diversion of tendency from the medical to the juridical faculty. Thus in 1886-87 there were 185 students of law and 698 of medicine, whereas in 1902-3 there were 459 studying law, and only 369 studying medicine. The percentage of Jews among the law students remained practically the same at 9 per cent, whereas that of medical students declined from 19.6 to 15. In philosophical faculties a rise in numbers took place from 246 in 1892–93 to 392 in 1902–3. In the latter year Jews formed 4.5 per cent of the students devoted to philosophy, 5.6 of mathematicians, 2.9 of economists, 9. of pharmacy, and 26.9 of dentistry.

The numbers of professors of the Jewish faith are rarely given authoritatively. Servi recorded that in Italy in 1867 there were seventeen Jewish professors at the Italian universities ("Statistica degli Israeliti," p. 298). About 1880 it was

Professors. said that there were six ordinary and twenty extraordinary professorships and twenty-nine readerships held by Jews at Berlin University, as compared with sixty-one, fifty-three, and fifty-seven respectively by Christians. Breslau records that there were seventy Jewish professors in German universities out of a total of 1,800, about the usual proportion ("Zur Judenfrage," p. 17, Berlin, 1880). About the same time six of the 259 chairs in the English universities were held by Jews. In 1903 it was declared that the University of Munich had ninety-nine Catholic, eighty-seven Protestant, and seventeen Jewish professors and privat-docents; Würzburg had thirty-eight Catholic, fifty Protestant, and one Jewish privat-docents; while Erlangen had twelve Catholic, fifty-three Protestant, and two Jewish professors (Bloch's "Wochenschrift," July 4, 1903). At Strasburg there were six Jewish professors (ib. Oct. 31, 1902). The only professing Jews who have ever held the rectorship of a Prussian university are Prof. Rosanes of Breslau and Prof. Julius Bernstein of Halle. Lazarus was rector at Bern; Gomperz at Vienna; Halberg at Czernowitz; and Zucker in Prague.

BIBLIOGRAPHY: Jacobs, *Jewish Statistics*, p. 47; Ruppin, *Juden der Gegenwart*, pp. 204–209; Thon and Ruppin, *Der Anteil der Juden am Unterrichtswesen in Preussen*, Berlin, 1903; *Zeitschrift für Jüdische Statistik*, passim, 1905.
J.

UNLEAVENED BREAD. See Mazzah.

UNNA, PAUL GERSON: German physician and dermatologist; born at Hamburg Sept. 8, 1850; son of Moritz Adolph Unna; educated at the universities of Heidelberg, Leipsic, and Strasburg (M.D. 1875). He was severely wounded in the Franco-Prussian war, in which he served as a private. After graduation he became assistant to Waldeyer at Strasburg, and in the following year he returned to Hamburg and established a practise. During 1877 he was assistant at the general hospital in that city. In 1881 he became interested in dermatology, and opened a private hospital for skin-diseases; and in 1884 he gave up his general practise and founded the well-known hospital for skin-diseases at Einisbüttel near Hamburg. This he enlarged in 1887 by adding a laboratory, which soon became the center for dermatological researches in Germany.

Unna is an untiring worker; he has written over one hundred essays in all fields of medicine and many standard works on his specialty. In 1882 he founded the semimonthly "Monatshefte für Praktische Dermatologie." He is collaborator for dermatology on Eulenburg's "Realencyklopädie der Gesammten Heilkunde"; on Baumgarten's "Jahresbericht über die Fortschritte in der Lehre von den Pathogenen Mikroorganismen"; and on Virchow-Hirsch's "Jahresbericht über die Fortschritte und Leistungen in der Medizin."

Among Unna's publications may be mentioned: "Kuno Fischer und das Gewissen," in "Zeitschrift für Völkerpsychologie und Sprachwissenschaft," 1875, ix.; "Anatomie der Haut," in Ziemssen's "Handbuch der Allgemeinen Therapie," 1882; "Histopathologie der Haut," in supplement to Orth's "Spezielle Pathologie," 1894, and "Allgemeine Therapie der Haut," 1898. All three are standard works. He publishes the "Histologischer Atlas zur Pathologie der Haut," and, together with Morris, Besnier, and Duhring, the "Internationaler Atlas Seltener Hautkrankheiten."

BIBLIOGRAPHY: Hirsch, *Biog. Lex.*; Pagel, *Biog. Lex.*
S.   F. T. H.

UNTERFÜHRER. See Marriage Ceremonies.

UR: A locality mentioned four times in the Bible (Gen. xi. 28, 31; xv. 7; Neh. ix. 7) with the qualification כשדים (= "of the Kasdim," or Chaldees), and described as the original home of Abram. Modern scholars, with few exceptions, are agreed that Ur is identical with the mound of ruins in southern Babylonia on the right bank of the Euphrates, known as Al-Muḳair or Al-Mughair. This was an ancient seat of lunar worship; and it was dominant as a political center as early as 3000 B.C. Those scholars who incline to establish a connection between moon-worship ("Sin" = "moon") and the monotheism of Israel ("Sinai") find a corroboration of their theory in the fact that Abram's original home was the seat of the worship of Sin (comp. Jensen in "Zeitschrift für Assyriologie," xi. 298 *et seq.*).

E. G. H.

URANIA: Daughter of Abraham the Precentor, of Worms, who herself acted as precentor in the women's synagogue in that city before 1275. See Sagerin.

A.   F. L. C.

URBINO: Italian city; capital of the province of Pesaro e Urbino; originally the capital of the duchy of Urbino, and later a portion of the States of the Church. Jews seem to have resided in the city as early as the thirteenth century, Abraham Abulafia having sojourned there; but existing documents make no mention of them until the following century, in the first decades of which a certain Maestro Daniele went from Viterbo to Urbino, where he opened a loan-office. Toward the close of the same century his son Isaac received privileges from Count Antonio. During the following century the Urbino Jews increased in prosperity; but their gain in numbers was small. The privilege of lending money at interest was reserved to the descendants of Maestro Daniele. Other Jews who

Maestro Daniele. wished to establish themselves in the business were obliged to obtain permission from the rulers and the privileged families. In 1430 Sabbatuccio di Alleuzzo, a Jew of Recanati, was obliged to guarantee the payment of a yearly tax of 500 scudi to these families before he was allowed to open a banking-house in Urbino. With these exceptions, the city contained only a few Jews, who were either physicians or were engaged in the humbler branches of trade.

Until the beginning of the sixteenth century the Jews of Urbino were permitted to buy, hold, and sell real estate; to deal in metals and paper, and to follow the trades of tailoring and tanning; to reside in all portions of the city; and to employ Christian servants. They were, however, subject to special taxation, for in addition to the ordinary taxes and the "impost of the Marches," levied on all the Jews of those districts, the money-lenders paid a separate tax, though one of them, Solomon of Urbino, stood high in the favor of Duke Frederick.

Toward the close of the fifteenth century and in the beginning of the sixteenth the Jews became the objects of popular persecution. In the year 1468 a MONTE DI PIETÀ was established in opposition to them; but as it loaned money to the very poor only, and allowed but 4 florins every six months to each person, the Jews still maintained their banks, and at the end of the century they obtained from Guido Ubaldo a ratification of their former privileges. So great was their increase in numbers and influence, moreover, that in 1507 an effort was made to check them. The sale of pledges outside the city was forbidden; and a committee was appointed to revise and limit their prerogatives. Then began the promulgation of a series of decrees against them, which, however, being issued merely to conciliate the papal see, produced little effect. On May 20, 1508, Duke Francesco Maria annulled all the privileges granted by his predecessors, and forbade the Jews to acquire real estate or to act as bankers. He compelled them to restore without interest all pledges in their possession, to wear the BADGE (which consisted of a yellow cap for men and a yellow veil for women), and to purchase food in the evening only.

Shortly afterward the Jews, who then numbered about 500, were obliged to take up their abode in a separate quarter, known as the "Androne delle Giudei," and were forbidden to employ Christians as servants. Despite these harsh measures, the

The Ghetto. Jewish bankers continued to prosper, increasing both in numbers and in influence. At length, in 1512, the municipal council resumed the practise of borrowing money from them, and sometimes, as in 1571, even pledged to them articles received from the monte di pietà. In 1598, however, a new decree was issued against lending money; but an edict published by the duke in the following year mentions the Jews of Urbino, "who conduct loan establishments," and laws enacted in the same year also allude to them.

In 1529 Solomon MOLKO was brought from Ancona to Urbino by the duke, who sought to shield him from the consequences of a dispute in which this protégé had been involved in the market-place of Urbino. A Jew named Moses was for many years the municipal physician of Urbino; and the court of Guido Ubaldo contained many Jewish courtiers, who were treated as the equals of their Christian confrères, although they were so unpopu-

lar with the people that it became necessary to promulgate special decrees for their protection (1549–1624).

In 1556 Guido Ubaldo offered asylum in his territories, especially at Pesaro, to the Maranos who had fled from Ancona on account of the persecutions there, hoping thus to attract to Pesaro the commerce of the East. When, however, he saw that his hopes were vain, he expelled the refugees in June, 1558. For the same reason he welcomed the Jews banished from the Pontifical States in 1569, only to drive them out in March, 1570, at the instance of Pius V.; and when some ventured to return, he banished them a third time (Aug. 16, 1571).

Urbino then entered upon a period of financial decay; and the Jews began to leave the city. The condition of those who remained became worse and worse; and the taxes levied upon them were gradually discontinued. At length, through the abdication of Francesco Maria II. della Rovere in 1627, the duchy of Urbino passed into the hands of the pope, thus precipitating the dissolution of the Jewish community. In 1718 the number of its members was reduced to 200, almost all being so sunk in poverty that they petitioned the pope to exempt them from contributing toward the payment of the debts of the Roman Jews, reminding him that on a former occasion, had he not extended aid to them, they would have been obliged to leave the city and seek their fortunes elsewhere. The history of the Jews of Urbino at that period was identical with that of their coreligionists throughout the Pontifical States. They obtained civic equality at the time of the French Revolution, but lost it at the restoration, receiving it again when the Marches were annexed to the kingdom of Italy (1866). The synagogue of Urbino was owned partly by Catholics until 1851, when it was acquired by the Jews, and, later, was restored and beautified. The decay of the community continued, however, until in the year 1870 there were but 181 Jews in the city, while in 1901 there were only 92.

Among the noted rabbis of Urbino may be mentioned the following: Solomon b. Abraham b. Solomon (15th and 16th cents.); Samuel b.

Rabbis. Abraham Corcos, Ephraim Mahalaleel Porto, Zechariah b. Ephraim Porto, Solomon b. Moses Rocca, Jedidiah b. Hezekiah Saba' (17th cent.); Jedidiah Ḥayyim Guglielmi (18th cent.); Mattithiah Nissim b. Jacob Israel Terni (18th and 19th cents.); and Isaac Joseph Cingoli (19th cent.).

BIBLIOGRAPHY: Ravà, in *Educatore Israelita*, 1870, p. 312; Vogelstein and Rieger, *Gesch. der Juden in Rom*, ii. 54, 108; Berliner's *Magazin*, xvii. 229; Güdemann, *Gesch.* ii. 179; Grätz, *Gesch.* 2d ed., ix. 350 *et seq.*, 361 *et seq.*, 382; *R. E. J.* xvi. 61 *et seq.*, xx. 47 *et seq.*; Joseph ha-Kohen, '*Emek ha-Baka*, ed. Wiener, p. 108; Luzzatto, *Banchieri Ebrei in Urbino nell' Età Ducale.*
D. U. C.

URBINO: Italian family, originating in the city of the same name. The following important members are cited in chronological order:

Solomon d'Urbino: Lived at Urbino in the early part of the fourteenth century, where he enjoyed the favor of Duke Frederick, and wrote a small work entitled "Yefeh Nof."

Isaac Saba' d'Urbino: Son of Solomon d'Urbino; mentioned by Moses Rieti in his "Miḳdash Me'aṭ" (ed. Goldenthal, p. 106b).

Solomon b. Abraham b. Solomon d'Urbino:
Flourished in the latter part of the fifteenth century and at the beginning of the sixteenth. In 1500 he completed his "Ohel Mo'ed," a work on Hebrew synonyms, which he dedicated to his teacher Obadiah. This book was printed at Venice in 1548, and reprinted by Willheimer with notes by Heidenheim and Dukes, Vienna, 1881; the "Yetad ha-Ohel," Isaac Berechiah Canton's commentary on it, has remained in manuscript.

Joseph Baruch b. Zechariah Jedidiah d'Urbino: Lived in the seventeenth century at Mantua, Modena, and Busseto. He was the author of the "Mizmor Shir Yedidot u-Benot ha-Shir" (Mantua, 1659), a collection of poems on various subjects. He gave his approbation to a decision of Hananiah Shullam (Modena,1636), and made a Hebrew translation of an Italian work on astronomy, which, however, has not been printed. He is probably identical with the Joseph Baruch d'Urbino who owned Codex Oxon. 911, and perhaps with Joseph Baruch b. Zerahiah Urbino of Busseto, who possessed Codex Oxon. 348.

Moses Judah b. Isaac d'Urbino: Flourished at Ancona in the seventeenth century. He is mentioned by Abraham Solomon Graziano in his annotations and novellæ on the Shulḥan 'Aruk (iii. 308 of the manuscript).

Jedidiah Zechariah d'Urbino: Nephew of Jehiel Trabotti; lived at Pesaro in the eighteenth century. He was the author of a manuscript volume of responsa; and a responsum of his is cited in the "Shemesh Ẓedaḳah" (ii. 24) of Samson Morpurgo.

Isaac d'Urbino: Son of Jedidiah d'Urbino; lived at Pesaro in the eighteenth century. Codex Montefiore 111 contains one of his letters ("J. Q. R." xiv. 185).

BIBLIOGRAPHY: Nepi-Ghirondi, *Toledot Gedole Yisrael*, pp. 107, 177, 210, 333; Steinschneider, *Cat. Bodl.* cols. 1538, 2391; Mortara, *Indice*, p. 67; Fürst, *Bibl. Jud.* iii. 461.
D.   U. C.

URI. See SWITZERLAND.

URI BEN DAVID BEN MOSES (קאלמייר):
Great-grandson of Samuel Edels (MaHaRSHA); rabbi of Pollno, Lithuania, and chief rabbi of the district; flourished in the middle of the seventeenth century. He was the author of "Or Torah" (Lublin, 1672), commentaries and sermons on the Pentateuch; and he included in his work several "peshaṭim" by his great-grandfather.

BIBLIOGRAPHY: Steinschneider, *Cat. Bodl.* col. 2692; Fuenn, *Keneset Yisrael*, p. 92; Sternberg, *Gesch. der Juden in Polen*, p. 185.
E. C.   S. O.

URI PHOEBUS BEN AARON HA-LEVI
(known also as **Uri Witzenhausen**): Dutch printer; born at Amsterdam 1623; died there Jan. 27, 1715 (not at Zolkiev in 1713, as Steinschneider records); son of Aaron ha-Levi, ḥazzan at the Neweh Shalom Synagogue, Amsterdam, and grandson of Moses Uri ha-Levi, founder and first ḥakam of the Spanish-Portuguese congregation in that city. After having first worked as a typesetter for Immanuel Beveniste, in whose establishment he printed Pappenheim's edition of the "Mishle Ḥakamim" in 1656,

Phoebus opened an establishment of his own in 1658 and carried on business as a printer till 1689. His imprint was a ewer and two fishes. In the first year he printed several books, among them a prayer-book of the German ritual. The last work he issued was a Sephardic Maḥzor, completed in 1689. Of more important works only two were printed by Phoebus, the Shulḥan 'Aruk, Ḥoshen Mishpaṭ, with the commentary "Sifte Kohen" of Shabbethai ha-Kohen (1663),and a Judæo-German translation of the Bible by Jekuthiel Blitz, who worked as a corrector in Phoebus' printing-house. In 1693 Phoebus opened a printing-house at Zolkiev, and there printed calendars and ritual and Judæo-German works till 1705.

It is doubtful whether Uri Phoebus was the author of the evening benediction in Judæo-German (Amsterdam, 1677) attributed to him; and he can scarcely have written the rare Spanish work "Memoria Para os Siglos Futuros" (*ib.* Kislew 10, 5471 = Dec., 1710), which was printed in Portuguese at the expense of Moses Levy Maduro under the title "Narracaõ da Vinda dos Judeos Espanhoẽs a Amsterdam" (*ib.* 1768), this version forming the basis of the Hebrew translation by Isaac ha-Kohen Belinfante.

BIBLIOGRAPHY: Fürst, *Bibl. Jud.* iii. 95; Steinschneider, *Hebr. Bibl.* iii. 6; idem, *Cat. Bodl.* cols. 3061 *et seq.*; Steinschneider and Cassel, *Jüdische Typographie*, in Ersch and Gruber, *Encyc.* section ii., part 28, pp. 65–66; Hillesum, in *Centraal Blad voor Israeliten in Nederland*, 1900, No. 13,599; Cardozo de Bethencourt, *Aankomst der Joden te Amsterdam*, pp. 10 *et seq.*, Amsterdam, 1904; Kayserling, *Bibl. Esp.-Port.-Jud.* p. 59.
J.   M. SEL.—M. K.

URI (ORI) BEN SIMEON: Scholar of the sixteenth century; born at Biel (ביל); resided at Safed. He made an abstract of a manuscript of 1537, giving a list of all the places said to contain the tombs of the Patriarchs, Prophets, Amoraim, and Tannaim, to which he added descriptive material gathered in the course of his extensive travels, as well as illustrations of various graves. To this work, which appeared in Venice in 1659 (2d ed. 1699) under the title "Yiḥus ha-Abot," was appended a description of a calendar compiled by him in 1575. The entire work was translated into Latin by Hottinger under the title "Cippi Hebraici, Genealogia Patriarcharum" (Heidelberg, 1659; 2d ed. *ib.* 1662); and E. Carmoly later translated the book into French under the title "Jichus ha-Abot, ou Tombeaux des Patriarches," and published it in his "Itinéraires de la Terre Sainte" ("Halikot Erez Yisrael"), together with a preface and twenty-seven illustrations from the first Venetian edition. The "Yiḥus ha-Abot" was rendered also into Judæo-German by an unknown translator, being published under the same title at Wilna in 1853.

Uri ben Simeon was likewise the author of a calendar ("luaḥ") covering a period of forty years. This work, which first appeared in Venice (1575), was translated into Latin by Jacob Christmann of Heidelberg, in which city it was published in 1594.

BIBLIOGRAPHY: Zunz, in *The Itinerary* of Benjamin of Tudela, pp. 275–276, notes a and b; E. Carmoly, *Itinéraires de la Terre Sainte*, pp. 419–496, Brussels, 1847; Steinschneider, *Cat. Bodl.* cols. 558, 815, 2693–2695; Benjacob, *Oẓar ha-Sefarim*, p. 221.
E. C.   S. O.

URIAH, URIJAH.—1. Biblical Data: A Hittite; husband of Bath-sheba, and one of David's picked warriors. The scanty Biblical allusions to him are of value as illustrating the taboo under which warriors were constrained to abstain from sexual intercourse (II Sam. xi. 7-15; see Schwally, "Kriegsaltertümer," p. 48), through which circumstance David's plan to cover his illicit relations with Bath-sheba was frustrated. Sent back to camp, Uriah was placed, by David's secret orders, "in the forefront of the hottest battle," and fell at the siege of Rabbah.

Josephus ("Ant." vii. 8, § 1) adds many embellishments to the account of the death of Uriah, declaring that when the Ammonites made a sortie and repulsed the besiegers, Uriah remained on the field with a few others, exposing himself to danger more than all his comrades, and maintaining his position until the enemy had surrounded the little band of heroes and completely destroyed them.

——In Rabbinical Literature: The Rabbis, who naturally could not admit the existence of any flaw in David's character, regarded Uriah as the one at fault. They claimed that he had defied David, since, when the king commanded him to go home, he replied, "My lord Joab is encamped in the open fields," thus disregarding the royal bidding (Shab. 56a; Tos. to Ḳid. 43a, above).

2. High priest during the reign of Ahaz. According to Isa. viii. 2, he was taken as a faithful witness by Isaiah when the prophet married the mother of Maher-shalal-ḥash-baz. II Kings xvi. 10-16 states that Ahaz sent Uriah the pattern of an altar seen by him at Damascus after the conquest of the city by Tiglath-pileser, directing the prophet to erect a similar one in the Temple, for the offering of certain sacrifices. In the list of high priests given in I Chron. v. 30-40 Uriah's name does not occur, although it is interpolated in Josephus, "Ant." x. 8, § 6.

3. Son of Shemaiah of Kirjath-jearim; a prophet of the reign of Jehoiakim. Like Jeremiah, in foretelling the destruction of Jerusalem by the Assyrians he brought upon himself the anger of the king and the princes. In fear of death he fled to Egypt, whereupon Jehoiakim sent an embassy headed by Elnathan b. Achbor, which seized the prophet and brought him to Jerusalem, where he was beheaded by the express command of the king, his body being thrown into the graves of the common people (Jer. xxvi. 20-23).

4. Son of Koz (Neh. iii. 4), probably of the seventh class of priests (comp. I Chron. xxiv. 10). On the fourth day after the return of the exiles to Jerusalem, his son Meremoth weighed the gold, silver, and vessels brought back from Babylon (Ezra viii. 33).

5. One of the men who stood at the right hand of Ezra while the latter read the Law to the people (Neh. viii. 4).

E. G. H.   S. O.

URIEL: Name of an archangel. Of the four chief angels, MICHAEL, GABRIEL, RAPHAEL, and Uriel, who preside over the four quarters of the globe (Jensen, "Kosmologie der Babylonier," p. 163), and who are frequently grouped together, Uriel is generally, but not invariably, mentioned last, although in this quartet his name is frequently re-

placed by that of another angel, thus showing the diversity of his nature (e.g., Fanuel, Enoch, xl. 9; Aniel, Stübe, "Jüdisch-Babylonische Zaubertexte," p. 26, Halle, 1895; Nuriel, "Seder Gan 'Eden we-Gehinnom," in Jellinek, "B. H." iii. 138). He is likewise one of the seven archangels, being the prince of the angels and of Tartarus (Enoch, xx. 2, where his name is given first in the list of the angels). According to Kautzsch ("Apokryphen," ii. 250), Lusken ("Michael," p. 36), and others, Uriel is the angel of thunder and earthquake, and is, moreover, the divine messenger who warns the son of Lamech of the end of the world, and bids him hide (Enoch, x. 1-2); he appears in a like capacity in II Esd. iv., where he propounds three difficult problems to Ezra and instructs him. Of these problems the first was, "Weigh me the weight of the fire," a demand closely connected in concept with the name "Uriel" (אור + אל = "the fire of God"), for its derivation from אל + אור (= "light of God," "glory of God"; Kohut, "Angelologie," p. 33) is erroneous, as is, consequently, the attempt to identify the angel with the Zoroastrian "Hvarenah" (= "glory"). The second question addressed to Ezra was concerned with the waters in the depths of the sea and above the firmament, and thus with the two "tehomot," as well as with the underworld (Sheol, Hades), this being in entire harmony with Enoch, xx. and designating Uriel as the archangel of fire and of GEHENNA, where flame is the chief element. In the passage under consideration this same spirit also speaks of the wind.

In medieval mysticism Uriel is represented as the source of the heat of the day in winter, and as the princely angel of Sunday, the first day of the week, thus agreeing fully with the explanation of his nature already given. Later authorities, however, brought his name into association with אור (= "light"), misled in part by the legend that Uriel instructed (enlightened) Ezra. "Why is he called Uriel? On account of the Torah, the Prophets, and the Hagiographa, since through him God makes atonement and brings light to Israel" (Num. R. ii. 10). Conforming to this view, subsequent writers identified him with Raphael, the revealer of secrets (Zunz, "S. P." p. 476), and his name was written on amulets intended to "illumine" the soul for sacred studies ("Sefer Raziel," p. 42b). Uriel is mentioned also in the magic papyri (Wessely, "Griechischer Zauberpapyrus," Index, Vienna, 1888; idem, "Neue Griechische Zauberpapyri," Index, ib. 1893; Lusken, l.c. p. 71), and in Babylonian incantations (Stübe, l.c. p. 23), while according to a French rabbi of the thirteenth century the repetition of Uriel's name ten times in one breath in the morning brings good fortune for the day (Schwab, "Vocabulaire de l'Angélologie," pp. 47, 304). On Uriel in the PIYYUṬ see Zunz, l.c., and on accounts of him in Christian writings comp. Lusken, l.c. p. 114. See also RAPHAEL for data concerning the four angels as a group.

BIBLIOGRAPHY: Kohut, Ueber die Jüdische Angelologie und Dämonologie in Ihrer Abhängigkeit vom Parsismus, pp. 33 et seq., Leipsic, 1866; Lusken, Michael, Index, Göttingen, 1898; Schwab, Vocabulaire de l'Angélologie d'Après les Manuscrits Hébreux de la Bibliothèque Nationale, pp. 47, 304, Paris, 1897.

s.   L. B.

URIEL D'ACOSTA. See Acosta.

URIEL VON GEMMINGEN. See Pfefferkorn; Reuchlin.

URIM AND THUMMIM.—Biblical Data:
Objects connected with the breastplate of the high priest, and used as a kind of divine oracle. Since the days of the Alexandrian translators of the Old Testament it has been asserted that אורים ותמים mean "revelation and truth" (δήλωσις καὶ ἀλήθεια), or "lights and perfections" (φωτισμοὶ καὶ τελεότητες); the τελειότης καὶ διδαχή of Symmachus (Jerome, "perfectio et doctrina"; Field, "Hexapla" on Deut. xxxiii. 8); and the φωτισμοί καὶ τελειώσεις of Aquila and Theodotion. The Vulgate has "doctrina [after Symmachus; Old Latin, "ostensio" or "demonstratio"] et veritas." There is, however, no foundation for such a view in the Bible itself. Ex. xxviii. 13–30 describes the high-priestly ephod and the breastplate with the Urim and Thummim. It is called a "breastplate of judgment" ("ḥoshen ha-mishpaṭ"); it is four-square and double; and the twelve stones were not put inside the ḥoshen, but on the outside. It is related in Lev. viii. 7–8 that when, in compliance with the command in Ex. xxix. 1–37, Moses consecrated Aaron and his sons as priests, "He [Moses] put upon him [Aaron] the coat, and girded him with the girdle, and clothed him with the robe, and put the ephod upon him, and he girded him with the cunningly woven band [A. V. "curious girdle"] of the ephod, and bound it unto him therewith. And he put the breastplate upon him: and in the breastplate he put the Urim and the Thummim." Deut. xxxiii. 8 (R. V.), in the blessing of Moses, reads: "And of Levi he said: Thy Thummim and thy Urim are with thy godly one, whom thou didst prove at Massah, with whom thou didst strive at the waters of Meribah" (see Steuernagel, "Deuteronomium," p. 125, Göttingen, 1898; Bertholet, "Deuteronomium," p. 106, Freiburg, 1899; Driver, "Deuteronomy," in "International Critical Commentary," p. 398, New York, 1895; Baudissin, "Gesch. des Alttestamentlichen Priesterthums," p. 76). The most important passage is I Sam. xiv. 41, where Wellhausen and Driver have corrected the text, on the basis of the Septuagint, to read as follows: "And Saul said: Lord, God of Israel, why hast thou not answered thy servant this day? If this iniquity be in me or in Jonathan my son, Lord, God of Israel, give Urim; but if it be in thy people Israel, give Thummim. Then Jonathan and Saul were taken by lot; and the people escaped" (Driver, "Notes on the Hebrew Text of the Books of Samuel," p. 89, Oxford, 1890; Budde, "The Books of Samuel," in Polychrome Bible, p. 63; H. P. Smith, "The Books of Samuel," p. 122; Kirkpatrick, "The First Book of Samuel," in "The Cambridge Bible for Schools and Colleges," 1891, p. 137).

I Sam. xxviii. 3–6 mentions three methods of divine communication: (1) the dream-oracle, of which frequent mention is made also in Assyrian and Babylonian literature; (2) the oracle by means of the Urim (here, undoubtedly, an abbreviation for "Urim and Thummim"); (3) the oracle by the word of the Prophets, found among all Semitic nations.

The only other mention of actual consultation of Yhwh by means of the Urim and Thummim found in the Old Testament is in Num. xxvii. 21. Eleazar was then high priest, and Moses was permitted by the Lord to address Him directly. But Joshua and his successors could speak to the Lord only through the mediation of the high priest and by means of the Urim and Thummim. It is quite probable that the age of Ezra and Nehemiah was no longer cognizant of the nature of the Urim and Thummim (Ezra ii. 63; Neh. vii. 65; see also I Macc. iv. 46, xiv. 41). Post-exilic Israel had neither the sacred breastplate nor the Urim and Thummim. Ezra ii. 63 tacitly contradicts the assertion of Josephus ("Ant." iii. 8, § 9, end) that the Urim and Thummim first failed in the Maccabean era (B. Niese, "Flavii Josephi Opera," i. 202; see also Soṭah ix. 12; Tosef., Soṭah, xiii. 2; Yer. Ḳid. iv. 1; Ryle, "Ezra and Nehemiah," p. 32). Ecclus. (Sirach) xxxiii. 3 may possibly prove a knowledge of the tradition concerning the use of the Urim and Thummim; but it can not be inferred that answers were received at that time by means of them (V. Ryssel, in Kautzsch, "Apokryphen," p. 394).

The Urim and Thummim are implied, also, wherever in the earlier history of Israel mention is made of asking counsel of the Lord by means of the ephod (Josh. ix. 14; Judges i. 1–2; xx. 18 [rejected as a later gloss from ib. i. 1 by most commentators], 26–28; I Sam. x. 22; xiv. 3, 18, 36 et seq.; xxii. 10, 13; xxiii. 2, 4, 6, 9–12; xxviii. 6; xxx. 7 et seq.; II Sam. ii. 1; v. 19, 23 et seq.; xxi. 1. On the nature of the ephod see G. F. Moore, "Judges," 1895, pp. 380–399, where copious references and the literature are given; idem, "Ephod," in Cheyne and Black, "Encyc. Bibl."; and especially T. C. Foote, "The Ephod," in "Jour. Bib. Lit." [1902] xxi. 1–48). In all cases except I Sam. x. 22 and II Sam. v. 23 et seq., the answer is either "Yes" or "No." It has been suggested by Riehm and others that these two passages have undergone editorial changes. After the death of David no instance is mentioned in the Old Testament of consulting the Lord by means of the Urim and Thummim or the ephod. This desuetude is undoubtedly occasioned by the growing influence of the Old Testament prophecy.

The ancient, and most of the modern, explanations of these mysterious instruments through which Yhwh communicated His will to His chosen people identify them with (a) stones in the high priest's breastplate, (b) sacred dice, and (c) little images of Truth and Justice such as are found round the neck of the mummy of an Egyptian priest (see Muss-Arnolt, "The Urim and Thummim," in "Am. Jour. Semit. Lang." July, 1900, pp. 199–204). The "Tablets of Destiny" which occur in the Assyro-Babylonian account of Creation and otherwise figure in Assyro-Babylonian conceptions suggest the correct explanation of the Hebrew Urim and Thummim. One of the functions ascribed to the Babylonian seer was to deliver oracles and to consult the god, whose answer was either "Yes" or "No." Quite often the god sends to his people an "urtu," a command to do, or not to do, something. "Urtu" belongs to the same

Biblical References.

Answer "Yes" or "No."

stem from which is derived "ertu," the "terminus technicus" for "oracle." The gods speak ("tamu, utammu") to the priest the oracle which they reveal; and the oracle is called "the mysterious word, revelation." Since God "at sundry times and in divers manners spake in time past," not only unto the fathers by the Prophets, but to all mankind in ways which it is now almost impossible to trace precisely, it is quite possible that the mythological account of the Tablets of Destiny and the Old Testament Urim and Thummim, both shaping the destiny of king and nation, revert to the same fountainhead and origin. Notwithstanding the fragmentary account of Babylonian literature and the scanty report of Old Testament writers, some points common to both may yet be gathered.

(1) According to Ex. xxviii. 30 and Lev. viii. 8, the Urim and Thummim rested within the breastplate, that is, on the breast of the high

Babylonian Accounts. priest; in the Babylonian account the Tablets of Destiny rested on the breast of their possessor. Only so long as they were resting on the breast of the god in the case of the one nation, and on the breast of the high priest in that of the other, were they efficacious.

(2) In the Babylonian accounts, only those gods who, in some way, were considered the messengers and mediators between the other gods and mankind were the lawful possessors of the Tablets of Destiny. In Israel the Urim and Thummim were entrusted by YHWH to Moses, and through him to the high priest as the representative of YHWH and as the mediator between God and the nation to whose decisions, through the Urim and Thummim, even kings bowed.

(3) There is, to be sure, in the Babylonian records no statement as to the exact number of the Tablets of Destiny. It is known that there were more than one; it may not be too hazardous to assume that there were only two, one lying on each breast: one revealing (or prognosticating?) good fortune; the other, misfortune. The Old Testament accounts of the Urim and Thummim indicate that there were only two objects (lots?).

(4) Marduk, after he had torn the Tablets of Destiny from the breast of his dead foe, sealed them with his own seal. There may be a reminiscence of this in Ex. xxviii. 21. The use of twelve stones, one for each of the twelve tribes, in addition to the two lots (of stone), is perhaps of some significance in this connection.

(5) Marduk, bearing on his breast the Tablets of Destiny, presided at the annual assembly of the gods, where the fate was determined and the lot was cast for king and nation. It is the general opinion that the Urim and Thummim were consulted only in cases where the safety of king or nation was concerned.

In Israel the development of a strict monotheism necessarily modified the conception of the Urim and Thummim. No description of them is found in the Old Testament; they are mentioned as something familiar both to Moses and to the people—an inheritance received from the time of their ancestors. The very fact that the Old Testament assumes that

XII.—25

Moses and the people were acquainted with the nature of the Urim and Thummim confirms the view that the latter were naturally connected with the functions of the high priest as the mediator between YHWH and His people.

The etymology of אורים and תמים, suggested by Zimmern and others, supports the explanation given here. The so-called plural ending of the two words expresses the "pluralis intensivus," plurals only in form, but not in meaning. "Urim" may be connected not with ארר = "curse, put under the ban," as

Etymology of the Words. Schwally and others have held, but with the Babylonian "u'uru," the infinitive of the "pi'el" of "a'aru," from which are derived also the nouns "urtu" = "command, order, decision" (usually of the gods) and "tertu" (originally with the same meaning). These words occur frequently in Assyro-Babylonian literature in sentences analogous in form to those in which "Urim and Thummim" are used in the Old Testament. The plural ארים ("fires") has no doubt had some influence in shaping the analogous form אורים = "urtu." תמים the present writer connects with the Assyrian "tamu," pi'el "tummu," verbal forms also belonging to the oracular language. "Urim and Thummim" correspond, then, to the Babylonian "urtu" and "tamitu," the latter a synonym of "piristu" = "oracle, oracular decision [of the gods]." That the original meaning of the two words and their significance were known even at the time when the Old Testament records, in which they are mentioned, were written is exceedingly doubtful; that they were not known either to the Greek translators or to the early Masorites is practically certain.

BIBLIOGRAPHY: In addition to works and articles mentioned in the body of the article, Buxtorf, *Historia Urim et Thummim,* in his *Exercitationes,* pp. 267 et seq., and in Ugolini, *Thesaurus,* vol. xii.; Spencer, *De Legibus Hebræorum Ritualibus,* 1685; Ludwig Diestel, *Gesch. des Alten Testamentes in der Christlichen Kirche,* Jena, 1869; idem, *Urim,* in Herzog-Haupt, *Real-Encyc.* xvi. 746 et seq., revised for 2d ed., xvi. 226 et seq., by Kautzsch; Bähr, *Symbolik,* ii. 134-141; W. Robertson Smith, *The Old Testament in the Jewish Church,* 2d ed., p. 292, London, 1895; Baudissin, *Die Geschichte des Alttestamentlichen Priesterthums Untersucht,* 1889, pp. 26, 27, 140, 141; Benzinger, *Arch.* 1894, pp. 382, 407, 408; Winer, *B. R.* 3d ed., ii. 643-648; Wittichen, in Schenkel's *Bibel-Lexikon* (1869), ii. 403; Steiner, *ib.* (1875) v. 851-853; G. Klaiber, *Das Priesterliche Orakel der Israeliten,* Stuttgart, 1865; Riehm, *Handwörterbuch,* 2d ed., i. 914-918; Stade, *Geschichte,* 2d ed., i. 156, 471-473, 505-506, 517-518. Additional literature is found in Knobel, *Der Prophetismus der Hebräer,* i. 5, No. 2; Hancock, *The Urim and the Thummim,* in *Old Testament Student,* March, 1884, iii. 252-256 (is quite unsatisfactory); Dosker, *The Urim and Thummim,* in *Presbyterian and Reformed Review,* Oct., 1892, pp. 717-736; and in T. Witton Davies, *Magic, Divination, and Demonology,* 1898. A very convenient summary is given by Kirkpatrick in *The First Book of Samuel,* pp. 217, 218, to which may be added the article *Urim and Thummim,* in Smith, *Dictionary of the Bible,* iii. 1600-1606, London, 1893; A. R. S. Kennedy, *Urim and Thummim,* in Hastings, *Dict. Bible,* iv. 835-841, New York, 1902; and Paul Haupt, *Babylonian Elements in the Levitical Ritual,* in *Jour. Bib. Lit.* 1900, xix. 58, 72 et seq.
E. G. H.   W. M.-A.

——In Rabbinical Literature: Tradition is unanimous in stating that the use of the Urim and Thummim ceased with the destruction of the First Temple, or, in other words, with the death of the Older Prophets; and they were among the five things lacking in the Second Temple (Soṭah ix. 10 [= 48b]; Yoma 21b; Yer. Ḳid. 65b). Josephus states ("Ant." iii. 8, § 9) that "this oracle had been silent" for 200 years before his time, or from the days of John Hyrcanus. The teachers of the Talmud, however, if their own statements may be believed, had never seen the Urim and Thummim, and regarded them as the "great and holy name of God" written on the breastplate of the high priest (Targ. pseudo-Jonathan to Ex. xxviii. 30); and they etymologize "Urim" as "those whose words give light," while "Thummim" is explained as "those whose words are fulfilled" (*ib.*; Yoma 73b; Yer. Yoma 44c).

The oracle was consulted in the following manner: The high priest donned his eight garments, and the person for whom he sought an answer **Mode of** stood facing him, while he himself **Con-** turned toward God (*i.e.*, the SHEKI- **sultation.** NAH). It was necessary that the question should be brief and that it should be pronounced, but not aloud; while the answer was a repetition of the query, either in the affirmative or in the negative. Only one question might be asked at a time; if more than one were put, the first alone received a reply. The answer was given by the letters of the names of the tribes which were engraved upon the high priest's breastplate (Yoma 73a, b; Yer. Yoma 44c; Sifre, Num. 141). If the question was not distinctly worded, the reply might be misunderstood, as in Judges xx. 18 *et seq.* (Sheb. 35b; Yoma 73b). A decision by the oracle might be demanded only by the king, or by the chief of the highest court, or by a prominent man within the community, such as a general of the army, and it might be sought only for the common weal (Yoma 7, end, 73a: "one anointed for war"; Targ. pseudo-Jonathan to Ex. xxviii. 30: "in case of need"). According to Targ. pseudo-Jonathan to Ex. xxviii., the breastplate was used to proclaim victory in battle. It was necessary that the high priest who questioned the oracle should be a man upon whom the Shekinah rested (Yoma 73b).

The characteristic feature of the Shekinah was radiance; and Josephus, who believed that God was present at every sacrifice, even when offered by Gentiles, states that the oracles were revealed through rays of light:

"But as to those stones, which we told you before, the high priest bare on his shoulders . . . the one of them shined out when God was present at their sacrifices . . . **Relation** bright rays darting out thence; and being seen **to the** even by those that were most remote; which **Shekinah.** splendor yet was not before natural to the stone. . . . Yet will I mention what is still more wonderful than this; for God declared beforehand, by those twelve stones which the high priest bare on his breast, and which were inserted into his breastplate, when they should be victorious in battle; for so great a splendor shone forth from them before the army began to march, that all the people were sensible of God's being present for their assistance. Whence it came to pass that those Greeks who had a veneration for our laws, because they could not possibly contradict this, called that breastplate *the Oracle*" ("Ant." iii. 8, § 9, Whiston's transl.).

The Talmudic concept seems to have been identical with the view of Josephus, holding that the reply of the Urim and Thummim was conveyed by rays of light. Two scholars of the third century, however, who had lost the vividness of the earlier concept, gave the explanation that those stones of the breastplate which contained the answer of the oracle either stood out from the others or formed themselves into groups (Yoma 73b).

The division of the country was made according to the Urim and Thummim, since the high priest, "filled with the Holy Spirit," proclaimed the tribe to which each division should belong. After this, lots were drawn from two urns, one containing the name of the tribe and the other that of the territory, and these were found to harmonize with the high priest's announcement (B. B. 122a; Sanh. 16a; comp. Yer. Yoma 41b, below). To enlarge the Holy City or the Temple court the orders of the king, of a prophet, and of the Urim and Thummim were necessary (Sheb. 2, 3, 16a; Yer. Sheb. 33d, below). In Yer. Sanh. 19b the question is propounded why the Urim and Thummim are needed when a prophet is present.

BIBLIOGRAPHY: Winer, *B. R.* ii. 644–645; Hamburger, *R. B. T.* i. 1002–1004; Herzog-Plitt, *Real-Encyc.* xvi. 226–233; Hastings, *Dict. Bible*, iv. 840–841; M. Duschak, *Josephus Flavius und die Tradition*, pp. 5–7, Vienna, 1864.
W. B. L. B.

URY, ADOLPHE (SIMON): Alsatian rabbi; born at Niederbronn, Lower Alsace, June 14, 1849. He was educated at the lyceum of Strasburg and the rabbinical seminary in Paris, receiving the degrees of doctor and chief rabbi, his thesis being " Les Arts et les Métiers chez les Anciens Juifs Selon la Bible et le Talmud." In 1875 he was appointed rabbi of Lauterburg, Lower Alsace, whence he was called ten years later to the rabbinate of Brumath, succeeding Solomon Levy. In the following year he became professor of Bible exegesis and Jewish history at the rabbinical school which had been established at Strasburg; and when, in 1890, that institution was closed for lack of funds, Ury was chosen chief rabbi of Lorraine, with his seat in Metz. In 1899 he became chief rabbi of Strasburg and Lower Alsace. He died before 1923.

S.

USAGE. See CUSTOM.

USHA. See SYNOD OF USHA.

USISHKIN, MICHAEL: One of the leaders of the Russian Zionists; born in 1863 in Dubrovna, government of Moghilef (Mohilev). In 1871 he went with his parents to Moscow. He studied the Bible and Talmud in the ḥeder till he was thirteen years old, and then passed successively through the professional and imperial technical schools, graduating from the latter in 1889 as an engineer. Since 1891 he has resided in Yekaterinoslav.

In addition to his secular instruction, Usishkin obtained a thorough Jewish education, and he has a good knowledge of the Neo-Hebrew literature. His public activity began while he was yet at school. He was one of the founders of the Bilu, the Jewish national students' organization, which formed the first Jewish colony in Palestine (see JEW. ENCYC. i. 248b); afterward he was one of the organizers of the students' Chovevei Zion and Bene Zion societies in Moscow. In 1887 he took part as delegate from Moscow in the Chovevei Zion conference at Drusgenik, government of Grodno; and in 1890 he was one of the founders of the Odessa Association for Aiding the Jewish Colonists in Palestine. After the Palestinian scheme had been transformed into the present political Zionist movement Usishkin became one of the most ardent followers and collaborators of Herzl, with whom he began a correspondence in 1896; and since then he has been one of the most energetic propagandists of Zionism among the Russian Jews. Usishkin has taken part in all the Zionist congresses except the sixth, and is one of the members of the Zionist Actions-Comité. In 1903 he was sent to Palestine by this committee and by the Chovevei Zion to purchase land for new colonies, and to organize the colonists and other Jews of Palestine.

Usishkin was a strong opponent of the Uganda project, and stood at the head of the party in Zionism which believed that the regeneration of the Jewish people can be accomplished in Palestine alone. In the twenty-four years of his activity as a leader of the Zionist movement he has contributed to the Jewish magazines many articles on different questions relating to Zionism; and his latest work is an account of the Zionist program, published by him in five languages (Hebrew, Yiddish, Russian, German, and English). See ZIONISM.

H. R. S. HU.

USQUE: Family deriving its name from the Spanish city of Huesca (the ancient **Osca;** Hebr. אושקה), where it originated, its members emigrating thence to Portugal, and finally to Italy, to escape the Inquisition.

Abraham Usque: Italian printer; born at Lisbon, where he was known as **Duarte Pinel;** son of Solomon Usque. Some time after 1543 he went to Ferrara, where he termed himself "Abraham Usque," and established a large printery, adopting as his imprint a globe with Isa. xl. 31 as the legend. His establishment published some Judæo-Spanish rituals and Portuguese works, and between 1551 and 1557 it issued about twenty-eight Hebrew books, including an unpointed Hebrew Bible, all of these works being edited by Samuel Zarfati, Isaac al-Ḥakim, Menahem b. Moses Israel, and Baruch Uzziel.

Usque's principal work was the valuable Ferrara Bible, bearing the title "Biblia en Lengua Española Traducida Palabra por Palabra de la Verdad Hebrayca por Muy Excelentes Letrados, Vista y Examinada por el Oficio de la Inquisicion. Con Privilegio del Ylustrissimo Señor Duque de Ferrara." This Bible, which is a revision of an earlier translation rather than a new version, was issued at the expense of the Spaniard Yom-Ṭob b. Levi Athias, who, as a Marano, assumed the name "Jeronimo de Vargas." Two slightly modified copies (not two editions) of this Bible were struck off, one of them being dedicated to Duke Ercole de Este, and the other, intended for the Jewish public, inscribed in honor of D. Gracia Nasi. New editions of the Ferrara Bible were published at Salonica in 1568, and at Amsterdam in 1611, 1630, 1646, 1661, 1695, etc. Before leaving Lisbon, Abraham Duarte Pinel published a "Latinæ Grammaticæ Compendium" and a "Tractatus de Calendis" (Lisbon, 1543).

The identity of Abraham Usque and Duarte Pinel, as well as of Yom-Ṭob b. Levi Athias and Jeronimo de Vargas, was first shown by Isaac da Costa in his "Israel und die Völker" (German transl. by Mann,

p. 282). See JEW. ENCYC. ii. 269b, *s.v.* YOM-ṬOB BEN LEVI ATHIAS.

BIBLIOGRAPHY: G. B. de Rossi, *De Typographia Hebræo-Ferrariensi,* ch. vi.; idem, *Dizionario* (German transl., p. 324); Steinschneider, *Hebr. Bibl.* ii. 28; Kayserling, *Sephardim,* p. 140; idem, *Bibl. Esp.-Port.-Jud.* pp. 28, 107.

Samuel Usque: Poet and historian; a near kinsman (but not a brother) of the printer Abraham Usque, whose contemporary he was at Ferrara, whence Samuel later went to Safed. No further details of his life are known, but he was a man of high culture, and one of the most interesting figures among the Jewish writers of the middle of the sixteenth century. He was thoroughly versed in the Bible, wrote Portuguese correctly, understood Spanish and Latin, and had a philosophical bent.

To confirm the Maranos in their faith and to prevent apostasy from Judaism, Usque wrote in Portuguese "Consolaçam as Tribulações de Ysrael" (Ferrara, 1553; 2d ed. Amsterdam, n.d.), a work on the trials and tribulations of the Jewish people, together with the causes of their various sorrows. This prose poem, which is dedicated to Gracia Mendesia, is divided into three dialogues between the patriarch *Icabo* (Jacob), who is introduced as a shepherd lamenting the fate of his children *Numeo* (Nahum) and *Zicareo* (Zechariah). In the first two dialogues, the author narrates the history of the Israelites down to the destruction of the Second Temple, and describes their sufferings under the Roman rule, basing his account on the Books of Maccabees and on Josephus. The work derives its importance, however, and its martyrologic character from the third dialogue, which, in thirty-seven numbers, recounts the sufferings of the Jews to the author's own time, and quotes the prophecies which were thereby fulfilled. The narrative begins with the persecution by Sisebut, which is followed by the story of the alleged desecrations of the host in France and Spain; the sufferings of the Jews in Persia, Italy, England, and Germany; the accusations against them in Spain and France; their persecution in Spain and Portugal; and the fortunes of those who were exiled from the last-named country. The story of these afflictions, most of them given in chronological order, concludes with words of consolation taken from the Bible.

Usque's chief sources for his history were Alfonso de Spina's "Fortalitium Fidei" (cited as "F. F." or "F. Fid."), which he attacked, and also the "Coronica de España," "Estorias de S. Denis de França" (ch. x.), "Coronica Dos Emperadores e Dos Papas," and other similar records. The abbreviations "L. I. E. B.," "E. B.," and "V. M." also occur frequently in Usque's work. The first two are supposed by Isidor Loeb to stand for "Liber Iehuda ibn Berga" (Verga), in which case they would denote the first edition of the "Shebeṭ Yehudah" of Judah ibn Verga. Grätz, however, thinks they connote "Liber Efodi," and he thus assumes that both Judah and Usque, who generally agree, drew upon the "Zikron ha-Shemadot" of Profiat Duran. The abbreviation "V. M." is as yet unexplained. Usque's "Consolaçam" was frequently used by Joseph ha-Kohen, author of the "'Emeḳ ha-Baka."

BIBLIOGRAPHY: De Rossi-Hamberger, *Hist. Wörterb.* pp. 324 *et seq.;* Rios, *Estudios,* pp. 496 *et seq.;* Grätz, *Gesch.* viii. 403 *et seq.,* ix. 346 *et seq.,* lxvii. *et seq.;* Julius Steinschneider, *R.*

Samuel Usque's Trost Israel's in Seinen Trübsalen, in *Festschrift zum Zehnten Stiftungsfest des Akademischen Vereins für Jüdische Gesch.* pp. 24–77, Berlin, 1893; Kayserling, *Bibl. Esp.-Port.-Jud.* p. 107; *R. E. J.* xvi. 211 *et seq.*, xvii. 270.

Solomon Usque (Salusque; called by Barbosa Machado Seleuco Lusitano; Marano name, Duarte Gomez): Poet and merchant; born in Portugal; lived at Ferrara, Venice, and Ancona in the middle of the sixteenth century; died after 1567. He made a Spanish translation of the poems of Petrarch, entitled "Sonetos, Canciones, Madrigales y Sextinas de Grande Poeta y Orador Francisco Petrarcha: Primiera Parte" (Venice, 1567), and dedicated to Alexander Farnese, Prince of Parma and Piacenza. It was greatly admired by his contemporaries for its artistic workmanship. Usque wrote also an Italian ode on the six days of Creation, dedicated to Cardinal Borromeo; and he collaborated with Lazaro Graziano in the composition of the Spanish drama "Esther," which was translated into Italian by Leon of Modena (Venice, 1619). He acted also as a business agent for Joseph Nasi, and enjoyed both his favor and that of Nasi's mother-in-law, Gracia Mendesia.

Another Solomon Usque (probably a native of Huesca, whence his name) was the father of the printer Abraham Usque; and a third was a typographer at Constantinople in 1561.

Bibliography: Barbosa Machado, *Bibliotheca Lusitana*, iii. 671, 705; Wolf, *Bibl. Hebr.* iii. 300, 1025; iv. 973; De Rossi-Hamberger, *Hist. Wörterb.* p. 324; Grätz, *Gesch.* ix., pp. lxii. *et seq.*; Kayserling, *Sephardim*, pp. 141, 340; idem, *Bibl. Esp.-Port.-Jud.* p. 107; Ersch and Gruber, *Encyc.* part ii., section 28, p. 39.
G.   M. K.

USURY: In modern language this term denotes a rate of interest greater than that which the law or public opinion permits; but the Biblical law, in all dealings among Israelites, forbids all "increase" of the debt by reason of lapse of time or forbearance, be the rate of interest high or low, while it does not impose any limit in dealings between Israelites and Gentiles. Hence in discussing Jewish law the words "interest" and "usury" may be used indiscriminately.

There are three Biblical passages which forbid the taking of interest in the case of "brothers," but which permit, or seemingly enjoin, it when the borrower is a Gentile, namely, Ex. xxii. 24; Lev. xxv. 36, 37; Deut. xxiii. 20, 21.

The Hebrew word for "usury" is "neshek," meaning literally "a bite," from its painfulness to the debtor; while in Lev. xxv. 36, 37 "increase" is the rendering of the Hebrew "marbit" or "tarbit" which denotes the gain on the creditor's side, and which in the later Hebrew becomes "ribbit." Lending on usury or increase is classed by Ezekiel (xviii. 13, 17) among the worst of sins. See also Ps. xv., in which among the attributes of the righteous man is reckoned the fact that he does not lend on usury.

The Talmud (B. M. 61b) dwells on Ezek. xviii. 13 (Hebr.): "He has lent on usury; he has taken interest; he shall surely not live, having done all these abominations"; on the words with which the prohibition of usury in Lev. xxv. 36 closes: "Thou shalt be afraid of thy God"; and on the further words in which Ezekiel (*l.c.*) refers to the usurer:

"He shall surely suffer death; his blood is upon him"; hence the lender on interest is compared to the shedder of blood.

The sages of the Mishnah knew full well that the forbearance of a debt causes a measurable loss. Thus the following case is put: A holds a demand on B for 1,000 zuzim payable by agreement in ten years; but two witnesses testify that **Loss on a**   B had agreed to pay in thirty days. **Debt.**   An alibi is proved against the witnesses; and they are condemned as "plotting witnesses" to pay the difference between 1,000 zuzim payable in ten years and the same sum payable in thirty days (Mak. i. 1). It often happens that money is paid to a husband in right of his wife, in which right he has an estate for life or during coverture. In modern times the money might be invested, and the husband would draw the interest or dividends; but in all such cases the Mishnah says: "Let ground be bought and the husband receive the income!" The Babylonians, from whom the post-exilic Jews learned much in the way of legal terms and forms, were accustomed to charge interest at the rate of 20 per cent per annum. Nearly, if not quite, all of their contract tablets show this rate of increase. (The first allusion in the Babylonian Talmud to a rate of interest [B. B. 60a] is to one of 20 per cent.) Yet with this knowledge, that the use of capital has a measurable value, and with the example of the Babylonians before them, the sages of the Mishnah not only do not mitigate the Scriptural injunction against interest, but carefully close many avenues of evasion, and forbid even all kinds of "moral usury."

The chapter on usury and increase (B. M. v.) commences thus: "What is usury ["neshek"] and what is increase ["tarbit"]?"; but by the latter word it seems to refer only to the rabbinical enlargement of the antiusury law. The former mode of dealing is easily illustrated; *e.g.*, "where one lends 4 denarii on a promise of the return of 5; or **Usury and**   2 bushels of wheat when 3 are to **Increase.**   be returned"; but the latter, an increase in "fruits" (*i.e.*, provisions which pass by quantity), is more complex and is put thus: "A has bought from B a kor of wheat for 25 denarii (=zuzim), which is the market price; afterward, when wheat has gone up to 30 denarii, A says: 'Deliver to me the wheat which I bought from you, as I wish to sell it and buy wine with the proceeds.' B answers: 'Very well, your wheat is sold to me for 30 zuzim, and you have wine [as much as 30 zuzim will buy at the ruling market price] in my hands'; when in fact B has no wine in his possession." Now the first deal, *i.e.*, B's buying the wheat back at a higher price than he had sold it for, is not objectionable as usury but his agreeing to deliver a named quantity of wine which is then worth 30 zuzim, but which he does not own, at some future time, when he might have to buy it in the open market at a higher price, is not indeed Scriptural but is rabbinical usury. The reason is given: B, who owes A 30 zuzim, takes the risk of having to pay it later on in wine, which may cost him more than 30 zuzim, in order to gain forbearance for his debt. This rule forbids, on the ground of usury, the sale of futures, made when the market price has not yet been fixed.

Some kinds of partnership dealings also are forbidden, because the partner without means is made to incur the risk of his time and labor besides that of loss by accidents or depreciation, in consideration of the capital furnished by the other. For instance, one may not give one's corn to a shopkeeper to sell at retail on half the profit over the wholesale price with which he is charged, nor may one give the shopkeeper money wherewith he may buy at wholesale and then sell on half the profits—because he runs the risk of fire and flood and robbery and of fall in price—unless he is paid wages for selling. And so with the breeding of chickens or the feeding of calves or colts on half profit; though the rule does not apply to cows or other grown beasts which "earn their keep." Commenting on B. M. v. 4, R. Judah (tanna of the 2d cent., pupil of Akiba) says (ib. 68b) that a nominal compensation, say a single dry fig, given to the working member of the special partnership is sufficient to exempt it from the usury laws. In modern Jewish practise this view has been followed. The contract between the moneyed man and the small trader is known as "sheṭar 'isḳa"; and in the well-known scrivener's handbook "Naḥalat Shib'ah" (Amsterdam, 1667) two forms of such an instrument are printed, which the compiler (Samuel ben David ha-Levi) follows up with an extract from an eminent rabbi of Lublin to this effect: "A man may say to his friend: 'Here are a hundred florins for thee in business [בעסקא], half profit and half loss. If thou shouldest say, "I have lost" or "I have not earned any money," thou must take a solemn oath to clear thyself.' But he must give him wages for his trouble; however, anything [כל שהוא] is enough for the purpose." Such special partnerships date back a very considerable time; for 4,000 years ago they were fully regulated by King Hammurabi in sections 100–107 of his code of laws for Babylon, and it seems that in quite modern times they have been common.

One may not give to an Israelite (money wherewith) to buy a certain quantity of corn before the market price ("sha'ar") is known; this restriction also is made in order that the man without means may not incur the risk of loss by higher prices in return for capital furnished. A landlord may lend to his metayers (tenants on shares) wheat for seed to be returned in kind, but not wheat for food. A man should not say to his neighbor, "Give me a kor of wheat and I will return it at thrashing-time"; but he may request such a loan "till my son comes home," or "till I find the key" (B. M. 75a). The reason is, that wheat might rise and the lender would profit. However, the Talmud abrogates this prohibition by allowing such a loan to be made when the borrower has some wheat of his own, though it be a much smaller quantity than that which he borrows. The Mishnah goes even so far as to forbid an exchange of work between neighboring farmers, where the later work is more laborious than the earlier. All these prohibitions are rabbinical only: that against a loan in kind might be called anti-Scriptural; for

the Bible, when it speaks of "usury of victuals" (Deut. xxiii. 29), contemplates a loan to be returned in kind, and forbids only the return of a greater quantity than that which was lent.

The lender should not lodge in the borrower's house free of rent, nor at less than the usual rent. The purchase-price must not be increased on account of delay in payment, such as an offer to sell a field at 1,000 zuzim if paid now, but at 1,200 zuzim in a year's time; but in charging rent the landlord may charge more when payable at the end of the year than when the rent is paid every month. It is improper for the seller of a field, after receiving part of the price, to say, "Bring me the rest of the money whenever you will and then take possession of your own"; for the income on the field would be interest on the deferred payment, and the purchaser is already a partial owner. But, what may turn out to be much more oppressive, a man may lend a sum of money upon a field on the terms "If you do not return me the money in three years, the field is mine"; and it actually becomes his. "Once Boethos, son of Zenon, did so under the advice of the learned" (B. M. 63a). It may thus be seen that the legal ban upon interest led to forfeitures which might give to the moneyed man more gain than even a high rate of interest. The mortgage in the English and American form is just such a contract as Boethos used to impose on borrowers. This form was contrived because the English law forbade loans upon interest; and in early times it was literally carried out, the land becoming the property of the mortgagee at once if the bond was not paid on the day appointed.

The Talmud and the codes distinguish between "fixed increase" ("ribbit ḳezuẓah") and the mere "dust ["abaḳ"] of increase." The Mishnah gives some instances of the latter; e.g., a man sends presents to a well-to-do neighbor, expecting to obtain a loan from him. This is interest in advance. Or after he has repaid his loans, he sends presents, "because your money was idle in my hands." Again, if A had not been in the habit of greeting B first, he should not do him this honor after he had obtained a loan from him; and, as the later authorities put it, if he was not in the habit of teaching B the Torah before the loan, he should not do it thereafter.

One difference between usury under the letter of the Law and rabbinical increase is this: the former, when collected by the creditor, may be reclaimed by action, while the latter may not. R. Johanan, one of the Palestinian amoraim, insists that even "definite usury," such as is forbidden by the written law, can not be recovered legally. In this view he is supported (B. M. 61b) by others on the grounds that in the Scriptural words quoted above the vengeance of Heaven is invoked upon the usurer, and that the rule that he who incurs the pain of death is not held to payment in a civil suit. The upshot of the dispute as laid down in the codes is this (Shulḥan 'Aruk, Yoreh De'ah, 161, 2): The rabbinical court will render judgment for the repayment of definite usury that has been collected, and will not enforce the judgment by levy on the lands or goods of the usurer's property, but only by force against his body.

When an Israelite lends money to a Gentile or to an "indwelling stranger" (a half-convert of foreign blood), he may and should charge him interest; and when he borrows from such a person he should allow him interest. It is the opinion of Maimonides that for Jews to charge Gentiles interest is a positive command of the written law. [The reason for the non-prohibition of the receipt by a Jew of interest from a Gentile, and vice versa, is held by modern rabbis to lie in the fact that the Gentiles had at that time no law forbidding them to practise usury; and that as they took interest from Jews, the Torah considered it equitable that Jews should take interest from Gentiles. Conditions changed when Gentile laws were enacted forbidding usury; and the modern Jew is not allowed by the Jewish religion to charge a Gentile a higher rate of interest than that fixed by the law of the land.—E. C.] The intervention of a Gentile may lead to an evasion of the law between Israelites. For example, one not standing in need of it has borrowed the money of a Gentile; the borrower lends it to another Israelite, he to pay the interest thereafter; this the first borrower may do only with the consent of the Gentile, if he will accept the other Israelite as his debtor, but not on his own responsibility, although the first borrower would pay to the Gentile the same interest which he should receive from his brother Israelite (B. M. v. 6).

In a baraita (ib. 71a) the other case is also put: "A lends money to a Gentile; the latter needs it no longer, but meets an Israelite who does. If the Gentile is willing to lend him the money on interest, he may do so, remaining bound to A; but A must not be a party to the change of debtor." However, it must have been easy to evade the usury law through the Gentile intermediary, even while maintaining these distinctions.

Case of a Gentile.

The guilt of breaking a Scriptural command falls not on the lender alone, but on the borrower as well (on the supposition that the verb referring to usury in Deut. xxiii. 20, "tashshik," stands in the causative form); also on the surety for the borrower, the witnesses, and, according to some opinions, the scrivener. The latter participants violate the precept "thou shalt not put a stumbling-block before the blind" (Lev. xix. 14).

Maimonides treats of interest in his "Yad" (Malweh, ch. v.), following the Gemara and the responsa of the Geonim. He to a certain extent mitigates the usury law; mitigation had indeed become a necessity in his time, as the Jews no longer dwelt in compact farming settlements like those of Palestine and Babylonia in the days of the Mishnah and the Talmud, but had been forced to become traders, brokers, and money-lenders. He says (ib. ch. xiv.): "There are things resembling interest that are allowed; e.g., a man may buy at a discount bonds belonging to his neighbor; a man may give his neighbor a denarius, on condition that he lends 100 denarii to a third person. A may give B a denarius to induce C to lend him (A) 100 denarii" (ib. ch. xv.). Some things are allowed by law, but have been forbidden by the Rabbis as a cunning evasion.

A says to B, "Lend me 100 zuzim." B says, "I have no money, but I have wheat worth that sum, which I can lend you." Then he buys the same wheat from him for 90 zuzim. He may afterward by law recover 100 zuzim because it is not even "dust of interest." Thus a man who has taken a field in pledge should not rent it back to the owner. But if such evasions are forbidden only by an appeal to the lender's conscience, very little is left of the enforceable law against usury.

The Shulḥan 'Aruk treats of usury not in the fourth or juridical part, but in the Yoreh De'ah, among moral and religious duties (§§ 159–177).

Views of Maimonides and the Shulḥan 'Aruk.

While Maimonides would restrict the lending of money to Gentiles within narrow limits, lest the lender should acquire a passion for taking usury, and practise it on his fellow Israelites, this later standard declares it "allowable nowadays in all cases" (ib. § 159). It allows also the money of orphans or of a poor- or a school-fund to be lent on terms which would be "rabbinical increase"; and if a guardian has improperly lent the money of his wards even at a fixed interest, the wards who have had the enjoyment of the income are not bound to restore it when they come of age. To save oneself in great need, however, one may borrow on interest (ib. § 160). The relaxation on behalf of infants and charities was unavoidable; for in numerous countries the Jews were precluded from the old plan of investing funds in land, which alone was permitted by the Talmud.

As a matter of jurisprudence it is found here (ib. § 160; Ḥoshen Mishpaṭ, § 52) that when a bond provides for principal and interest separately, it is enforceable as to the former, but not as to the latter; but if both are cast up into one sum, the bond is void in toto. When interest, even such as is forbidden by the written law, is once paid, it is said (Yoreh De'ah, § 161) that the courts may compel its restoration only by process of contempt (flogging until the defendant is willing to pay). When this power no longer rested with the Jewish courts, there was no remedy. If the lender died after he collected unlawful interest, it is here expressly said that his heirs are not even morally bound to make restitution.

E. C.   L. N. D.

——**Medieval Doctrine:** The Church, basing itself upon a mistranslation of the text Luke vi. 35 interpreted by the Vulgate "Mutuum date, nihil inde sperantes," but really meaning "lend, never despairing" (see T. Reinach in "R. E. J." xx. 147), declared any extra return upon a loan as against the divine law, and this prevented any mercantile use of capital by pious Christians. As the canon law did not apply to Jews, these were not liable to the ecclesiastical punishments which were placed upon usurers by the popes, Alexander III. in 1179 having excommunicated all manifest usurers. Christian rulers gradually saw the advantage of having a class of men like the Jews who could supply capital for their use without being liable to excommunication, and the money trade of western Europe by this means fell into the hands of the Jews. They were freed from all competition, and could therefore charge very high interest, and, indeed, were obliged to do so owing to the insecure tenure of their property. In almost every instance where large amounts were acquired by Jews through usurious transactions the property thus acquired fell either during their life or upon their death into the hands of the king. This happened to Aaron of Lincoln in England, Ezmel de Ablitas in Navarre, Heliot de Vesoul in Provence, Benveniste de Porta in Aragon, etc. It was for this reason indeed that the kings supported the Jews, and even objected to their becoming Christians, because in that case they could not have forced from them money won by usury. Thus both in England and in France the kings demanded to be compensated for every Jew converted. In the former country only in 1281 would the king give up his right to half the property of Jews who were converted. There was a continual conflict between the papal and the royal authority on this subject, and thus as early as 1146 the pope Eugenius declared all usury null and void, while the debtor was on a crusade, and Innocent XIII. made an indignant protest against usury, calling on all Christian princes to demand the return of the interest. Clement V. in 1311 protested against all civil law which permitted any form of usury by Christians.

It was impossible to carry out the canonical restrictions without stopping all progress in commerce, and numerous expedients were adopted to avoid the canonical laws. Especially the Cahorsins and Lombards invented methods by which usury was disguised in the form of payment for possible loss and injury, payment for delay, and so on. The competition of these Italian usurers—they were called the "pope's usurers"—rendered Jews less necessary to the kings in France and England in the middle of the thirteenth century, and both Louis IX. (1254) and Edward I. (1275) attempted to influence the Jews to avoid usury, but without effect (see ENGLAND). No other means of livelihood was open to them.

Very high interest was permitted the Jews in France under Philip Augustus, two deniers on the pound per week, or 43.3 per cent per annum, and King John in 1360 allowed this even to be doubled. In Sicily Frederick II. allowed 10 per cent in 1231. In Castile Alfonso X. allowed 25 per **Amount of** cent, while in Aragon the Cortes of **Interest.** Tarragona put 20 per cent as the maximum, and this was reduced to 12 per cent in the year 1231. In Navarre Philip III. established 20 per cent ("5 for 6") in 1330, while in Portugal Alfonso IV. (1350) fixed the maximum at 33⅓ per cent.

The enormously rapid increase of indebtedness due to this large interest caused ordinances to be passed to prevent interest being counted on interest, but without avail. As an instance of the extent to which interest could grow, the abbot of St. Edmund in 1173 borrowed about 40 marks from Benedict the Jew, and this had grown to £880 in seven years, though not entirely through interest (see Jacobs, "Jews of Angevin England," p. 60).

The loans were generally made upon PLEDGES, which could not be sacred vessels of the Church, to pledge which was punished as early as 814 by confiscation of goods. Almost all other objects could be

pledged, and it became a problem whether when a Jew had the pledge he could claim usury as well. This applied when lands were pledged for loans, when it was claimed the land or the produce thereof was sufficient to compensate for any loss of use of capital without further payment. Notwithstanding this the Jews claimed interest until both capital and interest were repaid.

Later on in the Middle Ages the doctrine of Aristotle that "money does not breed " was referred to usury, and forms the basis of Shylock's and Antonio's contention in "The Merchant of Venice," I., iii., and the casuists of Roman law drew a distinction between things consumable and fungible; that is, the use of which is exhausted by one using, and things which can be used over and over again. Interest or usury was allowed for the latter, but not for the former class, to which money was supposed to belong, because every passing of coin was regarded as a separate use. The lending of money with the expectation of any further return was still regarded as unnatural and disreputable, but in the later Middle Ages the Jews had been bereft of all capital, so that from the fifteenth century onward they are found mostly as dealers in second-hand clothing, rather than as usurers. Moreover a class of Christian merchants arose which evaded the canon law and lent money on interest without any opposition.

Notwithstanding this, the reputation of usurers has clung to the Jews even to modern times, though there is little evidence of their being more addicted to it than other persons who trade in money. In Russia the Christian "kulak" is regarded as being much more stringent in his demands than the Jewish moneylender, though in Bukowina the latter has proved to be somewhat of a plague. The poverty of the majority of Jews prevents them from any extensive addiction to this practise (see POVERTY).

BIBLIOGRAPHY: Endemann, *Die Nationalökonomischen Grundsätze der Kanonischen Lehre, 1863*, pp. 8 *et seq.*, 20 *et seq.*; Ashley, *English Commerce*, i. 152-154; Scherer, *Rechtsverhältnisse der Juden*, pp. 185-196.

J.

UTAH : One of the Western States of the United States of America; admitted into the Union in 1896. Jews first settled in Utah about 1860, among the earliest comers being Isidor Morris, Nicholas S. Ransohoff, Samuel Kahn, Fred Auerbach, Louis Cohn, Aaron Greenewald, Ichel Watters, and Emanuel Kahn.

Religious services were first conducted in **Salt Lake City** during the fall holidays of 1866. In the course of a few years Congregation B'nai Israel was established; and after its temporary dissolution it was reorganized in 1880. Its officiating ministers have been: J. Kaiser, L. Strauss, Hyman G. Elkin, Moses P. Jacobson, Gustave H. Lowenstein, Louis G. Reynolds, and Charles J. Freund.

Congregation Montefiore was organized March 20, 1899, and has occupied its present structure since 1903. Its officiating minister has been J. G. Brody. The Jewish Relief Society which was originally organized in 1873 was reorganized in the year 1888. The Council of Jewish Women has a large active section, mainly promoting the religious objects of the organization. Benjamin F. Peixotto Lodge 421 I. O. B. B. has been in existence since 1892, and at present has eighty members.

The Jews of Utah have from the time of their arrival taken a leading part in the development of its intellectual and industrial welfare. During Utah's existence as a state they have filled responsible government positions. Among those who have held public office have been: Simon Bamberger, state senator and chairman of the Democratic State Campaign Committee; Harry S. Joseph and Rudolph Kuchler, members of the state legislature; Joseph Oberndorfer, member of the board of education in Salt Lake City; Herman Bamberger, county commissioner of Salt Lake county; and Louis Cohn, councilman in Salt Lake City.

Besides those in Salt Lake City, the capital of the state, a few Jews are located in **Ogden, Provo, Price,** and **Logan.** The Jewish inhabitants of Utah number approximately 5,100 in a total population of about 373,351.

A.   C. J. F.

UTRECHT: Province of the Netherlands, with its capital of the same name. Jews resided in Utrecht prior to the expulsion from Spain and Portugal. In 1424 they were banished from the city; and their synagogue was transformed into the Church of the Blessed Virgin Mary. They evidently soon returned; for in 1444 the city council issued an ordinance directing that they be tortured on the wheel, imprisoned, and expelled. The reason for this procedure can no longer be determined with certainty; but it was due either to the fact that the Jews had championed the claims of Wolravus of Meurs to the bishopric, or to allegations made against them of insulting Christianity both publicly and privately. The ordinance of expulsion was quickly repealed, however, by the council itself; and Jews were permitted to settle in the village of Maarsen, near the city.

As early as 1664 a distinction was drawn between the German and Portuguese communities; the former consisting largely of the poorer classes, which earned a livelihood by peddling, while the Portuguese engaged in extensive commercial undertakings, and were wealthy and respected. An ordinance of Oct. 1, 1736, furthermore, gave the Portuguese the official right of residence in the province, and permitted them to conduct their business operations in the city itself. This privilege was renewed in 1777; and in 1789 it was extended to the German Jews on the condition that they assumed all communal duties.

After the uprising of the patriots against William of Orange and his expulsion by the French, France declared the Jews citizens, and granted them all civic rights and liberties. In 1796 a convention of the most prominent Jews of Holland assembled at Utrecht, before which the new constitution was solemnly read. Its text was translated into Hebrew by Zebi Hirsch Meilfeld, and published under the title "Dibre Negidim" (Utrecht, 1800).

BIBLIOGRAPHY: Koenen, *Geschiedenis der Joden in Nederland*, Utrecht, 1843. See also NETHERLANDS and the bibliography there given.

D.   S. O.

UZ (עוּץ): **1.** Son of Aram, and grandson of Shem, according to Gen. x. 23; but I Chron. i. 17 records him as a son of Shem.

2. Eldest son of Nahor by Milcah; nephew of Abraham (Gen. xxii. 21; A. V. has "Huz").

3. One of the sons of Dishan, and grandson of Seir the Horite (*ib.* xxxvi. 28; I Chron. i. 42).

4. Geographical name occurring three times in the Old Testament and connoting: (1) the native land of Job (Job i. 1); (2) a country northeast of Egypt, which it separated from Philistia, being one of the lands to which, at the command of YHWH, Jeremiah gave the wine-cup of fury to drink (Jer. xxv. 20); and (3) a country comprising part of Edom, summoned to rejoice over the destruction of the Temple (Lam. iv. 21).

According to modern investigators, who regard the names given in Genesis as geographical terms, the territory of Uz embraced the regions represented by the names of the persons mentioned above; and in like manner the brief notices in Jeremiah and Lamentations agree with those concerning the native country of Job's friends, as well as with other data concerning the land in the first chapter of Job. According to verses 15 and 17 of that chapter, the country was first invaded by the Sabeans from the south, and later by the Chaldeans from the north, which implies that the district lay on the northern edge of the great Arabian desert. Eliphaz, one of the friends of Job, was from Teman, a town of southern Edom; his companion, Bildad, came from Shuah (Gen. xxv. 2), which, according to the cuneiform inscriptions, lay south of Karkemesh (Carchemish); and Elihu was a native of Buz (comp. Jer. xxv. 23; Gen. xxii. 21). According to the cuneiform inscriptions, Shalmaneser II. received tribute from one Sasi, a son of the land of Uzza, from 859 to 831 B.C.; and the Midrash also identifies the name of Uz with the country, making Job a contemporary of Abraham (Yalḳ. Shim'oni, cii. 2; Gen. R. lvii. 3).

BIBLIOGRAPHY: Kautzsch, in Riehm's *Handwörterbuch*, s.v.; Delitzsch, *Wo Lag das Paradies?* p. 259.

E. G. H.   S. O.

UZÈS (אודיץ or אודים): Town of France, in the department of Gard, about 15 miles north-northeast of Nîmes. Jews were settled there as early as the fifth century. St. Ferréol, Bishop of Uzès, admitted them to his table and enjoyed their friendship. On this account complaint was made of him to King Childebert, whereupon the bishop changed his attitude toward the Jews, compelling all those who would not leave Uzès to become Christians. After his death (581) many who had received baptism returned to Judaism ("Gallia Christiana," vi. 613; Dom Vaissète, "Histoire Générale de Languedoc," i. 274, 545). Before the French Revolution there were seven Jewish families at Uzès, comprising forty-six individuals, who later settled either at Nîmes or at Pont-Saint-Esprit. Toward the end of the nineteenth century there was only one Jewish inhabitant in Uzès, namely, A. Mossé, an attorney. He was mayor of the town for several years (see Kahn, "Notice sur les Israélites de Nîmes," p. 31).

Among the scholars of Uzès were: the anonymous compiler (13th cent.) of the Talmudic collection mentioned in Steinschneider, "Cat. Bodl." No. 2343;

Samuel ben Judah, Gabriel of Milhauû, and Don Dieulosal ("R. E. J." xliii. 247).

BIBLIOGRAPHY: Gross, *Gallia Judaica*, pp. 23, 24.
S.   S. K.

UZIEL: Family name occurring principally among the Sephardim in Spain, where it is found as early as the fifteenth century. After the expulsion of the Jews from Spain and Portugal, the Uziels were scattered throughout northern Africa, Italy, and the Levant. The following are the more important members of the family:

Ḥayyim ben Abraham Uziel: Scholar and author of Spanish extraction; flourished in the latter half of the sixteenth century in Greece and Asia Minor. He wrote "Meḳor Ḥayyim" (3 vols., Smyrna, n.d.), an ethical work in Judæo-Spanish.
D.   S. O.

Isaac b. Abraham Uziel: Spanish physician and poet; born at Fez; died in Amsterdam April 1, 1622. At one time he held the position of rabbi at Oran; but late in life he left that city to settle in Amsterdam, where he opened a Talmudical school which counted among its pupils Manasseh ben Israel. Dissatisfied with the laxity in religious matters which he noticed among many members of the Sephardic community, Uziel delivered a series of lectures which led to the foundation of a new congregation under the name of "Neweh Shalom." In 1610, at the death of Judah Vega, the first rabbi of the new congregation, Uziel was called to the rabbinate. Uziel was the author of a Hebrew grammar, "Ma'aneh Lashon," edited by his pupil Isaac Nehemiah at Amsterdam in 1627 (2d ed. 1710). He left also in manuscript many Hebrew and Spanish poems ("Libros Poeticos en Declaracion de Todos los Equivocos de las Sagradas Letras"); these are highly praised by De Barrios, who represents the author as a great poet, an able musician, and a distinguished mathematician. Joseph Serrano dedicated a poem to Uziel; it is inserted in the "Temime Derek."

BIBLIOGRAPHY: Koenen, *Geschiedenis der Joden in Nederland*, pp. 144, 428; Jellinek, in *Orient, Lit.* viii. 264, 276; Kayserling, *Geschichte der Juden in Portugal*, p. 285; idem, *Bibl. Esp.-Port.-Jud.* p. 107; Steinschneider, *Cat. Bodl.* s.v.; Fuenn, *Keneset Yisrael*, p. 646.
G.   I. Br.

Jacob Uziel: Physician and poet of the seventeenth century; died at Zante 1630. He was of Spanish extraction, but emigrated to Italy at an early age, and settled in Venice, where he became famous for his medical skill. He was the author of "Dawid" (Venice, 1624), an epic poem in twelve cantos, written in Italian.

Joseph Uziel: Italian scholar and rabbi; died at Ferrara 1572. He was a pupil of Isaac Aboab of Castile, and left a responsum, which is included in the collection of Joseph di Trani (i. 39).

Judah Uziel: Italian scholar of the sixteenth century; born in Spain; died, probably at Venice, in 1634. He was the author of sixteen sermons on the Pentateuch, which were published under the title "Bet ha-'Uzzieli" (Venice, 1633-4).

Samuel Uziel: Talmudist and scholar of the seventeenth century; rabbi of Leghorn. He is mentioned in a responsum in the collection "Mayim Rabbim" (ii. 52) of Raphael Meldola.

Samuel ben Joseph Uziel: Rabbi and physi-

cian of Spanish extraction; lived in the sixteenth and seventeenth centuries. He officiated as rabbi at Salonica, where he also practised medicine.

BIBLIOGRAPHY: Steinschneider, *Cat. Bodl.* cols. 1158, 1376; Mortara, *Indice*, p. 67; Nepi-Ghirondi, *Toledot Gedole Yisrael*, p. 179; Conforte, *Ḳore ha-Dorot*, ed. Cassel, p. 45a; Jacobs, *Sources*, p. 200; Kayserling, *Gesch. der Juden in Portugal*, pp. 285, 294; idem, *Bibl. Esp.-Port.-Jud.* pp. 106, 107; Benjacob, *Oẓar ha-Sefarim*, p. 352; Zedner, *Cat. Hebr. Books Brit. Mus.* p. 384; Fürst, *Bibl. Jud.* iii. 462-463.
D.   S. O.

UZZA, UZZAH (עֻזָּא, עֻזָּה): **1.—Biblical Data:** Son of Abinadab. Together with his brother Ahio, he drove the new cart on which was placed the Ark of the Covenant when, accompanied by David and all the house of Israel, it was brought from Abinadab's house at Gibeah to Jerusalem. When they came to the thrashing-floor of Nachon, the oxen which drew the cart stumbled, and Uzza took hold of the Ark to steady it; whereupon he was slain by God "'al ha-shal" (= "for his error"). David, in memory of the event, called the place "Perezuzzah" (II Sam. vi. 3-8; I Chron. xiii. 7-11, where the thrashing-floor is called "Chidon"; comp. the commentaries of Budde, Löhr, and Nowack, *ad loc.*).

——In Rabbinical Literature: The Rabbis made various attempts to explain and palliate the death of Uzza. By an "argumentum a majore ad minus" proof is offered that if the Ark could bear those who bore it, so much the more could it bear itself. By not perceiving this, and thinking that the Ark might be prevented from falling by stopping the oxen, Uzza had brought death on himself. R. Johanan thought that "'al ha-shal" implied that he had died as a result of his act, while R. Eleazar drew from "shal" the inference that Uzza had eased himself near the Ark. He was, nevertheless, to share in the world to come: for it is expressly stated that he died "by" the Ark; and as the latter belonged to eternity, Uzza in like manner must be immortal (Soṭah 35a; Yalḳ., I Sam. 142, ed. Wilna, 1898).

2. Grandson of Ehud, and a member of the tribe of Benjamin (I Chron. viii. 7).

3. Head of a family of Nethinim who returned to Jerusalem with Zerubbabel (Ezra ii. 49; Neh. vii. 51).

4. Garden attached to the royal palace. According to Stade, "Gesch. des Volkes Israel," i. 569, ii. 679, "Uzza" should be corrected to "Uzziah," thus implying that the garden had been laid out by the king. It apparently contained a tomb in which Manasseh and his son Amon were buried (II Kings xxi. 18, 26).
E. G. H.   S. O.

UZZIAH (עֻזִּיָּה, עֻזִּיָּהוּ): **1.** Son of Amaziah; called also **Azariah** (comp. II Kings xv. 1, 13, 30). He was king of Judah, and began to rule, at the age of sixteen, in the twenty-seventh year of the reign of Jeroboam II. The Kings record (*ib.* xv. 2) states that his reign extended through fifty-two years (788-737 B.C.), and that he was righteous as his father had been, though he did not take away the high places, but allowed the people to sacrifice and burn incense at them. II Chron. xxvi. relates how Uzziah conquered the Philistines and the Arabians, and received tribute from the Ammonites; how he refortified his country, reorganized and reequipped his army, and personally engaged in agricultural pursuits. His success as king, administrator, and commander-in-chief of the army made him ruler over the largest realm of Judah since the disruption of the kingdom. His power and authority over the peoples of this realm help to explain to a certain extent the political situation in the reign of Judah's later kings, and probably also in 739, when Tiglath-pileser III. conquered nineteen districts in northern Syria which had belonged to Uzziah (Azri-ia-u).

Uzziah's strength became his weakness; for he attempted to usurp the power of the priesthood in burning incense in the Temple of YHWH. While in the act he was smitten with leprosy; and he was subsequently forced to dwell in a leper's house until the day of his death (II Chron. xxvi. 21). While he was in this condition Jotham, his son, ruled in his stead. The total number of years, fifty-two, attributed to Uzziah's reign include the period from his accession to his death.

E. G. H.   I. M. P.

UZZIEL (עזיאל): **1.** Son of Kohath and brother of Amram (Ex. vi. 18; I Chron. vi. 2). He was the father of Mishael, Elzaphan, and Zithri (Ex. vi. 22). The first two, at the bidding of Moses, carried from the Tabernacle the bodies of Nadab and Abihu, their cousins (Lev. x. 4). Elzaphan, moreover, was chief of the family of the Kohathites during the wandering in the wilderness (Num. iii. 30). Another son of Uzziel, named Amminadab, was one of the Levite chiefs selected to carry the Ark of the Covenant to the tent which David had pitched for it in Zion (I Chron. xv. 10). Two other sons of Uzziel were named respectively Micah and Jesiah (*ib.* xxiii. 20). His descendants were termed "Uzzielites" (Num. iii. 27; I Chron. xxvi. 23).

2. A Simeonite; son of Ishi; one of the chiefs who, during the reign of King Hezekiah, passed over the Jordan, annihilated the remnants of the Amalekites, and settled in their territory around Mount Seir (I Chron. iv. 41–43).

3. One of the eponymous heroes of the tribe of Benjamin; described as one of the five sons of Bela (*ib.* vii. 7).

4 (Called also **Azareel**). Son of Heman. He belonged to the eleventh order of those who were chosen by lot to serve as singers in leading the worship in the Temple during the reign of David (I Chron. xxv. 4, 18).

5. Son of Jeduthun; one of those who were chosen to resanctify the Temple during the reign of Hezekiah (II Chron. xxix. 14).

6. A goldsmith who repaired part of the walls of Jerusalem under Nehemiah (Neh. iii. 8).

E. G. H.   S. O.

V

VAEZ: Prominent family of Lisbon, whose foremost members, the four brothers Immanuel, Pedro, Ayres, and Salvador, resided in Portugal as Maranos during the sixteenth century.

Abraham Vaez: Ḥakam of the Portuguese congregation in Bayonne during the latter half of the seventeenth century. He was the author of a work on Jewish ritual laws entitled "Arbol de Vidas," to which was appended a lengthy treatise on rituals by Abraham Rodriguez Faro (Amsterdam, 1692). He wrote also several sermons on the Pentateuch, and a number of ethical treatises, which were collected under the title "Discursos Predicables y Avisos Espirituales" and published, at the expense of his son **Jacob Vaez,** by Isaac Aboab (Amsterdam, 1710), who himself wrote a long introduction.

BIBLIOGRAPHY: Fürst, *Bibl. Jud.* iii. 465; Kayserling, *Bibl. Esp.-Port.-Jud.* pp. 107–108.

Ayres Vaez: Physician to John III. of Portugal; brother of Immanuel Vaez; died at Rome about the middle of the sixteenth century. At the request of the King of Fez, with whom John, however, was not on terms of amity, Vaez was sent to Africa, where he succeeded in curing the monarch of a dangerous illness. Upon his return to Lisbon, Vaez devoted himself to the study of astronomy and astrology. In consequence of predicting to the king and queen the death of one of their children, a prediction which was fulfilled, he lost the royal favor. Thinking to regain the king's confidence, Vaez declared, in the course of a discussion, that astrology was an unreliable mode of divination, and that its practise was foolish and irreligious. The king, who had recently read a treatise expressing similar views, delivered Vaez to the Inquisition, charging him with being a heretic and a secret Jew. Vaez was ordered to defend himself before the inquisitors, and later to engage in a disputation with the theologian Sorao; but Capodiferro, the papal nuncio, succeeded in removing him from the jurisdiction of the Inquisition, and sent him to Rome to be tried by the Curia. Pope Paul, who was himself a believer in astrology, not only set Vaez at liberty, but even issued a bull (June 6, 1541) protecting the entire Vaez family, as well as the lawyers who had defended Ayres Vaez, against the Inquisition.

Daniel Vaez: Portuguese scholar; flourished at Amsterdam in the seventeenth century. Together with Joseph Athias, he published a prayer-book entitled "Orden de las Oraciones del Todo el Anno" (Amsterdam, 1677).

BIBLIOGRAPHY: Kayserling, *Bibl. Esp.-Port.-Jud.* p. 60.

Immanuel Vaez: Physician; eldest of the Vaez brothers. According to the account of Rodrigo de Castro ("De Universa Mulierum Morborum Medicina," ii. 47, 332, Hamburg, 1603), who was his nephew, and who settled in Hamburg in the sixteenth century, Immanuel was appointed physician to four kings of Portugal—John III., Sebastian, Henry, and Philip II. He won this distinction by virtue of his erudition and the experience which he had gathered in his extensive travels.

Pedro Vaez: Physician at ʻCovilhã, Portugal; second in age of the Vaez brothers. He is repeatedly mentioned in the "Medicorum Principum Historia" of Abraham Zacuto.

Salvador Vaez: Youngest of the Vaez brothers. He served as a page to the papal nuncio Hieronymo Ricenati Capodiferro in Lisbon, and was able to interest the prelate in the case of his brother Ayres, and to induce him to interfere in the latter's behalf. The result was that after the sessions of the Inquisition had begun, Salvador suddenly entered the hall and declared the sitting dissolved by order of the nuncio. Later he probably accompanied Capodiferro to Rome.

BIBLIOGRAPHY: Kayserling, *Gesch. der Juden in Portugal*, pp. 219–220.
D.   S. O.

VALABRÈGUE, ALBIN: French dramatist; born at Carpentras, Vaucluse, Dec. 17, 1853. He is one of the most prolific of modern French dramatists, producing about two plays a year and in addition acting as dramatic critic of the Paris "L'Illustration." Among his dramatic works are: "La Veuve Chapuzot," 1879; "Clarvin Père et Fils," Paris, 1880; "Le Crime" (with Bertol-Graivil), Dec., 1882; "Les Maris Inquiets," 1883; "La Flamboyante" (with Paul Ferrier), 1884; "Les Grippe-Sou," 1885; "La Nuit du 16," 1885; "L'Homme de Paille," 1885; "La Fille à Georgette," 1886; "Le Bonheur Conjugal," 1886; "Le Sens-Préfet," 1886; "Les Vacances du Mariage" (with Hennequin), 1887; "Durand et Durand" (with Ordonneau), 1887; "Clo-Clo" (with Decourcelle), 1887; "Les Saturnales," operetta (music by Lacombe), 1887; "Doit et Avoir" (with Felix Cohen), 1888; "La Sécurité des Familles," 1888; "Madame a Ses Brevets," 1890; "Les Moulinards," 1890; "Les Ménages Parisiens," 1890; "Le Pompier de Justine" (with Davril), 1890; "La Femme," 1891; "Les Vieilles Gens," 1891; "Le Commandant Laripète" (with Silvestre), 1892; "Le Premier Mari de France," 1893.

BIBLIOGRAPHY: Vapereau, *Dict. des Contemporains*; Larousse, *Dict.* Supplement, ii. 1968.
S.   E. Ms.

VALABRÈGUE,   MARDOCHÉE-GEORGES: French general; born at Carpentras, Vaucluse, Sept. 20, 1852. He was educated at the Ecole Polytechnique and the Ecole d'Application de l'Artillerie et du Génie; and, after reaching the rank of captain, he studied at the Ecole Supérieure de la Guerre from 1878 to 1880, when he was attached to the staff of the general of division in command of the artillery and fortifications of Paris. In 1884 he was made commandant of the third battery of the seventh battalion of artillery, and two years later was appointed officer of ordnance to General Boulanger, then minister of war. Valabrègue

Mardochée-Georges Valabrègue.

was made lieutenant-colonel in 1898, and colonel in 1902, when he became commandant of the Ecole Militaire de l'Artillerie et du Génie. In 1904 he was appointed "chef de cabinet" to the Ministry of War. In 1905 he became brigadier-general and was made commandant-in-chief of the Ecole Supérieure de Guerre and member of the technical committee of the general staff.

Valabrègue was created an officer of the Legion of Honor in 1904; and has been the recipient of numerous foreign decorations.
S.   J. Ka.

VALENCE: Chief town of the department of the Drome and former capital of the county of **Valentinois** in the ancient province of Dauphiné, France. Several Jewish families that had been expelled from the Comtat-Venaissin in 1323 sought refuge in Valence and its territories. Guillaume de Roussillon, Bishop of Valence, also brought a number into his diocese in 1330, and granted them important privileges. In 1441 there were eighteen Jewish families in Valence, each of which paid to the bishop, John of Poitiers, an annual pension of one gold florin ("R. E. J." ix. 238). The same prelate compelled them to wear the badge of the wheel (Jules Ollivier, "Dissertation Historique sur la Ville de Valence," p. 301).

The dauphin Louis showed much good-will toward the Jews of Valence and its territories. He confirmed the privileges which his predecessors had granted them, and invited all the Jews who wished to do so to settle within his dominions, promising them immunities and protection similar to those enjoyed by their coreligionists in other localities of Dauphiné, on condition that they paid the same dues. An anonymous writer of Valentinois in the fifteenth century composed a commentary on the astronomical tables of Immanuel Jacob Bonfils.

BIBLIOGRAPHY: Gross, *Gallia Judaica*, pp. 204, 263; Prudhomme, *Les Juifs en Dauphiné aux XIVe et XVe Siècles*, p. 67, Grenoble, 1883.
G.   S. K.

VALENCIA (בלינסיה): Capital of the former kingdom of the same name. During the dominion of the Moors, Valencia had a Jewish community eminent for its size and wealth. When James I. of Aragon made his entry into the conquered city on Oct. 9, 1238, the Jews went out to meet him with their rabbis and delegates at their head, and presented him with a roll of the Law in token of homage. As a reward for the important services which they had rendered him in the conquest of the strongly fortified city, he presented to some of them houses belonging to the Moors, as well as real estate in the city and its precincts. Among those who received such gifts after the "repartimiento de Valencia" were the secretaries and interpreters of the king, Maestros R. David, R. Solomon, and

James I. Makes Presents to the Jews.
R. Moses Bachiel; David Almadayan, secretary to the infante D. Fernando; Maestros (or Alfaquins) R. Joseph, Abraham ibn Vives (probably the father of the wealthy Joseph ibn Vives who in 1271 held a lease of the salt-works of Valencia, and who, as Amador de los Rios believes, was the ancestor of the Spanish hero Luis Vives, after whom

a street in Valencia is named), and R. Samson. Besides, presents were received by the gold-workers, merchants, and money-changers Moses Alconstantini (probably the same who in 1271 indiscreetly exhibited certain letters of the king), G. ibn Ya'ish, Simon Abenpesat (certainly a relative of Moses and Joseph Abenpesat of Tudela), and Astruc de Tortosa (without doubt the same that had possessions on the island of Majorca).

In 1239 King James assigned the Jews a commodious quarter for residence, extending from the wall Aben Xemi to 'Abd al-Malik; thence to the Puerto d'Exarea or Puerto de la Ley (= "gate of the law"); and from this gate to the "horno de Aben Nulid" and to the wall of Ibrahim al-Valenci. The Juderia or ghetto was first surrounded by a high wall in 1390, and was provided with three gates which were closed at night. The main gate was at the entrance of the long street which cut through the Juderia, hard by the Place de la Figuera (Higuera), where now the monastery of S. Thecla stands. Another gate, D'Exarea, was at the termination of the long street of the Jews; and a third gate led to the Place de la Olivera, now called "De Comedias." This restriction of the Jews met with opposition on many sides, especially from the Dominican friars, because by the establishment of the ghetto their church was wholly isolated.

Otherwise the Jews of Valencia enjoyed for a long time perfect freedom. They were not restrained in their trade or commerce; and they were not required to appear before the magistracy. They were subject solely to the city "baile," the representative of the crown. For several decades the baile-general was R. Judah (Jehudano), the king's confidant. The Jews were permitted to hold public office; but they were not allowed to execute justice upon a Christian. In 1283, however, this freedom was materially restricted. King Pedro decreed that no Jew should thenceforth hold any public office with which jurisdiction over Christians was connected. Moreover, Jews were to be admitted as sworn witnesses only in disputes involving sums not exceeding 5 sueldos.

Restrictions in 1283. The Jews in Valencia had a special formula, in Catalan, for an oath, which was not very different from that in Barcelona (see Rios, "Hist." i. 576 et seq.). They were not permitted to kill cattle in the public slaughter-house, and they were required to pay a special tax on the necessaries of life, merchandise, etc.

The Valencian Jews, who engaged in industrial pursuits and largely in commerce, aroused the envy of both nobles and citizens through the wealth and luxury displayed in their houses and apparel. In 1370 loud complaints were raised to the effect that the Jews had built houses outside the Juderia; and although they protested that this had been done with the consent of the king and by special permission of the queen, who received the Jewish taxes for rent, the king nevertheless decreed that the Jews should thereafter live only in the Juderia.

The inner government of the aljama was conducted by deputies ("adelantados"); and this body by royal permission had erected a school in 1264. Near the Jew street stood the large synagogue; and not far distant from this was a smaller one. The Jewish cemetery was outside the Juderia but within the city wall; and leading to it was the Puerta de los Judios, or Gate of the Jews.

The year of terror (1391) saw the abrupt dissolution of the flourishing Jewish community of Valencia. In the last third of the fourteenth century the city had sunk to a low level both morally and materially. The nobles wasted their property in excesses and indulged in the most extravagant luxury. Valencia, the beautiful garden of Spain, became the refuge of vagabonds and adventurers from all parts of the country. People were attacked, robbed, and even murdered in broad daylight; and the time was one of complete anarchy, the conditions being such that the Jews of Valencia trembled when they heard of the massacre in Seville in 1391. They sought protection from the magistracy and the city council, who took energetic measures for their defense. Quite unexpectedly, however, at noon on Sunday, July 9, 1391, St. Christopher's Day, a mob of between forty and fifty half-grown youths gathered in the market-place and formed themselves into a procession carrying a banner and several crosses. They marched to the main gate of the Juderia on the Place de la Figuera, shouting, "The Archdeacon of Seville comes to baptize all Jews," and tried to force their way into the quarter. The Jews hastily closed the gates, accidentally pulling in some of the youths. In an instant nobles and citizens, knights and clergy, strangers and the rabble generally made a rush upon the Juderia. In vain did the infante D. Martin, Duke of Montblanch, try to force back the crowd. The Jews defended themselves valiantly; and one of the youths was killed in the struggle. As soon as this became known the revengeful mob forced its way into the Juderia from the walls and roofs of the surrounding

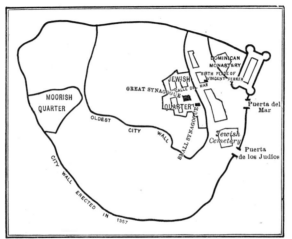

Plan of Valencia in the Fourteenth Century, Showing Position of Jewish Quarter.

houses. A frightful massacre ensued. Two hundred and thirty (according to another source, several hundred) Jews were killed, their
**Massacre
of
the Jews.** wives and daughters dishonored, and their houses plundered. Many, to escape death, accepted baptism. Don Samuel Abravallo, one of the richest Jews of Valencia, had the Marquis de Lombay as sponsor and took the name "Alfonso Fernandez de Villanova," from property belonging to him. Joseph Abarim, or Juan Perez de S. Jaime, as he called himself after baptism, declared in the criminal court (July 21, 1391) that notes due to him amounting to 30,000 gold gulden had been destroyed, that force had been used against his niece and against his son's nurse, and that his brother had been wounded.

After the catastrophe the magistracy did its utmost to punish the rioters; and ninety were taken prisoners. An order was issued to deliver up to the city all goods taken from the Jews; and soon the churches, the town-hall, and the neighboring
houses were filled with the most costly
**Dissolution
of the
Community.** objects. The city council demanded an exemplary punishment of the guilty parties; but owing to the fact that the most influential families of the city were implicated, the suit dragged along, and finally King John I. granted an amnesty to all concerned.

The Juderia was not reestablished. The community was destroyed: the large synagogue became a monastery (S. Cristobal); the smaller one was turned into a chapel; and the eight slaughtering-pens in the Juderia were sold (1393 and 1394). No Jew might enter the city without the permission of the baile; and even with this permit he might not stay longer than eight days. Each Jew entering the city without permission was liable to a fine of 50 maravedis. Only in places near Valencia, S. Thomas, S. Andres, and S. Esteban, might Jews reside even temporarily.

Several Jewish scholars lived in Valencia, among them Solomon ibn Gabirol, who also died there, and
Joseph Caspi. Isaac ben Sheshet was
**Scholars
and
Rabbis.** rabbi in Valencia for several years; and Amram ben Nathan Efrati occupied the rabbinate for four decades. The latter was widely respected for his learning, but was not on good terms with Ḥasdai ben Solomon (a friend of Isaac ben Sheshet), called from Tudela about 1380. Isaac Rocamora was born in Valencia. Several Jews adopted the name "Valensi," or "Alvalensi," after Valencia as the original home of their families; e.g., Samuel ben Abraham Valensi, a pupil of R. Isaac Campantons.

BIBLIOGRAPHY: Rios, *Hist.* i. 404, 413 *et seq.*; ii. 18 *et seq.*, 363 *et seq.*; iii. 400, 411; Jacobs, *Sources*, Nos. 315, 477, 483, 880, 1123; Isaac b. Sheshet, *Responsa*, Nos. 371, 387, 485. A plan of the Juderia is given in *R. E. J.* xiv. 264 *et seq.* On the massacre see the official report given in Rios, *Hist.* iii. 594 *et seq.* and in V. Boin, *Historia de la Ciudad de Valencia*, i. 440 *et seq.*; *Boletin Acad. Hist.* viii. 358 *et seq.*, xvi. 435; *R. E. J.* xiii. 239 *et seq.*; Grätz, *Gesch.* viii. 66.
s.　　　　　　　　　　　　　　　　　M. K.

VALENTIN, GABRIEL GUSTAV: German physiologist; born at Breslau July, 1810; died at Bern, Switzerland, May 24, 1883. He was educated at the University of Breslau (M.D. 1832), and estab-

lished himself as a physician in that city. In 1835 he received the Grand Prix of the Institut de France for his "Histiogenia Comparata," which is an able treatise on the evolution of animals and plants. In 1836 he was elected professor of physiology of the University of Bern, which chair he resigned in 1881.

Valentin was the author of several important works on the blood and its circulation, on the electricity of muscles and nerves, on digestion, on toxicology, on the physiology of the senses, etc. From 1836 to 1843 he published the "Repertorium für Anatomie und Physiologie," and collaborated on many professional journals. Of his numerous works the following may be mentioned: "Handbuch der Entwicklungsgeschichte des Menschen, mit Vergleichender Rücksicht der Entwicklung der Säugethiere und Vögel," Berlin and Paris, 1835 (see above); "Ueber den Verlauf und die Letzten Enden der Nerven," Bonn, 1836; "Ueber Mechanik des Blutumlaufs," Leipsic, 1836; "De Functionibus Nervorum Cerebralium et Nervi Sympathici," Bern, 1839; "Lehrbuch der Physiologie des Menschen," Brunswick, 1844, 2d ed. 1847–50; "Grundriss der Physiologie des Menschen," *ib.* 1846, 4th ed. 1854; "Der Einfluss des Vaguslähmung auf die Lungen und Hautausdünstung," Frankfort-on-the-Main, 1857; "Die Untersuchung der Pflanzen- und Thiergewebe im Polarisierten Licht," Leipsic, 1861; "Beiträge zur Anatomie und Physiologie des Nerven- und Muskelsystems," *ib.* 1863; "Der Gebrauch des Spektroskops," *ib.* 1863; "Versuch einer Physiologischen Pathologie der Nerven," *ib.* 1864; "Versuch einer Physiologischen Pathologie des Bluts und der Uebrigen Körpersäfte," *ib.* 1866–67.

BIBLIOGRAPHY: Pagel, *Biog. Lex.*; Hirsch, *Biog. Lex.*; Meyers Konversations-Lexikon.
s.　　　　　　　　　　　　　　　　　F. T. H.

VALENTINOIS. See VALENCE.

VALERIO, SAMUEL BEN JUDAH: Physician and author who lived in the Grecian Archipelago in the second half of the sixteenth century. He wrote the following works: "Yad ha-Melek," a commentary on the Book of Esther, completed at Corfu on the 6th of Feb., 1579, and published with the text at Venice, 1586; "Ḥazon la-Mo'ed," a philosophical commentary on the Book of Daniel, finished on the 7th of Feb., 1580, in a village near Patras, in the Morea, and published, with the text of the original, at Venice, 1586. There is an extract from the latter commentary in the rabbinical Bible of Amsterdam (1724–27). Valerio wrote also "'Emeḳ ha-Baka," "Pi Ḥakam," and "Bet ha-Malkut," still in manuscript.

BIBLIOGRAPHY: Fürst, *Bibl. Jud.* iii. 967; *Literaturblatt des Orients*, vi. (1845), 566, 606; Nepi-Ghirondi, p. 331; Steinschneider, *Cat. Bodl.* col. 2494.
s.　　　　　　　　　　　　　　　　　U. C.

VALI (VALLE), MOSES DAVID: Italian rabbi and physician; born at Padua; died there 1777. He was a cabalistic scholar of repute, and lectured before the Paduan association known as "Mebaḳeshe Adonai," in company with the two noted scholars Israel Hezekiah Treves and Jacob Ḥazaḳ. These lectures were attended by Moses Ḥayyim Luzzatto, who, becoming deeply interested in cabalistic research, began the study of it under Vali both with the association and in his own home, the acute intellect of Luzzatto exceeding that of his confrères. At the age of twenty-five Vali wrote a polemical work in Italian against Christianity, divided into seven parts, and entitled "I Sette Giorni della Verità." He wrote also, in Hebrew, seventy "tikḳunim" on Deut. xxxiv. 12. Between 1721 and 1767 he wrote eight large volumes in Hebrew (Almanzi MSS. Nos. 269-276), the greater part of them consisting of a commentary upon the entire Bible. They are still unpublished. Ephraim Luzzatto wrote a sonnet (No. 50 in his collection of poems) entitled "Eleh Bene ha-Ne'urim," praising the lectures of Vali and Treves.

BIBLIOGRAPHY: Kerem Ḥemed, iii. 119, 130, 131; Steinschneider, Hebr. Bibl. vi. 49-50.
S.   U. C.

VALLADOLID: Former residence of the kings of Castile and Spain; noteworthy for the numerous assemblies of the Cortes which were held there and which passed anti-Jewish laws. The city had a large Jewish community, which, together with the Jews of the neighboring towns of Zaratan, Portillo, Cigales, and Mucientes, paid 69,520 maravedis in taxes in the year 1290. Ferdinand IV., in opposition to the wishes of the town council, granted the Jews of Valladolid special privileges; but in the civil war between Pedro I. and Henry of Trastamara the inhabitants of the town rebelled against the king and supported D. Henry, taking advantage of this occasion to plunder and destroy the houses of the Jews and their eight synagogues, robbing the latter of their ornaments, and tearing the scrolls of the Law. Toward the end of the year 1411 Vicente Ferrer resided at Valladolid, and, not content with the results obtained from his sermons, induced the town council to confine the Jews within their circumscribed ghetto. In May, 1432, the great synod, composed of representatives of the different communities and of other influential men, held its sessions in the large synagogue in the Jewish quarter under the presidency of the court rabbi Abraham Benveniste. As in other places in Spain, during the year 1473 and in the following year many Jews who had renounced their religion were burned at the stake in Valladolid. The Jews of the city were so few that they, together with their coreligionists in the towns mentioned above, paid only 5,500 maravedis in taxes.

At the time of Asher ben Jehiel, Moses ben Ḥabib was rabbi in Valladolid, which was also the birthplace of the convert Abner of Burgos or Alfonso de Valladolid (Asher b. Jehiel, Responsa, § 107, No. 6). A few months before the expulsion, D. Abraham, physician in ordinary to D. Pedro Gonzalez de Mendoza, Primate of Spain, accepted baptism, as did also D. Abraham Senior and his two sons.

Valladolid was the seat of a tribunal of the Inquisition, which held many autos da fé there. See BENVENISTE; INQUISITION; SENIOR, ABRAHAM.

BIBLIOGRAPHY: Rios, Hist. ii. 55, 95, 429; iii. 594; Shebeṭ Yehudah, ed. Wiener, p. 133. Zarza is the only authority for the persecution of the Jews in Valladolid, the Christian chroniclers saying nothing about it. The introduction to the elegy edited by Jellinek in the Magen Abot (Leipsic, 1855), a commentary on the Pirḳe Abot of Simeon b. Zemaḥ Duran, alludes to the activity of Vicente Ferrer.
S.   M. K.

VALLENTINE, ISAAC: English journalist and communal worker; born in Belgium 1793; died in London 1868; son of the Rev. N. I. Vallentine. He founded the earliest Anglo-Jewish periodical, which at first was unsuccessful, but which afterward gave rise to the "Jewish Chronicle." He also took a prominent part in the foundation of the Jews' Orphan Asylum and other charitable and literary institutions in London. In 1848 Vallentine published "The Hebrew Almanack and Calendar," containing a table of holy days and fasts for the ensuing twenty-five years. This has been continued annually up to the present time, and has become the communal pocket calendar.

BIBLIOGRAPHY: Jew. Chron. Sept. 18, 1868; Jacobs and Wolf, Bibl. Anglo-Jud. No. 1321.
J.   G. L.

VALLS, RAPHAEL: Spanish Marano; burned at the stake by the Inquisition at Palma, Majorca, on May 6, 1691, as the "rabbi" of the CHUETAS, as were also his pupil, Raphael Terongi, and the latter's sister, Catalina Terongi, who adhered to Judaism. The popular poets of Majorca commemorated the death of these Maranos in verses which are still sung by the women of the island, one of them running as follows:

"En Valls duya se bandera,
Y en Terongi 's pano,
En sos Xuetas derrera,
Qui feyan se processo."

BIBLIOGRAPHY: A. de Castro, Historia de los Judios en España, pp. 214 et seq.; Kayserling, Gesch. der Juden in Spanien, i. 183 et seq.
S.   M. K.

VALUATION: Estimate of the value of the sacred gifts when a money substitute was required for them. The chief Biblical passage in relation to the subject of valuation is Lev. xxvii. 2 et seq., where ערך is probably a noun of action, as in Ex. xl. 4 (comp. König, "Syntax," § 277c). The particle ך, which in the cited passage often occurs suffixed to ערך, refers to the people of Israel, who are addressed, and in consequence also to the priest, who represents the people on every occasion. To assume a substantive, "'arkok" (ערכך), as does J. Halévy ("Journal Asiatique," 1899, p. 548), is not necessary, nor is it supported by tradition. This valuation was to be made by the priest, and his estimation was determined partly by fixed standards and partly by his individual judgment.

It might happen that some one made a vow that another person would become a Nazarite or would do service in the Sanctuary (comp. **Particular** Num. vi. 2 et seq.; I Sam. i. 22); and **Instances.** in case such a vow were not kept outwardly, the person in question had to be redeemed. For a male between twenty and sixty years of age, for instance, the sum to be paid was fifty shekels of silver (Lev. xxvii. 3-8).

It doubtless occurred very often that, moved by gratitude, some one would say, "I will consecrate this animal to the Lord." But if the animal in question did not reach the standard necessary in an animal destined for a sacrifice to the Lord, an equivalent in money was required. The value of the animal was estimated by the priest, and the person who had made the vow had to pay that sum and one-fifth more (Lev. xxvii. 9–13).

One might wish to give a house to YHWH, but since this could not be done literally, the donor would be directed to present the money-equivalent of the house. This, again, was to be estimated by the priest, and if the donor wished to buy back his house he was obliged to pay the estimated price and one-fifth in addition (Lev. xxvii. 14 et seq.).

The case became more complicated where any one wished to give a part of his land to YHWH. In such a case two possibilities had to be considered. (1) The land might have been inherited. In that case the price of the field was to be estimated according to the measure of seed it required; one homer of seed necessitated a payment of fifty shekels of silver. In addition, only the number of years which remained until the next year of jubilee was to be reckoned, for in that year the field re-

Valuation of Land. verted to its former possessor. If he who desired to give the field to YHWH nevertheless sold it afterward to some one, or leased it until the next year of jubilee, at the expiration of that term the field did not revert to its former owner, but belonged to YHWH forever (Lev. xxvii. 16–21). (2) The piece of land might have been purchased by the person wishing to make the gift, or leased by him until the next jubilee year. In such a case also, if he wished to redeem his field, he had to pay a sum estimated according to the amount of seed necessary for the field. This gift held good only for the number of years which remained until the next year of jubilee (Lev. xxvii. 22–25).

The first-born of unclean beasts (asses, for instance) were to be valued by the priest, though in Num. xviii. 16 five shekels of silver is mentioned as the price for the redemption of such an animal as soon as it should be one month old. The owner, however, might redeem such firstlings by paying the estimated price plus one-fifth (so in the case of the first-born of men, according to Ex. xiii. 13, xxxiv. 20; Num. xviii. 16), or else they were sold by the priest at the price fixed by him (Lev. xxvii. 26 et seq.). In the case of tithes, also, the obligatory fifth was added to the value if a part was to be redeemed by money (Lev. xxvii. 31). But such persons or things as were dedicated to the Lord in the form of the "ḥerem" (i.e., the ban) could be neither redeemed nor sold.

A comparison with other passages throws interesting light on these estimations. In the so-called Book of the Covenant the labor of a slave is valued at thirty shekels of silver (Ex. xxi. 32), while in Lev. xxvii. 3 the value of a strong man between twenty and sixty years of age is reckoned at fifty shekels of silver. Furthermore, in the Book of the Covenant no difference is made between a male and a female slave (Ex. xxi. 32), but according to Lev. xxvii. 3–8, a female is always reckoned at three-fifths the value of a male of the same age; in one case this three-fifths is reduced to one-half the value of a male (Lev. xxvii. 5). Moreover, the sum to be paid to the father of a dishonored virgin is fifty shekels of silver (Deut. xxii. 29), whereas in Ex. xxii. 15 no fixed sum is mentioned in such a case.

The number fifty, or half a hundred, is shown by these instances of its use to be a "round number" (a comparison of these numbers may be found in König, "Stilistik, Rhetorik, Poetik," p. 56).

A certain development may be traced in regard to valuation. In more ancient times persons were dedicated to the Lord, and then either

History of Valuation. they were actually obliged to do service in the Sanctuary, as in the case of the Gibeonites (Josh. ix. 23), and of Samuel (I Sam. i. 22), and of the women who, according to Ex. xxxviii. 8 and I Sam. ii. 22, did service at the door of the Tabernacle (this is König's interpretation of the fate of Jephthah's daughter; Judges xi. 39), or they lived as Nazarites and refrained from wine and other intoxicating drinks (Num. vi. 2 et seq.; Judges xiii. 7; Amos ii. 12 ["They caused my Nazarites to drink wine," Hebr.]). Later such persons were often redeemed (Lev. xxvii. 3–8).

A similar evolution is to be seen in the case of the first-born of unclean beasts. At first the neck of such an animal was broken (Ex. xiii. 13); but in later times, according to Lev. xxvii. 27 and Num. xviii. 15, redemption became allowable. The case of ḥerem also came to be treated more mildly in the course of time. This word (comp. the Arabic "ḥaram" = "to cut off") designated formerly a separation, or a setting aside to be destroyed (Ex. xxii. 19 et al.); but according to Num. xviii. 14 and Ezek. xliv. 29, the thing set aside belongs to the priest. Perhaps the passage Lev. xxvii. 28b designates a transition period in this idealization of the ḥerem (comp. Simon Mandl, "Der Bann," 1898, p. 13).

This valuation occurs once also in the history of Israel. King Jehoash, in II Kings xii. 5, mentions the money for the dedicated objects ("ḳodashim") which is brought into the house of YHWH. These ḳodashim are nothing else than persons or things given to YHWH and then redeemed with money, according to Lev. xxvii. 2 et seq. For in II Kings xii. 5 the valuation ("'erek") of the souls in question (i.e., of the persons) is spoken of, and nothing is said of the half-shekel which each male Israelite, according to a fixed rule, had to pay annually to the Temple as atonement money ("kofer"; Ex. xxx. 12–16). If the Chronicler in the parallel passage (II Chron. xxiv. 5) intended that, he was mistaken.

BIBLIOGRAPHY: Bertholet, Commentary on Lev. xxvii. in K. H. C. 1900; Baentsch, ib.
E. G. H. E. K.

VÁMBÉRY, ARMINIUS: Hungarian traveler and Orientalist; born at Duna-Szerdahely, on the island of Schütt, near Presburg, March 19, 1832. He was apprenticed at the age of twelve to a ladies' dressmaker; but after becoming tutor to the son of the village innkeeper, he was enabled by his friends to enter the gymnasium of St. George, near Presburg. In 1846 he went to Presburg, where he remained three years. Later he studied at Vienna, Kecskemet, and Budapest.

Vámbéry was especially attracted by the literature and culture of Turkey, and in 1854 he was enabled, through the assistance of Baron Joseph Eötvös, to go to Constantinople. There he became a private tutor, and thus entered the household of

Ḥusain Da'im Pasha, later becoming private secretary to Fuad Pasha. About this time he was elected a corresponding member of the Hungarian Academy of Sciences in recognition of his translations of Turkish historians. Returning to Budapest in 1861, he received a stipend of a thousand florins from the academy, and in the fall of the same year, disguised as a Sunnite dervish, and under the name of Rashid Effendi, he set out from Constantinople. His route lay from Trebizond to Teheran, via Erzerum, Tabriz, Zenjan, and Kazvin. He then went to Shiraz, through Ispahan, and in June, 1863, he reached Khiva, whence he went by way of Bokhara and Samarcand to Herat, returning through Meshed to Teheran and Trebizond.

Arminius Vámbéry.

This was the first journey of its kind undertaken by a European; and since it was necessary to avoid suspicion, Vámbéry could not take even fragmentary notes, except by stealth. He returned to Europe in 1864, and received in the next year the appointment of professor of Oriental languages in the University of Budapest, retiring therefrom in 1905. Vámbéry became known also as a publicist, zealously defending the English policy in the East as against that of the Russians.

The publications of Vámbéry, aside from magazine articles, are as follows: "Deutsch-Türkisches Taschenwörterbuch" (Constantinople, 1858); "Abuska," a Turkish-Chagatai dictionary (Budapest, 1861); "Reise in Mittelasien" (Leipsic, 1865, 2d ed. 1873); "Cagataische Sprachstudien" (ib. 1867); "Meine Wanderungen und Erlebnisse in Persien" (ib. 1867); "Skizzen aus Mittelasien" (ib. 1868); "Uigurische Sprachmonumente und das Kudatku-Bilik" (Innsbruck, 1870); "Uigurisch-Türkische Wortvergleichungen" (Budapest, 1870); "Geschichte Bocharas" (2 vols., Stuttgart, 1872); "Der Islam im Neunzehnten Jahrhundert" (Leipsic, 1875); "Sittenbilder aus dem Morgenlande" (Berlin, 1876); "Etymologisches Wörterbuch der Turkotatarischen Sprachen" (Leipsic, 1878); "Die Primitive Cultur des Turkotatarischen Volkes" (ib. 1879); "Der Ursprung der Magyaren" (ib. 1882); "Das Türkenvolk" (ib. 1885); "Die Scheïbaniade, ein Oezbegisches Heldengedicht," text and translation (Budapest, 1885); "Story of Hungary" (London, 1887); "A Magyarság Keletkezése és Gyarapodása" (Budapest, 1895); "Travels and Adventures of the Turkish Admiral Sidi Ali Reis in India, Afghanistan, Central Asia, and Persia During the Years 1553–1556," a translation from the Turkish (ib. 1899); and "Alt-Osmanische Sprachstudien" (Leyden, 1901).

On political subjects Vámbéry wrote: "Russlands Machtstellung in Asien" (Leipsic, 1871); "Zentralasien und die Englisch-Russische Grenzfrage" (ib. 1873); and "The Coming Struggle for India" (London, 1885). Many of his works have been translated into other languages, especially French. He wrote his autobiography under the titles "Arminius Vámbéry, His Life and Adventures" (ib. 1883) and "Struggles of My Life" (ib. 1904). He died Sept. 15, 1913.

BIBLIOGRAPHY: Meyers Konversations-Lexikon; Brockhaus Konversations-Lexikon.
s.   L. H. G.

VAN DEN ENDE, FRANZ. See SPINOZA.

VAN OVEN, ABRAHAM: Physician; died in England 1778; grandson of Samuel Basan, who, fleeing from Spain at the beginning of the eighteenth century, settled in Oven, Holland, whence the patronymic was derived. Abraham Van Oven received his medical diploma at Leyden Dec. 14, 1759. After residing for some time at Hamburg, he emigrated to England, and, settling in London, acquired an extensive and remunerative practise among the Jewish residents. He was a good Hebrew scholar, and wrote a Hebrew translation of Congreve's "Mourning Bride."

J.   G. L.

VAN OVEN, BARNARD: English physician and communal worker; born in London 1796; died there July 9, 1860; youngest son of Joshua Van Oven. He was brought up for the medical profession, studying under Sir William Blizard and receiving the degree of L.R.C.S. in 1818. He practised in London during his whole life, and had an extensive clientele among the Jewish community.

Van Oven was one of the pioneers in the movement for the removal of the disabilities of the Jews in England. In 1829 he wrote the first appeal which directed public attention to the subject, and which was entitled "An Appeal to the British Nation on Behalf of the Jews." He followed this up by organizing committees in support of the movement, and by convening public meetings, at which he was an indefatigable speaker. In 1847 he published the pamphlet "Ought Baron Rothschild to Sit in Parliament?" He was subsequently appointed chairman of the committee which celebrated the success of the agitation by the establishment of commemoration scholarships at several public schools. Van Oven served on the committees of most of the Jewish institutions of his day, and was instrumental in establishing the Jews' Infant Schools. In 1827 he had been appointed physician to the poor of the Great Synagogue, which position he filled for many years.

Van Oven was the author of a work entitled "The Decline of Life in Health and Disease" (London, 1853).

BIBLIOGRAPHY: Jew. Chron. July 13, 1860; Brit. Mus. Cat. s.v.
J.   G. L.

VAN OVEN, JOSHUA: English surgeon and communal worker; born in England 1766; died in Liverpool 1838; son of Abraham Van Oven. He was trained for the medical profession, being a pupil of Sir William Blizard. On receiving the degree of L.R.C.S. (1784) he established himself in London as a surgeon and apothecary, acquiring an extensive practise among the Jewish residents. Through unfortunate speculations he in 1830 found himself in monetary difficulties, and then removed to Liverpool, where he continued to reside till his death.

Van Oven was one of the most prominent workers in the Jewish community of his day, and was chiefly instrumental in establishing the Jews' Free School, the presidency of which he held for many years. His active participation was evinced in the weekly sermons he delivered to the pupils. He will, however, be chiefly remembered for his zeal in establish-

ing the Jews' Hospital in Mile End. There was at that time no institution for teaching handicrafts to Jewish lads; and its want was keenly felt and commented on. Van Oven therefore conceived the plan of erecting houses of industry and education, together with hospitals for the sick, whose maintenance was to be provided for by annual contributions from the sum paid according to the general poor-

Joshua Van Oven.

rates by Jewish householders. Opposition being shown to part of this plan, he was induced to modify it; and instead of several hospitals the Jews' Hospital in Mile End was erected from funds previously collected from the community.

Van Oven acted as honorary medical officer to the poor of the Great Synagogue, London, until his removal to Liverpool. In the latter city he took a prominent part in communal affairs, established schools and charitable organizations, and delivered in the synagogue sermons in the vernacular—at that time a novel proceeding.

Van Oven was a Hebrew scholar—perhaps one of the best of his day—and a voluminous writer, contributing articles on Jewish and medical subjects to the "European Magazine" and the "Liverpool Medical Gazette." He wrote also: "Letters on the Present State of the Jewish Poor in the Metropolis," London, 1802; a preface to "The Form of Daily Prayers," ib. 1822; and "A Manual of Judaism," ib. 1835.

BIBLIOGRAPHY: Picciotto, Sketches of Anglo-Jewish History, passim; European Magazine, 1815; Brit. Mus. Cat. s.v.
J.   G. L.

VAN PRAAGH, WILLIAM: Pioneer of lip-reading for deaf-mutes in England; born in Rotterdam June 11, 1845. Having studied under Dr. Hirsch, who had introduced into Holland from Germany the purely oral system of teaching the deaf and dumb, and who became principal of the Rotterdam Institute, Van Praagh became active in spreading his teacher's principles. When, in the early sixties, a Jews' Deaf and Dumb Home was established in London, Van Praagh was invited (1866) to take over the management of the institution. His application of the purely oral system at once attracted the notice of Miss Thackeray, daughter of the novelist, and others in the public press. In 1871 he published his "Plan for the Establishment of Day-Schools for the Deaf and Dumb." This pamphlet gave the first impulse in England to the establishment of day-schools and the boarding-out system.

The success of Van Praagh's work at the Jews' Deaf and Dumb Home led to the establishment by the late Baroness Mayer de Rothschild of an unsectarian institution on that system. It was termed "The Association for the Oral Instruction of the Deaf and Dumb." Lord Granville became president; Sir George Dasent, chairman; Sir John Lubbock (now Lord Avebury), treasurer; and Van Praagh, who severed his connection with the Jews' Deaf and Dumb Home, was appointed director (1870), which position he held almost until his death. In 1872 the association opened a Normal School and Training College for Teachers, as the head of which Van Praagh for more than a third of a century had charge of the training of the majority of English teachers in the lip-reading system.

Van Praagh's publications include (in addition to the above-mentioned pamphlet): "Lip-Reading for the Deaf" (6th ed. 1900); papers on the oral education of the deaf and dumb (including one read at the National Health Exhibition in 1884); "Lessons for the Instruction of Deaf and Dumb Children in Speaking, Lip-Reading, Reading, and Writing" (two parts, 1884); "Defective Articulation Resulting from Cleft Palate"; and various contributions to the medical and general press.

In consideration of Van Praagh's services to the deaf and dumb, M. A. Fallières, minister of public instruction and fine arts in France, created him "Officier d'Académie" in 1884. In 1887 Van Praagh gave evidence before the Royal Commission on the Blind, the Deaf and Dumb, etc. The teachers he trained have made known his system in every English-speaking country. He died June 28, 1907.

BIBLIOGRAPHY: Out of the Silence, in Cornhill Magazine, 1868; Proc. of Royal Commission on the Blind, the Deaf and Dumb, etc., 1887; Jew. Chron. Jan. 13, 1905; Jewish Year Book, 1905.
J.   I. H.

VAN STRAALEN, SAMUEL: English Hebraist and librarian; born at Gouda, Holland, 1845; died in London, England, 1902. In 1873 he was appointed Hebrew librarian at the British Museum. He translated many Dutch, German, and Hebrew books, and was the author of a catalogue of the Hebrew books in the British Museum (London, 1894) supplementary to that by Zedner, with an index to both volumes. He prepared also a subject catalogue of the Hebrew collection; but this was not published.

BIBLIOGRAPHY: Jacobs, in Publ. Am. Jew. Hist. Soc. xi.
J.   V. E.

VANCOUVER. See CANADA.

VANITIES. See IDOLS.

VARNHAGEN, RAHEL. See LEVIN, RAHEL.

VARUS, QUINTILIUS: Roman governor of Syria 6–4 B.C.; successor of Saturninus. He first became prominent in Jewish history when Herod the Great placed his own son ANTIPATER on trial before the tribunal over which Varus presided, and which condemned him. After Herod's death, however, his two sons, ARCHELAUS and ANTIPAS, went to Rome to make their pleas for the throne, while Varus remained in Jerusalem and quickly suppressed a revolt before he left for Antioch. When, however, SABINUS arrived at Jerusalem and oppressed the people, rebellion again raged throughout Judea, so that Varus was obliged to return with both his legions. Joined on the march by the Arabian king, Aretas, he first traversed Galilee, where Judas, whose father, Hezekiah, had been put to death by Herod, was at the head of the insurrectionists. Sepphoris, the capital, was burned, and all its inhabitants were sold as slaves, after which Varus marched on Emmaus in the west, and burned it likewise, the inhabitants saving themselves by flight. Traversing the entire district of Samaria, which he left undisturbed, he reached Jerusalem, where the Roman legion was besieged in the royal palace by the rebels. The news of his approach, however, so dispirited the latter that he was able to enter the city without resistance, whereupon the great majority of the people were pardoned, although the country was scoured by soldiers and about 2,000 of the insurgents were crucified. After the suppression of this revolt Varus returned to Antioch.

In an enumeration of the various wars, the Seder 'Olam Rabbah (end) alludes to this rebellion and its suppression as the "polemos shel Varos." According to Grätz, it exercised a great influence on Judaism, its direct results being the following: the rabbinical regulations (1) that emigration causes ritual defilement, since the people flee for refuge to foreign lands (Tosef., Mid. xviii. 3; Tosef., Kelim, B. Ḳ. i. 1, 5; Giṭ. 8a); and (2) that an agent delivering a geṭ must prove its authenticity through a messenger (Giṭ. i. 1); (3) the reception into the canon of Ecclesiastes, the Song of Solomon, and the Hagiographa (Yer. Shab. 3c); (4) the redaction of the Psalms (the majority of the daily Psalms contained lamentations and allusions to the Roman supremacy, and this was felt most keenly in the post-Herodian period); (5) the introduction of regular Psalms into the service of the Temple.

Bibliography: Josephus, Ant. xvii. 5, §§ 3–7; 10, §§ 7, 9–10; idem, B. J. i. 32, §§ 1–5; ii. 4, § 3; 5, §§ 1–3; Derenbourg, Hist. p. 194; Neubauer, M. J. C. i. 66; Grätz, in Monatsschrift, 1866, p. 80; idem, Gesch. 4th ed., iii. 235, 249, 252, 714–720; Schürer, Gesch. i. 322, 413, 420, 421, 669; iii. 215.

J. S. O.

VASHTI.—Biblical Data: The first wife of Ahasuerus; her disobedience and subsequent punishment furnish the theme for the introduction to the story of Esther. The name is held to be that of an Elamite goddess.

Bibliography: Wildeboer, Esther, p. 173, Freiburg, 1897.

E. G. H.

——**In Rabbinical Literature:** Among the women who ruled were: Jezebel and Athaliah in Israel; and Shemiramot (Semiramis), wife of Nebuchadnezzar (see Lev. R. xix., end), and Vashti in Gentile kingdoms (Esther R. i. 9). Vashti prepared a feast for women in the "royal house," where she served them with sweetmeats and other delicacies palatable to women; and she selected as the place of the banquet the royal chamber of Ahasuerus, where she might exhibit the artistic paintings which, according to R. Abin, women prefer to see to eating fattened birds (Yalḳ., ii., § 1049). Ahasuerus ordered Vashti to appear nude before him and his guests at the banquet with the queen's crown as her only ornament. R. Abba b. Kahana says Vashti was no more modest than Ahasuerus. R. Papa quotes a popular proverb: "He between the old pumpkins, and she between the young ones"; i.e., a faithless husband makes a faithless wife. According to R. Jose b. Ḥanina, Vashti declined the invitation because she had become a leper (Meg. 12b; Yalḳ., l.c.). Ahasuerus was "very wroth, and his anger burned in him" (Esth. i. 12) as the result of the insulting message which Vashti sent him: "Thou art the son of my father's stableman. My grandfather [Belshazzar] could drink before the thousand [Dan. v. 1]; but that person [Ahasuerus] quickly becomes intoxicated" (Meg. l.c.). Vashti was justly punished for enslaving young Jewish women and compelling them to work nude on the Sabbath (ib.).

E. C. J. D. E.

VATICAN LIBRARY: Papal library; originally housed, with its archives, in the Lateran Palace, where it was enriched, in the course of time, by many rare manuscripts. Transferred to the Torre Chartularia on the Palatine, it was taken to Avignon; but on the return of the Apostolic See to Rome it became known as the Biblioteca Avignonese. According to a catalogue published by P. Ehrle, this library contained 116 Hebrew manuscripts ("Historia Bibliothecæ Romanorum Pontificum," pp. 398, 754), and was probably the most ancient collection of its kind in any European library. The subsequent history of these manuscripts is uncertain, and they have been either wholly or partly lost. Such vicissitudes of fortune at length reduced the Vatican Library to a state of insignificance, until Martin V. (1417–31) and Nicholas V. (1447–55) endeavored to repair these losses, and founded the Biblioteca Apostolica in the Palace of the Vatican. This task was at length completed through the efforts of Sixtus IV., and from that time the Vatican Library has contained a large number of Hebrew codices. During the librarianship of Girolamo Aleandro (1519–38), who understood Hebrew, and of Marcello Cervini, afterward Marcellus II., the growth of this department was probably rapid; and it is clear that about 1550 the library must have contained a large number of Hebrew manuscripts, since after that date a special "scrittore" or copyist was employed for works in the Hebrew language. The actual number of manuscripts, however, is unknown, for the first catalogue, which was compiled by Carlo Federigo Borromeo, and which lists 173 books, is very imperfect, and is but little anterior to the middle of the seventeenth century.

Shortly afterward (1650) another catalogue was prepared by Bartolocci, with the assistance of Giovanni Battista Jonah, which contains a list of 584 Hebrew manuscripts and printed books. The manuscripts then in the Vatican had been acquired from two sources, the ancient Vatican collection, and the more modern Palatine foundation, which had formerly been in the library at Heidelberg, but which was presented by Duke Maximilian I. to Gregory XV., and placed in the Vatican by Urban VIII. in 1624. This Palatine collection contained 287 Hebrew manuscripts, which had originally belonged to Jews near the Rhine and the Neckar, from

Early Catalogues.

whom they had been taken during the persecution of 1391.

In 1658 the Vatican Library was enriched by the Urbino collection, which contained a number of valuable Hebrew manuscripts, including two ancient codices of the entire Bible. The second of these (not mentioned by Ginsburg in his "Introduction to the Massoretico-Critical Edition of the Hebrew Bible") was written, according to the colophon, in 976; this date is questionable; but the manuscript is undoubtedly very old. After these acquisitions, Bartolocci, assisted by Giulio Morosini, compiled a new catalogue of manuscripts; but all three lists are still unpublished.

The first printed catalogue is that of Stefano Evodio and Giuseppe Simone Assemani, issued in 1756, and in use at the present day. It contains numerous errors and discrepancies, however, some of them corrected by Berliner, Steinschneider (comp. "Die Hebräischen Uebersetzungen," p. xi.), and others. Thus, codex 133, which contains, according to the catalogue, a work by Isaac b. Jacob Alfasi, actually comprises a collection of treatises of Yerushalmi, and affords valuable material for the textual criticism of this Talmud. In his "Appendix ad Catalogum Codicum Hebraicorum Bibliothecæ Vaticanæ," Cardinal Mai gave a list of seventy-eight other manuscripts which were added to the library after the publication of the Assemani catalogue, thus raising the number of Hebrew manuscripts in the entire collection to 590.

In recent years three small libraries of Hebrew manuscripts have been added to the Vatican, these accretions comprising thirty-nine manuscripts from the Pia Casa dei Neofiti at Rome, deposited in the Vatican in 1892 and catalogued by Gustavo Sacerdote; eighteen manuscripts from the Museo Borgiano "De Propaganda Fide," added in 1902, together with the other Borgian codices; twelve manuscripts from the Barberini collection, placed in the Vatican in 1903, with the rest of the Barberini library. Neither the Borgian nor the Barberini manuscripts have as yet been accurately described and catalogued; and therefore the above estimate of their number is provisional. The Borgian collection contains a Bible of considerable antiquity; but the other manuscripts seem to be of little value. Among the Barberini codices is the famous tricolumnar Samaritan Pentateuch in Hebrew (Samaritan version), Arabic, and Samaritan (Targum), as well as the Pentaglot Psalter in Armenian, Arabic, Coptic, Aramaic, and Ethiopic.

Recent Accessions.

The Vatican Library was formerly governed by a cardinal librarian and a first and a second custodian; but in 1879 a sublibrarian was added to this staff, and in 1895 the position of second custodian was abolished. "Scrittori," or copyists, are employed in the library to copy and catalogue the manuscripts; but the statement that Sixtus IV. appointed a "scrittore" for Hebrew rests solely on a passage from Panvinio, and seems to be incorrect (comp. Müntz and Fabre, "La Bibliothèque du Vatican au Quinzième Siècle," p. 137, note 2), although it is certain that the library contained a Hebrew copyist about 1550, and that a second "scrittore"

was added by Paul V. (1605-21). The celebrated Bartolocci was a Hebrew copyist, as were many converted Jews, including Carlo Federigo Borromeo, Agostino Grimani, and Giovanni Battista Jonah, the last of whom went to Rome in 1638, and was a copyist at the Vatican until his death in 1668, when he was succeeded by Giulio Morosini, who held this office for the remainder of his life.

The Vatican Library includes also the Numismatic Cabinet and the "Pagan" and "Christian" museums. The last-named contains a glass vessel probably taken from a Jewish catacomb under the Via Labicana (see illustration, JEW. ENCYC. ii. 140b). This glass is especially valuable on account of its representation of the Temple of Jerusalem; it has been published by De Rossi ("Bollettino di Archeologia Cristiana," 1882, p. 137).

BIBLIOGRAPHY: S. E. and G. S. Assemani, *Bibliothecæ Apostolicæ Vaticanæ Codicum Manuscriptorum Catalogus*, Rome, 1756; Mai, *Scriptorum Veterum Nova Collectio*, vi. 83; Sacerdote, *I Manoscritti della Pia Casa dei Neofiti in Roma*, in *Atti della Regia Accademia dei Lincei*, 1893; De Rossi, *De Origine, Historia, Indicibus Scrinii et Bibliothecæ Sedis Apostolicæ*, Rome, 1886; Ehrle, *Historia Bibliothecæ Romanorum Pontificum*, Rome, 1890.
J. I. GI.

VATKE, JOHANN KARL WILHELM: Christian Hebraist; born March 14, 1806, at Behndorf, Saxony; died in Berlin April 19, 1882. After studying in Halle, Göttingen, and Berlin he became privat-docent in the University of Berlin in 1830, and assistant professor in 1837. In 1835 (Berlin) appeared his first important work, "Die Religion des Alten Testaments" (intended as part i. of a "Biblische Theologie"; but no more was published). After 1841 he published little; but his lectures on the Old Testament were edited after his death by H. Preiss under the title "Einleitung in das Alte Testament" (1886).

On the question of the origin of the Pentateuch, Vatke took the most advanced position, denying to Moses any share in the work, and regarding Deuteronomy as the earliest of the Pentateuchal books. He thus brought on himself the vigorous opposition of Hengstenberg; but his teaching exerted a lasting influence on a wide circle of hearers; and he is regarded as one of the predecessors of Graf, Kuenen, and Wellhausen.

BIBLIOGRAPHY: H. Benecke, *Wilhelm Vatke, Sein Leben und Seine Schriften*, Bonn, 1883; *Allg. Deutsche Biographie*.
T.

VAV. See WAW.

VÁZSONYI, WILHELM: Hungarian publicist and deputy; born at Sümegh (Sümeg) 1868. He was educated at Budapest, where his remarkable eloquence made him the leader of all student movements during his university career. After he had completed his studies the most vital social questions found in him an earnest investigator. He aroused a national sentiment against dueling, his success being proved by the numerous antidueling clubs in Hungary. Later he began a social and journalistic agitation in behalf of the official recognition of the Jewish religion, and kept the matter before the public until the law granting recognition was sanctioned (1895).

In 1894 Vázsonyi founded the first democratic club in Budapest, and became a common councilor. In 1900 he established the political weekly "Uj Század"

(="The New Century") for the dissemination of democratic ideas throughout the country; and at the same time he organized democratic clubs in all the large Hungarian cities. In 1901 Vázsonyi was elected deputy for the sixth district of the capital, on a democratic platform, of which he was the only public representative in the Hungarian Parliament; and at the election of Jan. 26, 1905, he defeated Hieronymi, minister of commerce, as a candidate for the deputyship from his district.

Besides numbers of articles in the daily press, Vázsonyi has written the following works: "Oenkormányzat" (1890), on autonomy; "A Választási elv a Külföldi Közigazgatásban" (1891), on the principle of election in foreign governments; "A Szavazás Deczentralizácziója" (1892), on decentralization in voting; and "A Királyi Placetum a Magyar Alkotmányban" (1893), on the royal veto in the Hungarian constitution.

BIBLIOGRAPHY: *Pallas Lex.* xviii.; Sturm, *Országgyülési Almanach*, 1901-6.
s.

L. V.

VECCHIO, DEL (דיל ויקייו, מאליויקיא): Italian family, tracing its descent from the period of the destruction of the Second Temple. Some members of this family were called also מהזקנים ("the old ones"). Its most important members were the following:

Abraham ben Shabbethai del Vecchio: Scholar of the seventeenth century; rabbi of Venice, Sassuolo, and Mantua. He was the author of the "Perush 'al ha-Ketubah," a work on marriage settlements. A commentary on this, entitled "Sheṭar Bi'urim," was in the possession of Joseph Almanzi. Abraham wrote also the "Sefer Zera' Abraham," on rituals, and a responsum included in the "Debar Shemuel" of Samuel Aboab (No. 19).

Samuel ben Mahalaleel del Vecchio: Rabbi of Ferrara in the sixteenth century. He was the author of "Tikkunim" (or "Haggahot ha-RIF"), on Alfasi's commentary on the Talmud, and of a responsum included in the collection of Jehiel ben Azriel Trabot (No. 19).

Shabbethai Elhanan ben Elisha del Vecchio (SHaBA): Rabbi of the seventeenth and eighteenth centuries; officiated at Lago, Leghorn, Ancona, and Casale. He was the author of all those responsa in Lampronti's "Paḥad Yiẓḥak" which bear the signature מלכת שבא: and he wrote also an approbation of that work. His correspondence with Morpurgo has been published in the latter's collection of responsa entitled "Shemesh Ẓedaḳah" (i., Nos. 15, 16; iv., No. 9), while his letters to Ḥayyim Joseph David Azulai are included in the latter's "Ḥayyim Sha'al" (i. 16). Shabbethai was also the author of the "'Ir Miḳlaṭ," responsa on the Biblical commandments, and of the "Da'at Zeḳenim," a work on ethics. The latter work is mentioned in the "Paḥad Yiẓḥak" (iv. 61b).

Solomon David ben Moses del Vecchio: Rabbi of Lugo; flourished in the latter part of the seventeenth and at the beginning of the eighteenth century. A responsum of his is printed in the "Paḥad Yiẓḥak" (i. 33a) of Lampronti, with whom he was on terms of intimate friendship, although the two were engaged in a literary contro-

versy concerning the question of damage to property (*ib.* iii. 37a). Solomon was also the author of a responsum on phylacteries, which is included in Samson Morpurgo's "Shemesh Ẓedaḳah" (i., § 4), and of a responsum in Motalia Terni's "Sefat Emet" (p. 19).

Solomon Moses del Vecchio: Rabbi at Sinigaglia in the eighteenth century.

BIBLIOGRAPHY: Mortara, *Indice*, p. 68; Fürst, *Bibl. Jud.* iii. 469-470; Steinschneider, *Hebr. Bibl.* v. 21; *She'elot u-Teshubot 'Afar Ya'aḳob*, No. 41; Nepi-Ghirondi, *Toledot Gedole Yisrael*, pp. 235, 321-323; *Mosé*, vi. 265, 338; Vogelstein and Rieger, *Gesch. der Juden in Rom*, i. 25.
E. C.
S. O.

VECINHO (VIZINO), JOSEPH: Portuguese court physician and scientist at the end of the fifteenth century. He was a pupil of Abraham Zacuto, under whom he studied mathematics and cosmography, on which latter subject he was regarded as an eminent authority by John II. of Portugal. He was sent by the king to the coast of Guinea, there to measure the altitude of the sun, doubtless by means of the astrolabe as improved by Jacob b. Machir.

When, in 1484, Columbus laid before the king his plan for a western route to the Indies, it was submitted to a junta, or commission, consisting of the Bishop of Ceuta, "Mestre Josepe" (Joseph Vecinho), the court physician Rodrigo, a Jewish mathematician named Moses, and Martin Behaim. The junta finally decided against Columbus' plans; and when the matter came up before the council of state Pedro de Menezes opposed them also, basing his arguments upon Joseph Vecinho's criticisms. Columbus attributed the refusal of the Portuguese monarch to adopt his plans chiefly to "the Jew Joseph." Though Vecinho did not favor Columbus, the latter had personal intercourse with him, and obtained from him a translation of Zacuto's astronomical tables. Columbus carried this translation with him on his voyage, and found it extremely useful; it was found in his library after his death.

Joseph Vecinho's translation of Zacuto's tables was published by the Jewish printer Samuel d'Ortas in Leiria under the title "Almanach Perpetuum," 1496.

BIBLIOGRAPHY: Kayserling, *Christopher Columbus*, pp. 9, 12-13, 16-18, 47-48.
s.
J.

VEGA, JOSEPH DE LA. See PENSO, JOSEPH.

VEGA, JUDAH: Rabbi and author; flourished in the sixteenth and seventeenth centuries. Vega was the first rabbi of the second synagogue of Amsterdam, Neweh Shalom, which was established in 1608. After a short time he resigned his office, and in 1610 went to Constantinople, where he is said to have written a work entitled "Jazania" (?), which treated of the life of the Jewish people from the time of the second destruction of Jerusalem. Conforte confounds this Judah Vega with another person of the same name (not Bizo), who lived at the same time, and who went from Salonica to Safed, where he conducted a Talmudic school and where he died. Judah Vega was a good preacher and haggadist; his small collection of sermons, entitled "Malke Yehudah," appeared at Lublin in 1616.

BIBLIOGRAPHY: Isaac Trani, *Responsa*, i. 139; De Barrios, *Vida de Ishak Husiel*, p. 42; Conforte, *Kore ha-Dorot*, p. 48a; De Rossi-Hamberger, *Hist. Wörterb.* p. 325; Grätz, *Gesch.* ix. 523.

E. C. M. K.

VEGETARIANISM: The theory according to which it is desirable to sustain the body with vegetables and fruits, and abstain from eating animal food or any product thereof. Rab said that Adam was prohibited from eating meat. "Dominion" in Gen. i. 28 is interpreted as the privilege of using the animals for labor only (Sanh. 59b). But after the Flood, when the animals were saved in Noah's ark, the right of consuming them was granted to man: "Every moving thing that liveth shall be meat for you; even as the green herb have I given you all things" (Gen. ix. 3). The only restriction was in the case of "flesh with the life thereof"; that is, flesh might not be taken for food from a living animal. Moses could with difficulty restrain the craving of the Israelites for the "flesh pots" of Egypt (Ex. xvi. 3). The manna, as a heavenly diet, could not satisfy them, and therefore Moses appointed a flesh meal for the evening (Yoma 75b). Again, the rabble among them "fell a lusting" and demanded more meat (Num. xi. 4). They were then supplied plentifully with quails from the sea, which caused an epidemic (Num. xi. 31-34; comp. Ps. lxxviii. 25-31). Moses limited the eating of flesh to certain kinds of animals, prohibiting those that were unclean (Lev. xi. 1-47). After the occupation of Palestine permission was given those who were too far from the Temple to eat the flesh of any clean animal that had been properly slaughtered (Deut. xii. 21). This is called "basar ta'awah" (= "meat of desire," or "meat of luxury"), meat not being considered a necessary of life. Daniel and his comrades were given pulse and water, and yet appeared in better health than those who were nourished with the king's meat and wine (Dan. i. 5-16). The prophet pictured a future when "the lion shall eat straw like the ox" (Isa. xi. 7). Isaac Abravanel, commenting on this passage, says that cruelty and ferocity are engendered in the animal that eats meat.

The Rabbis objected to meat-eating rather from an economic than from a moral standpoint. The advice of R. Judah ben Ilai was: "Sit in the shade and eat onions; but do not eat geese and **Rabbinic** chickens, though thy heart may crave **Views.** them" (Pes. 114a). A popular proverb in Palestine ran: "He who eats fat tails ["alita"] will be compelled to hide [from creditors] in the attic [" 'alita"]; but he who eats vegetables ["kakule"] may rest quietly on the bank of the river ["kikele"]" (*ib.*). The Rabbis, referring to Deut. xiv. 26, said, "The Torah teaches a lesson in moral conduct, that man shall not eat meat unless he has a special craving for it, and shall eat it only occasionally and sparingly." R. Eleazar b. Azariah thought that a man who is worth one maneh should provide his table with a pound of vegetables; ten manehs, with a pound of fish; fifty manehs, with a pound of meat; if he is worth 100 manehs, he may have a pot of meat every day. Rab followed the regulation of this tanna. R. Johanan, however, remarked that Rab came from a healthy family, but that people like himself must spend the last

peruṭa to purchase the best nourishment (Ḥul. 84a). Because he did not eat ox-meat in the evening R. Naḥman was not in a condition to render a correct decision to Raba until next morning (B. Ḳ. 72a). On Sabbaths and holy days fish and meat furnished the daintiest morsels. R. Abba spent every Friday thirteen silver coins at thirteen different butchers' shops in order to get the best meats in honor of Queen Sabbath (Shab. 119a). Rabbi, however, would prohibit an "'am ha-arez" from eating meat, quoting, "This is the law of the beasts, . . . that may be eaten," etc. (Lev. x. 46-47); one who is studying the Law may eat meat, but an ignoramus may not (Pes. 49b).

The modern question of vegetarianism is probably first discussed by I. B. Levinsohn, who justifies the strictness of the rules of "ṭerefah" on this account, and attributes the longevity of the generations from Adam to Noah to their vegetarian diet. The good morals and keen intellect of the Jews, he says, are largely due to their scant eating of meat ("Zerubbabel," iv., § 51). Dr. J. Kaminer, on the other hand, claims that the scarcity of meat among the Jews is directly responsible for many diseases peculiar to them; and he blames the exorbitant price of meat, due to the special Jewish meat-tax ("Seder Kapparot le-Ba'ale Ṭaḳsi," p. 77, note, Warsaw, 1878).

The principal reasons for upholding the theory of vegetarianism are summed up in an article by S. Rubin in connection with the prohibition of cruelty to animals (in Zederbaum, "Meliẓ Eḥad Minni-Elef," St. Petersburg, 1884).

An ardent advocate of vegetarianism was Aaron H. Frankel (b. Dec. 6, 1862, at Suwalki, Russia; d. Oct. 31, 1904, Brooklyn, N. Y.), who adopted a strict vegetarian diet and endeavored to organize vegetarian clubs. He expounded his theories in an English essay, "Thou Shalt Not Kill, or, the Torah of Vegetarianism" (p. 85, New York, 1896); and in order to arouse the interest of the Jewish masses and gain adherents he translated his essay into Yiddish under the title "Lo Tirẓah," adding chapters from time to time until he produced four large pamphlets on the subject. As a text for his work he took "He that killeth an ox is as if he slew a man" (Isa. lxvi. 3).

J. J. D. E.

VEIGELSBERG, LEO: Hungarian publicist; born at Nagy-Boldogasszony Jan. 18, 1846; educated at Kis-Körös, Budapest, and Vienna. For a short time he taught in the Jewish public school in Kecskemet, where he wrote noteworthy political articles for several newspapers, especially the "Politik" of Prague; in 1867 he became a member of the editorial staff of the "Neuer Freier Lloyd," and in 1872 he became editor-in-chief of the "Pester Lloyd." His political leaders, usually signed with two asterisks, always attracted great attention; and his services as a publicist were recognized by Francis Joseph I., who conferred upon him the decoration of the Order of the Iron Crown (3d class) on July 9, 1904.

Veigelsberg's son **Hugo,** born at Budapest Nov. 2, 1869, and educated at Kis-Körös, Kecskemet, Eperjes, and Budapest, is one of the most important authors of the younger generation, being distinguished for the lyric individuality of his poems, stories, and sociological works. He usually writes under one of the pseudonyms "Dixi," "Pató Pál," "Tar Lörincz," and "Ignotus." He has published: "A Slemil Keservei" (1891), "Versek" (1894), "Vallomások" (1900), and "Végzet," a translation of a novel by the Dutch author Couperus.

BIBLIOGRAPHY: *Pallas Lex.*
s. L. V.

VEIL: A cover for the face; a disguise. From the earliest times it has been a sign of chastity and decency in married women to cover their faces with veils in the presence of strangers. This custom is still in vogue in the Orient. The putting on of the veil marked the transition from girlhood to womanhood. Rebekah, the bride, covered herself with a veil on meeting Isaac, the groom (Gen. xxiv. 65). A widow did not wear a veil (*ib.* xxxviii. 19). The custom of dressing the virgin bride with a veil is mentioned in the Mishnah; covered with a veil ("hinuma") and seated on a litter, she was carried in the wedding-procession from her father's house to the nuptial ceremony (Ket. ii. 1). In modern times the bride is "covered" with a veil in her chamber in the presence of the groom, just before they are led under the canopy. In some countries the groom, and in others the rabbi, performs the ceremony of covering the bride.

Moses, when speaking to the people after he had come down from Mount Sinai, covered his face with a veil as his skin shone so brightly that the people feared to come nigh him (Ex. xxxiv. 29-35).

The veil was used as a disguise by Tamar to mislead Judah (Gen. xxxviii. 14). The prophet "disguised himself with his headband over his eyes" (I Kings xx. 38, R. V.).

A. J. D. E.

VEIT, JOHANNES: German painter; born in Berlin 1790; died at Rome 1854. He studied at Vienna and at Rome, where he especially took Vanucci for his model. Together with his brother Philipp VEIT he joined the neo-German school, but distinguished himself by his superior coloring. He painted an altar-piece for the cathedral at Liége and an "Adoration of the Shepherds" for a Catholic church at Berlin, as well as several famous portraits of the Madonna.

BIBLIOGRAPHY: Hans Wolfgang Singer, *Allgemeines Künstler-Lexicon*, Frankfort-on-the-Main, 1898; Bryan, *Dictionary of Painters and Engravers*, London, 1904.
s. F. C.

VEIT, PHILIPP: German portrait- and genre-painter; born Feb. 13, 1793, in Berlin; died Dec. 18, 1877, at Mayence. His father died while he was a child; and his mother, who was a daughter of Moses MENDELSSOHN, married Friedrich von Schlegel, who had the boy baptized.

The early part of his youth Veit spent at his step-father's home in Paris, but he was later sent to Dresden, where he studied under Friedrich Matthäi. He completed his education in Vienna, and in 1813 entered the army, taking part in the Napoleonic wars. He fought at Dresden, Kulm, and Leipsic, and was decorated with the Iron Cross for bravery in battle.

In 1815 he went to Rome, where he remained till 1830 and where he became identified with the neo-German religious school, joining Cornelius, Von Schadow, and Overbeck, together with whom he painted many important frescos; of these may be mentioned "Joseph with Potiphar's Wife" and "The Seven Fat Years" for the Casa Bartholdy, and "The Triumph of Religion" in the Vatican gallery. In Rome he painted also several subjects from Dante's "Divina Commedia" for the Villa Massimi, and a "Mary in Glory" for Santa Trinità de' Monti.

Returning to Germany in 1830, Veit became director of the Staedel Institute in Frankfort-on-the-Main. For this institute he painted the following large canvases: "The Triumph of Christianity," "The Introduction of Art into Germany by Christianity," "Italia," and "Germania." The last-named, which is an allegorical picture representing Germany as a young matron, did more than any of his other paintings toward establishing his reputation.

Veit resigned the directorate of the Staedel Institute in 1843, and settled in Sachsenhausen, where he painted his "Assumption of the Virgin" for the cathedral at Frankfort, and also several pictures for King Frederick William IV. In 1853 he was elected director of the Gallery of Art in Mayence. Here he designed for the cathedral a cycle of frescos, which were executed by his pupils, being completed in 1868.

Of Veit's other paintings the following may be mentioned: "St. George" (for the church at Bensheim); "The Marys at the Sepulcher" (Berlin National Gallery); "The Ascension of Christ" (1846; cathedral, Frankfort-on-the-Main); "Madonna" (Darmstadt Gallery of Art); "Christ" (cathedral of Naumburg).

Veit painted also for the Römersaal in Frankfort-on-the-Main several portraits of emperors of the Middle Ages, of which may be mentioned: "Charlemagne," "Otto IV.," and "Friedrich II."

To the "Vereinsschrift der Görres-Gesellschaft" he contributed "Zehn Vorträge über Kunst" (Cologne, 1891).

BIBLIOGRAPHY: *Meyers Konversations-Lexikon*; Bryan, *Dictionary of Painters and Engravers*, vol. ii., London, 1889; Hans Wolfgang Singer, *Allgemeines Künstler-Lexicon*, vol. iii., Frankfort-on-the-Main, 1898; Clement and Hutton, *Artists of the Nineteenth Century and Their Works*, Boston, 1880.
s. F. C.

VEITEL, EPHRAIM. See HEINE, HEINRICH.

VELLUM: Skins of animals constituted the ancient Oriental writing-material (Herodotus, v. 58; Strabo, xv. 1; Pauly-Wissowa, "Real-Encyc." ii. 944), and the Jews employed them as early as the Biblical period (Blau, "Das Althebräische Buchwesen," pp. 12-15), attaining great proficiency in their preparation (Letter of Aristeas, §§ 176-179). The Talmud was acquainted with three varieties, leather, parchment, and "doksostos," the last apparently a parchment obtained by scraping both sides of the skin (Blau, *l.c.* p. 28); in the case of leather the outside of the hide formed the writing-surface; in the case of parchment, the inside (Yer. Meg. 71a). The skins of domestic and of wild animals alike were used, although only those which were ritually clean might be chosen. The skins of fishes and birds were likewise prepared (Yer. Shab. 14c; Kelim 10; Blau, *l.c.* pp. 32 *et seq.*), but were not used for books. The most frequent writing-material was formed from the hide of the deer, although only half the skin was used (Blau, *l.c.* pp. 17, 30). While scrolls of the Law might be written on parchment (Yer. Meg. 71a, d; B. B. 14a, top), entire skins were the usual material, these being consequently of leather and called "gewil" (Blau, *l.c.* pp. 24–26). Parchment books are mentioned by Paul (II Tim. iv. 13), this phrase designating Greek manuscripts of Biblical writings on parchment ("Berliner Festschrift," p. 44). The Codex Sinaiticus of the fourth century is written on the skin of an antelope, and it is not impossible that the "Hexapla" of Origen was likewise inscribed on leather or parchment (Blau, *l.c.* pp. 45–47). The scribes manufactured their vellum themselves, and it formed an article of trade (Giṭ. 60a. Sanh. 28b). Babylonians were preeminent in the art of preparing leather (Meg. 17a, 19a), and doubtless displayed equal skill in the manufacture of leather and parchment for writing.

The distinctive writing-material of the ancient Hebrews was parchment, which alone may be used for the scrolls of the Law even at the present day; and parchment manuscripts which still exist show that this material continued to be employed after paper had come into general use for other purposes. References to examples of parchment and manuscript are given in JEW. ENCYC. viii. 305, *s.v.* MANUSCRIPTS, where the fact is also noted that the finest material came from Italy and Spain.

The statement is frequently made that the German Jews furnished parchment for the imperial chancery, and that when Charles IV. pawned the Jews of Frankfort to the citizens of that place, he reserved for himself and his descendants the right of obtaining parchment for the chancery from them. In 1354 a certain Smogil Perminter ("parchment-maker") is mentioned (Wattenbach, "Schriftwesen des Mittelalters," 3d ed., p. 131), and in the sixteenth century Moses Isserles declares that "our parchment is better for the preparation of scrolls of the Law than the leather ["gewil"] of the ancients." Books were printed on parchment, and phylacteries and mezuzot were made out of strips of parchment. Amulets were written on the same material; and medieval and modern cabalistic and magic writings contain directions for writing on parchment, with such added statements as that "it must be virginal." Colored parchment is not mentioned in the Talmud or Midrash, although the statement is made that parchment becomes black with age. See MANUSCRIPTS; SCROLL OF THE LAW.

BIBLIOGRAPHY: Blau, *Das Althebräische Buchwesen*, Strasburg, 1902; Löw, *Graphische Requisiten*, Leipsic, 1870.
J. L. B.

VENDOR AND PURCHASER. See SALE.

VENETIANER, LUDWIG: Hungarian rabbi and writer; born May 19, 1867, at Kecskemet. He studied at the rabbinical seminary and the University of Budapest, and at the Jewish Theological Seminary and the University of Breslau, 1888–89 (Ph.D. 1890, Budapest). Receiving his diploma as rabbi from the seminary of Budapest in 1892, he officiated as rabbi at Somogy-Csurgo from that year to 1895, holding at the same time the chair of Hun-

garian and German literatures at the Evangelical Reform Gymnasium of that city. In 1895 he was called to the rabbinate of Lugos, and in the following year to that of Ujpest near Budapest.

Venetianer was the author of: "A Fokozatok Könyve," on the sources of Shem-Ṭob ibn Falaquera (Szegedin, 1890); "A Felebaráti Szeretet a Zsidó Ethikában," on charity in Jewish ethics (Budapest, 1891); "Das Buch der Grade von Schemtob ibn Falaquera" (Berlin, 1894); "Die Eleusinischen Mysterien im Jerusalemischen Tempel" (Frankfort-on-the-Main, 1897); "A Héber-Magyar Oesszehasonlító Nyelvészet," a history of Hebrew-Hungarian philology (Budapest, 1898); "A Zsidóság Szervezete az Európai Államokban," a history of the Jewish communal constitution in Europe (*ib.* 1901); "A Magyar Zsidóság Szervezetéröl," a work treating of the organization of the Jews in Hungary (*ib.* 1903); "A Zsidóság Eszméi és Tanai," a treatise on the conceptions and doctrines of Judaism (*ib.* 1904). He has also contributed numerous articles to periodicals, including "Egyenlöség," "Társadalmi Lapok," "Jahrbuch des Litteraturvereins," "Pesti Napló," "Magyar-Zsidó Szemle," "Orientalistische Litteraturzeitung," "Ethnographia," and "Bloch's Festschrift" (supplement to the "Oesterreichische Wochenschrift"); and he has published some sermons in Hungarian. He died in 1922.

BIBLIOGRAPHY: A. Csurgoi, *Tanitó-Kepzö Jntézet Törtenete*, p. 45; *Gesch. des Jüdisch-Theologischen Seminars in Breslau*, p. 199.
S.

VENEZIANI, EMMANUEL FELIX: French philanthropist; born at Leghorn in 1825; died at Paris Feb. 5, 1889. At an early age he went to Constantinople, where he became the manager of the Banque Camondo and president of the committee of the Alliance Israélite Universelle; but after the close of the Franco-German war he went to Paris and became the associate of Baron Maurice de Hirsch in his philanthropic plans. In 1877 Veneziani traveled through Turkey and Bulgaria to relieve, without regard to creed, the distress of the poor who were suffering from the rigors of the Russo-Turkish war; and for his services he was rewarded with a commandership of the Order of the Nishan-i-Medjidie. In the following year, with Charles Netter and Sacki Kann, he went to the Berlin Congress to plead the cause of religious liberty, and in 1880 he and Netter made a similar plea for the Jews of Morocco at the Madrid Congress. Two years later he and Netter were sent by the Alliance to Brody to assist the Russian Jews and to aid them to emigrate, a million francs being set aside by the society, at his instance, for this purpose. On his election to the central committee of the Alliance in 1883, Veneziani made a tour of the Jewish colonies of Palestine, and it was decided, on his representation, to check the Russian emigration to that country. He made repeated visits to Vienna also, where he devoted himself to making the plans and laying the foundation of a charitable institution erected at the expense of Baron de Hirsch. Despite the shock resulting from the death of his son in 1882, Veneziani continued his activities to the last, dying only a few days after returning from a journey to Vienna.

BIBLIOGRAPHY: *Bulletin de l'Alliance Israélite Universelle,* Jan., 1889; Zadoc Kahn, *Souvenirs et Regrets,* pp. 278–283; *Univ. Isr.* Feb. 16, 1889.
S.   J. KA.

VENICE: Italian city; formerly capital of a republic embracing northeastern Italy and some islands in the Mediterranean. The first Venetian document, so far as known, in which Jews are mentioned is a decree of the Senate, dated 945, prohibiting captains of ships sailing in Oriental waters from taking on board Jews or other merchants — a protectionist measure which was hardly ever enforced. According to a census of the city said to have been taken in 1152 (Galliccioli, "Memoria Antiche Venete," ii. 279), the Jews then in Venice numbered 1,300, an estimate which Galliccioli himself believes to be excessive. An event which must have increased the number of Jews in Venice was the conquest of Constantinople by the allied Venetians and French in 1204, when the former took possession of several islands in the Levant, including Eubœa, where the Jews were numerous. At that time Jewish merchants went to Venice for the transaction of business, and some of them settled there permanently.

The first lasting settlement of Jews was not in the city itself, but on the neighboring island of Spinalunga, which was called "Giudeca" in a document dated 1252. For some unknown reason this island was afterward abandoned. For several centuries the ruins of two ancient synagogues were to be seen there (comp. Ravà in "Educatore Israelità," 1871, p. 47). At the beginning of the thirteenth century many Jews went to Venice from Germany, some seeking refuge from persecution, others attracted by the commercial advantages of this important seaport. A decree of the Senate, dated 1290,

Early Jewish Settlement. imposed upon the Jews of Venice a duty of 5 per cent on both imports and exports (Galliccioli, *l.c.* ii. 280). R. Simeon Luzzatto (1580–1663) speaks in his noteworthy "Discorso Circa il Stato degli Hebrei di Venetia" (p. 18) of the Jew who was instrumental in bringing the commerce of the Levant to Venice.

An ordinance of 1541, issued by the Senate on the advice of the Board of Commerce, to provide Jewish merchants with storehouses within the precincts of the ghetto, observes that "the greater part of the commerce coming from Upper and Lower Rumania is controlled by itinerant Jewish Levantine merchants" (Schiavi, "Gli Ebrei in Venezia e nelle Sue Colonie," p. 493). When the "Cattaveri" were commissioned in 1688 to compile new laws for the Jews, the Senate demanded that "the utmost encouragement possible should be given to those nations [referring to the various sections into which the whole Jewish community was divided] for the sake of the important advantages which will thus accrue to our customs duties" (comp. Ravà, *l.c.* 1871, p. 334).

Besides engaging in commerce, the Jews conducted loan-banks; and in the ancient decrees of the Senate in regard to them it is repeatedly declared that the operation of these banks, which was prohibited by the canonical law, was the chief reason for admitting Jews into Venice. Therefore, in deference to some remnant of scruple, it was ordained, at least at first,

that contracts relative to these transactions should not be drawn up in the city itself, but in the neighboring Mestre (Galliccioli, *l.c.* ii. 281). The interest on the loans was at first fixed by a decree of 1366 at 4 per cent, but it was raised afterward to 10 or 12 per cent, according to whether the loans were made on substantial security or on written obligations. The original object of these banks was solely to help the poor, but it soon became evident that it was neces-

The Ghetto, Venice.
(From a photograph.)

sary to provide for greater loans, some of which were made to the government itself. These banks, as well as Jewish affairs in general, were placed under the surveillance of special magistrates whose titles varied according to the times, as "consoli," "sopraconsoli," "provveditori," "sopraprovveditori," etc. (see Soave in "Corriere Israelitico," 1879, p. 56).

Despite all this, however, the right of the Jews to reside in Venice always remained precarious. Their

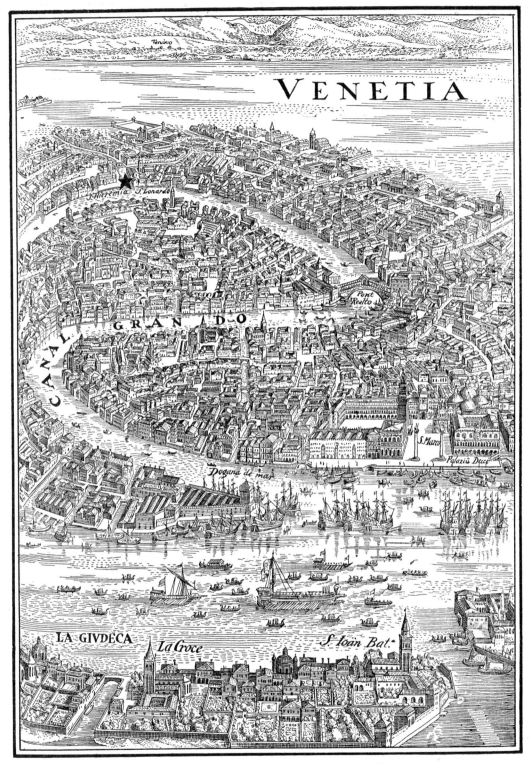

PLAN OF VENICE IN 1640. STAR SHOWS POSITION OF THE GHETTO,

(From Martin Zeiler, " Itineraria Italiæ.")

legal position was not regulated by law, but was determined, as in the case of other foreign colonies, by "condotte" (safe-conducts) granted for terms of years, and the renewal of which was sometimes refused (Lattes, in "Venezia e le Sue Lagune," vol. i., p. ii., Appendix, p. 177). The Jews, indeed, were twice expelled and compelled to retire to Mestre.

The first "condotta" for the Jews seems to have been issued in 1373; as a rule the duration of the condotte ranged between five and ten years. At one of the renewals, made in 1385, an annual tax of 4,000 ducats was imposed on them, but in compensation they were relieved from all other taxes except customs duties. In 1394 the **First** Senate, alleging that the Jews had not **"Condotta"** observed the legal regulations in their **for the** loan transactions, and that if these con- **Jews.** tinued all the movable property in Venice would pass into their hands, ordained that at the expiration of the current permit, in 1396, they should leave the city. When that date arrived they actually retired to Mestre (Galliccioli, *l.c.* ii. 282); but in the course of the same year, in view of the damage which resulted from their absence, the Senate recalled them (Ravà, *l.c.* 1871, p. 48). They were, however, not permitted to remain in Venice more than fifteen days at a time, and were obliged to wear on their breasts a distinguishing sign in the form of a round piece of yellow cloth, for which a yellow cap was later substituted, and still later a red cap. This odious regulation, although the degree of its observance varied at different times, and exceptions to it were permitted, continued in force for about two centuries, until advancing civilization did away with it; Galliccioli, writing at the end of the seventeenth century, says that in his day all such distinctions had ceased.

The restriction to fifteen days' residence does not seem to have been enforced long; being an isolated measure, it soon came to be disregarded. A decree of the year 1423 forbade all Jews of Venice to hold real estate ("pro Dei reverentia et pro utilitate et commodo locorum"; Galliccioli, *l.c.* ii. 291). Other repressive measures followed in 1434. The order to wear the badge, then little observed, was enforced with severity. Schools for games, singing, dancing, and other accomplishments ("di qualsiasi dottrina") were prohibited, and all association with Christian women was still more sternly forbidden (Ravà, *l.c.* 1871, p. 48). The practise of any of the higher professions was also forbidden, excepting that of medicine, which, notwithstanding various bulls prohibiting the treatment of Christians by Jews (Galliccioli, *l.c.* ii. 290), was always followed by the latter with credit. Other prohibitions followed; and in 1566 tailoring was specially included among the forbidden trades, "in order that Christian artisans may not be injured." For the same reason internal commerce was prohibited to the Jews, with the exception of the so-called "strazzaria," the trade in cast-off clothes (Ravà, *l.c.* 1871, p. 174).

It is noteworthy that despite all these restrictions the economic condition of the Jews in Venice was on the whole prosperous, which proves that in general the laws were by no means enforced to the letter. In 1386 Corfu submitted to Venice, and one of

the embassy charged with arranging the terms of the surrender was a Jew, who obtained for his coreligionists on the island privileges which were always faithfully observed; the Jews in their turn always gave proofs of their sincere devotion to the republic, winning from the commanders of the Venetian troops high praise for their valor in the frequent wars against the Turks (Schiavi, *l.c.* p. 487).

In the second half of the fifteenth century the Jews of the entire republic were menaced by the clerical agitation against Jewish money-lenders (see JEW. ENCYC. vii. 4, *s.v.* ITALY; x. 88, *s.v.* PLEDGES); and some cities of the mainland, terrorized by this agitation, requested permission of the Senate to expel the Jews. Cardinal Bessarione, when questioned on this subject by the Senate, replied that they might be tolerated "if the proper caution were observed," and the request was accordingly denied. Nevertheless a few cities persisted in their demands for the banishment of the Jews; and in the course of a few years some expulsions took place, as at Brescia (1463), Vicenza (1476), and Bergamo and Treviso (1479).

A much more serious fate befell the Jews of Trent when the monk BERNARDINUS OF FELTRE accused them of the murder of a Christian child (1475). Although the Doge of Venice, Mocenigo, issued a strong manifesto for the protection of the Jews, he could not prevent a similar trial for ritual murder from taking place in Venice itself a few years later, attended by the same atrocious methods of procedure. There was, however, one note- **Blood** worthy point of difference: the whole **Accusation.** trial was conducted as if for an individual crime, and the number of the victims was confined to the accused (Ciscato, "Gli Ebrei in Padova," p. 136).

The expulsion of the Jews from Spain (1492) and Portugal (1496) brought many exiles to Venice, and among them came, after many peregrinations, the celebrated Isaac Abravanel, who, during his residence in Venice, had occasion to use his diplomatic skill in settling certain difficulties between the republic and the King of Portugal (Grätz, "Gesch." ix. 9).

Times of peril now followed for the republic. In 1508 the famous League of Cambray was formed against it, in which nearly all the states of Europe, including Austria, France, Spain, the Papal States, and Naples, united. The common danger had the effect of relaxing the enforcement of the anti-Jewish laws and of drawing Jews and Christians together in more friendly relations. But peace was hardly concluded (1516) when the old policy was revived, and the better to insure the separation of Jews and Christians the institution of the ghetto was introduced. Venice thus became the mother of this institution. The decree which the Senate issued in regard to it referred to a decree of 1385; and this in turn referred to a still earlier decree which had not been carried out (Schiavi, *l.c.* p. 322). According to Galliccioli (*l.c.* ii. 301), however, all the Jews could not find homes in the ghetto, and many were obliged to live outside. Synagogues, formerly scattered throughout the city, were now permitted only in Mestre, but before long a new concession allowed them in Venice again, though only in the ghetto. At the same time, while Venice acquired the unenviable reputation of having introduced the ghetto, it became a potent factor in the spiritual life of Judaism through the famous printing establishment of Daniel BOMBERG, which published the most important works of rabbinical literature. In the later years of Bomberg's life other presses competed with him, as many as four existing in Venice at one time.

In 1553, however, the proscription of Hebrew literature by the Inquisition began, and all copies of the Talmud which could be found in Rome, Venice, Padua, and other cities were confiscated and burned.

In 1527 another expulsion took place, although it probably affected only the money-lenders, who withdrew to Mestre, but were permitted to return to Venice for the time necessary to sell their pledges. In 1534 they were recalled, and this time the Jews organized themselves into a corporation called "Università." Since each man wished to preserve his own nationality according to the country from which he came, the Università was divided into three national sections, Levantines, Germans, and Occidentals, the last name being applied to those who came from Spain and Portugal. The administration of the whole Università was in the hands of a coun-

RIO E PONTE DELLE GUGLIE, SHOWING HIGH HOUSES OF MODERN GHETTO.
(From a photograph.)

Later the prohibition was somewhat relaxed, though LEON OF MODENA, in his "Historia dei Riti Ebraici" (p. 38, Venice, 1638), declares: "To-day it [the Talmud] remains prohibited; and in Italy particularly it is neither seen nor read." In 1566 the Senate forbade the printing of Hebrew books; but either the prohibition affected Jews only or the decree was soon revoked, for Hebrew printing in Venice continued uninterruptedly or was resumed after a short interval, and many new works were published. Although these always appeared under the names of Venetian nobles as editors, the connection of the latter with such works ended there.

The Inquisition and Hebrew Literature.

cil of seven members, three chosen from the Levantines, three from the Germans, and one from the Occidentals. Many laws were passed, furthermore, to regulate the whole internal administration of the community. According to Schiavi, an internal tribunal was also established to adjudicate both civil and criminal suits; but later on the Council of Ten limited its powers to civil suits, and in these it could act only when the parties appealed to it (Schiavi, l.c. p. 329).

The most powerful weapon of which the heads of the community could avail themselves was that of excommunication, although it appears that legally at least the exercise of it was not left wholly in Jewish hands. Galliccioli records at length a successful appeal presented to the Patriarch of Venice by the heads of the Università, for permission to excommunicate those living in the ghetto who neglected their religious duties; and the author adds that the right to give this authority had been in the hands of the patriarch until 1671, when it passed to the "Cattaveri" (Galliccioli, *l.c.* ii. 301). It does not appear, however, from any subsequent documents that the Jews held strictly to this dependence.

Schools for study were naturally among the most important institutions of Jewish life in Venice at all times. In addition to Hebrew, secular branches of study were taught in them (Schiavi, *l.c.* p. 332). Although nominally restricted to the ghetto, the Jews lived in general throughout the city, and in the sixteenth century, when the vice of gambling raged in Venice, the ghetto also was infected, while Jews and Christians often played together. Although the government had already imposed penalties upon gambling, the heads of the Università saw that the measure remained ineffective, and they therefore pronounced excommunications in the synagogue against those who played certain games. Excommunication failed in its turn; and Leon of Modena, whose reputation was seriously stained because of his addiction to this vice, wrote a long protest against his own excommunication, which he declared illegal; the ban, he said, only drove people to worse sins. In all his long discussion there is no sign of the fact that the pronouncing of the excommunication was dependent on any but the Jews themselves. It appears from the disquisition of Leon of Modena that the number of Jews then in Venice was little more than 2,000. This agrees with other data of the time, so that it seems necessary to reject the number 6,000 given for that period in Luzzatto's "Discorso Circa il Stato degli Hebrei di Venetia." In 1659, according to an official census, their number had increased to 4,860 (Schiavi, *l.c.* p. 507). The struggle against gaming continued, and, in addition, regulations intended to check unnecessary luxury in dress and excessive display in banquets and family festivals were repeatedly published in the synagogue.

Prevalence of Gambling.

Among the various societies of the period there was in Venice, as probably in the majority of Jewish communities, one for the ransom of Jews who had been enslaved. Venice and Amsterdam were the two principal centers for the relief of such unfortunates, and consequently the societies of other communities as a rule made their headquarters in these two cities. Venice and Amsterdam, by mutual consent, divided the field of their activities. On the former devolved the task of effecting the ransom of those Jews who had sailed in Turkish ships from Constantinople and other Oriental ports, and had fallen into the hands of the Knights of St. John, who waged a fierce and continual warfare against such ships. The Jews taken captive in these frequent attacks were held in Malta in hope of a heavy ransom, and were most barbarously treated. The society at Venice had a permanent Christian delegate on the island, with the recognized title of consul, whose duty it was to alleviate the lot of the wretched captives as far as possible and

to conduct negotiations for their ransom (Soave, "Malta e gli Schiavi Ebrei," in "Corriere Israelitico," xvii. 54 *et seq.*).

In 1571, after the battle of Lepanto, in which the Venetians and Spaniards conquered the Turks in the contest for the island of Cyprus, the danger of expulsion again threatened the Jews of Venice. During this war much ill feeling had arisen in Venice against the Jews because one of their coreligionists, Joseph Nasi, was said to have suggested the war, and many Venetians suspected that the Jews of the city had sympathized with him. It was in consequence of this ill feeling, doubtless, that the Senate, in the first transports of its joy over the victory, issued a harsh decree in which, to show a proper gratitude to God for so great a victory, in which "they had conquered the enemies of His Holy Faith, as were the Jews also," it was ordained that in two years, on the expiration of the "condotta," all Jews should leave the city, never to return (Ravà, *l.c.* 1871, p. 176). This decree, however, was entirely revoked, either as a result of reflection or in deference to some powerful intervention.

Joseph Nasi.

In 1572 Sultan Salim II. sent the rabbi Solomon Ashkenazi, who, both as a physician and as a statesman, possessed great influence with the Divan, as a special ambassador to the Senate, charged with a secret mission to conclude an offensive and defensive alliance between the two states against Spain (Grätz, "Gesch." ix., note 7). The Senate received him with all the honors due the ambassador of a great power, and, although it did not accede to his proposals, it sent him back with presents. Ashkenazi availed himself of this opportunity to defend the cause of his coreligionists, and he seems to have obtained not only the revocation of the decree of expulsion, but also the promise that such expulsions should never again be proposed (Grätz, *l.c.* ix. 416).

An event, in itself of minor importance, yet noteworthy as one of the results of the great agitation aroused throughout the Jewish world by the Messianic claims of Shabbethai Ẓebi, was the brief stay in Venice of the visionary Nathan GHAZZATI. Even after the apostasy of Shabbethai Ẓebi had opened the eyes of the majority and calmed the excitement, Nathan continued to believe in him, or pretended to do so. He claimed to have had celestial visions, and proclaimed himself the prophet Elijah, the precursor of the Messiah, thus endeavoring to inflame the popular mind anew and revive the old excitement. Driven from Salonica and other cities, he went to Venice in 1668, where, in view of the credulity of the times, his presence might have been dangerous. Scarcely was his arrival known to the rabbis and heads of the Università when they called him before their tribunal and made him sign a document confessing the falsity of his claims to have had celestial visions, and denying that Shabbethai was the Messiah. This done, they warned him to leave at once and had him escorted to the frontier (Ravà, *l.c.* 1871, p. 307; Samuel Aboab, "Debar Shemuel," responsum No. 375, Venice, 1702).

While the administration of the Venetian republic

INTERIOR OF THE SYNAGOGUE, VENICE.

(From a photograph.)

was always under papal influence, a spirit of comparative tolerance prevailed there, as is usual in maritime and commercial cities, and the Jews, like all others, were free from restrictions in their worship. Well organized and strong, the republic always maintained order and fulfilled its compacts faithfully. The "condotte" were religiously observed, and the lives and property of Jews were protected. Local outbreaks against the Jews were of rare occurrence and were quickly followed by exemplary punishments (Osimo, "Narrazione della Strage Compita Contra gli Ebrei d' Asolo," Padua, 1875). The Inquisition existed at Venice, although it was not admitted until 1279, after long opposition; but its jurisdiction extended only over Christian heretics, and even over them its power was much restricted. In 1570 the inquisitors of Padua wished to compel the Jews to attend sermons in their churches. On this occasion the Senate recalled them to their proper province, but it appears that they succeeded at some later time, for the greater part of a sermon which was preached to the Jews in one of the churches in Padua in 1715 is still preserved (Ciscato, *l.c.* pp. 140–141). At all events, continual contact in daily life often led naturally to friendly relations between Jews and Christians, and the government was enlightened enough to encourage them. In 1553 the council granted Kalonymus, a Jewish physician, the means necessary to keep his son at his studies, " so that he may become a man useful in the service of this illustrious city " (Romanin, "Storia Documentata di Venezia," v. 337, note 3).

In the great financial stress in which the republic was placed during the long and expensive war with the Turks the Jews were obliged to pay heavy taxes. Nevertheless, their contributions, like those of the other citizens, were often spontaneous; and the names of the bankers Anselmo and Abramo, who had voluntarily contributed 1,000 ducats, with those of other contributors, were inscribed in a book of parchment " in everlasting remembrance " (Schiavi, *l.c.* p. 320). Most important of all, however, was the activity of the Jews in maritime commerce; in 1579, in the interest of this commerce, permission was extended to many Jews of Spanish and Portuguese extraction to remove from Dalmatia to Venice, where they received privileges which were obtained for them by their coreligionist Daniel Rodriguez, who was then Venetian consul in Dalmatia, and who was highly esteemed by the republic for his important services in furthering its commerce in the Orient (Ravà, *l.c.* 1871, p. 176).

Naturally, this maritime commerce continued to be favored by the government; and in 1686 the Portuguese Aronne Uziel was the first to obtain a patent for free commerce under the Venetian flag in the Orient and Occident. He was one of the first shipowners of the republic: he traded with Zante, Cephalonia, Corfu, and Constantinople; and his business was so great that in twenty years he paid 451,-000 ducats to Venice in duties (Schiavi, *l.c.* p. 514). Among other Jewish shipowners one of the most important was Abramo Franco, whose duty it was to provide for the loading of six merchantmen (*ib.*). To come down to more recent times, special mention should be made in this connection of the two brothers Baron Giuseppe Treves dei Bonfil, the ancestor of the present barons of that name, and Isaaco Treves, on account of the expedition which they undertook for the first time into the western hemisphere. They sailed under the Venetian flag with a cargo of flour and other goods, returning with coffee and sugar (Soave, in "Il Vessillo Israelitico," 1878, p. 115). Giuseppe Treves received the title of baron from Napoleon I. on account of his great services to the city, both commercially and otherwise (Maratti, "Venezia ed i Veneziani," iv. 256).

Domestic trade continued to be limited legally to second-hand goods, but as a matter of fact this nominal restriction counted for little, and with the growth of the city liberty of trade grew also. In the shops of the ghetto wares of all sorts were sold, among them glass, decorated crystal, gold ornaments, tapestries, embroideries, and books (Schiavi,

Title-Page of a Ritual Used by the Jewish Community of Tripoli, Printed at Venice 1680.
(From the Sulzberger collection in the Jewish Theological Seminary of America.)

l.c. p. 506). A trade of special importance, against which ineffectual prohibitions were several times issued, was that in precious stones; the sovereigns of Europe were the first to employ Jews for selling, buying, and exchanging gems (*ib.*). Jews were prominent also in engineering. In 1444 a decree of the Senate called "a certain Solomon, a Hebrew by race, to be present at conferences concerning the diversion of the Brenta, because he has great fame for skill in matters concerning water" (Zendrini, "Memorie dello Stato Antico e Moderno delle Lagune di Venezia," i. 102, Padua, 1811).

In 1490 an engineer, wishing to associate himself with some Jews in the mounting of a machine which he had invented, asked the Senate whether the laws concerning the granting of privileges to inventors were applicable to Jews as well as to others. To this the Senate replied that in such matters no distinction was made between Venetians and foreigners, between Jews and Christians (Romanin, *l.c.* v. 337, note C). One Zarfati, in the second half of the sixteenth century, invented certain improvements in the methods of silk-weaving, and his studies were published at Rome and obtained for him a privilege from Pope Sixtus V. (Schiavi, *l.c.* p. 504). In 1630 a certain Naḥman Judah obtained permission to manufacture cinnabar, sublimate, and similar compounds, on condition that the business should be carried on under the name of a Christian (Schiavi, *l.c.* p. 505). In 1718 another Zarfati was permitted to manufacture not only cinnabar and sublimate, but also aqua fortis, white lead, minium, etc. (*ib.*).

Under the restrictions placed upon them Jews could not contribute much to general literature; mention must be made nevertheless of the grammarian Elijah LEVITA, who spent a great part of his life in Venice (Ravà, *l.c.* 1871, p. 335; Grätz, *l.c.* ix. 225). Noteworthy also were the two rabbis already mentioned, LEON OF MODENA (1579–1649), at whose sermons even nobles and ecclesiastics were present, and Simeon (Simḥah) LUZZATTO (1590–1663), who, besides the "Discorso," wrote "Socrate, Ossia dell' Intendimento Humano," which he dedicated to the doge and Senate. Reference should also be made to the poetess Sara Copia SULLAM (1592–1641), who was regarded by several critics after her death as one of the most illustrious writers of verse in Italy (Soave, *l.c.* 1876, p. 198). Other authors of this period who usually wrote only in Hebrew were: David NIETO (1654–1728), author of the "Matṭeh Dan"; Moses GENTILI (d. 1711), author of "Meleket Maḥshabot"; his son Gershon (d. 1717, at the age of seventeen), author of the "Yad Ḥaruzim"; Rabbi Simeon Judah Perez; and Jacob SARAVAL (d. 1782). Among the physicians of the republican period the most distinguished were Jacob MANTINO (1490–1549), a native of Tortosa, who was directed by circumstances to Venice, and who became chief physician to Pope Paul III.; and Giuseppe Tamari, who held the office of city physician (Ravà, *l.c.* 1871, p. 334).

One of the conditions always imposed upon the Jews of Venice was that of keeping banks for lending money; and to insure their continuance the "condotta" of 1534 placed this obligation upon the Università as a body. Although these banks at first satisfied the requirements of the citizens and were at the same time a source of gain to those who kept them, they finally ended in a great financial disaster. The community, which formerly had been very rich, declined rapidly during and after the war with the Turks over the island of Candia (1645–55), the cause being the enormous burdens laid upon it by the expenses of the war. Many emigrated to escape these burdens; the plague of 1630, with the consequent stagnation of business, drove others out; and bad administration was responsible for other departures; so that in order to fulfil its obligations the community was forced to sink deeper and deeper into debt, which finally reached the sum of nearly a million ducats. As soon as the government saw the peril

of an institution which was considered a necessity to the state, it endeavored to remedy the evil by adopting more easy terms of payment and by making other arrangements within its power; but when all other methods had proved insufficient it was compelled finally to proclaim the Università a private corporation to enable it legally to announce its insolvency. In 1735 the Università suspended payments, and a compromise was effected with its creditors with the support and protection of the government. The banks continued to exist, however, even after the fall of the republic, and until 1806, when they were closed by an imperial decree. On that occasion the Jews gave the commune all the money and property in the banks, having a total value of 13,000 ducats, to be devoted solely to charity. The municipality publicly expressed its gratitude for this gift ("Gazetta di Venezia," Oct. 6, 1806).

The Università seems soon to have recovered from its failure; for in 1776, on the expiration of one of the "condotte," certain commercial restrictions were proposed as a check upon the excessive influence which the Jews had acquired. These proposals gave rise to many heated discussions. The majority sided with the Jews, and called attention to the fact that several Jewish families had acquired large fortunes by their thrift and were of service to industry, besides giving employment to many of the poor. The assistance they had rendered to the state was also called to mind, special emphasis being laid upon the noble conduct of Treves, who had loaned the treasury without interest the money necessary for the execution of the treaty of Barbary. After a long debate, however, the passions and influence of a few powerful reactionaries prevailed, and the proposals became law (Romanin, *l.c.* viii. 212).

Several years then passed without incident, when the republic, becoming involved in difficulties with

The Republic Becomes a Democracy.

Napoleon, reconstituted itself as a democracy. In consequence all citizens were declared equal in the eyes of the law, and all legal discriminations against the Jews became null and void.

Each strove to outdo the other in demonstrating his fraternity, and on July 11, 1797, amid great popular rejoicing, the gates of the ghetto were torn down and its name changed to "Contrada dall' Unione" (= "Street of Union"). Many speeches of lofty tone were made on this occasion, and even priests were present at the ceremony, setting the example in evidencing the feeling of fraternity, for which they were praised by the new municipality. The latter had been quickly constituted, and three Jews had at once taken their places in it (Romanin, *l.c.* x. 222).

Yet even this revolution, though made in the spirit demanded by the times, could not save the republic, which was powerless before the invading armies of France. In the very month in which this change of government took place Napoleon declared war on Venice, and the Senate, wishing at least to make an attempt at resistance, invited the Jews and the various religious corporations of the city to contribute all the available silver in their places of worship for the defense of the city against the impending attack. The Jews enthusiastically responded, among the first, to this appeal; and again they received from the Senate a gratifying letter of thanks (Soave, *l.c.* 1876, p. 38). The attack, however, was never delivered; for the Senate abandoned the republic on Oct. 17, 1797, and Austria and France signed the treaty of Campo Formio, by which the city was assigned to Austria. The latter took possession of it at once (Jan. 15, 1798), and the Jews by this change of government lost their civil equality. They regained it, however, in 1805, when the city became a part of Italy, but lost it once more in 1814, when, on the fall of Napoleon, the city again came under Austrian control.

When the news of the revolution at Vienna reached Venice in 1848 the city seized the opportunity to revolt, and, almost without bloodshed, forced the Austrian garrison to capitulate (March 22, 1848). It then proclaimed anew the republic of Saint Mark and elected a provisional government, of which two

**Equality
of Jews and
Christians
Estab-
lished.**

Jews formed a part — Isaaco Pesaro Maurogonato (appointed to the Ministry of Finance) and Leone Pincherle. Austria, however, reconquered the territory and held it until 1866, when it became part of the united kingdom of Italy; from that time the complete equality of Jews and Christians has been firmly established, as in all other parts of the country.

According to the last estimate, the Jewish community of Venice numbers 4,000; and it now bears the name of the Jewish Fraternity of Religion and Philanthropy. It possesses many institutions for study and benevolence, and is one of the most cultured Jewish communities in Italy. Among the Venetians of most recent times who have become distinguished are: Samuel Romanin, the learned historian of Venice, in whose honor a bust was placed in the Pantheon of Venice; I. P. Maurogonato, already mentioned, who for many years was vice-president of the Chamber of Deputies; Luigi Luzzatti, who was repeatedly minister of the treasury; the Treves dei Bonfili family, whose members still continue, as in the time of the republic, to be distinguished for their philanthropy and for their services to their fellow citizens; the poetess Eugenia Pavia Gentilomo Fortis; the physicians Namias and Asson; and the rabbi Abramo Lattes. In the industrial field also the Venetian Jews are well represented, being interested in many of the numerous factories and establishments on the islands around Venice, either as proprietors or as managers.

BIBLIOGRAPHY: Samuel Romanin, *Storia Documentata di Venezia*; Abraham Lattes, in *Venezia e le Sue Lagune*, vol. i., part ii., Appendix; Schiavi, *Gli Ebrei in Venezia e nelle Sue Colonie*, in *Nuova Antologia*, 3d series, vol. xlvii.; Vittore Ravà, in *Educatore Israelita*, 1871, 1872; Cesare Musatti, *Il Maestro Moise Soave*; M. Soave, *Malta e gli Schiavi Ebrei*, in *Corriere Israelitico*, xvii.; Ciscato, *Gli Ebrei in Padova*; Osimo, *Narrazione della Strage Compita Contra gli Ebrei di Asolo*; Grätz, *Gesch.* passim; Galliccioli, *Memoria Antiche Venete*; Simeon Luzzatto, *Discorso Circa il Stato degli Hebrei*, etc.; Leon of Modena, *Historia dei Riti Ebraici*, Paris, 1637.
D.   E. L.

VENTURA: Family of rabbis and scholars prominent in Italy and Greece in the sixteenth, seventeenth, and eighteenth centuries.

Eliezer ben Samuel Ventura: Italian scholar of the sixteenth century; born at Da Porta, prov-

ince of Perugia; died in 1534 at Ferrara, where he had officiated as rabbi. One of his manuscripts has been preserved in the collection of Marco Mortara (see "Mosè," vi. 134).

Elijah ben Abraham Ventura: Scholar of the eighteenth century; probably flourished in the Levant. He was the author of a work in three parts, entitled: (1) "Kokeba di-Shebiṭ," novellæ on various Talmudic sayings; (2) "Ḳonṭres," novellæ on the works of Elijah Mizraḥi; and (3) "She'elot u-Teshubot," responsa. The entire work appeared at Salonica in 1799.

BIBLIOGRAPHY: Steinschneider, *Cat. Bodl.* col. 952; Benjacob, *Oẓar ha-Sefarim*, p. 237.

Isaac Hananiah Ventura: Scholar of the seventeenth century; rabbi of Pesaro. He wrote a responsum which is published in the "Shelom ha-Bayit" of Menahem Cazes, and another which has been printed in Solomon Graziano's novellæ (ii. 123) on the Shulḥan 'Aruk.

Isaac ben Moses Ventura: Talmudist of the sixteenth and seventeenth centuries; rabbi at Ancona and Pesaro. One of his responsa is extant in Terni's "Sefat Emet" (p. 24), and another in Nethaneel Segre's "'Ezer Ya'aḳob" (No. 2).

Isaac Raphael Ventura: Rabbi of Pesaro in the seventeenth century. According to Mortara ("Indice," *s.v.*), he was a descendant of a family bearing the name אלמאורי הסטר; and he is mentioned in Graziano's novellæ (ii. 141) on the Shulḥan 'Aruk.

Jehiel Ventura: Rabbi of Romagna in the sixteenth century. He was related to MaHaRaM of Padua, who mentions him in his collection of responsa (ii., §§ 62, 83) as one of the foremost halakists of his time.

BIBLIOGRAPHY: Nepi-Ghirondi, *Toledot Gedole Yisrael*, p. 219, No. 258.

Jehiel Ventura: Liturgical poet of the first half of the seventeenth century; probably a resident of Ancona. He was the author of liturgical and elegiac poems, which Ghirondi of Padua possessed in manuscript (Zunz, "Literaturgesch." p. 440).

Moses ben Joseph Ventura (called also **Ventura of Tivoli** and **Ventura of Jerusalem**): Rabbi of Silistria, Bulgaria, in the latter half of the sixteenth century. He was educated at Jerusalem, but later settled in Silistria. Ventura was the author of "Yemin Mosheh" (Mantua, 1624; 2d ed., Amsterdam, 1718; 3d ed., The Hague, 1777), a commentary on the Shulḥan 'Aruk, Yoreh De'ah; and Aaron Alfandari, in his commentary entitled "Yad Aharon," ascribes to him the "Haggahot we-Hassagot 'al Bet Yosef," a commentary, as yet unpublished, on the four parts of the "Bet Yosef."

BIBLIOGRAPHY: Steinschneider, *Cat. Bodl.* col. 2008; Benjacob, *Oẓar ha-Sefarim*, p. 224; Fürst, *Bibl. Jud.* iii. 433.

Shabbethai ben Abraham Ventura: Scholar and rabbi of Spalato during the eighteenth century; one of the most prominent pupils of David Pardo. He was the author of the "Nehar Shalom" (Amsterdam, 1775), novellæ and notes on the Shulḥan 'Aruk, Oraḥ Ḥayyim.

BIBLIOGRAPHY: Steinschneider, *Cat. Bodl.* col. 2248; Azulai, *Shem ha-Gedolim*, ii. 90.
E. C.   S. O.

VENTURA, RUBINO : Soldier; born at Finale, Modena, 1795; died at Toulouse, France, April 5, 1858. At the age of seventeen he was enrolled as a volunteer in the militia of the kingdom of Italy. On the downfall of Napoleon he returned to his home; but in 1817, owing to a dispute between him and a local policeman, he was obliged to leave the country. He went first to Triest, and then to Constantinople, where he was for a time a ship-broker. Learning that Persia was seeking the services of European soldiers, he obtained an officer's commission, and helped to instruct the forces of the shah in European methods of warfare. He soon attained the rank of colonel. On the death of the shah in 1822, Ventura offered his services to his successor, 'Abbas Mirza. In the latter's service, however, were a number of English officers who were decidedly hostile to the French, with whom they classed Ventura on account of his having fought under Napoleon; and through their intrigues Ventura was dismissed. He then went to Lahore, India, accepting service in the army of Ranjit Sinh. A rebellion having arisen in Afghanistan, Ventura conducted successfully several campaigns of a difficult nature, and greatly enlarged the boundaries of the kingdom of Lahore.

Ventura married an Indian princess, by whom he had a daughter; but he was always desirous of returning to his native country. In 1837 he went on a diplomatic mission to Paris and London, but was recalled to Lahore before he had time to visit his family in Europe. On the death of Ranjit Sinh, Ventura took part in the contest for the succession, and remained in the service of the new raja, Dhulip Sinh. During the reign of the latter, Ventura continued his career of conquest; but later, feeling the approach of old age, he returned to Europe and settled in Paris, whence from time to time he visited his native country.

While in India, Ventura made numerous excavations. He presented Louis Philippe with a set of ancient Greek coins which he had unearthed, and which were evidences of the march through that country of Alexander the Great. In his later years he lost a part of his large fortune in unsuccessful commercial enterprises. According to Flaminio Servi, Ventura received baptism toward the end of his life.

BIBLIOGRAPHY: *Notizie Storiche e Biografiche de Generale Rubino Ventura, Finalese, Esposte da un Suo Concittadino,* Finale (Emilia), 1882; F. Servi, in *Corriere Israelitico,* x. 47 *et seq.;* idem, in *Vessillo Israelitico,* xxxi. 308 *et seq.*
s. U. C.

VENTURE, MARDOCHÉE : French scholar; flourished at Avignon in the latter part of the eighteenth century. In collaboration with Isaiah Vidal he composed the "Seder ha-Ḳonṭres" (Avignon, 1765), a collection of liturgical chants for the use of the Jews of the county of Venaissin. This compilation includes a piyyuṭ (p. 47; comp. Zunz, "Z. G." p. 473) composed by Venture, partly in Hebrew and partly in Provençal, which was translated into French by Sabatier in his "Chansons Hébraïco-Provençales des Juifs Comtadins" (Nîmes, 1876) and by Pedro II., of Alcantara, Emperor of Brazil, in his "Poésies Hébraïco-Provençales du Rituel Israélite Comtadin" (Avignon, 1891).

XII.—27

Venture himself translated into French: "Prières Journalières à l'Usage des Juifs Portugais ou Espagnols" (Nice, 1772); "Prières des Jours du Rosch-Haschana et du Jour de Kippour" (*ib.* 1773); "Prières des Jours de Jeûnes" (Paris, 1807); and "Prières des Fêtes de Pessach, Schebouot, et de Souccot" (*ib.* 1807; 2d ed., *ib.* 1845).
s. S. K.

VERA Y ALARCON, LOPE DE : Spanish martyr and knight ("caballero i mui emparentado," as he is designated by a contemporary) of noble family; born about 1619 at San Clemente la Mancha; died July 25, 1644, at Valladolid. Through his study of the Hebrew language and literature at Salamanca he was drawn toward Judaism; and he read the Psalms daily in the original text. When only twenty years of age he declared openly that he could not believe that the Messiah had appeared. According to the account of a contemporary, the Inquisition at Valladolid in 1638, on information furnished by De Vera's own brother, cast De Vera into prison, where he languished for six years. During this time he abstained from meat, circumcised himself, and called himself "Juda el Creyente" = "Judah the Believer." The most eminent theologians endeavored in vain to lead him back to the Church; and the entreaties of his father were equally unsuccessful. On July 25, 1644, he was tied to the stake, and, as Spinoza says, breathed his last with the Psalmist's words on his lips: "Into thine hand, Lord, I commit my spirit." His courage was universally admired, the inquisitor Moscoso writing to the Countess de Monterey thus: "Never has such firmness been witnessed as that displayed by this young man. He was well reared, scholarly, and otherwise blameless." The Marano poets Antonio Enriquez Gomez and Manuel de Pina mourned in their poems the death of the promising youth.

BIBLIOGRAPHY: Cardoso, *Las Excelencias de Israel,* p. 363; Manasseh b. Israel, *Spes Israelis,* ed. L. Wolf, p. 47; José de Pellicer, in the *Avisos,* Aug. 2, 9, 1644; A. de Castro, *Historia de los Judios de España,* p. 212; D. Levi de Barrios, *Govierno Popular Judayco,* p. 43; Kayserling, *Sephardim,* pp. 203 *et seq.;* Grätz, *Gesch.* x. 101.
J. M. K.

VERBAND DER VEREINE FÜR JÜDISCHE GESCHICHTE UND LITERATUR IN DEUTSCHLAND. See VEREIN FÜR JÜDISCHE GESCHICHTE UND LITERATUR.

VERBLOVSKI, GREGORI LEONTYEVICH : Russian jurist; born in the first quarter of the nineteenth century; died at Moscow 1900. He studied law at the University of St. Petersburg, from which he graduated in 1866. Verblovski was one of the first secretaries of the circuit court of St. Petersburg; he then became a member of that of Voronezh, and later of that of Moscow.

Verblovski's works include: "Sistematicheski Sbornik Polozheni i Izvlecheni iz Grazhdanskikh Kassatzionnykh Ryesheni za 1866–1875" (2 vols., Voronezh, 1879), a systematic collection of regulations and extracts of decisions of the Civil Court of Cassation for the period 1866–75, vol. i. being devoted to civil law, and vol. ii. to civil law cases; also similar collections for 1876–78 (*ib.* 1880), for 1879 (Moscow, 1881), for 1880 (*ib.* 1882), and for 1883–88 (St. Petersburg, 1889); "Dvizhenie Russkavo Grazhdanskavo Protzessa" (*ib.* 1883; 2d ed. 1889), on the proceedings in a Russian civil lawsuit; "Zakonopolozheniya o Poshlinakh s Imushchestv Perekhodyashchikh Bezmezdnymi Sposobami" (Voronezh, 1883), on laws concerning taxes; "Polozhenie o Sovyete po Zhelyeznodorozhnym Dyelam" (*ib.* 1886), the statute of the council on railway affairs; "Zakonopolozheniya o Preobrazovanii Myestnykh Krestyanskikh i Sudebnykh Uchrezhdeni" (*ib.* 1890); "Sudoproizvodstvo Grazhdanskoe i Ugolovnoe v Novykh Sudebno-Administrativnykh Uchrezhdeniyakh" (*ib.* 1891).

Besides, Verblovski published in the Russian juridical press a series of articles of practical interest; and, at the instance of the editorial commission instituted for the purpose of drawing up a new civil code, he translated into Russian the general civil code of 1811 of the Austrian empire (*ib.* 1885).

H. R.   V. R.

VERCELLI: City in the compartimento of Piedmont, Italy. The oldest document in existence concerning its Jews is dated Feb. 16, 1446, and consists of a permit granted by the city council to one Abramo della Vigneria and his son Angelo to open in Vercelli a banking and loan establishment, on condition of their lending the city 100 florins, when required, for a term of six months without interest, and for a longer period with interest. This is the first of a series of permits, granted for a set time only, but renewable, which authorized the residence of Hebrews within the city, and regulated their rights as well as their duties to the government. The Jews at this time were governed according to the harsh statutes of Amadeus VIII. promulgated June 17, 1430, which, among other regulations, obliged them to wear the customary badge, consisting of a piece of red cloth on the shoulder.

Under Emmanuel-Philibert the Piedmontese Jews were twice threatened by decrees of expulsion from the province. The first of these was promulgated July 19, 1560; but through the intercession of the duchess Margherita the Jews obtained a stay of four months. Then one of the duke's councilors persuaded him to renew the decree, fixing the time of the expulsion within ten days; but fortunately, through the efforts of an assistant physician attached to the ducal tribunal, a revocation of the edict was obtained. Later on (Oct., 1566) Emmanuel-Philibert ordered the immediate departure from his dominions of all the Jews, unless they consented to pay him the sum of 4,000 gold florins. They quitted the country, but shortly afterward were allowed to return on condition of paying down 2,000 florins and submitting to a yearly tax. On Sept.

Under Emmanuel-Philibert. 9, 1572, at the instance of one Vitale Sacerdoti, Emmanuel-Philibert published a decree which somewhat mitigated the severity of the laws of Amadeus VIII. When, in 1597, the Jews were banished from the Milanese territories, a number of the exiles took refuge in Vercelli, among whom was the continuator of the "'Emeḳ ha-Baka" of Joseph ha-Kohen. The anonymous historian relates that he and his family remained in Vercelli for some days, hoping to establish their abode in the city;

but, although Emmanuel-Philibert had promised the Jews but a short time before that they should remain unmolested in his dominions, his son, Charles Emmanuel, Duke of Savoy, was unwilling to afford an asylum in his territories to the Jewish exiles from other provinces, and when he learned that there were numerous Hebrew refugees in Vercelli, he issued a decree banishing them from that city also. Charles Emmanuel confirmed the privileges granted by his father to his own subjects (see TURIN).

Until the year 1600 the Italian ritual was used by the Jews of Vercelli. In that year one Abram Levi, having purchased the loan and banking establishment of Norzi and Sacerdote, settled in the city; and, owing to his influence and efforts, the

Italian Ritual Superseded by the German. German ritual was adopted, and it has remained in use until the present day. Rabbi Ḥayyim Segre, who in 1653 came from Casale Monferrato to reside in Vercelli, was sent with Samson Bachi and Jacob Pugliese to the East to investigate the theories and writings of Shabbethai Ẓebi, the expenses of his journey being defrayed by Jonah Clava (Ḳezigin).

During the eighteenth century, notwithstanding the general progress of the times, the condition of the Vercelli Jews did not improve. Indeed, it became worse, owing to the preponderating influence of the papal court. The constitutional laws of 1723, 1729, and 1770 were almost as inimical to the interests of the Jews as the ancient ducal statutes had been. Until the year 1724 the Jewish inhabitants were permitted to live in any portion of the city; but in that year they were restricted to a special quarter. Their concentration in the ghetto soon showed the need of a larger synagogue; and a new edifice was opened on the eve of Rosh ha-Shanah, 1740. The financial status of the Jews of Vercelli improved greatly after the death of Elijah Emmanuel Foa (July 20, 1796), who bequeathed his large fortune to the community for the aid and support of charitable societies and institutions, and particularly for the establishment of a Hebrew college in his own house. The Collegis Foa (Foa College) was opened Sept., 1829, and is still (1905) in existence. It has given many noteworthy rabbis and professors to the Italian Jewry.

With the outbreak of the French Revolution came indications of better times for the Jews of Piedmont; but the Austro-Russian provisional government of

Effects of the French Revolution. Piedmont at the restoration, in 1799, restored them to their former status. Later, by a patent of March 6, 1816, Victor Emmanuel I. definitely freed the Jews from the obligation of wearing a badge, and conferred on them leave to engage in merchandise, trade, and the fine arts. They were, however, still excluded from the universities, from public offices, and from the administration of charities. The law of Charles Albert, enacted June 19, 1848, completed the work of emancipation, and established the Jews on the footing of citizenship. In 1853 a Hebrew journal, the "Educatore Israelità," edited by Giuseppe Levi and Esdra Pontremoli, was founded in Vercelli. The "Vessillo Israelitico" of Casale Monferrato, founded by Flaminio Servi in 1878, is the successor of this review. In 1878 a new temple was dedicated.

The following is a list of the principal savants and rabbis of Vercelli: sixteenth century: Isaac Kohen (" R. E. J." xvi. 39 et seq.); seventeenth century: Jacob Bachi, Hananeel ben Aaron Asher Nantova; eighteenth century: Benjamin Segre, Elisha ben Ḥayyim Segre, Joshua Benzion ben Elisha Segre, Joshua Benzion ben Benjamin Segre; nineteenth century: Alessandro Foa, Giuseppe Levi Gattinara, Sabato Graziadio Treves, Jedidiah Levi, Michele Vita Treves, Isacco Sanguinetti, Felice Tedeschi, Giuseppe Raffaelle Levi.

In 1864 the city contained 600 Jews; shortly afterward their numbers began to diminish; in 1866 there were but 500; and to-day they number only 369.

Bibliography: F. Servi, in *Educatore Israelità*, xiv. 311 *et seq.*, xv. 36 *et seq.*; G. Volino, *Condizione Giuridica degli Israeliti in Piemonte Prima dell' Emancipazione*, Turin, 1904; M. Finzi, in *Rivista Israelitica*, i. 226 *et seq.*; Wiener, in his edition of '*Emek ha-Baka*, pp. 102, 105, 106; F. Servi, in *Corriere Israelitico*, pp. 172 *et seq.*; Mortara, *Indice*, passim.

S.   U. C.

VERDICT. See JUDGMENT.

VERDUN (Hebrew, ורדון): Capital of the department of Meuse, France. Jews resided there from the twelfth century; and among the scholars of the city may be mentioned the tosafist Samuel b. Ḥayyim (Tosef., Yeb. 65a, 66b; Tosef., M. Ḳ. 23a; Tosef., B. Ḳ. 77a, 89a), Samuel b. Joseph the Younger (Tosef., Niddah, 28a), and Jacob b. Joseph, brother of Samuel.

In 1433 Canon Guillaume Chaney made, on behalf of the chapter and the city, a fruitless request to the Council of Basel to relieve the strained financial situation by authorizing expelled Jews to return to Verdun; but until the annexation to France in 1559 of the three bishoprics of Toul, Metz, and Verdun, all rights of residence in the town and even of transit through it were forbidden to the Jews. Letters patent from Henry IV., Louis XIII., Louis XIV., and Louis XV., however, permitted the Jews of Metz to sojourn for very brief periods in Verdun to attend to business. In 1774 a Jew who had remained in the city for three days was expelled by order of De Watrouville, representative of the Marquis de Creil, the intendant. In 1748 the Jewish community of Metz addressed a petition to the intendant, asking that its members be allowed to visit Verdun, but this request was refused on account of the strong opposition of the merchants, goldsmiths, tailors, second-hand dealers, and, above all, the gild-wardens ("echevins") of the city, who were united in their hostility to the Jews. In 1752 and 1755 a number of Jews settled in the vicinity of Verdun, but were expelled by the intendant at the urgent demand of the gilds; and from that time until the Revolution of 1789 there are no traces of Jews in the city.

The community was founded in 1792, and of its remains there were left before the European War (1914–16) only forty-five families.

Bibliography: Documents in the municipal archives; Buvignier, *Notes sur les Archives de l'Hôtel-de-Ville de Verdun*, Metz, 1855; Carmoly, in *Revue Orientale*, i. 515; Gross, *Gallia Judaica*, pp. 205-207; R. E. J. xl. 126; Wassebourg, *Antiquités de la Gaule Belgique*, ii. 481, Paris, 1549; Zunz, Z. G. pp. 50, 55.

D.   S. K.

VEREIN ZUR ABWEHR DES ANTISEMITISMUS: Name of two societies for combating anti-Semitism. The first was formed in Berlin toward the end of 1890 by twelve men who issued an appeal to the German people, calling upon Jews and Christians alike to fight the excesses of anti-Semitism and especially all attempts to rob the Jews of their rights of equality. This appeal, issued in Jan., 1891, received 535 signatures from among the most prominent men of Germany. The poets Freytag, Heyse, and Sudermann (the first, on account of the Jewish characters in his novel "Soll und Haben" and in his drama "Die Journalisten," had been considered a partizan of anti-Semitism); scholars like Mommsen and Erich Schmidt; politicians like Von Forckenbeck and Baron von Stauffenberg; and Protestant clergymen like Dreyer and Zittel—these were among the signers (" Allg. Zeit. des Jud." Jan. 29, 1891; "Mittheilungen," etc., Jan. 30, 1901). A similar society was founded in Vienna July 20, 1891 ("Oesterreichische Wochenschrift," 1891, p. 526), of which the most prominent organizers were Baron and Baroness von Suttner and Professor Nothnagel.

These societies counted mostly upon Christians for support, although Jewish members were accepted. The Berlin society reported at its first general meeting, Nov. 28, 1893, a membership of 13,338 distributed in 963 localities. Its presidents were the eminent jurist and statesman Rudolf Gneist (up to 1895) and the liberal politicians Heinrich Rickert (up to 1902) and Theodor Barth. The propaganda of the societies was carried on chiefly by means of popular literature intended to check the growing anti-Semitic movement. Besides leaflets and pamphlets, the Berlin society published (1891) the "Antisemitenspiegel," a handbook of refutations of the slanderous assertions found in the "Antisemitenkatechismus," and (from Oct. 21, 1891) the weekly "Mittheilungen aus dem Verein zur Abwehr des Antisemitismus," which is a complete record of the anti-Semitic movement, containing valuable material for the refutation of anti-Semitic charges. Both societies have from time to time protested to the authorities against the unjust treatment of the Jews, and have therefore been called by their opponents "Judenschutztruppe" (Jew-guards). The Vienna society has established a "Rechtsschutzabtheilung," a bureau for legal advice to victims of anti-Semitism.

The foundation of the Berlin society coincided — hardly by accident — with the retirement of Court Chaplain Stöcker and a condemnation of anti-Semitism by Emperor William in a conversation with his Jewish classmate Judge Sommer. The effect of the society's agitation can not be measured with any degree of certainty, although in Germany the anti-Semitic movement has made no progress since 1892.

Bibliography: *Mittheilungen aus dem Verein zur Abwehr des Antisemitismus*, passim.

D.

VEREIN FÜR CULTUR UND WISSENSCHAFT DER JUDEN: Society founded at Berlin (Nov. 27, 1819) by Leopold Zunz, Eduard Gans, and Moses Moser. The objects of the society were to improve the social position of the Jews and to check the conversions to Christianity which at that time had alarmingly increased in the Berlin community. These aims were to be attained by spreading general culture among the Jews and by furthering the study of Jewish history and literature. About fifty intellectual members of the Berlin community joined the society, among them the philologist Ludwig MARKUS, to whose character Heinrich Heine paid a glowing tribute. On Aug. 4, 1822, Heine himself joined the society, and later some of the surviving members of Mendelssohn's circle, as David FRIEDLÄNDER and Lazarus BENDAVID, followed suit. Outside of Berlin the society was joined by about twenty members of the temple congregation at Hamburg (see JEW. ENCYC. vi. 193a), and also by individual Jews in other places.

The society, in spite of its very limited means, planned to establish a complete system of educational institutions, from primary to academic, including industrial schools. It actually opened a school in which Polish baḥurim, who came to Berlin in large numbers, were instructed in secular branches. At the same time the society prepared a program for a normal course of instruction in the Jewish religion. Heine proposed the founding of a women's auxiliary society which should promote the aims of the mother institution in the homes. However, on account of this manifold activity, no tangible results were accomplished, and hence it was decided to limit the work of the society to the furthering of "Jewish science." With this aim in view the society began in 1822 to publish a "Zeitschrift für die Wissenschaft des Judenthums," of which Leopold Zunz was the editor. The first number was headed by an article entitled "Ueber den Begriff einer Wissenschaft des Judenthums." Gans wrote on Talmudic law, and Zunz contributed an essay entitled "Salomon ben Isak, Genannt Raschi." As early as May, 1823, however, the editors felt obliged to ask the public to show greater interest in the periodical; this request being unheeded, the society had to cease its activity, a ceremonious farewell-meeting which had been suggested being tactfully omitted. Eduard Gans, who had been among the most active members of the society, was the first to desert the cause; he became converted to Christianity in order to obtain a professorship. Others followed him, and on account of the general lack of interest the rest despaired of attaining any measure of success.

BIBLIOGRAPHY: Grätz, Gesch. xi. 397 et seq.; Heinrich Heine, Ludwig Markus, Denkworte; G. Karpeles, Heinrich Heine: Aus Seinem Leben und aus Seiner Zeit, Berlin, 1901; Zeitschrift für die Wissenschaft des Judenthums, Berlin, 1823.
D.   E. Co.

VEREIN FÜR JÜDISCHE GESCHICHTE UND LITERATUR: Name of societies founded in many German cities since about 1890 for the spread of the study of Jewish history and literature. Although certain societies of the kind had existed earlier, the first impetus was given to the popular study of these subjects through the awakening of Jewish sensibilities by the growing anti-Semitic movement. It was chiefly felt in Jewish student circles. The growth of the movement began when Gustav Karpeles, after having founded such a society in Berlin (Jan. 2,

1892), organized the various societies into a union known as **Verband der Vereine für Jüdische Geschichte und Literatur in Deutschland** (Dec. 26, 1893). This association furnished lists of speakers to the constituent societies, issued pamphlets, and has published since 1898 the "Jahrbuch für Jüdische Geschichte und Literatur," of which up to 1905 seven volumes have appeared. These contain popular scientific essays and some fiction; and among the contributors are to be found the most eminent representatives of Jewish literature.

There are about 200 societies, with about 15,000 members, in Germany. The Jewish Chautauqua Society in the United States, the Jewish Study Circles in England, and the Université Juive in France have followed somewhat similar courses. An older organization of the same kind is the Afiḳe Yehudah of Prague.

BIBLIOGRAPHY: Jahrbuch für Jüdische Geschichte und Literatur, Berlin, 1898 et seq.
D.

VÉRITÉ ISRAÉLITE, LA. See PERIODICALS.

VERONA: Chief city of the Italian province of the same name. As early as the tenth century it numbered Jews among its inhabitants. They appear to have been treated with great harshness by Archbishop Raterio, and were later expelled from the city. Until 1408 they had apparently no recognized status or right of residence in Verona, although a few actually lived there and engaged in commerce. In that year (Dec. 31), shortly after Verona had passed under the government of the republic of Venice, the Jews obtained permission to live in the city and to lend money at interest. This concession met with strenuous opposition from a large number of the citizens; and all other professions were forbidden to the Jews. They lived among the Christians in the quarter of San Sebastiano, in the central part of the city, and built a synagogue in the Vicolo dei Crocioni, of which no traces now remain. In 1422 they were compelled to wear a badge, in the form of a yellow wheel, on the breast, or to pay a fine of 25 lire. The regulation, however, gradually came to be disregarded, but the ordinance decreeing the use of the badge was renewed. In 1443 the Jews were again refused permission to engage in the professions; and the shape of the badge was changed from a circle to a star. The original form was, however, restored in 1480.

By a resolution of the common council, dated March 11, 1499, the Jews were banished from the city and province of Verona, and their places were filled by Christian usurers, who so greatly oppressed the poor that the Jews were shortly afterward recalled. It is probable that some Jews remained in the city in spite of the decree of banishment; and it is certain that there were some scattered throughout the province, proof of their presence being afforded by a tombstone of this period, found in the neighboring village of Lonato. But, whether they never really quitted the province, or whether they gradually returned to it, in 1526 the citizens of Verona petitioned the Venetian republic to prohibit the Jews from lending money

Fifteenth and Sixteenth Centuries.

at interest in the city and territory of Verona. This request was granted, and the decree of prohibition was ratified on Dec. 4, 1548. In 1527 a yellow cap ("berretto") was substituted for the wheel-badge. An old manuscript, dated 1539, now in the possession of the Hebrew community of Verona, contains an account of the Jewish assemblies, of the amount of their taxes, of the fines levied on them, etc. In 1578 the Israelites were forbidden to pawn articles at the monte di pietà (see PLEDGES, HISTORICAL VIEW).

After their expulsion from the Milanese territory, some of the refugees settled in Verona (1597). In 1599 Agostino Valieri, Bishop of Verona, resolved to segregate the Jews in a ghetto; but, not finding a suitable location, he contented himself by enforcing the obligation of wearing the yellow cap. In the same year the Jews opened their cemetery, which remained in use until 1755. In 1604 the bishop carried out his designs, and enclosed the Jews in a ghetto, in a place called "Sotto i Tetti" (under the roofs). At this time they numbered about 400 and possessed twenty-five shops. All expenses for the improvement of the ghetto were borne by the Jews themselves; and they were obliged to borrow in order to build a synagogue. Finally they

The Ghetto. obtained a license, renewable every five years, to live in the city, on condition of the payment of a special tax. When the plague broke out in Verona in 1630, the Jews remained immune, which so enraged the Christians that they cast into the ghetto the garments infected by the sick, and thus spread the pestilence among its inhabitants.

At this epoch many Hebrew books were published at Verona, among them being Midrash Tanḥuma (1595), the Book of Isaiah (1625), the Psalms (1644), and "'En Yisrael" (1649). In 1645 the synagogue was supplied with an Ark of the Law of red marble and a beautiful and costly "tebah," also of marble. In 1655 a large number of Maranos, headed by Mosé Gaon and Giovanni Navarra, obtained leave to settle in Verona, for commercial purposes; and habitations were assigned them in what was known as the "Ghetto Nuovo" (New Ghetto). These Jews were called "Ponentini"; the others, "Levantines" or "Greeks." In 1766 there were two Jewish physicians in Verona; in 1790, four.

On the night of Oct. 30, 1786, a terrible conflagration accidentally broke out in the ghetto, and raged fiercely for three days, notwithstanding the efforts of Jews and Christians alike to extinguish it. During the course of the fire five Jews were killed and a great number injured. The painter Vita Greco has commemorated this disaster in one of his pictures.

During the occupation of Verona by the French in 1797, the gates of the ghetto were torn

The French Oc-cupation. down and burned in the public square; and thenceforth the Hebrews were permitted to reside in any portion of the city. On June 2 of that year a decree was issued, ordering that the Jews be represented in the council of commerce. On the restoration of the Austrian government a fanatical hatred of the Jews was fomented among the Christian population by the priests; and the Jews were so overwhelmed

with insults, affronts, and injuries that the Austrian governor of the province was obliged to interfere. A proclamation was issued Jan. 22, 1798, forbidding, under heavy penalties, the molestation of any citizen, by word or act; but the ill treatment of the Jews continued almost unabatedly until the issue of a second proclamation (Aug. 17, 1799), which definitely forbade all further molestation of them. They fared better on the resumption of French domination in 1805. Verona was represented by Israel Coen at the great Sanhedrin at Paris in 1806.

The community has now greatly diminished. In 1766 the Jews in Verona numbered 881; in 1770 there were 905; in 1864 they had increased to 1,200; while at the present day there are only about 600.

Many of the ancient Hebrew associations of Verona still exist, the principal ones being: La Misericordia (Hebrew name, "Gemilut Ḥasadim"), founded in 1599; the confraternity for the religious burial of the dead ("Gomel Dallim"), founded about 1599; the society for the aid of the sick poor ("Biḳḳur Ḥolim"), founded in 1610, with which the association for the proper attendance on the dead ("Liw-

Phil-anthropic As-sociations. yat Ḥen") was affiliated in 1765; "Shomerim la-Boḳer" (1610), and "Mishmeret ha-Ḥodesh" (1646), both devoted to the recitation of prayers; a confraternity for the recital of the "Tiḳḳun Ḥazot" (1655; see Zunz, "Ritus," p. 152); and "Limmude Adonai" (1703), for the pursuit of religious studies.

The following rabbis and scholars were natives or residents of Verona:

Twelfth and thirteenth centuries: Eleazar b. Samuel of Verona. Sixteenth century: Elihu Behr, Baruch Bassani, Joshua Jacob ben Johanan Heilpron, Moses Margalit, Abraham Menahem ben Jacob Porto, and Abraham ben Jehiel Porto. Seventeenth century: Judah Löb Ashkenazi, Hezekiah Mordecai ben Samuel Ḥayyim Bassani, Israel Hezekiah Bassani, Gershom ben Mordecai Bassani, Mordecai ben Jacob Bassani, Isaiah ben Mordecai Bassani, Isaac Cardoso, Simeon Cohen, Samuel ben Jacob Meldola, Samuel ben Raphael Meldola, Samuel Merari, Moses Abraham ben Moses Romanin, Joseph Shaliṭ ben Eliezer Richetti, Abraham Shalliṭ, Isaac ben Samuel Levi Valle, Judah ben Moses Fano, and Abraham Zemaḥ. Eighteenth century: Solomon ben Israel Bassani, Jacob ben Manasseh Gentili, Manasseh ben Jacob Gentili, Joseph Marin, Menahem Navarra, Uzziel Joel Pincherle, and Nethaneel ben Uzziel Joel Pincherle. Nineteenth century: Moses Shabbethai Beer, Abramo Mainster, David Samuel Pardo, Jacob Vita ben David Samuel Pardo, Samuel ben David Samuel Pardo, Jacob Ḥai Recanati, Emanuele (Menahem) Recanati, Abraham Grego, David Fortis, and Angelo Carpi.

BIBLIOGRAPHY: D. Fortis, in Educatore Israelita, xi. 199, 301 et seq., 392 et seq.; xii. 68 et seq., 110 et seq., 209 et seq.; S. Calabi, ib. xi. 78 et seq., 234 et seq.; Joseph ha-Kohen, 'Emeḳ ha-Baka, ed. Wiener, p. 135; Della Corte, Storia di Verona, 1592, book xiv., pp. 297 et seq.; Mortara, Indice, passim; Migne Patrologia, Latin series, clvi. 535; Güdemann, Gesch. ii. 32.
s.   U. C.

VERSE-DIVISION: The system of breaking up the Biblical text into verses may seem, both in the original and in the versions, to go hand in hand with its division into chapters. In truth, however, the chapter-division and the verse-division are of different origin. The division into chapters was employed first in the Vulgate, perhaps by Stephen Langton, Archbishop of Canterbury (d. 1228). It was adopted by Jewish scholars for purposes of reference — not only by ISAAC NATHAN BEN KALONYMUS in his great concordance, "Meïr Netib" (Venice, 1523), but, not long after its introduction into the Vulgate, by Solomon b. Ishmael (see "Theologisch Tijd-schrift," 1878, p. 104)—and was introduced into the printed editions of the Hebrew text,

Chapter-Divisions Christian. from the Bomberg Bible of 1521 downward. On the other hand, verse-division, with the elaborate systems of accentuation resting upon it, is in itself essentially a part of the Masoretic tradition, although notation by means of figures in the text, or on the margin, was employed first in the Latin Bibles of 1528 and 1555, and somewhat later (1571) by Arias Montanus in the Antwerp Bible: a figure on the margin corresponded to a cross in the text at the beginning of each verse. The Athias Bible (1659–61) was the first edition with verse-notation that could be used by Jews.

In all the manuscripts of the Hebrew Bible, except the scrolls used for the public lessons (see below), the end of a verse ("pasuḳ") is marked by the double point (:), which is called "sof pasuḳ." The next higher unit in the Pentateuch is the hebdomadal lesson ("parashah"), which is thus "treated as a chapter for the purpose of numbering the verses." At the end of each parashah the number of verses contained in it is given, together with a mnemonic sign. Thus at the end of the first pericope (Gen. i. 1–vi. 8) occurs קמ״ו (i.e., 146), followed by אמצי״ה, יחזקיה״ו, either of which words has the numerical value 146. Sometimes two pericopes which, in certain years, are read on one Sabbath, are computed together, in addition to the separate computation of the component parts (so נצבים וילך, Deut. xxix. 9–xxx. 20, xxxi. 1–30, in one MS., Ginsburg, No. 84; for the detailed items see Ginsburg, "Introduction," pp. 72–85; Blau, in "J. Q. R." 1897, pp. 479–482). Discrepancies occur in the various Masoretic sources available; according to Ginsburg, they point to different Masoretic schools, hence to a lack of fixity concerning the method of verse-division, while Blau holds that they are "for the most part errors in copying or in reading which are easily recognized and explained" (see also Baer, "Die Verszählung des Pentateuch," in "Orient, Lit." 1851, pp. 200 et seq.). There is complete agreement in the Masoretic sources as to the total number of verses in the Pentateuch, given as 5,845. In the other

Number Fixed. books of the Bible no subdivisions are marked as in the Pentateuch; while the separate figures given for the single books vary (see Ginsburg, l.c. pp. 87–105; Blau, l.c. pp. 486–487). The correct total figure for the verses in the prophetical books is proved by Blau to be 9,294; in the Hagiographa, 8,064. The total number of verses in the entire Scriptures is thus 23,203. With this computation agree the lists in a Yemen manuscript (Ginsburg, l.c. pp. 105 et seq.) and in "Diḳduḳe ha-Ṭe'amim" (ed. Baer-Strack, p. 55). Blau adduces a variety of proofs for the correctness of these totals. He proves also from a sufficient number of tests obtained from various Masoretic notes that the Masoretic verses were identical with those of the editions now used; i.e., they began and ended with the same words (l.c. pp. 471–474).

While the hebdomadal lessons are treated as "chapters" in the Masoretic computations of verses, the "chapters" of the traditional text are really the much shorter "open" and "closed" sections (Ginsburg, l.c. ch. ii.), which are necessarily coterminal with their concluding verses. The exceptions are the so-called "breaks in the middle of verses" ("pisḳa be-'emẓa' pasuḳ"; comp. Buhl, "Canon and Text of the Old Testament," 1892, p. 35, and the literature there noted). These exceptions, however, are only apparent. In Gen. xxxv. 22, for example, the portions before the break and after it are really separate verses, but are joined in reading for the purpose of slurring over the story concerning the misconduct of Reuben, or in order to suggest that, in spite of his misconduct, he was still counted

Breaks in Middle of Verses. with the other sons of Jacob (see Rashi, ad loc., and sources). The breaks are particularly numerous in the books of Samuel; in the majority of cases in the place of the break there seems to have been originally a reference to the priest's manipulation of the ephod.

With the Masoretic computation as given above that of an anonymous baraita in Ḳid. 30a is apparently at variance, which assigns to the Pentateuch 5,888 verses, to the Psalter 5,896, and to Chronicles 5,880. The repetition of the figure 8 and the divisibility of each number by 8 are not necessarily an evidence of artificiality. The frequently quoted statement of the amora Aḥa bar Ada (in the Talmudic passage referred to), that the Palestinians divided Ex. xix. 9 into three verses, and the avowal of another amora, Rab Joseph, in a discussion with Abaye, that "we are no experts in the counting of the verses," have been adduced by various scholars as a proof of the existence of different systems of verse-division in Talmudic times, and at all events of the absence of fixity in the pre-Masoretic period (comp. Frankel, "Vorstudien zu der Septuaginta," 1843, p. 217; Grätz, "Monatsschrift," 1885, pp. 97–100). It is true, of course, that the Eastern and Western schools varied from each other in the verse-division as in other matters (comp. the geonic statement, Blau, l.c. p. 141); such variation, however, it is contended by Blau, was only occasional, and was confined to a small number of places, which he enumerates. The contradiction between the Talmud and the Masorah is harmonized in a geonic responsum (Harkavy, "Responsa der Geonim," No. 3a) by the assertion that "the baraita refers to a Bible found in Jerusalem, which differed from other Bibles in respect to writing and number of verses." On the basis of an exhaustive induction from the Talmudic-Midrashic data tending to show that in the centuries immediately preceding the Masoretic period the verses began and ended practically in the same places as nowadays, Blau believes himself justified in minimizing the difficulty and in harmonizing the contradictory statements (l.c. pp. 471–474, 476, 483 et seq.).

Talmud Versus Masorah. According to the Yalḳuṭ on the Pentateuch, section 855, the Pentateuch contains 5,842 verses. The Talmud is equally at variance with the Masorah in counting Lev. xiii. 33, instead of Lev. viii. 8, as the middle verse of the Pentateuch, while Soferim ix. 3 gives Lev. viii. 23 as the middle verse.

·The Talmud credits the work of the verse-division to the scribes. This means that it antedates the Talmud. In medieval times Judah ha-Levi, Ibn Ezra, and Profiat Duran considered Ezra or the men of the Great Synagogue as the author or authors of this division (Bacher, "Ibn Ezra als Grammatiker," 1881, p. 38); but although an element of ancient tradition, the verse-division was not permitted to enter the scroll (Soferim iii. 7). It is clear that the verse-division occupies in the history of the Hebrew text a place posterior to the separation of words and the introduction of vowel-letters; with the verse-division there went hand in hand the accentuation which presupposes it; both antedated the vocalization. While on the Phenician monuments there is found continuous script, with no space to mark even the division of words, the Moabite Stone makes use of a single point for word-separation, and of a vertical stroke for the purpose of marking the end of a sense-unit corresponding somewhat to a Scriptural verse.

The beginnings of Scriptural verse-division must be sought in the poetical books. As can be seen from the Ecclesiasticus fragments as well as from certain poetical passages in the canon (e.g., Deut. xxxii.; see Harris in "J. Q. R." 1889, p. 225), it was customary to write each metrical (?) unit on a short line corresponding to what the Greeks called στίχος (in Latin, "versus"). In Hebrew poetry, two metrical units, or stichs, usually go to make one complete and rounded thought. The two stichs were therefore written opposite each other on one line, and together constituted a pasuḳ, a verse in the accepted sense. From the poetic **Stichoi of** passages the custom of verse-division **Verse.** spread to the other parts of Scripture. If Sievers may be believed ("Studien zur Hebräischen Metrik," p. 382, Leipsic, 1901), Gen. ii. 4-14 is metrical. Economy of space, of course, prevented the employment of broken lines even in the poetic passages. It was expensive to write "per cola et commata" (on the meaning of the phrase comp. Swete, "Introduction to the Old Testament in Greek," 1900, pp. 345 et seq.; the whole of ch. vi. will prove useful reading in connection with the present subject). Even in the scrolls many poetic pieces are written as prose. The manuscripts from which the Masoretic archetype immediately descends, as well as those from which the Greek translation was made, appear not to have been written in broken lines where one would expect such writing — e.g., in the Psalter (note the error in Ps. xlii. 6,7, פְּנֵי : אֱלֹהַי for פְּנֵי וֵאלֹהָי :), or in the alphabetical chapters of Lamentations (comp. Lam. i. 16, LXX.; Frankel, l.c. p. 218).

Saadia is criticized by Ibn Ezra for disregarding the traditional verse-division in ten Scriptural passages (Bacher, l.c. p. 39, note 14). More frequently this expedient is resorted to by modern commentators and editors. Examples may be found on the pages of Haupt's Bible, where a special sign (|) indicates the transposition of the Masoretic sof pasuḳ.

BIBLIOGRAPHY: C. D. Ginsburg, *Introduction to the Massoretico-Critical Edition of the Hebrew Bible*, 1897, ch. vi.; L. Blau, *Massoretic Studies*, in *J. Q. R.* 1897, pp. 122-144, 471-490. Older literature and special articles are enumerated by these two scholars.

T. M. L. M.

VERSICLE THEMES. See Ḳerobot; Seliḥah.

VERVEER, ELCHANAN: Dutch painter and vignette-engraver; born at The Hague April 19, 1826. He received instruction from his brother Samuel L. Verveer, and from H. F. C. Ten Kate. In 1845 he went to Brussels, where he engraved the vignette illustrations for Eugène Sue's "Le Juif Errant," and on his return to The Hague he was engaged for some time in drawing illustrations for "De Brillen van Onzen Tijd," which appeared first in "Nederlandsch Magazijn" and later as a separate publication.

Of Verveer's paintings may be mentioned "The First Pipe" and "Winter," both in the museum at Rotterdam, and "The Widow" and "Sufferers from Sea-Sickness," which belong to the Stadtmuseum in The Hague.

Verveer was a knight of the Lion of Nassau, and an officer of the Order of Leopold.

BIBLIOGRAPHY: A. Winkler Prins, *Geïllustreerde Encyclopædie*, Amsterdam, 1887; Hans Wolfgang Singer, *Allgemeines Künstler-Lexicon*, Frankfort-on-the-Main, 1898.

S. F. C.

VERVEER, SAMUEL LEONARDUS: Dutch landscape- and genre-painter; born at The Hague Nov. 30, 1813; died there Jan. 5, 1876. He was a pupil of B. J. van den Hove. Verveer traveled a great deal, visiting especially the art galleries of French cities; but the scenery of his native land was ever to his mind the most beautiful in the world, and he became a master in depicting views of Dutch towns and hamlets.

Of Verveer's paintings may be mentioned: "Afternoon at Katwijk on the Sea" (now in the museum at Rotterdam); "Nordwijk on the Sea" and "Scheveningen" (both in the Amsterdam Museum of Art). The last-named painting was exhibited at Philadelphia in 1876 and was awarded a silver medal. "Salmon Fishers" and "Departure for the Market" are two of the most representative of Verveer's genre-paintings. His works were also awarded prizes at Brussels in 1842 and 1851; and many of his paintings were bought by the art galleries of Ghent, The Hague, Hamburg, etc.

BIBLIOGRAPHY: Clement and Hutton, *Artists of the Nineteenth Century and Their Works*, Boston, 1880; A. Winkler Prins, *Geïllustreerde Encyclopædie*, Amsterdam, 1887; Hans Wolfgang Singer, *Allgemeines Künstler-Lexicon*, Frankfort-on-the-Main, 1898.

S. F. C.

VESOUL (Hebr. וזן or וושול) : Capital of the department of Haute-Saône, France. Jews first settled there in the latter part of the thirteenth century, under the leadership of Ḥayyim b. Jacob, who was a correspondent of Ḥayyim b. Isaac Or Zarua', one of the first pupils of Meïr of Rothenburg. The synagogue was situated within the city walls, on a site now occupied by the Chapelle de la Charité, on the Place du Palais-de-Justice; after the expulsion of the Jews in 1321 it was sold for the benefit of the public treasury.

In 1315 Héliot, a banker of Vesoul, was one of the Jewish syndics of the Langue d'Oïl who, together with Poncin de Bar, Joce de Pontoise, Cressent de Corbeil, and Morel d'Amboise, negotiated for the return of the Jews expelled from France by Philip the Fair. Three years later Countess Jeanne of Burgundy confiscated a house belonging to a Jew named Helget, and presented it to the prior and curé of Vesoul. In 1321 Philip V., the Tall, gave his wife, Queen Jeanne, the estate of Héliot and of his son Vivant as well as the property of other Jews of the county of Burgundy; and three years later Marguerite de Lambrez, one of the queen's ladies of the bedchamber, was allotted Héliot's house. In 1342 Michelet, a Jew of Vesoul, furnished the King of France with a subsidy of 187 livres.

In 1348 eighty Jews of Vesoul were arrested by order of Eudes IV., Duke of Burgundy, on the charge of well-poisoning. Renaud Joume de Chariez, provost of Vesoul, superintended the confiscation of their property, these seizures enriching the treasury to the amount of about 294 livres. Six of the prisoners were secretly put to the torture, and the twelve nobles appointed to pass judgment on them, in order to save them from the fury of the mob, sentenced them to banishment on the strength of confessions wrung from them in this manner. In 1360, however, Manecier or Menessier, a Jew of Vesoul, enjoyed the special favor of Charles V., whom he induced to permit the Jews to return to France. Twenty-four years later Philip the Bold authorized fifty-two Jewish families to settle in Burgundy, in consideration of the payment of an entrance-fee, and an annual tax to the treasury. They were, however, forbidden to loan money at a higher rate of interest than 4 deniers per livre, but their testimony was recognized in legal matters, even against Christians. Gui de la Trémouille, Sire de Joinville, a courtier, was appointed guardian of their rights and interests. From 1410 to 1419 Hacquin, a Jew of Vesoul, was physician to Duke John the Fearless.

At present there are twenty-five or thirty Jewish families in the city.

BIBLIOGRAPHY: Dom Plancher, *Histoire de Bourgogne*, iii.; Gross, *Gallia Judaica*, pp. 190–191; Gollut, *Mémoires des Bourguignons de la Franche-Comté*, p. 761; *R. E. J.* vii. 1; viii. 161; ix. 21, 187; xlix. 1, 244; Saige, *Les Juifs de Languedoc*, pp. 106, 330.

D.   S. K.

VESPASIAN: Emperor of Rome from 69 to 79; founder of the Flavian dynasty. The defeat of Cestius Gallus convinced Nero that the Jewish uprising was a serious matter, and he transferred the command of his army to the veteran Flavius Vespasianus, who had already fought courageously against the Britons. In the winter of 67 Vespasian made his preparations for war in Antioch, and in the following spring marched on Ptolemais. After joining his son Titus, who had advanced with an army from Alexandria, Vespasian found himself in command of a powerful force, consisting of the fifth, tenth, and fifteenth legions, twenty-three auxiliary cohorts, and six squadrons of horse, in addition to the troops of the native vassals, of the Jewish King Agrippa II., and of the kings of Commagene, Emesa, and Arabia (Josephus, "B. J." iii. 7, § 1). The entire Roman army must have mustered at least 60,000 men.

The first aim was the conquest of Galilee, a wealthy and populous district of Palestine, which was defended by Josephus. Upon the approach of Vespasian, however, the protecting army fled in confusion, and the city of Gadara fell into the **Gadara and** hands of the Romans. All its inhabit- **Jotapata** ants were put to the sword by order **Surrender.** of Vespasian, and Gadara and the neighboring towns and villages were burned (*ib.* iii. 7, § 1). These events were followed by the reduction of Jotapata in a siege which is described in detail by Josephus, who found himself compelled to surrender. Vespasian, like his son Titus, treated the captive as a friend. The operations were now interrupted by a brief truce, while the conqueror marched through Ptolemais to Cæsarea, where he rested his troops (*ib.* iii. 9, § 1). Vespasian himself went to Cæsarea Philippi, Agrippa's capital, where festivities in his honor were celebrated for twenty days. He then led his army against Tiberias, which willingly surrendered, and also against Taricheæ, which fell into his hands in the beginning of the month of Elul.

A terrible punishment awaited the conquered. Galilee was entirely depopulated; 6,000 youths were sent to Nero to work on the isthmus of Corinth; 1,200 old men were killed; and the remaining Jews, more than 30,400 in number, were sold as slaves, servitude being also the fate of those who were given to Agrippa (*ib.* iii. 10, § 10). There now remained only the fortress of Gamala, whose defenders repulsed the Romans so disastrously that Vespasian in person had to urge his soldiers on. The fortress was reduced at last, however, and the Romans massacred 4,000 Jews, the rest preferring death by their own hands. In the meantime the fort of Itabyrion at Tabor had surrendered, while the city of Giscala was reduced by Titus, so that Galilee was entirely subdued by Vespasian.

The simplest procedure would now have been an attack upon Jerusalem, as was desired by the Roman lieutenants, but Vespasian decided to leave the city to itself, knowing that Jewish factional strife would gradually weaken it (*ib.* iv. 6, §§ 2, 3). Notwithstanding the heavy rains, he advanced toward Perea, and occupied the Hellenistic city of Gadara, while Placidus, his second in command, was engaged in subduing the remainder of the district. Once more Vespasian marched from Cæsarea, and occupied in turn the cities of Antipatris, Lydda, Jamnia, and Emmaus, leaving the fifth legion in the last-named city, after which he scoured Edom, returning to Emmaus, and finally marching northward in the direction of Jerusalem through the district of Samaria. He met with little resistance in any of these places, even Jericho and Adida being easily taken by the Roman soldiers. Gerasa alone had to be conquered and destroyed by one of his generals (*ib.* iv. 9, § 1); this, however, can not have been the great Gerasa, which was a Hellenistic city.

Vespasian doubtless desired to pro- **Prolongs** long the campaign in Judea, since this **War for** left him in command of a large army **Political** which was desirable in view of the im- **Reasons.** perial succession. When he heard, however, that Simeon bar Giora had invaded and ravaged southern Palestine with his Jewish hordes, he determined to restore order there, and accordingly invaded and subdued the districts of Gophna and Acrobata in the month of Siwan, 69. He likewise captured the cities of Bethel and Ephraim, while Hebron was taken by his tribune Cerealis (*ib.* iv. 9, § 9). The Romans now had free access to Jerusalem from all sides, although some places, such as Emmaus, Herodium, Masada, and Machærus, still remained in the hands of the Jews.

In the meantime the imperial throne of Rome had been filled successively by Galba, Otho, and Vitellius; and the Oriental legions, following the example of the army of the Rhine, gave an emperor to Rome in the person of Vespasian. This event, which was to prove important for the history of the world, was doubtless planned in Palestine, where, according to Josephus, the proclamation was issued, although Tacitus and Suetonius assert that the Egyptian legions were the first to hail Vespasian emperor, on July 1, 69. Two personages of Jewish descent were particularly active in connection with this event—Berenice, the mistress of Titus, and Tiberius Julius Alexander, governor of Egypt. Josephus boasts that he foretold Vespasian's election to Vespasian himself and received his freedom as well as permission to accompany the emperor to Alexandria as a reward for his prophecy. According to Talmudic sources, however, Johanan ben Zakkai was the first to predict Vespasian's elevation to the imperial throne. The statement that he was unable to draw on one of his shoes for joy (Giṭ. 56b) may be explained by the fact that the phrase "calceos mutare" (to change the shoes) was used also to denote promotion to a higher rank ("Monatsschrift," 1904, p. 277). The fact that the proclamation of Vespasian was issued from Judea led Josephus, followed herein by Tacitus ("Hist." v. 13) and Suetonius ("Vespasianus," § 4), to interpret an ancient oracle foretelling that a ruler from Judea should acquire dominion over the entire world as an allusion to Vespasian (Josephus, *l.c.* vi. 5, § 4). The new emperor left his son TITUS in command of the army, while he himself hurried to Rome to take possession of the throne.

In the eyes of the Roman people Vespasian and Titus shared in the glory of the subjugation of Palestine, yet neither of them assumed the title "Judaicus," probably because this term referred to the religion as well as to the nationality of the Jews. In addition to the honors bestowed on Titus by the Senate, and the memorials erected to his praise, several decrees and monuments refer to Vespasian. The coins bearing the legend "victoria navalis" probably commemorate his pursuit of the Jews at Tarichæa on rafts, and the same circumstance doubtless explains why Titus brought a large number of ships with him when he entered Rome in triumph (*ib.* vii. 5, § 5). Together with his sons Titus and Domitian, Vespasian celebrated his own triumph in the year 71 (*ib.* vii. 5, § 7; Dio Cassius, lxvi. 7). In addition to the triumphal arch erected in honor of Titus, which still stands near the Roman Forum, another arch of Titus existed, until the fifteenth century, in the Circus Maximus, which bore an inscription expressly stating that Titus had conquered the Jewish people at the command and counsel of his father,

and under his auspices ("C. I. L." vi., No. 944; "R. E. J." i. 35).

The Judean Triumph and Medals. All three Flavian emperors struck coins with such legends as 'Ιουδαίας ἑαλωκυίας, "Iudæa devicta," or "Iudæa capta" (Madden, "Coins of the Jews," pp. 207–229), and numerous inscriptions furnish material for an exact determination of the names of the legions and officers that took part in the war; such lists have been compiled by Arsène Darmesteter and Joseph Offord.

The sacred vessels from the Temple at Jerusalem were deposited in the Temple of the Goddess of Peace, erected by Vespasian in commemoration of his victory, but destroyed by fire in 191; and other trophies were preserved in the imperial palace (Josephus, *l.c.* vii. 5, § 7; Jerome, "Comm. on Isaiah," xxix. 1). The Circus Maximus still exists, stained with the blood of Jewish martyrs. Vespasian instituted also the FISCUS JUDAICUS, and did not hesitate to claim all Judea as his property (Josephus, *l.c.* vi. 6, § 6). A papyrus from the Egyptian province of Arsinoe, preserved partly in London and partly in Vienna, gives detailed information concerning a special impost levied on the Jews in addition to the customary poll-tax. This papyrus is dated in the fifth year of Vespasian's reign, and shows that the tax was payable by every Jew and Jewess over three years of age. The annual amount of the special Jewish assessment was 8 drachmæ 2 oboles per individual, and to this was added an extra income tax of 1 drachma. The poll-tax itself amounted to 40 drachmæ, so that the Jews were heavily burdened, at least throughout Egypt. Christian sources further state that Vespasian caused all Jews of the house of David to be executed, and thus instigated a great persecution (Eusebius, "Hist. Eccl." iii. 12, based on Hegesippus). He also closed the Temple of Onias, in 73, and enlarged the pomerium of the city of Rome, which might be done only by an imperator who had increased the territories of the empire.

Talmudic References. Vespasian is frequently mentioned in rabbinical literature, the war, with which certain mourning customs were associated, being called "polemos shel Aspasyanos" (Soṭah ix. 14), and "Vespasian and his comrades" (*i.e.*, his sons) being accused of enriching themselves from the treasures of Israel (Midr. Teh. xvii. 2). When Vespasian came to Jerusalem he encamped outside the wall and made propositions of peace to the Jews which were rejected. According to Ab. R. N., Recension B, § 6, certain Jews in the city communicated treacherously with Vespasian by means of arrows; but this statement confuses Vespasian with Titus, while other passages confound him with Hadrian, or even with Nebuchadnezzar. "One of these will destroy the holy Temple, and that one is the miscreant Vespasian" (Midrash ha-Gadol on Gen. xxv. 23, ed. Schechter; in Gen. R. lxvii. the name of Hadrian is substituted). The passage "I have not despised them" was interpreted as meaning, "I have not despised them in the days of Vespasian" (Sifra, xxvi. 44; Esth. R., beginning); and it is clear from a statement of Jerome on Joel iii. 3 that several haggadic passages were likewise regarded as allusions to Vespasian. Various legends concerning this emperor appear in rabbinical literature, the first one being told by Josephus ("Ant." viii. 2, § 5), who relates how a Jewish exorcist displayed his skill to Vespasian. The shiploads of captive Jews are generally, and correctly, associated with the name of

Brass Coin of Vespasian, with Inscription "Iudaea Capta."
Struck in 72 C. E.

(From Madden, "History of Jewish Coinage.")

Titus; but according to a later legend (Buxtorf, "Synagoga Judaica," ix. 231; "J. Q. R." xv. 664), which apparently sought to attribute to Vespasian all the evils that befell the Jews, the future emperor guided three vessels filled with Hebrew prisoners to Lavanda, Arlada, and Bardeli.

Vespasian collected his memoirs of the Jewish war; and these were mentioned, and probably also used, by Josephus ("Vita," § 65; comp. "Contra Ap." i., § 10).

BIBLIOGRAPHY: Grätz, Gesch. 4th ed., iii. 494 et seq.; Schürer, Gesch. 3d ed., i. 610 et seq. (where further sources are given); Vogelstein and Rieger, Gesch. der Juden in Rom, i. 23; Mommsen, Römische Gesch. vol. v.; Darmesteter, in R. E. J. i. 40–56; Offord, in Proc. Soc. Bibl. Arch. 1902, xxiv. 325; Newton, The Epigraphal Evidence for the Reign of Vespasian and Titus, Ithaca, New York, 1901; Wessely, Die Epikrisis und das Ἰουδαίων τέλεσμα Unter Vespasian, in Studien zur Paleographie und Papyruskunde, Leipsic, 1901.
G.   S. KR.

VESSELS, SACRED. See TEMPLE, ADMINISTRATION OF.

VESSILLO ISRAELITICO, IL ("Hebrew Banner"): An Italian monthly; the continuation of the "Educatore Israelita" (founded 1853), which, upon the death of its editor Giuseppe Levi (July 10, 1874), passed under the new title into the control of Flaminio Servi, rabbi of Casale Monferrato, who transferred its headquarters from Vercelli to Casale. During the early years of its existence it contained essays from the pens of such men as Berliner, Benedetti, Perreau, Soave, and Steinschneider; but later its importance as a literary and scientific journal deteriorated. It is noteworthy as containing valuable biographical sketches of Italian Jews.

Flaminio Servi died Jan. 23, 1904, and was succeeded by his son Ferruccio, who has made considerable changes in the publication, giving it a distinctly modern character. In February, 1905, the "Lux," a review founded in Leghorn in 1904 under the editorship of Arrigo Lattes and Alfredo Toaff, was incorporated with the "Vessillo."
s.   U. C.

VÉSZI, JOSEPH: Hungarian editor and deputy; born at Arad Nov. 6, 1858. He was educated at the gymnasium of his native town, and studied philosophy, literature, and languages at Budapest.

In his early youth he was a poet, and in the seventies his lyrical productions were accepted by the best literary periodicals, while two volumes of his verses were published at Budapest in 1880 under the titles "A Bánat Dalaiból" and "Traviata, Dalok Egy Tévedt Nöhöz." Since 1877 he has devoted himself to journalism, advocating liberal views. He was for some time editor of the "Budapester Tagblatt," and contributed leaders and stories to the "Pester Lloyd." In 1894 he became editor-in-chief of the "Pesti Napló," and in 1896 he founded the "Budapesti Napló."

Vészi is president of the journalistic club of Budapest, and vice-president of the picture salon and of the club of amateur musicians in that city. He is also master of the masonic lodge "Reform." In 1899 he was elected to the Hungarian Parliament from the district of Szász Sebes; and in 1901, from the third district of the capital. In 1905 he represented the third district of Budapest. He takes an active interest in all Jewish affairs.

BIBLIOGRAPHY: Sturm, Országgyülési Almanach, 1901–6; Pallas Lex.
s.   L. V.

VICENTE, GIL. See GIL VINCENTE.

VICTORIA. See AUSTRALIA; BALLARAT; MELBOURNE.

VICTORIA. See CANADA.

VIDAL B. BENVENISTE IBN LABI. See LABI, JOSEPH IBN.

VIDAL, MENAHEM B. SOLOMON ME-IRI. See ME'IRI, MENAHEM.

VIDAL OF TOLOSA: Spanish scholar of the latter half of the fourteenth century. He resided in Catalonia, where he prepared his most important work, "Maggid Mishneh," a commentary on Maimonides' "Yad." This work covered the entire contents of the "Yad," but only those parts are extant which cover the following books: iii., iv., v. (ch. i.–ix. only), xi., xii. (ch. i.–iii. only), and xiii. The commentary was never published separately, but only together with the "Yad" (first at Constantinople, 1509). Vidal's second work was a commentary in Arabic on Al-Ghazali's "To'elet ha-Higgayon." This commentary was translated into Hebrew by Moses ben Joshua of Narbonne, and is extant in manuscript in the Library of the Vatican. From Joseph Caro's preface to his "Kesef Mishneh" it appears that Vidal was a personal friend of R. Nissim.

Vidal's son **Isaac** was also a prominent scholar; he lived in Alcala and corresponded with Isaac ben Sheshet (Responsa, No. 473).

BIBLIOGRAPHY: Michael, Or ha-Ḥayyim, pp. 360–361; Ibn Yaḥya, Shalshelet ha-Kabbalah, ed. Amsterdam, p. 45; Sefer Yuḥasin, ed. Filipowski, p. 225a; Conforte, Kore ha-Dorot, ed. Cassel, pp. 26a, 27a; Rosin, Compendium der Jüdischen Gesetzeskunde, p. 115, Breslau, 1871; De Rossi, Dizionario, p. 328; Steinschneider, Hebr. Uebers. i. 315, note 353; idem, Jüdische Literatur, p. 388, note 17; Wolf, Bibl. Hebr. i. 563, iii. 562; Bartolocci, Kiryat Sefer, ii. 804a–805b; Benjacob, Ozar ha-Sefarim, p. 384; Steinschneider, Cat. Bodl. cols. 2707–2708.
E. C.   S. O.

VIDAL-NAQUET, SAMUEL EMANUEL: French financier; born at Paris Aug. 22, 1859. Educated in his native city, he graduated from the Law Faculty and was admitted to the bar in 1882. In 1885 he entered the Banque des Fonds Publics et

Valeurs Industrielles, managed by his father, whom he succeeded as chief on the latter's death.

Since 1888 he has edited with his brother Charles the "Cote de la Bourse et de la Banque," for which paper he wrote many editorials. He is recognized as one of the leading French authorities on financial law.

BIBLIOGRAPHY: Curinier, *Dict. Nat.* iii. 34.
S.   F. T. H.

VIDAS, DE, ELIJAH B. MOSES. See ELIJAH B. MOSES DE VIDAS.

VIDAS, SAMUEL BEN ḤABIB DE: Spanish scholar and Bible commentator of the fifteenth century; it is said, but not known with certainty, that he was a physician also. He wrote a commentary on Lamentations, entitled "Perush Megillat Ekah," which appeared in Salonica, 1595. He was the author of the following works also, which have been preserved in manuscript: "Mebaḳḳesh ha-Shem," sermons on the weekly Torah lessons, beginning with Ki Tissa and continued to Niẓẓabim; and a commentary on Canticles, in which his name is given as Samuel Bibas (בבאש).

BIBLIOGRAPHY: Polak, in *Orient, Lit.* x. 276; Azulai, *Shem ha-Gedolim*, i. 174; Carmoly, *Histoire des Médecins Juifs*, pp. 121 *et seq.*; Schorr, in *He-Ḥaluẓ*, ii. 24; Dukes, in *Orient, Lit.* x. 707; Steinschneider, *Cat. Bodl.* cols. 2410–2411; Jacobs, *Sources*, p. 195.
J.   S. O.

VIENNA: Formerly capital of Austria-Hungary, now a province of Austria. Legend asserts that Jews settled in this city in the remotest antiquity, and it is alleged that some were among the first colonists that Rome sent to the Danube. In 905 decrees were issued fixing the toll to be paid by Jewish merchants in Austria; this, however, proves only that Jews traveled in that country. Although the document, dated 1156, which granted to Duke Leopold of Austria the privilege of admitting Jews into his dominions is a forgery originating two hundred years after its alleged date (O. Stobbe, "Die Juden in Deutschland," p. 12), Jews were undoubtedly living at that time in Austria, though not in great numbers. Under the protection of the liberal princes of the house of Badenberg they fared much better than the other German Jews of that period.

As early as 1194 Duke Leopold VI. of Austria placed a Jew of the name of Shlom (Solomon) at the head of the mint ("super officium **Shlom the** monetæ"), and Jewish officers of that **Minter.** mint had such influence as to give rise to bitter complaints. Two years later, when the Crusaders reached Vienna and heard that Solomon had imprisoned for theft one of his servants who was to join them, they rushed to the Jew's house, murdered him and fifteen other Jews, and liberated the imprisoned man. The duke was sufficiently just to execute two of the ringleaders (Joseph ha-Kohen, "Emeḳ ha-Baka," ed. Letteris, p. 46). The influence of the Jewish officials had become so great that after the expulsion of Duke Frederick the Belligerent, in 1237, the citizens of Vienna petitioned Emperor Frederick II. not to appoint any more Jews to official positions. Nevertheless Jews apparently continued to be employed as agents of the treasury. In 1235 they dictated the entire commer-

cial policy of Duke Frederick II. and induced him to forbid the export of grain into the "upper districts" (Pertz, "Monumenta Scriptores," ix. 786); and in 1257 the Jews Lublin and Nekelo, two brothers, were treasury agents ("Kammergrafen") "to the most illustrious Duke of Austria" (Steinschneider, "Hebr. Bibl." x. 44 *et seq.*). In Aug., 1238, Emperor Frederick II. took the Jews of Vienna under his protection ("servi cameræ nostræ"), granting them special privileges (see JEW. ENCYC. ii. 322, *s.v.* AUSTRIA). Of still greater importance is the charter that Duke Frederick II. granted to all Jews within his territory July 1, 1244; this afterward became the model by which the status of the Jews of Bohemia, Moravia, Hungary, Silesia, and Poland was regulated.

The Jews of Vienna, who had the right to own real estate and to buy houses, were engaged principally in lending money on security to the burghers

Gate Leading to the Old "Judenstadt" at Vienna.
(From an old print.)

and also to the impecunious princes. Frederick II. permitted the Jews to charge a weekly interest of eight heller on the pound (*i.e.*, 87 per cent); under his father they were permitted a still higher rate. Later the rate on loans by Jews was reduced to three heller on the pound. The rich Jew Techau in Vienna was in 1255 the bondsman of Duke Leopold VI. for a debt of 2,000 pounds of silver owed to King Andrew of Hungary (Steinschneider, *l.c.* x. 46). The "Muschlein Terhau" (Techau) mentioned in a document (Wiener, "Regesten," p. 117) was probably a son of this otherwise unknown person. The favorable position of the Jews changed when, in May,

The Church Council of 1267. 1267, the Council of Vienna revived the ancient ecclesiastical decrees concerning the Jews. These decrees fostered hatred against the Jews, but they could not be carried out to the letter, since the princes in their monetary difficulties could not get along without Jewish help. Emperor Rudolph, the first of the house of Hapsburg, who was indebted to a Jew by the name of Amschel Oppenheimer, confirmed in 1277 the Jews' statute of Duke Frederick the Belligerent; but a year later he declared the Jews ineligible for public office, a privilege which his successor, Duke Albert, confirmed to the citizens of Vienna in 1296.

The fourteenth century in general brought much misery to the Jews of Vienna. In 1337 outrages were committed against them, but Duke Albert and the nobles interfered to protect them from further injustice. In recognition of the good-will shown by the citizens of Vienna in time of distress, and in anticipation of its continuance, the Jews declared, in a document written in Hebrew and dated Vienna, June 19, 1338, that they

Plan of the Old "Judenstadt" at Vienna.

would lend to the citizens of Vienna, rich as well as poor, a pound of Vienna heller at a weekly interest of three heller. On the following day appeared the "Jews' decree" of the dukes Albert and Otto, and the endorsement of the Jewish document (G. Wolf, "Gesch. der Juden in Wien," p. 11; *idem,* "Studien zur Jubelfeier der Wiener Universität," pp. 170 *et seq.;* Wiener, *l.c.* p. 221).

The Jews of Vienna appear to have suffered during the persecutions consequent on the Black Death (1369), and in 1370 they were seized, deprived of their possessions, and expelled from the city. But in spite of these persecutions the Jews very soon returned to Vienna and other places. The dukes Albert and Leopold, who were continually in financial straits, needed the Jews, as did also their successors. At their pleasure they "killed the Jews' letters," that is, they canceled the debts of the burghers to the Jews, often those of an entire city. One of the

richest Jews of Vienna, called in the documents indifferently David the Steuzz, Von Steuzz, Steuzzel, or Steuzzlein (the Jew Hennlein von Neuenburg's son), who from 1350 to 1386 had business relations with the nobles and the burghers, often lent large sums to Duke Albert; and after his (Steuzz's) death his son Jonah entered upon his rights; only the duke himself could bring an action against him (Wiener, *l.c.* pp. 224 *et seq.;* according to Document No. 169 [p. 240] he should be called "Jonah the Steussen" instead of "Jonah the Russian").

In 1421 Duke Albert issued a decree that in future no Jew should be permitted to live in Austria; this decree was renewed by Duke Ladislaus in 1453 ("Monumenta Germaniæ," xi. 517; Wertheimer, "Die Juden in Oesterreich," i. 97; Wolf, Gesch., pp. 18 *et seq.;* Wiener, *l.c.* p. 239; Joseph ha-Kohen, "'Emek ha-Baka," p. 219; "Terumat ha-Deshen," responsa, No. 241). The houses of the Jews who had been burned or expelled were sold or given away by the duke, the synagogue at Tulln was presented to the convent of St. Dorothea in Vienna, and the synagogue at the latter place was torn down and the stones used for building a university. Notwithstanding these persecutions the spiritual activity of the Vienna Jews was considerable. One of the earliest rabbis of Vienna was Isaac b. Moses (called also Isaac "Or Zarua'," after the title of his work, or simply Isaac of Vienna). A ritual question was addressed to him in 1240 by Abigdor ha-Kohen, the son-in-law of the learned and rich Hayyim b. Moses of Wiener-Neustadt, who, together with his brother Eliezer, was at the head of the Viennese rabbinate. Another rabbi of Vienna was

Early Rabbis. Meïr ha-Levi ben Baruch, who restored the rabbinical ordination. His son probably was the "Judenmeister," Baruch of Vienna, with whom, together with Meïr b. Baruch, who died about 1400, the dukes Albert and Leopold came to an agreement in regard to security for 20,000 gulden (Wiener, *l.c.* p. 228, No. 82). Abraham Klausner filled the Vienna rabbinate; the last-named collected the various synagogal customs ("minhagim"), and was also a money-broker.

In spite of the decree of banishment Jews still remained in Vienna. In 1512 seven Jewish families were living there, the members of which interceded for their unfortunate coreligionists in Marchegg, who were in danger of being burned, like those of Bösing (Wolf, Gesch. pp. 23, 255). In 1528 Emperor Ferdinand issued a decree " for the Jewish residents of Austria, who are the property of the royal chancellery," and ordered that every Jew who came to Vienna should immediately report to the government office, where he would receive a "ticket"; he must wear the Jews' badge, a ring of yellow cloth, on his outer garment, "uncovered and unhidden"; and might stop only at the two houses set apart for Jews. The Jews of Vienna begged that their coreligionists who

The "Judenturm" at Vienna.
(From an old print.)

had been driven out of Presburg in this year might be allowed to settle in Lower Austria, but Ferdinand refused their request. In 1542 Emperor Ferdinand conceded to the Jew Moses the right to carry on in the country a small business and "trade," in recognition of his services at the mint; and in 1544 he granted to the Jew Lazarus, physician to his children, the privilege of living wherever he chose.

The decrees of banishment were renewed from time to time. A mandate of Jan. 2, 1554, ordered that the Jews should leave the territory of Lower Austria at the end of six months; but the period was several times prolonged. The same proceedings took place when the decrees of banishment were renewed in 1567 and 1572. However, toward the end of 1575 the Jews were really expelled; but they did not stay away very long, for the impecuniosity of the emperors and the interests of the state often inclined the monarchs to be favorably disposed toward them, outweighing religious hatred and the still stronger jealousy of the non-Jewish merchants. Yet the

condition of the Jews was permanently insecure, for they were without rights and privileges. When those of Vienna, who numbered in all thirty-one families, were not able, in 1599, to pay the 20,000 florins demanded of them, an order was issued, Feb. 5, 1600, that they should leave Vienna and Austria within fourteen days. All obeyed except eleven families and the physician Elias Aluanus (Ḥalfon), the "Erztney doctor"; but all the exiles soon returned, with others, to Vienna (Wolf, "Studien," pp. 173 *et seq.*).

The condition of the Jews improved under Emperor Ferdinand II. He renewed Emperor Matthias' decree that they could be driven from the cities only with the consent of the ruling emperor; he protected them against force and oppression, and expressly maintained their rights, so that the decree of general expulsion dated Jan.
Under Ferdinand II. 7, 1625, was not carried out (Wolf, "Die Juden Unter Ferdinand II." in "Jahrbuch für Gesch. der Juden," i. 218 *et seq.*). Those Jews whom the people of Vienna desired to expel in 1623 were assigned to the district of the Lower Wörth as a permanent place of residence, with protection "forever." A wall enclosed this new Jews' town, and here the wealthy ones among them acquired houses and gardens; they had their own shops, and soon a beautiful synagogue was built. They paid 600 florins a year in taxes to the city, and, apart from several imposts, 10,000 florins a year into the imperial treasury. After the death of Ferdinand II. (1637), to whose widow, the empress Eleonora, the Jews of Vienna were required to pay 2,500 gulden a year, the burghers addressed a petition to his successor, Ferdinand III., asking him "to drive out all of the Jews, no one excepted, three miles beyond this city, if not from the whole country" (Wolf, "Gesch. der Juden in Wien," pp. 261 *et seq.*). The emperor would not grant this request, but satisfied the burghers by depriving the Jews of the right to trade in the inner city, where the citizens had their shops. Free entrance into the city was henceforth denied the Jews. Trembling for their existence, the Jews of Vienna offered to assume a state debt of 8,000 gulden and to present the emperor with 15,000 gulden, and promised to trouble him no longer with their disputes.

In Vienna, where, in 1620, about fifty families were living—among them several court Jews—the community had two synagogues and a cemetery. Its first rabbi, mentioned in 1600, was **Abraham Flesch,** who was followed by **Isaac Ḥayyim of Opatow** (Sept., 1623); **Veit Munk; Yom-Ṭob Lipmann Heller,** of Nikolsburg; the physician **Leo Lucerna,** or **Judah Löb Ma'or Ḳaṭon** (d. 1635; built a synagogue at his own expense); and **Ḥayyim Menahem Mann.** The Vienna rabbinate, which supported higher Talmudic schools and philanthropic institutions, had among its more distinguished incumbents **R. Phöbus,** who emigrated to Palestine in 1655; he was succeeded by **Shabbethai Sheftel Hurwitz.** About this time **Zacharias Levi,** brother of Nathan Feitel (d. 1643), learned in rabbinical lore, built a third synagogue, in connection with a richly endowed Talmudic school, and Vienna became a center of Jewish learning and cabalistic speculation. The last rabbi of Vienna and of Lower Austria was **Gershon Ashkenazi**, whose colleagues were **Mordecai Löb Oettingen** (the friend of the Christian divine Wagenseil) and the preachers **Uri Lipmann Hirz Koma** and **Enoch Fränkel**.

The Jewish community of Vienna in 1660 numbered about 500 families, and in spite of the many taxes, assessments, and war duties was in a flourishing condition. But troublous times were in store for it. The hatred of the burghers increased with their intolerance, leading to difficulties in which the gov-

against them. The riots turned into wholesale looting expeditions, and the students and the mob attempted to fire the ghetto. The military guard had to be called out; but it was only on the third day of the riot that the emperor gave orders that no non-Jew was to set foot in the Jewry. In further evidence of the desirability of banishing the Jews, they were accused of being in secret communication with the Swedes. It was finally decided, July 26, 1669, to expel a number of Jews from Vienna and Lower Austria; 1,346 persons were affected by this decree of banishment. In their dire need the Jews of Vi-

Riot of 1668.

EXTERIOR OF THE LEOPOLDSTRASSE SYNAGOGUE, VIENNA.
(From a photograph.)

ernment had to interfere. When in May, 1665, the body of a woman was found in a pool in the Jewry, the Jews were accused of having murdered her, and their lives were in jeopardy. Unfortunately for them, Emperor Leopold, who was entirely in the hands of the Jesuits, married a Spanish infanta. When the crown prince died, in Jan., 1668, three months after his birth, the emperor and empress formed the thought of dealing with the Jews in Spanish fashion. A fire happened to break out in the newly built royal palace in February of the same year, and the populace accused the Jews of having kindled it. In April, 1668, delegates of the city of Vienna appeared before the emperor, praying him to destroy the Jews "root and branch"; and before the end of the month outrages began

enna once more sent a memorial to the emperor; but in vain, for the commission had attributed to them all kinds of crimes. On Monday, March 1, 1670, a solemn proclamation was made in all public places that "for the glory of God" all Jews should, on penalty of imprisonment and death, leave Vienna and Upper and Lower Austria before Corpus Christi Day, never to return. Hirz Koma and the physician of the community, Leo Winkler, in the name of the community made a last attempt to propitiate the emperor by offering him 100,000 florins and, in addition, 10,000 florins a year. In the meantime the period fixed for the exodus had been prolonged at the intercession of influential persons. In July the Jews began to leave, and by Aug. 1 not one Jew

Expulsion of 1670.

INTERIOR OF THE LEOPOLDSTRASSE SYNAGOGUE, VIENNA.

(From a photograph.)

was left in Vienna. The cemetery in the Rossau was protected by the city in consideration of the sum of 4,000 florins; the houses of the Jews became the property of the city; the large new synagogue was turned into a church, renamed the Leopoldskirche, and solemnly consecrated on Aug. 18; a Jew's house was turned into the parsonage. In place of the old synagogue, and out of its ruins, was built a little church—that of St. Margaret, since demolished. Many of the more prominent families settled in Berlin (D. Kaufmann, "Die Letzte Vertreibung der Juden aus Wien und Niederösterreich," Budapest, 1889; G. Wolf, "Die Juden in der Leopoldstadt im 17. Jahrhundert in Wien," Vienna, 1864).

Vienna only too soon regretted the expulsion of the Jews. The deficit in the state tax amounted, according to the report of the royal exchequer, to 40,000 florins a year; the "Landstände" also reported a loss of 20,000 florins owing to the departure of the Jews. The citizens of Vienna, who had undertaken

ber of the imperial household, the second as his assistant. But the hatred of the populace against the Jews was as bitter as it had been before the expulsion, leading to frequent riots, and, as in 1705 and 1710, to repeated demands for their banishment. Gradually more families settled there: the Schlesingers; Marcus and Meyer Hirschel, who contributed 150,000 florins to the building fund of the Church of St. Charles Borromeo; the Arnsteins and Eskeles; the Leidesdorfers; Diego d'Aguilar; and many others.

In 1753 there were 700 Jews in Vienna, who paid a yearly toleration tax amounting to 14,000 gulden.

"Jews' Decree," 1764. The plan, proposed repeatedly, to confine the Jews to a ghetto was not carried out; but they were huddled together in houses in certain streets, only a few court Jews being permitted to live among Christians. The precarious position of the Jews was in a way improved by the "Jews'

JEWISH ORPHAN ASYLUM, VIENNA.
(From a photograph.)

to pay the yearly Jews' tax of 14,000 florins, could hardly pay their own taxes. At a conference held in Wischaw, Moravia, Sept. 26, 1673, between representatives of the government and of the Jews it was agreed that 250 Jewish families might return to Vienna and occupy fifty business places in the inner city on payment of 300,000 florins and the former yearly tax of 10,000 florins. In view of the hopelessly depleted treasury, the royal exchequer considered this offer a "remarkable piece of good fortune," and on Feb. 28, 1675, the agreement was ratified; soon thereafter several Jews returned to Vienna. Samson Wertheimer, who, with his partner Samuel OPPENHEIMER, had rendered important services to the state, returned to the city in 1684, the first as a mem-

decree" of May 5, 1764, which permitted any Jew who could prove that he possessed a certain sum of ready money and "acceptable" papers, or that he had established a factory, etc., to live in Vienna. According to this decree no Jew could buy a house; a married Jew had to let his beard grow, that he might be readily distinguished; and no synagogue or other place for common worship was permitted. The empress Maria Theresa, who in her unbounded hatred of the Jews could conceive of "no greater pest for the state than this nation," was always considering how to "diminish the Jews; by no means to increase them."

Emperor Joseph II. also did not wish to favor the Jews or increase their numbers in his dominions;

POLISH SYNAGOGUE AT VIENNA.
(From a photograph.)

but he was at least the first Austrian ruler to recognize the Jew as a human being. The much-praised Edict of Toleration, published Jan. 2, 1782, permitted the Jews to learn all kinds of trades (without, however, granting the right to hold a master's certificate) and to lend money on real estate, though

Under Joseph II. they were not permitted to acquire any. The tolerated Jew—that is, the one who paid protection or toleration money—could live with his family wherever he chose in Vienna. Foreign Jews could sell their goods at the fairs, but could remain in Vienna no longer than was necessary to finish their

Jews and Jewesses in Vienna who were held in high esteem for their culture and wealth. The salons of Fanny von ARNSTEIN, wife of the banker Nathan von Arnstein, and of her sister Cecilia von Eskeles, wife of Bernhard von ESKELES, were at the time of the Congress of Vienna attended by princes and nobles, statesmen and high civic dignitaries, scholars and artists. After several unsuccessful petitions, the Jews of Vienna were allowed, in 1811, to fit up a "Betstube" (room for prayers) in a house they had bought on the old Dempfingerhof; twelve years later a synagogue was built, due to the efforts of M. L. Biedermann, I. L. von Hoffmannsthal, Joseph

"HOHE WARTE," THE JEWISH INSTITUTE FOR THE BLIND, VIENNA.
(From a photograph.)

business. All laws compelling differentiation in attire, as well as the prohibition against visiting public places of amusement, were repealed. The sixty-five families living in Vienna in 1784 were not allowed to form a congregation or to have a synagogue. In Vienna there were established at that time a Jewish physician (Samuel B. Oppenheimer), a Jewish lawyer (A. Joel), and a Jewish dramatist (David Benedict Arnsteiner). In 1788 Emperor Joseph decreed that the Jews were liable to military service, excepting only those of Vienna who were "protected."

Under Leopold II. the status of the Jews remained the same. He instituted the "Collectentaxe," a toll levied upon every Jew who went to Vienna. In spite of the harsh conditions under which they were compelled to live, there were even then

von Wertheimstein, and others, and Isaac N. MANNHEIMER was called as preacher and teacher of religion, and Salomon SULZER as cantor. The Jews of Vienna now possessed a synagogue, a hospital which had been fitted up in the eighteenth century, and a school of religion; the teachers in the last-named were Mannheimer, J. L. SAALSCHÜTZ, Leopold Breuer, and Gershon Wolf.

The number of tolerated families increased from year to year; in 1820 there were 135 **Statistics.** families, and 197 in 1847; in 1848 there were 4,000 Jews in the city. The congregation of Vienna built in 1855 a second synagogue, calling Adolf JELLINEK and later Moritz GÜDEMANN as preachers.

The restrictions placed upon the Jews in Vienna

INTERIOR OF THE "TURKISH TEMPLE" AT VIENNA.

(From a photograph.)

continued under Emperor Ferdinand. In 1846, the year in which the medieval OATH MORE JUDAICO was repealed, the representatives of the community of Vienna sent a petition to the emperor praying for a betterment of their condition; this petition was indorsed by the magistracy and the government, but it was not acted upon. Then came the Vienna revolution of March, 1848, during which the resolute Adolf FISCHHOF distinguished himself. The constitution of March 4, 1849, which recognized the equal rights of all citizens, regardless of creed, was repealed

ministered by a board of thirty-six members, elected by taxpayers. The expenses are defrayed by assessments and fees. The assessments are levied on each Jew according to his means, the lowest sum being 10 kronen ($2), and the highest, according to statute, 12,000 kronen, although occasionally this is voluntarily exceeded by individual members of the community. In 1903 communal taxes to the amount of 1,058,809 kronen were paid by 16,735 members.

The total receipts of the community for 1903

JEWISH GIRLS' ORPHANAGE, VIENNA.
(From a photograph.)

Dec. 31, 1851. On Jan. 18, 1860, the Jews of Lower Austria were permitted to acquire real estate.

BIBLIOGRAPHY: J. Wertheimer, *Die Juden in Oesterreich*, 2 vols., Leipsic, 1842; D. Kaufmann, *Die Letzte Vertreibung der Juden aus Wien und Niederösterreich*, Budapest, 1889; G. Wolf, *Die Juden in Oesterreich*, in *Die Völker Oesterreich-Ungarns*, vol. vii., Vienna, 1883; idem, *Die Juden in der Leopoldstadt im 17. Jahrhundert in Wien*, ib. 1864; idem, *Judentaufen in Oesterreich*, ib. 1863; idem, *Gesch. der Juden in Wien*, ib. 1876; idem, *Historische Notizen*, in *Allg. Zeit. des Jud.* 1861, vol. xxiii.; idem, *Zur Gesch. der Emancipation der Juden in Oesterreich*, in *Jüdisches Literaturblatt*, 1877, vol. vii.; idem, *Zur Gesch. der Juden in Wien*, in *Jahrb. für Israeliten*, pp. 73 et seq., Vienna, 1860; idem, *Das Hundertjährige Jubiläum der Israelitischen Cultusgemeinde in Wien*, pp. 132 et seq., Vienna, 1864.
J.   M. K.

——**Present Conditions:** The Jewish population of Vienna is organized, in accordance with the law of 1890, in one community, which embraces in its territory the municipal district of Vienna. It is ad-

amounted to 2,243,449 kronen, and the total expenditures to 2,147,506 kronen, the latter being itemized as follows:

	Kronen.
Synagogues and ritual institutions	419,900
Religious instruction and schools	260,235
Hospital	301,731
Almshouse	145,716
Charities	223,431
Cemetery and burials	332,364
Administration and miscellaneous	464,129

The records of Jewish births, marriages, and burials in Vienna are kept by the community. In 1921, the date of the latest census, there were 300,000 Jews in the city; and their increase in the course of the nineteenth and twentieth centuries, as well as their numerical relation to the total population, is shown in the following table:

Year.	Total Population.	Jewish Population.		
		Number.	Percentage to Total.	
1800.................	232,000	1,200	0.5	
1830.................	317,000	1,640	0.5	
1856.................	476,000	15,600	3.30	
1869.................	607,520	40,300	6.60	
1880.................	725,660	72,590	10.00	
1890.................	1,363,548	118,495	8.80	
1900.................	1,674,957	146,926	8.77	
1914.................	1,999,912	175,318	8.75	
1920.................	1,841,326	300,000	16.7	

The growth of the Jewish population, according to this table, was between 1830 and 1856, and between 1880 and 1890 and 1914–20; the former was due to the repeal, in 1848, of the law restricting Jewish residence in the city, and the latter to the annexation of suburban communities and religious liberty. While the first and last increases of number mark an actual rise in percentage, the second is a decrease, since the proportion of Jews in the nine incorporated suburbs was far lower than in the ten old districts.

The following table gives the annual number of births, marriages, and deaths among the Jews in comparison with those among the total population of Vienna according to the average of recent years:

	Total Population.		Jewish Population.	
	Number.	Percentage.	Number.	Percentage.
Births...............	55,000	3.43	3,300	2.36
Marriages..........	16,000	1.00	850	0.60
Deaths..............	33,000	2.06	1,900	1.36

It is clear from this table that the increase in the Jewish population is relatively less than among the other inhabitants, although a hopeful feature is the small proportion of deaths, which may be due to a more rational mode of life among the Jews. A proof of their unfavorable political situation in Austria is afforded by the large number of conversions to Christianity, which amounted to 559 in 1900, and 617 in 1904. The community provides for daily public worship in five synagogues erected and maintained by it. In addition to these synagogues, Vienna contains a large number of synagogal associations, which have their own places of worship and are subventioned in great part by the community. On the high festivals temporary synagogues are opened to meet the extra demands. The permanent synagogues of Vienna provide accommodations for about 7,000 men and 5,600 women.

Synagogues.

The liturgy used in the synagogues of the community, and in the majority of those associations mentioned above, is that introduced by I. N. Mannheimer and Salomon Sulzer; but in the Grosse Schiffgasse ('Adat Yisrael) synagogue, and in almost all the smaller ones, the old ritual is followed, and in the place of worship of the Turkish Jews (in the second district, Zirkusgasse), who form a community of their own, the Sephardic ritual is adhered to. The sheḥiṭah and the sale of kasher meat are under the supervision of the rabbinate of the community of Vienna, and in some stalls the sales are made under

the special control of the Orthodox community 'Adat Yisrael. There is also a miḳweh.

Religious instruction forms a part of the curriculum of the public schools of the lower and intermediate grades; the community provides for it entirely in the primary schools, while in the gymnasiums and real-schools, where the teachers are appointed and salaried by the state, it is supervised by inspectors commissioned by the community. In the primary schools the expenses of this instruction are borne by the community, with the aid of a fund contributed by the state in accordance with the law, although this covers only a small part of the actual disbursements; but in the secondary schools the entire expense of religious instruction falls on the state. Two hours weekly are allotted to this instruction in the curriculum, but the community maintains or subventions Hebrew schools for those who desire to acquire a more thorough knowledge of Bible and Talmud, while the large and valuable library of the Jewish community affords a wealth of material for students. The public schools of Vienna are non-sectarian, but the ruling majority have endeavored, partly with success, to enforce a sectarian division by evading the existing laws.

Educational Institutions.

The chief institutions of Jewish learning in Vienna are as follows: (1) the Israelitisch-Theologische Lehranstalt, founded in 1893 by the society for the establishment and maintenance of a Jewish theological institute in Vienna; (2) the Talmud Torah, founded in 1854, with an average attendance of 240; (3) the general Austro-Jewish institute for deaf-mutes, founded in 1853, with an average of 92 pupils and an annual expenditure of about 108,000 kronen; (4) the Jewish institute for the blind, founded in 1870, with an average of 60 pupils, and an annual expenditure of about 75,000 kronen; and (5) the Jewish kindergarten, founded in 1843, with an average of 330 children, and an annual expenditure of about 15,000 kronen. In 1900 a Jewish atheneum was established, in which evening lectures on various subjects are given to large Jewish audiences, composed especially of the poorer classes. Vienna is also the home office of the Baron de Hirsch fund for the promotion of popular education in Galicia and Bukowina and the seat of the Zionist Actions Comité.

The number of Jewish pupils in the various classes of schools as compared with the total number is given in the following table (p. 438), whose figures are cited partly according to the averages of recent years, and partly on the basis of the statistics of the school-year 1901–2. These figures are especially noteworthy when the percentage of Jewish inhabitants to the total population (8.8) is borne in mind.

Vienna's situation in the vicinity of Russia and Rumania, the great centers of Jewish emigration, has resulted in large accretions of impoverished foreign Jews; and the increased destitution of the native Israelites, due to anti-Semitic agitation, renders it readily intelligible that, despite the liberality of their more wealthy coreligionists and despite the existence of numerous societies and foundations, poverty is prevalent among the Viennese Jews. This

Class of School.	Total Number of Students.	Jewish Students.	
		Number.	Per-centage.
University.....................	6,300	1,560	24.74
Technical high schools.........	2,040	570	27.94
Gymnasia.....................	5,900	1,800	30.50
Real-schools...................	5,200	1,200	23.07
Girls' high schools	820	380	46.34
Industrial schools	24,000	1,100	4.58
Commercial high schools.......	53	17	32.07
Commercial colleges	680	280	41.17
Other commercial institutes....	8,300	1,800	21.68
Public schools.................	180,000	16,000	8.33
Schools for deaf-mutes	395	97	24.83
Schools for the blind	117	33	28.20
Schools for the feeble-minded ..	160	39	24.37
Schools for neglected children..	53		
Kindergartens	6,300	1,000	15.87

is intensified by an unfortunate division of forces among individual associations.

throne; the cost of its maintenance was about 145,000 kronen annually.

The following are devoted exclusively to the care of the poor: the asylum for orphan girls (60 inmates; annual expenditure about 40,000 kronen); the Lea Merores asylum for orphan girls (50 inmates; opened in 1904); the Baron Springer asylum for orphan boys (founded 1890; 50 inmates; the employment bureau for girls (accommodations for 180) and the employment bureau for boys (accommodations for 36), both institutions maintained by the Theresien Kreuzer Verein; the employment bureau for female apprentices (accommodations for 30), maintained by the Leopoldstadt Ladies' Club; the home for male apprentices, maintained by the Society for the Promotion of Handicrafts Among the Native Jews. Various forms of charitable work are also carried on by a large number of Jewish societies, of which the most important are given in the table on page 439.

PART OF OLD CEMETERY AT VIENNA.
(From a photograph.)

The community maintains a number of charities. A hospital was founded by the Vienna branch of **Benevolent Institutions.** the house of Rothschild, with 170 beds and an annual expenditure of about 300,000 kronen; it has later been endowed by Baron Nathaniel Rothschild with 2,000,000 kronen to render all its space available. A home for the aged and infirm, with 248 beds, was founded in honor of the fiftieth anniversary of the emperor's accession to the

Vienna is the seat of the following societies, which deserve mention here, although their sphere of activity is not restricted to this city, or else is not confined to philanthropic objects: the ISRAELITISCHE ALLIANZ (founded 1872); the OESTERREICHISCH-ISRAELITISCHE UNION (founded 1885); the Allgemeine Oesterreichisch-Israelitische Bund; the Association for the Aid of the Needy Jewish Population of Galicia; and the Baroness Hirsch Foundation for the Assistance of Boys and Girls in Austria.

Name of Organization.	Date of Foundation.	Approximate Annual Expenditures in Kronen. 1905
Hebra Kaddisha............................	1764	80,000
Women's Benevolent Society (first district)...................................	1816	40,000
Women's Benevolent Society (second district)................................	....	24,000
Society for the Poor......................	1821	140,000
Society for the Promotion of Handicrafts	1841	55,000
Orphans' Aid Society.....................	1860	64,000
Students' Aid Society....................	1861	12,000
Girls' Aid Society........................	1866	22,000
Society for the Aid of Consumptives.....	1871	14,200
Society for the Establishment of Public Kitchens...............................	1874	65,000
Fresh-Air Society.........................	1891	46,000
Baroness Hirsch Benevolent Foundation.	1898	200,000 (in loans) 30,000 (in donations)
Free Employment Bureau................	1899	27,000

An important factor in the care of the Jewish poor in Vienna is formed by the foundations, controlled, for the most part, by the community. The total capital of this class of funds amounts in round numbers to 8,500,000 kronen, although these figures include a number of foundations which are not benevolent, such as bequests for the care of graves and for memorial services.

The community provides for the maintenance of a cemetery, as well as for the preservation of the older cemeteries. In the Zentralfriedhof (communal cemetery) a portion is reserved especially for the Jews. Every Jew receives a separate grave, whether it is paid for or not, although nearly 70 per cent of all burials in Vienna are free. Two old cemeteries, now disused, exist in Vienna, one in the Seegasse, closed about 1783, and the Währinger graveyard, closed in 1879.

BIBLIOGRAPHY: Hickmann, *Wien im Neunzehnten Jahrhundert*; the statistical annuals of the city of Vienna, and the reports of the community and of individual societies.
D.   T. L.

VIENNE: Town in the ancient province of Dauphiné, France. Jews dwelt there as early as the tenth century (Gross, "Gallia Judaica," p. 191). They lived in a special quarter, known as "the Jewry," and in the thirteenth century had a beautiful synagogue (Carmoly, "Itinéraires," p. 187).

The following were the most noted scholars of Vienne: the tosafist Tobiah ben Elijah, author of a commentary on the Pentateuch and of liturgical poems (Zunz, "Z. G." pp. 56, 97; *idem*, "Literaturgeschichte," p. 303); Abraham ben Ephraim, a pupil of Tobiah and author of a work on casuistics; Yakar of Vienne, called also "Yakar ben Moses" of Burgundy (Vienne was for a time the capital of Burgundy), who composed posekim (legal decisions), fragments of which are still extant (Gross, *l.c.* p. 193).

BIBLIOGRAPHY: Gross, *Gallia Judaica*, pp. 191-194.
G.   S. K.

VILLEFRANCHE or **(VILLAFRANCA):** Town in the mountain district of the department of Rousillon, France; belonged formerly to Aragon. It was founded in 1095, and had a Jewish population as early as the middle of the thirteenth century, among the first settlers being Jews from Pro-

vence. In 1274 the small community was granted permission to lay out a cemetery; and in 1328 it was allowed to rebuild its synagogue, which had been destroyed about seven years previously. The edifice was presented in 1392 to the settlement of Monte de Pacht.

Villefranche, now called Villefranche de Confluent, was the birthplace of LEVI BEN ABRAHAM. It should not be confounded with **Villafranca de Panadés** in Catalonia, nor with **Villafranca** in Navarre, both of which towns had Jewish communities, the latter until 1498.

BIBLIOGRAPHY: Yanguas, *Antigüedades de Navarra*, iii. 258; Gross, *Gallia Judaica*, p. 199; *R. E. J.* xvi. 184; Rios, *Hist.* ii. 14, 163; Jacobs, *Sources*, Nos. 147, 541, 900, 1710.
J.   M. K.

VINE. See GRAPE.

VINEGAR: In the Biblical period vinegar was prepared either from wine or from cider, the former variety being termed "homez yayin," and the latter "homez shekar." It was used to moisten the flat loaves of the harvesters, and was also drunk when mixed with water, although thirst could not be quenched with it alone.

Since Jewish wine was not allowed to ferment, being intended for the altar, and therefore being necessarily clean Levitically, vinegar, which in Talmudic times was called also "the son of wine," was obtained from the lees or by the addition of barley to the wine or cider. The alteration usually required only three days, and the smell changed before the taste, although some wines were particularly liable to change. Though vinegar could become wine only by a miracle, the price of the former equaled that of the latter, and a fall in the value of the one depressed the rate for the other.

The chief varieties of vinegar were wine-vinegar and cider-vinegar, vinegar of late grapes, vinegar changed by barley, and soured vinegar. Pickles and meat were preserved in vinegar, and lettuce was dipped into it, while "The bitterer the salad of endives, the stronger must be the vinegar" was a Palestinian proverb. Vinegar was used with asafetida, the favorite condiment of antiquity and of the Middle Ages.

The effect of vinegar was astringent, but it was also used frequently because of its soothing and cooling effects. Medicinally, it might be employed for dandruff, and even for dressing wounds, while it was used as a gargle for toothache. Olives were sprinkled with vinegar to free them from their pits; it was used also in dyeing, and in adulterating oil. In view of the liability of wine to change, barrels containing 10 per cent of vinegar were deemed fit for purchase, but the dealer was responsible for a limited period only, except in the case of wine for the Temple, for which he was liable until the wine was used. The Halakah considered the question whether wine and vinegar were to be considered as one, and forbade the use of the vinegar of Gentiles, since it was prepared from forbidden wine. The question was raised whether wine which had turned to vinegar became subject to the prohibition when touched by a Gentile. On account of its calming effect vinegar was forbidden on the Day of Atone ment; and the prohibition of vinegar in the case of Nazarites was fully discussed in the Halakah.

The passage in which Ruth was bidden to dip her bread into vinegar (Ruth ii. 14) was interpreted by the Haggadah as referring to Manasseh, one of her descendants, whose deeds were sharp as vinegar. Among the proverbs concerning vinegar, in addition to Prov. x. 26 and xxv. 20, were the following: "Mayest thou have neither vinegar nor salt in thy house!" and "Much vinegar makes the wine cheap."

E. G. H.   I. Lö.

VINEYARDS. See GRAPE.

VINNITSA (VINITZA): Former Russian town in the government of Podolia, now Ukraine; situated on the banks of the Bug. Vinnitsa was founded in the fourteenth century on the left bank of the Bug, and was protected by two castles. The town suffered much in the sixteenth and seventeenth centuries from the depredations of the Tatars and the Cossacks. Jews lived probably in Vinnitsa in the fifteenth century, but 1532 is the date of the first documentary mention of them. In that year the local Jews carried on extensive business operations as cattle drovers, and one of them, Michael of Vinnitsa, paid customs duties on a single drove of 2,000 head of sheep and cattle. Reference is also made to a Jew (name not given) who in 1552 held the lease of the local customs duties. In 1616 there were only fifty Jews in Vinnitsa who paid taxes on their houses. During the COSSACK'S UPRISING the town was taken and pillaged by Chmielnicki's followers and its Jewish inhabitants were massacred. It was retaken by the Polish troops, and then fell again under the power of the Cossacks and Tatars, changing hands several times. It suffered severely from the HAIDAMACKS in the eighteenth century. The protecting castles had by that time disappeared, and the inhabitants, both Catholics and Jews, sought refuge in the Jesuit college founded by Ladislaus in 1649. In 1774 Vinnitsa was temporarily occupied by the Turks, and toward the end of the eighteenth century was almost entirely ruined.

Vinnitsa had 23,591 inhabitants in 1878, of whom 13,750 were Jews. The town was then an industrial center of some significance, possessing sixteen factories and other industrial establishments. Nine fairs were held there annually, though with but a limited volume of trade. The Jewish community possessed thirteen synagogues and houses of prayer, a Jewish two-class school, and a Jewish hospital. Most of the important distilleries (an ancient industry, to which the town owes its name) were owned by Jews. By 1879 the population of Vinnitsa had grown to 28,995, including more than 15,000 Jews. The town had in that year twenty-nine industrial establishments, and the Jewish community had added a Talmud Torah to its other communal institutions.

On April 3 (Old Style 16), 1905, the Jewish stores in the market-place in Vinnitsa were demolished by a drunken mob composed partly of reservists; several Jews caught on the streets were severely beaten. The conflict attracted the attention of a number of Jews organized for self-defense, who successfully repelled the assailants. Five soldiers and five Jews were injured. Order was restored by the police and the military.

BIBLIOGRAPHY: *Entziklopedicheski Slovar*; *Bolshaya Entziklopedia*; *Russko-Yevreiski Arkhiv*; *Regesty i Nadpisi*; *Voskhod*, 1905, No. 16, p. 28.
H. R.   J. G. L.

VIOL (נבל, lit. "skin"): Musical instrument; next to the "kinnor," it was the one most used by the Israelites. The Old Testament furnishes no description of it, and resort must therefore be had to conjectures regarding it. The viol is commonly identified with the santir (corresponding to the "pesanṭer" [= ψαλτήριον] of Dan. iii. 5), an instrument which is in use among the Arabs at the present time. The santir consists of a low, oblong box with a flat bottom and a somewhat convex sounding-board, over which the strings are stretched. The player sits on the ground, or on a low stool, and holds the viol in his lap.

A similar instrument is represented in a picture found in the palace of Kuyunjik, which shows a band of musicians, both men and women, who are followed by other women singing or beating time with their hands as they go to greet the returning conqueror, Assurbanipal. One of these musicians, with a plectrum in his right hand, plays an instrument consisting of a hollow box with strings stretched over it. Whether the left hand likewise plucks the strings (as is most probable), or presses them down to gain the desired pitch, is not clear. The name "nebel" would be very appropriate for such an instrument, with reference either to the convex shape of the sounding-board, or to the fact that the sounding-board consisted of animal membrane. The term "pi ha-nebel" in Amos vi. 5 would suggest the opening in the sounding-board across which the strings are stretched. Riehm, however, prefers to associate this term with the portable, many-stringed harp which is represented, on the picture at Kuyunjik, as having its sounding-box placed on the broad, upward-slanting upper portion of the frame. Yet Riehm himself points out that the shape of the Jewish nebel must have been somewhat different; for under any other hypothesis the name of this instrument becomes inexplicable. How many strings ("minnim") the instrument generally had is unknown. The "nebel 'asor" mentioned in Ps. xxxiii. 2 was probably different from the ordinary nebel; otherwise the additional word " 'asor" is superfluous. The instrument of later times is known to have had twelve strings (comp. Josephus, "Ant." vii. 12, § 3).

E. G. H.   W. N.

VIPER. See SERPENT.

VIRGINIA: One of the Middle Atlantic states and one of the thirteen original states of the United States of America; seceded from the Union April 17, 1861; readmitted 1870. As early as 1624 the names of Elias Lagardo, Joseph Moise, and Rebecca Isaacke are found in the "Musters of the Inhabitants of Virginia." In 1658 one Seignor Moses Nehemiah is mentioned as a party to a lawsuit ("Publ. Am. Jew. Hist. Soc.," xi. 70). It is probable that a number of Jews from Maryland removed to Richmond at an early date.

Nothing further is heard of Virginia Jews till 1754, when Michael Franks and Jacob Myer accompanied Washington in his expedition across the Alleghany Mountains, and received a reward for their gallant services in the campaign. In the list of Virginians who served in the Revolutionary army in the capacity of officers occurs the name of Isaac Israel, a lieutenant in the Eighth Virginia Regiment. The Congregation Beth-Shalom of Richmond, the oldest congregation in the state, was in existence prior to 1790, in which year it joined with the congregations of Philadelphia, New York, and Charleston in addressing a letter to President Washington. See RICHMOND.

Virginia has the following Jewish communities: **Alexandria** (Congregation Beth-El, founded June 3, 1878; a Hebrew Benevolent Society and a cemetery). **Berkley** (a congregation and a religious school). **Charlottesville** (Congregation Beth Israel, M. Kaufman being prayer-leader; and a cemetery). **Clifton Forge** (a congregation holding holy-day services). **Danville** (Congregation Beth Sholom). **East Radford** (congregation). **Fredericksburg** (Hebrew Aid Society, founded about 1880; had (1905) twelve members). **Hampton** (congregation). **Harrisonburg** (congregation). **Lynchburg** (congregation). **Newport News** (congregations Adath Yeshurum and Rodeph Sholom; and a Jewish Sunday-school). **Norfolk** (with a large Jewish community, supporting six congregations, a burial association, several charitable organizations, and a number of social and literary clubs). **Petersburg** (two congregations: the Orthodox congregation and the Rodeph Shalem, the latter founded in 1865). **Pocahontas** (has no organized congregation, but the community holds special services on Saturdays and holy days). **Radford** (community holding holyday services). **Richmond** (see JEW. ENCYC. x. 406). **Roanoke** (Congregation Emanu-El, founded 1890; and a cemetery). **Staunton** (a congregation and a benevolent society).

Virginia contributed 113 Jewish soldiers to the Civil war, and about thirty to the Spanish-American war. At present (1923) the number of its Jewish inhabitants is estimated at 16,020 in a total population of 2,309,187.

A.   A. M. Ho.

VIRTUE, ORIGINAL (Hebr. **Zekut Abot,** literally "merit of the Fathers"): A term invented by S. Levy as a contrast to the expression "original sin," and designating the specifically Jewish concept of the influence of the virtue of ancestors upon descendants. The doctrine asserts that God visits the virtues of the fathers upon the children for His name's sake and as a mark of grace; but it would appear, on the other hand, that the principle applies only when the children continue the piety of their parents. The Biblical basis for the doctrine is to be found in the second commandment (Ex. xx. 5), which states that God shows mercy unto thousands of generations that love Him and keep His commandments, and in Ps. ciii. 17–18, "the mercy of the Lord is from everlasting to everlasting upon them that fear him, and his righteousness unto children's children; to such as keep his covenant, and to those that remember his commandments to do

them." Thus Isaac was promised a blessing because Abraham had kept God's commandments (Gen. xxvi. 2–5); and the doctrine is also formulated in the first benediction of the "Shemoneh 'Esreh," which is technically known as the blessing of "Abot," or "the Fathers." The concept is intimately connected with the idea of the covenant with the PATRIARCHS, to which an appeal is made in Ex. xxxii. 13; Lev. xxvi. 42, 44, 45; and Deut. vii. 12, while an allusion to it is contained in the phrase "his great name's sake" (I Sam. xii. 22; comp. Ezek. xxxvi. 21, 23), which recalls the covenant. It thus forms part of the concept of the CHOSEN PEOPLE.

If the covenant is still kept with descendants, though they be unworthy, this is the result of God's grace ("ḥesed"); and it is possible that the original form of the expression was "ḥesed Abot" (= "grace of the Fathers." The Targum, however, uses

Result of Grace. "zekut" to translate the biblical Hebrew "zedakah" (comp. Gen. xv. 6; Deut. ix. 5, 6). The injunction of the second commandment is explained by the Targum and the Talmud (Sanh. 27b) on the principle that the sins of the fathers are visited upon the children only when they imitate the deeds of their parents (see Rashi and Ibn Ezra *ad loc.*). This doctrine underlies the Jewish conception of life, drawing its inspiration from an idealized past (comp. "Look unto Abraham your father, and unto Sarah that bare you," Isa. li. 2), and laying stress upon tradition and upon the ritual ceremonies intended to keep tradition alive. It is closely associated, moreover, with the idea of an organic or dynamic solidarity in Israel as a body existent through past, present, and future; and the principle that "all Jews are responsible one for another" is specifically connected in the Talmud with the idea of original virtue (Sanh. 27b; Shab. 39a; R. H. iii.).

The doctrine under consideration is limited by the concept of the reward of virtue, which, according

Virtues to the Virtuous. to Jewish teaching, is the opportunity of performing further virtuous acts. "The wages of virtue is virtue" (Ab. iv. 2), and "when the righteous do the will of God, they acquire strength and power to perform further acts of righteousness" (Yalḳ., Lam. 44). Special warning is given against depending upon original virtue, so that even one who is exceedingly righteous should not eat from (that is, depend upon) the merit of his fathers (Sanh. 81a). The passage Cant. i. 5: "I am black, but comely" is interpreted as meaning: Israel says: "I am black through my own works, but comely through the works of my fathers" (Cant. R. *ad loc.*; Ex. R. xxiii.), while "as a vine is supported by a prop, though made of dead wood, so Israel is supported by the merit of the Fathers, though it already sleeps in death." Original virtue is thus only an accessory. It would appear that the virtues of the fathers were believed to have acquired a right to a greater reward than could be given to them, and that this residue was therefore due to the children. Those who looked forward to an immediate reward were accordingly reproved, for if the Patriarchs had done so there would have been no store of original virtue for their descendants (Lev. R. xxxvi.; Ex. R. xliv.). See PATRIARCHS.

Like the Patriarchs, the later saints were regarded as a source of original virtue for their descendants or for Israel, and in addition to Moses, Joshua, David, Hezekiah, and Ezra, Hillel, Johanan b. Zakkai, and Meïr are especially mentioned as storing up works which shall speak for their descendants (Lev. R. ii.). On the other hand, the original virtue of the Patriarchs was regarded by some as lasting only till the time of Hosea (Shab. 55a) or until the days of Hezekiah (Lev. R. xxxvi.), though it was still operative in keeping exiled Israel in existence up to the time of redemption (Gen. R. lxx.); and in the Targum Yerushalmi to Deut. xxviii. 15 God assures "the Fathers of the world" that their merit will never cease to be efficacious.

The doctrine of original virtue is only the theological side of the principle of heredity, with the consequences and responsibilities which this involves. The community of interest between parents and children is emphasized in a special Jewish manner which at times leads to the diametrically opposite concept of the influence of descendants upon ancestors; so that the penalty of death is said to have been inflicted upon Adam because of the sins of Nebuchadnezzar and Hiram (Gen. R. ix.). The extension of the concept of God's grace even to unrighteous children of righteous parents is, moreover, an attribution to the Supreme Being of the ordinary attitude of men toward the degenerate children of distinguished or pious parents. The influence of a store of merit collected for the use of succeeding generations is the theological aspect of the concept of progress and civilization, which is practically a store of ancestral merits.

BIBLIOGRAPHY: S. Levy, The Doctrine of Original Virtue, in The Jewish Literary Annual, pp. 12-32, London, 1905; Weber, Jüdische Theologie, 2d ed., pp. 292-297; Lazarus, Ethics of Judaism, i. 34, ii. 289; I. Abrahams, in J. Q. R. xvi. 586.

J.

VISIGOTHS. See SPAIN.

VISONTAI, SOMA: Hungarian lawyer and deputy; born at Gyöngyös Nov. 9, 1854; educated at Budapest, where he became an attorney in 1882. While still a student he attracted much attention by his papers on political economy in the scientific journals of Hungary, and he also edited the "Vasút." He became widely known as a pleader in 1890, when he successfully defended the editor of the "Zasztava," the leader of the radical wing of the Servians in Hungary, in a trial for political murder. As a mark of gratitude, the people of Neusatz, being Servian sympathizers, elected Visontai in 1892 to the Hungarian Parliament as a supporter of Kossuth; and since 1899 he has represented his native town, Gyöngyös, in Parliament. He is an eminent authority on criminal law and was a member of the board of examiners for admission to the bar; and he prepared a large portion of the preliminary drafts for the criminal code.

BIBLIOGRAPHY: Pallas Lex.; Sturm, Osraggyülési Almanach, 1901-6.

S.   L. V.

VITA. See ḤAYYIM.

VITA DELLA VOLTA (SOLOMON ḤAY-YIM): Italian physician and Hebraist; born Sept. 24, 1772; died March 29, 1853; flourished in Mantua. He was the owner of a large Hebrew library, which, together with its 131 manuscripts, came into the possession of Marco Mortara. Vita della Volta was a contributor to the periodical "Kerem Ḥemed." A letter from I. S. Reggio to Della Volta appeared in "Oẓar Neḥmad" (iii. 25-27).

BIBLIOGRAPHY: Steinschneider, Cat. Bodl. col. 2709; Kerem Ḥemed, passim.

S.   S. O.

VITAL: Italian family, including several scholars, of whom the best known are:

Ḥayyim Vital: Cabalist; son of Joseph Vital; born at Safed in 1543; died at Damascus May 6, 1620. He was educated by Moses Alshech. His biography is full of legends; at the age of twelve, it is said, he was told by a chiromancer that when he reached the age of twenty-four years he would find himself standing before two roads, and would rise or fall according to his choice. Joseph Caro is said to have paid especial attention to Ḥayyim's talents by requesting Alshech in 1557 to take great pains with the education of a pupil who was destined to succeed his teacher in the world of learning. In the same year Ḥayyim became acquainted with Lapidot Ashkenazi, a cabalist, who was to influence him for the remainder of his life. The legend runs that after Ḥayyim's unhappy marriage to Hannah, the daughter of a certain Moses Saadia, the prophet Elijah appeared to him in a dream and led him to a beautiful garden, where he beheld the pious of all ages in the form of birds flying through the garden and studying the Mishnah. In the center of the garden was God Himself, seated on a throne and surrounded by the pious on rich tapestries.

This vision convinced the dreamer that he was destined to become a cabalist. After devoting himself to the study of alchemy for two years and a half, he had another vision of the prophet Elijah, who told him that he would succeed in his studies and would even write a commentary on the Zohar. In 1570 he became a pupil of Isaac Luria, and before he had studied under him a year Ḥayyim had already become known as one of the foremost cabalists, so that when, in 1572, Luria died at the early age of thirty-eight, in an epidemic which raged in Safed, Ḥayyim became his successor. Luria had left nothing in manuscript, and his pupil accordingly began to commit to writing what he had learned from his teacher. In 1576 he commenced to give cabalistic lectures, declaring himself to be the Messiah ben Joseph; and while wandering through Syria and Egypt, he is said to have performed many miracles, such as summoning spirits before him by the power of magic formulas.

In 1577 Ḥayyim arrived in Egypt, but evidently he met with a cool reception, since he soon returned to Palestine, where he settled, first in the little town of 'Ain Zaitun, and later in Jerusalem. There he remained until the governor, Abu Saifia, requested him to rediscover, by means of the Cabala, the aqueduct, leading from the River Gihon which had been built in the days of Hezekiah. This request so embarrassed Ḥayyim that he fled by night to Damascus, where he commenced his first cabalistic work on the patriarch Abraham, of which extracts are contained in the "Oẓerot Ḥayyim" (p. 54b). He submitted this work to Joshua ben Nun, the wealthy principal of the yeshibah at Safed. The greater part of the book consists of an exposition of the conjuring of clouds, and of a discourse on the seven fixed stars, the seven heavens, and their corresponding metals. After this Ḥayyim returned to Jerusalem, where his former teacher, Moses Alshech, appointed him rabbi in 1584. After a time, however, he left Jerusalem for Safed, where he fell sick and was obliged to keep his bed for an entire year.

During this illness Joshua, his closest follower, who had accompanied him on nearly every journey, succeeded in bribing Ḥayyim's younger brother, Moses, with 500 gold gulden to lend him the writings of the cabalist, which were locked in a box. Moses accordingly brought Joshua a large part of the manuscripts, and 100 copyists were immediately engaged, who, in the short space of three days, reproduced more than 600 pages. Although Ḥayyim maintained, when he learned of this, that the papers which had been copied were not his own writings, they were rapidly disseminated under the title "'Eẓ Ḥayyim." This work contains, in addition to a tribute to Isaac Luria, the bold assertion that it is one of the greatest pleasures of God to behold the promotion of the teaching of the Cabala, since this alone can assure the coming of the Messiah; that the old Cabala, however, covering the period from David to Naḥmanides, was valueless, since it was based merely on human intellect, and was not aided by the higher spirits. Ḥayyim asserted that he had received these teachings, like his other mystic theories, from the lips of his teacher Luria. His estimate of the value of the Cabala of Moses Cordovero was equally low, although he maintained that Moses had often appeared to him in dreams. One of the most prominent of Ḥayyim's opponents was Menahem di Lonzano, who publicly denounced him in his "Sefer Imre Emet." On the 20th of Elul, 1590, Ḥayyim was awarded the rabbinical diploma by his teacher Moses Alshech, and four years later he settled permanently in Damascus, where he lectured every evening on the Cabala and on the near advent of the Messiah. Despite the large following which Ḥayyim had in Damascus, Jacob Abulafia succeeded, by threats of excommunication, in compelling him to discontinue his lectures. In 1604 his sight began to fail; in 1620 he had prepared to return to Safed, when his death occurred.

Ḥayyim was the author of numerous works, which are collected under the title "Sefer 'Eẓ ha-Ḥayyim" (Zolkiev, 1772; Korzec, 1785; Shklov, 1800; Dobrowne, 1804; Sudzilkov, 1818; Laszow, 1818). They are as follows:

Sefer ha-Kawwanot, in two parts, the first being on the subject of benedictions and rituals, and the second on the ritual for Sabbaths and festivals. Venice, 1624; Hanau, 1624; Bragadini, n.d. There are five recensions of this work: (1) by Moses Vital, grandson of Ḥayyim; known especially in Egypt and Palestine; (2) by Zacuto, with glosses; (3) by Nathan Spira, with a commentary entitled "Me'orot Natan"; (4) by Abraham Azulai of Morocco, with glosses; (5) by M. Popper, under the title "Peri 'Eẓ Ḥayyim."

A piyyuṭ beginning "Dodi yarad le-ganno"; printed in "Sha'are Ẓiyyon." Amsterdam, 1671.

Nof 'Eẓ Ḥayyim, novellæ. Frankfort-on-the-Main, 1684; Zolkiev, 1772, 1775.

Sefer ha-Gilgulim, on the transmigration of souls. Frankfort-on-the-Main, 1684; Zolkiev, 1772.

Sha'are Ḳedushshah, on the rewards and punishments of the future world and on holiness. Constantinople, 1734; Sulzbach, 1758; Zolkiev, 1810.

Liḳḳuṭe Torah we-Ṭa'ame ha-Miẓwot, cabalistic exposition of the Bible according to Luria's teachings, with "ḥiddushim." Zolkiev, 1775.

Sha'ar ha-Yiḥudim we-Tiḳḳun 'Awonot, on the Prophets, on the Holy Spirit, and on repentance. Korzec, 1783.

Sefer Oẓerot Ḥayyim, edited by his pupil the Portuguese physician Joseph Ẓemaḥ. Korzec, 1783. (Besides the printed edition there exist two manuscripts, one with glosses by Moses Zacuto ["Codex Michael," No. 23], and the other with glosses by Nathan Spiro [ib. Nos. 27, 28]).

Liḳḳuṭe ha-Shas, cabalistic interpretations of Talmudic haggadot according to the teachings of Luria, with "ḥiddushim" by the author. Leghorn, 1785.

Arba' Me'ot Sheḳel Kesef, cabalistic treatise on the 400 shekels which Abraham paid for the cave of Machpelah. Korzec, 1804.

Joseph Vital: Writer of tefillin parchments; born in Calabria; flourished in the fifteenth and sixteenth centuries. On account of his accuracy his work, which was expensive, was highly esteemed, and was known everywhere as תפילין רב קלבראיש. He was also the author of responsa on the art of writing tefillin, which are frequently mentioned in the responsa of Menahem Azariah da Fano (§ 38 et passim).

Moses Vital: Rabbi at Safed; younger brother of Ḥayyim Vital; died in the middle of the seventeenth century. Like Ḥayyim, he was a great cabalist, and in addition to legends associating him with his brother and the prophet Elijah, a tradition is preserved which states that he predicted the famine which raged in Safed in 1632.

Moses Vital: Son of Samuel ben Ḥayyim Vital; rabbi in Egypt during the latter part of the seventeenth and at the beginning of the eighteenth century. He was a noted Talmudist and cabalist, but the only portion of his works which has been preserved is a responsum contained in Abraham ha-Levi's collection entitled "Ginnat Weradim."

Samuel ben Ḥayyim Vital: Cabalist; born in Damascus in the latter half of the sixteenth century; died in Egypt in the middle of the seventeenth. While still young he married a daughter of Isaiah Pinto, rabbi of Damascus. Poverty compelled him to emigrate to Egypt, where, through the influence of prominent men, he was placed in charge of the cabalistic society Tiḳḳune ha-Teshubah. After a brief residence there he went to Safed, where he instructed the physician Joseph Ẓemaḥ in Cabala. Later he returned to Egypt, where he died. Samuel Vital was the author of both cabalistic and rabbinical works. Among the former may be noted the "Shemonah She'arim," an introduction to the Cabala, later embodied in the "'Eẓ Ḥayyim" (Zolkiev, 1772; Korzec, 1785). Among his unpublished writings mention may be made of his "Sefer Toẓe'ot Ḥayyim," a commentary on the Bible, and his "Sefer Ta'alumot Ḥokmah," on the Cabala.

Bibliography: Steinschneider, Cat. Bodl. cols. 834-835, 2495; Conforte, Ḳore ha-Dorot, pp. 40b, 42a, 49b; Azulai, Shem ha-Gedolim; De Rossi, Dizionario; Kohn (Kahana), Eben Negef, Vienna, 1874; Fuenn, Keneset Yisrael; Benjacob, Oẓar ha-Sefarim; Fürst, Bibl. Jud. iii. 479-482.
D. S. O.

VITAL, DAVID B. SOLOMON VITAL HA-ROFE:

Spanish scholar; emigrated from Spain in the early part of the sixteenth century; died at Arta, or Narda, in Greece, after 1536. He went first to Turkey, and then settled at Patras in the Morea, remaining there until the fall of the city in 1532, when he lost almost his entire library. He then went to Arta, where he spent the remainder of his life.

Vital was the author of the following works: "Keter Torah" (Constantinople, 1536), the 613 commandments and prohibitions, and the seven regulations concerning Ḥanukkah, the Sabbath candle, Hallel, Megillah, ablutions, 'Erubin, and benedictions, including also the "Birkot ha-Nehenin" (the initial letters of the Ten Commandments are employed in this poem, an original feature of which is a complete drawing of a lung to illustrate the meaning); "Hilkot Bediḳah" (1570, 1682), rules for examinations concerning the eating of a slaughtered ox, with "Shir Ḥaruz be-Mishkal" (1687, 1712), a poetic composition on the same theme from a Maimonidean point of view (published with the responsa of Jacob Weil, Mantua, 1740); "Mihtam le-Dawid" (Venice, 1540), a versification of the thirteen articles of faith of Maimonides (one verse was published by Dukes in "Orient, Lit." xi. 272, note 6), printed with a poem entitled "Baḳḳashat ha-He'in," and consisting of a thousand words beginning with ה. He wrote also a poem on the divisions of the year (Zunz, "Ha-Palit," Berlin, 1850–51), and a number of piyyuṭim.

Bibliography: Orient, Lit. vii. 198, 780; ix. 272; De Rossi-Hamberger, Hist. Wörterb.; Benjacob, Shem ha-Gedolim, ii. 70; idem, Oẓar ha-Sefarim, pp. 138, 252, 329, 575; Zunz, Z. G. p. 231; idem, Literaturgesch. pp. 533 et seq.
J.   S. O.

VITALE (COEN), BENJAMIN ALESSANDRO.

See Coen, Benjamin Vitale.

VITEBSK:

Latvian city; formerly the Russian capital of a government of the same name, on the banks of the Düna. Probably founded before the tenth century, it was mentioned in Russian chronicles as early as 1021. Being included in the territory known as White Russia, it became a part of Lithuania in 1320, and about 1435 came into the possession of Casimir IV. This king restored many of its ancient privileges in 1441, particularly those concerning freedom of religious worship. Vitebsk suffered much in the wars between Lithuania, Poland, and Russia. Between 1502 and 1536 it was repeatedly pillaged by the different armies, and its commerce was greatly reduced. In 1654 after a siege of fourteen weeks the city was occupied by the Russian troops under Sheremetyev; it paid levies to Russian, Polish, and Swedish troops from 1700 to 1708; and it was finally burned in 1708 at the order of Peter the Great. In 1772 it became a part of Russia, and in 1802 it was made the capital of the government of Vitebsk.

Jewish traders undoubtedly came to Vitebsk in the fifteenth century and possibly much earlier, although it is uncertain whether a community existed there before the sixteenth century. Documentary evidence shows that the inns and taverns of the city were leased in 1522 to the Jew Michael Yesofovich of Brest. In 1551 the Jews of Vitebsk are mentioned among those exempted from the

Jewish Prosperity. payment of the Serebszczyzna, and reference is made to individual Jews of Vitebsk in 1555 and again in 1594.

In the grant of the Magdeburg Law to Vitebsk by King Sigismund III. in 1597 it was expressly stated that, in accordance with the ancient law, Jews could not become permanent residents of the town. As in many other places, the burghers of Vitebsk, in order to get rid of their formidable commercial competitors, evidently sought the aid of laws that had become obsolete. It is not known how successful this measure proved in excluding the Jews from Vitebsk, but from documents dated a few years later it appears that Jewish merchants continued to live in the city. Thus in the customs records of Vitebsk for 1605 mention is made of Matys Germanovich and Sir Jacob Ilinich, both local Jews, the latter evidently being a man of some distinction. The same archives also show that Jewish merchants from other localities resided in Vitebsk for more or less prolonged periods.

In 1627 the waywode Simeon Sangushko granted the Jews of the city permission to build a synagogue on their own land in the town or in its outskirts, this being in accord with royal privileges and in harmony with charters of former waywodes of Vitebsk, where the Jews had had synagogues in earlier times. This grant also provided for the exemption of the land and buildings of the synagogue from the payment of taxes. Formal entry of this privilege was made in the city records of Vitebsk in 1630 at the instance of the Jewish leaseholder Judah Yakubovich. It is clear, therefore, that, notwithstanding the Magdeburg Law of 1597, Jews continued to live in Vitebsk, and that they possessed an organized community there in the sixteenth and possibly also in the preceding century. The permanent residence of the Jews in the city was legalized in 1634 by an edict of Ladislaus IV., who issued it in response to the solicitations of Samuel and Lazar Moiseyevich, "the king's servants." It is expressly stated in this edict that the rights granted by it were only a confirmation of earlier privileges which permitted the Jews to buy and own land and houses in Vitebsk, and to have synagogues, cemeteries, and the like in the city. General Sheremetyev, who entered Vitebsk at the head of the Russian army in 1654, refers to the Jewish school

Siege of the City. (synagogue) in his enumeration of the Catholic and Unitarian churches of the city. The hardships of the siege which preceded his occupation of Vitebsk bore heavily on its Jewish inhabitants. They took an active part in the defensive operations by supplying men, provisions, ammunition, building materials, money, and houses for the quartering of the soldiers. As a punishment for their loyalty, they, together with the Shlyakhta, were imprisoned by Sheremetyev, and were later transported to Russia, where they suffered severely from ill treatment, many of them dying of hunger and cold. After a term of imprisonment at Novgorod the survivors were sent to different towns, and finally to Kazan on the Volga, whence they gradually found their way back to their native town. The property of some of those who died in captivity was presented to the churches of Vitebsk; there is a record, accordingly, of a house and parcel of ground which had formerly belonged to the Jew Mordecai who died in Moscow, and which was given by King John Casimir to a local church. Those who returned from Muscovite captivity complained in 1670 that much valuable personal property and many important documents had been left in the keeping of Christian citizens of Vitebsk, and that these had all disappeared during their absence. They were thus unable, in the absence of documentary evidence, to regain possession of their property.

In 1897 Vitebsk had a Jewish population of 39,-520 in a total of 65,871. The community possessed several synagogues, many houses of prayer, several schools for boys and girls, a rabbinical school, a Talmud Torah, and a Jewish hospital. Extensive trade was carried on by the Jewish merchants with Riga and foreign countries, the chief articles of export being breadstuffs, flax, hemp, beet-sugar, and timber. The Jews were also prominent in manufacturing industries. Hundreds of Jewish tailors were employed in the making of clothing sold in the stores of a number of large Russian cities. An important contribution to the Jewish industries was made in 1897, when a Jewish machinist established a small shop for the manufacture of plows. By 1905 the annual output was between 25,000 and 35,000 plows, all made by about 400 Jewish mechanics in five factories. Vitebsk also contained fifteen Jewish machine-shops, each employing from five to twenty-five men, and Jewish workmen were extensively engaged in the linen-mills operated by a Belgian corporation, as well as in the manufacture of eyeglasses, in cabinet-making, and similar occupations. In 1905 the Jews of Vitebsk informed the city council that their two representatives could not be considered delegates of the Jewish population, as they had not been elected, but had been appointed by the government. In the same year the Jews of the city, like those of many other communities, issued an appeal to the Russian people for more equitable legislation. In 1914 the Jewish population was about 60,000 in a total of 103,840.

Jewish Industries.

Vitebsk is the birthplace of B. I. Sobiesensky, author of "Ahabat Zaddiḳim" (Warsaw, 1881–82), and of the Talmudist David EPHRATI.

BIBLIOGRAPHY: Regesty i Nadpisi, i., s.v.; Bershadski, Litovskie Yevrei; Voskhod, 1901, xi. 52; 1905, iii. 72; 1905, No. 23, p. 16; No. 24, p. 22; Bershadski, Russko-Yevreiski Arkhiv, i.–ii., s.v.
H. R.   J. G. L.

VITORIA. See BASQUE PROVINCES.

VITRINGA, CAMPEGIUS (the Elder): Dutch Christian Hebraist; born at Leeuwarden May 16, 1669; died at Franeker March 31, 1722. He was educated at the universities of Franeker and Leyden, and became professor of Oriental languages at the former in 1681. His two chief works are his dissertation on the synagogue, "De Synagoga Vetere Libri Tres" (Franeker, 1685; 2d ed. 1696), which still has value; and his "Commentary on Isaiah" (Leeuwarden, 1714–20), which was frequently republished in the eighteenth century. The latter

was up to the time of Gesenius the most considerable contribution to the exegesis of Isaiah. There is also something of Jewish interest in his "Sacrarum Observationum Libri Sex" (Franeker, 1683–1708).

BIBLIOGRAPHY: McClintock and Strong, Cyc. s.v.
J.

VITRY, SIMḤAH B. SAMUEL. See MAHZOR.

VIZHAINY (VIZHUNY, VIZAN, VIZANY): Lithuanian town in the government of Suwalki. On Jan. 29, 1723, Moses Yefraimovich, an elder of the Grodno ḳahal, presented for entry in the municipal records of the city of Grodno the charter of privileges granted to the Jews of Vizhainy by King John III. The document was dated Cracow, Feb. 3, 1676, and was a confirmation of the privileges granted by King Michael at Warsaw Nov. 14, 1670. The king states in the latter that in consideration of the privileges granted to all the Jews living in the grand duchy of Lithuania by Ladislaus IV. at Warsaw Dec. 2, 1646, and confirmed by King John Casimir at the Cracow diet of Feb. 17, 1649, and in consideration also of the petition of the king's jeweler in Grodno, the Jew Isaac Faibishevich, acting in behalf of the Jews of Vizhainy, he, King Michael, promises to retain in force the rights of the said Jews in the possession of their houses, stores, and meat-markets, acquired by them in the past or to be acquired by them in the future, this applying also to their houses of prayer, cemeteries, and baths situated on land belonging to them and reserved for their own use. They are likewise accorded the right to sell liquor in their houses, to sell merchandise by weight or measure, and to sell meat in their butcher-shops to every Jewish artisan, provided they pay the proper tax on the cattle killed. Should the Jewish houses, stores, synagogue, meat-markets, or bath be destroyed by fire, the Jews retain the right to rebuild them. The Jewish artisans are given the right to pursue their avocations in accordance with the general privileges granted to the Jews of the grand duchy of Lithuania.

Further, the Jews of Vizhainy are exempted from municipal jurisdiction, but are subject to that of the local court, with the right of appeal to the king's tribunal. They may not be called to court on Saturdays or on other Jewish holy days; they may not be assessed in favor of the municipality (mir) and they are exempted from sentinel duty. They may not be made to do general work for their landlords, nor to supply conveyances, and shall be obliged only to pay the usual tax to the local court. In important matters they must take oath on the scroll of the Law, and in less important cases at the Ark, according to their Law. Suits concerning Jews alone are to be decided by their own elders according to Jewish Law. The Jews of Vizhainy are to have the right to use the town meadows for pasturing their cattle, and are permitted to make use of the neighboring woods on equal terms with the commoners of the town. In 1897 the population of Vizhainy numbered 2,274, mostly Jews.

BIBLIOGRAPHY: Entziklopedicheski Slovar; Regesty i Nadpisi, i. 506.
H. R.   J. G. L.

VOCALIZATION: All Semitic script, excepting Ethiopic and Assyro-Babylonian, the latter of which in its origin is held by many to be not Semitic, is purely consonantal, the reader being left to supply the vowels. The same feature is found in the Egyptian and Berber languages, not to speak of other tongues which have borrowed the Arabic alphabet. This circumstance renders the reading of Semitic script in many cases ambiguous even in a living language.

Semitic Skeleton Writing. To obviate such ambiguity the Semitic languages have developed three methods. The oldest method is to denote the vowels by the vowel-letters א ו י (also ה ע). The employment of vowel-letters shows a gradual development. At first used but sparingly to denote final vowels (Mesha Stone, Phenician inscriptions), they came to mark vowels long by nature (Arabic, early Hebrew), then, occasionally, tone-long vowels (Biblical Hebrew), and finally also short vowels (Aramaic dialects, later Hebrew). This method of vocalization has been retained in Mandean and partly in Samaritan. But since the vowel-letters were not sufficient to mark the exact shades of the vowel-sounds, some of the Semitic languages (i.e., those which were in possession of sacred books in whose recitation exactness was imperative) developed systems of vowel-signs. The employment of such signs proceeded along two lines. The Ethiopic, whose vowel-system probably dates from the fourth century c.e., has attached its vowel-signs to the body of the consonant, so that there are as many modifications of the form of each letter as there are vowels. Hebrew, Syriac, and Arabic, on the other hand, have their vowel-signs written independently, above, below, or within the letters.

It has hitherto been assumed that the Syriac system was the basis for the Hebrew and the Arabic, and that the Samaritan, which has no vowel-signs, was based on the latter. It has, however, been shown that such an assumption is groundless (Levias, "The Names of the Hebrew Vowels," in "Hebrew Union College Annual," 1894). All that is certain is that the composite Babylonian vocalization is the basis of all other systems. The exact interrelation, however, among these latter still awaits a careful examination.

The present Syriac and Arabic systems were preceded by a more primitive one consisting of dots. In the oldest manuscripts of the Koran a dot above a letter indicated *a*; below, *i-e*; at the side, *u*. In Syriac, a dot above indicated a stronger or fuller vocalization or pronunciation of a consonant, but when placed beneath the letter it denoted a weaker or thinner vocalization, a softer pronunciation of a consonant or its entire vowellessness. That primitive device is referred to as early as the fourth century c.e. by the Syriac Church father Ephraem, and is met with in Syriac manuscripts of the fifth century. The Arabic dot-system is later, having been introduced by Abu al-Aswad (689 c.e.). The question presents itself, Did Hebrew ever have such a system? Although no manuscripts with such notation have been handed down, it can be proved that such a notation

Rudimentary Systems.

did exist. The older Masorah subsumes all vowels under the two designations פתח and קמץ, the former denoting *a*, *ă*, *e*, *i*, the latter *u*, *ō̆*, *ē̆*. The former were evidently originally denoted by a dot above, the latter by a dot below, the letter. Moreover, the Masorah designates with "below" (מלרע) or "above" (מלעיל) the relative thinness or fulness of vowel-sound. Thus, *ă* is "below" when compared with *ā*, *ō*, *ū*; *ĕ* is "below" as compared with *ă*; similarly, *ĭ* as compared with *ă*, *ō*, *ū*; *ŏ* as compared with *ă*, *ō*; *ā* as compared with *ō*, *ū*; *ē* as compared with *ā*, *ō*, *ū* (comp. "Oklah we-Oklah," Nos. 5, 11); "shewa" is "below" when compared with a full vowel (comp. "Masorah Magna" to Isa. viii. 1). The same terminology is found in respect to chanting-notes and word-accent. The Masoretic terminology must have had a concrete basis, and that basis is discoverable only in the rudimentary use of the dot.

Until 1839 only one system of Hebrew vocalization was known, the Tiberian. In that year manuscripts were discovered in the Crimea representing a very different system. Since then a number of manuscripts from Yemen have come to light which

Systems of Hebrew Vocalization.

show that system in different stages of development. In 1894 a third system of vocalization was found, of which also several types are now known. The manuscripts of the last type, fragments, come from Syria and Egypt. Each of the three systems of vocalization has also a distinct system of accentuation. The different systems (and types) vary not only in the form and position of the vowel- and accent-signs, but to a greater or lesser extent also in pronunciation of the Hebrew. The greatest latitude of variation in pronunciation is exhibited in the Berlin MS. or. qu. 680, representing the (or a) Babylonian tradition.

The most marked difference between the usual system of vocalization and the one discovered in 1839 is in the position of the vowel-signs. In the former all but two are written below the letters, in the latter all are placed above the letters. The former was therefore called the "sublinear," the latter the "superlinear." With the discovery of the third system, which is also superlinear, this distinction has become impracticable, and more correct designations are desirable. On the basis of two passages in medieval literature, one a colophon to a Targum manuscript in Parma (comp. Berliner, "Targum Onḳelos," ii. 134), the other a passage in the Vitry Maḥzor (p. 462), the usual system is called the Tiberian (= T), the one discovered in 1839 the Babylonian (= B), and the third the Palestinian (= P). These designations are understood to denote the places where these systems were in vogue, implying nothing as to their place of origin. They may be used, for convenience' sake, just as are the terms "Semitic" and "Hamitic" as applying to languages. The objection that Tiberian is also Palestinian is not valid: the latter probably dates from a time when the Tiberian was not yet in existence, a supposition borne out by internal evidence. The Arabic system is designated by A, the Nestorian Syriac by Sy, the Samaritan by Sa.

The Babylonian system shows in the various manuscripts different stages of development, which can, however, be reduced to three leading types: the composite type (B¹), represented chiefly by the "Codex Petropolitanus," dated 916;

The Baby-lonian System. the simplified type (B²), found chiefly in Targum manuscripts and Neo-Hebrew texts; and the type (B³), represented by the Berlin MS. or. qu. 680. The first two types show not infrequently Tiberian influence. The ֻ in B¹ is Tiberian; so is the "dagesh"-point in B². B¹ denotes dagesh and vowellessness, not, as do all other types and systems, by a sign attached to the consonant, but by a modification of the preceding vowel. Its phonetic theory is evidently different from all the rest. One will not go far astray in seeing here the influences of the Hindu and the Greek grammatical system respectively. B² is a simplification of B¹ adapted to the needs of Aramaic. B³ is a modification of B¹ with the help of P, from which system it has borrowed its "rafe"-sign and the conception of dagesh.

The Palestinian system has come down in a few fragments, not all of which have yet been published. This system also shows a gradual development; the classification into types, however, must remain tentative until all the material shall have

The Pales-tinian System. been made accessible. According to Dr. Kahle ("Der Masoretische Text," p. 29, note 1), the fragments of the Cairo genizah, still unpublished, present the oldest type (P¹); an intermediate type was published by the writer in the "American Journal of Semitic Languages and Literature," vol. xv. (P²); the third type (P³) is contained in the texts published by Neubauer (in "J. Q. R." vii. 361) and Kahle (Stade's "Zeitschrift," xxi. 273). This system is based on B¹ and shows the transition to B³, T, Sa, Sy, and A. The position of the vowel-signs in P is, as in B, above the letters and thrown to the left, or, more correctly, over the space between the letters when the spelling is defective, and over the vowel-letters when the text is written "plene." The cases of plene writing have evidently determined the position of the vowel-sign. It is not impossible that the inventors of these two systems, like the later grammarians, supposed every vowel to be followed actually or virtually by a vowel-letter, so that the sign may always be intended for the latter. While the above is the rule, the vowels are at times found within the letter (B³) or beneath it; sometimes both below and over the letter; at other times the vowel-sign above the consonant is repeated over the following vowel-letter (P²). The dagesh-, mappiḳ-, and shewa-signs (see Notation Table, p. 448) may be placed on **the** consonant to which they belong or on the preceding consonant. P³ differs from P² chiefly by having differentiated the e-vowel into è and é.

The Tiberian system is based on B¹ (comp. Prætorius in "Z. D. M. G." liii. 195) and P.

The Tibe-rian and Accentual Systems. Like P³, it has differentiated the e-vowel. All its signs, with the exception of two within and one above the consonants, are written below the letters. The accentual system seems to have originated with P, since the vowel- and accent-signs in that system seem to have been cast in one mold. The accents were then transferred to B¹ and

mechanically supplemented by the conjunctive accents, which had later developed in T. As Prætorius has shown, these conjunctive accents are based on the Greek neumes of the early Middle Ages. The disjunctive accents, however, seem to have developed from the Greek interpunction-marks (comp. Kahle in "Z. D. M. G." lv. 167 et seq.; see also Consolo in "Verhandlungen des Internationalen Orientalisten-Kongresses," xiii. 214 et seq.).

In trying to determine the date when vocalization was first introduced the terminus a quo and the terminus ad quem must first be ascertained. Elijah LEVITA had already pointed out that the Talmudim and Midrashim do not mention vowel-signs or vowel-names, in spite of there having been abundant opportunity to do so. From this fact he

Date of In-troduction of Vocal-ization. concluded that vocalization and accentuation are post-Talmudic. The earliest dated mention of vocalization is that of Saadia Gaon and his contemporaries. Between the dates 500 and 900 the following data are to be considered: Even Aaron ben Moses ben Asher, whose ancestor in the sixth generation flourished in the second half of the eighth century, was ignorant of the origin of the vowel-points. A still older authority than Ben Asher the Elder, R. Phinehas, the head of the academy, is quoted as authority for T. If this R. Phinehas be identical with the payyeṭan mentioned after Ḳalir b. Saadia Gaon ("Agron," ed. Harkavy, p. 112), he must have lived early in the eighth century, or must have been contemporary with Khalil ibn Aḥmad (719–729), to whom the introduction of the Arabic system is attributed. Assuming that A and T were introduced about 750, these being based on P and B, the date for P must be about 700, since the age of P is conditioned by the zero-sign it uses, and that sign, together with the system of Arabic numerals to which it belongs, was first introduced by Mashallah (comp. NUMBERS AND NUMERALS). The date for B¹ must, therefore, be between 500 and 700; it is at present impossible to give the exact date. If vocalized manuscripts exist which go back to the seventh century (Harkavy's note to the Hebrew translation of Graetz's "Hist." iii. 160), then the date of B¹ must be about 600. The contention of C. D. Ginsburg ("Introduction to the Hebrew Bible," p. 451) that the late "Masseket Soferim" did not know the vowels is out of the question. How could it be ignorant of vowels when it knew the accents? The work is a compilation, and the passage Ginsburg quotes to prove his deduction is taken from older sources. The Nestorian Syriac vocalization is no doubt contemporary with A and T (comp. Duval, "Gram. Syr." § 71).

When in the course of time the origin of the vowel- and accent-signs was forgotten, some attributed their invention to Adam, others

Controver-sies About Age of Vo-calization. dated it from the Sinaitic revelation, while others traced it to Ezra or the Great Synagogue. Elijah Levita was the first to point out their post-Talmudic origin. The work in which he had embodied his views was soon translated into Latin by his pupil S. Münster (1539). Coming as it did in the time of the Reformation, Levita's theory was seized upon by the warring parties and led to numerous controversies. The most noted one was that between Cappellus and the Buxtorfs. On the Jewish side Levita was answered by Azariah dei Rossi in his "Me'or 'Enayim." S. D. Luzzatto published in 1852 his "Dialogues sur la Kabbale et le Zohar et sur l'Antiquité de la Punctuation et de l'Accentuation dans la Langue Hébraïque," placing himself on the side of Levita. That work called forth many answers, of which the most scholarly was that by Jacob Bachrach ("Ishtadalut 'im ShaDaL," Warsaw, 1896). Firkovich claimed to have discovered documents proving the invention of vocalization to be of Karaite origin; but these have been shown to be forgeries (comp. Harkavy's notes to

G. lv.; M. M. Kalish, *Hebr. Gram.* ii. 63 *et seq.*; M. Lenormant, *Essai sur la Propag. de l'Alph. Phén.* i. 307-326; C. Levias, in *Hebrew Union College Annual*, 1904; S. D. Luzzatto, *Dialogues sur la Kabbale et le Zohar et sur l'Antiquité de la Punctuation et de l'Accentuation dans la Langue Hébraïque*, Göritz, 1852; idem, in Pollak's *Halikot Kedem*, pp. 23 *et seq.*, Amsterdam, 1846; idem, in *Ha-Maggid*, iv., No. 24; G. Margoliouth, in *Proc. Soc. Bibl. Arch.* xv. 164-205; P. Mordel, in *Ha-Shiloaḥ*, v. 232 *et seq.*, x. 431 *et seq.*; J. Olshausen, in *Monatsberichte der Berliner Akademie*, July, 1865; S. Pinsker, *Einleitung in das Babylonisch-Hebräische Punktationssystem*, Vienna, 1863; F. Prætorius, *Ueber die Herkunft der Hebr. Accente*, Berlin, 1901; idem, *Die Uebernahme der Früh-Mittelgriechischen Neumen Durch die Juden*, Berlin, 1892; idem, in *Z. D. M. G.* liii. 195; S. L. Rapoport, *Hebräische Briefe*, pp. 75, 94; Roediger, in *Hall. Allgem. Literaturzeit.* 1848, No. 169.

Older literature on the subject is given in Wolf, *Bibl. Hebr.* ii. 475, iv. 214; Carpzov, *Critica Sacra*, p. 242; Gesenius, *Gesch. der Hebräischen Sprache*, §§ 48-56. Modern periodical literature is given in Schwab, *Répertoire*, Index.

On the controversy between Cappellus and Buxtorf comp. Diestel, *Gesch. des Alt. Test. in der Christl. Kirche*, s.v. *Vocalzeichen*; G. Schnedermann, *Die Controverse des L.*

VOWEL NOTATION.

	B¹	B²	B³	P	T	Sy	A	Sa
a	ז [ז̄] (ז̇)	ז̆, ז̄	ז̆	ז̇	ז	ז̇	ז́	'ז̇, ז̇, ז̣, ז̌
ä, ĕ	ז [ז̄] (ז̇)	ז̆, ז̄	ז̆	ז̇	ז	ז	ז́	—
å, a	ז [ז̄] (ז̇)	ז̆	ז	ז̇	ז̣, ז	ז̣, ז	ז́	'ז̇, ז̇, ז̣, ז̌
é	ז [ז̄] (ז̇)	ז̈	ז̇	ז̇ (P³ ז̇)	ז	ז, ז̣	ז̇	ז̇
è	ז [ז̄] (ז̇)	ז̣, ז	ז̆	ז̇	ז̣	ז, ז̣, ז̣	ז̣	ז̇
i	ז̇ [ז̄] (ז̇)	ז̇	ז̇	ז̇	ז	ז, ז̣, ז	ז̇	ז̇
u	ז̇ [ז̄] (ז̇)	ז̇	ז̇	ז̈	ז̣, בז	בז	ז̇	ז̇, ז̇
ō	ז̇	ז̣, ז̇	ז̇	ז̈	ז	בז	ז̇	ז̇, ז̇
ŏ	—[ז̄] (ז̇)	ז̇	ז̇	ז̇ (P² ז̇)	ז̇	בז	ז̇	
Vocal Shewa	ז̇	ז̇	ז̇	ז̇ (P² ז̇)	ז̣	~	ז̇	ז̇, 'ז̇, ז̇
Silent Shewa	—	—	—	(P² ז̇)	ז	—	ז̣, ז̇	
Ḥaṭef	ז̇ = a, ז̈ = e, ז̇ = o	ז̇	—	ז̇ (P² ז̇)	ז̣, ז, ז̣	—	—	—
Rafe	ז̄	—	ז̄	(P² ז̇)	ז̇	ז, ז̣	—	—
Dagesh	—	—	ז̇	(P² ז̇)	ב	ז̇	ז̇, ז̇, ז̇, ז̈	ז̇, ב
Mappiḳ	—	—	—	(P² ז̇)	ב		ז̣, ב	ז̇

The bracketed forms in B¹ are used before dagesh; the parenthetic forms before a vowelless consonant.

Graetz's "Hist." Hebr. transl., iii. 160, 175, 485). See PUNCTUATION.

BIBLIOGRAPHY: A. Ackermann, *Das Hermeneutische Element der Biblischen Accentuation*, pp. 1-30, Berlin, 1893; W. Bacher, *Die Anfänge der Hebräischen Grammatik*, in *Z. D. M. G.* xlix. 13-20; J. Bachrach, *Sefer ha-Yaḥas*, Warsaw, 1854; idem, *Ishtadalut 'im ShaDaL*, 2 vols., Warsaw, 1896; H. Barnstein, *The Targum of Onkelos to Genesis*, pp. 6 *et seq.*, Leipsic, 1896; S. Bernfeld, in *Oṣar ha-Sifrut*, iv. 347-360; A. Büchler, in *Sitzungsberichte der Wiener Akademie*, 1891, 1901; H. Ewald, in *Jahrbücher der Bibl. Wissenschaft*, i. 160-172; J. Fürst, *Gesch. des Karäert.* i. 19 *et seq.*, 134 *et seq.*; A. Geiger, *Urschrift*, pp. 484-490; I. Guidi, *Bolletino*, i. 430; P. Haupt, in *Journal American Oriental Soc.* vol. xxii.; Hupfeld, in *Theol. Stud. und Kritik.* 1837, pp. 57-130; P. Kahle, in Stade's *Zeitschrift*, xxi. 273 *et seq.*; idem, in *Z. D. M.*

Cappellus mit den Buxtorfen, Leipsic, 1879 (comp. I. Derenbourg in *Revue Critique*, 1879, pp. 455 *et seq.*); Hersmann, *Zur Gesch. des Streites über die Entstehung der Hebräischen Punktation*, Ruhrort, 1885. See also bibliographies to the articles ACCENTS and MASORAH.

T.

C. L.

VOGEL, SIR JULIUS: Agent-general in London for New Zealand; born in London Feb. 25. 1835; died there March 13, 1899. He was the son of Albert Lee Vogel, and was educated at University College School. Left an orphan, he emigrated to Australia in 1852. Disappointed with his progress at the gold-diggings, he fell back upon his literary ability and became editor and proprietor of several Victorian newspapers. He stood for Parliament in 1861, but was unsuccessful, and emigrated to Dunedin, New Zealand, where he bought a half interest in the "Otago Witness" and started the "Otago Daily Times," the first daily paper in New Zealand. In 1862 Vogel was elected to the provincial council of Otago, and four years later became the head of the provincial government, a post which he held till 1869. In 1863 he was elected a member of the New Zealand House of Representatives, and on retiring from the provincial government in 1869, he joined the Fox ministry as colonial treasurer, afterward becoming successively postmaster-general, commissioner of customs, and telegraph commissioner. The Fox ministry having been forced to resign, Vogel carried a vote of want of confidence in their successors, and in Oct., 1872, returned to power as leader in the Lower House, colonial treasurer, and postmaster-general. In 1873 Vogel became prime minister of the colony. In 1875–76 he visited England, and afterward resumed the premiership. From 1876 to 1881 he was agent-general for New Zealand in London, and in 1884 was again a member of the government of the colony. He finally gave up colonial office in 1887, from which date he resided in England. He was made C.M.G. in 1872, and K.C.M.G. in 1875, and received special permission to retain the colonial title of "Honorable" during his life. He unsuccessfully contested Penryn in 1880 as an Imperialist.

Sir Julius Vogel's principal achievement as a colonial statesman was the discovery that the savings of the mother country could, with mutual advantage, be obtained by the colonies and applied to the construction of railways and other public works. That his system of finance was on the whole successful was amply proved by the prosperous state of the Australasian colonies. Sir Julius Vogel was the author of the act by virtue of which Colonial stock has been inscribed at the Bank of England and has become a popular investment for trustees. His project of law was accepted by the imperial government to the equal benefit of all the colonies. His scheme of public borrowing for the colony of New Zealand was put into effect in 1870, and within the next ten years the colony borrowed £22,500,000 at diminishing rates of interest, the population rose from 250,000 to 500,000, the extent of land under cultivation increased from 1,000,000 to 4,000,000 acres, and the value of exports from £500,000 to £1,500,000. It is also stated that in the same ten years he introduced 100,000 immigrants and caused 1,200 miles of railway to be constructed. During a visit to England he established the existing mail service between New Zealand and San Francisco. In his first premiership he set on foot the government life-insurance system and organized the New Zealand Public Trusteeship. He was one of the first to advocate imperial federation.

Sir Julius Vogel wrote a novel entitled "Anno Domini 2000, or Woman's Destiny"; it was published in 1889, and passed through several editions. One of his sons, **Frank Leon Vogel,** was killed on Dec. 4, 1893, while serving with Major Wilson's force against the Matabele.

XII.—29

BIBLIOGRAPHY: *Jew. Chron.* March 18, 1899; Gisborne, *Hist. of New Zealand*; G. W. Rusden, *Hist. of New Zealand,* vols. ii., iii.
J.   G. L.

VOGELSTEIN, HERMANN : German rabbi and historian; born at Pilsen, Bohemia, Jan. 8, 1870. His father was **Heinemann Vogelstein,** rabbi of Stettin, and died Aug. 4, 1911. Vogelstein received his education at his native town, the gymnasium at Stettin, and the universities and Jewish theological seminaries at Berlin and Breslau (Ph.D. and rabbi 1894). In 1895 he became rabbi in Oppeln, and since 1897 he has been rabbi at Königsberg, East Prussia.

He is the author of "Die Landwirtschaft in Palästina zur Zeit der Mischnah" (Berlin, 1894) and, together with Rieger, of the first volume of "Geschichte der Juden in Rom," the second volume being written by Rieger alone (Berlin, 1896). The "Geschichte" gained one of the prizes offered by the Zunzstiftung.

s.   F. T. H.

VOICE OF HEAVEN. See BAT ḲOL.

VOICE OF ISRAEL. See PERIODICALS.

VOICE OF JACOB. See PERIODICALS.

VOID AND VOIDABLE CONTRACTS. See CONTRACT.

VOLOZHIN : Polish town in the government of Wilna; which in the year 1905 belonged to Prince Tishkewitz. As in most other Polish towns, the Jews constitute the greater part of the population. Jews settled there about the middle of the sixteenth century. Volozhin is celebrated for the rabbinical school which existed there until 1892. This school, or yeshibah, which was founded in 1803 by Ḥayyim b. Solomon, a pupil of the renowned Elijah, Gaon of Wilna, was in direct opposition to the Ḥasidic movement that spread through Lithuania in the second half of the eighteenth century. At the head of this conservative opposition, the members of which were styled "Mitnaggedim" (opponents), stood the Gaon of Wilna. He recognized that, in order to combat successfully the Ḥasidic movement, the love of Talmudic study must be aroused and strengthened. One way of doing this was to establish a great Talmudic academy, where the letter of the Law would be studied systematically. Death, however, removed him before his cherished plan could be carried out, and the task was left to his pupil Ḥayyim b. Solomon.

Wilna already had two yeshibot, and there was no room for a third; so Volozhin was chosen, where had lived a number of such men as the author of "Sha'agat Aryeh" and Zalman Volozhiner. In order to attract scholars to the institution two wise rules were laid down: (1) only those should be admitted who had distinguished themselves in Talmudic study, and (2) the medieval custom of assigning yeshibah students each day to a different family, in which they received their meals free, should be abolished; the students to be either self-supporting, or maintained by the institution. Thus scholars, both rich and poor, flocked to Volo-

The Yeshibah.

zhin from all parts of Russia and the rest of Europe. For nearly a century it held its reputation as a place of the highest Talmudic learning, until finally, in 1892, to the regret of all lovers of Judaism, the doors of the school were shut by order of the Russian government.

The very spirit in which the institution was founded was the cause of its downfall. It was, as stated before, ultraconservative, tolerating nothing that looked like an innovation, and strongly opposing all exoteric studies. For a long time it withstood the great wave of progress that swept over Russia in the middle of the nineteenth century. In 1887 Count Pahlen, who devoted a great deal of his time to the Jewish question, called together thirteen representative Jewish scholars of Russia in order to confer with them about the yeshibot. The conference drew up a set of regulations for the management of such institutions, the most important of which were: that each day not less than three hours should be devoted to the teaching of the Russian language and literature and to other secular studies; that the teachers in these branches should be appointed with the sanction of the government; that not more than twelve hours each day should be consumed in study; and that the chief rabbi should be responsible for the conduct of his pupils.

The chiefs of the yeshibot, fearing that secular studies would "poison the minds of the students and turn them away from the study of the Talmud," stubbornly refused to introduce these innovations; they feared also that Orthodox Jews would withhold their contributions from the school. In 1891 Count Delianov, then minister of education, submitted a similar plan to the authorities of the school in Volozhin; but, seeing that his instructions were not carried out, he closed its doors on Jan. 22, 1892.

BIBLIOGRAPHY: *Ha-Kerem* and *Ha-Meliz*, 1892; *Entziklopedicheski Slovar*, vol. vii.
H. R.   J. Go.

VOLTAIRE: French poet, historian, and essayist; born at Paris Nov. 21, 1694; died there May 30, 1778. His name was originally François Marie Arouet; but about 1718 he assumed the name of Voltaire. He is known to the world as one of the most active and popular champions of free thought and as an ardent advocate of religious as well as political liberty. It is the more surprising that he who, in his "Traité sur la Tolerance" (1766), vindicated Jean Calas, the victim of Catholic fanaticism, and who, in his "Lettres Chinoises," bitterly attacked religious bigotry, should have fostered anti-Jewish sentiments. His personal experiences with Jews would hardly suffice to explain such inconsistency. He alleges that, while an exile in London (1726), he had a letter of credit drawn on a Jewish banker, whom he refers to once as "Medina" and another time as "Acosta," and through whose bankruptcy he lost the greater part of 20,000 francs. In Potsdam, where he was the guest of Frederick the Great, he had a disagreeable experience with a Jew named Abraham Hirsch. In his treaty of peace with Saxony (1745) Frederick had stipulated that Saxon bonds ("Steuerscheine") held by his subjects should be redeemed at their face value, although they were then listed at 35 per cent below par. At the same time

it was ordered that no Prussian subject might purchase any of these bonds after the declaration of peace. Voltaire nevertheless ordered Hirsch to buy such bonds for him, giving him notes for the amount, while Hirsch deposited with Voltaire jewelry as security. Subsequently Veitel-Heine EPHRAIM offered Voltaire more favorable conditions, and he therefore withdrew his order from Hirsch. The last-named, who had already discounted Voltaire's notes, was arrested; but the enemies of the poet used the whole unsavory transaction as a means of attacking him. The king himself wrote a satire against Voltaire in the form of a drama entitled "Tantale en Procès"; and Hirsch was discharged after having paid a comparatively small fine. Voltaire himself refers to this incident in his humorous way, naturally presenting himself as having been duped. While it hardly had the effect of filling him with anti-Jewish sentiments, it inspired him, in his "Dictionnaire Philosophique Portatif" (1764), to make some unfavorable remarks about the Jews. He charges them with greed and selfishness, saying that their only ideals are children and money.

It seems that, aside from his desire to select any subject apt to furnish an opportunity to display his humorous satire and give him a chance to attack the Bible, Voltaire had no intention of antagonizing the Jews. In his reply to Isaac de PINTO, who wrote an apology for the Jews entitled "Apologie pour la Nation Juive," Voltaire admitted as much. He recognized the fact that there were respectable Jews, and he did not wish to wound the feelings of his opponent by references to the people of Israel as represented in the Bible. Antoine GUENÉ, who defended the Bible against the attacks of Voltaire, embodied in his "Lettres de Quelques Juifs" De Pinto's apology together with the correspondence to which it gave rise. Voltaire replied in a pamphlet, "Un Chrétien Contre Six Juifs" (1776), without taking up the Jewish question.

BIBLIOGRAPHY: Grätz, *Voltaire und die Juden*, in *Monatsschrift*, 1868, pp. 161–174, 201, 223; idem, *Gesch.* xi. 48–54; Becker, *Voltaire et les Juifs*, in *Archives*, xliii. 85 *et seq.*; Mathias Kahn, *ib.* xxxviii. 436 *et seq.*; Lazard, *Voltaire et les Juifs*, in *Univ. Isr.* xli. 1, 126; Bluemner, *Voltaire im Prozesse mit Abraham Hirsch*, in *Deutsches Museum*, 1863, No. 43.
D.

VOLTERRA, AARON ḤAI: Liturgical poet of the first half of the eighteenth century; rabbi of the Italian communities in Massa e Carrara. He was the author of a prayer entitled "Baḳḳashah," or "Elef Shin." The latter name, however, is misleading; for in the entire prayer, in which each word begins with the letter "shin," this letter occurs only 700 times, and not, as this title would indicate, 1,000 times. In his preface the author states that numerous difficulties obliged him to resort to artificial wordformations, in which he felt that the license of poetry justified him. The poem, which begins with the words "Shaddai shoken sheḥaḳim," is accompanied by a commentary containing a glossary of the Talmudic terms occurring in it. A second poem by Volterra, forming an eightfold acrostic of the author's name, commences "'Alekem ishim eḳra," and is written after the style of the poems of Jedaiah b. Abraham Bedersi. These two works were **published**

together under the title "Bakkashah Hadashah" (Leghorn, 1740).

BIBLIOGRAPHY: Zunz, *Z. G.* Index, *s. v.*; Nepi-Ghirondi, *Toledot Gedole Yisrael*, p. 30; Fuenn, *Keneset Yisrael*, p. 77; Benjacob, *Ozar ha-Sefarim*, p. 82; Mortara, *Indice*, p. 69.
E. C.　　　　　　　　　　　　　　　　S. O.

VOLTERRA, MESHULLAM BEN MENAHEM : Italian jeweler of the fifteenth century. He lived in Florence, where he and his father, Menahem ben Aaron Volterra (who in 1460 was worth 100,000 ducats), carried on a business in precious stones. According to Abraham Portaleone, Volterra wrote a book on jewelry. In 1481 he undertook a journey to the Orient, going by way of Rhodes to Alexandria, where there were at that time only sixty Jewish families. Here he saw a beautiful manuscript of the Hebrew Bible, which the natives claimed had been written by Ezra. In Cairo, where he bought gems, great honor was shown him by the nagid of the city, the wealthy Solomon ben Joseph, whose father also had been nagid, as well as body-physician to the sultan.

On July 29 Volterra reached Jerusalem, where at that time there were 250 Jewish families. Here both he and his companion became dangerously ill. He then passed through Jaffa and Damascus to Crete, where he was shipwrecked, lost his precious stones, and again became very ill. His life was saved only by the self-sacrificing care of a German Jewish physician. Volterra finally reached Venice in October. His account of the journey, which has been preserved in manuscript in the Laurentiana (cod. xi. 3, p. 128), was first published by Luncz in his "Jerusalem" (i. 166–219).

Volterra had a brother **Raphael,** who was engaged in the book-trade.

BIBLIOGRAPHY: Nepi-Ghirondi, *Toledot Gedole Yisrael*, p. 224; Portaleone, *Shilte ha-Gibborim*, p. 29a; Steinschneider, *Hebr. Bibl.* xxi. 76; Berliner, *Magazin*, vii. 119; Luncz, *Jerusalem*, iii. 50.
D.　　　　　　　　　　　　　　　　　M. K.

VOORSANGER, JACOB: American rabbi; born at Amsterdam, Holland, Nov. 13, 1852. He was educated at the Jewish Theological Seminary of Amsterdam, and received the degree of D.D. from the Hebrew Union College, Cincinnati, O. He officiated as rabbi at Philadelphia (1873–76), Washington, D. C. (1876–77), Providence, R. I. (1877–78), Houston, Tex. (1878–86), and, since 1886, at the Temple Emanu-El, San Francisco, Cal. In 1894 he was appointed professor of Semitic languages and literature at the University of California, which office he held until shortly before his death; he officiated also as chaplain and special lecturer at the Leland Stanford, Jr., University. He died April 27, 1908.

From 1881 to 1883 Voorsanger was editor of "The Jewish South" (Houston, Tex.), and from 1883 to 1886 of the "Sabbath Visitor" (Cincinnati, O.). In 1895 he founded "Emanu-El," of which paper he was editor until his death. He was the author of "Moses Mendelssohn's Life and Works."

BIBLIOGRAPHY: *The American Jewish Year Book*, 5664, p. 104.
A.　　　　　　　　　　　　　　　　　F. T. H.

VORARLBERG: Extreme western district of the Austrian empire. In the Middle Ages it was called "Vor dem Arlberg," and was divided into the estates of **Bregenz, Feldkirch,** and **Bludenz.** To these was added in 1560 the imperial county of **Hohenems.** The first three districts were held by the counts of Montfort-Werdenberg, but gradually came under Austrian control. Jews were in Vorarlberg as early as the fourteenth century. They were for the most part exiles from Switzerland and the German and Austrian countries bordering the Lake of Constance, and they ventured to settle only in the immediate neighborhood of the lord of Vorarlberg or his bailiffs. The "Stadtrecht" of Feldkirch (printed and discussed in "Zeit. für die Gesch. des Oberrheins," xxi. 129–171) contains four regulations referring to Jews (folios 3b, 13b, 15a). The statements made by modern historians regarding persecutions at Feldkirch in 1348–49 on account of the Black Death, and in 1443–44 because of an accusation of ritual murder, have been shown to be erroneous and due to the confusion of Feldkirch in Vorarlberg with Waldkirch in Baden, both of which were formerly called "Veltkilch" (Salfeld, "Martyrologium," p. 69, Berlin, 1898). It is known that the Black Death did not break out in Vorarlberg in 1348–49; and the episode of the ritual murder of 1443–44 took place in Baden, principally at Constance.

When Feldkirch became an Austrian dependency, at the end of the fourteenth century, the Jews left this district entirely. The account of the scattered settlements later found in various villages forms part of the history of the Jews of HOHENEMS, who founded in 1617, under Count Caspar, a community which still exists. Thus there was a settlement from 1676 to 1744 in the village of Sulz, near Feldkirch, the place whence the family of Prof. Salomon Sulzer originally came. Jews lived in the city and territory of Bregenz in the Middle Ages, but were all expelled from the country by an edict of 1559. Since 1617 Hohenems has had a Jewish community, to which all the Jews of Tyrol and Vorarlberg were assigned by the law of 1890. The Jews of Vorarlberg have frequently distinguished themselves in the history of the country, as, for instance, in the war with Napoleon in 1809, and have contributed much to the promotion of commerce and industry.

BIBLIOGRAPHY: Tänzer, *Gesch. der Juden in Tyrol und Vorarlberg*, vol. i.; idem, *Gesch. der Juden in Hohenems und dem Uebrigen Vorarlberg*, 1903–04.
D.　　　　　　　　　　　　　　　　　A. Tä.

VORSPIEL. See MARRIAGE.

VOSKHOD. See RUSSIA—PERIODICALS.

VOSSIUS, ISAAC. See MANASSEH BEN IS-RAEL.

VOWS (Hebr. "nedarim "): Promises made under religious sanction. In Talmudic law distinction is made between two principal kinds of vows: (1) A voluntary promise to bring a sacrifice which he who makes the vow is not otherwise in duty bound to bring; or a promise to give a certain sum to purposes of common charity or education. Such vows are called "nidre hekdesh" (="dedications "), and of these there are two specific kinds. (*a*) When he who promises points toward the object which he intends to give, and says, "This I dedicate to such and such a holy or charitable cause," then he is not bound to replace the thing if it is lost. (*b*) If, on the other hand, he says, "I promise such and such an object, or such and such a sum of money, to be devoted to that purpose," then he is bound to replace it if it becomes lost. The former kind of vows are called "nedabah" (= "gift"); the latter kind "neder" (="promise"). (2) The second chief kind of vows consists in promises made to abstain from the enjoyment of certain things, he who promises saying: "I deny myself the enjoyment of this thing, as of a thing sanctified." Such vows are called "nidre issar" (= "promises of prohibition or deprivation"). Such a vow is valid even if a second party imposes it upon the votary, he answering with an "Amen" and thereby accepting it.

A vow is valid only if made voluntarily, without any compulsion from without; and the votary must also be conscious of the scope or character of his vow. A promise made by mistake, or one exacted by compulsory measures, is invalid. The age of discretion with reference to promises is for men the beginning of the thirteenth year, for women the beginning of the twelfth, at which

Validity of Vows. ages the votaries are supposed to understand the importance of a vow (Maimonides, "Yad," Nedarim, xi. 1). A father may annul the vows made by his daughter; and a husband may annul those of his wife, if they be of such a nature that the keeping of them would cause distress to the wife. The father or the husband may, however, annul such vows only on the very day when he is informed of their having been given (Num. xxx. 2–17; Ned. x. 8; Maimonides, *l.c.* xii. 1 *et seq.*).

Any vow, be it a dedication ("neder heḳdesh"), or a promise of prohibition or deprivation ("neder issar"), can, in case the promisor regrets it, be declared void by an ordained teacher, or by three unordained teachers (Maimonides, "Yad," Shebu'ot, vi.; Shulḥan 'Aruk, Yoreh De'ah, 228, where the conditions are specified on which a vow can be annulled). To impose vows on oneself was discouraged by the sages of the Mishnah and the Talmud: "Do not form a habit of making vows," says an old baraita (Ned. 20a). Samuel said: "He who makes a vow, even though he fulfil it, commits a sin" (*ib.* 22a). The making of vows was tolerated only when it was done in order to rid oneself of bad habits, or in order to encourage oneself to do good; but even in such cases one should strive for the desired end without the aid of vows (Yoreh De'ah, 203, 207). More specific rules regarding vows are contained in Maimonides' "Yad," Nedarim, and in Shulḥan 'Aruk, Yoreh De'ah, 203–235. See also NEDARIM.

W. B.   J. Z. L.

VULGATE: Latin version of the Bible authorized by the Council of Trent in 1546 as the Bible of the Roman Catholic Church. It was the product of the work of Jerome, one of the most learned and scholarly of the Church leaders of the early Christian centuries. The earliest Latin version of the Scriptures seems to have originated not in Rome, but in one of Rome's provinces in North Africa. An Old Latin version of the New Testament was extant in North Africa in the second century C.E., and it is thought that a translation of the Old Testament into Latin was made in the

Earlier Latin Translations. same century. Indeed, Tertullian (*c.* 160–240) seems to have known a Latin Bible. There were at least two early Latin translations, one called the African and the other the European. These, based not on the Hebrew, but on the Greek, are thought to have been made before the text-work of such scholars as Origen, Lucian, and Hesychius, and hence would be valuable for the discovery of the Greek text with which Origen worked. But the remains of these early versions are scanty. Jerome did not translate or revise several books found in the Latin Bible, and consequently the Old Latin versions were put in their places in the later Latin Bible. These Old Latin versions are represented in the books of Esdras, Wisdom, Ecclesiasticus, Baruch, and Maccabees, and in the additions to Daniel and Esther. The Psalter also exists in a revised form, and the books of Job and Esther, of the Old Latin, are found in some ancient manuscripts. Only three other fragmentary manuscripts of the Old Testament in Old Latin are now known to be in existence.

Jerome was born of Christian parents about 340–342, at Stridon, in the province of Dalmatia. He received a good education, and carried on his studies at Rome, being especially fascinated by Vergil, Terence, and Cicero. Rhetoric and Greek also claimed part of his attention. At Trier in Gaul he took up theological studies for several years. In 374 he traveled in the Orient. In a severe illness he was so impressed by a dream that he dropped secular studies. But his time had not been lost. He turned his brilliant mind, trained in the best schools of the day, to sacred things. Like Moses and Paul, he retired to a desert, that of Chalcis, near Antioch, where he spent almost five years in profound study of the Scriptures and of himself. At this period he sealed a friendship with Pope Damasus, who later opened the door to him for the great work of his life. In 379 Jerome was ordained presbyter at Antioch. Thence he went to Constantinople, where he was inspired by the expositions of Gregory Nazianzen. In 382 he reached Rome, where he lived about three years in close friendship with Damasus.

For a long time the Church had felt the need of a good, uniform Latin Bible. Pope Damasus at first asked his learned friend Jerome to

Jerome's Bible-Revision Work. prepare a revised Latin version of the New Testament. In 388 the Four Gospels appeared in a revised form, and at short intervals thereafter the Acts and the remaining books of the New Testament. These latter were very slightly altered by Jerome. Soon afterward he revised the Old Latin Psalter simply by the use of the Septuagint. The name given this revision was the "Roman Psalter," in distinction from the "Psalterium Vetus." The former was used in Rome and Italy down to Pius V. (1566–72), when it was displaced by the "Gallican Psalter" (so called because first adopted in Gaul), another of Jerome's revisions (made about 387), based on many corrections of the Greek text by reference to other Greek versions. About the end of 384 Pope Damasus died, and Jerome left Rome to travel and study in Bible lands. In 389 he settled at Bethlehem, assumed charge of a monastery, and prosecuted his studies with great zeal. He secured a learned Jew to teach him Hebrew for still better work than that he had been doing. His revision work had not yet ceased, for his Book of Job appeared as the result of the same kind of study as had produced the "Gallican Psalter." He revised some other books, as Proverbs, Ecclesiastes, Song of Songs, and Chronicles, of which his revisions are lost, though their prefaces still exist.

But Jerome soon recognized the poor and unsatisfactory state of the Greek texts that he was obliged to use. This turned his mind and thought to the original Hebrew. Friends, too, urged him to translate certain books from the original text. As a resultant of long thought, and in answer to many requests, Jerome spent fifteen years, 390 to 405, on a new translation of the Old Testament from the original Hebrew text. He began with the books of Samuel and Kings, for which he wrote a remarkable preface, really an introduction to the entire Old Testament. He next translated the Psalms, and then the Prophets and Job. In 394–396 he prepared a translation of Esdras and Chronicles. After an interval of two years, during which he passed through a severe illness, he took up his arduous labors, and produced translations of Proverbs, Ecclesiastes, and Song of Songs. The Pentateuch followed next, and the last canonical books, Joshua, Judges, Ruth, and Esther, were completed by 404. The Apocryphal parts of Daniel and Esther, and Tobit and Judith, all translated from the Aramaic, completed Jerome's great task. The remainder of the Apocryphal books he left without revision or translation, as they were not found in the Hebrew Bible.

Jerome's Bible-Translation Work.

Jerome happily has left prefaces to most of his translations, and these documents relate how he did his work and how some of the earlier books were received. Evidently he was bitterly criticized by some of his former best friends. His replies show that he was supersensitive to criticism, and often hot-tempered and stormy. His irritability and his sharp retorts to his critics rather retarded than aided the reception of his translation. But the superiority of the translation gradually won the day for most of his work. The Council of Trent in 1546 authorized the Latin Bible, which was by that time a strange composite. The Old Testament was Jerome's translation from the Hebrew, except the Psalter, which was his Gallican revision; of the Apocryphal books, Judith and Tobit were his translations, while the remainder were of the Old Latin version. The New

Jerome's Translation in Later Times.

Testament was Jerome's revision of the Old Latin translation. These translations and revisions of translations, and old original translations, constitute the Vulgate. See also JEROME.

BIBLIOGRAPHY: Grützmacher, Hieronymus: eine Bibliographische Studie, vol. i., Leipsic, 1901; S. Berger, Histoire de la Vulgate Pendant les Premières Siècles du Moyen Age, Paris, 1893; H. J. White, Codex Amiatinus and Its Birthplace, in Studia Biblica et Ecclesiastica, vol. ii., Oxford, 1890; E. Nestle, Ein Jubiläum der Lateinischen Bibel, Tübingen, 1892; E. von Dobschütz, Studien zur Textkritik der Vulgata, Leipsic, 1894; Hastings, Dict. Bible. See fuller bibliography in S. Berger's work, mentioned above.

T.   I. M. P.

VULTURE : The Hebrew terms rendered in one or the other of the English versions by "vulture" are: "da'ah" (Lev. xi. 14) and its variant "dayyah" (Deut. xiv. 13 and Isa. xxxiv. 15 [R. V. "kite"]), "ayyah" (Lev. xi. 14; Deut. xiv. 13; Job xxviii. 7 [R. V. "kite" and "falcon"]), and "raḥam," "raḥamah" (Lev. xi. 18; Deut. xiv. 17 [A. V. "giereagle"]); all refer to unclean birds. The raḥam is identified with the Egyptian or Pharaoh's vulture (Neophron percnopterus), called also by the Arabs "raḥam"; it is a migratory bird, known in Palestine and Arabia, returning from the south in the spring. The Hebrew "nesher" (always rendered by "eagle" in the A. and R. V.) also denotes large birds of prey in general, and in some passages refers particularly to the vulture, or griffin-vulture, which belongs to the Vulturidæ family. So in Jer. xlix. 16 and Job xxxix. 27–30, where the nesher is described as making its nest in the highest cliffs, which is characteristic of the vulture; or in Micah i. 16, where the bald-headedness of the nesher is alluded to (this can only refer to the vulture, which is devoid of true feathers on the head and neck); or when it is used as an image of an invading army (comp. Deut. xxviii. 49; Jer. xlviii. 40; Hos. viii. 1; Hab. i. 8). The Romans also did not distinguish sharply between the eagle and the vulture (Pliny, "Nat. Hist." x. 3, xiii. 26). The griffin-vulture is most abundant in Palestine, where it breeds in colonies, while the kite is represented by four species.

Besides all the Biblical terms for the vulture, the Talmud uses the name "ra'ah" on account of the keenness of the vulture's sight, "for it can, while in Babylon, sight carrion in Palestine" (Ḥul. 63b; B. M. 24b [Rashi]). In the passage of Hullin it is said that there are a hundred kinds of unclean birds in the Orient, all belonging to the vulture tribe ("min ayyah"). The proper name of the raḥam is שרקרק; it is called raḥam because with its appearance mercy, that is, rain, is bestowed on the world, while the name שרקרק is due to its cry "shirḳrek" (Ḥul. 63a). In Ḥul. 25b is mentioned a bird of whose claws vessels were made, and which Rashi explains to be a griffin-vulture.

BIBLIOGRAPHY: Tristram, Nat. Hist. p. 172; Lewysohn, Z. T. p. 167.

E. G. H.   I. M. C.

W

WA'AD ARBA' ARAZOT. See COUNCIL OF FOUR LANDS.

WA-ANI TEFILLATI (Ps. lxix. 14 [A. V. 13]): The introduction to the reading of the lesson before the afternoon prayer on the Sabbath. Among the Ashkenazim it is chanted by the ḥazzan to the prayer-motive of the service (see MUSIC, SYNAGOGAL) like U-BA LE-ẒIYYON, which it follows in the Ger-

a shabua' ha-ben (B. Ḳ. 80a); and the author of the Vitry Maḥzor mentions a festal gathering on the eve of the day of circumcision as an ancient traditional custom (p. 627).

In Germany the pressure of business during the week finally fixed the gathering for the night of the Friday before the circumcision. The feast was then called "zakar" (male; comp. Isserlein, "Terumat

WA-ANI TEFILLATI

Wa- a - ni.... te- fil - la - ti........ le - ka, A - do - nai, 'el ra - zon:

E - lo - him,.... be-rob has- de - ka, 'a - ne - ni be- e - met yish - 'e - ka.

man ritual. In the later ritual tradition of the Sephardim, who sing it also in other portions of the liturgy, it is chanted by the congregation to the modern melody here transcribed.

A.   F. L. C.

WACHNACHT: The Judæo-German term for the night preceding the day of circumcision, spent in feasting and the recitation of hymns and prayers by the mohel, sandik, and members of the family. The ostensible object of the watch is to ward off the "evil spirit" and to drive away the "devils," especially LILITH, who is supposed to be inimical to the child about to enter into the covenant of Abraham. The cabalists deduce the peril of this time from the circumstances attending the circumcision of the son of Zipporah (Ex. iv. 24–26; Zohar, Lek Leka, 93b); but the real purpose was to inquire after the health and needs of the mother, for the Rabbis advised a similar procedure in the case of the sick (Ber. 54b), and preparations were also made for the ceremony and feasting accompanying the circumcision. Other plausible reasons for the watch were the repeated edicts of the Gentile governments in the early periods against circumcision and the persecutions by Hadrian, so that those who took part in the ceremony were obliged to adopt all precautions and to assemble on the night before it to prevent publicity. Since circumcision could be performed only by day, the same need of caution required that all doors and windows be closed and the daylight excluded, so that the ceremony was carried out by the light of lamps and candles. Different communities had secret signs and signals to announce the "Wachnacht," such as the grinding of a millstone or the lighting of a lamp. The eve of circumcision itself was disguised under the term "shabua' ha-ben" (week of the son; Sanh. 32b, and Rashi *ad loc.*). Even after the persecutions had ceased, the lights were still lit (Yer. Ket. i. 5). Rab, Samuel, and Rab Assi met at

ha-Deshen," responsum No. 269), and in modern times it is termed "shalom zakar," "shalom" meaning "peace," and both indicating the birth of a male child and also implying an inquiry after the health of the mother as well as safety from persecution. The festival is considered a feast of merit ("se'uddat miẓwah"; Shulḥan 'Aruk, Yoreh De'ah, 265, 12, note by Isserles).

In eastern Europe the small boys of the neighborhood are accustomed to assemble every night of the week before the circumcision and recite the "Shema'" and a few verses of the Bible, ending with "The Angel which redeemed" (Gen. xlviii. 16), for which they are given nuts and sweetmeats. The ceremony is more elaborate in the Orient, especially in Jerusalem, where, even at the birth of a girl, two women act as nurses of the mother during the entire week, while two men in another room recite and study the Scriptures and tik-kunim. The chief ceremony, however, is on the eve of the eighth day, when all who actually take part in the circumcision assemble together with the friends of the parents at the house of the latter and pass the entire night in celebration of the event, each guest bringing wine and cake as well as a lamp with olive-oil for illumination. The Sephardim decorate their lamps with wreaths of flowers, and march in the street to the beating of a drum until they reach the house, where the ḥakam delivers an address. The reading in the house consists of selections from the Bible, a few chapters of mishnayot, including the Mishnah Bekorot if the child is a first-born, and selections from the Zohar (Emden, "Siddur Bet Ya'aḳob," i. 99b–102a, Warsaw, 1881). In his "Ḥemdat Yamim" (i. 8, Leghorn, 1762) Nathan Benjamin Ghazzati transmits a rabbinical tradition that if the watch was observed with full ceremony throughout the eight days, or at least during the four preceding the circumcision, the child

In Modern Times.

would be destined to remain faithful to God; while Aaron Berechiah of Modena recommended the recitation of the "Piṭṭum ha-Ḳeṭoret" ("Ma'abar Yabboḳ," vi. 8, 5).

BIBLIOGRAPHY: Lewinsohn, *Meḳore Minhagim*, p. 65; Auerbach, *Berit Abraham*, 2d ed., pp. 35–38, Frankfort-on-the-Main, 1880; Glassberg, *Zikron Berit la-Rishonim*, Appendix, pp. 151–173, Cracow, 1892; Luncz, *Jerusalem*, i. 2; Abrahams, *Jewish Life in the Middle Ages*, p. 143, note.

A.   J. D. E.

WAGENSEIL, JOHANN CHRISTOPH: German Christian Hebraist; born at Nuremberg Nov. 26, 1633; died at Altdorf Oct. 9, 1705. In 1667 he was made professor of history at Altdorf, and was professor of Oriental languages at the same university from 1674 to 1697, after which he occupied the chair of ecclesiastical law until his death. For his knowledge of Hebrew he was chiefly indebted to Enoch Levi, who had come from Vienna to Fürth about 1670. Wagenseil devoted his learning to publishing anti-Christian works of Jewish authors, and undertook long journeys to gather his material. The fruit of this work is the collection entitled "Tela Ignea Satanæ, sive Arcani et Horribiles Judæorum Adversus Christum, Deum, et Christianam Religionem Libri" (Altdorf, 1681), which includes the apologetic "Ḥizzuḳ Emunah" of the Karaite Isaac b. Abraham of Troki. Becoming convinced by the "Toledot Yeshu" that the Jews were guilty of blaspheming Jesus, Wagenseil addressed to all high potentates his "Denunciatio Christiana de Blasphemiis Judæorum in Jesum Christum" (Altdorf, 1703), in which he implored them to restrain the Jews from mocking at Jesus, Mary, the cross, the mass, and Christian teachings. Although he would have been pleased to see the Protestant princes show greater zeal in the conversion of the Jews, Wagenseil was opposed to forcible baptism and similar measures, and devoted a special treatise to the refutation of the charge of ritual murder.

Wagenseil wrote, besides the above-mentioned books, "Hoffnung der Erlösung Israels" (Leipsic, 1705), which appeared in a second edition (Altdorf, 1707), augmented by a number of smaller works under the general title "Benachrichtigungen Wegen Einiger die Gemeine Jüdischheit Betreffenden Sachen." This collection contains the following treatises: (1) "Quomodo cum Judæo in Colloquio, Forte Fortuno Nato, Agendum"; (2) "Judæos non Uti Sanguine Christiano"; (3) "Quomodo Usura Judæorum Averti Possit"; (4) "De Precatione Judaica Olenu"; (5) "Denunciatio Christiana de Blasphemiis Judæorum in Jesum Christum"; (6) "Apologia"; (7) "Denunciatio ad Magistratus Christianos de Juribus Eorum a Judæis Violatis"; (8) "An Christianus Salva Religione Judæo Die Sabbati Inservire Possit." He wrote also: "Exercitationes Sex Varii Argumenti" (Altdorf, 1698); "Belehrung der Jüdisch-Deutschen Red- und Schreibart" (2d ed., Königsberg, 1699); "Disputatio Circularis de Judæis" (Altdorf, 1705); "Rabbi Moses Stendal's nach Jüdischer Rede-Art Vorlängst in Reimen Gebrachte Psalmen David's" (Leipsic, 1700); as well as an edition and Latin translation of the Talmudic treatise Soṭah (Altdorf, 1674).

BIBLIOGRAPHY: Wolf, *Bibl. Hebr.* ii. 1046; Grätz, *Gesch.* 3d ed., x. 274–276; Fürst, *Bibl. Jud.* iii. 489; Steinschneider, *Cat. Bodl.* cols. 2711–2713.

T.   E. N.

WAGER. See ASMAKTA; BETTING.

WAGES. See MASTER AND SERVANT.

WAGNER, WILHELM RICHARD (generally known as **Richard Wagner**): German composer of music; born at Leipsic May 22, 1813; died at Venice Feb. 13, 1883. He commenced the study of music at the University of Leipsic, but had a struggling existence till 1839, when he made the acquaintance of Meyerbeer, who assisted him in his attempts to have his operas produced in Paris. He came in contact also with Heine, who helped him with the libretto of "Der Fliegende Holländer." After much wandering he settled at Zurich in 1849, and there wrote an article, "Das Judenthum in der Musik," which appeared in the "Neue Zeitschrift" over the pen-name "K. Freigedenk." The article did not at first attract much attention, except a protest from eleven masters of the Leipsic Conservatorium to Brendel, the editor of the "Zeitschrift." Wagner protested against the tendency of music by Jewish composers like Mendelssohn and Meyerbeer to be sweet and tinkling without depth. In his "Oper und Drama" (1852) he makes the same protest against Meyerbeer. When the article "Das Judenthum in der Musik" was republished it drew forth numerous replies, among which may be mentioned: Joseph Engel, "Richard Wagner, das Judenthum in der Musik; eine Abwehr"; E. M. Oettinger, "Offenes Billetdoux an Richard Wagner," Dresden, 1869; and A. Truhart, "Offener Brief an Richard Wagner," St. Petersburg, 1869. Notwithstanding his public utterances against Jewish influence in music, Wagner had many Jewish friends; and his favorite choirmaster in later life was Herman Levi. See JEW. ENCYC. i. 643 b, *s.v.* ANTI-SEMITISM.

BIBLIOGRAPHY: Grove, *Dictionary of Music*, iv. 357–358; Glassenapp and Stein, *Wagner Lexikon*, s.v. *Judenthum*, Leipsic, 1883.

S.   J.

WAHB IBN MUNABBIH (Abu 'Abd Allah al-Ṣana'ani al-Dhimari): Mohammedan traditionist of Dhimar (two days' journey from Sanaa) in Yemen; died at the age of ninety, in a year variously given by Arabic authorities as 725, 728, 732, and 737 C.E. On his father's side he was descended from Persian knights, while his mother was a Himyarite. His father, whose name was Munabbih, had been converted to Islam in the lifetime of the Prophet, although a single authority, the "Al-Tibr al-Masluk" (ed. 1306 A.H., p. 41), states that Wahb himself had turned from Judaism to Mohammedanism. His other biographers, however, including Al-Nawawi and Ibn Ḥallikan, do not note that he was a Jew either in race or in religion. The fact that he was well versed in Jewish traditions, on which he wrote much, probably gave rise to the statement that he was a Jew, although he might have acquired his knowledge from his teacher Ibn 'Abbas. Wahb is said to have read more than seventy books on the prophets, and he was an extremely prolific narrator ("rawi") of stories regarding Mohammed and Biblical personages. Although the Mohammedans regarded him as a reliable authority in these accounts, many of them, such as Ibn Khaldun, declared that in his other writings he simply lied (comp. "Notices et Extraits des Manuscrits," xx.

part 1, p. 461; De Slane, Ibn Ḥallikan, iii. 673, note 2). Among Wahb's many writings may be mentioned his "Ḳiṣaṣ al-Anbiya" and "Kitab al-Isra'iliyat" ("Ḥajji Khalfa," iv. 518, v. 40). The former, which is believed to be his earliest literary work, is, as its title indicates, a collection of narratives concerning Biblical personages, the accounts being drawn from Jewish folk-lore though presented in Islamitic guise. Thus, like Ibn 'Abbas and Ka'b al-Aḥbar, he was an authority for many legends narrated by Al-Ṭabari, Mas'udi, and others. The "Kitab al-Isra'iliyat," or "Book of Jewish Matters," is lost, but was apparently a collection of Jewish stories, many of them incorporated by a Jewish compiler into the "Arabian Nights." In the latter collection there are indeed many stories that bear the Jewish stamp, and some of them, such as the "Angel of Death," are ascribed to Wahb by the author of "Al-Tibr al-Masluk." There are also other stories which are attributed to Wahb, and many more which, from their Jewish character, may be traced to him. His Jewish learning may be illustrated by his opinion of the Shekinah (Arabic, "Sakinah") as stated by different Arabic authors. According to Al-Baghawi in his "Ma'alim al-Tanzil" (Goldziher, "Abhandlungen zur Arabischen Philologie," i. 182, Leyden, 1896), Wahb believed that the Shekinah was the spirit of God. On the other hand, Al-Ṭabari ("Annals," i. 544), in recording the fact that the Israelites sometimes took the Ark of the Covenant into battle when they were at war with their enemies (comp. I Sam. iv. 4 et seq.), quotes Wahb as saying in the name of a certain Jewish authority that the Shekinah which rested in the Ark was a being in the shape of a cat, and that when the Israelites heard the mewing of cats coming from the interior of the Ark, they were sure of a victory. See also ARABIAN NIGHTS.

BIBLIOGRAPHY: V. Chauvin, La Récension Egyptienne des Mille et Une Nuits, pp. 31–32, 50 et seq., Brussels, 1899; Ibn Hallikan, French translation by De Slane, iii. 671 et seq.; Hammer-Purgstall, Literaturgesch. der Araber, ii. 177 et seq.; Brockelmann, Gesch. der Arabischen Litteratur, i. 64; Steinschneider, Die Arabische Literatur der Juden, § 14.

J.   M. SEL.

WAHL, ABRASKI. See WAHL, SAUL.

WAHL, MORITZ CALLMANN: German writer; born March 28, 1829, at Sondershausen; died Oct. 15, 1887. He studied Oriental languages at Leipsic under Julius Fürst and H. L. Fleischer. Later he taught for a time at an English school, and subsequently held the position of correspondent in a large business house at Lyons, France. Finally he settled at Erfurt, where he founded a business academy. Aside from his pedagogic activity Wahl pursued scientific studies. The following are the more important of his works: "Beiträge zur Vergleichenden Parömiologie"; "Das Sprichwort in der Hebräisch-Aramäischen Literatur"; "The Book of Merry Riddles"; "Das Sprichwort der Neueren Sprachen"; "Die Englische Parömiologie vor Shakespeare"; "Das Parömiologische Sprachgut bei Shakespeare."

S.   W. SA.

WAHL, SAUL: A remarkable personage who, according to tradition, occupied for a short time the throne of Poland. The story connected with his reign

is as follows: Prince Nicholas Radziwill, surnamed the Black, who lived in the sixteenth century, desiring to do penance for the many atrocities he had committed while a young man, undertook a pilgrimage to Rome in order to consult the pope as to the best means for expiating his sins. The pope advised him to dismiss all his servants and to lead for a few years the life of a wandering beggar. After the expiration of the period prescribed, Radziwill found himself destitute and penniless in the city of Padua, Italy. His appeals for help were heeded by nobody, and his story of being a prince was received with scorn and ridicule. He finally decided to appeal to Samuel Judah Katzenellenbogen, the rabbi of Padua. The latter received him with marked respect, treated him very kindly, and furnished him with ample means for returning to his native country in a manner befitting his high rank. When the time for departure came the prince asked the rabbi how he could repay him for his kindness. The rabbi then gave him a picture of his son Saul, who years before had left for Poland, and asked the prince to try and find the boy in one of the many yeshibot of that country. The prince did not forget the request. Upon his return to Poland he visited every yeshibah in the land, until finally he discovered Saul in that of Brest-Litovsk. He was so captivated by the brilliancy and depth of Saul's intellect that he took him to his own castle, provided for all his wants, and supplied him with all possible means for study and investigation. The noblemen who visited Radziwill's court marveled at the wisdom and learning of the young Jew, and thus the fame of Saul spread throughout Poland.

When King Bathori died (1586) the people of Poland were divided into two factions: the Zamaikis and the Zborowskis. There were quite a number of candidates for the throne, but the contending parties could agree upon no one. There existed at that time in Poland a law which stipulated that the throne might not remain unoccupied for any length of time, and that in case the electors could not agree upon a candidate an outsider should be appointed "rex pro tempore" (temporary king). This honor was then offered to Radziwill; but he refused, saying that there was a man who belonged to neither party, and who in wisdom and goodness was far superior to any one else he knew. That man possessed only one very slight shortcoming, and if the Diet would make his election unanimous, he (Radziwill) would acquaint it with his name. Accordingly, Saul's name was solemnly proposed; and amid great enthusiasm, and shouts of "Long live King Saul!" Wahl was elected to this high office. The name "Wahl" was given him from the German word "wahl" (= "election"). Traditions disagree as to the length of his reign. Some state that he ruled one night only; others make it a few days. All, however, are agreed that Saul succeeded in passing a number of very wise laws, and among them some that tended to ameliorate the condition of the Jews in Poland. Although this story can not be supported by any historical data, it gained a firm place in the belief of the people.

BIBLIOGRAPHY: Hirsch Edelman, Gedullat Sa'ul, London, 1844; S. A. Bershadski, Saul Wahl, in Voskhod, 1889; M. A.

Getzelten, *Po Povodu Legendi o Yevereie, Korolie Pols-kom*, in *Razsvjet*, 1880, No. 41; Eisenstadt, *Da'at Kedoshim*, p. 84; St. Petersburg, 1897-98; Karpeles, *Jewish Literature and Other Essays*, pp. 272-292, Philadelphia, 1895.
s.   J. Go.

WAHLTUCH, ADOLPHUS: English physician; born in Odessa, Russia, 1837. He studied medicine at Kiev, Prague, and London (M.D., L.R.C.P., 1863), and then settled in Manchester as a practising physician. He was known as a successful practitioner and as a prolific writer of professional works, among which may be mentioned: "A Dictionary of Materia Medica and Therapeutics," London, 1868; "On Catalepsy," *ib.* 1869; "Asthma Nervosum," Manchester, 1877; "Electro-Therapeutics," London, 1883; "Massage," 1889; "The Dead and the Living," 1891; "Treatment of Diseases by Energy," Manchester, 1900.

Wahltuch was consulting physician to the Victoria Jewish Hospital, and to the Hulme Dispensary, Manchester, and past president of the Clinical Society and of the Manchester Medico-Ethical Association. To the last-named association he has rendered valuable services as chairman of the Parliamentary Committee (1890–95). He was one of the founders of the Manchester Cremation Society, and was a frequent lecturer on hygiene and on scientific and historical subjects. He was an enthusiastic chess-player, edited the chess column in the "Manchester Weekly Times," and has founded several chess-clubs in the city of Manchester.

BIBLIOGRAPHY: De Gubernatis, *Diz. Biog.* Florence, 1879; *Manchester Faces and Places*, 1896.
J.   H. L. R.

WAHLTUCH, MARK: Russian philosopher and author; born at Odessa 1830; died at Pisa Jan. 27, 1901. He resided for many years in Ancona, Naples, Florence, Leghorn, and Pisa. He translated into Italian the works of A. Pushkin ("Poesie di A. Puschkin," Odessa, 1855), and wrote in Italian the following tragedies founded on Biblical subjects: "Assalonne," Odessa, 1857; "Sansone," *ib.* 1859; "Jefte," Milan, 1862; and "Giobbe," *ib.* 1872. He devoted himself to philosophical studies, and during his latter years to the investigation of spiritualism, the following works being the results of these activities: "Psicografia, Ossia Descrizione dell' Anima con Segni Sensibili, Preceduta da una Nuova Veduta Sopra Alcuni Punti Cardinali della Filosofia Obiettiva" (with illustrations), Naples, 1870; "L'Anima Umana nel Suo Stadio Oriundo, Terrestre e Futuro" (illustrated), Milan, 1875; "Antropobiotica Generale, Ossia la Vita dell' Anima e del Corpo nella Condizione Sana, Inferma, e Convalescente," Florence, 1879; and "Prove Incontestabili delle Pazzie d'un Pseudo-Alienista Appalesate" (against Cesare Lombroso), Leghorn, 1887.
s.   U. C.

WAHRHEIT, DIE. See PERIODICALS.

WAHRMANN, ISRAEL B. SOLOMON: Hungarian rabbi and Talmudist; born at Altofen, Hungary; died at Budapest June 24, 1824. He was called to the rabbinate of Pesth in 1799, and was the first officially recognized rabbi of the community, which developed rapidly under his leadership, its first statutes being drafted at his instance. The most important institution connected with his name

is the Nationalschule, an elementary school dedicated on Sept. 8, 1814, which was an important factor in raising the intellectual status of the community, its curriculum including Hungarian, modern science, and Hebrew. Wahrmann published only one sermon, in German and entitled "Andachtsübung der Israeliten der Königlichen Freistadt Pesth." The sorrow at his death found expression in Philip Weil's Hebrew and German poem "Evel Yisrael, oder Totenfeier."

BIBLIOGRAPHY: Reich, *Beth-El*, i. 123 *et seq.*; Büchler, *A Zsidók Története Budapesten*, pp. 380 *et seq.*
s.   E. N.

WAHRMANN, JUDAH: Hungarian rabbi; son of Israel WAHRMANN; born 1791; died at Pesth Nov. 14, 1868. He was appointed associate rabbi and teacher of religion at the gymnasium of Budapest on Feb. 9, 1851, and was the author of "Ma'areket ha-Ha'atakot" (Ofen, 1831) and "Dat Yehudah, Mosaische Religionslehre" (*ib.* 1861; 2d ed. 1868).

BIBLIOGRAPHY: Fürst, *Bibl. Jud.* iii. 490.
s.   E. N.

WAHRMANN, MORITZ: Hungarian politician; grandson of Israel WAHRMANN; born at Budapest Feb. 28, 1832; died there Nov. 26, 1892. He was educated at the Protestant gymnasium and the university of his native city, and entered his father's mercantile establishment in 1847, becoming its head after his father's death.

Wahrmann was closely associated with the development of Hungarian commerce and industry, the consolidation of the Hungarian finances, the growth of the educational and philanthropic institutions of Budapest, and preeminently with the progress of its Jewish community. Aiming to nationalize Hungarian commerce and to render his country independent of Austria, both financially and economically, he established large industrial and commercial enterprises.

Moritz Wahrmann.

In 1869 Wahrmann was elected to the Hungarian Parliament as the representative of the electoral district of the Leopoldstadt (at present the fifth district of Budapest), being the first Jew to be chosen a member of the Hungarian delegation, in which he energetically promoted the interests of Hungary. He was reelected six times, holding the office until his death. He spoke comparatively seldom, but was an active member of committees, in which his financial training frequently rendered him one of the most important figures. He was also president of the Chamber of Commerce and Industry of Budapest, and of the Lloyd Company.

Wahrmann was equally active in communal affairs, and was one of the foremost advocates of his coreligionists. He was a most zealous member of the Magyar Izraelita Egylet, and strove with tongue and pen for the emancipation of the Jews. In 1868 he was vice-president of the General Jewish Congress, and in this capacity headed a deputation to the king. As president of the community of Budapest he exercised a profound influence on its administration and institutions, and labored to establish unity of interest among the various political bodies. He also contributed generously from his ample means to scientific, educational, and philanthropic institutions.

His brother, **Alexander Wahrmann** (born 1839; died at Budapest in 1899), contributed much, together with Max Wirth, the Viennese political economist, toward the economic elevation of Hungary. He was especially noteworthy as a philanthropist, bequeathing 200,000 crowns to the benevolent societies of the capital, and 600,000 crowns for the erection of a Jewish gymnasium.

BIBLIOGRAPHY: Vasárnapi Ujság, 1892, pp. 825 et seq.; Magyar Zsidó Szemle, 1892, pp. 687 et seq.; 1893, pp. 7 et seq.; Pallas Lex. xvi. 973.
s. E. N.—L. V.

WAKRULKAR, SOLOMON ELIJAH: Beni-Israel soldier; enlisted in the Nineteenth Regiment Native (Indian) Infantry Sept. 25, 1838. He was promoted jemidar Jan. 1, 1853; subahdar, Jan. 22, 1858; subahdar-major, Jan. 1, 1872. In 1877 he was decorated with the first and second class Order of British India, with the titles of bahadur and sirdar-bahadur, the highest mark of approbation which the Indian government bestows on native officers. He fought in the Afghanistan campaign of 1839, including the capture of Ghazni and occupation of Kabul (medal); in the Punjab campaign, taking part in the siege of Multan, the battle of Gujarat, and the march to the mouth of the Khaibar Pass; and in the Central India campaign of 1858. In his various campaigns he marched up and down both banks of the Indus from Kurrachee to Kabul and Attock. Wakrulkar retired from active service Dec. 23, 1878.

J. J. HY.

WALDEN, AARON BEN ISAIAH NATHAN: Polish Talmudist, editor, and author; born at Warsaw about 1835. Walden, who was an ardent adherent of Hasidism, was known especially for his "Shem ha-Gedolim he-Ḥadash" (Warsaw, 1864), a work of the same nature as Azulai's "Shem ha-Gedolim." Like the latter, it consists of two parts: (1) "Ma'areket Gedolim," being an alphabetical list of the names of authors and rabbis, mostly those that lived after Azulai, but including also many of the seventeenth and eighteenth centuries who were omitted by Azulai; and (2) "Ma'areket Sefarim," an alphabetical list of book-titles. Walden himself says in his preface that he took Azulai's "Shem ha-Gedolim" as a model; and it is evident that he refers to Benjacob's edition of that work. It must be said that the alphabetical list in the first part is arranged only according to the first names of the persons mentioned. In many instances the names are accompanied by biographical sketches, especially of Ḥasidic rabbis, whose biographies contain records of the miracles wrought by them and in behalf of them. To the third edition of the work, published in 1882 by Walden's son Joseph Aryeh Löb, the latter added an appendix entitled "'En Zoker," con-

taining names and book-titles omitted in the two previous editions.

Another work by Walden, in which he has displayed great erudition, is the "Miḳdash Melek" (Warsaw, 1890), an edition of the Psalms in five volumes. In it are printed around the text: (1) "Bet ha-Midrash," a kind of yalḳuṭ after the model of the "Yalḳuṭ Shim'oni," Walden having gathered all the haggadot referring to the Psalms which were scattered in the Talmudim, in the midrashic literature, and in the Targum, as well as in the Zohar and other cabalistic works; (2) "Bet ha-Keneset," a fourfold commentary ("PaRDeS") consisting of material taken from the most prominent ancient commentators; and (3) "Bet Aharon," a reference index to the "Bet ha-Midrash," giving also variants and an explanation of difficult passages.

BIBLIOGRAPHY: Steinschneider, Hebr. Bibl. viii. 108; Zeitlin, Bibl. Post-Mendels. p. 403.
E. C. M. SEL.

WALDENBURG, LOUIS: German physician; born at Filehne, Posen, July 31, 1837; died at Berlin April 14, 1881; educated at the University of Berlin (M.D. 1860). After a postgraduate course at Heidelberg he established himself in Berlin as a specialist in diseases of the chest and throat. From 1864 to 1868 he was joint editor with H. Rosenthal of the "Allgemeine Medizinische Central-Zeitung." In 1865 he became privat-docent at the Berlin University, and from 1868 until his death he edited the "Berliner Klinische Wochenschrift." In 1871 he was appointed assistant professor, and in 1877 department physician, at the Charité.

Among Waldenburg's many works may be mentioned: "De Origine et Structura Membranarum, Quæ in Tuberculis Capsulisque Verminosis Involucrum Præbent," a prize essay at the University of Berlin, 1859; "Ueber Blutaustritt und Aneurysmenbildung, Durch Parasiten Bedingt," in "Archiv für Anatomie und Physiologie," 1860; "Ueber Structur und Ursprung der Wurmhaltigen Cysten," in "Archiv für Pathologische Anatomie und Physiologie und für Klinische Medizin," 1862; "Lehrbuch der Respiratorischen Therapie," Berlin, 1864 (2d ed. 1872); "Die Tuberkulose, die Lungenschwindsucht und Scrofulose," ib. 1869; and "Die Pneumatische Behandlung der Respirations- und Circulations-Krankheiten," ib. 1875 (2d ed. 1880).

BIBLIOGRAPHY: Pagel, Biog. Lex.
s. F. T. H.

WALDOW, B. See BLOCH, BIANCA.

WALDSTEIN, CHARLES (WALSTON): Anglo-American archeologist; born in New York March 30, 1856. He was educated at Columbia College, New York city (A.M. 1873), and studied also at Heidelberg (Ph.D. 1875) and finally at Cambridge, England (M.A. and Litt.D. 1878). In 1880 he became university lecturer on classical archeology at Cambridge University, and two years later university reader. From 1883 to 1889 he was director of the Fitzwilliam Museum; and in 1883 he was made a fellow of King's College. In 1889 he was called to Athens, Greece, as director of the American School of Classical Studies, which office he held until 1893, when he became professor at the same institution. In 1895 he returned to England as Slade professor of fine arts at the University of Cambridge; and he held this chair until 1901. During his stay in Athens he directed the excavations of the American Archeological Institute at the site of ancient Platæa, Eretria, where, he declared, he unearthed the tomb of Artistotle, the Heræum of Argos, etc. He has formed an international committee to promote the excavation of Herculaneum.

Waldstein is the author of: "Balance of Emotion and Intellect" (1878); "Essays on the Art of Phidias" (1885); "The Jewish Question and the Mission of the Jews" (1889, anon.; 2d ed. 1900); "The Work of John Ruskin" (1894); "The Study of Art in Universities" (1895); "The Expansion of Western Ideals and the World's Peace" (1899); "The Argive Heræum" (1902); "Art in the Nineteenth Century" (1903). He has written also in several journals numerous reports on his excavations, and has published, under the pseudonym "Gordon Seymour," three short stories which later appeared, under his own name, as "The Surface of Things" (1899).

BIBLIOGRAPHY: *American Jewish Year Book*, 5665.
J.   F. T. H.

WALDTEUFEL, EMILE: French composer; born at Strasburg Dec. 9, 1837. He commenced the study of music under the tuition of his father, a professional musician; later he became the pupil of Joseph Heyberger; and he completed his musical education at the Conservatoire in Paris. Here he pursued his studies on the piano in company with Massenet, a fellow pupil, who soon became his firm friend. About 1860, being obliged to discontinue his studies owing to lack of means, he turned his attention to dance-music. "Manolo," a waltz performed under his direction at a soirée given by the Prince of Sagan, was a great success; and it so delighted the Prince of Wales (later Edward VII.), who was present, that he requested the dedication of the piece to himself, and had it published in England. In a short time Waldteufel received brilliant offers from the English publishers of music; and his fame and fortune were thenceforth assured. His triumphs in London were soon followed by similar ones in Paris. In 1865 he was appointed pianist to the empress Eugénie. He became director of the court balls of the emperor Napoleon III., and organizer of the famous soirées at Compiègne and Biarritz. At the latter place he met Bismarck.

During the Franco-Prussian war (1870–71) Waldteufel enlisted as a volunteer in the legion of the Basses-Pyrénées. Upon the defeat of the French cause he returned to Paris and devoted himself with renewed ardor to his art. Of his most celebrated works may be mentioned: "Amour et Printemps," a waltz so universally popular that, after fourteen years of repeated publication by two firms, it was purchased by a third for the sum of 8,000 francs; "A Toi, Dolores"; "Dans les Nuages"; "Dans un Songe"; "Je T'Aime"; "Myosotis"; "Pour une Rose"; "Retour du Printemps"; "Sentiers Fleuris"; "Soir d'Amour"; "Les Sourires"; "Toujours ou Jamais"; "Doux Poëme"; "Les Violettes"; "L'Espace"; and the polka "Bella Bocca."

In 1885 Waldteufel was summoned to London to direct the performance of his compositions. There he met with a triumphant success, which was repeated four years later at Berlin, whither he went for a similar object. For three successive weeks the three great composers Fahrbach, Strauss, and Waldteufel personally directed the execution of their respective waltzes. Waldteufel has won renown also as an orchestra leader, particularly at the "Bals de l'Opéra." He was a chevalier of the Royal Order of Isabella the Catholic. He died in 1915.

BIBLIOGRAPHY: Le Petit *Poucet*, No. 12.
s.   J. KA.

WALEY, JACOB: English lawyer and professor of political economy; born in London March 17, 1819; died there June, 1873. He was the elder son of Solomon Jacob Levy (who adopted the name of Waley), and was educated at Neumegen's school at Highgate and at University College, London, where he was the first pupil to obtain the Flaherty Mathematical Scholarship. In 1839 he was graduated (B.A.) from the University of London, taking the first place in both mathematics and classics. He was entered as a student at Lincoln's Inn on Nov. 3, 1837, and was called to the bar Nov. 21, 1842, being the fourth Jew to be thus called.

Waley became one of the most eminent conveyancers of his day. His first studies in conveyancing were conducted in the chambers of Duval; and he was also a pupil of Holt, afterward lord chief justice. Waley practised as an equity draftsman; he acted as conveyancing counsel for the Bedford estates, and was named by the queen in 1867 a member of the royal commission appointed to consider the law on the transfer of real property. In this capacity he had a large share in framing the report on which was based the lord chancellor's bill passed in 1874. He was associate editor with Davidson of a work on conveyancing precedents, and attained the distinction of becoming (1870) one of the conveyancing counsel of the Court of Chancery.

Waley was president of the Jews' Orphan Asylum, and on the formation of the Anglo-Jewish Association he was elected its first president. His numerous engagements, however, compelled his early retirement from the latter position. He promoted the Hebrew Literary Society, was for a long period a member of the council of Jews' College, and aided materially in the organization of the Jewish Board of Guardians. But his greatest service to the Jewish community was his formation, in conjunction with Lionel Louis Cohen, of the United Synagogue, to which object he devoted his professional skill, eloquence, and careful judgment. He took much interest also in the treatment of Jews abroad; and in 1872 he wrote a brief preface to Israel Davis' "Jews in Rumania," in which he remonstrated against the persecution of his coreligionists.

In 1853 Waley was appointed professor of political economy at University College, London, which office he held until 1865, when the pressure of other engagements compelled him to resign. He was an active member of the governing body of the university, and was secretary of the Political Economy Club, as also of the Statistical Society. On his resignation he was named professor emeritus by the council of University College. Waley also acted as examiner for the University of London.

BIBLIOGRAPHY: *Times* (London), June 23, 1873; *Jew. Chron.* and *Jew. World*, June 27 and July 4, 1873; *Dictionary of National Biography*.
J.
G. L.

WALEY, SIMON WALEY: English merchant, musician, and communal worker; born in London Aug. 23, 1827; died there Dec. 30, 1875; younger son of Solomon Jacob Levy. He studied at University College, London, but left without taking a degree. At the age of seventeen he wrote a series of articles for the "Times" on the question of international traffic, and in 1858 he contributed to the "Daily News" a series of letters on "A Tour in Auvergne," afterward included in Murray's "Handbook to France." Waley entered the stock exchange and acquired an influential position, being elected a member of its committee. For nearly a quarter of a century he was honorary secretary of the Jews' Free School, and conducted the entire correspondence between the school and the government Board of Education. From 1843 he was the official correspondent for England of the chamber of commerce of Boulogne, in which city he took great interest.

Waley received instruction in piano from Moscheles, Sir William Sterndale Bennett, and G. Alexander Osborne, and in theory and composition from William Horsley and Molique. The first musical work published by Waley was "L'Arpeggio," a pianoforte study, which appeared in 1848. His other compositions include a pianoforte concerto, two pianoforte trios, many piano pieces and songs, and some orchestral pieces. He composed also hymns for Sabbaths and festivals, several of which were chanted for many years at the West London Synagogue. His songs include "Sing on, Ye Little Birds," "The Home of Early Love," and "Alpine Shepherds' Song."

BIBLIOGRAPHY: *Jew. Chron.* Jan. 7, 14, and 21, 1876; *Impartial* (Boulogne), Jan. 21, 1876; *Dict. National Biography*; Gross, *Dict. of Music and Musicians*.
J.
G. L.

WALLACHIA. See RUMANIA.

WALLERSTEIN, ABRAHAM BEN ASHER: German scholar and rabbi of the eighteenth century; officiated in Schnaittach, Bavaria. He was the author of the following works: "Ma'amar Abraham" (Fürth, 1757), Hebrew sermons on the weekly lessons of the entire Pentateuch; "Zera' Abraham" (*ib.* 1761), an ethical work in eighteen chapters, written according to Biblical as well as rabbinical principles; and "Maḥazeh Abraham" (*ib.* 1761), an index to the four ritual codices, arranged alphabetically. The last-named work was published in connection with the "Zera' Abraham."

BIBLIOGRAPHY: Steinschneider, *Cat. Bodl.* col. 711; Benjacob, *Oẓar ha-Sefarim*, p. 279.
E. C.
S. O.

WALLICH: German family which probably derived its name from the Hebrew transcription of "Falk" (וולק). The earliest known members of it are Joseph b. Meïr Wallich, a physician, and Moses Joshua Wallich, both of whom lived at Worms in the sixteenth century. A document relating to the purchase by Joseph b. Meïr Wallich of a Rashi and Rashbam manuscript (Worms, 1615) is signed by Joseph and by his two sons Eliezer and Solomon, all physicians and all surnamed Weibush (Phoebus?), and by thirteen other members of the Wallich family, among them the physicians Moses b. Lezer and Moses b. Moses Joshua (surnamed Weibelin). Many physicians of the Wallich family were prominent in Germany in the eighteenth century.

Subjoined is an abbreviated pedigree:

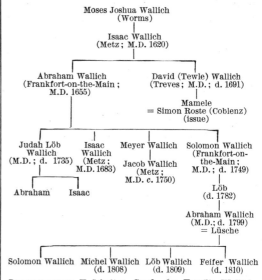

BIBLIOGRAPHY: H. Schultze, *Gesch. der Familie Wallich*; *Monatsschrift*, 1905, *passim*.
J.

The following are the more important members:

Abraham ben Isaac Wallich: Physician; born at Metz; flourished at Frankfort-on-the-Main in the second half of the seventeenth century. He went to Padua to study medicine, obtaining his diploma, "maxima cum laude," in 1655; and in 1657 he went to Frankfort to practise as a physician. He was the author of a Hebrew treatise on medicine entitled "Sefer Refu'ot," or, as he called it in Latin, "Harmonia Wallichis Medica" (published posthumously, Frankfort-on-the-Main, 1700). He tried to prove that the ailments of the soul correspond to those of the body and that they must be treated in the same way. In this work he speaks alternately as a physician and as a preacher of morals.

Immanuel Wallich: Rabbi and physician of Coblenz in the eighteenth century.

Joseph b. Meïr Wallich: Physician; the earliest known member of the family; flourished at Worms in the sixteenth and seventeenth centuries. He is known to have written in 1597, on a manuscript of Isaac Israeli's translation of Ibn al-Yazzar's "Zad al-Musafir," a bibliographical note in which he confounded the translator with Isaac ben Joseph Israeli. From this and from what has been said above it may be concluded that Joseph b. Meïr was a collector of medical and rabbinical manuscripts. He had in his possession also a copy of Bernard de Gordon's "Sefer ha-Gebulim" (see Neubauer, "Cat. Bodl. Hebr. MSS." No. 2125, 4), the first leaf of which was supplied in his own handwriting.

Judah ben Abraham Wallich: Physician; lived at Frankfort-on-the-Main in the seventeenth and eighteenth centuries. He was the author of: (1) "Dimyon ha-Refu'ot" or "Harmonia Wallichis Medica Animæ et Corporis" (Frankfort-on-the-Main, 1700), a Judæo-German compendium of his father's "Sefer Refu'ot," supplemented by a treatise on fever in children. (2) "Ẓori ha-Shamayemah" (Latin title, "Theriaca Cœlestis Wallichiana"; German, "Himmlischer Theriak"; *ib.* 1713). Of this work only the German preface and the first Hebrew section are extant; the remainder, which was destroyed by fire, was not published. (3) "Dankfest" (*ib.* 1716), a thanksgiving memorial in pure German with Hebrew characters; written on the occasion of the birth of Archduke Leopold of Austria (April 13, 1716).

Moses b. Eliezer Wallich: Scholar; lived at Worms in the seventeenth century. He was the author of "Sefer Meshalim" or "Kuh-Buch" (Frankfort-on-the-Main, 1687), a German collection of fables adapted from Berechiah ha-Naḳdan's "Mishle Shu'alim" and Isaac ibn Sahulah's "Mashal ha-Ḳadmoni." This book is not to be confounded with a similar work by ABRAHAM B. MATTATHIAS which bears the same title.

Naphtali Hirz b. Abraham Wallich: Physician; lived at Metz in the seventeenth century; brother of Judah ben Abraham Wallich. He is known as having been the competitor of Solomon b. Baruch of Lippstadt, who was appointed physician to the Jewish community of Metz. Solomon delayed his arrival, and consequently the community appointed Naphtali Hirz in his stead. When Solomon reached Metz a quarrel arose between the two physicians, Solomon urging his letter of appointment, and Naphtali Hirz his priority. They continued quarreling until 1695, when they were reconciled by R. Gabriel Eskeles of Metz.

Solomon Wallich: Physician of Mayence, where he died May 11, 1780; son of Immanuel Wallich. Like his father, Solomon received a rabbinical education in addition to his medical training.

BIBLIOGRAPHY: A. Berliner, in *Hebr. Bibl.* vii. 82–83; Carmoly, *Histoire des Médecins Juifs*, pp. 200, 207; Fürst, *Bibl. Jud.* iii. 492; Steinschneider, *Cat. Bodl.* cols. 1377–1378, 2008; idem, *Hebr. Uebers.* pp. 704, 959; Horovitz, *Jüdische Aerzte*, pp. 30–32; Landau, *Gesch. der Jüdischen Aerzte*, p. 116.

D.   M. SEL.

WALLIS (VALAIS). See SWITZERLAND.

WALLS (חיל, קיר, חמה): The walls erected by the Canaanites for the protection of their farmyards consisted of great unhewn blocks of stone, and remnants of them still exist, especially in the east-Jordan district. Walls of fortifications and towns were similar in structure, although many large cities may have had ramparts of hewn stone. Unburned bricks were also used for walls, and the excavations at Tell al-Ḥasi (Lachish) have brought to light brick walls between nine and ten feet thick. Less thick are the walls at Tell el-Mutasallim (Megiddo), which show a combination of both materials, the base being of unhewn stone, on which layers of brick are laid. The dimensions of the bricks at Megiddo are about 50 × 33 × 13 cm., and the size of the Canaanite walls filled the Israelites with alarm (Num. xiii. 28; Deut. i. 28).

The construction of walls of unhewn stone was long retained by the Israelites, so that, although Solomon built the outer wall of his palace of hewn stone (I Kings xii. 12), the description of the structure (*ib.* verses 9–11) shows that this was not the usual style of architecture, but an extraordinary innovation which aroused the admiration of his contemporaries. Herein, moreover, is seen the influence of the Tyrians, who designed the palace of Solomon, for Phenician architecture is characterized by its partiality for large blocks of hewn stone. The choice of material was doubtless conditioned primarily by the locality, since in the mountains there was no lack of stone, while in the plains bricks were used for houses and even for the walls.

The walls were generally broad, for the defenders stood on them (comp. Isa. xxxvi. 11; Neh. xii. 31; I Macc. xiii. 45), and engines of war were also placed thereon (II Chron. xxvi. 15). Battlements (שמשות, פנות [Isa. liv. 12] probably has a similar meaning) were likewise built to protect the guards (II Chron. *l.c.*). Strong towers were constructed at the corners and gates, as well as on the wall itself at intervals. The entrance was built in an angle, as may still be seen at Jerusalem; and the inner and outer gates were closed with doors covered with iron plates and fitted with iron bolts. A low bulwark (חיל; Isa. xxvi.; Ps. xlviii. 14 [A. V. 13]) with a protective glacis was frequently constructed at some distance before the main wall. See also FORTRESS; HOUSE; TOWER.

E. G. H.   I. BE.

WALOZIN. See VOLOZHIN.

WALTON, BRYAN: Christian Hebraist; born in 1600 at Hilton, Yorkshire, England; died in London Nov. 29, 1661; educated at Magdalene and Peterhouse colleges, Cambridge. He became a London clergyman and was involved in the question of tithes raised by John Selden, but was appointed king's chaplain, and, after being imprisoned by the Parliamentarians, went to Oxford to join the king. There he formed the project of issuing a polyglot Bible, better and cheaper than the one that had appeared at Paris as late as the year 1645. In 1652 he issued a circular on the subject, and subscriptions were obtained under the patronage of Selden and Ussher. The work, which was in six volumes, was published between 1654 and 1657 in nine languages, though no single book appears with more than eight versions. Much of the work was done by Castell, who compiled the Heptaglot Lexicon as a supplement to the Polyglot. Walton's prolegomena were printed as a separate work both in Germany (Leipsic, 1777) and in England (Canterbury, 1828).

The "Biblia Sacra Polyglotta" was one of the earliest books printed by subscription in England, the price being £10 for the six volumes. Walton dedicated his work to the Parliament; but when Charles II. came to the throne, the dedication was changed to one in honor of the king, who appointed Walton Bishop of Chester in 1660. Walton's Polyglot has been the standard work up to the present day; but its texts scarcely meet the requirements of modern scholarship.

BIBLIOGRAPHY: *Dict. National Biography.*

T. J.

WANDERING JEW: Imaginary figure of a Jerusalem shoemaker who, taunting Jesus on the way to crucifixion, was told by him to "go on forever till I return." The legend first appeared in a pamphlet of four leaves entitled "Kurtze Beschreibung und Erzählung von einem Juden mit Namen Ahasverus." This professes to have been printed at Leyden in 1602 by Christoff Crutzer, but no printer of that name has been discovered, and the real place and printer can not be ascertained. The legend spread quickly throughout Germany, no less than eight different editions appearing in 1602; altogether forty appeared in Germany before the end of the eighteenth century. Eight editions in Dutch and Flemish are known; and the story soon passed to France, the first French edition appearing in Bordeaux, 1609, and to England, where it appeared in the form of a parody in 1625 (Jacobs and Wolf, "Bibliotheca Anglo-Judaica," p. 44, No. 221). The pamphlet was translated also into Danish and Swedish; and the expression "eternal Jew" is current in Czech. The pretended existence of the Wandering Jew, who is stated to be met with from time to time in all of these countries, was eagerly seized upon amidst the religious disturbances caused by the Reformation, as furnishing an eye-witness of the crucifixion. The various appearances claimed for him were at Hamburg in 1547; in Spain in 1575; at Vienna, 1599; Lübeck, 1601; Prague, 1602; Lübeck, 1603; Bavaria, 1604; Ypres, 1623; Brussels, 1640; Leipsic, 1642; Paris, 1644; Stamford, 1658; Astrakhan, 1672; Frankenstein, 1676; Munich, 1721; Altbach, 1766; Brussels, 1774; and Newcastle, 1790. The last appearance mentioned appears to have been in America in the year 1868, when he was reported to have visited a Mormon named O'Grady (see "Deseret News," Sept. 23, 1868).

The figure of the doomed sinner, forced to wander without the hope of rest in death till the millennium, impressed itself upon the popular imagination, and passed thence into literary art, mainly with reference to the seeming immortality of the wandering Jewish race. These two aspects of the legend are represented in the different names given to the central figure. In German-speaking countries he is referred to as "Der Ewige Jude" (the immortal, or eternal, Jew), while in Romance-speaking countries he is known as "Le Juif Errant" and "L'Ebreo Errante"; the English form, probably because derived from the French, has followed the Romance. The Spanish name is "Juan Espera en Dios." The legend has been the subject of poems by Schubart, Schreiber (1807), W. Müller, Lenau, Chamisso, Schlegel, Julius Mosen (an epic, 1838), and Koehler; of novels by Franzhorn (1818), Oeklers, and Schucking; and of tragedies by Klinemann ("Ahasuerus," 1827) and Zedlitz (1844). Hans Andersen made his "Ahasuerus" the Angel of Doubt, and was imitated by Heller in a poem on "The Wandering of Ahasuerus," which he afterward developed into three cantos. Robert

Influence of Legend on Literature.

Hamerling, in his "Ahasver in Rom" (Vienna, 1866), identifies Nero with the Wandering Jew. Goethe had designed a poem on the subject, the plot of which he sketched in his "Dichtung und Wahrheit."

In France, E. Quinet published his prose epic on the legend in 1833, making the subject the judgment of the world; and Eugene Sue wrote his "Juif Errant" in 1844. From the latter work, in which the author connects the story of Ahasuerus with that of Herodias, most people derive their knowledge of the legend. Grenier's poem on the subject (1857) may have been inspired by Gustav Doré's designs published in the preceding year, perhaps the most striking of Doré's imaginative works. In England —besides the ballad given in Percy's "Reliques" and reprinted in Child's "English and Scotch Ballads" (1st ed., viii. 77)—there is a drama entitled "The Wandering Jew, or Love's Masquerade," written by Andrew Franklin (1797). William Godwin's novel "St. Leon" (1799) has the motive of the immortal man, and Shelley introduced Ahasuerus into his "Queen Mab." George Croly's "Salathiel," which appeared anonymously in 1828, treated the subject in an imaginative form; it has been recently reprinted under the title "Tarry Thou Till I Come" (New York, 1901).

According to L. Neubaur, the legend is founded on the words given in Matt. xvi. 28, which are indeed quoted in the earliest German pamphlet of 1602. So, too, from John xxi. 20 *et seq.* a legend arose in the Church that St. John would not die before the second coming of Jesus; while another legend declares that the attendant Malchus, whose ear St. Peter cut off in the garden of Gethsemane (John xviii. 10), was condemned to wander till the second coming. His action is associated in some way with the scoffing at Jesus, and is so represented in a broadsheet which appeared in 1584. An actual predecessor of the Wandering Jew is recorded in the "Flores Historiarum" by Roger of Wendover in the year 1228. An Armenian archbishop, then visiting England, was asked by the monks of St. Albans about the celebrated Joseph of Arimathea, who had spoken to Jesus, and was still alive. The archbishop answered that he had himself seen him in Armenia, and that his name was Cartaphilus; on passing Jesus carrying the cross he had said: "Go on quicker," Jesus thereupon answering: "I go; but thou shalt wait till I come." Matthew Paris included this passage from Roger of Wendover in his own history; and other Armenians appeared in 1252 at the Abbey of St. Albans, repeating the same story, which was regarded there as a great proof of the Christian religion (Matthew Paris, "Chron. Majora," ed. Luard, London, 1880, v. 340–341). The same archbishop is said to have appeared at Tournai in 1243, telling the same story, which is given in the "Chronicles of Phillip Mouskes," ii. 491, Brussels, 1839. According to Guido Bonnati, the astrologer known to Dante, this living witness of the crucifixion was known as Johannes Buttadæus because of his having struck Jesus. Under this name he appears at Mugello in 1413 and in Florence in 1415 (S. Morpurgo, "L'Ebreo Errante in Italia," Florence, 1891).

Origin of Legend.

It is difficult, however, to connect this Carta-philus, Buttadæus, or Buttadeo with the later Ahasuerus of the pamphlet of 1602, no trace being found either in popular legend or in literature during the intervening two centuries. Graetz supposes that the somewhat different picture given of the Wandering Jew in a book called "The Turkish Spy" (1644), in which work the Wandering Jew is called "Sieur Paule Marrana," and is said to have passed through the tortures of the Inquisition in Spain, Portugal, and Rome, was derived from a Marano author (see, however, Boswell's "Life of Johnson," under date April 10, 1783, and Malone's note). Moncure D. Conway attempts to connect the legend with others of immortal beings, as those of King Arthur, Frederick Barbarossa, and Thomas the Rhymer, not to speak of Rip Van Winkle. These again he connects with immortals visiting the earth; as Yima in Parsism, and the "ancient of days" in the books of Daniel and Enoch. Yima and Enoch, as well as Elijah, are also credited with immortality; but there is no evidence of any connection of these names with the legend of the Wandering Jew which, as stated above, was put into currency in 1602 in Germany, by some one who was acquainted with the earlier form of the story known only in literary sources from Matthew Paris.

BIBLIOGRAPHY: G. Paris, *Le Juif Errant*, Paris, 1881; M. D. Conway, *The Wandering Jew*, London, 1881; H. Graetz, in *Papers of the Anglo-Jewish Historical Exhibition*, pp. 1–4; Basnage, *Histoire des Juifs*, v. 1834–1836, Rotterdam, 1707; Graesze, *Der Tannhäuser und der Ewige Jude*, Dresden, 1861; Jacob Bibliophile, in *Curiosités des Croyances Populaires*, pp. 105–141, Paris, 1859; Neubaur, *Die Sage vom Ewigen Juden*, 2d ed., Leipsic, 1893.
J.

WANDSBECK: Town in Sleswick-Holstein, near Hamburg. About the year 1600 Count Breido Rantzau, owner of the estate of Wandsbeck, allowed Jews to settle there in consideration of a small yearly payment for protection. Many Jews availed themselves of this permission, attracted by the town's proximity to Hamburg, where Jews were not allowed to settle at that time. According to a document of Nov. 10, 1637, Berend of Hagen, called Geist, feudal tenant of the Danish crown estate of Wandsbeck, ceded to the Jews a plot for a cemetery and permitted them "to perform their prayers and other rituals according to their customs."

In 1674 the community of Wandsbeck formed together with those of Altona and Hamburg the "union of the three communities," acknowledging as its spiritual head the chief rabbi of Altona, the first being R. Hillel ben Naphtali. The three communities continued united until 1811 (see ALTONA; HAMBURG). Wandsbeck had to pay one-eighth of the chief rabbi's salary, Altona paying five-eighths, and Hamburg one-fourth. In 1688 the Jews of Wandsbeck obtained the right to receive into their congregation Jews living elsewhere, a payment being exacted for their protection. They made use of this privilege by forming a branch community in Hamburg, which soon became larger than the original community at Wandsbeck. Since 1710, when German Jews received unrestricted permission to settle in Hamburg, the community of Wandsbeck has diminished rapidly. Its relations with the communities of Altona and Hamburg were not always

the best. In 1773 the Wandsbeck community was put under ban for having evaded payment of its share of the communal expenses for the support of the poor. Rabbi Jacob Emden was called upon to settle this dispute.

For a list of the rabbis who officiated during the union of the three communities, from R. Solomon Mirels Neumark (d. 1706) to R. Zebi Hirsch Zamosz (d. 1807), see ALTONA. After the dissolution of the union in 1811, Wandsbeck remained under the rabbinate of Altona until the community in 1864 engaged Dr. Hanover (d. 1901) as its minister; he was succeeded by S. Bamberger, the present incumbent.

An official list of the members of the Wandsbeck community compiled in 1734 contains the names of 123 families (exclusive of unmarried members and widows). In 1905 there were about sixty Jewish families in the town.

BIBLIOGRAPHY: *Nachrichten von der Geschichte und Verfassung des Adlichen Gutes Wandsbeck*, Hamburg, 1773; Haarbleicher, *Zwei Epochen aus der Geschichte der Deutsch-Israelitischen Gemeinde Hamburgs*, ib. 1867; E. Dukesz, *Iwwah le-Moshab*, Cracow, 1903; M. Grunwald, *Hamburgs Deutsche Juden bis zur Auflösung der Dreigemeinden*, ib. 1903.
D. A. FE.

WANDSWORTH, LORD, SIDNEY STERN: English banker and peer; born in London 1845; son of Viscount de Stern, senior partner of the firm of Stern Brothers. He was educated at Magdalene College, Cambridge, and was for some time a member of the firm established by his father. He has, however, retired from business, and in 1905 he was a justice of the.peace for Surrey and London, an honorary colonel of the Fourth Volunteer Battalion of the East-Surrey Regiment, and vice-president of the London and Counties Radical Union. After several attempts to enter Parliament he was elected in May, 1891, by the Stowmarket division of Suffolk, which he represented until elevated to the peerage in 1895. He died Feb. 12, 1912. He was also a Portuguese viscount by hereditary right.

BIBLIOGRAPHY: *Jew. Chron.* Aug. 5, 1892; *Jewish Year Book*, 5665.
J. G. L.

WANEFRIEDEN, ELIAKIM GETSCHLIK: Dayyan and preacher in Amsterdam about the end of the eighteenth century. He published a pamphlet entitled "Megillat Sefer" (Amsterdam, 1790), containing some homilies, besides a eulogy of R. Saul Löwenstamm, chief rabbi of Amsterdam. His family name points to Wannfried in Hesse as his birthplace, but he is not identical with the Eliakim Getschlik Wanefrieden who was rabbi in Kanitz, Moravia, about 1760 ("Die Deborah," 1902, pp. 70–71). The latter was probably the father of Jeremiah ben Eliakim Getschlik Wanefrieden, rabbi in Rausnitz, Moravia, and one of those who defended Jonathan EYBESCHÜTZ against the charge of heresy ("Luḥot 'Edut," p. 29a, Altona, 1755).

BIBLIOGRAPHY: Fürst, *Bibl. Jud.* iii. 493.
D.

WAR.—Biblical Data: The earliest war recorded in the Old Testament is that of the Elamitic king Chedorlaomer and his allies against the five kings of Sodom and its adjacent cities (Gen. xiv. 1

et seq.). The result of the conflict was the destruction of the vanquished army in the field and the captivity of all the non-combatants, whose possessions became spoils of war. In the battle the troops were arranged in order (Gen. xiv. 8, R. V.), and the King of Sodom and his four allies displayed a certain degree of strategy by fighting in a valley, although their plan proved unsuccessful. Some modern scholars infer from the obscure passage II Sam. xi. 1 that wars were regularly begun in the spring.

Details. In many instances negotiations were carried on through messengers or ambassadors to avert bloodshed (Judges xi. 12–28; I Sam. xi. 1–10; I Kings xx. 2–11); and the Hebrews were expressly forbidden to make an attack without first demanding the surrender of the enemy (Deut. xx. 10 *et seq.*). The only instance in which war was declared without previous negotiations was that of the war between Amaziah, King of Judah, and Jehoash, King of Israel (II Kings xiv. 8).

In addition to the various modes of DIVINATION employed by all the nations before setting out for war (comp. Ezek. xxi. 26 *et seq.*), the Israelites consulted YHWH, who was not only their divinity, but also the war-god par excellence (comp. Ex. xv. 3, and the frequent phrase יהוה צבאות), deciding whether they should begin the war and whether they would be successful (Judges i. 1; xx. 18, 23). In these passages the manner of consultation is not indicated, but from other sections and from the Septuagint it may be inferred that the priest put on the ephod and stood before the Ark to consult the Urim and Thummim (Judges xx. 27–28; I Sam. xiv. 18, xxviii. 6, xxx. 7). Occasionally the divinities were consulted through dreams or prophets, or even through familiar spirits evoked by a witch (Judges vii. 13; I Sam. xxviii. 6 *et seq.*; I Kings xxii. 15). Troops were generally summoned by the blowing of a trumpet or the war-horn, which was likewise the signal that warned the people of an enemy's approach (Judges iii. 27; II Sam. xx. 1; comp. Ezek. xxxiii. 2–11), although sometimes banners were placed on the tops of high mountains or messengers were sent through the different tribes of Israel (Judges vii. 24; I Sam. xi. 7; Isa. xiii. 2). Occasionally extraordinary means were used to arouse a popular feeling of indignation which would ultimately impel the nation to make war, as in the case of the Levite who cut the body of his concubine into twelve parts and sent them to the other tribes of Israel, thus kindling between them and the Benjamites the war which resulted in the destruction of the latter tribe (Judges xix. 29 *et seq.*; comp. also I Sam. xi. 7).

The War-Priest. The army of the Israelites was always accompanied to the field by a priest, Phinehas having this post in the battle with the Midianites (Num. xxxi. 6). It was the duty of the priest to care for the spiritual welfare of the soldiers and, before the attack, to encourage them and to inspire martial enthusiasm in them (Deut. xx. 2–4). Sometimes, however, the high priest himself went upon the field, where he attended the Ark, which was carried into action quite as idols and images were borne into battle by the Philistines (I Sam. iv. 3–4; II Sam. v.

21, xi. 11). Like other Semites, the Israelites began a war with burnt offerings and fasting (Judges vi. 20, 26; xx. 26; I Sam. vii. 9, xiii. 10), this explaining the frequency of the phrase "to sanctify war," and the epithet "sanctified" as applied to warriors (Micah iii. 5; Isa. xiii. 3; Jer. vi. 4, xxii. 7). A single instance is recorded, though in obscure terms, of a human sacrifice as a burnt offering in a time of extreme danger (II Kings iii. 27). According to a passage of D, furthermore, the officers of the Hebrew troops were required to proclaim before a battle that whosoever had betrothed a wife and had not taken her, or had built a house and had not dedicated it, or had planted a vineyard and had not eaten of it, or was fearful and faint-hearted, should return home (Deut. xx. 5–9). This regulation was actually carried out under the Maccabees (I Macc. iii. 56), which shows that the document is of a post-exilic date.

From the geographical condition of Palestine, the raid was the favorite mode of warfare both among the Hebrews and among the other Semites (Gen. xlix. 19; I Sam. xiii. 17, xxvii. 8; II Sam. iii.

Raids. 22; II Kings xiii. 20), although in the course of time regular battles were fought, and in certain cases tactics of modern warfare were employed. The first instance recorded was in the battle of Gibeah between the tribes of Israel and the Benjamites (Judges xx. 30 *et seq.*). After laying an ambush behind the city, the Israelites pretended to flee from the Benjamites, thus enticing the latter from their fortified positions. Suddenly the Israelites wheeled, and the Benjamites found themselves outflanked on all sides. It is also probable that in the battle of Gilboa between the Philistines and the army of Saul, the Philistines resorted to strategy by striking northward at the plain of Esdraelon instead of attacking the Israelites by the shorter route from the southwest. By this device, which proved completely successful, the Philistines lured Saul's army from the valleys, where a stout defense could be offered, to the open plain, where the Israelites might be overwhelmed by sheer force of numbers (I Sam. xxviii. 1–xxxi. 7). A strong army was sometimes divided so that the enemy might be attacked from different directions (Gen. xiv. 15; II Sam. xviii. 2), and ambuscades were often used with success (Josh. xiii. 10–28; Judges xx. 30–44; II Kings vi. 8–9). Night marches were particularly in favor with the Hebrews; thus Joshua marched at night, Gideon assailed the Midianites about midnight, and Saul attacked the Ammonites before dawn (Josh. x. 9; Judges vii. 19; I Sam. xi. 11). It may be noted that night marches were made by other Semites as well, for Nebo was captured from the Israelites by Mesha, King of Moab, after such a march (Moabite Inscription, line 15). An instance is likewise recorded in which the Philistines chose a champion who challenged one of the opposing army to a duel to decide the fate of both forces (I Sam. xvii. 4 *et seq.*). Such proceedings were afterward much in vogue among the Arabs in their pre-Islamic tribal conflicts.

Fortresses played an important part in war, especially in defense. In early times the Israelites were unable to reduce the fortified cities of the inhabitants of the land, and consequently had no means of defense except to hide themselves in caves or mountains (Judges vi. 2; I Sam. xiii. 6; comp. Isa. ii. 21); but in the regal period they **Fortresses.** became so proficient in the art of warfare that they not only reduced the fortresses of the enemy, beginning with Jerusalem (II Sam. v. 7 *et seq.*), but also built many fortified cities. The chief method of reducing one of these towns seems to have been to throw up around the walls a bank, from which the archers might shoot their arrows into the place; while an instance is recorded from an earlier period in which the gates of a city were set on fire (Judges ix. 48 *et seq.*). According to a marginal note on I Kings xx. 12, R. V., the Syrians used engines in their effort to reduce Samaria, while similar machines were frequently employed in addition to the battering-ram for breaching walls in the time of Ezekiel (Ezek. iv. 2, xxvi. 8-9). The strength of the walls and the efficiency of the beleaguering army naturally conditioned the length of a siege. Thus Jericho, which fell in consequence of a miracle, was taken after a continuous onslaught of seven days (Josh. vi. 3 *et seq.*), but the Syrian sieges in Samaria were doubtless lengthy since they entailed terrible famines, and Jerusalem was captured by the Babylonians only after a siege of two years, despite the systematic operations of Nebuchadnezzar (II Kings xxv. 1-4). In their sieges the Hebrews were forbidden to fell fruit-trees for use in building bulwarks against the fortified city (Deut. xx. 19-20).

The accounts of wars in the patriarchal period show that the conquered peoples were reduced to captivity and their property was taken as spoils of war. In the case of the Shechemites, all the males were massacred by the sons of Jacob, while the women and children and all their possessions were carried off as booty (Gen. xxxiv. 25-29). Later, according to a document belonging to D (Deut. xx. 10-17), the Hebrews were commanded to make a wide distinction between the inhabitants of the land whom they were to replace and the Gentiles outside the land. Mildness was to be shown the latter in case they surrendered without fighting and submitted to pay tribute. If they were subdued by force of arms, however, every man was to be slain, **Treatment** while the women, children, cattle, and **of** all else should belong to the victors. **Captives.** Far different was to be the treatment of the inhabitants of the land, who were to be slaughtered without exception, not even the cattle being left alive. If this passage is of early date, it is evident that the command with regard to the inhabitants of the land was only partially executed, since, excepting the thirty-one kings enumerated in Josh. xii. 9-24, the greater part remained unconquered, and the Israelites were obliged to live with the very Gentiles whom they had been bidden to exterminate (comp. Josh. xviii. 2-3; Judges i. 21-35). Even when the Israelites proved victorious, they often granted the inhabitants their lives, and subjected them only to tribute (Judges i. 28, 30, 33, 35). At a later period, however, gross cruelty was practised both by the Hebrews and by the other nations. After having defeated the Moabites, David cast them down to the

XII.—30

ground and measured them with a line, putting to death two lines and keeping one alive (II Sam. viii. 2), while he put the Ammonites under saws, harrows, and axes of iron and made them pass through the brick-kiln (*ib.* xii. 31). Menahem, King of Israel, the Syrians, and the Ammonites are charged with the massacre of pregnant women (II Kings viii. 12, xv. 16; Amos i. 13); and Amaziah is described as causing ten thousand Edomite captives to be hurled from a cliff (II Chron. xxv. 12), while in some instances children were dashed against rocks (Ps. cxxxvii. 9).

There are instances of treaties of peace in which conditions were imposed by the victors on their defeated foes. The first treaty recorded is that which Nahash, King of Ammon, proposed to the people of Jabesh-gilead, and which was marked **Conditions** by the savagery of the Ammonite **of Peace.** king, the terms being that the right eye of every inhabitant of the city should be put out (I Sam. xi. 2). A treaty which might almost have been made in modern times, on the other hand, was drawn up between Ben-hadad and Ahab; by it the cities previously captured from Israel were to be restored, while Ahab had the right of making streets in Damascus, the same conditions having been previously imposed on the father of Ahab by Ben-hadad's father (I Kings xx. 34). Sennacherib, in the treaty with Hezekiah by which he withdrew his army from Judah, exacted a heavy indemnity from the Jewish king (II Kings xviii. 14). The victors generally returned home in triumphal processions and celebrated their victories with songs and festivals (Judges v. 1 *et seq.*, xi. 34, xvi. 23; comp. Prism Inscription, col. 1, line 53, in Schrader, "K. B.," ii. 141 *et seq.*).

The wars in the earlier period were religious in character and thus had the sanction of the Prophets. Deborah herself urged Barak to make war on Sisera and accompanied him into the field (Judges iv. 6 *et seq.*), while Elisha exhorted Joash, King of Israel, to prosecute the war with Syria and advised the allied kings to avail themselves of stratagem **Attitude of** against the Moabitish army (II Kings **the** iv. 16 *et seq.*, xiii. 14-19), and an anon- **Prophets.** ymous prophet encouraged Ahab to battle with Ben-hadad (I Kings xx. 13-14). Naturally the Prophets were opposed to war among the tribes of Israel, and when Rehoboam wished to resort to arms to recover his lost sovereignty over the ten tribes, he was prevented by the prophet Shemaiah (*ib.* xii. 21-24). In later times the Prophets considered war from a political point of view, and Jeremiah, seeing that hostilities against the Babylonians would be to the detriment of the Israelites, always advised the latter to submit to the stronger people and live in peace with them (Jer. xxvii. 12 *et passim*). War in general was represented by the Later Prophets only in its horrible aspect, and many of them, particularly Isaiah, longed for the time when there would be no more war, and when weapons should be transformed into agricultural implements (Isa. ii. 4; Micah iv. 3; and elsewhere). See ARMY; FORTRESS.

——**In Rabbinical Literature:** The Rabbis laid special stress on the distinction between obligatory war ("milḥemet miẓwah," or "milḥemet ḥobah") and voluntary war ("milḥemet ha-reshut"). The former category comprised the campaigns against the seven nations who inhabited the land, the battles against Amalek, and the repulse of an enemy attacking an Israelitish city; while the latter class denoted any war waged for the extension of Jewish territory. Obligatory war had the priority, nor was it necessary for the king to ask the permission of the Sanhedrin to levy troops, since he could compel the people to take the field. Voluntary war, on the other hand, could be declared only by the Great Sanhedrin of seventy-one members. Although certain persons were permitted by Deut. xx. 5 et seq. to leave the field before a battle began, this was allowed, according to rabbinical opinion, only in case of a voluntary war. No such leave of withdrawal was granted in an obligatory war, but, on the contrary, even a bridegroom and bride were obliged to leave their nuptial chamber and join the army (Soṭah 44b; Sanh. 2a, 20b; Maimonides, "Yad," Melakim, v. 1-2). The Rabbis differed greatly regarding the terms of peace to be offered the inhabitants of a beleaguered city (Deut. xx. 10 et seq.). According to Sifre, Deut. 199, which was followed by Rashi (on Deut. l.c.), peace might be proposed only in a voluntary war, while in an obligatory war no terms should be allowed. It would appear, however, from Lev. R. xvii. 6 and Deut. R. v. 13 that peace might be offered even in an obligatory war, and this was established as a law by Maimonides (l.c. vi. 1; comp. Naḥmanides on Deut. l.c.). According to both Maimonides and Naḥmanides, the command of extermination which was imposed regarding the seven nations (Deut. xx. 16-17) was applied only in case the beleaguered people refused to surrender. The submission in consideration of which the conquered were granted their lives had to be complete, since they were required to accept the seven commandments of the Noachidæ, and were obliged to pay tribute and to recognize their condition of servitude (Maimonides, l.c.).

In direct opposition to the obvious interpretation of Deut. xx. 5-9, the Rabbis declared that all the proclamations contained in that passage were made by the priest anointed as the chaplain of the army ("meshuaḥ milḥamah"), and the verses were interpreted as meaning that the priest made the proclamations and the officers repeated them to the troops, who could not hear the priest (Soṭah 43a; Maimonides, l.c. vii. 1, 4; comp. Sifre, Deut. 193). A Jewish army was forbidden to begin the siege of a Gentile city less than three days before the Sabbath, but it might continue its operations on that day even in a voluntary war. The army was permitted to encamp in any place, and the slain soldiers were to be buried in the place where they had fallen, since the combat had made it their own.

The Jewish soldiers enjoyed four privileges: they might take wood anywhere without incurring the charge of robbery; they were permitted to eat fruit even though it was not certain that it had been properly tithed ("demai"); and they were exempt from washing their hands and from " 'erube ḥazerot " (Shab. 19a; 'Er. 17a; Tosef., 'Er. iv. [iii.] 7; see also 'ERUB). In besieging a Gentile city, the troops

were commanded to invest it on three sides and to leave one side free so that any one who wished might escape from the town (Maimonides, l.c. vi. 7). During the seven years consumed by Joshua's conquest of Palestine the Israelitish soldiers were allowed to eat any food which they found in the houses of the Gentiles, even though such provisions were forbidden under all other circumstances (Ḥul. 17a; Maimonides, l.c. viii. 1).

E. C.   M. Sel.

WARBURG : Family whose members are widely spread throughout Germany, Denmark, Sweden, England, and America. There is a tradition that the family was originally settled at Bologna, but emigrated to the Westphalian town of Warburg, whence it removed to Altona, near Hamburg.

The earliest known bearer of the name is **Levi Joseph Warburg**, whose son **Jacob Samuel** died in 1667 at Altona. From him are descended two branches, one through **Samuel Moses Warburg** (died 1759), known also as "Frankfurter," and the other through **Samuel Reuben Warburg** (died 1756), whose grandson **R. D. Warburg** (1778-1847) founded the firm of Warburg in Hamburg. Samuel Moses Warburg had four sons: from the eldest, **Moses** (died 1752), are descended the present branch at Altona and the Copenhagen family of **Delbanco**, which adopted that surname. The second, **Gumprich** (died 1801), was the father of **Moses Marcus Warburg** (died 1830), who founded the firm of Moses Marcus Warburg & Co., of Hamburg. The third, **Elia Samuel Warburg**, said to have been a teacher of mathematics in Altona, took part in the Emden-Eybeschütz quarrel. He was the founder of two large branches of the Warburg family. **Samuel Elias Warburg** (died 1826) was the ancestor of most of the Hamburg and American Warburgs of to-day. The youngest son of Elia, **Simon Elias Warburg** (1760-1828), settled in Göteborg as a merchant, founding there a branch of his brother Samuel's firm at Hamburg. He was one of the founders of the Göteborg synagogue, and his two sons, **Samuel** (1800-81) and **Michael**, were the first Jews permitted to enter the public service in Sweden. The former married Emma Glückstadt, his cousin, and was a writer on economic subjects, and a member of the Board of National Debt Department from 1867 to 1879. He was decorated with the Order of the North Star in 1860 (" Nordisk Familjebok," xvii.).

The following members of the family have distinguished themselves: **Moritz Gumprecht Warburg**, who settled at Manchester as a merchant, but showed literary taste, and published Shakespeare's sonnets in German; **Carl Simon Warburg**, third son of Samuel Warburg (1835-65); he was the editor of "Svensk Monadsskrift," in which Mill's and Darwin's works were first presented to the Swedish public; **Frederick Elias Warburg**, second son of Samuel Warburg (born at Stockholm in 1832; died in London in 1899); as a director of the Electric Traction Company he was one of the founders of the Central London Electric Railway; **Moritz Warburg** (born in 1810 at Altona; died there in 1886), who was educated for the law, and ultimately became "Justizrat" and represented Altona in the

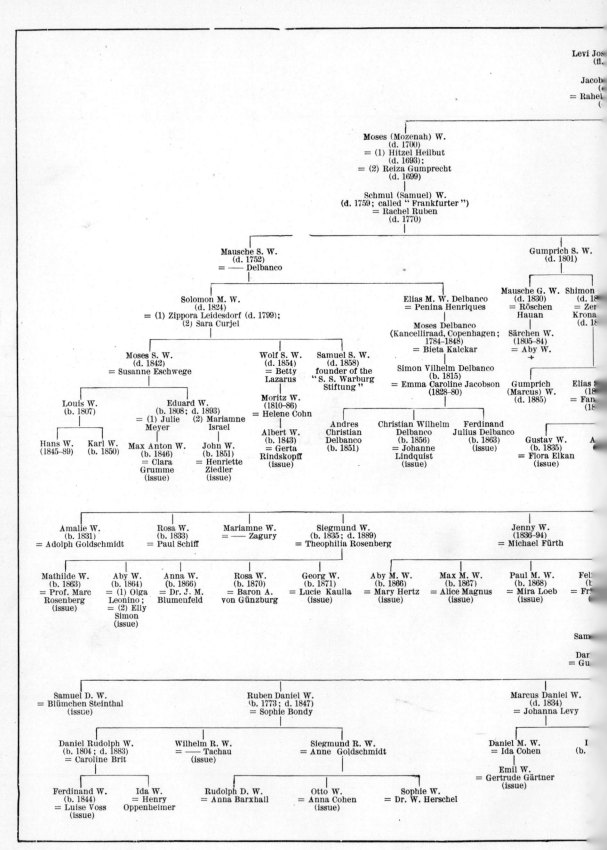

Levi Jos... (fl. ...)

Jacob... (...)
= Rahel... (...)

Moses (Mozenah) W.
(d. 1700)
= (1) Hitzel Heilbut (d. 1693);
= (2) Reiza Gumprecht (d. 1699)

Schmul (Samuel) W.
(d. 1759; called " Frankfurter ")
= Rachel Ruben (d. 1770)

Mausche S. W. (d. 1752) = —— Delbanco

Gumprich S. W. (d. 1801)

Solomon M. W. (d. 1824)
= (1) Zippora Leidesdorf (d. 1799); (2) Sara Curjel

Elias M. W. Delbanco = Penina Henriques
Moses Delbanco (Kancelliraad, Copenhagen; 1784–1848) = Bieta Kalckar
Simon Vilhelm Delbanco (b. 1815) = Emma Caroline Jacobson (1828–80)

Mausche G. W. (d. 1830) = Röschen Hauan
Särchen W. (1805–84) = Aby W. +

Shimon (d. 18...) = Zer... Krona... (d. 18...)

Moses S. W. (d. 1842) = Susanne Eschwege
Wolf S. W. (d. 1854) = Betty Lazarus
Samuel S. W. (d. 1858) founder of the "S. S. Warburg Stiftung"

Moritz W. (1810–86) = Helene Cohn
Albert W. (b. 1843) = Gerta Rindskopff (issue)

Gumprich (Marcus) W. (d. 1885)
Elias ... (18..) = Fan... (18..)

Louis W. (b. 1807)
Eduard W. (b. 1808; d. 1893) = (1) Julie Meyer (2) Mariamne Israel

Hans W. (1845–89)
Karl W. (b. 1850)
Max Anton W. (b. 1846) = Clara Grumme (issue)
John W. (b. 1851) = Henriette Ziedler (issue)

Andres Christian Delbanco (b. 1851)
Christian Wilhelm Delbanco (b. 1856) = Johanne Lindquist (issue)
Ferdinand Julius Delbanco (b. 1863) (issue)

Gustav W. (b. 1835) = Flora Elkan (issue)
A...

Amalie W. (b. 1831) = Adolph Goldschmidt
Rosa W. (b. 1833) = Paul Schiff
Mariamne W. = —— Zagury
Siegmund W. (b. 1835; d. 1889) = Theophilia Rosenberg
Jenny W. (1836–94) = Michael Fürth

Mathilde W. (b. 1863) = Prof. Marc Rosenberg (issue)
Aby W. (b. 1864) = (1) Olga Leonino; = (2) Elly Simon (issue)
Anna W. (b. 1866) = Dr. J. M. Blumenfeld
Rosa W. (b. 1870) = Baron A. von Günzburg
Georg W. (b. 1871) = Lucie Kaulla (issue)
Aby M. W. (b. 1866) = Mary Hertz (issue)
Max M. W. (b. 1867) = Alice Magnus (issue)
Paul M. W. (b. 1868) = Mira Loeb (issue)
Fel... (b...) = Fr... (...)

Sam...
Dar... = Gu...

Samuel D. W. = Blümchen Steinthal (issue)
Ruben Daniel W. (b. 1773; d. 1847) = Sophie Bondy
Marcus Daniel W. (d. 1834) = Johanna Levy

Daniel Rudolph W. (b. 1804; d. 1883) = Caroline Brit
Wilhelm R. W. = —— Tachau (issue)
Siegmund R. W. = Anne Goldschmidt
Daniel M. W. = Ida Cohen
I... (b....)

Emil W. = Gertrude Gärtner (issue)

Ferdinand W. (b. 1844) = Luise Voss (issue)
Ida W. = Henry Oppenheimer
Rudolph D. W. = Anna Barxhall
Otto W. = Anna Cohen (issue)
Sophie W. = Dr. W. Herschel

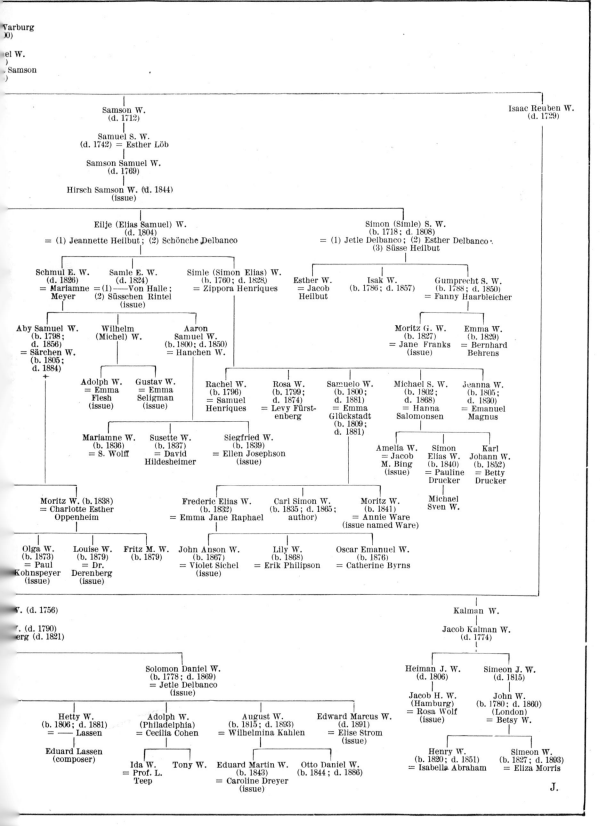

Reichstag· Moritz's second son, **Jacob** (born 1848), who was killed in battle during the Franco-Prussian war; and Moritz's eldest son, Albert (born 1843), who has been appointed "Commerzienrat."

Of the London branch, founded by **Mendel Martin Warburg** (born 1789; died 1877), the younger son, **James,** has settled at Manchester, where he is known as a musician. **Moses Delbanco** (born 1784; died 1848) attained the distinguished position of "Cancelliraad" at Copenhagen. **Aby Warburg** (born 1866) is known as an art critic and historian. **Karl Johann Warburg** (born in 1852 at Stockholm) is a historical and biographical writer of importance, has been appointed librarian of the Nobel Institute, and is a member of the Upper House of Sweden. **Otto Warburg** studied at Berlin, where he is now professor of natural history, and is prominent in the Zionist movement. **Emil Warburg** is a professor at Freiburg and Charlottenburg. One of the daughters of **Marcus Warburg** married R. Lassen, and her son was the composer and musical director, **Eduard Lassen.**

Felix M. Warburg (born in 1871 at Hamburg) settled in New York, where he joined the firm of Kuhn, Loeb & Co. He is at present (1905) commissioner of education in the city of New York, and is also one of the trustees of the Jewish Theological Seminary of America.

One of the striking features of the family history of the Warburgs is the practically world-wide extent of their wanderings and ultimate distribution, the following places being mentioned in their pedigree:

Altona	Melbourne	Stockholm
Glückstadt	Göteborg	Cassel
Grindel	Copenhagen	South America
Hamburg	Wandsbeck	Havana
London	Philadelphia	Leeds
India	Tokyo	Göttingen
Holstein	Shanghai	Hanau
Berlin	Lüneburg	Paris
Hanover	Manchester	New York
Freiburg		

Equally remarkable is the variety of occupations which the various members of this family have taken up or married into. Among those mentioned may be enumerated:

Saddlemaker	Paper manufacturer	"Commerzienrat"
"Cancelliraad"	Stationer	"Justizrat"
Merchant	Ribbon merchant	Soldier
Banker	Joiner (wholesale)	Photographer
Bookseller	Shoḥeṭ	Company director
Horsehair-dealer	Shawl manufacturer	Doctor
Clock manufacturer	Tobacconist	Librarian
Book censor	Lieutenant, R. N.	Editor
Art critic	Musician	Naturalist
Wool dyer		Professor
Author		Composer
Consul		

J.

Moritz Warburg: German jurist; born at Altona June 8, 1810; died there April 15, 1886. He studied at the colleges of Wolfenbüttel and Altona, and at the universities of Heidelberg and Kiel. His studies completed, he settled in Altona, where he practised law for over forty years; in 1879 he was appointed a counselor of justice. Warburg's name is connected with the stirring events of 1848, in which year he was elected to the Sleswick-Holstein constituent assembly, remaining a member of that body for twenty-two consecutive years.

Bibliography : *Jew. Chron.* April 23, 1886.
S.   L. R.

Otto Warburg: German botanist; born in Hamburg July 20, 1859. From 1879 to 1883 he studied at the universities of Bonn, Berlin, and Strasburg. Having graduated from the last-named university, he continued his studies at Munich and Tübingen; and from 1885 until 1889 he traveled through southern and eastern Asia. He settled in Berlin and became privat-docent in botany at the university in 1891. In the following year he was appointed teacher of tropical botany and agriculture at the Oriental Seminary, and received the title of professor in 1897. A few years ago Warburg began to interest himself in Jewish agricultural colonization, for which purpose he visited the East in 1900, 1901, and 1903; and he founded the first Jewish settlements in Asia Minor. He worked as an active administrative member of the Esra, an organization for the agricultural movement among the German Jews, and in connection therewith founded in Palestine the Neuhof Agricultural Society.

Warburg is the author of: "Monographie der Myristicaceen," in "Nova Acta Leopoldina," vol. 58 (1897)—the De Candolle prize essay; "Die Muskatnuss, Ihre Geschichte, Botanik, Kultur, Handel-Verwertung" (Leipsic, 1897); "Pandanaceæ," part iii. of "Pflanzenreich" (*ib.* 1900); "Die Kautschukpflanzen und Ihre Kultur" (Berlin, 1901); "Monsunia, Beiträge zur Kenntniss der Vegetation des Süd- und Ostasiatischen Monsungebietes" (Leipsic, 1901); "Die Kunene-Sambesi Expedition," 1903, published by the Colonial Agricultural Committee in Berlin.

From 1897 to 1903 Warburg was the publisher and editor of "Der Tropenpflanzer," a journal of tropical agriculture and the organ of the Colonial Agricultural Committee. He is besides one of the principal collaborators on the Zionistic periodicals "Palästina" and "Altneuland." Warburg is also chairman of the Palestine Commission of the Zionist Congress and a member of the smaller Actions Comité.

S.

WARNING. See Hatra'ah.

WARRANTY OF TITLE : The Hebrew term for warranty of title is אחריות (= "future"), the same word denoting the force of an attested deed which served as a mortgage on all lands owned by the debtor at the time of its delivery. Whenever lands or slaves were sold by deed, it was customary to insert a clause by which the seller bound himself to reimburse the buyer for any loss arising from a bad or defective title. The custom must have been very ancient; for similar clauses, which were frequently quite elaborate, are found in some of the oldest deeds of conveyance among the Assyrians and Babylonians. Warranty of title was implied, however, in every sale, whether of slaves, land, or chattels (Maimonides, "Yad," Mekirah, xix. 3; Shulḥan 'Aruk, Ḥoshen Mishpaṭ, 225), thus agreeing with the Talmudic saying (B. M. 15b) that an omission of the warranty was regarded as a mere oversight of the draftsman and was supplied by the courts. The parties to the sale were accordingly required to make a special agreement to exempt the seller from all responsibility, such a document releasing him from every claim against him, even if goods had been sold him which were later claimed by the true owner, who had been deprived of them by robbery. The most dangerous flaw in the title seems to have been an outstanding bond against the seller, or against his grantor or ancestor, thus affording an opportunity to levy for debt on the thing sold.

The warranty secured the buyer not only against the loss of his lands or slaves, but also against the payment of mesne profits (אכילת פירות), which he might otherwise have had to give the true owner for withholding possession; but the covenant of warranty, as far as it covered this uncertain and unliquidated liability, could be levied only on "free property," not on "subjected property" (see DEED). The Mishnah refers incidentally to mesne profits and to their inclusion in a warranty (Giṭ. v. 3), and thus limits the remedy (see TORT). The codes held that the ordinary and the implied warranty of title could be broken and give rise to a suit against the warrantor only in case the buyer was evicted or compelled to pay a bond debt by a Jewish court, although either the decision of a Gentile court or an adverse title appearing on the records kept by the Gentiles was to be deemed an overpowering force. Such a force might, however, have a special protective warranty, just as the seller might warrant against the loss of his field through the action of a neighboring river.

E. C.   L. N. D.

WARRENS, ROSA: Swedish poet and translator; born at Karlskrona Feb. 24, 1821; died at Copenhagen Nov. 8, 1878. At the age of five she went with her parents to Hamburg, where she remained until her father's death in 1861. She then moved to Berlin with her mother, and after the latter's death in the summer of 1878, she settled at Copenhagen. She devoted herself chiefly to Swedish literature and Norse mythology, translating into German the northern folk-songs in the original meters. The fruits of these studies were the following volumes: "Swedische Volkslieder der Vorzeit" (1856); "Dänische Volkslieder" (1858); "Schottische Volkslieder" (1861); "Zwei Lieder der Edden" (1863); "Norwegische Volkslieder," "Isländische Volkslieder," and "Finnische Volkslieder" (1868). A volume of her original poems appeared in 1873.

BIBLIOGRAPHY: *Allg. Deutsche Biographie*; Franz Brümmer, *Deutsche Dichter und Prosaisten des Neunzehnten Jahrhunderts*; Lina Morgenstern, *Die Frauen des Neunzehnten Jahrhunderts*.

S.   R. N.

WARS OF THE LORD, BOOK OF THE (ספר מלחמת יהוה): A work mentioned in a single passage of the Old Testament (Num. xxi. 14) in connection with the geographical position of Arnon. The title suggests that the book contained songs celebrating the victories of the Israelites led by YHWH, and it seems, therefore, to have been similar to the Book of JASHER or possibly even identical with it, though there is no evidence to support the latter hypothesis. Modern scholars regard Num. xxi. 17-18, 27 *et seq.* as extracts from the same book (comp. Naḥmanides on Num. xxi. 14); and since

some of the facts there mentioned refer to an epoch far subsequent to the Mosaic period, the last citation being supposed by Stade ("Gesch. des Volkes Israel," i. 50) to refer to the time of Omri's dynasty, the date of its composition is variously placed in the ninth century B.C. or in the reigns of David and Solomon (Reuss, "Gesch. der Heiligen Schrift," p. 172). It must be noted, however, that the Septuagint, reading מלחמת יהוה, renders the title of the book Πόλεμος τοῦ Κυρίου, and refers its contents to one particular war of YHWH. The verse which is said to be extracted from the book is extremely obscure, and the words את והב בסופה in particular are variously but unsatisfactorily interpreted. The Septuagint renders them τὴν Ζωὸβ ἐφλόγισε, apparently reading את זהב שרף, which is unintelligible in meaning, though it evidently contains some allusion to Dizahab. Jerome, following Onḳelos, translated את והב "he did," although it rather means "he gave." Among Jewish commentators only Ibn Ezra and Naḥmanides postulated the existence of a "Book of the Wars of YHWH"; according to the former the work had been written before the time of Abraham. They also advanced the theory that Waheb was the name of a place where the Israelites had waged wars against their enemies. The Targumim understood "the book" to denote the "Pentateuch" and interpreted the passage as meaning: "Therefore it is said in the Book, the wars which YHWH," etc., while Rashi and RaSHBaM translated בספר "in the act of narrating." Sayce ("The Academy," Oct. 22, 1892) follows the Targumim in the general translation of the passage, except that he adopts the Septuagint reading זהב instead of והב, and he accordingly disposes of the theory that such a book ever existed.

S.   M. SEL.

WARSAW: Former capital of the Russian government of the same name, and since 1918 the capital of the republic of Poland; situated on the left bank of the Vistula. According to Polish writers, the earliest settlement of Jews in Warsaw dates from the thirteenth century, and their influence at that time is indicated by a number of documents in Hebrew script preserved in the local archives. They at first resided on the Jewish street near the present Dunai street, whence they spread to other quarters of the city, acquiring houses and lands, possessing a cemetery, and owning a synagogue near St. John's Church.

As in other cities, their growing influence awakened commercial and social antagonism among the citizens. The Christian merchants endeavored to rid themselves of their Jewish competitors by insisting on the strict application of the MAGDEBURG LAW, and continued their propaganda with varying success until 1525, when Prince Janush of Mazovia issued a decree which forbade the Jews to reside in Warsaw or to pursue mercantile or industrial occupations in the city. This measure was not strictly enforced, however, for two years later Sigismund I. was obliged to issue a similar decree with an additional clause which debarred the Jews from residence even in the suburbs of Warsaw. This decree likewise proved ineffective, since the Jews who were driven from the city itself settled just beyond the walls, waiting for more favorable legislation which would permit them to return. By this expedient they were still enabled to secure an important portion of the city trade, but in 1570 Sigismund Augustus issued a more drastic decree containing the following provisions:

Provisions of Sigismund Augustus. (1) No Jew, Jewess, Jewish child or servant (be the latter Jewish or Christian) shall dwell with property or wares on any lands, municipal, royal, or clerical, within the limits of Old Warsaw or New Warsaw, nor may he or she remain there even during royal sojourns, excepting only at the time of the Diets, when Jews shall be permitted to visit Warsaw for business purposes. (2) The Jews who have business connections in Warsaw shall be allowed to sojourn there with the written consent of the magistrate; but they shall not have the right to engage in any trade or handicraft which may in any way interfere with the daily pursuits of the citizens. (3) The Jews shall have no right to reside on any grounds, or to trade or ply their handicrafts, within a radius of two miles from Warsaw on either bank of the Vistula, under penalty of confiscation. (4) It shall be the duty of the magistrates and their successors at Warsaw to enforce the removal of the Jews from the city and its environs without regard to any extenuating circumstances or even to letters of exemption from the king or his successors.

The commercial importance of the Jews as agents of the king and higher nobility, as well as the annual sessions of the Diets in Warsaw, rendered it impracticable to execute this ordinance, and the repeated protests and machinations of the Christian gilds were unavailing, at least so far as a large number of Jewish merchants was concerned. Petitions for the exclusion of the Jews from Warsaw and its suburbs were very frequent; and in 1580 King Stephen Bathori issued an edict forbidding the Jews to reside in Warsaw or to lease city taxes or property. Those Jews who were obliged to come to Warsaw on business had to secure a special permit from the city magistrates. It is evident that these laws were enforced under Ladislaus IV., for on July 16, 1646, Marcus Neckel obtained the title of " general Jewish delegate " in Warsaw. In 1648 Ladislaus reaffirmed the earlier restrictive decrees, although he made an exception in favor of Neckel, ordering that "Marcus, the Jewish delegate and royal agent, shall not be molested or ridiculed." The subsequent royal decrees of 1663, 1676, 1737, 1740, 1761, 1763, and 1770 confirmed the provisions of the earlier edicts. It is evident, therefore, that the exclusion of the Jews from Warsaw, like their expulsion from Riga and other cities, was never wholly effective. Deprived of the right of permanent residence, they secured immunity and exemption by purchasing the good-will of the city magistrates, while, on the other hand, the Christian merchants frequently paid bribes to the city magistrates for the exclusion of their Jewish competitors. Thus in 1691, when preparations were being made for the wedding of the crown prince Jacob Sobieski, which was to be attended by many guests, the merchants of Warsaw paid ten silver thalers to the great crown marshal, and gave lemons and oranges to the value of 54 Polish gulden, in order that intercession might be made with the king to withhold protection from the Jews.

Royal Decrees. In the reign of August III., Crown Marshal Franciszek Bielinski enforced the restrictive measures against the Jews, and during his incumbency they were permitted to enter Warsaw only during the sessions of the Diet. After his death the old order of things was restored. The great crown marshal Lubomirski issued special certificates at a cost of one silver groschen each, and every Jew wishing to stay in Warsaw was compelled to procure one of them under penalty of imprisonment, although they were good for five days only. The income from these tickets reached the sum of 200,000 Polish gulden annually. Large Jewish colonies were formed in the outskirts of the city on lands owned by members of the Polish nobility. The most noted of these settlements was " New Jerusalem," situated beyond the present Jerusalem gate. Notwithstanding a resolution of the city council which permitted Jews to reside in New Jerusalem, Marshal Lubomirski successively combated the legality of this right of settlement.

Destruction of " New Jerusalem," 1775. On Jan. 22, 1775, the marshal's guard invaded New Jerusalem, confiscated the merchandise found there, and demolished all the Jewish houses. The merchandise thus seized, which was valued at hundreds of thousands of gulden, was stored in the arsenal and was later sold at public auction, the proceeds being returned to the Jews.

In the following year the Jews secured permission to rebuild their houses, but had meanwhile settled in large numbers in the city itself. On May 25, 1784, however, Marshal Mniszek issued an ordinance expelling the Jews from Warsaw and its environs, though it should be noted that the better classes of Polish society condemned the ill treatment of the Warsaw Jews by the Christian merchant and artisan gilds. This is clear from the following paragraph, for example, in the Warsaw periodical " Pamietnik Historyczno-Politiczny " (1783, p. 5): " What terrible spectacles must we witness in the capital on solemn holidays! Students and even adults in noisy mobs persecute the Jews and sometimes beat them with sticks. We ourselves have seen a gang waylay a Jew, stop his horses, and give him such a cudgeling that he fell from the wagon. How can we look with indifference on such a survival of barbarism? "

An agreement was then made with Peter Tepper, the banker of King Stanislaus Augustus, permitting the Jews to reside in Rasin, Tepper's estate in the suburbs of Warsaw. The agreement was profitable to both. Rasin became a Jewish colony, and drew a large volume of trade from Warsaw. The city magistrates were alarmed at the commercial decline, however, and attempted to discourage the growth of the colony by threats and persuasion. They were finally forced to repeal the restrictive ordinances and gave permission to the Jews to reside in special districts. The new Jewish quarter of Warsaw was located on the square known as Marywil, the present theater-square. Subsequently the Pociej Palace was erected there and gave its name to the entire district.

The Jews gradually spread to Tlomacka, Klopocka, and Danilowicz streets, while some lived as far as Trinity Church, at the corner of Nalevki and Dluga streets. In March, 1790, members of the furriers' and tailors' gilds convened at the council-hall of Stare

Miasto, and in their fear of competition requested the magistrates to expel the Jews from the city. They

Action of the Gilds.

demanded that their request be presented to the Diet, threatening, in case of refusal, to take the matter into their own hands. John Deckert, president of the city council, referred the matter to the Diet, and the latter appointed a commission to investigate the grievances of the Christian gilds. The commission was informed that Jewish competition had forced the petitioners to resolve either to destroy themselves or to annihilate their competitors. The Diet acceded to the demand of the Christian craftsmen and ordered the expulsion of all Jewish traders and craftsmen, allowing only those merchants and manufacturers to remain who kept important establishments. As on former occasions, the Jews who had been expelled gradually returned in the course of a few weeks, and the Christian craftsmen, driven to desperation, organized an anti-Jewish riot.

A Christian tailor, Fox, meeting a Jewish tailor on the street, attempted to take from him some clothing which he was carrying. He pursued the Jew, who finally rallied around him some of his coreligionists and had Fox imprisoned, whereupon Fox's workmen raised the cry that the Jews had killed their master. This was the signal for a riot. A mob attacked the Jewish houses and stores, burning and pillaging everything in their way until forced to desist by the troops. The Polish authorities, fearing the outbreak of a revolution like the one which was then raging in Paris, forcibly restored order, arrested Fox and other leaders of the outbreak, enforced the old restrictive regulations against the Jews, and subjected the Jews transgressing these laws to corporal punishment. During the reign of Poniatowski the Jewish question received increased attention among liberal Poles; and at the sessions of the Four Years' Diet some reformers, including Butrymovicz, Czacki, and Kollontai, presented projects for its settlement.

The occupation of Warsaw by the Prussians brought about a beneficial change in the position of

Under Prussian Rule.

the Jews. The Prussian government, not recognizing the old city charters, allowed them to live in Warsaw, permitted them to organize a ḳahal for the regulation of local Jewish affairs, abolished rabbinical tribunals, and prohibited rabbinical anathemas under penalty of fifty thalers' fine and banishment for rabbis guilty of repeating this offense. The new administration led to an influx of Jews to Warsaw, thus giving rise to renewed complaints from the Christian merchants. A census of the Jewish population, ordered by the Prussian authorities in 1793, was largely evaded by the Jews, and the census returns of 6,997 were evidently much below the actual figures.

When the Russians invaded Poland in 1794 the Jews did their share in defending their Polish fatherland. Joselovich BEREK formed a light horse regiment of 500 Jews of Warsaw, which was almost annihilated during the siege of Praga (a suburb of Warsaw) by Suvarov.

Among the wealthy Jewish merchants of Warsaw at the end of the eighteenth century may be mentioned Hershka and Itzik, David and Nutka of Karolevetz, Hershko Markevich, Iosek and Hershko Salamonovich of Posen, Ivosan and Ḥayyim of Lutsk, Naftal of Sokhachov, Shmul Scheidazh and Abraham of Cracow, Josel Jankel and Schmul of Piotrkow. One of the most prominent Jews of the time was Samuel Zbitkover, who was also called Schmul Jacobovich. His name figures largely in official documents and in the correspondence of King Stanislaus Augustus, whose favorite he was; and a quarter of the suburb Praga was even called Schmulevizna in his honor. During the first partition of Poland he was the chief contractor in the Russian army, and traveled with an honorary convoy of Cossacks by permission of General Romanus.

Samuel Zbitkover.

Zbitkover was evidently a very influential man, and Stanislaus Augustus, in a memoir which he presented to Catherine II., mentions 7,000 ducats which the Russian army owed the contractor. The king also presented him with some lots in the suburb of Praga for a Jewish cemetery and synagogue. After the second partition of Poland, Zbitkover still continued to be the contractor of the Russian army, but after the Polish uprising under Kosciusko in April, 1794, the Polish party ("Rada Zastepeza") confiscated his money, which amounted to 757 ducats, and his leather factory. On Nov. 4, 1794, during the siege of Praga, Zbitkover, in his sympathy for the many victims of the war, issued a notice that any soldier or citizen who should bring him an inhabitant of Praga, whether Jew or Christian, would receive a ducat in gold, and whoever should bring him a dead citizen of Praga for burial, would be paid a ruble in silver. Two barrels, one filled with gold and the other with silver, stood before him, and both were emptied in a day. He died Sept. 3, 1800.

In 1797 an order was issued directing all the Jews of Warsaw to adopt family names selected by themselves or assigned them by local officials, and this ordinance accounts for the frequency of German names among the Polish Jews.

Family Names Adopted, 1797.

The increase of the Jewish population led the Prussian authorities to check the influx of Jews into Warsaw, and in March, 1798, a certain portion of the Jewish population was expelled from the city, and the remainder had to submit to increased taxation. All Jews who should arrive in Warsaw after that date were to pay a poll-tax of one gulden daily, while the "Nahrungssteuer," or tax collected from the permanent Jewish population, amounted to 210,000 Polish gulden annually. In addition to this, the Jews were obliged to pay a "Toleranzsteuer" amounting to 50 per cent of the total tax collected from the city population. Two years later the tax on kasher meat was again levied by the government, and in March, 1809, this tax, which formerly amounted to two groschen per pound, was raised to six groschen. The burdensome taxes did not, however, check the increase of the Jewish population. In May, 1804, another anti-Jewish riot broke out in Senatorski street, but was quelled by troops.

In 1826 a rabbinical school was established in

Warsaw under the direction of Anton Eisenbaum, some of the chief teachers being Aaron Moses Cylkow, father of the Judæo-Polish preacher of Warsaw, Jacob Cylkow (who translated the Psalms into Polish; Warsaw, 1883), A. Buchner (author of "Der Talmud und Seine Nichtigkeit"), and Isaac Kramsztyk. Eisenbaum, who was born at Warsaw in 1791 and died there in 1852, was educated under

mann, "Mo'ade 'Ereb," p. 84, Wilna, 1863; see also "Allgemeine Zeitung des Judenthums," 1851, No. 43).

The Reform movement of the early forties affected the Jewish community of Warsaw. Abraham Meyer Goldschmidt was its first German preacher (1842); and Mathias Rosen of the Jewish school board did much for the education of

EXTERIOR OF THE GREAT SYNAGOGUE AT WARSAW, POLAND.
(From a photograph.)

the supervision of his father, who instructed him in the Bible and Hebrew grammar in addition to his Talmudic studies. In the latter part

The Rabbinical School.

of 1823 he founded a Jewish weekly in Yiddish and Polish with the title "Der Beobachter an der Weichsel" (Polish title, "Dostrzegacz Nadwisianski").

A copy—the only one in existence—of this, the first Judæo-Polish periodical, is preserved in the library of the great synagogue of Warsaw. The school, however, did not produce many rabbis, since its real object was to impart secular knowledge rather than rabbinical learning, and it gradually became a Jewish high school ("Keneset Yisrael," i. 138; Reif-

the younger Jewish generation of Warsaw. When Count Uvarov, the Russian minister of public instruction, visited the rabbinical school of Warsaw in 1843, he was pleased with the results of the education of the Jews of the city; in that year the number of pupils was 221, as compared with 14 at the opening of the school in 1826. In 1861 the Warsaw rabbis Dob Berush MEISELS and Marcus JASTROW, suspected by the Russian government of sympathy with the Polish uprising, were expelled from the city, although Meisels was permitted to return in the following year. In 1861 Jewish artisans were admitted into the gilds of working men; and a Jewish weekly in the Polish language, entitled

"Jutrzenka" (Dawn), was founded by Daniel Neufeld. In 1878 Rabbi Jacob GESUNDHEIT, author of the "Tif'eret Ya'aḳob," died; and a new Jewish hospital was established by M. Bersohn, A. Kraushar, and others, and the great (reformed) synagogue was opened on Tłomacka street. In the following year a Hebrew technical school was established by L. Nathansohn, Lesser Levi, H. Reichmann, and others, and in 1881 a library, still in charge of Ignacy BERNSTEIN, was organized in connection with the great synagogue. In 1882 Jews were permitted to live in the streets which were formerly forbidden to them, and in 1889 a Jewish trade-school was founded by Ludwig Nathanson and others. In 1890 some foreign Jews were expelled from Warsaw.

In 1862 the Jews were accorded equal rights with the Christian inhabitants of Poland, largely owing to the efforts of Marquis Vyelepolski, **Equal Rights, 1862.** and the taxes on meat, baskets, and candles were then discontinued in Warsaw. The ḳahal was abolished in 1881, and in its place a committee was appointed to control Jewish religious affairs.

Serious anti-Jewish riots, instigated by the agents of Ignatiev, broke out in Warsaw on Dec. 25, 1881, and lasted for three days, during which time much property was destroyed, and twenty-four Christians and twenty-two Jews were injured. The sympathies of the soldiers sent to check the disorder were evidently with the rioters, for some of those arrested were allowed to escape, as was the case in other riots of the early eighties. A spirited protest against the indifference of the local administration was made by the Jews of Warsaw, including Mathias Bersohn, Ivan Blioch, Stanislas Brunn, Meczislav Epstein, Alexander Goldstand, Stanislas Kronenberg, Michael Landau, Stanislas Lesser, Ludwig Nathanson, and Julius Wienyavski.

The growth and proportion of the Jewish population of Warsaw since 1882 are shown by the following table:

	Jewish Population.	Total Population.
1876	98,698	307,451
1882	127,917	382,464
1886	136,234	406,965
1890	158,154	455,852
1897	231,678	638,208
1901	254,712	711,988
1914	298,137	821,369
1922	309,103	936,046
	Jewish Births.	Total Births.
1882	3,899	14,991
1901	4,744	15,416

BIBLIOGRAPHY: *Starozitne Polskie*, ii. 64; Sobiesczanski, *Rys Historicny m Warszawy*, p. 20; Przyborawski, *Z Przeszlosci Warszawy*, i. 246, Warsaw, 1899; Nussbaum, *Szkice Historyczne z Zycia Zydow w Warszawie*, ib. 1881; *Den*, 1870-1871.

H. R. J. G. L.

Following are lists of rabbis, dayyanim, and scholars of Warsaw and of its suburb Praga:

Rabbis and Dayyanim: Dob Berash ben Reuben (d. Feb. 27, 1819), rabbi of Praga; Simḥah ben Alexander Süsskind (d. Oct. 3, 1822), dayyan; Solomon ben Judah Löb (d. Feb. 24, 1832), dayyan, and author of "Shebile Torah" (Warsaw [?], 1804); Abraham Abele (d. April 14, 1832), dayyan for forty years; Aryeh Löb b. Moses Zunz (d. April 22, 1833), dayyan, and author of "Ya'alat Ḥen" (Praga, 1793) and "Geṭ Meḳushshar" (War-

saw, 1811); Mordecai b. Phinehas (d. May 7, 1837), rabbi of Praga; Solomon Zalman b. Isaac of Posen (d. March 26, 1839), first district rabbi of Warsaw and vicinity, and author of "Ḥemdat Shelomoh" (Warsaw, 1836); David Jedidiah b. Israel (d. April 14, 1842), dayyan for forty years; Ḥayyim Davidsohn b. David Tebele (d. March 17, 1854), rabbi for fifteen years (eulogy by Benjamin David Rabinowicz in "Ruaḥ Ḥayyim," Warsaw, 1854); Mordecai b. Nehemiah (d. July 1, 1855), dayyan, and author of "Mor Deror," a commentary on the Haggadah; Samuel b. Dob Bersohn (d. Feb. 27, 1856), dayyan for eighteen years; Meïr b. Eliezer (d. March 16, 1863), rabbi of Praga for thirty years; Israel Muschkat (d. Feb. 28, 1868), rabbi of Praga for twenty-eight years, and author of "Hare Besamim," a commentary on the prayers, and "Rashe Besamim," a commentary on the Bible and on the Talmudic Haggadah; Judah Aryeh Löbush, known as "the Holy" (d. Sept. 1, 1868), dayyan for thirty-three years; Dob Berush Meisels (d. Feb. 16, 1870), rabbi for fourteen years; Judah Heschel b. Gabriel Goldstadt (d. May 4, 1872), dayyan; Nathan b. Dob of Siemjaticz (d. July 22, 1873), dayyan for forty-three years; Solomon Hillel (d. May 25, 1874), dayyan, and author of "Aṭeret Shelomoh," on Eben ha-'Ezer and Masseket Ḳiddushin; Jacob b. Isaac Gesundheit (b. 1814; d. 1878), rabbi, and author of "Tif'eret Ya'aḳob," on Ḥoshen Mishpaṭ (Warsaw, 1842); Samuel S. Kleppisch (b. 1820; d. 1901), chief dayyan for forty years ("Ha-Ẓefirah," 1902, Nos. 225–227).

The list of rabbis of the modernized congregation, known as the "German" or "Choir" congregation, is as follows: Abraham Meïr Goldschmidt (b. 1812; d. Feb. 8, 1889), officiated until 1858, when he replaced A. Jellinek at Leipsic; Isaac Kramsztyk (b. 1814; d. Sept. 25, 1889); J. Cylkow, Polish translator of the Psalms, with notes (Warsaw, 1883); and Samuel Poznanski.

Scholars: Joseph b. Israel Löb (d. Aug. 25, 1794); Joseph Samuel b. Abigdor (d. in Praga Oct. 14, 1800), parnas of the Council of Four Lands; Benjamin Zeeb Wolf Cohen (d. April 23, 1808; first recorded burial in the Jewish cemetery in Warsaw, which was opened in 1807); Moses Solomon Zalman (d. Jan. 7, 1816), formerly rabbi of Cracow, and gabbai of the Holy Land Ḥaluḳḳah Fund; Baer Berksohn (d. March 12, 1831), left a legacy, the interest on which is to be distributed among the poor on his JAHRZEIT; Abraham Jacob Stern (d. Feb. 3, 1842), astronomer and mathematician, father-in-law of Ḥayyim Selig Slonimski; Jacob Moses b. Solomon Zalman Jerislawer (d. March 19, 1842), publisher of the works of R. Löw of Prague; Solomon ben Judah Blumberg (d. Oct. 2, 1850), parnas and philanthropist (left fund for a synagogue); Anton Eisenbaum (b. 1791; d. 1852), editor and publisher (1823–24) of "Der Beobachter an der Weichsel," the first Yiddish newspaper in Poland; Abraham Buchner, instructor in the Rabbinerschule, and author of "Doresh Ṭob" (Warsaw, 1830) and "Der Talmud" (2 vols., *ib.* 1848); Isaac Löb Peretz (born at Samoscz, May, 1851), the poet; Eleazar Thalgrün (d. April 2, 1857), German translator of the Psalms, with bi'ur "Tokaḥat Musar" (Warsaw, 1854); Ḥayyim Gershon b. Hillel Cohen Halle (d. Oct. 1, 1857), communal worker, and founder of the synagogue at the Iron Gate; Jacob David Schapiro (d. Aug. 5, 1863), formerly rabbi of Wiszagrod, and author of annotations on "Torat Kohanim"; Samuel b. Abraham Fliederbaum (d. April 6, 1867), gabbai of the burial society; Hillel Gleitstein (d. 1867), editor of the "Warschauer Jüdische Zeitung"; Zusze b. Wolf Ulrich (d. April 23, 1868), founder and leader of a synagogue; Solomon Baer (d. Dec. 1, 1868), formerly rabbi of Naszelsk, and author of "Dibre Shelomoh," Talmudic novellæ; Moses b. Eliezer Lippman Feinkind (d. May 17, 1869), gabbai of the Jewish hospital; Moses b. Enoch Zundel Endelman (b. 1808; d. Dec. 16, 1869), communal worker and gabbai; Jacob Tugendhold (b. 1791; d. April 20, 1871), author, translator, and censor of Hebrew books (see "Maggid Mishneh," i. 59); Joshua b. Solomon Löb of Ostrowa (d. April 25, 1873), author of "Toledot Adam"; Menahem Mendel b. Zeeb (d. May 13, 1873), rosh yeshibah; Bunem Wolf Zeeb Mendelssohn (d. Nov. 28, 1875), rosh yeshibah, and author of "Terumat Zahab"; Menahem Mendel Oettinger (d. July 6, 1878), bequeathed 10,000 rubles to the Jewish community; Jacob Joseph b. Mattithiah Ḥayyim (d. Aug. 3, 1878), publisher of Hebrew books, and author of "Sefer ha-Mizwot"; Simḥah b. Mordecai Posner (d. Oct. 17, 1878), author of "Ha-Ẓofeh be-Ereẓ Nod" ("The Wandering Jew"); Judah b. Zimel Epstein (d. Oct. 7, 1879), author of "Minḥat Yehudah"; Moses b. Mordecai Lipschitz (d. April 5, 1881), left legacy of 15,000 rubles to the community; Abraham b. Sussman Jabez (d. Feb. 28, 1882), author and publisher; Jacob Nathanson (d. 1882; d. Sept. 14, 1884), professor of chemistry; Gabriel Judah Lichtenfeld (b. 1811; d. March 22, 1887), author and mathematician; Isaac Goldmann (b. 1812; d. Jan. 13, 1888), Hebraist and author; Abraham Zuckerman (b. 1843; d. April 21, 1892), Hebrew publisher; Moses Cohen (b. 1820; d. Aug. 31, 1892), communal worker, and author of a Polish work in defense of the sheḥiṭah; Hilarius (Hillel) Nussbaum (b. 1820; d. 1895), Polish historian; Samuel Hirsch Peltin (b. 1831; d. Sept. 30, 1896), author; Abraham Shalom Friedberg (b. 1838; d. March 31, 1902), author and editor; Ḥayyim Selig Slonimski (b. 1810; d. May 15, 1904), author and scientist; Moses Forelle (b. 1814), calendarist and author (see "Sefer Zikkaron"); Stanislaus Kramsztyk (b. 1841), naturalist; Saul Pincus Rabinowitz (b. 1845), editor of "Keneset Yisrael," an illustrated Hebrew magazine, and translator of Grätz's "Geschichte der Juden"; Mordecai Spector (b. 1859), editor of the "Hausfreund" and the "Familienfreund"; Nahum Sokolow (b. 1859), editor of "Ha-Ẓefirah," the first Hebrew daily; Ben-Avigdor (b. 1867), founder of the two publishing-houses named respectively "Aḥiasaf" and "Tushiyyah."

BIBLIOGRAPHY: Samuel Jewnin, *Naḥalat 'Olamim*, Warsaw, 1882.
H. R.   J. D. E.

WARSCHAUER JÜDISCHE ZEITUNG. See PERIODICALS.

WARSHAWSKI, MARK SAMOILOVICH: Russian writer; born at Kherson in 1853. He received his early education at a gymnasium in St. Petersburg, and then studied engineering at the ministerial Institute for Engineers. Later he took up the study of law at the University of St. Petersburg, from which he was graduated in jurisprudence in 1879.

Since 1874 Warshawski has been a contributor to the St. Petersburg daily "Novosti," in which he has published a series of humoristic poems. In 1878 he wrote feuilletons for "Russki Mir," and he has been a contributor also to the humoristic weeklies "Pchela" and "Strekoza." He was one of the founders, and for some time associate editor, of the Russo-Jewish periodical "Razsvyet" (1879-81), to which he contributed various essays, as well as sketches of Jewish life. He has contributed also to the "Voskhod," and has published a collection of poems entitled "U Morya" (St. Petersburg, 1884).
H. R.   M. R.

WASHING: As compared with the Greeks and Romans, the Hebrews paid little attention to the care of the body; and the bath was a rarity in a land where water was relatively scarce. It was important, therefore, that personal cleanliness should have a religious basis, and that the cult should ordain frequent ablutions. Thus, for example, the ancient custom of washing before meals may have had its origin in ritualistic requirements; and water was an important factor in the Hebrew cult as in all other Semitic religions. A partial explanation of this phenomenon lies in the fact that springs and rivers were often worshiped by the Semites either as gods or as the dwelling-places of divinities. To bathe or wash in such waters was, therefore, in itself a ritualistic act, although this should not be taken to imply that all water was holy, and it must also be borne in mind that one who wished to take part in a ritualistic act had first to be in a condition appropriate to it, or, in other words, had to be ritually clean.

The original meaning of this concept can not be discussed here; for many things conditioned "purity," just as there were many things which made one ritually defiled. First of all, however, bodily cleanliness was requisite; for one could no more come unclean into the presence of God than before the king. Consequently a man washed not

only himself (Gen. xxxv. 2; Ex. xxx. 17 *et seq.*), but also his clothes (Ex. xix. 10 *et seq.*), while the camp of Israel, which was considered a holy place on account of the presence of YHWH, was defiled by any pollution (Deut. xxiii. 10 *et seq.*). It thus becomes plain how ablutions developed into symbolistic purifications, especially from ritualistic defilements. It is sufficient in this connection to allude to the ritual uncleanness connected with certain physical pollutions, as with touching a corpse, a leper, or his house, or with sexual intercourse. From this standpoint of symbolic purification ablutions were prescribed, in the course of the development of the Law, for a number of impurities which, since they could easily be removed by washing, were characterized as slight, in contradistinction to those graver states of defilement which required sacrifice and the like. Thus, the clothing of a leper (Lev. xiii. 6, 34, 54-58), one who had been in a leper's house (Lev. xiv. 47), and the house itself (Lev. xiv. 52) were to be washed, while washing also removed the pollution resulting from sexual intercourse and the like. See also ABLUTION.
E. G. H.   I. BE.

WASHINGTON: The extreme northwestern state on the Pacific coast, United States of America; originally a part of Oregon, but admitted to the Union in 1889. The first Jewish pioneers probably went to Washington about 1860, either from Victoria, B. C., which then contained a large Jewish settlement, or from Portland, at that time the only prominent American settlement north of San Francisco, or from Walla Walla, the largest post on the frontier trail from the East to the North-Pacific coast during the Civil war.

Seattle, which early became the metropolis of the state, was first visited by Jews about 1862, when the wholesale grocery house of Schwabacher & Co. was opened in Walla Walla. The members and representatives of the firm frequently went to Seattle; and they started a branch there in 1869. The first regular congregation, called Oheves Sholom, was organized in 1887, and a plot for a cemetery was purchased two years later. A synagogue was built and dedicated in 1891, but was sold, and the Reform Congregation Temple de Hirsch was organized May 29, 1899, chiefly through the efforts of Leo Kohn. The foundation and first story of the new temple were finished and dedicated Sept. 13, 1901. R. Brown (later in San Francisco) and R. Abrahamson (later in Portland) were the officiating rabbis of Congregation Oheves Sholom, and Theo. F. Joseph was the minister of Congregation Temple de Hirsch, followed by Samuel Koch. In addition to the Reform congregation there is an Orthodox organization, Bickor Cholem, which was founded in 1892. S. Toobin is hazzan and S. Glaser rabbi; the congregation worships in a synagogue. The Seattle Hebrew Benevolent Society owns the Hills of Eternity Cemetery, where members of the Reform congregation are interred, while Orthodox Jews are buried in Oak Park Cemetery, the property of Bickor Cholem congregation. Some of the charitable and educational societies in Seattle are: Seattle Hebrew Benevolent Society, Ladies' Hebrew Benevolent Society, Montefiore Society, Temple

Auxiliary, Council of Jewish Women, and Sons of Zion. The independent Order of B'nai B'rith is represented by two lodges, Seattle Lodge No. 342 (organized in 1883) and Hildesheimer Lodge No. 503 (organized in 1900). The Concordia Club, founded in 1903, is a flourishing social organization.

Next in size to the Jewish community of Seattle is that of **Spokane,** where the congregation Emanu-El, organized Sept. 28, 1890, had in 1905 a membership of about sixty. Rabbis E. Schreiber, A. Farber, Jacob Bloch have officiated as ministers, and the present incumbent is Rabbi J. Rosen. The communal societies are the Judith Montefiore Society (an auxiliary of the temple), the Ladies' Benevolent Society, and the Daughters of Israel (auxiliary of the semiorganized Orthodox community). Abraham Geiger Lodge No. 423, I.O.B.B., chartered in March, 1893, has about fifty members.

The Beth Israel congregation in **Tacoma** was organized in 1892 and completed its temple in 1893. The congregation, conservative in character, numbers about sixty-five members. There are several auxiliary societies, comprising the Lady Judith Montefiore Society, a section of the Council of Jewish Women, and the Hebrew Benevolent Society, which owns a large cemetery. A B'nai B'rith lodge formerly existed in the city, but the removal of many members resulted in the return of the charter to the grand lodge. Montague N. A. Cohen (now of York, Pa.) was the minister of the congregation during the year 1903-4.

A few Jewish families that are not regularly organized into congregations live in Walla Walla, Olympia (a cemetery plot was bought in 1872), Ellensburg, Aberdeen, Hoquiam, South Bend, Everett, and Bellingham.

Among the eminent Jews of Washington have been Gen. Edward S. Solomon, who was sent by President Grant to be governor of the territory of Washington from 1870 to 1872, and Bailey Gatzert, who was one of the pioneers of Seattle, and for several years one of the most prominent men of the Pacific coast, being president of the firm of Schwabacher & Co. from 1888 to 1893, the year of his death, and also the presiding officer of the Gatzert-Schwabacher Land Co.

In a total population of 1,356,621, according to the most recent—the fourteenth United States Census—1920, the Jews of Washington number approximately 10,030.

A.   T. F. J.

WASHINGTON, D. C.: Capital of the United States; situated in the District of Columbia, on the Potomac River. In 1849 there were in Washington six Jews, who were engaged in business on Pennsylvania avenue, and who went to Baltimore for the important holy-day services. On April 25, 1852, the First Washington Hebrew Congregation was organized; it numbered twenty-one members, and Solomon Pribram was elected its first president. Two years later the membership had increased to forty-two; and on Dec. 13, 1855, at the thirty-fourth session of Congress, a special act was passed, "that all the rights, privileges, and immunities heretofore granted by the law to the Christian churches in the city of Washington be and the same hereby are extended to the Hebrew Congregation of said city."

This marks the incorporation of the first Jewish institution in the District of Columbia. The congregation grew steadily in membership and in influence; and in 1863 it acquired for a place of worship the old Methodist church, which had been utilized by the government for hospital purposes during the Civil war. In 1898 the congregation moved into its present stately edifice, the corner-stone of which was laid by President McKinley in the presence of his entire cabinet, on Sept. 16, 1897. The First Washington Hebrew Congregation is the only Reform congregation in the District of Columbia. Its membership in 1920 was 395, and its religious school was attended by 255 children. The following readers and rabbis have officiated since 1854: S. M. Lansburgh, S. Weil, J. L. Jacobson, Herman Baar, Isaac Stampel, M. Goldberg, Louis Stern, and Abram Simon. Rabbis Simon and Stern are officiating conjointly.

In 1870 thirty-five members left the parent body to form an independent congregation, with Isaac Stampel as ḥazzan. This congregation, which was called Adath Israel, was organized as a protest against the Reform tendencies of the old congregation. In 1873 Adath Israel moved into its present home on the corner of Sixth and G streets, its synagogue being dedicated in the presence of President Grant and his cabinet. Its present membership includes 150 families, ministered to by Rabbi B. L. Grossman; and its religious school is attended by sixty-five pupils.

The Ahabai Shalom congregation was organized in 1902 as a result of the union of two smaller hebrot, the Chayai Odom (founded 1890) and the Agoodath Achim (1898). It has a membership of 125 families, and its ḥazzan was Robert Graffman, who conducted a day-school at 607 H street for twenty-five pupils. The Talmud Torah congregation (present rabbi, M. A. Horwitz) was founded in 1890, and meets on 4½ street, southwest. It has a membership of seventy persons, but no religious school. All four congregations maintain cemeteries on the same plot of ground on Harrison road.

The leading charitable, religious, and literary societies are: (1) The United Hebrew Charities (founded 1882; incorporated 1893; annual income in 1905, about $3,000; president, I. L. Blout, appointed 1894); (2) The Hebrew Free Inn, for the temporary care of the indigent; controlled by the executive board of the United Hebrew Charities; (3) The Hebrew Relief Society (founded 1905); (4) The Ladies' Auxiliary Society of Adath Israel; (5) The Old B'nai Zion; (6) The Rebecca Lodge (1863); (7) The Deborah Lodge (1875); (8) The Liberty Lodge No. 19, I.O.S.B. (1894); (9) The Friendship Circle (1897); (10) The Senior and Junior Councils of Jewish Women; (11) The Elijah, Grace Aguilar, and Argo lodges, I.O.B.B.; (12) The B'rith Abraham and the Independent B'rith Abraham; (13) The Sons of Judah; (14) The Mercantile Club; (15) The Hebrew Literary Society; (16) The Free Sons of Benjamin; (17) The Young People's Union of Zion.

While most of the Jews of Washington are engaged in commerce, the legal and medical professions are also creditably represented. Among the most prominent Jews may be mentioned: Commodore

Uriah P. Levy, Simon Wolf (publicist and author), Max Weyl (artist), Emile Berliner (inventor), Adolphus S. Solomons, Cyrus Adler (assistant secretary, Smithsonian Institution), and Dr. Milton J. Rosenau (director, Hygienic Laboratory, Marine Hospital Service). The Jewish population of the District of Columbia may be placed at 10,000.

A.   A. S.

WASKER, SILLEMAN ABAJEE (SOLOMON ABRAHAM): Beni-Israel soldier; died about 1850. He enlisted in the Third Regiment Native (Indian) Light Infantry, Jan. 1, 1809, and was present at the battles of Puna, Rusood, Khur, Multan, Kittoor, and Gujarat, rising ultimately to the highest rank open to a native soldier, that of sirdar bahadur; he was also decorated with the first class Order of the Star of British India. He retired from the army in March, 1846, after a service of thirty-seven years, during twenty-five of which he was native commander of the Beni-Israel regiment.

Bibliography: H. Samuel, *Sketch of Beni-Israel*, pp. 24-25.

J.

WASSERTRILLING, HERMANN (ZEBI HIRSCH BEN NATHAN): Austrian Hebraist; flourished in the nineteenth century; born at Boskowitz, Moravia. He officiated as teacher in the Jewish school of Hotzenplotz, Silesia, about 1850, and later as rabbi of Bojanowo, Posen. The following is a list of his works, all published at Breslau: "Hadrat Elisha'" (1857), an epic poem in nine cantos, describing the life of the prophet Elisha, and giving also a brief history of contemporary kings; "Nezer Ḥamudot" (1860), an epic poem in eight cantos, being a history of Daniel and his contemporaries under the reign of the Babylonian, Median, and Persian kings until the return of the Israelites to Jerusalem, and the building of the Second Temple; "Mattenat Naḥali'el" (part i., 1860; part ii., 1868), a collection of legends from the Talmud, Midrash, and the midrashic commentaries, arranged in verse in the order of the weekly lessons; "Torat ha-Berit" (1869), a treatise in reply to a question on circumcision addressed to the synod of Leipsic by Max Engel (July, 1869).

Bibliography: Fürst, *Bibl. Jud.* iii. 495; Lippe, *Bibliographisches Lexicon*, i. 518; Zeitlin, *Bibl. Post-Mendels.* pp. 404-405.

S.   M. Sel.

WASSERZUG, HAIM: English ḥazzan and composer; born at Sheritz, Prussian Poland, 1822; died at Brighton, England, Aug. 24, 1882. As a child he was endowed with a remarkably sweet voice, and at eighteen he was elected ḥazzan at Konin. His renown soon spread among the Jewish communities of Poland, and he received a call as ḥazzan to Novy-Dvor, where his introduction of choral singing and singing in harmony, instead of the then prevalent "ḥazzanut," aroused considerable opposition against him on the part of the Ḥasidim. Thirteen years later he was appointed to a post at Lonisa, near the Lithuanian frontier. Here he remained for five years, when he was elected cantor of the Wilna congregation. In 1867, on the opening of the North London Synagogue, he was elected its first reader, which office he held until his death in 1882.

During his ḥazzanship at Wilna, Wasserzug wrote some sacred compositions which, under the title "Sefer Shire Miḳdash," were published in London, 1878. These compositions received high commendation; and some of the principal cantors of the European continent and of America were numbered among his disciples. His son, **David Wasserzug,** was educated at Jews' College, London, and has officiated as rabbi at Cardiff in Wales, at Johannesburg in South Africa, and, since 1905, at the Dalston Synagogue, London.

Bibliography: *Jew. Chron.* and *Jew. World*, Sept. 1, 1882.

J.   G. L.

WATCH-NIGHT. See Wachnacht.

WATER: Water was looked upon by the Jews as extremely important and precious. The first thing placed before a guest was water to wash his feet (Gen. xviii. 4, xxiv. 32), and it was a duty of hospitality to give water to strangers coming into the house, or even passing by (*ib.* xxiv.

Water for Guests. 17, 43). The non-fulfilment of this duty often resulted in serious hostilities. Thus, when the Israelites were marching toward Palestine they were prevented from passing through Edom, Ammon, and Moab because the inhabitants refused to give them a drink of water, even for money. Two hundred years later this resulted in bitter warfare (see Ammon; Jephthah). During the wandering in the wilderness the lack of water caused the Israelites to murmur against their leader (Ex. xv. 22-25, xvii. 1-7; Num. xx. 1-13). On the other hand, the heroes of King David's guard won distinction by procuring water for the king at the risk of their lives (II Sam. xxiii. 16; I Chron. xi. 17-18).

Water was of great importance in purification, being used in cleansing the leper, in sickness, in

For Ritual Purposes. washing utensils, and in the cleansing of one who had been defiled by touching an unclean body (Lev. xv. 16-22, 27). The liability of plants and fruits to defilement was increased by contact with water (Lev. xi. 38), a contingency which formed a topic of much discussion in the Talmudic period, and became the subject of the treatise Makshirin.

The offering of water as a libation was an ancient institution, and even before the kingdom was established the Israelitish tribes, after having suffered repeated defeats at the hands of the Philistines, gathered together at Mizpeh at the command of the prophet Samuel, and poured water on the ground before Yhwh (I Sam. vii. 5-6). An apparent analogue to this is found in the story that at the great feast of Baal the prophet Elijah poured water in the trench which surrounded the altar (I Kings xviii. 35), possibly to enhance the miracle. The libation

Libations. at the Feast of Tabernacles, when the high priest sprinkled water upon the altar as a sacrifice, was a later development of the ancient offering; it was a feature of the ritual until the destruction of the Second Temple, and the disregard of it by Alexander Jannæus entailed terrible consequences (comp. Suk. 48b).

The word "water" was often used by the Jews

symbolically, especially in expressing grief, *i.e.*, tears (Jer. ix. 1, 18; Ps. cxix. 136). A misfortune of great magnitude, the full extent of which it seemed impossible to fathom, was likened to water (Lam. iii. 54; Ps. lxix. 2, cxxiv. 4–5), while the constant flow and unrest of water were symbolic of numerous descendants (Num. xxiv. 7). The forgiveness of sins and their complete remission were typified by sprinkling with clean water (Ezek. xxxvi. 25); and in Jer. ii. 13 God is compared to a fountain of living waters. It was customary in the Talmudic period, moreover, to use "water" symbolically for the divine teachings (see Mek., Beshallaḥ, Wayassa', 1); so that in several passages the term "water" is used without any amplification whatever (comp. Ḥag. 3a; B. M. 84b; Hor. 14a; Ab. i. 2).

Water prepared with the ashes of the RED HEIFER was especially important, since, even though unclean, it had the power of cleansing men and things infected with defilement. Still more important, however, was the "water of bitterness," the so-called

"**Water**
of Bitter-
ness."

"me ha-marim ha-me'arerim," which was prepared in the following manner: Into an earthen vessel the priest poured water which had stood in the Temple, and with this water he mixed dust taken from the Temple floor. If a woman was suspected of unfaithfulness toward her husband, the priest pronounced certain maledictions, which he afterward wrote on a little scroll. This was then dissolved in the water, which the accused woman was obliged to drink (Num. v. 17–24; see also the article SOṬAH).

Water was an important factor during the first three days of Creation. On the first day "the Spirit of God moved upon the face of the waters" (Gen. i. 2); on the second day the nether waters were divided from the upper, and the latter were transformed into the "raḳia'," or "firmament" (*ib.* verse 7); and on the third day the nether waters were assigned to their allotted place, which received the name of "sea" (*ib.* verse 10).

Through the influence of the Greeks, and especially of the Gnostics, who regarded water as the original element, similar beliefs gained currency among the Jews, so that Judah ben Pazi transmitted the following saying in the name of R. Ishmael (Yer. Ḥag. ii., beginning): "In the beginning the world consisted of water within water (Gen. i. 2); the water was then changed into ice (Ps. cxlvii. 17), and again transformed by God into earth (Job xxxvii. 6). The earth itself, however, rests upon the waters, and the waters on the mountains" (*i.e.*, the clouds; Ps. civ. 6). This teaching, however, was rejected by R. Akiba, who warned those scholars who devoted themselves to the study of cosmogony not to be led astray by Gnosticism, and not to cry "Water!" whenever they saw in their visions a sea of crystal around the throne of God (Ḥag. 14b). In the later Talmudic period the word "water" was used as a designation for mucus, which was called "water from the nose" (Tosef., Shab. viii.; Niddah 55d), while buttermilk was termed "water of milk," and unfermented grape-juice was called "water of the grape-vine" ('Orlah i. 7).

E. G. H.

WATER-DRAWING, FEAST OF (שמחת בית השואבה) :

At the morning service on each of the seven days of the Feast of Tabernacles (Sukkot) a libation of water was made together with the pouring out of wine (Suk. iv. 1; Yoma 26b), the water being drawn from the Pool of Siloam in a golden ewer of the capacity of three logs. It was borne in solemn procession to the water-gate of the Temple, where the train halted while on the SHOFAR was blown "teḳi'ah, teru'ah, teḳi'ah." The procession then ascended the "kebesh," or slanting bridge to the altar, toward the left, where stood on the east side of the altar a silver bowl for the water and on the west another for the wine, both having snout-like openings, that in the vessel for the wine being somewhat the larger. Both libations were poured out simultaneously (Suk. iv. 9).

Although there was no direct Mosaic law for the libation of water, it was claimed by R. Neḥunya of Beth-horon that the ordinance was a Mosaic tradition (Zeb. 110a), while R. Akiba deduced a Mosaic intimation ("remez") of the tradition from the plural form "u-nesakeha" ("drink-offerings"; Num. xxix. 31). R. Judah b. Bathyra drew a similar inference from the spellings נסביהם and נסכיה as compared with the usual נסכהם, and כמשפטם as compared with כמשפט (Num. xxix. 30, 31, 33), the superfluous letters forming מים ("water"; Shab. 103b); and R. 'Ena confirmed the tradition by quoting Isa. xii. 3: "Therefore with joy shall ye draw water out of the wells of salvation" (Suk. 48b). The treatise Sukkah also explains the offering as made in order that the rainy season, which begins at that time of the year, may be abundant (comp. R. H. i. 2, 16a; Ta'an. 2b).

A Mosaic Tradition.

Why the Rabbis laid such stress on the water-libation is not clear, unless there were weighty reasons which have not been recorded. It may have been emphasized to counteract the Gentile practise of offering wine only; or it may even have been intended as a temperance lesson. At all events, the Sadducees were strongly opposed to this interpretation of the Law, so that on one occasion ALEXANDER JANNÆUS poured the water on his feet instead of on the altar, thus affronting the Pharisaic sympathies of the people so bitterly that they threw at him the etrogim which they carried in celebration and nearly killed him, and the priest was accordingly required thenceforth to raise his hand when he poured out the water at the libation that his offering might be seen by all (Suk. 48b). To express their contempt of the Sadducees on the one hand and to strengthen their own position on the other, the Rabbis embellished the libation of water with so much ceremony that it became a favorite and distinctive rite on these occasions. On the night of the first day of the Feast of Tabernacles the outer court of the Temple was brilliantly illuminated with four golden lamps, each containing 120 logs of oil, in which were burning the old girdles and garments of the priests (Shab. 21a; Yoma 23a). These lamps were placed on high pedestals which were reached by ladders; and special galleries were erected in the court for the accommodation of women, while the men below held torches in their hands, sang hymns, and danced.

S. O.

On the fifteen steps of the Gate of Nicanor stood the Levites, chanting the fifteen "songs of degrees" (Ps. cxx.–cxxxiv.) to the accompaniment of their instruments, of which the most important was the "ḥalil," or flute, although it was used neither on the Sabbath nor on the first day of the feast (Suk. v. 1). The illumination, which was like a sea of fire, lit up every nook and corner of Jerusalem, and was so bright that in any part of the city a woman could pick wheat from the chaff. Whosoever did not see this celebration never saw a real one (Suk. 53a). Hillel the Elder encouraged general rejoicing and participated in the celebration that all might follow his example, while R. Simeon b. Gamaliel juggled with eight torches, throwing them in the air and catching them again, thus showing his joy at the feast. R. Joshua b. Hananiah states that the festival was celebrated throughout the night with songs, music, shouting, clapping of hands, jumping, and dancing.

Becomes a Favorite Rite.

After the destruction of the Temple the libation of water, being a portion of the sacrifice, was discontinued; but the custom of rejoicing was retained for some one day of the Feast of Sukkot other than the Sabbath or a full holy day. No "'am ha-arez" was permitted to join the celebration, although he was allowed to look on. Probably the ceremony originally included a symbolic form of prayer for rain in the winter season (see Zech. xiv. 16–19).

The feast of water-drawing is now celebrated in the bet ha-midrash on any night other than Friday in the middle of Sukkot. At Jerusalem each night of the semiholy days is observed in the bet ha-midrash or in the synagogue by chanting the fifteen "shire ha-ma'alot" and appropriate Bible verses, while the Sephardim have special piyyuṭim. After the service small parties are formed, and engage in feasting, singing, and dancing till midnight (Luncz, "Jerusalem," i. 40). In his "Die Eleusinischen Mysterien im Tempel von Jerusalem" (in Hungarian, in "Magyar-Zsidó Szemle," xii. 213; idem, in "Popular-Wissenschaftliche Monatsblätter," xvii. 121) L. Venetianer endeavors to prove that the feast of water-drawing bears traces of Greek influence.

E. C.   J. D. E.

WATER-RIGHTS. See RIPARIAN OWNERS.

WAVE-OFFERING. See SACRIFICE.

WAW (ו): Sixth letter of the Hebrew alphabet. The name possibly means "nail" or "hook," and the shape of the letter in the Phenician alphabet bears some resemblance to a hook. "Waw" is a labial spirant, identical in sound with the English "w." When preceded by the labial vowel "u," it blends with it ("uw"), the result being a long u-sound; and when an a-vowel precedes it, the two form the diphthong "au," which in Hebrew has passed into "o." At the beginning of a word (a position it rarely has in Hebrew) "waw" retains its consonantal value, except when followed by פ, ב, מ, or a letter with simple "shewa." As the first letter of verb-stems it has been replaced in Hebrew almost everywhere by "yod." As a numeral (in the later period) "waw" has the value of 6.

T.   I. BR.

WAWELBERG, HIPPOLITE HENRICH-OVICH: Russian banker; born at Warsaw 1844; died at St. Petersburg Oct. 20, 1901. After graduating from the real-gymnasium of Warsaw he studied at the university of that city, and later at the Agricultural College of Nova Alexandria, finally completing his studies in Germany. Upon his return to St. Petersburg he assumed the management of his father's banking establishment, and became a very successful financier. He took a lively interest in the communal affairs of St. Petersburg and of Warsaw, and contributed considerable sums of money toward the foundation and maintenance of industrial schools. He devoted large sums also to the improvement of the condition of the laboring classes. The Museum of Arts and Industries, the Technical School of Wawelberg and Rothwand, and the cheap lodging-houses of Warsaw owe their existence largely to his support.

Wawelberg contributed liberally to the publication in the Polish language of popular books on the applied sciences. It was his aim not only to raise the general economic and social condition of Poland, but also to elevate his coreligionists and to imbue them with a spirit of patriotism. He was a director of the Jewish community of St. Petersburg, and, from 1880, a member of the Society for the Promotion of Culture Among the Jews of Russia, and of the Society of Friends of Jewish Artisans and Farmers. After 1891 he was also an active member of the Jewish Colonization Association. Wawelberg was one of the trustees of the Industrial Company at Dubrovna, which endeavored to provide work for the poor Jewish artisans of that place.

BIBLIOGRAPHY: *Voskhod*, 1901, No. 57.
H. R.   J. G. L.

WAX (Hebr. "donag"): In the Old Testament wax is referred to only as a simile for something easily dissolved or evanescent (Ps. lxviii. 3); for compliance and submission (Judges xvi. 18; Micah i. 4; Ps. xcvii. 5); or for fear and discouragement (Ps. xxii. 15). In the Talmud mention is made of the use of wax ("sha'awah") for lighting purposes, probably in the form of candles (Shab. 20b; comp. Rashi). At present wax candles are frequently employed on the Feast of ḤANUKKAH in places where olive-oil is not easily obtainable. On the eve of the Day of Atonement and at the anniversary of the death of a relative (JAHRZEIT) it is customary to light in the synagogue large wax candles that will burn at least twenty-four hours. A candle made from braided wax tapers is used also for the HABDALAH ceremony.

E. G. H.   I. M. C.

WAY. See RIGHT OF WAY.

WAY, LEWIS: English clergyman; born at Denham, Bucks, England, Feb. 11, 1772; died in London Jan. 26, 1840. He was educated at Merton College, Oxford, and was called to the bar in 1797, but entered the Church and devoted to Church purposes a large legacy left him by a stranger named John Way. He was the founder, in 1808, of the London Society for Promoting Christianity Among the Jews, under the patronage of the Duke of Kent, father of Queen Victoria, and with the assistance of Prof. Simeon of Cambridge, Dr. Marsh of Birmingham, the convert J. F. Fry, and the preacher Leigh Richmond. Convinced that the Jewish nation would again arise, return to its ancestral home, embrace Christianity, and convert the Gentiles, Way traveled at his own expense through Holland, Germany, and Russia, in order to study the condition of the

such as the "Song by the Sea" (Ex. xv.; comp. ASHIRAH) or the "Journeys of the Standards" (Num. x. 14–16, 18–20, 22–24, 25–28; xxxiii. 11–13, 15–36, 41–47), the present chant is founded on a vocal imitation of a herald's trumpet-call. The accompanying transcription, based on that of Baer, shows the

WAYEHI 'EREB (Gen. i. 5)

Jews, ameliorate their social and political status, and urge the Christians to missionary work among them.

In 1817 Way induced Czar Alexander I. to issue two ukases assuring all baptized Jews of imperial protection and promising them land for farming. Further, he wrote a work entitled "Mémoires sur l'Etat des Israélites Dédiés et Présentés à Leurs Majestés Impériales et Royales, Réunies au Congrès d'Aix-la-Chapelle" (Paris, 1819), in which he emphasized the Messianic importance of the Jews, considered their relation to the Biblical promises and the ultimate fulfilment thereof, and pleaded for their emancipation in Europe. This was presented at the Congress of Aix-la-Chapelle (Oct., 1818) to the czar, who gave the memorandum to his plenipotentiaries, Nesselrode and Capodistrias, ordering them to bring it before the congress, together with the question of the emancipation of the Jews. It was accordingly entered on the minutes, but produced no further effect. In his own house Way used to entertain converted Jews, who sometimes ill repaid his hospitality, giving rise to a satirical epigram by Macaulay.

BIBLIOGRAPHY: Herzog-Hauck, *Real-Encyc.* xiii. 179; *Monatsschrift*, 1869, xviii. 234 *et seq.*, 334 *et seq.*, 477 *et seq.*, 551 *et seq.*; Grätz, *Gesch.* xi. 352 *et seq.*; *Dict. Nat. Biog.*; Trevelyan, *Life of Macaulay*, ch. i.

J.   E. N.

WAYEHI 'EREB ("And it was evening"): One of the "nedarim," or special declamatory variations from the strict CANTILLATION of the Pentateuch, according to the Northern use. This chant is introduced into the reading which reopens the yearly cycle of pericopes on the Rejoicing of the Law (see SIMḤAT TORAH); and it marks the verses which conclude the recital of the work of each of the six days of Creation (Gen. i. 5, 8, 13, 19, 23, 31). The reader pauses at the end of each verse; and after the congregation has loudly chanted the "Wayehi 'ereb," he repeats the intonation with florid amplification of the melody. Like other nedarim,

method of its rendering (comp. also "The Voice of Prayer and Praise," No. 168b, London, 1899).

A.   F. L. C.

WAYEKULLU ("Thus were finished"; Gen. ii. 1–3): The concluding verses of the story of Creation, deemed from Talmudic times an essential portion of the prayers for Friday night, as the eve of the Sabbath (Shab. 119b). While the whole congregation remained standing (Shulḥan 'Aruk, Oraḥ Ḥayyim, 268, 7), the "Wayekullu" was recited aloud in the synagogue after the silent repeating of the "'Amidah." In the homes it was recited before the domestic KIDDUSH. Thus the precentors were tempted to dwell upon it when chanting it; and in the course of time they developed for it, out of the simple CANTILLATION of the Law, an elaborately melismatic intonation in their most florid style, for an example of which see JEW. ENCYC. vi. 290.

A.   F. L. C.

WAYIḲRA RABBAH (called also **Haggadat Wayiḳra**): Haggadic midrash to Leviticus. Under the name "Wayiḳra Rabbah" this midrash is first referred to by Nathan, in his "'Aruk," *s.v.* מב, המה, and in several other passages, as well as by Rashi in his commentaries on Gen. xlvi. 26, Ex. xxxii. 5, Lev. ix. 24, etc. According to Zunz, however, Hai Gaon and Nissim knew and made use of this midrash; and Zunz dates its origin back to the middle of the seventh century. It originated in Palestine, and is composed largely of older works, its redactor having made use of Genesis Rabbah, Pesiḳta de-Rab Kahana, and the Jerusalem Talmud, in addition to other ancient sources. He appears to have referred also to the Babylonian Talmud, several expressions in the midrash being used in the sense in which only that work employs them (comp. Weiss, "Dor," iii. 261).

The Wayiḳra is not a continuous, explanatory midrash to Leviticus, but a collection of exclusive sermons or lectures on the themes or texts of that book; and it consists altogether of thirty-seven such homilies, each of which constitutes a separate chapter, or "parashah." The Scriptural passages on which the homilies are based are often referred to in the midrash as "parashiyyot," and are further designated according to their contents; as, for example, ch. i., "Parashat ha-Mishkan," on Lev. i. *et seq.*; ch. ix., "Parashah Ḳorbanot," on Lev. vii. 11 *et seq.*; ch. xv., "Parashat Negaʻim," on Lev. xiii. 1 *et seq.*; etc. Of the thirty-seven homilies, eight (1, 3, 8, 11, 13, 20, 26, 30) are introduced with the

Contents. formula "Pataḥ R." ("The teacher has commenced"); eight (2, 4-7, 9, 10, 19), with "Hada hu di-ketib" (lit., "As it is written"); and twenty-one (12, 14-18, 21-25, 27-29, 31-37), with "Zeh she-amar ha-katub" (lit., "This is what the Holy Scriptures say"). The fact that the redactor of the midrash selected only these thirty-seven texts for his exposition, is explained by Weiss (*l.c.*) as the existence of the Sifra, the halakic midrash to Leviticus: "The redactor of the Wayiḳra Rabbah had nothing to add to the halakic midrash; he collected therefore only those haggadic explanations which he found on various texts and passages." This surmise by Weiss is, however, refuted by the circumstance that nearly all the parashiyyot of the Wayiḳra Rabbah (with the exception of chapters 11, 24, 32, 35, and 36) refer to halakic passages. Thus, the redactor of the midrash collected haggadic expositions also of such texts as were treated in the Sifra. The conjecture of Theodor that in the older cycle of weekly lessons the passages on which the homilies of the Wayiḳra Rabbah were based consisted in certain paragraphs, or in lessons for certain festivals, seems therefore to be correct (comp. Theodor, "Die Midraschim zum Pentateuch und der Dreijährige Palestinensische Cyclus," in "Monatsschrift," 1886, pp. 307-313, 406-415; see also Jew. Encyc. viii. 560).

In its plan, as well as in the form of the several parashiyyot, the midrash bears great resemblance to the Pesiḳta de-Rab Kahana (see Jew. Encyc. viii. 559). Like the lectures in the Pesiḳta, the hom-

long pieces, in others brief sentences only, have been adduced in connection with the Scriptural passages, seemingly in accordance with the material at the redactor's disposal. Inasmuch, however, as the homilies in the Wayiḳra Rabbah treat largely of topics beyond the subject-matter of the Biblical text itself, the explanations of the individual verses are often replaced by series of haggadic quotations which refer to the theme considered in the homily (comp. ch. 8, 12-15, 18, 19, 23, 31-34, 36, 37). In

Relation to the Pesiḳta. this the Wayiḳra Rabbah differs from the Pesiḳta, for in the latter work the individual explanations are seldom lacking. Another difference between the two works is, that while the Pesiḳta rarely quotes lengthy haggadic excerpts after the proems, the Wayiḳra Rabbah quotes such after the conclusion of a proem, in the course of each parashah, and even toward the end of a chapter; these excerpts have often very slight reference to the context. But otherwise the Wayiḳra carefully follows the form of the Pesiḳta. The end of each parashah in the former work, in analogy with the usage followed in the Pesiḳta, consists of a passage containing a Messianic prophecy.

The extent of the present midrash is the same as that of the edition quoted by R. Nathan in the "ʻAruk," since he refers to passages from ch. xxxvi. (*s.v.* אחז) and xxxvii. (*s.v.* קלב) as "the end." Aside from some transpositions, eliminations, and glosses, the printed text of the midrash is noteworthy as containing, at the end of the first three parashiyyot, annotations from Tanna debe Eliyahu which were not contained in the older manuscripts.

Bibliography: Zunz, *G. V.* pp. 181-186; Weiss, *Dor*, iii. 261; Theodor, *Zur Composition der Agadischen Homilien*, in *Monatsschrift*, 1881, pp. 500-510.
S.　　　　　　　　　　　　　　　　　　J. Z. L.

WE-ADAR. See Adar Sheni.

WE-ʻAL KULLOM: The brief prayer which interrupts and divides into three sections the longer confession of sins enumerated in alphabetical order

WE-ʻAL KULLOM

Lento dolente.　　　　　　　　　　　　　　　　　　　　　　*piú moto.*

We - ʻal kul - lom, E - lo - ah se - li - hot, se - lah.........
And for them all, for - giv - - ing God, for - give.........

la - nu, me - hal......... la - nu, kap...... per........ la - nu.
us,............. par - don us,........ grant...... us re - mis - sion.

ilies in the Wayiḳra Rabbah begin with a larger or smaller number of proems on passages mostly taken from the Hagiographa. Thereupon follows the exposition proper of the passage to which the homily refers. The explanation often covers only a few verses, or even a few words of the first verse, of the passage on which the parashah is based. In some cases

(see ʻAl Ḥeṭ) in the prayers of the Day of Atonement. The traditional melody presents many variants besides the foregoing (comp. the Polish and German renderings given in Baer's "Baʻal Tefillah," No. 1357), all of which are based on the plaintive phrases of the wail which pervades the Seliḥah.

A.　　　　　　　　　　　　　　　　　　　F. L. C.

WEASEL (חלד): Unclean animal (Lev. xi. 29). Saadia, Bochart, and others render חלד by "mole," referring to the Arabic "ḥuld" and the Aramaic "ḥuldah." The family of the *Mustelidæ*, to which the weasel belongs, is represented in Palestine and Syria by several species.

In the Talmud the common weasel, *Mustela vulgaris*, is mentioned under the names חולדה and כרכושתא (Pes. 9a; Sanh. 105a). In Gen. R. xxiv. 6 also occurs the term נלא. The weasel lives on dung-heaps and in holes and chinks of walls, and it burrows in the ground (Pes. 8b, 118b; Niddah 15b; Suk. 20b). It kills animals larger than itself (Ṭoh. iv. 3), and even attacks corpses (Shab. 151b). It is especially dangerous to domestic fowl (Ḥul. 52b *et al.*); its bent and pointed teeth pierce the skulls of hens (*ib.* 56a; comp. Rashi on Deut. xxxii. 5).

It is above all dangerous to the cat. Hence the proverb "Weasel and cat wed," applied to simulated friendship (Sanh. 105a). Like all small beasts of prey, the weasel carries off glittering objects to its hole (Lev. R. clxxi. 4). The weasel alone of all land animals has no counterpart in the sea (Ḥul. 127a). It was employed in clearing the house of mice (B. Ḳ. 80a). On the use of the weasel in divination see Sanh. 66a; and for the pretty story of the weasel and the well which, as witnesses of a betrothal, avenged its breach, see Rashi on Ta'an. 8a.

BIBLIOGRAPHY: Tristram, *Nat. Hist.* p. 151; Lewysohn, *Z. T.* pp. 91, 366.
E. G. H.   I. M. C.

WEATHER-LORE: Popular prognostications regarding the weather. A certain number of these occur in the Talmud (B. B. 147a). If the weather at Shabu'ot is clear, sow wheat. If the smoke of the altar turns to the north on the last days of Tabernacles, there will be much rain in the following year. This was true for Jerusalem; the opposite, for Babylonia. If New-Year's day is warm, the whole year will be warm (comp. Yoma 21b).

Much importance was attributed to the "teḳufot," or changes of seasons. If the teḳufah of Ṭebet falls on a Wednesday or a Saturday, there will be famine. If the teḳufah of Nisan is on a Sunday, there will be war and death and snow. Some of these prognostications of later times were adapted from the Greeks. Thus, if the new moon of Ṭebet fell on a Sunday, it was taken to portend that the winter would be a good one. Moses ha-Darshan declared that if the teḳufah of Ṭebet fell within the first ten days of the month, grain would be dear. This is quoted by Issachar ibn Susan in his "'Ibbur Shanim" (pp. 123b, 124a, Venice, 1579), which contains other weather-lore. In some weather-signs the position of the planets is taken into account. Thus, if a new moon occurs in the mansion of Mars, the month will be warm and rainy; if in the mansion of Mercury, windy and dusty. If the teḳufah happens when the sun is in the zenith, the year will be a warm one; when Venus is in the ascendancy, a rainy one; etc.

Many of the larger Maḥzorim contain items of this kind; as, for example, the Roman Maḥzor edited by Luzzatto and the Vitry Maḥzor. So, too, in the "Sefer Yeraḥme'el" there is an elaborate treatise on meteorology, containing prognostications based on the occurrence of rain on certain days, or of thunder on such days. Thus, if it rains on the new moon of Nisan, there will be death among the cattle.

BIBLIOGRAPHY: M. Gaster, *Jewish Weather-Lore*, in *Jew. Chron.* Nov. 13, 1891, pp. 7-8.
S.   J.

WEAVING: As early as the nomadic period the Israelites understood the art of spinning the hair of camels and goats, and the wool of sheep, and of weaving therefrom rough stuffs for tents and clothing. Their method of weaving was probably quite as primitive as that of the Bedouins of Jabal Musa observed by E. H. Palmer, who describes the process, as carried on by a woman, thus: "Her loom was a primitive one, consisting only of a few upright sticks, upon which the threads were stretched; the transverse threads were inserted laboriously by the fingers without the assistance of a shuttle, and the whole fabric was pressed close together with a piece of wood" ("The Desert of the Exodus," i. 125).

In Palestine the Israelites became acquainted with somewhat better methods of weaving, although these must have remained very simple until a later period. This is shown by the fact that the Egyptian looms, although the Egyptian methods of weaving, like the Babylonian and Syrian, are spoken of as highly developed, were nevertheless exceedingly primitive. Herodotus narrates that the Egyptians wove at an upright loom. The threads were fastened below, and the weavers commenced their work at the bottom, unlike other peoples, who, according to the same authority, began at the top. This method of weaving was probably the one which was customary at the time of Herodotus, although the monuments prove that the Egyptians were acquainted also with horizontal looms. The well-known representation in one of the tombs at Beni Ḥasan (Wilkinson, "Ancient Egyptians," i. 317) shows a horizontal loom at which two women are seated. (The usual view that this is an upright loom has been refuted by Kennedy in Cheyne and Black, "Encyc. Bibl." iv.

Warp and Woof. 5279.) The warp was stretched over two sticks fastened to the ground by wooden pegs. Other representations show upright looms on which the warp runs from top to bottom, being held firm above and below by a cross-bar. Both kinds of loom may have been in use among the Hebrews also.

The Greeks and Romans used most commonly the upright loom, as described above, although at an earlier period both the upright and the horizontal loom may have been used side by side. Kennedy (*l.c.*) finds an indication of the existence of the horizontal loom in the story of Samson, where it is related that Delilah wove Samson's locks into the web of her loom while he was asleep (Judges xvi. 13 *et seq.*). In modern times only the horizontal loom is used in Palestine. Still another upright loom, differing from that described above, seems to have been in use. This corresponded to the old Grecian loom, having but one cross-bar at the top to fasten the web, while the threads were kept stretched apart at the bottom by weights instead of by a second cross-bar. With this kind of a loom it was necessary to begin at the top. Bliss claims to have found such looms in Tell al-Ḥasi ("A Mound of Many Cities," p. 113). The primitive

Looms. fashions of olden times made it possible to weave a whole garment in one piece, and the looms were adapted to the sizes of the products required. It was not customary to weave long strips of cloth from which the clothing was cut out later, although this was possible when the rods upon which the warp was stretched could be turned, as seems to have been sometimes the case with the Egyptian looms.

One of the most important problems of ancient weaving methods was the separation of the odd from the even threads of the warp, so that the woof could pass between them easily, and their interchange of positions (*i.e.*, respectively over and under the woof) after each stroke of the shuttle. This the ancient Egyptians effected by means of two sticks: one was pushed between the two layers of threads, keeping them separate, while the other, to which the threads of the lower layer were fastened by loops, made it possible to pull them up simultaneously, and thus to produce the interchange of positions. The insertion of the transverse thread was effected by means of a shuttle (ארג). There are no data by means of which the history of the development and perfection of this important discovery can be pursued any further.

Egyptian representations show that from the earliest times the Syrians delighted in variegated and gorgeous garments. The Hebrews must soon have learned how to manufacture many-colored stuffs, in addition to the most simple single-colored weaves. For example, the coarsest mantles of the modern peasants are striped black (or brown) and white, and they were probably the same in antiquity. The inweaving of gold was fashionable for elegant garments (Ex. xxviii. 5 *et seq.*, xxxix. 2 *et seq.*; Ps. xlv. 10), but it is not certain whether the stuff called רקמה, often mentioned in the description of the Tabernacle, was of variegated weave or an embroidery. It is doubtful whether the Hebrews understood how to weave figured textures.

The weaving of clothing, etc., for household use was originally a task which devolved upon the housewives; it is not known when weaving was first developed as a separate trade. In later times weavers held a position of high esteem among the people (comp. Delitzsch, "Jüdisches Handwerksleben," pp. 45 *et seq.*).

BIBLIOGRAPHY: Rieger, *Versuch einer Technologie und Terminologie der Handwerke in der Mischnah*, s.v. Spinnen, Weben, etc., Berlin, 1894; Cheyne and Black, *Encyc. Bibl.*
E. G. H. I. Be.

WECHSELMANN, IGNAZ: Hungarian architect and philanthropist; born at Nikolai, Prussian Silesia, in 1828; died at Budapest Jan. 17, 1903. He was educated at Berlin, and then went to Vienna, where he became the friend and assistant of the architect Ludwig Förster. In 1856 he removed to Budapest, where he, as Förster's representative, superintended the building of the great synagogue. Most of the monumental buildings erected in the Hungarian capital between 1870 and 1890 were designed by him, his work including palaces, mills,

factories, churches, and the famous Burg-Bazar. In 1886 he received the Order of the Iron Crown of the third class, and shortly afterward Francis Joseph I. elevated him to the Hungarian nobility.

Failing eyesight compelled Wechselmann to retire from active life in 1890, whereupon he devoted his time to philanthropic activity in Budapest. His greatest act of charity was embodied in two clauses in his will, by which he bequeathed one million kronen to the Institute for the Blind, and two millions for the support of meritorious teachers in the public schools. Half of these beneficiaries were to be Jews and the other half Christians; and the board of directors of the Jewish community was entrusted with the administration of the bequests.
s. L. V.

WECKER, DER. See PERIODICALS.

WEDDING and **WEDDING-GIFTS.** See MARRIAGE CEREMONIES.

WEEK (Hebr. "shabua'," plural "shabu'im," "shabu'ot"; Aramaic, "shabbeta," "shabba"; N. T. Greek, σάββατον, σάββατα): A division of time comprising seven days, thus explaining the Hebrew name. There are indications of the use of another system of reckoning time, in which the month was divided into three parts of ten days each, the decade being designated in Hebrew by the term "'asor" (Gen. xxiv. 55; comp. the commentaries of Dillmann and Holzinger *ad loc.*; Ex. xii. 3; Lev. xvi. 29, xxiii. 27, xxv. 9). This apparently represented one-third of the solar month, while the week of seven days was connected with the lunar month, of which it is, approximately, a fourth. The quadripartite division of the month was evidently in use among the Hebrews and other ancient peoples; but it is not clear whether it originated among

Connection with Lunar Phases. the former. It is unnecessary to assume, however, that it was derived from the Babylonians, for it is equally possible that observations of the four phases of the moon led the Hebrew nomads spontaneously and independently to devise the system of dividing the interval between the successive new moons into four groups of seven days each. There is ground, on the other hand, for the assumption that both among the Babylonians and among the Hebrews the first day of the first week of the month was always reckoned as coincident with the first day of the month. The emphasis laid on the requirement (Lev. xxiii. 15) that the weeks of PENTECOST should be "complete" ("temimot") suggests that weeks might be reckoned in such a way as to violate this injunction. This was the case as long as the first day of the first week of the month was made to coincide with the new moon. At the end of four weeks an interval of one or two days might intervene before the new week could begin. At an early date, however, this intimate connection between the week and the moon must have been dissolved, the chief cause of the fixed week of seven days being, in all probability, the predominance of the seventh day as the Sabbath (but see Meinhold, "Sabbat und Woche im O. T." Göttingen, 1905, according to whom Sabbath, originally only the full-moon day and the week are independent of each other). The week thus became a useful standard in the measurement of intervals of time (one week, Gen. xxix. 27 *et seq.*; two weeks, Lev. xii. 5; three weeks, Dan. x. 2; seven weeks, Deut. xvi. 9; Lev. xxiii. 15).

With the exception of the seventh day, which was called the SABBATH, the days of the week were designated by ordinal numerals, not by names. In post-Biblical and later Hebrew literature Friday is known as "'Ereb Shabbat" (Greek, παρασκευή or προσάββατον; Judith viii. 6; Mark xv. 42; Matt. xxvii. 62; Josephus, "Ant." xvi. 6, § 2). The Biblical writings contain no trace of any custom of naming the days of the week after the seven planets; nor had this custom, found among the Babylonians

**Week-
Days Not
Named.**
and the Sabeans, any bearing originally on the division of the week into seven days, since it was a mere numerical coincidence that seven planets were assumed in these primitive astrological conceits. In the Babylonian nomenclature the first day of the week was under the tutelage of Shamash, the sun; the second under that of Sin, the moon; the third under Nergal, Mars; the fourth under Nabu, Mercury; the fifth under Marduk (Bel), Jupiter; the sixth under Ishtar (Beltis), Venus; and the seventh under Ninib, Saturn (see, however, Schrader, "K. A. T." 3d ed., pp. 622 *et seq.*).

E. G. H.

WEEKBLAD VOOR ISRAELIETEN. See PERIODICALS.

WEEKS, FEAST OF. See PENTECOST.

WE-HIZHIR. See MIDRASH HAGGADAH.

WEHU RAHUM (והוא רחום = "But He, being full of compassion"): A prayer, beginning with Ps. lxxviii. 38, recited on Mondays and Thursdays before TAHANUN. It is composed chiefly of Biblical verses, and is divided into seven parts: (1) "Wehu Rahum"; (2) "Hatteh Elo'a Ozneka"; (3) "Habbet Na";(4) "Anna Melek"; (5) "El Rahum we-Hannun"; (6) "En Kamoka"; and (7) "Ha-Poteah Yad." From the repetitions in it, it may be inferred that the prayer is the work of more than one author. It was known in its present form to the compiler of the Vitry Mahzor, who quotes it in full; while in the Siddur of R. Amram it is given in three versions, one beginning with "Im 'Awonenu" (the seventh verse of the present form) and followed by the confession of sins (ASHAMNU; see Tur Orah Hayyim, § 134), another commencing with "We-Attah Adonai," and the third opening with "Wehu Rahum," but in much shortened form. In the Seder Tefillot of Maimonides (at the end of the second book of the "Yad") the prayer before "Tahanun" is given in a very different version and is to be recited every day, not merely on Mondays and Thursdays.

According to a legend, the "Wehu Rahum" was composed on the following occasion: After the destruction of the Temple many Jews were placed by Vespasian on three vessels and were abandoned by their captains in the open sea. Among those thus left to perish were Benjamin Yerushalmi, his brother Joseph, and their cousin Samuel. By a miracle the vessel bearing them and their companions reached Bordeaux in safety. They were kindly received by the ruler of the country, but at his death became the object of enmity. They accordingly instituted fasts for the cessation of the persecution, and during this period they recited the "Wehu Rahum," which had been composed by Benjamin, Joseph, and Samuel. Later, when the persecutions had ceased, the authors sent the prayer to their coreligionists of other countries.

Another legend of the origin of this prayer is given in the Vitry Mahzor, though it fails to mention the names of the authors. A prince is said to have notified three refugees from Jerusalem that he would throw them into a burning furnace to determine whether they were Jews. At the expiration of the respite which they requested, a pious old man told them he had heard in a dream a Biblical passage containing the word כי twice and the word לא thrice. One of them immediately recognized Isa. xliii. 2, from which they inferred that they would be saved. At the command of the prince a fire was kindled in the street, but the flames, as soon as the old man entered them, divided in three directions, and the Jews passed through uninjured. In commemoration of this miracle they composed the "Wehu Rahum," to which each of them contributed a portion.

BIBLIOGRAPHY: Zunz, *Literaturgesch.* p. 17; Gross, *Gallia Judaica*, p. 75.
J.   I. BR.

WEIBERDEUTSCH. See JUDÆO-GERMAN.

WEICHSELBAUM, ANTON: Austrian physician; born at Schiltern, Lower Austria, Feb. 8, 1845. Educated at the Josefs-Akademie and the University of Vienna (M.D. 1869), he joined the army as surgeon and remained in service until 1878, when he resigned and became privat-docent at the University of Vienna. In 1885 he was appointed assistant professor and in 1894 professor of pathological anatomy. In 1892 he was elected member of the Imperial Academy of Sciences at Vienna.

Weichselbaum has contributed more than a hundred essays to the professional journals, and is the author of "Grundriss der Pathologischen Histologie," Leipsic and Vienna, 1892.

BIBLIOGRAPHY: Eisenberg, *Das Geistige Wien*, vol. ii., Vienna, 1893.
S.   F. T. H.

WEIGERT, KARL: German pathologist; born at Münsterberg in Silesia March 19, 1845; died at Frankfort-on-the-Main Aug. 5, 1904. He received his education at the universities of Berlin, Vienna, and Breslau, graduating in 1868. After having taken part in the Franco-Prussian war as assistant surgeon he settled in Breslau, and for the following two years was assistant to Waldeyer; from 1870 to 1874 to Lebert, and then to Cohnheim, whom he followed to Leipsic in 1878. There he became assistant professor of pathology at the university in 1879. In 1884 he was appointed professor of pathological anatomy at the Senkenbergsche Stiftung in Frankfort-on-the-Main, and received the title of "Geheimer Medizinal-Rat" in 1899.

Weigert assisted Cohnheim in many of his researches, and wrote much on the staining of bacteria in microscopy. He contributed many **essays** to the medical journals. Among his works may be mentioned: "Zur Anatomie der Pocken" (Breslau, 1874); "Färbung der Bacterien mit Anilinfarben" (*ib.* 1875); "Nephritis" (Leipsic, 1879); "Fibrinfärbung" (1886); "Beiträge zur Kenntniss der Normalen Menschlichen Neuroglia" (Frankfort-on-the-Main, 1895); "Elastische Fasern" (*ib.* 1898).

BIBLIOGRAPHY: Pagel, *Biog. Lex.* s.v., Vienna, 1901; *Oesterreichische Wochenschrift*, 1904, pp. 533, 534.

s. F. T. H.

WEIGHTS AND MEASURES. — **Biblical Data:** While the references in the Old Testament are sufficient for a general knowledge of the ancient Hebrew system of weights and measures, and of the mutual relations of the several units, they are not adequate for an exact determination of the absolute standard of measurement. The rabbinical statements that a fingerbreadth equals seven barleycorns laid side by side, and that a log is equivalent to six medium-sized eggs, are as indefinite as the statement on the Siloam inscription that the Siloam canal (537.6 meters as measured by Conder) was **Derived** 1,200 ells long—evidently a round num**from Baby-** ber. Since, however, the entire system **lonia.** of measures corresponds almost exactly with the Babylonian, from which the Hebrew measures were in all probability derived, it may be assumed that the Hebrew system corresponded with the Babylonian with regard to the absolute standard as well. It is true that the Egyptian system may have exerted some influence here and there, as will be shown later, but it is now generally recognized that the culture of ancient Syria, even before the Israelites had migrated there, was almost wholly under Babylonian influence.

I. Measures of Length: The original measures of length were derived from the human body: the finger, hand, arm, span, foot, and pace. As these measures differ with each individual, they must be reduced to a certain definite standard for general use. The Hebrew system, therefore, had such a standard: the ell ("ammah") contained 2 spans ("zeret"), while each span was made up of 3 handbreadths ("ṭefaḥ") of 4 fingers ("ezba'") each. This division of the ell into 6 handbreadths was the one customarily employed in antiquity, but it was supplanted in Babylonia by the sexagesimal system. The Old Testament mentions two ells of different size. Ezekiel implies that in his measurement of the Temple the ell was equal to a "cubit and a handbreadth" (xl. 5, xliii. 13)—that is, one handbreadth larger than the ell commonly used in his time. Since among all peoples the ell measured 6 handbreadths, the proportion of Ezekiel's ell to the others was as 7 to 6. The fact that Ezekiel measured the Temple by a special ell **The Cubit.** is comprehensible and significant only on the assumption that this ell was the standard of measurement of the old Temple of Solomon as well. This is confirmed by the statement of the Chronicler that the Temple of Solomon was built according to "cubits after the first measure" (II Chron. iii. 3), implying that a larger ell was used at first, and that this was supplanted in the course of time by a smaller one.

The Egyptians in like manner used two kinds of ells in exactly the same proportion to each other, namely, the smaller ell of 6 handbreadths and the larger "royal" ell, which was a handbreadth longer. The latter measures 525–528 millimeters, and the former 450 millimeters, estimating a handbreadth as 75 millimeters. It would seem at first sight that the Egyptian system of measurement had influenced the Hebrew, and the two Hebrew ells might naturally be considered identical with the Egyptian measures. This assumption is, however, doubtful. Since all the other measures were derived from Babylon, in all probability the ancient Hebrew ell originated there also. The length of the Babylonian ell is given on the famous statue of King Gudea (beginning of 3d millennium B.C.), found in Telloh in southern Babylonia. A scale is inscribed on this statue, according to which the ell may be reckoned at 495 millimeters, a measurement which is confirmed by certain Babylonian tablets. These measure, according to the Babylonian scale, $\frac{2}{3}$ ell, or, according to the metric system, 330 millimeters (1 foot) on each side. The ell of 495 millimeters seems to have been used also in Phenicia in measuring the holds of ships, but these computations can not be discussed in detail here. The length of the ancient Hebrew ell can not be determined exactly with the data now controlled by science; but it was either 525 or 495 millimeters, and this slight difference between the two figures is scarcely appreciable in an estimate of the size of Hebrew edifices, etc.

II. Measures of Capacity: The Hebrew system here corresponds exactly with the Babylonian. In contradistinction to the Egyptian metrology, which shows the regular geometric progression—1, 10, 20, 40, 80, 160—the Hebrew and the Babylonian systems are based on the sexagesimal system. The unit of the Babylonian system was the "maris," a quantity of water equal in weight to a light royal talent. It contained, therefore, about 30.3 liters. The maris was divided into 60 parts, probably called "minæ" (=.505 liter). All the other measures are multiples of this mina: 12, 24, 60, 72 (60 + 12), 120, 720 minæ.

In the Hebrew system the log (Lev. xiv. 10) corresponds to the mina. Since the Hellenistic writers equate the log with the Græco-Roman sextarius, whatever these writers say on the rela**The Log.** tion of the sextarius to other measures applies also to the relation of these measures to the log. The log and the sextarius, however, are not equal in capacity. The sextarius is estimated at .547 liter, while there is no reason to regard the log as larger than the Babylonian mina, especially as other references of the Greek metrologists support the assumption that the log was equal to the mina. The fact that in the Old Testament the log is mentioned only as a fluid measure may be merely accidental, for the dry measures, which are distinguished in all other cases from the liquid measures, also have the log as their unit. The corresponding dry measure may, however, have been known under a different name. The same possibility must be borne in mind in the case of the cab, the next larger measure, containing four logs and mentioned only as a dry measure. A differentiation of the dry and liquid measures gives two simple systems, as follows:

DRY MEASURES.

1 homer=	10 ephahs=	30 se'aim=	180 cabs=	720 logs=	364.4 lit.
(cor)	1 ephah =	3 se'aim =	18 cabs =	72 logs =	36.44 lit.
		1 se'ah =	6 cabs =	24 logs =	12.148 lit.
			1 cab =	4 logs =	2.024 lit.
				1 log =	0.506 lit.

LIQUID MEASURES.

1 cor =	10 baths =	60 hins =	180 cabs =	720 logs =	364.4 lit.
	1 bath =	6 hins =	18 cabs =	72 logs =	36.44 lit.
		1 hin =	3 cabs =	12 logs =	6.074 lit.
			1 cab =	4 logs =	2.024 lit.
				1 log =	0.506 lit.

In these tables that homer has been omitted which is, according to Ex. xvi. 36, one-tenth of an ephah, and which is, therefore, identical with the "'issaron" (Num. xxviii. 5 *et al.*). The tenth part of a bath, for fluids, which is mentioned in Ezek. xlv. 14 without a special name, corresponds in content to the homer, or 'issaron, among the dry measures. The homer and its liquid equivalent do not belong to the original system, as may be seen by the proportion the homer bears to the other measures: $3\frac{1}{3}$ homers = 1 se'ah, $1\frac{2}{3}$ homers = 1 hin, 1 homer = $1\frac{1}{5}$ cabs = $7\frac{1}{5}$ logs. The

Babylonian Weight in the Form of a Lion with Inscription מנה מלך (= "royal maneh").

(From Madden, "History of Jewish Coinage.")

tenth part of a bath is, furthermore, mentioned only in Ezekiel and in the Priestly Code. The old division of the ephah and the bath was into three parts; Ezekiel mentions also the sixth part of an ephah. At a later period the se'ah and the cab disappear as dry measures, so that the Priestly Code refers simply to the tenth part of the ephah. This new division into tenths may be connected with the appearance of the decimal system, which can be traced elsewhere, especially in weights and coins.

Only one measure in addition to those enumerated above is mentioned in the Old Testament. This is the "letek," which occurs but once (Hosea iii. 2). It is a dry measure, and is uniformly designated in tradition as equal to $\frac{1}{2}$ homer, although it is doubtful whether a definite measure is implied by this term. The Septuagint translates "letek" in its single occurrence as $νέβελ$ $οίνου$ = "a skin of wine."

III. Measures of Weight: It is evident from inscriptions that the Babylonian system of weight was used in Syria and Palestine even before the entrance of the Israelites into the country. The Egyptian inscription of Karnak records the tribute which the kings of Egypt exacted from their Syrian vassals. Although the sums are given according to Egyptian weight, the odd numbers clearly indicate that the figures were computed originally by some

other system, which may easily be shown to have been the Babylonian.

The Babylonians reckoned weight in talents, minæ, and shekels. Layard found in the ruins of Nineveh several Babylonian units of weight, some in the form of a crouching lion and others in that of a duck, the former being twice as heavy as the latter. This proves that a heavy and

The Mina. a light talent were used in Babylon, the latter one-half the weight of the former. A heavy talent = 60,600 grams; 1 mina ($\frac{1}{60}$ talent) = 1,010 grams; 1 shekel = 16.83 grams; 1 light talent = 30,300 grams; 1 light mina = 505 grams; 1 light shekel = 8.41 grams. There was, in addition to this "royal" weight, another "common" weight which was somewhat lighter (compare the large "royal" ell and the "common" ell, mentioned above). According to this common weight the heavy talent weighed 58,944 grams; its mina 982.4 grams; its shekel 16.37 grams; and the light talent, mina, and shekel just one-half as much. The common heavy talent and its subdivisions were the weights current in Syria and Palestine, as Josephus expressly states ("Ant." xiv. 106, ed. Niese). According to him, 1 Jewish mina (of 50 shekels) was equal to $2\frac{1}{2}$ Roman pounds, or 818.62 grams; hence 1 shekel was equivalent to 16.37 grams, and 1 old mina of 60 shekels to 982.2 grams. There were also the half-shekel or bekah ("beḳa'").

In the course of time the sexagesimal system was superseded in Babylonia also, perhaps under Egyptian influence. The mina of 60 shekels was replaced throughout Asia Minor by the mina of 50 shekels. The shekel remained the same, forming the unit of weight, while the mina and talent were reduced, containing respectively 50 shekels = 818.6 grams and 3,000 shekels = 49,110 grams.

The period of these changes is unknown. In the Old Testament the first reference occurs in Ezekiel; if the Septuagint is correct in its translation of Ezek. xlv. 12, that passage reads, "You shall count the manhe [mina] as fifty shekels." There is other evidence in Ex. xxxviii. 25 (Priestly Code), where the tax levied upon 603,550 men at $\frac{1}{2}$ shekel each was computed to be 100 talents and 1,775 shekels, whence 1 talent equaled 3,000 shekels, and 1 mina was equivalent to 850 shekels. These measures were further changed in the currency, which was also reckoned in talents, minas, and shekels. In Jewish silver 1 shekel = 14.55 grams, 1 mina = 50 shekels = 727.5

Money. grams, 1 talent = 3,000 shekels = 43,-659 grams. What bearing this change —which was confined to silver—had upon the relative values of gold and silver, and how far it was conditioned by the demands of exchange day by day, can not be discussed in detail here (comp. Benzinger, "Arch." pp. 192 *et seq.*). With this silver shekel the shekel of weight must not be confounded. In the Pentateuch the heavy shekel of weight is called, in contradistinction to the silver shekel, the "holy shekel, the shekel of 20 gerahs" (Ex. xxx. 13; Lev. xxvii. 25; Num. iii. 47). This refers to the tax payable to the Sanctuary, which, it is expressly stated, must not be paid in silver shekels, but according to weight, conforming with ancient custom.

The division of the shekel into 20 gerahs is mentioned only in the passages just quoted and in Ezek. xlv. 12 (LXX.). Otherwise the Old Testament refers only to quarters and halves of shekels. See MONEY; NUMISMATICS.

BIBLIOGRAPHY: Brandis, *Das Münz-, Mass- und Gewichtswesen in Vorderasien bis auf Alexander den Grossen*, Berlin, 1866; Hultsch, *Griechische und Römische Metrologie*, 2d ed., Berlin, 1882; Lehmann, *Das Altbabylonische Mass- und Gewichtsystem als Grundlage der Antiken Gewicht-, Münz-, und Masssysteme*, in *Actes du 8ème Congr. Internat. des Orient.* vol. i., part 2, pp. 165 *et seq.*; Benzinger, *Arch.* pp. 178 *et seq.*, Leipsic, 1894; *Weights and Measures*, in Cheyne and Black, *Encyc. Bibl.*

E. G. H. I. BE.

——In Rabbinical Literature : The weights and measures of Talmudic literature are a combination of those of the ancient Hebrew system with foreign elements; and it was especially Greek and Roman metrology which became current among the Jews in the post-Biblical period. These two elements, the domestic and the foreign, were, however, so intimately fused that it is often **Domestic** difficult to distinguish between them. **and** In the course of time the Biblical **Foreign** weights and measures underwent vari-**Elements.** ous changes which are recorded in the Talmud, where an endeavor is made to determine the original values. The Talmudic system of metrology is especially important since it affords an evaluation of the Biblical units. Talmudic sources deduce the value of Biblical weights and measures by comparing them with those which were current in the period of the Talmud, and the units of this system may often be determined by a comparison with their Greek and Roman equivalents. Talmudic metrology is therefore of importance for the history of civilization, since it bears upon conditions prevailing among the classic peoples of ancient times. The weights and measures mentioned in Talmudic sources are as follows:

Gerah (גרה) or Ma'ah (מעה): In the Talmud the gerah is mentioned as a unit of weight only with reference to the Bible. Raba makes it the equivalent of a ma'ah, and names as an authority for this equation Onḳelos, the translator of the Pentateuch, who rendered the term "twenty gerahs" (Ex. xxx. 13) by "twenty ma'ot" (Bek. 50a). This ma'ah must be the Tyrian obol or ma'ah; for Bek. 50a says: "Six silver ma'ot are equal to a denarius." Inasmuch as four denarii are equivalent to one sela', it follows that twenty-four **Units of** ma'ot are also equal to one sela'; and **Weight.** this equation was used for the Tyrian sela' (comp. Boeckh, "Metrologische Untersuchungen über Gewichte, Münzfüsse, und Maasse des Alterthums in Ihrem Zusammenhange," p. 59, Berlin, 1838). The Talmud does not indicate the actual weight of the ma'ah, but from Tyrian silver coins still extant its value may be determined. The heaviest Tyrian silver coin in existence weighs 14.34 grams, and $\frac{1}{24}$ of this, or 0.5975 gram, is therefore the weight of a ma'ah. This deduction has been based upon the weight of the heaviest Tyrian silver coin because in those that are lighter the loss in weight is evidently due to handling and use.

Shekel (שקל; Greek, σίκλος, σίγλος): This is the next highest unit of weight. The Bible designates the value of the shekel as "twenty gerahs" (Ex. xxx. 13); whence, according to the weight already given for the gerah or ma'ah, the shekel should weigh 20×0.5975 gram, or 11.95 grams. The Jerusalem Talmud, however (Sheḳ. 46d), mentions another weight for the shekel, stating that half a shekel is equal to six גרמסין; and the same value is given in Tan., Ki Tissa, ed. Buber, p. 55a. The term גרמס designates a scruple (γραμμάριον), which is equal to $\frac{1}{24}$ ounce (comp. Mussafia, "Musaf he-'Aruk," *s.v.* גרמס). Inasmuch as the Roman pound contains twelve ounces, a half-shekel becomes the equivalent of $\frac{1}{48}$ Roman pound, and a whole shekel $= \frac{1}{24}$. According to Boeckh, the Roman pound weighed 327.434 grams, and a shekel would accordingly weigh 13.643 grams. In another passage of the Talmud the weight of a shekel is given as 14.34 grams, or the equivalent of the Tyrian silver coin already mentioned. The Talmud states that the silver coin recorded in the Pentateuch was identical with the Tyrian mintage (Bek. 50b); and the Tosefta likewise declares that the silver coin of Jerusalem was identical with that of Tyre (Tosef., Ket. xiii. 3). A shekel was therefore identical with the Tyrian sela' (Rashi on Bek. *l.c.*), and its weight was accordingly 14.34 grams. The difference between the weight given by the Jerusalem Talmud (13.643 grams) and that deduced by identifying the shekel with the Tyrian sela' (14.34 grams) amounts to 0.7 gram only; and it may be explained by assuming that the statement in the Jerusalem Talmud, which makes a half-shekel equal to six גרמסין, is only approximate. On the other hand, the difference between the weight of the shekel given in the Bible (11.95 grams), and that of the Tyrian sela' of 14.34 grams, with which the Biblical shekel is identified in the Mishnah (Bek. viii. 7) and the Babylonian Talmud (*ib.* 50a), as well as in Yerushalmi (Ḳid. 59d), is too large to be attributed to inaccuracy in reckoning. The divergence finds its explanation, however, in the Talmudic statement that the shekel was enlarged, the Biblical shekel being originally equivalent to 3⅓ denarii, and being later increased one-fifth, thus becoming equal to four denarii, so that, instead of its original value of twenty gerahs, it later became equivalent to twenty-four. The Biblical shekel weighed 11.95 grams, and the addition of one-fifth (2.39 grams) gives 14.34 grams as the weight of the later coin, which then became equal to the Tyrian sela'. In addition to this shekel, which was called "the shekel of the sanctuary," and which was equal to a sela', the Mishnah (Ned. iii. 1) and the Talmud (B. M. 52a) mention another shekel, which was the equivalent of half a sela', or half a "shekel of the sanctuary," and which was probably called the common shekel. This indicates that the value of the shekel varied at different times (on the reasons for these changes and the periods at which they took place see Frankel in "Monatsschrift," 1855, pp. 158 *et seq.*; Zuckermann, "Ueber Talmudische Gewichte und Münzen," p. 13).

Maneh or Mina (מנה; Greek, μινᾶ): In the Mishnah, as well as in the Talmud, the mina is often mentioned as a unit of weight for figs, spices, wool, meat, and the like (Ket. v. 8; 'Eduy. iii. 3; Ḥul. 137b; Ker. 6a; *et passim*). In the Mishnah it is sometimes called מנה איטלקי or "Italian mina" (Sheb. i. 2, 3), the designation "Iṭalḳi" helping to determine its weight. The Italian mina contained 100 denarii, while the Roman pound contained only ninety-six. A mina was therefore equivalent to $1\frac{1}{24}$ Roman pounds, and since the Roman pound equaled 327.434 grams, the Italian maneh was equal to 341.077 grams, the weight assigned it in the Talmud. From a passage in Ber. 5a it appears that a mina equaled twenty-five shekels; and since, according to the passage already cited from the Jerusalem Talmud (Sheḳ. 46d), a shekel was equal to twelve scruples, a mina was equivalent to 25×12, or 300 scruples. The Roman pound contained only 288 scruples, and the mina was therefore equal to $1\frac{1}{24}$ Roman pounds. Besides this mina of twenty-five shekels, the Talmud (Ḥul. 137b–138a) mentions another, which was equal to forty shekels or sela'im.

Liṭra (ליטרא; Greek, λίτρα): The liṭra, which originally corresponded to the Italian "libra," is mentioned in the Mishnah (Shebu. vi. 3; Bek. v. 1; Tem. iii. 5) and in the Talmud ('Er. 29a; Ket. 67b; *et passim*) as a unit of weight for figs, vegetables, meat, fish, gold, and silver. The Jerusalem Talmud (Ter. 47b) defines the liṭra as equal to 100 zinin, the zin (זין) being the same as the zuz (זוז), since the Mishnah (Ter. x. 8) uses the term "zuz" in the passage parallel to that in which the Tosefta (Ter. ix.) employs the word "zin." A liṭra was therefore equal to 100 zuzim. From this it follows that a liṭra was equivalent to a mina, since the Talmud also calls a denarius a zuz, which makes a liṭra = 100 zuzim = 100 denarii. As has been stated above, a mina equaled twenty-five shekels, and a shekel was equivalent to four denarii, thus making the mina = 100 denarii = 1 liṭra. In addition to the whole liṭra, pieces of weight of the value of a half, third, and quarter of a liṭra are also mentioned (Tosef., Kelim, B. M. ii.; B. B. 89a; Sifre, Deut. 294 [ed. Friedmann, p. 126b]).

Kikkar (ככר): The term "kikkar," generally rendered "talent" (Greek, τάλαντον), usually denotes in Talmudic sources a weight for gold and silver (Suk. 51b; 'Ab. Zarah 44a *et passim*). It is evident from the Talmud (Bek. 5a) that a kikkar contained sixty minæ. In the Jerusalem Talmud (Sanh. 19d) the value of the kikkar is given as sixty liṭras, which is the equivalent of sixty minæ; and the same passage refers to a kikkar as being equal to 100 minæ, although this statement must allude to the Attic mina, which was equal to $\frac{3}{5}$ Hebrew mina, rather than to the Hebrew weight itself.

Other Weights: Smaller weights also are indicated by coins, as, for example, the **denarius** (Tosef., Men. xii.; Shab. ix.) and the **zuz** (Shab. 110a). In the Jerusalem Talmud (Ta'an. 68a), as well as in Gen. R. (lxxix. 9) and other midrashic passages, the **ounce** (אונקיא) occurs. In the Mishnah (Sanh. viii. 2) mention is likewise made of the **tarṭimar** (תרטימר), which, according to the Talmud (Sanh. 70a), was equivalent to half a mina. The term is a corruption of the Greek τριτημόριον (= "one-third"), and probably indicated $\frac{1}{3}$ Alexandrian mina, which contained 150 denarii (comp. Boeckh, *l.c.* pp. 155 *et seq.*). One-third of this mina, or fifty denarii, was equal to half of the Hebrew mina, which

contained only 100 denarii (comp. Zuckermann, *l.c.* p. 8). A minute unit of weight, designated as one-sixteenth of a weight in Pumbedita, is also mentioned in the Talmud (Shab. 79a; Giṭ. 22a; B. M. 105b). Another small weight, the **riṭel** (ריטל), is mentioned in the Jerusalem Talmud (Yoma 41d). This was probably a small copper coin which derived its name from the red color (Latin, "rutilus") of the metal of which it was composed.

It must be borne in mind that the values of the weights often varied in different parts of the country. The Mishnah (Ter. x. 8; Ket. v. 9; etc.) accordingly states that the weights used in Judea had but half the value they possessed in Galilee, so that ten Judean sela'im were equal to five Galilean; and the same assertion is made by Sifre, Deut. 166, and by the Talmud (Ḥul. 137b; comp. Zuckermann, *l.c.* pp. 11–12).

Ezba' (אצבע = "fingerbreadth"): The smallest measure of length; it is mentioned as a unit even in the Biblical period (Jer. lii. 21; see WEIGHTS AND MEASURES, BIBLICAL DATA). The Mishnah often alludes to the ezba' as a measure (Kil. vii. 1; Yoma v. 2; Men. xi. 4; Oh. iv. 3; Miḳ. vi. 7), although no value is assigned it. Its length may, however, be deduced from a Talmudic passage; and Zuckermann has found by calculation that the Talmudic ezba' was equal to 2.33411 cm. In the Talmud the term "ezba'" refers to the thumb as well as to the middle and little fingers. The Talmud therefore draws a distinction between the breadth of the thumb and that of the middle and little fingers, by stating (Men. 41b): "The handbreadth ["ṭefaḥ"] mentioned in the Talmud is equal to four thumb-breadths, or six little-finger breadths, or five middle-finger breadths." The size of an ezba' as given above (2.33411 cm.) refers to the breadth of a thumb. From the proportionate dimensions of the thumb, middle finger, and little finger, according to the Talmudic passage already cited, the breadth of the middle finger would be 1.867288 cm., and that of the little finger 1.556 cm.

Ṭefaḥ (= "handbreadth"): The measure next in size to the ezba'; it was used as a measure of length in the Bible. The size of the handbreadth is described in the Talmud (Bek. 39b) as equal to four thumbbreadths; and in the passage previously quoted (Men. 41b) this statement is amplified by making it the equivalent of four thumbbreadths, or six little-finger breadths, or five middle-finger breadths. From this proportion of the ṭefaḥ to the breadth of the fingers, its size, according to the measurements given above, appears to have been 9.336443 cm. In addition to the normal handbreadth the Talmud mentions two others (Suk. 7a): one formed by holding the fingers loosely ("ṭefaḥ soḥeḳ"), and the other produced by pressing the fingers firmly together ("ṭefaḥ 'azeb"), although the divergence between these handbreadths and the normal is not determined.

Ell: In addition to the Mosaic ell, which was equal to the mean ell ("ammat benonit") and consisted of six handbreadths (comp. Zuckermann, *l.c.* p. 17), the Mishnah (Kelim xvii. 9) mentions two others, one of which was half a fingerbreadth and the other a whole fingerbreadth longer than the mean ell. The standards used for measuring both these ells were said to have been kept in a special place in the Second Temple. The Talmud explains the introduction of these two ells in addition to the mean or Mosaic ell (see Pes. 86a; Men. 98a), and mentions also an ell which contained only five handbreadths ('Er. 3b). The mean ell, equivalent to six handbreadths, was, according to the measurement of the handbreadth given above, equal to 56.018658 cm. The ell which was half a fingerbreadth longer was, therefore, 57.185375 cm. in length, and that which was a whole fingerbreadth longer was 58.352 cm. The Mishnah (Tamid iii. 6) mentions still another ell, called אמת שחי, which was measured from the tip of the middle finger to the armpit. Inasmuch as the ell which measured six handbreadths was equal to the length of the forearm, and the length of the latter is to the arm as 6 is to 10, it follows that the "ammat sheḥi" measured ten handbreadths, or 93.36443 cm. In the Midrash (Gen. R. xxxvii.) an ell is mentioned under the name אמה תביקין, by which the Theban ell (ϑηβαϊκόν) is probably meant. For another meaning of the term תביקין see Zuckermann, *l.c.* p. 21.

Garmida (גרמידא): Repeatedly mentioned in the Talmud (Shab. 110a; 'Er. 50b; Pes. 111b; *et passim*), without any indication of its size. It is noteworthy, however, that the Talmud (B. B. 27a) uses this term to indicate a square ell, without designating it as a square measure, while in 'Er. 14b "garmida" indicates a cubic ell, although the customary term denoting "cubic" is omitted.

Zeret (זרת = "span"): This measure, mentioned in the Bible (Ex. xxviii. 16) without any indication of its size, is described in the Tosefta (Kelim, B. M. vi. 12) as "half an ell of six handbreadths." Its measure was, accordingly, 28.009329 cm.

Hasiṭ (מלא הסיט, רוחב הסיט = "content and width of the hasiṭ"): This term occurs as a measure of length in the Mishnah ('Orlah iii. 2, 3; Shab. xiii. 4), in the Tosefta (Shab. ix.), and in the Talmud (Shab. 79a, 106a), without any indication of its size and without being compared with any other measure. According to Maimonides ("Yad," Shabbat, ix. 7–10), the breadth of the hasiṭ equals the opening between the thumb and the index-finger, which is about the equivalent of $\frac{2}{3}$ zeret, or two handbreadths. This appears to be correct, since a Greek measure called "dichas" (διχάς) equaled two handbreadths, and was called two-thirds of a span. The hasiṭ was identical with this dichas (comp. Zuckermann, *l.c.* p. 24), and its size was accordingly 18.672886 cm.

Hebel (חבל = "cord"): A measure described in the Mishnah ('Er. v. 4) as a cord of fifty ells in length, and in the Talmud ('Er. 58b) as one of four ells.

Teḥum Shabbat (תחום שבת = "Sabbath-way"): The extreme distance which a Jew might go in any one direction from his home on the Sabbath. It is defined in the Mishnah ('Er. iv. 3) and in the Talmud ('Er. 51a) as 2,000 Hebrew ells, and it was therefore equal to 112,037.316 cm. This was also the length of the mile (מיל), with which the Mishnah (Yoma vi. 18) and both Talmudim (Pes. 93b, 94a;

Yer. Yoma 40b) indicated distances. In the Talmud (Yoma 67a) it is explicitly stated that the mile is equal to the teḥum Shabbat; the Hebrew mile was therefore shorter than the Roman, with which it must not be confused.

Pesi'ah (פסיעה = "pace"): The pace is used as a measure of length in the Talmud ('Er. 42b), and its value is defined as one ell (56.018658 cm.).

Ris (ריס = "stadium"): The Mishnah uses the term "ris" to indicate distance, and defines its length as $\frac{2}{15}$ mile. The Talmud (B. M. 33a) also states that its length was $\frac{2}{15}$ mile, or 266$\frac{2}{3}$ ells. According to Frankel (in "Monatsschrift," 1856, p. 383), the term "ris" is Persian, as is also the term פרסה ("parasang"), used in the Talmud as a measure of length (comp. Tos. B. B. 23a, *s.v.* אלא), and defined as equal to four miles, or 8,000 ells (Pes. 93b–94a).

Day's Journey (דרך יום): The Talmud defines a day's journey for a man of medium gait as ten parasangs, or 80,000 ells.

Measurements of fields are generally indicated in the Talmud by the amount of seed sown in them. The term בית סאה, for example, indicates a field in which one se'ah can be sown; the term **Superficial** בית סאתים, one which requires two **Measures.** se'aim. The latter space is defined in the Talmud ('Er. 23b) as equal to 5,000 Hebrew square ells, or to 15,690,445.095 sq. cm., and this can be used as a basis for the determination of other superficial measures given in the Talmud.

The Talmud mentions separate systems of solid measures for dry and for liquid substances, although some units were used for both. The Mishnah states that the measures were enlarged at some time or other. In addition to the Biblical measure, which is called "desert measure" (מדה מדברית) in Talmudic sources, the Mishnah (Men. vii. **Solid** 1) mentions a "Jerusalem measure" **Measures.** (מדה ירושלמית), which was equal to 1$\frac{1}{5}$ "desert measures," and also alludes ('Er. 82a) to a "Sepphoric measure" (מדה צפורית), which was equal to 1$\frac{1}{5}$ "Jerusalem measures." One se'ah "desert measure" was therefore equal to $\frac{25}{36}$ se'ah "Sepphoric measure," and one se'ah "Jerusalem measure" equaled $\frac{30}{36}$ se'ah "Sepphoric measure." With regard to the names of the units, it must be noted that the hollow vessels used as measures also served as ordinary utensils; and the name of the vessel likewise designated the measure. The Biblical log is defined by the Talmud (Pes. 109a) as equal to the קסתא (= Greek ξέστης), and was therefore equivalent to 549.338184 cu. cm. (comp. Zuckermann, *l. c.* pp. 6–10); this aids in the evaluation of several other Talmudic measures.

Beẓah (ביצה = "egg"): The egg is often used in the Talmud as a standard of measurement; and in the Mishnah (Kelim xvii. 6) a method is given by which to determine its size. The Jerusalem Talmud (Ter. 43c) defines the egg as equal to $\frac{1}{24}$ cab; and the same value may be deduced from the Babylonian Talmud ('Er. 83a), where a se'ah is described as the equivalent of six cabs, or 144 eggs. Inasmuch as a cab was equal to four logs, it follows that an egg equaled $\frac{1}{6}$ log, or 91.565223 cu. cm. The expression ביצים שוחקות ("laughing eggs") occurs as a term for eggs of larger size ('Er. 83a), although the difference between these and ordinary eggs is not stated.

Cab (קב; Greek, χάβος): The cab is often mentioned as a measure in Talmudic sources (Kil. ii. 1; Ket. v. 8; Naz. 52b; Soṭah 8b *et passim*), and its halves, quarters, and eighths are frequently recorded (comp. RaSHBaM on B. B. 89b, *s.v.* תומן). The size of the cab is given in the Jerusalem Talmud (Ter. 47b), where it is said that a se'ah is equal to twenty-four logs. Since a se'ah is equal to six cabs, a cab is equivalent to four logs, or 2,197.406683 cu. cm. The Talmud (Pes. 48a) records also a large cab, containing $1\frac{1}{4}$ "Sepphoric cabs," and a "Nehardean cab" is likewise mentioned (Ket. 54a), although no indication of its size is given. The expression "ter-ḳab" (תרקב; Greek, τρίκαβος = "three cabs") also occurs frequently in the Talmud (Ḥag. 23b; Ta'an. 10a; Giṭ. 30a; *et passim*).

Ḳapiza (קפיזא): A small vessel often used as a measure and mentioned in several Talmudic passages (Shab. 10b; Pes. 48b; Giṭ. 70a; *et passim*). That the ḳapiza was smaller than the cab is clear both from Ḥul. 25a and from Shab. 103a, as well as from the discussion in B. B. 90b. The commentaries disagree as to its size, one defining it as a quarter, and another as three-quarters, of a cab, while in one passage in Menaḥot (78a) Rashi makes it equivalent to $\frac{1}{2}$ cab. In that case it would be identical with the Persian "kawiz" (Greek, καπίθη), which was equal to a choenix = 2 xestes = 2 logs = $\frac{1}{2}$ cab. The Talmud relates that a new measure which contained three ḳapizot was introduced by R. Papa b. Samuel into Pafonya, where it was called רוז פפא ("Papa's secret"; B. B. 90b).

Se'ah (סאה; Greek, σάτον): The Biblical se'ah recurs as a measure in the Mishnah, from which it appears (Parah i. 1; Ter. iv. 7; Men. vii. 1) that it was equal to six cabs, or 13,184.44 cu. cm. Another se'ah, which was used in Arbela and called an "Arbelian se'ah" (סאה ארבלית), is mentioned in the Jerusalem Talmud (Pe'ah 20a; Soṭah 17b), although no comparison is drawn between it and the ordinary se'ah.

Modius (מודיא): A measure mentioned in the Talmud, although its value is not designated (Giṭ. 57a; Yer. Shab. 13c; Pes. 30a). In one passage, however ('Er. 83a), the term is taken as a synonym of "se'ah" (comp. Zuckermann, *l.c.* pp. 40–41).

Tuman (תומן = "an eighth"): Mentioned in the Talmud as a dry measure (B. B. 89b), its value being defined as one-eighth of a cab.

'Ukla (עוכלא): A dry measure mentioned in the Talmud, its value being given by RaSHBaM as $\frac{1}{20}$ cab = $\frac{1}{5}$ log. According to another interpretation, the 'ukla was equal to $\frac{1}{32}$ cab, or $\frac{1}{8}$ log, as stated by Rashi ('Er. 29a, *s.v.* "'Ukla"). The first interpretation, however, is the correct one; and an 'ukla was therefore equal to $\frac{1}{5}$ log = 109.8743 cu. cm. (comp. Zuckermann, *l.c.* p. 42).

Ephah (איפה): The Biblical ephah is mentioned in the Mishnah (Men. vii. 1), where its value is defined as three se'aim.

Cor (כור): The Biblical cor is defined in the Talmud (B. B. 86b, 105a; comp. Men. 77a) as equal to thirty se'aim.

Letek (לתך): Although the letek is mentioned in the Bible as a measure, no value is assigned it. From examples given in the Mishnah (Sheb. vi. 3) and in the Talmud (Sheb. 43a; B. M. 80a, b), however, it appears that it was equal to $\frac{1}{2}$ cor = 15 se'aim (comp. Hos. iii. 2 in the Greek versions).

Pesiḳta (פסכתר; Greek, ψυκτήρ): A measure mentioned in the Mishnah (Tamid v. 5) as the equivalent of a letek.

Ardaba (ארדב, אדרב): Among its measures the Talmud alludes to the אדרב, which is the ארדב of the Shulḥan 'Aruk, and consequently the ardaba used by the Egyptians and Persians (or Medes). The context in the Talmudic passage (B. M. 80b) does not show which ardaba was equivalent to the אדרב there mentioned, but it is at least clear that the latter was not the ancient Egyptian measure (comp. Zuckermann, *l.c.* pp. 46–47).

Ḳomeẓ (קמץ) or **Kuna** (כונא): In the Talmud the handful is often mentioned as a measure, especially for medical purposes. The term varies, however, in the different passages. In Shab. 110b, 'Er. 29b, and Giṭ. 69b–70a it is called "buna," but in Giṭ. 69a, Ket. 99b, and 'Ar. 21b, "kuna." The hollow form of the hand was called "kuna," from כן (= "basin"), and this term designated the quantity which one could hold in the palm of his hand. The ḳomeẓ mentioned in the Bible (Lev. ii. 2, v. 12) connotes, according to the Talmud, the quantity one can grasp between the palm of the hand and the three middle fingers.

Geriwa (גריוא): A weight frequently mentioned in the Talmud as a measure for solids ('Er. 29b; Pes. 32a; Ned. 50b; B. Ḳ. 96a; *et passim*), but without any indication of its value. A single passage, however ('Er. 14b), states that 2,000 baths, which were equal to 6,000 se'aim, were equivalent to 6,000 geriwot. It would follow, therefore, that a geriwa was identical with a se'ah.

Gerib (גריב): This measure, which in name resembles the geriwa, is mentioned in the Talmud (Giṭ. 69b) as a measure for solids (comp. Rashi *ad loc.*, where he identifies it with the geriwa). A cask or a jar serving as a large measure for fluids also was called "gerib" (Shab. 13b), and the Mishnah (Ter. x. 8) mentions a גרב ("garab") containing two se'aim.

Liquid Measures.

Besides the log, the Talmud mentions also half-logs and quarter-logs, as well as eighths, sixteenths, and sixty-fourths of a log. The quarter-log was often called simply "quarter" ("rebi'it"; comp. RaSHBaM on B. B. 89b), and was likewise designated by the term טטרטון (*τέταρτον*; Yer. Pes. 37c, where "ṭeṭarṭon" or "rebia'" must be understood; comp. Zuckermann, *l.c.* pp. 48–49).

Anṭel (אנטל; Greek, ἀντλητής): A measure frequently mentioned in the Talmud as containing $\frac{1}{4}$ log (B. B. 58b). Ḥul. 107a alludes to a "naṭla" (= anṭel), which had the same capacity. "Anṭel" is the name of a utensil, which was also used as a measure.

Ambiga (אנפק, אנבג, or נבגא): In the Talmud the anpaḳ and anbag are compared with the anṭel (B. B. 58b), whence it may be inferred that, like it, they were equivalent to $\frac{1}{4}$ log.

MEASURES OF WEIGHT.

	Talent.	Mina.	Italian Mina.	Tarṭimar.	Shekel of the Sanctuary.	Common Shekel.	Zuz.	Gerah.
Talent.....................	1							
Mina......................	37½	1						
Italian Mina................	60	1¾	1					
Tarṭimar...................	120	3⅕	2	1				
Shekel of the Sanctuary.....	1,500	40	25	12½	1			
Common Shekel............	3,000	80	50	25	2	1		
Zuz.......................	6,000	160	100	50	4	2	1	
Gerah.....................	36,000	960	600	300	24	12	6	1
Grams.....................	21,510	573.6	358.5	179.25	14.34	7.17	3.585	.5975

MEASURES OF LENGTH.

	Day's Journey.	Ris (Parasang).	Sabbath Day's Journey.	Ris (Stadium).	Ammah (Pesi'ah).	Zeret.	Hasiṭ.	Ṭefaḥ.	Eẓba'.
Day's Journey........	1								
Ris (Parasang).......	10	1							
Sabbath Day's Journey	40	4	1						
Ris (Stadium)........	300	30	7½	1					
Ammah (Pesi'ah).....	80,000	8,000	2,000	266⅔	1				
Zeret	320,000	32,000	8,000	533⅓	2	1			
Hasiṭ	480,000	48,000	12,000	800	3	1½	1		
Ṭefaḥ................	960,000	96,000	24,000	1,600	6	3	2	1	
Eẓba'................	3,840,000	384,000	96,000	6,400	24	12	8	4	1
Centimeters..........	4,481,492.64	448,149.264	112,037.316	14,938.3088	56.018658	28.009329	18.672886	9.33644	2.33411

DRY MEASURES.

	Cor.	Letek (Pesiḳta).	Ephah.	Se'ah (Geriwa).	Cab.	Ḳapiza.	Log.	Tuman.	'Ukla.	Beẓah.
Cor	1									
Letek (Pesiḳta)..	2	1								
Ephah...........	10	5	1							
Se'ah (Geriwa) ..	30	15	3	1						
Cab.............	180	90	18	6	1					
Ḳapiza..........	360	180	36	12	2	1				
Log.............	720	360	72	24	4	2	1			
Tuman..........	1,440	720	144	48	8	4	2	1		
'Ukla	3,600	1,800	360	120	20	10	5	2½	1	
Beẓah...........	4,320	2,160	432	144	24	12	6	3	1⅕	1
Cubic Centimeters	395,533.2	197,766.6	39,553.32	13,184.44	2,197.406683	1,098.782676	549.391338	274.695669	109.8743	91.565223

LIQUID MEASURES.

	Meṭarta.	Kuza.	Log (Ḳaisa, Xestes).	Anṭel (Naṭla, Anpaḳ, Anbag, Kuza).	Barzina.	Ḳorṭab.
Meṭarta............................	1					
Kuza	12	1				
Log (Ḳaisa, Xestes)...............	72	6	1			
Anṭel (Naṭla, Anpaḳ, Anbag, Kuza)	288	24	4	1		
Barzina.........................	2,304	192	32	8	1	
Ḳorṭab	4,608	384	64	16	2	1
Cubic Centimeters................	39,553.32	3,296.11	549.391338	137.347834	17.168479	8.584239

Tamnita (תמניתא = "eighth"): In the Talmud (Pes. 109a) R. Joḥanan mentions the old "eighth" of Tiberias, which was about ¼ log larger than the new "eighth"; and the Jerusalem Talmud (Pes. 37c) likewise alludes to an old "eighth" of Sepphoris, which was equal to half the "eighth" of Tiberias.

Ḳorṭab (קורטב): A small measure mentioned in the Mishnah and in the Talmud (Men. xii. 4; Miḳ. iii. 1; R. H. 13a; B. B. 90a), its capacity being defined as $\frac{1}{64}$ log (Tosef., B. B. v. 10).

Ḳuṭit (קוטית) and **Zir** (זיר): In the Sifra, Ḳiddushin, a large measure is mentioned under the name of זיר, while a smaller one is designated as קוטית. The Romans had a large oblong cask, called "seria," which they used for wine and oil; while a small tub for the same purpose was termed "guttus." Both these vessels are mentioned in the Sifra as equivalents of the Biblical "mesurah."

Ḳaisa (קייסא): A measure mentioned in the Talmud (Ber. 44b), though without any indication of its value. According to Rashi ad loc., it was the equivalent of a log.

Hemina (המינא; Greek, ἡμίνα): A measure mentioned in Targum Sheni to Esther i. 8. It was probably identical with the Roman "termina," which was used for both liquids and solids (comp. Boeckh, l.c. pp. 201, 203).

Meṭarta (מטרתא; Greek, μετρητής): A measure mentioned in the Talmud ('Ab. Zarah 10b), and corresponding to the Attic metretes = 72 xestes. Although the metretes is a liquid measure, the meṭarta is mentioned in the Talmud (l.c.) as being used for dry substances, no strict distinction being drawn between dry and liquid measures.

Barzina (ברזינא): Mentioned in the Talmud (Shab. 109b) as a small measure, no value being indicated. The Shulḥan 'Aruk (s.v.) regards it as equal to $\frac{1}{32}$ log.

Kuza (כוזא; Greek, χοῦς): A measure mentioned both in the Mishnah (Tamid iii. 6) and in the Talmud (Shab. 33b; B. M. 40a; B. B. 96b), and probably equal to the Attic χοῦς. The Talmud records another kuza, which was introduced by R. Ashi in Huẓa, and was equivalent to ¼ log (Ḥul. 107a). There were accordingly two kuzot, one the equivalent of the χοῦς = 6 xestes = 3,296.11 cu. cm., and the other equal to ¼ log = ¼ xestes = 137.337917 cu. cm.

Ḳesusṭaban (קסוסטבן; Greek, ξεστίον): A measure mentioned in the Jerusalem Talmud (B. M. 10c), the context indicating that it was of small size. Its name is probably a diminutive of ξέστης.

Tarwad (תרוד): A measure mentioned several times in the Talmud, its size being indicated in Naz. 50b. According to one opinion it was the equivalent of a heaping handful, while according to another it equaled an ordinary handful.

Shorgash (שרגש): A measure mentioned in the Talmud ('Er. 29b). According to the 'Aruk it was well known in Pumbedita.

Kizba (כיזבא): A measure mentioned in the Talmud (Men. 69b), and, according to Rashi (ad loc.) and the Shulḥan 'Aruk (s.v.), equal to a handbreadth.

In addition to the units enumerated in this article, the Talmud employs several indefinite measures, such as the sizes of various fruits (olives, pomegranates, and the like), to indicate certain quantities.

The foregoing tables sum up the results reached in the present investigation.

BIBLIOGRAPHY: B. Zuckermann, Ueber Talmudische Gewichte und Münzen, Breslau, 1862; idem, Das Jüdische Maassystem und Seine Beziehungen zum Griechischen und Römischen, in Breslauer Jahresbericht, ib. 1867; Scheftel, 'Erek Millin, Berdychev, 1905.
J.
J. Z. L.

WEIL, ADOLF: German physician; born at Heidelberg Feb. 7, 1848. Educated at the universities of Heidelberg, Berlin, and Vienna (M.D. 1871), he settled in Heidelberg, where, in 1872, he became privat-docent in special pathology and therapy, and in 1876 assistant professor of syphilology. In 1886 he was called to Dorpat as professor of special pathology and therapy, from which position he resigned the following year on account of sickness. Since 1893 he has practised in Wiesbaden.

In 1886 he published in "Dorpater Archiv für Klinische Medizin," vol. xxxix., the essay "Ueber eine Eigenthümliche mit Milztumor, Icterus und Nephritis Einhergehende Acute Infectionskrankheit," treating of a disease which has since become known as Weil's disease.

Among his works the following may be mentioned: "Die Auscultation der Arterien und Venen" (Leipsic, 1875); "Handbuch und Atlas der Topographischen Percussion" (ib. 1877, 2d ed. 1880); "Zur Lehre vom Pneumothorax" (ib. 1882); "Zur Pathologie und Therapie des Typhus Abdominalis mit Besonderer Berücksichtigung der Recidive,

Sowie der Renalen und Abortiven Formen" (*ib.* 1885). He furthermore contributed to Virchow's "Archiv" (1884) the article "Ueber die Hereditäre Form des Diabetes Insipidus" and to Gerhardt's "Handbuch der Kinderkrankheiten" an essay on "Die Krankheiten der Bronchien."

BIBLIOGRAPHY : Pagel, *Biographisches Lexikon.*
s.   F. T. H.

WEIL, GUSTAV: German Orientalist; born in Sulzburg, Baden, April 25, 1808; died at Freiburg-im-Breisgau Aug. 29, 1889. Being destined for the rabbinate, he was taught Hebrew, as well as German and French; and he received instruction in

Latin from the minister of his native town. At the age of twelve he went to Metz, where his grandfather was rabbi, to study the Talmud. For this, however, he developed very little taste, and he abandoned his original intention of entering upon a theological career. In 1828 he entered the University of Heidelberg, devoting himself to the study of philology and history; at the same time

Gustav Weil.

he studied Arabic under Umbreit. Though without means, he nevertheless went to study under De Sacy in Paris in 1830, and thence followed the French military expedition to Algiers, acting as correspondent at Algiers for the Augsburger "Allgemeine Zeitung." This position he resigned in Jan., 1831, and journeyed to Cairo, where he was appointed instructor of French at the Egyptian Medical School of Abu-Zabel. He utilized the opportunity to study with the Arabic philologists Mohammed Ayyad al-Tantawi and Aḥmad al-Tunsi. Here also he acquired Neo-Persian and Turkish, and, save for a short interruption occasioned by a visit to Europe, he remained in Egypt till March, 1835.

Weil returned to Europe by way of Constantinople, where he remained for some time pursuing Turkish studies. In Germany he sought permission to establish himself as privat-docent in the University of Heidelberg, receiving it, however, only after great difficulties. Weil had attacked Joseph von Hammer-Purgstall in a translation of Zamakhshari's "Golden Necklaces" (Stuttgart, 1836), and the faculty of Heidelberg, being unable to judge the matter, hesitated to appoint him docent because of Hammer-Purgstall's high reputation. De Sacy's recommendation opened the way to him, which, however, was destined to remain rough and rugged. He gained his livelihood as assistant librarian, and was appointed librarian in 1838, which position he retained till 1861; in that year he became professor.

At Stuttgart in 1837 Weil published "Die Poetische Literatur der Araber," and later issued a translation of the "Thousand and One Nights," the first complete translation from the original text

into German (4 vols., 1837–41; 2d ed. 1866; 4th ed. 1871–72), which was, however, spoiled in the process of publication. Weil purposed to give a philologically exact version, which would have been highly desirable in many respects; but the Stuttgart publisher authorized August Lewald to change many objectionable passages, and thus made of it a popular and salable work. This perversion caused Weil much vexation. Weil's second great work was "Mohammed, der Prophet" (Stuttgart, 1843), a life of Mohammed, in the compilation of which he was the first to go back to the oldest accessible sources in Europe. It was not in his nature, however, to attempt a psychological reconstruction of the prophet's character, as was done later by Sprenger and Muir. Washington Irving in his "Life of Mohammed" used Weil's work as a source of information, and acknowledged his indebtedness to that author.

While pursuing these studies Weil published his "Historisch-Kritische Einleitung in den Koran" (Bielefeld and Leipsic, 1844 and 1878) as a supplement to Ullman's translation of the Koran, and the translation of one of the original sources of the biography of Mohammed, "Leben Mohammed's nach Muhammed ibn Isḥak, Bearbeitet von Abd el-Malik ibn Hischâm" (Stuttgart, 2 vols., 1864). Three additional essays remain to be mentioned: one on Mohammed's epilepsy ("Journal Asiatique," July, 1842); the second an investigation of a "Supposed Lie of Mohammed" (*ib.* May, 1849); and the third a discussion of the question whether Mohammed could read and write ("Proceedings of the Congress of Orientalists at Florence," i. 357). To these must be added "Biblische Legenden der Mohammedaner" (Frankfort, 1845), in which Weil proves the influence of the rabbinic legends upon the religion of Islam.

The most comprehensive work of Weil is his "Geschichte der Chalifen" (5 vols., Heidelberg and Stuttgart, 1846–51), which is virtually an elaboration of the original works of Mohammedan historians, whom he in large part studied from manuscripts; it treats also of the Egyptian and Spanish califates. This was followed by the "Geschichte der Islamischen Völker von Mohammed bis zur Zeit des Sultans Selim" (Stuttgart, 1866), an introduction to the medieval history of the Orient. After 1866 Weil confined his literary activity to the publication of reviews in the "Heidelberger Jahrbücher" and in the "Jenaische Litteratur-Zeitung." In later years he received honors from various states, including Baden and Prussia. Owing to continued illness he was pensioned in 1888.

Weil's collection of Arabic manuscripts was presented to the University of Heidelberg by his children.

BIBLIOGRAPHY : Von Weech, *Badische Biographien,* iv. 489-496, Carlsruhe, 1891; *Allgemeine Deutsche Biographie,* xli. 486-488, Leipsic, 1896; *Brockhaus Konversations-Lexikon*; *Meyers Konversations-Lexikon.*
s.   E. O. A. M.

WEIL, HENRI: Philologist; born at Frankfort-on-the-Main Aug. 26, 1818; educated at the universities of Bonn, Berlin, and Leipsic. He went to France, and continued his studies at Paris, graduating as "docteur ès lettres" in 1845, and becoming "agrégé" in 1848. Appointed professor of ancient literature at the University of Besançon, he was in 1872 elected dean of the faculty. In 1876 he was called to Paris to fill a vacancy as instructor in the normal high school and to assume charge of the Ecole Pratique des Hautes Etudes, both of which positions he resigned in 1891. In 1866 he was elected corresponding member of the Académie des Inscriptions et Belles-Lettres, becoming full member in 1882 as the successor of Dulaurier. In 1887 he received the cross of the Legion of Honor.

Henri Weil.

Weil edited the poems of Æschylus, eight tragedies of Euripides, and the orations of Demosthenes. Among his works may be mentioned: "De l'Ordre des Mots dans les Langues Anciennes Comparées aux Langues Modernes" (Paris, 1844; 3d ed. 1879); "De Tragædiarum Græcarum cum Rebus Publicis Conjunctione" (with L. Beuloew, Paris and Berlin, 1845); "Théorie Générale de l'Accentuation Latine" (*ib.* 1855); and "Etudes sur le Drame Antique" (*ib.* 1897). He died Nov. 24, 1909.

BIBLIOGRAPHY: Curinier, *Dict. Nat.* i. 142; *La Grande Encyclopédie.*
S.   F. T. H.

WEIL, JACOB: German rabbi and Talmudist; flourished during the first half of the fifteenth century. Of his life no details are known, but, according to Grätz, he died before 1456. He was one of the foremost pupils of Jacob Mölln (MaHaRIL), who ordained him in the rabbinate, and authorized him to officiate in Nuremberg. Weil, however, did not avail himself of this permission lest he should offend an older scholar, Solomon Cohen, who had been appointed rabbi of that city long before.

Weil was later called to the rabbinate of Erfurt; and congregations far and near, recognizing him as an authority, addressed their problems to him. He approved of the pilpulistic method only as an aid to study, but rendered legal decisions purely on the basis of logic (Responsa, No. 144).

Weil was especially severe on contemporary rabbis who regarded themselves as having peculiar privileges transcending the rights of the laity, declaring in a responsum (No. 163) that no rabbis of his time had any such prerogatives, and that, moreover, no man could be regarded as a scholar (TALMID ḤAKAM) in the Talmudic sense. Of Weil's works only a collection of opinions and decisions, "She'elot u-Teshubot" (Venice, 1549), has been preserved. To this work was added an appendix entitled "Sheḥiṭot u-Bediḳot," containing regulations for slaughtering and for the examination of slaughtered cattle. These rules have been regarded as authoritative by later rabbis, have run through seventy-

one editions, and have been the subjects of various commentaries and additions.

BIBLIOGRAPHY: Steinschneider, *Cat. Bodl.* cols. 1258–1265; Benjacob, *Oẓar ha-Sefarim*, No. 99, p. 558; No. 385, p. 570; Fuenn, *Keneset Yisrael*; Michael, *Or ha-Ḥayyim*, No. 1061; Grätz, *Gesch.* viii. 309 *et seq.*, 313 *et seq.*
E. C.   J. Z. L.

WEIL, JACOB: German educationist and writer; born at Frankfort-on-the-Main 1792; died there Nov. 18, 1864. His first work was "Fragmente aus Talmud und Rabbinen," Frankfort-on-the-Main (second edition of part i. appeared in 1809, of part ii. in 1811). He was an instructor at the Jewish school (Philanthropin) of Frankfort, and from 1818 until 1845 he conducted an educational institute.

In an address which he delivered, Oct. 18, 1816, in the chapel of the school, he expressed the hope that the new era would bring the emancipation of his coreligionists. He had, however, to defend the Jews against the attacks of Rühs and Fries, and refuted them in his pamphlet "Bemerkungen zu den Schriften der Herren Professoren Rühs und Fries über die Juden und Deren Ansprüche auf das Deutsche Bürgerrecht" (Frankfort-on-the-Main, 1816). Weil was one of the founders (1823) and for many years a member of the board of the Verein zur Beförderung der Handwerke Unter den Juden.

Various articles and numerous addresses on political, religious, and historical subjects written by him appeared in the Frankfort daily press. He supported Gabriel Riesser enthusiastically, and wrote his biography in Duller's "Männer des Volks" (vol. ii.). In addition Weil was the author of the following: "Das Junge Deutschland und die Juden" (Frankfort-on-the-Main, 1836), refuting the accusation that most of the young writers who agitated Germany were of the Jewish race; "Die Erste Kammer und die Juden in Sachsen" (Hanau, 1837); "Ueber die Idee des Christlichen Staats," in Karl Weil's "Konstitutionelle Jahrbücher" (i. 321 *et seq.*, Stuttgart, 1843). Other essays written by him in this periodical were: "Ueber die Verbindung des Staates mit der Kirche"; "Lamartine, über Kommunismus und Sozialismus"; "Gervinus, die Deutschkatholiken und die Glaubensfreiheit"; "Ueber die Stellung der Konstitutionellen Fürsten im Staate." Against the reactionary movement in Prussia Weil wrote "Wagener, Stahl, die Juden und die Protestantischen Dissidenten," in Stein's "Israelitischer Volkslehrer" (1857, pp. 209 *et seq.*; also printed separately, Frankfort-on-the-Main, 1857). Weil devoted himself to historic studies, and contributed a number of articles and essays to the "Magazin für die Literatur des Auslandes" (1843–1846) and to the "Blätter für Literarische Unterhaltung" (1850, 1851, 1854). His last production, "Die Alten Propheten und Schriftgelehrten und das Leben Jesu von David Strauss," criticized Strauss for his prejudices against Judaism.

A son of Jacob Weil, Henri WEIL, is professor at the University of Besançon.

BIBLIOGRAPHY: *Achawa*, ii. 33 *et seq.*; Grätz, *Gesch.* xi. 366; Jost, *Neuere Geschichte*, i. 57.
S.   S. MAN.

WEIL, KARL: Austrian physician; born at Altsattel, Bohemia, March 19, 1844. He studied medicine at the universities of Prague and Vienna

(M.D. 1867). From 1871 until 1873 he was assistant at the surgical hospital of Vienna University, and from 1873 to 1879 at the Prague German university. In 1877 he became privat-docent, and in 1879 assistant professor, of surgery at the latter university. Weil wrote "Beiträge zur Kenntniss des Genu Valgum" (1879) and "Untersuchungen über die Schilddrüse" (1889). For Maschka's "Handbuch der Gerichtlichen Medizin" he wrote "Beurtheilung der Verletzung und Narben." He died in 1922.

BIBLIOGRAPHY: Pagel, *Biographisches Lexikon.*
s.   F. T. H.

WEIL, KARL, RITTER VON: Austrian journalist; born in Württemberg, Germany; died at Vienna Jan. 7, 1878. He studied law at the University of Freiburg (LL.D. 1827), and afterward joined the staff of the "Allgemeine Zeitung," then published in Augsburg, now in Munich; from 1830 to 1832 he was its Paris correspondent. In 1832 he became editor of the "Württembergische Zeitung" in Stuttgart, holding that position until 1848, when he went to Berlin as associate editor of the "Constitutionelle Zeitung." During the following two years he resided in Stuttgart; and in 1851 he removed to Vienna, entering, as a journalist, the services of the Austrian government. In 1873 he was retired with the title of "Ministerial-Rath."

Weil took an active interest in Jewish affairs, and was a member of the executive board of the Israelitische Allianz from its foundation.

BIBLIOGRAPHY: *Allg. Zeit. des Jud.* 1878, pp. 57–58.
s.   F. T. H.

WEIL, NETHANEEL: Rabbi and Talmudist; born at Stühlingen in 1687; died at Rostadt May 7, 1769; son of Naphtali Hirsch Weil. His mother took him to Fürth when he was ten years old, and soon afterward to Prague, where his father's brother, Lippman Weil, adopted him. Although so young, Nethaneel was granted permission to attend the lectures of R. Abraham Brod, head of the yeshibah of Prague; and he soon won the favor of his teacher to such a degree that the latter proffered him the hand of his niece, Vögele. The wedding was celebrated in 1708; and when R. Abraham was called to the rabbinate of Mayence, his son-in-law accompanied him thither, remaining there until 1713, when he returned to Prague. Here he occupied himself with Talmudic studies and with teaching, his pupils being numbered by thousands. His only source of income was the scanty salary attached to his position as assistant rabbi.

Weil remained in Prague until the issue of the edict of Maria Theresa of Dec. 18, 1744, ordering the expulsion of all Jews from Bohemia. This proved to be the means of releasing Nethaneel from a burdensome existence; for he was then offered the rabbinate of the Black Forest, with headquarters in Mühringen. He assumed office in 1745, and held it for five years, writing the greater part of his commentary on Asher b. Jehiel during that time. In 1750 he was called as rabbi to Carlsruhe; and there he completed the commentary in the spring of 1754. It was published at Carlsruhe in 1755 under the title "Ḳorban Netan'el," and was later printed together with Asheri in editions of the Talmud, although it embraces only the orders Mo'ed and Nashim.

Nethaneel officiated in Carlsruhe for about twenty years. In addition to the "Ḳorban Netan'el," which was published by himself, he was the author of two works published posthumously by his son Simeon Hirsch: (1) "Netib Ḥayyim" (Fürth, 1779), containing critical notes on the Shulḥan 'Aruk, Oraḥ Ḥayyim, and its commentaries, the "Ṭure Zahab" and "Magen Abraham"; and "Torat Netan'el" (*ib.* 1795), in two parts, the first consisting of a collection of his responsa, and the second consisting of halakic derashot on the Pentateuch.

BIBLIOGRAPHY: L. Löwenstein, *Beiträge zur Gesch. der Juden in Deutschland,* ii., Frankfort-on-the-Main, 1898; Steinschneider, *Cat. Bodl.* col. 2053; Fürst, *Bibl. Jud.* iii. 501.
E. C.   J. Z. L.

WEIL, SIMEON HIRSCH: German scholar; son of Nethaneel Weil; lived in Carlsruhe in the eighteenth century. He published his father's "Netib Ḥayyim," "Torat Netan'el," and responsa, and wrote "Sefer Eldad ha-Dani" (with a German translation; 1769).

BIBLIOGRAPHY: Fürst, *Bibl. Jud.* iii. 501; Zedner, *Cat. Hebr. Books Brit. Mus.* pp. 217, 776.
E. C.   S. O.

WEIL, TIAH (JEDIDIAH): German rabbi; born at Prague Oct. 2, 1721; died at Carlsruhe Oct. 10, 1805. He was the son of Nethaneel Weil and received his early instruction from his father. In 1744 he married Gitel, daughter of Jacob Eger, a well-to-do resident of Prague; but the expulsion of the Jews from Prague ordered by Maria Theresa drove him to Metz in 1745, where he remained until 1748, continuing his studies under Jonathan Eybeschütz. Returning to Prague, he lived in great difficulties until, in 1754, he became rabbi of Wottitz, in Bohemia. In 1758 he again settled in Prague, which he left in 1770 to succeed his father in the rabbinate of Carlsruhe. Of his works only a commentary on the Passover Haggadah has been printed (Carlsruhe, 1791, published anonymously). Responsa of his are found in the collection of Ezekiel Landau and in his father's "Netib Ḥayyim" (Fürth, 1779). Numerous novellæ and homilies are preserved in manuscript. His will shows him to have been a man of genuine piety and a believer in the Cabala. Among his descendants there were several rabbis: his grandson R. Jacob Weil was the author of a compendium of Sabbath laws ("Torat Shabbat," Carlsruhe, 1839), and his great-grandson Nethaneel Weil was Klaus-rabbi at Carlsruhe (May 1, 1892).

BIBLIOGRAPHY: Löwenstein, *Beiträge zur Gesch. der Juden in Deutschland,* vol. ii., Frankfort-on-the-Main.
E. C.   D.

WEILL, ALEXANDRE (ABRAHAM): French writer; born at Schirhoffen, Alsace, May 10, 1811; died at Paris Oct. 18, 1898; grandson of R. Abraham Kellermeister. He was destined by his parents for a rabbinical career, and was sent to Frankfort to pursue his preparatory Talmudic studies. At the same time he studied German, French, English, Italian, Latin, and Greek literature. In 1837 he abandoned his rabbinical studies, and left Frankfort for Paris with a letter of introduction from

Heinrich Heine which procured him speedy admission into the salons and journalistic circles of the French capital. He became a contributor to the "Revue du Progrès" (edited by Louis Blanc), the "Démocratie Pacifique," the "Presse," the "Gazette de France," "L'Opinion Nationale," the "Figaro," and the "Temps," to various journals of Frankfort, Stuttgart, and Hamburg, and to the "Archives Israélites," the "Univers Israélite," etc. The publication of his "Histoires de Village" (1847), to which Heine wrote a preface, and of his "L'Ami Fritz" and "La Petite Fadette" marked his entrance into the field of romance. He was perhaps the first French writer to conceive the idea of depicting village scenes and writing rustic idyls. Among his numerous admirers may be mentioned Giacomo Meyerbeer and Victor Hugo.

Weill was a born polemic, and he wrote a number of brochures on some of the leading questions of the day; among these may be mentioned: "République et Monarchie," 1848; "Le Génie de la Monarchie," 1849; "Que Deviendront Nos Filles?" 1863; "Mes Batailles," 1867; and "Lettre de Vengeance d'un Alsacien," 1871. In the "Corsaire" of March 2, 1848, he addressed a remarkable letter to Hippolyte Carnot, the minister of public instruction and father of the late president of the French republic, Sadi Carnot. In this letter, which bore the heading "Une Révolution à Faire," he strongly urged a more general instruction in foreign languages in the public schools.

Weill was the author also of the following works: "Mes Contemporains" (1864; 2d ed., with an appendix, 1890); "Dix Mois de Révolution," 1868; "La Guerre des Paysans et des Anabaptistes," 1874; "Ludovic Boerne," 1878; "Souvenirs Intimes de Henri Heine," 1883; "Histoire Véridique et Vécue de la Révolution de 1848," 1887; "Le Centenaire de l'Emancipation des Juifs," 1888; "Mes Romans"; "Mon Théâtre"; "Fables et Légendes d'Or"; "Lamartine et Victor Hugo"; "La France Catholique" (in reply to Drumont's "La France Juive"); "Les Cinq Livres de Moïse" (translated from Hebrew, and supplied with etymological notes); "Moïse, le Talmud et l'Evangile"; "La Parole Nouvelle"; "Hommes Noirs, Qui Etes Vous?"; "L'Art Est une Religion"; "Lois et Mystères de la Création"; "Etude Comparative de la Langue Française avec l'Hébreu, le Grec, le Latin, l'Allemand, et l'Anglais"; "Rabbin et Nonne, Poésie et Realité"; "Le Nouvel Isaïe"; and a volume of poems entitled "Les Grandes Juives" (1882).

BIBLIOGRAPHY: Alexandre Weill, *Ma Jeunesse*, 1888; Maurice Bloch, *Alexandre Weill, Sa Vie et Ses Œuvres*, 1905.
s.   J. Ka.

WEILL, ANSELME: French physician; born at Bischheim, Alsace, Aug. 24, 1842. He received his education at the lyceum of Strasburg and the universities at Strasburg and Paris. Settling in the French capital, he took part, as assistant surgeon attached to the Lariboisière Hospital, during the defense of Paris in 1870–71. From 1871 to 1874 he was assistant physician at the Rothschild Hospital, and graduated as M.D. in 1874. He became chief physician of that institution in 1889; in the same year he was made "Officier d'Académie"; and in 1894 he received the cross of the Legion of Honor.

Weill has published many essays, especially on the treatment of tuberculosis.

BIBLIOGRAPHY: Curinier, *Dict. Nat.* iii. 195.
s.   F. T. H.

WEILL, EMANUEL: French rabbi; born at Ensisheim, Alsace, Oct. 21, 1841; educated at the bet ha-midrash of Colmar and the Séminaire Israélite de France in Paris (rabbi, 1861). In 1865 he was appointed rabbi at Versailles, and in 1876 he was called to Paris as assistant to the chief rabbi of that city. Since 1882 he officiated as rabbi of the Portuguese synagogue in Rue Buffault, Paris. He wrote "La Femme Juive Selon la Bible et le Talmud" (Paris; 2d ed. 1881) and "Judah Maccabée Suivi de Rabbi Akiba" (*ib.* 1888). He died Apr. 14, 1916.

s.   F. T. H.

WEILL, MATHIEU: French mathematician; born at Hagenau, Alsace, May 24, 1851; educated in the lyceums of Burg and Strasburg, at the Polytechnique in Paris, and at the military school in Fontainebleau. He attained the rank of lieutenant of artillery, but resigned in 1877. In 1881 he became teacher of mathematics in the Collège Chaptal at Paris, and in 1898 its principal.

Weill has published several essays in the mathematical journals of his country, and is the author of "Cours de Géométrie Analytique" and of "Précis d'Arithmétique, de Géométrie, d'Algèbre, de Trigonométrie," in four volumes.

BIBLIOGRAPHY: Curinier, *Dict. Nat.* iii. 72.
s.   F. T. H.

WEILL, MICHEL AARON: French rabbi; born at Strasburg July 19, 1814; died at Paris Jan. 6, 1889. He was educated at the Ecole Centrale Rabbinique at Metz, where he received the rabbinical diploma, and at the Sorbonne at Paris. After acting as a professor at the Ecole Consistoriale at Nancy, Weill was in 1845 appointed instructor at Algiers, where he became the first French chief rabbi (1846–64). His earnest efforts to inculcate French civilization in the Algerian Jews met, however, with little success, and he retired into private life until 1876, when he accepted the rabbinate of Toul. Nine years later he resigned this office and settled in Paris, devoting himself to literary pursuits.

Weill was the author of the following works: "Le Judaïsme, Ses Dogmes et Sa Mission" (Paris, 1866); "Théodicée" (*ib.* 1867); "La Révélation" (*ib.* 1868); "Providence et Rémunération" (*ib.* 1869); "La Morale du Judaïsme" (2 vols., *ib.* 1875–77); "La Parole de Dieu, ou la Chaire Israélite Ancienne et Moderne" (*ib.* 1880); and "Oraison Funèbre de M. Lazare Isidor, Grand-Rabbin" (*ib.* 1888).

Weill's son, **Georges Weill** (born at Algiers July 6, 1865), was educated at the Ecole Normale Supérieure, and in 1905 he occupied the chair of history at the Lycée Louis-le-Grand of Paris. He is the author of "Les Théories sur le Pouvoir Royal en France Pendant les Guerres de Religion" (Paris, 1892); "Saint-Simon et Son Œuvre" (*ib.* 1894); "L'Ecole Saint-Simonienne" (*ib.* 1896); "Histoire du Parti Républicain en France, 1814–1870" (*ib.* 1900);

"La France sous la Monarchie Constitutionelle" (*ib.* 1902); and "Histoire du Mouvement Social en France, 1852–1902" (*ib.* 1904).

s. J. KA.

WEILLER, LAZARE JEAN: French manufacturer and author; born at Schlettstadt, Alsace, July 20, 1858; educated at the Lycée Saint-Louis of Paris and at the University of Oxford. Devoting himself to electric metallurgy, he induced the French government to employ the various copper alloys which render the long-distance telephone possible; and in 1883 he was made a chevalier of the Legion of Honor in recognition of his treatise "Conducteurs Electriques." In 1889 he was the Republican candidate for deputy of the department of the Charente; he defeated the Boulangist Paul Déroulède, but the election went by a slight majority to the Bonapartist candidate. Weiller has been successively a member of the consulting committee of the railways of France, censor of the Bank of France, vice-president of the jury on electricity at the International Exposition at Paris (1900), and member of the superior colonial council.

In 1902 he was sent to the United States on an important diplomatic mission, and on his return published his impressions under the title "Les Grandes Idées d'un Grand Peuple," which ran through more than fifty editions in a few months. He has written also a number of scientific works, which are regarded as classics, notably his "Traité Général des Lignes et Transmissions Electriques"; and he has likewise been a contributor for many years to the "Revue des Deux Mondes." He is an enthusiastic art-collector.

Weiller took an active part in the Dreyfus case, and vainly endeavored, together with his old friend Scheurer-Kestner, to induce his uncle General Gonse, deputy chief-of-staff, to rehabilitate Dreyfus on his own responsibility. Weiller by marriage allied himself to a family of orthodox Catholics.

s. J. KA.

WEILLER, PAULINE (née **EICHBERG**): American pianist; born in Stuttgart April 22, 1839; died in Baltimore, Md., Dec. 28, 1874; eldest daughter of Moritz Eichberg, cantor in Stuttgart. The Eichberg daughters, of whom there were five, inherited musical talent from both parents. Under the tuition of Mathilde Ries, Pauline's gift for music developed so rapidly that she played in public before the age of ten. When she was thirteen Rubinstein heard her play, and introduced her to Meyerbeer, through whose influence she completed her musical education at the Leipsic Conservatorium, then under the direction of Moscheles. Later she played for a season with Rubinstein at Baden. Her greatest triumphs were won as a Chopin performer. Her technique was faultless and elegant, and her musical memory aroused the astonishment of critics. In 1859 she went to New York as a teacher of music, and two years later married Alexander Weiller of Baltimore.

BIBLIOGRAPHY: M. Kayserling, *Die Jüdischen Frauen in der Geschichte, Literatur und Kunst*, 1879, p. 326; Nahida Remy, *Das Jüdische Weib*, pp. 259–260.

A. H. S.

WEIMAR. See SAXON DUCHIES.

WEINBERG, PAUL: Russian writer; born at Odessa about 1840. His father, Isaiah Weinberg, adopted Christianity. Unlike his brothers, **Peter Weinberg,** a prominent writer, and **Jacob Weinberg,** a judge, Paul never studied at any institution of learning, and this lack of training is plainly shown in his literary works. From his early youth he devoted his time to caricaturing the Jews, whose lives, customs, and habits he never studied, knowing of them only through his uncle Billizer. These caricatures were published in three works: "Stzeny iz Yevreiskavo Byta" (St. Petersburg, 1870); "Novyya Stzeny i Anekdoty iz Yevreiskavo, Armyanskavo, Grecheskavo, Nyemetzkavo i Russkavo Byta" (*ib.* 1880); and¦ "Polny Sbornik Yumoristicheskikh Stzen iz Yevreiskavo i Armyanskavo Byta" (Moscow, 1883). These scenes are crudely humoristic.

BIBLIOGRAPHY: *Sistematicheski Ukazatel Literatury o Yevreyakh*, St. Petersburg, 1893; *Ha-Meliẓ*, 1878, No. 23.

s. J. Go.

WEINBERGE. See KÖNIGLICHE WEINBERGE.

WEINGAERTNER, FELIX ALPHONSE: French musician and composer; born at Nantes May 5, 1844. The son of a musician, he received his early education at home, later entering the Ecole des Beaux-Arts at Paris, where he became the pupil of Alard and of Vieuxtemps. Returning to his native city, he established himself as a teacher of music, and gave several very successful concerts. In 1884 he was appointed principal of the Conservatoire at Nantes, which position he held until 1894, when he moved to Paris. There he soon acquired a reputation as a violinist, appearing in many concerts. He traveled through France, giving concerts in the more important cities.

BIBLIOGRAPHY: Curinier, *Dict. Nat.* ii. 231.

s. F. T. H.

WEISEL, HIRZ. See WESSELY.

WEISS, ADOLPHE: French painter; born at Budapest May 11, 1838. He was educated at the School of Fine Arts in Vienna, and in 1860 went to Paris to complete his studies. His first exhibit at the Salon (1869) was a portrait of M. Marmontel. Becoming a French citizen in 1871, he settled in Paris, and has since then been a regular exhibitor at the Salons. Among his many paintings, which include also portraits of well-known people, may be mentioned: "La Corbeille de Mariage" (1874); "La Fiancée Slave" (1877; now in the Museum of Lisieux); "En 1815" (1878); "Le Lion Amoureux" (1883); "Tournesol" and "Nymphe Découvrant la Tête d'Orphée" (1886); "La Jeunesse" and "Fillette aux Pêches" (1891); "Judith" (1895); "Captifs" (1896; now in the Museum of Angers); and "Nouvelle Captive" (1901).

BIBLIOGRAPHY: Curinier, *Dict. Nat.* iii. 101.

s. F. T. H.

WEISS, ISAAC HIRSCH: Austrian Talmudist and historian of literature; born at Gross Meseritsch, Moravia, Feb. 9, 1815; died at Vienna June 1, 1905. After having received elementary instruction in Hebrew and Talmud in various ḥadarim of his native town, he entered, at the age of eight, the yeshibah of Moses Aaron Tichler (founded at Gross Meseritsch in 1822), where he studied Talmud for five years. He then studied at home under a tutor, and later in the yeshibah of Trebitsch, Moravia, under Ḥayyim Joseph Pollak, and in that of Eisenstadt under Isaac Moses Perles, returning to his home in 1837. From the tender age at which Weiss began to study Talmud and rabbinics it may

Isaac Hirsch Weiss.

be deduced that he was endowed with remarkable ability. He felt a keen desire for the pursuit of the secular sciences also, of which he was deprived in his youth, although he had been instructed in German by his private tutor. In some of the yeshibot which he attended instruction was given also in the Hebrew language and grammar; but that did not satisfy Weiss. It was for this reason that he changed from one yeshibah to another, hoping that he would ultimately find one in which his desire for learning would be satisfied. Influenced by Nachman Krochmal, by Rapoport, and by Zunz's "Gottesdienstliche Vorträge," Weiss devoted part of his time to the study of religious philosophy. Talmudic studies, however, occupied the greater part of his time, and during the years that he spent in his parents' home he wrote several pamphlets containing novellæ on Talmudic treatises, as well as on the Shulḥan 'Aruk, Yoreh De'ah and Ḥoshen Mishpaṭ. He also kept up a correspondence with many distinguished rabbis, particularly Joseph Saul NATHANSON, and contributed to Stern's "Kokebe Yizḥaḳ" and to Kobak's "Jeschurun." To the former he contributed articles on general subjects, as well as verses and a number of biographies, among which that of Rab (Abba Arika) deserves special notice. In the "Jeschurun" he published several articles on the origin of prayer.

His Early Ability.

In 1858 Weiss settled in Vienna, where he became corrector for the press in the printing establishment of Samarski and Dittmarsch. Six years later (1864) he was appointed lecturer in the bet ha-midrash founded by Jellinek, holding that position until his death. In Vienna, where Jellinek and other prominent Jewish scholars were congregated, Weiss found greater scope for his literary activity. He immediately turned his attention to a Vienna edition of the Talmud; and the notes with which he provided most of the treatises give evidence of his vast erudition. Then, at the request of Jacob Schlossberg, he wrote a compendium of the laws and observances relating to the ritual; this work, which was entitled "Oraḥ la-Ẓaddiḳ," was published by Schlossberg at the beginning of the "Seder Tefillat Ya'aḳob" (Vienna, 1861). In the following year Weiss edited the Sifra with the commentary of Abraham b. David of Posquières; to this work he added a historical and linguistic introduction in nine chapters, and he provided the text with critical and exegetical notes entitled "Masoret ha-Talmud," giving the variants of different manuscripts as well as an index showing the parallel passages in both Talmudim. In 1864 Weiss took a prominent part in the Kompert trial, publishing a pamphlet entitled "Neẓaḥ Yisrael" in support of the testimony of Horowitz and Mannheimer with regard to the belief in the Messiah. This work called forth a reply by Nissan Schidhoff, entitled "Neshek Bar" (Fürth, 1864). In the same year Weiss edited the mishnayot of the treatise Berakot, giving a list of variants in both Talmudim and a brief synopsis of the contents. A year later (1865) he founded a monthly magazine, "Bet ha-Midrash," of which, however, only five numbers appeared. In the same year he edited the Mekilta, to which he added an introduction dealing with the historical development of both Halakah and Haggadah, and a critical commentary entitled "Middot Soferim."

Activity at Vienna.

After the publication of his "Mishpaṭ Leshon ha-Mishnah" (1867), an essay on the mishnaic language, Weiss began to prepare his stupendous work, the "Dor Dor we-Dorshaw" (1871–91; see below). Although Weiss had not been successful with his "Bet ha-Midrash," he was more fortunate with the BET TALMUD, a monthly magazine which he founded in 1881 with Meïr FRIEDMANN. In this periodical Weiss published numerous articles of his own, most of them treating of the Talmud in general and of Talmudic subjects. No less important are his biographical sketches, among which are those of Maimonides, Rashi, and Jacob Tam ("Bet Talmud," i., ii., and iii., and reprinted in book form under the title "Toledot Gedole Yisrael"). In 1891, on the completion of his "Dor," Weiss reedited Isaac Campanton's "Darke ha-Gemara," a methodology of the Talmud. His last work in book form was his "Zikronotai" (Warsaw, 1895), a collection of his reminiscences from his childhood to his eightieth year. He continued to contribute to various Hebrew periodicals, writing mostly biographies, of which may be mentioned that of Saadia Gaon (in "Ha-Asif," ii. 275–293), published before Weiss had attained his thirtieth year, and that of Mannheimer (in "Mi-Mizraḥ umi-Ma'arab," iii. 17 et seq.). In his lectures Weiss was rather free with regard to the text of the Talmud and the Midrashim. He did not hesitate to declare the text faulty when it seemed so to him; but, on the other hand, he was very careful in making corrections. He held also that the words of the ancient rabbis should not be interpreted according to modern conception, such interpretation being liable to result in error.

Weiss's most important production, through which he acquired great renown, is his "Dor Dor we-Dorshaw," a work in five volumes. As its German title, "Zur Geschichte der Jüdischen Tradition," shows, it is a history of the Halakah, or oral law, from Biblical times until the expulsion of the Jews from Spain at the end of the fifteenth century. The first volume (1871) covers the history from the inception of the oral law to the destruction of the Second Temple; vol. ii. (1876) treats of the tannaitic period until the con-

His "Dor Dor we-Dorshaw."

clusion of the Mishnah; vol. iii. (1883), of the amoraic period till the completion of the Babylonian Talmud; vol. iv. (1887), of the geonic period until the end of the fifth millennium (= the middle of the thirteenth century); and vol. v., of the period of the casuists ("poseḳim") till the composition of the Shulḥan 'Aruk. As the oral law is in reality the interpretation of the Pentateuch, Weiss thinks that it originated immediately after the redaction of the latter by Moses. The apparent divergencies in the Pentateuch and the various books of the Prophets (as the well-known differences between the books of Ezekiel and Leviticus, and many others) are due only to different interpretations of the Pentateuch in different epochs. It will be seen that Weiss defended the unity of the Pentateuch and vindicated the authorship of Moses. But he believed that Moses himself followed certain traditions current in his time, as it is said that Abraham observed God's commandments and laws (Gen. xxvi. 5). He asserted also that while the Pentateuch contains no simple repetitions of the laws, it contains additions which amplify or limit the commandments laid down in the earlier books. In the second volume Weiss gives the history of the Mekilta, Sifra, Sifre, and Mishnah. This volume contains also monographs on the Tannaim which are invaluable to the Talmudic student; without concealing the failings of some, he defends them, especially the patriarchs, against the charges of Schorr and others. In the third volume much space is devoted to the Haggadah and the haggadists; and the author does not endeavor to find apologies for those seemingly strange passages in this part of the Talmud which serve as pretexts for those who seek to detract from its value. But he points out the many edifying sentences that are scattered throughout the Haggadah, and quotes a great number of them.

As was to be expected, this work, adopted by the majority of Talmudic scholars as the standard history of the oral law, called forth replies from some malcontents. Isaac Halevy is known to have written his "Dorot ha-Rishonim" mainly against Weiss's "Dor"; and Eleazar Zarkes published a criticism of the work in "Keneset ha-Gedolah" (iv., part 2, pp. 65 et seq.). Simḥah Edelmann issued a small pamphlet entitled "Ma'amar Doreshe Reshumot" (Warsaw, 1893), in which he endeavored to make evident Weiss's mistakes; and Simḥah Weissmann, in his pamphlet "Teshubot u-Ma'anot Nimraẓot," did not even abstain from personalities.

Bibliography: Chajes, in Rivista Israelitica, ii. 126-128; Ehrenpreis, in Ha-Maggid, xl., Nos. 5-7; Elbogen, in Ost und West, v. 499-502 Jewish Comment, xxi., No. 11; Louis Ginzberg, ib. xx., Nos. 18-20; N. Sokolow, in Ha-Asif, iv. 47; idem, Sefer Zikkaron, pp. 38-39; Weiss, Zikronotai, Warsaw, 1895. For the Dor Dor we-Dorshaw: Brüll, Jahrb. iv. 59 et seq., vii. 124 et seq., ix. 115 et seq.; Grätz, in Monatsschrift, xxvi. 92 et seq., 133 et seq.; Schechter, in J. Q. R. iv. 445 et seq.; P. Smolenskin, in Ha-Shaḥar, iii. 182-183.
s.   M. Sel.

WEISS, JOSEPH HIRSCH: Hungarian rabbi; born at Podola, Comitat Neutra, 1800; died at Erlau 1881. He was a descendant of a long line of rabbis resident in Moravia in the seventeenth and eighteenth centuries; the family name was originally Weissfeld. He officiated for some time as rabbi of the congregation of Sook-Szelocze, and in

1840 was appointed chief rabbi of Erlau, where he remained until his death. He was one of the leaders of the ultra-Orthodox party in Hungary, and one of the chief opponents of the founders of the Reform movement in Pesth. Identified with the Kossuth movement in 1848, he was obliged to seek refuge for a time in the monastery of Erlau under the protection of the resident archbishop. Later he was arraigned before the royal authorities at Vienna on a charge of sedition, but was ultimately acquitted. A considerable portion of his library, consisting mainly of responsa, was presented by his grandson Stephen S. Wise to Columbia University in New York.
s.   S. S. W.

WEISS, LEOPOLD W.: German ophthalmologist; born at Giessen 1849. He was educated at the universities of Giessen (M.D. 1874), Tübingen, and Vienna; and from 1875 to 1877 acted as an assistant at the ophthalmological institute of the University of Heidelberg, where he received the "venia legendi" in 1876. Since 1878 he has been a practising physician in Heidelberg and in Mannheim. Among his works may be mentioned: "Zur Bestimmung der Drehpunkte des Auges" (in Graefe's "Archiv," xxi.); "Beiträge zur Entwicklung der Myopie" (ib. xxii.); "Ueber die Tuberculose des Auges" (ib. xxiii.); "Ueber die Abflusswege der Intraoculären Flüssigkeiten" (ib. xxv.); and "Ueber den an der Innenseite der Pupille Sichtbaren Reflexstreif" (ib. xxxi.).

Bibliography: Hirsch, Biog. Lex.
s.   F. T. H.

WEISS, MARKUS NISSA (called also **Mardokai Ungvar**): Hungarian advocate of Reform. In 1792 he had a small business at Pesth, and in 1794 he leased an estate near Munkacs, where his oppressions gave rise to complaints among the Galician Jews. In 1802 he published a pamphlet entitled "Der Jude wie Er Ist," in which he pleaded with the Jews to accept the ideas of Reform. This work caused him to be bitterly attacked by the Hungarian Jews; and in order to defend his person and ideas he issued (Vienna, 1803) another pamphlet, which was entitled "Der Bedrängte Markus Nissa Weiss an die Menschen." Finding, however, that he could not overcome the antagonistic attitude of his coreligionists, he embraced Christianity.

After his conversion Weiss published his "In Neuerfundenen Tabellen Gegründete Praktische Vortheile der Rechnungskunst," Ofen, 1805; "Der Missverstandene Text und dessen Wahrer Sinn," ib. 1806. He has further published "Unparteiische Betrachtungen über das Grosse Jüdische Sanhedrin zu Paris" (ib. 1807).

Bibliography: Alexander Büchler, in Magyar Zsidó Szemle, xvii.
s.   A. Bü.

WEISS, MAX: Hungarian chess-player; born July 21, 1857, at Szered on the Waag. Removing to Vienna, he studied mathematics and physics at the university, and afterward taught those subjects. Having, however, learned to play chess in his twelfth year, his interest in the game increased as he grew older, and he entered many international competitions.

Weiss has acquitted himself well in tournaments, 1882–1890. Later Weiss was employed in Baron Rothschild's banking house at Vienna.

BIBLIOGRAPHY: C. T. Blanshard, *Examples of Chess Master-Play,* 1st series (transl. from the German of Jean Dufresne), Index, New Barnet, 1893.

s. A. P.

WEISS, MAYER SAMUEL: An American educator, Talmudic scholar, and author; born 1816, died at New York in 1892. As a leading London rabbi, he was sent to the United States by Baron Rothschild in 1870 and settled in Appleton, Wis., where he was first officiating rabbi. Later he conducted a Talmudic school in Milwaukee, and in 1877 a like institute in New York. He was the author of "Sermons to the Slumbering"; "The Psychology of Belief in Religion"; "Talmudic Tales"; etc. He left five sons and one daughter, all of whom are prominent in their professions.

E. C. F. H. V.

WEISS, WILHELM: Austrian mathematician; born at Ridka, Bohemia, Feb. 3, 1859; died at Prague June 18, 1904. He received his early education from his father, who was a teacher at Ridka; and from 1881 to 1887 he studied successively at the universities of Prague, Leipsic, and Erlangen (Ph.D. 1887). From 1887 to 1894 he was instructor in mathematics at the Deutsche Technische Hochschule at Prague, becoming lecturer in 1894, deputy professor in 1896, assistant professor in 1897, and professor in 1900. From 1901 to 1902 he was dean of the school of engineers at the same institution.

BIBLIOGRAPHY: *Prager Tageblatt* and *Bohemia,* June 19, 1904.

s. A. KI.

WEISSBERG, ISAAC JACOB: Russo-Hebrew writer and pedagogue; born at Polonki, government of Minsk, 1841; died at Kiev 1904. He received his preliminary training in various ḥadarim, and then attended the yeshibah of Slonim, where he came to be regarded as one of the best Talmudic students. Later he went to Minsk, where he became acquainted with various Hebrew scholars of the younger generation, especially with Joseph Brill, known also as Job of Minsk. While in Minsk, Weissberg devoted himself particularly to the study of Hebrew literature. In 1873 he established himself as a teacher of Hebrew in Kiev; many of his pupils have become prominent Hebrew writers.

In 1879 Weissberg began contributing articles to various Hebrew periodicals, and his literary activity was very extensive. The following is a list of his more important works: "Ga'on we-Shibro," a scholarly criticism of medieval and modern literature; "She'elat ha-Nashim 'al Pi ha-Talmud," a work written in Yiddish and treating of the status of women according to the Talmud, as well as of the prevailing opinion regarding the authority of the Talmud; "Peshuṭo shel Miḳra 'al Pi Da'at" (St. Petersburg, 1898), Talmudic explanations of Biblical passages; and "Mishle Ḳadmonim" (Nezhin, 1901), a collection of ancient proverbs. He was the author also of exegetic notes on the Pentateuch (published by Ezekiel Mandelstamm); and he collected and published letters by the poet J. L. Gordon (2 vols.), Isaac Bär Levinsohn, and Isaiah Tugendhold ("Dibre Yesha'yah"). Weissberg contributed numerous articles to "Ha-Meliẓ," "Ha-Maggid," "Ha-

Ẓefirah," "Ha-Shaḥar," "Ha-Boḳer Or," "Oẓar ha-Sifrut," "Aḥiasaf," "Ha-Shiloaḥ," "Ha-Goren," "Ha-Pisgah," and "Ha-Tiḳwah."

H. R. H. MA.

WEISSENBERG, SAMUEL ABRAMOWITCH: Russian physician and anthropologist; born in Yelizavetgrad, South Russia, Dec. 16, 1867. He attended the public school and the real-school of his native town; entered the Polytechnicum in Carlsruhe, Baden, in 1884; and received his medical degree in Heidelberg in 1890. His chief work has consisted of anthropological researches among the Jews of South Russia, the results of which he published in 1895 ("Die Südrussischen Juden," in "Archiv für Anthropologie," xxiii.). He has also published researches on the anthropology of the Karaites ("Die Karäer der Krim," in "Globus," lxxxiv., and in "Russki Antropologitcheski Zhurnal," 1904). Several other contributions were published in the "Zeitschrift für Ethnologie" and the "Mitteilungen der Anthropologischen Gesellschaft" of Vienna. Weissenberg has been a frequent contributor to the "Globus" on Jewish folk-lore, his articles on Jewish proverbs (vol. lxxvii.) and folksongs (vol. lxvii.) being particularly noteworthy. He has written also papers for the "Mitteilungen der Gesellschaft für Jüdische Volkskunde" on the "Purimspiel" (part xiii.), "Weddings" (part xv.), and kindred subjects.

J. M. FI.

WEISSMANN, ASHER (ARTHUR) SIMḤAH: Austrian scholar and publicist; born at Zelynia, Galicia, April 21, 1840; died at Vienna May 14, 1892. He received a rabbinical training in his native town and in the yeshibah of Rzeszow, whereupon he (1871) took up the study of foreign languages and secular sciences. After officiating for some time as director of the Jewish school of Galatz, Rumania, he went to Tysmenitz, Galicia, and finally settled in Vienna.

Weissmann's literary activity in Hebrew and German was considerable. In 1872 he edited the "Jüdische Freie Presse," a Judæo-German monthly with a Hebrew supplement entitled "Ha-Ḳohelet"; but only three numbers of it appeared. He contributed essays and novels to various Hebrew and Judæo-German periodicals, among which may be mentioned "Ha-Mabbiṭ," the "Israelit" of Mayence, the "Israelitische Wochenschrift," and the "Israelit" of Lemberg. Especially noteworthy were his novels "Ha-Neder" (in "Ha-Mabbiṭ," 1878, No. 15), treating of the moral status of the Jews; "Chajim Prostak" (in Rahmer's "Wochenschrift," 1880), dealing with Jewish life in Galicia; and "Folgen Verfehlter Erziehung" (in the "Israelit" of Lemberg). His "Chajim Prostak" was later translated into English.

In 1889 Weissmann founded in Vienna a German periodical, "Monatsschrift für die Litteratur und Wissenschaft des Judenthum," which was issued with a Hebrew supplement. To this publication, which existed for two years, he contributed numerous articles, among which may be mentioned essays on the redaction of the Psalms, and critical essays on the books of Esther and of Judith, the last-named being reprinted in book form. In the Hebrew supplement Weissmann published a work on the history of the formation of Jewish sects prior to the death of Simeon the Just. He was the author also of "Ḳonṭres 'al Debar Serefat ha-Metim" (Lemberg, 1878), a critical essay on cremation according to the Bible and Talmud, and "Ḳedushshat ha-Tenak" (Vienna, 1887), on the canonization of the books of the Old Testament. In 1891 he published at Vienna Jonathan Eybeschütz's "Shem 'Olam," together with notes of his own and an introduction by S. Rubin.

BIBLIOGRAPHY: Lippe, *Bibliographisches Lexicon*, i., *s.v.*; Sokolow, *Sefer Zikkaron*, pp. 39–40; *idem*, in *Ha-Asif*, vi. 1, 152; Zeitlin, *Bibl. Post-Mendels.* p. 412.

E. C.　　　　　　　　　　　　　　　　　　M. SEL.

WEISSMANN-CHAJES, MARCUS: Austrian scholar; born at Tarnow, Galicia, 1830. He was destined for a rabbinical career, and began early to receive instruction in the Talmud and in rabbinics, among his tutors being Israel Rapoport, then rabbi of Tarnow. When only ten years of age he commenced writing versified Hebrew letters, and five years later he wrote his "Mappalat ha-Mitḳashsherim," a metrical composition treating of the failure of the Polish revolt. Part of this work appeared in the "Maggid Mishneh" (1872) under the title "Aḥarit Mered."

In 1872 he founded in Lemberg the "Maggid Mishneh," a semimonthly periodical devoted to Jewish history and to Hebrew literature; of this publication, however, only four numbers appeared. In the following year he settled in Vienna, where he edited the thirty-seventh number of the "Kokebe Yiẓḥaḳ," founded by Stern, its previous editor. During the years 1874 to 1876 he edited the "Wiener Jüdische Zeitung," a Judæo-German weekly.

Weissmann-Chajes is the author of: "Mashal u-Meliẓah" (vol. i., Tarnow, 1860; vols. ii.–iii., Vienna, 1861–62; iv.–vi., Lemberg, 1863–64), an alphabetically arranged collection of Talmudic proverbs rendered into metrical rimes; "Allon Bakut" (Lemberg, 1863), elegies on the deaths of Mordecai Zeęb Ettinger and Jacob Gutwirth; "Mar'eh Maḳom we-Haggahot" (Krotoschin, 1866), index and glosses to the Jerusalem Talmud, appended to the Krotoschin edition; "Ḥokmah u-Musar" (Vienna, 1875), parables and legends rendered into metrical verse; "Ḥa-

Village Wells in Use in Palestine.
(From a photograph by the American Colony at Jerusalem.)

tan Bereshit we-Ḥatan Torah" (*ib.* 1883; a reprint from "Ha-'Ibri"), the 613 commandments derived by means of noṭariḳon from "bereshit," the initial word of the Pentateuch; and "Mille di-Bediḥuta" (*ib.* 1884), versified epigrams and humorous sayings. In 1893 a second edition of the "Mashal u-Meliẓah" appeared under the title "Dibre Ḥakamim we-Ḥidotam" (*ib.* 1893); in this edition the Talmudic proverbs are supplied with rimed explanations.

BIBLIOGRAPHY: Sokolow, *Sefer Zikkaron*, pp. 43–44; Zeitlin, *Bibl. Post-Mendels.* pp. 410–411.

S.　　　　　　　　　　　　　　　　　　M. SEL.

WEISZ, BERTHOLD: Hungarian deputy; born at Budapest 1845. He was educated at the gymnasium and commercial academy of his native city, devoting himself especially to the study of political economy. In 1876 he became a member of the arbitration committee of the Budapest exchange, and since then has contributed much toward promoting Hungarian commerce and industry. He was one of the founders (1879) of the suburban railroad system of Budapest, and in the following year took part in the framing of the industrial code. Since 1883 he established the Hungarian preserve-factory and factories for brassware and cartridges in Budapest and Berlin, as well as textile manufactories in Waitzen, Schmeczbanya, Közeg, and Rozsahegy. He was the originator also of the Danubius Dockyards in Budapest. The national pension bureau for employees in mercantile houses and the central hypothecary department of the provincial savings-banks owed their existence chiefly to his efforts.

Since 1896 Weisz has represented the district of Nagy Ajta in the Hungarian Parliament, and in 1903 he received the title of court councilor.

BIBLIOGRAPHY: *Pallas Lex.* xviii.; Sturm, *Orsszggyültési Almanach*, 1901–6.

S.　　　　　　　　　　　　　　　　　　L. V.

WELL: The Hebrew language distinguishes between two kinds of wells: (1) "be'er," an artificially constructed hollow in which the water of a spring or underground water collects, and "bor," a cistern in which rain-water is stored. Of the former, which were probably designated also as "wells of living water" (Gen. xxvi. 19), the best preserved is that at the foot of Gerizim, which in the time of Jesus was called "Jacob's Well," and is undoubtedly very old (comp. John iv. 2). It is 23 meters deep and 2½ meters in diameter. The shape of the cisterns for collecting rain-water of course differed. A number of such ancient cisterns are still well preserved. Those shaped like a bottle, round, broad at the bottom, and narrowing at the top, seem to have been the oldest. They were usually like chambers hewn out of rock, or built up with walls; and in their construction natural cavities were preferred. Sometimes they were of very considerable size. For instance, the largest of the celebrated cisterns on the Temple area, called the "sea" or the "king's cistern," had a circumference of 224 meters and a depth of 13 meters. These Temple cisterns were fed not only by rain-water but also, through large conduits, by spring-water. In distinction from open pools, cisterns and wells were wholly covered. Even the hole through which the water was drawn in leather buckets (Ex. ii. 16; Isa. xl. 15) was tightly closed with a large stone (Gen. xxix. 3 et seq.; comp. Ex. xxi. 33), in order to prevent any one from using the well without permission.

In a land so poor in springs and water, a well was always a valuable possession. In Jerusalem every house of the better sort had its own cistern. King Mesha of Moab in his inscription (line 23) boasts that by his command every house in the city of Ḳarḥah was provided with a cistern (comp. also II Sam. xvii. 18; Prov. v. 15). The wells outside of settlements formed the stations for caravans. To-day, as of old, strife among the wandering herdsmen, the Bedouins, arises chiefly from disputes over wells (comp. Gen. xxi. 25 et seq.; xxvi. 15, 19 et seq.). The importance of good wells is shown also by the situation of many cities near wells, after which they were named.

E. G. H.   I. BE.

Some of these wells and cisterns had their origin in the time of the Patriarchs. Abraham dug a well in Beer-sheba (Gen. xxi. 30), and Isaac restored the wells dug by his father, which had been filled up by the Philistines. Ordered by the king of the Philistines to leave the country, Isaac dug three wells in succession elsewhere; the first he called "Esek," the second "Sitnah," and the third "Rehoboth" (Gen. xxvi. 16–22).

Near Mosera, where Aaron died, were the wells "of the children of Jaakan" (Deut. x. 6 [R. V., margin]), and at the ford over the Arnon the Israelites found a very ancient well, which they celebrated in song as the work of princes and nobles (see WELL, SONG OF THE). The King of Edom refused to allow the Israelites to drink from his wells, even though they offered to recompense him for the privilege (Num. xx. 19). Eliezer, sent by Abraham to find a wife for Isaac, stopped at a well to rest and to await the course of events (Gen. xxiv. 11, 13).

In early times cisterns were used as dungeons, and even in later times, when prisons were built, they were still constructed for this purpose. Reuben counseled his brethren to throw Joseph into a cistern (Gen. xxxvii. 22); when Jeremiah was accused of having incited the people against the king, he was thrown into a miry dungeon in the court of the guard

(Jer. xxxviii. 6–13); and when a later prophet wished to picture a real deliverance, he described a liberation from a waterless cistern (Zech. ix. 11).

The well, or spring, was also used symbolically, as in Cant. iv. 12, where virginity is compared to a sealed fountain; but such symbolical interpretations are chiefly found in the Talmud and Midrash. Commenting on Prov. xx. 5 ("Counsel in the heart of man is like deep water"), the Midrash observes: "Only a man of understanding, who can join rope to rope, can draw from a deep well [the Law] full of water" (Cant. R. xciii.). When Johanan ben Zakkai wished to describe the ability of his pupils, he compared R. Eliezer b. Hyrcanus to "a cemented cistern that loses not a drop," and R. Eleazar b. 'Arak to "a rising well" (Ab. ii. 9, 10).

The cistern figured also in Biblical and Talmudic law. In case one opened a cistern and failed to cover it again, and a neighbor's animal fell into it, the owner of the cistern was required to make good the loss (Ex. xxi. 33–34). The Rabbis regarded a cistern in a public place as one of the four chief sources of danger, and determined upon various punishments for breaches of the regulations connected with it (B. Ḳ. i. 1).

BIBLIOGRAPHY: Herzog-Plitt, Real-Encyc. iv. 783; vi. 563; xiv. 296, 299; Hamburger, R. B. T. i. 198; Tobler, Dritte Wanderung nach Palæstina, pp. 206–217; Benzinger, Arch.
E. G. H.   S. O.

WELL, SONG OF THE: A poem which is quoted in Num. xxi. 17, 18. It is introduced in a list of the encampments made by Israel while crossing the wilderness. One of these camping-places was Beer. After this it is explained that Beer was the name of the well referred to when YHWH said to Moses, "Gather the people together, and I will give them water" (R. V.). Then Israel sang:

> "Spring up, O well,
> Sing ye to it:
> Thou well, dug by princes,
> Sunk by the nobles of the people,
> With the scepter, with their staves" (ib. Hebr.).

Budde ("New World," iv. 144 et seq.) points out that the word "midbar" (wilderness), which immediately follows, is never used as a proper name, and that in the present text it occurs awkwardly in the midst of a list of proper names. One would expect "from Beer" (they journeyed), and not "from the wilderness." He points out also that in an important group of manuscripts of the Septuagint the words "and from Mattanah," in verse 19, are omitted. He accordingly believes that "midbar" and "mattanah" were not intended as a part of the itinerary, but that they formed a part of the poem, which read:

> "Spring up, O well,
> Sing ye to it:
> Thou well, dug by princes,
> Sunk by the nobles of the people,
> With the scepter, with their staves,
> Out of the desert a gift!"

Cheyne concurs in this view of the text (Cheyne and Black, "Encyc. Bibl." s.v. "Beer"). The song belongs to a class of ancient popular poetry of which, unfortunately, only fragments survive. This poetry consisted of short snatches sung in honor of the vine in time of vintage, and of wells and springs. Ewald thought that they were popular songs accompanying the alternate strokes of hard labor

("Hist. of Israel" [English ed.], ii. 203). No complete vintage song survives, though probably a line from one is quoted in Isa. lxv. 8, and in the titles of Ps. lvii., lviii., and lix., and there are imitations of such songs in Isa. v. 1–7 and xxvii. 2–5.

The "song of the well" seems to be a complete popular song, addressed to a well. Budde and Cheyne, as is natural from their emended text, trace its origin to the Negeb, where wells were highly prized (comp. Gen. xxi. 25 *et seq.* and xxvi. 20 *et seq.*), and where indeed they were necessary to life (comp. Josh. xv. 19 and Judges i. 15). Budde believes that the song alludes to a custom by which, when a well or spring was found, it was lightly covered over, and then opened by the sheikhs in the presence of the clan and to the accompaniment of a song. In this way, by the fiction of having dug it, the well was regarded as the property of the clan. He thinks that a passage in Nilus (Migne, "Patrologia Græca," lxxix., col. 648) to which Goldziher had called attention confirms this view. Nilus says that when the nomadic Arabs found a well they danced by it and sang songs to it.

According to W. R. Smith, the use of the song was different: "The Hebrew women, as they stand around the fountain waiting their turn to draw, coax forth the water, which wells up all too slowly for their impatience" ("Brit. Quar. Rev." lxv. 45 *et scq.*). This would imply a Palestinian origin for the song, and suggests a use for it more in accord with Ewald's idea of the accompaniment to labor. Somewhat parallel to this conception of the purpose of the song is the statement of the Arabic writer Ḳazwini (i. 189), that when the water of the wells of Ilabistan failed, a feast was held at the source, with music and dancing, to induce it to flow again. The writer is inclined to accept Budde's view.

Bibliography: W. R. Smith, *Rel. of Sem.* 1894, pp. 169, 183; Budde, in *New World*, 1894, iv. 136–144; Gray, *Numbers*, in *International Critical Commentary*, 1903, pp. 288 *et seq.*
E. G. H. G. A. B.

WELL-POISONING. See Black Death.

WELLHAUSEN, JULIUS: German Biblical critic and Semitist; born at Hameln May 17, 1844; educated in theology and Semitics at Göttingen (Ph.D. 1870), where he became privat-docent in the theological faculty in 1870. Two years later he was called as professor to the theological faculty of Greifswald, and in 1874 received the degree of D.D. "honoris causa" from Göttingen. He was compelled to resign from the theological faculty, however, in 1882 in consequence of his views on the Bible, whereupon he entered the philosophical faculty of Halle as assistant professor of Semitics. Three years later he went as professor of Semitics to Marburg, and was called to Göttingen in 1892.

Wellhausen has written extensively on subjects of vital interest to the student of the Bible and of Judaism and other religions. Among his earliest publications was a dissertation on the tribal organization of ancient Israel ("De Gentibus et Familiis Judæis Quæ I Chron. ii. 4 Enumerantur," Göttingen, 1870). This was followed by a work on the text of Samuel (*ib.* 1871) and by an elaborate treatise on the Pharisees and Sadducees (Greifswald, 1874), in which he attempted, though without success, to weaken the discoveries of Geiger. The name of Wellhausen is more especially connected with Pentateuchal analysis, and on this basis he has reestablished and systematized the theory originally advanced by Vatke and Georg, and later by Graf, Reuss, and Kuenen, which assigns a post-exilic date to the Priestly Code and makes the Pentateuch, as it appears in the canon, posterior to the pre-exilic prophets. It is, consequently, the law-book of Judaism and the religion of the post-exilic congregation, the cult of the Israelites and Hebrews being held to have been a crude tribal Semitic nature-worship which culminated in a henotheistic Jahvistic nationalism, against which the Prophets, as the preachers of ethical righteousness, often had to protest. These critical views were expounded by Wellhausen in his "Composition des Hexateuchs und der Historischen Bücher des Alten Testaments" (3d ed., Berlin, 1901); "Prolegomena zur Geschichte Israels" (5th ed., *ib.* 1899); "Israelitische und Jüdische Geschichte" (4th ed., *ib.* 1901); and in his article "Israel" in "Encyc. Brit." 9th ed., xiii. 406–441. His series of "Skizzen und Vorarbeiten," which includes a commentary on the Minor Prophets, seeks in the third volume ("Reste Arabischen Heidenthums," Berlin, 1887) to elucidate and elaborate by a presentation of primitive Arabic paganism the analogies between the original Hebrew religion and the cults of the pre-Mohammedan Arabs. With the exception of his "Book of Psalms" (in "S. B. O. T." xiv.), the more recent researches of Wellhausen have been in the history of Islam and in the exegesis of the New Testament, his latest contributions being commentaries on the Gospels. Although his works are marvels of scholarship, they are marred by an unmistakable anti-Jewish bias and a consequent ignoring of the labors of Jewish writers. He died before 1922.

E. G. H.

WELT, DIE: Zionist periodical, published weekly at Vienna (as arranged it has removed its headquarters to Berlin in 1906). The first number appeared June 4, 1897, since which time the periodical has been issued regularly. At one time a Yiddish edition was published. There have been several editors—Uprimy, Feiwel, S. Werner, etc. It was for some years a private venture of Theodor Herzl, who sank much money in it. "Die Welt" is the official organ of the Zionist movement throughout the world, and contains articles dealing with Zionism in its various phases, the renascence of Hebrew literature, and Jewish conditions in different lands. It publishes also Judæo-national tales, and endeavors to encourage Jewish art. At the fifth Basel Congress it became the official organ of the Zionist movement.

J. A. M. F.

WELTSCH, SAMUEL: Austrian cantor; born at Prague Sept. 12, 1835; died in that city Aug. 5, 1901. Belonging to a family of ḥazzanim, he early entered the profession, and became cantor of the Meisel synagogue at Prague while quite a young man. He received his musical education at the Conservatory of Music at Prague. In 1865 he received a call from the Ahawath Chesed congregation in New York, and remained its cantor until 1880, when he resigned the position in order to return to his native city. During his stay in New York he was active in improving the musical service of the American synagogue, and was one of the collaborators on the first three volumes of the "Zimrat Yah," a fourth volume of which was later added by Alois Kaiser of Baltimore. This work contains the music for all the seasons of the year and is still extensively used. In addition Weltsch published Ps. xciii. with German words for solo and chorus, and "Todtenfeier," two hymns for the memorial service. He was a very prominent member of the order B'nai B'rith and took great interest in communal affairs in Prague, being the leading spirit in various charitable and educational organizations.

s.   A. KAI.

WERBER, BARUCH: Austrian Hebraist; born at Brody, Galicia, in the beginning of the nineteenth century; died there July 31, 1876. Werber, who was a follower of Isaac Erter and Nachman Krochmal, founded a Hebrew weekly, which was published in Brody from 1865 to 1890 under the names of "Ha-'Ibri" and "'Ibri Anoki." In addition to numerous articles which appeared in this magazine, Werber wrote: "Megillat Ḳohelet" (Lemberg, 1862; 2d ed., Warsaw, 1876), consisting of explanatory notes on Ecclesiastes, together with a long introduction; and "Toledot Adam" (Brody, 1870), a biography of Albert COHN of Paris.

BIBLIOGRAPHY: Zeitlin, Bibl. Post-Mendels. p. 413.
s.   S. O.

WERBER, JACOB: Austrian Hebraist; born at Brody, Galicia, Feb. 4, 1859; died there Aug. 20, 1890; son of Baruch WERBER. When only fifteen years of age Jacob could write and speak Hebrew fluently; and in 1874 he published in "Ha-'Ibri" a novelette of rare beauty, entitled "Galgal ha-Ḥozer ba-'Olam." In addition to several contributions to his father's magazine, he wrote articles on natural science for "Ha-Maggid" (1875, 1876) and for "Ha-Ẓefirah" (1876). Upon the death of his father in 1876, he became the editor of "Ha-'Ibri," and was active in this capacity until his death, when the paper ceased to appear. In 1890 Werber was attacked by a severe illness; and when he heard that his physician had given up hope of his recovery he wrote his own necrology, which appeared in the last number of "Ha-'Ibri," three days before his death.

BIBLIOGRAPHY: Ha-Asif, 1898, vi.140; Sefer Zikkaron, p. 40, Warsaw, 1890.
s.   S. O.

WERNER, ABRAHAM: Polish rabbi; born at Tels, Kovno, 1837. He received his early education in various ḥadarim, and at thirteen was well versed in Talmudic literature, whereupon he continued his studies under his father, who was government rabbi of Tels. In 1856 Werner received the HATTARAT HORA'AH from several eminent rabbis, and shortly after was appointed rabbi of Weger; later he succeeded his father as dayyan at Tels, subsequently becoming chief rabbi. He then accepted a call to Helsingfors as chief rabbi of the entire province of Finland, and finally, in 1891, was elected rabbi of the newly founded Maḥazike

Hadath congregation in London. Here he remained until July, 1901, when he settled in the Holy Land, and died Dec. 20, 1912.

BIBLIOGRAPHY: Young Israel, June, 1899; Jew. Chron., July 26, 1901.
J.   G. L.

WERNIKOVSKI, JUDAH: Russian Talmudical educator; born in Slonim, government of Grodno, 1823; died in Jerusalem Feb. 20, 1901. In his childhood he was known as an "'illui," or prodigy in Talmudical learning. He was married at the age of eleven; he was afterward sent to the yeshibah of Volozhin; and in 1840 he went to Wilna and studied under R. Israel Lipkin. Though ordained rabbi, he preferred to teach; and, settling in his native town, he gathered around him a number of men who studied Talmud under him. In 1861 he became "rosh yeshibah" in Slonim, and continued in that position until 1900, when he went to the Holy Land to spend his last days. He was the author of "Pene Yehudah," on the tractates Shabbat and Ketubot (Wilna, 1871–72); "Leḳeṭ Yehudah," sermons (ib. 1872); and "Pene Yehudah," on Baba Ḳamma and Keritot (Warsaw, 1890).

BIBLIOGRAPHY: Aḥiasaf, 5662, pp. 428–429.
E. C.   P. WI.

WERTHEIMER, JOHN: English printer; born in London at the close of the eighteenth century; died there Dec. 18, 1883; senior member of the firm of Wertheimer, Lea & Co. From 1820 until his death he was actively engaged as a printer in London; and many important educational, medical, and philological works were issued from his press. His firm printed most of the works needing Hebrew type, also commercial reports and the "Jewish Chronicle."

BIBLIOGRAPHY: Jew. Chron. Dec. 21, 1883.
J.   G. L.

WERTHEIMER, JOSEPH, RITTER VON: Austrian philanthropist and author; born at Vienna March 15, 1800; died there March 15, 1887. He was the descendant of an old and prominent Jewish family; and his father was an intimate friend of Joseph von Sonnenfels.

Joseph Wertheimer.

At the age of fifteen young Wertheimer entered the business of Freiherr von Stifft, and five years later that of his father, whose partner he became in 1821. During his leisure hours he devoted himself especially to the study of pedagogic works. In 1824, 1826, and 1828 he traveled through Germany, Italy, France, and England; and during a protracted sojourn in London made a special study of the kindergartens organized in that city in 1824. On his return he translated into German a work by the director of the London Central Infant School, publishing it under the title "Ueber Frühe Geistige Erziehung und Englische Kleinkinderschulen" (Vienna, 1826; 2d ed. 1828). At the same time he addressed to the government of Austria a letter advocating the establishment of similar institutions in that country. With the cooperation of Johann Lindner, a Catholic priest, Wertheimer opened in 1830 the first kindergarten in the Austrian capital. The success of this institution, and of others founded in the same year, led to the organization of a central society for the establishment of infant asylums, under the patronage of the empress Carolina Augusta, and with the active cooperation of the Catholic clergy. Wertheimer was one of the founders also of the Allgemeine Rettungsanstalt of Vienna, a society for the care of released criminals and neglected children.

Wertheimer began his labors in behalf of his coreligionists by founding in 1840 the Verein zur Förderung der Handwerke Unter den Israeliten, a society whose aim it was to afford Jewish children an opportunity of learning trades, and thereby to dispel the common belief in the Jews' dislike for manual work; this object was fully realized, thousands of apprentices being trained by the society. In 1843 Wertheimer founded a Jewish infant school in the Leopoldstadt, Vienna, to which a non-sectarian kindergarten was added in 1868. During the thirty-two years (1835-67) in which he was actively connected with the management of the Jewish community of Vienna, first as trustee and subsequently as president, he rendered signal services to Austrian Judaism by raising the social and political status of his coreligionists, and by advocating religious and educational reforms. Among other institutions founded by Wertheimer may be mentioned the Verein zur Versorgung Hilfsbedürftiger Waisen der Israelitischen Cultusgemeinde (1860), which led to the establishment of a girls' orphan asylum; and the Israelitische Allianz zu Wien (1872), of which he remained president for a number of years. In recognition of his labors the emperor conferred upon him the Order of the Iron Crown with the accompanying patent of nobility, and he was made an honorary citizen of Vienna. He took active part in the conferences of the second Jewish synod of Augsburg July 11-17, 1871.

Wertheimer's interest in the emancipation of his coreligionists led him to publish his work "Die Juden in Oesterreich vom Standpunkte der Geschichte, des Rechtes und des Staatsvortheiles" (2 vols., Leipsic, 1842), which is still considered a standard work. As such a work could not be issued in Austria at that time, and as Austrian subjects were forbidden to print interdicted works elsewhere, the writer's name had to be concealed from the authorities. Of other works by Wertheimer the following may be mentioned: "Therese. Ein Handbuch für Mütter und Kinderwärterinnen" (1835); "Dramatische Beiträge" (1838), consisting partly of translations from the English; "Die Stellung der Juden in Oesterreich" (Vienna, 1853); "Die Regelung der Staatsbürgerlichen Stellung der Juden in Oesterreich" (ib. 1859); "Jahrbuch für Israeliten" (11 vols., ib. 1854-64); "Die Emancipation Unserer Glaubensgenossen" (ib. 1882); and "Jüdische Lehre und Jüdisches Leben" (ib. 1883). From 1848 until his death he edited the "Wiener Geschäftsbericht";

and he contributed many political, economic, and historical essays to various periodicals.

BIBLIOGRAPHY: *Die Neuzeit*, March, 1887; Wurzbach, *Biog. Lex. der Oesterreichischen Monarchie*; *Jew. Chron.* March 25, 1887.
S.   S. SA.

WERTHEIMER, SAMSON: Austrian court Jew, financier, and rabbi; born at Worms Jan. 17, 1658; died at Vienna Aug. 6, 1724. He was the son of Joseph Josel Wertheimer (d. May 2, 1713, at the age of eighty-seven), and received his education at the yeshibot of Worms and Frankfort-on-the-Main. He went to Vienna Dec. 2, 1684, and associated himself with Samuel Oppenheimer, sharing the latter's privilege of residence. During the absence of Oppenheimer, Wertheimer represented him in transactions with the Austrian government. Wertheimer soon gained the confidence of Emperor Leopold I., who presented a portrait of himself to Wertheimer and his son Wolf, and on Dec. 15, 1701, followed this gift with another of 1,000 ducats for the financier's success in obtaining for the daughter of the King of Poland a dowry of 1,000,000 florins from her father upon her marriage to Leopold's brother-in-law Duke Charles Philip. In the Spanish War of Succession Wertheimer united with Samuel Oppenheimer to procure the money necessary for the equipment of the imperial army and for the supply of provisions. After Oppenheimer's failure, and his sudden death in 1703, Wertheimer maintained the credit of the state and found new sources of income. On Aug. 29, 1703, the emperor appointed him court factor, and extended for twenty years his privileges of free religious worship, denizenship, and immunity from taxation. Joseph I., who succeeded his father on May 5, 1705, confirmed Wertheimer's title and privileges.

Supplied the Imperial Army.

Under Emperor Joseph I., Wertheimer maintained his position as a financier and creditor of the state. He was in personal relations with Prince Eugene of Savoy, to whom he paid 300,000 florins promised by Joseph I., Charles VI. adding another 100,000 florins. During the Turkish war Wertheimer made large loans to the government. The title of "Landesrabbiner," which the Jews of Hungary had bestowed on Wertheimer, was made effective by Charles VI. (Aug. 26, 1711). Wertheimer, according to a contemporary account of one of his relatives, Abraham Levi, was called the "Juden Kaiser." Ten imperial soldiers stood as sentinels before his house. He possessed many of the palaces and gardens in Vienna, and numerous estates and houses in Germany, e.g., in Frankfort-on-the-Main, Worms, and other cities. He established schools, and distributed large amounts of money in Europe and in the Holy Land. Alien Jews were not allowed to remain over night in Vienna without a written permit from him.

Rabbinical Knowledge.

Wertheimer did not discontinue his rabbinical studies. In a manuscript volume he left a number of derashot that he had delivered in the private synagogue in his house; these show considerable Talmudic erudition. He delivered many funeral sermons on the deaths of distinguished rabbis, as Simḥah Cohen and David ben Israel, rabbi of Trebitsch and son-in-law of Menahem Krochmal. From far and near questions of religion, particularly of ritual, were submitted to him and to the rabbinical court over which he presided; and to the latter he called such great authorities as Jacob Eliezer Braunschweig, Simeon ben Judah Löb Jalles of Cracow, and Alexander ben Menahem ha-Levi of Prossnitz.

Moses Meïr Perls, for many years Wertheimer's secretary and almoner, mentions him in his "Megillat Sefer" (1709) as "a rabbi of great congregations in Israel." In some works Wertheimer is called "rabbi of Prague and Bohemia"; but he did not accept this title, as may be seen in an edition of Alfasi (Frankfort-on-the-Main, 1699–1700). His reputation spread

Tombstone of Samson Wertheimer at Vienna.
(From a photograph.)

even to the Orient, where he was described as a "prince of the Holy Land" and given the title of "rabbi of Hebron and Safed." His native city also honored him with the title of rabbi. Many authors sought his "approbation," but only in a few cases did he give it, e.g., in Moses ben Menahem's "Wa-Yakhel Mosheh," and Jair Bacharach's "Ḥawwot Yaïr." He contributed liberally toward the publication of such works as "Ḥawwot Yaïr" (in which his name appears with that of Samuel Oppenheimer), Judah ben Nisan's "Bet Yehu-

As Mæcenas. dah," Gershon Ashkenazi's "'Abodat ha-Gershuni" and "Tif'eret ha-Gershuni" (in which David Oppenheimer also is mentioned). He and his son-in-law Moses Kann bore the greater part of the expense of

printing the Babylonian Talmud at Frankfort-on-the-Main in 1712–22; this excellent edition was confiscated and for thirty years kept under lock and key (see Kann, Moses).

When Eisenmenger's "Entdecktes Judenthum" appeared at Frankfort in 1700, Wertheimer addressed to Emperor Leopold a petition in which he exposed the grave dangers which the malicious and slanderous attack of the unscrupulous author would bring upon the Jews. Accordingly the 2,000 copies of the book were confiscated, and for years its sale was forbidden.

When, in consequence of Rákóczy's insurrection (1708), the Jewish congregation of Eisenstadt had been dispersed and the wealthier members had taken refuge in Vienna, Wertheimer persuaded them to return or to help their poorer brethren rebuild the congregation. He himself built for them in Eisenstadt a house and a beautiful synagogue, still called "Samson's Schule." He lent his aid also in establishing about forty congregations in Hungary. In Frankfort-on-the-Main he founded and richly endowed a Talmudical school, at whose head was his son-in-law Moses Kann.

By the marriages of his children Wertheimer became connected with the most prominent families of Austria and Germany. His stepson Isaac Nathan Oppenheimer married a daughter of the wealthy purveyor Pösing; his eldest son, **Wolf**, married a daughter of Emanuel Oppenheimer. Wolf was an active agent in his father's financial transactions, and shared his dignity as court factor. He later experienced great reverses of fortune, however. Having invested a large part of his wealth in loans to the Bavarian government, the stipulated terms of repayment were not kept, and bankruptcy stared him in the face. For a time he was able to pay only half of the interest on the 150,000 florins which Samson Wertheimer had donated to charity, and of which Wolf was trustee. On his father's donation of 22,000 florins in favor of the German Jews in Palestine he did not pay any interest after 1733. His embarrassment was ended by Elector Maximilian, who liquidated his debts. In his will (1762) Wolf declared that, although entailing a great loss upon him, he accepted this liquidation in order to do justice to his creditors. Further, he enjoined his children to pay in full his father's donation of 22,000 florins, although in 1759 he (Wolf) had returned to the Frankfort congregation 10,000 florins which it had contributed to this fund. In 1769 the grandchildren of Samson Wertheimer secured the donation of 150,000 florins, and Wolf's heirs added thereto 40,000 florins, in compensation for unpaid interest. These two foundations at Vienna and Jerusalem still keep alive the name of Wertheimer.

Samson's second son, **Löb**, married a daughter of Issachar ha-Levi Bermann of Halberstadt, a relative of Leffman Behrens, court Jew of Hanover; thus the three great "shetadlanin" were closely connected. Samson's sons-in-law were: R. Moses Kann of Frankfort-on-the-Main; Issachar Berush Eskeles, father of the Vienna banker Bernhard Eskeles; Joseph, son of R. David Oppenheimer; and Seligmann Berend Kohn, called Solomon of Hamburg. His youngest son, **Joseph Josel** (b. 1718), married a daughter of his stepbrother Wolf. Joseph died in Vienna (1761), where he was greatly esteemed for his charity and Talmudic learning. See COURT JEWS.

BIBLIOGRAPHY: David Kaufmann, *Samson Wertheimer*, Vienna, 1888; idem, *Urkundliches aus dem Leben Samson Wertheimer's*, ib. 1892; Wurzbach, *Bibliographisches Lexicon*, lv. 130 et seq.
S.
S. MAN.

WERTHEIMER, SOLOMON AARON: Hungarian rabbi and scholar; born at Bösing Nov. 18, 1866. In 1871 he went with his parents to Jerusalem, where he was educated; and in 1890 he resided at Cairo, Egypt, where he collected ancient Jewish manuscripts. He is the author of the following works: "Ebel Mosheh" (1885), sermon delivered on the death of Sir Moses Montefiore; "Ḥiddushe Rabbi Nissim" (1888); "Pirḳe Hekalot" and "Ẓawwa'at Naftali" (1889); "Darke shel Torah" (1891), guide to the theory of the Talmud and to the fundamental principles of the Halakah and Haggadah; "Ḥatam Sofer" (1891), Talmudic studies, with notes; "Batte Midrashot" (4 parts, 1893–97), a collection of short midrashim from manuscripts, with glosses, notes, and introduction; "Ginze Yerushalayim" (3 parts, 1896–1902), a collection of scientific, literary, and poetic treatises, from rare manuscripts, with notes and introduction; "Midrash Ḥaserot wi-Yeterot" (1898), from the Parma manuscript, collated with three Egyptian manuscripts; "Leshon Ḥasidim" (1898), notes and introduction to the "Sefer Ḥasidim"; "Ḳohelet Shelomoh" (1899), a collection of geonic responsa, with notes and introduction, and with Hebrew translations of the Arabic responsa; and "'Abodat Ḥaleb" (1902), a commentary on the Jewish prayers.
S.

WESEL, BARUCH BENDET BEN REUBEN (called also **Benedict Reuben Gompertz**): German rabbi and scholar; born at Wesel in the latter half of the seventeenth century; died at Breslau in the latter part of 1753 or the beginning of 1754. He was a descendant of a prominent family which had ramifications in Germany, Austria, and Holland. His grandfather, Elijah Emmerich, was a confidential adviser of the Great Elector, and knew how to use his influence in behalf of his German coreligionists. Baruch's father, Reuben, was a rich merchant of Berlin, and was closely related to wealthy families in Breslau. In 1724 Baruch was one of the three members of the Breslau rabbinical court, and in that year he approved Solomon Hanau's "Sha'are Tefillah." On Jan. 30, 1728, the Council of Four Lands appointed him rabbi (*i.e.*, advocate) of the Polish congregation at Breslau. From his father he had inherited a fortune which made him financially independent; and he engaged in the trade of a money-broker, the rabbinate being unsalaried. Through poor business management, however, he soon lost his fortune, and in 1733 he was compelled to call a meeting of the wealthiest members of his congregation, who granted him a salary. Shortly afterward he requested the city authorities to strike his name from the tax-list of wholesale merchants, and to enroll him among the "Toleranz-Imposts," the second class of taxpayers. This petition was rejected; he was imprisoned, compelled to pay his arrears of first-class taxes, and deprived of the title of rabbi. After the issuance of the decree of expulsion by Maria Theresa (July 10, 1738), he was allowed to remain in the city as a "Plautzen Rabbiner" only. When Frederick II. invaded Silesia, Wesel wrote in his honor a eulogy, in the form of an acrostic (Breslau, 1741), of which only two copies have been preserved.

On the issuance of the new decree of May 6, 1744, which permitted only twelve families of Polish Jews, in addition to the privileged Polish merchants, to remain in Breslau, Wesel was appointed "'Landesrabbiner' without jurisdiction." In the same decree the Jews, who theretofore had buried their dead in Dyhernfurth, were ordered to purchase a site for a cemetery, but the congregation seemed unwilling to comply. Wesel thereupon suggested to the community that the money necessary for the purchase of the cemetery, as well as for the taxes on it, might be procured from a meat-tax. He died in the midst of these deliberations, and was buried in the cemetery at Dyhernfurth. His work "Meḳor Baruk," a collection of ten responsa, appeared in Dyhernfurth in 1755 (2d ed., published by his son Moses, Amsterdam, 1771).

BIBLIOGRAPHY: Benjacob, *Oẓar ha-Sefarim*, p. 366; Fuenn, *Keneset Yisrael*, p. 194; Zedner, *Cat. Hebr. Books Brit. Mus.* pp. 776–777; Azulai, *Shem ha-Gedolim*, s.v.; Steinschneider, *Cat. Bodl.* col. 776; Brann, *Gesch. des Landesrabbinats in Schlesien*, in *Grätz Jubelschrift*, pp. 237–251, Breslau, 1887.
D.
S. O.

WE-SHAMERU ("And the children of Israel shall keep the Sabbath"; Ex. xxxi. 16, 17): Quotation from the Pentateuch, recited before the "'Amidah" in the Sabbath evening service, and repeated in the domestic ḲIDDUSH on Sabbath morning after service. Nowadays it is usually chanted in a choral setting, or responsorially; but by the older precentors it was declaimed in a rhapsodical improvisation based on other melodies in the service, especially on the air

WE-SHAMERU (Ex. xxxi. 16, 17)

Recit. ad lib.

mf We - sha - me - ru   be - ne.............. Yis..... ra - el   et   ha - Shab -

cres.

bat,................... la - 'a - sot....   et   ha - Shab - bat....   le - do - ro -

tam be-rit 'o - lam. Be - ni.... u - ben be-ne Yis - ra - el

ot hi.... le-'o - lam, f ki she-shet ya-mim 'a - sah A - do - nai...

et ha - sha - ma - yim we - et ha - a - rez, u - ba - yom ha - she -

bi - 'i shab - - - - - - - -

bat wa - yin - na - - fash, wa - yin - na - fash.

for the "Ḳaddish" as rendered after the reading of
the Law on Sabbath, which is usually the one employed also before the " 'Amidah" on Friday evening, immediately following "We-Shameru." The
strains between A and B, C and D in the accompanying recitative, due to Naumbourg of Paris, may be
compared with the corresponding passages in the
JEW. ENCYC. vii. 404, s. v. ḲADDISH (AFTER THE
PENTATEUCHAL LESSON—SABBATH).

A.   F. L. C.

WESSELY, HARTWIG. See WESSELY,
NAPHTALI HIRZ.

WESSELY, MORITZ AUGUST: German
physician; born at Bleicherode, near Erfurt, Oct.
15, 1800; died at Nordhausen March 7, 1850; nephew
of Naphtali Hirz WESSELY. He was educated at the
universities of Halle and Göttingen (M.D. 1823); from
1823 to 1828 he studied at Paris; and in the latter
year, returning to Germany, settled in Nordhausen,
where he practised medicine until his death. Wessely received the title of "Geheimer Hofrath" from
the Duke of Nassau, and that of "Sanitätsrath" from
the King of Prussia. In 1849 he founded, together
with L. Blödan, the "Neue Zeitung für Medizin" and
the "Medicinal Reform," both of which journals he
edited until his death.

BIBLIOGRAPHY: Hirsch, Biog. Lex.
S.   F. T. H.

**WESSELY, NAPHTALI HIRZ (HART-
WIG):** German Hebraist and educationist; born
at Hamburg 1725; died there Feb. 28, 1805. One
of his ancestors, **Joseph Reis,** fled from Podolia
in 1648 on account of the CHMIELNICKI persecutions, during which his whole family had perished.
After a brief sojourn in Cracow, Reis settled in Am-

sterdam, where he acquired great wealth, and where
he, in 1671, was one of the signers of a petition to the
Dutch government requesting permission to erect a
synagogue. Together with his younger son, **Moses,**
Reis later settled in Wesel on the Rhine, whence the
family name "Wessely" originated. In the synagogue at Wesel are still preserved some ritual para-
phernalia presented to it by Moses Reis Wessely, who,
upon the advice of the Prince of Holstein, whose
purveyor he was, removed to Glückstadt, then the
capital of Sleswick. He established there a factory
of arms. King Frederick VI. of Denmark later sent
Moses to Hamburg as his agent; and while there he
transacted important business for Peter the Great
also. Moses' son, **Issachar Ber,** was the father of
Naphtali Hirz.

Naphtali Hirz Wessely passed his childhood at
Copenhagen, where his father was purveyor to the
king. In addition to rabbinical studies under Jonathan Eybeschütz, he studied modern languages. As
the representative of the banker Feitel, he later visited Amsterdam, where he published (1765–66) his
"Lebanon," or "Gan Na'ul," a philological investigation of Hebrew roots and synonyms. Although
prolix in style, and lacking scientific method, this
work established his reputation. After his marriage
at Copenhagen, he represented Feitel at Berlin, and
there became associated with Mendelssohn. Wessely
encouraged the latter in his labors by publishing
" 'Alim li-Terufah," a work advocating the "bi'ur"
and the translation of the Bible into German. To this
work Wessely himself contributed a commentary on
Leviticus (Berlin, 1782), having published, two years
previously, a Hebrew edition of the Book of Wisdom, together with a commentary.

Wessely was an ardent advocate of the educational and social reforms outlined in Emperor Joseph

II.'s "Toleranzedict." He even risked his reputation for piety by publishing a manifesto in eight chapters, entitled "Dibre Shalom we-Emet," in which he emphasized the necessity for secular instruction, as well as for other reforms, even from the points of view of the Mosaic law and the Talmud. This work has been translated into French as "Instructions Salutaires Adressées aux
His Works. Communautés Juives de l'Empire de Joseph II." (Paris, 1792); into Italian by Elia Morpurgo (Goerz, 1793); and into German by David Friedländer under the title "Worte der Wahrheit und des Friedens" (Berlin, 1798). By thus espousing the cause of reform, as well as by his support of Mendelssohn, Wessely incurred the displeasure of the rabbinical authorities of Germany and Poland, who threatened him with excommunication. His enemies, however, were finally pacified through the energetic intervention of the Italian rabbis, as well as by Wessely's pamphlets "Meḳor Ḥen," in which he gave evidence of his sincere piety. In 1788 Wessely published in Berlin his ethical treatise "Sefer ha-Middot," a work of great moral worth. He published also several odes, elegies, and other poems; but his masterwork is his "Shire Tif'e-ret" (5 vois.; i.-iv., Berlin, 1782-1802; v., Prague, 1829), describing in rhetorical style the exodus from Egypt. This work, through which he earned the admiration of his contemporaries, was translated into German (by G. F. Hufnagel and Spalding; 1789-1805), and partly into French (by Michel Berr; Paris, 1815). His commentaries on the Bible were published by the society Meḳiẓe Nirdamim (Lyck, 1868-75) under the title "Imre Shefer."

Naphtali Hirz Wessely.

Wessely influenced his contemporaries in various directions. As a scholar he contributed, by his profound philological researches, to the reconstruction of the language of the Bible, though his work is marred by prolixity and by his refusal to admit shades of meaning in synonyms. As a poet he possessed perfection of style, but lacked feeling and artistic imagination. No one exerted a greater influence than he on the dissemination of modern Hebrew; and no one, on the other hand, did more to retard the development of pure art and of poetic intuition. Because of the courageous battle which he fought in behalf of Jewish emancipation, Wessely may be regarded as a leader of the Maskilim.

BIBLIOGRAPHY: Abraham Meldola, *Ḳol ha-Zirim*, Altona, 1808; M. Mendelssohn, *Pene Tebel*, Amsterdam, 1872; *Ha-Asif*, iii. 404-416; N. Slouschz, *Renaissance de la Littérature Hébraïque*, ch. ii., Paris, 1903; David Friedrichsfeld, *Zeker le-Zaddik*, Amsterdam, 1809; W. A. Meisel, *Leben und Wirken des Naphtali Hirz Wessely*, Breslau, 1841; Zeitlin, *Bibl.*

Hebr.; A. Benesra, in *Ost und West*, May, 1905; D. Simonsen, *Hartvig Wessely's Todestag*, in *Monatsschrift*, 1905, pp. 205-208.
s.   N. Sl.

WESSELY, WOLFGANG: Austrian jurist and theologian; born at Trebitsch, Moravia, Oct. 22, 1801; died at Vienna April 21, 1870. At the age of fourteen he was sent to Prague to prepare himself for the rabbinate, graduating as Ph.D. in 1828, and as LL.D. in 1833. In 1831 he was appointed teacher of religion at the gymnasium, and in 1837 at the Jewish congregational school; in 1846 he received permission to lecture on Hebrew and rabbinical literature at the University of Prague. In the meantime he had made himself known by contributions to juristic literature; and when, in 1848, trial by jury was introduced into Austria, the minister of justice sent him on a mission through France, Rhenish Prussia, Holland, and Belgium to study the legal methods employed in these countries. In the following year he was appointed privat-docent of jurisprudence at the University of Prague; in 1852 he was made assistant professor; and in 1861 he was appointed ordinary professor, being the first Austrian Jew to hold such a position.

In addition to contributions to periodicals, Wessely was the author of the following works: "Wer Ist nach den Grundsätzen des Oesterreichischen Rechts zur Vornahme einer Jüdischen Trauung Befugt?" (Prague, 1839); "Netib Emunah" (*ib.* 1840; 8th ed. 1863), a catechism; "Tefillat Yisrael," a prayer-book with German translation in Hebrew characters (*ib.* 1841; 2d ed., with German characters, *ib.* 1844); "Ueber die Gemeinschaftlichkeit der Beweismittel im Oesterreichischen Civilprocesse" (*ib.* 1844); and "Die Befugnisse des Nothstands und der Nothwehr nach Oesterreichischem Rechte" (*ib.* 1862). As a theologian he had strong rationalistic tendencies; and he explains Bat Ḳol as being the voice of conscience (Jsidor Busch, "Jahrbuch," iii. 229).

BIBLIOGRAPHY: Wurzbach, *Biog. Lex.*; *Allg. Zeit. des Jud.* 1870, pp. 407-408; *Die Neuzeit*, 1870, pp. 186-188.
s.   D.

WEST: One of the "four skirts" (כנפות, Isa. xi. 12; Ezek. vii. 2; Job xxxvii. 3, xxxviii. 13) or "four corners," known also as the "four ends" (Jer. xlix. 36) or "four winds" (Ezek. xxxvii. 9; Dan. viii. 8, xi. 4), into which the Hebrews, following Assyrian analogies, divided heaven and earth. As the East was termed "ḳedem" (= "front"), the west was designated as "aḥor" (= "rear"; Isa. ix. 11; Job xxiii. 8). Since the Mediterranean Sea was west of Palestine, the noun ים (= "sea") became a favorite term to denote the west (Ex. x. 19, xxvii. 12, xxxviii. 12; Gen. xii. 8, xxviii. 14; Isa. xlix. 12; Ps. cvii. 3), another word being "ma'arab" (= "the point where the sun sets"; Ps. lxxv. 7 [A. V. 6], ciii. 12, cvii. 3; Isa. xliii. 5, xlv. 6).

In later Hebrew "ma'arab" is the common term for "west" (B. B. 25a). It may have been in opposition to the Babylonian belief that the entrance to the realm of death was situated in the west that R. Abbahu advanced the opinion that the SHEKINAH was in the west (ib.). The contrary assumption, attributed to the heretics ("minim"), who were said to maintain the doctrine that the Shekinah resided in the east, seems, therefore, to be a reminiscence of Babylonian influence. Since Palestine lay to the west of Babylon, it came to be designated as Ma'araba (Ber. 2b

obtained the assistance of Jewish residents, who were always antagonistic to the Spanish government.

The Portuguese were no less intolerant toward the Jews; and on their capture of Brazil from the Dutch in 1654 they exiled numbers of Jews. These sought refuge in the Dutch colonies, especially in Curaçao, to whose prosperity they have notably contributed until the present time. It was the tolerance shown by the Dutch and British governments which helped to build up the supremacy of those powers in the West Indies. France was nearly as intolerant as Spain; but prior to the promulgation of the "Code Noir" (1685) Jews were allowed, mainly through the policy of Colbert, to reside and trade in the French West Indies, despite the hostility of the Jesuits. In the eighteenth century laws

VIEW OF THE "JOODE SAVAANE," SURINAM, DUTCH GUIANA.
(From a seventeenth-century print.)

et seq.; Yeb. 17a et passim), and its inhabitants were called the "sons of the West" (Niddah 51b).

E. G. H.

WEST INDIES: Group of islands in the North Atlantic adjoining the Gulf of Mexico; so named because supposed by Columbus, who discovered them, to be India reached by the western route. For convenience the Dutch possessions in South America are known as the Dutch West Indies, and are treated here. Kayserling asserts that the Jew Luis de Torres, who accompanied Columbus in 1492, settled in Cuba and died there. Jewesses who had been forcibly baptized are known to have been sent to the West Indies by the Spanish government. Thus the Jews have been identified with these islands from the time of their discovery; but although families of Crypto-Jews are known to have lived in Cuba during four centuries, it was not until 1881 that they were legally admitted into the Spanish colonies; nor did they obtain full rights until the Spanish-American war. As late as the year 1783 the Inquisition claimed its victims from among the Cuban Maranos. It is probable that the buccaneers

were passed permitting some Jews to live in the West Indies; and in 1722 David GRADIS established a business at St. Pierre, Martinique, and two years later a branch office in Santo Domingo. He sent out merchantmen from Bordeaux, carrying cargoes of alcohol, meal, and pickled meat; and his family gradually grew so wealthy and powerful that the efforts of the colonial authorities to expel it were unavailing. Abraham Gradis, son of David, traded between Bordeaux, the French West Indies, and Canada, and was granted exceptional privileges, such as the right of acquiring real estate.

Jewish activity in the West Indies commenced in the middle of the seventeenth century, at a time when the exiled Spanish Jews had already made their influence felt in Amsterdam and in the Levant trade. Jews sent out by the government of the Netherlands had colonized Surinam and **Curaçao,** in which latter island there were twelve Jewish families in the year 1650. Governor Matthias Beck was directed to grant them land and to supply them with slaves, horses, cattle, and agri-

Curaçao and Surinam.

cultural implements. Their settlement was situated on the northern outskirts of the present district of Willemstad, and is still known as the Jodenwyk. In 1651 there was a large influx of Jews into Curaçao, under the leadership of Jan de Illan, who had the rights of patroon, and the contractor Joseph Nuñez de Fonseca, known also as David Nassi. The settlement was successful; and by reason of the tolerant attitude of the government large numbers of Jews went thither from Brazil after the Portuguese conquest of that country in 1654. The settlement became increasingly prosperous. A congregation was established in 1656, and a new synagogue built in 1692. In 1750 there were 2,000, in 1920, 650 Jewish inhabitants in the island. In 1905 the trade was almost entirely in the hands of Jews.

Jews had settled in **Surinam** prior to the occupation of that colony by the British (1665), when they were confirmed in all the privileges previously enjoyed by them, including full religious liberty. Summonses served on the Sabbath were declared to be invalid; and civil suits for less than the value of ten thousand pounds of sugar were to be decided by the Jewish elders, magistrates being obliged to enforce their judgments. Jews were permitted to bequeath their property according to their own laws of inheritance. In order to induce Jews to settle in Surinam it was declared that all who came thither for that purpose should be regarded as British-born subjects. In Feb., 1667, Surinam surrendered to the Dutch fleet, and in the treaty of Breda, which confirmed the Dutch in their possession, it was stipulated that all British subjects who desired to do so should be allowed to leave the country. In 1675 Charles II. despatched two commissioners with three ships to bring off those wishing to leave. The governor of Surinam, fearing that the emigration of the Jews would injure the prosperity of the country, refused to let them depart. According to a list which has been preserved, ten Jews, with 322 slaves, wished to go to Jamaica. The governor at first claimed that Jews could not be British subjects, and, being compelled to yield this contention, took advantage of the arrival of a frigate in the harbor to pretend that he had received fresh instructions from the Netherlands forbidding the migration of the Jews. Finally the British commissioners sailed away without having accomplished their purpose. The number of Jews in Surinam continued to increase, and a splendid synagogue was erected there in 1685; David Pardo of London, who officiated as its rabbi, died in Surinam in 1713. Maps still exist showing the position of the "Joodsche Dorp" and "Joode Savaane" in Surinam (see R. Gottheil in "Publ. Am. Jew. Hist. Soc." ix.). In 1785 the centennial of the synagogue was celebrated.

Jews were probably among the first colonizers of **Barbados**. In 1656 they were granted the enjoyment of the laws and statutes of the commonwealth of England relating to foreigners and **Barbados.** strangers. Schomburgk relates that Jews settled at Barbados in 1628 ("History of the Barbadoes"). In 1661 Benjamin de Caseres, Henry de Caseres, and Jacob Fraso petitioned the King of England for permission to live and trade in Barbados and Surinam. The petition,

supported by the King of Denmark, was referred to the Commissioners for Foreign Plantations, who reviewed the whole question of the advisability of allowing Jews to reside and trade in his Majesty's colonies, a matter which they said "hath been long and often debated." The request of the applicants was granted, but the principle was left undecided. About the time that this case was before the council, Jacob Josua Bueno Enriques, a Jew who had been for two years resident in Jamaica, petitioned the king for permission to work a copper-mine in that island. The result of this request is not known. In 1664 one Benjamin Bueno de Mesquita obtained letters of denization and relief from the provisions of the Navigation Act, but scarcely had these been obtained when he, with two sons and three other Jews, was banished from Jamaica for failure to find a promised gold-mine. His tomb has been discovered in New York. In 1671 Governor Lynch of Jamaica wrote to Secretary Arlington, opposing a petition requesting the expulsion of the Jews. Thenceforward their position became more secure. Despite special taxation in 1693, and a prohibition from employing indentured Christian servants (1703), the Jews' privileges were not afterward infringed. In 1802 an act of the Barbados legislature removed all the disabilities of the Jews.

There were Jewish colonists also in the **Leeward Islands.** A special act designed to prevent Jews from monopolizing imported commodities bears date of 1694. This was repealed in 1701 on the petition of the Jews, with the proviso that in case of war they should assist in the defense of the island to the utmost of their power, and further "behave themselves fairly and honestly for the future."

Spain and Portugal's loss was gain for the Dutch and British West-Indian colonies. For a few years the French possessions shared in the advantage. When France occupied **Martinique** in 1635 she found there a number of Jews whom the Dutch had brought with them as merchants or traders. For more than twenty years these were left unmolested, until their prosperity excited the envy of the colonists, and especially of the Jesuits, who caused various discriminating enactments to be issued from time to time against the Jews. Toward the year 1650 a Jew named Benjamin d'Acosta introduced into Martinique the cultivation of the sugar-cane. This benefit was rewarded with ingratitude; for when the epoch of toleration in France gave way to new persecutions under Louis XIV., an order of that king, dated Sept. 24, **Martinique.** 1683, commanded that the Jews should be expelled from the French possessions in America. The "Code Noir" of 1685, referred to above, repeated this injunction. In spite of occasional complaints, Jews continued to enter the island during the eighteenth century. They remained subject to the caprices of the colonial governors until the Revolution, when all discriminations against them were abolished.

There exists a Jewish congregation in the Danish island of **St. Thomas**. After the sacking of St. Eustatius by Rodney in 1781, a number of Jews emigrated thence and settled in St. Thomas, where they in 1796 built a synagogue under the appellation "Blessing and Peace." In 1803 the congregation numbered twenty-two families, having been augmented by arrivals from England, St. Eustatius, and Curaçao. In 1804 the synagogue was destroyed by fire. It was replaced by a small building erected in 1812; and in 1823 this was superseded by a larger one. Ten years later a still larger synagogue was erected, the community having in the meantime increased to sixty-four families. In 1850 King Christian VIII. sanctioned a code of laws for the government of the congregation. There were at that time about 500 Jewish inhabitants in the island, many of whom held civil offices. Among the ministers were B. C. Carillon of Amsterdam and M. N. Nathan and Mayer Meyers of England. In 1905, however, the Jewish community of St. Thomas numbered little more than fifty members. St. Thomas was included in the VIRGIN ISLANDS purchased by the United States from Denmark in 1916. See also BARBADOS; CUBA; CURAÇAO; JAMAICA; MARTINIQUE.

St. Thomas.

BIBLIOGRAPHY: L. Wolff, *American Elements in the Resettlement*, in *Transactions of the Jewish Historical Society of England*; Abraham Cahen, *Les Juifs dans les Colonies Françaises au 18e Siècle*, in *R. E. J.* iv., v.; G. A. Kohut, *Who Was the First Rabbi of Surinam?* in *Publ. Am. Jew. Hist. Soc.* No. 5, 1892; Dr. H. Friedenwald, *Material for the History of the Jews in the British West Indies*, ib. No. 5, 1897; B. Felsenthal, *The Jewish Congregation in Surinam*, ib. No. 2, 1894; B. Felsenthal and R. Gottheil, *Chronological Sketch of the History of the Jews in Surinam*, ib. No. 4, 1896; Herbert Cone, *The Jews in Curaçao*, ib. No. 10, 1902.
J.   V. E.

WEST VIRGINIA: One of the South Atlantic states of the American Union; formerly part of Virginia; made a separate state on June 19, 1863. While individual Jews went farther West as early as 1825, there seem to have been no communities before 1840 in the territory now constituting the state. On April 20, 1849, a Jewish Cemetery Association was incorporated in **Wheeling** by Samuel Kline, Meyer Heyman, Alexander Heyman, Julius Ballenberg, Isaac Horkheimer, Meyer Stein, Simon Stein, Seligman Oppenheimer, and Marx Graf. In the following month of the same year the Congregation Leshem Shomayim was organized, with Myer Mannheim as its rabbi. Since then nine ministers have occupied its pulpit, including Harry Levi, who was installed in 1897 and held the office several years. The congregation now has 110 members, a Ladies' Hebrew Benevolent Society (founded 1875), a Relief Society (1891), and a Rabbi Wise Personal Aid Gild (1899). The Mercantile Club, Wheeling's Jewish social organization, has a membership of forty-five.

Charleston, the capital of the state, contains the Congregation Bene Israel, which was organized in 1873, and which is now composed of forty-four members, the present rabbi being Israel Bettan; the city likewise has a small Orthodox congregation, a benevolent society, and a social club, the Germania, founded in 1874.

Parkersburg, the third largest city of the state, has a Ladies' Sewing Society, a Hebrew Aid Society, and the Progress club, and one congregation; before its organization, services were held on the fall holidays.

Huntington is one of the younger cities; but in 1887 the Congregation Ohev Shalom was organized

with eighteen members. Its charities are now in charge of the Ladies' Hebrew Benevolent Society.

Few in number as they are, the Jews of West Virginia have their fair share of prominent citizens, though they are not conspicious in high public positions. Joseph Shields, later residing in Cincinnati, was collector of internal revenue at Charleston during the Civil war, and Daniel Mayer was a commissioner of immigration under Governor Jacobs, prosecuting attorney twice in Logan and once in Boone county, a director of the hospital for the insane (1887), a member of the state legislature (1889), and for a number of years consul to Buenos Ayres. Charleston was represented in the army by Lieut. Samuel Frankenberger, and in the navy by his brother, Lieut. Hugo Frankenberger, who took high honors at Annapolis. Morris Horkheimer of Wheeling was a member of Governor Atkinson's staff, and commissary-general of the state under Governor White. Samuel Gideon of Huntington has run the whole gamut of public office in the south-western part of the state, being president of the Cabell County Court for six years, and Mike Broh was also a prominent citizen of Huntington, being the president of the Merchants' Association and a director of the Chamber of Commerce. For some years Albert Zillinzinger was a member of the Weston Asylum board.

Grafton, Fairmont, and **Sistersville** contain few Jews, but for some time have held annual services on New-Year and the Day of Atonement.

Wheeling has 1,000 Jews, all affiliated with the congregation; Charleston about 1,000; Parkersburg 1,000; and Huntington 310. In the entire state there are about 5,440 Jews in a total population of 1,463,701.
A.   H. L.

WETTE, WILHELM MARTIN LEBERECHT DE: Christian Biblical critic and theologian; born at Ulla, near Weimar, Jan. 12, 1780; died in Basel June 16, 1849. He took his doctorate in Jena, where he became privat-docent in 1806. The following year he was appointed professor of theology at Heidelberg, and in 1810 was called to the new University of Berlin, where he worked in harmony with Schleiermacher. A public expression of sympathy for Sand, the murderer of Kotzebue, occasioned his dismissal from the university (1819). After remaining three years in Weimar he was called (1822) as professor of theology to Basel, where he passed the rest of his life.

De Wette ranks among the foremost Old Testament scholars of the nineteenth century. His dissertation on Deuteronomy (1805) and his "Beiträge zur Einleitung in das Alte Testament" (1806–7) may be said to have laid the foundation (in conjunction with Vater's works) for the subsequent development of Old Testament criticism. In his commentary on the Psalms (1811) he called in question a number of the Davidic titles and the Messianic character of certain of the Psalms. His translation of the Old Testament (1809–11) had a wide circulation in Germany and elsewhere. In 1814 he published his "Lehrbuch der Hebräisch-Jüdischen Archäologie," which went through a number of editions. De Wette's critical work on the Old Testament was summed up in his "Lehrbuch der Historisch-Kritischen Einleitung in die Kanonischen und Apokryphischen Bücher des Alten Testaments" (1817), which was translated into English by Theodore Parker (1843), and was edited in revised form by Schrader (1869). Though later critics have departed in some points from his positions, his fundamental principle of historical development in the Old Testament has been the basis of all succeeding work. Besides the books mentioned above he wrote much on the New Testament, and on theology and ethics.

BIBLIOGRAPHY: Herzog, Real-Encyc.; Allgemeine Deutsche Biographie.
J.　　　　　　　　　　　　　　　　　　　　　T.

WETZLAR: Prussian city in the district of Coblenz; formerly a free city. Jews lived there probably as early as the twelfth century, since a young Jew of "Writschlar" is mentioned in connection with the murder of Alexander of Andernach (Aronius, "Regesten," No. 345, pp. 154 et seq.). The name of Wetzlar occurs also in a document of the year 1241, which contains the "taxes of the Jews" ("Monatsschrift," 1904, p. 71). On May 15, 1265, Archbishop Werner of Mayence entered into a compact of public peace with several counts and cities, including Wetzlar, to protect the Jews against all violence (Aronius, ib. No. 706, p. 291), and on July 9, 1277, Rudolph I. granted Siegfried von Runkel an income of ten marks from the 100 marks which the community of Wetzlar was required to pay as a yearly tax to the emperor (Wiener, "Regesten," No. 59, p. 10). In the beginning of the fourteenth century Emperor Louis the Bavarian transferred to Siegfried's son, Dietrich von Runkel, the entire yearly tax which the Jews of Wetzlar were required to pay the sovereign, while, in recognition of the services of Gerhard, of the house of Solms-Königsberg, Henry VII. granted him 300 marks in silver from the money paid by the Jews for protection. Finally, in a document dated Mayence, June 5, 1349, Charles IV., as a reward for faithful services on the part of Count John of Nassau, called "Von Merenberg," made to him a conditional transfer of the Jews of Wetzlar, with the taxes they paid into the imperial exchequer.

The community of Wetzlar was among those that suffered at the time of the Black Death in 1349 (Salfeld, "Martyrologium," pp. 78, 83 [German part, pp. 268, 284]); and in the same year, by a letter dated at Speyer on the Tuesday after Palm Sunday, Charles IV. confirmed all the privileges of the city of Wetzlar, adding that it should continue to levy the customary taxes on the Jews as servants of the royal treasury. Charles likewise confirmed the claim of Count John of Nassau-Weilburg to the Jewish taxes in a document dated March 17, 1362, but promised to impose no further burdens upon the Jews of that city. In 1382 King Wenzel granted Wetzlar the privilege of admitting Jews in order to enable the city to pay its debts, stipulating that they should be subject to the orders of the municipal council only. When the emperor, in 1491, levied a conscription upon the imperial cities, a valuation of 30 gulden was put upon the Jews of Wetzlar ("Blätter für Jüdische Geschichte und Li-

Allowed to Admit Jews.

teratur," supplement to "Israelit," 1900, i. 21). On Sept. 10, 1593, the municipal council decreed that within three months all Jews living in Wetzlar (including those from other cities) and holding notes against Christian citizens should renew them; otherwise the authorities would refuse to aid in collecting such notes. On March 20, 1604, the council enacted that the Jews should produce in court within a month all the notes they held against citizens. On Aug. 30, 1659, the Jews were forbidden to take as interest more than 4 pfennig per reichsthaler a week; and on June 4, 1661, they were prohibited from importing tobacco into Wetzlar. On the accession of Emperor Leopold (Aug. 30, 1661) the imperial commissioner, Count John Frederick of Hohenlohe, sent special envoys to receive the oath of allegiance of the Jews of Wetzlar in the town hall, in the presence of the council. Similar action was taken on the accession of Joseph I., in 1705; of Joseph II., in 1766; and of Leopold II., May 13, 1791.

About 1755 the Jews of Wetzlar were permitted to build a synagogue, which was dedicated in 1756; and a special tax of 10 kreuzer was imposed, to be paid to the messenger of the imperial supreme court of judicature at Wetzlar whenever he passed by on business ("Sulamith," 1807, ii. 407, note). Although the JUDENSTÄTTIGKEIT permitted only twelve Jewish families to live in Wetzlar, the town council admitted a larger number, that they might divide among themselves the 20 or 30 reichsthaler paid by each Jew for permission to reside in the city. This was set forth by the citizens in a complaint to the council in 1707. An "agreement" was accordingly made on July 18, 1712, that the number of resident Jews should again be reduced to twelve families. In 1836 there were 680 Jews living at Wetzlar, which had been incorporated with the kingdom of Prussia in 1815; but in 1904 only a little over 170 resided there, and the community, which supports a philanthropic society and a ḥebra ḳaddisha, has included itself in the rabbinate of Dr. Munk at Marburg ("Statistisches Jahrbuch des Deutsch-Israelitischen Gemeindebundes," 1903, p. 78).

Jews by the name of Wetzlar lived at Celle, in the province of Hanover (Neubauer, "Cat. Bodl. Hebr. MSS." pp. 529, 1145), at Emden (see the local "Memorbuch"), at Frankfort-on-the-Main (Horovitz, "Die Inschriften des Alten Friedhofs der Israelitischen Gemeinde zu Frankfurt-am-Main," p. 743), at Altona (Grunwald, "Hamburgs Deutsche Juden," 1904, p. 305), at Prague (Hock, "Familien Prags," p. 120), and elsewhere. R. Joel of Wetzlar died at Minden, Westphalia, in 1698, while Solomon b. Simeon Wetzlar of Fürth wrote the moral code entitled "Ḥaḳirot ha-Leb" (Amsterdam, 1731; Steinschneider, "Cat. Bodl." No. 6978), and a certain Wolf Wetzlar Ashkenazi is mentioned by Maggid ("Zur Gesch. und Genealogie der Günzburge," p. 195, St. Petersburg, 1899).

BIBLIOGRAPHY: Von Ulmenstein, Gesch. und Topographische Beschreibung der Kaiserlichen Freyen Reichsstadt Wetzlar, vol. i., Hadamar, 1802 (pp. 212 et seq., 250 et seq., 386 et seq., 493 et seq., 522); vol. ii., Wetzlar, 1806 (pp. 486, 534, 681, 730, 836); vol. iii., ib. 1810 (pp. 74, 76, 86 et seq., 154, 157 et seq.); Abicht, Der Kreis Wetzlar, Historisch, Statistisch und Topographisch Dargestellt, i. 5, 124, Wetzlar, 1836; Forschungen zur Deutschen Geschichte 1876, pp. 120, 134; Zeit. für die Gesch. der Juden in Deutschland, ii. 36, 43 et seq.
D.　　　　　　　　　　　　　　　　　　　　A. LEW.

WE-YE'ETAYU: A piyyuṭ by Eleazar Ḳalir (Zunz, "Literaturgesch." p. 21), chanted by the ḥazzan during the Musaf service on the days of New-Year and Atonement, according to the northern ritual; but omitted by many German congregations. The only music recognized as traditional is an eighteenth-century air, of distinct inferiority to the other

Washington, D. C., where he was a member of the Society of Washington Artists and of the Washington Water Color Club. Weyl's specialty was landscape-painting, and his work shows sympathy with the moods of nature. He was awarded the first prize at the exhibition of the Society of Washington Artists in 1891, has exhibited at the National Academy

WE-YE'ETAYU

inherited melodies of the Penitential season, but none the less firmly established in the tradition of many congregations, and prized for its quaintness.

s.   F. L. C.

WEYL, MAX: American painter; born at Mühlen, Württemberg, in 1837. At the age of fifteen he went to the United States, but returned to Europe to study art. He then made his home in

of Design in New York, and is represented in the Corcoran Gallery of Washington by a landscape entitled "Approaching Night." He was a protégé of Salvador de Mendonca, formerly Brazilian minister at Washington, and four of his paintings were in the Mendonca collection. He died in 1914.

BIBLIOGRAPHY: *American Art Annual*, New York, 1905.

A.   F. N. L.

WEYL, MEÏR B. SIMḤAH: German rabbi; born at Lissa 1744; died at Berlin 1826. He was a pupil of Hirsch Janow. In 1771 he became associate rabbi at Lissa, and in 1784 was called as associate rabbi to Berlin, where he was elected chief rabbi in 1800, receiving the title of acting chief district rabbi in 1809. He published no separate works, but his numerous opinions on questions of the Law, which prove the depth of his scholarship and judgment, are included in the collections of contemporary rabbis, as in those of Akiba Eger, Jacob Lissa, Salmon Cohen, Solomon Posner, Aryeh Löb Breslau, Ẓebi Hirsch Samoscz, Noah of Lubraniez, and Bendix Baruch Gompertz. A series of approbations, including those referring to the Jewish calendar, published with the sanction of the Berlin Academy of Sciences, show the importance attached to his opinion in learned circles. While he was opposed to innovations in ritual, he was the first advocate and in part the actual founder of seminaries for rabbis and teachers in Prussia.

BIBLIOGRAPHY: Lewin, *Gesch. der Juden in Lissa*, pp. 338–346, Berlin, 1904.
s.   L. LEW.

WEYL, WALTER EDWARD: American economist; born at Philadelphia, Pa., March 11, 1874. He was educated in the public schools of his native city and the University of Pennsylvania (Ph.B. 1892; Ph.D. 1897), and took postgraduate courses at the universities of Halle, Berlin, and Paris. Weyl has published several articles on railway labor, the passenger traffic of railways, etc. He was greatly interested in organized labor, and was connected with the United States bureaus of labor and statistics. He died Nov. 9, 1919.

BIBLIOGRAPHY: *American Jewish Year Book*, 5665 (1904–5).
A.   F. T. H.

WHALE: A cetaceous mammal. Several species of cetacea are found in the Mediterranean as well as in the Red Sea. In the Authorized Version of the Bible the Hebrew "tannin" is often rendered "whale"; while the Revised Version has "sea-monster" (Gen. i. 21; Job vii. 12), "dragon" (Ezek. xxxii. 12), and "jackal" (Lam. iv. 3).

The name "leviathan," which usually designates the fabulously great fish preserved for the future world, seems in certain passages of the Talmud to refer to some kind of whale; so, for instance, in Ḥul. 67b, where leviathan is said to be a clean fish, having fins and scales, and in B. B. 73b, where a fabulous description of its enormous size is given. In Shab. 7b the כלבית (meaning perhaps the porcupine) is said to be the vexer of the leviathan. See also LEVIATHAN AND BEHEMOTH.

BIBLIOGRAPHY: Tristram, *Natural History of the Bible*, p. 151; Lewysohn, *Zoologie des Talmuds*, pp. 155, 324.
E. G. H.   I. M. C.

WHEAT (Hebr. "ḥiṭṭah"; Deut. viii. 8 *et seq.*): The chief breadstuff of Palestine in both ancient and modern times. It has been observed that the cultivation of wheat indicates a higher stage of civilization than the cultivation of barley alone. Barley bread is, therefore, mentioned comparatively seldom (Judges vii. 13; II Kings iv. 42), and was probably the food of the common people only.

XII.—33

Among the Greeks and Romans, as in the Orient to-day, barley was less esteemed than wheat, which was therefore the preferred breadstuff. The loaves of bread used for divine sacrifice were naturally made only from the choicest wheat flour.

In Palestine the winter grain is sown in late autumn, when the early rains have loosened the soil and prepared it for plowing. Wheat is harvested somewhat later than barley, and generally at a time when the heavy rains have ceased (I Sam. xii. 17). The harvest season varies, according to the districts, between the end of April and the beginning of June. On harvesting, thrashing, and measuring the wheat see AGRICULTURE; BAKING; BREAD.

Wheat was an article of export from ancient times, Tyre (according to Ezek. xxvii. 17) obtaining wheat from Judah (comp. also Acts xii. 20). Galilee, according to Josephus, was the most fruitful district. At present the plains of Philistia and Jezreel produce chiefly wheat, but the Hauran district is still the great granary of Syria; and its grain is exported in large quantities by way of Haifa and Beirut.

Grains of wheat were eaten also roasted, a survival from the period when grinding and baking were not understood. Parched kernels ("ḳali") seem to have been very popular among the ancient Hebrews (I Sam. xvii. 17, xxv. 18; II Sam. xvii. 28), especially during harvesting (Ruth ii. 14; Lev. xxiii. 14), as is still the case to-day.
E. G. H.   I. BE.

WHEEL (אֹפָן, Ex. xiv. 25; גַּלְגַּל, Ezek. x. 2): In the Bible wheels are mentioned in connection with ordinary wagons, as well as with CHARIOTS. Mention is made also of the thrashing-wheel (Prov. xx. 26; Isa. xxviii. 27), and of the potters' wheel or disk (Jer. xviii. 3; see POTTERY).
E. G. H.   I. BE.

WHEELING. See WEST VIRGINIA.

WIDAL, FERNAND GEORGES: French physician; born at Paris March 9, 1862. From 1886 to 1888 he devoted himself to public demonstrations of the researches of the faculty of pathological anatomy, and during the two years following was in charge of a course in bacteriology in the laboratory of Professor Cornil. In 1895 he was appointed visiting physician to the hospitals of Paris, and in 1904 became an instructor in the faculty of medicine. In 1905 he was physician to the Hôpital Cochin, and is in charge of the medical clinics at the same institution.

Widal is the author of a remarkable series of essays on infectious diseases, erysipelas, diseases of the heart, liver, nervous system, etc., besides being a prolific contributor to various medical journals and encyclopedias.

BIBLIOGRAPHY: *Exposé des Travaux Scientifiques du Docteur Fernand Widal*, 3 vols., Paris, 1895–1904.
s.   J. KA.

WIDDIN: Bulgarian fortified town, situated at the confluence of the rivers Widd and Danube.

The beginnings of the Jewish community of Widdin were in the thirteenth century, its earliest members being some Byzantine and Hungarian Jewish settlers. At that time the city was a part of the territory of the waywode of Wallachia. According to several chroniclers, two celebrated rabbis went to Widdin in 1376—Moses Yewani ("the Greek") and R. Shalom of Neustadt. R. Shalom is said to have founded the first rabbinical school in Bulgaria, and to have been the first rabbi of the community; he was succeeded by R. Dosa Yewani, the son of Moses Yewani.

After the taking of Constantinople in 1453, during the campaigns of Mohammed the Conqueror in Anatolia, the waywode of Wallachia, Vladimir V., levied on every Jew of consequence a tribute of 1,000 silver aspers per head, fixing the loss of the right eye or the right ear as the penalty for failure in payment. The Jews of Constantinople appealed, in the name of their coreligionists, to the sultan Mohammed, who, according to the statement of Elijah Capsali, revoked the barbarous edict on his return from Anatolia. This was prior to his expedition into Transylvania in 1474. In spite of its final conquest by the Turks, Widdin remained under the immediate government of the rulers of the province of Wallachia, then tributaries or vassals of the Ottoman empire. In the seventeenth century the city passed for a time into the hands of the Hungarians, but was again surrendered to the Turks (1690).

In the interval Jews of different nationalities settled in the city. Among the principal families of Greek origin were the Pyzantes (or Byzantes), Pappos, and Polychrons; among those of German extraction were the Ashkenazis and Grünbergs; of Spanish origin (after the year 1492), the Peñaroya, Dueñas, Niño, and Rosañes families. There were also Portuguese Jews, as the Namias; Italian, as the Farḥis of Florence and Lecce; French, as the Yarḥis of Lunel and the Ḳimḥis of Provence; and even some natives of Barbary, *e. g.*, the Al-Ḳala‘is, the Al-Ajams, and others. A responsum of Samuel of Medina, dated 1558, reveals the fact that the Jews of Widdin were extensive cheese-makers, the principal manufacturers of that time being Joseph Tchillek and Solomon Uriel.

In the year 1784 the Ventura family removed from Spalatro, in Dalmatia, and settled in Widdin, where it founded a dynasty of spiritual rulers. The following members of this family were successively rabbis of Widdin: Shabbethai b. Abraham **The** Ventura, David Shabbethai Ventura **Venturas.** (1784–1806), Raḥamim Abraham Ventura (1806–10), Gedaliah Shabbethai Ventura, and Joseph ben David Ventura. Other rabbis later on were Benziyyon b. Shabbethai, Abraham Cohen, Bekor Eliakim, David Cohen, and Solomon Beḥar David.

Among the notable events in the history of the community of Widdin was the incident of the Jewish physician Cohen, falsely accused of poisoning his patron, Passvanoglu, the governor of the city, in 1807. This event, which came near being the cause of a wholesale slaughter of the entire community, occasioned the institution of an annual feast-day (4th—some say 9th—of Ḥeshwan), known as the PURIM OF WIDDIN, in thanksgiving for its escape. About 1830 one Conforte b. Eliakim, a native of Salonica, was the "ḥakim-bashi," or physician, to the governor. During the war between Servia and Bulgaria in 1885, when Widdin was being bombarded, the Jews of that town took refuge in Kalafat, Rumania. This occurred in midwinter; and the Jews, without means and wholly unprepared for flight, had no other refuge than the ancient synagogue.

Widdin was the first Bulgarian community to produce a Jewish writer of note; this was R. Dosa Yewani, author of "Perush-we-Tosafot," written about 1430 and still (1905) preserved at Wilna (Michael, "Or ha-Ḥayyim"; Benjacob, "Oẓar ha-Sefarim," **Literature.** *s.v.*). Two other writers who were natives of Widdin may be mentioned: Shabbethai b. Abraham Ventura, author of "Nehar Shalom" (Amsterdam, 1775), and David Shabbethai Ventura (brother of the former), author of "Kokba di-Shebiṭ," Salonica, 1799.

One of the relics of antiquity preserved in the local synagogue is a silver plate inscribed with the date 1658, given by the little Jewish community of the island of Adda-Kalessi, in the Danube, near Widdin.

At the present day Widdin contains about 2,000 Jews in a total population of 17,722. They include merchants and dealers in grain and cotton goods, together with tailors, shoemakers, tinsmiths, and makers of the "tcharik," or shoes worn by the peasantry. At the close of the Russo-Turkish war the community of Widdin built a magnificent synagogue, the finest in Bulgaria. Connected with the synagogue is a school containing 225 pupils (175 boys, 50 girls), and a number of charitable organizations and societies, among which are the Roḥezim (for the interment of the poor), the Biḳḳur Ḥolim (for the assistance of the sick), a Women's Society, and a Zionist Society.

BIBLIOGRAPHY: Grünwald, *Dibre Mordekai*, Sofia, 1894; Elijah Capsali, *Seder Eliyahu Zuṭa*, or *Debe Eliyahu* (MS. in Bodleian Library); *Bulletin de l'Alliance Israélite*, 1885–86, p. 21; *Anuarul Pentru Israelitzu*, Bucharest, 1889; Dezobry, *Dictionnaire de Biographie et d'Histoire*.
s. M. FR.

WIDDUI. See CONFESSION OF SIN.

WIDOW: The law of Israel treats the widow as a privileged person, and seeks to indemnify her in some degree for the loss of her natural protector. Thus the movable property of a widow can not be attached for debt (Deut. xxiv. 17), whether she be rich or poor, though the text speaks only of her garment (see EXECUTION). To meet the monition of Isaiah (i. 17), "Judge the fatherless, plead for the widow," it became the rule, in arranging the order of cases in a court, to take up the complaints of widows next after those of the fatherless (see PROCEDURE IN CIVIL CAUSES). The duty **Preroga-** of judges to do full justice to the **tives of a** complaining widow is emphasized by **Widow.** the assertion that God Himself "doth execute the judgment of the fatherless and widow" (Deut. x. 18), and that "a father of the fatherless, and a judge of the widows, is God in his holy habitation" (Ps. lxviii. 6). Widowhood "after marriage" gives to a daughter complete independence of her father; she becomes, in legal language, "an orphan during the father's lifetime." This principle is thus broadly laid down (Ket. iv. 2): "After he has given her in marriage the father has no power over her," though it is different where the husband dies after betrothal, but before marriage.

Under the sacerdotal law (Lev. xxi. 14) a widow

is not a suitable wife for the high priest, but she may marry an ordinary priest ("kohen hedyoṭ"). Yet, according to the Rabbis, where the latter has married a widow, and is thereafter appointed high priest, he may retain her as his wife (Yeb. 77a). Ezekiel (xliv. 22), in his scheme of a hierarchy, forbade to the ordinary priest marriage with a widow, unless her first husband had been a priest; but his scheme was never accepted as law.

In marrying again, a widow naturally is not favored as highly as a maiden. The smallest jointure for the latter is 200 zuzim; for the former, only a mina, or 100 zuzim (Ket. i. 2). Marriage with a maiden is generally celebrated on Wednesday; with a widow, on Thursday (Ket. i. 1). The rights of the widow in the husband's estate have, in the main, been set forth under KETUBAH, and are secured by the contract. The question of priority in

Re-marriage. payment between the widow's dues and the bond creditors of the husband, or between several widows of a polygamous husband, has been treated under PRIORITY. In the opinion of R. Akiba, prevailing over that of R. Ṭarfon, there is no "marshaling of assets" from outstanding deposits or demands in favor of the widow or of creditors; but the heirs are allowed to collect them, or to take possession (Ket. ix. 2, 3). The reason given is that no one can collect a demand against the decedent's estate without an oath (if such is required by the heirs) that he has not received it before, either in whole or in part.

Notwithstanding the difference between the customs of Jerusalem and Galilee on the one hand, and of Judea on the other, mentioned in Ket. iv. 12, the rule was recognized at an early day that the widow may dwell in her late husband's house, and receive her support from his estate, as long as she remains his widow and until she judicially demands payment of her dowry and jointure, or accepts such payment (see Bertinoro ad loc.).

The husband can not, at the time of entering upon the contract, confine the wife to any one fund out of which she may as a widow collect her ketubah; nor can he say to her, "Here, laid out on this table, is thy [due under the] ketubah"; for the whole of his estate is bound for it, including what he acquires by inheritance from his brothers after marriage.

Where the widow is, under the husband's appointment, guardian of his infant children, an oath can be demanded by the heirs as to her management, unless the husband has in writing freed her from rendering such an oath (Ket. ix. 5);

As Executrix. but if from her husband's grave she goes back to her father's house, or to the house of her father-in-law, and is not appointed guardian afterward, she owes an oath only as to the future, not as to her previous receipts (Ket. ix. 6). A widow who lessens her ketubah (i.e., collects a part thereof) can not thereafter demand further payments, except upon an oath as to the amount received; she must take the oath, also, if one witness testifies that she has been paid. So where land, sold or encumbered to third parties, is needed to satisfy the ketubah, the oath required in all these cases is taken in the most solemn form (Ket. ix. 7, 8).

Where the widow claims support from the estate in the hands of the heirs, her earnings belong to them. The husband's heirs are not bound for the expenses of her burial; these fall upon those who inherit her ketubah (Ket. xi. 1).

The widow, even if the husband died after betrothal, but before marriage, may, without the aid of a court, sell enough of his landed estate to satisfy her ketubah; and if the proceeds of the first sale are not sufficient, she may sell more until the full amount is realized. She may do the same thing to secure her support, if that is not given her. But this method of self-help seems not to have been practised in later times (Shulḥan 'Aruk, Eben ha-'Ezer, 96, 5). However, if she sells lands [that have a known value?] for less than their value, her sale is void; for in doing so she exceeds her powers, though the sale would hold good if it had been made under a decree of court (Ket. xi. 4, 5, where some dissenting views are recorded).

E. C.   L. N. D.

WIENER, ADOLF: German rabbi; born in Murowana-Goslin, Posen, 1811; died in Oppeln, Prussian Silesia, Aug. 25, 1895. Having acquired his diploma as Ph.D., he went as rabbi to Posen, where he introduced a modern synagogal service with German sermons. He met, however, strong opposition, headed by Solomon Eger; and the services could take place only under police protection. In 1845 Wiener was called as rabbi to Oppeln, where he officiated until his death. He was one of the most progressive rabbis of his time; and at the synods of Cassel (1844), Leipsic (1869), and Augsburg (1870) he advocated the following reforms in Judaism: revision of the prayer-book; employment of the organ in divine service; permission to travel on Sabbaths; and the abolition of all second days of festivals. His chief ambition, however, was to release the Jews from what he called the authority of the Talmud.

Wiener was the author of the following works: "Die Opfer- und Akeda-Gebete. Ein Beitrag zur Orientierung in der Cultusfrage" (Breslau, 1869); "Worte Gesprochen an der Bahre der Seligen Frau Rosalie Verwitwete Cohn" (Oppeln, 1871); and "Die Jüdischen Speisegesetze" (Breslau, 1895), a very radical criticism of the dietary laws.

BIBLIOGRAPHY: *Allg. Zeit. des Jud.* 1892, pp. 51-53; *Aḥiasaf,* 1896, p. 303; Lippe, *Bibliographisches Lexikon,* 1881, p. 532.
S.   S. O.

WIENER, ALOYS. See SONNENFELS, PERLIN LIPMANN.

WIENER ISRAELIT, DER. See PERIODICALS.

WIENER, JACQUES: Belgian engraver; born at Hoorstgen, Rhine Province, 1815; died at Brussels Nov. 3, 1899. When thirteen years of age he was sent to Aix-la-Chapelle to be instructed in drawing, modeling, and engraving by his uncle Baruch, who was an artist of considerable merit. In 1835 Wiener went to Paris for further study; and in 1839 he settled in Brussels as a medal-engraver. His work attained a high degree of perfection, and his reputation as a medalist spread to foreign countries, notably Germany. He was especially distinguished for his fidelity to the minutest details. The first Belgian postage-stamps were designed by Wiener, who also arranged for their manufacture, for which purpose he visited England in 1849. In 1872 he lost his eyesight through overwork, and was compelled to renounce his art, which, however, he had taught to his brothers **Karl Wiener** (d. 1867) and Leopold Wiener.

Wiener was decorated with the Order of the Knights of Leopold and with that of the Prussian Eagle. Upon his death the King of Belgium sent his family an autograph letter of condolence and also offered military honors at the funeral; these, however, the family declined.

BIBLIOGRAPHY: *Jew. Chron.* Nov. 10, 1899.
s.   F. C.

WIENER JAHRBUCH. See PERIODICALS.

WIENER JÜDISCHE ILLUSTRIRTE PRESSE. See PERIODICALS.

WIENER JÜDISCHE PRESSE. See PERIODICALS.

WIENER JÜDISCHE ZEITUNG. See PERIODICALS.

WIENER, LEO: American philologist; born at Byelostok, Grodno, Poland, July 27, 1862; studied in the gymnasia of Minsk and Warsaw, in the University of Warsaw, and in the Polytechnic of Berlin. Emigrating to the United States, he had for several years a varied career in New Orleans and in Kansas City, being obliged to work as a day-laborer and to peddle fruit in order to gain a livelihood. At length he was appointed teacher in Odessa, Mo., and later professor in the University of Kansas, where he remained until he was called to an assistant professorship in Slavic languages at Harvard University, which office he still holds.

Wiener is a prolific writer on philology, having contributed numerous articles to philological journals in America, England, Germany, Russia, and Austria. He has published also several articles on Jewish questions in the Jewish press of the United States, and has devoted especial attention to the study of Judæo-German in its philological aspects, having published several monographs on this subject in scientific journals. He is the author of "The History of Yiddish Literature in the Nineteenth Century" (New York, 1899), and has compiled an "Anthology of Russian Literature." He has translated numerous works from the Russian and from the Yiddish, including "Songs from the Ghetto" by Morris Rosenfeld, and the complete works of Leo Tolstoy.

A.   J. LEB.

WIENER, LEOPOLD: Belgian engraver and sculptor; born in Holland 1823; died at Brussels Jan. 24, 1891. He was a resident of Boitsfort, a small town near Brussels, of which he was several times elected mayor. In this place he devoted his undivided attention to engraving and sculpture; and several pieces of statuary sculptured by him are displayed in public squares throughout Belgium. In 1864 he was appointed engraver to the government, and soon after royal engraver, various titles of distinction being conferred upon him.

Wiener enjoyed a high reputation in musical circles also, and was at one time vice-president of the Conservatoire at Brussels. Many schools and institutions, notably a school of design for the working classes, owe their origin to his activity and energy.

BIBLIOGRAPHY: *Jew. Chron.* Jan. 30, 1891, p. 8.
s.   L. R.

WIENER, MEÏR: German teacher; born at Glogau June 3, 1819; died at Hanover March 31, 1880; head master of the religious school at Hanover. He made a German translation of the "Shebeṭ Yehudah" of Solomon ibn Verga (Hanover, 1855; 2d ed. 1856; reprinted, Königsberg, 1858; Warsaw, 1882). He made also a German version of the "'Emeḳ ha-Baka" of Joseph ha-Kohen, adding a sketch of the life and works of the author (Leipsic, 1858).

Further, Wiener was the author of "Regesten zur Geschichte der Juden in Deutschland Während des Mittelalters" (*ib.* 1862), in which he compiled all the data relating to the Jews; but his lack of independent study and his failure to make careful researches concerning the reliability of his sources seriously diminished the value of his work. He contributed numerous historical articles to the "Monatsschrift" (vols. ii.–xvii.), among which those treating of the Jews of Speyer and of Hanover deserve special mention. He likewise wrote for the "Ben Chananja" (iv.–viii.) and for the "Allgemeine Zeitung des Judenthums."

BIBLIOGRAPHY: *Monatsschrift*, xi. 153; Stobbe, *Die Juden in Deutschland Während des Mittelalters*, pp. 8–9, Brunswick, 1866; Steinschneider, *Cat. Bodl.* col. 2726; *Allg. Zeit. des Jud.* 1880, p. 231; Zeitlin, *Bibl. Post-Mendels.* p. 419.
s.   S. O.

WIENER MITTHEILUNGEN. See PERIODICALS.

WIENER MONATSBLÄTTER FÜR KUNST UND LITTERATUR. See PERIODICALS.

WIENER-NEUSTADT: City of Austria; situated thirteen miles south of Vienna. Jews settled in this city probably shortly after its foundation in the twelfth century, records showing that Duke Frederick II., on June 9, 1239, issued an order excluding them from holding those offices "in which they might cause inconvenience to Christians." Also in the spurious charter of the city, alleged to have been granted by Duke Leopold IV., the Jews are mentioned, their rights being based largely on the Austrian laws of 1244 and 1277 pertaining to Jews. The earliest tombstone discovered at Wiener-Neustadt bears date of 1285, and marks the grave of Guta, first wife of a certain Shalom. Tombstones from the years 1286, 1353, 1359, and 1370 have also been preserved.

During the time of the Black Death the Jews of Wiener-Neustadt were fully protected; but during the reign of Emperor Maximilian they were expelled from the city, their synagogue being transformed into a Catholic church (1497). Joseph I. permitted the city to admit the Jews who had fled from Hungary during the Kuruz rebellion; but these left the city again as soon as the uprising had been quelled. In 1848, Jews settled anew in Wiener-Neustadt; but at that time they were not allowed to bury their dead in the city, and had to take them to the cemeteries of the neighboring Hungarian or Austrian communities. They did not obtain a cemetery of their own until 1889.

Among the earlier rabbis of the Wiener-Neustadt congregation may be mentioned: Thirteenth century: Ḥayyim ben Moses, teacher of Ḥayyim ben Isaac, and author of " Or Zarua' ha-Ḳaṭon "; Moses Taku, author of the philosophical work "Ketab Tamim"; and Ḥayyim, son of Isaac of Vienna. Fourteenth century: Shalom (the teacher of Jacob Mölln), Isaac of Tyrnau, and Dossa of Widdin, the last-named of whom wrote a supercommentary on Rashi's work. Fifteenth century: Aaron Blumlein, one of the martyrs who were burned at Enns (1420) on a charge of desecrating the host; Israel Isserlein (d. 1460); and Josmann Cohen.

BIBLIOGRAPHY: Max Pollak, *A Zsidók Bécs-Ujhelyen*, Budapest, 1892.
E. C.   A. Bu.

WIENER VIERTELJAHRSSCHRIFT. See PERIODICALS.

WIENIAWSKI, HENRI: Russian violinist and composer; born at Lublin, Russian Poland, July 10, 1835; died at Moscow April 1, 1880; brother of Joseph WIENIAWSKI. He early showed himself in possession of great musical talent, and when only eight years of age he went to Paris, where he became a pupil of Claval and Massart at the Paris Conservatoire. At the age of eleven he was awarded the first prize for violin-playing. After one year's absence, during which he gave concerts at St. Petersburg and Moscow, he returned to Paris, where he studied harmony under Colet.

In 1850 Wieniawski toured with great success the principal cities of Poland, Russia, Germany, France, England, Belgium, and Holland. Ten years later he was appointed first violin to the Czar of Russia, and remained in St. Petersburg until 1872, when, together with Anton Rubinstein, he started on a prolonged tour through the United States. Upon his return to Europe in 1874 he accepted the post of professor of violin at the Conservatoire in Brussels as successor to Vieuxtemps. After a few years, however, he resigned this position and, in company with his brother Joseph, resumed his travels. A serious disease which he contracted forced him to abandon his journey and to hasten back to Russia. At Odessa he suffered a relapse; he was conveyed to Moscow, and died there.

Wieniawski was one of the greatest of modern violin-players, and possessed a striking individuality. His playing evinced an impetuous temperament mixed with a warmth and tenderness peculiar to himself. His compositions include two concertos for violin and orchestra; several polonaises, legends, and duets for pianoforte and violin; a fantasia on Russian airs; a "Fantaisie sur le Prophète"; and a set of studies.

BIBLIOGRAPHY: Champlin and Apthorp, *Cyclopedia of Music and Musicians*; Grove, *Dictionary of Music and Musicians*.
s.   J. Go.

WIENIAWSKI, JOSEPH: Russian pianist and composer; born at Lublin, Poland, May 23, 1837; brother of Henri WIENIAWSKI. He studied music under Zimmerman, Alkan, and Marmontel,

and harmony under Leccoppey, at the Paris Conservatoire. After his return to Russia in 1850, he frequently accompanied his brother Henri on his concert tours. In 1856 he studied music under Liszt at Weimar, and later theory under Marx, in Berlin. In 1866 he settled in Moscow, at first officiating as professor in the Conservatory of Music, and later opening a private school for pianoforte. From Moscow he went to Warsaw, where he often appeared in concerts. Among his compositions may be mentioned: two overtures for orchestra; a string quartet; a concerto for pianoforte and orchestra; a "Grand Duo Polonais" for pianoforte and violin; a "Valse de Concert"; fantasias; idyls; and several concert pieces. He died in November, 1912.

BIBLIOGRAPHY: Champlin and Apthorp, *Cyclopedia of Music and Musicians*.
s.   J. Go.

WIERNIK, PETER: Russo-American journalist; born at Wilna, Russia, in March, 1865. He received the customary Jewish education. From 1878 to 1882 he was in Riga; in 1882 he lived at Kovno; and in the following year he joined his parents at Byelostok, where he stayed for two years. His father, a maggid, instructed him in the Talmud and rabbinica, but otherwise he was self-taught. In 1885 he emigrated to the United States, where he settled in Chicago. Two years later he became a compositor on the "Jewish Courier," and in five years rose to be its editor. In 1898 he left for New York, where he has since resided. In that city he has been connected with the "Jüdisches Tageblatt," and in 1905 he was on the staff of "Das Morgen Journal."

In addition to his collaboration on several American and Yiddish journals and his contributions to THE JEWISH ENCYCLOPEDIA, Wiernik is the author of "History of the Jews," New York, 1901.

BIBLIOGRAPHY: *American Jewish Year Book*, 5665.
A.   F. T. H.

WIESBADEN: German town in the province of Hesse-Nassau; capital of the former duchy of Nassau. Schenk ("Gesch. der Stadt Wiesbaden") thinks that Jews lived there in the fourteenth century; but he gives no documentary evidence to support this view. There is no record of persecution of the Jews in Nassau, either in the ARMLEDER riots (1338) or during the Black Death (1348–49). In the public peace ("Landfrieden") promulgated in 1265 by Archbishop Wernher of Mayence, together with the lords of Epstein, Falkenstein, and others, an allusion is found to "certain undisciplined persons who have arisen against the Jews contrary to God's command," and who are to be punished as disturbers of the peace. It is not said, however, that such disturbances actually occurred in any place in the duchy. A "Judengasse" in Wiesbaden attests also the early presence of Jews there.

During the Thirty Years' war several Jewish families from the surrounding district, whose lives and property were in danger from the hostile soldiery, were received and sheltered in Wiesbaden; and when, soon after, their removal was insisted upon by the clergy, the latter were opposed by a considerable number of the citizens and officials, who protected the Jews. Indeed, a friendly sentiment toward the Jews seems to have found its way among the population. In 1700 a citizen of Wiesbaden—Heinrich Tillmann König—took such a liking to the Jewish religion that he faithfully observed its ceremonies, although he had to endure much at the hands of the clergy for so doing. It is strange that about the same time, as Schenk asserts, EISENMENGER composed part of his "Entdecktes Judenthum" in Wiesbaden.

For a long time the Jews of Wiesbaden formed only a small community and had no prominent rabbis, although now and again one is mentioned in collections of responsa. In 1832 Abraham Geiger was appointed to the rabbinate. He did good work in school and synagogue, and introduced confirmation and similar reforms. It was there that he published his "Wissenschaftliche Zeitschrift für Jüdische Theologie," and called together a meeting of rabbis (see CONFERENCES, RABBINICAL). Geiger resigned (1838) on account of some dissension in the community; and after a short interval, during which Benjamin HOCHSTÄDTER, at that time teacher in Wiesbaden, was in charge of the rabbinate, he was succeeded by Solomon Süsskind, district rabbi in Weilburg, who was transferred to Wiesbaden in 1844 and remained in office until 1884, when he retired on a pension. The next incumbent was Michael Silberstein, formerly district rabbi in Württemberg.

The congregation, which has greatly increased since 1886, now numbers about 2,000. Besides the main community there is the Altisraelitische Cultusgemeinde, an Orthodox congregation, with a membership of 300.

Weisbaden has a total population of 97,566.

BIBLIOGRAPHY: Schenk, *Gesch. der Stadt Wiesbaden.*
D. M. SI.

WIESNER, ADOLF: Austrian journalist and author; born in Prague 1807; died in New York Sept. 23, 1867. His name was originally Wiener, but, being desirous of pursuing a juridical career, which was not then possible for a Jew in Austria, he embraced Catholicism, assuming the name Wiesner. After practising law in the criminal court of Vienna for a short time, he devoted his endeavors to literary pursuits; and by the aid of Count Kolowrat, then home secretary, his historical drama "Inez de Castro" was staged at the Vienna Burgtheater in 1842. A second play, entitled "Die Geiseln und der Negersklave," and based on Emperor Charles V.'s expedition against Tunis, failed, however, of acceptance. He was the author of two more dramas: "Der Feind" and "Der Arzt und Seine Tochter."

In reply to the Russian privy councilor L. von Tengoborsky's work "Die Finanzen, der Oeffentliche Credit, die Staatschuld und das Besteuerungssystem des Oesterreichischen Kaiserstaates" (2 vols., Paris, 1843), which attracted considerable attention, Wiesner wrote his "Russisch Politische Arithmetik" (2 vols., Leipsic, 1844). In 1846, the political situation in Vienna becoming intolerable, he went to Frankfort, and shortly after his valuable historical work "Denkwürdigkeiten der Oesterreichischen Censur vom Zeitalter der Reformation bis auf die Gegenwart" (Stuttgart, 1847) appeared. In 1848 he was elected to the Frankfort Parliament, siding with the extreme Left; and during its session he edited the "Frankfurter Oberpostamts-Zeitung."

Seeing no future for himself in Germany, and being still unable to return home, Wiesner emigrated in 1852 to the United States. He settled in New York, and for some years was employed by railroad and steamship companies, besides doing literary work. It was due to his activity that the Schiller monument was erected in New York in 1859. In 1860 he edited the periodical "Geist der Weltliteratur," which enjoyed but a brief existence. He afterward moved to Baltimore, where he edited a "Turn-Zeitung." During the Civil war he devoted himself to the care of disabled Union soldiers; and at the close of the war the federal government acknowledged his good offices by appointing him to a post in the Baltimore custom-house, where he rendered himself helpful to the many German immigrants with whom he came in contact. Early in 1866 he became editor of the "Illinois-Staatszeitung." On learning of the imperial amnesty of June 8, 1867, Wiesner, though very ill, started for Germany. He reached New York exhausted, and suffered an attack of typhoid fever, from which he died.

BIBLIOGRAPHY: Wurzbach, *Biog. Lex.*; *Presse* (Vienna), 1867, Nos. 64, 184; *Fremden-Blatt*, 1867, No. 282; *Der Wanderer* (Vienna), 1867, No. 280; *Neues Wiener Tageblatt*, 1867, No. 213; *Neue Freie Presse*, 1867, No. 1118; Heinrich Laube, *Das Erste Deutsche Parlament*, i. 66, 283; ii. 99, 175, Leipsic, 1849.
S. N. D.

WIFE. See HUSBAND AND WIFE.

WIG (Judæo-German, **sheitel; peruk** [from the French "perruque"]): A covering for the head, consisting of false hair interwoven with or united to a kind of cap or netting. Wearing false hair on the head to supplement a scanty natural supply, or as an adornment, appears to have been a common custom among women in the Talmudic period. The Mishnah calls false hair "pe'ah nokrit" (a strange lock), and declares that on Sabbath a woman may wear a wig in the courtyard but not in the street, the apprehension in the latter case being that she might remove the wig and carry it from private to public premises, which is forbidden (Shab. vi. 5, 64b). The husband may object to a wife's vow if it involves shaving off her hair. One tanna thought she might wear a wig, but R. Me'ïr said the husband might object to the wig on the ground of uncleanliness (Naz. 28b). The question is discussed whether or not a wig may be considered as a part of the body of the wearer (Sanh. 112a; 'Ar. 7b).

The wearing of the hair loose and exposed in the street was forbidden to women as disorderly and immoral. A married woman who disobeyed this Jewish ordinance ("dat Yisra'el") established a legal cause for divorce and forfeited her dowry (Ket. vii. 6, 72a). This ordinance came to be scrupulously observed, and a married woman could be distinguished by her hair being entirely covered; if one went with uncovered head it was taken as evidence that she was a virgin (Sifre 11). For a woman, during the reading of the "Shema'," to leave visible hair which usually is covered is considered an impropriety (Ber. 24a). In the Middle Ages married women scrupulously cut or shaved off their hair, covering their heads with kerchiefs. Some women wore on the forehead a silk band resembling in color that of the hair. During the sixteenth century R. Judah Katzenellenbogen and R. David ha-Kohen of Corfu permitted a wig to be used under a cover (David ha-Kohen, Responsa, No. 90). Moses Alashkar permitted the side hair to be partly exposed (Responsa, No. 35). During the eighteenth and nineteenth centuries rich women wore wigs in various styles, more or less exposed. The "pe'ah nokrit" in the Mishnah was pointed out to prove the early custom, but the opponents of the innovation explained that the wig was covered, not exposed. R. Moses Sofer and his disciple Akiba Joseph were decidedly opposed to the wig ("Leb ha-'Ibri," pp. 129, 189, Lemberg, 1873).

In modern times Orthodox Jewesses in eastern Europe wear wigs, while in the Orient they still don the kerchief that covers all the hair. In America some of the women immigrants wear the wig; but the newly married women have all discarded it and wear their natural hair in the prevailing style. There is nothing in rabbinical literature to show that wigs were ever worn by men, aside, perhaps, from the statements that the Roman legions carried scalps with them ("ḳarḳefet"), and that Ishmael's scalp adorned the heads of the kings (Ḥul. 123a). The scalps appear to have been used in battle to insure good fortune and victory; and it is possible they were used as wigs. See HAIR IN RABBINICAL LITERATURE.

BIBLIOGRAPHY: Brüll's *Jahrb.* viii. 51–52, Frankfort-on-the-Main, 1887; Abrahams, *Jewish Life in the Middle Ages*, p. 281.
A.   J. D. E.

WIGA, JUDAH: Polish preacher of the sixteenth and seventeenth centuries. The name so written is given by Sternberg ("Gesch. der Juden in Polen," p. 183), apparently taken from Polish sources, and ascribed to a famous preacher of Lublin. Basnage ("Histoire des Juifs," ix. 993, The Hague, 1716), however, calls him Judah Vega, saying he must not be confounded with the Spanish rabbi of Amsterdam (see VEGA, JUDAH); and he refers to him as having published a collection of sermons toward the end of the sixteenth century during the reign of Sigismund. Wolf ("Bibl. Hebr." i., No. 709), though using the Hebrew form ויגא, agrees with Basnage, adding that the work was entitled "Derashot." On the other hand, this Judah Wiga may be identical with one Judah ben Moses בינה (transliterated "Biga" by Wolf, *l.c.* iii., No. 754; and "Bigo" by Zunz, "G. V." p. 430), the author of "Malke Yehudah" (Lublin, 1616), a collection of fifteen sermons.

BIBLIOGRAPHY: Steinschneider, *Cat. Bodl.* col. 1376.
E. C.   M. SEL.

WIHL, LUDWIG: German poet and philologist; born at Wevelingen, Prussia, Oct. 24, 1807; died at Brussels Jan. 16, 1882; educated at Krefeld, Cologne, Bonn, and Munich (Ph.D. 1830). In his "Anfänge der Kunst Unter den Griechen in Verbindung mit der Erklärung einer Phönicischen Inschrift," read before a learned society (1831), he advanced the theory that Phenician was a linguistic derivative of Hebrew, and that Phenicia had exercised a profound influence on the art of early Greece. Despite the efforts of his patron, the Archbishop of Cologne, and of others, Wihl's hopes for a university

career were doomed to failure, because he declined to be baptized.

Wihl then entered upon a journalistic career at Frankfort-on-the-Main and Hamburg, and published his first volume of poems at Mayence in 1837. During a trip to England two years later he wrote his "Englischer Novellenkranz"; but his account of Heine, written at Paris for the Hamburg "Telegraph," brought upon him the enmity of the poet. In 1840 he returned to Frankfort, where, with the help of funds advanced by a Catholic banker named Seufferheld, he established a boarding-school for boys; this school, however, existed for only eighteen months, because the authorities forbade him to admit Catholic pupils. During the next few years Wihl lived at Amsterdam and at Utrecht as a teacher and journalist, until he was called to Paderborn as an editor. A recklessly radical article which he published in a local paper during the Revolution of 1848, however, brought on him a sentence of a year's imprisonment in a fortress, and he fled to France, where he became professor of German at Paris and Grenoble. On the outbreak of the Franco-Prussian war he retired, from patriotic motives, to Brussels, where he resided for the remainder of his life on a pension.

Wihl was the author of the following works: "Geschichte der Deutschen National-Literatur von Ihren Ersten Anfängen bis auf Unsere Tage," 1840; "West-Oestliche Schwalben" (Mannheim, 1847; French translation, "Hirondelles Orientales," by Mercier, Paris, 1860), a collection of lyric poems; "Le Mendiant pour la Pologne" (Paris, 1864), a collection of French and German poems; and "Le Pays Bleu" (*ib.* 1865). He published also a number of "Portraits Poétiques," in which he gave free rein to his caustic sarcasm.

BIBLIOGRAPHY: Winter and Wünsche, *Die Jüdische Literatur*, iii. 884; Fränkel, in *Allgemeine Deutsche Biographie*, xxii. 469–472; *Ost und West*, i. 270–274.
S.   J. KA.

WILCZYNSKI, ERNEST JULIUS: American mathematician; born in Hamburg, Germany, Nov. 13, 1876. He went with his parents in 1885 to America, where he attended the Chicago high school. Returning to Germany in 1893, he studied astronomy and mathematics at the University of Berlin (Ph.D. 1897; thesis, "Hydrodynamische Untersuchungen mit Anwendungen auf die Theorie der Sonnenrotation"). In 1898 he became computer at the Nautical Almanac Office, Washington, D. C., and then instructor in mathematics successively at Columbian University Summer School there and at the University of California, being appointed assistant professor at the latter institution in 1902. From 1903 to 1905 he was absent on leave in Europe as research associate of the Carnegie Institution at Washington. Besides a large number of articles in mathematical and astronomical journals, he has published "Projective Differential Geometry of Curves and Ruled Surfaces," Leipsic, 1905.

A.   F. T. H.

WILD ASS: Rendering used in Gen. xvi. 12 (R. V.), Job vi. 5, xi. 12, xxiv. 5, xxxix. 5, Ps. civ. 11, Isa. xxxii. 14, Jer. xiv. 6, and Hos. viii. 9 for the Hebrew "pere," and in Jer. ii. 24 for "pereh";

in Job xxxix. 5 for the Hebrew "'arud"; and in Dan. v. 21 for the Aramaic "'arad." In all these passages the animal is depicted as extremely wild, shy, wary, and swift. At present it is rarely met with in Syria.

The wild ass, though it resembles in appearance the tame animal, is classed in the Talmud, in a ritual aspect, among the wild animals (Kil. i. 6, viii. 6). It is the only animal whose flesh underneath the muscles can be torn either way (Ḥul. 59a). It turned the mill in which grain was ground ('Ab. Zarah 16b), while its flesh was fed to the lions in the king's menagerie (Men. 103b). See also Ass.

BIBLIOGRAPHY: Tristram, *Nat. Hist.* p. 41; Lewysohn, *Z. T.* p. 143.
E. G. H.   I. M. C.

WILD BULL. See UNICORN.

WILD GOAT. See GOAT.

WILD OX. See ANTELOPE; UNICORN.

WILDA, WILHELM EDUARD: German jurist; born at Altona Aug. 17, 1800; died at Kiel Aug. 9, 1856; educated at the Johanneum of Hamburg and the universities of Göttingen, Heidelberg, Kiel, and Copenhagen. The year 1826 was passed partly in Berlin and partly in travel through Germany, France, and Switzerland. After practising as an attorney at Hamburg from 1826 to 1830, he was appointed assistant professor at Halle, where he remained until 1842, when he was called to Breslau as full professor. In 1854 he was transferred to Kiel. Wilda, who was the founder of comparative jurisprudence, was the author of the following works: "Das Gildewesen im Mittelalter" (Halle, 1831; 2d ed., Berlin, 1838); and "Das Strafrecht der Germanen" (Halle, 1842), a volume forming the second part of his "Geschichte des Deutschen Rechtes." In 1838 he founded, in collaboration with Reyscher, the "Zeitschrift für Deutsches Recht," which was published first at Tübingen and later at Leipsic, and was discontinued in 1861.

BIBLIOGRAPHY: *Jüdisches Athenœum*, pp. 244-245; *Meyers Konversations-Lexikon*; *Brockhaus Konversations-Lexikon*.
S.

WILDERNESS (Hebr. "ḥorbah" [Jer. vii. 34; Isa. xlviii. 21], "yeshimon" [Isa. xlviii. 19; Deut. xxxii. 10; Ps. lxxviii. 40], "midbar" [very frequently], "'arabah" [generally in poetic speech and as a parallel to "midbar"], "ẓiyyah" [Ps. lxxviii. 17], "tohu" [Ps. cvii. 40; Job xii. 24; Deut. xxxii. 10], "shammah," "shemamah" [Isa. v. 9; Jer. xlii. 18; Ezek. xxxv. 7], "sharab" [Isa. xxxv. 7; R. V., "glowing sand"]): An examination of the Hebrew terms rendered "wilderness" or "desert" in the English versions shows that these translations are inadequate and misleading. "Ḥorbah" implies violent destruction; and it is more exactly rendered by "waste places" (Ps. cii. 7 [A. V. 6]) or "desolation" (Jer. xliv. 2). The latter term also expresses more accurately the connotation of "yeshimon" and "shammah" or "shemamah," while "tohu" conveys the idea of chaotic confusion (Jer. iv. 23; Job xxvi. 7). "'Arabah" comes nearer to the meaning of the English "desert" (Isa. xxxv. 1; Jer. li. 43); "ẓiyyah" implies the absence or dearth of water (Ps. lxiii. 2 [A. V. 1]); while the more probable render-

ing of "sharab" is "mirage" (see Isa. xxxv. 7, R. V., marginal reading). In so far as the Hebrew terms do not imply artificial desolation and destruction, they connote a stretch of uncultivated land suitable for grazing and occupied by nomads (Num. xiv. 33), as is clear both from the etymology of the word "midbar," and from the fact that it and its synonyms usually denote the wilderness of the wandering or Exodus. Such a midbar occasionally existed in the very midst of land under tillage (Gen. xxxvii. 22), and again was found at the borders as a transition from cultivated to uncultivated districts (Deut. iv. 43; I Sam. xvii. 28).

This "wilderness" is described as without animate occupants (Deut. xxxii. 10), or as a district where no man is found (Jer. ii. 6; ix. 1, 11; Job xxxviii. 26) and where sowing is not carried on (Jer. ii. 2). It is an abandoned stretch (Isa. xxvii. 10; comp. vi. 12, vii. 16) without protection (Ps. lv. 8 [A. V. 7]), and a thirsty land (Ezek. xix. 13; Job xxx. 3, R. V.) devoid of vegetation (Hos. ii. 3; Isa. xli. 19). These terrors play upon the fancy of the people (Isa. xxx. 6; comp. "Z. D. P. V." iii. 114 *et seq.*). Some parts of the wilderness are characterized as "ne'ot" (Jer. xxiii. 10), or pastures, and others as "'arabot," or dry, barren stretches (II Sam. xv. 28), or as "ḥarerim," or stony table-lands (Jer. xii. 12, xvii. 6). The wilderness is the home of wild animals ("ẓiyyim"; Isa. xiii. 21, xxxiv. 14), including wild asses (Jer. ii. 24), and thorns grow there (Judges viii. 7, 16) as well as the heather (Jer. xvii. 6, xlviii. 6).

The term "midbar" is applied to the district of the Hebrews' wanderings between the Exodus and the conquest of Palestine. This region stretched south of Palestine in or on the border of the Negeb; separate parts of it are called the wildernesses of Sin, Shur, Kadesh, and the like. The wilderness between Canaan and the Euphrates is repeatedly mentioned in prophetic writings (Ezek. xx. 35; Isa. xl. 3), and some portions of it are named in Num. xxi. 11, 13 and Judges xi. 22. The wilderness referred to in Josh. xv. 61 is that of Judah, which comprised the eastern declivity of the mountainous region toward the Dead Sea. The character of this district illustrates most strikingly the great variety of localities designated in Biblical usage as wildernesses; for in it were pastures (II Chron. xxvi. 10), caves (I Sam. xxiv. 3), and cities (Josh. xv. 61), though it contained also barren rocks and precipices. This wilderness of Judah included the wildernesses of Maon (I Sam. xxiii. 24) and Ziph (*ib.* xxiii. 14). Connected with it to the north were the wildernesses of Gibeah (Judges xx. 42), Michmash (I Sam. xiii. 18), Ai (Josh. viii. 15), and Beth-aven (*ib.* xviii. 12).   E. G. H.

WILDERNESS, WANDERINGS IN THE.
—**Biblical Data:** Next to the Exodus, the remembrance of the wanderings in the desert for a period corresponding to the life of a generation (see FORTY) is central to the historic consciousness of Israel. Hence the scene of these migrations is often called "the" wilderness ("ha-midbar") par excellence (Ex. iii. 18, xiv. 11; Num. xxxii. 13; Deut. i. 31; comp. Judges xi. 16, 18; Amos ii. 10; *et al.*). This wil-

derness corresponds to that designated as Arabia
Petræa by the Greco-Roman geographers. The
story of the Hebrews' wanderings is related in: (1)
Ex. xiv.-xix. 24, 32, comprising the stations from
the time Israel left Egypt to the promulgation of
the Law on Sinai; and Num. x. 11–

**Stages of
Wan-
derings.**

xxii. 1, giving those from the revelation to the arrival of the people opposite Jericho; (2) Deut. i. 2, 19 *et seq.*;
ii.; iii. 6 *et seq.* (comp. xxxiv.), which
are without chronological order, but begin with the
desert of Sinai (Horeb) and extend to the incursion
into the land of the Amorites; (3) Num. xxxiii. 5–
50, cataloguing the camping stations on the march
from Rameses to Jericho. The last-mentioned list
differs from the data in Exodus and Numbers in so
far as it inserts eighteen stations between Hazeroth
(Num. xi. 35) and Kadesh or Sin (Num. xii. 16; xiii.
2, 21; xx. 1) that are not mentioned in the historical
narratives, while the stations enumerated in Num.
xi. 1 *et seq.*; xxi. 16, 19 are omitted. Other, smaller
divergences appear between Num. xxxiii. 30 *et seq.*
and Deut. x. 6, and between Num. xx. 22 *et seq.*
and the same passage of Deuteronomy.

——**Critical View:** The discrepancies just referred
to have been noticed by all commentators, and various theories have been advanced to account for them.
The favorite explanation of the precritical scholars
was that the historical narratives contain only the
names of the localities at which something occurred
worth chronicling, while the fuller list includes all
the points touched on the march. But this assumption was recognized as insufficient, especially by
Goethe ("Westoestl. Divan"), who urged the opin-

**Forty
Stations
in Forty
Years.**

ion that the eighteen stations were fic-
titious and were inserted merely to
carry out the theory that Israel wandered about in the wilderness forty
years and had one station for every
year. Most of the names of the sta-
tions can not be located topographically, and comparison of the data shows that the order of the stations varies as well as the events connected with
them.

In P a clearly chronological scheme is carried out,
the duration of the wanderings being calculated accurately by days, months, and years. On the fifteenth of the first month the Israelites started out
from Rameses (Num. xxxiii. 3); on the fifteenth of
the second month they reached the wilderness of
Sin (Ex. xvi. 1); in the third month they arrived at
that of Sinai (Ex. xix. 1), the exact day having been
expunged by a later hand (see Dillmann, Commentary, ed. Ryssel, p. 209); on the first of the first
month of the second year the Tabernacle was erected
(Ex. xl. 1, 17); etc. But these chronological data
conflict with Num. xiv. 34 (comp. Num. i. 1, x. 11,
xiii. 25, xx. 1, xxxiii. 38; and Paran; Sin). The
forty years correspond to the forty days of the spies,
and they are reckoned at one time from the Exodus,
and again from the return of the spies. Still, P did
not invent the number forty; it must have been
based on an old tradition that the generation of the
Exodus perished in the wilderness (Deut. i. 3; ii. 7;
viii. 2, 4; xxix. 4; Josh. xiv. 7, 10; Amos ii. 10, v.
25; Neh. ix. 21; Ps. xcv. 10).

But at the back of this tradition lies the historical
fact that before and after the exodus from Egypt
many of the tribes and clans of Israel moved about
as nomads in this region, and were

**Historical
Foun-
dation.**

only gradually welded together into a
union sufficiently close to give support
to the effort of some of their number
to gain a foothold across the Jordan.
Many of the names are those of stations in which
even in historic days the nomadic tribes would encamp, being connected with oases (*e.g.*, Elim). Other
names gave rise to legends, *e.g.*, Marah (Ex. xv. 23)
and Taberah (Num. xi. 3); and a few are explained
variously, *e.g.*, Massah and Meribah (Ex. xvii. 2,
7; Num. xx. 13; Deut. xxxiii. 8; see Paran and
Kadesh; comp. Num. xiii. 3, 26a and *ib.* xiii. 26b;
Deut. i. 19, Josh. xiv. 6, and Num. xx. 1; Deut. i.
46, Num. xiv. 25, and Deut. ii. 14, for the difficulties in the way of harmonizing the divergent statements of the sources [Wellhausen, "Prolegomena,"
iv. 349]). The religious or, to be more exact, irreligious anti-Moses and anti-Yhwh attitude of Israel
in the wilderness (Ex. xxxii.; Num. xi., xiv., xx.,
xxv.) reflects the conditions of a later historical
period. Many of the occurrences are outgrowths of
the natural tendency to impute greatness and miracles to the heroic generations (Ex. xvi., xvii. 5, xxiii.
20; Num. ix. 15 *et seq.*, xx. 8; Deut. viii. 4; see also
Manna; Quail; comp. Hosea ii. 16, 17; ix. 10;
Deut. xxxii. 10; Ezek. xvi. 8; Jer. ii. 2; Amos
v. 25).   E. G. H.

WILENKIN. See Minski, Nicolai Maksim-
ovich.

WILENKIN, GREGORY: Former Russian
government official; born at Tsarskoye-Selo, near
St. Petersburg, Russia, Feb. 22, 1864. He was a
member of an ancient Russian Jewish family which
has held landed estates for the last two centuries,
and he counted among his ancestors many who distinguished themselves for their charitable work.
The name of one of his female ancestors, Blema
Wilenkin, is still remembered in the Jewish community of Minsk, whence the family originally
came. At the end of the eighteenth century she bequeathed a house (still in existence) at Minsk to be
used as a "Klaus"; and she left another house for
the use of impoverished Russian Jews at Jerusalem.

After completing his studies in the gymnasium of
his native town, Wilenkin matriculated first at the
University of Dorpat and afterward at the University
of St. Petersburg, where he studied law. In 1887
he entered the government service in the Ministry of
Public Instruction, and was sent on a scientific mis-
sion to England to study the organization of the uni-
versities of Oxford and Cambridge; he went also to
Paris to investigate its system of primary schools.
His report on the schools was published, and the
French government bestowed on him the rank of
"Officier d'Académie" in recognition of this work.
On his return to St. Petersburg in 1895, Witte, then
minister of finance, invited Wilenkin to leave the
Ministry of Public Instruction for the Ministry of
Finance, and appointed him assistant financial agent
of the Russian government in London. Wilenkin
served in that post over nine years, and in May, 1904,

was appointed financial agent of the Russian government at Washington, D. C., being attached to the Russian embassy there. He died in 1918.

Wilenken's works include "Monometalism and Bimetalism" and "The Financial and Political Organization of Contemporary England and the Commercial and Political Organization of Contemporary Russia."

A.

WILKESBARRE: County-seat and principal city of Luzerne county, Pa. Evidence points to 1838 as the date of arrival of the first Jewish settlers, among whom Martin Long, a Bavarian, was the most prominent. Two years later a society was organized for occasional worship, and until 1849 the incipient congregation held its services in various rooms. In August of that year it dedicated its first synagogue under the auspices of Moses Strasser, Isaac Leeser of Philadelphia, and Samuel Isaacs of New York. In 1857 the community was incorporated as the Congregation B'nai B'rith. Its earlier pulpit history is practically the record of the service of Herman Rubin, reader and teacher from 1853 to 1882. His successors have been David Stern, Victor Rundbacken, Israel Joseph, and Marcus Salzman who has officiated for several years.

The rise of the younger generation gave a decided impetus to the growing tendency toward Reform, which resulted in the adoption of the Einhorn ritual. This yielded, in its turn, to the Union Prayer-Book. B'nai B'rith, the largest congregation in the city, is the only Reform organization.

Until 1871 B'nai B'rith was the only congregation in Wilkesbarre, but in that year the first efforts were made to unite the Orthodox Jews. The organization, little more than a minyan, became the parent of the congregations B'nai Jacob and Holche Yosher, which were formed in 1881, although their synagogues were not built until 1886 and 1887 respectively. In 1902 a fourth synagogue was dedicated to the use of the youngest congregation, Oheb Zedek (Anshe Ungarn).

The Jewish educational, philanthropic, and social activities of the city are entrusted to the following institutions: the religious and Hebrew schools, the Synagogue Industrial School, branch lodges of the leading Jewish orders, the Young Men's Hebrew Association, the social and literary clubs, four aid societies, a free loan association, and the Executive Committee of Jewish Congregations (which aids the work of the Industrial Removal Office).

With this equipment the community is an important center of Jewish activity in northeastern Pennsylvania, reaching out to Hazleton, Plymouth, Pittston, and the smaller towns in the vicinity. The Jews of Wilkesbarre numbered about 3,000 in a total population (1920), 73,833.

A. M. SAL.

WILL or **TESTAMENT** (Latin, "testamentum"; Greek, διαθήκη, which latter word is often found in the Mishnah and the Baraita [דייתיקי; see B. B. 152b: "One diatheke annuls another"]): The legal instrument by which a person disposes of his property, or of a part thereof, and which takes effect after his death, but the provisions of which may be changed or revoked at any time before death.

The ordinary substitute for the last will and testament in Jewish law answers to the "gift by reason of death," something like the "donatio causa mortis" of the Roman law, called in the Mishnah "gift of one lying sick" ("mattenat shekib mera'"), which has been briefly mentioned under GIFTS IN RABBINICAL LAW.

The notices of wills in the Mishnah (B. B. viii. 5, 6; ix. 6, 7) are scanty; and in the discussion upon them there are very few baraitot. The discrepancies as to details among later authorities are wide, and run back to the fundamental questions "How far can an owner of property, by his declaration, set aside or change the rules of succession laid down in Num. xxvii. ?" and, more particularly, "Can he abridge the rights of the first-born declared in Deut. xxi. 17?" This verse speaks of "the day when he gives their heritage to his sons," and only restrains the father from robbing the first-born of his double share;

Biblical Foundations. which implies that the father may make, otherwise, an unequal division among his sons or, when he has no sons, an unequal division among his daughters. As R. Johanan ben Baroka puts it in the Mishnah, "If the ancestor says, 'Such a person shall be my heir,' and such a person is capable of inheriting, his words are valid; if the person is not fit to inherit, his words are void" (B. B. viii. 5). The later Babylonian authorities (see B. B. 130a) follow R. Johanan's opinion, though he was in the minority.

But the Talmud nowhere defines how the choice among heirs of the same class may be made, whether in writing or by word of mouth; it is intimated (B. B. 113a) only that it should be done in daytime, not by night. The later authorities, while declaring that R. Johanan's opinion is the law, deprive it of almost all its force by restricting to persons dangerously sick this power of choosing an heir, that is, to those who can dispose of their property by gift "causa mortis." On the contrary, they require no written instrument for the purpose of giving to one son what belongs to all the sons; they here give greater weight to an oral command, holding that where a man "writes over" his estate to one son among several, he only makes him a trustee for all the sons (B. B. 130b); and if he makes a deed ("shetar") with a view to its taking effect only after his death, the effect may be nil, since a man's deed can not be delivered after his death. Thus particular precautions are necessary to avoid making the writing down of a testamentary disposition destructive of its purposes.

The Hebrew word corresponding to διαθήκη, whether written or spoken, is "zawwa'ah" (= "a command"); but it is hardly ever used in legal discussions, either in the Talmud or in the codes. Where the testator was the father of the beneficiaries, the will had, in addition to its legal effect, a great moral weight, it being deemed the duty of children to respect the desires of their deceased father, or even of more distant ancestors. That this principle originated in Biblical times is evi-

The "Zawwa'ah." denced by the faithful obedience of the Rechabites to the rules laid down for them by their ancestor Rechab (Jer. xxxv. 6–19). In this sense the written "zawwa'ah" became an important element in the Jewish literature of the Middle Ages, down even to the seventeenth century. But such an instrument, if written during good health, had only a moral sanction, even as to the disposal of property, which the civil judge could not enforce.

An owner of property can make a revocable disposition, taking effect after death, only in the form of a "gift of him who lies sick"; in other words, such a disposition can be made only when death is apparently very near; and if the danger present at the time of the gift passes away, the gift is ipso facto revoked. But this kind of gift differs very broadly from the "donatio causa mortis," which has been adopted by the probate and equity courts from the Roman law into the laws of England and America; for the latter gift is valid only when followed by delivery or such other formalities as the nature of the thing given demands in gifts "inter vivos," while the Talmudic gift "causa mortis" requires no formality whatever, not even an appeal to the bystanders, as, "You are my witnesses that I give this to NN."

There is this difference between the "gift of one lying sick" and a true testament: while the latter disposes of all that the testator owns at the moment of death, the other takes effect only on the property which the donor has at the time of the gift. Thus, if a man says, "My wife shall take a son's share," though the share may be increased or may be lessened by the subsequent death or birth of sons, it will be only a share in the property which the donor owned when he spoke the words (B. B. 128b). Says the Mishnah (B. B. viii. 5): "If one says, 'A, my first-born, shall not have a double share,' or, 'My son B shall not inherit among his brethren,' it is without effect; for he declares against what is written in the Torah. But if he divides his estate among his sons by his words, giving more to one than to another, or making the first-born equal to the others, his words are valid; only he must not speak of it as 'inheritance,' but must call it 'gift' somewhere in his spoken or written words."

The technical formula "gift of one lying sick" ("shekib mera'"; this Aramaic phrase is used in the Mishnah) really denotes the revocable gift; and **Gift "Causa** as the removal of the danger revokes **Mortis."** the gift, it was usual for the witnesses to it to draw up a minute containing the following or equivalent words: "This gift was made when he was sick and lay on his bed: and from this sickness he departed for his eternal home."

R. Eliezer, who represents in the Mishnah the position that the gift "causa mortis" is not effective without "kinyan," cites the well-known incident of a man of Meron (Galicia) at Jerusalem who wished to make a gift of movable property to an absent friend, and found no legal way except to buy a piece of land and then to make a deed conveying the land and the movable property together to his friend; he is told in answer that the man proposing to make the gift was evidently in good health (B. B. 156b; comp. Yer. Pe'ah 17d).

The gift of one who is sick is, as stated above, valid without the specific acts which ordinarily are necessary to pass a title; e.g., in the case of land or slaves, without deed, payment of price, or occupa-

tion; in the case of movable property, without "pulling"; in the case of demands, without the "meeting of three"; and the heirs can not release a demand that has been thus given away. While, according to the Mishnah, the majority uphold the position that such a gift can be made without kinyan and without writing only on the Sabbath, the contrary opinion, that the writing can be dispensed with on week-days also, prevailed afterward; and the Talmud declares that the words of the sick man must be deemed just as effectual as if they were written, sealed, and delivered. However, even the Mishnah cites the case of the "mother of Rokel's sons," who told her sons to give her valuable cloak to her daughter, the wish being enforced after her death.

Where the sick man gives away his whole estate with those formalities by which titles pass (kinyan), the act is nevertheless treated as revocable and as taking effect only on the donor's death; but, if he sets aside for himself "any land whatever" (according to the Mishnah) or "any movable property whatever" (according to later authorities), the gift is valid and irrevocable. The Talmud, however, provides that the part reserved must be sufficient to enable him to earn his living. Still the bystanders are encouraged to help the sick man in passing title to the donees whenever he desires to do so, on the ground that it will tend to calm his mind; and they may do this even on the Sabbath, so far as it can then be lawfully done; but it could hardly have been the intent of the sages to encourage a course of action which would leave the sick man penniless in case he should recover.

The most effective method of making a gift is to acknowledge the property right of the intended donee as already in force; e.g., one may acknowledge that one owes A a thousand zuzim, or such a horse, or such a slave; or that a certain sum in the hands of a named person (the sick man's debtor) belongs to A. If the sick man wishes to give anything to an idolater, he can do it only in this way, as a direct gift would not be enforced by a Jewish court. R. Marc, the son of Issur the convert, was begotten "not in holiness" (i.e., he was begotten before his father's conversion); therefore when Issur wished to leave him a sum of money then in the hands of a debtor, which money represented the bulk of his estate, he was told that it was against the policy of the Law to permit him to leave his estate by gift "causa mortis" to a son incapable of inheriting it (see DERELICTS). A way out of the difficulty was then shown him; this was to acknowledge before the witnesses that the sum of money already belonged to R. Marc. It seems that the heirs are estopped by the acknowledgment of the ancestor and can not question its truth.

A dispute may arise between a donor who wishes to resume his gift after possession thereof has been **Resump-** given or the title thereto has otherwise **tion** passed, and the donee, the former as- **of Gift.** serting that he was dangerously sick, and that the gift, being made "causa mortis," is revocable, while the donee says, "You were in good health, and your gift is irrevocable." A dispute may also arise between the donor's heirs and the donee, in the case of a gift not completed by ḳinyan, the former saying, "He recovered from the sickness in which he made the gift, and afterward died from another cause." The masters of the Mishnah differed as to the burden of proof; but finally the old rule of the Hillelites prevailed: "The estate remains according to its occupation," or, it might be said, "its presumption." That is, if the things given away remain in the possession of the donor or his heirs, the burden of proof is on the donee; if they are in the possession of the donee, the burden of proof is on the donor or his heirs. Where a testament in writing is found on the person of a dead man, in the absence of other evidence it amounts to nothing; for though the "gift of one lying sick" is good without delivery of the deed, the testator may have intended a delivery, and such delivery is impossible after his death.

The thing given "causa mortis" is as much subject to the donor's debts, or to his widow's jointure, as property that has descended to the heirs. If several sums are given in such words (spoken or written) as, "So much to A, afterward so much to B," etc., the last-named donee must first yield his gift to the testator's creditors; but in the absence of words of postponement, the several donees lose proportionately if, through the decedent's debts, or for any cause, the estate falls short of the necessary value.

Should a sick man send money or valuables to a person at a distance, and the messenger find such person dead, the gift is valid and goes to the heirs of the latter, if at the time of the delivery to the messenger the donee was alive; but if he was then dead, the gift is void, and the thing goes back to the donor's heirs.

BIBLIOGRAPHY: Maimonides, Yad, Zekiyyah, viii.-xii.; Caro, Shulḥan 'Aruk, Ḥoshen Mishpaṭ, 246, 250-258, 281 et seq.
E. C.   L. N. D.

WILLIAM OF AUVERGNE. See GUIL-LAUME OF AUVERGNE.

WILLIAM OF NORWICH: Alleged victim of ritual murder by Jews at Norwich in 1144. He may therefore claim to be the protomartyr of this class of pseudo-martyrdom. According to the boy's own family, he was enticed away on Monday, March 21, 1144, to become a scullion of the Archdeacon of Norwich, and was not heard of again till Saturday, March 26, when his uncle, cousin, and brother found his body, covered with sand, in Thorpe Wood, near Norwich, with the head shaven and with marks of puncture by thorns. Although there were signs of life in the body, it was reburied in the same place; and Godwin Sturt, the boy's uncle, at the next synod, accused the Jews of having murdered William, whereupon the prior of Lewis Priory claimed the body as that of a martyr, and the canons of Norwich Cathedral seized it for themselves. The boy's brother Robert and his uncle Godwin were appointed officials in the monastery on the strength of their relationship to the martyr; and his mother was buried in the graveyard of the monastery, somewhat to the scandal of the monks. No action was taken against the accused Jews, though it was asserted that the boy William had been seen entering the house of a Jew named Deusaie or Eleazar, and

a report was brought from Theobald, a converted Jew of Cambridge, that it was the custom of Jews to sacrifice a boy at Passover at some place chosen by lot, and that the lot for that year had fallen on Norwich. This is the first historical occurrence of the myth of the BLOOD ACCUSATION. The royal sheriff, in whose jurisdiction the Jews were, refused to take notice of the accusation, although he was himself indebted to the Jews, and would have been benefited personally if they had been proved guilty.

It has been suggested that the boy's relatives in a fit of religious exaltation attempted to gain increased sanctity for themselves and for the lad by making him undergo the form of crucifixion on Good Friday, March 25; that, during the process, the boy had fallen into a fit, which had alarmed his relatives, who thereupon buried him in Thorpe Wood, near their residence; and that, to divert suspicion, they accused the Jews, although the process of crucifixion would be quite unfamiliar to them, and obtained some sort of confirmation from the convert Theobald. Later, the legend of the martyr was considerably developed by Thomas of Capgrade (d. 1494). It was claimed that the Jews had been met as they were carrying the body in a bag to Thorpe Wood, on the opposite side from the Jewry outside the city, which they would have had to traverse. The person who thus encountered them kept silence, it was alleged, at the order of the sheriff, who had been bribed by the Jews. On his refusal to testify, a fierce light from heaven pointed out the place of martyrdom to a man, who found the lad's body disfigured with stigmata and hanging from a tree. Nothing of all this is found in the earliest form of the legend as related by Thomas of Monmouth, although the supernatural light appeared in Germany (Pertz, "Scriptores," vi. 472), whither the story was carried and where it had numerous repetitions. See BLOOD ACCUSATION.

BIBLIOGRAPHY: Jacobs, Jews of Angevin England, pp. 19-21, 256-258; idem, in J. Q. R. ix. 748-755; Jessop and James, The Life and Miracles of William of Norwich by Thomas of Monmouth, Cambridge, 1897.
J.

WILLOW: Any tree or shrub of the genus Salix. Willows and poplars are numerous in Palestine. In all regions the white willow (Salix alba) and the Euphrates poplar (Populus Euphratica) occur with great frequency, while the crack-willow (Salix fragilis) and the white poplar (Populus alba) are also common. On the banks of the Jordan and in the valleys of the Dead Sea grow the Salix safsaf and its variety, the Salix hierochuntica. The following species also occur, although less frequently: black willow (Salix nigricans) at Amanus, near Beirut; French willow (Salix triandra) at Al-Zib; Salix alba, var. latifolia, near Beirut and the Dead Sea; var. integrifolia near 'Aintab; goat-willow (Salix caprea) on Lebanon; Salix alba, var. Libanotica; Salix pedicellata near Damascus and in Cœle-Syria; black poplar (Populus nigra); weeping willow (Salix Babylonica); and Lombardy poplar (Populus pyramidalis). The "willows" of the Bible (ערבים, Isa. xv. 7, xliv. 4, and Ps. cxxxvii. 2; ערבי נחל, Lev. xxiii. 40 and Job xl. 22) were the Euphrates poplars, although the Mishnah interprets ערבים as "willows," despite the Talmudic traces that the willow had previously been termed צפצפה (comp.

Ezek. xvii. 5). לבנה (Gen. xxx. 37; Hos. iv. 13; the לבן of the Targum) is not the officinal storax (*Styrax officinalis*), but the white poplar (*Populus alba*). See PLANTS.

The Feast of Tabernacles requires, according to the Bible, "willows of the brook," the Karaites and recent exegetes regarding this as applying to the booths themselves, while rabbinical tradition refers it to the accessory decorations for the festival. One tannaitic tradition seems to show that the Biblical "willow of the brook" had leaves serrate like a sickle, while the variety with leaves dentate like a saw was rejected. Another tannaitic tradition, however, states that ערבים may be used only when they have red twigs and lanceolate leaves, they being unavailable if they have white twigs and round leaves. Babli combines these traditions, and identifies the former of the two varieties of willow with the ערבים, while the useless willow is the צפצפה (Euphrates poplar). The tannaitic description of the ערבים corresponds to the trembling poplar, or aspen (*Populus tremula*), and even more closely to the *Salix safsaf*, or the French willow (*Salix triandra*). Still another variety is the חילפא, a willow with red twigs and an oblong, sickle-shaped leaf, probably the white willow (*Salix alba*), and which answers to the tannaitic requirements.

The ruling of Babli concerning the available varieties of the willow was naturally adopted by the codifiers, such as Maimonides. Joseph Caro, however, followed by Mordecai Jaffe, dissented, claiming that the usage was at variance with the phraseology of the Halakah, since all willow twigs are green, although they become red after sufficient exposure to the sun, so that it is inadmissible to reject twigs because they are green, and not red.

In addition to the species of willow unavailable in themselves, twigs were forbidden which had been placed under the ban, or which had been stolen or cut, or had become dry, though twigs whose leaves had partly fallen or withered might be used. Willows were also used independently on the Feast of Tabernacles as a shield for the altar, and were carried in the processions which took place daily, or, after the destruction of the Temple, on the seventh day, the "willow of the brook" receiving the name of "hosanna" from the processional shout.

Willow twigs were used for weaving baskets and similar utensils, peeled twigs being employed for the finer grades; while the wood of the willow and poplar was made into troughs, etc. The galls on the leaves of the willow served to dye veils, and the cotton of the seeds of the female willow and poplar was made into an inferior grade of lamp-wick.

The Haggadah is concerned with the willow only so far as it forms part of the festal bush, in which the "willow of the brook" symbolizes: (1) God; (2) the impious and the ignorant of Israel, who have neither righteousness nor knowledge, as the willow has neither taste nor smell; (3) Joseph and Rachel, who, like the willow, faded before the rest; (4) the Sanhedrin, the pair of twigs typifying the two secretaries; (5) the mouth, on account of the labiate leaves. All four trees symbolize the beneficence of the rain which they cause; they fulfil their purpose when two fragrant and two scentless varieties of trees are combined. These metaphors are repeated frequently in synagogal poetry and in homiletic literature, with little change or addition, even in modern times.

E. G. H.   I. Lö.

WILMERSDÖRFFER, MAX, RITTER VON: Bavarian financier and philanthropist; born at Bayreuth April 8, 1824; died at Munich Dec. 26, 1903. At an early age he entered the Munich banking firm of his uncle, J. W. Oberndörffer, whose daughter he married. He was appointed consul-general of Saxony and decorated with the Bavarian cross of St. Michael and with the crosses of the Saxon Order of Merit and the Order of Albrecht, while in 1888 he was made a knight of the Order of the Bavarian Crown. He also received the title of privy commercial councilor from both Saxony and Bavaria. A man of high education, well read in the German classics, he was an authority on numismatics, as well as a patron of art and of many charitable institutions. As a strict Jew, he also took a great interest in the affairs of the Jewish congregation of Munich, whose president he was in 1864 and 1865.

BIBLIOGRAPHY: *Deutsche Israelitische Zeitung*, Regensburg, 1904, No. 1; *Allg. Zeit. des Jud.* 1904, No. 1.   D.

WILMINGTON. See NORTH CAROLINA.

WILNA: Ancient Lithuanian city, capital of the district of the same name; since 1918 the capital of the Lithuanian republic. Situated on the rivers Vilia and Vileika, about 200 miles southeast from Libau on the Baltic, and 436 miles southwest from St. Petersburg. A Jewish settlement existed there in the fourteenth century. The writer Narbutt, in his history of Wilna, states that as early as the reign of the Lithuanian chief Gedimin (1316–41) there was a large Jewish community in the place, and that the space occupied by the streets inhabited by

Earliest
Set-
tlement.

Jews was about one-fifth of the area of the whole city. From fully reliable data accessible to him, Narbutt even specified the names of the streets inhabited by Jews. The historian Bialinsky writes that under the reign of Olgerd (1345–1377) the Jewish community of Wilna was considerable. This opinion is expressed also by the writers Krashewsky, Kraushaar, Scherewsky (in his book upon the Jewish records of the city of Wilna), and Vassilievsky. The last-named historian claims that at the end of the sixteenth century the Jewish community of Wilna numbered from 10,000 to 15,000. Bershadski, in his historical sketch (in "Voskhod," 1881) of the Jewish community of Wilna, shows that the records preserved in the archives evidence the existence of a Jewish community at Wilna since the second half of the sixteenth century, but not before. He states authoritatively that he was unable to find any trace in official sources of the existence of a recognized Jewish congregation before that date. From scattered indications extant in various Hebrew writings the conclusion may be drawn that Bershadski's opinion, to the effect that a large Jewish community represented by a rabbi is traceable only to the second half of the sixteenth century, is nearer the truth than the others. In the responsa of R. Solomon Luria of Lublin (second half of 16th cent.) there is found the following:

"We, the undersigned, hereby certify and witness with our signatures that whereas we have been chosen as judges to decide the controversy which has taken place at Wilna between R. Isaac b. Jacob and R. Jonah b. Isaac, in the matter of the taxation of Polotzk, and whereas the disputant parties appeared before us, and the aforesaid R. Jonah has given to the aforesaid R. Isaac security in behalf of R. Abraham b. Jacob and his brother R. Menahem. . . .

"Signed at the city of Wilna, on the first day of the week, the 7th of Shebaṭ, in the year 5316 [1556]:

"Menahem b. Eliakim Triseash.
"Meshullam b. Jehiel.
"Meshullam b. Judah."

In none of the rabbinical writings is mention made of these rabbis; but the litigants, R. Jonah b. Isaac, R. Abraham b. Jacob and his brother Menahem (or Mendel), are mentioned in the official records, and are cited by Bershadski ("Russko-Yevreiski Arkhiv," No. 69) as the tax-farmers for certain localities, appointed by the Polish king in 1556. In the responsa of Joel ha-Levi Sirkes (BaḤ), second collection (Koretz 1785), the closing paragraph of section 75 has the following: "The above is the testimony given before us by Jacob b. R. Menahem Kaẓ. Signed in the city of Wilna, on the fourth day of the week, twenty-third day of Tammuz, in the year 5323 [1563]. Jonathan b. R. Samuel, Eliezer b. R. Joel, Menahem b. R. Samuel Margolis." In the exchange of correspondence on legal questions of MaHaRaM of Lublin (Metz, 1769), the closing paragraph of section 7 reads: "By this means the murderer was caught as set forth in full in the testimony taken at the city of Wilna, on the third day of the week, on the twentieth of Tammuz, in the year 5553 [1593]." The fact, therefore, that the Jewish community of Wilna was represented by several rabbis, and not by one, as small communities are, is conclusive proof that the community was at that time considerable.

There is evidence also that Jews resided in Wilna in still earlier periods. It is known that in 1490 the plenipotentiary of the Grand Duke of Moscow, in a letter to King Casimir, complained of the excessive tax imposed upon merchants traveling to and from Moscow through Wilna by the Jewish lessee of taxes Michael Danilow ("Regesty i Nadpisi," i., No. 208, St. Petersburg, 1899). In 1495 the grand duke presented to the city of Wilna some property which formerly had been owned by a Jew named Janischevsky (ib. No. 215). In 1507 King Sigismund wrote that he had bought various goods from the Jewish merchant Michael Rebinkowitz (Yesofovich; ib. No. 231). Under the date of 1508 there are statements of accounts of Jewish lessees of taxes in Wilna and Brest-Litovsk (ib. No. 234). In 1532 the Jew Joshua Paskowitz was appointed by King Sigismund as chief collector of taxes on wax in the market of Wilna (Bershadski, "Russko-Yevreiski Arkhiv," No. 140). In 1550 a certain Jewess, Fanna Kasparova, who resided at Wilna, refused to surrender to the Jewish court the Jew Chatzka Issakowitz, defying the Jewish court messenger sent to take him, although she had previously given bond for the appearance of the said Issakowitz (ib. No. 167). In 1555 King Sigismund granted to a certain Jew of Wilna a lease for three years of the privilege of stamping coins (ib. No. 45). The lessees, in 1560, of

Early Records.

the privilege of stamping coins in Wilna were the Jews Felix and Borodavka (ib. No. 125). In Sept., 1562, a Gentile brought before a magistrate a charge of assault against a Jew by the name of Israel, the defendant being described in the complaint as a physician (ib. No. 167). In 1568 King Sigismund issued an order commanding the Jewish community of Wilna to pay the taxes due to the treasury ("Regesty i Nadpisi," No. 557). In 1583 the Jew Judah Salamonowitz of Wilna paid taxes on goods brought by him from Lublin to Wilna, consisting of a truckload of wine, licorice, and linen ("Archeographicheski Sbornik," part iii., p. 289). The name of the Jew Moses Tomchamowitz of Wilna, secretary of the mint, is mentioned in the records of 1587 ("Regesty i Nadpisi," No. 660). In 1592 the citizens of Wilna attacked and destroyed the bet ha-midrash of Wilna ("Records of the Community of Wilna," part xxviii., p. 52, Wilna, 1901). In 1593 King Sigismund III. granted to the Jews of Wilna the privilege of buying real estate from the noblemen of that city; at the same time he made many other concessions to them, including permission to rebuild the bet ha-midrash (Bershadski, in "Voskhod," 1887). From the above data it is evident that there was a large Jewish community in Wilna in the middle of the sixteenth century, but that until then it was insignificant. The Jews' street in Wilna, the one formerly called by the name of St. Nicholas, which terminates at the Hospital of St. Mary, was known as the "Jews' street" in 1592 (Bershadski, "Istoria Yevreiskoi Obshchiny v Wilnye," in "Voskhod," 1887, p. 84), and is still so called.

In the seventeenth century the Jews in Wilna and in Lithuania generally enjoyed peace and prosperity. At the beginning of their settlement in that country their relations with the non-Jewish population were very friendly. Even from the orders given by Bogdan Chmielnicki to the Polish and Lithuanian magnates it is evident that up to that time the Lithuanian Jews lived in happiness and peace, and that only the Cossacks subjected them to oppression and maltreatment. But from that time on they gradually sank into misfortune. The conclusion to be drawn, therefore, from the study of the history of the Jews of Wilna during that period is that the kings and rulers of Poland and Lithuania were considerate toward them, but that the non-Jewish population was extremely hostile. In 1636 King Ladislaus IV. granted certain important concessions to the Jews of Wilna. In 1669 King Michael confirmed six privileges previously enjoyed by them. King John III., in 1682, permitted them to conduct their own census-taking. Five years later (1687) the same king wrote to the commander of his army and to the governor of Wilna warning them to see that the Jews of Wilna were not molested by the non-Jewish population, and telling them that they would be held personally responsible and punished severely for any violation of this order.

In the Seventeenth Century.

From the seventeenth century on the Wilna Jews passed from tragedy to tragedy, the differences being only in degree and extent, as may be seen from the series of restrictions and limitations imposed upon

INTERIOR OF THE OLD SYNAGOGUE AT WILNA.
(From a photograph.)

them, leading at times to riots and consequent destruction of property. In 1635 the populace, in a mood of frenzy, destroyed the newly erected and elaborately appointed Jewish prayer-house at Wilna, tearing to pieces eighteen scrolls of the Law, appropriating their golden handles and everything else of value, and not leaving a stone of the prayer-house unturned (Bershadski, in "Voskhod," May, 1887). In 1653 King John Casimir was induced to issue a circular prohibiting the Jews from engaging in certain businesses and from accepting employment as servants in the houses of Gentiles ("Regesty i Nadpisi," No. 940). In 1663 the trade-union of Wilna passed an ordinance prohibiting Jewish glaziers from entering that union, and forbidding glaziers to receive Jewish apprentices or to employ Jews in any other capacity (*ib.* No. 1019). In 1664 the fishermen's union of Wilna excluded the Jews from the fishing trade (*ib.*). In the same year the king yielded to the request of the citizens of Wilna and prohibited the Jews from engaging in the occupations of silversmiths and goldsmiths (*ib.* No. 1022). It seems also that two years later (1666) the Jews were excluded from the grain business (*ib.* No. 1041), in 1667 from tanning (*ib.* No. 1056),

Part of the Old Cemetery at Wilna. Star Shows Tombstone of Elijah Gaon.
(From a photograph.)

and in 1669 from the bristle manufacturing business (*ib.* No. 1078). But as long as Wilna remained under Polish and Lithuanian rulers all those restrictions and limitations were tolerable; the real and acute suffering began with the conquest of Wilna by the Russians in 1654, when the savage hordes of Cossacks, led by their barbaric chieftain Chmielnicki, destroyed everything destructible in the city, and killed every Jew they met (see "Entziklopedicheski Slovar," vol. vi., p. 384). The Jews that remained were banished from Wilna by order of the Russian king Alexis Mikhailovich ("Regesty," No. 971).

To this wholesale expulsion from Wilna reference is made in the preface of "Be'er ha-Golah" by R. Moses Ribkes: "And on the fourth day of the week, on the 23d of Tammuz, in 5415 [1655], the whole con-

gregation fled for its life from the city of Wilna, as one man. Those who had provided themselves with conveyances carried their wives,

Calamity of 1655. children, and their small belongings in them; but those who had no conveyances traveled on foot and carried their children on their backs." Further reference to that catastrophe is made in the "Bet Hillel" on Yoreh De'ah (section 21), and in the responsa collection "Zemah Zedek" (No. 101). Among the exiles from Wilna in that year were the following prominent rabbis: Aaron Samuel b. Israel Kaidanover (who afterward became rabbi of Cracow, and who used to supplement his signature with the words, "the exile from the city of Wilna"; see the preface to his "Birkat ha-Zebah"); Shabbethai b. Meïr ha-Kohen (author of "Megillah 'Afah," in which the Wilna catastrophe of that year is described); and Ephraim b. Aaron (author of "Sha'ar Efrayim"). Wilna remained in the hands of the Russians for about six years, when it again came under the rule of the kings of Poland; the lot of the Jews, however, remained as bad as ever.

The vernacular of the Jews of Wilna at that time seems to have been Russian. This conclusion is drawn from the following statement in the volume of responsa "Geburot Anashim" (p. 26): "It happened in the city of Wilna that a man, at the wedding ceremonies, used the Russian language in betrothing his bride, 'Ya tebja estum mekaddesh.'" The date following this is Dec. 26, 1636.

Nothing important of a favorable nature happened to the Jewish community of Wilna during the eighteenth century. In 1708, when Wilna was taken by Charles XII. of Sweden, more than 20,-

The Eighteenth Century. 000 died there from famine and pestilence in a comparatively short time; a great number of Jews being among these, the community became poverty-stricken, and many were compelled to leave the city ("Entziklopedicheski Slovar"). The author of the

יורה חג מד

PAGE FROM SHULḤAN 'ARUK, PRINTED AT WILNA, 1880.

"Rosh Yosef," in his memoirs (Preface), says: "The wrath of the oppressor compelled me to leave my place of residence, for his arm was stronger than ours, and the wo and terror which entered our locality deprived us of our resting-place in the country of Poland." The Jews now fell into such depths of poverty that they were unable to save their principal prayer-house from being sealed by creditors. In the "pinkes" of the Ẓedaḳah Gedolah (the principal charitable society), under date of the 2d of Elul, 5466 (Aug. 30, 1707), the following entry occurs: "In those days the synagogue was closed and sealed for almost a whole year. The cemetery also was closed." On the return to the throne of King August of Saxony in the year 1720, the populace of Wilna, mindful of its hatred toward the Jews, requested him to reduce the privileges heretofore granted to the latter in connection with the grain business. The king did not yield to the request at that time; but in 1742 the citizens secured the support of the magistrate, who compelled the representatives of the Jewish community to sign and execute an agreement in which they surrendered their former rights and privileges. Thus the Jewish community of Wilna continued to dwindle down to the time of the permanent occupation of Wilna by the Russians, when the position of the Jews improved somewhat—when, in fact, they lived under conditions much more favorable than those of the present day.

Following is a list of the more important known rabbis of Wilna: **Abraham Segal** (first rabbi of Wilna; mentioned by the author of "Sefer Toledot Yiẓḥaḳ," Prague, 1623); **Menahem Manus Hajes** (mentioned in "Etan ha-Ezraḥi," Koretz, 1636); **Feibush Ashkenazi** (mentioned in the "'Abodat ha-Gershuni," No. 67, and in other works); **Moses b. Isaac Judah Lima** (author of "Ḥelḳat Meḥoḳeḳ"); **Isaac b. Abraham of Posen**; **Naḥman b. Solomon Naphtali of Vladimir**; **Moses b. David** (known also as R. Moses Kremer); **R. Simson** (in his old age settled in Palestine); **Hillel b. Jonah ha-Levi**; **Baruch Kahana Rapoport**; **Joshua Heshel**; **Samuel** (the last head of the bet din). From R. Samuel's time the title "rosh bet din" was discarded, no rabbi subsequently elected being authorized to assume that title; since then the rabbi has been called "moreh ẓedeḳ." The reason for the abolition of the title was a quarrel in which R. Samuel was involved as a result of his having treated the community with disrespect. The rabbinic school or yeshibah, founded in 1847, but closed in 1873, was one of the most prominent in eastern Europe. Wilna is distinguished not only by its rabbis but also by the large number of eminent Hebrew scholars who have been born or have resided there. Among these may be mentioned: Judah Löb GORDON, LEBENSOHN, Reichenson, etc.

In 1875 the Jews of Wilna numbered 37,909 in a total population of 82,688. The census of 1902 showed about 80,000 Jews in a total population of 162,633. The explanation of this rapid increase, which is out of all proportion to the ordinary growth of urban populations, lies in the "May laws" of 1882, which prohibited Jews from living in rural districts, and thus brought a large number to Wilna, as to other cities. In Hebrew literature Wilna is described

as the "mother city in Israel," or the "Lithuanian Jerusalem": the latter term originated, probably, with Napoleon I., when he was in Wilna in 1812.

Wilna contains a teachers' institute (Jewish), the only one of the kind in the whole of Russia. To it four subordinate elementary schools for Jewish children are attached. After graduating from the higher school the students receive diplomas **Communal** as teachers; the number of such grad-**In-** uates is about twelve or thirteen annu-**stitutions.** ally. For the support of the institute, about 30,000 rubles per annum was appropriated by the government from the municipal meat-tax of Wilna, the burden of which fell mainly upon the poor class of the Jewish population, since members of the liberal professions and college graduates were exempt from that tax, and the well-to-do class, not being strictly Orthodox as a rule, were more or less indifferent to the use of kosher meat. There are about twenty elementary schools for Jewish children, called "people's schools." But neither in these schools nor in the teachers' institute and its subordinate schools is instruction given in even one specifically Jewish subject.

A soup-kitchen for Jews was maintained in Wilna, in which a substantial meal, consisting of bread, soup, and meat, could be had for 4 copecks (2 cents). The kitchen was much used by Jewish soldiers stationed in the city; the extremely poor received their meals free. It was supported by voluntary subscriptions, exclusively from Jews, and by the proceeds from certain Jewish balls and lectures. About 30,000 persons annually received meals from it, one-half being non-Jews. About 112 soldiers were annually recruited, under the general conscription laws, from the Jewish community of Wilna. The Jews are mostly engaged in the export of lumber and grain, and in shopkeeping. Poverty, prevalent throughout Russian Jewry, was especially marked in Wilna. It may safely be maintained, although no actual statistics are available, that fully 80 per cent of the Jewish population of Wilna did not know in the evening where they would obtain food the next morning. In former days a considerable number of people made their living by the liquor trade, keeping saloons and inns; but the Jews were excluded from that trade by government ordinances. Model tenement-houses have been erected for the Jewish workmen of Wilna by the Jewish Colonization Association.

The city of Wilna contained in 1914, 214,600 inhabitants, of whom 80,000 were Jews. Of the latter many were occupied in agriculture.

BIBLIOGRAPHY: *Regesty i Nadpisi*, St. Petersburg, 1899; Bershadski, *Russko-Yevreiski Arkhiv*; idem, *Ocherk Wilenskoi Yevreiskoi Obshchiny*; *Voskhod*, 1881-87; *Akty Wilenskoi Kommissi*, 1901-2.
H. R.   B. R.

—**Typography:** A Hebrew printing-press was established in Wilna in 1799 by Baruch ROMM, as a branch of his establishment at Grodno. Through the action of the Russian censorship this press had practically a monopoly of the Russian and Polish markets from 1845 onward, when the printing of Hebrew books was restricted to Wilna and Slavuta. Between 1847 and 1857 the Wilna press produced no less than 460 different works (enumerated by Benjacob in Steinschneider, "Hebr. Bibl." iv-v.). This yearly average of 41 works was raised to 63 in 1871 (E. Reclus, "Nouvelle Geographie," p. 436). Especially noteworthy were the Talmuds of 1835 and 1880, which have proved the standard editions for the east of Europe: a specimen page of the latter is given in illustration of the article TALMUD. Besides the many books printed by the Romms, the periodical "Ha-Karmel" was published at Wilna.

J.

WILNA, ABRAHAM. See ABRAHAM BEN ELIJAH OF WILNA.

WILNA GAON. See ELIJAH BEN SOLOMON.

WINAWER, SIMON: Russian chess-player; born in Warsaw 1839. In 1867 he was in Paris; and while watching some games at the Café de la Régence in that city he decided to enter a tournament to be held there. To the surprise of every one he gained the second prize, defeating, among several noted players, Samuel Rosenthal. He then applied himself to the game so assiduously that in 1878 he gained the second prize at the international tourney held at Paris, Zukertort being first and Blackburne third. In 1881 at Berlin he divided the third and fourth prizes with Tchigorin; and in 1882 at Vienna he divided the first and second prizes with Steinitz. In 1883, playing in the international tourney held in London, he, for the first time in his career, was not placed; but at Nuremberg (19 entries) in the same year he gained the first prize, defeating Blackburne, who gained second place.

From this time Winawer seems gradually to have declined as a tournament player. At Dresden in 1892 and again at Budapest in 1896 he succeeded in gaining sixth place only, while at Monte Carlo in 1901 he was unable to gain a prize.

BIBLIOGRAPHY: *Encyc. Brit.* supplementary vols., s.v. *Chess*; *Examples of Chess Master-Play* (transl. from the German of Jean Dufresne by C. T. Blanchard), New Barnet, 1893.

S.   A. P.

WINCHESTER: Ancient capital of England; county town of Hampshire. Jews appear to have settled there at an early date, one of the first entries in the pipe-rolls referring to a fine paid in 1160 by Gentill, a Jewess of Winchester, for the privilege of not marrying a certain Jew. The Jewry seems to have been located in Shorten street, afterward called Jewry street, leading to the North Gate. The synagogue was in Trussil, now Jail, street. The Jewry must have been a center of some importance, as Isaac of Chernigov was found there in 1182 (Jacobs, "Jews of Angevin England," p. 73). It has been conjectured that Moses b. Yom-Ṭob, who wrote the "Darke Niḳḳud" now found in the rabbinic Bibles, lived at Winchester (*ib.* p. 124).

When the massacres occurred in England (1189–1190), Winchester spared its Jews, though a couple of years later the blood accusation was raised against a Winchester Jew (see Richard of Devizes, "Chronicon," ed. Howlett, p. 435). A similar accusation was brought against the Winchester Jews in 1232 (Rigg, "Select Pleas," p. xiv.). In a description of the alleged murder of 1192 Winchester is called "the Jerusalem of the Jews" in those parts, and is stated to have had relations with Jews of France (probably Rouen). The most prominent Jew of Winchester in the eleventh century was probably Deulacresse or

Cresselin, who was an agent of AARON OF LINCOLN, and who obtained possession of some of the latter's lands after his death.

Several Jewesses are mentioned in the records as lending money at Winchester, notably Chera in the twelfth century, and Licorice in the thirteenth (*ib.* pp. 19–27). An elaborate list of transactions between the latter and Thomas of Charlecote about 1253 shows that Jewesses of those days had the right of holding land as security for payment of debt. Licorice agreed to pay the large fine of £5,000 on succeeding to the estate of her husband, David of Ox-

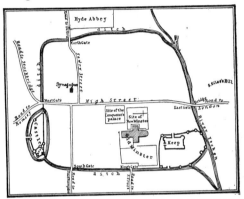

Plan of Winchester, England, in the Thirteenth Century, Showing the Position of the Jewish Quarter.

ford, in 1244 (*ib.* p. 27, note). Winchester had an ARCHA up to the time of the expulsion, and was, therefore, a licensed place of residence for the Jews while they remained in England. At the time of the expulsion a number of houses and outstanding debts fell into the hands of the king from the Jews of Winchester ("Trans. Jew. Hist. Soc. Eng." i. 137). The position of the Jews must have been exceptionally favorable in Winchester, because one of them was even received into the merchants' gild, a most unusual case, none other being known in early Anglo-Jewish history.

BIBLIOGRAPHY: Jacobs, *Jews of Angevin England*, pp. 133, 146–152, 380; Milner, *History of Winchester*, ii. 180; Kitchen, *Winchester*, p. 180; Norgate, *Angevin England*, i. 31.

J.

WINDOWS ("ḥallon," "arubbah"): The climate of Palestine and the customs of the ancient and the modern Orient alike rendered the house less important than it is in the Occident, since it was more a sleeping apartment than a place for work, or even for occupancy during the day (comp. HOUSE). Many large windows, therefore, were not desired, since they would admit heat in summer and rain and cold in winter. In like manner, the Assyro-Babylonian and the Egyptian house had few windows (comp. Perrot and Chipiez, "Art in Chaldea," i. 186 *et seq.*; Wilkinson, "Manners and Customs of the Ancient Egyptians," i. 362 *et seq.*). In this respect the houses of modern Palestine precisely resemble those of the ancient Hebrews, for the windows which look on the street are very small and are placed high in the wall, thus being analogous to the windows of the Temple of Solomon, which were narrow and high (I Kings vi.4). Large, wide windows were reserved, like panels of cedar-wood and mural paintings, for the luxurious palaces of the great (Jer. xxii. 14).

Although excavations show that GLASS was known to the Assyrians and Babylonians, as well as to the Egyptians, at a very early time, it was never used for windows in the ancient East. Openings for light and air were either left entirely free, as was often the case in the simple peasants' huts, or they had a shutter or wooden lattice; even the windows of the Temple had immovable gratings of wood (I Kings vi. 4, R. V.). Usually, however, these lattices were so constructed that they could be removed, or thrown apart like doors. The windows could be opened (II Kings xiii. 17), for Ahaziah fell through an open window (II Kings i. 2). Such means of closure were naturally very unsafe, and thieves could easily enter the house by means of the window (Joel ii. 9; comp. Jer. ix. 21).

E. G. H.   I. BE.

WINDS: Ancient Hebrew literature recognizes only four winds—north, south, east, and west, having no names for those from intermediate points, so that such a designation as "north" has a wide range of application. The dwelling-places of the winds were in the four corners of the earth ("ḳeẓot ha-areẓ"); there they were confined in storehouses, from which YHWH sent them forth (Jer. x. 13, xlix. 36, li. 16; B. B. vi. 7). According to Rev. vii. 1, these storehouses were guarded by four angels, who restrained the winds, as they continually strove to break loose (comp. Enoch, lxxvi. 1 et seq.: "At the ends of the earth I saw twelve doors opened toward all the quarters of heaven, and the winds came forth from them, and blew over the earth"). The ancient Hebrews had no conception of the nature and causes of winds; for them, as for every ancient people, the wind was a mysterious creation, whose paths were always unknown (Eccl. xi. 5 [R. V.]; John iii. 8). Indeed, in their action, as in their origin, the winds were phenomena wholly without the sphere of human knowledge (Ps. cvii. 25–27; Mark iv. 41), and YHWH's power appeared the greater in that it was He who created them (Amos iv. 13), causing them to come from out His treasuries (Ps. cxxxv. 7; Jer. x. 13, li. 16), and controlling their power and "weight" (Job xxviii. 25). He likewise made them His messengers and servants (Ps. civ. 4 [R. V.], cxlviii. 8), and used the "stormy winds" as instruments in the execution of His judgments (Isa. xxix. 6; Amos i. 14; Wisdom v. 23; Ecclus. [Sirach] xxxix. 28).

The Hebrews, as was natural, carefully distinguished the characteristics of the individual winds. The north wind was icy cold (Ecclus. [Sirach] xliii. 20; comp. LXX., Prov. xxvii. 16; Job xxxvii. 9), so that Jerome called it "ventus durissimus." When it came from the north it brought rain (Prov. xxv. 23), and, according to Josephus, the sailors on the coast called the stormy wind from the north, which scourges the waves, "the black north wind" ("B. J." iii. 9, § 3). The east wind, which came from the Syrian desert (Jer. iv. 11, xiii. 24; Job i. 19), was the hot wind, which parched the crops and blighted the trees (Gen. xli. 6, 23, 27; Ezek. xvii. 10, xix. 12; Hos. xiii. 15; Jonah iv. 8). Hence the **Septuagint** usually calls it καύσων ("the burner").

When it developed into a storm it was especially dangerous because of the violence of its blasts (Job i. 19, xxvii. 21; Isa. xxvii. 8; Jer. xviii. 17; Ezek. xxvii. 26; Ps. xlviii. 8 [A. V. 7]). The south wind also was a hot wind (Job xxxvii. 17; Luke xii. 55); although the due south wind blows but seldom in Palestine. From the west came the refreshing evening breeze which brought rain (Gen. iii. 8; Cant. ii. 17; I Kings xviii. 43 et seq.; Luke xii. 54; also Cant. iv. 16, where northwest and southwest winds are probably meant).

E. G. H.   I. BE.

WINE.—Biblical Data: The juice of the grape is the subject of special praise in the Scriptures. The "vine tree" is distinguished from the other trees in the forest (Ezek. xv. 2). The fig-tree is next in rank to the vine (Deut. viii. 8), though as food the fig is of greater importance (comp. Num. xx. 5) than the "wine which cheereth God and man" (Judges ix. 13; comp. Ps. civ. 15; Eccl. x. 19). Wine is a good stimulant for "such as be faint in the wilderness" (II Sam. xvi. 2), and for "those that be of heavy hearts" (Prov. xxxi. 6).

The goodness of wine is reflected in the figure in which Israel is likened to a vine brought from Egypt and planted in the Holy Land, where it took deep root, spread out, and prospered (Ps. lxxx. 9–11). The blessed wife is like "a fruitful vine by the sides of thy house" (Ps. cxxviii. 3). When peace reigns every man rests "under his vine and under his fig-tree" (I Kings v. 5 [A. V. iv. 25]). An abundance of wine indicates prosperity. Jacob blessed Judah that "he washed his garments in wine and his clothes in the blood of grapes" (Gen. xlix. 11).

Bread as an indispensable food and wine as a luxury represent two extremes; they were used as signs of welcome and good-will to Abraham (Gen. xiv. 18). A libation of wine was part of the ceremonial sacrifices, varying in quantity from one-half to one-fourth of a hin measure (Num. xxviii. 14).

Wine-drinking was generally accompanied by singing (Isa. xxiv. 9). A regular wine-room ("bet ha-yayin") was used (Cant. ii. 4), and wine-cellars ("oẓerot yayin"; I Chron. xxvii. 27) are mentioned. The wine was bottled in vessels termed "nebel" and "nod" (I Sam. i. 24, xvi. 20), made in various shapes from the skins of goats and sheep, and was sold in bath measures. The wine was drunk from a "miz-raḳ," or "gabia'" (bowl; Jer. xxxv. 5), or a "kos" (cup). The wine-press was called "gat" and "pu-rah"; while the "yeḳeb" was probably the vat into which the wine flowed from the press. The "vine of Sodom" (Deut. xxxii. 32), which probably grew by the Dead Sea, was the poorest kind. The "vine of the fields" (II Kings iv. 39) was a wild, uncultivated sort, and the "sorek" (Isa. v. 2) was the choicest vine, producing dark-colored grapes; in Arabic it is called "surik."

There were different kinds of wine. "Yayin" was the ordinary matured, fermented wine, "tirosh" was a new wine, and "shekar" was an old, powerful wine ("strong drink"). The red wine was the better and stronger (Ps. lxxv. 9 [A. V. 8]; Prov. xxiii. 31). Perhaps the wine of Helbon (Ezek. xxvii. 18) and the wine of Lebanon (Hos. xiv. 7) were white wines. The vines of Hebron were noted for their large clusters of grapes (Num. xiii. 23). Samaria was the center of vineyards (Jer. xxxi. 5; Micah i. 6), and the Ephraimites were heavy wine-drinkers (Isa. xxviii. 1). There were also "yayin ha-reḳaḥ" (spiced wine; Cant. viii. 2), "ashishah" (hardened sirup of grapes), "shemarim" (wine-dregs), and "ḥomeẓ yayin" (vinegar). Some wines were mixed with poisonous substances ("yayin tar'elah"; Ps. lx. 5; comp. lxxv. 9, "mesek" [mixture]). The "wine of the condemned" ("yen 'anushim") is wine paid as a forfeit (Amos ii. 8), and "wine of violence" (Prov. iv. 17) is wine obtained by illegal means.

E. G. H. J. D. E.

——**In Rabbinical Literature:** Wine is called "yayin" because it brings lamentation and wailing ("yelalah" and "wai") into the world, and "tirosh" because one that drinks it habitually is certain to become poor (תירוש=רש תהיא). R. Kahana said the latter term is written sometimes תירוש, and sometimes תירש; that means, if drunk in moderation it gives leadership (ראש = "head"); if drunk in excess it leads to poverty (Yoma 76b). "Tirosh" includes all kinds of sweet juices and must, and does not include fermented wine (Tosef., Ned. iv. 3). "Yayin" is to be distinguished from "shekar"; the former is diluted with water ("mazug"); the latter is undiluted ("yayin ḥai"; Num. R. x. 8; comp. Sifre, Num. 23). In Talmudic usage "shekar" means "mead," or "beer," and according to R. Papa, it denotes drinking to satiety and intoxication (Suk. 49b).

In metaphorical usage, wine represents the essence of goodness. The Torah, Jerusalem, Israel, the Messiah, the righteous—all are compared to wine. The wicked are likened unto vinegar, and the good man who turns to wickedness is compared to sour wine. Eleazar b. Simeon was called "Vinegar, the son of Wine" (B. M. 83b). The wine which is kept for the righteous in the world to come has been preserved in the grape ever since the six days of creation (Ber. 34b).

The process of making wine began with gathering the grapes into a vat ("gat"). There were vats hewn out of stone, cemented or potter-made vats, and wooden vats ('Ab. Zarah v. 11). Next to the vat was a cistern ("bor"), into which the juice ran through a connecting trough or pipe ("ẓinnor"). Two vats were sometimes connected with one cistern (B. Ḳ. ii. 2). The building containing or adjoining the wine-presses was called "bet ha-gat" (Tosef., Ter. iii. 7). The newly pressed wine was strained through a filter, sometimes in the shape of a funnel ("meshammeret"; Yer. Ter. viii. 3), or **Presses** through a linen cloth ("sudar"), in **and Recep-** order to remove husks, stalks, etc. A **tacles.** wooden roller or beam, fixed into a socket in the wall, was lowered to press the grapes down into the vat (Shab. i. 9; Ṭoh. x. 8).

The cistern was emptied by a ladle or dipper called the "maḥaẓ" (Ṭoh. x. 7), the wine being transferred to large receptacles known variously as "kad," "ḳanḳan," "garab," "danna," and "ḥabit." Two styles of ḥabit, the Lydian and the Bethlehemite (Niddah vi. 6), were used, the former being a smaller barrel or cask. All these receptacles were rounded earthen

vessels, tightly sealed with pitch. The foster-mother of Abaye is authority for the statement that a six-measure cask properly sealed is worth more than an eight-measure cask that is not sealed (B. Ḳ. 12a). New wine stood for at least forty days before it was admissible as a drink-offering ('Eduy. vi. 1; B. B. 97a). When the wine had sufficiently settled it was drawn off into bottles known as "lagin" or "leginah" and "ẓarẓur," the latter being a stone vessel with a rim and strainer, a kind of cooler (Sanh. 106a); an earthen pitcher, "ḥaẓab," was also used (Men. viii. 7). The drinking-vessel was the Biblical "kos." The wine was kept in cellars, and from them was removed to storerooms called "ḥefteḳ," or "apoṭiḳ" (ἀποθήκη), a pantry or shelves in the wineshop. Bottles of wine from this pantry were exposed for sale in baskets in front of the counter ('Ab. Zarah ii. 7, 39b).

The quality of a wine was known by its color and by the locality from which it came, red wine being better than white wine. Ḳeruḥim (probably the Coreæ of Josephus) in Palestine produced the best wine (Men. viii. 6), after which came the red wine of Phrygia (Perugita; Shab. 147b), the **Varieties.** light-red wine of Sharon (Shab. 77a), and "yayin Kushi" (Ethiopian wine; B. B. 97b). There were special mixtures of wine. Among these were: (1) "alunṭit," made of old wine, with a mixture of very clear water and balsam; used especially after bathing (Tosef., Dem. i. 24; 'Ab. Zarah 30a); (2) "ḳafrisin" (caper-wine, or, according to Rashi, Cyprus wine), an ingredient of the sacred incense (Ker. 6a); (3) "yen ẓimmuḳin" (raisin-wine); (4) "inomilin" (οἰνόμελι), wine mixed with honey and pepper (Shab. xx. 2; 'Ab. Zarah l.c.); (5) "ilyoston" (*ἡλιόστεον), a sweet wine ("vinum dulce") from grapes dried in the sun for three days, and then gathered and trodden in the midday heat (Men. viii. 6; B. B. 97b); (6) "me'ushshan," from the juice of smoked or fumigated sweet grapes (Men. l.c.); not fit for libation; (7) "enogeron" (οἰνόγαρον), a sauce of oil and garum to which wine was added; (8) "apiḳṭewizin" (ἀποκοτταβίζειν), a wine emetic, taken before a meal (Shab. 12a); (9) "ḳundiṭon" ("conditum"), a spiced wine ('Ab. Zarah ii. 3); (10) "pesinṭiṭon" ("absinthiatum"), a bitter wine (Yer. 'Ab. Zarah ii. 3); (11) "yen tappuḥim," made from apples; cider; (12) "yen temarim," date-wine. Wine made from grapes grown on isolated vines ("roglit") is distinguished from that made of the grapes of a vine suspended from branches or trained over an espalier ("dalit"); the latter was unfit for libation (Men. 86b).

During the time of fermentation the wine that was affected with sourness was called "yayin ḳoses" (Yer. Pe'ah ii., end), and when matured sour it was "ḥomeẓ" (vinegar). Good vinegar was made by putting barley in the wine. In former times Judean wine never became sour unless barley was put in it; but after the destruction of the Temple that characteristic passed to the Edomite (Roman) wine. Certain vinegar was called the "Edomite vinegar" (Pes. 42b).

Fresh wine before fermenting was called "yayin mi-gat" (wine of the vat; Sanh. 70a). The ordinary wine was of the current vintage. The vintage of the previous year was called "yayin yashan" (old wine). The third year's vintage was "yayin meyushshan" (very old wine). Ordinary, fermented wine, according to Raba, must be strong enough to take one-third water, otherwise it is not to be regarded as wine (Shab. 77a). R. Joseph, who was blind, could tell by taste whether a wine was up to the standard of Raba ('Er. 54a).

Wine taken in moderation was considered a healthful stimulant, possessing many curative elements. The Jewish sages were wont to say, "Wine is the greatest of all medicines; where wine is lacking, there drugs are necessary" (B. B. 58b). R. Huna said, "Wine helps to open the heart to reasoning" (B. B. 12b). R. Papa thought that when one could substitute beer for wine, it should be done for the sake of economy. But his view is opposed on the ground that the preservation of one's health is paramount to considerations of economy (Shab. 140b). Three things, wine, white bread, and fat meat, reduce the feces, lend erectness to one's bearing, and strengthen the sight. Very old wine benefits the whole body (Pes. 42b). Ordinary wine is harmful to the intestines, but old wine is beneficial (Ber. 51a). Rabbi was cured of a severe disorder of the bowels by drinking apple-wine seventy years old, a Gentile having stored away 300 casks of it ('Ab. Zarah 40b). "The good things of Egypt" (Gen. xlv. 23) which Joseph sent to his father are supposed by R. Eleazar to have included "old wine," which satisfies the elderly person (Meg. 16b). At the great banquet given by King Ahasuerus the wine put before each guest was from the province whence he came and of the vintage of the year of his birth (Meg. 12a). Until the age of forty liberal eating is beneficial; but after forty it is better to drink more and eat less (Shab. 152a). R. Papa said wine is more nourishing when taken in large mouthfuls. Raba advised students who were provided with little wine to take it in liberal drafts (Suk. 49b) in order to secure the greatest possible benefit from it. Wine gives an appetite, cheers the body, and satisfies the stomach (Ber. 35b). After bleeding, according to Rab, a substantial meal of meat is necessary; according to Samuel, wine should be taken freely, in order that the red of the wine may replace the red of the blood that has been lost (Shab. 129a).

The benefit derived from wine depends upon its being drunk in moderation, as overindulgence is injurious. Abba Saul, who was a grave-digger, made careful observations upon bones, and found that the bones of those who had drunk natural (unmixed) wine were "scorched"; of those who had used mixed wine were dry and transparent; of those who had taken wine in moderation were "oiled," that is, they had retained the marrow (Niddah 24b). Some of the rabbis were light drinkers. R. Joseph and Mar 'Ukba, after bathing, were given cups of inomilin wine (see above). R. Joseph felt it going through his body from the top of his head to his toes, and feared another cup would endanger his life; yet Mar 'Ukba drank it every day and was not unpleasantly affected by it, having taken it habitually (Shab. 140a). R. Judah did not take wine, except at religious ceremonies, such as "Ḳiddush," "Habdalah," and the Seder of Passover (four cups). The Seder wine affected him so seriously that he was

Medicinal Value.

Wine-Bibbing.

compelled to keep his head swathed till the following feast-day—Pentecost (Ned. 49b).

The best remedy for drunkenness is sleep. "Wine is strong, but sleep breaks its force" (B. B. 10a). Walking throws off the fumes of wine, the necessary amount of exercise being in the proportion of about three miles to a quarter-measure of Italian wine ('Er. 64b). Rubbing the palms and knees with oil and salt was a measure favored by some scholars who had indulged overmuch (Shab. 66b).

For religious ceremonies wine is preferable to other beverages. Wine "cheereth God" (Judges ix. 13); hence no religious ceremony should be performed with other beverages than wine (Ber. 35a). Over all fruit the benediction used is that for "the fruits of the tree," but over wine a special benediction for "the fruits of the vine" is pronounced (Ber. vi. 1). This latter benediction is, according to R. Eliezer, pronounced only when the wine has been properly mixed with water. Over natural wine the benediction is the same as that used for the "fruits of the tree" (Ber. 50b). The drinking of natural wine on the night of Passover is not "in the manner of free men" (Pes. 108b). "Ḳiddush" and "Habdalah" should be recited over a cup of wine. Beer may be used in countries where that is the national beverage (Pes. 106a, 107a). According to Raba, one may squeeze the juice of a bunch of grapes into a cup and say the "Ḳiddush" (B. B. 97b). The cup is filled with natural wine during grace, in memory of the Holy Land, where the best wine is produced; but after grace the wine is mixed.

The words introducing the grace, "Let us praise Him whose food we have eaten, and by whose goodness we live," are said over a cup of wine, part of which is passed to the hostess (Ber. 50a). Ulla, when the guest of R. Naḥman, was invited to pronounce the grace over wine, and the latter suggested the propriety of sending part of the wine to his guest's wife, Yalta; but Ulla demurred, declaring that the host is the principal channel of blessing, and passed it to R. Naḥman. When Yalta heard this she was enraged, and expressed her indignation by going to the wine-room ("be ḥamra") and breaking up 400 casks of wine (Ber. 51b). R. Akiba, when he made a feast in honor of his son, proposed, "Wine and long life to the Rabbis and their disciples!" (Shab. 67b).

Following the Scriptural precept, "Give strong drink unto him that is ready to perish, and wine unto those that be of heavy hearts" (Prov. xxxi. 6), the Rabbis ordered ten cups of wine to be served with the "meal of consolation" at the mourner's house: three cups before the meal, "to open the bowels," three cups between courses, to help digestion, and four cups after the grace. Later four cups were added in honor of the ḥazzanim, the parnasim, the Temple, and the nasi Gamaliel. So many cups producing drunkenness, the last four were afterward discontinued (Ket. 8b). Apparently this custom was in force when the Temple was in existence, and persisted in Talmudic times; it disappeared in the geonic period. R. Ḥanan declared that wine was created for the sole purpose of consoling the bereaved and rewarding the wicked for

In Mourning.

whatever good they may do in this world, in order that they may have no claim upon the world to come (Sanh. 70a). After the destruction of the Temple many Pharisees, as a sign of mourning, vowed to abstain from eating meat and drinking wine, but were dissuaded from issuing a decree which the public could not observe (B. B. 60b). R. Judah b. Bathyra said, "Meat was the principal accompaniment of joy in the time of the Temple, wine in post-exilic times" (Pes. 109a).

Rab said that for three days after purchase the seller is responsible if the wine turns sour; but after that his responsibility ceases. R. Samuel declared that responsibility falls upon the purchaser immediately upon the delivery of the wine, the rule being "Wine rests on the owner's shoulders." R. Ḥiyya b. Joseph said, "Wine must share the owner's luck" (B. B. 96a, b, 98a). If one sells a cellarful of wine, the purchaser must accept ten casks of sour wine in every hundred (Tosef., B. B. vi. 6). Whoever sells spiced wine is responsible for sourness until the following Pentecost (i.e., until the hot weather sets in). If he sells "old wine," it must be of the second year's vintage; if "very old wine" ("meyushshan"), it must be of the third year's vintage (B. B. vi. 2).

The question of responsibility on the part of carriers of wine ("sheḳulai") is discussed. When Rabbah bar Ḥana's hired carriers broke a cask he seized their overgarments; thereupon the carriers appealed to Rab, who ordered Rabbah to return their garments. "Is this the law?" asked Rabbah in astonishment. "It is the moral law," answered Rab, citing, "That thou mayest walk in the way of good men" (Prov. ii. 20). When the garments had been returned the carriers appealed again: "We are poor men; we have worked all day; and now we are hungry, and have nothing." Rab then ordered Rabbah to pay them their wages. "Is this the law?" inquired Rabbah. "It is the higher law," replied Rab, completing the verse previously cited—"and keep the paths of the righteous" (B. M. 83a).

As a commodity, wine has an important place in the business world. A large proportion of the trade in wine for the Feast of Passover is controlled by Jews. The agricultural activity of Palestine is directed mainly to viticulture. The Rothschild cellars at Rishon le-Ziyyon receive almost the entire produce of the Jewish colonists, which, through the Carmel Wine Company, is distributed throughout Russia, Austria, Holland, Switzerland, France, England, and the United States. The vintage of 1904 in the Rothschild cellars exceeded 7,000,000 bottles, of which 200,000 were sold in Warsaw. See AGRICULTURAL COLONIES IN PALESTINE.

Regarding the interdiction of wine prepared or handled by Gentiles see NESEK.

BIBLIOGRAPHY: C. H. Fowler, The Wine of the Bible, New York, 1878; W. Ebstein, Die Medizin im Neuen Testament und im Talmud, i. 36, 167; ii. 250, Stuttgart, 1903.
E. C. J. D. E.

WINKLER, MAX: American philologist; born at Cracow, Austria, Sept. 4, 1866; educated at the gymnasium of Cracow, Hughes High School (Cincinnati, Ohio), Harvard University (A.B. 1889), and the University of Michigan (Ph.D. 1892). He took a postgraduate course in the University of Berlin, and on returning to the United States was appointed instructor in German at the University of Michigan; in 1895 he became assistant professor, and in 1902 professor, of German language and literature. Winkler has edited the following works: Lessing's "Emilia Galotti," with introduction and notes, 1895; Goethe's "Egmont," 1898; Schiller's "Wallenstein," 1901; and Goethe's "Iphigenie," 1905.

BIBLIOGRAPHY: American Jewish Year Book, 5665.
A. F. T. H.

WINNIPEG: Capital of the province of Manitoba, Canada; situated at the junction of the Assiniboin and Red rivers. Jews had relations with Winnipeg when it was merely a small Hudson Bay post, but the first permanent Jewish settlers went thither about 1878. The Russian anti-Jewish outbreaks of 1881 and 1882 caused about three hundred Jews to settle there in the latter year, most of whom worked upon the Canadian Pacific Railway, then in the course of construction; and subsequent persecutions of the Jews in eastern Europe sent periodic waves of Jewish immigration to the Manitoban capital. In 1898 and 1899 there was an influx from Rumania, and from 1903 to 1905 there was a further considerable accession of settlers from Russia. The census of 1891 placed the Jewish population at 1,156, and according to the census report of 1921 the community numbers between 14,000 and 15,000 in a total population of 179,087. In professional, mercantile, and industrial pursuits the Jews of Winnipeg have done their full share toward the development of the city, and they are extensive holders of its real estate. In 1904 one of their number, Moses Finkelstein, was elected alderman for the most important and populous ward of the city, receiving a large majority. In 1892 and 1893, through the exertions of Asher, Charles and Michael Pierce, a number of Winnipeg Jews established a colony in Oxbow, without calling for outside aid. These colonists were afterward joined by others from eastern Canada and South Africa, and the colony is to-day in a flourishing condition.

Winnipeg now possesses nine Jewish congregations. The earliest was the B'nai Israel, established in 1883, and then came Congregation Beth-El, founded in 1885; in 1889 these two congregations amalgamated under the name "Shaary Zedek," and built a synagogue in King street. Congregation Rosh Pina was organized in 1890, with a synagogue on Martha street, Congregation B'nai Israel, in 1893, with a synagogue on Martha street; and Congregation Beth Jacob, in 1902, with a synagogue on Schultz street. In 1904 the Holy Blossom congregation came into existence, and was reorganized the following year under the name "Shaar Hashamoyim"; and Congregation Adas Yeshurun was founded in 1905.

The Jews of Winnipeg have established a number of communal societies, including the Dr. Gaster Benevolent Society, the Winnipeg Hebrew Benevolent Society, the Shaary Zedek Ladies' Aid Society, the Rosh Pina Ladies' Aid Society, the Winnipeg Hebrew Literary Society, and the Shaary Zedek Talmud Torah. The last-mentioned has erected a spacious building for educational purposes. In 1898 the first Winnipeg Zionist society was established, and at present there are in the city three large and active branches of the movement.

J.   C. I. DE S.

WINTER, SOLOMON: Hungarian philanthropist; born in the county of Zips, Hungary, in 1778; died at Hunsdorf, in the same county, Feb. 24, 1859, after laboring for sixty years for the advancement of the Jewish race in his locality. The erection of the synagogue in Hunsdorf about 1820, and the construction of the school in 1840, were due to him; and he was a representative of the collective communities of the county in the Budapest congress of Jewish notables.

BIBLIOGRAPHY: Wurzbach, *Biographisches Lexicon*, lvii. 81; Rosenberg, *Jahrbuch für die Israelitischen Cultusgemeinden*, i. 330.

S.   N. D.

WINTERNITZ, MORIZ: Austrian Orientalist; born at Horn Dec. 23, 1863. He received his earliest education in the gymnasium of his native town, and in 1880 entered the University of Vienna, receiving the degree of doctor of philosophy in 1886. In 1888 he went to Oxford, where until 1892 he assisted Max Müller in the preparation of the second edition of the Rig-Veda (4 vols., Oxford, 1890–92), collating manuscripts and deciding on the adoption of many new readings. Winternitz remained in Oxford until 1898, acting in various educational capacities, such as German lecturer to the Association for Promoting the Higher Education of Women (1891–98), librarian of the Indian Institute at Oxford (1895), and frequently as examiner in German and Sanskrit both for the university and for the Indian Civil Service. In 1899 he went to Prague as privat-docent for Indology and general ethnology, and in 1902 was appointed to the professorship of Sanskrit (made vacant by the retirement of Ludwig) and of ethnology in the German University of Prague. In addition to valuable contributions on Sanskrit and ethnology to various scientific journals, Winternitz edited the "Apastambiya Grihyasutra" (Vienna, 1887) and the "Mantrapaṭha, or the Prayer-Book of the Apastambins" (part i., Oxford, 1897); translated Müller's "Anthropological Religion" and his "Theosophy, or Psychological Religion" into German (Leipsic, 1894–95); and published "Das Altindische Hochzeitsrituell" (Vienna, 1892), which contains also valuable ethnological material; "A Catalogue of South Indian Manuscripts Belonging to the Royal Asiatic Society of Great Britain and Ireland" (London, 1902); and "Geschichte der Indischen Literatur" (part i., Leipsic, 1905).

J.   L. H. G.

WINTERNITZ, WILHELM: Austrian physician and hydropathist; born at Josefstadt, Bohemia, March 1, 1835; educated at Vienna and at Prague (M.D. 1857), where he settled and became an assistant at the institute for the insane. In 1858 he entered the Austrian navy, but resigned his position as surgeon in 1861 and established a practise in Vienna. There he became interested in hydropathy, and was soon regarded as one of the leading authorities. Admitted to the medical faculty of the University of Vienna as privat-docent for hydropathy in 1865, he was one of the founders of the General Vienna Dis-

pensary, where he was in 1905 departmental chief. In the same year he opened a private hospital near Vienna. In 1874 he became privat-docent in medicine, and was appointed assistant professor seven years later, becoming a full professor in 1899.

Winternitz was a collaborator for hydropathy on Von Ziemssen's "Handbuch der Allgemeinen Therapie" (ed. 1881), Eulenburg's "Realencyclopädie der Gesammten Heilkunde" (ed. 1897), and Eulenburg's "Lehrbuch der Allgemeinen Therapie und der Therapeutischen Methodik" (Berlin, 1898–99). In 1890 he founded the "Blätter für Klinische Hydrotherapie," of which he was the editor.

In addition to several essays and monographs in medical journals, Winternitz was the author of the following works: "Kaltenleutgeben und Meine Wasserheilanstalt" (Vienna, 1869); "Die Hydropathie auf Physiologischer und Klinischer Grundlage" (*ib.* 1877–80; 2d ed. 1890–92; translated into English, French, Italian, Spanish, and Russian); and "Cholera, Lungenphthise und Fieber: Klinische Studien" (*ib.* 1887–88). He died in Feb., 1917.

BIBLIOGRAPHY: Wurzbach, *Biographisches Lexicon*; Pagel, *Biog. Lex.*; Hirsch, *Biog. Lex.*

S.   F. T. H.

WINTERSTEIN, SIMON, FREIHERR VON: Austrian railroad magnate; born at Prague 1819; died at Vöslau June 11, 1883. The son of poor parents, he had to learn early to support himself. He chose a commercial career, and worked as a clerk in Prague and in Vienna, later establishing a business of his own in the latter city. After acting for some time as shipping agent for the Nordbahn, he entered the executive board of this railroad, and finally became its president. Through business connection with the house of Rothschild he became a member also of the boards of directors of the Südbahn and of the Creditanstalt. Winterstein was for a number of years president of the Jewish community of Vienna. He was a member of the Austrian House of Lords.

BIBLIOGRAPHY: *Allg. Zeit. des Jud.* 1883, p. 425.

S.   F. T. H.

WINTERTHUR. See SWITZERLAND.

WISCONSIN: State in the Upper Lake region of the United States of America; admitted to the Union in 1848. In 1792 a Jew named Jacob Franks went to Green Bay, and in 1805 he erected the first grist- and saw-mill in that section of the country. There were doubtless other Jews possessing business and other interests in the region which later became the state; but the early records are very scanty. The oldest congregation in the state is B'ne Jeshurun, in Milwaukee, organized in 1852 by Lobl Rindskopf, Leopold Newbauer, Solomon Adler, Emanuel Silverman, and others, all of whom were among the first Jewish settlers in that city.

Wisconsin contains the following Jewish communities: **Appleton,** with a congregation (Zion) comprising 34 members and founded in 1873, and a ladies' aid society having a membership of 32 and founded in 1878; **Ashland,** which has a congregation organized in 1887, an auxiliary society, a ladies' benevolent association, and a cemetery; **Duluth,** with a congregation, Adas Israel; **Eau Claire,** with a congregation, a religious school, and an aid society comprising 50 members; **Fond du Lac,** containing a congregation, Ḳehilatt Jacob; **Gilette** and **Green Bay,** each with a congregation; **Hurley** and **Ironwood,** which form a congregation jointly; **Kenosha,** with the Congregation B'nai Zedek, incorporated in 1904 and having 27 members; **La Crosse,** which has two congregations (Ansche Cheset, founded in 1856, and Shearith Israel, in 1899), a benevolent society, and a cemetery; **Madison,** possessing a congregation, **Agudas Achim,** and a cemetery; **Manitowoc,** whose congregation, Anshe Poelei Zedek, was founded in 1900; **Marinette,** which has a congregation (founded in 1888 and having 32 members), a religious school, and a cemetery; **Milwaukee** (see JEW. ENCY. viii. 594); **Monroe, Oshkosh** and **Racine,** each with a congregation; **Sheboygan** and **Superior,** which have three congregations each, all organized within the last twenty years.

The state had a Jewish population of 30,100 in 1920 in a total of 2,632,067.

J.

A. M. Ho.

WISDOM (Hebr. חכמה; Greek, σοφία): Practical intelligence; the mental grasp which observes and penetrates into the nature of things, and also the ability skilfully to perform difficult tasks. The former faculty is intuitive, the latter creative. Hence the word connotes both deep understanding and artistic skill. Wisdom is at once a human and a divine property.

All human wisdom and skill come from God. The spirit of God made Joseph discreet and wise (Gen. xli. 38–39), inspired and prepared Bezaleel and other artists for the work of the Tabernacle (Ex. xxxi. 3-6), and was also the source of the wisdom of Joshua (Deut. xxxiv. 9) and Solomon (I Kings iii. 12, 28). "The Lord giveth wisdom" (Prov. ii. 6; comp. Job xxxviii. 36; Ps. li. 8 [A. V. 6]; Dan. ii. 21), and He annuls the wisdom of the wise (Isa. xxix. 14). Great blame, therefore, attaches to those who disregard the di-
Wisdom in vine source of their wisdom and be-
the Bible. come conceited and sinful (Isa. v. 21, xxix. 14; Jer. iv. 22, viii. 8-9, ix. 22). Wisdom is acquired, moreover, by the observation of nature (Prov. vi. 6; Job xxxv. 11) and of history (Deut. xxxii. 29; Hos. xiv. 10 [A. V. 9]; Prov. viii. 33, xix. 20), as well as by study and by association with the wise (Prov. ix. 9, xiii. 20; Job xxxii. 7).

The wise were sought out for their counsel (Deut. i. 13, 15; II Sam. xiv. 20, xvi. 23; Prov. xii. 18, xiii. 14), so that, like the priest with his Torah and the prophet with his revealed word of God, they formed a special class (Jer. xviii. 18). In more primitive times "wise women" were consulted (II Sam. xiv. 2; xx. 16, 22), and at a later period females who were skilled in the art of music and song were called "wise women" (Jer. ix. 17).

As contrasted with the Law and the Prophets, which were intended for the people of Israel exclusively, wisdom was less restricted. "The children of the east country," as well as of Egypt and the south, were regarded as the possessors of wisdom from of old (comp. I Kings v. 10–11 [A. V. iv. 30-

31]; Jer. xlix. 7), and Daniel was considered a representative of them (Ezek. xxviii. 3). This spirit of universal wisdom was also typified by King Solomon (I Kings v. 9–14 [A. V. iv. 29–34], x. 1–24; Eccl. i. 13, 16); and to him, accordingly, was ascribed the entire Wisdom-literature preserved in the form of proverbs, secular songs (Song of Solomon), philosophic thought (Ecclesiastes), and, later, the Wisdom of Solomon. As soon as monotheism was firmly established as a result of the labors of the Prophets,
The sulted by Israel's sages, and questions
Ḥokmah concerning the origin of all things
Literature. could be answered, in both poetry and prose, far more intelligently than had been possible for the ancient Babylonians. This was done occasionally by the Deutero-Isaiah (xl. and elsewhere), by the interpolator of Amos iv. 13 and v. 8, by the authors of Proverbs (viii. 22–31), of Job (xxviii. and elsewhere), and of Ps. civ., and, most authoritatively of all, by the composers of Gen. i.–x. Wisdom, which dwelt, according to the Babylonian cosmology, in the depths of the sea with Ea, the creative deity, became in Biblical literature the all-encompassing intelligence of God, the helper of the Creator, the foundation of the world (comp. Jeremias, "Das Alte Testament im Lichte des Alten Orients," 1904, pp. 29, 80). In exact proportion as Israel's God was believed to be the God of the universe, wisdom was regarded as the cosmic power, God's master workman (Prov. viii. 30), the first of His works (*ib.* viii. 22), and His designer (*ib.* iii. 19; Ps. civ. 24), while at the same time wisdom became the law of life and the divine guide and ruler of man. Virtue, or the fear of God which is the avoidance of evil, was developed into the dominant teaching of the Proverbs and Job. The ceremonial laws are scarcely mentioned, and only the ethical side of religion is considered. At times the ethics assumes too worldly an aspect and becomes commonplace morality (Prov. vi. 34, xiv. 22, xxiv. 17–18, xxix. 3), although other passages point to high ideals (Job xxix. 15-16, xxxi.; Prov. x. 12).

The Book of Ecclesiastes, written by some Sadducean pessimist under the influence of Greek Epicureanism and skepticism, reflects the impressions made by a worldly wisdom no longer permeated by the spirit of the Torah, so that the Solomonic wisdom, which had lost sight of the ethical ideal, was mocked and shown to be a failure.

In the main, wisdom was greatly valued and eagerly sought during the Second Temple, and the wise became the teachers of the young and the models of the old. An extensive Wisdom-literature, of which large portions may have been lost, sprang up in continuation of the Proverbs of Solomon. Ecclesiasticus (SIRACH) proves, on analy-
Wisdom in sis, to be a compilation of writings
the Apoc- which belong in part to an older gen-
rypha. eration; and the TESTAMENTS OF THE TWELVE PATRIARCHS, which recent research has reclaimed for Jewish literature, may also be classed among these Wisdom-books. Concerning the Book of Wisdom see WISDOM, BOOK OF. The table-talk of the wise men of Jerusalem at the court of King Ptolemy of Egypt in the Letter

of Aristeas, §§ 187–300, as well as the answer of Zerubbabel, the page of King Darius (I Esdras ii.–iii.), indicates the Jewish longing to appear as wise men like Daniel and Joseph before the kings of the world.

In all these books wisdom is extolled and invested with divine attributes (Ecclus. [Sirach] i. 1–26, iv. 11–29, li. 13–30, and especially xxiv. 1–29, where it is identified with the law of Moses; Test. Patr., Levi, 13; Enoch, xlii. 1–2). The book on astronomy and cosmography in the writings of Enoch is described as celestial wisdom (Enoch, xxxvii. 2, xlix. 1–3, lxxxii. 2–3; comp. Book of Jubilees, iv. 17, xxi. 10), and Noah's book on healing (Book of Jubilees, x. 13) belongs to the same class.

Under the influence of Greek philosophy wisdom became a divine agency of a personal character (Wisdom vii. 22–30), so that Philo terms it the daughter of God, "the mother of the creative Word" ("De Profugis," §§ 9, 20), while as the creative principle of the world, wisdom occurs in Targ. Yer. to Gen. i. 1 (comp. Ḥag. 11b; Gen. R. i., where the Torah takes the place of wisdom; see also the midrash on Prov. iii. 19 in Jellinek, "B. H." ii. 23–39, v. 63–69). In Christian and Gentile Gnosticism, wisdom became the center of speculation (see GNOSTICISM). The so-called Fourth Book of Maccabees, a philosophical sermon on self-control with reference to the seven martyred sons of the Maccabean heroine, is another contribution to the Hellenistic Wisdom-literature.

Traces in Post-Biblical Literature.

"The wise man" was the title of the early master of the Law (Ab. i. 4, ii. 15), but at a later period the masters bore the epithet of "rabbi," and only those who had died retained the name of "the wise," while the learned were called "disciples of the wise" (see Levy, "Neuhebr. Wörterb." *s.v.* חכם). In general, "wisdom" ("ḥokmah") connotes universal or worldly wisdom, and is thus contrasted with the Torah (Ḳid. 49b; Niddah 69b; Sanh. 104b; Yer. Mak. ii. 31d). There are records of disputations between Jewish masters and Gentile sages, such as the one between R. Joshua b. Hananiah and the men of Athens (Bek. 8–9; Lam. R. i. 4 *et seq.* [comp. ATHENIANS]; Tamid 32a, b). In Pes. 94b (comp. R. H. 12a) the opinion of the wise men of the Gentiles is preferred to that of the Jewish sages. At the sight of Gentile sages one should recite the benediction: "Blessed art Thou, O Lord our God, King of the Universe, who hast imparted of Thy wisdom to flesh and blood" (Ber. 58b). "Ten measures of wisdom came down from heaven, and nine of them fell to the lot of the Holy Land" (Ḳid. 49b). "Since the destruction of the Temple the wise have taken the place of the Prophets" (B. B. 12a). "Who is wise? He who learneth from every one" (Ab. iv. 1). "The Shekinah rests only upon the wise, the strong, the rich, and the tall" (Shab. 92b); but the members of the Sanhedrin must possess universal wisdom (Sanh. 17a). Among the masters of the Mishnah, R. Johanan b. Zakkai and R. Akiba were considered the paragons of universal wisdom (Soṭah ix. 15, 49b). "Greek wisdom" was fostered in the house of Gamaliel, but was forbidden

elsewhere after the Hasmonean war (B. Ḳ. 82b–83a; Soṭah 49b). The sciences of music (R. H. 29b) and astronomy (Shab. 75a) are called "wisdom," and the midwife is termed the "wise woman" (Shab. xviii. 3), while the fourth benediction in the "Shemoneh 'Esreh" is called the "Benediction of Wisdom" (Ber. 33a).

In rabbinical and philosophical literature the various sciences are termed "ḥokmot"; and as the seven sciences of the medieval university ("trivia" and "quadrivia") were based on Prov. ix. 1, "Wisdom hath builded her house, she hath hewn out her seven pillars," so Jewish writers allude to the seven branches of wisdom (see Joseph Ḳimḥi on Prov. ix. 1; Steinschneider, "Jüdische Literatur," in Ersch and Gruber, "Encyc." section ii., part 27, pp. 424, 434–435, where the various "ḥokmot" are enumerated).

K.

WISDOM OF SOLOMON, BOOK OF THE (LXX. Σοφία Σολομῶνος; Vulgate, "Liber Sapientiæ"): Apocryphal book written in Alexandria about the middle of the first century B.C. That it was composed in Greek by an Alexandrian Jew has been conclusively shown by Freudenthal ("J. Q. R." iii. 722–753). The book has neither an introductory verse nor a regular conclusion. In fact, it consists of three independent parts which have no real connection, and which treat of subjects altogether different, a fact clearly recognized by Bretschneider, Eichhorn, and others, but disputed by Grimm ("Kurzgefasstes Exegetisches Handbuch zu den Apocryphen des Alten Testaments," vi. 9–24, Leipsic, 1860) and his followers.

The first six chapters of Wisdom form an address to the rulers of the earth (i. 1; comp. iii. 8; vi. 1–2, 9, 21). They accentuate the necessity of wisdom as indispensable to rulers (i. 6, vi. 9–25), although they are chiefly directed against the Epicureans, the ungodly who deny immortality, indulge in lust and incest, and mock the righteous and the learned, who in their turn upbraid them for their lawlessness and licentiousness (ii. 1–16). In contrast with them the "saints" (Ḥasidim) whom they expose to torture (ii. 19, iii. 1) and to a martyr's death (iii. 2) are called "sons of God," initiated into His mystery, promised an inheritance in eternal life (i. 14; ii. 13, 21, 23; iii. 4, 15; iv. 1; v. 15) like Enoch (iv. 10–16), and assured of a crown of glory in the world to come (v. 16). Finally, wisdom is introduced in vi. 9–25 as the speaker, and as the one who bestows the divine kingdom and confers immortality (vi. 20–21); whereas sin brings death, since "through envy of the devil came death into the world" (ii. 24). The second part (ch. vii.–ix. 17) contains an address of King Solomon, relating how his life was guided solely by wisdom, and closing with a prayer offered by him to God that he might obtain her. Here wisdom is represented as a mystic power which imparts not only knowledge of all mysteries and the spirit of prophecy (vii. 17–21, 27), but even immortality (viii. 13), while it is also a cosmic force invested with twenty-one divine attributes, this number being either a triple multiple of seven, or, if originally twenty-two instead of twenty-one, corresponding to the twenty-two letters of the Greek alphabet (vii.

Contents of the Book.

22–23). At the same time, wisdom, as in the Platonic system, is believed to teach the four cardinal virtues of temperance, prudence, justice, and fortitude (viii. 7). The prayer of Solomon refers to the heavenly tabernacle prepared from the beginning, and to his own predestination (ix. 7–8; see PREEXISTENCE). Wisdom is described as a cosmic principle dwelling on the throne of glory next to God, and as knowing and designing all things (ix. 1, 4, 10), being identical with the creative Word (ix. 1) and the Holy Spirit (ix. 17).

While these two portions of the book form a unity to some extent, and probably gave the entire work its title of "Wisdom of Solomon," the last section (ix. 18–xix. 22) is devoid of all connection with what precedes. The speaker is no longer Solomon, but the author or the saints (xvi. 28, xviii. 6 *et passim*), who recite the history of Israel's redemption from Egypt and other enemies. In like manner, the words are not addressed to the kings of the earth (ix. 18; x. 20; xi. 4, 9, 17, 21; *et passim*), but to God, the deliverer from the Red Sea. The whole appears on close observation to be part of a Passover Haggadah recited in Egypt with reference to Gentile surroundings, and it accordingly abounds in genuine haggadic passages of an ancient character. The tenth chapter serves as a connecting-link between the Solomonic Wisdom-book and this Passover-Haggadah fragment, and must, therefore, be taken with the last verse of the ninth chapter and the first of the eleventh, in both of which wisdom forms the theme. Here, however, it has nothing in common with the Solomonic wisdom, which, enabling the king to penetrate into all the mysteries of heaven and earth, to study the world of the spirits, and to learn the virtues of stones and roots, thus came **Hellenistic** very close to the Platonic wisdom (vii. **Passover** 17–26). The wisdom of the haggadist **Haggadah.** is exclusive and hostile to the Gentile world, rather than cosmopolitan and broad, saving only the righteous and bringing ruin upon the wicked (ix. 18, x. 1–21). From this point of view the lives of the Patriarchs are recounted to lead up to the story of the Exodus. Wisdom taught Adam to rise from his fall by repentance (comp. "Vita Adæ et Evæ," viii.; Pirḳe R. El. xx.); but it caused Cain and his generation to perish (x. 1–3). It saved Noah, Abraham, and Lot, but brought lasting doom upon the offenders (x. 4–9). It showed Jacob the kingdom of God in the vision of the ladder (comp. Gen. R. lxviii. 16; Targ. Yer. to Gen. xxviii. 12) and gave him victory over all his pursuers (x. 10–12). It preserved Joseph the righteous from sin, went with him into the pit and the prison, and raised him to the throne and to glory, but covered his detractors with shame (x. 13–15). It delivered Israel from its heathen oppressors, entered into the soul of Moses, enabling him to work all his miracles before Pharaoh, and, in the shape of a protecting pillar of cloud by day and of an illuminating fire by night, guided the people through the wilderness and through the Red Sea, while it drowned the Egyptians and cast them up again from the deep to enrich the Israelites with the spoils that floated upon the water (x. 15–20; comp. Mek., Beshallaḥ, 6; Targ. Yer. to Ex. xiii. 21; xv.

12, 20; Josephus, "Ant." ii. 16, § 6). It also opened the mouths of the dumb so that they joined in the song of the people in praise of God at the Red Sea (x. 21; comp. Mek. to Shirah [Song of Moses], 1), and it prospered the work of Moses in the wilderness (xi. 1–4).

This section is followed (xi. 5–xix. 21) by a haggadic discourse in the form of a prayer of thanksgiving on the Egyptian plagues and other miracles connected with the Exodus, obviously to be recited on the eve of the Passover (xviii. 6–9; comp. Josephus, "Ant." ii. 16, § 4; Book of Jubilees, xlix. 2–6). The fundamental principle of the ancient Haggadah is that God metes out the perfect justice expressed by the Rabbis in the phrase "middah ke-neged middah" (= "measure for measure"), so that the book declares: "Wherewithal a man sinneth, by the same also shall he be punished" (xi. 16). This was applied to the Egyptians with reference to Ex. xviii. 11 (see Targum *ad loc.*; Soṭah 11d). Here, however, the haggadist goes so far as to maintain that the very thing which proved an instrument of vengeance to the Egyptians became a means of safety for Israel (xi. 5). The water in which the Israelitish children were to be drowned was turned to blood for the parched Egyptians, while it flowed forth from the rock to quench the thirst of the children of Israel in the desert (xi. 4–7). In like manner, the animals worshiped by the Egyptians became the source of terror **Wonders of** and harm to them (xi. 15–19, xii. 24– **the** 27); "for these [the Israelites] thou **Exodus.** didst admonish and try, as a father: but the other [the Egyptian people], as a severe king, thou didst condemn and punish" (xi. 10), even though God loves all His creatures, and waits for the repentance of the sinner because He is the lover of souls (xi. 24–xii. 2). The real cause of the doom of such Gentile nations as the Canaanites was their commission of the capital sins of idolatry and murder (xii. 4–7; comp. Sibyllines, i. 150, 178; iii. 36–40, 585–605, 761–764; *et passim*). Yet even they were given time for repentance; wherefore God sent the wasps before Israel to destroy the Canaanites gradually, instead of killing them all at once (xii. 8–11; comp. Ex. xxiii. 28; Soṭah 36a); for God blends mercy with justice, to teach "that the just man should be merciful" (xii. 19; comp. i. 6), and unrepentant Egypt was thus severely punished until she acknowledged the God she had denied (xii. 27).

Egyptian (and Greek) idolatry is declared (xiii. 1–10) to be far less excusable than Babylonian star-worship, and it is therefore derided (xiii. 11–19) in terms borrowed from Isa. xliv. 13–20. Idolatry was first introduced by the giants who were descended from the fallen angels. Its purposes were corruption and fornication (xiv. 1–13); it owed its hold on mankind to the honor paid the images of dead sons (xiv. 14–21; comp. Book of Jubilees, xi. 4; **The Folly** Bezold, "Die Schatzhöhle," p. 31), and **of** it led to murder, adultery, theft, and **Idolatry.** perjury (xiv. 22–31). Knowledge of God alone guides to righteousness and immortality, while the enemies (the Romans and the Greeks of Alexandria, as well as the Egyptians) who hold Israel in subjection are termed foolish image-worshipers (xv. 1–15; comp. Ps. cxv., recited on the eve of the Passover). The Egyptian animal-worship again suggests to the haggadist the idea that while the beasts became a torment to Egypt, the quail became nourishing food for the people of God (xvi. 1–4); and though the serpents bit the Israelites in the wilderness, they were in the end a sign of salvation for them, admonishing them to look to God as the savior whose word heals all (xvi. 5–12; comp. R. H. iii. 8c). The fire which fell with both the hail and the rain (Ex. ix. 24; Tan., Wayera, ed. Buber, p. 22), as well as in the sea (Ex. xiv. 24; Targ. Yer. *ad loc.*; Josephus, "Ant." ii. 16, § 3), like the fire which would not destroy the frogs in the oven (xix. 21; Pes. 53b), manifested the wondrous power of God (xvi. 16–19). On the other hand, the manna, which fell like hoar frost and was flavored to suit every wish and taste, did not melt in the heat of the wilderness, but disappeared under the first rays of the sun that the people might offer their praise early in the morning (comp. Yoma 75a; Targ. Yer. to Ex. xvi. 21; Mek., Wayassa', 4 [ed. Weiss, p. 58a]; for the Essene prayer at sunrise see Josephus, "B. J." ii. 8, § 5; Ber. 9b; and comp. ESSENES). The Egyptian plague of darkness, in striking contrast to the light in the houses of the children of Israel (Ex. x. 21–23), is declared to have been a punishment for their imprisonment of the Israelites, the future bearers of the light of the Law, and for their pride in their intellectuality, besides being a token of their future doom (xvii. 1–xviii. 4). The last plague, the death of the first-born, was the punishment for the intended murder of the Israelitish children (xviii. 5). This same night of watching proved to be the doom of the Egyptians and the election of Israel, so that on the one side resounded cries of lamentation, and on the other were heard songs of thanksgiving (xviii. 7–17). The almighty "Word" carried the sword of death throughout Egypt, and by this same power Aaron, with his robe, his breastplate, and his diadem decked with divine mysteries, subdued the angel of death (xviii. 20–25). Finally, the destruction of the Egyptians in the Red Sea is described as a renewal of the miracle of Creation (xix. 1–6), since out of the sea rose a green field (comp. Targ. Yer. to Ex. xv. 19). The Egyptians had been more brutal in their treatment of the strangers than had the inhospitable Sodomites, thus accounting for the severity of their punishment (xix. 13–22). Here the Haggadah breaks off abruptly.

Plagues upon Egypt.

It is evident that these three parts, or at least the first two (i.–ix., x.–xix.), can not have emanated from the same author, for neither the style nor the views can be ascribed to one and the same person. This leads to the supposition that the original Wisdom of Solomon and the Passover-Haggadah fragment were probably joined together and then treated as one book. Grätz ("Gesch." 4th ed., iii. 382–385, 611–613) finds in the work allusions to the apotheosis of Caligula (38–40 C.E.), but the deification of the Ptolemies goes back to Egyptian custom. Ch. ii. and iii. refer to Jewish converts, not to Greeks in

Authorship and Date.

Alexandria. The character of the book as regards the creative Wisdom, Word, and Spirit indicates a stage prior to the Philonic system, and the Biblical story shows a haggadic form still fresh and not yet compressed into a rigid system, as in Philo (see Siegfried, "Philo von Alexandria," pp. 22–24, Jena, 1875). The apostle Paul (see Grafe, "Das Verhältniss der Paulinischen Schriften zur Sapientia Salomonis," Freiburg-im-Breisgau, 1892; comp. also SAUL OF TARSUS), the author of the Epistle to the Hebrews (Heb. i. 3, iv. 12; comp. Wisdom vii. 22, 26), and others have drawn from the Book of Wisdom. This places the date of the book, or at least that of the first part, with certainty in the first century B.C.

A Hebrew translation of the Wisdom of Solomon is mentioned by Naḥmanides in the preface to his commentary on the Pentateuch. A Hebrew version with a commentary was published by Hartwig Wessely (Berlin, 1780), and a German translation with notes, valuable for the references to rabbinical literature, was made by M. Gutmann (Altona, 1841).

BIBLIOGRAPHY: For the extensive literature see Schürer, *Gesch.* 3d ed., iii. 377–383. The chief editions, besides that contained in Fritzsche's *Apocryphi Græci,* are: Reusch, *Liber Sapientiæ Græce,* Freiburg-im-Breisgau, 1858; Deane, *Book of Wisdom,* Oxford, 1881. On the question of the original language see Margoliouth, *Was the Book of Wisdom Written in Hebrew?* in *J. R. A. S.* 1890, pp. 263 *et seq.*; answered by Freudenthal, *What Is the Original Language of the Wisdom of Solomon?* in *J. Q. R.* iii. 722–753.
K.

WISDOM OF GOD. See GOD.

WISE, AARON: American rabbi; born at Erlau, Hungary, May 2, 1844; died in New York March 30, 1896; son of Chief Rabbi Joseph Hirsch WEISS. He was educated in the Talmudic schools of Hungary, including the seminary at Eisenstadt, where he studied under Dr. Hildesheimer. Later he attended the universities of Leipsic and Halle, receiving his doctorate at the latter institution. He assisted Bernard Fischer in revising the Buxtorf lexicon, and was for several years a director of schools in his native town. He was for a time identified with the ultra-Orthodox party in Hungary, acting as secretary to the organization Shomere ha-Datt, and editing a Judæo-German weekly in its support. In 1874 Wise emigrated to the United States, and became rabbi of Congregation Beth Elohim in Brooklyn; two years later he was appointed rabbi of Temple Rodeph Shalom in New York, which office he held until his death.

Wise was the author of "Beth Aharon," a religious school handbook; and he compiled a prayer-book for the use of his congregation. He was for some time editor of the "Jewish Herald" of New York, and of the "Boston Hebrew Observer"; and he contributed to the year-books of the Jewish Ministers' Association of America, as well as to other periodical publications. He was one of the founders of the Jewish Theological Seminary, and the first vice-president of its advisory board of ministers. Wise founded the Rodeph Shalom Sisterhood of Personal Service, which established the Aaron Wise Industrial School in his memory.

BIBLIOGRAPHY: *American Jewess,* May, 1896, pp. 482–487; Markens, *Hebrews in America,* pp. 305–306.
A.   S. S. W.

WISE, ISAAC MAYER: American Reform rabbi, editor, and author; born at Steingrub, Bohemia, March 29, 1819; died at Cincinnati, Ohio, March 26, 1900. He was the son of Leo Wise, a schoolteacher, and received his early Hebrew education from his father and grandfather, later continuing his Hebrew and secular studies in Prague. He received the hattarat hora'ah from the Prague bet din, composed of Rabbis Rapoport, Samuel Freund, and E. L. Teweles. In 1843 he was appointed rabbi at Radnitz, Bohemia, where he remained for about two years, emigrating to the United States in 1846. He arrived in New York on July 23 of the same year, and in the following October was appointed rabbi of the Congregation Beth-El of Albany, New York. He soon began agitating for reforms in the service, and his was the first Jewish congregation in the United States to introduce family pews in the synagogue. Sermons in the vernacular, a mixed choir, and confirmation were also among the innovations introduced by Wise, who even went so far as to count women in forming a minyan or religious quorum.

In 1850 some unfortunate events caused a split in the Albany community, and the consequent formation of a new congregation, the Anshe Emeth, by the friends and supporters of the rabbi. Wise remained with this congregation until April, 1854, when he became rabbi of the Bene Yeshurun congregation of Cincinnati, Ohio, where he officiated for the remaining forty-six years of his life. Wise was active in so many directions, and was so great a power in the history of Judaism in the United States, that it is necessary to treat under distinct headings the various achievements of his long and successful career. He was above all an organizer, and the numerous institutions that he called into being attest to the great influence he wielded during his life.

In 1847, at the suggestion of Max Lilienthal, who was at that time stationed in New York, a bet din was formed, which was to act in the capacity of an advisory committee to the congregations of the country, without, however, exercising hierarchic powers. As members of this bet din, Lilienthal named Wise and two others, besides himself. At a meeting held in the spring of 1847 Wise submitted to the bet din the manuscript of a prayer-book, to

Prayer-Book.

be entitled the "Minhag America," and to be used by all the congregations of the country. He had noticed that nearly every prominent rabbi in Europe, and, later, in the United States, issued his own prayer-book, and in order to stem this individualistic tide he advocated the adoption of a common prayer-book. Nothing definite was done in the matter, however, until the Cleveland Conference of 1855, when a committee consisting of Wise, Rothenberg, and Kalisch was appointed to edit such a prayer-book. This book appeared under the title "Minhag America," and was practically Wise's work; it was adopted by most of the congregations of the Western and Southern states. So pronounced was Wise's desire for union, that when in 1894 the "Union Prayer-Book" was published by the Central Conference of American Rabbis, he voluntarily retired the "Minhag America" from his own congregation.

As early as 1848 Wise issued a call to the "ministers and other Israelites" of the United States, urging them to form a union which might put an end to the prevalent religious anarchy. His call appeared in the columns of the "Occident," and was ably seconded by its editor, Isaac Leeser. Wise suggested that a meeting be held in the spring of 1849 at Philadelphia, to establish a union of the congregations of the entire country. This meeting did not take place; but the originator of the idea never ceased advocating it, especially after he had established his own newspaper, "The Israelite" (July, 1854), in the columns of which he indefatigably expounded his views upon the subject. His persistence won its reward when in 1873, twenty-five years after he had first broached the idea, the UNION OF AMERICAN HEBREW CONGREGATIONS was organized at Cincinnati.

Earnest as he was in proclaiming the necessity for union among the congregations, he was equally indefatigable in insisting upon the pressing need of a theological seminary for the training of rabbis for American pulpits. In his "Reminiscences" he gives a vivid picture of the incompetency of many of the men who posed as spiritual guides of the congregations during the early days of his residence in the United States. He had scarcely arrived in Cincinnati when, with his characteristic energy, he set to work to establish a college in which young men could receive a Jewish

Hebrew Union College.

Isaac Mayer Wise.
(From a bust by Moses Ezekiel in the possession of A. S. Ochs.)

education. He enlisted the interest and support of a number of influential Jews of Cincinnati and adjacent towns, and in 1855 founded the Zion Collegiate Association. The venture, however, proved a failure, and the society did not succeed in opening a college. Nothing daunted, Wise entered upon a literary campaign, and year in and year out he presented the subject in the columns of "The Israelite." His indomitable perseverance was crowned with success when, on October 3, 1875, the HEBREW UNION COLLEGE opened its doors for the reception of students, four of whom were ordained eight years later.

The first outcome of Wise's agitation for union among the Jews was the Cleveland Conference held in 1855, and convened at his initiative. This conference was unfortunate, for, instead of uniting the rabbis of all parts of the country in a **Rabbinical** bond of fellowship, it gave rise to **Con-** strained relations between Wise and **ferences.** his followers on one side, and prominent rabbis in the eastern part of the country on the other side. These differences were partly removed during the rabbinical conference of Philadelphia (1869), which Wise attended. The New York conference of 1870, and the Cincinnati conference of 1871 were efforts in the same direction; but a controversy ensuing from the latter served only to widen the breach. Yet was the great "unionist" not discouraged. He continued agitating for a synod which was to be the central body of authority for American Judaism. In 1881 he submitted to the meeting of the Rabbinical Literary Association a report urging the formation of a synod; but the matter never passed beyond the stage of discussion. However, he lived to see the establishment of the Central Conference of American Rabbis in 1889, which was the third enduring offspring of his tireless energy and unfailing perseverance. During the last eleven years of his life he served as president of the conference which he had called into existence (see CONFERENCES, RABBINICAL).

Besides the arduous labors that the organization of these national institutions entailed, Wise was active in many other ways. In 1857, when a new treaty was to be concluded between the United States and Switzerland, he visited Washington as chairman of a delegation to protest against the ratification of this treaty unless Switzerland should cease its discriminations against American Jews. In his own city, besides officiating as rabbi of the Bene Yeshurun congregation and as president of the Hebrew Union College, he edited the "American Israelite" and the "Deborah," served as an examiner of teachers applying for positions in public schools, and was also a member of the board of directors of the University of Cincinnati. He traveled throughout the United States, lecturing, dedicating synagogues, and enlisting the interest of the Jewish communities in his plans and projects.

Wise was the author of the following works: "The History of the Israelitish Nation from Abraham to the Present Time," Albany, 1854; "The Essence of Judaism," Cincinnati, 1861; "The Origin of Christianity, and a Commentary on the Acts of the Apostles," 1868; "Judaism, Its Doctrines and Duties," 1872; "The Martyrdom of Jesus of Naza-

reth: a Historico-Critical Treatise on the Last Chapter of the Gospel," 1874; "The Cosmic God," 1876; "History of the Hebrews' Second Commonwealth," 1880; "Judaism and Christianity, Their Agreements and Disagreements," 1883; "A Defense of Judaism vs. Proselytizing Christianity," 1889; **His Works.** and "Pronaos to Holy Writ," 1891.

In his early years he wrote a number of novels, which appeared first as serials in the "Israelite," and later in book form; these were: "The Convert," 1854; "The Catastrophe of Eger," "The Shoemaker's Family," "Resignation and Fidelity, or Life and Romance," and "Romance, Philosophy, and Cabalah, or the Conflagration in Frankfort-on-the-Main," 1855; "The Last Struggle of the Nation," 1856; "The Combat of the People, or Hillel and Herod," 1858; and "The First of the Maccabees." He wrote also a number of German novels, which appeared as serials in the "Deborah"; among these may be mentioned: "Die Juden von Landshuth"; "Der Rothkopf, oder des Schulmeisters Tochter"; and "Baruch und Sein Ideal." In addition to all these works Wise published in the editorial columns of the "Israelite" numerous studies on various subjects of Jewish interest. He even wrote a couple of plays, "Der Maskirte Liebhaber" and "Das Glück Reich zu Sein."

During his lifetime Isaac M. Wise was regarded as the most prominent Jew of his time in the United States. His genius for organization was of a very high order; and he was masterful, rich in resources, and possessed of an inflexible will. More than of any of his contemporaries, it may be said of him that he left the impress of his personality upon the development of Judaism in the United States.

BIBLIOGRAPHY: I. M. Wise, *Reminiscences*, transl. from the German and ed. by David Philipson, Cincinnati, 1901; *Selected Writings of Isaac M. Wise*, with a biography by David Philipson and Louis Grossmann, *ib*. 1900; *The American Israelite*, 1854–1900, *passim*, and the Jubilee number, June 30, 1904.
A.   D. P.

WISE, LEO: American journalist and publisher; born at Albany Oct. 28, 1849; son of Isaac Mayer WISE. He was educated at St. Xavier College and Farmers College, Cincinnati; College Hill, Ohio; Trinity College, Hartford; and the University of Michigan (A.B., Farmers College, 1867; L.B., University of Michigan, 1869). In 1863 he served a brief term in the river flotilla of the United States navy, and in 1872 was one of the original prospectors in the diamond fields in South Africa, where at Dutoit's Pan he opened a new digging which was at first called "New Rush" and afterward became the famous "Colesburg Kopje," now in the Kimberley district.

From 1875 to 1890 Wise published "Die Deborah," and from 1884 to 1892 he owned the "Jewish Annual." In 1885 he established the "Chicago Israelite" at Chicago, and is still its publisher, in addition to being the managing editor and publisher of the "American Israelite" of Cincinnati, Ohio. Wise has also published most of the books written by his father.

BIBLIOGRAPHY: *American Jewish Year Book*, 5665 (1904–5).
A.   F. T. H.

WISE, STEPHEN SAMUEL: American rabbi; born at Budapest March 17, 1862; son of Aaron WISE. He studied at the College of the City of New York (1887–91), Columbia College (B.A. 1892), and Columbia University (Ph.D. 1901), and later pursued rabbinical studies under Gottheil, Kohut, Gersoni, Joffe, and Margolis. In 1893 he was appointed assistant to Rabbi Henry S. Jacobs of the Congregation B'nai Jeshurun, New York city, and later in the same year, minister to the same congregation. From 1900 to 1906 he was rabbi of the congregation Beth Israel, Portland, Ore. In 1907 he founded the Free Synagogue in New York, of which he is chief rabbi.

Wise was the first (honorary) secretary of the American Federation of Zionists; and at the Second Zionist Congress (Basel, 1898) he was a delegate, and secretary for the English language. He was a member also of the International Zionist Executive Committee in 1899. In 1902 he officiated as first vice-president of the Oregon State Conference of Charities and Correction; and in 1903 he was appointed Commissioner of Child Labor for the state of Oregon. He is the founder of the People's Forum of Portland. Wise is the editor of the Arabic original of "The Improvement of the Moral Qualities," an ethical treatise of the eleventh century by Solomon ibn Gabirol (New York, 1902), and of the "Beth Israel Pulpit." A.

WISMAR. See MECKLENBURG.

WISSENSCHAFTLICHE ZEITSCHRIFT FÜR JÜDISCHE THEOLOGIE. See PERIODICALS.

WISSOTZKY, KALONYMOS ZEEB WOLF: Russian philanthropist; born in Zhagory, government of Kovno, July 8, 1824; died at Moscow May 24, 1904. Wissotzky, whose father was a merchant of moderate means, received the usual Jewish education. He married at eighteen, and six months later left for the yeshibah at Volozhin, where he studied for a short period, settling afterward in Yanishki. At about this time the government organized a Jewish agricultural colony at Dubno, near Dvinsk, and Wissotzky became one of the colonists. The soil proving unproductive, he was obliged to return to Yanishki, where he engaged in business. His love of study, however, soon led him to Kovno, where he became a pupil of Israel LIPKIN. At the end of 1854 he returned to Yanishki, and in 1858 went to Moscow, where he engaged in the tea trade; this, however, did not prevent him from taking an active interest in the affairs of the local Jewish community.

Kalonymos Wissotzky.

He organized a Sabbath-school and Sabbath readings for the cantonists of the district, and had special meals prepared for the soldiers during Passover. He was instrumental also in restoring many a cantonist to Judaism and to his long-lost relatives. With his increasing wealth Wissotzky devoted constantly growing amounts of money to charity. He contributed 10,000 rubles to the Alliance Israélite at Paris, on condition that this sum be allowed to accumulate at compound interest for 100 years, when it would amount to 100 million francs, and that the money be then used for national purposes. Subsequently he made frequent and liberal additions to this fund, which now amounts to about half a million francs, and has become generally known as the "Wissotzky Fund."

The Wissotzky Fund.

Wissotzky was an enthusiastic believer in Zionism, and one of its prime movers in Russia. When, in the eighties of the nineteenth century, the idea of Jewish colonization in Palestine began to be realized, Wissotzky spent much time and money in effecting the organization of the Chovevei Zion. He journeyed to Palestine as a delegate, and laid there the foundation for future colonization. His letters from Palestine, together with other material, were published in book form. He made generous contributions to the Palestinian organizations, and furnished practically all the money necessary for the establishment and support of the Bet ha-Sefer school in Jaffa. When the publication of a Jewish encyclopedia was suggested to Wissotzky by Aḥad ha-'Am, he offered to give 20,000 rubles toward this purpose. When told that this sum would be but a small portion of the amount required for the colossal work, he decided to let the matter rest; he refused, however, to take back his contribution, and ordered the money to be transferred to the Society for the Promotion of Culture Among the Jews of Russia. At the instance of his son-in-law, Joseph Zeitlin, he gave 6,000 rubles toward the publication of a monthly magazine, "Ha-Shiloaḥ," under the editorship of Aḥad ha-'Am.

Aside from his gifts for literary enterprises and Palestinian affairs, Wissotzky expended large sums of money in contributions to yeshibot and Talmud Torahs. On the occasion of the marriage of his son, David Wissotzky, in 1898, he presented 70,000 rubles for the establishment in the city of Byelostok of a Talmud Torah with technical classes; this institution was opened in 1904. In his will Wissotzky bequeathed the sum of one million rubles for Jewish national purposes. Without specifying the manner in which this money was to be expended, he left it in charge of Aḥad ha-'Am, Rabbi Jacob Maze of Moscow, and the banker Shmelkin.

H. R. A. LU.

WITCHCRAFT: "Witchcraft" and "sorcery" are the terms used in the Bible to designate the practise of the arts of divination, which were tabooed by orthodox religious sentiment. As this orthodox sentiment was not a constant quantity, practises which at one time were regarded as innocent at another were relegated to the domain of sorcery or witchcraft. These practises were varied, and are denoted by several different Hebrew words.

One of the oldest of these practises was that of consulting the dead. The spirit of the dead was called "ob," and the consultation of such a spirit was accomplished through a woman who was called a "mistress of an ob" ("ba'alat ob"). The earliest and most famous instance of this on record is that of King Saul on the night before the fateful battle of Gilboa, in which he lost his life (comp. I Sam. xxviii. 3, 7 et seq.). It appears from the account that this method of gaining information was under the ban even at that early date. The "mistress of the ob" whom Saul found at En-dor is said to have been able to summon Samuel's spirit from the under world and to talk with it. The narrative represents her as able to call up any "ob" desired. Wherever "obot" are mentioned there also is found the term "yidde'oni" (R. V., incorrectly, "wizard"). It is, apparently, a synonym of "ob" as a designation of a departed spirit (comp. Lev. xix. 31; xx. 6, 27; Deut. xviii. 11; I Sam. xxviii. 3, 9; II Kings xxi. 6, xxiii. 24; Isa. viii. 19, xix. 3; II Chron. xxxiii. 6). "Ob" designated a subterranean spirit, but perhaps "yidde'oni" was a more general term. It is probable that the wizards who consulted the dead were ventriloquists, for Isaiah (comp. viii. 19) describes them as those that "chirp and . . . mutter." Probably the ventriloquist impersonated the dead as speaking in a faint voice from the ground, whence this description. Deut. xviii. 11 adds to consulting an ob or a yidde'oni, "inquiring of the dead," as though there were still another means of consulting them. If this be so, no information as to the method of consultation has been preserved.

The Ob and the Yidde'oni.

Another class of diviners is called "me'onenim" (comp. Judges ix. 37; II Kings xxi. 6; Isa. ii. 6; Mic. v. 12). This class also was very ancient. It appears from Judges ix. 26 that a sacred tree at Shechem was named from it. As this tree is probably identical with the "oak of Moreh" (Gen. xii. 6, R. V.), it is probable that the method of divination alluded to was also employed by the Canaanites. Isaiah (ii. 6) also alludes to the "me'onenim" as existing among the Philistines. It is evident, therefore, that this method of divination was common to Palestinian heathendom. W. R. Smith (in "Journal of Philology," xiv. 116 et seq.), who is followed by Driver, derives the word from עָנַן (comp. the Arabic "ghanna" = "to emit a hoarse, nasal sound"), and thinks that it denoted the "murmurer" or "hoarsely humming soothsayer"; he remarks that the characteristic utterances of an Arabic soothsayer are a monotonous croon called "saj'" and a low murmur, "zamzamah," or whisper, "waswasah."

An obscure class of soothsayers was called "mekashshefim" (comp. the "nomen abstractum" "kesha"; see Deut. xviii. 11; II Kings ix. 22; Mic. v. 12; Nah. iii. 4). W. R. Smith (l.c. p. 125) argues that the root "kashaf" means "to use magical appliances, or drugs"; and many interpreters follow him. Those who doubt the correctness of this explanation are unable to suggest an alternative. This interpretation receives some support from the facts that the Septuagint in Nah. iii. 4 gives φάρμακα, and that the belief in the use of drugs or herbs is very old, as is shown by the mention of mandrakes in Gen. xxx. 14–19. In the oldest code capital punishment is ordained for this class of sorcerers (comp. Ex. xxii. 18).

Drugs and Charms.

A further branch of witchcraft was "lahash," or charming (comp. Isa. iii. 3). In Jer. viii. 17 and Eccl. x. 11 the word is used of snake-charming.

Kindred in function to the "lahash" was the "hober" (comp. Deut. xviii. 11), which Ps. lviii. 5 makes parallel to "lahash." "Lahash," curiously, does not appear in Deut. xviii. 10–11, a passage which Ewald and W. R. Smith regard as an exhaustive list of forbidden enchantments. In its place there is "nahash" ("menahesh"). As ל and נ are both liquids, possibly the two roots are connected. In reality, however, "nahash" seems to have had a different meaning. Gen. xliv. 5 says that Joseph divined ("yenahesh") by means of a cup, perhaps by watching the play of light in a cup of liquid. Balaam (Num. xxiv. 1) is said to have occupied himself with enchantments ("nehashim"). Since Balaam observed omens on the hilltops, his oracles must have been deduced from some other natural phenomena. As the equivalent term in Syriac, "nāhshā," is one which covers portents from the flight of birds as well as other natural occurrences, "lahash" probably refers, as W. R. Smith concludes, to divination by natural omens and presages. If so, it was not always tabooed by the best men in Israel, for David once received an omen for a successful military attack from the sounds in the tops of certain trees (II Sam. v. 24).

Another term often used to describe sorcery is "kesem" (Num. xxiii. 23; Deut. xviii. 10; I Sam. xv. 23; II Kings xvii. 17; Isa. iii. 2; Ezek. xxi. 21). This method of divination is elucidated in Ezek. xxi., R. V., where the King of Babylon is represented as standing at the parting of the ways, and using divination to determine whether to proceed first against Rabbah of Ammon or against Jerusalem. "He shook the arrows to and fro, he consulted the teraphim, he looked in the liver." In verse 22 (Hebr.) it is declared that in "his right hand was the kesem for Jerusalem." It would appear, therefore, that "kesem" was a method of divination by arrows. Arabian analogy here throws much light upon the practise, as this system of drawing lots by means of arrows, and thus obtaining an oracle, was practised by the Arabs, and the details are quite well known (comp. W. R. Smith in "Journal of Philology," xiii. 277 et seq.). The lots were drawn with headless arrows in the presence of an idol, and were accompanied by a sacrifice. The method was thoroughly analogous to that which Ezekiel describes. The "kesem" was accordingly a method of casting lots. Among the Arabs judicial sentences were obtained in this way, so that it became a kind of ordeal. Such, probably, was the case in Israel, for Prov. xvi. 10 declares that "A divine sentence ["kesem"] is in the lips of the king: His mouth shall not transgress in judgment" (R. V.).

Indeed, all through the earlier period of Israel's history important matters were decided by lot. The land was assigned to the tribes by lot (Josh. xiv. 2); Saul is said to have been chosen king by lot (I Sam. x. 10); Jonathan, when he had violated a taboo, was detected by lot (I Sam. xiv. 41 et seq.); in fact, some form of casting lots was the one way of obtaining a divine decision (comp. Prov. xvi. 33). The EPHOD was probably an instrument for casting lots.

Ordeals and Lots.

Ewald and W. R. Smith have both observed that

Deut. xviii. 10–11 contains a formal list of all the important kinds of witchcraft or divination known at the time the passage was written. These various modes of obtaining oracles really diverted popular attention from spiritual prophecy. The Deuteronomist banished them from the realm of legitimate practise and promised in lieu of them a perennial succession of prophets. Among these various kinds of divination, "ḳesem" (by sacred lots in the presence of an idol) held a foremost place. It stands next in the list to making one's son or daughter "pass through the fire." This was a part of Moloch-worship, and was probably a means of obtaining an oracle: hence it was classed with witchcraft.

If the date of the Deuteronomic code given by modern critics is accepted (about 650 B.C.), the prominence given to "ḳesem" is easily understood. The Prophets were raising popular practises to a higher level; and arts which had before been esteemed innocent, or regarded as the handmaids of religion, were now condemned as witchcraft. It is probable that other forms of sorcery in the list had passed through a similar history. Isaiah (viii. 19) indicates that in the eighth century B.C. necromancy (consulting the dead by either an ob or a yidde'oni) was the most popular competitor of prophecy for popular favor. It can not be supposed, as Stade and others hold, that ancestor worship in a pronounced form ever existed among the Semites (comp. Frey, "Seelenglaube und Seelenkult im Alten Israel," Leipsic, 1898, and Grüneisen, "Der Ahnenkultus und die Urreligion Israels," Halle, **Relation to** 1900); yet, when it is borne in mind **Ancestor** how easily an ancestor or a departed **Worship.** sheik becomes a "wali" among the modern Arabs, it is not difficult to believe that the necromancy of ancient Israel had a semi-religious origin. The movement against necromancy was much older than that against "ḳesem," for it began as early as the reign of Saul (comp. I Sam. xxviii. 3); but old customs are persistent, and "seeking unto the dead" was still a popular practise in the time of Isaiah.

The denunciations of Isaiah and the Deuteronomist did not, however, annihilate witchcraft. It still existed in the time of the author of the Ethiopic Book of Enoch, although it was then in bad odor. This writer ascribes all kinds of sorcery and divination to the angels, who, in Gen. vi. 2–4, are said to have come down to earth and taken human wives (comp. Ethiopic Enoch, vii. 1, viii. 1, ix. 7, and xvi. 3). In this writer's view sin came into the world through these angels, and not through the eating of the fruit in paradise (viii. 1 et seq.). His idea of witchcraft as consisting of nefarious knowledge is expressed in ch. xvi. 3, where he says that the angels had been in heaven, and so knew "illegitimate mysteries."

The Book of Tobit represents even the pious Tobias as using a charm against evil spirits (vi. 4–8, viii. 2, xi. 11). This charm consisted of the smoke of the gall of a fish.

The Apocalypse of Baruch (lx. 1) regards the religion of the Amorites as "spells and incantations," but its author also remembers that Israel in the days of the Judges was polluted by similar sins.

XII.—35

Any foreign religion is here counted as witchcraft and a wicked mystery. This is analogous to the classification as sorcery, in Deut. xviii. 10–11, of Moloch-worship, which is attributed to the Ammonites. See Magic.

Bibliography: W. R. Smith, On the Forms of Divination and Magic Enumerated in Deut. xviii. 10–11, in Journal of Philology, xiii. 273–287, xiv. 113–128; Driver, Deuteronomy, in International Critical Commentary, 1895, pp. 223 et seq.; Grüneisen, Der Ahnenkultus und die Urreligion Israels, pp. 160 et seq., Halle, 1900.
E. G. H. G. A. B.

WITEBSK. See Vitebsk.

WITNESS. See Evidence.

WITTELSHÖFER, LEOPOLD: Austrian physician; born at Nagy-Kanizsa, Hungary, July 14, 1818; died at Vienna Jan. 8, 1889; educated at the University of Vienna (M.D. 1841). After practising medicine for ten years in Raab, Hungary, he moved to Vienna (1851) and became editor of the "Wiener Medizinische Wochenschrift," to which periodical he contributed many essays. He was the author also of "Wiener Heil- und Humanitäts-anstalten," Vienna, 1856.

Bibliography: Pagel, Biog. Lex.; Hirsch, Biog. Lex.
s. F. T. H.

WITTMANN, FRANZ: Hungarian electrician and physicist; born at Hod-Mező-Vasarhely Jan. 16, 1860. He was educated at the university of Budapest, and continued his studies in Vienna, Berlin, Paris, Frankfort-on-the-Main, Darmstadt, and Hanover. In 1892 he was appointed professor of physics at the polytechnic in Budapest; and five years later he became a member of the royal patent-bureau and secretary of the board of examiners for teachers in intermediate schools.

Wittmann's works, which have made him the leading Hungarian authority on electrotechnics, include the following: "Az Inductiv Taszításról" (on inductive repulsion); "Periodikus Áramok Optikai Vizsgálata" (optical tests of periodical currents); "Budapest Villamvilágításáról" (electric lighting of Budapest); "Az Erös Villamáramok Technikája" (technics of strong electric currents); "A Leydeni Batteriák és Induktoriumok Áramának Vizsgálata és Objektív Elöállítása" (objective production of currents from Leyden jars and inductors); "Kondensatorok Áramának Vizsgálata és Objectív Elöállítása" (test and objective production of currents from condensers); and "Akusztikai Kisérletek" (acoustic experiments). In addition to these works, Wittmann has published numerous articles on the technical uses of electricity and heat.
s. L. V.

WOCHENBLATT FÜR DIE FAMILIE. See Periodicals.

WODIANER, PHILIP: Hungarian communal worker; flourished in Szegedin during the latter part of the eighteenth and the beginning of the nineteenth century. He was president of the Jewish community there from 1793 to 1809, and presented the congregation with the site for its first synagogue, and with silver holy vessels for its ḥebra ḳaddisha.

His son **Cosman** (b. Veprovac 1788; d. at Györ-Sziget Aug. 18, 1831) studied Talmudics under Samuel

C. Brody and Lebusch Ḥarif in Szegedin, under R. Moses Sofer in Mattersdorf, and under R. Moses Minz in Alt-Ofen. In Györ-Sziget, where he settled after his marriage, he maintained a yeshibah of his own, which was usually frequented by forty to fifty pupils; and he enjoyed a high reputation as a Talmudist. His writings, left in manuscript, were published by his son **Arnold** (born in Raab 1817) under the editorship of Prof. W. Bacher. They appeared in 1890 in two volumes entitled "Sefer Naḥalat Yehoshua', Liber Hereditatis Josuæ, Commentationes in Plerosque Talmudi Babylonii Tractatus Additis Commentationibus in Pentateuchum," and consisted of Talmudic novellæ and of explanations of passages in the Torah.

Wodianer's son **Samuel**, who, after the death of his father, kept a large warehouse in Szegedin for tobacco, wool, and corn, was president of the community from 1812 to 1821. Later he settled in Pesth, where he and his children were baptized. His son **Albert** (born at Szegedin Aug. 13, 1818; died in Budapest July 17, 1898) studied technology in Pesth and Vienna, and was in 1867 appointed royal commissary of the Hungarian Northern Railroad. In 1869 he received the Iron Cross of the second class, and in 1870 the cross of the papal Order of St. George; and in 1886 he was elevated to the Hungarian nobility.

BIBLIOGRAPHY: Kulinyi-Löw, *A Szegedi Zsidók*; Sturm, *Országgyülési Almanach*, 1897.
s.
L. V.

WOGUE, JULES: French author; son of Lazare Wogue; born in Paris Dec. 4, 1863; educated at the Ecole Normale Supérieure in his native city ("agrégé ès lettres," 1885). After successive professorships at the lyceums of Saint Quentin and Reims, as well as at the Lycée Michelet and the Collège Rollin in Paris, he was appointed professor at the Lycée Buffon, a position he has held several years.

Wogue is the author of the following works: "Le Poète Gresset" (Paris, 1894); "Contes et Récits des Dix-Septième et Dix-Huitième Siècles"; "Les Portraits de La Bruyère"; and "Le Théâtre Comique aux Dix-Septième et Dix-Huitième Siècles" (Paris, 1905). He has published also editions of Racine's "Esther" and "Athalie," with historical introductions and commentaries, including copious Biblical notes. He is a contributor to the "Revue Bleue," the "Grande Revue," and "Le Temps."
s.
J. Ka.

WOGUE, LAZARE ELIEZER: French rabbi; born at Fontainebleau, Seine-et-Marne, July 22, 1817; died at Paris April 14, 1897; educated at the Lycée Charlemagne at Paris, and at the Collège Royal and the Ecole Centrale Rabbinique at Metz. Receiving his rabbinical diploma in 1843, he returned to Paris, and became assistant preacher under Marchand Ennery, chief rabbi of Paris. Eight years later Salomon Munk and Adolphe Franck established a chair of Jewish theology at the Ecole Centrale Rabbinique at Metz, to which Wogue was appointed, remaining in this position until his retirement, with the title of professor emeritus, in 1894. Upon the transfer of the college from Metz to Paris (1859) as the Séminaire Israélite de France, his duties were extended to embrace instruction in Hebrew

grammar, Biblical exegesis, and German. From 1879 to 1895 he was the director and editor-in-chief of the "Univers Israélite," being at the same time a member of the Imperial Academy of Metz, and of the Society of Archeology and History of the Moselle. On Jan. 11, 1885, he was made a chevalier of the Legion of Honor.

Wogue, who was a prolific writer, is best known for his translation of the Pentateuch, with notes which include the chief rabbinical interpretations and for his history of Bible exegesis. His works are as follows: "Sermon sur la Tolérance" (Metz, 1841); "Le Rabbinat Français au Dix-Neuvième Siècle" (Paris, 1843); "L'Avenir dans le Judaïsme" (*ib.* 1844); "Shomer Emunim, Le Guide du Croyant Israélite" (Metz, 1857; 2d ed., with a preface by Zadoc Kahn, Paris, 1898), a collection of prayers, hymns, and meditations in prose and verse; "Le Pentateuque" (Paris, 1860–69), a new translation, with Hebrew text and notes, and a version of the Haftarot; "L'Anthropomorphisme et les Miracles Selon le Judaïsme" (*ib.* 1867); a translation of the "Kol Kore" of Elijah Soloweyczyk (2 parts, *ib.* 1870–75), a harmony of the Bible, the Talmud, and the Gospels; a translation of Schleiden's "Bedeutung der Juden für Erhaltung und Wiederbelebung der Wissenschaften im Mittelalter" (*ib.* 1877); a revised and annotated edition of the "Sefer Sekiyyot ha-Ḥemdah" by D. Cahen (Mayence, 1877); a translation of Gabriel b. Joshua's "Petaḥ Teshubah," which appeared originally at Amsterdam in 1651 (Paris, 1879); a revised edition of letters A–C of Léon Hollaenderski's "Dictionnaire Universel Français-Hébreu" (*ib.* 1879); "Histoire de la Bible et de l'Exégèse Biblique Jusqu'à Nos Jours" (*ib.* 1881); a translation of the first two volumes of Grätz's "Geschichte der Juden" (*ib.* 1882–84); "Esquisse d'une Théologie Juive" (*ib.* 1887); and "La Prédication Israélite en France" (*ib.* 1890). In addition to these works, Wogue translated and annotated Lippmann Sofer's "Gan Raweh," and revised the "Semaine Israélite" of Baruch Créhange, the "Sentier d'Israël" and the "Rituel des Prières" of Elcan Durlacher (10 vols., with Hebrew text and French translation), and Ullmann's "Catéchisme."

BIBLIOGRAPHY: *Ozar ha-Sifrut*, v.; *Archives Israélites* and *Univers Israélite*, April, 1897.
s.
J. Ka.

WOHLLERNER, JETTY: Galician Hebrew writer; born at Lemberg in 1813; died there in 1891. When a little girl of eight, Jetty, after having passed her examination in primary instruction, was taken by her father, Michael Kehlmann, into his office as an accountant. She was so devoted to the study of Hebrew, however, that she always attended the Hebrew lessons given her brothers, and in her spare moments she used to read the Bible in Hebrew. The Hebrew letters of the Christian Anna Maria Schurmann stimulated her still more, and she induced her father to engage a teacher for her. The physician Goldschmied, then a student at Lemberg, was entrusted with her Hebrew education. At the age of fourteen she was betrothed to L. Rosanes of Brody, and carried on a correspondence with him which was styled by Rapoport "the echo of the Song of Songs." Her fiancé died, however; and she was married several years later to Samson Wohllerner. She continued to write her Hebrew letters notwithstanding; and the greater portion of her correspondence, which is noteworthy for its style and purity of language, was published in "Kokebe Yiẓḥaḳ" and "Ha-Boḳer Or," while two letters, one to Kayserling and one to Goldschmied, are found in "Oẓar ha-Sifrut" (i. 60–62).

BIBLIOGRAPHY: Kayserling, Die Jüdischen Frauen, pp. 309–311; Allg. Zeit. des Jud. 1891, p. 538; Weinberg, Ziyyurim me-Ḥayye 'Ammenu, Wilna, 1891; Jewish Chronicle, Nov. 13, 1891, p. 9.
s.   M. SEL.

WOLF (Hebr. "ze'eb"; for the rendering of "iyyim," Isa. xiii. 22, and "tannim," Lam. iv. 3, see Fox): The wolf (Canis lupus) is still found in Palestine, where the animals prowl in pairs or droves about sheepfolds at night. As a type of boldness, ferocity, and bloodthirstiness, it is mentioned in Gen. xlix. 27; Isa. xi. 6, lxv. 25; Jer. v. 6; Ezek. xxii. 27; Hab. i. 3; and Zeph. iii. 3.

According to the Talmud, the wolf (דיבא, זאב, and לוקום [= Greek λύπος]) resembles in external appearance the dog, with which it can copulate (Ber. 9b; Gen. R. xxxi. 6); and its period of gestation is three years (Bek. 8a). It is the enemy of flocks, and directs its attacks especially against the he-goats (B. Ḳ. 15b; Shab. 53b). The wound caused by the wolf's bite is oblong and ragged (Zeb. 74b). Although when pressed by hunger the wolf attacks even man (Ta'an. 19a), it can be tamed (Sanh. 15b). For a comparison of the otter with the wolf see Suk. 56b and Gen. R. cxii. 3; and for fables of which the wolf is the subject see Rashi on Sanh. 39a and 105a.

BIBLIOGRAPHY: Tristram, Nat. Hist. p. 152; Lewysohn, Z. T. p. 81.
E. G. H.   I. M. C.

WOLF, AARON BENJAMIN. See AARON B. BENJAMIN WOLF.

WOLF, ABRAHAM NATHAN: German scholar; born at Dessau in 1751; died there in 1784. On account of his liberal views he was highly esteemed by Moses Mendelssohn, but when he endeavored to harmonize the usual Jewish system of training with modern European culture, he was persecuted by the conservative element among the Jewish scholars, and even his friends nicknamed him "the backslider." Wolf was the author of the "Pesher Dabar" (Berlin, 1777), a comprehensive commentary on the Book of Job, which was highly praised by Moses Mendelssohn on account of the thorough rabbinical scholarship which it evidenced ("Der Sammler," 1785, p. 43). He also wrote "Grundzüge der Jüdischen Religion" (ib. 1782), in which he expounded the teachings of Judaism in simple language without reducing the moral and religious contents of Jewish law to arbitrary articles of faith. The latter work has been lost for the last fifty years. Wolf was likewise a contributor to "Ha-Meassef" and to the first three volumes of the "Bikkure ha-'Ittim."

BIBLIOGRAPHY: P. Philippson, Biographische Skizzen, pp. 153–154, Leipsic, 1865; Delitzsch, Zur Gesch. der Hebräischen Poesie, p. 107; Allg. Zeit. des Jud. 1837, p. 448; Steinschneider, Cat. Bodl. col. 2578.
s.   S. O.

WOLF, ADOLPH GRANT: American jurist; born at Washington, D. C., Jan. 11, 1869; educated at Johns Hopkins University (A.B. 1890) and at the George Washington (formerly Columbian) University of Washington, D. C. (LL.B. 1892; LL.M. 1893). He was admitted to the bar in 1893, and then took a postgraduate course at the University of Berlin. Upon his return to the United States (1895) he became financial secretary of the United Hebrew Charities at Washington; and in 1902 he was appointed associate justice of the Supreme Court of Porto Rico.

BIBLIOGRAPHY: American Jewish Year Book, 5665 (1904–5).
A.   F. T. H.

WOLF, EMMA: American authoress; born June 15, 1865, in San Francisco, Cal., to which city her parents had migrated from France, and where she received her education. In addition to several short stories, which appeared in various American magazines, she is the author of the following novels: "Other Things Being Equal," San Francisco, 1892; "A Prodigal in Love," ib. 1894; "The Joy of Life," ib. 1896; and "Heirs of Yesterday," ib. 1900. Her Jewish novels attracted particular attention.

BIBLIOGRAPHY: American Jewish Year Book, 5665 (1904–5).
A.   F. T. H.

WOLF, GEORGE GARCIA: South-African merchant, and member of the Cape Parliament; born at Great Yarmouth 1838; died in London March 18, 1899. He commenced business as an apprentice in Manchester, but soon emigrated to Montreal, where he became a general merchant. In 1860 he went to Kimberley, where he opened a general store. He then became associated with the leading men of the diamond fields, and in 1882 was elected representative for Kimberley in the Cape Parliament. He was presented by his constituents with a gold casket containing 500 guineas and accompanied by an illuminated address. Wolf held several other public offices in Kimberley for some years, until his return to England.

BIBLIOGRAPHY: Jew. Chron. March 24, 1899.
J.   G. L.

WOLF, GERSON: Austrian historian and educator; born at Holleschau, Moravia, July 16, 1823; died in Vienna Oct. 29, 1892. He began the study of Hebrew at a very early age, and later received instruction in German and in Latin from Dr. Egenter, then stationed in Holleschau as military surgeon. Intending to pursue a rabbinical career, he went in 1836 to Pohrlitz, and later to Nikolsburg, where he engaged in Talmudic studies, attending at the same time the gymnasium. Three years later (1839) he went to Vienna, where he attended the university, his studies embracing pedagogics, philosophy, and modern languages. In 1845 his first article, "Das Lustspiel des Aristophanes und das Lustspiel Unserer Zeit," appeared in Saphir's "Humorist." Three years later he published in Frankl's "Sonntagsblätter" his "Das Sterben eines Kindes," his only attempt in the field of fiction.

Wolf was personally engaged in the political struggles of 1848–49, his "Die Demokratie und der Socialismus" appearing in the latter year. On account of several radical articles published in "Die

Oesterreichische Zeitung" and in Die Zeit," he was ordered to leave Vienna; but owing to the intervention of influential friends the order was revoked. He then decided to abandon journalism, and presently accepted a position in a school for Jewish girls. In 1850 he was appointed religious instructor in the state industrial high school in the Leopoldstadt, one of the districts of Vienna, which position he held till 1876. In 1851, in response to a request from the mayor of Vienna for suggestions as to school reforms, he published his " Ueber die Volksschulen in Oesterreich," in which he advocated the elimination of religious instruction from all public schools. Toward the end of 1852, on account of a secret denunciation, his home was searched by the authorities, and Guizot's "La Démocratie en France," a work which had been placed under the ban, was found in his library. He was courtmartialed, held in custody for seventeen days during trial, and finally sentenced to four weeks' confinement in a fortress. In the same year he received his degree of Ph.D., and two years later was appointed religious instructor to the Jewish community of Vienna. Wolf was active in various public undertakings. In 1859 he founded a library for the young; and in 1861, together with Noah Mannheimer,

Johann Christoph Wolf.
(From Wolf, " Bibliotheca Hebræa," Hamburg, 1715.)

Baron Königswarter, and Julius von Goldschmidt, he organized a society for the aid of poor Jewish students in Vienna. This society, which is still (1905) in existence, has assisted more than 200 students annually since its foundation. Until 1872 Wolf officiated as pastor to the Jewish inmates of the houses of correction of Vienna and Stein-on-the-Danube; and from 1884 to 1892, as inspector of all the Jewish religious schools of Vienna.

Wolf is the author of the following works: " Geschichte Israels für die Israelitische Jugend " (Vienna, 1856), introduced as a text-book in various Jewish schools of the United States; " Ferdinand II. und die Juden " (*ib.* 1859; 2d ed., Leipsic, 1860); " Vom Ersten bis zum Zweiten Tempel. Geschichte der Israelitischen Cultusgemeinde in Wien, 1820-60 " (Vienna, 1860); " Zur Geschichte der Juden in Worms und des Deutschen Städtewe-

sens " (Breslau, 1862) ; " Judentaufen in Oesterreich " (Vienna, 1863) ; " Isaak Noah Mannheimer. Eine Biographische Skizze " (*ib.* 1863) ; " Die Juden in der Leopoldstadt " (*ib.* 1863) ; " Zur Geschichte der Jüdischen Aerzte in Oesterreich " (1864) ; " Zur Geschichte Jüdischer Tartüffe " (pseudonymously ; Leipsic, 1864) ; " Das Hundertjährige Jubiläum der Israelitischen Cultusgemeinde " (Vienna, 1864) ; " Zwei Geschichten der Israelitischen Cultusgemeinde in Wien " (*ib.* 1865) ; " Zur Lage der Juden in Galizien " (1867) ; " Joseph Wertheimer, ein Lebens- und Zeitbild " (Vienna, 1868) ; " Die Vertreibung der Juden aus Böhmen im Jahre 1744, und deren Rückkehr im Jahre 1748 " (Leipsic, 1869) ; " Kurzgefasste Religions- und Sittenlehre " (Vienna, 1870 ; 2d ed., *ib.* 1877), used as a text-book in Jewish schools of North America ; " Geschichte der Juden in Wien von 1156–1876 " (*ib.* 1876) ; " Joseph II." (*ib.* 1878) ; " Die Jüdischen Friedhöfe und die Chevrah Kadischah in Wien " (*ib.* 1879) ; " Die Alten Statuten der Jüdischen Gemeinden in Mähren, nebst den Darauffolgenden Synodalbeschlüssen " (*ib.* 1880) ; " Das Unterrichtswesen in Oesterreich Unter Kaiser Joseph II." (*ib.* 1880) ; " Aus der Zeit der Kaiserin Maria Theresia" (*ib.* 1888) ; " Josefína " (*ib.* 1890) ; and " Kleine Historische Schriften " (*ib.* 1892).

BIBLIOGRAPHY: Wurzbach, *Biog. Lex.*; *Allgemeine Deutsche Biographie*; *Mährens Männer der Gegenwart*, s.v. For Wolf's autobiography see *Notizenblatt der Historisch-Statistischen Section der Gesellschaft zur Beförderung des Ackerbaues*, ed. by Christian Ritter d'Elvert, 1875, Nos. 3 and 4.

s.   N. D.

WOLF, HENRY: American engraver, was born at Eckwersheim, Alsace, August 3, 1852; educated at Strasburg. He became a pupil of Jacques Lévy, an engraver of Strasburg. Wolf's work received honorable mention from the Paris Salon (1888, and a gold medal (1895). He exhibited at the World's Columbian Exposition, receiving a medal of the first class in 1893. Since then his work has been shown in various expositions, especially in Paris (1889, 1900). He received a medal from the St. Louis Exposition, 1904.

His principal works are engravings which illustrated the American Artist series and the Gilbert Stuart series of Women and Men for " The Century Magazine," and a series of portraits of women for " Harper's Magazine "; portraits of Thomas Jefferson and Carlyle; and " The Morning Star," " The Evening Star," and " A Duck Pond." He died in 1916.

BIBLIOGRAPHY: *Who's Who in America*, 1908-09.

F. H. V.

WOLF, HIRSCH W.: German physician; born at Lobsens, Posen, 1738; died at Hamburg April 14, 1820; studied at the University of Giessen (M.D. 1779). From 1786 to 1788 he acted as physician at the Hamburg poorhouse. He wrote "Abhandlung über das Spanische Fliegenpflaster," Altona, 1785; "Vertheidigung der Frühen Beerdigung der Juden," Hamburg, 1788; "Bemerkungen über die Blattern," ib. 1795; "Ideen über Lebenskraft, nebst Einigen Krankengeschichten und Bemerkungen," Altona, 1806; "Praktische Bemerkungen nebst Krankheitsgeschichten," Hamburg, 1811; "Ueber das Wesen des Fiebers, nebst einem Beitrag zum Thierischen Magnetismus," ib. 1815, 2d ed. 1818.

BIBLIOGRAPHY: Hirsch, Biog. Lex.
S.
F. T. H.

WOLF, JOHANN CHRISTOPH: Christian Hebraist and polyhistor, born at Wernigerode Feb. 21, 1683; died at Hamburg July 25, 1739. He came in contact with Vitringa, Surenhuis, Reland, and Basnage, and especially occupied himself with the study of Oriental languages and literature, of which he became professor at the Hamburg gymnasium in 1712. Wolf devoted himself to a description of Jewish literature based upon the Oppenheimer collection. His researches resulted in "Bibliotheca Hebræa" (4 vols., Hamburg, 1715–33). The first volume contains a list of Jewish authors; the second deals with the subject-matter under the headings "Bible," "Talmud," "Cabala," etc. The knowledge of Christendom about the Talmud was for nearly a century and a half derived from Wolf's statements. Vol. iii. is a supplement to vol. i.; vol. iv. to vol. ii. Wolf's work forms the basis of Steinschneider's catalogue of the Bodleian Library, which has references to it on nearly every page. He issued a history of Hebrew lexicons (for his doctor's dissertation; Wittenberg, 1705), and "Notitia Karæorum" (Hamburg, 1721).

BIBLIOGRAPHY: Steinschneider, Bibliographisches Handbuch, 1859, pp. xviii. et seq.; idem, Cat. Bodl. col. 2730; Fürst, Bibl. Jud. iii. 528; McClintock and Strong, Cyc.
T.
J.

WOLF BEN JOSEPH OF DESSAU: German scholar and author; born at Dessau in 1762; died there March 16, 1826. Left an orphan at an early age, he was educated by his father-in-law, Reb Gumpel; and in 1775 he lived with his uncle, Jacob Benscher, at Berlin, where he attended the communal school. He officiated as a teacher in Freienwalde-on-the-Oder from 1780 to 1782, was in Wriezen from 1782 to 1789, and lived in Sandersleben from 1789 to 1796, when he settled in Dessau, having been appointed tutor in the Herzog Franz Schule. At the same time he discharged the duties of secretary to the Jewish community of Dessau, and also officiated as preacher. Wolf was the author of the following works: "Minḥah Ṭehorah" (2 vols., Dessau, 1805), the Hebrew text of the Minor Prophets, with a German translation, and a Hebrew preface entitled "Solet la-Minḥah"; "Daniel" (ib. 1808), with the original text, a Hebrew commentary, and a German translation; a collection of sermons delivered in the synagogue, with a Hebrew translation (ib. 1812); "Shir" (ib. 1812), a eulogy on the Book of Esther, to which it was appended; a collection of sermons (ib. 1813); "Charakter des Judentums" (Leipsic,

1817), an apology written in collaboration with Gotthold Solomon; and "Yesode ha-Limmud" (Dessau, 1819), an elementary text-book of Hebrew, with a glossary. He was also a collaborator on the ninth and tenth volumes of "Ha-Meassef."

BIBLIOGRAPHY: P. Philippson, Biographische Skizzen, part ii., Leipsic, 1865; Benjacob, Ozar ha-Sefarim, p. 339; Zunz, in the introduction to Asher's English translation of Benjamin of Tudela, p. 293, London, 1840; Busch, in Jahrbuch für Israeliten, vi. 93; Zunz, G. V. p. 460; Delitzsch, Zur Gesch. der Hebräischen Poesie, pp. 107–108; Steinschneider, Cat. Bodl. cols. 2728–2729; Zeitlin, Bibl. Post-Mendels, p. 423.
E. C.
S. O.

WOLF, LUCIEN: English journalist and Anglo-Jewish historian; born in London Jan. 20, 1857. He began his journalistic career at a very early age on "The Jewish World," which he joined in 1874, and was principal leader-writer for that journal until 1893. He was assistant editor of the daily "Public Leader" in his twentieth year, and after other journalistic experience became foreign subeditor and leader-writer of the "Daily Graphic" in 1890, a position which he held until 1909. He is a fellow of the Institute of Journalists, and has held honorary positions in connection with it. For four years (1893–97) he was London correspondent of "Le Journal" of Paris. Wolf is one of the best-informed English writers on foreign politics, and for many years his articles signed "Diplomaticus" on that subject in the "Fortnightly Review" were one of the characteristic features of the magazine. In 1905 some communications by him to the London "Times" on Russian finance attracted international comment, and evoked the unique compliment of a disclaimer by the Russian Minister of Finance.

Wolf has shown a strong interest in Anglo-Jewish history. He was intimately connected with the Anglo-Jewish Historical Exhibition, compiling the official catalogue and the "Bibliotheca Anglo-Judaica," a bibliography of Anglo-Jewish history, both in collaboration with Joseph Jacobs. He suggested the Jewish Historical Society of England, and became its first president, in addition to editing for it the volume devoted to "Manasseh ben Israel's Mission to Oliver Cromwell" (London, 1901). He has devoted considerable attention to Anglo-Jewish pedigrees, of which he has made large collections, and wrote "Sir Moses Montefiore," a centennial biography (1885). He also contributed important articles on "Anti-Semitism" and "Zionism" to the "Encyclopædia Britannica," and on the latter subject wrote adversely in controversy with Israel Zangwill, with whom, however, he joined forces in 1905 for the Jewish Territorial Organization.
J.

WOLF, MAX: Austrian composer; born at Weisskirchen, Moravia, Feb., 1840; died in Vienna March 23, 1886. His father, a wealthy business man, desired him to pursue a commercial career, but Max early evinced a marked inclination for music. He began studying composition at the age of sixteen, later continuing his studies under A. B. Marx in Berlin and Otto Dessof in Vienna. It is told that General von Moltke, having heard one of Wolf's productions played at a concert in Berlin, requested the artist to compose a military march, "that a bit o' fire may get into the boys."

In his earlier compositions Wolf somewhat imitated the style of Offenbach; but later he acquired more originality and inventive talent. Among his works may be mentioned: "Die Schule der Liebe" (1868), a one-act operetta, which passed through thirty-four consecutive performances in Berlin under the title "Die Blaue Dame"; "Im Namen des Königs," an operetta, performed in Berlin and on various other German stages; "Die Porträtdame," staged at Gratz and in Vienna; "Die Pilger" (Vienna, 1872), a three-act opera; "Cesarine"; and "Rafaela."

BIBLIOGRAPHY: Scribner's Cyclopedia of Music and Musicians; Wurzbach, Biog. Lex.; Allgemeine Zeitung, 1886, p. 1262; Neue Freie Presse, 1886, No. 7750.
s.   N. D.

WOLF, SIMON: American jurist, publicist, and philanthropist; born at Hinzweiler, Bavaria, Oct. 28, 1836; emigrated to the United States in

1848 and settled as a merchant at Ulrichsville, Ohio. He studied law at the Ohio Law College, Cleveland, and was admitted to the bar at Mount Vernon, Ohio, in 1861. He practised law at New Philadelphia, in the same state, for a year, and then moved to Washington, where he opened an office. From 1869 to 1878 he was recorder of the District of Columbia. President Hayes appointed him one of the civil judges at Washington, but he resigned in 1881 to accept the appointment of consul-general of the United States to Egypt, from which office he retired the following year. He was appointed and reappointed member of the Board of Charities for the District of Columbia, and at present practises law in Washington.

Simon Wolf.

Wolf has been for many years chairman of the Board of Delegates of Civil and Religious Rights, and in that capacity has had many occasions for submitting to the federal government grave questions of Jewish interest. He has been very active in the Independent Order B'nai B'rith, of which he was president from 1903 to 1905. He was the founder and president of the Hebrew Orphans' Home at Atlanta, Ga., and is president of the Board of Children's Guardians, Washington.

He is a prominent freemason, an able lecturer, and a recognized orator who has devoted much time to philanthropic work among all classes.

Wolf is the author of "The American Jew as Patriot, Soldier, and Citizen" (Philadelphia, 1895) and of biographies of M. M. Noah and Com. U. P. Levy.

BIBLIOGRAPHY: American Jewish Year Book, 1905, p. 208.
J.   F. T. H.

WOLFENBÜTTEL: German city, particularly noted for its **Samson-Schule,** a school, originally at Brunswick, founded by Herz Samson, on a legacy by his father. On June 4, 1786, Philip, the brother of Herz, opened a Talmud school at Wolfenbüttel for boys. The funds of these schools were increased by subsequent gifts of the founders and their descendants. In 1805 the two foundations were combined as the "Samson Free School," and were transformed into a German seminary and school in charge of four teachers. Instruction was given in German, French, arithmetic, geography, history, and calligraphy, and the school consisted of one class with eight free scholars. In 1813 the Brunswick school was incorporated with the free school, and the funds were combined, with the condition that five additional free scholars should be admitted. As paying boarding pupils had also been received at the request of many parents, a second class was organized. Instruction in the Talmud was subsequently discontinued. In 1843 the institution was changed to a grammar-school with three classes, and was named "Samson-Schule." After 1871 it was gradually enlarged to a high school, and by 1903 it had gained the status of a real-school with six classes. It was under the direction and supervision of the ducal school-board of Brunswick, and was empowered to give certificates for one year's military service. Since 1881 Christian boys have been admitted as pupils and receive special religious instruction. In 1903 the faculty included the director, Ludwig Tachau, five teachers with university training, and three elementary teachers, one of whom also acts as resident teacher. The trustees were Counselor of Justice Magnus of Brunswick, Gustav Cohen of Hanover, and L. Samson of Wolfenbüttel. Among the former pupils of the institution may be mentioned M. I. Jost, Leopold Zunz, and Samuel Meyer Ehrenberg (1807–46), who was later its director. Although the institution was frequently enlarged, in 1895–96 a new and larger building with all modern improvements was erected to accommodate the constantly increasing attendance. There are twenty-five full and between eighteen and twenty partial scholarships, in addition to numerous foundations for the assistance of pupils, even after they have left the institution.

s.   L. K.

WOLFENSTEIN, MARTHA: American authoress; born at Insterburg, Prussia, Aug. 5, 1869. During her infancy her parents emigrated to the United States, settling in Cleveland, Ohio, in the public schools of which city she received her education. She died March 17, 1905.

Martha Wolfenstein contributed short stories to nearly all the leading Jewish journals, and to various other magazines. Among her writings may be mentioned: "A Priest from the Ghetto" and "A Sinner in Israel" (in "Lippincott's Magazine"); and "The Renegade" (in the "Outlook"). In 1901 the Jewish Publication Society of America published a book from her pen entitled "Idyls of the Gass" (German transl. in "Die Zeit" of Vienna).

BIBLIOGRAPHY: American Jewish Year Book, 1905.
A.   F. T. H.

WOLFF: American family which derives its origin from the Robles family of Surinam, Dutch Guiana. The following is the family tree:

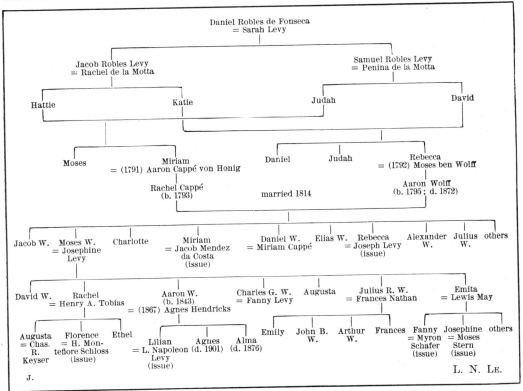

WOLFF PEDIGREE.

WOLFF, AARON : Danish merchant; born in the Island of Saint Christopher on Aug. 6, 1795; died in London, England, Jan. 12, 1872. He was a descendant of Daniel Robles de Fonseca. Soon after 1814 he removed to the Island of St. Thomas, Danish West Indies, where he was appointed to the office of "Stadthövidsmand" (mayor), which ranked him next to the governor of the island. He received from the King of Denmark the decoration of the Order of Dannebrog; and he was a member of the Royal Council; president of the Bank of St. Thomas, which he managed for thirty-two years; chairman of the Marine Slip; president of the St. Thomas Marine Insurance Company; and for many years president of the synagogue. Wolff anticipated the action of the King of Denmark by emancipating all his slaves previous to the Emancipation Proclamation of 1843.

J.   L. N. Le.

WOLFF, ABRAHAM ALEXANDER : German rabbi; born at Darmstadt April 29, 1801; died at Copenhagen Dec. 3, 1891. His first teacher was his father, Alexander Wolff, a merchant, who was well versed in the Talmud and who destined his son for a rabbinical career. At the age of six the boy astonished the scholars of Darmstadt by his knowledge of Hebrew. He continued his studies under Rabbi C. Meklenburg, and at the same time attended the gymnasium of his native city. In 1817 he went to Mayence, where he studied under Herz Scheyer and Michael Creizenach, the latter teaching him mathematics. He then pursued his education under Abraham Bing in Würzburg, and entered the university there. Three years after his graduation at Giessen (Ph.D. 1821), he was ordained rabbi, and in 1826 was appointed "Landesrabbiner" of the province of Oberhessen with a residence at Giessen. In 1828 he received a call from the community of Copenhagen; and he assumed office as chief rabbi of Denmark on May 16, 1829.

The synagogue of Copenhagen had been burned in 1795 and was still in ruins, so that the Jewish community—both Sephardim and Ashkenazim—was split into several congregations. Wolff, by his great energy, induced the Jews to build a new synagogue, which was dedicated on April 12, 1833; and in the same year Wolff published in Danish the agenda for the synagogal liturgy. He is credited also with improving the relations between the Jews and the Christians of Denmark. In recognition of his services in the organization of the Royal Library of Copenhagen he was created a knight of the Order of Dannebrog (Oct. 6, 1854), and was also awarded the title of professor.

Wolff was the father of Danish homiletics; and during his long rabbinical career of sixty-five years he delivered about 5,000 sermons, of which over forty in German and about 300 in Danish have been published. His works are as follows: "Der Prophet Habakkuk" (Darmstadt, 1822), the Book of Habakkuk with literal and metrical German translations, a critical commentary, and an introduction on prophecy; "Torat Yisrael" (German title, "Lehrbuch der

Israelitischen Religion"; Mayence, 1825), a text-book for instruction in Judaism in schools (an abridged Danish edition was published by Paul Martin Möller in "Bibliotheca Theologica," xvii. 67–81, and the entire work was translated into Swedish by M. Henrikes, Stockholm, 1844); "Einige Worte an das Publicum über Mein Israelitisches Religionsbuch" (*ib.* 1826); "Abhandlung über den Eid" (in Weiss, "Archiv für Kirchenrecht," 1830); "Drei Vorlesungen als Einleitung zu Vorträgen über das Judenthum" (Copenhagen, 1838); "Agende for det Mosaiske Trossamfunds Synagoge" (Leipsic, 1839); "'Ateret Shalom we-Emet" (first published under the pseudonym of "Aniam ben Schmida" in "Orient, Lit." ii., Nos. 23–26, and then, in enlarged form, as a book, Leipsic, 1857), a compilation of the opinions of ancient rabbis with regard to the piyyuṭim; "Tefillat Yisrael," the prayers with a Danish translation (*ib.* 1856); "Aufgefundener Briefwechsel Zwischen einem Hochgestellten Protestantischen Geistlichen und einem Rabbiner" (first in "Ben Chananja," 1860, and then in book form with additions and corrections, Leipsic, 1861); "Lærebog i den Israelitiske Religion" (*ib.* 1861); "Bibelhistorie for den Israelitiske Ungdom" (*ib.* 1862); "Bibelhistorie for Skole og Hjem" (*ib.* 1867); and "Talmudfjender" (*ib.* 1878). He also made a Danish translation of the Pentateuch, which was published on his ninetieth birthday.

BIBLIOGRAPHY: I. S. Gräber, in *Ozar ha-Sifrut*, v. 331–332; Kayserling, *Bibliothek Jüdischer Kanzelredner*, i. 329 *et seq.*; idem, *Gedenkblätter*, p. 85; *The Reformer*, x., No. 37, p. 1; N. Sokolow, *Sefer Zikkaron*, pp. 36–37; *idem*, in *Ha-Asif*, vi., part 1, pp. 147–148.

s.   M. SEL.

WOLFF, JOSEPH : Missionary and Oriental traveler; born at Weilersbach, near Bamberg, Germany, in 1795; died at Ile Brewers, Somerset, England, May 2, 1862. His father, who was rabbi at Württemberg, sent him to the Protestant Lyceum at Stuttgart, and while still a youth he learned Latin, Greek, and Hebrew. Leaving home on account of his inclination toward Christianity, he was converted after many wanderings, and was baptized on Sept. 13, 1812, by Leopold Zolda, abbot of the Benedictine monastery of Emmaus, near Prague. In 1813 he commenced to study Arabic, Syriac, and Aramaic, and in the following year attended theological lectures in Vienna. In 1815 he entered the University of Tübingen, and by the liberality of Prince Dalberg was enabled to study theology for nearly two years, as well as Arabic and Persian, Biblical exegesis, and ecclesiastical history. In 1816 he arrived in Rome, where he was introduced to Pope Pius VII. by the Prussian ambassador. He was soon afterward admitted as a pupil of the Collegio Romano, and later of the Collegio di Propaganda; but in 1818, having publicly attacked the doctrine of infallibility, he was expelled from the papal dominions on account of erroneous opinions. After a brief stay at the Monastery of the Redemptorists at Val Sainte, near Freiburg, he went to England to visit the eccentric Henry Drummond, M.P., whose acquaintance he had made at Rome. He soon declared himself a member of the Church of England.

Friendship with Henry Drummond.

At Cambridge he resumed the study of Oriental languages, with the purpose of visiting Eastern lands to prepare the way for missionary enterprises. Between 1821 and 1826 he traveled as a missionary in Egypt and the Levant, and was the first modern missionary to preach to the Jews near Jerusalem. He sent Christian boys from Cyprus to England for education, and then continued his travels through Persia, Mesopotamia, Tiflis, and the Crimea.

About 1828 Wolff commenced an expedition in search of the Lost Ten Tribes. After suffering shipwreck at Cephalonia and being rescued by Sir Charles Napier, whose friendship he retained through life, he passed through Anatolia, Armenia, and Khorassan, where he was made a slave, but ultimately set free. Undaunted, he traversed Bokhara and Balkh, and reached Cabul in a state of nudity, having walked six hundred miles through Central Asia without clothing. In 1836 he went to Abyssinia, and afterward to Sana in Yemen, where he preached to the Wahabites. His next journey was to the United States. He preached before Congress and received the degree of D.D. at Annapolis, Md., in 1836. He was ordained deacon by the Bishop of New Jersey, and in 1838 priest by the Bishop of Dromore. In 1843 he made another journey to Bokhara to ascertain the fate of Lieut.-Col. Charles Stoddart and Captain Connolly, a committee formed in London having raised the sum of £500 for his expenses. The men for whom he searched had been executed, and the same fate threatened Wolff. According to his own story he confronted the sovereigns of Central Asia with imperturbable audacity, refusing to conform to their court etiquette or to observe any ceremony in his speech; on being asked to become a Moslem he returned a defiant reply. The threat of execution was, however, a pretense, and he was ultimately rescued through the efforts of the Persian ambassador. In 1845 he was presented with the vicarage of Ile Brewers in Somerset, where he resided until his death.

Before joining the Church of England, Wolff had entertained all sorts of religious opinions. He was a member of the little band which met in Henry Drummond's house at Advent, 1826, for a six days' study of the Scriptures, which resulted in the origination of the Catholic Apostolic Church under the leadership of Irving. In his missionary travels he went fearlessly among the most fanatical peoples, and he may be said to have been one of the pioneers of modern missionary enterprise. His greatest opposition came from the Jews, and to overcome this he made use of extraordinary methods, as when, in Bombay, he wished to inspect the synagogue of the Beni-Israel. In spite of his education and his extensive travels, Wolff was possessed of many erratic ideas. In India he was considered a fanatic; in England he was at one time ostracized by the clergy; and he bent all facts to suit his theories of the lost tribes. He believed the East India Company to be the "kings of the east" (Rev. xvi. 12).

In 1827 Wolff married the sixth daughter of the Earl of Orford, Georgiana Mary Walpole, by whom he had a son, **Sir Henry Drummond Wolff,** the politician and diplomatist. After her death he married (1861) Louisa Decima, daughter of James King, rector of St. Peter-le-Poer, London. Wolff signed himself "Apostle of Our Lord Jesus Christ for Palestine, Persia, Bokhara, and Balkh." He was the author of the following works: "Missionary Journal" (London, 1824; 2d ed. 1827-29); "Sketch of the Life and Journal of Joseph Wolff" (Norwich, 1827); "Journal of Joseph Wolff for 1831" (London, 1832); "Researches and Missionary Labors Among the Jews, Mohammedans, and Other Sects Between 1831 and 1834" (Malta, 1835; 2d ed., London, 1835); "Journal of the Rev. Joseph Wolff Continued, An Account of His Missionary Labors for 1827-31 and from 1835 to 1838" (London, 1839); "A Narrative of a Mission to Bokhara to Ascertain the Fate of Colonel Stoddart and Captain Connolly" (London and New York; 7th ed. 1852); "Travels and Adventures of Joseph Wolff" (London, 1860; 2d ed. 1861; translated into German, 1863).

BIBLIOGRAPHY: *Travels and Adventures of Joseph Wolff*, London, 1861; *Dict. Nat. Biog.*
J. V. E.

WOLFF, JOSEPH: Russian historian; born at St. Petersburg; died at Heidelberg 1900. The son of a book-dealer, he early developed a passion for reading historical works. After completing a course of study at the gymnasium of his native city, he entered the University of Leipsic, where he devoted himself to the study of history, especially of Polish and Lithuanian affairs. Among his works the following may be mentioned: "Senatorowie i Dignitarze Wielkiego Ksiestwa Litewskiego, 1386-1795" (Cracow, 1885); "Syd Ministrem Króla Zygmunta" (*ib.* 1885), a historical sketch; "Ród Gedymina" (*ib.* 1886); and "Kniziowie Litewsko-Rusey od Końca xiv w." (Warsaw, 1895). Wolff was a corresponding member of the Academy of Cracow.

BIBLIOGRAPHY: *Encyklopedja Powszechna*, xv. 471; *Sistematicheski Ukazatel Literatury o Yevreyakh*, 1893.
s. J. Go.

WOLFF, JULIUS: German surgeon; born at Märkisch Friedland, West Prussia, March 21, 1836; died at Berlin Feb. 18, 1902. He received his education at the Grauekloster Gymnasium, and at the University of Berlin, graduating in 1860, whereupon he established himself as surgeon in the Prussian capital. He took part in the wars of 1864, 1866, and 1870-71, receiving the Iron Cross for non-combatants. In 1868 he was appointed privat-docent, and in 1884 assistant professor of surgery, at the University of Berlin. In 1890 he became chief surgeon of the newly founded orthopedic dispensary at the university. In 1899 he received the title of "Geheimer Medizinalrat."

Wolff contributed more than a hundred essays to medical journals, treating of orthopedics, osteopathy, and laryngology. He was the author also of "Das Gesetz der Transformation der Knochen" (Berlin, 1892), published by the Royal Prussian Academy of Sciences.

BIBLIOGRAPHY: Pagel, *Biog. Lex.*
s. F. T. H.

WOLFF, MAURICE: Swedish rabbi; born in 1824 at Meseritz, Prussia, where his father officiated as rabbi. He studied at the universities of Berlin and Leipsic, and was in 1849 appointed rabbi in

Culm, Prussia, whence he was called in 1857 to the rabbinate of Göteborg, Sweden. He is the author of the following works: "E Senusi's Begriffsentwickelung des Muhammedanischen Glaubensbekenntnisses" (Arabic and German), Leipsic, 1848; "Philonische Philosophie," *ib.* 1849 (2d ed., Göteborg, 1858); "Moses ben Maimon's Acht Capitel," Leipsic, 1863; "Muhammedanische Eschatologie," *ib.* 1872; "Bemerkungen zu dem Wortlaute der Emunot we-Deot," *ib.* 1878 (2d ed. 1880); "Philos Ethik," Göteborg, 1879; "Beiträge zur Philosophie der Historie," Stockholm, 1882; and "Zur Characteristik der Bibelexegese Saadia Alfajjumis," 1884-85.

BIBLIOGRAPHY: A. de Gubernatis, *Dictionnaire International des Ecrivains du Jour*; *Allg. Zeit. des Jud.* 1899, No. 45; *Jew. Chron.* Oct. 19, 1899.
s. F. C.

WOLFF, OSKAR LUDWIG BERNHARD: German improvisator and novelist; born at Altona July 26, 1799; died at Jena Sept. 13, 1851. He early manifested an unusual aptitude for acquiring languages, and while still in college he translated Shakespeare's "Macbeth" into German verse. In 1817 he entered the University of Berlin, where he devoted himself to the study of medicine, history, and literature, afterward settling in Hamburg, where he pursued a literary career. The success of the Italian improvisators Gianni and Spricci developed in him a desire to embrace a similar career; and in 1825 he started on his first tour, visiting Bremen, Hanover, Brunswick, Wolfenbüttel, Weimar, Leipsic, and Dresden, and meeting everywhere with marked success. Among his admirers were Goethe and Grand Duke Karl August, the latter of whom appointed him to a professorship in Weimar. At this period of his career Wolff embraced Christianity; and in 1829 he was appointed assistant professor of modern literature at the University of Jena, being promoted to a full professorship in 1837.

Among Wolff's works may be mentioned: "Sammlung Historischer Volkslieder und Gedichte der Deutschen" (1830); "Altfranzösische Volkslieder" (1831); "Poetischer Hausschatz des Deutschen Volkes" (1839; 15th ed. appeared before the author's death); "Die Geschichte des Romans von dessen Ursprung bis auf die Neueste Zeit" (1841); "Hausschatz der Deutschen Prosa" (1845); and "Handbuch Deutscher Beredsamkeit" (1846). A collection of his novels and stories was published in Jena in 1841-1842.

BIBLIOGRAPHY: O. L. B. Wolff's autobiography in his collected works, Jena, 1841-42; *Neuer Nekrolog der Deutschen*, 1851; Schröder, *Lexikon der Hamburger Schriftsteller*, ii. 707, Altona, 1830.
s. M. Z.

WOLFF, ULLA (pseudonym **Ulrich Frank**): German authoress; born at Gleiwitz, Silesia, April 2, 1850; daughter of Max Hirschfeld. She received her education at home and in Breslau and Vienna. In 1880 she took up her residence in Berlin, where she lived for years. In 1876 her first production, "Der Vampyr," appeared at the Lobetheater in Breslau, and was well received; in 1878 this was followed by "Der Herr Kollege," staged at the Nationaltheater in Berlin, but meeting with scant success. She thereupon gave up writing for the stage, and devoted her literary activity to stories and novels, among which may be mentioned: "Das Waldgeheimniss," Bremen, 1879; "Das Wunderkind," Berlin, 1884; "Frau Ottilie" and "Bettlers Heim," *ib.* 1886; "Weltliche Beichte," *ib.* 1887; "Der Kampf ums Glück," *ib.* 1888; "Rechtsanwalt Arnau," *ib.* 1891; "Der Kompagnon," *ib.* 1895; "Adelig," *ib.* 1896; "Gestern und Heute," *ib.* 1897; "Margarethe Eilert," *ib.* 1898; "Die Lene," *ib.* 1902; "Die Einsiedlerin"; "Die Geschichte Zweier Sabbathnachmittage" (appeared in English translation in "The New Era Illustrated Magazine," New York, Nov. and Dec., 1904); "Beim Patriarchen"; "Die Toten"; "Können Damen Allein Reisen?"; and "Die Frühlingsgnade."

BIBLIOGRAPHY: Gustav Karpeles, in *Nord und Süd*, part 327; Regine N(eisser), in *Deutsche Hausfrauen-Zeitung*, Sept. 11, 1904.
s.   F. T. H.

WOLFFSON, ISAAC: German jurist and politician; born Jan. 19, 1817; died at Hamburg Oct. 12, 1895. He was prominent in German politics, and prior to 1871 was a member of the North German Reichstag, being afterward elected to the German Reichstag. In the Jewish community he was a councilman for many years, and was known for his philanthropic deeds.

BIBLIOGRAPHY: *Jew. Chron.* Oct. 16, 1895, p. 9.
s.   F. S. W.

WOLFKAN OF RATISBON: Jewish convert to Christianity and traducer of the Jews; lived in the second half of the fifteenth century. He was prominent in the SIMON OF TRENT affair (1475), on which occasion he, in order to vent his spite against his former coreligionists, asserted that the Jews had very likely killed the child, since they needed Christian blood for the Passover festival. This affair, and particularly Wolfkan's testimony, a few months later afforded Bishop Henry a pretext for making a similar accusation against the Jews of Ratisbon, whom he charged with having eight years previously bought a Christian child, which they then murdered for ritual purposes.

BIBLIOGRAPHY: Grätz, *Gesch.* viii. 259, 267.
s.   M. SEL.

WOLFLEIN OF LOCHAMEN (LOCHHEIM): Medieval Bavarian litterateur; known for his compilation of the so-called "Lochheimer Liederbuch" (about 1450), a collection of medieval German folk-songs, numerically arranged. Under No. 15 appears the following dedication in Hebrew characters: "Der Allerliebsten Barbara Meinem Treuen Liebsten Gemaken," which seems to indicate that Wolflein was a Jew; as does also the expression "Vil guter Jar," which appears under No. 5, and which was used only by Jews. On the other hand, it is noteworthy that "Barbara" is not a current name among Jewish women, and that a Christian grace after meals appears under song No. 36.

BIBLIOGRAPHY: Arnold, in Chrysander's *Jahrbuch für Musikalische Wissenschaft*, ii. 12 *et seq.*; Güdemann, *Gesch.* iii. 160.
s.   M. SEL.

WÖLFLER, BERNARD: Austrian physician; born at Praschnoaugezd, Bohemia, Dec. 8, 1816. After having studied philosophy at the gym-

nasium of Prague, he attended the University of Vienna (1836–42), where he devoted himself to the study of medicine. From 1843 to 1845 he acted as assistant physician at the communal hospital of Vienna; from 1845 to 1849 he was a private practitioner in Prague; and in 1849 he was appointed director of the Jewish hospital of Vienna. When Baron Anselm von Rothschild, impressed by the efficiency of the hospital in spite of its limitations, erected a better building and presented it to the congregation, Wölfler devoted his whole energy to the new institution, and visited several hospitals of western Europe in order to study their methods.

Wölfler founded (1872) a society for the gratuitous care of consumptives, without distinction of creed. Two country houses at Kierling, near Klosterneuburg, were secured; and every summer a number of patients have enjoyed a stay there with proper professional attendance. Wölfler has been a curator, and for many years president, of the institute for the blind founded at the Hohe Warte by Dr. Ludwig August Frankl. In 1866 the government conferred upon him the Order of Francis Joseph, and in 1873 he received the title of imperial councilor. On the occasion of his eightieth birthday (1896) the committee of the Jewish community of Vienna hung his portrait, painted in oil by the Countess Adrienne Pötting, on the wall of the committee-room in the hospital, among the portraits of its benefactors.

BIBLIOGRAPHY: Wurzbach, *Biog. Lex.* vol. lvii., *s.v.*
s.   N. D.

WOLFNER, THEODORE: Former Hungarian deputy; born at Uj-Pest June 18, 1864; educated at the gymnasium and at the school of technology at Budapest. After spending some time in his father's tannery in order to acquire a practical knowledge of the manufacture of leather, he undertook an extensive journey, visiting Germany, Egypt, Palestine, and Turkey.

Wolfner was an alderman of Uj-Pest, a member of the county council of Pesth, president of the national association of leather manufacturers, director of the technological industrial museum, and a member of the chamber of commerce and industry in Budapest. In 1896 he represented Gödöllö in the Hungarian Parliament, a fact which is the more noteworthy because of the circumstance that this district was the favorite residence of Francis Joseph I., and was under the influence of court officials. In 1904 Wolfner was the recipient of a rare honor, when the king appointed him a captain of hussars in the reserves and elevated him to the Hungarian nobility.

BIBLIOGRAPHY: Sturm, *Országgyülési Almanach*, 1901.
s.   L. V.

WOLFSOHN, AARON. See HALLE, AARON BEN WOLF.

WOLFSOHN, WILHELM: German poet and essayist; born at Odessa Oct. 20, 1820; died at Dresden Aug. 13, 1865; studied medicine and philosophy at Leipsic. He began his literary career with translations from Latin into German under the pseudonym **Carl Maier.** In 1843 he traveled in Russia, lecturing on German literature with such success that he was offered a professorship on condition that he would embrace Christianity; this, however, he declined. Returning to Germany, he became assistant editor of the "Blätter für Literarische Unterhaltung," and later edited, in connection with Robert Prutz, "Das Deutsche Museum." In 1852 he moved to Dresden, where he continued his literary activity.

In addition to several volumes of poems, Wolfsohn was the author of the following works: "Jeschurun" (1841), a Jewish almanac; "Die Schönwissenschaftliche Literatur der Russen" (Leipsic, 1843); "Russlands Novellendichter" (3 vols., 1848-51), with an introduction; "Neues Laienbrevier" (1851), an anthology of German poetry; and "Schauspiele" (1857-59). Of his plays, "Nur eine Seele" became very popular, while "Die Osternacht," the plot of which was based on the blood accusation, was less successful. Besides contributing literary essays to the "Leipziger Zeitung," he edited a magazine of his own which from 1862 to 1864 appeared under the title "Russische Revue," and afterward under the title "Nordische Revue." His "Russische Geschichten" were published after his death by his son (Leipsic, 1884). Wolfsohn married outside of his faith, and his children were brought up as Christians.

BIBLIOGRAPHY: *Unsere Zeit,* 1865, p. 713; Georg Ebers, in *Ueber Land und Meer,* 1865, No. 50; *Allg. Zeit. des Jud.* 1865, pp. 537, 554, 602; *Allgemeine Deutsche Biographie.*
    S.   D.

WOLLEMBORG, LEONE: Italian economist; born at Padua 1859; graduated from the university of his native city (1878). He made a special study of political economy, and his most noteworthy achievement was the establishment of rural savings-banks for the peasantry and small farmers of Italy. He represented the city of Padua in the legislative assembly during several consecutive terms, and from 1900 to 1903 he held the portfolio of finance in Zanardelli's cabinet.

Wollemborg is the author of the following works: "Alcune Lettere Inedite" (Padua, 1880); "Il Costo di Produzione Come Norma per la Determinazione del Valore" (Bologna, 1882); "La Prima Cassa Cooperativa di Prestiti in Italia" (Padua, 1883); "L'Ordinamento delle Casse di Prestito" (Verona, 1884); "Le Casse Cooperative di Prestito"(*ib.* 1884); "Sull' Ordinamento Economico Giuridico delle Latterie Sociali Cooperative" (Bologna, 1887); "Sul Dazio Compensatore pei Cereali" (Padua, 1887); "Sull' Istituzione di un Consorzio fra gli Agricoltori del Friuli" (Udine, 1887); "Sull' Assicurazione in Generale e in Particolare sull' Assicurazione Contro i Danni della Mortalità del Bestiame (*ib.* 1887); "Sull' Assicurazione Contro i Danni della Mortalità del Bestiame e sui Modi di Ordinaria" (*ib.* 1887); "La Teoria della Cooperazione" (Bologna, 1887); "Les Caisses Rurales Italiennes, Rapport pour l'Exposition Universelle de Paris en 1889" (Rome, 1889); and "Che Cosa e una Cassa Rurale?" (Cuneo, 1895).

    S.   U. C.

WOLLHEIM, ANTON EDUARD W. DA FONSECA: German playwright and journalist; born in Hamburg Feb. 12, 1810; died in Berlin Oct. 24, 1884; studied at the University of Berlin (Ph.D. 1831). Shortly after the completion of his studies he removed to Paris, where he became infatuated with the daughter of a Portuguese nobleman who lived there in exile. In order to win her he enlisted in Don Pedro's regiment, and was wounded during an engagement. His fiancée having died in the meantime, Wollheim left Paris for Hamburg; and upon the death of his father he went to Copenhagen, where he was engaged in cataloguing the valuable Pali manuscripts in the royal library, being later appointed by King Frederick VI. secretary to the private council. In 1838 he went to Vienna, where he produced his first play, "Andrea," which represented the adventures of the French marshal Andrea Massena. Ten years later his "Raphael Sanzio" was staged in Vienna; while his "Rosen im Norden," or "Des Teufels Wette," was received with equal favor both in Berlin and in Hamburg. In 1849 he was appointed instructor in Oriental and modern languages at the University of Berlin, being at the same time engaged as the Berlin correspondent of the London "Morning Chronicle."

From 1854 to 1858 Wollheim was employed in the diplomatic service of the Austrian government; and during the following six years he edited at Hamburg a weekly journal, the "Controle," devoted to the promotion of Austrian interests. In 1868 he established his own summer theater at St. Georg, a suburb of Hamburg; and two years later he went to Berlin, where he became editor of the "Moniteur Officiel du Gouvernement Général." From 1871 to 1872 he was attached to the German embassy at Paris. Among his works may be mentioned: "National-Literatur der Skandinavier" (1876-77); "Deutscher Seehandel und die Französischen Prisengerichte"; "Indiscretionen" (1883); and "Neue Indiscretionen" (1884), containing many autobiographical data. He died in poverty in St. Hedwig's Hospital at Berlin.

BIBLIOGRAPHY: *Brümmer's Dichter-Lexikon; Schröder's Lexicon der Hamburger Schriftsteller;* Wurzbach, *Biog. Lex.;* Gottschall, *Deutsche National-Literatur des Neunzehnten Jahrhunderts;* Max Mendheim, *A. E. Wollheim da Fonseca.*
    S.   M. Z.

WOLOWSKI (Hebr. **Shor**): Polish family, several members of which became converted to Christianity. It flourished in southern Poland in the seventeenth and eighteenth centuries, and was directly descended from Osias Tebu'at-Shor. It was not until the family had become Christianized that it adopted the Polish form of the name, "Wolowski." Jewish members of this family bearing the name Twiaschor, and Christian members of the name of Wolowski are still living in Brody and Lemberg. The following are the more important members:

Elisha Shor: Rabbi of Rohatyn, Galicia, during the middle of the eighteenth century. He was a zealous adherent of the Shabbethaians, and, having become a follower of Jacob FRANK, he was a leader of the Frankists before that party joined the Catholic Church. When internal friction among the Frankists led to public proceedings against them (June 11, 1756), Elisha was charged with being the leader of those who seduced the people to lewdness. The prosecution failed, however, to make out a strong case against the Frankists, and Elisha returned to Rohatyn. Upon the death of Bishop Dembowski of Lemberg, which took place shortly after, the Frankists lost a stanch protector; they were outlawed, and the Polish rabble began murdering and pillaging among them, Elisha being one of the first victims (Nov., 1757).

Ḥayyah Wolowski: Daughter of Elisha. She played a conspicuous part among the Shabbethaians, and later among the Frankists. She had an excellent knowledge of the Zohar, and whenever she fell into one of her trances she would cite it from memory.

Nathan ben Elisha; after baptism, **Michael Wolowski:** Brother of Solomon, and like him prominently identified with the Frankists, although in a lesser degree.

Solomon ben Elisha; after baptism, **Lucas Franciszek Wolowski:** A son of Elisha, and a prominent figure in the Frankist movement in Poland, and later in Offenbach. Together with Judah Koysa, he was one of the chief delegates of the Frankists at the disputation held at Kamenetz-Podolsk (June 20, 1757) at the suggestion of Bishop Dembowski. Two years later (May 16, 1759) he went to Lemberg at Frank's request, in order to seek official recognition for the sect from Wratislav Lubienski, later primate of Gnesen. As a condition of the baptism of all Frankists, he asked that the newly appointed Archbishop Mikolsky should arrange a disputation between them and the rabbis, which request was granted (as to the time and result of this disputation see FRANK, JACOB, AND THE FRANKISTS). On Sept. 19, 1759, Solomon, together with 1,000 followers of Frank, embraced the Catholic faith in Lemberg, whereupon he assumed the name of Wolowski. Even after the death of Frank he was active as a mediator between Eve, Frank's daughter, and the Polish Jews. He died in Poland at the close of the eighteenth century, prior to the final division of Poland.

BIBLIOGRAPHY: Kleczewski, *Dissertacya Albo Mowa o Pismach Zydowskich*, Lemberg, 1759; Pikalski, *Zlosc Zydowska*, ib. 1760; J. Calmanson, *Essai sur l'Etat Actuel des Juifs de Pologne*, Warsaw, 1796; Skimborowicz, *Zywot Zkon in Nauka Jakoba Josefa Franka*, ib. 1866; Grätz, *Frank und die Frankisten*, Breslau, 1868.
s.   S. O.

WOLPER, MICHAEL: Russian educator and author; born in Wilna 1852; educated in the rabbinical school of his native city. He was graduated in 1872, since when he has been active as a teacher in Jewish elementary schools. Later in 1905 he officiated also as inspector of the Jewish seminary in Wilna, and as censor of Hebrew publications.

Wolper is the author of: "Pervaya Uchebnaya Knizhka po Zakonu Yevreiskoi Religii" (Wilna, 1880; 3d ed. 1882); "Mesillah Ḥadashah" (*ib.* 1888), a method for the study of Hebrew; and, in collaboration with Nemser, a catechism of Judaism. He has published also various other Russo-Jewish school-books.

BIBLIOGRAPHY: *Sistematicheski Ukazatel*, St. Petersburg, 1893.
H. R.   J. Go.

WOMAN, CREATION OF. See EVE.

WOMAN, RIGHTS OF: The problem of the rights of woman in Jewish law and custom is presented mainly in five phases: (1) the power of the father over his daughter; (2) woman's right of inheritance; (3) the powers and duties of the husband; (4) woman's opportunities for self-improvement and for following various occupations; and (5) the position of the mother.

(1) An early intimation of woman's freedom to choose her mate in life is found in Gen. xxiv. 58, where Rebekah, when her hand is sought for Isaac by the steward of Abraham, is asked:

Paternal Power. "Wilt thou go with this man?" Apparently, however, Isaac was not consulted at all as to whether he preferred a wife from Mesopotamia or a Canaanite or Hittite damsel. Although the story of Rebekah proves a deep-seated sentiment that a girl should not be coerced into marriage, the civil law gave no force to this sentiment, but recognized (Ex. xxi. 7) the power of the father to sell his daughter into bondage with the evident intention that she should become the wife of her master or of her master's son. The limitations to the rights of the father, as established by tradition, have been discussed under SLAVES AND SLAVERY. The daughter must be under the age of puberty, and the sale is justified only by extreme poverty, although the principle that the father can dispose of the daughter's hand remains intact, as is attested by expressions found elsewhere in the Torah, such as Deut. xxii. 16: "I gave my daughter to this man to wife." Tradition teaches (Ḳid. ii. 1), however, that a mature girl (בגרת), *i.e.*, one more than twelve and a half years of age, had the right to give herself in marriage, and the same privilege was allowed to a "widow from marriage," even in case she was immature. On the other hand, the father had the power to take a wife for his infant son without the son's consent (Ket. ix. 9).

Although marriages are celebrated between very young grooms and brides in Europe, it has for centuries been unusual, even in the eastern part of the Continent, to give immature girls in marriage. The form of the ketubah, as found in the "Naḥalat Shib'ah," published in 1666, speaks only of the bride as personally accepting the groom's proposal, and has no alternative form by which the father might accept for her.

The father is entitled to the work of his daughter's hands, and to what she finds (Ket. iv. 4), until she attains the age of maturity, which is reached very early; and he has the same rights over his infant son, the term here lasting six months longer.

The father was empowered to release his daughter from her vows (Num. xxx.), although, according to the Mishnah (Ned. x. 2), this power ceased when she attained her majority. This power of loosing vows was a great step in the progress of woman's freedom, marking an advance over both Babylonian and Roman law, under which the father could impose vows on his daughter even against her will.

(2) While in some systems of ancient law daughters or sisters were excluded from all rights of inheritance, and while in other systems they were put on an equality with sons or brothers, the Mosaic law gave the inheritance to the daughter or daughters when there were no sons, and, by

Female Inheritance. analogy, to sisters or paternal aunts when there were no brothers (see AGNATES). In no case, however, either under Mosaic or under rabbinic law, did an inheritance go to the mother (B. B. viii. 1). The institution of maintenance for minor daughters, and the rule that the father's estate must provide a dowry for the younger daughters which should equal the portion received by their elder sisters (unless the father had become impoverished, when the minimum dowry should be fifty zuzim), show that in the great majority of cases the daughters fared better than the sons (see B. B. ix. 1; Ket. iv. 11; and the clause concerning "benan nuḳban," or "female children," in the ketubah). No such favor was shown, on the other hand, to sisters or other kinswomen of the decedent, and traditional law sought merely to soften the hardships of agnatic succession in accordance with the natural feelings of a dying father, instead of setting the inheritance aside, as was done by the one hundred and eighteenth novel in the Roman Code and by American statutes enacted since the Revolution.

The position of the daughter or sister in regard to the right of inheritance was at least no worse than it is now under the law of England in case of landed estates.

(3) The position of married women in Israel was naturally improved when the wife brought a dowry to her husband instead of being purchased. שלוחים, the word for "dowry," appears for the first time in the arrangements for the

Relations to Husband. wedding between King Solomon and Pharaoh's daughter (I Kings ix. 16). The literal meaning of the term is "dismissal," since it was the father's present to his daughter when she left his house. The use of the word in this place proves the existence of a custom of bestowing on the daughter such gifts as would inure to the husband's benefit. In later times the Babylonian word "nedunya" was substituted for the Hebrew term. The "moḥar," or "price," which the groom had to weigh out according to the Pentateuch, was originally the sum paid for the bride, like the "tirḥatu" of Babylonian law; but in Israel, as in Babylon, it early became customary for the bride's father to restore this price to the husband at the wedding, whereupon it was secured by contract (the ketubah) to the wife as a jointure, payable upon the death of the husband or in case of divorce. Thus the moḥar was no longer incompatible, either in Babylonia or in Canaan, with the dowry bestowed upon the bride from her father's house. The obligation to return the dowry and to pay the jointure (ketubah) served as a good security against divorce on insufficient grounds.

POLYGAMY must have been very rare during the period of the Mishnah and Gemara; for though the wives of many rabbis are mentioned, there are no allusions to plural marriages. Among the personages named by Josephus, King Herod is almost the only polygamist. Concubinage, or the taking of an inferior wife (see PILEGESH), was no longer practised in mishnaic times.

The husband's duties to the wife are set forth in detail under KETUBAH. In the body of that instrument he binds himself to work for her, and to honor, support, and maintain her. The wife, if she brings no dowry, is bound to do such housework for the husband as grinding, baking, washing, cooking, suckling her child, spreading the bed, and working in wool (spinning, knitting, and the like). If she brings one slave woman, or the means to buy one, she need not grind, bake, nor wash clothes; if two, she need not cook, nor suckle her child; if three, she need not spread the bed nor work in wool; if four, she may "sit still in her chair" (Ket. v. 5). She must, however, do certain small services for her husband which it would be improper for any but the wife to perform, such as washing his hands and face (comp. the Talmud *ad loc.*). R. Eliezer maintained, however, that though she brought a hundred slaves, the husband might insist on her working in wool, lest idleness should lead her into intrigues; and R. Simeon ben Gamaliel declared the husband should not allow idleness in his wife, as it would drive her into melancholia. It is noteworthy that a married woman was never bound to work in the field.

As shown under ASSAULT AND BATTERY, the husband must not strike his wife; if he does, he is liable for "damage, pain, and shame," the same as to a stranger. The legal remedy was less effectual as a protection to the wife, however, than the religious warning (B. M. 59a), which ran: "A man should always be careful lest he vex his wife: for as her tears come easily, the vexation put upon her comes near [to God]; since, though all other gates be shut, the gate of tears is never closed."

(4) The fear that an idle wife would fall either into intrigues or into melancholia shows that study or reading was not a common diversion of women. The Talmud (*ad loc.*) suggests that they might maintain cheerfulness by playing chess ("nardeshir"). On

Woman and Culture. the other hand, it would appear from a passage of the Mishnah (Ned. iv. 3), that it was usual to teach girls to read, which of course meant to read the Bible, though it was regarded as highly improper to instruct them in the oral law.

The tone which pervades the Bible and the Talmud, however, is not very different from that which runs through the literature of other nations, showing that woman was held of less account than man. Leah boasts of the many sons she has borne to Jacob; Hannah prays to the Lord for a man child; and the Mishnah speaks of him who prays that his wife may bring forth a son rather than a daughter. In Hebrew law women were not competent witnesses either in civil or in criminal cases. It was a disgrace to a warrior to be killed or disabled by a woman, while a woman who could not find a man to marry her was held in contempt. Recognition was won, however, by women of high talent, such as Deborah in Israel's heroic epoch, the prophetess Huldah in the later days of the kingdom of Judah, and R. Meïr's wife in the mishnaic period; while the nine years' reign of Queen Salome was a golden age in Jewish history. The last chapter of Proverbs could not have been written among a nation which despised its women. Wives were frequently empowered by their husbands to manage a shop or store ("ḥanut"), and widows were appointed guardians for their infant children; so that business was not an unknown field to them (Ket. ix. 4-5.) In modern times much of the retail trade of the Jews, and not a little even of wholesale commerce, has been carried on by women, while their husbands have been poring over the Bible or Talmud, either at home or in the bet ha-midrash.

(5) The position of the mother is higher under the Mosaic law than under any other system of antiquity. By the fifth commandment the mother is to be honored equally with the father, while in the moral law (Lev. xix. 3) the command to "fear" the mother, that is, to treat her with re-

Woman as Mother. spect, is placed even before the duty of "fearing" the father. Death is threatened him who strikes or who curses his mother, as well as him who thus offends against his father. The Talmud, in showing under what extreme provocation the righteous man will maintain an outward regard for his parents (Ḳid. 30b–32a), gives stories of outrageous mothers who were treated with the utmost respect. This sentiment was not shown by the Greeks toward even the best of mothers; for in the first book of the "Odyssey" Telemachus reproves Penelope, and imperiously sends her away to her own apartment to mind her own womanly business. In the so-called Sumerian family laws, the Babylonian code goes farther than Mosaic legislation, for the son must leave the parental house at his mother's bidding. The Book of Proverbs is full of expressions of reverence for the mother, who is the teacher of all virtues. It states that King Lemuel was taught wisdom by his mother. A curse is foretold for the man who forgets to reverence his mother.

The Baraita teaches the influence of the mother on her offspring through simple heredity when it says: "Most sons follow the nature of the mother's brothers" (B. B. 110a). This very belief that the mother gave her child a legacy of good or evil qualities which, though hidden in her, appeared in her brothers, must have raised the standing of mothers and of womankind in general.

See also DAUGHTER IN JEWISH LAW; HUSBAND AND WIFE; MAJORITY; MARRIAGE; MOTHER; WIDOW.

E. C.   L. N. D.

WOOD FESTIVAL, THE. See AB, FIFTEENTH DAY OF.

WOODBINE: Borough in Cape May county, New Jersey; established as an industrial village Aug. 28, 1891; incorporated as a borough in April, 1903. It is situated on a tract of land which originally comprised 5,300 acres, and was purchased by the trustees of the Baron de Hirsch Fund as a site for an agricultural and industrial colony. The primary intention of the founders of Woodbine was the establishment of an agricultural colony for Jewish immigrants from eastern Europe. Farming was to be the chief occupation, but, to make it more remunerative, it was decided at the same time to reserve a certain portion of the tract as

Early Development. a site for the future village of Woodbine, which should contain a local market for farm produce as well as factories to give employment to members of the farmers' families.

By the summer of 1892 about fifty farmhouses were completed, and all were occupied in the fall of

that year. In the same year the firm of Meyer Jonasson & Co. opened a cloak-factory which gave employment to more than one hundred persons. Almost all of these employees lived on farms, some of them residing at a distance of three miles from the village. Unfortunately, the economic depression of 1893 affected the cloak industry unfavorably, and the decreased demand led to a partial suspension of work in the Woodbine factory. The discontent among the operatives and the strikes which followed caused the factory to shut down; and the firm finally removed from the village. In addition to this, many of the farmers, unable to earn a living either from the land or in the factory, left for New York or Philadelphia. A large number of those who remained were employed to cut cord-wood; and others were engaged in clearing the town lots of stumps, while the young people picked huckleberries, or sought work in the tomato-canning factory in Ocean View near Sea Isle City.

In 1894 and 1895 the outlook became much brighter. A clothing-factory was established in the

Factories Established. village by Daniel & Blumenthal of Philadelphia; and the population began to increase. This was followed by the establishment of several other manufactories in Woodbine; and these additions, though gradual, were accompanied by an almost uninterrupted growth of population. While the early settlers were mostly from southern Russia, later arrivals increased the proportion of Lithuanians and added to the number from the government of Kherson, the latter immigrants being chiefly from Odessa. A small group of Rumanians also went to Woodbine.

The early plans of the founders of Woodbine have not been realized. Instead of becoming an agricultural colony with an industrial adjunct, it is an industrial village with a few farmers. In 1905 there were probably only twenty farmers who derived a part or all of their income from the soil; and, although many of the villagers cultivated small gardens, a number of the more distant farms were entirely unoccupied. Considerable farming skill and capital are required to bring about much improvement in the soil; and the Woodbine farmers possess

Failure of Farms. but a limited amount of either. Notwithstanding all these drawbacks, however, the farmers of Woodbine have made real progress within recent years. Those who supply the local demand for milk have learned something of balanced rations and of economy in feeding, while the truck-gardeners and the fruit-growers have acquainted themselves with market conditions and have increased the fertility of their soil. Grapes, which were once sold in Woodbine itself, now find a market at Vineland; and garden-truck, which formerly could not be disposed of at a profit, is sold to advantage at Ocean City and Sea Isle City.

The farmers of Woodbine have profited unmistakably from the Baron de Hirsch Agricultural School, which was established in 1895 and has gradually extended the cultivated area of the school farms. It has a model poultry-plant and an apiary, as well as orchards, vineyards, and greenhouses, and covers in all about 300 acres of land. The establishment of the school was largely due to the efforts of H. L. Sabsovich. Its curriculum is chiefly practical, attention being given primarily to various branches of applied husbandry and to farm mechanics, while the theoretical instruction is mainly directed toward familiarizing the pupils with the principles underlying modern farming. A considerable number of the alumni of the school are devoting themselves to practical agriculture. One of them is the successful manager of the Allivine farm near Vineland, N. J.; three are farming for themselves in Connecticut, two in Colorado, one in northern New Jersey, one in New York state, and two in Woodbine. A much larger number are working for other farmers. The alumni include four college graduates, two graduates of a medical school, one lawyer, twelve college students, three members of the United States navy, one of the United States army, and a number of machinists.

Agricultural School.

The four local public schools had in 1905 an enrolment of over 500, and the average attendance in 1904 was 450. At first included in the school district of Dennis township, the Woodbine schools were organized into a separate district in April, 1903, and temporary trustees were appointed until the spring of 1904. Woodbine has also a kindergarten and a Talmud Torah. The public buildings include two synagogues, a bath-house, a hospital (formerly a hotel), and an engine-house and meeting-hall for the volunteer fire-company. The local industries are housed in five brick buildings, while water and electric lighting are supplied to most of the houses in the borough from the central pumping-station.

Schools and Synagogues.

In 1901 the average individual income was $7.30 per week, and the average earnings per family were $675 per annum. There were in that year 175 single and double cottages in Woodbine, of which 14 were owned by the Baron de Hirsch Fund and 161 by the people; of the latter only 23 were rented. Seventy per cent of the cottages varied in cost of construction between $575 and $1,000, the remainder being erected at a cost of over $1,000 each. Their estimated total cost was $157,450, of which $58,200 had been paid in 1901. In 1905 the borough proper had 223 private houses, these and the outlying farmhouses being inhabited by 325 families. Jacob Kotinsky, entomologist for the territory of Hawaii, Joseph W. Pincus, agriculturist of the Baron de Hirsch School, and Jacob G. Lipman, soil chemist and bacteriologist of the New Jersey State Experiment Station, were among the early settlers in Woodbine. The population in 1920 was 1,406, of whom 95 per cent were Jews. See also JEW. ENCYC. i. 262, s.v. AGRICULTURAL COLONIES.

A. 　　　　　　　　　　　　　　　　　　　J. G. L.

WOOLF, ALBERT EDWARD: American chemist and inventor; born in New York Sept. 26, 1846; educated in the public schools of that city and at the College of the City of New York. Among Woolf's achievements may be mentioned: the introduction of peroxid of hydrogen for bleaching ostrich-feathers and for use as an antiseptic (1876), and the discovery (1889) of the antiseptic properties of sea-water decomposed by electrolysis (electrozone), a discovery now widely applied in the treatment of drinking-water, garbage, and sewage, and used by the United States authorities in suppressing yellow fever in Havana, Cuba (1899). Woolf was a member of the American Institute of Electrical Engineers, and of the Society of Arts, London, England. He died Apr. 19, 1920.

BIBLIOGRAPHY: *Who's Who in America*, 1903–5.
A. 　　　　　　　　　　　　　　　　　　　F. H. V.

WOOLF, EDWARD: American musician and novelist; born in London, England, Sept., 1803; died in New York March 14, 1882. After acting as a musical conductor in his native city, he emigrated (1839) to New York, where his abilities were soon recognized, and where he was engaged as orchestral leader, musical instructor, and choirmaster. He contributed many novels to "The Jewish Messenger" during the early part of the existence of that periodical; among these may be mentioned "The Jewess of Toledo," "The Vicomte d'Arblay," and "Judith of Bohemia."

Woolf's sons all attained more or less prominence: **Solomon,** as a professor of art and drawing for forty years in the College of the City of New York; **Benjamin E.** (born in London Feb., 1836; died in Boston, Mass., Feb. 6, 1901), as a dramatist and composer ("The Mighty Dollar" and "The Doctor of Alcantara"); **Michael Angelo** (born in London 1837; died in New York March 4, 1899), famous for his street caricatures; **Philip** (born in New York Feb. 7, 1848; died in Boston 1903), as a physician and novelist; and **Albert Edward,** as an inventor.

BIBLIOGRAPHY: Isaac S. Isaacs, *Edward Woolf*, in *Publ. Am. Jew. Hist. Soc.* 1904.
A. 　　　　　　　　　　　　　　　　　　　A. S. I.

WOOLF, SIDNEY: English lawyer; born in London 1844; died March 12, 1892; educated at Neumegen's school and at University College, London. After passing the examination of the Incorporated Law Society, he joined his brother as a partner in a firm of solicitors. Then, after having been a pupil of Murphy, queen's counsel, he was called to the bar by the Middle Temple in 1873. He began to practise in mercantile and criminal cases, and later became the leading advocate of his day in bankruptcy matters. On Jan. 24, 1890, he was appointed queen's counsel.

Woolf's first legal book dealt with the law on adulteration of food (1874). He afterward wrote, in collaboration with Middleton, on the law and practise of compensation, as well as on the liquidation of business firms by the court. He was active as a communal worker, was one of the principal supporters of the Westminster Jews' Free School; and served as warden and as council member of the Berkeley Street Synagogue. He was a member also of the council of the Anglo-Jewish Association.

BIBLIOGRAPHY: *Jew. Chron.* and *Jew. World*, March 18, 1892.
J. 　　　　　　　　　　　　　　　　　　　G. L.

WORM: "Rimmah" and "tole'ah" are the terms most frequently employed in the Bible to connote not only the earthworm, but any elongated crawling creature, such as the maggot, caterpillar, larva of an insect, and the like. Thus, in the account of the "worms" which appeared in the manna (Ex. xvi. 20, 24) the terms evidently refer to caterpillars which feed on putrefying matter, while the "worms" described as destroying vineyards and the gourd (Deut. xxviii. 39; Jonah iv. 7) were some variety of beetle or insect larva, and the "worms" in Isa. xiv. 11, Job xvii. 14, xxi. 26, and similar passages were maggots or larvæ which feed on dead bodies. For the meaning of "zoḥale ereẓ" (Mic. vii. 17) see SERPENT.

Metaphorically, the worm symbolizes lowliness and helplessness (Isa. xli. 14; Ps. xxii. 7 [A. V. 6]; Job xxv. 6), but in Isa. lxvi. 24 the worm and fire together connote eternal pain.

There are several species of earthworm (*Lumbricus*) in Palestine, and *Myriapoda* abound.

In the Talmud also "rimmah" and "tole'ah" are found as general terms for "worm," while the generic denomination for all crawlers is "sheḳaẓim u-remasim" (see REPTILES). Several species are mentioned under special names, such as בחש, a kind of water-worm (*Nais tulifex*; Zeb. 22a); שילשול, rainworm (Ḥul. 67b); מורנא, the worm which lives in the tracheæ of sheep and causes them to cough (*Strongulus filaria*; *ib.* 49a); and קוקאני, worms found in the intestines of fishes (*Lingula cingulum*; *ib.* 67b). Since the raven is heartless toward its young, Providence, according to B. B. 8a, takes care of them by causing maggots to arise from their excrement, thus furnishing them with food (comp. Rashi on 'Er. 22a). With the worms which arose from rotten bran Noah fed the chameleon in the ark (Sanh. 108b). A host of worms infest the human body, both living and dead (Tem. 31a; Ab. iii. 1). There are worms in the liver (ארקתא; Shab. 109b) and in the belly (כירצא), a remedy for the latter being the milk of an ass mixed with the leaves of the bay, or bread and salt taken with fresh water before breakfast (Giṭ. 69b; B. M. 107b). Garlic is a cure for worms in the great intestine (Bek. 82b), while the tapeworm is driven out by the raw meal of barley or by hyssop (Ber. 36a; Shab. 109b). מורנא is the name of a worm which finds lodgment between the prepuce and glans penis and is removed by circumcision, so that even Gentiles submitted to the operation ('Ab. Zarah 26b). From the mouths of the false spies whom Moses sent to Canaan came forth worms (Soṭah 35a), and Yer. Yoma 39a records similar phenomena proceeding from the nose of a heretic (comp. also Yoma 19b; B. M. 84b).

BIBLIOGRAPHY: Tristram, *Natural History of the Bible*, p. 300; Lewysohn, *Zoologie des Talmuds*, p. 334.

E. G. H.   I. M. C.

WORMS: Town in Rhein-Hesse, former grand duchy of Hesse, Germany. Like Mayence and Cologne it has one of the oldest Jewish communities in Germany. A legend relates that the Jews of Worms were descended from the Benjamites who had migrated from Palestine to Germany (Brüll's "Jahrbücher," 1879, iv. 34 *et seq.*). It is possible that there was a congregation there in the time of the Romans, but the first historical reference is the statement that Jews from this city visited the fair at Cologne about the year 1000 (Aronius, "Regesten," No. 149; Kober, "Studien zur Mittelalterlichen Geschichte der Juden

in Köln am Rhein," p. 9, note 3, Breslau, 1903). The earliest authentic information regarding the community, however, dates back only to 1034.

Early History. On Jan. 18, 1074, Emperor Henry IV. granted the "Jews and other citizens of Worms" exemption from customs duties in the royal-customs ports of Frankfort, Boppard, Dortmund, Goslar, etc., as a reward for their fidelity. Already at this time the Jews lived in a special quarter of the city. About 1090 Henry IV. granted the community, which was represented by the Jew-bishop Solomon, the privileges of free commerce and exemption from taxation; he designated

Exterior of the Old Synagogue at Worms.
(From a drawing by C. Gross Mayer.)

the Jews as "subjects of his treasury," and placed them under his immediate protection, so that neither royal nor episcopal functionaries could exercise any jurisdiction over them, their only authority being the BISHOP OF THE JEWS, appointed by themselves, and confirmed in his office by the emperor. These privileges were renewed by the emperors Frederick I., Barbarossa (April 6, 1157), and Frederick II. (about 1236).

On May 18 and 25, 1096, the Crusaders murdered all the Jews of Worms—about 800 in number—with the exception of some who committed suicide and a few who were forcibly baptized. Later a new community was formed in Worms; and this suffered during the Second Crusade (1146), and again in 1196, when the victims included Dulcina, wife of R. Eleazar, his daughters Belat and Hannah, and his son Jacob. During the division of the kingdom at the close of the twelfth century Worms was besieged by King Otto, and the Jews, who sided with Philip of Swabia, took part in the defense. On July 8, 1230, Pope Honorius III. issued from San Rieti an order directing the Archbishop of Mayence to compel the community to pay the sum of 1,620 marks before the following Easter, threatening it with exclusion from all

Taxation. dealings with Christians if it failed to raise the amount. In 1241 the state taxes of the Jews of Worms amounted to 130 marks in silver, and on Feb. 28, 1255, Bishop Richard of

Worms transferred to the chapter of the local cathedral, among other revenues from the city, the sum of 40 pounds heller which the congregation was obliged to pay annually on St. Martin's Day (Nov. 11). Between 1254 and 1271 the Jews of Worms were taxed 2,870 pounds heller and 250 marks in silver for the public peace insured by the Rhenish Alliance; and from 1269 to 1275 they were compelled to pay 200 marks annually to King Richard of Cornwall. In 1294 orders were issued by King Adolphus and by the bishop, forbidding the Jews to acquire real estate in the parish of St. Martin. By an edict dated March 9, 1316, Louis the Bavarian granted the city of Worms the privilege of levying on the Jewish community a yearly tax of 100 pounds heller in addition to the 300 pounds it had thitherto paid; and on May 1, 1338, he informed the council of Worms that the Jews of that city were bound by agreement to pay the sum of 2,000 gulden toward the king's contemplated expedition against France, and that, if necessary, force might be employed in collecting this sum.

By an edict dated at Speyer Jan. 4, 1348, the emperor Charles IV. surrendered the Jews of Worms to the city government, but on March 1, 1349, at the time of

Exterior of the Old Synagogue at Worms.
(From a photograph.)

the Black Death, the community was practically annihilated, the Jews setting fire to their houses, and more than 400 persons perishing in the flames. The women's wing of the synagogue, added in 1213 through the munificence of Meïr and his wife, Judith, was also destroyed. An edict of Charles IV., dated March 29, 1349,

Fourteenth and Fifteenth Centuries. gave to the citizens of Worms the property left by the Jewish community; but a few years later (1353) the city desired to again admit Jews, and on Nov. 20, 1355, Charles IV. allowed it to grant them the right of residence. In May, 1377, the Jewish community of Worms, numbering

XII.—36

thirty-six persons, pledged itself, in a Hebrew document addressed to the city council, to pay in "voluntary" taxes the sum of 20,000 gulden; and in the following year (Aug. 28, 1378) the city was granted the right of extending protection to the Jews. This privilege was renewed by King Wenceslaus on May 5, 1400, after he had already ordered the city (by edict dated April 22, 1391) to afford protection to his "Kammerknechte," as he styled the Jews. On March 17, 1398, the city council enacted that every Jew or Jewess over twelve should pay one old tournois in LEIBZOLL, but not one farthing more. On Oct. 31, 1400, King Ruprecht confirmed the privileges granted the Jews of Worms by Henry IV., by virtue of which they were allowed to exchange money in any part of the city, except in front of the mint or in the minters' offices of exchange. The same king enacted also, by a decree dated at Heidelberg July 29, 1406, that the Jews of Worms might be tried only by the municipal court, a privilege which was at first granted for a period of six years only, but was extended by King Sigismund (1414).

In 1409 the Jews of Worms were accused of the murder of a Christian child, but as there was no evidence against them, they were acquitted by the council, although they lost part of their property. In 1422 the community, encouraged by the council, refused to pay the "Hussite taxes," and was therefore outlawed by King Sigismund, who, through the margrave of Baden, confiscated and sold the houses vacated by the Jews. On Aug. 1, 1431, King Sigismund assured the Jews of Worms that all edicts annulling the outstanding debts owed them would be declared invalid upon the payment by each Jew of an indemnity. This caused an uprising among the peasantry, which was, however, speedily quelled, the ringleaders being punished. Two years later (1433) the community presented Sigismund with the sum of 20 florins as a coronation tribute, and promised to pay an additional 100 florins in the middle of the following Lent. On Nov. 6, 1441, regulations referring to the Jews were enacted by the gilds of the bakers, butchers, and marketmen. About 1470 the Jews of Worms occupied thirty-two houses, for which they paid the city a ground rent of 960 gulden. In 1484 the citizens of Worms wished to expel the Jews, but this was prevented by the emperor, and ten years later (June 14, 1494) Maximilian confirmed the Jews in all their privileges, while on April 4, 1500, he forbade the city to encroach upon the imperial prerogative concerning them. In 1495, and again in 1496, the palsgrave Philip and his son, **Sixteenth** Duke Ludwig, visited the "Juden-**Century.** schul" at Worms (Boos, "Urkundenbuch der Stadt Worms," iii. 395, 401). In 1509 complaint was lodged against the Jews of Worms charging them with violence against mes-

pecially Dr. Chemnitz, advocated the expulsion of the Jews from Worms, whereupon the elector Frederick took the congregation under his protection; the opposition of the gilds, however, forced the Jews to emigrate (April 20, 1615), after which their synagogue was demolished, the cemetery laid waste, and the tombstones destroyed. After the suppression of the uprising by the troops of Frederick, an imperial decree was promulgated (Jan. 19 or 20, 1616) ordering both the palsgrave and the Bishop of Speyer to readmit the Jews; in commemoration of this event the eve of the Feast of Shebat was designated as a fast-day for the community of Worms. During the Thirty Years' war the Jews of the city were compelled to pawn even the silver of the synagogue in order to raise the manifold contributions exacted from them. At the same time they suffered from a pestilence which raged in the Jewish quarter in 1632 and

CEMETERY AT WORMS.
(From a photograph.)

sengers of the imperial court. In the following year (1510) Emperor Maximilian gave the community permission to hold a public meeting in Worms ("Sulamith," 1811, iii. 416 *et seq.*; Hormayr's "Archiv," 1812, iii., Nos. 11, 12). On Nov. 22, 1559, Ferdinand I. issued from Vienna an order to the city council of Worms, directing it, under penalty of heavy punishment, to protect the Jews in all their privileges during the quarrel between the city and Bishop Dietrich, and forbidding the levying of any special taxes. Ordinances regulating Jewish affairs were issued by the council of Worms on Dec. 6, 1570; Nov. 1, 1584; Dec. 23, 1605; as well as in later years.

In 1615 some members of the city magistracy, es-

1635; and Emperor Ferdinand II. therefore issued an edict (Vienna, May 16, 1636) directing the council of Worms to be lenient in levying **During the** taxes upon the Jews, and ordering **Thirty** the release of Jews who had been im-**Years'** prisoned on account of inability to **War.** pay. Three years later Ferdinand III. gave his nephew Anselm Casimir, Elector of Mayence, full authority to appoint a committee consisting of the Bishop of Worms, the Prince of Dalberg, and the council and Jews of Worms, or their representatives, for the purpose of framing new Jewish regulations. On May 31, 1689, the city of Worms was invaded by the French under Melac, and at the same time a terrible catastrophe visited the Jews. The entire Jewry, which displayed the imperial arms on both gates, was burned, together with the interior of the synagogue, and the so-called Rashi Chapel. The ruins of the synagogue were used as a stable and storehouse. In 1698 a committee was formed for the purpose of restoring the Jewish community of Worms, which had been broken up by the French invasion. By an agreement dated June 7, 1699, the council of Worms pledged itself to grant the Jews certain concessions, and this arrangement was confirmed by Joseph I. (April 19, 1707) in order to protect the Jews against any infringements of their rights on the part of the council; it was later approved also by Emperor Charles VI. (Oct. 26, 1714).

In 1751 one-fifth of the revenues of the city of Worms was furnished by the Jewish taxes. The treaty of 1699 was again confirmed by a decree dated at Vienna March 10, 1766 ("Jeschurun," iv. 99 *et seq.*). In 1872 a Jew named Edinger represented Worms in the Hessian Diet, while Levy was second mayor. In 1874, prior to the enactment of the new liberal school law, S. Rothschild was appointed teacher in the non-sectarian school.

The Jewish community of Worms, which in 1875 numbered 1,000 members, consisted in 1910 of about 1,500. In addition to a large number of other institutions, the city has a Jewish hospital, a ḥebra ḳaddisha, a society for the support of sick women, an endowment society, a society for the distribution of fuel, and an association for the support of school children. There is also the Dalberg Lodge of the Order B'nai B'rith.

D.   A. LEW.

Until the close of the twelfth century the Jews of Worms engaged in extensive and remunerative business enterprises, but through restrictive measures these were gradually rendered unprofitable, and at length only trading in money was left open to them. In 1165 even this branch of business was denied them, and during the thirteenth century more and more of them engaged in usury. In 1255 orders were issued regulating the interest on loans, and the Jews were thereby prohibited, under pain of severe punishment, from charging more than 33⅓ per cent per annum.

Social Condition.

Michael Gernsheim, a Judenbischof of Worms, Seventeenth Century.
(From a drawing in possession of M. Gernsheim, New York.)

During the Middle Ages the Jews, as citizens of Worms, were permitted to acquire real estate; they might even occupy the commons (that is, territory belonging to the commonwealth), until Adolf of Nassau on July 28, 1294, issued an order against this. In spite of their various privileges, however, the Jews might not dwell among the Christians, but were assigned a special quarter of the town, separated from the Christians by walls and gates. These gates had various names, of which may be mentioned "Porta Judæorum," "Juden Borter," and "Juden Burgetor." The synagogue formed the center of the Jewish quarter. It was erected in 1034 through the munificence of a wealthy Jew, Mar Jacob, and his wife, Rachel; and in spite of the many accidents that have befallen it in the course of time its appearance has changed but little. It is built in early Moorish style, and was originally intended for men only. It had three entrances. The apse for the Torah scrolls consisted of a semicircular protuberance of the wall. The women's wing of the synagogue, connecting with the northern wall of the older structure, was built in 1213. The men's synagogue had five inscriptions; the women's, four.

Prominent in the legendary and historic accounts of the Jews of Worms is the so-called Rashi Chapel, built in 1624 by David ben Isaac Joseph Oppenheim. This building was erected so close to the synagogue that it prevented the use of one of the entrances of the latter. The fact that Rashi lived for a short while in Worms, where he was a pupil of Isaac ha-Levi, gave rise to the legend that he taught in the edifice erected 500 years after his death. According to a report by Juspa Shammes (1648–78), in which mention is made of a "prayer-house of Rashi," the congregation took occasion to place an inscription in the building, which they termed the Rashi Chapel. Abraham Epstein of Vienna discovered in a niche of the Rashi Chapel an inscription designating the niche as the seat of David Oppenheim. The synagogue and the chapel stand in a court, and are surrounded by one wall. Inside this court is a square space enclosed by a wall two meters high, and in which there formerly grew a nut-tree. The use and purpose of this space can no longer be deter-

Rashi Chapel.

mined. From the chapel a path inside the courtyard led to the Judenbäder, which were located underground. In 1895 the work of excavating them was begun, but they are not yet accessible.

The cemetery dates from the first half of the eleventh century, and is located on the left side of the present Andreasstrasse, near the old Andreas gate. The oldest tombstone bears date of 1077, and is that of one Jacob Baḥur. Of other tomb-

Cemetery. stones may be mentioned a monument erected in honor of twelve elders of whom a legend reports that, during the Crusade of 1096, they asked the town councilors for protection, and, on being refused, murdered the councilors, whereupon they all committed suicide in the cemetery. There are also the tombstones of Jekuthiel ben Jacob (1261); Baruch ben Meïr, father of Meïr of Rothenburg (1275); and Meïr of Rothenburg (1307); a tombstone of four sisters, with inscriptions arranged in four rows (1419); and also those of Jacob Mölln (1427) and Juspa Shammes (1678). Mention may be made also of thirteen inscriptions relating to members of the Bacharach family (seventeenth and eighteenth centuries). The Jewish congregation of Worms had its own public park, for the care of which each member had to contrib-

Interior of the Old Synagogue at Worms.
(From an old lithograph.)

ute a yearly sum fixed by the Jewish council. The guarding and keeping of the park devolved upon the communal servant, who officiated as "schulklopfer" and sexton also.

The internal affairs of the community were arranged by a Jewish council of twelve members headed by the BISHOP OF THE JEWS. This institution dated back to the eleventh century. The Jew-

Organiza- ish bishop was elected by the council, and his appointment originally had to

tion. be sanctioned by the emperor. On July 25, 1312, however, Bishop Emerich ordered that the Jew-bishop should no longer be confirmed in his office by the emperor, but by the bishop of the diocese; and also that a Jew-bishop once appointed should retain his title until his death, although his official duties should each year

devolve on another member of the council. On the death of a Jew-bishop the new appointee was to pay to the bishop 60 pounds Worms pfennigs; this stipulation, however, was changed by Bishop Frederick (Feb. 8, 1439), who ordered that the Jewish community should pay 20 florins each year on St. Martin's Day, in lieu of the former payment.

Next to the communities of Mayence and Speyer, that of Worms occupied the most prominent place in the fields of science and literature, and many of the foremost Lorrainese savants were born in Worms; it was from that city also that the most famous "taḳḳanot Shum" were issued. Among the most prominent rabbis and scholars of Worms may be mentioned:

Isaac ben Eleazar ha-Levi, Rashi's teacher (11th cent.); Isaac ben Judah, a contemporary of Rashi; Eleazar ben Judah Roḳeaḥ (13th cent.); Moses ben Aaron, teacher of the last-named (d. 1240); Baruch ben Meïr, father of Meïr of Rothenburg (d. 1275); Nathan ben Isaac (d. 1333); Jacob Mölln (d. 1427); Meïr ben Isaac (1511); Abraham Samuel Bacharach (d. 1615); Elijah Loanz (d. 1636); Simson Bacharach (d. 1670); Aaron Teomim (rabbi until 1687; d. Cracow, 1690); Jair Ḥayyim Bacharach (rabbi, 1689–1702); Naphtali Hirsch Spitz (d. 1712); Menahem Mendel Rothschild (d. 1732); Moses Broda of Ungarisch-Brod (d. 1742); Hirsch Auerbach of Brody (1743–78).

Worms had the distinction of having the first Jewish mayor in Germany in the person of Ferdinand Eberstadt (born there Oct., 1808; died at Mannheim March 10, 1888). He was elected to the mayoralty in 1848, having proved himself a leader in the liberal movement of the time. He held office till 1851, when, owing to the reaction, he resigned, and later removed to Mannheim. He represented the same district, Alzey-Worms-Oppenheim, in the upper house of the Hessian Landtag.

A man of considerable importance in the history of the Jews of Worms was the sexton and "schulklopfer" Jephthah Juspa ben Naphtali, known also by

Juspa the name **Juspa Shammes.** He was born in Fulda in the beginning of

Shammes. the seventeenth century, and studied until 1623 under R. Phinehas Horwitz in his native town. In that year he went to Worms, where he remained until his death in 1678.

He was the author of the following works: (1) "Shir Musar" (Amsterdam, 1690), a poem on morals; printed on one folio sheet. (2) "Ma'ase Nissim" (Frankfort-on-the-Oder, 1702), a Hebrew work in which history and fiction are intermingled, and of which only one copy is extant (in Oxford). It was translated into Judæo-German (Amsterdam, 1723; Homburg, 1725; Fürth, 1767). (3) A "Teḥinnah"

Interior View of Women's Section in the Old Synagogue at Worms.
(From an old lithograph.)

for the eve of the first day of the month of Adar; still recited in Worms on that day. His work on the internal organization of the Jewish community of Worms, written in Hebrew and in Judæo-German, is in the possession of A. Epstein of Vienna.

BIBLIOGRAPHY: Zunz, Z. G. pp. 29-60, 304-459; Lewysohn, Nafshot Zaddiḳim, Frankfort-on-the-Main, 1855; Rothschild, Die Judengemeinden zu Mainz, Speyer und Worms, Berlin, 1904; Carlebach, Die Rechtlichen und Sozialen Verhältnisse der Jüdischen Gemeinden Speyer, Worms, und Mainz, Leipsic, 1901; Jellinek, Worms und Wien, Vienna, 1880; Epstein, Jüdische Alterthümer in Worms und Speyer, pp. 1-13, Breslau, 1896; Aronius, Regesten; Saalfeld, Martyrologium; Breslau, in Hebr. Bibl. x.; G. Wolf, Zur Gesch. der Juden in Worms und des Deutschen Städtewesens, Breslau, 1862; Wiener, in Israelitisches Literaturblatt, 1878, No. 16; Berliner, Aus dem Inneren Leben, 1871, p. 9.
J.   S. O.

WORMS: Frankfort and English family, tracing its descent from Aaron Worms of Frankfort-on-the-Main in the middle of the eighteenth century. Aaron's great-great-grandson was created hereditary baron of the Austrian empire April 23, 1871; and a later descendant, Baron Henry de Worms, was raised to the British peerage as Lord Pirbright (see pedigree below).   J.

WORMS, AARON. See AARON WORMS.

WORMS, ASHER ANSHEL: German physician, mathematician, and Hebraist; born at Frankfort-on-the-Main toward the end of the seventeenth century; died there in 1769. Worms was graduated as Ph.D. and M.D. in 1723, and shortly afterward was appointed physician at the Jewish hospital of his native town, holding that position for more than forty-five years. Before graduating Worms published his "Mafteaḥ ha-Algebra ha-Ḥadashah" (Offenbach, 1722), a manual of algebra, with problems and their solutions. Four years later he published in Frankfort-on-the-Main a revised edition of the "Ma'adanne Melek," a chess manual (wrongly ascribed to Jedaiah Bedersi), adding to it a preface and a German poem. After graduation he occupied himself with mathematics, astronomy, natural history, philosophy, and music, the result of his studies being a number of unpublished scientific works, all of which are enumerated in his "Seyag la-Torah" (ib. 1766), a Masoretic commentary on the Pentateuch followed by a commentary on Saadia Bekor Shor's poem on the number of letters in the Bible. Before its publication this work circulated among rabbis and other

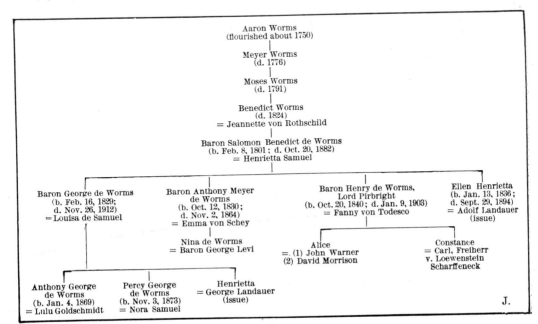

Aaron Worms
(flourished about 1750)
|
Meyer Worms
(d. 1776)
|
Moses Worms
(d. 1791)
|
Benedict Worms
(d. 1824)
= Jeannette von Rothschild
|
Baron Salomon Benedict de Worms
(b. Feb. 8, 1801; d. Oct. 20, 1882)
= Henrietta Samuel

Baron George de Worms
(b. Feb. 16, 1829;
d. Nov. 26, 1912)
= Louisa de Samuel

Baron Anthony Meyer
de Worms
(b. Oct. 12, 1830;
d. Nov. 2, 1864)
= Emma von Schey
|
Nina de Worms
= Baron George Levi

Baron Henry de Worms,
Lord Pirbright
(b. Oct. 20, 1840; d. Jan. 9, 1903)
= Fanny von Todesco

Alice
=. (1) John Warner
(2) David Morrison

Ellen Henrietta
(b. Jan. 13, 1836;
d. Sept. 29, 1894)
= Adolf Landauer
(issue)

Constance
= Carl, Freiherr
v. Loewenstein
Scharffeneck

Anthony George
de Worms
(b. Jan. 4, 1869)
= Lulu Goldschmidt

Percy George
de Worms
(b. Nov. 3, 1873)
= Nora Samuel

Henrietta
= George Landauer
(issue)

J.

WORMS PEDIGREE.

Hebrew scholars, who plagiarized much of its contents; and Wolf Heidenheim discovered that Joseph Heilbronn's "Mebin Ḥidot," although printed before the "Seyag la-Torah," contained much material taken from the latter, several passages being not even paraphrased.

BIBLIOGRAPHY: Berliner, in his *Magazin*, xiii. 62; Carmoly, *Histoire des Médecins Juifs*, pp. 210-211; Fuenn, *Keneset Yisrael*, p. 157; M. Horovitz, *Frankfurter Rabbinen*, iii. 63; idem, *Jüdische Aerzte in Frankfurt-am-Main*, p. 35.

s. M. SEL.

WORMS, ÉMILE: French jurist; born at Frisange, Luxembourg, May 23, 1838; educated at the University of Heidelberg and at Paris (LL.D. 1864). In 1863 he received a prize from the Institut de France for an essay on the commercial history of the Hanseatic League; and in 1867 he was again awarded a prize. In that year he was appointed assistant professor of law at the University of Paris; and later in the same year he received a call as professor of law at the University of Rennes, which position he held until 1898, when he removed to Paris.

Worms represented the French government at the statistical congresses of Florence (1867), The Hague (1869), St. Petersburg (1872), and Budapest (1876). He is the author of the following works: "Histoire Commerciale de la Ligue Hanséatique," 1864; "Sociétés par Actions et Opérations de Bourse," 1867; "Théorie et Pratique de la Circulation Monétaire et Fiduciaire," 1869; "Les Rapports du Droit Pénal avec l'Economie Politique," 1870; "L'Allemagne Economique, ou Histoire du Zollverein Allemand," 1874; "Sociétés Humaines et Privées," 1875; "Exposé Elémentaire de l'Economie Politique," 1880; "Nouveau Catéchisme d'Economie Politique," 1881; "De l'Etat au Regard des Erreurs Judiciaires," 1884; "Les Ecarts Législatifs," 1886; "De la Liberté d'Association au Point de Vue du Droit Public à Travers les Ages," 1887; "De la Propriété Consolidée, ou Tableau Historique et Critique de Tous les Systèmes les Plus Propres à la Sauvegarde de la Propriété Foncière et de Son Démembrement," 1888; "Une Association Douanière Franco-Allemande, avec Restitution de l'Alsace-Lorraine," 1888; "Les Attentats à l'Honneur," 1890; "Doctrine, Histoire, Pratique et Reforme Financière, ou Exposé Elémentaire et Critique de la Science des Finances," 1891; "Les Condamnations Conditionelles Suivant la Loi Française et Etrangère," 1891; "Essai de Législation Financière; le Budget de la France dans le Passé et le Présent," 1894; "La Politique Commerciale de l'Allemagne," 1895.

s. F. T. H.

WORMS, GUSTAVE-HIPPOLYTE: French actor; born in Paris March 21, 1837. He was graduated from the Conservatoire in 1857, winning the first prize for tragedy and the second for comedy. Soon afterward he was engaged at the Théâtre Français, where he made his début in 1859 as *Achille* in "Duc Job." In 1862 Léon Laya, appreciating the clever comedy work of Worms, engaged him to create the part of *Horace* in "Loi du Cœur," and his success was so marked that he secured a contract with the Théâtre-Michel, St. Petersburg, where he repeated his French successes. In 1875 he returned

to Paris, making his reappearance at the Gymnase as *Armand Duval* in "La Dame aux Camélias" with great success. After a short sojourn in Russia Worms was called to the Comédie-Française, Paris, in 1877, and elected a "sociétaire" in the following year. He retired from the stage in 1901.

Worms's original creations are: *Elie Mareau* in "Anne de Kerviller," *Georges* in "Les Rantzau," *Issarts* in "Service en Campagne," *Lude* in "Portraits et la Marquise," *Henri* in "Les Maucroix," *André de Bardannes* in "Denise," *Capitain Olivier* in "Antoinette Rigaud," *Stanislas de Grand-Redon* in "Francillon," *Marquis de Simiers* in "La Souris," *Jacquemin* in "Le Flibustier," and *François* in "Margot." He died Nov. 19, 1910.

BIBLIOGRAPHY: Vapereau, *Dict. des Contemporains*, p. 1606; *Nouveau Larousse Illustré*, s.v.

s. E. Ms.

WORMS, BARON HENRY DE. See PIRBRIGHT, HENRY DE WORMS, BARON.

WORMS, JULES: French physician; born in Paris Jan. 24, 1830; died there April 15, 1898; educated at the University of Strasburg (M.D. 1852). From 1853 to 1854 he acted as an assistant at the military medical school in Paris, and from 1854 to 1858 as first assistant surgeon of an infantry regiment. He took part in the Crimean war as a surgeon; was from 1858 to 1864 assistant physician at the Gros-Caillou Hospital in Paris; and from 1865 to 1875 was surgeon at the Rothschild Hospital. From 1870 to 1880 he officiated as statistician of the board of health of Paris, and in 1875 was appointed chief physician to the Northern Railroad (Chemin du Fer du Nord). Of his works may be mentioned "De l'Extirpation des Cystes de l'Ovaire," Paris, 1860.

BIBLIOGRAPHY: Pagel, *Biog. Lex.*

s. F. T. H.

WORMS, JULES: French genre painter; born in Paris Dec. 16, 1832. He studied under Philippon and Lafosse, and made his début at the Salon of 1859, his first painting, "Dragoon Making Love to a Nurse on a Bench in the Place Royale," auguring his success in the humorous vein. In 1861 he exhibited the painting "Arrest for Debt," and thereafter visited various countries, sojourning for some time in Spain, where he made several sketches of the manners and costumes of the people.

Worms was awarded medals for his exhibits at the Salons of 1867, 1868, 1869, and 1878, and was in 1876 created a chevalier of the Legion of Honor. Following is a list of his paintings, several of which were purchased at high prices by American collectors: "Fountain in Burgos" (1863; Laval Museum); "Tavern in the Asturias" and "Departure of Smugglers" (1865); "Kitchen in Valencia" (1866); "Scene in Old Castile" (1867); "Romance à la Mode" (1868; Luxembourg Museum); "Welcome Visitor" and "Precocious Talent" (1869); "Sale of a Mule" and "A Letter Box" (1870); "Sheep-Shearing in Granada" (1872); "An Aunt-in-Law" (1873); "The Little Cabinet-Maker" (1874); "A Sensational Novel" and "One's Vocation" (1875); "The Dance of the Vito at Granada" and "Going to the Review" (1876); "The Bull Fountain in Granada" (1877); "Distracted Barber" and "Every Age Its Pleasures" (1878); "Pastoral Tournament" (1879); "Before the Alcalde" (1880); "Public Writer" (1882); and "Politicians" (1883).

BIBLIOGRAPHY: Champlin and Perkins, *Cyclopedia of Painters and Paintings*, New York, 1892; Singer, *Allgemeines Künstler-Lexicon*, Frankfort-on-the-Main, 1901; Clement and Hutton, *Artists of the Nineteenth Century and Their Works*, Boston, 1880.
s. F. C.

WORMS, MAURICE BENEDICT DE: English financier and agriculturist; born in Frankfort-on-the-Main 1805; died in London 1867; grandson of Meyer Anselm de Rothschild, and son of Benedict de Worms, a distinguished member of the Jewish community of Frankfort. On a visit to the Far East in 1841, Maurice and his brother **Gabriel de Worms** purchased a large estate in Ceylon, which became known as the Rothschild Estate. Acre by acre was added to this estate, which was among the best-cultivated tracts of land in the island; and when the Worms brothers in 1865 disposed of their holdings, they had no less than 2,000 acres under cultivation, and more than 6,000 acres of forest land to be reclaimed. The brothers were among the pioneer settlers in Ceylon, and contributed largely to its prosperity. In his will Maurice de Worms bequeathed large sums of money to various Jewish charitable institutions.

BIBLIOGRAPHY: *Jew. Chron.* June 14, 1867.
J. G. L.

WORMS, RENÉ: French auditor of the council of state; son of Emile WORMS; born at Rennes Dec. 8, 1869; educated at the lyceum of his native city and at the Lycée Charlemagne and the Ecole Normale Supérieure in Paris ("docteur en droit," 1891; "docteur ès lettres," and "docteur ès sciences politiques et economiques," 1896). Worms, who is a laureate of the French Institute (Académie des Sciences Morales et Politiques), became a member of the higher statistical board in 1897 and of the consulting committee for agricultural statistics in 1903, besides being a member of many learned societies. He began his legal career as an advocate at the Court of Appeals in Paris in 1891, and was appointed auditor of the council of state three years later. He has been on the examining board for commercial high schools since 1897. In 1904 he was the secretary of the extra-parliamentary board of marine investigation, and in the following year was appointed recording secretary of the French colonial congress. His talents found university recognition in 1895, when he was appointed lecturer on political economy in the faculty of law of the University of Paris. He held this position until 1897, when he was chosen associate professor in the same faculty at Caen, remaining there until 1902; he was instructor in the faculty of law, section of economic sciences, and in the Ecole Normale Supérieure in 1897, and was appointed in 1902 honorary professor of political economy at the Commercial Institute, Paris, which position he still held in 1905.

In 1893 Worms established the "Revue Internationale de Sociologie," of which he became the editor, and later founded the "Bibliothèque Sociologique Internationale," besides organizing the Institut International de Sociologie and the Société de Sociologie de Paris. He is, furthermore, a prolific writer, his principal works being as follows: "De la Volonté Unilatérale Considérée Comme Source d'Obligations" (Paris, 1891); "Précis de Philosophie" (3d ed. 1905); "Eléments de Philosophie Scientifique et de Philosophie Morale" (*ib.* 1891); "La Morale de Spinoza" (crowned by the Académie des Sciences Morales et Politiques; *ib.* 1892); "De Natura et Methodo Sociologiæ" (*ib.* 1896); "Organisme et Société" (*ib.* 1896; Russian translation, St. Petersburg, 1897); "La Science et l'Art en Economie Politique" (Paris, 1896); and "Philosophie des Sciences Sociales" (3 vols., *ib.* 1903–5). In addition he has contributed briefer studies to technical magazines.

Worms is a devoted adherent of Judaism, and was chosen as its apologist at the Mole conference, where he twice defended the decree of Crémieux regarding the Jews of Algeria against those members who demanded its repeal. He was created a chevalier of the Legion of Honor Feb. 18, 1905.

s. J. KA.

WORMS, BARON SOLOMON BENEDICT DE: English financier; born at Frankfort-on-the-Main Feb. 5, 1801; died at Brighton, England, Oct. 20, 1882; son of Benedict de Worms of Frankfort. He was taken to England at an early age, and eventually went to Ceylon, where, by his judgment and perseverance, he contributed greatly to the advancement of the colony. He was a generous benefactor to various Jewish charities, was a life-member of the council of the United Synagogue, and acted as a trustee of several metropolitan synagogues. In 1871 he was created a baron of the Austrian empire in recognition of services rendered that country; and in consideration of the efforts made by him and his brothers in developing the colony of Ceylon, Queen Victoria granted him and his heirs, by royal warrant of 1874, the right of using the title in England.

BIBLIOGRAPHY: *Jew. Chron.* and *Jew. World*, Oct. 27, 1882.
J. G. L.

WORMS, VICTOR: French lawyer; younger brother of Emile WORMS; born at Luxembourg Nov. 16, 1853; educated at Paris and Rennes ("docteur en droit," 1878). In 1880 he was appointed "conseiller de préfecture" for the department of Ille-et-Vilaine, and at Rennes made the acquaintance of Waldeck-Rousseau, who appointed him his private secretary when he entered Gambetta's cabinet as minister of the interior. On the retirement of Waldeck-Rousseau, Worms returned to his former post, but when his patron accepted a portfolio in the cabinet of Jules Ferry, Worms was made president of the "conseil de préfecture" for the department of Seine-et-Marne. On the fall of this ministry Worms retired from the administrative magistracy and entered the judiciary. Appointed a judge in the civil tribunal of Reims in 1886, he was transferred three years later in a similar capacity to Versailles, where he was made vice-president of the tribunal by a decree of Nov. 22, 1904.

s. J. KA.

WORMSER, ANDRÉ ALPHONSE: French composer; born in Paris Nov. 1, 1851; studied at the Paris Conservatoire under Bazin and Marmontel. In 1875 he was awarded the Prix de Rome. Besides a great number of concert overtures, piano compositions, operettas, farces, and ballets, he has written two operas, "Adèle de Ponthière" (Aix-la-Chapelle, 1887) and "Rivoli" (Paris, 1896).

BIBLIOGRAPHY: Riemann, *Musik-Lexikon*, 1900.

S.

WORSHIP, IDOL-: All idolatrous cults are condemned by the Biblical insistence on worship of YHWH only. The Decalogue begins with the command to reverence the one true God and to recognize no other deities. On this theme the Pentateuch dilates from every point of view, and the efforts of the Prophets were chiefly directed against idolatry and against the immorality connected with it. To recognize the true God meant also to act according to His will, and consequently to live a moral life. The thunderings of the Prophets against idolatry show, however, that the cults of other deities were deeply rooted in the heart of the Israelitish people, and they do not appear to have been thoroughly suppressed until after the return from the Babylonian exile. There is, therefore, no doubt that Jewish monotheism was preceded by a period of idolatry; the only problem is that which concerns the nature of the cults (comp. the articles ADRAMMELECH; ANAMMELECH; ASHERAH; ASS-WORSHIP; ASTARTE WORSHIP AMONG THE HEBREWS; ATARGATIS; BA'AL AND BA'AL-WORSHIP; BAAL-PEOR; BAAL-ZEBUB; BAAL-ZEPHON; BAMAH; CALF, GOLDEN; CALF-WORSHIP; CHEMOSH; DAGON; HIGH PLACE; MOLOCH; STAR-WORSHIP; STONE AND STONE-WORSHIP; TAMMUZ; TERAPHIM; and WITCHCRAFT).

I. Biblical Data: The narratives in Genesis presuppose monotheism as the original religion. After its decline Abraham was called to spread the true knowledge of God (Gen. xii.; Josh. xxiv.), but the prophetical books still reflect the struggle against idols and idolatry. Even Jeremiah, who lived to see the end of the Jewish state, complains: "According to the number of thy cities are thy gods, O Judah" (ii. 28). The various terms, sometimes expressive of scorn and disdain, which were applied to idols and idolatry are indicative of the wide diffusion of polytheistic cults and of the horror with which they filled the Biblical writers. Thus idols are stigmatized "non-God" (Deut. xxxii. 17, 21; Jer. ii. 11), "things of naught" (Lev. xix. 4 *et passim*), "vanity" (הבל, Deut. xxxii. 21 *et passim*; frequently in Jer.), "iniquity" (און, I Sam. xv. 23 *et passim*), "wind and confusion" (Isa. xli. 29), "the dead" (Ps. cvi. 28), "carcasses" (Lev. xxvi. 30; Jer. xvi. 18), "a lie" (Isa. xliv. 20 *et passim*), and similar epithets. They are made of gold, silver, wood, and stone, and are graven images, unshapen clods, and, being the work of men's hands, unable to speak, see, hear, smell, eat, grasp, or feel, and powerless either to injure or to benefit (Scholz, "Götzendienst und Zauberwesen," pp. 45 *et seq.*).

Idols were either designated in Hebrew by a term of general significance, or were named according to their material or the manner in which they were made. They were placed upon pedestals, and fastened with chains of silver or nails of iron lest they should fall over or be carried off (Isa. xl. 19, xli. 7; Jer. x. 14; Wisdom xiii. 15), and they were also clothed and

Historical Outlines.

Origin, Extent, Name.

colored (Jer. x. 9; Ezek. xvi. 18; Wisdom xv. 4) At first the gods and their images were conceived of as identical; but in later times a distinction was drawn between the god and the image. Nevertheless it was customary to take away the gods of the vanquished (Isa. x. 10 *et seq.*, xxxvi. 19, xlvi. 1; Jer. xlviii. 7, xlix. 3; Hosea x. 5; Dan. xi. 8), and a similar custom is frequently mentioned in the cuneiform texts.

Temples, altars, and statues were erected to the gods, and figures of oxen and of other animals are also mentioned (Ezek. viii. 10 *et seq.*). In Israel the worship of high places was a favorite form of polytheistic cult, as is shown by the Book of Kings, where the reign of each monarch is judged chiefly from the standpoint of his participation in the worship of idols, so that the words "but the high places were not removed" form a stereotyped phrase. Prayer was offered to the gods (Ex. xx. 5, xxiii. 24, *et passim*), the hands were stretched out to them (Ps. xliv. 21 [A. V. 20]), they were invoked by name (I Kings xviii. *et seq.*, xxiv.), their names were praised (Josh. xxiii. 7), knees were bent before them (I Kings xix. 18), incense was burned in their honor (I Kings xi. 8 *et passim*), they were invoked in the taking of oaths, and sacrifices were immolated to them (Jer. vii. 18; Ex. xxxiv. 15), the victims including even human beings, such as the offerings made to Moloch. The custom of worshiping stars and idols by throwing kisses to them is mentioned in Job xxxi. 13. The exchange of clothes, by which men put on women's clothes and women donned men's garments, was an idolatrous custom, and was consequently forbidden (Deut. xxii. 5). Human hair also served as a sacrifice, and the prohibition against shaving the head or having writing burned into one's body (Lev. xix. 18, 27; xxi. 5; comp. Jer. ix. 26, xxv. 23, xlix. 32) was recognized by the Talmud (Mak. iii. 6) and by Maimonides ("Moreh," iii. 37; "Yad," 'Ab. Zarah xii. 5) as connected with idol-worship. There were, moreover, many other forms of worship, and numerous commandments of the Pentateuch, even though they omit the term "abomination" as a synonym of idolatry, refer to polytheistic worship; for idolatry was deeply rooted in the national character, as is shown by the many proper names compounded with names of idols, so that it became necessary to make every effort for its eradication.

Forms of Idol-Worship.

II. Post-Biblical Period: It is generally supposed that idolatry was completely crushed in Israel after the return from the Exile. This assertion is somewhat exaggerated, however, as is evident from the continual warnings against idols and idolatry both in the Apocrypha (Kautzsch, "Apokryphen," Index, *s.v.* "Götzen") and in Jewish tradition. The Talmud has a special treatise on idolatry (see 'ABODAH ZARAH), and also discusses the subject elsewhere in many passages, so that its data concerning this matter would fill a volume. The gods of the Greco-Roman epoch, especially those of the Oriental world, appear in its pages in variegated profusion. "If one wished to write all the names of idols, all the skins [parchment scrolls] would be insufficient" (Sifre, Deut. 43). The monotheism of the masses, it is true, was

Survivals in Talmudic Times.

not endangered, for when it was threatened by the Syrians and Romans, the Jews revolted, refusing to permit Roman troops to enter their territory with flags; they even detected idols in the portraits of the Cæsars stamped on coins, and this was not unjustifiable, in view of the divine worship paid the emperors (see ZEALOTS). Despite this fear of idols and images, the danger of inroads among the Jews by idolatrous customs and usages, which permeated the whole ancient world around them, was so great that the scholars could not invent too many "fences." They accordingly aimed at making intimate association with the heathen impossible, and thereby succeeded in protecting the Jewish people from the evil which threatened them.

The ancient world regarded the Jews as atheists because of their refusal to worship visible gods. "Whosoever denies idols is called a Jew" (Meg. 13a, b). To statements such as this the Jew responded: "Whosoever recognizes idols has denied the entire Torah; and whosoever denies idols has recognized the entire Torah" (Sifre, Deut. 54 and parallel passages). "As soon as one departs from the words of the Torah, it is as though he attached himself to the worship of idols" (Sifre, Num. 43).

Although the Jews were forbidden in general to mock at anything holy, it was a merit to deride idols (Meg. 25b), and Akiba decreed that the names of the gods be changed into de- **Attitude of Jews Toward Idolatry.** rogatory names (Sifre, Deut. 61, end, *et passim*). Thus, Baal-zebub (II Kings i. 2, 6) is called Beel-zebul (בעל זבול = "dominus stercoris") in Matt. xii. 24, 27, and elsewhere, and the word with which the Talmud designates sacrifice to idols (זבח; Yer. Ber. 13b) literally means "to manure." The Hellenistic Jews also observed this custom, so that they applied the term εἰδωλόθυτος to what the Gentiles called ἱερόθυτος (Deissmann, "Die Hellenisierung des Semitischen Monotheismus," p. 5, Leipsic, 1903). It was forbidden to look upon images (Tosef., Shab. xvii. 1 [ed. Zuckermandel, p. 136] and parallels), and even thinking of idolatrous worship was prohibited (Ber. 12b); if one saw a place where an idol had once stood, he was commanded to utter a special prayer (Ber. 61a). Sacrifice to an idol or anything which in any way might be associated with idolatry was forbidden. It was even insufficient to reduce an idol to powder and scatter it to the winds, since it would fall to earth and become a fertilizer; but the image must be sunk in the Dead Sea, whence it could never emerge ('Ab. Zarah iii. 3); nor might the wood of the "asherah" be used for purposes of healing (Pes. 25a; see MAGIC). Among the three cardinal sins for which the penalty was death, idolatry stood first (Pes. 25a and parallels). "Dust of idolatry" is a technical expression for the prohibition of anything related to idol-worship (" 'abodah zarah").

To prevent any possible inducement to idolatry, all association of Jews with Gentiles was rendered difficult. For three days before a Gentile feast-day no Jew might have any commercial dealings with the idolaters ('Ab. Zarah i. 1), and it was forbidden to attend the fairs connected with such festivals, or even to go on a road which led to the image of a deity, or

to arrange a meeting in the vicinity of such a statue. No cattle might be housed in the stalls ('Ab. Zarah ii. 1). The Jews were driven to this intolerance partly through the wickedness and immorality of the Gentiles.

III. Post-Talmudic Period: In the century between the return from the Exile and the termination of the Babylonian Talmud, the Jews were thoroughly weaned from all belief in idols, although superstition itself can never be wholly eradicated. **Survivals of Idol-Worship.** Through mysticism and magic many polytheistic ideas and customs again found their way among the people, and the Talmud confirms the fact that idolatrous worship is seductive (Sanh. 102b). The fight for a pure belief in one God and worship of Him was waged by the religious philosophers, while the authorities on rabbinical law strove for purity of worship. Philosophy and law were united by Maimonides, who in his philosophical "Moreh Nebukim" and in his legal "Yad ha-Ḥazaḳah" devoted separate sections to idolatry and thoroughly exposed its teachings. The Shulḥan 'Aruk, Yoreh De'ah, also has a separate section on idolatry.

BIBLIOGRAPHY: See, in general, works on the history of Israel and on Biblical theology. Special works of this nature are: Baudissin, *Studien zur Semitischen Religionsgeschichte*, i.-ii., Leipsic, 1876-78; Dillmann, *Alttestamentliche Theologie*, ib. 1895; Hastings, *Dict. Bible*, ii. 445-448; Cheyne and Black, *Encyc. Bibl.* ii. 2146-2158; Hamburger, *R. B. T.* i. 460-465; Herzog-Hauck, *Real-Encyc.* vi. 750-757 (gives extensive bibliography and special treatment of idolatry in the N. T.; *ib.* iii. 217-221, on idolatry in the O. T); Scholz, *Götzendienst und Zauberwesen bei den Alten Hebräern*, Regensburg, 1877; Smend, *Alttestamentliche Religionsgeschichte*, 2d ed., Freiburg-im-Breisgau, 1899; Stade, *Geschichte des Volkes Israel*, Berlin, 1887; F. Weber, *Jüdische Theologie*, 2d ed., Leipsic, 1897, Index, s.v. *Götzendienst*; Wellhausen, *I. J. G.* 4th ed., Berlin, 1901; Winer, *B. R.* 3d ed., i. 433-436; Bousset, *Religion des Judenthums im Neutestamentlichen Zeitalter*, Berlin, 1903.

K. L. B.

WREATH: Garland placed on the head as a token of honor. The wealthy bridegroom and bride, on the day of their nuptials, were ornamented with crowns of precious metal and jewels, while the poor adorned themselves with twisted bands of roses, myrtles, and olive-leaves. The Mishnah mentions wreaths made from vine-branches and from ears of corn ('Ab. Zarah iv. 2). When Jerusalem was besieged the Rabbis forbade the wearing of crowns, but permitted wreaths of flowers (Soṭah 49a, b). R. Jeremiah as a groom wore a wreath of olive-leaves, while Samuel regarded the prohibition as including wreaths also, as a sign of mourning for the destruction of Jerusalem (Yer. Soṭah ix. 15). When Rabina discovered Mar bar R. Ashi in the act of twisting a wreath for his daughter, Ashi claimed that women were exempted from the prohibition (Giṭ. 7a).

The first-fruit offerings were tastefully arranged, and the ox which the people took to Jerusalem for a sacrifice was crowned with a wreath of olive-leaves on its horns (Bik. iii. 3). A scholar, on being ordained, was garlanded with a wreath known as "the crown of the ḥakam" ('Er. 53b; Tan., Ki Teẓe, 6). In Talmudic times the cup of wine for grace was decorated with a wreath (Kohut, "Aruch Completum," vi. 189). The "vine" referred to in Gen. xl. 10 is symbolic of Israel, and the "three branches," or wreaths, represent the Temple, the king, and the high priest (Ḥul. 92a). See CROWN.

BIBLIOGRAPHY: Abrahams, *Jewish Life in the Middle Ages*, p. 195.

E. G. H.   J. D. E.

WRESCHEN: A town in Posen, Poland, three miles from the Russian frontier. Its Jewish community formerly ranked among the largest of southern Prussia, and is mentioned as one of the congregations which suffered severely during the persecutions of the years 1648-51. Unluckily, however, all the early documents were destroyed in the conflagration of 1873, in which the synagogue, a beautiful old wooden building, also was burned. The gravestones of the ancient cemetery, which has been closed for about forty years, afford no historical data, since the great majority of the older inscriptions have been obliterated.

Among the members of the community special mention may be made of Rabbi Ẓebi Hirsch b. Aaron Mirels, Rabbi Aaron Mirels (Kaufmann, "Die Letzte Vertreibung der Juden aus Wien und Niederösterreich," pp. 79 *et seq.*, Vienna, 1889), and the Bible commentator Rabbi Meïr Löb Malbim. Ẓebi Mirels, who was called also Hirsch Aaron London, was the author of the "Mispar Ẓeba'am," and presented a Hebrew hymn to General Möllendorf when the latter was sent by the Prussian king Frederick William II. to receive the allegiance of the new province of southern Prussia ("Das Jahr 1793," p. 16, note, Posen, 1895). Rabbi Aaron Mirels, the author of the "Bet Aharon," is buried in the cemetery at Hirschberg in Silesia. In Wreschen, Malbim wrote his first work, the collection of annotations on the first chapters of the Shulḥan 'Aruk, Oraḥ Ḥayyim, which laid the foundation of his renown as a scholar. In Wreschen, moreover, the musical director Louis Lewandowski was born April 3, 1821.

The population of Wreschen in 1905 numbered 5,435, of whom 490 were Jews. The rabbi then was Dr. M. Lewin. The community has a religious school and a public school, the former having an attendance of forty and the latter of thirty-five.

D.   M. Lw.

WRITING. See ALPHABET; MANUSCRIPTS; SCRIBES; SCROLL OF THE LAW.

WRITTEN INSTRUMENTS. See DEED; SHEṬAR.

WUNDERBAR, REUBEN JOSEPH: Russian pedagogue and author; born at Mitau Sept. 12, 1812; died there Aug. 16, 1868. He received the usual Jewish education under a private teacher, and at the age of eighteen entered his father's business. In 1834 he married, and, having lost his fortune, supported himself as a private tutor. At the beginning of the colonization movement inaugurated by Czar Nicholas (see JEW. ENCYC. i. 252), Wunderbar wrote an address to the colonists who went from Courland to Kherson ("Betrachtungen über die aus Kurland nach dem Cherson'schen Gouvernment Auswandernden Israelitischen Kolonisten-Familien," Mitau, 1840); this address attracted the attention of Max LILIENTHAL, who appointed him teacher at the Riga school under his management. After Lilien-

thal had been called to St. Petersburg, Wunderbar acted temporarily as principal of the school and as rabbi. In 1848 he was called to Mitau as teacher of religion and as Hebrew interpreter to the government, acting occasionally as rabbi also; this position he held until his death.

In addition to various pamphlets and sermons, as well as articles contributed to the "Orient" and to the "Allgemeine Zeitung des Judentums," Wunderbar was the author of the following works: "Biblisch-Talmudische Medizin" (3 vols., Riga and Leipsic, 1850-60); "Geschichte der Juden in der Provinz Liv- und Kurland" (Mitau, 1853); and "Immerwährender Kalender der Juden" (Dessau, 1854). A bibliography of his earlier writings is given in his history of the Jews in Livonia and Courland.

BIBLIOGRAPHY: *Allg. Zeit. des Jud.* 1869, pp. 19-20, 37-38.

H. R.   D.

WÜNSCHE, AUGUST: German Christian Hebraist; born at Hainewalde July 22, 1839. He has devoted his attention almost exclusively to rabbinic literature. After completing his commentaries on Hosea (1868) and Joel (1872), he wrote "Neue Beiträge zur Erläuterung der Evangelien aus Talmud und Midrasch" (1878), the most complete collection of the parallel passages of the Talmud and the New Testament since the works of Lightfoot and Schöttgen. In his "Bibliotheca Rabbinica" (Leipsic, 1880-85) he made a German translation of the whole of the Midrash Rabbah and the Midrash to the Five Megillot, and he has also translated haggadic portions of the Jerusalem Talmud (1880) and of the Babylonian Talmud (1886-89), as well as the Pesiḳta (1885) and the Midrash to the Psalms (1891). Smaller works of his are: "Die Rätselweisheit bei den Hebräern" (1883); "Die Freude im Alten Testament" (1896); "Naturbildersprache des Alten Testaments" (1897); and "Die Schönheit der Bibel" (Leipsic, 1905). Together with Winter he compiled the "Geschichte der Jüdischen Litteratur" (3 vols., Leipsic, 1892-95), the best existing anthology of Jewish literature in a modern language. He died in 1916.

BIBLIOGRAPHY: Kürschner, *Deutscher Literatur-Kalender*.

S.   J.

WÜRTTEMBERG: Republic of southwestern Germany; formerly a kingdom. Jews were found in this country in Bopfingen (1241), Ulm (1243), Esslingen (1253), Oehringen (1253), Calw (1284), and Weil (1289); and their numbers, as well as the places where they lived, may be ascertained by investigating the persecutions to which they were subjected by Rindfleisch and his followers (1298). Albrecht I. of Austria had been chosen King of Germany, and Ulrich I. and Eberhard I. were ruling in Württemberg, when RINDFLEISCH and his wild hordes attacked the Jews in Creglingen, Ellwangen, Forchtenberg, Gartach, Göglingen, Ingelfingen, Künzelsau, Leonberg, Mockmühl, Mergentheim, Stetten, Sindringen, Sontheim, Waldenburg, Weinsberg, Widdern, and Weikersheim. In the large community of Heilbronn alone there were 200 martyrs, among them Johanan ben Eliakim, the rabbi, and R. Asher, the president of the community. There was at that time a large community also in Ulm, which had its own cemetery,

*Distribu-
tion and
Per-
secution.*

and which enjoyed certain privileges granted it by a municipal law of 1274, this law being in force in Ravensburg also. In the fourteenth century there were Jews also in Baldern, Geislingen, Göppingen, Schwäbisch Hall, Rohrbach, Hohenburg, Horb, Reutlingen, Rottweil, Stuttgart, Sulm, Tübingen, Vaihingen, and Wolfegg. The counts of Württemberg owed money to the Jews of Colmar and Schlettstadt, but Louis IV. canceled their indebtedness (1346), as had also Henry VII. and Louis the Bavarian (1311 and 1316) in the case of the citizens of Esslingen.

During the night of April 19, 1316, the Bavarian party of Ulm succeeded in introducing Bavarian troops into the city, aided, as alleged, by a Jew. In the same night, however, the Austrian party, which was in the majority, appeared and drove out the Bavarians. In commemoration of this event a mass was instituted to recall the treachery of the Jews; but this was abolished in 1322, when the Bavarians gained possession of Ulm. New persecutions soon broke out, however, the Jews being charged with being enemies of the Christians, and with stealing and desecrating the host. The community of Esslingen was almost annihilated in 1334; and two years later the Jews in Hohenburg, Landenbach, Mergentheim, Weikersheim, and Widdern were persecuted. The situation became still worse toward the end of 1348, when the plague and fanaticism combined brought destruction upon the Jewish communities of Baldern, Bopfingen, Ellwangen, Esslingen, Göppingen, Geislingen, Schwäbisch Hall, Heilbronn, Hohebach, Horb, Krailsheim, Mengen, Mergentheim, Nagold, Oehringen, Ravensburg, Reutlingen, Rottweil, Stuttgart, Sulgen, Sulm, Ulm, Vaihingen, Waldenburg, Weilderstadt, and Widdern.

For the protection afforded them the Jews of Ulm had to pay large sums to the municipal council, to the citizens, and to the counts of Helfenstein. The plunder taken from the Jews became a bone of contention among the cities, the emperor, and the counts; and their disputes led to renewed despoliations of the Jews. As the latter still

Ulm. found advocates, some counts and rulers united against them; and when the emperor's demand for a share of the plunder was unheeded, he made war against the cities, confiscated their possessions, and compelled them to pay high taxes. The city of Ulm being unable to raise the exorbitant sums demanded, the Jews came forward to aid it in its distress (1374), chief among them being Säcklin, son-in-law of Moses of Ehlingen, who was a citizen of Ulm. In order to exact money from the few wealthy Jews still residing in the city, the emperor declared them to be under the ban, and they had to pay large sums to have the edict revoked. In 1385 the federation of cities declared void all promissory notes held by the Jews within its jurisdiction; and in some cases it released the Christian debtors from paying interest on their loans, while in other cases it annulled part of the debt. Two years later the federation issued a decree that no German or Italian merchant might thenceforth have money transactions with the Jews. Emperor Wenceslaus, following the example of the federation, canceled in 1390 all the debts owing to the Jews, demanding,

however, that the debtors pay him. All these measures were explained and justified on the grounds that the Jews were body and soul the property of the emperor, with which he could do as he pleased, and that the usury of the Jews had become intolerable. In spite of this, the counts of Württemberg permitted the Jews to reside in Stuttgart (1434), Kirchheim (1435), Tübingen (1459), Cannstadt, and Göppingen (1462), on definitely stated conditions, and on payment of large taxes for protection. Count Ulrich (1433–80) was commissioned by the emperor to protect the Jews, and at the same time rigorously to suppress their usury; the fines imposed were to be sent to the imperial treasury. Thus money flowed into the coffers of the count and of the emperor.

Count Eberhard im Bart (1459–96) was a pronounced enemy of the Jews. He removed them from Tübingen in 1477; and in 1495 he decreed that they should be expelled from his dominions. This order was confirmed by decree of June

Expulsion, 14, 1498; and the Jews of Ulm, who **1498.** were wealthy and well educated, had to leave the city on Aug. 6 of that year. The exiles were deprived of their property; and the emperor demanded that the people of Ulm should mention him in their prayers because he had delivered them of the Jews.

The fifteenth century was ominous also for the Jews of Ravensburg. A blood accusation brought against them induced Emperor Sigismund to burn some of the Jews of that city, and to expel others. The Jews were expelled from Esslingen in 1438; but ten years later they were again admitted, only to be expelled a second time in 1490. From Heilbronn, where Jews had settled anew in 1414, a number of them were expelled in 1469; and seven years later the city council insisted on a general expulsion, notwithstanding the imperial order to protect the Jews. The Jews expelled from the cities scattered among the villages; but in many cases they returned to the urban communities. Thus, there were Jews in Gmünd and Reutlingen in 1433; in Brackenheim, 1434; in Nersheim, 1454; in Giengen, 1486; and in Lauterburg, Pflaumloch, and Uzmemmingen, 1491. Between the end of the fifteenth century and 1806 no Jews settled in Ulm; individual Jews were permitted to enter the city only temporarily, and the citizens were warned against having any business transactions with them. When Württemberg became a dukedom, the treatment of the Jews remained on the whole the same; all money transactions with them were forbidden. These ordinances were frequently renewed and enforced; not even JOSEL OF ROSHEIM, the great advocate of the Jews, was permitted to travel through the country. Strict ordinances were issued regarding the commercial and religious status of the Jews (1536). Jews traveling through the country were subjected to many annoyances, and no attention was paid to the repeated imperial edicts for their protection. Josel of Rosheim had succeeded in regulating by a compact the convoy charges of traveling Jews; but Duke Christoph, from whom he had obtained this agreement, was so inimical to the Jews that in the Reichstag of Augsburg in 1559 he advocated their expulsion from Germany. Frederick I. (1593–1608) tried in the face of the most violent opposition to establish a Jewish mercantile association under the direction of Maggino Gabrieli and a Jewish magician, Abraham Calorno; the attempt, however, was an absolute failure.

During the reign of Eberhard Ludwig (1677–1733) a favorable change of attitude toward the Jews took place; and they were now permitted to frequent the fairs (1706) and to trade in horses (1707). The Countess of Würben procured the privilege of free trade for the Jews of Freudenthal (1728) and for those of Gochsheim (1729). Under Carl Alexander (1733–37), Joseph Süss OPPENHEIMER was appointed privy factor, and subsequently financial councilor, to the duke; and through

Joseph Süss Oppenheimer. his influence several Jews were permitted to settle at Stuttgart and Ludwigsburg. Oppenheimer's subserviency to the duke brought upon him the enmity of the people, and after his master's death (1737) he fell into disgrace. He was executed in 1738, and in the following year all the Jews were mercilessly expelled. They were soon permitted to return, but they were severely restricted in the exercise of their religion, as well as in their business; and the people were warned against having any dealings with them in monetary affairs. Court factors were treated more leniently, and important government contracts were given to them (1759, 1761, 1764) in spite of the objections of the populace. Karl Eugen, as also his successors, Ludwig (1793–1795) and Friedrich (1795–97), treated the Jews considerately. These rulers were the last of the line of Catholic dukes; and under the succeeding Protestant régime a new era dawned for the Jews of Württemberg.

With the nineteenth century the whole country received an entirely new political constitution. It was not only made a kingdom, but considerable territory was added to it (1806); and its Jewish population increased until in 1828 it numbered 8,918 souls. King Frederick I. (1797–1816) took the first steps toward the emancipation of the Jews. He annulled the body-tax and admitted the Jews into the army (1807); instituted family registers; included the Jews in the general taxation (1808); opened up to them all trades;

Emancipation. and regulated the organization and government of their communities. The Jews so treated showed themselves loyal citizens during the Napoleonic wars.

The work of ameliorating the condition of the Jews was continued by William I. (1816–64), and completed under Charles I. in 1869. King William instituted the Israelitische Oberkirchenbehörde; and, by a law enacted in 1828, he regulated the constitution of the Jewish communities, and made it obligatory upon Jewish parents to let their children receive a common-school education as provided by the general school-law of 1825. In the work of purifying the worship from the neglect and irregularities that had crept in, Dr. Maier, as theological member of the Oberkirchenbehörde, was most active. His aim was to eliminate completely all non-German elements, and to approach as closely as possible to the culture of the time, maintaining the idea of Jewish unity and morality, while abandoning the specifically Jewish laws of exclusion. Similar ideas actuated his successor, Church Councilor Dr. von Wassermann (1872–1893). Most of the communities in the northern part of the country clung, however, to the Hebrew language and to the Biblical and Talmudic rules of life; and at present the majority of the Jewish children are instructed in Hebrew, while the form of worship has remained almost unchanged.

According to the census of 1910, the Jews in the kingdom of Württemberg numbered 11,982 in a total population of 2,437,574. They thus constituted

Present Status. 0.49 per cent of the population, distributed among the four districts, as follows: (1) **Neckar**, 6,276; (2) **Black Forest**, 1,359; (3) **Jagst**, 2,412; and (4) **Danube**, 1,935. Total population in 1919, 2,526,171.

The Neckar district is divided into five rabbinates, the seat of which is in Stuttgart; the Black Forest district constitutes one rabbinate, the seat of which is in Mühringen; the Jagst district embraces the rabbinates of Heilbronn, Oberdorf, Mergentheim, Braunsbach, and Weikersheim; and the Danube district, the rabbinates of Göppingen, Laupheim, Buchau, and Ulm, making a total of fifteen rabbinates for the kingdom. Laws and decrees regulating the communal affairs were issued as follows: April 25, 1828; Oct. 27, 1831; Jan. 31, 1834 (rabbinical examinations); 1838 (rituals), 1841 (duties of rabbis and choir-leaders); March 25, 1851; March 26, 1873; Feb. 22, 1875; and Feb. 18 and April 24, 1876 (taxation); Aug. 5, 1875; and April 23, 1900 (pensioning of rabbis); and July 8, 1878; and March 25, 1900 (qualifications of choir-leaders).

According to the school statistics of 1900–1, the thirteen rabbinates had under their care 61 school districts, with 1,757 Jewish pupils, of whom 1,523

Statistics. (736 boys and 787 girls) were under fourteen, and 234 (92 boys and 142 girls) more than fourteen, years of age. They are instructed in part in twenty-seven Jewish parochial schools, receiving their specifically religious instruction in thirty-one religious schools. In some places the religious instruction is given also in evening-schools and Sunday-schools. All but 140 children receive religious instruction. According to the statistics of the penal institutions of the country for 1900–1, fourteen Jews were sentenced in the course of the year, ten of whom were of Württemberg. The criminal status of the entire population of 2,169,480 is 0.089 per cent; that of the Jews, 0.083 per cent.

There are in Württemberg the following Jewish philanthropic institutions: the orphan asylum Wilhelmspflege at Esslingen; the Society for the Relief of Teachers, Widows, and Orphans; and the District Asylum and Relief Society. Since 1896 the rabbis of the country, as well as the Jewish teachers and choir-leaders, have been holding yearly conventions in Stuttgart. Among the most noteworthy synagogues are those at Stuttgart, Heilbronn, Ulm, Buchau, and Unterdeufstetten. There are very old cemeteries at Aufhausen, Oberdorf, Esslingen, Affaltrach, Unterbalbach, Neckarsulm, Wankheim, and Laibach. The Israelitische Oberkirchenbehörde, which is under the immediate supervision of the ministry for ecclesiastical and educational affairs, regulates the affairs of all the Jewish communities of the country. This body is composed of a Jewish theologian, a Jewish lawyer, and four Jewish associates, with a Christian ministerial counselor at their head. In all communities there are institutions for the instruction of adults, as well as burial societies, dispensaries, and societies for the relief of the resident and traveling poor. Stuttgart and Hall have societies for the promotion of a knowledge of rabbinical literature. The ancient ritual is observed in most of the communities, though some innovations have been introduced in Stuttgart, Heilbronn, Ulm, and Göppingen. See also HEILBRONN; STUTTGART; ULM.

s.　　　　　　　　　　　　　　　　T. K.

WÜRZBURG : Capital of Lower Franconia, Bavaria, Germany. It ranked as a city in 741, and had a Jewish community as early as the eleventh century, although the first documentary evidence of the existence of Jews in the town is dated in 1119. The Crusade of 1147 brought much suffering on the Jews, and they were also persecuted in 1298, and again in 1349, when in their synagogue the men, together with their wives and children, met a voluntary death in the flames. Bishop Julius continued the work begun by Bishop Friedrich, who had expelled the Jews of Würzburg in 1565, and banished the community from the city. The cemetery was, accordingly, no longer used, and Bishop Julius confiscated it by illegal means, even ignoring the emperor's admonition to treat the Jews with justice.

After the expulsion from Würzburg the Jewish community of the neighboring town of Heidingsfeld flourished greatly, and to it were transferred the rabbinate of Würzburg and the Jewish court. The rabbinical office of Würzburg has always been held by prominent men, including Eliezer ben Nathan, Isaac Or Zarua‘, Meïr of Rothenburg, Israel Koppel Fränkel and his son Samson Fränkel, Jacob of Reckendorf, Aryeh Löb Rapoport, and Levin Fahrenbach. Under Fahrenbach's successor the Jews were again permitted to settle in Würzburg; and Rabbi Abraham Bing, who was appointed chief rabbi of Franconia in 1798, took up his residence in the city. When Bing retired from active service in 1839 the chief rabbinate was abolished, and a district rabbinate was created in its place. The first district rabbi of Würzburg was Seligmann Baer BAMBERGER, who died in 1878 and was succeeded by his son Nathan Bamberger. Seligmann Baer Bamberger founded various important institutions, including a Jewish school, a teachers' seminary, and a yeshibah. He also originated the movement for the establishment of a Jewish hospital.

Würzburg has numerous societies which support all forms of Jewish activity, among them being four associations for the promotion of the study of the Torah. The Jews of Würzburg numbered in 1919 4,000 out of a total population of 86,571, and constituted one of the most important communities in Bavaria.

BIBLIOGRAPHY: M. L. Bamberger, *Ein Blick auf die Gesch. der Juden in Würzburg,* Würzburg, 1905; idem, *Beiträge zur Gesch. der Juden in Würzburg-Heidingsfeld*; Heffner, *Juden in Franken,* Nuremberg, 1855; Himmelstein, *Zeitschrift des Historischen Vereins für Unterfranken und Aschaffenburg,* vol. xii.; Salfeld, *Martyrologium*; Stern-Neubauer, *Hebräische Berichte über die Judenverfolgungen Während der Kreuzzüge,* Berlin, 1892; Stumpf, *Denkwürdigkeiten,* part i.; Wegele, *Vorträge und Abhandlungen.*
D.　　　　　　　　　　　　　　　M. L. B.

WÜRZBURGER, JULIUS : American journalist; born in Bayreuth, Germany, 1819; died in New York city Sept. 14, 1876; studied at the University of Erlangen. In 1848, the year of the revolution, he was editor of the "Bayreuth Tageblatt." Removing to Munich, his liberal views and writings attracted the attention of the government; and in 1849 he was banished from Bavaria. He went to Italy and France, where he acted as correspondent, and finally emigrated to America, where he became connected with the "New-Yorker Staats-Zeitung" (1856–75), editing its Sunday supplement with marked ability and success.

A.　　　　　　　　　　　　　　　　A. S. I.

WYSBER, LUDWIG : Hungarian journalist and author; born 1817. Originally a street pedler in Pesth, he obtained employment as a chorus singer in the German theater of that city, and afterward held minor positions on several local newspapers. At the outbreak of the March Movement in 1848, he obtained permission to publish "Der Patriot," while Julian Chownitz, or Chowanetz, a Jew who had been active as a revolutionist, was given permission to publish "Die Opposition." These two journals represented Kossuth's party, and acquired considerable influence. Between 1850 and 1870 Wysber appears to have been guilty of numerous peculations among the merchants and clergy of Hungary, extending his operations even to Vienna. He employed various aliases, as "Arthur von Alaven," "Jonas Földváry," and "Wysbersi"; and warrants were issued for his arrest. He was the author of "Lebensbilder aus Ungarn," mentioned in Von Helfert's "Geschichte Oesterreichs vom Ausgange des Wiener October Aufstandes 1848" (Prague, 1876; Appendix, p. 135, note 311).

BIBLIOGRAPHY: Wurzbach, *Biog. Lex.*; Janstyckh von Adlerstein, *Die Letzten Zwei Jahre Ungarns,* ii. 176, 181 *et seq.,* Vienna, 1850; *Evangelisches Wochenblatt,* Pesth, 1858, No. 37, p. 599; *ib.* 1861, No. 7, p. 110; *Fremden-Blatt,* 1861, No. 111.
s.　　　　　　　　　　　　　　　　N. D.

X

XABILLO. See Ḥabillo.

XANTEN: Town of Rhenish Prussia, in the district of Düsseldorf. Like most Rhenish towns, Xanten had a Jewish community in early medieval times. Two massacres of Jews occurred during the First Crusade (June 1 and 27, 1096). On the latter occasion some Jews committed suicide in order to escape the fury of the Crusaders (Aronius, "Regesten," p. 89, No. 188; p. 92, No. 195). In 1187 the martyrs of Neuss were brought to Xanten to be buried by the side of those martyred in 1096 (*ib*. p. 144, No. 322).

In the latter part of the nineteenth century the attention of the Jewish world was attracted to the small congregation of Xanten by a blood accusation. On June 29, 1891, John Hegemann, the five-year-old son of a local cabinetmaker, was found dead in a neighbor's barn, with his throat cut from ear to ear. Anti-Semitic agitation connected **Blood Ac-** the Jewish butcher and former shoḥeṭ **cusation.** Adolf Buschoff with this crime; and the local priest Bresser lent support to this rumor by publishing articles on ritual murder in the "Bote für Stadt und Land," of which he was the editor. The agitation in the anti-Semitic press, as well as at anti-Semitic meetings, where it was insinuated that the Jews had bribed or intimidated the authorities in order to prevent the discovery of the truth, compelled the government to arrest Buschoff and his family (Oct. 14, 1891). The evidence against the man, who had always borne a good reputation, was so flimsy, however, that he was discharged (Dec. 20). This action aroused the anti-Semites to still stronger agitation, which culminated in a heated debate in the Prussian Diet; in the course of this argument Stoecker, the ex-court chaplain, cleverly repeated the accusation of ritual murder, and hinted at Jewish influence as the cause of the failure to find the murderer (Feb. 7, 1892). Under pressure of this agitation Buschoff was rearrested (Feb. 8), and tried before a jury at Cleve (July 4-14, 1892). During this trial it was found that the accusations were based on mere hearsay, and contained absolutely impossible assertions. The prosecuting attorney himself moved for the dismissal of the charge, and the jury rendered its verdict accordingly. The real murderer was never discovered, and the possibility that the death of the child was due to an accident was not entirely disproved. The agitation had the effect of reducing the Jewish population of the city, and Buschoff himself had to leave. Xanten has about thirty Jews in a population aggregating 5,000.

BIBLIOGRAPHY: *Mittheilungen aus dem Verein zur Abwehr des Antisemitismus*, 1892, Index, s.v. *Xanten* and *Buschoff*; *Allg. Zeit. des Jud.* 1892, Nos. 29-31; *Der Prozess Buschoff*, Leipsic, 1892; Nathan, *Der Prozess Buschoff*, Berlin, 1892; *Der Prozess Xanten-Cleve*, ib. 1892; *Der Xantener Knabenmord vor dem Schwurgericht zu Cleve, 4-14 Juli, 1892*, Berlin, 1893 (a complete stenographic record).

J.
D.

XERES (JEREZ) DE LA FRONTERA: City in the Spanish province of Cadiz. It had a Jewish community with a separate Juderia as early as the time of the Moors. When Alfonso X., the Wise, conquered the city in Oct., 1264, he assigned houses and lands to the Jews. The Juderia, which was located near S. Cristobal street and extended along the city wall, included ninety-six houses, large and small, and had two synagogues and two "casas de la merced," institutions for aiding and housing the poor. Near one synagogue were the "casas del reab" (houses of the rabbi); Don Todros, father of Don Yuçaff, is mentioned as being the occupant in 1264. Near the other synagogue was the house of Rabbi Yuçaff. Upon the conquest of the city the following persons received houses by command of the king: Don Yehuda Mosca (as he is several times expressly called in the list drawn up in 1338), who made translations from Arabic into Spanish for the king; the "almoxarife" Don Mayr, or rather Mür de Malhea, and his son Çag (Isaac); Çimha (Simḥah) Xtaruçi, whose father lost his life and the whole of his large fortune during the rebellion of the city; Don Vellocid (Vellecid), "ballestero del rey a caballo"; Solomon Ballestero; and Axucuri Ballestero—the last three being in the king's army.

Among the richest and most influential Jews in Jerez were the following: Çag aben Açot, who was the representative of the community at the repartition of the taxes in 1290, and his relatives Judah aben Açot, Bonet aben Açot, Abraham aben Açot; likewise Samuel de Cadiz, Jacob Castellano, Çag aben Colmiel or Calamiel, Samuel Barrach, Levi de Faro, Abraham Saltos, Vellido de Castro, and Abraham de Carrion. The Jews of Jerez engaged in business. One Yuçaff Alcaçabi, who had laid in large quantities of salt pork in his houses and lost everything he possessed, because he had favored the Moors, did not receive the house which had first been assigned him. The Jews engaged in viticulture also, Jerez wine being the most valued wine of Spain. There were also tailors (Cedillo Alfayate is mentioned), rope-makers (Çag el Cordonnero), and shoemakers among them. The Jerez Jews, who in 1294 paid King D. Sancho IV. 5,000 maravedis in taxes, were freed by the king from the payment of tolls throughout the kingdom, and were assured of the same favor as was enjoyed by Christians and other inhabitants of the city—a privilege which was confirmed by Kings Fernando IV. and Alfonso XI. (Dec. 30, 1332).

In the second half of the fifteenth century the Jews of Jerez suffered from the enmity of the Christian population. In 1459 the city council gave a portion of the Jewish cemetery to a Christian inhabitant; and in spite of the protests of Joseph de Paredes and Samuel Corcos, who represented the Israelite community, and regardless of their appeal to a decree of May 25, 1455, issued by King Henry IV., according to which the synagogues and Jewish cemeteries were not in any way to be violated, the council in March, 1460, granted another portion of the cemetery to a Christian who desired to build a house upon it. At the same time the following incident, related by Abraham Arama, took place in Jerez: Certain monks who appealed to a rich Jew for alms and received blows instead, desired to avenge themselves on the whole community. They accordingly exhumed the body of a baptized Jew that had been buried in the Christian cemetery, and took it to the Jewish burial-ground, hoping to create the impression that the act had been committed by the Jews. The affair came before the duke or the governor, who wished to have the king's opinion on the subject and to keep all the Jews in the city under arrest until the king's decision should arrive. The influential Judah ibn Verga of Seville exerted himself in behalf of the terrified Jews; and as the innocence of those who had been slandered was soon proved, two of the monks were burned at the stake, while the others, at the intercession of the people, were banished for life. See SPAIN.

BIBLIOGRAPHY: *Boletin Acad. Hist.* x. 465 *et seq.*, xii. 65 *et seq.*; *R. E. J.* xv. 125 *et seq.*, xvii. 138 *et seq.*; *Shebeṭ Yehudah*, pp. 66 *et seq.*
G.   M. K.

XERXES: Son of Darius, King of Persia (485–465 B.C.). His name, which is Khshayarsha in Persian, Ikhshiyarshu (with variants) in Babylonian, and Ξέρξης in Greek, frequently occurs in the Old Testament. It is often written with ו instead of י, as in the Masoretic text, where it is spelled אחשורש (Aḥashwerôsh) instead of אחשירש (Ayḥashyarsh), with the prothetic vowel indispensable in Semitic before initial double consonants. Xerxes is mentioned in the Book of Ezra (iv. 6) in connection with a complaint lodged against the Jews by the Samaritans (comp. Meyer, "Entstehung des Judenthums," pp. 16 *et seq.*). He is the "king" of the Esther romance, and in the Book of Daniel (ix. 1) he is mentioned as the father of Darius, "of the seed of the Medes."

E. G. H.   E. ME.

XIMENES DE CISNEROS: Spanish priest, statesman, regent, and grand inquisitor; born 1436; died 1517. He studied in Rome, and upon his return to Spain was appointed confessor to Queen Isabella of Castile. In 1507 the pope invested him with the dignity of a cardinal, and at the same time he was appointed grand inquisitor, being the third to hold that office in Spain. Two years later he accoutered an army at his own expense, and invaded North Africa in order to forcibly introduce Christianity. It is said that he succeeded in conquering the city of Oran by employing some Jewish spies. Upon his return to Spain he founded the University of Alcalá de Henares, with the establishment of which is connected the publication of the first polyglot Bible. Ximenes was dismissed from the government service by Charles V. in 1517.

During the beginning of his incumbency as grand inquisitor, De Cisneros was less severe than his predecessors, Torquemada and Diaz. When, however, Charles V., in accordance with the advice of his Flemish councilors, began negotiating with the Ma-

ranos, offering them religious liberty on payment of 800,000 gulden (gold), the grand inquisitor proceeded mercilessly against both Maranos and Jews; and 2,500 persons were given over to autos da fé during his inquisitorship.

When the University of Alcalá de Henares was founded, Ximenes commenced the work of compiling the polyglot Bible, which was completed in 1517. and published in Alcala under the title "Biblia Hebraica, Chaldaica, Græca et Latina." Volume iv. of this work was supplied with a Hebrew grammar, "Introductio Artis Grammaticæ Hebraicæ," adapted from Reuchlin's grammar; while a glossary entitled "Lexicon Hebraicum et Chaldaicum" was appended to the last volume.

BIBLIOGRAPHY: Hefele, *Der Cardinal Ximenes*, Tübingen, 1851; Leorente, *Histoire de l'Inquisition en Espagne*, i. 345 *et seq.*; *Meyers Konversations-Lexikon*, ix. 567–568; Grätz, *Gesch.* ix. 14, 218; Fürst, *Bibl. Jud.* iii. 559.
J.   S. O.

XIMENES, SIR MORRIS (MOSES): Born at London about 1762; died there after 1830. He was a member of the London Exchange, where he made a large fortune. In 1802 he was elected a warden of the Bevis Marks Synagogue, but declined to accept; and on being fined he resigned from the community and became converted to Christianity. He appears afterward to have adopted a military career, and was known as Captain Ximenes; he was knighted, and became a high sheriff of the county of Kent.

His son, **Sir David Ximenes,** had no connection with the Jewish community.

BIBLIOGRAPHY: Picciotto, *Sketches of Anglo-Jewish History*, pp. 303–304.
S.   J.

XYSTUS: A building in Jerusalem, erected, as is shown by the name, in the Hellenistic period, probably under the Herodians. The term properly denotes a covered colonnade in the gymnasia, although the Romans employed the word "xystus" to designate open terraces before the colonnades of their country-houses. That the Xystus of Jerusalem was an open terrace, as Buhl rightly assumes, is clear from the fact that from it Titus conducted his negotiations with the leaders of the Jews while they stood in the upper city, a proceeding which would scarcely have been possible had it been a covered building. The translation "colonnade" is erroneous. It was artificially formed by erecting on the western edge of Mount Moriah a structure supported by pillars, the roof, which was practically level with the Temple area, constituting the Xystus. Similar buildings, also called Xysti, were found in a number of Greek cities, as in Elis.

The site of the Xystus of Jerusalem can be approximately, though not definitely, determined. The first wall on the north, beginning at the so-called tower of Hippicus, extended to the Xystus, then skirted the council-house (βουλή), **Site.** and ended at the western cloister of the Temple (Josephus, "B. J." v. 4, § 2). Both the Xystus and the council-house were, therefore, situated within the wall, the former lying to the north and the latter to the south. When Titus negotiated with the Jews concerning their surrender, he stood on the western side of the outer Temple, facing the upper city, taking this position on account of the gates upon the Xystus, and also being influenced in his choice by the bridge which connected the upper city with the Temple and which lay between the Jewish leaders and himself (*ib.* vi. 6, § 2). The Xystus was, moreover, the scene of an assembly of the people before the outbreak of the rebellion, when Agrippa II. addressed them while his sister Berenice remained in sight of the populace in the house of the Hasmoneans, which overlooked the Xystus (*ib.* ii. 16, § 3). In his account of this conference, Josephus states, curiously enough, that the bridge connected the Temple with the Xystus and not with the upper city. This can be explained only on the assumption that the Xystus, as was natural, lay below Mount Moriah itself, and was, perhaps, separated from the hill by a ravine. A bridge running from the upper city would, therefore, connect the Xystus with Mount Moriah, and this agrees with the assumption that the bridge, like the gates, was constructed "above the Xystus." During the factional strife between Simeon bar Giora and John of Giscala a fortified tower was built on the Xystus (*ib.* iv. 9, § 12), and this edifice later marked the limit set by Titus for the burning of the Temple cloister (*ib.* vi. 3, § 2).

It thus becomes evident that the Xystus formed a portion of the western cloister of the Temple, while the council-house lay to the south, but in the same direction and probably built into the cloister. The Hasmonean palace, raised still higher by Agrippa II. (Josephus, "Ant." xx. 8, § 11), stood opposite, on the western heights of the upper city, which was at that point connected with the Xystus by a bridge. Many investigators regard "Robinson's Arch," which

is still preserved, as an anchorage for this bridge, but the absence of any corresponding structure on the western hill opposite inclines others to identify "Robinson's Arch" with the remains of the stair-tower mentioned by Josephus (*ib.* xv. 11, § 5). An additional argument against any identification of "Robinson's Arch" with the Xystus is found in the fact that it lies in the lowest portion of the wall and almost in the bottom of the valley, while the Xystus evidently equaled Mount Moriah in height. It must have been situated, moreover, where the first wall joined the cloister of the Temple and turned toward the south. Mommert's hypothesis that the lower city, which was called Akra and which was leveled and graded by the Maccabees, included the open space of the Xystus, is disproved by the fact that the Temple, on which the Xystus bordered, did not extend to the lower city.

Connection with "Robinson's Arch."

Equally erroneous is the theory of Schürer, supported by Buhl, that the so-called hall of hewn stone ("lishkat ha-gazit"), in which the Sanhedrin held its sessions, was built on the Xystus and that נזית is identical with ξυστός; because, according to the Mishnah, this body deliberated within the precincts of the Temple, and not in the buildings which surrounded it, so that this hypothesis is rightly rejected by Bacher and Büchler.

Bibliography: Schürer, *Gesch.* 3d ed., ii. 211 (opposed by Bacher, in Hastings, *Dict. Bible,* iv. 399); Büchler, *Das Synedrion in Jerusalem,* p. 15, Vienna, 1902; Buhl, *Geographie des Alten Palästina,* pp. 135, 144, 146, Freiburg-im-Breisgau, 1896; *Z. D. P. V.* x. 243; Baedeker, *Palästina und Syrien,* 6th ed., pp. 28, 59, Leipsic, 1904; Mommert, *Topographie des Alten Jerusalem,* i. 67, *ib.* 1900.

G.   S. Kr.

Y

[Note: For topics beginning with **Y** not found in alphabetical place see under **J.**]

YA'ABEẒ. See Emden, Jacob Israel ben Ẓebi Ashkenazi.

YA'ALEH: The introductory hymn prefixed to the seliḥot which follow the evening service proper of the Day of Atonement (comp. Kol Nidre) in the northern rituals. The author of the hymn has not been identified with certainty. It consists of eight strophes in reverse alphabetical order, each composed of three lines, with the twenty-second Hebrew letter thrice repeated to complete the twenty-four lines. The scheme of construction is as follows:

> "Let our Z ascend from eventide,
> And our Y approach from morning,
> And our X appear till eventide."

The verbs are drawn from the prayer "Ya'aleh we-yabo we-yeraeh," etc., specially inserted before the three concluding benedictions of the "'Amidah" (see Shemoneh 'Esreh), and in the grace after meals, on all festal days (comp. Shab. 24a), including the Day of Atonement. The thought, if not the form, is the basis of G. Gottheil's hymn "To Thee we give ourselves . . . from eventide to eventide" ("Union Hymnal," No. 103), for which, however, a

tune from another section of the penitential services (see Kerobot—Ḳaliric strophic hymn) was selected.

A fine eighteenth-century melody for "Ya'aleh" has been preserved as a general setting through its adaptation by Isaac Nathan in 1815 to Lord Byron's verses "The Harp the Monarch Minstrel Swept," which was published, with pianoforte accompaniment, in the "Hebrew Melodies," issued in that year. The melody as now usually sung is somewhat less elaborate than in Nathan's version. It has been traditional in the Great Synagogue, London, since 1750 at least, and is well known on the Continent also. Its expressive swing had made it widely known and treasured in connection with the Atonement hymn even before it received a further appreciation from the fascination with which it appealed to Louis Lewandowski, the premier synagogue musician of his generation. In his "Todah w'Zimrah" (Berlin, 1876) he not only includes it with its original text for the service of the Day of Atonement (vol. ii., No. 94), but he has set it also to the chief hymn chanted by the ḥazzan in the "dew" and "rain" supplications on the Passover and Tabernacle festivals (see Geshem).

The melody is here transcribed with Byron's Eng-

YA'ALEH

Hazzan.

Andante maestoso.

mf

1. Ya - 'a - leh...
1. The harp................ the mon - arch min - strel swept, the
3. It told................ the tri - umphs of our King, the

ta - ha - nu - - - - - - - - - ne - nu me - 'e - reb,...
mon - - arch min - strel swept, The King of men, the loved of heaven,
tri - - umphs of our King; It waft - ed glo - ry to our God;

We - - ya - bo...... shaw - - - - - 'a - te - nu
Which.......... mu - sic hal - lowed while she wept O'er tones her heart of
It.............. made our glad - dened val - leys ring, The ce - dars bow, the

mi - bo - ker..... Wĕye - ra - 'eh.... rin - nu - ne - nu 'ad 'e - reb.
hearts had given,.... Re - doub - led be her tears, its chords are riven!
moun - tains nod,..... Its sound as - pired to heaven and there a - bode.

2. Ya - 'a - leh........ ko - - - - le - nu me - 'e - reb, We -
2. It.... sof - tened, sof - tened men of i - ron mold; It
4. Since then, since then, though heard on earth no more, De -

ya - - bo...... zid - ka - te - nu mi - bo - ker;...... We -
gave.... them, it gave them vir - tues not..... their own; No
vo - - tion, de - vo - tion and her daugh - ter Love, Still

Meshorerim.

Hazzan.

dim.

ye - ra - 'eh, ah!............... ah!.................... pid - yo -
ear so dull, no ear so dull, no...... soul so cold, That felt not
bid the soul, the burst - ing soul, still..... bid the soul, To sounds that

XII.—37

ne - nu, ah!...................................... We - ye - ra - 'eh, we
fired.... not................. to the bone,.... Till Da - vid's lyre, till
seem.... as................. from a - bove..... In dreams, in dreams, in

ye - ra - 'eh, we - ye - ra - 'eh, pid - yo - ne -
Da - vid's lyre grew might - i - er than................. his
dreams that day's, that day's broad light can................ not re -

nu,...... pid - yo - ne - nu, ah!................. 'ad - 'e - reb.
throne, till Da - vid's lyre grew might - i - er, grew........... might - i - er than his throne.
move, that day's.... broad.... light........ can..................... not re - move.

lish verses, as presented in 1815. It extends to two stanzas of the Hebrew hymn. This application and the manner in which the old-time vocal accompanists rather than choristers, the "meshorerim," otherwise known as "singer and bass" (see MUSIC, SYNAGOGAL), would alternate with and imitate the solo of the precentor, are further shown in the transcription by the addition of the Hebrew text of the opening strophes.

BIBLIOGRAPHY: A. Baer, Baal Tefillah, No. 1306, Frankfort-on-the-Main, 1883; Israel, ii. 183, London, 1898.
A.   F. L. C.

YAD (lit. "hand"; Judæo-German, **teitel**): A pointer to guide the reading in public of the text of the Sefer Torah. During the reading of the Law in the synagogue the reader stands on the right side, the one "called up" being in the center, and the "segan," or deputy representing the congregation, on the left. The segan points out with the "yad" the text for the reader to follow.

From the remotest times the Hebrew teacher used a pointer somewhat similar to the tapering stick employed by the professional lecturer in modern times to point out places, figures, or words on a map or blackboard. The earliest reference to **Origin** its use is in connection with the schools **from the** of BETHAR before the destruction of **School.** that place in the war of Bar Kokba (132-135). Bethar had a larger number of schools and scholars than any other town in Judea; when an enemy forced himself into one of the schools the teachers stabbed him with their pointers (Giṭ. 58a). The use of the "teitel" by the teacher of primary classes in the ḥeder or Talmud Torah is still common in the eastern countries of Europe.

The use of the yad by the segan for guiding the reader of the Sefer Torah is not obligatory, as the reader may guide himself with it, or it may be dispensed with entirely. It is for the convenience of the reader only, and it is handled by a second person, the segan, perhaps in order to impress the ceremony upon the reader, and to prevent errors in the reading. It serves also to keep the reader from touching the text with his fingers in a desire to guide his reading; for touching the bare Sefer Torah with the hands without a "mappah" rendered them impure for handling "terumah," the priests' share of the heave-offering (Yad. iii. 2). This is one of the eighteen enactments or "gezerot" (Shab. 14a); and the motive of the edict was doubtless to compel the priests, who had easy access to the Sefer Torah, to handle it with special care.

There are various styles of yad for the Sefer Torah. The usual size is about 12 inches long. It is made in the fashion of a staff or scepter, narrowed down at the end, which is in the shape of a closed hand with the index-finger extended. Most frequently the staff is made of silver, ornamented sometimes with a gold hand and sometimes even with jewels; but hard wood also is used, preferably the olive-wood of the Holy Land, with an ivory hand. Often the yad is inscribed with an appropriate Biblical verse, such as "The law of the Lord is perfect, converting the soul" (Ps. xix. 7), or with the name of the donor. There is a ring attached to the top of the staff, with a chain by which to hang it to the rollers (= "'eẓ ḥayyim") of the scroll after the latter has been rolled up. The yad is one of the "kele ḳodesh" (= "holy vessels") ornamenting the Torah. See SCROLL OF THE LAW.

BIBLIOGRAPHY: Jacobs, Year Book, 5659, p. 314.
J.   J. D. E.

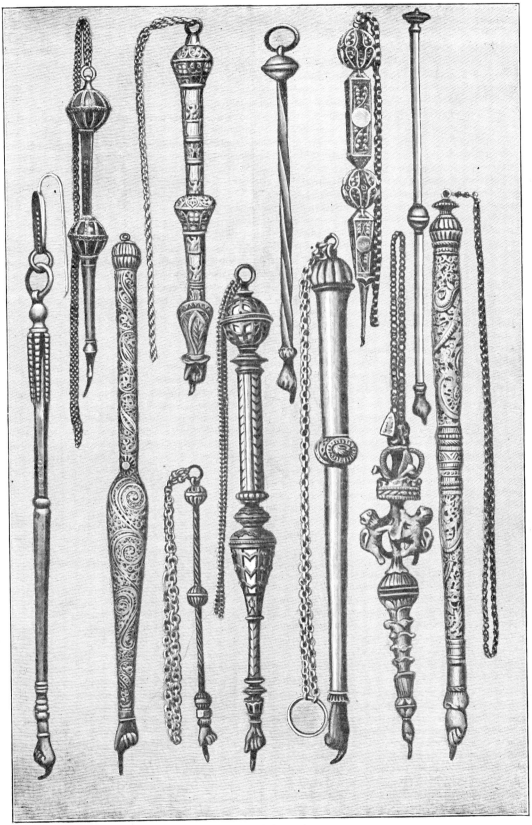

VARIOUS SPECIMENS OF THE YAD.

(In the Victoria and Albert Museum, London ; Cluny Museum, Paris ; Temple Emanu-El, New York ; Temple Shearith Israel, New York ; and in the possession of Sir Samuel Montagu, London ; E. A. Franklin, London ; Maurice Herrmann, New York.)

YADAYIM ("Hands"): Treatise of the Mishnah and the Tosefta, dealing with the uncleanness of the hands and their ablution. It stands eleventh in the order Ṭohorot in most editions of the Mishnah, and is divided into four chapters, containing twenty-two paragraphs in all.

Ch. i.: The quantity of water necessary to cleanse the hands by pouring it over them (§ 1); the vessels from which the water may be poured over the hands (§ 2); kinds of water which may not be used to cleanse the hands, and persons who may perform the act of manual ablution (§§ 3–5).

Ch. ii.: How the water should be poured over the hands, and the first and second ablutions (§§ 1–3); the hands are regarded as clean in all cases where doubt exists as to whether the ablution was properly performed (§ 4).

Ch. iii.: Things which render the hands unclean; the canonical books make the hands unclean. The holy writings were kept together with the equally sacred heave-offering ("terumah") of the priests, and were injured by mice; to prevent this it was enacted that the holy writings defiled the hands as well as the heave-offering, thus leading to a discontinuance of the custom of keeping them together; discussion of the question whether the Song of Solomon and Ecclesiastes are canonical, and thus render the hands unclean; on the day of the election of Eleazar b. Azariah as nasi these books were declared canonical.

Ch. iv.: Other verdicts rendered on the same day in which the Song of Solomon and Ecclesiastes were declared canonical, these rulings being corollaries of that decision (§§ 1–4); the Aramaic language in Ezra and Daniel, the ancient Hebrew writing ("ketab 'Ibri"), and dissensions between Pharisees and Sadducees (§§ 5–8).

The Tosefta to this treatise is divided into two chapters, and contains, in addition to amplifications of the mishnaic sayings, various interesting maxims, of which the following may be mentioned: "The book of Ben Sira (Ecclesiasticus [Sirach]) and all books of later date are no longer canonical" (ii. 13). The "Ṭobele Shaḥarit" (= "Morning Baptists"; see JEW. ENCYC. v. 230) said to the Pharisees: "We reproach you for uttering the Holy Name before your bodies have been cleansed of their impurities" (ii. 20).

J.   J. Z. L.

YAH SHIMEKA: Hymn of five long stanzas which forms the introduction to the Ḳaddish before "Bareku" in the morning service of the second day of New-Year in the ritual of the Sephardim; it is signed with the acrostic "Yehudah," and is attributed to Judah ha-Levi (Zunz, "Literaturgesch." p. 413). The refrain, "Yishtabbah," etc., is quoted from the Ḳaddish mentioned, and suggests by its rhythm the shaping of the whole hymn in one of the favorite rhythmic figures of Arab music. As with so many other melodies of the Sephardic tradition, and particularly with those for the penitential season, its ancient Oriental tune is also utilized for other hymns. Such are the verses "Shinannim" by Solomon ibn Gabirol, occupying a similar position in the Atonement services, and Judah ha-Levi's other hymn, "Yede rashim," which takes its place on the first day of New-Year, as well as the following Ḳaddish itself and the more familiar hymns EN KELO-

YAH SHIMEKA

Allegretto.

Yah shim-eka,.... a-ro-mi-me-ka, we-zid-ka-te-ka.........
lo a kas-seh;........ He-'e-zan-ti we-he-e-man-ti,......
We-ek yo-mer..... ye-zir.......... ho-mer, e-
De-rash-ti-hu, pe-gash-ti-hu, le-
Ha-ba-hir,...... we-or mas-hir........ be-

Last time.

lo esh-'al.... we-lo a-nas-seh;
le yo-zěro........ ma ta-'a-seh;
mig-dal 'oz.... we-zur mah-seh;
en ma-sak.... we-en mik-seh;   Yish-tab-bah,...... we-

più lento.   rit.

yit-pa-'ar, we-yit-ro-mam, we-yit-----nas-se.

HENU and ADON 'OLAM at the close of the devotions on the same solemn days. The melody thus becomes in the Spanish and Portuguese ritual a "representative theme" for the New-Year festival. The quaint tune presents several antique and Oriental features. One is the repetition of the middle phrase as many times as the varying length of the texts to which it is chanted may render necessary. The presence in the same melody of a note sometimes natural and sometimes flat is explained by the fact that the scale is that of the "immutable system" of the ancients (see Gevaert, "Histoire et Théorie de la Musique de l'Antiquité," i. 105 *et seq*.). A very similar peculiarity in a parallel melody from Asia Minor is exhibited and discussed in Bourgault-Ducoudray, "Trente Mélodies Populaires de Grèce et d'Oriente," No. 16.

A.   F. L. C.

YAHBI'ENU. See NE'ILAH (HYMN TUNES, 1).

YAHYA: Portuguese family of the Middle Ages, members of which were prominent in Portugal, Spain, Italy, and Turkey. Certain individuals of the family bore the additional cognomen "Negro," with reference to the Moors, from whom several of their estates had been obtained. The more prominent members of the family are as follows:

1. Yahya ibn Ya'ish (יעיש): Flourished in Lisbon in the eleventh century; died about 1150. He was held in high esteem among the Jews, and King Alfonso I. honored him for his courage. After the conquest of Santarem the king presented him with two country houses that had belonged to the Moors, wherefore he assumed the name "Negro."

2. Joseph ibn Yahya ha-Zaken: Grandson of Yahya ibn Ya'ish (No. 1); lived in Lisbon in the middle of the thirteenth century, and was so wealthy that he built a synagogue at his own expense. He was the author of a Talmudic commentary that is no longer extant.

3. Solomon ibn Yahya ha-Zaken: Son of Joseph ibn Yahya (No. 2); died before 1300. He endeavored to check the growing love of luxury among his coreligionists, in order that they might not incur the hatred and envy of the Christians.

4. Gedaliah ibn Yahya ha-Zaken ben Solomon: Body-physician to King Ferdinand until 1370, when he lost the favor of his master. He thereupon entered the service of Henry of Castile, who made him the head of the Jewish communities of his realm; and he enjoyed a yearly income of 5,000 gold ducats, which sum was levied as a tax. He died at a ripe age in Toledo.

5. Joseph ibn Yahya ben Solomon: Brother of Gedaliah (No. 4); famous for his physical beauty and also for his poetic ability. He left Portugal with his brother and settled in Castile. He was the author of some liturgical poems, but they were destroyed in a conflagration. Joseph was a pupil of Solomon ben Adret, at whose death he wrote an elegy in so-called echo rime that has often been reprinted. He defrayed the cost of repairing a synagogue built in Calatayud by one of his ancestors, **Aaron ibn Yahya.**

6. David ibn Yahya Negro ben Gedaliah (ha-Rab shel Sefarad): A prominent figure during the war between the kings of Castile and Portugal. By divulging a secret he succeeded in frustrating the plot of Queen Leonora to murder her son-in-law, and as a reward he was appointed chief rabbi of Castile, while King João of Portugal disposed of his estates in that country. At the time of his death, which occurred at Toledo in Oct., 1385, he held the post of "almoxarife" for King Ferdinand of Castile. His tombstone has been preserved.

7. Judah ibn Yahya Negro ben David: Born in Toledo in the middle of the fourteenth century. Together with his brother Solomon he emigrated to Portugal in the year of terror, 1391. Judah was employed for a long time in the service of Queen Philippa, the consort of João I., and he had also considerable influence with the king. When Vicente Ferrer asked permission to carry on a propaganda against the Jews in Portugal, the king, at the instigation of Judah, informed him (Ferrer) that his request would be granted on condition that he place a red-hot crown upon his head. Judah was one of the most prominent poets of his time, and wrote several elegies deploring the unhappy fate of his Spanish brethren. Among these poems may be mentioned: (1) an elegy beginning with the words יהודה וישראל and written in continuous rime; (2) one beginning with the words אל אל אשר ברא; (3) an elegy on the persecutions of 1319 in Seville, Andalusia, Castile, Provence, and Aragon (printed in Landshuth's "'Ammude ha-'Abodah," p. 30); (4) three poems that have been printed in Carmoly's "Dibre ha-Yamim li-Bene Yahya," p. 12; (5) an elegy for the Ninth of Ab. He was also the author of responsa and of several piyyuṭim; among the latter are a hymn to be recited before the prayer ברוך שאמר, and another which appeared in "Sheḳel ha-Ḳodesh," pp. 67, 68.

8. Gedaliah ibn Yahya ben Solomon (Mestre Guedelha Fysico e Astrologo): Portuguese philosopher and astrologer; born in Lisbon about 1400. Before he was thirty years of age he was appointed court astrologer to João I. Upon the death of that king (1433) the latter's son Duarte prepared for his coronation, but Gedaliah warned him against it; and when the prince insisted on assuming the crown the astrologer prophesied that his reign would be brief and unhappy. Later, when Duarte fell sick he attributed his illness to this evil prophecy, and the oppressive measures against the Jews were made still more severe.

9. Solomon ibn Yahya ben David: A person of prominence during the reign of Alfonso V. of Portugal, he and his entire family being admitted at court. He was rabbi of the Lisbon community, and forbade his children and relatives to accumulate property because he foresaw the coming persecutions. His death occurred before that of Alfonso V.

10. Solomon ibn Yahya ben David: Prominent scholar who was highly honored by Alfonso V. He was the father of the author of "Leshon Limmudim"; he died in Lisbon, where his grave is still shown.

11. Joseph ibn Yahya ben David: Born 1425; was an intimate friend of Alfonso V., who called him "the wise Jew." He was blamed by the king for not dissuading the Jews from indulging their love of luxury. When some of the exiled Spanish Jews settled in Portugal, they were regarded with disfavor by the Portuguese Jews, and Joseph did his best to remove this animosity. King João at the beginning of his reign allowed the Jews to settle in the kingdom, and when he endeavored later to convert them to Christianity he chose Joseph as the first to receive baptism (1495). Joseph thereupon fled, together with his sons David Meïr and Solomon, taking with him 100,000 crusados. He cruised in the Mediterranean for some time, and finally landed in Castile, where he was sentenced to be burned at the stake. Through the intervention of Duke Alvarez de Bragança he was permitted to continue his journey; and after a five months' voyage he landed in Pisa, Italy, where he and his family were put in irons by the troops of Charles VIII., who was about to invest that city. By sacrificing enormous sums of money he obtained his liberty, and placed himself under the protection of the Duke of Ferrara. In the beginning he was well treated, but later he was accused of endeavoring to induce the Maranos to return to Judaism and was tortured. He freed himself from this charge by paying 7,000 gold pieces, but he died as a result of the tortures he had endured (1498). A legend relates that his tomb was located near that of the prophet Hosea. It is said that a copy of Maimonides' "Yad" was made for him in 1472 by Solomon ben Alsark, or Alsarkon.

12. Dinah Yaḥya: Wife of David ibn Yaḥya ben Joseph (No. 15). Disguised in masculine attire she fled from Portugal together with her father-in-law and her husband; and during the flight she abstained from meat, subsisting on bread and water only. Arriving in Pisa, she sought refuge from the French troops on top of a tower twenty meters high; and when discovered she is said to have leaped to the ground without suffering injury. She fled to Florence, where she gave birth to her son Joseph.

13. Gedaliah ibn Yaḥya ben David: Philosopher; born in Lisbon 1437; died at Constantinople in Oct., 1487. He was the author of "Shib'ah 'Enayim," on the seven cardinal virtues of the Jews, which appeared in Constantinople in 1543, and later in Venice. During a sojourn in Constantinople he advocated a union of the Karaites and Rabbinites.

14. David ibn Yaḥya ben Solomon: Born 1455; died 1528. He was rabbi of the Lisbon community in 1476. Accused of inducing the Maranos to relapse into Judaism, he was sentenced by King João II. to be burned at the stake. He fled to Naples with his family, but was captured; and he was compelled to sell his library in order to secure sufficient money to purchase his liberty. On his release he fled to Corfu, and later went to Larta, where he died in extreme poverty. He was the author of a Hebrew grammar entitled "Leshon Limmudim," which was published in Constantinople (1506, 1528) and in Venice (1542). While at Larta he wrote to the wealthy Jew Isaiah Messene, asking his aid; and this letter was copied by Joseph David Sinzheim, and later published by Grätz ("Gesch." viii. 482–483). According to Carmoly, David was the author of the following works also: "Ḳab we-Naḳi" (Lisbon, n.d.), a commentary on the Mishnah; a selection of the best explanations by various commentators on the Bible

(2d ed., Venice, 1518; 4th ed., Salonica, 1522); "Sheḳel ha-Ḳodesh" (Constantinople, 1520), on the rules for Hebrew poetry; "Tehillah le-Dawid," an uncompleted commentary on the Psalms; "Hilkot Ṭerefot" (ib. 1520); and a commentary on Maimonides' "Moreh," appended to his above-mentioned letter of supplication to Messene.

15. David ibn Yaḥya ben Joseph. See JEW. ENCYC. vi. 553.

16. Solomon ibn Yaḥya ben Joseph: A Portuguese exile who fled with his family to Pisa. He left his relatives and went to Rhodes, where he died in 1533.

17. Meïr ibn Yaḥya ben Joseph: Author of a poetic introduction to the "Cuzari" (Fano, 1506). He lived at Pisa, and later settled in Oulina (אולינא), Italy, where he died in 1530.

18. Joseph ibn Yaḥya ben David. See JEW. ENCYC. vi. 553.

19. Judah ibn Yaḥya ben Joseph: Physician; born in Imola, Italy, 1529; died in Bologna 1560. He studied medicine at Padua, and was at the same time a pupil of Meïr Katzenellenbogen. Receiving his medical degree in 1557, he settled as a practitioner in Bologna.

20. David ibn Yaḥya ben Joseph: President of the Jewish community of Naples; died in 1565. He was a cousin of David ibn Yaḥya (No. 14), the author of "Leshon Limmudim," under whom he studied, and was the author of a eulogy which appeared in that work.

21. Gedaliah ibn Yaḥya ben Joseph: Talmudist; born at Imola, Italy, 1515; died, probably in Alexandria, about 1587. He studied in the yeshibah at Ferrara under Jacob Finzi and Abraham and Israel Rovigo. In 1549 he settled in Rovigo, where he remained until 1562, in which year the burning of the Talmud took place in Italy. He then went to Codiniola, and three years later to Salonica, whence he returned in 1567 to his native town. Expelled with other Jews by Pope Pius V., and suffering a loss of 10,000 gold pieces, he went to Pesaro, and thence to Ferrara, where he remained till 1575. During the ensuing eight years he led a wandering life, and finally settled in Alexandria. His chief work was the "Sefer Shalshelet ha-Ḳabbalah," called also "Sefer Yaḥya," on which he labored for more than forty years. This work is not without defects, having suffered either by reason of the author's itinerant mode of life or through faulty copying of the original manuscript. Its contents are as follows: (1) history and genealogy of the Jews from the time of Moses until that of Moses Norzi (1587); (2) account of the heavenly bodies, Creation, the soul, magic, and evil spirits; (3) history of the peoples among which the Jews have dwelt, and a description of the unhappy fate of the author's coreligionists up to his time. The value of this work is, however, lessened considerably by the facts that the writer has included many oral narratives which he gathered partly in his home, partly in Salonica and Alexandria, and that he often lacks the ability to distinguish truth from fiction. For these reasons the book has been called "The Chain of Lies"; but Loeb has proved that it is more accurate than many have supposed it to be. The "Shalshelet ha-Ḳabbalah" was

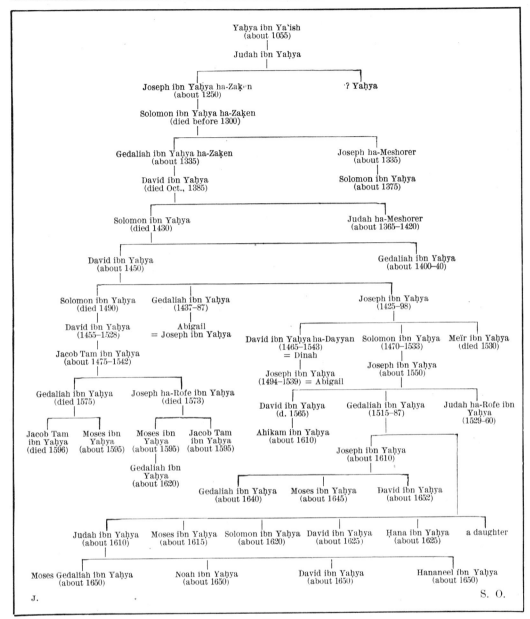

YAḤYA PEDIGREE.

published at Venice, 1587; Cracow, 1596; Amsterdam, 1697; Zolkiev, 1802, 1804; Polonnoye, 1814; and Lemberg, 1862.

Gedaliah was the alleged author of twenty-one other works, which he enumerates at the end of his "Shalshelet," and which are mentioned also in Benjacob's "Oẓar ha-Sefarim" (pp. 590-591).

22. Jacob Tam ibn Yaḥya ben David: Turkish rabbi; lived from about 1475 to 1542. He was probably rabbi of Salonica, and was a Talmudist of repute. Benjamin ben Abraham Muṭal, in the preface to his "Tummat Yesharim," mentions Jacob Tam as the author of the following works: a commentary on Alfasi; the completion of Nissim Gerondi's halakot entitled "Ma'aseh Nissim"; a commentary on R. Nissim's halakot entitled "'Al ha-Nissim"; controversial writings against R. Nissim; Talmudic decisions; and responsa and derashot. All these works were destroyed in a fire at Constantinople. Jacob Tam published Leon ben Massoni's "Sefer Yosippon" (1510), and wrote an opinion of Abraham ben Solomon Treves's "Birkat Abraham" (1512). He was a member of the rabbinical conference which convened in May, 1520, to dissolve the ban placed on Shaltiel, "kahijalik" ("præfectus aulæ") to Sultan Sulaiman, on account of which Shaltiel had been discharged from his office.

23. Joseph ibn Yahya bar Jacob Tam: Born in Constantinople; body-physician to Sultan Sulaiman. Joseph was obliged to be in constant attendance during the sultan's travels and in time of war; and he met his death in battle (1573). The poet Saadia Lougo wrote an elegy in Joseph's honor which was printed in the "Seder Zemannim." Joseph defrayed the cost of publishing the "Shib'ah 'Enayim," the "Leshon Limmudim," and the "Sheḳ-el ha-Ḳodesh," all written by his ancestors.

24. Gedaliah ibn Yahya ben Jacob Tam: Physician and scholar; born in Constantinople; died there 1575. He officiated as rabbi and teacher in Salonica and Adrianople until 1548, in which year he went to Constantinople and devoted himself to Hebrew literature. He left numerous manuscripts, several of which are still extant in the Orient.

25. Tam ibn Yahya ben Gedaliah: Born in Constantinople in the middle of the sixteenth century. He inherited a large fortune from his father, and used his wealth to promote Jewish literature. Upon the death of his father he settled in the neighborhood of Salonica, where he was intimate with several well-known poets, among them Abraham Reuben and Saadia Lougo. His own literary efforts consisted in compiling the commentaries left by his forefathers on the writings of Alfasi, R. Nissim, and Moses ben Naḥman. He completed this task in 1595, but died before the work was published. Eliezer Shoshan and Meïr Yizḥaḳi were called to his deathbed and entrusted with the task of publishing the work, which appeared at Venice in 1622, under the title "She'elot u-Teshubot Ohole Shem."

26. Moses ibn Yahya ben Gedaliah: Turkish physician of the latter half of the sixteenth century. He resided in Constantinople, and during an epidemic of the plague he not only devoted a large part of his fortune to aiding the sufferers, but also rendered medical assistance at the risk of his life. He was known throughout Turkey for his generous hospitality.

27. Gedaliah ibn Yahya ben Moses: Born at Salonica in the latter half of the sixteenth century; son of Moses ibn Yahya (No. 26). He was a liberal patron of letters, and gathered about him no less than thirty-two littérateurs in order to cultivate Hebrew poetry. Among the most prominent members of this circle were Judah Zarḳa and Israel Najara. The names of these poets and some of the verses written by them in Gedaliah's honor have been printed in Carmoly's "Dibre ha-Yamim."

Other members of the Yahya family whose relationship to the persons mentioned above has not been established are as follows:

28. Bonsenior ibn Yahya (called also **Maestro ibn Yahya**): Author of a poem on chess. It appeared first at Mantua (1549) and later in a Latin translation at Oxford (1702), Frankfort-on-the-Main (1767), and Presburg.

29. Judah ibn Yahya ben Gedaliah: Italian scholar of the eighteenth century; lived in Padua and in Venice. He sought the advice of Meïr Katzenellenbogen with regard to intimate family affairs,

the incident being mentioned in Meïr's responsa (No. 53).

30. Reuben ibn Yahya ben Solomon Hezekiah: Born in Lugo, Italy, at the close of the seventeenth century. He was a pupil of Isaac Fano, and was appointed rabbi of Lugo during the lifetime of his teacher. He was the author of a haskamah which appears in the preface to Lampronti's "Paḥad Yizḥaḳ."

31. Samuel ibn Yahya: Rabbi in Amsterdam in the sixteenth and seventeenth centuries; author of "Trinta Discursos" (Amsterdam, 1629), thirty sermons in Spanish.

32. Solomon ibn Yahya: A Portuguese exile who settled in Ancona, where he was burned at the stake by order of Pope Paul IV.

33. Zerahiah ibn Yahya: Scholar of Lugo, Italy; flourished about 1730. In his latter years he held the office of ab bet din in his native town. He is mentioned in Lampronti's "Paḥad Yizḥaḳ" (iii. 20a).

BIBLIOGRAPHY: Zunz, Z. G. pp. 223, 233, 381, 394, 409, 461, 465, 499, 531; idem, G. V. p. 434; De Rossi, Dizionario; Luzzatto, Prolegomena, p. 35; Geiger, Melo Chofnajim, p. 72; Conforte, Ḳore ha-Dorot, ed. Cassel; Azulai, Shem ha-Gedolim, i. 92; ii. 11, 15, 33, 46; Orient, Lit. vii. 542, 561; xii. 455; Jost's Annalen, ii. 26; Carmoly, Histoire des Médecins Juifs, pp. 123, 164, Brussels, 1844; Ersch and Gruber, Encyc. ii.; xxxi. 60, 80; Nepi-Ghirondi, Toledot Gedole Yisrael, pp. 132, 148, 149; Dukes, Naḥal Ḳedumim, p. 53; Gedaliah ibn Yahya, Shalshelet ha-Ḳabbalah; Delitzsch, Zur Gesch. der Jüdischen Poesie, pp. 3, 67, 70, 76, 77, 158, 174; Bass, Sifte Yeshenim, ed. Zolkiev, 1800, p. 18d; J. Loeb, in R. E. J. xvii. 93–95; Frankel, in Zeitschrift für die Religiösen Interessen des Judenthums, ii. 78; Reifmann, in Ha-Maggid, 1864, viii. 190–191; Hebr. Bibl. ii. 110, vi. 458-459, xvi. 40; Manasseh ben Israel, Nishmat Ḥayyim, iii. 21; Landshuth, 'Ammude ha-'Abodah, xxx.; Carmoly, Dibre ha-Yamim li-Bene Yahya, Frankfort-on-the-Main, 1850; Kayserling, Gesch. der Juden in Portugal; idem, Bibl. Esp.-Port.-Jud. p. 53a; Steinschneider, Cat. Bodl. cols. 804, 864-866, 1002, 1475-1476, 2256-2467, 2665; idem, Schach bei den Juden.
J.   S. O.

YA'ISH, DAVID B. ABRAHAM IBN: Representative of the community of Seville and contemporary of Asher b. Jehiel. He was probably a brother of Solomon b. Abraham ibn Ya'ish and the father of the Solomon b. David ibn Ya'ish mentioned by Judah b. Asher ("Zikron Yehudah," p. 12a).

BIBLIOGRAPHY: Ibn Verga, Shebeṭ Yehudah, pp. 18, 31; Grätz, Gesch. vii. 541 et seq.; Steinschneider, Hebr. Uebers. pp. 686, 939; Hebr. Bibl. vi. 115 (on the identity), xvii. 119, xix. 93 et seq.; Jost's Annalen, i. 231, 302; Asher b. Jehiel, Responsa, Nos. 13, 2; 18, 1.
D.   M. K.

YAKIM. See ALCIMUS.

YAKINI, ABRAHAM. See ABRAHAM HA-YAKINI.

YAḲḲAR BEN SAMUEL HA-LEVI I.: German scholar of the eleventh century; lived for a short time in Speyer. He was a pupil of Kalonymus of Rome, and questions addressed by him to Kalonymus have been preserved ("Shibbole ha-Leḳeṭ," viii.); several of these referred to a custom observed among the Jews of Speyer only. The same subject is treated by Mordecai ("B. M." ix.).

BIBLIOGRAPHY: Kohn, Mordekai ben Hillel, pp. 126, 127, and notes, Breslau, 1878; Fuenn, Keneset Yisrael, pp. 669-670; Gross, Gallia Judaica, p. 567.
E. C.   S. O.

YAḲḲAR BEN SAMUEL HA-LEVI II.: German scholar and liturgical poet of the second half of the thirteenth century; flourished in Cologne and in Mayence. He was related to Meïr of Rothenburg, in whose responsa he is several times mentioned; and he was a pupil of R. Jehiel of Paris. His marginal glosses to Abot are still preserved in manuscript. He was, besides, the author of the following liturgical poems: a "yozer" for a Sabbath festival; an "ofan"; a "zulat," poem to be sung before the recital of the "Shemoneh 'Esreh"; a "Ḳedushshah," to be sung at the repetition of the "Shemoneh 'Esreh"; a zulat, poem beginning with the words "Ezkerah Elohim" and meant for the Sabbath following the 20th of Tammuz, in memory of the martyrs of Pforzheim, 1267; a Ḳedushshah, poem in eleven lines, with continuous rime; a "Ge'ullah" of three cantos, each consisting of two stanzas of five lines; and an elegy on Zion, in which the author's name is twice mentioned. As Yaḳḳar and his father, Samuel ben Abraham, fell victims in the butchery of 1271, the zulat in memory of the Pforzheim martyrs must have been written shortly before his death.

BIBLIOGRAPHY: Zunz, S. P. p. 32; idem, Literaturgesch. pp. 487–488; idem, Z. G. pp. 100, 101, 105, 193; Landshuth, 'Ammude ha-'Abodah, p. 132; Gross, Gallia Judaica, pp. 566–568; Kohn, Mordekai ben Hillel, pp. 127–128; Fuenn, Keneset Yisrael, p. 670.

E. C. S. O.

YALḲUṬ ("Compilation"); called also **Yalḳuṭ Shim'oni** ("The Compilation of Simeon"): A haggadic compilation on the books of the Old Testament. From such older haggadot as were accessible to him, the author collected various interpretations and explanations of Biblical passages, and arranged these according to the sequence of those portions of the Bible to which they referred. The individual elucidations form an organic whole only in so far as they refer to the same Biblical passage.

Contents. Lengthy citations from ancient works are often abridged or are only partially quoted, the remainder being cited elsewhere. Since the interpretations of the ancient exegetes usually referred to several passages, and since the Yalḳuṭ endeavored to quote all such explanations, repetitions were inevitable, and haggadic sayings relating to two or more sections of the Bible were often duplicated. In many instances, however, only the beginning of such an explanation is given, the reader being referred to the passage in which it is recorded in its entirety.

The work is divided into sections, which are numbered from Genesis to the end of Deuteronomy, and are numbered anew from the beginning of Joshua, the first non-Pentateuchal book, so that the Yalḳuṭ falls into two parts. The first division treats of the Pentateuch and contains 963 sections, of which §§ 1–162 relate to Genesis; §§ 163–427 to Exodus; §§ 428–682 to Leviticus; §§ 683–788 to Numbers; and §§ 789–963 to Deuteronomy. The second part deals with the non-Pentateuchal books (the Prophets and the Hagiographa), and contains 1,085 sections. In this part the redactor followed the Talmudic order of the prophetic books (B. B. 14b), §§ 1–252 being devoted to the first prophets (Joshua, Samuel, and Kings); §§ 253–335 to Jeremiah; §§ 336–384 to Ezekiel; §§ 385–514 to Isaiah; §§ 515–595 to the twelve minor prophets; §§ 596–609 to Ruth; §§ 610–890 to Psalms; §§ 891–928 to Job; §§ 929–965 to Proverbs; §§ 966–979 to Ecclesiastes; §§ 980–994 to The Song of Solomon; §§ 995–1043 to Lamentations; §§ 1044–1059 to Esther; §§ 1060–1066 to Daniel; §§ 1067–1071 to Ezra and Nehemiah; and §§ 1072–1085 to Chronicles.

In the arrangement of the Hagiographa the author deviates from the Talmudic order (B. B. l.c.) by placing Esther before Daniel, while the reverse order is followed in the Talmud. The division into sections is arbitrary, and the sections are very unequal in length; Deut. 818, for example, in the Wilna edition containing only five lines, while Deut. 938 comprises eighteen columns. In his **Order and** exegesis of each passage, often in the **Arrange-** text itself, the author indicates the **ment.** sources from which his explanations are derived. In the Salonica edition they are given at the beginning of each corresponding Biblical passage, although in later editions they were placed in the margin. In many instances, however, the sources are given in an inconvenient place or are entirely eliminated; while some references are even indicated by a later redactor, as, for example, Job 921, where the source (Ex. R.) is a later addition, the original redactor being unacquainted with Exodus Rabbah (comp. Epstein, "Rabbi Shimeon Ḳara weha-Yalḳuṭ Shim'oni," in "Ha-Ḥoḳer," i. 137). The sources embrace not only the major portion of halakic and haggadic literature during the ancient and geonic epochs, but also the haggadic literature as late as the twelfth century. The author made use of the older midrashic works, such as Seder 'Olam, Sifra, Sifre, Sifre Zuṭa, Mekilta, the Baraita on the Thirty-two Middot, the Baraita on the Forty-nine Middot, and **Sources.** the Baraita on the Erection of the Tabernacle ("Meleket ha-Mishkan"); and he availed himself also of the Mishnah, both Talmudim, and Semaḥot, Ḳallah, and Soferim. He drew from the ethical and historical Haggadah, such as Abot de-Rabbi Natan, Tanna debe Eliyahu (Rabbah and Zuṭa), Derek Ereẓ, Masseket Gan 'Eden, Midrash Wayissa'u, the Chronicle of Moses, and the Midrash on the Death of Moses. The author's chief source, however, was the explanatory midrashim, such as the rabbot on Pentateuch (with the exception of Exodus Rabbah), Pesiḳta, Pesiḳta Rabbati, Yelammedenu, Tanḥuma, Debarim Zuṭa, Midrash Abba Gorion, Esfa, Tadshe, Abkir, Pirḳe Rabbi Eli'ezer, and the midrashim on Samuel, Psalms, Proverbs, and Job. The latter works are often cited simply as "Midrash," without any more definite identification. In that portion of the Yalḳuṭ which treats of the books of Samuel, Psalms, and Proverbs, the term "Midrash" designates the midrash on the respective books. The term "Midrash" is used also to indicate the source of passages which belong to older or more recent works. In these few instances the author was apparently either uncertain of his references or he used an older collection known under the name of "Midrash," but did not have access to the original documents. It must also be borne in mind that the redactor failed to use various sources, such as the Midrash on the Ten Commandments and the Midrash on the Death of Aaron, and that he likewise ignored the Targumim and writings relating to esoteric doctrines, with the exception of the "Otiyyot de-R. Akiba," to which he alludes in Gen. 1., § 1.

The author of the Yalḳuṭ can not be determined with certainty. The title-page of the Venice edition ascribes the composition of the work to R. Simeon of Frankfort, "the chief of exegetes" ("rosh ha-darshanim"), and this was accepted by Conforte and Azulai, who called him Simeon Ash-
Author kenazi of Frankfort. Rapoport (in **and Date.** "Kerem Ḥemed," vii. 7 et seq.), on the other hand, maintained that R. Simeon (the father of R. Joseph Ḳara), who flourished in the eleventh century, was its author; but this assertion is untenable since the compiler of the Yalḳuṭ used midrashim of a later date. If the Yalḳuṭ was so old, moreover, it would be difficult to explain why no mention of it is made by R. Nathan b. Jehiel, the author of the "'Aruk," or by Rashi. All the proofs advanced by Rapoport have been refuted by Epstein, who inclines to agree with Zunz that the author of the Yalḳuṭ flourished in the early part of the thirteenth century. According to Zunz, the work was written by R. Simeon Ḳara, who lived in southern Germany at that period, and the title "ha-Darshan" was bestowed upon him probably at a later date. It is certain that a manuscript of the Yalḳuṭ, mentioned by Azariah dei Rossi, existed in 1310 (comp. Zunz, "G. V." pp. 295–303); but despite this, there is scarcely any allusion to the work during the fourteenth and fifteenth centuries. This may be ascribed, however, to the unhappy position of the German Jews and to the repeated persecutions of the period; for peace and prosperity were necessary for the copying of so extensive a work, and the Jews of Germany had neither. After the beginning of the fifteenth century, on the other hand, the work must have been disseminated in foreign countries, for it was used by Spanish scholars of the latter half of that century, Isaac Abravanel being the first to mention it (comp. Epstein, l.c. p. 134).

The editio princeps of the Yalḳuṭ was printed in Salonica in 1521, the latter part of the work, relating to the Prophets and the Hagiographa, appearing first. The part treating of the Pentateuch appeared between 1526 and 1527, and the entire work was later published in Venice (1566) with certain emendations and deviations from the Salonica edition. All later texts are
Editions. merely reprints of the Venetian edition, with the exception of one published at Leghorn (1650–59), which contained additions and corrections as well as a commentary by R. Abraham Gedaliah. The latest text (Wilna, 1898) is based on the editions of Lublin, Venice, and Leghorn, and contains foot-notes giving the sources, a glossary of difficult words, and an index of the chapters and verses of Biblical passages. To this edition is appended a brief commentary by Abraham Abele Gumbiner of Kalisz entitled "Zayit Ra'anan."

BIBLIOGRAPHY: Zunz, G. V. pp. 295–303; Rapoport, in Kerem Ḥemed, vii. 4 et seq.; Abraham Epstein, Rabbi Shimeon Ḳara weha-Yalḳuṭ Shim'oni, in Ha-Ḥoḳer, i. 85–93, 129–137; Schürer, Gesch. 3d ed., i. 146.
J.   J. Z. L.

YANNAI: Palestinian amora of the third century; father-in-law of Ammi. According to his own statement, he had a grandson of the same name (Ḥul. 111a). He is known as having taken part in a controversy regarding the succession of the writings of King Solomon, he himself maintaining that the book Ḳohelet is the last one written by him (Cant. R. i. 1).

BIBLIOGRAPHY: Bacher, Ag. Pal. Amor. ii. 145a, iii. 573–574; Heilprin, Seder ha-Dorot, ii. 116d.
J.   S. O.

YANNAI: First payyeṭan to employ rime and introduce his name in acrostics; flourished, probably in Palestine, in the first half of the seventh century. He was apparently a very prolific poet, for reference is made to "the liturgical poems of Yannai"; he is also said to have composed "ḳerobot" for the "orders of the year" (perhaps for the weekly lessons). Most of his poems are lost; some are perhaps still extant, but they can not be recognized with certainty as Yannai's work. The following fragments alone remain to show his style:

1. אוני פטרי רחמתים: A "ḳerobah" for Sabbath ha-Gadol. It is said to include also אז רוב נסים הפלאת בלילה, found in the Pesaḥ Haggadah.

2. שיר השירים נא לידידי: A "shib'ata" for the seventh day of Pesaḥ. The middle portion is missing. It is designated as דרמושה (this reading must be substituted for the senseless לרמושה in the superscription), i.e., "bolt" or "beam" (δρόμος, otherwise called רהיט), and forms a sort of textual variation of Canticles, following the conception and interpretation of that book in the Midrash.

3. תעו אז בפתרוס: A "silluḳ" for Sabbath Shim'u, i.e., the second Sabbath before the Ninth of Ab.

Yannai, like his predecessor Jose b. Jose, is not as obscure in his vocabulary and in his metaphors as is Ḳalir, who is said to have been Yannai's pupil and to have been killed by his master out of jealousy. The extant examples of Yannai's work do not indicate any great poetic talent.

BIBLIOGRAPHY: Rapoport, in Bikkure ha-'Ittim, 1829, p. 111; idem, in Kerem Ḥemed, 1841, vi. 25; Luzzatto, Mebo, p. 10; Zunz, Literaturgesch. p. 28; Landshuth, Ammude ha-'Abodah, p. 102; Harkavy, Studien und Mittheilungen, v. 106; S. A. Wertheimer, Ginze Yerushalayim, ii. 18b.
D.   H. B.

YANNAI (known also as **Yannai Rabbah** = "the Great"): Palestinian amora of the first generation (2d and 3d cent.). A genealogical chart found at Jerusalem traced his descent from Eli (Yer. Ta'an. iv. 2; Gen. R. xcviii. 13). Yannai was very wealthy; he is said to have planted four hundred vineyards (B. B. 14a) and to have given an orchard to the public (M. Ḳ. 12b). His first residence was at Sepphoris (Yer. Ber. iv. 6 et al.), where he seems to have held a public office, since at the death of R. Judah ha-Nasi I. (Rabbi) he gave an order that even priests might attend the funeral of the great teacher (ib. iii. 1). Halevy, however, has concluded that Yannai always lived at 'Akbarah, or 'Akbari, where he established a school (see below).

Yannai was prominent both as halakist and haggadist. He was a pupil of Rabbi, in whose name he transmitted several halakic sayings (Yer. Ḥag. iii. 2; Yer. Ḳid. iii. 14; et al.). The best known of his senior fellow pupils was Ḥiyya Rabbah, who, as an assistant teacher in Rabbi's school, sometimes acted as

Yannai's tutor (Yer. Dem. vii. 1; Yeb. 93a). But several discussions between Ḥiyya and Yannai (Yer. Ber. iv. 5, and Babli *passim*) show the real relationship. Their friendship was afterward cemented by the marriage of Yannai's daughter to Ḥiyya's son Judah (Yer. Bik. iii. 3; Ket. 62b). Yannai transmitted also some halakot in the name of the council ("ḥaburah") of the last tannaim (Mak. 21b). He established an important school at 'Akbarah (Yer. 'Er. viii. 4), often mentioned in both Talmuds and in the Midrash as the "debe R. Yannai" or the "bet R. Yannai," and which continued after his death. His school differed from others in that the pupils were treated as belonging to the master's family; they worked on

His School.

Yannai's estate, took their share of the revenue, and lived under his roof (comp. Yer. Sheb. viii. 6). His chief pupil, of whom he thought highly, was R. Johanan, who transmitted most of his halakot (Yer. Kil. viii. 1; Soṭah 18b; Ḳid. 64b). Others of his many pupils were Simeon b. Laḳish (Yer. Yoma iii. 10; Ta'an. ii. 6; Ḥul. 82a), R. Aibu (Ḳid. 19), and R. Hoshaiah (Ket. 79a).

In regard to the Mishnah of Rabbi he shared the opinion of Ḥiyya. In fact, Yannai ascribed no greater authority to the Mishnah than to the collections of halakot or baraitot compiled by Ḥiyya and other disciples of Rabbi (comp. Yer. Pes. i. 5; Yer. Yoma iv. 2). When his pupil R. Johanan remarked that the Mishnah rendered a decision different from his, he answered, "The Mishnah gives only the decision of a single tanna, while I decide conformably to the Rabbis as a whole" (Shab. 140a). He was independent in his decisions, and sometimes had all his contemporaries against him (Yer. Niddah iii. 4; Shab. 65a). His decisions were generally rigid as regards private persons (Yer. Ber. ii. 6; Yer. Ket. i. 10; Shab. 14a), but liberal when the whole community was concerned. Yannai's disregard of R. Judah Nesi'ah (Judah II.), Rabbi's grandson, was notorious (B. B. 111a, b), and so was his attitude toward R. Ḥanina, an ardent believer in Rabbi's Mishnah (Yer. Kil. ix. 7; Ber. 30a; *et al.*). Referring to Ḥanina, Yannai said, "He who studies the Law under only one teacher sees no sign of blessing" ('Ab. Zarah 19a).

Yannai is conspicuous in both Talmud and Midrash as a prolific haggadist, and he occupies an important place among the Biblical exe-

His Haggadah.

getes of his time. In reference to a man who studied much but did not fear God, he said: "Wo to the man who, before he gets a house, makes the door" (Shab. 31b). He recommended submission to the government (Zeb. 102a; Men. 98a). When old age had impaired his sight he requested Mar 'Uḳba to send him some collyrium prepared by Samuel (Shab. 108b). He enjoined his children to bury him neither in white nor in black clothes, as they would not know whether his place would be in paradise or in hell (Shab. 114a; Yer. Kil. ix. 4).

Bibliography: Bacher, *Ag. Pal. Amor.* i. 35–47; Frankel, *Mebo*, p. 103a, b, Breslau, 1870; Grätz, *Gesch.* 3d ed., iv.; Halevy, *Dorot ha-Rishonim*, ii. 273–282; Heilprin, *Seder ha-Dorot*, ii.; Weiss, *Dor*, iii. 50, 51.
G. M. Sel.

YANNAI BEN ISHMAEL: Palestinian amora of the third century; a contemporary of

Ze'era and of Abba bar Kahana. There exist a few halakot transmitted in his name, among them one referring to the prayer "Shomea' Tefillah" (Ta'an. 14a). A question, likewise referring to the "Shemoneh 'Esreh," is addressed to Yannai by Ze'era through R. Nahum (Yer. Ber. 5a). R. Zeriḳan quotes a halakah in the name of Yannai, referring to the circumcision of slaves (Yer. Yeb. 8d). Several haggadot of Yannai's have been preserved, among which may be mentioned one treating of Adam's meeting with the angels (B. M. 86b), and a farewell address based on the verse Judges i. 15 (Soṭah 46b). Once, during an illness, Yannai was visited by Ze'era and Abba bar Kahana (Yer. Ter. 45c), with the latter of whom he engaged in a controversy relating to Solomon's plantations.

Bibliography: Bacher, *Ag. Pal. Amor.* iii. 572–573; Heilprin, *Seder ha-Dorot*, ii. 117a; Frankel, *Mebo*, p. 103b; *Yuḥasin*, ed. Filipowski, p. 15b.
J. S. O.

YANNAI THE YOUNGER: Palestinian amora of the fourth generation; called "the Younger" ("ze'era") to distinguish him from Yannai b. Ishmael. When his father-in-law died Yannai was exempted from the priestly laws of purity in order that he might attend to the interment of the dead (Yer. Ber. 6a; Yer. Naz. 6i). A sentence treating of the importance of an oath and how it is to be made has been preserved in Lev. R. vi. It appears that at Yannai's funeral his pupils did not follow current customs, for which reason they were reproved by R. Mani (Yer. M. Ḳ. 82c).

Bibliography: Bacher, *Ag. Pal. Amor.* ii. 442, note 5; iii. 448, 623; Frankel, *Mebo*, pp. 103b–104a; Heilprin, *Seder ha-Dorot*, p. 116d.
J. S. O.

YARḤI, ABRAHAM. See ABRAHAM BEN NATHAN.

YARMOUTH: Seaport of Norfolk, England. Jews must have resided in this town at an early date. In the Lansdowne MS. under date of 1280 mention is made of a certain Ysaac de Gernemutha, and in "Hebrew Deeds" ("Sheṭarot"), edited by M. D. Davis, there is an allusion to one Isaac of Yarmouth who resided at Norwich. Row 42 has been known traditionally as Jews' or Synagogue Row, and in 1847 a synagogue which had been erected there was consecrated by Rev. M. B. Levy of the Brighton congregation, the building taking the place of an older one which had become dilapidated. In 1877 the synagogue was closed in consequence of the decrease in the Jewish population, and it is at present used as a parish mission-room. For some time after its closing, services were held at the house of Michael Mitchell. The first minister was probably Rabbi I. Cohen; the second was Levi Levenberg, who died in 1870.

A plot of land for a cemetery was granted by the town council on April 7, 1801, on the petition of Simon Hart, a silversmith, who had resided in Yarmouth for forty years and who was the first to be interred there, in the following year. The cemetery is in the Alma road and contains sixteen tombstones and one headstone, all bearing inscriptions in Hebrew or English.

Among other relics of former days existing in the parish church are an illuminated Hebrew scroll of

Esther, said to date back to the end of the fifteenth century; a copy of the Yosippon in pointed characters and printed at Basel in 1541; and a Hebrew and Latin Bible printed at Antwerp in 1584.

J.
V. E.

YARMUK (modern **Shari'at al-Manaḍirah**): River of Palestine; its various sources rise in the mountains of Hauran and Jaulan; it flows generally west and empties into the Jordan four English miles south of the Lake of Gennesaret. Although it is narrow and shallow throughout its course, at its mouth it is nearly as wide as the Jordan, measuring thirty feet in breadth and five in depth. The Matthew Bridge, which crosses the Yarmuk at its confluence with the Jordan, and which is built of volcanic stones, is celebrated. According to R. Johanan, the Yarmuk was the second largest river in Palestine (B. B. 74b), but its water was not to be used for the water of atonement with the ashes of the red heifer (Parah viii. 10).

BIBLIOGRAPHY: Sepp, *Jerusalem und das Heilige Land*, ii. 287 *et seq.*, Regensburg, 1876; Schwartz, *Palestine*, p. 53, Philadelphia, 1850; Neubauer, *G. T.* p. 31; Ritter, *Comparative Geography of Palestine*, ii. 299 *et seq.*

E. G. H.
S. O.

YAROSLAV (JAROSLAW): Town in Galicia, known as one of the principal seats of the COUNCIL OF FOUR LANDS. The fair of Yaroslav, at which the Council decided matters regarding the various communities, and at which also the heads of yeshibot used to discuss Talmudic themes ("shiṭṭot") with their pupils, was held toward the end of the summer. It is known that in the second half of the seventeenth century Yaroslav began to supplant the other towns with regard to the Council of Four Lands; so that Moses Ḥagiz, in his "Mishnat Ḥakamim," No. 349, mentions only the Yaroslav fair, where the rabbis used to assemble once every three years. In 1671 the Council decided to meet in a place a few miles from Yaroslav, as the town was deemed unsafe; but the decision was soon revoked. It was at the fair of Yaroslav that the Council gave judgment in the eighteenth century in the dispute between Jonathan Eybeschütz and Jacob Emden. Among other important acts of the Council was the giving of approbations of literary works, and many of these were issued at Yaroslav. Thus, in the autumn of 1677, under the presidency of Issachar Bärusch b. Höschel, at this town, permission was granted to print Jekuthiel Blitz's German translation of the Bible; and on the eighth of Tishri, 5452 (= Oct. 1, 1691), under the presidency of Löb Ḥasid, a similar approbation was granted for the Midrash Rabbah.

BIBLIOGRAPHY: Friedberg, *Luḥot Zikkaron*, pp. 17, 36, 65, *et passim*; Grätz, *Gesch.* 3d ed., ix., note 9; x. 51; Schudt, *Jüdische Merckwürdigkeiten*, i. 209.

H. R.
M. Sel.

YASHAR, SEFER HA-: One of the latest works of the midrashic Haggadah; known also under the titles "Toledot Adam" and "Dibre ha-Yamim he-'Aruk." It is written in correct and fluent Hebrew, and treats of the history of the Jews from the time of Adam to that of the Judges. Three-fourths of the work is devoted to the pre-Mosaic period, one-fifth to the Mosaic period, and only three pages to later history. In his endeavors to explain

all Biblical subjects the author invented entire narratives, interweaving them with certain passages of the Bible.

Among such narratives and additions originating with the author may be especially mentioned an explanation of the murder of Abel by Cain, and also an extended and ingenious genealogy of the descendants of Shem, Ham, and Japheth. In this genealogy the origin of Seir, which Ibn Ezra states to be shrouded in obscurity, is explained by the assertion that Seir was the son of Hur, the grandson of Hori, and the great-grandson of Cainan. The life of Abraham is described at great length, the account beginning with his birth and the appearance of the star (viii. 1–35), and including the smallest details, such as, for example, his two journeys to his son Ishmael (xxi. 22–48). Similar minuteness is displayed with regard to the last days of Sarah and her funeral, which, according to the author, was attended not only by Shem, Eber, Aner, Eshkol, and Mamre, but also by Canaanitish kings with their retinues (xxii. 41–44). The enumeration of the doctrines which the three Patriarchs received through Shem and Eber also occupies considerable space; and the life of Joseph is depicted in an especially impressive manner (xxxvii.–xli.).

In connection with the different "blessings" which Jacob before his death gave to his sons, the author depicts the bloody warfare waged between the kings of Canaan and the sons of Israel on account of the violation of Dinah, the war ending with the victory of Israel (xxxiv.–xxxv.). In the history of the sojourn of the Israelites in Egypt and of their exodus from that country are also interwoven several legends, though these lack the completeness that marks the narratives of the pre-Mosaic history (part ii.). The author, moreover, gives an entire song of Joshua, which is merely indicated in the book of that prophet (x. 13); but this consists only of Biblical passages artistically put together.

In the compiling of the work the following sources were made use of, namely: the Babylonian Talmud; Bereshit Rabbah; Pirḳe R. Eliezer; the Yalḳuṭ; the Chronicle of Moses; Yosippon; Midrash Abkir; and various Arabic legends. As to the place and time of the work's origin various legendary accounts are given in the preface of the first edition (Naples, 1552).

Sources.

In 1750 the London printer Thomas Ilive issued an English translation of the work, asserting that he had published the real "Book of Yashar" mentioned in the Bible; and in 1828 the London "Courier" (Nov. 8) reported that a man from Gazan in Persia, by name Alcurin (Noah has "Alcuin"), had discovered the book named after Joshua, and brought it with him to London. Eleven days later (Nov. 19) a Jew of Liverpool named Samuel reported in the same paper that he was working on a translation of this work, which he had obtained in North Africa. Zunz thereupon found himself compelled to assert, in the "Berliner Nachrichten" of Nov. 29, 1828, that the work mentioned was the same as that published in Naples in 1552 or 1613; and in his "Gottesdienstliche Vorträge," 1832, the

Modern Translations.

same author declared that the book originated in Spain in the twelfth century. That Italy, however, was the land of its origin seems evident from the author's knowledge of Italian names, as Tuscany, Lombardy, and the Tiber (x. 7–36), and also from the description of the rape of the Sabines (xvii. 1–14). The appearance of Arabic names, such as Sa'id, Allah, Abdallah, and Khalif, only tends to show that the book was written in southern Italy, where Arabic influence was strongly felt even in the eleventh century.

The " Yashar " has appeared in the following editions: Naples, 1552; Venice, 1625; Cracow, 1628; Prague, 1668; Frankfort-on-the-Main, **Editions.** 1706; Amsterdam, 1707; Constantinople, 1728; Fürth, 1768; Koretz, 1785; Frankfort-on-the-Oder, 1789; Grodno, 1795; Lemberg, 1816 and 1840; Warsaw, 1846; Wilna, 1848; Lemberg, 1850; Wilna, 1852; Warsaw, 1858. It was translated into Judæo-German by Jacob ha-Levi, and published with various annotations and Arabic glosses (Frankfort-on-the-Main, 1674; Sulzbach, 1783). A Latin version by Johann G. Abicht appeared in Leipsic in the middle of the eighteenth century under the title " Dissertatio de Libro Recti." The work was first translated into English by Thomas Ilive, as mentioned above, and later by M. M. Noah under the title " The Book of Yashar " (New York, 1840).

BIBLIOGRAPHY: The passages mentioned in this article refer to the New York edition, since the Hebrew editions are not divided into either chapters or paragraphs. See also Zunz, *G. V.* 2d ed., pp. 162–165 and notes ; Carmoly, in Jost's *Annalen*, 1839, i., No. 19, pp. 149–150 ; M. M. Noah, in preface to *The Book of Yashar*, New York, 1840; Benjacob, *Ozar ha-Sefarim*, p. 233 ; Fürst, *Bibl. Jud.* ii. 111 ; Israel Lévi, *Une Anecdote sur Pharaon*, in *R. E. J.* xviii. 130.

J.   S. O.

YATES PEDIGREE. See SAMUEL AND YATES PEDIGREE.

YATES, BENJAMIN ELIAKIM. First minister of the congregation at Liverpool, England; died there 1798. He was the elder son of Eliakim Getz (Goetz) of Strelitz, and he himself also appears to have been a native of Strelitz. On going to England he became an itinerant seal-engraver, and probably settled in one of the southwestern counties. Subsequently he located in Liverpool, where he became an engraver and working jeweler; and with this calling he combined that of minister or rabbi of the infant Liverpool congregation, acting also as ḥazzan, shoḥeṭ, and mohel. His residence, at 109 Frederick street, is believed to have been the first regular synagogue of the Liverpool Jews. Its small garden was used as a burial-ground, and Benjamin Yates was the last person interred in it.

After Benjamin's death his younger brother, **Samuel,** settled in Liverpool, probably in order to manage the engraving and jewelry business left by his brother, and to look after the latter's young and helpless family. Samuel Yates became, by his marriage with Martha Abrahams, of Shaftesbury, Somersetshire, a progenitor of the leading families of the Liverpool community (see SAMUEL AND YATES).

BIBLIOGRAPHY : Lucien Wolf, *History and Genealogy of the Jewish Families of Yates and Samuel of Liverpool*, London, 1901 ; Gore, *Liverpool Directory*, 1790, 1796, and 1800; Margoliouth, *Jews of Great Britain*, iii. 110–112 (to be cor-

rected by Wolf) ; *Jewish World*, August 10, 1877; Isaac Leeser, *History of the Jews and Their Religion*, in Griffin's *Cyclopædia of Religious Denominations*, p. 11, London, 1853.

J.   I. H.

YAWAN. See JAVAN.

YIDDISH. See JUDÆO-GERMAN.

YEAR-BOOK (German, *Jahrbuch*): An annual publication that contains not only a calendar and a review of the year, but also articles of literary interest, and communal information, being thus distinguished from the almanac, though the line of distinction can not be very sharply drawn. The earliest work of this kind seems to have been that of J. Heineman (Berlin, 1818–20), entitled " Almanach für die Israelitische Jugend." This, however, lasted only a couple of years, whereas the " Jahrbuch " of Isidore Busch was published in Vienna for six years (1842–47), with contributions from the most distinguished Jewish scholars of the time, including Zunz, Rapoport, Picciotto, Sachs, Ludwig Frankl, Kompert, and L. Löw; the latter work was followed by Wertheimer's (1854–68) ; and Klein's " Jahrbuch " was published in Breslau for nineteen years (1841–61). For two or three years the Institut für Förderung der Jüdischen Wissenschaft issued a year-book on Jewish history, and the Société des Etudes Juives also produced an " Annuaire " for four years after its establishment (1880–84).

A somewhat different variety of this class of publications was started by J. Jacobs in the " Jewish Year Book " (1896), which contained statistics, lists of communal institutions and of communal celebrities, a glossary, and a " Who's Who." " The American Jewish Year Book," edited by Cyrus Adler (1899 *et seq.* ; later with Henrietta Szold), has some of these features, together with other characteristics (see ALMANAC). It may here be mentioned that in M. H. Myer's " Calendar and Diary," which appeared in London (1876–96), I. Zangwill produced some of his earliest sketches under the pseudonym " Baroness von S."

The Hebrew year-books deserve special mention, as in a measure they precede the rest in the twelve volumes of " Bikkure ha-'Ittim," which were published in Vienna from 1820 to 1831; these were edited chiefly by I. S. Reggio, and included many articles by Rapoport that were of great value. A kind of supplement was produced at Vienna in 1845, and two volumes of " Bikkurim " were edited by N. Keller in the same place (1864–65). Still more recently two series have appeared in Warsaw: " Ha-Asif " (1894–1903), edited by N. Sokolow; and " Aḥiasaf," begun in 1893 and still in progress. A Hebrew and Dutch " Muzen Almanak " was produced by G. Pollak at Amsterdam in 1844, but appeared only one year. The Jüdischer Verlag of Berlin issued in 1904 the first volume of a " Jüdische Almanach " that was mainly devoted to Zionistic literature, although it contained also much decorative work by E. M. Lilien. The Austrian Jewish Union produces a calendar which often includes literary matter, and which therefore comes under the year-book category (Vienna, 1892; still in progress). A somewhat curious year-book entitled " Bethlehem " was produced in Budapest in 1871, being entirely restricted to the promotion of agriculture among the Jews of Hungary; it was edited by I. Reich, and appeared for one year only. A still earlier Hungarian example was the "Jahrbuch für die Israelitischen Cultusgemeinden in Ungarn," edited by Leopold Rosenberg and published at Budapest in 1860. The Israelitisch-Ungarische Literaturgesellschaft, since its foundation in 1895, has published a year-book of literary contents. In Rumania, Julius Barasch produced a historical year-book at Bucharest, and this is still continued under the title "Anuarul Pentru Israelitzi."

BIBLIOGRAPHY: A. S. Freidus, in *Bulletin of the New York Public Library*, vii. 263–265, New York, 1903.

J.

YEDAYA. See BEDERSI or BEDARESI, JEDAIAH BEN ABRAHAM.

YEHUDAI BEN NAHMAN (usually cited as **Yehudai Gaon**): Gaon of Sura from 760 to 764. After the office of the gaonate was left vacant by the death of Mar Aha, the exilarch Solomon, departing from the usual custom, decided to appoint a scholar of the Pumbedita Academy, Yehudai ben Nahman, as gaon of Sura. Shortly afterward Yehudai's brother Dodai was appointed gaon of Pumbedita (761–767). Yehudai was blind, and was perhaps so afflicted, as I. H. Weiss suggests, at the time when he was appointed gaon. If this was the case his appointment was contrary to Sanh. 49a, according to which a man blind in both eyes is incapable of acting as a judge or as president of a court. It is interesting, however, that it was Yehudai Gaon who decided that blindness should not act as a bar to the appointment as hazzan of a man otherwise irreproachable ("Or Zarua'," i. 116). As far as is known, Yehudai had one son, Joseph (see "Halakot Pesukot," ed. Schlossberg, p. 122); Mar Ahinai is mentioned as his pupil.

Yehudai was highly respected as a halakic authority, and later geonim as well as rabbis hesitated to decide against his opinion (comp. "Teshubot ha-Geonim," ed. Lyck, No. 43, end; Jacob Emden, "She'elat Ya'bez," i., No. 145). His responsa, generally written in Aramaic, are precise and usually very short; they sometimes consist of only one or two words, giving merely the decision. But when he was asked to explain Talmudical passages his responsa naturally went more into detail; and there are also some long responsa dealing with property rights. Some Hebrew responsa are supposed to have been translated by his pupils or by the compiler. The majority of Yehudai's responsa deal with the order of the prayers and the readings from the Scriptures; with traveling on board a vessel and disembarking on the Sabbath, and various laws concerning the observance of the Sabbath and of holy days; with the tefillin (see Hayyim M. Horowitz, "Halachische Schriften der Geonim," i. 45 *et seq.*); and with dietary laws, divorce, and halizah cases of Jews who had embraced Islam and returned to Judaism (comp. especially "Teshubot ha-Geonim," ed. Lyck, No. 45; Müller, "Mafteah le-Teshubot ha-Geonim," pp. 66 *et seq.*).

Alfasi in his "Halakot" (Nedarim, end) asserts that it was Yehudai Gaon who did away with absolution from vows ("hattarat nedarim"), which was so carelessly granted by the rabbis of his time that it gave occasion for Karaite attacks. He even went

so far as to abolish the study of the Talmudical treatise Nedarim ("Vows"), and his successors were anxious to adhere to this reform (see L. Löw, "Gesammelte Schriften," iii. 363).

Yehudai Gaon, however, is best known as the author of halakot, which are quoted under the titles of: "Halakot de-R. Yehudai Gaon," "Halakot Pesukot" or "Hilkot Re'u," "Halakot Ketu'ot," and "Halakot Kezubot" or "Halakot Ketannot" (as distinguished from the "Halakot Gedolot" of Simeon Kayyara). The relation to one another of these several versions, which are obviously adaptations from one and the same original work, is not yet quite clear, and indeed forms a very difficult problem in literary criticism. According to A. Epstein, who devoted an important study to the problem, this work was a collection of legal decisions (halakot), mainly in Aramaic, which first appeared in Yehudai's short responsa or were taken down from his lectures by his pupils and probably arranged by them later. Owing to the fact that the responsa are so short and confine themselves to a mere statement of the decision in question they were called "Decisive Laws" ("Halakot Pesukot" or, according to a more Arabic mode of speech, "Halakot Ketu'ot"). Of the numerous evidences brought forward by Epstein to prove that the responsa were **His** actually called thus, only one may be **Responsa.** indicated here. At the end of a collection of Meïr of Rothenburg's "She'elot u-Teshubot" (MS. Prague) some "Halakot Kezubot de-R. Yehudai" are given. Soon after this heading occurs the stereotyped form for "responsa," וששאלתם or ושאמרתם, etc. These halakot have been published according to this manuscript by Joel Müller under the title "Handschriftliche, Jehudai Gaon Zugewiesene Lehrsätze." Besides, there must have been incorporated into these "Halakot Pesukot" or "Halakot Ketu'ot" a collection of "dinim," arranged according to the order of the Talmud or according to subject-matter; for such dinim are quoted by geonim and later rabbis as "Halakot Pesukot" and "Halakot Ketu'ot," sometimes with and sometimes without a mention of the authorship of Yehudai Gaon or his pupils (for the reference see Epstein, "Ma'amar 'al Sefer Halakot Gedolot," in "Ha-Goren," iii. 57 *et seq.*).

Simeon Kayyara, author of the "Halakot Gedolot," as well as R. Amram, author of the well-known "Siddur," borrowed largely from these halakot of Yehudai Gaon, for which, as Epstein points out, the two terms "Halakot Pesukot" and "Halakot Ketu'ot" were used promiscuously in the geonic period; only later, when the varying recensions of them increased in number, were the titles distinguished as designating two different recensions.

Yehudai's halakot were translated from Aramaic into Hebrew, including even the Aramaic quotations from the Talmud. This translation has been preserved in an Oxford manuscript **His** under the original title "Halakot Pe-**Halakot.** sukot," being also known, according to the first word of the text, as "Hilkot Re'u"; and it was published by A. L. Schlossberg, Versailles, 1886. It was probably made in a Greek-speaking country, as Halberstam showed in his introductory letter to Schlossberg's edition, and was brought thence to Babylonia. A very great part of it, however, is taken from the "Halakot Gedolot" in an abridged form, so that Epstein did not recognize it as being a translation of the "Halakot Pesuḳot," but rather deemed it a compilation of the "Halakot Gedolot," containing at the same time Hebrew quotations from the Aramaic "Halakot Pesuḳot."

The "Halakot Ḳezubot" seem to be a compilation from the "Halakot Pesuḳot" and the "Halakot Gedolot." They are preserved in a Parma manuscript that has been published by Ḥayyim M. Horowitz in "Halachische Schriften der Geonim," first part, pp. 14 *et seq.*, Frankfort-on-the-Main, 1881. According to the beginning of the text, however, these "Halakot Ḳezubot" are ascribed to Yehudai Gaon. Since the term "Ḳezubot," a synonym of "Pesuḳot," seems to have been prevalent in Western countries (see "Sefer we-Hizhir," **The** ed. Freimann, ii., Introduction; "Ha-**"Halakot** lakot Gedolot," ed. Hildesheimer, p. **Ḳezubot."** 469; "She'elot u-Teshubot Sha'are Ẓedeḳ," p. 29a; Zunz, in Steinschneider, "Hebr. Bibl." viii. 20), and as the "Halakot Ḳezubot" are not quoted in geonic literature, Epstein supposes Palestine or Italy to have been the birthplace of this compilation, which afterward was widely known in Germany and France, and was often copied and enlarged by additions. It is quoted especially in the "Sefer ha-Pardes," in the Vitry Maḥzor, in the "Sefer Issur we-Hetter" (Merzbacher MS. No. 6), and others.

Much has been written about the relation between the "Halakot Pesuḳot" and the "Halakot Gedolot" and their respective authors. The note in Abraham ibn Daud's "Sefer ha-Ḳabbalah" ("M. J. C." i. 63) that Yehudai Gaon gathered his "Halakot Pesuḳot" from the "Halakot Gedolot" of Simeon Ḳayyara, and the supposition of the medieval Jewish scholars of Germany and northern France that Yehudai Gaon was the author of the "Halakot Gedolot," caused great confusion regarding the authorship, and also regarding the dates of these two authors. Recently, however, the disputed points have gradually been cleared up.

The writing of halakic compendiums was always censured by those who were afraid that such works might displace the study of the Talmud itself, the mass of the people being perfectly satisfied to know the final halakic decision without caring for its development in the Talmud. It is interesting to observe that as old a compendium as the "Halakot Pesuḳot" of Yehudai Gaon met with the disapproval of Palṭoi, gaon of Pumbedita (842–858), for the very same reason (see Epstein, *l.c.* p. 57).

BIBLIOGRAPHY: Brüll, in *Jahrbücher für Jüdische Geschichte und Litteratur*, ii. *et seq.*, v. 158 *et seq.*; Grätz, *Gesch.* v. 165, 174; *idem*, in *Monatsschrift*, vii. 217 *et seq.*; A. Harkavy, *Responsen der Geonim*, Index; A. Neubauer, in *Ha-Maggid*, 1873, pp. 125 *et seq.*; *idem*, in *Letterbode*, iv. 55 *et seq.*; S. Sachs, in *Ha-Naḥalat Shedal*, in *Oẓar Ṭob*, 1878, p. 17; S. Sachs, in *Ha-Maggid*, 1878, Nos. 31–34; I. Halevy, *Dorot ha-Rishonim*, iii. 194, 200; Weiss, *Dor*, iv. 31–40; Winter and Wünsche, *Die Jüdische Litteratur*, ii. 16 *et seq.*; Epstein, in *Ha-Goren*, iii. 55 *et seq.*; Schorr, in *He-Ḥaluẓ*, xii. 81 *et seq.*; Ḥayyim M. Horowitz, *Halachische Schriften der Geonim*, Preface, Frankfort-on-the-Main, 1881; Steinschneider, *Jewish Literature*, pp. 26, 67; Zunz, *G. V.* p. 60; Buber, *Sefer ha-Orah*, pp. 20, 75, 82, 114, Lemberg, 1905.

s.   M. Sc.

YEKATERINOSLAF (YEKATERINOSLAV):

Former Russian city, now Ukraine, founded in 1787 during the reign of Catherine II.; capital of the government of the same name. It is one of the most important commercial and industrial centers of southern Russia, the census of 1911 crediting it with a population of 217,848 persons, including 36,600 Jews. The latter were actively identified with the trades and industries of the city, about one-third of the entire Jewish population (2,388 families; in all 11,157 persons) deriving its income from commercial pursuits, and another third (2,712 master artisans and 480 apprentices) being engaged in industrial occupations. The city had more than thirty shops and factories, mainly grist-mills, lumber-mills, foundries, machine shops, and tobacco-factories. Almost all of these establishments were owned by Jews, but the number of Jewish factory employees was comparatively low, although in one cigarette-paper factory and in one tobacco-factory the workmen were all Jews. There were 847 Jewish day-laborers, mainly drivers, porters, etc.

On account of its busy commercial and industrial life, Yekaterinoslaf serves as a center of attraction for the population of a very extensive region. The concentration in this city of such a considerable number of Jews, for the most part impecunious, was stimulated by a series of government measures enacted during the last twenty years of its regime, which limited the sphere of Jewish economic activity. Among these were the so-called temporary measures of 1882; the exclusion of the Don region (1880) and of Rostov and Taganrog from the Pale of Settlement; and the establishment of a government monopoly in the manufacture of alcoholic beverages (1896). All of these measures led to the increase in Yekaterinoslaf of a Jewish proletariat which, for lack of employment, became dependent on charity. Thus, in 1898, 1,830 families, representing 9,000 persons, were given aid for Passover. In the same year the local Jews supported the following charitable organizations: a hospital, a maternity home, a dispensary, a free-loan association ("gemilut ḥasadim"), and a clerks' mutual aid society. The expenditures of these institutions, amounting to about 74,000 rubles, were defrayed mainly from the basket-tax (43,067 rubles) and from voluntary contributions and membership fees. In the year 1905 the most important charitable organization was the Association for the Aid of Poor Jews, founded toward the end of 1898; its income in 1900 was 52,509 rubles, and its expenditures 47,611. The society maintains a free employment bureau.

Yekaterinoslaf in 1905 had the following Jewish educational institutions: ten private schools, a Talmud Torah (400 pupils) founded in 1857, a yeshibah (74 students), and ninety-two ḥadarim (855 pupils). The Zionistic movement has made great progress in the city, the propaganda being carried on by several societies under the leadership of Michael Usishkin. The attitude of the Christian population toward the Jews was expressed in 1881 in the decisions of the provincial commission concerning the Jewish question, formed here as in other government cities in order to determine the causes of the anti-Jewish outbreaks. This commission saw a way to the solution of the Jewish question in the passing of a series of regulations limiting the rights of the Jews in commerce, in the acquisition of real estate, in the participation in local government, etc. The anti-Jewish outbreaks did not spare Yekaterinoslaf. On July 20, 1883, a mob invaded the Jewish houses and wrought great destruction. Many ruined families were compelled to seek safety in flight.

BIBLIOGRAPHY: *Razsvyet*, 1881, No. 45; *Russki Yevrei*, 1883, No. 32; *Otchot Pravleniya Obschestva Posobiya Byednym Yevreyam za 1889 God*, Yekaterinoslaf, 1900; *ib.*, *za 1900 God*, 1901.
H. R.   S. J.

YELAMMEDENU. See TANHUMA MIDRASH.

YELISAVETGRAD (ELIZABETHGRAD): Town in the government of Kherson, Ukraine. It was founded in 1754, and soon became one of the most important cities of southern Russia. The name of Yelisavetgrad recalls sad memories to the Russian Jews; for from that town issued the signal for the riots which brought upon them incalculable affliction and misery. As soon as Alexander III. had ascended the throne rumors of a rising against the Jews reached Yelisavetgrad, which caused the leaders of the Jewish community to apply to the governor for special protection. No notice was taken of the appeal, and on Wednesday, April 27, 1881, the dreaded outbreak took place.

A religious dispute in an inn concerning the use of Christian blood by the Jews served as a pretext for the rioters, who proceeded to the Jewish quarter and commenced a systematic destruction of Jewish shops and warehouses. At first the Jews attempted to protect their property; but, seeing that this only served to increase the violence of the mob, and that the soldiers, who were called to protect them, took part in the pillage, they barricaded themselves in their houses. For two days the rioters perpetrated, under the very eyes of the officials, and with the cooperation of the soldiers, the most barbarous and hideous deeds. Synagogues were wrecked and Jewesses outraged. Two young girls, in dread of violation, threw themselves from windows. An old man named Pelikov, who attempted to save his daughter, was thrown from the roof by the enraged soldiery. Many persons were killed; 500 houses and 100 shops were demolished; and 2,000,000 rubles' worth of property was stolen or destroyed.

In the revolutionary uprisings of 1905 the town was burned, and the mob killed the Jews and plundered their quarter.

BIBLIOGRAPHY: Jacobs, *Persecution of Jews in Russia*, 1881, p. 4; *Russkaya Mysl*, June, 1881, pp. 96–99; Sychewski, *Protivo Yevreiskiya Bezobraziya*; H. Rosenthal, in JEW. ENCYC. i. 347, s.v. *Alexander III.*; Semenov, *Geographical-Statistical Dictionary of the Russian Empire* (in Russian), *s.v.*
H. R.   I. BR.

According to the census of 1910, Yelisavetgrad had a population of 75,800, including 30,000 Jews. The latter were prominent in the city's commerce, trade, and industries, and three-fourths of its factories were controlled by them. The number of factories exceeds eighty, among them being grist-mills, machine- and tool-factories, foundries, soap-factories, brick-yards, vinegar-distilleries, and tobacco-factories. Only tobacco manufacture, however, engages any considerable number of Jewish workers. There were in all 522 Jewish factory-laborers, 363 day-laborers, and 3,164 artisans.

The Jewish community supports a number of charitable institutions, among which may be mentioned a society for the aid of the poor (founded 1899), a loan society which lends money to the poor at a low rate of interest, and a Jewish dispensary with infirmary attached. More than 1,000 Jewish families have recourse to charity. In the winter of 1898, 1,100 families received fuel from charitable organizations, while 1,300 families applied for aid for Passover.

Institutions.

The Jewish children are sent either to the general or to the Jewish schools, although Jewish boys are not freely admitted to the former. The Jewish schools include a Talmud Torah with industrial classes, two government schools (one with industrial classes), several private schools, a school founded by the local Zionists, and 122 ḥadarim, including a free ḥeder with sixty pupils. Early in 1881 there was organized among the Jews of Yelisavetgrad a Bible Brotherhood (see BIBLEITZY).
H. R.   S. J.

YEMEN: Province comprising the southwestern part of Arabia. Various traditions trace the earliest settlement of Jews in this region back to the time of Solomon, and the Sanaite Jews have a legend to the effect that their forefathers settled there forty-two years before the destruction of the First Temple. Under the prophet Jeremiah 75,000 Jews, including priests and Levites, are said to have gone to Yemen; and when Ezra commanded the Jews to return to Jerusalem they disobeyed, whereupon he pronounced an everlasting ban upon them. Tradition states, however, that as a punishment for this hasty action Ezra was denied burial in Palestine. As a result of this tradition, which is devoid of historicity, no Jew of Yemen gives the name of Ezra to a child, although all other Biblical appellatives are found there.

The actual immigration of Jews into Yemen appears to have taken place about the beginning of the second century C.E., although the province is mentioned neither by Josephus nor by the Mishnah or Talmud. According to Winckler, the Jews of Yemen enjoyed prosperity until the sixth century C.E., and the fourth sovereign before Dhu Nuwas was a convert to Judaism. The kingdoms of Sheba, Raidan, Ḥaḍramaut, and Yamanat (Yemen) were united under the hegemony of the Yemenite kings, who were as follows:

First Settlements.

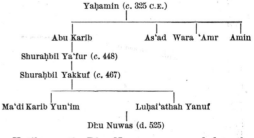

Until recently Dhu Nuwas was regarded as the first king who was zealous for Judaism, but a chronicle of saints in the British Museum gives the name of the martyr Arḳir, who was condemned to death by Shuraḥbil Yakkuf at the instigation of his counselors, the rabbis. Although all these legends are extremely biased and are chiefly devoted to the portrayal of the persecution of Christians by the Jews, it is evident that Judaism had in the fourth century taken a firm hold upon the royal house. In this legend, as in others, the city of Najran is important. Two Jewish youths are said to have been killed there, whereupon Dhu Nuwas conquered the city and executed the king after offering him his choice between Judaism and death. The effect of these traditions was a bitter oppression of the Jews, first by the Christians and later by the Arabs.

The average Jewish population of Yemen for the first five centuries c.e. is said to have been about 3,000. The Jews were scattered throughout the country, but carried on an extensive commerce and thus succeeded in getting possession of many Jewish books. When Saladin became sultan in the last quarter of the twelfth century and the Shiites revolted against him, the trials of the Yemenite Jews began. There were few scholars among them at that time, and a false prophet arose, proclaiming the amalgamation of Judaism and Mohammedanism, and pretending to be able to prove the truth of his teachings from the Bible. In this hour of need the greatest Jewish scholar of Yemen, Jacob ben Nathan-
Yemen and ael al-Fayyumi, wrote for counsel to
Mai- Maimonides, who replied in a consola-
monides. tory epistle entitled "Iggeret Teman."
This letter made such an impression on the Jews of Yemen that, according to Saphir, they included the name of Maimonides in the Ḳaddish prayer. The false prophet was condemned to death and died in his illusion. Although Benjamin of Tudela did not personally visit Yemen, he gives certain data concerning the Yemenite Jews. Their capital was Teima and they called themselves Rechabites, while at their head stood the nasi Ḥanan. They were in constant strife with their Ismaelitic neighbors, from whom they won many victories and took much booty.

At the beginning of the nineteenth century the condition of the Jews of Yemen was miserable. They were under the jurisdiction of the Imam, and were forbidden to wear new or good clothes, nor might they ride an ass or a mule, being compelled to make the longest journeys on foot when occasion required it. They were prohibited, moreover, from engaging in money transactions, and were all mechanics, being employed chiefly as carpenters, masons, and smiths. At the beginning of the nineteenth century they are said to have numbered 30,000, and to have lived principally in Aden (200), Sana (10,000), Sada (1,000), Dhamar (1,000), and the desert of Beda (2,000). In recent times there have been no Jews in the Tahama (the low coast-land) nor in Hodeida, but they now reside in the interior of the plateau. Settlements of considerable size are found in the vicinity of Sana, and are divided between Manakhah, with 3,000 Jews, and Sana, which has a separate quarter containing about 8,000. The Jews have also special sections of the city in Kaukaban, Weilan, and Dhamar. Special mention should likewise be made of the Jewish village of Al-Gharaba, two kilometers from

XII.—38

Reda'. The chief industry of the Jews of Yemen is the making of pottery, which is found in all their settlements and which has rendered them famous throughout the East. They engage very little in commerce. An important personage among the Yemenite Jews in the last quarter of the nineteenth century was Aaron Chehip, known as the "Coffee King." He came to a violent end, however, being murderously assaulted and robbed by the natives.

According to the most recent investigations, there is no longer any doubt that the Jews of Yemen
whatever the date of their settlement,
Literature. brought with them the Bible and a
large part of the traditional Haggadah, which also had an influence on the Koran. The Talmud, or at least a part of it, was likewise known in Yemen, and the fact that it was less widely distributed there than in Europe was due solely to the poverty of the people, which made it impossible to buy more copies. The Jews of Yemen must have been in close touch with Babylonia, since they reckoned time according to the Seleucidan era, and this chronology is found on tombstones as early as the ninth century. All the Hebrew manuscripts of Yemen, moreover, show the superlinear, or Babylonian, system of punctuation. It is clear from the "Iggeret Teman" that though the Yemenite Jews were not Talmudists, they acted according to the decisions of Rab Ashi in traditional law, at least after they had come under the influence of Maimonides. The "Yad," which they called "Ḥibbur," and the Shulḥan 'Aruk of Joseph Caro were regarded by them as the highest authorities in Jewish law.

The oldest Yemenite manuscripts are those of the Bible, which the Yemenite Jews call "Taj" (= "crown"). They date from the ninth century, and each of them has a short Masoretic introduction, while many contain Arabic commentaries. The Masorah was highly valued by the Jews of Yemen, and a special compilation, made by Yaḥya Saliḥ, was called by Ginsburg the "Masorah of Teman." They were acquainted with Saadia, Rashi, Ḳimḥi, Naḥmanides, and Isaac Arama, besides producing a number of exegetes from among themselves. In the fourteenth century **Nathanael b. Isaiah** wrote an Arabic commentary on the Bible, full of haggadot and almost wholly destitute of any real Biblical hermeneutics, while in the second half of the fifteenth century **Saadia b. David al-'Adani** was the author of a com-
Writers. mentary on Leviticus, Numbers, and
Deuteronomy, and **Abraham b. Solomon** wrote on the Prophets (British Museum). Of the Talmud the following treatises are now known to exist in manuscript: Beẓah, Pesaḥim, Mo'ed Ḳatan, Megillah, and Zebaḥim. The Yemenite **Abner b. Ker ha-Shoshani** wrote a double commentary in Hebrew on the "'En Ya'aḳob" of Jacob Ḥabib, and between 1478 and 1483 Saadia b. David al-'Adani composed a gloss on the "Yad" of Maimonides. Among the midrashim compiled in Yemen mention should be made of the "Midrash ha-Gadol" of **David bar Amram al-'Adani** (vol. i., ed. Schechter, 1902). Between 1413 and 1430 the physician **Yaḥya Zechariah b. Solomon** wrote a compila-

tion entitled "Midrash ha-Ḥefeẓ," which included the Pentateuch, Lamentations, Esther, and the haftarot, while between 1484 and 1493 **David al-Lawani** composed his "Midrash al-Wajiz al-Mughni." In the thirteenth and fourteenth centuries supercommentaries on the "Yad" were written by **Saliḥ Musa al-Ḥadhari, Isaac b. Abraham,** and **David b. Solomon.**

The Cabala was and is very popular among the Yemenite Jews, who are familiar with the Zohar and with the work of all the European cabalists. One of them, Solomon b. Dawid ha-Kohen, has written a cabalistic treatise in thirteen chapters, entitled "Leḥem Shelomoh."

Among the Yemenite poets who wrote Hebrew

Manuscripts of the Yemen Siddur are in the British Museum. The prayers agree in part with the Sephardic and in part with the Ashkenazic liturgy, and their language is partly Hebrew and partly Aramaic and Arabic, while the daily so-called "Ma-'amadot" prayers are written in Aramaic. The Yemenite Siddur appeared in Jerusalem 1892 (2d ed. 1898), and in Vienna 1896.

BIBLIOGRAPHY: Benjamin of Tudela, ed. Asher, p. 70, London, 1840; Burchard, in *Ost und West*, ii. 337–341; Deinard, *Or Me'ir*, pp. 20–28, New York, 1896; Greenburg, *The Hagadah According to the Rite of Yemen*, i.–iv., London, 1896; Grätz, *Gesch.* iv.–vi. (Index); Harkavy, *Studien und Mittheilungen*, pp. 202, 217, Berlin. 1887; Neubauer, in *J. Q. R.* iii. 22; idem, in *R. E. J.* xxiii. 122 et seq.; idem, in *Monatsschrift*, iii. 42–44; Saphir, *Eben Safir*, i. 99–116; Steinschneider, *Verzeichniss der Hebräischen Handschriften der Königlichen*

GROUP OF YEMEN JEWS.
(From a photograph by Elkan N. Adler.)

and Arabic hymns modeled after the Spanish school, mention may be made of **Yaḥya al-Dhahri** and the members of the Al-Shabbezi family. A single non-religious work, inspired by Ḥariri, was written in 1573 by **Zechariah b. Saadia** (identical with the Yaḥya al-Dhahri mentioned above), under the title "Sefer ha-Musar." The philosophical writers include: **Saadia b. Jabeẓ** and **Saadia b. Mas'ud,** both at the beginning of the fourteenth century; **Ibn al-Ḥawas,** the author of a treatise in the form of a dialogue written in rimed prose, and termed by its author the "Flower of Yemen"; **Hasan al-Dhamari;** and **Joseph ha-Levi b. Jefes,** who wrote the philosophical treatises "Ner Yisrael" (1420) and "Kitab al-Masaḥah."

Bibliothek zu Berlin, ii. 71 et seq.; idem, in *Israelitische Monatsschrift*, 1891, No. 2; idem, in *Monatsschrift*, 1894, pp. 79 et seq.; Winckler, *Altorientalische Forschungen*, iv. 329–337; W. Bacher, *Der Süd-Arabische Siddur*, in *J. Q. R.* xiv. 581–621; idem, *Ein Hebräisch-Arabisches Liederbuch aus Jemen*, in *Berliner-Festschrift*, 1903, pp. 10–32; S. Poznanski, *Zum Schrifthum der Süd-Arabischen Juden*, in *J. Q. R.* xiv. 752–757; P. Heinrich, *Fragment eines Gebetsbuches aus Jemen*, Vienna, 1902; idem, in *J. Q. R.* xv. 330–333.

J.   S. O.

YERUSHALMI, SOLOMON B. MENAHEM (called also **Solomon Isaac [Sekel] Ashkenazi**): Scholar of the early part of the sixteenth century. He wrote a commentary on the Book of Ruth which he entitled "Perush 'al Rut" (Salonica, 1551; 2d ed. [together with the "Pardes Rimmonim"], Sabbionetta, 1554).

BIBLIOGRAPHY: Ersch and Gruber, *Encyc.* section 2, xxviii. 40; Benjacob, *Oẓar ha-Sefarim*, p. 474.

E. C.   S. O.

YESHIBAH : A high school; a rabbinical college. It is the oldest institution of Jewish learning, and ranks higher than the ḤEDER or the TALMUD TORAH. The term "yeshibah" and the Aramaic equivalent "metibta" (both found in the Talmud) originally meant a session, a council, or a meeting of scholars, over which presided the "elder." The Patriarchs were all elders of a yeshibah (Yoma 28b). R. Pappa was elected "rosh yeshibah" (or "resh metibta"), *i.e.*, president of the yeshibah, and it was his duty to deliver a lecture and discussion before the yeshibah of a large and mixed assembly (Ber. 57a and Rashi *ad loc.*; B. Ḳ. 117a). At first the bet ha-midrash was the place where the yeshibah assembled, one or two (morning and afternoon) sessions being held daily. Later, when the number of students increased, it became necessary to hold the sessions in a separate large hall adjoining the bet ha-midrash, and this hall was known by the name of "yeshibah." The general term for the lecture was probably "pesiḳta" or "mekilta," which, like the modern term "shi'ur," means "measure," indicating the fixed and limited time occupied by the rosh yeshibah in delivering the discourse—from two to three hours.

During the Talmudic period the principal Palestinian yeshibot were at Sepphoris, Tiberias, and Cæsarea, while the leading Babylonian ones were at Maḥuza, Nehardea, Sura, and Pumbedita. Those at the last two towns were maintained in the geonic period (see ACADEMIES). The principal seat of the Rabbis after the days of the Second Temple was Pumbedita ("Iggeret Rab Sherira Gaon," ed. Goldberg, p. 32, Mayence, 1873). The attendance at the Babylonian yeshibot gradually decreased. Rab had 1,200 students at his yeshibah; R. Huna had 800 students, with 13 amoraim as interpreters; Rabbah and R. Joseph each had 400; and R. Ashi had only 200 (Ket. 106a). The sessions of the Babylonian yeshibot were interrupted on several occasions, and were finally suspended by the Persian persecutions, the last being held at Bagdad. Benjamin of Tudela (1160–73) found ten yeshibot there, and he enumerates the names of every rosh yeshibah, the principal one being R. Samuel b. Eli. The "rosh ha-golah" (president of the Captivity) bestowed "semikah" (ordination) upon the graduates of the yeshibah (Benjamin of Tudela, "Itinerary," ed. Asher, p. 60, London, 1840). Pethahiah of Regensburg, in his "Sibbub" (travels), written in the same century, describes the Bagdad yeshibah as follows: "The rosh yeshibah [R. Samuel ha-Levi b. Eli] has about 2,000 students at a time, and there are over 500 around him who are well informed. The students receive lessons from other teachers before they are admitted to the yeshibah. The rosh ha-golah is R. Eliezer, and under him is the rosh yeshibah. The latter occupies a large house covered with tapestry. He is dressed in a gold-trimmed garment and sits on high, while the students sit on the ground. He discourses through an interpreter or explainer ["meturge-

In Babylon.

man"], who answers all questions asked by the students, and if he does not know inquires of the rosh yeshibah. Sometimes there are several interpreters, each expounding a treatise in a different part of the yeshibah. The whole study is with an intonation" (ed. Benisch, p. 16, London, 1861). Toward the end of the eleventh century an important yeshibah at Bagdad was under the guidance of Isaac ibn Sakin, and later it was under Samuel b. David ha-Kohen, who defended Maimonides against the edict of excommunication (1289).

The example of the yeshibot of Babylon was followed throughout the Levant. It is curious that even the Karaites carried along with them the title of "rosh yeshibah," bestowing it in the tenth century on Jacob ha-Tamani (= "of Taman," on the Bosporus) (d. 958; see Pinsker, "Liḳḳuṭe Ḳadmoniyot," Appendix, p. 86; the date is disputed by Deinard in "Ha-Shaḥar," viii. 452). Until the ninth century the Jews in European countries and elsewhere depended entirely upon the decisions of the authorities in the yeshibot of Babylon, which they supported liberally. It was largely due to the encouragement of Charlemagne that the learned men of Babylon emigrated and later established yeshibot in France and Germany. During the tenth century three new yeshibot were founded: the first by Shemariah b. Elhanan at Miẓr (Cairo), Egypt; the second by Ḥushiel at Kairwan in North Africa; and the third by Moses b. Enoch (d. 965) at Cordova (Abraham ibn Daud, "Sefer ha-Ḳabbalah").

The yeshibah of Narbonne was perhaps the most famous of its time, drawing eager students from all parts of France and Germany. Benjamin the traveler says: "R. Abraham [ibn Daud] is rosh yeshibah at Narbonne, whence the study of the Law spreads over all countries. At Lunel the foreign students who attend the yeshibah are supplied with food and raiment at the public expense. At Beaucaire there is a grand yeshibah under the presidency of Abraham ibn Daud, an eminent scholar of the Scriptures and Talmud, who attracts students from distant countries, and who provides for them from his private means, which are quite considerable. At Marseilles, in the upper city near the fortress, is a great yeshibah which boasts of very learned scholars, headed by R. Simon Anatolio, Abba Mari b. Isaac [author of the "'Iṭṭur"], and others. The scholars and descendants of Rashi hold yeshibot at Troyes and Ramerupt. Paris contains many learned men whose equals are not to be found anywhere upon earth" ("Massa'ot," pp. 4, 6, 112). The yeshibah of Paris was closed by order of King Philip Augustus (1181), but the yeshibah at Champagne, where the tosafists pursued their work, still flourished, as did also that at Dampierre, where a grandson of Rashi conducted a yeshibah of considerable authority. R. Isaac, a nephew of R. Tam, guided a yeshibah of sixty pupils, each one studying for himself a different treatise of the Talmud, and all together taking up one treatise at a time in rotation under the rosh yeshibah ("Ẓedah la-Derek," Introduction, ed. Ferrara, 1554, p. 4a). A yeshibah was reopened at Paris for a short time in the thirteenth century by R. Jehiel, who emigrated to the

In France.

Holy Land. Mattithiah b. Joseph of Provence reestablished a yeshibah at Paris in the fourteenth century, and Jacob of Orleans (d. 1189), a pupil of R. Tam, crossed the Channel and opened a yeshibah in London.

The first yeshibah in Spain was established at Cordova, and attracted the scholars of the Levant. Later were founded the yeshibah of Granada and that of Lucena, the latter being successively conducted by Isaac Alfasi (1090) and his pupil Ibn Migash. These examples were followed by Jehiel ben Asher at Toledo, where he changed the whole tone of Spanish Judaism; by Solomon ben Adret at Barcelona in 1305; and by R. Nissim at the same city in 1372. R. Gershom (960–1028) emigrated from France to Mayence, where he founded a yeshibah and gathered many students from Germany and Italy. This yeshibah flourished for more than eighty years and became a center of Talmudic activity. Joseph Colon (1420–80), the author of a collection of responsa, had a yeshibah at Pavia, Italy; and Judah Minz of Mayence founded a yeshibah at Padua (1504–26). Joseph Ottolenghi opened a yeshibah in Cremona, northern Italy, prior to the public burning of the Talmud in 1559. The yeshibah 'Eẓ Ḥayyim in Amsterdam flourished during the eighteenth century, and its publications of responsa under the title "Peri 'Eẓ Ḥayyim" extended from 1733 to 1792. In the same century there were celebrated yeshibot at Altona-Hamburg, Frankfort-on-the-Main, Fürth, and Metz. At Nikolsburg Mordecai Benet had a yeshibah with from 300 to 400 students.

In Spain, Germany, Italy, and Holland.

Jacob Pollak (1460–1541), the founder of "ḥilluḳim" (the sophistic method of Talmudic discussions), was the first to transfer the rabbinical science from Germany to Poland; he opened a yeshibah at Cracow, which later was presided over by Moses Isserles and became the most celebrated school throughout the whole European Jewry. All who sought sound learning betook themselves thither; and the fact that a man had been educated in the yeshibah of Poland was of itself a high recommendation if he sought to obtain a position as rabbi. Other German scholars settled in Lithuania, Ruthenia, and Volhynia and founded new centers of rabbinic study.

In Poland.

The three documents mentioned below describe the yeshibah at various times and in various countries, and illustrate the life, methods, regulations, and course of studies in the old yeshibah. A document called "Ḥuḳḳe ha-Torah" (= "the laws of the Torah," i.e., rules or bylaws regulating the teaching of the Torah), and appended to the "Semaḳ" of Isaac Corbeil under date of 1309, throws light on the attitude and conditions of the yeshibah in northern France in the thirteenth century. There were two schools, one called "midrash gadol" and the other "midrash ḳaṭon," corresponding respectively to the Christian cathedral school and parochial school at that time; the lower schools were known also as "petites écoles," and in some paragraphs the "higher midrash" is referred to as

Curriculum, 13th Century.

"yeshibah." The "Ḥuḳḳe ha-Torah" is composed of three different collections, and may have been added to from time to time, as the occasion required, to complete and perfect the regulations. The rules for the higher and lower schools are mixed indiscriminately. The students of the higher midrash were called "perushim" (= "Pharisees"), a title still retained by married students in the yeshibah. The length of the term was seven years, during which time the pupils dwelt in the midrash, food and lodging being provided for them. The head teacher, called "rosh yeshibah," also lodged there during the week, but returned to his home on Friday night. Interpreters were employed, one for every ten students, to explain the lecture of the rosh yeshibah (Güdemann, "Gesch. des Erziehungswesens," etc., i., note 3; Jacobs, "Jews of Angevin England," pp. 343 et seq.).

The following is a summary of the chief provisions of this important code of education. The separate sections sometimes occur in more than one of the three recensions, here indicated by the letters A, B, C. Jacobs ("Jews of Angevin England") is of the opinion that A was composed in England in the thirteenth century, on account of the references to the capital and to the long winter nights:

(i.) Every first-born male is to be set apart ("separated") for the study of the Law from the eighth day after circumcision (A 1, B 5).

(ii.) At five years of age every Jewish boy is to be brought in the month Nisan to the small school of the province, and taught to read; then put to Leviticus, then to read the weekly portion in Hebrew, then in the vernacular, and then in the Targum (A 7, 8; B 6; C 1).

(iii.) At ten years he studies the Mishnah, beginning with the tractate Berakot of the Talmud, and going through the smaller tractates of the order Mo'ed in the next three years (B 6, C 2).

(iv.) At thirteen years the education of the ordinary boy is completed; that of the separated continues in the same school till the lad is sixteen, when he decides for himself whether he will devote his life to the Law, and, if so, goes up to the great school of the separated in the capital for another seven years (A 2, 3; C 3).

(v.) The small school of the province is to be held in a two-story house, capable of holding 100 pupils, 10 teachers, and a rector to supervise. No teaching is to be done at home, and the rector must not reside at the school with his family, but must go home every Sabbath (B 6, A 5, B 3).

(vi.) The rector gives two lectures—one in the morning, one in the afternoon. The teachers go over each lesson twice with their classes [this probably refers to the great school of the capital]. At the end of each week there is repetition of the week's work; similarly at the end of the month, and at the end of the summer and of the winter session. No teacher may take more than ten pupils, nor may he have any other calling than teaching (B 7; A 6, 10, 12).

(vii.) The lads are encouraged to examine one another every evening in the day's lessons. Dull scholars are to be sent away, so as not to keep back the more forward. Teaching is to be by book, not from memory. In winter the evening lessons are to be short, on account of the light (A 5, 7, 9, 11).

(viii.) Every member of the community pays twelve pence yearly as school-fees, instead of the half-shekel of old. The great school is to be bought, and then let out to the separated. The separated pay for their lodging, and a share of the teachers' salaries. The rector gets 20 marks yearly, a teacher 8 (A 4; B 1, 6).

Nathan Hannover, in "Yewen Meẓulah" (ed. Venice, 1653, end), relates the history of the Chmielnicki massacres and describes the yeshibah at that period: "Nearly all communities in Poland supported a yeshibah. They maintained the students and gave them out of the public funds fixed sums weekly for ordinary expenses. The baḥurim taught the smaller boys. A community consisting of fifty 'ba'ale battim' [= "householders"] supported about thirty students. In addition to receiving fixed stipends the students were invited as guests to the tables of the community, every household having invariably one or more such guests from the yeshibah. Consequently the number of ḥakamim increased to such an extent that very often there were found twenty ḥakamim bearing the title of 'morenu' or 'ḥaber' in a community of fifty householders. The rosh yeshibah was above all in rank. The terms of study were as follows: in summer from the 1st of Iyyar to the 15th of Ab, and in winter from the 1st of Ḥeshwan to the 15th of Ṭebet, the intervals being devoted to private studies. In the first part of each season, namely, from the 1st of Iyyar to Pentecost, and from the 1st of Ḥeshwan to Ḥanukkah, the studies in the yeshibah consisted of Gemara with Rashi and tosafot, one page daily. This was called one halakah. The rosh yeshibah sat on a chair, and the students stood around him. The students prepared themselves beforehand by carefully studying the halakah of the day, and then asked the rosh yeshibah to explain the difficult passages. After he had answered, all kept silence, and he then discussed a 'ḥilluḳ,' a pilpulistic review of the halakah in detail. This lasted till noon or a little later. The second half of the term was devoted to the study of Alfasi and the poseḳim [decisions and codes], particularly the four volumes of the Ṭurim with commentaries. A few weeks before the term expired the rosh yeshibah permitted the best students to deliver a discourse, in order to familiarize them with the art of delivering a ḥilluḳ. The Talmud was studied in the order of the sedarim. Every rosh yeshibah had a 'shammash' [= "attendant"], whose business was to see that the students in every class attended strictly to their studies. Every Thursday the students were ushered into the presence of the gabbai, who examined them. For failure in the examination the student was sometimes chastised with a rod by the shammash and sometimes admonished in the presence of the other students. In the last days of the term the pupils reviewed what they had learned during the term. When the session ended the students traveled with the rosh yeshibah to the fairs on market-days ["yerid"]: in summer to the fairs of Zaslav and Yaroslav, and in winter to the fairs of Lemberg and Lublin. The students were allowed to choose any yeshibah in those places during the fairs. The gathering of so many students at the fairs, where merchants congregated to sell or purchase goods, was the occasion of making hundreds of marriage engagements; the best students were selected on the recommendation of the rosh yeshibah, and the amount of dowry offered varied according to the student's knowledge of the Talmud and his skill in delivering a ḥilluḳ. Both the students and the rosh yeshibah were held in high esteem by rich and poor alike. The rosh yeshibah received many presents in money and goods; if neither a Kohen nor a Levite, he was entitled to the third portion ["shelishi"] in the order of persons called up to read the sidra. In leaving the synagogue, the rosh yeshibah led the students, who were followed by the people. On Sabbaths and holy days he was visited by the prominent members of the community."

Yeshibah Culture, 17th Century.

Yeshibot began to flourish again in the Holy Land in the sixteenth century—in Safed under Berab and Caro, and in Jerusalem under Levi ibn Ḥabib. Some private yeshibot were supported by individual donors from abroad; and this became the prevailing fashion. Two brothers named Vega in Leghorn supported the yeshibah of Jacob Ḥagiz in the seventeenth century. A document dated 1758 and copied by Hazan in his bibliography "Ha-Ma'alot li-Shelomoh" (p. 102b, Alexandria, 1898) gives a list of the yeshibot in Jerusalem at that time and shows that a majority of them were supported by private charity. The list is interesting as to the details of management and the courses of study in the eighteenth century among the Sephardim, and is as follows:

In Palestine.

Yeshibat Jacob Pereira : Subsidized by Jacob Pereira of Holland ; income 1,200 piasters per annum ; rosh yeshibah, Ḥakam Meyuḥas b. Samuel, author of " Peri ha-Adamah," aged 53 ; 30 baḥurim, 3 melamedim. Order of study : each student separately one halakah ; in the afternoon same halakah by all together, and also one chapter of Mishnah with commentaries.

Yeshibat Neweh Shalom : Supported by Isaac di Mayo & Co. of Constantinople ; income 700 piasters ; rosh yeshibah, Raphael Moses Bulah, author of " Geṭ Mekushshar," etc.; 20 students, 2 melamedim. Order of study : in the forenoon halakah ; in the afternoon 5 folios of [Di Vida's] " Reshit Ḥokmah," and Ṭur with " Bet Yosef."

Yeshibat Yefa'er 'Anawim : Supported by Joseph and Raphael Franco of Leghorn ; income 600 piasters ; rosh yeshibah, Abraham ibn Asher, etc. Order of study : in the forenoon 3 chapters of Mishnah with commentaries.

Yeshibat Ḥesed le-Abraham u-Binyan Shelomoh : Income 1,000 piasters ; rosh yeshibah, R. Ẓemaḥ, etc.; 6 baḥurim. Order of study : in the forenoon 3 hours halakah, in the afternoon 3 hours Ṭur.

Yeshibat Dameseḳ Eliezer : Supported by Eliezer Ashkenazi ; income 450 piasters ; rosh yeshibah, Judah Nabon, etc.; 8 students. Order of study : all together one halakah lasting 1½ hours ; the rest of the day each one studies for himself ; on Wednesday the pupils review what they have studied during the past week.

Yeshibat Keneset Yisrael : Organized by Ḥayyim ibn 'Aṭṭar and supported by donations from abroad ; income 600 piasters ; rosh yeshibah, Ḥayyim Mundichi, etc.; 4 baḥurim. Study : halakah.

Yeshibat Mordecai Taluk : Supported by Mordecai Taluk; income 400 piasters ; rosh yeshibah, Jonah Nabon, etc.; 4 baḥurim.

Yeshibat Abraham Meyuḥas : income 1,000 piasters ; rosh yeshibah, Meïr Sornaga, etc.; 5 baḥurim. Study : halakah 7 hours daily.

Midrash ha-Ḥasidim : Rosh yeshibah, Shalom Sherebi, etc.

Among the rabbis was Abraham ha-Kohen Eskir, who never let midnight pass without study, and who studied all night on Sabbaths and holy days. Three other yeshibot were composed of laymen ("ba'ale battim"), who studied the Bible, Mishnah, and Musar (ethics). The Midrash ha-Ḥasidim is now called "Bet El," and is a congregation of cabalists who study the Zohar and the works of Luria. The other yeshibot of the Sephardim are still subsidized by individual donors abroad. The yeshibot of the Ashkenazim were not established before the latter part of the nineteenth century.

The drift of the Reform movement in Germany from the time of Mendelssohn, when the need of secular knowledge became apparent, caused the gradual decline of the yeshibot, until they were

partly replaced by the rabbinical and theological seminaries. There is now no trace of the great yeshibot in France or elsewhere in western
Decline of the Yeshibah. Europe. When civil rights were granted to the Jews by France in 1831 there remained only the yeshibah in Metz, officially named "Collège Rabbinique," which, like all other religious institutions, was supported out of the public budget. The yeshibah still existed in Bohemia and Moravia, but had lost many of its former characteristics.

The Reform movement on one side and the ensnaring Ḥasidic tendencies on the other caused the pupils of the Wilna Gaon to deliberate how they might preserve the true Jewish learning and perpetuate the method and style of study inaugurated by the Gaon, who was rather opposed to pilpul and the ḥilluḳim as practised in the yeshibot of Poland. With this aim, R. Ḥayyim, the chief disciple of the Gaon, organized in 1803 the celebrated yeshibah of
Volozhin Yeshibah. Volozhin, a small town in the government of Wilna, and his own birthplace. His chief object was to make the students independent of private charity; and, being a merchant and possessing considerable wealth, he provided at first for the comfort of the students out of his own means, maintaining some at his table and paying for the board and lodging of others. He started with ten students, and when the number became too large for his means, he issued appeals for assistance to the neighboring communities, which were promptly responded to. At the time of his death in 1828 the number of students was about 100. The yeshibah was continued under the leadership of his son R. Isaac and his son-in-law R. Hillel; and in 1854 Naphtali Ẓebi Berlin, a son-in-law of R. Isaac, succeeded to the position of rosh yeshibah of Volozhin. The Maskilim advocated the introduction into the yeshibah of secular sciences and modern methods of pedagogy; and the attention of the government having been drawn to the matter, it decided to close the yeshibah in 1879. Two years later Berlin succeeded in inducing the government to revoke the edict, and reopened the yeshibah, which he conducted with renewed energy till 1891; it was then closed again by the government, which accused some of the students of having joined the revolutionary movement. After Berlin's death in 1893 the yeshibah was reopened under the management of Joseph Baer Soloveichik. In 1905 there were about 200 students, and the rosh yeshibah was Raphael Schapiro.

Under the leadership of Berlin the Volozhin yeshibah attained its highest efficiency, having nearly 400 students, among whom were about 60 perushim. The cost of its maintenance was about 40,000 rubles annually, which sum was collected by meshullaḥim in Russia and America. Poor and rich students alike flocked to this yeshibah from all parts of Europe and even from America. The rich students simply followed the advice of the Mishnah: "Wander forth to a home of the Torah" (Ab. iv. 18). Those students who received a regular allowance from home and paid their own expenses were known as "köstnikers" (= "easy boarders"), while the poor students who depended on the weekly allowance of the ḥaluḳḳah from the yeshibah fund were called "wochernikers" (= "weeklies"). The amount ranged from 60 to 75 copecks per week for the baḥurim, and from 2 to 3 rubles per week for the perushim, who sent about two-thirds of the allowance home to support their families. A special fund created by Brodsky draws an income which provides 20 perushim with 4 rubles each per week. Books were furnished free by the yeshibah. The small stipend was not sufficient to provide food, lodging, and clothing for the indigent students, and the majority of them were obliged to lodge in the class-rooms of the yeshibah or its annex, sleeping on the floor, on the seats, or on the tables in both summer and winter, and having as bedding sacks of straw seldom furnished with linen. They endured great privation, as described in the injunction: "Eat a morsel of bread with salt, drink water by measure, sleep upon the ground, and live a life of tribulation whilst thou toilest in the Torah" (Ab. vi. 4). Some students were invited to board free one day in the week in the houses of the charitably disposed. In fact, the charitable spirit of the town was remarkable; the poorest washerwoman deemed it her duty to give board to one or two students systematically during one or two days a week, and there was hardly a Jewish family in the town that did not shelter in its house one or more students every night, these lodgers taking regular turns one night a week. The days for free lodging were called in the yeshibah vernacular "eating days."

The students in the yeshibah were grouped according to the cities whence they came. Thus one would be known as "Itzel der Kovner" (Isaac of Kovno) and another as "Getzil der Warsawer." Some received the title "'illui" (= "the excellent") or "matmid" (= "diligent student"), such a one being known, for example, as "Der Kovner
Organization. 'Illui" or "Der Lomzer Matmid," assuming that only one from a town was so designated. The title was given by the general consent of the students. They studied singly or in pairs, there being no classes in the general sense of the term; the single pupils or pairs studied according to their grade of learning, asking explanations of difficult passages from those of a higher grade or from the rosh yeshibah. Nearly all studied the Talmud and posḳim, and more especially the laws relating to civil and religious matters in common practise. The Haggadah of the Talmud was excluded from their studies. The only occasion on which the students were together was when the rosh yeshibah delivered his lecture, called "shi'ur," for a certain "sugya" (lesson) on a halakic subject, which lasted about two hours; after this the students discussed the subject among themselves and with the rosh yeshibah. This generally took place in the afternoon session, but sometimes the assistant rosh yeshibah delivered a similar lecture in the forenoon. The rest of the session was spent in studying the subject of the shi'ur beforehand, or in private study.

Sometimes the rosh yeshibah would call in to see if the students attended to their studies. Besides there were "mashgiḥim" (supervisors), whose duty was to watch the class-rooms as monitors and keep the students from idling. They served also in the capacity of censors or inquisitors, especially to see that no student smuggled into the yeshibah Neo-Hebrew books or modern literature, such as novels or works that developed "liberal" views on religion. Such books were characterized by the "mash-giah" as "terefah" and "pasul," i.e., not fit to be read. When a student was detected reading such a book he was reprimanded, fined, or suspended by the rosh yeshibah. The Volozhin mashgihim, however, did not go beyond the enclosure of the school, and the student was not interfered with outside of the yeshibah when reading "sefarim hizonim" (books outside of the Jewish sphere). These supervisors even encouraged the students to acquire secular knowledge in private, but those in other yeshibot were more strict in this respect.

The official hours of study extended from sunrise to sunset, time being allowed for prayers and meals; but the enthusiasm of some students knew no bounds, and they often studied till midnight. The yeshibah was open all night, and the cost of candles was a large item in its expenditure. Usually, however, the night sessions were suspended between the 15th of Iyyar and the 15th of Ab (three summer months) in compliance with the advice of R. Judah he-Hasid ("Sefer Hasidim," § 565, old ed.). Vacation time was in the holiday months of Nisan and Tishri, when the perushim went home to their families and the bahurim to their parents to enjoy the holidays. Those who remained in Volozhin visited the house of the rosh yeshibah and entertained themselves by singing "zemirot" and drinking "le-hayyim," i.e., toasting long life to the rosh yeshibah. "At the conclusion of every 'zemer' [song] a student knocks with his fist on the table and cries, 'Hurrah for the rabbi!' and all answer, 'Hurrah, hurrah, hurrah!'" ("Ha-Shahar," viii. 166, note). Another enjoyable occasion was at the completion of a "masseket" or "seder" (SIYYUM), when all students and invited guests participated in an elaborate meal.

In almost every Russian town with a large Jewish population there are yeshibot under the immediate supervision of the local rabbis, but account is taken here only of those which established a wide reputation and attracted students from the neighboring towns and foreign countries.

Other Yeshibot in Russia. The yeshibah of Minsk, presided over first by Aryeh Loeb, author of "Sha'agat Aryeh" (d. 1785), and later by Joshua Eisik Harif, preceded the yeshibah of Volozhin. In 1831 a yeshibah was founded at Wilna by a band of forty young scholars, and was known as the "Ferziglach" (= "party of forty"). The rosh yeshibah was David Cohen, the "Kosover." In the same year a yeshibah named after R. Maila was organized there under the presidency of R. Mordecai and R. Eliezer Teitz. The Maila yeshibah still existed in 1905; and its cost of maintenance was about 5,000 rubles annually ("Ozar ha-Sifrut," iv. 532; "Ha-Asif," 1885, p. 149). Two other yeshibot, one founded by Mordecai Melzer (Klatzki) and the other by Israel Salanter, were opposed to each other in the mode of learning, the former adopting the style of pilpul and the latter that of peshat (logical reasoning).

Other noted yeshibot are at Slonim, Mir, and Eisheshok. The yeshibah of Slobotka was organized by Israel Salanter. The yeshibah at Kovno was opened in 1872 by Isaac Blazer (now in Jerusalem) under the auspices of Isaac Elhanan Spector, being attended mainly by perushim. In 1877 a banker of Berlin named Lachman donated 75,000 rubles in property for the maintenance of this yeshibah (see "Ha-Meliz," 1888, Nos. 177, 186). The yeshibah at Vitebsk conducted by Zalman Landau, later rabbi in St. Petersburg, was noted for the method by which its students learned in company every halakah in Talmud according to the decision in the codes (= מסקנתא אליבא דהלכתא‎). At Chelm (government of Kovno) Simhah Süssel conducted a yeshibah with a somewhat more modern method (about 1880). In 1882 Isaac Jacob Reines proposed to meet the demands of the government by establishing a yeshibah with a ten-year course, during which the student was to acquire the rabbinical knowledge necessary for ordination as a rabbi, and at the same time secure the secular education required of a government rabbi. The plan met with opposition, however, and after an experiment of four years the yeshibah was closed by the authorities. Reines opened at Lida in 1885 a regular yeshibah on the lines of that at Kovno.

The Hasidim, who were always opposed to the yeshibah for spending time on dry legalism instead of in "devotion," later showed a conciliatory spirit and change of opinion by recognizing the worth of the yeshibah; and under the leadership of their "rebbe" and "zaddik," Menahem Mendel of Lubavitz, they organized the society Tomeke Temimim, which supported no less than four yeshibot. They were located at Lubavitz, Zembin, Dokshitz (government of Minsk), and Horoditch (government of Vitebsk), and were attended by a total of 200 students, with an expenditure of nearly 40,000 rubles per annum.

Hungary is noted for its yeshibot, the most prominent of which is that of Presburg established by Moses Sofer, author of "Hatam Sofer." Others are

In Hungary. at Eisenstadt (Kis-Marton), Nyitra, Papa, Mattersdorf (Nagy-Marton), Szik-Udvarhely, Grosswardein (Nagy-Varad), Szatmár, Huszth, and twenty other places. These, however, have not established so high a reputation as have the Russian yeshibot. Ruben Brainin compares the type of the Russian yeshibah bahur with that of Hungary, and gives his opinion that "the former is more improved internally [in mind] and the latter externally [in dress]" ("Ha-Zofeh," i., No. 219).

Among the modern yeshibot in Jerusalem is the 'Ez Hayyim, organized in 1851, with Eliezer Dan, son-in-law of Joseph SCHWARZ, as rosh yeshibah. This yeshibah has about 100 students and is connected with a Talmud Torah. It is patronized by Rabbi Samuel Salant (see Luncz, "Luah," 5664, pp. 121–167). The yeshibah at Me'ah She'arim, a suburb of Jerusalem, has about 100 students. The rosh yeshibah is Rabbi S. H. Hurwitz, known as the "Dubrowner." Yeshibat Ohel Mosheh has about 35 students, and Jacob Urnstein is its rosh yeshibah. It was founded by R. Diskin. The principal yeshibah is the Torat Ḥayyim, with about 150 students, and Isaac Winegrad as rosh yeshibah. The Sephardim maintain the Tif'eret Yerushalayim and other private yeshibot.

The yeshibah system was transplanted in America by the Russian immigrants. The first school, 'Eẓ Ḥayyim (Talmudical academy), was organized in 1886 in New York, and owns its school property at 85 Henry street. Its general expense is $5,000 per annum, and the average attendance about 175 students, with 6 melammedim teaching as many classes; namely, 2 for Ḥumesh (Pentateuch) and 4 for Talmud, consisting of the three Babot (B. Ḳ., B. M., B. B.) with Rashi. The hours of study are from 9 A.M. to 12 M. and from 1 to 4 P.M. for Hebrew, and from 4 to 6 P.M. for English secular subjects. Saturday is review day for the Hebrew studies of the week. The course of study requires from three to four years.

Yeshibat Rabbenu Jacob Joseph, located at 197 Henry street, New York, was organized in 1902. The president and general superintendent is Samuel Isaac Andron, and the principal R. Meïr Hecht. There are about 250 students, with 8 teachers and as many classes, including 2 in English and 2 in Talmud. Hebrew studies last from 8.30 A.M. to 12 M. and from 1 to 3.30 P.M.; English studies from 4 to 7 P.M. The course occupies three years. The English students are prepared for entrance examinations for public grammar-school and college.

The most important yeshibah in New York is Yeshibat Rabbi Isaac Elhanan (Theological Seminary Association), organized in 1897 and located at 156 Henry street. It has about eighty students, ranging in age from thirteen to twenty-three. Dr. Philip (Hillel) Klein is president, and Nahum Dan Barhon is mashgiaḥ, with Moses Löb Schapiro as rosh yeshibah and Solab and Hirschberg as his assistants. Each student receives a stipend of $3 per week and clothing; expenditure about $15,000 per annum. The Talmud and poseḳim are the only subjects taught there, chief attention being given the treatises of the three Babot, Giṭṭin, Ketubot, and Ḳiddushin. Of the Shulḥan 'Aruk only Yoreh De'ah, Ḥoshen Mishpaṭ, and Eben ha-'Ezer are studied. After a course of three or four years the graduates receive semikah. One of the graduates, Naphtali Rosenberg, was elected rabbi of Syracuse, N. Y. This yeshibah is planned on the model of that of Volozhin. Other yeshibot of less importance are in Boston, Philadelphia, Pittsburg, and Chicago.

The advocates of the yeshibah system contend that it is still necessary to produce a true rabbinical training. Thus Isaac Hirsch Weiss says that it requires at least ten years of diligent study, and scrupulous and strict examination, before the hattarat hora'ah is issued to a candidate. Weiss admits, however, the need for a modern rabbi to be familiar with modern knowledge and literature ("Zikronotai," pp. 73–83). Isaac Rabbinowitz, the Hebrew poet, remarks that experiments with the Rabbinerschule in Wilna and Jitomir have proved the impossibility of producing in the modern schools

of learning acceptable rabbis for the old-fashioned Russian congregations ("Ha-Kerem," p. 33, Warsaw, 1887). See TALMUD TORAH.

BIBLIOGRAPHY: Moses Reines, Aksaniyot shel Torah, Cracow, 1890; Smolenskin, Ha-To'eh be-Darke ha-Ḥayyim, ii. 20–68 (a sketch); Ha-Shaḥar, viii. 112, 119, 161. For the Volozhin yeshibah: M. Hurwitz, Derek 'Eẓ ha-Ḥayyim, Cracow, 1885; Schechter, Studies in Judaism, pp. 94–97; Eisenstadt and Zevin, in Jewish Comment, 1903, Nos. 24–26; Ha-Zefirah, 1901, No. 247; Barditchewski, in Ha-Asif, 1887, p. 242; Ha-Kerem, pp. 33–82. For New York yeshibot: S. Lederhändler, in New Era Ill. Magazine, March and April, 1905.

J.   J. D. E.

YESHU'AH (JESHUAH) BEN ELIJAH HA-LEVI: African scholar and, perhaps, liturgical poet; of unknown date. He collected the poems of JUDAH HA-LEVI into a diwan, providing the volume with an Arabic introduction and heading most of the poems with superscriptions in which both the contents and the occasion of each poem are indicated. In the introduction, which was translated into German by Geiger ("Nachgelassene Schriften," iii. 154), Yeshu'ah says that he utilized three collections of his predecessors, Ḥiyya al-Ma'arabi, David b. Maimon, and Abu Sa'id ibn Alḳash; but he added many more poems, for which he does not guarantee Judah's authorship. Sachs ("Religiöse Poesie," p. 290, note 2) identifies the subject of this article with the author of the two poems found in the Tripolitan Maḥzor, one a "pizmon" beginning "Ye'erab siḥi lifne ḳadosh" and signed "Yeshu'ah," and the other a "mustajab" beginning "Emune lebab habinu" and signed "Yeshu'ah Ḥazzan." Both are to be recited on Yom Kippur night.

BIBLIOGRAPHY: Fuenn, Keneset Yisrael, p. 671; Landshuth, 'Ammude ha-'Abodah, p. 132; Zunz, Literaturgesch. pp. 567–568.

E. C.   M. SEL.

YESHU'AH (JESHUAH) BEN JOSEPH HA-LEVI: Algerian Talmudist of the fifteenth century; born at Tlemçen. In 1467, owing to the massacres of the Jews of Tlemçen committed by the Spaniards at that time, Yeshu'ah, still a young man, fled from his native town, with the intention of returning thither when the troubles should be over. He arrived at Toledo about 1469, and there received the hospitality of Don Vidal ibn Labi, the head of a flourishing school in that city. Perceiving that the young Algerian possessed a profound knowledge of the Talmud, Don Vidal requested him to write a methodology of the Talmud, which he would establish as the standard manual for the yeshibot. Yeshu'ah accordingly wrote the "Halikot 'Olam" (Lisbon or Spain, c. 1490), a methodology of the Talmud in five "gates" ("she'arim") or parts, each divided into chapters. The first gate treats of the order of the Mishnah and the manner of its composition; the second, of the method of the Gemara; the third, of the method of the Mishnah; the fourth, of the hermeneutic rules; and the fifth, of the method of the halakic decisions. In his preface Yeshu'ah praises his principal teacher, Jacob ha-Kohen Ashkenazi, and his benefactor, Don Vidal, whom he also eulogizes in a metrical poem at the end of the preface. This work was republished several times; and in 1634 an edition was issued in Leyden with a Latin translation made by L'Empereur. Later, Henry Jacob Bashuysen reedited it with L'Empereur's Latin translation and with notes of his own (Hanau, 1714). Finally, an adaptation from it was made by J. J. Struve under the title "Logicæ Hebraicæ Rudimenta" (Jena, 1697).

BIBLIOGRAPHY: Fuenn, *Keneset Yisrael*, p. 672; Fürst, *Bibl. Jud.* ii. 64–65; Steinschneider, *Cat. Bodl.* cols. 1392–1393.
E. C.　　　　　　　　　　　　　　　　M. SEL.

YEVREISKAYA BIBLIOTEKA. See RUSSIA, PERIODICALS.

YEZER HA-RA': Evil inclination or impulse, popularly identified with the lusts of the flesh. The idea is derived from Gen. viii. 21: "the imagination of the heart of man is evil from his youth." Yet from the use of the two "yods" in Gen. ii. 7, the Rabbis deduced that there are in man two Yezarim: the good (**Yezer Ṭob**) and the evil (Ber. 61a). Cain defended himself before God for having slain Abel by arguing that God had implanted in him the Yezer ha-Ra' (Tan., Bereshit, 25 [ed. Buber, p. 10]). "It lies at the door of the heart like a fly" (Ber. 61a; comp. BEELZEBUB). Yet in a way the Yezer ha-Ra', like all things which God made (Gen. i. 31), is good. Without it, for example, a man would never marry, beget, build a house, or trade (Gen. R. ix. 9). Therefore, man is enjoined to love God with both the Yezarim implied in "with all thy heart" of the Shema' (Sifre, Deut. 32 [ed. Friedmann, p. 73a]). It would appear that the Yezer Ṭob comes with reflection, and at the age of bar mizwah or confirmation, because it is said to be thirteen years younger than the Yezer ha-Ra', which is an inborn impulse (Eccl. R. ix. 14). The Yezer Ṭob delivers the citadel of the body from the Yezer ha-Ra' by means of temperance and good works (Ned. 32b). The "little city" of Eccl. ix. 14, 15 is interpreted by the Targum and Eccl. R. (*ad loc.*) as the kingdom of the heart, and the "great king" who comes against it as the Yezer ha-Ra'.

According to the Rabbis, the Yezer ha-Ra' has seven different epithets in the Bible: evil (Gen. viii. 21); uncircumcised (Deut. x. 16); unclean (Ps. li. 12); the enemy (Prov. xxv. 21); stumbling-block (Isa. lvii. 14); stone (Ezek. xxxvi. 26); and hidden (Joel ii. 20).

The greater the man the greater his Yezer ha-Ra'; and it is among the four things which God regretted to have created (Suk. 52a, b). It is identified with Satan and with the angel of death (B. B. 16a; comp. Maimonides, "Moreh," ii. 12, iii. 22). Against the Yezer ha-Ra' the Torah is the great antidote (Suk. 52b; Ḳid. 30b; Ab. R. N. 16). The Yezer ha-Ra' grows with a man, as is deduced from the parable in II Sam. xii. 4. At first it is a mere traveler; then it becomes a guest; and at last it is the man himself (Suk. 52b). Yet the heart of man contains both the Yezer ha-Ra' and the Yezer Ṭob, as is deduced by Midrash Tehillim from Ps. ix.

"Yezer ha-Ra'" does not refer exclusively to the body; this can be inferred from its close association with the Yezer Ṭob. It undoubtedly leads to sensual sins with great power; hence
Charac-　　both Akiba and Meïr were saved from
teristics.　its influence only by heavenly intercession (Ḳid. 81a). It was to avoid the temptations of the Yezer ha-Ra' that women were ordered to take separate seats in the galleries of synagogues (Suk. 51b). Revenge and avarice are also given as the outcome of the Yezer ha-Ra' (Sifre, Deut. 33 [ed. Friedmann, p. 74a]); and anger is another of its manifestations. Ps. lxxxi. 10 (A. V. 9) is interpreted as referring to the Yezer to whose influence one should not yield (Shab. 105b), submission being, therefore, compared to idolatry (Yer. Ned. 41b). It is with reference to anger that he is called mighty who overcomes his Yezer ha-Ra' (Ab. iv. 2). Vanity is still another form in which the Yezer ha-Ra' displays itself. When the Yezer sees a conceited man it says: "He is mine" (Gen. R. xxii. 13). The Yezer ha-Ra' belongs only to this world, and does not exist in angels or other higher beings (Lev. R. xxvi.). It is for this reason that there is no eating or drinking, procreation or barter, envy or hatred, in the world to come (Ber. 17a; comp. Mark xii. 25, and synoptic parallels).

In a discussion between Rabbi and the emperor Antoninus, the latter contends that the Yezer ha-Ra' comes to man at birth, and not before, and Rabbi agrees (Sanh. 91b). All the sportive deviltry of young children is attributed to the Yezer ha-Ra' (Eccl. R. iv. 13). The Yezer ha-Ra' was not due to man, but to God as the Creator of all; but man is responsible for yielding to its influence, since he, as has been seen above, is able to put it to a good use. Hence the Yezer ha-Ra' is placed on a level with the woman and the child: the left hand should reject it, while the right hand draws it near (Soṭah 47a; Sanh. 107b). Under the Second Temple the Yezer ha-Ra' continued to exist because needed in the world. The Rabbis interpret Neh. ix. 4 as referring to the call of the people: "Wo, wo, it is the Yezer ha-Ra'. He destroyed the sanctuary, killed the righteous, drove the Israelites out of their land, and still dances among us. Why was he given unto us? Only that we may receive reward for conquering him." The Israelites are then reported to have got rid of the Yezer of idolatry and of the grosser forms of unchastity, but found it necessary to preserve the Yezer ha-Ra' lest the world should come to an end (Yoma 69b; comp. Sanh. 64a). It has been conjectured by Taylor that the clause in the Lord's Prayer, "Deliver us from evil," is probably "Deliver us from the evil Yezer" ("Sayings of the Jewish Fathers," pp. 128–130, 186–192).

There is a tendency to give personality and separate activity to the Yezer, as in the case of the angel of death and of Satan, with each of whom, indeed, it is identified (B. B. 16a).
Personifi-　Objections to the Law which in Sifra
cation.　　86a are attributed to the Yezer are in Yoma 67b attributed to Satan. According to R. Jonathan, the Yezer, like Satan, misleads man in this world, and testifies against him in the world to come (Suk. 52b). Hence in the prayers one asks to be delivered "from evil man and from evil act, from evil Yezer, from evil companion, from evil neighbor, and from Satan" (Ber. 16b). Here, however, the Yezer is clearly distinguished from Satan. On other occasions it is made exactly parallel to sin. Thus, in Gen. R. xxii. 11 the parable of II Sam. xii. 4 is applied to sin, though elsewhere it is applied to the Yezer (see above). Similarly, Akiba interprets Isa. v. 18 as

applying to sin, while Rab Ashi applies it to the Yezer (Suk. 52a). "At the beginning they are like the thread of the spinning web, at the end like a cart rope." The connection of the Yezer with habit is exactly parallel to the growth of sin through habit. Man's Yezer overpowers him every day (Kid. 30b). At first it befools him; then it dwells in him (comp. Hos. iv. 12, v. 4). So too Ps. xxxvi. 2, "sin speaks to the wicked," is applied to the Yezer ha-Ra' (Ab. R. N. 32). In the same passage all men are divided into three classes: the righteous, under the rule of the Yezer Tob; the wicked, under the rule of the Yezer ha-Ra'; and the middle class, ruled now by one, now by the other. According to others, there are only two classes: the righteous with the good Yezer; and the wicked, who submit to the evil Yezer (Eccl. R. iv. 15, 16). The first part of Eccl. xi. 9 is said to relate to the joy of youth derived from the Yezer ha-Ra'; the latter part indicates that God will bring all transgressors under judgment to the Yezer Tob (Shab. 63a).

Just as iron can be made into all sorts of vessels if cast into the fire, so one can make the Yezer ha-Ra' useful by words of the Law; for it is learned from Prov. xxv. 21 that "if thine enemy be hungry [that is, "when the Yezer ha-Ra' prompts thee"] give him bread to eat" (i.e., bread of the Law; Pesik., ed. Buber, 80b). Both Yezarim are to be utilized; similarly a man having two oxen, one meant for plowing and the other not, puts the yoke upon both. The promise of Gen. iv. 7 is applied to the Yezer ha-Ra' (Kid. 30b). There is a contrast of strength between the two Yezarim; hence, "Blessed is he that considereth the poor" (Ps. xli. 2) is applied to him who makes the poor and weak Yezer Tob rule over the Yezer ha-Ra' (Lev. R. xxxiv.). Though the latter is seemingly so powerful, resistance easily overcomes it, as Abraham found after it had brought about the Flood and the dispersion of the nations (Gen. xxii. 12). If a man find that the Yezer ha-Ra' is too strong for him, he should go to a place where he is not known, and not profane the name of heaven openly (Hag. 16a). The Law is like a plaster to the wound made by the Yezer ha-Ra'; if the plaster is taken away, an evil ulcer will come forth (Kid. 30b). Or, again, the Law will wear away the Yezer as water wears away stone (Suk. 52b). As the Law is called a stone (Ex. xxiv. 12), and the Yezer ha-Ra' also is called a stone (ib. xxxvi. 26), let one stone guard the other stone (Cant. R. vi. 11). The stone of Gen. xxix. 2 is also compared to the Yezer ha-Ra': as the stone is rolled away from the mouth of the well, so the Yezer ha-Ra' departs when men go into the synagogue to drink of the Law (Gen. R. lxx. 8); hence, the night prayer said in connection with the "Shema'" includes the clause "let not the Yezer ha-Ra' rule in me" (Ber. 60b).

God will finally destroy the Yezer ha-Ra', as is promised in Ezek. xxxvi. 26. Yet to the righteous who have struggled against it, it will appear like a high mountain; but to the wicked, like a hair (Suk. 52a). It is because the Yezer ha-Ra' anticipates this final punishment that it brings man to destruc-

The Law the Antidote.

tion (Ab. R. N. 16). Meanwhile, like a stone (see above), it gradually crumbles away until it no longer forms a stumbling-block.

While the expression "yezer" is used both in Deut. xxxi. 21 and in Isa. xxvi. 3 for the disposition or mind, "heart" or "evil heart" usually takes its place in Biblical theology as the seat and power of temptation and sin in man. The first definitive passage in which the term occurs is in the lately recovered Hebrew text of Ecclus. (Sirach) xv. 14: "God created man from the beginning . . . and gave him into the hand of his Yezer." And in vi. 22 (Heb.) man is compared to the fruit of a tree, while his thoughts are according to his Yezer. So, too, the "wicked heart" referred to in Ezra iv. 18 is analogous to the Yezer ha-Ra' in being offset by the Law and in not having power to overcome the Law, and also because God will ultimately remove it. This is an approach to the dualism of Paul (Rom. vii. 7–24), but the contrast between the flesh and the spirit nowhere exists in Jewish theology, and is probably derived from Plato.

Rise of the Idea.

BIBLIOGRAPHY: F. C. Porter, The Yeçer Hara, in Yale Biblical and Semitic Studies, pp. 91–156, New York, 1901; Taylor, Sayings of the Jewish Fathers, 2d ed., pp. 37, 63 et seq., 70, 77, 82, 98, 128–130, 140, 147–152, 186–192; Lazarus, Ethics of Judaism, § 238.
E. C.   J.

YEZIRAH, SEFER (ספר יצירה = "Book of Creation"): The title of two esoteric books. Of these the older is also called "Hilkot Yezirah" (Rules of Creation), and is a thaumaturgical work that was popular in the Talmudic period. "On the eve of every Sabbath, Judah ha-Nasi's pupils, Rab Ḥanina and Rab Hoshaiah, who devoted themselves especially to cosmogony, used to create a three-year-old calf by means of the 'Sefer Yezirah,' and ate it on the Sabbath" (Sanh. 65b, 67b). According to the tradition given by Rashi on both passages, this miracle was accomplished by the letters of the Holy Name ("zeruf otiyyot"), and not by witchcraft. In like manner, according to Rab, Bezaleel, the architect of the Tabernacle in the wilderness, worked by the permutations of the letters with which God created heaven and earth (Ber. 55a). All the miraculous creations attributed to other amoraim in Sanh. 65b and Yer. Sanh. 52d are ascribed by the commentators to the use of the same thaumaturgical book. Such a work, entitled Κοσμοποιΐα ("Creation of the World"), circulated in many forms among the Gnostics of the second century B.C., and was a combination, as Dieterich ("Abraxas," pp. 3–31) has shown, of many Jewish, Greek, and Egyptian names and elements. It formed also part of magic papyri. Its basal idea is that the same mystic powers that were at work in the creation of the world should also aid the magician in performing his miraculous feats (ib. pp. 136 et seq.). While in the cosmogony of ABRAXAS, however, the seven worlds were created by the emission of seven sounds followed by three others, the older cosmogonies, which were nearer their Egyptian sources, make the twenty-eight letters corresponding to the twenty-eight days of the astrological calendar the creative elements constituting both the names and the essence of the Deity (Reizenstein, "Poimandres,"

The Power of the Name.

pp. 256–291). Both the macrocosm (the universe) and the microcosm (man) are viewed in this system as products of the combination and permutation of these mystic characters (*ib.* pp. 261, 267), and such a use of the letters by the Jews for the formation of the Holy Name for thaumaturgical purposes is attested by magic papyri that quote an "Angelic Book of Moses," which was full of allusions to Biblical names (Reizenstein, *l.c.* pp. 14, 56).

While the mystic use of letters and numbers undoubtedly points to a Babylonian origin, the idea of the creative power of the various sounds is Egyptian, as well as the division of the letters into the three classes of vowels, mutes, and sonants is Hellenic, although this classification necessarily underwent certain changes when applied to

Origin. the Hebrew letters. The origin of the "Sefer Yeẓirah" is accordingly placed by Reizenstein (*l.c.* p. 291) in the second century B.C. Some data regarding the age of this system may also be derived from the work of Philo of Byblos on the Phenician letters, in which they are explained as symbols of the (Egyptian) gods and at the same time as cosmic "elements" (see Baudissin, "Studien zur Semitischen Religionsgeschichte," i. 18, 270). How far these mystic uses of the alphabet influenced the rabbis of the Talmudic period is still a problem. Rab of Babylonia combined the ten creative potencies with the Forty-two-Lettered Name and the twelve letters which constitute the Holy Name (see Bacher, "Ag. Bab. Amor." pp. 17–20), and R. Akiba in particular was credited with a knowledge of the mystic significance of the letters (Bacher, "Ag. Tan." i. 347–348). When, therefore, the rationalistic "Sefer Yeẓirah" was developed from the thaumaturgical work of the same name, which was known only to a few, the authorship was ascribed to Akiba. The closing mishnah (vi. 15), however, expressly declares that Abraham was the recipient of the divine revelation of mystic lore; so that the oldest geonim (see Hai Gaon in the responsum cited in "Kerem Ḥemed," viii. 57) and such philosophers as Saadia, Donnolo, and Judah ha-Levi ("Cuzari," iv. 25) never doubted that Abraham was the author of the book.

It is noteworthy that in a manuscript (see Margoliouth, "Catalogue of the Hebrew and Samaritan Manuscripts of the British Museum," part II., p. 190) the "Sefer Yeẓirah" is called "Hilkot Yeẓirah" and declared to be treated as esoteric lore not accessible to any but the really pious (comp. *ib.* p. 255, where it is mentioned as being used by Naḥmanides for cabalistic purposes). K.

The later "Sefer Yeẓirah" is devoted to speculations concerning God and the angels. The ascription of its authorship to R. Akiba, and even to Abraham, shows the high esteem which it enjoyed for centuries. It may even be said that this work had a greater influence on the development of the Jewish mind than almost any other book after the com-

Influence. pletion of the Talmud. The Aristotelian Saadia, the Neoplatonist Ibn Gabirol, the speculative cabalists of France, and the mystics of Germany deemed themselves justified in deriving their doctrines from this remarkable work, although it often suffered the same treatment as other sacred books, since its commentators read into it far

more than the text implied. The "Sefer Yeẓirah" is exceedingly difficult to understand on account of its obscure, half-mystical style, and the difficulty is rendered still greater by the lack of a critical edition, the present text being admittedly much interpolated and altered. Hence there is a wide divergence of opinion regarding the age, origin, contents, and value of the book, since it is variously regarded as pre-Christian, Essene, Mishnaic, Talmudic, or geonic.

As the book is the first speculative treatise in Hebrew, and at the same time the earliest known work on the Hebrew language, the philological part may

The Phonetic System. be discussed first, since it is necessary for an elucidation of the philosophical speculations of the work. The twenty-two letters of the Hebrew alphabet are classified both with reference to the position of the vocal organs in producing the sounds, and with regard to sonant intensity. In contrast to the Jewish grammarians, who assumed a special mode of articulation for each of the five groups of sounds, the "Sefer Yeẓirah" says that no sound can be produced without the tongue, to which the other organs of speech merely lend assistance. Hence the formation of the letters is described as follows: אחה"ע with the tip of the tongue and the throat; בומ"ף between the lips and the tip of the tongue; גיכ"ק in the middle ([?] על שלישיתה) of the tongue; דטלנ"ת by the tip of the tongue; and זסש רץ"ץ by the tongue, which lies flat and stretched, and by the teeth (ii. 3). The letters are distinguished, moreover, by the intensity of the sound necessary to produce them, and are accordingly divided into: mutes, which are unaccompanied by sound, such as מ, which the book calls מ'דוממת; sibilants, such as ש, which is therefore called ש'שורקת, the "hissing shin"; and aspirates, such as א, which holds a position between the mutes and sibilants, and is designated as the "airy א, which holds the balance in the middle" (iv. 1; in some eds. ii. 1). Besides these three letters (אמ"ש), which are called "mothers," a distinction is also drawn between the seven "double" letters (בגדכפרת) and the twelve "simple" letters (פשוטות), the remaining characters of the alphabet.

The linguistic theories of the author of the "Sefer Yeẓirah" are an integral component of his philosophy, its other parts being astrological and Gnostic cosmogony. The three letters אמ"ש are not only the three "mothers" from which the other letters of the alphabet are formed, but they are also symbolical figures for the three primordial elements, the substances which underlie all existence. The mute מ is the symbol of the water in which the mute fish live; the hissing ש corresponds to the hissing fire; and the airy א represents the air; while as the air occupies a middle position between the fire which reaches upward and the water which tends downward, so the א is placed between the mute מ and the hissing ש. According to the "Sefer

Cosmogony. Yeẓirah," the first emanation from the spirit of God was the רוח (= "spirit," "air") that produced fire, which, in its turn, formed the genesis of water. In the beginning, however, these three substances had only a potential existence, and came into actual being only by means of the three letters אמ"ש; and as these are the principal parts of speech, so those three substances are the elements from which the cosmos has been formed. The cosmos consists of three parts, the world, the year (or time), and man, which are combined in such a way that the three primordial elements are contained in each of the three categories. The water formed the earth; heaven was produced from the fire; and the רוח produced the air between heaven and earth. The three seasons of the year, winter, summer, and the rainy season (רויה), correspond to water, fire, and רוח in the same way as man consists of a head (corresponding to fire), torso (represented by רוח), and the other parts of the body (equivalent to water). The seven double letters produced the seven planets, the "seven days," and the seven apertures in man (two eyes, two ears, two nostrils, and one mouth). Again, as the seven double letters vary, being pronounced either hard or soft, so the seven planets are in continuous movement, approaching or receding from the earth. The "seven days," in like manner, were created by the seven double letters because they change in time according to their relation to the planets. The seven apertures in man connect him with the outer world as the seven planets join heaven and earth. Hence these organs are subject to the influence of the planets, the right eye being under Saturn, the left eye under Jupiter, and the like. The twelve "simple" letters created the twelve signs of the zodiac, whose relation to the earth is always simple or stable; and to them belong the twelve months in time, and the twelve "leaders" (מנהיגים) in man. The latter are those organs which perform functions in the body independent of the outside world, being the hands, feet, kidneys, gall, intestines, stomach, liver, pancreas, and spleen; and they are, accordingly, subject to the twelve signs of the zodiac. In its relation to the construction of the cosmos, matter consists of the three primordial elements, which, however, are not chemically connected with one another, but modify one another only physically. Power (δύναμις) emanates from the seven and the twelve heavenly bodies, or, in other words, from the planets and the signs of the zodiac. The "dragon" (תלי) rules over the world (matter and the heavenly bodies); the sphere (גלגל) rules time; and the heart rules over the human body. The author sums up this explanation in a single sentence: "The dragon is like to a king on his throne, the sphere like a king traveling in his country, and the heart like a king at war."

While the astrological cosmogony of the book contains few Jewish elements, an attempt is made, in the account of the creation, to give a Jewish coloring to the Gnostic standpoint. To harmonize the Biblical statement of the creation "ex nihilo" with the doctrine of the primordial elements, the "Sefer Yezirah" assumes a double creation, one ideal and the other real. The first postulate is

The Creation. the spirit of God, from which the prototypes of matter emanated, the world being produced, in its turn, by the prototypes of the three primordial substances when they became realities. Simultaneously with the prototypes, or at least before the real world, space was produced, and it is here conceived as the three di-

mensions with their opposite directions. The spirit of God, the three primordial elements, and the six dimensions of space form the "ten Sefirot," which, like the spirit of God, exist only ideally, being "ten Sefirot without reality" as the text designates them. Their name is possibly derived from the fact that as numbers express only the relations of two objects to each other, so the ten Sefirot are only abstractions and not realities. Again, as the numbers from two to ten are derived from the number one, so the ten Sefirot are derived from one, the spirit of God. The spirit of God, however, is not only the commencement but also the conclusion of the Sefirot, "their end being in their beginning and their beginning in their end, even as the flame is connected with the coal" (i. 7). Hence the Sefirot must not be conceived as emanations in the ordinary sense of the word, but rather as modifications of the spirit of God, which first changes to רוח, then becomes water, and finally fire, the last being no further removed from God than the first. Besides these abstract ten Sefirot, which are conceived only ideally, the twenty-two letters of the alphabet produced the material world, for they are real, and are the formative powers of all existence and development. By means of these elements the actual creation of the world took place, and the ten Sefirot, which before this had only an ideal existence, became realities. This is, then, a modified form of the Talmudic doctrine that God created heaven and earth by means of letters (Ber. 58a). The explanation on this point is very obscure, however, since the relation of the twenty-two letters to the ten Sefirot is not clearly defined. The first sentence of the book reads: "Thirty-two paths, marvels of wisdom, hath God engraved . . . ," these paths being then explained as the ten Sefirot and the twenty-two letters. While the Sefirot are expressly designated as "abstracts" (בלי מה), it is said of the letters: "Twenty-two letters: He drew them, hewed them, combined them, weighed them, interchanged them, and through them produced the whole creation and everything that is destined to come into being" (ii. 2). The basal theory of the letters apparently regards them neither as independent substances nor yet as mere forms, so that they are, as it were, the connecting-link between essence and form. They are designated, therefore, as the instruments by which the real world, which consists of essence and form, was produced from the Sefirot, which are merely formless essences.

In addition to the doctrine of the Sefirot and the letters, the theory of contrasts in nature, or of the syzygies ("pairs"), as they are called by the Gnostics, occupies a prominent place in the "Sefer Yezi-

Syzygies. rah." This doctrine is based on the assumption that the physical as well as the moral world consists of a series of contrasts mutually at war, yet pacified and equalized by the unity, God. Thus in the three prototypes of creation the contrasting elements fire and water are equalized by רוח; corresponding to this are the three "mothers" among the letters, the mute מ contrasting with the hissing ש, and both being equalized by א. Seven pairs of contrasts are enumerated in the life of man: life and death, peace and strife, wisdom and folly, wealth and poverty, beauty and ugliness, fertility and sterility, lordship and servitude (iv. 3). From these premises the "Sefer Yeẓirah" draws the important conclusion that "good and evil" have no real existence, for since everything in nature can exist only by means of its contrast, a thing may be called good or evil according to its influence over man by the natural course of the contrast. The Jewish bent of the author's mind comes out, however, in the concession that as man is a free moral agent, he is rewarded or punished for his actions. It must be noted, on the other hand, that the conceptions of heaven and hell are foreign to the book, the virtuous man being rewarded by a favorable attitude of nature, while the wicked finds it hostile to him. Notwithstanding the seeming unity of the book, its system is composed of divergent elements, and the differences of opinion regarding it can never be harmonized so long as emphasis is laid on any one component rather than on the book as a whole. The doctrine of the three primordial substances is doubtless an element of ancient Semitic theosophy, and was probably adopted by the Greeks from the Semites. In the seventh chapter of the "Timæus" Plato has the following statement, which is very similar to the views expressed in the "Sefer Yeẓirah" (iii. 3): "And thus God placed water between fire and earth, and air in the middle . . . and connected and thus joined heaven so that it became sensible to touch and sight." Even the expression "mother" (אם) is found in Plato (l.c. xix.), who speaks of the "nurse" of creative force. The idea of the three substances is likewise found in mythological form in the Midrash (Ex. R. xv. 22) and in other midrashim of the geonic period (Midr. Konen, in Jellinek, "B. H." ii. 23).

Far more important is the similarity of the "Sefer Yeẓirah" to various Gnostic systems, to which Grätz has called special attention. As the "Sefer Yeẓirah" divides the Hebrew alphabet into three groups, so the Gnostic Marcus divided the Greek letters into three classes, regarded by him as the symbolic emanations of the three powers which include the whole number of the upper elements. Both systems attach great importance to the power of the combinations and permutations of the letters in explaining the genesis and development of multiplicity from unity (comp. Irenæus, "Adversus Hæreses," i. 16). The Clementine writings present another form of gnosis which agrees in many points with the "Sefer Yeẓirah." As in the latter, God is not only the beginning but also the end of all things, so in the former He is the ἀρχή and τέλος of all that exists; and the Clementine writings furthermore teach that the spirit of God is transformed into πνεῦμα (= רוח), and this into water, which becomes fire and rocks, thus agreeing with the "Sefer Yeẓirah," where the spirit of God, רוח (= πνεῦμα), water, and fire are the first four Sefirot (Uhlhorn, "Homilien und Recognitionen," pp. 181–182; the rocks in the Clementine writings correspond to the אבנים in the "Sefer Yeẓirah," i. 11). The remaining six Sefirot, or the limitations of space by the three dimensions in a twofold direction, are also found in the Clementina, where God is described as the boundary of the universe and as the

Gnostic Elements.

source of the six infinite dimensions (Hom. xvii. 9; comp. Lehman, "Die Clementinischen Schriften," p. 377). Regarding points of contact between the "Sefer Yeẓirah" and Buddhistic doctrines see Epstein in "R. E. J." xxviii. 101; and Rubin, "Yesod Mistere ha-'Akkum," pp. 19–20. The "dragon," which plays such an important part in the astrology of the book, is probably an ancient Semitic figure; at all events its name is not Arabic, as scholars have hitherto assumed, but either Aramaic or possibly a Babylonian loan-word (A. Harkavy, "Teli Atlia," reprinted from "Ben 'Ammi," i. 27–35).

The essential elements of the book are characteristic of the third or fourth century; for a work of this nature, composed in the geonic period, before the Jews had become acquainted with Arabic and Greek learning, could have been cast only in the form of Jewish gnosis, which remained stationary after the fourth century, if indeed it had not already become extinct. The date of the book, as regards its present form, resolves itself, therefore, into a problem of literature; for the contents were certainly derived from ancient sources. It must be borne in mind, however, that the Talmudic period contains absolutely nothing to show how abstract philosophical questions were treated in Hebrew; and since, moreover, the "Sefer Yeẓirah" contains many new expressions that are not found in the earlier literature, there is nothing to disprove that the book was written in the sixth century. It may be noted that Ḳalir, who certainly lived before the ninth century, used not only the "Sefer Yeẓirah," but also the Baraita of Samuel, which was written about the same time. Saadia advanced the view (end of the preface to his commentary on the "Sefer Yeẓirah") that the book was circulated orally for a long time before it was reduced to writing, his statement being somewhat more than an excuse for his free treatment of the text.

Date.

As already stated, the date and origin of the book can not be definitely determined so long as there is no critical text of it. The editio princeps (Mantua, 1562) contains two recensions, which were used in the main by the commentators of the book as early as the middle of the tenth century. The shorter version (Mantua I.) was annotated by Dunash ibn Tamim or by Jacob b. Nissim, while Saadia and Donnolo wrote commentaries on the longer recension (Mantua II.). The shorter version was also used by most of the later commentators, such as Judah b. Barzillai and Naḥmanides, and it was, therefore, published in the ordinary editions. The longer recension, on the other hand, was little known, the form given in the editio princeps of the "Sefer Yeẓirah" being probably a copy of the text found in Donnolo's commentary. In addition to these two principal recensions of the text, both versions contain a number of variant readings which have not yet been examined critically. As regards the relation of the two recensions, it may be said that the longer form contains entire paragraphs which are not found in the shorter, while the divergent arrangement of the material often modifies the meaning essentially. Although the longer recension

History of the Text.

doubtless contains additions and interpolations which did not form part of the original text, it has many valuable readings which seem older and better than the corresponding passages in the shorter version, so that a critical edition of the text must consider both recensions.

The history of the study of the "Sefer Yeẓirah" is one of the most interesting in the records of Jewish literature. With the exception of the Bible, scarcely any other book has been the subject of so much annotation. Aristotelians, Neoplatonists, Talmudists, and cabalists have used the book as a source, or at least thought they did so. Two points must be taken into consideration in judging the importance of the work: the influence which it exerted on the development of Jewish philosophy, especially on its mystic side, and the reputation which it enjoyed for more than a thousand years in most Jewish circles. This may best be illustrated by the following chronological list of authors who have interpreted the book or tried to do so: Saadia; Isaac Israeli; Dunash ibn Tamim (Jacob b. Nissim); Donnolo; Judah b. Barzillai; Judah ha-Levi; Abraham ibn Ezra; Eleazar of Worms; pseudo-Saadia (time and school of Eleazar); Abraham Abulafia; (pseudo-?) Abraham b. David; Naḥmanides (although the work may be ascribed to him incorrectly); Judah b. Nissim of Fez; Moses Botarel; Moses b. Jacob ha-Goleh; Moses b. Jacob Cordovero; Isaac Luria; Elijah b. Solomon of Wilna; Isaac Ḥaber; and Gershon Enoch b. Jacob. To these twenty commentators, who represent the period from the beginning of the tenth to the end of the nineteenth century and include scholars of the highest rank, must be added men like Hai Gaon, Rashi, and others who diligently studied the book.

Jewish Study of the Book.

If Botarel's statement may be credited, many commentaries were written on the "Sefer Yeẓirah" in the geonic period. It is far more difficult, however, to decide how many of the opinions and doctrines contained in the book influenced the views of later Jewish thinkers. The fact that scholars of so many different views quoted it in support of their theories justifies the assumption that none of them really based his hypotheses on it, and this view is adopted by most modern scholars. It must be borne in mind, however, that an intimate relation exists between the "Sefer Yeẓirah" and the later mystics, and that, although there is a marked difference between the Cabala and the "Sefer Yeẓirah" as regards the theory of emanations, yet the system laid down in the latter is the first visible link in the development of cabalistic ideas. Instead of the immediate creation "ex nihilo," both works postulate a series of emanations of mediums between God and the universe; and both consider God as the first cause only, and not as the immediate efficient cause of the world. Although the Sefirot of the cabalists do not correspond to those of the "Sefer Yeẓirah," yet the underlying problem is identical in both. The importance of the "Sefer Yeẓirah" for mysticism, finally, lies in the fact that the speculation about God and man had lost its sectarian character. This book, which does not even mention such words as "Israel" and "revelation," taught the cabalists to reflect on "God," and not merely on the "Ruler of Israel."

A book of the same name, which, however, had nothing else in common with the "Sefer Yeẓirah," was circulated among German mystics between the eleventh and thirteenth centuries. Judging from the examples collected by Epstein in "Ha-Ḥoker," ii. 1–5, it was a mystic and haggadic work on the six days of creation, and corresponded in part to the small Midrash Seder Rabbah de-Bereshit which was edited by Wertheimer ("Batte Midrashot," i. 1–31).

BIBLIOGRAPHY: Editions and translations: Editio princeps, Mantua, 1562; other important editions: Amsterdam, 1642; Zolkiev, 1745; Korzec, 1779; Constantinople, 1791; Grodno, 1806 (five commentaries); Warsaw, 1884 (nine commentaries); Goldschmidt, *Das Buch der Schöpfung . . . Kritisch Redigirter Text*, Frankfort-on-the-Main, 1894 (the edition, however, by no means represents a critical text). Translations: Latin: Postell, *Abraham Patriarchæ Liber Iezirah*, Paris, 1552; Pistor, *Liber Iezirah*, in *Ars Cabalistica*, Basel, 1557; Rittangel in the Amsterdam edition of 1642; German: Johann F. von Meyer, *Das Buch Yezira*, Leipsic, 1830; English: I. Kalisch, *A Sketch of the Talmud*, New York, 1877; W. W. Westcott, *Sepher Yezirah*, London, 1893; French: Karppe, *Etude sur les Origines . . . du Zohar*, pp. 139–158, Paris, 1901. Literature: Castelli, *Il Commento di Sabbatai Donnolo*, Florence, 1880; Epstein, *Studien zum Jezira-Buche*, in *Monatsschrift*, xxxvii.; idem, *Pseudo-Saadia*, ib.; idem, *Recherches sur le Sefer Yeçira*, in *R. E. J.* xxviii.-xxix. (both articles also published separately); idem, in *Monatsschrift*, xxxix. 46–48, 134–136; Grätz, *Gnosticismus und Judenthum*, pp. 102–132, Breslau, 1846; Franck, *La Kabbale*, pp. 53–66, 102–118, Paris, 1843 (German translation by Jellinek, pp. 57–65, Leipsic, 1844); Hamburger, *R. B. T.* Supplement, iii. 98–102; Jellinek, *Beiträge*, i. 3–16; Rosenthal, in *Keneset Yisrael*, ii. 29–68; Steinschneider, in Berliner's *Magazin*, xix. 79–85; idem. *Cat. Bodl.* cols. 552–554; Zedner, *Cat. Hebr. Books Brit. Mus.* p. 13; Fürst, *Bibl. Jud.* i. 27–28; Bacher, *Die Anfänge der Hebräischen Grammatik*, pp. 20–23, Leipsic, 1895.

K.　　　　　　　　　　　　　　　　　　L. G.

YIBBUM. See LEVIRATE MARRIAGE.

YIGDAL: The hymn which in the various rituals shares with ADON 'OLAM the place of honor at the opening of the morning and the close of the evening service. It is based on the thirteen ARTICLES OF FAITH (usually called the Thirteen Creeds) formulated by Moses ben Maimon, and was written by Daniel ben Judah Dayyan (Zunz, "Literaturgesch." p. 507), who spent eight years in improving it, completing it in 1404 (S. D. Luzzatto, "Mebo," p. 18). This was not the only metrical presentment of the Creeds; but it has outlived all others, whether in Hebrew or in the vernacular. A translation is to be found in the Daily Prayer-Book.

With the Ashkenazim only thirteen lines are sung, one for each creed; and the last, dealing with the resurrection of the dead, is solemnly repeated to complete the antiphony when the hymn is responsorially sung by ḥazzan and congregation. The Sephardim, who sing the hymn in congregational unison throughout, use the following line as the fourteenth: "These be the thirteen bases of the Rule of Moses and the tenets of his Law."

"Yigdal" far surpasses "Adon 'Olam" in the number of its traditional tunes and the length of time during which they have been traditional. In the Spanish ritual, in its Dutch- and English-speaking tradition, the hymn is often sung, according to the general Sephardic custom (comp. e.g., YAH SHIMEKA), to some "representative" melody of the particular day.

Sephardic Tunes.

Thus, for example, it is chanted at the close of evening service on New-Year to the tune of 'ET SHA'ARE RAẒON. On Friday evening the Sab-

YIGDAL—A (Sephardic Festival)

Yig - dal E - lo - him hay, we - yish - tab - bah,

Nim - za we - en 'et el.......... me - zi - 'u - to. *Other verses similarly.*

YIGDAL—B ("Leoni")

HAZZAN: Yig - dal E - lo - him hay, we - yish - tab - bah, Nim - za we - en 'et

el...... me - zi - 'u - to. CONGREGATION: E - had, we - en ya - hid ke -

yi - hu - do, Ne' - lam, we - gam en sof..... le - ah' - du - to.

YIGDAL—C (Penitential, "Polish")

HAZZAN: Me - tim ye - hay - yeh El be - rob has - do: Ba - ruk...... 'a - de 'ad

shem te - hil - la - to. CONGREGATION: Me - tim ye - hay - yeh El.... be -

rob has - do: Ba - ruk 'a - de 'ad shem te - hil - la - to.

YIGDAL—D (Penitential, "South German")

HAZZAN: Yig - dal E - lo - him hay, we - yish - tab - bah, Nim - za we - en....

'et el me - zi - 'u - to. CONGREGATION: E - had, we - en ya - hid...... ke -

yi - hu - do,. Ne'- lam we - gam en sof...... le - ah - du - to. HAZZAN: En

lo de - mut ha - guf,.... we - e - no guf, Lo na - 'a - rok e -

law.... ke - dush - sha - to. CONGREGATION: Kad-mon le - kol da - bar a - sher nib -

ra, Ri - shon we - en re - shit.... le - re - shi - to.

YIGDAL—E (Passover)

Allegretto.

HAZZAN: Yig - dal E - lo - him hay, we - yish - tab - bah,.... Nim - za we - en

'et el me - zi - 'u - to.... CONGREGATION: E - had,.... we - en ya - hid ke -

yi - hu - do,.... Ne'- lam.... we - gam en sof le - ah - du - to.....

Last verses. Lento.   *tempo primo.*
pp

HAZZAN: Me - tim ye - hay - yeh El,.... be - rob has - do: Ba - ruk 'a -

de....... 'ad.... shem te-hil-la-to..... Choir: Me - tim ye-hay-yeh

El,..... be - rob..... has-do..... (Ba - ruk 'a - de...... 'ad), Ba -

ruk 'a - de... 'ad, Ba - ruk 'a - de..... 'ad shem te - hil - la - to.

YIGDAL—F (Pentecost)

Andantino.

cres.

Yig - dal.... E - lo - him hay, we - yish...... tab - bah,......... Nim -

za...... we - en.... 'et.... el me - zi - - 'u - to.

E - had,.... we - en ya - hid ke - yi - - hu - do,... Ne' -

lam.......... we - gam.... en sof le - ah - - du - to......

YIGDAL—G (Tabernacles)

mf Con spirito.

Hazzan: Yig - dal E - lo - him hay,.. we - yish - tab - bah, Nim - za we - en

mf

'et el me - zi - 'u - to. Congregation: E - chad, we - en ya - hid... ke -

XII.—39

yi - hu - do, Ne' - lam we - gam en sof le - ah - du - to......

HAZZAN: En..... lo de - mut ha - guf,.. we - e - no guf, Lo na.......... 'a -

rok...... e - law ke - dush - sha - to. CONG.: Kad - mon le - kol da - bar, a -

sher nib - ra, Ri - shon we - en re - shit le - re - shi - to......

bath "Yigdal" is customarily sung to the same melody as are "Adon 'Olam" (see JEW. ENCYC. i. 206, melody A) and EN KELOHENU. On the three festivals the melody here transcribed under A is the tune favored. Its old Spanish character is evident.

In the Ashkenazic ritual "Yigdal," though always commencing the morning prayer, is not invariably sung at the close of the evening service on Sabbaths and festivals, being often, especially in Germany, replaced by "Adon 'Olam." In Polish use, however, it is more regularly employed as the closing hymn, while in the synagogues of northwestern Germany, Holland, and England, where the influence of the Sephardic ritual has been felt by that of the Ashkenazim, "Yigdal" is considered an integral portion of the Sabbath and **Ashkena-** festal evening prayer; and in London **zic Tunes.** for fully two centuries there has been allotted to the hymn, according to the occasion, a definite tradition of tunes, all of which are antiphonal between hazzan and congregation. The most familiar of these tunes is the Friday evening "Yigdal," transcribed here under B. It has passed into the repertory of the Anglican and Nonconformist churches under the title of "Leoni" (see JEW. ENCYC. viii. 229). It is utilized also in Germany and in some parts of Poland and Bohemia as a festival "Yigdal." The melody may date from the seventeenth century or perhaps earlier. Next in importance comes the beautiful and plaintive air reserved for the solemn evenings of New-Year and Atonement, and introduced, in the spirit of Ps. cxxxvii. 6, into the service of the Rejoicing of the Law. This melody, here transcribed under C, is constructed in the Oriental chromatic scale (EFG ♯ ABCD ♯ E) with its two augmented seconds (see MUSIC, SYNAGOGAL), and is the inspiration of some Polish precentor, dating perhaps from the early seventeenth century, and certainly having spread westward from the Slavonic region. In the German use of Bavaria and the Rhineland the old tradition has preserved a contrasting "Yigdal" for New-Year and Atonement that is of equally antique character, but built on a diatonic scale and reminiscent of the morning service of the day. This interesting melody is here transcribed under D.

For the evenings of the three festivals the old London tradition has preserved, from at least the early eighteenth century, three characteristic melodies, probably brought from north Germany or Bohemia. That for the Passover, here transcribed under E, illustrates the old custom according to which the precentor solemnly dwells on the last creed, that on the resurrection of the dead (in this case to a "representative" theme common to Passover and to Purim), and is answered by the choristers with an expression of confident assurance. The choral response here given received its final shaping from Mombach. The "Yigdal" for Pentecost, transcribed under F, is of a solemn tone, thus strikingly contrasting with those for the other festivals.

The tune for Tabernacles, here transcribed under G, displays a gaiety quite rare in synagogal melody. It was employed by Isaac Nathan, in 1815, as the air for one of Lord Byron's "Hebrew Melodies," being set by him to the verses "The Wild Gazelle" in such a manner as to utilize the contrasting theme then chanted by the hazzan to the last line as in the Passover "Yigdal." Other old tunes for the hymn, such as the melody of Alsatian origin used on the "Great Sabbath" before Passover, are preserved in local or family tradition (comp. ZEMIROT).

BIBLIOGRAPHY: A. Baer, Ba'al Tefillah, Nos. 2, 432–433, 760–762, 774, 988–993, Frankfort-on-the-Main, 1883; Cohen and Davis, Voice of Prayer and Praise, Nos. 28–29, 139–142, 195, London, 1899.

A.   F. L. C.

YIMLOK ADONAI: The tenth and final verse of Ps. cxlvi., which opens the series of Halleluiah

Psalms that conclude the Psalter. The verse is employed as a response at prominent points in the liturgy, and is always the concluding response in the KEDUSHSHAH. In the rite of the Ashkenazim it also introduces (in association with Ps. xxii. 4 [3]) the responsory hymns in the KEROBOT. In the ritual of the Sephardim it is chanted four times, by officiant and congregation alternately, before the scroll is returned to the Ark during the singing of the processional MIZMOR LE-DAWID. The melody to which it is thus chanted is a quaint strain long preserved by tradition and doubtless of Peninsular origin.

also a pupil of Saadia, and was the author of a commentary on Chronicles, some fragments of which were united by a compiler with writings of other commentators, among them Judah ibn Ḳuraish, the whole being edited by Kirchheim under the title "Ein Kommentar zur Chronik aus dem 10. Jahrhundert" (Frankfort-on-the-Main, 1874). There are extant only three fragments of Yir'am's commentary: the first is taken from Saadia's commentary; the second is a haggadic explanation of certain words; and the third is an interpretation of the subject-matter, as to which Yir'am is charged by the compiler

YIMLOK ADONAI

(A)—OF THE SEPHARDIM (Before the Scroll Is Returned to the Ark)

Yim - lok A - do - nai le - 'o - - - - lam, E - lo-
ha - yik Zi - yon le - dor........ wa - dor: Ha - le - lu - yah!

(B)—OF THE ASHKENAZIM (as Closing Response on Festivals)

Yim - lok A - do - nai.... le - 'o - lam, E - lo - ha - yik
Zi - yon le - dor wa - dor: Ha - le - lu - yah!

Among the Ashkenazim the tradition, handed down from the Middle Ages, was to recite "Yimlok" in a monotone, closing with the cadence of the prayer-motive to which the remainder of the benedictions in the Standing Prayer were intoned by the precentor (comp. MUSIC, SYNAGOGAL, Prayer-Motives). But on the festive days on which the HALLEL is chanted this monotone has long since developed into a tuneful phrase shaped on the melody-type of the festival intonation. The two strains alluded to are given herewith.

                                          F. L. C.
A.

YIR'AM OF MAGDIEL: Italian Biblical commentator; lived at Rome in the tenth century. Yir'am was styled "of Magdiel" in conformity with the rabbinical interpretation which refers the name "Magdiel" (Gen. xxxvi. 43) to Rome (comp. Rashi *ad loc.*). He was a junior contemporary and perhaps

with not having thoroughly penetrated into the meaning of the passage.

BIBLIOGRAPHY: Vogelstein and Rieger, *Gesch. der Juden in Rom*, i. 184.
    T.   M. SEL.

YISHAI (JESSE) BEN HEZEKIAH: Exilarch of Damascus toward the end of the thirteenth century. He was a very prominent defender of the writings of Maimonides against the attacks of the anti-Maimonists. Thus, when he was informed of the agitation of the mystic Solomon Petit against the "Moreh," he warned him, under the penalty of the ban, to cease vilifying Maimonides. Solomon Petit paid no heed to the threats of Yishai, and the latter convoked several rabbis, among them those of Safed, and in the month of Tammuz, 1286, wrote a formal excommunication of the agitator of Acre and his followers (see "Kerem Ḥemed," iii. 169 *et* *seq.*, where Yishai's letter is published; Halberstam, in Kobak's "Jeschurun," vi. 66, however, declares that the year was 1291). The letter of excommunication was stamped with the seal of the exilarch, representing a crouching lion with a hand raised over its head, and was signed by Yishai and twelve rabbis. It declared that whoever was in possession of any writing hostile to Maimonides should deliver it immediately to David Maimuni or to his son.

Bibliography: Besides the sources mentioned by F. Lazarus, in Brüll's *Jahrb.* x. 51; Fuenn, *Keneset Yisrael*, p. 681; Grätz, *Gesch.* 3d ed., vii. 158, 166–167, note 8.

J.   M. Sel.

YISHAR KOḤEKA ("May thy strength be firm"): A frequent exclamation and expression of thanks. The first part of the formula is derived by Levy and Kohut from "yashar" = "to be firm or healthy." The phrase occurs in the Talmud in the Hebrew form " yishar koḥeka " (Shab. 87a) and in the Aramaic form " yishar ḥeylak " (Shab. 53a, 62b; Lam. R. 52b; Gen. R. 54), and is now used, for example, as a response to the preacher after the sermon, to the ḥazzan after the prayer, and to the priest after the priestly blessing, while it serves as a formula of thanks also.

A.   S. O.

YISRAEL NOSHA': A hymn composed by an early medieval writer named Shephatiah (Zunz, "Literaturgesch." p. 235), and forming the pizmon, or chief responsory verses, in the seliḥot of one of the mornings in the week preceding the New-Year festival. It is chanted on the Monday in the Polish use and on the Tuesday in the German. The initial verse is employed also in the Ne'ilah service of the former ritual. The melody is of particular interest as one of the few metrical airs of medieval German

YISRAEL NOSHA'

origin which were constructed in scales of an Eastern character. Such were more familiar to those Jews resident in the region of the Greek Church, who came under the influence of the Byzantine rather than of the Roman plain-song. The melody exists in four parallel variants. In the English tradition the singing of the first verse in the closing service of the Day of Atonement has led to the modification of the concluding phrases of the tune by attraction into the melody employed for several other hymns similarly used in that service (comp. Neʿilah [Hymn Tunes] and see "The Voice of Prayer and Praise," No. 286, London, 1899). Of the other traditional forms of the air, that used in northern Germany appears nearest to the original. It falls in the key of the dominant of the minor scale, recalling the fourth Byzantine mode (in the variety entitled λέγετος; comp. Bourgault-Ducoudray, "Etudes sur la Musique Ecclésiastique Grècque"). In the Polish and South-Russian traditions the consistent sharpening of the leading note of the minor, so familiar in Hungarian Gypsy melody, brings the tonality with a form of the Oriental chromatic mode (see Music, Synagogal) and lends the air the wailing plaintiveness favored by the Jews of northeastern Europe.

A.   F. L. C.

*YIẒḤAḲ (ISAAC): Tanna of the early post-Hadrianic period (2d cent. C.E.); a halakic exegete whose Biblical exegesis mostly belongs to the Mekilta and the Sifre. In the Tosefta he transmits sayings in the name of Eliezer ben Hyrcanus (Ter. i. 1, 15; ii. 5). He was a disciple of Ishmael, but associated also with the pupils of Akiba, with one of whom, named Nathan, he originated a halakah (Mek., Ex. xii. 2). He was also intimate with Jonathan and with the proselyte sons of Judah in the yeshibah of Simeon ben Yoḥai (Gen. R. xxxv.; M. Ḳ. 9a; Pesiḳ. 87b). Of his non-halakic exegeses may be mentioned: on Ex. xii. 7: "The blood upon the doors at Passover shall serve the Egyptians as tortures for their souls" (Mek.); on Ex. xx. 9: "Count the days of the week after the Sabbath" (*l.c.*); on Deut. xiv. 11: "Unclean birds are called עוף, while clean are called either עוף or צפור" (Sifre); on Ezek. i.: "The paragraph treating of the chariot of God

extends to the word חשמל only" (Ḥag. 13a). Another of his sayings is: "The prayer in need is adapted to all occasions" (R. H. 18a).

Bibliography: Bacher, *Ag. Tan.* ii. 387–399; Weiss, *Einleitung zur Mekilta*, p. 33, Vienna, 1865; Frankel, *Hodegetica in Mischnam*, p. 203, note 3.
J.   S. O.

YIẒḤAḲ BAR ADDA: Palestinian amora of uncertain period. He interpreted Ps. xcii. 13 as meaning that even as the shade of the palm-tree extends far and wide, so shall the reward of the pious extend to the future world (Shoḥer Ṭob to Ps. xcii.; Gen. R. xl., beginning). With reference to Ps. lvii. 9, he said that David procured an eolian harp in order that its tones might awaken him for midnight prayer (Ber. 4a).

Bibliography: Bacher, *Ag. Pal. Amor.* iii. 767 and note 7.
J.   S. O.

YIẒḤAḲ HA-BABLI: Palestinian amora. His period is unknown. Two haggadot of his are extant. The king Melchizedek, who went to meet Abraham, was called Salem, says Yiẓḥaḳ, because he was perfect; that is, he had early submitted to circumcision (Gen. R. xliii. 7). With reference to Jacob's promise, the amora interprets the words "Which my lips have uttered, and my mouth hath spoken when I was in trouble" (Ps. lxvi. 14) by saying that one makes a vow when in need, in order to keep the commandments of the Torah (Gen. R. lxx. 1; Midrash Shemuel ii.).

Bibliography: Bacher, *Ag. Pal. Amor.* ii. 209, iii. 768.
J.   S. O.

YIẒḤAḲ OF CARTHAGE: In an edition of the Pesiḳta Rabbati by Buber (xiv. 64a) occurs the word קרטיקי, written incorrectly for קטדיקי = καταδίκη ("punishment," "penance"). Buber, however, in his preface (p. 80) attempts to identify this with the name of one Yiẓḥaḳ of Carthage mentioned in Ber. 29a; but according to Bacher such a person never existed. The confusion may have arisen from the fact that Yer. Ber. 8a and Taʿan. 65c mention an Abba of Carthage who transmitted in the name of R. Yiẓḥaḳ.

Bibliography: Bacher, *Ag. Pal. Amor.* ii. 218, 225.
J.   S. O.

YIẒḤAḲ B. ELEAZAR OF CÆSAREA: Palestinian amora of the fourth century. He was a teacher of law in the old synagogue of Cæsarea, where he was so loved by pupils and friends that

Jacob of Kefar Nibburaya placed him as high in this synagogue as is God Himself in the Temple of Zion (Yer. Bik. 65d; Midrash Shemuel vii. 6). The following halakic decisions of his may be mentioned: one concerning sale and purchase, rendered to his pupil Hoshaiah b. Shammai (Yer. M. Ḳ. 81b); another on religious law in a case referred to him by Samuel bar Abdimi (Yer. Shab. 16d); a ruling concerning fraud (Suk. 35b); instruction in regard to the writing of a letter of divorce (B. B. 163a); halakic deduction to the effect that, although a tithe of dates need not be rendered, honey made from them must be tithed (Yer. Bik. 63d); decision concerning marital law (Yer. Ḳid. 63b); regarding signs for detecting murder upon finding a corpse (Yer. Naz. 57d); and a halakah concerning the lifting of the terumah (Yer. Dem. 26b). He appears as a traditionist of Jeremiah (Lev. R. xxxiii. 2) and of Naḥman bar Jacob (Yer. Shab. 9a), and was famed for his gastronomical art (Lam. R. to iii. 17; Yer. Ber. 61c; Yer. Ḥag. 78a). He gives examples of the ban from the Mishnah (Yer. M. Ḳ. 81a), and a prescription in accordance with them (Yer. Ta'an. 69b).

In the vicinity of Cæsarea is a cliff extending into the sea. One day as Yizḥak was walking along this cliff he saw a large bone on the ground, and tried several times to cover it with earth, so that no one should stumble over it; but his efforts were unsuccessful, as the bone became uncovered as fast as he heaped the earth upon it. He accordingly considered the bone to be an instrument of God, and waited patiently to see what would happen. Soon afterward an imperial messenger named Veredarius came that way, stumbled on the bone, and died as a result of his fall; this messenger had been sent to Cæsarea bearing malicious edicts against the Jews (Gen. R. x. 7; Lev. R. xxii. 4; Num. R. xviii.; Eccl. R. to v. 8). In answer to a question as to how it came about that two great prophets like Jeremiah and Daniel should suppress attributes of God which had been given Him by Moses himself, he said that these prophets knew that God was a lover of truth, and that any dissimulation on their part would have been punishable (Yer. Ber. 13c; Meg. 74c). He made a comparison between wisdom and humility (Yer. Shab. 3c); and he explained the expression הלעיטני in Gen. xxv. 30 by a comparison with the insatiability of Rome, saying that Esau sat like a camel with jaws wide open and that Jacob had to fill his mouth with food (Pesiḳ. R. xvi.; Pesiḳ. 59a). Yizḥak, moreover, connected the expression וישטם in Gen. xxvii. 41 with the word "senator," in order more clearly to express Rome's hatred of Judah (Yer. 'Ab. Zarah 39c).

Yizḥak must be distinguished from an amora of the same name who lived half a century earlier, and in whose house Ḥiyya bar Abba, Ammi, and Yizḥak Nappaḥa used to assemble to study (Ḥag. 26a; 'Ab. Zarah 24a; M. Ḳ. 20a). This earlier amora delivered a funeral address at the death of Johanan (M. Ḳ. 25b; but see Bacher ["Ag. Pal. Amor." iii. 718, note 4] for different version).

BIBLIOGRAPHY: Frankel, Mebo, p. 107a; Heilprin, Seder ha-Dorot, ii. 238; Bacher, Ag. Pal. Amor. iii. 717–719.
J. S. O.

YIZḤAḲ BEN ḤAḲOLA: Palestinian amora of the third century. He was a contemporary of Joshua ben Levi and Johanan, and belonged to the school of Eleazar ben Pedat. He transmitted halakot in the names of Abba ben Zabda, Judah II. (Yer. 'Er. 24d), Hezekiah ('Orlah i. 2), and Simeon (Yer. Suk. i., end; Ket. ii. 8). There has been preserved a haggadah by him dealing with the quarrel between the shepherds of Abimelech and those of Abraham, and with the settlement of the dispute (Gen. R. liv., end).

BIBLIOGRAPHY: Bacher, Ag. Pal. Amor. i. 109, ii. 206, iii. 588–589; Frankel, Mebo, 107a; Heilprin, Seder ha-Dorot, ii. 238.
J. S. O.

YIZḤAḲ BEN ḤIYYA THE SCRIBE: Palestinian amora of the fourth century; contemporary of Mani. He was well known as a scribe, and was the author of a halakah in which he asserted that Torah scrolls might be written on various parchments, but that this rule did not apply in the case of tefillin and mezuzot (Yer. Meg. p. 71c). In the name of Johanan he transmitted a halakah relating to the marriage law (Yer. Yeb. 14a). Three other haggadot by him have been preserved: (1) on the future fate of the good and the wicked (Gen. R. lxiv. 4); (2) explaining why Saul did not consult the Urim and Thummim instead of the witch of En-dor (Lev. R. xxvi. 7; Midr. Shemuel xxiv. 6); and (3) setting forth that the Torah is compared to the tree of life (Prov. iii. 18) because it is equal in value to all living men (Midr. Shoḥer Ṭob to Ps. i. 19).

BIBLIOGRAPHY: Bacher, Ag. Pal. Amor. iii. 449 (note 8), 716–717; Heilprin, Seder ha-Dorot, ii. 241.
J. S. O.

YIZḤAḲ BAR JOSEPH: Palestinian amora of the third and fourth centuries. He was a pupil of Abbahu and of Johanan, and transmitted almost entirely in the name of the latter. It is related that he was once about to be killed by a spirit to which he was speaking, when a cedar-tree saved him (Sanh. 101a; Rashi on the passage). It was said to be due to him that the Samaritans were declared to be a heathen people, the following narrative being told in this connection: "Yizḥak was once sent into the Samaritan district to purchase wine, and met there an old man who told him that no one in that region observed the laws. The amora returned with this report to Abbahu, and the latter, together with Ammi and Assi, declared the Samaritans to be heathens" (Ḥul. 6a; comp. also Rashi and the Tosafot on the passage).

In his teacher's company Yizḥak often visited Usha, by whom the taḳḳanot were enacted; he attended lectures in a yeshibah in that city (Ḳid. 50a; Pes. 72a). It was he who brought most of these taḳḳanot to the knowledge of the Babylonians; he was in fact one of the most prominent intermediaries between Palestine and Babylonia in matters pertaining to religious decisions, and was greatly respected in the latter country, being on terms of intimate friendship with Abaye (Ber. 42b).

Thirteen halakic decisions transmitted by Yizḥak in the name of Johanan have been preserved: regarding circumcision on Yom Kippur (Yeb. 64b); on an undecided question (Shab. 45b); on the difference between Palestine and Babylonia with reference to 'erub ('Er. 22a); on the ḥaliẓah (Yeb. 104a); on the testimony of two witnesses before a court of law (Sanh. 4a); five sentences regarding ṭerefah (Ḥul. 43a); on sexual intercourse (Niddah 65b); on sacrifices (Tem. 26a); and on the gall and liver of slaughtered animals (Ḥul. 48a). He transmitted also three halakic maxims in the name of Yannai: two on the custom of washing the hands (Ḥul. 105b) and one on Nazir (Naz. 42b).

In addition to his occasional journeys in Palestine in the company of Abbahu, Yiẓḥaḳ is once mentioned as undertaking a journey to Babylonia, where he associated with Abaye, as well as with Rabin and Pappa, the sons-in-law of Yiẓḥaḳ Nappaḥa (Ḥul. 110a). Yiẓḥaḳ relates that Judah I. had a private entrance to his yeshibah in order to spare his pupils the inconvenience of rising when he entered (Men. 33a).

BIBLIOGRAPHY: Bacher, *Ag. Pal. Amor.* i. 420; ii. 96, 211; iii. 99, 402, 520; Heilprin, *Seder ha-Dorot*, ii. 240.
J.   S. O.

YIẒḤAḲ BAR JUDAH: Babylonian amora of the fourth century; a junior contemporary of Ulla. He was educated at his father's house in Pumbedita; and once when Ulla visited there the latter expressed displeasure at the fact that Yiẓḥaḳ was not yet married (Ḳid. 71b). Yiẓḥaḳ was once told by his father to go to Nehardea in order to see how Ulla pronounced the Habdalah benediction at the close of the Sabbath; but Yiẓḥaḳ sent Abaye in his place, and for so doing was severely reprimanded by his father (Pes. 104b). Yiẓḥaḳ was a pupil of various scholars. First he attended the lectures of Rabbah (Sheb. 36b), and later those of Rami bar Ḥama, whom he soon left in order to study under R. Sheshet, Rami bitterly reproaching him for the slight. Among Yiẓḥaḳ's nearest friends and companions may be mentioned Aḥa bar Ḥana; Samuel, son of Rabbah bar bar Ḥana (Sheb. 36b); and Rami bar Samuel.

BIBLIOGRAPHY: Bacher, *Ag. Pal. Amor.* ii. 299; Heilprin, *Seder ha-Dorot*, ii. 242b.
J.   S. O.

YIẒḤAḲ OF MAGDALA: Palestinian amora of the third century. He engaged in various midrashic controversies. Among them was one with Levi concerning I Kings vii. 50 (Cant. R. on iii. 10), and another with Kahana concerning Joseph's abstention from wine after his imprisonment by his brothers (Shab. 139a; Gen. R. xcii., xcviii.). With reference to the saying that the curse inflicted upon the world consists in the bringing forth of gnats, flies, and other insects, Yiẓḥaḳ states that even these creatures are of use in the world (Gen. R. v. 9).

BIBLIOGRAPHY: Bacher, *Ag. Pal. Amor.* i. 443, ii. 448, iii. 588; A. Perles, in *Bet Talmud*, i. 153; Heilprin, *Seder ha-Dorot*, p. 241a.
J.   S. O.

YIẒḤAḲ BEN MARYON: Palestinian amora of the third century; contemporary of Eleazar ben Pedat (Yer. Suk. 53a). He transmitted some haggadic maxims in the names of Ḥanina (Eccl. R. ix. 12) and Jose ben Ḥanina (Pesiḳ. 99a). With reference to Gen. ii. 4 and 8 he remarked that since

God is proud of His creation, no one may venture to find fault with it (Gen. R. xii. on xv. 5). Commenting on II Sam. xx. 21, he states that he who offends a great man is just as guilty as he who offends the king himself (Eccl. R. on ix. 18). Other haggadic maxims of his have been preserved as follows: on Gen. xxxi. 36 and I Sam. xx. 1 (Gen. R. lxxiv. 10); on Ezek. xxi. 21 (Shoḥer Ṭob to Ps. lxxviii. 19); on Job ii. 4 (Eccl. R. to iii. 9); and on Ruth ii. 14 (Lev. R. xxxiv. 8).

BIBLIOGRAPHY: Bacher, *Ag. Pal. Amor.* i. 10, 286, 327, 427; iii. 589–591; Heilprin, *Seder ha-Dorot*, p. 241a.
J.   S. O.

YIẒḤAḲ BAR NAḤMAN: Palestinian amora of the third century; a friend of Jacob bar Idi, together with whom he officiated as poor-law commissioner (Yer. Sheḳ. 49a). The two friends often engaged in halakic controversies (Yer. Shab. 14d). Yiẓḥaḳ twice transmits sayings by Joshua ben Levi on the conversion of purchased slaves, Ze'era having addressed a question to him on this point (Yer. Yeb. 8d). He had a dispute with Abdima of Ḥaifa concerning some question of religious law (Yer. Niddah 50a), and also engaged in a controversy with Simeon ben Pazzi (Meg. 23a). Jacob bar Aḥa transmits a saying in his name (Yer. Yeb. 12a).

BIBLIOGRAPHY: Bacher, *Ag. Pal. Amor.* i., ii., iii.; Heilprin, *Seder ha-Dorot*, ii. 241a.
J.   S. O.

YIẒḤAḲ NAPPAḤA: Palestinian amora of the third and fourth centuries. He is found under the name "Nappaḥa" only in the Babylonian Talmud, not in the Palestinian. As a haggadist he stands in the foremost rank of his contemporaries. In the Babylonian Talmud he is identified with various other Yiẓḥaḳs (Pes. 113b), and since that was due to the arbitrary action of a later amora, the real name of his father can no longer be determined. As regards the name "Nappaḥa" (the smith), there had been an older Yiẓḥaḳ of the same name, who was rich and who is said to have owned five courts in Usha; it has not yet been possible, however, to ascertain any relationship between the two, and if the elder was an ancestor of this Yiẓḥaḳ, the latter could well have inherited the name without ever having practised the trade. In the later midrashic literature he is called Yiẓḥaḳ Nappaḥa, whereas the older works call him only R. Yiẓḥaḳ.

Although he was a pupil of Johanan, his associations with the latter are indicated in only one passage (B. M. 24b), which tells of his once appearing before Johanan. As a traditionist of the haggadah of Johanan, he appears only in the **Relations** Babylonian Talmud (Ber. 62b). He **with** was in Babylonia only temporarily, **Johanan.** probably soon after the death of Johanan; and while there he visited in the house of the exilarch (M. Ḳ. 24b), together with Sheshet (*ib.* 24b) and Joseph (R. H. 3b; Shab. 52b). Raba quoted in his name (Ber. 32a; Tem. 15a); but sometimes tradition maintains that it is uncertain whether the sayings originated with Yiẓḥaḳ or with Raba (Sanh. 94a; Ned. 39a; Naz. 23b). Rabbin bar Adda also cites in his name (Ber. 6a; Pes. 8b). His

home was originally in Cæsarea, but he afterward
went to Tiberias to live. He associated intimately
with Ammi, with whom he often discussed halakic
questions (Soṭah 34a; Men. 11b; Ḥag. 26a; Ber. 41a;
Yoma 42b); and together they sometimes rendered
decisions in matters pertaining to religious law (Ḥul.
48b; Ned. 57b; Ber. 27a). Yiẓḥaḳ, Abbahu, and
Ḥanina bar Pappai constituted a board of judges
(Ket. 84b; 'Ab. Zarah 39b; Ber. 38a, b; B. Ḳ.
117b; Giṭ. 29b). Ḥelbo referred to Yiẓḥaḳ two
liturgical questions addressed to him from Galilee:
the first question he answered immediately; the second he expounded publicly in the seminary (Giṭ.
60a). A thesis on the creation of light, formulated
anonymously, was made public by R. Yiẓḥaḳ (Gen.
R. iii., beginning). He also engaged in haggadic discussions with the celebrated Levi (Gen. R. xix. 14;
Pesiḳ. R. xxiii., beginning; Ber. 4a; Yer. Ta'an. 65b);
with Abba b. Kahana (Gen. R. xliii. 7; Lev. R. ii.
1; Midr. Teh. to Ps. xlix. 1); with Aḥa (Pesiḳ. R.
xv.; Gen. R. v. 7; Yer. Pe'ah 15d); and with Ḥiyya
bar Abba (Lev. R. xx. 7; Pesiḳ. R. xxii.). Among
those who transmitted in the name of Yiẓḥaḳ were
the famous halakist Haggai, the latter's sons Jonathan and Azariah (Gen. R. xxii. 18, xl. 6; Midr.
Shemuel xxii., end), and Luliani ben Ṭabrin (Gen.
R. passim; Midr. Teh. to Ps. xxiv. 4; Yer. Meg.
75c).

That Yiẓḥaḳ was a great authority on the Halakah, as well as on the Haggadah, is shown by an
anecdote which is told and according to which Ammi
and Assi would not let him speak, because the one
wished to hear Halakah and the other Haggadah
(B. Ḳ. 60b). So after telling them the celebrated story
of the man who had two wives, one of whom pulled
out all his white hairs because she was young,
whereas the other extracted his black hairs because
she was old, R. Yiẓḥaḳ presented to them a haggadah with a halakic background, in order to satisfy
both at the same time. Yiẓḥaḳ, however, devoted
himself to the Haggadah with more zeal, because
he regarded it as a necessity in the adverse circumstances of the Jews. The poverty of the Palestinians had increased to such an extent that people no
longer waited for the harvest, but ate the green ears
of wheat (Gen. R. xx. 24); consequently they were
in need of comfort and refreshment of soul (Pes.
101b). Yiẓḥaḳ tried to make his lectures as effective as possible, and they show him to have been an
unusually forceful rhetorician and a skilful exegete.

Yiẓḥaḳ's haggadic material may be divided according to contents into the following four groups:
I. Proverbs and dicta: concerning sins (Suk. 52a,
b; Ḥag. 16a; Ḳid. 31a; Ber. 25a; R. H. 16b; Yoma
87a; B. B. 9b; Pes. 190b); concerning the relation
of man to God (Ned. 32a; Soṭah 48b);
His on the relation of man to
Sayings. his fellow beings (B. M. 42a; Meg.
28a; B. Ḳ. 93a); concerning prayer
(Pes. 181a; Lev. R. xxx. 3; Midr. Shemuel i. 7; R.
H. 16b; Yer. Ḳid. 61b; Yer. Ned. 41b); concerning
study and the Law (Pes. 193a, b; Meg. 6b; Lev. R.
ii. 1; Sanh. 21b, 24a; Ḥul. 91a; Yoma 77a); concerning Israel (Pes. 165a; Gen. R. lxiii. 8); concerning the nations (Esther R. i. 10; Lev. R. i. 14; Ex.
R. xxxviii. 3); concerning Jerusalem (Pesiḳ. R. xli.

1; Pes. 6a). II. Exegesis: general (Sanh. 82a, 89a,
95b; Tem. 16a; Yer. R. H. 57c; Gen. R. liii. 20;
Ḥul. 91b; Soṭah 48b; B. B. 16a); halakic (Ber. 13b;
Giṭ. 59b; Pes. 31b; Yoma 77a; Yer. Soṭah 17a); Biblical personages (Gen. R. xxxiv. 11, xxxix. 7, lviii.
7; Yeb. 64a); Biblical narratives (Soṭah 34a; Deut.
R. xi. 2; B. B. 91a; Midr. Teh. to Ps. vii. 13; Sanh.
106b; Men. 53b; Esther R. iii. 9; Pesiḳ. R. xxxv. 1).
III. Homiletics (Gen. R. xix. 6, xxxviii. 7; Sanh.
96a; B. M. 87a; Yer. Soṭah 17b; Ex. R. xliii. 4; Sanh.
102a; Ber. 63b; Eccl. R. iii. 19; Tem. 16a; Yer.
Ta'an. 65b; Hor. 10b). IV. Proems (Gen. R. iii. 1,
lix. 2, lxv. 7; Pes. 101b; Ex. R. xxxii. 5; Lev. R.
xii. 2); maxims (Gen. R. lvi. 1; Deut. R. ii. 27;
Lev. R. xxxiv. 8); similes (Yer. R. H. 57b; Lev.
R. v. 6; Ex. R. xv. 16; Yer. Ber. 13a; B. B. 74b);
Messianic subjects (Eccl. R. i. 11; Deut. R. i. 19;
'Ab. Zarah 3b); eschatology (Lev. R. xiii. 3; Midr.
Teh. to Ps. xlix. 1; Shab. 152a; B. M. 83b).

According to the unanimous testimony of several
writers of the tenth century, the gaon Hai b. David
ascribed to Yiẓḥaḳ Nappaḥa the calculation of the
Rabbinite calendar. The only fact known concerning Yiẓḥaḳ's family is that his daughter married the
Babylonian amora Pappa (Ḥul. 110a).

BIBLIOGRAPHY: Bacher, Ag. Pal. Amor. ii. 205–295; Frankel,
  Mebo, pp. 106b–107a; Heilprin, Seder ha-Dorot, ii., s.v.; S.
  Pinsker, Liḳḳuṭe Ḳadmoniyyot, ii. 148–151; Al-Ḳirḳisani,
  ed. Harkavy, in Publ. Kaiserliche Russische Archæolo-
  gische Gesellschaft, 1894, vii. 293; Weiss, Dor, iii. 98 et seq.
J.   S. O.

YIẒḤAḲ BEN PARNAK: Palestinian amora
of uncertain period. He is named as the author of an
apocryphal work entitled פרק ר' יצחק בן פרנך מניהנם,
which describes the events that take place at the
death of a human being. When a man is dying
three angels come to his bedside—the angel of death,
the recording angel, and the guardian angel; and
these three review his entire life. If he has been a
pious man, three more angels appear; and while the
struggle with death is going on one of these angels
recites Isa. lvii. 1, the second ib. lvii. 2, and the
third ib. lviii. 8. At last four more angels descend
to the bedside; and when the dying man cries out
to the earth to help him, the first angel answers him
with the words of Ps. xxiv. 1; when he implores
the aid of his relatives, the second angel recites Ps.
xlix. 8 (A. V. 7); when he turns to his money for
solace, the third angel answers him with Ps. xlix. 9
(A. V. 8); and when he appeals to his good deeds, the
fourth angel recites Isa. lviii. 8. There is clearly
some influence here of the Buddhist legend of "The
Three Friends" (comp. "Barlaam and Josaphat," ed.
Jacobs, Appendix). Yiẓḥaḳ's father, Parnak, transmitted in the name of Johanan (Gen. R. liii., end;
M. Ḳ. 9a; Shab. 14a; B. M. 85a).

BIBLIOGRAPHY: Bacher, Ag. Pal. Amor. i. 219, note 3; iii.
  767–768; Jellinek, Bet ha-Midrash, v. 48–49, Vienna, 1873.
J.   S. O.

YIẒḤAḲ BAR REDIFA: Palestinian amora
of the fourth century; the transmitter of the haggadah of R. Ammi (Lev. R. xii., beginning; Ex. R.
xlii., end; Yer. Sheḳ. 48a; Ex. R. iii. to Ex. iii. 14).
He once requested the amora Jeremiah to decide a
question, but received only an evasive reply (Yer.
Sheb. 39a). He was the author of several explanations of the stories concerning Samson (Soṭah 9b).

Especial mention should be made of his interpretation of the word תעכסנה in Isa. iii. 16, which he derives from the Greek ἔχις ("serpent"), saying: "The women used to place myrrh and balsam in their shoes, and when meeting young men in the streets they stamped their feet so that a strong odor arose which awakened evil impulses in the youths, as though they were under the influence of a serpent's poison" (Shab. 62b).

Yiẓḥaḳ transmitted dissertations on the salvation of the tribe of Benjamin, with reference to Judges xxi. 7 (B. B. 116a); on the list of idolatrous priests referred to in Hosea xiii. 2 (Sanh. 62a); on the pronunciation of the words "Praised be the name of His glorious kingdom" (ב"ש"כ מל"ו) after the "Shema'" (Pes. 56a); on the act of rising when the name of God is uttered, as deduced from Judges iii. 20 (Sanh. 60a); and on the assumption of the sex of an expected child, with reference to Lev. xii. 2 (Ber. 60a; Niddah 25b, 31a).

BIBLIOGRAPHY: Bacher, *Ag. Pal. Amor.* i. 518, note 1; ii. 151, note 6; iii. 719–720; Rabbinovicz, *Diḳduḳe Soferim*, ix. 169; Heilprin, *Seder ha-Dorot*, ii. 241; Frankel, *Mebo*, pp. 90a, 107b.

J.   S. O.

YIẒḤAḲ BEN SAMUEL BEN MARTA: Babylonian amora of the third and fourth centuries. He was a pupil of R. Naḥman, to whom he directed questions relating to sacrifice (Men. 81a) and to differentiation between sanctified and unsanctified things (Ḥul. 35a). In the name of Rab he transmitted sayings relating to the presentation of letters of divorce (Giṭ. 13a, 63b), and to Rab's method of pronouncing the Sabbatical benediction (Pes. 166a). Rabbah transmitted sayings of Yiẓḥaḳ's (Meg. 16b); Ze'era addressed him as "Rabbenu" (Ḥul. 30b); and Rami bar Ḥama directed a question to him (*ib.* 35a). Yiẓḥaḳ once met Simlai in Nisibis, where he heard the latter denounce the free use of oil among the Jews; and he later furnished a report of this denunciation ('Ab. Zarah 36a; comp. Yer. 'Ab. Zarah 41d).

BIBLIOGRAPHY: Bacher, *Ag. Pal. Amor.* i. 569; Heilprin, *Seder ha-Dorot*, ii. 239–240.

J.   S. O.

YIẒḤAḲ BEN ṬABLAI: Palestinian amora of the fourth century; a contemporary of Jacob ben Zabdai and Ḥelbo, together with both of whom he was called upon to decide a question of religious law (Yer. Niddah 50a). When asked whether the law of Demai applied to the Syrian leek, he was unable to decide the question by himself, and had to seek the advice of R. Jose (Yer. Dem. 22d); and on another occasion, when a question relating to the divorce law was addressed to him, he had to refer it to Eleazar (Yer. Ḳid. 63c). A tradition handed down from the above-mentioned Eleazar was differently transmitted by the amoraim Jonah and Jose (Yer. Sheb. 33d).

In the Babylonian Talmud (Pes. 113b) Yiẓḥaḳ has been identified with five other amoraim of similar name, but this has been refuted by Bacher, who disproved also the allegation of S. Krauss that the names חקלא and טבלא are identical. The Babylonian Talmud (Ned. 81b) mentions Yiẓḥaḳ as the transmitter of an interpretation of Mal. iii. 20. To him is ascribed also the haggadic explanation identifying the name לבנן with the Temple, with reference to the paro-

nomasia on לבנן and מלבין, which latter word, meaning "to make white," has been used with regard to the Temple in the sense of "atone." Yiẓḥaḳ was the author, moreover, of haggadot on Deut. xxix. 10 and Josh. x. 4 (Midr. Tan. to Deut. xxix.) and of a haggadah comparing Israel to the stubborn princess (Pesiḳ. R. xxviii.; Midr. Teh. to Ps. cxxxviii. 5).

BIBLIOGRAPHY: Bacher, *Ag. Pal. Amor.* iii. 720–722; idem, *Ag. Tan.* i. 26, note 2; S. Krauss, *Lehnwörter*, i. 77, 246; Frankel, *Mebo*, p. 107; Heilprin, *Seder ha-Dorot*, pp. 237–238.

J.   S. O.

YIẒḤAḲ BEN ZE'ERA: Palestinian amora of the fourth century. He interpreted the word ארה in Ps. xix. 6, in connection with Gen. xviii. 11, as signifying that the descending sun resembles a drop of blood not larger than a mustard-seed (Lev. R. xxxi. 9). He is credited also with an interpretation of a verse of the Song of Solomon (vii. 10); but some confusion exists with regard to the name, that of Bar Nazira occurring instead of his in some passages (Yeb. 97a; Bek. 31b).

BIBLIOGRAPHY: Bacher, *Ag. Pal. Amor.* i. 121, note 1; iii. 722; Heilprin, *Seder ha-Dorot*, p. 242.

J.   S. O.

YIẒḤAḲI. See Rashi.

YIẒḤAḲI, ABRAHAM: Turkish Talmudist; lived at Salonica toward the end of the sixteenth century. He was dayyan under Rabbi Solomon ha-Levi, after whom Yiẓḥaḳi signed third under a decision issued in 1597, and second under a decision of 1598. Yiẓḥaḳi was the author of the work "Aḥot Ḳeṭannah," which is quoted in Joseph Almosnino's "'Edut bi-Yehosef" (i., No. 54) and in Ḥasdai Peraḥya's "Torat Ḥesed" (No. 65), and printed at the end of Jacob Ḥagiz's "Halakot Ḳeṭannot," and which is erroneously ascribed by Heilprin ("Seder ha-Dorot," iii., *s.v.*) to Michael b. Moses ha-Kohen. It is a work in four parts on the laws relative to the "geṭ" of a minor.

BIBLIOGRAPHY: Benjacob, *Oẓar ha-Sefarim*, p. 34, No. 646; Fuenn, *Keneset Yisrael*, p. 30; Michael, *Or ha-Ḥayyim*, No. 141.

J.   M. Sel.

YIẒḤAḲI, ABRAHAM BEN DAVID: Palestinian rabbi and anti-Shabbethaian; born in 1661; died at Jerusalem June 10, 1729; on his mother's side a grandson of Abraham Azulai. He was a pupil of Moses Galante, and was in his turn the teacher of Moses Ḥagiz. Yiẓḥaḳi was prominent in opposition to the followers of Shabbethai Ẓebi, and exhorted the rabbis of Smyrna to investigate the writings of Miguel Cardoso. He signed the letter of excommunication launched against Nehemiah Ḥayyun by the rabbinate of Jerusalem in 1708. Later, Yiẓḥaḳi was sent to Europe to collect contributions, and when at Constantinople he wrote a preface to Jacob Sason's "Bene Ya'aḳob." In 1711 he arrived at Leghorn, where he agitated strongly against Ḥayyun; and he did the same at Amsterdam in the following year, together with Ẓebi Ashkenazi. On his way back to Jerusalem in 1714 Yiẓḥaḳi passed through Constantinople, where he joined the other rabbis in the excommunication of Ḥayyun.

Of Yiẓḥaḳi's works, only the "Zera' Abraham," responsa on the four Ṭurim, was published (vol. i., on Oraḥ Ḥayyim and Yoreh De'ah, Smyrna, 1733; vol. ii., on Eben ha 'Ezer and Ḥoshen Mishpaṭ, Constantinople, 1732). His other works are: "Iggeret Shib-buḳin" and "Ketobet Ḳa'aḳea'," both on Ḥayyun's heresies; a work on Maimonides' "Yad"; and no-vellæ on the Shulḥan 'Aruk.

BIBLIOGRAPHY: Fuenn, Keneset Yisrael, p. 30; Grätz, Gesch. 3d ed., x. 311, 317, 320; Fürst, Bibl. Jud. ii. 78; Michael, Or ha-Ḥayyim, No. 81.
J.
M. SEL.

YIZIDRO (YSIDRO), ABRAHAM GAB-BAI. See GABBAI.

YOD (י): Tenth letter of the Hebrew alphabet. The name seems to be connected with "yad," mean-ing "hand"; the Phenician "yod" remotely resembles a hand in form. The letter is a palatal semivowel, identical in sound with the English "y." Preceded by the cognate vowel "i" (= Eng. "ee"), it blends with it, the resulting combination being long "i." With a preceding a-vowel it forms the diphthong "ai," which in Hebrew (that language having pre-served no diphthongal sounds) has become "ē" (= Eng. "ay"). As a radical, "yod" sometimes inter-changes with "waw." As a numeral, it has in the later usage the value 10. The Tetragrammaton is some-times represented by "yod," its first letter.

T.
I. BR.

YOKE. See AGRICULTURE.

YOM, HA-. See PERIODICALS.

YOM KIPPUR. See ATONEMENT, DAY OF.

YOM KIPPUR ḲAṬAN: The "Minor Day of Atonement"; observed on the day preceding each Rosh Ḥodesh or New-Moon Day, the observance con-sisting of fasting and supplication, but being much less rigorous than that of Yom Kippur proper. The custom is of comparatively recent origin and is not mentioned in the Shulḥan 'Aruk. It appears to have been inaugurated in the sixteenth century at Safed by the cabalist Moses Cordovero (Da Silva, "Peri Ḥadash," Rosh Ḥodesh, § 417), who called the fast "Yom Kippur Ḳaṭan"; and it was in-cluded by Isaac Luria in his "Seder ha-Tefillah." R. Isaiah Horowitz refers to it by that name, and says it should be observed by fasting and repentance: "Following the custom of the very pious, one must repent of his ways and make restitutions both in money and in personal acts, in order that he may enter the new month as pure as a new-born infant" ("Shelah," ed. Amsterdam, 1698, pp. 120b, 140a, 179a). When Rosh Ḥodesh occurs on a Sabbath or Sunday, Yom Kippur Ḳaṭan is observed on the pre-ceding Thursday. The fasting is not obligatory, and only the very pious observe that act of self-denial.

The liturgy of the day, which consists of seliḥot, is recited at the Minḥah prayer in the afternoon. Ṭallit and tefillin are adjusted, and if there are among the congregation ten persons who have fasted, they read from the scroll "Wa-Yeḥal" (Ex. xxxii. 11 et seq.). The seliḥot are taken partly from the collection used on the general fast-days and Yom Kippur, with the "Widdui ha-Gadol" (the great confession of sin by Rabbenu Nissim) and "Ashamnu," and also a beau-tiful poem written for the occasion by Leon of Mo-dena and beginning with "Yom zeh." Some congre-gations add "Abinu Malkenu." The fast ends with the Minḥah prayer. For the text see Baer, "'Abo-dat Yisrael," pp. 317–319; Emden's Siddur "Bet Ya'aḳob," ed. Warsaw, pp. 212a–216b.

BIBLIOGRAPHY: Moses Bruck, Pharisäische Volkssitten und Ritualien, pp. 42–44, Frankfort-on-the-Main, 1840.
J.
J. D. E.

YOM-ṬOB BEN ABRAHAM ISHBILI (called also **RITBA**, from the initials of his name, ריטבא): Famous Talmudic commentator of the first half of the fourteenth century. He received his name from the city of Seville; but was living at Alcolea de Cinca in 1342. He was gifted with a clear, acute mind, and was a pupil of Aaron ha-Levi and Solo-mon Adret at Barcelona, although it is doubtful whether he studied under Meïr ha-Levi Abulafia also, as some scholars think (Perles, "R. Salomo b. Abraham b. Adret," p. 59, Breslau, 1863). He was engaged in a controversy with Rabbi Dan Ashke-nazi, who had emigrated to Spain. Yom-Ṭob's vo-luminous works include valuable novellæ on many of the Talmudic treatises, and commentaries on the writings of Alfasi and certain works of Naḥmani-des. His published novellæ include those on 'Eru-bin, Ta'anit, Mo'ed Ḳaṭan, Ketubot, and Baba Meẓi'a (Amsterdam, 1729; Prague, 1810), Ta'anit and Mo'ed Ḳaṭan (Prague, 1811), Ḥullin (ib. 1734), Giṭṭin (Salonica, 1758), Yebamot (Leghorn, 1787), Shabbat (Salonica, 1806), Yoma (Constantinople, 1754; Berlin, 1860), 'Abodah Zarah (Ofen, 1824), and Rosh ha-Shanah (Königsberg, 1858). Most of the novellæ have been collected under the title "Ḥiddushe ha-Riṭba" (Lemberg, 1860–61), while extracts from his commentaries on haggadic pas-sages are quoted by the author of the "'En Ya'aḳob" (Berlin, 1709; Fürth, 1766; etc.). The "Migdal 'Oz" of Shem-Ṭob ibn Gaon and the "Maggid Mishneh" of Vidal of Tolosa have been erroneously ascribed to him.

BIBLIOGRAPHY: Malachi b. Jacob ha-Kohen, Yad Mal'aki, ed. Berlin, p. 131; Azulai, Shem ha-Gedolim, i. 72 et seq.; Steinschneider, Cat. Bodl. col. 1406; Cassel, Lehrbuch der Jüdischen Gesch. und Literatur, p. 302; Fürst, Bibl. Jud. i. 248; Zedner, Cat. Hebr. Books Brit. Mus. pp. 784 et seq.
E. C.
M. K.

YOM-ṬOB BEN ISAAC OF JOIGNY (called also **ha-Ḳodesh**): Tosafist and liturgical poet who suffered martyrdom at York, England, in March, 1190, as has been proved by Grätz ("Gesch." vi. 455). The Jews of York sought refuge in the for-tress from the fury of the populace; and after offer-ing a vain resistance for several days the most of them, on the advice of Yom-Ṭob ben Isaac, joined him in voluntary death.

Yom-Ṭob was a pupil of R. Tam, and was promi-nent as a tosafist, being frequently mentioned with the epithet "ha-Ḳodesh" (= "the Holy" or "the Martyr"). He also was a Biblical exegete and a liturgical poet. His best-known productions are OMNAM ḲEN, a hymn sung on the eve of the Day of Atonement, and a penitential prayer in fourteen stanzas. He wrote also an elegy beginning with the words "Yah tishpok" and lamenting the death of the Jews of Blois who perished in 1071.

BIBLIOGRAPHY: Zunz, Z. G. pp. 52, 100; idem, Literatur-gesch. pp. 286 et seq.; Grätz, Gesch. vi. 265; Gross, Gallia Judaica, p. 252; R. E. J. iii. 5; Tr. Jew. Hist. Soc. Eng. iii. 9 et seq.; Jacobs, Jews of Angevin England, pp. 109–112, 125, 421 (bibliography).
J.
M. K.

YOMA: A treatise in the Mishnah, in the To-sefta, and in both Talmudim, treating of the divine service on the Day of Atonement, of the fasting ceremony on that day, and of other regulations pertaining to the occasion. In the Tosefta this treatise is entitled "Yom ha-Kippurim" (Day of Atonement), while in the Mishnah (ed. Lowe), as well as by Sherira Gaon, it is called simply "Kippurim" (Atonement). The Day of Atonement was known also as "Yoma Rabba" (The Great Day), often shortened to "Yoma" (The Day); hence this treatise was given the name of "Yoma" in the Mishnah as well as in the Talmudim. In most Mishnah editions the treatise is the fifth in the order of Mo'ed. It is divided into eight chapters, containing a total of sixty-one paragraphs.

Ch. i.: On the high priest's seven days of preparation for his service on the Day of Atonement; how the stipulated order of the sacrificial ceremony was read to him, and how the elders impressed upon him that he should proceed only according to the prescribed order, and not in harmony

Contents:
Ch. i.-viii. with Sadducean customs (§§ 1–5); regarding the night of the Day of Atonement; if the high priest was a wise man and a scholar, he preached a sermon; if not, the sages present delivered a lecture or read from Holy Script, choosing only passages from the Hagiographa; how the young priests watched to see that the high priest did not fall asleep (§§ 6–7); on the removal of the ashes from the altar upon the Day of Atonement and upon other days (§ 8).

Ch. ii.: In connection with the rules regarding the removal of the ashes (i. 8), it is said that this duty originally devolved on all priests without any specific allotment, such distinction being introduced only in the course of time (§§ 1–2); other allotments made in order to distribute the Temple duties among the priests (§§ 3–4); when the daily sacrifice ("tamid") was offered, and regulations concerning other sacrifices (§§ 5–7).

Ch. iii.: Further regulations regarding the divine service in the Temple on the Day of Atonement; how the high priest was to bathe five times and wash himself ten times on that day; regarding the various dresses he should wear for the different services (§§ 1–7); the presentation to the high priest of a bullock, and the confession of sin he was to speak while holding his hands on the bullock's head (§ 8); the casting of lots for the two he-goats; Ben Gamla had made two golden dice for this purpose, and was therefore mentioned with words of praise (§ 9), as were also Ben Ḳaṭṭina, King Monobaz, Queen Helene, and Nicanor, who had all introduced improvements or embellishments in the sanctuary (§ 10); words of blame directed against the family of Garmu for being unwilling to teach others how to prepare the showbread; similar comment on the family of Abtinas for refusing to teach the method of compounding the incense ("ḳeṭoret"), and on Hugros (or Hugdos) ben Levi and Ben Ḳamẓar, who refused to give instruction in singing and writing respectively (§ 11).

Ch. iv.: How lots were cast by the high priest over the two he-goats, one of which was slaughtered, while the other was sent to Azazel; how the high priest marked the he-goats by placing a red ribbon upon the head of one and around the neck of

the other; the confession of sin pronounced by the high priest for the priestly caste (§§ 1–2); particulars of the incense-offering on the Day of Atonement; the ascension of the high priest to the altar, and his washing of hands and feet (§§ 3–6).

Ch. v.: What was done in the sanctuary; the incense-offering; the sprinkling of the blood, first of the bullock, and later of the he-goat; the short prayer spoken by the high priest; the foundation-stone ("eben shetiyah") in the most holy part of the Temple, upon which the high priest, in the absence of the Ark of the Covenant from the Second Temple, placed the incense; the purification of the golden altar; and other regulations regarding the order of service on the Day of Atonement.

Ch. vi.: What was done with the he-goat sent to Azazel; the confession of sin pronounced by the high priest for all Israel while he held his hands upon the head of the Azazel goat; who might lead the animal to Azazel (§§ 1–3); how the Babylonians present in Jerusalem used to pluck hair from Azazel's goat; how the aristocratic Jerusalemites accompanied the goat to the first halting-place; regarding the ten stations in the journey from Jerusalem to the mountain-top from which the animal was thrown down; how it was thrown; how color-signals were used to make it known in Jerusalem and in the Temple that Azazel's goat had reached the wilderness; how to the door of the Hekal was tied a red ribbon, which turned white when the goat had arrived in the wilderness (§§ 4–8).

Ch. vii.: The ceremony attending the high priest's reading from the Law; the paragraphs read by him, and what he repeated; the benediction pronounced by him; the remainder of his duties; the eight articles of dress which he had to wear when conducting the service and when questioning the Urim and Thummim; on what occasions the Urim and Thummim were consulted.

Ch. viii.: Regulations concerning fasting on the Day of Atonement; from what enjoyments one must abstain; the means by which atonement is made—through sin-offering, guilt-offering, death, Day of Atonement, and penance; cases in which no atonement takes place; sins against God are expiated through the Day of Atonement, while sins against one's fellow men can be blotted out only when pardoned by those trespassed against. On the original form of this mishnaic treatise see Joseph Derenbourg, in "R. E. J." vi. 41 et seq.

The Tosefta to this treatise is divided into five chapters, and contains additions to and amplifications of the Mishnah, and also several haggadic and ethical maxims, among which the following may be mentioned: "Ben 'Azzai used to say, ' What belongs to you [i.e., "What you have deserved"] is given to you; by your name [i.e., "the name

Tosefta and Gemara. you have made for yourself"] you are called; and on the place to which you are entitled you are stationed. God forgets no one; and no man can take to himself that which is intended for another'" (ii. 8). "He who induces others to lead good and pious lives will be prevented from committing any sin, in order that he may not be excluded from the future world while those taught by him partake therein.

On the other hand, he who leads others to sin is prevented from doing penance, that he may not partake of the eternal life from which those seduced by him are excluded" (v. 10–11). The Tosefta defends those who in the Mishnah are blamed for refusing to give instruction, saying they did so because they feared that, if they imparted their knowledge, those whom they taught might use their attainments in the service of a temple of idolatry (ii. 5–8). Other items of interest in the Tosefta are an account of the miraculous saving of the Gate of Nicanor (ii. 4), and R. Jose's assertion that he had seen in Rome the curtain from the sanctuary of the Temple in Jerusalem, and that it still had upon it stains caused by the sprinkling of blood by the high priests on the Day of Atonement (iii. 8).

Both the Babylonian and the Palestinian Gemara discuss and explain the various mishnaic maxims, and contain in addition a wealth of haggadic explanations and proverbs, as well as many interesting parables and narratives. The following passages from the Babylonian Gemara may be quoted here: "If one is told anything by another, he must keep it secret even though not explicitly requested to do so; only when he has received express permission may he relate it further" (4b). "The First Temple stood for 410 years, during which time 18 high priests officiated successively; the Second Temple stood 420 years, and during that time more than 300 high priests officiated" (9a). "During the time of the Second Temple the people studied the Law, observed the commandments, and did deeds of charity; only the causeless hatred between the factions brought about the destruction of the Temple and the fall of the state" (9b). It is told how Hillel endeavored to study the Law in spite of his poverty, and how he, with danger to his life, attempted to attend the lectures of Shemaiah and Abṭalion. It is likewise related of Eleazar ben Ḥarsum that, in spite of his wealth, he led a life of self-denial in order that he might study the Law (35b). Another interesting passage narrates how the Jews, on their return from Babylonia, succeeded in rooting out from among themselves the existing tendency to idolatry (69b). A description is given (73b) of the mode of questioning the Urim and Thummim, and of the manner in which their replies became visible upon the stones; the passage §§ 75a–76b tells how the manna fell, how thick it lay upon the ground, and how it tasted. It is related in § 83b that once when R. Meïr, R. Judah, and R. Jose visited an inn the first-named formed a correct estimate of the innkeeper's character.

J.   J. Z. L.

YORK: Capital town of Yorkshire, England, and seat of a metropolitan see. In the Angevin period it was the second city in the kingdom, and Jews flocked thither in considerable numbers. It is recorded that at the coronation of Richard I. two "noble" Jews of York, Joce and Benedict, went up to London, probably as a deputation from the York community. During a riot which followed the festivities Benedict was forced to submit to baptism, but was permitted by Richard to revert on the following day (Howden, "Chronica," ed. Stubbs, iii. 14); he died shortly afterward at Northampton. Joce es-

caped and returned to his home in York, which was looked upon as a royal residence on account of its strength and magnificence. He had been one of the agents of Aaron of Lincoln, among whose debtors was one Richard de Malbis, who in 1182 had paid £4 out of the great debt which he owed to Aaron.

De Malbis and others of the York nobles who were contemplating joining Richard in the Third Crusade took advantage of a fire that broke out in the city to raise a tumult against the Jews. The houses of Benedict and Joce were attacked, and the latter obtained the permission of the warden of York Castle to remove his wife and children and the rest of the Jews into the castle, where they were probably placed in Clifford's Tower. This was surrounded by the mob, and when the warden left the castle the Jews in fear would not readmit him. He appealed to the sheriff, who called out the county militia; and Clifford's Tower was surrounded for several days. A certain Premonstratensian monk paced the walls each morning and took the sacrament, as if the work of hounding on the mob was a holy office. He was crushed by a stone thrown by the besieged Jews; this changed the wrath of the mob to a frenzied madness. When the Jews in Clifford's Tower found that they had no alternative but to submit to baptism or perish at the hands of the mob, YOM-ṬOB OF JOIGNY, who had become their chief rabbi some time before, recalled the practise of their ancestors, and urged that they should kill themselves rather than surrender to the cruelty of their enemies. Those who disagreed were permitted to withdraw; and the remainder, having set fire to their garments and goods that these might not fall into the hands of the mob, found refuge in death. Joce with his own hand cut the throat of

<table>
<tr><td rowspan="2">The Massacre.</td><td>his wife, Hannah, with the knife used in sheḥiṭah; and finally Joce was killed by Yom-Ṭob, who then stabbed him-</td></tr>
</table>

self, being the only person of the number to take upon himself the crime of suicide. In the morning the few who had withdrawn summoned the besiegers, who killed most of them, sending the remainder to London in the hands of the sheriff. The mob searched the castle for the Jews' deeds of indebtedness, and, not finding them, hastened to the minster and took the deeds from the cathedral treasury, thus showing the real motive of their acts.

William de Longchamp, the ruler of the kingdom in Richard's absence, was much incensed at this insult to the royal dignity, the Jews being under the king's protection. He accordingly marched to York, imposed heavy fines on fifty-two of the chief citizens, and banished Richard de Malbis and various members of the Percy, Faulconbridge, and Darrel families, who had clearly been the leaders of the riot, and each of whom, according to unimpeachable evidence, was indebted to the Jews. Richard de Malbis returned from Scotland ten years later, when he "obtained warren" for his land at Acaster Malbis, five miles south of York, the name of which still recalls the arch villain of the York tragedy.

For some time after this there is no record of Jews at York. Among the contributions to the Northampton donum of 1194 none are mentioned as coming from York, although it was the second city in the kingdom; but in the early part of the thirteenth century Jews began again to settle there. In 1208 a Jewess of York was murdered, three Christians being suspected of the crime; a charge of murder was brought against them by Milo, her husband, while her brother Benedict brought a similar charge against Milo himself ("Select Pleas of the Crown," Selden Society, i., Nos. 59, 103). Joce's son, AARON OF YORK, became the chief Jew of the kingdom in the reign of Henry III., being presbyter, or chief rabbi, of England for a short time in 1237. The widow of Aaron of York claimed dower from Thomas Kyme of Northampton, and in 1270 attempted to recover a considerable number of debts due to her deceased husband (Rigg, "Select Pleas of the Jewish Exchequer," pp. 52-53, London, 1902). When the regulation was issued permitting Jews to reside only in certain towns where archæ were kept for the preservation of Jewish deeds, York was included in the list, showing that it was still an important center of Jewish commerce in 1272. Among the eminent Jews of London mentioned at the time of the expulsion was Bonamy of York. On the expulsion of the Jews from England the lands and chattels of those living in York fell into the king's hands. The Jewish burial-ground at York was between St. Morris and the River Fosse, and the synagogue was on the north side of the Jubbergate, in close proximity to the castle, under the warden of which the Jews of the city were placed by the king's authority.

Since the return of the Jews to England there has been no congregation at York, but a. few Jewish tailors have settled there in recent years (E. S. Rowntree, "Poverty, a Study of Town Life," p. 11, London, 1903), and for their benefit a synagogue was erected in the Aldwark in 1892.

BIBLIOGRAPHY: Drake, *Eboracum*, pp. 57, 94-96, 228, 253-254, 265, 277, 322; Raines, *York*, London, 1892, Index; Hargrave, *York*, ii. 386-388, 558; Twyford and Griffiths, *Records of York Castle*, pp. 25-35; R. Davies, *The Medieval Jews of York*, in *Yorkshire Archæological and Topographical Journal*, iii. 147-197; J. T. Fowler, *Certain Starrs*, ib. pp. 53-63; Jacobs, *Jews of Angevin England*, pp. 101, 112, 116-130, 238, 392.

J.

YOSIPPON. See JOSEPHUS.

YOUNG MEN'S HEBREW ASSOCIATION : Communal institution organized in various cities of the United States for the mental, moral, social, and physical improvement of Jewish young men. The first established was that in New York, which was organized on March 22, 1874, at the house of Dr. Simeon N. Leo. The board of directors was elected on May 3, 1874, and included Isaac S. Isaacs, Adolph L. Sanger, Oscar S. Straus, Lewis May, and others. The first president was Lewis May (1874-76). On March 27, 1876, the association removed from its temporary quarters to the Harvard Rooms, Forty-second street and Sixth avenue.

The functions of the New York branch are philanthropic and benevolent. The social work includes public lectures by prominent citizens, literary and debating meetings, free classes in Bible, Hebrew, stenography, bookkeeping, mechanical drawing, and other subjects, as well as in physical culture. A library was founded, and in 1886 became the basis of the Aguilar Free Library, which was later merged into the New York Public Library. For about ten years (1875-85) the association had rather varying fortunes; and in the following decade its affairs became so unsatisfactory that the question of disbanding was considered. A downtown branch was opened on the East Side, out of which in 1891 grew the Educational Alliance. In 1895, however, a reorganization took place; and on Jan. 10, 1897, Jacob H. Schiff presented the association with a new home at 861 Lexington avenue, which gift was followed on Dec. 20, 1898, by the donation of a new building at Ninety-second street and Lexington avenue. This structure, which was dedicated on May 30, 1900, is provided with all modern requisites, including a library, reading-rooms (containing more than 9,000

Clifford's Tower, York, England.
(From a photograph.)

volumes for reference), a gymnasium, and rooms for recreation. In addition to evening classes in a large number of subjects, the association holds religious services on Friday evenings, and has established a vacation camp. For the year ending April 30, 1905, the total attendance was no less than 166,-289; the income was $39,423.21; and the disbursements amounted to $38,673.32. Percival S. Menken has been president of the association since 1895.

The Young Men's Hebrew Association of New York city is the parent institution of similar organizations that have been established throughout the United States. In 1875 there was founded in the city of Philadelphia, Pa., a Young Men's Hebrew Association, which has continued in existence to the present time. It is located in a rented building; and its activities consist principally in the delivery of public lectures during the winter season, an annual ball, and the encouragement of literature and of debating societies, besides numerous classes, a gymnasium, and entertainments. It also awards prizes for essays; and several periodicals have been issued under its auspices. Joint public debates have been held at various times between the Philadelphia association and that of New York. The former has a small library for the use of members.

The Young Men's Hebrew Association of New Orleans, La., has been established for a number of years. It is largely devoted to social purposes, and therefore performs for the most part the functions of a club. The handsome building occupied by the association for a number of years was recently destroyed by fire; it contained a ballroom, a billiard-room, parlors, meeting-rooms, and a library. This is one of the principal Jewish organizations of the city.

In St. Louis, Mo., there is a Young Men's Hebrew Association of considerable size and importance. It attempts to combine the features of both the New Orleans and the New York organization; social purposes, however, predominate, and in its functions and activities it is a club rather than a philanthropic association like the New York branch.

San Francisco, Cal., has a Young Men's Hebrew Association with a considerable membership. It is conducted practically on the lines of the organization in New Orleans, being confined largely if not exclusively to club features.

In Louisville, Ky., there is a Young Men's Hebrew Association; but it is not in a flourishing condition, and it seems to be very difficult to arouse interest in its welfare.

In Washington, D. C., there was for a number of years a Young Men's Hebrew Association; but for causes similar to those which affect the organization in Louisville, Ky., it was some time ago abandoned, and has not since been revived.

Chicago, Ill., has a Young Men's Hebrew Association of great significance.

In addition to those mentioned above, there are numerous other Young Men's Hebrew **Smaller** Associations of more or less impor-**Institu-** tance throughout the United States. **tions.** In Springfield, Mass., there is an association which was established some years ago and which is principally a social and literary organization. Memphis, Tenn., has for a num-

ber of years supported a Young Men's Hebrew Association, which follows closely in its methods the branch in New Orleans. It is one of the principal Jewish organizations in Memphis, and performs to a large extent the functions of a social club, dramatic performances being among the entertainments provided by its members.

The Young Men's Hebrew Association of Boston, Mass., is now located in a home of its own, the gift of a public-spirited Jewish citizen, and has recently been reorganized, being devoted chiefly to philanthropic and benevolent work. It maintains public classes, debating and literary societies, religious work, a library, reading-rooms, and other features, in all of which it follows closely the lead of the New York organization.

In the following cities Young Men's Hebrew Associations have been established on a small scale, confining themselves principally to social activities and serving as small social clubs: Nashville, Tenn.; Mobile, Ala.; Savannah, Ga.; Stamford, Conn.; Chelsea, Mass.; Wilkesbarre, Pa.; Salem, Mass.; Milwaukee, Wis.; Baltimore, Md.; Newport News, Va.; Fort Worth, Tex.; and Newark, N. J.

J.   P. S. M.

YOẒEROT : The collective name for the piyyuṭim introduced in the recitation of the morning service on the festivals and on special Sabbaths throughout the year in the Northern rituals (see Zunz, "S. P." *passim*). These hymns are termed ḲEROBOT if intercalated in the repetition of the 'AMIDAH, but are called in turn "Yoẓer" (creator), "Ofan" (angel), "Me'orah" (light), "Ahabah" (love), "Zulat" (besides), and "Ge'ullah" (redemption) if introduced in the blessings which precede and follow the SHEMA' at the points where these respective words or subjects occur in the ordinary liturgy. The benediction "Yoẓer" coming first, its title has been extended to cover the whole class of introduced hymns, and, even further, the section of the service itself that centers around the "Shema'" as a whole. The modern tendency is to omit the "Yoẓerot" because their recitation results in excessive prolongation of the services (comp. ḤAZZAN and LITURGY).

Owing to the comparative lateness of their adoption into the ritual, there is much less uniformity in the traditional melodies for these piyyuṭim than for any other section of the synagogal melody which dates from before the modern period. The scheme discussed under ḲEROBOT is sometimes followed; but more generally the ḥazzan founds his intonation, with much freedom of treatment, on the prayer-motive or model musical interpretation of the particular service in which he is engaged (see MUSIC, SYNAGOGAL). When he departs from it, his florid melody is conceived in the spirit of modern instrumental virtuosity (comp. 'AL HA-RISHONIM) or closely reproduces the old-world folk-song of northern Europe (comp. MA'OZ ẒUR). But while following the local tradition, he draws a sharp distinction not merely between the jubilant praise of the three festivals and the pleading supplication of the Days of Penitence, but also between the historical reminiscence of the Sabbaths preceding Passover, with their proud reference to the glories of the Temple ritual, and the agonized lament of those coming between Passover and Pentecost, with their distressful memory of the barbarity of the Crusaders and other persecutors of the dark Middle Ages. This latter sentiment often makes itself felt even amid the joyous melody of the festival days (comp. BERAḤ DODI).

Whatever may have been the melodies to which such piyyuṭim were chanted when first introduced, the great number of them in the Northern liturgies produced so much inconvenience by lengthening the service that the tunes were soon ignored, and the verses themselves were quickly read through in an undertone, only the concluding stanza being intoned by the ḥazzan (comp. ḲEROBOT). In the Sephardic ritual, however, the number of "Yoẓerot" is so small that the originally chosen musical settings, also usually of a folk-song character, have been retained in living tradition till the present (comp. ADONAI BE-ḲOL SHOFAR; 'ET SHA'ARE RAẒON; YAH SHIMEKA).

A.   F. L. C.

YSIDRO, ABRAHAM GABBAI. See GABBAI.

YUDAN : Palestinian amora of the fourth century. His name does not occur in the Babylonian Talmud, whereas it is often mentioned in the older Palestinian midrashim, as well as in the Jerusalem Talmud, where he is repeatedly referred to as a halakist (Pe'ah 16b; Dem. 25d; Kil. 29b; Ma'as. Sh. 52c; 'Er. 20d; etc.). He was a pupil of Abba (Yer. Soṭah 16c), and became a colleague of Jose, the principal of the school at Tiberias, with whom he often engaged in halakic controversies (Yer. Pe'ah 16c; Sheb. 36d; Suk. 52a; etc.). He appears to have held the office of judge simultaneously with Jose, it being stated (Yer. Ket. 34b) that the latter once rendered alone a decision on a question of civil law at a time when Yudan had fled to Nawe. This statement concerning Yudan's flight from Tiberias to Nawe, in Peræa, is the only biographical datum known with regard to his career, no mention being made of his family relations, of his native place, or even of the name of his father. His own references to older contemporaries throw but little light upon his personality.

Relations with Ze'era. Mention is made of an objection relating to a halakic thesis which Yudan personally brought to the attention of Ze'era (Yer. Sanh. 24d); and several comments which Yudan made upon Ze'era's halakic maxims have been preserved (Yer. Suk. 54a; Yer. R. H. 57d; Yer. Ber. 61b). Of his pupils, Mana, the son of Jonah, is the only one known (Yer. Pes. 33a; Ta'an. 66a). On a certain day Yudan did not visit the school, and Mana referred to him the halakic questions which had been brought up during the session (Yer. Giṭ. 47a).

This amora is one of the best-known transmitters of haggadic literature, he having handed down maxims of many of the older amoraim, as Ḥanina, Johanan, Ḥama ben Ḥanina, Simeon b. Laḳish, and Joshua ben Levi. He often transmitted also tannaitic maxims. In many instances maxims originating with older amoraim have been ascribed to him (comp. Bacher, "Ag. Pal. Amor." p. 242, note 8); and he often places transmitted maxims side by side with his own (Yer. Ber. 13a; Gen. R. ix. 1). Together with his own

haggadic maxims there are often handed down the divergent expositions of other haggadists on the same subjects. Among the haggadists whose opinions are thus given by Yudan may be mentioned Huna, Berechiah, Phinehas, and Azariah (comp. Bacher, l.c.). His maxims extend to all branches of the Haggadah, and include exegetic and homiletic explanations of Biblical passages, as well as comments on Biblical personages and narratives, sentences relating to the study of the Law, and eschatological and Messianic sayings.

Some of Yudan's haggadic maxims may be mentioned here. With reference to the atoning power of suffering, he remarks that if a slave is liberated because of pain inflicted upon a single member of his body (Ex. xxi. 20), how much more entitled to liberty in the world to come is a man who has been afflicted with sufferings in his whole body?

Haggadic Maxims. (Gen. R. xcii. 1). He who publicly teaches the Torah shall be found worthy to have the Holy Spirit rest upon him, even as it rested on Solomon, who, because he had preached the Torah, was thought worthy to write the books of Proverbs, Ecclesiastes, and the Song of Solomon (Cant. R., Introduction, § 9). The words "the law of the Lord" in Isa. v. 24 refer to the written law, while "the word of the Holy One" in the same verse means the oral law (Pesiḳ. 121b). To "the nations" —by which term the Christians are probably meant— the Sabbath has been given with the word "Remember" (Ex. xx. 8), because, although they remember that day, they do not keep it; but to Israel it was given with the word "Observe" (Deut. v. 12; Pesiḳ. R. xxiii. 115b). The visit to Seir promised by Jacob (Gen. xxxiii. 14) is meant for the future, when the "saviors shall come up on Mount Zion" (Obadiah, verse 21; Yer. 'Ab. Zarah 40c). The words "and man became a living ["ḥayyah"] soul" (Gen. ii. 7) are explained by Yudan as meaning that man was originally created with a rudimentary tail, so that he resembled an animal ("ḥayyah"); later, however, God removed this appendage in order that man's dignity should not suffer (Gen. R. xiv., where the name "Judah" occurs erroneously for "Yudan").

Yudan often interpreted Biblical words according to their consonantal formation, without referring to their vowel-sounds (Gen. R. xxxv. 1, xxxviii. 8); and he also used the numerical values of the letters as a basis for explanations (ib. xxxix. 11, lxxix. 1). He interpreted numbers in other ways, asserting, for instance, that the fact that the name of Barzillai occurs five times in II Sam. xix. 31–40 (corresponding to the five books of the Torah), teaches that he who supports the pious with the necessaries of life, as Barzillai sustained David (II Sam. xvii. 27), is regarded as having kept all the precepts of the five books (Gen. R. lviii.). With regard to the sentence "I saw your fathers as the firstripe in the fig-tree at her first time" (Hosea ix. 10), he remarked that even as one plucks first one fig from the fig-tree, then two, then three, and at length a whole basketful, so at first "Abraham was one" (Ezek. xxxiii. 24), then there were two (Abraham and Isaac), then three (Abraham, Isaac, and Jacob), and at length "the children of Israel were fruitful, and increased abundantly" (Ex. i. 7; Gen. R. xlvi. 1).

Many of Yudan's exegetic interpretations give the correct and simple meanings of the words or passages to which they refer. Thus he explains, with regard to Ps. ix. 18, that the word לא in the first part of the verse refers to the word תאבד in the **Exegetic** second part: "For even as the needy **Inter-** shall not always be forgotten, so shall **pretations.** not the expectation of the poor perish forever" (Midr. Teh. to Ps. ix.). In I Sam. xxiii. 27 the word מלאך denotes a messenger, and not an angel (Midr. Shemuel xvii. 2); and the word עפאים in Ps. civ. 12 is to be interpreted "leaves" in analogy with the word עפיה in Dan. iv. 9 (Midr. Teh. to Ps. civ. 9). Yudan also frequently employs parables, the following being a representative example: "Every one has a patron; and when he is in need he may not suddenly enter into the presence of his benefactor to ask for aid, but must wait at the door while a slave or an inmate of the house carries his request before the master. God, however, is not such a patron; when man is in need he shall call neither upon Gabriel nor upon Michael, but upon God direct, who will hear him without any mediators" (Yer. Ber. 13a).

BIBLIOGRAPHY: Bacher, *Ag. Pal. Amor.* iii. 237–272.
J.   J. Z. L.

YUDAN BEN ISHMAEL: Palestinian amora of the third century; probably a brother of Yannai ben Ishmael. He solved the question whether instructors in the Law should be paid for their services, by declaring that they ought to be remunerated for the time during which they might have earned something by other work (Yer. Ned. 38c). The words "he weigheth the waters by measure" (Job xxviii. 25) were interpreted by him as implying the law of God, which is compared to water. The words of the Law are given to each individual by measure; one is accorded a knowledge of the Bible, another of the Mishnah, a third of the Halakah, and a fourth of the Haggadah, while many are learned in all (Lev. R. xv. 2, where "ben Ishmael" should be read instead of "ben Samuel").

BIBLIOGRAPHY: Frankel, *Mebo*, p. 95a; Bacher, *Ag. Pal. Amor.* iii. 603–604.
J.   J. Z. L.

YUDAN BEN MANASSEH: Palestinian amora of the third century. One of his halakic maxims has been preserved in the Jerusalem Talmud (Kil. 27a), and the Babylonian Talmud contains two haggadic sayings by him, both based on the interpretation of a Biblical word with varied vocalization, and both referring to I Sam. ii. 2 (Meg. 14a; Ber. 10a; see "Dikduke Soferim" on both passages). In emphasizing the decorous mode of expression adopted in the Bible, Yudan declared that "even those passages which enumerate the characteristics of the unclean animals first give the marks of their cleanness" (comp. Lev. xi. 4–7); and this aphorism is frequently quoted in midrashic literature (Lev. R. xxvi. 1; Pesik. iv. [ed. Buber, p. 31a]; Num. R. xix. 1).

BIBLIOGRAPHY: Bacher, *Ag. Pal. Amor.* iii. 604.
J.   J. Z. L.

YUDAN BEN SIMEON (called **Judah ben Simeon** in the Babylonian Talmud): Palestinian

amora of the third century; a contemporary of Johanan, who in his name transmits a ruling relating to the law of inheritance, as well as a discussion which took place between them (B. B. 114b–115a). Reference is often made to a controversy between Johanan and Yudan ben Simeon concerning written and oral law (Yer. Pe'ah 17a; Meg. 74d; Hag. 76d).

Several haggadic interpretations of Yudan's have been preserved; and of these many are of cosmogonic and cosmological content, while others refer to questions of natural history. Among the latter may be mentioned the following explanation of Job xxix. 18: "The phenix lives a thousand years; and at the end of that period its body shrinks, its feathers fall off, and only a kind of egg remains. From this egg new members grow, and the phenix returns to life" (Gen. R. xix. 5). The giant animals behemoth and leviathan, according to him, were created in order to serve as quarries for the pious in the future world. Those who have not seen the hunts and animal contests among the heathen peoples in this world will be found worthy to view the chase in the world to come (Lev. R. xiii. 3). In his haggadic interpretations Yudan employs parables also, explaining, for example, Hosea xii. 4 by a beautiful allegory (Lev. R. xxvii. 6; Num. R. x. 1). Moreover, he made use of the system of NOTARIKON, interpreting the first word of the Decalogue, לא, by decomposing the letters, so that it read למד אלף, *i.e.*, "learn thousands," that is, "study the numberless words of the Law" (Pesik. xxii.).

BIBLIOGRAPHY: Bacher, *Ag. Pal. Amor.* iii. 604–607.
J.   J. Z. L.

YUDGHANITES: Members of the Jewish sect called "Al-Yudghaniyyah," after the name of its founder, Yudghan or Judah of Hamadan, a disciple of Abu 'Isa al-Isfahani. Shortly after the defeat of Abu 'Isa and his followers, the 'Isawites, at Rai (the ancient Rhagæ) early in the eighth century, Yudghan conceived the project of forming a new sect from the scattered followers of his master. More prudent than the founder of the 'Isawite sect, Yudghan did not pretend to have been entrusted by God with the mission of delivering the Jews from the rule of the Gentiles and of making them politically independent, but confined himself to the rôle of a prophet and teacher, assuming the surname of "al-Ra'i" (= "the Shepherd"; not "al-Da'i," as given erroneously by Shahrastani in his "Kitab al-Milal wal-Nihal," ed. Cureton, p. 168).

Influenced by the doctrines of SUFISM, which at that time began to spread among the Mohammedans in the land of the Magi, Yudghan set aside the literal meaning of the words of the Torah in **Influence** favor of a mystic or spiritual inter- **of Sufism.** pretation. Like the Sufis, he taught that all religious beliefs, such as those relating to paradise, hell, etc., are allegories; but, on the other hand, he opposed the Sufic doctrine of predestination, and declared that man is absolutely free in the choice of good and evil and is therefore responsible for his actions. From among the tenets of the 'Isawites Yudghan retained the prohibition of wine and animal food, and probably also the institution of seven daily prayers instead of the three rabbinical ones. In opposition to the ancient traditional view, according to which the Biblical accounts of God's deeds and thoughts must be taken literally, he asserted, probably under the influence of the Motazilites, that one is not allowed to represent God with material attributes, *i.e.*, anthropomorphically. Yudghan attached more importance to praying and fasting than to the observance of the ceremonial laws. He held that the laws concerning the Sabbath and the festivals were not binding in the Diaspora, but were observed merely as a remembrance.

Like Abu 'Isa, Yudghan declared that Jesus and Mohammed were prophets, and that each was sent as a missionary to his nation. According to Ḳirḳisani, both Abu 'Isa and Yudghan took this attitude for diplomatic reasons; for had they not recognized the post-Biblical prophets, their own claim to prophetic inspiration would very likely have been challenged. Yudghan gained many followers, who maintained their beliefs long after the death of their master. Their faith in him was so great that they declared he had not died, but would appear again in order to bring a new doctrine with him. Shahrastani relates that after the death of Yudghan a follower of his named Mushka founded a new sect called "Al-Mushkaniyyah." The tenets of the new sect were the same as those of the Yudghanites, with the single addition of an injunction to forcibly impose the doctrines of Yudghan upon all Jews. Mushka marched out of Hamadan with a troop of followers, but they were all killed in the vicinity of Koom (east of Hamadan and southwest of Teheran).

"Al-Mushka-niyyah."

According to some scholars, Saadia, in criticizing in his "Emunot we-De'ot" (vi.) the belief in metempsychosis of "the so-called Yehudim" (ממי שנקראים יהודים), had reference to the Yudghanites, who were still in existence in his time. Although this is not impossible, as maintained by Rapoport (introduction to the "Hegyon ha-Nefesh" of Abraham bar Ḥiyya, p. lii.), it is highly improbable, since no mention is made by either Shahrastani or Ḳirḳisani of such a belief among the tenets of the Yudghanites. It is more probable that Saadia referred not to a special Jewish sect, but to all those, among either the Karaites or the Rabbinites, who held to the doctrine of Pythagoras.

BIBLIOGRAPHY: Shahrastani, *Kitab al-Milal wal-Niḥal*, ed. Cureton, p. 168, London, 1846; Judah Hadassi, *Eshkol ha-Kofer*, § 79; Ḳirḳisani, in Harkavy, *Le-Ḳorot ha-Ḳittot be-Yisrael*, in Graetz, *Hist.* Hebr. ed., iii. 503; Jellinek, *Beiträge*, p. 53; Grätz, *Gesch.* v. 191.
J. I. Br.

YUḤASIN, SEFER HA-. See Zacuto, Abraham.

YULEE, DAVID LEVY: American politician; born in St. Thomas, West Indies, in 1811; died in New York city Oct. 10, 1886. He went to Richmond, Va., where he applied himself to classical studies and the law. Later he removed to Florida and became a planter. He was elected as a delegate from Florida to the 27th and 28th Congresses as a Democrat, at that time bearing the name of Levy. He was later known as David Levy Yulee, and under this name was a delegate to the first state constitutional convention of Florida. He was twice elected United States senator from Florida as a Democrat, serving from Dec., 1845, to 1851, and again from 1855 until his retirement on Jan. 21, 1861. He served also in the Confederate Congress, and was a prisoner of state at Fort Pulaski in 1865. After the Civil war he was president of the Atlantic and Gulf Railroad of Florida, and was interested in the financial and commercial growth of Fernandina and Cedar Keys, Fla.

BIBLIOGRAPHY: *American Jewish Year Book*, 5661 (1901), p. 524; *Biographical Congressional Dictionary*, p. 651, Washington, D. C., 1903.
A. A. S. I.

YULY (YULEE), SAMUEL: Moorish envoy to England; born in Mogador, Morocco, at the end of the eighteenth century; died at Portsea, England, in Jan., 1872. He was connected with the Guedella family, agents for the Sultan of Morocco and one of the wealthiest merchant firms in Mogador. In 1820 Yuly went to England, as the accredited representative of the Sultan of Morocco, with letters to the British government. He afterward resided permanently in England, but kept up a trading connection with Mogador. See Morocco.

J. G. L.

YUSUF IBN NUḤ, ABU YA'ḲUB. See Joseph b. Noah ha-Baṣri.

YUSUF IBN TESHUFIN: Almoravid king of Spain in the eleventh and twelfth centuries. He was the only Almoravid ruler hostile to the Jews, and he once endeavored to force Islam upon them. Passing through Lucena in 1105, he noticed the flourishing Jewish community there, and convoked its representatives, telling them that Mohammed had granted the Jews religious freedom only on condition that the Jewish Messiah should come within five hundred years after the Hegira, and that the Jews had agreed to embrace Islam if at the end of the half-millennium the Messiah had not appeared. He informed them further that as the term was then just at an end, he would withdraw from them his protection and declare them outlaws if they did not accept the religion established by the Prophet. The Jews of Lucena averted the danger, however, by presenting Yusuf, through his vizier 'Abd Allah ibn 'Ali, with large sums of money.

BIBLIOGRAPHY: Grätz, *Gesch.* 3d ed., vi. 99.
J. M. Sel.

Z

ZABARA, JOSEPH. See JOSEPH ZABARA.

ZABDAI BEN LEVI: Palestinian amora of the first generation (third century). He belonged to the scholarly group of which Hoshaiah Rabbah was the chief (Yer. Dem. vii. 26a), and his halakot were transmitted by R. Johanan (Zeb. 28b; Ker. 5a). Zabdai was particularly prominent in the Haggadah and in Biblical exegesis, in both of which he disputed with Rab, Joshua b. Levi, and Jose b. Petrus. Thus the words "le-ruaḥ ha-yom" (Gen. iii. 8; A. V., "in the cool of the day") are explained by Zabdai to mean "the side of the setting of the sun," in opposition to Rab's interpretation, "the side of the rising of the sun" (Gen. R. xix. 8). The phrase "Ka-'et ḥayyah" (Gen. xviii. 14; A. V., "At the time appointed") is explained by Zabdai as meaning "in a year from hence." God made a scratch on the wall, saying that when a year later the sun should arrive at that mark Sarah would bear a son (Pesiḳ. R. 6 [ed. Friedmann, p. 24b]; Tan., Wayera, 36; see also Pesiḳ. xxv. 158a; Gen. R. lxxiv. 11; Lev. R. vii. 2).

Two proems to Lam. R. (Nos. 29 and 30) are by Zabdai; in the second of them he contrasts the different prayers of four kings with regard to their enemies. David prayed to God that he might overtake his foes and defeat them (Ps. xviii. 38); and his prayer was granted (I Sam. xxx. 8). Asa prayed to God that he might pursue the enemy, but that God would smite him; and it was so (II Chron. xiv. 12). Jehoshaphat said that he was too feeble to pursue the enemy, and prayed God to exterminate the foe while he would sing the praises of his divine helper; and his prayer was satisfied (ib. xx. 22). Finally, Hezekiah said that he had no strength even to sing the praises of God, but he prayed that his enemy might be routed while he himself would lie in his bed; and it so happened (II Kings xix. 35). It is related that Zabdai, having survived Joshua b. Levi, wished to see him in a dream. Joshua accordingly appeared to him, and showed him people with faces raised and people with faces cast down. When Zabdai asked the reason for the difference in posture, Joshua answered that those who arrived there with the study of the Law in their memories had their faces raised, while those who had forgotten it had their faces cast down (Eccl. R. ix. 10).

BIBLIOGRAPHY: Bacher, *Ag. Pal. Amor.* iii. 640–642; Heilprin, *Seder ha-Dorot*, ii.

J. M. SEL.

ZABIM ("Sufferers from Discharges"): Ninth tractate in the Mishnah and Tosefta of the sixth Talmudic order Ṭohorot. It deals with the uncleanness caused by discharges from either man or woman, the regulations concerning which form the subject of Lev. xv. According to the Pentateuchal law, when a man has a running issue out of his flesh, or when a woman has a discharge of her blood beyond the time of her menstruation, such person is unclean. Anything upon which the sufferer sits, lies, or rides is unclean; so that any person sitting in the same seat, lying in the same couch, or riding in the same vehicle with one thus afflicted, or carrying any vessel which the sufferer has used, is unclean until the evening and must wash himself and his clothes in water. If a person having a discharge touches any one without having previously washed his or her hands, the individual so touched is unclean until the evening. An earthen vessel that has been touched by the sufferer must be broken; a wooden one that has been similarly defiled must be rinsed with water. After the discharge has ceased the afflicted one must count seven days, and at the end of that term must wash his or her clothes and must take a bath in running water; and on the eighth day an offering of two doves must be brought, one for a sin-offering and one for a burnt offering.

The treatise consists of five chapters, divided respectively into six, four, three, seven, and twelve paragraphs or mishnayot. It gives in detail all particulars of uncleanness and purification, specifies the degrees of the discharges which render an individual subject to the laws stated above, and mentions what persons are subject to those laws and in what way they cause vessels or other people to become unclean. The contents of the respective chapters may be summarized as follows:

Ch. i.: In order to be liable to all the laws mentioned above, a "zab" must have his discharge three times, either all on one day or on two or three consecutive days; consideration of the length of the intervals between the discharges.

Ch. ii.: All are subject to the laws of Zabim, including proselytes, slaves, minors, deaf-mutes, and eunuchs; description of the different methods by which the zab is examined, and an explanation of the manner in which he makes people and things unclean by his touch.

Ch. iii. and iv.: Specification of the different ways in which a man or a woman suffering from a discharge makes unclean another person. For instance, if a zab and a clean person sit together in a small boat or ride together on a beast, even though their garments do not come in contact the clean person becomes unclean by the pressure; but, according to R. Judah, if both of them sit on a tottering bench, the clean person does not become unclean.

Ch. v.: The ways in which a person becomes unclean by touching a zab, and also in which things become unclean through the touch of the zab and by touching other unclean things.

J. M. SEL.

ZABLUDOWSKI, ISRAEL (ISIDOR): Russian physician; born at Byelostok, in the government of Grodno, July 30, 1850. At the age of twelve he wrote a Hebrew novel entitled "Ha-Yaldut we-ha-Shaḥarut" (Wilna, 1863). In 1869 he was admitted to the military academy of medicine at St. Petersburg (M.D. 1874), and seven years later was appointed physician in one of the military hospitals of southern Russia. During the Russo-Turkish war he served as chief physician of a Cossack regiment near Plevna, and so distinguished himself by his work that Alexander II. awarded him the second rank of the Order of Saint Stanislas.

In the field-hospital Zabludowski's attention was attracted to the massage treatment practised by a Bulgarian monk named Makari, and, adopting this as his specialty, he was sent abroad by the Russian government at the close of the war to perfect himself in the theory of massage. After visiting Vienna, Munich, Paris, Amsterdam, and Berlin, he returned to St. Petersburg in 1881, and was soon appointed chief physician in the hospital of the Preobrazhenski regiment of the imperial guards. He then began to make experiments in massage on persons in sound health, and published a voluminous treatise on this subject in the "Voyenno-Meditzinski Zhurnal" (St. Petersburg, 1882). In the same year Zabludowski settled in Berlin at the request of Bergmann, whose clinical assistant he became. There he published several essays on massage, and in 1884 lectured on this subject before the medical congress of Copenhagen. He is also the author of a long series of articles on his specialty, including a description of a machine invented by him for the cure of writers' cramp ("Berliner Klinische Wochenschrift," 1886, Nos. 26 et seq.). In 1896 he was appointed titular professor of massage in the University of Berlin, a position which he still held in 1905.

BIBLIOGRAPHY: Liebermann, in Ha-Meliz, xxviii., Nos. 213–214; Wohlener, ib. No. 62; Wrede, Das Geistige Berlin, iii., s.v.
J.   M. SEL.

ZABLUDOWSKI, JEHIEL MICHAEL BEN ḤAYYIM: Russian Hebrew scholar and author; born at Byelostok, government of Grodno, in 1803; died there Nov. 14, 1869. He devoted himself especially to the study of the Haggadah; and in addition to a long series of exegetical notes which he published in various periodicals, such as "Ha-Maggid," "Ha-Meliz," and "Ha-Karmel," he wrote two books: "Mish'an Mayim" (Wilna, 1861), a guide to the true meaning of the haggadic passages in the Talmud and Midrashim; and "Me Mikal" (ib. 1872), a commentary and critical notes on difficult passages in the Midrash Rabbot.

BIBLIOGRAPHY: Ha-Meliz, ix. 320; Zeitlin, Bibl. Post-Mendels. p. 325.
J.   M. SEL.

ZACHARIAH OF KIEV. See JUDAIZING HERESY.

ZACUTO, ABRAHAM BEN SAMUEL: Spanish astronomer, mathematician, and historian; born at Salamanca about 1450; died in Turkey after 1510. An astronomer of wide-spread reputation, he was appointed professor at the university of his native city, and later at that of Saragossa. After the Spanish exile, Zacuto settled at Lisbon, where he was soon appointed court astronomer and historiographer to John II. He retained his office under D. Manuel, and in this capacity he was consulted by the king regarding the practicability of the projected expedition of Vasco da Gama, which he approved and encouraged. The ships fitted out for the expedition were provided with Zacuto's newly perfected astrolabe, which was the first to be made of iron instead of wood. The great services rendered by Zacuto did not protect him, however, from

the persecutions inaugurated by Manuel at the instigation of Ferdinand and Isabella; and he and his son Samuel were forced to seek safety in flight. After an eventful voyage in which he was twice taken prisoner, Zacuto reached Tunis, where he lived until the Spanish invasion, when he fled to Turkey, residing there for the remainder of his life. In 1504, during his sojourn at Tunis, he wrote a chronological history of the Jews from the Creation to 1500, making constant reference to Jewish literature, and entitling his book "Sefer ha-Yuḥasin." In this work Zacuto gives an account of the oral law as transmitted from Moses through the elders, prophets, sages, and the like, and also records the acts and monuments of the kings of Israel, as well as of some of the surrounding nations. In like manner space is given to the Babylonian captivity,

His "Yu- the events which occurred during the
ḥasin."   period of the Second Temple, the char-
          acteristics of that period, the princes
of the Captivity, and the rectors of the academies of Sura and Pumbedita. Although the author was far from discriminating as to his sources, and thus fell into many errors, his work is of great value to the student of Jewish literary history.

The "Sefer ha-Yuḥasin" was edited by Samuel Shalom with many omissions and additions of his own (Constantinople, 1566), and was reprinted at Cracow in 1581, at Amsterdam in 1717, and at Königsberg in 1857, while a complete edition was published by Filipowski in London in 1857. In 1473, while still at Salamanca, Zacuto wrote his "Bi'ur Luḥot," which was published in a Latin translation under the title "Almanach Perpetuum" by Joseph Vecinho (Leiria, 1496), who also rendered it into Spanish and appended it to his "She'erit Yosef." Zacuto was likewise the author of three other works: "Sefer Tekunat Zakkut," an astronomical work which is believed to be still extant in manuscript (see "Ha-Shaḥar," i., No. 12); "Arba'im la-Binah," a treatise on astrology; and "Hosafot le-Sefer ha-'Aruk," a rabbinic Aramaic lexicon, of which an account is given by A. Geiger in "Z. D. M. G." xii. 144.

BIBLIOGRAPHY: De Rossi, Dizionario, s.v.; Lindo, The History of the Jews of Spain and Portugal, p. 267; Fuenn, Sephardim, p. 452; Da Costa, Israel and the Gentiles, p. 284; Steinschneider, Cat. Bodl. col. 706; idem, Hebr. Uebers. p. 984; Jost, Gesch. des Judenthums und Seiner Sekten, iii. 113; Grätz, Gesch. ix. 18 et seq.; Fuenn, Keneset Yisrael, p. 22; Fürst, Bibl. Jud. iii. 200–201.
J.   I. BR.

ZACUTO, MOSES BEN MORDECAI (abbreviated רמ״ז = **Rabbi Moses Zacuto**): Cabalistic writer and poet; born about 1625; died at Mantua Oct. 1, 1697. It is generally supposed that his birthplace was Amsterdam, although, like the Amsterdam rabbi Saul Levi MORTEIRA, he probably lived in Venice, the residence of a brother named Nehemiah. He was a pupil of Morteira, on whose death he composed a long elegy (edited by Kaufmann in "R. E. J." xxxvii. 115 et seq.), and he was also a fellow student of Baruch SPINOZA. He was inclined to mysticism from his youth, and at one time fasted forty days that he might forget the Latin which he had learned, since, in his opinion, it could not be reconciled with cabalistic truths. To continue his Talmudic studies he went from Amsterdam to Posen or Poland, as is clear from the letter of recommendation which he gave at Venice in 1672 to the delegates who had come to Italy to collect money for the oppressed Polish communities. It was his intention to make a pilgrimage to Palestine, but on the way he was persuaded to remain as rabbi in Venice, where he stayed, with the exception of a short residence in Padua, from 1645 until the summer of 1673. He was then called to Mantua at a fixed salary of 300 ducats, and remained there until his death, twenty-four years later. His epitaph is given by Wolf ("Bibl. Hebr." iv. 1200) and by Landshuth ("'Ammude ha-'Abodah," p. 215).

Zacuto applied himself with great diligence to the study of the Cabala under Ḥayyim Vital's pupil Benjamin ha-Levi, who had come to Italy from Safed; and this remained the chief occupation of his life. He established a seminary for the study of the Cabala; and his favorite pupils, Benjamin ha-Kohen and Abraham Rovigo, often visited him for months at a time at Venice or Mantua, to investigate cabalistic mysteries. Zacuto was not without poetic talent, but his verses seldom rise above mediocrity. He composed forty-seven liturgical poems, chiefly cabalistic, enumerated by Landshuth (l.c. pp. 216 et seq.). Some of them have been printed in the festal hymns "Hen Ḳol Ḥadash," edited by Moses Ottolenghi (Amsterdam, 1712), and others have been incorporated in different prayer-books. He wrote also penitential poems ("Tiḳḳun Shobabim," Venice, 1712; Leghorn, 1740) for the service on the evening before the day of New Moon, as well as prayers for Hosha'na Rabbah and similar occasions, all in the spirit of the Cabala. Zacuto was, moreover, the author of a poem containing a thousand words, each beginning with the letter "alef" ("Elef Alpin"; printed with a commentary at the end of the "Iggerot ha-ReMeZ," pp. 43 et seq.); a long poem, "Tofteh 'Aruk," or "L'Inferno Figurato" (Venice, 1715, 1744), in which he depicts the punishments of hell; and the oldest dramatic poem in the Hebrew language, which A. Berliner first edited under the title "Yesod 'Olam" (Berlin, 1874).

Other published works of Zacuto's are "Shudda de-Dayyane," a guide for decisions on commercial law (Mantua, 1678; reprinted in "Ha-Goren," iii. 181 et seq.); "Ḳol ha-ReMeZ" (published posthumously), a commentary on the Mishnah (which he knew by heart), with elucidations of the commentaries of Bertinoro and others (Amsterdam, 1719); a collection of responsa with the decisions of contemporaries (Venice, 1760); and "Iggerot ha-ReMeZ," containing letters of cabalistic content written by himself and others (Leghorn, 1780). He edited and emended also the Zohar (Venice, 1663) and other writings. A considerable number of his works, such as a commentary on the Jerusalem Talmud, homilies, and cabalistic writings, are still unpublished.

BIBLIOGRAPHY: Azulai, Shem ha-Gedolim, i. 153; De Barrios, Arbol de las Vidas, p. 78; Delitzsch, Zur Geschichte der Jüdischen Poesie, pp. 72 et seq.; Ha-Goren, iii. 175 et seq.; Grätz, Gesch. ix. 201 et seq., x. 170; Nepi-Ghirondi, Toledot Gedole Yisrael, p. 225; Steinschneider, Cat. Bodl. cols. 1989–1992; Zunz, Literaturgesch. pp. 440 et seq.; Fürst, Bibl. Jud. iii. 201 et seq.; Zedner, Cat. Hebr. Books Brit. Mus. pp. 588 et seq.

J.   M. K.

ẒADDIḲ. See ḤASIDIM.

ẒADDUḲIM. See SADDUCEES.

ZADOK: 1. A priest, perhaps the high priest during the reign of David. He was the son of Ahitub (II Sam. viii. 17), but the attempt to trace his genealogy back to Eleazar, the third son of Aaron, as opposed to Abiathar, his contemporary and colleague, who was regarded as a descendant of Eli and considered a member of the house of Ithamar, was first made by the Chronicler (I Chron. v. 30–34 [A. V. vi. 4–8]; comp. vi. 35–38 [A. V. vi. 50–53]), thus assuring the preeminence of the Zadokites over the descendants of Eli. In the beginning of his career he was associated with Abiathar (II Sam. xx. 25) and with his son (ib. viii. 17; I Chron. xxiv. 3, 6, 31). The hypothesis has accordingly been advanced that Zadok officiated in the Tabernacle at Gibeon (I Chron. xvi. 39; comp. I Kings iii. 4), while the sons of Eli were stationed as high priests at Jerusalem or, more probably, at Shiloh (comp. Keil on I Kings i. 8). Such a division of functions is very doubtful, however; and it is more plausible to suppose that Zadok gradually won equality of rank with the sons of Eli by his good fortune in gaining the favor of David.

According to the somewhat improbable statement of the Chronicler, a certain Zadok, as a young man, had been one of those who joined David at Hebron and helped him win the crown of all Israel, his house then including twenty-two captains (I Chron. xii. 29); and Josephus expressly identifies this Zadok with the high priest of the same name ("Ant." vii. 2, § 2). During the rebellion of Absalom, Zadok gained still greater prominence. He and the Levites wished to accompany the fleeing David with the Ark of the Covenant, but the king begged them to remain at Jerusalem, where they could do him better service (II Sam. xv. 24–29; comp. 35), so that it actually happened that Ahimaaz, the son of Zadok, and Jonathan, the son of Abiathar, brought the king an important message (ib. xvii. 21). In all these passages Zadok is mentioned before Abiathar. According to the Hebrew text of II Sam. xv. 27, David addressed the priest with the words "ha-ro'eh attah," and the Vulgate consequently regards Zadok as a seer, although this interpretation is incorrect. These two difficult words are emended by Wellhausen to הכהן הראש אתה, thus implying the promise of the high-priesthood to him. On the suppression of the rebellion, the king sent Zadok and Abiathar to the elders of Judah, urging them to hasten to bring the monarch back (ib. xix. 12). Zadok again manifested his loyalty to the king when he espoused the cause of Solomon against Adonijah (I Kings i. 8 et seq.), and in his gratitude the new king appointed him sole high priest (ib. ii. 35). In his account of this event Josephus states ("Ant." viii. 1, § 3) that Zadok was a scion of the house of Phinehas, and consequently a descendant of Eleazar.

Reliable historical data show that the high-priesthood remained in the hands of the Zadokites from this time until the rise of the Maccabees. The descendants of Zadok increased in rank and influence, so that his son Azariah was one of the princes of Solomon (I Kings iv. 2), and the Ahimaaz who married a daughter of Solomon was probably another of Zadok's children (*ib.* iv. 15). Either Zadok himself or his grandson was the ruler of the Aaronites (I Chron. xxvii. 17), and Jerusha, the mother of Jotham, is apparently termed the daughter of Zadok to emphasize her noble lineage, since her father may have been a descendant of the first Zadok (II Kings xv. 33; II Chron. xxvii. 1). A Zadok is also mentioned in the genealogy of Joseph, the father of Jesus (Matt. i. 14).

G.   S. Kr.

2. Sadducean leader. The only data concerning the origin of the Sadducees are based on certain deductions drawn from their name, for a late rabbinical source alone appears to be founded on actual knowledge. Two pupils of ANTIGONUS OF SOKO are said to have misinterpreted their teacher's statement that God should be worshiped without hope of reward as meaning that there is no recompense, either for good or for evil, in the world to come. These two scholars, Zadok and Boethus, are accordingly regarded as the founders of the heresies of the SADDUCEES and the BOETHUSIANS (Ab. R. N. recension A, 5; recension B, 10). This statement is devoid of historicity, however, since it incorrectly postulates denial of the future life as the cardinal doctrine of the Sadducees, while it betrays also its lack of authenticity by making the origin of the Boethusians synchronous with the rise of Sadduceeism, although the former sect derived its name from the high priest Boethus, who flourished during the reign of Herod.

The only historical portion of this legend is the part which connects the origin of each of these heresies with a personal name, for the Hebrew צדוקים is derived from צדוק just as are ביתוסים from ביתום and אפיקורסים from אפיקורום, while Herod was the eponym of the party of the HERODIANS.

Geiger's theory of the derivation of the name of the Sadducean party from the Biblical appellative "Zadok" is, therefore, the most probable one. This name צדוק, which occurs ten times in Ezekiel, Ezra, and Nehemiah, is transliterated Σαδδούκ throughout by the Septuagint in these books, as well as in other passages in Lucian's version of the Septuagint. The same form appears in Josephus; and even a manuscript of the Mishnah (Codex De Rossi No. 138) vocalizes the name of the rabbi Zadok צָדּוּק (= "Ẓadduḳ"). The only moot point is the problem whether the appellation of the sect is to be derived from a Zadok who is no longer known or from the priestly family of the Zadokites. An unknown Zadok was assumed to be the founder of the Sadducees by Kuenen (though he later adopted the opposing theory), Graetz, Montet, and Lagarde, while the second hypothesis, which is the more probable, was maintained by Geiger and Schürer, and is now confirmed by the Hebrew Ben Sira (see Schechter's note in "The Wisdom of Ben Sira," 1899, p. 35). A third conjecture, deriving the word from the adjective צדיק, which was advocated in ancient times by Jerome and Epiphanius, and was defended more recently by Joseph Derenbourg and Hamburger, is untenable both on linguistic and on historical grounds.

From the days of Solomon the descendants of the priest Zadok were regarded with great reverence, which must have been much increased by the Deuteronomic legislation concentrating all cults at Jerusalem. In Ezekiel's prophetic vision the "sons of Zadok" are described as the only priests worthy to discharge their holy office (Ezek. xl. 46, xliii. 19, xliv. 15, xlviii. 11); and although in the Second Temple certain prerogatives were allowed the sons of Ithamar, the Zadokites alone formed the priestly aristocracy, so that the Chronicler assigns twice as many priestly divisions to the Zadokite descendants of Eleazar as to the Ithamarites (I Chron. xxiv.). In Ecclesiasticus (Sirach), in like manner, the Zadokites alone receive praise (li. 12 [9], Hebr.). Despite the fact that those members of this powerful family who adopted the Sadducean doctrines were but few, they gave the teachings such support that the entire sect bore their name, and Josephus expressly states that scions of the priestly aristocracy, *i.e.*, the Zadokites, were preeminently adherents of Sadduceeism. See SADDUCEES.

BIBLIOGRAPHY: Geiger, *Urschrift*, pp. 20, 102; Wellhausen, *I. J. G.* 4th ed., p. 294; idem, *Pharisäer und Sadducäer*, Göttingen, 1874; Schürer, *Gesch.* 3d ed., ii. 408–411.

J.   S. Kr.

3. Tanna of priestly descent; father of Eleazar. He flourished in the years preceding and following the beginning of the common era. According to an account which must refer to him in the prime of life, he was taken as a captive to Rome, where he was sold to an aristocratic house. Its mistress attempted to force him to marry one of her beautiful slaves, but Zadok refused, claiming that not only did he belong to one of the most influential families of Jerusalem, but that he was of priestly lineage, whereupon his mistress gave him his freedom (Ab. R. N., ed. Schechter, p. 32a and note 11; Ḳid. 40a). A historical account dating from the time of the Temple vouches for the fact that he was a priest. During a sacrifice a strife broke out between two priests, perhaps brothers, because one had taken precedence of the other at the altar, and one of them was stabbed. There was great excitement among the congregation, whereupon Zadok ascended the steps of the "ulam," from which the priests were accustomed to give the benediction, and there calmed the people by an address based on Deut. xxi. 1 *et seq.* Since, however, it has been proved that only priests were allowed to mount the ulam, Zadok must have been a priest (Yoma 23a; Tosef., Yoma, i. 12; Yer. Yoma ii. 39d).

Together with Eliezer b. Hyrcanus and Joshua b. Hananiah, Zadok was present at the marriage of the son of Gamaliel II. in Jabneh. On that occasion Gamaliel II. himself poured out the wine and handed it round. Joshua and Eliezer began to praise Gamaliel, whereupon **Zadok and Gamaliel.** Zadok became angry, declaring that they should not turn away from the worship of God, who had created everything for man, and worship a mortal (Ḳid. 32a). According to Bacher, however, this incident occurred not at a wedding, but at another feast, which Gamaliel gave to the scholars of Jabneh.

The whole life of this tanna fell within the period of the dissolution of the Jewish state, and he declared that he had fasted forty years in his endeavor to prevent the destruction of the Temple. When this took place, however, Zadok had become so weak that Johanan b. Zakkai was obliged to appeal for him to Titus, who had him treated by a physician (Giṭ. 56b; Lam. R. i. 5). Zadok moved to Jabneh together with Johanan b. Zakkai and other scholars, and his few halakot, found in 'Eduy. vii. 1–5, date from this period. He was the most influential personality in Gamaliel's tribunal, and always sat at the right of the latter (Yer. Sanh. 19c), while on one occasion he was present at the eating of the sacrificial lamb in Gamaliel's house (Pes. 74a). Together with Johanan b. Zakkai and Gamaliel, he rendered a decision on the conditions under which food might be eaten outside the Tabernacle during the Feast of Weeks (Suk. 26b). Although he was theoretically an adherent of the principles of the Bet Shammai, in practise he always made his rulings in accordance with the Bet Hillel (Yeb. 15b). His motto in ethical matters was, "Do not make learning a crown to make thyself great thereby, nor a spade to dig with it" (Ab. iv. 5). The thirtieth chapter of the Tanna debe Eliyahu Rabbah relates that Zadok once came to the place where the Temple had formerly stood. In his grief at the desolation he reproached God Himself, whereupon he fell into a sleep in which he saw God and the angels mourning over the destruction of Zion. The Pirḳe de-Rabbi Eli'ezer ascribes to Zadok haggadic sayings concerning the descendants of the giants (ch. xxii.), the sacrifices of Cain and Abel (ch. xxi.), the Flood (ch. xxiii.), and Noah's prayer in the ark (ib.).

BIBLIOGRAPHY: Bacher, Ag. Tan. i. 43–46; Derenbourg, Hist. pp. 342–344; Zacuto, Sefer Yuḥasin ha-Shalom, ed. Filipowski, pp. 32a, 76a, b; Frankel, Darke ha-Mishnah, pp. 70–71; Heilprin, Seder ha-Dorot, ii. 319–320; Büchler, Die Priester und der Cultus, p. 126, note 1, Vienna, 1895; Neubauer, G. T. p. 375.
J.   S. O.

ZADOK GAON (called also **Isaac b. Ashi**): Gaon of Sura from 820 to 821. On the basis of a responsum quoted in the "Sha'are Ẕedeḳ" (iv. 311, No. 2), Weiss refers to him as follows in his "Dor": "If a case was brought before him and he found the defendant guilty, but was unable to inflict an adequate punishment, he would say to him: 'I charge thee to go to the man thou hast injured and implore his pardon or give him an indemnity.' If the accused did not obey this injunction, he was excommunicated." Zadok was one of the first geonim to take exception to many of the Talmudic regulations, although he inclined toward rigor rather than leniency in their application.

BIBLIOGRAPHY: Grätz, Gesch. 3d ed., v. 196; Weiss, Dor, iv. 27, 43–45.
S.   S. O.

ZADOK 'IMANI or **'AMANI** (עמאני): African liturgical poet, who wrote the following eight poems that are found in the Tripolitan Maḥzor: (1) "El hekal ḳodsho"; (2) "Le-bet el banu"; (3) "La-Adonai et yom ha-shebi'i berak"; (4) "Meholel kol be-ḳaw yashar"; (5) "Ezri yabi el me-'ayin"; (6) "'Al rob 'awoni"; (7) "'Ammeka le-shaḥareka ḳamu"; (8) "Ki bo Elohim dibber be-ḳodsho." No. 3 consists of thirteen strophes, and each of the others consists of five strophes. Nos. 3, 4, 7, and 8 are to

be recited on the Sabbaths of the month of Elul. Only No. 3 bears the complete signature צדוק עמאני; No. 7 is signed עמאני, while all the others show only the name צדוק. Nos. 3 and 8 are both "mustajabs"; in the former every strophe begins with "la-Adonai" and terminates with "Adonai," while in the latter the strophes begin with "ki bo" and rime in "to."

BIBLIOGRAPHY: Zunz, Literaturgesch. pp. 598–599.
J.   M. SEL.

ZAG. See BENVENISTE, ISAAC; MALEA, MEÏR DE; ISAAC IBN SID; ALFONSINE TABLES.

ZAHALON (צהלון): A family of Spanish origin; represented by members who, after the exile from Spain, settled in Italy and the Orient, where they distinguished themselves as rabbis and scholars.

Abraham ben Isaac Ẓahalon: Talmudist and cabalist of the second half of the sixteenth century. He was the author of: "Yad Ḥaruẓim," on the Jewish and Mohammedan calendars (Venice, 1594–95); "Yesha' Elohim," interpretations of Esther compiled from earlier commentators (ib. 1595); and "Marpe la-Nefesh," a cabalistic dissertation on ethics, especially on penitence, according to the system of Isaac Luria (ib. 1595).

BIBLIOGRAPHY: Fürst, Bib. Jud. iii. 541; Steinschneider, Cat. Bodl. col. 711; Fuenn, Keneset Yisrael, p. 58.

Jacob ben Isaac Ẓahalon: Italian rabbi and physician; born at Rome 1630; died at Ferrara 1693. Acquiring early a high reputation both as physician and Talmudist, he was called to the rabbinate of Ferrara and held this position until his death. He was the author of the "Oẓar ha-Ḥayyim," a medical work in thirteen parts, the last of which remained unpublished for lack of funds (Venice, 1683), and of the "Margaliyyot Ṭobot," an abridgment of the "Ḥobot ha-Lebabot" of Baḥya b. Joseph ibn Paḳuda, divided into thirty chapters corresponding to the number of days of the month, each chapter being followed by prayers for various occasions (ib. 1665). In his preface Jacob enumerates the following works which he left in manuscript: "Morashah Ḳehillat Ya'aḳob," on Maimonides; "Yeshu'ot Ya'aḳob," a commentary on Isaiah; "Titten Emet le-Ya'aḳob," homilies on the Pentateuch; "Ḳol Ya'aḳob," an index to the Yalḳuṭ, called also "Or ha-Darshanim" ("Oẓrot Ḥayyim," No. 30); "Zahalah u-Rinnah," on the Song of Solomon; "Ḳohelet Ya'aḳob," on Ecclesiastes; "Derushim 'al-Daniel," on Daniel; "Milḥemet Ya'aḳob," subject unknown; "Oẓar ha-Shamayim," on theology and philosophy; and "Shubu Elai," on the SHEMA' and the benedictions which accompany it.

Jacob was much consulted on halakic questions by his contemporaries. His decisions and responsa are found in the "Teshubot ha-Remez" of Moses Zacuto (§ 36), in the "Paḥad Yiẓḥaḳ" (s.v. בן ין שנה ויום אחז) of Isaac Lampronti, and in the "'Afar Ya'aḳob" of Nathanael Segre; the last-named declares that Jacob was one of the three most learned men of his generation.

BIBLIOGRAPHY: Nepi-Ghirondi, Toledot Gedole Yisrael, p. 130; Steinschneider, Cat. Bodl. col. 1265; Fuenn, Keneset Yisrael, p. 569; Fürst, Bibl. Jud. iii. 541.

Mordecai ben Jacob Ẓahalon: Physician and rabbi of Ferrara; died there Nov. 30, 1748. He wrote the following works: "Megillat Naharot," describing the miraculous rescue of the Jewish community of Ferrara from the inundation that occurred in 1707 (Venice, 1707); "She'elot we-Teshubot Meẓiẓ u-Meliẓ," a lecture delivered at the Talmud Torah of Ferrara on the modulation of the priestly blessing (*ib.* 1715); and halakic decisions quoted by Lampronti in the "Paḥad Yiẓḥaḳ," by Samson Morpurgo in his "Shemesh Ẓedaḳah" ("Yoreh De'ah," § 61), and by Raphael Meldola in his "Mayim Rabbim" ("Yoreh De'ah," § 7). Mordecai was a talented Hebrew poet, and several of his religious verses on local events are still recited in the synagogue of Ferrara, while one of his sonnets is also found at the head of the poem "'Eden 'Aruk."

BIBLIOGRAPHY: Nepi-Ghirondi, *Toledot Gedole Yisrael*, pp. 228, 235; Carmoly, *Histoire des Médecins*, p. 239; Steinschneider, *Cat. Bodl.* col. 1675.

Yom-Ṭob ben Akiba Ẓahalon: Talmudic scholar of Constantinople in the second half of the seventeenth century; grandson of Yom-Ṭob ben Moses. He was the author of "She'elot u-Teshubot," containing 296 responsa and novellæ on the fifth and sixth chapters of the treatise Baba Meẓi'a (Venice, 1694). This collection includes many decisions made by his grandfather, to whom the author ascribes also a commentary on the Abot de-Rabbi Natan which is probably identical with that given by Azulai under the title "Magen Abot."

BIBLIOGRAPHY: Conforte, *Ḳore ha-Dorot*, p. 42a; Azulai, *Shem ha-Gedolim*, i. 74; Steinschneider, *Cat. Bodl.* col. 1414; Fuenn, *Keneset Yisrael*, p. 444.
  J.   I. BR.

Yom-Ṭob ben Moses Ẓahalon: Palestinian Talmudist; rabbi at Safed; born in 1557; died about 1638. At the early age of twenty-five he was requested by Samuel Yafeh, a rabbi of Constantinople, to decide a difficult and complicated problem which had been referred to himself (Ẓahalon, Responsa, No. 40); and he corresponded with most of the authorities of his time, one of his chief antagonists being the elder Moses Galante. Although a Sephardi, Ẓahalon rendered a decision in favor of an Ashkenazic congregation in a controversy which arose between the Sephardim and Ashkenazim at Jerusalem, and in his love of truth he did not spare even his teacher, Joseph Caro (*ib.* No. 238), declaring that the Shulḥan 'Aruk was written for children and laymen (*ib.* No. 76). Ẓahalon was the author of a commentary on Esther, entitled "Leḳaḥ Ṭob" (Safed, 1577). He was the author of responsa and novellæ which were published with a preface by his grandson Yom-Ṭob (Venice, 1694), and he mentions also a second part (*ib.* No. 102), of which nothing more is known. He likewise wrote a commentary on the Abot de-Rabbi Natan, entitled "Magen Abot," which is still extant in manuscript. In his preface to this latter work Ẓahalon terms himself Yom-Ṭob b. Moses ha-Sefardi, whence it is clear that the family came originally from Spain, although it is not known when it emigrated or where Ẓahalon was born.

BIBLIOGRAPHY: De Rossi, *Dizionario*, s.v.; Nepi-Ghirondi, *Toledot Gedole Yisrael*, p. 206; Dukes, in *Orient, Lit.* ix. 346; Steinschneider, *Cat. Bodl.* col. 1414.
  E. C.   L. GRÜ.

ZAKKAI: 1. Palestinian tanna of the second century; contemporary of Judah ha-Nasi I. and apparently a pupil of Simeon b. Yoḥai. He is mentioned as having transmitted a halakah of R. Jacob and one of Simeon b. Yoḥai (Tosef., Yad. ii. 9; Shab. 79b); and he had a halakic controversy with Simeon b. Gamaliel and Simeon b. Eleazar, the former being the father and the latter the companion of Judah ha-Nasi (Ber. 25b). Zakkai was prominent in the Haggadah, where he is styled "Zakkai Rabbah" (Zakkai the Great). He interpreted the words "we-yidgu la-rob" (Gen. xlviii. 14) as referring to the haggadic statement that 600,000 children were once thrown into the river by command of Pharaoh, but were saved through the merits of Moses (Gen. R. xcvii. 5; comp. Cant. R. vii. 5; Yalḳ., Isa. 472). Zakkai attained to a very great age, and when his pupils asked him through what virtue he lived so long, he said that he never called his neighbor by a nickname and never neglected to buy wine for the Ḳiddush of the Sabbath. His aged mother even once sold her cap to purchase wine for him, and when she died she left him 300 kegs of wine, while he himself bequeathed to his children 3,000 kegs (Meg. 27b).

2. Babylonian amora of the third century. He emigrated to Palestine, where he was the chief lecturer in R. Johanan's school ('Er. 9a; Yeb. 77b; Sanh. 62a; and elsewhere). In Sanh. 62a and in Yer. Shab. vii. 2, R. Johanan calls him "the Babylonian." The press-house (מעצרתא) which he left in Babylon was the meeting-place of certain rabbis ('Er. 49a; B. B. 42b). From Palestine he sent a halakah to the exilarch Mar 'Uḳba (Ket. 87a), who transmitted a haggadah of Zakkai (Sanh. 70a). The latter seems to have been a good preacher; and in one of his sermons he gives an interpretation of Micah iv. 10 (Yer. Suk. 54c).

BIBLIOGRAPHY: Bacher, *Ag. Pal. Amor.* iii. 642–643; Heilprin, *Seder ha-Dorot*, ii.
  J.   M. SEL.

ZALINSKI, EDMUND LOUIS GRAY: American soldier and inventor; born at Kurnich, Prussian Poland, Dec. 13, 1849. In 1853 his parents emigrated to the United States and settled in Seneca Falls, N. Y. He was educated at the public school there and at the Syracuse high school. In 1864 he entered the army as a volunteer, was promoted second lieutenant, Second New York Heavy Artillery, for gallantry at the battle of Hatcher's Run, and served till the close of the war in 1865. Appointed second lieutenant, Fifth United States Artillery, in 1866, in the following year he was promoted first lieutenant. He was professor of military science at the Massachusetts Institute of Technology from 1872 to 1876. In 1880 he graduated from the United States Artillery School at Fort Monroe, Va., and from the School of Submarine Mining at Willets Point, N. Y. He became captain in 1887, and in 1889 and 1890 traveled in Europe to study military affairs. He did garrison duty at San Francisco in 1892, and retired from the service in 1894.

Zalinski invented the pneumatic dynamite torpedo-gun, an intrenching tool, a ramrod-bayonet, a telescopic sight for artillery, and a system of range-

and position-finding for seacoast and artillery firing. He died March 10, 1909.

BIBLIOGRAPHY: *Who's Who in America*, 1905; Kipling, *The Captive*, in *Traffics and Discoveries*, London, 1904.
A.   F. T. H.

ZALINSKI, MOSES G.: American soldier; born in New York city Jan. 23, 1863; educated in the public schools. He joined the regular army as a private in 1885, and was appointed second lieutenant, Second Artillery, in 1889. Graduating from the Artillery School in 1894, he became first lieutenant, Fourth Artillery, in 1895, and was transferred to the Second Artillery in the same year. In 1898 he was promoted captain and quartermaster; he was stationed at Washington, D. C., first as major-quartermaster, and later as colonel. He now lives in Atlanta, Ga.

BIBLIOGRAPHY: *American Jewish Year Book*, 5665, p. 2.
A.   F. T. H.

ZALMUNNA: Midianite king defeated and slain by Gideon (Judges viii. 5-7, 10, 12, 15, 18, 21; Ps. lxxxiii. 12 [A. V. 11]). Zalmunna is always mentioned together with Zebah, who was also a Midianite king.

E. G. H.   B. P.

ZAMENHOF, LAZARUS LUDWIG: Founder of the universal language "Esperanto"; born at Byelostok in Dec., 1859. His father, **Markus Zamenhof,** and his grandfather, Fabian Zamenhof, were teachers of French and German, the latter being the pioneer of general culture among the Jews of Byelostok. In 1873 Markus Zamenhof removed to Warsaw, where he became professor of German, first at the Veterinary Institute, and subsequently at the real-gymnasium. He was one of the three Jews of his time who held such an official appointment, and he became a state councilor. He compiled many text-books, and was the author of a rabbinical phrase-book in Hebrew (i., Warsaw, 1905) and a polyglot phrase-book (i., *ib.* 1905).

Zamenhof pursued general medical studies at Warsaw and Moscow (M.D. 1884), and settled in Warsaw as an oculist. He later practised at Kherson and Grodno, but in 1897 returned to Warsaw, where he practised among the poorer Jews in 1905.

Zamenhof's reputation is due to the fact that he was the founder of Esperanto, the new universal language which took the place of Volapük. The idea of an international form of speech was suggested to him by the polyglot character of his native town; four different languages were spoken there, and to this fact he attributed the constant dissensions and misunderstandings which disturbed the city. In the gymnasium and at the university he threw himself heart and soul into the study of languages while pursuing his medical work; but the idea of Esperanto did not dawn on him at once. At one time he entertained the idea of mathematical construction, and later the claim of the dead languages, especially Hebrew, appealed to him. For three years he worked at Yiddish and compiled a grammar which was still unpublished in 1905, hoping that, since Judæo-German was a modern tongue in use among millions of his coreligionists, it might be universalized. Discarding this idea in its turn, he

Esperanto.

finally reached the conclusion that no language could ever become a universal medium of communication if it identified itself with any individual nationality or country; it must be neutral. In 1878 he succeeded in building up such a language on the basis of the Romance and Teutonic roots of modern European tongues, but it was not until 1887 that, after several unsuccessful attempts to find a publisher, he gave to the world his first brochure, published anonymously under the pen-name of "Doktoro Esperanto" (Dr. Hopeful).

The success of his pamphlet was immediate, and from that time to the present Esperanto has steadily increased in popularity. In the following year the Volapük Society at Nuremberg ceased to exist, and its place was taken by the first Esperanto club. In 1891 a second club was founded at Upsala, in Sweden; St. Petersburg followed, with branches at Odessa and in Siberia; France and Denmark joined the movement in 1897; and Brussels and Stockholm were included in the following year. The first Esperantist group in Paris was started in 1900, and the next year Esperanto made its first official appearance on American soil in the city of Montreal. Since then associations for its study have been founded in all parts of the world.

Spread of the Movement.

There are now about 120 societies in existence, and the language is spoken by at least 200,000 persons. At the St. Louis Exposition it was accorded official recognition by the French sectional committee. There is a large and constantly increasing literature in Esperanto, and more than twenty journals are in circulation, including a braille monthly magazine for the blind, a Roman Catholic organ, a Socialist paper, and an "International Scientific Review." Two plays of Shakespeare, "Hamlet" and "The Tempest," have been rendered into Esperanto, the former by Zamenhof himself; and the language is also coming into commercial use.

In compiling his universal language Zamenhof appears to have regarded primarily the needs of his Yiddish-speaking coreligionists, whom he has described as "speechless, and therefore without hope of culture, scattered over the world, and hence unable to understand one another, obliged to take their culture from strange and hostile sources."

In other writings and labors, unconnected with Esperanto, Zamenhof has manifested great interest in Jewish affairs. At one time he was an ardent Zionist, and established at Warsaw the first Zionist association (Friends of Zion). More mature reflection, however, caused him to abandon the idea of a Jewish political nationality, and in 1901 he published a Russian pamphlet on Hillelism as a project for solving the Jewish question. The main contention of this work is that the troubles of the Jewish people are due to "the pseudo-Palestinian character of their religion"; Judaism should reform itself and become Hillelism, or, in other words, a pure monotheism with no other law than that of love of one's neighbor. The new Jewish sect should, however, retain its ancient manners and customs, but as traditions, not as laws. It should also acquire some simple medium of intercommunication, which must not be Hebrew; and it should obtain a geographical center, which would be the seat of a Jewish synod. He died in 1917.

BIBLIOGRAPHY: *Esperanto and Its Originator*, in *New Era Illustrated Magazine*, Jan., 1905.
J.　　　　　　　　　　　　　　　　　　　　　I. H.

ZAMOSZ, ABRAHAM BEN ISAAC HA-KOHEN: Polish rabbi and anti-Shabbethaian of the eighteenth century; rabbi of Tarly. He was very prominent in persecuting the Shabbethaians who had established themselves in Podolia, and on this subject he corresponded with Jacob Emden in 1759 and 1760. In the quarrel between Jacob Emden and Jonathan Eybeschütz, Zamosz, as is evident from his letters reproduced in Emden's "Shoṭ la-Sus," sided with Emden. Zamosz was the author of "Bet Abraham" (Berlin, 1753), a work containing two responsa followed by novellæ on the Talmud.

BIBLIOGRAPHY: Fuenn, *Keneset Yisrael*, p. 22.
J.　　　　　　　　　　　　　　　　　　　　M. SEL.

ZAMOSZ, ISRAEL BEN MOSES HA-LEVI: Polish Talmudist and mathematician; born at Buberki about 1700; died at Brody April 20, 1772. He was appointed one of the lecturers in the yeshibah of Zamosz, but at the same time he occupied himself with the study of secular sciences, particularly with mathematics, and while there wrote many notes on the "Yesod 'Olam" of Isaac Israeli and on the "Elim" of Joseph Delmedigo. During his residence at Zamosz he also wrote his "Arubbot ha-Shamayim" (still unpublished), a work on descriptive geometry, in which many haggadot relating to cosmogony are explained, with a vindication of their accuracy. About 1742, after he had published his "Neẓaḥ Yisrael," Zamosz went to Berlin, where he remained several years. There he instructed Moses Mendelssohn in mathematics and logic, and his scholarship was much appreciated by Lessing (see Levinsohn, "Zerubbabel," i. 68).

Zamosz was a versatile writer, his knowledge comprising rabbinics, religious philosophy, and secular sciences. The only works of his published during his lifetime were the "Neẓaḥ Yisrael" (Frankfort-on-the-Oder, 1741) and his edition of the "Ruaḥ Ḥen" of Ibn Tibbon or Jacob Anatolio, to which he appended a commentary of his own (Jessnitz, 1744). After his death appeared the "Nezer ha-Dema'" (Dyhernfurth, 1773), a work in poetical prose on man's desire for luxury; the "Oẓar Neḥmad" (Vienna, 1796), a commentary on the "Sefer ha-Kuzari" of Judah ha-Levi; and the "Ṭub ha-Lebanon" (*ib.* 1809), a commentary on the "Ḥobot ha-Lebabot" of Baḥya b. Joseph. Like the "Arubbot ha-Shamayim," his "Eben Yisrael," a collection of responsa, is still unpublished (comp. Levinsohn, "Te'uddah be-Yisrael," ch. xlv.).

BIBLIOGRAPHY: Carmoly, in *Revue Orientale*, ii. 333–334; D. Cassel, introduction to his edition of the *Cuzari*, p. xxxiii.; Fuenn, *Keneset Yisrael*, pp. 670 *et seq.*; Steinschneider, *Cat. Bodl.* col. 1169; Zunz, in Liebermann's *Deutsches Volkskalender*, 1853, p. 69.
J.　　　　　　　　　　　　　　　　　　　　M. SEL.

ZAMOSZ, JOSEPH BEN JACOB ISAAC: Polish rabbi of the eighteenth century; rabbi of Zamosz. He was the author of "Mishnat Ḥakamim" (Lemberg, 1792), an analytical work on the commandments, based on the ancient authorities and

showing which laws were derived from the Pentateuch ("mi-dibre Torah") and which were added by the scribes ("mi-dibre soferim"). It is divided into two parts: "Yabin Shemu'ah," explaining the words of the ancients; and "Ẓofnat Pa'neaḥ," casuistic novellæ. The work is followed by an appendix entitled "Ma'alot ha-Middot" and composed of notes on the "Sefer ha-Madda'" of Maimonides. In this book Zamosz mentions his "Otot le-Mo'adim," which contained the laws, expressed in the form of responsa, concerning the Sabbath and holy days.

BIBLIOGRAPHY: Benjacob, *Oẓar ha-Sefarim*, p. 385; Fuenn, *Keneset Yisrael*, p. 469; Steinschneider, *Cat. Bodl.* col. 1477.
J.　　　　　　　　　　　　　　　　　　　　M. SEL.

ZAMOSZ, ẒEBI HIRSCH BEN BENJAMIN: German rabbi; born in 1740; died at Altona in 1807. He was rabbi of several communities, including Brody and Glogau, and from 1803 until his death he held the rabbinate of the three communities of Altona, Hamburg, and Wandsbeck. He was the author of several works, which consist for the most part of responsa and of notes on the Bible, Talmud, and casuists ("posḳim"); but his only publication was a collection of his responsa on the Shulḥan 'Aruk, Oraḥ Ḥayyim and Yoreh De'ah, entitled "Tif'eret Ẓebi" (Lemberg, 1811). Some of his responsa are also included in Meshullam Zalman's "Bigde Kehunnah" and in Isaac Abraham's "Keter Kehunnah," No. 9.

BIBLIOGRAPHY: Fuenn, *Keneset Yisrael*, pp. 281–282; Steinschneider, *Cat. Bodl.* col. 2751.
J.　　　　　　　　　　　　　　　　　　　　M. SEL.

ZAMZAM: A sacred well in the mosque of Mecca; identified by Islamitic legend with the spring from which Hagar and Ishmael drank (Gen. xvi. 14; see Abraham ibn Ezra's commentary *ad loc.* and HAGAR IN ARABIC LITERATURE). Some Mohammedan Arabists explain the name as a reduplication of "zamm" (= "fill, fill"), since Hagar commanded Ishmael to fill the jar as soon as she saw the water. Sale (quoted by Hughes, "A Dictionary of Islam," *s.v.*) interpreted it similarly, but thought that its etymology was Egyptian and meant "stay, stay," since Hagar had bidden Ishmael to cease his wandering when she found the well. The spring is naturally regarded as miraculous, and the water, which is held in high esteem, is used for drinking and ablutions. It is exported to distant countries, and religious Moslems break their fasts with it; it is also applied to the eyes to brighten the sight, thus presenting a close analogy to the beverage of the Habdalah cup, with which many Jews moisten their eyes on the night of the Sabbath. The water of Zamzam is likewise thought to aid students in the pronunciation of Arabic in non-Arabic countries.

BIBLIOGRAPHY: Hughes, *Dictionary of Islam*, s.v.
S.　　　　　　　　　　　　　　　　　　　　M. SEL.

ZANGWILL, ISRAEL: English man of letters; born in London Feb. 14, 1864. When he was young his parents moved to Bristol, where he attended the Red Cross School; and after their return to London he entered the Jews' Free School, later becoming a teacher there and taking the degree of B.A. at London University. A misunderstanding with the directors of the school caused him to resign his position, and he then devoted himself to literature. He had already shown considerable taste in this direction, having edited and partly written as early as 1880 an annual called "Purim"; and shortly after leaving the Free School he published, under the pseudonym "J. Freeman Bell," an elaborate novel written in collaboration with Lewis Cowen and entitled "The Premier and the Painter"

Israel Zangwill.

(1888), a work somewhat in the style of Lord Beaconsfield, but with passages of Dickensian humor and with an entirely original plot. He had been appointed editor of "Ariel," and for a time was associated with a number of young literati like Jerome K. Jerome and Robert Barr, who represented what was known as the "new humor." This phase of his work was represented by his "Bachelors' Club," issued in 1891, and by "The Old Maids' Club," produced in the following year, each of these books being a series of fantastic sketches replete with the wit and humor of topsyturvydom.

Meanwhile Zangwill had been contributing to the "Jewish Standard" (edited by H. S. Lewis) a weekly causerie under the pseudonym "Marshalik," commenting with freakish humor on communal incidents. He gave evidence also of higher powers and touched

His Jewish Novels. a deeper note in two sketches, "Satan Mekatrig" and "The Diary of a Meshumad," contributed to M. H. Myers' "Diary" (1888–89) under the pseudonym "Baroness von S.," and afterward reprinted in his "Ghetto Tragedies." These and his other works (including a remarkable analysis of modern English Judaism in "J. Q. R." i.) drew to him the attention of the Jewish Publication Society of America, and it requested him to write a novel on modern Jewish life, which commission he executed in the well-known "Children of the Ghetto, Being Pictures of a Peculiar People" (Philadelphia and London, 1892), a work that at once made him famous. The author's profound knowledge of the life and problems of the ghetto, his command alike of pathos and of humor (especially in the first part of the book), his scintillating style, and the evidence of the application of a keenly logical intellect to the perplexities of modern Judaism place this book of Zangwill's at the head of artistic presentations of the ghetto. It attracted very general attention, and was translated into German, Russian, Hebrew (in part), and Yiddish. This work was followed by "The King of Schnorrers" (London, 1894), which also was translated into Yiddish, and by "The Dreamers of the Ghetto" (1898); the former work applying to the London ghetto life of the eighteenth century the bizarreries of the "new humor," the latter work dealing with a series of his-

toric scenes ranging from the times of Shabbethai Ẓebi and Spinoza to those of Lassalle and Disraeli. In "The Dreamers of the Ghetto" Zangwill is not altogether successful in reproducing the past, but he shows a keen insight into the characters of such men as Solomon Maimon, Heine, and Beaconsfield.

In general literature also Zangwill has achieved considerable success. His novels "The Master" (1895), dealing with art life, and "The Mantle of Elijah" (1901), treating of imperialism and the political problems connected therewith, have been widely read; and various shorter sketches, published by him in

In General Literature. volumes entitled "They That Walk in Darkness" (1899) and "Gray Wig" (1903), show remarkable versatility and brilliance. He contributed to "The Pall Mall Gazette" a series of critical causeries, part of which were republished under the title "Without Prejudice" (London, 1896); and these perhaps show Zangwill's powers in their most characteristic form. He has also published many poems and verses, including some striking translations from the medieval Jewish poets that are now being included in the authorized festival prayers of the English Jewish congregations. Most of these poems have been collected under the title "Blind Children" (London, 1903).

Zangwill has written several dramatic sketches which have been produced with more or less success, among them curtain-raisers like "Six Persons," "Three Penny Bits," "The Revolting Daughter," and "The Moment of Death," a striking and original melodramatic study produced at Wallack's Theater, New York, 1901. In addition he dramatized his "Children of the Ghetto," which was produced with success in the United States, where it ran for nearly a year. It was likewise produced at the Adelphi in London (1899); but the Boer war diverted public attention, and the play was withdrawn. Zangwill's dramatization of his Christmas story "Merely Mary Ann," written in 1893, was very well received both in England and in America (1904–5), and was followed by "Jinny the Carrier," in the United States (1905).

Zangwill has been a successful lecturer, traveling in that capacity in the United States (1898), through Great Britain, Ireland, and Holland, and to Jerusalem, which he visited in 1897. He has taken great

As Lecturer and Zionist. interest in Zionism, and has attended most of the congresses at Basel, at first merely as a critic and onlooker, but later being drawn into the movement, of which he has become one of the leading spirits. He has written and lectured much on the subject, advocating in the United States (1904) and elsewhere the acceptance of the British government's offer of an autonomous settlement in British East Africa. On the refusal of the Seventh Zionist Congress to consider any further offer of the kind, Zangwill formed a separate body, the **Jewish Territorial Organization**, intended to obtain, preferentially from the British government, an adequate tract of country in which persecuted Jews can live their own life under Jewish conditions. Among those whom he has attracted to his views is Lucien Wolf, with whom he had previously had a somewhat sharp controversy on Zionism in the "Jewish Quarterly Review."

Zangwill was one of the "Wandering Jews" who met at the house of Asher I. Myers, and was one of the founders of the Maccabæans.

BIBLIOGRAPHY: *Who's Who*, 1905; *New International Encyclopedia*; Brainin, in *Ha-Meliz*, 1897, p. 233; J. Lebowich, in *Menorah*, 1904, pp. 256-258; G. B. Burgin, in *The Critic*, New York, March, 1903; D. Philipson, *The Jew in English Fiction*, 2d ed., 1902.

J.

ZANGWILL, LOUIS: English novelist; born at Bristol, England, July 25, 1869; brother of Israel ZANGWILL. He was educated at Jews' Free School, and for a time acted as teacher there, but left together with his brother, and set up a printing establishment. Afterward, however, he turned to literature, and produced, under the pseudonym "Z. Z.," "A Drama in Dutch" (London, 1895), which attracted some attention for its local color. It was followed by "The World and a Man" (1896), "The Beautiful Miss Brook" (1897), and "Cleo the Magnificent" (1899), all distinguished by a certain realistic vividness and somewhat cynical humor. More recently he has produced a more sympathetic study, "One's Womenkind" (London, 1903).

Zangwill is a chess-player of high rank.

BIBLIOGRAPHY: *Who's Who*, 1905.

J.

ZANTE: Island in the Mediterranean Sea. According to an unpublished study by Leonidas Zoë, publisher of Zante, Jews did not settle there as a community until 1498; this statement is confirmed by the silence of Benjamin of Tudela. In that year, however, the republic of Venice offered special privileges to those who wished to reside in the island, which had become depopulated as a result of the frequent Turkish invasions; and many Jews of Corfu, Patras, Lepanto, and other parts of Greece welcomed the opportunity. The Jewish families mentioned in the earliest published documents are those of Abdela (1499) and Mila (1510). In 1527 the Jewish population of the island was 240, but by 1555 it had dwindled to 140, although it had risen to 300 in 1809. Although the Jewish names of Zante are Romance in type, the Jews have always spoken Greek; and their features, like those of their coreligionists of Chalcis, are so purely Hellenic that Carres asserts that they "are genuine Greeks."

At present the community of Zante has no spiritual head, and the people in their poverty are constantly emigrating, so that there are almost as many Zantiots in Corfu as in their native island. In both places the Zante Jews are usually tinsmiths. The Zante community possessed two synagogues, one Zantiot and the other Candiot, but the latter was destroyed by an earthquake some years ago. The Zantiot synagogue was built in the latter part of the seventeenth century by Cretan Jews who had sought refuge in Zante from a revolution. Abraham Coen (b. 1670; d. 1729) is the only well-known rabbinical author of the island. He was a Cretan by ancestry, but was born in Zante, and graduated as a physician at the University of Padua. In 1700 he published his "Derashot 'al ha-Torah," which was followed by his "Kehunnat Abraham," a paraphrase of the Psalms in various meters (Venice, 1719). In 1879

M. Ventura of Corfu found a Hebrew poem by Coen inscribed on the wall of the Candiot synagogue, and later edited his discovery.

During the period of Venetian dominion the Jews of Zante were subjected to the same restrictions as were their coreligionists throughout the republic, being obliged to wear the BADGE, and losing all rights of citizenship, while they were forced to bear all civic burdens and to live in a ghetto. English control (1815-64) improved their status greatly, but they were still forbidden to become citizens, and the gates of the ghetto were not torn down until 1862. In 1864, however, when the island was annexed to Greece, the Jews of Zante were granted all civil and political rights.

In connection with the riots of CORFU in 1891, serious excesses were committed against the Jews of Zante on May 1 of that year, during an ecclesiastical procession. The blood accusation of Corfu had excited the population to such an extent that many Jews left the island. Archbishop Latas of Zante took occasion at the Parliament of Religions in Chicago, Sept. 23, 1893, to make a declaration against this calumny, and he even appealed to the congress to give his protest its official sanction.

D.   M. C.

ZANTE, ABRAHAM. See ABRAHAM BEN SHABBETHAI COHEN OF ZANTE.

ZAPATEIRO, JOSEPH. See ÇAPATEIRO, JOSEPH.

ZAPHNATH-PAANEAH: Name given by Pharaoh to Joseph (Gen. xli. 45). It seems to be an Egyptian name, but its etymology is in doubt. It is not plain on what (Hebrew ?) etymology the earliest explanations of Hebrew scholars were founded. Targum Onḳelos gives the meaning of the name as "the man to whom mysteries are revealed"; pseudo-Jonathan, "one who reveals mysteries"; Josephus ("Ant." ii. 6, § 1), "a finder of mysteries." Many other old writers offer similar definitions, and even the A. V. has in the margin: "Which in the Coptic signifies, 'A revealer of secrets,' or 'The man to whom secrets are revealed.'" There is, however, no Egyptian etymology by which these guesses can be supported. Jerome claims that his suggestion, "savior of the world," rests on the Egyptian, and possibly the reading of the Septuagint has been followed by the authors of this etymology; the Coptic "eneh" = Egyptian "nḥ" (= "eternity," "eternal"), seems to be discernible, to which erroneously the later meaning of the Hebrew "'olam" ("eternity," "age"; later, "world") has been given, overlooking the "'ayin." Thus this inadmissible interpretation, which is accepted even by Jablonski, clearly betrays rabbinical influence.

Modern Egyptologists have tried a great many untenable etymologies for the element "Zaphnath," but have mostly agreed that "paaneah" contains the Egyptian "p-'ônḥ," meaning "the life" (thus first Lepsius, "Chronologie," i. 382). Steindorff's explanation (in "Zeitschrift für Aegyptische Sprache," xxvii. 42; modifying Krall's etymology in "Trans. 7th Orientalist. Congr." p. 110) differs somewhat; it is "ṣe(d)-p-nute(r)-ef-onḥ" = "the god speaks, [and] he lives." This has become popular, and is philologically possible; however, it does not convey the allusion to Joseph's office or merits which we should expect. "P-'ônḥ" (= "the life") would still answer better in this respect; only "Zaphnath" does not admit a quite convincing explanation. The Septuagint (Ψον[or Ψομ]θομφανήχ) and the Hexaplaric versions, however, differ so widely from the Hebrew in the first half of the name that it may have been disfigured by copyists.

BIBLIOGRAPHY: Marquardt, *Philologus*, vii. 676; Cheyne and Black, *Encyc. Bibl.* col. 5379 (where a disfigured Hebrew original is suspected); *Zeitschrift für Aegyptische Sprache*, 1883, p. 59; *Proc. Soc. Bibl. Arch.* xx. 208 (where the other theories have been collected).

E. G. H. W. M. M.

ZAPPERT, BRUNO: Austrian dramatist and journalist; born in Vienna Jan. 28, 1845; died there Jan. 31, 1892. The Zappert family, many members of which have gained prominence as merchants, originally settled in Bohemia, and spread thence to Hungary and lower Austria. Bruno, who was the son of August Zappert, a manufacturer, received his early education at the gymnasium; and, though desiring a university training, he entered the Vienna commercial academy in 1862 with a view to fitting himself to continue the business of his father. The latter's untimely death, however, caused him to change his plans, and he engaged in the publishing business in Vienna, beginning with Wallishauser, and in 1869 assuming the sole management of Hügel's house, which he conducted till 1877. He then took up dramatic literature, becoming secretary and artistic director of the Presburg theater, and later dramatist of the Carltheater in Vienna, where he worked for two years under Director Steiner, and for three years under Tatarczy.

Zappert edited the "Wiener Leben" (from 1879), Langer's "Hans Jörgel" (1885-86), and the illustrated "Wiener Wespen" (1886-87); and he collaborated on other Vienna journals as feuilletonist. He also frequently collaborated for the theater, working with Robert Genée, Costa, Jul. Rosen, Mannstädt, Oeribaner, and others; and he wrote many comic and topical songs for the stage, as well as celebration plays and prologues.

His principal plays were: "Zwischen Zwei Uebeln," musical farce in one act, with music by Franz Roth (1870; acted and published under the pseudonym "Zeno Brunner"); "Die Czarin," operetta in three acts, with music by Max Wolf (1872); "Ein Hochgeborener," popular piece in three acts, with music by H. Delin (1877); "Ein Junger Drahrer," musical farce in three acts, with music by Paul Mestrozi (1878); "Rinicherl," parody in one act, with music by Gothov-Grüneke (1878); "Cri-cri," musical picture from life in one act (1879); "Die Glöckerln am Kornfeld," parody on Robert Planquette's "Les Cloches de Corneville," with music by Gothov-Grüneke (1879); "Eine Parforcejagd Durch Europa," extravaganza in three tableaux, with music by Jul. Hopp (1879); "Ein Böhm in Amerika," musical burlesque in six tableaux, with music by Gothov-Grüneke (1880); "Moderne Weiber," musical farce in three tableaux, with music by Gothov-Grüneke (1880); "Pressburger Luft," musical local farce in five tableaux (1882); "Der Para-

graphenritter," musical farce in four acts (1883; published as "Doctor Schimmel"); "Pamperl's Abenteuer," musical farce in three acts (1883); "Theaterblut," musical farce in three acts (1883); "Papa Palugyay," farce in one act (1884); Reschfesch," musical farce in one act (1884); "Sein Spezi," musical farce in five acts, with music by Franz Roth (1884); "Beim Sacher," musical farce in one act, with music by Paul Mestrozi (1887); (with Genée and Mannstädt) "Der Glücksritter," operetta in three acts, with music by Alf. Czibulka (1887); (with Genée) "Der Freibeuter," operetta in three acts from the French, with music by Planquette (1888); (with Genée) "Ein Deutschmeister," operetta in three acts, with music by C. M. Ziehrer (1888-89); "Johann Nestroy," musical popular piece in six tableaux (1888); (with Genée) "Die Jagd nach dem Glücke," operetta in three acts and an introduction, with music by Franz von Suppé (1888; printed as a text-book and translated into five languages); "Das Lachende Wien," farce in six tableaux, with introduction; (with Genée) "Die Herzogin von Newfoundland," operetta in three acts, with music by Ludwig Engländer; (with Genée) "Prinz Eugen," operetta in three acts, with music by I. R. Kral; "Im Flug um die Welt," fairy extravaganza (1891); etc.

BIBLIOGRAPHY: Eisenberg, *Das Geistige Wien*, i. 657; Wurzbach, *Biographisches Lexikon*, vol. 59; *Allg. Zeit. des Jud.* Nov. 2, 1888, No. 305, p. 4493.

S. N. D.

ZAPPERT, GEORGE: Hungarian historian and archeologist; born in Alt-Ofen Dec. 7, 1806; died in Vienna Nov. 23, 1859. The son of well-to-do parents, Zappert was educated at the Pesth gymnasium and at the University of Vienna. He began the study of medicine, but relinquished it after renouncing Judaism for Roman Catholicism in 1829, then taking up theology. This too he was forced to abandon in the second year, owing to deafness caused by a severe illness; and after this disappointment, which he felt keenly, he devoted himself to what became his life-work, namely, the study of the Middle Ages. He led a retired life in Vienna; and it is noteworthy that he foretold the time of his death to the minute three days before it occurred, and that there have been in his family several cases of similar premonition. The Imperial Academy of Sciences elected him corresponding member on July 28, 1851.

Zappert published: "Gravure en Bois du XII. Siècle" (Vienna, 1837 *et seq.*); "Vita B. Petri Acotanti" (*ib.* 1839); and the following memoirs: "Ueber Antiquitätenfunde im Mittelalter" (in "Sitzungsberichte der Kaiserlichen Akademie der Wissenschaften," Nov., 1850); "Epiphania, ein Beitrag zur Christlichen Kunstarchäologie" (*ib.* xxi. 291-372); "Ueber Badewesen in Mittelalterlicher und Späterer Zeit" (in "Archiv für Kunde Oesterreichischer Geschichtsquellen," xxi. 5); "Ueber Sogenannte Verbrüderungsbücher in Nekrologien im Mittelalter" (in "Sitzungsberichte der Kaiserlichen Akademie der Wissenschaften," x. 417-463, xi. 5-183); "Ueber ein für den Jugendunterricht des Kaisers Max I. Abgefasstes Lateinisches Gesprächsbüchlein" (*ib.* xxviii. 193-280); etc.

BIBLIOGRAPHY: Wurzbach, *Biographisches Lexikon*, vol. 59;
Larousse, *Dict.*; *Acte der Kaiserlichen Akademie* (auto-
biog.); *Wiener Zeitschrift*, 1859, No. 299; *Fremden-Blatt*
(Vienna), 1867, No. 110.
S.   N. D.

ZAPPERT, ISRAEL L. : Austrian philanthropist; elder brother of George and grandfather of
Bruno Zappert; born at Prague in 1795; died there
in 1865. He was a grandson of **Wolf Zappert**, who
was the founder of the family, and who was twice
court jeweler, the second time to Emperor Joseph II.
(1765–90). Wolf, who was distinguished for both
uprightness and business ability, made two fortunes,
the first of which he expended to secure the revocation of an order expelling the Jews from Trebitsch;
and when his coreligionists were driven out of
Prague he alone was allowed to remain. In his will
he founded twenty-two charitable institutions endowed with considerable funds, which were administered by his son and, after him, by his grandson,
the subject of this article. I. L. Zappert was also a
director of many Jewish benevolent institutions in
Prague, and himself founded several more, among
them one for providing poor girls with dowries and
trousseaux, and another for the care of the sick.

BIBLIOGRAPHY: Wurzbach, *Biographisches Lexikon*, vol. 59.
S.   N. D.

ZARA'AT. See LEPROSY.

ZARFÁTI, ZAREFATI ("French"): Epithet
frequently applied in rabbinical literature to Jews
of French birth or descent. Among those so called
may be mentioned: **Meïr Zarfati**, whom Carmoly
sought to identify with the Meïr ha-Kohen of Narbonne who emigrated to Toledo, dying there in
1263 ("Ha-Karmel," vii. 58); **Abraham Zarfati**,
author of the "Tamid ha-Shaḥar," copied by Abraham of Chinon about 1370; Perez טרבוט, called
הצרפתי קטלאנו, which probably indicates that he
emigrated from his native country, France, to Catalonia; the physician **Jacob b. Solomon Zarfati**;
and the mathematician **Joseph b. Moses Zarfati**.
By far the most important Zarfati family, however,
was that of TRABOT (Trabotti), which seems to
have originated in Trévoux in the department of the
Ain, and to have settled in Italy in the second half
of the fifteenth century.

BIBLIOGRAPHY: Azulai, *Shem ha-Gedolim*, ed. Leghorn, pp.
8a, 20b, 41a; Berliner's *Magazin*, ii. 16, 96; Conforte, *Ḳore
ha-Dorot*, p. 39b *et passim*; Gross, *Gallia Judaica*, pp. 220–
222, 538, 576; Renan-Neubauer, *Les Ecrivains Juifs Français*, pp. 710, 801; *R. E. J.* iv. 114, 208; Steinschneider, *Cat.
Bodl.* col. 2052; Zunz, *Z. G.* p. 166.
E. C.   S. K.

Jacob ben Solomon Zarfati : Physician who
lived, probably at Avignon, in the second half of
the fourteenth century. He was a native of northern France, and is believed to have settled at Avignon after the banishment of the Jews. He was the
author of a work entitled "Mishkenot Ya'aḳob,"
which is still extant in manuscript (Bibliothèque
Nationale, Paris, MS. No. 137). This work is divided into three books, which bear separate titles, as
follows: (1) "Bet Ya'aḳob," containing allegorical
interpretations of certain passages of the Pentateuch; (2) "Yeshu'ot Ya'aḳob," a treatise on the
ten plagues of Egypt; (3) "Ḳehillat Ya'aḳob," a
theological treatise on the laws, other than the Ten
Commandments, which are believed to have been
given on Mount Sinai. An appendix, entitled "Ebel
Rabbati," contains an account of the deaths of three
children whom Zarfati lost in the space of three
months during the plague of 1395. He was also the
author of a treatise on the headache called in medical works "vertigine" (Neubauer, "Cat. Bodl." No.
2583, 2).

BIBLIOGRAPHY: Renan-Neubauer, *Les Ecrivains Juifs Français*, pp. 364 *et seq.*
E. C.   I. Br.

Joseph ben Samuel Zarfati (called by Christian
writers **Josiphon, Giosifante, Giuseppo Gallo**) :
Italian physician; lived at Rome in the fifteenth and
sixteenth centuries. He acquired early in life a great
reputation in his profession; and the privileges that
had been granted (1504) to his father by Pope Julius II. were extended to him. These were renewed
in 1524 by Leo X., who expressed himself toward the
Jewish physician in the most flattering terms. He
was the more willing, said he in his patent, to grant
these privileges as Joseph was no less magnanimous
and no less skilful in his profession than was his
father.

Joseph was well versed in Hebrew, Aramaic, and
Arabic, and was an accomplished Latinist and Hel-
lenist; he possessed also a wide knowledge of mathematics and philosophy. He was the teacher of
Teseo Ambrogio, subsequently professor of Oriental
languages at the University of Bologna. In the latter part of his life Joseph met with many misfortunes.
An unfaithful servant fled to Constantinople with all
his savings. Joseph pursued him thither, but was
accused by the thief as a spy of the pope, and had
to seek safety in flight. During the siege of Rome
in 1527 Joseph was attacked by four robbers. He
succeeded in escaping; but while endeavoring to
reach Vicovaro he was stricken with the plague. Refused entrance to the city, he died without assistance
in the open field.

BIBLIOGRAPHY: Perio Valeriano, *De Litteratorum Infelici-
tate Libri Duo*, pp. 19 *et seq.*, Venice, 1620; Vogelstein and
Rieger, *Geschichte der Juden in Rom*, ii. 85 and Index.
G.   I. Br.

Samuel Zarfati. See JEW. ENCYC. xi. 31b.

ZARFATI : Oriental Jewish family, traced by
the bibliographer Azulai to a line of French rabbis
descended from Rashi through his grandson Rabbenu
Tam.

Elijah Zarfati : Moroccan Talmudist; chief
rabbi of Fez about 1770; grandson of Samuel Zarfati.

Joseph Zarfati : Turkish rabbinical scholar;
lived at Adrianople in the early part of the seventeenth century. He was the author of a collection
of sermons entitled "Yad Yosef" (1617).

Samuel Zarfati : Chief rabbi of Fez in the eighteenth century; died 1713; grandson of Vidal Zarfati
II. He wrote a work entitled "Nimmuke Shemu'el,"
in which he defended the opinions of Maimonides.

Vidal Zarfati I. : Moroccan Talmudist; lived
at Fez in the sixteenth century. He is the earliest
known member of the family.

Vidal Zarfati II. : Chief rabbi of Fez; grandson of Vidal Zarfati I.; lived about 1660. He was
the author of "Ẓuf Debash," a commentary on the
Talmud.

Ẓemaḥ Ẓarfati: Talmudic author and chief rabbi of Tunis in the early part of the eighteenth century; remarkable for the number of his pupils. In the latter part of his life he dwelt for several years at Damascus; but his last days were passed at Jerusalem. Some of his manuscript notes were published in the latter part of the eighteenth century by Joseph Cohen Tanugi in his "Bene Yosef."

BIBLIOGRAPHY: Azulai, Shem ha-Gedolim, s.v.
D.　　　　　　　　　　　　　　　　　　M. FR.

ZARIFA: Name of a goddess mentioned in a single passage of the Talmud ('Ab. Zarah 12a) as having been worshiped at Ashkelon. Kohut, Levy, and other Jewish lexicographers identify her with Serapis; but the Hebrew spelling would seem to imply that the deity was the goddess Sarapia or Serapia, another name of Isis Pharia, whose festival was celebrated in April (Preller, "Römische Mythologie," 3d ed., ii. 382, Berlin, 1883). It is possible, however, since Ẓarifa is mentioned in connection with Ashkelon, that she is to be identified with Derceto, who was worshiped in that city (Diodorus Siculus, i. 4; Ovid, "Metamorphoses," iv. 3), the term "ẓarifa" (= "composite") being especially fitting for a goddess represented with a human head and the body of a fish. Joseph Halévy, on the other hand, suggests ("Revue Sémitique," vi. 177) that Ẓarifa represents the Babylonian divinity Zarpanit, wife of Marduk. For a variant view see ASHKELON.

BIBLIOGRAPHY: Krauss, Lehnwörter, ii., s.v.; Neubauer, G. T. p. 69.
S.　　　　　　　　　　　　　　　　　　M. SEL.

ZARKA. See ACCENTS IN HEBREW.

ZARKO, JUDAH BEN ABRAHAM: Hebrew poet distinguished for the elegance of his style; flourished at Rhodes in the sixteenth century. During a residence at Constantinople he wrote his "Leḥem Yehudah" (Constantinople, 1560), which contains an allegory on the soul, metrical and nonmetrical poems, and epigrams directed against various celebrities, including Maimonides and Judah Sabara. A letter written by him to congratulate Joseph Hamon on his marriage is given at the beginning of the anonymous Hebrew style-book "Yefeh Nof," and some of his shorter poems have been published by Edelmann in his "Dibre Ḥefez" (London, 1853).

BIBLIOGRAPHY: Steinschneider, Cat. Bodl. cols. 1371 et seq.; Grätz, Gesch. ix. 395; Fuenn, Keneset Yisrael, p. 395.
J.　　　　　　　　　　　　　　　　　　I. BR.

ZARZA, SAMUEL IBN SENEH: Spanish philosopher; lived at Valencia in the second half of the fourteenth century. According to Zunz, his surname is derived from the Spanish town Zarza (= "thorn-bush"), and is accordingly synonymous with the Hebrew "seneh." Of his life no details are known; for while in his notes on the "Sefer ha-Yuḥasin" (ed. Filipowski, p. 226) Samuel Shalom states that Zarza was burned at the stake by the tribunal of Valencia on the denunciation of Isaac CAMPANTON, who accused him of denying the creation of the world, historians have proved this assertion a mere legend. Although a comparatively unimportant writer, if his two works may serve as a criterion, Zarza ranked high in the estimation of his contemporaries, so that the poet Solomon Reubeni

of Barcelona and the astronomer Isaac ibn Al-Ḥadib composed poems in his honor.

Zarza was the author of the "Meḳor Ḥayyim," a philosophical commentary on the Pentateuch (Mantua, 1559); and of the "Miklol Yofi," a philosophical commentary devoted to the haggadot found in both Talmudim and divided into 151 chapters and seven parts (Neubauer, "Cat. Bodl. Hebr. MSS." No. 1296). In the introduction to the latter work Zarza draws a melancholy picture of the state of the Jews of Castile in his time, stating that in Toledo alone 10,000 perished in the course of the war between Don Pedro and his brother Henry. In his "Meḳor Ḥayyim," Zarza mentions four other writings of his which are no longer in existence: "Ṭaharat ha-Ḳodesh," on the principles of religion; "'Ezem ha-Dat"; "Ẓeror ha-Mor"; and "Magen Abraham."

BIBLIOGRAPHY: Steinschneider, Cat. Bodl. cols. 2496-98; Grätz, Gesch. 3d ed., viii. 16, 23, 25-26.
K.　　　　　　　　　　　　　　　　　　I. BR.

ZARZAL, ABRAHAM IBN (called Zarzar by Arabic chroniclers): Spanish physician and astronomer; flourished in the first half of the fourteenth century at the court of the Nasserites in Granada, where a certain Pharez ben Abraham ibn Zarzal, who may have been his father, was physician in ordinary ("Monatsschrift," xxxiii. 479; Steinschneider, "Hebr. Uebers." p. 272); died after 1369. Fearing that he might become involved in the murder of the minister Reduan, he retired to Castile, where his medical and astrological fame, as well as the recommendation of Mohammed IV. of Granada, who was in friendly relations with the King of Castile, won him the appointment of astrologer and physician in ordinary to Pedro the Cruel. Abraham, who gained the favor of the king and was constantly near him, took every opportunity of smoothing over the difficulties between Castile and Granada. It is said that he, like other astrologers, prophesied to Pedro that the horoscope of his nativity destined him to become the mightiest king of Castile, to conquer the Moors everywhere, and to capture Jerusalem. At Seville, a few weeks before his death, Pedro summoned Zarzal and said: "Abraham, why have the events of my life been opposite to all that you and other astrologers have prophesied to me? I bid you tell me the entire truth of all that I ask, concealing nothing." Abraham replied: "Your Majesty, if I tell the whole truth, may I be certain that you will not be offended thereby?" Having been reassured on this point, he continued: "Will one perspire who takes a very hot bath on a very cold day in January?" "Certainly," replied the king. "Such a result would be contrary to the governing constellation," said Abraham; "and it is the same with the horoscope of your nativity: your sins and your government have brought about the direct opposite."

Abraham was actively interested in the religious and philosophic movements of the time; and he endeavored to gain recognition for Judaism.

BIBLIOGRAPHY: Juan Rodriguez de Cuenca, Sumario de los Reyes de España, p. 75, Madrid, 1781; Rios, Hist. ii. 232 et seq., 255 et seq.; Grätz, Gesch. 3d ed., vii. 356; Gedaliah ibn Yaḥya, Shalshelet ha-Kabbalah, 83b (ed. Amsterdam); Jeschurun, ed. Kobak, vi. 201 et seq.; Monatsschrift, xxxiii. 477 et seq.
S.　　　　　　　　　　　　　　　　　　M. K.

ZARZAL, MOSES IBN : Spanish physician and poet; physician in ordinary to Henry III. of Castile; flourished in the latter half of the fourteenth and the first part of the fifteenth century; son of Abraham ibn Zarzal. On March 6, 1405, he was at Toro, where he celebrated the birth of John II. in a poem which is given in the "Cancionero de Baena" (p. 222); and in 1389, 1400, and 1409 he resided in the Calle de Rehoyo at Segovia. The date of his death can not be determined; the epitaph found at Carmona stating that he died in 1432 is a forgery.

BIBLIOGRAPHY : Juan Rodriguez de Cuenca, *Sumario de los Reyes de España*, p. 75, Madrid, 1781 ; Kayserling, *Sephardim*, pp. 53 *et seq.*, 333 ; Grätz, *Gesch.* viii. 47 ; Rios, *Estudios*, p. 419 ; idem, *Hist.* ii. 423 ; Kayserling, *Bibl. Esp.-Port.-Jud.* p. 111 ; Fidel Fita, *Historia Hebrea*, i. 213 *et seq.*; *Boletin Acad. Hist.* ix. 316, 349 ; xvii. 172 *et seq.*

s. M. K.

ZAUSMER, JACOB DAVID BEN ISAAC : Polish Masorite of the sixteenth and seventeenth centuries; rabbi of Zausmer, near Cracow; died before 1644. He was the author of the "Perush ha-Massorah" and of the "Ṭa'ame ha-Massorah" (Lublin, 1616); the former work elucidating Masoretic problems and forming a supplement to the "Sha'ar Shibre Luḥot" of Elijah Levita's "Massoret ha-Massoret," while the "Ṭa'ame ha-Massorah" was a commentary on the Masorah. A revised and augmented edition was published by his son **Judah Isaac Darshan** (*ib.* 1644), who speaks of his father as having died.

BIBLIOGRAPHY : Fuenn, *Keneset Yisrael*, p. 570 ; Fürst, *Bibl. Jud.* iii. 545 ; Steinschneider, *Cat. Bodl.* cols. 1266–68.

J. M. SEL.

ZAUSMER, JACOB BEN SAMUEL : Polish rabbi and preacher; flourished at Zausmer in the seventeenth century. He was the author of the "Bet Ya'aḳob" (Dyhernfurth, 1696), a work containing 174 responsa. In the preface he says that he wrote also "Toledot Ya'aḳob," homilies on the Pentateuch arranged in the order of the parashiyyot.

BIBLIOGRAPHY : Fuenn, *Keneset Yisrael*, p. 570 ; Fürst, *Bibl. Jud.* iii. 545 ; Steinschneider, *Cat. Bodl.* col. 1268.

J. M. SEL.

ZAYIN (ז) : Seventh letter of the Hebrew alphabet. The meaning of the name is uncertain. In sound the letter is a sonant sibilant, its phonetic value corresponding to the English "z." It interchanges with the surd sibilant ("s"), and occurs only as a radical, never as a formative element. In the later period it has the numerical value 7.

T. I. BR.

ZBARAZER. See EHRENKRANZ, BENJAMIN WOLF.

ZBITKOVER, SAMUEL. See WARSAW.

ZEALOTS (Hebrew, **Ḳanna'im**) : Zealous defenders of the Law and of the national life of the Jewish people; name of a party opposing with relentless rigor any attempt to bring Judea under the dominion of idolatrous Rome, and especially of the aggressive and fanatical war party from the time of Herod until the fall of Jerusalem and Masada. The members of this party bore also the name SICARII, from their custom of going about with daggers ("sicæ") hidden beneath their cloaks, with which they would stab any one found committing a sacrilegious act or anything provoking anti-Jewish feeling.

Following Josephus ("B. J." ii. 8, § 1; "Ant." xviii. 1, §§ 1, 6), most writers consider that the Zealots were a so-called fourth party founded by Judas the Galilean (see Grätz, "Gesch." iii. 252, 259; Schürer, "Gesch." 1st ed., i. 3, 486).

Origin and Meaning of the Name. This view is contradicted, however, by the fact that Hezekiah, the father of Judas the Galilean, had an organized band of so-called "robbers" which made war against the Idumean Herod ("B. J." i. 10, § 5; "Ant." xiv. 9, § 2), and also by the fact that the system of organized assassination practised by the Zealots was in existence during the reign of Herod, if not long before (see below). The name "Ḳanna'im" (קנאים; not "Kenaim" as given in Herzog-Hauck, "Real-Encyc." 1886, *s.v.* "Zeloten") occurs twice in the Talmud: in Sanh. ix. 11 and in Ab. R. N. vi. (where the other version has סקרין ["Sicarii"]; see Schechter's edition, pp. 31 and 32). The former passage contains a statute, evidently of the Maccabean time, declaring that "Whosoever steals the libation cup [Num. iv. 7] or curses one with the aid of the Holy Name [Lev. xxiv. 16, Sifra] or has sexual intercourse with a Syrian [heathen] woman shall be felled by the Ḳanna'im or Zealots." This is explained in the Talmud (Sanh. 82a, b; Yer. Sanh. ix. 27b) to mean that, while the acts mentioned are not causes for criminal procedure, they fall into the same category as did the crime of Zimri the son of Salu, whom Phinehas, because "he was zealous for his God," slew flagrante delicto (Num. xxv. 11–14). Phinehas is set up as a pattern, being called "Ḳanna'i ben Ḳanna'i" (a Zealot, the son of a Zealot), inasmuch as he followed the example of Levi, the son of Jacob, who avenged the crime perpetrated upon Dinah by killing the men of Shechem (Sifre, Num. 131; Sanh. 82b; comp. Book of Jubilees, xxx. 18, 23, where Levi is said to have been chosen for the priesthood because he was zealous in executing vengeance upon the enemies of Israel, and Judith ix. 2–4, where Simeon as ancestor of Judith is praised for his zealous act).

This unfailing "zeal for the Law" became the standard of piety in the days of the Maccabean struggle against the Hellenizers. Thus it is asserted that when Mattathias slew the Jew whom he saw sacrificing to an idol, "he dealt zealously for the law of God, as did Phinehas unto Zimri the son of Salu"; and Mattathias' claim of descent from Phinehas implies that, like the latter, he obtained for his house the covenant of an everlasting priesthood (I Macc. ii. 24, 26, 54). Mattathias' call, "Whosoever is zealous of the Law, and maintaineth the covenant, let him follow me" (*ib.* verse 27; comp. verses 43–45), whether authentic or not, is practically a recognition of a league of Ḳanna'im or Zealots, no matter when or by whom the First Book of Maccabees was written. Similarly Elijah

Phinehas the Model Zealot. also is lauded for his zeal for the Law (*ib.* verse 58; comp. I Kings xix. 10, 14; Ecclus. [Sirach] xlviii. 2); and later haggadists declared Phinehas and Elijah to have been the same person (Targ. Yer. to Ex. vi. 18; Pirḳe R. El. xxix., xlvii.). That Phinehas was regarded during the Maccabean reign as the type of true (priestly) piety, in contradistinction to the Hellenizing Sadducees typified by Zimri, may be learned from the warning said to have been addressed by King Jannæus on his deathbed to his wife: "Fear not the Pharisees nor the Sadducees [non-Pharisees], but the hypocrites who conduct themselves like Zimri and expect the reward of Phinehas" (Soṭah 22b).

Originally the name "Ḳanna'im" or "Zealots" signified religious fanatics; and as the Talmudic traditions ascribe the rigorous laws concerning marriage with a non-Jewess (Sanh. 82a) to the Hasidæan bet din of the Hasmoneans, so probably to the Zealots of the Maccabean time are due the rabbinical laws governing the relations of Jews to idolaters, as well as those concerning idols, such as the prohibition of all kinds of images (Mek., Yitro, 6) and even the mere looking upon them, or of the use of the shadow of an idol (Tosef., Shab. xvii.; 'Ab. Zarah iii. 8), or of the imitation of heathen (Amorite) customs (Shab. vi. 10; Tosef., Shab. vi.). The divine attribute "El ḳanna" (= "a jealous God"; Ex. xx. 5; Mek., Yitro, l.c.) is significantly explained as denoting that, while God is merciful and forgiving in regard to every other transgression, He exacts vengeance in the case of idolatry: "As long as there is idolatry in the world, there is divine wrath" (Sifre, Deut. 96; Sanh. x. 6; comp. I Macc. iii. 8).

Regarding the original Zealots or Ḳanna'im, the source from which Josephus derived his description of the Essenes, and which has been preserved in more complete form in Hippolytus, "Origenis Philosophumena sive Omnium Hæresium Refutatio," ix. 26 (ed. Dunker, 1859, p. 482; comp. JEW. ENCYC. v. 228–230), has the following:

"Some of these [Essenes] observe a still more rigid practise in not handling or looking at a coin bearing an image, saying that one should neither carry nor look at nor fashion any image; nor will they enter a city at the gate of which statues are erected, since they consider it unlawful to walk under an image [comp. Sifra, Ḳedoshim, i.; Shab. 149a; Yer. 'Ab. Zarah iii. 42b–43b]. Others threaten to slay any uncircumcised Gentile who listens to a discourse on God and His laws, unless he undergoes the rite of circumcision [comp. Sanh. 59a; Sifre, Deut. 345]; should he refuse to do so, they kill him instantly. From this practise they have received the name of 'Zealots' or 'Sicarii.' Others again call no one Lord except God, even though one should torture or kill them."

It is only this last point which Josephus singles out as the doctrine of the Zealots of his day ("B. J." ii. 8, § 1; "Ant." xviii. 1, §§ 1–6) in order to give them the character of political extremists; the rest he omits. But even here he misstates the facts. The principle that God alone is King is essentially a religious one. It found expression in the older liturgy (comp. "Beside Thee we have no King," in "Emet we-Yaẓẓib"; "Rule Thou alone over us," in the eleventh benediction of the "Shemoneh 'Esreh"; "And be Thou alone King over us," in "U-Beken Ten Paḥdeka"; "We have no King besides Thee," in "Abinu Malkenu" and in "Yir'u 'Enenu"). Expressed in I Sam. viii. 7, and deemed by the Rabbis to be expressed also in Num. xxiii. 21 and Deut. xxxiii. 5 (see Targ. to Sifre, Deut. 346; Musaf of Rosh ha-Shanah; comp. also III Sibyllines, ii.; III Macc. ii. 4), it was to be pronounced in the "Shema'" twice a day (Ber. ii. 1; Friedmann in his edition of

Sifre, p. 72b, note, erroneously ascribes the institution to the time of the Roman oppression). As early as 63 B.C. the Pharisaic elders in the name of the nation declared to Pompey that it was not befitting for them to be ruled by a king, because the form of government received from their forefathers was that of subjection to the priests of the God they worshiped, whereas the present descendants of the priests (Hyrcanus and Aristobulus) sought to introduce another form of government which would make slaves of them (Josephus, "Ant." xiii. 3, § 2). The kingship of God is indeed especially accentuated in the Psalms of Solomon, composed at that time (ii. 36; v. 22; vii. 8; xvii. 1, 32, 38, 51). "Either God is your king or Nebuchadnezzar" (Sifra, Ḳedoshim, at the close); "Whoso takes upon himself the yoke of the Torah will have the yoke of the worldly power removed from him," says R. Neḥunya ben ha-Ḳanah ("the Zealot"; see Geiger's "Zeitschrift," ii. 38; comp. Ab. R. N. xx. [ed. Schechter, p. 72]); "My mother's sons were incensed against me" (Cant. i. 6); "These are Sanhedrin" ["Boulai"] of Judea who cast off the yoke of the Holy One and set over themselves a human king." See also Philo's description of the Essenes in "Quod Probus Liber Est," §§ 12–13: "They condemn masters; even their most cruel and treacherous oppressor [Herod] could not but look upon them as free men."

The reign of the Idumean Herod gave the impetus for the organization of the Zealots as a political party. Shemaiah and Abṭalion (Ptollion), as members of the Sanhedrin, at first opposed Herod, but seem to have preferred a passive resignation in the end

Organization as a Political Party. (Josephus, "Ant." xiv. 9, § 4; xv. 1, § 1; xv. 7, § 10; xv. 10, § 4); though there were those who "could by no torments be forced to call him [Herod] king," and who persisted in opposing his government. Hezekiah and his so-called "band of robbers," who were the first to fall as victims under Herod's bloodthirsty rule ("B. J." i. 10, § 5; "Ant." xiv. 9, §§ 2–3), were by no means common robbers. Josephus, following his sources, bestows the name of "robbers" upon all the ardent patriots who would not endure the reign of the usurper and who fled with their wives and children to the caves and fortresses of Galilee to fight and to die for their conviction and their freedom ("Ant." xiv. 15, §§ 4–6; xv. 8, §§ 3–4; xvii. 10, §§ 5–8; xx. 8, §§ 5–6; "B. J." i. 18, § 1; ii. 13, §§ 2–4; iv. 4, § 3; and elsewhere). All these "robbers" were in reality Zealots. Josephus relates of one of them that he slew his wife and his seven sons rather than allow them to be slaves to the Idumean Herod ("Ant." xiv. 15, § 5; "B. J." i. 16, § 4); this man is possibly identical with TAXO, the Levite mentioned in the "Assumptio Mosis," ix. 1–7, as undergoing a martyr's death in a cave with his seven sons, saying: "Let us die rather than transgress the commands of the Lord of Lords, the God of our fathers; for if we do this our blood will be avenged before the Lord" (comp. Charles, "The Assumption of Moses," 1897, p. 36, who suggests the original reading הקנא ["the Zealot"] in place of חסקא, which he considers a corruption of the copyist; see also Schürer, "Gesch." 1st ed., iii. 3, 217, and Charles, l.c. pp. lv.–lviii.). Sepphoris in

Galilee seems to have been the main fortress in which the Zealots concentrated their forces ("Ant." xiv. 15, § 4; xvii. 10, § 5).

It was for the sake of punishing the crimes of idolatry and bloodshed committed by Herod that the Zealots of Jerusalem first appeared with daggers ("sicæ") hidden underneath their cloaks, bent upon slaying the Idumean despot. Josephus relates ("Ant." xv. 8, §§ 1-4) that it was the introduction

The Sicarii.
of Roman institutions entirely antagonistic to the spirit of Judaism, such as the gymnasium, the arena, and, above all, the trophies (that is, images to which homage was to be paid), which provoked the indignation of the people. Ten citizens of Jerusalem swore vengeance against Herod as an enemy of the nation, and, with concealed daggers, went into the theater, where Herod was supposed to be, in order to slay him there. Owing, however, to his system of espionage, Herod was informed of the conspiracy in time, and so escaped, while the conspirators suffered death with great torture, but gloried in their martyrdom. The people sympathized with them, and in their wrath tore to pieces the spy who had discovered the plot. Another outburst of indignation on the part of the Zealots occurred when Herod, toward the end of his life, placed a large golden eagle over the great gate of the Temple. Two masters of the Law, Judah ben Sarifai and Matthias ben Margalot, exhorted their disciples to sacrifice their lives rather than allow this violation of the Mosaic law, which forbids as idolatry the use of such images; and forty young men with these two teachers at their head pulled down the golden eagle, for which act the entire company suffered the cruel penalty of death by fire inflicted by order of Herod ("B. J." i. 33, § 2; "Ant." xvii. 6, §§ 2-4).

The spirit of this Zealot movement, however, was not crushed. No sooner had Herod died (4 c.e.) than the people cried out for revenge ("Ant." xvii. 9, § 1) and gave Archelaus no peace. Judea was full of robber bands, says Josephus (l.c. 10, § 8), the leaders of which each desired to be a king. It was then

Judas, the Zealot Leader.
that Judas, the son of Hezekiah, the above-mentioned robber-captain, organized his forces for revolt, first, it seems, against the Herodian dynasty, and then, when Quirinus introduced the census, against submission to the rule of Rome and its taxation. Little reliance, however, can be placed upon Josephus regarding the character of Judas: at one point this author describes him as a leader "desirous only of the royal title" and bent upon "pillaging and destroying people's property" with the aid of "a multitude of men of profligate character"; elsewhere ("B. J." ii. 8, § 1; "Ant." xviii. 1, §§ 1, 6; comp. "B. J." ii. 17, § 8) he mentions Judas as "the founder of the fourth sect of Jewish philosophy, who taught that God is the only Ruler and Lord, and neither death nor any dread should make them call any man Lord"; and at the same time he says, "The nation was infected with their doctrine to an incredible degree, which became the cause of its many misfortunes, the robberies and murders committed." Judas the Galilean, the son of Hezekiah, is spoken of in Eccl. R. i. 11 as one of the scholarly Ḥasidim to whom in the world to come God shall join a band of the righteous to place him at His side because he had failed to receive due homage as a martyr (see Derenbourg, "Palestine," p. 161).

It was under the leadership of Judas and of his sons and grandson that the Zealots became an aggressive and relentless political party which would brook no compromise and would have no peace with Rome. They were those who would bring about "the kingdom of heaven," that is, the kingship of God, "by force and violence" (Matt. xi. 12). Of Judas' three sons, Jacob and Simon fell as martyrs to their cause in opposing the Roman rule under Tiberius Alexander ("Ant." xx. 5, § 2); his other son, Menahem, was the chief leader of the revolt in 66, and was slain on account of his tyranny by rivals in his own party when, surrounded with royal pomp, he went up to the Temple to be crowned ("B. J." ii. 17, §§ 8-9; comp. ib. § 3 and "Vita," § 5). Rabbinical tradition alludes to Menahem's Messiahship when stating that the Messiah's name is Menahem the son of Hezekiah (Sanh. 98b); and according to Geiger ("Zeitschrift," vii. 176-178), he is the one who went up with eighty couples of disciples of the Law equipped with golden armor and crying out: "Write upon the horn of the ox, 'Ye [yielding Pharisees] have no share in the God of Israel!'" (Yer. Ḥag. ii. 77b). His kinsman and successor at Masada was the Zealot leader Eleazar ben Jair ("B. J." ii. 17, §§ 9-10; vii. 9). In the speech attributed to him he declares that it is a glorious privilege to die for the principle that none but God is the true Ruler of mankind, and that rather than yield to Rome, which is slavery, men should slay their wives and children and themselves, since their souls will live forever (ib. 8, §§ 6-7). This is certainly not the language and conduct of the leader of a band of "robbers," as Josephus persists in calling this party. In their opposition to Rome the Zealots were clearly inspired by religious motives (Geiger, "Zeitschrift," v. 268 et seq.; Grätz, "Gesch." iii. 4, 259, 795-797).

As stated by Josephus ("B. J." iv. 3, § 9), they boastfully called themselves by the name of "Ḳanna'im" (Zealots) on account of their religious zeal. The right of the Ḳanna'im to assassinate any non-Jew who dared to enter the consecrated parts of the Temple was officially recognized in a statute inscribed upon the Temple wall and discovered by Clermont-Ganneau in 1871 (see Schürer, "Gesch." 1st ed., ii. 3, 274; comp. Josephus, "B. J." vi. 2, § 4; both Derenbourg and Grätz ["Gesch." iii. 4, 225] misunderstood the passage). "Ḳanna'im" was the name for those zealous for the honor and sanctity of the Law as well as of the sanctuary, and for this reason they at first met with the support and encouragement of the people and of the Pharisaic leaders, particularly those of the rigid school of Shammai. It was only after they had been so carried away by their fanatic zeal as to become wanton destroyers of life and property throughout the land that they were denounced as heretic Galileans (Yad. iv. 8) and "murderers" (הרצחנים; Soṭah ix. 9) and that their principles were repudiated by the peace-loving Pharisees.

When, in the year 5, Judas of Gamala in Galilee

started his organized opposition to Rome, he was joined by one of the leaders of the Pharisees, R. Zadok, a disciple of Shammai and one of the fiery patriots and popular heroes who lived to witness the tragic end of Jerusalem ("Ant." xviii. 11; Giṭ. 56a; Grätz, "Gesch." iii. 4, 259, 796, and I. H. Weiss, "Dor Dor we-Dorshaw," i. 177, against Geiger, "Zeitschrift," v. 268). The

Their History. taking of the census by Quirinus, the Roman procurator, for the purpose of taxation was regarded as a sign of Roman enslavement; and the Zealots' call for stubborn resistance to the oppressor was responded to enthusiastically. The anti-Roman spirit of the Zealots, as Grätz has shown (*l.c.*), found its echo chiefly in the school of Shammai, whose members did not shrink from resorting to the sword as the ultimate authority in matters of the Law when anti-heathen measures were to be adopted (Shab. 17a; Weiss, *l.c.* p. 186). A great many of the laws that are so strikingly hostile to idols and idolaters ('Ab. Zarah 20a; Tosef., 'Ab. Zarah, iii. 3; Sanh. 63b; and elsewhere) appear to have emanated from these times of warfare against Rome (Grätz, "Gesch." iii. 4, 471), though such views were expressed as early as the time of John Hyrcanus (see JUBILEES, BOOK OF).

The call for political activity was renewed with greater force when, after the death of Agrippa I. in the year 44, Judea became more emphatically a province of Rome and the Sanhedrin at Jerusalem was again deprived of its jurisdiction. Numerous bands of Zealots under the leadership of Tholomy, Amram, Hanibas (Taḥina ?), and Eleazar (see below) roamed through the land, fanning local strifes into wars of rebellion; but in every case they were ultimately defeated, and their leaders were either beheaded or banished for a time ("Ant." xx. 1, § 1). Soon afterward Jacob and Simon, sons of Judas the Galilean, as mentioned above, organized a revolt against Tiberius Alexander, and paid the penalty of crucifixion (47). But matters reached a climax under the procurators Cumanus, Felix, and Florus (49–64), who vied with one another in bloodthirsty cruelty and tyranny when the Zealot leaders, in their desperate struggle against the overwhelming power of an implacable enemy, resorted to extreme measures in order to force the people to action.

Three men are singled out by Josephus and in rabbinical tradition as having shown boundless ferocity in their warfare against Rome and Romanizers: ELEAZAR B. DINAI, Amram ("Ant." xx. 1, § 1; 8, § 5), and Taḥina (Josephus has "Hanibas," not "Hannibal" as Grätz reads, and in "B. J." ii. 8, § 4, "Alexander"; comp. Soṭah ix. 9; Cant. R. iii. 5; Grätz, "Gesch." iii. 4, 431). Of Eleazar ben Dinai and Amram it is said in the last-cited passage that "they desired to urge the Messianic deliverance of Israel, but fell in the attempt." Regarding Eleazar ben Dinai (comp. Kil. v. 10) and Tahina (called also the "Pharisaic saint"), R. Johanan b. Zakkai relates in Soṭah *l.c.* that, on account of the frequent murders committed by them and which won them the epithet of "murderers," the Mosaic law concerning expiation for unknown slain ones (" 'eglah 'arufah ") was set in abeyance. Obviously Josephus misrep-

resents these Zealot leaders, who, while tyrannical and cruel, were certainly no "robbers." However,

Misrepresented by Josephus. their dealings with property, especially that belonging to those suspected of friendliness to Rome, created anarchy throughout the land, as may be learned from the rabbinical legislation concerning the "siḳariḳon" (Giṭ. v. 6, 55b; Yer. Giṭ. v. 47b). One of these, named Doras and mentioned by Josephus (*l.c.*), has become, like Eleazar ben Dinai, proverbial in rabbinical literature (Men. 57a; Yer. Shab. 14a, where he is mentioned as a type of a voracious eater).

As the oppression of the Roman procurators increased, so also the passion and violence of the Zealots grew in intensity, affecting all the discontented, while one pseudo-Messiah after another appeared arousing the hope of the people for deliverance from the Roman yoke ("Ant." xx. 5, § 1; 9, § 10; "B. J." ii. 13, § 5). It was quite natural that under the name of Sicarii all kinds of corrupt elements, men eager for pillage and murder, should join the party, spreading terror through the land. Finally the barbarities of Albinus and, above all, of Gessius Florus precipitated the crisis and played into the hands of the terrorists ("Ant." xx. 9–11; "B. J." ii. 14–15). The issue was between the peace party, which was willing to yield to cruel Rome, and the war party, which, while relying on God's help, demanded bold action; and under the leadership of the priestly governor of the Temple, Eleazar ben Anania, who refused to receive gifts from or offer sacrifice on behalf of Rome, the latter party prevailed ("B. J." ii. 17, § 2), another priest belonging to the Shammaite party, Zachariah b. Amphicalos, having decided in favor of Eleazar (Tosef., Shab. xvii. 6; Giṭ. 56a; Grätz, "Gesch." iii. 4, 453–458, 818). At this opportune time Menahem, the son of Judas the Galilean, seized the fortress Masada in Galilee, killed the Roman garrison, and then drove the Romans out of other fortresses; and finally his kinsman and successor as master of Masada, Eleazar ben Jair, took up the war of rebellion against Rome and carried it to the very end ("B. J." ii. 17, §§ 2, 7, 10). True to the Shammaite principle that warfare against the heathen possessors of Palestine is permitted even on the Sabbath (Shab. 19a; Grätz, *l.c.* pp. 796–797), the war was carried on by the Zealots on that day ("B. J." ii. 19, § 2), and the Romans were everywhere overpowered and annihilated, Simon bar Giora being one of the heroic leaders whom none could resist. The whole army of Cestius, who had brought twelve legions from Antioch to retrieve the defeat of the

Zealots Annihilate Cestius' Army. Roman garrison, was annihilated by the Zealots under the leadership of Bar Giora and Eleazar ben Simon the priest. The Maccabean days seemed to have returned; and the patriots of Jerusalem celebrated the year 66 as the year of Israel's deliverance from Rome, and commemorated it with coins bearing the names of Eleazar the priest and Simon the prince (Bar Giora [?], or Simon ben Gamaliel as Grätz has it; "B. J." ii. 19, §§ 1 *et seq.*, 20, §§ 1–5; Grätz, *l.c.* pp. 469–470, 509, 818–841).

The news of the victory of the Zealots in Jerusalem set the whole province of Galilee ablaze. Always a hotbed of revolution, it at once began an insurrection, and its thousands soon rallied round the fiery Zealot leaders John ben Levi of Giscala ("Gushḥalab"), Justus the son of Pistus, Joshua ben Saphia of Tiberias, and Joseph of Gamala ("B. J." ii. 21, § 1; iv. 4, § 13; "Vita," §§ 12, 27, 35–36). Only Sepphoris, a city full of aliens, obstinately refused to join the revolution. Josephus was sent by the Jerusalem Sanhedrin, composed chiefly of Zealots, for the purpose of prevailing upon the Sepphorites to abandon the cause of Agrippa II. and Rome, and to help Galilee work hand in hand with the authorities at Jerusalem in the liberation of Judea; but he deceived the Zealots and played into the hands first of Agrippa and then of Rome. His "De Bello Judaico" and his "Vita," written for the purpose of pleasing his Roman masters, are full of aspersions upon the character of the Zealots and their leaders.

The year 67 saw the beginning of the great war with the Roman legions, first under Vespasian and then under Titus; and Galilee was at **The Final** the outset chosen as the seat of war. **Stage.** The Zealots fought with almost superhuman powers against warriors trained in countless battles waged in all parts of the known world, and when they succumbed to superior military skill and overwhelming numbers, often only after some act of treachery within the Jewish camp, they died with a fortitude and a spirit of heroic martyrdom which amazed and overawed their victors. Josephus' own description of the tragic end of the last great Zealot leader, Eleazar ben Jair, and his men after the siege and final capture of Masada ("B. J." vii. 8–9) is the best refutation of his malicious charges against them.

At the siege of Jerusalem the Zealots were not deterred even by the defeat in Galilee and the terrible massacre of their compatriots; their faith in the final victory of the Holy City and its massive walls remained unshaken. But there were too much enmity and strife between them and the ruling body, the Sanhedrin, which they distrusted; and their own leaders were also divided. Instead of working after the clearly mapped-out plan of one powerful leader, they had their forces split up into sections, one under Simon bar Giora, another under Eleazar ben Simon and Simon b. Jair (Ezron), a third under John of Giscala, and a fourth, consisting chiefly of semibarbarous Idumeans, under Jacob ben Sosas and Simon ben Kathla ("B. J." v. 6, §§ 2–3; vi. 1). In order to force the wealthy and more peaceably inclined citizens to action, the Zealots in their fury set fire to the storehouses containing the corn needed for the support of the people during the siege ("B. J." v. 1, § 4). This tragic event is recorded in Ab. R. N. vi. (ed. Schechter, p. 32), the only Talmudical passage that mentions the Ḳanna'im as a political party. The second version (ed. Schechter, p. 31) has "Sicarii" instead, and agrees with Giṭ. 56, Lam. R. i. 5, and Eccl. R. vii. 11 in mentioning three rich men of Jerusalem who, being inclined to make peace with the Romans, had their storehouses burned by the Zealots: namely, Ben Kalba Shabua', Ben Ẓiẓit ha-Kassat, and Nicodemus (Nikomedes ben

Gorion; see Grätz, *l.c.* pp. 527–528; Derenbourg, *l.c.* p. 284). In Eccl. R. vii. 11 the instigation of the burning of the storehouses is ascribed to the leader of the Zealots ("Resh Barione"; see the articles ABBA SAḲḲARA and BEN BAṬIAḤ).

Simon bar Giora and John of Giscala survived the fall of Jerusalem, and were taken as captives to Rome to glorify Titus' triumph; the former, with a rope around his head, was dragged to the Forum and cast down from the Tarpeian rock ("B. J." v. 5, § 6). Most of the Zealots fell under the sword or other instruments of death and torture at the hands of the Romans, and such as fled to Alexandria or Cyrenaica roused by their unyielding hostility to Rome the opposition of those eager for peace, until they too finally met the same tragic fate ("B. J." vii. 6, §§ 1–5; 10, §§ 1–4). It was a desperate and mad spirit of defiance which animated them all and made them prefer horrible torture and death to Roman servitude. History has declared itself in favor of the Pharisees, who deemed the schoolhouse (see JOHANAN BEN ZAKKAI) of more vital importance to the Jews than state and Temple; but the Zealot, too, deserves due recognition for his sublime type of steadfastness, as George Eliot points out in her "Impressions of Theophrastus Such" (1879, p. 212).

Among the disciples of Jesus there is mentioned a Simon the Zealot (Luke vi. 15; Acts i. 13); for the same person Matt. x. 4 and Mark iii. 18 have "the Canaanite," obviously a corruption of הקנאי ("ha-Ḳanna'i" = "the Zealot").

BIBLIOGRAPHY: Hamburger, *R. B. T.* ii. 1286–1296; Grätz, *Gesch.* iii. 4 and Index.

K.

ZEBAḤIM ("Animal Sacrifices"): Treatise in the Mishnah, the Tosefta, and the Babylonian Talmud, dealing mainly with the laws and regulations to be observed in making animal offerings. In the Tosefta this treatise is called "Ḳorbanot" (Sacrifices), while its older name, used in the Talmud (B. M. 109b), is "Sheḥiṭat Ḳodashim" (Slaughtering of Consecrated Animals). It is the first treatise in the order Ḳodashim, and consists of fourteen chapters divided into 101 paragraphs.

Ch. i.: Setting forth the intention necessary in the bringing of a sacrifice; the Passover sacrifice must be slaughtered at the proper time; by what acts performed with improper intention **Mishnah.** the sacrifice becomes unfit ("pasul"). **Contents:** Ch. ii.: What makes a sacrifice un- **i.-vii.** fit, and what makes it an abomination ("piggul"); a sacrifice becomes piggul when the one who brings it intends to partake of it or to offer a part thereof later than the time prescribed by law.

Ch. iii.: Enumerating oversights in spite of which the sacrifice remains fit; the only wrongful intentions that can render the sacrifice unfit are the intentions to eat of the sacrifice later than the lawful time or in a place other than that stipulated by law. Passover sacrifices and sin-offerings are rendered unfit when not slaughtered with the proper intentions of making them Passover sacrifices or sin-offerings.

Ch. iv.: The sprinkling of the blood; the points of distinction between a sacrifice consecrated by heathen and one consecrated by Israelites; definition of the correct intentions necessary in the bringing of a sacrifice.

Ch. v.: Where the various animals are slaughtered according to their different degrees of holiness; where and how their blood must be sprinkled; where and for how long their flesh may be eaten.

Ch. vi.: Continuation of ch. v.; on the preparation and delivering of a sin-offering consisting of birds.

Ch. vii.: Further regulations concerning the sacrifice of birds.

Ch. viii.: Rules governing cases in which different animals or parts of different animals have been mingled, or in which the blood of one sacrifice has been mixed with that of another.

Contents:
viii.-xiv.

Ch. ix.: In which cases that which has been placed on the altar may not be removed; things which in some instances the altar, the ladder, and the sanctified vessels render holy, and the cases in which they have no sanctifying powers.

Ch. x.: The order of the various sacrifices; which sacrifices precede others with regard to time, and also in degree of holiness; thus, the daily burnt offering (" tamid ") precedes the additional offering (" musaf ") brought on Sabbaths and festivals; how the priests partake of the sacrificial meat.

Ch. xi.: Cases in which a garment or utensil stained by the blood of a sacrificed animal may be washed, and when it may not be washed; on the cleansing of the vessels according to the flesh of different sacrifices which has been prepared in them.

Ch. xii.: Priests who do not partake of the flesh of the sacrifices; in which cases the skins belong to those who bring the sacrifices, and in which to the priests; exceptions among the latter cases; where the bullocks and he-goats are burned, and under what conditions the garments of those who attend to the burning are rendered unclean.

Ch. xiii.: Various offenses that may occur in connection with sacrifices.

Ch. xiv.: Regulations concerning the bringing of a sacrifice outside of the Temple in Jerusalem; before the erection of the Tabernacle it was permitted to sacrifice on the high places (" bamot "), and the first-born officiated as priests; but after the erecting of the Tabernacle this was forbidden, and the priests of the family of Aaron officiated; the sacrificing on high places was again permitted in Gilgal, but was anew prohibited in Shiloh; in Nob and in Gibeon permission was once more granted, but the practise was finally forbidden when the Temple was built in Jerusalem; description of the sanctuary in Shiloh.

The Tosefta to this treatise is divided into thirteen chapters, and contains not only elucidating amplifications of the Mishnah, but also several interesting maxims. Mention may be made of R. Ṭarfon's acknowledgment of the wisdom of R. Akiba (i. 8), to whom he says: " I have heard, but did not know how to explain; you, however, explain, and your interpretation is in accord with the traditional Halakah. Therefore, he who disagrees with you is as though he had parted with life." Ch. vi. 11 contains a description of the altar; and xi. 1 interprets the name of the meal-offering (" shelamim ")

The Tosefta.

as being derived from " shalom " (peace), explaining that at this sacrifice the altar, the priests, and the offerer of the sacrifice all receive a part thereof, so that all are satisfied. Ch. xiii. 6 sets forth the length of the various periods during which the sanctuary was in the wilderness, in Gilgal, in Shiloh, in Nob and Gibeon, and in Jerusalem.

The Gemara of the Babylonian Talmud discusses and explains the several mishnayot, and contains besides some interesting haggadic interpretations and maxims. A description is given of the manner in which David decided upon the place where the Temple should be built (§ 54b). When the Jews returned from the Babylonian exile there were among them three prophets: one pointed out to the people the place where the altar had formerly stood and where it should again be erected; the second told them that they might sacrifice, although the Temple had not yet been built; and the third instructed them that the Torah should be written in square characters (§ 62a). A description is also given of how, during the revelation on Mt. Sinai, the voice of God was heard by all the nations, and how they became frightened and went to Balaam, who explained to them the import of the noise (§ 116a).

J.   J. Z. L.

ẒEBA'OT ADONAI. See ADONAI.

ZEBEDEE (Ζεβεδαῖος; apparently from the Hebrew זבדיה = " the gift of YHWH "): Father of the apostles James and John, and husband of Salome; a native of Galilee and a fisherman by calling (Matt. iv. 21, xxvii. 56; Mark xv. 40). It seems from the mention of his boat and hired servants (ib. i. 20) that Zebedee was a man of some means, although he had to work himself.

J.   M. Sel.

ẒEBI BEN AARON. See KAIDANOVER, ẒEBI HIRSCH.

ẒEBI ASHKENAZI. See ASHKENAZI, ẒEBI HIRSCH BEN JACOB.

ẒEBI HIRSCH BEN ḤAYYIM: Dayyan and ḥazzan at Posen toward the end of the seventeenth century. Under the title " Sefer Or Yashar " he edited (Amsterdam, 1709) an Ashkenazic ritual, to which he appended notes of his own, various commentaries collected from ancient authorities, the annotations of Isaac Luria, the dinim that are in daily use, and ethical dissertations taken from the " Ḥobot ha-Lebabot," " Reshit Ḥokmah," and " To-ze'ot Ḥayyim." Ẓebi Hirsch is not to be confounded with a printer of Wilmersdorf of similar name.

BIBLIOGRAPHY: Nepi-Ghirondi, *Toledot Gedole Yisrael*, p. 298; Steinschneider, *Cat. Bodl.* col. 2751.
J.   I. Br.

ẒEBI HIRSCH BEN ISAAC JACOB: Shoḥet at Cracow in the sixteenth century; a pupil of Moses Isserles. He was the author of " Haggahot le-Sefer Sheḥiṭah u-Bediḳah " (Cracow, 1631; n.p. 1723; Amsterdam, 1745; Zolkiev, 1793), annotations appended to Jacob Weil's work on the laws governing the slaughtering of animals and the examination of the lungs.

BIBLIOGRAPHY: Nepi-Ghirondi, *Toledot Gedole Yisrael*, p. 298; Fürst, *Bibl. Jud.* i. 396; Steinschneider, *Cat. Bodl.* col. 2753.
J.   I. Br.

ZEBI HIRSCH BEN JOSEPH BEN ZEBI HA-KOHEN: Polish Talmudist of the seventeenth century; studied for some time at Cracow under Yom-Ṭob Lipmann Heller. He was the author of "Naḥalat Ẓebi" (Venice, 1661), a commentary on Joseph Caro's Shulḥan 'Aruk, Eben ha-'Ezer, and of "'Aṭeret Ẓebi," a commentary on Oraḥ Ḥayyim. Ẓebi left several works in manuscript, among which are commentaries on the two remaining parts of the Shulḥan 'Aruk.

BIBLIOGRAPHY: Fürst, *Bibl. Jud.* i. 395; Steinschneider, *Cat. Bodl.* col. 2755.
J. I. BR.

ZEBI HIRSCH B. SIMON: Lithuanian Talmudist; lived in the middle of the eighteenth century. He was dayyan and preacher in the community of Vitebsk during the rabbinates of R. Isaiah and R. Löb, and was known as one of the first Talmudic authorities in that part of Lithuania. He corresponded with many rabbis who consulted him on difficult ritual questions. Of his numerous writings only one has been printed: "Hadrat Zeḳenim" (Dubrovna, 1802), edited by his grandsons Joshua and Abraham b. Meïr. This work, intended as a codification of the halakot enacted during the period following the compilation of the Shulḥan 'Aruk, does not treat the subject fully, the printed part developing inadequately the subjects contained in the first 200 paragraphs of the Shulḥan 'Aruk, Yoreh De'ah. The unpublished part of the "Hadrat Zeḳenim" contains novellæ on Berakot and on all treatises of the order Mo'ed.

BIBLIOGRAPHY: *Hadrat Zeḳenim*, Introduction and notes of approbation.
E. C. L. G.

ZEBID: 1. Babylonian amora of the fourth century; a contemporary of Abaye, whose halakot he transmitted, and of whom he was perhaps a pupil (Ber. 46b; Soṭah 32b; *et passim*). Zebid also transmitted the halakot of Raba and R. Naḥman (B. Ḳ. 84a; B. M. 17a), but he particularly preferred the decisions of Abaye, and it is narrated ('Ab. Zarah 38b) that his adherence to Abaye caused his death. When the people of the exilarch once questioned R. Ḥiyya Parwa'ah regarding a certain halakah, he answered that Hezekiah and Bar Ḳappara had interpreted it, while R. Johanan had decided to the contrary, and that as the authorities thus stood two to one, the law would have to be interpreted according to the majority. Zebid said, however, "Do not listen to him, for Abaye decided according to R. Johanan"; whereupon the people of the exilarch forced Zebid to drink a cup of vinegar, which caused his death. R. Ḥinena b. R. Iḳa is recorded as his opponent in halakic decisions (Me'i. 19a). Zebid particularly explained to his pupils the baraitot of R. Hoshaiah or Oshaya ("bi-debe R. Osha'ya"; 'Ab. Zarah 6b, 56a; B. M. 92b; *et passim*).

2. Contemporary of the preceding, and generally called Zebid of Nehardea (Ḳid. 72b; comp. Rashi *ad loc.*). He was for eight years head of the yeshibah of Pumbedita; and among his pupils were Amemar, Huna b. Nathan, and R. Kahana (Ḳid. *l.c.*; B. M. 73b; Yeb. 18b; and elsewhere). At his death R. Kahana delivered his funeral oration at Pum Nahara (M. Ḳ. 27b).

BIBLIOGRAPHY: Heilprin, *Seder ha-Dorot*, ii.
J. M. SEL.

ZEBU'IM. See HYPOCRISY.

ZEBULUN: The sixth son of Leah (Gen. xxx. 20), and hence the name of the tribe descended from him (Num. i. 9, vii. 24, x. 16; Ps. lxviii. 28 [A. V. 27]). In the division of the land Zebulun was assigned districts north of Issachar (Josh. xix. 11) and west and south of Naphtali (*ib.* verse 34) and east of Asher (*ib.* verse 27). Still, Gen. xlix. 13 and Deut. xxxiii. 18 *et seq.* suggest that Zebulun must have possessed also territory bordering on the sea; and, indeed, the boundaries detailed in Josh. xix. are unintelligible. Zebulun's possessions were not extensive, but were fertile and were crossed by important roads from the Jordan to the Mediterranean. This fact explains the reference to Zebulun's commerce with other clans, even such as were not Hebrews ("'ammim"; Deut. xxxiii. 19; see Josephus, "Ant." v. 1, § 22), with whom at Mount TABOR Zebulun entered into commercial covenant relations (Deut. *l.c.*) = "zibḥe-ẓedeḳ," allusion to which the author of the verse seemingly recognizes by assonance in the name "Zebulun" (with "zebaḥ"). Reported as rather populous while in the wilderness (Num. i. 30, xxvi. 26), Zebulun seems later to have had within its borders numerous Canaanites (Judges i. 30; Isa. viii. 23). Its prowess is mentioned in the song of Deborah (Judges v. 14, 18; comp. *ib.* iv. 6, 10; vi. 35). One of the judges, Elon, is said to have been of the tribe (Judges xii. 11). It is probable that Zebulun at a comparatively early period was incorporated in Issachar or Asher (see omission of Zebulun in I Kings iv., xv. 20; II Kings xii. 18). The territory was annexed to the Assyrian empire in 734-733 by Tiglath-pileser. E. G. H.

ZECHARIAH: One of the Minor Prophets, to whom is attributed the collection of prophecies and apocalyptic visions constituting the book bearing his name. He was a son of Berechiah and a grandson of Iddo (Zech. i. 1), and was loosely called the son of Iddo (Ezra v. 1, vi. 14); the latter was possibly identical with the Iddo mentioned as high priest in Neh. xii. 4, which would make the prophet himself the high priest named in Neh. xii. 16. Zechariah was probably born during the Captivity, but was brought back early to Palestine. He began his prophetic ministry in the second year of King Darius Hystaspes, a little later than HAGGAI (Zech. i. 1; Hag. i. 1), his preoccupation being the rebuilding of the Temple. According to the contents of that part of the book which without doubt is by him (i.–viii.; see ZECHARIAH, BOOK OF—CRITICAL VIEW), Zechariah received YHWH's messages largely through the medium of visions (i. 8; ii. 2, 5; and elsewhere), which excited his curiosity, and which, in answer to his inquiries, were interpreted to him as significant monitions bearing on the condition of the colony and the timeliness of proceeding with the rearing of the sanctuary (i. 16, ii. 14). He appeals for loyalty on the part of Joshua the high priest toward the Messianic prince, the "Branch" (iii. 8) or ZERUBBABEL (iv. 9). As the mediator of his visions, the prophet names an angel of Y<small>HWH</small>, called sometimes "the" angel, and it is he who introduces also "the" S<small>ATAN</small> in the rôle of a mischief-maker confirming the people's hesitation and discouraged mood (iii. 1, 2). His method thus borders on the apocalyptic. His style is not lacking in directness in some passages, but in others it leans toward involved obscurity. Zechariah, however, proves himself to be an uncompromising critic of the ritual substitutes for true piety, such as fasting and mourning (vii. 5); and he reiterates the admonitions for mercy and righteousness, which according to the Prophets constitute the essence of the service of Y<small>HWH</small> (vii. 8, 9). For neglect of this service Israel was visited with the sufferings that befell it (vii. 13, 14). Jerusalem is to be called the city of truth (viii. 3), and shall dwell in peace, so that old men and old women shall be found in its streets (verse 4), together with boys and girls (verse 5), and prosperity shall abound in the land (verses 7 et seq.).

While Zechariah lacks originality, he is distinguished from his contemporaries by the "gift of plain speech" (G. A. Smith). But while some of the obscurities and repetitions which mark his visions are probably due to other hands, there remain enough of these defects that come from him to indicate that the visions were not the spontaneous outflow of ecstasy, but the labored effort of a strained and artificial imagination. He was a prophet, but of a period when prophecy was rapidly running to its own extinction. E. G. H.

ZECHARIAH, BOOK OF.—**Biblical Data:** Prophetical book composed of fourteen chapters; the eleventh in the order of the Minor Prophets, following Haggai and preceding Malachi. Ch. i.–viii. comprise three prophecies: (1) an introduction (i. 1–6); (2) a complex of visions (i. 7–vi.); and (3) the seed of Peace (vii.–viii.).

(1) The introduction, dated in the eighth month of the second year of King Darius, is an admonition to repentance addressed to the people and rendered impressive by reference to the consequences of disobedience, of which the experience of the fathers is a witness.

(2) This introductory exhortation is followed on the twenty-fourth day of the month of Shebaṭ by eight symbolic visions: (*a*) angel-horsemen (i. 7–17); (*b*) the four horns and the four smiths (i. 18–21 [English], ii. 1–4 [Hebrew]); **Contents.** (*c*) the city of peace (ii. 1–5 [English]); (*d*) the high priest and the Satan (iii.); (*e*) the Temple candlestick and the olive-trees (iv.); (*f*) the winged scroll (v. 1–4); (*g*) the woman in the barrel (v. 5–11); (*h*) the chariots of the four winds (vi. 1–8). To these is added a historical appendix, in which the prophet speaks of the divine command to turn the gold and silver offered by some of the exiles into a crown for Joshua (or Zerubbabel ?), and reiterates the promise of the Messiah (vi. 9–15).

(3) The next two chapters (vii.–viii.) are devoted to censuring fasting and mourning (vii.) when obedience to God's moral law is essential, and to describing the Messianic future.

Ch. ix.–xiv. contain:

(1) A prophecy concerning the judgment about to fall upon Damascus, Hamath, Tyre, Zidon, and the cities of the Philistines (ix.).

(2) Exhortation of the people to seek help not from T<small>ERAPHIM</small> and diviners but from Y<small>HWH</small>.

(3) Announcement of war upon unworthy tyrants, followed by an allegory in which the faithless people is censured and the brotherhood between Israel and Judah is declared to be at an end; fate of the unworthy shepherd (xi.). To this chapter xiii. 7–9 seems to belong, as descriptive of a process of purification by the sword and fire, two-thirds of the people being consumed.

(4) Judah versus Jerusalem (xii. 1–7).

(5) Results, four in number, of Jerusalem's deliverance (xii. 8–xiii. 6).

(6) The judgment of the heathen and the sanctification of Jerusalem (xiv.).

——**Critical View:** Inspection of its contents shows immediately that the book readily divides into two parts; namely, i.–viii. and ix.–xiv., each of which is distinguished from the other by its method of presenting the subject and by the range of the subject presented. In the first part Israel is the object of solicitude; and to encourage it to proceed with the rearing of the Temple and to secure the recognition of Zerubbabel and Joshua are the purposes of the prophecy. Visions, which are described and construed so as to indicate Y<small>HWH</small>'s approval of the prophet's anxiety, predominate as the mediums of the prophetic message, and the lesson is fortified by appeals to Israel's past history, while stress is laid on righteousness versus ritualism. The date is definitely assigned to the second year of King Darius Hystaspes. The historical background is the condition which confronted the Jews who first returned from the Exile (see, however, Koster's "Herstel von Israel," 1894). Some event—according to Stade, the revolt of Smerdis; but more probably the second conquest of Babylon under Darius—seems to have inspired buoyant hopes in the otherwise despondent congregation in Jerusalem, thus raising their Messianic expectations (Zech. ii. 10 [A. V. 6] *et seq.* vi. 8) to a firm belief in the reestablishing of David's throne and the universal acknowledgment of the supremacy of Y<small>HWH</small>. Angels and Satan are intermediaries and actors.

In the second part the method is radically different. Apocalyptic visions are altogether lacking, **The Second** and historical data and chronological **Zechariah.** material are absent. The style is fantastic and contains many obscure allusions. That the two parts are widely divergent in date and authorship is admitted by all modern critics, but while there is general agreement that the first part is by the prophet Zechariah, no harmony has yet been attained concerning the identity or the date of the second part.

Many recent commentators regard the second part as older than the first, and as preexilic in date. They would divide it, furthermore, into at least two parts, ix.–xi. and xii.–xiv., the former by an author contemporary with Amos and Hosea. This assignment is based on the facts that both Israel and Judah are mentioned, and that the names of Assyria, Egypt, and the contiguous nations are juxtaposed, much as they are in Amos. The sins censured are false prophecy and idolatry (xiii. 1-6). This group of chapters (xii.-xiv.), containing the denunciations familiar in all preexilic prophets, is regarded as later than the other division, since only Judah is mentioned. It is therefore assigned to the period after the fall of the Northern Kingdom, and more specifically, on account of xii. 11, to the last days of the Southern Kingdom after the battle of Megiddo and the death of King Josiah.

Other scholars have argued with much plausibility for the hypothesis that the second part belongs
Date of the to a very late period of Jewish history.
Second In the first place, the theology (see
Zechariah. ESCHATOLOGY) of these chapters shows tendencies which are not found in Amos, Hosea, Isaiah, or Jeremiah, but are due to Ezekiel's influence, such as the war on Jerusalem preceding the Messianic triumph. Again, the Temple service (xiv.) is focal even in the Messianic age, and this suggests the religious atmosphere of the Sadducean and Maccabean theocracy with Zion as its technical designation. A mixture of races is also mentioned, a reminiscence of conditions described by Nehemiah (Neh. xiii. 23 *et seq.*), while deliverance from Babylonian exile underlies such promises as occur in ix. 12. The advent of a king is expected, though as yet only a Davidic family is known in Jerusalem (xii. 7, 12).

The second part of the book may thus be recognized to be a compilation rather than a unit, all its components being post-exilic in character. Two groups, ix.-xi. and xii.-xiv., are clearly indicated. The second group (xii.-xiv.) is eschatological and has no individual coloring, although from the contrast between Jerusalem and the country of Judah a situation may be inferred which recalls the conditions of the early stages of the Maccabean rebellion. The first group may likewise be subdivided into two sections, ix. 1-xi. 3 and xi. 4-17 and xiii. 7-9. The Greeks (see JAVAN) are described in ix. 13 as enemies of Judea, and the Assyrians and Egyptians are similarly mentioned in x., these names denoting the Syrians (SELEUCIDÆ) and the Ptolemies. In ix. 1-2 Damascus, Hamath, and Hadrach are seats of the Seleucid kings, a situation which is known to have existed in 200-165 B.C. The internal conditions of the Jewish community immediately before the Maccabean uprising appear in the second subdivision, where the shepherds are the tax-farmers (see TOBIADS; MENELAUS). In xi. 13 there seems to be an allusion to HYRCANUS, son of Tobias, who was an exception among the rapacious shepherds.

BIBLIOGRAPHY: Wright, *Zechariah and His Prophecies*, 2d ed., London, 1879, which gives earlier literature; Stade, *Deuterozachariah*, in *Zeitschrift für Alttestamentliche Wissenschaft*, 1881-82; the commentaries by Marti, Nowack, and Wellhausen; G. A. Smith, *Twelve Prophets*, ii.; Bredenkamp, *Der Prophet Sacharja*, 1879; Sellin, *Studien zur Entstehungszeit der Jüdischen Gemeinde*, 1901; Stärk, *Untersuchungen über die Komposition und Abfassungszeit von Zachariah*, 1891, ix.-xiv.

E. G. H.

ZECHARIAH BEN ABKILUS (Amphika-los): Palestinian scholar and one of the leaders of the ZEALOTS; lived in Jerusalem at the time of the destruction of the Second Temple. According to the Talmud, the authority which he enjoyed among the rabbis of Jerusalem was the cause of the downfall of the city. Zechariah was present at the banquet famous for the affair of KAMẒA and BAR KAMẒA (comp. Josephus, "Vita," § 10); and though his influence might have prevented the disgrace of Bar Kamẓa, he did not exercise it. Again, when the emperor sent a blemished calf as an offering to the Temple, the Hillelites would have accepted it to frustrate Bar Kamẓa, had not Zechariah, acting in the interest of the school of Shammai, given a casting vote, or (according to Lam. R. iv. 2) refrained from voting, and thus rendered the decision negative. The people wished to kill Bar Kamẓa so that he should not be able to tell the emperor of the refusal, but Zechariah once more restrained them from carrying out their design. R. Johanan, on the other hand, or, according to another source, R. Jose, declared that the humility of Zechariah b. Abkilus, in refusing to cast his vote, caused the destruction of the Temple (Giṭ. 56a; Tosef., Shab. xvi. [xvii.] 6; Lam. R. iv. 2). He is recorded as following neither the Bet Hillel nor the Bet Shammai with regard to holding date-stones on the Sabbath (Shab. 143; Tosef., Shab. *l.c.*). He is probably referred to by Josephus ("B. J." ii. 17, §§ 2-3).

BIBLIOGRAPHY: Grätz, *Gesch.* iii. 458, 509, 817-819; Derenbourg, *Hist.* p. 257.

E. C. M. SEL.—K.

ZECHARIAH BEN JEHOIADA.—Biblical Data: A reforming priest who lived under King Joash of Judah. He reproved the idolaters, announcing God's judgment against them; and a conspiracy was formed against him that resulted in his being stoned in the court of the Temple at the command of the king, who "remembered not the kindness which Jehoiada his father had done to him" (II Chron. xxiv. 22). Zechariah's dying words were: "YHWH look upon it, and require it" (*ib.* verses 20-22).

E. G. H. B. P.

——In Rabbinical Literature: According to the Rabbis, Zechariah was the son-in-law of the king, and, being also a priest, prophet, and judge, he dared censure the monarch. He was killed in the priests' courtyard of the Temple on a Sabbath which was likewise the Day of Atonement. Later, when NEBUZAR-ADAN came to destroy the Temple, Zechariah's blood began to boil. The Assyrian asked the Jews what that phenomenon meant, but when they replied that it was the blood of sacrifices, he proved the falsity of their answer. The Jews then told him the truth, and Nebuzar-adan, wishing to appease Zechariah's blood, slew in succession the Great and Small Sanhedrins, the young priests, and school-children, till the number of the dead was 940,000. Still the blood continued to boil, whereupon Nebuzar-adan cried: "Zechariah, Zechariah! for thee have I slain the best of them; wouldst thou that I destroy them all?" And at these words the blood ceased to effervesce (Giṭ. 57b; Sanh. 96b; Lam. R. iv. 13).

E. C. M. SEL.

ZECHARIAH HA-KOHEN: Greek or Turkish Biblical commentator and liturgical poet of the fifteenth century; maternal grandfather of Menahem ben Moses Tamar. According to the latter ("Tanḥumot El," ch. x.), Zechariah wrote a pamphlet ("ḳonṭres") in which he refutes Naḥmanides' strictures on Ibn Ezra's commentary on the Pentateuch, citations from which relating to the weekly lesson Wayiggash are made by Menahem in his commentary on Ruth. Hebrew MS. No. 249, 1 of the Vatican Library is a work by a certain Zechariah ha-Kohen refuting Naḥmanides' strictures ("hassagot") on Maimonides' "Sefer ha-Miẓwot," and its author is probably identical with the subject of this article. In this work, written in 1451, Zechariah is styled "the philosopher." He wrote two "taḥanunim" beginning respectively "Anan adon 'olam" and "Zebaḥ u-minḥah ne'edaru," both to be recited on Rosh ha-Shanah before the blowing of the shofar; and he produced also a metrical poem beginning "Be-'iḳḳarim yeḳarim la-beḳarim," on the thirteen Articles of Faith, all the words riming in רים. Moreover, a manuscript formerly in the possession of Osias Schorr contains several poems by Zechariah ha-Kohen. One poem beginning "Torat emet amun" and published by Schorr (in "He-Ḥaluẓ," ii. 162) and by Geiger (in his "Jüdische Dichter," p. 28, Hebr.) is also Zechariah's, although both scholars, misled by a difference in handwriting, ascribed it to another poet.

BIBLIOGRAPHY: Fuenn, *Keneset Yisrael*, p. 314; Steinschneider, *Cat. Leyden*, p. 143, note 1, Leyden, 1858; Zunz, *Literaturgesch.* pp. 378–379, 650.
J.   M. SEL.

ZECHARIAH MENDEL BEN ARYEH
LÖB: Polish Talmudist of the eighteenth century; a native of Cracow, and in later life chief rabbi and head of the yeshibah at Belz, Galicia. He was the author of "Be'er Heṭeb," a well-known commentary on the Shulḥan 'Aruk, Yoreh De'ah, and Ḥoshen Mishpaṭ (first edition of the first part, Amsterdam, 1754; of the second, *ib.* 1764); the work is principally a compendium of the "Sifte Kohen" and "Ṭure Zahab."

BIBLIOGRAPHY: Azulai, *Shem ha-Gedolim*, ii., s.v. *Be'er Heṭeb*; Fuenn, *Keneset Yisrael*, p. 318.
J.   M. SEL.

ZECHARIAH MENDEL BEN ARYEH
LÖB: Galician and German preacher and scholar; born at Podhaice in the early part of the eighteenth century; died at Frankfort-on-the-Oder Dec. 20, 1791. He was of the same family as Solomon Luria and Moses Isserles, who traced their genealogy to Rashi. Zechariah Mendel's principal teacher was Jacob Joshua, author of "Pene Yehoshua'." Zechariah Mendel was preacher in the Talmud Torah at Frankfort-on-the-Oder. He left many writings, of which only the following three have been published (at Frankfort-on-the-Oder): "Menorat Zekaryah" (1776), a work containing novellæ on the treatise Shabbat and homilies for the Sabbath and holy days; "Zekaryah Meshullam" (1779), a sequel to the preceding work, and containing novellæ on the Talmud; "Zekaryah ha-Mebin" (1791), a guide to religious philosophy and to the knowledge of the true Cabala.

BIBLIOGRAPHY: Fuenn, *Keneset Yisrael*, p. 315; Fürst, *Bibl. Jud.* iii. 305.
J.   M. SEL.

ZECHARIAH IBN SA'ID AL-YAMANI:
Author of an Arabic version of the "Yosippon"; flourished in the tenth or eleventh century. His version exists in three recensions: (1) in several manuscripts which yet await thorough examination; (2) an abbreviated text printed in the Paris and London polyglots (1645, 1657) as II Maccabees ("Kitab al-Maḳabiyyin"), the term "Maccabees" here connoting the entire Hasmonean dynasty, since the book begins with the death of Alexander the Great and ends with the destruction of Jerusalem by Titus; and (3) an abstract printed under the title "Ta'rikh Yosippus al-Yahudi" (Beirut, 1873). According to a manuscript at Leyden (No. 1982), Ibn Ḥazm (d. 1063) was acquainted with the Arabic translation from the Hebrew. From an investigation of the Arabic version as contained in two Parisian manuscripts (No. 1906; De Slane, No. 287), Wellhausen has reached the conclusion ("Der Arabische Josippus," in "Abhandlungen der Königlichen Gesellschaft der Wissenschaften zu Göttingen," new series, i. 1–50, Berlin, 1897) that the translator was an Egyptian Jew who made his Arabic version from the Hebrew. Wellhausen believes, furthermore, that the Arabic and existing Hebrew texts have a common origin, and that the Arabic of the manuscripts is nearer to II Maccabees than to the Hebrew version; while all three are to be considered independent recensions and valueless as historical documents. Despite Wellhausen's researches, however, the relation of the Arabic "Yosippon" to the Hebrew text is a problem still unsolved. The Arabic recension was probably the source of the Ethiopic "Ziena Aihud" (comp. Goldschmidt, "Die Aethiopischen Handschriften der Stadtbibliothek zu Frankfurt-am-Main," pp. 5 *et seq.*, Berlin, 1897; Wright, "Catalogue of Ethiopic Manuscripts in the British Museum," No. ccclxxviii.).

BIBLIOGRAPHY: Steinschneider, *Die Arabische Literatur der Juden*, § 71, Frankfort-on-the-Main, 1902; Vogelstein and Rieger, *Gesch. der Juden in Rom*, i. 483. See also JOSEPH BEN GORION.
S.   M. Sc.

ZECHARIAH BEN SOLOMON ZEBSIL
(= "Shabbethai") **ASHKENAZI:** German Talmudist of the sixteenth century; rabbi of the Ashkenazic community at Jerusalem, where he died. He was the father-in-law of Joseph Caro, who speaks of him as of one well versed in rabbinics (Joseph Caro, "Abḳat Rokel," No. 29). His signature has been found with that of David b. Zimra under a halakic decision (*ib.* No. 115). In 1565 a case of ḥaliẓah was the occasion of a controversy between Zechariah and his companions on the one side and David b. Zimra on the other. The brother of the deceased, an Ashkenazic Jew who lived in Palestine and who already had a wife, married the widow instead of performing the rite of ḥaliẓah, which was contrary to the Ashkenazic custom; and Zechariah and his companions put him under the ban. David b. Zimra, on the contrary, argued that as the man lived in a country where polygamy was not forbidden, the Ashkenazic rabbis had no right to excommunicate him. The other Sephardic rabbis, however, declared that Zechariah and his companions were right ("Bet Yosef," Hilkot "Yibbum wa-Ḥaliẓah").

BIBLIOGRAPHY: Azulai, *Shem ha-Gedolim*, i.; S. Frumkin, *Eben Shemuel*, p. 60; Fuenn, *Keneset Yisrael*, p. 314.
J.   M. SEL.

ẒEDAḲAH BOX:
A receptacle in which voluntary charitable contributions are deposited. The

earliest mention of such a device is in connection with Jehoiada the priest, who prepared a chest with a hole in the lid and placed it beside the altar opposite the general entrance at the south side of

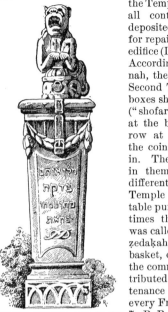

Wooden Ẓedaḳah Box in the Synagogue at Lutomiersk, Russia.
(From Bersohn, "Kilka Slow.")

the Temple; in this chest all contributions were deposited to form a fund for repairing the sacred edifice (II Kings xii. 10). According to the Mishnah, there were in the Second Temple thirteen boxes shaped like a horn ("shofar"), being broad at the bottom and narrow at the top, where the coins were dropped in. The money placed in them was used for different sacrifices in the Temple and for charitable purposes. In later times the charity box was called "kuppah shel ẓedaḳah," *i.e.*, charity basket, or receptacle for the communal fund contributed to provide sustenance for the poor every Friday (Pe'ah viii. 7; B. B. 8b).

From time immemorial the synagogue and bet ha-midrash were provided with sets of charity boxes, each bearing an inscription designating the purpose for which the money was collected. Among these boxes were one for "bedeḳ ha-bayit" (repairs of the synagogue), one for candles in the bet ha-midrash, a third for the Talmud Torah, a fourth for "malbish

Ẓedaḳah Box.
(Designed by Leo Horovitz.)

'arummim" (= "to clothe the naked," *i.e.*, to provide clothing for the poor), and a fifth for "gemilat ḥasadim" (loans without interest to the poor). One special box was marked "mattan ba-seter" (= "a gift in secret"; comp. Prov. xxi. 14), in which large sums were often placed by anonymous donors, who some-

times specified how the money should be distributed. The charity boxes were under the supervision of a board of trustees called "gabba'im." A charity box is carried in front of a funeral by the shammash (beadle), who recites "Ẓedaḳah taẓẓil mi-mawet" (= "Righteousness [charity] delivereth from death"; Prov. x. 2). Charity boxes are also placed in private houses for the support of the yeshibot, hospitals, orphan asylums, etc., of the Holy Land, the funds being collected by the meshullaḥim of the various institutions. See CHARITY; ḤALUḲḲAH.

J.　　　　　　　　　　　　　　　J. D. E.

ẒEDEḲ, JOSEPH KOHEN-: Austro-English rabbinical scholar and preacher; born in Lemberg 1827; died in London 1903. His family claimed to trace its ancestry back to the exilarchs through Solomon Luria and Moses Isserles. Ẓedeḳ was instructed by Joseph Saul Nathansohn, chief rabbi of Lemberg, and attended also the yeshibah of Joseph Yekeles, rabbi of Yavorov. While at Lemberg he produced a number of Hebrew poems of a patriotic character, and edited a volume of collectanea in honor of Sir Moses Montefiore, entitled "Neweh Tehillah" (Lemberg, 1869). He likewise edited at Lemberg the Hebrew periodicals "Meged Yeraḥim" (1855–57), "Oẓar Ḥokmah" (1859–65), and "Ha-Yehudi ha-Niẓḥi" (1866). Ẓedeḳ was a fluent preacher in Hebrew, and occupied temporary positions at Cracow and Altona, as well as at Frankfort-on-the-Main, where he issued the first numbers of another Hebrew periodical, "Or Torah" (1874). He went to London in 1875, and in that city he published the following works: "Mussar Haskel" (1878), a collection of his sermons; "Or Ḥadash" (1881); "Ha-Torah weha-Miẓwah" (1884); and a collection of responsa entitled "Urim we-Tummim." He moreover edited Joseph Cohen's "Dibre ha-Yamim" (1859), Kalonymus' "Eben Boḥan" (1865), and a curious account of a blood accusation at Granada in 1845 under the title "Ohole Shem" (London, 1883). During his later years this scholar collected a mass of material for a biographical and literary history of English rabbis, and published a volume of "Biographical Sketches of Eminent Jewish Families" (*ib.* 1897).

BIBLIOGRAPHY: Zeitlin, *Bibl. Post-Mendels.* pp. 179–182; *The Jewish Year Book,* 5663, p. 308.

J.

ẒEDEKIAH: **1.** One of the four hundred prophets (I Kings xxii. 11, 24, 25) whom Ahab summoned to inquire of them before Jehoshaphat whether he should attack the Syrians in battle at Ramoth-gilead. Zedekiah appeared as a rival of Micaiah, whom Ahab always feared, and who on this occasion ironically foretold Israel's defeat. Zedekiah struck him on the cheek because he explained by a figure that the words of the four hundred prophets were inspired by a lying spirit. Micaiah's reply was that his rival should see a verification of the adverse prophecy with his own eyes.

2. One of the evil men of Israel in the Captivity, whose false utterances and immoral acts aroused even Nebuchadrezzar, King of Babylon, to such a pitch of wrath that he ordered them to be roasted in the fire (Jer. xxix. 21–23), probably in some such fiery furnace as that mentioned in Daniel.

3. The last king of Judah. He was the youngest

son of Josiah and full brother of Jehoahaz (II Kings xxiii. 31, xxiv. 18), the first son of Josiah to reign, who was carried captive to Egypt by Pharaoh-Necho in 608 B.C. (*ib.* xxiii. 33). Zedekiah's real name was "Mattaniah" (*ib.* xxiv. 17), but Nebuchadrezzar, who enthroned him (in 597) in the place of the rebellious and captive Jehoiachin, his nephew, changed it to "Zedekiah" (= "righteousness of Jah"). The new king assumed the throne under the sovereignty of Nebuchadrezzar; and an abundance of material descriptive of the events of his reign is furnished in II Kings (xxiv. 17–xxv. 7), in II Chronicles (xxxvi. 10–21), and in more than a dozen chapters of Jeremiah. The eleven years of Zedekiah's reign were notable for a steady decline in Judah's power and for the desperate efforts of Jeremiah to avert the coming disaster. As a ruler he was pliant in the hands of his princes and of Jeremiah, yielding readily to the influence of any adviser, whether prince or prophet. He made a journey to Babylon in the fourth year of his reign to assure Nebuchadrezzar that he would stand by his oath (Jer. li. 59); but the undying ambitions of the Egyptian kings kept turning toward Asia, and Zedekiah, with his usual wavering policy, could no longer resist the persuasions of Hophra (Apries), King of Egypt (589–569 B.C.), and in 588 B.C. broke off his allegiance to Nebuchadrezzar. This brought the Babylonian army against Jerusalem; but it had no sooner settled down to a siege than Judah's Egyptian ally appeared from the southwest. The Babylonians hastily raised the siege and gave Hophra's army such a blow that it retired to the land of the Nile. The siege of Jerusalem was then resumed, and after an investment of one and one-half years the walls yielded. Zedekiah and his retinue escaped through some hidden gate and fled toward the Jordan; but the Babylonians overtook him on the plains of Jericho, and carried him captive to the King of Babylon, whose headquarters were at Riblah. Here Zedekiah's sons, heirs to the throne, were slain in his presence, his own eyes were put out, and he was bound with fetters and taken to Babylon as an ignominious rebel prisoner. As a result of his conspiracies Jerusalem was taken, plundered, and burned; its best population was deported to Babylon as captives; the Jewish kingdom perished; and Israel ceased to exist as an independent nation. Zedekiah passed the remainder of his days in a Babylonian dungeon.

E. G. H. I. M. P.

ZEDEKIAH BEN ABRAHAM. See ANAW, ZEDEKIAH BEN ABRAHAM.

ZEDEKIAH BEN BENJAMIN: Italian Talmudist and liturgist; lived in Rome in the thirteenth century; died after 1280; elder cousin of Zedekiah b. Abraham ANAW, by whom he is often quoted in the "Shibbole ha-Leḳeṭ." Zedekiah b. Benjamin was a pupil of Meïr b. Moses at Rome; and he later went to Germany and studied under the tosafist Abigdor b. Elijah ha-Kohen, whom he often consulted afterward ("Shibbole ha-Leḳeṭ," i. 266, ii. 40). Abraham of Pesaro speaks of Zedekiah as his companion (*ib.* ii. 6). As Abraham Abulafia mentions one Zedekiah among his disciples and fol-

lowers, certain scholars suppose that this was Zedekiah b. Benjamin. He was the author of several seliḥot found in MS. No. 42 of the Foa collection.

BIBLIOGRAPHY: Vogelstein and Rieger, *Gesch. der Juden in Rom*, i. 249, 267, 273, 376, 378; Zunz, *Literaturgesch.* p. 357.
J. M. SEL.

ZEDERBAUM, ALEXANDER OSSYPO-VITCH: Russian Hebrew journalist; born in Samostye, Lublin, 1816; died in St. Petersburg 1893; founder and editor of "Ha-Meliz," and other periodicals published in the Russian and Yiddish languages. A son of poor parents, he was in his early youth apprenticed to a tailor, but through energy and assiduity he succeeded in acquiring a knowledge of Hebrew literature, and of the Russian, Polish, and German languages. He married in Lublin, and in 1840 left his native town for Odessa, then the "Mecca" of the HASKALAH movement. He obtained there a commercial position, made the acquaintance of the Maskilim of the city, and in his leisure hours continued to work for his self-education. Later he opened a clothing-store, and was himself cutter in his tailoring-shop.

In 1860 Zederbaum succeeded in obtaining the government's permission to publish "Ha-Meliz," the first Hebrew periodical issued in Russia; and three years later he began publishing the pioneer Yiddish journal "Ḳol Mebasser." After an existence of eight years the latter paper was suppressed by the government, whereupon Zederbaum went to St. Petersburg, obtaining permission to transfer the headquarters of "Ha-Meliz" to that city. He was also granted permission to do his own printing, and to publish, besides "Ha-Meliz," a Russian weekly ("Vyestnik Ruskich Yedreed"), which, however, enjoyed only a short existence, as did also the "Razsvyet," which he started a few years later. In 1881 he founded the "Volksblatt," a daily Yiddish journal which existed for eight years, although Zederbaum was its editor for only a few years.

Zederbaum was the author of "Keter Kehunnah" and "Ben ha-Meẓarim," but neither of these works met with any success. His chief significance lies in the fact that he was a champion of the Haskalah. His Yiddish periodical "Ḳol Mebasser" offered an opportunity for many of the best jargon-writers to develop their talents; and among these may be mentioned Linetzky, Abramowitch, Spector, and Sholem Aleichem.

Zederbaum exercised considerable influence in government circles, and it was due to his intercession that an impartial judgment was obtained for many Jewish families accused of ritual murder in Kutais; he disclosed also the ignorance of the Russian anti-Semite Lutostansky, whose pamphlets threatened to become dangerous for the Russian Jews. The Palestine Association of Odessa, which aids the Jewish colonists in Syria and Palestine, owes its existence to Zederbaum's activity.

BIBLIOGRAPHY: *Khronika Voskhoda*, 1893, Nos. 35–36; Sokolow, *Sefer ha-Zikkaron*, 1890; Wiener, *History of Yiddish Literature*; Brainin, *Zikronot*, 1899; Friedberg, in *Sefer ha-Shanah*, 1900.
J. S. HU.

ZEDNER, JOSEPH: German bibliographer and librarian; born at Gross-Glogau Feb. 10, 1804; died at Berlin Oct. 10, 1871. After completing his education, he acted as teacher in the Jewish school in Strelitz (Mecklenburg), where the famous German lexicographer Daniel Sanders was his pupil. In 1832 he became a tutor in the family of the bookseller A. Asher in Berlin, and later engaged in the book-trade himself; but being unsuccessful he accepted in 1845 a position as librarian of the Hebrew department of the British Museum in London, where he remained till 1869, when ill health compelled him to resign and to retire to Berlin, where he spent the last two years of his life. Shortly after his appointment, the British Museum acquired the library of the bibliophile Heimann J. Michael of Hamburg, which Zedner catalogued.

Zedner was the author of the following works: "Auswahl Historischer Stücke aus Hebräischen Schriftstellern vom Zweiten Jahrhundert bis in die Gegenwart, mit Vocalisiertem Texte, Deutscher Uebersetzung und Anmerkungen" (Berlin, 1840); "Catalogue of the Hebrew Books in the Library of the British Museum" (London, 1867); and "Ein Fragment aus dem Letzten Gesange von Reineke Fuchs" (Berlin, 1871), a poetical satire on Napoleon III. He contributed to Asher's edition of the Travels of Benjamin of Tudela (London, 1840), and wrote poems on two collections of portraits ("Ehret die Frauen," and "Edelsteine und Perlen," Berlin, 1836–45). While in London, he published a second edition of Ibn Ezra's commentary on the Book of Esther, to which he wrote an introduction entitled "Wa-Yosef Abraham."

BIBLIOGRAPHY: Steinschneider, in *Magazin für die Literatur des Auslandes*, 1871, No. 44, abstracts of which are given in *Allg. Zeit. des Jud.* 1871, pp. 116–118, and in *Generalanzeiger für die Gesammten Interessen des Judentums*, Berlin, Feb. 22, 1904.
s. D.

ZEEBI, ISRAEL : Prominent Talmudist; son of Benjamin Zeebi, and on his mother's side a grandson of Abraham Azulai; born at Hebron in 1651; died in 1731. Benjamin dying when Israel was but four years old, the latter was educated by his mother; and at the age of eighteen he married a daughter of Abraham Cuençui (see Grätz, "Gesch." x. 463, note 6). For about thirty years he officiated as chief rabbi of Hebron. It is said that he was a partizan of Nehemiah Ḥiyya Ḥayyun. He corresponded with Abraham Yizḥaḳi, Moses Ḥayyun, Ephraim Nabon, Jeshua Shababo, and other authorities. Zeebi's full name was Abraham Israel; the first prænomen he seems to have assumed in later years, probably after an illness. At his death he left one son, **Isaac,** who published at Smyrna in 1758 "Urim Gedolim," a volume of responsa, and "Or li-Yesharim," a collection of homilies, both works being by his father.

BIBLIOGRAPHY: Azulai, *Shem ha-Gedolim*, s.v. *Abraham, Azulai*, and *Israel Zeebi*.
E. C. L. GRÜ.

ZE'ENAH U-RE'ENAH or TEUTSCH ḤUMESH : Judæo-German paraphrase of the Pentateuch, the Hafṭarot, and the Five Megillot, written by **Jacob b. Isaac of Janow,** who flourished in the sixteenth and seventeenth centuries. The work is enriched with many haggadot taken either directly from the Midrash or from such homiletic commentaries as the "Toledot Yizḥak," "Ẓeror ha-Mor,"

"Ḥazeḳuni," and others. Very often the weekly lesson begins with a verse from Proverbs and is supplemented by extracts from the commentary of Baḥya b. Asher and narratives found in various midrashim and other "Ma'aseh" collections. It is very likely that such a paraphrase was originally entitled "Teutsch Ḥumesh," as it is still often called; but as the first printer placed on the title-page as a motto the words of Cant. iii. 11: "Ẓe'enah u-re'enah benot Ẓiyyon" (= "Go out and see, ye daughters of Zion"), and as the book was particularly intended for use by women, it came to be known by the first two words of this motto. Although a work of this kind had been compiled previously by ISAAC B. SAMSON HA-KOHEN at Prague, yet the "Ze'enah u-Re'enah" of Jacob b. Isaac far surpassed it in popularity, and it has continued until the present to be the most favored literary work with Jewish women. Neither the date nor the place of the first edition can be determined with certainty, but the edition of Cracow, 1620, seems to have been the second, and two years later the book was reedited in Basel, which shows that the editions were soon exhausted. Since then it has been very often reedited, and in the later editions (from that of Amsterdam, 1711, onward) there were added the Targum of Shir ha-Shirim in Judæo-German by Issachar Bermann ha-Kohen, and Targum Sheni in Judæo-German by Simeon ben Meshullam. John Saubert translated into Latin the first parashah or Bereshit (Helmstedt, 1660; reproduced by Wolf in "Bibl. Hebr." iii. 474 *et seq.*), and Alexandre Créhange adapted from it his "La Semaine Israélite, ou le Tseena Ourena Moderne," etc. (Paris, 1846). As to Jacob b. Isaac, the author, Steinschneider thinks ("Cat. Bodl." col. 1216) that he died at Janow shortly before 1623. Jacob b. Isaac wrote besides: "Sefer ha-Maggid" (Prague, 1576), a work of the same kind as the "Ze'enah u-Re'enah," and treating of the Prophets and the Hagiographa, with the exception of Chronicles; "Shoresh Ya'aḳob" (Cracow, 1585), a reference index for the laws contained in the Shulḥan 'Aruk, Yoreh De'ah; "Meliẓ Yosher" (Lublin, 1622), Judæo-German homilies on the Pentateuch, being a supplement to the "Ze'enah u-Re'enah."

BIBLIOGRAPHY: Fürst, *Bibl. Jud.* ii. 19–20; Steinschneider, *Cat. Bodl.* cols. 1215 *et seq.*; idem, *Jewish Literature*, p. 238.
J. M. SEL.

ZE'ERA : Palestinian amora of the third generation; born in Babylonia, where he spent his early youth. He was a pupil of Ḥisda (Ber. 49a), of Huna (*ib.*), and of Judah b. Ezekiel in Pumbedita. He associated also with other prominent teachers of the Babylonian school, as Naḥman b. Jacob (Yer. Ber. 8c), Hamnuna (Zeb. 105b; Ber. 24b), and Sheshet, who called him a great man (gabra rabba"; 'Er. 66a). His love for the Holy Land led him to decide upon leaving his native country and emigrating to Palestine. This resolve, however, he kept secret from his teacher Judah, who disapproved of any emigration from Babylonia. Before leaving, he spied upon Judah while the latter was bathing, and the words which he then overheard he took with him as a valuable and instructive memento (Shab. 41a; Ket. 110b). A favorable dream, in which he

Love of Holy Land.

was told that his sins had been forgiven, encouraged him to undertake the journey to the Holy Land (Ber. 57a); and before starting he spent a hundred days in fasting, in order to forget the dialectic method of instruction of the Babylonian schools, that this might not handicap him in Palestine (B. M. 85a). His journey took him through Akrokonia, where he met Ḥiyya b. Ashi ('Ab. Zarah 16b), and through Sura (ib.). When he reached the River Jordan he could not control his impatience, but passed through the water without removing his clothes. When jeered at by an unbeliever who stood by, he answered, "Why should not I be impatient when I pursue a blessing which was denied even to Moses and Aaron?" (Yer. Sheb. 35c).

Ze'era's arrival in Palestine and his first experiences there have been recorded in various anecdotes. He was small of stature and of dark complexion, for which reason Assi called him "Black Pot" ('Ab. Zarah 16b), according to an expression current in Babylonia (comp. Meg. 14b; Pes. 88a; Ber. 50a); this name probably also contained an allusion to his sputtering manner of speech. With reference to a malformation of his legs, he was called "the little one with shrunken **Arrival in** legs," or "the dark, burned one with **Palestine.** the stubby legs" (comp. Bacher, "Ag. Pal. Amor." iii. 7, note 2). With these nicknames is connected a legend which throws light upon Ze'era's ascetic piety (B. M. 85a). In Palestine he associated with all the prominent scholars. Eleazar b. Pedat was still living at the time (Niddah 48), and from him Ze'era received valuable instruction (Yer. Ter. 47d). His most intimate friends were Assi and Ḥiyya b. Abba. In his intercourse with Assi he was generally the one who asked questions; and on one occasion Assi made known his approval of one of Ze'era's questions by saying: "Right you are, Babylonian; you have understood it correctly" (Yer. Shab. 7c). Ze'era especially acknowledged the authority of Ammi, the principal of the school at Tiberias; and it is related that he asked Ammi to decide questions pertaining to religious law that had been addressed to himself (Yer. Dem. 25b; Yer. Shab. 8a; Yer. Yeb. 72d). Ze'era was highly esteemed by Abbahu, the rector at Cæsarea, of whom he considered himself a pupil. He was ordained rabbi, a distinction usually denied to members of the Babylonian school; and though in the beginning he refused this honor (Yer. Bik. 65c), he later accepted it on learning of the atoning powers connected with the dignity (Sanh. 14a). His insignificant appearance was humorously referred to when at his ordination he was greeted with the words of a wedding-song: "Without rouge and without ornament, but withal a lovable gazel" (Ket. 17a).

With regard to Ze'era's private vocation, the only facts known are that he once traded **Social Con-** in linen, and that he asked Abbahu **dition and** how far he might go in improving the **Family** outward appearance of his goods with **Life.** out rendering himself liable in the slightest degree to a charge of fraud (Yer. B. M. 9d). Information regarding his family relations is also very scanty; it is asserted that he became an orphan at an early age (Yer. Pe'ah 15c), and

that his wedding was celebrated during the Feast of Tabernacles (Suk. 25b); and he had one son, Ahabah or Ahava, who has become well known through various haggadic maxims (comp. Bacher, l.c. iii. 651–659).

Ze'era occupies a prominent place in the Halakah as well as in the Haggadah; with regard to the former he is especially distinguished for the correctness and knowledge with which he transmits older maxims. Among his haggadic sayings the following may be mentioned as throwing light upon his high moral standpoint: "He who has never sinned is worthy of reward only if he has withstood temptation to do so" (Yer. Ḳid. 61d); "One should never promise a child anything which one does not intend to give it, because this would accustom the child to untruthfulness" (Suk. 46b). On account of his lofty morals and piety Ze'era was honored with the name "the pious Babylonian." Among his neighbors were several people known for their wickedness, but Ze'era treated them with kindness in order to lead them to moral reformation. When he died, these people said, "Hitherto Ze'era has prayed for us, but who will pray for us now?" This reflection so moved their hearts that they really were led to do penance (Sanh. 37a). That Ze'era enjoyed the respect of his contemporaries is evidenced by the comment upon his death written by an elegist: "Babylonia gave him birth; Palestine had the pleasure of rearing him; 'Wo is me,' says Tiberias, for she has lost her precious jewel" (M. Ḳ. 75b).

BIBLIOGRAPHY: Bacher, Ag. Pal. Amor. iii. 1–34; Heilprin, Seder ha-Dorot, ii. 117–120.
J.   J. Z. L.

ZEFIRAH, HA-. See PERIODICALS.

ZE'IRI: Amora of the third century; born in Babylonia. He sojourned for a long time in Alexandria, and later went to Palestine, where he became a pupil of Rabbi Johanan. In the name of Ḥanina b. Ḥama he transmitted the maxim that he who in the presence of a teacher ventures to decide a legal question, is a trespasser ('Er. 3a). He also transmitted a saying by Ḥanina to the effect that the Messiah would not arrive until all the arrogant ones had disappeared (Sanh. 98a). During his sojourn in Alexandria he purchased a mule which, when he led it to water, was transformed into a bridge-board, the water having lifted the spell which rested on the animal. The purchase-money was refunded to Ze'iri, and he was advised to apply the water-test thenceforth to everything he purchased, in order to ascertain whether it had been charmed (ib. 67b). When Eleazar arrived in Palestine he sought information from Ze'iri concerning men known in ancient traditions (B. B. 87a). Ze'iri was praised by Raba as an exegete of the Mishnah (Zeb. 43b). He was proffered the daughter of Rabbi Johanan for a wife, but refused because he was a Babylonian and she a Palestinian (Ḳid. 71b). Among those who transmitted in his name may be mentioned Rabbi Ḥisda (Ber. 43a), R. Judah ('Ab. Zarah 61b; Men. 21a), R. Joseph (Ned. 46b), R. Naḥman ('Ab. Zarah 61b), and Rabbah (Ned. 46a).

BIBLIOGRAPHY: Bacher, Ag. Pal. Amor. iii. 644; Heilprin, Seder ha-Dorot, ii. 123a; Blau, Altjüdisches Zauberwesen, p. 158, note 5, Strasburg, 1898; Yuḥasin, ed. Filipowski, p. 134b.
J.   S. O.

ZEISEL, SIMON: Austrian chemist; born at Lomnitz, Moravia, April 11, 1854; educated at the German gymnasium of Brünn and at the University of Vienna (Ph.D. 1879). He established himself as privat-docent for chemistry at the same university in 1887, and in 1892 was appointed assistant professor of general and agricultural chemistry at the agricultural high school of Vienna, where he became full professor seven years later (1899). In addition to monographs in technical periodicals, Zeisel is the author of "Die Chemie in Gemeinverständlicher Darstellung" (Vienna, 1890).

BIBLIOGRAPHY: Eisenberg, *Das Geistige Wien*, ii. 574, Vienna, 1893.
S.   F. T. H.

ZEISLER, SIGMUND: American jurist; born at Bielitz, Austria, April 11, 1860; educated at the University of Vienna and at the Northwestern University, Chicago. He was admitted to the Chicago bar, and was associate counsel for the defense in the anarchist cases of 1886 and 1887. In 1893 he was elected chief assistant corporation counsel for Chicago, but resigned his position in 1894 on account of ill health. After traveling for several months in Europe, he returned to Chicago, where he has since been engaged in private practise. Zeisler is a prominent Democrat, and took an active part in the presidential campaigns of 1896 and 1900. He has contributed to reviews and law journals.

BIBLIOGRAPHY: *American Jewish Year Book*, 5665, p. 211.
A.   F. T. H.

ZEISSL, HERMANN VON: Austrian dermatologist; born at Vierzighuben near Zwittau, Moravia, Sept. 22, 1817; died at Vienna Sept. 23, 1884; educated at the University of Vienna (M.D. 1846). In 1846 he was appointed assistant in the ophthalmological, surgical, and dermatological hospitals of the University of Vienna, and four years later he established a practise and was admitted to the medical faculty of the university as privat-docent. He soon became an authority on skin-diseases and syphilis. In 1861 he was appointed assistant professor, and in 1869 he became professor and chief physician, of the second department for syphilis at the general hospital. These positions he held until his resignation in 1883. He was knighted by the Austrian emperor.

Zeissl wrote many essays for the medical journals, and was the author of the following works: "Compendium der Pathologie und Therapie der Tertiären Syphilis und Einfachen Venerischen Krankheiten" (Vienna, 1850); "Lehrbuch der Constitutionellen Syphilis für Aerzte und Hörer der Medizin" (Erlangen, 1864); "Lehrbuch der Syphilis und der mit Dieser Verwandten Oertlichen Venerischen Krankheiten" (Stuttgart, 1875); and "Grundriss der Pathologie und Therapie der Syphilis" (*ib.* 1876). The last two works have been translated into Russian, Dutch, English, and Italian.

BIBLIOGRAPHY: Hirsch, *Biog. Lex.* s.v.
S.   F. T. H.

ZEIT, DIE. See PERIODICALS.

ZEITGEIST, DER. See PERIODICALS.

ZEITLIN, JOSHUA: Russian rabbinical scholar and philanthropist; born at Shklov in 1742; died

at Kherson Aug. 18, 1822. He was a pupil of the casuist Aryeh Loeb, the author of "Sha'agat Aryeh"; and, being an expert in political economy, he stood in close relations with Prince Potemkin, the favorite of Catherine II. During the Turko-Russian war Zeitlin furnished the Russian army with various supplies, and managed that business so cleverly that he was afterward appointed imperial court councilor ("nadvorny sovyetnik").

On retiring from business Zeitlin resided on his estate Ustzia, where he was consulted by the rabbis with regard to rabbinical questions. He rendered pecuniary assistance to many Talmudists and scholars, and supported a magnificent bet ha-midrash, in which many Jewish writers were provided with all the necessaries of life, so that they could pursue their vocations without trammel of any kind. Among writers who benefited by his generosity may be mentioned: R. Nahum, author of "Tosafot Bikkurim"; Mendel Lepin, author of "Ḥeshbon ha-Nefesh"; and the physician Baruch Schick. Zeitlin was the author of annotations to the "Sefer Miẓwot Ḳaṭan," printed with the text (Kopys, 1820), and supplemented by some of his responsa.

BIBLIOGRAPHY: Fuenn, *Ḳiryah Ne'emanah*, p. 277; idem, *Keneset Yisrael*, p. 431.
J.   M. SEL.

ZEITLIN, JOSHUA B. AARON: Russian scholar and philanthropist; born at Kiev Oct. 10, 1823; died at Dresden Jan. 11, 1888. While he was still young his parents removed to Chernobyl, where he associated with the ḤASIDIM, later devoting himself to the study of secular sciences as well as the Hebrew language and literature. He was married at Slutsk, where he studied for some time with Samuel Simchowitz, with whom he later engaged in business. Leaving Slutsk, Zeitlin resided for several years in St. Petersburg, and afterward settled in Moscow, where he became prominent as a benefactor of Talmudic students and Maskilim. During the Russo-Turkish war he was a contractor for the Russian army, and on Aug. 1, 1879, Czar Alexander II. awarded him a medal in recognition of his services.

In 1883 Zeitlin left Russia and settled in Dresden, where he collected a large library, which he placed at the disposal of Talmudic students. In the beginning of 1887 he undertook a journey to the Holy Land, where he celebrated the Passover. He visited Jerusalem and Hebron, and took great interest in the Jewish antiquities, as well as in the agricultural colonies of Palestine, to which he bequeathed 50,000 francs, in addition to many bequests to educational institutions.

BIBLIOGRAPHY: I. Gräber, in *Oẓar ha-Sifrut*, ii., part 2, pp. 279–280; S. Mandelkern, in *Keneset Yisrael*, iii. 219 *et seq.*; *Ha-Meliẓ*, xxviii. 44.
J.   M. SEL.

ZEITLIN, WILLIAM: Russian scholar and bibliographer; born at Homel, government of Moghilef, about the middle of the nineteenth century. He is known especially as the author of "Ḳiryat Sefer," or "Bibliotheca Hebraica Post-Mendelssohniana" (Leipsic, 1891–95), a bibliographical dictionary of modern Hebrew literature from the beginning of Mendelssohn's epoch until 1890. The compilation of this work occupied Zeitlin for twenty years. He made extensive use of Benjacob's "Oẓar ha-Sefarim" and of Fürst's "Bibliotheca Judaica," and visited Wilna and Warsaw, the centers of the Hebrew book market, as well as many university cities—as Königsberg, Berlin, Geneva, and Paris—from the libraries of which he gathered additional material for his work. The "Kiryat Sefer" indexes not only works in book form, but also important periodical articles, biographical sketches, and scientific essays, in addition to giving biographical notes on several authors. Zeitlin had previously prepared an index of works written on the Jewish calendar, in which he enumerates seventy-seven Hebrew works; this index was published by Ḥayyim Jonah Gurland in "Yevreiski Kalendar" (St. Petersburg, 1882). In the "Zeit. für Hebr. Bibl." (ix. 3–4) Zeitlin later published an alphabetical list of anagrams and pseudonyms of modern Hebrew writers; and he is a contributor to several Hebrew periodicals, writing mostly biographical articles.

J.   M. Sel.

ZEITSCHRIFT FÜR DIE GESCHICHTE DER JUDEN IN DEUTSCHLAND. See Periodicals.

ZEITSCHRIFT FÜR DIE RELIGIÖSEN INTERESSEN DES JUDENTHUMS. See Periodicals.

ZEITSCHRIFT FÜR DIE WISSENSCHAFT DES JUDENTHUMS. See Periodicals.

ZEITUNG. See Periodicals.

ZEKOR BERIT: A poem by Gershom ben Judah (960–1040), the "Light of the Exile" (Zunz, "Literaturgesch." p. 239); it is chanted in the Seliḥot of the Northern rituals as the central hymn of the early penitential prayers on the eve of New-Year, to which day the hymn has given its name in familiar Jewish parlance. Other hymns with the same commencement, which bases an appeal for the redemption of the remnant of Israel on the remembrance of the merits of the Patriarchs, were afterward written by Kalonymus ben Judah and Samuel ben Majo (Zunz, *l.c.* pp. 255, 263), and were also adopted into some rituals. The hymn of Gershom is specially honored in the Polish ritual by being placed at the head of the extracts from the hymns in the seliḥot quoted in the course of the Ne'ilah service. It is there always chanted to an old air which obviously originated in western Europe, and which presents points of resemblance to some of the minnelieder of the twelfth century. The commencement of the second verse, on which the others are modeled, should be compared with the melodies transcribed under Shofet Kol ha-Areẓ.

s.   F. L. C.

ZELAZOWSKA, CATHERINE: Polish convert to Judaism; born in 1460; martyred at Cracow in 1540. She was the widow of an alderman of Cracow; and at the time when, influenced by the Bible, Polish Christendom was divided into different sects, she followed the example of the daughter of Nicholas Radziwill and embraced Judaism. Peter Gamrat, Bishop of Cracow, condemned her to be burned, and, though eighty years old, she went gladly to meet a martyr's death.

Bibliography: Grätz, *Gesch.* 3d ed., ix. 454; Sternberg, *Gesch. der Juden in Polen*, p. 56.

J.   M. Sel.

ZELMAN, SAMUELE VITA: Austro-Italian poet; born at Triest in 1808; died there in 1885. He was educated at the rabbinical college of Padua, where he was the favorite pupil of Samuel David Luzzatto. He was the author of the following works: "Kinah on the death of S. D. Luzzatto" (Padua, 1865); "Primi Discorsi di Rab Melza" (Triest, 1854); "Le Parole di un Ignorante ai Dotti," directed against demagogic writers (*ib.* 1855); Ha-Niẓẓanim," a collection of Hebrew poems (*ib.* n.d.). A complete edition of his Hebrew essays, hymns, letters, elegiac poems, etc., was published by Vittorio Castiglione under the title "Ne'im Zemiro,

ZEKOR BERIT

ma - 'an - ka fe - de - nu; Re - 'eh.... ki a - ze - lat.... ya - de - nu;
Thine own sake re - lease us; *Be - hold,... how weak - ness doth... de - crease us;*

SHur, ki a - be - du ha - si - de - nu; Maf - gi - a' a - - yin
See,.... how now our saints do.... cease us; And none is left...... whose

ba - - 'a - de - nu: We - shub be - ra - ha - mim 'al she - 'e -
help...... should ease us: Then turn in mer - cy to Is - ra - el's

rit Yis - ra - el, We - ho - shi - 'e - nu le - ma - 'an she - me - ka.
rit Yis - ra - el, And do Thou save us for Thy.... great Name's.... sake.

Shemu'el o Yelid Kinnor" (*ib.* 1866). Some of his Hebrew poems are contained in the periodicals "Bikkure ha-'Ittim" (vol. xi.) and "Mosé" (vols. v. and viii.).

BIBLIOGRAPHY: *Corriere Israelitico,* xxiv. 188; Fürst, *Bibl. Jud.* iii. 748; *Mosé,* viii. 415; *Oẓar Neḥmad,* i. 63; Steinschneider, *Cat. Bodl.* col. 2760.
s.   U. C.

ZELOPHEHAD (צלפחד).—**Biblical Data:** A Manassite who in one passage is called the son of Hepher, the son of Gilead, the grandson of Manasseh (Num. xxvi. 29–33), and in another is set down as the second son of Manasseh (I Chron. vii. 15). The etymology of the name is very doubtful; some scholars think that the root is Syriac and means "first rupture," indicating that he was a first-born son (comp. ZELOPHEHAD IN RABBINICAL LITERATURE). But the Septuagint Σαλπαάδ or Σαλφαάδ (B in Chron., Σαπφαάδ) shows that the Hebrew was vocalized צֶלְפָחָד (= "the shadow [or "protection"] of terror"). Zelophehad died in the wilderness and left five daughters, who subsequently claimed the inheritance of their father. Knowing that those who took part in the revolt of Korah were exceedingly objectionable to Moses, Zelophehad's daughters argued that their father was not of Korah's assembly, but that he "died in his own sin." Moses consulted YHWH about the matter, and was ordered to satisfy the daughters' demand. Thus after the conquest of the land under Joshua, Zelophehad's daughters obtained their father's lot (Num. xxvii. 1-7, xxxvi. 2-12; Josh. xvii. 3).
J.   M. SEL.

——**In Rabbinical Literature:** Zelophehad and his father, Hepher, were among those who went out from Egypt, and consequently each of them had his part in the land. Zelophehad, as the first-born

son, had two parts in his father's lot, so that his daughters inherited "three shares" in the land (Sifre, Num. 133; B. B. 116b; Num. R. xxi. 13). The Rabbis interpret Num. xxvii. 3 as meaning that Zelophehad was not among those who murmured against God (Num. xi. 1 *et seq.*), nor among those who revolted against Him at the time of the spies (*ib.* xiv. 1 *et seq.*), nor of the company of Korah; for none of these three classes had a part in the land (Sifre, *l.c.*; B. B. 18b). The Rabbis, however, do not agree as to whether Zelophehad himself was a good man; for while he was righteous according to the anonymous opinion of the Sifre, R. Nathan concludes that he was wicked (Sifre, *l.c.*). In any case, the words "died in his own sin" (Num. xxvii. 3) are interpreted as meaning that while he did not induce others to sin, he himself sinned, for which he was punished. According to R. Akiba, Zelophehad was the man who was stoned to death for gathering sticks upon the Sabbath-day (Num. xv. 32–36), while according to Judah b. Bathyra, he was one of those who "presumed to go up unto the hilltop," and who were smitten by the Amalekites and Canaanites (*ib.* xiv. 44–45; Sifre, Num. 113, 133; Shab. 96b). As both events took place in the second year after the Exodus, the youngest of Zelophehad's daughters at the time they claimed their father's inheritance was at least forty years old. They were not yet married (comp. Num. xxxvi. 6, 11) because they had been waiting for men suitable to be their husbands (B. B. 119b).
J.   M. SEL.

ZEMAḤ BEN ḤAYYIM: Gaon of Sura from 889 to 895. He was the stepbrother and successor of Nahshon ben Zadok, and has become known especially through the reply which he made to the inquiry of the Kairwanites regarding Eldad ha-Dani. This responsum, which appeared in part in the first edition of the "Shalshelet ha-Ḳabbalah" (Venice, 1480), was republished as completely as possible by A. Epstein in Vienna in his "Eldad ha-Dani." It embraces nine points and concludes with an apology for Eldad's forgetfulness. According to Epstein, only one other responsum by Zemah has been published; it is given in the Constantinople edition of the "Pardes," and ends with the same words as does the first-mentioned responsum: לנטות ימין ושמאל. Weiss, however, ascribes to this gaon also the authorship of responsa in "Sha'are Ẓedeḳ" (iv., No. 14) and in the compilation "Ḥemdah Genuzah" (Nos. 58–61, 111–131). Nothing is known of the gaon's personal career.

BIBLIOGRAPHY: A. Epstein, Eldad ha-Dani, pp. 6–10, Presburg, 1891; Reifmann, in Ha-Karmel, viii., No. 32; Monatsschrift, 1874, p. 553; Frankel, ib. 1878, p. 423; Grätz, Gesch. v. 243–245; Weiss, Dor, iv. 124, 264.
J.   S. O.

ẒEMAH, JACOB BEN ḤAYYIM: Portuguese cabalist and physician; died at Jerusalem in the second half of the seventeenth century. He received a medical training in his native country as a Marano, but fled about 1619 to Safed and devoted himself to the Talmud and the casuists ("poseḳim") until 1625; then he went to Damascus, where for eighteen years he studied the Cabala from the Zohar and the writings of Isaac Luria and Ḥayyim Vital. He finally settled at Jerusalem and opened a yeshibah for the study of the Zohar and other cabalistic works, David CONFORTE being for some time one of his pupils ("Ḳore ha-Dorot," pp. 36a, 49a). Jacob Ẓemaḥ was one of the greatest cabalists of his period and was a prolific author, his works including treatises of his own as well as compilations of the writings of Ḥayyim Vital. He produced twenty works, of which only two have been published. The first of these is the "Ḳol ba-Ramah" (Korez, 1785), a commentary on the "Idra," which he began in 1643, and for which he utilized the commentary of Ḥayyim Vital. In the preface to this work he maintained that the coming of the Messiah depended on repentance ("teshubah") and on the study of the Cabala from the Zohar and the writings of Isaac Luria, the delay in the advent of the Messiah being due to the fact that schools for such study had not been established in every town. His second published work is the "Nagid u-Meẓawweh" (Amsterdam, 1712), on the mystical meaning of the prayers, this being an abridgment of a compendium which Ẓemaḥ composed on the basis of a more comprehensive treatise. Among his unpublished works, special mention may be made of the "Ronnu le-Ya'aḳob," in which he calls himself "the

proselyte" ("ger ẓedeḳ"; "Cat. Oppenheimer," No. 1062 Q). This treatise consists of notes recorded while studying under Samuel Vital and supplemented by his own additions. In his compilation of Ḥayyim Vital's writings, Ẓemaḥ pretended to have discovered many works of Vital which were unknown to the latter's son Samuel.

BIBLIOGRAPHY: Azulai, Shem ha-Gedolim, i., ii. s.v. Gilgulim, et passim; Carmoly, in Revue Orientale, ii. 287; Fuenn, Keneset Yisrael, p. 570; Steinschneider, Cat. Bodl. col. 1268.
E. C.   M. SEL.

ẒEMAH BEN KAFNAI: Gaon of Pumbedita from 936 to 938, at the time when Saadia had been reinstated in the gaonate of Sura after his excommunication. Nothing is known concerning his life or his works.

BIBLIOGRAPHY: Letter of Sherira, in Neubauer's Anecdota Bronicusa, i. 40; Grätz, Gesch. v. 276–277; Weiss, Dor, iv. 160.
J.   S. O.

ZEMATUS, MAGISTER. See MICHAEL B. SHABBETHAI.

ZEMIROT ("songs"): A term applied by the Sephardim to the Psalms in the earlier sections of the morning service. The Ashkenazim, on the other hand, style them "pesuḳe de-zimra" (= "verses of song"), and the term "zemirot" more especially designates the Hebrew hymns chanted in the domestic circle, particularly those which precede or follow the grace after the chief meal on the eve and the afternoon of the Sabbath. Music at table was a regular feature in ancient Jewish life, and the Mishnah expressly states (Soṭah ix. 11) that it was discontinued only as a mark of mourning for the abolition of the Sanhedrin. Even then the later Rabbis found it necessary to insist emphatically on abstention from such domestic melodies (comp. Soṭah 48a), although there were never serious objections to them when they were devotional in character (comp. MUSIC, SYNAGOGAL). The singing of hymns at the table (probably selected psalms like Ps. cxxvi. and cxxxvii., which are now used on Sabbaths and on week-days respectively) seems to have been known in the days of the later Midrash, but the ancient custom afterward received a powerful impetus from the spread of the CABALA and the belief in the visits of celestial guests on the Sabbath (comp. Zohar, pp. 252b, 272b, et passim). In the sixteenth century many compilations of such hymns were published, especially at Amsterdam and Constantinople. Gradually, however, two favorite collections were formed, one for the Sabbath evening meal and the other for the Sabbath afternoon. A third group was selected for chanting at the close of the Sabbath in order that the "sacred season" might be prolonged at the expense of the "profane" (Shab. 118b; Shul-

Sabbath Hymns.

ZEMIROT—Melodies at Grace.

GRACE AFTER MEALS

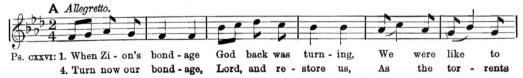

Ps. CXXVI: 1. When Zi - on's bond - age God back was turn - ing, We were like to
          4. Turn now our bond - age, Lord, and re - store us, As the tor - rents

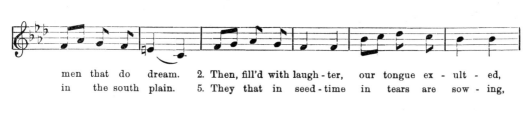

men that do dream. 2. Then, fill'd with laugh - ter, our tongue ex - ult - ed,
in the south plain. 5. They that in seed - time in tears are sow - ing,

And our eyes with glad smiles did gleam: Then did they de - clare a - mong the
Joy in reap - ing - time yet may gain. 6. When he go - eth forth, the sow - er

na - tions: "Great things hath the Lord for these men wrought!" Great things hath the
weep - eth, In his hands a store of pre - cious seed; When he com - eth

D. C.

Lord wrought for His peo - ple, Joy to faith - ful ones by them is wrought.
back, he shall be sing - ing, Good - ly sheaves be bear - ing for his meed.

B *Moderato.*

SHORT VERSICLES: Bo neh be - ra - ḥa - maw Ye - ru - sha - la - yim: A - men.

C *Moderato.*

LONG VERSICLES: ⎰ Mig - dol ye - shu - 'ot mal - ko; we - 'o - seh he - sed
(II SAM. XXII. 51) ⎱

lime - shi - ḥo, le - Da - wid u - le - zar - 'o.... 'ad 'o - lam. 'O -

seh sha - lom bime - ro - maw, Hu ya - 'a - seh sha - lom 'a -

le - nu we - 'al kol Yis - ra - el, we - im - ru: A - men.

XII.—42

SABBATH REST

1. This day is to our race   Of all sea-sons the best,   Re - plete with ev - 'ry
2. The lives torn with dis - tress,   With sweet sol - ace it heals,   With fresh spir - it doth
3. This day, more than all - else,   Did God ho - ly de - clare,   When He whose love it

grace,   The day that brings us rest;   O come, most wel-come guest,   Re -
bless   The soul that an - guish feels;   A - way sor - row it steals   From
tells,   Com - pleted His work so fair.   The hearts full of de - spair   In

fresh each wea - ry breast!   A light and a joy to us is Sab-bath rest.
hearts sad - ly op - pressed: A light and a joy to us is Sab-bath rest.
its qui - et are blessed: A light and a joy to us is Sab-bath rest.

AIRS OF THE ḤASIDIM

A *Allegretto con moto.*

Ai! di - di - dy did - dy did - dy di!   Ai! did - dy did - dy did - dy did - dy di!

Ai! di - di - dy did - dy did - dy di!   Ai! did - dy did - dy did - dy did - dy di!

B *Andantino.*

Ai, ai, ai! ai, ai, ai, ai, ai! ai, ai, ai! ai, ai, ai, ai, ai!

rit - - -

Ai, ai, ai! ai, ai, ai, ai, ai! ai, ai, ai! ai, ai, ai, ai, ai!

KI ESHMERAH SHABBAT

p Andante.   *mf*   *dolce.*

REFRAIN. If the Sab - bath I shall keep, God will then.... my guardian be: An e - ter - nal

cov - e - nant and sign, 'Twixt Him and me. There - on one must not trade, Nor

go...... on.... jour - ney, Nor talk on mat - ters of the state, Nor of the

sea, Nor of one's own af - - fairs, Nor of..... one's pay or

fee. So let me speak of God's great Law.... to........ make wise me.

han 'Aruk, Orah Hayyim, 293, 1), and that the departing Queen Sabbath might be escorted on her way with protracted song (comp. Zohar, p. 208a). These collections of hymns are still published in such old-fashioned prayer-books as the one containing the "Derek ha-Hayyim" of JACOB BEN JACOB MOSES OF LISSA. The authors are among the latest of the payyetanim, and the only early medieval hymn in the collections is the "Baruk Adonai Yom Yom" of SIMEON B. ISAAC B. ABUN.

Even later in origin than the hymns are the melodies. Indeed, the ordinary head of a household could scarcely be expected to do more than repeat in the domestic circle the folk-songs which he heard in the workaday world outside. With the growing elaboration of the florid chant of the hazzan, it would be difficult for the children at the table even to approximate the intricate ornamental vocalization heard in the synagogue; nor

Melodies. would they be able to analyze the intonations and detect the basis on which they were constructed. Jewish characteristics are manifested chiefly in occasional phrases of synagogal character in which the traditional melody diverges from its folk-song model (comp. EN KELOHENU). It was the introduction of these occasional Hebraic phrases into the popular melodies of Gentile neighbors which Chopin deplored when he wrote (F. Niecks, "Chopin," i. 183): "Poor Polish airs! you do not in the least suspect how you will be interlarded with Majufes" (the Judæo-Polish pronunciation of "Mah Yafit," the opening words of a hymn by Mordecai ben Isaac for the eve of the Sabbath, one of the most popular zemirot). The most wide-spread melodies for the zemirot are those short phrases introduced into the chanting of the grace after meals when three or more adult males are present (comp. 'AL HET). They are South-German in origin, and recall many of the snatches of tune built into the fabric of the Passover home-service. Even

where other zemirot are not sung, the psalm preceding the grace is at least chanted. One of the best-known melodies for it is here transcribed. Its instrumental model may perhaps be identified in a violin composition of the eighteenth century.

When the whole collection of zemirot is used, they are not chanted to definite melodies, but are read in a sort of cantillation (comp. OREN), and where a selection is made, the most frequent air is a German melody employed either with the "Yom Zeh le-Yisrael" of Isaac LURIA or with the anonymous "Zur mi-Shello Akalnu."

A favorite melody, often used with "Mah Yafit," may be added as an example of the Sabbath-melody popular among the HASIDIM of southern Poland and Galicia. Together with the melody which follows it, it was first transcribed by Lewandowski (comp. his "Hebräische Melodien," op. 32, Berlin, 1882) as typical of its class.

The Hasidim affect the chanting both of zemirot and of "songs without words," or melodies set to meaningless sounds; nor are these cantillations restricted to the Sabbath table, since they aim at expressing the joy of the spirit upon all occasions. Two such airs, one from Russia and the other from Jerusalem, are here transcribed. Their recent Slavonic origin is obvious.

The Sephardic tunes for the zemirot are sung in a more florid fashion than is usual among German or even Polish Jews. They include many tender airs, of which that for "Ki Eshmerah Shabbat" (a poem often incorrectly attributed to Abraham IBN EZRA) may be instanced.

Sephardic tradition is particularly rich in melodies for the conclusion of the Sabbath. One has already been given elsewhere (see HA-MABDIL), and another, the air to BEMOZA'E MENUHAH, also is well worth presentation.

Some of the original melodies for the zemirot may well have been composed or adapted by the authors of the verses, especially in the case of Israel ben Moses NAJARA, whom Delitzsch calls the founder of the Jerusalem rite, and who wrote no less than 650 hymns after selecting from the folk-songs of the Levant the melodies for his verses. In his compilations, first published at Safed in 1587, the zemirot are arranged according to the order of the Perso-Arabic modes in which fall the melodies to which they were set, while the original Arabic, Turkish, Greek, Rumanian, Spanish, and Italian titles are prefixed to his Hebrew verses. His hymns "Yah Ribbon 'Olam" and "Yiggaleh Kebod Malku-teka" are frequently chanted as zemirot, especially among the Ḥasidim, but are set to melodies of much later date. Indeed, for the reasons stated at the beginning of this article, there are few zemirot which retain the same melody for more than two generations.

BIBLIOGRAPHY: Zunz, *Literaturgesch.* pp. 306, 364, 419, 484–486, 490, 511, 540, 546, 555, 565, 579, 583, 584, 591, 595, 597.

J.   F. L. C.

ZEND-AVESTA. See AVESTA.

ZENOBIA SEPTIMIA:
Empress of Palmyra; regent (from 267 to 273) for her minor son Vollaba-thus, who had been appointed imperator by the emperor Aurelian. Zenobia appears to have been friendly to the Jews; and according to some accounts, which, however, lack authentication, she was herself of Jewish descent. That she came into close relations with the Jews is shown by Yer. Ta'an. viii. 46b (see also PALMYRA). Within a brief space of time she so extended her dominion over the whole of Egypt and Syria that Aurelian feared lest she should renounce her allegiance to Rome, and he accordingly made war on her in 272, conquered her, and led her and her son in golden chains in triumph through Rome, although he treated her with leniency and gave her a villa on the Tiber.

BIBLIOGRAPHY: Grätz, *Gesch.* 3d ed., iv. 273–276; Hamburger, *R. B. T.* i., s.v. *Thadmor.*

S.   S. O.

ZEPHANIAH:
One of the twelve Minor Prophets who describes himself as "the son of Cushi, the son of Gedaliah, the son of Amariah, the son of Hezekiah, in the days of Josiah, the son of Amon, King of Judah" (Zeph. i. 1). He seems, therefore, to have been a descendant of Hezekiah, King of Judah, since otherwise only the name of his father would have been given (comp. Isa. i. 1; Ezek. i. 3; Joel i. 1). If he was of royal descent, he probably lived in Jerusalem; and evidence of this is seen in his prophecies, where he describes various parts of the city. According to the first verse of the book which bears his name, he flourished during the reign of Josiah, and on the basis of his utterances the majority of modern scholars date his activity prior to the reforms so rigorously inaugurated and promulgated after 621, the pictures of corruption and the approaching foe being most appropriately referred to the situation in Judah during the early years of Josiah and the Scythian invasion.

The contents of the book of this prophet fall into two parts: i. 1–iii. 8, the coming judgment on the world, including Israel and the nations; and iii. 9–20, a promise of universal salvation. Zephaniah's special denunciations are directed against false worship and irreligion. The calamity will find every one, even in the hiding-places of Jerusalem; Philistia, Moab, Ammon, Cush, and Assyria shall be overwhelmed by punishment and disaster; Jerusalem in particular, being rebellious, corrupt, and disobedient to the word of YHWH, shall fall under the divine wrath. Yet, on the other hand, God's promise is made known to the nations, that He will so purify them that they may call on Him, and all shall bring Him offerings. After the storm of judgment Israel shall be humble, and shall trust in YHWH alone. New social conditions shall arise, and justice and righteousness shall prevail, so that the redeemed shall rejoice in the Lord.

Zephaniah is a forceful book. Its language is vigorous and picturesque, and betrays an acquaintance with the Earlier Prophets. The ideas most emphasized are the providential control of the nations of the world, the necessity of purity and justice as opposed to the prevalent corruption and injustice of the day, and the refining value of judgment and suffering.

BIBLIOGRAPHY: Davidson, *Nahum, Habakkuk, and Zephaniah,* in *The Cambridge Bible for Schools,* 1896; Nowack, *Die Kleinen Propheten,* in *Handkommentar zum Alten Testament,* 1897; Smith, *The Book of the Twelve Prophets,* ii., in *The Expositor's Bible,* 1898.

E. G. H.   I. M. P.

ZEPHANIAH BEN MORDECAI TROKI:
Karaite scholar and author; flourished during the latter part of the sixteenth century; brother of Joseph b. Mordecai Troki. He was the author of "Ḳiddush ha-Ḥodesh we-Sod ha-'Ibbur," a work on the calendar, and of responsa on the laws governing SHEḤIṬAH. Both works are mentioned by Simḥah Luzki in his "Oraḥ Ẓaddiḳim."

BIBLIOGRAPHY: Fürst, *Gesch. des Karäerthums,* iii. 39; idem, *Bibl. Jud.* iii. 448; Gottlober, *Biḳḳoret le-Toledot ha-Ḳara-'im,* p. 209.

J.   M. SEL.

ZERAHIAH BEN ISAAC HA-LEVI GERONDI (known as ZeRaH and ReZBI):
Talmudic author and liturgical poet of the twelfth century; disciple of Moses ben Joseph of Narbonne. Azulai and many others, influenced by the statement of Zacuto ("Sefer ha-Yuḥasin," ed. Filipowski, p. 218) that Zerahiah completed in 1150 his "Sefer ha-Ma'or," which he is known to have begun at the age of nineteen, give 1131 as the year of his birth. This date can scarcely be correct, however, since the "Sefer ha-Ma'or" mentions the commentaries of Jacob Tam and Samuel ben Meïr, which could not have been known so early in Provence. It is equally improbable that he died in 1186, as is asserted by Judah ibn Verga ("Shebeṭ Yehudah," ed. Hanover, p. 112). Zerahiah belonged to a prominent Spanish family called Yiẓhari of Gerona, but early in life he left his native place, where he seems to have had many enemies, and settled at Lunel. There he appears to have devoted himself to teaching, his pupils including Samuel ibn Tibbon, son of Judah ibn Tibbon, who, in his ethical will, freely recognized Zerahiah as a greater scholar than himself. Zerahiah was not only a thorough Talmudist of great erudition, with an analytic and synthetic mind, but he was also deeply versed in Arabic literature, in philoso-

phy, and in astronomy, and was, above all, a gifted poet, combining elegance of style with elevation of sentiment.

Zerahiah's chief work was the "Sefer ha-Ma'or," which he began at the age of nineteen and completed late in life. It contains a critique of Alfasi as well

as additions to his Halakot, and is divided into two parts, the first, entitled **The "Sefer** "Ha-Ma'or ha-Ḳaṭan," comprising the **ha-Ma'or."** Seder Mo'ed and the treatises Berakot and Ḥullin, and the second, called "Ha-Ma'or ha-Gadol," embracing the Sedarim Nashim and Neziḳin. In this work the author displays great erudition and a fine critical sense which recognizes no other authority than logical reasoning. His independence displeased the conservatives, however, and refutations of his criticisms were written by Naḥmanides under the title "Milḥamot Adonai," and by Abraham ben David of Posquières (RABaD), who alluded in his harsh fashion to Zerahiah as an immature youth who had had the audacity to criticize his master, and even accused him of having appropriated some of his (RABaD's) own interpretations without mentioning the author. A justification of Zerahiah's critique was written by Ezra Malki under the title "Shemen la-Ma'or," and since 1552 the "Sefer ha-Ma'or" has always been printed together with Alfasi.

As a sequel to his "Sefer ha-Ma'or" Zerahiah composed the "Sefer ha-Ẓaba," in which he expounded the methodology of the Talmud, and at the same time endeavored to show that Alfasi had not observed the principles laid down in the Talmud for halakic interpretation. This work, like its prede-

cessor, was criticized by Naḥmanides, **Other** who justified Alfasi. Both the "Sefer **Works.** ha-Ẓaba" and the criticism of Naḥmanides were inserted in the "Sefer Temim De'im" (§§ 225, 226, Venice, 1622), and were also published separately at Shklov in 1803. Zerahiah was likewise the author of the following works: "Hilkot Sheḥiṭah u-Bediḳah," mentioned in the "Sefer ha-Ma'or" at the end of the first chapter on the treatise Ḥullin; "Hassagot 'al Ba'ale ha-Nefesh," a critique of RABaD's treatise on the laws relating to women, published in part with the "Ba'ale ha-Nefesh" (Venice, 1741; Berlin, 1762); "Dibre Ribot," a controversy with RABaD on civil jurisprudence, mentioned in the "Sefer ha-Ma'or" on Baba Meẓi'a and cited in part by Bezaleel Ashkenazi in his "Shiṭṭah Meḳubbeẓet" on Baba Meẓi'a, p. 98a; "Sela' ha-Maḥaloḳot," mentioned in the "Sefer ha-Ma'or" at the end of the first chapter of Shebu'ot; "Piṭḥe Niddah," quoted by the author's grandson in his "Bedeḳ ha-Bayit" (vii. 3); a dissertation on the Mishnah Kinnim, published at Constantinople in 1795; and responsa, mentioned in the "Sefer ha-Ma'or" at the end of the second chapter of Giṭṭin and quoted in the "Sefer ha-Terumot" (xlv. 1). Zerahiah was the author of numerous liturgical poems, eighteen of which are found in the Sephardic Maḥzor.

BIBLIOGRAPHY: Zunz, Z. G. p. 476; idem, in Allg. Zeit. des Jud. iii. 679; Sachs, Religiöse Poesie, p. 257; Dukes, in Orient, Lit. ix. 760; Landshuth, 'Ammude ha-'Abodah, p. 63; Reifmann, Toledot R. Zeraḥyah ha-Lewi, Prague, 1853; Carmoly, La France Israélite, p. 107; Steinschneider, Cat. Bodl. cols. 2589–2593; Fuenn, Keneset Yisrael, p. 570; Gross, Gallia Judaica, pp. 255, 282; Michael, Or ha-Ḥayyim, p. 367, No. 826.
J.   I. BR.

ZERAHIAH HA-YEWANI (RaZaH): Byzantine ethical writer of the thirteenth or fourteenth century. Of his life no details are known, except that he was the author of an ethical work entitled "Sefer ha-Yashar," which was confused with Jacob Tam's halakic work of the same name and erroneously attributed to the renowned tosafist. This error was detected by Menahem of Lonzano, who, in his poem "Derek Ḥayyim" ("Shete Yadot," p. 122), expressly states that the ethical work in question belonged to Zerahiah. Lonzano did not succeed, however, in correctly establishing the identity of its author, for a second error immediately arose. Since Zerahiah ha-Yewani had the same initials as Zerahiah ha-Levi Gerondi, the author of the well-known "Sefer ha-Ma'or," the "Sefer ha-Yashar" was attributed by some bibliographers to the latter.

The "Sefer ha-Yashar" is divided into eighteen short chapters, and treats of the ethical principles which underlie the relation of man to God. It is an imitation of Baḥya's "Ḥobot ha-Lebabot," which Zerahiah acknowledges in his preface that he had studied, although he found it too long and too profound for the average reader. The indebtedness of the "Sefer ha-Yashar" to the "Ḥobot ha-Lebabot" is especially evident in the first chapter, entitled "Sod Beri'at 'Olam," which is simply a brief summary of the chapters called "Sha'ar ha-Yiḥud" and "Sha'ar ha-Beḥinah" in Baḥya's work. The "Sefer ha-Yashar" was first published at Constantinople in 1526, and since then has passed through twenty-four editions.

BIBLIOGRAPHY: De Rossi, Dizionario, s.v. Tam, Jacob; Nachman Krochmal, in Kerem Ḥemed, iv. 272; Carmoly, in Jost's Annalen, i. 155; Steinschneider, Cat. Bodl. cols. 2586–2588.
J.   I. BR.

ZERA'IM ("Seeds"): The first order of the Mishnah, containing eleven treatises: Berakot, Pe'ah, Demai, Kil'ayim, Shebi'it, Terumot, Ma'aserot, Ma'aser Sheni, Ḥallah, 'Orlah, and Bikkurim. With the exception of the first, all these treatises, as is implied by the name of the order, deal with the laws governing agriculture and farm products.

E. C.   J. Z. L.

ZERED, BROOK or **VALLEY OF:** One of the stations of the Israelites in the wilderness, indicated as the end of the thirty-eighth year of wandering (Num. xxi. 12; Deut. ii. 13–14). The Targum of pseudo-Jonathan renders the name by "valley where willows grow," and thus apparently etymologizes it by the Talmudic זרדתא, which is confirmed by the Septuagint reading Ζάρετ. The location of Zered is given as east of the Jordan on the border between Moab and Edom before one crosses the River Arnon. Most modern scholars, including Dillmann, identify it with the Wadi Karak, a deep and narrow ravine running northwest to the Dead Sea.

J.   M. SEL.

ZERFFI, GUSTAV (real name, **Hirsch**): Hungarian journalist and revolutionist; born in Hungary about 1820. He was the author of "Wiener Lichtbilder und Schattenspiele," with twelve caricatures (Vienna, 1848); and as editor of "Der Ungar" in 1848, he became conspicuous by his attacks upon the Germans and the imperial family.

With Csernatoni, Stancsits, Zanetti, Steinitz, and others he set the tone for the revolutionists, and in 1848 he was Schweichel's captain and adjutant in the honved army. On the failure of the revolution he fled to Belgrade (1849), where he entered the service of the French consul. In 1850 he translated Kossuth's complete works into German for the "Europäische Bibliothek der Neuen Belletristischen Litteratur" (cccxxii., cccxlvii., cccxlix.), and two years later he visited Paris, going in 1853 to London, where he became a member of the Royal Medical College, and afterward secretary of the German National Association. He resigned this post under suspicion, however, although he was still in London in 1863.

Bibliography: Wurzbach, *Biographisches Lexikon*, lix., s.v.; *Die Presse*, No. 355, feuilleton (Vienna, 1863); *Die Geissel*, No. 155 (Vienna, July 3, 1849).

s. N. D.

ZERIKA:

Palestinian amora of the fourth century; a pupil of Eleazar, whose halakic maxims he transmitted (Soṭah 4b; Zeb. 93b; Men. 7b, 86b), and of Ammi (see Ḥul. 46a). He was a colleague of Abba, with whom he decided the controversy of Judah I. and Nathan on the problem whether the night should be divided into three or four watches (Yer. Ber. 2d), and by whom he was informed of a correction in a halakic tradition given by Ammi (B. B. 130b). He was also acquainted with Ze'era (Yer. Beẓah 60c), and especially with Jeremiah (Men. 88b; Suk. 37b). In Babylonia it was said that he had called Safra's attention to the difference between the modesty of "pious Palestine" and the audacity of "bold Babylonia" on the occasion of the prayer for rain (Ta'an. 23b). No haggadic maxims of Zerika's have been preserved, the only saying ascribed to him being one belonging really to Hidka, whose name was incorrectly transliterated "Zerika" (comp. Ḥag. 16a, where the correct name, "Ḥidka," is given).

Bibliography: Bacher, *Ag. Pal. Amor.* iii. 754–755.

E. C. J. Z. L.

ẒEROR, RAPHAEL JEDIDIAH SOLOMON BEN JESHUA:

Algerian rabbi; born at Algiers Sept. 8, 1681; died there Dec. 21, 1737. He was a descendant of a family of distinguished Talmudists, and his grandfather, **Solomon Ẓeror**, was, like himself, chief rabbi of Algiers. Together with the other rabbis of his city he signed the ban against Nehemiah Ḥayyun (comp. Nepi-Ghirondi, "Toledot Gedole Yisrael," p. 280). Ẓeror studied secular sciences, devoting himself especially to logic, physics, and geography, and he likewise occupied himself much with poetry in addition to acquiring a reputation as a skilful physician and carrying on an extensive commerce by both sea and land. Some of his responsa and novellæ were collected by his pupil Judah 'Ayyashi, and were published under the title "Peri Ẓaddiḳ" (Leghorn, 1748), the edition being preceded by a preface written by Ẓeror's pupils and contemporaries.

Bibliography: Bloch, *Inscriptions Tumulaires*, pp. 45 *et seq.*, Paris, 1888; Steinschneider, *Cat. Bodl.* col. 2126.

J. M. Sel.

ZERUBBABEL:

Son of Shealtiel (Ezra iii. 2, 8; Hag. i. 1; "Pedaiah" in I Chron. iii. 19 is probably a scribal error) and grandson of Jehoiachin. The name is either the Hebrew זרוע בבל (= "begotten of [in] Babylon"), although compounds with the passive participle, frequent in Assyrian, are rarely, if ever, found in Hebrew; or, more probably, it is the Assyro-Babylonian "Zeru-Babel" (= "seed or offspring of Babylon"). It is a moot question whether or not he was identical with SHESHBAZZAR, "the prince of Judah" and leader of the first great band of exiles returning to Jerusalem from Babylon under Cyrus (Ezra i. 8). On the one hand, it is urged that he is regarded as the head of the community of returned exiles (Ezra iv. 2), that he is associated in this capacity with the high priest Jeshua in the general administration (Ezra iii. 2, 8; iv. 3; v. 2; Hag. i. 1; Zech. iii.–iv.), and that the same title of governor ("peḥah") of Judah is given him by the prophet Haggai (i. 1; ii. 2, 21) as is attributed to Sheshbazzar by Ezra (v. 14); while it is supposed that he, like Daniel, bore a double name, the Hebrew "Zerubbabel" and the Babylonian "Sheshbazzar." In opposition to this view it is pointed out that "Zerubbabel" is in all probability a Babylonian name, and that no hint of this identity is given in those portions of Ezra in which both names occur. It has been suggested that "Sheshbazzar" may be identical with "Shenazar" (I Chron. iii. 18), one of the sons of Jehoiachin and an uncle of Zerubbabel. In that case it might be supposed that the nephew took a prominent part in the reorganization of the community and shortly afterward succeeded to the governorship. At all events, Zerubbabel was governor of Judah in the second year of Darius Hystaspis (520 B.C.; Hag. i. 1, 14; ii. 2). According to the story of the chronicler in Ezra iii.–iv. 5, Zerubbabel, together with the high priest Jeshua and others, erected an altar for burnt offerings in the seventh month, offered morning and evening sacrifices, and kept the Feast of Tabernacles. In the second month of the second year of the return they laid the foundation of the Temple, but the opposition of "the adversaries of Judah and Benjamin" (either descendants of Jews who had not gone into exile or interlopers who showed hostility to the returning exiles) caused a delay of seventeen years. Roused to fresh activity by the prophets Haggai and Zechariah, work was resumed in the second year of Darius (520 B.C.), but fresh obstacles were encountered in the suspicions of Tatnai, "governor beyond the river" (R. V.), and an appeal was made to Darius, who promulgated a decree authorizing the completion of the work. The Temple was finished and dedicated four years later (Ezra v.–vi.). Nothing further is certainly known of Zerubbabel, although a Jewish tradition says that he returned to Babylon and died there. His sons are named in I Chron. iii. 19, and in Ecclus. (Sirach) xlix. 11 his name appears in the list of the famous men of Israel.

In I Esdras iv. 13–63, followed by Josephus ("Ant." xi. 3, §§ 5–9), a story, which appears to lack historicity, is told to the effect that Zerubbabel was a soldier in the body-guard of Darius Hystaspis and commended himself to the king's notice by his ready wit, receiving as his reward permission to go to Jerusalem and rebuild the Temple. In recent times interest has been aroused by the ingenious hypothesis of Sellin ("Serubbabel: ein Beitrag zur Geschichte der Messianischen Erwartung," 1898), who endeavors to show that Zerubbabel was actually made King of Judah, but was overthrown and put to death by the Persians. This kingdom, he believes, was regarded as Messianic, and in Isa. liii. he sees an allusion to Zerubbabel's martyrdom.

BIBLIOGRAPHY: Ryle, *Ezra and Nehemiah*, in *The Cambridge Bible for Schools*, Cambridge, 1893; Van Hoonacke, *Zorobabel et le Second Temple*, Paris, 1892; Sayce, *Higher Criticism and the Verdict of the Monuments*, pp. 539 et seq., London, 1894; Wellhausen, *I. J. G.* 3d ed.; Schrader, *Die Dauer des Zweiten Tempelbaues*, in *Studien und Kritiken*, 1867, pp. 460–504; Koster's *Het Herstel van Israel in het Perzische Tijdvak*, 1894.

E. G. H. J. F. McL.

ZEVAST. See WILL.

ZHIDOVSTVUYUSHCHAYA YERES. See JUDAIZING HERESY.

ZHITOMIR (JITOMIR): Former Russian city; capital of the government of Volhynia, now belonging to Ukraine. It is one of the oldest towns in European Russia, having become part of Lithuania in 1320 and being one of its prominent towns in the middle of the fifteenth century. As late as the middle of the seventeenth century, however, there were probably no Jews there, or else their number was very small, for the destruction of the city during the uprising under CHMIELNICKI in 1648 is not mentioned in the records of the Volhynian massacres of that year. When Zhitomir became part of Russia in 1778, it had a large Jewish community, and was a center of the Ḥasidic movement. In 1861 it had 13,299 Jews in a total population of 40,564, and owned one large synagogue and twenty-six small ones. In 1920 the Jews numbered about 22,000 out of a population of 65,452, there were three synagogues, and 46 batte ha-midrashoth.

The Russian government regarded Zhitomir as the central point of the Jewish population of southwestern Russia, as Wilna is considered the Jewish center of the northwestern part of the country. The printing of Hebrew books was permitted only in these two cities during the monopoly of Hebrew printing from 1845 to 1862, and both of them were also chosen as the seats of the two rabbinical schools which were established by the government in 1848 in pursuance of its plans to force secular education on the Jews of Russia in accordance with the program of the Teutonized Russian HASKALAH movement. The rabbinical school of Zhitomir was considered the more Jewish, or rather the less Russianized, of the two (see "Ha-Meliẓ," 1868, No. 40). Its first head master was Jacob EICHENBAUM, who was succeeded by Ḥayyim Selig SLONIMSKI in 1862. The latter remained at the head of the school until it was closed (together with the one at Wilna) in 1873 because of its failure to provide rabbis with a secular education who should be acceptable to the Jewish communities. Suchastover, Gottlober, Lerner, and Zweifel were among the best-known teachers of the rabbinical school at Zhitomir, while Goldfaden, Mandelkern, and Paperna were among the students who later became famous in the Jewish world.

The teachers' institutes which were substituted for the rabbinical schools were scarcely more satisfactory, and the one in Zhitomir, which was probably the worst-managed Jewish institution in Russia of which there is any record (see Prelooker, "Under the Czar and Queen Victoria," pp. 8–21, London, 1895), and of which Jonas Gurland was inspector from 1873 to 1880, was closed in 1885. The educational institutions of the Jewish community included a Talmud Torah, a "government school" for boys, a girls' school, and several admirable private schools for both sexes. The other Jewish communal institutions of Zhitomir were considered to rank above the average in excellence.

Wolf (d. 1800), author of the "Or ha-Meïr" (Koretz, 1795), a pupil of Bär of Meseritz and one of the leaders of early Ḥasidism, and Abraham Bär Mavruch, "rosh bet din" or acting rabbi of Zhitomir in the first half of the nineteenth century and author of the "Bat 'Ayin" (Zhitomir, 1850), are two of the few noteworthy rabbinical authorities of Zhitomir; indeed, the town has never been a center of rabbinical learning. Its best-known "crown rabbis" have been Lev Bienstok, Kulisher, and the 1905 incumbent, S. Skomorovsky, who has held this position for nearly fifteen years. Ḥayyim Naḥman Bialik (b. in Radi, Volhynia, 1873), who is considered the ablest of the younger Neo-Hebrew poets, was educated in Zhitomir.

About twenty Jews were killed and a large number were wounded during the disturbances which occurred in Zhitomir on May 7 and 8, 1905, when the section of the city known as "Podol" was devastated. Among the dead was Nicholas Blinov, a Christian student, who fell while defending the Jews, and thus acted in real life the part of "Boris" in Chirikev's drama "Yevrei," which he had often played as an amateur on the stage. Ten young Jews who started from a neighboring town to assist the Jews of Zhitomir were killed in the village of Troyanov, near the city. After the massacre of Zhitomir a committee was organized to collect money for the families of those who had been killed; it received about 33,000 rubles from Russia, 9,500 from England, 1,500 from Germany, and 6,000 from the United States.

The district of Zhitomir outside the city contained 22,636 Jews in a population of 281,378 in 1897.

——**Typography:** The earliest Hebrew book printed in Zhitomir bears the date of 1804. After the misfortune which befell Moses SCHAPIRO at Slavuta (comp. Hillel Noah Steinschneider, "'Or Wilna," pp. 21–27, Wilna, 1900) and the suppression, by the Russian government, of all Hebrew printing-offices in Russia, excepting Wilna, about eight years passed before the brothers Hanina Lippa, Aryeh Loeb, and Joshua Heschel, "grandchildren of the rabbi of Slavuta," were permitted to establish a Hebrew printing-office in Zhitomir which was a revival of the Slavuta office, with the same beautiful type for which that establishment had been famous. In the sixties the Schapiros published at Zhitomir the finest edition of the Babylonian Talmud which had appeared in Russia until that time. Abraham Shalom Shadow and Isaac Moses BAKST also conducted printing establishments in Zhitomir in the second half of the nineteenth century.

BIBLIOGRAPHY: Fuenn, *Keneset Yisrael*, p. 9; *Ha-Shaḥar*, vi. 585–586; *Razsvyet*, 1880, No. 26; Sokolow, *Sefer ha-Shanah*, pp. 60 et seq.; Zweifel, *Shalom 'al-Yisrael*, i. 69–73 (quotations from the *Or ha-Meïr* of Wolf of Zhitomir).

H. R. P. WI.

ZIDON (SIDON): 1, Eldest son of Canaan (Gen. x. 15; I Chron. i. 13).

2. According to Strabo (xvi. 2), the oldest city of Canaan; situated twenty miles south of Beirut. Its territory extended from the slopes of the Lebanon to the coast, and was bounded on the south by Asher and Zebulun (Gen. xlix. 13; Josh. xix. 25). In its flourishing period the city had a winter and a summer harbor, which are now filled with sand. The city is said to have been called after the eldest son of Canaan (Gen. x. 19; Josephus, "Ant." i. 10, § 2); but the name may also have been derived from the extensive fisheries (צוד) in which the inhabitants engaged. It was ruled by independent kings (Jer. xxvii. 3), and had its own cult (Judges x. 6; II Kings xxiii. 13). It had this advantage over Tyre, that it entered into relations with the Israelites when its king, Ethbaal, married his daughter Jezebel to Ahab (I Kings xvi. 31).

The prophets of Israel were continually referring to the great importance of Zidon as a commercial city (Isa. xxiii. 2, 4, 12; Joel iv. [A. V. iii.] 4-7). It lost this position when Nebuchadnezzar conquered Palestine and part of Phenicia. Ezekiel's prophecy referring to it (Ezek. xxviii. 20-24) dates from a later time. Isaiah (xxiii. 1-14, according to Duhm; xxiv. 10, according to Cheyne) refers to the destruction of the city by Artaxerxes Ochus in 351 B.C. There are also various references in the Talmud to the city. Ze'era says (Meg. 6a): "The tribe of Zebulun, which borders upon Sidon, complains of its mountainous country, with its superabundance of streams and seacoast, and is answered by reference to Deut. xxxiii. 19, pointing out the advantages of this region": "sefune" is said to mean the murex from which the purple dye חלזון is obtained; "te-mune" is said to be an allusion to the abundance of fish; and "ḥol" is said to refer to the Phenician glass which is made from the sands. In the seventh century Zidon was identified with Zeboud in Galilee or with Bagdal of·Yo דיו בגדל; Gen. R. xcviii. 16).

Down to the middle of the nineteenth century the population did not exceed 8,000 inhabitants, but this number has increased to 15,000 within the last fifty years; of this number about 10,000 are Mohammedans, and 800 Jews. The latter are very poor, and are dependent almost entirely upon the ḤALUKKAH. Zidon is still considered to be outside the Pale of Palestine; and pious Jews direct their bodies to be taken after death to a more southerly city.

BIBLIOGRAPHY: Sepp, *Jerusalem und das Heilige Land*, ii. 450-466, Ratisbon, 1876; Neubauer, *G. T.* pp. 294-295; Schwarz, *The Holy Land*, p. 174. For data on the ḥalukkah see *Die Jüdische Presse* (Mayence), 1897, *passim*.
J.   S. O.

ZIEGLER, IGNAZ: Austrian rabbi; born at Also-Kubin, Hungary, Sept. 29, 1861; educated at the Rabbinical Seminary and at the University of Budapest (Ph.D. 1888). Immediately after his graduation he was called to the rabbinate of Carlsbad, a position which he still held in 1905. Through his efforts the Kaiser Franz Josef Regierungs-Jubiläum Hospiz was erected at Carlsbad, át a cost of 500,000 Austrian crowns, to provide food, shelter, and medical treatment for indigent Jews who come to that city in large numbers in search of health. This institution was opened May 1, 1903. Ziegler's works are as follows: a Hungarian dissertation on the prophet Malachi (Budapest, 1888); "Religiöse Disputationen im Mittelalter" (Frankfort-on-the-Main, 1894); "Geschichte des Judentums" (Prague, 1900); and "Die Königsgleichnisse im Midrasch" (Breslau, 1903).

s.   H. M.

ZIKLAG: Simeonitic town which, after the union of the tribes of Simeon and Judah, became Judean; first mentioned in the account of the territory and borders of the individual tribes (Josh. xv. 31, xix. 5). In the early part of the regal period Ziklag came into the possession of the Philistines, who retained it until King Achish gave it to his vassal David as a place of residence (I Sam. xxvii. 6; II Sam. i. 1, iv. 10; I Chron. xii. 1, 20). It was invaded and burned by the Amalekites when David joined the Philistine king in war (I Sam. xxx. 1-26), and after the return from the first Exile it was one of the towns assigned to the Judeans (Neh. xi. 28). The town has not yet been identified, although Conder and Kitchener believe that its ruins are represented by the remains called Zuḥailika, discovered by them in 1877, and lying on three low hills east-southeast of Gaza and four miles north of Wadi al-Shari'ah.

BIBLIOGRAPHY: Riehm, *Handwörterbuch*, 2d ed., p. 1866b; Buhl, *Geographie des Alten Palästina*, Berlin, 1896.
J.   S. O.

ZILZER, ANTAL (ANTON): Hungarian painter; born at Budapest in 1861. He was a pupil of Rauscher, Gregusz, and Szekely at the national model school of design, and later studied at the Munich Academy under Raupp, Hackl, Seitz, and Herterich, completing his education at Berlin, Paris, and London. He devoted himself especially to portraits, and received the Munich gold medal in 1887. His paintings include: "Alone in the Woods"; "Ludwig II. on His Funeral Bier"; "Forest Idyls"; and "Sunset on the Lake of Constance."

BIBLIOGRAPHY: Singer, *Allgemeines Künstler-Lexicon*, v., *s.v.*
s.   N. D.

ZIMMER, NATHAN LÖB DAVID: English pietist and scholar; born at Fürth, Bavaria, in March, 1831; died at London Jan. 10, 1895. He was noted in London for his intense piety, which he probably inherited from his father, who was a fervent ẓaddiḳ. Zimmer went to England about 1850 and entered business. He was primarily engrossed with the study of the Law, however, and especially with the more occult commentaries, every moment not absolutely needed for worldly objects being devoted to contemplation and to study of the higher life as revealed in the Cabala. His knowledge of the Cabala, and especially of gemaṭria, was profound, and astronomical calculations also had a strong attraction for him. He compiled an elaborate genealogical table of the chief rabbis of England and was a frequent contributor to the Jewish periodical press on questions of astronomical calculation and of ritual. He was one of the original founders of the London Federation of Synagogues, and is

supposed to be the original of *Karlkammer* in Zangwill's "Children of the Ghetto."

BIBLIOGRAPHY: *Jew. Chron.* Jan. 14, 1895; *Jew. World*, Jan.
14, 1895.
J. G. L.

ZIMMERN, HELEN: German authoress; born
at Hamburg March 25, 1846. She went to England
at an early age, and resided there till 1887, when she
removed to Florence. She has written lives of Scho-
penhauer (1873), Maria Edgeworth (1883), and Sir
Laurence Alma-Tadema (1902), and has also translated "Tales from the Eddas" (1882), "The Epic of
Kings" (1882), "Comedies of Goldoni" (1892), and
the "Pentamerone" (1893). She likewise contributed
a volume on the Hansa towns to "The Story of the
Nations" series (1899).

BIBLIOGRAPHY: *Who's Who*, 1905; *New International Encyclopedia*, s.v.
S. J.

ZIMRAT HA-AREZ. See PERIODICALS.

ZIMRI: 1. Son of Zerah and grandson of Judah
(I Chron. ii. 6), identical with Zabdi (Jos. vii. 1).

2. Son of Salu, a prince of the Simeonites. In
the wilderness the Israelites were smitten at Shittim
for worshiping Baal-peor, and while they were
weeping before the door of the Tabernacle, Zimri
took a Midianite woman named Cozbi, the daughter of Zur, in the presence of Moses and all the people. Thereupon Phinehas, the grandson of Aaron,
seized a javelin, went into Zimri's tent, and slew
the guilty pair (Num. xxv. 6–14).

3. Son of Jehoadah or Jarah (I Chron. viii. 36, ix.
42). He was a Benjamite and a descendant of Saul.

4. King of Israel for seven days; originally the
captain of half the chariots of King Elah. He
gained the throne by the murder of his master as Elah
was reveling in the house of Arza, his steward, at
Tirzah. In the midst of the festivity Zimri killed
the king and all the house of Baasha, the predecessor of Elah; but when the army, then engaged in
the siege of the Philistine town of Gibbethon, heard
of the assassination, it immediately proclaimed its
general OMRI king. He marched at once against
Tirzah and took the city, whereupon Zimri retreated
to the royal palace, set it on fire, and perished in the
flames (I Kings xvi. 9–20).

5. In Jer. xxv. 25 "kings of Zimri" are mentioned together with Elamitic and Median sovereigns. This Zimri may be identical with Zimran, a
son of Abraham by Keturah (Gen. xxv. 2).

E. G. H. B. P.

ZIN (צִן): Frontier post of Judah on the south,
mentioned in the description (Num. xxxiv. 4; Josh.
xv. 3) of the frontier between the "ascent of
AKRABBIM" and Kadesh-barnea. The desert of Zin
derived its name from this place. Kadesh-barnea
was situated in this desert (Num. xiii. 2, xxxiii.
36; Deut. xxxii. 51; Josh. xv. 1, 3; comp. Num.
xx. 1, xxvii. 14; Deut. xxxii. 51); and one passage (Num. xxxiii. 36) reads, "the wilderness of
Zin which is Kadesh." The phrase "the wilderness
of Kadesh," which occurs only once (Ps. xxix. 8),
refers possibly not to any definite geographical
locality, but to the region around Kadesh. The
statement found in Num. xiii. 26, that Kadesh is
situated in the wilderness of Paran, is due to the

fact that, of the two sources combined in that chapter, one (P) says that the spies started from the
wilderness of Paran, and the other (JE) that they
set out from Paran. The wilderness of Zin adjoined the wilderness of Paran on the north;
hence it must be assigned to a locality immediately
south of the southern part of Judah, on the plateau
or on the mountain region (Josephus mentions the
"mountains of Sin") in which the 'Azazime Bedouins now pitch their tents.

E. G. H. I. BE.

ZINC. See BRASS.

ZION. See JERUSALEM.

ZION. See PERIODICALS.

ZIONIDES or **SONGS OF ZION** (Hebr. **Shire
Ziyyon**): The songs of Zion, *i.e.*, the lyrical hymns
which express the longing of the Jewish nation to
see the hill of Zion and the city of Jerusalem shine
again in all their former glory, date back to the
time immediately after the destruction of Solomon's
Temple. Since that period the poets and singers of
Israel have devoted their best talent to painting in
the most brilliant colors the ancient glories of Zion.
By far the greater number of these songs unite in
voicing a heartfelt desire to see the nation, the city
of Jerusalem, Mount Zion, and the Temple restored
to their former splendor. The oldest song of Zion
in Jewish literature was written in the fifth century
B.C., and is a lamentation that the enemy compels
Israel to live on foreign soil; this is the celebrated
Ps. cxxxvii. 1–3. A similar Zionide of the same
period is Ps. cxxvi.; in it the poet, full of hope,
sings of the day when the Captivity shall be over
and the joyfully returning exiles shall sing a new
song of Zion. The elegy ending with a desire for
deliverance, which is found in the fifth chapter of
Lamentations, dates probably from the first pre-
Christian century.

During the Middle Ages, Zionides from the pens
of the greatest poets formed the chief comfort and
consolation of the people. As early as the time of
Ibn Gabirol (11th cent.) songs of Zion
were incorporated in the liturgy,
partly as lamentations for the Ninth of
Ab and partly as tefillot and piyyuṭim.
Among the songs of lamentation for Zion which are
sung on the Ninth of Ab the following may be specially referred to: a song beginning with the words
בליל זה יבכיון ויילילו בני and giving a vivid description of the destruction of Zion; the well-known song
which begins with the words שמרון קול תתן מצאוני
עוני, and in which Samaria and Jerusalem try to ex-
cel each other in the description of the misfortune
which has fallen upon them; and, above all, the song
with the refrain:

אלי ציון ועריה
כמו אשה בצריה
וכבתולה חגורת שק
על בעל נעוריה

("Zion and her cities wail like a woman in childbirth,
and like a virgin clothed in sackcloth for the man of
her youthful choice"). Of other tefillot and piyyuṭim may be mentioned the song beginning:

קול ברמה נשמע בילָלה
אבן הראשה לעים ולחרישה

and several strophes of the song "Lekah Dodi,"
composed by Solomon ha-Levi and incorporated in
the Sabbath eve service.

The most important of Ibn Gabirol's Zionides are
the poem beginning with the words:

שלח מנזר
לעם נגזר
אשר הפזר
הן והן

("Send a prince to the condemned people which is
scattered hither and thither") and that beginning:

שעה נאסר
אשר נמסר
ביד בבל
ונם שעיר

("Turn thy face, O God, to the conquered, who is
delivered up into the hand of Babel and of Seir").

Judah ha-Levi (1140) was the author of the Zionide beginning:

> " Zion, wilt thou not send a greeting to thy captives,
> Who greet thee as the remnant of thy flocks?
> From West to East, from North to South, a greeting,
> From far and near, take thou on all sides.
> A greeting sends the captive of desire, who sheds his tears
> Like dew on Hermon ; would they might fall on thy hills."

Besides this song, which has been translated into
nearly all European languages in prose and in verse,
Judah wrote several shorter songs, chief of which
are מערב בסוף ואנכי במזרח לבי ("My heart is in the
East, although I am at the end of the West") and
ירושלים האנחי ודמעך ציון הסכי ("Sigh, O Jerusalem, and shed thy tears, O Zion ").

Among other medieval writers of this class may
be mentioned Abraham ibn Ezra, who composed the
Zionide אלהי קדם מעונה ישובב יונה הללה ("O God,
who art enthroned in the East, appease the mourning dove"); Judah al-Ḥarizi (13th cent.), author of
the song שלום לעיר שלם ("Peace be

**Various
Authors.** to the city of Salem [Jerusalem] ");
and Israel Najara (16th cent.), who
wrote the song יפרח כתמר ציון ישע
("May the flower of salvation bloom like a palm ").
In more modern times Samuel David Luzzatto wrote:

לבי לבי
רב מכאובי
הנה עצבי
ישן נושן

("My heart, my heart is full of pain; see, my
grief is an ancient one "); and equally well known
is Joseph Almanzi's

מכל פנה
תבוא רנה
בקרא מקרא
אל אל כי טוב

("From all corners comes rejoicing on the day of
celebration to God, who is good ").

The most prominent Hebrew poets have written
Zionides, among the number being M. S. Rabener,

Micah Levisohn, Judah Loeb Gordon, S. Mandelkern, M. M. Dolitzky, and N. H. Imber. Countless
songs have been produced under the influence of
Zionism: of these may be mentioned the song
adopted by all the Zionists of the world as their
national song, and beginning with the words
"There, where a slender cedar kisses the clouds";
the song of the academic society Kadimah in Austria, "Knowest thou whence freedom comes?"; the
song of the united Zionists, "Sluchajcie bracia
gueśni tij"; and "Ha-Tiḳwah" (Hope), composed
by N. H. Imber, which has the refrain:

עוד לא אבדה תקותינו
תקוה הנושנה
לשוב לארץ אבותינו
עיר בה דוד תנה

("Our hope has not yet gone, the old hope to return
to the land of our fathers, to the city where David
lived ").

BIBLIOGRAPHY: *Kinnor Ẓiyyon*, Warsaw, 1900 (collection of all
the Zionides from the oldest times to the present day [Hebr.]);
Yevreiskyie Motivy, Grodno, 1900; Heinrich Loewe, *Liederbuch für Jüdische Vereine*, Cologne, 1898; Jacobs, *Jewish
Ideals*, p. 131.

J.
S. O.

ZIONISM : Movement looking toward the segre-
gation of the Jewish people upon a national basis
and in a particular home of its own; specifically, the
modern form of the movement that seeks for the
Jews "a publicly and legally assured home in Palestine," as initiated by Theodor Herzl in 1896, and
since then dominating Jewish history. It seems
that the designation, to distinguish the movement
from the activity of the Chovevei Zion, was first used
by Matthias Acher (Birnbaum) in his paper "Selbst-
emancipation," 1886 (see "Ost und West," 1902, p.
576; Aḥad ha-'Am, "'Al Parashat Derakim," p. 93,
Berlin, 1903).

The idea of a return of the Jews to Palestine has
its roots in many passages of Holy Writ. It is an
integral part of the doctrine that deals with the

**Biblical
Basis.** Messianic time, as is seen in the constantly recurring expression, "shub
shebut" or "heshib shebut," used both
of Israel and of Judah (Jer. xxx. 7, 1;
Ezek. xxxix. 25; Lam. ii. 14; Hos. vi. 11; Joel
iv. 1 *et al.*). The Dispersion was deemed merely
temporal: "The days come . . . that . . . I will
bring again the captivity of my people of Israel, and
they shall build the waste cities and inhabit them;
and they shall plant vineyards, and drink the wine
thereof . . . and I will plant them upon their land,
and they shall no more be pulled up out of their
land " (Amos ix. 14; comp. Zeph. iii. 20); and "I will
bring them again also out of the land of Egypt, and
gather them out of Assyria; and I will bring them
into the land of Gilead and Lebanon " (Zech. x. 10;
comp. Isa. xi. 11). In like strain the Psalmist sings,
"O that the salvation of Israel were come out of Zion!
When the Lord bringeth back the captivity of his
people, Jacob shall rejoice, and Israel shail be glad "
(Ps. xiv. 7; comp. cvii. 2, 3). According to Isaiah
(ii. 1-4) and Micah (iv. 1-4), Jerusalem was to be a
religious center from which the Law and the word of
the Law were to go forth. In a dogmatic form this
doctrine is more precisely stated in Deut. xxx. 1-5.

The belief that the Messiah will collect the scattered hosts (גליותיו של ישראל) is often expressed in Talmudic and midrashic writings; even though more universalistic tendencies made themselves felt, especially in parts of the Apocryphal literature (see JEW. ENCYC. viii. 507, *s.v.* MESSIAH). Among Jewish philosophers the theory held that the

Relation to Mes-sianism. Messiah b. Joseph "will gather the children of Israel around him, march to Jerusalem, and there, after overcoming the hostile powers, reestablish the Temple-worship and set up his own dominion" (*ib.* p. 511b). This has remained the doctrine of Orthodox Judaism; as Friedländer expresses it in his "Jewish Religion " (p. 161): " There are some theologians who assume the Messianic period to be the most perfect state of civilization, but do not believe in the restoration of the kingdom of David, the rebuilding of the Temple, or the repossession of Palestine by the Jews. They altogether reject the national hope of the Jews. These theologians either misinterpret or wholly ignore the teachings of the Bible and the divine promises made through the men of God."

The Reform wing of the Synagogue, however, rejects this doctrine; and the Conference of Rabbis that sat in Frankfort-on-the-Main July 15–28, 1845, decided to eliminate from the ritual " the prayers for the return to the land of our forefathers and for the restoration of the Jewish state." The Philadelphia Conference, Nov. 3–6, 1869, adopted as the first section of its statement of principles the following: " The Messianic aim of Israel is not the restoration of the old Jewish state under a descendant of David, involving a second separation from the nations of the earth, but the union of all the children of God in the confession of the unity of God, so as to realize the unity of all rational creatures, and their call to moral sanctification." This was re-

Rejected by Reform Judaism. affirmed at the Pittsburg Conference, Nov. 16–18, 1885, in the following words: " We consider ourselves no longer a nation, but a religious community; and we therefore expect neither a return to Palestine, nor a sacrificial worship under the sons of Aaron, nor the restoration of any of the laws concerning a Jewish state."

Historically, the hope of a restoration, of a renewed national existence, and of a return to Palestine has existed among the Jewish people from olden times. After the first Exile, the Jews in Babylonia looked forward continually to the reestablishment of their ancient kingdom. However much the Jews spread from land to land, and however wide the dispersion and consequent Diaspora became, this hope continued to burn brightly; and from time to time attempts were made to realize it. The destruction of the Temple by Titus and Vespasian (70 C.E.) was perhaps the most powerful factor in driving the Jews east, south, and west. Nevertheless, in a short time the hope of a restoration was kindled anew. The risings under Akiba and Bar Kokba (118) soon followed; and the Jews drenched the soil of Palestine with their blood in the vain attempt to regain their national freedom against the heavy hand of the Roman power. Despite these checks, the idea of the restoration persisted and became a matter of dogmatic be-

lief; as such it finds expression in Jewish literature, both prose and poetic. The Talmudic writings as a whole, while making suitable provision for the actual circumstances under which the Jews lived, are based upon the idea that at some time the ancient order of things will be reestablished, and the old laws and customs come again into vogue. These hopes found expression in numerous prayers which

In Talmudic Times. from time to time were inserted in the ritual. Various calculations were made as to when this time would arrive, *e.g.*, in the eighth century (" Revelations of R. Simeon b. Yoḥai ") and in the eleventh century (Apoc. Zerubbabel; see Zunz, "Erlösungsjahre," in " G. S." iii. 224; Poznanski in "Monatsschrift," 1901). The idea was given a philosophic basis by those who treated of Jewish theology. And the singers, both of the Synagogue and the home, were fervid in their lament for the glory that was past and in their hopes for the dignity that was to come (see ZIONIDES).

But the outward condition in which the Jews lived so many centuries made it impossible for them to think of realizing in fact that which they hoped and prayed for. The supernatural accessories with which theology had clothed the idea of the restoration also palsied any effort that might have been made. The Deity was supposed to lead the way; and the hand of man remained inert. From time to time, it is true, individual Jews or bands of Jews journeyed to Palestine, there either to lay their bones in sacred soil or to await the coming of the Messiah (see PILGRIMAGE). Only fitfully and at periods far distant from one another was any attempt made to anticipate Providence and to venture such a restoration on a practical basis. And even in such cases it was not always Palestine that was selected for the first attempt, because of the practical diffi-

Joseph Nasi. culties which were known to inhere in any such a scheme. An attempt of this kind was that of Joseph NASI in the middle of the sixteenth century, both in his endeavor to gain from the Republic of Venice an island to which the Portuguese Jews might emigrate and in his proclamation to the Jews of the Roman Campagna asking them to emigrate to Palestine.

By the side of such projects there were others of a more fantastic character. In 1540 an Augsburg Jew attempted to form a Jewish state upon a Messianic basis (see " Anzeiger des Deutschen Nat. Museums," 1894, p. 103). Of schemes based upon Messianic speculations and purely religious hopes, the most important was that of SHABBETHAI ZEBI (1626–76), who, personating the Messiah, announced that he would restore Israel to the Promised Land. How ardent and true the belief in the restoration was in the hearts of the Jews may be seen from the fact that numerous communities were ready to follow the impostor's lead. Even such men as Spinoza believed in the possibility of the accomplishment of the project; and after Zebi's fraud had been discovered, the belief in the impending restoration lingered for many years.

The problem, however, was attacked also from the philanthropic point of view. The condition of the Jews in many parts of Europe occasioned well-meaning and charitable persons to seek some means of settling them under such conditions as would insure to them repose and freedom from persecution. Of such a kind was the project elaborated in England about 1654, an account of which is contained in the Egerton collection of manuscripts in the British Museum. This account is entitled "Privileges Granted

Colonizing Attempts Outside Palestine. to the People of the Hebrew Nation That Are to Goe to the Wilde Cust," and, according to Lucien Wolf, has reference to a Jewish settlement in Surinam. Such colonies as these with far-reaching administrative rights had

been established in Curaçao in 1652 under the authority of the Dutch West India Company, and in 1659 in Cayenne by the French West India Company ("Tr. Jew. Hist. Soc. Eng." iii. 82). In 1749 Maurice de Saxe, a natural son of August II. of Poland, had in mind a project to make himself king of a Jewish state which was to be founded in South America (M. Kohler, in "Menorah," June, 1892). The invitation of Napoleon to the Jews of Asia and Africa to settle again in Jerusalem under his egis (see "Moniteur Universelle," No. 243) was a political document and not meant to be taken seriously. Even Mendelssohn was approached with a proposal of a similar nature made by an unknown friend in the year 1770. He refused to entertain the project on the ground that the oppression under which the Jews had been living for so many centuries had robbed their spirit of all "vigueur," that they were too scattered to work in common, that the project would cost too much money, and that it would need a general consent of the great powers of Europe ("Gesammelte Schriften," v. 493, Leipsic, 1844). A like measure was elaborated in 1819 by W. D. Robinson, who proposed the formation of a Jewish settlement in the upper Mississippi and Missouri territory; and in 1850 the American consul in Jerusalem, Warder Cresson, a convert to Judaism under the name of Michael C. Boaz Israel, established a Jewish agricultural colony near Jerusalem, enlisting in its support the Rev. Isaac Leeser of Philadelphia, and L. Philippson of Magdeburg (M. Kohler, in "Publ. Am. Jew. Hist. Soc." No. viii., p. 80). The most persistent advocate, however, of such schemes was Mordecai M. NOAH (see also ARARAT). As early as the year 1818 he actively propagated the idea of the necessary restoration of the Jews to Palestine. In a "Discourse on the Restoration of the Jews," delivered in 1845 before a Christian audience in the city of New York, he

Mordecai Noah. showed the wide range of his political views, and laid down the chief principles upon which a return of the Jews to Palestine could be effected.

In developing this idea, he conceived a plan for a preliminary settlement named "Ararat" on Grand Island in the Niagara River, near Buffalo. On Jan. 19, 1820, Noah's memorial to the New York legislature, praying for the sale to him of Grand Island, was presented. This project aroused much interest in Europe also. Of course nothing definite came of it (*ib.* No. viii., pp. 84 *et seq.*; No. x., p. 172; No. xi., p. 132); though in 1873 the London "Jewish Chronicle"

editorially suggested a Jewish colony in the United States upon a plan similar to that of Noah (July 4, p. 233).

All these projects of the preliminary stage were bound to fail because the Jewish people had not been educated to understand their true position in the modern world, nor had they been sufficiently stimulated by the great waves of feeling that had swept through Europe. The two influences that made themselves felt in such manner as to form the first stage in the development of modern Zionism were the rise of a strong nationalistic sentiment and the development of anti-Semitism. The last part of the eighteenth century and the first half of the nineteenth are characterized in Europe by a strong sentiment of cosmopolitanism which even exceeded the bounds of rational development. It was a natural reaction against the arbitrary grouping of nationalities which ignored all racial affiliations and was based simply upon political necessities. The swing of the pendulum went too far; and the counter-reac-

Rise of Nationalist Sentiment. tion in favor of personal freedom made itself felt throughout the whole of the first half of the nineteenth century. The idea of personal freedom brought

in its wake the desire for racial freedom. The action of Switzerland, Hungary, and the various Balkan states, the attempt of Ireland to free itself from British rule, the unification of Italy and Germany upon racial lines, were bound to react upon the Jews. Upon the continent of Europe many of them had been in the front ranks of those who had fought for this racial freedom. The Jews little thought that the weapons which they had used against others would be turned against themselves, and would create within their own ranks a longing for racial unity and a communal life.

Under these influences there arose gradually, especially among the younger generation in eastern Europe, a sentiment in favor of Jewish national existence, which carried in its wake many of the brightest and most advanced Jews of the day. And the opening up of the Eastern question brought the needs of certain parts of the Ottoman empire prominently before Europe. The historian Joseph Salvador as early as 1830 believed in the possibility that a congress of European powers might restore Palestine to the Jews; and the founders of the Alliance Israélite Universelle had a similar idea in their minds when, under Albert COHN and Charles NETTER, the work of colonizing Jews in Palestine was taken up, and the agricultural school Miḳweh Yisrael was founded near Jaffa.

In 1852 Hollingsworth, an Englishman, urged the establishment of a Jewish state, because of the necessity of safeguarding the overland route to India; and in 1864 there appeared in Geneva a pamphlet entitled "Devoir des Nations de Rendre au Peuple Juif Sa Nationalité," which occasioned a lengthy discussion in the "Archives Israélites."

French Anticipations. It was ascribed to Abraham Pétavel, a Christian clergyman and professor in Neuchâtel. Pétavel was a member of the Alliance Israélite Universelle, although he was openly and honestly interested in the conversion of the Jews. Though he denied the authorship of the pamphlet, it was generally believed to have been his work, especially as he published at the same time a long poem, " La Fille de Sion ou la Rétablissement d'Israël " (Paris, 1864). The " Archives " declared itself strongly opposed to the project ; but Lazar Lévy-Bing, a banker of Nancy and later a member of the legislature (July 2, 1871), wrote warmly in favor of Jewish nationalism, with no thought of the economic condition of the Jews of his day. Jerusalem, he hoped, might become the ideal center of the world. Undoubtedly influenced by Pétavel, a Jew, J. Frankel, published in Strasburg in 1868 a pamphlet with the title " Du Rétablissement de la Nationalité Juive." The author, impressed on the one hand by the national movements of his time and on the other by the insecure conditions under which the Jews of eastern Europe lived, pleaded boldly and openly for the reconstitution of a Jewish state in Palestine by the purchase of the country from Turkey. "Should Palestine prove to be impossible," he adds, "we must seek elsewhere in any part of the globe some fixed home for the Jews ; for the essential point is that they be at home and independent of other nations," thus approaching in a measure the modern territorialists (see below).

Various schemes with a similar end in view were elaborated. Between 1835 and 1840 Moritz Steinschneider was among those who founded in Prague a student society for the purpose of propagating the idea of a Jewish state in Palestine ; and in the latter year an anonymous writer in the " Orient " (No. xxvi., p. 200) published an appeal to his brethren to make an attempt to procure Syria for the Jews under Turkish sovereignty while the blood persecution in Damascus was still fresh in memory ; and in 1847 Barthélémy published in " Le Siècle " a lengthy poem inviting the Rothschilds to restore the kingdom of Judah to its former glory. Judah ben Solomon Alkalai, rabbi in Semlin, Croatia, published his " Goral Ladonai," Vienna, 1857 (2d ed., Amsterdam, 1858), in which he advocated the formation of a joint-stock company for the purpose of inducing the sultan to cede Palestine to the Jews as a tributary state. In similar manner Luzzatto, in Padua, wrote in 1854 to Albert Cohn, " Palestine must be colonized and worked by the Jews in order that it may live again commercially and agriculturally." The journeys of Sir Moses MONTEFIORE and Adolphe CRÉMIEUX to Palestine increased the interest of the Jews in their ancient home, and brought the matter prominently before the public. The founder of the Geneva Convention, Henry Dunant, worked incessantly with a similar object in view. He tried to interest in such projects the Alliance Israélite Universelle (1863), the Anglo-Jewish Association in London, and the Jews of Berlin (1866), even founding two societies for that purpose, the International Palestine Society and, in 1876, the Syrian and Palestine Colonization Society. All his efforts failed to evoke a response. A like fate befell both the project of Sir Moses Montefiore, who in 1840 laid before Mohammed Ali a plan to colonize Jews in Palestine, and that of Lord Shaftesbury, associated with the Society for the Relief of Persecuted Jews. In the year 1870 Benedetto

In Austria.

Musolino, a Christian and a fervent Italian patriot, worked out a complete plan for the establishment of a Jewish state in Palestine, demonstrating the advantage of such a state not only to the Jews, but also to the Ottoman empire and to England. In vain he tried to interest Lord Palmerston and the Rothschilds in the plan. Even his work " La Gerusalemme e il Popolo Ebreo " remained unpublished (" The Maccabæan," 1905, p. 225). Nor was Laurence Oliphant (1829–88), the English traveler and politician, more successful. In 1879, after having vainly attempted to procure from the Porte the concession of the Euphrates Valley Railway, on the sides of which he had proposed to settle Russian Jews, he conceived the idea of a Jewish settlement in Palestine, in the land of Gilead. A society was to be formed with a capital of 10,000,000 rubles. Upon 1,000,000 to 1,500,000 acres the Jewish proletariat of Poland, Lithuania, Rumania, and Asiatic Turkey were to be colonized, and an agrarian bank was to be founded. Oliphant failed both in 1879 and in 1882 to obtain the permission of the sultan to such a plan.

Among the early writers who pleaded for the repatriation of Palestine by the Jews were David b. Dob Baer GORDON (1826–86), Ẓebi Hirsch KALISCHER (1795–1874), Elijah Guttmacher, Moses HESS, and the historian Heinrich GRAETZ. This movement in course of time assumed the name of CHOVEVEI ZION. Gordon and Hess were its intellectual leaders, the first publishing in the year 1871 in his paper " Ha-Maggid " a number of articles on the colonization of Palestine as the basis for the future regeneration of Judaism. Hess wrote his " Rom und Jerusalem " in 1862, which book has remained one of the foundation works in Zionist literature ; though a later edition of the work was burned by his family, in order to rid the world of this " scandal " (" Die Welt," ii., No. 9, p. 16). He confidently hoped for the assistance of France in the founding of such colonies. Kalischer, who lived in Thorn, was perhaps the first practical Zionist. His " Derishat Ẓiyyon " (Lyck, 1862) deals with the religious and theological problems involved. He advocated the colonization of Palestine, the cultivation of land there, and the founding of an agricultural school and of a Jewish military guard. He held that the salvation promised by the Prophets could come only gradually and by self-help on the part of the Jews. He traveled extensively in aid of these ideas ; caused the first colonization society to be established in Frankfort-on-the-Main in 1861 ; and had some influence in the work that Charles Netter did in Palestine. Many Orthodox rabbis joined in this movement, e.g., J. Schwarz, S. Schwarz, and Hildesheimer. Rabbi Goldschmidt of Leipsic, writing in the " Allg. Zeit. des Jud.," referred to the colonization of the Holy Land as a " tatsächlich heilige Sache " ; and in such cities as Brody, Tarnopol, and Vienna societies were founded for the purpose of studying the Hebrew language.

Moses Hess.

Two years after the appearance of Hess's " Rom und Jerusalem," and undoubtedly influenced by it, Graetz published in the " Jahrbuch für Israeliten " (1863–64) an essay entitled " Die Verjüngung des Jüdischen Stammes," in which he tried to show historically that the Jewish nation was its own Messiah, and should bring about its own rejuvenescence and redemption, without waiting for the coming of a single person as redeemer. The violent conflict engendered by this essay reechoed even in the courts of law (see T. Zlocisti in "Jüdischer Volkskalender," pp. 9 *et seq.*, Brünn, 1903-4, where Graetz's essay has been reproduced).

Heinrich Graetz.

Toward the end of the seventies in the nineteenth century the national movement commenced to gain ground still further among the Jews. This was due to a recrudescence of national sentiment in Europe, as a result of which the Servians, the Bulgarians, and the Rumanians had gained complete liberty. Pinsker had not looked specifically to Palestine as a possible home for the Jews; but Jewish sentiment quickly led others in that direction. Ben Yehudah published in "Ha-Shaḥar" (1879) a series of articles proposing the colonization of the Holy Land and the gradual centralization of the Jews there as the only means to save both Jews and Judaism; and Isaac RÜLF in 1883 wrote his standard work "Aruḥat Bat 'Ammi" on the same lines. Christian writers also became affected with the idea, which was thus brought prominently before the world. The rise of this national sentiment in Russia is closely connected with the names of Moses Löb LILIENBLUM and Perez SMOLENSKIN. The riots of 1880 and 1881 turned the attention of these authors to the Jewish question. The first in his "Derek la-'Abor Golim" and the second in his "'Am 'Olam," and in his journal "Ha-Shaḥar" (even before 1880), gave literary expression to the national hopes. To these names must be added that of Lev Osipovitch Levanda. In England Disraeli had already declared that "race is the key of history," and George Eliot wrote her "Daniel Deronda" in 1876, and in 1879 her "Impressions of Theophrastus Such," the last chapter of which is entitled "The Modern Hep! Hep! Hep!" (republished by the Federation of American Zionists, 1899). In this she makes the Jew say, "The effect of our separateness will not be completed and have its highest transformation unless our race takes on again the character of a nationality. That is the fulfilment of the religious trust that molded them into a people." "Daniel Deronda" was enthusiastically reviewed in the "Monatsschrift" (1877, pp. 172 *et seq.*) by David Kaufmann, who added, "Who will dare to say what may not result from this rising flood of feelings in the heart of the Jews, who will dare to insist that the imponderable mass of indefinite feelings and vague impulses which in the march of centuries has rather increased than decreased in the soul of the Jewish people, will pass off without leaving any trace?" In like manner Joseph Jacobs reviewed the work, adding, "And Mordecai's views of the resumption of the soil of the Holy Land by the holy people are the only logical position of a Jew who desires that the long travail of the ages shall not end in the total disappearance of the race" ("Jewish Ideals," p. 80). Influenced by "Daniel Deronda," Gustav Cohen of Hamburg privately printed his "Die Judenfrage und die Zukunft"

George Eliot's "Daniel Deronda."

(1891, 1896), in which he developed the theory there expounded to its logical Zionistic conclusion. In the United States, a Jewess, Emma LAZARUS, moved by the immigration of large numbers of Russian Jews to America, wrote a stirring series of articles in the "American Hebrew" (1882, 1883) pleading for an independent Jewish nationality and a Jewish home in Palestine ("An Epistle to the Hebrews"; republished by the Federation of American Zionists, 1900).

The result of all this agitation was the founding of various colonization societies, not only in Russia (under the leadership of S. P. Rabinowitz, Pinsker, H. Schapira, Lilienblum, Max Mandelstamm, and Kalonymus Wissotzky), but also in Germany, France, England, and America; *e.g.*, the Central Committee at Galatz, the Esra at Berlin, the Chovevei Zion in London, the Shawe Zion in the United States, and the Yishshub Erez Yisrael in Paris. The first Palestinian colony was founded in 1874; but the work did not commence in earnest till 1879. At the conference of the Chovevei Zion and of other societies, held at Kattowitz on Nov. 6, 1884, to regulate the help sent to the colonists, no less than fifty bodies were represented. A second conference was held in Drusgenik on June 15, 1887; and a third in Wilna, in 1889, at which thirty-five societies were represented and thirty-eight delegates were present. In 1891–92 Paul Friedmann made an unsuccessful attempt to establish a Jewish colony in Midian (see JEW. ENCYC. v. 519, *s.v.* FRIEDMANN, PAUL). The growth of the colonization movement upon philanthropic principles reached its height in 1894, when it was arrested largely by the fact that the Turkish authorities made it difficult for Jews to enter Palestine (see JEW. ENCYC. iv. 47, *s.v.* CHOVEVEI ZION). Even Baron de Hirsch was not in principle opposed to colonization in the Holy Land, as he told a deputation on July 22, 1891; he desired that a searching inquiry should first be made into its feasibility. He promised to aid any negotiations that should be undertaken in Constantinople if the report of a commission proved favorable ("The Maccabæan," p. 118, New York, 1904).

The Chovevei Zion.

The second influence working to produce the modern Zionist movement was the rise and extension of ANTI-SEMITISM. The Jews had imagined that with their political emancipation, and, with the destruction of the walls of the ancient ghettos, their entrance into the comity of nations, the complete subsidence of the ancient "odium Judaicum" would result. In this they were sadly disappointed. Political liberty did not give them social equality; and the newly arisen nationalistic sentiment turned fiercely against them. At the very moment when their own dormant national feeling had been aroused, and when the work of colonization in Palestine had sent a thrill of fervor through the Jewish masses, the anti-Semitic movement grew in intensity. From 1881 it pursued its victorious march through Europe. The strength of the movement in eastern Europe was at first underrated in the hope that it would give way before the advance of culture and education in those countries.

Influence of Anti-Semitism.

This hope was doomed to failure; and when states like Germany, Austria, and France joined in it actively, with the more or less overt cooperation of the governments of the day, a reaction among Jews was bound to take place. Most of the latter, it is true, continued to hope that the phenomenon was but a passing one; but a small band in western Europe and in America sought its cause in sources that were deeper than a passing whim. They thought to find it in the impossibility felt by various peoples to assimilate the Jews and at the same time to allow them that measure of individual and collective freedom which the Jews considered necessary for the preservation of their individual character. In addition, they had witnessed the results of the attempt made by many of their brethren to meet fully the demands of the outside world. The consequence had been the almost complete conversion to Christianity of many of the leading families in the Mendelssohn epoch, and the loosening of the bonds that held the Jews together, which meant, if continued, the absorption of the Jews in the general population and the disappearance of Judaism as a distinctive faith. To meet anti-Semitism the great Jewish communities, contenting themselves with an attempt to ward off the blows as they fell successively, offered in general a passive resistance, to which many noble-minded Christians contributed in the German and Austrian societies for repelling anti-Semitism (see VEREIN ZUR ABWEHR DES ANTI-SEMITISMUS). On the other hand, the small band referred to above took up a more positive attitude, and found the answer to militant anti-Semitism in a recurrence to what they considered the basis of Jewish life—the idea of the continued national existence of the Jews as a people. This current among the Jews of modern Western culture combined with the two other currents, that of the national Jewish revival and that of the philanthropic colonization of Palestine, to form the modern Zionist movement.

It was at this time that Theodor HERZL, brooding over the strong rise of anti-Semitism in his own Austrian home and in Paris, in which city he was then living, wrote his "Judenstaat." According to his own statement, it was conceived and written during the last two months of his stay in Paris in the year 1895, as a private expression of his opinion, and to be shown only to a small circle of his friends. One of these friends, after reading the pamphlet, declared its author to be of unsound mind. Any active agitation or discussion of the principles laid down in the book was far from Herzl's purpose. It was only in the spring of 1896 that the "Judenstaat" was published in Vienna. Translations of it were soon made into French, English, and Hebrew; and the original German has now (1905) gone through five editions (see also "Theodor Herzl's Zionistische Schriften," Berlin, 1905). The theories here laid down and the propositions made for their realization may be summed up in the following statement:

Starting with the fact that anti-Semitism is a continually growing menace both to the Jews and to the world at large and is ineradicable, that the Jews are a people that are not permitted to merge into the social life around them, that true assimilation is possible only by means of intermarriage, he comes to the conclusion that it is necessary for the Jews, if they wish to preserve themselves, to have as their own some portion of the globe large enough for them to foregather therein and to build up a definite home. For the accomplishment of this object he suggests the formation of a "Society of Jews," which shall take up the preliminary scientific and political work, and of a "Jewish Company" similar to the great English and French trading companies, with a capital of £50,000,000 and having its center in London. The company was to develop the work prepared by the Society of Jews, and to organize the new community. As a possible territory for such an ingathering Herzl suggested either Argentina or Palestine; the incoming was to be brought about not by infiltration, but by organized immigration; and if Palestine was to be chosen, the sanctuaries of other religious faiths were to be made extraterritorial. It will be seen that the religious sanction, which had been the mainspring of the Orthodox Jewish hope in the restoration, was entirely wanting. The problem was attacked simply from its economic and political sides. In course of time, and as Herzl came into closer contact with his Jewish brethren than he had been before, he began to recognize the value of the religious sanction, as far as a large section of the Jewish people was concerned, and to see that the Jewish national consciousness was bound indissolubly to Palestine. The absolute separation, however, of church and state remained one of the fundamental ideas of his project; the arrangements between the Ottoman government and the Jews was to be in the form of a charter granted to the latter upon a purely political and mercantile basis.

It was largely through the instrumentality of Israel Zangwill that Herzl was induced to present his project publicly to the Jewish world. He was received by the Maccabæans in London Nov. 24, 1895. In a preliminary letter to the "Jewish Chronicle" (London, Jan. 17, 1896) he laid down the principal features of his plan; and on July 6, 1896, he was able to present the project in person to the Maccabæans. Although his "Judenstaat" had been translated (by Sylvie d'Avigdor) into English, and despite the publicity given to it by his appearance in London, the Jews in England, and even the old Chovevei Zion, refused to approve the new expression given to the old hope. On the Continent, however, such men as Max Nordau and Alexander Marmorek in Paris, Dr. Max Bodenheimer in Cologne, Prof. M. Mandelstamm in Kiev, and a number of other intellectuals came to his support.

However much Herzl had wished to remain in his purely literary career as feuilletonist, dramatist, and journalist, circumstances proved too strong. He had touched the core of the Jewish question as many of his brethren saw it, and reached the heart of the Jewish people. The wave of enthusiasm gradually pushed him forward and bore him high upon its crest. The first to take up the "Judenstaat" as a realizable program was the Zion Society in Vienna. Several thousand names were subscribed to an address sent out by Drs. M. T.

Schnirer and Oser Kokesch calling for the formation of a "Society of Jews" to be founded in July, 1896, in London; and a letter of adhesion to Herzl's principles was forwarded in the month of May to Herzl by the above-named as representing their society. According to Lucien Wolf ("Encyc. Brit." *s.v.* "Zionism") the Sultan of Turkey, having heard of Herzl's publication, sent a private messenger, the Chevalier de Newlinsky, in May, 1896, with the offer of a charter of Palestine for the Jews if they would use their influence to stop the agitation consequent upon the Armenian massacres. The offer was refused.

Herzl's call for the First Zionist Congress, which was to have been held in Munich in 1898, brought the whole subject prominently and forcibly before the Jewish public. In some quarters it was supposed that the gathering was to deal with general Jewish questions, and not specifically with Zionism (Bambus, in "Allg. Zeit. des Jud." April 23, 1897)—a misconception which could not possibly be due to those who had issued the call. But misconceptions were apt to occur, since feeling ran high on the part of both those who favored and those who opposed the Zionist proposition. It may be said at the outset that the Jewish people did not answer to the call of Dr. Herzl as he and his followers had expected. Only in certain quarters did there gather around him Jews who had been in a measure prepared for his coming. Those who had been affected by the Jewish national idea naturally looked to him as their standard-bearer. The Jewish masses, groaning under oppression in eastern Europe, saw in him their possible savior; and those of them who had escaped to western Europe and America were not slow to follow the lead of their brethren left behind. In addition to these a comparatively small number of intellectuals came to Herzl's aid. Some were moved thereto either by the results of the academic discussion of the questions involved, or by a reawakened feeling of attachment to old scenes and thoughts from which they had become estranged. Others in their own persons or in their immediate surroundings had felt the sting of anti-Semitism; while a large number were attracted to the new movement from a feeling of benevolent compassion for the sufferings of their more unfortunate brethren.

Opposition to Zionism arose from many quarters; and even as the movement embraced within its fold Jews of various religious convictions, so did the opposition emanate from different points of the horizon. Orthodox Judaism in Europe at first held severely aloof, believing that because some of the leaders were non-observants of Jewish ceremonial, the whole movement set rather away from than toward positive Judaism. It was supposed to be forcing the **Opposition.** hand of Providence and to be contrary to the positive teachings of Orthodox Judaism in regard to the coming of the Messiah and the providential work of God in bringing about the restoration. In Russia the extreme Orthodox synagogue, not content with a simple protest, organized an active opposition which had for its center the Poltava rabbi Akiba Rabinowitz and the magazine "Ha-Peles" in Wilna. A library opened there by the

Zionists on April 14, 1902, had to be closed for a time. In common parlance this opposition was spoken of as the "Black Cabinet" (Lishkah ha-Sheḥorah).

A more theological aspect was given to the opposition by some of the European rabbis. Dr. Güdemann, chief rabbi of Vienna, in his "National-Judenthum" (Leipsic and Vienna, 1897) says that Israel has been since the Dispersion a purely religious community, a leader of peoples; that its historical task has consisted in opposing the idea of nationalism; and that if Judaism should reawaken in all its adherents the endeavor again to become a nation, it would be committing suicide. According to Güdemann, the vocation of Israel lies in the spiritual impress that it has been able to put upon humanity and in its endeavor to further the Messianic time which shall conciliate nations to one another. He holds that Judaism has acclimatized itself everywhere; that Zion is only a symbol of its own and mankind's future; that in this sense the word is used in the prayer-book of the Synagogue, and that true Zionism can not be separated from the future of humanity. In a similar spirit K. Kohler formulates his opposition to Zionism. He does not call himself an anti-Zionist; but believes that in a positive way Judaism has another future before it. For him Judaism is a religious truth entrusted to a nation destined to interlink all nations and sects, classes and races of men; its duty is to be a cosmopolitan factor of humanity, basing itself upon the Biblical passage, "Ye shall be unto Me a kingdom of priests and a holy nation." "The mission of the Jew is not only spiritual or religious in character; it is social and intellectual as well, and the true Zionism demands of the Jews to be martyrs in the cause of truth and justice and peace until the Lord is one and the world one." He repudiates the idea that Judea is the home of the Jew—an idea which "unhomes" the Jew all over the wide earth—and holds the entire propaganda a Utopian dream because even if Turkey were willing, none of the great powers of Christendom would concede the Holy Land to the Jew; that the high temperature of Palestine would no longer afford him a congenial and healthful soil; that Palestine has poor prospects of ever becoming a leading state and of attracting Jewish capital; that the incongruous elements of which a Jewish state would be composed would militate against a harmonious blending into one great commonwealth; and that so petty a commonwealth would be unable to cope successfully with the hostile forces arrayed against it. However, he looks with favor upon the colonization of Palestine by the Jews, and sees the "possibility of Zionism leading to a united Judaism and a pan-Judean congress" (see "The Judæans," pp. 68 *et seq.*, New York, 1899). Claude Montefiore proclaimed himself a convinced and determined antagonist of the plan on the ground that Zionism is calculated to beget and foster anti-Semitic feelings, more especially when it is looked upon as a glorious ideal instead of a mournful necessity. The Jews, he thinks, are to fight the good fight, not to despair, but with self-purification and brave endurance to await the better time that civilization will shortly bring, when their fellow citizens will claim them as their own (*ib.* pp. 86 *et seq.*).

Strong denunciations of Zionism were heard, especially in Germany. The appearance of the party organ "Die Welt" was declared to be a misfortune ("Allg. Zeit. des Jud." June 11, 1897); G. Karpeles maintaining even that Judaism was no religion, but a "sittliche Weltanschauung und geschichtliche Thatsache" ("Die Welt," 1905, No. viii.). In the name of the Association of Jewish Rabbis of Germany, S. Maybaum (Berlin) and H. Vogelstein (Stettin) issued a protest against the Zionists, who were declared to be "fanatics from Russia and youthful, hot-headed students." In a preliminary communication the protesters laid down the following principles: that the Jews are nothing more than a religious body, and those in Germany national Germans, though as such faithful to the divine religion of Sinai. They demanded a united protest of all the German congregations against political Zionism; anti-agitation to counteract that of the Zionists; and a public declaration of all societies composed of rabbis and teachers against the movement. Dr. Leimdörfer (Hamburg) associated himself with this protest (ib. June 11 and July 2, 1897). In Hanover the advocate Dr. Meyer proposed in addition an anti-Zionist meeting in Berlin at which the Jews should proclaim their German patriotic sentiments and in this way disarm the Zionists (ib.). No such action, however, seems to have been taken; though, in England, several rabbis were inhibited by the chief rabbi from preaching on Zionism, and the haham M. Gaster was prevented by the Mahamad of the Spanish and Portuguese congregation from touching on the subject in his official capacity (1899). The

Protest of German Rabbis. formal protest appeared in the "Allgemeine Zeitung des Judenthums," July 16, 1897, signed by the Board of Ministers. It states, first, that the attempts of the Zionists to found a Jewish national state in Palestine are contrary to the Messianic promises of Judaism as laid down in Holy Writ and in the later religious authorities; secondly, that Judaism demands of its adherents to serve the state in which they live and in every way to further its national interests; thirdly, that no opposition thereto can be seen in the noble plan to colonize Palestine with Jewish agriculturists, because that plan has no connection with the founding of a national state. In the same spirit the Conference of American Rabbis, which met at Richmond, Va., on Dec. 31, 1898, declared itself as opposed to the whole Zionist movement on the ground (as one of the members stated) "that America was the Jews' Jerusalem and Washington their Zion."

A like uncompromising attitude against Zionism has been taken in England by Lucien Wolf. Starting with a bias not indistinctly favorable to the plan as formulated by Herzl, he has come to hold not only the impracticability of the scheme, but the untenableness of its premises. He believes that the Jews are of Aryan origin and that they are not anthropologically a separate race (a view held also by Solomon Reinach; see "R. E. J." xlvii. 1), and that at a later time only a centrietal anthropological movement set in; that there is peril in Zionism, in that it is the natural and abiding ally of anti-Semitism and its most powerful justification; that it is

an attempt to turn back the course of modern Jewish history; that it is "an ignorant and narrow-minded view of a great problem—ignorant because it takes no account of the decisive element of progress in history; and narrow-minded because it confounds a political memory with a religious ideal." As a means of alleviating Jewish distress in eastern Europe, Wolf considers it inadequate and in a certain sense unnecessary. The chances of emancipation in Russia he holds to be by no means desperate; and the Rumanian Jewish question he thinks is greatly improved and "a manageable one." The mission of the

Lucien Wolf and Laurie Magnus. Jew is the Mendelssohnian one: to show an example to the nations, to take its stand on lofty toleration and real universalism, and "its highest traditional ideal is undoubtedly national, but it is not the nation of a kept principality but the holy nation of a kingdom of priests" ("The Zionist Peril," in "J. Q. R." xvii. 1–25).

From the point of view of its effect upon the status of Jews in western Europe and America, Zionism has been strongly criticized by Laurie Magnus. This criticism may be summed up in the following extract:

"A flight which is no flight, an abandonment, and an evacuation—this is the modern rendering of the Messianic hope: instead of Gentiles coming to the light, Dr. Herzl offers the petty picture of Jews content, like foreign visitors, with a 'favorable welcome and treatment.' We have called this a travesty of Judaism. But it is more than satire—it is treason. Dr. Herzl and those who think with him are traitors to the history of the Jews, which they misread and misinterpret. They are themselves part authors of the anti-Semitism which they profess to slay. For how can the European countries which the Jews propose to 'abandon' justify their retention of the Jews? And why should civil equality have been won by the strenuous exertion of the Jews, if the Jews themselves be the first to 'evacuate' their position, and to claim the bare courtesy of 'foreign visitors'?" ("Aspects of the Jewish Question," p. 18, London, 1902).

This is also practically the position taken by Prof. Ludwig Geiger, the leader of the liberal Jews in Berlin, though with more special reference to the particular country in which he lives. He says:

"Zionism is as dangerous to the German spirit ["Deutschthum"] as are social democracy and ultramontanism. It has something of each: of the one its radicalism, of the other its ultramontanism ["Jenseitige"], the desire for a fatherland other than that belonging to it by language and culture. . . . Zionism may be able to raise its army up to hundreds of thousands, if no hindrance is placed in its way. Just as we are warned against ultramontane works on history and Social-Democratic teachings, so must we be warned against Zionistic sophisms ["Afterweisheit"]. The German Jew who has a voice in German literature must, as he has been accustomed to for the last century and a half, look upon Germany alone as his fatherland, upon the German language as his mother tongue; and the future of that nation must remain the only one upon which he bases his hopes. Any desire to form together with his coreligionists a people outside of Germany is, not to speak of its impracticability, downright thanklessness toward the nation in whose midst he lives —a chimera; for the German Jew is a German in his national peculiarities, and Zion is for him the land only of the past, not of the future."

No opponent of Zionism has dared to say what Geiger adds:

"The withdrawal of citizen's rights appears to be the necessary consequence of German legislation against Zionism, the only answer that the German national conscience can give" (see "Stimmen der Wahrheit," pp. 165 et seq., Berlin, 1905).

While criticisms such as these touched upon the basal principles of Zionism, other criticisms dealt in charges which are evidence of the strong feeling raised on all sides in Jewry by the successive progress of the Zionist movement. The "Univers Israélite" summed up the matter in saying:

Minor Objections.

" The long and short of it is, Zionists and anti-Semites are one and the same." The "Reform Advocate" of Chicago spoke of the "Anti-Semites, his [Herzl's] friends" (March 12, 1898). A rabbi in Marburg classed Zionism as "Messiasschwärmerei"; and the traveler Edward Glaser believed that Zionism was put forward by the British government in order to break up Turkey and form a buffer state. The ḥakam bashi in Constantinople posted a notice in the synagogue putting the Hebrew paper "Ha-Ẓefirah" under the ban; and Dr. Bloch, editor of the Vienna "Wochenschrift," first endeavored to procure a subvention from the Zionists, offering to give up eight pages of his newspaper to the cause, if "Die Welt" ceased to appear ("Die Welt," ii., No. 48); failing which, he became a most determined opponent. S. Bernfeld's "Am Ende des Jahrhunderts" (1899) has a bare mention of Zionism and the congresses; while that portion of the year's review by Martin Philippsohn in the "Jahrbuch für Jüdische Geschichte," 1898, mentioning the Basel Congress of 1897, was stricken out by the editor, G. Karpeles. When the "Trust" was founded, the report was spread that each of the directors was to have a bonus of 100,000 marks for passing the statutes, and that the sole object of the corporation was to combat Orthodoxy. The London "Financial News" (April 28, 1899, p. 872) spoke of the "harebrained and irresponsible promoters of the ridiculous Trust."

In the United States, too, the opposition grew apace.

The "Reform Advocate" in Chicago suggested editorially that the real object of Herzl and Nordau was to possess themselves of the savings of their poorer brethren. Isaac M. Wise, president of the Hebrew Union College, thought that the Zionists were "traitors, hypocrites, or fantastic fools whose thoughts, sentiments, and actions are in constant contradiction to one another" ("Hebrew Union College Journal," Dec., 1899, p. 47); while Rabbi Samfield wrote in the "Jewish Spectator" that "Zionism is an abnormal eruption of perverted sentiment." Prof. Louis Grossman held that the "Zionistic agitation contradicts everything that is typical of Jews and Judaism," and that the "Zionistic movement is a mark of ingenuity, and does not come out of the heart of Judaism, either ancient or contemporary" ("Hebrew Union College Journal," Dec., 1899, p. 72).

On the other hand, the attitude of the Christian world toward Zionism has been in nearly every case one of cordial attention; in some quarters, even one of active furtherance. While those of the more important daily papers that were in Jewish hands either accorded the movement scanty attention or were absolutely silent (the Vienna "Neue Freie Presse," of which Herzl was feuilleton editor, never mentioned the word "Zionism" as long as Herzl lived), the other great dailies of the world freely opened their columns to news of the movement, as did also the great monthlies and quarterlies in England and the United States (e.g., "Contemporary Review," "Nineteenth Century," "Forum," "Fortnightly Review," "North American Review," "International Review," and "Century"). In Oct., 1897, the London "Daily Chronicle" and the "Pall Mall Gazette" publicly accepted the Zionist program and advocated the calling of a general European Congress. Many Christians, it is true, were led to such a course by religious hopes of a Messianic return of the Jews to Palestine and their possible conversion there; although the German "Allgemeine Missions Conferenz" declared that

Christian Attitude.

"Zionism will not hasten the conversion of Israel, but rather delay it" ("Nathaniel," 1901). Others, however, had a sincere desire to advance this attempt at Jewish self-help.

In addition to those mentioned above who had been actively engaged in one project or another, there are a large number who by their voice and otherwise have encouraged Zionism. As early as 1885 Prof. K. Furrer of Zurich University spurred on the Russian Jewish students to work for the colonization of Palestine by the Jews; and in 1904 Secretary John Hay of the United States declared in an interview that Zionism was in his opinion quite consistent with American patriotism. The Grand Duke of Baden on Aug. 4, 1899, uttered these words to Dr. A. Berliner: "The movement is an important one and deserves vigorous assistance." The Preraphaelite painter Holman Hunt was one of the first to greet Herzl's proposal in London (1896) with friendly assistance. He has done the same (1905) to Israel Zangwill and the Territorialists. The Rev. W. H. Hechler of Vienna has been a constant attendant at the congresses, and has been of actual assistance in other directions. Prof. F. Heman of Basel, the author of "Das Aufwachen der Jüdischen Nation" (Basel, 1899), also deserves mention, as he sees in Zionism a conciliatory force, bringing Jews and Christians nearer to each other. Among those who have publicly pronounced themselves in favor of Zionism may be mentioned Leon Bourgois, the Rumanian premier Stourdza, Baron Maxim Manteuffel, Bertha von Suttner, Felix Dahn, Karl Peters, Prof. T. A. Masaryk, Björnstjerne Björnsen, Rider Haggard, Hall Caine, Maxim Gorki, and Prof. Thomas Davidson. The philosopher Edward von Hartmann, however, is of opinion that Zionism plays into the hands of the anti-Semites, and August Rohling in his "Auf nach Zion" (1901) did indeed give color to this idea; but the conference of political anti-Semites in Hamburg in the year 1899 declared it necessary to oppose the movement, as it awakened sympathy for the Jews among the Christian population. The theological faculty of the University of Geneva set as the subject for the prize essay of the year 1905 the theme "Le Sionisme et Ses Aspirations Actuelles." A collection of opinions has been published by Emil Kronberger, "Zionisten und Christen," Leipsic, 1900, and by Hugo Hoppe, "Herrvorragende Nichtjuden über den Zionismus," Königsberg, 1904.

Though the number of shekel-paying Zionists has increased largely year by year, the opposition sketched above has hardly diminished, except in the case of those whose spokesman has been Lucien Wolf (see below). A large section of Orthodox Jewry still sees in Zionism or rather in its promoters a danger to established custom and time-honored rites, despite the fact that a specific resolution of the Second Basel Congress declared that Zionism would do nothing to militate against such customs and such rites. The Orthodox rabbis at Grodno in 1903 declared themselves opposed to the movement, as did a number of Hungarian rabbis in 1904. On the other hand, the Ḥaside Ẓiyyon of Lodz is made up of Ḥasidim; and such men as Samuel Mohilewer, Chief Rabbi J. H. Dünner in Holland, the haham M. Gaster in England, and H. Pereira Mendes in

New York have joined the Zionist ranks. The stumbling-block has been the "Kultur-Frage," the question of the relation of Zionism to modern education and to the modern point of view. The use of the word "Kultur" in this connection was unfortunate, as the east-European Jew had been led to regard this term as connoting certain distinctive and anti-religious tendencies of modern society. The doubt has remained, despite all attempts to clear up the difficulty by definition. The question was mooted at the First Basel Congress (on the proposition of Birnbaum), but was really taken up at the Third, Fourth, and Fifth Congresses, at the last of which it was made part of the party's program. The advocacy of physical and mental advancement upon modern lines, has provoked the opposition of a large body of Orthodox Jews, who otherwise might have joined the Zionist body, as the idea of the restoration still forms a part of their theological equipment. The Jews connected with Reform synagogues, and those outside any distinctively Jewish organization, in most cases still look upon Zionism as a reaction, not only from a theological point of view, but from the standpoint of general culture as well; and this last, despite the reiterated pronouncements made at various congresses. In his opening address at the First Congress Herzl said: "We have no thought of giving up even one foot of the culture that we have acquired; on the contrary, we wish to broaden that culture," and at the Third Congress he added, "We desire to lift ourselves up to a higher moral plane, to open up new means of communication between nations and prepare the way for social justice. Just as the poet weaves songs out of his own pain, so shall we prepare from out of our own suffering the advancement of mankind in whose service we are." In fact, a formal resolution was adopted at the Second Congress to this effect: "Zionism seeks not only the economic and political but also the spiritual rebirth of the Jewish people and must ever remain upon the stand of modern culture, whose achievements it highly values."

To a still larger number of Jews, who might perhaps sympathize with Zionism, the seeming impracticability of carrying out the platform and the supposed insuperable difficulties in finding a home for the Jews in and around Palestine, coupled with the peculiar political circumstances which render those countries the bone of contention among the European powers, stand in the way; though some of those who now stand aloof have shown a readiness to join the Zionist ranks if another, and to their eyes more practical, policy should be evolved—*e.g.*, that connected with the offer of territory in East Africa (see below).

In spite of all opposition Herzl continued the elaboration of the policy set forth in the "Judenstaat." The first part of his program was the calling of a congress of such Jews and such Jewish organizations as sympathized with the new movement. This congress was to have been held in Munich; but the Kultusvorstand of the Munich Congregation memorialized the committee that had

it in charge, asking them to change its venue. In face of this determined attitude on the part of the leaders of the community, the place of meeting was changed in July to Basel. At this congress there were 204 delegates. It is notable that the B'nai B'rith lodges in Rumania sent two delegates; while the English Chovevei Zion organizations were not represented, on the ground that the congress was "dangerous." Additional difficulties attended the holding of this congress. Part vii. of the first volume of "Die Welt" had been confiscated by the Austrian authorities. Most of the Jewish newspapers of Europe had been actively opposed to Zionism, while that part of the daily press which was in any way controlled by Jews pursued a consistent policy of silence. Among the delegates there were representatives of the various Jewish national bodies, though most of the members came in their private capacity. The great Jewish beneficiary organizations of Europe and America were entirely without representation; and, with one or two exceptions, they kept themselves entirely free from any connection with Zionism. However, a number of noted Christians, whose interest was either purely humanitarian or theological, testified by their attendance to the kindly interest which large sections of the non-Jewish world brought to the new movement. Among such were Dunant, the founder of the Red Cross Society; the Rev. M. Mitchell; the Rev. Mr. Hechler, chaplain to the British embassy in Vienna; Baron Manteuffel; Col. Count Bentinck; and Dr. Johannes Lipsius, the editor of "Der Christliche Orient." This First Congress was in the main a manifestation; though the organization of the movement was commenced there and a number of propositions made which were carried out at a subsequent period; *e.g.*, the promotion of the study of the Hebrew language and literature, in the discussion of which the plan for a proposed Jewish high school in Jaffa or Jerusalem was brought forward; the formation of a general Hebrew school organization and a special literature commission (Chief Rabbi Ehrenpreis of Bulgaria); the formation of a Jewish national fund (Professor Shapira of Heidelberg). At this congress the Basel Program was drawn up, which states the object of Zionism to be "the establishing for the Jewish people a publicly and legally assured home in Palestine" (see Th. Herzl in the "Contemporary Review," 1897, pp. 587-600; German translation, "Der Baseler Congress," Vienna, 1897).

Between the First and Second Congresses the Actions Committee elected at the former busied itself with furthering the propaganda by means of a number of pamphlets, such as the addresses of Herzl and Nordau at the First Congress; "Das Ende der Juden Noth," by York-Steiner, in German, Hebrew, and Yiddish; Nordau's "Ueber die Gegner des Zionismus"; and a pamphlet setting forth the aims of Zionism, printed in Hebrew, Arabic, and French for use in the East. It furthered also the organization of the various groups that had sprung up; and it took the first measures for the founding of the Jewish Colonial Trust. A prefatory conference of the Actions Committee, together with some of the leaders from various countries, was held in Vienna in April, 1898; and the Second Congress met in Basel Aug. 28–31 of that year. The spread of the movement may be gaged by the number of Zionist societies and groups that had come into being since the First Congress:

Country.	New.	Old.	Total.	Country.	New.	Old.	Total.
Russia..........	350	23	373	France.........	3	..	3
Austria..........	176	42	218	Belgium.........	2	..	2
Hungary........	32	228	260	Turkey..........	2	..	2
Rumania........	100	27	127	Denmark........	1	..	1
England........	12	14	26	Servia.........	1	..	1
Germany........	25	....	25	Greece.........	1	..	1
Italy	12	9	21	Egypt.........	2	..	2
Bulgaria........	15	1	16	The Transvaal..	6	..	6
Switzerland	6	....	6	*America........	50	10	60

* New York, 26; Chicago, 8.

A Russian preliminary conference had been held in Warsaw at which about 140 delegates took part, and a second one was held at Basel, those attending being Orthodox rabbis, presided over by Haham M. Gaster of London. More than forty telegrams of adhesion were received from Orthodox rabbis; and besides a number of crown rabbis of Russia, there were also present representatives of the Ḥasidim. A special colonization committee was appointed with a view to furthering colonization on the basis of the consent of the Turkish government; and an agreement was reached as to the formation of the Jewish Colonial Trust, a committee of nine being appointed for that purpose, with D. Wolfssohn of Cologne at the head. The founding of a general Hebrew-speaking nation was proposed by Chief Rabbi Ehrenpreis of Bulgaria; and the resolution on "Kultur," proposed by Haham Gaster, to which reference has been made above, was accepted.

The Third Congress likewise met in Basel, Aug. 15–18, 1899. It was here that Herzl announced that his endeavors were centered upon re-

The Third and Fourth Congresses. ceiving a charter from the sultan. The report of the Actions Committee showed that the number of societies in Russia (877) had increased by 30 per cent and in other countries by 25 per cent. The shekel-payers numbered more than 100,-000, which meant that probably a quarter of a million Jews were actively identified with the Zionist movement. All the Chovevei Zionists in Rumania had become members of the congress. A new scheme of organization was submitted, which had for its object the building up of the inner structure of the movement. The "Kultur" question was further discussed, in the attempt to make it clear that "Kultur" in no way militated against Judaism in any form. The question of colonization in Cyprus was brought up by Davis Trietsch, who had held a preliminary conference to consider the proposal; but he was not allowed to proceed with the question in open congress, the great majority of the members being decidedly averse to even a consideration of the proposal.

The Fourth Congress was transferred to London, where it met in Queen's Hall Aug. 13–16, 1900. The transfer was made with a view to influencing British public opinion still further, as in no country had the Zionist propaganda been received by the general public with more understanding or with greater sympathy. During the year that had elapsed the Russian societies had increased to 1,034, those of England to 38, and those of the United States to 135; while in a small country like Bulgaria there were no less than 42 such societies.

The hopes of the Zionist body in regard to Palestine and the good intentions of the sovereign power there were somewhat dampened by the instructions sent by the Porte in Nov., 1900, making it impossible for Jewish visitors to Palestine to remain there for a period longer than three months. The Italian government immediately protested that it made no difference between its Jewish and its Christian subjects; and the matter having been brought to the attention of Secretary Hay, the American ambassador in Constantinople was on Feb. 28, 1901, instructed to make a similar protest in the name of the United States government. This action by the Porte, which was merely the revival of a regulation that had been issued about fifteen or twenty years previously, was in many quarters said to have been due to the renewed Zionist activity; but on May 17, 1901, the sultan himself received Herzl in audience, the latter being accompanied by two other mem-

Herzl's Interview with the Sultan. bers of the Actions Committee, David Wolfssohn and Oscar Marmorek. Herzl was received on two further occasions; and upon leaving, the sultan conferred upon him the grand cordon of the Order of the Mejidie. From Constantinople Herzl went to London, where on June 11, 1901, he was again received by the Maccabæans, on which occasion he spoke with much confidence of the success of his mission to the sultan and asked the Jewish people for £1,500,000 in addition to the money in the bank for the purpose of obtaining the charter. But the Jewish people kept silent; and the negotiations which had proceeded so far were for the moment in abeyance.

The Fifth Congress was held at Basel in 1901, this time during the winter, Dec. 26–30. The new organization statutes were here finally accepted. They called for a meeting of the congress once every two years; and in the interval between the congresses a meeting of the Larger Actions Committee and the leaders in the various countries was to be held. It was also decided that a new territorial organization could be founded in any land if 5,000 shekel-payers demanded the same. All arrangements for opening the bank had been made; resolutions were passed to give a subvention to the National Library in Jerusalem, and as to the necessity of a Hebrew encyclopedia and the founding of a statistical bureau. A severe criticism of the Baron de Hirsch Trust was made by I. Zangwill, but his motion was not put before the congress. There was again a long "Kultur" debate, which ended in the following pronouncement: "The

Zangwill at the Fourth Congress. congress declares spiritual amelioration ["kulturelle Hebung"], i.e., the education of the Jewish people along national lines, to be one of the chief elements of the Zionist program, and lays it as a duty upon every Zionist to work toward that end." During this congress thirty-seven delegates, comprising the Democratic Fraction,

headed by Berthold Feiwel, being dissatisfied with the ruling of the president, left the congress in a body, but returned after the demonstration had been made.

On July 10, 1902, Herzl appeared before the Royal Immigration Commission, sitting in London, to determine what measures, if any, should be taken to prevent the large influx of a foreign proletariat into England. Herzl's plea was for a regulation of immigration, as far as the Jews were concerned, rather at its source in eastern Europe than at its outlet in western Europe and America. In the summer of the same year a deputation of the German Zionist body was received in audience at Carlsruhe by the Grand Duke of Baden, who has on several occasions testified to his deep interest in the movement.

In the autumn of 1898 and after preliminary audiences in Potsdam and Constantinople, Emperor William II. of Germany publicly received a Zionist deputation in Palestine. The delegation consisted of Dr. Theodor Herzl, Dr. M. T. Schnirer, D. Wolffsohn, Dr. M. Bodenheimer, and Engineer Seidener, president of the Zionist groups in Germany; and, after an introductory greeting on Oct. 28 at the Colony Miḳweh Yisrael near Jaffa, it was received on Nov. 2 in the imperial tent in Jerusalem, State Secretary von Bülow being present. In answer to the address presented, the emperor said that "all such endeavors, as aiming at the promotion of Palestinian agriculture to the weal of the Turkish empire, and having due respect to the sovereignty of the sultan, might be sure of his good-will and interest."

Both at this time and subsequently Herzl had interviews with the sultan. His original program meant an understanding with that ruler upon the basis of a regulation of the Turkish finances (" Die Welt," i., No. 1). He tried also to impress upon the sultan the perfect loyalty of the Zionist body, as shown in the public manner in which it dealt with the problem and in its opposition to any form of small colonization which meant the smuggling in of Jews to Palestine against the wishes of the sovereign power, as well as the value to Turkey of an industrious, law-abiding, and progressive element in the country. The concessions on the part of the sultan were to be in the form of a charter, the Turkish government affording the Jews a large amount of municipal self-government, the Jews on their part paying a certain sum upon the delivery of the concession and a yearly tribute after that. The status was to be similar to that of the Island of Samos, which, on account of the part it had taken in the liberation of Greece in 1821, was accorded on Dec. 11, 1832, through the intervention of England, France, and Russia, a Christian autonomous prince, having his own army, flag, and congress, and paying to the sultan a yearly tribute of 300,000 piasters (W. Miller, in "The Speaker," 1898, p. 579). Though upon several occasions Herzl believed himself near to the realization of his policy, it failed because of the lack of monetary support from the Jews. At a later period the sultan proposed a scattered colonization of the Jews in the Turkish empire, which Herzl was bound to refuse, as being incompatible with the Basel Program and the needs of the Jewish national movement ("Protokoll" of the Sixth Zionist Congress, p. 6).

In October of the same year (1898) negotiations were opened with some members of the English government for a land concession in the Sinai Peninsula. These negotiations were continued in Cairo by L. J. Greenberg with Lord Cromer and the Egyptian government. A commission, consisting of Engineer Kessler, Architect Marmorek, Captain Goldsmid, Engineer Stephens, Professor Laurant, Dr. S. Soskin,

Interview Between William II. of Germany and Theodor Herzl Outside of Jerusalem, 1902.
(From a photograph.)

Dr. Hillel Joffe, and Mr. Humphreys, representing the Egyptian government, left Egypt at the beginning of 1903 to make an exhaustive study of the territory under consideration; and it returned toward the end of March. The Egyptian government, although in part agreeing to the demands for a Jewish administration and extended municipal powers in the proposed settlement at Al 'Arish, felt itself not warranted in agreeing to the concession on account of the lack of water, which would necessitate the use of a certain portion of the Nile. It may be added that the Jewish Colonization Association had shown itself not unwilling to lend its assistance, had the concession been granted ("Die Welt," 1904, No. 1).

Russia having furnished the greatest number of Zionists, the trend of sentiment in that country may briefly be indicated. At the Minsk **Zionism in** Congress held in Sept., 1902, 500 dele- **Russia.** gates attended, representing the Orthodox Party, the Democratic Fraction, a so-called Center Party, and the socialistic Bund. At this meeting the relation of orthodoxy to radicalism, the "Kultur" question, and especially colonization in Palestine were discussed. The congress was not indisposed to unite with non-Zionist colonization societies for the immediate purchase of land in Palestine, thus making the first break in the rigidity of the Basel Platform. Resolutions were passed to the effect that all moneys belonging to the National Fund should be used only for the purchasing of land in Palestine, and that the paragraphs of the National Fund statutes should be so changed as to preclude the collection of capital to which restrictions were attached (see M. Nurock, "Der i. Allrussische Zionisten-Congress in Minsk," Riga, 1902).

The year 1903 is memorable in the annals of Zionism. On June 24, Von Plehve, the Russian minister of the interior, issued a secret circular to the governors, city prefects, and chiefs of police, putting a ban upon all Zionist meetings and forbidding all collections for Zionist purposes. The moneys belonging to the Trust and to the Jewish National Fund, and the shekel collections were to be turned over to the Odessa society for assisting Jewish agriculturists in Palestine. The reason given for this action was the supposed impossibility of realizing the Zionist program except in the distant future; but the real motive was the fear that Jewish Socialists might make use of the Zionist platform for the propagation of their theories ("The Times," London, Sept. 2 and 11). This, together with the distressing condition of the Jews in general in that country, induced Herzl to visit Russia early in Aug., 1903. He there had interviews with Witte and Von Plehve, and was joyfully acclaimed by the Jewish prole- **Herzl's** tariat of the cities through which he **Interview** passed. The result of his interview **with Von** with Von Plehve is given in a letter **Plehve.** to Herzl dated Aug. 12, and published at the Sixth Zionist Congress. In it Von Plehve promises that if the Zionistic movement confines its agitation to the creation of an independent state in Palestine and to the organized emigration from Russia of a certain number of Jewish inhabitants, the Russian government will give its moral and material support to Zionist negotiations at Constantinople, and will facilitate the work of the emigration societies with certain moneys contributed by the Jews of Russia ("Die Welt," Aug. 25, 1903).

Ever since the negotiations in regard to Al 'Arish, Herzl and his agents had kept in contact with the English government. The project to effect a Jewish colonization in the East-African Protectorate seems not to have been an entire surprise. In the "Jewish Chronicle" of July, 1903, it was mooted by Robert T. Yates. It was, however, in no way sought by the Zionist leaders, but was spontaneously offered to Dr. Herzl by Joseph Chamberlain, after the latter's visit to South Africa upon the close of the Boer war. In an official letter dated from the Foreign Office, Aug. 14, 1903, Clement Hill wrote to L. J. Greenberg in regard to "the form of an agreement which Dr. Herzl proposes should be entered into between His Majesty's government and the Jewish Colonial Trust, Ltd., for the establishment of a Jewish settlement in East Africa." Hill was directed by the Marquis of Lansdowne to say:

"That he has studied the question with the interest which His Majesty's government must always take in any well considered scheme for the amelioration of the position of the Jewish race . . . If a site can be found which the Trust and His Maj- **The East-** esty's Commissioner consider suitable and **African** which commends itself to his government, **Project and** Lord Lansdowne will be prepared to entertain **the Sixth** favorably proposals for the establishment of **Congress.** a Jewish colony or settlement on conditions which will enable the members to observe their national customs . . . the details of the scheme comprising as its main features the grant of a considerable area of land, the appointment of a Jewish official as the chief of the local administration, and permission to the colony to have a free hand in regard to municipal legislation as to the management of religious and purely domestic matters, such local autonomy being conditional upon the right of His Majesty's government to exercise general control."

The Sixth Congress drew near without a shadow to presage the storms that were coming. It was held in Basel Aug. 23-28, 1903. It is true that on Aug. 22 a preliminary meeting was convened, in which the Government Party was severely criticized by Alfred Nossig, who pleaded for "national education" as being more important and of more immediate necessity than the acquisition of territory; but such criticism on the part of the opposition was expected. Although the basis of representation had been raised to 200 shekel-payers, no less than 592 delegates and more than 2,000 spectators were present. The announcement by Herzl of his interview with Von Plehve created a sensation among the Russian delegates, especially among those of Socialistic proclivitities; while the offer made by the British government was received with very varied feelings. In his address Herzl distinctly said: "East Africa is indeed not Zion and can never become it"; and in an eloquent oration Max Nordau spoke of such a possible settlement simply as a "Nachtasyl." The Democratic Fraction as a whole was against the proposition, as were the majority of the Russian delegates. Feeling ran very high, and at one time threatened even to disrupt the meeting. The proposition before the congress was that a commission should be sent out to examine the territory in East Africa, and that before a final vote was taken on the merits of the question a special congress should be called for that purpose. After several days of argument a vote was taken which showed 295 affirmative and 178 negative, 90 withholding their votes entirely. This vote represented the view of the congress not as to the advisability of accepting the offer of the British government, but merely as to the proper spirit in which so generous an offer ought to be received and upon the political necessities of the moment. Nevertheless, it was taken to have a much wider meaning; and although a rider was attached to the resolution prohibiting the use of any shekel moneys or any property of the Trust for the purpose of the expedition, the Russian members of the Actions Committee and a number of Russian delegates persisted in misunderstanding the purport of the vote and created a demonstration by publicly leaving the congress.

The East-African proposal acted like a firebrand in the Zionist camp. It threatened to divide the party into two opposed halves, and meetings of protest and discussion were everywhere

The East-African Commission.
held. The misunderstanding would not down. On the one hand, some groups in Rumania went so far as to commence preparations to leave for East Africa; and a special warning had to be issued by the Actions Committee. On the other hand, the inhibition placed upon Zionist moneys for the purposes of the commission caused a long delay in the formation and despatch of that body. In Sept., 1903, the Jewish Colonization Association was asked to bear one-half of the expense of the commission; and it consented to do so on the understanding that any settlement made in East Africa should be only in the way of simple colonization, and should have no political character whatsoever. This necessitated the withdrawal of the request, the greater part of the expense of the commission being at a later time borne by Christian friends of the movement. It was also noted that a strong opposition manifested itself in East Africa. Lord Delamere, the high commissioner, sent a cable protest (" Times," London, Aug. 28), which protest was endorsed by Lord Hindlip and Sir Harry H. Johnston (ib. Sept. 2); the latter, however, changed his position later on (" Die Welt," 1904, p. 42). Popular feeling had been so roused among the Jews that on Dec. 19, 1903, a Russian student of unsound mind, Haim Selik Loubau, made an attempt upon the life of Max Nordau at the Zionist ball given in the Salle Charras in Paris.

Simultaneously with the Sixth General Congress the first Jewish congress was held in Palestine. It was organized and led by Usishkin. Seventy delegates and sixty teachers met in the colony Zikron Ya'aḳob. It was intended to be a Basel congress in miniature.

An organization was founded, to which all Jews in Palestine were to belong who were above eighteen years of age and who paid one franc a year. The delegates were to meet once a year, chosen by groups of fifty, for which purpose Palestine was divided into six sections :

1. Jerusalem, Hebron, Moẓah, and Artuf.
2. The colonies around Ramleh.
3. Jaffa and Petaḥ Tiḳwah.
4. Nazareth, Tiberias, and the colonies in the neighborhood.
5. Ḥudairiyah, Zikron Ya'aḳob, and Haifa.

6. Safed and the Galilean colonies.

There was to be an actions committee of twenty-three members and an extra-Palestinian committee containing representatives of the Odessa body, the Jewish Colonization Association, the Alliance Israélite, the Esra, and Baron Edmond Rothschild. It is not known that the organization was perfected or that either it or its committees ever held further meetings.

The Russian members of the Actions Committee when they returned home were not inactive. In Oct., 1903, most of them held a secret conference at Kharkof, at which they resolved to send a committee to Vienna to demand of Herzl a written promise to relinquish the East-African project before the convening of the Seventh Congress, and in his capacity as a leader of the Zionists to engage in no further territorial projects. He was formally to promise also to take up the work in Palestine and the acquisition of land there and in Syria with the moneys of the National Fund. An organization of the Russian Actions Committee was determined upon in order to give it greater weight in the Zionist deliberations. If Herzl should refuse to give the promises demanded, the Russians were to

Rise of Territorialism.
refrain from sending further contributions to Vienna and to commence an active propaganda against the Government Party. It was this conference that invented the name "Territorialism." This undoubted revolutionary action on the part of many members of the Larger Actions Committee living in Russia was received with an outburst of protests from Zionist organizations throughout the world, some of which came from St. Petersburg, Odessa, Warsaw, and Baku. The delegation of the Kharkof Conference, consisting of A. A. Belkowsky, S. J. Rosenbaum, and W. J. Temkin, went to Vienna and met a session of the Larger Actions Committee on April 11, 1904. Everything was done to convince the Russian members not only of the illegality of the position they had taken, but also of the groundlessness of their fears that either Herzl or the Actions Committee had swerved one iota from the Basel Platform; and the resolutions of the Kharkof Conference were allowed to pass without action.

They were, however, to leave an indelible mark upon the Zionist movement as a whole. The opposition to the proposed offer of the English government in many quarters turned into opposition against the president of the congress. He was bitterly attacked, notably by Haham M. Gaster of London; and he felt deeply the exposed position in which he had been placed. For some time past the cares of the great Zionist movement had weighed too heavily upon him. At the Sixth Congress he had complained that his physical powers were unequal to the task, and that an affection of the heart made the great work more difficult than it otherwise would have been. Still he was unremitting in his labors. On Oct. 11, 1903, the King of Italy received Rabbi S. Margulies of Florence in the interests of Zionism, and on Jan. 25 following Herzl had

Death of Herzl.
audience both of the king and of Tittoni, the Italian Minister of Foreign Affairs. On this occasion he saw also the pope and Cardinal Merry del Val. On July 3, 1904, Herzl breathed his last, a martyr to the Jewish cause. There is no doubt that the discussions

and misrepresentations consequent upon the East-African proposal aggravated the disease that was slowly mastering his body. Perhaps the only Jewish statesman of modern times who had devoted himself to the service of his people, he had done more than any single person or group of persons to give the cause dignity and standing. He had been able to unite upon a common ground factors of varying opinions and divergent interests. His fascinating personality and his diplomatic tact had made him the spokesman of his brethren. He had found the Jewish question a philanthropic and at best an agricultural one. He left it an economic and diplomatic one. Whatever his merit as a German litterateur may have been (and this was testified to most bountifully at his death), as an upholder of Jewish ideals and a liberator of his people from mental and moral serfdom he stands almost unique in Jewish annals.

The death of Herzl naturally created consternation within the Zionist body. He had united so much in his own person that he took upon himself alone many of the burdens that others should have borne with him. The question of his successor as chairman of the Actions Committee and as president of the congress naturally preoccupied all minds. On Aug. 16, 1904, a meeting of the Larger Actions Committee was called to take over the affairs of the organization, and on the 17th the annual conference was held. An additional commission to the Smaller Actions Committee was elected, consisting of Nordau, Wolffsohn, Katzenelensohn, Warburg, Tschlenow, Usishkin, Alexander Marmorek, Bodenheimer, and Greenberg, although no provision for such a commission was contained in the constitution. On Nov. 18, 1904, a Zionist deputation, consisting of N. Katzenelensohn, J. Jasinowsky, Tschlenow, and Belkowsky, had an interview with Sviatopolk-Mirsky, the new Russian Minister of the Interior; and on Dec. 4 and 5 Dr. N. Bodenheimer and others, representing the Actions Committee, attended a meeting in Frankfort-on-the-Main for the purpose of regulating the emigration of Jews from Russia. In Jan., 1905, the Larger Actions Committee again sat in Vienna, and it was resolved to legalize the National Fund in London under the control of the Jewish Colonial Trust. The Russian Zionists meanwhile commenced to arm themselves for the struggle which it was foreseen would arise at the Seventh Congress. On Jan. 14, 1905, a conference of forty-seven persons was held in Wilna, at which it was resolved that "as regards the view which considers it possible to realize the ultimate aim of Zionism in a country other than Palestine, it is agreed that such a view is opposed to both the historic ideal of Zionism and the Basel Platform."

The East-African Commission of Inquiry which had been sent out on Dec. 25, 1902, after the committee of nine members appointed by the congress of that year had examined the project in Europe, was composed of Major A. St. H. Gibbons, Prof. Alfred Kaiser, and Engineer M. Wilbusch. The British government had proposed to leave the delimitation of the proposed Jewish settlement to the commission and to the authorities in British East Africa. Herzl, however, preferred that the government should offer a definite territory, which it did after communicating with the high commissioner. This

Question of the Guas Ngishu Plateau. territory is known as the Guas Ngishu Plateau, covering "an area of about 6,000 square miles, bounded in the north by a line running parallel to the equator, and the starting-point of which is the Keremkie, a western tributary of the Kerio River, which flows into Lake Rudolf. In the west it is bounded by the line of the meridian, which is to be counted from the Kissimchanga Mountain to the equator, and which terminates at the Maragolia Hills. In the south the boundary-line as far as the main slope of the so-called Rift Valley, the great East-African depression, is formed by the equator, from which point the eastern boundary-line is drawn almost due north along the Elgeyo escarpment as far as the above-mentioned Keremkie River." The report of the commission was presented to the Actions Committee May 16, 1903, and has been printed as a Zionist Blue Book in English and German (London, 1905). The opinions of the members of the commission were divided; but in general the territory offered was found to be insufficient for a large number of Jewish settlers, and to be fit rather for grazing than for agriculture.

The Seventh Congress met in Basel on July 27, 1905, the first anniversary of the funeral of Theodor Herzl. Over 800 delegates had been elected, of whom more than 600 attended. As had been anticipated, the sessions were particularly

The Seventh Congress. exciting; indeed, at times they became turbulent. The various parties had previously made preparations, the Ziyyone Zionists having held a preliminary conference in Freiburg. Dr. Max Nordau was elected president. Perhaps the most interesting report presented to the congress was that of the Palestine Commission. It told of the publication of its organ "Altneuland," of a geological expedition, of meteorological observation stations established, of the mission of Dr. S. Soskin to Palestine and Syria in the interests of the culture of cotton there, and of the lecture courses on colonization held at Köthen (March 27–April 8, 1905) in connection with the local technical institute. The real interest of the congress lay, however, in the vote that was to be taken on the report of the East-African Commission. Several days were spent in its discussion, and on July 30 the special congress was held provided for in the resolution of the Sixth Congress. The conclusion was foregone. The Actions Committee had, upon receipt of the commission's report, given its opinion that the proffered land was not sufficient in extent and resources for colonization on a large scale; and the Government Party, together with the Ziyyone Zionists and the Mizraḥi faction, was known to be largely in the majority. Various resolutions dealing with the subject were offered; and the following compromise was finally proposed by Alexander Marmorek in the name of the Actions Committee:

"The Seventh Zionist Congress declares: The Zionist organization stands firmly by the fundamental principle of the Basel Program, namely, 'The establishment of a legally secured, publicly recognized home for the Jewish people in Palestine,' and it rejects, either as an end or as a means of colonizing, activity outside Palestine and its adjacent lands. The Congress resolves to thank the British government for its offer of a territory in British East Africa, for the purpose of establishing there a Jewish settlement with autonomous rights. A commission having been sent out to examine the territory, and having reported thereon, the Congress resolves that the Zionist organization shall not engage itself further with the proposal. The Congress records with satisfaction the recognition accorded by the British government to the Zionist organization in its desire to bring about a solution of the Jewish problem, and expresses a sincere hope that it may be accorded the further good offices of the British government where available in any matter it may undertake in accordance with the Basel Program. The Seventh Zionist Congress recalls and emphasizes the fact that, according to article I. of the statutes of the Zionist organization, the Zionist organization includes those Jews who declare themselves to be in agreement with the Basel Program."

In the final trial of strength on this motion the Territorialists abstained from voting, while Dr. Syrkin, in the name of twenty-eight delegates belonging to the Poale Zion, presented a protest against the decision, and together with his party left the hall, refusing to take further part in the congress.

The future work of the Zionist body in Palestine was also the subject of long discussion between the Government Party and the Ẓiyyone Zionists. A compromise resolution was likewise effected in this regard, to wit:

Proposed Work in Palestine. "The Seventh Zionist Congress resolves that, concurrently with political and diplomatic activity, and with the object of strengthening it, the systematic promotion of the aims of the movement in Palestine shall be accomplished by the following methods: 1. Exploration. 2. Promotion of agriculture, industry, etc., on the most democratic principle possible. 3. Cultural and economic improvement and organization of Palestine Jews through the acquisition of new intellectual forces. 4. Acquisition of concessions. The Seventh Zionist Congress rejects every aimless, unsympathetic, and philanthropic colonization on a small scale which does not conform to the first point in the Basel Program."

It was further voted that no land in Palestine was to be bought with the moneys of the National Fund until this could be done in a judicial way.

It is difficult to estimate the number of Zionist societies at present (1905) in existence. They run up into many thousands, and the work they do is of varying complexions according to the needs of Jews living under different conditions. Some are purely national Jewish gatherings, others are literary, while others again are devoted to a development of social intercourse among their members. Many have libraries attached to their places of meeting, and do a certain amount of settlement work.

Present Condition of the Movement. All have one object in view: to foster the national Jewish sentiment, and to band their members together in the further development of Jewish character. The payment of the shekel (25 cents) confers the right to vote for delegates to the congress. Yearly or half-yearly meetings are held by all the societies within a certain district, and federations are gradually being formed in the various countries. The first such organization was the FEDERATION OF AMERICAN ZIONISTS, founded in 1898 for the purpose of gathering into one body the societies in and around New York, but gradually including within its scope all the societies in the United States and the Philippine Islands. In 1905 this federation comprised 238 socie-

ties, with eighty societies in a second organization, the Knights of Zion (Chicago), only loosely connected with the federation. The English Zionist Federation, into which most of the older Chovevei Zion societies were merged after a conference held at Clerkenwell Town Hall, March 6, 1898, was founded in Feb., 1899, and to it were soon added the Canadian and South-African federations, the Societati Sion Istilor diu Rominia, the Zionistische Vereinigung für Deutschland, the Niederlandsch Zionistenbund, and the Dansk Zionistisk Forening. Russia is divided into thirteen "rayons," each one of which is presided over by a member of the Larger Actions Committee.

Constitution. The constitution of the whole Zionist organization is democratic in its very foundations. Full authority resides only in the congresses, in whose hands lie the direction of all Zionist affairs and the election of all officers. While Theodor Herzl was alive the chairman of the Smaller Actions Committee was at the same time president of the congress. At the Seventh Congress the two offices were separated, and it was made impossible for a member of the Actions Committee to be an executive officer of a congress. The congress has its own manual of procedure, which has been modified from time to time. Representation at the congress is upon the basis of one delegate for every 200 shekel-paying Zionists. Up to the Seventh Congress the president carried on the affairs of the organization with six other members living in the same city, who with him formed the Smaller Actions Committee. By the side of this there was a Larger Actions Committee, composed of the leaders of the various organizations in different countries, proposed by their own territorial organizations and elected by the congress. The number of members in this larger committee has continually grown; in 1898 it was 37, in 1900 it was 42, and in 1905 it reached 53. In this last year the Larger Actions Committee was made the executive body of the congress, while the Smaller Actions Committee, consisting of David Wolfssohn, Professor Warburg, Jacobus Kann, Kohen-Bernstein, M. Usishkin, L. J. Greenberg, and Alexander Marmorek, was simply a committee of the larger body. Wolfssohn is at present (1905) chairman of the Smaller Actions Committee, which has its seat in Cologne. The annual budgets of this committee from 1898 to the present time are given in the following table:

Year.	Value in Francs.	Year.	Value in Francs.
1898–1899.....	158,212	1902–1903	158,637
1899–1900.....	173,018	1903–1904 ...	114,911
1900–1901.....	146,631	1904–1905	170,119

Jewish Colonial Trust. The founding of the JEWISH COLONIAL TRUST has been described elsewhere (JEW. ENCYC. vii. 176). Its purposes are not financial but political. As a body with corporate rights, it is the practical instrument of the Zionist organization. The original memorandum declared its purpose to be to work in Palestine, in Syria, or, when in the opinion of the advisory council the interests of the Jewish people should demand it, in any other manner (than specified) and in any other part of the world. Fear was soon felt that this latitude was too great and opened the door to a possible misuse of the funds. The bank's activity was therefore circumscribed. At the Third Congress (Aug. 17, 1899) the clause was changed so as to read " to promote, develop, work, and carry on colonization schemes in the East, by preference in Palestine and Syria; further, to promote, develop, and carry on industries and undertakings in Palestine, in Syria, or in any other part of the world." At the Seventh Congress (Aug. 1, 1905), under the influence of the anti-territorial majority present, the action of the Trust was further circumscribed, and the clause amended so as to read " in Palestine, Syria, any other part of Asiatic Turkey, the Sinai Peninsula, and the Island of Cyprus"; but at the second special meeting called in London, Aug. 31, 1905, the proper voting power was not present and the necessary resolution could not be passed. The shares of the Trust are largely held in very small numbers, the shareholders numbering in the neighborhood of 300,000. Various means have been employed to make their purchase possible in this manner; e.g., the Joint Share Clubs which were founded in London in 1901. The funds in the Trust amounted in Dec., 1903, to £296,887, and in Dec., 1904, to £321,345. Dividends of 2 per cent in 1903 and 2½ per cent in 1904 have been paid. In order to prosecute the work of the Trust in Palestine, and to give stability to Jewish interests there, it was proposed at the Fifth Congress to open up a branch at Jaffa. This was done in 1903, a new corporation, the Anglo-Palestine Company, being established, all the shares of which are held by the Jewish Colonial Trust. In Aug., 1904, a branch of the Anglo-Palestine Company was founded in Jerusalem, which is to be followed by one in Haifa. The Anglo-Palestine Company paid in 1904 a dividend of 4 per cent. The Jewish Colonial Trust has also joined in the foundation of the Palästina Handels Gesellschaft (1903, 22,500 M.) and the Deutsch Levant Baumwoll Gesellschaft (1903, 25,-000 M.). At one time an attempt was made to ruin the Trust, the "Israelite" of Mayence (March 20, 1902) and a correspondent in the "Jewish Chronicle" of London (March 21, 1902) charging it with making false entries. The accusation was reproduced by Dr. Bloch in his "Wochenschrift" (Vienna). The "Jewish Chronicle," upon receipt of better information, of its own accord withdrew the charges; the other two journals were forced to do so by process of law ("Wochenschrift," Feb. 10, 1903). In 1905 the Bezalel society was formed in Germany for the purpose of introducing a more artistic development into Palestinian industries. Together with the Anglo-Palestine Company and the Palästina Handels Gesellschaft, many Jews not affiliated with Zionism have joined hands with them in this attempt to elevate Jewish workmanship in Palestine. Boris Schatz and E. M. Lilien have gone there in order to introduce a " Kunstgewerbeschule."

At the First Congress, in 1897, the idea of a Jewish National Fund (Territorial Fund) was mooted by Prof. Herman Shapira. At the Fourth (1900) it was accepted in principle. The purpose of the Fund is to produce a permanent capital which shall be the property of the Jewish people for the exclusive purpose of buying land in Palestine. It is not to be touched until it reaches $1,000,000, half of which sum is always to remain on hand. The statutes as laid down by the National Fund Commission were accepted by the Fifth Congress (1901); and in 1904 the Fund (" Ḳeren Ḳayyemet") was legally domiciled in London, its moneys being placed in possession of the Jewish Colonial Trust. The Fund is derived from the use of stamps placed on Zionist letters, invitations, and the like, from free-will offerings, and from payments made to inscribe persons and societies in the "Golden Book" ("Sefer ha-Zahab"). Since June 1, 1902, these collections have produced a little over $205,000. The resolution to refrain from using the Fund until it has reached a certain point was violently opposed by the Ẓiyyone Zionists, and a resolution against the statute was adopted by the Minsk Convention; but the Jews in Palestine themselves pleaded (1903) for the original form.

Jewish National Fund.

In its intellectual and spiritual influence upon the Jewish people Zionism has specifically and in many various ways influenced Jewish life. Education has been one of the principal objects in view. Thus, in the district around Yelisavetgrad it has founded about forty-eight model ḥadarim; and it has established reading-rooms, evening courses, and the like. In 1903 Zionists founded a school in Temir Khan Shusa in Daghestan, and the national school for girls (Bet ha-Sefer) in Jaffa receives an annual subvention from the society. The same is true of the Jewish Central Library (Abarbanel Library; see JEW. ENCYC. i. 27) founded by an ardent Zionist, Joseph Chazanowicz of Byelostok. A complete program for a Jewish university was elaborated by Buber and Weizman and published by the Jüdischer Verlag (Berlin, 1901). In Paris the Université Populaire Juive owes its existence to the Zionist societies there, headed by Alexander Marmorek; and the Jewish Toynbee halls in Vienna (opened Dec. 2, 1900), Brünn, Hamburg, Lemberg, Amsterdam, and Tarnopol have had a similar origin.

Educational Work.

In attempting to estimate the effect of the Zionist upheaval it must not be forgotten that, though it tended to consolidate previous efforts in various directions, and to create new efforts along similar lines, the movement itself was merely the culminating point of a previous development. It brought to a head the Jewish Renaissance and provided a channel into which the various activities of this renaissance might flow and find a concerted expression. This is seen, for instance, in the student organizations in Austria and partly in Germany.

Even before the rise of anti-Semitism in the former country, as early as 1882, Jewish students in Vienna, from Russia, Galicia, and Rumania, had banded together for the purpose of conserving Jewish feeling and of cherishing Jewish literature. Perez Smolenskin gave this society its name, "Kadimah," which, meaning both "Forward" and "Eastward," indicated the direction of its activity. Pinsker's "Autoemancipation" became its Bible, and its practical

Jewish Students' Societies.

interest was enlisted in the colonization of Palestine. Its first announcement in Hebrew and German upon the blackboard of the university created consternation. It was strongly opposed by the great mass of Vienna Jews, but in spite of this it continued to further the physical and mental advance of its members. The ordinary "Burschenschaften," "Corps," and "Landsmanschaften" gradually became "Judenrein," under strong pressure from without, even going so far as to declare the Jewish students unworthy of satisfaction by duel. The answer on the part of the Jewish students was the formation of further societies: in 1892 the "Unitas" for students coming from Moravia, and the "Ivria" for students from northern Moravia and Silesia (reorganized 1894); in 1895 the "Libanonia," at first for veterinary students, and later on for students at large; in 1897 the "Bar Kochba" for those coming from Galicia, in which Hebrew courses of instruction were established; and in 1898 the "Maccabaea" for technical students, and the "Bar Giora" for students from the south-Slavic countries. The "Rede- und Lesehalle Jüdischer Hochschüler" and the "Vereinigung der Zionistischen Finkenschaft an der Wiener Universität" are open to all comers. At other universities and high schools similar societies were founded, e.g., the "Ferialverbindungen": the "Emunah" in Bielitz, the "Astra" in Kanitz, the "Massada" in Vienna, the "Severitas" in Loschitz. To these must also be added the "Veritas" in Brünn, the "Charitas" in Graz, the "Kolko Akademickie" in Kolomea, the "Hasmonea" and "Zephirah" in Czernowitz, the "Bar Kochba" in Prague, the "Przedsnt" ("Ha-Shaḥar") in Cracow, the "Akademische Verbindung" in Yaroslaw, the "Makkabaea" in Breslau, the "Hasmonae" in Berlin, the "Herzl" in Königsberg, the "Zionist Society" at Columbia University, New York, and the "Jüdische Studentenverbindung Zionah" at Giessen. At various times general meetings of delegates of these societies have been held, e.g., the "Zionistischen Studententag" in Lemberg on July 25, 1899, and the "Studententag" in Vienna, June 30, 1903, and in June, 1905. In general, see "Ost und West," 1901, p. 415; Albert M. Friedenberg, "Zionist Studies," p. 23, New York, 1904.

Along similar lines were founded a large number of "Turnvereine" (gymnastic societies), which had as their object the development of Jewish muscle and the strengthening of Jewish conscience in the rising generation. The movement in this direction commenced even before the First Zionist Congress,

JEWISH GYMNASTIC SOCIETIES.

Date of Foundation.	Place.	Name of Society.
1894....	Constantinople.	
1898....	Berlin (Oct. 22)..	Bar Kochba.
	Philippopolis..........	Makabi.
1899....	Vienna................	Wiener Jüd. Turnverein.
	Biala.................	Bialäer Jüd. Turnverein.
	Bucharest.............	Aurora.
	Sofia.................	Samson.
1900....	Halberstadt	Turnklub Junger Jüd. Kaufleute.
	Vienna...............	Zion.
	Privitz	Jüd. Turnverein.
	Mährisch-Ostrau.......	Jüd. Turnverein.
1901....	Ungarisch-Hradisch ...	Moravia.
	Olmütz...............	Jüd. Turnklub.
1902....	Rustchuk (Bulg.)......	Makabi.
	Kustendil (Bulg.)......	Samson.
	Troppau..............	Jüd. Turnklub.
	Cologne	Jüd. Turnverein.
	Hamburg..............	Jüd. Turnerschaft.
	Mannheim.............	Jüd. Turnverein.
	Frankfort-on-the-Oder .	Jung-Juda.
	Freiburg	Jüd. Turnverein.
	Posen.................	Neuen Posener Turnverein.
	Leipsic...............	Jüd. Turnverein.
	Munich...............	Ezra.
	Breslau...............	Jüd. Turn- und Sport-Verein.

Gymnastic Societies. such a society having been founded in Constantinople in the year 1894. It received a great moral support from the national spirit engendered by the Zionist propaganda, and the outward impulse to the formation of such separate societies was given by the exclusion of Jewish students from the "Bundesgenossenschaft" of gymnasts in Austria and from the academic "Turnvereine" in Germany. It was in the latter country that these Jewish societies were most sharply attacked, notably by a Jew,

Rathenau, and by the "Kölnische Zeitung." The governing body of the "Jüdische Turnerschaft" in Germany answered the attack (Sept. 2, 1903) in order to assure the public that there was nothing anti-German in their action. Whereupon the "Kölnische Zeitung" and the "Frankfurter Zeitung" changed in a measure their attitude; but the "Allgemeine Zeitung des Judenthums" hoped that such "extravagances" could not be laid at the door of German Jews; while the "Mittheilungen zur Abwehr des Anti-Semitismus" fought the movement tooth and nail, looking upon it only as a means of Zionistic propaganda. On the other hand, such Jewish weeklies as the "General Anzeiger" of Berlin, the "Israelitisches Familienblatt" of Hamburg, and the "Israelitisches Gemeindeblatt" reflected the sentiments of a part of the Jewish community by heartily welcoming the new movement. As the foregoing table will show, the work of the "Turnvereine" has grown apace, and at the Third Basel Congress, in 1899, a public exhibition was given by societies from Berlin, Cologne, Freiburg, Mannheim, Mährisch-Ostrau, Prossnitz, Ungarisch-Hradisch, and Vienna, and a second Jewish "Turnertag" was held in Berlin April 23 and 24, 1905. The "Bar Kochba" of Berlin has printed a collection of songs ("Vereins Liederbuch"), and since 1902 it has published the monthly "Jüdische Turnzeitung."

In addition there are societies (the dates of whose foundation are not known) at Hanover, Frankfort-on-the-Main ("Jung-Juda"), Brünn, Bern, Samokoff, Bazardjik, Dubnitza, Cracow, and Lemberg.

In accord with the democratic basis of the Zionist organization, women have from the first been admitted to a voice and a vote in the congress. This has occasioned the formation of a large number of women's societies, which bear such names as "Benoth Zion" (Jassy, Sofia, New York), "Hadassa" (Vienna, Braila, New York), "Jehudith" (Brünn), "Moria" (Vienna), "Zion" (Lemberg), "Jüdisch Nationale Frauen Vereinigung" (Frankfort-on-the-Main). The work of these societies is of a literary, educational, and social character.

The inspiration that Zionism has given to the furtherance of modern Jewish Renaissance is seen in various directions. From its ranks have come most of those sturdy students, writers, poets, painters, and sculptors who have done so much to make the modern artistic development available for Jewish life (see Buber in the "Protocol of the Fifth Congress," pp. 151 et seq.). Not only has the cultivation of the Hebrew language been foremost in their program, but especially the furtherance of art with a distinctive Jewish bent. Ephraim Moses Lilien, Lesser Ury, Judah Epstein, and Herman Struck have worked in line and color; Frederic Beer, Henryk Glitzenstein, Alfred Nossig, and Boris Schatz in marble and bronze. In 1901 Alfred Nossig, Davis Trietsch, Buber, Feiwel, and Lilien started the Jüdische Verlag in Berlin, which has attempted to substitute artistic book-making for the inelegant presswork of former times. Besides publishing a "Jüdischer Almanach" and the "Jüdische Statistik," it has printed a number of highly artistic volumes dealing with modern Jewish literature and art. The Jüdischer Künstler Verlag Phoenix (1902) in Berlin owes its origin to the same circle, as does also the Jüdischer Künstler Aesthetik in Warsaw.

Influence on Literature and Art.

One of the most potent factors of Zionist propaganda has been its press. Only a few of the older Jewish papers were inclined toward the new movement, e.g., "Ha-Meliz" and "Ha-Ẓefirah" in Russia, the "Jewish World" in England, the "Corriere

Israelitico" in Italy, the "Jewish Exponent" in Philadelphia, and the "Jewish Comment" in Baltimore. The "Jewish Chronicle" of

Zionistic Press. London, though editorially unfavorable, has always given the widest publicity to Zionist news and to correspondence anent the movement.

On the other hand, the majority of Jewish weeklies have shown themselves more or less violently inimical, especially the "Voskhod" in St. Petersburg, the "Allgemeine Zeitung des Judenthums" in Berlin, "Bloch's Wochenschrift" in Vienna, and "The American Israelite" in Cincinnati. It therefore became necessary for the society to create a press of its own. In 1898 Theodor Herzl founded "Die Welt," which he carried on at his own expense until the Fifth Basel Congress officially accepted it as the organ of the party. Simultaneously there grew up a great number of Zionist periodicals in Hebrew, Yiddish, Judæo-Spanish, German, French, English, Italian, Russian, Rumanian, Bulgarian, Arabic, etc. Many of these are official publications of Zionist Territorial and other organizations, e.g., the "Maccabæan," of the Federation of American Zionists; "L'Echo Sioniste," of the French Federation; "Israelitische Rundschau" (Berlin), of the German Zionist Union; "Israel's Messenger," of the Shanghai Zionists. Of the others only a few can be mentioned: "Der Jüdische Arbeiter" (Vienna); "Jüdische Zukunft" (London); "Zionistische Monatshefte" (Geneva); "Jüdische Post" (Pittsburg); "Ha-Mizpah" (Cracow); "Ha-Shaḥar" (Sofia); "Ha-Shiloaḥ" (Berlin); "Degel Maḥaneh Yehudah" (Jassy); "Buduschnost" (St. Petersburg); "El Dia" (Philippopolis); "Idea Sionista" (Ferrara); "El-Miṣrayim" (Cairo). "Ost und West" (Jüdischer Verlag, Berlin) is the first attempt at an artistic Jewish journal; and in the "Schlemiel" the Jew—perhaps for the first time—refuses to take himself seriously. "Unsere Hoffnung" (Vienna) is a Zionist juvenile publication.

The extent to which the Zionist idea has spread among the Jewish people may be seen not only in the number of Jews affiliated with the Zionist organization and congress, but also in the fact that there is hardly a nook or corner of the Jewish world in which Zionistic societies are not to be found. Even where no such organizations exist expressions of approval and adhesion have come from bodies of Jews who have lived practically cut off from all connection with the course of Jewish

Wide Spread of Zionism. life. Notable were communications, together with subscriptions for the fund, from a band of descendants of Portuguese Jews in Manecoré in Amazonas, Brazil (March 12, 1901), from Jews settled in Chile, and from the Jadid al-Islam in Khorasan (1901); while societies exist in Tshita (Siberia, on the Manchurian border), Tashkent, Bokhara, Rangoon (Burma), Nagasaki, Tokyo, Hongkong, Singapore, and among the American soldiers in the Philippines. The Shanghai Zionist Association was founded in 1903; the Dr. Herzl East Africa Zionist Association in Nairobi (East-African Protectorate) in 1904. In Australia there are four Zionist federations: New South Wales, Victoria, South Australia, and West Australia. Queensland has its own federation with its center in Brisbane, and New Zealand has several societies. Even among the Russian Jews settled by the Jewish Colonization Association in Argentina, there is a federation comprising four societies. A Zionist congress was held there May 16, 1904, comprising delegates of 1,150 shekel-paying members. In every country of Europe, in the United States, along the North-African coast, and in Palestine similar societies are to be found. At the St. Louis Exposition, 1904, the Zionist flag (blue and white stripes, with a "Magen Dawid" in the center) floated from one of the buildings together with those of other nationalities.

This topographical diversity runs parallel with the variety of Jews to whom the Zionist movement has appealed; and it is therefore natural that a great divergence of opinion is manifest within its own ranks. This could not be otherwise, considering that the movement is a national one. Several parties and factions have accordingly grown up

Parties in Zionism. within the body, and have made themselves felt during some of the congresses. In fact, the discussions, very violent at times because they are based on radical differences of principle both in the congress and outside, are the natural concomitants of this as of all world-movements. Of the parties or groups within the Zionist body the following may be specifically enumerated:

The group composed of the immediate followers of Theodor Herzl and of those that stood by him during his seven years of work may be called the Government Party. Their program is that enunciated by the president of the congress at its various sittings. They desire a legally assured home for the Jewish people in Palestine and neighboring countries, and take their stand upon the Basel Platform pure and simple. They are politico-diplomatic Zionists, though not opposed to strengthening the position of the Jews in Palestine by bettering their condition and by conducting experiments in farming and industrial enterprises.

The second group is that of the Mizraḥi, an alliance of the Orthodox Jews within the Zionist body. The Mizraḥi was formed at the time of the Fifth Congress as an offset to the Radical Fraction. Its head is Rabbi Isaac Jacob Reines of Lida, Russia, where its first yearly meeting was held Feb. 23, 1903. It claimed then a membership of 11,000, but has largely gained since that time. In 1903 it had founded 125 societies, not only in Russia, but in Germany, England, Galicia, and Palestine. A world conference of Mizraḥists was held in Presburg Aug. 21–24, 1904, and a special conference of the English societies in London July 19, 1904. The group has spread also to the United States, where it has held two meetings, Jan. 5–7, 1905, in New York, and June 17, 1905, in Philadelphia. The American branch maintains an organ, "The Sabbath Journal." The Mizraḥists, forming the Jewish Center Party, were stanch adherents of Theodor Herzl, and since his death have remained true to his principles. To these they have added, as a special feature, the conservation of Orthodox Jewish practises. At the congress they usually vote with the Government Party. According to their program, they are "an organization of Orthodox Zionists who, on the basis of the Basel Program, believe a faithful adherence to the Torah and the tradition in all matters pertaining to Jewish life, and a longing for the land of the fathers, to constitute the task of the Jewish people and the conditions favorable to its preservation."

The Po'ale Zion, or the Democratic "Fraction," represents the Jewish Left. Its members claim to speak for the proletariat in eastern Europe, and have a number of pronounced Socialists in their ranks. Though comparatively a small body, they made themselves felt at the Second Congress, when the motion of Professor Mandelstamm to exclude them was lost. They are organized in Austria and in Switzerland; and one faction calls itself openly "The Zionistic Socialist Workingmen's Party, London–Paris." They organized in America in 1903, and held their first convention April 29, 1904, twelve societies being represented and maintaining an organ, "Die Neue Stimme." In the United States they are affiliated with the Federation of American Zionists. The Po'ale Zion holds that the Jewish proletariat will be driven into its ranks as the pressing, practical need for emigration from eastern Europe becomes greater. The members are therefore largely Territorialists, and claim to be forced in a measure to be opposed to Palestinian colonization on whatever scale, because of its apparent impossibility. On the other hand, they are believed in some quarters to have their Socialist propaganda more at heart than their Zionist work, and to threaten to compromise the movement with certain European governments. The Bund in Russia was at first opposed to Zionism, accusing the latter society of refusing to aid the Rumanian Jews in 1897. Since then it has made sensible approaches to Zionism, its members becoming Nationalist Jews and working for national Jewish autonomy.

A very large party within the general body consists of the so-called Ẓiyyone Zionists, a product of the discussions raised by the Sixth Congress. They are practically led by Usishkin of Yekaterinoslav. At the time of the Sixth Congress he was **Ẓiyyone** presiding over a congress in Palestine, **Zionists.** and declared himself not only against the East-African project, but also against the binding character of the vote taken at the congress. In a pamphlet, "Unser Programm" (Vienna, 1905), he has laid down the principles of the new group. Holding that the diplomatic actions of Herzl have proven a failure, it demands immediate work in Palestine, without waiting for the granting of a charter. Land there should be bought at once with a certain portion of the National Fund; and whatever diplomatic actions are to accompany Zionist work should be carried out by a collegium. For the purposes of colonization a special society, Geullah, has been formed; and the assistance of the ICA and other colonization societies is to be sought. A Palestine Zionist Association was founded in London in May, 1905, with Haham M. Gaster as its president, to work along similar lines. Since the Sixth Congress, Usishkin has been ceaselessly active in gathering his forces together. Before the Seventh Congress a preliminary conference was held in Freiburg, and at the congress itself the Ẓiyyone Zionists polled a vote of 360, practically controlling the voting power. There can be no doubt that the Ẓiyyone Zionists are made up largely of the old Chovevei Zion groups; and though they have protested strongly against the imputation, the Political Zionists see in their rise a danger of the movement falling back into the rut of the old beneficent colonization.

Diametrically opposed to the Ẓiyyone Zionists are the Territorialists. The new organization was formed largely of those who wished the congress to accept the offer of the English government; but in a very short while it developed into a body seeking a territory upon an autonomous basis **Terri-** in any part of the world where such **torialists;** territory might be available. The **Israel** Zionistische Territoriale Verbindung **Zangwill.** in Bern issued a call in "Die Welt" (1905, No. 12), but the new group was really formed as the Jewish Territorial Organization during the Seventh Congress. Israel Zangwill has been its leader and its president. Despite his protest that the minority at the congress must always bow to the majority (speech in London, 1900), he felt that the need of the wandering mass of Jews, and consequent emigration called for a more rapid solution than political Zionism was able to afford. According to Zangwill, the majority at the Sixth Congress was for Territorialism; but this is a misstatement, inasmuch as a large majority of those who voted in the affirmative on that occasion voted merely for the sending of the commission, and not upon the merits of the proposition as a whole. Ignoring completely the vote taken at the Seventh Congress, he put himself at the head of the Jewish Territorial Organization, and, joined by the radical element which cut itself off from the Zionist body, and by a number who, like himself, remained Zionists although they believed it inopportune to refuse the offer of the English government, he fashioned the new organization in Basel. In the "Jewish Chronicle," London, Aug. 25, 1905, he issued a manifesto in which he stated that the Jewish Territorial Organization

"makes as a body no opposition toward Zionism, its members being left free to determine their individual relations to that movement. Naturally no land whatever is excluded from our operations, provided it be reasonably good and obtainable."

The object of the organization was said to be:

"1. To procure a territory upon an autonomous basis for those Jews who cannot or will not remain in the lands in which they at present live. 2. To achieve this end the organization proposes: to unite all Jews who are in agreement with this object; to enter into relations with governments and public and private institutions; and to create financial institutions, labor bureaus, and other instruments that may be found necessary."

The large mass of Zionists saw in this new organization a breaking away from the larger body, and, practically, Zionism minus Zion.

Israel Zangwill has (Sept., 1905) joined hands with Lucien Wolf, who now seems more willing to accept the idea of a British colony with Jewish autonomous rights—the very proposition made to Theodor Herzl by the British government—though he still proclaims himself as far from the Zionist position as he ever was. In furtherance of these plans Zangwill in the name of the Jewish Territorial Organization memorialized the Hon. Alfred Littleton (Sept. 8, 1905), asking that the original concession in British East Africa remain open for a while longer. However, on Sept. 16 Littleton replied in the negative, stating that the territory in question had already been thrown open to colonization, but renewing the assurance contained in the letter of Clement Hill (see above) that his government follows with the same interest any attempt to ameliorate the condition of the Jewish people.

Several less clearly defined groupings have sprung

up of late years. The so-called Political Zionists held their own conference at Warsaw in June, 1905, Prof. M. Mandelstamm presiding. These are on some points opposed to the Territorialists, who are in a sense anti-Palestinian; but they are willing to make certain concessions in their desire to conserve the large mass of Jews emigrating out of eastern Europe from complete assimilation **Other** and demoralization. They are willing **Groups.** to cooperate with other bodies in concentrating this emigration in an autonomous national territory other than Palestine. They desire, however, that the work in and for Palestine shall continue; and they agree that no Zionist moneys are to be employed for other than Palestinian purposes. They claim to have had forty-five delegates at the Fifth Congress, and at the Seventh they formed a special group, their spokesman being Prof. N. Slouschz of Paris. They are opponents of the Ẓiyyone Zionists and gravitate naturally toward the Territorialists.

A second minor group is that of the Practical Political Party ("Real Politische Partei"), led by Nossig and Trietsch, with some of whose views Professor Warburg, Dr. Franz Oppenheimer, and others of the Palestine Commission coincide. They are opposed to both the Ẓiyyone Zionists and the Territorialists. They hold that the importance of autonomy in a Jewish ingathering is exaggerated; and they demand that the Zionists further a legal colonization in Palestine and the neighboring countries, a systematic economic advance in the near East, the purchase of land in and around Palestine, the investigation of both its agricultural and commercial possibilities, the founding of experimental farming and other stations, and diplomatic measures only in so far as their ends are attainable. They also lay great stress upon the organization of the Jews and upon Jewish culture (see Nossig in "Die Stimme der Wahrheit," pp. 11 *et seq.*). The leaders of this small group have been severe critics of the diplomatic activity of Theodor Herzl. They favor colonization in Cyprus and have done successful work in furthering the intellectual side of the Jewish Renaissance.

Very different from those above mentioned are the followers of Aḥad ha-ʿAm (Asher Ginsberg). This leader of what is called "Moral Zionism," though now opposed both to Chovevei Zionism and to Political Zionism, was one of the moving forces in the early days of the former. In 1889 **Moral** he formed in Odessa the Bene Mo- **Zionism of** sheh, a secret organization, lodges of **Aḥad ha-** which are to be found in many Rus- **ʿAm** sian cities, and which has ramifications **(Asher** in Palestine, Great Britain, Paris, and **Ginsberg).** Berlin. For three or four years this society supplied the material and the enthusiasm that established the colony Reḥobot, the Carmel Wine Company, the Aḥiasaf Publication Society, the monthly "Ha-Shiloaḥ," and the Bet ha-Sefer in Jaffa. According to Aḥad ha-ʿAm, Judaism is in greater need than are the Jews, and a national spiritual center is necessary in Palestine to act as a centrifugal force against the disintegrating tendencies within the Jewish ranks. A "Renais-

sance of the heart" must come, and gradually, through a process of development. Only when the spirit of the people has been centralized can the work of centralizing the people themselves be begun. Aḥad ha-ʿAm is the philosopher of the Jewish Renaissance; and as he has severely attacked Political Zionists, he has been as severely attacked by them in return. Many Zionist leaders and workers subscribe to Aḥad ha-ʿAm's principle as a theory, while furthering the practical works of the organization; and many theoretic Zionists look to him as their leader, as such adhesion leaves them uncompromised in their affiliations. Nor must it be forgotten that much of his program is that of all Zionists. At the opening of the Second Congress, Herzl proclaimed that Zionism meant "a return to Judaism as preparatory to a return to a Jewish land" (see Henrietta Szold in "Jewish Comment," May 12, 1905; Matthias Acher, "Aḥad ha-ʿAm," Berlin, 1903).

It can not be denied that these various currents have had an effect upon the general trend of Zionism as officially expressed in the discussions and resolutions of succeeding congresses. While any violation of the fundamental principles of the Basel Platform is sternly rejected, there has been manifest a greater readiness to undertake work in Palestine upon a practical basis without first waiting for the final results of diplomatic and political action, the while carefully pursuing these actions and preventing a recurrence of the older and worthless Chovevei Zionism.

BIBLIOGRAPHY: The bibliography on Zionism, which is extremely large, has been collected in a Russian publication, *Ukazatel Literatury o Sionizmě*, St. Petersburg, 1903. Only a few works can be mentioned here. A history of Zionism has been attempted by Sapir, *Der Zionismus*, Brünner Jüdischer Verlag, 1903. The files of *Die Welt* and the stenographic *Protokoll* of the seven congresses furnish the most reliable material; an index to them has been drawn up by Hugo Schachtel, *Register zu den Protokollen der Zionistenkongresse*, i.-vi., Berlin, 1905. See also R. Gottheil, *The Aims of Zionism*, in *Publ. Am. Fed. of Zionists*, New York, 1899; C. Levias, *The Justification of Zionism*, in *Hebrew Union College Journal*, Cincinnati, April, 1899; R. Gottheil, *The Zionist Movement*, in *North American Review*, 1902; J. de Haas, *Zionism*, London, 1901; Max Nordau, in the *International Quarterly*, 1902, No. 1; Israel Zangwill, in *Lippincott's Magazine*, Oct., 1899; *Theodor Herzl's Zionistische Schriften*, ed. Leon Kellner, Berlin, 1905; Heinrich Sachse (Löwe), *Zionistenkongress und Zionismus, Eine Gefahr?* Berlin, 1897; Ephraim Deinard, *Dibre ha-Yamim le-Ziyyon be-Russia*, Kearny, N. J., 1904; F. Heman, *Das Erwachen der Jüdischen Nation*, Basel, 1897; Max Jaffé, *Die Nationale Wiedergeburt der Juden*, Berlin, 1897; D. Farbstein, *Der Zionismus und die Judenfrage*, Bern, 1898; Ben Eliezer, *Die Judenfrage und der Socialer Judenstaat*, Bern, 1898; Aron Sandler, *Anthropologie und Zionismus*, Brünn, 1904; *Was Will der Zionismus?* Berlin (Zion. Verein. f. Deutschland), 1903. A collection of essays will be found in *Die Stimme der Wahrheit*, ed. E. Nossig, Berlin, 1905, and in the *Publications of the Federation of American Zionists*.
G.

ZIONIST, DER. See PERIODICALS.

ZIPPOR: Father of Balak, King of Moab, who hired Balaam to curse Israel. All the passages which mention Zippor name him together with his son Balak (Num. xxii. 2, 4, 10, 16; xxiii. 18; Josh. xxiv. 9; Judges xi. 25). An allusion to him may be contained in "the former king of Moab" in Num. xxi. 26.
E. G. H.   B. P.

ZIPPORAH.—Biblical Data: Daughter of Jethro and wife of Moses. According to the Bible,

Moses met the daughters of Jethro when they were being driven away from a well by shepherds; he assisted them, and was invited into the house of Jethro, who gave him Zipporah to be his wife (Ex. ii. 21). On his return to Egypt, Moses was accompanied by his wife, who saved him from great danger during their journey (*ib.* iv. 24–26). She appears to have returned with her children to her father's house; for after the exodus from Egypt, Jethro brought Zipporah and her children out to Moses in the wilderness (*ib.* xviii. 2–5). Zipporah is mentioned only once more in the Bible; namely, in Numbers xii. 1, where she is referred to as "the Ethiopian woman," for having married whom Moses is upbraided by Miriam and Aaron.

——**In Rabbinical Literature**: Zipporah is mentioned by the Rabbis alternately with praise and with blame. Her name (= "bird") is explained as having been given her because, when questioned by her father as to the man who had rescued her, she flew out of the house like a bird and returned with Moses (Yalḳ., Shim'oni, i. 169). R. Joshua was of the opinion that Zipporah and Moses were always estranged, and that the latter did not love his wife (*ib.* 268). The name "Cushite" was given to her, it is said, because she was distinguished from other women by her beauty, even as the Ethiopians differed from other people in their complexions. The circumstance that she is twice referred to in one verse as "the Ethiopian" (Num. xii. 1) is explained as indicating that her actions were as distinctive as her beauty, and that she conducted herself no less royally while in her father's house than when she became the wife of Moses (Yalḳ., Shim'oni, 1238; comp. also M. Ḳ. 16b; Yer. Sanh. x. 28d).

J.   S. O.

ZIPSER, MAIER: Hungarian rabbi; born at Balassa-Gyarmath Aug. 14, 1815; died at Rechnitz Dec. 10, 1869. He studied in various yeshibot, among his teachers being Wolf Boskowitz and Maier Eisenstadt; and he acquired a secular education partly through the assistance of Löw Schwab and partly through his own endeavors. In 1844 he was chosen rabbi at Stuhlweissenburg, where, however, he became involved in a controversy with the Orthodox members of the community on account of a divorce which he had granted without a precedent. In his defense he wrote a pamphlet entitled "Me ha-Shiloaḥ: Rabbinisches Gutachten über Jüdische Ehescheidung" (Budapest, 1853). About 1850 he went to England, where he published a pamphlet entitled "The Sermon on the Mount," defending Judaism against the parliamentary speeches of Inglis (London, 1852). In 1858 Zipser was elected rabbi of Rechnitz, and he held this position until his death. In addition to the two pamphlets already mentioned, he published various sermons and made numerous contributions to the Jewish press, especially to the "Orient," the "Allgemeine Zeitung des Judenthums," and the "Neuzeit," winning the reputation of being one of the most scholarly Hungarian rabbis of his day.

BIBLIOGRAPHY: *Allg. Zeit. des Jud.* 1870, p. 8; *Neuzeit*, 1869, pp. 603–605; Fürst, *Bibl. Jud.* iii. 552–554.
S.   D.

ZIRNDORF, HEINRICH: German poet and rabbinical scholar; born at Fürth, Bavaria, May 7, 1829; died at Cincinnati, Ohio, Dec. 17, 1893; educated privately. His parents intended him for a commercial career, and for a short time he was employed as a clerk by a firm in Fürth, but his early studies of German and English classics inspired him to continue studying, and at the age of nineteen he went to Munich, where he attended the gymnasium until 1855. He then moved to Vienna, and remained there until 1857. These two years were chiefly devoted to poetry, and some of his best verse was written during that time, his "Kassandra," a tragedy in five acts, being published at Vienna in 1856. In 1857 he obtained the position of rabbi of Lipto-Szent-Miklos, Hungary, but soon resigned and moved to Frankfort-on-the-Main; there he made the personal acquaintance of Isaac Marcus Jost (1859), whose reminiscences he published under the title "Isaak Markus Jost und Seine Freunde" (Cincinnati, 1886). In 1860 he published a selection of his poems at Leipsic, and in the fall of the same year he accepted an invitation to go to London as a private tutor. There he lived for thirteen years, writing and teaching, and mingling with the best society of the capital. In 1873 he returned to Germany as rector of the Hebrew Teachers' Institute at Münster, and three years later accepted a call to the rabbinate of the Congregation Beth-El, Detroit, Mich. In 1884 he became professor of history in the Hebrew Union College at Cincinnati, being succeeded in Detroit by Louis Grossmann, now rabbi of the Plum Street Temple and professor in the Hebrew Union College. About this time Zirndorf began to contribute to the "Deborah," of which he subsequently became associate editor. In 1889 he was chosen rabbi and preacher of the Ahabath Achim congregation in Cincinnati, and held this position until his death. In 1892 a translation of a number of his sketches contributed to the "Deborah" appeared at Philadelphia under the title "Some Jewish Women."

BIBLIOGRAPHY: Zirndorf, *Isaak Markus Jost und Seine Freunde*, pp. 6–9, Cincinnati, 1886; idem, *Some Jewish Women*, p. vi., Philadelphia, 1892; Brümmer, *Deutsches Dichter-Lexikon*, i. 545 *et seq.*; *American Israelite*, xl., No. 25.
S.   M. Z.

ZIZIT. See FRINGES.

ZNAIM: City in Moravia, Czecho-Slovakia. Jews probably settled there during the twelfth century; for in a document of Ottocar I. dated 1225 a Jews' street in Znaim is mentioned. During the ARMLEDER PERSECUTIONS in 1338 and the Black Death in 1349 the Jews of this place were among the sufferers. Upon the complaint of the butchers in 1401, Margrave Prokop forbade the Jews to engage in the retailing of meat. King Sigismund, who was constantly in financial difficulties, borrowed from the city 905 florins, which the Jews in the royal cities of Moravia had to pay; of this sum the Jews of Znaim paid 400 florins, and those of Brünn only 300, proving that the former city had the larger Jewish population. The chief occupation of the Jews of Znaim in those early days was money-lending; in 1437 they were forbidden to charge a higher rate of interest than $3\frac{1}{2}$ pfennigs per shock groschen, and in 1453 the rate was reduced to $\frac{1}{2}$ pfennig. In 1454 the fanatic Franciscan monk

John of CAPISTRANO aroused the population against the Jews, and on July 25 of the same year they were expelled. From that time until 1848 Jews were not permitted to reside in Znaim; and those who went thither on business had to pay a LEIB-ZOLL, which in 1708 was fixed at 18 or 7 kreuzer, according to certain conditions. In 1785 Jacob FRANK spent some time in the city.

After the constitution of 1848 had declared freedom of residence, Jews began to settle in the city, but they did not hold religious services until 1858. A Jewish society for worship was formed in 1866, and two years later a cemetery was acquired, where were deposited the remains of those buried in the old cemetery (confiscated in 1454), and also three tombstones from the same ancient burial-ground. In 1870 the society received the rights of a corporation ("Cultusgemeinde"), and in 1888 a new synagogue was dedicated. The congregation numbers 160 families, of which 120 live in the city and the remainder in the outlying district. The community was originally under the spiritual direction of teachers only, and not until 1894 was it permitted to appoint a rabbi. The following ministers have officiated in Znaim: H. Barth, Joseph Paschkes (1869), Samuel Mühsam (1870–72), Jacob Wittenberg (1872–77), Samuel Grün (1878–82), Ignaz Holzer (1884–99), and Isidor Kahan, the incumbent in 1905.

The community supports three charitable societies: a ḥebra ḳaddisha, a women's benevolent society, and a Talmud Torah society which provides poor school-children with text-books. The Jews of Znaim are mostly commission-merchants, but there are among them also physicians, lawyers, civil engineers, and some industrial workers. The annual expenditure of the congregation is about $2,800.

D.   I. K.

ZOAN: An important Egyptian city of great antiquity, almost as old as Hebron (Num. xiii. 22). The "princes of Zoan" are ranked in Isa. xix. 11, 13 with those of Noph (Memphis), and the city itself is mentioned in Ezek. xxx. 14 together with No (Thebes). The Israelitish embassies to it (Isa. xxx. 4) may imply that it was the residence of Pharaoh, and a similar allusion may possibly be traced in Ps. lxxviii. 12, 43, unless "the field of Zoan" is a poetic designation of Egypt in general.

Zoan (Hebr. צֹעַן; the Egyptian "Za'ne" [older form, "Ẓa'net"]; the Coptic "Ja[a]ne," "Jani"; and the "Tanis" of the Greeks) was situated in the Delta on the Tanitic branch of the Nile, not far from the modern lake of Menzelah and the northeastern frontier of Egypt. The ruins, excavated by Mariette in 1860 and, more thoroughly, by Petrie in 1883, have yielded monuments ranging from the sixth dynasty to the Roman period, when the city, once a royal residence, especially of the twenty-first or "Tanitic" dynasty, began to degenerate into the fishing-village represented by the modern Ṣan al-Ḥajar.

BIBLIOGRAPHY: Petrie, *Tanis*, London, 1885–87.
E. G. H.   W. M. M.

ZODIAC: An imaginary zone of the heavens containing the twelve signs within which lie the paths of the principal planets, and through which the sun passes in its annual course. The signs, mostly representing symbols of animals, extend for thirty degrees each, and the entire zodiac is divided into twelve equal parts, six north and six south of the equator. When Hipparchus observed the constellations at Rhodes, those which bore the same names coincided approximately in position with the divisions of the sun's path which they designated and which agree with the signs according to the Talmudic tradition. The precession of the equinoxes, however, gradually shifted the series, and the discrepancy now amounts to an entire sign. The signs are used by astronomers, while the constellations are employed by astrologers. Menahem ibn Zeraḥ (fourteenth century) says that the zodiac moves very slowly from east to west, one degree in 100 years, making 36,000 years for the cycle, and that some authorities believe the movement to be eccentric ("Ẓedah la-Derek," p. 21b, Ferrara, 1554).

The duodecimal division of the zodiac is first mentioned in the "Sefer Yeẓirah," which is of unknown antiquity, and in which the constellations ("mazzalot") are named in the following order: Ṭaleh, Shor,
The Twelve Signs. Te'omim, Sarṭan, Aryeh, Betulah, Moznayim, 'Aḳrab, Ḳeshet, Gedi, Deli, and Dagim, corresponding to Aries, Taurus, etc., and to the twelve months beginning with Nisan. The constellations are also said to correspond to the twelve organs of the body: two hands, two feet, two kidneys, the gall, intestines, liver, throat, stomach, and pancreas ("Sefer Yeẓirah," v. 4). This order of the constellations harmonizes with the theory of the Assyrian astronomers, who supposed that at the moment of crossing the equator toward the north the sun was at the first point of Aries, and that about thirty days later it entered Taurus, and so on. They also designated the signs according to the organs of the body, which they arranged in the sequence of head, neck, arms, breast, heart, bowels, kidneys, loins, thighs, knees, legs, and feet.

The twelve constellations represent the twelve tribes, while each station of the zodiac has thirty paths, and each path has thirty legions (of stars) (Ber. 32b). The standards of the tribes corresponded to the zodiacal signs of the constellations, so that in the east was the standard of Judah, with Issachar and Zebulun beside it, these three being opposite Aries, Taurus, and Gemini; in the south was the standard of Reuben, with Simeon and Gad, opposite Cancer, Leo, and Virgo; in the west was the standard of Ephraim, with Manasseh and Benjamin, opposite Libra, Scorpio, and Sagittarius; and in the north was the standard of Dan, with Asher and Naphtali, opposite Capricornus, Aquarius, and Pisces (Yalḳ., Num. 418).

The motives underlying the choice of the symbolic signs are obvious in the case of some and only conjectural in the case of others. All may be traced to Assyrian mythology and influence. The Jews during
Symbolism. the Babylonian exile adopted Hebraicized forms of the Assyrian names of the months and constellations. In some instances the Rabbis endeavored to explain the origin of these names. Thus they said that the Temple could not be destroyed in the

first month (Nisan) since the sign Aries is a reminder of the 'AḲEDAH, Isaac representing the sacrificial "ṭaleh" (= "lamb"). In the second month (Iyyar) the sign Taurus or Shor (= "ox") recalls the "calf tender and good" (Gen. xviii. 7) which Abraham provided for the angels; and in the third month (Siwan) the sign Gemini (= "twins") represents Esau and Jacob. In the fourth month (Tammuz) the sign Cancer (= "crab"), which lives in water, represents Moses, who was saved from water, while in the fifth month (Ab), which is designated by the sign of Leo, "the lion is come up from his thicket" (Jer. iv. 7), the Temple named "Ariel" (= "the lion of God") was destroyed (Isa. xxix. 1; Pesiḳ. R. 27–28 [ed. Friedmann, p. 133b]). The constellations represent the Creation: Aries is light and Taurus is darkness; Gemini represents the two sexes; Cancer symbolizes

marriage would be a failure. A detailed description of the influence of the several planets and constellations is given in the "Zedah la-Derek" of Menahem ibn Zeraḥ (i., §§ 28–29), as well as in the "'Abbi'ah Ḥidot" of Abraham Ḥamawi (pp. 49b–62a, ed. Leghorn, 1874), but all agree that the righteous Jew is above the "mazzal" (constellation or planet) and need not fear any evil fate. In support of this teaching the passage "be not dismayed at the signs of heaven; for the heathen are dismayed at them" (Jer. x. 2) is frequently quoted, and it is contrary to the Jewish religion to consult the predictions of astrologers or to depend on them (Deut. xviii. 11).

The dates at which the sun enters the signs of the zodiac in the course of a year are specified in the accompanying table.

J.   J. D. E.

Sun Enters	Hebrew Name.	Approximate Date.	First of Hebrew Month.	Approximate Hebrew Date.	Jewish Constellation.	Astronomical Signs.
Aries	Ṭaleh	March 21	Nisan	March 27	♓	♈
Taurus	Shor	April 21	Iyyar	April 26	♈	♉
Gemini..........	Te'omim	May 22	Siwan	May 25	♉	♊
Cancer	Sarṭan	June 22	Tammuz	June 24	♊	♋
Leo.............	Aryeh	July 23	Ab	July 23	♋	♌
Virgo...........	Betulah	Aug. 24	Elul	Aug. 23	♌	♍
Libra	Moznayim	Sept. 24	Tishri	Sept. 22	♍	♎
Scorpio.........	'Aḳrab	Oct. 24	Ḥeshwan	Oct. 22	♎	♏
Sagittarius	Ḳeshet	Nov. 23	Kislew	Nov. 19	♏	♐
Capricornus	Gedi	Dec. 22	Ṭebet	Dec. 18	♐	♑
Aquarius	Deli	Jan. 20	Shebaṭ	Jan. 16	♑	♒
Pisces	Dagim	Feb. 19	Adar	Feb. 15	♒	♓

man, who first retreats to nooks and corners like the crab, but eventually becomes as brave as a lion (= "Leo"); Virgo is a symbol of marriage; Libra weighs all the deeds of man, who, if found guilty, is punished by Scorpio, a symbol of Gehinnom; after purification in Mercy, however, he is cast forth as quickly as an arrow from a bow, represented by Sagittarius, and becomes as innocent as a kid and is purified as by water poured by Aquarius (Pesiḳ. R. 20 [ed. Friedmann, p. 97b]).

Since each of the planets was supposed to rule a certain hour of the day, while every constellation governed a certain month of the year, the fate of an infant was predicted according to the heavenly bodies that presided over the hour and the month of its birth. The conjunction of the planets and constellations was accordingly manipulated to determine the fortunes of the person whose horoscope was thus drawn. A "good" planet might synchronize with a "bad" constellation to some extent.

Astrologic Use. Both planets and constellations indicated certain characteristics in the person born at that time, and care had likewise to be taken to marry only such a mate as had been born under a harmonizing planet and constellation, since otherwise the

XII.—44

ZOHAR (called also in the earlier literature **Midrash ha-Zohar** and **Midrash de-Rabbi Shim'on ben Yoḥai**): A pseudepigraphic work which pretends to be a revelation from God communicated through R. Simeon ben Yoḥai to the latter's select disciples. Under the form of a commentary on the Pentateuch, written partly in Aramaic and partly in Hebrew, it contains a complete cabalistic theosophy, treating of the nature of God, the cosmogony and cosmology of the universe, the soul, sin, redemption, good, evil, etc. It first appeared in Spain in the thirteenth century, being made known through the agency of the cabalistic writer Moses ben Shem-Ṭob de Leon, who ascribed it to the miracle-working tanna Simeon ben Yoḥai. The

Source. fact that it was launched by such an unreliable sponsor as Moses de Leon, taken together with the circumstance that it refers to historical events of the post-Talmudical period, caused the authenticity of the work to be questioned from the outset. After the death of Moses de Leon, it is related, a rich man of Avila, named Joseph, offered the widow, who had been left without means, a large sum of money for the original from which her husband had made the copy; and she then confessed that her husband himself was the author of the work. She had asked him several times, she said, why he had chosen to credit his own teachings to another, and he had always answered that doctrines put into the mouth of the miracle-working Simeon ben Yoḥai would be a rich source of profit (see "Sefer ha-Yuḥasin," ed. Filipowski, p. 89). Incredible as this story seems —for it is inconceivable that a woman should own that her deceased husband had committed forgery for the sake of lucre—it at least proves that shortly after its appearance the work was believed by some to have been written entirely by Moses de Leon. This seems to have been the opinion of the cabalistic writer Joseph ibn Waḳar, and he cautioned the public against the work, which he asserted to be full of errors.

The general opinion, however, was in favor of its authenticity, this view being held not only by the cabalists, for whom the book opened new paths in the field of mysticism, but also by eminent Talmudists. It was quoted by Todros Abulafia, by Menahem Recanati, and even by Isaac of Acco, in whose name the story of the confession of Moses de Leon's widow is related. Isaac evidently ignored the woman's alleged confession in favor of the testimony of Joseph ben Todros and of Jacob, a pupil of Moses de Leon, both of whom assured him on oath that the work was not written by Moses ("Sefer ha-Yuḥasin," *l.c.*). The only objection worthy of consideration by the believers in the authenticity of the Zohar was the lack of references to the work in Jewish literature; and to this they answered that Simeon ben Yoḥai did not commit his teachings to writing, but transmitted them orally to his disciples, who in turn confided them to their disciples, and these to their successors, until finally the doctrines were embodied in the Zohar. As to the references in the book to historical events

Authenticity. of the post-Talmudic period, it was not deemed surprising that Simeon ben Yoḥai should have foretold future happenings. The first attack upon the accepted authorship of the Zohar was made by Elijah Delmedigo. Without expressing any opinion as to the real author of the work, he endeavored to show, in his "Beḥinat ha-Dat," that it could not be attributed to Simeon ben Yoḥai. The objections advanced by him were as follows: (1) were the Zohar the work of Simeon ben Yoḥai, it would have been mentioned by the Talmud, as has been the case with the Sifre and other works of the Talmudic period; (2) the Zohar contains names of Talmudists who lived at a later period than that of Simeon; (3) were Simeon ben Yoḥai the father of the Cabala, knowing by divine revelation the hidden meaning of the precepts, his halakic decisions would have been adopted by the Talmud; but this has not been done; (4) were the Cabala a revealed doctrine, there would have been no divergence of opinion among the cabalists concerning the mystic interpretation of the precepts ("Beḥinat ha-Dat," ed. Vienna, 1833, p. 43).

These arguments and others of the same kind were used by Leon of Modena in his "Ari Nohem" (pp. 49 *et seq.*, Leipsic, 1840). A work exclusively devoted to the criticism of the Zohar was written, under the title "Miṭpaḥat Sefarim," by Jacob Em-den, who, waging war against the remaining adherents of the Shabbethai Ẓebi movement, endeavored to show that the book on which the pseudo-Messiah based his doctrines was a forgery. Emden demonstrates that the Zohar misquotes passages of Scripture; misunderstands the Talmud; contains some ritual observances which were ordained by later rabbinical authorities; mentions the crusades against the Mohammedans (ii. 32a); uses the expression "esnoga" (iii. 232b), which is a Portuguese corruption of "synagogue," and explains it in a cabalistic manner as a compound of the Hebrew words אש and נוגה; gives a mystical explanation of the Hebrew vowel-points, which were introduced long after the Talmudic period (i. 24b, ii. 116a, iii. 65a).

These and other objections of Emden's, which were largely borrowed from the French ecclesiastic Jean Morin ("Exercitationes Biblicæ," pp. 359 *et seq.*, Paris, 1669), were refuted by Moses ben Menahem Kunitz, who, in a work entitled "Ben Yoḥai" (Budapest, 1815), endeavors to show the following characteristics: that the vowel-points were known in Talmudic times; that the rites which Emden claimed to have been ordained by later rabbinical authorities were already known to the Talmud; and that Simeon ben Yoḥai, who before taking refuge in the cave was designated only by the name of Simeon, is credited in the Talmud with many miracles and mystic sayings. Another work in favor of the antiquity of the Zohar was published by David Luria under the title "Ḳadmut ha-Zohar" (Königsberg, 1855 [?]). It is divided into five chapters, in which the author gives proofs that Moses de Leon did not compile the Zohar; that the Geonim in Babylonia cite cabalistic doctrines from a certain "Midrash Yerushalmi," the language of which strongly resembles that of the Zohar; that the work was compiled before the completion of the Talmud; that a great part of it was written in the period of Simeon ben Yoḥai; and, finally, that the Aramaic language was used in Talmudic times as well as in the geonic period. Of these proofs only those showing the inadmissibility of the authorship of Moses

Moses de Leon Not the Author. de Leon deserve consideration, the others being mere quibbles; for even if it be conceded that the Talmud knew of the vowel-points and that the Aramaic was commonly used, there is no evidence whatever that Simeon ben Yoḥai or his immediate disciples were connected with the Zohar. As to the identification of the Zohar with the so-called "Midrash Yerushalmi," the single fact that most of the passages quoted are not found in the Zohar, as Luria himself admits, is a sufficient proof that the two works can not be identical. However, Luria has quite as much warrant for asserting, on the ground of his proofs, that a great part of the Zohar was written by Simeon ben Yoḥai as have Jellinek, Grätz, Ginsburg, and many others for maintaining that it was wholly composed by Moses de Leon on the ground that in the works of the last-named there are passages which are found verbatim in the Zohar. These scholars seem to shrink from the idea that Moses de Leon should have been guilty of plagiarism, but they are not afraid to charge him with forgery, and that of so clumsy a nature as to arouse at once the suspicions of the reader. For Moses de Leon could not have supposed for a moment that the insertion in the middle of an Aramaic sentence of two verses from Ibn Gabirol's "Keter Malkut" (which, being recited in the synagogues, were known to every Jew) could have escaped detection; nor could he have thought that a quotation from the Cuzari, which was so much read and commented upon at that time, would pass unperceived by his contemporaries.

Had Moses de Leon, who was a talented writer and an able scholar, wished for mercenary purposes to forge a work in the name of Simeon ben Yohai, he would have been more careful in his statements and would certainly have employed the Hebrew language, first, because the tanna would have written in that language, and, second, because a work in Hebrew, being easier to understand, would have gained a far wider circle of readers, and consequently a larger number of purchasers, than would one written in a peculiar Aramaic dialect that was accessible to only a few. Were the pseudepigraphic "Sefer Yezirah," "Pirke de-Rabbi Eli'ezer," "Sefer Hekalot," "Sefer ha-Bahir," etc., any the less believed to be the works of those to whom they were attributed simply because they were written in plain Hebrew and not in Aramaic? But apart from all these considerations, the contents of the Zohar clearly indicate that the work is the production not of a single author or of a single period, but of many authors, periods, and civilizations; for

Not the Work of a Single Author or Period. it combines the most puzzling incongruities and irreconcilable contradictions with lofty ideas and conceptions which would do honor to a genius of modern times, and also mystic teachings of the Talmudic period with those of the Geonim and later Cabala. To determine the country in which the work originated and the time at which its teachings began to develop, it is necessary to ascertain where and when the Jews became intimately acquainted with the Hindu philosophy, which more than any other exercised an influence on the Zohar. As an instance of Hindu teachings in the Zohar may be quoted the following passage:

"In the book of Hamnuna the Elder we learn through some extended explanations that the earth turns upon itself in the form of a circle; that some are on top, the others below; that all creatures change in aspect, following the manner of each place, but keeping in the same position. But there are some countries on the earth which are lighted while others are in darkness; and there are countries in which there is constantly day or in which at least the night continues only some instants. . . . These secrets were made known to the men of the secret science, but not to the geographers" (Zohar, iii. 9b).

The theory that the earth is a sphere revolving on its own axis, which immortalized Copernicus, was previously known only to the Hindus, who were instructed in the truth of it by Aryabhatta in the first century before the common era. As far as is known, the Vedanta school of the Hindu philosophers found nowhere, outside of its place of origin, so many admirers as in Persia in the eighth century. Under its influence the Mohammedans of Persia founded many mystic sects, among them being that of the Sufis, who for many centuries were very numerous. This mystic movement did not fail to exercise an influence upon the Persian Jews, and there arose among them various sects, such as the 'Isawites, the Yudghanites, etc., the tenets of which, so far as can be ascertained from the scanty information concerning them that is available, bore more or less the stamp of the Vedanta philosophy. Thus the Yudghanites abstained from meat, led ascetic lives, set aside the literal meaning of the Torah for a supposed mystic interpretation, and believed in metempsychosis, etc. All these sects had their sacred writings, which they kept secret; and

The Germ Probably in Persia. these writings probably formed the nucleus of the Zohar, which is a mystic commentary on the Pentateuch, as the upanishads are the mystic interpretation of the Vedas and other Brahmanic scriptures. In its peregrinations from Persia to Spain the Zohar probably received many additions and interpolations, among which may have been the various names of the Tannaim and Amoraim, as well as the allusions to historical events.

The Zohar is not considered complete without the addition of certain appendixes, which are attributed either to the same author or to some of his immediate disciples. These supplementary portions are printed as part of the text with separate titles, or in separate columns. They are as follows: "Sifra di-Zeni'uta," consisting of five chapters, in which are chiefly discussed the questions involved in the Creation, such as the transition from the infinite to the finite, that from absolute unity to multifariousness, that from pure intelligence to matter, etc.; "Idra Rabbah," in which the teachings of the preceding portion are enlarged upon and developed; and "Idra Zuṭa," giving a résumé of the two preceding sections. The characteristic features of these portions are the absence of the doctrine of the EN SOF, and the use of the appellation "Zaddik" for the ninth Sefirah, which show that these writings are of an earlier period. To the larger appendixes are added the following fragments: "Raze de Razin," dealing with the physiognomy of the Cabala and the connection of the soul with the body; "Sefer HEKALOT," describing the seven heavenly halls, paradise, and hell; Ra'ya Mehemna," giving a conversation between Moses, the prophet Elijah, and Simeon ben Yohai on the allegorical import of the Mosaic commandments and prohibitions, as well as of the rabbinical injunctions; "Sitre Torah," on various cabalistic topics; "Midrash ha-Ne'elam," explaining passages of Scripture mystically by way of "remazim" and gemaṭria; "Saba," containing a conversation between the prophet Elijah and Simeon ben Yohai about the doctrine of metempsychosis; "Yanuḳa," on the importance of washing the hands before meals and on similar subjects, written in the name of a child of Hamnuna Saba, whence the title "Yanuḳa" (child); "Tosefta" and "Matnitin," in which are sketched the doctrines of the Sefirot, the emanation of the primordial light, etc. Besides the Zohar proper, there are also a "Zohar Ḥadash," on Canticles, and "Tiḳḳunim," both new and old, which bear a close resemblance to the original work.

The Zohar repeatedly endeavors to impress upon the mind of the reader that the Biblical narratives and ordinances contain higher truths in addition to the literal meaning.

"Wo unto the man," says Simeon ben Yoḥai, "who asserts that this Torah intends to relate only commonplace things and

Mysticism of the Zohar.

secular narratives; for if this were so, then in the present times likewise a Torah might be written with more attractive narratives. In truth, however, the matter is thus: The upper world and the lower are established upon one and the same principle; in the lower world is Israel, in the upper world are the angels. When the angels wish to descend to the lower world, they have to don earthly garments. If this be true of the angels, how much more so of the Torah, for whose sake, indeed, the world and the angels were alike created and exist. The world could simply not have endured to look upon it. Now the narratives of the Torah are its garments. He who thinks that these garments are the Torah itself deserves to perish and have no share in the world to come. Wo unto the fools who look no further when they see an elegant robe! More valuable than the garment is the body which carries it, and more valuable even than that is the soul which animates the body. Fools see only the garment of the Torah, the more intelligent see the body, the wise see the soul, its proper being; and in the Messianic time the 'upper soul' of the Torah will stand revealed" (Zohar, iii. 152).

"The man," it is said in the "Sifra di Ẓeni'uta," "who is not acquainted with this book is like the savage barbarian who was a stranger to the usages of civilized life. He sowed wheat, but was accustomed to partake of it only in its natural condition. One day this barbarian came into a city, and good bread was placed before him. Finding it very palatable, he inquired of what material it was made, and was informed that it was made of wheat. Afterward one offered to him a fine cake kneaded in oil. He tasted it, and again asked: 'And this, of what is it made?' and he received the same answer, of wheat. Finally, one placed before him the royal pastry, kneaded with oil and honey. He again asked the same question, to which he obtained a like reply. Then he said: 'At my house I am in possession of all these things. I partake daily of them in root, and cultivate the wheat from which they are made.' In this crudeness he remained a stranger to the delights one draws from the wheat, and the pleasures were lost to him. It is the same with those who stop at the general principles of knowledge because they are ignorant of the delights which one may derive from the further investigation and application of these principles."

The Zohar assumes four kinds of Biblical exegesis: "Peshaṭ" (literal meaning), "Remez" (allusion), "Derash" (anagogical), and "Sod" (mystic). The initial letters of the words "Peshaṭ," "Remez," "Derash," and "Sod" form together the word "PaRDeS" (Paradise), which became the designation for the fourfold meaning of which the mystical sense is the highest part. The mystic allegorism is

"PaRDeS."

based by the Zohar on the principle that all visible things, the phenomena of nature included, have besides their exoteric reality an esoteric reality also, destined to instruct man in that which is invisible. This principle is the necessary corollary of the fundamental doctrine of the Zohar. The universe being, according to that doctrine, a gradation of emanations, it follows that the human mind may recognize in each effect the supreme mark, and thus ascend to the cause of all causes. This ascension, however, can only be made gradually, after the mind has attained four various stages of knowledge; namely: (1) the knowledge of the exterior aspect of things, or, as the Zohar calls it (ii. 36b), "the vision through the mirror that projects an indirect light"; (2) the knowledge of the essence of things, or "the vision through the mirror that projects a direct light"; (3) the knowledge through intuitive representation; and (4) the knowledge through love,

since the Law reveals its secrets to those only who love it (ii. 99b).

After the knowledge through love comes the ecstatic state which is applied to the most holy visions. To enter the state of ecstasy one had to remain motionless, with the hand between the knees, absorbed in contemplation and murmuring prayers and hymns. There were seven ecstatic stages, each of which was marked by a vision of a different color. At each new stage the contemplative entered a heavenly hall ("hekal") of a different hue, until he reached the seventh, which was colorless, and the appearance of which marked both the end of his contemplation and his lapse into unconsciousness. The Zohar gives the following illustration of an ecstatic state:

"Once," says R. Simeon ben Yoḥai, "I was plunged in a contemplative ecstasy, and I beheld a sublime ray of a brilliant light which illumined 325 circles, and amid which something dark was bathing. Then the dark point, becoming bright, began to float toward the deep and sublime sea, where all the splendors were gathering. I then asked the meaning of this vision, and I was answered that it represented the forgiveness of sins."

The Zohar spread among the Jews with remarkable celerity. Scarcely fifty years had passed since its appearance in Spain before it was quoted by many cabalists, among whom was the Italian mys-

Spread of the Zohar.

tical writer Menahem Recanati. Its authority was so well established in Spain in the fifteenth century that Joseph ibn Shem-Ṭob drew from it arguments in his attacks against Maimonides. It exercised so great a charm upon the cabalists that they could not believe for an instant that such a book could have been written by any mortal unless he had been inspired from above; and this being the case, it was to be placed on the same level with the Bible. Even representatives of Talmudic Judaism began to regard it as a sacred book and to invoke its authority in the decision of some ritual questions. They were attracted by its glorification of man, its doctrine of immortality, and its ethical principles, which are more in keeping with the spirit of Talmudical Judaism than are those taught by the philosophers. While Maimonides and his followers regarded man as a fragment of the universe whose immortality is dependent upon the degree of development of his active intellect, the Zohar declared him to be the lord of the Creation, whose immortality is solely dependent upon his morality. Indeed, according to the Zohar, the moral perfection of man influences the ideal world of the Sefirot; for although the Sefirot expect everything from the En Sof, the En Sof itself is dependent upon man: he alone can bring about the divine effusion. The dew that vivifies the universe flows from the just. By the practise of virtue and by moral perfection man may increase the outpouring of heavenly grace. Even physical life is subservient to virtue. This, says the Zohar, is indicated in the words "for the Lord God had not caused it to rain" (Gen. ii. 5), which mean that there had not yet been beneficent action in heaven because man had not yet given the impulsion.

These and similar teachings appealed to the Talmudists and made them overlook the Zohar's disparities and contrasts and its veiled hostility to the Talmud. The influences of the Zohar on Judaism were both beneficial and deleterious. On the one hand, the Zohar was praiseworthy because it op-

Ethical System.
posed formalism, stimulated the imagination and feelings, and restored prayer (which had gradually become a mere external religious exercise) to the position it had occupied for centuries among the Jews as a means of transcending earthly affairs for a time and placing oneself in union with God; and on the other hand, it was to be censured because it propagated many superstitious beliefs, and produced a host of mystical dreamers, whose overheated imaginations peopled the world with spirits, demons, and all kinds of good and bad influences. Its mystic mode of explaining some commandments was applied by its commentators to all religious observances, and produced a strong tendency to substitute a mystic Judaism for the rabbinical cult. Thus the Sabbath, with all its ceremonies, began to be looked upon as the embodiment of the Divinity in temporal life, and every ceremony performed on that day was considered to have an influence upon the superior world. Zoharic elements even crept into the liturgy of the sixteenth and seventeenth centuries, and the religious poets not only used in their compositions the allegorism and symbolism of the Zohar, but even adopted its style, the characteristic features of which were the representation of the highest thoughts by human emblems and human passions, and the use of erotic terminology to illustrate the relations between man and God, religion being identical with love. Thus, in the language of many Jewish poets the beloved one's curls indicate the mysteries of the Deity; sensuous pleasures, and especially intoxication, typify the highest degree of divine love as ecstatic contemplation; while the wine-room represents merely the state through which the human qualities merge or are exalted into those of the Deity.

The enthusiasm felt for the Zohar was shared by many Christian scholars, such as Pico de Mirandola, Reuchlin, Ægidius of Viterbo, etc., all of whom believed that the book contained proofs of the truth of Christianity. They were led to this belief by the analogies existing between some of

Influence on Christian Mysticism.
the teachings of the Zohar and certain of the Christian dogmas, as for instance the fall and redemption of man, and the dogma of the Trinity, which is expressed in the Zohar in the following terms: "The Ancient of Days has three heads. He reveals himself in three archetypes, all three forming but one. He is thus symbolized by the number Three. They are revealed in one another. [These are:] first, secret, hidden 'Wisdom'; above that the Holy Ancient One; and above Him the Unknowable One. None knows what He contains; He is above all conception. He is therefore called for man 'Non-Existing' ["'Ayin"]" (Zohar, iii. 288b). This and also the other doctrines of Christian tendency that are found in the Zohar are now known to be much older than Christianity; but the Christian scholars who were deluded by the similarity of these teachings to certain Christian dogmas deemed

it their duty to propagate the Zohar. Shortly after the publication of the work (Mantua and Cremona, 1558) Joseph de Voisin translated extracts from it which deal with the soul. He was followed by many others, among whom was Knorr, Baron von Rosenroth, who rendered into Latin the introduction, the "Sifra di-Zeni'uta," the "Idra Rabbah," and the "Idra Zuṭa" ("Kabbala Denudata," Sulzbach, 1677).

The disastrous effects of the Shabbethai Zebi movement, which was greatly fostered by the obnoxious influences of the Zohar, damped the enthusiasm that had been felt for the book, and the representatives of Talmudic Judaism began to look upon it with suspicion. Especially was this the case when the Shabbethaian movement had degenerated into religious mysticism and had produced the anti-Talmudic sectaries who styled themselves "Zoharites," and who, under the leadership of Jacob Frank, finished by embracing Christianity. However, the Zohar is still held in great reverence by many Orthodox Jews, especially the Ḥasidim, who, under its influence, assign the first place in religion not to dogma and ritual, but to the sentiment and the emotion of faith.

Among the numerous commentaries written on the Zohar the most important are: "Torat Emet," containing corrections and explanations of words for the section on Genesis, by David ben

Commentaries.
Abraham Shemariah (Salonica, 1604); "Yesh Sakar," on the religious prescriptions of the Zohar, by J. Bär ben Petahiah, who published also "Meḳor Ḥokmah" and "Imre Binah," on the foreign words in the Zohar (Prague, 1610, 1611); "Yesha' Yah," explanation of the foreign words in the Zohar, by Solomon Isaiah ben Eliezer Ḥayyim Nizza (Venice, 1630); "Ḥiḅbur 'Ammude Sheba'," by Aaron Selig Zolkiev (Cracow, 1636); "Amarot Ṭehorot," explaining the difficult words of the Zohar, by Wolf Leitmeritz (Lublin, 1645); "'Emeḳ ha-Melek," commentaries on various sections of the Zohar, by Naphtali Herz ben Jacob Elhanan (Amsterdam, 1648); "Sha'ar ha-Shamayim," introduction to and rules of the cabalistic system of the Zohar, by Abraham Herrera (ib. 1655); "Ḥesed la-Abraham," novellæ on the Zohar, by Abraham Azulai (ib. 1685); "Wayaḳhel Mosheh," by Moses ben Menahem (Dessau, 1699); "Or Yisrael," by Israel Jaffe (Frankfort-on-the-Oder, 1711). For the cabalistic system of the Zohar see ADAM ḲADMON ; AMULET ; ASCENSION ; AZILUT ; CABALA ; CREATION ; EMANATION ; SEFIROT ; SOUL.

BIBLIOGRAPHY: Modern sources: Zunz, *G. V.* 2d ed., pp. 415 *et seq.*; A. Franck, *La Kabbale*, Paris, 1843; 2d ed., *ib.* 1889; German transl. by Ad. Jellinek, Leipsic, 1844; Landauer, in *Orient, Lit.* vi. 178 *et seq.*; Ignatz Stern, in *Ben Chananja*, i.-vi.; D. H. Joël, *Midrash ha-Zohar, Die Religionsphilosophi edes Sohar*, Leipsic, 1849; Jellinek, *Moses de Leon und Sein Verhältniss zum Zohar*, ib. 1851; Steinschneider, *Jewish Literature*, § xiii.; Jost, *Geschichte des Judenthums*, ii., iii., Index; Ginsburg, *The Kabbalah*, London, 1865; Hamburger, *R. B. T.* s.v. *Geheimlehre, Kabbala* and *Mystik*; Hermann Beer, *Historische Daten in dem Zohar*, in *Monatsschrift*, v. 158; Duschak, *Platonische Mythe in dem Zohar*, in *Orient, Lit.* x. 181; Rapoport, in *Kerem Ḥemed*, i. 154; Grätz, *Gesch.* vii., Index (compare also the notes by Harkavy to the Hebrew translation of Grätz in vol. v.); Bacher, *L'Exegèse Biblique dans le Zohar*, in *R. E. J.* xxii. 33 *et seq.*; idem, in *J. Q. R.* iii. 781; Karppe, *Etude sur les Origines du Zohar*, Paris, 1891; Isaac Myer, *Qabbalah*, Philadelphia, 1888; Flugel, *Philosophy, Kabbala and Vedanta*, Baltimore, 1902. See also the bibliography to the article CABALA.

J.　　　　　　　　　　　　　　　　　　　　I. Br.

ZOLA, EMILE: French novelist; born in Paris April 2, 1840; died there Sept. 29, 1902. It was only in his last years, when anti-Semitism had reached an acute stage in France, that he took up the cause of the Jewish community against its assailants; but several Jewish charac-

His Novels. ters, almost invariably connected with the French financial world, had appeared in some of his novels. Thus, in his "Son Excellence Eugène Rougon," he delineated a certain *Kahn*, an unscrupulous deputy, railway-contractor, and ironmaster, son of a Jewish banker at Bordeaux; in "Nana" he portrayed a German Jew named *Steiner*, whom he represented as amassing millions by his acumen and as squandering them in gross dissipation until he was at last completely ruined by the woman whose name furnishes the title of the book; and in "L'Argent" (1890-91) he introduced various Jewish characters, such as bankers, stock-jobbers, and speculators. But it should be said that if Zola placed various bitter diatribes in the mouths of some of the Jew-haters figuring in the last-named novel, this was simply because his subject required it, the diatribes in question being in no sense representative of the author's personal sentiments.

It is curious to observe that his book "Paris," in which he presents in a not quite favorable light a great number of Jewish characters, and which was published in volume form in March, 1898 (that is, immediately after the author's trial in Paris in connection with the DREYFUS CASE),

Attitude on Jewish Question. gives no indication whatever of his intervention in that famous affair, or of the various attempts he had made, while writing the volume, to stem the progress of anti-Semitism in France. In the early part of 1896 he contributed to the pages of the Paris "Figaro" a very vigorous and much-noticed article entitled "Pour les Juifs," the key-note of which was sounded in the opening paragraph:

"For some years I have been following with increasing surprise and disgust the campaign which some people are trying to carry on in France against the Jews. This seems to me monstrous, by which I mean something foreign to all common sense, truth, and justice, something blind and foolish, which would carry us back several centuries, and which would end in the worst of abominations, religious persecution. . . ."

In this article Zola dealt with anti-Semitism from a general point of view, making no mention of Captain Dreyfus, the agitation for whose release had not yet begun. At a later date, when Zola had espoused the cause of the unfortunate prisoner, he frequently referred to the general question of anti-Semitism, which he denounced as odious and foolish, both in his articles "M. Scheurer-Kestner," "Le Syndicat," and "Procès Verbal," published in "Le Figaro" in the autumn of 1897, and in his subsequent pamphlets "Lettre aux Jeunes Hommes" and "Lettre à la France." His adversaries thereupon accused him of venality, asserting that he had been bought by the Jews.

When his active participation in the Dreyfus case had ceased, he chose the affair as the subject of what was destined to be his last novel, "Vérité," largely transferring the action, however, from mili-

tary spheres to the teaching world, in such wise that in his pages Captain Alfred Dreyfus became a

His Last Work. French provincial schoolmaster called *Simon*, with a brother named *David* (M. Mathieu Dreyfus), while the notorious Major Esterhazy was transformed into a certain *Brother Gorgias*. Other Jewish characters figured in the volume; for instance, *Simon's* wife, *Rachel* (Mme. Alfred Dreyfus); their children *Joseph* and *Sarah*; the *Lehmanns*, a family of penurious Jewish tailors; and *Baron Nathan* and his daughter *Lia*, who became a Catholic, like *Eve* in "Paris," and married a violent anti-Semite, the *Count de Sanglebœuf*. *Nathan* is not described as having formally renounced the Jewish faith, but Zola treats him as a renegade, one of those who, having risen to affluence and rank, not only cast off the ancestral traditions, but even join the persecutors of their race. From first to last "Vérité" is a vigorous denunciation of anti-Semitism in its various forms, its growth and diffusion in France being chiefly attributed by Zola to the action of the Roman Catholic priesthood. The writing of the book was only just finished when Zola died by accidental suffocation. Sincere regret for his death was expressed by Jewish communities all over the world, for they recognized that they had lost an able and perfectly disinterested friend in the deceased writer. A considerable part of the large sum of money subsequently raised for the erection of a monument to him in Paris was contributed by Jewish subscribers, several of whom had previously given liberally when a superb gold medal was struck in his honor.

BIBLIOGRAPHY: Zola, *Son Excellence Eugène Rougon*, Paris, 1876; idem, *Nana*, ib. 1880; idem, *L'Argent*, ib. 1891; idem, *Vérité*, ib. 1903; idem, *Nouvelle Campagne*, ib. 1897; idem, *La Vérité en Marche*, ib. 1901 (in the last-named volume will be found the various articles, letters, and addresses written by Zola in connection with the Dreyfus case; of some of these there is an English translation, *Zola's Letters to France*, with introduction, by L. F. Austin, New York and London, n. d.). On Zola's attitude toward the Jews: Ernest Vizetelly, *Emile Zola, Novelist and Reformer*, New York and London, 1904.

s. E. A. V.

ZOMBER, BERNHARD (BÄR): Polish scholar; born at Lask in 1821; died at Berlin in 1884. Having acquired a fair knowledge of rabbinical literature in his native country, he went to Germany, where he studied successively under Joseph Shapiro and Jacob Ettinger. Later he attended the universities of Würzburg and Berlin, and in 1871 he was appointed principal teacher of the Bet ha-Midrash of Berlin, a position which he held until his death. His works are as follows: "Hilkot Pesaḥim," on Passover laws compiled by Isaac ibn Ghayyat, supplemented by a commentary of his own entitled "Debar Halakah" (Berlin, 1864); "Ma'amar," a dissertation on Rashi's commentary on Nedarim and Mo'ed Ḳaṭan (ib. 1867); "Moreh Derek," the commentaries of Gershon Me'or ha-Golah and of Rashi on Mo'ed Ḳaṭan (ib. 1870); and "Shiṭṭah Meḳubbeẓet," Bezalel Ashkenazi's novellæ on Nedarim. In addition to these works, Zomber contributed several valuable articles to Jewish scientific periodicals, including a study on Judah ben Yaḳar, the commentator of the Yerushalmi, which was translated from German into Hebrew by Abraham Abele Ehrlich ("Ha-Karmel," iii. 294).

BIBLIOGRAPHY: Fürst, *Bibl. Jud.* iii. 542; Zedner. *Cat. Hebr. Books Brit. Mus.* p. 791; Zeitlin, *Bibl. Post-Mendels.* p. 428; Fuenn, *Keneset Yisrael*, p. 187.
J. I. Br.

ZOR. See Tyre.

ZOREF, SAMUEL HA-LEVI: Rabbi at Posen; died between 1710 and 1716. He was the author of "Maẓref la-Kesef" (Frankfort-on-the-Oder, 1681), containing extracts from and an index to the "Shene Luḥot ha-Berit" ("SHeLaH") of Isaiah Horowitz, with two appendixes, one entitled "Kur la-Zahab" and giving extracts from Gabirol's "Mibḥar ha-Peninim," and the other entitled "Teshubot Shib'im Zeḳenim" and containing maxims. A separate edition of the "Kur la-Zahab" was published at Offenbach in 1710, and in 1716 it was printed with the "Teshubot Shib'im Zeḳenim."

BIBLIOGRAPHY: Fürst, *Bibl. Jud.* iii. 555; Steinschneider, *Cat. Bodl.* col. 2499.
J. I. Br.

ZOROASTRIANISM: The religion of ancient Persia as founded by Zoroaster; one of the world's great faiths that bears the closest resemblance to Judaism and Christianity. According to the tradition in the Parsee books, Zoroaster was born in 660 B.C. and died in 583; but many scholars claim that he must have flourished at a much earlier time. All investigators, however, are agreed that his teachings were generally in force throughout Iran before the time of the Jewish Captivity. His name in its ancient form in the Avesta is "Zarathustra," and in later Persian, "Zardusht"; the form "Zoroaster," which is now common, has been adopted from the Greek and Latin "Zoroastres." The native country of the prophet is now believed to have been Media, in western Iran, and there are reasons for claiming that his birthplace was in the province of Atropatene, the modern Azerbaijan; but much of his ministry, or rather most of his prophetic career, was passed in eastern Iran, especially in the region of Bactria, where he won a powerful patron for his religion. This defender of the faith was a king named Vishtaspa, or Gushtasp, a name identical with that of Hystaspes, the father of Darius, although the two personages are not to be confounded, as has sometimes been done.

Zoroaster was originally a Magian priest, but he appears to have reformed or purified the creed of the Magi. His religious teachings are preserved in the Avesta. The character of the Persian religion before Zoroaster's time is not known, but a comparison with that of India shows that it must have had much in common with the early religion of the Hindus. It may be presumed that it was a modified nature-worship, with polytheistic features and some traces of demonistic beliefs. Herodotus ("Hist." i. 131 *et seq.*) states that the Persians from the earliest times worshiped the sun, moon, stars, and earth, and the waters and wind, and he intimates in precise words that they had borrowed certain religious elements from the Assyrians. One or two superstitious practises which he describes, such as the propitiation of the powers of evil (*ib.* iii. 35, vii. 114), show survivals of demoniacal rites, against which Zoroaster so strongly inveighed; and the account

Tenets of the Faith.

which he gives of the Magian ceremonies is quite in accordance with Zoroastrianism.

One of the characteristic features of Zoroastrianism is the doctrine of dualism, recognizing the powers of good and evil as two personified principles at war with each other. Ahuramazda, or Ormuzd ("the Wise Lord"), leads the forces of good; Angra-Mainyu, or Ahriman ("the Spiritual Enemy"), heads the hosts of evil. Bands of angels and archangels follow the divine leader, while troops of demons and archfiends hasten after the evil lord. The archangels are six in number and are called by the general name Amesha Spentas ("Immortal Holy Ones"); they are personifications of virtues and abstract ideas, and are named Vohu Manah ("Good Mind"), Asha Vahishta ("Perfect Righteousness"), Khshathra Vairya ("Wished-for Kingdom"), Spenta Armaiti (a feminine personification of harmony and the earth), Haurvatat ("Health," "Salvation"), and Ameretat ("Immortality"). The angels and lesser divine beings are termed Yazatas ("Worshipful Ones") and are very numerous, although twenty-one of them are more prominent than the rest; these include divine embodiments of the sun, moon, stars, fire, earth, water and air, the spirits of the righteous (called "fravashis"), and also several abstract concepts, like victory, religion, kingly glory, and the divinity known as Mithra, an incarnation of light and truth. The rabble of hell, led by Ahriman, is ill organized, and the chief archfiend, after Ahriman himself, is the demon Aeshma (Dæva), a name which is thought to be found in the Book of Tobit as Asmodeus, although this view is not accepted by some (see Asmodeus). In addition to the six archfiends there is a legion of minor fiends and demons ("dæva," "druj").

The Kingdoms of Good and Evil.

The conflict between the opposing kingdoms of light and darkness forms the history of the world, which lasts for 12,000 years and is divided into four great eons. The first 3,000 years is the period of spiritual existence. Ormuzd knows of Ahriman's coexistence, and creates the world first in a spiritual state before giving it a material form, the "fravashis" being the models of the future types of things. Ahriman is ignorant of his great rival's existence, but on discovering this he counter-creates the hosts of demons and fiends. In the second 3,000 years, while Ahriman and his host have been confounded by Ormuzd, the latter creates the world in its material form, and the world is then invaded by Ahriman. The third 3,000 years is the period of conflict between the rival powers and the struggle for the soul of man, until Zoroaster comes into the world. His birth inaugurates a new era, and the fourth and last 3,000 years begins. These final millennial eras are presided over by Zoroaster himself and his three posthumous sons, who are to be born in future ages in an ideal manner, the last being the Messiah called Saoshyant ("Savior," "Benefactor"; lit. "he who will benefit and save the world"). In its general bearings this dualistic scheme of the universe is theologically monotheistic in so far as it postulates the final predominance of

Millennial Doctrines.

Ormuzd; and it is optimistic in its philosophy, inasmuch as it looks for a complete regeneration of the world.

In all this struggle man is the important figure; for the ultimate triumph of right depends upon him. He is a free agent according to Zoroaster ("Yasna," xxx. 20, xxxi. 11), but he must ever be on his guard against the misguidance of evil. The purpose of Zoroaster's coming into the world and the aim of his teaching are to guide man to choose aright, to lead him in the path of righteousness, in order that the world may attain to ultimate perfection. This perfection will come with the establishment of the Good Kingdom (Avesta, "Vohu Khshathra"), the Wished-for Kingdom (Avesta, "Khshathra Vairya"), or the Kingdom of Desire (Avesta, "Khshathra Ishtōish"). When this shall come to pass the world will become regenerate (Avesta, "Ahūm Frashem Kar"; or "Frashōkereti"); a final battle between the powers of good and evil will take place; Ahriman and his hosts will be routed; and good shall reign supreme ("Yasht," xix. 89–93; Bundahis, xxx. 1–33). The advent of the Messiah (Saoshyant) will be accompanied by the resurrection of the dead and the general judgment of the world, which thenceforth will be free from evil and free from harm.

The motto of the Zoroastrian religion is "Good thoughts, good words, good deeds" (Avesta, "Humata, hūkhta, hvarshta"). Man in his daily life is enjoined to preserve purity of body and soul alike.

He is to exercise scrupulous care in **Ethical** keeping the elements earth, fire, and **Teachings** water free from defilement of any **and** kind. Truth-speaking and honest **Religious** dealing are made the basis of every **Practises.** action; kindliness and generosity are virtues to be cultivated; and agriculture and cattle-raising are prescribed as religious duties. Marriage within the community of the faithful, even to wedlock with blood relatives, is lauded; and according to the Avesta ("Vendīdād," iv. 47), "he who has a wife is to be accounted far above him who has none; and he who has children is far above the childless man."

In disposing of the dead, it is unlawful to burn or bury the body or to throw it into water, as any of these modes of disposal would defile one of the sacred elements; the dead must therefore be exposed in high places to be devoured by birds and dogs, a custom which is still observed by the Parsees and Gabars in their "Towers of Silence."

In religious matters the priesthood was supreme in authority, and the sacerdotal order was hereditary. The Mobeds and Herbeds were the **Priesthood** Levites and Kohanim of Zoroastrian- **and** ism. The name for priest, "athaur- **Ritual.** van," in the Avesta corresponds to "atharvan" in India; the Magi were a sacerdotal tribe of Median origin. In acts of worship (Avesta, "Yasna") animal sacrifices were sometimes offered, especially in more ancient times, but these immolations were subordinate and gave place more and more to offerings of praise and thanksgiving accompanied by oblations of consecrated milk, bread, and water. The performance of these

rites was attended by the recitation of long litanies, especially in connection with the preparation of the sacred drink "haoma," made from a plant resembling the Indian "sōma," from which an exhilarating juice was extracted. It has been thought that the twigs (Avesta, "baresman"; modern Persian, "barsom") employed by the Zoroastrian priests in their ritual are alluded to as the "branch" held to the nose by the sun-worshipers in the vision of Ezekiel (viii. 16–17); and the consecrated cake (Avesta, "draonah"; modern Persian, "darūn") has been compared with the Hebrew showbread.

The points of resemblance between Zoroastrianism and Judaism, and hence also between the former and Christianity, are many and striking. Ahuramazda, the supreme lord of Iran, om- **Resem-** niscient, omnipresent, and eternal, en- **blances** dowed with creative power, which he **Between** exercises especially through the me- **Zoroastri-** dium of his Spenta Mainyu ("Holy **anism and** Spirit"), and governing the universe **Judaism.** through the instrumentality of angels and archangels, presents the nearest parallel to YHWH that is found in antiquity. But Ormuzd's power is hampered by his adversary, Ahriman, whose dominion, however, like Satan's, shall be destroyed at the end of the world. Zoroastrianism and Judaism present a number of resemblances to each other in their general systems of angelology and demonology, points of similarity which have been especially emphasized by the Jewish rabbinical scholars Schorr and Kohut and the Christian theologian Stave. There are striking parallels between the two faiths and Christianity in their eschatological teachings—the doctrines of a regenerate world, a perfect kingdom, the coming of a Messiah, the resurrection of the dead, and the life everlasting. Both Zoroastrianism and Judaism are revealed religions: in the one Ahuramazda imparts his revelation and pronounces his commandments to Zarathustra on "the Mountain of the Two Holy Communing Ones"; in the other YHWH holds a similar communion with Moses on Sinai. The Magian laws of purification, moreover, more particularly those practised to remove pollution incurred through contact with dead or unclean matter, are given in the Avestan Vendīdād quite as elaborately as in the Levitical code, with which the Zoroastrian book has been compared (see AVESTA). The two religions agree in certain respects with regard to their cosmological ideas. The six days of Creation in Genesis find a parallel in the six periods of Creation described in the Zoroastrian scriptures. Mankind, according to each religion, is descended from a single couple, and Mashya (man) and Mashyana are the Iranian Adam (man) and Eve. In the Bible a deluge destroys all people except a single righteous individual and his family; in the Avesta a winter depopulates the earth except in the Vara ("enclosure") of the blessed Yima. In each case the earth is peopled anew with the best two of every kind, and is afterward divided into three realms. The three sons of Yima's successor Thraetaona, named Erij (Avesta, "Airya"), Selm (Avesta, "Sairima"), and Tur (Avesta, "Tura"), are the inheritors in the Persian account; Shem, Ham, and Japheth, in the Semitic story. Likenesses in minor matters, in certain details of ceremony and ritual, ideas of uncleanness, and the like, are to be noted, as well as parallels between Zoroaster and Moses as sacred lawgivers; and many of these resemblances are treated in the works referred to at the end of this article.

It is difficult to account for these analogies. It is known, of course, as a historic fact that the Jews and the Persians came in contact with each other at an early period in antiquity and remained in more or less close relation throughout their history (see AVESTA; MEDIA; PERSIA). Most scholars, Jewish as well as non-Jewish, are of the opinion that Judaism was strongly influenced by Zoroastrianism in views relating to angelology and demonology, and probably also in the doctrine of the resurrection, as well as in eschatological ideas in general, and also that the monotheistic conception of YHWH may have been quickened and strengthened by being opposed to the dualism or quasi-monotheism of the Persians. But, on the other hand, the late James DARMESTETER advocated exactly the opposite view, maintaining that early Persian thought was strongly influenced by Jewish ideas. He insisted that the Avesta, as we have it, is of late origin and is much tinctured by foreign elements, especially those derived from Judaism, and also those taken from Neoplatonism through the writings of Philo Judæus. These views, put forward shortly before the French scholar's death in 1894, have been violently combated by specialists since that time, and can not be said to have met with decided favor on any side. At the present time it is impossible to settle the question; the truth lies probably somewhere between the radical extremes, and it is possible that when knowledge of the Assyrian and Babylonian religion is more precise in certain details, additional light may be thrown on the problem of the source of these analogies, and may show the likelihood of a common influence at work upon both the Persian and Jewish cults.

Causes of Analogies Uncertain.

BIBLIOGRAPHY: For general works on the subject consult bibliographies under articles AVESTA, MEDIA, and PERSIA. Special works on Zoroaster and the religion: Jackson, *Zoroaster the Prophet of Ancient Iran*, New York, 1899; idem, *Die Iranische Religion*, in Geiger and Kuhn, *Grundriss der Iranischen Philologie*, Leipsic, 1904; Justi, *Die Aelteste Iranische Religion und Ihr Stifter Zarathustra*, in *Preussische Jahrbücher*, lxxxviii. 55-86, 231-262, Berlin, 1897; Lehmann, *Die Parsen*, in Chantepie de la Saussaye, *Lehrbuch der Religionsgeschichte*, 3d ed., Tübingen, 1905; idem, *Zarathustra, en Bog om Persernes Gamle Tro*, pp. 1-2, Copenhagen, 1899, 1902; Tiele, *Geschichte der Religion: Die Religion bei den Iranischen Völkern*, vol. ii., section 1, translated by Gehrich, Gotha, 1898 (English transl. by Nariman in *Indian Antiquary*, vols. xxxii. *et seq.*, Bombay, 1903). Particular treatises on the analogies between Zoroastrianism and Judaism: Schorr, in *He-Ḥaluz*, ii.-v.; Kohut, *Ueber die Jüdische Angelologie und Dämonologie in Ihrer Abhängigkeit vom Parsismus*, Leipsic, 1866; idem, *Was Hat die Talmudische Eschatologie aus dem Parsismus Aufgenommen?* in *Z. D. M. G.* xxi. 552-591; De Harlez, *Avesta*, Introduction, pp. ccv.-ccvi., ccix., Paris, 1881; Spiegel, *Eranische Alterthumskunde*, ii. 17, 19, 26, 34, 40, 50 *et seq.*, 63-65, 75, 117, 166 *et seq.*, 169-171, Leipsic, 1878; Darmesteter, *La Zend-Avesta*, iii., Introduction, pp. lvi.-lxii., Paris, 1893; *S. B. E.* 2d ed., iv., Introduction, pp. lvii.-lix.; Cheyne, *Origin and Religious Concepts of the Psalter*, London, 1891; Aiken, *The Avesta and the Bible*, in *Catholic University Bulletin*, iii. 243-291, Washington, 1897; Stave, *Einfluss des Parsismus auf das Judenthum*, Haarlem, 1898; Söderblom, *La Vie Future d'Après le Mazdeisme*, Paris, 1901; Böklen, *Verwandschaft der Jüdisch-Christlichen mit der Parsischen Eschatologie*, Göttingen, 1902; Moulton, in *Expository Times*, ix. 351-359, xi. 257-260, and in *Journal of Theological Studies*, July, 1902, pp. 514-527; Mills, *The Avesta, Neoplatonism and Philo Judæus*, i., Leipsic, 1904; Moffat, *Zoroastrianism and Primitive Christianity*, in *Hibbert Journal*, 1903, i. 763-780.

K.   A. V. W. J.

ZOX, EPHRAIM LAMEN: Communal worker of Melbourne, Australia; born in London 1837; died Oct. 23, 1899. He was thirteen years old when he arrived in Melbourne, and he engaged successively in gold-digging, auctioneering, and the clothing business, and also operated for many years as a financier. Zox was closely associated with almost every charitable movement in Melbourne, and the Jewish community there long regarded him as its leader. He was successively treasurer, president, and trustee of the Hebrew congregation; supported the Jewish Philanthropic Society; was president of the Melbourne branch of the Anglo-Jewish Association; and took a special interest in the Discharged Prisoners' Aid Society. He was, moreover, one of the most popular of Victorian politicians, and was a member of the legislature, entering the Assembly in May, 1877, as a representative of East Melbourne, and retaining his seat for that electorate for twenty-one years. He served also as chairman of the Charities Commission.

BIBLIOGRAPHY: *Jew. Chron.* Dec., 1899.

J.   G. L.

ZSIDÓ HIRADÓ. See PERIODICALS.

ZUCKER, ALFRED: Chemist and manufacturer of Dresden, Germany; born Aug. 17, 1871, in Uffenheim, Bavaria. He studied pharmacy and chemistry at the universities of Würzburg and Erlangen; and while he was still a student the Württemberg government, at the suggestion of the Würzburg professor of botany, Geheimrat Sachs, placed him on a commission for fighting a destructive vine-bug, the efforts of which body he directed to a successful conclusion. He was later appointed military apothecary of the Bavarian Home for Pensioned Soldiers ("Invalidenhaus"), and while holding that position he published several short pharmaceutical treatises which attracted the attention of specialists. His larger publications are "Beitrag zur Direkten Beeinflussung der Pflanzen Durch die Kupfervitriolkalkbrühe," Stuttgart, 1896, and "Repertorium der Photochemie," Vienna, Leipsic, and Budapest, 1901; and he contributed to "Hager's Pharmaceutisch-Technisches Manuale. Encyclopädische Vorschriftensammlung für Aerzte, Apotheker, etc.," 7th ed., Leipsic and Berlin, 1902.

S.

ZUCKER, MARCUS: German librarian and author; born May 1, 1841. He was for some time chief librarian at the University of Erlangen, and has made a specialty of the history of art. Among his writings are: "Dürers Stellung zur Reformation" (1886); "Michelangelo" (1888); "Die Holländische Malerei des 17ten Jahrhunderts" (1892); "Albrecht Dürer" (1900). With J. Merz he edited the "Christliches Kunstblatt." He died in 1915.

S.   N. D.

ZUCKERKANDL, EMIL: Austrian anatomist; born at Raab, Hungary, in 1849; educated at the University of Vienna (M.D. 1874). In 1875 he became privat-docent of anatomy at the University of Utrecht, and he was appointed assistant professor at the University of Vienna in 1879, being made professor at Graz in 1882. After 1888 he was the professor of descriptive and topographical anatomy at the University of Vienna.

Zuckerkandl contributed many monographs to medical journals. Among his works the following may be mentioned: "Zur Morphologie des Gesichtschädels" (Stuttgart, 1877); "Ueber eine Bisher noch Nicht Beschriebene Drüse der Regio Suprahyoidea" (*ib.* 1879); "Ueber das Riechcentrum" (*ib.* 1887); and "Normale und Pathologische Anatomie der Nasenhöhle und Ihrer Pneumatischen Anhänge" (Vienna, 1892). He died May 28, 1910.

BIBLIOGRAPHY: Pagel, *Biog. Lex.* s.v.
s.
F. T. H.

ZUCKERMANDEL, MOSES SAMUEL: German rabbi and Talmudist; born at Ungarisch-Brod, Moravia, April 24, 1836. He became a rabbi in Pleschen, Prussia, and was appointed lecturer on the Mora-Leipziger foundation at Breslau April 1, 1898. He published: "Die Erfurter Handschrift der Tosefta" (1876); "Die Tosefta nach den Erfurter und Wiener Handschriften" (1880–82); "Spruchbuch Enthaltend Biblische Sprüche aus dem Gebetbuche" (1889); and "Volkabularium und Grammatik zu den Hebräischen Versen des Spruchbuches I." (1890). He died in 1917.

BIBLIOGRAPHY: Kürschner, *Literatur-Kalender*, 1898, s.v.; Frankl-Grün, *Gesch. der Juden in Ungarisch Brod*, Vienna, 1905, pp. 56–57.
s.
N. D.

ZUCKERMANN, BENEDICT: German scientist; born at Breslau Oct. 9, 1818; died there Dec. 17, 1891. He received a thorough Hebrew and secular education at the institutions of his native city, and devoted himself at the university to the study of mathematics and astronomy. In 1845 he joined Graetz in agitating for an address to Zacharias Frankel to congratulate him on the conservative stand which he had taken against the Frankfort Conference; and when Frankel assumed the management of the Breslau seminary he appointed Zuckermann on the teaching staff. He gave instruction in mathematics to those of the students who had not had a regular school training, and taught calendric science in the academic department, at the same time acting as librarian and administrator of the stipendiary fund. He wrote: "Ueber Sabbathjahrcyclus und Jubelperiode," Breslau, 1859 (translated into English by A. Loewy, London, 1866); "Ueber Talmudische Münzen und Gewichte," Breslau, 1862; "Katalog der Seminarbibliothek," part i., *ib.* 1870 (2d ed., *ib.* 1876); "Das Mathematische im Talmud," *ib.* 1878; "Tabelle zur Berechnung des Eintrittes der Nacht," *ib.* 1892; "Anleitung und Tabellen zur Vergleichung Jüdischer und Christlicher Zeitangaben," *ib.* 1893. He also contributed occasionally to the "Monatsschrift für Geschichte und Wissenschaft des Judenthums."

Zuckermann's religious attitude was strictly Orthodox. Regularly twice a day he attended the synagogue maintained by him in the house which he had inherited from his father, although he lived in the seminary building, where daily services were held in the chapel. He never married; and while genial

and kindly in nature, he was strongly opposed to anything savoring of ostentation. On his seventieth birthday he fled from Breslau to escape all ovations, and in his will he forbade the delivering of a funeral address.

BIBLIOGRAPHY: *Allg. Zeit. des Jud.* 1892, Nos. 1 and 2; *Die Deborah*, Feb. 4, 1892; *Jahresbericht des Jüdisch-Theologischen Seminars Fränckelscher Stiftung*, Breslau, 1892.
s.
D.

ZUENZ, ARYEH LOEB HARIF B. MOSES: Polish rabbi; born at Pinczow about 1773; died at Warsaw 1833. He was a thorough Talmudic scholar, and was also well versed in the Cabala. Holding first the rabbinate of Plock and then that of Prague, he later settled at Warsaw, where he died. The author of "Shem ha-Gedolim he-Ḥadash" narrates that Aryeh Loeb promised on his deathbed to be a good advocate in heaven for those who should publish his writings, and that this promise was engraved upon his tombstone. The rabbi was the author of many works, most of which are still in manuscript, only the following two having been published: "Ya'alat Ḥen" (Prague, 1793), responsa; and "Ṭib Giṭṭin" (Warsaw, 1812), discussions on the "Geṭ Meḳushshar" of R. M. Bala. The "Ṭib Giṭṭin" was written when the author was eighteen years of age, and its decisions have been accepted in many places.

BIBLIOGRAPHY: Walden, *Shem ha-Gedolim he-Ḥadash*, i. 80, ii. 17, Warsaw, 1882; Kohn, *Kine'at Soferim*, p. 102a, Lemberg, 1892; Fürst, *Bibl. Jud.* iii. 102; Steinschneider, *Cat. Bodl.* col. 745; Zedner, *Cat. Hebr. Books Brit. Mus.*
H. R.
A. S. W.

ZUG. See SWITZERLAND.

ZUGOT (lit. "pairs"): Name given to the leading teachers of the Law in the time preceding the Tannaim. The period of the Zugot begins with Jose b. Joezer and ends with Hillel. The name "Zugot" (comp. Latin "duumviri") was given to these teachers because, according to the tradition in Ḥagigah, two of them always stood at the same time at the head of the Sanhedrin, one as president ("nasi") and the other as vice-president or father of the court ("ab bet din"; see SANHEDRIN). There were five pairs of these teachers: (1) Jose b. Joezer and Jose b. Johanan, who flourished at the time of the Maccabean wars of independence; (2) Joshua b. Peraḥyah and Nittai of Arbela, at the time of John Hyrcanus; (3) Judah b. Ṭabbai and Simeon b. Sheṭaḥ, at the time of Alexander Jannæus and Queen Salome; (4) Shemaiah and Abtalion, at the time of Hyrcanus II.; (5) Hillel and Shammai, at the time of King Herod.

J.
J. Z. L.

ZUKERTORT, JOHANNES HERMANN: Chess-player and physician; born at Lublin, Russian Poland, Sept. 7, 1842; died in London June 20, 1888; son of a Jewish convert to Christianity who was a clergyman at Lublin. He was educated at the gymnasium of Breslau and at the university of that city, whence he graduated in medicine in 1866. As a member of the medical corps of the German army he saw service in 1866, and again in the Franco-Prussian war of 1870–71.

Zukertort, who was destined to be one of the most

eminent exponents of the game, learned to play chess in Breslau when he was about nineteen. Entering a tournament in that city, and receiving the odds of the queen, he lost every game, whereupon he took up the study of Bilguer's "Handbuch," with the result that in 1862 he won games from Anderssen at the odds of a knight. Within a very few years he became one of the strongest players in Germany; and in 1871 he defeated Anderssen in a set match.

In 1872 Zukertort went to London and won third prize in the tourney there, Steinitz and Blackburne gaining first and second respectively. His reception in England was so cordial that he decided to make that country his home; and he accordingly became naturalized, and thenceforth played as an English representative in international competitions. From this time forward his career was one of unprecedented success. In 1878 he gained the first prize at the Paris Exhibition tournament; in 1880 he beat Rosenthal in a match; in 1881 he took second prize at Berlin (Blackburne first); the same year he beat Blackburne in a match; in 1882 he was fifth at Vienna (Steinitz first); and in 1883 at the London international tournament he gained the first prize of £300 ($1,500), Steinitz being second, and Blackburne third. In this last competition he won twenty-two games and lost only one. Of a highly nervous temperament, Zukertort unfortunately had recourse to drugs to brace himself for his contests, and their ill effects became manifest toward the close of the tournament. He never fully recovered; and he very unwisely persisted in challenging Steinitz to a match, of which seven games were to be played in New York, seven in St. Louis, and seven in New Orleans. Zukertort took four games out of five in the first set (March, 1886), but was altogether outplayed in the remaining ones; and he returned to England a mere wreck of his former self. On June 19, 1888, while taking part in a game at Simpson's Divan in London, he was seized with apoplexy. He was removed to the Charing Cross Hospital, where he died on the following day.

Perhaps Zukertort's greatest achievements were in blindfold play, in which he has been surpassed only by Pillsbury.

Zukertort, at first with Anderssen and afterward alone, edited the "Neue Berliner Schachzeitung" (1867-71); and he collaborated with Jean Dufresne on the "Grosses Schach-Handbuch" (2d. ed., Berlin, 1873). He was the author of "Leitfaden des Schachspiels" (Berlin, 1869; 5th ed. 1897) and "Sammlung der Auserlesensten Schachaufgaben, Studien und Partiestellungen" (*ib.* 1869). From 1873 to 1876 he was one of the principal contributors to the "Westminster Papers," the official organ of the St. George's Chess Club, London; and in 1879, together with L. Hoffer, he founded "The Chess Monthly," which for seventeen years was the leading chess magazine in England.

BIBLIOGRAPHY: *Dictionary of National Biography*; *The Chess Monthly,* July, 1888; L. Hoffer, in *The Field* (London), June 23, 1888; *Brockhaus Konversations-Lexikon*; *Meyers Konversations-Lexikon.*
s.   A. P.

ZUKUNFT, DIE. See Periodicals.

ZUNDER, MAIER. See Connecticut.

ZUNSER, ELIAKIM: Russian "badḥan" and poet; born at Wilna in 1845. At the age of sixteen he had gained a local reputation as a poet, and after setting his rimes to music of an Oriental character for voice, orchestra, and piano, he sang at weddings and other entertainments, where his talent was always liberally rewarded, his fee being at one time as high as 200 rubles. He thus introduced a new and more refined method of amusing wedding guests; and since the publication of his "Shirim Ḥadashim" (Wilna, 1861) he has composed over 600 songs, some of which he translated into a Hebrew which is not always rigid in its accuracy. In 1889 Zunser went to America, touring the country under the management of an impresario, and singing and reciting his repertoire. He finally settled in New York as a printer and publisher, and died Sept. 22, 1913. Most of Zunser's poems are national in tendency, while the remainder are nearly all panegyrics of civilization, this category including "Die Eisenbahn," "Licht," "Die Sokhe," "Die Pyramiden," "Columbus und Washington," and "Das Goldene Land." In addition he wrote for the Yiddish stage, for which he produced the best version of the "Sale of Joseph." Many of his poems have been published in the "Jewish Daily News" and the "Volksadvokat," while an edition of a large number of his songs with their music has also appeared (New York, 1891). His seventieth birthday was the occasion of a celebration in New York.

BIBLIOGRAPHY: Minikes, *Hebrew Holiday Papers,* v., No. 37; Wiener, *Yiddish Literature,* pp. 91-93, 120, 232-233, 377; Zunser, *Selbstbiographie,* New York, 1905.
J.   G. Se.

ZUNTZ, NATHAN: German physiologist; born at Bonn Oct. 6, 1847; educated at the university of his native city (M.D. 1868). Becoming an assistant at the physiological institution of the university, he was appointed privat-docent in 1871, and three years later became prosector and assistant professor of anatomy. In 1881 he was appointed professor of animal physiology at the Landwirtschaftliche Hochschule at Berlin. Zuntz made many contributions on physiology, nutrition, respiration, etc., to the medical journals. He died in 1920.

BIBLIOGRAPHY: Pagel, *Biog. Lex.*
s.   F. T. H.

ZUNZ, LEOPOLD (Hebrew name, **Yom-Ṭob Lippmann**): Founder of the modern "science of Judaism" and pioneer in the history of Jewish literature, religious poetry, and the ritual of the synagogue; born at Detmold Aug. 10, 1794; died at Berlin March 18, 1886. The genealogy of his family can be traced continuously for three centuries (comp. Kaufmann in "Monatsschrift," 1894, p. 481), and members are known to have been prominent in the Jewish community of Frankfort-on-the-Main, the cognomen "Zunz" being a modification of "Zons," the name of a place on the Rhine.

His Family. Zunz's father, **Mendl Emanuel** (b. 1761; d. July 3, 1802), was a "baḥur," or Talmudic student, who earned a precarious livelihood as a teacher at the bet ha-midrash and by giving private lessons in Hebrew and Talmud until a pulmonary affection compelled him to relinquish this occupation almost entirely and to conduct a small grocery. His mother, **Hendel Behrens** (b. 1773; d. Nov. 9, 1809), was also delicate, and died at the age of thirty-six in Hamburg, whither she and her husband had removed the year after Lippmann's birth. Although his constitution was extremely delicate in boyhood, Lippmann outlived not only his twin sister, who died in infancy, but also his other sisters and brothers. His early youth was spent under the clouds of physical discomfort and material poverty. His first teacher was his father, who began to instruct his son in Hebrew verbs, Rashi, and the Mishnah as early as 1799. The father's sudden death was a great blow to the struggling family, and obliged Lippmann to accept a free scholarship in the Samson school at Wolfenbüttel, which he entered just a year after his father died. At this school he attracted the notice of his instructors by his remarkable aptitude for mathematics, though at first he seems to have been little amenable to discipline. The appointment of S. M. Ehrenberg as the director of the school in 1807 marked an epoch in the mental and moral development of the lad. As early as 1805 Zunz had tried his hand at making a key to an elementary text-book on arithmetic, while in 1806 a Hebrew satire from his pen, in which he spared neither teachers nor fellow pupils, was consigned to the flames to atone for the wickedness of its author. Ehrenberg, however, took care that this gifted pupil should pursue his studies methodically, and such was his success that in July, 1810, fifteen months after Zunz had been admitted to the highest grade of the Wolfenbüttel gymnasium (which he was the first Jew to enter), Ehrenberg entrusted to him the temporary supervision of the Samson school. His mother had died in the previous year, and Zunz was thus left without a near relative. His free scholarship was about to expire, moreover, and in order to remain at Wolfenbüttel he began to act as an instructor at the Samson school in return for board and lodging. He was particularly interested in algebra and optics, and perfected his mastery of Hebrew by translating various historical essays from the German and other languages.

Early Training. The summer of 1811 is noteworthy as the time when Zunz made his first acquaintance with Wolf's "Bibliotheca Hebræa," which, together with David Gans's "Ẓemaḥ Dawid," gave him his first introduction to Jewish literature and the

Leopold Zunz.

first impulse to think of the "science of Judaism." In the same year (1811) he proceeded to write a book which he intended to be for Palestine what the "Anacharsis" of Klotz had been for Greece. Though he finished the curriculum of the gymnasium in 1811, his intention of taking up university studies could not be carried out until more than four years had elapsed. He remained at Wolfenbüttel until Sept. 25, 1815, when he set out for Berlin, arriving there Oct. 12, and accepting a tutorship in the Hertz family. At the university, where he matriculated while Schleiermacher was rector, he took up mathematical, philosophical, historical, and philological studies, among his professors being Boeckh, Fr. A. Wolf, Savigny, De Wette, and Wilken, the last two inducting him into Semitics and Biblical branches. In Aug., 1817, he wrote his first sermon. Of far greater importance, as showing the bent of his mind, is the fact that during this period he copied the manuscript of Shem-Ṭob ibn Falaquera's "Sefer ha-Ma'alot" and occupied himself with the study of Hebrew manuscripts from Palestine and Turkey shown him by a Polish Jew named David ben Aaron. In Dec., 1817, he wrote an essay entitled "Etwas über die Rabbinische Litteratur; Nebst Nachrichten über ein Altes bis Jetzt Ungedrucktes Hebräisches Werk." It was published in 1818 ("Gesammelte Schriften," i. 1–31, Berlin, 1875). This little book marks an epoch in the history of modern Jewish scholarship. It is a plea for the recognition of Judaism and its literature in university research and teaching. It exposed the ignorance which marked the books written by non-Jewish scholars on Judaism and the Jews, showing at the same time that Judaism had made valuable contributions to many sciences and therefore had a place in their history. This booklet may be said to have been the first to trace the outlines of Jewish science.

The Foundation of Jewish Science.

Shortly after writing the book, but before its publication, Zunz resigned his position with Hertz (March 28, 1818) and revisited his home. During this time he was invited to become a candidate for the position of preacher in the Hamburg Temple, and would have obtained it had he not withdrawn upon learning that Büschenthal was willing to accept the call. In June, Zunz returned to Berlin and resumed his university studies, which he completed in 1819, though it was not till Jan. 2, 1821, that he took his degree of Ph.D. at the University of Halle.

In the interval, while privately continuing his studies and eking out a livelihood by tutoring in German, Latin, and mathematics, he founded, together with Eduard Gans and Moses Moser, the Verein für Cultur und Wissenschaft der Juden (Nov. 17, 1819), a society intended "through culture and education to bring the Jews into harmonious relations with the age and the nations in which they live." This association, of which Zunz was the leading spirit, from the very first attracted the best and brightest among the Jews of Germany, including Heinrich Heine, Ludwig Markus, David Friedländer, Israel Jacobson, and Lazarus Bendavid. In 1822 the "Zeitschrift für die Wissenschaft des Judenthums,"

The Verein für Cultur der Juden. edited by Zunz, appeared under the auspices of this society. According to the program written by Wohlwill, the new "science" comprised a study of the historical development and the philosophical essence of Judaism, although these two methods must be based on a critical understanding of Jewish literature. Zunz's contributions justified this program. In addition to his article on "Hispanische Ortsnamen," mention should be made of his biography of Rashi, which is a veritable classic, illustrating the method which should be pursued, and serving as a brilliant example of what the result must be when all the modern principles of historical and literary research are devoted to a critical study of the data buried in Jewish literature. Another remarkable essay which he published in the "Zeitschrift" was his "Grundlinien zu einer Künftigen Statistik der Juden." The ideas which he there enunciated are by no means antiquated even at this day. The hopes aroused by the Verein were doomed to disappointment, however, and the "Zeitschrift" ceased to appear after the first volume. "Young Palestine," as Heine called the members, lacked religious enthusiasm; Gans became a Christian, and the Verein died. But the "science of Judaism" which it had founded did not share the fate of its first foster-parents, for it lived, thanks to Zunz. "A man of word and deed, he had created and stimulated and brought to pass, while others dreamed and then sank down despondent." As characteristic of him Heine coined the phrase which Karpeles deems so pregnantly descriptive of Zunz's disposition that he repeats it: "he remained true to the great caprice of his soul," believing in the regenerative power of the "Wissenschaft," while the weaker associates of those enthusiastic days deserted, and found preferment by way of baptism.

Other grievous disappointments awaited him at this same period. He preached in the so-called "Beer's Temple" (the new synagogue) from May, 1820, to the spring of 1822, receiving toward the end of this epoch a small stipend from the Berlin congregation. He married Adelheid Beermann May 9, 1822,

Marriage and Journalistic Career. the union remaining childless. Soon after his marriage his position as preacher became distasteful to him, and, feeling that preaching in the face of official arrogance and communal apathy was incompatible with his honor, he resigned his office on Sept. 13, 1822. The masterly sermons he had preached, and which were published

in April, 1823, did not treat of specifically Jewish matters. In 1822 Zunz became a member of the editorial staff of the "Haude und Spener'sche Zeitung," giving besides private lessons in the afternoon hours. He was not freed from this irksome task until Jan. 3, 1826, when he entered upon his duties as director of the Jewish communal elementary school. He remained at the head of the school four years; but again feeling that he was not permitted to bring about needed changes, he relinquished his post, disregarding the sacrifices the step entailed for him and his wife, and receiving but slight recognition for his devotion in a nomination to membership on the board of trustees of the Talmud Torah Institute of the congregation. He was doomed to still greater drudgery on the "Spener'sche Zeitung," part of his work consisting in making excerpts and translations from foreign journals.

In 1831 a difference of political opinion with the management induced him to resign. Though fraught with grave economic difficulties for Zunz, this step may be said to have been providential for Jewish literature. In 1825 he had drafted a plan for a work in four divisions on the "Wissenschaft des Judenthums." On Aug. 25, 1828, he paid his first visit to the famous Oppenheim Library, then in Hamburg but now in Oxford. Through Heine he had even begun to correspond with prominent publishers concerning his intended work; but on Oct. 15,

The "Gottesdienstliche Vorträge." 1831, he began to write in earnest, and on July 21, 1832, the "Gottesdienstliche Vorträge der Juden" appeared, destined to be the most important Jewish work published in the nineteenth century. In the preface, which was no less remarkable than the contents, the German authorities were arraigned for their refusal to grant the Jews the justice due them by right and for their reluctance to accord them liberty instead of special rights and privileges. The Jews were entitled to be citizens of Germany. Jewish science too ought no longer to be excluded from governmental patronage, but should have institutions provided for its development. In the synagogues the living word was once more to resound, for the sermon had always been an institution of Judaism. The book afforded the proof, and its purpose was to trace the historic growth of this synagogal institution. This preface was suppressed by the government and cut out from most copies of the first edition. The work itself was a masterly exposition of the gradual growth and evolution of homiletic literature, traced through the Midrash, the Haggadah, and the prayer-book. It was the first book to assign dates and to disclose the relative interdependence of the various documents. Besides showing that the sermon was thoroughly Jewish, the book demonstrated that Judaism had a science which could justly claim equality with the studies admitted to university standing. It proved, furthermore, that Judaism was a growing force, not a crystallized law. Scientific throughout, the book had a powerful influence in shaping the principles of Reform Judaism, especially as applied to the prayer-books. For all time to come the "Gottesdienstliche Vorträge" fixed the method which the literary exploration of Jewish literature must follow to a certain degree, even though the merely formal criterion of the mention of a literary document is urged too strongly as decisive in assigning to it its date and place. With this book Zunz rose at once to the pinnacle of recognized leadership. His discriminating insight, his power of combination, his sound scholarship, his classic reserve, and his dignity of presentation proclaimed him master. No second edition of the "Gottesdienstliche Vorträge" was prepared by the author, but it was reprinted after his death (Frankfort-on-the-Main, 1892; comp. E. G. Hirsch, "Die Jubiläen Zweier Werke," in "Der Zeitgeist," 1882).

While Zunz's reputation as a pioneer was readily spread abroad by the "Gottesdienstliche Vorträge," no material benefits accrued to him from its publication. In Sept., 1832, he went to Hamburg, where he met H. I. Michael, the owner of rare manuscripts. The old struggle for bread awaited him upon his return to Berlin. He did not receive the appointment as head master of the Veitel-Heine Ephraim foundation as some friends had hoped he would, and he was even unsuccessful in his efforts to obtain employment as a bookkeeper, although willing to accept such a position. He advertised for pupils in Hebrew, rabbinics, and mathematics through the medium of the University Bulletin Board, but again with slight results. His friends proposed him for the vacant post of rabbi at Darmstadt, Aaron Chorin having conferred on him the hattarat hora'ah; but though Gabriel Riesser had recommended him (Oct. 9, 1833) as the first scholar of the day in Jewish literature, he was not elected. In consequence of this he could not be induced to be a candidate for Cassel and other places, though suggestions to apply came to him from various quarters, among them, it is interesting to note, one from New York. He continued to meet his friends on Sabbaths at Gumpertz's, and in 1835 he delivered a course of lectures on the Psalms, attended by Gans, Bellermann (the latter eighty years of age), M. Sachs, Zedner, Moser, and Gumpertz. In the same year he was called to Prague as preacher to the Society for Improving the Mode of Worship, a call which at last promised to deliver him from the drudgery for mere bread. When he **In Prague.** arrived at Prague, however (Sept. 16, 1835), it did not require many days to convince him that he had found no compensation for his sacrifice in leaving Berlin. In Prague he met scarcely one that understood him. He thought himself lost "in China." He missed "books, periodicals, men, liberty." He regretted his "Wissenschaft." Before fifty days had elapsed he resolved to leave this city of petrified irresponsiveness. The people misjudged him, and called his firmness stubbornness and his principles eccentricities. His discontent did not help to improve the situation, and on Jan. 1, 1836, he gave notice that he wished to resign. He rejoiced like one delivered from prison when on July 8 he again arrived in Berlin. Soon after his return he found another opportunity of utilizing his scholarship in behalf of his German coreligionists. A royal edict forbade the Jews to assume Christian names. In this predicament the administration of the congregation bethought itself of Zunz, and on Aug. 5

he was commissioned to write a scientific treatise on the names of the Jews based upon original investigations. On Dec. 7, 1836, his "Die Namen der Juden" ("G. S." ii. 1–82) was published. It demonstrated that the names which had been classed as non-Jewish were an ancient inheritance of Judaism, and this proof, which rested on indisputable evidence and which was presented with the calm dignity of the scholar, made a deep impression. Tributes of admiration and gratitude were offered the author from all sides, Alexander von Humboldt being among those who felt impelled to thank Zunz. The congregation itself informed him soon afterward (July, 1837) of its intention of founding a "Lehrerseminar" to be directed by him. This seminary was opened Nov. 16, 1840, after protracted negotiations with Zunz, who became its first director. Even while the preparations for the founding of the normal school were in **Director of the "Lehrerseminar."** progress, Zunz had organized a staff of scholars for the translation of the Bible which has since borne his name, he himself acting as editor-in-chief and translating the Book of Chronicles (comp. Jew. Encyc. iii. 193). With this entrance upon a secure position, Zunz at last found himself freed from the struggle for existence. Thenceforth he had the leisure to concentrate his energies; his pen was busy enriching periodicals and the works of others with his contributions. Noteworthy among these was a study on the geographical literature of the Jews from the remotest times to the year 1841, which appeared in an English translation in Asher's edition of Benjamin of Tudela (ii. 230 *et seq.*). He also gave expert opinions on problems arising from the agitation for Reform, such as "Gutachten über die Beschneidung" (Frankfort-on-the-Main, 1844).

Although his "Gottesdienstliche Vorträge" was the very rampart behind which Reform could securely and calmly beat back the attacks of its opponents, Zunz showed little sympathy with the movement, because he suspected its leaders of ecclesiastic ambitions, and feared that rabbinical autocracy would result from the Reform crusade. **Attitude Toward Reform.** He regarded much of the professional life of the rabbis as a "waste of time," and in a very late letter (see "Jahrbuch für Jüdische Geschichte," 1902, p. 171) he classed rabbis with soothsayers and quacks. The point of his protest against Reform was directed against HOLDHEIM and the position maintained by this leader as an autonomous rabbi, as is evident from Geiger's answer to Zunz's strictures (Geiger, "Nachgelassene Schriften," v. 184–185). The violent outcry raised against the Talmud by some of the principal spirits of the Reform party was repugnant to Zunz's historic sense, while he himself was temperamentally inclined to assign a determinative potency to sentiment, this explaining his tender reverence for ceremonial usages. His position was by no means Orthodox in the usual sense, however, even in regard to the ritual practises, which he called symbols (see among others his meditation on tefillin, reprinted in "Gesammelte Schriften," ii. 172–176), denying them the validity of divine ordinances which the faithful are bound to observe without inquiry into their meaning. His position accordingly approached that of the symbolists among the reformers who insisted that symbols had their function, provided their suggestive significance was spontaneously comprehensible. He emphasized most strongly the need of a moral regeneration of the Jews.

Zunz's sympathies with the science of Judaism were too dominant to allow him to lay aside his reserve and take a part in the active endeavors to recast the framework of the Synagogue, but in his chosen field, during this very period of agitation and unrest, he garnered a new harvest. In 1845 he published in Berlin another volume, "Zur Geschichte und Literatur," which comprises studies in all the departments of Jewish literature and life. The introductory chapter is a philosophical presentation of the essence of Jewish literature and its right to existence, its connection with the culture of the peoples among which the Jews have lived, and its bearing upon the civilizations amid which it developed. Zunz makes an earnest protest against the neglect of this literature, and caustically exposes its underlying motives—indolence, arrogance, and prejudice. A rapid survey of the treatment accorded Hebrew books serves as a prelude to the unsparing castigation administered to the conceit of the Christian scholars of the nineteenth century, and as a protest against the outrage perpetrated by the exclusion of Jewish studies from the universities. The volume itself was a proof that Jewish science had a right to citizenship in the academic republic of letters. Apparently disjointed, the various subjects treated in this volume found their unity in the methodical grasp of the author, who made it clear that underlying all these diverse interests was a distinct unity of purpose, the pulse-beat of a life striving for expression and realization. Bibliography, ethics, and culture were among the departments into which the book ushered the student, while long periods of time, of which little had been known or understood, were there set forth in all their bearings and ambitions. Zunz had, indeed, earned the title of the Jewish Boeckh. Under his touch every detached fact appeared as symptomatic of the life of a vitalized organism. Superficially examined, the book seemed to be a collection of incoherent names, dates, and details, but when rightly taken as a whole, it won distinction as the result of studies undertaken to reveal the unifying thought manifest in all the various fragments of information, whether old or new. Once more Zunz had proved his supreme mastership in the wide field of Jewish literature; and that he had also the rare art of popular presentation was shown by the lectures which he delivered in 1842.

"Zur Geschichte und Literatur."

The year 1848 brought Zunz an opportunity to utilize his rare gifts of mind, tongue, and heart in the political arena. His oration in honor of the victims of the March uprising in Berlin attracted universal attention to him; and he was chosen elector in the 110th precinct both for the deputy to the Prussian legislature and for the representative in the German Diet. He addressed many a meeting of his fellow citizens, his lucidity of diction, clarity of thought, eloquence of speech, readiness of wit, and thorough familiarity with the subject of the discussion distinguishing him among the many men of parts and power who were his colleagues. He was called to act as vice-chairman (Aug. 9, 1849) and later as chairman (Oct. 4) of the eighth Berlin Volksverein. On Nov. 6 he delivered the memorial address on Robert Blum; and at the same time he strove to reorganize the Jewish community on a liberal basis. He was likewise busy in conferences and private interviews with influential men, endeavoring to carry into effect the emancipation of the Jews; for in 1847 high functionaries of the court and state had sought his opinion on the proposed legislation regulating the status of the Prussian Jews.

The office of director of the normal school now seemed to him to consume too much of his time, and he severed his connection with this institution on Feb. 25, 1850. A small pension was voted him by the congregation, and assured him the liberty he craved for the completion of the labors which had come to fruition only in part in his "Gottesdienstliche Vorträge." The prayers and prayer-books of Judaism still awaited his presentation, but the material for this purpose was widely scattered in inaccessible manuscripts and distant libraries. Zunz had already gone in Sept., 1846, to the British Museum, and his visit had confirmed him in his plan of writing the history of Jewish hymnology and synagogal poetry as incorporated in the various liturgies of the Synagogue. He soon realized, however, that such a work would fill several volumes, and he accordingly resolved to write first the story of the poetry and then that of the poets. The "Synagogale Poesie des Mittelalters" was published March 2, 1855, and discussed the various kinds of poetry incorporated in the Jewish services, their external forms, their inner motive, and the circumstances, hopes, experiences, and sufferings that had evoked them. To trace the development of the Hebrew language in these monuments of the Jewish spirit was another of the preoccupations of Zunz, who showed, especially in his introductory chapter, that he who woke to new life the Jewish hymnal handled the German tongue with a mastership equaled only by the greatest writers, while his German translations helped to illustrate and vitalize the story. This introductory chapter has, indeed, become a classic, George Eliot deeming its phrases worthy of incorporation in "Daniel Deronda." Under the necessity of abbreviating the services at public worship the piyyuṭim had been attacked for years by those who strove for a reform of the ritual. Zunz's work gave the proof that these hymns were the slow accretion of centuries and were unequal in value. Yet, on the other hand, his book showed what wealth of feeling and fervor of faith lay hidden in these outbursts of lament, penitence, and expectancy. He demonstrated that the jewel-casket of the medieval Synagogue contained many a priceless gem in addition to several of inferior value.

The "Synagogale Poesie."

Zunz now realized that without personal inspection of the manuscripts he could go no further in his history of the poets and the liturgy. On April

26, 1855, he set out on his journey of exploration, spending twelve days in the British Museum, twenty in the Bodleian at Oxford, and three in Paris, and inspecting 280 manuscripts and 100 rare books. After paying a visit to Heinrich Heine (June 26–28), he returned on July 4, 1855. In the following year he inspected and excerpted eighty manuscripts in the Hamburg Library (June 18–July 27, 1856), and after his return he resumed his lectures on Jewish literature. In 1856, moreover, he wrote his "Ueber die Eidesleistungen der Juden," a defense of the Jews against the charge of perjury and a protest against the OATH MORE JUDAICO, which appeared in the same year as his "Die Ritus des Synagogalen Gottesdienstes Geschichtlich Entwickelt" (1859). In conciseness of presentation and wealth of content this volume has scarcely a peer. He brought order out of chaos by grouping the several components of the liturgy according to various countries, exhibiting the growth of a liturgical literature developing through two millennia from small beginnings to the final compilations of fixed cycles ("maḥzorim") and rites.

Scientific Journeys.

During his studies preparatory to the concluding volume of his monumental work, Zunz continued his activity in public affairs, being entrusted with the presidency of the electoral assembly of his district (April 25, 1862). His main energy, however, was devoted to his scholarly pursuits, and, becoming daily more deeply impressed with the necessity of inspecting the Hebrew collections in Italy, he went to Parma (May 20, 1863), where he examined about 120 codices in the De Rossi Library; but he was not allowed to visit the Vatican. One of the fruits of this Italian trip was his "Hebräische Handschriften in Italien, ein Mahnruf des Rechts." He crowned the labors to which he had consecrated his life by his volume on the "Literaturgeschichte der Synagogalen Poesie," the preface of which is dated Sept. 26, 1865. This was his thanks to the friends who had remembered his seventieth birthday (Aug. 10, 1864) by the founding of the Zunzstiftung, the initiative having been taken by Salomon Neumann. This concluding volume was of the greatest importance not only for the history of Jewish poetry, but also for that of the Jews, revealing the intellectual life of the Jews in Italy, Spain, and Germany. Once more an enormous mass of material was made intelligible as to conditions of time and place, and amorphous detail again assumed shape and function within the circle of correlated circumstance, thus becoming part of a living and growing organism. In 1867 a supplement appeared, adding to the 1,500 poets and their numerous productions, 80 new versifiers and 500 new poems.

The Germany of 1870 found in Zunz as an elector a loyal cooperator in its destiny. In 1872 he raised his voice in his "Deutsche Briefe" in defense of the purity of the German language, menaced by the journalism and vulgarism then rampant. The same year he wrote his "Monatstage des Kalenderjahres," a memorial calendar recording the days on which Israel's great sons and martyrs had died, and giving characteristic details concerning their labors and lives.

A new field now began to attract his attention, that of Bible criticism; and in his studies on Deuteronomy, Ezekiel, Leviticus, and Esther ("Z. D. M. G." xxvii. 669–689) he reached conclusions diametrically opposed to those deduced by the traditionists and even by the conservatives, proving the untenability of the dogma of the Mosaic authorship of the Pentateuch. In his "Gesammelte Schriften" these essays have been reproduced, and others on Exodus, Numbers, and Genesis have been added ("G. S." i. 217–270), proof sufficient that Zunz did not discredit his own studies in spite of the outcry raised against them. In his letters addressed to David Kaufmann he took occasion to declare his indifference toward "babblers and hypocrites." "It is not my business to defend religion, but to defend human rights." "Opinions on books are not subject to the authority of religion." "Why do they not inquire whether it be true or false? Miserable men they who desire not to be disturbed." "My first critical studies go back to 1811, long before Hengstenberg's day and the splendor of other 'critic-astra.'"

Attitude Toward Higher Criticism.

The light of his life was now to fail him. On Aug. 18, 1874, his Adelheid, known to their friends as "Die Zunzin" (="female Zunz"), passed away. From this blow Zunz never recovered. His entire literary activity was limited to superintending the publication of his "Gesammelte Schriften." Though the ninetieth anniversary of his birthday was celebrated throughout the world and brought to him messages of love from the four quarters of the globe, even being marked by the publication of a "Zunz Jubelschrift," he felt that few remembered his existence. David Kaufmann alone seems to have succeeded in arousing in him the old interest for Jewish studies; and Steinschneider was perhaps the only one with whom he maintained personal intercourse. His thoughts dwelt with her who had been his companion.

While all parties in Judaism have claimed Zunz for their own, his Bible-critical epilogue to his labors (in a letter to David Kaufmann) justifies the assumption that, if he is to be classified at all, he must be assigned a place with Geiger, with whom he was on terms of closest intimacy, and to whose "Zeitschrift" he was a regular contributor. The end, superinduced by a fall, came on March 18, 1886. To the last he was clear in mind and in the full possession of his faculties.

BIBLIOGRAPHY: Letters and manuscripts in the possession of the Lehranstalt für die Wissenschaft des Judenthums, Berlin; *Das Buch Zunz*, a manuscript autobiography in the possession of the Zunzstiftung; Kaufmann, *Zunz*, in *Allgemeine Deutsche Biographie*; idem, in *Monatsschrift*, xxxviii.; Strodtmann, *H. Heine's Leben und Werke*, i.; Maybaum, *Aus dem Leben von Leopold Zunz*, Berlin, 1894; *Jahrbuch für Jüdische Geschichte*, 1902–3; Zunz, *G. S.* i.–iii.

S.   E. G. H.

ZUPH: 1. A Levite, and one of the ancestors of the prophet Samuel (I Sam. i. 1); in the parallel passage, I Chron. vi. 11 (A. V. 26), he is called **Zophai.**

2. A country, perhaps so called because it was inhabited by the family of Zuph (I Sam. ix. 5). It seems to have been connected with Ramathaim-zophim (I Sam. i. 1), since both places are mentioned together with Mount Ephraim (comp. *ib.* ix. 4–5).

E. C.   M. Sel.

ZUPNIK, AARON HIRSCH: Galician Hebrew and Judæo-German writer; born at Drohobycz c. 1850. In addition to editing the "Drohobyczer Zeitung," a Judæo-German weekly begun in 1883, and the "Ẓiyyon," a periodical which was at first devoted to Hebrew literature (irregularly from 1885 to 1888) and later became a monthly scientific publication (1896–97), Zupnik published the following works: "Ḳedushshat ha-Shem" (Brody, 1867), a historical novel depicting Jewish life in Spain and adapted from Ludwig Philippson's "Jacob Tirado"; "Toledot Abraham" (Lemberg, 1869), biography of Abraham Cohn, a preacher of Lemberg; "Emet u-Mishpaṭ" (Drohobycz, 1883), a Hebrew translation of Joseph von Wertheimer's "Jüdische Lehre und Jüdisches Leben" (also published in Polish under the title "Nauka Zydowska"); "Vom Ḥeder zur Werkstätte" (ib. 1884), a Judæo-German novel dealing with Jewish life in Galicia; "Zur Lösung der Judenfrage Durch die Juden" (Berlin, 1885).

BIBLIOGRAPHY: Lippe, *Bibliographisches Lexicon*, new series, i.; Zeitlin, *Bibl. Post-Mendels.* p. 431.

J.   M. Sel.

ZURICH: Capital of the Swiss canton of the same name. Jews first settled there in the early part of the fourteenth century, and soon acquired considerable wealth by lending money. They paid high taxes for toleration, but were allowed to buy and own houses, including the castle of Manegg on the Utliberg and an estate in the Beckenhof. On the whole, they were treated justly by the government, although they were subject to medieval restrictions, being obliged to wear the JUDENHUT, and probably also the BADGE. Of Talmudic authors only Moses of Zurich, the annotator of the "Semaḳ" of ISAAC BEN JOSEPH OF CORBEIL, is known (Neubauer, "Cat. Bodl. Hebr. MSS." pp. 183–184).

In 1348 the Black Death brought about a change in the condition of the Jews, who were accused of having poisoned the wells. At the same time they were charged with the murder **The Black** of a boy, and in 1349 a number **Death.** of Jews were burned in consequence of these two calumnies. Soon afterward, however, Jews again settled in Zurich, and in 1401, when those of Schaffhausen and Winterthur were burned on account of the murder of a Christian boy at Diessenhofen, their colleagues of Zurich were protected by the city council against the citizens and gilds, although, for their own security, they were kept in confinement until all danger was over. The hostility of the people and of the gilds made it impossible, however, for the council to keep the Jews in the town any longer, and in the years 1424, 1435, and 1436 decrees of expulsion were issued against them. Two centuries later a Frankfort Jew named Samuel Eiron made a remark derogatory to the founder of Christianity, and was beheaded, whereupon it was solemnly proclaimed throughout the town that no Jew should again be allowed to settle within it unless he had first received special permission.

From that date, 1634, until the middle of the nineteenth century no Jews lived in Zurich; nor was it until the emancipation of their coreligionists of Aargau in 1863 that the gates of the city were

opened to them. Shortly before this, however, a few Jews, mostly Alsatians, lived in the suburbs of Zurich, where they founded a cemetery. After the emancipation Jews from Endingen and Lengnau, the only two villages in Switzerland **Emancipa-** in which Jews had always been allowed **tion.** to live, migrated to Zurich in greater numbers, being followed by their coreligionists from other countries, especially from the neighboring German states. Among the well-known German Jews who lived and died in Zurich was Solomon L. STEINHEIM. About 1870 the congregation had increased sufficiently to employ a rabbi, the first incumbent being Moritz Levin (now with the Reform Congregation of Berlin); the second, Alexander Kisch (now in Prague). In 1883 a synagogue was built in Löwenstrasse. In 1920 the Jewish population of Zurich was about 4,000 in a total of 207,161, and, like the whole town, it is of an international character. In Zurich, as in the rest of Switzerland, the Jews are absolutely free politically, but social life is not yet devoid of prejudices. The Cantonal University and the Swiss Polytechnic School are attended by many foreign Jews and Jewesses, especially from Russia, and there are several Jewish professors and privat-docents in the two faculties. The gymnasium likewise has a Jewish teacher, and two Jewish representatives sit in the Cantonal Council, although no Jew is yet a member of the municipal government.

The Zurich Jews are chiefly merchants, while the Polish and Russian immigrants are mostly pedlers. The chief community is the Israelitische Kultusgemeinde, directed since 1893 by Dr. Littmann, and containing 330 households. In addition to this is the Orthodox Israelitische Religionsgesellschaft, which has a room for worship in a private house, and also owns a cemetery. A Jewish library of several thousand volumes (including incunabula and manuscripts) has been purchased by the Israelitische Kultusgemeinde from a bequest of the historian Heidenheim (who died in Zurich), and presented to the municipal library.

BIBLIOGRAPHY: Ulrich, *Sammlung Jüdischer Geschichten in der Schweiz*, Basel, 1748; Bär, *Die Juden Zürichs im Mittelalter*, in *Zürcher Taschenbuch auf das Jahr 1896*; Steinberg, *Studien zur Geschichte der Juden in der Schweiz Während des Mittelalters*, Zurich, 1903; *Israelitisches Wochenblatt für die Schweiz*, i., Nos. 30, 36.

D.   E. Sc.

ZURIEL, MOSES BEN SAMUEL: Mathematician of the seventeenth century; author of "Meḥaddesh Ḥodashim" (Venice, 1653), a calendar for 5414–34 (= 1654–74).

BIBLIOGRAPHY: Steinschneider, in *Monatsschrift*, xlix. 495.

E. C.   M. Sel.

ZURISHADDAI: The father of Shelumiel, a chief of the tribe of Simeon, who was chosen to aid Moses in numbering the people (Num. i. 6; ii. 12; vii. 36, 41; x. 19).

E. G. H.   B. P.

ZURITA: Fortified city of Castile on the River Tajo, one and one-half miles from Pastrana. It had a Jewish community as early as 1137, when King Alfonso VII. won it from the Moors; and during the Almohade persecutions many Jews sought refuge there. In the charter granted the city by Alfonso

VIII. in 1180, no distinctions were drawn between Jews and Christians, and on Dec. 20, 1215, the aljama in Zurita was exempted from all taxation by Henry I. of Castile in view of the pecuniary sacrifices made by its members during the war, and in recognition of its faithful defense and improvement of the fort entrusted to it. In 1474 this same aljama, which was so wealthy that it gave the king a thousand doubloons (" mille aureos "), paid, together with the aljamas of Pastrana and Almequera, two thousand maravedis in taxes.

BIBLIOGRAPHY: *Boletin Acad. Hist.* xl. 166 *et seq.*; Rios, *Hist.* i. 356, iii. 599.
J.   M. K.

ZUTRA, MAR, I. : Exilarch from 401 to 409. He was the successor of Mar Kahana and a contemporary of R. Ashi, whose enactments he had to follow in spite of his exalted position. He was obliged to leave Nehardea and take up his residence in Sura, where he held an annual reception at the opening of the harvest season for the delegates of all Babylonian communities, the receptions being called " rigli " (ריגלא דרישי גלוותא). In addition Mar Zutra received various other delegations at Sura. Nothing further is known about his career.

BIBLIOGRAPHY: Grätz, *Gesch.* iv. 351, note 3; Neubauer, *Anecdota*, i. 32–33; Heilprin, *Seder ha-Dorot*, i. 167a.
J.   S. O.

ZUTRA, MAR, II. : Exilarch; born about 496; died about 520; ruled from 512 to 520. He was the son of Huna, who was appointed exilarch under Firuz; and he was born at the time when Mazdak endeavored to introduce communism in all Persia. The opposition against Mar Zutra, his imprisonment, and his early death have given rise to a number of legends. The following anecdote is told about his birth and the events preceding it: Mar Zutra's father was engaged in constant strife with his father-in-law, the school principal Mar Hanina, because the latter refused to obey the orders issued by the exilarch. Hanina was accordingly punished for his disobedience; and, being embittered and humiliated, he went into the prayer-house at night, and there shed a dishful of tears, whereupon he fell asleep. He dreamed that he was in a cedar forest, engaged in felling the trees; and when he came to the last cedar-tree King David appeared and forbade him to fell it. On awakening, Hanina learned that the entire house of the exilarch had perished, except his daughter, who was pregnant and had been spared. Soon afterward she gave birth to a son, whom the grandfather named Mar Zutra, at the same time assuming personal charge of his training. During Mar Zutra's infancy the exilarchate was administered by his brother-in-law Mar Pahra, or Pahda. The latter bribed King Kobad in order that he might remain in office; but when Mar Zutra had reached the age of fifteen, his grandfather presented him to the king as the legitimate ruler, whereupon the monarch installed him as exilarch. Mar Pahda opposed this, but was killed by a fly which entered his nostril; and after that event the exilarchs had a fly on their seal.

Mar Zutra took up arms against the Persians, and organized an uprising to oppose the introduction of communism, although the king himself was in favor thereof. The immediate cause of the uprising, however, was the assassination of the school principal Isaac, regarding which no accurate information exists. From the fact that Mar Hanina took part in the struggle, it may be deduced that it was of a religious character. At the head of a company of 400 Jewish warriors Mar Zutra advanced against the opposing Persian forces; and the battles fought by him have furnished material for various legends. It is told that a pillar of fire always preceded his army; and it is further stated that Mar Zutra founded an independent Jewish state, with Mahoza as his residence. He ruled as an independent king, and imposed heavy taxes on all non-Jews. In spite of his able government, however, immorality spread among his people, whereupon the pillar of fire disappeared. In a subsequent battle between Mar Zutra and the Persians the former was defeated; and both he and his grandfather Hanina were taken prisoners and decapitated, their bodies being suspended from crosses on the bridge at Mahoza.

The account of Mar Zutra's life is based on a mixture of historic facts and legendary narratives. Thus, the description of the uprising of the Jews against Persian reforms, the statement regarding the prominent position held by Mar Zutra, and the account of his death are all based on historical data, whereas the stories of the extinction of the exilarchal house are legendary, as are also the dream of Hanina (which corresponds with that of Bostanai) and the account of the pillar of fire. All those legends, however, which tend to prove that the later rulers of Babylonia were usurpers have a basis of truth, inasmuch as Mar Zutra's only son emigrated to Jerusalem.

BIBLIOGRAPHY: Grätz, *Gesch.* v. 4–6, note 1; Neubauer, *Anecdota*, ii. 76; Heilprin, *Seder ha-Dorot*, i. 167.
J.   S. O.

ZUTRA, MAR, BAR MAR ZUTRA : Palestinian scholar. On the day of his birth his father was crucified, and his mother fled with him to Palestine, where he was later appointed archipherecite (see ARCHIPHERECITES). According to Brüll, he was active in causing the scientific material collected in Palestine to be gathered together and examined; and the Palestinian Talmud is said to have been completed in his lifetime. During his term of office the order of Justinian in relation to reading from Holy Scripture was promulgated; and the first opposing utterance is said to have been made by Mar Zutra. His place of residence was probably Tiberias, and by virtue of his title he was the official leader of the Palestinian Jews.

BIBLIOGRAPHY: Brüll's *Jahrb.* v. 94–96; Heilprin, *Seder ha-Dorot*, i. 173; *Yuhasin*, ed. Filipowski, p. 93; Weiss, *Dor*, iv. 2, 304; Grätz, *Gesch.* iii. 386.
J.   S. O.

ZUZIM : Name of an ancient people mentioned in Gen. xiv. 5 as residing in Ham, the territory east of the Jordan, and as having been smitten by Chedorlaomer. The narrator must have supposed that the Zuzim were well known, for he prefixes the definite article to their name, though its use may also imply that even to him the nation was somewhat nebulous. This prefix induced the Septuagint and the

Peshiṭta (or the scribe of the copy underlying their version) to read the name as an appellative. They therefore translate it as "the strong" (= "ha-'izzuzim") or "the mighty" (= "ha-'ezuzim"), and thus identify the people with the Rephaim, the giants who occupied the district and who are said to have been called "Zamzummim" by the Ammonites (Deut. ii. 20). The rendering of Symmachus results from a combination of the two names Zuzim and Zamzummim (Σοαζομμειν), and thus anticipates those modern scholars who maintain that the names are identical, the variance being due to scribal errors. Sayce ("Higher Criticism and the Verdict of the Monuments," pp. 160 et seq.; "Expository Times," viii. 463), proceeding on the theory that Gen. xiv. is a translation of a Babylonian document, advances the hypothesis that the double spelling of the name arose from the identity of the characters "m" and "w" in Babylonian. It has also been proposed to connect the name with Ziza, a military post of the Roman period (Dillmann, "Genesis," ad loc.).

E. G. H.

ZWEIFEL, LAZAR (ELIEZER ẒEBI B. DAVID HA-KOHEN): Russian apologist and critical compiler from rabbinical works; born at Moghilef April 15, 1815; died at Gluchof Feb. 18, 1888. He was a lecturer in the rabbinical seminary of Jitomir from 1853 until the institution was closed in 1874. Zweifel was a collector of excerpts and quotations from rabbinical literature, which he used in all his works to such an extent that they comprise about three-quarters of the text. One large "yalḳuṭ" of his compilation was burned, and only about a tenth of the original work was saved from the fire that once destroyed his house. Zweifel acted as a mediator and peace-maker between the various Jewish sects, and was especially prominent as a protector of the ḤASIDIM. He also defended the Karaites against the attack of Deinard, and even had a good word for Reform ("Sanegor," pp. 38–41, 43). He endeavored also to give a Jewish coloring to Spinoza's philosophy, and quoted fifty opinions, most of which, including that of Besht (BA'AL SHEM-ṬOB), were in harmony with the philosopher, while he himself contended that the only difference lay in the fact that Spinoza used words without careful discrimination to explain his system ("Shalom 'al-Yisrael," iii. 43, ed. Wilna, 1873).

Zweifel was a prolific writer and one of the first to use Talmudic and idiomatic Hebrew for the modern poetry which he frequently composed, stanzas being interspersed throughout his works. He was also a talented and epigrammatic Yiddish author, and some of his productions in that field were published in Spector's "Hausfreund."

Zweifel is best known through his apologetic "Shalom 'al-Yisrael," a work in four volumes, two of which are marked "part true." He based his defense on the ground that "Beshtism" (בעשטנות) is the development of the views expressed in the "Moreh Nebukim" of Maimonides, the "Ḥobot ha-**Defense of** Lebabot" of Baḥya, and the "Mesillat **Ḥasidism.** Yesharim" of Moses Luzzatto. He showed also that similar ideas were found in Luria's cabalistic system, and demonstrated that the Ḥasidic minhagim were mere repetitions of what had already been recognized in the Talmud and in early literature by Philo and other Alexandrian Jews ("Shalom 'al-Yisrael," i. 47a). He claimed, moreover, that the prejudice against the Ḥasidim and the persecutions which they were forced to endure at the hands of their opponents were as unjust as the oppression of Jews by Christians (ib. vi. 59). He admitted, however, that Ḥasidism had changed somewhat since the time of Besht, and that the rank and file of those who professed Ḥasidism no longer strictly followed the ancient path. He accordingly urged the leading rabbis or ẓaddiḳim, especially R. Mordecai of Czernobel, R. Israel of Razun, and R. Mendel of Lubawicz, to instruct their thousands of adherents to weed out the idlers among them, and to refrain from denunciations and appeals to the government in their petty quarrels, likewise imploring them to cease introducing innovations into minhagim (ib. iii., end, ed. Wilna).

Zweifel was bitterly criticized by the Maskilim for his apologetics and panegyrics of the Ḥasidim. Ḥayyim Selig Slonimski, his colleague in the rabbinical **Replies to** seminary, made a public protest, de-**Zweifel.** claring that Zweifel's opinion was not shared by the faculty and that he trusted it would make no impression on the students ("Ha-Meliẓ," viii., No. 37; comp. also Nos. 42–45, 47). Some remarked that his name Zweifel (= "doubt") was indicative of his wavering and unbalanced mind, and J. L. Gordon hesitated to take Zweifel seriously ("Iggerot Yeleg," ii. 277), while Isaac Hirsch Weiss regarded his efforts to harmonize the factions as unavailing, all refutation of false accusations against Jews in general being superfluous or useless, though he admitted Zweifel's good intentions and the value of his works taken as a whole ("Ha-Asif," iii. 152).

The works of Zweifel are as follows: (1) "Minnim we-'Ugab," containing a poetical introduction in which the numerical value of the let-**Works.** ters of each line is 1,856 (the year of issue), notes on various passages of the Bible and Talmud, poems, and a collection of sayings entitled "Pirḳe de R. Eliezer ha-Ḳaṭan" (Wilna, 1858); (2) "Musar Ab," containing the letter of admonition addressed by Maimonides to his son Abraham, the ethical will of Judah ibn Tibbon to his son Samuel, together with notes and explanations, and 150 proverbs (Jitomir, 1865); (3) "Pardes Rimmonim," explanations of legendary haggadot in the Talmud, by Shem-Ṭob Shaprut (first ed., Sabbionetta, 1554), edited with an introduction and remarks (Jitomir, 1866); (4) "Liḳḳuṭe Ẓebi," a collection of remarks on the Bible and Midrash by Hirsch Ẓebi Segall of Kovno, edited with introduction and notes (ib. 1866); (5) "Tushiyyah," stories and poems, chiefly translations from Russian and German (ib. 1867); (6) "Ḥomer be-Yad ha-Yoẓer," an ethico-philosophical commentary on Pappenheim's liturgical hymn "Ki Hinne Ka-Ḥomer" for the eve of Yom Kippur, with notes, a eulogy on Solomon Löb Rapoport, and similar material (ib. 1868); (7) "Shalom 'al-Yisrael" (i.–iii., part 1, ib. 1868–70; iii., part 2, Wilna, 1873; iv., Jitomir, 1873; comp. J. S. Trachtmann in "Ha-Karmel," 1873, No. 11); (8) "Bet Middot," moral and ethical teachings by

Jacob Löb Margolioth, with notes (Jitomir, 1870); (9) "Ḥeshbon shel 'Olam," on theodicy (Warsaw, 1878); (10) "Nezaḥ Yisrael," the vitality of the Jewish nation explained by the teachings of Judaism (St. Petersburg, 1884; reprint from Zederbaum's "Meliẓ Eḥad Minni Elef"); (11) "Sanegor," a defense against the accusation of materialism and Talmudic Judaism, divided into five sections and giving historical explanations (Warsaw, 1885; 2d ed., Wilna, 1894; comp. J. L. Freidkin in "Keneset Yisrael," i. 242; Berdyczewski, in "Bet ha-Midrash," i. 87); and (12) "'Olam Ḳaṭan," or "Klein Weltel," a Yiddish poem reprinted from "Ha-Zofeh" (London, 1894). Zweifel wrote also numerous articles for the Hebrew weeklies and magazines.

Zweifel's granddaughter **Pauline Zweifel** is an opera-singer of international reputation. She graduated from the Warsaw Conservatorium, made her début at Milan, and sang at the opera house in Rio de Janeiro in 1905.

Bibliography: *Ha-Maggid*, xxxii., Nos. 41–45; *Ha-Meliẓ*, 1888, No. 38; *Ha-Asif*, v. 214; *Oẓar ha-Sifrut*, iv. 273–276; Paperna, in *Sefer ha-Shanah*, 1900, pp. 63 *et seq.*; Zeitlin, *Bibl. Post-Mendels.* p. 431.

H. R.   J. D. E.

ZWEIFEL, PAUL: German gynecologist; born at Höngg, near Zurich, Switzerland, June 30, 1848; educated at the University of Zurich (M.D. 1871). In 1871 he received the "venia legendi" at the University of Strasburg, where he had already become assistant in the gynecological institute. In 1876 he was appointed professor of gynecology at the University of Erlangen, and in 1887 he was transferred to Leipsic. He has the title "Geheimer Medizinal-Rat."

Zweifel has contributed over one hundred monographs to medical journals. Among his many works may be mentioned: "Ueber den Verdauungsapparat der Neugeborenen" (Strasburg, 1874); "Lehrbuch der Operativen Geburtshülfe" (Stuttgart, 1881; appeared as "Lehrbuch der Geburtshülfe," *ib.* 1887, 5th ed. 1901); "Der Einfluss der Aerztlichen Thätigkeit auf die Bevölkerungsbewegung" (*ib.* 1887); "Die Symphyseotomie" (*ib.* 1893); and "Aetiologie, Prophylaxis und Therapie der Rachitis" (*ib.* 1900).

Bibliography: Pagel, *Biog. Lex.*; *Meyers Konversations-Lexikon*; *Brockhaus Konversations-Lexikon*.

S.   F. T. H.

THE END.

LIST OF PATRONS

LIST OF PATRONS.

With this the concluding volume of THE JEWISH ENCYCLOPEDIA the FUNK & WAGNALLS COMPANY fulfil the promise made to their subscribers nearly eight years ago to supply the world at large with a full account of the history, views, and sociology of the Jewish people from their appearance in history down to the present day. The publishers feel that they may claim to have carried out their promise unstintingly, and with sole regard to thoroughness of workmanship. A few figures, which may be interesting in themselves, will suffice to substantiate this claim. The promise was made to provide twelve volumes containing 8,000 pages supplied by 400 contributors, and embellished by 2,000 illustrations. The twelve volumes contain 8,572 pages, written by 605 contributors, and supplemented by 2,464 illustrations, a large number of them full-page, with a considerable number of photogravures, and 23 reproduced in facsimile by lithographic process in colors. Of the merits of the work it is scarcely the publishers' place to speak, but the universal verdict of the press of the world has been that it presents its subjects in fulness of detail and with perfect impartiality of treatment. It has been the aim of the editorial board to present all sides of Jewish life from every standpoint held by any important section of the Jewish community. Imperfections there must needs be in a work of this scope, which has absolutely no forerunners by which it can be checked; but care has been taken to reduce these to a minimum by every device that has been suggested by the ingenuity of the editorial board or the experience of the publishing-house. In cases of doubt resort was had to the advice of the boards of consulting editors in Europe and America, especially on matters of general policy. During the making of the Encyclopedia the American board was unfortunately decreased by the regretted deaths of Dr. M. Mielziner and Dr. M. Jastrow, the latter of whom to the end of the second volume was editor of the Talmudic Department, and who showed his interest in the work by remaining a consulting editor till his death. The foreign board lost Prof. Moritz Lazarus, Dr. Eude Lolli, and Dr. Kayserling, the last of whom, besides acting as a consulting editor, contributed the largest number of articles to the Encyclopedia of all contributors other than the office staff.

The 8,168,957 words the presentation of which this volume completes have been selected for the reader from the 9,630,211 that were supplied by the contributors; or, in other words, one word out of every six has been eliminated in order to present the fullest amount of information within the space limits. By this use of the pruning-knife the alphabetical division of the volumes was made to coincide almost exactly with the schedule laid down before the first volume was issued. In this way alone it became possible to treat subjects in the later letters of the alphabet with just as much fulness as those in the earlier volumes.

As promised in the first volume, the Funk & Wagnalls Company repeat herewith the list of stanch friends of THE JEWISH ENCYCLOPEDIA who by their loyal trust have rendered the production of these volumes practicable. In an enterprise of this kind, addressed in the first place to a special public, the support of that public during the progress of the work is as necessary for its adequate completion as is the literary ability of the editorial board or the executive capacity of the publishing-house. The promises of the list of patrons contained in the first volume encouraged the Funk & Wagnalls Company to undertake the work; the fulfilment has enabled them to carry it through to what may be fairly termed a triumphant conclusion. They hereby render their thanks to those who throughout this arduous undertaking have stood by their side as silent but very efficacious helpers.

Unfortunately, great discrepancies exist between the former list and that now presented to the reader. Through misunderstanding, through ill health, or through failure of means, a number of the original subscribers found themselves unable to carry out their engagements, and at one time the Funk & Wagnalls Company had in view the suspension of the work owing to this lack of support. At this juncture a number of public-spirited gentlemen in America undertook to guarantee the sale of a certain number of copies of the Encyclopedia, and others in England, headed by Sir Isidore Spielmann, made an earnest and successful appeal for increased subscription. Thus encouraged, the Funk & Wagnalls Company determined to continue in a task which, if it promised no adequate profit, seemed to them a worthy contribution to the higher life of America and of the world. Sustained by the support of these gentlemen, the Funk & Wagnalls Company have spared no pains or expense to carry out the plans of the editorial board in their entirety, and trust that the work now presented to the reader is a worthy outcome of American constructive scholarship and of American publishing enterprise.

The names of the American public-spirited gentlemen referred to above are as follows:

NATHAN BIJUR
CHARLES S. HENRY
PHILIP S. HENRY
L. N. HERSHFIELD
ADOLPH LEWISOHN
*LEONARD LEWISOHN

LOUIS MARSHALL
M. WARLEY PLATZEK
*JACOB H. SCHIFF
JAMES SPEYER
LEOPOLD STERN

*LOUIS STERN
*ISIDOR STRAUS
C. L. SULZBERGER
MAYER SULZBERGER
FELIX M. WARBURG

*Deceased.

New York, Dec., 1905.

NORTH AND SOUTH AMERICA

A

Aaron, Isaac M................New York City
Aaron, Rev. Israel, D.D................Buffalo, N. Y.
Aaron, Louis I................Allegheny City, Pa.
Aaron, Marcus................Pittsburg, Pa.
Aaronsohn, Samuel J................Paterson, N. J.
Aaronson, Reuben................Baltimore, Md.
Aaronstamm, A. Stephen................New York City
Abeles, Charles T................Little Rock, Ark.
Abelman, Mayer................New York City
Abels, S................Brooklyn, N. Y.
Abelson, Rev. Alter................Jersey City, N. J.
Aberle, Daniel................St. Paul, Minn.
Ablowich, Rachel................New York City
Abraham, A................Brooklyn, N. Y.
Abraham, M................Brooklyn, N. Y.
Abrahams, Abe................Sheridan, Wyo.
Abrahams, Colman................Cincinnati, Ohio
Abrahams, Joseph B................New York City
Abrahams, Julius................Philadelphia, Pa.
Abrahams, M................Denver, Colo.
Abrahams, R., M.D................New York City
Abrahams, William................Philadelphia, Pa.
Abrahamson, Julius................Duluth, Minn.
Abrahamson, Rev. Robert................Portland, Ore.
Abrahamson, Mrs. W. M................Duluth, Minn.
Abramovitz, Louis................New York City
Abramowitz, A................Providence, R. I.
Abramson, Louis................Shreveport, La.
Abramson, Max................New York City
Acker, Henry F................New York City
Ackerman, Leon, M.D................New York City
Ackerman, S., Ph.G................New York City
Ackerman, Samuel................New York City
Adam, Hugo................New York City
Adams, Lionel................New Orleans, La.
Adams, Saul................Stamford, Conn.
Addelston, William M................New York City
Adelberg, A................Brooklyn, N. Y.
Adelman, L................Providence, R. I.
Adelsheimer, E................Minneapolis, Minn.
Adelstein, Hyman................New York City
Adelstein, Michael................Montreal, Canada
Adler, Chas. S................New York City
Adler, Cyrus, Ph.D................New York City
Adler, E. A................Rochester, N. Y.
Adler, Prof. Felix................New York City
Adler, Harris B., M.D................New York City
Adler, Isaac J................New York City
Adler, Jacob P................New York City
Adler, Levi................Rochester, N. Y.
Adler, Mrs. M. D................New York City
Adler, Max................New York City
Adler, Max................New Haven, Conn.
Adler, Paul................St. Louis, Mo.
Adler, Simon................New York City
Adler, William................New Orleans, La.
Agat, Rev. Isaiah, Ph.B................Chicago, Ill.
Agoos, L................Chelsea, Mass.
Aiken, Rev. S. J., D.D................New York City
Aisenman, Wolf................Manila, P. I.
Aizenman, Ralph................New York City
Albert, Charles................Cincinnati, Ohio
Albertstamm, Jacob D................Boston, Mass.
Alexander, A................New York City
Alexander, Abraham................New York City
Alexander, Bernard, A.M................New York City
Alexander, David................Toledo, Ohio
Alexander, E................New York City
Alexander, Henry................New York City
Alexander, Hugo................New York City
Alexander, James R................Orange Valley, N. J.

Alexander, Leo................New York City
Alexander, M................Ft. Worth, Tex.
Alexander, Nestor A. (deceased)................New York City
Alexander, W. M. F................New Orleans, La.
Algase, Harry D................New York City
Alkus, Isaac................Philadelphia, Pa.
Alkus, Morris................Philadelphia, Pa.
Allen, Isaac................New York City
Allen, Joseph E................Augusta, Ga.
Allenton, D. D................New York City
Alpern, Aaron H................Pittsburg, Pa.
Alpern, D................Pittsburg, Pa.
Alsberg, Irving N................New York City
Alter, Rev. M. A................Pittsburg, Pa.
Alterman, N................New York City
Altheimer, Ben................St. Louis, Mo.
Altman, A................New York City
Altman, Charles................New York City
Altman, Mrs. Louis................Portland, Ore.
Altman, Max................New York City
Altman, Max, M.D................New York City
Altman, Moritz................New York City
Altmayer, Max................New York City
Altschul, Samuel................New York City
Altschuler, Jacob................New York City
Altshul, Victor I................Jersey City, N. J.
Amdur, Rev. Bernard................Buffalo, N. Y.
Amdur, Louis................New York City
Amdursky, B................Pittsburg, Pa.
Amdursky, Henry................Pittsburg, Pa.
American, Sadie................New York City
Amman and Mackel................New York City
Amram, Miss Carrie E................Philadelphia, Pa.
Amram, David Werner................Philadelphia, Pa.
Amsinck, G................New York City
Amster, Moses................Richmond, Va.
Anable, E. Nott................Morristown, N. J.
Anauer, Henry F................New York City
Andrews, Rev. R. M................Kittrell, N. C.
Anrade, Jacob A................Jamaica, W. I.
Anspacher, Rev. Abraham S................Scranton, Pa.
Apfel, Ignace Irving................New York City
Apfel, M. Marion, M.D................Brooklyn, N. Y.
Apfelbaum, Edward E................New York City
Apfelbaum, Herman................New York City
Apfelbaum, Isidor................New York City
Apotheker, D................Philadelphia, Pa.
Applebaum, A. C................Detroit, Mich.
April, J................New York City
Apt, Morris................Philadelphia, Pa.
Arbib, Alexander................New York City
Arent, Herman................Jersey City, N. J.
Argow, Rev. William................Toledo, Ohio
Arkin, F................New York City
Arkin, Henry................Washington, D. C.
Arkin, M................New York City
Arkin, Raphael................New York City
Arkin, Simon................Chicago, Ill.
Arkin, William, D.D.S................New York City
Arkush, Reuben................New York City
Arnold, Arthur Straus................Philadelphia, Pa.
Arnold, Mrs. Miriam................Philadelphia, Pa.
Arnstein, Emanuel................New York City
Arnstein, Henry................New York City
Arnstein, I................New York City
Arnstein, Max................Knoxville, Tenn.
Aronowitz, M................Albany, N. Y.
Arons, Morris................New York City
Aronsohn, Samuel J................Paterson, N. J.
Aronson, H. D................New York City
Aronson, H. J................New York City
Aronson, I. Leonard................Pittsburg, Pa.

Aronson, Joseph	Boston, Mass.
Aronson, M.	Niagara Falls, N. Y.
Aronson, M.	New York City
Aronson, Morris	Boston, Mass.
Aronson, Oscar	New York City
Aronson, S.	New York City
Aronson, Saul	Brooklyn, N. Y.
Aronstam, J.	Springfield, Mass.
Aschaffenburg, A.	New Orleans, La.
Ascher, Simon	New York City
Aschheim, Mayer S.	New York City
Ash, Louis	New York City
Ash, Mark	New York City
Asher, Mrs. Joseph Mayor	New York City
Asher, Maurice, M.D.	Newark, N. J.
Asikowitz, E.	Boston, Mass.
Asinof, Mrs. Morris	New York City
Ast, J.	Newport News, Va.
Atkins, H. I.	Boston, Mass.
Atlas, S.	Washington, D. C.
Audenried, Charles Y.	Philadelphia, Pa.
Auer, M.	Cincinnati, Ohio
Auerhaim, S.	Bradford, Pa.
Auguss, Samuel	New York City
Augustus, N. G.	Okolona, Miss.
Augyal, Sam	New York City
Averbach, H.	Pittsburg, Pa.
Avner, Maurice Louis	Pittsburg, Pa.
Avrutine, J.	New York City
Avrutis, A.	New York City
Axilrod, J.	Cumberland, Wis.

B

Baar, Herman N.	New York City
Babad, Nathan M., M.D.	New York City
Babb, Joseph	New York City
Bache, Mrs. Semon	New York City
Bacher, Rudolph C.	New York City
Bachlin, David	Brooklyn, N. Y.
Bachrach, Julius	New York City
Bachrach, L.	Rondout, N. Y.
Bachrach, S. L.	New York City
Bachrach, Simon	Oakland, Cal.
Bachs, Herman	New York City
Backer, George	New York City
Bacon, Col. Alex. S.	New York City
Badanes, B. B.	New York City
Baehr, Herman	New York City
Baer, Harry E.	New York City
Baer, J. M.	Finleyville, Pa.
Baer, Morris	Pittsburg, Pa.
Baer, Paul	New York City
Baermann, J. B.	New York City
Baitler, Charles A.	Boston, Mass.
Baker, H. D.	New York City
Baker, Isaac	Erie, Pa.
Baker, Joseph E.	New Rochelle, N. Y.
Bakst, Joseph	New York City
Balchowsky, C. H.	Frankfort Station, Ill.
Baldauf, Morris	Henderson, Ky.
Baldwin, A.	New Orleans, La.
Balser, Joshua S.	Baltimore, Md.
Balter, Joseph	Cleveland, Ohio
Bamberger, Jacob	Baltimore, Md.
Bamberger, Jacob	Baltimore, Md.
Bamberger, Mrs. Jacob	Salt Lake City, Utah
Bamberger, Louis	Newark, N. J.
Bamberger, Max	Philadelphia, Pa.
Bamberger, Mrs. Simon	Salt Lake City, Utah
Bame, Abram	Brooklyn, N. Y.
Bandman, Albert, D.D.S.	New York City
Bank, A. M.	New York City
Barash, Pincus J.	New York City
Barcus, Dr. A. L.	Philadelphia, Pa.
Barkhouse, Louis	Louisville, Ky.
Barkman, A.	East Tawas, Mich.
Barnet, H. M.	St. Paul, Minn.
Barnett, Hyman I., LL.B.	New York City
Barnett, J., M.D.	New Orleans, La.
Barnett, Miss Ray	New York City
Barnstein, Rev. H., Ph.D.	Houston, Tex.
Baron, Paul	New York City
Barondess, Joseph	New York City
Barr, Nathan M.	Brooklyn, N. Y.
Barron, Hyman	Boston, Mass.
Barth, Leopold	New York City
Bartler, Chas. A.	Boston, Mass.
Barton, George A.	Bryn Mawr, Pa.
Baruch, B. M.	New York City
Baruth, Herman	New York City
Barwell, Jno. W.	Waukegan, Ill.
Basch, G.	New York City
Basch, Joseph	Columbus, Ohio
Bash, Henrietta	Philadelphia, Pa.
Bashlow, Louis	New York City
Bass, Mayer	Brooklyn, N. Y.
Bassel, M.	New York City
Batchelor, J. M., M.D.	New Orleans, La.
Bath, A. A.	Shreveport, La.

Bauer, Madame Julie H.	Portland, Ore.
Bauer, S.	Somerville, N. J.
Bauer, Rev. Sol	Chicago, Ill.
Bauerberg, Paul J., M.D.	Yonkers, N. Y.
Baum, Henry	New York City
Baum, Joseph	Fort Wayne, Ind.
Baum, Joseph, M.D.	New York City
Baum, Rev. Solomon	New York City
Baum, Soma, M.D.	Passaic, N. J.
Baumgarden, Ben	Chicago, Ill.
Baumgart, Isidor	Brooklyn, N. Y.
Baumgarten, Herman	Washington, D. C.
Baumgarten, Julius	Washington, D. C.
Bayard, Harris	Chelsea, Mass.
Bazel, Rev. Jacob M.	Braddock, Pa.
Beck, Charles	New York City
Becker, A. G.	Chicago, Ill.
Beckhardt, Moses	New York City
Beckman, S.	Beaver Falls, Pa.
Beer, Bertrand	New Orleans, La.
Beer, Sophia	New York City
Beerger, Bernhard	Philadelphia, Pa.
Behren, A. H.	New York City
Behren, Louis D.	New York City
Behrend, Jacob	Philadelphia, Pa.
Behrman, J.	Portland, Ore.
Beisman, Joseph, M.D.	Detroit, Mich.
Belais, David	New York City
Belasco, David	New York City
Belber, M. Y., D.D.S.	Philadelphia, Pa.
Belkowsky, Isidor, M.D.	Cleveland, Ohio
Bell, Victor C.	New York City
Beller, A.	New York City
Beller, Jacob	New York City
Beller, M.	New York City
Beller, Wolf	New York City
Benari, S. L.	Brooklyn, N. Y.
Benatar, Louis	Newark, N. J.
Benchman, S.	New York City
Bendheim, Ferdinand	Altoona, Pa.
Bendit, Sig. L.	New York City
Bendon, George	Brooklyn, N. Y.
Benedict, Julian	New York City
Benedict, W. S.	New Orleans, La.
Benerofe, Abraham	New York City
Benisch, Miss Leah	Brooklyn, N. Y.
Benjamin, E. V.	New Orleans, La.
Benjamin, F. D.	Toronto, Ont., Canada
Benjamin, M. M.	Minneapolis, Minn.
Benjamin, Morris W.	New York City
Benn, Marcus A.	Philadelphia, Pa.
Benno, Joseph	Buffalo, N. Y.
Bensdorf, Herman	Memphis, Tenn.
Bentson, B. L.	Fargo, N. Dak.
Bercinsky, D., M.D.	New Haven, Conn.
Bercou, J.	New Rochelle, N. Y.
Bercovitch, Peter	Montreal, Canada
Berdy, Louis	New York City
Berenberg, Bernhard	Brooklyn, N. Y.
Berg, Gertrude	Philadelphia, Pa.
Berg, Max	Philadelphia, Pa.
Berg, Simon	New York City
Bergen, Samuel	Yonkers, N. Y.
Berger, B. H.	New York City
Berger, Samuel	New York City
Bergman, J.	New York City
Bergman, Joseph L.	Boston, Mass.
Bergman, M.	New Orleans, La.
Bergmann, Max	New York City
Bergstein, S.	Youngstown, Ohio
Beringer, Leopold	New York City
Berkenstein, H.	Charleston, W. Va.
Berkman, Simon	Pittsburg, Pa.
Berkovitz, H.	Somerville, N. J.
Berkovitz, Joseph	Philadelphia, Pa.
Berkowich, Louis I.	New York City
Berkowitz, Adolph	Philadelphia, Pa.
Berkowitz, Armin	Hamilton, Ohio
Berkowitz, Emil	New York City
Berkowitz, G. D.	New York City
Berkowitz, Rev. Henry	Philadelphia, Pa.
Berkowitz, James	New York City
Berkowitz, Leon	New York City
Berkowitz, Leon M.	Newark, N. J.
Berkowitz, Wm. J.	Kansas City, Mo.
Berkson, Henry	New York City
Berlin, Joseph	Roxbury, Mass.
Berlin, S. M.	Brooklyn, N. Y.
Berliner, David	New York City
Berliner, Julius	Brooklyn, N. Y.
Berliner, Lazar	Brooklyn, N. Y.
Berliner, M.	New York City
Berlinger, Rabbi	New York City
Berman, Adolph	Corinth, Ky.
Berman, Adolph	Findlay, Ohio
Berman, B.	Detroit, Mich.
Berman, Isidor	New York City
Berman, M.	Altoona, Pa.
Berman, Nathan A.	New York City

Berman, Tobias	Boston, Mass.
Bermann, Leon	New York City
Bermann, Philip	New York City
Bermon, Monist	New York City
Bernays, Ely	New York City
Bernhard, Abraham	Brooklyn, N. Y.
Bernheim, B	Louisville, Ky.
Bernheim, Chas. S	New York City
Bernheim, Gustave	New York City
Bernheim, Isaac W	Louisville, Ky.
Bernheimer, Beatrice	New York City
Bernheimer, Chas. S	Philadelphia, Pa.
Bernheimer, Max E	New York City
Bernheimer, Mayer S	New York City
Bernkopf, David	Providence, R. I.
Bernstein, A	Chicago, Ill.
Bernstein, A	New York City
Bernstein, A. M	Rochester, N. Y.
Bernstein, Adolph	Marshalltown, Iowa
Bernstein, Alex	Portland, Ore.
Bernstein, Barnet	New York City
Bernstein, Bernard	New York City
Bernstein, C	New York City
Bernstein, C. L	Utica, N. Y.
Bernstein, Charles	Marshalltown, Iowa
Bernstein, D. S	Evansville, Ind.
Bernstein, Ernest Ralph	Shreveport, La.
Bernstein, Eugene A	New York City
Bernstein, H	New York City
Bernstein, H	New York City
Bernstein, H. A., M.D	New York City
Bernstein, Henry	Philadelphia, Pa.
Bernstein, I	Chelsea, Mass.
Bernstein, Isaac	New York City
Bernstein, Julius A	New York City
Bernstein, L. I., D.D.S	Philadelphia, Pa.
Bernstein, M. M	Charleston, S. C.
Bernstein, Morris	New York City
Bernstein, Myer	New York City
Bernstein, Robt. B	New York City
Bernstein, S. I	New York City
Berrent, Abraham	New York City
Bertzer, Max	New York City
Berxon, J. B	New York City
Better, Alexander	New York City
Beyer, L. H	New York City
Bialosky, Louis	Cleveland, Ohio
Bialostosky, S	New York City
Biegeleisen, A., M.D	New York City
Bieher, Leopold	New York City
Bienenfeld, Bernard	San Francisco, Cal.
Bienenfeld, Chas	New York City
Bierman, A. E	New York City
Bijur, Nathan	New York City
Binswanger, Barnett	Philadelphia, Pa.
Binswanger, S. J	New York City
Biolostosky, S	New York City
Birkenfeld, Ben	New York City
Birkhahn, Charles D	New York City
Birkhahn, Max S	New York City
Bischof, Louis	Crawfordsville, Ind.
Biscow, B	New York City
Bishop, Rev. Hutchins C	New York City
Biskind, I. J., M.D	Cleveland, Ohio
Blachschleger, Abe	Cincinnati, Ohio
Black, E. Martin	New York City
Black, Geo. N	Los Angeles, Cal.
Black, Harris	Chicago, Ill.
Black, Julius	Nashville, Tenn.
Black, N. & Co	Norfolk, Va.
Blain, John	New York City
Blaine, L	New York City
Blank, Jacob C	Camden, N. J.
Blankfurst, Bernard	New York City
Blatt, Isidor	San Francisco, Cal.
Blatt, Rev. Joseph	Columbus, Ga.
Blattner, I. S	McKeesport, Pa.
Blau, William	New York City
Blaustein, Solomon	Baltimore, Md.
Blaustein, Solomon	Montreal, Canada
Blectstein, M	New York City
Bleiman, A., M.D	New York City
Blender Brothers	Chicago, Ill.
Bleyer, Leo	New York City
Blieden, Gustave L	Philadelphia, Pa.
Blinnauer, Louis	Portland, Ore.
Bliss, Barnett, D.D.S	New York City
Blitzer, Bernhard	New York City
Bloch, Abe	Cincinnati, Ohio
Bloch, B. B	Philadelphia, Pa.
Bloch, Bernhard	New York City
Bloch, Edward	New York City
Bloch, H	Yonkers, N. Y.
Bloch, Israel	New York City
Bloch, Rev. Dr. J	Portland, Ore.
Bloch, Joseph C	Cleveland, Ohio
Bloch, Louis	Philadelphia, Pa.
Bloch, Moses L	Philadelphia, Pa.
Bloch, N	St. Louis, Mo.
Bloch, Simon L	Philadelphia, Pa.
Blochman, A	San Diego, Cal.
Block, Alexander, M.D	Pueblo, Colo.
Block, B	Houston, Tex.
Block, Bernhard	New York City
Block, David	New York City
Block, H	Chicago, Ill.
Block, Harris	Chicago, Ill.
Block, S	Brooklyn, N. Y.
Blondheim, Solomon	Baltimore, Md.
Bloom, A	Rochester, N. Y.
Bloom, Benjamin	New York City
Bloom, M	New York City
Bloom, M. L	Baltimore, Md.
Bloom, Max J	Brooklyn, N. Y.
Bloom, Moses	New York City
Bloom, R	New York City
Bloom, Dr. S. N	Louisville, Ky.
Bloom, Simon	Fall River, Mass.
Bloomfield, M	Boston, Mass.
Bloomingdale, Lyman G. (deceased)	East Des Moines, Iowa
Blotcky, Joseph	East Des Moines, Iowa
Bluestone, J. I., M.D	New York City
Blum, Benj	Calumet, Mich.
Blum Brothers	Bellaire, Ohio
Blum, C. H	Nitta Yuma, Miss.
Blum, Edward C	Brooklyn, N. Y.
Blum, Gabriel	Philadelphia, Pa.
Blum, Leon	Galveston, Tex.
Blumauer, Louis	Portland, Ore.
Blumauer, Simon	New York City
Blumberg, Siegfried	New York City
Blumberg, Wm	Shreveport, La.
Blume, Max	Scranton, Pa.
Blumenberg, Marc A	New York City
Blumenfeld, M	Cleveland, Ohio
Blumenstein, Isaac L	New Haven, Conn.
Blumenstiel, A	New York City
Blumenthal, D	Detroit, Mich.
Blumenthal, E. E	New York City
Blumenthal, H	Memphis, Tenn.
Blumenthal, H. B	Philadelphia, Pa.
Blumenthal, H. S	Detroit, Mich.
Blumenthal, Herman	Washington, D. C.
Blumenthal, Sol	Philadelphia, Pa.
Blumgart, Louis	New York City
Blumrosen, B	Sault Ste. Marie, Mich.
Blumrosen, M	Detroit, Mich.
Blunn, F. S. M	New York City
Bodenheimer, H	Shreveport, La.
Bodesch, Adolf	New York City
Bodys, A. C	Washington, D. C.
Boehm, A	New York City
Boehm, Samuel C	New York City
Bogart, John	New York City
Bogen, B., Ph.D	Cincinnati, Ohio
Bohys, A. C	Washington, D. C.
Bojarsky, E. H	Berwick, La.
Bollack, M	Oregon City, Ore.
Bolland, L	Manistee, Mich.
Bolstow, Louis	Providence, R. I.
Bomash, Louis	Chicago, Ill.
Bomfild, Philip	New York City
Bondi, August	Salina, Kan.
Bondy, Adolph	Chicago, Ill.
Bondy, Eugene	New York City
Bonner, Adolph, M.D	New York City
Bonnheim, A	Sacramento, Cal.
Bonnheim, Benjamin A	Las Vegas, N. Mex.
Bonoff, Elias M	New York City
Bonwit, Paul J	New York City
Borchardt, Benj	Brunswick, Ga.
Borchardt, M	New York City
Borcherd, Henry	New York City
Borg, Mrs. Simon	New York City
Borgenicht, Louis	New York City
Born, M	Chicago, Ill.
Bornstein, Moses	New York City
Bornstein, S	Denver, Colo.
Borofsky, Samuel H	Boston, Mass.
Borovsky, Hyman	Boston, Mass.
Borsodi, William	New York City
Borsuk, Max	New York City
Bortin, Morris	Brooklyn, N. Y.
Botealin, Henry L	Middletown, Conn.
Botein, H. W., D.D.S	New York City
Bottigheimer, Rev. S. G	Natchez, Miss.
Bouder, Rev. A. T	Pittsburg, Pa.
Boudin, L. Boudianoff	New York City
Boyers, J. H	Troy, N. Y.
Brady, F	Lancaster, Pa.
Brager, Albert A	Baltimore, Md.
Brager, Sam A	New York City
Bragin, Aaron S	New York City
Brainin, S. M., M.D	New York City
Brand, Chas	New York City
Brand, Robt	New York City
Brandon, D. H	Panama, C. Am.
Brandon, Emanuel	North Beach, L. I., N. Y.

Brandon, Isaac....................New York City
Brandon, James....................New York City
Brandstadter, H...................New York City
Brandt, Louis.....................New York City
Braneman, Isidore....................Clifton, N. J.
Brann, Herman.....................New York City
Branner, B........................New York City
Brash, Edward M...................Lancaster, Pa.
Braslan, A., M.D..................New York City
Braude, Rev. Moses J.............Syracuse, N. Y.
Braude, Paul......................Chicago, Ill.
Brauer, Robert....................New York City
Braun, Henry A., D.D..............New York City
Braun, Herman.....................New York City
Braun, Max......................New Orleans, La.
Braun, Philip......................Pittsburg, Pa.
Braunfeld, Julius...............New Orleans, La.
Braunstein, W. S..................New York City
Brav, Herman A., M.D............Philadelphia, Pa.
Breakstone, Isaac.................New York City
Brechhoefer, Charles..............St. Paul, Minn.
Breitstein, Elias.............San Francisco, Cal.
Brener, Jacob...................New Orleans, La.
Brenner, George....................Pittsburg, Pa.
Brenner, Jacob.................Newport News, Va.
Brenner, S. H...................Kansas City, Mo.
Brenner, Victor...................New York City
Breschel, Adolph.................Syracuse, N. Y.
Breslauer, L......................New York City
Bresler, Simon L., Ph.D., Ph.G......Denver, Colo.
Bressler, David M.................New York City
Breyer, Fritz.....................New York City
Brez, Colman...................Washington, D. C.
Brice, A. G.....................New Orleans, La.
Bricks, Fritz.....................New York City
Brieger, Adolph...................New York City
Brill, Rev. Abram..................Helena, Ark.
Brill, Rev. Nathan.................Helena, Ark.
Brilleman, Isaac...................Albany, N. Y.
Brilling, Harry....................Detroit, Mich.
Brinn, Simon......................New York City
Briodo, George....................New York City
Britner, E. M.....................Pittsburg, Pa.
Brobston, Edwin.................Jacksonville, Fla.
Brodey, Ike.....................Toronto, Canada
Brodezky, Rudolph.................New York City
Brodie, Israel B..................Baltimore, Md.
Brodkey, Sol.......................Omaha, Neb.
Brody, Bertha R...................New York City
Brody, E. J......................Boston, Mass.
Brody, F......................Des Moines, Iowa
Brody, Henry A....................New York City
Bromberg, Dr. Bernard B..........New York City
Bromberg, Boris...................Newark, N. J.
Bromberg, I. G...................Mineola, Tex.
Bromberg, M.......................Chicago, Ill.
Bromberg, Sol...................Galveston, Tex.
Brond, Adolph.....................New York City
Bronde, Joseph....................Pittsburg, Pa.
Brondy, Ely.......................New York City
Bronenberg, Abraham ....Philadelphia, Pa.
Bronner, Harvey....................Keyport, N. J.
Bronner, Leonard ....New York City
Bronstein, Max....................Baltimore, Md.
Brook, H., M.D....................St. Louis, Mo.
Brooks, George B...............Providence, R. I.
Broomberg, Abram..................New York City
Browarsky, Marks..................Pittsburg, Pa.
Browarsky, Sol.....................Chicago, Ill.
Brown, A. B........................Pittston, Pa.
Brown, Abe.....................McKeesport, Pa.
Brown, Albert......................Pittston, Pa.
Brown, Charles R...............Galveston, Tex.
Brown & Co.....................Brunswick, Ga.
Brown, Emanuel ....Buffalo, N. Y.
Brown, George.....................New York City
Brown, Dr. Israel.................Norfolk, Va.
Brown, W.......................Brooklyn, N. Y.
Browne, Edw. B. M..............Columbus, Ga.
Brownstein, J. B..............New Haven, Conn.
Brownstein, S., M.D................Chicago, Ill.
Brozen, I.........................New York City
Bruce, David D. B..............Philadelphia, Pa.
Bruck, George.....................New York City
Brucke, Charles H.................New York City
Bruckheimer, Samuel...............New York City
Bruder, Joseph, M.D...............New York City
Bruenn, Bernard................New Orleans, La.
Bruenn, Louis L...................New York City
Brunn, A. W.......................New York City
Bruno, Herman.....................Lincoln, Neb.
Bry, Louis.........................St. Louis, Mo.
Bryan, Rev. D.................Albuquerque, N. Mex.
Bryan, W. J.......................Lincoln, Neb.
Bucbaum, Sam......................New York City
Buchanan, Chas. J.................Albany, N. Y.
Buchanan, S. H., D.D............McGregor, Tex.
Buchman, R........................New York City
Buchsbaum, Aaron ....New York City

Buckbinder, Harry................Newark, N. J.
Budge, Henry......................New York City
Budwin, Mrs. Theo..............Spokane, Wash.
Buechler, H....................Morristown, N. J.
Buegeleisen, Samuel...............New York City
Buhr, Fannie...................Philadelphia, Pa.
Burg, S., M.D..................San Antonio, Tex.
Burger, L.........................New York City
Burger, Sam I.................Texarkana, Ark.
Burgheim, J.......................Houston, Tex.
Burk, Charles....................Baltimore, Md.
Burke, Dr. Harris..............Brooklyn, N. Y.
Burke, Bishop T. M. A.............Albany, N. Y.
Burkes, Leon......................New York City
Burnce, M. L. (deceased)........Boston, Mass.
Burner, George A..............Minneapolis, Minn.
Burnstine, Bernard.............Washington, D. C.
Burros, Joseph......................Scranton, Pa.
Burstein, S. P., M.D...........New Haven, Conn.
Burstein, Samuel H................New York City
Burtsell, Rev. Richard L., D.D......Rondout, N. Y.
Busch, S..........................Chicago, Ill.
Bussner, Albert...................New York City
Bussner, Simon....................New York City
Buttenwieser, Joseph L............New York City
Buttenwieser, Dr. Moses.........Cincinnati, Ohio.
Butter, Samuel...................Boston, Mass.
Buttner, S........................New York City
Buttner, Simon....................New York City
Bychower, Victor, M.D...........Boston, Mass.
Byer, Alexander.................Cincinnati, Ohio
Byron, Marcus..................Brooklyn, N. Y.

C

Cabelinsky, Simon................Boston, Mass.
Cahan, S. H....................Philadelphia, Pa.
Cahan, Mrs. Leopold...............New York City
Cahn, Bertrand I...............New Orleans, La.
Cahn, Edgar M..................New Orleans, La.
Cahn, Sigmund............Richmond Hill, L. I., N. Y.
Cain, J. L.....................New Orleans, La.
Caldwell, Aaron................Tiptonville, Tenn.
Calisch, Rev. Edward N...........Richmond, Va.
Callmann, Carl....................New York City
Calmenson, Moses...............St. Paul, Minn.
Calthrop, Rev. S. R............Syracuse, N. Y.
Caminez, Jacob.................Brooklyn, N. Y.
Camnitzer, A., M.D...............New York City
Canister, P., M.D.................New York City
Cannold, H.....................Brooklyn, N. Y.
Cantarow, Jacob................Hartford, Conn.
Cantor, B......................Brooklyn, N. Y.
Cantor, David................San Francisco, Cal.
Cantor, Jacob A...................New York City
Cantor, Samuel, M.D...............New York City
Caplan, G..........................Pittsburg, Pa.
Caplan, H...................Montreal, Quebec, Canada
Caplan, H. L...................Baltimore, Md.
Caplan, M. L....................Denver, Colo.
Caplin, Myer....................Baltimore, Md.
Caplin, Stephen...................New York City
Cardozo, Michael H.............New York City
Carey, Rev. Joseph............Saratoga Springs, N. Y.
Carlos, A.........................New York City
Carmin, M...................Montreal, Quebec, Canada
Caro, Rev. V.....................Milwaukee, Wis.
Carpenter, E. Z...............Schenectady, N. Y.
Carr, Sydney H.................Brooklyn, N. Y.
Casanowiez, I. M..............Washington, D. C.
Caspe, A., M.D....................New York City
Caspe, M., M.D....................New York City
Cassel, Sam.......................New York City
Castelberg, Joseph...............Baltimore, Md.
Cator, George...................Baltimore, Md.
Chajes, Herman..................Bayonne, N. J.
Chalmers, Rev. Thomas M........Leipsic, Germany
Chandler, Walter M................New York City
Chapman, Halla Finley, D.D.S.....Fort Scott, Kan.
Chapman, Rev. J. Wilbur, D.D.....Winona Lake, Ind.
Charak, Isaac...................Boston, Mass.
Charosh, Israel ....New York City
Chase, Isidore.................Waterbury, Conn.
Chaska, S.....................Fort Wayne, Ind.
Chattanooga Public Library.......Chattanooga, Tenn.
Chavin, Morris....................New York City
Chelimer, Morris B................New York City
Chertoff, J.....................Cleveland, Ohio
Chetkin, Philip, M.D...........Brooklyn, N. Y.
Chuck, R. W.......................New York City
Ciner, Emanuel....................New York City
Cisin, M., M.D....................New York City
Citron, Dr. G. B..................New York City
Clark, Mrs. L., Jr................New York City
Clarkson, A. V....................New York City
Claybrook, Rev. Willoughby N........Tyler, Tex.
Clegg, Hon. John...............New Orleans, La.
Clemhalert, Abraham............New Haven, Conn.
Clemons, Miss Julia...............New York City
Clifford, Rev. Cornelius.......Morristown, N. J.

Clint, Hon. Chas. F....................Dallas, Tex.
Cobe, M. H......................Boston, Mass.
Coffee, Rudolph I.................New York City
Cogan, Henry, LL.B...............New York City
Cohen, A........................New York City
Cohen, A.................Montreal, Quebec, Canada
Cohen, A. A.....................Florence, S. C.
Cohen, Aaron....................New York City
Cohen, Alfred M.................Cincinnati, Ohio
Cohen, B.....................Washington, D. C.
Cohen, Benjamin.................Baltimore, Md.
Cohen, Benjamin L................Boston, Mass.
Cohen, Benno..................Jersey City, N. J.
Cohen, D......................New York City
Cohen, D. Solis..................Portland, Ore.
Cohen, E. T....................New York City
Cohen, Emanuel................Minneapolis, Minn.
Cohen, Ephraim..................Boston, Mass.
Cohen, Rev. Fred................Omaha, Neb.
Cohen, H.....................Meriden, Conn.
Cohen, Harry....................New York City
Cohen, Henry...................St. Louis, Mo.
Cohen, Rev. Henry...............Galveston, Tex.
Cohen, Herman..................New York City
Cohen, Hyman..................New York City
Cohen, I....................Newport News, Va.
Cohen, I. B.................New Rochelle, N. Y.
Cohen, Rev. Isaac J..................Dallas, Tex.
Cohen, Isidor..................Sacramento, Cal.
Cohen, Isidor......................Miami, Fla.
Cohen, J. (deceased)..............Chelsea, Mass.
Cohen, J. M.......................Cardiff, Ill.
Cohen, J. Solis, M.D............Philadelphia, Pa.
Cohen, Jacob.....................Chicago, Ill.
Cohen, Jacob G..................Yonkers, N. Y.
Cohen, James..................Somerville, Mass.
Cohen, James...................Pittsburg, Pa.
Cohen, Joseph...............Port Chester, N. Y.
Cohen, Joseph H.................New York City
Cohen, Josiah...................Pittsburg, Pa.
Cohen, Julius...................New York City
Cohen, Julius C.................Pittsburg, Pa.
Cohen, L......................New York City
Cohen, L. I....................New York City
Cohen, Lewis..................Bloomsburg, Pa.
Cohen, Lewis J.................Baltimore, Md.
Cohen, Louis...................New York City
Cohen, Louis B................Philadelphia, Pa.
Cohen, Lyon.............Montreal, Quebec, Canada
Cohen, M. A....................Norfolk, Va.
Cohen, M. H...................Nashua, N. H.
Cohen, M. W...................Boston, Mass.
Cohen, Mark...................Toronto, Canada
Cohen, Marks I.................Boston, Mass.
Cohen, Miss Mary M. ....Philadelphia, Pa.
Cohen, Maurice.................Toronto, Canada
Cohen, Max...................Cleveland, Ohio
Cohen, Max....................New York City
Cohen, Mendes..................Baltimore, Md.
Cohen, Meyer................Washington, D. C.
Cohen, Rev. Montague N. A........Sacramento, Cal.
Cohen, Morris...............New Haven, Conn.
Cohen, Morris..................Worcester, Mass.
Cohen, Morris..................New York City
Cohen, Moses S.................Baltimore, Md.
Cohen, N....................Waupaca, Wis.
Cohen, Nathaniel ....New York City
Cohen, Mrs. Robert I............Galveston, Tex.
Cohen, S......................Windbor, Pa.
Cohen, S. J....................Boston, Mass.
Cohen, Selig..................Wilkesbarre, Pa.
Cohen, Siegfried ....New York City
Cohen, Rev. Simon R..............Norfolk, Va.
Cohen, Solomon Solis............Philadelphia, Pa.
Cohen, The Misses...............Baltimore, Md.
Cohn, Abe....................New York City
Cohn, Alfred E..................New York City
Cohn, Emanuel..................New York City
Cohn, Rev. Frederick, M.A........Omaha, Neb.
Cohn, George..................New York City
Cohn, H.....................Nashville, Tenn.
Cohn, Harris.................Philadelphia, Pa.
Cohn, Harry..................New York City
Cohn, Herman..................Chicago, Ill.
Cohn, Isidore..................New York City
Cohn, J.....................Seattle, Wash.
Cohn, Jacob...................St. Louis, Mo.
Cohn, Kaspar E................Los Angeles, Cal.
Cohn, Leopold.................Brooklyn, N. Y.
Cohn, M.....................St. Louis, Mo.
Cohn, M.....................New York City
Cohn, Mark M.................Little Rock, Ark.
Cohn, Max...................Los Angeles, Cal.
Cohn, Michael A., M.D..........Brooklyn, N. Y.
Cohn, Morris..................New York City
Cohn, Morris M................Little Rock, Ark.
Cohn, Nathan.................Nashville, Tenn.
Cohn, S.....................Detroit, Mich.
Cohn, Samuel ....New York City

Cohn, William H.................Pittsburg, Pa.
Coleman, Nathan ....New York City
Colwell, Irving S................Auburn, N. Y.
Conay, M....................New York City
Cone, Mrs. Herman..............Baltimore, Md.
Conheim, Hermann...............New York City
Considine, Rev. M. J.............New York City
Content, H...................New York City
Coons, Mrs. Eva ....Philadelphia, Pa.
Coons, Joseph D................Wilkesbarre, Pa.
Cooper, Leon..................New York City
Cooper, Levi..................Shreveport, La.
Cooper, Michael ....New York City
Coplin, Meyer.................Baltimore, Md.
Corbly, Pres. L. J...............Huntington, W. Va.
Cordish, I...................Baltimore, Md.
Corn, Samuel..................New York City
Cornell University Library..........Ithaca, N. Y.
Covitz, A. Pascal ....Chicago, Ill.
Cowen, Mrs. Bertha..............Chicago, Ill.
Cowen, Israel ....Chicago, Ill.
Cowen, Leo ....New York City
Cowen, N....................New York City
Craiger, Sherman Montrose.........Washington, D. C.
Crockin, Emil.................Baltimore, Md.
Crockin, H...................Norfolk, Va.
Cronin, Rev. Edmund W...........New York City
Crunden, F. M.................St. Louis, Mo.
Crystal, J...................Baltimore, Md.
Cukor, Morris ....New York City
Cullian, A...................Lawrence, Mass.
Cummings, Martin B.............Brooklyn, N. Y.
Cunnion, Rev. M. A.............New York City
Curran, Rev. Edward F.........St. Johns, Newfoundland
Currick, Max C.................Erie, Pa.
Curry, Rev. James B........Cornwall-on-Hudson, N. Y.
Cusack, Bishop Thos. F............New York City
Cusher, Louis M................Cincinnati, Ohio
Cutler Bros...................Brooklyn, N. Y.
Cutner, S. A..................New York City

D

Daland, Rev. Wm. C., D.D..........Milton, Wis.
Daly, Rev. William J. B............New York City
Dana, Myer...................Boston, Mass.
Danciger, Mrs. Annie............Kansas City, Mo.
Danenbaum, M. C...............New York City
Daniels, Abraham G.............Boston, Mass.
Dannenberg, Adolph.............Bridgeport, Conn.
Danson, B...................Toronto, Canada
Danzis, M., M.D................Newark, N. J.
Dart, William P...............New Orleans, La.
Daub, William.................New York City
Daus, F. F...................New York City
Daust, Adolph.................St. Louis, Mo.
Davidow, A. D., M.D.............Florida, N. Y.
Davidson, David ....New York City
Davidson, David ....Sioux City, Iowa
Davidson, Mrs. E...............Minneapolis, Minn.
Davidson, Isaac................Baltimore, Md.
Davidson, Isaac T..............San Diego, Cal.
Davidson, K. M., M.D...........Boston, Mass.
Davidson, L. L., M.D............Newark, N. J.
Davidson, L. S.................New York City
Davidson, M. I.................Brooklyn, N. Y.
Davidson, Rev. R...............Pittsburg, Pa.
Davidson, S...................New York City
Davis, B....................Pittsburg, Pa.
Davis, Benjamin ....Chicago, Ill.
Davis, D. S..................San Francisco, Cal.
Davis, David..................Syracuse, N. Y.
Davis, David T................New York City
Davis, E....................New York City
Davis, H. I., M.D...............Chicago, Ill.
Davis, Ike..................Las Vegas, N. Mex.
Davis, James..................Chicago, Ill.
Davis, M....................New York City
Davis, Mrs. S.................Pittsburg, Pa.
Davis, Solomon...............Washington, D. C.
Dawedoff, Max................Denver, Colo.
De Groot, Benjamin E.............Troy, N. Y.
Degutz & Schnitzer ....Brooklyn, N. Y.
Deinstag, Mrs. B................Chicago, Ill.
De Lee, Solomon T..............Chicago, Ill.
Dembitz, Lewis N...............Louisville, Ky.
De Meza, J. E.................New Orleans, La.
Denigre, George................New Orleans, La.
Dent, Hon. Marmaduke H..........Charleston, W. Va.
De Pinna, Alfred ....New York City
Deues, Rev. Francis C............New York City
Deutelbaum, Leopold ....Chicago, Ill.
Deutsch, Prof. Gotthard, Ph.D.......Cincinnati, Ohio
Deutsch, Leo..................New York City
Deutsch, S...................Chicago, Ill.
Deutschman, Selig..............San Antonio, Tex.
De Watloff, Dr. D..............Brooklyn, N. Y.
De Wolf, Edwin A..............St. Louis, Mo.
Dey, Anthony..................New York City
Diamond, Harry................Pittsburg, Pa.

Diamond, J.............................Montreal, Canada
Diamond, Julius........................Tallahassee, Fla.
Dickelman, L. H..............................Forest, Ohio
Dickinson, Charles H..............Grand Rapids, Minn.
Dilsheimer, F..........................Philadelphia, Pa.
Dine, Joseph...............................Boston, Mass.
Dine, Philip.............................Cincinnati, Ohio
Dischler, M.................................Baltimore, Md.
Disston, Mrs. R. A....................Philadelphia, Pa.
Dittenhoefer, A. J.....................New York City
Dittenhofer, Jacob......................St. Paul, Minn.
Dittman, Charlotte.....................New York City
Dix, Henry A................................Millville, N. J.
Dixon, William A.........................Covington, La.
Dlugasch, M.............................New York City
Doering, William George............Cincinnati, Ohio
Doktorsky, H..............................Chicago, Ill.
Dominger, E...............................New York City
Doniger, Henry...........................New York City
Doob, Irving Ephraim..................New York City
Dorfmann, S. A., M.D..................New York City
Douglas, Charles.........................New York City
Douglass, S. D., M.D...................New York City
Dover, Max.................................Shreveport, La.
Dowie, Rev. John Alexander........Zion City, Ill.
Drachman, Benjamin....................Jersey City, N. J.
Drachman, Rev. Bernard, Ph.D.......New York City
Draifuss, Isaac..............................Danville, Pa.
Draper, Mrs. Henry.....................New York City
Dreeben, M. B............................Henderson, Tex.
Dreinel, Adolph..........................Brooklyn, N. Y.
Dreyer, Moritz W., M.D...............Brooklyn, N. Y.
Dreyfus, Edward.............................Oakland, Cal.
Dreyfus, Louis..........................New Iberia, La.
Dreyfus, Mrs. Moise......................Chicago, Ill.
Dreyfus, William, D.Sc................New York City
Dreyfuss, Sol................................Paducah, Ky.
Dropsie, Moses A.......................Philadelphia, Pa.
Drucker, A. P.............................Woodville, Miss.
Druckerman, Max........................Brooklyn, N. Y.
Druckerman, Samuel A.................Brooklyn, N. Y.
Druckman, B............................Montreal, Canada
Druckman, S..............................New York City
Dryer, Dr. Moritz.......................Brooklyn, N. Y.
Dubman, Charles.........................New York City
Ducey, Rev. Thomas I..................New York City
Ducker, Sol...............................New York City
Duckman, B.........................Montreal, Quebec, Canada
Duckman, Moses, M.D..................New York City
Dudley, Charles B...........................Altoona, Pa.
Dukas, Julius J..........................New York City
Dunkirk, Miss Wolphine................New York City
Du Pont, Mrs. F. G....................Montchanin, Del.
Durbacher, Jonas F.....................New York City
Dushkind, Charles.......................New York City
Dutcher, S. B............................Brooklyn, N. Y.
Dvorkin, J................................New York City
Dworetzky, M............................New York City
Dwork, J. H., & Brother...............New York City
Dworsky, Abraham......................New York City

E

East, William Palmer....................Yonkers, N. Y.
Echikson, L................................Newark, N. J.
Eckstein, Louis..............................Chicago, Ill.
Edelman, Samuel L.....................New York City
Edelson, N.............................Washington, D. C.
Edelstein, A...............................Paterson, N. J.
Edelstein, Adler........................New York City
Edelstein, B...........................Rockaway Beach, N. Y.
Edelstein, Isidore.........................El Paso, Tex.
Edelwirth, Alfred.......................New York City
Edlaviteh, Levi...........................Baltimore, Md.
Edlis, Adolph...............................Pittsburg, Pa.
Edman, Morris L........................New York City
Edmon, Solomon.........................New York City
Egelskie, S................................Rochester, N. Y.
Ehrenreich, Rev. Bernard C..........Philadelphia, Pa.
Ehrich, Hon. Louis R..............Colorado Springs, Colo.
Ehrich, Mrs. W. J.......................New York City
Ehrlich, Abraham.......................Springfield, Mass.
Ehrlich, Adolph..........................Brookline, Mass.
Ehrlich, Joseph.........................Philadelphia, Pa.
Ehrlich, Julius........................Greenwood, Brit. Col.
Ehrlich, M.............................Philadelphia, Pa.
Eichberg, Joseph T.........................Atlanta, Ga.
Eichhold, Charles.......................New York City
Eichler, Rev. M. M....................Philadelphia, Pa.
Eichold, Emanuel..............................Mobile, Ala.
Eidman, N. H. S........................New York City
Eigler, Emil................................Chicago, Ill.
Einfeld, William J.....................Philadelphia, Pa.
Einhorn, Isaac..........................New York City
Einstadt, S................................New York City
Einstein, Edwin.........................New York City
Einstein, I. D............................New York City
Einstein, Mrs. William.................New York City
Eiseman, Aaron.........................New York City
Eisemann, E..............................New York City

Eisen, Nathan...........................St. Joseph, Mo.
Eisenberg, Isidor C., M.D............New York City
Eisenberg, Joseph.......................New York City
Eisenberg, Louis........................New York City
Eisenberg, Rev. Maurice...............Butte, Mont.
Eisenberg, William.....................New York City
Eisendrath, B. D........................Woodbine, N. J.
Eisendrath, Henry J.......................Chicago, Ill.
Eisendrath, W. M...........................Chicago, Ill.
Eisenstadt, S............................New York City
Eisenstaedt, Isidore.......................Chicago, Ill.
Eisenstaedt, S. H..........................Chicago, Ill.
Eisenstein, Harry......................New York City
Eisenstein, J. D.........................New York City
Eisler, Isaac.............................New York City
Eisler, Morris...........................New York City
Eisner, T. D..............................Brooklyn, N. Y.
Elder, Paul, & Company...........San Francisco, Cal.
Eldridge, S. C......................San Antonio, Tex.
Eletz, Sam...............................New York City
Elias, Ely...............................Cincinnati, Ohio
Eliassof, Herman..........................Chicago, Ill.
Elisberg, E...............................New York City
Elk, Wolf.................................Boston, Mass.
Elkin, Rev. M............................Hartford, Conn.
Elkins, B. J............................Worcester, Mass.
Elkus, Abram I.........................New York City
Ellbogen, M.................................Chicago, Ill.
Ellenbogen, M...........................New York City
Ellenbogen, M. H........................Paterson, N. J.
Ellinger, Rev. Emil........................Austin, Tex.
Ellinger, M..............................New York City
Ellis, James M......................San Francisco, Cal.
Ellis, Hon. T. C. W...................New Orleans, La.
Ellison, H...............................Montreal, Canada
Elmaleh, Rev. Leon H................Philadelphia, Pa.
Eloman, G. M...........................New York City
Elovitz, W..............................Providence, R. I.
Elsas, Herman.........................New York City
Elsner, Charles T.........................Chicago, Ill.
Elsner, Prof. John, M.D................Denver, Colo.
Elzas, Barnett A......................Charleston, S. C.
Emanuel, Henry........................New York City
Emanuel, Nathan........................Brunswick, Ga.
Embrocht, S.............................New York City
Emelin, Mark J., D.D.S...............New York City
Enelow, Rev. H. G., D.D...............Louisville, Ky.
Engel, J. G.............................Brooklyn, N. Y.
Englander, B............................New York City
Englander, Rev. Henry.................Providence, R. I.
Englander, Herman.....................New York City
Englander, S...........................Philadelphia, Pa.
Engleman, S............................Des Moines, Iowa
Enowitz, C. L..........................Colchester, Conn.
Eppstein, Rev. E............................Quincy, Ill.
Epstein, David..........................New York City
Epstein, Elias.............................Chicago, Ill.
Epstein, E. W. Lewin...................New York City
Epstein, H.............................Brooklyn, N. Y.
Epstein, Jacob...........................Baltimore, Md.
Epstein, Samuel........................New York City
Epstein, Samuel...........................St. Louis, Mo.
Epstein, Simon..........................New York City
Epstein, Solomon.......................Brooklyn, N. Y.
Erb, Newman............................New York City
Erlanger, A.............................New York City
Ernst, Myron C.........................Jersey City, N. J.
Ernst, N. H................................Chicago, Ill.
Eron, J. E...............................New York City
Erschler, Rev. Abraham H...........Philadelphia, Pa.
Eschwege, S............................Brooklyn, N. Y.
Essenson, O. S., M.D...................New York City
Ettelson, Henry........................New York City
Ettinge, Rev. J. E......................New York City
Ettinger, I. B...........................New York City
Evon, J. E..............................New York City
Ewing, Hampton D......................Yonkers, N. Y.

F

Faber, Rev. M.............................Tyler, Tex.
Fabian, Jacob...........................Paterson, N. J.
Faeber, R................................Stockton, Cal.
Faggen, Nathan........................Philadelphia, Pa.
Falck, Adolph...........................New York City
Falk, B. J..............................New York City
Falkenstein, M.........................New York City
Fansey, Rev. J. S.......................Syracuse, N. Y.
Farber, Rev. R...........................Detroit, Mich.
Farley, Most Rev. Archbishop John M.....New York City
Farrar, Edgar H......................New Orleans, La.
Fass, Jacob A...........................Plainfield, N. J.
Fay, Rev. John J.......................New York City
Feder, Marcus..........................Cleveland, Ohio
Federleicht, Louis......................Baltimore, Md.
Feibleman, E.........................New Orleans, La.
Feigelson, Hayman...................Montreal, Canada
Feinberg, Barnet.......................New York City
Feinberg, David........................Brooklyn, N. Y.
Feinberg, Israel L., M.D...............New York City

Feinberg, Max	Pittsburg, Pa.
Feinberg, S. E., M.D	Scranton, Pa.
Feiner, Adolph	Pittsfield, Mass.
Feiner, Benj. F	New York City
Feingold, David	Boston, Mass.
Feingold, Simon	Philadelphia, Pa.
Feinstein, Jacob	Providence, R. I.
Feinstein, S	Baltimore, Md.
Feist, Gustave	Galveston, Tex.
Feldenheimer, A	Portland, Ore.
Feldman, Dr. B. M	New York City
Feldman, David	Philadelphia, Pa.
Feldman, Israel	Brooklyn, N. Y.
Feldman, Jacob	Woodbine, N. J.
Feldmann, D	Cincinnati, Ohio
Feldmann, Jonas	Chillicothe, Ohio
Feldstein, Charles	Pittsburg, Pa.
Feldstien, Mrs. Clara	Pittsburg, Pa.
Feller, Albert	New York City
Fellheimer, L	Cincinnati, Ohio
Fellman, Jacob	Detroit, Mich.
Fels, D	Montreal, Canada
Fels, Maurice	Philadelphia, Pa.
Felsenthal, M	New York City
Felser, Joseph	Baltimore, Md.
Felstiner, M	New York City
Fendig, Albert	Brunswick, Ga.
Ferberger, Henry	Philadelphia, Pa.
Ferguson, H. B	Pittsburg, Pa.
Fergusson, David	Seattle, Wash.
Fernberg, Harry	Plainfield, N. J.
Feuerlicht, Rev. J	Chicago, Ill.
Feuerlicht, Rev. Morris M	Indianapolis, Ind.
Feurlicht, A. S	Owensboro, Ky.
Feustmann, Mrs. B. H	Philadelphia, Pa.
Fichman, J	St. Joseph, Mo.
Fielding, Louis	Worcester, Mass.
Fierkel, David B	Philadelphia, Pa.
Finberg, Benjamin	Philadelphia, Pa.
Fine, M	Maxton, N. C.
Fine, Morris	New York City
Fine, Samuel	Boston, Mass.
Fine, A., & Sons	New York City
Finegold, Louis	Pittsburg Pa.
Fineman, Leon	Baltimore, Md.
Fineman, Solomon	Baltimore, Md.
Fineshriber, Rev. William H	Davenport, Iowa
Fink, R. L	Brooklyn, N. Y.
Finkel, S	Boston, Mass.
Finkelpearl, H., M.D	Pittsburg, Pa.
Finkelpearl, Joseph	Pittsburg, Pa.
Finkelstein, Emil, M.D	New York City
Finkelstein, Mrs. H. P	Peoria, Ill.
Finkelstein, Harry	New York City
Finkelstein, Isadore	Scranton, Pa.
Finkelstein, M., M.D	New York City
Finkelstein, Sam	New York City
Finkelstein, William	Binghamton, N. Y.
Finkelstien, Mrs. H. V	Peoria, Ill.
Firestone, Henry	McKeesport, Pa.
Firestone, Samuel	McKeesport, Pa.
Fisch, Adolph	Newark, N. J.
Fisch, Joseph	Newark, N. J.
Fischel, Mrs. A. A	New York City
Fischel, Harry	New York City
Fischelis, Philipp, M.D	Philadelphia, Pa.
Fischer, I. F	Brooklyn, N. Y.
Fischer, Wolf	Mt. Vernon, N. Y.
Fischlowitz, Abram	Brooklyn, N. Y.
Fischlowitz, Gustav G., M.D	New York City
Fischlowitz, Isidore	St. Louis, Mo.
Fischman, S	Chicago, Ill.
Fischman, William	New York City
Fish, W	New York City
Fishberg, B	New York City
Fishberg, Maurice, M.D	New York City
Fishel, Louis	New Orleans, La.
Fisher, Charles	Montreal, Canada
Fisher, Rev. Charles	Kiowa, Kan.
Fisher, Gabriel	New York City
Fisher, H. S	New Haven, Conn.
Fisher, Louis I	Wilkesbarre, Pa.
Fishmann, Arthur, M.D	New York City
Fisik, S	New York City
Fiterman, Sam	Minneapolis, Minn.
Fitzgerald, Rev. Joseph N. (deceased)	Albany, N. Y.
Flaxman, Max	Houston, Tex.
Fleck, Samuel, Jr	New York City
Flegenheimer, Adolph	New York City
Fleigelman, Victor	New York City
Fleischer, Rev. Charles	Cambridge, Mass.
Fleischer, Nathan	Paterson, N. J.
Fleischer, Sigmund L	New York City
Fleischman, S. M	Philadelphia, Pa.
Fleischner, I. N	Portland, Ore.
Fleischner, M	Portland, Ore.
Fleisher, Mrs. A	Philadelphia, Pa.
Fleisher, Simon B	Philadelphia, Pa.
Flersheim, A. S	Kansas City, Mo.

Flesch, Berthold, M.D	New York City
Florsheim, Mrs. B	Chicago, Ill.
Florsheimer, S	New York City
Florsheimer, Simon	Chicago, Ill.
Floster, William	New York City
Flursheim, Max	New York City
Fogler, Henry	Toronto, Ontario, Canada
Folda, Louis	Demopolis, Ala.
Folkoff, Samuel H	New York City
Forcimmer, M	Montreal, Canada
Foreman, E. G	Chicago, Ill.
Foreman, Oscar G	Chicago, Ill.
Foss, Israel I	Savannah, Ga.
Foster, Solomon	Newark, N. J.
Fox, Aaron	Troutdale, Ore.
Fox, Alfred	Boston, Mass.
Fox, Bertram A	Birmingham, Ala.
Fox, Emanuel E	New York City
Fox, F., M.D	Baltimore, Md.
Fox, George	Cincinnati, Ohio
Fox, Isaac	Stamford, Conn.
Fox, J	New York City
Fox, Leo	New York City
Fox, Louis	Atlanta, Ga.
Fox, Michael	Denver, Colo.
Fox, Sol	Cincinnati, Ohio.
Fraad, D	New York City
Frailey, H	Reno, Nev.
Frailey, Moses	St. Louis, Mo.
Frank, Alexander	Baltimore, Md.
Frank, Mrs. B	Buffalo, N. Y.
Frank, Eli	Baltimore, Md.
Frank, Ferdinand	Alabama City, Ala.
Frank, Gustave	New York City
Frank, Henry	Natchez, Miss.
Frank, Rev. Henry	New York City
Frank, Henry L	Chicago, Ill.
Frank, I. J	Akron, Ohio
Frank, I. S	New York City
Frank, Isaac W	Allegheny, Pa.
Frank, Ivan	New York City
Frank, J. H	Pittsburg, Pa.
Frank, Jacob L	Chicago, Ill.
Frank, Jacob S	Philadelphia, Pa.
Frank, Julius	Zanesville, Ohio
Frank, Nathan	Ogdensburg, N. Y.
Frank, Mrs. Rose	Philadelphia, Pa.
Frankel, A	New York City
Frankel, B	New York City
Frankel, Lee H., Ph.D	New York City
Frankel, Louis	New York City
Frankel, M	Toronto, Canada
Frankel, M. J	Philadelphia, Pa.
Frankel, Mandel	New York City
Frankel, Nathan	New York City
Frankel, Perry	Philadelphia, Pa.
Frankel, S	New York City
Frankel, Samuel M	New York City
Franken, Louis	New York City
Frankenberg, Solomon	New York City
Frankenstein, W. B	Chicago, Ill.
Frankfort, Frank	New York City
Frankfurt, Levy	New York City
Frankfurter, Leopold	New York City
Frankl, Albert A	New York City
Frankle, A. M	Youngstown, Ohio
Franklin, Julius	New York City
Franklin, Rev. Leo M	Detroit, Mich.
Franklin, M., M.D	Philadelphia, Pa.
Franklin, S	New York City
Franks, J	Dorchester, Mass.
Frau, Gustave	Pittsburg, Pa.
Frechie, A. M	Philadelphia, Pa.
Fredland, A	Pittsburg, Pa.
Freed, L. A	San Antonio, Tex.
Freedberger, Henry	New York City
Freedman, Arthur	Hoboken, N. J.
Freedman, B	Baltimore, Md.
Freedman, Charles I	New York City
Freedman, D	Boston, Mass.
Freedman, Ernest	Brooklyn, N. Y.
Freedman, F	Montreal, Canada
Freedman, H	New York City
Freedman, Harry	Baltimore, Md.
Freedman, Julius	Forest City, Pa.
Freedman, Louis	New York City
Freedman, M	New York City
Freedman, Morris	Schenectady, N. Y.
Freedman, Robert Samuel, M.D	New York City
Freedman, S	Montreal, Canada
Freedman, S. N	New York City
Freedman, Victor	New York City
Freedman, Will	Chicago, Ill.
Freedman, N., & Brother	Boston, Mass.
Freedom, Adolph G., M.D	Baltimore, Md.
Freeman, Dudley	Boston, Mass.
Freiberg, Mrs. Julius	Cincinnati, Ohio
Freicks, Samuel L	New York City
Freidberg, S	Topeka, Kan.

Freiman, Edward......................New York City
Fremer, S.........................Toronto, Canada
Freudenheim, H. W..................New York City
Freund, Rev. Charles J.............Salt Lake City, Utah
Freund, Gustav.......................Chicago, Ill.
Freund, H. W......................Cincinnati, Ohio
Freund, Henry......................New York City
Freund, Isidor.....................New York City
Freundlich, Isidor.................New York City
Freusdorf, Sigmund.................Syracuse, N. Y.
Frey, Philip W.....................Evansville, Ind.
Fried, Isaac.......................Newark, N. J.
Fried, J. S........................New York City
Fried, Rev. Michael................Pittsburg, Pa.
Fried, Samson......................New York City
Friedberg, M. S....................Philadelphia, Pa.
Friedberg, S.......................Topeka, Kan.
Friedberger, Benjamin..............New York City
Friedberger, Simon.................Philadelphia, Pa.
Friedburg, Herman..................New York City
Friede, J. S.......................New York City
Friede, Marcus Sergey..............New York City
Friedelson, Sam....................New York City
Friedenberg, Charles A.............New York City
Friedenberg, M. I..................Philadelphia, Pa.
Friedenheit, Isaac.................New York City
Friedenstein, Simon................New York City
Friedenthal, Solomon...............Seattle, Wash.
Friedenwald, Harry, M.D............Baltimore, Md.
Friedenwald, Herbert...............Philadelphia, Pa.
Frieder, H.........................New York City
Friedland, Elias J., M.D., D.D.S...New York City
Friedland, F.......................Newport News, Va.
Friedlander, Chas..................Norfolk, Va.
Friedlander, Rev. E................Montreal, Canada
Friedlander, Rev. H................Albany, N. Y.
Friedlander, Isidor................New York City
Friedlander, M.....................San Francisco, Cal.
Friedler, J. L., M.D...............New York City
Friedman, B. C.....................Philadelphia, Pa.
Friedman, Ben, M.D.................New York City
Friedman, Chas. J..................New York City
Friedman, D. S.....................Montreal, Canada
Friedman, David L..................New York City
Friedman, Edward...................New York City
Friedman, Fritz....................New York City
Friedman, H., M.D..................New York City
Friedman, H. S.....................Philadelphia, Pa.
Friedman, Harris...................New York City
Friedman, Harry....................Baltimore, Md.
Friedman, Hyman....................New York City
Friedman, Hyman....................Las Vegas, N. Mex.
Friedman, I........................San Francisco, Cal.
Friedman, Isaac....................New York City
Friedman, J. A.....................Mobile, Ala.
Friedman, J. L.....................Albany, N. Y.
Friedman, J. L.....................Paducah, Ky.
Friedman, Josef....................New York City
Friedman, Joseph...................New York City
Friedman, Julius...................Detroit, Mich.
Friedman, L........................Brooklyn, N. Y.
Friedman, Lee H....................Boston, Mass.
Friedman, Leo......................New York City
Friedman, Louis....................Pensacola, Fla.
Friedman, M. E.....................Tawas City, Mich.
Friedman, Max......................Pittsburg, Pa.
Friedman, Max H....................New York City
Friedman, Morris...................Providence, R. I.
Friedman, Morris...................Schenectady, N. Y.
Friedman, Myer.....................Las Vegas, N. Mex.
Friedman, Nathan...................New York City
Friedman, S........................Yonkers, N. Y.
Friedman, Samuel...................Cleveland, Ohio
Friedman, Samuel...................New York City
Friedman, Rev. Samuel..............Harrisburg, Pa.
Friedman, Samuel, M.D..............New York City
Friedman, Sig. C...................Boston, Mass.
Friedman, Rev. Dr. William S.......Denver, Colo.
Frieman, Edward....................New York City
Friger, J..........................New York City
Frinblatt, B.......................New York City
Frisch, Frederick..................New York City
Froehlich, Joseph..................Davenport, Iowa
Frohman, Daniel....................New York City
Fromberg, M........................Sumter, S. C.
Frosch, U. S.......................Houston, Texas
Frost, S. W........................Cincinnati, Ohio
Früh, Carl D. S....................Philadelphia, Pa.
Fry, Moses.........................New York City
Fryslie, Mrs. J....................Black River Falls, Wis.
Fuholske, Dr. H....................St. Louis, Mo.
Fuhrman, Abe.......................Camden, N. J.
Fuhs, J., M.D......................Brooklyn, N. Y.
Fuirman, Leon......................Baltimore, Md.
Fulchinsky, W......................New York City
Furman, M. M.......................Chicago, Ill.
Furst, Michael.....................Brooklyn, N. Y.
Furth, Emanuel.....................Philadelphia, Pa.

G

Gabriel, Robt......................Brooklyn, N. Y.
Gaebelein, Rev. A. C...............New York City
Gaeldgaeler, M.....................Toronto, Canada
Galantiere, J......................Chicago, Ill.
Galbenewitz, Benjamin G., M.D......Boston, Mass.
Galinski, B........................New York City
Galinsky, A. L.....................Sioux City, Iowa
Gall, Charles G....................Brooklyn, N. Y.
Gallert, Mark......................Brookline, Mass.
Gamson, Emil, M.D..................Bayonne, N. J.
Ganz, A............................New York City
Garbelein, Rev. H. C...............New York City
Gardner, M.........................Montreal, Canada
Garfiel, Charles...................New York City
Garfunkel, Aaron...................New York City
Gartenstein, Jacob.................Milwaukee, Wis.
Gartman, Leo N., M.D...............Philadelphia, Pa.
Gartner, Isidore...................New York City
Gassner, L.........................New York City
Gates, Ferdinand...................Memphis, Tenn.
Gatzert, August....................Chicago, Ill.
Gaulsic, Max.......................New York City
Gaus, Leo..........................New York City
Gautscher, A.......................New York City
Geiger, S..........................New York City
Geilich, S.........................New York City
Gelber, L..........................Toronto, Canada
Gelbwaks, Elias....................New York City
Geldzaeler, M......................Toronto, Canada
Gelin, William H...................Springfield, Mass.
Geller, Emanuel....................Pittsburg, Pa.
Gellis, Henry......................New York City
Gemeiner, S........................New York City
Genser, Miss Bessie B..............Montreal, Canada
Germansky, A. L....................New York City
Germansky, H. B....................Philadelphia, Pa.
Germansky, L.......................New York City
Germanus, D........................Portland, Ore.
Gernsbacher, H.....................Fort Worth, Texas
Gernsheimer, R.....................New York City
Gershel, George....................New York City
Gershel, Henry.....................East Orange, N. J.
Gerson, B..........................Pensacola, Fla.
Gerstle, Mrs. Hannah...............San Francisco, Cal.
Gerstley, Mrs. Henry...............Philadelphia, Pa.
Gerstley, Louis....................Philadelphia, Pa.
Gerstley, William..................Philadelphia, Pa.
Gerzog, George.....................New York City
Getlag, Selig Richard..............New York City
Gevurz, Philip.....................Portland, Ore.
Ghinger, Joe.......................New York City
Gibbons, His Eminence James Cardinal..Baltimore, Md.
Gidden, Herman M...................Boston, Mass.
Gilbert, John Mills................New York City
Gilbman, M.........................New York City
Gillman, Bernard...................New York City
Gilmore, Samuel L..................New Orleans, La.
Gimbel, Ben........................Philadelphia, Pa.
Gimbel, Isaac......................Philadelphia, Pa.
Ginsberg, A........................New York City
Ginsberg, Adolph...................Baltimore, Md.
Ginsberg, David....................New York City
Ginsberg, George...................New York City
Ginsberg, H........................New York City
Ginsberg, J........................Springfield, Mass.
Ginsberg, J........................Sacramento, Cal.
Ginsberg, S........................Baltimore, Md.
Ginsburg, Abraham..................New York City
Ginsburg, Bernard..................Detroit, Mich.
Ginsburg, Joshua, M.D..............Chicago, Ill.
Ginsburg, M. Ph....................Chicago, Ill.
Ginsburger, Emil...................New York City
Gintzler, H........................Buffalo, N. Y.
Ginzberg, Albert A.................Boston, Mass.
Ginzberg, Louis, Ph.D..............New York City
Ginzburg, Alexander................New York City
Girsdansky, Max, M.D...............New York City
Gitkin, Joseph.....................Bethlehem, Pa.
Gittelson, A. D....................Cleveland, Ohio
Gittelson, N. L....................Montreal, Canada
Gladstone, D. H....................Durham, N. C.
Gladstone, David...................New York City
Glaser, Rev. Hyman.................Boston, Mass.
Glaser, M..........................Boston, Mass.
Glass, Henry.......................New York City
Glass, M...........................St. Louis, Mo.
Glattke, Max.......................Pittsburg, Pa.
Glauber, M.........................Chicago, Ill.
Glick, Bernard.....................New York City
Glickman, M........................New York City
Glickman, Moses....................Montreal, Canada
Glickman, P........................Montreal, Canada
Glickman, T........................Montreal, Canada
Glicksman, Nathan..................Milwaukee, Wis.
Globus, James......................Brooklyn, N. Y.
Glottstein, Joseph.................Pittsburg, Pa.
Glou, Isidor.......................Plymouth, Pa.

Glover, Rev. A. Kingsley	Auburn, Cal.
Gluces, David	New York City
Gluck, Rev. Dr. B	Newark, N. J.
Glück, Sam.	New York City
Gluck, Samuel	New York City
Gluckman, Saul (deceased)	Jersey City, N. J.
Gluskin, E., D.D.S.	New York City
Gluttstein, Joseph G	Pittsburg, Pa.
Godchaux, Albert	New Orleans, La.
Godchaux, Mrs. Charles	New Orleans, La.
Godchaux, Emil	New Orleans, La.
Godfrey, Frank	Memphis, Tenn.
Goding, J. Q.	Worcester, Mass.
Godinski, S. M.	Worcester, Mass.
Goebricher, M.	Conneaut, Ohio
Goepp, Judith	Philadelphia, Pa.
Goes, George W	Milwaukee, Wis.
Goetz, Joseph	Newark, N. J.
Gold, Isidore	Jersey City, N. J.
Gold, Louis	New York City
Gold, Morris	New York City
Goldansky, H	Denver, Colo.
Goldberg, A.	Brooklyn, N. Y.
Goldberg, Aaron	Malden, Mass.
Goldberg, Abraham	New York City
Goldberg, Abraham	New Orleans, La.
Goldberg, Albert A	East Boston, Mass.
Goldberg, Ben	Chicago, Ill.
Goldberg, Frank	Springfield, Ohio
Goldberg, G	Oklahoma City, O. T.
Goldberg, H.	Chicago, Ill.
Goldberg, H. S. W	Chicago, Ill.
Goldberg, Harris	Boston, Mass.
Goldberg, Henry, M.D.	New York City
Goldberg, I	New York City
Goldberg, I	Trenton, N. J.
Goldberg, Isaac	Kalamazoo, Mich.
Goldberg, Isaac	New York City
Goldberg, Jacob A	Chicago, Ill.
Goldberg, Joseph	Charleston, S. C.
Goldberg, Joseph M	Alexandria, La.
Goldberg, Lewis	New York City
Goldberg, M.	Brooklyn, N. Y.
Goldberg, M. A., M.D.	New York City
Goldberg, Manuel	New York City
Goldberg, Max	New York City
Goldberg, Max	Pittsburg, Pa.
Goldberg, Robert	New York City
Goldberg, S.	New York City
Goldberg, S. W	East Orange, N. J.
Goldberg, Samuel	Cincinnati, Ohio
Goldberg, Samuel B	Chicago, Ill.
Goldberg, W.	Hamilton, Canada
Goldberg, William Victor	New York City
Goldberger, M., M.D.	New York City
Goldberger, Samuel	New York City
Goldblum, K.	Minneapolis, Minn.
Goldburg, E.	Cincinnati, Ohio
Goldburg, Morris L	Chicago, Ill.
Golde, Morris.	New York City
Golden, Albert A	Boston, Mass.
Goldenberg, Mrs. Moses	Baltimore, Md.
Goldenberg, Mrs. Rose	New York City
Goldenkranz, Solomon, M.D.	New York City
Goldenstein, I. S.	Montreal, Canada
Goldfarb, Rev. Jacob	Washington, Pa.
Goldfogle, Hon. Henry M.	New York City
Goldish, S	St. Paul, Minn.
Goldman, A.	Minneapolis, Minn.
Goldman, Aaron	Detroit, Mich.
Goldman, B. L.	New York City
Goldman, Charles, M.D.	New York City
Goldman, Edwin W	New York City
Goldman, Henry	Little Rock, Ark.
Goldman, Henry C	New York City
Goldman, Henry E.	New York City
Goldman, Herman	New York City
Goldman, I	Kansas City, Kan.
Goldman, J	Charleston, S. C.
Goldman, Joseph	Baltimore, Md.
Goldman, Louis J	Cincinnati, Ohio
Goldman, M.	New York City
Goldman, Marcus	New York City
Goldman, S.	Philadelphia, Pa.
Goldman, S. L.	Bradford, Pa.
Goldman, Simon	Philadelphia, Pa.
Goldman, T.	Torras, La.
Goldmark, Leo	Paterson, N. J.
Goldring, N.	Pensacola, Fla.
Goldschmidt, Abraham	New York City
Goldschmidt, Bernhard	New York City
Goldschmidt, William	New York City
Goldsmith, Adolph	New York City
Goldsmith, August	New York City
Goldsmith, B. M.	Carnegie, Pa.
Goldsmith, Benjamin J	Saratoga Springs, N. Y.
Goldsmith, F.	New York City
Goldsmith, Frederick	New York City
Goldsmith, Henry	New York City
Goldsmith, J	Cleveland, Ohio
Goldsmith, Joseph	Harrisburg, Pa.
Goldsmith, Mrs. L	Chicago, Ill.
Goldsmith, M	Cleveland, Ohio
Goldsmith, Meyer B	Baltimore, Md.
Goldsmith, Milton	New York City
Goldsmith, Theresa	New York City
Goldsmith, Z. A.	Troy, N. Y.
Goldstein, Aaron	Dallas, Texas
Goldstein, Charles J	New York City
Goldstein, David	New York City
Goldstein, H. I.	Pittsburg, Pa.
Goldstein, I. S.	Montreal, Canada
Goldstein, Jacob	New York City
Goldstein, Jacob, M.D.	New York City
Goldstein, Jacob W	Minneapolis, Minn.
Goldstein, Joseph	Gulfport, Miss.
Goldstein, Louis	Boston, Mass.
Goldstein, Louis	New York City
Goldstein, Louis L	New York City
Goldstein, M. A.	Binghamton, N. Y.
Goldstein, Max	Brooklyn, N. Y.
Goldstein, Max	Youngstown, Ohio
Goldstein, Meyer A	New York City
Goldstein, Nathan	Greenville, Miss.
Goldstein, Philip	Newark, N. J.
Goldstein, Rubein	Rochester, N. Y.
Goldstein, S.	Detroit, Mich.
Goldstein, Rev. S	Montreal, Canada
Goldstein, Sam.	Rochester, N. Y.
Goldstein, Sam I	Worcester, Mass.
Goldstein, Samuel L	Youngstown, Ohio
Goldston, Israel J	Homestead, Pa.
Goldstone, D.	New Haven, Conn.
Goldstone, Harry	Cohoes, N. Y.
Goldstone, J. A.	Utica, N. Y.
Goldstone, Morris R.	Pittsburg, Pa.
Goldwasser, J. Edwin	New York City
Goldwater, Ephraim Bert	New York City
Goldwater, Morris	Prescott, Ariz.
Golilbery, Samuel	Cincinnati, Ohio
Golland, M., M.D.	St. Louis, Mo.
Gomberg, Max B., M.D.	Providence, R. I.
Gombotz, Ignatz	New York City
Gonsior, Nathan	Chicago, Ill.
Goodfellow, L. M.	New York City
Goodfried, Ignatius L., M.D.	New York City
Goodfriend, Jacob	New York City
Goodfriend, M. H.	Philadelphia, Pa.
Goodfriend, Meyer	New York City
Goodhart, P. J	New York City
Goodheart, Lawrence	Brooklyn, N. Y.
Goodman, David N	Cleveland, Ohio
Goodman, E.	Seattle, Wash.
Goodman, H., Jr.	Chattanooga, Tenn.
Goodman, Jacob	New York City
Goodman, Jos. J	Coatesville, Pa.
Goodman, M.	Youngstown, Ohio
Goodman, Maurice	New York City
Goodman, Max P.	Cleveland, Ohio
Goodman, Mrs. Samuel	Boston, Mass.
Goodstein, A.	Denver, Colo.
Goodstein, Esther	Philadelphia, Pa.
Goodstone, Morris A., M.D.	Pittsburg, Pa.
Goorin, C. B.	Pittsburg, Pa.
Gordo, Isaac	New York City
Gordon, Abraham	New London, Conn.
Gordon, Rev. B.	Chicago, Ill.
Gordon, Benjamin L., M.D.	Philadelphia, Pa.
Gordon, George J., M.D.	Minneapolis, Minn.
Gordon, H. B.	Boston, Mass.
Gordon, Harry	Boston, Mass.
Gordon, Jacob	Boston, Mass.
Gordon, Moses	Cincinnati, Ohio
Gordon, Paul	Baltimore, Md.
Gordon, Phineas	New York City
Gordon, Samuel	Philadelphia, Pa.
Gorfinkel, S.	Providence, R. I.
Gorfinkell, L.	Allegheny, Pa.
Gorfinkle, Joseph I	Chelsea, Mass.
Gothberg, H.	New York City
Gottdiener, H.	Galion, Ohio
Gottesman, M., M.D.	New York City
Gotthelf, Philip	New York City
Gottlieb, A.	Flushing, N. Y.
Gottlieb, Abraham,	New York City
Gottlieb, Edward	New York City
Gottlieb, Edward O.	New York City
Gottlieb, Henry	New York City
Gottlieb, Herman	New York City
Gottlieb, J.	New York City
Gottlieb, Louis S.	New York City
Gottschall, Simon	New York City
Gottscher, Simon	New York City
Gottstein, K.	Seattle, Wash.
Gottstein, M.	Seattle, Wash.
Gouldie, Max	New York City
Goward, George	Philadelphia, Pa.
Grabenheimer, H.	New Orleans, La.

Hano, Philip	New York City
Hanower, Louis N	Arlington, N. J.
Hanser, J	Galveston, Tex.
Hansher, M	Montreal, Canada
Harburger, Hon. Julius	New York City
Harburger, Leo	New York City
Hark, Joseph	New York City
Harkavy, Alexander	New York City
Harkavy, Dr. Samuel	New York City
Harlowe, David	Milwaukee, Wis.
Harmel, Paul	Washington, D. C.
Harmon, S., M.D.	Norfolk, Va.
Harper, William H	Brewton, Ala.
Harris, A	Ottawa, Canada
Harris, Benjamin	New York City
Harris, Bernard	Philadelphia, Pa.
Harris, Charles N	New York City
Harris, D	New York City
Harris, E. H	Chicago, Ill.
Harris, Mrs. F	Chicago, Ill.
Harris, George W	Cincinnati, Ohio
Harris, H	Baltimore, Md.
Harris, Harry	Pittsburg, Pa.
Harris, Isaac	Boston, Mass.
Harris, Jacob	Kingston, N. Y.
Harris, Jacob	Montclair, N. J.
Harris, Louis	Montclair, N. J.
Harris, Rev. Dr. Maurice H	New York City
Harris, Max	Philadelphia, Pa.
Harris, Simon	Portland, Ore.
Harrison, Aaron E	New York City
Harrison, Jacob	New York City
Harrison, Joseph H	Denver, Colo.
Harriss, Herman	New York City
Harsh, Mrs. M. A	Baltimore, Md.
Hart, Albert	Philadelphia, Pa.
Hart, Byerly	Philadelphia, Pa.
Hart, Frederick A	Bath Beach, N. Y.
Hart, H	Bridgeport, Conn.
Hart, Harry	Chicago, Ill.
Hart, John I., D.D.S.	New York City
Hart, Joseph S	Grand Rapids, Mich.
Hart, Max	Chicago, Ill.
Hart, Robert	New York City
Hartfeld, David	New York City
Hartman, B	New York City
Hartman, Simon	Chicago, Ill.
Hartmann, F. E	New York City
Hartmann, J. S	Chicago, Ill.
Hartzell, E	Youngstown, Ohio
Harvitt, Joseph, D.D.S.	New York City
Haskell, A. H	New York City
Hass, Sam	Louisville, Ky.
Hassell, Sylvester	Williamston, N. C.
Hassenbusch, Samuel	St. Joseph, Mo.
Hassler, Isaac	Philadelphia, Pa.
Hast, A. M	Pittsburg, Pa.
Hatch, Nathan	Albany, N. Y.
Hatowski, Benjamin	Chicago, Ill.
Hatowski, Phillip	Chicago, Ill.
Hatowski, Phillip	Chicago, Ill.
Hatter, M. A	Norfolk, Va.
Hatton, B	New York City
Hausburg, Max	New York City
Hauser, Rev. George P	Denison, Tex.
Hausher, M	Montreal, Canada
Hausman, D. S	Montgomery, Ala.
Haydn, Rev. H. C., D.D	Cleveland, Ohio
Hayes, Rev. James M	Dallas, Tex.
Hays, Daniel P	New York City
Hecht, Adolph	New York City
Hecht, Ernest	Laurium, Mich.
Hecht, Jacob	New York City
Hecht, Jacob H	Boston, Mass.
Hecht, Monie	Baltimore, Md.
Hecht, Rev. Dr. Sigmund	Los Angeles, Cal.
Hefler, Louis	New York City
Heflich, Sam	New York City
Heichman, Max	Boston, Mass.
Heilbron, Henry H	Philadelphia, Pa.
Heilbron, Louis	Texarkana, Tex.
Heilbrun, David	New York City
Heilferin, Louis	Shreveport, La.
Heim, George	New York City
Heim, Marcus	New York City
Heim, Moritz	St. Paul, Minn.
Heiman, Gus	Philadelphia, Pa.
Heimann, Julius	New York City
Heimann, Leopold	Milwaukee, Wis.
Heimberger, D	Denver, Colo.
Heimlich, Daniel, M.D.	Cleveland, Ohio
Heinberg, Mrs. C. J	Pensacola, Fla.
Heinberg, Rev. Israel	Monroe, La.
Heine, Morris	New York City
Heineman, Sam	Baltimore, Md.
Heinemann, Herman	New York City
Heiner, Charles	New York City
Heinsheimer, Edward L	Cincinnati, Ohio
Heinz, Maurice	Wilkesbarre, Pa.
Heiser, S. A	Albany, N. Y.
Heisey, Geo. R	Lancaster, Pa.
Heisman, A. M	Little Rock, Ark.
Heisne, Isaac	Philadelphia, Pa.
Heksch, Alfred	Philadelphia, Pa.
Held, Charles	New York City
Held, John A	Tyler, Tex.
Held, Joseph	New York City
Hellenstein, Herman	New York City
Heller, Abraham A	New York City
Heller, Isaac	East Boston, Mass.
Heller, Jacob, M.D.	New York City
Heller, Max	New Orleans, La.
Heller, Richard	New York City
Heller, Robert	New York City
Heller, S.	New York City
Heller, S. W	New York City
Hellerman, Benjamin	New York City
Hellinger, Leopold	New York City
Hellinger, Paul	New York City
Hellman, I	Canton, Ohio
Hellman, Isaias W	San Francisco, Cal.
Helschman, Charles	Brooklyn, N. Y.
Henderson, Mrs. D	San Francisco, Cal.
Henderson, Joseph J	Brooklyn, N. Y.
Henderson Public Library	Henderson, Ky.
Hendricks, Mrs. A. S.	New York City
Hendricks, Henry H	New York City
Henly, Elkan	Philadelphia, Pa.
Henry, Philip S	New York City
Henry, William	New York City
Hepler, Joseph	Charleston, S. C.
Herbst, George	New York City
Herman, David	New York City
Herman, H. F	Schenectady, N. Y.
Herman, Jacob	Bayonne, N. J.
Herman, Meyer	Bayonne, N. J.
Herman, Robt	Greenwood, Miss.
Hermann, Eschel	Boston, Mass.
Hermann, S	New York City
Hermann, Solomon, M.D.	New York City
Hernbute, Bernhard	New York City
Hernsheim, Isidore	New York City
Herold, Simon	Shreveport, La.
Herringer, I	New York City
Herrmann, Maurice	New York City
Hershfield, David	New York City
Hershfield, Isidore	New York City
Hershfield, Levi	New York City
Hershick, Sam	Bridgeport, Conn.
Herskovits, Albert	New York City
Herskovits, Ludwig	New York City
Hertz, Emanuel	New York City
Herz, Rev. Joseph	Columbus, Miss.
Herzberg, Jos. A	New York City
Herzberg, L. L	Gadsden, Ala.
Herzberg, Max	Philadelphia, Pa.
Herzmark, D	Washington, D. C.
Herzog, Louis	New York City
Herzog, Max	New York City
Herzog, Sam	Chicago, Ill.
Herzog, Solomon	Chicago, Ill.
Hess, Ferdinand	New York City
Hess, Isabella R	Troy, N. Y.
Hess, Julius	New York City
Hess, Simon	New York City
Hess, Simon	New London, Conn.
Hessberg, Albert	Albany, N. Y.
Hewitt, Hon. Abram S. (deceased)	New York City
Heyman, Emanuel S	Chicago, Ill.
Heyman, Henry	Philadelphia, Pa.
Heyman, Henry W	New York City
Heyman, Rev. Dr. Hugo	Brooklyn, N. Y.
Heyman, N. D	New York City
Heymann, Max	New York City
Hickey, W. D	Dayton, Ohio
Hill, Rev. J., D.D.	Brooklyn, N. Y.
Hillis, Rev. Newell D	Brooklyn, N. Y.
Hillkowitz, Philip	Chicago, Ill.
Hillkowitz, Philip, M.D.	Denver, Colo.
Hillman, I. N	San Francisco, Cal.
Hillman, J	Baltimore, Md.
Hillman, Louis	Baltimore, Md.
Hilton, Joseph	Newark, N. J.
Hinchmann, Leopold, M.D.	New York City
Hirsch, Alfred C	Philadelphia, Pa.
Hirsch, Benjamin	Lafayette, Ind.
Hirsch, Benjamin	Pittsburg, Pa.
Hirsch, Celia R	Des Moines, Iowa
Hirsch, Henry	Archbold, Ohio
Hirsch, Hugo	Brooklyn, N. Y.
Hirsch, Isaac	New York City
Hirsch, Jacob F	Altoona, Pa.
Hirsch, Joseph	Vicksburg, Miss.
Hirsch, Jules	Houston, Tex.
Hirsch, Leon	New York City
Hirsch, M	Holyoke, Mass.
Hirsch, Max	Philadelphia, Pa.
Hirsch, Nathan	New York City

Hirsch, N. N.............................Columbus, Ga.
Hirsch, Samuel.....................Wilkesbarre, Pa.
Hirsch, Solomon.......................Portland, Ore.
Hirschberg, A. S....................Roxbury, Mass.
Hirschberg, Abram......................Chicago, Ill.
Hirschberg, B.....................Youngstown, Ohio
Hirschberg, David,.................New York City
Hirschberg, Hon. M. H...........Newburgh, N. Y.
Hirschberg, Rev. Samuel...............Milwaukee, Wis.
Hirschberg, Solomon......................Waco, Tex.
Hirschheimer, A.....................La Crosse, Wis.
Hirschhorn, Rudolph..................New York City
Hirschman, David, M.D................New York City
Hirschman, Joseph S.................Baltimore, Md.
Hirschman, L. B....................Pensacola, Fla.
Hirschman, Leopold, M.D.............New York City
Hirschman, Moses...................Cincinnati, Ohio
Hirsdansky, Simon...................New York City
Hirsh, Alfred Curtin................Philadelphia, Pa.
Hirsh, B.............................Akron, Ohio
Hirsh, B. W........................Memphis, Tenn.
Hirsh, George.........................Austin, Minn.
Hirsh, Hugo........................Brooklyn, N. Y.
Hirsh, Jacob F........................Altoona, Pa.
Hirshberg, Leonard Keene...........Baltimore, Md.
Hirshberg, S.....................E. Boston, Mass.
Hirshberg, Rev. Samuel.............Milwaukee, Wis.
Hirshick, Sam...................Bridgeport, Conn.
Hirshman, Harry..................New Haven, Conn.
Hoban, M. J..........................Scranton, Pa.
Hochheimer, Emanuel, M.D...........New York City
Hochman, S........................New York City
Hochman, Samuel J...................Easton, Pa.
Hochman, T........................New York City
Hochstadter, Albert F...............New York City
Hochstein, Mrs. J.................New Orleans, La.
Hoedemaker, Henry..................New York City
Hoff, Max.........................Baltimore, Md.
Hoffman, Charles...................New York City
Hoffman, I..........................Chicago, Ill.
Hoffman, I.......................New York City
Hoffman, I. M....................Manistique, Mich.
Hoffman, Mark.....................New York City
Hollander, Isidore.................Shreveport, La.
Hollander, J. H...................Baltimore, Md.
Hollander, S. C...................Baltimore, Md.
Holley, Enoch.....................New York City
Holtz, Jacob......................New York City
Holtz, Lipman.....................Rochester, N. Y.
Holtzoff, S. S...................New York City
Holzman, A........................New York City
Holzman, Benjamin M...............New York City
Holzman, Joseph, M. D..............Boston, Mass.
Holzman, N........................New York City
Holzmark, W....................Kansas City, Mo.
Hood, Myer S......................Newark, N. J.
Hopp, Louis.......................New York City
Horchow, Samuel..................Portsmouth, Ohio
Horn, Bernhard....................New York City
Horn, Henry.......................New York City
Horn, Pincus.....................Philadelphia, Pa.
Hornbein, J..........................Chicago, Ill.
Hornbein, J..........................Denver, Colo.
Hornbein, Samuel...................Denver, Colo.
Hornik, M. J....................Charleston, S. C.
Horowitz, A.......................New York City
Horowitz, Israel...................Brooklyn, N. Y.
Horowitz, J.......................New York City
Horowitz, Joseph..................New York City
Horowitz, Prof. Moses.............Brooklyn, N. Y.
Horowitz, Z. M., M.D..............Newburgh, N. Y.
Horschdorfer, A...................New York City
Hortfeldt, David..................New York City
Horvitz, B.........................Pittsburg, Pa.
Horwich, B..........................Chicago, Ill.
Horwich, Henry J....................Chicago, Ill.
Horwitz, Harry....................Boston, Mass.
Horwitz, Israel...................New York City
Horwitz, Jennie G.................Baltimore, Md.
Horwitz, Judah....................Rochester, N. Y.
Hostetter, Louis....................Omaha, Neb.
Hourwich, I. A....................New York City
Houston Instalment Company...........Houston, Tex.
Howitz, B..........................Pittsburg, Pa.
Hughes, Rev. Thomas P.............New York City
Huhns, Rev. F.....................Houston, Tex.
Hummel, A. H......................New York City
Hummelfarb, Morris................Baltimore, Md.
Hurowitz, Samuel..................New York City
Hurwitz, Abraham J., Ph.G..........Boston, Mass.
Hurwitz, David....................New York City
Hurwitz, Max......................New York City
Hurwitz, Samuel...................New York City
Husch, Daniel.....................New York City
Hutkoff, Nathan...................New York City
Huttner, Samuel J..................Pittsburg, Pa.
Hutzler, A. G.....................Baltimore, Md.
Hutzler, Charles...................Richmond, Va.
Hyams, C. H.....................New Orleans, La.

Hyams, William....................New York City
Hyland, C. A......................Yokena, Miss.
Hyman, A..........................Syracuse, N. Y.
Hyman, D. J., M.D.................New York City
Hyman, Gerson.....................New York City
Hyman, Joseph.....................New York City
Hyman, Julius.....................Louisville, Ky.
Hyman, Maurice S..................New York City
Hyman, Mortimer...................New York City
Hyman, Samuel.....................New York City
Hyman, Samuel I...................New York City
Hyman, Samuel L...................New York City
Hyman, Silas I...................New Orleans, La.
Hyman, Sol........................Summit, Miss.
Hymanson, A., M.D.................New York City
Hyneman, Samuel M................Philadelphia, Pa.
Hyvernat, Henry..................Washington, D. C.

I

Igel, Charles M...................Allegheny, Pa.
Ilfeld, Charles................Las Vegas, N. Mex.
Illch, Julius.....................Albany, N. Y.
Ingber, Jacob M.................Philadelphia, Pa.
Ingersoll, Charles E.............Philadelphia, Pa.
Isaac Brothers..................Los Angeles, Cal.
Isaac, Levi.......................Cleveland, Ohio
Isaac, William B..................New York City
Isaacs, A. S......................Paterson, N. J.
Isaacs, Isaac S...................New York City
Isaacs, Joseph....................New York City
Isaacs, M. S......................New York City
Isaacs, Max, & Brother............Louisville, Ky.
Isaacs, Moses.....................New York City
Isaacs, N. E......................New York City
Isaacson, Jacob...................Brooklyn, N. Y.
Isacowitz, Julius....................Chicago, Ill.
Iseman, D. V...................Newport News, Va.
Isenberg, Israel..................Wheeling, W. Va.
Israel, Julius...................Lancaster, N. Y.
Israels, Charles H................New York City
Israelson, Isaac S...............Brooklyn, N. Y.
Isseks, Abraham B..................Bayonne, N. J.

J

Jaches, Joseph J., M.D............New York City
Jaches, Leopold...................New York City
Jackles, A. H...................Binghamton, N. Y.
Jackson, Henry...................Pittsburg, Pa.
Jackson, Rev. S. M................New York City
Jacob, J. T......................Brooklyn, N. Y.
Jacob, Jay.....................San Francisco, Cal.
Jacob, Louis.....................Charleston, S. C.
Jacob, M.......................New Haven, Conn.
Jacob, M..........................New York City
Jacob, Meyer......................Tacoma, Wash.
Jacobi, Henry.....................New York City
Jacobi, A...........................Detroit, Mich.
Jacobs, Jacob.....................New York City
Jacobs, Jacob....................Brooklyn, N. Y.
Jacobs, James I., C.E.............Brooklyn, N. Y.
Jacobs, James S..................Brooklyn, N. Y.
Jacobs, Jos., M.D................Yonkers, N. Y.
Jacobs, Max........................Oil City, Pa.
Jacobs, P.........................Huntsville, Ala.
Jacobs, Rev. P..............Albuquerque, New Mex.
Jacobs, Rev. S....................Toronto, Canada
Jacobs, S........................Montreal, Canada
Jacobs, S. R......................New York City
Jacobs, S. W.....................Montreal, Canada
Jacobs, Samuel K..................New York City
Jacobson, B. W....................New York City
Jacobson, H. M...................Philadelphia, Pa.
Jacobson, Jacob...................New York City
Jacobson, Joseph (deceased).......New York City
Jacobson, L. B....................New York City
Jacobson, R......................Montreal, Canada
Jacobson, S........................Buffalo, N. Y.
Jacobson, S......................Pittsburg, Pa.
Jacobson, Samuel...............Charlestown, Mass.
Jacoby, Herman....................New York City
Jacoby, Morris....................New York City
Jaffa, Nathan...................Roswell, New Mex.
Jaffe, A..........................New York City
Jaffe, M.........................Memphis, Tenn.
Jaffe, Dr. M. S..................Sacramento, Cal.
Jaffe, Max........................New York City
Jaffe, Moses......................New York City
Jaffe, Simon......................New York City
James, Peter H...................Jersey City, N. J.
Jancower, Joseph.................Jersey City, N. J.
Janko, Nehemiah, M.D..............New York City
Janowitz, H........................Titusville, Pa.
Jarkow, Jacob S..................Brooklyn, N. Y.
Jarmulowsky, Louis................New York City
Jarmulowsky, Meyer................New York City
Jarmulowsky, Meyer................New York City
Jarsawitz, Louis..................New York City
Jastrow, Mrs. Bertha.............Germantown, Pa.

Jastrow, Morris J.	Philadelphia, Pa.
Jay, Leopold.	Newark, N. J.
Jedel, Aaron.	Newark, N. J.
Jellenik, Felix.	New York City
Jensen, Ove.	Brooklyn, N. Y.
Jeshurun, George, D.D.S.	New York City
Jewel, Horace R.	Newport, R. I.
Jewish Hospital Fair of Brooklyn	Brooklyn, N. Y.
Joachim, B.	Brooklyn, N. Y.
Joffe, A.	New York City
Joffe, Harris.	Rochester, N. Y.
Joffe, Joseph.	New York City
Joffe, Joseph, M.D.	Woodbine, N. J.
Joffe, Julius.	Chicago, Ill.
Joffe, Leon S., D.D.S.	Philadelphia, Pa.
Joffie, Leo.	Paterson, N. J.
Jolineck, E. L.	Buffalo, N. Y.
Jolles, Charles.	Boston, Mass.
Jolles, Edward.	Boston, Mass.
Jolles, Leo S.	Boston, Mass.
Jolles, Louis.	Boston, Mass.
Jonap, H.	Cincinnati, Ohio
Jonas, Henry.	Butte, Mont.
Jonas, Marcus.	Oakland, Cal.
Jones, D. (deceased).	New York City
Jones, H. P., M.D.	New Orleans, La.
Jones, Morris.	New York City
Jones, Samuel.	New York City
Jordan, Rev. Louis H.	Toronto, Canada
Jordon, D. E.	Philadelphia, Pa.
Jorsch, Abel, D.D.S.	New York City
Joseph, Mrs. Frederick.	New York City
Joseph, I.	Houston, Tex.
Joseph, Isaac.	Cleveland, Ohio
Joseph, Isaac.	Cincinnati, Ohio
Joseph, Jacob.	Tacoma, Wash.
Joseph, Solomon.	New York City
Joseph, Rev. Theodore F.	Seattle, Wash.
Josephi, Isaiah.	New York City
Josephs, Isaiah.	New York City
Judis, Irving.	New York City
Jufe, Isidore.	New York City
Jurim, Tobias, M.D. (deceased).	New York City
Jurist, Louis.	Philadelphia, Pa.

K

Kadisa, Dr. A. P.	Chicago, Ill.
Kaffeman, Frederick.	New York City
Kahanowitz, F.	Greensburg, Pa.
Kahn, E. M.	Dallas, Tex.
Kahn, Emanuel.	Easton, Pa.
Kahn, Rev. Emanuel.	Grand Rapids, Mich.
Kahn, Emil.	Galveston, Tex.
Kahn, J.	Houston, Tex.
Kahn, Joseph.	Harrisburg, Pa.
Kahn, Joseph M.	New York City
Kahn, Julius.	New York City
Kahn, Julius.	Chicago, Ill.
Kahn, Leon I.	Shreveport, La.
Kahn, Louis.	New York City
Kahn, Ludwig, M.D.	New York City
Kahn, Maurice L.	New York City
Kahn, Moses H.	New York City
Kahn, Solomon.	Philadelphia Pa.
Kahn, William.	Charlestown, W. Va.
Kahnheimer, Joseph.	Cardington, Ohio
Kaisen, B.	Jamaica, N. Y.
Kaiser, Alois.	Baltimore, Md.
Kaiser, M.	Burnside, Ga.
Kaiser, Mrs. Maria.	New Orleans, La.
Kalisch, Samuel.	Newark, N. J.
Kalish, Louis P.	Chicago, Ill.
Kaliski, Hyman.	New York City
Kallman, Charles.	Boston, Mass.
Kalmon, Fried.	Newark, N. J.
Kamaiky, Leon.	New York City
Kamber, J.	New York City
Kamber, Minnie.	New York City
Kamin, Meyer.	Brooklyn, N. Y.
Kaminer, R.	East St. Louis, Ill.
Kaminski, Edward.	New York City
Kamm, William, D.D.S.	Chicago, Ill.
Kampert, Dr. Gustav.	New York City
Kandell, George.	Philadelphia, Pa.
Kane, H., M.D.	Brooklyn, N. Y.
Kann, Albert, M.D.	New York City
Kann, M. M.	Pittsburg, Pa.
Kanner, Gabriel.	New York City
Kanrich, S.	New York City
Kantor, David.	New York City
Kantor, Leon.	New York City
Kantor, William L., M.D.	New York City
Kantrowitz, Sigmund.	New York City
Kaplan, A.	Trenton, N. J.
Kaplan, Rev. Bernard M.	San Francisco, Cal.
Kaplan, C.	Philadelphia, Pa.
Kaplan, Isaac M.	Brooklyn, N. Y.
Kaplan, J. H.	San Francisco, Cal.
Kaplan, J. H.	Albuquerque, New Mex.

Kaplan, L.	New York City
Kaplan, L. H.	Anniston, Ala.
Kaplan, Louis.	Chicago, Ill.
Kaplan, Morris.	Chicago, Ill.
Kaplan, Paul, M.D.	New York City
Kaplansky, A. L.	Montreal, Canada
Kaplowitz, Abraham, M.D.	New York City
Kappelbaum, I.	New York City
Kargen, Jonah.	Philadelphia, Pa.
Karpas, Morris J., M.D.	New York City
Karr, Jacob A.	Philadelphia, Pa.
Kaskel, Paul.	New York City
Kassel, Abe.	New York City
Kassel, S.	New York City
Kassler, F.	New York City
Kastenbaum, Nathan.	Brooklyn, N. Y.
Kastor, I.	Evanston, Wyo.
Katchen, Julius L., Ph.G.	Newark, N. J.
Katlinsky, Lemuel.	Chicago, Ill.
Katowsky, Phillip.	Chicago, Ill.
Katten, A.	Hartford, Conn.
Katten, Levi.	Allegheny Pa.
Katz, H.	Dermott, Ark.
Katz, Harris.	Albany, N. Y.
Katz, Jacob.	Philadelphia, Pa.
Kätz, Mark J.	New York City
Katz, Samuel.	Omaha, Neb.
Katzel, Leon J., Ph.G.	Denver, Colo.
Katzenberg, I.	Philadelphia, Pa.
Katzenelenbogen, J.	New York City
Katzenstein, Leopold.	New York City
Katzinger, Edward.	Chicago, Ill.
Kauders, Ignatz.	New York City
Kauffman, Abe.	Galveston, Tex.
Kauffman, Jacob.	Portsmouth, Va.
Kauffman, Morris.	Detroit, Mich.
Kauffman, Moses.	Detroit, Mich.
Kauffman & Krueger.	Sioux City, Iowa
Kaufman, Albert, M.D.	Wilkesbarre, Pa.
Kaufman, David J.	New York City
Kaufman, Edward.	Brooklyn, N. Y.
Kaufman, Gustave.	New York City
Kaufman, I., M.D.	Brooklyn, N. Y.
Kaufman, Isaac.	Portland, Ore.
Kaufman, Mrs. Jennie.	New York City
Kaufman, L.	Lake Charles, La.
Kaufman, M.	Lexington, Ky.
Kaufman, Maurice B.	Brooklyn, N. Y.
Kaufman, William.	Montreal, Canada
Kaufmann, Albert.	New York City
Kaufmann, Isaac.	Pittsburg, Pa.
Kaufmann, Theodore.	Pittsburg, Pa.
Kaul, Leo.	Chicago, Ill.
Kaun, M.	Washington, D. C.
Kaush, William M.	Charleston, S. C.
Kauvar, Rev. C. H.	Denver, Colo.
Kayser, Leopold.	New York City
Kayton, Harmon.	New York City
Kearney, Rev. John F.	New York City
Kehlmann, L.	New York City
Keifer, Louis.	Chicago, Ill.
Keiffer, Mrs. Julius.	New Orleans, La.
Keiler, John W.	Paducah, Ky.
Keiner, William.	Lock Haven, Pa.
Keiser, L.	Buffalo, N. Y.
Keller, A. M.	Philadelphia, Pa.
Keller, Charles E.	Shelbyville, Ill.
Keller, Jacob.	Houston, Tex.
Kellert, S.	Montreal, Canada
Kempe, Samuel D.	New York City
Kemper, S. A.	Jersey City, N. J.
Kempner, Adolph.	Chicago, Ill.
Kempner, I. H.	Galveston, Tex.
Kenner, Elijah.	Duluth, Minn.
Kent, Charles F.	New Haven, Conn.
Kentucky University.	Lexington, Ky.
Kepelman, Rev. H.	Hartford, Conn.
Kepold, V. H.	Brooklyn, N. Y.
Kert, L.	Montreal, Canada
Kesner, J. L.	Chicago, Ill.
Kessler, Aaron.	New York City
Kessner, M. L.	New York City
Kest, Max.	New York City
Kesterbaum, Nathan.	Brooklyn, N. Y.
Kestler, Joseph.	Passaic, N. J.
Kiernan, Peter.	New Orleans, La.
King, Dr. M.	New York City
King, M., D.D.S.	New York City
King, Maxwell Benedict, M.D.	Boston, Mass.
King, Simon.	Lafayette, Ind.
Kingsbacher, A.	Pittsburg, Pa.
Kingsbacher, M.	Allegheny, Pa.
Kinkead, Rev. Thomas L.	Peekskill, N. Y.
Kinsky, J.	New York City
Kirschbaum, Max.	New York City
Kirschberg, J.	Montreal, Canada
Kirsh, Mrs. A.	Shreveport, La.
Kirshberg, Elias.	New York City
Kiss, Frank.	New York City

Kissick, W. A..........................Brooklyn, N. Y.
Kitay, H. B...........................Paterson, N. J.
Klasky, A.........................Newport News, Va.
Klatt, Friedrich........................Milford, Conn.
Klatzko Brothers......................New York City
Klauber, S. J.............................Orange, N. J.
Klebansky, K...........................Pittsburg, Pa.
Klebansky, Wolf.....................Philadelphia, Pa.
Klein, Rev. David, B.Ph., M.A..........Columbus, Ohio
Klein, E.............................Cincinnati, Ohio
Klein, Gutman......................Philadelphia, Pa.
Klein, Herman.......................New York City
Klein, Israel..........................Helena, Mont.
Klein, Jacob..........................Cleveland, Ohio
Klein, Joseph Alexander...............New York City
Klein, L.............................New York City
Klein, Leo W.........................New York City
Klein, Moses......................Philadelphia, Pa.
Klein, Rev. Dr. Philip................New York City
Klein, Solomon.......................New York City
Klein, William.......................New York City
Kleiner, Nathan I...................New Haven, Conn.
Kleinert, A.............................Chicago, Ill.
Kleinert, I. B........................New York City
Kleinfeld, Rev. A. S..................Paterson, N. J.
Kleinfeld, Rev. Dr. Solomon...........New York City
Kleinhaus, Samuel.................Jersey City, N. J.
Kleinman, M., M.D....................New York City
Klemer, A..........................Providence, R. I.
Klendman, Emanuel...................New York City
Kline, Charles.......................Allentown, Pa.
Kline, Henry........................Anguilla, Miss.
Kline, Henry S.....................Philadelphia, Pa.
Klingenstein, Jacob..................New York City
Knittschnitt, E. W.................New Orleans, La.
Knobloch, I..........................New York City
Knoch, Ike...........................Susanville, Cal.
Knopf, Samuel........................New York City
Kobacker, Morris......................Toledo, Ohio
Kobre, Max...........................New York City
Koch, Henry..........................New York City
Koch, Samuel.........................Pensacola, Fla.
Koefeman, Fred.......................New York City
Koenig, Samuel W.....................New York City
Koff, Jacob..........................New York City
Koffler, Samuel......................New York City
Kofka, Jacob.........................New York City
Kohen, Samuel.....................Christiansburg, Va.
Kohler, Max J.......................Cincinnati, Ohio
Kohler, Max J........................New York City
Kohlman, W., M.D...................New Orleans, La.
Kohn, A. B.........................Philadelphia, Pa.
Kohn, Aaron..........................Louisville, Ky.
Kohn, Arnold......................Philadelphia, Pa.
Kohn, D.............................New York City
Kohn, David.......................Philadelphia, Pa.
Kohn, Edmund.........................New York City
Kohn, Emerich........................New York City
Kohn, Leo............................Seattle, Wash.
Kohn, S. B........................Philadelphia, Pa.
Kohn, Samuel......................Philadelphia, Pa.
Kohn, Simon I.....................Philadelphia, Pa.
Kohns, Lazarus.......................New York City
Kohns, Lee...........................New York City
Kohut, Rev. George A.................New York City
Kolasky, M...........................New York City
Kolber, S...........................Montreal, Canada
Komie, Emanuel.........................Chicago, Ill.
Kommel, B............................New York City
Kommel, Isaac........................New York City
Kompert, Gustav, M.D.................New York City
Koplan, H..............................Chicago, Ill.
Koplik, Joseph B.....................New York City
Koplik, Philip.......................New York City
Koplin, J.........................Philadelphia, Pa.
Kopold, Joseph.......................New York City
Kops, Daniel.........................New York City
Kopstein, Emil.......................New York City
Koransky, Dr. H......................New York City
Koref, Ignatz........................New York City
Kornfeld, Joseph Saul...............Montreal, Canada
Korngut, Samuel D...................Elizabeth, N. J.
Kornholz, Frederick W.............Philadelphia, Pa.
Kornick, G............................Boston, Mass.
Kors, Charles H...................Philadelphia, Pa.
Kory, Sol. S..........................Vicksburg, Miss.
Kotlowitz, Morris....................Brooklyn, N. Y.
Kottarsky, Samuel.................Philadelphia, Pa.
Kottek, Jacob D......................New York City
Kraft, William.......................Cleveland, Ohio
Krakauer, Jacques....................New York City
Krakower, Max........................Brooklyn, N. Y.
Kram, Louis..........................New York City
Kramer, H..............................Chicago, Ill.
Kramer, S............................New York City
Kramer, S. W.........................Cadillac, Mich.
Krane, B.............................New York City
Krasnowetz, Rev. Nathan..............Owensboro, Ky.
Kraus, Adolph..........................Chicago, Ill.

Kraus, Dan...........................New York City
Kraus, S.............................New York City
Krause, Adolph.......................New York City
Krause, J.............................St. Louis, Mo.
Krauskopf, Joseph.................Philadelphia, Pa.
Krauskopf, Rev. Marcus...............New York City
Krauss, T............................Pittsburg, Pa.
Krehbiel, Herman.....................New York City
Kreinson, J..........................Bradford, Pa.
Kremen, Julius J.....................New York City
Kridel, Samuel.......................New York City
Krieger, Leon......................Providence, R. I.
Krimsky, G...........................New York City
Kristeller, Julius...................Newark, N. J.
Kritt, I.............................Baltimore, Md.
Krivulin, Arnold.....................New York City
Krolik, Henry A......................Detroit, Mich.
Kroll, E. L..........................New York City
Kroll, Herman........................New York City
Kroll, Lazar.........................New York City
Krone, Joel..........................New York City
Kronengold, Adolph...................Brooklyn, N. Y.
Kronengold, Philip...................New York City
Krueger, Herman......................Baltimore, Md.
Krulewitch, Bernard..................New York City
Krulewitch, Isaac A..................New York City
Kubie, Samuel........................New York City
Kuder, M. A......................Parkersburg, W. Va.
Kudlich, H. C........................New York City
Kuff, M. S...........................Baltimore, Md.
Kugel, Julius J......................New York City
Kuhn, Isaac..........................Champaign, Ill.
Kuldell, Rev. A. R..................Allegheny, Pa.
Kulla, Jacob.........................New York City
Kunestlich, D., M.D..................New York City
Kuposky, Barnett.....................Boston, Mass.
Kuppenheimer, Louis B.................Chicago, Ill.
Kupperman, L.........................New York City
Kurtz, Gustavus E....................Roxbury, Mass.
Kurtz, R. M.........................Cleveland, Ohio
Kurzman, Charles.....................New York City
Kussy, Miss Sarah....................Newark, N. J.

L

Lachman, Hon. Samson.................New York City
Lack, Morris.........................New York City
Lackheim, G..........................Baltimore, Md.
Ladinski, L. J., M.D.................New York City
Lamakay, J...........................New York City
Lambert, Jules J.....................New York City
Lambert, Richard..................New Orleans, La.
Lambie, Mrs..........................Pittsburg, Pa.
Lamendorf, Jacob.....................New York City
Lampel, Sam..........................New York City
Lamport, S. Charles..................New York City
Landau, Rev. E. A.....................Albany, Ga.
Landau, K.............................Chicago, Ill.
Landau, Samuel.....................Wilkesbarre, Pa.
Landauer, H...........................Chicago, Ill.
Landberg, Max......................Rochester, N. Y.
Lande, Marcus........................New York City
Landes, Leonard, M.D.................New York City
Landfried, C. J., M.D.............New Orleans, La.
Landman, Louis H., M.D.............Cincinnati, Ohio
Lando, M.............................Pittsburg, Pa.
Landon, Amos W.......................Baltimore, Md.
Landon, Charles W....................Baltimore, Md.
Landsberg, Louis.....................Detroit, Mich.
Landsberg, Max, Ph.D...............Rochester, N. Y.
Landsman, S. M., M.D.................New York City
Langfeld, A. M.....................Philadelphia, Pa.
Lanrowitz, Leon......................New York City
Lapidus, H...........................New York City
Larner, John B....................Washington, D. C.
Lascoff, J. Leo......................New York City
Lasday, Max..........................Pittsburg, Pa.
Lasdusky, Joseph.....................Homestead, Pa.
Lasker, Hyman M........................Troy, N. Y.
Lasker, Isidore.......................Chicago, Ill.
Lasky, H............................Haverhill, Mass.
Lasting, Samuel....................Portsmouth, Va.
Laubheim, Julius.....................New York City
Lauchheim, Jacob M...................Baltimore, Md.
Lauchheimer, Sylvan Hayes............Baltimore, Md.
Lauer, E. H..........................Portland, Ore.
Lauer, Leon..........................Baltimore, Md.
Laufman, G..........................Cleveland, Ohio
Laufman, T..........................Cleveland, Ohio
Lauterbach, Edward...................New York City
Laventall, Julius.....................Albany, N. Y.
Lavitt, Max..........................Norfolk, Va.
Lawrence, Benjamin B., M.D........Philadelphia, Pa.
Lazarus, David M..................Allegheny, Pa.
Lazarus, Frederick..................Columbus, Ohio
Lazarus, Henry L..................New Orleans, La.
Lazarus, Leon.........................Bayonne, N. J.
Lazdon, Jacob E.......................Troy, N. Y.
Lazear, P..............................Atlanta, Ga.
Lear, Solomon......................New Haven, Conn.

Leavitt, S.	Montreal, Canada
Lebovitz, Bernhard	Brooklyn, N. Y.
Lebovitz, Jacob	Chicago, Ill.
Lebowich, Max	Boston, Mass.
Lebowitz, Henry	New York City
Lechner, Richard L.	Brooklyn, N. Y.
Lederer, Ephraim	Philadelphia, Pa.
Leeberman, G., M.D.	Brooklyn, N. Y.
Leesersohn, Leonard	New York City
Lefkovits, Dr. M.	East Las Vegas, N. Mex.
Lefkowitz, Rev. David	Dayton, Ohio
Lefkowitz, Hyman B.	New York City
Lehman, A.	Peru, Ind.
Lehman, Edgar	New York City
Lehman, Irving	New York City
Lehman, Isidore	Ft. Wayne, Ind.
Lehman, Israel J.	Cleveland, Ohio
Lehovitz, Bernhard	Brooklyn, N. Y.
Lehrhaupt, David	Detroit, Mich.
Lehring, William	New York City
Leiber, S. Philip, D.D.S.	Pittsburg, Pa.
Leibowitch, Leon, M.D.	New York City
Leibson, Joseph	Wilkesbarre, Pa.
Leichtentritt, M.	Plainfield, N. J.
Leiler, Max	New York City
Leinkin, Morris	Lowell, Mass.
Leipziger, Emil William	Terre Haute, Ind.
Leiser, Rev. Joseph	Lafayette, Ind.
Lelewer, D.	Chicago, Ill.
Lemann, Isaac Ivan	New Orleans, La.
Lemelson, Joseph	New York City
Lenchner, S.	Pittsburg, Pa.
Leo, J. S.	Montreal, Canada
Leon, Albert	Newark, N. J.
Leon, David	New York City
Leopold, Isaac, M.D.	Philadelphia, Pa.
Leopold, M.	Millville, N. J.
Leopold, Simon	Berwick, La.
Lerner, Leo	New York City
Leroy, B. M.	New York City
Lesinsk, A.	Birmingham, Ala.
Lesser, E.	New York City
Lesser, George, M.D.	New York City
Lesser, Henry	New York City
Lesser, Julius	St. Louis, Mo.
Lesser, L.	Baltimore, Md.
Lesser, S.	Augusta, Ga.
Leszynsky, J.	New York City
Leucht, Rev. I. L.	New Orleans, La.
Leucht, Rev. Joseph	Newark, N. J.
Levanthal, Abraham M.	New York City
Levantine, Solomon	Albany, N. Y.
Levenberg, Dr. B.	Cleveland, Ohio
Levensohn, Max	Worcester, Mass.
Levenson, Abe	Pittsburg, Pa.
Levenson, Henry H.	Boston, Mass.
Levenson, Joseph	New York City
Levenson, Julius	Boston, Mass.
Leventhal, M.	Kansas City, Mo.
Leventhal, M	New York City
Leventritt, W. R.	New York City
Levi, B	Scranton, Pa.
Levi, Berth	New York City
Levi, Rev. Dr. Charles S.	Peoria, Ill.
Levi, David	St. Paul, S. C.
Levi, Emil S.	New York City
Levi, Ferdinand	Sumter, S. C.
Levi, Gershon B.	Philadelphia, Pa.
Levi, Rev. Harry	Wheeling, W. Va.
Levi, Henlein	New York City
Levi, Isaac	Cleveland, Ohio
Levi, Joseph	Oil City, Pa.
Levi, Leo N. (deceased)	New York City
Levi, Leon	New York City
Levi, Louis	New York City
Levi, Paul	Toronto, Canada
Levi, Solomon W	Cincinnati, Ohio
Levias, Prof. C.	Cincinnati, Ohio
Levien, Douglas A.	New York City
Levin, Abraham	Montreal, Canada
Levin, Charles J.	Baltimore, Md.
Levin, Ellis	New Haven, Conn.
Levin, Hyman	New York City
Levin, J., & Son	Baltimore, Md.
Levin, J. S.	Bayonne, N. J.
Levin, L. S.	Pittsburg, Pa.
Levin, Louis H.	Baltimore, Md.
Levin, Louis H.	New York City
Levin, Louis L.	New York City
Levin, Mendil	Brooklyn, N. Y.
Levin, S. I.	Duluth, Minn.
Levin, William	Brooklyn, N. Y.
Levin, Z., M.D.	San Francisco, Cal.
Levine, A.	Holyoke, Mass.
Levine, Abram	Chicago, Ill.
Levine, Albert	New York City
Levine, D.	Norfolk, Va.
Levine, Isaac	Schenectady, N. Y.
Levine, L.	Cincinnati, Ohio
Levine, Leopold E.	New York City
Levinsky, Irene Ida	New York City
Levinsky, L.	Toronto, Canada
Levinson, Alexander	New York City
Levinson, D.	New York City
Levinson, James	Cincinnati, Ohio
Levinson, Joseph	New York City
Levinson, Leo	New York City
Levinson, Louis	New York City
Levinson, M. Z.	New York City
Levinson, Samuel	Cincinnati, Ohio
Levinstein, Israel	Baltimore, Md.
Levinthal, Rev. B. L.	Philadelphia, Pa.
Levinthal, Rev. Isidore	Nashville, Tenn.
Levison, Isaac	New York City
Levison, Isidore	New York City
Levison, J. G.	Wilkesbarre, Pa.
Levison, S.	Springfield, Mass.
Levitan, Isidor S.	Baltimore, Md.
Leviton, A. H., M.D.	Chicago, Ill.
Leviton, Aaron	New York City
Levitt, M. J., M.D.	New York City
Levkowitz, S.	New York City
Levor, G.	Gloversville, N. Y.
Levor, Mrs. L. S.	Attica, Ind.
Levoy, B. M.	New York City
Levy, A., M.D.	Perth Amboy, N. J.
Levy, Rev. Dr. A. R.	Chicago, Ill.
Levy, Aaron	Brooklyn, N. Y.
Levy, Abraham	New York City
Levy, Abram	Augusta, Ga.
Levy, Achille	Chicago, Ill.
Levy, Arthur G.	Rutland, Vt.
Levy, B. H.	Savannah, Ga.
Levy, Benjamin F.	Elmira, N. Y.
Levy, Charles S.	New York City
Levy, D.	Baltimore, Md.
Levy, D.	New Orleans, La.
Levy, D. B.	Wilmington, Del.
Levy, David	New York City
Levy, Rev. Edward I.	Selma, Ala.
Levy, Elias Henry	New York City
Levy, F. L.	New Orleans, La.
Levy, Ferdinand	New York City
Levy, H., M.D.	Rochester, N. Y.
Levy, H. H.	New York City
Levy, Harry	New York City
Levy, Henry	New York City
Levy, Herman	New York City
Levy, Hiram	Montreal, Canada
Levy, I. D.	New York City
Levy, Isaac	Washington, D. C.
Levy, Isaac	Brooklyn, N. Y.
Levy, Isaac	New York City
Levy, Isaac	New York City
Levy, Israel	New York City
Levy, J. F.	New Orleans, La.
Levy, J. H.	Pittsburg, Pa.
Levy, Rev. J. Leonard	St. Louis, Mo.
Levy, Jacques	Rutland, Vt.
Levy, Joseph	Scranton, Pa.
Levy, Joseph	Brooklyn, N. Y.
Levy, Julius	Scranton, Pa.
Levy, Kalman	New York City
Levy, L. Napoleon	Natchitoches, La.
Levy, Leopold	Denver, Colo.
Levy, Lesser	Cincinnati, Ohio
Levy, Lipman	Denver, Colo.
Levy, Louis	Mt. Vernon, N. Y.
Levy, Louis A	Albany, N. Y.
Levy, Louis D.	New York City
Levy, Louis Eduard	Philadelphia, Pa.
Levy, M., M.D.	New Orleans, La.
Levy, M. A.	Chicago, Ill.
Levy, M. B.	San Francisco, Cal.
Levy, M. G.	New York City
Levy, M. M.	Allegheny, Pa.
Levy, M. M.	Galveston, Tex.
Levy, Rev. M. S.	San Francisco, Cal.
Levy, Max	Rockaway Beach, N. Y.
Levy, Max	New York City
Levy, Michael S.	Baltimore, Md.
Levy, Moe	New York City
Levy, Moe	Norfolk, Va.
Levy, Morris	New York City
Levy, Morris	Omaha, Neb.
Levy, Morris, M.D.	New York City
Levy, N.	New York City
Levy, N. B.	Scranton, Pa.
Levy, Nathan	McKeesport, Pa.
Levy, Oscar	St. Joseph, La.
Levy, Paul S.	Baltimore, Md.
Levy, Ralph, M.D.	New York City
Levy, Robert, M.D.	Denver, Colo.
Levy, Robt. D.	New York City
Levy, S. Lionel	New York City
Levy, S. W.	Galveston, Tex.

Levy, Samuel................Nashville, Tenn.	Lipschutz, Emil................Brooklyn, N. Y.
Levy, Samuel................Lake Charles, La.	Lipsky, Rev. J................Rochester, N. Y.
Levy, Rev. Dr. Samuel................Waco, Tex.	Lipstate, J................Tyler, Tex.
Levy, Samuel D................New York City	Lisk, Matthew................New York City
Levy, Simeon S................**Titusville**, Pa.	Lisle, Rev. James..................Gandy, Neb.
Levy, Simon................Philadelphia, Pa.	Lissman, Leonard................Brooklyn, N. Y.
Levy, Tobias................New York City	Lissmon, Edward................Brooklyn, N. Y.
Levy, William................Baltimore, Md.	Lit, Jacob D................Philadelphia, Pa.
Levy, Wm. I................New York City	Lithgow, James R................Halifax, Nova Scotia
Levyn, Jacob................Alpena, Mich.	Litowich, B. A................Salina, Kan.
Lewengood, Lewis................New York City	Littauer, N. L................New York City
Lewenthal, M................Kansas City, Mo.	Littauer, Nathan C................New York City
Lewi, F. L................Newark, N. J.	Littmann, M................St. Louis, Mo.
Lewi, William J., M.D................Albany, N. Y.	Litz, Daniel................New York City
Lewin, S................Washington, D. C.	Livenright, Florence K................Philadelphia, Pa.
Lewine, Fisher................New York City	Liveright, Henry................Philadelphia, Pa.
Lewine, Julius................New York City	Livingston, H. H................Pittsburg, Pa.
Lewine, Leopold E., M.D................New York City	Livingston, Louis D................New York City
Lewinnek, Lesser................Denver, Colo.	Livingston, Rev. William................Poughkeepsie, N. Y.
Lewinsky, J. C., M.D................New York City	Lobel, Abraham D................New York City
Lewinsohn, Lewis................Chicago, Ill.	Loble, Henry................Helena, Mont.
Lewinsohn, Salomon................New York City	Loeb, Adolph................Chicago, Ill.
Lewinson, Benno................New York City	Loeb, Edward................Philadelphia, Pa.
Lewinthal, Rev. Isidore................Nashville, Tenn.	Loeb, Ernest M................New Orleans, La.
Lewinthal, Max................Brookhaven, Miss.	Loeb, Hanau A., M.D................St. Louis, Mo.
Lewis, Alphons................New York City	Loeb, Herman................Shreveport, La.
Lewis, E. S................New Orleans, La.	Loeb, Jacob F................Philadelphia, Pa.
Lewis, George................Chicago, Ill.	Loeb, Jacques................Montgomery, Ala.
Lewis, Henry I................New York City	Loeb, James................New York City
Lewis, I. W................Salt Lake City, Utah	Loeb, L................Akron, Ohio
Lewis, Isaac................Brooklyn, N. Y.	Loeb, Mrs. L................Philadelphia, Pa.
Lewis, M. A................Washington, D. C.	Loeb, Leo................Philadelphia, Pa.
Lewis, Samuel................New York City	Loeb, Leo A................Chicago, Ill.
Lewis, Samuel................Toronto, Canada	Loeb, Louis................New York City
Lewisohn, Miss A................New York City	Loeb, Marx B................Philadelphia, Pa.
Lewisohn, Adolph (deceased)................New York City	Loeb, Maurice................New York City
Lewisohn, Philip................New York City	Loeb, Morris................New York City
Lewison, Alexander................New York City	Loeb, S. S................Seattle, Wash.
Lewy, B................Scranton, Pa.	Loeb, Solomon................New York City
Lewy, Solomon................New York City	Loeber, F., M.D................New Orleans, La.
Liachowitz, Aaron................Shamokin, Pa.	Loeser, David................Montclair, N. J.
Liberman, I................New York City	Loevy, H................Easton, Pa.
Liberman, Myron S................Utica, N. Y.	Loewe, Jacques, M.D................Brooklyn, N. Y.
Liberstein, M................St. Louis, Mo.	Loewenberg, W. B................Wabash, Ind.
Lichtbach, D................Texarkana, Ark.	Loewenberg, Rev. William................Philadelphia, Pa.
Lichten, William................Philadelphia, Pa.	Loewenheim, Frederick................New York City
Lichtenberg, August................New York City	Loewenheitz, Leo................Columbus, Ga.
Lichtenstein, D................Richmond, Va.	Loewenstein, Isaac................Charleston, W. Va.
Lichtenstein, Isaac................New York City	Loewenstein, J................Houston, Tex.
Lichtenstein, J................Richmond, Va.	Loewenstein, Louis................Troy, N. Y.
Lichtenstein, Joseph................Richmond, Va.	Loewenstein, Morris................New York City
Lichtenstein, Mayer................Philadelphia, Pa.	Loewenthal, J................New York City
Lichtig, Henry................New York City	Loewenthal, Philip, M.D................New York City
Lidschin, I................Chicago, Ill.	Loewenthau, Max, M.D................New York City
Lidschin, J................New York City	Loewithan, M., M.D................New York City
Lidz, Israel................New York City	London, I................Salem, Mass.
Lidz, Max................New York City	London, Meyer................Selma, Ala.
Lieberman, David H................New York City	London Brothers................New York City
Lieberman, G., M.D................Brooklyn, N. Y.	Londoner, Jacob, M.D................Brooklyn, N. Y.
Lieberman, H................Chicago, Ill.	Long, Bernhard................Wilkesbarre, Pa.
Lieberman, Isaac................New York City	Longs, Dora................Wilkesbarre, Pa.
Lieberman, J................Atlanta, Ga.	Lorentz, Moses L................Brooklyn, N. Y.
Lieberman, Rev. M................Kansas City, Mo.	Lorie, S................Toronto, Canada
Lieberman, Samuel................St. Joseph, Mo.	Lorinez, Simon................New York City
Lieberman, Schloma................Philadelphia, Pa.	Lorsch, Henry................New York City
Liebeskind, Abraham................New York City	Lorsch, Solomon................New York City
Liebman, L................Hamilton, Ohio	Loth, M................Cincinnati, Ohio
Liebman, Mrs. L................Shreveport, La.	Loucks, Leonard, M.D................New York City
Liebman, Louis................Youngstown, Ohio	Louis, Julius P................Kansas City, Mo.
Liebman, Rudolph................Dallas, Tex.	Louis, Mrs. Minnie D................New York City
Liebovitz, S................New York City	Louria, Leon, M.D................Brooklyn, N. Y.
Lieser, Rev. Joseph................Kingston, N. Y.	Lourie, David A................Boston, Mass.
Light, Benjamin................New York City	Lovatskin, Joseph D................Lowell, Mass.
Lightstone, H., M.D................Montreal, Canada	Loveman, A. B................Birmingham, Ala.
Likes, Albert H................Baltimore, Md.	Lowenheim, A. A., M.D................Chicago, Ill.
Liknaitz, Rev. David................Leavenworth, Tex.	Lowenstein, Isaac................Newark, N. J.
Lilienthal, Joseph................Pottsville, Pa.	Lowenstein, Max................New York City
Lindau, J. W................Greensboro, N. C.	Lowenstein, Max, M.D................New York City
Lindenberger, Robert................Astoria, Ore.	Lowenstein, N. A................New York City
Linder, William, M.D................Brooklyn, N. Y.	Lowenthal, H................Philadelphia, Pa.
Lindner, Walter................New York City	Lowenthal, J................New York City
Lindwall, Max................New York City	Lowenthal, L................Philadelphia, Pa.
Linenthal, Julius................Chicago, Ill.	Lowenthal, Max................Rochester, N. Y.
Linetzky, Hirsch................New York City	Lowentritt, Rachel................Oil City, Pa.
Linkin, Morris................Lowell, Mass.	Lowery, Rev. John F., LL.D................Troy, N. Y.
Linkman, M., M.D................New York City	Lowinstein, E................Wilkesbarre, Pa.
Lintherman, M................Albany, N. Y.	Lowman, I. L................Los Angeles, Cal.
Lipetz, Abraham................Binghamton, N. Y.	Lowy, Philip................Newark, N. J.
Lipinsky, S................Asheville, N. C.	Lubarsky, A................New York City
Lippe, Charles................New York City	Lubetkin, Max................New York City
Lippman, Israel................New York City	Lubin, David................New York City
Lippman, J. M................St. Louis, Mo.	Ludins, David G................New York City
Lippman, Louis................New York City	Ludwig, L................Brunswick, Ga.
Lippman, Morris L................New York City	Ludwig, Samuel D................New York City
Lippman, S. L................New York City	Luhler, A................Waco, Tex.
Lippman, S. L................New York City	Luintz, Jacob................New York City
Lippmann, Louis L................Seattle, Wash.	Luntz, Charles J................Brooklyn, N. Y.
Lipschitz, L................Montreal, Canada	Lupin, E. J., M.D................Philadelphia, Pa.
Lipschutz, B................Philadelphia, Pa.	Luria, Samuel................New York City

Lurie, Abraham.........................New York City
Lurie, Herman I.........................New York City
Lurie, Louis............................New York City
Lurie, Morris...........................New York City
Lurrie, Marcus S........................Boston, Mass.
Lustberg, M............................New York City
Luster, Max............................Chicago, Ill.
Lustig, Joseph..........................Denver, Colo.
Lustig, Joseph.........................New York City
Lustig, Joseph.....................Youngstown, Ohio
Lutzky, Louis..........................Baltimore, Md.
Lyman, Isidor, D.D.S..................Cleveland, Ohio
Lyon, A. H............................New York City
Lyon, B...............................New York City
Lyon, Mrs. D. T..........................Chicago, Ill.
Lyon, Harry..........................Providence, R. I.
Lyon, J. L..............................Chicago, Ill.
Lyon, Mark T...........................Chicago, Ill.
Lyons, Rev. Alexander..................New York City
Lyons, D...............................New York City
Lyons, E...............................New York City
Lyons, Joseph.......................Washington, D. C.
Lyons, M............................Appleton, Wis.
Lyons, Max.............................Utica, N. Y.
Lyons, Phillip..........................Marion, Ind.
Lyons, Solomon.......................Huntsville, Ala.

M

McAleer, Rev. P........................New York City
McAllister, Wm. K......................Denver, Colo.
McCabe, Right Rev. Charles C............Evanston, Ill.
McCarthy, Hon. John Henry.............New York City
McClosky, Hon. Bernard...............New Orleans, La.
McCready, Rev. Charles, LL.D...........New York City
McDevitt, Cora E.......................New York City
McDonnell, Right Rev. Charles E.........Brooklyn, N. Y.
McGinnis, Rev. William F., D.D...Westbury Station, N. Y.
McKee, Rev. F. W..................Pattersonville, N. Y.
McKim, Rev. Randolph H............Washington, D. C.
McLaughlin, J. F....................Toronto, Canada
McNamara, John W......................Albany, N. Y.
McNamara, Rt. Rev. Mgr. P. J., V.G.....Brooklyn, N. Y.
McNulty, P. J..........................Pittsburg, Pa.
Maaget, Israel H.......................New York City
Maas, Rev. A. J., S.J..................Woodstock, Md.
Maas, Louis...........................New York City
Maas, S................................Selma, Ala.
Machol, M., M.D......................Cleveland, Ohio
Macht, David I........................Baltimore, Md.
Mack, Jacob W.........................New York City
Mackay, F. F..........................Brooklyn, N. Y.
Mackey, Mrs. H. E......................New York City
Macowsky, Isaac...................San Francisco, Cal.
MacRae, Rev. D......................Calgary, Canada
MacRae, Rev. D., D.D................St. John, N. B.
Madill, George A. (deceased).............St. Louis, Mo.
Madoedoff, M. E.......................New York City
Maduro, Mrs. Esther L.................Panama, C. Am.
Magid, Louis B.........................Tallulah, Ga.
Magil, Rev. Julius M., Ph.D...........Ligonier, Ind.
Magner, Morris A.......................New York City
Magrill, Rev. Joseph..................Cincinnati, Ohio
Mahler, Abraham.......................New York City
Maimin, H...........................Philadelphia, Pa.
Mainoff, Louis.........................Denver, Colo.
Mainthow, S. M........................New York City
Maisel, A. J..........................New York City
Maisel, J. J., M.D....................New York City
Maisel, Louis..........................Buffalo, N. Y.
Makover, Bernard......................Baltimore, Md.
Malkan, H.............................New York City
Malter, Henry, M.D...................Cincinnati, Ohio
Maltinsky, S...........................Braddock, Pa.
Maltzer, B............................New York City
Mamlok, L.............................Boston, Mass.
Manam, Emanuel.......................New York City
Manasha, A............................New York City
Mandel, Adolf.........................New York City
Mandel, Edward.......................New York City
Mandel, Mrs. Emanuel...................Chicago, Ill.
Mandel, Rev. Morris...................Allentown, Pa.
Mandel, Samuel.....................Philadelphia, Pa.
Mandelbaum, M., M.D................Brooklyn, N. Y.
Mandelbaum, Seymour...................Baltimore, Md.
Mandelberg, Max......................Brooklyn, N. Y.
Mandelkern, J.........................New York City
Mandell, M.......................Albuquerque, N. Mex.
Mandelstam, Isaac W.................East Boston, Mass.
Mandelstamm, L........................New York City
Mandelstamm, M.......................New York City
Mandelstamm, N., M.D..................New York City
Mandelstone, Isaac W................East Boston, Mass.
Mandl, Nicholas M., M.D...............New York City
Manishewitz, Miss Mamie F...........Cincinnati, Ohio
Mann, Benjamin A......................Albany, N. Y.
Mann, Emerson.......................Fargo, N. Dak.
Mann, Samuel..........................New York City
Mannheimer, S.......................Cincinnati, Ohio
Manovitch, M..........................New York City

Manson, Lewis.........................Syracuse, N. Y.
Marcus, Aaron..........................Pittsburg, Pa.
Marcus, Adolph.........................Scranton, Pa.
Marcus, Emanuel.......................New York City
Marcus, I.............................Pittsburg, Pa.
Marcus, Rev. Jacob.....................Elmira, N. Y.
Marcus, Joseph S......................New York City
Marcus, Lewis.....................So. Bethlehem, Pa.
Marcus, Louis W........................Buffalo, N. Y.
Marcus Brothers.......................New York City
Marcuson, Rev. Isaac E...............Sandusky, Ohio
Margoles, Louis L...................Montreal, Canada
Margolies, M.........................Cleveland, Ohio
Margolies, S..........................Portland, Ore.
Margolin, Abraham J................Philadelphia, Pa.
Margolis, Abraham......................Chicago, Ill.
Margolis, Elias....................Cincinnati, Ohio
Margolis, Jacob........................Chicago, Ill.
Margulies, Irving, M.D................New York City
Margulies, M..........................New York City
Margulies, William, M.D..............Brooklyn, N. Y.
Mark, Louis H.........................New York City
Markel, Max...........................New York City
Markell, W...........................Chelsea, Mass.
Markewich, Samuel.....................New York City
Markowitz, Benjamin...................New York City
Markowitz, H..........................New York City
Markowitz, M..........................Chicago, Ill.
Marks, Albert S....................Philadelphia, Pa.
Marks, Harris.........................Brooklyn, N. Y.
Marks, Isaac D........................New York City
Marks, Isaac L.....................Philadelphia, Pa.
Marks, M., M.D.....................Philadelphia, Pa.
Marks, M. L...........................New York City
Marks, Martin A.....................Cleveland, Ohio
Marmor, Jacob D.......................Baltimore, Md.
Marrus, Philip......................Providence, R. I.
Marshall, Louis.......................New York City
Martin, Hon. John Mc. C............Port Gibson, Miss.
Martin, Prof. W. R...................Hartford, Conn.
Martinache, M.........................Yonkers, N. Y.
Martindale, Jr., S...................La Crosse, Wis.
Martinson, Julius, M.D................New York City
Marx, Albert T........................Albany, N. Y.
Marx, Rev. David......................Atlanta, Ga.
Marx, Emanuel........................New York City
Marx, M...............................Chicago, Ill.
Marx, M..............................Galveston, Tex.
Marx, Samuel..........................New York City
Marx, Simon...........................Tuskegee, Ala.
Marx, W. Bennett..........Weehawken Heights, N. J.
Marx & Jacobson......................New York City
Marymont, A...........................Detroit, Mich.
Mascovitz, Albert..................New Haven, Conn.
Masliansky, Rev. H....................New York City
Massell, Joseph, M.D..................Boston, Mass.
Master, Harris.....................Philadelphia, Pa.
Mathany, H............................New York City
Mathews, H............................New York City
Matshak, S............................New York City
Matthews, Rev. M. A., D.D............Seattle, Wash.
Matz, Israel..........................New York City
Matzke, A.............................New York City
Maurer, Emil, M.D..................Philadelphia, Pa.
Mautner, Sigfried......................Chicago, Ill.
Mavison, Joseph.......................Boston, Mass.
May, Leon V.......................Charleston, W. Va.
May, Moses...........................Brooklyn, N. Y.
Mayer, A. A., M.D....................Baltimore, Md.
Mayer, Andrew........................Brooklyn, N. Y.
Mayer, Mrs. B.........................New York City
Mayer, Benjamin R..................Baton Rouge, La.
Mayer, C. O........................Philadelphia, Pa.
Mayer, Charles........................Lincoln, Neb.
Mayer, David..........................New York City
Mayer, Eli.........................Cincinnati, Ohio
Mayer, Fred..........................Brooklyn, N. Y.
Mayer, Gabriel H...................Philadelphia, Pa.
Mayer, Harry H.....................Kansas City, Mo.
Mayer, Henry..........................New York City
Mayer, Ike........................New Orleans, La.
Mayer, Isaac..........................New York City
Mayer, Jacob.......................Cleveland, Ohio
Mayer, Joseph.........................New York City
Mayer, Leo..........................Cambridge, Mass.
Mayer, Levi.......................Philadelphia, Pa.
Mayer, Lewis.........................Demopolis, Ala.
Mayer, Prof. M........................New York City
Mayer, Max............................New York City
Mayer, Morris.......................Demopolis, Ala.
Mayer, Morris.........................New York City
Mayer, Oscar J........................New York City
Mayer, S. Julius.......................Portland, Ore.
Mayer, S. N...........................New York City
Mayer, Theodore....................Cincinnati, Ohio
Mayerwitz, Rev. B......................Atlanta, Ga.
Mazer, Joseph.........................New York City
Meadow, Jacob........................Brooklyn, N. Y.
Meadow, Samuel........................New York City

Medvedev, Paul..........................New York City
Mehrenlender, A. N., M.D..............New York City
Meier, Mrs. A. J.......................Portland, Ore.
Meisels, Raphael.......................Brooklyn, N. Y.
Melinger, Paul.........................New York City
Melitzer, M. L.........................New York City
Meller, A. R...........................Philadelphia, Pa.
Mellors, Joseph........................Philadelphia, Pa.
Meltsner, Joseph.......................New York City
Meltzer, J.............................New York City
Meltzer, Mark A........................New York City
Melzer, Joseph.........................New York City
Mendelowitz, J.........................New York City
Mendelsohn, Benjamin E.................Chicago, Ill.
Mendelsohn, Herman T...................New York City
Mendelsohn, Isador.....................Boston, Mass.
Mendelsohn, Rev. Dr. S.................Wilmington, N. C.
Mendelsohn, Sigmund....................New York City
Mendelson, J...........................New York City
Mendelson, Meyer.......................New York City
Mendelson, Moses.......................Chicago, Ill.
Mendes, Rev. Frederick de Sola, Ph.D....New York City
Mendes, Mrs. Isaac P...................Savannah, Ga.
Mendine, W. K..........................New Orleans, La.
Menken, Percival S., Ph.D., LL.B.......New York City
Menline, Joseph Spencer................New York City
Merksamer, Julius......................New York City
Merksamer, Leopold.....................New York City
Merritt, Max J.........................Evansville, Ind.
Merz, Daniel...........................Philadelphia, Pa.
Meseritz, Isaac........................Brooklyn, N. Y.
Mesirow, E. B., M.D....................Chicago, Ill.
Messing, Jr., Rev. A. J................Montgomery, Ala.
Messing, Aaron J., Ph.D................Chicago, Ill.
Messing, Rev. Henry J..................St. Louis, Mo.
Messing, M.............................Indianapolis, Ind.
Messmer, S. G..........................Green Bay, Wis.
Metzenbaum, Joseph.....................Cleveland, Ohio
Metzger, David.........................New York City
Metzger, N. A..........................New York City
Meyer, Adolph H........................Nashville, Tenn.
Meyer, Mrs. Alice......................Monroe, La.
Meyer, Ely.............................Rochester, N. Y.
Meyer, Harrison........................Denver, Colo.
Meyer, Isaac...........................Chicago, Ill.
Meyer, Rev. Julius H...................Milwaukee, Wis.
Meyer, Karl............................Brooklyn, N. Y.
Meyer, Leo B., A.M., M.D...............New York City
Meyer, Leopold.........................Chicago, Ill.
Meyer, Levy............................New York City
Meyer, Louis...........................New York City
Meyer, Martin..........................New York City
Meyer, Rabbi...........................New York City
Meyer, Rev. Martin A...................Albany, N. Y.
Meyer, Max.............................New York City
Meyer, O...............................New York City
Meyer, Samuel..........................Macon, Ga.
Meyer, Samuel..........................New York City
Meyer, Rev. Samuel.....................New York City
Meyer, Sigmund T.......................Long Branch, N. J.
Meyer, Theodore, M.D...................Salt Lake City, Utah
Meyers, Aaron..........................Buffalo, N. Y.
Meyers, D..............................New York City
Meyers, Harold.........................New York City
Meyers, Louis..........................Buffalo, N. Y.
Meyers, M..............................Cincinnati, Ohio
Meyerson, L. B.........................New York City
Meyerson, Meyer........................Philadelphia, Pa.
Michael, Elias.........................St. Louis, Mo.
Michael, Isaac L.......................New York City
Michael, Jacob.........................Brooklyn, N. Y.
Michael, M.............................Mobile, Ala.
Michael, M. G..........................Athens, Ga.
Michael, Oscar.........................Newark, N. J.
Michaelis, Michael.....................New York City
Michaels, L. P.........................New York City
Michel, H..............................New Orleans, La.
Michinard, P., M.D.....................New Orleans, La.
Mielziner, Benjamin....................Cincinnati, Ohio
Mielziner, Benjamin G..................Cleveland, Ohio
Mielziner, Rev. Jacob..................Cincinnati, Ohio
Mierenberg, Harry......................New York City
Mihalovitch, B.........................Cincinnati, Ohio
Milch, David...........................New York City
Miller, A..............................New York City
Miller, B..............................Kansas City, Mo.
Miller, Baruch K.......................New Orleans, La.
Miller, General Charles................Franklin, Pa.
Miller, D. Knox........................Pittsburg, Pa.
Miller, Geo. I., M.D...................New York City
Miller, H..............................Philadelphia, Pa.
Miller, I..............................Paterson, N. J.
Miller, Isaac..........................Washington, D. C.
Miller, Isidore........................New York City
Miller, Mrs. J. B......................Newark, N. J.
Miller, Louis..........................Baltimore, Md.
Miller, Louis..........................Jamaica, N. Y.
Miller, Louis M........................Baltimore, Md.
Miller, Raphael W., M.D................Cincinnati, Ohio

Miller, S..............................Montreal, Canada
Miller, Sam............................Cleveland, Ohio
Miller, Simon..........................Philadelphia, Pa.
Miller, Solomon F......................Baltimore, Md.
Miller, Mrs. William K.................Philadelphia, Pa.
Millman, L.............................Montreal, Canada
Milnis, August.........................New York City
Mincer, S..............................Chicago, Ill.
Mincowsky, Philip......................Cincinnati, Ohio
Mindlin, H.............................New York City
Mintz, Jacob J., D.D.S.................New York City
Mintz, Nathan..........................New York City
Mirontz, Julius........................New York City
Misch, Mrs. Cæsar......................Providence, R. I.
Misel, Nathan..........................Brooklyn, N. Y.
Mishkin, H.............................Portchester, N. Y.
Mishkin, I.............................New York City
Mitchell, Edwin Knox...................Hartford, Conn.
Mitchell, Harley B.....................La Grange, Ill.
Mitchell, J............................New York City
Mitshkun, M............................Detroit, Mich.
Mittelman, Israel......................Middletown, Conn.
Mittleman, J. H., M.D..................New York City
Moch, M. E.............................Cincinnati, Ohio
Moeller, Herman........................New York City
Mogulesko, Sigmund.....................New York City
Moise, Marion..........................Sumter, S. C.
Moldawer, M............................Philadelphia, Pa.
Molner, H..............................Chicago, Ill.
Monash, I. Morris......................Charleston, S. C.
Monfried, Max..........................New York City
Monosewitz, F..........................New York City
Mooney, Rt. Rev. Mgr. Joseph F., V.G...New York City
Moore, Geo. F..........................Montgomery, Ala.
Moore, Prof. George F..................Cambridge, Mass.
Mord, M................................New Brighton, S. I., N. Y.
Mord, R................................Stapleton, S. I., N. Y.
Mordecai, F. Moultrie..................Charleston, S. C.
Morgan, Rev. D. Parker.................New York City
Morgan, Samuel.........................Baltimore, Md.
Moriarty, John S.......................New York City
Morocco, J.............................New York City
Morris, H..............................Memphis, Tenn.
Morris, Isaac..........................Brooklyn, N. Y.
Morris, L. Z...........................Richmond, Va.
Morris, M..............................Trenton, Tenn.
Morris, M. L...........................Montreal, Canada
Morris, N. L...........................Salt Lake City, Utah
Morris, W..............................Philadelphia, Pa.
Morrison, Isidore D....................New York City
Morse, Godfrey.........................Boston, Mass.
Morse, Jessie Arine....................Boston, Mass.
Morton, E. S...........................New York City
Moscovits, Albert......................New Haven, Conn.
Moscovitz, Albert......................New Haven, Conn.
Moscovitz, M...........................New York City
Moscovitz, M...........................Brooklyn, N. Y.
Moses, Adolph..........................Chicago, Ill.
Moses, Rev. Adolph.....................Louisville, Ky.
Moses, Alfred F........................Mobile, Ala.
Moses, Miss Hannah.....................New York City
Moses, J. B., M.D......................Crestline, Ohio
Mosessohn, Rev. Dr. N..................Portland, Ore.
Mosesson, S., M.D......................New York City
Moshkowitz, Z., M.D....................New York City
Moskovitz, David.......................New York City
Moskovitz, Morris......................New York City
Moss, H. W. (deceased).................Akron, Ohio
Moss, Hartwig..........................New Orleans, La.
Mosson, Hermann........................New York City
Muhlfelder, David......................Albany, N. Y.
Muhlhauser, Henry......................New York City
Muhr, Fannie...........................Philadelphia, Pa.
Muldberg, Moritz, M.D..................New York City
Muldberg, S., M.D......................New York City
Muller, Alfred.........................Denver, Colo.
Muller, Andre..........................New York City
Muller, H..............................Philadelphia, Pa.
Muller, Isaias.........................New York City
Muller, Mrs. J. L......................Los Angeles, Cal.
Mureck, William........................Brooklyn, N. Y.
Mushneis, Isaac........................New York City
Myers, Mrs. A. L.......................New York City
Myers, A. W............................Montreal, Canada
Myers, Angelo..........................Philadelphia, Pa.
Myers, I. H............................New York City
Myers, Rev. Isidore....................Los Angeles, Cal.
Myers, Mandel K........................Colorado Springs, Colo.
Myers, Martin J........................New York City
Myers, Nathaniel.......................New York City
Myers, Simon P.........................Montreal, Canada
Myerson, L. B..........................New York City
Myres, Aaron...........................New York City
Myres, Max M...........................New York City

N

Nachman, D.............................Augusta, Ga.
Nachman, Israel........................Albany, N. Y.
Naftalin, D............................Fargo, N. Dak.

Naiman, N..............................Baltimore, Md.
Naphtaly, Joseph....................San Francisco, Cal.
Napplebaum, I.......................New York City
Nasanowitz, Abraham (deceased).........Baltimore, Md.
Nassauer, B............................New York City
Nassauer, F............................Baltimore, Md.
Nathan, Clarence A.....................New York City
Nathan, David.........................Boston, Mass.
Nathan, Edgar J.......................New York City
Nathan, Edward I.....................Philadelphia, Pa.
Nathan, Frederick.....................New York City
Nathan, Isidore.......................Brooklyn, N. Y.
Nathan, Jacob..........................Troy, N. Y.
Nathan, Philip.........................Omaha, Neb.
Nathan, Robert F......................New York City
Nathan, S.............................New York City
Nathan, Samuel.........................Chicago, Ill.
Nathansohn, Osias.....................New York City
Nathanson, H..........................New York City
Nathanson, H. N.......................Philadelphia, Pa.
Natkin, Dr. David.....................Boston, Mass.
Nauhaus, Louis.........................Mars, Pa.
Nauheim, Benjamin.....................New York City
Naumberg, Elkan.......................New York City
Navison, Joseph.......................Boston, Mass.
Neethe, John..........................Galveston, Tex.
Negbaur, Max..........................Newark, N. J.
Neiman, Bennie........................Pittsburg, Pa.
Neiman, M. S..........................McKeesport, Pa.
Nelson, John..........................Providence, R. I.
Nelson, Rev. Leon M...................Cincinnati, Ohio
Nemser, William.......................New York City
Netzorg, Mrs. Ray S...................Detroit, Mich.
Neuberger, H. P.......................Chicago, Ill.
Neuberger, J. B., M.D.................Brooklyn, N. Y.
Neufeld, A. W.........................New York City
Neugass, C............................Brooklyn, N. Y.
Neuman, A.............................New York City
Neuman, Emanuel.......................New York City
Neuman, H.............................Pittsburg, Pa.
Neuman, Ignace........................Chicago, Ill.
Neuman, Michael.......................Brooklyn, N. Y.
Neuman, Moritz........................New York City
Neuman, Sol...........................New York City
Neumann, Solomon, M.D.................New York City
Neumark, S. E.........................New York City
Neuschatz, A..........................New York City
Neustadt, Joseph......................New York City
Neustaedter, M., M.D..................New York City
New Albany Public Library.............New Albany, Ind.
Newberger, Louis......................Indianapolis, Ind.
Newburger, Bernhard...................St. Joseph, Mo.
Newburger, J. M.......................New York City
Newburger, Hon. Joseph E..............New York City
Newburger, Max........................New York City
Newburger, Morris.....................Philadelphia, Pa.
Newfield, Morris......................Birmingham, Ala.
Newhall, Daniel H.....................Yonkers, N. Y.
Newman, A.............................New York City
Newman, Abraham L.....................New York City
Newman, Edward D......................New York City
Newman, H.............................Pittsburg, Pa.
Newman, H.............................Baltimore, Md.
Newman, H. J..........................New York City
Newman, Jacob.........................Tarrytown, N. Y.
Newman, Joseph........................New York City
Newman, Rev. Julius...................Chicago, Ill.
Newman, Leo H.........................Albany, N. Y.
Newman, Moritz........................New York City
Newman, Nathan........................New York City
Newman, Sig...........................Chicago, Ill.
Newmark, Benjamin.....................New York City
Newmark, Harris.......................Los Angeles, Cal.
Newmark, Rev. Hyman...................New York City
Niedlinger, Lewis.....................New York City
Nierenberg, M. B......................Brunswick, Md.
Nieto, A. H...........................New York City
Nieto, Rev. Jacob.....................San Francisco, Cal.
Niflot, Adolph........................New York City
Nightingale, James, M.D...............Worcester, Mass.
Nodell, Charles.......................Paterson, N. J.
Noot, Rev. Isaac C....................New York City
Noot, Rev. M..........................Troy, N. Y.
Norden, Felix A.......................Chicago, Ill.
Norden, Jennie H......................Chicago Ill.
Norden, Leopold.......................New York City
Norden, Max...........................New York City
Northshield, Charles..................New York City
Notes, Marcus.........................Washington, D. C.
Nourse, Edward E......................Berlin, Conn.
Novack, J. L., M.D....................Philadelphia, Pa.
Nuffler, A............................New York City
Nunn, R. J............................Savannah, Ga.
Nusbaum, Philip.......................Bradford, Pa.
Nusbaum, Sidney L.....................Norfolk, Va.
Nussbaum, M...........................New York City
Nussbaum, Myer........................Albany, N. Y.
Nye, Simon L..........................Wilkesbarre. Pa.

Oberfelder, Max.......................New York City
Obernauer, Herman.....................Pittsburg, Pa.
Ochs, Adolph S........................New York City
Ochser, S., M.D.......................New York City
Ockooneff, Solomon....................New London, Conn.
O'Connor, Rt. Rev. J. J...............So. Orange, N. J.
O'Donovan, Rev. John F., S.J..........New York City
Oechsner, John F......................New Orleans, La.
Oesterlein, Jacob.....................New York City
Oestreicher, Isaac....................New York City
Oettinger, Mrs. Henry.................Baltimore, Md.
Offenberg, Samuel.....................Brooklyn, N. Y.
Ognus, Louis..........................Chicago, Ill.
Ogusky, J.............................Uniontown, Pa.
Ohavei Zion Congregation..............New Orleans, La.
Oldstein, H. J., M.D..................Philadelphia, Pa.
Olivein, Ben Zion D...................Philadelphia, Pa.
O'Malley, D. C........................New Orleans, La.
Oppenheim, D..........................Pittsburg, Pa.
Oppenheim, Gustavus...................Washington, D. C.
Oppenheim, Isaac......................Toledo, Ohio
Oppenheim, Jacob......................New York City
Oppenheim, Louis......................New York City
Oppenheim, Samuel.....................New York City
Oppenheim, William....................New York City
Oppenheimer, Mrs. Anton...............New York City
Oppenheimer, Harry D..................Chicago, Ill.
Oppenheimer, Isaac, M.D...............New York City
Oppenheimer, Julius M.................San Antonio, Tex.
Oppenheimer, Sigmund (deceased).......New York City
Oppenheimer, Simon....................Washington, D. C.
Oransky, L............................Des Moines, Iowa
Orently, A............................New York City
Orently, D............................New York City
Orler, Solomon........................Brooklyn, N. Y.
Ornstein, Simon.......................New York City
Orth, Henry...........................Washington, D. C.
Oser, Harris E........................Philadelphia, Pa.
Oser, Harry...........................San Francisco, Cal.
Oser, Maurice Henry, D.D.S............New York City
Osgood, S.............................Pittsburg, Pa.
Oshinsky, Joseph......................New York City
Oshlag, J., M.D.......................New York City
Osk, Marcus L.........................New York City
Osterberg, Max E. E., A.M.............New York City
Otesky, Morris........................Newark, N. J.
Ottenberg, Adolphus...................New York City
Ottinger, Marx........................New York City
Ottinger, Moses.......................New York City
Ozersky, Louis A......................Youngstown, Ohio

P

Packard Brothers......................Syracuse, N. Y.
Pain, S...............................St. Louis, Mo.
Paley, Herman.........................New York City
Paley, John...........................Brooklyn, N. Y.
Paley, Peretz.........................New York City
Palley, Samuel........................Brooklyn, N. Y.
Palmbaum, George......................Charlestown, W. Va.
Palter, Ephraim.......................Toronto, Canada
Paper, Lewis..........................St. Paul, Minn.
Parelhoff, Rev. Samuel................Baltimore, Md.
Parges, B. F..........................Chicago, Ill.
Parham, F. W., M.D....................New Orleans, La.
Parn, Hugo............................Chicago, Ill.
Parnas, M.............................New York City
Paton, Prof. Lewis B..................Hartford, Conn.
Patton, Walter M......................Baldwin, Kan.
Pearlman, Jacob.......................New York City
Pearlman, William.....................Pittsburg, Pa.
Pearlstein, I. M......................Charleston, S. C.
Peck, Leopold.........................New York City
Peinstein, N..........................Worcester, Mass.
Peiser, Louis, M.D....................New York City
Peiser, Rev. Simon....................Cleveland, Ohio
Peixotto, Raphael.....................San Francisco, Cal.
Pellman, Louis........................New York City
Pellman, S. M.........................New York City
Pels, Julius..........................Baltimore, Md.
Peltz, H. M...........................Newport News, Va.
Penny, Rev. William L., LL.D..........New York City
Pereles, James M......................Milwaukee, Wis.
Peres, Israel H.......................Memphis, Tenn.
Perezel, Adelbert.....................New York City
Peritz, Prof. Ismar J., Ph.D..........Syracuse, N. Y.
Perla, Joseph.........................New York City
Perlberg, S...........................Philadelphia, Pa.
Perlman, Abraham......................New York City
Perlman, Louis R......................New York City
Perlman, William......................Pittsburg, Pa.
Perls, Emanuel........................New York City
Perlstein, Rev. M.....................Chicago, Ill.
Perlstein, W. P.......................New York City
Perry, Edwin..........................Providence, R. I.
Pesenberg, Abraham....................New York City
Peskind, A., M.D......................Cleveland, Ohio
Peters, Rev. Madison C., D.D..........Brooklyn, N. Y.

Pevitz, Osmer J.....................Syracuse, N. Y.
Peyser, George B...................New York City
Peyser, Julius J...............Washington, D. C.
Peyser, Nathan.....................New York City
Pfaelzer, Bernhard...................Chicago, Ill.
Pfaelzer, David......................Chicago, Ill.
Pfaelzer, David M....................Chicago, Ill.
Pfaelzer, Eli........................Chicago, Ill.
Pfaelzer, Morris................Philadelphia, Pa.
Pfeifer, Simon...................New Orleans, La.
Phelps, E...........................Shreveport, La.
Philip, Maximilian..................New York City
Philipson, Rev. David, D.D.........Cincinnati, Ohio
Phillips, Adeline I................New York City
Phillips, D. H.....................New York City
Phillips, Harry......................Chicago, Ill.
Phillips, Isidor....................Boston, Mass.
Phillips, N. Taylor................New York City
Phillips, Nathan...................Seattle, Wash.
Phillipson, Joseph..................Chicago, Ill.
Phillipson, Samuel..................Chicago, Ill.
Philo, Rev. Isador E..................Akron, Ohio
Pian, S.............................St. Louis, Mo.
Pick, Richard.......................Chicago, Ill.
Pierce, A.......................Montreal, Canada
Pierson, Rev. Arthur T., D.D......Brooklyn, N. Y.
Pincus, A............................Mobile, Ala.
Pincus, Bernard.................Philadelphia, Pa.
Pincus, Paul.......................New York City
Pines, J. & D......................Boston, Mass.
Pinsler, P......................Montreal, Canada
Pirosh, Berthold, M.D................Chicago, Ill.
Pitkowsky, Max.....................New York City
Pius, Alexander S..................New York City
Plant, Isaac....................Philadelphia, Pa.
Platzek, M. Warley................New York City
Plaut, Louis........................Newark, N. J.
Plotz, Joseph....................Brooklyn, N. Y.
Plumer, Samuel.....................New York City
Pockrass, Bernard...............Philadelphia, Pa.
Pokrony, Dave...................New Orleans, La.
Polacsek, Maurice..................New York City
Pollachek, John....................New York City
Pollack, Isaac...................Brooklyn, N. Y.
Pollak, Emil......................Cincinnati, Ohio
Polley, Jacob......................New York City
Pollock, Jacob......................Mobile, Ala.
Polstein, Joseph...................New York City
Ponch, A...........................New York City
Popkin, Isaac.......................Franklin, La.
Popper, Simon......................New York City
Popper, Stephen.......................Macon, Ga.
Popper, Dr. William................New York City
Porges, B. F........................Chicago, Ill.
Porter, F. C......................New Haven, Conn.
Porthory, Baron A..................New York City
Posert, Henry, M.D................Memphis, Tenn.
Posner, Leo......................Galveston, Tex.
Posner, Samuel.....................Tacoma, Wash.
Poss, Jacob.......................Milwaukee, Wis.
Poss, Louis........................New York City
Post, J. L.........................New York City
Potashinsky, Rev. Louis M.........Loveland, Colo.
Potsdamer, J. B., M.............Philadelphia, Pa.
Potter, Rt. Rev. Henry C., D.D....New York City
Powell, Rev. Herbert E..........Santa Clara, Cal.
Poyas, A.......................St. John, N. B., Canada
Poziski, S. C.......................Ashland, Wis.
Praeger, Albert...................Baltimore, Md.
Prager, William....................New York City
Prago, William L...................New York City
Prensky, Joseph....................New York City
Prensky, Nathan..................Brooklyn, N. Y.
Present, Philip....................Rochester, N. Y.
Press, Jacob.....................New Haven, Conn.
Press, Max.......................Middletown, Conn.
Price, Barnett.....................New York City
Price, Barnet......................New York City
Price, Ira Maurice...................Chicago, Ill.
Price, Rev. John...................Pittsburg, Pa.
Price, John A., M.D...............New York City
Price, Morris J....................New York City
Price, Abraham......................Chicago, Ill.
Price, H............................Houston, Tex.
Price, Henry.......................New York City
Price, Dr. John Dyneley............New York City
Printz, M.........................Cleveland, Ohio
Prinz, Emanuel...................Brooklyn, N. Y.
Pritzker, Nicholas..................Chicago, Ill.
Prockter, J. M..................Montreal, Canada
Proctor, George H..................Hastings, Fla.
Prokcimer, Ed......................Newark, N. J.
Prokesch, Jacob...................New York City
Prokesch, Samuel J................New York City
Prowler, David.....................New York City
Pruyn, Robert C......................Albany, N. Y.
Pruzan, I. M.......................Baltimore, Md.
Public Library..................New London, Conn.
Pulaski, M. H......................New York City

Pullan, E........................Ottawa, Canada
Putzler, Gibson....................New York City
Pye, Saul M........................New York City

Q

Quickmire, Samuel................San Mateo, Cal.
Quigley, Rt. Rev. Archbishop James E...........Chicago, Ill.

R

Rabinoff, M..........................Chicago, Ill.
Rabinovich, F........................Chicago, Ill.
Rabinovitch, Joseph M..............Paterson, N. J.
Rabinowitz, A...................Stamford, Conn.
Rabinowitz, David.................Brooklyn, N. Y.
Rabinowitz, H.....................Baltimore, Md.
Rabinowitz, H......................New York City
Rabinowitz, H. A...................New York City
Rabinowitz, J......................New York City
Rabinowitz, J...................San Francisco, Cal.
Rabinowitz, Louis..................New York City
Rabinowitz, Samuel.......St. John, N. B., Canada
Rabinowitz, Zelig................Kansas City, Mo.
Rachlin, David...................Brooklyn, N. Y.
Rachlin, Morris....................Newark, N. J.
Rachlin, William, M.D...........Brooklyn, N. Y.
Radcliffe College................Cambridge, Mass.
Radin, Adolph M., Ph.D.............New York City
Radin, Matthias....................New York City
Radin, Oscar.......................Pittsburg, Pa
Raff, Henry D......................Chicago, Ill.
Raffel, Jacob M...................Baltimore, Md.
Rahenovitch, Joseph M.............Paterson, N. J.
Rains, H. S........................New York City
Raisin, Jacob S....................Butte, Mont.
Raisin, Max.......................Meridian, Miss.
Raken, Simon C..................Philadelphia, Pa.
Raker, M...........................Olyphant, Pa.
Rambach, Hyman M.................Boston, Mass.
Rappaport, Rev. A................Petoskey, Mich.
Rappaport, D. M...................New York City
Rappaport, Solomon.................New York City
Rappoport, Rev. Julius..............Chicago, Ill.
Rapport, Samuel....................Durham, N. C.
Rascovar, James....................New York City
Raske, J. L........................Chicago, Ill.
Ratkowsky, Morris B...............New York City
Ratner, Aaron......................New York City
Ratner, Leo, M.D.................Brooklyn, N. Y.
Ratnoff, Nathan....................New York City
Raub, Marcus......................Pittsburg, Pa.
Raub, Solomon........................Dayton, Ohio
Rauch, Max......................Charleston, W. Va.
Ravitch, M. L., M.D................Lexington, Ky.
Rayfel, Hyman...................Brooklyn, N. Y.
Raymond, Rev. Andrew V. V.......Schenectady, N. Y.
Rayner, Albert W.................Baltimore, Md.
Reader, Meyer......................New York City
Reder, Ike..........................Akron, Ohio
Reder, Jake.......................Crestline, Ohio
Reed, D. F.......................Cleveland, Ohio
Reese, Abraham..................Wilkesbarre, Pa.
Reesfield, David................Newport News, Va.
Rehlberger, Moritz.................New York City
Reich, Morris......................St. Joseph, Mo.
Reich, S. Moses....................Bradford, Pa.
Reichbart Brothers.................New York City
Reichert, Rev. Isador..............Uniontown, Pa.
Reichman, William.................New York City
Reichstein, B......................Pittsburg, Pa.
Reigelhaupt, S., M.D.............Cleveland, Ohio
Reiner, Isidor................So. Bethlehem, Pa.
Reinerff, P........................New York City
Reinhardt, A.......................New York City
Reinherz, I. B.....................Boston, Mass.
Reinherz, P........................New York City
Reinthaler, Jonas E., M.D..........New York City
Reis, Benedict.....................New York City
Reis, Isidor.....................Brooklyn, N. Y.
Reis, M............................New York City
Reisman, M.........................Buffalo, N. Y.
Reismann, David, M.D...........Philadelphia, Pa.
Reiss, Jacob, M.D..................New York City
Reiter, A. F.......................Bluffton, Ohio
Reiter, Louis......................New York City
Reshower, J........................New York City
Resnik, Philip....................Hartford, Conn.
Rice, Abraham......................New York City
Rice, Henry........................New York City
Rice, Isaac L......................New York City
Rice, Max..........................Scranton, Pa.
Rice, S. M......................Wheeling, W. Va.
Rich, Joseph S.....................New York City
Rich, Mrs. Matilda.................New York City
Rich, William S....................Newark, N. J.
Richard, William V., M.D.........New Orleans, La.
Richardson, Rev. H. G...........Clarksburg, W. Va.
Richman, Jacob M.................Hartford, Conn.
Richman, Miss Julia................New York City
Richmond, Joseph...................Boston, Mass.

Richter, Charles J.	New York City
Richter, Daniel.	New York City
Richter, Max.	New York City
Riegelhaupt, S., M.D.	Cleveland, Ohio
Rieger, Frank.	New York City
Riemer, William.	Brooklyn, N. Y.
Rieser, A. L.	New York City
Rifkin, A., & Co.	Wilkesbarre, Pa.
Riglander, M. M.	New York City
Ringolsky, I. J.	Kansas City, Mo.
Ripkin, D.	New York City
Ripple, Ezra H.	Scranton, Pa.
Risnicoff, Morris.	Brooklyn, N. Y.
Ristner, Max.	New York City
Ritay, H. B.	Paterson, N. J.
Ritch, Morris.	Philadelphia, Pa.
Rittenberg, S.	Charleston, N. C.
Robb, Rev. G. M.	Philadelphia, Pa.
Robbin, Samuel B.	Washington, D. C.
Robbins, Barnet R.	New York City
Robbins, Benjamin.	New York City
Robbins, Bernard.	New York City
Robbins, Samuel.	Boston, Mass.
Robert, Simon.	Chelsea, Mass.
Roberts, Harry.	Boston, Mass.
Roberts, S.	Boston, Mass.
Robin, Peter.	Pittsburg, Pa.
Robinovitz, J.	New York City
Robinowich, Julius.	New York City
Robinowitz, Louis.	New York City
Robinson, A.	New York City
Robinson, J.	Detroit, Mich.
Robinson, J. A.	Providence, R. I.
Robinson, J. L.	Los Angeles, Cal.
Robison, Gerson.	New York City
Robison, Lazarus (deceased).	New York City
Robitsek, Sam.	New York City
Rochomowitz, David.	New York City
Rodenberg, George L.	Providence, R. I.
Rodman, H., M.D.	New York City
Roedel, Charles F.	New York City
Roedel, Max F.	New York City
Roeder, Mrs. Geraldine.	New York City
Rogers, Gustavus A.	New York City
Rogers, J.	New York City
Rogers, J.	Roxbury, Mass.
Rogers, Mark H.	New York City
Rogers, Prof. Robert W.	Madison, N. J.
Roggen, Nathan.	New York City
Rohrheimer, Moses.	Philadelphia, Pa.
Romain, Armand.	New Orleans, La.
Romain, S.	Montreal, Canada
Roman, David.	Waco, Tex.
Romansky, J.	Greenville, Miss.
Romm, I. W.	New York City
Romm, M., M.D.	New York City
Roos, Isidore.	New York City
Roos, Rev. J. S. (Rabbi).	Dutch Guiana, S. Am.
Ropes, James H.	Cambridge, Mass.
Rosahnsky, Herman, M.D.	Brooklyn, N. Y.
Rosanburg, H.	Minneapolis, Minn.
Rose, A. James.	Providence, R. I.
Rose, Abie and Willie.	New York City
Rose, Adolph.	Vicksburg, Miss.
Rose, Harry.	Manistique, Mich.
Rose, Ike.	Providence, R. I.
Rose, Isaac.	Montreal, Canada
Rose, Jacob.	New York City
Rose, M.	New York City
Rose, Morris.	New York City
Rose, Oscar B.	Toronto, Canada
Rose, Samuel.	Newark, N. J.
Rose, Solomon.	Rochester, N. Y.
Rosebault, W. M.	New York City
Roseman, William, M.D.	Baltimore, Md.
Rosen, A.	New York City
Rosen, H.	Toledo, Ohio
Rosen, Max.	New York City
Rosen, Nathan.	Baltimore, Md.
Rosenau, Rev. Dr. William.	Baltimore, Md.
Rosenbach, Abr.	Philadelphia, Pa.
Rosenbaum, Henry W.	New York City
Rosenbaum, Morris.	New York City
Rosenbaum, S. D.	New York City
Rosenbaum, Samuel.	Laurium, Mich.
Rosenbaum, Walter S.	Chicago, Ill.
Rosenberg, Abraham.	New York City
Rosenberg, Abraham H.	New York City
Rosenberg Brothers.	Everett, Mass.
Rosenberg, C.	Montreal, Canada
Rosenberg, D.	McKeesport, Pa.
Rosenberg, E.	Seattle, Wash.
Rosenberg, Dr. E.	Cleveland, Ohio
Rosenberg, Rev. Erwin.	Brooklyn, N. Y.
Rosenberg, J.	New York City
Rosenberg, J.	Pittsburg, Pa.
Rosenberg, Jacob.	New York City
Rosenberg, Jacob, & Sons.	Pittsburg, Pa.
Rosenberg, James.	Cleveland, Ohio
Rosenberg, Joseph.	New York City
Rosenberg, Mrs. Joseph.	Bradford, Pa.
Rosenberg, K.	Pittsburg, Pa.
Rosenberg, L. & M.	New York City
Rosenberg, Morris.	Baltimore, Md.
Rosenberg, Morris.	Philadelphia, Pa.
Rosenberg, Simon.	Rochester, N. Y.
Rosenblatt, J.	Baltimore, Md.
Rosenblatt, J.	New York City
Rosenblatt, Rev. Levi.	St. Louis, Mo.
Rosenbloom, Daniel.	Syracuse, N. Y.
Rosenbloom, Henry.	New York City
Rosenbloom, Max Z.	Rochester, N. Y.
Rosenbloom, Solomon J.	Brooklyn, N. Y.
Rosenblum, William.	Philadelphia, Pa.
Rosendale, Simon W.	Albany, N. Y.
Rosener, Sol.	New York City
Rosenfeld, B.	Tucson, Ariz.
Rosenfeld, Bertie.	New York City
Rosenfeld, Chas. H.	Woodbine, N. J.
Rosenfeld, J. H.	New York City
Rosenfeld, M. E.	New York City
Rosenfeld, Mrs. Maurice.	Chicago, Ill.
Rosenfeld, Mrs. Rosa W.	Baltimore, Md.
Rosenfeld, S. M.	New York City
Rosenfeld, William I.	New York City
Rosenfelt, J. H.	New York City
Rosenfield, Benjamin.	Elmira, N. Y.
Rosenfield, I.	New York City
Rosenfield, Louis.	Pittsburg, Pa.
Rosengard, H.	Chicago, Ill.
Rosenheck, I.	Brooklyn, N. Y.
Rosenheimer, D.	Chicago, Ill.
Rosenholz, J. W.	Tompkinsville, N. Y.
Rosenstein, A.	New York City
Rosenstein, Henry.	Brooklyn, N. Y.
Rosenstein, Joseph.	Philadelphia, Pa.
Rosenstein, Louis.	Moline, Ill.
Rosenstein, M.	Philadelphia, Pa.
Rosenstein, Rev. Marcus.	New York City
Rosenstock, Morris.	Greenville, Miss.
Rosenthal, A.	Mt. Vernon, N. Y.
Rosenthal, Adolph.	Boston, Mass.
Rosenthal, Alexander.	New York City
Rosenthal, Eliazer Lieberman.	Montreal, Canada
Rosenthal, Rev. F. L.	Baton Rouge, La.
Rosenthal, George D.	St. Louis, Mo.
Rosenthal, Harris L.	New York City
Rosenthal, Harry.	New York City
Rosenthal, Herman.	Charlestown, Mass.
Rosenthal, Isidore.	Lancaster, Pa.
Rosenthal, J.	St. Joseph, Mo.
Rosenthal, Lazarus.	Manistique, Mich.
Rosenthal, Levi M.	Montreal, Canada
Rosenthal, Max, M.D.	New York City
Rosenthal, Meyer.	Pittsburg, Pa.
Rosenthal, Michael, M.D.	New York City
Rosenthal, Mitchell.	Cohoes, N. Y.
Rosenthal, Moses.	Petoskey, Mich.
Rosenthal, Philip.	Au Sable, Mich.
Rosenthal, S.	New York City
Rosenthal, Mrs. S.	Detroit, Mich.
Rosenthal, S. C.	Binghamton, N. Y.
Rosenthal, William H.	New York City
Rosenthorn, Herin.	New York City
Rosentreter, A.	St. Louis, Mo.
Rosenwald, D. S.	Albuquerque, N. Mex.
Rosenwald, Julius.	Chicago, Ill.
Rosenwald, L. S.	Salina, Kan.
Rosenwasser, H.	New York City
Rosenwasser, M., M.D.	Cleveland, Ohio
Rosenwasser, Max.	New York City
Rosenwasser, Morris.	New York City
Rosenzweig, J.	Detroit, Mich
Rosett, Moritz.	New York City
Rosing, Jacob.	Buffalo, N. Y.
Rosner, Sam.	New York City
Rosnick, J.	St. Joseph, Mo.
Rosnosky, Isaac.	Boston, Mass.
Rosow, I. P.	Brooklyn, N. Y.
Ross, James.	Montreal, Canada
Rosskam, Isaac (deceased).	Philadelphia, Pa.
Rostow, Clarence, M.D.	Newark, N. J.
Roth, A. L.	New York City
Roth, Adolph.	Brooklyn, N. Y.
Roth, B.	Marshall, Tex.
Roth, Edward.	New York City
Roth, Emery.	New York City
Roth, Fred.	San Francisco, Cal.
Roth, Henry, M.D.	New York City
Roth, Ignatz.	New York City
Roth, M. L.	New York City
Roth, William B.	Brooklyn, N. Y.
Rothause, S.	Texarkana, Tex.
Rothberg, Benjamin.	New York City
Rothblum, Saul.	Cleveland, Ohio
Rothchild, S.	New York City
Rothenberg, Leon.	New York City
Rothkowitz, Harri B.	New York City

Rothschild, D. M.	Chicago, Ill.
Rothschild, Edward L.	Philadelphia, Pa.
Rothschild, Jacob.	New York City
Rothschild, Jacob.	Cawker City, Kan.
Rothschild, Meyer D.	New York City
Rothschild, S. F.	Brooklyn, N. Y.
Rothstein, Isidore.	Pittsburg, Pa.
Rothstein, Rev. Leonard J.	Kalamazoo, Mich.
Rothstein, Myer.	Johnstown, Pa.
Rottenberg, Dr. Ignatz Morvay.	New York City
Rovinsky, Alexander, M.D.	New York City
Rovno, Pinkas.	Philadelphia, Pa.
Ruben, A.	Charleston, S. C.
Ruben, Maurice.	Pittsburg, Pa.
Rubenstein, C. A.	Baltimore, Md.
Rubenstein, Jacob.	Boston, Mass.
Rubin, Edward.	New York City
Rubin, Jacob.	New York City
Rubin, Joseph H.	Philadelphia, Pa.
Rubin, Max.	New York City
Rubin, S.	Brooklyn, N. Y.
Rubin, W. B.	Milwaukee, Wis.
Rubinger, Charles.	New York City
Rubinson Brothers.	Brooklyn, N. Y.
Rubinstein, Everett, Ph.G.	Cleveland, Ohio
Rudawsky, S.	St. Paul, Minn.
Rudolph, A.	Montreal, Canada
Rushman, Townsend.	Plainfield, N. J.
Ruslander, Moses.	McKees Rocks, Pa.
Rutenberg, Charles.	New York City
Ruth, Abraham.	New York City
Rypins, Rev. Isaac L.	St. Paul, Minn.
Ryskind, Matthew H.	New York City

S

Sabbathai, Lieberman.	St. Joseph, Mo.
Sabsevitz Brothers.	New York City
Sabsovich, Prof. H. L.	New York City
Sachs, Charles H.	Pittsburg, Pa.
Sachs, E.	Chicago, Ill.
Sachs, H.	New York City
Sachs, Isidor.	New York City
Sachs, Julius.	New York City
Sachs, Moses A.	New York City
Sachs, Philip.	Baltimore, Md.
Sachs, Philip.	New York City
Sacks, Harris.	New York City
Sacks, I.	Lynchburg, Va.
Sacks, Perress.	Rolling Fork, Miss.
Sacks, Samuel.	Philadelphia, Pa.
Sadvoransky, J.	Brooklyn, N. Y.
Safowitz, S.	New York City
Safro, Aaron.	New York City
Sahud, Dr. M.	Danville, Ill.
Sakowitz, Solomon.	New York City
Saks, J.	Norfolk, Va.
Salamont, Oscar H.	Boston, Mass.
Salaway, A. M.	Boston, Mass.
Sale, Rev. S.	St. Louis, Mo.
Salinger, Julius.	New York City
Salinger, Lewis.	Centerville, Iowa
Salinger, N.	Goshen, Ind.
Salit, Michael.	Brooklyn, N. Y.
Salk, M.	Chicago, Ill.
Saller, Isaac.	Philadelphia, Pa.
Saller, Louis.	Philadelphia, Pa.
Salmon, M.	Beaver Falls, Pa.
Salomon, H. A.	New York City
Salomon, L.	New York City
Salomon, M. L.	Greenville, Miss.
Salomonsky, Louis.	New York City
Salpeter, Jacob.	Brooklyn, N. Y.
Salsburg, Abram.	Wilkesbarre, Pa.
Saltz, Max.	New York City
Salzberg, Louis.	New York City
Salzman, Rev. Marcus.	Wilkesbarre, Pa.
Salzman, Rev. Tobias.	Baltimore, Md.
Salzman, William.	New York City
Sameth, Max.	New York City
Sameth, N. M.	Bluefield, W. Va.
Samett, M. W., & Brother.	Canisteo, N. Y.
Samett, Sol.	New York City
Samuel, John.	Philadelphia, Pa.
Samuel, L.	Portland, Ore.
Samuels, Peter.	New York City
Samuelson, Jacob.	New York City
Sanders, Frank K.	New Haven, Conn.
Sanders, Leon.	New York City
Sanders, Louis.	Brooklyn, N. Y.
Sandfield, A.	San Antonio, Tex.
Sanditen, Mordecai Hirsh.	Brooklyn, N. Y.
Sanger, Philip.	Dallas, Tex.
Sanger, Sam.	Waco, Tex.
Sanguinetti, Percy A.	New York City
Santer, Bernard.	New York City
Santz, Simson V., M.D.	Philadelphia, Pa.
Saperston, Julius L.	Buffalo, N. Y.
Sapirstein, N. L., M.D.	Pittsburg, Pa.
Sarasohn, Sam.	Detroit, Mich.

Sarasohn & Son.	New York City
Sarason, B.	New Haven, Conn.
Sarnoff, Mrs. Irene Ida.	New York City
Sass, Samuel.	New York City
Sauber, Morris.	New York City
Sauber, Robert.	Syracuse, N. Y.
Saudomire, P.	Pittsburg, Pa.
Sauer, Adolph.	Baltimore, Md.
Saukstone, J. I.	Arcola, Miss.
Saul, Marx.	Allegheny, Pa.
Saul, Max M.	Allegheny, Pa.
Saul, Samuel.	Allegheny, Pa.
Saulson, William.	Detroit, Mich.
Saunders, E. D.	New Orleans, La.
Saunders, Ernest.	Toronto, Canada
Saunders, Julius.	Toronto, Canada
Savage, Moses, M.D.	Baltimore, Md.
Sawin, Rev. T. P.	Troy, N. Y.
Sax, Joe W.	South Bend, Ind.
Sax, Louis.	Chicago, Ill.
Saxon, Louis.	Binghamton, N. Y.
Schaap, Michael.	New York City
Schachne, Moritz.	Chillicothe, Ohio
Schafer, Samuel M.	New York City
Schafner, Mrs. H.	Chicago, Ill.
Schalbe, S.	New York City
Schamberg, Jay F., M.D.	Philadelphia, Pa.
Schanberg, Lewis M.	Philadelphia, Pa.
Schanfarber, Rev. T.	Mobile, Ala.
Schapiro, Rudolph.	Brooklyn, N. Y.
Scharff, Monroe.	Natchez, Miss.
Scharlin, J. A.	San Francisco, Cal.
Scharlin, S.	New York City
Schaul, Lewis J.	Augusta, Ga.
Schechter, Prof. Solomon.	New York City
Scheff, Jonas S.	New York City
Scheib, Henry.	New York City
Schein, Jacob.	Pittsburg, Pa.
Scheinberg, Joseph R.	New York City
Scheinman, I. L.	Detroit, Mich.
Schellenberg, Charles B.	Brooklyn, N. Y.
Schem, Simon.	New York City
Schenkes, Israel W.	New York City
Schenthal, Sylvan.	Baltimore, Md.
Schepper, Abraham.	New York City
Scherbel, A.	New York City
Scherer, Jacob.	New York City
Scheuer, E.	Toronto, Canada
Scheuer, Jacob.	Cincinnati, Ohio
Scheuer, Simon.	Newark, N. J.
Schick, Philip I.	New York City
Schiff, Jacob H.	New York City
Schiff, Simon.	New York City
Schiffer, Alfred.	New York City
Schiffer, Joseph.	New York City
Schiffer, Walter A.	New York City
Schiller, E. B.	New York City
Schiller, L.	New York City
Schiller, Mark.	New York City
Schiller, Dr. Michael.	New York City
Schinasi Brothers.	New York City
Schinze, N.	New York City
Schlachter, M.	New York City
Schlang, Aaron.	Brooklyn, N. Y.
Schlein, S.	Philadelphia, Pa.
Schleistein, M.	New York City
Schlesinger, A.	St. Louis, Mo.
Schlesinger, Anthony.	New York City
Schlesinger, H.	New York City
Schlesinger, Jacob.	Newark, N. J.
Schlesinger, Le Roy.	San Francisco, Cal.
Schlesinger, Louis.	Newark, N. J.
Schlesinger, M.	Albany, N. Y.
Schlesinger, Morris, M.D.	New York City
Schlesinger, Simon.	New York City
Schleuker, Rudolph.	New York City
Schlockow, Oswald.	New York City
Schloesing, J. H.	Chicago, Ill.
Schloessinger, Max, M.D.	New York City
Schloss, Herman.	Philadelphia, Pa.
Schloss, Jonas.	Baltimore, Md.
Schloss, Max.	New York City
Schloss, Nathan.	Baltimore, Md.
Schloss, Seligman.	Detroit, Mich.
Schmeidler, Leopold.	New York City
Schmidt, Nathaniel.	Ithaca, N. Y.
Schmidt, Rev. S.	Providence, R. I.
Schmidt, S. H.	Manor, Pa.
Schmookler, Henry B., M.D.	Philadelphia, Pa.
Schmultz, Samuel D.	Victoria, B. C., Canada
Schneider, C. H.	Augusta, Ga.
Schnitzer, Henry J.	New York City
Schnitzer, Marcus.	New York City
Schnur, B.	New York City
Schoen, Adolph, M.D. (deceased).	Yankton, S. D.
Schoen, B.	New York City
Schoen, Henry.	New York City
Schoenberg, Isidor.	Baltimore, Md.
Schoenberg, L.	Providence, R. I.

Schoenberg, M.	St. Louis, Mo.
Schoenberger, W. J.	Cleveland, Ohio
Schoenfeld, Benj. P.	New York City
Schoenfeld. L.	Seattle, Wash.
Schoenkopf. Rev. S.	Elizabeth, N. J.
Schoenthal, Henry	Washington, Pa.
Schomer, Abraham S.	New York City
Schonthal, Joseph	Columbus, Ohio
Schooner, Joseph Y.	Boston, Mass.
Schreiber, Rev. Dr. Emanuel	Chicago, Ill.
Schreiber, Max.	New York City
Schrier, Benjamin.	New York City
Schulang, Philip.	New York City
Schulman, Abraham	Brooklyn, N. Y.
Schulman, David.	Brooklyn, N. Y.
Schulman, I.	Minneapolis, Minn.
Schulman, Joseph	Brooklyn, N. Y.
Schulman, Louis.	Brooklyn, N. Y.
Schulman, Louis.	New York City
Schulman, Rev. Samuel.	Olyphant, Pa.
Schultz. J.	Chicago, Ill.
Schultz, M.	Vancouver, B. C., Canada
Schultz, Samuel D.	New York City
Schumack, Rev. Ambrose	New York City
Schuman, Edgar.	Brooklyn, N. Y.
Schurr, Mark J.	New York City
Schvartz, S.	New York City
Schwab, Adolph.	Chicago, Ill.
Schwab, Charles H.	Cleveland, Ohio
Schwab, Mrs. Flora	St. Louis, Mo.
Schwab, Isaac.	Chicago, Ill.
Schwab, Louis.	San Francisco, Cal.
Schwabacher, Mrs. A.	New Orleans, La.
Schwabacher, Mrs. Max.	New York City
Schwan, L. M.	Brooklyn, N. Y.
Schwarcz, Max M.	Brooklyn, N. Y.
Schwartz, Mrs. A.	Plymouth, Pa.
Schwartz, Aaron.	New York City
Schwartz, Adolph.	New York City
Schwartz, B. M.	Philadelphia, Pa.
Schwartz, Charles	Lafayette, Ind.
Schwartz, D.	New York City
Schwartz, David.	Knoxville, Tenn.
Schwartz, L.	New York City
Schwartz, Louis	Utica, N. Y.
Schwartz, M.	New York City
Schwartz, Mrs. M. M.	New York City
Schwartz, Max.	New York City
Schwartz, Meyer.	New York City
Schwartz, Moritz, M.D.	New York City
Schwartz, Natin.	New York City
Schwartzberg, Max.	Shreveport, La.
Schwartzberger, J. B., & Co.	Mobile, Ala.
Schwarz, Mrs. R. M.	New York City
Schwarzkopf, Gustave.	New York City
Schwarzschild, Samuel.	Somerville, N. J.
Schwed, Charles.	San Francisco, Cal.
Schweitzer, Mrs. Jacob	New York City
Schweitzer, Julius.	Chicago, Ill.
Schweitzer, Samuel.	New York City
Schwob, Adolphe.	Newport News, Va.
Scott. M.	Montreal, Canada
Scrimger, Joseph S.	New York City
Scrivin, J. A.	New York City
Scully. P. J.	New York City
Seadler, B. F.	Cincinnati, Ohio
Seasongood, A. J.	Pittsburg, Pa.
Seder, I.	Allegheny, Pa.
Sedler, Barnet.	New York City
Seelig, Henry.	Northumberland, Pa.
Seff, Harris.	Baltimore, Md.
Seff, Samuel.	Philadelphia, Pa.
Segal, A.	Philadelphia, Pa.
Segal, Bernhard, M.D.	New York City
Segal, Isaac.	Portland, Ore.
Segal, Myer.	Portsmouth, Va.
Segall, H.	Baltimore, Md.
Seidenman, Selig, & Brother	New York City
Seidman, Nathan H.	Newark, N. J.
Seidmann, Marcus, M.D.	Brooklyn, N. Y.
Seifter, Frederick.	New York City
Seigel, Max A.	New York City
Seigsmeister, William.	Cincinnati, Ohio
Seinsheimer, Henry A.	Binghamton, N. Y.
Seitman, S.	New York City
Seitz, Daniel.	New York City
Seldin, Nathan A.	Philadelphia, Pa.
Selig, B.	Chicago, Ill.
Selig, L. M.	Baltimore, Md.
Seliger, Solomon.	New York City
Seligman, Aaron.	New York City
Seligman, Edwin R. A.	New York City
Seligman, Isaac N.	New York City
Selikovitz, Adolph.	Morrillton, Ark.
Sellers, J. F.	Lynn, Mass.
Sellers, Maurice M	Hartford, Conn.
Seltzer, Barnett.	Chicago, Ill.
Selz, Morris.	St. Louis, Mo.
Seman, Philip L.	

	Erie, Pa.
Semuel, S.	New York City
Sensheimer, Charles.	Niverville, Manitoba, Canada
Serkau, Louis.	New York City
Serwer, Morris.	New York City
Sessler, Arnold.	New Haven, Conn.
Setlow, Joseph H.	Chicago, Ill.
Shabad, A. M., M.D.	Chicago, Ill.
Shabad, Henry M.	Nashua, N. H.
Shaber, S.	Pittsburg, Pa.
Shaeffer, David.	Chicago, Ill.
Shaeffer, Samuel J.	New York City
Shaff, Carl.	New York City
Shaine, B. M.	Louisville, Ky.
Shapinsky, S.	Montreal, Canada
Shapira, D.	Winston-Salem, N. C.
Shapiro, A.	New York City
Shapiro, Aaron S.	New York City
Shapiro, Adolph.	New Haven, Conn.
Shapiro, Ch.	Montreal, Canada
Shapiro, D.	New York City
Shapiro, H.	Chicago, Ill.
Shapiro, H.	Colorado Springs, Colo.
Shapiro, Mrs. Helen	Cleveland, Ohio
Shapiro, I.	Chicago, Ill.
Shapiro, Isaac.	Salt Lake City, Utah
Shapiro, J.	Brooklyn, N. Y.
Shapiro, Jacob.	New York City
Shapiro, Jenny	New York City
Shapiro, Julius.	Montreal, Canada
Shapiro, M.	New York City
Shapiro, Morris.	New York City
Shapiro, S.	Washington, D. C.
Shappiro, Jacob.	Philadelphia, Pa.
Shar, Aaron.	New York City
Sharfin, Z., M.D.	Philadelphia, Pa.
Shatz, Lewis A.	Brooklyn, N. Y.
Shatzkin, N. J.	New York City
Shatzkin, S. M.	Millville, N. J.
Sheffer, Harry.	New York City
Sheffield, Herman B., M.D.	San José, Cal.
Sheffler, Samuel.	Norfolk, Va.
Shefsky, Lewis	Philadelphia, Pa.
Sheftelson, Solomon.	New York City
Sheifer, V. S.	Pittsburg, Pa.
Sheinberg, B.	Philadelphia, Pa.
Shenken, Julius, M.D.	New York City
Shenkman, Samuel.	Toronto, Canada
Sheppard, E. E.	Pittsburg, Pa.
Sher, Bennett.	New York City
Sher, Edward.	Philadelphia, Pa.
Sherbow, Rev. Jacob S.	Binghamton, N.Y.
Sherman, H. J.	New York City
Sherman, Louis I.	Albany, N. Y.
Sherman, M.	Jersey City, N. J.
Sherman, Oscar.	Fredericktown, Mo.
Sherman, Samuel.	St. Louis, Mo.
Sherman, Samuel.	Warsaw, Ind.
Shield, Jacob S.	New York City
Shiller, S.	New York City
Shinkman, Samuel.	Montreal, Canada
Ship, F.	New York City
Shlachetsky, Louis, M.D.	Chicago, Ill.
Shless, A. L.	Brooklyn, N. Y.
Shlevin, H. S., M.D.	Brooklyn, N. Y.
Shlivek, Hyman	Chicago, Ill.
Shoffner, Charles.	Charlestown, Mass.
Shoolman, Joseph.	Newark, N. J.
Shorr, Rev. Israel.	Rat Portage, Canada
Shragg, Alexander.	New York City
Shramek, Carl.	New York City
Shufro, Jacob J.	New Castle, Pa.
Shuklansky, Jacob I.	New York City
Shuldiner, David.	Montreal, Canada
Shulhof, R. L.	New Haven, Conn.
Shulman, M.	Baltimore, Md.
Shulman, Nathan	New York City
Shumberg, George.	Boston, Mass.
Shurdut, Phillip.	Chicago, Ill.
Shure, Mandel.	Cincinnati, Ohio
Shwartz, Simon.	New York City
Shweitzer, Julius.	New York City
Sichel, Maurice.	Portland, Ore.
Sichel, Sigmund.	Newark, N. J.
Sickles, Gustavus.	Philadelphia, Pa.
Sickles, Louis.	New York City
Sidenberg, Charles.	Cincinnati, Ohio
Siebler, Bernard H.	New York City
Siegel, A.	New York City
Siegel, Henry.	New York City
Siegel, Isaac.	Salt Lake City, Utah
Siegel, Rachel U.	Newark, N. J.
Siegel, Samuel.	Cleveland,
Siegelstein, L. E., M.D.	New York
Sigmund, S.	New York
Silberberg, David.	Bradford
Silberberg, Fred.	New
Silberberg, Siegfried.	New
Silberblatt, S.	New
Silberfeld, Rev. Julius.	Ne

Silberman, David	New York City
Silberman, I.	New York City
Silberman, Jacob	New York City
Silberman, Jacob L.	Philadelphia, Pa.
Silberman, Max	New York City
Silberman, Morris	New York City
Silbe man, Samuel J.	New York City
Silberman, Tanchum	Baltimore, Md.
Silberstein, Bernard	Duluth, Minn.
Silberstein, Solomon	Philadelphia, Pa.
Silberstein, Solomon D.	New York City
Silk, Charles I.	Perth Amboy, N. J.
Silver, George	Chicago, Ill.
Silver, Isidor	Augusta, Ga.
Silver, J. C.	New York City
Silver, Moritz	Austin, Tex.
Silverberg, E. Myers	Pittsburg, Pa.
Silverglade, M.	Cincinnati, Ohio
Silverman, A.	Brooklyn, N. Y.
Silverman, George Morris	Uniontown, Pa.
Silverman, Rev. Herman	New York City
Silverman, I.	New York City
Silverman, Joseph, D.D.	New York City
Silverman, K.	New York City
Silverman, Louis	Quebec, Canada
Silverman, M. J., M.D.	New York City
Silverman, Moses	Boston, Mass.
Silverman, Samuel	New Haven, Conn.
Silverman, S.S.	Syracuse, N. Y.
Silverson, Abraham	New York City
Silverstein, E.	New York City
Silverstein, J.	New York City
Silverstein, Louis	New York City
Silverstein, Morris	St. Louis, Mo.
Silverstone, Louis	New York City
Simmons, David	New York City
Simmons, Rev. G.	New York City
Simmons, G. H.	Columbus, Ohio
Simmons, Nathan	New York City
Simon, A.	Detroit, Mich.
Simon, Rev. Abram	Washington, D. C.
Simon, E.	Nashua, N. H.
Simon, Gustav (deceased)	Altoona, Pa.
Simon, H.	Manchester, N. H.
Simon, Hon. Joseph	Portland, Ore.
imon, Kassel	New York City
mon, Sig.	Salt Lake City, Utah
mon, Solomon	New York City
nonoff, H.	New York City
ons, A.	Bradford, Pa.
ons, B. R.	Philadelphia, Pa.
ns, David W.	Detroit, Mich.
ns, Louis	Chicago, Ill.
sky, S.	Toronto, Canada
on, Alexander	Jersey City, N. J.
n, Joseph S., M.D.	Philadelphia, Pa.
I.	New York City
A.	Baltimore, Md.
r. B. L.	Montreal, Canada
ritz	Philadelphia, Pa.
	New York City
nry B.	New York City
dor	New York City
	Toronto, Canada
b.	Philadelphia, Pa.
	Norfolk, Va.
	New York City
	New York City
	New York City
M	Baltimore, Md.
eph.	New York City
	Baltimore, Md.
	Pittsburg, Pa.
	New York City
S.	Pittsburg, Pa.
lsky, Simon S.	Philadelphia, Pa.
ch, Max	Baltimore, Md.
er, H.	Altoona, Pa.
ky, John J.	Boston, Mass.
Rev. Dr. Thomas R.	New York City
er, Mrs. A.	St. Paul, Minn.
odien, Joseph	Perth Amboy, N. J.
odkin, Harris A.	Boston, Mass.
mensky, I.	Ottawa, Canada
mka, Adolf	New York City
mka, Adolph	New York City
mka, Jacob	New York City
mowitz, Samuel	Billings, Mont.
oss, Mrs. M. C.	San Francisco, Cal.
oss, Sarah	San Francisco, Cal.
te, Samuel H., M.D.	Brooklyn, N. Y.
kin & Praglin	New York City
s, N.	Montreal, Canada
Daniel	Augusta, Ga.
r, H.	Altoona, Pa.
Adolph S.	Brooklyn, N. Y.
Solomon	Cincinnati, Ohio
lman	New York City
	New York City
Smith, Robert	New York City
Smith, Rev. Samuel G.	St. Paul, Minn.
Smolinsky, I. D.	New York City
Smukler, H.	Philadelphia, Pa.
Smyth, John	New Orleans, La.
Snellenberg, Joseph W.	Philadelphia, Pa.
Snellenberg, Nathan	Philadelphia, Pa.
Sobel, Isador	Erie, Pa.
Sobel, Jacob	Brooklyn, N. Y.
Sobel, Jacob, M.D.	New York City
Sobel, S. R.	Pittsburg, Pa.
Sobel, Samuel	Brooklyn, N. Y.
Soble, N. H., M.D.	Elmira, N. Y.
Sohn, L.	New York City
Sokolower, J.	New York City
Sola, Clarence I. de	Montreal, Canada
Sola, Rev. Meldola de	Montreal, Canada
Solinger, Lewis	Centerville, Iowa
Solis, Isaac N.	New York City
Sollod, Nathan	Baltimore, Md.
Soloborsky, Joseph	Brooklyn, N. Y.
Solomon, A. A.	Philadelphia, Pa.
Solomon, A. L.	Pittsburg, Pa.
Solomon, Aaron	Detroit, Mich.
Solomon, Alden	Boston, Mass.
Solomon, Rev. E. L.	Paterson, N. J.
Solomon, George	Savannah, Ga.
Solomon, Mrs. Henry	Chicago, Ill.
Solomon, J.	Allegheny, Pa.
Solomon, L.	New York City
Solomon, Louis	New York City
Solomon, M. H.	New York City
Solomon, Mark	Rochester, N. Y.
Solomon, Marx	New York City
Solomon, Max	Beaver Falls, Pa.
Solomon, Oscar	Cedar Rapids, Iowa
Solomon, S.	Scranton, Pa.
Solomon, S. D., A.B.	Syracuse, N. Y.
Solomon, Sam	New York City
Solomon, Samuel	New York City
Solomon, Samuel E.	New York City
Solomon, Saul	Montreal, Canada
Solomons, A. S.	Washington, D. C.
Solomons, Joseph R., D.D.S.	New York City
Solomont, Simon	Boston, Mass.
Solon, Moses	Chicago, Ill.
Solotar, Jacob	New York City
Solotaroff, H., M.D.	New York City
Soloweitzik, Solomon	Westerly, R. I.
Solus, Joseph W.	Philadelphia, Pa.
Solzman, H.	New Haven, Conn.
Sommer, Henry	New York City
Sommer, M.	New York City
Sommer, Rudolph	New York City
Sommerfeldt, M.	Yonkers, N. Y.
Somolsky, Jacob	Washington, Pa.
Sondheim, Julius	Philadelphia, Pa.
Soneborn, S. B.	Baltimore, Md.
Sonenberg, Adolf	Montreal, Canada
Sonneborn, Henry	Baltimore, Md.
Sonneborn, Jonas	New York City
Sonneborn, Mrs. Leo	New York City
Sonneborn, M.	Wheeling, W. Va.
Sonnenschein, Rev. S. H.	St. Louis, Mo.
Sonstein, I.	McKeesport, Pa.
Sockne, Joseph, D.D.S.	New York City
Sophian, Michael, M.D.	New York City
Sossnitz, Isaac, M.D.	New York City
Souenberg, Adolf	Montreal, Canada
Souie, George	New Orleans, La.
Sparenberg, E.	New York City
Sparger, Rev. William	New York City
Speaker, Henry M.	Philadelphia, Pa.
Spear, N.	Pittsburg, Pa.
Spector, Joseph	New York City
Spektorsky, Hyman	New York City
Spektorsky, Joseph	New York City
Sperber, David	Montreal, Canada
Speyer, James	New York City
Speyer, Leo	New York City
Spiegel, Rev. Adolph	New York City
Spiegel, Judge Frederick S.	Cincinnati, Ohio
Spiegel, Julius	New York City
Spiegel, Samuel, M.D.	New York City
Spiegel, Wolf Max	Elmira, N. Y.
Spiegelberg, F.	New York City
Spiegelberg, I. N.	New York City
Spiegelberg, Levi	New York City
Spigil, Julius	New York City
Spiro, Abraham C. (deceased)	New York City
Spiro, Abraham I.	New York City
Spiro, M., M.D.	Allegheny, Pa.
Spiro, Max	New York City
Spitz, Samuel	Chicago, Ill.
Spivak, C. D., M.D.	Denver, Colo.
Sporborg, Celia May, Pres.	Albany, N. Y.
Srolovitz, Max L.	Monongahela City, Pa.
Stadecker, Leopold	New York City
Stahl, S.	Albany, N. Y.

Staller, Max, M.D.	Philadelphia, Pa.
Stander, Anna.	New York City
Stark, Joseph.	New York City
Starr, Hyman.	New York City
Starr, Robert.	New York City
Starr, Rev. William E.	Baltimore, Md.
Staub, J. A.	New York City
Stearns, Benjamin.	New Rochelle, N. Y.
Stecker, Louis.	Philadelphia, Pa.
Steckler, Alfred.	New York City
Steif, W.	Chicago, Ill.
Stein, Abram.	New York City
Stein, Adolf.	Chicago, Ill.
Stein, Charles I.	Greenwood, Miss.
Stein, David.	Chicago, Ill.
Stein, Fred M.	New York City
Stein, H.	Lancaster, Pa.
Stein, Isidor.	New York City
Stein, J. M.	Washington, D. C.
Stein, Joseph.	New York City
Stein, Joseph.	New York City
Stein, Julius.	Brooklyn, N. Y.
Stein, Leo.	New York City
Stein, M., M.D., D.D.S.	New York City
Stein, M. B.	Stockton, Cal.
Stein, M. H.	Philadelphia, Pa.
Stein, S.	New York City
Stein, W. D.	Chicago, Ill.
Steinbach, A. B.	New York City
Steinbach, L. W., M.D.	Philadelphia, Pa.
Steinberg, Charles J.	Pensacola, Fla.
Steinberg, D.	New Haven, Conn.
Steinberg, Jacob.	Carteret, N. J.
Steinberg Brothers.	Toledo, Ohio
Steinberger, F.	Bradford, Pa.
Steindler, Max.	New York City
Steinem, Mrs. Joseph.	Toledo, Ohio
Steiner, Alfred.	Brooklyn, N. Y.
Steiner, Benjamin.	New York City
Steiner, David.	Youngstown, Ohio
Steiner, I.	Hampton, Va.
Steiner, Jacob.	Newark, N. J.
Steiner, Louis.	Brooklyn, N. Y.
Steinfeld, Julius.	New York City
Stengel, Emil.	Pittsburg, Pa.
Stern, A.	New York City
Stern, Benjamin.	New York City
Stern, Charles M.	Albany, N. Y.
Stern, Daniel.	Brooklyn, N. Y.
Stern, David.	Chicago, Ill.
Stern, David.	Philadelphia, Pa.
Stern, David F.	New York City
Stern, Eugene M.	Philadelphia, Pa.
Stern, G.	Newark, N. J.
Stern, Harry.	Boston, Mass.
Stern, Isaac.	New York City
Stern, Isador.	New York City
Stern, J.	New York City
Stern, J. L.	Cumberland, Md.
Stern, Jake.	Las Vegas, N. Mex.
Stern, Josef.	New York City
Stern, Joseph.	New York City
Stern, Joseph.	Montreal, Canada
Stern, Mrs. L. M.	Brooklyn, N. Y.
Stern, Leopold.	New York City
Stern, Leopold H.	New York City
Stern, Louis.	Brooklyn, N. Y.
Stern, Louis.	New York City
Stern, Louis.	Philadelphia, Pa.
Stern, Rev. Louis.	Washington, D. C.
Stern, M.	Rochester, N. Y.
Stern, M. H.	Philadelphia, Pa.
Stern, Maurice.	New Orleans, La.
Stern, Moses.	Allentown, Pa.
Stern, Nathan.	New York City
Stern, Nathan.	Trenton, N. J.
Stern, Philip H.	Montgomery, Ala.
Stern, Samuel.	Uniontown, Pa.
Sternbach, A. B.	Portland, Ore.
Sternbach, Charles (deceased).	New York City
Sternbach, Morris.	New York City
Sternberg, H.	Columbus, Ga.
Sternberger, Mrs. Pauline.	New York City
Sternberger, Samuel.	Philadelphia, Pa.
Sterne, Simon (deceased).	New York City
Sternlicht, Isaac, M.D.	New York City
Sterns, Charles.	Rutland, Vt.
Stettauer, Mrs. D.	Chicago, Ill.
Stewart, E. B.	Chicago, Ill.
Stiefel, Mrs. H.	New York City
Stien, Max.	New York City
Stifft, Charles S.	Little Rock, Ark.
Stine, Albert.	New York City
Stine, Marcus.	New York City
Stiner, Max.	New York City
Stix, William.	St. Louis, Mo.
Stoerger, Sigmund.	Brooklyn, N. Y.
Stol, Sebastian, M.D.	Chicago, Ill.
Stolaroff, A.	El Paso, Tex.

Stoll, Harry.	New York City
Stolz, Benjamin.	Syracuse, N. Y.
Stolz, Rev. J. H.	Cumberland, Md.
Stolz, Joseph.	Chicago, Ill.
Stone, Alfred Holt.	Washington, D. C.
Stone, Charles.	Toronto, Canada
Stone, J. W.	Boston, Mass.
Stone, Rev. John Timothy.	Baltimore, Md.
Stone, Mrs. Julius.	Chicago, Ill.
Stone, Nathan H.	New York City
Stoneman, David.	Boston, Mass.
Stotter, Dr. Henry B.	Cleveland, Ohio
Stotter, J., M.D.	Cleveland, Ohio
Strasbourger, Samuel.	New York City
Strashower, Max.	Cleveland, Ohio
Strashun, A., M.D.	Cincinnati, Ohio
Strasser, Ike.	Albany, N. Y.
Stratton, Asa E.	Montgomery, Ala.
Straulman, A.	New York City
Straus, A.	Las Vegas, N. Mex.
Straus, A. D.	New York City
Straus, Alexander L.	Baltimore, Md.
Straus, Eli M.	Chicago, Ill.
Straus, F. A.	New York City
Straus, Isidor.	New York City
Straus, J.	Philadelphia, Pa.
Straus, Joseph L.	Baltimore, Md.
Straus, Julius.	Richmond, Va.
Straus, Leopold.	Montgomery, Ala.
Straus, Louis.	St. Louis, Mo.
Straus, Nathan.	New York City
Straus, Hon. Oscar S.	New York City
Straus, S. D.	New York City
Straus, Simon W.	Chicago, Ill.
Strauss, B.	Newark, N. J.
Strauss, Julius.	New York City
Strauss, Meyer.	Hamilton, Ohio
Strauss, S. J.	Wilkesbarre, Pa.
Strauss, Samuel.	New York City
Straussberg, Dr. M.	Newark, N. J.
Stream, Louis.	New York City
Streicher, M.	Providence, R. I.
Streitfeld, Harry A.	Philadelphia, Pa.
Strelitz, Henry.	Chattanooga, Tenn.
Strook, Sol. M.	New York City
Strouse, A. L.	Freeport, Pa.
Strouse, Mrs. Hennie.	Baltimore, Md.
Strouse, Isaac.	Baltimore, Md.
Strouse, Leopold.	Baltimore, Md.
Strouse, Samuel.	Baltimore, Md.
Strouss, Isaac.	Youngstown, Ohio
Strunsky, Elias.	San Francisco, Cal.
Stulman, M.	Baltimore, Md.
Stumer, Louis M.	Chicago, Ill.
Sturtz, Samuel.	New York City
Suesskind, Adolph.	New York City
Sugarman, Martin L.	Omaha, Nebr.
Sullivan, Rev. J. W.	Centerview, Mo.
Sullivan, P. F.	Lowell, Mass.
Sulzbacher, Joseph H.	New York City
Sulzbacher, Louis.	Braddock, Pa.
Sulzberger, Cyrus L.	New York City
Sulzberger, Ferdinand.	New York City
Sulzberger, Hon. Mayer.	Philadelphia, Pa.
Sulzberger, S. L.	Chicago, Ill.
Sulzberger, Solomon.	New York City
Summerfield, H. G.	Little Rock, Ark.
Summerfield, Moses.	St. Louis, Mo.
Sumner, Philip S., M.D.	Boston, Mass.
Sundelson, Adolph, M.D.	New York City
Sunstein, A. J.	Pittsburg, Pa.
Sunstein, C.	Allegheny, Pa.
Supowitz, M.	Pittsburg, Pa.
Suravitz, N.	Scranton, Pa.
Suskind, Harris.	New York City
Susskind, S. J.	Philadelphia, Pa.
Sussman, I.	Youngstown, Ohio
Svarcz, Mano.	Baltimore, Md.
Swartz, Miss Anna.	Pittsburg, Pa.
Swartz, Fred. M.	Providence, R. I.
Sweeney, Thomas S.	Brackettville, Tex.
Swett, Z.	Portland, Ore.
Switz, Rev. M.	Pittsburg, Pa.
Sydeman, A.	Boston, Mass.
Syrkin, Arnold.	New York City
Szold, Miss Henrietta.	New York City

T

Taledano, Albert.	New Orleans, La.
Talpes, S.	Montreal, Canada
Talpis, Ralph T.	El Paso, Tex.
Tamor, Abraham I.	New York City
Tandlich, Samuel, M.D.	New York City
Tannenbaum, A.	New York City
Tannenbaum, L.	New York City
Tannenbaum, L.	New York City
Tannenbaum, Simon, M.D.	New York City
Tanner, Joseph M.	Salt Lake City, Utah
Taplitzky, Jacob.	Toronto, Canada

Tapolsky, Harry..................Pittsburg, Pa.
Tarnowski, Samuel.................New York City
Tarshis, Isaac...................Brooklyn, N. Y.
Tattarsky, M.....................Brooklyn, N. Y.
Tauber, A........................New York City
Tauber, Bernard..................New York City
Tausend, Felix...................New York City
Tausig, Emil.....................New York City
Tausig, Joseph...................Myles, Miss.
Tausig, William..................Chicago, Ill.
Taylor, David....................Seattle, Wash.
Taylor, John A...................New York City
Teideman, Leo....................New York City
Teitelbaum, H....................New York City
Teller, lbert....................Philadelphia, Pa.
Teller, Benjamin F...............Philadelphia, Pa.
Teller, William H................Philadelphia, Pa.
Tennenbaum, S. (deceased).........Cincinnati, Ohio
Teplitz, Benjamin................Pittsburg, Pa.
Tepper, Martin, D.D.S............New York City
Terr, Jacob......................New York City
Terr, Louis......................Philadelphia, Pa.
Tessler, M., M.D.................St. Paul, Minn.
Teven, Louis.....................New York City
Thacher, Hon. John Boyd..........Albany, N. Y.
Thaler, Jacob....................New York City
Thalheimer, Gates................Syracuse, N. Y.
Thalheimer, H....................New Orleans, La.
Thalheimer, Mrs. L. S............Philadelphia, Pa.
Thalheimer, Sam..................Baltimore, Md.
Thomashefsky, B..................New York City
Thompson, T. P...................New Orleans, La.
Thurman, Jacob...................East Boston, Mass.
Thurnauer, Charles M.............Cincinnati, Ohio
Tiche, Edward....................Dallas, Tex.
Ticktin, Charles.................Chicago, Ill.
Tiefenbrun, B....................Baltimore, Md.
Tierkel, David B.................Philadelphia, Pa.
Tilzer, A., M.D..................Portland, Ore.
Tintner, Leonard.................Pittsburg, Pa.
Tischler, Adolph.................New York City
Tischler, Samuel.................New York City
Titlebaum, Nathan J..............Boston, Mass.
Tivol, Nathan....................Kansas City, Mo.
Tobias, Francis H................New York City
Tobias, Julius D.................New York City
Tobriner, Leon...................Washington, D. C.
Toch, Henry M....................New York City
Todes, Solomon...................Baltimore, Md.
Tolzers, A. M....................Montreal, Canada
Tonkonogy, Nathaniel, M.D........New York City
Topaz, Lionel....................New York City
Toplitzky, Jacob.................Toronto, Canada
Tosky, Jacob.....................St. Louis, Mo.
Tour, Jacob......................Pueblo, Colo.
Toy, Prof. C. H., D.D., LL.D......Cambridge, Mass.
Tracy, Samuel G..................Hartford, Conn.
Trager, Isidore..................Cincinnati, Ohio
Traitel, Benjamin D..............New York City
Trapp, Edward A..................New York City
Trau, Gus........................Pittsburg, Pa.
Traugott, Rev. Abraham...........Springfield, Ill.
Travis, P. H.....................College, Ga.
Tre Fethren, E. B................Waubay, S. Dak.
Treichlinger, David..............St. Louis, Mo.
Treuhold, Morris.................New York City
Triedberg, A.....................New York City
Triest, Montague.................Charleston, S. C.
Trosky, Bernard..................Brooklyn, N. Y.
Trost, Edward....................Pittsburg, Pa.
Trost, Samuel W..................Cincinnati, Ohio
Trouse, Paul.....................New York City
Tryor, Rev. S....................Petersburg, Va.
Tuch, Michael....................Brooklyn, N. Y.
Tuedberg, A......................New York City
Turkel, B........................New York City
Turner, A........................Chicago, Ill.
Turner, Rev. J. W................Evansville, Ind.
Turtletaub, J....................Charleston, S. C.
Tutelman, Nathan.................Philadelphia, Pa.
Tutelman, William................Philadelphia, Pa.
Twining, Prof. N. C..............Nipomo, Cal.
Tworger, Philip..................Boston, Mass.

U

Ufland, Abraham..................New York City
Ufland, W........................New York City
Uhlmann, Simon...................New York City
Ulanov, Prof. Nathan.............New York City
Ullman, Adolph...................Cincinnati, Ohio
Ullman, Nathan...................New York City
Ullman, Sigmund..................New York City
Ulman, Alfred J..................San Francisco, Cal.
Ulmann, Albert...................New York City
Una, G...........................New York City
Ungar, Max.......................Halifax, N. S.
Unger, David.....................New York City
Unger, Henry W...................New York City
Unger, Samuel J..................Plainfield, N. J.

Ungerleider, M., M.D.............Chicago, Ill.
Unterberg, Israel................New York City

V

Valenstein, M....................New York City
Valentine, S.....................New York City
Vanamee, William.................Middletown, N. Y.
Van de Water, Geo. R.............New York City
Van Leer, Charles................Seaford, Del.
Van Leer, Mrs. Hannah............Baltimore, Md.
Van Raalte, E....................New York City
Van Taube, G.....................Montvale, N. J.
Van Wagner, Mrs. M. F............Troy, N. Y.
Varady, Samuel...................New York City
Vehon, L. S......................Chicago, Ill.
Velleman, Joshua.................New York City
Vendig, Charles H................New York City
Vetter, Henry H..................Philadelphia, Pa.
Vineberg, Hiram N., M.D..........New York City
Vineberg, M. (deceased)..........Winnipeg, Manitoba, Canada
Vinissky, B. W...................Chicago, Ill.
Vinson, R. E.....................Austin, Tex.
Vogel, Heinrich, M.D.............New York City
Vogel, Joseph....................New York City
Vogelstein, L....................New York City
Volmer, Leon.....................Charleston, W. Va.
Volpé, Arnold D..................New Rochelle, N. Y.
Volpe, Harold D..................New York City
Volter, Adolph...................New York City
Voorsanger, Jacob................San Francisco, Cal.
Vorhaus, Louis J.................New York City

W

Wachs, A.........................Philadelphia, Pa.
Wachsman, Isidore................Albany, N. Y.
Wacht, Samuel....................New York City
Wagner, Isidor...................Brooklyn, N. Y.
Wainzimer, Philip................New York City
Waisman, M.......................New York City
Walb, Lasar......................Philadelphia, Pa.
Walcoff, Harry...................New York City
Wald, H., M.D....................New York City
Waldheim, H......................St. Louis, Mo.
Waldman, Louis...................Toronto, Canada
Waldman, Louis I.................Albany, N. Y.
Waldstein, Abraham S.............Boston, Mass.
Walker, Adolph...................Brooklyn, N. Y.
Wallach, Karl W..................New York City
Wallach, Moses...................New York City
Wallenstein, Max.................Troy, N. Y.
Waller, H........................Philadelphia, Pa.
Walsey, Rev. Louis...............Little Rock, Ark.
Walsh, Rev. John.................Troy, N. Y.
Walter, Abraham..................Baltimore, Md.
Walter, Bernhard.................New York City
Walter, M. R.....................Baltimore, Md.
Waltman, Abe.....................Philadelphia, Pa.
Waltoff, D. de, M.D..............Brooklyn, N. Y.
Warburg, Felix M.................New York City
Ward, M..........................Bridgeport, Conn.
Wartell, Isaac...................New York City
Wartell, S. H....................New York City
Wartelsky, Miss J................Chicago, Ill.
Wasserman, Henry.................New York City
Watman, Alexander................Bayonne, N. J.
Watman, George...................New York City
Waxelbaum, E. A..................Macon, Ga.
Waxman, J........................New York City
Weber, David.....................Philadelphia, Pa.
Webster, Jacob...................New York City
Wechselman, Solomon..............New York City
Wechsler, A. H...................Brooklyn, N. Y.
Wechsler, Isaac..................New York City
Weeden, P. H.....................New York City
Wehart, Mrs. Charles.............Peoria, Ill.
Wehlau, L., M.D..................Scranton, Pa.
Weil, A. Leo.....................East Liberty, Pa.
Weil, Abraham....................Fort Wayne, Ind.
Weil, D..........................Montgomery, Ala.
Weil, David L....................New York City
Weil, E..........................Brooklyn, N. Y.
Weil, Edmond.....................New York City
Weil, Henry......................Pelham, N. Y.
Weil, Henry......................Goldsboro, N. C.
Weil, J. B.......................Los Angeles, Cal.
Weil, Jacob......................Philadelphia, Pa.
Weil, Jacob A....................New York City
Weil, Jonas......................New York City
Weil, L. P.......................San Francisco, Cal.
Weil, Leo A......................East Liberty, Pa.
Weil, Leon.......................Montgomery, Ala.
Weil, Leopold....................New York City
Weil, Leopold....................New York City
Weil, Louis......................Chicago, Ill.
Weil, N. J.......................New York City
Weil, R..........................Spokane, Wash.
Weil, Samuel.....................Youngstown, Ohio

Weil, Samuel.	New York City
Weill, L. W.	New York City
Weiller, L.	New York City
Weinberg, Benjamin L.	Minneapolis, Minn.
Weinberg, Jacob.	Lancaster, Pa.
Weinberg, James.	Brooklyn, N. Y.
Weinberg, Joseph.	Greenville, Miss.
Weinberg, Julius.	Atlantic City, N. J.
Weinberg, Morris.	Baltimore, Md.
Weinberg, Nicholas J.	New York City
Weinberg, B.	New York City
Weinberger, Emma.	New Orleans, La.
Weinberger, F.	New York City
Weinberger, Henry.	New York City
Weinberger, Jonas.	Plainfield, N. J.
Weinberger, M.	Rockaway Beach, N. Y.
Weiner, Alexander.	Philadelphia, Pa.
Weiner, Jacob.	New York City
Weiner, Leopold S.	New York City
Weiner, Richard.	Montreal, Canada
Weinfield, Henry.	New York City
Weingart, S.	Scranton, Pa.
Weingart, Sol.	New York City
Weinhandler, Adolph.	New York City
Weinhandler, M.	New York City
Weinreb, Arthur.	New York City
Weinshel, Jacob.	Chicago, Ill.
Weinshenker, Tobias.	New York City
Weinstein, A.	Chicago, Ill.
Weinstein, B.	Goshen, Ind.
Weinstein, Rev. E.	New York City
Weinstein, Henry.	New York City
Weinstein, I., M.D.	New York City
Weinstein, Joseph, M.D.	New York City
Weinstein, Morris.	New York City
Weinstein, S.	Sacramento, Cal.
Weinstock, Harris.	Brooklyn, N. Y.
Weinstock, Louis.	Sacramento, Cal.
Weinstock, Lubin, & Co.	New Orleans, La.
Weis, Julius.	Boston, Mass.
Weis Brothers.	Pittsburg, Pa.
Weisberg, S.	Minneapolis, Minn.
Weiskopf, Henry.	New Haven, Conn.
Weisman, Abraham.	New York City
Weisman, Isaac.	Minneapolis, Minn.
Weisman, Isidore.	Boston, Mass.
Weisman, Mayer.	New York City
Weisman, S.	Brooklyn, N. Y.
Weiss, A.	Los Angeles, Cal.
Weiss, A. E.	New York City
Weiss, Abraham.	Philadelphia, Pa.
Weiss, Alter.	Philadelphia, Pa.
Weiss, Charles.	Macon, Ga.
Weiss, Rev. Harry.	Philadelphia, Pa.
Weiss, Isaac.	Chicago, Ill.
Weiss, Isadore.	Mobile, Ala.
Weiss, J. W.	New York City
Weiss, Jacob.	New York City
Weiss, Joseph.	Galveston, Tex.
Weiss, Robert.	New York City
Weissbrot, Samuel.	New York City
Weissman, Reuben.	New York City
Weltner, Moritz.	Pana, Ill.
Welvart, Chas.	Montreal, Canada
Wener, H.	New York City
Wener, J.	Olmus, Tex.
Wenning, Gottfried.	Brooklyn, N. Y.
Werbelowsky, A.	Brooklyn, N. Y.
Werbelowsky, David.	New York City
Werdenschlag, David.	New York City
Werner, Edward M.	New York City
Werner, H.	New York City
Wertheim, B., & Son.	New York City
Wertheim, Sol.	Allegheny, Pa.
Wertheimer, Isaac.	New York City
Wertheimer, Jacob.	New York City
Weslock, Morris.	New Orleans, La.
Westfeldt, P. M.	St. Joseph, Mo.
Westheimer, Samuel.	New York City
Westin, M. H.	Montreal, Canada
Wetstein, R.	New York City
Wexler, S. W.	New Orleans, La.
Wexler, Solomon.	Philadelphia, Pa.
Weyl, Maurice N.	Allegheny, Pa.
White, C.	Philadelphia, Pa.
White, Rev. H. F.	Chicago, Ill.
White, H. O., M.D.	Exeter, N. H.
White, Philip.	Philadelphia, Pa.
Whitehill, Edward.	New York City
Whitelaw, Jonas.	Pittsburg, Pa.
Whitestone, Simon.	Richmond, Va.
Whitlock, Philip.	Boston, Mass.
Whitman, Esther.	Amsterdam, N. Y.
Whitteker, Rev. W. F.	New York City
Whitul, Fr.	New York City
Widder, Simon.	Pittsburg, Pa.
Wiener, David.	New York City
Wiener, Henry.	New York City
Wienstein, H.	New York City
Wiernik, Peter.	New York City
Wies Brothers.	Boston, Mass.
Wilbush, Benjamin.	Houston, Tex.
Wilcox, E. L.	Peoria, Ill.
Wilder, Charles.	New York City
Wilder, Morris, M.D.	New York City
Wilder, V. A.	Warwick, N. Y.
Wildman, S.	New York City
Wile, Herman.	Buffalo, N. Y.
Wile, Julius M.	Rochester, N. Y.
Wilenzig, Myer.	Baltimore, Md.
Wilfson, D.	Baltimore, Md.
Wilk, L. J.	Minneapolis, Minn.
Wilkes, Morris, M.D.	New York City
Wilkoff, William.	Youngstown, Ohio
Williams, J. G.	Worcester, Mass.
Williams, Rev. Dr. Leighton.	New York City
Willner, Rev. W.	Meridian, Miss.
Wilner, Samuel.	New York City
Wilson, Rev. George.	Gibson City, Ill.
Wilson, Jerome J.	Birmingham, Ala.
Wilzin, J. M.	New York City
Winchel, Geo. C.	New York City
Wineburgh, Henry.	Philadelphia, Pa.
Wineland, Elias.	Olean, N. Y.
Winer, Elias.	New York City
Winer, Harry.	Chattanooga, Tenn.
Winer, Herman L.	New York City
Winkelman, Samuel.	Manistique, Mich.
Winkleman, Sol.	Rochester, N. Y.
Winkler, Isaac.	Cincinnati, Ohio
Winstein, Louis.	Portland, Me.
Winter, Morris.	Boston, Mass.
Winterfield.	New York City
Winternitz, David.	Las Vegas, N. Mex.
Winternitz, Samuel L.	Chicago, Ill.
Wintner, Rev. Leopold, Ph.D.	Brooklyn, N. Y.
Wintrob, J. M.	Philadelphia, Pa.
Wisdom, M. N.	New Orleans, La.
Wise, August.	Philadelphia, Pa.
Wise, Barnat.	Pittsburg, Pa.
Wise, Henry E.	New York City
Wise, Otto Irving.	San Francisco, Cal.
Wise, Rev. Jonah B.	Chattanooga, Tenn.
Wise, Rev. Dr. Stephen S.	Portland, Ore.
Wise, Solomon.	Abbeville, La.
Wise Brothers.	Yazoo City, Miss.
Wiseman, Harry S.	Indianapolis, Ind.
Witmark, Isidor.	New York City
Witt, Rev. Louis.	Pueblo, Colo.
Witt, Samuel.	New York City
Witte, Max.	New York City
Wittenberg, Rev. David H.	Jacksonville, Fla.
Wittenberg, Joseph, M.D.	New York City
Wittenberg, Louis.	Philadelphia, Pa.
Woelfkin, Rev. Cornelius.	Brooklyn, N. Y.
Wohl, L.	New York City
Wohlgemuth, M. J.	New York City
Wolbach, S.	Grand Island, Nebr.
Wolbarsht, Hyman.	Baltimore, Md.
Wolberg, Enoch.	New York City
Wolf, A.	New Orleans, La.
Wolf, Mrs. Abraham S.	Philadelphia, Pa.
Wolf, Albert.	Philadelphia, Pa.
Wolf, Alexander I., M.D.	St. Louis, Mo.
Wolf, August.	Philadelphia, Pa.
Wolf, Benjamin.	Philadelphia, Pa.
Wolf, Bernard H.	Boston, Mass.
Wolf, Clarence.	Philadelphia, Pa.
Wolf, D.	Pittsburg, Pa.
Wolf, Edward.	Philadelphia, Pa.
Wolf, Edwin.	Philadelphia, Pa.
Wolf, Edwin E.	Chicago, Ill.
Wolf, Emanuel.	Bayou Sara, La.
Wolf, Gessel, M.D.	New York City
Wolf, Henry M.	Chicago, Ill.
Wolf, Herman.	Yonkers, N. Y.
Wolf, I. B.	New York City
Wolf, Mrs. L. J.	Cleveland, Ohio
Wolf, Louis.	Philadelphia, Pa.
Wolf, M., M.D.	Yonkers, N. Y.
Wolf, Miriam H.	Philadelphia, Pa.
Wolf, P.	Pittsburg, Pa.
Wolf, Simon.	Philadelphia, Pa.
Wolf, Hon. Simon.	Washington, D. C.
Wolfe, Adolphe.	Portland, Ore.
Wolfe, Frank.	Hamilton, Canada
Wolfe, Menko H.	New York City
Wolfe, Morris.	Brooklyn, N. Y.
Wolfe, P.	New York City
Wolfenstein, Dr. S.	Cleveland, Ohio
Wolff, A. N.	New York City
Wolff, Emil.	New York City
Wolff, Harris.	New York City
Wolff, Henry.	Allendale, S. C.
Wolff, Isaac.	New York City
Wolff, Mrs. Robert.	Chicago, Ill.
Wolff, Samuel.	Chicago, Ill.
Wolff, Solomon.	New Orleans, La.

Wolffner, Henry L., M.D.............St. Louis, Mo.
Wolfneir, Mrs. W. F....................Peoria, Ill.
Wolfsfeld, Simon.....................New York City
Wolfsohn, Jacob M.....................Chicago, Ill.
Wolfsohn, M..........................New York City
Wolfson, David.....................Billings, Mont.
Wolfson, Rev. G.....................Lowell, Mass.
Wolfson, Dr. J.....................Philadelphia, Pa.
Wolfson, L., M.D...................Philadelphia, Pa.
Wolfson, Meyer E...................New York City
Wolfson, Morris.....................New York City
Wollstein, Louis....................New York City
Wolper, A...........................Boston, Mass.
Wolpert, Mayer....................Minneapolis, Minn.
Wolsey, Rev. Louis...............Little Rock, Ark.
Wolsey, William.......................Clare, Mich.
Woodward, Frederick E............Washington, D. C.
Woolf, Louis........................New York City
Woolf, M. J. H., M.D............San Francisco, Cal.
Woolfson, L.........................Brooklyn, N. Y.
Woolner, Mrs. Samuel, Sr...........Peoria, Ill.
Worman, Max N.....................Brooklyn, N. Y.
Wormser, David......................Chicago, Ill.
Wormser, E. L.......................Scranton, Pa.
Wormser, Mrs. Isidor................New York City
Wright, Sophie B..................New Orleans, La.
Wrubel, S.........................Middletown, Conn.
Wyman, S...........................Cleveland, Ohio

Y

Yedeikin, Nathan....................New York City
Yeidel, I...........................Denison, Tex.
Yewell, Horace R...............Albuquerque, N. Mex.
Yog, Isidor.........................New York City
Yogg, Moses........................Newark, N. J.
Yohalem, Benny.....................New York City
Yorkel, A...........................New York City
Young, Charles.....................Yonkers, N. Y.
Young, Rev. Ed. J..................Waltham, Mass.
Young, Horace G.....................Albany, N. Y.
Young, Max L.......................New York City
Young, Rev. S. Edward..............Pittsburg, Pa.
Youngerman, Moses..............Somerville, Mass.
Younker, A........................Des Moines, Iowa

Younker, Falk......................New York City
Yudelson, A. B......................Chicago, Ill.
Yungel, E..........................New York City
Yutzy, Rev. Jacob................Selinsgrove, Pa.

Z

Zadekow, L.........................New York City
Zakon, Louis I.....................Pittsburg, Pa.
Zander, Gustav.....................New York City
Zander, Herman.....................Nashville, Tenn.
Zarach, Isaac, M.D.................New York City
Zarembowitz, A.....................New York City
Zausmer, Wolff.....................New York City
Zechnovitz, Samuel.................New York City
Zederbaum, A., M.D.................Denver, Colo.
Zeisler, Samuel....................New York City
Zeitz, H...........................Brooklyn, N. Y.
Zelenko, Joseph....................New York City
Zelezny, Morris....................New York City
Zéliqzon, Dr. Maurice.............Cleveland, Ohio
Zepin, Rev. George................Cincinnati, Ohio
Zetlin, B..........................New York City
Zetner, Charles...................Philadelphia, Pa.
Zielonka, Rev. Martin...............El Paso, Tex.
Zimmerman, C. L., D.D.S.............Chicago, Ill.
Zimmerman, Hyman...................New York City
Zimmerman, M. L., D.D.S..........Philadelphia, Pa.
Zimmerman, Morris..................New York City
Zindler, T..........................New York City
Zinman, Morris....................Philadelphia, Pa.
Zipkin, M. W.......................New York City
Ziporkes, J........................New York City
Zippert, Max.......................New York City
Zirn, Harry........................Brooklyn, N. Y.
Zoffer, Henry......................Rochester, Pa.
Zoline, Elijah N., LL.B............Chicago, Ill.
Zolotkoff, Leon, LL.B..............Chicago, Ill.
Zuosmer, Wolff.....................New York City
Zucker, L..........................New York City
Zuckermann, Manfred................New York City
Zukor, Adolph......................New York City
Zundelowitz, A..................Wichita Falls, Tex.
Zussman, Samuel, M.D...........San Francisco, Cal.
Zwetow, Samuel R....................Denver, Colo.

EUROPE, ASIA, AFRICA, AND AUSTRALIA

A

Aaron, D. H.....................London, England
Aaron, Harry...................Lancaster, England
Aaron, J...........................Hull, England
Abarbanel Library...............Jerusalem, Palestine
Abelheim, A., M.D.........Johannesburg, So. Africa
Abelson, Rev. Joshua, B.A..........Bristol, England
Aberdeen Public Library.........Aberdeen, Scotland
Aberdeen, University of..........Aberdeen, Scotland
Aboaf, A...........................Cairo, Egypt
Abraham, D. E. J..................Shanghai, China
Abraham, James...................London, England
Abrahams, B. Lionel.............London, England
Abrahams, Daniel...............Glasgow, Scotland
Abrahams, H. A...................London, England
Abrahams, Israel, M.A..........Cambridge, England
Abrahams, L......................London, England
Abrahams, Louis B., B.A..........London, England
Abrahams, M..........Port Elizabeth, So. Africa
Abrahams, Rev. M..................Leeds, England
Abrahams, Morris.................London, England
Abrahamson, A. D................Cardiff, Wales
Abrahamson, Joshua...............Cardiff, Wales
Abrahamson, L. S................Newport, Wales
Abrahamson, Max..................Leeds, England
Académie Impériale des Sciences....St. Petersburg, Russia
Académie des Inscriptions et Belles Lettres..Paris, France
Académie Royale des Sciences..........Brussels, Belgium
Accademia dei Sienza...............Milan, Italy
Adelman, Joseph..............Manchester, England
Adler, Elkan N., M.A.............London, England
Adler, Dr. Herman, Chief Rabbi British Empire,
        London, England
Adler, Marcus Nathan, M.A...........London, England
Adler, Rev. Michael, B.A...........London, England
Adler, Solomon.................Glasgow, Scotland
Aguilar, The Misses..............London, England
Ailion, Max......................London, England
Aitchison, G., R.A...............London, England
Alcaley, Dr. D...................Belgrade, Servia
Alexander, B.............Johannesburg, So. Africa
Alexander, Henry........Newcastle-upon-Tyne, England
Alexander, Louis.................Sheffield, England
Alexander, Morris.............Cape Town, So. Africa
Alfandary, M.....................London, England
Alford, Rev. George, M.A.......Leamington Spa, England
Alliance Israélite School..........Constantinople, Turkey
Alliance Israélite Universelle..............Paris, France
All Souls' College.................Oxford, England
Alprovich, H.....................Southsea, England

Altaras, E.....................Manchester, England
Altman, Albert L...................Dublin, Ireland
Altof, Colonel A.................London, England
Amsterdam, Univ. of, Biblio. Rosenthaliana,
        Amsterdam, Holland
Andrade, Jacob A. P. M..........Spanish Town, Jamaica
Andrade, Mrs. Rebecca da Costa.......London, England
Andrade, S. V. da Costa..............London, England
Annenberg, Mark..................London, England
Ansell, J. M.....................London, England
Aria College......................Portsea, England
Arnhold, Philipp.................London, England
Aschkenasi, Israel I.............London, England
Ascoli, E.......................Manchester, England
Ash, H............................Cardiff, Wales
Ash, Michael...................Abertillery, Wales
Ass'n for Study of Jewish Relig.............Puna, India
Auerbach, Isidore................London, England
Auerbach, S.....................Liverpool, England
Austrian Imperial Library............Vienna, Austria
Avner, Mark......................London, England

B

Bacher, Prof. Dr. Wilhelm..........Budapest, Hungary
Baden, The Grand Duke of.........Carlsruhe, Germany
Baker, Mrs. D..................Manchester, England
Baker, Percy P..................Glasgow, Scotland
Bala Theological College...............Bala, Wales
Balfour, Rt. Hon. Arthur J.........London, England
Balkind, A..............Newcastle-upon-Tyne, England
Balon, R.......................Manchester, England
Bambus, W.........................Berlin, Germany
Baptist College................Manchester, England
Baranov, Herman...............Vryheid, So. Africa
Barber, Rev. W. T. A...........Cambridge, England
Barbican Mission to Jews..........London, England
Barder, Samuel....................Bristol, England
Barnett, Aaron..................Barry Dock, Wales
Barnett, Lionel..............Birmingham, England
Barnett, Max...............Cape Town, So. Africa
Barnett, S.......................London, England
Barnett, Solomon.................Newport, Wales
Baron, Bernhard..................London, England
Baron, Rev. David................London, England
Baron, H.........................London, England
Barrett, Wilson (deceased).........London, England
Barry, Rev. William, D.D.......Dorchester, England
Barsht, A........................London, England
Barth, Dr. Jacob.................Berlin, Germany
Basch, E.....................Buluwayo, So. Africa

Bash, Phillip ... Birmingham, England
Battersea, Lord ... London, England
Bauer, G. M ... London, England
Bauer, Le Chevalier de ... Brussels, Belgium
Baumann, Max ... Johannesburg, So. Africa
Baumberg, A. H ... Sydney, Australia
Baur, Charles ... Paris, France
Baur, Leon ... Paris, France
Beirnstein, Harris M ... London, England
Beirnstein, Mrs. Jane ... London, England
Belilios, Hon. Emanuel R., C.M.G., etc ... London, England
Belisha, Albert Isaac ... London, England
Belisha, Barrow Isaac ... Manchester, England
Belkind, Israel ... Rishon-le-Zion, Palestine
Benas, Baron L., J.P ... Liverpool, England
Bendon, George ... London, England
Bendry, Rev. A. P ... Cape Town, So. Africa
Benjamin, Hyman ... Middlesborough, England
Benjamin, Isaac ... Llanelly, Wales
Benjamin, Richard ... Nottingham, England
Ben-Oliel, Rev. Maxwell M ... London, England
Benscher, Martin ... London, England
Benscher, W ... London, England
Bensusan, The Messrs ... Bexhill-on-Sea, England
Bentwich, Herbert, LL.B ... London, England
Benzinger, Dr. Immanuel ... Jerusalem, Palestine
Berkhamsted Gram. School, Rev. Dr. Fry, Berkhamsted, England
Berlin, University of ... Berlin, Germany
Berliner, A ... Berlin, Germany
Berlinski, Solomon J ... London, England
Berlowitz, L ... London, England
Berlyn, M ... Birmingham, England
Bern, University of ... Bern, Switzerland
Bernard, O. L ... E. Northam, W. Australia
Berner Hochschul Bibliothek ... Bern, Switzerland
Bernfeld, Dr. Simon ... Berlin, Germany
Bernfield, S ... London, England
Bernstein, J ... Johannesburg, So. Africa
Bernstein, Max ... Glasgow, Scotland
Bernstein, Solomon ... Manchester, England
Bertish, Marcus ... Bristol, England
Berwitz, Louis ... Belfast, Ireland
Besso, Moses ... Manchester, England
Besso, R ... Manchester, England
Besso, Samuel ... Manchester, England
Betesh, Joseph ... Manchester, England
Bethencourt, C. de ... Paris, France
Betts, Mrs. K. M ... London, England
Bevan, T., D.L., J.P ... London, England
Bhinjekar, Elias R ... Bombay, India
Bibliothèque des Bollandistes ... Brussels, Belgium
Bickersteth, Rt. Rev. Edward Henry, D.D. . Exeter, England
Bigio, S. B ... Southport, England
Birks, H ... Manchester, England
Birmingham Public Library ... Birmingham, England
Birnbaum, Bernard ... London, England
Birnbaum, E ... Königsberg, Germany
Birnstingl, Avigdor L ... London, England
Bischoffsheim, Mrs. C ... London, England
Bishop of Bangor, The ... Menai Bridge, Wales
Bishop of Exeter, The ... Exeter, England
Bishop of Lichfield, The ... Lichfield, England
Bishop of London, The ... London, England
Bishop of Newcastle, The . . Newcastle-upon-Tyne, England
Bishop of Ripon, The ... Ripon, England
Bishop of Stepney, The ... London, England
Bitton, J ... London, England
Black, William George, F.S.A ... Glasgow, Scotland
Blaiberg, S ... London, England
Blau, Dr. Ludwig ... Budapest, Hungary
Blaustein, M ... London, England
Blaustein, Tobias ... London, England
Bles, A. J. S ... Manchester, England
Bloch, Rev. Arm., Grand Rabbin de Belgique, Brussels, Belgium
Bloch, Rev. Dr. Philipp ... Posen, Germany
Bloom, Abraham ... Middlesborough, England
Bloom, Rev. E ... Merthyr-Tydvil, Wales
Bloom, Goodall ... Beel Water, So. Africa
Bloom, Isadore ... Middlesborough, England
Bloom, Mrs. Louis ... West Hartlepool, England
Bloom, S ... Chester, England
Blumberg, Harris ... Manchester, England
Blumberg, Isaac ... Manchester, England
Blumenau, Louis ... Dublin, Ireland
Bodleian Library ... Oxford, England
Bojanowo, Dr. J. Theodor ... Posen, Germany
Bolloten, Joseph ... Upper Bangor, Wales
Bomash, T. S ... Cardiff, Wales
Bootle Free Public Library and Museum . . Liverpool, England
Bowman, L. G. M. A ... London, England
Box, Rev. George H., M.A ... Chingford, England
Bradford Free Library ... Bradford, England
Bradford, Mayor of ... Bradford, England
Bradshaw, R ... Dublin, Ireland
Brainin, Dr. R ... Charlottenburg, Germany
Brandes, Dr. Eduard ... Copenhagen, Denmark
Brann, M., Ph.D ... Breslau, Germany
Bransky, Ellis ... Newcastle-upon-Tyne, England
Brighton Public Library ... Brighton, England
Brill, N ... London, England
Brilliant, H ... London, England
Briscoe, A. W ... Dublin, Ireland
Bristol Public Library ... Bristol, England
British and Foreign Bible Society ... London, England
Brody, H., Ph.D ... Nachod, Austria
Brodziak, A ... Sydney, Australia
Bromley House Library ... Nottingham, England
Brown, A ... Manchester, England
Brown, Bernard ... Sheffield, England
Brown, H. L ... Sheffield, England
Brown, Lewis ... Newcastle-upon-Tyne, England
Brown, Morris ... Edinburgh, Scotland
Brown, Philip ... Edinburgh, Scotland
Browne, Rev. W. J ... Rathfriland, Down, Ireland
Browning, Prof. Oscar . . . King's College, Cambridge, England
Brüll, Rev. Dr. Adolf . . . . . Frankfort-on-the-Main, Germany
Brussels Bollandists Society ... Brussels, Belgium
Btesh, M. A ... Manchester, England
Buber, Solomon ... Lemberg, Austria
Büchler, Dr. Adolf ... Vienna, Austria
Bucks, Morris ... London, England
Budge, Henry ... Hamburg, Germany
Buetow, Max ... South Shields, England
Bugeisky, Louis ... Dudley, England
Buhl, Dr. Franz ... Copenhagen, Denmark
Bulley, B ... Belgrade, Servia
Buluwayo Chovevei Zion Association . . Buluwayo, So. Africa

C

Cabrol, Rev. Fernand ... Farnborough, England
Cadbury, R ... Worcester, England
Cahen, Isidore ... Paris, France
Caiden, Michael ... London, England
Cambridge Free Library ... Cambridge, England
Camrass, Hyman ... Leeds, England
Cansino, Isaac ... Manchester, England
Cantor, L ... London, England
Caplan, Isaac ... Johannesburg, So. Africa
Cardiff Free Library ... Cardiff, Wales
Caro, Dr. Jacob ... Breslau, Germany
Carpenter, Rev. J. Estlin ... Oxford, England
Carpenter, Rt. Rev. William Boyd ... Ripon, England
Cassell, John ... Birmingham, England
Castello, James ... London, England
Castiglione, Dr ... Triest, Austria
Cazalet, Rev. A. M ... London, England
Chaikin, George, B.A ... Sheffield, England
Chamberlain, F ... Barnsley, England
Chaplin, Rev. A ... Chelmsford, England
Chapman, Rev. John ... London, England
Charles, Prof. R. H., D.D ... Oxford, England
Cheetham Free Reference Library . . . . Manchester, England
Chelsea Public Library ... London, England
Cheyne, Rev. T. K., D.D ... Oxford, England
Chief Rabbi of Austria, The ... Prague, Bohemia
Chief Rabbi of Belgium, The ... Brussels, Belgium
Chief Rabbi of the British Empire, The . . . London, England
Chief Rabbi of Bulgaria, The ... Sofia, Bulgaria
Chief Rabbi of Denmark, The ... Copenhagen, Denmark
Chief Rabbi of France, The ... Paris, France
Chief Rabbi of Holland, The ... Amsterdam, Holland
Chief Rabbi of Hungary, The ... Budapest, Hungary
Chotzner, Dr. J., Ph.D ... Ramsgate, England
Christ Church Library ... Oxford, England
Christ's College ... Cambridge, England
Church House Library, Westminster ... London, England
Claff, Samuel ... Manchester, England
Clenowich, Judah ... London, England
Clozenberg, Isaac ... London, England
Cobban, James MacLaren ... London, England
Coe, Rev. C. C., F.R.G.S ... Bournemouth, England
Cohen, Rev. Aaron ... London, England
Cohen, Alfred L., L.C.C ... London, England
Cohen, Arakie ... London, England
Cohen, B., J.P ... Bradford, England
Cohen, Barnett ... London, England
Cohen, Benjamin L., M.P ... London, England
Cohen, Charles ... Leeds, England
Cohen, E. Arakie ... London, England
Cohen, E. M. D ... Calcutta, India
Cohen, Eli E ... Manchester, England
Cohen, Rev. Francis L ... London, England
Cohen, H. B ... Saratoga, So. Africa
Cohen, Hon. Henry E ... Sydney, Australia
Cohen, Mrs. Herbert ... London, England
Cohen, Dr. Hermann ... Marburg, Germany
Cohen, Hyman ... Stockton-on-Tees, England
Cohen, Israel ... Cardiff, Wales
Cohen, Israel Wolfe ... Manchester, England
Cohen, J. B ... Manchester, England
Cohen, Jacob E ... Hull, England
Cohen, James de Lara ... London, England
Cohen, Joseph ... Birmingham, England
Cohen, Joseph M ... London, England
Cohen, Mrs. Julia M ... London, England
Cohen, Leonard ... London, England

Cohen, Louis S., J.P................Liverpool, England
Cohen, M........................Sunderland, England
Cohen, Rev. M. I., B.A...........Buluwayo, So. Africa
Cohen, Morris...........Newcastle-upon-Tyne, England
Cohen, Nathaniel L................London, England
Cohen, Neville.............New South Wales, Australia
Cohen, Philip..................Birmingham, England
Cohen, Philip.........Newcastle-upon-Tyne, England
Cohen, S., & Co....................Batavia, Java
Cohen, Samuel....................London, England
Cohen, Samuel..................Manchester, England
Cohen, Samuel I...................London, England
Cohen, Samuel J................Manchester, England
Cohen, Rev. Susman.............London, England
Cohen, W. R............Merthyr-Tydvil, Wales
Cohen, W. R...............Walgett, Australia
Cohen, Woolf H...................London, England
Cohn, Albert....................London, England
Cohn, Dr. Heinrich Meyer.........Berlin, Germany
Cohn, Joshua....................London, England
Collins, H. H...................London, England
Constitutional Club..............London, England
Conybeare, F. C.................Oxford, England
Cope, I. G.....................London, England
Copenhagen Jewish Congregation ....Copenhagen, Denmark
Copenhagen Library.........Copenhagen, Denmark
Corfield, Prof. W. H., M.A..........London, England
Cornill, Dr. Karl Heinrich........Breslau, Germany
Cotton, Aaron..............Birmingham, England
Cotton, B. M...............Birmingham, England
Coudenhove, Dr. Heinrich, Count von....Ronssperg, Austria
Cowen, David....................Wigan, England
Cowen, J........................London, England
Cowen, L........................Derby, England
Cowen, Maurice................Manchester, England
Cowley, Arthur E...............Oxford, England
Craigie, Mrs. P. M. T. ("John Oliver Hobbes"),
                                London, England
Crown, Zalig..............Walthamstow, England
Croydon Public Libraries..............London, England

D

Daltroff, Albert...................Paris, France
Dampier, Miss Margaret G...........Beccles, England
David, D. A..................Calcutta, India
David, Salem S..................Bombay, India
Davids, A.....................London, England
Davidson, David.........East London, So. Africa
Davidson, Rev. George ....Edinburgh, Scotland
Davidson, H. R..........Barrow-in-Furness, England
Davis, D. H.................Birmingham, England
Davis, D. L.................Manchester, England
Davis, David M.................London, England
Davis, Mrs. Eliza...............London, England
Davis, Rev. G. E., M.A...............Bath, England
Davis, Harris..................Walsall, England
Davis, Isaac....................London, England
Davis, Israel, M.A................London, England
Davis, Morris...........Newcastle-upon-Tyne, England
Davison, Rev. W. T., D.D..........Birmingham, England
Dawson, E. B....................Lancaster, England
Derby, Earl of..................Prescot, England
Derby Public Library...............Derby, England
Derenbourg, Prof. Hartwig...........Paris, France
Deutsch, Felix.................Berlin, Germany
Deutsch, Franz.................London, England
Deutsch-Jüdischer Gemeindebund......Berlin, Germany
Deutsch, Victor.............Magdeburg, Germany
Devonport Free Public Library......Devonport, England
Dickamp, Dr. Franz..............Münster, Germany
Dickons, J. Norton...............Bradford, England
Divinity School..............Cambridge, England
Doffman, Jacob.................Leicester, England
Donald, Macalister, M.D...........Cambridge, England
Doniger, Hy..................Southport, England
Dorchester Missionary College.......Wallingford, England
Dorchi Zion Association.........Manchester, England
D'Ore, B. Cola...............Birmingham, England
Dorfmann, N. Isaac..............Liverpool, England
Dorshei Zion Association.........Cape Town, So. Africa
Dresden, George.................London, England
Dreyfus, Charles, Ph.D..............London, England
Dreyfuss, Dr. Robert.........Manchester, England
Driver, Rev. S. R., D.D............Oxford, England
Dryer, Jacob.................Manchester, England
Dunner, Rev. Dr., Chief Rabbi ....Amsterdam, Holland
Duparc, M....................London, England
Durban Public Library............Durban, So. Africa
Durham, University of............Durham, England
Duveen, J. J..................London, England

E

Eaidan, M....................London, England
Eckstein, Rev. Dr. A..............Bamberg, Germany
Ecole Speciale des Langues Orientales Vivantes, Paris, France
Edells, A. H..................London, England
Edelman, Albert..............Broken Hill, Australia
Edelshain, Adam.................Glasgow, Scotland
Edinburgh Jewish Public Library......Edinburgh, Scotland

Edinburgh Public Library..........Edinburgh, Scotland
Edinburgh University..........Edinburgh, Scotland
Edwards, Rev. Thomas Charles, D.D.........Bala, Wales
Ehrenberg, Israel...............Reading, England
Ehrmann, Willy................London, England
Eisiski, S....................Rhyl, Wales
Elkind, Dr. Arcadius.............Moscow, Russia
Ellison, Louis...............Manchester, England
Elsner, A....................London, England
Emanuel, Ald. A. Leon, J.P.......Portsmouth, England
Emanuel, Barrow, M.A., J.P.......London, England
Emanuel, Rev. G. J., B.A........Birmingham, England
Emanuel, Mrs. G. J............Birmingham, England
Englander, A..................London, England
Epler, Adolf............Johannesburg, So. Africa
Epler, J....................Brünn, Austria
Eprile, Joseph.............Edinburgh, Scotland
Epstein, A..................Cardiff, Wales
Epstein, J..................Derby, England
Epstein, P..................London, England
Erdberg, Abraham.....Newcastle-upon-Tyne, England
Erlangen, University of...........Erlangen, Germany
Erman, W....................Breslau, Germany
Errera, Prof. Leo..............Brussels, Belgium
Esterman, Joseph................London, England
Esterson, Rev. Wolffe.............London, England
Euting, J..................Strasburg, Germany
Ezekiel, Dr. Abraham.............Bombay, India
Ezekiel, Joseph................Bombay, India
Ezra, Edward I................Shanghai, China
Ezra, N. E. B.................Shanghai, China

F

Fabian, Levi...................Breslau, Germany
Faculté de Théologie Protestante........Paris, France
Faith, Charles.........Newcastle-upon-Tyne, England
Falkirk Public Library...............Falkirk, Scotland
Farkas, Dr. Emile.............Budapest, Hungary
Fay, Rev. D..................London, England
Fedderman, Lionel................Manchester, England
Feilitzen, Capt. O. V., R.S.N........Stockholm, Sweden
Felber, Morres.................London, England
Feldman, Rev. A., B.A............London, England
Feldman, Abraham..............Leeds, England
Feldman, H....................Hull, England
Feldman, S. J..................Hull, England
Fersht, Barnett Abraham...........London, England
Fiers, L...................Birmingham, England
Finburgh, Samuel ....Manchester, England
Fine, Israel...........Merthyr-Tydvil, Wales
Fine, J................Penrhiwceiber, Wales
Fine, L. L., J.P................Rhymney, Wales
Fine, Louis..................Bristol, England
Fine, Mark...........Johannesburg, So. Africa
Finestone, David..............Southport, England
Finestone, Louis..............Southport, England
Finkelstein, Dr. S............Manchester, England
Finn, Samuel............South Shields, England
Finsbury Public Library...........London, England
Fisher, M....................London, England
Fisher, Moss................Birmingham, England
Fishout, M................Pont-y-pridd, Wales
Flatow, Jacobi Wronker.........Dewsbury, England
Fleming, Isidor...............London, England
Fligelstone, Frank.............Rhymney, Wales
Flinberg, H. M.............Manchester, England
Florence Jewish Theological Seminary.......Florence, Italy
Florentin, Meise J...........Manchester, England
Follick, Coleman...............Cardiff, Wales
Fowler, Rev. J. T., D.C.L., University Library,
                                Durham, England
Franco, M................Shumla, Bulgaria
Frank, Rev. Dr. S............Cologne, Germany
Fränkel, Dr. Sigmund..........Breslau, Germany
Frankenburg, Alderman, J.P.......Manchester, England
Frankenstein, Louis...........Manchester, England
Frankenstein, S..............Southport, England
Frankenthal, Adolph L.........Bern, Switzerland
Frankfurt-am-Main Stadtbibliothek,
                        Frankfort-on-the-Main, Germany
Frankfort-Loge.........Frankfort-on-the-Main, Germany
Franklin, Ellis A..............London, England
Franklin, Ernest L..............London, England
Franklin, Frederick S............London, England
Franklin, Henry A...............London, England
Franklin, Jacob Hyman..........London, England
Franks, Arnold................Wigan, England
Franks, Lawrence...............London, England
Franks, Michael...............London, England
Franzos, Dr. Karl Emil..........Berlin, Germany
Fraser, Israel...............Manchester, England
Frauenberger, Dr. H.......Düsseldorf-am-Rhine, Germany
Free Church College..............Glasgow, Scotland
Freecorn, A...............Perth, W. Australia
Freedman, A. I................Dowlais, Wales
Freedman, Rev. David I., B.A........Perth, W. Australia
Freedman, George..............Glasgow, Scotland
Freedman, Isaac................Stockport, England
Freedman, L...................London, England

Freedmann, Herman.................Manchester, England
Freeman, Samuel.........................Belfast, Ireland
Freiburg, University of..............Freiburg, Germany
Freimann, Dr. A.........Frankfort-on-the-Main, Germany
Freudenthal, Dr. Jacob................Breslau, Germany
Friedbinder, M........................London, England
Friedeberg, Rev. S., B.A............Liverpool, England
Friedlander, H. L.....................London, England
Friedlander, Dr. M.....................Vienna, Austria
Friedländer, Dr. Michael...............London, England
Friedlander, Mrs. Wulf...............De Aar, So. Africa
Friedman, Aaron........................Leeds, England
Friedrich-Loge XXIX, No. 444......Heidelberg, Germany
Friend, Capt. B. J....................London, England
Friend, Henry.......................Sunderland, England
Fürst, Rev. J.....................Edinburgh, Scotland
Fyne, Rev. S...........................Swansea, Wales

G

Gabriel, H. Wallace...................Pagham, England
Gabriesen, G. P......................Liverpool, England
Garson, David S.....................Manchester, England
Gartman, Mrs. R......................London, England
Gaster, Very Rev. M., Ph.D..........London, England
Gautier, Prof. Lucien, Ph.D........Geneva, Switzerland
Geffen, Rev. J. L.....................London, England
Gelbert, Maurice J., Ph.D..............Bristol, England
Gellmann, Bernard....................London, England
Gembitski, E. D....................Manchester, England
Gembitski, William.................Manchester, England
Geneva Public Library.............Geneva, Switzerland
Genussow, M. L..............Cape Town, So. Africa
Gerson, H.................Johannesburg, So. Africa
Gestetner, David....................London, England
Gesundheit, S.......................Brighton, England
Gidney, Rev. W. T...................London, England
Ginzberg, I.......................Amsterdam, Holland
Ginzberg, U...........................Odessa, Russia
Gittlesohn, Herrmann..........Merthyr-Tydvil, Wales
Glasgow, University of...............Glasgow, Scotland
Glaskin, W...........................Warsaw, Russia
Glass, H...........................Hartlepool, England
Glass, Harris......................Manchester, England
Gleitzmann, Henry....................London, England
Gluckstadt, I..................Copenhagen, Denmark
Gluckstein, Myer....................London, England
Gobits, Dr. P. J..................Amsterdam, Holland
Goldberg, Barnett....................Swansea, Wales
Goldberg, E. H......................London, England
Goldberg, H.........................London, England
Goldberg, Harris......................Bristol, England
Goldberg, Hyam.......................Swansea, Wales
Goldberg, J.................Buluwayo, So. Africa
Goldberg, L.......................Manchester, England
Goldberg, Louis.............Durban, So. Africa
Goldman, A.................Johannesburg, So. Africa
Goldman, Henry....................Sunderland, England
Goldreich, S................Johannesburg, So. Africa
Goldring, Jacob......................Tulcea, Rumania
Goldschmidt, A....................Hamburg, Germany
Goldsmid, Colonel Albert E. W.........London, England
Goldsmid, Captain L. C................London, England
Goldsmid, L. Lionel..........Johannesburg, So. Africa
Goldsmid, O. E. d'Avigdor............Tunbridge, England
Goldstein, A. E......................Sydney, Australia
Goldstein, Jacob........................Hull, England
Goldstein, Rev. Julius A...............London, England
Goldstein, Rev. S. A..........Auckland, New Zealand
Goldston, Rev. Nehemiah................London, England
Goldstone, Alfred.................Birmingham, England
Goldstone, H...........................Hull, England
Goldzicher, Edouard..................Brussels, Belgium
Goldziher, Ignaz, Ph.D..............Budapest, Hungary
Gollancz, Rev. H., M.A., Litt.D........London, England
Goodman, Barnett...................Birmingham, England
Goodman, David...............Wolverhampton, England
Goodman, H.................Johannesburg, So. Africa
Goodman, M..........................Preston, England
Goodman, Moses...........Merthyr-Tydvil, Wales
Goodman, Paul......................London, England
Goodman, S.........................London, England
Goodman, S..........................Preston, England
Goodman, Solomon Joseph.............London, England
Gordon, E...................Londonderry, Ireland
Gordon, Jonas.................Birmingham, England
Gordon, L......................Edinburgh, Scotland
Gordon, Samuel.................Birmingham, England
Gore, Rt. Rev. Charles, M.A., Bishop of Birmingham, England
Göteborgs Stadtbibliothek.............Göteborg, Sweden
Gotliffe, Solomon Lewis...........Manchester, England
Gotthelf, Moritz.....................Sydney, Australia
Göttingen, University of............Göttingen, Germany
Göttinger Gesellschaft der Wissenschaften,
                       Göttingen, Germany
Gouldstein, Rev. Julius A...........London, England
Gow, Rev. James, M.A., Litt.D........London, England
Green, Michael A...................London, England
Greenberg, Charles L.........Johannesburg, So. Africa
Greenberg, Israel S...............Birmingham, England

Greenberg, Leopold J..................London, England
Greenberg, S. Z.............Johannesburg, So. Africa
Griqualand W. Hebrew Congreg'n....Kimberley, So. Africa
Groot, Laurence de.....................Dublin, Ireland
Gross, Dr. P., L.R.C.P. Lond...........London, England
Gross, William.......................London, England
Grossberg, Solomon...................London, England
Grosvenor Gallery Library.............London, England
Grün, Maurice.......................London, England
Grunwald, Dr. M...................Hamburg, Germany
Gubbay, Reuben.........................Paris, France
Gudansky, Rev. Abraham...............Dublin, Ireland
Güdemann, M., Ph.D., Chief Rabbi........Vienna, Austria
Guinsberg, B................Johannesburg, So. Africa
Guinsberg, J. H............Johannesburg, So. Africa
Guinsburg, A...............Johannesburg, So. Africa
Gundelfinger, Prof. Dr............Darmstadt, Germany
Günzburg, Baron D. von............St. Petersburg, Russia
Guttmann, Rev. Dr. J................Breslau, Germany
Guttmann, Dr. Michael...............Csongrad, Hungary

H

Haas, Henri...........................Paris, France
Haas, J. de.........................London, England
Haggard, H. Rider...............Ditchingham, England
Haileybury College....................Hertford, England
Halévy, Joseph.........................Paris, France
Hallenstein, H....................Holstein, Germany
Hallgarten, Chas. L......Frankfort-on-the-Main, Germany
Halpern, S............................Preston, England
Hamburger, Fritz..................Carlsruhe, Germany
Hamburger, Rev. Dr. J..................Strelitz, Austria
Hampstead Public Libraries............London, England
Hanson, Rev. G., D.D..................London, England
Harbour, Charles....................London, England
Harkavy, A., Ph.D............St. Petersburg, Russia
Harrasowitz, Otto....................Leipsic, Germany
Harris, A...........................Glasgow, Scotland
Harris, Lieut.-Col. D...........Kimberley, So. Africa
Harris, Ephraim, M.A...........Manchester, England
Harris, Herman......................London, England
Harris, Rev. Isidore, M.A.............London, England
Harris, J. Rendel.................Cambridge, England
Harris, Lionel.......................Tredegar, England
Harris, Marcus........................Blaina, Wales
Harris, Merton....................Manchester, England
Harris, N...........................Landport, England
Harris, Nathaniel....................London, England
Harris, Rev. Raphael.................London, England
Harris, S. Louis....................Tredegar, England
Harris, Simon.....................Edinburgh, Scotland
Harris, Wolf........................London, England
Harris, Woolf.............Cape Town, So. Africa
Hart, Henry.........................London, England
Hart, Henry, J.P.....................Dover, England
Hart, Sir Israel, J.P..............Leicester, England
Hart, J. H. A........................Derby, England
Hart, Joshua......................Plumstead, England
Hart, Philip.....................Manchester, England
Hassid, J. Albert...................Salonica, Turkey
Hatchard, Messrs....................London, England
Hatvany-Deutsch, Alexander de.......Budapest, Hungary
Hatvany-Deutsch, Josef de...........Budapest, Hungary
Hawkins, C. W.................Dunedin, New Zealand
Hayman, H..........................London, England
Headingly College....................Leeds, England
Hebrew School....................Birmingham, England
Hechler, Prof. W. H...................Vienna, Austria
Heidelberg, University of...........Heidelberg, Germany
Heilbron, David.................Glasgow, Scotland
Heimann, Sigmund.........Johannesburg, So. Africa
Heming, Isidor......................London, England
Henriques, Alfred G., J. P............Hove, England
Henry, Charles S....................London, England
Henry, Philip S.....................London, England
Hepker, H.................Buluwayo, So. Africa
Herbert, R. J........................London, England
Hermann, Sigmund.........Johannesburg, So. Africa
Herson, S...........................London, England
Hertz, Rev. Dr. Joseph H........Johannesburg, So. Africa
Hertzberg, A......................Brisbane, Australia
Hertzberg, A. M....................Brisbane, Australia
Herzl, Dr. Theodor (deceased)........Vienna, Austria
Herzog, Rev. Rabbi....................Leeds, England
Heymann, Hermann.........Johannesburg, So. Africa
Heymann, Maurice....................London, England
Hildesheimer, Rev. Dr. Hirsch........Berlin, Germany
Hill, Rev. W. B...............Blandford, England
Hillman, Selig............Norvals Pont, So. Africa
Hilson, S...............Johannesburg, So. Africa
Himann, Sigmund.........Johannesburg, So. Africa
Himmelsfarb, Dr. G...................Odessa, Russia
Hinds, Henry......................Ramsgate, England
Hirsch, Benjamin................Halberstadt, Germany
Hirsch, Joseph......................London, England
Hirschfeld, Professor H...............London, England
Hoffman, Gustav....................London, England
Hoffmann, Dr. David..................Berlin, Germany
Hoffnung, A........................London, England

Hogan, Rev. R................Lochgelly, Scotland
Hogg, Prof. H. W......Fallowfield, Manchester, England
Holberg, Frederick................Birmingham, England
Horovitz, Dr. S....................Leipsic, Germany
Horovitz, Rev. Dr. M....Frankfort-on-the-Main, Germany
Hoster, Mrs. Constance.................London, England
House of Lords Library.................London, England
Hudson, G. J......................London, England
Hull Public Libraries....................Hull, England
Hull Subscription Library................Hull, England
Humanitätsverein Wien, "Bnai Brith".....Vienna, Austria
Hyam, Joseph C....................Algiers, No. Africa
Hyamson, A. M....................London, England
Hymans, Henry....................London, England

I

Iago-Trelawny, Major-Gen.............Liskeard, England
Isaacs, Abraham.....................London, England
Isaacs, D.....................Cape Town, So. Africa
Isaacs, Ellis.....................Glasgow, Scotland
Isaacs, Rev. Harris................Kimberley, So. Africa
Isaacs, Henry.....................Leeds, England
Isaacs, Sir Henry A..................London, England
Isaacs, Isaac A................Manchester, England
Isaacs, Isaac A..................Melbourne, Australia
Isaacs, Isaac Judah...............Manchester, England
Isaacs, J......................London, England
Isaacs, Maurice..................London, England
Isaacs, Maurice..................Edinburgh, Scotland
Isaacs, Moss.....................Brighton, England
Isaacs, Rufus D., K.C., M.P...........London, England
Isaacs, Solomon..................Stockport, England
Isaakowitz, A......................London, England
Isacowitz, A..........Orange River Colony, So. Africa
Israel, Shalom B....................Bombay, India
Israel. Theolog. Lehranstalt............Vienna, Austria
Israelite School.....................Bombay, India
Israelitische Allianz................Vienna, Austria
Israelitische Cultusgemeinde............Brünn, Austria
Israelitische Cultusgemeinde...........Vienna, Austria
Israelitische Gemeindebibliothek........Prague, Bohemia
Israelitisches Lehrerseminar..........Budapest, Hungary
Israelstam, A...............Johannesburg, So. Africa
Izckowitz, Lazarus J.............Muizenberg, So. Africa

J

Jacob, Rev. Dr. B..................Göttingen, Germany
Jacob, Rt. Rev. Edgar, D.D. Oxon.,
                              Newcastle-upon-Tyne, England
Jacobs, A......................London, England
Jacobs, Rev. A. C..................Brighton, England
Jacobs, Abe....................Sunderland, England
Jacobs, B. S.....................Hull, England
Jacobs, Barnet.....................Cardiff, Wales
Jacobs, Benjamin..................Sheffield, England
Jacobs, Bertram, LL.B...............London, England
Jacobs, D. Montague..............Salisbury, So. Africa
Jacobs, Herbert Levi................London, England
Jacobs, Israel...................Sunderland, England
Jacobs, Lesser R..................London, England
Jacobs, M. E....................Cwmbran, Wales
Jacobs, Maurice..................London, England
Jacobs, Morris....................Aberdare, Wales
Jacobs, Morris.................West Kirby, England
Jacobs, Nathan....................London, England
Jacobs, S......................Newport, Wales
Jacoby, S....................Buluwayo, So. Africa
Jaffé Brothers...................Limerick, Ireland
Jaffé, John.......................Nice, France
Jaffé, Sir Otto, J.P................Belfast, Ireland
Janovsky, S...............St. Petersburg, Russia
Japan, The Emperor of................Tokyo, Japan
Japhet, S......................London, England
Jaré, Rev. Giuseppe, Chief Rabbi..........Ferrara, Italy
Jena, University of..................Jena, Germany
Jessel, Albert H., M.A...............London, England
Jewish Colonial Trust................London, England
Jewish Literary and Social Society......Tredegar, England
Jewish Theological Seminary..........Budapest, Hungary
Jews' College.....................London, England
Jews' Hospital....................London, England
Joffe, Max F................Johannesburg, So. Africa
Joffe, R...................Krugersdorp, So. Africa
John Rylands Library............Manchester, England
Jonas, I......................Birmingham, England
Jones, Albert Victor................London, England
Jones, Rev. R. Eifion................Anglesey, Wales
Joseph, D.....................London, England
Joseph, Rev. D....................Berlin, Germany
Joseph, Dr. Hans H................Newport, Wales
Joseph, Leo.....................Cardiff, Wales
Joseph, Lewis....................London, England
Joseph, Rev. M....................London, England
Joseph, Moritz G..................London, England
Judah, Miss K..................Calcutta, India

K

Kahn, A., M.A....................London, England
Kahn, Rev. Rabbin Jacques..............Paris, France

Kahn, Zadoc, Grand Rabbin de France......Paris, France
Kais. Universitäts- und Landesbibliothek, Strasburg, Ger.
Kaiserman, L....................Manchester, England
Kaitcer, Hyman....................Dublin, Ireland
Kaliski, Isaac....................London, England
Kanin, N., M.D...............Johannesburg, So. Africa
Karpeles, Emil....................Vienna, Austria
Karpeles, Dr. G....................Berlin, Germany
Katz, Oscar..................Manchester, England
Kaufman, S....................Hartlepool, England
Kaufmann, A. J....................London, England
Kayserling, Dr.M.,Chief Rabbi (deceased),Budapest, Hungary
Keble College....................Oxford, England
Kelvin, Lord, G.C.V.O., etc.............London, England
Kennard, Mrs. E. A..............Hampton Wick, England
Kersh, Myer..................Manchester, England
Kessler, Leopold............Johannesburg, So. Africa
Kilburn Public Library................London, England
Kindler, Isaac..................Manchester, England
King's College..................Cambridge, England
King's College, Wilson Library.........Aberdeen, Scotland
Kingston-upon-Thames Public Library...Kingston, England
Kirschbaum, Isaac..................London, England
Kisch, Benjamin..................London, England
K. K. Hof-Bibliothek................Vienna, Austria
Klein, Hermann, F.J.I..............London, England
Klein, Louis....................London, England
Kleinfeld, Oisia..................London, England
Kletz, Louis..................Manchester, England
Klingenstein, William..............London, England
Koder, S. S.....................Cochin, India
König, Dr. Eduard........University of Rostock, Germany
Königl. Akad. der Wissenschaften.........Berlin, Germany
Königl. Oeffentliche Bibliothek..........Dresden, Germany
Königl. Universitäts-Bibliothek..........Berlin, Germany
Kornfeld, Sigmund................Budapest, Hungary
Krailsheimer, Julius................London, England
Krakauer, Solomon..................Barnsley, England
Krauss, Dr. Samuel................Budapest, Hungary
Kriegsfeld, Benjamin................London, England
Kroner, Dr. Theodor................Stuttgart, Germany
Kulisher, M. I...............St. Petersburg, Russia

L

Lambert, Baron..................Brussels, Belgium
Lambert, Mayer....................Paris, France
Lancashire Independent College......Manchester, England
Landau, Annie E., Rothschild School, Jerusalem, Palestine
Landau, Hermann..................London, England
Landau, Marcus..................London, England
Landauer, Dr. S..................Strasburg, Germany
Lander, Julius....................London, England
Landman, D......................Odessa, Russia
Landman, Judah..................Leeds, England
Langermann, Max.............Johannesburg, So. Africa
Lapine, E................Buenos Ayres, So. America
Lara, Isidore de....................Paris, France
Laredo, M......................London, England
Larkinson, Samuel............Wolverhampton, England
Laserson, Morris M......Newcastle-upon-Tyne, England
Laserson, S. M..................Manchester, England
Laski, Nathan..................Manchester, England
Lasry, Solomon....................Tunis, Algeria
Lawrence, Rev. Z..................Sunderland, England
Lawton, W. F.....................Hull, England
Lazare, Bernard....................Paris, France
Lazarus, Abraham................London, England
Lazarus, Prof. M., Geh. Reg. Rath...........Meran, Austria
Lazarus, Maurice......Newcastle-upon-Tyne, England
Lazarus, S....................Londonderry, Ireland
Lazarus, S. L....................London, England
Lebus, Harris....................London, England
Lediker, M...............Johannesburg, So. Africa
Lee, Edward....................London, England
Lee, Samuel....................Dudley, England
Leeds Free Public Libraries............Leeds, England
Leeds Library (Commercial Street)........Leeds, England
Leef, Edward de..................London, England
Lees, Rev. Robert James.............Plymouth, England
Lehberg, L.......................Bolton, England
Lehmann, H....................London, England
Leicester Public Library.............Leicester, England
Leighs, H....................Aldershot, England
Leipsic, University of..................Leipsic, Germany
Lemberger, A..................Manchester, England
Leroy-Beaulieu, Anatole................Paris, France
Lessmann, M..................Hamburg, Germany
Lessner, S. D....................Nagasaki, Japan
Letter, L....................Manchester, England
Lettman, Dr. M..................Zurich, Switzerland
Leuw, Sidney....................London, England
Levene, John M..................London, England
Levene, Myer....................Belfast, Ireland
Levene, Rev. Samuel................Ramsgate, England
Levenson, M..................Ammanford, Wales
Levenstein, A..................Birmingham, England
Lévi, Israel......................Paris, France
Levi, J. L.....................Cardiff, Wales
Levi, Louis......................Hull, England

Levi, P. .... Manchester, England
Levi, S. M. .... Edgbaston, England
Levin, Joseph .... Dublin, Ireland
Levin, Julius .... London, England
Levin, Rev. Dr. M. .... Berlin, Germany
Levinshon, M. .... London, England
Levinson, Aaron .... Manchester, England
Levinson, Rev. Abraham .... Brighton, England
Levinson, Rev. Isaac .... London, England
Leviseur, M. .... Bloemfontein, So. Africa
Levy, A. .... Middlesborough, England
Levy, Abraham .... London, England
Levy, B. .... Brighton, England
Levy, B. W. .... London, England
Levy, J. H. .... London, England
Levy, Jacob .... Newcastle-upon-Tyne, England
Levy, Joseph .... Manchester, England
Levy, Joseph .... London, England
Levy, Jos. H. .... London, England
Levy, Judah .... London, England
Levy, L. A. .... Alexandria, Egypt
Levy, M. C. .... London, England
Levy, Moses .... South Shields, England
Levy, S. .... London, England
Levy, S. .... South Shields, England
Levy, Rev. S., M.A. .... London, England
Levy, S. A. .... Southsea, England
Levy, Saul .... Middlesborough, England
Levy, Simon .... Glasgow, Scotland
Lewin, Maurice .... London, England
Lewinsky, Rabbi .... Hildesheim, Germany
Lewis, Lady .... London, England
Lewis, Harry Reginald .... London, England
Lewis, Jacob .... Cardiff, Wales
Lewis, Leon .... Cape Town, So. Africa
Lewis, Leon .... Johannesburg, So. Africa
Lewis, Mrs. Moss .... Manchester, England
Lewis, Solomon J. .... Manchester, England
Leyden, University of .... Leyden, Holland
Leyton Public Libraries .... London, England
Liberman, H. .... Cape Town, So. Africa
Libraire Durlacher .... Paris, France
Lieberthal, W. .... Vosburg, So. Africa
Liebster, L., M.D., L.S.A. .... London, England
Liggi, M. .... Scarborough, England
Lightman, Victor .... Leeds, England
Liknaigtry, Dr. B. .... Johannesburg, So. Africa
Lintine, D. F. .... Birmingham, England
Lipinski, David .... Hull, England
Lipkind, Rev. G. .... London, England
Lipshytz, Rev. C. T. .... Mitcham, England
Lisbona, Raphael H. .... Manchester, England
Littmann, Dr. M. .... Zurich, Switzerland
Liverman, Philip .... Birkenhead, England
Liverpool Free Public Library .... Liverpool, England
Loewe, James H. .... London, England
Lolli, Eude, D.D., Chief Rabbi (deceased) .... Padua, Italy
Loopuit, S. W. .... Amsterdam, Holland
Lorie, M. .... Pentre, Wales
Lotery, Mrs. M. .... London, England
Lotinga, M. .... Newcastle-upon-Tyne, England
Löw, Emmanuel .... Szegedin, Hungary
Löwy, Ernest D. .... London, England
Lubash, S. .... London, England
Luby, L. .... London, England
Lucas, Henry .... London, England
Lumley, Maitland .... London, England
Luntz, M. .... Birmingham, England
Lyon, H. .... London, England
Lyons, Abraham .... Swansea, Wales
Lyons, Frank I. .... London, England
Lyons, H. .... Liverpool, England
Lyons, M. A. .... Johannesburg, So. Africa
Lyons, Marks .... Monmouth, England
Lyons, Councilor Marks J. S. .... Ebbw Vale, Wales
Lyons, Soloman .... Swansea, Wales
Lyttelton, Rev. Hon. Canon E., M.A. .... Hertford, England

M

Macdonald, Rev. Frederick William .... London, England
McDonald, W. .... Maynooth, Ireland
Mack, Joseph .... Wrexham, Wales
McKilliam, Robert, M.D. .... London, England
Madras Literary Society .... Madras, India
Magnus, Sir Philip, B.A. .... London, England
Maizels, Joseph .... London, England
Malits, Morris .... Pont-y-pridd, Wales
Manchester College .... Oxford, England
Manchester Free Ref'ce. Library (4 copies), Manchester, Eng.
Manchester Zionist Association .... Manchester, England
Mandelkern, Dr. Solomon .... Leipsic, Germany
Mandelstamm, Dr. .... Kiev, Russia
Marcus, Joseph .... London, England
Marcus, Theodore .... Liverpool, England
Margowski, Max .... London, England
Margulies, Dr. .... Florence, Italy
Margulies, S. H. .... Bad Aussee, Austria
Marks, Charles .... Stockport, England
Marks, Daniel .... London, England
Marks, G. S. .... London, England
Marks, Harry H., J.P., M.P. .... London, England
Marks, Jacob .... Cape Town, So. Africa
Marks, Jacob .... Edgbaston, England
Marks, M. .... Manchester, England
Marks, Morris .... Newcastle-upon-Tyne, England
Marks, Moss .... London, England
Marmorek, Dr. Alexander .... Paris, France
Marmorek, Oskar .... Vienna, Austria
Marsden, Maurice I. .... Bagnères-de-Bigorre, France
Marsden, Rodolph I. .... London, England
Marshall, Rev. J. T., M.A. .... Manchester, England
Martin, Richard B., M.A., M.P. .... London, England
Martinez, E. N. .... London, England
Marx, Herman .... London, England
Marx, Herrmann .... London, England
Marx, L. .... London, England
Masterman, Dr. Ernest W. G. .... Jerusalem, Palestine
Maybaum, Rev. Dr. S. .... Berlin, Germany
Mayer, Naphtali .... London, England
Mayor, Rev. J. B., M.A. .... Kingston, England
Melbourne Public Library .... Melbourne, Australia
Melcher, Lewis .... Cardiff, Wales
Meltzer, N. .... Newcastle-upon-Tyne, England
Mendelsohn, L. .... Dunedin, New Zealand
Mendelsohn, M. .... Birmingham, England
Mendelson, M. D. .... Newcastle-upon-Tyne, England
Mendelssohn, E. .... London, England
Mentz, C. V. .... London, England
Mer, M. F. .... London, England
Merkel, A. .... Newcastle-upon-Tyne, England
Mesquita, D. Bueno de .... London, England
Meyer, Eduard, Ph.D. .... Halle, Germany
Meyerstone, Hymann .... Manchester, England
Michael, Gustave, M.B. .... London, England
Michaels, Maurice A. .... Manchester, England
Michaelson, C. P. .... Edinburgh, Scotland
Michaelson, H. .... Birmingham, England
Michaelson, J. .... Cardiff, Wales
Michelson, Asher .... Stockton-on-Tees, England
Michelson, M. D. .... Grätz, Austria
Mickler, Aba .... Newcastle-upon-Tyne, England
Mildmay Mission to Jews .... London, England
Miles, Rev. F. J. .... Freemantle, Australia
Miller, Wolfe .... London, England
Mindelsohn, Justinian .... Birmingham, England
Mindelsohn, M. .... Birmingham, England
Missionary College .... Dorchester, England
Mitchell Library .... Glasgow, Scotland
Mitchell, Mark .... Sydney, Australia
Mocatta, Frederick D. .... London, England
Montagu, Sir Samuel, Bart. .... London, England
Montefiore, Claude G., M.A. .... London, England
Montefiore College .... Ramsgate, England
Montgomery, Mrs. .... Bray, Ireland
Moore, J. T. .... London, England
Moosa, J. .... Shanghai, China
Moro, Arthur .... London, England
Morris, B. .... Durham, England
Morris, I. .... London, England
Morris, J. .... Carlisle, England
Moser, Jacob, J.P. .... Bradford, England
Moses, David .... London, England
Moses, Mark .... London, England
Moses, Samuel, M.A. .... London, England
Moses, Hon. Silas Meyer .... Bombay, India
Moss, A. .... London, England
Moss, Eric .... London, England
Moss, N. .... London, England
Mudie's Select Library .... London, England
Muhsam, Rev. Dr. .... Grätz, Austria
Mundy, A. .... London, England
Myer, Ernest Alex .... London, England
Myers, Arthur M. .... Auckland, New Zealand
Myers, Asher I. (deceased) .... London, England
Myers, H. S. .... Gateshead-on-Tyne, England
Myers, Isaac .... Birmingham, England
Myers, Rev. J. E. .... Belfast, Ireland
Myers, M. E. .... Middlesborough, England
Myers, Moses .... Leeds, England
Myers, Moss S. .... London, England
Myers, Phineas .... Hove, England
Myers, S. .... Hanley, England
Myers, Samuel Peel, J.P. .... Ilkley, England
Myers, Solomon .... London, England
Myers, Victor .... London, England
Myers, Wolf .... London, England

N

Nachim, Rev. Michael .... London, England
Nahon, Raphael .... London, England
Nahum, Victor di H. .... Manchester, England
Napier, Rev. F. P. .... Guildford, England
Naples National Library .... Naples, Italy
Nathan, J. E. .... London, England
Nathan, Myer S., LL.B. .... London, England
Nathan, Nathan Alfred .... Auckland, New Zealand
Nathan, S. J. .... Singapore, Straits Settlements
Nathanson, Leopold .... Copenhagen, Denmark

National Library of Ireland................Dublin, Ireland
Nelson Public Library..................Nelson, England
Neubauer, Prof. Adolf..................Oxford, England
Neuenburg, Ernest........Newcastle-upon-Tyne, England
Neumann, Dr........................Ossmannstedt, Germany
Neumann, Dr. E., Chief Rabbi.....Nagy-Kanizsa, Hungary
Newcastle Public Library...Newcastle-upon-Tyne, England
Newcastle-upon-Tyne Literary and Philosophical Society,
        Newcastle-upon-Tyne, England
New College.......................Edinburgh, Scotland
Newgass, B.......................London, England
Niman, Alfred.....................Wigan, England
Niman, Isaac...................Blackburn, England
Nordau, Max, M.D.....................Paris, France
Norfolk and Norwich Library...........Norwich, England
Norwich Free Library.............Norwich, England
Nottingham Central Free Public Library, Nottingham, Eng.
Nowack, Dr. Wilhelm.............Strasburg, Germany
Nutt, Alfred.......................Harrow, England

O

Ochs, James F.......................London, England
O'Connor, His Honour Arthur, K.C......Durham, England
Odessa Society of Jewish Clerks...........Odessa, Russia
Olswang, D. A.....................Sunderland, England
Olswang, Simon..................Sunderland, England
Oort, Dr. H........................Leyden, Holland
Oppenheim, Samuel S..................London, England
Oppenheimer, A..................London, England
Oppert, Prof. Gustav................Berlin, Germany
Oppert, Dr. Jules.....................Paris, France
Orelli, Dr. Konrad von.............Basel, Switzerland
Orkin, Heyman...................London, England
Osterley, Rev. W. O. E., B.D.........London, England
Owens College, Christie Library.....Manchester, England

P

Padua, University of.....................Padua, Italy
Palestrant, M.......................Leeds, England
Palmer, George William, M.P.........Newbury, England
Paris, Leon.....................London, England
Paris, University of.....................Paris, France
Pariser, Lewis A...................Manchester, England
Parker, Rev. Joseph, D.D. (deceased)....London, England
Parsons, Rev. L. H..................London, England
Pass, A. E. de...................London, England
Pass, Charles de..................London, England
Pass, Daniel de..................London, England
Pearlman, Benno....................Hull, England
Pearlman, J.....................South Shields, England
Pelican, H.......................London, England
Penkar, Samuel S., L.C.E............Bombay, India
Perles, Rev. Dr. Felix............Königsberg, Germany
Perreau, Abbé Pietro..................Padua, Italy
Phibbs, Owen.....................Sligo, Ireland
Philippson, Francis.................Brussels, Belgium
Philippson, Martin, Ph.D.............Berlin, Germany
Phillips, A........................Leeds, England
Phillips, Rev. Isaac................Portsea, England
Phillips, Rev. Jacob.............Port Elizabeth, So. Africa
Phillips, Joseph..................London, England
Phillips, M. David.................London, England
Phillips, Phil......................Cardiff, Wales
Phillips, S.......................Cardiff, Wales
Pinn, Benjamin..............Johannesburg, So. Africa
Pinn, L........................Cape Town, So. Africa
Pinna, Montague I. de.................London, England
Platt, Samuel....................Stockport, England
Plotzker, David..................Manchester, England
Plotzker, Lesser..................Manchester, England
Plotzker, Marcus..................Manchester, England
Plymouth Free Public Library........Plymouth, England
Polack, Rev. J., B.A................Bristol, England
Politzer, Joseph..................London, England
Porges, Rev. Dr. N................Leipsic, Germany
Poznanski, Dr. Samuel..............Warsaw, Russia
Pozner, Montague..................London, England
Prag, Joseph.....................London, England
Prag, Julius.................Merthyr-Tydvil, Wales
Preece, Sir William H., K.C.B., etc......London, England
President of Switzerland, The......Bern, Switzerland
Pretoria Zionist Library..............Pretoria, So. Africa
Price, Louis.......................Preston, England
Pritchard, Wm. H............Johannesburg, So. Africa
Pruss, I........................Tir Phil, Wales
Pyke, Joseph......................London, England

R

Rabinovitz, I.......................Eden, Australia
Rabinowitz, Rev. J. (deceased)......Cape Town, So. Africa
Raffalowich, I....................Manchester, England
Ramsay, Prof. W. M., King's College....Aberdeen, Scotland
Ramsden, Sir John W., Bart.............Slough, England
Raphael, A.............Jews' Hospital, London, England
Raphael, Albert P.................Cape Town, So. Africa
Raphael, Miss H........Jews' School, Manchester, England
Rashkovski, N.....................Odessa, Russia
Ratner, B.......................Wilna, Russia
Ratzker, Joseph.............Johannesburg, So. Africa

Razsovich, Jacques....................Paris, France
Reading Public Library...............Reading, England
Reale Biblioteca Nazionale Centrale.......Florence, Italy
Reeback, Wolf.....................Leeds, England
Reform Club.....................London, England
Reinach, Salomon.....................Paris, France
Reinach, Theodor.....................Paris, France
Reiniger, Prof. Ad.....................Paris, France
Reitlinger, Albert.....................Brünn, Austria
Reitlinger, Alfred H.................London, England
Reitlinger, Frederic.....................Paris, France
Reitlinger, Sigismond.....................Paris, France
Ricado, B. Israel................Amsterdam, Holland
Ricardo, Joseph..................London, England
Richards, D. M.................Aberdare, Wales
Richardson, Harry..................London, England
Ricker, K. L.................St. Petersburg, Russia
Rieger, Rev. Dr. Paul.............Potsdam, Germany
Rigal, D.....................Birmingham, England
Ring, Maurice....................London, England
Ripon, Marquis of.................London, England
Rittenberg, B..........Newcastle-upon-Tyne, England
Robertson, Prof. James, D.D..........Glasgow, Scotland
Romain, S................Cape Town, So. Africa
Rooth, Edward..................Pretoria, So. Africa
Rosefield, Adolph H..............Longford, Ireland
Rosen, J................Johannesburg, So. Africa
Rosenbacher, Dr. Arnold.............Prague, Bohemia
Rosenbaum, D..................Liverpool, England
Rosenbaum, Henry..................London, England
Rosenbaum, Rev. M......Newcastle-upon-Tyne, England
Rosenbaum, Sol..................Tredegar, England
Rosenberg, J.....................London, England
Rosenberg, Louis.................Manchester, England
Rosenberg, Mark..................Liverpool, England
Rosenberg, Morris Levy...........Brighton, England
Rosenberg, Simeon........Newcastle-upon-Tyne, England
Rosenbloom, S...................Manchester, England
Rosenheim, Herman..................London, England
Rosenschein, J. L..................London, England
Rosenstock, Julius..................London, England
Rosenthal, Dr. F.................Breslau, Germany
Rosenthal, Falke..................London, England
Rosenthal, Israel..................London, England
Rosenthal, John D., LL.D.............Dublin, Ireland
Rosenthal, M............Newcastle-upon-Tyne, England
Rosenthal, Rev. M..................London, England
Rosenthal, Mark A............Johannesburg, So. Africa
Rosenthal, Vasili..................Poltava, Russia
Rosenthall, A...................Manchester, England
Rosenzweig, Rev. J..................Bangor, Wales
Rossdale, Mrs. Nellie.................London, England
Rostock, University of.............Rostock, Germany
Roth, Joseph.....................London, England
Rothschild, Rt. Hon. Lord.............London, England
Rothschild, Alfred..................London, England
Rothschild, The Hon. Charles.........London, England
Rothschild, Baron Edmond de.............Paris, France
Rothschild, Leopold de, C.V.O.........London, England
Rowland, S......................Cardiff, Wales
Rowley, Rev. W. E.............Cape Town, So. Africa
Royal and University Library.........Breslau, Germany
Royal Danish Academy of Sciences..Copenhagen, Denmark
Royal Dublin Society.................Dublin, Ireland
Royal Library.....................Berlin, Germany
Royal Library.....................Munich, Germany
Royal Library.................The Hague, Holland
Royal Library.................Stockholm, Sweden
Royal Library of Belgium.............Brussels, Belgium
Royal University..................Berlin, Germany
Royal University..................Ghent, Belgium
Royal University.................Göttingen, Germany
Royal University..................Halle, Germany
Rubenstein, Harris.................Upsala, Sweden
Rubinstein, M............Johannesburg, So. Africa
Ryland, C. J.................Southerndown, England

S

Saalfeld, A.....................Manchester, England
Sachs, Leopold Katzenelbogen..........London, England
Sacker, I........................Odessa, Russia
Sadig, Mufti M..........Quadian, Gurdaspur, India
Saffer, Nathan...................Leeds, England
Safferty, A.....................Charlton, England
Sagar, A.............Newcastle-upon-Tyne, England
Sager, Judah L...................Cambridge, England
St. Andrew's, University of.......St. Andrew's, Scotland
St. Deiniol's, Library.............Hawarden, England
St. Patrick's, College.............Maynooth, Ireland
St. Paul's Cathedral Library..........London, England
Salaman, Mrs. Myer..................London, England
Salfeld, Rev. Dr. Sigismund.........Mayence, Germany
Salinger, M. S....................London, England
Salmen, Albert Berl.................London, England
Salomon, B.....................Manchester, England
Salomon, Rev. Dr. Berendt.........Manchester, England
Salomon, Fr. E..............Copenhagen, Denmark
Salomon, Frederick..................Southport, England

Salomon, Louis.........................London, England
Samson, Samuel........................London, England
Samuel, Albert B......................Bourgas, Bulgaria
Samuel, Charles.......................London, England
Samuel, Haeem.........Israelite School, Bombay, India
Samuel, Isaac.........................Cardiff, Wales
Samuel, Rev. Isaac....................London, England
Samuel, L.............................Southsea, England
Samuel, Sir Marcus, Knt...............London, England
Samuels, Simon H......................Manchester, England
Sanday, Rev. William..................Oxford, England
Sandeman, Albert G....................Ware, England
Saqui, Horatio........................London, England
Sassoon, Charles Isaac................Brooklands, England
Sassoon, Sir Edward, Bart., M.P.......London, England
Sauerbach, Roger......................Paris, France
Saul, David...........................Morriston, Wales
Saunders, Solomon, J.P................Adelaide, Australia
Saxe, Edward A. de....................London, England
Sayers, M.............................Cork, Ireland
Sayers, P.............................Cork, Ireland
Schachter, Prof. Dr. Max..............Budapest, Hungary
Schapiro, Max.........................Odessa, Russia
Schatunowsky, Gregory.......Kamenetz-Podolsk, Russia
Schechter, Dr. Solomon.....(late of) Cambridge, England
Scheier, J. L.........................London, England
Schishka, David.......................London, England
Schlom, Morris........................Folkestone, England
Schmidl, Dr. Maximilian, Chevalier.....London, England
Schmidt, A. Schmitoff.................Hull, England
Schneideman, Marx.......Newcastle-upon-Tyne, England
Schreiner, Dr. Martin.................Berlin, Germany
Schürer, Dr. Emil.....University of Göttingen, Germany
Schwab, Dr. Moïse.....................Paris, France
Schwabadorf, Dr. Neumann.......Ossmannstedt, Germany
Schwartz, Woolf.......................London, England
Schwarz, Rev. Dr. Adolf...............Carlsruhe, Germany
Schwarz, Arthur.......................Bradford, England
Schwarz, M............................London, England
Schwarzfeld, Dr. E....................Paris, France
Schwarzman, M.........................London, England
Scott, Very Rev. Archibald, D.D......Edinburgh, Scotland
Seeligmann, Sigmund...................Amsterdam, Holland
Segal, Solomon...........Newcastle-upon-Tyne, England
Seligman, Isaac.......................London, England
Selver, Rev. Dr.......................Darmstadt, Germany
Semo, Santo...........................Paris, France
Servi, Chev. F., Chief Rabbi.......Casale Monferrato, Italy
Setof, Colonel A......................London, England
Seymour, J. A.........................London, England
Shaffer, Louis........................Preston, England
Shaffer, M............................Bolton, England
Shaffer, Mendle.......................Manchester, England
Shaffer, Nathan.......................Manchester, England
Shalom, Ezra..........................Manchester, England
Shane, A..............................Brynmawr, Wales
Shane, Isaac Minden...................Stroud, England
Shapiro, Max..................Mossel Bay, So. Africa
Shapiro, Morris A.....................Carnarvon, Wales
Shapiro, S..................Johannesburg, So. Africa
Sharp, Rev. J.........................London, England
Sharpe, Rev. T. W.....................London, England
Shatz, B..............................Cardiff, Wales
Shepherd, M. A........................Swansea, Wales
Sherwinter, Jacob.....................Edinburgh, Scotland
Shonman, S. J.........................London, England
Shrimski, Daniel, M.L.C., J.P......Auckland, New Zealand
Shrimksi, S. E...................Auckland, New Zealand
Sieff, Ephraim........................Manchester, England
Siegfried, Dr. Carl...................Jena, Germany
Siemms, F. D. Samson-.................London, England
Signet Library........................Edinburgh, Scotland
Silvera, David........................Manchester, England
Silverman, M..........................London, England
Silverstone, Mark.....................London, England
Simmons, Bernard Rintel...............Birmingham, England
Simmons, George Alexander.............London, England
Simmons, Henry........................Bristol, England
Simon, Rev. Isidore...................Manchester, England
Simons, J.............................Abertillery, Wales
Simons, Moss..........................London, England
Simons, S.............................London, England
Simonsen, Rev. D., Chief Rabbi.....Copenhagen, Denmark
Singer, Rev. Simeon...................London, England
Sklovsky, S...........................Edinburgh, Scotland
Slijper, E............................Amsterdam, Holland
Sliufko, E............................Middlesborough, England
Smith, Rev. George Adam, M.A........Glasgow, Scotland
Snowman, J., M.D......................London, England
Society of Antiquaries................London, England
Society of Biblical Archæology........London, England
Society for Promoting Christianity Among Jews,
                                      Dublin, Ireland
Sollas, A. M..................Jamaica, West Indies
Solomon, David........................London, England
Solomon, Harriss B.......Newcastle-upon-Tyne, England
Solomon, James H......................London, England
Solomon, Joseph.......................London, England
Solomon, Joseph Bernard...............London, England

Solomon, Solomon J., A.R.A...........London, England
Solomons, Maurice E., J.P............Dublin, Ireland
Somech, David E.......................Manchester, England
Sonenfeld, R..........................London, England
Soudier, H. le........................Paris, France
Speculand, Isaac Mayer................Glasgow, Scotland
Speculand, M..........................Edinburgh, Scotland
Spencer, Herbert (deceased)..........Brighton, England
Spielmann, Miss Miriam................London, England
Spielmann, Sir Isidore, F.S.A........London, England
Spielmann, M. A.......................London, England
Spielmann, Marion H., F.S.A..........London, England
Spiers, F. S..........................London, England
Spiers, Lionel........................Birmingham, England
Spiro, S..............................Cork, Ireland
Spolianski, Frol. Ossipovich..........Odessa, Russia
Stade, B..............................Hesse, Germany
State University......................Leyden, Holland
Stave, Dr. Erik.........University of Upsala, Sweden
Steel, B..............................Manchester, England
Stein, C. A...........................London, England
Stein, Ludwig, Ph.D...................Bern, Switzerland
Steinart, M...........................Manchester, England
Steindorff, Prof. Geo......University of Leipsic, Germany
Steinhart, B..........................London, England
Steinschneider, Dr. Moritz............Berlin, Germany
Stern, Edward David, B.A..............London, England
Stern, Gustav.........................Hove, England
Stern, Rev. Joseph F..................London, England
Sternheim, E..........................London, England
Stettauer, C..........................London, England
Stewart, Rev. Alexander...............Aberdeen, Scotland
Stock, E..............................London, England
Stockholm Society of Jewish Literature..Stockholm, Sweden
Stoloff, Rev. W.......................London, England
Stone, Rev. Darwell...................Wallingford, England
Stone, S..............................Manchester, England
Stone, S..............................Halifax, England
Stoneyhurst College, Browne, Rev. J..Blackburn, England
Story, Rev. Adam, D.D.................Durham, England
Strack, Prof. Hermann L...............Berlin, Germany
Strasburg, University of..........Strasburg, Germany
Stratton, Stephen S...................Birmingham, England
Strisower, Dr. Leo......University of Vienna, Austria
Strump, Benjamin......................Glasgow, Scotland
Stungo, M.............................Edinburgh, Scotland
Stungo, Solomon S.....................Edinburgh, Scotland
Stuttgart Kgl. Israel. Oberkirchenbehörde,
                                      Stuttgart, Germany
Summerfield, D..........Newcastle-upon-Tyne, England
Summerfield, Isidor...................London, England
Sumner, Isaac.........................Birmingham, England
Surowicz, Saul Severin..........Ciechanowiec, Russia
Susman, Joseph........................Manchester, England
Sutro, L...................Johannesburg, So. Africa
Sutton, C. W..........................Manchester, England
Swaab, M..............................Amsterdam, Holland
Swete, Prof. Henry Barclay, D.D......Cambridge, England
Sydney, Algernon E....................London, England
Synagogengemeinde zu Breslau.........Breslau, Germany

T

Tachau, Prof. Dr. L...................Brunswick, Germany
Talegamkar, I. A......................Bombay, India
Tannenbaum, A.........................London, England
Tate Central Library..................London, England
Taylor, Col., R.A.....................Hounslow, England
Taylor, Rev. Charles, D.D., LL.D......Cambridge, England
Tedeschi, R...........................Batavia, Java
Tennant, J. C.........................Norwich, England
Thomas, Isaac.........................Birmingham, England
Thomas, S.............................Leicester, England
Thomas, Rev. William..................Aberdare, Wales
Tobias, Mark..........................London, England
Tobins, J.............................London, England
Tom, M................................London, England
Toohey, Philip Marcus.................Limerick, Ireland
Torres, E. D..........................Manchester, England
Trefecca College......................Tagarth, Wales
Treissmann, David.........Johannesburg, So. Africa
Trietsch, Davis.......................Berlin, Germany
Trilling, N...........................Byelostok, Russia
Trinity College.......................Cambridge, England
Trinity College.......................Dublin, Ireland
Tuck, Adolph..........................London, England
Tuck, Gustave.........................London, England
Tuck, Herman..........................London, England
Turin National Library................Turin, Italy
Turok, H..................Woodstock, So. Africa

U

Unitarian Home Missionary College ...Manchester, England
University Hall.......................London, England
Utrecht, University of................Utrecht, Holland

V

Vámbéry, Dr. Arminius.................Budapest, Hungary
Vandamm, George.......................London, England
Van Mentz, Abraham....................London, England

Van Thal, M........................London, England
Vatican Library.........................Rome, Italy
Vaughan, His Eminence Cardinal (deceased),
                                    London, England
Venetianer, Dr. L.................Neupesth, Hungary
Ventura, Martin J..................Leeds, England
Vesterman, C...................Yekaterinaslaf, Russia
Visetti, Chevalier Albert............London, England
Vivante, M. di Sabbatai...........Manchester, England
Vogelstein, Rev. Dr. Hermann.......Königsberg, Germany
Von Günzburg, Baron David.........St. Petersburg, Russia
Vredenberg, J.....................Amsterdam, Holland

W

Wace, Very Rev. Henry, D.D..Dean of Canterbury, England
Waislowitsh, Dr. Joseph.......Kamenetz-Podolsk, Russia
Waley, A. S....................Chantilly, Oise, France
Waley, Alfred J.....................Reigate, England
Wallach, Siegfried....................Essen, Germany
Wansker, Joseph................Manchester, England
Wansker, Morris................Manchester, England
Warburg, M....................Hamburg, Germany
Warburg, M. M., & Co...........Hamburg, Germany
Wartski, Isidore...................Bangor, Wales
Wartski, Morris....................Bangor, Wales
Warwick, Countess of........Warwick Castle, England
Wasserzug, Rev. D., B.A..........London, England
Watson, Sir John...................Hamilton, Scotland
Wechsler, B....................London, England
Weil, B. B.....................London, England
Weil, Major S....................London, England
Weill, Rev. Julien...................Paris, France
Weinberg, H. J.................Nottingham, England
Weinberg, Israel..................London, England
Weinberg, Marcus.................London, England
Weiner, H.......................Dublin, Ireland
Weiner, Samuel...................London, England
Weissberg, C.....................Dublin, Ireland
Weisz, Rev. Dr. Max.............Budapest, Hungary
Wellhausen, Prof. J........Göttingen University, Germany
Wernikoff, S...................Johannesburg, So. Africa
Wertheimer, A....................London, England
Westminster College.............Cambridge, England
Wharman, Samuel...............London, England
Wiener, S........................Belfast, Ireland
Wigoder, Dr. George S..............Dublin, Ireland
Wilenski, Henry....................London, England
Wilkes, Sam.............Gateshead-on-Tyne, England
Wilkinson, Rev. Samuel H..........Brentwood, England
Wilks, J.....................Middlesborough, England

Williams, Rev. A. L., M.A............Royston, England
Williams, Louis..................Stockport, England
Williams's Library, Dr.............London, England
Wilmers, E.......................London, England
Winberg, S.....................Landport, England
Wineberg, Reuben.................Walsall, England
Winter, J......................London, England
Winter, Rev. Dr. J...............Stockport, England
Wolf, Rev. A., M.A...............Dresden, Germany
Wolf, Albert....................Manchester, England
Wolf, Haman....................Dresden, Germany
Wolf, Lucien....................Leeds, England
Wolf, W.......................London, England
Wolfe, Abraham..................Bradford, England
Wolfe, Alexander................Sunderland, England
Wolfe, Baron....................Manchester, England
Wolfe, I. J.....................Penygraig, Wales
Wolfe, Jonas....................London, England
Wolfers, Rev. Philip.............Cardiff, Wales
Wolffe, David...................Birmingham, England
Wolfman, Samuel.................Chester, England
Wolfsbergen, Henry...............London, England
Wolfsohn, D.....................Cologne, Germany
Wolfson, S......................Leeds, England
Woolf, Abraham..................London, England
Woolf, Albert M.................London, England
Woolf, B. A.....................London, England
Woolf, Gabriel........Newcastle-upon-Tyne, England
Woolf, Leopold M................London, England
Woolf, Lewis...................Birmingham, England
Woolf, Rev. William......Johannesburg, So. Africa
Woolfe, John....................London, England
Woolfe, Max L..................Wrexham, Wales
Woolff, Joseph.................Manchester, England
Woolstone, Eugene...............London, England
Workmen's Library and Literary Institute, Tredegar, England
Worms, Baron de, F.S.A., V.P.R.S.L....London, England
Wright, W. Aldis, M.A., Trinity College, Cambridge, England
Württemberg, University of.........Tübingen, Germany

Z

Zangwill, Israel...................London, England
Zara, R. J.......................Cairo, Egypt
Zeffert, Isaac...................Portsmouth, England
Zeffert, Isaac David..............Leicester, England
Ziegler, Dr. T....................Carlsbad, Bohemia
Ziman, Harris....................London, England
Zlocisti, Dr. Theo.....................Germany
Zossenheim, Maximilian...........Harrogate, England
Zuckermann, A.....................Warsaw, Russia

LIBRARIES, CLUBS, SOCIETIES, INSTITUTIONS, ETC.

A

Abarbanel Library............Jerusalem, Palestine
Aberdeen Public Library...........Aberdeen, Scotland
Aberdeen, University of............Aberdeen, Scotland
Abraham Lincoln Lodge, I. O. B. B., No. 190,
                                    Bloomington, Ill.
Académie Impériale des Sciences.....St. Petersburg, Russia
Académie des Inscriptions et Belles Lettres..Paris, France
Académie Royale des Sciences..........Brussels, Belgium
Accademia dei Sienza...................Milan, Italy
Adas Israel Congregation.............Louisville, Ky.
Adath Yeshurun Congregation Sunday-School,
                                    Syracuse, N. Y.
Aguilar Free Library.....................New York City
Alameda Public Library.................Alameda, Cal.
Alliance Israélite School........Constantinople, Turkey
Alliance Israélite Universelle...............Paris, France
All Souls' College...................Oxford, England
Altoona Mechanics, Library..............Altoona, Pa.
American Geographical Society..........New York City
American Israelite Club...............Troy, N. Y.
American School for Oriental Study and Research,
                                    Jerusalem, Palestine
Amsterdam, Univ. of, Biblio.Rosenthaliana,
                                    Amsterdam, Holland
Ancient and Accepted Scottish Rite Library..Portland, Ore.
Andover Theological Seminary...........Andover, Mass.
Appleton Library, Lawrence University..Appleton, Wis.
Aria College...................Portsea, England
Association for Study of Jewish Religion......Puna, India
Auburn Theological Seminary............Auburn, N. Y.
Augustinian College of St. Thomas of Villanova,
                                    Villanova, Pa.
Austrian Imperial Library..............Vienna, Austria

B

Bala Theological College.................Bala, Wales
Bangor Theological Seminary............Bangor, Me.
Baptist College................Manchester, England
Barbicau Mission to Jews............London, England
Baylor University..................Waco, Tex.
Berkeley Divinity School Library..Middletown, Conn.
Berkhamsted Grammar School.....Berkhamsted, England
Berkshire Athenæum.................Pittsfield, Mass.

Berlin, University of...............Berlin, Germany
Bern, University of..............Bern, Switzerland
Berner, Hochschul Bibliothek.........Bern, Switzerland
Beth-Ahaba Sunday-School...........Richmond, Va.
Beth Elohim Sunday-School........Brooklyn, N. Y.
Beth-El Sabbath-School.............New York City
Beth-Emeth Sunday-School..........Albany, N. Y.
Beth-Israel Congregation............Houston, Tex.
Beth Israel Congregation.............Macon, Ga.
Bibliotheca Rosenthaliana.........Amsterdam, Holland
Bibliothèque des Bollandistes.......Brussels, Belgium
Birmingham Lodge, I. O. B. B........Birmingham, Ala.
Birmingham Public Library........Birmingham, England
Blackstone, James, Memorial Library.....Branford, Conn.
B'nai B'rith Library..............San Francisco, Cal.
B'nai Israel Congregation............Kalamazoo, Mich.
B'nai Israel Congregation........Sacramento City, Cal.
B'nai Israel Sunday-School...........Natchez, Miss.
B'nai Jehudah Sunday-School........Kansas City, Mo.
B'nai Jeshurun Congregation..........New York City
B'nai Jeshurun Religious School........New York City
B'nai Yeshurun Congregation Sunday-School,
                                    Des Moines, Iowa
B'nai Yeshurun (Kahal Kadosh)..........Dayton, Ohio
B'ne Jeshurun Library.............Milwaukee, Wis.
Board of Education.................Newburg, N. Y.
Bodleian Library...................Oxford, England
Bootle Free Public Library and Museum..Liverpool, England
Boston Athenæum..................Boston, Mass.
Boston Public Library...............Boston, Mass.
Boston University..................Boston, Mass.
Bowdoin College...................Brunswick, Me.
Braddock Lodge, I. O. B. B. No. 516.....Braddock, Pa.
Bradford Free Library..............Bradford, England
Brattleboro Free Library............Brattleboro, Vt.
Brighton Public Library............Brighton, England
Bristol Public Library...............Bristol, England
British and Foreign Bible Society.......London, England
Bromley House Library...........Nottingham, England
Brooklyn Library, The.............Brooklyn, N. Y.
Brooklyn Public Library............Brooklyn, N. Y.
Brooklyn Y. M. C. A................Brooklyn, N. Y.
Brown University Library............Providence, R. I.
Brussels Bollandists Society...........Brussels, Belgium

Buffalo Public Library, The..............Buffalo, N. Y.
Buluwayo Chovevei Zion Association..Buluwayo, So. Africa
Bureau of American Ethnology.........Washington, D. C.
Bureau of Education....................Washington, D. C.
Bureau of Rolls and Library, Department of State,
            Washington, D. C.
Butte Free Public Library.................Butte, Mont.

C

California State Library...............Sacramento, Cal.
Cambridge Free Library.............Cambridge, England
Cambridge Library....................Cambridge, Mass.
Cardiff Free Library.....................Cardiff, Wales
Carnegie Free Library....................Allegheny, Pa.
Carnegie Free Library.....................Bradford, Pa.
Carnegie Free Library....................Charlotte, N. C.
Carnegie Free Library....................Nashville, Tenn.
Carnegie Library.........................Pittsburg, Pa.
Case Memorial Library....................Hartford, Conn.
Cathedral Library Association, The........New York City
Century Club, The....................New York City
Century Co., The.....................New York City
Charleston Library....................Charleston, S. C.
Chattanooga Public Library.........Chattanooga, Tenn.
Cheetham Free Reference Library......Manchester, England
Chelsea Public Library..............London, England
Chicago American.......................Chicago, Ill.
Chicago Public Library...................Chicago, Ill.
Chicago Theological Seminary, Hammond Library,
             Chicago, Ill.
Children of Israel Congregation.........Memphis, Tenn.
Christ Church Library................Oxford, England
Christ's College.....................Cambridge, England
Church House Library, Westminster....London, England
Cincinnati Club, The..................Cincinnati, Ohio
Cincinnati Public Library...............Cincinnati, Ohio
City Library.............................Lowell, Mass.
City Library Association, The...........Springfield, Mass.
Cleveland Public Library...............Cleveland, Ohio
Colgate University.....................Hamilton, N. Y.
College of the City of New York.........New York City
College of St. Francis Xavier.............New York City
Columbia Seminary....................Columbia, S. C.
Columbia University....................New York City
Columbus Public Library...............Columbus, Ohio
Congregational Library.................Boston, Mass.
Connecticut State Library...............Hartford, Conn.
Constitutional Club....................London, England
Copenhagen Jewish Congregation......Copenhagen, Denmark
Copenhagen Library................Copenhagen, Denmark
Cornell University........................Ithaca, N. Y.
Crerar Library, The John................Chicago, Ill.
Croydon Public Libraries..............London, England
Crozer Theological Seminary, Bucknell Library,
             Chester, Pa.

D

Dallas Public Library....................Dallas, Tex.
Dayton Public Library....................Dayton, Ohio
Derby Public Library...................Derby, England
Detroit Public Library....................Detroit, Mich.
Deutsch-Jüdische Gemeindebund.......Berlin, Germany
Devonport Free Public Library......Devonport, England
Dickinson College.......................Carlisle, Pa.
Divinity School....................Cambridge, England
Divinity School of the Protestant Episcopal Church,
            Philadelphia, Pa.
Dorchester Missionary College......Wallingford, England
Dorchi Zion Association..........Manchester, England
Dorshei Zion Association.........Cape Town, So. Africa
Drew Theological Seminary Library.....Madison, N. J.
Durban Public Library..............Durban, So. Africa
Durham, University of.............Durham, England

E

East Orange Free Library..........East Orange, N. J.
Ecole Speciale des Langues Orientales Vivantes..Paris, France
Edinburgh Jewish Public Library....Edinburgh, Scotland
Edinburgh Public Library..........Edinburgh, Scotland
Edinburgh University..............Edinburgh, Scotland
Elmira Public Library....................Elmira, N. Y.
El Paso Public Library...................El Paso, Tex.
Emanu-El Congregation...................Dallas, Tex.
Emek Branch Lodge, No. 61, I. O. B. B..Fort Wayne, Ind.
Enoch Pratt Free Library...............Baltimore, Md.
Episcopal Theological School Library....Cambridge, Mass.
Erlangen, University of..............Erlangen, Germany
Esras Chovevi Zion.....................Baltimore, Md.
Evelina de Rothschild School.......Jerusalem, Palestine

F

Faculté de Théologie Protestante.........Paris, France
Falkirk Public Library...............Falkirk, Scotland
Fall River Public Library.............Fall River, Mass.
Finsbury Public Library..............London, England
Florence Jewish Theological Seminary.....Florence, Italy
Forbes Library.....................Northampton, Mass.
Frankfurt-am-Main Stadtbibliothek,
      Frankfort-on-the-Main, Germany

Frankfurt-Loge.........Frankfort-on-the-Main, Germany
Franklin and Marshall College.........Lancaster, Pa.
Free Church College...............Glasgow, Scotland
Free Library of Philadelphia, The......Philadelphia, Pa.
Free Public Library..................New Haven, Conn.
Free Public Library.................St. Joseph, Mo.
Free Public Library.................Worcester, Mass.
Freiburg, University of.............Freiburg, Germany
Freundschaft Society, The...............New York City
Friedrich-Loge XXIV No. 444......Heidelberg, Germany
Friends of Zion....................Philadelphia, Pa.

G

General Theological Seminary...........New York City
Geneva Public Library..............Geneva, Switzerland
Georgia State Library....................Atlanta, Ga.
Glasgow, University of............Glasgow, Scotland
Göteborgs Stadtbibliothek............Göteborg, Sweden
Göttingen, University of..........Göttingen, Germany
Göttinger Gesellschaft der Wissenschaften,
          Göttingen, Germany
Gratz College........................Philadelphia, Pa.
Griqualand W. Hebrew Congregation..Kimberley, So. Africa
Grosvenor Gallery Library...........London, England
Grosvenor Library.......................Buffalo, N. Y.

H

Hailsyburg College.................Hertford, England
Hampstead Public Libraries...........London, England
Harlem Library.........................New York City
Harmonie Club...........................New York City
Harris Institute Library.............Woonsocket, R. I.
Hartford Public Library...............Hartford, Conn.
Harvard University..................Cambridge, Mass.
Haverford College....................Haverford, Pa.
Headingly College....................Leeds, England
Hebrew Circle of Women................Troy, N. Y.
Hebrew Educational Society............Brooklyn, N. Y.
Hebrew Educational Society............Philadelphia, Pa.
Hebrew Literary Association.............Chicago, Ill.
Hebrew Literature Society............Philadelphia, Pa.
Hebrew National Association...........Boston, Mass.
Hebrew Orphan Asylum.................Baltimore, Md.
Hebrew Orphan Asylum.................Brooklyn, N. Y.
Hebrew Orphan Asylum..................New York City
Hebrew Orphan Home....................Atlanta, Ga.
Hebrew School, The.............Birmingham, England
Hebrew Sheltering Guardian Society......New York City
Hebrew Union College...............Cincinnati, Ohio
Heidelberg, University of.........Heidelberg, Germany
Helena Public Library..................Helena, Mont.
Henderson Public Library...............Henderson, Ky.
Hiram College Library.................Hiram, Ohio
Hot Springs Council of Jewish Women..Hot Springs, Ark.
House of Lords Library.............London, England
Howard Memorial Library..........New Orleans, La.
Hull Public Libraries..................Hull, England
Hull Subscription Library...............Hull, England
Humanitätsverein "B'nai B'rith".......Vienna, Austria

I

Illinois State Library...................Springfield, Ill.
Independent Order B'nai B'rith........New York City
Indianapolis Hebrew Congregation Sabbath-School,
          Indianapolis, Ind.
Indianapolis Public Library..........Indianapolis, Ind.
Indiana University Library...........Bloomington, Ind.
I. O. B. B. Lodge No. 434.............Houston, Tex.
I. O. B'nai B'rith....................New York City
Iowa Masonic Library............Cedar Rapids, Iowa
Iowa State Library.................Des Moines, Iowa
Iroquois Social Club...................Utica, N. Y.
Isaiah Congregation Sabbath-School........Chicago, Ill.
Israel. Theolog. Lehranstalt..............Vienna, Austria
Israelite School.......................Bombay, India
Israelitische Allianz..................Vienna, Austria
Israelitische Cultusgemeinde............Brünn, Austria
Israelitische Cultusgemeinde............Vienna, Austria
Israelitische Gemeindebibliothek.......Prague, Bohemia
Israelitisches Lehrerseminar.........Budapest, Hungary

J

Jackson Street Synagogue...............Mobile, Ala.
Jacksonville Public Library...........Jacksonville, Fla.
Jefferson Club, The....................Richmond, Va.
Jena, University of.....................Jena, Germany
Jewish Colonial Trust..............London, England
Jewish Congregation, The..........Copenhagen, Denmark
Jewish Foster Home and Orphan Asylum..Philadelphia, Pa.
Jewish Literary and Social Society....Tredegar, England
Jewish Orphans' Home................New Orleans, La.
Jewish Theological Seminary.........Budapest, Hungary
Jewish Theological Seminary of America....New York City
Jews' College.....................London, England
Jews' Hospital.....................London, England
John Rylands Library................Manchester, England
Johns Hopkins University...............Baltimore, Md.

K

Kais. Universitäts- und Landesbibliothek,
                Strasburg, Germany
Kansas City Public Library.............Kansas City, Mo.
Kansas State Historical Society..........Topeka, Kan.
Keble College............................Oxford, England
Kellogg Hubbard Library..............Montpelier, Vt.
Keneseth Israel Free Library..........Philadelphia, Pa.
Kilburn Public Library..................London, England
King's College.........................Cambridge, England
King's College, Wilson Library.......Aberdeen, Scotland
Kingston-upon-Thames Public Library..Kingston, England
K. K. Hof-Bibliothek..................Vienna, Austria
Königl. Akad. der Wissenschaften.......Berlin, Germany
Königl. Oeffentliche Bibliothek........Dresden, Germany
Königl. Universitäts-Bibliothek........Berlin, Germany

L

Lancashire Independent College.....Manchester, England
Lane Theological Seminary..............Cincinnati, Ohio
Lasker Lodge, The Ed.....................Tyler, Tex.
Leeds Free Public Libraries..............Leeds, England
Leeds Library (Commercial Street).......Leeds, England
Legislative Assembly Library...........Quebec, Canada
Leicester Public Library...........Leicester, England
Leipsic, University of..................Leipsic, Germany
Lexington Public Library................Lexington, Ky.
Leyden, University of..................Leyden, Holland
Leyton Public Libraries.................London, England
Libraire Durlacher......................Paris, France
Library of Supreme Court.............Montgomery, Ala.
Lincoln Library........................Springfield, Ill.
Liverpool Free Public Library........Liverpool, England
Long Island Historical Society..........Brooklyn, N. Y.
Los Angeles Public Library.............Los Angeles, Cal.
Louisville Public Library..............Louisville, Ky.
Lynn Public Library.......................Lynn, Mass.

M

McClelland Library.......................Pueblo, Colo.
McCormick Theological Seminary...........Chicago, Ill.
McMillan Free Library, Reuben......Youngstown, Ohio
Macon Public Library.......................Macon, Ga.
Madras Literary Society.................Madras, India
Maimonides Free Library...............New York City
Maine State Library.......................Augusta, Me.
Manchester City Library.............Manchester, N. H.
Manchester College.....................Oxford, England
Manchester Free Reference Library (4 copies),
               Manchester, England
Manchester Zionist Association......Manchester, England
Marietta College.........................Marietta, Ohio
Maryland Historical Society............Baltimore, Md.
Masonic Library Association...........Des Moines, Iowa
Meadville Theological School............Meadville, Pa.
Melbourne Public Library...........Melbourne, Australia
Mercantile Library........................St. Louis, Mo.
Mercantile Library.....................New York City
Mercantile Library...................Philadelphia, Pa.
Meriden High School.....................Meriden, Conn.
Metropolitan Museum of Art..............New York City
Michigan State Library..................Lansing, Mich.
Mickva Israel Sunday-School..............Savannah, Ga.
Mildmay Mission to Jews................London, England
Milwaukee Public Library..............Milwaukee, Wis.
Minneapolis Athenæum Library.....Minneapolis, Minn.
Minnesota Historical Society, The.......St. Paul, Minn.
Missionary College..................Dorchester, England
Mitchell Library.......................Glasgow, Scotland
Montclair Public Library..............Montclair, N. J.
Montefiore Club.......................Montreal, Canada
Montefiore College, The.............Ramsgate, England
Montefiore Congregation................Marshall, Tex.
Montefiore Home.......................New York City
Mudie's Select Library................London, England

N

Naples National Library..................Naples, Italy
National Farm School...................Doylestown, Pa.
National Library of Ireland............Dublin, Ireland
Nelson Public Library...................Nelson, England
Nevada State Library................Carson City, Nev.
New Albany Public Library...........New Albany, Ind.
Newberry Library, The...................Chicago, Ill.
Newcastle Public Library....Newcastle-upon-Tyne, England
Newcastle-upon-Tyne Literary and Philosophical Society,
           Newcastle-upon-Tyne, England
New College...........................Edinburgh, Scotland
Newcomb College, H. Sophie..........New Orleans, La.
New London Public Library..........New London, Conn.
New Rochelle Public Library........New Rochelle, N. Y.
Newton Free Library.......................Newton, Mass.
Newton Theological Institution.....Newton Center, Mass.
New York Public Library (Astor, Lenox, and Tilden
    Foundations), The...................New York City
New York State Library..................Albany, N. Y.
Norfolk Library..........................Norfolk, Va.

Norfolk and Norwich Library..........Norwich, England
Normal University...................Las Vegas, N. Mex.
Northampton Public Library.........Northampton, Mass.
Norwich Free Library..................Norwich, England
Nottingham Central Free Public Library,
               Nottingham, England

O

Odessa Society of Jewish Clerks..........Odessa, Russia
Ohavei Zion Society.......................New York City
Ohaway Zion Literary Association, The.Minneapolis, Minn.
Omaha Public Library.......................Omaha, Neb.
Osterhout Free Library.................Wilkesbarre, Pa.
Owens College Christie Library, The..Manchester, England

P

Pacific Hebrew Orphan Asylum......San Francisco, Cal.
Padua, University of......................Padua, Italy
Paris, University of......................Paris, France
Peabody Institute.......................Baltimore, Md.
Penn College..........................Oskaloosa, Iowa
Pennsylvania State College...........State College, Pa.
Pennsylvania State Library.............Harrisburg, Pa.
Pensacola Library Association...........Pensaco'a, Fla.
People's Institute......................New York City
Peoria Public Library......................Peoria, Ill.
Plainfield Public Library...............Plainfield, N. J.
Plant Memorial Hebrew Free School, The..Newark N. J.
Plymouth Free Public Library........Plymouth, England
Portland Library Association............Portland, Ore.
Pratt Institute Free Library............Brooklyn, N. Y.
Presbyterian College....................Halifax, N. S.
Pretoria Zionist Library............Pretoria, So. Africa
Princeton Theological Seminary.........Princeton, N. J.
Princeton University...................Princeton, N. J.
Progress Club.........................New York City
Progress Club.......................Philadelphia, Pa.
Protestant Episcopal Divinity School.....Philadelphia, Pa.
Providence Public Library.............Providence, R. I.
Public Library and Reading Room......Bridgeport, Conn.

Q

Queen's University....................Kingston, Canada

R

Radcliffe College....................Cambridge, Mass.
Reading Public Library................Reading, England
Reale Biblioteca Nazionale Centrale........Florence, Italy
Reform Club, The.....................London, England
Religious School of Ohib Sholim Congregation,
               Baltimore, Md.
Religious School Temple Beth Israel........Portland, Ore.
Religious School Temple Emanu-El......New York City
Residence Library University Settlement...New York City
Reynolds Library.......................Rochester, N. Y.
Riggs Library, Georgetown University..Washington, D. C.
Rochester Theological Seminary Library..Rochester, N. Y.
Rockford Public Library..................Rockford, Ill.
Rodef Sholem Congregation Sabbath-School,
               Youngstown, Ohio
Rodeph-Shalom Congregation.........Philadelphia, Pa.
Rosenberg Library.....................Galveston, Tex.
Rosenwald Lodge No. 545.............Las Vegas, N. Mex.
Rostock, University of................Rostock, Germany
Royal and University Library..........Breslau, Germany
Royal Danish Academy of Sciences..Copenhagen, Denmark
Royal Dublin Society...................Dublin, Ireland
Royal Library.........................Berlin, Germany
Royal Library.........................Munich, Germany
Royal Library.......................The Hague, Holland
Royal Library.......................Stockholm, Sweden
Royal Library of Belgium.............Brussels, Belgium
Royal University......................Berlin, Germany
Royal University......................Ghent, Belgium
Royal University....................Göttingen, Germany
Royal University......................Halle, Germany
Royal University......................Upsala Sweden

S

Sabbath-School Congregation Temple Israel.Jonesboro, Ark.
Sabbath-School Indianapolis Hebrew Congregation,
               Indianapolis, Ind.
Sage Library, Gardner A.............New Brunswick, N. J.
St. Agnes Free Library.................New York City
St. Andrew's College Library..........Toronto, Ontario
St. Andrew's, University of........St. Andrew's, Scotland
St. Deiniol's Library.................Hawarden, England
St. Louis Public Library.................St. Louis, Mo.
St. Louis University.....................St. Louis, Mo.
St. Michael's Passionist Monastery..West Hoboken, N. J.
St. Patrick's College.................Maynooth, Ireland
St. Paul's Cathedral Library...........London, England
St. Paul Public Library.................St. Paul, Minn.
San Francisco Public Library........San Francisco, Cal.
Scranton Public Library.................Scranton, Pa.
Seattle Public Library.................Seattle, Wash.
Signet Library......................Edinburgh, Scotland
Sir Montefiore Association............Cincinnati, Ohio

Skinner Library, The Mark............Manchester, N. H.
Smith College, The Philander...........Little Rock, Ark.
Smithsonian Institution, U. S. National Museum
                                    Washington, D. C.
Society for Promoting Christianity Among Jews,
                                    Dublin, Ireland
Society of Antiquaries................London, England
Society of Biblical Archæology..........London, England
Society Library......................New York City
Somerville Public Library.............Somerville, Mass.
Southern Baptist Theological Seminary....Louisville, Ky.
Spokane City Library..................Spokane, Wash.
Standard Club........................Uniontown, Pa.
State Library........................Boston, Mass.
State Library........................Raleigh, N. C.
State Universtiy.....................Leyden, Holland
Stockholm Society of Jewish Literature..Stockholm, Sweden
Stoneyhurst College...................Blackburn, England
Strasburg, University of..............Strasburg, Germany
Stuttgart Kgl. Israel, Oberkirchenbehorde
                                    Stuttgart, Germany
Sunday-School Board, Congregation B'nai Yeshurun,
                                    Des Moines, Iowa
Swarthmore College Library............Swarthmore, Pa.
Synagogengemeinde zu Breslau..........Breslau, Germany
Syracuse Public Library...............Syracuse, N. Y.

T

Tacoma Public Library................Tacoma, Wash.
Tate Central Library.................London, England
Temple Emanu-El Sabbath-School........New York City
Temple Beth-El Sabbath-School..........Detroit, Mich.
Temple Emanu-El Sabbath School.........New York City
Temple Emanu-El Sunday-School Library Spokane, Wash.
Temple Emanu-El Sunday-School Library Milwaukee, Wis.
Temple Emanu-El Sunday-School Library Milwaukee, Wis.
Temple Emanu-El Sunday-School Library Birmingham, Ala.
Temple Israel East Side School..........New York City
Temple Israel Sabbath-School...........St. Louis, Mo.
Temple Library......................Norfolk, Va.
Temple Library, The..................Cleveland, Ohio
Temple Sinai Congregation.............New Orleans, La.
Terre Haute Section Council of Jewish Women,
                                    Terre Haute, Ind.
Theological College..................Bala, N. Wales
Theological Seminary.................Gettysburg, Pa.
Theological Seminary Library....Theological Seminary, Va.
Theological Seminary of the Reformed Church in the
    United States....................Lancaster, Pa.
Tiphereth Zion Society................Pittsburg, Pa.
Toledo Public Library................Toledo, Ohio
Toronto Public Library...............Toronto, Canada
Traverse Public City Library..........Traverse City, Mich.
Trefecca College....................Talgarth, Wales
Trinity College.....................Cambridge, England
Trinity College.....................Dublin, Ireland
Trowbridge Reference Library, Yale Divinity School,
                                    New Haven, Conn.
Tulane University...................New Orleans, La.
Turin National Library...............Turin, Italy

U

Union Theological Seminary.............New York City
Unitarian Home Missionary College....Manchester, England
United Hebrew Charities...............New York City
University of California (Semitic)........Berkeley, Cal.
University of Chicago Press, The.........Chicago, Ill.
University Hall......................London, England
University of Kansas.................Lawrence, Kan.
University of Leyden.................Leyden, Netherlands
University Library..................Durham, England
University of Michigan...............Ann Arbor, Mich.
University of Pennsylvania, The.........Philadelphia, Pa.
University of Rostock, The............Rostock, Germany
University of Toronto Library..........Toronto, Canada
University of Wisconsin...............Madison, Wis.
Utica Public Library.................Utica, N. Y.
Utrecht, University of...............Utrecht, Holland

V

Vanderbilt University................Nashville, Tenn.
Vassar College......................Poughkeepsie, N. Y.
Vatican Library.....................Rome, Italy
Vine Street Temple Sabbath-School......Nashville, Tenn.

W

Washington and Jefferson College.........Washington, Pa.
Washington Public Library............Washington, D. C.
Wellesley College...................Wellesley, Mass.
Wells College Library................Aurora, N. Y.
Wesleyan University Library...........Middletown, Conn.
Western Reserve University (College for Women),
                                    Cleveland, Ohio
Western Theological Seminary..........Allegheny, Pa.
Westminster College.................Cambridge, England
Wheeling Public Library...............Wheeling, W. Va.
William's Library ,Dr.................London, England
Wilmington Institute Free Library.......Wilmington, Del.
Wolf Lodge, Simon, I. O. B. B..........Savannah, Ga.
Workmen's Library and Literary Institute,
                                    Tredegar, England
Wurttemberg, University of..........Tubingen, Germany

Y

Yale University.....................New Haven, Conn.
Yonkers Public Library...............Yonkers, N. Y.
Young Hebrew Zionists................Syracuse, N. Y.
Young Men's Gymnastic Club...........New Orleans, La.
Young Men's Hebrew Association........Atlanta, Ga.
Young Men's Hebrew Association........Bradford, Pa.
Young Men's Hebrew Association........Memphis, Tenn.
Young Men's Hebrew Association........New Orleans, La.
Young Men's Hebrew Association........New York City
Young Men's Hebrew Association........Philadelphia, Pa.
Young Men's Hebrew Association........Wilmington, Del
Young Zionists of St. Paul............St. Paul, Minn.

Z

Zion Library........................New Haven, Conn.
Zion Society of Rochester.............Rochester, N. Y.

SUPPLEMENTARY LIST, UNITED STATES.

A

Aronson, Mayr.......................Brooklyn, N. Y.
Ascherman, T. E.....................Chicago, Ill.
Auerbach, Louis,....................New York City

B

Balleisen, Wolf.....................Brooklyn, N. Y.
Baskin, Julius......................New York City
Beard, Newman......................Philadelphia, Pa.
Beatman, William....................Hartford, Conn.
Benjamin, A., M.D....................Newport, Ky.
Bergman, A.........................Philadelphia, Pa.
Bergman, Morris.....................Brooklyn, N. Y.
Berkowitz, Isaac....................New York City
Berkowitz, Max.....................New York City
Berkowitz, Samuel...................New York City
Berman, Max D.....................Hartford, Conn.
Bisgeier, Jacob.....................New York City
Bleichrode. J. B....................New York City
Bloom, David.......................New York City
Bookstader, Peyser..................New York City
Brandstein, Herman I.................Bensonhurst, N. Y.
Brown, Louis.......................Brooklyn, N. Y.
Buegeleisen, H. D...................Brooklyn, N. Y.

C

Cahn, Louis D......................New York City
Catholic University of America........Washington, D. C.
Cohen, Adolph......................New York City
Cony, Rudolph......................Chicago, Ill.

D

Deschamps, J. M....................Anamosa, Iowa
DeSola, Moses......................Curaçao, D. W. I.
Dombek, Samuel.....................Brooklyn, N. Y.
Drucker, Ephraim...................New York City

E

Earl, Jr., George H.................Bryn Mawr, Pa.
Eisenstaedt, A. L...................Mt. Vernon, N. Y.
Ellner, Saul.......................New York City
Elsass, Otto.......................New York City

F

Faggen, Solomon....................Philadelphia, Pa.
Farbish, Max F.....................New York City
Fitz Public Library.................Chelsea, Mass.
Fleischman, Samuel..................New York City
Fowler, Bishop C. H.................New York City
Freiberger, David...................New York City
Freid, Isidor......................New York City
Freilander, Max....................Hazelton, Pa.

G

Glazer, Samuel.....................Hartford, Conn.
Glotzer, Samuel J...................Hartford, Conn.
Goldberg, Hiram....................Philadelphia, Pa.
Goldberg, Michael...................Hartford, Conn.
Goldblum, H........................New York City
Golden, Max.......................Philadelphia, Pa.
Goldman, Selig.....................Worcester, Mass.
Goldschmidt, Herman E...............New York City
Goodman, Max......................Brooklyn, N. Y.
Gottfried, Harry...................New York City
Gouled, Peter......................New York City
Greenberg, Rev. D..................New York City
Greenhoot, A. A....................New York City
Guggenheimer, Sig. S................New York City

H

Hamburger, B.......................New York City
Heilprin, William A.................New York City
Heineman, Rebecca..................New York City

Henriques, Edward.................Brooklyn, N. Y.
Herz, A........................Terre Haute, Ind.
Hirsch, Isaac L., M.D..............New York City
Hirschhorn, Lewis................Cincinnati, Ohio
Holloway, Rev. E. S................New York City

I

Immergut, L.....................New York City
Indiana State Normal School........Terre Haute, Ind.
Isaacs, Isidor R...................New York City

J

Jonas, L........................Nashville, Tenn.
Joseph, Irving J..................New York City
Joseph, Louis....................New York City

K

Kassel, M.......................Hoboken, N. J.
Katz, Max E.....................Cleveland, Ohio
Katz, Michael, M.D...............New York City
Kaufmann, Nathan.................Toledo, Ohio
Kessler, Max....................New York City
Klee, Benj......................New York City
Klein, Adolph...................Los Angeles, Cal.
Klotz, Jacob....................New York City
Kone, Samuel C..................Hartford, Conn.
Koppleman, H. P.................Hartford, Conn.
Krause, Herman..................New York City
Krause, Louis...................New York City

L

Landau, Maurice..................New York City
Langer, Samuel..................New York City
Lefkowitz, I....................New York City
Lehman, Charles.................New York City
Levi, Mrs. J....................Oil City, Pa.
Levin, Boris....................Philadelphia, Pa.
Levine, Charles.................New York City
Levine, Joseph R................Brooklyn, N. Y.
Levy, Benjamin..................New York City
Levy, Davis....................Brooklyn, N. Y.
Levy, H. P.....................Hartford, Conn.
Levy, Israel N..................New York City
Levy, Julius...................Brooklyn, N. Y.
Levy, Louis J...................New York City
Lewy, Arthur...................New York City
Lichter, Abraham................New York City
Lieber, Max....................Philadelphia, Pa.
Lindheim, Reuben................New York City
Lippman, Samuel.................New York City
Loewith, Sigmund................Bridgeport, Conn.

M

Mandel, Chas r..................Brooklyn, N. Y.
Mann, Sigmond..................New York City
Marcuse, Alex. I................New York City
Margolies, Hyman S..............Philadelphia, Pa.
Marks, Henry...................Pittsburg, Pa.
Marx, Prof. Alex................New York City
Mayer, Max H...................Brooklyn, N. Y.
Mayer, Paul....................New York City
Mehr, S. N.....................Toronto, Can.
Miller, Michael.................Brooklyn, N. Y.
Miller, Sidney F................Brooklyn, N. Y.
Moss, Isaac....................Bridgeport, Conn.

N

Nathan, Marvin..................Philadelphia, Pa.
Naumburg, Elkan.................New York City
Newman, Serenus L., M.D..........New York City

O

Offen, Morris...................Philadelphia, Pa.
Ortleff, Rev. E. E...............Greenville, Ohio

P

Parsell, Henry V. A...............New York City
Peikes, J......................New York City

Perlo, Samuel...................New York City
Polstein, Isaac..................New York City
Pomerantz, Max.................Philadelphia, Pa.
Porris, R......................Hartford, Conn.
Pritz, Carl....................Cincinnati, Ohio

R

Rickman, Samuel J...............Hartford, Conn.
Rod, Barnet W...................New York City
Rose, Louis S...................New York City
Rosen, H. B....................Hartford, Conn.
Rosenbaum, M...................Bonham, Tex.
Rosenblatt, C. H................New York City
Rosenthal, J. S.................New York City
Roth, Dr. Herman................New York City
Roth, L........................New York City
Rothstein, Sam..................New York City
Rubovits, Toby..................Chicago, Ill.

S

Sadowsky, R....................New York City
Salamon, William................New York City
Samuels, H. C..................Brooklyn, N. Y.
Sapolsky, Abr..................New York City
Sarfaty, Joseph.................New York City
Schlager, Simon.................New York City
Schleifer, Morris...............New York City
Schoenbaum, M. S...............New York City
Schnitzer, Wm. M...............New York City
Schultz, Philip.................Worcester, Mass.
Schwartz, Jacob.................Philadelphia, Pa.
Schwartz, Michael...............New York City
Seideman, Adolph D..............Philadelphia, Pa.
Seidenberg, Henry C.............Brooklyn, N. Y.
Selig, Arthur Louis..............New York City
Seligman, Selig.................Brooklyn, N. Y.
Shalek, Fred. J.................New York City
Shapiro, David.................Brooklyn, N.Y.
Shedinsky, Harris...............New York City
Siegfried, Reuben...............New York City
Silver, Wolf...................New Haven, Conn.
Simons, B. Berry................New York City
Skora, Philip..................Evansville, Ind.
Slater, Joseph P................New York City
Sloat, Louis J..................New York City
Solomon, J. F..................New York City
Souweine, Adolphe...............New York City
Spicehandler, Chas..............New York City
Stearns, Wallace N..............Grand Forks, N. D.
Steinhaus, Isaac................New York City
Stern, Mrs. I...................New York City
Strauss, Annie J................New York City
Strauss, Samuel.................Danville, Ind.
Suisman, Marx..................Hartford, Conn.

T

Tracy, Ira D...................Brooklyn, N. Y.
Tufts College..................Tufts College, Mass.

U

Ullman, Jacob B.................New Haven, Conn.
University Club.................Philadelphia, Pa.

W

Webster, Mrs. Myer S............New York City
Weisman, L....................Farwell, Mich.
Werner, Samuel.................New York City
White, Augusta.................Brookline, Mass.
Williamson, M..................New York City
Wolf, Abraham..................New York City
Wolf, Lillie...................New York City
Wolfman, Philip................New York City

Z

Zucker, Dr. Morris..............New York City
Zweighaft, S...................New York City